WHO WAS WHO ON SCREEN

WHO WAS WHO ON SCREEN

Second Edition

EVELYN MACK TRUITT

R. R. BOWKER COMPANY
New York & London, 1977

This book is dedicated to all my friends,
and especially to my boss, who "tolerated"
me during this literary effort.

Published by R. R. Bowker Co.
1180 Avenue of the Americas, New York, N.Y. 10036

Printed and bound in the United States of America

Library of Congress Cataloging in Publication Data

Truitt, Evelyn Mack, 1931-
  Who was who on screen.

  Bibliography: p.
  1. Moving-picture actors and actresses—Biography.
I. Title.
PN1998.A2T73   1977   791.43′028′0922 [B]   77-22651
ISBN 0-8352-0914-8

The first edition of *Who Was Who on Screen* covered over 6,000 screen personalities, primarily American, British, and French, who died between the years 1920 and 1971. This, the second edition, has been revised to span the years 1905 to 1975. It now includes some 9,000 names, and many original listings have been significantly expanded.

This book is concerned with the players—not only the greats and the near-greats, but the bit players in important features and the headliners in lesser known films. Also listed are persons who, while they appeared at least briefly on screen, are better known for other achievements —fighter James J. Corbett, Senator Everett Dirkson, artist Pablo Picasso, and authors Somerset Maugham and George Bernard Shaw, for example. Animal performers are not forgotten and the efforts of Rin Tin Tin (Jr. and Sr.), Trigger, Petey, and others are recognized.

Because screen appearances are what this book is all about, directors, producers, and other behind-the-scene luminaries are included only if they also appeared in front of the camera. Marriage and family data have usually been included only if industry-related or relevant to a well known performer's career.

For ease of reference, performers are listed alphabetically. Each entry is comprised of a brief biographical sketch, together with a full list of screen credits, if available, rather than the summary or highlighted version found in most reference works.

For consistency, *Film Daily* has been used for release dates, thus avoiding the discrepancy between East Coast *vs.* West Coast and foreign opening dates. Because early films seldom exceeded four reels in length, shorts are distinguished from features only after 1920. For the purposes of this book, a short is defined as a film of less than five reels and a feature as one of five reels or more.

In its coverage of both well-remembered and obscure performers, this book brings together information from hundreds of sources. This information has been carefully cross-checked to assure accuracy, and vital records and living sources have been consulted wherever possible to resolve conflicting or inadequate data. The keen memory of J. Patrick O'Malley, in one instance, helped make it possible to distinguish his films from those of Patrick O'Malley; Brenda Forbes helped determine in which films her mother, Mary Forbes, appeared, rather than Mary Elizabeth Forbes; and without the assistance of Frances Delmar, widow of Victor Daniels (Chief Thundercloud), and Anne Bauer, widow of Scott T. Williams (the other Chief Thundercloud), it would not have been possible to accurately credit each actor. Where name duplications or similarities could not be resolved, screen credits are not given and this is noted in the individual entries.

The cataloging of foreign film credits presents a special problem for several reasons: the limited availability of source material, the discrepancy between foreign and U.S. release dates, and title changes or translations. British films, more than most, undergo a variety of title changes before being imported to Hollywood. Therefore, in many instances, the listing of the original British title and release date is followed by the title and date of release in the United States. Foreign language films, if released in the United States, are listed primarily by their retitled or translated names.

Since publication of the first edition of *Who Was Who on Screen,* I have been the happy recipient of countless letters from a variety of people offering suggestions and advising me of their interest and support. It is mind-boggling to think of the time and effort these people have spent to provide me with extensive additional information or miscellaneous corrections. I will forever be grateful to them for their contributions on my behalf: Robert Crawford, Robert Evans, Lillian Tudiver, and William C. Wilson; also Helen Brady, Richard Braff, R. W. Brilhante, Harold Flasker, Steven Garneau, John P. Hiestand, Arthur Hill of the Screen Actors Guild, James Powers, Bruce Saver, Bob Tamkin, Zoe Voigtsberg Truitt, John F. Rengstorff, and Roi A. Uselton; and Sam Gill and Anthony Slide of the Academy of Motion Picture Arts & Sciences Library.

And then, a very special note of appreciation is due to a new friend, Barry Brown, who devoted endless hours of research to submit numerous additions to the first edition, and offered unfailing encouragement for this, the second, edition of *Who Was Who on Screen*.

It is impossible to research and finalize a book such as this without the benefit of true and dedicated assistance. For such superb support, thank you Margaret Breckenridge, Elaine Langwell Decker, Suzanne Goodwin, Bea Humbird, Michael P. Kelly, Pat McDonald, and Kathleen Moser. I really doubt that I could have assembled this myriad of data without the untiring and capable help of Sue Fisher and my friend, neighbor, research assistant, and film historian, Carol Cullen. They truly worked above and beyond the call of duty. Words of thanks are inadequate. And, once again, I must thank my dear friend, Charles Pollock, who convinced me to get the initial project from the hobby stage to reference book status.

Every effort has been made to provide you—whether film scholar or film buff—with as comprehensive, functional, and reliable a book as possible. Conflicting data have been noted along with the verifiable information. Since mystery—sometimes intended, sometimes merely clouded by the past—continues to surround many performers, additional or supplementary information is welcome and can be submitted via the publisher.

E.M.T.

WHO WAS WHO ON SCREEN

AASEN, JOHN

Born: 1887, Minnesota. Died: Aug. 1, 1938, Mendocino, Calif. Screen actor and circus giant.

Appeared in: **1923** Why Worry? **1927** Legionnaires in Paris; Two Flaming Youths. **1928** Should Married Men Go Home?

ABBE, CHARLES S.

Born: 1860. Died: June 16, 1932, Darien, Conn. (blood poisoning). Stage and screen actor.

Appeared in: **1915** Niobe. **1921** Cappy Ricks; The Conquest of Canaan. **1922** Back Home and Broke. **1923** Homeward Bound. **1924** West of the Water Tower.

ABBOTT, AL

Born: 1884. Died: Sept. 4, 1962, Reseda, Calif. (heart attack). Screen and vaudeville actor.

Appeared in: **1929** Small Town's Ramblers (short).

ABBOTT, BUD (William A. Abbott)

Born: Oct. 2, 1896, Asbury, N.J. Died: Apr. 24, 1974, Woodland Hills, Calif. (cancer). Screen, stage, television, radio, vaudeville and burlesque actor. Was part of comedy team of Abbott and Costello. For films they appeared in together see Lou Costello (dec. 1959).

Appeared in (without Costello): **1946** The Ghost Steps Out. **1950** The Real McCoy. **1967** Voice only used for cartoon shorts.

ABBOTT, DOROTHY

Died: Dec. 5, 1968. Screen actress.

Appeared in: **1962** Sergeants Three. **1963** A Gathering of Eagles.

ABBOTT, FRANK

Born: 1879. Died: 1957, Los Angeles, Calif. Screen actor. Entered films during early silents.

Appeared in: **1925** The Wild Bull's Lair.

ABBOTT, JAMES FRANCIS

Born: 1873. Died: Jan. 19, 1954, North Hollywood, Calif. Screen actor.

ABEL, ALFRED

Born: Mar. 12, 1880, Leipzig, Germany. Died: Dec. 12, 1937. Screen actor and film producer. Known as "The Louis Stone of German pictures."

Appeared in: **1918** Colomba; Sundiege Mutter (Sinning Mothers). **1919** Rausch. **1921** Doktor Mabuse, der Spieler (Dr. Mabuse, the Gambler—US 1927). **1922** Der Brennende Acker; Sappho; Die Flamme; Das Phantom. **1923** Die Buddenbrooks; Die Finanzen des Grossherzogs. **1924** Die Frau im Feuer. **1925** Prinzessin Suwarin. **1926** Metropolis (US 1927). **1927** Das Tanzende Wien. **1928** L'Argent; Rasputin's Liebesabenteuer (aka Rasputin und die Frauen). **1929** Cagliostro; Narkose; Strauss, the Waltz King. **1931** Dolly Macht Karriere (Dolly's Way to Stardom); Das Schicksal der Renate Langen; Der Herzog von Reichstadt; Die Koffer des Herrn O.F.; Manolescu, der Furst der Diebe; Der Kongress Tanzt (Congress Dances—US 1932). **1932** Das Madel von Montparnasse; Das Schone Abenteuer; 1941: The Last Days Before the War; Der Herr Buerovorsteher. **1933** Brennendes Geheimnis; Eine Siebzehnjahrige; Das Schicksal der Renate Langen (The Fate of Renate Langen); Die Galavorstellung; Die Frau von der Man Spricht. **1935** Viktoria. **1936** Kater Lampe; Ein Seltsamer Gast (US 1937); Marie, die Magd (US 1937); Und Du, Mein Spiel an Bord. **1937** Millionen Erbschaft; Unter Ausschluss der Offentlichkeit; Sieben Ohrfeigen (Seven Slaps —aka Boxes on the Ear—US 1938); Salon Dora Green. **1938** Frau Sylvelin; Kater Lampe. **1940** Alle Stehen Kopf (General Confusion).

ABELES, EDWARD

Born: 1870. Died: July 10, 1919, New York, N.Y. (pneumonia). Stage and screen actor.

Appeared in: **1914** Brewster's Millions; Ready Money. **1915** After Five; Under Two Flags. **1918** Opportunity.

ABINGDON, WILLIAM L.

Born: May 2, 1859, Tewcester-Hertheontes, England. Died: May 17, 1918, New York, N.Y. Screen actor. Father of stage director William Abingdon.

Appeared in: **1914** Manon Lescaut. **1916** Panthea. **1918** Fedora.

ABRAHAMIAN, AROUSIAK (Arousiak Hashashian)

Born: 1890, Ankara, Turkey. Died: July 2, 1973, Philadelphia, Pa. Screen actress. Mother of actor Val Avery.

ABURTO, ARMANDO

Born: 1910, Mexico. Died: July 1, 1955, Mexico City, Mexico. Stage and screen actor.

ACE, JANE (Jane Sherwood)

Born: 1900. Died: Nov. 11, 1974, New York, N.Y. Screen and radio actress. Married to writer Goodman Ace.

Appeared in: **1935** Easy Aces (short); an RKO short.

ACKERMAN, WALTER

Born: 1881. Died: Dec. 12, 1938, Hollywood, Calif. Screen actor. Entered films in 1907.

Appeared in: **1925** Rugged Water. **1926** Man of the Forest. **1927** Aflame in the Sky; Back to God's Country. **1929** Bride of the Desert.

ACORD, ART

Born: 1890, Stillwater, Minn. Died: Jan. 4, 1931, Chihuahua, Mexico (suicide—poison). Screen actor. Entered films in 1912. Divorced from actresses Edythe Sterling and Louise Lorraine.

Appeared in: **1914** The Squaw Man. **1915** A Man Afraid of His Wardrobe. **1920** The Moon Riders (serial). **1921** The White Horseman (serial); Winners of the West (serial). **1922** In the Days of Buffalo Bill (serial). **1923** The Oregon Trail (serial). **1924** Fighting for Justice; Looped for Life. **1925** The Scrappin' Kid; The Call of Courage; Three in Exile; The Circus Cyclone; Pals; Triple Action; The Wild Girl. **1926** Lazy Lightning; The Man from the West; The Ridin' Rascal; Rustler's Ranch; The Set-Up; The Silent Guardian; Sky High Corral; The Terror; Western Pluck. **1927** Hard Fists; Loco Luck; Set Free; Spurs and Saddles; The Western Rover. **1928** Two Gun O'Brien. **1929** The Arizona Kid; Bullets and Justice; Fighters of the Saddle; An Oklahoma Cowboy; The White Outlaw; Wyoming Tornado.

ACOSTA, RODOLFO

Born: 1920, Mexico. Died: Nov. 7, 1974, Woodland Hills, Calif. Screen, stage and television actor.

Appeared in: **1948** The Fugitive. **1950** One Way Street; Poncho Villa Returns. **1951** The Bullfighter and the Lady (aka Torero). **1952** Yankee Buccaneer; Horizons West. **1953** Destination Gobi; Wings of the Hawk; Appointment in Honduras; City of Bad Men; San Antone; Hondo. **1954** Drum Beat; Passion. **1955** A Life in a Balance; The Littlest Outlaw. **1956** Bandido; The Proud Ones. **1957** The Tijuana Story; Apache Warrior; Last Stagecoach West; Trooper Hook. **1958** From Hell to Texas. **1960** Flaming Star (aka Black Star, Flaming Heart, Flaming Lance); Walk Like a Dragon; Let No Man Write My Epitaph. **1961** One-Eyed Jacks; The Second Time Around; Posse from Hell; The Last Rebel; How the West Was Won. **1963** Savage Sam. **1964** Rio Conchos. **1965** The Sons of Katie Elder; The Reward; The Greatest Story Ever Told. **1966** Return of the Seven. **1967** V¿˙¹·y of Mystery. **1968** Dayton's Devils.

1969 Impasse; Young Billy Young. **1970** Flap (aka Nobody Loves Flapping Eagle); The Great White Hope.

ACUFF, EDDIE

Born: 1908, Caruthersville, Mo. Died: Dec. 17, 1956, Hollywood, Calif. (heart attack). Stage and screen actor.

Appeared in: **1935** I Found Stella Parish; Shipmates Forever; Miss Pacific Fleet. **1936** The Petrified Forest; The Black Legion; Crash Donovan; Boulder Dam; The Law in Her Hands; Jail Break; The Case of the Velvet Claws; The Golden Arrow; The Walking Dead. **1937** Talent Scout; The Go-Getter; The Outer Gate; They Won't Forget; The Singing Marine; Love Is On the Air; Without Warning; The Missing Witness; Hollywood Hotel; Back in Circulation; What Price Vengeance; Laughing at Trouble; Guns of the Pecos; Behind Prison Bars. **1938** How to Watch Football (short); Four Daughters; Smashing the Rackets; Law of the Underworld; She Loved a Fireman; Ladies in Distress; Rhythm of the Saddle; The Invisible Menace. **1939** Blondie Meets the Boss; Help Wanted (short); The Mysterious Miss X; Rough Riders' Roundup; Two Bright Boys; Cowboy Quarterback; Meet Doctor Christian; Backfire; Lawyer Woman. **1940** Shooting High; Cafe Hostess; One Night in the Tropics; The Boys from Syracuse. **1941** Robin Hood of the Pecos; Texas Rangers Ride Again; Blondie Goes Latin; The Great American Broadcast; The People vs. Dr. Kildare; Here Comes Happiness; Rags to Riches; Blondie for Victory; Hellzapoppin. **1942** Yankee Doodle Dandy; Bells of Capistrano; Dr. Gillespie's New Assistant; Pardon My Sarong; Mr. District Attorney in the Carter Case; The Traitor Within; The Lady is Willing; Dr. Kildare's Victory; Mississippi Gambler; Girl Trouble; War against Mrs. Hadley; Army Surgeon. **1943** He Hired the Boss; Headin' for God's Country; Guadalcanal Diary. **1944** Carolina Blues; South of Dixie; Weekend Pass; In the Meantime, Darling; It Happened Tomorrow. **1945** Sergeant Mike; The Frozen Ghost; The Hidden Eye; She Gets Her Man; Don Juan Quilligan; Diamond Horseshoe; Honeymoon Ahead; Her Lucky Night; Leave It to Blondie; Shadow of Terror; Jungle Captive. **1946** The Notorious Lone Wolf; Flying Serpent; Wake up and Dream; Night Train to Memphis. **1947** Bandits of Dark Canyon; Blondie's Holiday; Buck Privates Come Home; Bells of San Angelo; Helldorado; Blondie's Big Moment; G-Men Never Forget (serial); Swing the Western Way; Blondie in the Dough; Slippy McGee. **1948** Blondie's Reward. **1949** Blondie's Big Deal; Blondie's Secret.

ADAIR, JACK

Born: 1894. Died: Sept. 22, 1940, Hollywood, Calif. Screen actor.

Appeared in: **1935** Peter Ibbetson. **1936** Lady Be Careful. **1937** 52nd Street; Manhattan Merry-Go-Round.

ADAIR, JEAN

Born: 1873. Died: May 11, 1953, New York, N.Y. Screen, stage, and vaudeville actress.

Appeared in: **1922** In the Name of the Law. **1933** Advice to the Lovelorn. **1944** Arsenic and Old Lace. **1946** Something in the Wind. **1947** Living in a Big Way.

ADAIR, JOHN

Born: 1885. Died: Jan. 22, 1952, New York. Screen, stage, radio and television actor.

Appeared in: **1936** Muss 'Em Up. **1940** The Ramparts We Watch.

ADAIR, ROBERT

Born: Jan. 3, 1900, San Francisco, Calif. Died: Aug. 10, 1954, London, England. Screen, stage, television and vaudeville actor.

Appeared in: **1925** Raffles. **1930** Journey's End. **1933** King of the Jungle; The Kiss Before the Mirror. **1934** Where Sinners Meet; Limehouse Blues; The Crusades. **1935** The Last Outpost; Peter Ibbetson; The Girl Who Came Back. **1937** The Prince and the Pauper. **1948** Noose (aka The Silk Noose—US 1950). **1953** Park Plaza (aka Norman Conquest—US). **1954** Eight O'Clock Walk (US 1955).

ADALBERT, MAX (Max Krampf)

Born: 1874, Danzig, Germany. Died: 1933, Munich, Germany. Stage and screen actor.

Appeared in: **1915** Der Schirm mit dem Schwan. **1919** Konig Nicolo oder So Ist das Leben; Die Verfuhrten. **1920** Der Dummkopf. **1921** Der Mude Tod (aka Between Worlds/Destiny); Dr. Mabuse der Spieler (Dr. Mabuse, the Gambler—US 1927). **1922** Die Flamme; Lebenshunger; Sein Ist das Gericht. **1925** Vorderhaus und Hinterhaus. **1930** Das Gestohlene Gesicht; Hans in Allen Gassen. **1931** Die Schlacht von Bademunde; Der Hauptmann von Kopenick (Captain of Koepenick); Das Ekel; Mein Leopold; Hurra! Ein Junge!; Der Herr Finanzdirektor; Kyritz—Pyritz; Drei Tage Mittelarrest (Three Days in the Guard-House); Der Hellseher (aka Mein Herz Sehnt Sich Nach Liebe). **1932** Ein Toller Einfall (A Mad Idea); Der Schutzenkonig; Die Galavorstellung der Fratellinis (aka Spione im Savoy-Hotel). **1933** Lachende Erben. **1934** Tante Gusti Kommandiert. Other German film: So Und Die Drei.

ADAMS, CONSTANCE

Born: 1893. Died: July 17, 1960, Hollywood, Calif. Screen actress. Married to producer/director Cecil B. DeMille (dec. 1959).

Appeared in silent films.

ADAMS, EDITH

Born: 1879. Died: Jan. 10, 1957, New York, N.Y. Screen and stage actress.

ADAMS, ERNEST S.

Born: 1885. Died: Nov. 26, 1947, Hollywood, Calif. Screen and stage actor.

Appeared in: **1919** A Regular Girl. **1924** Curlytop; Hutch of the U.S.A.; The Beloved Brute. **1925** The Best People; The Pony Express; Where the Worst Begins. **1926** Hair Trigger Baxter; The Jazz Girl; Pals in Paradise; The Valley of Bravery; The Black Bird. **1927** Jewels of Desire; The Main Event; Men of Daring; The Gay Defender; Nevada; Melting Millions (serial). **1928** So This is Love; Stool Pigeon; What a Night; A Woman's Way; Tenth Avenue. **1929** One Splendid Hour; The Saturday Night Kid. **1930** The Fighting Legion; Shadow Ranch; The Storm; For the Defense. **1931** The Gang Buster; The Tip Off. **1932** Panama Flo; The Big Broadcast; Hold 'Em Jail. **1933** West of Singapore; Breed of the Border; Secrets of Hollywood. **1934** Here Comes the Groom; We're Not Dressing. **1935** Men of the Hour; The Miracle Rider (serial); The Ruggles of Red Gap; The Perfect Clue. **1936** Three on the Trail; Hopalong Cassidy Returns. **1937** San Quentin; Hopalong Rides Again; Stars over Arizona; Colorado Kid; Two Gun Law. **1938** The Purple Vigilantes; The Painted Trail. **1939** Trigger Pals. **1940** The Man with Nine Lives. **1941** The Invisible Ghost. **1942** The Pride of the Yankees; Cactus Makes Perfect (short). **1947** The Perils of Pauline; The Pretender; Buck Privates Come Home.

ADAMS, HOWARD

Born: 1909. Died: Sept. 29, 1936, Chicago, Ill. (plane crash). Screen actor, film director and radio announcer.

ADAMS, ISABEL

Born: 1856. Died: Sept. 22, 1936, Englewood, N.J. Screen and stage actress.

ADAMS, JEFF (Carol Wayne Adams)

Born: 1936. Died: May 21, 1967, Hawthorne, Calif. (plane crash). Screen, stage and television actor.

ADAMS, JOHN WOLCOTT

Born: 1874, Worcester, Mass. Died: June 3, 1925, New York, N.Y. (appendicitis). Artist, illustrator and screen actor.

Appeared in: **1913** Saved by Parcel Post.

ADAMS, KATHRYN

Born: 1894. Died: Feb. 17, 1959, Hollywood, Calif. Screen actress.

Appeared in: **1920** The Forbidden Woman; The Best of Luck. **1921** The Silver Car. **1922** The Man from Downing Street. **1924** Borrowed Husbands. **1925** Pampered Youth. **1931** The Squaw Man. **1939** Fifth Avenue Girl. **1940** Argentine Nights; If I Had My Way; Ski Patrol; Black Diamonds. **1941** The Invisible Woman; Bachelor Daddy; Meet the Chump; Unfinished Business; Saboteur; Sky Raiders (serial).

ADAMS, LESLIE

Born: 1887. Died: Mar. 26, 1936, New York, N.Y. Screen, stage, vaudeville and burlesque actor.

Appeared in: **1934** Crime without Passion.

ADAMS, MARY

Died: Nov. 30, 1973. Screen actress.

Appeared in: **1948** For the Love of Mary. **1954** Executive Suite. **1956** Rebel in Town; The Mountain. **1957** Blood of Dracula. **1962** The Clown and the Kid. **1963** Diary of a Madman.

ADAMS, NICK (Nicholas Aloysius Adamshock)

Born: July 10, 1932, Nanticoke, Pa. Died: Feb. 5, 1968, Beverly Hills, Calif. (drug overdose). Screen and television actor. Nominated for 1963 Academy Award for Best Supporting Actor in Twilight of Honor.

Appeared in: **1952** Somebody Loves Me. **1955** Rebel without a Cause; Strange Lady in Town; Picnic; The Jagged Edge; Mr. Roberts. **1956** Our Miss Brooks; The Last Wagon; A Strange Adventure; Frankenstein Meets the Giant Devil Fish. **1957** Fury at Showdown. **1958** No Time for Sergeants; Teacher's Pet; Sing, Boy, Sing. **1959** The FBI Story; Pillow Talk. **1962** The Interns; Hell Is for Heroes. **1963** Twilight of Honor; The Hook. **1964** The Young Lovers. **1965** Die, Monster, Die; Young Dillinger. **1966** Invasion of the Astro Monsters (aka Battle of the Astros, Invasion of the Astros and Monster Zero—US 1970); Frankenstein Conquers the World; Don't Worry, We'll Think of a Title. **1968** Fever Heat; Mission Mars.

ADAMS, STELLA
Died: Sept. 17, 1961. Screen actress and comedienne.

Appeared in: **1907** The Power of the Sultan. **1915** Jimmy's Little Kid; Almost a King; All in the Same Boat. **1916** A Seminary Scandal. **1926** Uppercuts (short); Honeymoon Hospital (short). **1928** Me, Gangster. **1932** Bachelor Mother. **1933** The Vampire Bat; Sister to Judas; Sing, Sinner, Sing; The Whirlwind.

ADAMS, TOMMYE (Abigail Adams)
Died: Feb. 13, 1955. Screen actress.

Appeared in: **1943** Tahiti Honey.

ADAMS, WILLIAM PERRY
Born: 1887, Tiffin, Ohio. Died: Sept. 29, 1972, New York. Screen, stage, radio, television actor and stage director. Married to actress Eleanor Wells.

Appeared in: **1945** The House on Ninety-Second Street. **1959** Odds Against Tomorrow.

ADAMSON, JAMES (William James Adamson)
Born: June 12, 1896, Calif. Died: Jan. 29, 1956, Los Angeles, Calif. (heart attack). Black screen actor.

Appeared in: **1933** Lone Cowboy. **1942** Jungle Siren. **1948** A Letter to Three Wives. **1951** The Lion Hunters. **1954** The Golden Idol. **1956** Lord of the Jungle.

ADLER, JACOB P.
Born: 1855. Died: Apr. 1, 1926, New York, N.Y. Yiddish screen, stage actor and stage producer.

Appeared in: **1914** Michael Strogoff.

ADLON, LOUIS
Died: Mar. 31, 1947, Los Angeles, Calif. (heart attack). Screen actor.

Appeared in: **1938** Dramatic School. **1939** Confessions of a Nazi Spy. **1940** Mystery Sea Raider. **1945** Counter-Attack.

ADOLFI, JOHN G. (aka JOHN ADOLPHI)
Born: Feb. 19, 1888, New York. Died: May 11, 1933, Canoe River, British Columbia (stroke). Screen, stage actor and film director. Entered films as an actor in 1909 and became director approximately 1912.

Appeared in: **1909** Napoleon, The Man of Destiny. **1912** Apartment No. 13; His Day.

ADOREE, RENEE (Renee LaFonte)
Born: Sept. 30, 1898, Lille, France. Died: Oct. 5, 1933, Tujunga, Calif. (tuberculosis). Screen actress and circus performer.

Appeared in: **1920** The Strongest. **1921** Made in Heaven. **1922** Daydreams; Monte Cristo; Honor First; Mixed Faces; A Self-Made Man; West of Chicago. **1923** The Eternal Struggle; The Six-Fifty. **1924** The Bandolero; Defying the Law; A Man's Mate; Women Who Give. **1925** The Big Parade; Exchange of Wives; Excuse Me; Parisian Nights; Man and Maid. **1926** Tin Gods; La Boheme; Blarney; The Exquisite Sinner; The Flaming Forest; The Black Bird. **1927** Mr. Wu; On Ze Boulevard; The Show; Back to God's Country; Heaven on Earth. **1928** Forbidden Hours; The Cossacks; Show People; A Certain Young Man; The Mating Call; The Michigan Kid; The Spieler. **1929** The Pagan; His Glorious Night; Tide of Empire. **1930** The Spoiler; The Singer of Seville; Redemption; Call of the Flesh.

ADRIAN, MAX (Max Cavendish)
Born: Nov. 1, 1903, Ireland. Died: Jan. 19, 1973, Surrey, England. Screen, stage and television actor.

Appeared in: **1930** The Primrose Path. **1934** Eight Cylinder Love. **1936** A Touch of the Moon; To Catch a Thief; The Happy Family; Nothing Like Publicity. **1937** Why Pick on Me?; Macushla (US 1940); When the Devil Was Well. **1938** Merely Mr. Hawkins. **1941** Kipps (aka The Remarkable Mr. Kipps —US 1942); Penn of Pennsylvania (aka The Courageous Mr. Penn—US 1944). **1942** The Young Mr. Pitt; Talk About Jacqueline. **1945** Henry V (US 1946). **1950** Her Favourite Husband (aka The Taming of Dorothy—US). **1951** Pool of London. **1952** The Pickwick Papers (US 1953). **1964** Dr. Terror's House of Horrors (US 1965). **1966** The Deadly Affair (US 1967). **1967** The Terrornauts. **1970** Julius Caesar; The Music Lovers. **1971** The Devils; The Boy Friend.

AFRIQUE (Alexander Witkin)
Born: 1907, South Africa. Died: Dec. 17, 1961, London, England. Stage and screen actor, vocalist and impersonator.

Appeared in: **1937** Let's Make a Night of It.

AGAR, JANE
Born: 1889. Died: June 10, 1948, Lakewood, Ohio. Screen and stage actress.
Appeared in silent films.

AGUGLIA, MIMI
Born: 1885, Italy. Died: July 31, 1970, Woodland Hills, Calif. Stage and screen actress.

Appeared in: **1924** The Last Man on Earth. **1933** El Eltimo Varon Sobre la Tierra; Su Ultimo Amor. **1934** Tres Amores. **1937** The Lady Escapes. **1945** A Bell for Adano. **1947** Carnival in Costa Rica; The Outlaw. **1948** Cry of the City. **1949** That Midnight Kiss. **1950** Black Hand; Deported; The Man Who Cheated Himself; Right Cross. **1951** Cuban Fireball. **1952** When in Rome. **1955** The Rose Tattoo. **1957** The Brothers Rico.

AGUIRRE, MANUEL B.
Born: 1907, Mexico. Died: Dec. 3, 1957, Mexico City, Mexico. Screen actor.

AHEARNE, TOM
Born: 1906, Boston, Mass. Died: Jan. 5, 1969, New York, N.Y. (influenza). Screen, stage and television actor.

Appeared in: **1949** Project X; The Window. **1950** Cry Murder. **1951** Mister Universe. **1968** Three in the Attic.

AHERNE, PATRICK
Born: 1901, Ireland. Died: Sept. 30, 1970, Hollywood, Calif. (cancer). Screen, stage and television actor.

Appeared in British films prior to 1933: City of Play; Oh, What a Duchess; Bindle; A Daughter in Revolt; Silver Lining; Huntingtower; Auld Lang Syne; Virginia's Husband; Carry On; The Game Chicken; Come into My Parlor. **1936** Trouble Ahead. Entered U.S. films in 1946.

Appeared in: **1947** Green Dolphin Street. **1948** The Paradine Case. **1952** Bwana Devil. **1953** Botany Bay; Rogue's March; The Royal African Rifles. **1956** The Court Jester; The Man Who Knew Too Much.

AHLERS, ANNY
Born: 1906, Germany. Died: Mar. 1933, London, England. Screen and stage actress.

Appeared in: **1931** Der Wahre Jakob. **1936** Die Marquise von Pompa-dour.

AHLM, PHILIP E.
Born: 1905. Died: July 5, 1954, Hollywood, Calif. (shot). Screen actor.

AINLEY, HENRY H.
Born: Aug. 21, 1879, Morley, England. Died: Oct. 31, 1945, London, England. Stage and screen actor. Father of actor Richard Ainley (dec. 1967).

Appeared in: **1914** A Bachelor's Love Story; She Stoops to Conquer; Called Back. **1915** The Prisoner of Zenda; Rupert of Hentzau (US 1916); Sweet Lavender; The Outrage; Iris; The Great Adventure; Brother Officers; Jelf's (aka A Man of His Word—US). **1916** The Marriage of William Ashe; Sowing the Wind; The Manxman. **1919** Quinneys. **1920** Build Thy House. **1921** Money; The Prince and the Beggarmaid. **1923** The Royal Oak; Sally Bishop. **1926** The Inscrutable Drew, Investigator (serial). **1929** Armistice (narration). **1932** The First Mrs. Fraser. **1933** The Good Companions (narration). **1936** As You Like It. **1941** Battle of the Books (short-narration).

AINLEY, RICHARD (aka RICHARD RIDDLE)
Born: Dec. 22, 1910, Stanmore, Middlesex, England. Died: May 18, 1967, London, England. Screen, stage and radio actor. Son of actor Henry Ainley (dec. 1945). Occasionally used the name of Richard Riddle on stage.

Appeared in: **1936** As You Like It. **1937** The Gang Show; Our Fighting Lady (aka Torpedoed—US 1939); The Frog (US 1939). **1938** Lily of Laguna; Old Iron. **1939** There Ain't No Justice; An Englishman's Home (aka Madmen of Europe—US); A Stolen Life. **1940** Lady with Red Hair. **1941** Singapore Woman; Bullets for O'Hara; The Smiling Ghost; Shining Victory. **1942** White Cargo. **1943** Three Hearts for Julie; I Dood It; Above Suspicion. **1949** Passage to Hong Kong.

AINSLEY, NORMAN
Born: May 4, 1881, Edinburgh, Scotland. Died: Jan. 23, 1948, Hollywood, Calif. Stage and screen actor.

Appeared in: **1930** Scotland Yard. **1933** International House, Horseplay. **1934** The Notorious Sophie Lang. **1936** Too Many Parents; Modern Times; Drawing Roomers; Tale of Two Cities; Lost Horizon; Sworn Enemy; Libeled Lady; Captains Courageous. **1937** Shall We Dance; The Shadow Strikes. **1940** Adventure in Diamonds. **1943** The Good Fellows. **1944** Man in Half Moon Street. **1945** Kitty.

AINSWORTH, SIDNEY (aka SYDNEY AINSWORTH)
Born: 1872, England. Died: May 1922, Madison, Wisc. Screen and stage actor. Entered films in 1909.

Appeared in: **1915** The White Sister. **1916** The Strange Case of Mary Page (serial). **1919** A Man and His Money; The Crimson Gardenia; Heartsease; The Girl from Outside. **1920** Madame X. **1921** Boys Will Be Boys; Hold Your

Horses; The Invisible Power; A Poor Relation; Doubling for Romeo. **1922** Mr. Barnes of New York.

AITKEN, FRANK "SPOTTISWOODE"
Born: 1869. Died: Feb. 26, 1933, Los Angeles, Calif. Screen and stage actor.

Appeared in: **1911** The Battle. **1915** Birth of a Nation. **1919** Captain Kidd, Jr.; The White Heather; Hay Foot, Straw Foot; Her Kingdom of Dreams. **1920** Nomads of the North. **1921** At the End of the World; Beyond; Reputation; The Unknown Wife. **1922** A Dangerous Game; Man of Courage; Manslaughter; Monte Cristo; One Wonderful Night; The Price of Youth; The Snowshoe Trail; The Trap; The Young Rajah. **1923** Around the World in 18 Days (serial); The Love Pirate; Merry-Go-Round; Six Days. **1924** The Fire Patrol; Lure of the Yukon; Gerald Cranston's Lady; Triumph; Those Who Dare. **1925** The Eagle; The Coast Patrol; Accused; The Goose Woman. **1926** The Power of the Weak; The Two-Gun Man. **1927** God's Great Wilderness; Roaring Fires.

AKED, MURIEL
Born: Nov. 9, 1887, Bingley, Yorkshire, England. Died: Mar. 23, 1955, Settle, Yorkshire, England. Stage and screen actress. Entered films approx. 1920.

Appeared in: **1922** A Sister to Assist 'Er. **1926** Bindle Series, incl: Bindle's Cocktail. **1930** Bed and Breakfast; The Middle Watch. **1932** Goodnight Vienna (aka Magic Night—US); The Mayor's Nest; Her First Affaire; Rome Express. **1933** Yes, Madam; The Good Companions; Trouble; Friday the Thirteenth (US 1934); No Funny Business. **1934** The Queen's Affair (aka Runaway Queen—US 1935); Evensong; Josser on the Farm; The Night of the Party; Autumn Crocus. **1935** Can You Hear Me Mother? **1936** Don't Rush Me!; Fame; Public Nuisance No. 1; Royal Eagle. **1937** Mr. Stringfellow Says No. **1939** The Girl Who Forgot; The Silent Battle (aka Continental Express—US 1942). **1941** Cottage to Let (aka Bombsight Stolen—US). **1943** The Life and Death of Colonel Blimp (aka Colonel Blimp—US 1945); The Demi Paradise (aka Adventure for Two—US 1945). **1944** 2,000 Women. **1945** They; The Wicked Lady (US 1946). **1947** Just William's Luck. **1948** William Comes to Town; So Evil My Love; It's Hard to be Good (US 1950); Accidental Spy (reissue of Mr. Stringfellow Says No—1937); A Sister to Assist 'Er (and 1922 version). **1950** The Happiest Days of Your Life. **1951** Flesh and Blood; The Wonder Kid. **1953** The Story of Gilbert and Sullivan (aka The Great Gilbert and Sullivan—US).

AKERS, HENRY CARL "HANK"
Born: 1908. Died: Aug. 22, 1967, Hollywood, Fla. Screen actor and stand-in for Johnny Weismuller.

ALADDIN (Aladdin Abdullah Achmed Anthony Pallante)
Born: 1913, New York. Died: June 9, 1970, Van Nuys, Calif. (heart disease). Screen, radio, television actor and comic singer.

ALARIE, AMANDA
Born: 1889, Canada? Died: Dec. 9, 1965. Screen actress.

ALBERNI, LUIS
Born: 1887, Spain. Died: Dec. 23, 1962, Hollywood, Calif. Stage and screen actor.

Appeared in: **1921** Little Italy. **1922** The Man from Beyond. **1923** The Bright Shawl; The Valley of Lost Souls. **1930** The Santa Fe Trail. **1931** Men in Her Life; Side Show; Svengali; Monkey Business in Africa (short); The Mad Genius; The Last Flight; I Like Your Nerve; Sweepstakes; Children of Dreams. **1932** Girl in the Tonneau; Woman in Room 13; First in War (short); The Cohens and the Kellys in Hollywood; Working Wives; Hypnotized; Guilty or Not Guilty; Crooner; The Kid from Spain; Manhattan Parade; Week-End Marriage; Cock of the Air; Big Stampede; A Parisian Romance; High Pressure. **1933** The Last Trail; Topaze; Artists Muddles (short); Sherman Said It (short); Child of Manhattan; Men Must Fight; I Love that Man; The Sphinx; When Ladies Meet; Trick for Trick; California Trial; The Man From Monterey; Above the Clouds. **1934** The Black Cat; The Captain Hates the Sea; When Strangers Meet; Goodbye Love; La Ciudad de Carton; Count of Monte Cristo; La Buenaventura; I Believed in You; Glamour; One Night of Love. **1935** Love Me Forever; Bad Boy; Roberta; The Gilded Lily; Goin' to Town; The Winning Ticket; Let's Live Tonight; In Caliente; The Gay Deception; Music is Magic; Metropolitan; Public Opinion; Manhattan Moon. **1936** Colleen; Anthony Adverse; Dancing Pirate; Ticket to Paradise; Follow Your Heart; Hat's Off. **1937** Sing and Be Happy; Two Wise Maids; Manhattan Merry-Go-Round; When You're in Love; Under Suspicion; The King and the Chorus Girl; The Great Garrick; Easy Living; Hitting a New High; Madame X. **1938** I'll Give a Million; Love on Toast. **1939** The Great Man Votes; Naughty but Nice; The Housekeeper's Daughter. **1940** Enemy Agent; Public Deb No. 1; Scatterbrain; Santa Fe Trail. **1941** They Met in Argentina; The Lady Eve; They Met in Bombay; Road to Zanzibar; San Antonio Rose; World Premier; Babes on Broadway; That Hamilton Woman. **1942** Mexican Spitfire's Elephant; Obliging Young Lady; Two Weeks to Live. **1943** Here Comes Kelly; Submarine Base; Nearly Eighteen; Here Comes Elmer; Harvest Melody; My Son, the Hero. **1944** When the Lights Go on Again; In Society; Men on Her Mind; Voice in the Wind; Machine Gun Mama. **1945** A Bell for Adano. **1946**

In Fast Company. **1950** Captain Carey, U.S.A.; When Willie Comes Marching Home. **1952** What Price Glory.

ALBERS, HANS
Born: 1892, Hamburg, Germany. Died: July 24, 1960, Munich, Germany. Screen, stage, vaudeville and circus actor.

Appeared in: **1917** Mut Zur Sunde; Rache des Gefallenen; Rauschgold. **1918** Baronesschen auf Straufurlaub; 1001 Nacht (1001 Nights). **1919** Die Prinzessin von Urbino; Der Furst. **1920** Berlin W. (aka Der Weg ins Verderben Fuhrt); Die Marquise von O. **1921** Die Grosse und die Kleine Welt; Der Falschspieler; Madeleine. **1922** Lumpaci Vagabundus; Lyda Ssanin; Menschenopfer. **1923** Fraulein Raffke. **1924** Auf Befehl der Pompadour; Das Schone Abenteuer; Gehetzte Menschen (aka Taumel); Guillotine. **1925** Der Bankkrasch unter den Linden (aka Der Herr auf der Galgenleiter); Der Konig und die Kleinen Madchen; Der Mann aus dem Jenseits (aka Feldgrau); Deutsche Herzen am Deutschen Rhein (aka Liebe und Heimat); Die Gesunkenen; Die Venus vom Montmarte; Ein Sommernachtstraum; Halbseide; Luxusweibchen (aka Ein Zeitbild Berlin-W); Mein Freund—der Chauffeur (My Friend, the Chauffeur). **1926** An der Schonen Blauen Donau; Bara en Danserska; Der Lachende Ehemann; Der Prinz und die Tanzerin (aka Der Prinz und Die Drei Probier-mamsells); Die Frau, Die Nicht "Nein" Sagen Kann; Die Versunkene Flotte (aka Die Seeschlacht Beim Skagerak); Die Villa im Tiergarten (aka Die Dame aus der Cittage-Villa); Die Warenhausprinzessin; Eine Dubarry von Heute; Es Blasen die Trompeten (aka Husarenliebe); Ich Hatt Einen Kameraden; Jagd auf Menschen; Kussen ist Keine Sunde; Nixchen; Schatz, Mach Kasse; Wir Sind um K.U.K. Infanterie-Regiment. **1927** Der Goldene Abgrund; Die Dollarprinzessin und Ihre 6 Freier (aka Die Liebeszentrale); Die Gluhende Gassie; Drei Seelen und ein Gedanke; Eine Kleine Freundin Braucht Jeder Mann; En Perfekt Gentleman; Der Grosste Gauner des Jahrhunderts; Primanerliebe; Rinaldo Rinaldini (aka Abenteuer Eines Heimgekehrten). **1928** Das Fraulein aus Argentinien (aka Das Madchen Argentinien); Der Rote Kreis (aka Rund um Europa); Dornenweg Einer Furstin (aka Zerstorte Heimat); Frauenarzt Dr. Schafer (aka Der Frauenarzt); Herr Meister und Frau Meisterin; Heut War Ich bei der Frieda; Prinzessin Olala; Rasputin's Liebesabenteuer (aka Rasputin und die Frauen); Saxophon-Susie; Weib in Flammen (aka Die Geschichte Einer Leidenschaft); Wer das Scheiden Hat Erfunden (aka Die Juwelen der Furstin Ljuba). **1929** Ja, Ja, Die Frauen Sind Meine Schwache Seite; Mascottchen (aka Bist du es Lachendes Gluck); Moblierte Zimmer (aka Der Sturmfreie Junggeselle); Teure Heimat (aka Drei Machen ihr Gluck); Vererbte Triebe; der Kampf ums Neue Geschlecht (aka Erbsunde). **1930** Der Greifer; Hans in Allen Gassen; Der Blaue Engel (The Blue Angel); Die Nacht Gehoert Uns (The Night Belongs to Us—US 1932). **1931** Bomben Auf Monte Carlo (Monte Carlo Madness); Der Draufganger (The Daredevil); Der Sieger (The Victor); Drei Tage Liebe (Three Days of Love). **1932** Liebe Ist Lieb (Love is Love); Koenigin der Unterwelt; Heut Kommts Drauf An (US 1933); Quick, Koenig der Clowns (US 1933); Der Weisse Damon (aka Rauschgift). **1933** Ein Gewisser Herr Gran; F.P.I. Antwortet Nicht (German version only); Fluchtlinge (German propaganda film). **1934** Gold; Peer Gynt (US 1939). **1935** Variete; Henker, Frauen und Soldaten (Hangmen, Women and Soldiers—US 1940). **1936** Casanova; Mord im Savoy (Savoy-Hotel 217); Der Mann, der Sherlock Holmes War; Unter Heissem Himmel. **1937** Fahrendes Volk (aka Gehetzter Gaukler); Die Gelbe Flagge. **1938** Sergeant Berry. **1939** Zwei Lustige Abenteurer (Two Merry Adventurers); Wasser fur Cantoga; Ein Mann auf Abwegen. **1940** Trenck, der Pandur. **1941** Carl Peters (German propaganda film). **1942** Munchhausen (US 1943). **1944** Gross Freiheit Nr. 7 (aka La Paloma); Shiva und die Galgenblume. **1947** . . . und Uber uns der Himmel. **1950** City of Torment; Fohn. **1951** Blaubart. **1952** Nachts auf den Strassen; Kapt'n Bay-Bay. **1953** Johnny Rettet Nebrador; Auf der Reeperbahn Nachts um Halb Eins; The White Hell of Pitz Palu. **1954** An Jedem Finger Zehn. **1955** Der Letzte Mann (The Last Laugh).

ALBERT, DAN
Born: 1890, Nashville, Tenn. Died: Aug. 1919, Nashville, Tenn. Screen actor.

ALBERTSON, ARTHUR W.
Born: Jan. 6, 1891, Waycross, Georgia. Died: Oct. 20, 1926, New York, N.Y. Stage and screen actor. Married to actress Esther Howard (dec. 1965).

Appeared in: **1916** It Happened in Honolulu. **1917** The Argyle Case.

ALBERTSON, FRANK
Born: Feb. 2, 1909, Fergus Falls, Minn. Died: Feb. 29, 1964, Santa Monica, Calif. Screen, stage and television actor. Entered films in 1922.

Appeared in: **1928** Prep and Pep; The Farmer's Daughter. **1929** Salute; Words and Music; Blue Skies; Happy Days. **1930** Son of the Gods; The Big Party; Born Reckless; Men without Women; So This Is London; Wild Company; Just Imagine; Spring Is Here. **1931** The Connecticut Yankee; The Brat; The Tiger's Son; Big Business Girl; Old Greatheart; Traveling Husbands. **1932** Lost Special (serial); The Cohens and the Kellys in Hollywood; Way Back Home; Huddle. **1933** King for a Night; Ann Carver's Profession; Dangerous Crossroads; Midshipman Jack; Ever in My Heart; Racing Youth; Impossible Lover; Air Mail; Billion Dollar Scandal; The Cohens and the Kellys in Trouble; Rainbow Over Broadway. **1934** The Last Gentleman; The Life of Vergie Winters; Bachelor of

Arts; Hollywood Hoodlum; Enter Madame. 1935 Doubting Thomas; Alice Adams; Ah, Wilderness; Personal Maid's Secret; East of Java; Kind Lady; Waterfront Lady. 1936 The Farmer in the Dell; Fury; The Plainsman. 1937 Navy Blue and Gold. 1938 Hold That Kiss; Spring Madness; The Shining Hour; Mother Carey's Chickens; Fugitives for a Night; Room Service. 1939 Bachelor Mother. 1940 Framed; Dr. Christian Meets the Women; The Ghost Comes Home; When the Daltons Rode; Behind the News. 1941 Man-Made Monster; Louisiana Purchase; Ellery Queen's Penthouse Mystery; Citadel of Crime; Flying Cadets; Father Steps Out; City Limits; Burma Convoy. 1942 Wake Island; Underground Agent; Shepherd of the Ozarks; The Man From Headquarters; Junior G-Men of the Air (serial); City of Silent Men. 1943 Keep 'Em Slugging; Here Comes Elmer; O, My Darling Clementine; Mystery Broadcast. 1944 And the Angels Sing; I Love a Soldier; Rosie the Riveter. 1945 Arson Squad; How Do You Do? 1946 They Made Me a Killer; Gay Blades; It's A Wonderful Life; Ginger. 1947 Killer Dill; The Hucksters. 1948 Shed No Tears. 1956 Nightfall. 1957 The Enemy Below. 1958 The Last Hurrah. 1960 Psycho. 1961 Girl on the Run; Man-Trap. 1962 Don't Knock the Twist. 1963 Johnny Cool; Bye Bye Birdie.

ALBRIGHT, BOB "OKLAHOMA"
Born: 1884. Died: Apr. 30, 1971, Hollywood, Calif. (heart attack). Screen, stage, vaudeville actor and orchestra leader.

Appeared in: 1929 Oklahoma Bob Albright and His Rodeo Do Flappers (short).

ALBRIGHT, HARDIE (Hardy Albrecht)
Born: Dec. 16, 1903, Charleroi, Penn. Died: Dec. 7, 1975, Mission Viejo, Calif. (heart failure). Screen, stage, television actor and writer. Divorced from actress Martha Sleeper and later married to Arnita Wallace.

Appeared in: 1931 Heartbreak; Hotel Continental; Young Sinners; Skyline. 1932 The Purchase Price; Jewel Robbery; The Crash; A Successful Calamity; Cabin in the Cotton; This Sporting Age; So Big; Match King. 1933 The Working Man; Song of Songs; Three-Cornered Moon; The House on 56th Street. 1934 The Scarlet Letter; The Ninth Guest; White Heat; Nana; Beggar's Holiday; Two Heads on a Pillow; Silver Streak; Sing Sing Nights. 1935 Red Salute; Women Must Dress: Calm Yourself; Ladies Love Danger; Champagne for Breakfast. 1940 Ski Patrol; Granny Get Your Gun; Carolina Moon. 1941 Flight from Destiny; Marry the Boss's Daughter; Men of Timberland; Bachelor Daddy. 1942 The Pride of the Yankees; The Loves of Edgar Allen Poe; Lady in a Jam. 1944 Army Wives. 1945 Jade Mask; Sunset in Eldorado; Captain Tugboat Annie. 1946 Angel on My Shoulder. 1947 The Gangster.

ALCALDE, MARIO
Born: 1927. Died: Apr. 22, 1971, Los Angeles, Calif. (cancer). Screen, stage and television actor.

Appeared in: 1956 Crowded Paradise. 1960 All the Young Men. 1964 Dead Ringer. 1969 Hail, Hero!

ALCOCK, DOUGLAS
Born: 1908. Died: Oct. 14, 1970, Cinecitta, Italy (heart attack). Screen, stage actor and film director.

ALDEA, MERCEDES
Born: Spain. Died: Oct. 28, 1954, Sabadell, Spain (killed when struck by airplane propeller while filming What Never Dies). Screen actress.

ALDEN, BETTY
Born: 1898. Died: Apr. 1948, Beverly Hills, Calif. Screen and stage actress.

Appeared in: 1930 Lightnin'. 1934 The Fountain. 1935 The Nut Farm.

ALDEN, MARY (Mary Maguire Alden)
Born: 1883, New Orleans, La. Died: July 2, 1946, Woodland Hills, Calif. Stage and screen actress.

Appeared in: 1915 Birth of a Nation. 1916 Hell-to-Pay; Austin. 1919 The Unpardonable Sin. 1920 Milestone; Honest Hutch. 1921 The Old Nest; Snowblind; Trust Your Wife; Parted Curtains; The Witching Hour. 1922 Man with Two Mothers; A Woman's Woman; The Bond Boy; The Hidden Woman; Notoriety. 1923 Pleasure Mad; The Eagle's Feather; The Empty Cradle; Has the World Gone Mad!; The Steadfast Heart; The Tents of Allah. 1924 Babbitt; A Fool's Awakening; Painted People; The Beloved Brute; When a Girl Loves; Soiled. 1925 Faint Perfume; The Happy Warrior; Siege; Under the Rouge; The Plastic Age; The Unwritten Law. 1926 April Fool; Brown of Harvard; The Earth Woman; Lovely Mary. 1927 The Potters; The Joy Girl; Twin Flappers. 1928 Ladies of the Mob; The Cossacks; Fools for Luck; Sawdust Paradise; Someone to Love. 1929 Girl Overboard. 1932 Hell's House; Strange Interlude.

ALDERSON, ERVILLE
Born: 1883. Died: Aug. 4, 1957, Glendale, Calif. Screen actor.

Appeared in: 1921 The Good-Bad Wife. 1923 The Exciters; The White Rose. 1924 America; Isn't Life Wonderful. 1925 Sally of the Sawdust. 1926 The White Black Sheep. 1927 The Girl from Chicago; The Heart of Maryland; The

Price of Honor; Salvation Jane. 1928 A Thief in the Dark; The Fortune Hunter; Fazil; Fleetwing. 1929 Speakeasy. 1930 The Bad Man; Guilty?; Redemption; The Dawn Trail. 1931 Too Many Cooks; The Lash; Arrowsmith; Shanghaied Love. 1932 Alias the Doctor; Cabin in the Cotton; They Call It Sin; I Am a Fugitive from a Chain Gang. 1933 To the Last Man. 1934 Lazy River; The Scarlet Empress. 1935 Square Shooter; The County Chairman; Woman Wanted; Pursuit; Public Opinion; The Virginia Judge; Seven Keys to Baldpate. 1936 Educating Father; Career Woman; Jungle Princess. 1937 The Mighty Treve; Small Town Boy. 1938 Love Finds Andy Hardy. 1939 Jesse James; Mr. Smith Goes to Washington; Romance of the Redwoods; Andy Hardy Gets Spring Fever; The Hardys Ride High; Outside These Walls; Nancy Drew—Trouble Shooter; Vitaphone short. 1940 Santa Fe Trail; Dr. Kildare Goes Home. 1941 Sergeant York; Bad Men of Missouri; Parachute Battalion. 1942 The Commandos Strike at Dawn; My Favorite Blonde; The Postman Didn't Ring; The Loves of Edgar Allan Poe; You Can't Escape Forever; Careful; Soft Shoulders. 1943 First Comes Courage. 1945 Along Came Jones. 1947 Smash-Up; The Story of a Woman. 1948 Shanghai Chest; The Feathered Serpent. 1949 Mr. Whitney Had a Notion (short). 1952 Something to Live For.

ALDRICH, MARISKA
Born: March 27, 1881, Mass. Died: Sept. 28, 1965, Los Angeles, Calif. (acute intestinal obstruction). Opera singer and screen actress.

Appeared in: 1934 Lady by Choice. 1939 At the Circus. 1941 You're the One; Whistling in the Dark.

ALDRIDGE, ALFRED
Born: 1876, New Orleans, La. Died: May 4, 1934, Hollywood, Calif. Stage and screen actor.

Appeared in: 1921 It Can Be Done.

ALEXANDER, A. L.
Born: 1906, Boston, Mass. Died: Feb. 24, 1967. Screen actor, radio announcer and screenwriter.

Appeared in: 1934 War Is a Racket. 1937 Private Life of the Gannets (short).

ALEXANDER, BEN (Nicholas Benton Alexander)
Born: May 26, 1911, Goldfield, Nev. Died: June, 1969, Westchester, Calif. (natural causes). Screen, television actor, radio emcee and announcer.

Appeared in: 1916 Each Pearl a Tear (film debut). 1918 Hearts of the World. 1919 The Turn in the Road; The White Heather. 1921 The Heart Line. 1922 In the Name of the Law. 1923 Penrod and Sam; Boy of Mine. 1924 Jealous Husbands; A Self-Made Failure. 1925 Pampered Youth; Flaming Love; The Shining Adventure; Frivolous Sal. 1926 Scotty of the Scouts (serial); The Highbinders. 1927 Fighting for Fame (serial). 1930 All Quiet on the Western Front. 1931 A Wise Child; Many a Slip; Are These Our Children?; Mystery Ship; Suicide Fleet. 1932 The Strange Love of Molly Louvain; Tom Brown of Culver; The Vanishing Frontier; High Pressure. 1933 What Price Innocence?; This Day and Age; Stage Mother. 1934 Once to Every Woman; The Most Precious Thing in Life; The Life of Vergie Winters. 1935 Reckless Roads; Splendor; Grand Old Girl; Annapolis Farewell; Born to Gamble; The Fire Trap. 1936 Hearts in Bondage. 1937 Red Lights Ahead; The Outer Gate; Behind Prison Bars; Western Gold. 1938 The Spy Ring; Mr. Doodle Kicks Off. 1939 Convicts' Code. 1940 The Leather Pushers. 1954 Dragnet. 1957 Pay the Devil; Man in the Shadow.

ALEXANDER, CLAIRE
Born: 1898. Died: Nov. 16, 1927, Alhambra, Calif. (double pneumonia). One of the first Mack Sennett bathing beauties and was in early Keystone films.

Appeared in: 1917 Jerry's Big Mystery; Jerry's Brilliant Scheme; Jerry's Triple Alliance; Jerry's Romance; Minding the Baby; Be Sure You're Right; The Lady Detective; The Ransom; Jerry's Picnic; Jerry's Finishing Touch; Jerry Joins the Army; Jerry's Master Stroke; Jerry and the Bully; Jerry's Soft Snap; Jerry's Lucky Day; Jerry and the Vampire; Jerry's Running Fight; Jerry's Victory; Jerry and the Burglars; Jerry Takes Gas; Jerry's Boarding House; Jerry's Best Friend. 1920 The Fatal Sign (serial).

ALEXANDER, EDWARD
Born: 1888. Died: Aug. 15, 1964, Dearborn, Ohio (heart attack). Screen actor and film producer. Entered films in 1910.

Appeared in: 1915 The Terror of the Fold; Bait; Curse of the Black Pearl. 1917 Chosen Prince (aka The Friendship of David and Jonathan); North of 53. 1918 The Wild Strain. 1919 The Island of Intrigue. 1920 The Heart of Youth.

ALEXANDER, FRANK "FATTY"
Born: 1879. Died: Sept 8, 1937, North Hollywood, Calif. Screen actor. Entered films in 1913 with Keystone.

Appeared in: 1923 Cyclone Jones. 1925 SOS Perils of the Sea. 1926 Oh, What a Night! 1927 Play Safe.

ALEXANDER, GEORG (Werner Louis Georg Luddeckens)
Born: 1889, 1892 or 1895 (?), Hannover, Germany. Died: 1945, Berlin, Germany. Stage and screen actor. Entered films in 1919.

Appeared in: 1919 Fahrt ins Blaue; Die Platonische Ehe. 1920 Falscher Start; Der Mann ohne Namen (The Man Without a Name). 1921 Das Madchen aus der Fremde. 1922 Der Film ohne Name; Lady Hamilton; Das Madchen aus dem Goldenen Westen; Das Spiel mit dem Weibe; Stubbs, der Detektiv; Die Tanzerin des Konigs; Vanina oder die Galgenhochzeit; Der Frauenkonig. 1923 Die Frau mit den Millionen; Liebe macht Blind (Love Makes One Blind); Das Milliardensouper; Das Paradies im Schnee. 1924 Die Grosse Unbekannte; Komodianten des Lebens; Mein Leopold; Das Schone Abenteuer; Die Schonste Frau der Welt. 1925 Eifersucht (Jealousy); Herrn Filip Collins Abenteuer; Der Herr ohne Wohnung; Husarenfieber. 1926 Gasthaus zur Ehe; Die Insel der Verbotenen Kusse; Die Kleine vom Variete; Die Muhle von Sanssouci; Nanette macht Alles; Die Welt will Belogen Sein; Colonialskandal (aka Liebe im Rausch). 1927 Die Dame mit dem Tigerfell; Die Dollarprinzessin und Ihre sechs Freier; Eins plus Eins Gleich Drei; Flucht vor Blonde; Die Frau Ohne Namen; Die Indiskrete Frau; Die Jagd nach der Braut; Der Kampf um den Mann; Der Orlow; Venus im Frack. 1928 Dyckerpott's Erben; Er geht Rechts-Sie Geht Links; Die Grosse Abenteurerin; Leontines Ehemanner; Liebe im Schnee; Die Lustigen Vagabunden; Mikosch Rucht; Prinzessin Olala; Sechs Madchen Suchten Nachtquartier; Unmoral; Was Ist los mit Nanette. 1929 Autobus Nr. 2; Die Garde-Diva; Der Leutnant ihrer Majestat; Das Recht auf Liebe; Schwarzwaldmadel; Ehestreik. 1930 Die Singende Stadt; Liebeswalzer (Love Waltz); Zartlichkeit; Leutnant Warst du Einst bei den Husaren; Geld auf der Strasse. 1931 Die Brautigamswitwe (Bridegroom for Two); Der Liebesexpress; Wiener Liebschaften; Trara um Liebe; Opernredoute; Der Verjungte Adolar; Die Fledermaus; Hurrarein Junge!; Nitouche; Ehe G.m.b.H. 1932 Das Testament der Cornelius Gulden; Wie sag' ich's Meinem Mann; Durchlaucht Amusiert Sich; Ein Bisschen Liebe fur Dich; Flucht nach Nizza (Ein Ganz Verflixter Kerl); Wenn die Liebe Mode Macht; Moderne Mitgift; Liebe, Scherz und Ernst. 1933 Und wer Kusst Mich?; Mein Liebster Ist ein Jagersmann; Madame Wunscht Keine Kinder; Eine Frau wie Du; Der Zarewitsch; Ist Mein; Mann Nicht Fabelhaft?; Liebe Muss Verstanden Sein. 1934 Das Blumenmadchen vom Grande-Hotel; Zigeunerblut; Der Doppelganger; G'schichten aus dem Wienerwald; Die Englische Heirat; Alles Hort auf Mein Kommando. 1935 Tanzmusik; Der Alte und der Junge Konig; Ein Falscher Fullziger; Ein Idealer Gatte; Der Schlafwagenkontrolleur; Ein Madel aus Guter Familie; Ein Teufelskerl; Der Vogelhandler; Rendezvous am Rhein. 1936 Martha; Das Frauenparadies; Das Schloss in Flandern; Donaumelodien; Madchen in Weiss; Eskapade. 1937 Abenteuer in Warschau; Eine Nacht mit Hindernissen; Die Fledermaus (and 1931 version); Krach und Gluck bei Kunnemann; Hahn im Korb; Karussell; Zwei mal Zwei im Himmelbett. 1938 Verliebtes Abenteuer; Das Madchen von Gestern Nacht; Der Fall Deruga; Gelt Fallt vom Himmel; Heimat; Die Frau am Scheidewege; Kleiner Mann; Ganz Gross; Unsere Kleine Frau; Gastspiel im Paradies. 1939 Wenn Manner Verreisen; Leinen aus Irland; Frau am Steuer; Der Arme Millionar; Die Kluge Schwiegermutter. 1940 Was Will Brigitte?; Der Kleinstadtpoet. 1941 Das Himmelblaue Abendkleid; Oh Diese Manner; Frau Luna; Frauen sind doch Bessere Diplomaten. 1942 Ein Zug Fahrt Ab. c. 1943 Abenteuer im Grandhotel; Die Beiden Schwestern; Und die Musik Spielt Dazu. 1944 Die Frau Meiner Traume; Der Meisterdetektiv.

ALEXANDER, JAMES "JIMMY" (James Burnel Alexander)
Born: Apr. 25, 1902, Indiana. Died: Jan. 31, 1961, Hollywood, Calif. (diabetes, arteriosclerosis). Screen, stage and television actor. Do not confuse with James Alexander who appeared in later films.

Appeared in: 1952 Jack and the Beanstalk. 1955 Las Vegas Shakedown; Treasure of Ruby Hills.

ALEXANDER, JOHN
Born: 1865. Died: Apr. 5, 1951, Ontario, Calif. Screen and stage actor. In recent years a stand-in for Guy Kibbee and Donald Meek. Do not confuse with John Alexander born in 1897.

ALEXANDER, LOIS A.
Born: 1891, Warsaw, Indiana. Died: May 3, 1962, Washington, D.C. (stroke). Screen, television actress and dancer. Do not confuse with silent screen actress Lois Alexander.

ALEXANDER, MARA (Mara Levine)
Born: Feb. 7, 1914, New York. Died: May 23, 1965, San Francisco, Calif. (pneumonia). Stage and screen actress.

Appeared in: 1939 The Rains Came.

ALEXANDER, RENE
Died: 1914, France. Screen actor.

Appeared in: 1915 The Old Thespian.

ALEXANDER, ROSS
Born: July 27, 1907, Brooklyn, N.Y. Died: Jan. 2, 1937, Los Angeles, Calif.

(suicide—gun). Stage and screen actor. Married to actress Anna Nagel (dec. 1966).

Appeared in: 1932 The Wiser Sex. 1934 Flirtation Walk; Gentlemen Are Born; Loudspeaker Lowdown; Social Register. 1935 A Midsummer Night's Dream; Captain Blood; We're in the Money; Shipmates Forever; Going Highbrow; Maybe It's Love. 1936 Brides Are Like That; I Married a Doctor; Boulder Dam; China Clipper; Hot Money; Here Comes Carter! 1937 Ready, Willing and, Able.

ALEXANDER, SARA
Born: 1839. Died: Dec. 24, 1926, New York, N.Y. Screen and stage actress.

ALEXANDER, SUZANNE
Died: Sept. 21, 1975. Screen actress.

Appeared in: 1953 Cat Women of the Moon. 1954 Down Three Dark Streets; Princess of the Nile. 1955 The Girl in the Red Velvet Swing.

ALEXANDER THE GREAT
Died: Aug. 1933, Bridgeport, Ohio (old age and excessive heat). Stage and screen animal performer (German police dog).

Appeared in 241 films.

ALGARO, GABRIEL
Born: 1888. Died: Oct. 1951, Sargozza, Spain. Screen, stage actor and film director.

ALGIER, SIDNEY H.
Born: Dec. 5, 1889, Shamokin, Pa. Died: Apr. 24, 1945, West Los Angeles, Calif. (heart attack). Screen, stage, vaudeville, burlesque actor, film director and screenwriter. Entered films as an actor in 1915.

ALI, GEORGE
Born: 1866. Died: Apr. 26, 1947, Freeport, N.Y. Screen actor and animal impersonator.

Appeared in: 1924 Peter Pan.

ALIPPI, ELIAS
Died: May 4, 1942, Buenos Aires, Argentina. Screen actor.

Appeared in: 1939 Viento Norte (North Wind); Cadetes de San Martin. 1940 Asi es la Vida (Such Is Life). 1942 Viejo Hucha.

ALLBEURY, DAISY
Born: 1885. Died: Oct. 1961, London, England. Screen film extra.

ALLEBORN, AL
Born: 1892. Died: June 14, 1968, Hollywood, Calif. (leukemia). Retired studio executive and former assistant director who entered films as a stuntman.

ALLEGRET, MARC
Born: 1900, France. Died: Nov. 3, 1973, Paris, France. Screen actor, film director and screenwriter.

Appeared in: 1960 Et Mourir de Plaisir (aka Blood and Roses—US 1961).

ALLEN, ALFRED
Born: 1866, Alfred, N.Y. Died: June 18, 1947. Screen actor.

Appeared in: 1916 The Yoke of Gold; The Unattainable; The Price of Victory; A Child of Mystery. 1917 The Price of a Good Time (aka The Whim). 1918 The Lion's Claw (serial). 1919 The Red Glove (serial). 1920 An Old Fashioned Boy. 1921 The New Disciple; O'Malley of the Mounted; The Sage Hen. 1922 The Pride of Palomar; Colleen of the Pines; Shattered Idols. 1923 Desert Driven; A Gentleman of Leisure; The Grub Stake; The Miracle Baby; A Noise in Newboro; Shootin' for Love. 1924 Abraham Lincoln; Stolen Secrets; A Girl of the Limberlost. 1925 Bustin' Thru; Dangerous Innocence; Speed. 1926 The Mystery Club; Rolling Home. 1927 Singed; The Outlaw Dog; The Golden Yukon; Out all Night; The Magic Garden. 1928 Anybody Here Seen Kelly?; Hot News; The Fifty-Fifty Girl; Under the Tonto Rim. 1929 The Flying Fleet; Sunset Pass.

ALLEN, ARTHUR B.
Born: 1881. Died: Aug. 25, 1947, New York, N.Y. Screen, stage actor and radio emcee.

Appeared in: 1937 Ebb Tide. 1940 Our Town; Rangers of Fortune.

ALLEN, BAMBI
Died: Jan. 21, 1973. Screen actress.

Appeared in: 1968 Someone. 1969 The Ribald Tales of Robin Hood; The Fabulous Bastard from Chicago; The Hanging of Jake Ellis; Satan's Sadists; Wild Outtakes. 1970 Angels Die Hard!; The Bang Bang Gang; Hell's Bloody Devils'; How to Succeed with Sex.

ALLEN, DOROTHY
Born: 1896. Died: Sept. 30, 1970, N.Y. Stage and screen actress.

Appeared in: 1921 Beyond Price; The Power Within; Dynamite Allen. 1922 The Broken Silence; Free Air. 1923 If Winter Comes. 1924 Second Youth; The Hoosier Schoolmaster. 1925 Pearl of Love; School for Wives.

ALLEN, ETHAN
Born: 1882. Died: Aug. 21, 1940, Hollywood, Calif. Screen, stage actor, film director and screenwriter.

Appeared in: 1930 The Border Legion. 1931 The Flood. 1939 Trigger Pals.

ALLEN, FRED (John Florence Sullivan)
Born: May 31, 1894, Cambridge, Mass. Died: Mar. 17, 1956, New York, N.Y. (heart attack). Screen, stage, vaudeville actor, columnist, radio emcee and film director. Billed in vaudeville as "Fred St. James," "Freddie James, World's Worst Juggler" and "Paul Huckle, European Entertainer." In 1927 was part of emcee team "Allen and York."

Appeared in: 1929 Fred Allen's Prize Playettes (short). 1930 The Still Alarm (short). 1935 Thanks a Million. 1938 Sally, Irene and Mary. 1940 Love Thy Neighbor. 1945 It's in the Bag (aka The Fifth Chair). 1952 We're Not Married; O. Henry's Full House. 1956 Fabulous Hollywood (film clips).

ALLEN, GRACIE (Grace Ethel Cecile Rosale Allen)
Born: July 26, 1906, San Francisco, Calif. Died: Aug. 28, 1964, Los Angeles, Calif. (heart attack). Screen, vaudeville, radio and television actress. Married to actor George Burns and was half of comedy team "Burns and Allen." She was known as "the smartest dumbbell in the history of show business."

Appeared with Burns in: 1929 Lamb Chops (short). 1930 Pulling a Bone (short); Fit to Be Tied (short). 1931 Burns and Allen (short); The Antique Shop (short); Once over Lightly (short); One Hundred Percent Service (short). 1932 The Big Broadcast of 1932; Oh, My Operation (short); The Babbling Book (short); Hollywood on Parade #2 (short). 1933 International House; College Humor; Walking the Baby (short); Let's Dance (short). 1934 Six of a Kind; Many Happy Returns; We're Not Dressing; College Rhythm. 1935 Love in Bloom; Here Comes Cookie; The Big Broadcast of 1936. 1936 College Holiday; The Big Broadcast of 1937. 1937 A Damsel in Distress. 1938 College Swing. 1939 Honolulu. 1944 Hollywood on Parade. 1954 Hollywood Grows Up (film clips); Hollywood Fathers (film clips). Appeared without Burns in: 1939 Gracie Allen Murder Case. 1941 Mr. and Mrs. North. 1944 Two Girls and a Sailor.

ALLEN, HUGH (Hugh Clifford Allen)
Born: Nov. 19, 1886, Canada. Died: Sept. 13, 1966, Los Angeles, Calif. (suicide—jumped from building). Screen actor. Do not confuse with actor Hugh Allan, born 1903.

ALLEN, JANE MARIE
Born: 1916. Died: Feb. 16, 1970, Santa Monica, Calif. Screen actress and dancer.

ALLEN, JOE
Born: 1888. Died: Jan. 31, 1955, Hollywood, Calif. Screen actor.

ALLEN, JOSEPH, JR.
Born: Mar. 30, 1918, Boston, Mass. Died: Nov. 9, 1962, Patchogue, N.Y. Screen, stage and television actor. Son of actor Joseph Allen, Sr. (dec. 1952).

Appeared in: 1936 Motor Madness. 1939 Lucky Night; Our Leading Citizen. 1942 Who Is Hope Schuyler?; Death of Champion; Right to the Heart; It Happened in Flatbush; The Night before the Divorce. 1946 Dangerous Money. 1947 I Cover Big Town; Road to the Big House. 1948 The Time of Your Life.

ALLEN, JOSEPH, SR.
Born: 1872. Died: Sept. 9, 1952, Newton, Mass. Screen and stage actor. Father of actor Joseph Allen, Jr. (dec. 1962).

Appeared in: 1912 Essaney films. 1929 Seven Keys to Baldpate.

ALLEN, LESTER
Born: 1891, England. Died: Nov. 6, 1949, Hollywood, Calif. (struck by auto). Screen, stage, vaudeville, minstrel, burlesque, circus actor and film director.

Appeared in: 1930 Leave It to Lester. 1932–33 Paramount shorts. 1943 The Heat's On. 1945 The Great Flamario; The Dolly Sisters. 1946 The Dark Mirror. 1948 Crime on Their Hands (short); The Pirate; That Lady in Ermine. 1949 Ma and Pa Kettle.

ALLEN, MAUDE (Maude Allen Giannone)
Died: Nov. 7, 1956, Washington. Stage and screen actress.

Appeared in: 1930 La Grande Mare (The Big Pond). 1931 The Smiling Lieutenant. 1935 The Cowboy Millionaire; It's in the Air; Whispering Smith Speaks. 1936 The Captain's Kid. 1937 Secret Valley. 1938 Painted Desert. 1939 The Women. 1940 Black Diamonds. 1942 Juke Box Jennie; I Married an Angel.

ALLEN, PHYLLIS
Born: 1861. Died: Mar. 26, 1938, Los Angeles, Calif. Screen and vaudeville actress.

Appeared in: 1914 Caught in a Cabaret (reissued as The Jazz Waiter); The Property Man; The Rounders; Dough and Dynamite (reissued as The Doughnut Designers); Gentlemen of Nerve (reissued as Some Nerve); Fatty's Jonah Day; Getting Acquainted. 1915 Giddy, Gay and Ticklish (reissued as A Gay Lothario); Gussle's Wayward Path; Fickle Fatty's Fall; A Submarine Pirate; A Movie Star; The Judge.

ALLEN, SAM
Born: 1861, Md. Died: Sept. 13, 1934, Los Angeles, Calif. Stage and screen actor. Entered films with Biograph in 1910.

Appeared in: 1921 The Conflict. 1922 Forget-Me-Not; The Son of the West; Confidence. 1923 Are You a Failure?; The Virginian. 1925 Timber Wolf: Bashful Buccaneer; Midnight Limited. 1926 The Call of the Klondike; Man Rustlin'; The Sea Beast. 1927 Blackjack; Death Valley; Mother; Woman's Law. 1928 Burning Bridges. 1930 The Sea Wolf. 1934 The Last Round-Up.

ALLEN, VIOLA
Born: 1869. Died: May 9, 1948, New York, N.Y. Screen and stage actress. Daughter of stage actor C. Leslie Allen (dec.).

Appeared in: 1915 The White Sister.

ALLENBY, THOMAS
Born: 1861, Australia. Died: Dec. 19, 1933, Hollywood, Calif. Screen actor.

ALLERTON, LITTLE HELEN (aka HELEN KILDUFF and HELEN SCHWEISTHAL)
Born: 1888. Died: Nov. 4, 1959, Golf, Ill. Screen, stage and vaudeville actress. Appeared in vaudeville as part of "May and Kilduff" team. Entered films with Essanay and Selig Studios in Chicago and appeared in films from 1910 to 1916.

ALLGOOD, SARA
Born: Oct. 31, 1883, Dublin, Ireland. Died: Sept. 13, 1950, Woodland Hills, Calif. (heart attack). Stage and screen actress.

Appeared in: 1929 Blackmail (film debut); Juno and the Paycock (aka The Shame of Mary Boyle—US). 1932 The World, the Flesh and the Devil. 1933 The Fortunate Fool. 1934 Irish Hearts (aka Norah O'Neale—US); Lily of Killarney (aka Bride of the Lake—US). 1935 The Passing of the Third Floor Back; Lazybones; Peg of Old Drury (US 1936); Riders to the Sea. 1936 Pot Luck; Southern Roses; It's Love Again. 1937 Storm in a Teacup; The Sky's the Limit; Kathleen Mavourneen (aka Kathleen—US 1938). 1938 The Londonderry Air. 1939 On the Night of the Fire (aka The Fugitive—US 1940). 1941 That Hamilton Woman; How Green Was My Valley; Dr. Jekyll and Mr. Hyde; Lydia. 1942 The War Against Mrs. Hadley; Roxie Hart; This Above All; It Happened in Flatbush; Life Begins at 8:30. 1943 City Without Men. 1944 The Lodger; Between Two Worlds; Jane Eyre; Keys of the Kingdom. 1945 The Strange Affair of Uncle Harry. 1946 Cluny Brown; Kitty; The Spiral Staircase. 1947 Mother Wore Tights; The Fabulous Dorseys; Ivy; Mourning Becomes Electra; My Wild Irish Rose. 1948 One Touch of Venus; The Man from Texas; The Girl from Manhattan; The Accused. 1949 Challenge to Lassie. 1950 Sierra; Cheaper by the Dozen.

ALLISON, STEVE
Born: 1916. Died: Mar. 6, 1969, Hollywood, Calif. (lung cancer). Screen actor, radio emcee and singer.

Appeared in: 1957 The Burglar.

ALLISTER, CLAUD (Claud Palmer)
Born: Oct. 3, 1893, London, England. Died: July 26, 1970, Santa Barbara, Calif. Stage and screen actor. Entered films in 1929.

Appeared in: 1929 The Trial of Mary Dugan; Bulldog Drummond; Three Live Ghosts; Charming Sinners. 1930 Monte Carlo; The Floradora Girl; The Czar of Broadway; Slightly Scarlet; In the Next Room; Such Men Are Dangerous; Murder Will Out; Ladies Love Brutes. 1931 On the Loose (short); Captain Applejack; Reaching for the Moon; Meet the Wife; Papa Loves Mamma; I Like Your Nerve; Rough-House Rhythm (short); Platinum Blonde. 1932 The Midshipman; Two White Arms (aka Wives Beware—US 1933); Diamond Cut Diamond (aka Blame the Woman—US); The Return of Raffles. 1933 The Medicine Man; That's My Wife; Sleeping Car; The Private Life of Henry VIII; Excess Baggage. 1934 The Lady is Willing; Those Were the Days; The Return of Bulldog Drummond; The Private Lives of Don Juan. 1935 The Dark Angel; Three Live Ghosts (and 1929 version). 1936 Dracula's Daughter; Yellowstone. 1937 Bulldog Drummond at Bay; Danger—Love at Work; Radio Parade of 1937; The Awful Truth; Let's Make a Night of It (US 1938). 1938 Men Are Such Fools; Storm Over Bengal; Kentucky Moonshine; The Blonde Cheat. 1939 Arrest Bulldog Drummond; Captain Fury. 1940 Lillian Russell. 1941 Charley's Aunt; The Reluctant Dragon; A Yank in the RAF; Confirm or Deny. 1943 Forever and a Day; Hundred Pound Widow. 1944 Kiss the Bride Goodbye. 1945 Don Chicago; Dumb Dora Discovers Tobacco. 1946 Gaiety

George (US 1948). **1947** Fag End (reissue of Dumb Dora Discovers Tobacco—US 1945). **1948** Quartet (US 1949). **1949** Ichabod and Mr. Toad. **1951** Hong Kong. **1953** Kiss Me, Kate; Down Among the Sheltering Palms.

ALLYN, LILLY (Elizabeth A. Tatu)
Born: 1866. Died: May 5, 1944, Philadelphia, Pa. Screen, stage, vaudeville actress and light opera performer.

ALMAR THE CLOWN. *See* ALBERT A. MARX

ALONSO, JULIO
Born: 1906. Died: Feb. 9, 1955, Hollywood, Calif. Screen actor. Brother of actor Gilbert Roland.

ALSEN, ELSA
Born: 1881, Obra, Poland. Died: Jan. 31, 1975, New York, N.Y. Screen actress and opera singer.

Appeared in: **1930** The Rogue Song.

ALSTRUP, CARL
Born: 1877. Died: 1942. Stage and screen actor.

Appeared in: **1911** The Actor as Soldier; Buttons and Hooks; His First Monacle; The Twins.

ALTHOFF, CHARLES R.
Born: 1890. Died: Oct. 14, 1962, Irvington, N.J. Screen, vaudeville and radio actor.

ALTHOUSE, EARL F.
Born: 1893. Died: Feb. 6, 1971, Gladwyne, Pa. Screen cowboy actor. Entered films with Lubin Studios.

ALVARADO, DON (Jose Paige)
Born: Nov. 4, 1900, Albuquerque, N.M. Died: Mar. 31, 1967, Los Angeles, Calif. (cancer). Screen and television actor. Also known professionally as Don Page.

Appeared in: **1925** The Pleasure Buyers; Satan in Sables; The Wife Who Wasn't Wanted. **1926** A Hero of the Big Snows; The Night Cry; His Jazz Bride. **1927** Loves of Carmen; Breakfast at Sunrise; Drums of Love; The Monkey Talks. **1928** The Battle of the Sexes; No Other Woman; The Scarlet Lady; Driftwood. **1929** Rio Rita; The Apache; The Bridge of San Luis Rey. **1930** Free and Easy; The Bad One; Forever Yours. **1931** Beau Ideal; Captain Thunder; Reputation. **1932** The Bachelor's Affair; La Cucaracha; Lady With a Past; The King Murder. **1933** Under Secret Orders; Contraband; Black Beauty; Morning Glory. **1934** Demon for Trouble; No Sleep on the Deep; Once to Every Bachelor. **1935** The Devil Is a Woman; Red Wagon; I Live for Love; Sweet Adeline. **1936** Rosa de Francia; Federal Agent; Rio Grande Romance; Put on the Spot; Rose of the Rancho; Spy 77. **1937** Nobody's Baby; The Lady Escapes; Love under Fire. **1938** Rose of the Rio Grande. **1939** Cafe Society. **1940** One Night in the Tropics. **1949** The Big Steal.

AMARANTE, ESTEVAO
Born: 1890. Died: Jan. 1952, Oporto, Portugal. Stage and screen actor. During 1930s did first talkies in Portuguese language for Paramount in Paris.

AMATO, GIUSEPPE (Giuseppe Vasaturo)
Born: 1899, Italy. Died: Feb. 3, 1964, Rome, Italy (heart attack). Screen actor, film producer/director and screenwriter.

AMAYA, CARMEN
Born: 1913. Died: Nov. 19, 1963, Bagur, Spain (kidney ailment). Screen, stage actress and flamenco dancer.

Appeared in: **1944** Follow the Boys; Knickerbocker Holiday. **1945** See My Lawyer (with her dancing company). **1963** Los Tarantos (US 1964).

AMBLER, JOSS
Born: 1900, England. Died: 1959. Screen actor.

Appeared in: **1937** Captain's Orders; The Last Curtain. **1938** Meet Mr. Penny; Break the News (US 1941); The Citadel; The Claydon Treasure Mystery. **1939** Trouble Brewing; Come on George; Secret Journey (aka Among Human Wolves—US 1940). **1940** Contraband (aka Blackout—US); Fingers. **1941** Penn of Pennsylvania (aka The Courageous Mr. Penn—US 1944); Once a Crook; The Black Sheep of Whitehall. **1942** The Big Blockade; The Peterville Diamond; Gert and Daisy Clean Up; Flying Fortress; The Next of Kin (US 1943); Much Too Shy. **1943** Happidrome; The Silver Fleet (US 1945); Rhythm Serenade; Battle for Music; Somewhere in Civvies; Headline. **1944** The Halfway House (US 1945); A Canterbury Tale; Candles at Nine; Give Me the Stars. **1945** The Agitator; Here Comes the Sun. **1946** The Years Between (US 1947). **1947** Mine Own Executioner (US 1949). **1952** Ghost Ship; Who Goes There! (aka The Passionate Sentry—US 1957). **1953** The Captain's Paradise. **1954** The Harrassed Hero. **1955** Miss Tulip Stays the Night. **1956** The Long Arm

(aka The Third Key—US 1957); The Feminine Touch (aka The Gentle Touch—US 1957); Soho Incident (aka Spin a Dark Web—US).

AMES, ADRIENNE
Born: Aug. 3, 1909, Fort Worth, Tex. Died: May 31, 1947, New York, N.Y. (cancer). Screen, stage actress and radio commentator. Divorced from actor Bruce Cabot (dec. 1972).

Appeared in: **1931** Girls About Town; Twenty-Four Hours; The Road to Reno. **1932** Husband's Holiday; Two Kinds of Women; Merrily We Go to Hell; Sinners in the Sun. **1933** Broadway Bad; The Death Kiss; From Hell to Heaven; A Bedtime Story; Disgraced; The Avenger. **1934** You're Telling Me; George White's Scandals. **1935** Abdul the Damned; Black Sheep; La Fiesta de Santa Barbara (short); Gigolette; Woman Wanted; Harmony Lane; Ladies Love Danger. **1938** Slander House; City Girl; Fugitives for a Night. **1939** Zero Hour; Panama Patrol.

AMES, GERALD
Born: 1881, Blackheath, England. Died: July 4, 1933, London, England (accident—fall). Screen, stage actor and film director.

Appeared in: **1914** The King's Minister; The Kitchen Countess; The Cage; The Revenge of Thomas Atkins; England's Menace; The Fringe of War; She Stoops to Conquer; The Black Spot; A Highwayman's Honour; The Difficult Way; On His Majesty's Service (aka A Message from the Sky—US). **1915** Rupert of Hentzau (US 1916); The Prisoner of Zenda; The Middleman; "1914"; The King's Outcast (aka His Vindication—US); Brother Officers; The Christian; The Sons of Satan; Whoso Diggeth a Pit; The Shulamite; The Derby Winner; Love in a Wood; Jelf's (aka A Man of His Word—US). **1916** Arsene Lupin; The Princess of Happy Chance; You; The Game of Liberty (aka Under Suspicion—US); Paste; Me and Me Moke (aka Me and My Pal—US); The Greater Need; The Morals of Weybury (aka The Hypocrites); When Knights Were Bold; The King's Daughter. **1917** A Gamble for Love; The Ragged Messenger; Masks and Faces. **1918** Adam Bede; A Fortune at Stake; Missing the Tide; A Peep Behind the Scenes; Red Pottage; A Turf Conspiracy. **1919** Sunken Rocks; The Nature of the Beast; Comradeship (aka Comrades in Arms); The Forest on the Hill; The Irresistible Flapper; Possession; Sheba. **1920** Alf's Button; The Amazing Quest of Ernest Bliss (serial); Anna the Adventuress; Aylwin; Helen of Four Gates; John Forest Finds Himself; Mrs. Erricker's Reputation. **1921** Wild Heather; Tansy; Mr. Justice Raffles. **1923** The Loves of Mary Queen of Scots (aka Marie, Queen of Scots); A Royal Divorce; Within the Maze; The Woman Who Obeyed; God's Prodigal. **1924** Fights Through the Ages (series). **1926** The Little People. **1927** The King's Highway. **1928** A Light Woman; The Rising Generation.

AMES, HARRY
Born: 1893. Died: Aug. 11, 1969, Hollywood, Calif. Screen and stage actor.

AMES, JIMMY
Born: 1915. Died: Aug. 14, 1965, Hollywood, Calif. (heart attack). Screen and television actor.

Appeared in: **1946** Whistle Stop; The Kid from Brooklyn; The Best Years of Our Lives. **1949** The Lucky Stiff.

AMES, PERCY
Born: 1874, England. Died: Mar. 29, 1936, New York, N.Y. Screen and stage actor.

Appeared in: **1923** Adam and Eva. **1925** Soul Fire. **1934** Gambling.

AMES, ROBERT
Born: Mar. 23, 1898, Hartford, Conn. Died: Nov. 27, 1931, New York, N.Y. (bladder hemorrhage). Stage and screen actor. Entered films in 1925.

Appeared in: **1925** Without Mercy; The Wedding Song. **1926** Three Faces East; The Crown of Lies. **1929** Voice of the City; Marianne; Rich People; Black Waters; Nix on Dames; The Trespasser. **1930** Holiday; Madonna of the Streets; Double Cross Roads; Not Damaged; A Lady to Love; War Nurse. **1931** Rebound; Millie; Behind Office Doors; Smart Woman; Rich Man's Folly. **1932** The Slippery Pearls (short).

AMORES, ADELINA
Born: 1883, Spain. Died: Mar. 10, 1958, Madrid, Spain. Screen and stage actress.

AMUANARRIZ, RAUL CANCIO
Born: 1911, Spain. Died: Oct. 23, 1961, Madrid, Spain. Screen and stage actor who appeared in more than 100 Spanish films.

ANALLA, ISABEL
Born: 1920. Died: Jan. 17, 1958, San Francisco, Calif. (cancer). Screen and television actress.

Appeared in: **1957** Pal Joey; Kiss Them for Me. **1958** Vertigo.

ANDERSON, AUDLEY (Audley Lloyd Anderson)
Born: Mar. 5, 1885, Louisiana. Died: Dec. 19, 1966, Hollywood, Calif. (pulmonary edema). Screen actor.

Appeared in: **1957** Outlaw's Son.

ANDERSON, CLAIRE
Born: 1896, Detroit, Mich. Died: Mar. 23, 1964, Venice, Calif. Screen actress. Was one of the original Mack Sennett beauties.

Appeared in: **1916** Cinders of Love; The Lion and the Girl; A Male Governess; Bath Tub Perils; She Loved a Sailor. **1917** A Clever Dummy; Her Finishing Touch; The Late Lamented; The Hidden Spring. **1920** The Palace of Darkened Windows. **1921** The Road Demon; When We Were Twenty-One; Who Am I; The Servant in the House. **1922** The Yellow Stain. **1923** The Clean-Up. **1925** The Meddler.

ANDERSON, GENE
Born: 1931, London, England. Died: May 5, 1965, London, England (cerebral hemorrhage). Screen, stage and television actress. Married to actor Edward Judd.

Appeared in: **1953** Background (aka Edge of Divorce); The Intruder (US 1955); **1956** Doublecross. **1957** Yangtse Incident (aka Battle Hell—US); The Long Haul. **1960** The Shakedown. **1961** The Day the Earth Caught Fire (US 1962). **1962** The Break (US 1963).

ANDERSON, GEORGE
Born: 1891. Died: Aug. 28, 1948, Los Angeles, Calif. Screen and stage actor.

Appeared in: **1937** Under Suspicion. **1938** Born to Be Wild. **1939** Our Neighbors, The Carters; King of Chinatown; The Lady's from Kentucky; Union Pacific; A Woman Is the Judge. **1940** Santa Fe Marshal; Hidden Gold; The Secret Seven. **1942** The Palm Beach Story. **1943** Henry Aldrich Haunts a House. **1944** Wilson; Murder, My Sweet. **1945** Mildred Pierce; Nob Hill.

ANDERSON, GILBERT M. "BRONCHO BILLY" (Max Aronson)
Born: Mar. 21, 1882, Little Rock, Ark. Died: Jan. 20, 1971, South Pasadena, Calif. Screen, stage, vaudeville, television actor, film director and screenwriter. In 1907 he co-founded Essanay Film Manufacturing Co. Won 1958 Special Academy Award for his pioneer contribution to the film industry. He appeared in "Broncho Billy" series, beginning in 1908 with The Bandit Makes Good; "Snakeville Comedy" series, beginning in 1911; and "Alkali Ike" series, beginning in 1912.

Appeared in: **1902** The Messenger Boy's Mistake (film debut). **1903** The Great Train Robbery. **1907** An Awful Skate. **1908** The Bandit Makes Good. **1909** The Heart of a Cowboy; The Indian Trailer; A Western Maid; The Ranchman's Rival; The Spanish Girl; His Reformation; Judgment; The Best Man Wins; A Tale of the West; The Black Sheep; A Mexican's Gratitude. **1910** Away Out West; The Cowboy and the Squaw; The Cowpuncher's Ward; The Flower of the Ranch; The Forest Ranger; The Mistaken Bandit; The Outlaw's Sacrifice; The Ranch Girl's Legacy; The Ranchman's Feud; The Sheriff's Sacrifice; The Bandit's Wife; Western Chivalry; Take Me Out to the Ball Game; The Bad Man's Last Deed; The Unknown Claim; Trailed by the West; The Desperado; Under Western Skies; The Dumb Half Breed's Defense; The Deputy's Love Affair; The Millionaire and the Girl; An Indian Girl's Love; The Pony Express Rider; The Tout's Remembrance; Patricia of the Plains; The Bearded Bandit; A Cowboy's Mother-in-Law; Pals of the Range; The Silent Message; A Westerner's Way; The Marked Trail; A Western Woman's Way; A Cowboy's Vindication; The Tenderfoot Messenger; A Gambler of the West; The Bad Man's Christmas; Broncho Billy's Redemption. **1911** The Girl from the Triple X; Last Round-Up; The Cowboy Coward; When Love and Honor Called; A Girl of the West; The Border Ranger; The Two Reformations; The Bad Man's Downfall; On the Desert's Edge; The Romance of Bar O; The Faithful Indian; A Thwarted Vengeance; Across the Plains; Carmenita the Faithful; The Sheriff's Chum; The Indian Maiden's Lesson; The Puncher's New Love; The Lucky Card; The Infant at Snakeville; The Tribe's Penalty; The Sheriff's Brother; The Hidden Mine; The Corporation and the Ranch Girl; The Count and the Cowboy; The Outlaw and the Child; Broncho Billy's Adventure. **1912** Broncho Billy's Outwitted; The Outlaw's Sacrifice; The Shotgun Ranchman; The Tomboy on Bar Z; The Ranch Girl's Trial; The Mother of the Ranch; An Indian Friendship; Cutting California Redwoods; Broncho Billy's Heart; The Dance at Silver Gulch; Broncho Billy's Mexican Wife; The Boss of the Katy Mine; Western Girls; Broncho Billy's Promise; The Prospector; The Sheriff's Luck; The Sheriff's Inheritance; The Reward for Broncho Billy; The Smuggler's Daughter; Alkali Ike Plays the Devil; Alkali Ike Stung!; Alkali Ike's Boarding House; Alkali Ike's Pants; Love on Tough Luck Ranch; Alkali Ike's Close Shave; Alkali Ike's Motorcycle. **1913** Oath; Alkali Ike's Misfortunes; Alkali Ike's in Jayville; Alkali Ike's Homecoming; Alkali Ike's Auto; Broncho Billy and the Maid; Broncho Billy and the Outlaw's Mother; Broncho Billy's Gun Play; The Sheriff's Child; The Making of Broncho Billy; The Sheriff's Story; Broncho Billy's Last Deed; Broncho Billy's Ward; Broncho Billy and the Squatter's Daughter; Broncho Billy and the Step-Sisters; Broncho Billy's Sister; Broncho Billy's Gratefulness; Broncho Billy's Way; The Sheriff's Honeymoon; Broncho Billy's Secret; Broncho Billy's First Arrest; Broncho Billy's Squareness; Broncho Billy's Christmas Deed; The Three Gamblers. **1914** The Treachery of

Broncho Billy's Pal; Broncho Billy and the Rattler; Broncho Billy's True Love; Broncho Billy's Close Call; Broncho Billy Gun-Man; Broncho Billy's Sermon; Broncho Billy's Leap; Broncho Billy's Cunning; Broncho Billy's Duty; Broncho Billy's Jealousy; Broncho Billy and the Mine Shark; Broncho Billy Outlaw; Red Riding Hood of the Hills; Broncho Billy's Punishment; Broncho Billy and the Sheriff; The Redemption of Broncho Billy; Snakeville's New Doctor; Broncho Billy Guardian; Broncho Billy and the Bad Man; Broncho Billy and the Settler's Daughter; Broncho Billy and the Red Man; The Calling of Jim Barton; The Interference of Broncho Billy; Broncho Billy's Bible; Broncho Billy and the Sister; The Good-for-Nothing; Broncho Billy and the Claim Jumpers; Broncho Billy and the Escaped Bandit. **1915** Broncho Billy and the Land Grabber; Broncho Billy and the Lumber King; Broncho Billy and the Posse; Broncho Billy Evens Matters; Broncho Billy's Love Affair; Broncho Billy Well Repaid; Broncho Billy's Marriage; Broncho Billy and the False Note; Broncho Billy and the Vigilante; Broncho Billy's Parents; Broncho Billy's Protege; Broncho Billy's Sentence; Broncho Billy's Teachings; Broncho Billy and the Baby; Broncho Billy Begins Life Anew; Broncho Billy Sheepman; Broncho Billy's Brother; Broncho Billy's Greaser Deputy; Broncho Billy's Surrender; Broncho Billy's Word of Honor; Broncho Billy's Vengeance; Broncho Billy's Cowardly Brother; Broncho Billy Steps In. **1918** Shootin' Mad.

ANDERSON, IVIE
Born: 1909, Gilroy, Calif. Died: Dec. 28, 1949, Los Angeles, Calif. Black singer and screen actress.

Appeared in: **1937** A Day at the Races; The Hit Parade.

ANDERSON, JAMES
Born: 1872. Died: Mar. 22, 1953, Glasgow, Scotland (burns received in fire). Screen, stage and radio actor.

Appeared in: **1925** The Freshman. **1926** Butterflies in the Rain; The College Boob; Flying High. **1928** Fleetwing. **1929** Welcome Danger. **1930** The Runaway Bride. **1949** Whiskey Galore (aka Tight Little Island—US and Mad Little Island).

ANDERSON, JAMES "JIM"
Born: 1921. Died: Sept. 14, 1969, Billings, Mont. Screen actor. Entered films in 1951.

Appeared in: **1951** Hunt the Man Down; Along the Great Divide; Five. **1952** The Last Musketeer; Duel at Silver Creek; Ruby Gentry. **1953** China Venture; The Great Jesse James Raid; Flight to Tangier. **1954** Drums Across the River; Dragnet; Riot in Cell Block 11. **1955** The Violent Men; The Marauders; Seven Angry Men. **1956** Fury at Gunsight Pass; Running Target; The Rawhide Years. **1957** The Big Land. **1958** I Married a Monster from Outer Space; The Thing That Couldn't Die. **1962** To Kill a Mocking Bird; The Connection; Pressure Point. **1965** The Brig. **1969** Take the Money and Run. **1970** The Ballad of Cable Hogue; Little Big Man.

ANDERSON, JOAN
Died: 1974. Screen actress.

Appeared in: **1963** Lonnie.

ANDERSON, LAWRENCE
Born: 1893, London, England. Died: Mar. 28, 1939, London, England (pneumonia). Stage and screen actor. Entered films in 1920.

Appeared in: **1921** Innocent; Bluff. **1922** The Recoil. **1932** Threads. **1933** The Stickpin; Mayfair Girl; The Fire Raisers; The Right to Live. **1934** Nell Gwyn. **1936** Living Dangerously; His Lordship (aka Man of Affaires—US 1937). **1937** O.H.M.S. (aka You're in the Army Now—US); Make Up; Gangway.

ANDERSON, LILLIAN
Born: Aug. 6, 1881, Indiana. Died: Aug. 25, 1962, Los Angeles, Calif. Screen actress and drama coach.

ANDRA, FERN (aka FERN ANDRE)
Born: Feb. 24, 1893, Watseka, Ill. Died: Feb. 8, 1974, Aiken, S.C. (cancer). Screen, stage, vaudeville actress, film director, producer and screenwriter. Appeared in German, British and U.S. films. Entered films in Vienna.

Appeared in: **1916** Little Eve Edgarton; Des Lebens Ungemischte Freude (serial). **1917** Uncle Tom's Cabin. **1918** Um Krome und Peitsche. **1920** Genuine. **1923** L'incubo di Za-La-Vie. **1924** L'Ergastolano Innocente. **1925** Und es Lockte der Ruf der Sundigen Welt. **1928** Spangles; The Burgomaster of Stilemonde. **1930** The Lotus Lady; Eyes of the World.

ANDRE, GABY
Died: Aug. 9, 1972, Rome, Italy (cancer). Screen actress. Mother of actress Carol Andre.

Appeared in: **1939** Fin du Jour (End of a Day). **1950** Please Believe Me; Hoboes in Paradise; Highway 301. **1952** The Green Glove; L'Ingiusta Condanna (Guilt Is Not Mine—US 1968). **1957** The Life and Music of Giuseppe Verdi. **1958** Incognito; The Crawling Terror. **1959** The Cosmic Monsters (aka Strange World of Planet X). **1960** Goliath and the Dragon. **1962** East of Kilimanjaro (aka La Grande Caccia [The Big Hunt] and The Big Search). 1970 Pussycat, Pussycat, I Love You. Other foreign films: Stage Door; Paradise Lost; The Heir of Mondesir; Strange Suzy; L'Ange de la Nuit; Un Seul Amour; $2,000,000 Bank Robbery; The Victim; Angel of Sin; Donatella; Verde; Moglie e Amante.

ANDRE, GWILI
Born: 1908, Copenhagen, Denmark. Died: Feb. 5, 1959, Venice, Calif. (apartment fire). Screen actress.

Appeared in: 1932 The Roar of the Dragon; Secrets of the French Police. 1933 No Other Woman. 1937 The Girl Said No; Meet the Boy Friend. 1941 A Woman's Face. 1942 The Public Be Damned; The Falcon's Brother.

ANDREWS, BART
Died: July 31, 1969, New York, N.Y. Screen actor.

Appeared in: 1965 Superman vs. the Gorilla Gang (short). 1966 Rocketman Flies Again (short).

ANDREWS, LAVERNE
Born: July 6, 1915, Minneapolis, Minn. Died: May 8, 1967, West Los Angeles, Calif. (cancer). Screen, radio, television actress and vaudeville singer. One of the "Andrews Sisters" trio.

Appeared in: 1940 Argentine Nights. 1941 Buck Privates; In the Navy; Hold that Ghost; Private Buckaroo. 1942 What's Cookin'?; Give Out, Sisters. 1943 How's About It?; Always a Bridesmaid. 1944 Swingtime Johnny; Moonlight and Cactus; Follow the Boys; Hollywood Canteen. 1945 Her Lucky Night. 1946 Make Mine Music. 1947 Road to Rio. 1948 Melody Time.

ANDREWS, LOIS (Lorraine Gourley)
Born: Mar. 24, 1924, Huntington Park, Calif. Died: April 1968, Encino, Calif. (lung cancer). Stage and screen actress. Divorced from entertainer George Jessel.

Appeared in: 1943 Dixie Dugan; Roger Touhy, Gangster. 1949 Rustlers. 1950 The Desert Hawk. 1951 Meet Me after the Show.

ANDREWS, ORVILLE
Born: Nebr. Died: Mar. 29, 1968, Hartford, Conn. Screen, television actor and radio comedy singer.

ANDREWS, STANLEY
Born: 1892. Died: June 23, 1969, Los Angeles, Calif. Screen and television actor.

Appeared in: 1935 All the King's Horses; Private Worlds; People Will Talk; The Crusades; Nevada; Wanderer of the Wasteland; Drift Fence; Hold 'Em Yale; Escape from Devil's Island; The Big Broadcast of 1936. 1936 Wild Brian Kent; Desire; Foolproof (short); In His Steps; Happy Go Lucky. 1937 John Meade's Woman; High, Wide and Handsome; The Devil's Playground; Easy Living; The Man Who Found Himself; Nancy Steele Is Missing. 1938 The Buccaneer; Cocoanut Grove; Spawn of the North; The Mysterious Rider; Prairie Moon; When G-Men Step In; Blondie; Adventure in Sahara; Alexander's Ragtime Band; I'll Give a Million; Kentucky; The Lone Ranger (serial); Stablemates. 1939 Mr. Smith Goes to Washington; Homicide Bureau; Beau Geste; Union Pacific; Geronimo. 1940 The Blue Bird; Little Old New York; Brigham Young-Frontiersman; Kit Carson. 1941 In Old Colorado; Play Girl; Meet John Doe; Strange Alibi; Mr. and Mrs. North; Wild Geese Calling; Time Out for Rhythm. 1942 North to the Klondike; The Major and the Minor; Canal Zone; My Gal Sal; The Postman Didn't Ring; Ten Gentlemen from West Point. 1943 Crash Dive. 1944 Murder, My Sweet; Tucson Raiders; Princess and the Pirate. 1946 The Virginian. 1947 Robin Hood of Texas; Michigan Kid. 1948 Sinister Journey; The Dead Don't Dream; The Valiant Hombre; Dock of New Orleans; The Paleface; Northwest Stampede. 1949 Blondie's Big Deal; Brothers in the Saddle; Man from Colorado; Trail of the Yukon; The Last Bandit; Brimstone; Tough Assignment. 1950 Across the Badlands; Arizona Cowboy; Blonde Dynamite; Mule Train; The Nevadan; Outcast of Black Mesa; Salt Lake Raiders; Short Grass; Streets of Ghost Town; Trigger, Jr.; Two Flags West; Tyrant of the Sea; Under Mexicali Stars; West of Wyoming. 1951 Al Jennings of Oklahoma; Saddle Legion; Silver Canyon; Utah Wagon Train; Vengeance Valley. 1952 Fargo; Kansas Territory; The Man from Black Hills; Montana Belle; Talk about a Stranger; Thundering Caravans; Waco. 1953 Appointment in Honduras; Dangerous Crossing. 1954 Dawn at Socorro; Southwest Passage; The Steel Cage. 1955 Treasure of Ruby Hills. 1956 Frontier Gambler.

ANDREWS, TOD
Born: 1920. Died: Nov. 6, 1972, Beverly Hills, Calif. (heart attack). Screen, stage and television actor.

Appeared in: 1950 Outrage. 1956 Between Heaven and Hell. 1957 From Hell It Came. 1965 In Harm's Way. 1968 Hang 'em High. 1969 Changes. 1970 Beneath the Planet of the Apes.

ANGELI, PIER (Anna Maria Pierangeli)
Born: June 19, 1932, Sardinia, Italy. Died: Sept. 10, 1971, Beverly Hills, Calif. (overdose of drugs). Screen, stage and television actress. Twin sister of actress Marisa Pavan. Divorced from singer/actor Vic Damone.

Appeared in: 1951 Teresa; The Light Touch. 1952 The Devil Makes Three; Tomorrow Is Too Late. 1953 The Story of Three Loves (aka Equilibrium); Sombrero. 1954 Flame and the Flesh. 1955 The Silver Chalice. 1956 Port Afrique; Somebody up There Likes Me. 1957 The Vintage. 1958 Merry Andrew. 1960 S.O.S. Pacific; The Angry Silence. 1962 White Slave Ship. 1963 Sodom and Gomorrah. 1964 Banco a Bangkok (aka OSS 17 and Shadow of Evil—US 1967). 1965 The Battle of the Bulge. 1966 Spy in Your Eye. 1968 Rey de Africa (aka King of Africa and One Step to Hell—US 1969); Kol Mamzer Melech (aka Every Bastard a King—US 1970).

ANGELO, JEAN
Born: 1888. Died: Nov. 26, 1933, Paris, France. Screen and stage actor.

Appeared in: 1928 Une Java. 1929 Nana; La Vierge Folle. 1930 The Strange Case of District Attorney M. 1932 L'Atlantide.

ANGOLD, EDIT (Edit Goldstandt)
Born: 1895, Berlin, Germany. Died: Oct. 4, 1971, Los Angeles, Calif. Screen, stage, radio and television actress.

Appeared in: 1944 Tomorrow the World! (stage and film versions). 1946 Suspense. 1949 Ringside; Tough Assignment. 1950 The White Tower; Molly (aka The Goldbergs, film and radio versions). 1952 Woman in the Dark. 1953 Murder without Tears. 1956 The Birds and the Bees. 1957 Bernardine. 1959 The Blue Angel.

ANKRUM, MORRIS (Morris Nussbaum aka STEPHEN MORRIS)
Born: Aug. 28, 1897, Danville, Ill. Died: Sept. 2, 1964, Pasadena, Calif. (trichinosis). Screen, stage actor and film director.

Appeared in: 1933 Reunion in Vienna. 1936 Hopalong Cassidy Returns; Trail Dust. 1937 Borderland; Hills of Old Wyoming; North of the Rio Grande; Rustler's Valley. 1940 Buck Benny Rides Again; Knights of the Range; The Showdown; Three Men from Texas; Light of the Western Stars; Cherokee Strip. 1941 I Wake up Screaming; This Woman Is Mine; The Roundup; In Old Colorado; Border Vigilantes; Wide Open Town; Doomed Caravan; Pirates on Horseback; Road Agent; The Bandit Trail. 1942 Tales of Manhattan; Roxie Hart; Ride 'Em Cowboy!; Ten Gentlemen from West Point; The Loves of Edgar Allen Poe; The Omaha Trail; Time to Kill; Tennessee Johnson. 1943 Let's Face It; Reunion in France; Swing Fever; Dixie Dugan; The Heavenly Body. 1944 Marriage Is a Private Affair; Barbary Coast Gent; Meet the People; Rationing; Gentle Annie; The Thin Man Goes Home; plus the following shorts: Dark Shadows; Radio Bugs; and Return from Nowhere. 1945 The Hidden Eye. 1946 The Harvey Girls; Courage of Lassie; Little Mr. Jim; Cockeyed Miracle; Lady in the Lake; The Mighty McGurk. 1947 Undercover Maisie; Cynthia; Good News; Desire Me; High Wall; Sea of Grass. 1948 The Fabulous Fraud (short); Joan of Arc; For the Love of Mary; Fighting Back; Bad Men of Tombstone. 1949 We Were Strangers; Colorado Territory; Slattery's Hurricane. 1950 Borderline; Chain Lightning; The Damned Don't Cry; Redhead and the Cowboy; Rocketship XM; In a Lonely Place; Short Grass; Southside 1-000. 1951 Tomorrow Is Another Day; My Favorite Spy; Fighting Coast Guard; Along the Great Divide; The Lion Hunters; Flight to Mars. 1952 The Raiders; The Man Behind the Gun; Hiawatha; Mutiny; Red Planet Mars; Son of Ali Baba; Fort Osage. 1953 Arena; Devil's Canyon; The Moonlighter; Invaders from Mars; Fort Vengeance; Sky Commando; Mexican Manhunt. 1954 Vera Cruz; Southwest Passage; Apache; The Three Young Texans; Taza, Son of Cochise; Silver Lode; Drums Across the River; The Steel Cage; Cattle Queen of Montana; Two Guns and a Badge; The Outlaw Stallion; The Saracen Blade. 1955 Chief Crazy Horse; The Eternal Sea; The Silver Star; Tennessee's Partner; No Man's Woman; Crashout; Jupiter's Darling; Abbott and Costello Meet the Mummy; Jujin Yukiotoko (Half Human). 1956 Fury at Gunsight Pass; Quincannon, Frontier Scout; Earth vs. The Flying Saucers; Death of a Scoundrel; Walk the Proud Land; When Gangland Strikes. 1957 Omar Khayyam; Hell's Crossroads; Drango; Zombies of Mora-Tau; Kronos; The Giant Claw; Beginning of the End. 1958 Badman's Country; Tarawa Beachhead; From the Earth to the Moon; Twilight for the Gods; Young and Wild; The Saga of Hemp Brown; Frontier Gun; How to Make a Monster; Giant from the Unknown. 1961 The Most Dangerous Man Alive; The Little Shepherd of Kingdom Come. 1963 The Man With the X-Ray Eyes.

ANSELMI, ROSINA
Born: 1880, Italy. Died: May 23, 1965, Cantania, Sicily. Stage and screen actress.

Appeared in: 1935 The Rich Uncle; L'Eredita dello Zio; L'Aria del Continente (Continental Atmosphere—US 1939); Milizia Territoriale. 1937 El Feroce Saladino; Signora Fortuna (Lady Luck); Gat Ci Cova; Lasciate Ogni Speranza. 1939 El Marchese De Rivolito (The Marquis of Rivolito); L'Ha Fatto Una Signora (A Woman Did It); Re di Danari (Money King). 1940 El Paraninfo (The Matchmaker).

ANSON, A. E.

Born: 1879, England. Died: June 25, 1936, Monrovia, Calif. Stage and screen actor.

Appeared in: **1931** Arrowsmith; The Road to Singapore.

ANSON, LAURA

Born: 1892. Died: July 15, 1968, Woodland Hills, Calif. Screen actress. Married to actor Philo McCullough. She was a leading lady of Roscoe "Fatty" Arbuckle.

Appeared in: **1921** The Easy Road; Crazy to Marry; The Little Clown. **1922** Bluebeard, Jr.; If You Believe It, It's So; The Great Alone. **1923** Flames of Passion; Skid Proof; The Call of the Canyon; The Silent Partner; The Way of the Transgressor.

ANTRIM, HARRY

Born: 1895, Chicago, Ill. Died: Jan. 18, 1967, Hollywood, Calif. (heart attack). Screen, stage, television and vaudeville actor.

Appeared in: **1947** Miracle on 34th Street (film debut). **1948** The Luck of the Irish; Larceny; Let's Live a Little; Words and Music; Act of Violence. **1949** Free for All; Johnny Allegro; Thelma Jordan; Intruder in the Dust; Prison Warden; The Heiress; Chicago Deadline; Ma and Pa Kettle. **1950** Devil's Doorway; I'll Get By; Outside the Wall; No Man of Her Own; Side Street; There's A Girl in My Heart. **1951** Appointment with Danger; Night into Morning; Meet Me after the Show; Tomorrow Is Another Day; Follow the Sun; Mr. Belvedere Rings the Bell; I'll See You in My Dreams. **1952** The Lion and the Horse; Mutiny. **1954** The Bounty Hunter. **1955** A Lawless Street. **1956** The Solid Gold Cadillac. **1958** Teacher's Pet. **1959** Gunmen from Laredo. **1965** The Monkey's Uncle.

AOKI, TSURU

Born: 1893. Died: Nov. 1961, Tokyo, Japan (acute peritonitis). Stage and screen actress. Married to actor Sessue Hayakawa (dec. 1973).

Appeared in: **1914** The Typhoon; The Wrath of the Gods (aka The Destruction of Sakura-Jima); The Vigil. **1916** Alien Souls; The Honorable Friend. **1917** Each to His Kind; The Call of the East. **1918** The Bravest Way; His Birth Right. **1919** Bonds of Honor; A Heart in Pawn; The Courageous Coward; The Gray Horizon (aka A Dead Line); The Dragon Painter; The Rajah's Amulet (reissue of 1917 Each To His Kind). **1920** The Breath of the Gods. **1921** Black Roses. **1922** Night Life in Hollywood; Five Days to Live. **1923** La Bataille. **1924** The Danger Line; The Great Shan; Sen Yan's Devotion. **1960** Hell to Eternity.

APFEL, OSCAR C.

Born: Cleveland, Ohio. Died: Mar. 24, 1938, Hollywood, Calif. (heart attack). Screen, stage actor, film, stage director and stage producer. Entered films with Edison and Reliance in 1911.

Appeared in: **1922** Ten Nights in a Bar Room; Auction of Souls; The Man Who Paid; The Wolf's Fangs. **1923** A Man's Man; In Search of a Thrill; The Social Code. **1924** The Heart Bandit; Trail of the Law. **1925** Borrowed Finery; The Thoroughbred; The Sporting Chance. **1926** Perils of the Coast Guard; Somebody's Mother; The Call of the Klondike; The Last Alarm; Midnight Limited; Race Wild. **1927** When Seconds Count; Cheaters; Code of the Cow Country. **1928** The Valley of Hunted Men; The Heart of Broadway; Romance of the Underworld. **1929** Marianne; Not Quite Decent; True Heaven; Halfway to Heaven; Smiling Irish Eyes; Hurdy Gurdy. **1930** The Texan; Misbehaving Ladies; The Spoilers; Virtuous Sin; The Right to Love; Man Trouble; Abraham Lincoln. **1931** Men in Her Life; Huckleberry Finn; Helping Grandma (short); Five-Star Final; Finger Points; Wicked; Big Business Girl; The Maltese Falcon; Sidewalks of New York; The Bargain; Sooky; Inspiration. **1932** State's Attorney; High Pressure; Woman from Monte Carlo; Hot Saturday; Shopworn; East Side; Cardigan's Last Case; The Silent Voice; Business and Pleasure; Woman in Room 13; You Said a Mouthful; Heart of New York; It's Tough To Be Famous; Old Greatheart; The World and the Flesh; Alias the Doctor; When a Fellow Needs a Friend; Two against the World; Mad Masquerade; Sporting Widow; Way Back Home; The Man Who Played God; Make Me a Star; Hell's Highway; False Faces; Madame Racketeer. **1933** Pick Up; Story of Temple Drake; Tomorrow at Seven; Emergency Call; One Man's Journey; Before Dawn; Ladies Must Love; Only Yesterday; The Bowery; The World Changes; Hold the Press. **1934** Fifteen Wives; The Old-Fashioned Way; Take the Stand; I Am a Thief; Romance in Manhattan; Beloved; Madame Spy; It Happened One Day (short); You Said a Hateful (short); The House of Rothschild; Are We Civilized?; White Lies; Whirlpool. **1935** Border Town; Two Faces; Death Flies East; The Nut Farm; Mary Jane's Pa; The Man on the Flying Trapeze; Cappy Ricks Returns; O'Shaughnessey's Boy; His Night Out; Another Face; The Fire Trap. **1936** Murder at Glen Athol; Sutter's Gold; Bridge of Sighs; Every Saturday Night; The Criminal Within; Hearts in Bondage; Bulldog Edition; And Sudden Death; Hollywood Boulevard; We Who Are About to Die; The Plot Thickens; Crack-Up. **1937** Fifty Roads to Town; The Soldier and the Lady; Conquest; Shadows of the Orient; History Is Made at Night; Trouble in Morocco; Jim Hanvey-Detective; The Toast of New York.

APPEL, ANNA

Born: 1888. Died: Nov. 19, 1963, New York, N.Y. Screen, stage, and television actress.

Appeared in: **1926** Broken Hearts. **1932** The Heart of New York; Symphony of Six Million; Faithless. **1937** Green Fields; The Singing Blacksmith.

APPLEGARTH, JONAS

Born: 1920. Died: July 23, 1965, Bashaw, Alberta, Canada (auto accident). Screen actor.

Appeared in: **1954** Saskatchewan. **1955** Battle Cry. **1959** The Sheriff of Fractured Jaw.

APPLEGATE, HAZEL

Born: 1886. Died: Oct. 20, 1959, Chicago, Ill. Screen actress. Entered films in Chicago with Essaney.

APPLEWHITE, "RIC" (Eric Leon Applewhite)

Born: 1897. Died: May 29, 1973, Miami, Florida. Screen and television actor.

Appeared in: **1954** Dial M for Murder. **1961** X-15.

AQUISTAPACE, JEAN

Born: 1882, France. Died: Oct. 20, 1952, Nice, France. Screen actor and opera singer. Appeared in a number of French films.

ARBENZ, ARABELLA

Born: 1945. Died: Oct. 5, 1965, Bogota, Colombia (suicide—gun). Screen actress.

Appeared in: A Pure Soul (played dual lead role, in Mexico and N.Y., in the experimental film).

ARBUCKLE, MACKLYN

Born: July 9, 1866, San Antonio, Tex. Died: Apr. 1, 1931, Waddington, N.Y. Stage and screen actor.

Appeared in: **1915** The County Chairman. **1922** The Prodigal Judge; Squire Phin; Welcome to Our City; Mr. Potter of Texas; Mr. Bingle; The Young Diana. **1923** Broadway Broke. **1924** Yolanda; Janice Meredith. **1925** That Old Gang of Mine; Lure of the Track; The Thoroughbred. **1926** The Gilded Highway.

ARBUCKLE, ROSCOE "FATTY"

Born: Mar. 24, 1887, San Jose, Calif. Died: June 29, 1933, New York, N.Y. (heart attack). Screen, stage, vaudeville, burlesque actor, film director and producer. Directed under name of William Goodrich. Married to actress Addie McPhail. Divorced from actresses Doris Deane (dec. 1974) and Minta Durffee (dec. 1975).

Appeared in: **1909** Ben's Kid; Mrs. Jones' Birthday; Making It Pleasant for Him. **1910** The Sanitarium. **1913** Alas! Poor Yorick; The Gangsters (aka The Feud); Passions, He Had Three (aka He Had Three and Possums, He Had Three); Help! Help! Hydrophobia!; The Waiters' Picnic; A Bandit; Peeping Pete; For the Love of Mabel; The Telltale Light; A Noise from the Deep; Love and Courage; Professor Bean's Removal; The Riot; Mabel's New Hero (aka Fatty and the Bathing Beauties); Fatty's Day Off; Mabel's Dramatic Career (aka Her Dramatic Debut); The Gypsy Queen; The Fatal Taxicab (aka The Faithful Taxicab); When Dreams Come True; Mother's Boy (aka Mother's Boys); Two Old Tars (aka The Sea Dogs); A Quiet Little Wedding; The Speed Kings; Fatty at San Diego (aka A Jealous Husband); Wine (aka Wine Making); Fatty Joins the Force; The Woman Haters (aka The Woman Hater); Ride for a Bride; Fatty's Flirtation (aka The Masher); His Sister's Kids; He Would a Hunting Go. **1914** A Misplaced Foot; The Under Sheriff; A Flirt's Mistake; In the Clutches of the Gang; Rebecca's Wedding Day; A Robust Romeo; Twixt Love and Fire; A Film Johnnie (aka Movie Nut; Million Dollar Job); Tango Tangles (aka Charlie's Recreation; Music Hall); Her Favorite Pastime (aka The Bonehead; Charlie is Thirsty); A Rural Demon; Barnyard Flirtations; Chicken Chaser (aka New Yard Lovers); A Suspended Ordeal; The Water Dog (aka The Rescue); The Alarm (aka Fireman's Picnic); The Knockout (aka Counted Out; The Pugilist); Fatty and the Heiress; Fatty's Finish; Love and Bullets (aka The Trouble Mender); A Rowboat Romance; The Sky Pirate; Those Happy Days; That Minstrel Man; Those Country Kids; Fatty's Gift; The Masquerader (aka Putting One Over; The Female Impersonator; The Picnic; His New Profession; Charlie at the Studio; Charlie the Actor); A Brand New Hero; The Rounders (aka Revelry; Two of a Kind; Oh, What a Night); Lover's Luck; Fatty's Debut (aka Fatty Butts In); Fatty Again (aka Fatty the Fourflusher); Their Ups and Downs; Zip, the Dodger; Lovers' Post Office; An Incompetent Hero; Fatty's Jonah Day (aka Fatty's Hoodoo Day); Fatty's Wine Party; The Sea Nymphs; Leading Lizzie Astray; Shotguns That Kick; Fatty's Magic Pants (aka Fatty's Suitless Day); Fatty and Minnie-He-Haw. **1915** Mabel and Fatty's Wash Day; Fatty and Mabel's Simple Life; Fatty and Mabel at the San Diego Exposition; Mabel, Fatty and the Law; Fatty's New Role; Mabel and Fatty's Married Life; Fatty's Reckless Fling; Fatty's Chance Acquaintance; Love in Armor; That Little Band of Gold; Fatty's Faithful Fido (aka Fatty's Fatal Fido); When Love Took Wings; Wished on

Mabel; Mabel and Fatty Viewing the World's Fair at San Francisco; Mabel's Wilful Way; Miss Fatty's Seaside Lovers; The Little Teacher (aka Small Town Bully); Fatty's Plucky Pup (aka Foiled by Fido); Fatty's Tintype Tangle; Fickle Fatty's Fall; The Village Scandal; Fatty and the Broadway Stars. **1916** Fatty and Mabel Adrift; He Did and He Didn't; The Bright Lights (aka The Lure of Broadway); His Wife's Mistake; The Other Man; The Waiters' Ball; A Reckless Romeo; A Creampuff Romance. **1917** The Butcher Boy; The Rough House; His Wedding Night; Oh, Doctor!; Fatty at Coney Island; A Country Hero. **1918** Out West; The Bell Boy; Moonshine; Good Night, Nurse!; The Cook; The Sheriff; United States Fourth Liberty Loan Drive; Canadian Victory Loan Drive; Camping Out; The Pullman Porter; Love; The Bank Clerk; A Desert Hero; Back Stage; The Hayseed. **1920** The Garage; The Round Up; The Life of the Party. **1921** Brewster's Millions; The Dollar a Year Man; The Traveling Salesman; Gasoline Gus; Crazy to Marry; Leap Year (aka This is So Sudden; Skirt Shy); Freight Prepaid (aka The Fast Freight; Handle with Care). **1923** Hollywood. **1925** Go West. **1932** Hey, Pop (short). **1933** The following shorts: Buzzin' Around; How've You Bean?; Close Relations; In the Dough; Tomalio. **1951** Memories of Famous Hollywood Comedians (film clips). **1960** When Comedy Was King (doc.). **1961** Days of Thrills and Laughter (doc.).

ARBURY, GUY

Born: 1907. Died: Dec. 26, 1972, New York, N.Y. (stab wounds). Screen, stage and television actor.

Appeared in: **1970** Kremlin Letter. **1971** They Might Be Giants. **1972** Lady Liberty.

ARCHAINBAUD, GEORGE

Born: May 7, 1890, Paris, France. Died: Feb. 20, 1959, Beverly Hills, Calif. (heart attack). Screen, stage actor, film, television director and film producer.

ARCHER, ANNE

Born: 1912. Died: Aug. 5, 1959, Los Angeles, Calif. Screen actress.

ARDELL, JOHN E.

Born: 1881. Died: Apr. 26, 1949, Hollywood, Calif. (monoxide gas). Screen actor.

ARDEN, EDDIE

Born: 1908. Died: June 23, 1952, Hollywood, Calif. (heart attack). Stage and screen actor.

ARDEN, EDWIN

Born: Feb. 13, 1864, St. Louis, Mo. Died: Oct. 2, 1918, New York, N.Y. (heart attack). Stage and screen actor.

Appeared in: **1915** Eagle's Nest; The New Exploits of Elaine (serial); The Beloved Vagabond; Simon, the Jester; The Grey Mask. **1917** The Iron Heart. **1918** Virtuous Wives. **1919** Ruling Passions.

ARDEN, VICTOR

Born: 1893, Ill. Died: July 30, 1962, New York, N.Y. Screen actor, orchestra leader, musician and radio performer.

ARENAS, MIGUEL

Born: 1902, Alicante, Spain. Died: Nov. 3, 1965, Mexico City, Mexico (heart attack). Stage and screen actor.

Appeared in: **1933** In Fraganti. **1936** Mas Alla de la Muerta. **1937** El Misterio del Rostro Palido. **1938** No Basta ser Madre (Motherhood Is Not Enough); Abnegacion. **1939** Un Domingo en la Tarde (On a Sunday Afternoon); Maria. **1940** Herencia Macabra (A Macabre Legacy); Vivire Otra Vez (I Shall Live Again); El Conde de Monte Cristo. **1944** La Dama de las Camelias. **1951** Toast to Love.

ARGYLE, PEARL

Born: Nov. 7, 1910, Johannesburg, So. Africa. Died: Jan. 29, 1949, Calif. (cancer). Screen, stage actress and ballet dancer. Married to screen actor/director Curtis Bernhardt.

Appeared in: **1934** Chu Chin Chow. **1936** Things to Come.

ARLEDGE, JOHN (Johnson Lundy Arledge)

Born: Mar. 12, 1906, Crockett, Tex. Died: May 15, 1947. Screen, stage and vaudeville actor.

Appeared in: **1930** The King of Jazz. **1931** Young Sinners; Daddy Long Legs; Heartbreak; Spider. **1932** Careless Lady; Huddle; Week Ends Only. **1933** Jimmy and Sally. **1934** Olsen's Big Moment; Flirtation Walk. **1935** Devil Dogs of the Air; Mary Jane's Pa; Old Man Rhythm; Shipmates Forever. **1936** We're Only Human; You May Be Next; Two in Revolt; Murder on a Bridle Path; Don't Turn 'Em Loose; The Big Game. **1937** Saturday's Heroes; County Fair; The Big City. **1938** Prison Nurse; Numbered Woman; Campus Confessions. **1939** Twelve Crowded Hours; Gone with the Wind; You Can't Cheat an Hon-

est Man; 6,000 Enemies. **1940** The Grapes of Wrath; All Women Have Secrets; Strange Cargo; Ski Patrol; Flight Angels; City of Conquest. **1941** Cheers for Miss Bishop. **1947** I Wonder Who's Kissing Her Now.

ARLEN, BETTY

Born: 1904. Died: 1966. Screen actress. Was a Wampas Baby Star of 1925.

ARLEN, JUDITH (Laurette Rutherford)

Born: Mar. 18, 1914, Hollywood, Calif. Died: 1968. Screen actress. Was a Wampas Baby Star of 1934. Sister of actress Ann Rutherford. Daughter of opera singers Juan Gilberti and Pauline Daly (aka Actress Mary Lou Mansfield).

Appeared in: **1934** Kiss and Make Up; Young and Beautiful.

ARLEY, CECILE. See CECILE ARNOLD

ARLISS, FLORENCE

Died: Mar. 11, 1950, London, England. Screen actress. Married to actor George Arliss (dec. 1946).

Appeared in: **1921** The Devil; Disraeli. **1929** Disraeli (and 1921 version). **1932** The Millionaire. **1933** The King's Vacation. **1934** The House of Rothschild.

ARLISS, GEORGE

Born: Apr. 10, 1868, London, England. Died: Feb. 5, 1946, London, England (bronchial trouble). Stage and screen actor. Married to actress Florence Arliss (dec. 1950). Won 1929 Academy Award for Best Actor in Disraeli and nominated for 1930 Academy Award for Best Actor in The Green Goddess.

Appeared in: **1921** The Devil; Disraeli. **1922** Man Who Played God. **1923** The Green Goddess; The Ruling Passion. **1924** $20 a Week. **1929** Disraeli (and 1921 version). **1930** The Green Goddess (and 1923 version); Old English. **1931** The Millionaire; Alexander Hamilton. **1932** Man Who Played God (and 1922 version); A Successful Calamity. **1933** The Working Man; A King's Vacation; Voltaire; The Adopted Father. **1934** The House of Rothschild; The Last Gentleman. **1935** The Tunnel (aka Transatlantic Tunnel—US); Cardinal Richelieu; The Guv'nor (aka Mr. Hobo—US 1936); Iron Duke. **1936** His Lordship (aka Man of Affairs—US 1937); East Meets West. **1937** Dr. Syn.

ARMAND, TEDDY V. (Edwin C. Winscott)

Born: 1874. Died: July 12, 1947, Los Angeles, Calif. Screen and stage actor.

ARMENDARIZ, PEDRO

Born: May 9, 1912, Mexico City, Mexico. Died: June 18, 1963, Los Angeles, Calif. (cancer and suicide—gun). Screen and stage actor. Father of actor Pedro Armendariz, Jr.

Appeared in: **1936** Rosario. **1937** Jalisco Nuca Pierde (Jalisco Never Loses). **1938** Mi Candidato (My Candidate). **1939** El Indio, La China Hilaria. **1940** Los Olvidados de Dios (Those Forgotten by God); La Reina del Rio (The Queen of the River). **1941** Isle of Passion (aka Passion Island—U.S. 1943). **1943** Maria Candeleria (U.S. 1944); Guadalajara; The Life of Simon Bolivar. **1944** Tierra de Passiones. **1945** Flor Sylvestre. **1947** The Fugitive; Juan Charrasqueado. **1948** The Pearl; Three Godfathers; Fort Apache; Maclovia. **1949** La Masquereda; Tulsa; We Were Strangers; Enamorada. **1950** The Torch. **1951** Ella y Yo. **1952** Lucretia Borgia. **1954** Border River; Lovers of Toledo; El Bruto; Street Corner (aka Both Sides of the Law—US 1954). **1955** The Littlest Outlaw; Diane. **1956** Viva Revolution; Sins of the Borgias; The Conqueror. **1957** The Big Boodle (aka A Night in Havana); Manuela (aka Stowaway Girl—US). **1958** Conqueror of the Desert. **1959** The Little Savage; The Wonderful Country. **1960** Soldiers of Pancho Villa. **1961** Beyond All Limits (aka Flowers of Mayo); La Cucaracha; Francis of Assisi. **1962** La Bandida (The Bandit). **1963** My Son, the Hero (aka The Titans); Captain Sinbad. **1964** From Russia with Love.

ARMETTA, HENRY

Born: July 4, 1888, Palermo, Italy. Died: Oct. 21, 1945, San Diego, Calif. (heart attack). Screen, stage and television actor.

Appeared in: **1923** The Silent Command. **1928** Street Angel. **1929** Lady of the Pavements; In Old Arizona; Homesick; Love, Live and Laugh; Jazz Heaven. **1930** A Lady to Love; The Climax; The Little Accident; Lovin' the Ladies; Romance; Sins of the Children; Die Sehnsucht Jeder Frau. **1931** Strangers May Kiss; A Tailor Made Man; Five and Ten; Hush Money; The Unholy Garden; Speak Easily. **1932** Scarface; Arsene Lupin; The Passionate Plumber; The Doomed Battalion; Impossible Lover; Tiger Shark; Weekends Only; Penalty of Fame; Central Park; Cauliflower Alley; Steady Company; Huddle; They Just Had to Get Married; Prosperity; Farewell to Arms; Uptown New York; Okay, America; Men of America. **1932–33** Universal shorts. **1933** Fra Diavolo (The Devil's Brother); The Cohens and the Kellys in Trouble; Her First Mate; Too Much Harmony; Laughing at Life; Deception; What! No Beer?; So This Is Africa; Don't Bet on Love. **1934** Cat and the Fiddle; Cross Country Cruise; One Night of Love; Viva Villa!; Poor Rich; Hide-Out; Embarrassing Moments; Gift of Gab; Two Heads on a Pillow; Wake up and Dream; Imitation of Life; The Merry Widow; The Man Who Reclaimed His Head; Kiss and Make Up; Cheating Cheaters; Romance in the Rain; Let's Talk It Over; Universal shorts. **1935** Straight from the Heart; Vanessa, Her Love Story; Night Life of the Gods; After Office Hours; I've Been Around; Dinky; Princess Ohara; Unknown Woman; Three Kids and a Queen; The Show Goes On; Magnificent Obsession; Manhattan Moon. **1936** Let's Sing Again; The Crime of Dr. Forbes; Poor Little Rich Girl; The Magnificent Brute; Two in a Crowd. **1937** Top of the Town; Make a Wish; Manhattan Merry-Go-Round; Seventh Heaven. **1938** Everybody Sing; Speed to Burn; Road Demon; Submarine Patrol. **1939** Fisherman's Wharf; The Lady and the Mob; My Pop; Winner Take All; I Stole a Million; The Outsider; Dust Be My Destiny; The Escape. **1940** Three Cheers for the Irish; We Who Are Young; You're Not So Tough; The Man Who Talked Too Much. **1941** Caught in the Act; The Big Store; Slick Chick; Stage Door Canteen; Good Luck, Mr. Yates. **1943** Thank Your Lucky Stars. **1944** Allergic to Love; The Ghost Catchers. **1945** Penthouse Rhythm; A Bell for Adano; Col. Effingham's Raid; Anchors Aweigh.

ARMITAGE, WALTER W.
Born: 1907, South Africa. Died: Feb. 22, 1953, New York, N.Y. Screen, stage actor, playwright and screenwriter.

Appeared in: **1931** The Love Habit. **1934** Bombay Mail; Where Sinners Meet; British Agent.

ARMSTRONG, CLYDE
Born: 1879. Died: Sept. 30, 1937, N.Y. Screen, stage and vaudeville actor.

ARMSTRONG, LOUIS "SATCHMO" (Daniel Louis Armstrong)
Born: July 4, 1900, New Orleans, La. Died: July 6, 1971, Queens, N.Y. Black screen, stage, television actor and jazz trumpeter. Winner of Down Beat Hall of Fame Award in 1952.

Appeared in: **1930** Ex-Flame. **1932** Paramount shorts. **1936** Pennies from Heaven. **1937** Artists and Models; Every Day's a Holiday. **1938** Going Places; Doctor Rhythm. **1940** The Philadelphia Story. **1943** Cabin in the Sky. **1944** Jam Session; Atlantic City. **1945** Pillow to Post. **1947** New Orleans. **1948** A Song Is Born. **1951** Glory Alley; The Strip; Here Comes the Groom. **1954** The Glenn Miller Story. **1956** High Society. **1957** The Five Pennies; The Beat Generation. **1960** Jazz on a Summer's Day. **1961** Paris Blues. **1965** When the Boys Meet the Girls (aka Girl Crazy). **1966** A Man Called Adam. **1969** Hello, Dolly; On Her Majesty's Secret Service.

ARMSTRONG, ROBERT
Born: Nov. 20, 1896, Saginaw, Mich. Died: Apr. 20, 1973, Santa Monica, Calif. Screen, stage, television and vaudeville actor. Divorced from actresses Ethel Kent and Gladys Dubois and later married to Louise Armstrong.

Appeared in: **1927** The Main Event (film debut). **1928** Celebrity; The Baby Cyclone; A Girl in Every Port; Square Crooks; The Cop; The Leopard Lady; Show Folks; Ned McCobb's Daughter. **1929** Big News; The Leatherneck; The Woman from Hell; The Shady Lady; Oh, Yeah!; The Racketeer. **1930** Dumbbells in Ermine; Be Yourself!; Danger Lights; Big Money. **1931** Paid; Iron Man; The Tip-Off; Suicide Fleet; Ex-Bad Boy. **1932** Panama Flo; The Lost Squadron; Is My Face Red?; Radio Patrol; The Most Dangerous Game; Hold 'Em Jail; The Penguin Pool Murder. **1933** The Billion Dollar Scandal; King Kong; Fast Workers; I Love that Man; Behind Adventure; Son of Kong; Above the Clouds. **1934** Flirting with Danger; Search for Beauty; Palooka; She Made Her Bed; The Hell Cat; Kansas City Princess; Manhattan Love Song. **1935** Sweet Music; G Men; Gigolette; Little Big Shot; Remember Last Night; The Mystery Man; **1936** The Ex-Mrs. Bradford; Dangerous Waters; Public Enemy's Wife; Without Orders; All-American Chump. **1937** Nobody's Baby; Three Legionnaires; It Can't Last Forever; The Girl Said No. **1938** She Loved a Fireman; The Night Hawk; There Goes My Heart. **1939** Unmarried; Call a Messenger; The Flying Irishman; Man of Conquest; Winter Carnival; Flight at Midnight. **1940** Enemy Agent; Forgotten Girls; Framed; Behind the News. **1941** Mr. Dynamite; The Bride Wore Crutches; Dive Bomber; Sky Raiders (serial); Outside the Law; San Francisco Docks; Citadel of Crime. **1942** My Favorite Spy; It Happened in Flatbush; Baby Face Morgan; Let's Get Tough. **1943** The Kansan; The Mad Ghoul; Adventures of Flying Cadets (serial); Around the World. **1944** Action in Arabia; Mr. Winkle Goes to War; Goodnight, Sweetheart; The Navy Way; Belle of the Yukon. **1945** Blood on the Sun; The Falcon in San Francisco; Gangs of the Waterfront; Arson Squad. **1946** Decoy; Criminal Court; Gay Blades; G.I. War Brides; Blonde Alibi. **1947** The Sea of Grass; The Fugitive; The Fall Guy; Exposed. **1948** The Paleface; Return of the Bad Men. **1949** The Lucky Stiff; Mighty Joe Young; Streets of San Francisco; The Crime Doctor's Diary; Captain China. **1950** Sons of New Mexico; Destination Big House. **1952** The Pace That Thrills. **1955** Las Vegas Shakedown. **1956** The Peacemaker. **1957** The Crooked Circle. **1963** Johnny Cool. **1964** For Those Who Think Young.

ARMSTRONG, WILL H.
Born: 1869. Died: July 28, 1943, Hollywood, Calif. Screen and vaudeville actor.

Appeared in: **1927** Clancy's Kosher Wedding; A Boy of the Streets.

ARNA, LISSY
Born: Germany. Died: Jan. 22, 1964, Berlin, Germany (cancer). Screen and

television actress. Entered films in German silents and entered U.S. films in 1930.

Appeared in: **1928** The Physician. **1929** The Prince of Rogues. **1930** Der Tanz Geht Weiter (Those Who Dance). **1931** Beyond Victory. **1932** Der Ungetreue Eckehart. **1933** Theodor Koerner. **1937** Die Schwebende Jungfrau. Other German films: The Yellow Flag; Mountains in Flames.

ARNAUD, YVONNE
Born: Dec. 20, 1892, Bordeaux, France. Died: Sept. 20, 1958, London, England. Screen, stage, television actress and pianist.

Appeared in: **1920** The Magic Skin (aka Desire); The Temptress. **1930** Canaries Sometimes Sing (stage and film versions); On Approval (stage and film versions). **1931** Tons of Money. **1933** A Cuckoo in the Nest. **1934** Princess Charming (US 1935); Lady in Danger. **1935** Widow's Might; Stormy Weather (US 1936). **1936** The Improper Duchess; The Gay Adventure. **1940** Neutral Port. **1942** Tomorrow We Live (aka At Dawn We Die—US 1943). **1946** Woman to Woman. **1947** The Ghosts of Berkeley Square.

ARNHEIM, GUS
Born: 1899. Died: Jan. 19, 1955, Beverly Hills, Calif. (heart attack). Screen, television actor, bandleader and songwriter.

Appeared with his orchestra in: **1928** Gus Arnheim and His Ambassadors (short); Gus Arnheim and His Cocoanut Grove Orchestra (short). **1929** Broadway; Half Marriage; Street Girl; Gus Arnheim and His Ambassador Hotel Orchestra (short). **1934** Gift of Gab. **1937** Paramount short.

ARNO, SIG (Siegfried Arno)
Born: 1895, Hamburg, Germany. Died: Aug. 17, 1975, Woodland Hills, Calif. (Parkinson's disease). Screen, stage actor and cabaret performer.

Appeared in: **1925** Pandora's Box; Manon Lescaut. **1933** The Big Attraction. **1935** The Star Maker. **1940** A Little Bit of Heaven; The Mummy's Hand; Diamond Frontier; Dark Streets of Cairo; The Great Dictator. **1941** This Thing Called Love; New Wine; Two Latins from Manhattan; Gambling Daughters; It Started With Eve. **1942** Pardon My Sarong; Tales of Manhattan; Juke Box Jenny; Palm Beach Story; The Devil With Hitler; Two Yanks in Trinidad. **1943** The Crystal Ball; Larceny With Music; His Butler's Sister; Taxi, Mister. **1944** Once Upon a Time; Song of the Open Road; Up in Arms. **1945** A Song to Remember; Roughly Speaking; Bring on the Girls. **1946** One More Tomorrow. **1949** The Great Lover; Holiday in Havana. **1950** Duchess of Idaho; The Toast of New Orleans. **1952** Diplomatic Courier. **1953** Fast Company; The Great Diamond Robbery.

ARNOLD, CECILE (aka CECILE ARLEY)
Died: 1931, Hong Kong (influenza). Screen actress. Was a Sennett bathing beauty.

Appeared in: **1914** The Face on the Barroom Floor; The Masquerader; Those Love Pangs; Dough and Dynamite; Getting Acquainted; His Prehistoric Past. **1915** Gussle's Day of Rest; A Game Old Knight. **1916** His Last Scent.

ARNOLD, EDWARD (Guenther Schneider)
Born: Feb. 18, 1890. Died: Apr. 26, 1956, Encino, Calif. (cerebral hemorrhage). Screen, stage and television actor. Father of actor Edward Arnold, Jr. Entered films in 1915 with Essanay.

Appeared in: **1916** The Primitive Strain. **1927** Sunrise—a Song of Two Humans. **1932** Man of the Nile; Rasputin and the Empress; The White Sister; Afraid to Talk; Okay America; Three on a Match. **1933** Whistling in the Dark; I'm No Angel; Gennie Gerhardt; The Barbarian; Her Bodyguard; Secret of the Blue Room; Roman Scandals. **1934** The President Vanishes; Unknown Blonde; Thirty Day Princess; Madame Spy; Million Dollar Ransom; Hide-Out; Sadie McKee; Wednesday's Child. **1935** Remember Last Night?; Biography of a Bachelor Girl; The Glass Key; Crime and Punishment; Diamond Jim; Cardinal Richelieu. **1936** Meet Nero Wolf; Sutter's Gold; Come and Get It. **1937** The Toast of New York; Easy Living; Blossoms on Broadway; John Meade's Woman. **1938** The Crowd Roars; You Can't Take It with You. **1939** Idiot's Delight; Mr. Smith Goes to Washington; Let Freedom Ring; Man About Town. **1940** Slightly Honorable; Johnny Apollo; The Earl of Chicago; Lillian Russell. **1941** Unholy Partners; All That Money Can Buy; Meet John Doe; The Penalty; The Lady from Cheyenne; Johnny Eager; Nothing but the Truth; Design for Scandal. **1942** The War against Mrs. Hadley; Eyes in the Night. **1943** The Youngest Profession. **1944** Kismet; Mrs. Parkington; Standing Room Only; Janie; Main Street after Dark. **1945** The Hidden Eye; Weekend at the Waldorf. **1946** Janie Gets Married; Ziegfeld Follies; Three Wise Fools; No Leave, No Love; My Brother Talks to Horses; The Mighty McGurk. **1947** Dear Ruth; The Hucksters. **1948** Three Daring Daughters; The Big City; Wallflower. **1949** John Loves Mary; Command Decision; Big Jack; Take Me out to the Ball Game; Honest John (Horner); Dear Wife. **1950** Annie Get Your Gun; The Yellow Cab Man; The Skipper Surprised His Wife. **1951** Dear Brat. **1952** Belles on Their Toes; The Devil and Daniel Webster (reissue and retitle of All That Money Can Buy—1941). **1953** Man of Conflict; Money From Home; City That Never Sleeps. **1954** Living It Up. **1956**

Miami Expose; The Huston Story; The Ambassador's Daughter. **1974** That's Entertainment (film clips).

ARNOLD, JESSIE (Jessie Gertrude Arnold)
Born: June 29, 1877, Mich. Died: June 10, 1971, Los Angeles, Calif. (heart attack). Screen actress.

Appeared in: **1916** A Social Slave; The Masked Woman; Cross Purposes; He Became a Regular Fellow; Mixed Blood; Circumstantial Justice; The Light of Love; The Losing Winner; The Pointed Finger. **1921** The Idol of the North. **1923** Fury. **1925** Playing With Souls. **1930** Brothers. **1932** Stranger in Town; Hot Saturday. **1933** The Bitter Tea of General Yen. **1934** We Live Again. **1935** Southern Exposure (short); The Four-Star Boarder (short). **1940** The Ape; The Haunted House. **1946** The Strange Woman. **1949** Air Hostess. **1951** Golden Girl.

ARNOLD, MABEL
Born: 1889. Died: Jan. 7, 1964, Hollywood, Calif. Screen actress.

ARNOLD, MARCELLA
Born: 1911. Died: Mar. 1937, Pasadena, Calif. (auto accident). Screen actress.

Appeared in: **1928** Trial Marriage. **1929** Unguarded Girls.

ARNOLD, PHIL
Born: 1909, Hackensack, N.J. Died: May 9, 1968, Van Nuys, Calif. Screen, stage, television and vaudeville actor.

Appeared in: **1939** King of the Turf. **1940** Drafted in the Depot (short). **1941** Sis Hopkins. **1942** Men of San Quentin. **1947** Buffalo Bill Rides Again. **1949** I Cheated the Law. **1951** G.I. Jane; Yes Sir, Mr. Bones; Kentucky Jubilee. **1953** The Jazz Singer; plus the following shorts: Tricky Dicks; Pardon My Backfire; and Rip, Sew and Stitch. **1954** The Big Chase; Money From Home; A Star Is Born; So You Want to Be Your Own Boss (short). **1955** It's Always Fair Weather; The Court Martial of Billy Mitchell; Illegal. **1957** Jet Pilot; My Gun Is Quick. **1958** Damn Yankees. **1960** Studs Lonigan. **1962** The Errand Boy. **1963** The Three Stooges Go around the World in a Daze; Under the Yum Yum Tree. **1964** Robin and the Seven Hoods; Three Nuts in Search of a Bolt; The Candidate; What a Way to Go. **1965** Zebra in the Kitchen. **1966** Hold On! **1967** The Cool Ones; Good Times. **1968** Skiddo.

ARNOLD, SETH
Born: 1885, London, England. Died: Jan. 3, 1955, New York, N.Y. Screen, stage actor and stage director.

Appeared in: **1949** Lost Boundaries.

ARNOLD, WILLIAM R.
Born: 1883. Died: July 20, 1940, Hollywood, Calif. (streptococcus infection). Screen, stage and vaudeville actor.

Appeared in: **1931** Oh! Oh! Cleopatra (short); Gun Smoke; The Vice Squad; Rich Man's Folly. **1932** The Crowd Roars. **1934** In Love with Life; Cain and Mabel. **1937** Four Days' Wonder. **1938** The Overland Express. **1940** Edison, The Man; The Great Dictator.

ARNOUX, ROBERT
Born: 1900, France? Died: Mar. 15, 1964. Screen actor.

Appeared in: **1935** Lilliom. **1939** Mademoiselle ma Mere. **1940** Whirlpool. **1950** Between Eleven and Midnight. **1951** Au Grand Balcon. **1953** The Night Is My Kingdom. **1957** Four Bags Full; Deadlier Than the Male. **1961** Il Suffit d'Aimer (aka Bernadette of Lourdes—US 1962).

ARQUETTE, CLIFF (aka CHARLEY WEAVER)
Born: Dec. 28, 1905, Toledo, Ohio. Died: Sept. 23, 1974, Burbank, Calif. (heart attack). Screen, vaudeville, radio and television actor.

Appeared in: **1940** Comin' 'Round the Mountain. **1965** Saturday Night Bath in Apple Valley. **1966** Don't Worry, We'll Think of a Title. Appeared in vaudeville as part of "The Three Public Enemies" team.

ARRAS, HARRY
Born: 1882. Died: Jan. 28, 1942, Hollywood, Calif. (heart attack). Screen actor. Entered films approximately 1918.

Appeared in: **1922** Blind Circumstances. **1942** Escape from Crime.

ARRUZA, CARLOS "EL CICLON"
Born: 1920, Mexico. Died: May 20, 1966. Mexico (auto accident). Matador and screen actor.

Appeared in: Mi Reino por un Torero (My Kingdom for a Bullfighter, film debut). **1957** Torero! **1960** The Alamo.

ARTAUD, ANTONIN
Born: 1896, Marseille, France. Died: Mar. 4, 1948, Ivry-sur-Seine, France (cancer). Screen, stage actor, film director, screenwriter and author.

Appeared in: **1927** Napoleon (US 1929). **1928** La Passion de Jeanne d'Arc (The Passion of Joan of Arc—US 1929). **1934** Le Serment.

ARTEMAL, TALAT
Born: 1902, Turkey. Died: Aug. 1957, Bolu, Turkey (heart attack). Stage and screen actor.

ARTHUR, JOHNNY (John Williams)
Born: 1883, Scottsdale, Pa. Died: Dec. 31, 1951, Woodland Hills, Calif. Stage and screen actor. Appeared in silent "Christie" comedies.

Appeared in: **1923** The Unknown Purple. **1924** Mlle. Midnight; Daring Love. **1925** The Monster. **1928** On Trial. **1929** The Desert Song; The Gamblers; Show of Shows; Divorce Made Easy; Lover's Delight; Adam's Eve; The Aviator; Stimulation (short). **1930** Cheer up and Smile; Personality; She Couldn't Say No; Scrappily Married; Down with Husbands; Paper Hanging (short); Bridal Night (short). **1931** Penrod and Sam, Going Wild; It's a Wise Child. **1933** Convention City; Easy Millions. **1934** Twenty Million Sweethearts; Many Happy Returns; Hell in Heaven. **1935** Anniversary Trouble (short); Traveling Saleslady; Doubting Thomas; The Ghost Walks; It's in the Air; The Bride Comes Home; Crime and Punishment; Too Tough to Kill. **1936** Freshmen Love; Murder of Dr. Harrigan; The King Steps Out; All American Toothache (short); Stage Struck. **1937** The Hit Parade; Exiled to Shanghai; Pick a Star; Night 'n' Gales (short); Make a Wish; Blossoms on Broadway; It Had to Happen Out West; Something to Sing About. **1938** Danger on the Air; Feed 'Em and Weep (short). **1940** Road to Singapore. **1941** Mountain Moonlight. **1942** Shepherd of the Ozarks. **1943** The Nazty Nuisance; The Masked Marvel (serial).

ARTHUR, JULIA
Born: 1869, Hamilton, Ontario, Canada. Died: Mar. 28, 1950, Boston, Mass. Stage and screen actress.

Appeared in: **1918** The Common Cause; The Woman the Germans Shot.

ARVIDSON, LINDA (Linda Johnson)
Born: 1884. Died: July 26, 1949, New York, N.Y. Screen, stage actress and author. Divorced from film producer David Wark Griffith (dec. 1948).

Appeared in: **1908** When Knighthood Was in Flower; When Knights Were Bold; A Calamitous Elopement; Balked at the Altar; Where Breakers Roar; An Awful Moment; The Adventures of Dollie; The Greaser's Gauntlet; The Man and the Woman; The Barbarian, Ingomar; The Planter's Wife; The Curtain Pole. **1909** Edgar Allan Poe; The Cricket on the Hearth; Lines of White on a Sullen Sea; At the Altar; The Cord of Life; The Salvation Army Lass; Tragic Love; Politician's Love Story; The Deception; A Drunkard's Reformation; Her First Biscuits; A Convict's Sacrifice; The Mills of the Gods; 1776, or The Hessian Renegades; Comata, the Sioux; Pippa Passes; The Death Disc. **1910** The Unchanging Sea; The Broken Doll; White Roses. **1911** Enoch Arden; Fisher Folks; Heartbeats of Long Ago.

ASCHE, OSCAR
Born: 1871, England. Died: Mar. 23, 1936, London, England. Screen, stage actor, playwright and screenwriter. Married to actress Lily Brayton (dec. 1953).

Appeared in: **1914** Kismit. **1933** Don Quixote; My Lucky Star. **1934** Two Hearts in Waltztime. **1935** Scrooge; The Private Secretary. **1936** Eliza Comes to Stay; Robber Symphony (US 1937).

ASH, RUSSELL (Russell Harvey Ash)
Born: Dec. 12, 1910, Ohio. Died: June 3, 1974, Los Angeles, Calif. (cancer). Screen actor. Entered films in 1937.

Appeared in: **1956** Around the World in 80 Days.

ASH, SAMUEL HOWARD
Born: 1884. Died: Oct. 20, 1951, Hollywood, Calif. Screen and stage actor.

Appeared in: **1929** Unmasked. **1933** Girl without a Room. **1934** Kiss and Make Up. **1935** Four Hours to Kill; Paris in the Spring. **1936** A Man Betrayed. **1939** Some Like It Hot. **1943** The Dancing Master; The Heat's On. **1947** Saddle Pals. **1949** Oh, You Beautiful Doll.

ASHE, WARREN
Born: New York. Died: Sept. 19, 1947, Madison, Conn. (auto accident). Screen, stage and radio actor.

Appeared in: **1940** Military Academy. **1941** The Face Behind the Mask; Naval Academy; Harmon of Michigan. **1942** Smith of Minnesota. **1943** What's Buzzin' Cousin?; Destroyer. **1947** Monsieur Verdoux.

ASHER, MAX
Born: 1880. Died: Apr. 15, 1957, Hollywood, Calif. Screen actor.

Appeared in: **1913** Mike and Jake at the Beach; The Cheese Special; Lazy Louis; Mike and Jake in the Wild West; Mike and Jake in Mexico; Mike and Jake as Heroes; Mike and Jake as Pugilists; Mike and Jake at College; Mike and Jake Among the Cannibals; Jake and Mike go Fishing; The Stingers Stung, or Mike and Jake in the Oil Fields. **1914** Love Disguised; The Tender-

Hearted Sheriff; In the Clutch of Circumstance; Mike Searches for His Long-Lost Brother; Across the Court; In the Clutches of the Villain; Their First Anniversary; The Diamond Nippers; Love and Electricity; Love and Graft; O, What's the Use?; Well! Well! Well!; The Mystery of a Taxicab; In the Year 2014; A Freak Temperance Wave; Love and Politics. **1915** Lady Baffles and Detective Duck; Saved by a Shower; Back to School Days; Schultz's Lady Friend; Wedding Bells Shall Ring; The Way he Won the Widow; The Fatal Kiss; Over the Bounding Waves; No Babies Allowed; A Millionaire for a Minute; Pete's Awful Crime; Dad's Awful Deed; Chills and Chickens; Their Bewitched Elopement; A Dip in the Water; When Hiram Went to the City; At the Beach Incognito; He Couldn't Fool His Mother-in-Law; The Sign of the Sacred Safety Pin; A Day at the San Diego Fair; Hiram's Inheritance; The Lover's Lucky Predicament; When Schultz Led the Orchestra; How Billy Got His Raise; At the Bingville Barbecue; The Mechanical Man; Mrs. Prune's Boarding House; The Opera Singer's Romance; Slightly Mistaken; The Ore Mystery; Lemonade Aids Cupid. **1916** You Want Something. **1917** Suds of Love; A Wise Dummy; Kicked in the Kitchen; Rainstorms and Brainstorms. **1918** Maimed in the Hospital. **1919** A Yankee Princess. **1921** Rip Van Winkle; The Silver Car. **1922** The Ladder Jinx. **1923** The Courtship of Miles Standish. **1924** Trigger Finger; The Shooting of Dan McGrew. **1925** Heir-Loons; The Snob Buster. **1926** Beyond the Rockies; The Carnival Girl; The Call of the Wilderness; What Happened to Jane (series); We're in the Navy Now. **1927** Avenging Fangs; Galloping Fury; Painting the Town; She's My Baby; Lost at the Front. **1928** Burning up Broadway. **1929** Show Boat; Kid's Clever. **1930** Trigger Tricks; Sweethearts on Parade. **1931** Bag O' Tricks; Talking Picture Epics (short). **1933** The Perils of Pauline (serial). **1934** Little Man, What Now?

ASHLEY, BEAULAH

Died: July 6, 1965, Hollywood, Calif. Screen actress.

ASHTON, DORRIT

Born: 1873. Died: July 25, 1936, Los Angeles, Calif. Screen, stage and vaudeville actress. Entered films in 1915 with American Films. Married to actor Charles Newton (dec. 1926).

ASHTON, SYLVIA

Born: 1880. Died: Nov. 17, 1940, Los Angeles, Calif. Screen and stage actress.

Appeared in: **1917** The Nick of Time Baby; Her Fame and Shame; Secrets of a Beauty. **1919** The Lottery Man; Men, Women and Money; Don't Change Your Husband. **1920** Jenny Be Good; Conrad in Quest of His Youth. **1921** The Blushing Bride; Garments of Truth; Her Sturdy Oak; Hold Your Horses; The Love Charm; Sham; The Love Special; A Prince There Was. **1922** Manslaughter; Is Matrimony a Failure?; For the Defense; Borderland; Saturday Night; Our Leading Citizen; A Daughter of Luxury; Youth to Youth; While Satan Sleeps. **1923** Desire; The White Flower; Souls for Sale. **1924** Greed. **1926** Dancing Days. **1927** Cheating Cheaters; Red Signals; Woman's Wares. **1928** Bachelor's Paradise; The Head Man; The Leopard Lady; Ladies' Night in a Turkish Bath; Queen Kelly; The Barker; The Crash.

ASHTON, VERA

Died: Apr. 28, 1965, Hollywood, Calif. Screen actress. Doubled for Viola Dana in silent films and also appeared in talkies.

ASKAM, EARL

Born: 1899. Died: Apr. 3, 1940, Los Angeles, Calif. (heart attack). Stage and screen actor.

Appeared in: **1930** Madam Satan. **1936** Empty Saddles; Cain and Mabel; Trail Dust. **1938** Pride of the West. **1940** Northwest Mounted Police; Pioneer of the West.

ASKAM, PERRY

Born: Aug. 31, 1898, Seattle, Wash. Died: Oct. 22, 1961, San Francisco, Calif. Screen, stage actor and opera singer.

Appeared in: **1930** Sweet Kitty Bellairs (film debut). **1935** The Crusaders.

ASQUITH, ANTHONY

Born: 1902, London, England. Died: Feb. 20, 1968, London, England. Screen actor, film director and screenwriter. Son of first Earl of Oxford, British W.W.I Prime Minister. Doubled in blonde wig for Phyliss Neilson Terry in: **1926** Boadicea.

ASTANGOV, MIKHAIL (aka LAURENCE ASTAN)

Born: 1901, Russia. Died: Apr. 21, 1965, Moscow, Russia. Stage and screen actor. Winner of three Stalin Awards.

Appeared in: **1937** Prisoners. **1949** The First Front. **1950** The Victors and the Vanquished. **1953** Sadko (rereleased as The Magic Voyage of Sinbad—US 1962); Maximba.

ASTOR, JUNIE

Born: 1918, France. Died: Aug. 23, 1967, Avalon, France (auto accident). Screen actress.

Appeared in: **1937** The Lower Depths; Club des Femmes (Girls' Club). **1939**

Entente Cordiale. **1940** Il Carnevale di Venezia (The Carnival of Venice). **1948** L'Eternel Retour (The Eternal Return).

ATCHLEY, HOOPER

Born: 1887, Tenn. Died: Nov. 16, 1943, Hollywood, Calif. (suicide—gun). Stage and screen actor.

Appeared in: **1929** Love at First Sight. **1930** The Santa Fe Trail. **1931** Millie; Men in Her Life; The Secret Witness; Branded Men; Sundown Trail; Clearing the Range; Arizona Terror. **1932** Hell's House. **1933** The Sphinx; Gambling Ship; Big Time or Bust; Gun Justice; Speed Wings. **1934** Mystery Mountain (serial). **1935** Hot Money (short); Behind the Green Lights; The Sagebrush Troubadour. **1936** The Return of Jimmy Valentine; Hearts in Bondage; Navy Born; Roarin' Lead! **1937** A Day at the Races; Portia on Trial. **1938** Little Tough Guy; Penny's Picnic (short); The Old Barn Dance; Cipher Bureau; Hunted Men; Mr. Wong, Detective. **1939** Think First (short); Chicken Wagon Family; Mountain Rhythm; East Side of Heaven. **1940** The Gay Caballero. **1941** In the Navy. **1942** Are Husbands Necessary?; Rings on Her Fingers; In Old California; Fingers at the Window; Gentleman Jim.

ATES, ROSCOE

Born: Jane. 20, 1892. Died: Mar. 1, 1962, Hollywood, Calif. (lung cancer). Screen, stage, vaudeville and television actor. Married to actress Barbara Ray (dec. 1955).

Appeared in: **1929** South Sea Rose. **1930** The Lone Star Ranger; Billy the Kid; The Big House; Caught Short; Love in the Rough; City Girl. **1931** The Great Lover; Cimarron; A Free Soul; The Champ; Politics; Too Many Cooks; Cracked Nuts. **1932** Shampoo the Magician (short); Freaks; Ladies of the Jury; Rainbow Trail; The Optimist; Roadhouse Murder; Young Bride; Deported; The Big Shot; Come on Danger; Hold 'Em Jail. **1933** Renegades of the West; What! No Beer?; Lucky Devils; The Scarlet River; Past of Mary Holmes; Cheyenne Kid; Golden Harvest; Alice in Wonderland. **1934** Woman in the Dark; She Made Her Bed; Merry Wives of Reno. **1935** The People's Enemy; a Vitaphone short. **1936** God's Country and the Woman; Fair Exchange. **1937** Universal and Columbia shorts. **1938** Riders of the Black Hills; Wild Bill Hickok (serial). **1939** Three Texas Steers; Gone With the Wind. **1940** Rancho Grande; A Cowboy from Sundown; Fireman, Save My Choo Choo (short); Untamed; Captain Caution; Chad Hannah. **1941** I'll Sell My Life; Mountain Moonlight; Bad Men of Missouri; Robin Hood of the Pecos; One Foot in Heaven; Reg'lar Fellers. **1942** Palm Beach Story; Affairs of Mimi Valentine. **1946** Colorado Serenade; Down Missouri Way; Driftin' River; Stars over Texas. **1947** Wild Country; West to Glory; Range Beyond the Blue. **1948** Black Hills; Inner Sanctum; Tumblewood Trail. **1949** Thunder in the Pines. **1950** Hills of Oklahoma; Father's Wild Game. **1951** Honeychile. **1952** The Blazing Forest. **1953** The Stranger Wore a Gun; Those Redheads from Seattle. **1955** Lucy Gallant; Abbott and Costello Meet the Keystone Kops. **1956** The Birds and the Bees; Come Next Spring. **1957** The Big Caper; Short Cut to Hell. **1961** The Silent Call; The Ladies' Man.

ATKINS, ALFRED

Born: 1900. Died: June 1941, London, England (air raid). Screen and stage actor.

ATKINS, ROBERT

Born: Aug. 10, 1886, Dulwich, England. Died: Feb. 9, 1972, London, England. Screen, stage actor and stage director.

Appeared in: **1935** Peg of Old Drury (US 1936). **1936** The Cardinal; Everything Is Thunder. **1942** The Great Mr. Handel (US 1943). **1946** A Matter of Life and Death (aka Stairway to Heaven—US). **1949** Black Magic; That Dangerous Age (aka If this Be Sin—US 1950). **1951** The House in the Square (aka I'll Never Forget You—US).

ATKINSON, EVELYN

Born: 1900. Died: Dec. 16, 1954, Seattle, Wash. Screen and stage actress.

Appeared in: **1926** The Boy Friend.

ATKINSON, FRANK

Born: Mar. 19, 1893, Blackpool, England. Died: Feb. 23, 1963, Pinner, England. Screen, stage, vaudeville, television actor, circus performer and screenwriter. Married to actress Jeanne D'Arcy. Entered films in U.S.

Appeared in: **1931** Ladies' Man; Along Came Youth; Ambassador Bill. **1932** The Woman in Room 13; The Man from Yesterday; Devil's Lottery; Sherlock Holmes. **1933** The Right to Live; Sailor's Luck; Pleasure Cruise; Cavalcade. **1934** The Great Defender; The Third Clue; Rolling in Money; Freedom of the Seas; The Path of Glory. **1935** Barnacle Bill; Death Drives Through; Night Mail; Play Up the Band; The Morals of Marcus (US 1936); Be Careful Mr. Smith. **1936** Shipmates O' Mine; The Limping Man; A Woman Alone (aka Two Who Dared—US 1937). **1937** A Romance in Flanders (aka Lost on the Western Front—US 1940); Knights for a Day; The Schooner Gang; The Green Cockatoo (US 1947 aka Four Dark Hours). **1938** I've Got a Horse. **1939** Ten Days in Paris (aka Missing Ten Days—US); Two Days to Live; The Body Vanishes. **1942** Mrs. Miniver; Hard Steel. **1948** The Last Load. **1953** Time Bomb (aka Terror on a Train—US). **1954** Lease of Life; The Green Buddha

(US 1955). **1955** Track the Man Down; Before I Wake (aka Shadow of Fear—US 1956). **1956** Wicked as They Come (US 1957); Three Men in a Boat (US 1958). **1957** At the Stroke of Nine (US 1958); High Flight (US 1958); Cat Girl; Just My Luck. **1959** Left, Right and Centre (US 1961). **1960** Trouble with Eve (aka In Trouble with Eve—US 1964). **1961** The Kitchen.

ATKINSON, GEORGE A.
Born: Dec. 15, 1877, Liverpool, England. Died: May 1, 1968, Woodland Hills, Calif. (arteriosclerosis). Screen actor, screenwriter and film critic.

Appeared in: **1921** The Conquering Power. **1923** Times Have Changed. **1924** Racing for Life. **1928** The Crimson Canyon.

ATMAR, ANN
Born: Mar. 10, 1939, Tex. Died: Oct. 14, 1966, Hollywood, Calif. (suicide). Screen and television actress.

Appeared in: **1959** Street Fighter. **1961** A Cold Wind in August. **1966** Incubus.

ATWELL, ROY
Born: 1880, Syracuse, N.Y. Died: Jan. 6, 1962, New York. Screen, stage, vaudeville and radio actor.

Appeared in: **1922** The Heart Specialist; South of Suva; Red Hot Romance; Grand Larceny; Don't Get Personal. **1923** Souls for Sale. **1926** The Outsider. **1933** A Universal short; Strike Me Pink. **1936** The Harvester. **1937** Varsity Show; Behind the Mike. **1942** The Fleet's In. **1956** People Are Funny; Gentleman Joe Palooka.

ATWILL, LIONEL (Lionel Alfred William Atwill)
Born: Mar. 1, 1885, Croydon, England. Died: Apr. 22, 1946, Pacific Palisades, Calif. (pneumonia). Stage and screen actor. Divorced from Phyllis Ralph; Elsie MacKay and Louise Stolesbury. Married to radio writer Paula Pruter.

Appeared in: **1919** The Marriage Price. **1921** The Highest Bidder; Indiscretion. **1932** Silent Witness; Mystery of the Wax Museum; Dr. X. **1933** Solitaire Man; The Sphinx; Song of Songs; Secret of the Blue Room; Vampire Bat; Secret of Madame Blanche; Murders in the Zoo. **1934** Beggars in Ermine; Nana; The Firebird; Age of Innocence; One More River; Stamboul Quest. **1935** The Devil Is a Woman; Mark of the Vampire; Captain Blood; Murder Man; The Man Who Reclaimed His Head; Rendezvous; Lives of a Bengal Lancer. **1936** Lady of Secrets; 'Til We Meet Again; Absolute Quiet. **1937** High Command; Last Train from Madrid; The Road Back; Lancer Spy; The Wrong Road; The Great Garrick. **1938** The Three Comrades; The Great Waltz. **1939** The Mad Empress; The Sun Never Sets; The Gorilla; The Hound of the Baskervilles; The Three Musketeers; Son of Frankenstein; Mr. Moto Takes a Vacation; Balalaika; The Secret of Dr. Kildare. **1940** Johnny Apollo; Boom Town; Charlie Chan's Murder Cruise; The Girl in 313; The Great Profile; Charlie Chan in Panama. **1941** Man-Made Monster. **1942** Strange Case of Dr. X; Cairo; Night Monster; Junior G-Men of the Air (serial); Pardon My Sarong; Sherlock Holmes and the Secret Weapon; The Mad Doctor of Market Street; The Ghost of Frankenstein; To Be or Not To Be. **1943** Captain America (serial); Frankenstein Meets the Wolf Man. **1944** Raiders of Ghost City (serial); Secrets of Scotland Yard; Lady in the Death House. **1945** House of Dracula; Fog Island; Crime, Inc.; House of Frankenstein. **1946** Lost City of the Jungle (serial); Genius at Work. **1953** Return of Captain America (reissued serial).

AUBREY, GEORGES
Born: 1928, Verviers, Belgium. Died: Nov. 1, 1975, Brussels, Belgium (acute bronchitis). Stage and screen actor.

Appeared in: **1966** Le Depart (US 1968). **1975** On the Tip of the Lips.

AUBREY, WILL
Born: 1894, Lithuania. Died: Jan. 3, 1958, San Francisco, Calif. Screen, vaudeville actor and radio emcee. Entered films in 1927 and appeared in Vitaphone shorts.

Appeared in: **1934** The Thin Man. **1936** After the Thin Man.

AUBURN, JOY. *See* ALYCE McCORMICK

AUDRAN, EDMOND
Born: 1919. Died: July 1951, Lyons, France (injuries from auto accident). Screen actor, dancer and choreographer.

Appeared in: **1948** The Red Shoes. **1951** Tales of Hoffman.

AUER, ANNA *See* ANNA WILLIS BAKER

AUER, FLORENCE
Born: 1880, Albany, N.Y. Died: May 14, 1962, New York, N.Y. Screen, stage actress and screenwriter. Entered films in 1908 with Biograph.

Appeared in: **1912** His Auto's Maiden Trip. **1922** Fair Lady. **1925** The Beautiful City; Heart of a Siren; That Royal Girl. **1948** State of the Union; Eight-Ball Andy (short); Michael O'Halloran. **1949** Bad Boy; Knock on Any Door; Hold

that Baby. **1950** Blonde Dynamite. **1954** Silver Lode. **1956** Andy Goes Wild (short); Pardon My Nightshirt (short).

AUER, MISCHA (Mischa Ounskowski)
Born: Nov. 17, 1905, St. Petersburg, Russia. Died: Mar. 5, 1967, Rome, Italy (heart attack). Screen, stage and television actor.

Appeared in: **1928** Something Always Happens (film debut). **1929** Marquis Preferred. **1930** Just Imagine; The Benson Murder Case; Inside the Lines; Paramount on Parade. **1931** This Unholy Garden; Delicious; Women Love Once; The Yellow Ticket. **1932** Rasputin and the Empress; No Greater Love; The Midnight Patrol; Scarlet Dawn. **1933** Infernal Machine; Dangerously Yours; Sucker Money; Corruption; Tarzan, the Fearless; After Tonight; Cradle Song; Girl without a Room; Woman Condemned. **1934** Crosby Case; Wharf Angel; Bulldog Drummond Strikes Back; Stamboul Quest. **1935** Lives of a Bengal Lancer; I Dream Too Much; The Crusaders; Clive of India; Mystery Woman; Murder in the Fleet. **1936** We're Only Human; The House of a Thousand Candles; One Rainy Afternoon; The Gay Desperado; Sons O'Guns; The Princess Comes Across; My Man Godfrey; Winterset; That Girl from Paris; Tough Guy. **1937** Three Smart Girls; We Have Our Moments; Top of the Town; One Hundred Men and a Girl; Prescription for Romance; Pick a Star; Marry the Girl; Merry-Go-Round of 1938; Vogues of 1938. **1938** It's All Yours; Rage of Paris; Service De Luxe; Little Tough Guys in Society; Sweethearts; You Can't Take It with You. **1939** East Side of Heaven; Unexpected Father; Destry Rides Again. **1940** Seven Sinners; Trail of the Vigilantes; Alias the Deacon; Sandy Is a Lady; Margie; Spring Parade; Public Deb No. 1. **1941** Moonlight in Hawaii; Sing Another Chorus; Cracked Nuts; Flame of New Orleans; Hold That Ghost; Hellzapoppin'. **1942** Don't Get Personal. **1943** Twin Beds; Around the World. **1944** Up in Mabel's Room; Lady in the Dark. **1945** A Royal Scandal; Czarina; And Then There Were None; Brewster's Millions. **1946** She Wrote the Book; Sentimental Journey. **1947** For You I Die. **1948** Sofia. **1952** Song of Paris (aka Bachelor in Paris—US 1953); Fame and the Devil; The Sky Is Red. **1953** Confidential Report. **1957** The Monte Carlo Story. **1958** Foxiest Girl in Paris; Mam'zelle Pigalle; That Naughty Girl. **1960** Au Pied, au Cheval et par Sputnik (A Dog, a Mouse and a Sputnik); Futures Vedettes (aka School for Love—US). **1962** We Joined the Navy; Mr. Arkadin. **1963** Ladies First; Dynamite Girl. **1966** Arrivederci, Baby!; The Christmas That Almost Wasn't.

AUERBACH, ARTHUR
Born: 1903, N.Y. Died: Oct. 3, 1957, Van Nuys, Calif. (heart attack). Screen, stage, television and radio actor.

Appeared in: **1937** An MGM short.

AUERBACH, HENRY L.
Died: Aug. 22, 1916, Oakland, Calif. Screen, stage and vaudeville actor.

AUGUST, EDWIN (Edwin August Philip Von der Butz)
Born: 1883. Died: Mar. 4, 1964, Hollywood, Calif. Screen, stage actor, film director and author. Brother of actor Hal August (dec. 1918). Entered films in 1908 with Biograph.

Appeared in: **1910** The Fugitive; Simple Charity; Winning Back His Love; His Daughter; Madame Rex. **1911** A Tale of the Wilderness; A Blot on the 'Scutcheon. **1912** The Girl and Her Trust; The Lesser Evil; The Old Actor; The School Teacher and the Waif; The Sands of Dee. **1918** The Lion's Claw (serial). **1921** The Idol of the North. **1922** The Blonde Vampire. **1925** Scandal Sheet. **1929** Side Street. **1930** Romance of the West. **1942** Over My Dead Body.

AUGUST, HAL
Born: 1890. Died: Sept. 21, 1918, Great Lakes, Ill. Screen actor. Brother of actor Edwin August (dec. 1964).

Appeared in: **1914** The Romance of an Actor. **1916** Beyond the Trail.

AULT, MARIE (Marie Cragg)
Born: Sept. 2, 1870, Wigan, England. Died: May 9, 1951, London, England. Stage and screen actress.

Appeared in: **1922** Class and No Class; The Wee MacGregor's Sweetheart; A Prince of Lovers (US 1927 aka Life of Lord Byron); The Grass Orphan; If Four Walls Told. **1923** Paddy-the-Next-Best-Thing; The Monkey's Paw; The Starlit Garden; Woman to Woman (US 1924). **1924** The Colleen Bawn; The Prude's Fall. **1925** The Rat; Children of the Night Series #2. **1926** The Triumph of the Rat; The Lodger (aka The Case of Jonathan Drew—US 1928); Mademoiselle from Armentieres. **1927** A Daughter in Revolt; Roses of Picardy; Hindle Wakes (aka Fanny Hawthorne—US 1929); The Rolling Road; The Silver Lining; Madame Pompadour. **1928** Dawn; Virginia's Husband; Yellow Stockings; Troublesome Wives (aka Summer Lightning); Life (aka Juan Jose); Victory; God's Clay; Hell Cat. **1929** Kitty; Little Miss London; The Return of the Rat; Downstream; The Alley Cat. **1931** Third Time Lucky; The Speckled Band; Contraband Love; Peace and Quiet. **1932** Little Fella. **1933** Money for Speed; Daughters of Today; Their Night Out; Maid Happy. **1935** Windfall; Swinging the Lead; Lend Me Your Wife. **1936** Tropical Trouble. **1941** Major Barbara; Love on the Dole. **1942** The Missing Million. **1943** We Dive at Dawn. **1944** It

Happened One Sunday. **1945** They Knew Mr. Knight. **1948** The Three Weird Sisters. **1949** Madness of the Heart (US 1950). **1951** Cheer the Brave.

AUSTIN, ALBERT
Born: 1882. Died: Aug. 17, 1953, North Hollywood, Calif. Screen actor, film director and screenwriter. Entered films in 1910.

Appeared in: **1921** The Kid; My Boy. **1922** Trouble. **1923** A Prince of a King. **1925** Keep Smiling.

AUSTIN, CHARLES
Born: 1878. Died: Jan. 14, 1944, London, England. Screen and stage actor.

Appeared in: **1937** Another Dawn.

AUSTIN, GENE (Eugene Lucas)
Born: 1901. Died: Jan. 24, 1972, Palm Springs, Calif. (cancer). Screen actor, singer and songwriter.

Appeared in: **1933** Melody Cruise. **1934** Sadie McKee; Gift of Gab. **1935** An RKO short. **1936** An RKO short. **1940** My Little Chickadee. **1944** Moon Over Las Vegas.

AUSTIN, JERE
Born: 1876. Died: Nov. 12, 1927, Hollywood, Calif. (cancer). Screen actor.

Appeared in: **1914** The School for Scandal; Nina of the Theatre; The Lynbrook Tragedy. **1915** The White Goddess; Unfaithful to His Trust. **1916** The Romance of the Hollow Tree; For Uncle Sam's Navy. **1918** Fedora. **1927** King of Kings.

AUSTIN, JOHANNA (Anna R. Austin)
Born: 1853. Died: June 1, 1944, Hollywood, Calif. Screen actress. Appeared in early Edison Co. films.

AUSTIN, LOIS
Born: 1909. Died: Apr. 26, 1957, Hollywood, Calif. (cachexia). Screen actress. Married to film director Charles Barton.

Appeared in: **1942** Swamp Woman; Down Texas Way. **1946** The Spider Woman Strikes Back; Centennial Summer. **1947** The Trap. **1949** Night Unto Night; Henry, the Rainmaker. **1950** Father Makes Good; The Fuller Brush Girl. **1952** Night Stage to Galveston. **1957** Mom and Dad.

AUSTIN, STEPHEN E.
Born: 1891. Died: May 12, 1955, Dallas, Tex. (heart attack). Screen and radio actor.

AVALIER, DON
Died: May 29, 1973. Screen actor.

Appeared in: **1954** Playgirl.

AVERY, PATRICIA
Born: 1902. Died: 1973. Screen actress. Was Wampas Baby Star of 1927. Married to art director Merrill Pye.

Appeared in: **1927** A Light in the Window; Annie Laurie; Night Life. **1928** Alex the Great.

AVERY, TOL
Born: 1915. Died: Aug. 27, 1973, Calif. (heart attack). Screen and television actor.

Appeared in: **1952** Scarlet Angel. **1955** It Came from Beneath the Sea; I'll Cry Tomorrow. **1957** The Unholy Wife. **1958** Buchanan Rides Alone; The Case Against Brooklyn. **1961** Twist Around the Clock; The George Raft Story; Man-Trap. **1963** Ticklish Affair. **1964** A Tiger Walks. **1965** Satan Bug. **1966** Follow Me, Boys! **1967** Hotel. **1969** A Dream of Kings. **1970** W.U.S.A.

AVOLO, ROSALIE. *See* ROSALIE AVOLO WINCOTT

AYE, MARYON
Born: 1906. Died: July 21, 1951, Hollywood, Calif. (suicide—poison). Stage and screen actress.

Appeared in: **1921** Montana Bill; The Vengeance Trail. **1923** The Meanest Man in the World; The Eternal Three. **1924** The Last Man on Earth; The Roughneck. **1926** Irene.

AYLESWORTH, ARTHUR
Born: Aug. 12, 1884, Apponaug, R.I. Died: June 26, 1946. Screen actor.

Appeared in: **1932–33** Paramount shorts. **1934** Babbitt; St. Louis Kid; Gentlemen Are Born; Six Day Bike Rider; Dames; Midnight Alibi; The Dragon Murder Case; The Key; Desirable; The Man With Two Faces; Case of the Howling Dog; British Agent. **1935** I Am a Thief; The Secret Bride; The Nitwits; Men Without Names; The Man on the Flying Trapeze; The Big Broadcast of 1936; The Virginia Judge; Escape from Devil's Island; Forced Landing. **1936** Rose of the Rancho; Woman Trap; The Petrified Forest; King of the

Pecos; Girl of the Ozarks; Love Begins at Twenty; Arizona Raiders; Down the Ribber (short); To Mary With Love; Mister Cinderella; Dimples; The Man I Marry; The Plot Thickens; The President's Mystery. **1937** Sandflow; Marked Woman; Fifty Roads to Town; That Man's Here Again; I Cover the War; Slave Ship; Escape by Night; Marry the Girl. **1938** Test Pilot; Of Human Hearts; Blockade; Outside the Law; Spawn of the North. **1939** The Oklahoma Kid; King of the Underworld; Jesse James; The Return of the Cisco Kid; 6,000 Enemies; Beau Geste; Drums Along the Mohawk; What a Life; The Return of Dr. X; Dust Be My Destiny. **1940** Little Old New York; The Grapes of Wrath; Edison the Man; Young People; Brigham Young—Frontiersman; The Westerner. **1941** Dancing on a Dime; The Smiling Ghost. **1942** Moontide; Sin Town; Scattergood Rides High. **1944** The Adventures of Mark Twain; Home in Indiana; Roger Touhy Gangster. **1945** Scared Stiff.

AYLING, ROBERT
Died: Aug. 28, 1919, New York, N.Y. Screen actor.

AYLMER, DAVID
Born: 1933. Died: July 20, 1964, London, England (suicide). Screen, stage and television actor. Son of actor Felix Aylmer.

Appeared in: **1957** Yangtse Incident (aka Battle Hell—US). **1958** Gideon's Day (aka Gideon of Scotland Yard—1959); The Man Who Wouldn't Talk (US 1960). **1962** The Iron Maiden (aka The Wingin' Maiden—US 1963).

AYRES, AGNES (Agnes Hinkle)
Born: Apr. 4, 1898, Carbondale, Ill. Died: Dec. 25, 1940, Los Angeles, Calif. (cerebral hemorrhage). Screen, stage, radio, and vaudeville actress.

Appeared in: **1920** The Furnace; Held by the Enemy; Go and Get It. **1921** Affairs of Anatole; Forbidden Fruit; The Sheik; Cappy Ricks; The Love Special; Too Much Speed. **1922** Clarence; The Ordeal; The Lane That Had No Turning; Bought and Paid For; Borderland; A Daughter of Luxury. **1923** The Ten Commandments; Tess of the Storm Country; Racing Hearts; The Heart Raider; Hollywood; The Marriage Maker. **1924** The Story Without a Name; When a Girl Loves; Bluff; Don't Call It Love; The Guilty One; Worldly Goods. **1925** Tomorrow's Love; Morals for Men; The Awful Truth. **1926** The Son of the Sheik; Her ket Value. **1928** The Lady of Victory; Into the Night. **1929** Bye, Bye, Buddy; The Donovan Affair; Broken Hearted; Eve's Love Letters. **1937** Morning Judge (short).

AYRES, MITCHELL "MITCH"
Born: 1911, Milwaukee, Wisc. Died: Sept. 5, 1969, Las Vegas, Nev. (auto accident). Orchestra leader and screen actor.

Appeared in: **1944** Swingtime Johnny; Moonlight and Cactus; Lady, Let's Dance!

AYRES, ROBERT
n: 1914, Mich. Died: Nov. 5, 1968, Hemel Hempstead, England (heart attack). Screen, stage and television actor.

Appeared in: **1949** They Were Not Divided. **1951** The Black Widow; To Have and to Hold. **1952** Cosh Boy; 24 Hours in a Woman's Life (aka Affair in Monte Carlo). **1953** A Night without Stars; The Slasher. **1954** A Prize of Gold; River Beat. **1955** Contraband Spain; It's Never Too Late. **1956** The Baby and the Battleship; Depraved. **1957** The Story of Esther Costello; The Cat Girl; Operation Murder. **1958** A Night to Remember. **1959** First Man into Space; John Paul Jones; Time Lock. **1962** The Road to Hong Kong; Two and Two Make Six. **1963** The Sicilians. **1965** The Heroes of Telemark (US 1966). **1968** Battle beneath the Earth. **1969** Isadora (aka The Loves of Isadora—US).

AYRES, SYDNEY
Died: Sept. 9, 1916, Oakland, Calif. Screen actor, nenwriter and film producer.

Appeared in: **1911** Captain Brand's Wife; Blackbeard; The Heart of John Barlow. **1912** The Foreign Spy. **1913** Trapped in a Forest Fire; An Innocent Informer. **1914** The Power of Light; The Rose of San Juan; Destinies Fulfilled; The Son of Thomas Gray; The Cricket on the Hearth; The Crucible; The Turning Point; The Last Supper; The Story of the Olive. **1915** Fifty Years Behind; The Stranger; Around the Corner; The Honor of Kenneth McGrath; On Desert Sands; The Love That Lasts; Love and Handcuffs; The Law o' The Parent; The Hearts of Fate; Haunting Winds; Every Man's Money; The Shot; The Vengeance of Guido; A Pure Gold Partner; The Man from Argentine; Honor Thy Husband; His Good Name; The Mirror of Justice; The Third Partner. **1919** The Stolen Melody; As in a Dream; The String of Conscience.

"BABY LAURENCE" (Lawrence Jackson)
Born: 1921, Baltimore, Md. Died: Apr. 2, 1974, New York, N.Y. (cancer). Black screen, stage, vaudeville, television actor and tap dancer.

BACCALONI, SALVATORE
Born: 1900, Rome, Italy. Died: Dec. 31, 1969, New York, N.Y. Screen actor and operatic comedian.

Appeared in: **1956** Full of Life (film debut). **1958** Rock-A-Bye Baby; Merry

Andrew. **1961** Operation Bottleneck; Fanny. **1962** The Pigeon That Took Rome.

BACH. See CHARLES "BACH" PASQUIER

BACH, MRS. RUDI
Died: Apr. 11, 1960, Buffalo, N.Y. Stage and screen actress.

BACKUS, GEORGE
Born: 1858. Died: May 22, 1939, Merrick, N.Y. Screen, stage actor and playwright.

Appeared in: **1921** The Price of Possession. **1923** The Exciters. **1924** Her Own Free Will; The Warrens of Virginia.

BACLANOVA, OLGA
Born: 1899? Moscow, Russia. Died: Sept. 6, 1974, Vevey, Switzerland. Screen, stage, radio actress and ballet dancer. Married to actor Nicholas Soussanin (dec. 1975); married to theatre owner Richard Davis.

Appeared in: **1927** The Dove (film debut). **1928** The Street of Sin; Forgotten Faces; Docks of New York; Avalanche; Three Sinners; The Man Who Laughs. **1929** A Dangerous Woman; The Wolf of Wall Street; The Man I Love. **1930** Are You There?; Cheer Up and Smile. **1931** The Great Lover. **1932** Downstairs; Freaks. **1933** The Billion Dollar Scandal. **1935** Broadway Brevities (short); a Universal short. **1943** Claudia.

BACON, BESSIE (Bessie Bacon Allen)
Born: 1886. Died: Dec. 7, 1952, Los Angeles, Calif. Screen actress and writer.

BACON, DAVID (David Gaspar Griswold Bacon)
Born: Mar. 24, 1914, Jamaica Plains, Mass. Died: Sept. 13, 1943, Los Angeles, Calif. (stab wounds). Screen actor.

Appeared in: **1942** Ten Gentlemen from West Point. **1943** The Masked Marvel (serial); Crash Dive; Gals Inc.

BACON, FAITH
Born: 1909. Died: Sept. 26, 1956, Chicago, Ill. (suicide—jump from window). Screen and vaudeville actress.

Appeared in: **1938** Prison Train.

BACON, FRANK
Born: 1864, Marysville, Calif. Died: July 21, 1922, Chicago, Ill. (heart attack). Stage and screen actor.

Appeared in: **1915** The Silent Voice.

BACON, IRVING
Born: Sept. 6, 1893, St. Joseph, Mo. Died: Feb. 5, 1965, Hollywood, Calif. Screen, stage and television actor. Entered films with Mack Sennett.

Appeared in: **1927** California or Bust. **1928** Head Man; The Good-Bye Kiss. **1929** Half Way to Heaven; Side Street; Dane and Arthur series; Louise Fazenda series; Two Sisters; The Old Barn (short); The Saturday Night Kid. **1930** Street of Chance. **1931** Alias the Bad Man; Branded Men. **1932** Union Depot; No One Man; This Is the Night; Gentleman for a Day; Central Park; File 113; Million Dollar Legs. **1933** He Learned About Women; Hello, Everybody!; Private Detective 62; Big Executive. **1934** Shadows of Sing Sing; You Belong to Me; Hat, Coat and Glove; Ready for Love; The Pursuit of Happiness; Lone Cowboy; Miss Fane's Baby Is Stolen; Six of a Kind; It Happened One Night; The Hell Cat; No Ransom. **1935** West of the Pecos; Powdersmoke Range; Here Comes Cookie; Private Worlds; Goin' to Town; The Glass Key; The Virginia Judge; Ship Cafe; Two-Fisted; It's a Small World; Diamond Jim; Manhattan Moon; Bright Leaves. **1936** Petticoat Fever; Earthworm Tractors; Drift Fence; Hollywood Boulevard; Lady Be Careful; Murder with Pictures; Wives Never Know; Valiant Is the Word for Carrie; Hopalong Cassidy Returns; It's a Great Life; Big Town Girl; Three Cheers for Love; The Big Broadcast of 1937. **1937** Let's Make a Million; Interns Can't Take Money; Exclusive; Seventh Heaven; Arizona Mahoney; Big City; Marry the Girl; It's Love I'm After. **1938** Passport Husband; Blondie; Mr. Moto's Gamble; The Big Broadcast of 1938; The Texans; There Goes My Heart; The Cowboy and the Lady; You Can't Take It with You; Midnight Intruder; Exposed; The First Hundred Years; The Chaser; Tip-Off Girls; Sing, You Sinners; Spawn of the North; Kentucky Moonshine; The Amazing Dr. Clitterhouse; The Sisters. **1939** Too Busy to Work; Blondie Meets the Boss; Hollywood Slaves; Tailspin; Lucky Night; Second Fiddle; Hollywood Cavalcade; Gone with the Wind; I Stole a Million; Blondie Takes a Vacation; Rio; Blondie Brings up Baby; The Gracie Allen Murder Case; The Oklahoma Kid; Torchy Runs for Mayor. **1940** Indianapolis Speedway; Heaven with a Barbed Wire Fence; The Grapes of Wrath; The Man Who Wouldn't Talk; Young People; Dr. Ehrlich's Magic Bullet; Blondie on a Budget; Manhattan Heartbeat; The Return of Frank James; Gold Rush Maisie; The Howards of Virginia; Dreaming Out Loud; Blondie Has Servant Trouble; Michael Shayne, Private Detective; Star Dust; You Can't Fool Your Wife; Blondie Plays Cupid. **1941** Blondie Goes Latin; She Couldn't Say No; Western Union; Ride on, Vaquero; Caught in the Draft; Accent on Love; Too Many Blondes; Moon over Her Shoulder; It Started with Eve;

Never Give a Sucker an Even Break; Blondie in Society; Remember the Day; Meet John Doe; A Girl, a Guy and a Gob; Great Guns; Henry Aldrich for President; Cadet Girl; Tobacco Road. **1942** The Bashful Bachelor; Pardon My Sarong; Through Different Eyes; Juke Girl; Young America; Give Out, Sister; Between Us Girls; Get Hep to Love; Blondie for Victory; Holiday Inn; Footlight Serenade. **1943** It's a Great Life; Footlight Glamour; Shadow of a Doubt; Johnny Come Lately; Hers to Hold; Follow the Band; King of the Cowboys; Two Weeks to Live; Happy Go Lucky; So's Your Uncle; The Good Fellows; In Old Oklahoma; Action in the North Atlantic; The Desperados; Stranger in Town; Dixie Dugan. **1944** Weekend Pass; Chip Off the Old Block; Her Primitive Man; Since You Went Away; Heavenly Days; Pin Up Girl; Wing and a Prayer. **1945** Under Western Skies; Roughly Speaking; Patrick the Great; Out of This World; Guest Wife; Hitchhike to Happiness. **1946** Night Train to Memphis; One Way to Love; Wake up and Dream. **1947** My Brother Talks to Horses; Saddle Pals; Monsieur Verdoux; The Bachelor and the Bobby-Soxer. **1948** Albuquerque; Moonrise; Adventures in Silverado; State of the Union; The Velvet Touch; Good Sam; Rocky; Family Honeymoon. **1949** Night unto Night; John Loves Mary; The Green Promise; The Big Cat; Dynamite; It's a Great Feeling; Manhandled; Woman in Hiding. **1950** Wabash Avenue; Born to Be Bad; Emergency Wedding; Dear Wife; Sons of New Mexico. **1951** Honeychile; Cause for Alarm; Katie Did It; Desert of Lost Men. **1952** O. Henry's Full House; Room for One More. **1953** Fort Ti; Devil's Canyon; Kansas Pacific; Sweethearts on Parade. **1954** Ma and Pa Kettle at Home; Black Horse Canyon; Duffy of San Quentin; A Star Is Born; The Glenn Miller Story. **1955** Run for Cover; At Gunpoint. **1956** Hidden Guns; The Dakota Incident. **1958** Ambush at Cimarron Pass; Fort Massacre.

BACON, LLOYD
Born: Jan. 16, 1890, San Jose, Calif. Died: Nov. 15, 1955, Burbank, Calif. (cerebral hemorrhage). Screen, stage, vaudeville actor and film director. Entered films with Essanay Co.

Appeared in: **1915** Broncho Billy and the Lumber King; Broncho Billy Misled; Wine, Women and Song; Snakeville's Champion; Broncho Billy's Cowardly Brother; The Burglar's Godfather; Broncho Billy and the Cardsharp; A Quiet Little Game; Broncho Billy Begins Life Anew; A Christmas Revenge. **1917** His Thankless Job; A Hotel Disgrace; His Fatal Move; His Taking Ways; A Dark Room Secret. **1919** Square Deal Sanderson. **1921** The Great Profit; Hands Off; Hearts and Masks; The Road Demon. **1922** Smudge.

BACON, WALTER SCOTT
Born: 1891. Died: Nov. 7, 1973, Hollywood, Calif. (heart attack). Screen actor and assistant film director. Married to actress Sybil Bacon.

BACUS, LUCIA. See LUCIA SEGAR

BAER, ARTHUR "BUGS"
Born: 1886, Philadelphia, Pa. Died: May 17, 1969, New York, N.Y. (cancer). Screen actor and newspaper columnist.

Appeared in: **1924** The Great White Way. **1926** Oh, Baby! **1930** They Learned About Women.

BAER, MAX
Born: 1909. Died: Nov. 21, 1959, Hollywood, Calif. (heart attack). Screen, stage, radio and vaudeville actor and former heavyweight boxing champion of the world. Divorced from actress Dorothy Dunbar.

Appeared in: **1933** The Prizefighter and the Lady. **1938** Fisticuffs (short). **1942** The Navy Comes Through. **1943** Ladies' Day; Buckskin Frontier. **1944** The Iron Road. **1949** Africa Screams; Bride for Sale. **1950** Riding High. **1951** Skipalong Rosenbloom. **1956** The Harder They Fall. **1957** Utah Blaine. **1958** Once upon a Horse; Over She Goes.

BAER, THAIS
Born: 1929. Died: Sept. 8, 1930, Painted Desert, Ariz. Fourteen-month-old baby girl making fourth screen appearance when she died during filming of Painted Desert.

Appeared in: **1931** Painted Desert.

BAGDAD, WILLIAM
Died: Nov. 20, 1975. Screen actor.

Appeared in: **1967** She Freak. **1968** The Girl in Gold Boots; The Astro-Zombies; Head.

BAGDASARIAN, ROSS S. (aka DAVID SEVILLE)
Born: 1920. Died: Jan. 16, 1972, Beverly Hills, Calif. (natural causes). Composer, orchestra leader and screen actor.

Appeared in: **1952** Viva Zapata. **1953** Destination Gobi. **1954** Alaska Seas; Rear Window. **1956** Three Violent People; The Proud and the Profane. **1957** The Devil's Hairpin. **1958** The Deep Six. **1959** Stalag 17.

BAGGETT, LYNNE

Born: 1928. Died: Mar. 22, 1960, Hollywood, Calif. (overdose of barbiturates). Screen actress. Divorced from film producer Sam Spiegel.

Appeared in: **1941** Manpower. **1944** The Adventures of Mark Twain; Hollywood Canteen. **1946** The Time of Their Lives. **1950** D.O.A.; Flame and the Arrow. **1951** The Mob.

BAGGOT, KING

Born: 1874, St. Louis, Mo. Died: July 11, 1948, Los Angeles, Calif. (stroke). Screen, stage actor, film director and screenwriter. Entered films in 1910 as an actor.

Appeared in: **1911** The Scarlet Letter. **1912** Lady Audley's Secret. **1913** Dr. Jekyll and Mr. Hyde; Ivanhoe. **1915** The Corsican Brothers. **1916** Lovely Mary. **1918** The Eagle's Eye (serial). **1920** Dwelling Place of Light; The Cheater; The Hawk's Trail (serial). **1921** Moonlight Follies; Snowy Baker; The Shadow of Lightning Ridge; The Fighting Breed; The Butterfly Girl; The Girl in the Taxi. **1922** Going Straight. **1923** His Last Race; The Thrill Chaser. **1925** Tumbleweeds. **1926** Lovely Mary. **1927** The Notorious Lady. **1930** Once a Gentleman; The Czar of Broadway. **1931** Scareheads; Sweepstakes. **1932** The Big Flash (short); Fame Street. **1934** Beloved. **1935** It Happened in New York; Father Brown, Detective; I've Been Around; Mississippi; Chinatown Squad; She Gets Her Man. **1941** Come Live with Me. **1945** Abbott and Costello in Hollywood.

BAGLEY, SAM (Samuel Borken)

Born: 1903. Died: July 3, 1968, Hollywood, Calif. (heart ailment). Screen actor. Entered films approx. 1930.

Appeared in: **1955** The Lieutenant Wore Skirts.

BAGNI, JOHN

Born: 1911. Died: Feb. 13, 1954, Hollywood, Calif. (heart attack). Screen, stage actor, screen, radio and television writer.

Appeared in: **1942** Bombay Clipper. **1943** Mug Town. **1945** A Bell for Adano. **1946** The Phantom Thief. **1947** The Pretender. **1950** Captain China.

BAILEY, ALBERT

Born: 1891. Died: July 31, 1952, Hollywood, Calif.(suicide—gun). Western screen actor and trainer of film horses.

BAILEY, EDWARD LORENZ

Born: 1883. Died: Oct. 16, 1951, Lima, Ohio. Stage and screen actor.

BAILEY, EDWIN B.

Born: 1873. Died: July 22, 1950, Santa Monica, Calif. Screen, stage and vaudeville actor. Married to actress Grace Lockwood (dec. 1955).

BAILEY, FRANKIE (Frankie Walters)

Born: 1859, New Orleans, La. Died: July 8, 1953, Los Angeles, Calif. Screen, stage and burlesque actress. Known at the turn of the century as "The Girl with the Million Dollar Legs." Entered films in 1922.

Appeared in: **1923** The Famous Mrs. Fair. **1925** Flower of Night; Thank You. **1926** The Crown of Lies.

BAILEY, WILLIAM (William Norton Bailey)

Born: 1886. Died: Nov. 8, 1962, Hollywood, Calif. Screen actor and film director.

Appeared in: **1913** The Snare. **1918** The Eagle's Eye (serial). **1920** The Phantom Foe (serial). **1921** The Yellow Arm (serial). **1923** Is Money Everything? **1924** Three O'Clock in the Morning; The Cyclone Rider; The Desert Hawk; The Uninvited Guest; Against All Odds; The Flaming Forties; Gold Heels; Winner Take All. **1925** Big Pal; My Neighbor's Wife; Bustin' Thru; The Desert Flower; Fighting Youth; Lazybones; Top Hand; You're Fired. **1926** House without a Key (serial); Queen O'Diamonds; Ranson's Folly; The Stolen Ranch; Fighting Jack; Lash of the Law. **1927** Melting Millions (serial); Wild Beauty; High School Hero; The Fighting Three. **1928** Waterfront; The Flyin' Cowboy; The Lone Patrol; Burning Bridges; Hit of the Show; Man in the Rough; The Stronger Will; The Way of the Strong. **1929** The Aviator. **1930** Back Pay; Today. **1932** The Midnight Patrol. **1933** The Lone Avenger. **1934** Search for Beauty. **1935** George White's Scandals; Thunder Mountain; One Hour Late. **1936** Charlie Chan's Secret; Too Many Parents. **1944** Movie Pests (short). **1949** Brand of Fear; Across the Rio Grande. **1950** Lightning Guns.

BAINES, BEULAH

Born: 1905. Died: Aug. 1930, Banning, Calif. Stage and screen actress.

Appeared in: **1921** The Charm School.

BAINTER, FAY

Born: Dec. 7, 1891, Los Angeles, Calif. Died: Apr. 16, 1968, Los Angeles, Calif. Screen, stage and television actress. Mother of actor Reginald Venable (dec. 1974). Won 1938 Academy Award for Best Supporting Actress in Jezebel and

was nominated for Best Actress in White Banners—did not win. A change in the Academy Awards nominating and voting rules was made because of confusion of her two nominations in 1938.

Appeared in: **1934** This Side of Heaven (film debut). **1937** The Soldier and the Lady; Make Way for Tomorrow; Quality Street. **1938** Mother Carey's Chickens; Jezebel; White Banners; The Arkansas Traveler; The Shining Hour. **1939** Daughters Courageous; The Lady and the Mob; Yes, My Darling Daughter; Our Neighbors, The Carters. **1940** A Bill of Divorcement; Our Town; Young Tom Edison; Maryland. **1941** Babes on Broadway; Love Crazy. **1942** Journey for Margaret; Mrs. Wiggs of the Cabbage Patch; The War against Mrs. Hadley; Woman of the Year. **1943** Cry Havoc; The Human Comedy; Salute to the Marines; Presenting Lily Mars; The Heavenly Body. **1944** Three Is a Family; Dark Waters. **1945** State Fair. **1946** The Virginian; The Kid from Brooklyn. **1947** The Secret Life of Walter Mitty; Deep Valley. **1948** June Bride; Give My Regards to Broadway. **1951** Close to My Heart. **1953** The President's Lady. **1962** The Children's Hour; Bon Voyage.

BAIRD, CORA

Born: 1913. Died: Dec. 7, 1967, New York, N.Y. Screen, stage, and television actress. Partner in puppet team of Bil and Cora Baird.

BAIRD, DOROTHY. See DOROTHY VERNON

BAIRD, LEAH

Born: c. 1891. Died: Oct. 3, 1971, Hollywood, Calif. (anemia). Screen, stage actress, screenwriter and film producer. Entered films with Vitagraph in New York.

Appeared in: **1912** Stenographers Wanted; Chumps; The Black Sheep; The Extension Table; The Foster Child; The Miracle; The Way of a Man; Counsel for the Defense; Working for Hubby; The Nipper's Lullaby; Adventure of the Italian Model; Lord Browning and Cinderella; The Dawning; The Red Barrier; The Days of Terror; All For a Girl. **1913** Ivanhoe; Sue Simpkins' Ambition; The Anarchist; Mr. and Mrs. Innocence Abroad; The Two Purses; A Woman; The Birthday Gift; The Locket; A Soul in Bondage; A Vampire of the Desert; The Heart of Mrs. Robbins; My Lady Idleness; Time is Money; Cutey and the Chorus Girls; Hearts of the First Empire. **1914** Neptune's Daughter; The Old Rag Doll; The Price of Sacrilege; The Flaming Diagram; Fine Feathers Make Fine Birds; The Man Who Knew; Love and a Lottery Ticket; His Last Chance; His Dominant Passion; Out of the Far East; The Upper Hand; Love or a Throne; Watch Dog of the Deep. **1915** Tried for His Own Murder; The Ruling Power; Dorothy; Saints and Sinners; The Gods Redeem; A Question of Right or Wrong; The Romance of a Handkerchief. **1916** The Eyes of Love; The Primal Instinct; The Bond of Blood; Would You Forgive Her? **1917** A Sunset; The Old Toymaker; The Devil's Pay Day; One Law for Both; The Doctor's Deception; A Woman of Clay; Sins of Ambition. **1918** Wolves of Kultur (serial); The Fringe of Society; Moral Suicide. **1919** The Echo of Youth; As a Man Thinks. **1921** The Heart Line. **1922** Don't Doubt Your Wife; When the Devil Drives; The Bride's Confession; When Husbands Deceive. **1923** Destroying Angel; Is Divorce a Failure?; The Miracle Makers. **1924** The Law Demands; The Radio Flyer. **1925** The Unnamed Woman. **1942** Lady Gangster; Yankee Doodle Dandy. **1956** Around the World in 80 Days.

BAKER, ANNA WILLIS (Anna Auer)

Born: 1860. Died: Apr. 2, 1944, Fort Lee, N.J. Screen and stage actress.

BAKER, ART

Born: 1898, New York, N.Y. Died: Aug. 26, 1966, Los Angeles, Calif. (heart attack). Screen, radio and television actor.

Appeared in: **1944** Once upon a Time. **1945** Spellbound. **1946** Abie's Irish Rose. **1947** The Beginning of the End; Dark Delusion; Daisy Kenyon; The Farmer's Daughter. **1948** Silver River; A Southern Yankee; Walk a Crooked Mile; The Decision of Christopher Blake; State of the Union; The Walls of Jericho. **1949** Easy Living; Take One False Step; Any Number Can Play; Night Unto Night; Massacre River; Cover Up; Impact; Task Force. **1950** The Underworld Story; Hot Rod. **1951** Cause for Alarm; Only the Valiant. **1954** Living It Up. **1955** Artists and Models. **1960** Twelve Hours to Kill. **1962** Swingin' Along. **1965** Young Dillinger. **1966** The Wild Angels.

BAKER, BELLE

Born: 1895, New York, N.Y. Died: Apr. 29, 1957, Los Angeles, Calif. (heart attack). Screen, stage, vaudeville and television actress.

Appeared in: **1929** Song of Love. **1944** Atlantic City.

BAKER, BOB (Leland T. Weed)

Born: Nov. 8, 1901, Forest City, Iowa. Died: Aug. 29, 1975, Prescott, Ariz. (stroke). Screen actor and singing cowboy.

Appeared in: **1937** Courage of the West. **1938** Border Wolves; The Last Stand; Outlaw Express; Black Bandit; Singing Outlaw. **1939** Desperate Trails; Oklahoma Frontier. **1940** Chip of the Flying U; West of Carson City; Riders of Pasco Basin; Bad Man from Red Butte. **1943** Wild Horse Stampede. **1944** Mystery Man.

BAKER, EDDIE (Edward King)
Born: Nov. 17, 1897, Davis, W.Va. Died: Feb. 4, 1968, Hollywood, Calif. Screen actor. Entered films as a prop boy with Biograph in 1914. Was one of the original Keystone Kops and appeared in early "Joker" comedies, "Gale Henry" comedies, Hal Roach films and Christie shorts.

Appeared in: **1924** Hold Your Breath. **1929** All at Sea. **1930** The Big Kick (short). **1931** City Lights; Monkey Business; plus the following shorts: One of the Smiths; Call a Cop; and Come Clean. **1932** The following shorts: Free Eats; Choo Choo; Now We'll Tell One; and Too Many Women. **1933** The following shorts: Beauty and the Bus; Kickin' the Crown Around; Sons of the Desert; His Silent Racket; Arabian Tights; Midsummer Mush; Tired Feet; Knight Duty; Tired for Life; and Feeling Rosy. **1934** Elmer and Elsie; Babes in Toyland (aka The March of the Wooden Soldiers); plus the following shorts: Them Thar Hills; It Happened One Day; Something Simple; The Chases of Pimple Street; and Petting Preferred. **1950** Revenge Is Sweet (reissue of Babes in Toyland—1934). **1955** Land of Fury.

BAKER, ELSIE
Born: 1893, Chicago, Ill. Died: Aug. 16, 1971, Hollywood, Calif. (heart attack). Screen, stage, vaudeville, radio and television actress. Made stage debut at age of ten months.

Appeared in: **1952** No Room for the Groom.

BAKER, FLOYD
Born: 1906. Died: Mar. 17, 1943, Hollywood, Calif. Screen actor.

BAKER, JOSEPHINE
Born: June 3, 1906, St. Louis, Mo. Died: Apr. 12, 1975, Paris, France (cerebral hemorrhage). Black screen, stage actress and singer-dancer. Divorced from painter Count Heno Abatino and orchestra leader Jo Bouillon.

Appeared in: **1923** Black Shadows (documentary); **1944** Moulin Rouge. **1959** The French Way. **1975** Black Shadows on the Silent Screen (documentary-rerelease of 1923 film).

BAKER, LEE
Born: 1876, Ovid, Mich. Died: Feb. 24, 1948, Los Angeles, Calif. Stage and screen actor.

Appeared in: **1923** The Fighting Blade. **1925** Soul Fire. **1947** Mourning Becomes Electra.

BAKER, PHIL
Born: Aug. 24, 1898, Philadelphia, Pa. Died: Dec. 1, 1963, Copenhagen, Denmark. Screen, stage, radio and vaudeville actor. Appeared in vaudeville with Ben Bernie (dec. 1943) as part of "Bernie and Baker" team.

Appeared in: **1929** A Bad Boy from a Good Family (short); In Spain (short). **1934** Gift of Gab. **1938** The Goldwyn Follies; Start Cheering. **1943** The Gang's All Here. **1944** Take It or Leave It.

BAKER, WILLIAM
Died: Dec. 21, 1916, New York, N.Y. Screen actor.

BALDRA, CHARLES M.
Born: 1899, Albany, Ore. Died: May 14, 1949, Hollywood, Calif. (train–auto accident). Stage and screen actor. Entered films in 1920.

Appeared in: **1936** The Law-less Nineties.

BALDWIN, GEORGE
Died: Feb. 28, 1923, Manila, Philippine Islands (poisoned). Screen and vaudeville actor.

BALDWIN, KITTY
Born: 1853. Died: June 27, 1934, Buffalo, N.Y. Stage and screen actress.

BALFOUR, LORNA
Born: 1913, England. Died: Mar. 2, 1932, Hollywood, Calif.(complications following surgery). Stage and screen actress.

Appeared in: **1931** Merely Mary Ann.

BALIEFF, NIKITA
Born: 1877. Died: Sept. 3, 1936, New York, N.Y. Screen and stage actor.

Appeared in: **1936** Once in a Blue Moon.

BALIN, MIREILLE
Born: 1911, France. Died: Nov. 8, 1968, Paris, France. Screen actress.

Appeared in: **1933** Don Quixote. **1936** Pepe Le Moko. **1938** Gueurde d'Amour. **1940** The Kiss of Fire.

BALL, SUZAN (Susan Ball)
Born: Feb. 3, 1933, Buffalo, N.Y. Died: Aug. 5, 1955, Beverly Hills, Calif. (cancer). Screen actress. Married to actor Richard Long (dec. 1974). Injured her right knee while filming East of Sumatra in 1952; injury developed into cancer.

Appeared in: **1952** Untamed Frontier (film debut); Yankee Buccaneer. **1953** East of Sumatra; City beneath the Sea. **1954** War Arrow. **1955** Chief Crazy Horse.

BALLANTINE, E. J.
Born: 1888, Edinburgh, Scotland. Died: Oct. 20, 1968, London, England. Stage and screen actor.

Appeared in: **1943** The Moon Is Down. **1944** Tampico.

BALLANTYNE, NELL
Died: Feb. 19, 1959, Glasgow, Scotland. Screen, stage and radio actress.

Appeared in: **1954** Scotch on the Rocks. **1958** Rockets Galore. **1959** The Bridal Path.

BALLIN, MRS. MABEL
Born: 1885. Died: July 24, 1958, Santa Monica, Calif. Screen actress.

Appeared in: **1917** The Spreading Dawn; For Valour; Just What Bobby Wanted; When Bobby Broke His Arm. **1921** East Lynne; Pagan Love; Jane Eyre; The Journey's End. **1922** Other Women's Clothes; Married People. **1923** Vanity Fair; Souls for Sale. **1925** Barriers Burned Away; Beauty and the Bad Man; Code of the West; Riders of the Purple Sage; The Shining Adventure.

BALLOU, MARION
Born: 1871. Died: Mar. 25, 1939, Hollywood, Calif. Screen and stage actress.

Appeared in: **1930** Night Work; The Big Pond. **1933** Little Women; Cradle Song. **1935** David Copperfield; The Melody Lingers On. **1936** Camille. **1937** Portia on Trial.

BAMATTRE, MARTHA
Born: 1892. Died: July 12, 1970, Glendale, Calif. Screen and stage actress. Entered films in 1927.

Appeared in: **1951** An American in Paris. **1955** To Catch a Thief.

BAMESTER, KATHERINE
Died: Oct. 16, 1919, Chicago, Ill. (injuries from auto accident). Screen actress.

BANCROFT, CHARLES (Fred Bently)
Born: 1911. Died: May 17, 1969, Woodland Hills, Calif. (cancer). Screen actor. Entered films approx. 1930.

BANCROFT, GEORGE
Born: Sept. 30, 1882, Philadelphia, Pa. Died: Oct. 2, 1956, Santa Monica, Calif. Stage and screen actor. Father of actress Anne Bancroft.

Appeared in: **1921** The Journey's End. **1922** Driven; The Prodigal Judge. **1924** The Deadwood Coach; Teeth. **1925** The Pony Express; Code of the West; The Rainbow Trail; The Splendid Road. **1926** Old Ironsides; The Enchanted Hill; The Runaway; Sea Horses. **1927** White Gold; Underworld; The Rough Riders; Tell It to Sweeney; Too Many Crooks. **1928** The Dragnet; The Docks of New York; The Showdown. **1929** The Wolf of Wall Street; Thunderbolt. **1930** The Mighty; Ladies Love Brutes; Derelict; Nuits de Chicago (French release of Underworld—1927); Paramount on Parade. **1931** Scandal Sheet; Rich Man's Folly; The Skin Game. **1932** The World and the Flesh; Lady and Gent. **1933** Blood Money; Hello, Everybody!; A Lady's Profession; Under the Tonto Rim; Sunset Pass; Mama Loves Papa; This Day and Age; Turn Back the Clock; Love, Honor and Oh, Baby!; Tillie and Gus. **1934** Elmer and Elsie; Miss Fane's Baby Is Stolen; Journal of a Crime; Many Happy Returns; Merry Widow; She Loves Me Not; The Cat's Paw; Ladies Should Listen; College Rhythm. **1936** Mr. Deeds Goes to Town; Hell Ship Morgan; Wedding Present. **1937** John Meade's Woman; Racketeers in Exile. **1938** A Doctor's Diary; Submarine Patrol; Angels with Dirty Faces. **1939** Stagecoach; Each Dawn I Die; Rulers of the Sea; Espionage Agent. **1940** Green Hell; When the Daltons Rode; Northwest Mounted Police; Little Men; Young Tom Edison. **1941** Texas; The Bugle Sounds. **1943** Whistling in Dixie; Syncopation.

BANDO, MITSUGORO
Died: Jan. 16, 1975, Kyoto, Japan (food poisoning). Screen and Kabuki actor.

BANDO, TSUMASABURO
Born: 1898, Japan. Died: July 7, 1953, Kyoto, Japan (cerebral hemorrhage). Screen and Kabuki actor. Entered films approx. 1923.

BANJAMIN, GLADYS (Gladys Lanphere)
Died: 1948. Screen actress.

BANKHEAD, TALLULAH
Born: Jan. 31, 1902, Huntsville, Ala. Died: Dec. 12, 1968, New York, N.Y. (double pneumonia). Screen, stage, radio and television actress. Divorced from actor John Emery (dec. 1964).

Appeared in: **1918** When Men Betray; Thirty a Week. **1928** His House in

Order. **1929** Her Cardboard Lover. **1931** Tarnished Lady; The Cheat; My Sin. **1932** Thunder Below; The Devil and the Deep; Faithless; Make Me a Star (guest without billing). **1943** Stage Door Canteen. **1944** Lifeboat. **1945** A Royal Scandal. **1953** Main Street to Broadway. **1965** Fanatic (aka Die! Die! My Darling—US). **1966** The Daydreamer (voice only).

BANKS, LESLIE
Born: June 9, 1890, Liverpool, England. Died: Apr. 21, 1952, London, England. Screen, stage actor, stage director and stage producer.

Appeared in: **1932** The Most Dangerous Game (film debut aka The Hounds of Zaroff). **1933** Strange Evidence; The Fire Raisers. **1934** Night of the Party; Red Ensign (aka Strike!—US); I Am Suzanne; The Man Who Knew Too Much. **1935** Sanders of the River; The Tunnel (aka Transatlantic Tunnel—US). **1936** The Three Maxims (aka The Show Goes On—US 1938); Debt of Honour. **1937** Fire Over England; Farewell Again (aka Troopship—US 1938); Wings of the Morning; The First and the Last (aka 21 Days Together—US 1940). **1939** Jamaica Inn; Dead Man's Shoes; The Arsenal Stadium Mystery; Sons of the Sea; Guide Dogs for the Blind (short). **1940** The Door with Seven Locks (aka Chamber of Horrors—US 1941); Neutral Port; Busman's Honeymoon (aka Haunted Honeymoon—US). **1941** Cottage to Let (aka Bombsight Stolen—US); Ship with Wings (US 1942); Give Us More Ships (short). **1942** The Big Blockade; Went the Day Well? (aka 48 Hours—US 1944). **1945** Henry V (US 1946). **1947** Mrs. Fitzherbert (US 1950). **1949** The Small Back Room (US 1952). **1950** Your Witness (aka Eye Witness—US); Madeleine.

BANKS, MONTY (Mario Bianchi aka MONTAGUE BANKS)
Born: 1897, Casene, Italy. Died: Jan. 7, 1950, Arona, Italy (heart attack). Screen, stage actor, film director and film producer. Married to actress Gracie Fields. Divorced from actress Gladys Frazin (dec. 1939). Appeared in early Mack Sennett films.

Appeared in: **1921** Monty Banks series. **1924** Racing Luck. **1925** Keep Smiling. **1926** Atta Boy. **1927** Flying Luck; Horse Shoes; Play Safe. **1928** Adam's Apple (aka Honeymoon Ahead—US); Weekend Wives (US 1929); A Perfect Gentleman. **1929** Atlantic. **1930** The Compulsory Husband. **1932** Tonight's the Night; For the Love of Mike. **1933** You Made Me Love You. **1934** The Girl in Possession; Church Mouse (US 1935). **1935** So You Won't Talk; Man of the Moment. **1936** Honeymoon Merry-Go-Round (aka Olympic Honeymoon). **1941** Blood and Sand. **1945** A Bell for Adano. **1961** Days of Thrills and Laughter (doc.).

BANNER, JOHN
Born: 1910, Austria. Died: Jan. 28, 1973, Vienna, Austria (abdominal hemorrhage). Screen, stage and television actor.

Appeared in: **1942** Once Upon a Honeymoon; Seven Miles from Alcatraz. **1943** The Moon Is Down; Tonight We Raid Calais; The Fallen Sparrow. **1946** Black Angel; Rendezvous. **1948** My Girl Tisa; To the Victor; The Argyle Secrets. **1949** Guilty of Treason. **1953** The Juggler. **1955** The Rains of Ranchipur. **1958** The Beast of Budapest. **1959** The Blue Angel. **1960** The Story of Ruth. **1961** Operation Eichmann; 20,000 Eyes. **1962** Hitler; The Interns. **1963** The Yellow Canary. **1964** 36 Hours. **1968** The Wicked Dreams of Paula Schultz. **1970** Togetherness.

BANNISTER, HARRY
Born: 1889, Holland, Mich. Died: Feb. 26, 1961, N.Y. Screen, stage and television actor. Divorced from actress Ann Harding.

Appeared in: **1921** The Porcelain Lamp. **1929** Her Private Affair. **1930** The Girl of the Golden West. **1931** Suicide Fleet; Husband's Holiday. **1961** Girl on the Run.

BANZET, JANET
Died: c. 1970, New York, N.Y. Screen actress.

Appeared in: **1964** Lilith. **1966** Teen Age Gang Debs. **1967** To Turn a Trick; Teach Me How to Do It; Cool It, Baby; Mini-Skirt Love; Julie Is No Angel; Venus in Furs. **1968** Come Play with Me.

BAO, MIGUEL GOMEZ
Born: Argentina. Died: 1961, Argentina. Screen actor.

Appeared in: **1939** Madreselva (Honeysuckle).

BAPTISTA, CARLOS
Born: 1900. Died: Jan. 7, 1950, Lisbon, Portugal. Screen and stage actor.

BARA, THEDA (Theodosia Goodman aka THEODOSIA DE COPPETT)
Born: 1890, Cincinnati, Ohio. Died: Apr. 7, 1955, Los Angeles, Calif. (cancer). Stage and screen actress. Married to actor and director Charles J. Brabin (dec. 1957).

Appeared in: **1915** The Two Orphans; The Clemenceau Case; The Stain; A Fool There Was; Sin; Carmen; Kreutzer Sonata; The Devil's Daughter; Lady Audley's Secret; The Galley Slave. **1916** Romeo and Juliet; Destruction; The Light; Gold and the Woman; The Serpent; The Eternal Sappho; East Lynne; Her Double Life; Under Two Flags; The Vixen. **1917** Cleopatra; Camille; Heart and Soul; The Tiger Woman; The Darling of Paris; Her Greatest Love.

1918 Salome; When a Woman Sins; The Forbidden Path; The She Devil; Rose of the Blood; Madame DuBarry; The Soul of Buddha; Under the Yoke. **1919** Kathleen Mavourneen; La Belle Russe; The Light; When Men Desire; The Siren's Song; A Woman There Was; The Lure of Ambition. **1921** The Prince of Silence; Her Greatest Love. **1923** The Hunchback of Notre Dame. **1925** The Unchastened Woman. **1926** Madame Mystery; The Dancer of Paris.

BARAGREY, JOHN
Born: April, 1919, Haleyville, Ala. Died: Aug. 4, 1975, New York, N.Y. (cerebral hemorrhage). Screen, stage and television actor. Married to actress Louise Larabee.

Appeared in: **1948** The Loves of Carmen; The Saxon Charm; The Creeper; The Fabulous Fraud (short). **1949** Shockproof. **1950** Four Days Leave. **1955** Tall Man Riding. **1956** Pardners. **1958** The Colossus of New York. **1959** The Fugitive Kind. **1965** Daikaiju Gamma Ray (aka Gamma Ray the Invisible—U.S. 1966).

BARBANELL, FRED
Born: 1931. Died: Sept. 11, 1959, Hollywood, Calif. (following surgery). Screen and television actor.

BARBAT, PERCY (Percy Dewitt Barbat)
Born: 1883. Died: June 20, 1965, San Antonio, Tex. Screen, vaudeville and radio actor.

Appeared in: **1925** Peter Pan. **1934** Tubal-Cain. **1964** No Man's Land.

"BARBETTE" (Vander Barbette)
Born: 1906, Round Rock, Tex. Died: Aug. 5, 1973, Austin, Tex. Screen actor and circus performer.

Appeared in: **1932** Le Sang d'un Poete (Blood of a Poet).

BARBIER, GEORGE W.
Born: 1865, Philadelphia, Pa. Died: July 19, 1945, Los Angeles, Calif. (heart attack). Stage and screen actor.

Appeared in: **1924** Monsieur Beaucaire. **1930** The Big Pond; The Sap from Syracuse. **1931** The Smiling Lieutenant; 24 Hours; Girls about Town; Touchdown. **1932** Skyscraper Souls; Evenings for Sale; No Man of Her Own; No One Man; Strangers in Love; The Broken Wing; One Hour with You; The Strange Case of Clara Deane; Million Dollar Legs; Madame Racketeer; The Phantom President; The Big Broadcast. **1933** Hello, Everybody!; Mama Loves Papa; Sunset Pass; Under the Tonto Rim; This Day and Age; Tillie and Gus; Turn Back the Clock; A Lady's Profession; Love, Honor and Oh, Baby! **1934** Miss Fane's Baby Is Stolen; Many Happy Returns; Ladies Should Listen; She Loves Me Not; College Rhythm; Elmer and Elsie; The Notorious Sophie Lang; Journal of a Crime; The Merry Widow. **1935** McFadden's Flats; Hold 'Em Yale; The Crusades; Here Comes Cookie; Millions in the Air; Life Begins at 40; Broadway Gondolier; Old Man Rhythm; The Cat's Paw. **1936** The Milky Way; Preview Murder Mystery; Wife vs. Secretary; The Princess Comes Across; Spendthrift; Early to Bed; Three Married Men. **1937** On the Avenue; Waikiki Wedding; Hotel Haywire; It's Love I'm After; A Girl with Ideas. **1938** Tarzan's Revenge; Little Miss Broadway; My Lucky Star; Hold That Coed; Straight, Place and Show; Thanks for Everything; Hold That Kiss; Sweethearts; The Adventures of Marco Polo. **1939** Wife, Husband and Friend; SOS Tidal Wave; News Is Made at Night; Smuggled Cargo; Remember? **1940** Village Barn Dance; The Return of Frank James. **1941** Repent at Leisure; The Man Who Came to Dinner; Million Dollar Baby; Marry the Boss's Daughter; Weekend in Havana. **1942** The Magnificent Dope; Thunder Birds; Song of the Islands; Yankee Doodle Dandy. **1943** Hello, Frisco, Hello. **1944** Weekend Pass. **1945** Blonde Ransom; Her Lucky Night.

BARBOUR, DAVE (David Michael Barbour)
Born: May 28, 1912, New York, N.Y. Died: Dec. 11, 1965, Hollywood, Calif. (hemorrhaged ulcer). Jazz musician, composer and screen actor. Divorced from singer Peggy Lee.

Appeared in: **1950** Secret Fury.

BARBOUR, EDWIN WILBOUR
Died: Sept. 14, 1914. Screen actor and screenwriter. Appeared in early Lubin films.

BARCLAY, DELANCEY
Born: New York, N.Y. Died: Dec. 10, 1917, New York, N.Y. Screen actor.

BARCLAY, DON (Don Van Tassel Barclay)
Born: 1892, Ashland, Ore. Died: Oct. 16, 1975, Palm Springs, Calif. Screen, stage actor and artist. Member of Hal Roach's "All Star" trio of the mid-1930s.

Appeared in: **1914** The Cannon Ball (aka The Dynamiter). **1915** That Little Band of Gold (aka For Better or Worse); The Wrong Address. **1918** All Stuck Up; Check Your Hat, Sir? **1933** Air Fright (short); Backs to Nature (short); Beauty and the Bus (short). **1934** Honkey Donkey (short); Soup and Fish (short); Maid in Hollywood (short). **1936** Man Hunt; Treachery Rides the

Range; The Murder of Dr. Harrigan; The Lion's Den; Bengal Tiger; The White Legion. **1937** Fugitive in the Sky; Navy Spy; Border Phantom; Sweetheart of the Navy; I Cover the War. **1938** The Spy Ring; Accidents Will Happen; Thunder in the Desert; Outlaw Express. **1940** Badlands of Dakota. **1942** The Falcon's Brother; Mexican Spitfire Sees a Ghost; Sing Your Worries Away; The Big Street. **1943** Frankenstein Meets the Wolfman; Good Morning, Judge. **1944** In Society. **1948** Whispering Smith; Mr. Perrine and Mr. Traill. **1955** The Long Gray Line. **1961** The Hundred and One Dalmatians (voice). **1964** Mary Poppins. **1968** Half a Sixpence.

BARCROFT, ROY (Howard H. Ravenscroft)
Born: Sept. 7, 1902, Crab Orchard, Nebr. Died: Nov. 28, 1969, Woodland Hills, Calif. (cancer). Screen, stage and television actor.

Appeared in: **1932** Mata Hari (film debut); SOS Coast Guard (serial). **1938** Heroes of the Hills; Stranger from Arizona; The Frontiersman; Flaming Frontiers. **1939** Silver on the Sage; Mexicali Rose; The Renegade Trail. **1940** Rancho Grande; Hidden Gold; Bad Men from Red Butte; Yukon Flight; Stage to Chino; Ragtime Cowboy Joe; Trailing Double Trouble; The Showdown. **1941** Pals of the Pecos; The Bandit Trail; Wide Open Town; Jessie James at Bay; Outlaws of the Cherokee Trail; The Masked Rider; West of Cimarron; King of the Texas Rangers (serial); Riders of Death Valley; Sheriff of Tombstone; White Eagle. **1942** Stardust on the Sage; Dawn on the Great Divide; Land of the Open Range; West of the Law; Romance on the Range; Sunset on the Desert; Below the Border; Sunset Serenade; Pirates of the Prairie. **1943** Hoppy Serves a Writ; False Colors; Riders of the Rio Grande; Cheyenne Roundup; Calling Wild Bill Elliott; Carson City Cyclone; The Stranger from Pecos; Bordertown Gun Fighters; Wagon Tracks West; Raiders of Sunset Pass; The Old Chisholm Trail; Sagebrush Law. **1944** Call of the South Seas; The Girl Who Dared; The Laramie Trail; Hidden Valley Outlaws; Code of the Prairie; Lights of Old Santa Fe; Stagecoach to Monterey; Firebrands of Arizona; Sheriff of Sundown; Cheyenne Wildcat; Haunted Harbor (serial). **1945** Wagon Wheels Westward; The Vampire's Ghost; Marshal of Laredo; The Big Bonanza; Bells of Rosarito; Sunset in El Dorado; Dakota; Along the Navajo Trail; Manhunt of Mystery Island (serial); The Purple Monster Strikes (serial); Santa Fe Saddlemates. **1946** Daughter of Don Q; Home on the Range; The Phantom Rider (serial); Alias Billy the Kid; Sun Valley Cyclone; My Pal Trigger; Night Train to Memphis; Traffic in Crime; Stagecoach to Denver. **1947** Oregon Trail Scouts; The Web of Danger; Stage Coach to Reno; Vigilantes of Boomtown; Spoilers of the North; Rustlers of Devil's Canyon; Springtime in the Sierras; Wyoming; Marshal of Cripple Creek; Blackmail; Along the Oregon Trail; The Wild Frontier; Bandits of Dark Canyon; Last Frontier Uprising; The Fabulous Texan; Jesse James Rides Again (serial); Son of Zorro (serial). **1948** The Bold Frontiersman; Old Los Angeles; The Main Street Kid; Madonna of the Desert; Lightnin' in the Forest; Oklahoma Badlands; Secret Service Investigator; The Timber Trail; Train to Alcatraz; Out of the Storm; Eyes of Texas; Sons of Adventure; Grand Canyon Trail; Renegades of Sonora; Desperadoes of Dodge City; Marshal of Amarillo; Sundown at Santa Fe; G-Men Never Forget (serial); The Gallant Legion. **1949** The Far Frontier; Sheriff of Wichita; Prince of the Plains; Frontier-Investigator; Law of the Golden West; South of Rio; Down Dakota Way; San Antone Ambush; Ranger of Cherokee Strip; Outcasts of the Trail; Powder River Rustlers; Ghost of Zorro (serial); Federal Agents vs. Underworld (serial). **1950** Pioneer Marshal; Gunmen of Abilene; The Arizona Cowboy; The Vanishing Westerner; Rock Island Trail; Federal Agent at Large; Code of the Silver Sage; Salt Lake Raiders; The Savage Horde; Vigilante Hideout; Rustlers on Horseback; West of the Great Divide; Surrender; The Missourians; Under Mexicali Skies; North of the Great Divide; Tyrant of the Sea. **1951** Wells Fargo Gunmaster; In Old Amarillo; Insurance Investigator; Night Riders of Montana; The Dakota Kid; Rodeo King and the Senorita; Fort Dodge Stampede; Arizona Manhunt; Utah Wagon Train; Street Bandits; Honeychile; Pals of the Golden West; Flying Disc Man from Mars (serial); Desert of Lost Men; Rhythm Inn; Don Daredevil Rides Again (serial); Pirates Harbor (rerelease of Haunted Harbor serial—1941). **1952** Radar Men from the Moon (serial); Leadville Gunslinger; Oklahoma Annie; Hoodlum Empire; Border Saddlemates; Wild Horse Ambush; Black Hills Ambush; Thundering Caravans; Oklahoma Plains; Desperadoes' Outpost; Ride the Man Down; The WAC from Walla Walla; South Pacific Trail; Captive of Billy the Kid; Montana Belle. **1953** Marshal of Cedar Creek; Down Laredo Way; Iron Mountain Trail; Bandits of the West; Savage Frontier; Old Overland Trail; El Paso Stampede; Shadows of Tombstone. **1954** The Desperado; Two Guns and a Badge; Rogue Cop; The Man with the Steel Whip (serial). **1955** Man Without a Star; Oklahoma; The Spoilers; Commando Cody (serial). **1957** The Kettles on Old MacDonald's Farm; Domino Kid; Last Stagecoach West. **1959** Escort West; Ghost of Zorro. **1960** Freckles. **1961** When the Clock Strikes. **1962** Six Black Horses. **1966** Gunpoint; Texas Across the River; Billy the Kid vs. Dracula; Destination Inner Space. **1967** The Way West. **1968** Bandolero! **1969** Gaily, Gaily; The Reivers.

BARD, MARIA (aka MIGO BARD)
Born: 1901, Germany. Died: Apr. 1944, Germany. Screen and stage actress.

Appeared in: **1932** Mensch Ohne Namen (Man without a Name). **1933** Berlin-Alexanderplatz. **1938** Liebe im Gleitflug (Love in Stunt Flying). Other film: Emperor of America.

BARKER, BRADLEY
Born: 1883, Hempstead, N.Y. Died: Sept. 29, 1951, New York, N.Y. Screen, radio actor, film producer and animal imitator (original screen voice of Leo the Metro lion).

Appeared in: **1919** Erstwhile Susan. **1920** The Master Mind. **1921** Coincidence; Devotion; God's Crucible. **1922** Insinuation; The Secrets of Paris. **1923** Adam and Eva; The Fair Cheat; The Fighting Blade; The Leavenworth Case; Twenty-One. **1924** The Man without a Heart; Playthings of Desire; Into the Net (serial). **1925** The Crackerjack; The Early Bird; Ermine and Rhinestones; The Live Wire; The Police Patrol. **1926** The Brown Derby; Rainbow Riley. **1927** Combat; His Rise to Fame; The Potters; Rubber Heels. **1928** The Ape; Inspiration.

BARKER, FLORENCE
Born: Nov. 22, 1891, Calif. Died: Feb. 15, 1913, Los Angeles, Calif. (pneumonia). Screen actress.

Appeared in: **1908** An Awful Moment. **1909** A Fool's Revenge; The Girls and Daddy. **1910** Faithful; The Dancing Girl of Butte; Her Terrible Ordeal; The Newlyweds; The Last Deal; The Call; The Oath and the Man; His Sister-in-Law; The Love of Lady Irma; The Kid; Up a Tree; An Affair of Hearts; The Implement; A Knot in the Plot; A Child's Impulse: A Child's Faith; The Tenderfoot's Triumph. **1911** A Wreath of Orange Blossoms; The Diamond Star; Priscilla and the Umbrella. **1912** That Jane Shore; His Madonna; The Burglar and the Rose; Just a Woman; What the Milk Did; The Golden Rule; Two Women; On the Danger Line; A Dreamland Tragedy; The First Glass.

BARKER, LEX (Alexander Crichlow Barker, Jr.)
Born: May 8, 1919, Rye, N.Y. Died: Apr. 11, 1973, New York, N.Y. (heart attack). Screen, stage and television actor. Divorced from Constance Thurlow, Irene Labhart, Maria del Carmen Cervera and actresses Lana Turner and Arlene Dahl. Won Germany's Bambi Award for Best Foreign Actor of 1966. Was the 10th actor to portray "Tarzan" in film series.

Appeared in: **1945** Doll Face (film debut). **1946** Two Guys from Milwaukee; Do You Love Me? **1947** Under the Tonto Rim; Crossfire; The Farmer's Daughter; Dick Tracy Meets Gruesome; Unconquered. **1948** The Velvet Touch; Return of the Badmen; Mr. Blandings Builds His Dream House. **1949** Tarzan's Magic Fountain. **1950** Tarzan and the Slave Girl. **1951** Tarzan's Peril (aka Tarzan and the Jungle Goddess). **1952** Tarzan's Savage Fury (aka Tarzan, the Hunted); Battles of Chief Pontiac. **1953** Tarzan and the She-Devil; Thunder Over the Plains; The Last of the Renegades. **1954** The Yellow Mountain. **1955** The Man from Bitter Ridge; Duel on the Mississippi; Mystery of the Black Jungle; Black Devils of Kali. **1956** Away All Boats; The Price of Fear. **1957** The Deerslayer; The Girl in Black Stockings; War Drums; The Girl in the Kremlin; Jungle Heat. **1958** Female Friends (aka The Strange Awakening—US 1960). **1959** Mission in Morocco; Terror of the Red Mask; Capitano Fuoco; La Scimitarra del Saraceno (aka La Vengeance du Sarrasin and The Pirate and the Slave Girl—US 1961). **1960** Robin Hood and the Pirates; Pirates of the Barbary Coast; Caravane pour Zagota; La Dolce Vita (US 1961). **1961** Marco Polo; Il Secreto Dello Sparviera Nero (The Secret of the Black Falcon); Im Stahlnetz des Dr. Mabuse (The Return of Dr. Mabuse—US 1966). **1962** Die Unsichtbaren Krallen des Dr. Mabuse (The Invisible Dr. Mabuse—US 1965). **1963** Le Tresor du lac d'Argent (Treasure of Silver Lake—US 1965); Breakfast in Bed; Knight of the 100 Faces; Son of the Red Corsair; Winnetou I Teil (aka Apache Gold—US 1965). **1964** Winnetou II Teil (aka Last of the Renegades—US 1966); Old Shatterhand (aka Shatterhand—US 1967); Captain Falcon; Goddess of Vengeance (aka Kali-Yug or Kali-Yug, Goddess of Vengeance). **1965** Die Holle von Manitoba (aka A Place Called Glory—US 1966); Winnetou III Teil (aka The Desperate Trail—US 1967); Code 7, Victim 5. **1966** The Apaches' Last Battle; 24 Hours to Kill; Savage Kurdistan (aka Attacks of the Kurds); "3". **1967** Sept Fois Femme (Woman Times Seven); Die Schlangengrube und das Pendel (aka The Blood Demon—US 1969). **1968** The Longest Day In Kansas City; Devil May Care.

BARKER, REGINALD
Born: 1886, Bothwell, Scotland. Died: Feb. 23, 1945, Los Angeles, Calif. (heart attack). Screen, stage actor, film and stage director. Entered films as an actor in 1913.

BARLOW, REGINALD
Born: 1867, Mass. Died: July 6, 1943, Hollywood, Calif. Screen, stage and minstrel actor. Entered films temporarily in 1916 and permanently in 1931. Married to actress Zelma Rose (dec. 1933).

Appeared in: **1925** Clothes Make the Pirate. **1932** The Washington Masquerade; Age of Consent; If I Had a Million; Night Court; World and the Flesh; Wet Parade; Blessed Event; I Am a Fugitive from a Chain Gang; Sinners in the Sun; Mata Hari; This Reckless Age; Alias the Doctor; Afraid to Talk; Horse Feathers. **1933** His Private Secretary; The Big Cage; Grand Slam; Flying Down to Rio. **1934** You Can't Buy Everything; Romance in Manhattan; Half a Sinner. **1935** Cardinal Richelieu; Strangers All; The Bride of Frankenstein; Mutiny Ahead. **1936** Little Lord Fauntleroy; The Last of the Mohicans; O'Malley of the Mounted; Lloyds of London. **1937** It Happened Out West.

1939 Rovin' Tumbleweeds; The Witness Vanishes. **1940** The Courageous Dr. Christian.

BARNELL, NORA ELY
Born: 1882. Died: July 10, 1933, Los Angeles, Calif. (cerebral hemorrhage). Screen actress and casting director. Entered films as an actress with Thomas Ince.

BARNES, BARRY K. (Nelson Barnes)
Born: 1906, Chelsea, England. Died: Jan. 12, 1965, London, England. Stage and screen actor. Married to actress Diana Churchill.

Appeared in: **1936** Dodging the Dole. **1937** The Return of the Scarlet Pimpernel (US 1938). **1938** Who Goes Next?; This Man is News; You're the Doctor; Prison Without Bars (US 1939); The Ware Case (US 1939). **1939** Spies of the Air (US 1940); This Man in Paris; The Midas Touch. **1940** Two for Danger; Law and Disorder; The Girl in the News (US 1941). **1946** Bedelia (US 1947). **1947** Dancing With Crime.

BARNES, EDNA REMING
Born: 1883. Died: Mar. 7, 1935, Los Angeles, Calif. (cancer). Screen character actress.

BARNES, FLORENCE "PANCHO" (Florence Lowe)
Born: 1902, Calif. Died: Mar. 1975, Boron, Calif. Screen stunt pilot.

Appeared in: **1929** Hell's Angels.

BARNES, FRANK (Richard Allen)
Died: Nov. 1, 1940, Bronx, N.Y. Stage and screen actor. Entered films prior to 1917.

Appeared in: **1927** The General.

BARNES, GEORGE
Born: 1890. Died: Nov. 18, 1949, Hollywood, Calif. (cancer). Stage and screen actor.

Appeared in: **1903** The Great Train Robbery.

BARNES, JUSTUS D.
Born: 1862. Died: Feb. 6, 1946, Weedsport, N.Y. Screen and stage actor.

Appeared in: **1915** The Country Girl.

BARNES, T. ROY
Born: Aug. 11, 1880, Lincolnshire, England. Died: Mar. 30, 1937, Hollywood, Calif. Screen, stage and vaudeville actor. Appeared in vaudeville with his wife, Bessie Crawford, in an act billed as "Package of Smiles."

Appeared in: **1920** Scratch My Back; So Long Letty. **1921** See My Lawyer; Exit the Vamp; Her Face Value; A Kiss in Time. **1922** The Old Homestead; Is Matrimony a Failure?; Don't Get Personal; Too Much Wife. **1923** Adam and Eva; The Go-Getter; Hollywood; Souls for Sale. **1924** The Great White Way; Butterfly; Reckless Romance; Young Ideas. **1925** Seven Chances; The Crowded Hour; The Price of Pleasure; The Re-Creation of Brian Kent. **1926** Dangerous Friends; Ladies of Leisure; A Regular Scout; The Unknown Cavalier. **1927** Body and Soul; Chicago; Smile, Brother, Smile; Tender Hour. **1928** A Blonde for a Night; The Gate Crasher. **1929** Sally; Dangerous Curves. **1930** Wide Open; Caught Short. **1931** Alpha; Women of All Nations. Prior to **1933** the following shorts: How's My Baby?; His Error; Carnival Revue. **1934** Kansas City Princess; It's a Gift. **1935** Village Tale; The Virginia Judge; Doubting Thomas; The Four-Star Boarder (short).

BARNES, V. L.
Born: 1870. Died: Aug. 9, 1949, Los Angeles, Calif. Screen actor.

Appeared in: **1921** Cold Steel. **1924** Crossed Trails. **1925** Peggy of the Secret Service. **1926** The Fighting Cheat.

BARNETT, CHESTER A.
Born: 1885. Died: Sept. 22, 1947, Jefferson City, Mo. (pneumonia). Stage and screen actor.

Appeared in: **1912** The Girl in the Next Room; Her Dressmaker's Bills; The Gypsy Flirt; Locked Out; A Tangled Marriage. **1913** Where Charity Begins; Pearl's Mistake; Dress Reform; The Woman and the Law; His Rich Uncle; Robert's Lesson; Girls Will Be Boys; The Cabaret Singer; Hubby's New Coat; The Convict's Daughter; A Woman's Revenge; Pearl's Hero. **1915** Trilby. **1916** La Boheme. **1919** The Wishing Ring.

BARNETT, GRIFF
Born: 1885. Died: Jan. 12, 1958, Hollywood, Calif. (heart condition and pneumonia). Screen actor.

Appeared in: **1942** Stardust on the Sage. **1943** Shadows on the Sage. **1946** To Each His Own. **1947** Possessed; Gunfighters; Cass Timberlane; Wild Harvest; The Millerson Case; Daisy Kenyon. **1948** Fighting Father Dunne; Fury at Furnace Creek; The Walls of Jericho; Tap Roots; For the Love of Mary;

Apartment for Peggy. **1949** Criss Cross; The Doolins of Oklahoma; Mother Is a Freshman; Pinky. **1950** Customs Agent; No Man of Her Own; Peggy; Sierra. **1951** Cattle Drive; Passage West; Two of a Kind; When I Grow Up. **1952** Scandal Sheet; The Sellout. **1953** Angel Face.

BAROUX, LUCIEN
Born: 1889, Toulouse, France. Died: May 21, 1968, Toulouse, France. Stage and screen actor.

Appeared in: **1931** Un Soir de Rafle (Night Raid). **1932** Levy and Co. **1933** Le Petit Ecart. **1934** Ces Messieurs de la Sande. **1935** Bacara; Charlemagne. **1936** Le Mioche. **1937** Les Mysteres de Paris; L'Enfant de Troupe. **1938** Forty Little Mothers. **1939** Champs Elysees; Behind the Facade. **1943** Fire in the Straw. **1944** 32 Rue de Montmartre; Moulin Rouge. **1952** The French Way; Father's Dilemma. **1953** Naughty Martine. **1958** Lovers and Thieves. **1962** Le Diable et les Dix Commandments (The Devil and the Ten Commandments—US 1963).

BARR, BYRON
Born: 1917. Died: Nov. 3, 1966. Screen actor. Do not confuse with actor Gig Young who appeared in early films under his real name, Byron Barr.

Appeared in: **1940** Misbehaving Husbands. **1941** Navy Blues. **1942** The Man Who Came to Dinner; You're in the Army Now. **1944** Double Indemnity. **1945** Follow that Woman; Tokyo Rose; Love Letters; The Affairs of Susan. **1946** They Made Me a Killer. **1947** Seven Were Saved; Big Town. **1948** The Pitfall; The Main Street Kid. **1949** Down Dakota Way. **1950** Thelma Jordon (aka File on Thelma Jordon); There's a Girl in My Heart; Tarnished; Covered Wagon Raiders (aka Covered Wagon Raid).

BARR, JEANNE
Born: 1932. Died: Aug. 10, 1967, New York, N.Y. Screen, stage, and television actress.

Appeared in: **1960** The Fugitive Kind. **1962** Long Day's Journey into Night. **1964** Lilith.

BARRAT, ROBERT
Born: July 10, 1891, New York, N.Y. Died: Jan. 7, 1970, Hollywood, Calif. Screen, stage and television actor.

Appeared in: **1933** Baby Face; Major of Hell; The Picture Snatcher; The Silk Express; Heroes for Sale; The Kennel Murder Case; Wild Boys of the Road; Lily Turner; Captured; King of the Jungle; I Loved a Woman; The Secrets of the Blue Room; From Headquarters; Ann Carver's Profession. **1934** Dark Hazard; Massacre; Wonder Bar; Fog Over Frisco; Friends of Mr. Sweeney; Dames; Here Comes the Navy; A Very Honorable Guy; Midnight Alibi; Hi, Nelli; Gambling Lady; Upper World; The Dragon Murder Case; Housewife; Return of the Terror; Big-Hearted Herbert; The St. Louis Kid; I Sell Anything; The Firebird. **1935** Devil Dogs of the Air; Captain Blood; Moonlight on The Prairie; While the Patient Slept; Bordertown; The Florentine Dagger; Stranded; Dr. Socrates; Village Tale; Special Agent; Dressed to Thrill; The Murder Man; I Am a Thief. **1936** The Last of the Mohicans; Exclusive Story; The Country Doctor; I Married a Doctor; Sons O'Guns; Draegerman Courage; Charge of the Light Brigade; God's Country and the Woman; The Black Legion; Trail of the Lonesome Pine; Trailin' West; Mary of Scotland. **1937** Mountain Justice; Life of Emile Zola; Confessions; Love Is on the Air; The Barrier. **1938** Bad Man of Brimstone; Penitentiary; The Texans; Charlie Chan in Honolulu; Breaking the Ice; Shadows over Shanghai; The Buccaneer; Forbidden Valley. **1939** Colorado Sunset; Allegheny Uprising; Conspiracy; Bad Lands; The Cisco Kid and the Lady; The Return of the Cisco Kid; Man of Conquest; Heritage of the Desert; Union Pacific. **1940** The Man from Dakota; Northwest Passage; Laddie; Go West; Captain Caution; Fugitive from a Prison Camp. **1941** Parachute Battalion; Riders of the Purple Sage; They Met in Argentina. **1942** The Girl from Alaska; American Empire; Fall In. **1943** Johnny Come Lately; The Bomber's Moon; They Came to Blow up America; A Stranger in Town; Dr. Paul Joseph Goebbels. **1944** The Adventures of Mark Twain; Enemy of Women. **1945** They Were Expendable (He portrayed General Douglas MacArthur as he did in American Guerilla in the Philippines—1950); Road to Utopia; Grissly's Millions; Dakota; The Great John L; Strangler of the Swamp; San Antonio; Wanderer of the Wasteland. **1946** The Magnificent Doll; Dangerous Millions; Sunset Pass; Just Before Dawn; The Time of Their Lives. **1947** Sea of Grass; Fabulous Texan; Road to Rio. **1948** Joan of Arc; I Love Trouble; Relentless; Bad Men of Tombstone. **1949** Riders of the Range; The Lone Wolf and His Lady; Canadian Pacific; Song of India; The Doolins of Oklahoma. **1950** An American Guerilla in the Philippines; Baron of Arizona; Davy Crockett, Indian Scout; The Kid from Texas; Double Crossbones. **1951** Darling, How Could You?; Distant Drums; Flight to Mars; The Pride of Maryland. **1952** Denver and the Rio Grande; Son of Ali Baba. **1953** Cow Country. **1955** Tall Man Riding.

BARRETT, CHARLES C.
Born: 1871. Died: Feb. 11, 1929, Baltimore, Md. Screen, stage, vaudeville and burlesque actor.

BARRETT, IVY RICE
Born: 1898. Died: Nov. 8, 1962, Hollywood, Calif. Screen and stage actress. In Sennett films as a bathing beauty from 1915 to 1920.

BARRETT, JANE
Born: May 7, 1923, Highgate, London, England. Died: July 20, 1969, England. Screen, stage, radio and television actress.

Appeared in: **1938** The Citadel (film debut). **1946** The Captive Heart (US 1947). **1948** Colonel Bogey. **1949** Eureka Stockade. **1952** Time Gentlemen Please! **1953** The Sword and the Rose. **1956** Bond of Fear.

BARRETT, PAT
Born: 1889. Died: Mar. 25, 1959. Screen and radio actor.

Appeared in: **1940** Comin' Round the Mountain.

BARRETT, TONY
Born: May 24, 1916, New York, N.Y. Died: Nov. 16, 1974, Los Angeles, Calif. (cancer). Screen, radio actor, screenwriter and television writer-producer. Married to writer Steffi Barrett.

Appeared in: **1946** The Falcon's Adventure; San Quentin; Seven Keys to Baldpate; Under the Tonto Rim; Wild Horse Mesa. **1947** Born to Kill; Dick Tracy's Dilemma; Dick Tracy Meets Gruesome. **1948** Western Heritage; Mystery in Mexico. **1949** Impact; Flame of Youth. **1950** Prisoners in Petticoats. **1955** It's a Dog's Life.

BARRI, MARIO
Died: Nov. 21, 1963, Manila, Philippine Islands. Screen actor and film producer.

Appeared in: **1956** Huk. **1961** The Steel Claw. **1962** Out of the Tiger's Mouth; No Man Is an Island; Samar. **1964** A Yank in Viet-Nam.

BARRIE, SIR JAMES MATTHEW
Born: May 9, 1860, Kirriemuir, Scotland. Died: June 19, 1937, London, England (bronchial pneumonia). Playwright, novelist and screen actor.

Appeared in: **1918** Masks and Faces.

BARRIER, EDGAR
Born: Mar. 4, 1907, New York, N.Y. Died: June 20, 1964, Hollywood, Calif. (heart attack). Stage and screen actor.

Appeared in: **1940** Escape; Comrade X. **1941** The Penalty; They Dare Not Love. **1942** Eagle Squadron; Danger in the Pacific; Arabian Nights; Journey into Fear. **1943** We've Never Been Licked; Flesh and Fantasy; Phantom of the Opera. **1944** The Cobra Woman; Secrets of Scotland Yard. **1945** Nob Hill; A Game of Death (US 1946); Song of Mexico. **1946** Cornered; Tarzan and the Leopard Woman. **1948** Adventures in Silverado; Rocky; To the Ends of the Earth; Port Said; Macbeth; Rogues' Regiment. **1949** The Secret of St. Ives. **1950** Last of the Buccaneers; The Squared Circle; Cyrano de Bergerac. **1951** The Whip Hand; Hurricane Island. **1953** Count the Hours; The Stand at Apache River; Destination Gobi; The Prince of Pirates; Eyes of the Jungle; The Golden Blade. **1954** The Saracen Blade; Princess of the Nile. **1956** Rumble on the Docks. **1957** The Giant Claw. **1959** Juke Box Rhythm. **1961** On the Double; Snow White and the Three Stooges; Pirates of Tortuga. **1963** Irma la Douce.

BARRINGER, BARRY (A. B. Barringer)
Born: June 25, 1888, Mobile, Ala. Died: May 21, 1938, Los Angeles, Calif. Screen actor, screenwriter and director. Entered films as an actor during silents.

BARRINGTON, HERBERT (Herbert Barrington Hollingsworth)
Born: 1872. Died: Oct. 26, 1933, Tarrytown, N.Y. Screen and stage actor. Entered films in Yonkers, N.Y. with Pilot Films.

Appeared in: **1912** Souls in the Shadow. **1913** The Streets of New York; Hoodman Blind. **1915** The Undying Fire; Jean the Faithful; The Girl and the Matinee Idol; The Woman Who Paid. **1916** Broken Chains; The Way of the World. **1917** Maternity; Shall We Forgive Her? **1918** The Spurs of Sybil; His Royal Highness.

BARRIS, HARRY
Born: 1905. Died: Dec. 14, 1962, Burbank, Calif. (cancer). Screen actor, singer and songwriter. Member of "The Rhythm Boys" singing group. Divorced from singer Lois Whiteman and later married to Esther Margie Barris. Father of singer Marti Barris.

Appeared in: **1930** Two Plus Fours (short). **1931** The Spirit of Notre Dame. **1932** Now's the Time (short); He's a Honey (short); That Rascal (short). **1934** Hollywood Party. **1935** Every Night at Eight; Love Me Forever; After the Dance. **1936** The Man I Marry; Showboat. **1937** Something to Sing About; Double or Nothing. **1938** Cowboy from Brooklyn. **1939** Some Like It Hot; The Shining Hour. **1940** Rhythm on the River. **1941** Birth of the Blues. **1942** Priorities on Parade; The Fleet's In. **1944** Practical Joker (short). **1945** Penthouse Rhythm; Steppin' in Society. **1947** Pet Peeves (short).

BARRISCALE, BESSIE
Born: 1884, New York. Died: June 30, 1965, Kentfield, Calif. Screen, stage and vaudeville actress. Married to actor/director Howard Hickman (dec. 1940).

Appeared in: **1914** The Rose of the Rancho. **1916** Home, Plain Jane; Not My Sister. **1917** Wooden Shoes. **1919** A Trick of Fate. **1921** The Broken Gate; The Breaking Point. **1923** Girl of the Golden West. **1928** Show Folks. **1933** Above the Clouds. **1934** Beloved. **1935** The Man Who Reclaimed His Head.

BARRON, FREDERICK C.
Born: 1888, Melbourne, Australia. Died: Oct. 9, 1955, Central Islip, N.Y. Screen, stage and television actor. Entered films in U.S. in 1898.

BARROWS, HENRY A.
Born: 1875 or 1885 (?), Maine. Died: Mar. 25, 1945. Screen and stage actor. Entered films in 1913.

Appeared in: **1916** Fires of Conscience. **1917** The World Apart; The Heir of the Ages; The Bride's Silence; Charity Castle; Her Country's Call; The Sunset Trail; Lost in Transit; The Stainless Barrier. **1919** The Lion Man (serial). **1920** The Veiled Mystery (serial). **1921** Tiger True; It Can be Done. **1922** The Great Night; Putting It Over; Rent Free; The Law and the Woman; A Tailor Made Man; Yellow Men and Gold; The Woman's Side; The Wise Kid. **1923** Broadway Gold; The Footlight Ranger; Jazzmania; Long Live the King; The Shock. **1924** The Reckless Age; Between Friends; Captain Blood; The Marriage Cheat; Sporting Youth; The Sea Hawk. **1925** Cobra; Drusilla with a Million; His Majesty, Bunker Bean; The Man on the Box; Crack O'Dawn. **1926** Footloose Widows; The Little Irish Girl; The Lost Express; Mistaken Orders; Oh, What a Nurse!; Skinner's Dress Suit; Atta Boy. **1927** All Aboard; Horse Shoes; The Sunset Derby; The Lost Limited; White Pants Willie; Three's a Crowd; The Return of the Riddle Rider (serial). **1928** A Perfect Gentleman; The Wright Idea; Burning Brides; Women Who Dare. **1929** Some Mother's Boy; The Drake Case. **1930** The Kibitzer. **1931** Guilty Hands.

BARROWS, JAMES O.
Born: 1853. Died: Dec. 7, 1925, Hollywood, Calif. (heart attack). Stage and screen actor.

Appeared in: **1921** Silent Years. **1922** Pawned; The Pride of Palomar; When Love Comes; The Call of Home; Hurricane's Gal; White Shoulders. **1923** The Old Fool; Cause for Divorce; Shadows of the North; Stephen Steps Out. **1924** Her Night of Romance; The Tomboy; The Gaiety Girl; The Signal Tower; Young Ideas. **1925** The Goose Woman; Daddy's Gone A-Hunting; The Price of Pleasure. **1926** The Sea Beast.

BARRY, JOE
Died: July 8, 1974. Screen actor. Do not confuse with assistant film director Joe Barry.

Appeared in: **1955** Man With the Gun. **1958** Bell, Book and Candle.

BARRY, ROBERT
Born: 1901. Died: Mar. 21, 1931, Santa Monica, Calif. (auto accident). Screen actor.

BARRY, TOM (Hal Donahue)
Born: 1884. Died: Nov. 7, 1931, Hollywood, Calif. (heart trouble). Screen, stage, vaudeville actor, playwright, screenwriter and newspaperman.

Appeared in: **1931** The Cisco Kid (his only film).

BARRY, VIOLA
Born: 1894. Died: Apr. 2, 1964, Hollywood, Calif. Screen, stage actress, screenwriter, stage producer and stage director.

Appeared in: **1913** The Mothering Heart. **1920** Sea Wolf.

BARRYE, EMILY
Born: 1896. Died: Dec. 15, 1957, Hollywood, Calif. Screen actress. Entered films in 1915 with Universal.

Appeared in: **1924** Fast and Fearless. **1925** The Bloodhound; Border Intrigue; Fast Fightin'. **1926** The Bonanza Buckaroo; Speedy Spurs; Volcano. **1927** King of Kings. **1929** The Godless Girl.

BARRYMORE, DIANA (Diana Blanche Barrymore Blythe)
Born: Mar. 3, 1921, New York, N.Y. Died: Jan. 25, 1960, New York, N.Y. (natural causes). Screen, stage actress and author. Married to actor Robert Wilcox (dec. 1955). Divorced from actor Bramwell Fletcher and tennis pro John Howard. Daughter of actor John Barrymore (dec. 1942) and Blanche Oelrichs who wrote under the pen name of Michael Strange. Regarding family, see John Barrymore.

Appeared in: **1941** Manpower. **1942** Eagle Squadron; Between Us Girls; Nightmare. **1943** Fired Wife; Frontier Badman; When Ladies Fly. **1944** The Ghost Catchers; Ladies Courageous; The Adventures of Mark Twain; Hollywood Canteen. **1950** D.O.A; Flame and the Arrow. **1951** The Mob.

BARRYMORE, ETHEL (Ethel Blythe)

Born: Aug. 15, 1879, Philadelphia, Pa. Died: June 18, 1959, Beverly Hills, Calif. (heart condition). Screen, stage and television actress. Regarding family, see John Barrymore. Won 1944 Academy Award for Best Supporting Actress in None but the Lonely Heart. Nominated for 1946 Academy Award for Best Supporting Actress in The Spiral Staircase and for 1949 Academy Award for Best Supporting Actress in Pinky.

Appeared in: 1914 The Nightingale (film debut). 1915 The Final Judgement. 1916 Kiss of Hate. 1917 The Awakening of Helen Ritchie; The Lifted Veil; The Call of Her People; The White Raven; The American Widow. 1918 Our Mrs. McChesney; The Whirlpool. 1919 The Divorcee. 1932 Rasputin and the Empress. 1933 All at Sea (short). 1935 Peter Ibbetson. 1944 None but the Lonely Heart. 1946 The Spiral Staircase. 1947 Night Song; Moss Rose; The Farmer's Daughter. 1948 Portrait of Jenny; The Paradine Case; Moonrise. 1949 Pinky; The Great Sinner; That Midnight Kiss; The Red Danube. 1951 Kind Lady; The Secret of Convict Lake; Daphne, the Virgin of the Golden Laurels (narr.). 1952 Deadline U.S.A.; Just for You; It's a Big Country. 1953 The Story of Three Loves; Main Street to Broadway. 1954 Young at Heart. 1957 Johnny Trouble. 1974 That's Entertainment (film clips).

BARRYMORE, JOHN (John Blythe)

Born: Feb. 15, 1882, Philadelphia, Pa. Died: May 29, 1942, Los Angeles, Calif. Stage and screen actor. Son of stage actor Maurice Barrymore (dec. 1905) and stage actress Georgia Drew (dec.). Brother of actor Lionel Barrymore (dec. 1954) and actress Ethel Barrymore (dec. 1959); father of actress Diana Barrymore (dec. 1960) and actor John Drew Barrymore, Jr. Divorced from Katherine Harris, Blanche Oelrichs (aka Michael Strange) and actresses Dolores Costello and Elaine Barry.

Appeared in: 1908 The Boys of Company B. 1914 The Man from Mexico; An American Citizen. 1915 The Dictator; Incorrigible Dukane; Are You a Mason? 1916 The Lost Bridegroom; The Red Widow. 1917 Raffles; The Empress. 1918 On the Quiet; Here Comes the Bride. 1919 Test of Honor. 1920 Dr. Jekyll and Mr. Hyde. 1921 The Lotus Eaters. 1922 Sherlock Holmes. 1924 Beau Brummel. 1926 The Sea Beast; When a Man Loves; Don Juan. 1927 The Beloved Rogue. 1928 Tempest. 1929 The Show of Shows; Eternal Love; General Crack. 1930 Moby Dick; The Man from Blankley's; Handsome Gigolo, Poor Gigolo. 1931 Svengali; The Mad Genius. 1932 Arsene Lupin; Rasputin and the Empress; A Bill of Divorcement; Grand Hotel; State's Attorney. 1933 Dinner at Eight; Counsellor at Law; Reunion in Vienna; Topaze; Night Flight. 1934 Long Lost Father; Twentieth Century. 1936 Romeo and Juliet. 1937 Maytime, True Confession; Night Club Scandal; Bulldog Drummond Comes Back; Bulldog Drummond's Revenge. 1938 Bulldog Drummond's Peril; Romance in the Dark; Spawn of the North; Marie Antoinette; Hold That Co-Ed. 1939 The Great Man Votes; Jesse James; Midnight. 1940 The Great Profile. 1941 The Invisible Woman; Playmates; World Premiere.

BARRYMORE, LIONEL (Lionel Blythe)

Born: Apr. 28, 1878, Philadelphia, Pa. Died: Nov. 15, 1954, Van Nuys, Calif. (heart attack). Screen, stage, radio, vaudeville actor, film producer and screenwriter. Divorced from Doris Rankin. Married to stage actress Irene Fenwick. Acted from wheelchair from 1940 due to the effects of arthritis and hip injury. Regarding family, see John Barrymore. Won 1931 Academy Award for Best Actor in A Free Soul.

Appeared in: 1908 The Paris Hat. 1911 Fighting Blood; The Battle. 1912 Friends; The One She Loved; The Musketeers of Pig Alley; Gold and Glitter; My Baby; The Informer; The New York Hat; My Hero; Oil and Water; The Burglar's Dilemma; A Cry for Help; The God Within; Fate; An Adventure in the Autumn Woods. 1913 The Sheriff's Baby; The Perfidy of Mary; A Misunderstood Boy; The Wanderer; The House of Darkness; Just Gold; The Yaqui Cur; The Ranchero's Revenge; A Timely Interception; Death's Marathon; Judith of Bethulia. 1915 The Expoits of Elaine; The Romance of Elaine; The Yellow Streak. 1916 The Brand of Cowardice; The Quitter. 1917 His Father's Son. 1918 The Yellow Ticket. 1920 The Copperhead; The Master Mind. 1921 Jim the Penman; The Devil's Garden; The Great Adventure. 1922 The Face in the Fog; Unseeing Eyes. 1924 I Am the Man; America; Decameron Nights (US 1928); Wedding Women. 1925 The Little Colonel; The Wrongdoers; Wildfire; The Iron Man; Fifty-Fifty; The Girl Who Wouldn't Work; Children of the Whirlwind. 1926 The Bells; The Splendid Road; The Barrier; The Temptress; Brooding Eyes; The Lucky Lady; Paris at Midnight. 1927 Love; The Show; The Thirteenth Hour; Body and Soul; Women Love Diamonds. 1928 The River Woman; Drums of Love; Sadie Thompson; Alias Jimmy Valentine; The Lion and the Mouse; Road House; West of Zanzibar. 1929 Stark Mad; The Mysterious Island; The Hollywood Revue of 1929. 1930 Free and Easy. 1931 A Free Soul; Guilty Hands; The Yellow Ticket (and 1918 version). 1932 Mata Hari; Broken Lullaby; Grand Hotel; Rasputin and the Empress; Arsene Lupin; Washington Masquerade; The Man I Killed. 1933 Sweepings; One Man's Journey; Christopher Bean; Should Ladies Behave?; Reunion in Vienna; Dinner at Eight; The Stranger's Return; Night Flight; Looking Forward. 1934 Treasure Island; This Side of Heaven; The Girl from Missouri; Carolina. 1935 Mark of the Vampire; David Copperfield; The Return of Peter Grimm; Ah, Wilderness!; Public Hero Number One; The Little Colonel. 1936 The Devil Doll; The Gorgeous Hussy; The Road to Glory; The Voice of Bugle Ann;

Camille. 1937 A Family Affair; Saratoga; Captains Courageous; Navy Blue and Gold. 1938 Young Doctor Kildare; You Can't Take It with You; A Yank at Oxford; Test Pilot. 1939 Let Freedom Ring; Calling Dr. Kildare; The Secret of Dr. Kildare; On Borrowed Time. 1940 Dr. Kildare Goes Home; Dr. Kildare's Strangest Case; Dr. Kildare's Crisis. 1941 The Bad Man; The Penalty; The People vs. Dr. Kildare; Lady Be Good; Dr. Kildare's Victory; Dr. Kildare's Wedding Day; Invisible Woman. 1942 Dr. Gillespie's New Assistant; Calling Dr. Gillespie; Tennessee Johnson. 1943 Dr. Gillespie's Criminal Case; Thousands Cheer; A Guy Named Joe; The Last Will and Testament of Tom Smith (short). 1944 Three Men in White; Since You Went Away; Dragon Seed (narr.). 1945 Valley of Decision; Between Two Women. 1946 Duel in the Sun; It's a Wonderful Life; The Secret Heart; Three Wise Fools. 1947 Dark Delusion; Cynthia. 1948 Key Largo. 1949 Down to the Sea in Ships; Malaya; Some of the Best (documentary). 1950 Right Cross. 1951 Bannerline. 1952 Lone Star. 1953 Main Street to Broadway. 1964 Big Parade of Comedy (documentary). 1974 That's Entertainment (film clips).

BARTELL, RICHARD

Born: 1898. Died: July 22, 1967, Woodland Hills, Calif.(cancer). Stage and screen actor.

Appeared in: 1941 Design for Scandal. 1942 My Sister Eileen; Sabotage Squad. 1951 Abbott and Costello Meet the Invisible Man; The Enforcer. 1953 The Vanquished.

BARTELS, LOUIS JOHN

Born: 1895, Bunker Hill, Ill. Died: Mar. 4, 1932, Hollywood, Calif. (stomach disorder). Stage and screen actor.

Appeared in: 1927 Broadway Nights; Dance Magic. 1929 The Canary Murder Case; Nothing but the Truth. 1930 The Floradora Girl; The Cohens and the Kellys in Africa; Sin Takes a Holiday. 1931-32 Pathe shorts. 1931 The Prodigal. 1932 The Big Shot.

BARTER, TEDDY

Born: 1889. Died: Oct. 10, 1939, Hollywood, Calif. (auto accident). Screen actor and stage manager.

BARTHELMESS, RICHARD

Born: May 9, 1897, New York, N.Y. Died: Aug. 17, 1963, Southampton, N.Y. (cancer). Screen actor and film producer. Son of stage actress Carolina Harris (dec. 1958). Won 1927 Special Academy Award for The Patent Leather Kid.

Appeared in: 1916 War Brides. 1917 The Seven Swans; Bab's Burglar; The Eternal Sin. 1918 Hit-the-Trail-Haliday; Rich Man, Poor Man. 1919 The Girl Who Stayed Home; Three Men and a Girl; I'll Get Him Yet; Scarlet Blossoms; Boots; The Hope Chest; Peppy Poppy. 1920 The Love Flower; Way down East; The Idol Dancer. 1921 Experience; Tol'able David. 1922 The Seventh Day; Sonny; The Bond Boy; Just a Song at Twilight. 1923 The Bright Shawl; Fury; Twenty-One; The Fighting Blade. 1924 The Enchanted Cottage; Classmates. 1925 Soul Fire; Shore Leave; The Beautiful City; New Toys. 1926 Ransom's Folly; Just Suppose; The White Black Sheep; The Amateur Gentleman. 1927 The Drop Kick; The Patent Leather Kid. 1928 Wheel of Chance; Out of the Ruins; Scarlet Seas; Little Shepherd of Kingdom Come; The Noose. 1929 Weary River; Drag; Young Nowheres; The Show of Shows; Adios. 1930 The Dawn Patrol; Son of the Gods. 1931 The Lash; The Last Flight; The Finger Points. 1932 The Cabin in the Cotton; Alias the Doctor; Cock of the Air; The Putter (short); The Slippery Pearls (short). 1933 Central Airport; Heroes for Sale. 1934 Massacre; A Modern Hero; Midnight Alibi. 1935 Four Hours to Kill. 1936 Spy of Napoleon. 1939 Only Angels Have Wings. 1940 The Man Who Talks Too Much. 1942 The Mayor of 44th Street; The Spoilers. 1963 The Great Chase (film strip); Hallelujah the Hills (film clip from Way Down East).

BARTHOLOMEW, AGNES

Born: Scotland. Died: Sept. 10, 1955, Glasgow, Scotland. Stage and screen actress. Married to actor Holmes Herbert (dec. 1956).

Appeared in: 1955 A Man Called Peter.

BARTLETT, CLIFFORD

Born: 1903, England. Died: Dec. 1936, London, England. Screen and stage actor.

BARTON, JAMES

Born: Nov. 1, 1890, Gloucester, N.J. Died: Feb. 19, 1962, Mineola, N.Y. (heart attack). Screen, vaudeville and burlesque actor.

Appeared in: 1923 Why Women Re-Marry. 1930 The Underdog (short). 1935 Captain Hurricane; His Family Tree. 1938 Universal short. 1941 The Shepherd of the Hills. 1944 Lifeboat. 1948 The Time of Your Life; Yellow Sky. 1950 The Dungeon; Daughter of Rosie O'Grady; Wabash Avenue. 1951 Here Comes the Groom; The Scarf; Golden Girl. 1956 The Naked Hills. 1957 Quantez. 1961 The Misfits.

BARTON, JOE
Born: 1883. Died: July 5, 1937, Los Angeles, Calif. (following surgery). Screen actor. Entered films approx. 1930.

Appeared in: **1933** Lone Cowboy. **1935** McFadden's Flats.

BARTON, JOHN
Born: May 1, 1872, Germantown, Pa. Died: Dec. 23, 1946, New York, N.Y. Screen, stage and vaudeville actor. Married to Anne Ashley with whom he appeared in vaudeville in an act billed as "Barton and Ashley."

BARTOSCH, CHESTER
Born: 1899. Died: Oct. 31, 1967, San Diego, Calif. (heart ailment). Screen and television actor.

BARTY, JACK
Born: 1889, London, England. Died: Nov. 25, 1942, Streatham, London, England. Screen, stage, vaudeville actor, screenwriter and film producer.

Appeared in: **1933** This is the Life (US 1935). **1934** My Song Goes Round the World; plus the following shorts: Maid in Hollywood; Babes in the Goods; and Oliver the Eighth. **1935** In Town Tonight. **1936** All In; It's in the Bag. **1937** Take a Chance; Talking Feet. **1938** Stepping Toes. **1939** What Would You Do Chums?

BARZELL, WOLFE
Born: 1897, Poland. Died: Feb. 14, 1969, off Acapulco, Mexico (heart attack). Stage and screen actor.

Appeared in: **1957** Street of Sinners. **1958** Frankenstein's Daughter. **1959** The Blue Angel. **1961** Homicidal; Atlantis, The Lost Continent. **1962** The Scarface Mob. **1963** Love with the Proper Stranger. **1964** Judith. **1965** Mordei Haor (aka Sands of Beersheba—US 1966).

BASCH, FELIX
Born: 1889. Died: May 17, 1944, Los Angeles, Calif. Screen actor, film producer and director.

Appeared in: **1942** Destination Unknown; Desperate Journey; Once upon a Honeymoon; Pacific Rendezvous; Enemy Agents Meet Ellery Queen. **1943** Hitler—Dead or Alive; Mission to Moscow; The Falcon in Danger; Bomber's Moon; Hostages; The Cross of Lorraine; Chitnicks; Desert Song. **1944** Woman in Bondage; Uncertain Glory.

BASKETT, JAMES
Born: 1904, Indianapolis, Ind. Died: Sept. 9, 1948, Los Angeles, Calif. (heart ailment). Black screen, stage and radio actor. Won 1946 Special Academy Award for his performance as Uncle Remus in Song of the South.

Appeared in: **1946** Song of the South.

BASSERMANN, ALBERT
Born: Sept. 7, 1865, Mannheim, Germany. Died: May 15, 1952, Zurich, Switzerland (heart attack). Stage and screen actor. Married to actress Else Bassermann-Schiff (dec. 1961). Nominated for 1940 Academy Award for Best Supporting Actor in Foreign Correspondent.

Appeared in: **1931** Vorunter Suchung (Inquest). **1932** 1914: The Last Days before the War. **1933** Kadetten. **1934** Ein Gewisser Herr Gran; Alraune. **1938** Letzte Liebe (Last Love). **1939** Le Famille Lefrancois (aka Heroes of the Marne). **1940** The Story of Dr. Ehrlich's Magic Bullet; Foreign Correspondent; A Dispatch from Reuters; Moon over Burma; This Man Reuter; Knute Rockne, All American; Escape. **1941** The Shanghai Gesture; The Great Awakening; New Wine; A Woman's Face. **1942** The Moon and Sixpence; Invisible Agent; Once upon a Honeymoon; Fly by Night; Desperate Journey. **1943** Good Luck, Mr. Yates; Passport to Heaven; Reunion in France. **1944** Madame Curie; Since You Went Away. **1945** Rhapsody in Blue. **1946** Strange Holiday; The Searching Wind. **1947** Private Affairs of Bel Ami; Escape Me Never. **1948** The Red Shoes.

BASSERMANN-SCHIFF, ELSE
Born: Jan. 14, 1878, Leipzig, E.Germany. Died: May 30, 1961, Baden-Baden, W.Germany. Screen, stage actress, author and playwright. Married to actor Albert Bassermann (dec. 1952).

Appeared in: **1938** Letzte Liebe (Last Love). **1940** Escape. **1941** Captain of Koepenick. **1942** Desperate Journey. **1944** Madame Curie.

BASSETT, RUSSELL
Born: 1846, Milwaukee, Wisc. Died: May 2, 1918, New York, N.Y. (brain hemorrhage). Stage and screen actor. Married to stage actress Carlotta E. M. Bassett (dec. 1952) and father of actor Albert Bassett.

Appeared in: **1911** The Best Man Wins. **1912** Young Wild West Leading a Raid. **1913** The New Clerk. **1914** The Eagle's Mate; Behind the Scenes; Such a Little Queen; Those Persistent Old Maids; One of the Finest; What a Baby Did. **1915** Sold; Jim the Penman; Little Pal; The Commanding Officer; The Fatal Card; Masquerades; May Blossom; The Morals of Marcus; The Heart of Jennifer. **1916** Hulda from Holland; Less than the Dust; The Quest of Life; A

Coney Island Princess; Diplomacy. **1917** The Public Be Damned; Broadway Jones; The Honeymoon; Seven Keys to Baldpate. **1918** Hit the Trail Holiday. **1919** The Traveling Salesman.

BASSETT, TONY (Albert Anthony Bassett)
Born: 1885. Died: Aug. 4, 1955, Hollywood, Calif. Screen and vaudeville actor.

BATEMAN, VICTORY
Born: 1866. Died: Mar. 2, 1926, Los Angeles, Calif. (bronchial asthma). Stage and screen actress. Entered films approx. 1920.

Appeared in: **1921** The Idle Rich; Keeping up with Lizzie; A Trip to Paradise. **1922** Captain Fly-By-Night; A Girl's Desire; If I Were Queen. **1923** Can a Woman Love Twice?; The Eternal Three; Human Wreckage. **1924** Tess of the D'Urbervilles; The Turmoil.

BATES, BARBARA
Born: Aug. 6, 1925, Denver, Colo. Died: Mar. 18, 1969, Denver, Colo. Screen actress.

Appeared in: **1945** Salome, Where She Danced; This Love of Ours. **1946** A Night in Paradise; Strange Holiday. **1947** The Fabulous Joe. **1948** June Bride. **1949** The House across the Street; One Last Fling; The Inspector General. **1950** All about Eve; Quicksand; Cheaper by the Dozen. **1951** The Secret of Convict Lake; I'd Climb the Highest Mountain; Let's Make It Legal. **1952** Belles on Their Toes; The Outcasts of Poker Flat. **1953** All Ashore; The Caddy. **1954** Rhapsody. **1956** House of Secrets. **1957** Town on Trial; Triple Deception. **1958** Campbell's Kingdom; Apache Territory.

BATES, BLANCHE
Born: 1873, Portland, Ore. Died: Dec. 25, 1941, San Francisco, Calif. (following stroke). Stage and screen actress.

Appeared in: **1914** The Seats of the Mighty. **1918** The Border Legion.

BATES, FLORENCE (Florence Rabe)
Born: Apr. 15, 1888, San Antonio, Tex. Died: Jan. 31, 1954, Burbank, Calif. (heart attack). Screen, stage, television actress and attorney.

Appeared in: **1937** The Man in Blue. **1940** Rebecca; Calling All Husbands; Son of Monte Cristo; Hudson's Bay; Kitty Foyle. **1941** Road Show; Love Crazy; The Chocolate Soldier; Strange Alibi; The Devil and Miss Jones. **1942** The Tuttles of Tahiti; The Moon and Sixpence; My Heart Belongs to Daddy; Mexican Spitfire at Sea; We Were Dancing. **1943** Slightly Dangerous; His Butler's Sister; They Got Me Covered; Mister Big; Heaven Can Wait; Mr. Lucky; Whistle Stop at Eaton Falls. **1944** Since You Went Away; The Mask of Dimitrios; Kismet; The Belle of the Yukon; The Racket Man. **1945** Saratoga Trunk; Tahiti Nights; Tonight and Every Night; San Antonio; Out of This World. **1946** Claudia and David; Cluny Brown; The Diary of a Chambermaid; Whistle Stop; The Time, the Place and the Girl. **1947** The Brasher Doubloon; Love and Learn; Desire Me; The Secret Life of Walter Mitty; The High Window. **1948** Texas, Brooklyn and Heaven; Winter Meeting; A Letter to Three Wives; The Inside Story; River Lady; My Dear Secretary; Portrait of Jennie; I Remember Mama. **1949** The Judge Steps Out; The Girl from Jones Beach; On the Town. **1950** Belle of Old Mexico; County Fair. **1951** The Second Woman; Lullaby of Broadway; The Tall Target; Havana Rose; Father Takes the Air. **1952** San Francisco Story; Les Miserables. **1953** Paris Model; Main Street to Broadway.

BATES, GRANVILLE
Born: 1882, Chicago, Ill. Died: July 8, 1940, Hollywood, Calif. (heart attack). Stage and screen actor.

Appeared in: **1929** Jealousy. **1930** The Sap from Syracuse. **1934** The Smiling Lieutenant; Midnight; Warner Bros. newspaper shorts. **1935** Woman Wanted; Pursuit; O'Shaughnessey's Boy. **1936** Here Comes Trouble; Poppy; Chatterbox; 13 Hours by Air; The Plainsman; The Captain's Kid; Times Square Playboy; Sing Me a Love Song; Beloved Enemy; Under Suspicion. **1937** When's Your Birthday?; Let's Get Married; It Happened in Hollywood; Green Light; They Won't Forget; The Perfect Specimen; Larceny on the Air; Nancy Steel Is Missing; Waikiki Wedding; Wells Fargo; Mountain Justice; Back in Circulation. **1938** The Jury's Secret; Youth Takes a Fling; Mr. Chump; Go Chase Yourself; The Affairs of Annabel; A Man to Remember; Next Time I Marry; Gold Is Where You Find It; Romance on the Run; Cowboy from Brooklyn; Garden of the Moon; Hard to Get. **1939** The Great Man Votes; Blackwell's Island; Twelve Crowded Hours; Naughty but Nice; Pride of the Blue Grass; Our Neighbors, the Carters; Fast and Furious; Internationally Yours; Sweepstakes Winner; Of Mice and Men; Charlie McCarthy, Detective; Indianapolis Speedway; Jesse James. **1940** Millionaire Playboy; Thou Shalt Not Kill; My Favorite Wife; The Mortal Storm; Private Affairs; Men against the Sky; Flowing Gold; Brother Orchid.

BATES, LESLIE A. (aka LES BATES)
Born: 1877. Died: Aug. 8, 1930, Hollywood, Calif. (auto accident). Screen actor.

Appeared in: **1921** A Broken Doll. **1922** Belle of Alaska; Big Stakes; Deserted at the Altar; My Dad; Strength of the Pines. **1923** Blood Test; Vanity Fair. **1924** Martyr Sex; Shackles of Fear. **1925** Once in a Lifetime; Triple Action. **1926** Beyond All Odds; Blue Blazes; In Search of a Hero; Lure of the West; The Texas Streak; While London Sleeps. **1927** Irish Hearts. **1928** Buck Privates; The Glorious Trail. **1930** The Fighting Legion; Mountain Justice.

BATIE, FRANKLYN A.

Born: 1880, Norwich, N.Y. Died: Dec. 31, 1949, Norwich, N.Y. Screen, stage and vaudeville actor.

Appeared in: **1930** Big Boy.

BATLEY, ERNEST G.

Died: c. 1917. Screen actor, producer, director and screenwriter. Married to film producer, director and actress Ethyle Batley. Father of actress Dorothy Batley.

Appeared in: **1912** A Child's Strategy; The Heavenly Twins; Peggy Gets Rid of the Baby; Through the Flames. **1913** The Broken Chisel (aka Escape from Broadmoore—US); Through the Clouds; A Tragedy in the Alps; The Child Mother (aka The Little Mother); Guy Fawkes and the Gunpowder; The Two Father Christmases; There's Good in the Worst of Us; The Battle of Waterloo; In Fate's Grip; Bess the Detective's Daughter (aka To Save Her Dad). **1914** The Tattooed Will; The Midnight Wedding; The Drawn Blind; The Master Crook Turns Detective; The Master Crook Outwitted by a Child; An Englishman's Home; Retribution; The Price of her Silence. **1915** Dewdrop Braves the Floods of Maidenhead; Honour Among Thieves; Instruments of Fate; Bulldog Grit; Remember Belgium; Across the Wires.

BATTIER, ROBERT

Born: 1887. Died: Dec. 16, 1946, Hollywood, Calif. Screen actor.

Appeared in: **1937** Love and Hisses.

BATTY, ARCHIBALD

Born: 1887. Died: Nov. 24, 1961, Budleigh, Salterton, England. Screen, stage actor and playwright.

Appeared in: **1938** I See Ice; The Drum (aka Drums—US). **1939** Four Feathers.

BAUDIN, GINETTE

Born: 1921, France. Died: Mar. 1971, France. Screen, stage actress, dancer and singer.

Appeared in: La Briseur de Chaines; L'Escalier sans Fin; Seul Dans la Nuit; Une Femme par Jour; Les Amants Maudits; Lady Paname.

BAUER, DAVID

Born: 1918, Chicago, Ill. Died: Feb. 13, 1973, London, England. Screen, stage and television actor. Married to singer Stella Tanner.

Appeared in: **1963** The Winston Affair (aka Man in the Middle—US 1964); Live It Up (aka Sing and Swing—US 1964); Walk a Tightrope (US 1964). **1965** The Spy Who Came in from the Cold. **1967** Danger Route (US 1968); The Double Man; Torture Garden (US 1968). **1968** Inspector Clouseau; The Mercenaries (aka Dark of the Sun—US). **1969** Crooks and Coronets (aka Sophie's Place—US 1970); Royal Hunt of the Sun. **1970** Patton; Tropic of Cancer.

BAUERSFELD, MARJORIE "MIRANDY"

Born: 1890, Springfield, Mo. Died: July 22, 1974, Santa Barbara, Calif. Screen, stage, radio and television actress. Appeared in Mack Sennett comedies.

BAUM, MRS. H. WILLIAM

Born: 1882. Died: Mar. 9, 1970, Farmingdale, N.Y. Screen and radio actress. Was the model for the U.S. Liberty 25-cent piece.

Appeared in: **1915** Birth of a Nation.

BAUM, HARRY

Born: 1916. Died: Jan. 31, 1974, Hollywood, Calif. (heart attack). Screen actor, stand-in and stuntman. Son of actress Lily Teitelbaum.

BAUR, HARRY

Born: 1881, France. Died: Apr. 1943, Paris, France. Screen, stage and radio actor.

Appeared in: **1913** Shylock. **1923** La Voyante. **1932** David Golder. **1933** Poil de Carotte; Les Trois Mousquetaires; The Red Head. **1934** Golgotha. **1935** Moscow Nights (US 1938); Le Cap Perdu; Les Miserables; Crime et Chatiment (Crime and Punishment); Cette Vielle Canaille; Taras Bulba. **1936** I Stand Condemned. **1937** The Golem; The Life and Loves of Beethoven; Le Juif Polonaise. **1938** Un Carnet de Bal; Dark Eyes; Rothschild; The Rebel Son; Moscow Nights; Rasputin. **1939** A Man and His Wife. **1941** Volpone; Hatred; The Mad Empress.

BAXTER, JAMES C. "JIMMY"

Born: 1923. Died: Apr. 20, 1969, Dallas, Tex. Screen actor and singer.

Appeared in: **1935** The Dark Angel.

BAXTER, LORA

Born: 1908. Died: June 16, 1955, New York, N.Y. Screen, stage, vaudeville, television actress and screenwriter.

BAXTER, WARNER

Born: Mar. 29, 1891, Columbus, Ohio. Died: May 7, 1951, Beverly Hills, Calif. Stage and screen actor. Married to actress Winifred Bryson. Won 1929 Academy Award for Best Actor for In Old Arizona.

Appeared in: **1914** Her Own Money. **1918** All Woman. **1919** Lombardi, Ltd. **1921** Cheated Hearts; First Love; The Love Charm; Sheltered Daughters. **1922** If I Were Queen; The Girl in His Room; A Girl's Desire; The Ninety and Nine; Her Own Money (and 1914 version). **1923** Blow Your Own Horn; In Search of a Thrill; St. Elmo. **1924** Alimony; Christine of the Hungry Heart; The Female; The Garden of Weeds; His Forgotten Wife; Those Who Dance. **1925** The Golden Bed; The Air Mail; The Awful Truth; The Best People; Rugged Water; A Son of His Father; Welcome Home. **1926** Mannequin; Miss Brewster's Millions; Mismates; Aloma of the South Seas; The Great Gatsby; The Runaway. **1927** The Telephone Girl; The Coward; Drums of the Desert; Singed. **1928** Danger Street; Three Sinners; Ramona; Craig's Wife; The Tragedy of Youth; A Woman's Way. **1929** Linda; Far Call; Thru Different Eyes; Behind That Curtain; Romance of the Rio Grande; In Old Arizona; West of Zanzibar; Happy Days. **1930** The Arizona Kid; Such Men Are Dangerous; Renegades. **1931** The Cisco Kid; Squaw Man; Doctor's Wives; Their Mad Moment; Daddy Long Legs; Surrender. **1932** Six Hours to Live; Man about Town; The Slippery Pearls (short); Amateur Daddy. **1933** Paddy, the Next Best Thing; Forty-Second Street; Dangerously Yours; I Loved You Wednesday; Penthouse. **1934** Stand up and Cheer; Broadway Bill; As Husbands Go; Such Women Are Dangerous; Grand Canary; Hell in the Heavens. **1935** Under the Pampas Moon; One More Spring; La Fiesta de Santa Barbara (short); King of Burlesque. **1936** The Prisoner of Shark Island; Road to Glory; To Mary, with Love; White Hunter; Robin Hood of El Dorado. **1937** Slave Ship; Vogues of 1938; Wife, Doctor and Nurse. **1938** Kidnapped; I'll Give a Million. **1939** Wife, Husband and Friend; Barricade; The Return of the Cisco Kid. **1940** Earthbound. **1941** Adam Had Four Sons. **1943** Crime Doctor; Crime Doctor's Strangest Case. **1944** Lady in the Dark; Shadows in the Night. **1945** The Crime Doctor's Courage; The Crime Doctor's Warning. **1946** Just before Dawn; The Crime Doctor's Man Hunt; The Razor's Edge; Smoky. **1947** The Millerson Case; The Crime Doctor's Gamble. **1948** A Gentleman from Nowhere. **1949** Prison Warden; The Devil's Henchman; The Crime Doctor's Diary. **1950** State Penitentiary.

BAY, TOM (aka TOMMY BAY)

Born: 1901. Died: Oct. 13, 1933, Burbank, Calif. (shooting). Screen actor.

Appeared in: **1922** The Better Man Wins. **1926** The Dead Line; The Devil's Gulch; The Fighting Boob; The Valley of Bravery. **1927** Drifting On; Tearin' into Trouble; White Pebbles. **1928** Desperate Courage; Devil's Tower; Lightnin' Shot; Mystery Valley; Painted Trail; Trail Riders; Trailin' Back. **1929** The Oklahoma Kid; Pioneers of the West; Code of the West; Fighters of the Saddle; The Fighting Terror; The Lone Horseman. **1930** The Parting of the Trails.

BAYER, CHARLES W.

Born: 1893. Died: Nov. 28, 1953, Hollywood, Calif. (cancer). Screen actor. Entered films with Vitagraph.

BEAL, FRANK

Born: 1864. Died: Dec. 20, 1934, Hollywood, Calif. Screen actor and film director. Married to actress Louise Lester (dec. 1952) and father of actor/director Scott Beal (dec. 1973) and actress Dolly Beal.

Appeared in: **1922** A Question of Honor. **1923** Playing It Wild; Soft Boiled; When Odds Are Even. **1924** The Arizona Express; The Cyclone Rider; Hook and Ladder; The Lone Chance. **1925** The Best Bad Man; The Golden Strain; Marriage in Transit. **1926** The Dead Line; Man Four Square. **1927** The Final Extra; Galloping Fury; The Stolen Bride. **1928** The Danger Rider; Women Who Dare. **1929** Broken Barriers; The Big Diamond Robbery; Senor Americano. **1930** Wide Open. **1931** Everything's Rosie (short); Cimarron.

BEAL, ROYAL

Born: 1900. Died: May 20, 1969, Keene, N.H. (cancer). Screen, stage and television actor.

Appeared in: **1949** Lost Boundaries. **1951** Death of a Salesman. **1953** The Joe Lewis Story. **1959** Anatomy of a Murder.

BEAL, SCOTT

Born: 1890. Died: July 10, 1973, Hollywood, Calif. (cancer). Screen actor, film director and cameraman. Son of actress Louise Lester (dec. 1952) and film director Frank Beal (dec. 1934). Brother of actress Dolly Beal. Entered films with Selig in 1910.

BEAMISH, FRANK
Born: 1881, Memphis, Tenn. Died: Oct. 3, 1921, New York, N.Y. Stage and screen actor.

Appeared in: 1922 The Blonde Vampire; The Faithless Sex.

BEAR, MARY
Died: 1972. Stage and screen actress. Married to actor Don Shelton (dec. 1976).

Appeared in: 1948 That Lady in Ermine. 1949 Bride for Sale. 1950 Mother Didn't Tell Me; Singing Guns; Stella.

BEATON, MARY (Mary Louise Beaton)
Died: Jan. 25, 1962. Screen actress.

Appeared in: 1920 Clothes. 1921 The Man Who; A Message from Mars.

BEATTY, CLYDE R.
Born: June 10, 1903, Chillicothe, Ohio. Died: July 19, 1965, Ventura, Calif. (cancer). Screen actor, circus performer, animal trainer and circus owner.

Appeared in: 1933 The Big Cage. 1934 The Lost Jungle (serial). 1936 Darkest Africa (serial). 1937 Paramount short. 1940 Cat College (short). 1949 Africa Screams. 1954 Ring of Fear.

BEATTY, GEORGE
Born: Sept. 5, 1895, Steubenville, Ohio. Died: Aug. 6, 1971, Hollywood, Calif. (stroke). Screen, stage, vaudeville, radio actor, screenwriter and radio writer.

Appeared in: 1943 Hi' Ya, Sailor; Crazy Horse. 1944 Johnny Doesn't Live Here.

BEATTY, MAY
Born: 1881, Christchurch, New Zealand. Died: Apr. 1, 1945, Covina, Calif. Stage and screen actress. Married to stage actor William Lauri (dec.).

Appeared in: 1930 The Benson Murder Case; The Boudoir Diplomat. 1931 Ex-Flame. 1934 Horse Play. 1935 Night Life of the Gods; Becky Sharp; Mad Love; Here Comes the Band; The Girl Who Came Back; Bonnie Scotland. 1936 Little Lord Fauntleroy; Show Boat; Private Number; Lloyds of London. 1937 Four Days' Wonder; She Loved a Fireman. 1938 If I Were King. 1939 The Women; Eternally Yours; We Are Not Alone; The Adventures of Sherlock Holmes; Union Pacific. 1940 Pride and Prejudice; My Son, My Son. 1943 Forever and a Day.

BEAUBIEN, JULIEN (Julien A. Dolenzai)
Born: 1896. Died: Oct. 18, 1947, Long Branch, N.J. Screen and stage actress.

Appeared in: 1919 The Winning Stroke; Checkers. 1923 Main Street.

BEAUDET, LOUISE
Born: 1862. Died: Dec. 31, 1947, New York. Screen, stage, opera and vaudeville actress.

Appeared in: 1913 Sauce for the Goose; Which? 1914 Jerry's Uncle's Namesake. 1915 The Battle Cry of Peace; A Price for Folly; On Her Wedding Night. 1916 The Law Decides. 1917 The Price She Paid. 1921 Her Lord and Master. 1923 The Gold Diggers. 1925 Sally.

BEAUDINE, WILLIAM, SR.
Born: Jan. 15, 1892, New York, N.Y. Died: Mar. 18, 1970, Canoga Park, Calif. (complications of euremic poisoning). Screen actor, director and television director. Father of film producer William Beaudine, Jr. Entered films in 1909 as an actor and turned director in 1914.

Appeared in: 1909 Pippa Passes. 1910 The Broken Doll. 1912 A Close Call.

BEAUMONT, CHARLES
Born: 1929. Died: Feb. 21, 1967, Woodland Hills, Calif. (rare disease of nervous system). Screen actor, screenwriter, television writer and author.

Appeared in: 1962 The Intruder.

BEAUMONT, DIANA MURIEL
Born: May 8, 1909, London, England. Died: June 21, 1964, London, England. Stage and screen actress.

Appeared in: 1928 Adam's Apple (aka Honeymoon Ahead—US) (film debut). 1931 Alibi; The Old Man. 1932 A Lucky Sweep. 1933 Mannequin. 1934 Autumn Crocus. 1935 A Real Bloke; Birds of a Feather. 1936 The Secret Voice; They Didn't Know; While London Sleeps. 1937 Stage Struck. 1938 Black Limelight (US 1939); Luck of the Navy (aka North Sea Patrol—US 1940). 1939 Murder in Soho (aka Murder in the Night—US 1940); Old Mother Riley MP. 1940 Let George Do It. 1941 Hi Gang!; 1942 Let the People Sing. 1943 Millions Like Us. 1944 Out of Chaos. 1952 Home at Seven (aka Murder on Monday—US 1953); Stolen Face. 1958 I Was Monty's Double (aka Hell, Heaven or Hoboken).

BEAUMONT, HARRY
Born: Feb. 10, 1888, Abilene, Kans. Died: Dec. 22, 1966, Santa Monica, Calif. Screen actor, film director and screenwriter.

Appeared in: 1912 How Father Accomplished His Work; Linked Together; Their Hero; The Butler and the Maid; How the Boys Fought the Indians; Uncle Mun and the Minister; Annie Crawls Upstairs; The Totville Eye; The Third Thanksgiving. 1913 Leonie; False to Their Trust; The Photograph and the Blotter; The Elder Brother; The Golden Wedding; Mother's Lazy Boy; It Wasn't Poison After All; For Her; Over the Back Fence. 1914 Treasure Trove; The Witness to the Will; A Transplanted Prairie Flower; Who Goes There?; The Ever-Gallant Marquis; The Shattered Tree. 1915 The Stoning; Poisoned by Jealousy; A Thorn Among Roses; Jack Kennerd, Coward; That Heavenly Cook. 1916 Putting It Over; The Grouch; His Little Wife; The Discards.

BEAUMONT, LUCY
Born: May 18, 1873, Bristol, England. Died: Apr. 24, 1937, New York, N.Y. Screen, stage and radio actress.

Appeared in: 1923 Ashes of Vengeance; Enemies of Children; Lucretia Lombard; Cupid's Fireman. 1924 The Family Secret; The Last of the Duanes; Good Bad Boy. 1925 The Man without a Country; The Trouble with Wives. 1926 The Greater Glory; The Old Soak; The Fighting Failure; Men of the Night; Torrent. 1927 The Beloved Rogue; Closed Gates; The Love Wager; Resurrection; Hook and Ladder No. 9; Stranded; Savage Passions. 1928 Stool Pigeon; The Crowd; A Bit of Heaven; Branded Man; The Little Yellow House; Outcast Souls; Comrades. 1929 The Greyhound Limited; Knights Out (short); One Splendid Hour; The Ridin' Demon; Hard Boiled Rose; The Girl in the Show; Sonny Boy. 1931 A Free Soul; Caught Plastered; Get Rich Quick Wallingford. 1932 Union Depot; Three Wise Girls; Parlor, Bedroom and Wrath (short); Cheaters at Play; Midnight Lady; Movie Crazy; Thrill of Youth. 1934 His Double Life. 1935 False Pretenses; Temptation. 1936 The Devil Doll. 1937 The Maid of Salem.

BEAUMONT, VERTEE
Born: 1889. Died: June 27, 1934, Hollywood, Calif. (heart disease). Screen, stage and vaudeville actress. Married to stage actor Jack Arnold (dec.) with whom she appeared in vaudeville as part of "Beaumont and Arnold" team.

BEAVERS, LOUISE
Born: 1898, Cincinnati, Ohio. Died: Oct. 26, 1962, Hollywood, Calif. (heart attack). Black screen, television and minstrel actress. Entered films in 1924.

Appeared in: 1927 Uncle Tom's Cabin. 1929 The Glad Rag Doll; Gold Diggers of Broadway; Barnum Was Right; Coquette; Nix on Dames; Wall Street. 1930 Back Pay; Wide Open; She Couldn't Say No; Safety in Numbers. 1931 Party Husbands; Reckless Living; Sundown Trail; Annabell's Affairs; Six Cylinder Love; Good Sport; Up for Murder; Girls about Town. 1932 You're Telling Me (short); Ladies of the Big House; Old Man Minick; The Expert; Freaks; Night World; Street of Women; What Price Hollywood?; Unashamed; Young America; Divorce in the Family; Wild Girl; Too Busy to Work; It's Tough to Be Famous; We Humans; Jubilo. 1933 Girl Missing; What Price Innocence; Her Bodyguard; Bombshell; Her Splendid Folly; Notorious but Nice; Pick Up; She Done Him Wrong; A Shriek in the Night. 1934 In the Money; Glamour; I Believed in You; I Give My Love; Merry Wives of Reno; A Modern Hero; Registered Nurse; Imitation of Life; I've Got Your Number; Bedside; The Merry Frinks; Cheaters; Hat, Coat and Glove; Dr. Monica. 1935 West of the Pecos; Annapolis Farewell. 1936 Bullets or Ballots; General Spanky; Wives Never Know; Rainbow on the River. 1937 Make Way for Tomorrow; Wings over Honolulu; Love in a Bungalow; The Last Gangster. 1938 Scandal Sheet; Peck's Bad Boy with the Circus; The Headleys at Home; Life Goes On; Brother Rat; Reckless Living. 1939 The Lady's from Kentucky; Reform School; Made for Each Other. 1940 I Want a Divorce; Women without Names; Parole Fixer; No Time for Comedy. 1941 Shadow of the Thin Man; The Vanishing Virginian; Sign of the Wolf; Belle Starr; Virginia. 1942 Holiday Inn; Reap the Wild Wind; The Big Street; Seven Sweethearts (aka Tulip Time); Tennessee Johnson. 1943 Good Morning, Judge; DuBarry Was a Lady; All by Myself; There's Something about a Soldier; Jack London; Top Man. 1944 South of Dixie; Dixie Jamboree; Follow the Boys; Barbary Coast Gent. 1945 Delightfully Dangerous. 1946 Lover Come Back; Young Widow. 1947 Banjo. 1948 Mr. Blandings Builds His Dream House; For the Love of Mary; Good Sam. 1949 Tell It to the Judge. 1950 My Blue Heaven; Girls' School; The Jackie Robinson Story. 1952 Colorado Sundown; I Dream of Jeannie; Never Wave at a WAC. 1956 Goodbye, My Lady; You Can't Run Away from It; Teenage Rebel. 1957 Tammy and the Bachelor. 1958 The Goddess. 1960 The Facts of Life; All the Fine Young Cannibals.

BEBAN, GEORGE
Born: 1873, San Francisco, Calif. Died: Oct. 5, 1928, Los Angeles, Calif. (fall from horse). Screen, stage, vaudeville, minstrel actor, screenwriter and film director.

Appeared in: 1915 The Alien. 1916 Pasquale. 1917 Lost in Transit. 1921 One Man in a Million. 1922 The Sign of the Rose (stage and film versions). 1924 The Greatest Love of All. 1926 The Loves of Ricardo. 1928 The Loves of Ricardo (and 1926 version).

BECH, LILI

Born: 1885, Denmark. Died: 1939, Sweden. Stage and screen actress. Married to actor Victor Seastrom (dec. 1960).

Appeared in: The Talisman; The Gardener; The Black Masks; The Vampire; The Child; Because of Her Love; The Stormy Petrel; Children of the Street; Daughter of the High Mountain; When Artists Love; One Out of Many; Expiated Guilt; The Playmates; His Wife's Past; Ace of Thieves; The Dagger; The Mine-Pilot; The Governor's Daughters; Ships that Meet; She Was Victorious; The Wings; The Gold Spider; Therese.

BECHTEL, WILLIAM A. "BILLY"

Born: 1867, Germany. Died: Oct 27, 1930, Hollywood, Calif. Stage and screen actor. Entered films approx. 1907.

Appeared in: 1921 Idle Hands. 1924 Meddling Women. 1929 Spite Marriage; Jazz Age. 1930 The Social Lion; Die Sehnsucht jeder Frau.

BECK, DANNY

Born: 1904. Died: Nov. 8, 1959, Hollywood, Calif. Screen actor.

Appeared in: 1941 Birth of the Blues. 1957 Man of a Thousand Faces.

BECK, JAMES

Born: 1932. Died: Aug. 6, 1973, London, England. Screen, stage and television actor.

BECK, NELSON C.

Born: 1887. Died: Mar. 3, 1952, Hollywood, Calif. (overdose of sleeping pills). Screen actor.

BECKER, JACQUES

Born: 1906, Paris, France. Died: 1960, Paris, France. Screen actor, screenwriter and film director.

Appeared in: 1932 Boudu Sauve des Eaux (Boudu Saved from Drowning). 1937 La Grande Illusion (The Grand Illusion—US 1938).

BECKETT, SCOTTY (Scott Hastings Beckett)

Born: Oct. 4, 1929, Oakland, Calif. Died: May 10, 1968, Los Angeles, Calif. Screen actor. Was in "Our Gang" films during early 1930s at age of three.

Appeared in: 1934 Gallant Lady; Stand Up and Cheer; I Am Suzanne; Sailor Made Widow; Whom the Gods Destroy; George White's Scandals; plus the following shorts: Mike Fright; Hi Neighbor; For Pete's Sake; First Round-Up; Honkey Donkey; Washee Ironee; Mama's Little Pirates; Shrimps for a Day. 1935 Dante's Inferno; Pursuit; I Dream Too Much; plus the following shorts: Anniversary Trouble; Beginner's Luck; Teacher's Beau; Sprucin' Up; Little Papa; Our Gang Follies of 1936. 1936 Anthony Adverse; Charge of the Light Brigade; The Case Against Mrs. Ames; The Lucky Corner (short). 1937 Life Begins with Love; Conquest. 1938 Marie Antoinette; Listen, Darling; You're Only Young Twice; The Devil's Party; Four's a Crowd; Marie Walewska; Bad Man from Brimstone. 1939 The Flying Irishman; Mickey the Kid; Our Neighbors, the Carters; The Escape; Days of Jesse James; Blind Alley; plus the following shorts: Cousin Wilbur; Dog Daze; Royal Rodeo. 1940 Street of Memories; Gold Rush Maisie; My Favorite Wife; The Blue Bird; My Son, My Son. 1941 Aloma of the South Seas; Father's Son; The Vanishing Virginian; Kings Row. 1942 Between Us Girls; It Happened in Flatbush. 1943 Good Luck, Mr. Yates; The Youngest Profession. 1944 Ali Baba and the Forty Thieves; The Climax. 1945 Junior Miss; Circumstantial Evidence. 1946 The Jolson Story; My Reputation; White Tie and Tails; Her Adventurous Night. 1947 Cynthia; Dangerous Years. 1948 Michael O'Halloran; A Date with Judy. 1950 Battleground; Nancy Goes to Rio; The Happy Years; Louisa. 1951 Corky of Gasoline Alley. 1952 Savage Triangle. 1953 Hot News. 1956 Three for Jamie Dawn. 1974 That's Entertainment (film clips).

BECKWITH, REGINALD

Born: 1908, York, England. Died: June 26, 1965, Bourne End, England. Screen, stage, television actor, stage director, playwright and screenwriter.

Appeared in: 1941 Freedom Radio (aka A Voice in the Night—US). 1948 Scott of the Antarctic (US 1949). 1950 Miss Pilgrim's Progress; The Body Said No! 1951 Mr. Drake's Duck; Circle of Danger; Another Man's Poison (US 1952). 1952 Whispering Smith Hits London (aka Whispering Smith vs. Scotland Yard—US); Brandy for the Parson; You're Only Young Twice!; Penny Princess. 1953 The Titfield Thunderbolt; Innocents in Paris (US 1955); Genevieve (US 1954). 1954 Don't Blame the Stork; The Million Pound Note (aka Man with a Million—US); Fast and Loose; The Runaway Bus; Lease on Life; Men of Sherwood Forest (US 1956); Aunt Clara. 1955 The Lyons in Paris; Break in the Circle (US 1957); They Can't Hang Me; A Yank in Ermine. 1956 The March Hare; It's a Wonderful World (US 1961); A Touch of the Sun; Charley Moon. 1957 Carry on Admiral (aka The Ship Was Loaded—US 1959); These Dangerous Years (aka Dangerous Youth—US 1958); Light Fingers; Lucky Jim; Night of the Demon (aka Curse of the Demon—US 1958). 1958 Up the Creek; Law and Disorder; Next to No Time (US 1960); Rockets Galore; Mad Little Island. 1959 The Captain's Table (US 1960); The Horse's Mouth; The 39 Steps (US 1960); The Ugly Duckling; The Navy Lark; Friends and Neigh-

bors (US 1963); Desert Mice; Expresso Bongo. 1960 Bottoms Up!; Dentist in the Chair (US 1961); Doctor in Love (US 1962); There Was a Crooked Man (US 1962). 1961 The Girl on the Boat; Five Golden Hours; Double Bunk; Dentist on the Job (aka Get on with It!—US 1963); The Day the Earth Caught Fire (US 1962). 1962 Hair of the Dog; The Prince and the Pauper; Night of the Eagle (aka Burn Witch Burn—US); The Password is Courage (US 1963). 1963 The King's Breakfast; Just for Fun; Lancelot and Guinevere (aka Sword of Lancelot—US); The VIPS; Doctor in Distress (US 1964); Never Put it in Writing (US 1964). 1964 Mister Moses (US 1965); A Shot in the Dark; The Yellow Rolls Royce (US 1965). 1965 Gonks Go Beat; The Amorous Adventures of Moll Flanders; Where the Spies Are; The Secret of My Success; Thunderball; The Big Job.

BECKWITH, ROGER. See WILHELM VON BRINCKEN

BECWAR, GEORGE (George Jerome Becwar)

Born: Sept. 16, 1917, Ill. Died: July 9, 1970, Santa Monica, Calif. (heart attack). Screen and television actor.

Appeared in: 1956 Bride of the Monster. 1958 Attack of the Fifty-Foot Woman; War of the Colossal Beast.

BEDOYA, ALFONSO

Born: 1904, Vicam, Sonora, Mexico. Died: Dec. 15, 1957, Mexico City, Mexico. Screen actor.

Appeared in: 1948 The Treasure of Sierra Madre (Hollywood film debut); Angel of the Amazon; The Pearl; Angel in Exile. 1949 Border Incident; Streets of Laredo. 1950 Fortunes of Captain Blood; The Black Rose. 1951 The Man in the Saddle. 1952 California Conquest; Stronghold. 1953 Sombrero; The Stranger Wore a Gun. 1954 Ricochet Romance; Border River; The Black Pirates; Street Corner (aka Both Sides of the Law—US). 1955 Ten Wanted Men. 1958 The Big Country.

BEECHER, ADA

Born: 1862. Died: Mar. 30, 1935, Hollywood, Calif. Screen actress.

BEECHER, JANET (J. B. Meysenburg)

Born: 1884, Jefferson City, Mo. Died: Aug. 6, 1955, Washington, Conn. Stage and screen actress.

Appeared in: 1933 Gallant Lady. 1934 The Last Gentleman; The Mighty Barnum; The President Vanishes; Once a Gentleman. 1935 Let's Live Tonight; Village Tale; The Dark Angel; So Red the Rose. 1936 Love before Breakfast; I'd Give My Life; The Longest Night. 1937 Give Till it Hurts (short); The Good Old Soak; The Thirteenth Chair; Between Two Women; Big City; My Dear Miss Aldrich; Beg, Borrow or Steal; Rosalie. 1938 Judge Hardy's Children; Yellow Jack; Woman against Woman; Say It in French. 1939 The Story of Vernon and Irene Castle; I Was a Convict; Man of Conquest; Career; Laugh It Off. 1940 Slightly Honorable; The Gay Caballero; All This and Heaven Too; Bitter Sweet; The Mark of Zorro. 1941 The Man Who Lost Himself; The Lady Eve; A Very Young Lady; West Point Widow; The Parson of Panamint; For Beauty's Sake. 1942 Hi, Neighbor; Silver Queen; Reap the Wild Wind; Men of Texas. 1943 Mrs. Wiggs of the Cabbage Patch; Henry Aldrich Gets Glamour.

BEECROFT, VICTOR R.

Born: 1887, London, England. Died: Mar. 25, 1958, Newport News, Va. Screen, stage, television and radio actor.

Appeared in: 1915 A Dawn of Tomorrow.

BEERY, NOAH, SR.

Born: Jan. 17, 1884, Kansas City, Mo. Died: Apr. 1, 1946, Los Angeles, Calif. (heart attack). Stage and screen actor. Brother of actor Wallace Beery (dec. 1949) and father of actor Noah Beery, Jr. Married to actress Marguerita Lindsay (dec. 1955).

Appeared in: 1918 The Mormon Maid. 1919 The Red Lantern; In Mizzoura; The Woman Next Door; Louisiana. 1920 The Sea Wolf; The Mark of Zorro; The Fighting Shepherdess; Go and Get It; Dinty. 1921 Beach of Dreams; Bits of Life; The Call of the North; Lotus Blossom; Bob Hampton of Placer. 1922 I Am the Law; The Heart Specialist; The Lying Truth; Omar the Tentmaker; Good Men and True; Flesh and Blood; Belle of Alaska; Ebb Tide; The Crossroads of New York; The Power of Love; Youth to Youth; Tillie; Wild Honey. 1923 The Spoilers; Wandering Daughters; When Law Comes to Hades; Dangerous Trails; The Call of the Canyon; The Destroying Angel; Stephen Steps Out; Stormswept; To the Last Man; Forbidden Lover; His Last Race; Main Street; Hollywood; Quicksands; The Spider and the Rose; Soul of the Beast; Tipped Off. 1924 The Heritage of the Desert; North of 36; The Female; The Fighting Coward; Lily of the Dust; Wanderer of the Wasteland; Welcome Stranger. 1925 The Coming of Amos; East of Suez; Lord Jim; The Thundering Herd; Contraband; The Light of Western Stars; Old Shoes; The Spaniard; Wild Horse Mesa; The Vanishing American. 1926 Beau Geste; The Crown of Lies; Padlocked; Paradise; The Enchanted Hill. 1927 The Rough Riders; The Dove; Evening Clothes; The Love Mart. 1928 Two Lovers; Beau Sabreaur; Hellship Bronson. 1929 False Feathers; Noah's Ark; Passion Song; Linda; Careers; Two O'Clock in the Morning; The Isle of Lost Ships; Four Feathers; Love in the Desert; The Show of Shows; The Godless Girl; Glorifying the American Girl. 1930 Murder Will Out; Sin Flood; Song of the Flame; The Way of All Men; Under a Texas Moon; Golden Dawn; Big Boy; El Dorado; Isle of Escape; Feet First; The Love Trader; Renegades; Tol'able David; Oh, Sailor, Behave!; Mammy. 1931 Bright Lights; Honeymoon Lane; Lost Men; Millionaire; In Line of Duty; Soldiers Plaything; Homicide Squad; Shanghai Love; Riders of the Purple Sage. 1932 Stranger in Town; The Stoker; No Living Witness; Big Stampede; Long Loop Laramie; The Drifter; The Kid from Spain; Out of Singapore; Heroes of the West (serial). 1933 The Flaming Signal; Cornered; Man of the Forest; Easy Millions; Sunset Pass; She Done Him Wrong; To the Last Man (and 1923 version); Laughing at Life; The Woman I Stole. 1934 David Harum; Kentucky Kernels; Madame Spy; Happy Landing; The Trail Beyond; Caravan; Mystery Liner; Cockeyed Cavalier; The Thundering Herd (and 1925 version). 1935 Sweet Adeline. 1936 King of the Damned; The Crimson Circle; The Avenging Hand; Strangers on a Honeymoon (US 1937); Live Again; The Marriage of Corbal (aka Prisoner of Corbal—US 1939); Someone at the Door. 1937 Our Fighting Navy (aka Torpedoed—US 1939); The Frog; Zorro Rides Again (serial). 1938 Bad Man of Brimstone; The Girl of the Golden West; Panamints Bad Man. 1939 Mexicali Rose; Mutiny on the Blackhawk. 1940 A Little Bit of Heaven; The Tulsa Kid; Pioneers of the West; Grandpa Goes to Town; Adventures of Red Ryder (serial). 1941 A Missouri Outlaw. 1942 Isle of Missing Men; Tennessee Johnson. 1943 Clancy Street Boys; Salute to the Marines. 1944 Block Busters; Barbary Coast Gent; The Million Dollar Kid; Gentle Annie; The Honest Thief. 1945 This Man's Navy; Sing Me a Song of Texas.

BEERY, WALLACE

Born: Apr. 1, 1885, Kansas City, Mo. Died: Apr. 15, 1949, Los Angeles, Calif. (heart attack). Screen, stage, circus actor, and film director. Entered films with Essanay in 1913. Brother of actor Noah Beery, Sr. (dec. 1946). Divorced from Areta Gillman and actress Gloria Swanson. Won a 1934 foreign award for Viva Villa! and won 1931 Academy Award for Best Actor in The Champ.

Appeared in: 1914 "Sweedie" series. 1916 A Dash of Courage; Teddy at the Throttle. 1917 Cactus Nell. 1919 The Unpardonable Sin; The Love Burglar; The Life Line; Victory. 1920 Behind the Door; Virgin of Stamboul; The Mollycoddle. 1921 The Four Horsemen of the Apocalypse; The Last of the Mohicans; A Tale of Two Worlds; The Golden Snare; The Last Trail; The Rookie's Return. 1922 Only a Shop Girl; The Sagebrush Trail; Hurricane's Gal; Robin Hood; Wild Honey; I Am the Law; The Man from Hell's River; The Rosary; Trouble. 1923 The Three Ages; Patsy; Ashes of Vengeance; White Tiger; The Spanish Dancer; Richard the Lion-Hearted; Drifting; The Eternal Struggle; Bavu; The Flame of Life; The Drums of Jeopardy; Stormswept. 1924 The Signal Tower; The Red Lily; Another Man's Wife; Dynamite Smith; Madonna of the Streets; The Sea Hawk; Unseen Hands. 1925 The Lost World; The Wanderer; Rugged Water; Adventure; The Devil's Cargo; The Great Divide; The Pony Express; So Big; Coming Through; The Night Club; In the Name of Love; Let Women Alone. 1926 Old Ironsides; Behind the Front; We're in the Navy Now; Volcano. 1927 We're in the Air Now; Fireman, Save My Child; Casey at the Bat. 1928 The Big Killing; Partners in Crime; Wife Savers; Beggars of Life. 1929 Stairs of Sand; River of Romance; Chinatown Nights. 1930 The Big House; Min and Bill; Way for a Sailor; A Lady's Morals; Billy the Kid; Derelict; Soul Kiss. 1931 The Champ; Jenny Lind; The Secret Six; Hell Divers; Stolen Jools (short). 1932 Grand Hotel; Flesh; The Slippery Pearls (short). 1933 Tugboat Annie; Dinner at Eight; The Bowery. 1934 Treasure Island; Viva Villa!; The Mighty Barnum. 1935 China Seas; West Point of the Air; O'Shaughnessy's Boy; Ah, Wilderness! 1936 A Message to Garcia; Old Hutch. 1937 Slave Ship; Good Old Soak. 1938 Stablemates; Bad Man from Brimstone; Port of Seven Seas. 1939 Stand up and Fight; Thunder Afloat; Sergeant Madden. 1940 Two Gun Cupid; Wyoming; The Man from Dakota; Twenty-Mule Team. 1941 Barnacle Bill; The Bugle Sounds; The Bad Man. 1942 Jackass Mail. 1943 Salute to the Marines. 1944 Barbary Coast Gent; Rationing; Gold Town; The Honest Thief; Airship Squadron. 1945 This Man's Navy. 1946 The Mighty McGurk; Bad Bascomb. 1948 A Date with Judy; Alias a Gentleman. 1949 Big Jack. 1960 When Comedy Was King (documentary). 1964 Big Parade of Comedy (documentary). 1974 That's Entertainment (film clips).

BEGGS, LEE

Born: 1871. Died: Nov. 18, 1943, New York, N.Y. Screen, stage actor and film director. Father of actor Malcolm Lee Beggs (dec. 1956).

Appeared in: 1911 His Musical Soul. 1912 A Terrible Lesson; Mignon; A Solax Celebration; The Gold Brick; Making an American Citizen; Father and the Boys; Phantom Paradise; Canned Harmony; The Equine Spy; The Idol Worshipper; Billy's Shoes; Saved by a Cat; The Child of the Tenements; Mickey's Pal; The Wooing of Alice; The Detective Dog; For the Love of the Flag. 1914 Eats; Father's Timepiece; The Egyptian Mummy. 1915 Forcing Dad's Consent; A Mix-Up in Dress-Suit Cases; The Green Cat. 1921 The Iron Trail. 1924 America; Janice Meredith; Playing for Desire. 1926 Stepping Along.

BEGGS, MALCOLM LEE

Born: 1907. Died: Dec. 10, 1956, Chicago, Ill. (beaten to death). Screen, stage, television actor and stage director. Son of actor Lee Beggs (dec. 1943).

Appeared in: 1952 It Grows on Trees; Love Island. 1953 Botany Bay; Houdini. 1958 Edge of Fury.

BEGLEY, ED

Born: Mar. 25, 1901, Hartford, Conn. Died: Apr. 28, 1970, Hollywood, Calif. (heart attack). Screen, stage, radio and television actor. Won 1962 Academy Award for Best Supporting Actor in Sweet Bird of Youth.

Appeared in: 1947 Boomerang; The Web; The Roosevelt Story (narr.); Big Town. 1948 Sorry, Wrong Number; Sitting Pretty; Deep Waters; The Street with No Name. 1949 It Happens Every Spring; The Great Gatsby; Tulsa. 1950 Stars in My Crown; Saddle Tramp; Dark City; Backfire; Wyoming Mail; Convicted. 1951 The Lady from Texas; You're In the Navy Now (aka U.S.S. Teakettle); On Dangerous Ground. 1952 Boots Malone; Lone Star; Deadline U.S.A.; The Turning Point; What Price Glory. 1956 Patterns. 1957 Twelve Angry Men. 1959 Odds against Tomorrow. 1961 The Green Helmet. 1962 Sweet Bird of Youth. 1964 The Unsinkable Molly Brown. 1966 The Oscar. 1967 The Warning Shot; Billion Dollar Brain. 1968 Firecreek; A Time to Sing; Hang 'Em High; Wild in the Streets. 1969 The Monitors. 1970 The Dunwich Horrors.

BEHRENS, FREDERICK

Born: 1854. Died: Jan. 5, 1938, Los Angeles, Calif. Screen and stage actor.

BEHRLE, FRED

Born: 1891, San Diego, Calif. Died: May 20, 1941, San Fernando Valley, Calif. (heart attack). Screen actor. Entered films with Vitagraph Co.

Appeared in: 1923 The Midnight Alarm. 1927 Through Thick and Thin. 1929 Big News. 1941 Texas.

BELASCO, GENEVIEVE

Born: 1871, London, England. Died: Nov. 17, 1956, New York, N.Y. Screen, stage and radio actress.

Appeared in: 1923 Ten Commandments. 1924 The Sainted Devil.

BELCHER, ALICE

Born: 1880. Died: May 9, 1939, Hollywood, Calif. Screen and stage actress.

Appeared in: 1922 Second Hand Rose. 1926 Mistaken Orders; Pals First. 1927 Blondes by Choice. 1928 The Cowboy Kid.

BELCHER, FRANK H.

Born: 1869, San Francisco, Calif. Died: Feb. 27, 1947, Brentwood, N.Y. Stage and screen actor.

Appeared in: 1916 Gloria's Romance. 1921 Coincidence.

BELL, DIANA

Born: Queensland, Australia. Died: Oct. 30, 1965, Melbourne, Australia. Screen, stage and television actress.

BELL, GASTON

Born: 1877, Boston, Mass. Died: Dec. 11, 1963, Woodstock, N.Y. Stage and screen actor. Appeared in silents.

BELL, GENEVIEVE

Died: Oct. 3, 1951, Los Angeles, Calif. (after surgery). Screen actress. Entered films during silents.

Appeared in: 1952 Phone Call from a Stranger.

BELL, GEORGE O.

Died: Oct. 2, 1969. Screen actor.

BELL, HANK (Henry Bell)

Born: 1892. Died: Feb. 4, 1950, Hollywood, Calif. (heart attack). Screen actor.

Appeared in: 1923 Don Quickshot of the Rio Grande. 1925 The Pony Express; Gold and Grit. 1926 Double Daring; The Terror; Twin Triggers; Ace of Action; The Scrappin' Kid. 1927 Code of the Cow Country; Between Dangers. 1928 Saddle Mates. 1929 The Fighting Terror; The Last Roundup; 'Neath Western Skies. 1930 Trails of Peril; Abraham Lincoln. 1935 Westward Ho. 1936 Red River Valley; Comin' 'Round the Mountain; Disorder in the Court (short); Three Troubledoers (short); The Trail of the Lonesome Pine. 1937 Goofs and Saddles (short). 1939 Geronimo; Teacher's Pest (short). 1941 Border Vigilantes. 1942 Valley of the Sun. 1944 Mystery Man. 1945 Flame of the Barbary Coast. 1949 Loaded Pistols.

BELL, JAMES

Born: Dec. 1, 1891, Suffolk, Va. Died: Oct. 26, 1973. Screen and stage actor.

Appeared in: 1932 I Am A Fugitive from a Chain Gang. 1933 King's Vacation; Infernal Machine; Private Detective 62; Day of Reckoning; White Woman;

Storm at Daybreak. **1943** I Walked with a Zombie; My Friend Flicka; Gangway for Tomorrow; The Leopard Man; So Proudly We Hail! **1944** I Love a Soldier; Step Lively; Secret Mission. **1945** Thunderhead—Son of Flicka; Blood on the Sun; The Girl of the Limberlost. **1946** The Spiral Staircase; The Unknown. **1947** Dead Reckoning; Blind Spot; The Sea of Grass; Brute Force; Romance of Rosy Ridge; Driftwood; Killer McCoy; Philo Vance's Secret Mission; The Millerson Case. **1948** I, Jane Doe; Sealed Verdict; Black Eagle. **1949** Streets of Laredo; Roughshod. **1950** Dial 1119; The Company She Keeps; Buckaroo Sheriff of Texas; The Violent Hour. **1951** The Dakota Kid; Flying Leathernecks; Arizona Manhunt; Red Mountain. **1952** Japanese War Bride; Wild Horse Ambush; Ride the Man Down; Million Dollar Mermaid. **1953** Devil's Canyon; All the Brothers Were Valiant; The Last Posse. **1954** The Glenn Miller Story; Riding Shotgun; Crime Wave; About Mrs. Leslie; Black Tuesday. **1955** Strategic Air Command; Lay that Rifle Down: Teen-age Crime Wave; Sincerely Yours; A Lawless Street; Texas Lady; Stranger on Horseback. **1956** Huk; Four Girls in Town; The Search for Bridey Murphy; Tribute to a Bad Man. **1957** The Lonely Man; Back from the Dead; Johnny Trouble; The Tin Star. **1958** In Love and War. **1959** 30. **1961** Claudelle Inglish; Posse from Hell. **1963** Twilight of Honor.

BELL, LOLA

Died: Jan. 6, 1967. Screen actress.

BELL, MONTA

Born: Feb. 5, 1891, Washington, D.C. Died: Feb. 4, 1958, Hollywood, Calif. Screen, stage actor, screenwriter, film producer and film director. Divorced from screen actress Betty Lawford (dec. 1960).

Appeared in: **1923** The Pilgrim.

BELL, RALPH W.

Born: 1883. Died: July 14, 1936, San Francisco, Calif. (pneumonia). Screen, stage actor and stage director.

Appeared in: **1930** Clancy in Wall Street; Cock o' the Walk. **1931** Connecticut Yankee.

BELL, REX

Born: Oct. 16, 1905, Chicago, Ill. Died: July 4, 1962, Las Vegas, Nev. (coronary occlusion). Screen actor. Married to actress Clara Bow (dec. 1965) and was Lieutenant Governor of Nevada from 1954 to 1962.

Appeared in: **1928** Wild West Romance; The Girl-Shy Cowboy; The Cowboy Kid. **1929** Taking a Chance; Joy Street; Pleasure Crazed; Salute; They Had to See Paris; Happy Days. **1930** Courage; True to the Navy; Harmony at Home; Lightnin'. **1931** Battling with Buffalo Bill (serial). **1932** Forgotten Women; Law of the Sea; From Broadway to Cheyenne; The Man from Arizona; Arm of the Law; Crashin' Broadway; Diamond Trail; Lucky Larrigan; The Fighting Texans. **1935** Fighting Pioneers; Fun Fire; Saddle Acres. **1936** Too Much Beef; The Idaho Kid; West of Nevada; Men of the Plains; Stormy Trails. **1942** Tombstone, The Town Too Tough to Die; Dawn on the Great Divide. **1952** Lone Star.

BELL, RODNEY

Born: 1916. Died: Aug. 3, 1968. Screen actor.

Appeared in: **1945** The Strange Affair of Uncle Harry; An Angel Comes to Brooklyn; Scarlet Street. **1951** Meet Me After the Show; So You Want to Be a Handyman (short); So You Want to Be a Paperhanger (short); So You Want to be a Plumber (short). **1952** Something for the Birds; So You Want to Get It Wholesale (short); So You're Going to the Dentist (short). **1953** The Hitchhiker; So You Want a Television Set (short). **1954** So You're Having Neighbor Trouble (short); So You Want to Be Your Own Boss (short); So You're Taking in a Roomer (short). **1956** The Phantom from 10,000 Leagues. **1958** The Missouri Traveler; Wink of an Eye. **1960** The Rookie. **1961** Go Naked in the World.

BELL, RUTH

Born: 1907. Died: June 17, 1933, Los Angeles, Calif.(suicide—poison). Screen actress.

BELLEW, COSMO KYRLE

Born: 1886. Died: Jan. 25, 1948, Hollywood, Calif. Screen and stage actor. Son of actor Kyrle Bellew (dec. 1911).

Appeared in: **1926** Summer Bachelors; **1927** The Magic Flame. **1928** Black Butterflies; Midnight Life; Hit of the Show. **1929** The Devil's Apple Tree; Strange Cargo; Disraeli. **1930** Lummox. **1931** The Lady Who Dared. **1934** Beloved; Norah O'Neill.

BELLEW, KYRLE

Born: 1857, Calcutta, India. Died: Nov. 3, 1911, Salt Lake City, Utah (pneumonia). Stage and screen actor. Father of actor Cosmo Kyrle Bellew (dec. 1948).

Appeared in: **1904** A Gentleman of France.

BELMAR, HENRY

Born: 1849. Died: Jan. 12, 1931, New Castle, Pa. Screen, stage actor, playwright and stage producer. Appeared in silents. Married to actress Laurel Love (dec.).

BELMONT, JOE A.

Born: 1860. Died: Mar. 28, 1930, Toledo, Ohio. Screen actor double and circus acrobat. Do not confuse with screen actor Joseph Belmont.

BELMONT, MICHAEL

Born: 1915. Died: Nov. 9, 1941, Beverly Hills, Calif. (injuries—fall from horse). Screen actor.

BELMONT, RALF

Born: 1892. Died: Sept. 21, 1964, Hollywood, Calif. (struck by car). Screen actor.

BELMONTE, HERMAN

Born: 1891. Died: Sept. 15, 1975, Woodland Hills, Calif. (stroke). Screen actor, dance director and dancer.

BELMORE, BERTHA

Born: Dec. 22, 1882, Manchester, England. Died: Dec. 14, 1953, Barcelona, Spain. Stage and screen actress.

Appeared in: **1934** Going Gay; Are You a Mason?; Over the Garden Wall. **1935** Give Her a Ring; So You Won't Talk; You Never Can Tell; In the Soup. **1936** Broken Blossoms. **1937** Let's Make a Night of It. **1938** Over She Goes. **1939** Discoveries; The Midas Touch; Yes, Madam. **1941** She Couldn't Say No; Pirates of the Seven Seas.

BELMORE, DAISY (Daisy Garstin)

Born: 1874, London, England. Died: Dec. 12, 1954, New York, N.Y. (heart attack). Stage and screen actress. Entered films with Famous Players in N.Y. in 1912.

Appeared in: **1928** We Americans. **1930** Seven Days' Leave; Alias French Gertie; Scarlet Pages; All Quiet on the Western Front; Way for a Sailor. **1931** Fifty Million Frenchmen; My Past; Born to Love.

BELMORE, LIONEL

Born: 1867, England. Died: Jan. 30, 1953, Woodland Hills, Calif. Stage and screen actor.

Appeared in: **1920** Jes' Call Me Jim; Madame X. **1921** Courage; A Shocking Night; Guile of Women; Moonlight Follies; Two Minutes to Go; The Sting of the Lash. **1922** Oliver Twist; The Barnstormer; The Galloping Kid; Iron to Gold; Head over Heels; Enter Madame; The Kentucky Derby; Kindred of the Dust; The World's Champion; Peg o' My Heart. **1923** Within the Law; Jazzmania; Forgive and Forget; Red Lights; Quicksands; Railroaded. **1924** A Boy of Flanders; A Lady of Quality; The Sea Hawk; Try and Get It; A Fool's Awakening; The Man Who Fights Alone; Racing Luck; The Silent Watcher. **1925** Madame Behave; Without Mercy; Eve's Secret; Never the Twain Shall Meet; The Storm Breaker. **1926** Bardelys the Magnificent; The Return of Peter Grimm; The Black Bird; The Checkered Flag; Shipwrecked; Stop, Look and Listen. **1927** The Student Prince in Old Heidelberg; Sorrell and Son; Roaring Fires; Winners of the Wilderness; The Sunset Derby; The Demi-Bride; The Dice Woman; The King of Kings; The Tender Hour; Wide Open. **1928** The Play Girl; Rose Marie; The Circus Kid; The Matinee Idol; The Wife's Relations; The Good-Bye Kiss; Heart Trouble. **1929** The Redeeming Sin; The Love Parade; The Yellowback; The Unholy Night; Evidence; From Headquarters; Stark Mad. **1930** Love Comes Along; The Rogue Song; Hell's Island; Monte Carlo; Sweet Kitty Bellairs; The Boudoir Diplomat; Queen of Scandal; Playing Around; One Heavenly Night; Captain of the Guard. **1931** Ten Nights in a Barroom; Shanghai Love; Frankenstein; Alexander Hamilton. **1932** So Big; Vanity Fair; Police Court; Malay Nights. **1933** The Vampire Bat; Oliver Twist (and 1922 version); The Constant Wife; Warrior's Husband. **1934** Cleopatra; The Count of Monte Cristo; Caravan; I Am Suzanne; Jane Eyre. **1935** Red Morning; Dressed to Kill; Forced Landing; Vanessa, Her Love Story; Hitch Hike Lady; Bonnie Scotland; Cardinal Richelieu; Clive of India. **1936** Little Lord Fauntleroy; The Last of the Mohicans; Mary of Scotland. **1937** It's Love I'm After; Maid of Salem; The Prince and the Pauper; The Toast of New York. **1938** If I Were King; Pie a la Maid (short). **1939** Tower of London; Son of Frankenstein. **1940** My Son, My Son; Diamond Frontier.

BELOKUROV, VLADIMIR V.

Born: 1904, Russia. Died: Jan. 30, 1973, Moscow, Russia. Stage and screen actor.

Appeared in: 1932 House of Death. **1937** Paris Commune. **1941** Wings of Victory. **1963** Optimisticheskaya Tragediya (The Optimistic Tragedy—US 1964).

BELSON, EDWARD

Born: 1898. Died: Dec. 1, 1975, Hollywood, Calif. (kidney failure). Screen actor. Married to former dancer Billie Belson.

BELTRAN, RAYMOND "RAY"
Born: 1892. Died: Oct. 17, 1967. Screen actor.

Appeared in: **1941** This Woman is Mine. **1949** The Cowboy and the Indians. **1953** Treasure of the Golden Condor.

BELTRI, RICARDO
Born: 1899, Mexico. Died: June 1962, Mexico City, Mexico. Screen and stage actor. Appeared in silents.

BELWIN, ALMA
Born: c. 1894, San Francisco, Calif. Died: May 3, 1924, Boston, Mass. Stage and screen actress.

Appeared in: **1915** The Ivory Snuff Box.

BENADERET, BEA
Born: Apr. 4, 1906, New York, N.Y. Died: Oct. 13, 1968, Los Angeles, Calif. (cancer). Screen, stage, television and radio actress.

Appeared in: **1962** Tender Is the Night.

BEN-ARI, RAIKIN
Born: 1904, Russia. Died: Jan. 2, 1968, Moscow, Russia. Screen, stage actor and stage director.

Appeared in: **1959** Gangster Story.

BENASSI, MEMO
Born: 1886, Italy. Died: Feb. 24, 1957, Bologna, Italy. Stage and screen actor.

Appeared in: **1936** La Signora di Tutti. **1937** Signora Paradiso. **1939** Scipio Africanus. **1948** Rossini.

BENCHLEY, ROBERT
Born: Sept. 15, 1889, Worcester, Mass. Died: Nov. 21, 1945, New York, N.Y. (cerebral hemorrhage). Screen, radio actor, writer, critic and film director. Won 1935 Academy Award for his short, How to Sleep.

Appeared in: **1928** The Sex Life of the Polyp; The Treasurer's Report (short); The Spellbinder (short). **1929** The following shorts: Lesson No. 1; Furnace Trouble; Stewed, Fried and Boiled. **1932** Sport Parade. **1933** Headline Shooter; Dancing Lady; Your Technocracy and Mine (short). **1934** Rafter Romance; Social Register. **1935** China Seas; How to Sleep (short); How to Break 90 at Croquet (short). **1936** Piccadilly Jim; plus the following shorts: How to Behave; How to Train a Dog; How to Vote; How to be a Detective. **1937** Live, Love and Learn; plus the following shorts: Broadway Melody of 1938; The Romance of Digestion; How to Start the Day; A Night at the Movies. **1938** The following shorts: How to Figure Income Tax; Music Made Simple; An Evening Alone; How to Raise a Baby; The Courtship of the Newt; How to Read; How to Watch Football; Opening Day; Mental Poise. **1939** The following shorts: How to Sub-Let; An Hour for Lunch; Dark Magic; Home Early; How to Eat; The Day of Rest; See Your Doctor. **1940** Hired Wife; Foreign Correspondent; plus the following shorts: That Interior Feeling; Home Movies; The Trouble with Husbands. **1941** Nice Girl?; The Reluctant Dragon; You'll Never Get Rich; Three Girls About Town; Bedtime Story; plus the following shorts: Waiting for Baby; Crime Control; The Forgotten Man; How to Take a Vacation. **1942** Take a Letter, Darling; The Major and the Minor; I Married a Witch; plus the following shorts: But Nerves; The Witness; Keeping in Shape; The Man's Angle. **1943** Flesh and Fantasy (narr.); Young and Willing; The Song of Russia; The Sky's the Limit; My Tomato (short); No News Is Good News (short). **1944** Her Primitive Man; The National Barn Dance; See Here, Private Hargrove; Practically Yours; Janie; Important Business (short); Why, Daddy? (short). **1945** Pan-Americana; It's in the Bag; Weekend at the Waldorf; Kiss and Tell; Duffy's Tavern; Stork Club; The Road to Utopia; Boogie Woogie (short); I'm a Civilian Here Myself (short). **1946** The Bride Wore Boots; Snafu; Janie Gets Married; Blue Skies. **1964** Big Parade of Comedy (documentary).

BENDER, CHIEF (Charles Albert Bender)
Born: May 5, 1883, Brainerd, Minn. Died: May 22, 1954. Professional baseball player and screen actor.

Appeared in: **1911** The Baseball Bug.

BENDER, RUSSELL "RUSS" (Russell Richard Bender, Jr.)
Born: Jan. 1. 1910, New York, N.Y. Died: Aug. 16, 1969, Woodland Hills, Calif. Screen, television actor and screenwriter.

Appeared in: **1956** It Conquered the World. **1957** The Amazing Colossal Man; Badlands of Montana; Dragstrip Girl; Invasion of the Saucer Men; The Joker Is Wild; Motorcycle Gang; I Bury the Living; War of the Colossal Beast; Suicide Battalion. **1959** Ghost of Dragstrip Hollow; Compulsion; No Name on the Bullet. **1960** Vice Raid. **1961** Anatomy of a Psycho; The Purple Hills; The Little Shepherd of Kingdom Come. **1962** Air Patrol; Panic in Year Zero!; That Touch of Mink. **1963** A Gathering of Eagles. **1964** Raiders from Beneath the Sea; The Strangler. **1965** The Satan Bug; Wild on the Beach; The End of the World (rerelease of Panic in Year Zero!—1962). **1966** The Navy vs. the Night Monsters. **1967** Devil's Angels. **1968** Maryjane; The Young Animals (aka Born Wild).

BENDIX, WILLIAM
Born: Jan. 14, 1906, New York, N.Y. Died: Dec. 14, 1964, Los Angeles, Calif. (lobar pneumonia and complications). Screen, stage, television and radio actor.

Appeared in: **1941** Woman of the Year (film debut). **1942** Brooklyn Orchid; Wake Island; The Glass Key; Star Spangled Rhythm; Who Done It? **1943** The McGuerins from Brooklyn; Guadalcanal Diary; China; The Crystal Ball; Taxi, Mister; Hostages. **1944** Lifeboat; The Hairy Ape; Abroad with Two Yanks; Greenwich Village; Skirmish on the Home Front (short). **1945** It's in the Bag; Don Juan Quilligan; A Bell for Adano. **1946** The Blue Dahlia; Two Years before the Mast; Sentimental Journey; The Dark Corner; White Tie and Tails. **1947** Blaze of Noon; The Web; I'll Be Yours; Calcutta; Where There's Life; Variety Girl. **1948** Race Street; The Babe Ruth Story; The Time of Your Life. **1949** Life of Riley; Streets of Laredo; Cover Up; The Big Steal; Connecticut Yankee in King Arthur's Court. **1950** Johnny Holiday; The Gambling House; Kill the Umpire. **1951** Submarine Command; Detective Story. **1952** Macao; Blackbeard the Pirate; A Girl in Every Port. **1954** Dangerous Mission. **1955** Crash Out. **1956** Battle Stations. **1958** The Deep Six. **1959** Idle on Parade; The Rough and the Smooth. **1961** Portrait of a Sinner. **1962** Boys' Night Out. **1963** The Young and the Brave; For Love or Money. **1964** Law of the Lawless (aka Invitation to a Hanging); The Phony American. **1965 Young Fury; Johnny Nobody.**

BENEDICT, BROOKS
Born: Feb. 6, (?), New York, N.Y. Died: Jan. 1, 1968. Screen and stage actor.

Appeared in: **1923** Cupid's Fireman. **1924** The Only Woman. **1925** The Freshman; His Master's Voice; The Love Gamble: Shoes. **1926** College Days; Going the Limit; Ranson's Folly; Tramp, Tramp, Tramp; Why Girls Go Back Home; Officer of the Day. **1927** Backstage; Casey Jones; The Drop Kick; The Gorilla; The Kid Sister; Orchids and Ermine; Lost at the Front; White Flannels; Three's a Crowd. **1928** The Cowboy Kid; Moran of the Marines; Speedy. **1929** Clear the Decks; The Sophomore; The Garden of Eatin'. **1930** Derelict; The Office Wife; Recaptured Love; The Street of Chance; The Widow from Chicago. **1931** Six Cylinder Love (stage and film versions); Gun Smoke; Reckless Living. **1932** Girl Crazy; What Price Hollywood? **1933** No Other Woman; Pick Up; Cheating Blondes; Don't Bet on Love; Sons of the Desert. **1934** Belle of the Nineties; Picture Brides. **1935** Murder on a Honeymoon; Hot Money (short); Slightly Static (short). **1936** Follow the Fleet; Vamp till Ready (short); Early to Bed; Life Hesitates at 40 (short). **1937** Midnight Madonna; Love Takes Flight; Pick a Star. **1940** I Take This Oath. **1943** Hi' Ya, Chum; Jack London. **1946** Man Who Dared; Out California Way. **1947** Three on a Ticket.

BENEDICT, JEAN
Born: 1876. Died: July 28, 1943, Woodland Hills, Calif. Screen and stage actress. Married to actor Kingsley Benedict.

Appeared in: **1938** A Slight Case of Murder; The Patient in Room 18; Blondes at Work; Little Miss Thoroughbred.

BENELL, JOHN THOMAS
Born: 1915. Died: Aug. 12, 1940, Beverly Hills, Calif. Screen and stage actor.

BENGE, WILSON
Born: 1875, Greenwich, London, England. Died: July 1, 1955, Hollywood, Calif. Screen, stage actor and stage producer.

Appeared in: **1922** Robin Hood. **1923** Ten Commandments. **1925** Alias Mary Flynn; The Road to Yesterday. **1926** A Trip to Chinatown; The Midnight Message. **1927** King of Kings; Fast and Furious; The Lone Eagle. **1928** Anybody Here Seen Kelly?; A Gentleman Preferred; Freedom of the Press; That's My Daddy. **1929** A Most Immoral Lady; Bulldog Drummond; Untamed; Cynara; This Thing Called Love. **1930** Raffles; Her Wedding Night; Charley's Aunt; The Bat Whispers. **1931** Men in Her Life. **1933** Big Executive; By Appointment Only. **1934** Twin Husbands. **1935** Cardinal Richelieu; The Ghost Walks; False Pretenses. **1936** Dancing Feet; Murder at Glen Athol. **1937** The Shadow Strikes; Easy Living; Mr. Boggs Steps Out. **1938** Trade Winds.

BENHAM, DOROTHY
Born: Sept. 6, 1910, Boston, Mass. Died: Sept. 19, 1956, Watertown, Wis. (Hodgkin's disease). Screen actress. Daughter of actor Harry Benham (dec. 1969) and actress Ethyle Cook (dec. 1949). Sister of actor Leland Benham.

Appeared in: **1912** The Wrecked Taxi; Don't Pinch My Pup; The Country's Prize Baby. **1915** Mr. Meeson's Will; The Commuted Sentence. **1916** The Path of Happiness.

BENHAM, HARRY
Born: Feb. 26, 1886, Valparaiso, Ind. Died: 1969, Sarasota, Fla. Stage and screen actor. Entered films with Thanhouser in 1911. Married to actress Ethyle Cook (dec. 1949) and father of actress Dorothy Benham (dec. 1956) and actor Leland Benham.

Appeared in: **1911** Their Burglar; The Tomboy. **1912** Dr. Jekyll and Mr. Hyde; Her Ladyship's Page; When a Count Counted. **1913** For Another's Sin; The Head of the Ribbon Counter; The Girl of the Cabaret; Louie the Life Saver. **1914** Henry's Waterloo; The Runaway Princess; Zudora, the Twenty

Million Dollar Mystery (serial). **1915** The Country Girl; The Heart of Princess Mirsari; The Girl of the Sea; A Freight Car Honeymoon; Daughters of Kings; When the Fleet Sailed; When Hungry Hamlet Fled; The Scoop at Belleville; Helen's Babies; His Two Patients; Madame Blanche. **1916** The Man Inside; The Doll Doctor; The Capital Prize; Mignonette; Through Flames to Love; Her Wonderful Secret; Peggy and the Law; Clever Mrs. Carter; The Little Gray Mouse; The Intruder; A College Boomerang; Love's Masquerade; The Angel of the Attic; The Heart Wrecker; The Girl Who Didn't Tell; Pamela's Past; Toto of the By-Ways; Path to Happiness; Mischief Makers. **1917** The Outsider; Souls United; When Thieves Fall Out; The Dancers Peril; Warfare of the Flesh; When You and I Were Young. **1918** Cecilia of the Pink Roses; Convict 993; The Frame-Up. **1920** Polly with a Past; The Dangerous Paradise; The Prey. **1921** Hush Money. **1922** The Road to Mandalay; The Town That Forgot God; Your Best Friend.

BENNETT, ALMA

Born: 1904, Seattle, Wash. Died: Sept. 16, 1958. Screen actress.

Appeared in: **1922** Flaming Hearts; Without Compromise; Smiling Jim. **1923** The Face on the Barroom Floor; The Grail; Man's Size; Three Jumps Ahead. **1924** The Cyclone Rider; Lilies of the Field; Triumph; The Dawn of a Tomorrow; Why Men Leave Home; The Silent Watcher. **1925** The Lost World; The Light of the Western Stars; A Fool and His Money; The Price of Success. **1926** Brooding Eyes; Don Juan's Three Nights; The Silent Lover; The Thrill Hunter. **1927** Long Pants; Orchids and Ermine; Compassion. **1928** The Goodbye Kiss; The Grain of Dust; The Head of the Family. **1929** My Lady's Past; New Orleans; Painted Faces; Two Men and a Maid; Girl Crazy (short); Midnight Daddies. **1930** Woman Who Was Forgotten; Hail the Princess (short); Jack White talking shorts.

BENNETT, BARBARA

Born: 1911. Died: Aug. 8, 1958, Montreal, Canada (heart attack). Stage and screen actress. Sister of actresses Constance Bennett (dec. 1965) and Joan Bennett and daughter of actor Richard Bennett (dec. 1944) and actress Adrianne Morrison. Divorced from singer Morton Downey. Married to actor Addison "Jack" Randall (dec. 1945).

Appeared in: **1927** Black Jack. **1929** Syncopation; Mother's Boy. **1930** Love among the Millionaires.

BENNETT, BELLE

Born: 1891, Milaca, Minn. Died: Nov. 4, 1932, Los Angeles, Calif. Screen, stage and vaudeville actress.

Appeared in: **1916** Sweet Kitty Bellairs. **1917** Fuel of Life. **1918** A Soul in Trust. **1920** The Courage of Marge O'Doone. **1922** Flesh and Spirit; Robin Hood; Your Best Friend. **1924** In Hollywood with Potash and Perlmutter. **1925** Stella Dallas; Playing with Souls; East Lynne; His Supreme Moment; If Marriage Fails. **1926** The Lily; Reckless Lady; Fourth Commandment; The Amateur Gentleman. **1927** Wild Geese; Mother; Way of all Flesh. **1928** The Devil's Skipper; The Devil's Trademark; The Sporting Age; Mother Machree; Battle of the Sexes; The Power of Silence. **1929** The Iron Mask; Molly and Me; My Lady's Past; Big Money; Fashions in Love. **1930** Their Own Desire; Courage; Recaptured Love; Night Work; One Romantic Night; The Woman Who Was Forgotten. **1932** The Big Shot.

BENNETT, CHARLES

Died: July 1925, New York, N.Y. (hemorrhage). Screen actor and scenery designer.

BENNETT, CHARLES J.

Born: 1891. Died: Feb. 15, 1943, Hollywood, Calif. Screen actor.

Appeared in: **1914** Tillie's Punctured Romance. **1919** The Adventures of Ruth (serial). **1922** The Top of New York. **1924** America.

BENNETT, CONSTANCE

Born: Oct. 22, 1905, New York, N.Y. Died: July 24, 1965, Ft. Dix, N.J. (cerebral hemorrhage). Screen, stage actress and film producer. Daughter of actor Richard Bennett (dec. 1944) and actress Adrianne Morrison. Sister of actresses Barbara (dec. 1958) and Joan Bennett. Married to John Coulter. Divorced from Chester Moorhead, Philip Plant, film producer Marquis de la Falaise de la Coudray and actor Gilbert Roland.

Appeared in: **1922** Reckless Youth; What's Wrong with Women?; Evidence. **1924** Cytherea; The Forbidden Way; Into the Net. **1925** My Wife and I; Sally, Irene and Mary; The Pinch Hitter; Code of the West; The Goose Hangs High; The Goose Woman; My Son; Wandering Fires. **1926** Should a Woman Tell; Married. **1929** This Thing Called Love. **1930** Three Faces East; Common Clay; Rich People; Sin Takes a Holiday; Son of the Gods. **1931** The Common Law; The Easiest Way; Born to Love; Bought. **1932** What Price Hollywood?; Lady with a Past; Two against the World; Rockabye. **1933** Our Betters; Bed of Roses; After Tonight. **1934** The Affairs of Cellini; Moulin Rouge; Outcast Lady. **1935** After Office Hours. **1936** Everything Is Thunder; Ladies in Love. **1937** Topper. **1938** Merrily We Live; Service de Luxe; Topper Takes a Trip. **1939** Tail Spin. **1940** Escape to Glory (aka Submarine Zone). **1941** Two-Faced Woman; Law of the Tropics; Wild Bill Hickok Rides. **1942** Sin Town; Ma-

dame Spy. **1945** Madame Pimpernel; Paris Underground. **1946** Centennial Summer. **1947** The Unsuspected. **1948** Smart Woman; Blonde Ice. **1949** Angel on the Amazon. **1951** As Young as You Feel. **1954** It Should Happen to You. **1966** Madame X.

BENNETT, ENID

Born: Jan. 2, 1895, Australia. Died: May 14, 1969, Malibu, Calif. (heart attack). Stage and screen actress. Entered films in 1917.

Appeared in: **1917** Princess in the Dark. **1918** The Biggest Show on Earth; The Vamp; Fuss and Feathers. **1919** The Haunted Bedroom; Stepping Out. **1920** The Woman and the Suitcase; Hairpins. **1921** Her Husband's Friend; Keeping up with Lizzie; Silk Hosiery. **1922** Robin Hood; The Bootlegger's Daughter; Scandalous Tongues. **1923** The Bad Man; The Courtship of Miles Standish; Strangers of the Night; Your Friend and Mine. **1924** The Sea Hawk; The Red Lily; A Fool's Awakening. **1926** A Woman's Heart. **1927** The Wrong Mr. Wright. **1929** Good Medicine. **1931** Skippy; Waterloo Bridge; Sooky. **1939** Meet Dr. Christian; Intermezzo: A Love Story. **1940** Strike up the Band.

BENNETT, FRANK

Born: 1891. Died: Apr. 1957. Screen actor. Appeared in silent films.

BENNETT, JOE (Joseph Bennett Aldert)

Born: 1889, Charleston, S.C. Died: Aug. 31, 1967, Amityville, N.Y. Screen, vaudeville, minstrel actor and dancer. Appeared in vaudeville as part of "The Dark Clouds" team with Edward Richards and later in a vaudeville act billed as "The Georgia Trio," both blackface acts.

BENNETT, JOSEPH

Born: 1896, Los Angeles, Calif. Died: Dec. 4, 1931, Hollywood, Calif. Screen actor. Entered films in 1917.

Appeared in: **1921** Love Never Dies; The Night Horsemen; A Daughter of the Law; The Home Stretch. **1922** Elope If You Must. **1924** Barbara Frietchie; The Breed of the Border; Trigger Finger; Flashing Spurs. **1925** Cold Nerve. **1926** The Sign of the Claw; The Man in the Shadow. **1927** God's Great Wilderness; Shooting Straight; Men of Daring; Straight Shootin'; Wolf's Trail; Three Miles Up; Somewhere in Sonora; The Valley of Hell. **1928** The Shepherd of the Hills; Vultures of the Sea (serial); Won in the Clouds. **1929** The Lariat Kid. **1930** After the Fog.

BENNETT, LEE

Born: 1911. Died: Oct. 10, 1954, Chicago, Ill. Screen, radio actor, singer and orchestra leader.

Appeared in: **1937** Hold 'Em Navy. **1947** The Last Round-Up; Spirit of West Point. **1950** At War with the Army. **1951** The Dakota Kid; Three Desperate Men (aka Three Outlaws).

BENNETT, MICKEY

Born: 1915, Victoria, B.C., Canada. Died: Sept. 6, 1950, Hollywood, Calif. (heart attack). Screen actor and assistant film director.

Appeared in: **1922** The Man Who Played God; Reported Missing. **1923** Big Brother; The Empty Cradle; The Last Moment; Loyal Wives; Marriage Morals. **1924** The New School Teacher; Second Youth. **1926** Big Pal; The Cohens and the Kellys; Grabbing Grabbers (short); It's the Old Army Game; There Ain't No Santa Claus (short); Honesty—The Best Policy. **1927** A Boy of the Streets; Babe Comes Home; Slaves of Beauty. **1928** Tillie's Punctured Romance; United States Smith; The Vanishing West (serial); The Head of the Family. **1929** The Dummy; Footlights and Fools; The Ghost Talks. **1930** Strictly Modern; Swing High; Father's Son. **1931** Big Business Girl. **1932** Laughter in Hell. **1933** The Mayor of Hell.

BENNETT, RAY

Born: 1895. Died: Dec. 17, 1957, Hollywood, Calif. (heart attack). Screen actor.

Appeared in: **1937** Public Cowboy No. 1. **1938** The Old Barn Dance; Prairie Moon. **1942** The Spoilers; Call of the Canyon. **1948** Canon City; Northwest Stampede. **1949** Song of Surrender; Rimfire; Ma and Pa Kettle; The Dalton Gang. **1951** Apache Drums. **1952** The Man from Black Hills; Waco. **1953** The Redhead from Wyoming; The Great Sioux Uprising. **1956** The Wrong Man. **1957** African Manhunt.

BENNETT, RED (William Houghton)

Born: 1873. Died: May 10, 1941, Hollywood, Calif. Screen actor.

BENNETT, RICHARD

Born: May 21, 1873, Deacon's Mills, Cass County, Ind. Died: Oct. 22, 1944, Los Angeles, Calif. (heart attack). Screen, stage and vaudeville actor. Married to actress Adrianne Morrison. Father of actresses Constance (dec. 1965), Barbara (dec. 1958) and Joan Bennett.

Appeared in: **1915** Damaged Goods. **1923** The Eternal City. **1924** Youth for Sale. **1925** Lying Wives. **1928** The Home Towners. **1931** Five and Ten; Arrowsmith; Bought. **1932** No Greater Love; Stange Justice; This Reckless Age; If I Had a Million; Madame Racketeer. **1933** The Woman Accused; The Song of

Songs; Big Executive. **1934** Nana. **1935** This Woman Is Mine. **1942** Journey into Fear; The Magnificent Ambersons.

BENNETT, SAM
Born: 1887. Died: Aug. 25, 1937, Hollywood, Calif. Screen and stage actor.

BENNETT, TOMMY
Died: Oct. 1943. Screen actor.

BENNETT, WILDA
Born: 1894. Died: Dec. 20, 1967, Winnemucca, Nev. Screen and stage actress.

Appeared in: **1939** What a Life; The Women. **1940** Those Were the Days.

BENNISON, ANDREW
Born: 1887. Died: Jan. 7, 1942, Oxnard, Calif. Screen, stage actor, screenwriter and film director.

BENNISON, LOUIS
Born: 1884. Died: June 9, 1929, New York, N.Y. (suicide—gun). Screen actor and playwright.

Appeared in: **1921** Lavender and Old Lace.

BENNY, JACK (Benjamin Kubelsky)
Born: Feb. 14, 1894, Waukegan, Ill. Died: Dec. 26, 1974, Holmby Hills, Calif. (stomach cancer). Screen, stage, burlesque, vaudeville, radio, television actor, film producer, violinist and orchestra leader. Married to actress Mary Livingstone.

Appeared in: **1928** Bright Moments (short). **1929** Hollywood Revue of 1929; The Road Show. **1930** Chasing Rainbows; The Medicine Man; The Song Writers Revue (short); plus Paramount shorts. **1931** Taxi Tangle (short). **1933** Mr. Broadway. **1934** Transatlantic Merry-Go-Round. **1935** Broadway Melody of 1936; It's in the Air. **1936** The Big Broadcast of 1937; College Holiday. **1937** Artists and Models. **1938** Artists and Models Abroad. **1939** Man About Town. **1940** Love Thy Neighbor; Buck Benny Rides Again. **1941** Charley's Aunt (aka Charley's American Aunt). **1942** George Washington Slept Here; To Be or Not to Be. **1943** The Meanest Man in the World. **1944** Hollywood Canteen. **1945** The Horn Blows at Midnight; It's in the Bag (aka The Fifth Chair). **1946** Without Reservations. **1949** The Great Lover. **1952** Somebody Loves Me. **1954** Susan Slept Here. **1957** Beau James. **1961** You Have to Run Fast. **1962** Gypsy. **1963** It's a Mad, Mad, Mad, Mad World. **1967** A Guide for the Married Man.

BENSON, JOHN WILLIAM
Born: 1862. Died: July 12, 1926, New York, N.Y. (complications of diseases). Screen, stage and vaudeville actor.

BENSON, JULIETTE V. P.
Born: 1875. Died: Dec. 22, 1962, Hollywood, Calif. Screen actress. Entered films approx. 1933.

BENSON, MAY
Died: Sept. 29, 1916. Stage and screen actress.

Appeared in: **1915** Mariana.

BENSON, SANDFORD
Born: 1914. Died: Feb. 4, 1935, Hollywood, Calif. (injuries from auto accident). Stage and screen actor.

BENT, MARION
Born: Dec. 23, 1879, Bronx, N.Y. Died: July 28, 1940, Bronx, N.Y. Screen, stage actress and dancer. Married to actor Pat Rooney (dec. 1962).

Appeared in: **1915** I'll Get You Yet.

BENT, PHILIP
Born: 1941. Died: June 12, 1966, La Jolla, Calif. (plane crash). Screen actor.

Appeared in: **1966** How to Stuff a Wild Bikini; Dr. Goldfoot and the Bikini Machine.

BENTLEY, IRENE (Alexina Bentley)
Born: Nov. 12, 1904, New York, N.Y. Died: Nov. 24, 1965, Fla. (heart attack). Screen actress. Divorced from Kenneth Niemann (dec.); stockbroker George S. Kent (dec.) and actor Richard C. Hemingway (dec.).

Appeared in: **1933** My Weakness. **1934** Smoky; Frontier Marshall.

BENTLEY, ROBERT
Born: 1895. Died: Apr. 19, 1958, Benton Harbor, Mich. Screen, stage and radio actor.

Appeared in: **1921** The Power Within. **1923** None So Blind. **1924** The New School Teacher.

BENTON, BESSIE
Died: Jan. 1917, Los Angeles, Calif. Screen actress.

BERANGER, GEORGE (George Andre de Beranger)
Born: Mar. 27, 1895, Sydney, Australia. Died: 1973. Screen, stage actor and film director.

Appeared in: **1915** Birth of a Nation; The Stab. **1916** Flirting with Fate; Pillars of Society; Manhattan Madness; The Good-Bad Man; Should She Have Told?; In the Dead O'Night; Mixed Blood. **1917** Those Without Sin. **1918** Sandy; A Bum Bomb. **1923** The Leopardess; Dulcy; The Bright Shawl; The Extra Girl; Ashes of Vengeance; Tiger Rose; The Man Life Passed By. **1924** Beau Brummel. **1925** Grounds for Divorce; Beauty and the Bad Man; Are Parents People?; A Woman's Faith; The Man in Blue; Confessions of a Queen. **1926** The Grand Duchess and the Waiter; So This is Paris; The Bat; Miss Brewster's Millions; The Popular Sin; The Eagle of the Sea; Fig Leaves; The Lady of the Harem. **1927** Altars of Desire; Paradise for Two; If I Were Single; The Small Bachelor. **1928** Powder My Back; Beware of Bachelors; Five and Ten-Cent Annie. **1929** Stark Mad; Strange Cargo; The Glad Rag Doll. **1930** Lillies of the Field; The Boudoir Diplomat. **1931** Annabelle's Affair; Surrender; Ladies of the Jury. **1933** Mama Loves Papa. **1934** Young and Beautiful; Kiss and Make Up. **1935** The Pay-Off. **1936** Love Before Breakfast; The Noise; Walking on Air; Down the Stretch; Colleen; Hot Money; King of Hockey. **1937** Hollywood Round-Up; Gilding the Lily (short). **1939** Beauty for the Asking. **1942** Over My Dead Body.

BERANGERE, MME.
Born: France. Died: Nov. 1928, Paris, France. Screen actress.

BEREGI, OSCAR, SR.
Born: 1875, Hungary. Died: Oct. 18, 1965, Hollywood, Calif. Hungarian screen and stage actor. Father of screen actor Oscar Beregi, Jr. (dec. 1976).

Appeared in: **1926** Butterflies in the Rain; The Love Thief; The Flaming Forest. **1927** Camille; Moon of Israel. **1933** A Key Balvany (A Blue Idol). **1934** Iza Neni; Rakoczi Indulo.

BERESFORD, HARRY
Born: 1864, London, England. Died: Oct. 4, 1944, Los Angeles, Calif. Screen, stage actor, screenwriter and novelist.

Appeared in: **1926** The Quarterback. **1931** Charlie Chan Carries On; Sob Sister; Heaven on Earth; Sooky; Finn and Hattie; Scandal Sheet; Up Pops the Devil; The Secret Call. **1932** Ambition; High Pressure; Scandal for Sale; So Big; Strange Love of Molly Louvain; Prosperity; Dr. X; The Match King; Dance Team; Forgotten Commandments; The Sign of the Cross. **1933** Murders in the Zoo; The Mind Reader; I Cover the Waterfront; Dinner at Eight; Night Flight; Bureau of Missing Persons; Ever in My Heart; College Coach. **1934** Friends of Mr. Sweeney; Cleopatra; The Little Minister; Fashions of 1934; The Merry Frinks. **1935** Seven Keys to Baldpate; Anna Karenina; David Copperfield; A Dog of Flanders; I'll Love You Always; Page Miss Glory; I Found Stella Parrish. **1936** Klondike Annie; Follow the Fleet; Grand Jury; Postal Inspector; In His Steps. **1937** The Prince and the Pauper; The Go-Getter; She's No Lady; She Asked for It; They Won't Forget. **1944** The Sign of the Cross (revised version of 1932 film).

BERG, GERTRUDE
Born: Oct. 3, 1900, New York, N.Y. Died: Sept. 14, 1966, N.Y. (heart ailment). Screen, stage, television, radio actress, author and screenwriter.

Appeared in: **1951** Molly. **1953** Main Street to Broadway.

BERG, STINA
Born: 1869, Sweden. Died: 1930, Sweden. Screen actress.

Appeared in: The Tyrannical Fiance; On the Fateful Roads of Life; The Modern Suffragette; People of the Border; Halfbreed; The Birthday Present; King Solomon's Judgment; The Way to the Man's Heart; The Chamberlain; Children of the Street; Expiated Guilt; The Playmates; Revenge Is Sweet; Keep to Your Trade; The Consequences of Jealousy; His Wedding Night; Her Royal Highness; The Lucky Brooch; Love and Journalism; The Million Inheritance; Sir Arne's Treasure (1919); Erotikon; Mrs. Anderson's Charlie; Gunnar Hede's Saga; The Norrtull Gang; Constable Paulus's Easter Bomb; Her Little Majesty; Two Kings; Ebberod's Bank; The Gyurkovics Girls; The Queen of Pellagonia; His English Wife; Sealed Lips; Sin (1928); Jansson's Temptation; Say It With Music; People of Norrland; For Her Sake; Gentlemen in Uniform; Charlotte Lowenskold; Motley Leaves; 33.333.

BERGER, NICOLE
Born: 1934, France. Died: Apr. 1967, Rougen, France (following auto accident). Screen, stage and television actress.

Appeared in: **1955** The Game of Love. **1956** Bold Adventure. **1957** Julietta. **1958** He Who Must Die; Premier Mai (The First Day of May). **1959** Filles de la Nuit (Girls of the Night). **1960** The Siege of Sidney Street (US 1961); The Chasers (aka Les Dragueurs [The Dredgers]). **1962** La Denonciation (The Denunciation—aka The Immoral Moment—US 1967); Love Is My Profession;

Shoot the Piano Player. **1963** The Girl from Flanders; Char de Poule (aka Highway Pick Up—US 1965). **1968** La Permission (aka The Story of a Three Day Pass—US).

BERGERE, RAMONA
Born: 1902. Died: Apr. 26, 1941, Glendale, Calif. Screen actress.

BERGERE, VALERIE
Born: Feb. 2, 1875, Alsace-Lorraine, France. Died: Sept. 16, 1938, Hollywood, Calif. Screen, stage and vaudeville actress.

Appeared in: **1937** The Singing Marine; It's Love I'm After.

BERGMAN, HENRY
Born: 1870, San Francisco, Calif. Died: Oct. 22, 1946, Hollywood, Calif. (heart attack). Screen actor, circus and opera performer, screenwriter and assistant film director. Entered films with Pathe-Lehrman in 1913.

Appeared in: **1915** His New Job; A Night Out; The Champion; In the Park; The Jitney Elopement; The Tramp; By the Sea; Work; A Woman; The Bank; Shanghaied; A Night in the Show. **1916** Carmen; Police; Triple Trouble; The Floorwalker; The Fireman; The Vagabond; One A.M.; The Count; The Pawnshop; Behind the Screen; The Rink. **1917** Easy Street; The Cure; The Immigrant; The Adventurer. **1918** A Dog's Life; The Bond; Shoulder Arms. **1919** Sunnyside; A Day's Pleasure. **1920** The Idle Class. **1921** The Kid. **1922** Pay Day; The Pilgrim. **1923** A Woman of Paris. **1925** The Gold Rush. **1928** The Circus. **1931** City Lights. **1936** Modern Times. **1940** The Great Dictator.

BERISTAIN, LEOPOLDO
Born: 1883, Mexico. Died: Jan. 5, 1948, Tijuana, Mexico (diabetes). Screen actor.

Appeared in: **1939** Mexico Lindo.

BERISTAIN, LUIS
Born: 1918, Mexico. Died: Apr. 1, 1962, Mexico City, Mexico (heart attack). Screen and television actor.

Appeared in: **1955** This Strange Passion. **1962** El Angel Exterminador (The Exterminating Angel—US 1967).

BERK, SARA
Born: 1898. Died: Apr. 21, 1975, New York, N.Y. (heart attack). Screen actress.

Appeared in: **1962** Light Fantastic.

BERKELEY, ARTHUR
Born: 1896. Died: July 29, 1962, Hollywood, Calif. Screen actor.

Appeared in: **1957** Teenage Monster.

BERKELEY, REGINALD
Born: 1882, London, England. Died: Mar. 20, 1936, Hollywood, Calif. Screen actor, screenwriter and author.

BERKES, JOHN PATRICK
Born: 1897. Died: July 5, 1951, Hollywood, Calif. Screen and stage actor.

Appeared in: **1947** The Corpse Came C.O.D.; The Egg and I. **1948** Romance on the High Seas. **1949** My Dream is Yours. **1950** Branded. **1951** Journey into Light; The Big Carnival.

BERLE, SANDRA (Sarah Glanz)
Born: 1877, New York, N.Y. Died: May 31, 1954, New York, N.Y.(cerebral hemorrhage). Screen and television actress. An occasional extra at Biograph Studios in youth. Mother of actor Milton Berle and often in his various acts.

BERLINER, MARTIN
Born: 1896, Germany. Died: Jan. 26, 1966, Berlin, Germany (heart attack). Screen, stage and television actor.

Appeared in: **1962** The Counterfeit Traitor. **1964** Three Penny Opera.

BERN, PAUL (Paul Levy)
Born: 1889, Wandabeck, Germany. Died: Sept. 4, 1932, Beverly Hills, Calif. (suicide—gun). Screen, stage actor, film producer, film director and screenwriter. Married to actress Jean Harlow (dec. 1937).

BERNARD, AL
Born: 1888. Died: Mar. 6, 1949, New York, N.Y. Screen, television, radio, vaudeville, minstrel actor, singer, author, and songwriter.

BERNARD, BARNEY
Born: Aug. 17, 1877, Rochester, N.Y. Died: Mar. 21, 1924, New York, N.Y. (bronchial pneumonia). Screen, stage and vaudeville actor. He and Alexander Carr (dec. 1946) created the roles of Potash and Perlmutter on stage.

They appeared in: **1923** Potash and Perlmutter.

BERNARD, DOROTHY
Born: 1890. Died: Dec. 14, 1955, Hollywood, Calif. (heart attack). Stage and screen actress.

Appeared in: **1909** The Cricket on the Hearth; "Jonsey" series. **1910** Fate's Turning. **1911** The Failure; Sunshine through the Dark; A Tale of the Wilderness; A Sister's Love; A Blot on the 'Scutcheon; The Root of Evil. **1912** The Girl and Her Trust; The Female of the Species; A Siren of Impulse; The Goddess of Sagebrush Gulch; His Lesson; Heaven Avenges. **1916** A Man of Sorrow. **1918** Little Women; Les Miserables. **1921** The Wild Goose.

BERNARD, HARRY
Born: 1878. Died: Nov. 4, 1940, Hollywood, Calif. Screen and vaudeville actor. Appeared in Keystone films in 1915.

Appeared in: **1915** Crossed Love and Swords; Dirty Work in a Laundry; The Battle of Ambrose and Walrus; Our Daredevil Chief. **1928** Two Tars (short). **1929** The following shorts: Berth Marks; Liberty; Wedding Again; That's My Wife; Men O'War; A Perfect Day. **1930** The following shorts: Night Owls; Blotto; Another Fine Mess. **1931** The following shorts: Laughing Gravy; Bargain Days; Shiver My Timbers; Dogs Is Dogs; The Pip from Pittsburgh; Rough Seas; One of the Smiths; The Panic Is On; Skip the Maloo!; The Hasty Marriage; High Gear; Call A Cop; Mama Loves Papa; The Kickoff. **1932** The following shorts: Any Old Port; Readin' and Writin'; Free Eats; Choo Choo; A Lad an' a Lamp; Pooch; In Walked Charley; Young Ironsides; Mr. Bride; Love Pains; The Knock-Out; Too Many Women; Sneak Easily. **1933** The following shorts: Maids a la Mode; The Bargain of the Century; Forgotten Babies; Kid from Borneo; Bedtime Worries; The Midnight Patrol; Fallen Arches; The Silent Racket; Sherman Said It; Luncheon at Twelve. **1934** Sons of the Desert; plus the following shorts: Three Chumps Ahead; The Live Ghost; The Neighbor; The Cracked Iceman; Another Wild Idea; Something Simple; You Said a Hateful; The Chases of Pimple Street. **1935** Ruggles of Red Gap; plus the following shorts: Top Flat; Sprucin' Up; Okay Toots!; Poker at Eight; Southern Exposure; Manhattan Monkey Business. **1936** The Bohemian Girl; Our Relations; plus the following shorts: On the Wrong Trek; Life Hesitates at 40; Neighborhood House. **1937** New Faces of 1937. **1939** Rattling Romeo (short).

BERNARD, IVOR
Born: June 13, 1887, London, England. Died: June 30, 1953. Stage and screen actor.

Appeared in: **1931** The Skin Game; Sally in Our Alley. **1932** The Good Companions. **1933** Illegal; Sleeping Car; Waltz Time; The Crime of Blossoms; The Wandering Jew. **1934** Princess Charming. **1935** Death at Broadcasting House; The Roof; Mr. Hobo; Behind the Mask. **1936** Double Exposure; Foreign Affairs; The House of the Spaniard; Secret Lives; Farewell to Cinderella. **1937** What a Man; Victoria the Great; Storm in a Teacup; The Mill on the Floss. **1938** Pygmalion. **1941** Stars Look Down; The Saint's Vacation. **1944** Hotel Reserve (aka Epitaph for a Spy); Escape to Danger; Undercover. **1945** The Silver Fleet. **1946** Great Day; The Wicked Day; Caesar and Cleopatra. **1947** Appointment with Crime; Princess Fitz; Great Expectations; So Well Remembered; Murder in Reserve. **1948** London Belongs to Me (aka Dulcimer Street). **1949** Don't Take It to Heart; Queen of Spades; Paper Orchid. **1950** Madeline; Mrs. Fitzherbert. **1951** Oliver Twist; Sin of Esther Waters. **1952** Time, Gentlemen, Please. **1953** Malta Story; Sea Devils. **1954** Beat the Devil.

BERNARD, LOIS
Born: 1898. Died: Apr. 25, 1945, Los Angeles, Calif. (suicide—jumped from building). Screen actress. Married to actor Joseph Bernard.

BERNARD, PAUL
Born: France. Died: May 1958, Paris, France. Stage and screen actor.

Appeared in: **1936** Pension Mimosas. **1947** Panic! **1948** Les Maudits (The Damned); Un Ami Viendra Ce Soir (A Friend Will Come Tonight). **1954** Caroline Cherie. **1956** Les Dames du Bois du Boulogne (Women of the Bois du Boulogne).

BERNARD, PETER
Born: 1888, U.S. Died: Dec. 22, 1960, Huddersfield, England. Screen, vaudeville actor, vocalist and songwriter.

BERNARD, SAM
Born: 1889. Died: July 5, 1950, Hollywood, Calif. Screen and stage actor.

Appeared in: **1931** Wanted by the Police; Prison Train. **1941** Tumbledown Ranch in Arizona. **1942** Let's Get Tough; Today I Hang; Smart Alecks; Baby Face Morgan; Ice Capades Revue. **1943** The Crime Smashers. **1945** Thoroughbreds. **1948** The Vicious Circle; When My Baby Smiles at Me. **1949** The Big Sombrero.

BERNARD, SAM (aka SAMUEL BARNET)
Born: 1863, Birmingham, England. Died: May 16, 1927, on board ship in the Atlantic (apoplexy). Screen, stage and vaudeville actor. Entered films with Triangle Film Corp. in 1915. Appeared in vaudeville under name of Samuel Barnet.

Appeared in: **1915** Fatty and the Broadway Stars. **1916** Because He Loved Her; The Great Pearl Tangle.

BERNARDI, NERIO

Born: 1899. Died: Jan. 12, 1971, Italy. Screen actor.

Appeared in: **1922** Nero. **1923** The Shepherd King. **1935** Il Delitto di Mastrovanni. **1936** Tempo Massimo; Fiat Voluntas Dei. **1937** Loyalty of Love. **1938** Adventura di Giacomo Casanova. **1939** Il Corsaro Nero (The Black Corsair). **1948** La Traviata (The Lost One). **1950** Heart and Soul. **1952** Never Take No for an Answer; I Cadetti di Guascogna. **1953** Fanfan the Tulip; The Young Caruso. **1954** Theodora, Slave Empress. **1959** Ballerina e Buon Dio (aka Ballerina and the Good God and Angel in a Taxi—US 1963). **1960** La Donna dei Faraoini (The Pharaoh's Woman—US 1961); Les Nuits de Raspoutine (The Night They Killed Rasputin—US 1962); Le Passage du Rhin (Tomorrow Is My Turn—US 1962); Prisoner of the Volga. **1961** La Guerra di Trois (aka The Trojan Horse—US 1962); Tesco Contro il Minotauro (aka The Minotaur—The Wild Beast of Crete and The Minotaur—US); Liane Die Weisse Sklavin (Nature Girl and the Slaver and The White Slave). **1962** La Leggenda di Enea (The Avenger—US 1964); Col Ferro e Col Fuoco (aka Daggers of Blood and Invasion 1700—US 1965). **1963** Giulio Casare il Conquistatore delle Gallie (aka Caesar the Conqueror—US). **1964** Ercole Contro Molock (Conquest of Mycene—US 1965). **1966** Se Tutte le Donne del Mondo (Kiss the Girls and Make Them Die—US 1967).

BERNES, MARK

Born: 1912, Russia. Died: Aug. 25, 1969, Moscow, Russia. Screen, television actor and singer.

Appeared in: **1943** Diary of a Nazi. **1944** Two Soldiers. **1945** The Ural Front. **1946** The Turning Point. **1952** Taras Shevchenko. **1953** Maximka. **1955** The Boys from Leningrad; The Frigid Sea. **1957** School of Courage. **1965** Zvonyat Otkrdyte Dver (aka The Girl and the Burglar—US 1967).

BERNHARDT, SARAH (Rosalie Bernard)

Born: Oct. 22, 1844, Paris, France. Died: Mar. 26, 1923, Paris, France (uremic poisoning and weak heart). Screen, stage and vaudeville actress.

Appeared in: **1900** Hamlet (title role). **1910** La Dame aux Camelias (Camille—US 1912); Queen Elizabeth. **1915** Sarah Bernhardt at Home; Jeanne Dore. **1917** Mothers of France. **1931** Stars of Yesterday (short—film clips).

BERNIE, BEN (Benjamin Anzelvitz)

Born: 1891, Bayonne, N.J. Died: Oct. 20, 1943, Hollywood, Calif. Screen, vaudeville, radio actor and bandleader. Appeared in vaudeville with Phil Baker (dec. 1963) as part of "Bernie and Baker" team.

Appeared in: **1930** Ben Bernie and His Orchestra (short). **1934** Shoot the Works. **1935** Stolen Harmony. **1937** Wake Up and Live; Love and Hisses.

BERNIVICI, COUNT (aka COUNT BERNAVICI and COUNT BERNI VICI)

Born: 1884. Died: July 12, 1966, Hollywood, Calif. Screen and vaudeville actor.

BERRELL, GEORGE (aka GEORGE BURRELL)

Born: 1849, Philadelphia, Pa. Died: Apr. 20, 1933. Screen and stage actor.

Appeared in: **1916** The People vs. John Doe. **1917** The Girl in the Garret; Swede Hearts; Double Suspicion; The Lair of the Wolf. **1920** The City of Masks. **1921** The Fire Eater; The Girl from God's Country; The Barbarian. **1922** Tracks. **1923** The Grub Stake; Crimson Gold. **1925** The Everlasting Whisper; The Trail Rider. **1926** The Sea Beast. **1927** Black Jack.

BERRY, ALINE

Born: 1905. Died: Apr. 3, 1967, Hollywood, Calif. (heart attack). Screen, stage and radio actress.

Appeared in: **1925** Soul Fire.

BERRY, ARTHUR NELSON

Born: 1887. Died: June 12, 1945, Hollywood, Calif. Screen and vaudeville actor. Married to actress Elizabeth Berry with whom he appeared in vaudeville.

BERRY, JULES (Jules Peaufichet)

Born: 1883, France. Died: Apr. 25, 1951, Paris, France (heart ailment). Stage and screen actor.

Appeared in: **1929** Crossroads; Le Four Se Leve. **1940** Daybreak. **1942** Les Visiteurs du Soir. **1944** 32 Rue de Montmartre. **1947** Etoile Sans Lumiere (Star without a Light); The Devil's Own Envoy; La Symphonie Fantastique. **1954** Dreams of Love. **1964** The Crime of Monsieur Lange.

BERRY, NYAS

Died: Oct. 6, 1951. Screen actor and dancer. Brother of actor-dancer Walter Berry, with whom he appeared in an act billed as "The Berry Brothers."

Appeared in: **1941** Lady Be Good. **1942** Panama Hattie. **1949** You're My Everything.

BERTRAM, VEDAH (Adele Buck)

Born: Dec. 4, 1891, Boston, Mass. Died: Aug. 27, 1912, Oakland, Calif. (appendicitis). Screen actress. Entered films with Essanay in 1911.

Appeared in: **1912** Broncho Billy's Adventure; The Bandit's Child; A Road Agent's Love; Broncho Billy and the Bandits; Broncho Billy and the Indian Maid; A Moonshiner's Heart; On the Cactus Trail; The Smuggler's Daughter; Broncho Billy's Gratitude; The Desert Sweetheart; Broncho Billy's Pal; The Deputy's Love Affair; Western Hearts; Broncho Billy Outwitted.

BERTRAM, WILLIAM (Benjamin Switzer)

Born: Jan. 19, 1880, Walkerton, Ont., Canada. Died: May 1, 1933, Los Angeles, Calif. Screen, stage actor, film, stage director and screenwriter. Entered films in 1903 with Pathe.

Appeared in: **1922** The Long Chance. **1924** The Dramatic Life of Abraham Lincoln; The Smoking Trail. **1925** Fangs of Fate. **1926** Twisted Triggers; Under Fire. **1927** The Swift Shadow; Wanted—A Coward. **1928** The Boss of Rustler's Room; Little Shepherd of Kingdom Come. **1930** Spurs. **1931** Trails of the Golden West; Lightnin' Smith's Return.

BERTRAND, MARY

Died: May 12, 1955, Woodland Hills, Calif. Screen actress. Appeared in silents.

BESOZZI, NINO

Born: Italy. Died: Feb. 1971, Italy. Screen actor.

Appeared in: **1935** Il Serpente a Sonagli. **1936** Vivere (To Live). **1937** Tre Anni Senza Donna; Destino di Donna; Trenta Second d'Amore; I Due Misantropi; Nina Non Far La Stupida. **1938** Come le Foglie (Like the Leaves); Amore in Quarantena (Love in Quarantine); Duetta Vagabondo (Vagabond Duet); La Donna Bianca (The White Woman aka The Lady in White—US 1948). **1939** Eravamo Sette Sorelle (We Were Seven Sisters); Ho Perduto Mio Marito (I Have Lost My Husband). **1940** Amicizia (Friendship). **1948** Rossini. **1960** Holiday Island.

BESSENT, MARIE

Born: 1898. Died: Oct. 12, 1947, Los Angeles, Calif. Screen, stage and vaudeville actress. Double for actress Mabel Normand.

BESSERER, EUGENIE

Born: 1870. Died: May 30, 1934, Los Angeles, Calif. Screen and stage actress. Entered films in 1910.

Appeared in: **1912** The Count of Monte Cristo. **1915** The Ingratitude of Liz Taylor. **1919** Scarlet Days; The Greatest Question. **1920** The Fighting Shepherdess. **1921** Molly O; The Sin of Martha Queed; The Light in the Clearing; The Breaking Point; Good Women; What Happened to Rosa? **1922** The Hands of Nara; June Madness; The Rosary; Penrod; The Stranger's Banquet. **1923** Anna Christie; Her Reputation; Enemies of Children; The Rendezvous; The Lonely Road. **1924** Bread; The Price She Paid. **1925** A Fool and His Money; Friendly Enemies; Bright Lights; The Circle; Confessions of a Queen; The Coast of Folly; Wandering Footsteps. **1926** The Millionaire Policeman; The Skyrocket. **1927** The Jazz Singer; When a Man Loves; Flesh and the Devil; The Fire Brigade; Captain Salvation; Slightly Used; Wandering Girls. **1928** The Yellow Lily; Two Lovers; Drums of Love; Lilac Time. **1929** Seven Faces; The Bridge of San Luis Rey; A Lady of Chance; Madame X; Fast Company; Illusion; Thunderbolt; Mister Antonio; Speedway; Whispering Winds. **1930** In Gay Madrid; A Royal Romance. **1933** To the Last Man.

BEST, DOLLY

Born: 1899. Died: Oct. 6, 1968, Los Angeles, Calif. Screen and stage actress. Appeared in silents.

BEST, EDNA (Edna Hove)

Born: Mar. 3, 1900, Hove, Sussex, England. Died: Sept. 18, 1974, Geneva, Switzerland. Screen, stage and television actress. Divorced from actors Seymour Beard and Herbert Marshall (dec. 1966) and later married to agent Nat Wolff (dec.). Mother of actress Sarah Best Marshall.

Appeared in: **1921** Tilly of Bloomsbury. **1923** A Couple of Down and Outs. **1930** Sleeping Partners; Loose Ends; Escape; Beyond the Cities. **1931** Michael and Mary (US 1932); The Calendar (aka Bachelor's Folly—US 1932). **1932** The Faithful Heart (aka Faithful Hearts—US 1933). **1934** The Man Who Knew Too Much. **1938** South Riding; Prison Without Bars (US 1939). **1939** Intermezzo; A Love Story. **1940** The Swiss Family Robinson; A Dispatch from Reuters (aka This Man Reuter). **1947** The Ghost and Mrs. Muir; The Late George Apley. **1948** The Iron Curtain.

BEST, WILLIE (aka "SLEEP 'N EAT")

Born: May 27, 1916, Miss. Died: Feb. 27, 1962, Woodland Hills, Calif. (cancer). Black screen and television actor.

Appeared in: **1932** The Monster Walks. **1934** Little Miss Marker; Kentucky Kernels; several RKO shorts. **1935** West of the Pecos; Murder on a Honeymoon; The Nitwits; The Arizonian; Hot Tip; The Littlest Rebel. **1936** Murder on the Bridle Path; The Bride Walks Out; Mummu's Boys; Racing Lady; Make Way for a Lady; Thank You, Jeeves!; General Spanky; Two in Revolt; Down the Stretch. **1937** Meet the Misses; Breezing Home; The Lady Fights Back; Super Sleuth; Saturday's Heroes. **1938** Vivacious Lady; Gold Is Where You Find It; Merrily We Live; Goodbye Broadway; Blondie; Youth Takes a Fling. **1939** Nancy Drew—Trouble Shooter; Mr. Moto Takes a Vacation; The Covered Trailer; At the Circus. **1940** Money and the Woman; Who Killed Aunt Maggie?; I Take This Woman; The Ghost Breakers. **1941** Road Show; High Sierra; The Lady from Cheyenne; Nothing but the Truth; Flight from Destiny; Scattergood Baines; Highway West; The Smiling Ghost. **1942** Juke Girl; Whispering Ghosts; Busses Road; The Hidden Hand; Scattergood Survives a Murder; The Body Disappears; A-Haunting We Will Go. **1943** Cabin in the Sky; Thank Your Lucky Stars; The Kansan; Cinderella Swings It. **1944** Adventures of Mark Twain; Home in Indiana; The Girl Who Dared. **1945** Hold that Blonde; The Red Dragon; Pillow to Post. **1946** The Bride Wore Boots; The Face of Marble; Dangerous Money. **1947** The Red Stallion; Suddenly It's Spring. **1948** The Smart Woman; Half Past Midnight; The Shanghai Chest. **1949** Jiggs and Maggie in Jackpot Jitters; The Hidden Hand. **1950** High and Dizzy (short). **1951** South of Caliente.

BETTS, WILLIAM E.
Born: 1856. Died: Apr. 6, 1929, New York, N.Y. (pneumonia and heart disease). Stage and screen actor.

Appeared in: **1924** A Sainted Devil.

BETZ, MATTHEW (Matthew Von Betz)
Born: 1881, St. Louis, Mo. Died: Jan. 26, 1938, Los Angeles, Calif. Screen, stage and vaudeville actor.

Appeared in: **1915** The Parson of Pine Mountain. **1917** A Social Climber; An Actress's Romance; The Evil Sag; The Love of Princess Olga. **1921** Salvation Nell; Burn 'Em Up Barnes; The Single Track. **1922** My Old Kentucky Home; Boomerang Bill. **1923** The Self-Made Wife; Let's Go; Sawdust; Luck. **1924** Those Who Dance; The Heart Bandit; Love's Whirlpool; The Only Woman; The Siren of Seville. **1925** The Way of a Girl; The Lighthouse by the Sea; My Lady's Lips; The White Desert; The Unholy Three; Lights of Old Broadway; White Fang. **1926** The Flame of the Yukon; The Exquisite Sinner; Oh, What a Nurse!; The Little Irish Girl; Shipwrecked. **1927** The Patent Leather Kid; Broadway after Midnight. **1928** The Wedding March; Sins of the Fathers; The Big City; Shepherd of the Hills; The Terror; The Crimson City; Telling the World. **1929** Girls Gone Wild; Fugitives; The Girl in the Glass House. **1930** The Big House; Shooting Straight; The Squealer; See America Thirst; Her Man. **1931** Salvation Nell (and 1921 version); Side Show. **1932** The Big Flash (short); The Fighting Marshal; Alias Mary Smith; Dynamite Denny; From Broadway to Cheyenne; Speed Madness; Gold. **1933** Knight Dry (short); Western Code; Via Pony Express; The Big Chance; Silent Men; Under Secret Orders; State Trooper; The Whirlwind; Tarzan the Fearless; I Have Lived. **1934** Fighting Rookie; Circus Hoodoo (short); The Woman Who Dared; Countess of Monte Cristo; The House of Rothschild. **1935** Men of the Night; Mississippi; On Probation; Let 'Em Have It; The Tin Man (short); Reckless Roads; Mutiny Ahead; The Girl Who Came Back. **1936** Just My Luck; The Last Assignment; Racing Blood; Florida Special. **1937** Jail Bait (short); Outcast. **1938** Fury Below.

BEVAN, BILLY (William Bevan Harris)
Born: Sept. 29, 1897, Orange, Australia. Died: 1957. Screen, stage actor and opera singer.

Appeared in the following shorts, unless otherwise noted: **1920** Let 'Er Go; The Quack Doctor; It's a Boy; My Goodness; Love, Honor and Behave (feature); A Fireside Brewer. **1921** A Small Town Idol (feature); Be Reasonable; By Heck; Astray from the Steerage. **1922** The Duck Hunter; On Patrol; Oh, Daddy; Gymnasium Jim; Ma and Pa; When Summer Comes; The Crossroads of New York. **1923** Nip and Tuck; Sinbad the Sailor; The Extra Girl. **1924** One Spooky Night; Wall Street Blues; Lizzies of the Field; Wandering Waistlines; The Cannon Ball Express; The White Sin. **1925** Honeymoon Hardships; Giddap; The Lion's Whiskers; Butter Fingers; Skinners in Silk; Super-Hooper-Dyne Lizzies; Sneezing Beezers; The Iron Nag; Over There-Abouts; From Rags to Britches. **1926** Whispering Whiskers; Trimmed in Gold; Circus Today; Wandering Willies; Hayfoot, Strawfoot; Fight Night; Muscle Bound Music; Ice Cold Cocos; A Sea Dog's Tale; Hubby's Quiet Little Game; Masked Mamas; Hoboken to Hollywood; The Divorce Dodger; Flirty Four-Flushers. **1927** Should Sleepwalkers Marry?; Peaches and Plumbers; A Small Town Princess; The Bull Fighter; Cured in the Excitement; The Golf Nut; Gold Digger of Weepah; Easy Pickings. **1928** The Beach Club; The Best Man; The Bicycle Flirt; His Unlucky Night; Caught in the Kitchen ("Tired Businessman's" series); Motorboat Mamas; Motoring Mamas; Hubby's Latest Alibi; Hubby's Weekend Trip; The Lion's Roar; His New Steno; Riley the Cop. **1929** Calling Hubby's Bluff; Button My Back; Foolish Husbands; Pink Pajamas; Don't Get Jealous. The following are features unless so noted: **1929** High Voltage; Sky Hawk. **1930** Scotch (short); Journey's End; For the Love O' Lil; Temptation; Peacock Alley. **1931** Transatlantic. **1932** Sky Devils; Spot on the Rug; Honeymoon Beach; The Silent Witness; Vanity Fair; Payment Deferred; Honey-

moon Beach (short). **1933** Alice in Wonderland; Big Squeal (short); Looking Forward; Midnight Club; Too Much Harmony; A Study in Scarlet; Cavalcade; Luxury Liner; Peg O' My Heart; The Way to Love. **1934** The Lost Patrol; Shock; Caravan; Limehouse Blues. **1935** Mystery Woman; Black Sheep; The Last Outpost; A Tale of Two Cities. **1936** The Song and Dance Man; Lloyds of London; Private Number; Dracula's Daughter; Piccadilly Jim; God's Country and the Woman. **1937** Slave Ship; Another Dawn; The Sheik Steps Out; The Wrong Road. **1938** Bringing Up Baby; The Mysterious Mr. Moto; Girl of the Golden West; Shadows over Shanghai. **1939** Captain Fury; Let Freedom Ring; Grand Jury Secrets; We Are Not Alone. **1940** Earl of Chicago; The Long Voyage Home; Tin Pan Alley. **1941** Shining Victory; Dr. Jekyll and Mr. Hyde; Confirm or Deny. **1942** Mrs. Miniver; The Man Who Wouldn't Die; London Blackout Murders; Counter Espionage. **1943** Forever and a Day; The Return of the Vampire; Young and Willing. **1944** The Lodger; National Velvet; The Invisible Man's Revenge; South of Dixie. **1945** The Picture of Dorian Gray; Tonight and Every Night. **1946** Cluny Brown; Devotion; Terror by Night. **1947** Moss Rose; It Had to be You; Swordsman. **1948** The Black Arrow; Let's Live a Little. **1949** The Secret of St. Ives; The Secret Garden. **1950** Rogues of Sherwood Forest; Fortunes of Captain Blood. **1960** When Comedy Was King (documentary). **1963** Thirty Years of Fun (documentary).

BEVANS, CLEM
Born: 1880, Cozaddle, Ohio. Died: Aug. 11, 1963, Woodland Hills, Calif. Screen, stage, television and vaudeville actor.

Appeared in: **1935** Way Down East (film debut). **1936** Rhythm on the Range. **1937** Riding on Air; Big City; Idol of the Crowds. **1938** Miracle Money (short); Of Human Hearts; Young Fugitives; Comet over Broadway; Tom Sawyer, Detective; Hold That Coed. **1939** Help Wanted (short); Ambush; Zenobia; Hell's Kitchen; Night Work; Thunder Afloat; Main Street Lawyer; The Cowboy Quarterback. **1940** Abe Lincoln in Illinois; Go West; Young Tom Edison; 20 Mule Team; Half a Sinner; The Captain Is a Lady; Untamed; Girl from God's Country; Calling All Husbands; Granny Get Your Gun. **1941** Sergeant York; She Couldn't Say No; Midnight Angel; The Parson of Panamint; The Smiling Ghost. **1942** Tombstone, the Town Too Tough to Die; The Forest Rangers; Captains of the Clouds; Mrs. Wiggs of the Cabbage Patch; Saboteur. **1943** The Human Comedy; The Kansan; Lady Bodyguard; Happy Go Lucky; The Woman of the Town. **1944** Night Club Girl. **1945** Grissly's Millions; Captain Eddie. **1946** Wake Up and Dream; Gallant Bess; The Yearling. **1947** The Yankee Fakir; The Millerson Case; Mourning Becomes Electra. **1948** Texas, Brooklyn and Heaven; Highway 13; Portrait of Jenny; Paleface; The Relentless. **1949** Loaded Pistols; Big Jack; Streets of Laredo; Rim of the Canyon; The Gal Who Took the West; Deputy Marshal; Moonrise; Tell It to the Judge. **1950** Joe Palooka Meets Humphrey; Harvey. **1951** Gold Raiders; Silver City Bonanza; Man in the Saddle. **1952** Captive of Billy the Kid; Hangman's Knot. **1953** The Stranger Wore a Gun. **1954** Boy from Oklahoma. **1955** Ten Wanted Men; The Kentuckian. **1956** Davy Crockett and the River Pirates.

BEVANS, LIONEL
Born: 1884. Died: Feb. 17, 1965, Los Angeles, Calif. Screen, stage actor and stage director.

BEVANS, PHILIPPA
Born: 1913, London, England. Died: May 10, 1968, New York, N.Y. Screen, stage and television actress.

Appeared in: **1962** The Notorious Landlady. **1964** The World of Henry Orient. **1966** The Group. **1968** Madigan.

BIANCHETTI, SUZANNE
Born: 1894, Paris, France. Died: 1936, Paris, France. Screen actress.

Appeared in: **1921** Les Mysteres de Paris (The Mysteries of Paris); Le Pere Goriot. **1922** Jocelyn. **1925** Madame Sans-Gene. **1927** Napoleon; Loves of Casanova (US 1929). **1930** Verdun Vision d'Histoire. **1935** L'Appel du Silence; La Violetera.

BIANCHI, GEORGIO
Born: 1904. Died: Feb. 9, 1968, Rome, Italy. Screen actor, film director and film producer.

Appeared in: **1932** Il Miracolo di Sant' Antonio.

BIAS, CHESTER
Born: 1917. Died: Mar. 1, 1954, Woodland Hills, Calif. Screen actor.

BIBY, EDWARD
Born: 1885. Died: Oct. 3, 1952, Los Angeles, Calif. Screen actor.

Appeared in: **1947** The Strange Woman.

BICKEL, GEORGE L.
Born: 1863, Saginaw, Mich. Died: June 5, 1941, Los Angeles, Calif. Screen, stage, circus and vaudeville actor. Entered films approx. 1915 with Edison Feature Film Co.

Appeared in: **1929** Beneath the Law (short); In Holland (short). **1930** Soup to Nuts; Maybe It's Love; Recaptured Love. **1931** One Heavenly Night. **1932** The Man I Killed.

BICKFORD, CHARLES

Born: Jan. 1, 1889, Cambridge, Mass. Died: Nov. 9, 1967, Los Angeles, Calif. (emphysema). Screen, stage, television and burlesque actor. Married to actress Beatrice Loring. Nominated for 1943 Academy Award for Best Supporting Actor in Song of Bernadette; in 1947 for The Farmer's Daughter; and 1948 for Johnny Belinda.

Appeared in: **1929** Dynamite (film debut); South Sea Rose; Hell's Heroes. **1930** Anna Christie; The Sea Bat; The Passion Flower. **1931** The Squaw Man; East of Borneo; The Pagan Lady; River End; Men in Her Life. **1932** Ambition; Scandal for Sale; Vanity Street; The Last Man; Thunder Below; Devil and the Deep; Panama Flo. **1933** No Other Woman; Song of the Eagle; This Day and Age; White Woman. **1934** Little Miss Marker; Red Wagon (US 1935); A Wicked Woman. **1935** Under Pressure; A Notorious Gentleman; The Farmer Takes a Wife; East of Java; The Littlest Rebel. **1936** Rose of the Rancho; The Plainsman; Pride of the Marines. **1937** High, Wide and Handsome; Thunder Trail; Night Club Scandal; Daughter of Shanghai. **1938** Gangs of New York; Valley of the Giants; The Storm. **1939** Stand Up and Fight; Street of Missing Men; Mutiny in the Big House; Romance of the Redwoods; Our Leading Citizens; One Hour to Live; Of Mice and Men. **1940** Thou Shalt Not Kill; Girl from God's Country; South to Karango; Queen of the Yukon. **1941** Burma Convoy; Riders of Death Valley (serial). **1942** Reap the Wild Wind; Tarzan's New York Adventure. **1943** The Song of Bernadette; Mr. Lucky. **1944** Wing and a Prayer. **1945** Fallen Angel; Captain Eddie. **1946** Duel in the Sun. **1947** The Farmer's Daughter; The Woman on the Beach; Brute Force. **1948** The Babe Ruth Story; Johnny Belinda; Four Faces West; Command Decision. **1949** Guilty of Treason; Roseanna McCoy; Whirlpool. **1950** Branded; Riding High. **1951** Elopement; Jim Thorpe All-American. **1952** The Raging Tide; Man of Bronze. **1953** The Last Posse. **1954** A Star is Born. **1955** Prince of Players; Not as a Stranger; The Court-Martial of Billy Mitchell. **1956** You Can't Run Away from It. **1957** Mister Cory. **1958** The Big Country. **1960** The Unforgiven. **1962** Days of Wine and Roses. **1966** A Big Hand for the Little Lady.

BIEGEL, ERWIN

Born: 1896. Died: May 24, 1954, Berlin, Germany (heart ailment). German screen and stage actor.

Appeared in: **1938** Wenn Du eine Schwiegermutter hast (When You Have a Mother-in-Law). **1949** Palace Scandal. **1952** The Berliner. **1959** Das Tanzende Herz (The Dancing Heart).

BIG MAYBELLE (Mabel Smith)

Born: 1924, Jackson, Tenn. Died: Jan. 23, 1972, Cleveland, Ohio. Black jazz singer and screen actress.

Appeared in: **1960** Jazz on a Summer's Day.

BILDT, PAUL

Born: 1885, Germany. Died: Mar. 16, 1957, Berlin, Germany. Stage and screen actor.

Appeared in: **1927** Slums of Berlin. **1933** The Rebel. **1935** Schwarzer Jaeger Johanna; Die Toerichte Jungfrau. **1939** Der Schritt vom Were (The False Step). **1940** The Dreyfus Case. **1948** Razzia. **1949** Somewhere in Berlin; The Affair Blum. **1950** Our Daily Bread. **1956** As Long as You're Near Me; Anastasia. **1958** International Counterfeiters. **1959** Himmel Ohne Sterne (Sky without Stars).

BILLINGS, ELMO

Born: 1913. Died: Feb. 6, 1964, Los Angeles, Calif. (stroke). Screen actor. Freckle-faced urchin of early "Our Gang" comedies.

Appeared in: **1925** Locked Doors; The Midnight Flyer. **1927** Tumbling River.

BILLINGS, GEORGE A.

Born: 1871. Died: Apr. 15, 1934, West Los Angeles, Calif. Stage and screen actor.

Appeared in: **1924** Barbara Frietchie; Abraham Lincoln. **1925** The Man without a Country. **1926** Hands Up!; The Greater Glory. **1929** Woman to Woman. **1930** Night Work; The Third Alarm; Traffic (short); "Folly Comedies" second series. **1933** King for a Night. **1934** As the Earth Turns; The Pursuit of Happiness. **1935** The Gilded Lily.

BING, GUS (aka GEORGE BINGHAM)

Born: 1893. Died: Aug. 4, 1967, Los Angeles, Calif. (leukemia). Screen, stage, vaudeville and burlesque actor. Brother of actor Herman Bing (dec. 1947).

BING, HERMAN

Born: Mar. 30, 1889, Germany. Died: Jan. 9, 1947, Los Angeles, Calif. (suicide—gun). Screen actor, film producer and opera performer. Brother of actor Gus Bing (dec. 1967).

Appeared in: **1929** A Song of Kentucky; Married in Hollywood. **1930** Show Girl in Hollywood; The Three Sisters; Menschen Hinter Gettern. **1931** The Great Lover; The Guardsman; Women Love Once. **1932** Silver Dollar; Hypnotized; Jewel Robbery; Flesh. **1933** The Nuisance; Dinner at Eight; The Bowery; My Lips Betray; Fits in a Fiddle (short); Footlight Parade; The Great Jasper; The College Coach. **1934** The Hide-Out; Embarrassing Moments; Love Time; The Crimson Romance; When Strangers Meet; The Mighty Barnum; Mandalay; Melody in Spring; The Merry Widow; Manhattan Love Song; I'll Tell the World; The Black Cat; Twentieth Century. **1935** Night Is Young; It Happened in New York; Thunder in the Night; Hands across the Table; Great Hotel Murder; Redheads on Parade; Call of the Wild; The Florentine Dagger; Don't Bet on Blondes; Calm Yourself; In Caliente; Every Night at Eight; His Family Tree; Three Kids and a Queen; Fighting Youth; A Thousand Dollars a Minute; The Misses Stooge (short). **1936** Laughing Irish Eyes; The Music Goes 'Round; Tango; Come Closer Folks; Rose Marie; The Great Ziegfeld; Three Wise Guys; Human Cargo; Dimples; The King Steps Out; Adventure in Manhattan; Champagne Waltz; That Girl from Paris. **1937** Maytime; Beg, Borrow or Steal; Every Day's a Holiday. **1938** Paradise for Three; Vacation from Love; The Great Waltz; Sweethearts; Bluebeard's Eighth Wife; Four's a Crowd. **1940** Bitter Sweet. **1942** The Devil with Hitler. **1945** Where Do We Go from Here? **1946** Rendezvous 24; Night and Day.

BINGHAM, GEORGE. *See* GUS BING

BINNS, GEORGE H.

Born: 1886, England. Died: Oct. 27, 1918, Glendale, Calif. (Spanish influenza, pneumonia). Screen actor.

Appeared in: **1916** Tubby Turns the Tables; The Telephone Belle. **1917** The Late Lamented; A Dog's Own Tale; The Camera Cure; Innocent Sinners; His Marriage Failure; His Bitter Fate; An Innocent Villain; Their Domestic Deception; His Baby Doll.

BIRCH, PAUL

Died: May 24, 1969. Stage and screen actor.

Appeared in: **1952** Assignment Paris. **1953** The War of the Worlds. **1954** Ride Clear of Diablo. **1955** Rebel Without a Cause; Apache Woman; Strange Lady in Town; The Fighting Chance; Five Guns West. **1956** The Fastest Gun Alive; Beast With 1,000,000 Eyes; When Gangland Strikes; The White Squaw; Everything but the Truth. **1957** Gun for a Coward; Not of This Earth; The Twenty-Seventh Day; The Tattered Dress; Joe Dakota. **1958** The World Was His Jury; Gunman's Walk; Wild Heritage; The Gun Runners; Queen of Outer Space. **1959** Gunmen from Laredo. **1960** The Dark at the Top of the Stairs; Pay or Die; Portrait in Black. **1961** Two Rode Together. **1962** The Man Who Shot Liberty Valance; A Public Affair. **1963** The Raiders; It's a Mad, Mad, Mad, Mad World. **1967** Welcome to Hard Times; A Covenant With Death.

BIRKETT, VIVA

Born: 1887, England. Died: June 27, 1934, London, England. Screen and stage actress. Married to actor Philip Merivale (dec. 1946).

Appeared in: **1927** The Prince of Lovers.

BISHOP, CHESTER

Born: 1858. Died: May 23, 1937, Los Angeles, Calif. Screen and stage actor.

Appeared in: **1923** Lights Out. **1924** Missing Daughters.

BISHOP, RICHARD

Born: 1898. Died: May 28, 1956, Sharon, Conn. Screen, stage, radio and television actor.

Appeared in: **1942** Native Land. **1948** Call Northside 777. **1951** Teresa. **1955** The Long Gray Line.

BISHOP, STARK, JR.

Born: 1932. Died: July 9, 1945, Hollywood, Calif. Screen actor.

BISHOP, WILLIAM

Born: July 16, 1917, Oak Park, Ill. Died: Oct. 3, 1959, Malibu, Calif. (cancer). Screen, stage, television and radio actor.

Appeared in: **1943** A Guy Named Joe. **1946** Pillow to Post. **1947** Romance of Rosy Ridge; Song of the Thin Man; Devil Ship. **1948** Thunderhoof; Untamed Breed; Coroner Creek; Adventures in Silverado; Port Said; Black Eagle. **1949** Walking Hills; Anna Lucasta. **1950** The Tougher They Come; Harriet Craig; Killer That Stalked New York. **1951** Lorna Doone; The Texas Ranger; The Frogmen; Basketball Fix. **1952** Cripple Creek; Breakdown; The Raiders; The Redhead from Wyoming. **1953** Gun Belt. **1954** Overland Pacific. **1955** Top Gun; Wyoming Renegades. **1956** The White Squaw; The Boss. **1957** The Phantom Stagecoach; Short Cut to Hell. **1959** The Oregon Trail.

BITTNER, WILLIAM W.

Born: 1866. Died: July 6, 1918, New York, N.Y. Screen and stage actor.

Appeared in: **1917** Runaway Romany. **1918** My Four Years in Germany.

BJORNE, HUGO

Born: 1886, Sweden. Died: Feb. 14, 1966, Stockholm, Sweden. Screen, stage, radio and television actor. Married to actress Gerda Bjorne.

Appeared in: **1912** Lojen och Tarar (film debut). **1938** Karl Fredrik Reigns; Sun over Sweden; Frun Tillhanda (Servant Girl). **1944** Himlaspelet. **1947** Torment. **1948** Crime and Punishment.

BLACK, BILL

Born: 1927. Died: Oct. 21, 1965, Memphis, Tenn. Screen actor and musician. Leader of "Bill Black's Combo."

Appeared in: **1961** Teenage Millionaire.

BLACK, MAURICE

Born: Warsaw, Poland. Died: Jan. 18, 1938, Hollywood, Calif. Stage and screen actor. Entered films approx. 1923.

Appeared in: **1928** Marked Money. **1929** Leaping Love (short); Broadway Babies; Dark Streets; The Carnation Kid. **1930** Numbered Men; The Chumps (short); Little Caesar; Playing Around; The Street of Chance; Live and Learn; Brothers; The Sea God; Framed; The Runaway Bride. **1931** Front Page; Oh! Oh! Cleopatra (short); Women Go On Forever; Smart Money; Sob Sister; While Paris Sleeps. **1932** High Pressure; Dancers in the Dark; The Strange Love of Molly Louvain; Scarlet Dawn. **1933** The Cohens and the Kellys in Trouble; Grand Slam; A Shriek in the Night; I Cover the Waterfront; Flying Down to Rio; Ship of Wanted Men; Murder on the Campus. **1934** Sixteen Fathoms Deep; The Great Barnum; Twin Husbands; Wake Up and Dream; West of the Pecos; Down to Their Last Yacht. **1935** The Crusades; Bonnie Scotland; Stars over Broadway. **1936** Laughing Irish Eyes. **1937** Three Legionnaires; The Californian; Adventure's End.

BLACKFORD, MARY

Born: 1914, Philadelphia, Pa. Died: Sept. 24, 1937, Santa Monica, Calif. (results of auto accident). Screen actress.

Appeared in: **1933** The Sweetheart of Sigma Chi.

BLACKMER, SIDNEY (aka SYDNEY BLACKMER)

Born: July 13, 1896, Salisbury, N.C. Died: Oct. 5, 1973, New York, N.Y. (cancer). Screen, stage, television, radio and vaudeville actor. Divorced from actress Lenore Ulric and married to actress Suzanne Kaaren.

Appeared in: **1914** Perils of Pauline (film debut). **1927** Million Dollar Mystery (serial). **1929** A Most Immoral Lady. **1930** The Love Racket; Strictly Modern; Kismet; Sweethearts and Wives; The Bad Man; Mother's Cry; Little Caesar; One Adventurous Night. **1931** Woman Hungry; It's a Wise Child; The Lady Who Dared; Daybreak; Once a Sinner. **1933** From Hell to Heaven; Cocktail Hour; The Deluge; The Wrecker. **1934** The Count of Monte Cristo; Goodbye Love; This Man Is Mine; Down to Their Last Yacht; Transatlantic Merry-Go-Round; The President Vanishes. **1935** Forced Landing; False Pretenses; A Notorious Gentleman; The Little Colonel; The Firetrap; Behind Green Lights; Great God Gold; Smart Girl; Streamline Express; The Girl Who Came Back. **1936** Woman Trap; Florida Special; Early to Bed; Missing Girls; The President's Mystery; Heart of the West. **1937** A Doctor's Diary; John Meade's Woman; House of Secrets; Girl Overboard; Shadows of the Orient; The Last Gangster; Charlie Chan at Monte Carlo; Thank You, Mr. Moto; This Is My Affair; Wife, Doctor and Nurse; Heidi; The Women Men Marry; Michael O'Halloran. **1938** Straight, Place and Show; Speed to Burn; Suez; Sharpshooters; While New York Sleeps; Orphans of the Street; Trade Winds; In Old Chicago. **1939** The Convict's Code; Unmarried; Law of the Pampas; Trapped in the Sky; Fast and Loose; Within the Law; It's a Wonderful World; Hotel for Women. **1940** Maryland; I Want A Divorce; Third Finger, Left Hand; Framed; Dance, Girl, Dance. **1941** Cheers for Miss Bishop; The Great Swindle; Rookies on Parade; Love Crazy; Ellery Queen and the Perfect Crime; The Officer and the Lady; The Feminine Touch; Murder Among Friends; Angels With Broken Wings; Down Mexico Way; Obliging Young Lady. **1942** Always in My Heart; Nazi Agent; Sabotage Squad; Quiet Please, Murder; Gallant Lady; Prison Girls; The Panther's Claw. **1943** Murder in Times Square; In Old Oklahoma; I Escaped From the Gestapo. **1944** The Lady and the Monster; Buffalo Bill; Wilson; Broadway Rhythm. **1946** Duel in the Sun. **1948** My Girl Tisa; A Song Is Born (narr.); The Hero (narr.). **1950** Farewell to Yesterday. **1951** Saturday's Hero; People Will Talk. **1952** Washington Story; The San Francisco Story. **1954** Johnny Dark; The High and the Mighty. **1955** The View from Pompey's Head (aka Secret Interlude). **1956** Accused of Murder; High Society; Beyond a Reasonable Doubt. **1957** Tammy and the Bachelor. **1965** Joy in the Morning; How to Murder Your Wife. **1967** A Covenant With Death. **1968** Rosemary's Baby.

BLACKMORE, E. WILLARD

Born: 1870. Died: Nov. 20, 1949, East St. Louis, Mo. Screen and stage actor. Aided Thomas A. Edison in making the first talking film.

BLACKTON, J. STUART

Born: Jan. 5, 1875, Sheffield, England. Died: Aug. 13, 1941, Hollywood, Calif. (auto accident). Screen actor, film director, producer and screenwriter. One of founders of Vitagraph Pictures. Worked with Thomas Edison on first ten films ever made—he drew sketches. Married to actress Evangeline Russell and to Paula Hunt. Father of actress Violet Virginia Blackton, screenwriter Marian Constance Blackton and Charla Blackton.

Appeared in: **1902** The Twentieth Century Tramp (aka Happy Hooligan and His Airship). **1912** A Vitagraph Romance.

BLACKWELL, CARLYLE

Born: 1888, Troy, Pa. Died: June 17, 1955, Miami, Fla. Screen, stage actor, stage and film producer. Entered films in 1909 with Vitagraph. Father of actor Carlyle Blackwell, Jr. (dec. 1974).

Appeared in: **1909** Uncle Tom's Cabin. **1910** A Dixie Mother. **1912** A Bell of Penance. **1913** Perils of the Sea. **1914** Such a Little Queen; The Spitfire; The Key to Yesterday. **1916** A Woman's Way. **1917** The Burglar. **1918** His Royal Highness; The Road to France. **1920** The Restless Sex. **1923** Bulldog Drummond; The Virgin Queen; The Beloved Vagabond; Good for Nothing. **1924** The Shadow of Egypt. **1925** Monte Carlo; Racing Dramas (shorts); She. **1927** One of the Best; The Rolling Road. **1928** The Wrecker (US 1929); The Crooked Billet.

BLACKWELL, CARLYLE, JR.

Born: 1913. Died: Sept. 20, 1974, North Hollywood, Calif. Screen and television actor. Son of actor Carlyle Blackwell (dec. 1955).

Appeared in: **1935** The Goose and the Gander. **1936** The Calling of Dan Matthews; Romeo and Juliet. **1941** All-American Co-Ed. **1945** Docks of New York.

BLACKWOOD, BONNIE

Born: 1909. Died: Feb. 18, 1949, Burbank, Calif. Screen and stage actress.

BLACKWOOD, DIANA

Died: Mar. 1961, London, England. Screen, stage and television actress.

BLAGOI, GEORGE

Born: 1898, Russia. Died: June 23, 1971, Hollywood, Calif. Screen actor. Married to actress Tina Blagoi.

Appeared in: **1926** Into Her Kingdom. **1928** Four Sons. **1935** Crime and Punishment.

BLAINE, JOAN

Died: Apr. 19, 1949, New York. Screen, stage and radio actress.

BLAIR, ELLA S.

Born: 1895. Died: Dec. 11, 1917, New York, N.Y. Screen actress.

BLAISE, PIERRE

Born: 1951. Died: Aug. 31, 1975, near Montauban, France (auto accident). Screen actor.

Appeared in: **1974** Lacombe, Lucien (film debut).

BLAISELL, CHARLES "BIG BILL"

Born: 1874. Died: May 10, 1930, Hollywood, Calif. Screen and vaudeville actor. Appeared in early Christie Comedies.

BLAKE, AL (Alva D. Blake aka A. D. BLAKE)

Born: 1877, Manitou, Colo. Died: Nov. 5, 1966, Los Angeles, Calif. (heart attack). Screen actor.

Appeared in: **1916** The Trap; The Jungle Flashlight; Father of Her Child; Where Are My Children?

BLAKE, ANNE

Died: Feb. 17, 1973. Screen actress.

Appeared in: **1951** The Second Mate. **1956** Murder Reported (US 1960). **1957** The Curse of Frankenstein. **1958** Orders to Kill; The Secret Place. **1961** Taste of Fear (aka Scream of Fear–US); The Curse of the Werewolf; Saturday Night and Sunday Morning. **1965** The Spy Who Came In From the Cold. **1966** Sky West and Crooked (aka Gypsy Girl–US 1966). **1970** The Private Life of Sherlock Holmes.

BLAKE, MADGE

Born: 1900. Died: Feb. 19, 1969, Pasadena, Calif. (heart attack). Screen and television actress.

Appeared in: **1950** Between Midnight and Dawn; A Life of Her Own. **1951** The Prowler; Queen for a Day; An American in Paris. **1952** Singin' in the Rain; Something for the Birds. **1954** Rhapsody; The Long, Long Trailer; Fireman, Save My Child! **1956** Please Murder Me; Glory. **1962** Sergeants Three. **1966** Batman; Follow Me, Boys!

BLAKE, PAUL
Died: Jan. 28, 1960, London, England. Stage and screen actor.

Appeared in: **1937** Cafe Colette. **1940** The Lilac Domino.

BLAKECLOCK, ALBAN
Died: Dec. 6, 1966, London, England. Screen, stage, radio, and television actor.

Appeared in: **1952** Murder in the Cathedral.

BLAKENEY, OLIVE
Born: Aug. 21, 1903, Newport, Ky. Died: Prior to 1972. Stage and screen actress. Married to actor Bernard Nedell (dec. 1972).

Appeared in: **1934** Mr. What's His Name (film debut); Leave it to Blanche; Give Her a Ring. **1935** Hello Sweetheart (aka The Butter and Egg Man–US); Come Out of the Pantry. **1936** Excuse My Glove; The Three Maxims (aka The Show Goes On–US 1938); Two's Company. **1937** Don't Get Me Wrong; Gangway. **1941** Glamour Boy; That Uncertain Feeling. **1942** Henry and Dizzy; Henry Aldrich, Editor; Random Harvest. **1943** Henry Aldrich Haunts a House; Henry Aldrich Gets Glamour; Henry Aldrich Swings It. **1944** Henry Aldrich Plays Cupid; Henry Aldrich's Little Secret; Henry Aldrich, Boy Scout; The Ghost Catchers; Experiment Perilous. **1945** Dakota; Leave Her to Heaven. **1946** Sentimental Journey; The Strange Woman. **1947** Time out of Mind. **1948** Sealed Verdict. **1954** Roogie's Bump. **1957** The Green-Eyed Blonde; Three Brave Men.

BLANCARD, RENE
Born: 1897, France. Died: Nov. 5, 1965, Paris, France. Screen actor.

Appeared in: **1947** La Cage aux Rossignols (A Cage of Nightingales); Au Bonheur des Dames (Shop-Girls of Paris). **1948** Jenny Lamour. **1951** Marie Du Port. **1952** Under the Paris Sky. **1954** Marchandes d'Illusions (aka Nights of Shame–US 1961). **1955** To Catch a Thief. **1958** The Lovemaker; Diary of a Bad Girl. **1959** Julie La Rouge (Julie the Redhead–US 1963). **1960** Sin and Desire; La Verite (The Truth–US 1961).

BLANCHAR, PIERRE
Born: 1893, Philippeville, Algeria. Died: Nov. 21, 1963, Paris, France. Stage and screen actor.

Appeared in: **1923** Jocelyn. **1929** La Marche Nuptiale. **1930** The Chess Player. **1931** L'Atlantide. **1932** La Courtourierre de Luneville. **1933** Le Diable en Bouteille. **1934** Crime et Chatiment (Crime and Punishment). **1936** A Royal Divorce. **1937** The Late Mattia Pascal; L'Affaire du Courrier de Lyon (US 1938); Mademoiselle Docteur. **1935** Cette Vieille Canaille. **1938** Un Carnet de Bal; The Volga Boatman. **1940** Two Women. **1942** Poncarral. **1944** La Dame de Pique. **1946** La Symphonie Pastorale (US 1948). **1948** They Are Not Angels; Street of Shadows. **1958** Riff Raff Girls (US 1962 aka Rififi for Girls and Rififi among the Women). **1963** Magnificent Sinner.

BLANCHARD, MARI
Born: 1927. Died: May 10, 1970, Woodland Hills, Calif. (cancer). Screen and television actress.

Appeared in: **1951** On the Riviera; Ten Tall Men; No Questions Asked; The Unknown Man; The Overland Telegraph. **1952** The Brigand; Assignment—Paris; Back at the Front. **1953** Abbott and Costello Go to Mars; The Veils of Bagdad. **1954** Destry; Rails into Laramie; Black Horse Canyon. **1955** The Return of Jack Slade; Son of Sinbad; The Crooked Web. **1956** Stagecoach to Fury; The Cruel Tower. **1957** Jungle Heat; She Devil. **1958** Machete; No Place to Land. **1962** Don't Knock the Twist. **1963** Twice Told Tales; McLintock.

BLANCHE, FRANCIS
Born: 1922, France. Died: July 7, 1974, France. Screen actor and songwriter.

Appeared in: **1954** Ah! Les Belles Bacchantes (aka Peek-a-Boo–US 1961). **1959** La Jument Verte (The Green Mare–US 1961). **1960** La Francaise et l'Amour (Love and the Frenchwoman–US 1961); L'Ours (The Bear–US 1963); Babette Goes to War; Au Pied, Au Cheval, et Par Spoutnik (A Dog, a Mouse and a Sputnik). **1961** Les Menteurs (The Liars–US 1964 aka Twisted Lives). **1962** Le Septieme Jure (The Seventh Juror–US 1964); Les Petits Matins (Early Mornings); La Planque (The Hideout). **1963** Dragees au Poivre (Sweet and Sour–US 1964); Un Drole de Paroissien (aka Deo Gratias, The Funny Parishioner); Heaven Sent (aka Thank Heaven for Small Favors–US 1965); Les Tontons Flingueurs (The Gentle Gunmen). **1964** La Chasse a l'Homme (Male Hunt–US 1965); Les Barbouzes (aka The Great Spy Chase–US 1966); Les Plus Belles Escroqueries du Monde (The Beautiful Swindlers–US 1967); La Tulipe Noire (The Black Tulip). **1967** Belle du Jour (US 1968); La Grande Sauterelle (aka Femmina–US 1968); Le Plus Vieux Metier du Monde (The Oldest Profession–US 1968).

BLAND, JOYCE
Born: 1906, England. Died: Aug. 24, 1963, Bournemouth, England. Stage and screen actress.

Appeared in: **1932** Goodnight Vienna (aka Magic Night—US). **1935** The Right Age to Marry. **1936** A Touch of the Moon; Spy of Napoleon (US 1939).

1937 Dreaming Lips. **1938** Sixty Glorious Years (aka Queen of Destiny—US); The Citadel.

BLANDICK, CLARA
Born: 1881, aboard American ship in harbor of Hong Kong, China. Died: Apr. 15, 1962, Hollywood, Calif. (suicide). Stage and screen actress.

Appeared in: **1911** The Maids' Double. **1914** Mrs. Black Is Back. **1916** The Stolen Triumph. **1929** Men Are Like That; Poor Aubrey. **1930** Wise Girls; Burning Up; The Girl Said No; Sins of the Children; Romance; Last of the Duanes; Tom Sawyer. **1931** Once a Sinner; The Easiest Way; Dance, Fools, Dance; Inspiration; Drums of Jeopardy; Daybreak; It's a Wise Child; Laughing Sinners; I Take This Woman; Bought; Murder at Midnight; Huckleberry Finn; New Adventures of Get-Rich-Quick Wallingford; Possessed. **1932** Shopworn; The Strange Case of Clara Deane; The Pet Parade; Life Begins; Two against the World; The Expert; Three on a Match; Rockabye. **1933** Bitter Tea of General Yen; Child of Manhattan; The Mind Reader; Three-Cornered Moon; One Sunday Afternoon; Turn Back the Clock; Charlie Chan's Greatest Case; Ever in My Heart. **1934** The President Vanishes; Broadway Bill; Jealousy; Beloved; As the Earth Turns; Harold Teen; The Show-Off; The Girl from Missouri; Sisters under the Skin; Fugitive Lady. **1935** The Winning Ticket; Straight from the Heart; Princess O'Hara; Party Wire. **1936** Transient Lady; The Trail of the Lonesome Pine; Anthony Adverse; The Case of the Velvet Claws; Hearts Divided; The Gorgeous Hussy; In His Steps; Make Way For a Lady. **1937** A Star Is Born; Wings Over Honolulu; The Road Back; The League of Frightened Men; Small Town Boy; You Can't Have Everything; Her Husband's Secretary. **1938** My Old Kentucky Home; Tom Sawyer, Detective; Professor Beware; Swing, Sister Swing; Crime Ring. **1939** Drums along the Mohawk; Swanee River; I Was a Convict; Adventures of Huckleberry Finn; The Wizard of Oz; The Star Maker. **1940** Alice in Movieland; Tomboy; Anne of Windy Poplars; Dreaming Out Loud; Youth Will Be Served; Northwest Mounted Police. **1941** The Big Store; Enemy Within; Private Nurse; One Foot in Heaven; It Started with Eve; The Nurse's Secret; The Wagons Roll at Night. **1942** Lady in a Jam; Gentleman Jim; Rings on her Fingers. **1943** Heaven Can Wait; DuBarry Was a Lady; Dixie. **1944** Shadow of Suspicion; Can't Help Singing. **1945** Frontier Gal. **1946** She-Wolf of London; Pillow of Death; People Are Funny; Claudia and David; So Goes My Love; A Stolen Life. **1947** Philo Vance Returns; Life with Father. **1948** Bride Goes Wild. **1949** Mr. Soft Touch; Roots in the Soil. **1950** Love that Brute; Key to the City.

BLANEY, MAY
Born: 1874, England. Died: Feb. 10, 1953, Wepener, Orange Free State, South Africa. Stage and screen actress.

BLANKMAN, GEORGE
Born: 1877. Died: Mar. 13, 1925, Los Angeles, Calif. Screen actor.

Appeared in: **1925** Don Q.

BLATCHFORD, WILLIAM
Born: 1886, Pittsburgh, Pa. Died: Dec. 30, 1936, Los Angeles, Calif. Stage and screen actor.

Appeared in: **1934** The Old Fashioned Way.

BLEDSOE, JULES
Born: 1899. Died: July 14, 1943, Hollywood, Calif. Black screen, stage actor and singer.

Appeared in: **1929** Show Boat. **1942** Drums of the Congo.

BLEIBTREAU, HEDWIG
Born: 1868, Austria. Died: Jan. 24, 1958, Vienna, Austria. Stage and screen actress.

Appeared in: **1933** Ein Maedel der Strasse. **1937** Das Maedchen Irene. **1939** Hotel Sacher. **1940** Waldrausch (Forest Fever); Maria Ilona; Wiener Geschichten (Vienna Tales). **1950** The Third Man.

BLICK, NEWTON
Born: 1899, Bristol, England. Died: Oct. 1965, Dublin, Ireland. Screen, stage and television actor.

Appeared in: **1954** Carrington VC (aka Court-Martial—US 1955). **1956** The Feminine Touch (aka The Gentle Touch—US 1957); Charlie Moon; The Long Arm (aka The Third Key—US 1957). **1957** Town on Trial; Barnacle Bill (aka All at Sea—US 1958). **1958** The Gypsy and the Gentleman; Bachelor of Hearts (US 1962). **1960** Man in the Moon (US 1961). **1961** Flame in the Streets (US 1962). **1962** Term of Trial (US 1963). **1963** Ring of Spies (aka Ring of Treason—US 1964). **1965** Lord Jim. **1966** Morgan—A Suitable Case for Treatment (aka Morgan—US).

BLINN, BENJAMIN F.
Born: 1872. Died: Apr. 28, 1941, Hollywood, Calif. Screen and stage actor.

Appeared in: **1923** Danger. **1925** Quicker'n Lightnin'.

BLINN, GENEVIEVE (Genevieve Namary)

Born: St. John, New Brunswick, Canada. Died: July 20, 1956, Ross, Calif. Stage and screen actress.

Appeared in: 1921 Queen of Sheba; Crazy to Marry; Don't Tell Everything; The Witching Hour. 1922 If I Were Queen; The Call of Home. 1924 Abraham Lincoln. 1930 Common Clay.

BLINN, HOLBROOK

Born: 1872, San Francisco, Calif. Died: June 24, 1928, Crotan, N.Y. (fall from horse). Screen, stage actor and film producer.

Appeared in: 1915 The Boss; McTeague; The Butterfly on the Wheel. 1916 The Weakness of Man; Husband and Wife. 1921 Power. 1923 The Bad Man; Rosita. 1924 Janice Meredith; Yolanda. 1925 Zander the Great; The New Commandment. 1926 The Unfair Sex. 1927 The Masked Woman; The Telephone Girl.

BLOCKER, DAN

Born: 1929, Texas. Died: May 13, 1972, Hollywood, Calif. (pulmonary embolus). Screen, stage and television actor.

Appeared in: 1957 Outer Space Jitters (short). 1961 The Errand Boy. 1963 Come Blow Your Horn. 1968 Lady in Cement. 1970 The Cockeyed Cowboys of Calico County.

BLOMFIELD, DEREK

Born: 1920. Died: July 23, 1964, Brittany, France. Screen, stage, television actor and playwright. Entered films in 1932.

Appeared in: 1935 Emil and the Detectives (aka Emil—US 1938); Turn of the Tide. 1936 Shipmates O'Mine. 1941 Ghost of St. Michael's. 1942 Alibi. 1950 Night and the City. 1953 The Floating Dutchman. 1954 Hobson's Choice. 1956 It's Great to Be Young (US 1958); It's a Wonderful World (US 1961). 1957 Carry on Admiral (aka The Ship Was Loaded—US 1959). 1964 East of Sudan.

BLORE, ERIC

Born: Dec. 23, 1887, London, England. Died: Mar. 2, 1959, Hollywood, Calif. (heart attack). Screen, stage actor and songwriter. Married to actress Clara Mackin.

Appeared in: 1926 The Great Gatsby. 1930 Laughter. 1931 My Sin; Tarnished Lady. 1933 Flying Down to Rio. 1934 Gay Divorcee (stage and film versions); Limehouse Blues. 1935 Follies-Bergere; The Good Fairy; Diamond Jim; The Casino Murder Case; I Live My Life; Top Hat; I Dream Too Much; Old Man Rhythm; To Beat the Band; Seven Keys to Baldpate; Glitter; Behold My Wife. 1936 Two in the Dark; The Ex-Mrs. Bradford; Swing Time; Smartest Girl in Town; Sons O' Guns; Piccadilly Jim. 1937 The Soldier and the Lady; Quality Street; Shall We Dance?; Breakfast for Two; Hitting a New High; It's Love I'm After; Michael Strogoff. 1938 The Joy of Living; Swiss Miss; A Desperate Adventure. 1939 $1,000 a Touchdown; Island of Lost Men; A Gentleman's Gentleman. 1940 The Man Who Wouldn't Talk; The Lone Wolf Meets a Lady; The Boys from Syracuse; Earl of Puddlestone; South of Suez. 1941 Road to Zanzibar; The Lone Wolf Keeps a Date; The Lady Eve; The Lone Wolf Takes a Chance; Red Head; New York Town; Lady Scarface; Three Girls about Town; Confirm or Deny; The Shanghai Gesture; Sullivan's Travels; Secrets of the Lone Wolf. 1942 The Moon and Sixpence; Counter Espionage. 1943 Forever and a Day; Submarine Base; Holy Matrimony; One Dangerous Night; Passport to Suez; The Sky's the Limit; Happy Go Lucky. 1944 San Diego, I Love You. 1945 Penthouse Rhythm; Easy to Look At; Men in Her Diary. 1946 Kitty; The Notorious Lone Wolf; Abie's Irish Rose; Two Sisters from Boston. 1947 Winter Wonderland; The Lone Wolf in London; The Lone Wolf in Mexico; Love Happy. 1948 Romance on the High Seas. 1949 Adventures of Ichabod and Mr. Toad (voice). 1950 Fancy Pants. 1952 Babes From Bagdad. 1955 Bowery to Bagdad.

BLUE, BEN (Ben Bernstein)

Born: Sept. 12, 1901, Montreal, Canada. Died: Mar. 7, 1975, Los Angeles, Calif. Screen, stage, vaudeville, radio and television actor. Married to actress Axie Dunlap. Divorced from Mary Blue.

Appeared in: 1926 Vitaphone shorts. 1927 The Arcadians. 1932 Strange Innertube (short); What Price Taxi (short). 1933 Wreckety Wreck (short); Call Her Sausage (short); College Rhythm. 1934 A Vitaphone short. 1936 College Holiday; Follow Your Heart. 1937 Top of the Town; High, Wide and Handsome; Turn Off the Moon; Artists and Models; Thrill of a Lifetime. 1938 College Swing; The Big Broadcast of 1938; Cocoanut Grove. 1939 Paris Honeymoon. 1942 Panama Hattie; For Me and My Gal. 1943 Thousands Cheer. 1944 Two Girls and a Sailor; Broadway Rhythm. 1945 Badminton (short). 1946 Two Sisters from Boston; Easy to Wed. 1947 My Wild Irish Rose. 1948 One Sunday Afternoon (aka The Strawberry Blonde). 1963 It's a Mad, Mad, Mad, Mad World. 1966 The Russians are Coming, The Russians are Coming. 1967 A Guide for the Married Man; The Busy Body. 1968 Where Were you When the Lights Went Out?

BLUE, MONTE

Born: Jan. 11, 1890, Indianapolis, Ind. Died: Feb. 18. 1963, Milwaukee, Wis. (coronary attack). Screen actor, screenwriter, and circus performer. Entered films as a screenwriter and stuntman with Griffith.

Appeared in: 1915 Birth of a Nation. 1916 Intolerance. 1918 Till I Come Back to You. 1919 In Mizzoura; Every Woman; Pettigrew's Girl. 1920 Jucklins; Something to Think About. 1921 Moonlight and Honeysuckle; The Affairs of Anatole; A Broken Doll; A Perfect Crime; The Kentuckians. 1922 Orphans of the Storm; Peacock Alley; My Old Kentucky Home. 1923 Loving Lies; Defying Destiny; Main Street; Lucretia Lombard; Brass; The Tents of Allah; The Purple Highway; Loving Lies. 1924 Being Respectable; Revelation; The Lover of Camille; The Marriage Circle; Daddies; The Dark Swan; Daughters of Pleasure; Her Marriage Vow; How to Educate a Wife; Mademoiselle Midnight. 1925 Kiss Me Again; Red Hot Tires; Hogan's Alley; The Limited Mail; Recompense. 1926 Across the Pacific; So This Is Paris; The Man Upstairs; Other Women's Husbands. 1927 Bitter Apples; The Black Diamond Express; Brass Knuckles; The Brute; The Bush Leaguer; Wolf's Clothing; One-Round Hogan. 1928 Across the Atlantic; White Shadows of the South Seas. 1929 Tiger Rose; Conquest; From Headquarters; The Greyhound Limited; No Defense; Skin Deep; The Show of Shows. 1930 Isle of Escape; Those Who Dance. 1931 The Flood. 1932 The Stoker; The Valley of Adventure. 1933 The Nectors; Her Forgotten Past; The Intruder; Officer 13. 1934 The Last Round-Up; Come On Marines!; The Thundering Herd; Student Tour; Wagon Wheels; College Rhythm. 1935 Hot off the Press; Trails of the Wild; Nevada; G-Men; Lives of a Bengal Lancer; Wanderer of the Wasteland; On Probation. 1936 Ride, Ranger, Ride; Undersea Kingdom; Treachery Rides the Range; Mary of Scotland; Song of the Gringo; Desert Gold. 1937 The Outcasts of Poker Flat; Rootin' Tootin' Rhythm; Thunder Trail; Souls at Sea; High, Wide and Handsome. 1938 Hawk of the Wilderness; Tom Sawyer, Detective; Spawn of the North; Big Broadcast of 1938; The Mysterious Rider; Illegal Traffic; Wild Bill Hickok; Born to the West; Rebellious Daughters; Cocoanut Grove. 1939 Dodge City; Geronimo; Frontier Pony Express; Days of Jesse James; Juarez; Port of Hats; Our Leading Citizen. 1940 A Little Bit of Heaven; Mystery Sea Rider; Young Bill Hickok; Texas Rangers Ride Again. 1941 The Great Train Robbery; Arkansas Judge; Law of the Timber; Scattergood Pulls the Strings; New York Town; Sunset in Wyoming; Bad Man of Deadwood. 1942 The Palm Beach Story; Gentleman Jim; The Road to Morocco; North to the Klondike; Secret Enemies; Across the Pacific; Panama Hattie. 1943 Truck Busters; Edge of Darkness; Northern Pursuit; Mission to Moscow; Thank Your Lucky Stars; Secret Enemies; Thousands Cheer. 1944 The Mask of Dimitrios; The Conspirators; Passage to Marseille; The Adventures of Mark Twain. 1945 Saratoga Trunk; San Antonio. 1946 Cinderella Jones; Shadow of a Woman; Two Sisters from Boston; Easy to Wed. 1947 Bells of San Fernando; Life with Father; Speed to Spare; That Way with Women; Cheyenne; Possessed; My Wild Irish Rose. 1948 Silver River; Two Guys from Texas; Key Largo; Johnny Belinda. 1949 The Younger Brothers; Ranger of Cherokee Strip; Flaxy Martin; Homicide; South of St. Louis. 1950 Dallas; This Side of the Law; The Tomahawk Trail; The Blonde Bandit; Backfire; Montana; The Iroquois Trail. 1951 Warpath; Snake River Desperadoes; Three Desperate Men; Gold Raiders; The Sea Harvest. 1952 Rose of Cimarron; Hangman's Knot. 1953 The Last Posse. 1954 Apache.

BLUETTE, ISA

Born: 1898, Italy. Died: Nov. 10, 1939, Turin, Italy. Screen and stage actor.

BLUM, MAX

Born: 1874. Died: Jan. 10, 1944, Hollywood, Calif. Screen actor.

BLUM, SAMMY

Born: 1889, New York, N.Y. Died: June 1, 1945, Hollywood, Calif. (heart attack). Stage and screen actor. Entered films in 1905.

Appeared in: 1925 Galloping Jinx. 1926 The Winning of Barbara Worth; Black Paradise; Siberia. 1927 Smile, Brother, Smile; The Wheel of Destiny. 1929 Rio Rita; The Delightful Rogue; The Prince of Hearts. 1930 More Sinned against Than Usual (short); The Grand Parade; Party Girl. 1931 Iron Man. 1932 Night World. 1937 Lodge Night (short). 1945 The following shorts: Alibi Baby; Sleepless Tuesday; What, No Cigarettes?; It's Your Move; Let's Go Stepping.

BLYDEN, LARRY (Ivan Lawrence Blieden)

Born: June 23, 1925, Houston, Tex. Died: June 6, 1975, Agadir, Morocco (auto accident). Screen, stage, television and radio actor, stage director and producer. Divorced from actress Carol Haney (dec. 1962).

Appeared in: 1957 The Bachelor Party; Kiss Them for Me. 1970 On a Clear Day You Can See Forever.

BLYSTONE, STANLEY "STAN" (William Stanley Blystone)

Born: Aug. 1, 1894, Wisc. Died: July 16, 1956, Hollywood, Calif. (heart attack). Screen and television actor.

Appeared in: 1924 Darwin Was Right; Excitement. 1925 Under the Rouge. 1927 The Circus Ace. 1928 Four Sons; Wildcat Valley (short); Always a Gentleman (short); His Maiden Voyage (short); Ladies Preferred (short). **1929** Synthetic Sin; Through Different Eyes; Waltzing Around (short). **1930** The Fighting Legion; Parade of the West; Young Eagles; The Laurel-Hardy Murder Case (short). **1931** Dancing Dynamite; Man From Death Valley; Sundown Trail. **1932** Galloping Through; Honor of the Mounted; Sunkissed Sweeties (short); The Golden West; Hold 'Em Jail. **1933** Strange People; Man of Action; Infernal Machine; Cross Fire; Lucky Larrigan; The Fighting Parson. **1934** Burn 'Em Up Barnes (serial and feature); We're Not Dressing; Lemon Drop Kid; Hips, Hips Hooray; In Old Santa Fe; Sons of the Desert. **1935** The Three Musketeers; Fighting Pioneers; Ladies Crave Excitement; Smart Girl; Code of the Mounted; Trail's End; Saddle Aces; The Ivory Handled Gun; The Phantom Empire (serial); Restless Knights (short); A Night at the Opera. **1936** Strike Me Pink; Ace Drummond (serial); The Vigilantes Are Coming (serial); Here Comes Trouble; The Riding Avenger; Half-Shot Shooters (short); False Alarms (short). **1937** Edgar and Goliath (short); Armored Car; Goofs and Saddles (short); Two Wise Maids; Windjammer; Galloping Dynamite; Headin' East; Boots and Saddles. **1938** California Frontier; Stranger from Arizona; Swiss Miss. **1939** The Lone Ranger Rides Again (serial); Trigger Pals; Crashing Through; Three Texas Steers; Torture Ship; Mr. Moto Takes a Vacation. **1940** The Tulsa Kid; A Chump at Oxford; Remedy for Riches; Pony Post. **1941** King of the Texas Rangers (serial); Sea Raiders (serial); Tall, Dark and Handsome; Sunset in Wyoming; Buck Privates. **1942** Through Different Eyes; Piano Mooner (short); Jesse James, Jr.; Even As I.O.U. (short); Carry Harry (short). **1943** Spook Louder (short); Three Little Twerps (short). **1945** Navajo Kid. **1946** King of the Forest Rangers (serial); Six Gun Man; Moon Over Montana. **1947** The Sea Hound (serial); Out West (short). **1948** Eyes of Texas; I Wouldn't Be in Your Shoes. **1949** Ride, Ryder, Ride; Deputy Marshal; Rustlers; Loaded Pistols; Powder River Rustlers. **1950** Desperados of the West (serial); Six Gun Mesa; County Fair; Square Dance Katy; Slap Happy Sleuths (short). **1951** Silver Canyon. **1952** Road Agent. **1953** Jack McCall, Desperado; Abbott and Costello Go to Mars. **1954** Living It Up. **1955** You're Never Too Young. **1956** Pardners.

BLYTHE, BETTY (Elizabeth Blythe Slaughter)
Born: Sept. 1, 1893, Los Angeles, Calif. Died: Apr. 7, 1972, Woodland Hills, Calif. Stage and screen actress. Married to film director Paul Scardon (dec. 1954). In 1938 was presented a Special Academy Award for her pioneer contributions to the motion picture industry. Entered films with Vitagraph Studios.

Appeared in: **1916** Slander. **1917** His Own People. **1918** Miss Ambition; Over the Top; Tangled Lives; The Green God. **1919** Dust of Desire; Undercurrent. **1920** Nomads of the North; Silver Horde; Third Generation. **1921** Charge It; Just Outside the Door; Mother O'Mine; The Queen of Sheba; The Truant Husband; Disraeli. **1922** Fair Lady; His Wife's Husband; How Women Love. **1923** Darling of the Rich; Sinner or Saint; Truth About Wives; Chu Chin Chow (US 1925). **1924** In Hollywood with Potash and Perlmutter; The Spitfire; The Breath of Scandal; The Folly of Vanity; The Recoil; Southern Love (aka A Woman's Secret—US). **1925** She; Speed; Percy. **1927** Snowbound; Eager Lips; A Million Bid; The Girl from Gay Paree. **1928** Sisters of Eve; Domestic Troubles; Glorious Betsy; Into No Man's Land; Daughter of Israel. **1929** Stolen Love. **1931** Stars of Yesterday (short). **1932** Tom Brown of Culver; Lena Rivers; Back Street. **1933** Pilgrimage; Only Yesterday; Before Midnight. **1934** The Scarlet Letter; Ever Since Eve; Money Means Nothing; Badge of Honor; Girl of the Limberlost; Two Heads on a Pillow; Night Alarm. **1935** Cheers of the Crowd; The Perfect Clue; The Spanish Cape Mystery. **1936** Murder at Glen Athol; The Gorgeous Hussy; Yours for the Asking; Rainbow on the River. **1938** Romance of the Limberlost; Gangster's Boy. **1940** Misbehaving Husbands; Earl of Puddlestone. **1941** Honky Tonk; Federal Fugitives; Top Sergeant Mulligan; Tuxedo Junction. **1942** The Miracle Kid; House of Errors; Dawn on the Great Divide; Piano Mooner (short). **1943** Girls in Chains; Bar 20; Sarong Girl; Spotlight Scandals; Where Are Your Children?; Farmer for a Day (short). **1944** The Chinese Cat. **1945** Docks of New York; Abbott and Costello in Hollywood. **1946** Joe Palooka, Champ; The Undercover Woman. **1948** Jiggs and Maggie in Society; Madonna of the Desert. **1949** Jackpot Jitters (aka Maggie and Jiggs in Jackpot Jitters). **1964** My Fair Lady.

BOARDMAN, TRUE (William True Boardman)
Born: Apr. 21, 1882, Oakland, Calif. Died: Sept. 28, 1918, Norwalk, Calif. Screen and stage actor. Married to actress Virginia True Boardman (dec. 1971). Starred in "Stingaree" series; "The Girl from Frisco" series; "The Social Pirates" series; "The Hazards of Helen" series from 1915-1917.

Appeared in: **1911** The New Editor. **1912** The Outlaw's Sacrifice. **1914** The Calling of Jim Barton; The Conquest of Man; Broncho Billy and the Sheriff; Single-Handed; Sophie Gets Stung. **1915** When Thieves Fall Out; Broncho Billy's Sentence; The False Clue; The Dream Seekers; Mysteries of the Grand Hotel; The Man in Irons; Stingaree; A Voice in the Wilderness; The Pitfall; An Enemy of Mankind; A Bushranger at Bay. **1916** On the Brink of War; The Purification of Mulfera; The Moth and the Star; The Villain Worshipper; The Duel in the Desert; The Darkest Hour; The Trapping of Peeler White; The Record Run; The Race For a Siding; The Governor's Special; The Fighting Heiress; The Oil Field Plot; The Turquoise Mine Mystery; Tigers Unchained; The Treasure of Cibola; The Web of Guilt; The Reformation of Dog Hole; The Yellow Hand; The Harvest of Gold; A Battle in the Dark; Mystery of the Brass

Bound Chest; The Fight For Paradise Valley; The Son of Cain; The Witch of the Dark House; The Poisoned Dart; The Stain of Chuckawalla. **1917** The False Prophet; The Resurrection of Gold Bar; Wolf of Los Alamos; The Homesteader's Feud; The Jackaroo; The Fugitive Passenger; The Tracking of Stingaree. **1919** Tarzan of the Apes; Molly Go Get 'Em; The Doctor and the Woman.

BOARDMAN, VIRGINIA TRUE
Born: 1889. Died: June 10, 1971, Hollywood, Calif. Screen and stage actress. Entered films in 1911 with Selig Studios in Chicago. Appeared on stage as Virginia Eames. Married to actor True Boardman (dec. 1918).

Appeared in: **1922** The Village Blacksmith; Where Is My Wandering Boy Tonight?; A Blind Bargain; Penrod; The Third Alarm. **1923** The Town Scandal; The Barefoot Boy; The Gunfighter; Pioneer Trails; Three Jumps Ahead; The Mailman; Michael O'Halloran. **1924** Girl of the Limberlost; The Tomboy. **1925** The Home Maker; The Red Rider. **1926** The Test of Donald Norton. **1927** Down the Stretch; King of the Jungle (serial); Speedy Smith. **1929** The Lady Lies. **1931** Scareheads. **1933** One Year Later. **1934** The Road to Ruin. **1934** "Baby Burlesque" series. **1936** The Fugitive Sheriff.

BODEL, BURMAN
Born: 1911. Died: July 17, 1969, Calif. Stage and screen actor.

BOESE, JOACHIM
Born: 1933, Germany. Died: Apr. 25, 1971, Germany (?) (auto accident). Stage and screen actor.

BOESEN, WILLIAM
Born: 1924. Died: Mar. 25, 1972, New York, N.Y. Screen and stage actor.

Appeared in: **1969** Putney Swope. **1971** The Gang Who Couldn't Shoot Straight.

BOETIGER, JULIA
Born: 1852. Died: Oct. 28, 1938, Los Angeles, Calif. Screen actress.

BOGART, HUMPHREY (Humphrey DeForest Bogart)
Born: Dec. 25, 1899, New York, N.Y. Died: Jan. 14, 1957, Los Angeles, Calif. (cancer). Stage and screen actor. Married to actress Lauren Bacall. Divorced from actresses Helen Menken (dec. 1966), Mary Phillips (dec. 1975) and Mayo Methot (dec. 1951). Nominated for 1942 Academy Award for Best Actor in Casablanca and in 1954 for The Caine Mutiny. Won 1952 Academy Award for Best Actor in The African Queen.

Appeared in: **1930** A Devil with Women (film debut); Broadway's Like That (short); Up the River. **1931** Body and Soul; Bad Sister; Women of all Nations; A Holy Terror. **1932** Love Affair; Big City Blues; Three on a Match. **1934** Midnight. **1935** Black Fury; The Petrified Forest (stage and film versions); Two against the World; Bullets or Ballots; China Clipper; Isle of Fury. **1937** The Great O'Malley; Black Legion; San Quentin; Marked Woman; Kid Galahad; Dead End; Stand-In. **1938** Swing Your Lady; Men Are Such Fools; Crime School; The Amazing Dr. Clitterhouse; Racket Busters; Angels with Dirty Faces. **1939** King of the Underworld; You Can't Get Away with Murder; Dark Victory; The Oklahoma Kid; The Return of Dr. X; The Roaring Twenties; Invisible Stripes; Arizona Kid. **1940** Virginia City; It All Came True; Brother Orchid; They Drive by Night. **1941** High Sierra; The Wagons Roll at Night; The Maltese Falcon. **1942** All Through the Night; The Big Shot; Across the Pacific; Casablanca; In This Our Life (unbilled). **1943** Action in the North Atlantic; Thank Your Lucky Stars; Sahara. **1944** Passage to Marseille. **1945** Conflict; To Have and Have Not; Hollywood Victory Canteen (short). **1946** The Big Sleep; Two Guys from Milwaukee (unbilled). **1947** The Two Mrs. Carrolls; Dead Reckoning; Dark Passage; Always Together. **1948** The Treasure of Sierra Madre; Key Largo. **1949** Knock on Any Door; Tokyo Joe. **1950** Chain Lightning; In a Lonely Place. **1951** The Enforcer; Sirocco; Saving Bond (short); The African Queen. **1952** Road to Bali (film clip); Deadline—U.S.A. **1953** Battle Circus. **1954** Beat the Devil; The Caine Mutiny; Sabrina; The Barefoot Contessa; Love Lottery (unbilled). **1955** We're No Angels; The Desperate Hours; The Left Hand of God. **1956** The Harder They Fall.

BOHANNON, E. J. "BO"
Born: 1896. Died: Feb. 14, 1966, Sacramento, Calif. Screen actor and stuntman.

BOHNEN, MICHAEL
Born: May 2, 1887, Cologne, Germany. Died: Apr. 26, 1965, Berlin, Germany (heart attack). Screen actor and opera singer. Entered films in 1919. Divorced from singer Mary Lewis and later married to dancer La Jana.

Appeared in: **1929** Sajenko the Soviet. **1930** Zwei Kravatten (Two Neckties). **1933** Viktoria und Ihr Husar (Victoria and her Hussar); Wiener Blut. **1934** Gold. **1936** The Private Life of Louis XIV. **1937** August der Starke. **1938** Solo Per Te (Only for Thee). **1939** Das Unsterbliche Herz (The Immortal Heart).

BOHNEN, ROMAN

Born: Nov. 24, 1894, St. Paul, Minn. Died: Feb. 24, 1949, Hollywood, Calif. (heart attack). Stage and screen actor.

Appeared in: **1937** 52nd Street; Vogues of 1938. **1939** Of Mice and Men. **1940** The Living Dead. **1941** They Dare Not Love; The Bugle Sounds; Appointment for Love; So Ends Our Night. **1942** Young America; The Hard Way; Grand Central Murder; Affairs of Jimmy Valentine. **1943** Edge of Darkness; Mission to Moscow; The Mask of Dimitrios; The Song of Bernadette. **1944** The Hitler Gang; None but the Lonely Heart; The Hairy Ape. **1945** A Bell for Adano; Counter-Attack. **1946** Deadline at Dawn; The Hoodlum Saint; Mr. Ace; The Strange Love of Martha Ivers; Miss Susie Slagle's; Two Years Before the Mast; California; The Best Years of Our Lives. **1947** Brute Force; For You I Die; Winter Wonderland; Song of Love. **1948** Arch of Triumph; Joan of Arc; Open Street; The Night Has a Thousand Eyes. **1949** Kazan; Mr. Soft Touch.

BOLAND, EDDIE

Born: 1883, San Francisco, Calif. Died: Feb. 3, 1935, Santa Monica, Calif. (heart attack). Screen actor. Entered films in 1913.

Appeared in: **1922** Oliver Twist. **1923** Within the Law; Long Live the King. **1924** Little Robinson Crusoe. **1926** Hard Boiled; Unknown Dangers; A Gentleman Roughneck. **1927** Sunrise; The Kid Brother. **1928** Manhattan Knights; Shorts prior to 1929: Nobody's Business; Nothing Matters; and Who's My Wife? **1929** Last Performance. **1930** Wings of Adventure; City Girl. **1931** The Miracle Woman. **1932** Mother-In-Law's Day (short); Giggle Water (short); Vanity Street. **1933** I Have Lived.

BOLAND, MARY

Born: Jan. 28, 1880, Philadelphia, Pa. Died: June 23, 1965, New York, N.Y. Screen, stage and television actress.

Appeared in: **1916** The Edge of the Abyss (film debut); The Stepping Stone. **1918** His Temporary Wife. **1931** Personal Maid; Secrets of a Secretary. **1932** If I Had a Million; The Night of June Thirteen; Trouble in Paradise; Evening for Sale; Night after Night. **1933** Mama Loves Papa; Three-Cornered Moon; The Solitaire Man. **1934** Six of a Kind; Stingaree; Down to Their Last Yacht; Four Frightened People; Melody in Spring; Here Comes the Groom; The Pursuit of Happiness. **1935** People Will Talk; Two for Tonight; The Big Broadcast of 1936; Ruggles of Red Gap. **1936** Wives Never Know; Early to Bed; College Holiday; A Son Comes Home. **1937** Marry the Girl; There Goes the Groom; Mama Runs Wild; Danger—Love at Work. **1938** Little Tough Guys in Society; Artists and Models Abroad. **1939** The Magnificent Fraud; The Women; Boy Trouble; Night Work. **1940** He Married His Wife; The Hit Parade of 1941; One Night in the Tropics; New Moon; Pride and Prejudice. **1944** Nothing but Trouble; In Our Time. **1945** The Right to Live; They Shall Have Faith. **1948** Julia Misbehaves. **1950** Guilty Bystander.

BOLDER, ROBERT "BOBBIE"

Born: 1859, London, England. Died: Dec. 10, 1937, Beverly Hills, Calif. Stage and screen actor.

Appeared in: **1919** Strictly Confidential. **1921** The Fighting Lover; The Silent Call; Black Beauty; The House that Jazz Built; The Marriage of William Ash; Beyond the Rocks; The Lane that Had No Turning. **1923** Grumpy; The Christian; The Love Piker. **1924** Abraham Lincoln; Captain Blood; What Three Men Wanted; Vanity's Price; The Sea Hawk. **1925** Raffles, the Amateur Cracksman; Stella Maris; The Handsome Brute; Blue Blood. **1926** Butterflies in the Rain. **1927** The Wise Wife; Woman's Wares; Tarzan and the Golden Lion. **1929** The Tip Off. **1930** Grumpy (and 1923 version); Lady of Scandal; Charlie's Aunt. **1931** Get-Rich-Quick Wallingford; The Miracle Woman; East Lynne.

BOLES, JOHN

Born: Oct. 1895, Greenville, Tex. Died: Feb. 27, 1969, San Angelo, Tex. (heart attack). Stage and screen actor. During W.W. I he was a U.S. spy in Germany, Bulgaria and Turkey.

Appeared in: **1925** So This Is Marriage; Excuse Me. **1927** The Love of Sunya. **1928** Shepherd of the Hills; Bride of the Colorado; What Holds Men?; We Americans; Fazil; The Water Hole; Virgin Lips; Man-Made Woman. **1929** The Desert Song; The Last Warning; Rio Rita; Scandal; Romance of the Underworld; She Goes to War. **1930** Song of the West; Captain of the Guard; Queen of Scandal; King of Jazz; One Heavenly Night. **1931** Seed; Good Sport; Resurrection; Frankenstein. **1932** Careless Lady; Back Street; Six Hours to Live. **1933** Hollywood on Parade (short); Child of Manhattan; My Lips Betray; Only Yesterday; Beloved. **1934** I Believed in You; Age of Innocence; Bottoms Up; Stand Up and Cheer; Life of Vergie Winters; The White Parade; Music in the Air; Wild Gold. **1935** Orchids to You; Curly Top; Redheads on Parade; The Littlest Rebel; Masquerade (aka Escapade). **1936** Rose of the Rancho; A Message to Garcia; Craig's Wife. **1937** As Good as Married; Stella Dallas; Fight for Your Lady. **1938** Romance in the Dark; She Married an Artist; Sinners in Paradise. **1942** Road to Happiness; Between Us Girls. **1943** Thousands Cheer. **1952** Babes in Bagdad.

BOLEY, MAY

Born: Washington, D.C. Died: Jan. 7, 1963, Hollywood, Calif. (cancer). Stage and screen actress.

Appeared in: **1928** The Wagon Show. **1929** Dangerous Curves; Dance of Life; Beneath the Law (short); Hail the Princess; Woman from Hell. **1930** Lillies of the Field; Moby Dick; Children of Pleasure. **1931** Going Wild. **1932** A Woman Commands; The Expert. **1933** Advice to the Lovelorn. **1934** The Mighty Barnum. **1935** The Informer. **1936** Without Orders. **1937** Ready, Willing and Able; Tovarich. **1938** Reckless Living; Cowboy from Brooklyn; Prison Farm. **1939** Persons in Hiding; Death of a Champion; Undercover Doctor; The Women.

BOLGER, ROBERT "BO" (Robert Erin Bolger)

Born: 1937. Died: Aug. 23, 1969, Oceanside, Calif. (killed while skydiving). Screen, television actor and stuntman.

BOMBARD, LOTTIE GERTRUDE

Born: 1908. Died: Nov. 1913, Saranac Lake, N.Y. Child actress featured in Pathe films.

BONANOVA, FORTUNIO

Born: Jan. 13, 1893, Palma de Mallorca, Spain. Died: Apr. 2, 1969, Woodland Hills, Calif. (cerebral hemorrhage). Screen, stage, television actor, opera singer and playwright.

Appeared in: **1924** Don Juan (film debut). **1932** Careless Lady; A Successful Calamity. **1936** El Desaparecido; Podoroso Caballer. **1938** Tropic Holiday; Romance in the Dark; Bulldog Drummond in Africa. **1939** La Immaculada. **1940** I Was an Adventuress; Down Argentine Way. **1941** They Met in Argentina; Moon over Miami; A Yank in the R.A.F.; Two Latins from Manhattan; Mr. and Mrs. North; Obliging Young Lady; Citizen Kane; That Night in Rio; Blood and Sand. **1942** Sing Your Worries Away; Girl Trouble; Larceny, Inc.; The Black Swan. **1943** The Sultan's Daughter; For Whom the Bell Tolls; Five Graves to Cairo. **1944** Double Indemnity; My Best Gal; Ali Baba and the Forty Thieves; Falcon in Mexico; Mrs. Parkington; Brazil; Going My Way. **1945** Where Do We Go from Here?; A Bell for Adano; Hit the Hay; Man Alive; The Red Dragon. **1946** Monsieur Beaucaire. **1947** Rose of Santa Rosa; Fiesta; The Fugitive. **1948** Bad Men of Tombstone; Angel on the Amazon; Romance on the High Seas; Adventures of Don Juan. **1949** Whirlpool. **1950** Nancy Goes to Rio; September Affair. **1951** Havana Rose. **1953** So This is Love; Conquest of Cochise; Second Chance; Thunder Bay; The Moon Is Blue. **1955** New York Confidential; Kiss Me Deadly. **1956** Jaguar. **1957** An Affair to Remember. **1958** The Saga of Hemp Brown. **1959** Thunder in the Sun. **1963** The Running Man. **1967** The Million Dollar Collar.

BOND, JACK (Alfred Welch)

Born: 1899. Died: Apr. 29, 1952, Hollywood, Calif. Screen and stage actor.

Appeared in: **1946** The Kid from Brooklyn.

BOND, LYLE

Born: 1917. Died: Apr. 14, 1972, San Diego, Calif. (heart attack). Screen, radio, television actor, newscaster and television sportscaster.

BOND, WARD

Born: Apr. 9, 1903, Denver, Colo. Died: Nov. 5, 1960, Dallas, Tex. (heart attack). Screen, stage and television actor. Entered films in 1928 while attending U.S.C.

Appeared in: **1929** Salute (film debut); Words and Music. **1930** Born Reckless; The Big Trail. **1932** High Speed; White Eagle; Rackety Rax; Hello Trouble; Virtue. **1933** Obey the Law; The Sundown Rider; Heroes for Sale; Wild Boys of the Road; When Strangers Marry; The Wrecker; Whirlpool; Unknown Valley; Police Car 17. **1934** Straightaway; Most Precious Thing in Life; Tall Timber; The Fighting Code; The Voice in the Night; A Man's Game; The Crime of Helen Stanley; Girl in Danger; The Human Side; Kid Millions; Against the Law; The Poor Rich; The Frontier Marshal; It Happened One Night; The Defense Rests; The Fighting Ranger; Here Comes the Groom. **1935** Western Courage; Men of the Night; Justice of the Range; Too Tough to Kill; Devil Dogs of the Air; Little Big Shot; The Crimson Trail; She Gets Her Man; His Night Out; Black Fury; Fighting Shadows; Guard that Girl; Murder in the Fleet; Headline Woman; Waterfront Lady; The Informer. **1936** Cattle Thief; Pride of the Marines; Avenging Waters; Muss 'Em Up; The Bride Walks Out; Second Wife; Without Orders; Crash Donovan; Conflict; They Met in a Taxi; The Man Who Lived Twice; The Legion of Terror; The Leathernecks Have Landed. **1937** The Wildcatter; A Fight to the Finish; You Only Live Once; Dead End; Park Avenue Logger; The Devil's Playground; 23 1/2 Hours' Leave; Night Key; Escape by Night. **1938** Bringing Up Baby; Hawaii Calls; Born to be Wild; Flight into Nowhere; Reformatory; Gun Law; The Law West of Tombstone; Professor Beware; Mr. Moto's Gamble; Submarine Patrol; Prison Break; Numbered Woman; Over the Wall; The Amazing Dr. Clitterhouse. **1939** Mr. Moto in Danger Island; They Made Me a Criminal; Made for Each Other; Dodge City; Waterfront; Gone with the Wind; Trouble in Sundown; The Return of the Cisco Kid; Frontier Marshall (and 1934 version); The Girl from Mexico; The Kid from Kokomo; The Oklahoma Kid; Drums along the Mohawk; Dust Be My Destiny; Young Mr. Lincoln. **1940** Heaven with a Barbed Wire Fence; Virginia City; The Cisco Kid and the Lady; The Grapes of Wrath; Little Old New York; Santa Fe Trail; Buck Benny Rides Again; The Mortal Storm; Kit Carson; The Long Voyage Home. **1941** The Shepherd of the Hills; A Man Betrayed; Sergeant York; Manpower; Doctors Don't Tell; Swamp Water; Wild Bill Hickok Rides; Tobacco Road; The Maltese Falcon. **1942** In This Our Life; The Falcon Takes Over; Gentleman Jim; Sin Town; Ten Gentlemen from West Point. **1943** Slightly Dangerous; They Came to Blow Up America; Cowboy Commandos; Hello, Frisco, Hello; Hitler, Dead or Alive; A Guy Named Joe. **1944** Home in Indiana; The Sullivans; Tall in the Saddle. **1945** Dakota; They Were Expendable. **1946** Canyon Passage; My Darling Clementine; It's a Wonderful Life. **1947** The Fugitive; Unconquered. **1948** Fort Apache; The Time of Your Life; Joan of Arc; Tap Roots; Three Godfathers. **1950** Riding High; Wagonmaster; Singing Guns; Kiss Tomorrow Goodbye; Dodge City; Great Missouri Raid. **1951** Operation Pacific; Only the Valiant; On Dangerous Ground. **1952** The Quiet Man; Hellgate; Thunderbirds. **1953** Blowing Wild; The Moonlighter; Hondo. **1954** Gypsy Colt; The Bob Mathias Story; Johnny Guitar. **1955** Mr. Roberts; A Man Alone; The Long, Gray Line. **1956** The Searchers; Dakota Incident; Pillars of the Sky. **1957** Halliday Brand; The Wings of Eagles. **1958** China Doll. **1959** Rio Bravo; Alias Jesse James.

BONDHILL, GERTRUDE (Gertrude Schafer)
Born: 1880. Died: Sept. 15, 1960, Chicago, Ill. Screen, stage and radio actress. Appeared in early silents made at Essanay Studios in Chicago.

BONIFACE, SYMONA
Born: 1894. Died: Sept. 2, 1950, Woodland Hills, Calif. Screen, stage actress, stage producer and playwright. Daughter of stage actor George C. Boniface and stage actress Nona Ferner. Married to actor Frank Pharr Sims.

Appeared in: **1932** Strictly Unreliable (short). **1934** Washee Ironee (short). **1936** Girls Dormitory. **1938** Ankles Away (short). **1940** A-Plumbing We Will Go (short); No Census, No Feeling (short). **1941** The following shorts: All the World's a Stooge; An Ache in Every Stake; In the Sweet Pie and Pie. **1942** Unexpected Riches (short). **1943** Spook Louder (short). **1944** Crash Goes the Hash (short). **1945** Micro Phonies (short). **1946** G. I. Wanna Go Home (short). **1947** Half-Wits Holiday (short). **1949** Who Done It (short); Vagabond Loafers (short). **1950** Pirates of High Seas (serial). **1951** The Pest Man Wins (short). **1955** Bedlam in Paradise (short). **1956** Scheming Schemers (short). **1958** Pies and Guys (short).

BONIFANT, CARMEN
Born: 1890, Mexico. Died: Aug. 1, 1957, Mexico City, Mexico. Screen actress.

BONILLAS, MYRNA
Born: 1890. Died: Nov. 13, 1959, Hollywood, Calif. (heart attack). Screen actress.

Appeared in: **1922** Shackles of Gold; A Stage Romance. **1923** The Custard Cup. **1927** The Claw; The Gingham Girl. **1930** Lummox; Asi es la Vida.

BONN, FRANK
Born: 1873. Died: Mar. 4, 1944, Los Angeles, Calif. Screen actor.

Appeared in: **1926** Old Ironsides.

BONN, WALTER
Born: 1889. Died: Sept. 8, 1953, Hollywood, Calif. Stage and screen actor.

Appeared in: **1938** International Crime; Cipher Bureau. **1948** All My Sons.

BONNARD, MARIO
Born: 1889, Italy. Died: Mar. 22, 1965, Rome, Italy (heart attack). Screen actor, film director and screenwriter. Entered films as actor and director in 1909.

BONNER, ISABEL
Born: 1908. Died: July 1, 1955, Los Angeles, Calif. (brain hemorrhage). Screen, stage, television and radio actress.

Appeared in: **1955** The Shrike.

BONNER, JOE
Born: 1882. Died: Apr. 13, 1959. Screen actor.

Appeared in: **1922** The Man Who Waited; Affinities. **1923** Slow as Lightning. **1924** Western Grit. **1927** Face Value; Is Your Daughter Safe?

BONUCCI, ALBERTO
Born: 1919, Italy. Died: Apr. 7, 1969, Rome, Italy (heart attack). Screen actor and film director.

Appeared in: **1954** Fugitive in Trieste. **1956** The Magnificent Seven (Japan). **1961** Neapolitan Carousel; Blood and Roses. **1963** Love and Larceny. **1966** The

Little Nuns. **1967** The Taming of the Shrew. Other Italian Films: The Tenor from Oklahoma; Walter and His Cousins.

BOOKER, HARRY
Born: 1850. Died: June 28, 1924, San Diego, Calif. Screen, vaudeville actor and film director. Played in vaudeville as part of "Canfield and Booker" team. Entered films with Mack Sennett in Keystone comedies.

Appeared in: **1915** The Great Vacuum Robbery; Her Painted Hero; A Game Old Knight. **1916** The Feathered Nest (aka Girl Guardian—reissued 1920 as Only a Farmer's Daughter); Her Marble Heart; The Judge; His Hereafter (aka Murray's Mix-Up); Maid Mad (aka The Fortune Teller); A Love Riot; Pills or Peril; Bombs. **1917** Maggie's First False Step; Her Fame and Shame; Her Torpedoed Love; She Needed a Doctor; His Uncle Dudley. **1921** Skirts. **1922** The Hottentot.

BOOT, GLADYS
Born: 1890. Died: Oct. 16, 1964, London, England. Screen, stage and television actress.

Appeared in: **1949** The Blue Lagoon. **1956** Murder Reported. **1958** Gypsy and the Gentleman; Harry Black and the Tiger; Virgin Island (US 1960).

BOOTH, ELMER (W. Elmer Booth)
Born: Dec. 9, 1882, Los Angeles, Calif. Died: June 16, 1915, Los Angeles, Calif. (auto accident). Screen actor.

Appeared in: **1912** Brutality; So Near, Yet So Far; The Narrow Road; Gold and Glitter; In the North Woods; An Unseen Enemy; The Musketeers of Pig Alley; An Interrupted Elopement. **1913** The Unwelcome Guest; Drink's Lure. **1914** Mrs. Black Is Back. **1915** Mr. Wallack's Wallet; A Chase by Moonlight; Mixed Values; Ethel's Deadly Alarm Clock; Gasoline Gus; Beppo the Barber; Two Daughters of Eve.

BOOTH, HELEN
Died: Feb. 5, 1971, England. Screen, stage and television actress.

Appeared in: **1967** The Family Way.

BOOTH, NESDON (Nesdon Foye Booth)
Born: Sept. 1, 1918, Baker, Ore. Died: Mar. 25, 1964, Hollywood, Calif. (heart attack). Screen, stage and television actor.

Appeared in: **1949** City Across the River (film debut). **1952** The Girl in White; Sally and Saint Anne. **1953** The Glass Wall; I Love Melvin; Executive Suite. **1954** Rogue Cop. **1955** I'll Cry Tomorrow; Pete Kelly's Blues; I Died a Thousand Times. **1956** He Laughed Last; The Price of Fear; These Wilder Years. **1957** The Shadow on the Window; Funny Face; Reform School Girl; Escape from Red Rock; Mister Cory; The Brothers Rico. **1958** Cattle Empire; Space Master X-7; Damn Yankees; Too Much, Too Soon; Sing, Boy, Sing. **1959** Rio Bravo; The Big Circus; The FBI Story; Yellowstone Kelly. **1960** Bells Are Ringing; Let No Man Write My Epitaph; The Rise and Fall of Legs Diamond. **1961** The Wackiest Ship in the Army; Claudelle Inglish; Gun Street; Ada; One-Eyed Jacks. **1962** Walk on the Wild Side; Jumbo. **1963** Critic's Choice. **1964** What a Way to Go! **1965** The Greatest Story Ever Told.

BORDAS, EMILIA F.
Born: 1874, Spain. Died: 1958, Madrid, Spain. Stage and screen actress.

BORDEAUX, JOE (aka JOE BORDEAU)
Born: 1894. Died: Sept. 10, 1950, Hollywood, Calif. Screen actor. Entered films with Keystone in 1913.

Appeared in: **1916** Fatty and Mabel Adrift; The Other Man; The Moonshiners; The Waiter's Ball; Bright Lights. **1929** Hurricane. **1930** The Man Hunter. **1932** High Speed. **1936** The Lucky Corner (short); On the Wrong Trek.

BORDEN, EDDIE
Born: 1888, Deer Lodge, Tenn. Died: July 1, 1955, Hollywood, Calif. Screen, stage and vaudeville actor. Entered films in 1921.

Appeared in: **1922** Back Home and Broke. **1925** Bad Boy (short). **1926** Hold Everything (short); Battling Butler. **1927** The Show Girl; One Chance in a Million. **1928** The Dove. **1930** The Rampant Age; Rough Romance. **1932** Breach of Promise. **1933** Jungle Bride. **1934** The Chases of Pimple Street (short). **1935** The Devil Is a Woman. **1936** Early to Bed; Conflict. **1938** Give Me a Sailor. **1939** The Day the Bookies Wept. **1940** A Chump at Oxford; Secrets of a Model. **1943** Unlucky Dog (short).

BORDEN, EUGENE
Born: Mar. 21, 1897, Paris, France. Died: July 21, 1972. Stage and screen actor.

Appeared in: **1917** Draft 258. **1921** The Barricade; The Porcelain Lamp. **1922** Forget Me Not. **1924** Revelation. **1925** Blue Blood. **1926** The Jade Cup. **1928** Gentlemen Prefer Blondes. **1929** Hold Your Man; Rampant Age; Rough Romance. **1930** The Woman Racket. **1937** I Met Him in Paris; Charlie Chan on Broadway; The Firefly; Thin Ice; Cafe Metropole. **1940** The Mark of Zorro. **1941** Charlie Chan in Rio; Scotland Yard. **1942** Dr. Renault's Secret. **1943**

Song of Bernadette; Mission to Moscow; Adventure in Iraq. **1944** Dark Waters; Our Hearts Were Young and Gay. **1945** The Caribbean Mystery. **1946** Do You Love Me?; So Dark the Night; The Thrill of Brazil; The Return of Monte Cristo. **1947** Cigarette Girl; Jewel of Brandenburg; The Bishop's Wife. **1948** Glamour Girl; Saigon. **1950** Under My Skin; All About Eve; Last of the Buccaneers. **1951** Silver Canyon; An American in Paris; On the Riviera. **1952** Happy Time. **1953** Saginaw Trail; A Blueprint for Murder. **1955** The Far Country; Pirates of Tripoli. **1956** The Best Things in Life Are Free. **1957** The Tarnished Angels. **1958** The Fly; Me and the Colonel; The Perfect Furlough. **1960** Can-Can.

BORDEN, OLIVE (Sybil Trinkle)

Born: July 14, 1907, Richmond, Va. Died: Oct. 1, 1947, Los Angeles, Calif. (stomach ailment). Screen actress. Entered films as a Sennett bathing beauty in 1922 and was one of the twelve Wampas Baby Stars of 1925.

Appeared in: **1925** Dressmaker from Paris; The Happy Warrior; The Overland Limited. **1926** Three Bad Men; Fig Leaves; Yellow Fingers; The Country Beyond; My Own Pal; The Yankee Senor. **1927** Monkey Talks; The Joy Girl; Come to My House; Pajamas; The Secret Studio. **1928** The Albany Night Boat; Sinners in Love; Gang War; Stool Pigeon; Virgin Lips. **1929** The Eternal Woman; Love in the Desert; Half Marriage; Dance Hall. **1930** Wedding Rings; The Social Lion; Hello Sister. **1933** Hotel Variety.

BORDONI, IRENE

Born: 1895, Ajaccio, Corsica. Died: Mar. 19, 1953, New York, N.Y. Screen, stage, radio and vaudeville actress.

Appeared in: **1929** Paris (film debut); The Show of Shows. **1936** A Vitaphone short. **1942** Louisiana Purchase (stage and film versions).

BORELL, LOUIS

Born: Oct. 6, 1906, Amsterdam, Holland. Died: Apr. 1973, Amsterdam, Holland. Screen, stage and television actor.

Appeared in: **1936** The Crosspatch; The Avenging Hand; House Broken. **1937** Head Over Heels in Love; Over the Moon. **1938** Queer Cargo. **1941** Pirates of the Seven Seas. **1942** London Blackout Murders. **1943** Paris After Dark. **1944** A Night of Adventure.

BORELLI, LYDA

Born: 1888, Genoa, Italy. Died: June 2, 1958, Rome, Italy. Stage and screen actress.

Appeared in: **1913** Ma l'Amore Mio Non Muore (My Love Never Dies); Memorie Dell 'Altro. **1914** La Donna Nuda. **1915** Il Bosco Dacr; Fior di Male; Rapsodia Satanica; Marcia Nuziale (Wedding March). **1916** La Falena; Malombra; Madame Tallian. **1917** Carnevalesca (Carnival); Il Dramma di una Notte; La Storia dei Tredici. Other Italian film: Vergine Folle (Foolish Virgin).

BORELLO, MARCO

Born: 1899. Died: Jan. 21, 1966, Santa Cruz, Calif. Screen actor and stuntman. Appeared in silents.

BOREO, EMIL

Born: 1885. Died: July 27, 1951, New York, N.Y. Screen, stage and vaudeville actor.

Appeared in: **1938** The Lady Vanishes. **1947** Carnegie Hall.

BORG, VEDA ANN

Born: Jan. 15, 1915, Boston or Roxbury, Mass. (?). Died: Aug. 16, 1973, Hollywood, Calif. Screen actress. Divorced from film director Andrew McLaglen.

Appeared in: **1936** Three Cheers for Love (film debut). **1937** Men in Exile; Marry the Girl; Public Wedding; Kid Galahad; The Singing Marine; San Quentin; Confession; It's Love I'm After; Submarine D-1; The Missing Witness; The Case of the Stuttering Bishop; Varsity Show. **1938** Alcatraz Island; She Loved a Fireman; Over the Wall. **1939** The Law Comes to Texas. **1940** Bitter Sweet; Cafe Hostess; Behind the News; A Miracle on Main Street; I Take This Oath; Dr. Christian Meets the Women; Laughing at Danger; Glamour for Sale; Melody Ranch; The Shadow (serial). **1941** Arkansas Judge; The Penalty; The Pittsburgh Kid; Honky Tonk; The Corsican Brothers; Down in San Diego; The Get-Away. **1942** Two Yanks in Trinidad; Duke of the Navy; I Married an Angel; About Face; She's In the Army; Lady In a Jam. **1943** Something to Shout About; Murder in Times Square; The Isle of Forgotten Sins; Revenge of the Zombies; The Girl from Monterey; The Unknown Guest; False Faces. **1944** Standing Room Only; The Big Noise; Irish Eyes Are Smiling; The Falcon in Hollywood; Smart Guy; Detective Kitty O'Day; Marked Trails; The Girl Who Dared. **1945** Rough, Tough and Ready (aka Men of the Deep); Don Juan Quilligan; Love, Honor and Goodbye; What a Blonde; Fog Island; Bring on the Girls; Scared Stiff; Nob Hill; Dangerous Intruder; Jungle Raiders (serial); Mildred Pierce. **1946** Avalanche; Life With Blondie; Accomplice; Wife Wanted; The Fabulous Suzanne; I Love My Husband, But! (short). **1947** Mother Wore Tights; Blonde Savage; Big Town; The Pilgrim Lady; The Bachelor and the Bobby-Soxer. **1948** Julia Misbehaves; Chicken Every Sunday. **1949**

One Last Fling; Forgotten Women; Mississippi Rhythm. **1950** The Kangaroo Kid; Rider From Tucson. **1952** Aaron Slick from Punkin Crick; Big Jim McLain; Hold That Line. **1953** Mister Scoutmaster; Three Sailors and a Girl; Hot News; A Perilous Journey. **1954** Bitter Creek. **1955** I'll Cry Tomorrow; You're Never Too Young; Guys and Dolls; Love Me or Leave Me. **1956** Frontier Gambler. **1958** The Naked Gun; The Fearmakers. **1959** Thunder in the Sun. **1960** The Alamo.

BORGATO, AGOSTINO

Born: 1871, Venice, Italy. Died: Mar. 14, 1939, Hollywood, Calif. (heart attack). Screen actor. Entered films in 1913.

Appeared in: **1925** The Street of Forgotten Men. **1926** The Love Thief. **1927** Magic Flame; Kiss in a Taxi; Helen of Troy; Hula; Fashions for Women; Horse Shoes. **1928** A Perfect Gentleman. **1929** Romance of the Rio Grande; She Goes to War; Hot for Paris. **1930** Behind the Make-Up; Redemption. **1931** The Maltese Falcon; Transgression. **1932** Bird of Paradise.

BORGSTROM, HILDA

Born: 1871, Sweden. Died: Jan. 2, 1953, Stockholm, Sweden. Stage and screen actress.

Appeared in: **1912** En Sommarsaga (film debut). **1939** Du Fria, Du Gamla (Thou Old, Thou Free); Familjen Andersson (The Anderson Family). **1948** Musik I Morker (Night Is My Future–US 1963).

BOROS, FERIKE

Born: 1880, Nagvarad, Hungary. Died: Jan. 16, 1951, Hollywood, Calif. Screen, stage actress and playwright.

Appeared in: **1930** Born Reckless; Little Caesar; Ladies Love Brutes. **1931** Bought; Gentlemen's Fate; Svengali. **1932** The World and the Flesh; Huddle. **1933** Humanity; Rafter Romance. **1934** Eight Girls in a Boat; The Fountain. **1935** Symphony of Living. **1937** Make Way for Tomorrow. **1939** Love Affair; Stronger than Desire; Bachelor Mother; Fifth Avenue Girl; Dust Be My Destiny; Rio; The Light That Failed. **1940** Argentine Nights; Three Cheers for the Irish; La Conga Nights; Girl from God's Country; Christmas in July. **1941** Sleepers West; Caught in the Draft; Private Nurse. **1942** Once upon a Honeymoon; The Pied Piper; The Talk of the Town. **1943** Margin for Error; Princess O'Rourke. **1944** The Doughgirls. **1945** This Love of Ours; A Tree Grows in Brooklyn. **1946** Specter of the Rose.

BORZAGE, DANIEL "DANNY"

Died: June 17, 1975, Los Angeles, Calif. Screen actor and musician. Brother of director-actor Frank Borzage (dec. 1962).

Appeared in: **1952** What Price Glory. **1955** Mister Roberts. **1957** The Wings of Eagles. **1958** The Last Hurrah. **1961** Two Rode Together. **1963** McLintock! **1964** Cheyenne Autumn.

BORZAGE, FRANK

Born: Apr. 23, 1893, Salt Lake City, Utah. Died: June 19, 1962, Hollywood, Calif. (cancer). Screen, stage actor and film director. Divorced from actress Rena Rogers (dec. 1966). Brother of actor Daniel Borzage (dec. 1975).

Appeared in: **1914** The Typhoon. **1915** His Mother's Portrait; The Hammer; In the Switch Tower; The Spark in the Embers; Her Alibi; The Girl of the Sea; A Friend in Need; Alias James—Chauffeur; Touring with Tillie; One to the Minute; Anita's Butterfly; Almost a Widow; Cupid Beats Father; Two Hearts and a Thief; The Papered Door; Settled Out of Court; Nobody's Home; The Pitch of Chance; Aloha Oe; The Cactus Blossom; The Clean-Up. **1916** That Gal of Burk's; Immediate Lee; Land O'Lizards; Mammy's Rose; The Forgotten Prayer; The Courtin' of Calliope Clew; That Gal of Burke's; Nugget Jim's Partner. **1917** A Mormon Maid; A School for Husbands; Fear Not. **1918** The Curse of Iku. **1922** Hair Trigger Casey (reissue of Immediate Lee–1916).

BOS, ANNIE

Born: 1887. Died: Aug. 3, 1975. Screen actress. One of the top stars of Dutch silent films.

BOSSICK, BERNARD B.

Born: 1918. Died: Nov. 10, 1975, Hollywood, Calif. (heart attack). Screen actor, film producer, director and television writer.

Appeared in: **1970** The Golden Box.

BOSTON, NELROY BUCK

Born: 1911. Died: Feb. 28, 1962, Van Nuys, Calif. (auto accident). Stage and screen actor. Entered films approx. 1940.

BOSWELL, MARTHA

Born: 1905. Died: July 2, 1958, Peekskill, N.Y. Screen, stage, radio actress and singer. Was one of the three singing Boswell Sisters including Connee (dec. 1976) and Helretia Boswell.

Appeared in: **1932** The Big Broadcast; Universal shorts; a Paramount short. **1934** Radio Star. **1937** A Paramount short.

BOSWORTH, HOBART

Born: Aug. 11, 1876, Marietta, Ohio. Died: Dec. 30, 1943, Glendale, Calif. (pneumonia). Screen, stage actor, film producer, director and screenwriter. Formed Bosworth Film Company approx. 1913.

Appeared in: 1908 The Roman. 1909 The Sultan's Power. 1912 The Count of Monte Cristo. 1913 Sea Wolf. 1914 The Country Mouse; Odessy of the North. 1916 Joan the Woman; Oliver Twist. 1917 The Little American. 1919 The Border Legion. 1920 Behind the Door. 1921 The Foolish Matrons; The Brute Master; Below the Surface; His Own Law; A Thousand to One; Blind Hearts; The Cup of Life. 1922 The Sea Lion; White Hands; The Stranger's Banquet. 1923 Man Alone; The Common Law; The Eternal Three; Little Church Around the Corner; In the Place of the King; Vanity Fair; The Man Life Passed By; Rupert of Hentzau; Souls for Sale. 1924 Captain January; Bread; The Silent Watcher; Name the Man; Hearts of Oak; Nellie, the Beautiful Cloak Model; Sundown; Through the Dark; The Woman on the Jury. 1925 The Big Parade; Zander the Great; My Son; Chickie; The Half-Way Girl; Winds of Chance; The Golden Strain; If I Marry Again. 1926 Steel Preferred; The Nervous Wreck; Spangles; The Far Cry. 1927 The Blood Ship; Annie Laurie; My Best Girl; Three Hours. 1928 Chinese Parrott; Annapolis; Hangman's House; After the Storm; Freckles; The Sawdust Paradise; The Smart Set; A Man of Peach (short). 1929 The Show of Shows; Hurricane; King of the Mountain; A Woman of Affairs; Eternal Love; General Crack. 1930 Just Imagine; The Office Wife; Sit Tight; The Third Alarm; DuBarry, Woman of Passion; The Devil's Holiday; Mammy; Abraham Lincoln; A Man of Peace. 1931 Dirigible; Shipmates; This Modern Age; Fanny Foley Herself; Bad Timber. 1932 Carnival Boat; No Greater Love; Phantom Express; The Miracle Man; County Fair. 1933 Divine Love; Last of the Mohicans; Lady for a Day. 1934 Music in the Air; Whom the Gods Destroy. 1935 The Crusades; Keeper of the Bees; Steamboat Round the Bend. 1937 Portia on Trial. 1938 The Secret of Treasure Island (serial); Wolves of the Sea. 1941 One Foot in Heaven; Law of the Tropics. 1942 Sin Town; I Was Framed; Bullet Scars.

BOTELER, WADE

Born: 1891, Santa Ana, Calif. Died: May 7, 1943, Hollywood, Calif. (heart attack). Screen, stage actor and screenwriter.

Appeared in: 1919 Twenty-Three and a Half Hours' Leave; An Old Fashioned Boy. 1921 Blind Hearts; One Man in a Million; Stranger than Fiction; Ducks and Drakes; Fifty Candles; The Home Stretch. 1922 At the Sign of the Jack O'Lantern; Second Hand Rose; Ridin' Wild; Afraid to Fight; The Lying Truth; The Woman's Side; Deserted at the Altar; While Satan Sleeps; Through a Glass Window; The Unfoldment; Don't Shoot; The Great Night. 1923 Going Up; A Man of Action; The Ghost Patrol; Around the World in 18 Days (serial); Alias the Night Wind (serial). 1924 Through the Dark; The Whipping Boss; Never Say Die; The Phantom Horseman. 1925 Capital Punishment; Introduce Me; Seven Keys to Baldpate; Marriage in Transit; Winds of Chance; Havoc; Jimmie's Millions; The Last Edition. 1926 Hold That Lion; That's My Baby. 1927 Let It Rain; High School Hero; Soft Cushions. 1928 Let 'Er Go Gallagher; Sporting Goods; Warming Up; Just Married; A Woman Against the World; The Toilers; The Baby Cyclone; Top Sergeant Mulligan; The Crash. 1929 Close Harmony; The New Halfback (short); Big News; The Leatherneck; The Godless Girl. 1930 Navy Blues; The Devil's Holiday; Soldiers and Women; Way of All Men; College Lovers; Top Speed; Derelict. 1931 Painted Desert; Beyond Victory; Fainting Lover (short); Kick In; Silence; Twenty-Four Hours; Bad Company; Penrod and Sam; The Way Back Home; Local Boy Makes Good. 1932 For the Love of Ludwig (short); Night Mayor; Painted Woman; Speed Madness; Manhattan Tower; Central Park; Death Kiss; The Man Who Played God. 1933 Duck Soup; End of the Trail; Come On Danger; She Done Him Wrong; Speed Demon; Humanity; This Day and Age; College Humor; Unknown Valley; King for a Night. 1934 Melody in Spring; Charlie Chan's Courage; A Man's Game; Among the Missing; Belle of the Nineties; The Richest Girl in the World; The Crosby Case; Operator 13; Fugitive Lady. 1935 Love in Bloom; Goin' to Town; The Leather Necker (short); Baby Face Harrington; O'Shaughnessey's Boy; Black Fury; The Goose and the Gander; Headline Woman; The Three Musketeers; Cheers of the Crowd; Freckles; Melody Trail; Streamline Express. 1936 Whipsaw; Riff Raff; Exclusive Story; The Return of Jimmy Valentine; The President's Mystery; The Country Gentleman; Here Comes Trouble; Charlie Chan at the Circus; Human Cargo; The Bride Walks Out; Alibi for Murder; Poppy. 1937 The Great Hospital Mystery; The Frame-Up; A Fight to the Finish; The Mandarin Mystery; You Only Live Once; Hold 'Em Navy; 52nd Street; Dead Yesterday; Find the Witness; Jim Hanvey—Detective; Dangerous Holiday; Youth on Parole; It Can't Last Forever; Borrowing Trouble. 1938 Passport Husband; The Marines Are Here; Little Miss Roughneck; In Old Chicago; Peck's Bad Boy with the Circus; Spawn of the North; Valley of the Giants; Billy the Kid Returns. 1939 Dog Daze (short); Southward Ho!; Sabotage; The Man from Down Under; Days of Jesse James; Everything's on Ice; Missing Daughters; The Mysterious Miss X; Thunder Afloat; Ambush; Chicken Wagon Family. 1940 Double Alibi; Torrid Zone; Gaucho Serenade; Three Faces West; Castle on the Hudson; Young Buffalo Bill; Hot Steel; The Leather Pushers; The Howards of Virginia; Under Texas Skies; Till We Meet Again; My Little Chickadee; Three Cheers for the Irish. 1941 Where Did You Get That Girl?; A-Hunting We Will Go; Shanghai Alibi; It Started with Eve; Kathleen; The

Singing Hill; The Kid from Kansas; The Body Disappears. 1942 Blue, White and Perfect; Bombay Clipper; Ride 'Em Cowboy; I Was Framed; Escape from Crime; Moonlight in Havana; Mississippi Gambler; Gentleman Jim. 1943 It Ain't Hay; Hi, Buddy; The Good Fellows; Find the Blackmailer; Hit the Ice; Eyes of the Underworld. 1944 The Last Ride.

BOTHWELL, JOHN F.

Born: 1921. Died: Mar. 1967, Long Branch, N.J. Screen actor. Known as "Freckles" in "Our Gang" comedies.

BOTKIN, PERRY, SR.

Born: 1907. Died: Oct. 14, 1973, Van Nuys, Calif. Guitarist, songwriter and screen actor.

Appeared in: 1941 Birth of the Blues.

BOTTOMLEY, ROLAND

Born: Sept. 23, 1880, Liverpool, England. Died: Jan. 5, 1947, New York, N.Y. Stage and screen actor.

Appeared in: 1916 The Tricksters; The Grip of Evil (serial). 1917 The Neglected Wife (series). 1921 The Charming Deceiver; The Devil; A Man's Home. 1923 Does It Pay?; Modern Marriage. 1924 The Dawn of a Tomorrow. 1925 Enticement; Raffles, the Amateur Cracksman.

BOUCHER, VICTOR

Born: France. Died: Feb. 1942, France. Stage and screen actor.

Appeared in: 1931 La Douceur D'Aimer. 1942 Nine Bachelors.

BOUCICAULT, DION G.

Born: 1859, England (?). Died: June 25, 1929, Hurley, Berkshire, England. Screen, stage actor, stage director and playwright. Son of actor-playwright Dion Boucicault (dec. 1890). Brother of actress Nina Boucicault (dec. 1950). Father of screenwriter Dion Boucicault. Married to actress Irene Vanbrugh (dec. 1949).

Appeared in: 1917 Masks and Faces.

BOUCICAULT, NINA

Born: 1867, England. Died: Aug. 4, 1950, Ealing, England. Stage and screen actress. Daughter of stage actor Dion Boucicault (dec. 1890) and sister of actor Dion G. Boucicault (dec. 1929).

Appeared in: 1923 Daddy-the-Next-Best-Thing. 1924 Miriam Rozella. 1937 Juggernaut.

BOUCOT, LOUIS

Born: 1889. Died: Mar. 30, 1949, Paris, France. Screen and stage actor.

BOULTON, MATTHEW

Born: Jan. 20, 1893, Lincoln, England. Died: Feb. 12, 1962. Screen, stage actor and screenwriter.

Appeared in: 1927 His Rest Day. 1930 The Man From Chicago (US 1931); Bed and Breakfast. 1931 Potiphar's Wife (aka Her Strange Desire–US 1932); Third Time Lucky; Keepers of Youth; Creeping Shadows (aka The Limping Man–US 1932); The Flying Fool; The Ghost Train. 1936 Sabotage (aka The Woman Alone–US). 1937 Night Must Fall; The Thirteenth Chair; The Firefly. 1938 Bulldog Drummond's Peril; Lord Jeff; Bulldog Drummond in Africa. 1940 Adventure in Diamonds; Phantom Raiders; Mystery Sea Raider. 1941 Rage in Heaven; They Met in Bombay. 1942 Counter-Espionage; The Undying Monster. 1944 Secrets of Scotland Yard; The Man in Half Moon Street; Nothing But Trouble. 1945 Molly and Me; The Brighton Strangler; The Woman in Green; Love Letters. 1947 Stallion Road; Bulldog Drummond Strikes Back. 1948 Tarzan and the Mermaids; The Woman in White; Enchantment. 1949 The Secret Garden; Barbary Pirate. 1952 Last Train From Bombay.

BOURKE, FAN

Born: 1886, Brooklyn, N.Y. Died: Mar. 9, 1959, Norwalk, Conn. Screen, stage, vaudeville actress and screenwriter. Entered films in 1915.

Appeared in: 1930 Lummox.

BOURNE, WILLIAM PAYNE

Born: 1936. Died: Oct. 8, 1972, Hollywood, Calif. (suicide—gun). Screen actor and screenwriter.

BOURVIL (Andre Raimbourg)

Born: 1913, Normandy, France. Died: Sept. 23, 1970, Paris, France. Screen, stage and radio actor.

Appeared in: 1945 La Ferme du Pendu. 1946 Pas Si Bete. 1947 Blanc Comme Neige. 1948 Le Coeur Sur la Maine. 1949 Miguette et Sa Mere. 1950 Le Rosier de Madame Husson. 1951 Garou-Garou au Passe-Murail-le; Seul dans Paris; Miquette; Mr. Peek-A-Boo. 1952 The Price. 1953 Les Trois Mousquetaires (The Three Musketeers–US 1954). 1954 Le Cadet Rousselle; Poisson d'Avril. 1955 Les Hussards. 1956 La Traversee de Paris (The Crossing of Paris–aka

Four Bags Full–US 1957). **1957** Le Chanteur de Mexico. **1959** La Jumet Verte (The Green Mare–US 1961); The Mirror Has Two Faces. **1960** Crazy for Love. **1962** Tout l'Or du Monde; The Longest Day. **1963** Les Culottes Rouges (The Red Pants); Les Bonnes Causes (The Good Causes); Heaven Sent. **1964** La Cuisine au Beurre (Cooking with Butter); Don't Tempt the Devil. **1965** Les Grandes Gueles (The Wild Guys–US 1969); The Secret Agents; Thank Heaven for Small Favors; My Wife's Husband. **1966** La Grande Vadrouille (The Big Spree); The Dirty Game; The Sucker. **1967** Don't Look Now (US 1969). **1968** Le Verveau (The Brain–US 1969). **1969** Monte Carlo or Bust; L'Albero di Natale (The Christmas Tree); Those Daring Young Men in Their Jaunty Jalopies. Other French films: The Atlantic Wall; Le Corniaud (The Dumbbell).

BOW, CLARA

Born: Aug. 25, 1905, Brooklyn, N.Y. Died: Sept. 27, 1965, Los Angeles, Calif. (heart attack). Screen actress. Married to Rex Bell, former actor and Lt. Gov. of Nevada (dec. 1962). She was known as the "It" Girl.

Appeared in: **1922** Beyond the Rainbow. **1923** Enemies of Women; Down to the Sea in Ships; The Daring Years; Maytime. **1924** Black Oxen; Black Lightning; Grit; Daughters of Pleasure; Poisoned Paradise; Empty Hearts; This Woman; Wine. **1925** Helen's Babies; Free to Love; Keeper of the Bees; The Plastic Age; Kiss Me Again; The Scarlet West; Capital Punishment; The Primrose Path; Eve's Lover; The Adventurous Sex; The Best Bad Man; Lawful Cheaters; My Lady's Lips; Parisian Love. **1926** The Ancient Mariner; Dancing Mothers; Kid Boots; Fascinating Youth; My Lady of Whims; Mantrap; Two Can Play; The Runaway; The Shadow of the Law. **1927** Hula; Rough House Rosie; Get Your Man; Children of Divorce; It; Wings. **1928** Red Hair; The Fleet's In; Three Week Ends; Ladies of the Mob. **1929** Dangerous Curves; The Saturday Night Kid; The Wild Party. **1930** Love among the Millionaires; Paramount on Parade; True to the Navy; Her Wedding Night. **1931** Kick In; No Limit. **1932** Call Her Savage. **1933** Hoopla.

BOWERS, JOHN

Born: Dec. 25, 1899, Garrett, Ind. Died: Nov. 17, 1936, Santa Monica, Calif. (drowned). Stage and screen actor. Entered films in 1916. Divorced from actress Marguerite de la Motte (dec. 1950).

Appeared in: **1916** Hulda from Holland; Madame X. **1919** Sis Hopkins; Through the Wrong Door; Strictly Confidential. **1921** Roads of Destiny; The Silent Call; The Sky Pilot; The Ace of Hearts; Bits of Life; Godless Men; The Night Rose; An Unwilling Hero; The Poverty of Riches. **1922** Quincy Adams Sawyer; Affinities; South of Suva; The Bonded Woman; The Golden Gift. **1923** Lorna Doone; The Woman of Bronze; Desire; The Barefoot Boy; What a Wife Learned; Crinoline and Romance; The Destroying Angel; Divorce; Richard, the Lion-Hearted. **1924** When a Man's a Man; Code of the Wilderness; The White Sin; Those Who Dare; Empty Hearts; So Big. **1925** Confessions of a Queen; Chickie; Flattery; Daughters Who Pay; Off the Highway; The People vs. Nancy Preston. **1926** Pals in Paradise; The Danger Girl; Whispering Smith; Hearts and Fists; Rocking Moon; Laddie. **1927** The Dice Woman; For Ladies Only; Ragtime; The Heart of the Yukon; Heroes in Blue; The Opening Night; Three Hours; Jewels of Desire. **1929** Skin Deep; Say It with Songs. **1931** Mounted Fury.

BOWERS, LYLE

Born: 1896. Died: Mar. 8, 1943, Hollywood, Calif. Screen actor. Entered films approx. 1923.

BOWES, MAJOR EDWARD

Born: 1874, San Francisco, Calif. Died: June 13, 1946, Rumson, N.J. Screen, radio actor and composer. Married to actress Margaret Illington (dec. 1934). Began radio career in 1925 and originated Major Bowes Amateur Radio Hour in 1934.

Appeared in: **1936** Amateur Parade (short); Amateur Theatre of the Air (short). Other shorts he appeared in are as follows: Musical Varieties; Variety Review; Radio Revels; Stars of Tomorrow; Harmony Broadcast and Melody Maker.

BOWMAN, LAURA

Born: 1881. Died: Mar. 29, 1957. Screen actress.

Appeared in: **1940** Son of Ingagi.

BOWMAN, LEWIS EDWARD

Born: 1886. Died: 1961. Screen actor and stuntman. Appeared in silents.

BOWMAN, PALMER

Born: 1883. Died: Sept. 25, 1933, Chicago, Ill. (heart disease). Screen, stage, vaudeville actor, film director, and screenwriter. Appeared in early Selig and Essanay Company productions.

BOYCE, JACK

Born: 1885. Died: Dec. 13, 1923, New York, N.Y. Screen and stage actor.

BOYD, BLANCHE "DEEDEE"

Born: 1889. Died: Apr. 14, 1959, Laguna Beach, Calif. (heart attack). Stage and screen actress.

BOYD, WILLIAM

Born: June 5, 1895, Hedrysburg, Ohio. Died: Sept. 12, 1972, South Laguna, Calif. (combination of Parkinson's disease and congestive heart failure). Screen and television actor. Married to actress Grace Bradley. Divorced from actresses Ruth Miller, Elinor Fair and Dorothy Sebastian (dec. 1957). Star of "Hopalong Cassidy" film and television series. Entered films in 1915.

Appeared in: **1918** Old Wives for New. **1920** Why Change Your Wife? **1921** Brewster's Millions; Moonlight and Honeysuckle; A Wise Fool; Exit the Vamp. **1922** Bobbed Hair; Nice People; On the High Seas; Manslaughter; The Young Rajah. **1923** Enemies of Children; The Temple of Venus; Michael O'Halloran; Hollywood. **1924** Tarnish; Changing Husbands; Triumph. **1925** Forty Winks; The Road to Yesterday; The Midshipman; Golden Bed. **1926** The Last Frontier; Her Man O'War; The Volga Boatman; Steel Preferred; Eve's Leaves. **1927** King of Kings; Wolves of the Air; Two Arabian Knights; Dress Parade; Jim the Conqueror; Yankee Clipper. **1928** The Night Flyer; Power; The Cop; Skyscraper. **1929** High Voltage; Lady of the Pavements; The Flying Fool; The Leatherneck; Wolf Song. **1930** Those Who Dance; His First Command; Officer O'Brien; The Frame (short). **1931** Suicide Fleet; Beyond Victory; Gang Buster; Big Gambler. **1932** The Wiser Sex; Carnival Boat; Painted Woman; Sky Devils; Madison Square Garden. **1933** Men of America; Midnight Warning; Lucky Devils; Emergency Call; The Great Decision. **1934** Cheaters; Flaming Gold. **1935** Hopalong Cassidy (aka Hopalong Cassidy Enters); The Eagle's Brood; Bar 20 Rides Again; Racing Luck; Port of Lost Dreams. **1936** Call of the Prairie; Three on the Trail; Heart of the West; Hopalong Cassidy Returns; Trail Dust; The Last Frontier; Federal Agent; Burning Gold; Go Get 'Em Haines. **1937** Borderland; Borrowed Trouble; North of the Rio Grande; Rustler's Valley; Hopalong Rides Again; Texas Trail; Partners of the Plains; Hills of Old Wyoming; Men Have to Fight. **1938** Cassidy of Bar 20; Heart of Arizona; Bar 20 Justice; Pride of the West; In Old Mexico; The Sunset Trail; Deputy Sheriff; The Frontiersman. **1939** Range War; Law of the Pampas; Silver on the Sage; Renegade Trail. **1940** Santa Fe Marshall; The Showdown; Hidden Gold; Stagecoach War; Three Men from Texas; War Along the Stage Trail. **1941** Doomed Caravan; In Old Colorado; Border Vigilantes; Pirates on Horseback; Wide Open Town; Twilight on the Trail; Riders of the Timberline; Stick to Your Guns; Outlaws of the Desert (aka Arabian Desert Outlaws); Secrets of the Wasteland. **1942** Undercover Man. **1943** Border Patrol; The Leather Burners; Lost Canyon; Hoppy Serves a Writ; Colt Comrades; Bar 20; False Colors; Riders of the Deadline. **1944** Forty Thieves; Mystery Man; Texas Masquerade; Lumberjack; Frontier Marshal in Prairie Pals. **1946** The Devil's Playground; Fool's Gold; The Unexpected Guest. **1947** Dangerous Venture; Hoppy's Holiday; The Marauders. **1948** Silent Conflict; Sinister Journey; The Dead Don't Dream; Borrowed Trouble; False Paradise; Strange Gamble. **1952** The Greatest Show on Earth.

BOYD, WILLIAM "STAGE"

Born: 1890. Died: Mar. 20, 1935, Hollywood, Calif. (liver ailment). Do not confuse with William "Hopalong Cassidy" Boyd (dec. 1972). Screen, stage actor and circus rider. Divorced from actress Clara Joel.

Appeared in: **1930** The Locked Door; The Spoilers; Derelict. **1931** Gun Smoke; City Streets; The Road to Reno. **1932** The False Madonna; State's Attorney. **1933** The House on 56th Street; Oliver Twist; The Chief; Laughing at Life. **1934** Transatlantic Merry-Go-Round. **1935** The Lost City (serial).

BOYNE, SUNNY

Born: 1883, Boston, Mass. Died: Aug. 27, 1966, Van Nuys, Calif. Screen actress and dancer.

Appeared in: **1941** All That Money Can Buy. **1950** Born to be Bad. **1952** The Devil and Daniel Webster (reissue of All That Money Can Buy–1941). **1958** King Creole.

BOYNTON, CHARLES "TED"

Born: 1921. Died: Sept. 19, 1968. Screen and television actor.

BOZO, LITTLE. *See* LITTLE BOZO

BOZYK, MAX (aka MAX BOZHYK)

Born: 1899. Died: Apr. 5, 1970, Town Hall, N.Y. (heart attack). Yiddish stage and screen actor. Married to actress Reizel Bozyk with whom he appeared in an act billed as "Max and Reizel Bozyk."

Appeared in: **1937** Yiddle With His Fiddle; Der Purimspieler. **1938** The Dybbuk; Tkies Khal (The Vow); Mamele (Little Mothers). **1939** A Brivele der Mamen (A Letter to Mother). **1950** God, Man and Devil; Catskill Honeymoon.

BRABIN, CHARLES J.

Born: Apr. 17, 1882, Liverpool, England. Died: Nov. 4, 1957, Santa Monica, Calif. (heart attack). Screen actor, film director and screenwriter. Married to actress Theda Bara (dec. 1955). Entered films with Edison in 1908 as an actor.

BRACEY, CLARA T. (aka CLARA BRACY)

Born: 1847. Died: Feb. 22, 1941, Los Angeles, Calif. Screen, stage actress and stage producer. Married to concert tenor Henry Bracey (dec. 1917). Mother of actor Sidney Bracey (dec. 1942). Made early films with Kinemacolor and later Biograph.

Appeared in: **1909** Eloping with Auntie; The Awakening. **1910** Three Sisters; A Decree of Destiny. **1924** Her Night of Romance.

BRACEY, SIDNEY (aka SIDNEY BRACY)

Born: 1877, Melbourne, Australia. Died: Aug. 5, 1942, Hollywood, Calif. Stage and screen actor. Son of actress Clara T. Bracey (dec. 1941) and concert tenor Henry Bracey (dec. 1917). Entered films in 1910.

Appeared in: **1914** Zudora (The Twenty Million Dollar Mystery—serial). **1920** The Invisible Ray (serial). **1921** An Amateur Devil; The Outside Woman; Passion Fruit; Crazy to Marry; The March Hare; Morals. **1922** Manslaughter; The Dictator; The Radio King (serial); Is Matrimony a Failure?; Midnight; One Wonderful Night. **1923** Merry-Go-Round; Nobody's Bride; The Wild Party; The Social Buccaneer (serial); Ruggles of Red Gap. **1924** Being Respectable; By Divine Right; Her Night of Romance; So This Is Marriage?; Why Men Leave Home. **1925** Her Market Value; The Merry Widow; Wandering Footsteps; A Slave of Fashion. **1926** A Man Four-Square; The Mystery Club; The Black Bird; My Official Wife; You Never Know Women. **1927** Birds of Prey; Painting the Town; The Thirteenth Juror; The Woman on Trial. **1928** Show People; Haunted House; The Cameraman; Queen Kelly; The Wedding March; Win That Girl; Home James; Man-Made Women. **1929** His Captive Woman; Sioux Blood; The Bishop Murder Case. **1930** Second Floor Mystery; Anybody's Woman; Outside the Law; Free Love; Monte Carlo; Redemption. **1931** What a Bozo (short); Thundering Tenors (short); The Avenger; Parlor, Bedroom and Bath; Lion and the Lamb; A Dangerous Affair; Subway Express; Shanghaied Love; The Deceiver. **1932** The Monster Walks; The Greeks Had a Word for Them; Tangled Destinies; No More Orchids; Little Orphan Annie. **1933** The Intruder; Corruption; Broken Dreams. **1934** The Poor Rich; The Ninth Guest; I've Been Around; Anna Karenina. **1936** Magnificent Obsession; Second Childhood (short); Sutter's Gold; Isle of Fury; Preview Murder Mystery. **1937** Three Smart Boys (short). **1938** Mr. Chump; Dawn Patrol; The Baroness and the Butler; Merrily We Live; My Bill. **1939** On Trial; Smashing the Money Ring; Everybody's Hobby; Sweepstakes Winner. **1940** My Love Came Back; Devil's Island; Tugboat Annie Sails Again. **1941** Bullets for O'Hara; Shadows on the Stairs. **1942** The Gay Sisters.

BRADBURY, JAMES, SR.

Born: Oct. 12, 1857, Old Town, Me. Died: Oct. 12, 1940, Clifton, Staten Island, N.Y. Stage and screen actor. Father of actor James Bradbury, Jr.

Appeared in: **1924** Manhattan. **1926** Fascinating Youth; The High Flyer. **1927** The Blood Ship; The Fair Co-Ed; Babe Comes Home; The Circus Ace; Romantic Rogue; The Racing Fool. **1928** Skinner's Big Idea; Blockade; Waterfront; Scarlet Seas; Hot Heels; The Leopard Lady; Walking Back; Midnight Madness. **1929** Tide of the Empire; Woman from Hell. **1930** The Matrimonial Bed; Tol'able David; Abraham Lincoln. **1934** The Silver Streak.

BRADFORD, CHARLES AVERY

Born: 1873. Died: July 23, 1926, Hollywood, Calif. (possible suicide). Screen actor.

BRADFORD, LANE

Born: 1923. Died: June 7, 1973, Honolulu, Hawaii (cerebral hemorrhage). Screen and television actor. Son of actor John Merton (dec. 1959) and brother of actor Robert La Varre.

Appeared in: **1946** Silver Range; Ghost Town Renegades; Pioneer Justice. **1947** Prairie Raiders; Riders of the Lone Star; Black Hills; Shadow Valley; Swing the Western Way; Return of the Lash. **1948** The Hawk of Powder River; Black Hills; Tornado Ridge; Check Your Guns; Frontier Agent; Sundown at Santa Fe. **1949** The Far Frontier; The Wyoming Bandit; South of Rio; San Antone Ambush; Prince of the Plains; Law of the Golden West; Bandit King of Texas; The Fighting Redhead; Death Valley Gunfighter. **1950** Bells of Coronado; Frisco Tornado; Hills of Oklahoma; The Missourians; The Old Frontier; Cowboy and the Prizefighter; Code of the Silver Sage. **1951** Stage from Blue River; Whistling Hills; Texas Lawmen; The Lady from Texas; Lawless Cowboys; Don Daredevil Rides Again. **1952** African Treasure; Dead Man's Trail; Desperados' Outpost; Fort Osage; Texas City; Waco; Gunman; Kansas Territory; The Man from the Black Hills; Night Raiders; The Raiders; Rose of Cimarron; Zombies of the Stratosphere (serial); Target; Desert Passage. **1953** Savage Frontier; Son of Belle Starr. **1954** Drums Across the River; The Forty-Niners; Ride Clear of Diablo; The Golden Idol. **1956** Showdown at Abilene. **1957** Apache Warrior; The Phantom Stagecoach. **1958** The Lone Ranger and the Lost City of Gold; Satan's Satellites; Toughest Gun in Tombstone. **1963** The Gun Hawk. **1964** A Distant Trumpet. **1965** The Slender Thread. **1968** Journey to Shiloh.

BRADFORD, MARSHALL

Born: 1896. Died: Jan. 11, 1971, Hollywood, Calif. (heart attack). Screen, stage and television actor.

Appeared in: **1949** Western Renegades. **1950** Texas Dynamo. **1951** Ghost Chasers; Night Raiders of Montana; Colorado Ambush. **1952** Hellgate. **1954** Yukon Vengeance. **1957** I Was a Teenage Frankenstein. **1958** Teenage Caveman. **1962** Terror at Black Falls.

BRADLEY, AMANDA

Died: Dec. 13, 1916, New York, N.Y. (auto accident). Screen actress.

BRADLEY, BENJAMIN R.

Born: 1898. Died: Sept. 29, 1950, St. Louis, Mo. (heart disease and complications). Screen actor and magician. Appeared in silents.

BRADLEY, HARRY C.

Born: Apr. 15, 1869, San Francisco, Calif. Died: Oct. 18, 1947, Hollywood, Calif. (heart attack). Stage and screen actor.

Appeared in: **1933** Frozen Assets (short); I Love That Man; This Day and Age; I Have Lived. **1934** It Happened One Night; Heat Lightning; The Merry Frinks; The Last Gentleman; City Limits; White Lies. **1935** Love in Bloom; Private Worlds; Way Down East. **1936** Cain and Mabel; It Had to Happen; Three of a Kind; Gold Diggers of 1937. **1937** New Faces of 1937; Trouble at Midnight. **1938** Women Are Like That; The Little Adventures. **1939** When Tomorrow Comes. **1940** Slightly Tempted. **1941** The Big Store. **1942** Busses Roar; Hi, Neighbor; Get Hep to Love; Mrs. Wiggs of the Cabbage Patch. **1944** Henry Aldrich's Little Secret; Make Your Own Bed; Henry Aldrich Plays Cupid.

BRADLEY, LOVYSS

Born: 1906. Died: June 21, 1969, Woodland Hills, Calif. (cancer). Screen and television actress.

Appreared in: **1950** Outrage. **1951** Golden Girl; The Blue Veil. **1968** Up Tight.

BRADLEY, TRUMAN

Born: 1905. Died: July 28, 1974, Los Angeles, Calif. Screen, television and radio actor.

Appeared in: **1938** Vacation From Love; Spring Madness; Young Doctor Kildare. **1939** The Hardys Ride High; On Borrowed Time; Money to Loan (short); Help Wanted (short). **1940** Millionaires in Prison; Yesterday's Heroes; Northwest Passage; A Night at Earl Carroll's. **1941** Murder Among Friends; Dead Men Tell; Keep 'Em Flying; Charlie Chan in Rio; Last of the Duanes; Mob Town; Burma Convoy. **1942** Treat 'Em Rough; Night Before the Divorce; Lone Star Ranger; Bombay Clipper. **1945** The Horn Blows at Midnight. **1947** I Wonder Who's Kissing Her Now.

BRADSHAW, EUNICE

Born: 1893. Died: 1973. Screen actress. Appeared in silents.

BRADSHAW, LIONEL M.

Born: May 10, 1892, Lima, Ohio. Died: Dec. 17, 1918, Los Angeles, Calif. (Spanish influenza). Stage and screen actor.

Appeared in: **1915** The Black Box; Carmen. **1916** Peg O' the Ring (series); Lady Raffles Returns.

BRADY, ALICE

Born: Nov. 2, 1892, New York, N.Y. Died: Oct. 28, 1939, New York, N.Y. (cancer). Stage and screen actress. Daughter of stage producer William A. Brady and dancer Rose Marie Rene. Divorced from actor James Lyon Crane. Won 1938 Academy Award for Best Supporting Actress for In Old Chicago.

Appeared in: **1914** As Ye Sow. **1915** The Boss; The Cup of Chance; The Lure of Woman. **1916** La Boheme; Bought and Paid For; The Gilded Cage; The Rack; The Ballet Girl; The Woman in 47; Then I'll Come Back to You; Tangled Fates; Miss Petticoats. **1917** Betsy Ross; A Woman Alone; A Hungry Heart; The Dancer's Peril; Darkest Russia; Maternity; The Divorce Game; A Self-Made Widow; A Maid of Belgium. **1918** Woman and Wife; Her Silent Sacrifice; The Knife; The Spurs of Sybil; At the Mercy of Men; The Trap; The Whirlpool; The Death Dance; The Ordeal of Rosetta; The Better Half; In the Hollow of Her Hand; Her Great Chance. **1919** The Indestructible Wife; The World to Live In; Marie, Ltd.; The Redhead; His Bridal Night. **1920** Fear Market; The New York Idea; Sinners; A Dark Lantern. **1921** Out of the Chorus; Little Italy; The Land of Hope; The Dawn of the East; Hush Money. **1922** Anna Ascends; Missing Millions. **1923** The Leopardess; The Snow Bride. **1933** When Ladies Meet; Beauty for Sale; Broadway to Hollywood; Stage Mother; Should Ladies Behave? **1934** Miss Fane's Baby is Stolen; The Gay Divorcee; False Faces. **1935** Gold Diggers of 1935; Let 'Em Have It; Lady Tubbs; Metropolitan. **1936** The Harvester; My Man Godfrey; Go West, Young Man; Mind Your Own Business. **1937** Three Smart Girls; One Hundred Men and a Girl; Mama Steps Out; Call It a Day; Mr. Dodd Takes the Air; Merry-Go-Round of

1938. **1938** In Old Chicago; Joy of Living; Goodbye Broadway. **1939** Zenobia; Young Mr. Lincoln.

BRADY, EDWARD J.
Born: 1888, New York, N.Y. Died: Mar. 31, 1942, Hollywood, Calif. (heart attack). Screen, stage and vaudeville actor.

Appeared in: **1915** Who Pays?; Neal of the Navy (serial). **1919** The Great Radium Mystery (serial). **1921** The Rough Diamond; The Silent Call; Cheated Love; The Kiss. **1922** The Old Homestead; The Pride of Palomar; Over the Border; The Siren Call; Boy Crazy; If You Believe It, It's So; A Question of Honor. **1923** To the Last Man; The Broken Wing; Racing Hearts; The Trail of the Lonesome Pine; The Eternal Struggle. **1924** The Dancing Cheat; The Fighting American; The Rose of Paris; The Price She Paid; Stolen Secrets; Fool's Highway. **1925** Marry Me; The Thundering Herd; A Child of the Prairie; Flower of Night. **1926** Three Faces East; Whispering Canyon. **1927** The Rose of Kildare; Hoof Marks; Lost at the Front; King of Kings; Clancy's Kosher Wedding. **1928** Harold Teen; The Noose; Do Your Duty; The Code of the Scarlet; The Bushranger; Dressed to Kill. **1929** The Delightful Rogue; Stewed, Fried and Boiled (short); Alibi. **1930** The Texan; City Girl; Cameo Kirby. **1931** The Squaw Man; The Sin of Madelon Claudet; Shanghaied Love; The Conquering Horde. **1932** Union Depot; The Night Club Lady. **1933** The Lone Avenger; Son of Kong. **1934** Redhead; In a Pig's Eye (short). **1935** It's a Small World. **1938** Blockade; If I Were King. **1940** Shooting High; Saps at Sea (short).

BRADY, FRED (Frederick Kress)
Born: Mar. 29, 1912, New York, N.Y. Died: Nov. 11, 1961, Los Angeles, Calif. (heart failure). Screen actor and screenwriter.

Appeared in: **1943** Stage Door Canteen; Swing Shift Maisie. **1944** Why, Daddy? (short); Three Is a Family; Dancing in Manhattan. **1946** Meet Me On Broadway; The Cat Creeps; Little Miss Big; Slightly Scandalous.

BRADY, PAT
Born: Dec. 31, 1914, Toledo, Ohio. Died: Feb. 27, 1972, Green Mountain Falls, Colo. Screen, stage, television actor and musician. Member of the "Sons of the Pioneers" singing group.

Appeared in: **1938** West of Cheyenne. **1939** Man From Sundown. **1940** Two-Fisted Rangers; The Durango Kid. **1943** Song of Texas; The Man From Music Mountain. **1949** Down Dakota Way; The Golden Stallion. **1950** Bells of Coronado; Trigger, Jr.; Twilight in the Sierras. **1951** South of Caliente.

BRAGA, EURICO
Born: 1894, Rio de Janeiro, Brazil. Died: Nov. 19, 1962, Lisbon, Portugal (cancer). Screen, stage actor and newspaper columnist.

BRAHAM, HARRY
Born: 1874, London, England. Died: Sept. 21, 1923, Staten Island, N.Y. Stage and screen actor. Appeared in Griffith films.

BRAHAM, HORACE
Born: 1893. Died: Sept. 7, 1955, New York, N.Y. Screen, stage, radio and television actor. Married to actress Gladys Feldman (dec. 1974).

Appeared in: **1922** The Prodigal Judge. **1923** Sinner or Saint.

BRAHAM, LIONEL
Born: 1879, England. Died: Oct. 6, 1947, Hollywood, Calif. (heart attack). Stage and screen actor.

Appeared in: **1916** Diane the Huntress. **1925** I'll Show You the Town. **1926** Skinner's Dress Suit; Don Juan. **1927** Night Life; Out All Night. **1936** As You Like It. **1937** Personal Property; The Prince and the Pauper; Wee Willie Winkie. **1938** A Christmas Carol. **1939** The Little Princess. **1948** Macbeth.

BRAITHWAITE, DAME LILIAN
Born: 1873, England. Died: Sept. 17, 1948, London, England (heart attack). Stage and screen actress. In 1943 she was made Dame Commander of Order of the British Empire.

Appeared in: **1915** The World's Desire (aka The Lord Gave); The Climax (aka Motherhood). **1917** The Woman Who Was Nothing; Dombey and Son; Justice; The Gay Lord Quex; Masks and Faces. **1918** Because. **1919** The Chinese Puzzle. **1920** General Post; Castles in Spain; Garry Owen. **1921** Mary-Find-The-Gold. **1927** Downhill (aka When Boys Leave Home–US 1928). **1931** Carnival (aka Venetian Nights–US); Man of Mayfair. **1932** The Chinese Puzzle (and 1919 version). **1947** A Man About the House (US 1949).

BRANDON, ARTHUR F.
Born: 1925. Died: June 27, 1975, near Barton, Vt. (heart attack). Screen, stage actor and composer.

Appeared in: **1938** Life Goes On.

BRANDON, DOLORES
Born: 1917. Died: Aug. 9, 1959, Hollywood, Calif. Screen and vaudeville actress.

BRANDON, FLORENCE
Born: 1879. Died: Oct. 11, 1961, London, England. Screen and stage actress. Appeared in silents.

BRANDON, FRANCIS
Born: 1886. Died: Oct. 3, 1924, Bronx, N.Y. Stage and screen actor.

BRANDT, CHARLES
Born: 1864. Died: June 9, 1924, Philadelphia, Pa. Screen and stage actor.

Appeared in: **1912** A Matter of Business; A Child's Devotion; The Heavenly Voice. **1913** The Power of the Cross; The District Attorney's Conscience; The Insurance Agent; Dr. Maxwell's Experiment; John Arthur's Trust; A Timely Rescue; Annie Rowley's Fortune; When John Brought Home His Wife; The Sea Eternal; The School Principal. **1914** The Fortune Hunter; A Daughter of Fire. **1915** The Sporting Duchess; The District Attorney; The Great Ruby Mystery; The Rights of Man; Think, Mothers; Sweeter Than Revenge; The Road of Strife (serial). **1916** The Soul Market; Friday the Thirteenth. **1919** The Misfit Earl. **1920** The Master Mind.

BRANDT, LOUISE
Born: 1877. Died: July 13, 1959, San Diego, Calif. Screen actress.

BRANNIGAN, OWEN
Born: 1909, England. Died: May 9, 1973, Newcastle, England. Screen, stage actor and singer.

Appeared in: **1953** The Story of Gilbert and Sullivan (aka Gilbert and Sullivan–US).

BRASFIELD, ROD
Died: Sept. 12, 1958. Screen and radio actor.

Appeared in: **1956** A Face in the Crowd. **1958** Country Music Holiday.

BRASSEUR, PIERRE (Pierre Espinasse)
Born: 1903, Paris, France. Died: 1972, Italy. Screen, stage actor, playwright, screenwriter, film director and stage producer. Married to actress Odette Joyeux and father of actor Claude Brasseur.

Appeared in: **1928** Claudine a l'Ecole. **1933** Cafe de Paris. Other films prior to 1936: Circulez; Papa Sans le Savoir; Vainqueur; La Reve Blonde; Moi et l'Imperatrice; Voyage de Noce; Chanson d'une Nuit; Le Sexe Faible; Incognito; Garnison Amoureuse; Oncle de Pekin; Je Suis un As; Patte de Mouche; Debauche. **1938** Le Quai des Brumes (The Foggy Quay). **1939** Mademoiselle ma Mere; Port of Shadows; Last Desire. **1940** Claudine. **1942** Lumiere d'ete. **1944** Les Enfants du Paradis (The Children of Paradise–US 1947). **1946** Jericho; Les Portes de la Nuit (Gates of the Night–US 1950). **1950** Julie de Carneilhan; Noah's Ark. **1951** The Lovers of Verona; Barbe Bleu (Bluebeard). **1953** Le Plaisir (aka House of Pleasure and The House of Madame Tellier); Maitre Apres Dieu (aka Skipper Next to God). **1954** Dirty Hands. **1955** Portes des Lilas. **1957** Oasis. **1958** Gates of Paris. **1959** The Processors; Sans Famille. **1960** Candide (US 1962); Il Bell'Antonio (Bell Antonio–US 1962); Cartagine en Flamme (Carthage in Flames–US 1961); Where the Hot Wind Blows (aka Le Legge-The Law); Les Yeux Sans Visage (aka The Horror Chamber of Dr. Faustus–US 1962). **1962** Le Crime ne Paie Pas (Crime Does not Pay). **1963** Les Bonnes Causes (The Good Causes aka Don't Tempt the Devil–US 1964). **1964** Liola (aka A Very Handy Man–US 1966). **1965** Deux Heures a Tuer; La Metamorphose des Cloportes (Cloportes–US 1966). **1966** Un Monde Nouveau (A Young World–US); Le Roi de Coeur (King of Hearts–US 1967). **1968** Les Oiseaux vont Mourir au Perou (Birds in Peru).

BRASWELL, CHARLES
Born: 1925. Died: May 17, 1974, Bronx, N.Y. Stage and screen actor.

Appeared in: **1957** Bail Out at 43,000. **1960** Pretty Boy Floyd. **1970** The Only Game in Town.

BRATANOV, IVAN
Born: 1920, Bulgaria. Died: 1968, Bulgaria. Screen actor.

Appeared in: **1954** Septembrists (Septemvriitsi); Pessen za Choveka (Song for Man). **1955** Nespokoen Pat (Troubled Road). **1956** Dimitrovgradtsi (People of Dimitrovgrad). **1960** Parvi Urok (First Lesson); Stubenskite Lipi (The Stoublen Lindens). **1967** Nai Dalgata Nosht (The Longest Night).

BRAVO, JAMIE
Born: 1932. Died: Feb. 2, 1970, Zacatecas, Mexico (auto accident). Matador and screen actor.

Appeared in: **1965** Love Has Many Faces.

BRAWN, JOHN P.
Born: 1869, New York, N.Y. Died: June 16, 1943, New York, N.Y. Stage and screen actor.

BRAY, JOHN F.
Born: 1906. Died: May 3, 1955, Gladewater, Tex. Screen actor.

Appeared in: **1948** Paleface. **1949** Mr. Belvedere Goes to College. **1951** Here Comes the Groom. **1952** Viva Zapata!

BRAYFIELD, GEORGE
Died: Feb. 17, 1968. Screen actor. Appeared in early westerns.

BRAYTON, LILY
Born: June 23, 1876, Hindley, Lancs, England. Died: Apr. 30, 1953, Dawlish, England, Screen, stage actress and stage producer. Married to actor/producer Oscar Asche (dec. 1936) and later married to Douglas Chalmers Watson.

Appeared in: **1914** Kismet.

BREAKSTON, GEORGE P.
Born: Jan. 22, 1920, Paris, France. Died: May, 1973, Paris, France. Screen, stage, television, radio actor, film director, producer and screenwriter.

Appeared in: **1933** Wild Boys of the Road. **1934** It Happened One Night; No Greater Glory; Mrs. Wiggs of the Cabbage Patch; A Successful Failure; Great Expectations. **1935** The Dark Angel; The Return of Peter Grimm; Life Returns. **1936** Second Wife; Boulder Dam. **1938** Love Finds Andy Hardy; A Criminal Is Born (short). **1939** Jesse James; Andy Hardy Gets Spring Fever; Boy Slaves; Swanee River. **1940** Judge Hardy and Son; Andy Hardy Meets the Debutante; Grapes of Wrath. **1941** Andy Hardy's Private Secretary. **1942** The Courtship of Andy Hardy; Men of San Quentin.

BREAMER, SYLVIA
Born: 1903. Died: June 7, 1943, New York, N.Y. Screen actress.

Appeared in: **1918** Missing. **1921** The Devil; Not Guilty; Doubling for Romeo; The Roof Tree; A Poor Relation. **1922** Wolf Law; Money to Burn; The Man Who Married His Own Wife; The Man with Two Mothers; The Man Unconquerable; Calvert's Valley; The Face Between; Money to Burn; Sherlock Brown. **1923** Bavu; The First Degree; Flaming Youth; The Barefoot Boy; Her Temporary Husband; The Girl of the Golden West; Thundergate. **1924** Lillies of the Field; The Woman on the Jury; Reckless Romance; Robes of Sin. **1925** Too Much Youth; Women and Gold. **1926** Up in Mabel's Room; Lightning Reporter. **1936** Too Many Parents.

BRECHER, EGON
Born: Feb. 16, 1885, Czechoslovakia. Died: Aug. 12, 1946, Hollywood, Calif. (heart attack). Screen, stage actor, and stage director.

Appeared in: **1929** The Royal Box. **1933** To the Last Man. **1934** As the Earth Turns; No Greater Glory; Many Happy Returns; The Black Cat; Now and Forever. **1935** Black Fury; The Florentine Dagger; Here's to Romance. **1936** Charlie Chan's Secret; Boulder Dam; Till We Meet Again; Sins of Man; Ladies in Love; The White Angel; Stolen Holiday; Alibi for Murder. **1937** The Black Legion; Heidi; I Met Him in Paris; Love under Fire; Thin Ice. **1938** I'll Give a Million; Suez; Cocoanut Grove; You and Me; Spawn of the North; The Spy Ring; Invisible Enemy. **1939** While America Sleeps (short); Devil's Island; The Three Musketeers; Nurse Edith Cavell; Judge Hardy and Son; Juarez; Angels Wash Their Faces. **1940** Pound Foolish (short); Four Sons; The Man I Married; I Was an Adventuress. **1941** Out of Darkness (short); Kings Row; They Dare Not Love; Underground; Manpower. **1942** Isle of Missing Men; For a Common Defense (short); Berlin Correspondent. **1944** The Hairy Ape; U-Boat Prisoner. **1945** A Royal Scandal; White Pongo. **1946** The Wife of Monte Cristo; OSS; So Dark the Night.

BRECKNER, GARY
Born: 1896. Died: June 25, 1945, Redlands, Calif. (auto accident). Screen, stage and radio actor.

Appeared in: **1937** Wake Up and Live; Love and Hisses. **1938** Thanks for Everything; Rebecca of Sunnybrook Farm. **1940** Johnny Apollo. **1941** The Great American Broadcast.

BREEN, HURLEY "RED"
Born: 1913. Died: Sept. 8, 1963, Hollywood, Calif. Screen actor and boxer. Double for James Cagney.

Appeared in: **1952** Boots Malone.

BREEN, MARGARET
Died: Dec. 5, 1960, Santa Monica, Calif. Screen, stage and vaudeville actress. Was part of the "Breen Family" vaudeville act.

Appeared in: **1930** Heads Up.

BREESE, EDMUND
Born: June 18, 1871, Brooklyn, N.Y. Died: Apr. 6, 1936, New York, N.Y. (peritonitis). Screen, stage actor and playwright. Entered films in 1914.

Appeared in: **1915** The Song of the Wage Slave. **1916** The Spell of the Yukon. **1921** Burn 'Em up Barnes. **1922** Beyond the Rainbow; Sure-Fire Flint; The Curse of Drink. **1923** Luck; The Little Red Schoolhouse; You are Guilty; Bright Lights of Broadway; The Fair Cheat; Jacqueline of Blazing Barriers; Marriage Morals. **1924** Three O'Clock in the Morning; The Early Bird; The Shooting of Dan McGrew; Damaged Hearts; Restless Wives; Playthings of Desire; The Sixth Commandment; The Speed Spook; Those Who Judge. **1925** The Police Patrol; Wildfire; The Live Wire. **1926** Stepping Along; Woman Handled; The Brown Derby; The Highbinders. **1927** Paradise for Two; Back to Liberty; Home Made. **1928** Finders Keepers; Burning Daylight; Perfect Crime; The Wright Idea; On Trial; The Haunted House. **1929** Sonny Boy; Fancy Baggage; Conquest; Girls Gone Wild; From Headquarters; The Gamblers; The Hottentot; Girl Overboard; In the Headlines. **1930** Hold Everything; The Sea Bat; Rough Waters; Top Speed; Tol'able David; All Quiet on the Western Front; Kismet; The Czar of Broadway; Playboy of Paris. **1931** Bright Lights; Playthings of Hollywood; Oh! Oh! Cleopatra (short); Public Defender; Wicked; Chinatown after Dark; Mother's Millions; Millie; The Last Parade; Defenders of the Law; Young Sinners; The Good Bad Girl; The Painted Desert; Platinum Blonde; Morals for Women; Bad Girl. **1932** Cross Examination; The Hatchet Man; Mata Hari; Police Court; The Reckoning; Love Bound; Drifting Souls; Alias Mary Smith; Cabin in the Cotton; Golden West; Madame Butterfly; The Match King. **1933** Women Won't Tell; Billion Dollar Scandal; International House; Laughing at Life; Man of Sentiment; Ladies Must Love; Duck Soup; Above the Clouds. **1934** Come on Marines; Beloved; Treasure Island; Broadway Bill; The Dancing Man; Lost in the Stratosphere. **1935** The Marriage Bargain.

BRENDEL, EL (Elmer G. Brendel)
Born: Mar. 25, 1890, Philadelphia, Pa. Died: Apr. 9, 1964, Hollywood, Calif. (heart attack). Screen, stage, vaudeville, and television actor. Married to Sophie Flo Bert with whom he appeared in vaudeville. Entered films in 1926.

Appeared in: **1926** The Campus Flirt; You Never Know Women. **1927** Ten Modern Commandments; Too Many Crooks; Wings; Arizona Bound; Rolled Stockings. **1929** The Cock-Eyed World; Sunny-Side Up; Frozen Justice; Hot for Paris; Beau Night (short). **1930** Happy Days; The Big Trail; The Golden Calf; Just Imagine; New Movietone Follies of 1930. **1931** Mr. Lemon of Orange; Spider; Delicious; Women of All Nations; Six Cylinder Love. **1932** West of Broadway; Disorderly Conduct; Handle with Care. **1933** Hot Pepper; My Lips Betray; The Last Trail. **1934** The Meanest Gal in Town; Olsen's Big Moment. **1935** Broadway Brevities (short). **1936** Career Woman; Lonesome Trailer (short); God's Country and the Woman. **1937** The Holy Terror; Blonde Trouble. **1938** Happy Landing; Little Miss Broadway; Valley of Giants. **1939** Code of the Streets; House of Fear; Risky Business; Spirit of Culver; Call of a Messenger. **1940** If I Had My Way; Captain Caution; Gallant Sons. **1944** I'm From Arkansas; Machine Gun Mama; Defective Detectives (short); Mopey Dope (short). **1945** Pistol Packin' Nitwits (short), Snooper Service (short). **1949** The Beautiful Blonde from Bashful Bend. **1953** Paris Model. **1956** The She-Creature.

BRENDLIN, ANDRE
Born: 1911, France. Died: Oct. 6, 1934, Marne, France (drowned). Screen actor.

BRENEMAN, TOM
Born: 1902. Died: Apr. 28, 1948, Encino, Calif. Screen actor and radio emcee of "Breakfast in Hollywood."

Appeared in: **1946** Breakfast in Hollywood.

BRENNAN, JOHN E.
Born: 1865, Springfield, Mass. Died: Dec. 27, 1940, Los Angeles, Calif. (heart attack). Screen actor.

Appeared in: **1912** Strong Armed Nellie; The Landlubber; The Chaperon Gets a Ducking. **1916** Vindication.

BRENNAN, ROBERT
Born: 1892. Died: Apr. 17, 1940, Los Angeles, Calif. Stage and screen actor. Entered films during silents.

BRENNAN, WALTER
Born: July 25, 1894, Swampscott or Lynn, Mass. (?). Died: Sept. 21, 1974, Oxnard, Calif. (emphysema). Screen, stage, vaudeville and television actor. Father of Arthur, Ruth and film producer Walter Brennan, Jr. Won 1936 Academy Award for Best Supporting Actor in Come and Get It; in 1938 for Kentucky; and in 1940 for The Westerner. Nominated for 1941 Academy Award as Best Supporting Actor in Sergeant York. Entered films as an extra in the early 1920s.

Appeared in: **1927** The Ridin' Rowdy; Tearin' Into Trouble. **1928** Ballyhoo Buster. **1929** The Lariat Kid; The Long, Long Trail; Shannons of Broadway;

Smilin' Guns; One Hysterical Night. **1930** The King of Jazz. **1931** Scratch as Catch Can (short); Dancing Dynamite; Neck and Neck. **1932** The Iceman's Ball (short); Law and Order; Texas Cyclone; Two-Fisted Law; All American. **1933** One Year Later; Parachute Jumper; Man of Action; Fighting for Justice; Sing, Sinner, Sing; Strange People. **1934** Woman Haters (short); Good Dame; Half a Sinner. **1935** Restless Knights (short); The Wedding Night; Northern Frontier; Lady Tubbs; The Man on the Flying Trapeze; Barbary Coast; Seven Keys to Baldpate; Law Beyond the Range; Bride of Frankenstein; Metropolitan; Bric-a-Brac (short). **1936** Three Godfathers; These Three; Come and Get It; Fury; Banjo on My Knee; The Moon's Our Home; The Prescott Kid. **1937** When Love Is Young; The Affairs of Cappy Ricks; Wild and Wooly; She's Dangerous. **1938** The Adventures of Tom Sawyer; The Buccaneer; Kentucky; The Texans; Mother Carey's Chickens; The Cowboy and the Lady. **1939** Stanley and Livingstone; The Story of Vernon and Irene Castle; They Shall Have Music; Joe and Ethel Turp Call on the President. **1940** The Westerner; Northwest Passage; Maryland. **1941** Sergeant York; Meet John Doe; Swampwater; This Woman Is Mine; Nice Girl?; Rise and Shine. **1942** The Pride of the Yankees; Stand By for Action. **1943** The North Star; Slightly Dangerous; Hangmen Also Die; The Last Will and Testament of Tom Smith (short). **1944** The Princess and the Pirate; To Have and Have Not; Home in Indiana. **1945** Dakota. **1946** My Darling Clementine; Centennial Summer; A Stolen Life; Nobody Lives Forever. **1947** Driftwood. **1948** Scudda Hoo! Scudda Hay!; Red River; Blood on the Moon. **1949** Brimstone; The Green Promise; Task Force; The Great Dan Patch. **1950** Curtain Call at Cactus Creek; Ticket to Tomahawk (aka The Sheriff's Daughter); Singing Guns; Surrender; The Showdown. **1951** Best of the Bad Men; The Wild Blue Yonder; Along the Great Divide. **1952** Lure of the Wilderness; Return of the Texan. **1953** Sea of Lost Ships. **1954** Drums Across the River; Four Guns to the Border; Bad Day at Black Rock. **1955** The Far Country; At Gunpoint. **1956** Glory; Come Next Spring; Good-Bye, My Lady; The Proud Ones. **1957** Tammy and the Bachelor; The Way to the Gold; God Is My Partner. **1959** Rio Bravo. **1962** How the West Was Won; Shoot Out at Big Sag. **1964** Those Calloways. **1966** The Oscar. **1967** The Gnome-Mobile; Who's Minding the Mint? **1968** The One and Only, Genuine, Original Family Band. **1969** Support Your Local Sheriff. **1973** The Love Bug Rides Again.

BRENON, HERBERT
Born: Jan. 13, 1880, Dublin, Ireland. Died: June 21, 1958, Los Angeles, Calif. Screen, stage, vaudeville actor, film director, film producer and screenwriter. Married to Helen Oberg (dec.) with whom he appeared in vaudeville.

Appeared in: **1911** Blind Musician; The Strike. **1913** Ivanhoe. **1915** The Heart of Maryland; Two Orphans.

BRENT, EVELYN (Mary Elizabeth Riggs aka DOROTHY RIGGS and BETTY RIGGS)
Born: Oct. 20, 1899, Tampa, Fla. Died: June 4, 1975, Los Angeles, Calif. (heart attack). Screen, stage and television actress. Entered films as an extra with World Film Studio in 1914. Divorced from director/producer Harry Edwards and Bernard P. Fineman. Later married vaudeville actor Harry Fox (dec. 1959).

Appeared in: **1914** A Gentleman from Mississippi; The Heart of a Painted Woman; The Pit. **1915** The Shooting of Dan McGrew. **1916** Lure of Heart's Desire; The Soul Market; The Spell of the Yukon; The Iron Woman; Playing With Fire; The Weakness of Strength. **1917** The Millionaire's Double; Who's Your Neighbor?; To the Death; Raffles, the Amateur Cracksman. **1918** Daybreak. **1919** Fool's Gold; The Other Man's Wife; Help, Help, Police; The Glorious Lady; Into the River; The Border River. **1920** The Shuttle of Life; The Law Divine. **1921** Demos (aka Why Men Forget—US); The Door That Has No Key (US 1922); Sybil; Sonia (aka The Woman Who Came Back—US 1922); Laughter and Tears; Circus Jim. **1922** Trapped by the Mormons; The Spanish Jade; The Experiment; Married to a Mormon; Pages of Life. **1923** Held to Answer; Loving Lies. **1924** The Arizona Express; The Cyclone Rider; The Dangerous Flirt; The Desert Outlaw; The Lone Chance; My Husband's Wives; The Plunderer; Silk Stocking Sal; The Shadow of the East (aka Shadow of the Desert and Shadows of the East). **1925** Alias Mary Flynn; Broadway Lady; Forbidden Cargo; Lady Robinhood; Midnight Molly; Smooth as Satin; Three Wise Crooks (aka Three of a Kind). **1926** The Flame of the Argentine; The Imposter; The Jade Cup; Love 'Em and Leave 'Em; Queen of Diamonds; Secret Orders. **1927** Blind Alley; Love's Greatest Mistake; Underworld; Women's Wares. **1928** Beau Sabreur; The Drag Net; His Tiger Lady; The Last Command; The Mating Call; A Night of Mystery; The Showdown; Interference; The Mormon Peril (reissue of Trapped by the Mormons—1922); Broadway; Darkened Rooms; Fast Company; Why Bring That Up?; Woman Trap. **1930** Framed; Madonna of the Streets; Paramount on Parade; The Silver Horde; Slightly Scarlet; Nuits de Chicago (French release of Underworld—1927). **1931** Traveling Husbands; Mad Parade (aka Forgotten Women); The Pagan Lady. **1932** High Pressure; Attorney for the Defense; The Crusader. **1933** The World Gone Mad (aka The Public Be Damned). **1935** Home on the Range; The Nitwits; Symphony of Living. **1936** It Couldn't Have Happened; The President's Mystery (aka One for All); Hopalong Cassidy Returns; Jungle Jim (serial); Penthouse Party (aka Without Children); Song of the Trail. **1937** King of the Gamblers; Night Club Scandal; Daughter of Shanghai (aka

Daughter of the Orient); Last Train from Madrid. **1938** Tip-Off Girls; Law West of Tombstone; Mr. Wong, Detective; Sudden Bill Dorn; Speed Limited. **1939** Daughter of the Tong; Juarez and Maximilian (aka The Mad Empress); Panama Lady. **1940** The Fighting 69th; Adventure in Diamonds; 'Til We Meet Again. **1941** Emergency Landing; Dangerous Lady; Wide Open Town; Forced Landing; Holt of the Secret Service (serial); Ellery Queen and the Murder Ring. **1942** Wrecking Crew; The Pay-Off; Westward Ho. **1943** The Seventh Victim (aka Attorney for the Defence and The Silent Witness); Spy Train. **1944** Bowery Champs. **1946** Raiders of the South. **1947** Robin Hood of Monterey. **1948** The Mystery of the Golden Eye (aka The Golden Eye); Stage Struck. **1950** Again, Pioneers.

BREON, EDMUND (E. McLaverty)
Born: Dec. 12, 1882, Hamilton, Scotland. Died: 1951. Screen and stage actor.

Appeared in: **1930** The Dawn Patrol; On Approval. **1931** The Love Habit; Uneasy Virtue; I Like Your Nerve; Born to Love; Chances. **1932** Women Who Play; Wedding Rehearsal; Leap Year. **1933** Waltz Time; No Funny Business; Three Men in a Boat. **1934** Mister Cinders; The Private Life of Don Juan. **1935** The Divine Spark; Night Mail; The Scarlet Pimpernel; She Shall Have Music (US 1942). **1936** Love in Exile; Strangers on a Honeymoon (US 1937). **1937** Keep Fit; The Return of the Scarlet Pimpernel (US 1938); French Leave. **1938** A Yank at Oxford; Dangerous Medicine; Owd Bob (aka To the Victor—US); Premiere (aka One Night in Paris—US 1940); Crackerjack (aka The Man With a Hundred Faces—US); Luck of the Navy (aka North Sea Patrol—US 1940); Many Tanks Mr. Atkins. **1939** The Outsider (US 1940); Goodbye, Mr. Chips. **1940** Gentleman of Venture (aka It Happened to One Man—US 1941). **1944** Casanova Brown; Man in Half Moon Street; Hour before the Dawn; Our Hearts Were Young and Gay; Gaslight. **1945** Saratoga Trunk; The Corn Is Green; Woman in the Window. **1946** Devotion; Six Gun Man; Outlaw of the Plains; Dressed to Kill; Sherlock Holmes and the Secret Code. **1947** The Imperfect Lady. **1948** Forever Amber; Hills of Home. **1949** Challenge to Lassie; Enchantment. **1951** Sons of the Musketeers. **1952** At Sword's Point.

BRERTON, TYRONE
Born: 1894. Died: Apr. 25, 1939, Hollywood, Calif. Screen actor.

Appeared in: **1925** Secrets of the Night. **1928** The Canyon of Adventure.

BRESSART, FELIX
Born: 1880, Eydtkuhnen, Germany. Died: Mar. 17, 1949, Los Angeles, Calif. (leukemia). Stage and screen actor.

Appeared in: **1931** Die Drei von der Tankstelle; Der Wahre Jakob, Das Alte Lied; Nie Wieder Liebe (No More Love); Eine Freundin so Goldig wie Du. **1932** Der Schrecken der Garnison; Hirsekorn Greift Ein; Der Herr Buerovorsteher. **1933** Holsapfel Weiss Alles; Drei Tage Mittelarrest; Der Sohn der Weissen Berg. **1934** Der Gluecksylinder. **1935** Und Wer Kuesst Mich? **1939** Swanee River; Ninotchka; Three Smart Girls Grow Up; Bridal Suite. **1940** Third Finger, Left Hand; The Shop around the Corner; Edison the Man; Bitter Sweet; It All Came True; Comrade X. **1941** Married Bachelor; Kathleen; Mr. and Mrs. North; Blossoms in the Dust; Ziegfeld Girl; Escape. **1942** Iceland; Crossroads; To Be or Not to Be. **1943** Song of Russia; Three Hearts for Julia; Above Suspicion. **1944** The Seventh Cross; Greenwich Village; Secrets in the Dark; Blonde Fever. **1945** Dangerous Partners; Without Love. **1946** I've Always Loved You; Ding Dong Williams; The Thrill of Brazil; Her Sister's Secret. **1947** Concerto. **1948** A Song Is Born; Portrait of Jennie. **1949** Take One False Step; My Friend Irma.

BREWER, MONTE
Born: 1934. Died: Apr. 21, 1942, Hollywood, Calif. (stomach ailment). Screen actor and radio singer.

Appeared in: **1941** Mr. Dynamite.

BRIAN, DONALD
Born: 1871, St. Johns, Newfoundland, Canada. Died: Dec. 22, 1948, Great Neck, N.Y. Screen, stage actor and singer. Married to actress Virginia O'Brien.

Appeared in: **1915** The Voice in the Fog. **1916** The Smugglers. **1929** America's Foremost Musical Comedy Star (short). **1930** My Mistake (short). **1931** Squaring the Triangle (short).

BRIANT, GEORGE HAMILTON
Born: 1922. Died: Oct. 22, 1946, near San Antonio, Tex. (died during filming of Blaze at Noon in air accident). Screen actor and stunt flyer.

Appeared in: **1947** Blaze at Noon.

BRICE, BETTY (aka ROSETTA BRICE)
Born: 1892, Sunbury, Pa. Died: Feb. 15, 1935, Van Nuys, Calif. Stage and screen actress. Married to concert singer, John L. Pratt.

Appeared in: **1914** The Fortune Hunter. **1921** The Spenders. **1922** The Green Temptation; Heart's Haven. **1924** Beau Brummell.

BRICE, FANNY (Fanny Borach)

Born: Oct. 29, 1891, New York, N.Y. Died: May 29, 1951, Beverly Hills, Calif. (cerebral hemorrhage). Screen, stage, radio, vaudeville and burlesque actress. Divorced from Nick Arnstein and producer Billy Rose (dec. 1966).

Appeared in: **1928** My Man (film debut). **1929** The Man From Blankleys'. **1930** Be Yourself. **1936** The Great Ziegfeld. **1938** Everybody Sing. **1946** Ziegfeld Follies.

BRICKER, BETTY

Born: 1890. Died: Feb. 15, 1954, Hollywood, Calif. Screen actress. Entered films approx. 1914.

BRICKERT, CARLTON

Born: 1891. Died: Dec. 23, 1943, New York, N.Y. Screen, stage and radio actor.

Appeared in: **1921** The Rider of the King Log. **1923** You Are Guilty.

BRICKLEY, CHARLES E.

Born: 1891. Died: Dec. 28, 1949, New York, N.Y. (heart attack). Professional athlete and screen actor.

Appeared in: **1915** The Hero of the Gridiron.

BRIDGE, ALAN "AL"

Born: Feb. 26, 1891, Pa. Died: Dec. 27, 1957. Screen actor.

Appeared in: **1931** Ridin' Fool; Rider of the Plains; Rose of the Rio Grande; God's Country and the Man. **1932** Galloping Thru; Spirit of the West; Wyoming Whirlwind; A Man's Land; The Forty-Niners. **1933** Drum Taps; When a Man Rides Alone; Cowboy Counsellor; Sucker Money; Sunset Pass; Black Beauty; Lone Avenger; Cheyenne Kid; Son of the Border; Fighting Texans. **1934** Thundering Herd; Public Stenographer; Mystery Mountain. **1935** Melody Trail; The Good Fairy; Burn 'Em Up Barnes; New Frontier; Valley of Wanted Men; A Night at the Opera. **1936** Call of the Prairie; Fast Bullets; The Lawless Nineties; Public Enemy's Wife; Three Mesquiteers; The Trail Dust. **1937** Jungle Jim (serial); Borderland; Western Gold; Two-Gun Law; Woman Chases Man; Springtime in the Rockies; Partners of the Plains. **1938** Two-Gun Justice; Highway Patrol; Little Miss Roughneck; Adventure in Sahara; Down in Arkansas; Colorado Trail; Crime School. **1939** Blue Montana Skies; Man from Sundown; Romance of the Redwoods; No Place to Go; Blazing Six Shooters; Pioneers of the Frontier; Christmas in July. **1940** The Courageous Dr. Christian. **1941** The Lady from Cheyenne; Law of the Range; The Little Foxes; The Kid's Last Ride; Sullivan's Travels. **1942** Fighting Bill Fargo; Bad Men of the Hills; Bells of Capistrano. **1943** Tenting Tonight on the Old Camp Grounds; Seeing Nellie Home (short). **1944** The Miracle of Morgan's Creek; Hail the Conquering Hero; The Unwritten Code. **1945** Thunderhead, Son of Flicka; A Tree Grows in Brooklyn; A Guy, a Gal and a Pal; The Jade Mask. **1946** The Virginian; The Falcon's Alibi; My Pal Trigger; Below the Deadline; Singin' in the Corn; Cowboy Blues; The Sin of Harold Diddlebock; Cross My Heart; Shadows Over Chinatown. **1947** The Hal Roach Comedy Carnival; Alias Mr. Twilight; Robin Hood of Texas; Last Days of Boot Hill; Black Gold. **1948** Silver River; Unfaithfully Yours; That Wonderful Urge. **1949** The Beautiful Blonde from Bashful Bend; The Devil's Henchman. **1950** The Traveling Saleswoman; The Tougher They Come. **1951** Oh, Susanna; All That I Have; Mad Wednesday. **1952** The Last Musketeer; We're Not Married. **1953** Iron Mountain Trail. **1954** Hell's Outpost.

BRIDGE, LOIE

Born: 1890. Died: Mar. 8, 1974, Glendale, Calif. (natural causes). Screen, stage and television actress.

Appeared in: **1932** Single-Handed Sanders; Wyoming Whirlwind. **1943** O, My Darling Clementine. **1949** Riders of the Whistling Pines; Riders of the Sky.

BRIGGS, HAL

Born: 1881. Died: Apr. 28, 1925, Rockville, New York (heart failure). Screen actor and film director.

BRIGGS, HARLAN

Born: 1880. Died: Jan. 26, 1952, Woodland Hills, Calif. (stroke). Stage and screen actor.

Appeared in: **1936** Dodsworth; Mad Holiday; Happy-Go-Lucky; Easy Money. **1937** A Family Affair; Easy Living; Interns Can't Take Money; Live, Love and Learn; Beg, Borrow or Steal; Riding on Air; Exclusive. **1938** That's My Story; Reckless Living; The Missing Guest; Opening Day (short); Dynamite Delaney; One Wild Night; You and Me; Meet the Girls; Quick Money; Trouble at Midnight; Having a Wonderful Time; A Man to Remember. **1939** Calling Dr. Kildare; Tell Me No Tales; Flight at Midnight; The Mysterious Miss X; The Wizard of Oz; Mr. Smith Goes to Washington; Maisie; Blondie Takes a Vacation. **1940** Abe Lincoln in Illinois; Young as You Feel; The Man Who Wouldn't Talk; The Bank Dick; My Little Chickadee; Charlie Chan's Murder Cruise. **1941** Among the Living; One Foot in Heaven. **1942** Lady Bodyguard; The Remarkable Andrew; The Vanishing Virginian; Tennessee Johnson. **1945**

State Fair. **1946** A Stolen Life. **1947** Cynthia; Ladies' Man. **1948** A Double Life. **1949** Rusty Saves a Life. **1952** Carrie.

BRIGGS, MATT

Born: 1883. Died: June 10, 1962, Seattle, Wash. Screen and stage actor.

Appeared in: **1933** Advice to the Lovelorn. **1934** Hips, Hips, Hooray; Born to Be Bad. **1943** The Ox-Bow Incident; The Dancing Master; Meanest Man in the World. **1944** Roger Touhy, Gangster; Coney Island; Buffalo Bill. **1948** The Babe Ruth Story.

BRIGGS, OSCAR

Born: 1877, Wis. Died: Jan. 17, 1928, Hollywood, Calif. (paralysis-stroke). Screen, stage and vaudeville actor.

BRIGHTON, ALBERT

Born: 1876. Died: July 11, 1911, Grassmere, N.Y. (drowned while filming). Stage and screen actor. Entered films with Edison Co.

BRILL, PATTI (Patricia Brilhante aka PATSY PAIGE)

Born: Mar. 8, 1923, San Francisco, Calif. Died: Jan. 18, 1963, Calif. Screen, stage actress and dancer.

Appeared in: **1928** Lillies of the Field. **1929** The Vagabond Lover. **1938** Mad about Music. **1939** 1,000 Men and a Girl. **1940** Best Foot Forward. **1942** Star Spangled Rhythm; The Petty Girl. **1943** Lady of Burlesque; Henry Aldrich Gets Glamour; Adventures of a Rookie; Salute for Three; Pan-Americana; The Falcon Strikes Back; The Falcon and the Co-Eds. **1944** Music in Manhattan; Girl Rush; Cocktails for Two. **1945** Sing Your Way Home. **1949** Incident. **1955** Not as a Stranger.

BRINDLEY, MADGE

Died: Aug. 28, 1968, near Brighton, England (auto accident). Stage and screen actress.

Appeared in: **1949** The Spider and the Fly (US 1952). **1954** Hobson's Choice. **1955** The Ladykillers (US 1956). **1956** The Feminine Touch (aka The Gentle Touch—US 1957). **1957** The Long Haul. **1969** A Nice Girl Like Me.

BRINDMOUR, GEORGE

Born: 1870. Died: July 21, 1941, Los Angeles, Calif. Screen and vaudeville actor. Married to Helen Hilliard with whom he appeared in vaudeville. He was known as the "Handcuff King."

BRINKMAN, ERNEST

Born: 1872. Died: Dec. 28, 1938, Los Angeles, Calif. Screen, stage and vaudeville actor. Married to Mary Steele with whom he appeared in vaudeville in an act billed as "Brinkman and the Steele Sisters."

BRISCOE, LOTTIE

Born: 1881. Died: Mar. 19, 1950, New York, N.Y. Screen, stage and radio actress.

Appeared in: **1911** Getting Sister Married. **1912** An Amateur Iceman; The Sporting Editor; The Heavenly Voice; The Country School Teacher; The Samaritan of Coogan's Tenement; A Little Family Affair; A Child's Devotion; A Leap Year Lottery Prize; The Violin's Message; The Wooden Bowl; A Bachelor's Waterloo; Her Gift; The Spoiled Child; The Power of Conscience; A College Girl; A Matter of Business; In After Years; The Convalescent. **1913** His Better Self; Two Boys; John Arthur's Trust; The Sea Eternal; Her Husband's Wife; The District Attorney's Conscience; Annie Rowley's Fortune; Dr. Maxwell's Experiment; The Artist's Romance; The School Principal; The Gift of the Storm; A Timely Rescue; When John Brought Home His Wife; The Power of the Cross; The Pawned Bracelet; His Niece from Ireland; A Jealous Husband; The Insurance Agent. **1914** The Beloved Adventurer (serial); Lord Algy; The Girl from the West; The Question and Answer Man; The Shadow of Tragedy; The Parasite. **1915** Comrade Kitty; Who Violates the Law; When Father Interfered; Her Martyrdom; On the Road to Reno; The Cornet; Winning Winsome Winnie; Socially Ambitious; Country Blood; The Last Rose. **1918** The House of Mirth.

BRISSON, CARL (Carl Brisson Petersen)

Born: Dec. 24, 1893, Copenhagen, Denmark. Died: Sept. 24, 1958, Copenhagen, Denmark (jaundice). Screen, stage actor and singer. Married to actress Cleo Willard (dec. 1975). Father of film producer Frederick Brisson.

Appeared in: **1917** De Mysteske Fodspor. **1927** The Ring. **1928** Hjaratas Triumf. **1929** The Manxman; The American Prisoner; Chelsea Nights (short). **1930** Knowing Men; Song of Soho. **1933** Prince of Arcadia. **1934** Two Hearts in Waltztime. **1935** All the King's Horses; Ship Cafe.

BRISSON, CLEO (Cleo Willard)

Born: 1894, Denmark. Died: Nov. 28, 1975, Copenhagen, Denmark. Screen, stage actress and singer. Married to actor Carl Brisson (dec. 1958). Mother of producer Frederick Brisson.

BRISTER, ROBERT S.
Born: 1889. Died: Mar. 2, 1945, Hollywood, Calif. Screen, stage and radio actor.

Appeared in: **1937** Night Club Scandal. **1938** Dangerous to Know.

BRITT, ELTON (James Britt Baker)
Born: July 7, 1912, Marshall, Ark. Died: June 23, 1972, Connellsville, Pa. Country singer, screen, television and radio actor.

Appeared in: **1949** Laramie.

BRITTON, ETHEL
Born: 1915. Died: Feb. 26, 1972, New York, N.Y. Screen, stage and television actress. Married to stage producer/director Frank McCoy (dec. 1947).

Appeared in: **1956** Patterns.

BRITTON, KEITH (Eli Britza)
Born: Aug. 3, 1919, Pa. Died: Oct. 23, 1970, Woodland Hills, Calif. (heart disease). Screen actor.

Appeared in: **1956** Storm Fear.

BRITTON, MILT (Milton Levy)
Born: 1894, Winston-Salem, N.C. Died: Apr. 29, 1948, New York, N.Y. (heart attack). Screen, stage, vaudeville actor, and bandleader. His band was known as "America's Craziest Orchestra"; "The Brown Derby Band" and "The Mad Musical Maniacs."

Appeared in: **1933** Moonlight and Pretzels. **1935** Sweet Music. **1937** A Vitaphone short. **1945** Riding High.

BRITTON, PAMELA
Born: 1923. Died: June 17, 1974, Arlington Heights, Ill. (brain tumor). Screen, stage and television actress. Daughter of radio actress Ethel Owens.

Appeared in: **1945** Anchors Aweigh. **1946** A Letter From Evie. **1949** D.O.A. **1950** Key to the City; Watch the Birdie. **1969** If It's Tuesday, This Must Be Belgium. **1970** Suppose They Gave a War and Nobody Came?

BROADLEY, EDWARD
Died: Nov. 24, 1947, New York, N.Y. Stage and screen actor.

Appeared in: **1938** The Jury's Secret; Women Are Like That.

BROCK, TONY
Died: Nov. 26, 1924, New York, N.Y. (auto accident while filming stunt in The Great Circus Mystery).

Appeared in: **1925** The Great Circus Mystery (serial).

BROCKWELL, GLADYS
Born: 1894, Brooklyn, N.Y. Died: July 2, 1929, Hollywood, Calif. (peritonitis as result of auto accident injuries). Stage and screen actress.

Appeared in: **1916** Sins of the Parent. **1918** The Devil's Wheel. **1921** The Sage Hen. **1922** Paid Back; Double Stakes; Oliver Twist. **1923** The Drug Traffic; Penrod and Sam; The Darling of New York; His Last Race; The Hunchback of Notre Dame. **1924** So Big; The Foolish Virgin; Unmarried Wives. **1925** The Ancient Mariner; Chickie; Stella Maris; The Necessary Evil; The Reckless Sex; The Splendid Road. **1926** The Carnival Girl; Spangles; Her Sacrifice; The Skyrocket; Twinkletoes; The Last Frontier. **1927** Seventh Heaven; The Satin Woman; The Country Doctor; Long Pants; Man, Woman and Sin. **1928** The Law and the Man; My Home Town; Lights of New York; Home Towners; Woman Disputed; Hollywood Bound. **1929** From Headquarters; Hard-Boiled Rose; The Hottentot; The Argyle Case; The Drake Case.

BRODERICK, HELEN
Born: 1891, Philadelphia, Pa. Died: Sept. 25, 1959, Beverly Hills, Calif. Screen, stage, vaudeville and radio actress. Mother of actor Broderick Crawford.

Appeared in: **1924** High Speed. **1926** The Mystery Club. **1930** Nile Green (short); For Art's Sake (short). **1931** Fifty Million Frenchmen; The Spirits of 76th Street (short); Court Plastered (short). **1932** Cold Turkey (short). **1935** Top Hat; To Beat the Band. **1936** Love on a Bet; Murder on the Bridle Path; The Bride Walks Out; Swing Time; Smartest Girl in Town. **1937** We're on the Jury; Meet the Missus; The Life of the Party. **1938** She's Got Everything; Radio City Revels; The Rage of Paris; The Road to Reno; Service Deluxe. **1939** Stand Up and Fight; Honeymoon in Bali; Naughty but Nice. **1940** The Captain Is a Lady; No, No, Nanette. **1941** Virginia; Father Takes a Wife; Nice Girl. **1942** Are Husbands Necessary? **1943** Stage Door Canteen. **1944** Her Primitive Man; Three Is a Family; Chip Off the Old Block. **1945** Love, Honor and Goodbye. **1946** Because of Him.

BRODIE, BUSTER
Born: 1886. Died: Apr. 9, 1948, Hollywood, Calif. (heart attack). Screen, stage and vaudeville actor. Entered films approx. 1926.

Appeared in: **1927** All Aboard.

BRODY, ANN (Ann Brody Goldstein)
Born: Aug. 29, 1884, Poland. Died: July 16, 1944, New York, N.Y. Stage and screen actress. Entered films with Vitagraph Co. in 1912.

Appeared in: **1921** Shams of Society. **1923** Lost in a Big City. **1924** A Sainted Devil. **1925** The Manicure Girl; Red Love. **1926** Too Much Money. **1927** Alias the Lone Wolf; Clancy's Kosher Wedding; Jake the Plumber; Heroes in Blue. **1928** Turn Back the Hours; My Man. **1929** Times Square; So This Is College; The Case of Lena Smith; The Wolf Song; Alpine Tale; The Man from Blankley's. **1930** Fall Guy; A Royal Romance; Playing Around. **1931** Oh! Oh! Cleopatra (short); Drums of Jeopardy. **1932** The Drifter; Lawyer Man; Heart of New York. **1933** High Gear; Bloody Money. **1934** Money Means Nothing.

BROKAW, CHARLES
Born: 1898. Died: Oct. 23, 1975, New York, N.Y. Screen and stage actor.

Appeared in: **1926** Fascinating Youth. **1937** I Cover the War; Idol of the Crowd; Behind Prison Bars. **1938** The Buccaneer; Air Devils; Convicts at Large. **1940** Murder in the Air.

BROMBERG, J. EDWARD
Born: Dec. 25, 1903, Temesvar, Hungary. Died: Dec. 6, 1951, London, England (natural causes). Stage and screen actor.

Appeared in: **1936** Under Two Flags; Reunion; Stowaway; Sins of Man; The Crime of Dr. Forbes; Girls' Dormitory; Star for a Night; Ladies in Love. **1937** Fair Warning; That I May Live; Seventh Heaven; Charlie Chan on Broadway; Second Honeymoon. **1938** Mr. Moto Takes a Chance; The Baroness and the Butler; One Wild Night; Four Men and a Prayer; Sally, Irene and Mary; Rebecca of Sunnybrook Farm; I'll Give a Million; Suez. **1939** Wife, Husband and Friend; Hollywood Cavalcade; Jesse James; The Mark of Zorro. **1941** Hurricane Smith; Midnight Angel; Dance Hall. **1942** Life Begins at 8:30; Invisible Agent; Pacific Blackout; Reunion in France; Tennessee Johnson; The Devil Pays Off; Halfway to Shanghai. **1943** Sons of Dracula; Lady of Burlesque; Phantom of the Opera. **1944** Chip Off the Old Block; A Voice in the Wind. **1945** Salome, Where She Danced; The Missing Corpse; Easy to Look At; Pillow of Death. **1946** Tangier; The Walls Came Tumbling Down; Cloak and Dagger. **1947** Queen of the Amazon. **1948** Arch of Triumph; A Song is Born. **1949** I Shot Jesse James. **1950** Guilty Bystander.

BRONSON, BETTY (Elizabeth Ada Bronson)
Born: Nov. 17, 1907, Trenton, N.J. Died: Oct. 19, 1971, Pasadena, Calif. Screen, stage and television actress.

Appeared in: **1922** Anna Ascends. **1923** Java Head; His Children's Children; Twenty-One. **1924** The Great White Way; The Eternal City. **1925** Are Parents People?; Not So Long Ago; The Golden Princess; Peter Pan. **1926** The Cat's Pajamas; Everybody's Acting; A Kiss for Cinderella; Paradise; Ben Hur. **1927** Brass Knuckles; Paradise for Two; Open Range; Ritzy. **1928** The Singing Fool; The Companionate Marriage (aka The Jazz Bride). **1929** Bellamy Trial; Sonny Boy; One Stolen Night. **1930** The Medicine Man; A Modern Sappho; The Locked Door. **1931** Lover Come Back. **1932** The Midnight Patrol. **1937** Yodelin' Kid from Pine Ridge (aka The Hero of Pine Ridge). **1961** Pocketful of Miracles. **1964** The Naked Kiss. **1968** Blackbeard's Ghost. **1971** Evel Knievel.

BROOK, CLIVE (Clifford Hardman Brook)
Born: June 1, 1887, London, England. Died: Nov. 17, 1974, London, England. Screen, stage, television actor and film director. Married to actress Mildred Evelyn. Father of actress Faith and actor/playwright Clive Lyndon Brook.

Appeared in: **1920** Trent's Last Case; Kissing Cup's Race. **1921** Her Penalty; The Loudwater Mystery; Daniel Deronda; A Sportsman's Wife; Sonia; Christie Johnstone. **1922** Tense Moments with Great Authors series including: Vanity Fair and A Tale of Two Cities; Master Song Scenes series including: Whispering and The Sheik; Famous Poems by George R. Sims series including: Sir Rupert's Wife and The Parson's Wife; Tense Moments from Opera series including: Rigoletto and La Traviata; Shirley; Married to a Mormon; The Experiment; A Debt of Honour; Love and a Whirlwind. **1923** Through Fire and Water; This Freedom; Out to Win; The Reverse of the Medal; The Royal Oak; Woman to Woman (US 1924). **1924** The Money Habit; The White Shadow (aka White Shadows—US); The Recoil (aka Recoil); The Wine of Life; The Passionate Adventure; Human Desires; Christine of the Hungry Heart; The Mirage. **1925** When Love Grows Cold; Enticement; Declassee (aka The Social Exile); Playing with Souls; If Marriage Fails; The Woman Hater; Compromise; Seven Sinners; The Home Maker; The Pleasure Buyers. **1926** Three Faces East; Why Girls Go Back Home; For Alimony Only; You Never Know Women; The Popular Sin. **1927** Afraid to Love; Barbed Wire; Underworld; Hula; The Devil Dancer; French Dressing. **1928** Midnight Madness; The Yellow Lily; The Perfect Crime; Forgotten Faces. **1929** Interference; A Dangerous Woman; The Four Feathers; Charming Sinners; Return of Sherlock Holmes;

The Laughing Lady. **1930** Slightly Scarlet; Paramount on Parade; Sweethearts and Wives; Anybody's Woman. **1931** Scandal Sheet; East Lynne; Tarnished Lady; The Lawyer's Secret; Silence; Twenty-Four Hours (aka The Hours Between); Husband's Holiday. **1932** Shanghai Express; The Man from Yesterday; The Night of June 13th; Sherlock Holmes; Make Me a Star (cameo appearance). **1933** Cavalcade; Midnight Club; Gallante Lady. **1934** If I Were Free (aka Behold, We Live); Where Sinners Meet (aka The Dover Road); Let's Try Again (aka The Marriage Symphony). **1935** The Love Affair of the Dictator (aka The Dictator and The Loves of a Dictator—US); Dressed to Thrill. **1936** The Lonely Road (aka Scotland Yard Commands—US 1937); Love in Exile. **1937** Action for Slander (US 1938). **1938** The Ware Case (US 1939). **1940** Return to Yesterday; Convoy. **1941** Freedom Radio (aka A Voice in the Night—US); Breach of Promise (aka Adventure in Blackmail—US 1943). **1943** The Flemish Farm; The Shipbuilders; For the Love of a Queen (rerelease of The Love Affair of the Dictator-1935). **1944** On Approval (US 1945). **1963** The List of Adrian Messenger.

BROOKE, CLAUDE
Born: 1853. Died: Dec. 14, 1933, Leonia, N.J. Screen and stage actor.

Appeared in: **1922** Silver Wings. **1923** Does It Pay? **1924** Pied Piper Malone; Classmates. **1926** Great Gatsby; Sorrows of Satan; God Save Me Twenty Cents.

BROOKE, CLIFFORD
Born: 1872, England. Died: Dec. 28, 1951, Santa Monica, Calif. (injuries sustained after struck by auto). Screen and stage actor. Entered films approx. 1939.

Appeared in: **1941** A Woman's Face. **1944** Wilson. **1945** Hangover Square; Molly and Me; The Suspect. **1946** Three Strangers; Black Beauty. **1948** The Woman in White. **1951** The First Legion.

BROOKE, MRS. MYRA
Born: 1865. Died: Feb. 9, 1944, Amityville, N.Y. Screen and stage actress.

BROOKE, RALPH (Ralph Tweer Brooks)
Born: 1920. Died: Dec. 4, 1963, Hollywood, Calif. Screen, stage actor, screenwriter and film producer/director. Entered films with the Max Reinhardt Co. in Hollywood.

Appeared in: **1935** A Shot in the Dark. **1944** The Thin Man Goes Home. **1950** Mystery Submarine. **1953** The Charge at Feather River. **1960** The Third Voice.

BROOKE, TYLER (Victor Huge de Biere)
Born: 1891, New York, N.Y. Died: Mar. 2, 1943, North Hollywood, Calif. (suicide-carbon monoxide poisoning). Stage and screen actor.

Appeared in: **1927** Rich, but Honest; Stage Madness; The Cradle Snatchers. **1928** Fazil; None But the Brave. **1929** Dynamite; Van Bibber Fox comedies. **1930** Playboy of Paris; Madame Satan; The Furies; The Divorcee; Monte Carlo; Lilies of the Field. **1931** The Magnificent Lie; Oh! Oh! Cleopatra (short); A Dangerous Affair. **1932** Love Me Tonight. **1933** Hallelujah, I'm a Bum; Child of Manhattan; Morning Glory. **1934** Blind Date; Belle of the Nineties; Imitation of Life. **1935** Call of the Wild; Reckless; Times Square Lady; Here Comes the Band. **1936** The Poor Little Rich Girl; To Mary—With Love; Two in a Crowd. **1937** This Is My Affair; You Can't Have Everything. **1938** Tom Sawyer, Detective; Bluebeard's Eighth Wife; In Old Chicago; Alexander's Ragtime Band. **1940** Tin Pan Alley; Little Old New York; One Night in the Tropics. **1942** Lucky Legs; I Married an Angel; The McGuerins from Brooklyn.

BROOKE, VAN DYKE (aka VAN DYKE BROOKS)
Born: Detroit, Mich. Died: Sept. 17, 1921, Saratoga Springs, N.Y. Screen, stage actor, film director, stage director and screenwriter. Entered films with Vitagraph.

Appeared in: **1911** Captain Barnacle's Courtship; My Old Dutch; Captain Barnacle's Baby; Captain Barnacle, Diplomat. **1912** The First Violin; Captain Barnacle, Reformer; For the Honor of the Family; The Law or the Lady; Winning Is Losing; The Diamond Brooch; On the Pupil of His Eye; Captain Barnacle's Legacy; The Old Silver Watch; Nemesis; Counsel for the Defense; Dr. Lafleur's Theory; The Foster Child; The Spider's Web; Their Golden Anniversary; Flirt or Heroine; Lord Browning and Cinderella; Captain Barnacle's Waif; O'Hara, Squatter and Philosopher; Mrs. 'Enry 'Awkins; Mrs. Lirriper's Lodger. **1913** O'Hara and the Youthful Prodigal; A Modern Psyche; O'Hara as Guardian Angel; Ida's Christmas; O'Hara Helps Cupid; An Elopement at Home; Fanny's Conspiracy; O'Hara's Godchild; The Mouse and the Lion; Wanted: A Strong Hand; Tim Grogan's Foundling; An Old Man's Love Story; Better Days. **1914** A Wayward Daughter; His Little Page; The Memories in Men's Souls; Politics and the Press; Under False Colors; Goodbye Summer; Fogg's Millions; Officer John Donovan; The Vavasour Ball. **1915** The Romance of a Handkerchief; Dorothy; The Fortune Hunter; A Question of Right or Wrong; Elsa's Brother; Saints and Sinners; A Daughter's Strange Inheritance. **1916** The Primal Instinct; The Bond of Blood; Would You Forgive Her? **1919** The Moonshine Trail. **1921** Midnight Bell; The Passionate Pilgrim; The Son of Wallingford; The Crimson Cross; Straight Is the Way.

BROOK-JONES, ELWYN
Born: Dec. 11, 1911, Borneo. Died: Sept. 4, 1962, Reading, England. Screen, stage and television actor.

Appeared in: **1941** Pimpernel Smith (aka Mister V—US 1942); Dangerous Moonlight (aka Suicide Squadron—US 1942). **1942** Tomorrow We Live (aka At Dawn We Die—US 1943). **1943** The Night Invader. **1947** Odd Man Out. **1948** The Three Weird Sisters; Good Time Girl (US 1950); It's Hard to be Good (US 1950); Bonnie Prince Charlie. **1951** I'll Get you for This (aka Lucky Nick Cain—US); Life in Her Hands; The Wonder Kid. **1952** Judgment Deferred; The Night Won't Talk. **1953** Three Steps in the Dark. **1954** Beau Brummell; The Harrassed Hero. **1955** The Gilded Cage. **1956** Assignment Redhead (aka Million Dollar Manhunt—US 1962). **1957** Rogue's Yarn. **1958** The Duke Wore Jeans. **1959** Passport to Shame (aka Room 43—US); The Ugly Duckling. **1961** The Pure Hell of St. Trinians.

BROOKS, ALAN (Irving Hayward)
Born: 1888. Died: Sept. 1936, Saranac, N.Y. Screen, vaudeville actor, stage and vaudeville producer.

Appeared in: **1926** Red Dice; Young April; Pals in Paradise. **1927** King of Kings; Home Struck; Ladies Beware; Shanghaied; South Sea Love. **1929** Mr. Intruder (short); The Hole in the Wall. **1932-33** Paramount shorts. **1937** The League of Frightened Men.

BROOKS, HANK
Died: Dec. 3, 1925, Los Angeles, Calif. Screen actor. Entered films with Sennett in 1915.

BROOKS, JESS LEE
Born: 1894. Died: Dec. 13, 1944, Hollywood, Calif. (heart attack). Black screen and stage actor.

Appeared in: **1941** Sullivan's Travels. **1942** Drums of the Congo; Jungle Siren. **1945** Wilson; The Lost Weekend.

BROOKS, PAULINE
Born: 1913. Died: June 7, 1967, Glendale, Calif. (cancer). Stage and screen actress.

Appeared in: **1933** Beauty for Sale. **1934** Student Tour. **1935** Age of Indiscretion; Make a Million; Alibi Ike.

BROOKS, RANDY
Born: 1918. Died: Mar. 21, 1967, Springvale, Me. (result of smoke inhalation). Band leader, trumpeter and screen actor. Do not confuse with screen actor with same name.

Appeared in: **1945** A Columbia short (with his orchestra).

BROPHY, EDWARD
Born: Feb. 27, 1895, New York, N.Y. Died: May 30, 1960, Los Angeles, Calif. Screen actor. Entered films in 1919.

Appeared in: **1920** Yes or No (film debut). **1927** West Point. **1929** The Cameraman. **1930** Our Blushing Brides; Free and Easy; Those Three French Girls; Paid; Doughboys; Remote Control. **1931** Parlor, Bedroom and Bath; A Dangerous Affair; A Free Soul; The Champ. **1932** Speak Easily; Freaks; Flesh; The Big Shot. **1933** What, No Beer?; Broadway to Hollywood. **1934** Hide-Out; Death on the Diamond; Evelyn Prentice; I'll Fix It; The Thin Man; Paris Interlude. **1935** I Live My Life; $1,000 a Minute; Naughty Marietta; The Whole Town's Talking; Shadow of Doubt; Mad Love; China Seas; People Will Talk; She Gets Her Man; Remember Last Night?; Show Them No Mercy. **1936** Mr. Cinderella; The Soldier and the Lady; Strike Me Pink; Woman Trap; The Case against Mrs. Ames; Spendthrift; Wedding Present; All American Chump; Kelly the Second; Here Comes Trouble; Career Woman; Great Guy. **1937** Hideaway Girl; Michael Strogoff; The Great Gambini; Blossoms on Broadway; Varsity Show; Jim Hanvey—Detective; The Hit Parade; Oh, Doctor!; The Last Gangster; The Girl Said No; The River of Missing Men; Trapped by G-Men. **1938** A Slight Case of Murder; Romance on the Run; Come On, Leathernecks!; Gambling Ship; Hold That Kiss; Vacation from Love; Passport Husband; Pardon Our Nerve; Golddiggers in Paris. **1939** You Can't Cheat an Honest Man; For Love or Money; Society Lawyer; The Kid from Kokomo; Golden Boy; The Amazing Mr. Williams; Kid Nightingale. **1940** The Big Guy; Dance, Girl, Dance; Sandy Gets Her Man; Calling Philo Vance; Alias the Deacon; Golden Gloves; The Great Profile. **1941** Sleepers West; A Dangerous Game; The Invisible Woman; Dumbo (voice); Thieves Fall Out; Nine Lives Are Not Enough; Steel against the Sky; The Bride Came C.O.D.; Buy Me That Town; The Gay Falcon. **1942** Broadway; Lady Bodyguard; Air Force; Madame Spy; One Exciting Night; Destroyer; Larceny, Inc.; All Through the Night. **1944** It Happened Tomorrow; A Night of Adventure; The Thin Man Goes Home; Cover Girl. **1945** I'll Remember April; Wonder Man; See My Lawyer; The Falcon in San Francisco; Penthouse Rhythm. **1946** Swing Parade of 1946; Girl on the Spot; The Falcon's Adventure; Sweetheart of Sigma Chi. **1947** It Happened on Fifth Avenue. **1949** Arson, Inc. **1951** Pier 23; Danger Zone; Roaring City. **1956** Bundle of Joy. **1958** The Last Hurrah.

BROSIG, EGON

Born: 1890, Germany. Died: May 23, 1961, Berlin, Germany. Screen, stage and radio actor.

Appeared in the following German films: The Old and the Young King; The Strange Adventures of Mr. Fridolin; The Cold Heart; The Subject.

BROTHER BONES See FREEMAN DAVIS

BROUGH, MARY

Born: Apr. 16, 1863, London, England. Died: Sept. 30, 1934, London, England (heart trouble). Stage and screen actress.

Appeared in: 1914 The Bosun's Mate; A Christmas Carol; Lawyer Quince; Mrs. Scrubbs' Discovery; Beauty and the Barge. 1915 His Lordship. 1917 Masks and Faces. 1920 Fordington Twins; John Forest Finds Himself; Judge Not; London Pride; The Amazing Quest of Ernest Bliss (serial); The Law Divine; Enchantment. 1921 Squibs; The Will; The Adventures of Mr. Pickwick; The Bachelor's Club; The Diamond Necklace; Demos (aka Why Men Forget—US); The Golden Dawn; The Old Wives' Tale; The Night Hawk (aka The Haven); The Tinted Venus; All Sorts and Conditions of Men. 1922 A Sister to Assist 'Er; Squibs Wins the Calcutta Sweep; Tit for Tat. 1923 Lights of London; The School for Scandal; Lily of the Alley; Married Love (aka Married Life and Maisie's Marriage). 1924 The Alley of Golden Hearts; His Grace Gives Notice; Not for Sale; The Passionate Adventure; Tons of Money. 1925 The Only Way. 1926 Safety First. 1927 A Sister to Assist 'Er (and 1922 version). 1928 Dawn; The Passing of Mr. Quin; The Physician (US 1929); Sailors Don't Care; Wait and See; When We Were Young series, including: Nursery Chairs and The King's Breakfast. 1929 The Broken Melody; Master and Man. 1930 Rookery Nook (aka One Embarassing Night—US); On Approval. 1931 Tons of Money (and 1924 version). 1932 A Night Like This; Thark. 1933 Turkey Time; A Cuckoo in the Nest; Up to the Neck.

BROWER, OTTO

Born: Dec. 2, 1895, Grand Rapids, Mich. Died: Jan. 25, 1946, Hollywood, Calif. (heart failure). Screen actor and film director.

Appeared in: 1922 On the High Seas. 1923 All the Brothers Were Valiant.

BROWER, ROBERT

Born: July 14, 1850, Point Pleasant, N.Y. Died: Dec. 8, 1934, West Hollywood, Calif. Screen, stage actor and screenwriter.

Appeared in: 1911 Foul Play; How Mrs. Murray Saved the American Army; A Conspiracy Against the King; The Reform Candidate; The Living Peach; The Bo'sun's Watch; Uncle Hiram's List; The Trapper's Five Dollar Bill; The New Church Carpet; The Captain of Fort Ticonderoga; Maiden of the Piefaced Indians; The Hair Restorer and the Indians; His First Trip; The Declaration of Independence; The Three Musketeers; A Cure for Crime; The Death of Nathan Hale. 1912 The Third Thanksgiving; How the Boys Fought the Indians; For the Commonwealth; The Convict's Parole; Blinks and Jinks; Attorneys at Law; The Bank President's Son; The Sunset Gun; The Usurer's Grip; Helping John; The Father; The Harbinger of Peace; Under False Colors; A Baby's Shoe; The Dam Builder. 1919 The Lottery Man; Hawthorne of the U.S.A.; The Beauty Market. 1920 City Sparrow; Held by the Enemy; A Cumberland Romance; Jack Straw; The Jucklins. 1921 The Faith Healer; The Little Minister; The Lost Romance; What Every Woman Knows. 1922 Fools First; Is Matrimony a Failure?; The Man Who Saw Tomorrow; Singed Wings; Thirty Days. 1923 Adam's Rib; Long Live the King; Racing Hearts. 1924 Riders Up. 1925 Fifth Avenue Models; The Thoroughbred. 1926 The Honeymoon Express; Wild Oats Lane. 1927 The Gay Defender; The Last Trail. 1928 Beggars of Life. 1930 Abraham Lincoln.

BROWN, BARBARA

Died: July 7, 1975. Screen actress.

Appeared in: 1942 The Wife Takes a Flyer; You Were Never Lovelier. 1943 Reveille With Beverly; Falcon and the Co-Eds; Wedtime Stories (short); Mission to Moscow; Never a Dull Moment; Top Man. 1944 The Sullivans; Janie; The Ghost That Walks Alone; Hey, Rookie; The Doughgirls; Hollywood Canteen. 1945 Roughly Speaking; Pillow to Post; Too Young to Know; Mildred Pierce. 1946 Janie Gets Married; Personality Kid; White Tie and Tails; The Beast With Five Fingers. 1947 That Way With Women; High Barbaree; Love and Learn; That Haggen Girl. 1948 Arthur Takes Over; Wallflower. 1949 Henry, the Rainmaker; Miss Mink of 1949; Yes, Sir, That's My Baby; Leave it to Henry. 1950 Father Makes Good; Born Yesterday; Father's Wild Game. 1951 Ma and Pa Kettle Back on the Farm; Home Town Story; Father Takes the Air; The Lady and the Bandit. 1952 Jack and the Beanstalk; The Brigand; You for Me. 1953 Ma and Pa Kettle on Vacation. 1955 Sincerely Yours; Annapolis Story; My Sister Eileen. 1970 The Red, White and Black.

BROWN, BLY

Born: 1898. Died: Dec. 19, 1950, Los Angeles, Calif. Screen and stage actress.

BROWN, CHARLES D.

Born: July 1, 1887, Council Bluffs, Iowa. Died: Nov. 25, 1948, Hollywood, Calif. (heart ailment). Stage and screen actor.

Appeared in: 1921 The Man of Stone; The Way of a Maid. 1929 The Dance of Life; Dangerous Curves. 1931 The Road to Reno; Twenty-Four Hours; Murder by the Clock; Touchdown. 1933 The Woman I Stole. 1934 It Happened One Night. 1936 Golddiggers of 1937. 1937 Thoroughbreds Don't Cry. 1938 Think it Over (short); Island in the Sky; Mr. Moto's Gamble; Speed to Burn; Inside Story; Up the River; Exposed; Algiers; Duke of West Point; Shopworn Angel; The Crowd Roars; Barefoot Boy; Five of a Kind. 1939 Tell No Tales; Mr. Moto in Danger Island; Charlie Chan in Reno; Hotel for Women; Kid Nightingale; Smashing the Money Ring; Ice Follies of 1939; Little Accident; Disbarred. 1940 Know Your Money (short); Brother Orchid; Pier 13; The Santa Fe Trail; The Grapes of Wrath; He Married His Wife; Sailor's Lady. 1941 Glamour Boy; Tall, Dark and Handsome; Reaching for the Sun; International Lady. 1942 Fingers at the Window; Roxie Hart; Sweater Girl. 1943 A Lady Takes a Chance. 1944 Up in Arms; The Fighting Seabees; The Contender; Jam Session; Secret Command. 1945 Having a Wonderful Crime; Don Juan Quilligan; Apology for Murder; Sunbonnet Sue. 1946 Wake Up and Dream; The Killers; Just Before Dawn; The Last Crooked Mile; The Big Sleep; Night Editor; The Strange Loves of Martha Ivers. 1947 Smash-Up; The Story of a Woman; Merton of the Movies; The Senator Was Indiscreet. 1948 A Miracle Can Happen; In This Corner. 1949 Follow Me Quietly. 1951 Sealed Cargo.

BROWN, HARRY W. (Harry William Brown)

Born: Feb. 27, 1918. Died: May 26, 1966, Pacoima, Calif. (lung cancer). Screen actor. Do not confuse with actor Harry J. Brown.

BROWN, HELEN "MINA"

Born: 1916. Died: Sept. 9, 1974, Calif. (cancer). Screen and television actress.

Appeared in: 1935 Diamond Jim. 1936 Three Godfathers; Collegiate; Big Brown Eyes; To Mary—With Love. 1937 This Is My Affair. 1939 Hidden Power; Should A Girl Marry; Hotel for Women. 1940 Babies for Sale; Out West With the Peppers; Five Little Peppers in Trouble. 1941 Mr. District Attorney. 1943 She's For Me. 1944 Tampico. 1946 Danny Boy. 1947 Nora Prentiss. 1948 The Walls of Jericho. 1949 Holiday Affair; Arctic Manhunt. 1950 Shadow on the Wall; Molly (aka The Goldbergs); Dancing in the Dark. 1951 Al Jennings of Oklahoma. 1952 Dream Boat. 1953 Shane. 1955 Strategic Air Command; Teen-Age Crime Wave. 1958 The Missouri Traveler.

BROWN, JOE E. (Joseph Even Brown)

Born: July 28, 1892, Holgate, Ohio. Died: July 17, 1973, Brentwood, Calif. Screen, stage, circus, vaudeville actor and author.

Appeared in: 1928 Crooks Can't Wait (film debut); Me, Gangster; Road House; Dressed to Kill; The Circus Kid; Hit of the Show; Take Me Home; Burlesque; Don't Be Jealous. 1929 In Old Arizona; Sunny Side Up; Molly and Me; Sally; My Lady's Past; On With the Show; Painted Faces; The Cock-Eyed World; The Ghost Talks; Protection. 1930 Up the River; Maybe It's Love; Song of the West; Born Reckless; City Girl; Hold Everything; The Lottery Bride; Top Speed. 1931 Going Wild; Local Boy Makes Good; Broad-Minded; Sit Tight. 1932 The Tenderfoot; Fireman, Save My Child; The Slippery Pearls (short); You Said a Mouthful; The Putter (short). 1933 Elmer the Great; Son of a Sailor. 1934 The Circus Clown; Six Day Bike Rider; A Very Honorable Guy. 1935 A Midsummer Night's Dream; Alibi Ike. 1936 Bright Lights; Polo Joe; Sons O'Gun; Earthworm Tractors. 1937 Fit for a King; When's Your Birthday?; Riding on Air (aka All is Confusion). 1938 Flirting with Fate; The Gladiator; Wide Open Faces. 1939 Beware Spooks!; $1,000 a Touchdown. 1940 So You Won't Talk. 1942 Shut My Big Mouth; The Daring Young Man; Joan of the Ozarks. 1943 Chatterbox. 1944 Pin-Up Girl; Hollywood Canteen; Casanova in Burlesque. 1947 Riding on Air. 1949 The Tender Years. 1951 Showboat; Memories of Famous Hollywood Comedians (short—narrator). 1954 Hollywood Fathers (short). 1956 Around the World in 80 Days. 1959 Some Like it Hot. 1963 A Comedy of Terrors (doc.); It's a Mad, Mad, Mad, Mad World.

BROWN, JOHN

Died: May 16, 1957. Screen and radio actor. Do not confuse with actor John Brown who entered films during the 1950's.

BROWN, JOHNNY MACK

Born: Sept. 1, 1904, Dothan, Ala. Died: Nov. 14, 1975, Woodland Hills, Calif. (cardiac condition). Screen actor and All American college football player.

Appeared in: 1927 The Bugle Call; Fair Co-Ed. 1928 Our Dancing Daughters; Divine Woman; Soft Living; Square Crooks; Play Girl; Annapolis; Lady of Chance. 1929 Woman of Affairs; Coquette; The Valiant; Single Standard; Hurricane; Jazz Heaven. 1930 Undertow; Montana Moon; Billy the Kid. 1931 Secret Six; Great Meadow; Lasca of the Rio Grande; Last Flight; Laughing Sinners. 1932 Flames; 70,000 Witnesses; Vanishing Frontier; Malay Nights. 1933 Saturday's Millions; Female; Son of a Sailor; Fighting With Kit Carson (serial); Hollywood on Parade. 1934 Marrying Widows; Three on a Honeymoon; Belle of the Nineties; Cross Streets; Against the Law. 1935 St. Louis Woman; Between Men; Courageous Avenger; The Rustlers of Red Dog; The

Right to Live. **1936** The Desert Phantom; Rogue of the Range; Every Man's Law. **1937** Lawless Land; Bar Z Bad Man; Guns in the Dark; A Lawman is Born; Boothill Brigade; Wells Fargo; Wild West Days (serial). **1938** Born to the West; Flaming Frontiers (serial). **1939** Desperate Trails; Oklahoma Frontier; The Oregon Trail (serial). **1940** Chip of the Flying U; West of Carson City; Riders of Pasco Basin; The Bad Man from Red Butte; Son of Roaring Dan; Ragtime Cowboy Joe; Law and Order; Pony Post. **1941** Law of the Range; The Masked Rider; Man from Montana. **1942** Ride 'Em Cowboy; Arizona Cyclone; Fighting Bill Fargo; Stagecoach Buckaroo; The Silver Bullet; Deep in the Heart of Texas; The Boss of Hangtown; Little Joe, the Wrangler. **1943** Tenting Tonight on the Old Camp Ground; The Old Chisholm Trail; Cheyenne Roundup; The Ghost Rider; The Stranger from Pecos; Lone Star Trail. **1944** Range Law; Land of the Outlaws; Raiders of the Border; West of the Rio Grande; Partners of the Trail; Law of the Valley; Law Men. **1945** They Shall Have Faith; Law of the Valley; Flame of the West. **1946** Drifting Along; The Haunted Mine; Under Arizona Skies; Shadows on the Range; Raiders of the South; Gentleman from Texas; Trigger Fingers; Silver Range. **1947** Land of the Lawless; Valley of Fear; Trailing Danger; The Law Comes to Gunsight; Flashing Guns; Prairie Express; Code of the Saddle; Gun Talk. **1948** Triggerman; Frontier Agent; Overland Trails; Cross Trails; The Fighting Ranger; Backtrail; The Sheriff of Medicine Bow; Hidden Danger; Gunning for Justice. **1949** Stampede; Trails End; Law of the West; Western Renegades; West of El Dorado; Range Justice. **1950** Over the Border; West of Wyoming; Short Grass; Six Gun Mesa; Outlaw Gold; Law of the Panhandle. **1951** Man from Sonora; Blazing Bullets; Colorado Ambush; Montana Desperado; Texas Lawmen; Whistling Hills. **1952** Man from the Black Hills; Canyon Ambush; Dead Man's Trail; Texas City. **1954** Hollywood Fathers (short). **1965** Requiem for a Gunfighter; The Bounty Killer. **1966** Apache Uprising.

BROWN, MAXINE VELENA
Born: 1897, Denver, Colo. Died: Dec. 1956, Alameda, Calif. (burns). Screen, stage, vaudeville and radio actress. Divorced from vaudeville performer George Maines. Married to vaudeville actor Clarence Willard. Appeared in Famous and Warner films.

BROWN, MELVILLE
Born: 1888, Portland, Ore. Died: Jan. 31, 1938, Hollywood, Calif. (heart attack). Screen, stage, vaudeville actor, film, stage director and screenwriter. Entered films in 1916.

BROWN, PAMELA (aka PAMELA BROWNE)
Born: July 8, 1917, London, England. Died: Sept. 18, 1975, London, England. Screen, stage and television actress. (Do not confuse with Pamela Brown, writer/producer, etc., born 1924).

Appeared in: **1942** One of Our Aircraft Is Missing. **1945** I Know Where I'm Going (US 1947). **1951** The Tales of Hoffman. **1952** The Second Mrs. Tanqueray (US 1954). **1953** Personal Affair (US 1954). **1955** Richard III (US 1956). **1956** Lust For Life. **1959** The Scapegoat. **1963** Cleopatra. **1964** Becket. **1965** Gonks Go Beat. **1966** A Funny Thing Happened on the Way to the Forum. **1967** Half a Sixpence (US 1968). **1968** Secret Ceremony. **1970** Wuthering Heights; On a Clear Day You Can See Forever. **1972** Lady Caroline Lamb.

BROWN, PHIL
Died: July 11, 1973. Screen actor. Do not confuse with screen child actor Philip Brown.

Appeared in: **1941** I Wanted Wings; H. M. Pulham, Esq. **1942** Calling Dr. Gillespie; Pierre of the Plains; Hello Anapolis. **1944** Weird Woman; The Impatient Years. **1945** Jungle Captive; Over 21; State Fair. **1946** Without Reservations; The Killers. **1947** Johnny O'Clock. **1948** If You Knew Susie; The Luck of the Irish. **1949** Moonrise. **1950** The Hidden Room (aka Obsession). **1955** The Green Scarf. **1958** The Camp on Blood Island. **1959** John Paul Jones. **1962** The Counterfeit Traitor. **1965** The Bedford Incident. **1966** The Boy Cried Murder. **1969** The Adding Machine; Operation Cross Eagles. **1970** Land Raiders; Tropic of Cancer. **1971** Valdez Is Coming.

BROWN, RAYMOND "RAY"
Born: Aug. 16, 1880, Champaign, Ill. Died: July 30, 1939, Los Angeles, Calif. Stage and screen actor. Entered films in 1929.

Appeared in: **1933** My Woman. **1934** Jealousy; It's the Cats (short); I'll Fix It; Blind Date; Whom the Gods Destroy; White Lies; Successful Failure; Mystery Liner. **1935** Million Dollar Baby; Baby Face Harrington; The Flame Within; Dr. Socrates; Moonlight on the Prairie. **1936** The Story of Louis Pasteur; Laughing Irish Eyes; Comin' Round the Mountain; Down the Stretch; The Magnificent Brute; Career Woman. **1937** The Holy Terror; Two Wise Maids; We Have Our Moments; Parole Rackets; Back in Circulation. **1939** They Made Me a Criminal; King of the Underworld; The Family Next Door.

BROWN, RONALD C.
Born: 1911. Died: Oct. 27, 1962, Hollywood, Calif. Screen actor and dancer. Entered films approx. 1937.

BROWN, RUSS
Born: May 30, 1892, Philadelphia, Pa. Died: Oct. 19, 1964, Englewood, N.J. Screen, stage and vaudeville actor. Divorced from screen actress Gertrude Whitaker. Appeared in vaudeville in an act with Bert Wheeler and later with Gertrude Whitaker in an act billed as "Brown and Whitaker."

Appeared in: **1928** "Brown and Whitaker" appeared in the following shorts: A Laugh or Two; In the Park. Brown later appeared in: **1933** Moulin Rouge; My Woman. **1934** The Love Captive; Let's Talk It Over. **1958** South Pacific; Damn Yankees. **1959** Anatomy of a Murder; It Happened to Jane. **1962** Advise and Consent. **1963** The Cardinal.

BROWN, TROY, JR.
Died: Nov. 18, 1944. Screen actor.

Appeared in: **1936** Can This Be Dixie? **1937** Nothing Sacred. **1940** Dreaming Out Loud.

BROWN, WALLY
Born: Oct. 9, 1904, Malden, Mass. Died: Nov. 13, 1961, Los Angeles, Calif. Screen, vaudeville, radio and television actor. Was part of film comedy team of "Brown and Carney" with Alan Carney.

Appeared in: **1943** Petticoat Larceny; Radio Runaround (short); Mexican Spitfire's Blessed Event; The Seventh Victim; Gangway for Tomorrow; Around the World. **1944** The Girl in the Case. **1946** From This Day Forward; Notorious; Vacation in Reno. **1948** Backstage Follies (short); Bachelor Blues (short); Family Honeymoon. **1949** Come to the Stable. **1951** As Young as You Feel. **1954** The High and the Mighty. **1956** The Wild Dakotas. **1957** Untamed Youth; The Joker is Wild. **1958** The Wink of an Eye; The Left-Handed Gun. **1959** Westbound; Holiday for Lovers. **1961** The Absent Minded Professor. Brown and Carney films: **1943** The Adventures of a Rookie (their film debut together) and Rookies in Burma. **1944** Girl Rush; Seven Days Ashore; Step Lively. **1945** Radio Stars on Parade; Zombies on Broadway. **1946** Genius at Work.

BROWNE, EARLE
Born: 1872. Died: Nov. 28, 1944, Hollywood, Calif. Screen and stage actor.

Appeared in: **1922** Sherlock Holmes. **1926** Sparrows. **1927** Love of Sunya. **1929** The Iron Mask; The Locked Door; Taming of the Shrew. **1930** DuBarry, Woman of Passion. **1932** Mr. Robinson Crusoe.

BROWNE, IRENE
Born: 1893, London, England. Died: July 24, 1965, London, England (cancer). Stage and screen actress.

Appeared in: **1929** The Letter. **1933** Cavalcade (stage and film versions); Berkeley Square; My Lips Betray; Peg O'My Heart; Christopher Strong. **1936** The Amateur Gentleman. **1938** Pygmalion. **1941** The Prime Minister; Kipps (aka The Remarkable Mr. Kipps—US 1942). **1947** Meet Me at Dawn (US 1948). **1948** The Red Shoes; Quartet. **1950** Madeleine. **1951** The House in the Square (aka I'll Never Forget You—US). **1953** The Gay Duellist (rerelease of Meet Me at Dawn-1947). **1957** Barnacle Bill (aka All at Sea—US 1958). **1958** Rooney. **1959** Serious Charge (aka Immoral Charge—US 1962). **1963** The Wrong Arm of the Law. **1964** A Touch of Hell (rerelease of Serious Charge-1959).

BROWNE, W. GRAHAM
Born: 1870, Ireland. Died: Mar. 11, 1937, London, England (pneumonia). Stage and screen actor. Married to actress Marie Tempest (dec. 1942).

Appeared in: **1915** Mrs. Plumb's Pudding. **1934** The Lady Is Willing. **1937** Moonlight Sonata.

BROWNING, TOD
Born: July 12, 1882, Louisville, Ky. Died: Oct. 6, 1962, Hollywood, Calif. (cancer). Screen, stage actor, film director and screenwriter. Married to actress Alice Browning.

Appeared in: **1914** Billy Takes a Lady to Lunch; Bill Saves the Day; The Deceiver; An Interrupted Seance; A Race for a Bride; The White Slave Catchers; Bill Squares It with the Boss. **1915** Cupid and the Pest; Bill and Ethel at the Ball.

BROWNING, WILLIAM E.
Died: Dec. 21, 1930, Middle Village, N.Y. Screen, stage, and radio actor.

Appeared in: **1929** Applause; plus numerous shorts.

BROWNLEE, FRANK
Born: Oct. 11, 1874, Dallas, Tex. Died: Feb. 10, 1948. Screen actor.

Appeared in: **1919** Brass Buttons; Miss Adventure; The Brute Breaker. **1920** Shore Acres; Riders of the Dawn; The Lincoln Highwayman; The Man Who Dared; Under Crimson Skies; The Valley of Tomorrow; Hearts Are Trumps. **1921** His Own Law; The Hole in the Wall; Love Never Dies; Soul and Body; The Whistle. **1922** The Face Between; Fools of Fortune. **1923** Boston Blackie;

Nobody's Bride; Romance Land; Sawdust. **1924** The Beloved Brute. **1925** The Desert Flower; The Ridin' Streak; Straight Through. **1926** The Social Highwayman; King of the Pack. **1927** Wanted—A Coward; Sailors Beware. **1928** Sawdust Paradise; Midnight Rose. **1929** Beggars of Life. **1931** Rough Seas (short). **1932** Pack Up Your Troubles; Tombstone Canyon. **1933** The Midnight Patrol (short); Terror Trail. **1935** Man's Best Friend.

BRUCE, BELLE
Died: June 15, 1960. Screen actress.

Appeared in: **1917** The Great Secret (serial).

BRUCE, BETTY
Born: 1920. Died: July 18, 1974, New York, N.Y. Screen, stage actress, singer, dancer.

Appeared in: **1962** Gypsy (stage and film versions). **1963** Island of Love (aka Not on Your Life). **1969** Potpourri.

BRUCE, BEVERLY
Died: July, 1925, Bryn Mawr, Calif. Screen, stage and vaudeville actress.

Appeared in: **1920** Empty Arms.

BRUCE, CLIFFORD
Born: 1885, Toronto, Canada. Died: Aug. 27, 1919, West Camp, N.Y. Stage and screen actor.

Appeared in: **1914** A Page From Yesterday; The Perils of Pauline (serial). **1915** A Woman's Past; A Fool There Was; Lady Audley's Secret; Princess Romanoff. **1916** The Fourth Estate; The Devil at His Elbow; The Weakness of Strength. **1917** The Siren; The Barricade; Blue Jeans; Seven Deadly Sins; Passion. **1918** The Winding Trail; A Weaver of Dreams; Breakers Ahead; Riders of the Night. **1919** The Racing Strain; Woman! Woman!

BRUCE, KATE
Born: 1858. Died: Apr. 2, 1946. Screen actress. Entered films in 1908.

Appeared in: **1908** In Old Kentucky; An Awful Moment. **1909** At the Altar; The Golden Louis; Choosing a Husband; The Girl and the Daddy; In the Hempen Bag. **1910** The Two Brothers; A Gold Necklace; The Fugitive; The Rocky Road; A Romance of the Western Hills; Willfull Peggy; Examination Day at School; The Fugitive Waiter. **1912** Death's Marathon; The Leading Man; Home Folks; An Indian Summer; The Punishment; One Is Business, the Other Is Crime; The Informer; A Dash Through the Clouds; The Would-Be Shriner; Death's Marathon. **1913** My Hero; Just Gold; Look Up; The Yaqui Cur; A Tender-Hearted Boy; The Sheriff's Baby. **1914** Judith of Bethulia; The Battle at Firebush Gulch; A Nest Unfeathered; The Scar; Her Mother's Weakness; A Soldier Boy. **1915** Betty of Greystone; Suzan Rocks the Boat; Gretchen the Greenhorn; The Microscope Mystery. **1917** Betsy's Burglar. **1918** Hearts of the World; The Hun Within. **1919** A Romance of Happy Valley; The Girl Who Stayed at Home; Scarlet Days. **1920** Mary Ellen Comes to Town; Flying Pat; The Idol Dancer; Way Down East; Jacqueline of the Blazing Barriers. **1921** The City of Silent Men; Orphans of the Storm; Experience. **1923** The White Rose. **1924** His Darker Self. **1925** I Want My Man. **1927** A Bowery Cinderella; Ragtime; The Secret Studio.

BRUCE, LENNY (Leonard Alfred Schneider)
Born: 1926, Mineola, N.Y. Died: Aug. 3, 1966, Hollywood, Calif. (drug overdose). Nightclub comic, screenwriter and screen actor. Divorced from actress Honey Harlow.

Appeared in: **1953** Dance Hall Racket. **1967** Lenny Bruce (aka Lenny Bruce Concert). **1974** Lenny Bruce Performance Film.

BRUCE, NIGEL
Born: Feb. 4, 1895, Ensenada, Mexico. Died: Oct. 8, 1953, Santa Monica, Calif. (heart attack). Screen, stage and radio actor. Married to actress Violet Campbell (dec. 1970). Best known for his long film and radio portrayal as Dr. Watson in "Sherlock Holmes" series.

Appeared in: **1929** Red Aces. **1930** Birds of Prey (aka The Perfect Alibi—US 1931). **1931** The Squeaker; The Calendar (aka Bachelor's Folly—US 1932); Escape. **1932** Lord Camber's Ladies; I Was a Spy (US 1934); The Midshipmaid. **1934** Channel Crossing; Stand Up and Cheer; Coming Out Party; Murder in Trinidad; The Lady is Willing; Springtime for Henry; Treasure Island. **1935** Jalna; She; The Man Who Broke the Bank at Monte Carlo; The Scarlet Pimpernel; Becky Sharp. **1936** Follow Your Heart; Make Way for a Lady; The Man I Marry; The Trail of the Lonesome Pine; The Charge of the Light Brigade; The White Angel; Under Two Flags. **1937** Thunder in the City; The Last of Mrs. Cheyney. **1938** The Baroness and the Butler; Kidnapped; Suez. **1939** The Adventures of Sherlock Holmes; The Hound of the Baskervilles; The Rains Came. **1940** Adventures in Diamonds; Lillian Russell; A Dispatch from Reuters; Hudson's Bay; The Blue Bird; Rebecca; Susan and God. **1941** Play Girl; Free and Easy; The Chocolate Soldier; This Woman is Mine; Suspicion. **1942** Roxie Hart; Eagle Squadron; Sherlock Holmes and the Voice of Terror; Journey for Margaret; Sherlock Holmes and the Secret Weapon; This Above All. **1943** Sherlock Holmes in Washington; Forever and a Day; Sherlock Holmes Faces Death; Crazy House; Lassie, Come Home. **1944** The Scarlet Claw; The Pearl of Death; Follow the Boys; Sherlock Holmes and the Spider Woman; Gypsy Wildcat; Frenchman's Creek. **1945** Son of Lassie; The House of Fear; The Corn is Green; Pursuit to Algiers; The Woman in Green. **1946** Terror by Night; Dressed to Kill; Two Mrs. Carrolls. **1947** Exile. **1948** Julia Misbehaves. **1950** Vendetta. **1951** Hong Kong; B'wana Devil; Limelight. **1954** World for Ransom.

BRUCE, PAUL
Died: May 2, 1971, Hollywood, Calif. (heart attack). Screen, stage and television actor.

Appeared in: **1967** The Born Losers. **1969** The Harem Bunch: or War and Piece (aka Dessert Odyssey).

BRUCE, TONIE EDGAR. *See* TONI EDGAR-BRUCE

BRUGGEMAN, GEORGE
Born: Nov. 1, 1904, Belgium. Died: June 9, 1967, North Hollywood, Calif. Screen actor.

Appeared in: **1933** I'm No Angel. **1952** What Price Glory? **1954** Demetrius and the Gladiators. **1956** Around the World in 80 Days. **1962** Bachelor Flat. **1963** Forty Pounds of Trouble; Wives and Lovers.

BRUNDAGE, BERTHA
Born: 1860. Died: May 7, 1939, Long Beach, Calif. Screen actress.

BRUNDAGE, MATHILDE
Born: 1871, Louisville, Ky. Died: May 6, 1939. Screen actress.

Appeared in: **1914** The Crucible. **1915** Wormwood; Dr. Rameau; Emmy of Stork's Nest; The Corsican Brothers. **1916** The Lords of High Decision; Half a Rogue; The City of Illusion. **1917** Wife Number Two; Thou Shalt Not Steal; Bridges Burned; The Soul of a Magdalen; The Little Terror; Enlighten Thy Daughter; Reputation. **1921** The Good-Bad Wife; The Lady from Longacre; Hail the Woman; Lovetime; My Boy; No Defense; The Rage of Paris; The Unknown Wife; Too Much Married. **1922** Conquering the Woman; Don't Doubt Your Wife; A Front Page Story; A Self-Made Man; Shirley of the Circus; The Primitive Lover. **1923** Blinky; Fashion Row; Refuge; Strangers of the Night; The Midnight Guest. **1924** One Glorious Night; Oh, You Tony!; Westbound. **1925** Anything Once; Seven Sinners; Border Intrigue; The Charmer; The Spaniard. **1926** Men of the Night; Racing Romance; Midnight Limited; The Midnight Message; Coming an' Going; Dangerous Friends; Cupid's Knockout. **1927** The Denver Dude; Tongues of Scandal; Silver Comes Through. **1928** That's My Daddy; Love Me and the World Is Mine.

BRUNETTE, FRITZI
Born: 1890. Died: Sept. 28, 1943, Hollywood, Calif. Stage and screen actress.

Appeared in: **1912** A Waiter of Weight; The Consequences; The Foolishness of Oliver; It Happened Thus; The Professor's Dilemma. **1913** The Hypocrite; The Lie; Sunny Smith; The Grouch; The Appeal; The Ring of Sorrow; For the Sins of Another. **1916** Unto Those Who Sin; At Piney Ridge. **1919** The Woman Thou Gavest Me. **1920** The Devil to Pay; Live Sparks; Thirty Thousand Dollars. **1921** The Butterfly Girl; Sure Fire; The Man from Lost River; Tiger True; Discontented Wives; A Wife's Awakening. **1922** Give Me My Son; Bells of San Juan; The Boss of Camp 4; While Satan Sleeps; The Crusader; The Other Side. **1923** The Footlight Ranger; Cause for Divorce. **1925** Camille of the Barbary Coast; The Pace that Thrills. **1928** Driftwood. **1937** Maid of Salem.

BRUNETTI, MIRO
Born: 1908, Italy. Died: July 3, 1966, Hollywood, Calif. Screen actor. Married to actress Argentina Brunetti.

BRUNIUS, JACQUES (Jacques-Bernard Brunius)
Born: 1906, Paris, France. Died: 1967. Screen actor, film director and screenwriter.

Appeared in: **1930** L'Age d'Or (The Age of Gold—US 1964). **1932** L'Affaire est Dans le Sac. **1935** Le Crime de M. Lange. **1936** Une Partie de Campagne (US 1937). **1951** The Lavender Hill Mob. **1952** 24 Hours of a Woman's Life (aka Affair in Monte Carlo—US 1953); South of Algiers (aka The Golden Mask—US 1954). **1953** Sea Devils; Always a Bride (US 1954); Laughing Anne (US 1954). **1954** Forbidden Cargo (US 1956). **1955** To Paris With Love; The Cockleshell Heroes (US 1956). **1956** The Lieutenant Wore Skirts; Wicked As They Come (US 1957). **1957** True as Turtle; Dangerous Exile (US 1958). **1958** Orders to Kill. **1961** The Greengage Summer (aka Loss of Innocence—US). **1964** The Yellow Rolls-Royce (US 1965). **1965** Return from the Ashes.

BRUNIUS, JOHN W.
Born: 1884, Stockholm, Sweden. Died: 1937, Sweden (?). Screen actor and director.

Appeared in: **1918** Masterkatten i Stovlar (Puss in Boots). **1930** Roeda Dagen (Red Day); Longing For the Sea. **1937** Happy Vestkoping.

BRUNOT, ANDRE

Born: 1880, France. Died: Aug. 6, 1973, Paris, France. Stage and screen actor.

Appeared in: **1939** The Curtain Rises. **1940** Hotel du Nord. **1941** Personal Column. **1948** Portrait of Innocence. **1957** The Virtuous Scoundrel. **1958** Rouge et Noir (The Red and the Black). **1960** Picnic on the Grass. **1962** Maxine.

BRYAN, ARTHUR Q.

Born: 1899. Died: Nov. 30, 1959, Hollywood, Calif. Screen, television and radio actor.

Appeared in: **1932** The Big Shop; Fast Life; The Mummy. **1933** 20,000 Years in Sing Sing; Tonight is Ours; Gabriel over the White House; The Silk Empress; Mayor of Hell; Private Detective 62; College Coach. **1934** House of Rothschild; Two Alone; Fog over Frisco; The Notorious Sophie Lang; The Man with Two Faces; That's Gratitude!; The President Vanishes; Marie Gallante. **1935** Secret Brides; The Casino Murder Case; Shadow of a Doubt; The Whole Town's Talking; Oil for the Lamps of China; Murder in the Fleet. **1936** Prisoner of Shark Island. **1940** South of the Boudoir (short); Millionaire Playboy. **1941** Devil Bat. **1943** Swing Out the Blues. **1944** Mopey Dope (short); I'm from Arkansas. **1946** Dark Horse. **1949** Samson and Delilah. **1954** Broken Lance. **1955** Hell's Outpost. **1956** The Lieutenant Wore Skirts.

BRYAN, GEORGE

Born: 1910. Died: June 27, 1969, New York. Radio announcer, screen and radio actor.

Appeared in: **1948** Will It Happen Again? (narrator). **1957** Lost Continent (narrator). **1961** Ritual of Love (narrator).

BRYAN, JACKSON "JACK" LEE

Born: 1909. Died: Sept. 14, 1964, Hollywood, Calif. (following surgery). Screen, stage and television actor.

BRYANT, CHARLES

Born: 1879, England. Died: Aug. 7, 1948, Mt. Kisco, N.Y. Screen, stage actor, film director and stage producer. Divorced from actress Alla Nazimova (dec. 1945).

Appeared in: **1918** Eye for Eye; Revelation. **1919** The Brat; Out of the Fog; The Red Lantern. **1920** Stronger than Death; The Heart of a Child.

BRYANT, NANA

Born: 1888, Cincinnati, Ohio. Died: Dec. 24, 1955, Hollywood, Calif. Screen, stage and television actress.

Appeared in: **1935** Guard that Girl (film debut); Crime and Punishment; Unknown Woman; One Way Ticket; A Feather in Her Hat. **1936** Lady of Secrets; The Blackmailer; The Lone Wolf Returns; You May Be Next; The King Steps Out; The Man Who Lived Twice; Theodora Goes Wild; Pennies from Heaven; Meet Nero Wolf; Panic on the Air. **1937** Let's Get Married; The League of Frightened Men; The Devil is Driving; Counsel for Crime. **1938** Man Proof; Midnight Intruder; Mad about Music; The Adventures of Tom Sawyer; Sinners in Paradise; Swing, Swing, Swing; Give Me a Sailor; Always in Trouble; Out West with the Hardys; Peck's Bad Boy with the Circus. **1939** Espionage Agent; Streets of Missing Men; Parents on Trial; Our Neighbors, the Carters. **1940** Brother Rat and the Baby; If I Had My Way; A Little Bit of Heaven; Father is a Prince. **1941** Thieves Fall Out; Nice Girl?; One Foot in Heaven; Public Enemies; The Corsican Brothers. **1942** Youth on Parade; Thunder Birds; Calling Dr. Gillespie; Get Hep to Love; The Reluctant Dragon (voice); Madam Spy. **1943** The West Side Kid; Hangmen Also Die; Get Going; The Song of Bernadette; Princess O'Rourke. **1944** The Adventures of Mark Twain; Take It or Leave It; Bathing Beauty; Jungle Woman; Marriage Is A Private Affair. **1945** Black Market Babies; Weekend at the Waldorf; Brewster's Millions. **1946** The Virginian; The Runaround. **1947** The Perfect Marriage; Millie's Daughter; Big Town; The Big Fix; Possessed; Her Husband's Affair; The Hal Roach Comedy Carnival; The Unsuspected; The Fabulous Joe. **1948** Stage Struck; The Eyes of Texas; Lady at Midnight; Dangerous Years; Return of October; Inner Sanctum. **1949** Hideout; State Department File-649; Ladies of the Chorus; The Lady Gambles. **1950** The Blonde Bandit; Modern Marriage; Harvey. **1951** Follow the Sun; Bright Victory; Only the Valiant. **1954** About Mrs. Leslie; The Outcast; Geraldine. **1955** The Private War of Major Benson.

BUCHANAN, JACK

Born: Apr. 2, 1891, Glasgow, Scotland. Died: Oct. 20, 1957, London, England (spinal arthritis). Screen, stage, television actor, screenwriter, stage director, film producer and director.

Appeared in: **1917** Auld Lang Syne. **1919** Her Heritage. **1923** The Audacious Mr. Squire. **1925** Bulldog Drummond's Third Round (aka The Third Round); Settled Out of Court (aka Evidence Enclosed); The Happy Ending. **1927** Confetti. **1928** Toni. **1929** Paris; The Show of Shows. **1930** The Glee Quartette (short); Monte Carlo. **1931** Man of Mayfair. **1932** Goodnight Vienna (aka Magic Night—US). **1933** Yes Mr. Brown; That's a Good Girl. **1935** Brewster's

Millions; Come Out of the Pantry. **1936** When Knights Were Bold (US 1942); This'll Make You Whistle (US 1938); Limelight (aka Backstage—US). **1937** Smash and Grab; The Sky's the Limit. **1938** Break the News (US 1941); Cavalcade of the Stars. **1939** The Gang's All Here (aka The Amazing Mr. Forrest—US); The Middle Watch. **1940** Bulldog Sees It Through. **1952** Giselle (short—voice). **1953** The Bank Wagon. **1955** Josephine and Men; As Long as They're Happy (US 1957). **1957** The French Are a Funny Race (aka The French They Are a Funny Race). **1974** That's Entertainment (film clips).

BUCHANAN, MEG (Margaret Buchanan)

Born: Scotland. Died: July, 1970, Uddingston, Scotland. Screen, stage and radio actress.

Appeared in: **1952** The Brave Don't Cry. **1954** The Maggie (aka High and Dry—US).

BUCHANAN, STUART

Born: 1894. Died: Feb. 4, 1974, Cleveland, Ohio. Screen, radio actor, radio, television director and announcer. One of the founders of American Federation of Radio Artists.

Appeared in: **1937** Snow White and the Seven Dwarfs (voice of Grumpy).

BUCK, ELIZABETH

Born: 1912. Died: Mar. 31, 1934, Van Nuys, Calif. (hit by auto). Screen dancer.

BUCK, FORD (Ford Lee Washington)

Died: Jan. 31, 1955, New York, N.Y. Black screen, stage, and radio comedian.

BUCK, FRANK

Born: Mar. 17, 1888, Gainesville, Tex. Died: Mar. 25, 1950, Houston, Tex. (lung ailment). Screen actor, circus performer, film director and producer.

Appeared in: **1932** Bring 'Em Back Alive. **1934** Wild Cargo. **1935** Fang and Claw. **1937** Jungle Menace (serial). **1943** Jacare. **1949** Africa Screams.

BUCK, INEZ

Born: 1890, Oetrichs, S.D. Died: Sept. 6, 1957, Oakland, Calif. Stage and screen actress. Entered films with Lubin Studios.

Appeared in: **1915** Sorrows of Happiness.

BUCKLER, HUGH

Born: 1870, Southgate, England. Died: Oct. 1936, Lake Malibu, Calif. (auto accident). Stage and screen actor. Father of actor John Buckler (dec. 1936).

Appeared in: **1919** The Garden of Resurrection. **1920** Duke's Son; The Lure of Crooning Water. **1921** A Gentleman of France; The Place of Honour. **1923** Guy Fawkes. **1936** Crash Donavan; The Last of the Mohicans; The Jungle Princess. **1937** Lost Horizon.

BUCKLER, JOHN

Born: 1896, London, England. Died: Oct. 30, 1936, Lake Malibu, Calif. (auto accident). Stage and screen actor. Son of actor Hugh Buckler (dec. 1936).

Appeared in: **1935** David Copperfield; Eight Bells; Black Room Mystery. **1936** Tarzan Escapes; The Unguarded Hour.

BUCKLEY, FLOYD

Born: 1874. Died: Nov. 14, 1956, New York, N.Y. (heart attack). Screen, stage, vaudeville, radio actor, film producer, director and stuntman.

Appeared in the following serials: **1914** Exploits of Elaine. **1916** Pearl of the Army. **1917** The Fatal Ring; Patria; The Seven Pearls. **1918** The House of Hate. **1919** The Fatal Fortune; The Master Mystery.

BUCKLEY, JOSEPH

Born: 1875. Died: Dec. 2, 1930, Van Nuys, Calif. Screen actor.

BUCQUET, HAROLD S.

Born: 1891, England. Died: Feb. 13, 1946, Hollywood, Calif. Screen actor and film director. Entered films as an extra.

BUFFINGTON, SAM

Died: May 15, 1960. Screen actor.

Appeared in: **1957** Invasion of the Saucer Men. **1958** The Light in the Forest; The Rawhide Trail; Damn Citizen; Unwed Mother. **1959** They Came to Cordura.

BUHLER, RICHARD

Born: 1876, Washington, D.C. Died: Mar. 27, 1925, Washington, D.C. Stage and screen actor. Entered films with Lubin Co. in 1913.

Appeared in: **1915** The Rights of Man; A Man's Making. **1916** Gods of Fate.

BULGAKOV, LEO
Born: Mar. 22, 1889, Moscow, Russia. Died: July 20, 1948, Binghamton, N.Y. Screen, stage actor, stage director, film producer and director.

Appeared in: **1943** This Land Is Mine; For Whom the Bell Tolls. **1944** Song of Russia; And Now Tomorrow.

BULLOCK, DICK
Died: Dec. 1, 1971, Kan. (hit by auto). Screen actor/stuntman.

Appeared in: **1969** Hell's Belles. **1972** The Culpepper Cattle Company; Bad Company.

BUMP, EDMOND
Born: 1877. Died: Nov. 6, 1938, Hollywood, Calif. Stage and screen actor.

BUMPAS, H. W. "BOB"
Born: 1911. Died: Dec. 9, 1959, Gulf of Mexico (airline crash). Screen, stage, television actor, screenwriter, and radio writer.

Appeared in: **1951** The Big Carnival.

BUNCE, ALAN
Born: 1903, Westfield, N.J. Died: Apr. 27, 1965, New York, N.Y. Screen, stage, radio and television actor.

Appeared in: **1930** She's My Weakness. **1959** The Last Mile. **1960** Sunrise at Campobello. **1961** Homicidal.

BUNKER, RALPH
Born: 1889, Boston, Mass. Died: Apr. 28, 1966, New York, N.Y. (stroke). Stage and screen actor.

Appeared in: **1921** Scrambled Wives. **1922** That Woman. **1924** Another Scandal. **1936** The Ghost Goes West. **1947** The Hucksters.

BUNNY, GEORGE
Born: 1870, New York, N.Y. Died: Apr. 16, 1952, Hollywood, Calif. (heart attack). Stage and screen actor. Brother of actor John Bunny (dec. 1915).

Appeared in: **1921** "If Only" Jim; Danger Ahead. **1922** The Super Sex. **1925** The Dark Angel; The Lost World; Enticement; Lights of Old Broadway. **1926** Thrilling Youth. **1927** Tender Hour; Laddie Be Good. **1928** Breed of the Sunsets; Heroes in Blue; The Love Mart. **1929** The Man and the Moment; The Locked Door.

BUNNY, JOHN
Born: Sept. 21, 1863, New York, N.Y. Died: Apr. 26, 1915, Brooklyn, N.Y. (Bright's disease). Screen, stage, vaudeville actor and stage director. Brother of actor George Bunny (dec. 1952). Entered films with Vitagraph in 1910. He made 260 shorts with Flora Finch (dec. 1940) between 1910 and 1915. They appeared as Mr. and Mrs. Bunny and/or Mr. and Mrs. Brown, and fans referred to these shorts as "Bunnygraphs," "Bunnyfinches," and "Bunnyfinchgraphs." See Flora Finch regarding the films they appeared in together.

Other films he appeared in: **1910** Jack Fat and Jim Slim at Coney Island (film debut); He Who Laughs; Cupid and the Motor Boat. **1911** Doctor Cupid; A Queen for a Day; Captain Barnacle's Courtship; The Widow Visits Springtown; An Unexpected Review; Winsor McCay's Drawings; In the Arctic Night; The Return of "Widow" Pogson's Husband; Treasure Trove; Intrepid Davy; The Wrong Patient; Her Sister's Children; Ups and Downs; Kitty and the Cowboys; Madge of the Mountains; The Gossip; In the Clutches of a Vapor Bath; The Leading Lady; Vanity Fair; The Old Doll; The Latent Spark; The Hundred Dollar Bill; Captain Barnacle's Baby; The Tired Absent-Minded Man; Her Hero; The Missing Will; Hypnotizing the Hypnotist; A Slight Mistake; Bachelor Buttons. **1912** The First Violin; His Mother-in-Law; The Unknown Violinist; Burnt Cork; Leap Year Proposals; Chased by Bloodhounds; A Persistent Lover; Lovesick Maidens of Cuddleton; Cork and Vicinity; Ida's Christmas; The Troublesome Stepdaughters; Chumps; Who Stole Bunny's Umbrella?; Captain Jenks' Dilemma; Captain Barnacle's Messmate; I Deal, the Diver; The Honeymooners; Mr. Bolter's Infatuation; At Scroggineses Corner; Captain Jenks' Diplomacy; Working for Hubby; Who's to Win?; An Eventful Elopement; Bunny and the Dogs; Michael McShane, Matchmaker. **1913** Mr. Bolter's Niece; The Three Black Bags; Ma's Apron Strings; And His Wife Came Back; The Man Higher Up; Seeing Double; Bunny and the Bunny Hug; A Millinery Bomb; John Tobin's Sweetheart; Autocrat of Flapjack Junction; Bunny of the Derby; Bunny's Mistake; Bunny for the Cause; Flaming Hearts; Suspicious Henry; Bunny Blarneyed; The Fortune; Bunny's Honeymoon; Bunny Versus Cutey; Bunny as a Reporter; His Tired Uncle; One Good Joke Deserves Another; The Pirates; Pickwick Papers series including: The Honourable Event, The Adventure of Westgate Seminary and The Adventure of the Shooting Party. **1914** The Misadventures of a Mighty Monarch; Bunny's Mistake; Mr. Bunny in Disguise; Pigs Is Pigs; The Locked House; Personal Introductions; Bachelor Buttons; Bunny Attempts Suicide; Love, Luck and Gasoline; Setting the Style; Sheep's Clothing. **1915** Bunny at Bunnyland; To John Bunny's.

BUNSTON, HERBERT
Born: 1874. Died: Feb. 27, 1935, Los Angeles, Calif. (heart attack). Stage and screen actor.

Appeared in: **1929** The Last of Mrs. Cheyney. **1930** The Lady of Scandal. **1931** Dracula; Always Good-Bye; Once a Lady. **1932** Charlie Chan's Chance; File No. 113. **1933** Trick for Trick. **1934** Long Lost Father; Doctor Monica; The Richest Girl in the World; The Little Minister. **1935** A Shot in the Dark; Cardinal Richelieu; After Office Hours; Clive of India.

BUQUOR, ROBERT
Born: 1935. Died: July 27, 1966, Malibu, Calif. (parachute failed to open while filming Don't Make Waves). Screen actor/stuntman.

Appeared in: **1967** Don't Make Waves.

BURANI, MICHELETTE
Born: 1882, Paris, France. Died: Oct. 27, 1957, Eastchester, N.Y. Screen, stage, opera, radio and television actress.

Appeared in: **1926** Aloma of the South Seas. **1935** Enter Madame; The Gilded Lily. **1936** Give Us This Night. **1938** Fools for Scandal; Everybody Sing.

BURBANK, GOLDIE
Born: 1880. Died: Mar. 1, 1954, Toledo, Ohio. Screen and vaudeville actress. Appeared in vaudeville as part of "Melville Sisters" and later as part of "Sutherland Sisters" acts. Was in films from 1910 to 1913.

BURCH, BETTY EVANS
Born: 1888. Died: May 30, 1956, Pasadena, Calif. Screen actress.

BURCH, JOHN
Born: Aug. 17, 1896, Chicago, Ill. Died: July 29, 1969, Honolulu, Hawaii. Screen actor, film and television director.

Appeared in: **1925** White Fang. **1947** Great Expectations.

BURGESS, DOROTHY
Born: Mar. 4, 1907, Los Angeles, Calif. Died: Aug. 20, 1961. Stage and screen actress.

Appeared in: **1929** In Old Arizona; Pleasure Crazed; Protection; Song of Kentucky; Beyond Victory. **1930** Recaptured Love; Swing High; Lasca of the Rio Grande; The Voice of Hollywood (short series in 1930 and 1931). **1931** Oh! Oh! Cleopatra (short). **1932** The Stoker; Malay Nights; Taxi; Play Girl; Out of Singapore. **1933** Strictly Personal; Ladies They Talk About; What Price Decency; I Love That Man; Hold Your Man; It's Great to Be Alive; The Important Witness; Easy Millions; Rusty Rides Alone; Headline Shooter; Ladies Must Love; From Headquarters. **1934** Fashions of 1934; Orient Express; Miss Fane's Baby Is Stolen; A Modern Hero; Black Moon; The Circus Clown; Registered Nurse; Affairs of a Gentleman; Hat, Coat, and Glove; Friends of Mr. Sweeney; Gambling. **1935** Village Tale; Manhattan Butterfly. **1940** I Want a Divorce. **1941** Lady For a Night. **1942** The Lone Star Ranger. **1943** Man of Courage; Girls in Chains.

BURGESS, HAZEL
Born: 1910. Died: Dec. 11, 1973, Hollywood, Calif. (following surgery). Screen actress. Entered films in 1936 as an extra and stand-in.

BURGESS, HELEN
Born: 1918. Died: Apr. 7, 1937, Beverly Hills, Calif. (lobar pneumonia). Stage and screen actress.

Appeared in: **1936** The Plainsman. **1937** A Doctor's Diary; King of Gamblers; A Night of Mystery.

BURGESS, WILLIAM
Born: 1867. Died: Oct. 30, 1948. Screen actor.

Appeared in: **1937** Wild Money.

BURGHER, FAIRFAX
Born: 1897. Died: Sept. 20, 1965, New York, N.Y. Screen and stage actor.

BURIAN, VLASTA
Born: 1891. Died: Feb. 5, 1962, Prague, Czechoslovakia. Stage and screen actor. Barred from appearing in public for ten years after W.W. II for allegedly collaborating with Nazis.

Appeared in: **1931** Versuchen Sie Meine Schwester. **1932** Der Falsche Feldmarschall. **1934** Der Adjutant Seiner Hoheit. **1937** The Inspector General.

BURKE, BILLIE (Mary William Ethelberg Appleton Burke)
Born: Aug. 7, 1885, Washington, D.C. Died: May 14, 1970, Los Angeles, Calif. Stage and screen actress. Married to stage producer Flo Ziegfeld (dec. 1932).

Appeared in: **1915** Peggy. **1916** Gloria's Romance (serial). **1917** The Land of Promise. **1918** Eve's Daughter; Let's Get a Divorce; In Pursuit of Polly; The

Make-Believe Wife. **1919** Good Gracious, Annabelle; The Misleading Widow; Sadie Love. **1921** The Education of Elizabeth; Frisky Mrs. Johnson. **1930** Ranch House Blues. **1932** A Bill of Divorcement. **1933** Dinner at Eight; Only Yesterday; Christopher Strong. **1934** Forsaking All Others; Finishing School; We're Rich Again; Where Sinners Meet. **1935** Becky Sharp; Only Eight Hours; Society Doctor; After Office Hours; Doubting Thomas; She Couldn't Take It; Splendor; A Feather in Her Hat. **1936** Craig's Wife; My American Wife; Piccadilly Jim; The Great Ziegfeld. **1937** Topper; Navy, Blue and Gold; The Bride Wore Red; Parnell. **1938** Merrily We Live; Everybody Sing; The Young in Heart. **1939** The Wizard of Oz; Topper Takes a Trip; Bridal Suite; Remember?; Eternally Yours; Zenobia. **1940** The Captain Is a Lady; The Ghost Comes Home; And One Was Beautiful; Irene; Dulcy; Hullabaloo. **1941** Topper Returns; The Man Who Came to Dinner; Wild Man of Borneo; One Night in Lisbon. **1942** In This Our Life; They All Kissed the Bride; Girl Trouble; What's Cooking? **1943** Hi Diddle Diddle; So's Your Uncle; Gildersleeve on Broadway; You're a Lucky Fellow, Mr. Smith. **1944** Laramie Trail. **1945** Swing Out, Sister; The Cheaters. **1946** Breakfast in Hollywood; The Bachelor Daughter. **1949** Billie Gets Her Man (short); The Barkleys of Broadway. **1950** Father of the Bride; Three Husbands; The Boy from Indiana; And Baby Makes Three. **1951** Father's· Little Dividend; Darling, How Could You. **1953** Small Town Girl. **1959** The Young Philadelphians. **1960** Sgt. Rutledge; Pepe.

BURKE, J. FRANK
Born: Apr. 1867, Hartland, Vt. Died: Jan. 23, 1918, Los Angeles, Calif. (arteriosclerosis). Screen, stage and vaudeville actor.

Appeared in: **1915** The Ace of Hearts; The Toast of Death; Aloha Oe. **1916** The Beckoning Flame; The Waifs; The No-Good Guy; The Vagabond Prince; The Dawn Maker. **1917** The Iced Bullet; Bawbs o' Blue Ridge; Princess of the Dark; The Square Deal Man. **1918** The Bargain.

BURKE, JAMES
Born: 1886, New York, N.Y. Died: May 28, 1968, Los Angeles, Calif. Married to actress Elinor Durkin (dec.); they appeared in vaudeville together in an act billed as "Burke and Durkin."

Appeared in: **1929** Tete-a-Tete in Songs (short with Durkin). **1932** Hollywood Handicap. **1933** Torch Singer; A Lady's Profession; Girl in 419; College Humor; To the Last Man; Lady Killer. **1934** Little Miss Marker; Wharf Angel; City Limits; Treasure Island; Scarlet Empress; Love Time; The Lemon Drop Kid; Lady by Choice; Six of a Kind; It's a Gift; It Happened One Night. **1935** The Case of the Missing Man; Hot Money (short); Ruggles of Red Gap; Mystery Man; Mississippi; Dinky; Call of the Wild; Make a Million; Here Comes Cookie; Affairs of Susan; Coronado; Frisco Waterfront; Man on the Flying Trapeze; Welcome Home; Broadway Gondolier; So Red the Rose. **1936** Rhythm on the Range; 36 Hours to Kill; Can This Be Dixie; Song and Dance Man; Dancing Feet; The Leathernecks Have Landed; Klondike Annie; Forgotten Faces; Old Dutch; The Great Guy. **1937** Champagne Waltz; Laughing at Trouble; Dead End; High, Wide and Handsome; The Perfect Specimen; Life Begins with Love. **1938** The Mad Miss Manton; Dawn Patrol; The Joy of Living; Flight into Nowhere; Affairs of Annabel; Men with Wings; Orphans of the Street; Little Orphan Annie. **1939** I'm from Missouri; The Saint Strikes Back; Within the Law; On Borrowed Time; Beau Geste; At the Circus; Fast and Furious. **1940** The Way of all Flesh; No Time for Comedy; The Cisco Kid and the Lady; Double Alibi; Charlie Chan's Murder Cruise; Buck Benny Rides Again; Opened by Mistake; The Saint Takes Over; The Golden Fleecing; Little Nellie Kelly; Ellery Queen, Master Detective. **1941** The Maltese Falcon; Pot O' Gold; Ellery Queen's Penthouse Mystery; Ellery Queen and the Perfect Crime; Ellery Queen and the Murder Ring; Reaching for the Sun; Million Dollar Baby. **1942** It Happened in Flatbush; Enemy Agents Against Ellery Queen; Army Surgeon; All Through the Night. **1943** A Night to Remember; Riding High; No Place for a Lady; Dixie. **1945** Anchors Aweigh; The Horn Blows at Midnight; I Love a Bandleader; Shady Lady; How Do You Do. **1946** Two Years Before the Mast; Bowery Bombshell; California; The Virginian. **1947** The Gashouse Kids in Hollywood; Easy Come, Easy Go; Philo Vance's Gamble; Body and Soul; Down to Earth; Nightmare Alley; Blaze of Noon. **1948** The Timber Trail; Night Wind; June Bride. **1949** Shamrock Hill. **1950** Mrs. O'Malley and Mr. Malone; Copper Canyon. **1951** Raton Pass; The Last Outpost. **1952** Denver and Rio Grande; Lone Star. **1953** Arrowhead. **1954** Lucky Me. **1955** You're Never Too Young. **1956** The Birds and the Bees. **1957** Public Pigeon No. 1; The Unholy Wife. **1962** Geronimo. **1965** The Hallelujah Trail.

BURKE, JOSEPH
Born: 1884, New York, N.Y. Died: Dec. 17, 1942, New York, N.Y. Screen, stage and vaudeville actor. Do not confuse with actor Joe Burke.

Appeared in: **1918** Kidnapped; Independence, By Gosh. **1920** The Fortune Teller; Heritage; The Perfect Woman. **1921** Worlds Apart; Princess Jones; The Wakefield Case. **1922** The Prophet's Paradise. **1923** His Children's Children; The White Rose. **1924** The Law and the Lady; Two Shall be Born; Pied Piper Malone; West of the Water Tower. **1925** The Adventurous Sex; The Fool; Lucky Devil; The Pinch Hitter; Share and Share Alike; Too Many Kisses. **1926** Fascinating Youth; Striving for Fortune; The Kick-Off. **1928** Hangman's

House; Manhattan Knights; Obey Your Husband; South of Panama. **1929** The Royal Rider.

BURKE, THOMAS F.
Died: Mar. 25, 1941, Los Angeles, Calif. Screen actor.

Appeared in: **1932** Carmen. **1938** Kathleen; Father O'Flynn.

BURKHARD, CHARLES
Died: Feb. 1927. Screen actor.

BURLANDO, CLAUDE
Born: 1918. Died: Sept. 25, 1938, Hollywood, Calif. (traffic injuries). Screen actor and extra.

BURMASTER, AUGUSTA
Born: 1860, Hamburg, Germany. Died: Mar. 28, 1934, Los Angeles, Calif. Screen actress.

Appeared in: **1915** Stop Thief. **1917** Mary Moreland. **1929** The Greene Murder Case.

BURNABY, DAVE "DAVY"
Born: Apr. 7, 1881, Buckland Herts, England. Died: Apr. 18, 1949, Angmering, Sussex, England. Screen, stage, radio actor, songwriter and author.

Appeared in: **1929** The Co-Optimists (US 1930). **1933** Just My Luck; The Wishbone; That's My Wife; Cleaning Up; Three Men In a Boat; Strike It Rich; A Shot In the Dark (US 1935); The Right to Live. **1934** On the Air; Murder At the Inn; The Man I Want; Keep It Quiet; How's Chances; Are You a Mason?; Radio Parade of 1935 (US 1935); Screen Vaudeville Number One (short). **1935** Equity Musical Revue Series; Dandy Dick; Boys Will Be Boys; While Parents Sleep; We've Got to Have Love; When the Cat's Away. **1936** The Marriage of Corbal (aka Prisoner of Corbal—US 1939). **1937** Feather Your Nest; Leave It to Me; Song of the Forge; Calling All Stars; Talking Feet. **1938** Chips; Many Tanks Mr. Atkins; Second Best Bed; Kicking the Moon Around. **1939** The Diplomatic Lover (reissue of 1934 How's Chances); Come on George.

BURNE, NANCY
Born: 1913, England. Died: Mar. 25, 1954, Maidstone, England. Screen, stage and vaudeville actress.

Appeared in: **1933** Facing the Music (US 1934); The Love Nest; Little Napoleon. **1934** Song at Eventide; Irish Hearts (aka Norah O'Neale—US); The Warren Case. **1935** Trust the Navy; Lend Me Your Husband; Old Roses; Once a Thief; Royal Eagle. **1936** A Wife or Two; Reasonable Doubt; Skylarks. **1937** Thunder in the City; Knights for a Day; When the Poppies Bloom Again; Feather Your Nest. **1938** John Halifax, Gentleman. **1939** Flying Fifty Five.

BURNETT, AL
Born: 1906, England. Died: Apr. 19, 1973, London, England. Screen actor and comedian.

Appeared in: **1959** Sweet Beat (aka The Amorous Sex—US 1962).

BURNETTE, "SMILEY" (Lester Alvin Burnett)
Born: Mar. 18, 1911, Summum, Ill. Died: Feb. 16, 1967, Los Angeles, Calif. (leukemia). Screen, television, radio actor and songwriter. Married to screenwriter Dallas McDonald (dec. 1976). Entered films in 1934. Appeared in Roy Rogers, Gene Autry and Charles Starrett (as Durango Kid) series.

Appeared in: **1934** In Old Santa Fe; Mystery Mountain (serial). **1935** Tumbling Tumbleweeds; Waterfront Lady; Melody Trail; Sagebrush Troubadour; The Singing Vagabond; The Phantom Empire (serial); Hitch Hike Lady; Rex and Rinty; Streamline Express; Harmony Lane. **1936** Doughnuts and Society; Hearts in Bondage; Oh, Susannah; Ride, Ranger, Ride; Comin' 'Round the Mountain; Red River Valley; The Singing Cowboy; Guns and Guitars; A Man Betrayed; The Border Patrolman. **1937** The Old Corral; The Big Show; Round Up Time in Texas; Springtime in the Rockies; Larceny on the Air; Dick Tracy (serial); Git Along Little Dogies; Rootin' Tootin' Rhythm; Yodelin' Kid from Pine Ridge; Meet the Boy Friend; Public Cowboy No. 1; Manhattan Merry-Go-Round; Boots and Saddles. **1938** Prairie Moon; The Old Barn Dance; Hollywood Stadium Mystery; Under Western Stars; Gold Mine in the Sky; Man from Music Mountain; Billy the Kid Returns; Rhythm of the Saddle; Western Jamboree. **1939** Home on the Prairie; Blue Montana Skies; Mountain Rhythm; Colorado Sunset; In Old Monterey; Rovin' Tumbleweeds; South of the Border; Mexicali Rose. **1940** Rancho Grande; Men with Steel Faces; Gaucho Serenade; Carolina Moon; Ride, Tenderfoot, Ride. **1941** Ridin' on a Rainbow; Back in the Saddle; The Singing Hill; Sunset in Wyoming; Under Fiesta Stars; Down Mexico Way; Sierra Sue. **1942** Cowboy Serenade; Heart of the Rio Grande; Home in Wyomin'; Stardust on the Sage; Call of the Canyon; Bells of Capistrano; Heart of the Golden West. **1943** Beyond the Last Frontier; Idaho; King of the Cowboys; Silver Spurs. **1944** Beneath Western Skies; The Laramie Trail; Call of the Rockies; Code of the Prairie; Pride of the Plains; Bordertown Trail; Firebrands of Arizona. **1946** The Desert Horseman; The

Fighting Frontiersman; The Galloping Thunder; Gunning for Vengeance; Land Rush; Roaring Rangers; Two-Fisted Stranger; Hunting West. **1947** The Lone Hand Texan; Terror Trail; West of Dodge City; Law of the Canyon; Prairie Raiders; Riders of the Lone Star; South of Chisholm Trail. **1948** Buckaroo from Powder River; Last Days of Boot Hill; Phantom Valley; Six-Gun Law; West of Sonora; Whirlwind Raiders; Trail to Laredo. **1949** Quick on the Trigger; Laramie; Eldorado Pass; Desert Vigilante; Challenge of the Range; Horsemen of the Sierras; Blazing Trail; South of Death Valley; Bandits of El Dorado; Renegades of the Sage. **1950** Outcast of Black Mesa; Texas Dynamo; Trail of the Rustlers; Streets of Ghost Town; Across the Badlands; Raiders of Tomahawk Creek; Lightning Guns; Frontier Outpost. **1951** Whirlwind; Riding the Outlaw Trail; Prairie Roundup; Snake River Desperadoes; Fort Savage Raider; Bonanza Town; Cyclone Fury; The Kid from Amarillo; Pecos River. **1952** Smoky Canyon; The Hawk of Wild River; The Kid from Broken Gun; The Rough, Tough West; Junction City; Laramie Mountains. **1953** Winning of the West; Goldtown Ghost Riders; On Top of Old Smoky; Pack Train; Saginaw Trail; Last of the Pony Riders.

BURNEY, HAL (Harold Burmeister)
Born: 1900. Died: Nov. 11, 1933, Eureka, Calif. Screen, stage, vaudeville and radio actor.

BURNHAM, NICHOLAS
Born: 1860. Died: Jan. 30, 1925, Bernardsville, N.Y. Screen and stage actor.

Appeared in: **1920** Uncle Sam of Freedom Ridge.

BURNS, BOB "BAZOOKA"
Born: Aug. 2, 1893, Van Buren, Ark. Died: Feb. 2, 1956, San Fernando Valley, Calif. Screen, vaudeville, radio, and carnival actor. Known as "The Arkansas Philosopher."

Appeared in: **1931** Quick Millions. **1935** The Phantom Empire (aka Radio Ranch and Men with Steel Faces); The Singing Vagabond; The Courageous Avenger; Restless Knights (short). **1936** Rhythm on the Range; Guns and Guitars. **1937** The Big Broadcast of 1937; Waikiki Wedding; Wells Fargo; Git Along, Little Dogies; Public Cowboy No. 1; Yodelin' Kid from Pine Ridge; Hit the Saddle; Mountain Music. **1938** The Arkansas Traveler; Tropic Holiday; Radio City Revels. **1939** Our Leading Citizen; I'm From Missouri; Rovin' Tumbleweed. **1940** Alias the Deacon; Comin' Round the Mountain; Prairie Schooner. **1942** Call of the Canyon; The Hillbilly Deacon. **1944** Belle of the Yukon; Mystery Man. **1947** Twilight on the Rio Grande; Saddle Pals.

BURNS, DAVID
Born: June 22, 1901, New York, N.Y. Died: Mar. 12, 1971, Philadelphia, Pa. (heart attack). Screen, stage and television actor.

Appeared in: **1939** The Saint in London. **1954** Knock on Wood; Deep in My Heart. **1960** Let's Make Love. **1967** The Tiger Makes Out. **1970** More. **1971** Who Is Harry Kellerman and Why Is He Saying Those Terrible Things about Me?

BURNS, DOROTHY See DOROTHY VERNON

BURNS, EDDIE
Died: Sept. 1, 1957. Screen actor. Do not confuse with other actors with variations of the same name.

BURNS, HARRY
Born: 1885. Died: July 9, 1948, Santa Monica, Calif. (heart attack). Screen, stage and vaudeville actor.

Appeared in: **1935** A Vitaphone short. **1936** Hot Money. **1937** Two Wise Maids. **1939** Kid Nightingale. **1940** Northwest Mounted Police. **1941** Redhead. **1942** Tortilla Flat; What's the Matador (short).

BURNS, HARRY
Born: 1884. Died: Jan. 9, 1939, Los Angeles, Calif. (heart attack). Screen actor and film director. Married to actress Dorothy Vernon and father of actor Bobby Vernon (dec. 1939).

BURNS, IRVING
Born: 1914. Died: Sept. 21, 1968, Hollywood, Calif. (heart attack). Screen actor.

BURNS, JAMES "JIM"
Died: July 16, 1975. Screen actor.

Appeared in: **1925** O. U. West.

BURNS, LULU. See LULU BURNS JENKS

BURNS, NAT (Nat Burden Haines)
Born: 1887, Philadelphia, Pa. Died: Nov. 8, 1962, New York, N.Y. Screen, stage and television actor.

BURNS, PAUL E.
Born: Jan. 26, 1881. Died: May 17, 1967, Van Nuys, Calif. (heart attack). Screen and television actor.

Appeared in: **1930** Framed; Hell Harbor. **1932** Renegades. **1939** The Return of the Cisco Kid; Rose of Washington Square; Jesse James. **1940** Shooting High; Little Orvie; New Moon; Chad Hanna; Seventeen. **1941** Men of Timberland; Belle Starr; Swamp Water. **1942** Mystery of Marie Roget; Timber; The Mummy's Tomb. **1943** Dixie Dugan; Crash Dive; The Ox-Bow Incident; The Meanest Man in the World. **1944** Dragon Seed; Barbary Coast Gent; Seventh Cross. **1945** State Fair; Fallen Angel. **1946** Crime Doctor's Man Hunt; Mysterious Intruder; Night Editor; Devil's Mask; Gallant Journey; Sing While You Dance; Shadowed; My Pal Trigger. **1947** Desperate; Saddle Pals; Framed (and 1930 version); Smoky River Serenade; Exposed; Blind Sport. **1948** Relentless; Hollow Triumph. **1949** Johnny Allegro; Look for the Silver Lining; I Married A Communist; Arctic Manhunt; Cover Up; Hideout; Lust For Gold. **1950** Montana; Father Makes Good; It's a Small World; Sunset in the West; Tarnished; The Woman on Pier 13. **1951** The Big Gusher; Frenchie; Santa Fe; Storm Warning. **1952** Son of Paleface; Sound Off. **1956** Fury at Gunsight Pass. **1958** Gunman's Walk. **1959** Face of a Fugitive. **1960** Guns of the Timberland. **1961** A Pocketful of Miracles. **1964** Stage to Thunder Rock. **1967** Barefoot in the Park.

BURNS, ROBERT
Born: Montana. Died: Aug. 20, 1947. Screen actor and wild west performer. Do not confuse with actors with variations of the same name.

BURNS, ROBERT E.
Born: 1885. Died: Mar. 14, 1957. Screen actor and screenwriter. Do not confuse with actors with variations of the same name.

BURNS, ROBERT PATRICK
Born: 1929. Died: June 8, 1955, Los Angeles, Calif. Screen actor.

Appeared in: **1930-1935** "Our Gang" comedies.

BURNS, WILLIAM JOHN
Born: Oct. 19, 1861, Baltimore, Md. Died: Apr. 14, 1932, Sarasota, Fla. (heart attack). Detective and screen actor.

Appeared in: **1914** The Five Million Dollar Counterfeiting Plot.

BURR, EDMUND
Died: July 16, 1975. Screen actor.

Appeared in: **1928** Chinese Parrot. **1931** Sea Devils; Devil Plays. **1932** Western Limited; Air Mail; Death Kiss.

BURR, EUGENE "GENE"
Born: Leavenworth, Kans. Died: June 7, 1940, Los Angeles, Calif. (pulmonary edema). Screen actor.

Appeared in: **1917** Fanatics; Fuel of Life. **1918** Captain of His Soul; Old Hartwell's Cab; Modern Sphinx; The Painted Lily; Alias Mary Brown; The Atom; Daughter Angele; An Heiress For a Day; Nancy Comes Home. **1919** The Girl With No Regrets; Restless Souls; The Final Closeup. **1920** The Son of Tarzan (serial). **1921** Her Face Value. **1922** Life's Greatest Question; The Broadway Madonna. **1923** Bell Boy 13; Jungle Trail of the Son of Tarzan.

BURROUGH, TOM
Born: 1869, Clinton County, Ill. Died: Sept. 8, 1929. Stage and screen actor.

Appeared in: **1916** Caprice of the Mountains; Unwelcome Mother; Sins of Men. **1917** Miss U.S.A. **1921** Heedless Moths.

BURROUGHS, ERIC
Died: Aug. 1960, New York. Stage and screen actor.

Appeared in: **1959** Odds Against Tomorrow.

BURT, FREDERIC
Born: Feb. 12, 1876, Onarga, Ill. Died: Oct. 2, 1943, Twenty-Nine Palms, Calif. Stage and screen actor. Entered films in 1930. Married to actress Helen Ware (dec. 1939).

Appeared in: **1930** The Shadow of the Law; The Eyes of the World; Outside the Law. **1931** Cimarron; The Yellow Ticket; The Cisco Kid; The Royal Bed; Up For Murder.

BURT, LAURA
Born: 1872. Died: Oct. 17, 1952. Screen actress.

Appeared in: **1905** The House Thief.

BURT, WILLIAM P. (William Presley Burt)
Born: Feb. 11, 1873, St. Peter, Minn. Died: Feb. 23, 1955, Denver, Colo. Screen, stage, minstrel, circus actor, film director, radio and screenwriter. Entered films with the Thanhouser Picture Co. in 1915.

Appeared in: **1920** Pirate Gold (serial). **1927** King of Kings. **1928** The Leopard Lady; Night of Mystery. **1930** Girl of the Port; Danger Lights; Midnight Mystery; Rogue of the Rio Grande. **1931** Sally of the Subway; Cimarron. **1933** Her Splendid Folly.

BURTIS, JAMES
Born: May 12, 1893. Died: July 24, 1939, Calif. Screen actor.

Appeared in: **1930** Jazz Cinderella; Ladies in Love. **1931** The Lawless Woman. **1932** Strangers of the Evening. **1933** The Bargain of the Century (short); Trick for Trick; One Sunday Afternoon. **1934** Here Comes the Groom; Burn 'Em Up Barnes (serial); Hips Hips Hooray; Twentieth Century; Young and Beautiful; The Case of the Howling Dog. **1935** Mystery Man; Wings in the Dark; One Hour Late; Mister Dynamite; Keeper of the Bees; Stormy; $1,000 a Minute; Sprucin' Up (short); Bonnie Scotland. **1936** The Return of Jimmy Valentine; Dancing Feet; Ghost Patrol; General Spanky; The Criminal Within. **1937** Arizona Mahoney; That Man's Here Again.

BURTON, CHARLOTTE
Born: 1882. Died: Mar. 28, 1942, Los Angeles, Calif. (heart attack). Screen actress. Entered films in 1911 with American Film Mfg. Co.

Appeared in: **1913** Trapped in a Forest Fire. **1915** The Diamond from the Sky (serial); A Man's Way. **1916** The Sequel to the Diamond from the Sky (serial).

BURTON, CLARENCE
Born: May 10, 1882, Fort Lyons, Mo. Died: Dec. 2, 1933, Hollywood, Calif. (heart attack). Stage and screen actor. Entered films in 1912.

Appeared in: **1916-17** American Film Mfg. Co. films. **1921** Miss Lulu Bett; Forbidden Fruit; Crazy to Marry; Fool's Paradise; High Gear Jeffrey; The Lost Romance; The Love Special. **1922** Manslaughter; The Ordeal; The Beautiful and Damned; The Crimson Challenge; One Glorious Day; The Law and the Woman; A Daughter of Luxury; Her Husband's Trademark; Her Own Money; The Impossible Mrs. Bellew; The Man Unconquerable. **1923** The Ten Commandments; Adam's Rib; Mr. Billings Spends His Dime; Sixty Cents an Hour; Garrison's Finish; Hollywood; Nobody's Money; Salomy Jane; The Satin Girl. **1924** The Navigator; No More Women; Bluff; The Guilty One; The Mine with the Iron Door. **1925** The Coming of Amos; Flyin' Thru; The Wedding Song; The Million Dollar Handicap; The Road to Yesterday; Savages of the Sea. **1926** The Danger Girl; The Nervous Wreck; Red Dice; Three Faces East; Shipwrecked; The Warning Signal. **1927** King of Kings; The Angel of Broadway; Chicago; The Fighting Eagle; The Yankee Clipper; A Harp in Hock; Rubber Tires. **1928** Stool Pigeon; Submarine; Square Crooks; Midnight Madness; Stand and Deliver. **1929** Godless Girl; Barnum Was Right; Dynamite. **1930** The Unholy Three; Love Trader; The Love Racket; Only Saps Work. **1932** The Sign of the Cross. **1944** The Sign of the Cross (revised version of 1932 film).

BURTON, FREDERICK
Born: Oct. 20, 1871, Indianapolis, Ind. Died: Oct. 23, 1957, Woodland Hills, Calif. Screen, stage actor and opera performer.

Appeared in: **1919** Anne of Green Gables. **1920** Yes or No; Heliotrope. **1921** Bits of Life; If Women Only Knew; The Education of Elizabeth. **1922** The Man She Brought Back; Anna Ascends; Back Home and Broke. **1923** Broadway Broke; The Fighting Blade. **1924** The Rejected Woman. **1925** Back to Life. **1927** Running Wild. **1930** The Big Trail. **1931** Sweepstakes; Secret Service; An American Tragedy. **1932** Woman From Monte Carlo; Fireman Save My Child; Alias the Doctor; Mata Hari; The Wet Parade; State's Attorney; Okay America; One Way Passage; Too Busy to Work. **1933** No Other Woman; Broadway Baby; The Working Man; Golden Harvest; Counsellor-at-Law. **1934** Smarty; Love Birds; Belle of the Nineties; Flirtation Walk. **1935** Transient Lady; McFadden's Flats; Shipmates Forever. **1936** The Calling of Dan Matthews; Theodora Goes Wild; Everybody's Old Man; Mummy's Boys; The Voice of Bugle Ann. **1937** The Man in Blue; Love is News; Nancy Steele Is Missing; The Duke Comes Back. **1938** Air Devil; The Saint in New York; My Lucky Star; Kentucky. **1939** Hollywood Cavalcade; Old Maid; Mr. Smith Goes to Washington; Silver on the Sage; Confessions of a Nazi Spy. **1940** The Man from Dakota; Go West Brigham Young. **1941** Bowery Boys; Washington Melodrama. **1942** Silver Queen; Babes on Broadway; Tennessee Johnson; Gentleman After Dark. **1944** Town Went Wild.

BURTON, GEORGE H.
Born: 1900. Died: Dec. 8, 1955, Los Angeles, Calif. (heart attack). Bird trainer, screen, stage and television actor.

Appeared in: **1934** In Old Santa Fe; **1935** Ruggles of Red Gap; The Miracle Rider (serial). **1937** Come On Cowboys. **1947** Bill and Coo.

BURTON, NED
Born: c. 1850. Died: Dec. 11, 1922, New York, N.Y. Screen, stage and vaudeville actor.

Appeared in: **1921** Jim the Penman. **1922** Back Home and Broke.

BURTON, ROBERT
Born: Aug. 13, 1895. Died: Sept. 29, 1964, Woodland Hills, Calif. (lung cancer). Screen actor.

Appeared in: **1952** The Bad and the Beautiful; Fearless Fagan; Everything I Have Is Yours; My Man and I; Sky-Full of Moon; Desperate Search; Above and Beyond. **1953** Latin Lovers; Code Two; The Band Wagon; The Girl Who Had Everything; A Slight Case of Larceny; Cry of the Hunted; Fast Company; All The Brothers Were Valiant; Inferno; The Big Heat; Confidentially Connie; Taza, Son of Cochise. **1954** Hit the Deck; Rogue Cop; Riot in Cell Block 11; The Siege of Red River; Broken Lance. **1955** The Road to Denver; Soldier of Fortune; Count Three and Pray; Lay That Rifle Down; The Left Hand of God; The Last Command; A Man Called Peter. **1956** Reprisal!; The Brass Legend; Slander; Ransom; Jubal; The Rack. **1957** Three Brave Men; No Down Payment; The Spirit of St. Louis; The Hired Gun; The Tall T; Domino Kid; The Hard Man; I Was a Teenage Frankenstein. **1958** Man or Gun; Mardi Gras; Too Much, Too Soon. **1959** The Story on Page One; The Thirty Foot Bride of Candy Rock; Compulsion; A Private's Affair. **1960** Seven Days from Sundown; Wake Me When It's Over; Gallant Hours. **1961** The Young Savages. **1962** Sweet Bird of Youth; Invasion of the Animal People; Jumbo; Bird Man of Alcatraz; Manchurian Candidate. **1963** The Slime People.

BURTON, WILLIAM H.
Born: 1845. Died: Mar. 15, 1926, New York, N.Y. Screen and stage actor.

Appeared in: **1923** Radio Mania. **1924** Born Rich. **1925** Makers of Men.

BUSBY, AMY
Born: 1872, Rochester, N.Y. Died: July 13, 1957, East Stroudsberg, Pa. Stage and screen actress.

BUSCAGLIONE, FRED
Born: 1921, Italy. Died: Feb. 3, 1960, Rome, Italy (auto accident). Screen, stage actor, singer and composer.

Appeared in: I Ragazzi del Juke Box (The Jukebox Boys); A Qualcuno Piace Fred (Someone Likes Fred).

BUSCH, MAE
Born: Jan. 20, 1891, Melbourne, Australia. Died: Apr. 19, 1946, Woodland Hills, Calif. Screen, stage and vaudeville actress. Entered films with Mack Sennett.

Appeared in: **1915** A One Night Stand; Settled at the Seaside; The Rent Jumpers; A Rascal of Wolfish Ways (reissued as A Polished Villain); The Best of Enemies; A Favorite Fool. **1916** The Worst of Friends; Because He Loved Her; Better Late Than Never (aka Getting Married); Wife and Auto Trouble; A Bath House Blunder; Sisters of Eve. **1919** The Grim Game. **1920** The Devil's Passkey. **1921** The Love Charm; A Parisian Scandal. **1922** Foolish Wives; Brothers under the Skin; Her Own Money; Only a Shop Girl; Pardon My Nerve! **1923** The Christian; Souls for Sale. **1924** Broken Barriers; Bread; Married Flirts; Nellie, the Beautiful Cloak Model; The Shooting of Dan McGrew; Name the Man; A Woman Who Sinned; The Triflers. **1925** Camille of the Barbary Coast; The Unholy Three; Frivolous Sal; Time, the Comedian. **1926** Nutcracker; Fools of Fashion; The Miracle of Life. **1927** San Francisco Nights; Tongues of Scandal; The Truthful Sex; Love 'Em and Weep (short); Husband Hunters; Perch of the Devil. **1928** Fazil; The Beauty Shoppers; Sisters of Eve; Black Butterflies; While the City Sleeps. **1929** Alibi; Unaccustomed as We Are (short); A Man's Man. **1930** Young Desire. **1931** Defenders of the Law; Wicked; plus the following shorts: Fly My Kite; Chickens Come Home; Come Clean. **1932** Their First Mistake (short); Without Honor; Man Called Back; Doctor X; Heart Punch; Scarlet Dawn; Rider of Death Valley; Racing Strain. **1933** Women Won't Tell; Blondie Won't Tell; Blondie Johnson; Sucker Money; Lilly Turner; Cheating Blondes; Secrets of Hollywood; Picture Brides; Dance, Girl, Dance (short); Sons of the Desert. **1934** Going Bye Bye (short); The Live Ghost (short); Beloved; The Road to Ruin; I Like It That Way; Oliver the Eighth (short); Them Thar Hills (short). **1935** Tit for Tat (short); The Fixer Uppers (short); Affairs of Susan; Stranded. **1936** The Bohemian Girl. **1937** Daughter of Shanghai. **1938** Prison Farm; Nancy Drew, Detective. **1940** Women without Names. **1942** Hello, Annapolis; The Mad Monster. **1945** Stork Club; Masquerade in Mexico. **1947** Ladies' Man.

BUSH, ANITA
Born: Washington. Died: Feb. 16, 1974, New York. Black screen, stage and vaudeville actress. Appeared in vaudeville as part of "Williams and Walker" team.

Appeared in: **1921** The Crimson Skull. **1922** The Bulldogger.

BUSH, GEORGE
Born: 1858, Janesville, Wis. Died: Nov. 23, 1937, Culver City, Calif. Screen actor.

Appeared in: **1938** The Adventures of Tom Sawyer.

BUSH, PAULINE

Born: May 22, 1886, Lincoln, Nebr. Died: Nov. 1, 1969, San Diego, Calif. (pneumonia). Screen actress.

Appeared in: 1911 The Brand of Fear; The Poisoned Flume; The Sheriff's Sister; Objection Over-ruled. 1912 The Thief's Wife; A Life For a Kiss; An Innocent Grafter; Maiden and Men; A Bad Investment; The Outlaw Colony; The Jealous Rage; The Reformation of Sierra Smith; The Power of Love; The Agitator; The Ranchman's Marathon; The Promise; The New Cowpuncher; The Haters; The Brand; The Man and the Maid; Fidelity; Under False Pretenses; Nell of the Pampas; Driftwood; The Land of Death; Her Mountain Home; The Coward; The Girl of the Manor; The Pensioners; For the Good of Her Men; The Intrusion at Lompoc; The Stranger at Coyote. 1913 The Embezzler; Love Is Blind; An Eastern Flower; The Angel of the Canyon; The Lamb, the Woman, The Wolf; The End of the Feud; Red Margaret—Moonshiner; The Lie; The Wishing Seat; The Wall of Money; The Spirit of the Flag; Jewels of Sacrifice. 1914 The Honor of the Mounted; Remember Mary Magdalen; Discord and Harmony; The Menace of Carlotta (aka Carlotta, the Bead Stringer); The Tragedy of Whispering Creek; The Unlawful Trade; The Higher Law; The Cross; Her Bounty; The Hopes of Blind Alley; The Forbidden Room; The Oubliette; Richelieu; The Pipes of Pan; Virtue Is Its Own Reward; Lights and Shadows; A Night of Thrills; The Sin of Olga Brandt. 1915 Star of the Sea; The Measure of a Man; The Threads of Fate; The Girl Who Couldn't Go Wrong; Such Is Life; Where the Forest Ends; Outside the Gates; The Desert Breed; The Maid of the Mist; The Grind; Girl of the Night; For Cash; An Idyll of the Hills; The Stronger Mind; Steady Company; The Chimney's Secret; The Trap; Her Escape. 1916 The Capture of Rattlesnake Ike. 1917 Double Revenge; Nature's Calling; The Old Sheriff; The Man Who Saved the Day; Bloodhounds of the North. 1924 The Enemy Sex.

BUSHMAN, FRANCIS X. (Francis Xavier Bushman)

Born: Jan. 10, 1883, Baltimore, Md. Died: Aug. 23, 1966, Pacific Palisades, Calif. (heart attack due to fall). Screen, stage, radio and television actor. Father of screen actor Francis Bushman, Jr. Divorced from actress Beverly Bayne. Entered films with Essannay.

Appeared in: 1911 Last Year (film debut). 1912 When Soul Meets Soul; The Magic Wand; A Good Catch. 1913 The Spy's Defeat. 1914 One Wonderful Night; Blood Will Tell; Under Royal Patronage. 1915 Graustark; The Return of Richard Neal; The Silent Voice. 1916 The Great Secret; Romeo and Juliet. 1917 Red, White and Blue Blood. 1918 Social Quicksands. 1921 Smiling All the Way. 1922 According to Hoyle; Making the Grade. 1923 Modern Marriage. 1924 Marriage Circle. 1925 The Masked Bride. 1926 Ben Hur; The Marriage Clause. 1927 The Lady in Ermine; The Thirteenth Juror. 1928 The Grip of the Yukon; Man Higher Up; Midnight Life; Say It with Sables; The Charge of the Gauchos. 1930 The Call of the Circus; The Dude Wrangler; Once a Gentleman. 1931 Spell of the Circus (serial); Ben Hur (rerelease of 1926 film). 1933 The Three Musketeers (serial). 1936 Hollywood Boulevard. 1937 Dick Tracy (serial). 1944 Wilson. 1951 David and Bathsheba. 1952 Apache Country. 1954 Sabrina. 1957 The Story of Mankind. 1960 Twelve to the Moon. 1962 The Phantom Planet. 1965 Peer Gynt. 1966 The Ghost in the Invisible Bikini.

BUSLEY, JESSIE

Born: 1869, Albany, N.Y. Died: Apr. 20, 1950, New York, N.Y. Stage and screen actress.

Appeared in: 1930 Seeing Off Service (short); Home Made (short). 1931 Personal Maid. 1938 Brother Rat. 1939 King of the Underworld. 1940 It All Came True; Brother Rat and a Baby; Escape to Glory (aka Submarine Zone).

BUSQUETS, JOAQUIN

Born: 1875, Mexico. Died: Dec. 4, 1942, Mexico City, Mexico. Screen, radio actor and radio producer. Entered films during silents.

Appeared in: 1934 La Sangre Manda; Enemigos. 1935 Tierra, Amor y Dolor. 1936 La Mujer del Puerto. 1937 El Misterio del Rostro Palido; La Gran Cruz (The Heavy Cross).

BUSSEY, HANK

Born: 1891. Died: Jan. 14, 1971, Hollywood, Calif. Screen, stage and vaudeville actor. Member of vaudeville team of "Bussey and Case."

BUSTER, BUDD (Budd Leland Buster aka BUD BUSTER)

Born: June 14, 1891, Colo. Died: Dec. 22, 1965, Los Angeles, Calif. (heart attack). Screen actor.

Appeared in: 1935 The Cyclone Ranger; The Texas Rambler; The Vanishing Riders. 1936 Blazing Justice; Desert Guns; Desert Justice; The Riding Avenger; Cavalry; Headin' for the Rio Grande. 1937 Arizona Days; Sing, Cowboy, Sing; The Gun Ranger; Old Louisiana; The Trusted Outlaw; Drums of Destiny; Colorado Kid; Hit the Saddle. 1938 Code of the Rangers; Paroled—to Die; Thunder in the Desert; Song and Bullets; Desert Patrol; Stranger From Arizona; Frontier Scout. 1939 Zorro's Fighting Legion; Daughter of the Tong. 1940 King of the Royal Mounted; The Courageous Dr. Christian; Straight Shooter; Covered Wagon Trails; Murder on the Yukon; I Take This Oath; Marked Men; West of Pinto Basin. 1941 Billy the Kid's Fighting Pals; Secret Evidence;

The Lone Rider in Ghost Town; Texas Marshal; Gangs of Sonora; Thunder Over the Prairie; The Lone Star Vigilantes; Sierra Sue; Billy the Kid Wanted; West of Cimarron. 1942 Heart of the Rio Grande; Call of the Canyon; Westward, Ho; West of Tombstone; Billy the Kid Trapped; The Yukon Patrol; Down Rio Grande Way; Billy the Kid's Smoking Guns; Texas Bataan. 1943 The Old Chisholm Trail; Cheyenne Roundup; Cowboy Commandos; Daredevils of the West; The Black Trail; Santa Fe Scouts. 1944 Trail of Terror; Wolves of the Range; Frontier Outlaws; Hidden Valley Outlaws; Call of the South Seas; Trigger Trail; Brand of the Devil; Guns of the Law; Thundering Gun Slingers; The Pinto Bandit; Outlaw Roundup; Wild Horse Phantom; Riders of the Santa Fe; Saddle Leather Law. 1945 Navajo Kid; Border Badmen; Jungle Raiders. 1946 Six-Gun Man; The Flying Serpent; Gentlemen With Guns; Ambush Trail; Home on the Alamo; Terrors on Horseback; Sheriff of Redwood Valley; Texas Panhandle; Outlaw of the Plains; Terror Trail; Rainbow Over the Rockies; Songs of the Sierras. 1947 Vigilantes of Boomtown; The Wild Frontier; Shadow Valley; Cheyenne Takes Over. 1948 The Westward Trail. 1949 Loaded Pistols.

BUTCHER, ERNEST

Born: 1885. Died: June 8, 1965, London, England. Screen, stage and radio actor. Divorced from actress Muriel George (dec. 1965) and later married to actress Miss Brough.

Appeared in: 1935 Key to Harmony; Wedding Eve; The Small Man; Lieutenant Darling, RN. 1937 Overcoat Sam; Talking Feet; Song of the Road. 1938 Stepping Toes. 1939 Me and My Pal. 1940 Pack Up Your Troubles; Old Mother Riley in Business. 1942 Variety Jubilee. 1943 The Tawny Pipit (US 1947); It's in the Bag; When We are Married. 1944 Candles at Nine; It Happened One Sunday. 1945 Men of the Mines. 1946 The Years Between (US 1947); Appointment With Crime (US 1950). 1947 Dear Murderer (US 1948); While I Live. 1948 My Brother Jonathan (US 1949). 1949 Meet Simon Cherry. 1950 Highly Dangerous (US 1951). 1953 Time Bomb (aka Terror on a Train—US); Background (aka Edge of Divorce). 1959 The Desparate Man.

BUTI, CARLO

Born: 1902. Died: Nov. 16, 1963, Florence, Italy. Screen actor and singer.

Appeared in: 1938 I Due Gemelli (The Twins). 1939 Per Uomini Soli (For Men Only).

BUTLER, EDDIE

Born: 1888. Died: May 31, 1944, Hollywood, Calif. Screen actor.

BUTLER, FRANK

Born: Dec. 28, 1890, Oxford, England. Died: June 10, 1967, Hollywood, Calif. Screen, stage actor and screenwriter. Was in early "In-Law" series.

Appeared in: 1921 The Sheik; The Great Moment. 1922 A Tailor-Made Man; Beyond the Rocks; My American Wife. 1923 The Self-Made Wife; The Tiger's Claw; Bluebeard's Eighth Wife; The Call of the Wild. 1924 The King of the Wild Horses. 1925 Tol'able Romeo (short); Compromise; Satan in Sables. 1926 Made for Love; The Passionate Quest; The Fighting Buckaroo; Thirty Below Zero.

BUTLER, JAMES "JIMMY"

Born: 1921. Died: Feb. 18, 1945, France (killed in action, W. W. II). Screen actor. One of the original "Dead End Kids."

Appeared in: 1933 Only Yesterday; Beloved. 1934 No Greater Glory; Romance in Manhattan; Mrs. Wiggs of the Cabbage Patch; Manhattan Melodrama. 1934 I'll Fix It. 1935 When a Man's a Man; Laddie; Dinky; The Dark Angel. 1936 Battle of Greed; Stella Dallas; County Fair. 1937 Wells Fargo. 1938 Boys Town. 1939 The Escape; Nurse Edith Cavell; Winter Carnival. 1940 Military Academy. 1941 Naval Academy. 1942 Tough as They Come.

BUTLER, JOHN A. (aka JOHNNY BUTLER)

Born: 1884. Died: Oct. 9, 1967. Screen actor.

Appeared in: 1922 John Smith. 1923 Wet Gold. 1936 Make Way For a Lady. 1937 Some Blondes Are Dangerous; Expensive Husbands. 1938 Accidents Will Happen; Exposed; What Price Safety (short); How to Watch Football (short); Opening Day (short); Mental Poise (short). 1939 Torchy Runs for Mayor; The Day of Rest (short); Think First (short); Money to Loan (short). 1940 We Who Are Young; That Inferior Feeling (short). 1941 Mob Town. 1941 Silent Conflict; Sinister Journey. 1949 That Wonderful Urge; It Happens Every Spring. 1950 The Yellow Cab Man; Convicted; Code of the Silver Sage. 1951 Branded. 1952 The Pride of St. Louis. 1953 The Farmer Takes a Wife.

BUTLER, LOUISE (Estelle Louise Fiske)

Died: Dec. 8, 1958, Chicago, Ill. Stage and screen actress.

BUTLER, ROYAL "ROY" (Royal Edwin Butler)

Born: May 4, 1895, Atlanta, Ga. Died: July 28, 1973, Desert Hot Springs, Calif. Screen, stage and vaudeville actor. Entered films in 1911 with Photo Drama Co.

Appeared in: **1941** Sierra Sue. **1942** Home in Wyomin'; Heart Burn (short); House of Errors. **1947** Land of the Lawless; Gun Talk. **1948** Overland Trails; Range Renegades. **1949** Sky Liner; Deputy Marshal; Stallion Canyon. **1950** Bandit Queen; Fast on the Draw; Indian Territory; One Too Many. **1951** Fingerprints Don't Lie; Gene Autry and the Mounties; Texans Never Cry. **1952** Night Raiders.

BUTLER, WILLIAM J. "DADDY"

Born: 1860. Died: Jan. 27, 1927, Staten Island, N.Y. Stage and screen actor.

Appeared in: **1909** 1776, or The Hessian Renegades; In Old Kentucky; One Night and Then—. **1910** The Purgation; A Flash of Light; The Usurer. **1911** The Two Sides; A Romany Tragedy; The Last Drop of Water; Fighting Blood; The Unveiling; Dan the Dandy; A Blot on the 'Scutcheon. **1912** Man's Lust for Gold. **1913** The Hero of Little Italy; A Timely Interception. **1917** The Great Secret (serial).

BUTTERFIELD, HERBERT

Born: 1896. Died: May 2, 1957, Los Angeles, Calif. Screen and television actor.

Appeared in: **1950** Never Fear; The Young Lovers. **1951** House on Telegraph Hill. **1953** A Blueprint for Murder. **1954** Shield for Murder. **1956** The Ten Commandments.

BUTTERWORTH, CHARLES

Born: July 26, 1896, South Bend, Ind. Died: June 14, 1946, Los Angeles, Calif. (auto accident). Screen, stage, vaudeville and radio actor.

Appeared in: **1930** Life of the Party (film debut); Illicit. **1931** Side Show; The Bargain; The Mad Genius. **1932** Beauty and the Boss; Love Me Tonight; The Slippery Pearls (short); Manhattan Parade. **1933** The Nuisance; Penthouse; My Weakness. **1934** The Cat and the Fiddle; Hollywood Party; Student Tour; Forsaking All Others; Bulldog Drummond Strikes Back; Ruggles of Red Gap. **1935** The Night Is Young; Baby Face Harrington; Orchids to You. **1936** The Magnificent Obsession; The Moon's Our Home; Half Angel; We Went to College; Rainbow on the River. **1937** Swing High, Swing Low; Every Day's a Holiday. **1938** Thanks for the Memory. **1939** Let Freedom Ring. **1940** Second Chorus; The Boys from Syracuse. **1941** Blonde Inspiration; Sis Hopkins; There's Nothing to It (short); Road Show. **1942** Love Me Tonight; Night in New Orleans; Give Out, Sisters; What's Cooking? **1943** Always a Bridesmaid; The Sultan's Daughter; This Is the Army. **1944** Bermuda Mystery; Follow the Boys; Dixie Jamboree.

BUTTERWORTH, WALTER T.

Born: 1893. Died: Mar. 10, 1962, Hollywood, Calif. Screen, stage and vaudeville actor.

BUZZI, PIETRO

Died: Feb. 16, 1921, Los Angeles, Calif. Screen actor and opera performer. Entered films approx. 1910.

BYFORD, ROY

Born: 1873. Died: Jan. 31, 1939, London, England. Screen and stage actor.

Appeared in: **1916** The Little Damozel; On the Banks of Allen Water. **1918** The Happy Warrior. **1920** The Twelve Pound Look. **1921** The Night Hawk (aka The Haven); The Double Event. **1922** Treasure Trove; The Spanish Jade; A Master of Craft; Perpetua (aka Love's Boomerang—US). **1923** The Gems of Literature series including: Falstaff the Tavern Knight. **1924** Tons of Money. **1935** Immortal Gentleman. **1937** Museum Mystery. **1938** Horse Sense.

BYINGTON, SPRING

Born: Oct. 17, 1893, Colorado Springs, Colo. Died: Sept. 7, 1971, Hollywood, Calif. Screen, stage, radio and television actress.

Appeared in: **1931** Papa's Slay Ride (short). **1933** Little Women. **1935** Mutiny on the Bounty; The Werewolf of London; Love Me Forever; Orchids to You; Way Down East; Ah, Wilderness; Broadway Hostess; The Great Impersonation. **1936** The Charge of the Light Brigade; Every Saturday Night; Educating Father; Back to Nature; The Voice of Bugle Ann; Palm Springs; Stage Struck; The Girl on the Front Page; Dodsworth; Theodora Goes Wild. **1937** Green Light; Penrod and Sam; Off to the Races; Big Business; Hot Water; Borrowing Trouble; Hotel Haywire; The Road Back; It's Love I'm After; Clarence; A Family Affair. **1938** You Can't Take It with You; Love on a Budget; A Trip to Paris; Safety in Numbers; The Buccaneer; Penrod and His Twin Brother; Jezebel; Down on the Farm; The Adventures of Tom Sawyer. **1939** Everybody's Baby; The Jones Family in Hollywood; Quick Millions; The Story of Alexander Graham Bell; Chicken Wagon Family; Too Busy to Work; Jones Family at the Grand Canyon. **1940** A Child Is Born; The Bluebird; On Their Own; My Love Came Back; Lucky Partners; Laddie; Young As You Feel; The Ghost Comes Home. **1941** Arkansas Judge; Meet John Doe; The Devil and Miss Jones; When Ladies Meet; Ellery Queen and the Perfect Crime; The Vanishing Virginian. **1942** Roxie Hart; Once Upon a Thursday; The War Against Mrs. Hadley; Rings on Her Fingers; The Affairs of Martha. **1943** Heaven Can Wait; Presenting Lily Mars; The Heavenly Body. **1944** I'll Be Seeing You. **1945** Thrill of a Romance; Captain Eddie; Salty O'Rourke; The Enchanted Cot-

tage; A Letter for Evie. **1946** Dragonwyck; Meet Me on Broadway; Little Mr. Jim; Faithful in My Fashion; My Brother Talks to Horses. **1947** Living in a Big Way; Singapore; It Had to Be You; Cynthia; The Rich Full Life. **1948** B. F.'s Daughter. **1949** The Big Wheel; In the Good Old Summertime. **1950** Please Believe Me; Devil's Doorway; Louisa; Walk Softly, Stranger; The Skipper Surprised His Wife; The Reformer and the Redhead (voice only). **1951** Angels in the Outfield; Bannerline; According to Mrs. Hoyle. **1952** No Room for the Groom; Because You're Mine. **1954** The Rocket Man. **1960** Please Don't Eat the Daisies.

BYLES, BOBBY

Born: 1931. Died: Aug. 26, 1969, Hollywood, Calif. (heart attack). Screen and television actor.

Appeared in: **1958** Onionhead. **1964** War is Hell.

BYRAM, RONALD

Born: Brisbane, Australia. Died: Apr. 1919, Calgary, Canada. Stage and screen actor.

Appeared in: **1919** Out of the Shadow; A Gentleman of Quality.

BYRD, RALPH

Born: Apr. 22, 1909, Dayton, Ohio. Died: Aug. 18, 1952, Tarzana, Calif. (heart attack). Screen and television actor. Starred as Dick Tracy in film and television series.

Appeared in: **1936** Hell-Ship Morgan; Border Caballero; Swing Time. **1937** S.O.S. Coast Guard (serial); Motor Madness; The Trigger Trio; Paid to Dance; Blake of Scotland Yard (serial); Dick Tracy (serial); Criminals of the Air. **1938** Down in "Arkansaw"; Born to be Wild; Army Girl; Dick Tracy Returns (serial). **1939** Mickey, the Kid; Dick Tracy's G-Men (serial); Fighting Thoroughbreds; S.O.S. Tidal Wave. **1940** Misbehaving Husbands; The Howards of Virginia; Drums of the Desert; The Golden Fleecing; The Son of Monte Cristo; Dark Streets of Cairo; Northwest Mounted Police. **1941** Dick Tracy vs. Crime, Inc. (serial); The Penalty; Desperate Cargo; A Yank in the RAF. **1942** Broadway Big Shot; Jungle Book; Careful, Soft Shoulders; Time to Kill; Moontide; Duke of the Navy; Ten Gentlemen from West Point; Manila Calling. **1943** They Came to Blow Up America; Guadalcanal Diary. **1944** Tampico. **1947** The Vigilante (serial); Dick Tracy's Dilemma; Dick Tracy Meets Gruesome; Stallion Road; Mark of the Claw. **1948** Jungle Goddess; Thunder in the Pines; Canon City; Stage Struck; The Argyle Secrets. **1950** Radar Secret Service. **1951** The Redhead and the Cowboy. **1952** Dick Tracy vs. The Phantom Empire (serial).

BYRENS, MYER

Born: 1840. Died: June 29, 1933, Los Angeles, Calif. Screen and stage actor.

BYRNES, NANCY ROSENBLUTH

Born: 1915. Died: June 15, 1962, Union. N.J. Screen actress and singer.

BYROADE, GEORGE

Born: 1883. Died: Mar. 5, 1975. Screen stuntman and stand-in.

BYRON, ARTHUR

Born: Apr. 3, 1872, Brooklyn, N.Y. Died: July 17, 1943, Hollywood, Calif. Stage and screen actor.

nared in: **1929** A Family Affair (short). **1932** Twenty Thousand Years in Sing Sing; The Mummy; Fast Life. **1933** Gabriel over the White House; Tonight Is Ours; Silk Express; Mayor of Hell; Private Detective 62; College Coach. **1934** The Man with Two Faces; Marie Galante; Two Alone; Notorious Sophie Lang; The House of Rothschild; The President Vanishes; Stand Up and Cheer; The Secret Bride; Fog over Frisco. **1935** The Whole Town's Talking; Shadows of Doubt; The Casino Murder Case; Murder in the Fleet; Oil for the Lamps of China. **1936** The Prisoner of Shark Island.

BYRON, KATY (Catherine Byron)

Born: 1918. Died: Feb. 22, 1970, New Haven, Conn. Screen and radio actress. Married to radio producer-director Edward A. Byron (dec.).

Appeared in: **1929** A Funny Affair (short).

BYRON, PAUL

Born: 1891. Died: May 12, 1959, San Diego, Calif. Screen and stage actor. Entered films with Universal in 1915.

BYRON, ROYAL JAMES

Born: 1887. Died: Mar. 4, 1943, Trenton, N.J. Screen, stage and vaudeville actor. Entered films with Vitagraph.

Appeared in: **1926** The Palm Beach Girl. **1930** Unmasked.

BYSTROM, WALTER E.

Born: 1894. Died: Sept. 13, 1969, San Diego, Calif. Screen actor. Entered films as an extra before joining Sennett as a Keystone Kop.

CABANNE, WILLIAM CHRISTY
Born: 1888, St. Louis, Mo. Died: Oct. 15, 1950, Philadelphia, Pa. (heart attack). Film director, screen, stage actor, and screenwriter.

Appeared in: **1909** The Cord of Life; One Touch of Nature; The Song of the Shirt. **1912** Under Burning Skies; The Punishment; A Temporary Truce; A String of Pearls. **1913** Judith of Bethulia.

CABOT, BRUCE (Jacques Etienne Pellissier de Bujac)
Born: Apr. 20, 1904, Carlsbad, N.Mex. Died: May 3, 1972, Woodland Hills, Calif. (lung and throat cancer). Screen, stage and television actor. Divorced from Grace Mary Mather Smith and actresses Adrienne Ames (dec. 1947) and Franchesca de Scaffa.

Appeared in: **1932** What Price Hollywood?; Roadhouse Murder. **1933** Lucky Devils; King Kong; Great Jasper; Midshipman Jack; Ann Vickers; Disgraced!; Flying Devils. **1934** Shadows of Sing Sing; Murder on the Blackboard; Finishing School; His Greatest Gamble; Redhead; Night Alarm; Their Big Moment. **1935** Men of the Night; Without Children; Let 'Em Have It!; Show Them No Mercy. **1936** Don't Gamble with Love; Legion of Terror; Three Wise Guys; Fury; Sinner Take All; The Last of the Mohicans; Don't Turn 'Em Loose; The Big Game; Robin Hood of Eldorado; Penthouse Party. **1937** Love Takes Flight; Bad Guy. **1938** Bad Man of Brimstone; Sinners in Paradise; Smashing the Rackets; 10th Avenue Kid. **1939** You and Me; Homicide Bureau; Dodge City; Traitor Spy; Mickey the Kid; Mystery of White Room. **1940** My Son Is Guilty; Susan and God; Captain Caution; Girls Under 21. **1941** The Flame of New Orleans; Wild Bill Hickok Rides; Sundown. **1942** Pierre of the Plains; Silver Queen. **1943** The Desert Song. **1945** Divorce; Salty O'Rourke; Fallen Angel. **1946** Smoky; The Avalanche. **1947** The Angel and the Badman; Gunfighters (aka The Assassin). **1948** The Gallant Legion. **1949** Sorrowful Jones. **1950** Fancy Pants; Rock Island Trail (aka Transcontinental Express). **1951** Best of the Badmen. **1952** Lost in Alaska; Kid Monk Baroni. **1955** El Mantello Rosso (The Red Cloak—US 1961). **1956** Il Tesoro di Rommel (Rommel's Treasure—US 1963). **1958** The Quiet American; The Sheriff of Fractured Jaw. **1959** The Love Specialist; John Paul Jones; Goliath and the Barbarian. **1961** The Comancheros. **1962** Hatari! **1963** McLintock! **1964** Law of the Lawless. **1965** In Harm's Way; Cat Ballou; Black Spurs; Town Tamer. **1966** The Chase. **1967** The War Wagon. **1968** The Hellfighters; The Green Berets. **1969** The Undefeated; A Hall of Mirrors. **1970** WUSA; Chisum. **1971** Big Jake; Diamonds are Forever.

CADELL, JEAN
Born: Sept. 13, 1884, Edinburgh, Scotland. Died: Sept. 1967, London, England. Screen, stage and television actress.

Appeared in: **1912** David Garrick. **1915** The Man Who Stayed at Home. **1920** Alf's Button; Anna the Adventuress. **1923** The Naked Man. **1930** The Loves of Robert Burns. **1932** Two White Arms (aka Wives Behave—US 1933); Fires of Fate (US 1933). **1933** Timbuctoo. **1934** Little Friend; The Luck of a Sailor. **1935** David Copperfield. **1937** Love from a Stranger; Whom the Gods Love (aka Mozard—US 1940). **1938** Pygmalion. **1939** Confidential Lady. **1941** Quiet Wedding. **1942** Young Mr. Pitt. **1943** Dear Octopus (aka The Randolph Family—US 1945). **1945** I Know Where I'm Going (US 1947). **1947** Jassy (US 1948). **1949** That Dangerous Age (aka If This be Sin—US 1950); Marry Me (US 1951); Whisky Galore (aka Tight Little Island—US and Mad Little Island). **1950** Madeleine; The Reluctant Widow (US 1951); No Place for Jennifer (US 1951). **1951** The Late Edwina Black (aka Obsessed—US). **1952** I'm a Stranger. **1953** Meet Mr. Lucifer. **1956** Keep It Clean. **1957** The Little Hut; The Surgeon's Knife; Let's Be Happy. **1958** Rockets Galore; Mad Little Island. **1959** Upstairs and Downstairs (US 1961); Serious Charge (aka Immoral Charge—US 1962). **1960** A Taste of Money. **1964** A Touch of Hell (rerelease of Serious Charge-1959).

CAHILL, LILLY
Born: 1886. Died: July 20, 1955, San Antonio, Tex. Screen, stage and television actress. Married to actor Blandon Tynan (dec. 1967).

Appeared in: **1910** The Fugitive. **1931** My Sin. **1939** So This Is London (US 1940).

CAHILL, MARIE
Born: 1874, Brooklyn, N.Y. Died: Aug. 23, 1933, N.Y. (heart trouble). Screen, stage and vaudeville actress.

Appeared in: **1915** Judy Forgot. **1917** Gladys' Day Dreams and three two-reel comedies.

CAHILL, THOMAS M.
Born: 1889, Chillicothe, Ohio. Died: Apr. 3, 1953, near Washington, D.C. Screen, stage, television actor, and newspaper reporter.

Appeared in government-made short documentary films.

CAHOON, MILLIAN BENEDICT
Born: 1860. Died: Jan. 28, 1951, Darien, Conn. Screen and stage actor.

CAIN, ROBERT
Born: 1887. Died: Apr. 27, 1954, New York, N.Y. Screen, stage, television and radio actor.

Appeared in: **1916** My Lady Incog. **1918** He Comes Up Smiling. **1919** In Mizzoura; Male and Female. **1921** The Witching Hour; Man-Woman-Marriage. **1922** The Impossible Mrs. Bellew; The Crossroads of New York; Burning Sands; Reported Missing. **1923** Children of Jazz; Hollywood; Drums of Fate; Racing Hearts; The Tiger's Claw. **1924** Three Weeks; Conductor 1492; Soiled; The Rose of Paris. **1925** The Everlasting Whisper; The Golden Bed; When the Door Opened; Every Man's Wife; Wings of Youth. **1926** The Danger of Paris; Too Much Money; The Wilderness Woman. **1927** Husband Hunters; Rich Men's Sons.

CAINE, GEORGIA
Born: 1876, San Francisco, Calif. Died: Apr. 4, 1964, Hollywood, Calif. Stage and screen actress.

Appeared in: **1930** Good Intentions; Night Work. **1933** The Cradle Song. **1934** Call It Luck; Love Theme; I Am Suzanne; Once to Every Woman; Count of Monte Cristo; The Crusades; The White Angel. **1935** Hooray for Love. **1936** One Rainy Afternoon; Sing Me a Love Song; Navy Born. **1937** Time Out for Romance; It's Love I'm After; Bill Cracks Down; The Affairs of Cappy Ricks. **1938** Women Are Like That; His Exciting Night. **1939** Dodge City; Juarez; No Place to Go; Honeymoon in Bali; Tower of London. **1940** Remember the Night; Babes for Sale; Nobody's Children; The Lone Wolf Meets a Lady; Christmas in July. **1941** The Nurse's Secret; The Great Lie; Ridin' on a Rainbow; Hurry, Charlie, Hurry. **1942** Hello, Annapolis; The Wife Takes a Flyer; Yankee Doodle Dandy; Gentleman Jim; Are Husbands Necessary? **1944** The Miracle of Morgan's Creek; Hail the Conquering Hero. **1947** Mad Wednesday; A Double Life. **1948** Give My Regards to Broadway; Unfaithfully Yours. **1949** The Beautiful Blonde from Bashful Bend.

CAIRNES, SALLY
Born: 1920. Died: Feb. 9, 1965, Hollywood, Calif. Screen actress and singer.

CAITS, JOSEPH
Born: 1889. Died: Mar. 9, 1957, New York, N.Y. Screen, stage and vaudeville actor. Appeared in vaudeville with his brother Louis in an act billed as "The Caits Brothers."

Appeared in: **1937** Hollywood Cowboy; Youth on Parole. **1938** A Slight Case of Murder; Reformatory. **1939** Lady and the Mob; Babes in Arms. **1940** Brother Orchid.

CALDER, KING
Born: 1900. Died: June 28, 1964, Los Angeles, Calif. (heart attack). Screen, stage and television actor.

Appeared in: **1956** Timetable; On the Threshold of Space; The Rains of Ranchipur. **1958** Hong Kong Confidential; Mardi Gras. **1960** Three Came to Kill. **1961** Everything's Ducky. **1964** Ready for the People.

CALDWELL, JACK
Died: Oct. 21, 1944, Honolulu, Hawaii. Screen actor.

CALDWELL, ORVILLE R.
Born: 1896, Oakland, Calif. Died: Sept. 24, 1967, Santa Rosa, Calif. Stage and screen actor.

Appeared in: **1923** The French Doll; The Lonely Road; The Six-Fifty; The Scarlet Lily. **1924** Daughters of the Night. **1925** Sackcloth and Scarlet. **1926** The Wives of the Prophet; Flame of the Argentine. **1927** The Harvester; Judgment of the Hills. **1928** The Patsy; The Little Yellow House. **1938** Just around the Corner; The Last Warning.

CALHERN, LOUIS (Carl Henry Vogt)
Born: 1895, Brooklyn, N.Y. Died: May 12, 1956, Tokyo, Japan (heart attack). Screen, stage, vaudeville and burlesque actor. Divorced from actresses Ilka Chase, Julia Hoyt (dec. 1955), Natalie Schaefer and Marianne Stewart.

Appeared in: **1921** The Blot; Too Wise Wives; What's Worth While? **1922** Woman, Wake Up! **1923** The Last Moment. **1931** Stolen Heaven; Road to Singapore; Blonde Crazy. **1932** Okay, America; They Call It Sin; Night After Night; Afraid to Talk. **1933** Strictly Personal; 20,000 Years In Sing Sing; Frisco Jenny; The Woman Accused; Diplomaniacs; The World Gone Mad; Duck Soup. **1934** The Affairs of Cellini; The Count of Monte Cristo; The Man with Two Faces. **1935** The Arizonian; The Last Days of Pompeii; Woman Wanted; Sweet Adeline. **1936** The Gorgeous Hussy. **1937** Her Husband Lies; The Life of Emile Zola. **1938** Fast Company. **1939** Juarez; 5th Avenue Girl; Charlie McCarthy, Detective. **1940** I Take This Woman; Dr. Erlich's Magic Bullet. **1943** Up in Arms; Nobody's Darling; Heaven Can Wait. **1944** The Bridge of San Luis Rey. **1946** Notorious. **1948** Arch of Triumph. **1949** The Red Danube; The Red Pony. **1950** Annie Get Your Gun; The Asphalt Jungle; Two Weeks with Love; Devil's Doorway; A Life of Her Own; Nancy Goes to Rio. **1951** The Man with a Cloak; The Magnificent Yankee (stage and film versions). **1952** The Invitation; The Washington Story; We're Not Married; The Prisoner of Zenda. **1953** Julius Caesar; Confidentially Connie; Remains to Be Seen; Main Street to Broadway; Latin Lovers. **1954** Executive Suite; The Student Prince; Men of the Fighting Lady; Betrayed; Athena; Rhapsody. **1955** High Society; The Blackboard Jungle; The Prodigal. **1956** Forever, Darling; The Teahouse of the August Moon.

CALHOUN, ALICE

Born: Nov. 24, 1904, Cleveland, Ohio. Died: June 3, 1966, Los Angeles, Calif. (cancer). Screen actress. Entered films with Vitagraph in N.Y.

Appeared in: **1920** Human Collateral; Deadline at Eleven. **1921** The Charming Deceiver; Closed Doors; Peggy Puts It Over; Princess Jones. **1922** Angel of Crooked Street; Girl in His Room; The Little Minister; Matrimonial Web; The Rainbow; A Girl's Desire; Little Wildcat; Blue Blood. **1923** The Man from Brodney; The Man Next Door; The Midnight Alarm; One Stolen Night; Masters of Men; Pioneer Trails. **1924** Between Friends; Code of the Wilderness; Flowing Gold. **1925** Pampered Youth; The Other Woman's Story; The Part Time Wife; The Everlasting Whisper; The Happy Warrior; The Man on the Box. **1926** Flying High; Hero of the Big Snows; The Power of the Weak; Kentucky Handicap; Tentacles of the North. **1927** The Down Grade; Savage Passions; The Trunk Mystery; Hidden Aces; In the First Degree; Isle of Forgotten Women. **1929** Bride of the Desert.

CALL, JOHN

Born: 1907. Died: Apr. 3, 1973, New York, N.Y. Screen and stage actor.

Appeared in: **1952** Hangman's Knot; Boots Malone; Fearless Fagan; Indian Uprising; Young Man With Ideas. **1964** Santa Claus Conquers the Martians.

CALLAHAN, BILLY

Born: 1911. Died: Feb. 21, 1964, Queens, N.Y. (heart attack). Screen and vaudeville actress. Appeared in vaudeville with Louise Brooks in an act billed as "Brooks and Callahan." Doubled for Thelma Todd.

CALLAHAN, CHARLES S. "CHUCK"

Born: 1891. Died: Nov. 12, 1964, New York, N.Y. Screen, stage, radio, television and vaudeville actor. Brother of actor Bobby Callahan (dec. 1938), with whom he appeared in vaudeville in an act billed as "Bob and Chuck Callahan."

Appeared in: **1937** Grips, Grunts and Groans (short).

CALLAHAN, ROBERT "BOBBY"

Born: 1896. Died: May 15, 1938, West Los Angeles, Calif. Screen and vaudeville actor. Brother of actor Chuck Callahan (dec. 1964) with whom he appeared in vaudeville in an act billed as "Bob and Chuck Callahan."

Appeared in: **1929** The Champion Golfer (short). **1930** Wild Company. **1934** Men in Black (short). **1937** Battle of Greed.

CALLEIA, JOSEPH (Joseph Spurin-Calleia)

Born: Aug. 4, 1897, Malta. Died: Oct. 31, 1975, Malta. Screen, stage actor, singer and screenwriter.

Appeared in: **1931** His Woman. **1935** Public Hero No. 1; Riffraff. **1936** Exclusive Story; Tough Guy; Sworn Enemy; His Brother's Wife; Sinner Take All; After the Thin Man. **1937** Man of the People. **1938** Bad Man of Brimstone; Algiers; Marie Antoinette; Four's a Crowd. **1939** Juarez; The Gorilla; Five Came Back; Golden Boy; Full Confession. **1940** My Little Chickadee; Wyoming. **1941** The Monster and the Girl; Sundown. **1942** The Glass Key; Jungle Book. **1943** For Whom the Bell Tolls; The Cross of Lorraine. **1944** The Conspirators. **1946** Gilda; Deadline at Dawn. **1947** The Beginning of the End; Lured. **1948** The Noose Hangs High; Four Faces West. **1950** Palomino; Captain Carey, U.S.A.; Branded; Vendetta. **1951** Valentino; The Light Touch. **1952** Yankee Buccaneer; The Iron Mistress; When in Rome. **1953** The Caddy. **1955** Underwater; The Treasure of Pancho Villa; The Littlest Outlaw. **1956** Hot Blood; Serenade. **1957** Wild Is the Wind. **1958** Touch of Evil; The Light in the Forest. **1959** Cry Tough. **1960** The Alamo. **1963** Johnny Cool.

CALLIS, DAVID

Born: 1888. Died: Sept. 10, 1934, Los Angeles, Calif. Stage and screen actor.

Appeared in: **1929** The Sin Sister; What's Your Racket?

CALTHROP, DONALD

Born: Apr. 11, 1888, England. Died: Aug. 1940, England (heart attack). Stage and screen actor.

Appeared in: **1916** Wanted a Widow; Altar Chains. **1917** Masks and Faces; The Gay Lord Quex. **1918** Nelson; Goodbye. **1928** Shooting Stars. **1929** Atlantic; Blackmail; The Clue of the New Pin; The Flying Squad; Up the Poll (short); Juno and the Paycock (aka The Shame of Mary Boyle—US). **1930** Two Worlds; Murder; Loose Ends; Elstree Calling; Almost a Honeymoon (US 1931); Song of Soho; The Night Porter; Spanish Eyes; We Take Off Our Hats; Star Impersonations (short); The Cockney Spirit in the War Series including All Riot on the Western Front and The Cockney Spirit in the War. **1931** The Ghost Train (US 1933); Uneasy Virtue; Cape Forlorn (aka The Love Storm—US); The Bells; Many Waters. **1932** Money for Nothing; Rome Express; Fires

of Fate (US 1933); Number Seventeen. **1933** Friday the Thirteenth (US 1934); The Acting Business; F.P.T.; Orders Is Orders (US 1934); I Was a Spy; Early to Bed; Sorrell and Son. **1934** Red Ensign (aka Strike!—US); Nine Forty-Five; It's a Cop. **1935** Man of the Moment; Scrooge; The Phantom Light; The Clairvoyant; The Divine Spark. **1936** The Man Behind the Mask; Broken Blossoms; The Man Who Changed His Mind (aka The Man Who Lived Again—US). **1937** Cafe Colette (aka Danger in Paris—US); Dreaming Lips; Fire Over England; Love from a Stranger. **1939** Shadow of Death. **1940** Band Wagon; Let George Do It. **1941** Major Barbara.

CALVERT, CATHERINE (Catherine Cassidy)

Born: 1891, Baltimore, Md. Died: Jan. 18, 1971, Uniondale, N.Y. Stage and screen actress.

Appeared in: **1918** A Romance of the Underworld. **1919** Fires of Faith; The Career of Catherine Bush. **1920** Dead Men Tell No Tales. **1921** The Heart of Maryland; Moral Fibre; You Find It Everywhere. **1922** That Woman; The Green Caravan. **1923** The Indian Love Lyrics; Out to Win.

CALVERT, ELISHA H.

Born: June 27, 1873, Alexandria, Va. Died: Oct. 5, 1941, Hollywood, Calif. Screen, stage, vaudeville actor, film director and producer.

Appeared in: **1911** The Love Test (film debut). **1912** Giuseppe's Good Fortune. **1913** The Boomerang; Tapped Wires; The Sign; The Love Theft; Broken Threads United; The Heart of the Law; In Convict Garb; The Pay-as-You-Enter Man; The Melburn Confession; Seeing Is Believing; The Heiress; Bill Mixes With His Relations; The Unknown; The Misjudging of Mr. Hubby; The Little Mother; Love Through a Lens; The Road of Transgression; Odd Knots; The Hero-Coward; Hypnotism in Hicksville; What George Did; The Price of Gold; The Rival Salesman. **1914** The Grip of Circumstance; The Counter-Melody; One Wonderful Night; Ashes of Hope. **1923** Inez from Hollywood. **1924** Bluff; The Only Woman; Why Men Leave Home; Inez from Hollywood. **1925** Havoc; Sally; East of Suez; The Talker. **1926** Ella Cinders; The Girl from Montmarte. **1927** Melting Millions (serial); The First Auto; Lonesome Ladies; The Wizard; Rookies. **1928** Moran of the Marines; The Man Without a Face (serial); The Legion of the Condemned; Let 'Er Go Gallagher; Why Sailors Go Wrong; Prop and Pep. **1929** The Greene Murder Case; Darkened Rooms; The Mighty; The Virginian; Dark Street; The Studio Murder Mystery; The Canary Murder Case; Fast Company; The Love Parade; Thunderbolt. **1930** Half Shot at Sunrise; Behind the Makeup; The Benson Murder Case; The Border Legion; The Kibitzer; Ladies Love Brutes; A Man from Wyoming; Men Are Like That; Only the Brave; The Widow from Chicago; The Social Lion; Peacock Alley. **1932** Beyond Victory; Horse Feathers. **1933** Wild Horse Mesa; The Mysterious Rider; Duck Soup. **1934** Here Comes the Groom; The Mighty Barnum. **1936** The Glory Trail.

CALVERT, LOUIS

Born: 1859, England. Died: July 9, 1923, England? Screen and stage actor.

Appeared in: **1913** David Garrick.

CALVIN, HENRY (Wimberly Calvin Goodman, Jr.)

Born: 1918, Dallas, Tex. Died: Oct. 6, 1975, Dallas, Tex. (cancer). Screen, television, radio and stage actor.

Appeared in: **1956** The Broken Star; Crime Against Joe. **1960** Toby Tyler; The Sign of Zorro. **1961** Babes in Toyland. **1965** Ship of Fools.

CAMELIA, MURIEL

Born: 1913. Died: Nov. 15, 1925, Miami, Fla. (motor bus accident). Stage and screen actress. Appeared in D. W. Griffith films.

CAMERON, BRUCE (Paul Brachard, Jr.)

Born: 1910. Died: Apr. 10, 1959, Los Angeles, Calif. Screen actor and circus acrobat.

CAMERON, DONALD

Born: 1889. Died: July 11, 1955, West Cornwall, Conn. Stage and screen actor.

Appeared in: **1921** The Education of Elizabeth.

CAMERON, GENE

Died: Nov. 16, 1928, Yuma, Ariz. Screen actor.

Appeared in: **1922** The Sign of the Rose. **1923** An Old Sweetheart of Mine. **1924** Circe, The Enchantress. **1925** Excuse Me. **1926** The Midnight Kiss. **1927** Chain Lightning; The Gay Retreat.

CAMERON, HUGH

Born: 1879, Duluth, Minn. Died: Nov. 9, 1941, New York, N.Y. Stage and screen actor.

Appeared in: **1921** Cappy Ricks. **1923** Homeward Bound. **1924** Pied Piper Malone. **1925** The Man Who Found Himself. **1927** For the Love of Mike. **1931** One Heavenly Night; Papa's Slay Ride (short). **1932** The Emergency Case. **1939** One Third of a Nation; Back Door to Heaven.

CAMERON, RUDOLPH "RUDY" (Rudolph Cameron Brennan)
Born: Oct. 24, 1894, Washington, D.C. Died: Feb. 17, 1958, Los Angeles, Calif. (hemorrhage). Stage and screen actor.

Appeared in: **1917** The More Excellent Way; Clover's Rebellion; **1918** My Husband's Friend. **1922** Rose o' the Sea. **1923** Shattered Faith. **1927** For the Love of Mike. **1928** Coney Island; Three-Ring Marriage. **1930** Song of the West; Queen High.

CAMP, SHEPPARD
Born: 1882, West Point, Ga. Died: Nov. 20, 1929, Hollywood, Calif. (injuries from fall). Stage and screen actor.

Appeared in: **1929** The Greene Murder Case. **1930** Playing Around; Song of the Flame.

CAMPBELL, ALAN
Born: 1905. Died: June 14. 1963, West Hollywood, Calif. Screen, stage actor and screenwriter. Married to writer Dorothy Parker (dec. 1967).

CAMPBELL, COLIN
Born: 1883, Falkirk, Scotland. Died: Mar. 27, 1966, Woodland Hills, Calif. Screen, stage actor and film producer. Entered films in 1915. Do not confuse with film director Colin Campbell (dec.).

Appeared in: **1915** Tillie's Tomato Surprise; Toodles, Tom and Trouble; Bing Bang Brothers. **1916** Belinda's Bridal Breakfast. **1920** Nothing But the Truth. **1921** Where Lights Are Low; The Girl from Nowhere; The Man of Stone. **1922** Cardigan. **1925** The White Monkey. **1930** Big Boy; The Road to Singapore; Unwanted; The Gay Diplomat. **1931** The Deceiver. **1933** Alice in Wonderland. **1934** Eight Girls in a Boat. **1941** San Francisco Docks. **1942** Life Begins at 8:30; Mrs. Miniver; This Above All; The War Against Mrs. Hadley. **1944** The Lodger. **1945** The Fatal Witness; Scotland Yard Investigator. **1947** Moss Rose; The Wife of Monte Cristo; Exposed; The Two Mrs. Carrolls. **1948** Texas, Brooklyn and Heaven. **1949** The Fan; Mr. Belvedere Goes to College; Adventure of Icabod and Mr. Toad (voice). **1955** Abbott and Costello Meet the Keystone Kops. **1954** Sabrina. **1960** The Lost World. **1963** The Three Stooges Go Around the World in a Daze; The Leather Boys (US 1965). **1964** Saturday Night Out; The High Bright Sun (aka McGuire Go Home!—US 1966).

CAMPBELL, ERIC (Eric Alfred Campbell)
Born: Apr. 26, 1879, Scotland. Died: Dec. 20, 1917, Los Angeles, Calif. (auto accident). Screen, stage actor and screenwriter.

Appeared in: **1914** Between Showers; Cruel, Cruel Love; Mabel At the Wheel; Caught In a Cabaret; The Fatal Mallet; Her Friend the Bandit; The Knockout. **1916** The Floorwalker; The Fireman; The Vagabond; The Count; The Pawnshop; The Rink; Behind the Screen. **1917** Easy Street; The Cure; The Immigrant; The Adventurer. **1963** 30 Years of Fun (documentary).

CAMPBELL, FRANK
Born: 1847. Died: Apr. 30, 1934, Hollywood, Calif. Screen and stage actor.

Appeared in: **1929** Frozen River.

CAMPBELL, MARGARET
Born: 1873. Died: June 27, 1939, Los Angeles, Calif.(murdered—hammer attack; son confessed to crime). Screen actress. Divorced from actor Josef Swickard (dec. 1940).

Appeared in: **1921** Lying Lips; Eden and Return; The Girl in the Taxi. **1922** Don't Shoot; Confidence; The Top O' the Morning. **1923** The Clean Up; Legally Dead; His Mystery Girl. **1924** The Dangerous Blonde; The Fast Worker. **1925** Home Maker. **1926** The Better Man; Monte Carlo; The Lady from Hell. **1927** Children of Divorce; Wages of Conscience. **1929** One Hysterical Night. **1930** Take the Heir.

CAMPBELL, MRS. PATRICK (Beatrice Stella Tanner)
Born: Feb. 1865, Kensington, London, England. Died: Apr. 10, 1940, Pau, France. Stage and screen actress.

Appeared in: **1930** The Dancers (film debut). **1934** Riptide; Outcast Lady; One More River. **1935** Pygmalion; Crime and Punishment.

CAMPBELL, VIOLET (Violet Shelton)
Born: 1893. Died: Jan. 1970, London, England. Screen and stage actress. Married to actor Nigel Bruce (dec. 1953).

Appeared in: **1941** Suspicion (her only film).

CAMPBELL, WEBSTER (William Webster Campbell)
Born: 1893, Kansas City, Mo. Died: Aug. 28, 1972, Liberty, Kans. Screen actor, film director, screenwriter and author. Divorced from actress Corinne Griffith. Married to Beatrice Campbell.

Appeared in: **1914** The Secret Marriage. **1915** Oh, Daddy and Kay-Bee films. **1917** The Clock Struck One; Satan's Private Door; The Fettered Woman; Local Color; The Love Doctor; The Renaissance at Charleroi. **1918** The Count and the Wedding; The Girl of Today. **1920** Human Collateral; The Tower of

Jewels. **1921** It Isn't Being Done This Season. **1930** The Love Racket; In the Next Room.

CAMPEAU, FRANK
Born: 1864, Detroit, Mich. Died: Nov. 5, 1943, Woodland Hills, Calif. Stage and screen actor.

Appeared in: **1915** Jordan In a Hard Road. **1917** Reaching for the Moon; Man from Painted Post. **1918** Bound in Morocco; Light of the Western Stars; Headin' South; Arizona. **1919** Cheating Cheaters; The Knickerbocker Buckaroo; His Majesty the American. **1920** The Life of the Party. **1921** The Kid; The Killer; For Those We Love. **1922** The Sin of Martha Queed; The Crimson Challenge; Just Tony; The Lane That Had No Turning; The Yosemite Trail; The Trap; Skin Deep. **1923** Isle of Lost Ships; To the Last Man; Modern Matrimony; North of Hudson Bay; Quicksands; The Spider and the Rose; Three Who Paid. **1924** Hoodman Blind; Those Who Dance; The Alaskan; Not a Drum Was Heard. **1925** Battling Bunyon; Heir-Looms; Coming Through; The Man from Red Gulch; The Saddle Hawk; The Pleasure Buyers; Manhattan Madness; The Golden Cocoon. **1926** The Three Bad Men; The Frontier Trail; No Man's Gold; Sea Horses; Whispering Wires. **1927** The First Auto; Let it Rain; The Heart of the Yukon. **1928** Across the Border (short); The Candy Kid. **1929** In Old Arizona; In the Headlines; Sea Fury; Points West; The Gamblers; Frozen River; Say It with Songs. **1930** Hideout; The Last of the Duanes; Abraham Lincoln; Captain Thunder; The People Versus (short); Lightnin'; Trifles (short); Danger (short). **1931** Fighting Caravans; Soldier's Plaything; Lasco of the Rio Grande. **1932** Girl of the Rio; White Eagle; The Dove. **1933** Smoky. **1935** Hopalong Cassidy. **1936** Everyman's Law; Empty Saddles. **1937** Black Aces. **1938** Border Wolves; The Painted Trail.

CANE, CHARLES
Born: 1899. Died: Nov. 30, 1973, Woodland Hills, Calif. Screen actor.

Appeared in: **1933** The Mayor of Hell. **1942** All Through the Night; The Man in the Trunk; Bells of Capistrano; Beyond the Blue Horizon. **1943** Hello, Frisco, Hello; Henry Aldrich Haunts a House; Gildersleeve's Bad Day; Dixie; True to Life. **1944** The Hairy Ape; The Lady and the Monster. **1945** Nob Hill; Circumstantial Evidence; Don Juan Quilligan. **1946** The Kid From Brooklyn; Crime of the Century; Valley of the Zombies; It Shouldn't Happen to a Dog. **1947** Dead Reckoning; The Guilt of Janet Ames. **1948** Fighting Mad; Tenth Avenue Angel; Adventures in Silverado; Bodyguard. **1949** The Dark Past; Prison Warden; Streets of San Francisco; Calamity Jane and Sam Bass. **1950** Southside 1-1000; The Blonde Bandit. **1951** Belle le Grand; Native Son; The Birds and the Bees. **1952** Scandal Sheet; Lone Star; Models, Inc.; Ruby Gentry. **1953** No Escape. **1955** Prince of Players; Revenge of the Creature. **1957** Gun Battle at Monterey. **1961** The Gambler Wore a Gun.

CANFIELD, WILLIAM F.
Died: Feb. 14, 1925, New York, N.Y. Screen, stage and vaudeville actor.

CANSINO, EDUARDO
Born: 1895. Died: Dec. 23, 1968. Screen actor/dancer. Brother of dancer Elisa Cansino, father of actress Rita Hayworth and actor Eduardo Cansino, Jr. (dec. 1974). Leader of the "Dancing Cansino" group.

Appeared in: **1926** A Vitagraph short. **1936** The Dancing Pirate.

CANSINO, EDUARDO, JR.,
Born: 1920. Died: Mar. 11, 1974, Hollywood, Calif. (cancer). Screen actor/dancer. Brother of actress Rita Hayworth and son of actor Eduardo Cansino, Sr. (dec. 1968).

Appeared in: **1926** Vitagraph short. **1953** The Great Adventures of Captain Kidd (serial).

CANTER, LYNN. *See* LYNN CASTILE

CANTOR, CHARLES
Born: 1898. Died: Sept. 11, 1966, Hollywood, Calif. (heart attack). Screen, stage and radio actor. Brother of actor Nat Cantor (dec. 1956).

Appeared in: **1952** Stop, You're Killing Me.

CANTOR, EDDIE (Edward Israel Iskowitz)
Born: Jan. 31, 1892, New York, N.Y. Died: Oct. 10, 1964, Beverly Hills, Calif. (heart attack). Screen, stage, vaudeville, burlesque, radio, television actor and screenwriter. Received a 1956 Special Academy Award for distinguished service to the film industry. Married to actress Ida Cantor (dec. 1962).

Appeared in: **1926** Kid Boots (film debut). **1927** Special Delivery; Follies. **1929** Glorifying the American Girl. **1930** Insurance (short); Whoopee. **1931** Palmy Days. **1932** The Kid from Spain. **1933** Roman Scandals. **1934** Kid Millions. **1936** Strike Me Pink. **1937** Ali Baba Goes to Town. **1940** Forty Little Mothers. **1943** Thank Your Lucky Stars. **1944** Hollywood Canteen; Show Business. **1945** Rhapsody in Blue. **1948** If You Knew Susie. **1952** The Story of Will Rogers.

CANTOR, HERMAN

Born: 1896. Died: Oct. 12, 1953, Jersey City, N.J. Screen actor.

Appeared in: **1948** Trouble Makers.

CANTOR, IDA (Ida Tobias)

Born: 1892, New York, N.Y. Died: Aug. 8, 1962, Beverly Hills, Calif. (heart attack). Screen actress. Married to actor Eddie Cantor (dec. 1964).

Appeared in: **1953** The Eddie Cantor Story (cameo).

CANTOR, NAT

Born: 1897. Died: Mar. 15, 1956, Queens, N.Y. Screen, stage, vaudeville, burlesque, radio and television actor. Brother of screen actor Charles Cantor (dec. 1966).

CANTWAY, FRED R.

Born: 1883. Died: Mar. 12, 1939, Hollywood, Calif. Screen and stage actor.

CANZONERI, TONY

Died: Dec. 10, 1959. Professional boxer and screen actor.

Appeared in: **1933** Mr. Broadway. **1949** Ringside.

CAPRICE, JUNE

Born: 1899. Died: Nov. 9, 1936, Los Angeles, Calif. Screen actress. Married to actor and film director Harry Millarde (dec.).

Appeared in: **1916** Caprice of the Mountains. **1917** A Modern Cinderella; Unknown 274. **1918** The Camouflage Kiss; Blue-Eyed Mary; Miss Innocence; The Heart of Romance. **1921** Rogues and Romance.

CARD, KATHRYN

Born: 1893. Died: Mar. 1, 1964, Costa Mesa, Calif. (heart attack). Screen, stage, radio and television actress.

Appeared in: **1945** Kiss and Tell. **1946** It Shouldn't Happen to a Dog; Undercurrent. **1947** The Hucksters; Born to Kill; That Hagen Girl. **1948** Three Daring Daughters; The Sainted Sisters. **1949** The Dark Past; A Kiss for Corliss; Mother Is a Freshman. **1950** Harriet Craig; The Skipper Surprised His Wife. **1951** Never Trust a Gambler. **1952** Paula; The Girl in White; You for Me; The Model and the Marriage Broker; The Pride of St. Louis. **1953** Remains to Be Seen; It Happens Every Thursday. **1955** Daddy Long Legs. **1956** Hollywood or Bust; The Birds and the Bees. **1958** Home Before Dark; Good Day for a Hanging. **1960** Because They're Young. **1962** Walk on the Wild Side. **1964** The Unsinkable Molly Brown.

CARDWELL, JAMES (Albert James Cardwell)

Born: Nov. 21, 1921, Camden, N.J. Died: Feb. 4, 1954, Hollywood, Calif. (suicide-gun). Screen actor.

Appeared in: **1944** The Sullivans; Sweet and Low Down. **1945** The Shanghai Cobra; Voice of the Whistler. **1946** Fear; A Walk in the Sun; Behind the Mask; The Missing Lady. **1947** Devil on Wheels. **1948** Harpoon; He Walked by Night. **1949** Daughter of the Jungle; Down Dakota Way; San Antone Ambush; Tokyo Joe; And Baby Makes Three. **1950** Arizona Cowboy.

CARELL, ANNETTE

Died: Oct. 20, 1967, London, England. Screen, stage, and television actress. Appeared in U.S., British and German films.

Appeared in: **1953** Martin Luther. **1962** The Tell-Tale Heart. **1965** Darling. **1967** Our Mother's House; The Vulture.

CARELSEN, FIE

Born: 1890. Died: July 21, 1975. Dutch screen and stage actor.

CARETTE (Julien Carette)

Born: Dec. 23, 1897, France. Died: July 20, 1966, Paris, France (burns). Stage and screen actor.

Appeared in: **1932** L'Affaire est dans le Sac; L'Amour a l'Americaine; Les Gaites de l'Escadron. **1933** Adieu les Beaux Jours; Le Billet de Mille; Georges et Georgette; Je te Confie ma Femme; Gonzague; Moi et l'Imperatrice; Ganster Malgre; Le Greluchon Delicat. **1934** Quadrille d'Amour; La Marraine; Paris-Camargue; Marinella. **1935** Fanfare d'Amour; Et Moi j' te Dis Qu'elle t'a Fait d' l'Oeil; Fernand le Noceur; Dora Nelson; Les Soeurs Hortensias; Une Nuit de Noce. **1936** Mon Coeur t'appelle; Adventure a Paris; Les Rois du Sport. **1937** Gribouille; La vie Est Belle; 27 Rue de la Paix; La Grand Illusion. **1938** Cafe de Paris; Entree des Artistes; La Marseillaise; La Bete Humaine; La Route Enchantee; L'accroche-coeur. **1939** Le Monde Tremblera; Sixieme Etage; Tempete sur Paris; Menaces; La Famille Duraton; Je Chante; Battements de Coeur; Derriere la Facade; La Regle du Jeu; Le Recif de Corail. **1940** 24 Heures de Perm; Soyez les Bienvenus. **1941** Parade en Sept Nuits; Fromont Jeune et Risler Aine. **1942** Fou d'amour; Une Etoile au Soleil; Croisteres Siderales; Lettres d'amour; Monsieur des Lourdines. **1943** Coup de Tete; Adieu Leonard; Service de Nuit; Bonsoir Mesdames, Bonsoir Messieurs; Le bal des Passants. **1944** L'enquete sur le 58; Le Merle Blanc. **1945** Impasse; Sylvie et le Fantome. **1946** Les Portes de la Nuit; Histoire de Chanter; Monsieur Ludovic;

L'ampir Autor de la Maison; Le Chateau de la Derniere Chance. **1947** La Mannequin Assassine; La Fleur de l'age. **1948** Une si Jolie Petite Plage. **1949** Branquigno!; Amedee; Premieres Armes; La Marie du Port; Occupe-toi d'Armelie; Ronde de Nuit; Oh, Amelia. **1950** Sans Laisser d'Address. **1951** L'auberge Rouge (The Red Inn—US 1954); Pour l'amour du Ciel; Ovvero E' piu Facile Che un Cammello; Rome-Paris-Rome Ovvero Signori in Carrozza! **1952** Drole de Noce; Agence Matrimoniale. **1953** Au Diable la Vertue; La Fete a Henriette; Gli Uomini che Mascalzoni; Le bon Dieu sans Confession. **1954** Chateaux en Espagne; Sur le Banc; Pas de Coup dur Par Johnny; Si Paris Nous Etait Conte; Ces Sacrees Vacances; Elena et les Hommes. **1955** La Mome Pigalle (aka The Maiden—US 1961). **1956** Coup dur Chez les Mous; Je Reviendrai a Kandara; Paris-Palace-Hotel. **1957** Crime et Chatiment. **1959** La Jument Verte (The Green Mare—US 1961); The Mirror Has Two Faces; Archimede, Le Clochard (Magnificent Tramp—US 1962). **1961** Rules of the Game. Other French film: A Nous la Liberte.

CAREW, ARTHUR EDMUND (aka ARTHUR EDMUND CAREWE)

Born: 1894, Trebeizond, Armenia. Died: Apr. 23, 1937, Santa Monica, Calif. Stage and screen actor.

Appeared in: **1920** Rio Grande. **1921** Bar Nothin'; Her Mad Bargain; The Easy Road; Sham; The Mad Marriage. **1922** The Ghost Breaker; His Wife's Husband; My Old Kentucky Home; The Prodigal Judge. **1923** Trilby; Refuge; Daddy. **1924** The Song of Love; The Price of a Party. **1925** Sandra; Phantom of the Opera; The Only Thing; The Boomerang; A Lover's Oath. **1926** The Torrent; The Silent Lover; Diplomacy; Volcano. **1927** Uncle Tom's Cabin; A Man's Past; The Cat and the Canary; The Claw. **1930** The Matrimonial Bed; Sweet Kitty Bellairs; The Life of the Party. **1931** God's Gift to Women; The Gay Diplomat. **1932** Doctor X. **1933** The Mystery of the Wax Museum. **1935** Thunder in the Night. **1936** Charlie Chan's Secret.

CAREW, JAMES

Born: Feb. 5, 1876, Goshen, Ind. Died: Apr. 4, 1938, London, England. Screen, stage and radio actor. Entered films in England. Married to actress Ellen Terry (dec. 1928).

Appeared in: **1913** The Fool; The Suffragette. **1914** The Flight of Death; The Rajah's Tiara; The Corner House Burglary. **1915** The Polo Champion. **1917** Justice; The Profit and the Loss. **1919** Sheba; The Kinsman; The Forest on the Hill; The Nature of the Beast; Spinner O'Dreams; Sunken Rocks; Twelve: Ten. **1920** Alf's Button; Anna the Adventuress; Helen of Four Gates; Mrs. Erricker's Reputation. **1921** Dollars in Surrey; Mr. Justice Raffles; The Narrow Valley; Tansy; Wild Heather. **1923** The Naked Man; Mist in the Valley; Comin' Thro' the Rye; Strangling Threads. **1924** Eugene Aram; The Love Story of Aliette Brunton; Owd Bob; The Wine of Life. **1925** Children of the Night (series); Satan's Sister. **1926** One Colombo Night. **1927** A Woman Redeemed; The House of Marney; The King's Highway; One of the Best. **1928** Love's Option (aka A Girl of Today); A Window in Piccadilly (aka Lady of the Lake—US 1930). **1929** House of Play; High Seas; High Treason. **1931** To Oblige a Lady; Mischief; Guilt. **1932** Brother Alfred. **1933** You Made Me Love You; Mayfair Girl. **1934** Freedom of the Seas; Too Many Millions. **1935** Come Out of the Pantry; The Mystery of the Mary Celeste (aka Phantom Ship—US 1937); Oh! What a Night!; All at Sea; Who's Your Father?; Royal Cavalcade (aka Regal Cavalcade—US). **1936** The Improper Duchess; Living Dangerously; David Livingstone; Murder at the Cabaret; Midnight at Madame Tussaud's (aka Midnight at the Wax Museum—US); Not Wanted on Voyage (aka Treachery on the High Seas—US); You Must Get Married. **1937** Rhythm Racketeer; Thunder in the City; Wings Over Africa; Strange Experiment; Jericho (aka Dark Sands—US 1938). **1938** Glamour Girl.

CAREW, ORA (Ora Whytock)

Born: 1893, Salt Lake City, Utah. Died: Oct. 26, 1955, Los Angeles, Calif. Screen, stage and vaudeville actress. Entered films with Sennett in 1915.

Appeared in: **1915** Saved by the Wireless; The Martyrs of the Alamo. **1916** A La Cabaret; The Torrent of Vengeance; Dollars and Sense (aka The Twins); Love Comet; Wings and Wheels. **1917** Her Circus Knight (aka The Circus Girl); Oriental Love; Skidding Hearts. **1918** Too Many Millions; Go West Young Man. **1919** The Terror of the Range (serial); Loot; Under Suspicion. **1920** The Peddler of Lies. **1921** The Big Town Roundup; Little Fool; Ladyfingers; Alias Ladyfingers; A Voice in the Dark; After Your Own Heart. **1922** Sherlock Brown; Beyond the Crossroads; The Girl from Rocky Point; Smiles Are Trumps; Smudge. **1924** Paying the Limit; Getting Her Man; Three Days to Live; Waterfront Wolves; The Torrent. **1925** Cold Fury.

CAREWE, EDWIN (Jay J. Fox)

Born: Mar. 5, 1883, Gainesville, Tex. Died: Jan. 22, 1940, Los Angeles, Calif. (heart attack). Screen, stage actor, film, stage director and film producer. Entered films as an actor with Lubin Company in 1910. Father of actress Rita Carewe (dec. 1955).

Appeared in: **1916** The Snow Bird.

Baby; Born: 1908. Died: Oct. 22, 1955, Torrance, Calif. Screen actress. Daughter of screen actor/director Edwin Carewe (dec. 1940). Appeared in: **1925** Joanna. **1926** High Steppers. **1928** Revenge; Ramona; The Stronger Will. **1930** Radio Kisses (short).

CAREY, HARRY
Born: Jan. 16, 1878, New York, N.Y. Died: Sept. 21, 1947, Brentwood, Calif. (coronary thrombosis). Screen, stage actor and playwright. Father of actor Harry Carey, Jr. Married to actress Olive Golden.

Appeared in: **1912** An Unseen Enemy; The Musketeers of Pig Alley; In the Aisles of the Wild; Friends; Heredity; The Informer; The Unwelcome Guest; An Adventure in the Autumn Woods. **1913** Love in an Apartment Hotel; Broken Ways; The Sheriff's Baby; The Ranchero's Revenge; The Left Handed Man; The Hero of Little Italy; Olaf—An Atom; Judith of Bethulia. **1915** Graft (serial). **1917** Straight Shooting. **1919** The Outcasts of Poker Flat; The Blind Husband. **1921** Freeze-Out; Hearts Up; If Only Jim; Sundown Slim; The Wallop; West Is West; The Fox; Desperate Trails. **1922** Man to Man; Good Men and True; Kickback. **1923** Canyon of the Fools; Crashin' Thru; Desert Driven; Miracle Baby. **1924** The Lightning Rider; The Night Hawk; The Man from Texas; Tiger Thompson; Roaring Rails; The Flaming Forties. **1925** Beyond the Border; Soft Shoes; The Texas Trail; Silent Sanderson; Bad Lands; The Prairie Pirate; The Man from Red Gulch; Wanderer. **1926** The Frontier Trail; Satan Town; Driftin' Thru; The Seventh Bandit. **1927** Slide, Kelly, Slide; A Little Journey. **1928** Trail of '98; The Border Patrol; Burning Bridges. **1931** Cavalier of the West; Trader Horn; Bad Company; The Vanishing Legion (serial); Across the Line; Double Sixes; Horseshoofs; The Hurricane Rider; Border Devils. **1932** Without Honor; Law and Order; The Devil Horse (serial); Last of the Mohicans (serial); Night Rider. **1933** Man of the Forest; Sunset Pass. **1934** Thundering Herd. **1935** Rustler's Paradise; Powdersmoke Range; Barbary Coast; The Last of the Clintons; Wild Mustang; The Last Outpost; Wagon Trail. **1936** The Last Outlaw; The Prisoner of Shark Island; Little Miss Nobody; Sutter's Gold; Valiant Is the Word for Carrie; The Accusing Finger; The Three Mesquiteers; The Man Behind the Mask; Ghost Town. **1937** Kid Galahad; Born Reckless; Souls at Sea; Border Cafe; Annapolis Salute; Danger Patrol; Aces Wild. **1938** The Port of Missing Girls; You and Me; King of Alcatraz; Sky Giant; The Law West of Tombstone; Gateway. **1939** Burn 'Em Up O'Connor; Mr. Smith Goes to Washington; Street of Missing Men; Inside Information; Code of the Streets. **1940** They Knew What They Wanted; My Son Is Guilty; Outside the 3-Mile Limit; Beyond Tomorrow. **1941** Shepherd of the Hills; Sundown; Among the Living; Parachute Battalion. **1942** The Spoilers. **1943** Air Force; Happy Land. **1944** The Great Moment. **1945** China's Little Devils. **1946** Duel in the Sun. **1947** Sea of Grass; The Angel and the Badman. **1948** So Dear to My Heart; Red River.

CARLE, RICHARD (Charles Nicholas Carleton)
Born: July 7, 1871, Somerville, Mass. Died: June 28, 1941, North Hollywood, Calif. (heart attack). Screen, stage actor and playwright.

Appeared in: **1925** Zander the Great; The Mad Marriage; The Coming of Amos. **1926** Eve's Leaves. **1927** Soft Cushions; The Understanding Heart; Stranded (short). **1928** Fleet's In; While the City Sleeps; Habeus Corpus (short); Sunny California (short); The Worrier (short). **1928** It Can Be Done; Madam X; His Glorious Night. **1930** Brothers; The Grand Parade; A Lady to Love; Free and Easy. **1931** Flying High. **1932** One Hour with You; Fireman, Save My Child!; Night of June 13th; other shorts prior to 1933: Rich Uncles; Hold the Babies; Some Babies. **1933** Private Jones; Man Hunt; Diplomaniacs; Morning Glory; Ladies Must Love; Golden Harvest. **1934** Hollywood Party (short); The Witching Hour; Wake Up and Dream; Caravan; Beloved; Last Round Up; Old Fashioned Way; Harold Teen; George White Scandals; Such Women Are Dangerous; Sing and Like It; Affairs of a Gentleman. **1935** Life Returns; Home on the Range; The Ghost Walks; When a Man's a Man; The Gay Deception; Love in Bloom; Here Comes Cookie; The Bride Comes Home; Night Life of the Gods; Baby Face Harrington; Moonlight on the Prairie; Dangerous. **1936** Little Red Schoolhouse; Easy to Take; The Man I Marry; College Holiday; The Trail of the Lonesome Pine; Love before Breakfast; Nevada; Anything Goes; The Case against Mrs. Ames; Drift Fence; Spendthrift; The Texas Rangers; The Arizona Raiders; Let's Sing Again; One Rainy Afternoon; Three of a Kind. **1937** She's Dangerous; Top of the Town; She Asked for It; Outcast; Arizona Mahoney; True Confession; The Man in Blue; Love in a Bungalow; Racketeers in Exile; It's All Yours; I'll Take Romance; Rhythm in the Clouds; 45 Fathers. **1939** Persons in Hiding; It's a Wonderful World; Undercover Doctor; Maisie; Ninotchka; Remember? **1940** Ma, He's Making Eyes at Me; Parole Fixer; Lillian Russell; The Great McGinty; Comin' Round the Mountain; One Night in the Tropics; Seven Sinners; The Golden Fleecing; The Ghost Comes Home. **1941** A Dangerous Game; That Uncertain Feeling; Buy Me That Town; Moonlight in Hawaii; New Wine; The Devil and Miss Jones; My Life with Caroline; Million Dollar Baby.

CARLES, ROMEO
Born: 1896, France. Died: Sept. 1971, France. Screen actor.

Appeared in: Chouchou; Bancede Princess; Au Fil des Ondes.

CARLETON, GEORGE
Born: 1885. Died: Sept. 23, 1950, Hollywood, Calif. (heart attack). Stage and screen actor.

Appeared in: **1942** Just Off Broadway; Tennessee Johnson; The Great Gildersleeve; Over My Dead Body. **1943** Henry Aldrich Haunts a House. **1944** And Now Tomorrow; Henry Aldrich's Little Secret. **1945** A Tree Grows in Brook-

lyn. **1946** Sioux City Sue. **1947** The Last Round-Up; Ladies' Man. **1949** Prince of the Plains.

CARLETON, LLOYD B.
Born: 1872. Died: Aug. 8, 1933, N.Y. Screen, stage actor, and film director.

Appeared in: **1910** The Fugitive. **1927** Tongues of Scandal.

CARLETON, WILL C.
Born: 1871. Died: Sept. 21, 1941, Los Angeles, Calif. Stage and screen actor and screenwriter. Appeared in silents.

CARLETON, WILLIAM P.
Born: 1873. Died: Apr. 6, 1947, Hollywood, Calif. (injuries from auto accident). Stage and screen actor.

Appeared in: **1921** A Wife's Awakening; Behind Masks; Good Women; Morals; The Inside of the Cup; Straight from Paris; What No Man Knows. **1922** Bobbed Hair; The Danger Point; Our Leading Citizen; The Law and the Woman; The Worldly Madonna; Domestic Relations. **1923** Homeward Bound; Sinner or Saint; The Truth about Wives; The Tie That Binds. **1924** Half-a-Dollar Bill. **1932** Charlie Chan's Chance. **1933** Girl without a Room; Ann Vickers. **1935** The Perfect Clue. **1936** The Bohemian Girl; The Border Patrolman. **1938** La Zandunga.

CARLETON, WILLIAM T.
Born: 1859, England. Died: Sept. 28, 1930, St. John, New Brunswick, Canada. Screen, stage actor and stage director.

Appeared in: **1909** Lines of White On a Sullen Sea. **1916** Gloria's Romance; Pearl of the Army. **1917** A Daughter of Maryland. **1918** Eye for Eye; The Danger Mark. **1919** Home Wanted; His Father's Wife; Me and Capt. Kidd; A Society Exile. **1920** The Copperhead; The Amateur Wife. **1921** The Inside of the Cup; Sinners; Straight From Paris; Good Women.

CARLIE, EDWARD
Born: 1878. Died: Nov. 25, 1938, Hollywood, Calif. (heart attack). Screen and vaudeville actor.

Appeared in: **1924** Racing Luck. **1939** I'm from Missouri (died while dancing during filming).

CARLISLE, ALEXANDRA (Alexandra Swift)
Born: Jan. 15, 1886, Yorkshire, England. Died: Apr. 21, 1936, New York, N.Y. Stage and screen actress.

Appeared in: **1934** Half a Sinner.

CARLYLE, HELEN
Born: 1893. Died: June 30, 1933, Hollywood, Calif. (complications of ailments). Stage and screen actress.

Appeared in: **1932** Forgotten Commandments.

CARLYLE, RICHARD
Born: May 21, 1879, Guelph, Ontario, Canada. Died: June 12, 1942, San Fernando, Calif. Stage and screen actor. Married to stage actress Mirza Marston. Entered films in 1913.

Appeared in: **1920** The Copperhead. **1921** The Inside of the Cup; Out of the Chorus; Ten Nights in a Barroom. **1922** Women Men Marry; Back Home and Broke. **1923** Haldane of the Secret Service. **1927** Shootin' Irons. **1928** Brotherly Love; Lingerie. **1929** Taking a Chance; The Valiant; Children of the Ritz; The Girl in the Show; It Can Be Done; In Old California; Hearts in Dixie. **1930** Guilty?; Mountain Justice; Playing Around; Tol'able David; Hideout; The Girl of the Golden West; Kismet. **1931** West of Broadway; Oh! Oh! Cleopatra (short); Quick Trigger Lee. **1932** Saddle Buster; Unholy Love. **1933** Midnight Club. **1935** When a Man's a Man; Sons of Steel; Public Opinion; Happiness C.O.D.

CARMI, MARIA
Born: 1880, Germany. Died: Aug. 1957, Myrtle Beach, S.C. Screen actress. Appeared in early UFA films.

CARMICHAEL, MYRA
Died: Oct. 22, 1974. Screen actress.

CARMINATI, TULLIO (Count Tullio Carminati de Brambilla)
Born: Zara, Dalmatia, Italy. Died: Feb. 26, 1971, Rome, Italy (stroke). Stage and screen actor.

Appeared in: **1926** The Bat; The Duchess of Buffalo. **1927** Stage Madness; Honeymoon Hate. **1928** Three Sinners. **1933** Gallant Lady. **1934** Moulin Rouge; One Night of Love. **1935** Let's Live Tonight; Paris in Spring. **1936** The Three Maxims; The Wedding March; London Melody (aka Girl in the Street—US 1938); Sunset in Vienna (aka Suicide Legion—US 1940); La Marcia Nuzialf. **1938** The Show Goes On. **1940** Safari. **1949** The Golden Madonna. **1952** Beauty and the Devil. **1953** Roman Holiday; The Secret Conclave. **1956**

War and Peace. **1960** A Breath of Scandal. **1961** El Cid. **1962** Swordsman of Siena; Hemingway's Adventures of a Young Man. **1963** The Cardinal.

CARNERA, PRIMO

Born: Oct. 25, 1906, Sequals, Italy. Died: June 29, 1967, Sequals, Italy (liver ailment). World heavyweight boxing champion, circus performer, wrestler and screen actor.

Appeared in: **1933** Mr. Broadway; The Prizefighter and the Lady. **1949** Iron Crown. **1954** Prince Valiant; Casanova's Big Night. **1956** A Kid for Two Farthings. **1960** Hercules Unchained.

CARNEY, ALAN (David Bougal)

Born: Dec. 22, 1911, Brooklyn, N.Y. Died: May 2, 1973, Inglewood, Calif. (heart attack). Screen, stage and vaudeville actor. Partner in vaudeville and film comedy team of "Brown and Carney" with Wally Brown (dec. 1961).

Appeared in: **1941** Convoy. **1942** In Which We Serve. **1943** Mr. Lucky; Adventures of a Rookie (with Brown); Rookies in Burma (with Brown); Around the World; Mexican Spitfire's Blessed Event; Gangway For Tomorrow; Gildersleeve's Bad Day. **1944** Step Lively; The Girl Rush; Seven Days Ashore. **1945** Radio Stars on Parade; Zombies on Broadway. **1946** Genius at Work; Vacation in Reno. **1947** The Pretender. **1949** Hideout. **1959** Lil' Abner. **1960** North to Alaska. **1961** The Absent-Minded Professor; Double Trouble. **1962** Swingin' Along. **1963** Son of Flubber; It's a Mad, Mad, Mad, Mad World. **1965** Sylvia. **1967** Monkeys, Go Home!; The Adventures of Bullwhip Griffin. **1968** Blackbeard's Ghost. **1973** The Love Bug Rides Again.

CARNEY, DON "UNCLE DON" (Howard Rice)

Born: 1897. Died: Jan. 14, 1954, Miami, Fla. (heart trouble). Screen, stage, radio and vaudeville actor. Appeared in films briefly prior to 1928.

CARNEY, GEORGE

Born: Nov. 21, 1887, Bristol, England. Died: Dec. 9, 1947. Screen, stage and vaudeville actor.

Appeared in: **1916** Some Waiter! **1933** The Television Follies; Commissionaire. **1934** Say It With Flowers; Music Hall; Lest We Forget; Hyde Park; Flood Tide; Night Club Queen; Easy Money; A Glimpse of Paradise. **1935** A Real Bloke; The Small Man; Variety; The City of Beautiful Nonsense; Windfall; Cock O' the North. **1936** Land Without Music (aka Forbidden Music–US 1938); It's in the Bag; Tomorrow We Live. **1937** Dreaming Lips; Father Steps Out; Little Miss Somebody; Lancashire Luck; Beauty and the Barge. **1938** Easy Riches; Weddings are Wonderful; Paid in Error; Kicking the Moon Around; Miracles Do Happen; Consider Your Verdict. **1939** Come on George; A Window in London (aka Lady in Distress–US 1942); The Stars Look Down (US 1941); Young Man's Fancy (US 1943). **1940** Convoy; The Briggs Family. **1941** Love on the Dole; The Common Touch; Kipps (aka The Remarkable Mr. Kipps–US 1942). **1942** Thunder Rock (US 1944); In Which We Serve; Hard Steel; Unpublished Story; Rose of Tralee. **1943** When We Are Married; The Night Invader; Schweik's New Adventures. **1944** Tawny Pipit (US 1947); Welcome Mr. Washington. **1945** Waterloo Road; The Agitator; I Know Where I'm Going (US 1947). **1946** Spring Song (aka Springtime–US); Woman to Woman; Wanted for Murder. **1947** The Root of All Evil; The Little Ballerina ((US 1951); Brighton Rock; Fortune Lane. **1948** Good Time Girl (US 1950).

CARNEY, HARRY (Harry Howell Carney)

Born: 1910, Boston, Mass. Died: Oct. 8, 1974, New York, N.Y. Black musician and screen actor.

Appeared in: **1937** The Hit Parade. **1943** Reveille With Beverly.

CAROL, DIANE

Born: 1940. Died: Sept. 30, 1966. Screen actress.

CAROL, JOHN

Born: 1910, England. Died: Oct. 1968, London, England. Stage and screen actor. Do not confuse with U.S. actor John Carroll.

Appeared in: **1937** We live and Learn; The Windmill; The Perfect Crime. **1938** The Dark Stairway. **1943** The Silver Fleet (US 1945); The Dummy Talks. **1945** Pink String and Sealing Wax (US 1950). **1947** It Always Rains on Sunday (US 1949). **1949** The Spider and the Fly (US 1952).

CAROL, MARTINE (Marie-Louise de Mourer aka MARYSE MOURER)

Born: 1921, France. Died: Feb. 6, 1967, Monte Carlo (heart attack). Screen, stage and radio actress. Known on stage as Catherine Arley and appeared in "Caroline" film series as Carol Martine.

Appeared in: **1943** La Femme aux Loups. **1944** The Wolf Farm. **1945** Bifur III; L'extravagante Mission; Trente et Quarante. **1946** En Etes-Vous Bien Sur? **1947** La Fleur de l'age ou L'ile des Enfants Perdus; Voyage. **1948** Les Souvenirs ne Sont pas a Vendre. **1949** Les Amants de Verone (Lovers of Verone–US 1954); Je N'aime que Toi. **1950** Une Nuit de Noces; Mefiez-vous des Blondes; Caroline Cherie (US 1954); Nous Irons a Paris. **1951** El Deseo y el Amor; Nana (US 1957). **1952** Adorable Creature (US 1956); A Night with Caroline; Les Belles de Nuit (Beauties of the Night—US 1954). **1953** Un Caprice de Caroline Cherie; Lucrece Borgia; Destinees Destini di Donne; The Bed (US 1955). **1954** Secrets d'Alcove; Il Letto Della Pompadour; La Spiaggia (The Beach); Madam DuBarry. **1956** Le Carnet du Major Thompson (Defendo il Mio Amour (Defend My Love–US 1959); Around the World in 80 Days; Austerlitz. **1957** Le Passager Clandestin; The French Are a Funny Race (US 1958); Action of the Tiger. **1958** Sins of the Borgias; The Foxiest Girl in Paris (aka Nathalie). **1959** Ten Seconds to Hell. **1960** The Sins of Lola Montes; La Francoise et l'Amour (Love and the Frenchwoman–US 1961). **1961** La Cave Se Rebiffe (The Sucker Strikes Back–aka The Counterfeiters of Paris and Money, Money, Money–US 1962). **1966** Hell Is Empty.

CARPENTER, GLORIA

Born: 1927. Died: Sept. 11, 1958, Hollywood, Calif. Screen actress.

CARPENTER, HORACE B.

Born: 1875. Died: May 21, 1945, Hollywood, Calif. (heart attack). Screen, stage actor and screenwriter. Entered films with Famous Players-Lasky Co.

Appeared in: **1914** The Virginian. **1923** King's Creek Law. **1924** Headin' Through; The Silent Stranger; Travelin' Fast. **1928** Texas Tommy. **1929** False Feathers; Riders of the Rio Grande; West of the Rockies; Bride of the Desert. **1930** South of Sonora. **1934** In Old Santa Fe. **1937** Range Defenders; Git Along Little Dogies; The Big Show; Gunsmoke Ranch. **1939** Rovin' Tumbleweeds. **1944** Belle of the Yukon.

CARPENTER, PAUL

Born: 1921, Montreal, Canada. Died: June 12, 1964, London, England. Screen, television actor and singer with Ted Heath's band. Married to actress Kim Parker.

Appeared in: **1946** School for Secrets. **1948** Uneasy Terms. **1949** Landfall. **1953** Albert RN (aka Break to Freedom–US 1955). **1954** The House Across the Lake (aka Heatwave–US); Face the Music (aka The Black Glove–US); Five Days (aka Paid to Kill–US); Duel in the Jungle; The Young Lovers (aka Chance Meeting–US 1955); The Stranger Came Home (aka The Unholy Four–US); The Sea Shall Not Have Them (US 1955); Diplomatic Passport; Johnny on the Spot. **1955** Shadow of a Man; One Jump Ahead; The Hornet's Nest; Stock Car. **1956** Fire Maidens from Outer Space; The Iron Petticoat; The Narrowing Circle; Women Without Men (aka Blonde Bait–US); Behind the Headlines. **1957** No Road Back; Action Stations (aka Hi-Jack); Murder Reported (US 1960); The Hypnotist (aka Scotland Yard Dragnet–US 1958); Black Ice (US 1958). **1958** Undercover Girl; Intent to Kill. **1959** Jet Storm (US 1961). **1960** Date at Midnight. **1962** Dr. Crippen (US 1964). **1963** Call Me Bwana; Panic (US 1966). **1964** First Men on the Moon; The Beauty Jungle (aka Contest Girl–US 1966). **1965** Miss Tulip Stays the Night.

CARPENTIER, GEORGES

Born: Jan. 12, 1894, Lens, France. Died: Oct. 28, 1975, Paris, France. Professional heavyweight fighter, screen and vaudeville actor.

Appeared in: **1912** The Romance of Carpentier (film debut). **1913** Carpentier vs. Bombadier Wells Fight. **1920** The Wonder Man; Le Match Criqui-Ledoux. **1922** A Gypsy Cavalier (aka My Lady April). **1928** La Symphonie Pathetique. **1929** The Show of Shows. **1930** Hold Everything; Georges Carpentier in Naughty But Nice (short). Other French films: The Adventures of a Champion; The Treasure of Keriolet.

CARR, ALEXANDER

Born: 1878, Rumni, Russia. Died: Sept. 19, 1946, Los Angeles, Calif. Screen, stage, burlesque actor and circus performer. He was "Perlmutter" in the "Potash and Perlmutter" series on screen and stage with Barnie Bernard (dec. 1924).

Appeared in: **1923** Potash and Perlmutter. **1924** In Hollywood with Potash and Perlmutter. **1926** Partners Again; The Beautiful Cheat; April Fool. **1929** The End of the World (short). **1932** Uptown New York; No Greater Love; Hypnotized; Pathe comedies. **1933** The Death Kiss; Constant Woman; Her Splendid Folly; Out All Night. **1934** I Hate Women. **1940** Christmas in July.

CARR, GEORGIA

Born: 1925. Died: July 4, 1971, Los Angeles, Calif. (stroke). Black singer, screen, stage and television actress. Sang with bands during 1950s and early 1960s.

Appeared in: **1957** Will Success Spoil Rock Hunter? **1964** Handle with Care.

CARR, GERALDINE

Born: 1917. Died: Sept. 2, 1954, near Hollywood, Calif. (auto accident). Screen and television actress.

Appeared in: **1950** The Great Jewel Robbery; The Company She Keeps. **1952** The Sniper.

CARR, GINNA

Born: 1937. Died: July 13, 1972, Hollywood, Calif. (cancer). Screen, stage and burlesque actress. Married to comedian Joey Faye. Daughter of vaudeville performers known as "The Dancing Alexanders."

CARR, JACK
Born: 1899. Died: Feb. 2, 1968, Calexico, Calif. Screen and television actor. Do not confuse with black actor Jack Carr (dec. 1951).

Appeared in: 1957 Chicago Confidential. 1958 Seven Guns to Mesa; Bullwhip; Toughest Gun in Tombstone. 1960 Platinum High School.

CARR, JACK
Died: 1951. Black screen actor. Do not confuse with Jack Carr (dec. 1968).

CARR, JANE (Rita Brunstrom)
Born: Aug. 1, 1909, Whitley Bay, Northumberland, England. Died: Sept. 29, 1957. Stage and screen actress.

Appeared in: 1932 Let Me Explain Dear; Love Me, Love My Dog. 1933 Taxi to Paradise; Orders is Orders (US 1934); Dick Turpin. 1934 On the Air; Oh No Doctor!; Murder at the Inn; Night Club Queen; Keep It Quiet; The Outcast; Those Were the Days; The Church Mouse (US 1935); Lord Edgware Dies; Youthful Folly. 1935 The Ace of Spades; The Triumph of Sherlock Holmes; Night Mail; Hello Sweetheart; Get Off My Foot. 1936 The Interrupted Honeymoon; Millions; It's You I Want. 1937 The Lilac Domino; Little Miss Somebody; Melody and Romance; Captain's Orders. 1942 Sabotage at Sea; Lady from Lisbon. 1949 It's Not Cricket. 1953 The Saint's Return (aka The Saint's Girl Friday–US). 1954 Thirty-Six Hours (aka Terror Street–US).

CARR, MARY K.
Born: 1874, Philadelphia, Pa. Died: June 24, 1973, Woodland Hills, Calif. Stage and screen actress. Married to actor/producer William Carr (dec. 1937). Mother of directors Thomas and Stephen Carr.

Appeared in: 1919 Mrs. Wiggs of the Cabbage Patch. 1920 Over the Hill. 1921 Thunderclap. 1922 Silver Wings. 1923 Broadway Broke; Loyal Lives; The Daring Years; You Are Guilty; The Custard Cup; On the Banks of the Wabash; Three O'Clock in the Morning. 1924 Damaged Hearts; On the Stroke of Three; Roulette; East of Broadway; For Sale; Why Men Leave Home; The Woman on the Jury; The Mine with the Iron Door; Painted People; A Self-Made Failure; The Spirit of the USA; Three Women. 1925 Red Kimona; The Wizard of Oz; Big Pal; Hogan's Alley; The Re-creation of Brian Kent; A Slave of Fashion; Capital Punishment; Drusilla with a Million; Easy Money; The Fighting Cub; Flaming Waters; Go Straight; Gold Hunters; His Master's Voice; The Night Ship; The Parasite. 1926 Atta Boy; The Night Patrol; The Night Watch; Stop, Look and Listen; Dame Chance; Whom Shall I Marry?; The Wise Guy; Frenzied Flames; Her Own Story; The False Alarm; The Hidden Way; The King of the Turf; The Midnight Message; Pleasures of the Rich; Somebody's Mother. 1927 Blonde or Brunette; Special Delivery; The Show Girl; Better Days; Paying the Price; The Swell-head; False Morals; The Fourth Commandment; God's Great Wilderness; On Your Toes; Jesse James. 1928 Love over Night; Lights of New York; A Million for Love. 1929 Sailor's Holiday; Some Mother's Boy. 1930 Just Imagine; Second Wife; Hot Curves; Ladies in Love; The Utah Kid; The Midnight Special. 1931 Primrose Path; Law of the Tongs; Kept Husbands; Beyond Victory; Honeymoon Lane; One Good Turn (short); Stout Hearts and Willing Hands (short). 1932 The Fighting Marshall; Pack Up Your Troubles. 1933 Forbidden Trails; Gun Law; Police Call. 1934 Love Past Thirty; Change of Heart; Loud Speaker. 1935 The World Accuses; Fighting Lady; I Don't Remember (short). 1936 East Side of Heaven. 1940 Manhattan Heartbeat. 1942 Eagle Squadron. 1956 Friendly Persuasion. 1957 Dino.

CARR, MICHAEL (Michael Cohen)
Born: Mar. 17, 1900, Leeds, Yorkshire, England. Died: Sept. 16, 1968, London, England. Screen actor and composer. Do not confuse with Michael Carr, US actor.

Appeared in: 1937 Let's Make a Night of It.

CARR, NAT
Born: Aug. 12, 1886, Russia. Died: July 6, 1944, Hollywood, Calif. Screen, stage, vaudeville, burlesque actor and screenwriter.

Appeared in: 1925 His People. 1926 The Cohens and the Kellys; Private Izzy Murphy; Millionaires; Kosher Kitty Kelly; April Fool; Her Big Night; The Mystery Club; Watch Your Wife. 1927 The Jazz Singer; The Love Thrill; Popular Comedian (short). 1929 Madonna of the Sleeping Cars; Wall Street; "Ginsburg" series including One Gun Ginsburg, Gunboat Ginsburg and General Ginsburg. 1930 Red Heads; The Talk of Hollywood; plus the following shorts: Traffic; Two Plus Fours. 1931 Fifty Million Frenchmen; His People; plus the following shorts: Night Class; Campus Champs; Open House; Humanette. 1932 Union Depot; High Pressure. 1933 What Fur (short); The Merchant of Menace (short); Big Time or Bust. 1934 Wrong Direction (short); Hey Nanny Nanny (short). 1935 Pardon My Scotch (short). 1936 Next Time We Love. 1937 Portia on Trial. 1938 Comet Over Broadway; Torchy Gets Her Man. 1939 On Trial; Everybody's Hobby; Torchy Plays with Dynamite. 1940 King of the Lumberjacks; Granny Get Your Gun.

CARR, PERCY
Born: 1865, England. Died: Nov. 22, 1926, Saranac Lake, N.Y. Stage and screen actor.

Appeared in: 1922 One Exciting Night. 1923 The Ragged Edge.

CARR, SADE (Sade Latham)
Born: 1889, London, England. Died: Nov. 17, 1940, Carmel, Calif. Stage and screen actress. Appeared in early Essaney films.

CARR, WILLIAM
Born: 1867. Died: Feb. 13, 1937, Los Angeles, Calif. Screen actor and film director. Entered films as an actor with Lubin Company in 1907. Married to actress Mary Carr (dec. 1973).

Appeared in: 1921 Get-Rich-Quick Wallingford.

CARRE, BARTLETT A.
Born: July 10, 1897, Melrose, Mass. Died: Apr. 26, 1971, Hollywood, Calif. (respiratory ailment). Screen actor, stuntman, assistant film production manager.

Appeared in: 1924 Behind Two Guns. 1925 Flying Hoofs.

CARRICO, CHARLES
Born: 1888. Died: Jan. 18, 1967, Desert Hot Springs, Calif. Screen actor. Appeared in films during the 1920s.

CARRIGAN, THOMAS J. (aka THOMAS J. CORRIGAN)
Born: 1886. Died: Oct. 2, 1941, Lapeer, Mich. (cerebral hemorrhage). Stage and screen actor. Entered films during experimental days with Powers in New York and later with Selig. Divorced from stage actress Mabel Taliaferro.

Appeared in: 1911 Two Orphans; Cinderella. 1919 Checkers. 1921 Room and Board. 1923 Crooked Alley; Salomy Jane; You Can't Fool Your Wife. 1925 The Making of O'Malley. 1927 Wings. 1932 The Big Broadcast.

CARRILLO, LEO
Born: Aug. 6, 1881, Los Angeles, Calif. Died: Sept. 10, 1961, Santa Monica, Calif. (cancer). Screen, stage and vaudeville actor.

Appeared in: 1927 The following shorts: Italian Humorist; At the Ballgame. 1928 The Dove; plus the following shorts: The Hell Gate of Soissons; The Foreigner. 1929 Mister Antonio. 1931 Lasca of the Rio Grande; Homicide Squad; Guilty Generation; Hell Bound. 1932 Lost Men; Broken Wing; Second Fiddle; Cauliflower Alley; Girl of the Rio. 1933 Parachute Jumper; City Streets; Deception; Men Are Such Fools; Moonlight and Pretzels; Obey the Law; Racetrack; Before Morning. 1934 The Barretts of Wimpole Street; Band Plays On; Four Frightened People; The Gay Bride; Manhattan Melodrama; Viva Villa. 1935 If You Could Only Cook; In Caliente; Love Me Forever; La Fiesta de Santa Barbara (short); The Winning Ticket. 1936 The Gay Desperado; It Had to Happen; Moonlight Murder. 1937 The Barrier; History Is Made at Night; Hotel Haywire; I Promise to Pay; Manhattan Merry-Go-Round; 52nd Street. 1938 Arizona Wildcat; Blockade; Flirting with Fate; Girl of the Golden West; Little Miss Roughneck; Too Hot to Handle; City Streets. 1939 The Girl and the Gambler; Society Lawyer; Chicken Wagon Family; Rio; Fisherman's Wharf. 1940 Twenty-Mule Team; One Night in the Tropics; Wyoming; Captain Caution; Bad Man of Wyoming; Lillian Russell. 1941 Horror Island; Riders of Death Valley (serial); Tight Shoes; The Kid from Kansas; Road Agent; Barnacle Bill. 1942 What's Cooking?; Unseen Enemy; Escape from Hong Kong; Men of Texas; Top Sergeant; Danger in the Pacific; Timber; Sin Town; American Empire. 1943 Crazy House; Screen Snapshort #5 (short); Frontier Badmen; Larceny with Music; Follow the Band; Phantom of the Opera. 1944 Babes on Swing Street; Bowery to Broadway; The Ghost Catchers; Gypsy Wildcat; Merrily We Sing; Moonlight and Cactus. 1945 Crime, Inc.; Mexicana; Under Western Skies. 1947 The Fugitive. 1948 The Valiant Hombre. 1949 The Gay Amigo; The Daring Caballero; Satan's Cradle. 1950 The Girl from San Lorenzo; Pancho Villa Returns. 1964 Big Parade of Comedy (doc.).

CARRINGTON, EVELYN
Born: 1876. Died: Nov. 21, 1942, Hollywood, Calif. Screen and stage actress.

Appeared in: 1920 In Search of a Sinner. 1921 Salvation Nell. 1937 Living on Love.

CARRINGTON, FRANK
Born: 1902. Died: July 3, 1975, Millburn, N.J. Screen, stage actor and stage producer.

CARRINGTON, HELEN
Born: 1895. Died: Oct. 22, 1963, Morristown, N.J. Screen and stage actress.

Appeared in: 1930 Heads Up; Queen High (stage and film versions).

CARROLL, EARL

Born: Sept. 16, 1893, Pittsburgh, Pa. Died: June 17, 1948, Mt. Carmel, Pa. (plane crash). Stage, film producer, playwright and screen actor.

Appeared in: 1941 A Night at Earl Carroll's.

CARROLL, LEO G.

Born: 1892, Weedon, Northants, England. Died: Oct. 16, 1972, Hollywood, Calif. Screen, stage and television actor.

Appeared in: 1934 Sadie McGee; Outcast Lady; Stamboul Quest; Barretts of Wimpole Street. 1935 Murder on a Honeymoon; The Right to Live; Clive of India; The Casino Murder Case. 1937 London by Night. 1938 A Christmas Carol. 1939 Wuthering Heights; The Private Lives of Elizabeth and Essex; Bulldog Drummond's Secret Police; Charlie Chan in City in Darkness; Tower of London. 1940 Charlie Chan's Murder Cruise; Rebecca; Waterloo Bridge. 1941 Suspicion; Scotland Yard; Bahama Passage; This Woman Is Mine. 1945 Spellbound; The House on 92nd Street. 1947 Forever Amber; Time Out of Mind; Song of Love. 1948 So Evil My Love; Enchantment; The Paradine Case. 1950 Father of the Bride; The Happy Years. 1951 The First Legion; The Desert Fox; Strangers on a Train. 1952 The Snows of Kilimanjaro; Rogue's March; The Bad and the Beautiful. 1953 Treasure of the Golden Condor; Young Bess. 1955 Tarantula; We're No Angels. 1956 The Swan. 1959 North by Northwest. 1961 One Plus One (Exploring the Kinsey Reports); The Parent Trap. 1963 The Prize. 1965 That Funny Feeling. 1966 The Spy with My Face; One of our Spies is Missing; One Spy too Many. 1969 From Nashville with Music.

CARROLL, NANCY (Ann Veronica La Hiff)

Born: Nov. 19, 1906, New York, N.Y. Died: Aug. 6, 1965, New York, N.Y. (natural causes). Screen, stage and television actress. Married to C. H. J. Groen. Divorced from playwright Jack Kirkland and magazine editor Bolton Mallory.

Appeared in: 1927 Ladies Must Dress (film debut). 1928 Chicken a la King; Abie's Irish Rose; Easy Come, Easy Go; The Water Hole; Manhattan Cocktail. 1929 The Shopworn Angel; The Wolf of Wall Street; The Sin Sister; Close Harmony; The Dance of Life; Illusion; Sweetie. 1930 Dangerous Paradise; The Devil's Holiday; Honey; Paramount on Parade; Follow Thru; Laughter; Two against Death. 1931 Revolt; Stolen Heaven; Personal Maid; The Night Angel. 1932 The Man I Killed; Broken Lullaby; Wayward; Scarlet Dawn; Hot Saturday; Under Cover Man. 1933 I Love That Man; Child of Manhattan; The Woman Accused; The Kiss Before the Mirror. 1934 Transatlantic Merry-Go-Round; Jealousy; Springtime for Henry; Broken Melody. 1935 I'll Love You Always; After the Dance; Atlantic Adventure. 1938 There Goes My Heart; That Certain Age.

CARROLL, WILLIAM A.

Born: 1876. Died: Jan. 26, 1928, Glendale, Calif. (cancer). Stage and screen actor. Entered films with Selig and Vitagraph.

Appeared in: 1912 Black Sheep. 1916-1918 American Film Mfg. Co. films. 1919 Bill Henry; Trail of the Octopus (serial). 1920 The Branded Four (serial); The Screaming Shadow (serial). 1921 Fifty Candles. 1922 A Motion to Adjourn; Confidence; Chain Lightning; Remembrance; Yellow Men and Gold; Gas, Oil and Water. 1924 North of 36; Women First; Alimony; Wanderer of the Wasteland; K—The Unknown; Stolen Secrets; Sporting Youth. 1925 The Unwritten Law; The Ancient Highway; I'll Show You the Town. 1926 Born to the West; College Days; Joselyn's Wife; The Fighting Edge. 1927 Snowbound; Beauty Shoppers.

CARRON, GEORGE

Born: 1930, Canada. Died: Apr. 23, 1970, Montreal, Canada (heart attack). Screen, stage, television and radio actor.

Appeared in the following Canadian films: Footsteps in the Snow; Entre la Mer et l'Eau Douce.

CARRUTHERS, BRUCE C.

Born: 1901, Bedeque, Prince Edward Island, Canada. Died: Jan. 1954, Woodland Hills, Calif. Screen actor and film technical advisor.

Appeared in: 1951 Gene Autry and the Mounties.

CARSEY, MARY

Born: 1938. Died: Aug. 27, 1973, Dallas, Texas. Screen, stage, television actress, model and stage producer.

Appeared in: 1964 The Pink Panther.

CARSON, JACK

Born: Oct. 27, 1910, Carmen, Canada. Died: Jan. 2, 1963, Encino, Calif. (cancer). Screen, stage, television and vaudeville actor. Married to Sandra Tucker. Divorced from actress Lola Albright and singer Kay St. Germain.

Appeared in: 1937 Stage Door (film debut); Stand-In; A Rented Riot (short); You Only Live Once; Too Many Wives; Music for Madame; It Could Happen to You; High Flyers; The Toast of New York; Reported Missing. 1938 The Saint in New York; Vivacious Lady; Mr. Doodle Kicks Off; Crashing Hollywood; Bringing Up Baby; She's Got Everything; Night Spot; Go Chase Yourself; Law of the Underworld; This Marriage Business; Maid's Night Out; Hav-

ing a Wonderful Time; Carefree; Everybody's Doing It; Quick Money. 1939 Destry Rides Again; The Kid from Texas; Mr. Smith Goes to Washington; Legion of Lost Flyers; The Escape; The Honeymoon's Over. 1940 The Girl in 313; I Take This Woman; Shooting High; Young As You Feel; Enemy Agent; Parole Fixer; Typhoon; Alias the Deacon; Queen of the Mob; Sandy Gets Her Man; Love Thy Neighbor; Lucky Partners. 1941 Mr. and Mrs. Smith; Love Crazy; The Bride Came C.O.D.; Navy Blues; Blues in the Night; The Strawberry Blonde. 1942 Larceny, Inc.; Wings for the Eagle; Gentleman Jim; The Hard Way; The Male Animal. 1943 Thank Your Lucky Stars; Princess O'Rourke. 1944 The Dough Girls; Make Your Own Bed; Hollywood Canteen; Shine on Harvest Moon; Arsenic and Old Lace; Road to Glory (short). 1945 Mildred Pierce; Roughly Speaking. 1946 The Time, the Place and the Girl; One More Tomorrow; Two Guys from Milwaukee. 1947 Love and Learn; Royal Flush. 1948 Two Guys from Texas; April Showers; Romance on the High Seas. 1949 John Loves Mary; My Dream Is Yours. 1950 Bright Leaf; The Good Humor Man. 1951 Mister Universe; The Groom Wore Spurs. 1953 Dangerous When Wet. 1954 Red Garters; Phffft; A Star Is Born. 1955 Ain't Misbehaving. 1956 The Bottom of the Bottle; Magnificent Roughnecks. 1957 The Tattered Dress; The Tarnished Angels. 1958 Rally 'Round the Flag, Boys!; Cat On a Hot Tin Roof. 1960 The Bramble Bush; Circus of Horrors. 1961 The Big Bankroll; King of the Roaring 20's. 1962 Sammy the Way-Out Seal.

CARSON, JAMES B.

Born: 1885. Died: Nov. 18, 1958, Los Angeles, Calif. Screen, stage and vaudeville actor.

Appeared in: 1930 Everything Happens to Me (short). 1933 Moonlight and Pretzels. 1935 Harmony Lane; Coronado. 1938 Secrets of an Actress; Crime School; The Girls Downstairs. 1939 The Gracie Allen Murder Case; Disputed Passage.

CARTER, BEN F.

Born: Feb. 10, 1911, Fairfield, Iowa. Died: Dec. 11, 1946. Black screen, radio actor and singer. Do not confuse with musician Benny Carter.

Appeared in: 1935 Ben Carter and his Pickaninny Choir (short). 1939 Gone with the Wind; Little Old New York. 1940 Maryland; Tin Pan Alley; Chad Hanna; South to Karanga; Earl of Puddlestone; Safari. 1941 Sleeps West; Ride on Vaquero; Dressed to Kill; Reap the Wild Wind; Young America; Born to Sing; Her Cardboard Lover; Happy Go Lucky. 1943 Crash Dive. 1944 Bowery to Broadway; Dixie Jamboree. 1945 Lady on a Train. 1946 The Harvey Girls.

CARTER, BOAKE

Born: Baku, Russia. Died: Nov. 16, 1944, Hollywood, Calif. Radio announcer and screen actor.

Appeared in: 1937 The Dead March (narrator).

CARTER, CHARLES CALVERT

Born: 1859. Died: Aug. 29, 1932, Long Beach, Calif. (heart ailment). Screen actor. Entered films in 1912.

Appeared in: 1921 The Smart Set; Lying Lips. 1923 The Bolted Door; Slave of Desire. 1924 Abraham Lincoln. 1929 Broadway Fever.

CARTER, FRANK

Died: May 9, 1920, Grantville, Md. Screen actor.

Appeared in: 1922 Foolish Lives.

CARTER, MRS. LESLIE (Caroline Louise Dudley)

Born: June 10, 1862, Lexington, Ky. Died: Nov. 12, 1937, Los Angeles, Calif. (heart disease). Screen, stage and vaudeville actress.

Appeared in: 1915 The Heart of Maryland (stage and film versions), Du Barry (stage and film versions). 1934 The Vanishing Pioneer. 1935 Rocky Mountain Mystery.

CARTER, LOUISE

Born: 1875, Denison, Iowa. Died: Nov. 10, 1957, Hollywood, Calif. Stage and screen actress and playwright.

Appeared in: 1924 The Truth about Women. 1925 The Lost Chord; Scandal Street; The Substitute Wife. 1926 Striving for Fortune; In Borrowed Plumes. 1932 Broken Lullaby; The Strange Case of Clara Deane; Madame Butterfly; Week-End Marriage; Two Against the World; Blondie of the Follies; The Last Mile; Tess of the Storm Country. 1933 Jennie Gerhardt; This Day and Age; Pilgrimage; East of Fifth Avenue; Beauty for Sale; The Right to Romance; The Monkey's Paw. 1934 Beloved; You're Telling Me; Ready for Love. 1935 Straight from the Heart; The Mystery of Edwin Drood; Paddy O'Day; Reckless Roads. 1936 Rose of the Rancho. 1938 Inside Story. 1939 Nancy Drew and the Hidden Staircase.

CARTER, MONTE

Born: 1886, San Francisco, Calif. Died: Nov. 14, 1950, San Francisco, Calif. Screen, stage, burlesque, vaudeville actor, film director and stage director.

Appeared in: 1928 Midnight Life. 1929 Melody Lane. 1931 The Vice Squad.

1934 Redhead. 1935 Make a Million; Confidential. 1936 Give Us This Night. 1937 Million Dollar Racket.

CARTIER, INEZ GIBSON
Born: 1918. Died: Aug. 4, 1970, Hollywood, Calif. Screen actress and film stunt pilot.

CARTON, PAULINE
Born: 1885, France. Died: June 17, 1974, France? Screen and stage actress.

Appeared in: **1927** The Living Dead Man. **1931** The Parisian. **1937** Meet Miss Mozart. **1938** Story of a Cheat; Indiscretions; The Pearls of the Crown; Forty Little Mothers. **1939** The Affair la Font. **1940** Louise. **1948** Private Life of an Actor. **1951** Miquette. **1952** The Prize; Armoire Volante (The Cupboard was Bare). **1956** Fruits of Summer. **1957** The Virtuous Scoundrel. **1958** Lovers and Thieves. **1960** Au Pied, au Cheval et par Sputnik (aka A Dog, a Mouse and a Sputnik).

CARUSO, ENRICO
Born: Feb. 25, 1873, Naples, Italy. Died: Aug. 2, 1921, Naples, Italy (peritonitis). Opera singer and screen actor.

Appeared in: **1917** Webb Singing Pictures. **1918** My Cousin; The Splendid Romance (not released).

CARVER, KATHRYN (aka KATHRYN HILL)
Born: 1906, New York, N.Y. Died: July 17, 1947, Elmhurst, N.Y. (gastric ulcer). Screen actress. Appeared under both names. Divorced from actor Adolphe Menjou (dec. 1963).

Appeared in: **1925** When Love Grows Cold. **1926** The Wanderer; The Yankee Senor. **1927** Beware of Widows; Service for Ladies; Serenade. **1928** His Private Life; Outcast. **1929** No Defense.

CARVER, LOUISE (Louise Spilger Murray)
Born: June 9, 1869, Davenport, Iowa. Died: Jan. 18, 1956, Hollywood, Calif. Screen, stage, opera and vaudeville actress. Appeared in Mack Sennett silent films. Married to actor Tom Murray (dec. 1935).

Appeared in: **1923** The Extra Girl; Main Street; Scaramouche. **1924** The Breed of the Border. **1926** Shameful Behavior? **1927** Blondes by Choice; Backstage; The Fortune Hunter. **1929** The Redeeming Sin; The Sap; Must We Marry?; Tonight at Twelve; The Bride's Relations (short); Wolves of the City. **1930** Back Pay; The Man from Blankley's; Big Trail. **1931** One of the Smiths (short); Side Show. **1932** The Monkey's Paw. **1933** Hallelujah, I'm a Bum. **1935** Every Night at Eight; Southern Exposure (short); I'm a Father (short). **1937** Dizzy Doctors (short); Lodge Night (short). **1941** Some More of Samoa (short).

CARVER, LYNN (Virginia Reid Sampson)
Born: Sept. 13, 1909. Died: Aug. 12, 1955, New York, N.Y. Screen, stage and television actress.

Appeared in: **1935** Strangers All; Roberta; Old Man Rhythm; To Beat the Band. **1937** Maytime; The Bride Wore Red; Madame X. **1938** Young Dr. Kildare; Everybody Sing; A Christmas Carol. **1939** Huckleberry Finn; Calling Dr. Kildare; Within the Law. **1940** Sporting Blood; A Door Will Open; Broadway Melody of 1940; Pound Foolish (short); Dulcy; Bitter Sweet. **1941** Mr. District Attorney in the Carter Case; County Fair; Blood and Sand; Charley's Aunt; Sucker List (short). **1942** Man from Cheyenne; Yokel Boy; Sunset on the Desert. **1943** Tennessee Johnson. **1944** Law of the Valley. **1945** Flame of the West. **1946** Drifting Along. **1948** Crossed Trails. **1953** One Came Home.

CASADESUS, MATHILDE
Born: May 15, 1921, Paris, France. Died: Aug. 30, 1965, Minorca Island, Spain (heart attack). Stage and screen actress.

Appeared in: **1943** La Boite aux Reves. **1945** Le Part de L'ombre. **1946** L'ediota. **1948** Marlene. **1949** Au Royaume des Cieux; Branguignol. **1950** Boniface Sonnambule. **1951** Le Plaisir. **1953** La Dame aux Camelias. **1955** Gervaise (US 1957). **1956** Ce soir les Jupons Volent. **1960** Candide (US 1962); Meutre en 45 Tours (Murder at 45 R.P.M.–US 1965). **1962** Love Is My Profession. **1963** Five Miles to Midnight. Other French film: L'Air de Paris.

CASALEGGIO, GIOVANNI
Born: 1880, Italy. Died: Nov. 11, 1955, Turin, Italy, Italian screen actor and film director.

Appeared in: **1913-1914** Cabiria.

CASALS, PABLO (Pau Carlos Salvador Defillo de Casals)
Born: Dec. 29, 1876, Vendrell, Spain. Died: Oct. 22, 1973, Rio Pedras, Puerto Rico (heart attack). Cellist, conductor, composer and screen actor. Divorced from soprano Susan Metcalfe. Married to Marta Montanez.

Appeared in: **1958** Windjammer.

CASE, PAUL
Born: 1895. Died: March 29, 1933, Los Angeles, Calif.(injuries from fall from horse). Screen actor.

CASEY, DOLORES (Margaret Dolores Katherine Casey)
Born: 1917, New York, N.Y. Died: May 11, 1945, Hollywood, Calif. Screen actress.

Appeared in: **1936** Big Brown Eyes. **1937** Artists and Models Abroad. **1938** Cocoanut Grove; Doctor Rhythm.

CASEY, KENNETH
Born: 1899, N.Y. Died: Aug. 10, 1965, Newburg, N.Y. (heart condition). Screen actor and songwriter.

Appeared in: **1911** Daddy's Boy and Mammy; Wig-Wag; The Little Spy. **1912** How Tommy Saved His Father; The Higher Mercy; Xenophon, A Story of the Circus; Tom Tillin's Baby; Bumps; Ingenuity; The Eavesdroppers; Fate's Awful Jest; An Innocent Theft; The Man Under the Bed; A Juvenile Love Affair; The Old Silver Watch. **1913** When Bobby Forgot; In the Shadow. **1919** Heartsease. **1935** An MGM short.

CASEY, STUART F.
Born: 1896, London, England. Died: Jan. 23, 1948, Saratoga, N.Y. Stage and screen actor.

Appeared in: **1935** Reckless; The Age of Indiscretion; Captain Blood.

CASH, WILLIAM F.
Born: c. 1880. Died: April 15, 1963, New York, N.Y. (stroke). Stage and screen actor.

CASHER, IZADORE (aka ISIDORE CASHIER)
Born: 1887, Russia. Died: Apr. 15, 1948, Savannah, Ga. (heart ailment). Yiddish screen and stage actor.

Appeared in: **1926** Broken Hearts. **1937** Green Fields. **1939** The Light Ahead.

CASHMAN, HARRY
Died: Dec. 14, 1912, Chicago, Ill. Screen actor.

Appeared in: **1911** Bill Bumper's Bargain. **1912** The Tale of a Cat; The Voice of Conscience; The Iron Heel; The Warning Hand; The End of a Feud; Almost a Man; When a Man's Married; Down Jayville Way; Sunshine; The Moving Finger; The Eye that Never Sleeps; Lonesome Robert; Getting a Hired Girl. **1913** The Farmer's Daughter.

CASON, JOHN
Died: July 7, 1961. Screen actor.

Appeared in: **1941** Buck Privates. **1947** The Last Round-Up. **1949** Ringside; Rimfire; The Blazing Trail; Red Desert; Tough Assignment; The Big Sombrero; Range Land. **1950** Desperadoes of the West (serial); Crooked River; Redwood Forest Trail; Fast on the Draw; Marshal of Heldorado; West of the Brazos; Colorado Ranger; Traveling Saleswoman; Streets of Ghost Town; Hostile Country; Rustlers on Horseback. **1951** Don Daredevil Rides Again (serial); Prairie Round-up; Savage Raider. **1952** The Hawk of Wild River; Black Hills Ambush; Wagon Team; Voodoo Tiger. **1953** Jungle Drums of Africa (serial); From Here to Eternity; Gun Fury; The Lost Planet (serial); Savage Frontier. **1954** Saskatchewan; Red River Shore. **1955** Wyoming Renegades; Count Three and Pray. **1956** He Laughed Last; Over-Exposed. **1957** The Storm Rider. **1958** Snowfire. **1960** Cimarron.

CASS, GUY (Caster Abney Gay, Jr.)
Born: 1921. Died: Sept. 28, 1959, near Hollywood, Calif. (auto accident). Screen actor.

CASS, MAURICE
Born: Oct. 12, 1884, Vilna, Lithuania. Died: June 8, 1954, Hollywood, Calif. (heart attack). Screen, stage actor and playwright.

Appeared in: **1923** Experimental picture (sound-on-film) by Dr. Lee De Forest, exhibited at Rivoli Theatre in N.Y. **1930** Wife vs. Secretary. **1935** Two for Tonight; Millions in the Air; Whispering Smith Speaks. **1936** Arbor Day (short); Professional Soldier; Everybody's Old Man; Pepper; Charlie Chan at the Opera; Give Us This Night; Champagne Waltz. **1937** Maytime; Women of Glamour; This Is My Affair; The Lady Escapes; She Had to Eat; Thin Ice; Wife, Doctor and Nurse; Danger—Love at Work; Life Begins in College; Ali Baba Goes to Town; Big Town Girl; Exiled to Shanghai. **1938** Making the Headlines; The Lone Wolf in Paris; Gangs of New York; Walking Down Broadway; The Baroness and the Butler; When Were You Born?; Josette; Sunset Trail; Gold Diggers in Paris; A Desperate Adventure; Exposed; Breaking the Ice. **1939** Second Fiddle; Mr. Smith Goes to Washington. **1940** Florian. **1941** Chocolate Soldier; Charley's Aunt; Glamour Boy (short); Blood and Sand. **1942** My Heart Belongs to Daddy. **1943** Mission to Moscow. **1944** Up in Arms; Mrs. Parkington. **1945** Easy to Look At; Hit the Hay; Paris Underground; Her Lucky Night; Wonder Man. **1946** The Notorious Lone Wolf; Angel on My Shoulder; Catman of Paris; Spook Busters. **1947** High Conquest;

Spoilers of the North; Saddle Pals. **1948** Song of My Heart. **1949** Once More My Darling. **1952** We're Not Married. **1953** So You Want to be a Musician (short).

CASSADY, JAMES (James J. Cassidy)
Born: 1869, Philadelphia, Pa. Died: Mar. 23, 1928, Spokane, Wash. Screen actor.

Appeared in: **1915** Siren of Corsica.

CASSEL, SID
Born: 1897, Leeds, England. Died: Jan. 17, 1960, Hollywood, Calif. Screen, stage and television actor.

CASSIDY, BILL (William E. Cassidy)
Born: 1876. Died: April 6, 1943, Cincinnati, Ohio. Screen and stage actor.

Appeared in: **1915** Birth of a Nation. **1916** Intolerance.

CASSIDY, ED (Edward Cassidy)
Born: 1893. Died: Jan. 1968, Woodland Hills, Calif. Screen actor.

Appeared in: **1935** Toll of the Desert; Commodore. **1937** Borderland; Hit the Saddle; Come on, Cowboys. **1938** Frontier Town; The Purple Vigilantes; Man from Music Mountain; Cassidy of Bar 20; Rawhide; The Mexicali Kid; Starlight Over Texas. **1939** Wild Horse Canyon; Silver on the Sage; Mountain Rhythm; Rovin' Tumbleweeds; Desperate Trails; Cowboys from Texas. **1940** Riders of Pasco Basin; Ragtime Cowboy Joe; Gaucho Serenade. **1941** Wide Open Town; Robbers of the Range; Wyoming Wildcat; Ridin' on a Rainbow; The Gang's All Here. **1942** House of Errors; The Mad Monster; Stardust on the Sage; Pirates of the Prairie. **1943** Thundering Trails; Cowboy in the Clouds; The Avenging Rider. **1944** Boss of Rawhide; Brand of the Devil; Frontier Outlaws; Fuzzy Settles Down; The Great Mike; The Pinto Bandit; Saddle Leather; Rustlers' Hideout; Trigger Law; Tucson Raiders. **1945** Along the Navajo Trail; Arson Squad; Corpus Christi Bandits; The Gangster's Den; Sheriff of Cimarron; Stagecoach Outlaws; Sunset in Eldorado; Three in the Saddle. **1946** Alias Billy the Kid; Ambush Trail; Days of Buffalo Bill; Trigger Fingers; The El Paso Kid; The Navajo Kid; Prairie Badmen; Roaring Rangers; Roll on Texas Moon; Sun Valley Cyclone. **1947** Homesteaders of Paradise Valley; Oregon Trail Scouts; Son of Zorro (serial); Valley of Fear; Stagecoach to Denver; Buffalo Bill Rides Again; Border Feud. **1948** The Bold Frontiersman; Desperadoes of Dodge City. **1949** Roughshod. **1950** Fence Riders; Trail of Robin Hood; Buckaroo Sheriff of Texas. **1951** Million Dollar Pursuit. **1952** Desperadoes' Outpost; Black Hills Ambush; Night Raiders; And Now Tomorrow; Talk about a Stranger. **1956** The First Traveling Saleslady.

CASSON, SIR LEWIS
Born: 1876. Died: May 16, 1969, London, England. Screen, stage, television actor, stage producer and director. Married to actress Dame Sybil Thorndyke (dec. 1976) and father of actors John and Christopher and actresses Ann and Mary Casson.

Appeared in: **1930** Escape. **1936** Rhodes of Africa (aka Rhodes–US); Calling the Tune. **1937** Victoria the Great. **1938** South Riding; Sixty Glorious Years (aka Queen of Destiny–US). **1951** Men of the Sea. **1959** Shake Hands With the Devil.

CASTAGNA, JOE
Born: 1934. Died: Aug. 22, 1970, Los Angeles, Calif. (heart attack). Screen actor and stuntman.

Appeared in: **1957** Johnny Trouble. **1969** That Tender Touch.

CASTIGLIONI, IPHIGENE
Born: 1901. Died: July 30, 1963, Hollywood, Calif. Screen, stage and television actress.

Appeared in: **1935** Story of Louis Pasteur. **1937** Life of Emile Zola; Maytime. **1953** Greatest Show on Earth. **1954** Rear Window. **1955** Conquest of Space. **1957** Funny Face; Wild Is the Wind; Valerie. **1961** Comancheros. **1962** Rome Adventure.

CASTILE, LYNN (aka LYNN CANTER)
Born: 1898. Died: Apr. 8, 1975, Los Angeles, Calif. Screen, stage, radio actress and singer.

Appeared in: **1948** Marshal of Amarillo.

CASTLE, DON
Born: Sept. 29, 1917, Beaumont, Tex. Died: May 26, 1966, Hollywood, Calif. (overdose of medication). Screen actor.

Appeared in: **1938** Love Finds Andy Hardy (film debut); Rich Man, Poor Girl; Out West with the Hardys. **1939** These Glamour Girls. **1940** I Take This Woman. **1941** Power Dive; World Premiere. **1942** Tombstone, the Town Too Tough To Die. **1947** The Invisible Wall; The Guilty; High Tide; Roses Are Red. **1948** Perilous Waters; I Wouldn't Be in Your Shoes; Strike It Rich; Who Killed "Doc" Robbin? **1949** Stampede. **1950** Motor Patrol. **1957** The Big Land; Gunfight at the O.K. Corral.

CASTLE, IRENE (Irene Foote)
Born: 1893, New Rochelle, N.Y. Died: Jan. 25, 1969, Eureka Springs, Ark. Screen, stage actress and dancer. Married to Vernon Castle (dec. 1918) with whom she appeared on stage and screen.

Appeared in: **1914** Mr. and Mrs. Vernon Castle Before the Camera (with Vernon Castle). **1915** The Whirl of Life (with Vernon Castle). **1917** Patria (serial); Vengeance is Mine; Sylvia of the Secret Service; Stranded in Arcady; The Mark of Cain; Convict 999. **1918** The Hillcrest Mystery; The First Law; The Mysterious Client; The Girl from Bohemia; The Common Cause. **1919** The Firing Line; The Invisible Bond. **1920** The Amateur Wife. **1921** The Broadway Bride. **1922** French Heels; No Trespassing; Slim Shoulders. **1924** Broadway After Dark.

CASTLE, LILLIAN
Born: 1865. Died: Apr. 24, 1959, Los Angeles, Calif. Screen and vaudeville actress.

Appeared in: **1935** Confidential.

CASTLE, NICK
Born: Mar. 21, 1910, Brooklyn, N.Y. Died: Aug. 18, 1968, Los Angeles, Calif. (heart attack). Screen, vaudeville dancer, film and television dance director.

Appeared in: **1955** Artists and Models.

CASTLE, PEGGY (aka PEGGIE CASTLE)
Born: Dec. 22, 1926, Appalachia, Va. Died: Aug. 11, 1973, Hollywood, Calif. (cirrhosis of the liver and heart condition). Screen and television actress. Divorced from film producer William McGarry.

Appeared in: **1949** Mr. Belvedere Goes to College (film debut). **1950** Buccaneer's Girl. **1951** Payment on Demand (aka Story of Divorce); Air Cadet; The Prince Who Was a Thief; The Golden Horde. **1952** Invasion USA; Harem Girl; Wagons West. **1953** I, The Jury; 99 River Street; Cow Country; Son of Belle Starr. **1954** The Long Wait; Jesse James' Women; The White Orchid; The Yellow Tomahawk; Overland Pacific; Southwest Passage. **1955** Finger Man; Target Zero; Tall Man Riding. **1956** Two Gun Lady; Miracle in the Rain; Oklahoma Woman; Quincannon—Frontier Scout. **1957** Beginning of the End; The Counterfeit Plan; Hell's Crossroads; Back from the Dead (aka Bury Me Dead). **1958** The Seven Hills of Rome.

CASTLE, VERNON
Born: May 2, 1887, England. Died: Feb. 15, 1918, Houston, Texas (plane crash). Screen, stage actor and dancer. Married to Irene Castle (dec. 1969) with whom he appeared on stage and screen.

Appeared in: **1914** Mr. and Mrs. Vernon Castle Before the Camera (with Irene Castle). **1915** The Whirl of Life (with Irene Castle).

CASTRO, STEVEN
Born: 1864. Died: Nov. 19, 1952, Hollywood, Calif. Screen cowboy actor and rodeo rider.

CATLETT, WALTER
Born: Feb. 4, 1889, San Francisco, Calif. Died: Nov. 14, 1960, Woodland Hills, Calif. (stroke). Screen, stage, opera, vaudeville actor and screenwriter.

Appeared in: **1924** Second Youth. **1926** Summer Bachelors. **1929** Married in Hollywood; Why Leave Home?; The Gay Nineties. **1930** The Floradora Girl; Let's Go Places; Happy Days; The Big Party; The Golden Calf; Stage Struck; Aunts in the Pants. **1931** Front Page; Cock of the Air; Platinum Blonde; Yellow; Camping Out (short); Palmy Days; Gold Fish Bowl; The Maker of Men. **1932** The Expert; It's Tough to Be Famous; Big City Blues; The Penalty of Fame; Sky Devils; Back Street; Rain; Free, White and 21; Rockabye; Okay America; Sport Parade. **1933** Private Jones; Only Yesterday; Mama Loves Papa; Arizona to Broadway. **1934** Unknown Blonde; The Captain Hates the Sea; Olsen's Big Moment; Lightning Strikes Twice. **1935** Every Night at Eight; A Tale of Two Cities; Affair of Susan. **1936** I Loved a Soldier; Mr. Deeds Goes to Town; We Went to College; Follow Your Heart; Sing Me a Love Song; Cain and Mable; Banjo on My Knee. **1937** Four Days' Wonder; On the Avenue; Love is News; Wake Up and Live; Love Under Fire; Danger—Love at Work; Varsity Show; Every Day's a Holiday; Come Up Smiling. **1938** Bringing Up Baby; Going Places. **1939** Kid Nightingale; Exile Express; Zaza. **1940** Pop Always Pays; Remedy for Riches; Comin' 'Round the Mountain; Spring Parade; Half a Sinner; Pinocchio (voice); Li'l Abner; The Quarterback. **1941** You're the One; Honeymoon for Three; Horror Island; It Started with Eve; Wild Man of Borneo; Million Dollar Baby; Hello Sucker; Manpower; Mad Men of Missouri; Unfinished Business; Steel Against the Sky; Wild Bill Hickok Rides. **1942** Star Spangled Rhythm; My Gal Sal; Maisie Gets Her Man; Yankee Doodle Dandy; Give Out Sisters; Heart of the Golden West; Between Us Girls. **1943** West Side Kid; Hit Parade of 1943; How's About It?; Cowboy in Manhattan; Get Going; They Got Me Covered; Fired Wife; His Butler's Sister. **1944** Her Primitive Man; Pardon My Rhythm; The Ghost Catchers; Hat Check Honey; Up in Arms; Lady, Let's Dance!; Three Is a Family; Hi, Beautiful; My Gal Loves Music; Lake Placid Serenade. **1945** The Man Who Walked Alone; I Love a Bandleader. **1946** Riverboat Rhythm; Slightly Scandalous.

1947 I'll Be Yours. 1948 Mr. Reckless; Are You With It?; The Boy with Green Hair. 1949 Henry, the Rainmaker; Look for the Silver Lining; Dancing in the Dark; The Inspector General; Leave It to Henry. 1949 Father Makes Good. 1950 Father's Wild Game. 1951 Father Takes the Air; Honeychile; Here Comes the Groom. 1956 The Gay Nineties; Davy Crockett and the River Pirates; Friendly Persuasion. 1957 Beau James.

CAULKINS, RUFUS

Died: July 15, 1935, Los Angeles, Calif. (auto accident). Screen actor.

CAVALIERI, LINA

Born: Dec. 25, 1874, Rome, Italy. Died: Feb. 8, 1944, near Florence, Italy. Screen, opera and stage actress.

Appeared in: 1914 Manon Lescaut. 1917 The Eternal Temptress. 1918 A Woman of Impulse. 1919 The House of Granada; Two Brides; Mad Love.

CAVANAGH, PAUL

Born: Dec. 8, 1895, Chislehurst, Kent, England. Died: Mar. 15, 1964. Screen, stage, radio actor and author.

Appeared in: 1928 Tesha; Two Little Drummer Boys. 1929 A Woman in the Night; The Runaway Princess. 1930 Strictly Unconventional; Grumpy; The Storm; The Devil to Pay; The Virtuous Sin. 1931 Born to Love; Unfaithful; Transgression; Always Goodbye; The Squaw Man. 1932 Heartbreak; Tonight is Ours; The Devil's Lottery; The Crash; A Bill of Divorcement. 1933 The Sin of Nora Moran; The Kennel Murder Case. 1934 Tarzan and His Mate; Shoot the Works; Menace; The Notorious Sophie Lang; Curtain at Eight; Uncertain Lady; Escapade; One Exciting Adventure. 1935 Goin' to Town; Splendor; Wings in the Dark; Without Regret; Thunder in the Night. 1936 Champagne Charlie; Crime over London (US 1938). 1937 A Romance in Flanders (aka Lost on the Western Front–US 1940) (aka Danger in Paris–US). 1939 Reno; Within the Law; The Under-pup. 1940 I Take This Woman. 1941 The Case of the Black Parrot; Maisie was a Lady; Shadows on the Stairs; Passage from Hong Kong. 1942 Eagle Squadron; Captains of the Clouds; The Strange Case of Dr. Rx; Pacific Rendezvous; The Hard Way; The Gorilla Man. 1943 Adventures in Iraq. 1944 The Scarlet Claw; Maisie Goes to Reno; Marriage is a Private Affair; The Man in Half Moon Street. 1945 The House of Fear; The Woman in Green. 1946 Night and Day; Night in Paradise; The Verdict; Club Havana; Humoresque. 1947 Ivy; Dishonored Lady. 1948 The Black Arrow; The Babe Ruth Story; The Secret Beyond the Door; You Gotta Stay Happy. 1949 Madame Bovary. 1950 The Iroquois Trail; Hit Parade of 1951; Rogues of Sherwood Forest; Hi-Jacked. 1951 Desert Fox; All That I Have; The Strange Door; Hollywood Story; The Son of Dr. Jekyll; Tales of Robin Hood; The Highwayman. 1952 The Golden Hawk; Plymouth Adventure. 1953 The Mississippi Gambler; House of Wax; The All American; The Bandits of Corsica; Flame of Calcutta; Port Sinister; Charade. 1954 The Raid; Casanova's Big Night; The Iron Glove; Magnificent Obsession; The Law vs. Billy the Kid; Khyber Patrol. 1955 The Purple Mask; The King's Thief; The Prodigal; The Scarlet Coat; Diane. 1956 Francis in the Haunted House; Blonde Bait. 1957 She-Devil; God is My Partner; The Man Who Turned to Stone. 1958 In the Money. 1959 The Four Skulls of Jonathan Drake; The Beat Generation.

CAVANAUGH, HOBART

Born: 1887, Virginia City, Nev. Died: Apr. 27, 1950, Woodland Hills, Calif. Screen, stage and vaudeville actor.

Appeared in: 1928 San Francisco Nights. 1929 Sympathy (short). 1930 The Poor Fish (short); The Headache Man (short). 1932 Close Friends (short). 1933 Footlight Parade; Picture Snatcher; Death Watch; Study in Scarlet; Gold Diggers of 1933; Goodbye Again; Mary Stevens, M.D.; The Mayor of Hell; Private Detective 62; Kennel Murder Case; From Headquarters; Broadway Thru a Keyhole; Lilly Turner; Havana Widows; Convention City; Headline Shooter; No Marriage Ties; The Devil's Mate; My Woman; I Cover the Waterfront. 1934 Wonder Bar; Mandalay; The Firebird; Dark Hazard; I Sell Everything; Madame Du Barry; I am a Thief; St. Louis Kid; Housewife; A Lost Lady; Fashions of 1934; Kansas City Princess; Moulin Rouge; Hi Nellie; Easy to Love; I've Got Your Number; Harold Teen; Jimmy the Gent; Merry Wives of Reno; The Key; A Very Honorable Guy; A Modern Hero; Now I'll Tell. 1935 Wings in the Dark; While the Patient Slept; Captain Blood; Broadway Breveties (short); Don't Bet on Blondes; We're in the Money; Border Town; Broadway Gondolier; Page Miss Glory; Dr. Socrates; A Midsummer Night's Dream; I Live for Love. 1936 The Lady Consents; Love Letters of a Star; Colleen; Love Begins at Twenty; Two against the World; Hearts Divided; Sing Me a Love Song; Cain and Mabel; Here Comes Carter; The Golden Arrow; Stage Struck; Wife vs. Secretary. 1937 The Great O'Malley; Three Smart Girls; Mysterious Crossing; The Mighty Treve; Night Key; Girl Overboard; Love in a Bungalow; Reported Missing. 1938 That's My Story; Cowboy from Brooklyn; Orphans of the Street. 1939 Zenobia; Career; Tell No Tales; Chicken Wagon Family; Reno; That's Right, You're Wrong; The Covered Trailer; The Day of Rest (short); See Your Doctor (short); The Honeymoon's Over; Adventures of Jane Arden; Rose of Washington Square. 1940 You Can't Fool Your Wife; A Child Is Born; Home Movies (short); I Stole a Million; Shooting High; An Angel from Texas; Street of Memories; Stage to Chino; Public Deb. No. 1; The

Great Plane Robbery; Santa Fe Trail; Charter Pilot; Love, Honor and Oh Baby!; The Ghost Comes Home; Hired Wife. 1941 Horror Island; Meet the Chump; Thieves Fall Out; Land of the Open Range; I Wanted Wings. 1942 A Tragedy at Mid-Night; Jackass Mail; Whistling in Dixie; Stand by for Action; My Favorite Spy; The Magnificent Dope. 1943 Skylark; Dangerous Blondes; The Meanest Man in the World; The Kansan; Gildersleeve on Broadway; Man from Down Under. 1944 The Immortal Blacksmith (short); Louisiana Hayride; Sweet Rosie O'Grady; Jack London; Kismet. 1945 House of Fear; Roughly Speaking; Don Juan Quilligan; I'll Remember April; Lady on a Train. 1946 Cinderella Jones; The Spider Woman Strikes Back; Faithful in My Fashion; Black Angel; Little Iodine; Margie. 1947 Driftwood. 1948 Best Man Wins; You Gotta Stay Happy; Up in Central Park; The Inside Story. 1949 A Letter to Three Wives. 1950 Stella.

CAVANNA, ELISE

Born: 1902. Died: May 12, 1963, Hollywood, Calif. (cancer). Screen, stage actress, author and painter.

Appeared in: 1926 Love 'Em and Leave 'Em. 1931 A Melon-Drama (short). 1932 The Dentist (short). 1933 The Barber Shop (short); The Pharmacist (short). 1934 You're Telling Me. 1938 I Met My Love Again; Everybody Sing. 1946 Ziegfeld Follies.

CAVEN, ALLAN

Born: Mar. 25, 1880, Concord, Calif. Died: Jan. 19. 1941, Hollywood, Calif. Stage and screen actor. Entered films in 1919.

Appeared in: 1921 The Primal Law. 1923 When Odds are Even. 1927 London After Midnight; Shanghai Bound. 1928 The Terrible People (serial); The Man Who Laughs. 1929 Leave It to Gerry; The Million Dollar Collar. 1934 Opened by Mistake (short); The Mighty Barnum. 1935 Thicker Than Water (short). 1936 Rebellion. 1937 Old Louisiana; Nation Aflame. 1938 I Am A Criminal.

CAVENDER, GLEN W.

Born: 1884. Died: Feb. 9, 1962, Hollywood, Calif. Screen actor and film director. One of the original Keystone Kops.

Appeared in: 1915 Fickle Fatty's Fall; A Submarine Pirate. 1916 Fatty and Mable Adrift; Because He Loved Her; The Village Blacksmith; The Surf Girl. 1917 A Dog Catcher's Love; The Pawnbroker's Heart. 1921 Hearts of Youth; The Primal Law; Skirts; Little Miss Hawkshaw; Straight from the Shoulder; What Love Will Do. 1922 Iron to Gold. 1923 Main Street. 1925 Keep Smiling; Manhattan Madness. 1927 The General. 1929 Ships of the Night. 1935 G-Men. 1938 Penrod's Double Trouble. 1942 Yankee Doodle Dandy.

CAVENDISH, DAVID

Born: 1891. Died: Oct. 8, 1960, Hollywood, Calif. (heart attack). Stage and screen actor.

Appeared in: 1942 Random Harvest.

CAVENS, FRED (Frederic Adolphe Cavens)

Born: Aug. 30, 1882, Belgium. Died: Apr. 30, 1962, Woodland Hills, Calif. (uremia). Screen actor, stuntman and fencing master.

Appeared in: 1922 The Three-Must-Get-Theres. 1927 King of Kings. 1933 Breed of the Border. 1938 Kidnapped. 1939 The Man in the Iron Mask. 1952 Lydia Bailey.

CAWTHORN, JOSEPH

Born: Mar. 29, 1868, N.Y. Died: Jan. 21, 1949, Beverly Hills, Calif. (stroke). Married to actress Queenie Vass (dec. 1960). Stage and screen actor.

Appeared in: 1927 Very Confidential; Two Girls Wanted; The Secret Studio. 1928 Silk Legs; Hold 'Em Yale. 1929 Street Girl; Jazz Heaven; Dance Hall; The Taming of the Shrew; Speakeasy. 1930 Dixiana; The Princess and the Plumber; 1931 Kiki; The Runaround; Peach O'Reno; A Tailor Made Man. 1932 White Zombie; Love Me Tonight; They Call It Sin. 1933 Whistling in the Dark; Blondie Johnson; Grand Slam; Men Are Such Fools; Made on Broadway; Best of Enemies; Broken Dreams; Radio short. 1934 Housewife; Young and Beautiful; The Human Side; Lazy River; The Last Gentleman; Twenty Million Sweethearts; Glamour; Music in the Air; The Cat and the Fiddle. 1935 Adeline; Maybe It's Love; Go into Your Dance; Sweet Music; Page Miss Glory; Bright Lights; Harmony Lane; Gold Diggers of 1935; Naughty Marietta; Smart Girl. 1936 Freshman Love; Hot Money; The Great Ziegfeld; One Rainy Afternoon; Brides are Like That; Crime Over London. 1940 Lillian Russell; Scatterbrain. 1941 So Ends the Night. 1942 The Postman Didn't Ring.

CAZENUVE, PAUL

Born: France. Died: June 22, 1925, Hollywood, Calif. Screen, stage actor and film director.

Appeared in: 1921 Big Town Ideas; The Queen of Sheba. 1923 Six Days; The French Doll.

CECCARELLI, VINCENZO

Born: 1889. Died: Aug. 8, 1969, Los Angeles, Calif. Screen actor and singer.

CECIL, EDWARD

Born: Sept. 1888, San Francisco, Calif. Died: Dec. 13, 1940, Los Angeles, Calif. Screen, stage and vaudeville actor.

Appeared in: 1921 Big Game; The Greater Claim; Parted Curtains; There Are No Villains; The Off-Shore Pirate. 1922 The Guttersnipe; The Love Gambler; My Wild Irish Rose; The Top of New York. 1923 The Scarlet Car. 1924 Wolves of the North (serial); The Sword of Valor. 1925 The Phantom of the Opera; Hidden Loot; Secrets of the Night; What Happened to Jones? 1926 Vanishing Millions (serial); The Crown of Lies; The Stolen Ranch; The Smoke Eaters. 1927 Woman's Law; Hoof Marks; Cheaters; The Desert of the Lost. 1928 Jazzland; The Sky Rider; Saddle Mates; A Midnight Adventure. 1929 Silent Sentinel; The Black Book (serial). 1930 Guilty?; Lotus Lady. 1931 Resurrection.

CECIL, MARY

Born: 1885, N.Y. Died: Dec. 21, 1940, New York, N.Y. (pneumonia). Screen, stage and radio actress.

Appeared in: 1939 The Women (stage and film versions).

CEDAR, DAYNA

Died: June 10, 1974. Screen actress.

CEDAR, IVAN

Died: Nov. 1937, Tucson, Ariz. (auto accident). Screen actor and stuntman.

CELESTE, OLGA

Born: 1887, Sweden. Died: Aug. 31, 1969, Burbank, Calif. (heart attack after treatment for pneumonia). Screen, circus, vaudeville actress and animal trainer.

Appeared in: 1934 Cleopatra.

CELLIER, FRANK

Born: Feb. 23, 1884, Surbiton, Surrey, England. Died: Sept. 27, 1948, London, England. Stage and screen actor.

Appeared in: 1931 Her Reputation; Tin Gods. 1933 The Golden Cage; Soldiers of the King (aka The Woman in Command–US 1934); Doss House; Hearts of Oak; The Fire Raisers. 1934 Colonel Blood. 1935 Lorna Doone; The Love Affair of the Dictator (aka The Dictator and The Loves of a Dictator–US); The 39 Steps; The Guv'nor (aka Mister Hobo–US 1936); The Passing of the Third Floor Back. 1936 Rhodes of Africa (aka Rhodes–US); Tudor Rose (aka Nine Days a Queen–US); The Man Who Changed His Mind (aka The Man Who Lived Again–US); 1937 O.H.M.S. (aka You're in the Army Now–US); Take My Tip; Action for Slander (US 1938); Non-Stop New York. 1938 Kate Plus Ten; Sixty Glorious Years (aka Queen of Destiny–US); A Royal Divorce; The Ware Case (US 1939). 1939 The Midas Touch. 1941 Quiet Wedding; Love on the Dole; Ships with Wings (US 1942); The Black Sheep of Whitehall; Cottage to Let (aka Bombsight Stolen–US); Jennie. 1942 The Big Blockade. 1944 Give Us the Moon. 1946 Quiet Weekend (US 1948); The Magic Bow (US 1947). 1948 Easy Money (US 1949); The Blind Goddess (US 1949).

CERVI, GINO

Born: May 3, 1901, Bologna, Italy. Died: Jan. 3, 1974, Punta Ala, Italy (pulmonary stroke). Screen, stage, television actor, stage director, stage producer and political figure. Father of film producer Tonino Cervi.

Appeared in: 1934 Frontier (film debut). 1935 Amore; Aldebaran. 1936 I Due Sergenti. 1937 Gli Uomini non Sono Ingrati; Voglio Vivere Con Letizia; Il Ponto di Vetro. 1938 L'Argine (The River Bank). 1939 Un Matrimonio Ideale (An Ideal Marriage). 1940 Un Aventura di Salvator Rosa (An Adventure of Salvator Rosa). 1942 Four Steps in the Clouds (US 1948). 1947 Fabiola (US 1951); Revenge. 1948 Anna Karenina; Four Steps in the Clouds; Eternal Melodies; The Spirit and the Flesh. 1948 Iron Crown (US 1949); His Young Wife. 1950 My Widow and I. 1951 Women Without Names. 1952 Little World of Don Camillo (US 1953—first of the Don Camillo series); Les Miserables; Malia; The Cliff of Sin; O.K. Nero (US 1953). 1953 Tre Storie Proibite (Three Forbidden Stories); Maddalena (US 1955); Queen of Sheba; Strange Deception (aka The Forbidden Christ). 1954 Indiscretion of an American Wife. 1955 Moglie per una Notte (Wife for a Night–US 1957). 1956 The Return of Don Camillo. 1958 Los Amantes del Desierto (aka Amanti del Desierto and La Figlia Dello Sceicco aka Desert Warrior–US 1961). 1959 The Naked Maja; Sans Famille; Sign of the Gladiator. 1960 L'Assedio di Siracusa (Siege of Syracuse–US 1962 aka Archimede); Femmine di Lusso (Love, the Italian Way–US 1964); Gli Inamorati (Wild Love–US 1962); Agguato a Tangier (Trapped in Tangiers aka Ambush in Tangiers). 1961 La Rivolta degli Schiavi (The Revolt of the Slaves). 1962 Le Crime ne Paie Pas (Crime Does not Pay). 1963 La Smania Addosso (The Eye of the Needle–US 1965). 1964 Becket; Volles Herz und Leere Taschen (A Full Heart and Empty Pockets).

CESANA, RENZO

Born: Oct. 30, 1907. Died: Nov. 8, 1970, Hollywood, Calif. (lung cancer). Screen and television actor.

Appeared in: 1950 A Lady without a Passport; Stromboli. 1951 Mark of the Renegade; Try and Get Me. 1952 California Conquest. 1959 For the First

Time; The Naked Maja. 1960 Fast and Sexy. 1961 Francis of Assisi. 1965 The Art of Love. 1966 Three on a Couch.

CESAR, M.

Died: Sept. 1921. Screen actor.

CHABRIER, MARCEL

Born: 1888, France. Died: Aug. 18, 1946, Piedmont, Canada (drowned). Screen, stage, radio actor and painter.

Appeared in: 1943 Le Pere Chopin.

CHADWICK, HELENE

Born: Nov. 25, 1897, Chadwick, N.Y. Died: Sept. 4, 1940, Los Angeles, Calif. (injuries from fall). Stage and screen actress. Divorced from film director William Wellman (dec. 1975). Entered films in 1916.

Appeared in: 1919 Heartsease. 1920 Scratch My Back; Cupid; The Cowpuncher; Long Arm of Mannister; The Cup of Fury. 1921 The Sin Flood; From the Ground Up; Godless Men; The Old Nest; Dangerous Curve Ahead; Made in Heaven. 1922 Yellow Men and Gold; Glorious Fool; Dust Flower; Brothers under the Skin. 1923 Quicksands; Gimme. 1924 Her Own Free Will; Reno; The Border Legion; Her Dark Swan; Love of Women; The Masked Dancer; The Naked Truth; Trouping with Ellen; Why Men Leave Home. 1925 Re-Creation of Brian Kent; The Woman Hater; The Golden Cocoon. 1926 Dancing Days; Hard Boiled; Pleasures of the Rich; The Still Alarm. 1927 The Rose of Kildare; The Bachelor's Baby; Stage Kisses; Stolen Pleasures. 1928 Modern Mothers; Say It with Sables; Women Who Dare. 1929 Father and Son; Confessions of a Wife. 1930 Men Are Like That. 1931 Hell Bound. 1935 Mary Burns, Fugitive.

CHALIAPIN, FEODOR

Born: Feb. 13, 1873, Kazan-Kazan, Russia. Died: Apr. 12, 1938, Paris, France (anemia brought on by kidney ailment). Screen, opera and vaudeville actor. Father of actor Feodor Chaliapin, Jr.

Appeared in: 1933 Don Quixote.

CHALMERS, THOMAS

Born: Oct. 20, 1890, New York, N.Y. Died: June 12, 1966, Greenwich, Conn. Screen, opera, television, radio actor, film director and producer of industrial and documentary films.

Appeared in: 1923 Puritan Passions. 1927 Blind Alleys. 1938 The Rivers (narr.). 1961 Romanoff and Juliet. 1963 All the Way Home. 1964 The Outrage.

CHALZEL, LEO

Born: 1901. Died: July 16, 1953, Westport, Conn. (heart ailment). Screen, stage, vaudeville and television actor.

Appeared in: 1934 Men in White; Come on Marines.

CHAMBERLIN, FRANK

Born: 1870. Died: Aug. 29, 1935, Los Angeles, Calif. Cowboy screen actor and songwriter.

CHAMBERLIN, RILEY C.

Born: 1854, Grand Rapids, Mich. Died: Jan. 24, 1917, New Rochelle, N.Y. Stage and screen actor. Entered films with Thanhouser in 1912.

Appeared in: 1912 Why Tom Signed the Pledge; Old Dr. Judd; Conductor 786; Now Watch the Professor; Please Help the Pope; Six-Cylinder Elopement; Dottie the Dancer; In a Garden; Brains vs. Brawn. 1913 Rosie's Revenge; Waiting for Hubby; The Official Goat Protector; What Might have Been; How Philmy Won his Sweetheart. 1914 Mrs. Pinkhurst's Proxy; Coals of Fire; The Strategy of Conductor 786; The Benovolence of Conductor 786; The Touch of a Little Hand. 1915 Capers of College Chaps; Film Favorite's Finish; Madame Blanche—Beauty Doctor; Tracked Through the Snow; P. Henry Jenkins and Mars; Freddie Fink's Flirtation; Three Roses; Truly Rural Types; Help! Help!; That Poor Damp Cow; Biddy Brady's Birthday Coos; The Car Conductor; Simon's Swimming Soul-Mate; The Dead Man's Keys; When William's Whiskers Worked; The Conductor's Classy Chassis; Clarence Cheats at Croquet; Una's Useful Uncle; Cousin Clare's Cook Book; Bing-Bang Brothers; Tille the Terrible Typist; The Dog Catcher's Bride; The Actor and the Rube. 1916 Ruining Randall's Reputation; The Optimistic Oriental Occults; The Sailor's Smiling Spirit; Dad's Darling Daughters; Lucky Larry's Lady Love; Snow Storm and Sunshine; Grace's Gorgeous Gown; Maud Muller Modernized; Theodore's Terrible Thirst; Perkins' Peace Party; The Kiddie's Captain Kidd; Politickers; Prudence the Pirate; Doughnuts.

CHAMBERS, J. WHEATON

Born: 1888. Died: Jan. 31, 1958, Hollywood, Calif. Screen and stage actor. Entered films in 1929.

Appeared in: 1940 Drums of Fu Manchu. 1942 Reap the Wild Wind; Even as I.O.U. (short); The Wife Takes a Flyer; They All Kissed the Bride. 1943 This Land Is Mine. 1944 The Falcon out West; Tall in the Saddle. 1945 The Clock; That's the Spirit; Marshal of Laredo. 1946 South of Monterey; People Are

Funny. **1947** Crime Doctor's Gamble. **1949** Deputy Marshal; I Can't Remember (short); Not Wanted; Mississippi Rhythm. **1950** Baron of Arizona; Between Midnight and Dawn. **1951** The Prowler; The Well; The Cimarron Kid; The Day the Earth Stood Still. **1952** Wagons West; Slaves of Babylon. **1954** The Big Chase. **1956** The Peacemaker.

CHAMBERS, MARGARET
Died: Oct. 6, 1965, Hollywood, Calif. Screen actress.

Appeared in: **1929** Woman to Woman.

CHAMBERS, MARIE
Born: 1889. Died: Mar. 21, 1933, Paris, France. Screen and stage actress.

Appeared in: **1925** That Royal Girl.

CHAMBERS, RALPH
Born: 1892. Died: Mar. 10, 1968. Screen actor.

Appeared in: **1924** Another Scandal. **1957** The Pajama Game.

CHAN, MRS. PON Y.
Born: 1870. Died: Apr. 1, 1958, Hollywood, Calif. Screen character actress.

CHANCE, ANNA
Born: Oct. 25, 1884, Oxford, Md. Died: Sept. 11, 1943, Hollywood, Calif. Screen, stage and vaudeville actress. Married to actor Charles Grapewin (dec. 1956) with whom she appeared in Christie Comedies. Entered films in 1929.

Appeared in: **1929** Jed's Vacation; Ladies' Choice; That Red Headed Hussy. Prior to 1930 was in The Wanderlust (short).

CHANCE, FRANK (Frank Leroy Chance)
Born: Sept. 19, 1879, Fresno, Calif. Died: Sept. 14, 1924. Professional baseball player and screen actor.

Appeared in: **1913** Baseball's Peerless Leader.

CHANDLER, ANNA
Born: 1887. Died: July 10, 1957, El Sereno, Calif. Screen, vaudeville actress and singer.

Appeared in: **1928** Popular Songs (short). **1932** The Big Broadcast. **1942** Tennessee Johnson.

CHANDLER, HELEN
Born: Feb. 1, 1906, Charleston, S.C. Died: Apr. 30, 1965, Hollywood, Calif. (following surgery). Stage and screen actress. Divorced from actor Branwell Fletcher and writer Cyril Hume.

Appeared in: **1927** The Joy Girl; The Music Master. **1929** Salute; Mother's Boy; The Sky Hawk. **1930** Outward Bound; Rough Romance; Mother's Cry. **1931** Fanny Foley Herself; Daybreak; Salvation Nell; The Last Flight; A House Divided; Dracula. **1932** Cock of the Air; Vanity Street; Behind Jury Doors. **1933** Goodbye Again; Alimony Madness; Dance Hall Hostess; The Worst Woman in Paris?; Christopher Strong. **1934** Long Lost Father; Lover Divine; Midnight Alibi; Unfinished Symphony. **1935** Radio Parade of 1935; It's a Bet. **1938** Mr. Boggs Steps Out.

CHANDLER, JAMES ROBERT
Born: 1860. Died: Mar. 17, 1950, East Islip, N.Y. Stage and screen actor.

Appeared in: **1921** Home Stuff. **1925** Hurricane Horseman. **1927** Hawk of the Hills (serial). **1928** Quick Triggers. **1929** Hawk of the Hills (rerelease of 1927 serial as a feature film).

CHANDLER, JEFF (Ira Grossel)
Born: Dec. 1918, Brooklyn, N.Y. Died: June 17, 1961, Culver City, Calif. (blood poisoning following surgery). Screen, stage and radio actor.

Appeared in: **1947** Johnny O'Clock; The Invisible Wall; The Roses Are Red. **1949** Sword in the Desert; Mr. Belvedere Goes to College; Abandoned. **1950** Deported; Two Flags West; Broken Arrow. **1951** The Iron Man; The Bird of Paradise; Flame of Araby; Smuggler's Island. **1952** The Battle at Apache Pass; Red Ball Express; Yankee Buccaneer; Meet Danny Wilson (unbilled); Because of You. **1953** East of Sumatra; The Great Sioux Uprising; War Arrows. **1954** The Sign of the Pagan; Taza, Son of Cochise (unbilled); Yankee Pasha. **1955** Foxfire; Female on the Beach; The Spoilers. **1956** Away All Boats; Pillars of the Sky; Toy Tiger. **1957** Jeanne Eagles; The Tattered Dress; Drango; Pay the Devil. **1958** The Lady Takes a Flyer; Raw Wind in Eden. **1959** Ten Seconds to Hell; Stranger in My Arms; The Jayhawkers; Thunder in the Sun. **1960** A Story of David; The Plunderers. **1961** Mad Dog Coll; Return to Peyton Place. **1962** Merrill's Marauders.

CHANEY, FRANCES (Frances Cleveland Bush aka CLEVA CREIGHTON)
Born: 1889, Oklahoma. Died: Nov. 21, 1967, Sierra Madre, Calif. (stroke). Stage and screen actress. Divorced from actor Lon Chaney, Sr. (dec. 1930) and mother of Lon Chaney, Jr. (dec. 1973).

Appeared in: **1950** The Underworld Story (aka The Whipped).

CHANEY, LON, JR. (Creighton T. Chaney)
Born: Feb. 10, 1905, Oklahoma City, Okla. Died: July 12, 1973, San Clemente, Calif. Screen, stage and television actor. Son of actor Lon Chaney (dec. 1930) and actress Frances Chaney (dec. 1967). Married to model Patsy Beck. Entered films in 1932 as a stuntman.

Appeared in: **1932** Bird of Paradise; Girl Crazy. **1933** Son of the Border; The Three Musketeers (serial); Lucky Devils; The Last Frontier (serial); Scarlet River. **1934** Girl O'My Dreams; Sixteen Fathoms Deep; The Life of Vergie Winters. **1935** Accent on Youth; Captain Hurricane; Hold 'Em Yale; Shadow of Silk Lennox; The Marriage Bargain; Scream in the Night. **1936** Ace Drummond (serial); The Singing Cowboy; Rhythm on the Range; Undersea Kingdom (serial); Killer at Large. **1937** The Old Corral; Life Begins in College; Angel's Holiday; Wild and Woolly; Midnight Taxi; Wife, Doctor and Nurse; Charlie Chan on Broadway; Secret Agent X-9 (serial); The Lady Escapes; Love and Hisses; One Mile from Heaven; Second Honeymoon; That I May Live; City Girl; Slave Ship; Born Reckless; Thin Ice. **1938** Mr. Moto's Gamble; Passport Husband; Road Demon; Josette; Alexander's Ragtime Band; Straight, Place and Show; Walking Down Broadway; Submarine Patrol; Speed to Burn; Happy Landing. **1939** Jesse James; Union Pacific; Frontier Marshal; Charlie Chan in City in Darkness; Of Mice and Men. **1940** One Million B.C.; Northwest Mounted Police. **1941** Man-Made Monster (aka The Electric Man); Billy the Kid; Badlands of Dakota; The Wolf Man; Too Many Blondes; San Antonio Rose; Riders of Death Valley (serial). **1942** North of the Klondike; The Ghost of Frankenstein; The Mummy's Tomb; The Overland Mail (serial). **1943** Crazy House; Frankenstein Meets the Wolf Man; Son of Dracula; Frontier Badmen; Calling Dr. Death; Eyes of the Underworld. **1944** Ghost Catchers; Weird Woman; Cobra Woman; The Mummy's Ghost; Dead Man's Eyes; Follow the Boys; The Mummy's Curse. **1945** House of Frankenstein; Here Come the Co-Eds; The Frozen Ghost; Strange Confession; The Daltons Ride Again; House of Dracula; Pillow of Death. **1947** My Favorite Brunette. **1948** Abbott and Costello Meet Frankenstein; Albuquerque; 16 Fathoms Deep (rerelease of 1934 film); The Counterfeiters. **1949** There's a Girl in My Heart; Captain China. **1950** Once a Thief. **1951** Inside Straight; Only the Valiant; Behave Yourself; Flame of Araby; Bride of the Gorilla. **1952** Thief of Damascus; High Noon; Springfield Rifle; The Black Castle; The Bushwackers. **1953** A Lion in the Streets; Raiders of the Seven Seas. **1954** The Black Pirates; The Boy from Oklahoma; Jivaro; Casanova's Big Night; Passion; The Big Chase. **1955** Big House U.S.A.; Not as a Stranger; I Died a Thousand Times; The Indian Fighter; The Silver Star. **1956** Manfish; Pardners; The Black Sleep; The Indestructible Man; Daniel Boone—Trail Blazer. **1957** Cyclops. **1958** Money, Women and Guns; The Defiant Ones. **1959** La Casa del Terror (aka Face of the Screaming Werewolf—US 1965); The Alligator People; No. 13 Demon Street (aka The Devil's Messenger—US 1962). **1961** Rebellion in Cuba (aka Chivato). **1963** The Haunted Palace. **1964** Witchcraft; Stage to Thunder Rock; Law of the Lawless (aka Invitation to a Hanging and The Day of the Hanging); Long Rifle and the Tomahawk; The Pathfinder and the Mohicans. **1965** Black Spurs; Young Fury; Town Tamer. **1966** Johnny Reno; Apache Uprising. **1967** Dr. Terror's Gallery of Horrors (aka The Blood Suckers and Return from the Past); Welcome to Hard Times; Hillbillys in a Haunted House; The Vulture. **1968** Spider Baby (aka Cannibal Orgy, or The Maddest Story Ever Told and The Liver Eaters); Buckskin (aka The Frontiersman). **1969** Fireball Jungle (aka Jungle Terror). **1971** Dracula vs. Frankenstein.

CHANEY, LON, SR. (Alonzo Chaney)
Born: Apr. 1, 1883, Colorado Springs, Colo. Died: Aug. 26, 1930, Los Angeles, Calif. Screen, stage actor, film director, screenwriter and stage producer. Father of actor Lon Chaney, Jr. (dec. 1973). Divorced from actress Frances Chaney (aka Cleva Creighton) (dec. 1967).

Appeared in: **1913** Poor Jake's Demise; The Sea Urchin; The Trap; Almost an Actress; Back to Life; Red Margaret, Moonshiner; Bloodhounds of the North. **1914** The Lie; The Honor of the Mounted; Remember Mary Magdalen; Discord and Harmony; The Menace to Carlotta; The Embezzler; The Lamb, the Woman, the Wolf; The End of the Feud; The Tragedy of Whispering Creek; The Unlawful Trade; The Forbidden Room; The Old Cobbler; A Ranch Romance; Her Grave Mistake; By the Sun's Rays; The Oubliette; The Higher Law; A Miner's Romance; Her Bounty; The Pipes of Pan; Richelieu; Virtue Is Its Own Reward; Her Life's Story; Lights and Shadows; The Lion, the Lamb, the Man; A Night of Thrills; Her Escape; Where the Forest Ends. **1915** The Sin of Olga Brandt; Star of the Sea; Threads of Fate; The Measure of a Man; When the Gods Played a Badger Game; Such is Life; Where the Forest Ends; All For Peggy; The Desert Breed; Outside the Gates; The Grind; Maid of the Mist; The Girl of the Night; The Stool Pigeon; An Idyll of the Hills; For Cash; The Stronger Mind; The Oyster Dredger; Steady Company; The Violin Maker; The Trust; Bound on the Wheel; Mountain Justice; Quits; The Chimney's Secret; The Pine's Revenge; The Fascination of the Fleur de Lis; Alas and Alac; A Mother's Atonement; Lon of the Lone Mountain; The Millionaire Paupers; Father and the Boy; Under a Shadow; Stronger Than Death. **1916** The Grip of Jealousy; Dolly's Scoop; Tangled Hearts; The Gilded Spider; Bobbie of the Ballet; Grasp of Greed; The Mark of Cain; If My Country Should Call; Place Beyond the Winds; Felix on the Job; The Price of Silence; The Piper's Price. **1917** Hell Morgan's Girl; The Mask of Love; The Girl in the Checkered Coat; The Flashlight Girl; A Doll's House; Fires of Rebellion; Vengeance of the West; The Rescue; Triumph; Pay Me; The Empty Gun; Anything Once; Bondage; The Scarlet Car. **1918** The Grand Passion; Broadway Love; The Kaiser, the Beast of Berlin; Fast Company; A Broadway Scandal; That Devil Bateese; The Talk of the Town; Riddle Gawne; Danger—Go Slow. **1919** The Wicked Darling; The False Faces; A Man's Country; Paid in Advance; The Miracle Man; When Bearcat Went Dry; Victory. **1920** Daredevil Jack; Treasure Island; The Gift Supreme; Nomads of the North; The Penalty. **1921** Outside the Law; The Ace of Hearts; Bit of Life; For Those We Love; The Night Rose. **1922** The Trap; Quincy Adams Sawyer; Shadows; A Blind Bargain; Flesh and Blood; Voices of the City; The Light in the Dark; Oliver Twist. **1923** The Hunchback of Notre Dame; The Shock; All the Brothers Were Valiant; While Paris Sleeps. **1924** He Who Gets Slapped; The Next Corner. **1925** The Phantom of the Opera; The Tower of Lies; The Monster; The Unholy Three. **1926** The Black Bird; The Road to Mandalay; Tell It to the Marines. **1927** Mr. Wu; The Unknown; Mockery; London After Midnight. **1928** The Big City; Laugh, Clown, Laugh; While the City Sleeps; West of Zanzibar. **1929** The Thunder; Where East Is East. **1930** The Unholy Three (and 1925 version).

CHANEY, NORMAN "CHUBBY"

Born: Jan. 18, 1918, Baltimore, Md. Died: May 30, 1936, Baltimore, Md. (glandular trouble). Screen actor. Entered the "Our Gang" series in 1926 and appeared in part of Joe Cobb until he outgrew his role in 1934.

Appeared in: **1929** The following shorts: Railroadin'; Lazy Days; Boxing Days; Moan and Groan. **1930** The following shorts: Shivering Shakespeare; The First Seven Years; When the Wind Blows; Bear Shooters; A Tough Winter; Pups Is Pups; Teacher's Pet; School's Out. **1931** The following shorts: Helping Grandma; Love Business; Little Daddy; Bargain Days; Fly My Kite; The Stolen Jools (short).

CHAPIN, ALICE

Born: 1858. Died: July 6, 1934 (injuries from a fall). Stage and screen actress.

Appeared in: **1921** Anne of Little Smoky. **1924** Argentine Love; Daughters of the Night; Manhattan; Youth for Sale. **1925** The Crowded Hour; The Pearl of Love.

CHAPIN, BENJAMIN (Benjamin Chester Chapin)

Born: 1875. Died: June 2, 1918, New York, N.Y. (tuberculosis). Screen actor. Famous for his Abraham Lincoln impersonation.

Appeared in: **1917** The Lincoln Cycle films including: My Mother; My Father; Myself; The Call to Arms.

CHAPLIN, CHARLES, JR.

Born: 1925, Beverly Hills, Calif. Died: Mar. 20, 1968, Hollywood, Calif. (blood clot). Screen, stage and television actor. Son of actor Charles Chaplin and actress Lita Grey Chaplin.

Appeared in: **1952** Limelight. **1954** Follow the Hunter; Fangs of the Wild. **1958** High School Confidential. **1959** Night of the Quarter Moon; The Beat Generation; Girls' Town; The Big Operator.

CHAPLIN, SYDNEY

Born: Mar. 17, 1885, Capetown, South Africa. Died: Apr. 16, 1956, Nice, France. Screen, stage actor and film producer. Half brother of actor Charles Chaplin. Entered films with Sennett.

Appeared in: **1914** Fatty's Wine Party; Tillie's Punctured Romance; Gussle, the Golfer (in which he appeared as "Gussle" in the series). **1915** Hushing the Scandal (reissued as Friendly Enemies); A Steel Rolling Mill; The United States Army in San Francisco; Giddy, Gay and Ticklish (aka A Gay Lothario); That Springtime Feeling; Gussle's Day of Rest; Gussle's Wayward Path; Gussle Rivals Jonah; Gussle's Backward Way; Gussle Tied to Trouble; A Lover's Lost Control (aka Looking Them Over); A Submarine Pirate. **1918** Shoulder Arms; A Dog's Life. **1921** King, Queen, Joker. **1922** Pay Day. **1923** Her Temporary Husband; The Rendezvous; The Pilgrim. **1924** The Perfect Flapper; Galloping Fish. **1925** The Man on the Box; Charley's Aunt. **1926** Oh, What a Nurse; The Better 'Ole. **1927** The Missing Link. **1928** A Little Bit of Fluff; The Fortune Hunter. **1955** Land of the Pharaohs. **1963** Thirty Years of Fun (doc.).

CHAPMAN, BLANCHE

Born: 1851, Covington, Ky. Died: June 7, 1941, Rutherford, N.J. Screen, stage and radio actress. Appeared in silents and talking films.

CHAPMAN, EDYTHE

Born: Oct. 8, 1863, Rochester, N.Y. Died: Oct. 15, 1948, Glendale, Calif. Stage and screen actress. Married to actor James Neill (dec. 1931).

Appeared in: **1916** Oliver Twist. **1917** The Little American; The Evil Eye. **1919** Everywoman. **1920** Huckleberry Finn; Double Dyed Deceiver. **1921** Alias Ladyfingers; Ladyfingers; Bits of Life; The Night Rose; Bunty Pulls the Strings; Dangerous Curves Ahead; Just Out of College; One Wild Week; A Tale of Two Worlds; A Wife's Awakening. **1922** Manslaughter; Beyond the Rocks; Her Husband's Trademark; Youth to Youth; My American Wife; North of the Rio Grande; The Sleepwalker; Saturday Night; Tailor-Made Man. **1923** The Ten Commandments; Divorce; The Miracle Makers; The Girl I Loved; Hollywood. **1924** Chastity; Broken Barriers; Worldly Goods; The Breaking Point; Daugh-

ters of Pleasure; The Shadow of the East; The Wise Virgin. **1925** Lightnin'; Soul Mates; Classified; Havoc; The Pride of the Force; Daddy's Gone A-Hunting; In the Name of Love; Lazybones; Learning to Love. **1926** Faithful Wives; The Runaway; Three Faces East; One Minute to Play. **1927** King of Kings; American Beauty; The Student Prince in Old Heidelberg; The Crystal Cup; Naughty but Nice. **1928** Man Crazy; Happiness Ahead; Shepherd of the Hills; The Count of Ten; Love Hungry; Three Week Ends; The Little Yellow House; Sally's Shoulders. **1929** Twin Beds; Synthetic Sin; The Idle Rich. **1930** Double Cross Roads; Take the Heir; Navy Blues; Up the River; Man Trouble.

CHAPMAN, THOMAS H. (Maj. Gen.)

Born: 1896. Died: June 7, 1969, Boerne, Tex. Screen actor and pilot.

Appeared in: **1927** Wings (flew the plane in Buddy Rogers' role).

CHARBENEAU, OSCAR

Died: Sept. 1915, Los Angeles, Calif. (killed while on film location). Screen actor.

CHARLESON, MARY

Born: May 18, 1893, Dunganon, Ireland. Died: Dec. 3, 1961, Woodland Hills, Calif. Stage and screen actress. Married to actor Henry B. Walthall (dec. 1936).

Appeared in: **1912** Bill Wilson's Gal; When California Was Young; The Spirit of the Range; Timid May; Natoosa. **1913** A Bit of Blue Ribbon; The Winning Hand; Matrimonial Maneuvers; The Whispered Word; A Corner in Crooks; The Two Brothers; The Transition; The Actor; Bedelia Becomes a Lady; After the Honeymoon; The Silver Skull; A Matter of Matrimony; The Deceivers; The Spell. **1914** Etta of the Footlights; Iron and Steel; The Acid Test; The Honeymooners; Her Great Scoop (aka Her Biggest Scoop); The Barnes of New York; The Evil Men Do; The Education of Aunt Georgiana; Dr. Smith's Baby. **1915** The Raven; Road of Strife (serial); What Happened to Jones?; The Iron Hand of Law; The Sacrifice; The Call of Motherhood; Polly of the Pots and Pans; Think, Mothers; Sealed Lips; Tony and Marie; Greater Love; Cutting Down Expenses; When Youth is Ambitious; The Silent Accuser. **1916** Passers By; The Country God Forgot; A Prince Chap. **1917** The Truant Souls; Little Shoes; The Saint's Adventure; Satan's Private Door. **1918** His Robe of Honor; With Hoops of Steel; Humdrum Brown. **1919** The Long Lane's Turning; Upstairs and Down. **1920** Human Stuff.

CHARLESWORTH, JOHN

Born: 1935, England. Died: Apr. 2, 1960, Birmingham, England (suicide). Screen, stage and television actor.

Appeared in: **1951** Scrooge; Tom Brown's Schooldays; The Magic Box (US 1952). **1954** The Horse's Mouth; John of the Fair. **1956** A Question of Adultery (US 1959); Blonde Sinner (aka Yield to the Night). **1957** Yangtse Incident (aka Battle Hell–US). **1959** Blue Peter; The Angry Silence (US 1960); The Man Upstairs.

CHARLOT, ANDRE

Born: July 26, 1882, Paris, France. Died: May 20, 1956, Woodland Hills, Calif. Screen, stage, radio actor, stage producer and manager.

Appeared in: **1942** Here We Go Again; The Falcon's Brother; Arabian Nights. **1943** The Constant Nymph; The Falcon Strikes Back; Above Suspicion; The Fallen Sparrow; The Man from Down Under; They Came to Blow Up America; Melody Parade; The Song of Bernadette. **1944** Action in Arabia; Summer Storm. **1945** Delightfully Dangerous; This Love of Ours; Paris Underground. **1946** Temptation.

CHARON, JACQUES

Born: 1920, Paris, France. Died: Oct. 15, 1975, Paris, France (heart attack). Screen, stage actor, film and stage director.

Appeared in: **1950** The Paris Waltz. **1960** The Would-Be Gentleman. **1962** Cartouche (US 1964). **1963** In the French Style. **1968** A Flea in Her Ear.

CHARRIERE, HENRI

Born: 1907. Died: July 29, 1973, Madrid, Spain (throat cancer). Author and screen actor.

Appeared in: **1974** Popsy Pop.

CHARSKY, BORIS

Born: May 28, 1893, Petrograd, Russia. Died: June 1, 1956, Hollywood, Calif. Stage and screen actor.

Appeared in: **1928** The Red Dance. **1929** Captain Lash.

CHARTERS, SPENCER

Born: 1875, Ducannon, Pa. Died: Jan. 25, 1943, Hollywood, Calif. (suicide—pills and carbon monoxide). Stage and screen actor.

Appeared in: **1923** Little Old New York. **1924** Janice Meredith. **1930** Whoopee (stage and film versions). **1931** Lonely Wives; The Front Page; Traveling Husbands; Palmy Days; The Bat Whispers. **1932** Movie Crazy; Central Park; Hold 'Em Jail; The Match King; The Tenderfoot; Jewel Robbery; The Crooked Circle. **1933** 20,000 Years in Sing Sing; Broadway Bad; So This Is Africa;

Gambling Ship; Female; The Kennel Murder Case. **1934** The Firebird; Wake Up and Dream; The St. Louis Kid; It's a Gift; Million Dollar Ransom; Blind Date; Wonder Bar; Pursuit of Happiness; Fashions of 1934; The Circus Clown; Hips, Hips Hooray; Half a Sinner; Loud Speaker. **1935** $1000 a Minute; Alibi Ike; Murder on a Honeymoon; In Person; The Nut Farm; The Ghost Walks; The Raven; Welcome Home; Don't Bet on Blondes; The Goose and the Gander; Whispering Smith Speaks. **1936** F-Man; Colleen; Postal Inspector; The Farmer in the Dell; The Lady from Nowhere; Love on a Bet; Murder on the Bridle Path; Career Woman; Banjo on My Knee; Preview Murder Mystery; The Moon's Our Home; 'Til We Meet Again; Spendthrift; Don't Get Personal; The Mine with the Iron Door; Mr. Deeds Goes to Town; The Harvester; All American Chump; Libeled Lady; Fugitive in the Sky. **1937** Dangerous Number; Wells Fargo; The Mighty Treve; Girl Loves Boy; Venus Makes Trouble; The Prisoner of Zenda; Behind the Mike; The Hurricane; Four Days' Wonder; Back in Circulation; Fifty Roads to Town; Wife, Doctor and Nurse; Danger—Love at Work; Big Town Girl; Checkers; Pick a Star; Mountain Music; Mr. Boggs Steps Out. **1938** The Joy of Living; Forbidden Valley; Mr. Chump; The Texans; Five of a Kind; In Old Chicago; One Wild Night; Three Blind Mice; Inside Story; Professor Beware; Breaking the Ice; The Road to Reno; Lady Behave; Crime School. **1939** Woman Doctor; I'm from Missouri; Women in the Wind; Young Mr. Lincoln; Second Fiddle; Drums Across the Mohawk; Yes, My Darling Daughter; Topper Takes a Trip; The Covered Trailer; The Flying Irishman; In Name Only; They Made Her a Spy; Two Thoroughbreds; The Hunchback of Notre Dame; Exile Express; They Asked for It; The Under-Pup; Unexpected Father; Jesse James. **1940** Friendly Neighbors; Maryland; The Refuge; Remember the Night; He Married His Wife; Our Town; Alias the Deacon; The Girl from God's Country; The Golden Fleecing; Meet the Missus; Blondie Plays Cupid; Santa Fe Trail. **1941** Moon over Miami; Tobacco Road; Glamour Boy; Petticoat Politics; High Sierra; So Ends Our Night; She Couldn't Say No; The Lady from Cheyenne; Mr. District Attorney in the Carter Case; Midnight Angel; Look Who's Laughing; Man at Large; The Singing Hill. **1942** The Remarkable Andrew; Born to the Heart; The Night Before the Divorce; The Postman Didn't Ring; The Affairs of Jimmy Valentine; Scattergood Survives a Murder; Juke Girl; Pacific Blackout; Yankee Doodle Dandy.

CHASE, ARLINE
Born: 1900. Died: Apr. 19, 1926, Sierra Madre, Calif. (tuberculosis). Screen, vaudeville actress and dancer. Was a Mack Sennett bathing beauty.

CHASE, CHARLEY (Charles Parrott)
Born: Oct. 20, 1893, Baltimore, Md. Died: June 20, 1940, Hollywood, Calif. (heart attack). Screen and vaudeville actor. Under name of Charles Parrott he was a film producer, director and screenwriter. Brother of actor James Parrot (dec. 1939). Entered films in 1912.

Appeared in: **1914** Our Country Cousin; The Knock-Out (reissued as The Pugilist); Mabel's New Job; The Masquerader; Her Last Chance; His New Profession (reissued as The Good-For-Nothing); The Rounders; Dough and Dynamite (reissued as The Doughnut Designer); Gentlemen of Nerve (reissued as Some Nerve); Cursed By His Beauty; Tillie's Punctured Romance. **1915** Love in Armor; Only a Farmer's Daughter; Hash House Mashers; Settled at the Seaside; Love, Loot and Crash; A Versatile Villain; His Father's Footsteps; The Rent Jumpers; The Hunt. **1917** Her Torpedoed Love; Chased Into Love. **1918** Hello Trouble (short). **1919** Ship Ahoy (short). **1920** Kids Is Kids (short). **1923** Long Live the King. **1924** His Wooden Wedding (short). **1925** Appeared in the following shorts: The Rat's Knuckles; Hello Baby; Fighting Fluid; The Family Entrance; Bad Boy; Is Marriage the Bunk; Big Red Riding Hood; Looking for Sally; What Price Goofy; Isn't Life Terrible; Innocent Husbands; No Father to Guide Him; Hard Boiled; The Caretaker's Daughter; The Uneasy Three; His Wooden Wedding. **1927** One Mama Man; The Call of the Cuckoo (short). **1929** Modern Love; You Can't Buy Love!; plus the following shorts: The Big Squawk; Leaping Love; Snappy Sneezer; Crazy Feet; Stepping Out; Great Gobs. **1930** The following shorts: The Real McCoy; Whispering Whoopee; All Teed Up; Fifty Million Husbands; Fast Work; Girl Shock; Dollar Dizzy; Looser Than Loose; High C's. **1931** The following shorts: Thundering Tenors; The Pip from Pittsburgh; Rough Seas; One of the Smiths; The Panic Is On; Skip the Maloo!; What a Bozo!; The Hasty Marriage. **1932** The following shorts: The Tabasco Kid; The Nickel Nurser; In Walked Charley; First In War; Young Ironsides; Girl Grief; Now We'll Tell One; Mr. Bride. **1933** The following shorts: Fallen Arches; Nature in the Wrong; His Silent Racket; Arabian Tights; Sherman Said It; Midsummer Mush; Luncheon at Twelve. **1934** The Sons of the Desert; plus the following shorts: The Cracked Iceman; Four Parts; I'll Take Vanilla; Another Wild Idea; It Happened One Day; Something Simple; You Said a Hateful; Fate's Fathead; The Chases of Pimple Street. **1935** The following shorts: Okay Toots!; Poker at Eight; Southern Exposure; The Four-Star Boarder; Nurse to You; Manhattan Monkey Business; Public Ghost No. 1. **1936** Kelly the Second; plus the following shorts: Life Hesitates at Forty; The Count Takes the Count; Vamp Till Ready; On the Wrong Trek; Neighborhood House. **1937** The following shorts: The Grand Hooter; From Bad to Worse; The Wrong Miss Wright; Calling All Doctors; The Big Squirt; Man Bites Lovebug. **1938** The following shorts: Time Out for Trouble; The Mind Needer; Many Sappy Returns; The Nightshirt Bandit; Pie a la Maid. **1939** The following shorts: Mutiny On the Body; The Sap Takes a Rap; The Chump Takes a Bump; Rattling Romeo; Skinny the Moocher; Teacher's Pest; The Awful Goof. **1940** The following shorts: The Heckler; South of the Boudoir; His Bridal Fright. **1957** The Golden Age of Comedy (documentary). **1960** When Comedy Was King (documentary). **1961** Days of Thrills and Laughter (documentary). **1963** Thirty Years of Fun (documentary). **1965** Laurel and Hardy's Laughing 20's (documentary). **1968** The Further Perils of Laurel and Hardy (documentary).

CHASE, COLIN
Born: 1886. Died: Apr. 24, 1937, Los Angeles, Calif. (paralysis attack). Stage and screen actor.

Appeared in: **1923** Bucking the Barrier; Snowdrift. **1924** The Iron Horse. **1926** Silver Fingers. **1927** King of Kings. **1929** The Air Legion; Big News; The Godless Girl. **1930** Renegades; The Lone Star Ranger. **1935** The Cyclone Ranger; The Vanishing Riders.

CHASE, GEORGE WASHINGTON
Born: 1890, Spokane, Wash. Died: July 29, 1918, Woodhaven, N.Y. Stage and screen actor.

Appeared in: **1915** Between Father and Son. **1916** Four Narratives. **1917** Doing Her Bit; Flame of the Yukon; Flying Colors.

CHASE, HAL (Harold W. Chase)
Born: Feb. 13, 1883, Los Gatos, Calif. Died: May 18, 1947, Colusa, Calif. (kidney ailment). Professional baseball player and screen actor.

Appeared in: **1911** Hal Chase's Home Run.

CHASEN, DAVE
Born: July 18, 1899, Odessa, Russia. Died: June 16, 1973, Los Angeles, Calif. (cancer). Restaurateur, stage, vaudeville and screen actor.

Appeared in: **1930** Rain or Shine. **1935** Millions in the Air; Old Man Rhythm; Warner Bros. shorts. **1937** Arizona Mahoney.

CHATTERTON, RUTH
Born: Dec. 24, 1893, New York, N.Y. Died: Nov. 24, 1961, Norwalk, Conn. Screen, stage actress, film producer, and novelist. Married to stage actor Barry Thomson (dec. 1960). Divorced from actors Ralph Forbes (dec. 1951) and George Brent.

Appeared in: **1928** Sons of the Fathers (film debut). **1929** The Doctor's Secret; Madame X; Charming Sinners; The Dummy; The High Road. **1930** The Laughing Lady; Sarah and Son; The Right to Love; Paramount on Parade; The Lady of Scandal; Anybody's Woman. **1931** Once a Lady; Unfaithful; Magnificent Lie. **1932** The Rich are Always with Us; Tomorrow and Tomorrow; The Crash. **1933** Frisco Jenny; Female; Lilly Turner. **1934** Journal of a Crime. **1936** Dodsworth; Girl's Dormitory; The Lady of Secrets. **1938** The Rat; A Royal Divorce.

CHATTERTON, THOMAS "TOM"
Born: Feb. 12, 1881, Geneva, N.Y. Died: Aug. 17, 1952, Hollywood, Calif. Stage and screen actor.

Appeared in: **1915** American Film Mfg. Co. and Kay-Bee films. **1916** The Secret of the Submarine. **1921** The Price of Silence. **1937** A Fight to the Finish; Sandflow. **1938** Under Western Stars. **1939** Arizona Legion; Rovin' Tumbleweeds. **1940** Covered Wagon Days; The Trail Blazers!; Drums of Fu Manchu. **1941** Outlaws of the Cherokee Trail. **1942** Raiders of the Range. **1943** Santa Fe Scouts. **1947** Smash-Up, The Story of a Woman. **1949** Gun Law Justice; Highway 13.

CHATTON, SYDNEY
Born: 1918, Bolton, England. Died: Oct. 6, 1966, Berkeley, Calif. (coronary). Screen, stage, radio and television actor. Known as "the man of 1,000 voices."

Appeared in: **1938** The Rangers Roundup. **1958** Once Upon a Horse.

CHAUTARD, EMILE
Born: 1881, Paris, France. Died: Apr. 24, 1934, Westwood, Calif. (organic trouble). Screen, stage actor and film director. Entered films in Paris, in 1907.

Appeared in: **1926** Bardely's, the Magnificent; The Flaming Forest; My Official Wife; Broken Hearts of Hollywood; Paris at Midnight. **1927** Blonde or Brunette; Now We're in the Air; Seventh Heaven; Upstage; Whispering Sage. **1928** Love Mart; Lilac Time; Out of the Ruins; Caught in the Fog; The Olympic Hero; Adoration; The Noose; His Tiger Lady. **1929** Times Square; Marianne; South Sea Rose; Tiger Rose; The House of Horrors. **1930** Just Like Heaven; Morocco; A Man from Wyoming; Estrellados (Spanish version of Free and Easy); Contre-Enquete; L'Enigmatique Monsieur Parkes. **1931** Le Petit Cafe; Road to Reno. **1932** Cock of the Air; Blonde Venus; Man from Yesterday; Shanghai Express. **1933** California Trail; The Devil's in Love; Design for Living. **1934** Man of Two Worlds; Wonder Bar.

CHAUVEL, CHARLES E.

Born: 1897. Died: Nov. 11, 1959, Sydney, Australia. Screen actor, screenwriter, film producer and film director. Worked as an extra in Hal Roach comedies during the 1920s.

CHEATHAM, JACK (John Preston Cheatham)

Born: Dec. 28, 1894, Miss. Died: Mar. 30, 1971, La Mirada, Calif. (heart failure). Screen actor.

Appeared in: **1934** Something Simple (short). **1935** Fighting Pilot; Gunners and Guns; His Fighting Blood. **1937** Bank Alarm. **1941** Holt of the Secret Service (serial). **1942** Broadway Big Shot; Men of San Quentin; Quiet Please—Murder.

CHECCHI, ANDREA

Born: Oct. 21, 1916, Italy. Died: Mar. 31, 1974, Rome, Italy (rare virus infection). Screen, stage, television actor and painter.

Appeared in: **1933** 1860 (film debut). **1938** Luciano Serra. **1939** Grandi Magazzini (US 1941); Piccolo Hotel; L'Assedio Dell'Alcazar (Siege of Alcazar). **1940** Ragazza che Dorme; Senza Cielo. **1941** Ore 9 Lezione di Chimica; Via delle Cinque Lune. **1942** Malombra; Giacomo L'Idealista. **1943** Tempesta sul Golfo; La Velle del Diavolo. **1945** Due Lettere; Un Americano in Vacanza. **1946** Le Vie del Peccato; Roma Citta Libera; La Notte Porta Consiglio; L'Ultimo Amore. **1947** Caccia Tragica (Tragic Hunt–US 1948). **1948** Eleanora Duse. **1949** Le Mura di Malapaga (The Walls of Malapaga–US 1950); El Grido Della Terra (The Earth Cries Out). **1950** Atto D'Accusa. **1951** L'Eroe Sono Io; Altri Tempi (Times Gone By–US 1953). **1952** La Signora Senza Camelie. **1953** Amori di Mezzo Secolo; Pieta per chi Cade. **1954** Casa Ricordi (House of Ricordi–US 1956); Tempi Nostri; Siluri Umani. **1955** Operazione Notte; Buonanotte Avvocato. **1956** Il Tesoro di Rommel (Rommel's Treasure–US 1963); I Quattro del Getto Tonante; Parola di Ladro. **1959** Il Nemico di Mia Moglie (My Wife's Enemy–US 1967). **1960** L'Assassino (aka The Lady Killer of Rome–US 1965). **1963** Finche dura la Tempesta (aka Beta Som and Torpedo Bay–US 1964). **1965** Italiano Brava Gente; Made in Italy (US 1967). **1967** Quien Sabe? (aka A Bullet for the General–US 1968). **1968** El Che Guevara (US 1969).

CHEF MILANI (Joseph L. Milani)

Born: 1892. Died: Nov. 30, 1965, San Juan Capistrano, Calif. (auto accident). Television and radio cooking-show host and screen actor.

Appeared in: **1943** The Seventh Victim. **1944** Hollywood Canteen.

CHEFEE, JACK (aka JACK CHEFE)

Born: Apr. 1, 1894, Kiev, Russia. Died: Dec. 1, 1975, Hollywood, Calif. Stage and screen actor.

Appeared in: **1917** Veiled Lady. **1919** Tailor Made Romance. **1921** Who's Who. **1928** Runaway Girls. **1929** Alibi; Madame X; Men Without Women; Redeeming Sin. **1930** Son of the Gods; Her Wedding Night. **1931** Hot and Bothered (short); Lonely Wives; Nice Women. **1932** Last Ride; One Hour with You. **1939** The Flying Deuces. **1940** The Perfect Snob. **1942** Tales of Manhattan. **1943** Dixie Dugan. **1944** Bermuda Mystery; That's My Baby! **1945** It's a Pleasure. **1948** Appointment with Murder. **1951** Double Dynamite (aka It's Only Money); Payment on Demand (aka The Story of a Divorce); Target Unknown; Magic Carpet. **1954** So You Want to Go to a Nightclub (short). **1956** Around the World in 80 Days.

CHEIREL, JEANNE (Jeanne Leriche)

Born: Mar. 18, 1869, Paris, France. Died: Nov. 2, 1934, Paris, France. Screen, stage and vaudeville actress.

Appeared in: **1909** Le bal Noir. **1922** Crainquebille. **1931** Hardi les Gars!; Ma Tante d'Honfleur. **1932** La Petite de Montparnasse. **1933** Les Deux "Monsieurs" de Madame; Touchons du Bois; Le Sexe Faible; Je te Confie ma Femme; Les Surprises du Sleeping. **1934** Le Voyage de Monsieur Perrichon; Miquette et sa Mere; La Jeune Fille d'une Nuit; Les Filles de la Concierge; Le Monde ou l'on S'ennuie.

CHEKHOV, MICHAEL

Born: Aug. 29, 1891, Leningrad, Russia. Died: Sept. 30, 1955, Beverly Hills, Calif. Screen, stage actor, film and stage director. Nephew of author Anton Chekhov.

Appeared in: **1944** In Our Time; Song of Russia. **1945** Spellbound. **1946** Specter of the Rose. **1947** Cross My Heart. **1948** Arch of Truimph. **1952** Holiday for Sinners; The Invitation. **1954** Rhapsody.

CHERKASSOV, NIKOLAI

Born: 1903, Russia. Died: 1966. Screen actor.

Appeared in: **1937** Baltic Deputy; Peter the First. **1938** Ski Battalion. **1939** Friends; Captain Grant's Children; The Man with the Gun; Alexander Nevsky; Lenin in 1918; The Conquests of Peter The Great. **1941** General Suvorov. **1942** Ivan the Terrible Part I (US 1947); In the Name of Life. **1948** Spring. **1949** The First Front. **1950** Ivan Pavlov. **1951** Moussorgsky. **1954** Rimsky Korsakov. **1959** Ivan the Terrible Part II. **1961** Don Quixote.

CHERRYMAN, REX

Born: 1898. Died: Aug. 10, 1928, Le Havre, France (septic poisoning). Stage and screen actor.

Appeared in: **1920** Madame Peacock. **1921** Camille. **1923** The Sunshine Trail.

CHESEBRO, GEORGE (George Newell Chesebro)

Born: July 29, 1888, Minneapolis, Minn. Died: May 28, 1959, Hermosa Beach, Calif. (arteriosclerosis). Stage and screen actor.

Appeared in: **1918** Hands Up (serial). **1920** Wanted at Headquarters; The Lost City (serial). **1921** The Recoil; The Diamond Queen (serial); The Hope Diamond Mystery (serial). **1922** Blind Circumstances; Diamond Carlisle; For Love of Service; The Hate Trail; The Menacing Pact. **1924** Safe Guarded. **1925** Wolf Blood. **1926** Money to Burn; Rustler's Ranch; The Block Signal; Hearts and Spangles; The Mile-a-Minute Man. **1927** Mountains of Manhattan; The Silent Avenger. **1929** Should a Girl Marry?; Handcuffed; Show Boat; Brothers. **1931** Air Police; Sheriff's Secret; First Aid; Sky Spider; Lariats and Six Shooters. **1932** 45 Calibre Echo; Mark of the Spur; Behind Stone Walls; County Fair; Gorilla Ship; Tex Takes a Holiday; Fighting Camp. **1933** Lucky Larrigan. **1934** Mystery Ranch; Rawhide Mail; Fighting Hero; In Old Santa Fe; Mystery Mountain. **1935** Unconquered Bandit; Danger Ahead; Tumbling Tumbleweeds; Wild Mustang; Never Too Late; Man from Guntown; Confidential. **1936** The Lawless Nineties; The Return of Jimmy Valentine; Caryl of the Mountains; The Speed Reporter; Roamin' Wild; Trail Dust; Gallant Defender; Red River Valley. **1937** Borderland; Hills of Old Wyoming; Roarin' Lead; Two-Fisted Sheriff; Springtime in the Rockies. **1938** Outlaws of Sonora; The Purple Vigilantes; The Mexicali Kid; Starlight Over Texas. **1940** Frontier Crusader; Land of Six Guns; Wild Horse Range; Gun Code; The Kid from Santa Fe; West of Pinto Basin. **1941** Trail of the Silver Spurs; Billy the Kid's Fighting Pals; Law of the Wild; The Lone Rider in Ghost Town; The Pioneers; Wrangler's Roost; The Medico of Painted Springs; The Lone Rider Ambushed. **1942** SOS Coast Guard; Perils of the Royal Mounted (serial). **1943** Two-Fisted Justice; Fugitive of the Plains; The Renegade; Black Market Rustlers. **1944** The Drifter; Arizona Whirlwind; Boss of Rawhide; Thundering Gunslingers. **1946** Gentlemen with Guns; Sun Valley Cyclone; That Texas Jamboree; Days of Buffalo Bill; Two Fisted Stranger; Gunning for Vengeance; Texas Panhandle; Overland Riders; The Fighting Frontiersman; South of the Chisholm Trail; Singin' in the Corn; Terror Trail; Landrush; Daughter of Don Q (serial). **1947** Stage Coach to Denver; The Lone Hand Texan; Vigilantes of Boomtown; Over the Santa Fe Trail; West of Dodge City; Wyoming; Song of the Wasteland; Riders of the Lone Star; Law of the Canyon; Black Hills; Return of the Lash; Shadow Valley; The Fighting Vigilantes; Cheyenne Takes Over; Stage to Mesa City; Code of the Plains; Homesteaders of Paradise Valley; Out West (short). **1948** Tornado Range; Black Hills; Check Your Guns; West of Sonora. **1949** Death Valley Gunfighter; Trails End; Desert Vigilante; Challenge of the Range; Renegades of the Sage; Horseman of the Sierra. **1950** Gunslingers; Gunmen of Abilene; Salt Lake Raiders; Hostile Country; Texas Dynamo; Streets of Ghost Town; West of the Brazos; Marshal of Heldorado; Colorado Ranger; Crooked River; Fast on the Draw; Tornado; Lightning Guns; Trail of Robin Hood; Frisco Tornado. **1951** Blonde Atom Bomb (short); Night Riders of Montana; Snake River Desperadoes; Kentucky Jubilee; Cyclone Fury; The Kid from Amarillo. **1952** Montana Territory; Junction City. **1953** Winning of the West. **1954** Pals and Gals (short).

CHESHIRE, HARRY V. "PAPPY"

Born: 1892. Died: June 16, 1968. Screen actor.

Appeared in: **1940** Barnyard Follies. **1942** Hi, Neighbor. **1943** Swing Your Partner; O, My Darling Clementine. **1944** Sing, Neighbor, Sing. **1946** Smooth as Silk; Child of Divorce; Affairs of Geraldine; Traffic in Crime; If I'm Lucky; Sioux City Sue. **1947** The Invisible Wall; Shoot to Kill; Springtime in the Sierras; Sport of Kings; Tender Years; The Flame; Luckiest Guy in the World (short). **1948** Slippy McGee; Black Eagle; 16 Fathoms Deep; Incident; Moonrise; Adventures of Gallant Bess; For the Love of Mary; Racing Luck. **1949** Sand; Riders of the Whistling Pines; It Happens Every Spring; Miss Grant Takes Richmond; I Married a Communist; Fighting Man of the Plains; Brimstone. **1950** County Fair; Girls' School; The Woman on Pier 13; No Sad Songs for Me; Lucky Losers; Lonely Heart Bandits; Chain Gang; The Arizona Cowboy; Square Dance Katy. **1951** Blue Blood; Thunder in God's Country. **1952** Phone Call from a Stranger; The Sniper; Dreamboat. **1954** Fireman Save My Child; Pride of the Blue Grass; Dangerous Mission. **1956** The Boss; The First Traveling Saleslady. **1957** My Man Godfrey; Lure of the Swamp; The Restless Breed. **1960** Let's Make Love. **1961** The Errand Boy.

CHESNEY, ARTHUR

Born: 1882, England. Died: Aug. 27, 1949, London, England. Stage and screen actor. Brother of actor Edmund Gwenn (dec. 1959). Divorced from actress Estelle Winwood.

Appeared in: **1920** The Lure of Crooning Water. **1926** The Lodger. **1931** French Leave. **1933** Fires of Fate. **1934** Sensation; Sorrell and Son. **1936** O.H.M.S. (aka You're in the Army Now–US 1937). **1938** Girl in the Street.

CHESTER, ALMA
Born: 1871. Died: Jan. 22, 1953, Woodland Hills, Calif. Stage and screen actress.

Appeared in: **1931** Beloved Bachelor. **1934** Dude Ranger.

CHESTER, BROCK
Born: 1947. Died: Apr. 28, 1971. Screen actor.

CHEVALIER, ALBERT
Born: Mar. 21, 1861, London, England. Died: July 10, 1923, London, England. Screen, stage, vaudeville actor, playwright, stage, film producer and screenwriter.

Appeared in: **1915** The Middleman; The Bottle; My Old Dutch. **1916** The Fallen Star.

CHEVALIER, MAURICE (Maurice Auguste Chevalier)
Born: Sept, 12, 1888, Menilmontante, France. Died: Jan. 1, 1972, Paris, France (heart attack following kidney surgery). Screen, stage, television actor and writer. Divorced from actress Yvonne Vallee. Nominated for 1929-30 Academy Award as Best Actor in The Love Parade and The Big Bond. In 1958 received Special Academy Award for his contributions to the world of entertainment for more than half a century.

Appeared in: **1908** Trop Credule. **1911** Un Mariee qui se Fait Attendre; La Mariee Reclacitrante; Par Habitude. **1914** La Valse Renversante. **1917** Une Soiree Mondaine. **1921** Le Mauvais Garcon. **1922** Gonzague; Le Match Criqui-Ledoux (short); L'Affaire de la Rue de Lourcine; Par Habitude (and 1911 version). **1928** Bonjour New York! **1929** Innocents of Paris; The Love Parade. **1930** The Big Pond; Playboy of Paris; Le Grande Mere; Paramount on Parade. **1931** The Smiling Lieutenant; Le Petit Cafe; El Cliente Seductor (short); The Stolen Jools (short—aka The Slippery Pearls). **1932** One Hour With You; Love Me Tonight; Toboggan (short—aka Battling Georges); Make Me a Star. **1933** A Bedtime Story; The Way to Love. **1935** Folies Bergere. **1936** The Beloved Vagabond (US 1937); L'Homme du Jour (The Man of the Hour—US 1940); Avec le Sourir (With a Smile—US 1939). **1938** Break the News (US 1941). **1941** Personal Column. **1945** Le Silence est D'Or (Man About Town–US 1947). **1947** The Little Cafe. **1949** Le Roi (aka A Royal Affair–US 1950). **1950** Ma Pomme (aka Just Me); Paris 1900 (doc.). **1953** Un Siecle d'Amour; Schlager Parade. **1955** Cento Anni d'Amour; J'Avais Sept Filles (My Seven Little Sins–US 1956). **1957** Love in the Afternoon; The Happy Road; Rendezvous avec Maurice Chevalier. **1958** Gigi. **1959** Count Your Blessings. **1960** Can-Can; A Breath of Scandal; Pepe; Un, Deux, Trois, Quatre! (narr.; aka Black Tights–US 1962). **1961** Fanny. **1962** In Search of the Castaways; Jessica. **1963** A New Kind of Love. **1964** Panic Button; I'd Rather be Rich. **1967** Monkeys, Go Home! **1970** The Aristocats (sang). **1972** Le Chagrin et la Pitie (The Sorrow and the Pity–documentary). **1976** Singing Under the Occupation (documentary).

CHIEF BLACK HAWK (Elmer Attean)
Died: May 15, 1975. Screen actor.

Appeared in: **1922** Suzanna. **1927** Painted Ponies.

CHIEF JACK
Born: 1877. Died: Jan. 9, 1943, Los Angeles, Calif. Screen and vaudeville actor.

CHIEF JOHN BIG TREE (Isaac Johnny John)
Born: 1865. Died: July 1967, Onondaga Reservation, N.Y. Screen actor. Posed for artist James Fraser for the profile which became the famous Indian head nickel.

Appeared in: **1922** The Primitive Lover. **1923** The Huntress. **1924** The Iron Horse. **1925** The Red Rider. **1926** The Desert's Toll; The Frontier Trail; Ranson's Folly. **1927** Painted Ponies; Winners of the Wilderness; The Frontiersman; Spoilers of the West. **1928** Wyoming. **1929** The Overland Telegraph; Sioux Blood. **1935** The Singing Vagabond. **1937** Hills of Old Wyoming. **1939** Stagecoach; Susannah of the Mounties; Drums Along the Mohawk. **1940** Brigham Young, Frontiersman; Hudson's Bay. **1941** Western Union; Las Vegas Nights. **1947** Unconquered. **1949** She Wore a Yellow Ribbon. **1950** Devil's Doorway.

CHIEF MANY TREATIES (William Hazlett)
Born: 1875. Died: Feb. 29, 1948, Los Angeles, Calif. (heart attack). Screen actor and rodeo performer.

Appeared in: **1937** Drums of Destiny. **1941** Go West Young Lady.

CHIEF NIPO STRONGHEART (Nee-hah-pouw Tah-che-num)
Born: May 15, 1891, Wakima (Indian reservation), Wash. Died: Dec. 30, 1966, Woodland Hills, Calif. Stage and screen actor. Entered films with Lubin Co. in 1905.

Appeared in: **1925** Braveheart; The Road to Yesterday. **1926** The Last Frontier. **1947** Canyon Passage; Black Passage; Black Gold. **1950** The Outriders; Young Daniel Boone. **1951** The Painted Hills; Across the Wide Missouri; Westward the Women. **1952** Lone Star; Pony Soldier. **1953** Charge at Feather Riv-

er; Take the High Ground. **1954** Rose Marie. **1955** Fox Fire; Seven Cities of Gold. **1960** Ten Who Dared. **1963** Savage Sam.

CHIEF STANDING BEAR
Died: Feb., 1939. Screen actor.

Appeared in: **1930** Santa Fe Trail. **1931** Conquering Horde. **1935** The Miracle Rider (serial).

CHIEF THUNDERCLOUD (Victor Daniels)
Born: Apr. 12, 1889, Muskogee, Okla. Died: Nov. 30, 1955, Ventura, Calif. (cancer). Screen, radio actor, singer and rodeo performer. Married to singer/dancer Frances Delmar. Entered films as a stuntman in 1929.

Appeared in: **1935** Rustler's Paradise; The Singing Vagabond; The Farmer Takes a Wife. **1936** Ramona; Silly Billies; The Plainsman. **1937** Renfrew of the Royal Mounted. **1938** The Lone Ranger (serial); The Great Adventures of Wild Bill Hickok (serial); Flaming Frontier (serial). **1939** Geronimo; Union Pacific; The Lone Ranger Rides Again (serial). **1940** Young Buffalo Bill; Hi-Yo Silver; Typhoon; Wyoming; Northwest Mounted Police; Hudson's Bay; Murder on the Yukon. **1941** Western Union; Silver Stallion. **1942** My Gal Sal; Shut My Big Mouth; King of the Stallions. **1944** The Falcon Out West; Black Arrow (serial); Fighting Seabees; Buffalo Bill; "The Trail Blazers" series, incl. Sonora Stage-Coach; An Outlaw Trail. **1946** Romance of the West; Badman's Territory. **1947** The Senator Was Indiscreet; Unconquered. **1948** Blazing Across the Pecos; Renegade Girl. **1949** Ambush; Call of the Forest. **1950** Colt .45; Ticket to Tomahawk; The Traveling Saleswoman; Indian Territory; Davy Crockett—Indian Scout; I Killed Geronimo. **1951** Santa Fe. **1952** Buffalo Bill in Tomahawk Territory; The Half-Breed.

CHIEF THUNDERCLOUD (Scott T. Williams)
Born: Dec. 20, 1898, Cedar, Mich. Died: Jan. 31, 1967, Chicago, Ill. Was great, great, great grandson of Chief Pontiac of the Ottawa Tribe. Screen and radio actor. Portrayed "Tonto" on early Lone Ranger radio program and appeared in numerous western films during the 1930s but should not be confused with Victor Daniels, also known as "Chief Thundercloud."

CHIEF YOWLACHIE (Daniel Simmons)
Born: Aug. 15, 1891, Wash. Died: Mar. 7, 1966, Los Angeles, Calif. (pneumonia). Screen actor.

Appeared in: **1925** Tonio, Son of the Sierras. **1926** Ella Cinders; Moran of the Mounted; Forlorn River; War Paint. **1927** The Red Raiders; Sitting Bull at the Spirit Lake Massacre. **1929** The Glorious Trail; Hawk of the Hills; The Invaders. **1930** The Girl of the Golden West; The Santa Fe Trail. **1940** Winners of the West (serial). **1941** White Eagle (serial). **1942** King of the Stallions. **1947** The Senator was Indiscreet; Red River; The Paleface. **1949** El Paso; Ma and Pa Kettle; Mrs. Mike; The Cowboy and the Indians. **1950** A Ticket to Tomahawk; Cherokee Uprising; Indian Territory. **1951** The Painted Hills. **1952** Buffalo Bill; Son of Geronimo (serial). **1953** The Pathfinder. **1954** Rose Marie; Gunfighters of the Northwest (serial).

CHILDERS, NAOMI
Born: Nov. 15, 1893, Pottstown, Penn. Died: May 9, 1964, Hollywood, Calif. Screen actress.

Appeared in: **1914** The Ageless Sex; The Rose and the Thorn; The Wrong Flat. **1915** The Price of Fame; The Juggernaut. **1919** Lord and Lady Algy. **1920** Earthbound. **1921** Hold Your Horses; Courage. **1922** Mr. Barnes of New York. **1923** Success. **1924** Restless Wives; Virtuous Liars. **1934** White Heat; The Mighty Barnum.

CHILDS, MONROE (J. Monroe Rothschild)
Born: 1891. Died: Nov. 7, 1963, Santa Monica, Calif. Screen and stage actor.

CHINNAPPA, P.U.
Died: Sept. 23, 1951. South Indian screen actor.

CHIRELLO, GEORGE "SHORTY"
Born: 1897. Died: Feb. 9, 1963, Honolulu, Hawaii. Screen actor. Formerly Orsen Welles' cook and chauffeur.

Appeared in: **1948** Macbeth.

CHITTISON, HERMAN
Died: Mar. 8, 1967, Cleveland, Ohio. Screen, radio actor and jazz pianist.

Appeared in: French film Pepe Le Moko.

CHIVVIS, CHIC
Born: 1884. Died: Oct. 26, 1963, Hollywood, Calif. Screen actor and stuntman. Entered films during silents.

CHRISTENSEN, BENJAMIN
Born: 1879, Viborg, Denmark. Died: 1959, Sweden? Screen, stage actor, film director and screenwriter. Appeared in U.S., Danish, German and Swedish films.

CHRISTIAN, JOHN
Born: 1884. Died: Aug. 29, 1950, Hollywood, Calif. Screen and stage actor.

CHRISTIANO, ELEANOR IRENE
Born: 1912. Died: 1932. Screen, stage actress and dancer.

CHRISTIANS, MADY
Born: 1900, Vienna, Austria. Died: Oct. 28, 1951, Norwalk, Conn. (cerebral hemorrhage). Screen, stage and radio actress. Appeared in U.S., Austrian, German, French and British films.

Appeared in: 1926 The Waltz Dream. 1929 Slums of Berlin; The Runaway Princess (aka Princess Priscilla's Fortnight). 1930 Because I Love You; The Burning Heart. 1932 Leutnant Warst Du Einst bei den Husaren; Der Schwartze Husar (The Black Hussars). 1933 One Year Later; The Only Girl (aka Heart Song—US 1934); Die Frau von der Man Spricht; Friederike; Das Schicksaal der Renate Langen (The Fate of the Renata Lancer). 1934 Wicked Woman. 1935 Escapade; Ship Cafe; Ich Und die Kaiserin. 1936 Come and Get It. 1937 Seventh Heaven; Heidi; Salon Dora Green (House of Dora Green); The Woman I Love. 1943 Tender Comrade. 1944 Address Unknown. 1948 All My Sons; Letter from an Unknown Woman. Other European films: Cinderella; Glass of Water; Finances of the Archduke; Queen Louise; Duel; Priscilla's Fortnight; Meet My Sister; Dich-halder Gelieb; Mon Amour.

CHRISTIANS, RUDOLPH
Born: 1869. Died: Feb. 7, 1921, Pasadena, Calif. (pneumonia). Screen actor.

Appeared in: 1922 Foolish Wives.

CHRISTIE, GEORGE (George Stuart Christie)
Born: 1873, Philadelphia, Pa. Died: May 20, 1949, Tom's River, N.J. Stage and screen actor.

Appeared in: 1917 Duchess of Doubt; Sowers and Reapers.

CHRISTY, BILL
Born: 1925. Died: Feb. 25, 1946, Los Angeles, Calif. (form of paralysis). Screen and radio actor.

Appeared in: 1944 Song of the Open Road. 1946 Live Wires; Behind the Mask.

CHRISTY, IVAN
Born: 1888. Died: May 9, 1949, Burbank, Calif. (heart attack). Screen actor.

Appeared in: 1921 Rainbow. 1922 Island Wives; The Madness of Love. 1926 Man of the Forest. 1927 Nevada; The Mysterious Rider. 1929 Seven Footprints to Satan. 1930 Son of the Gods.

CHRISTY, KEN
Born: 1895. Died: July 23, 1962, Hollywood, Calif. Screen, stage, vaudeville, radio and television actor.

Appeared in: 1940 Dr. Kildare Goes Home; plus the following shorts: He Asked for It; Tattle Television; Soak the Old; and You the People. 1941 Burma Convoy; Harmon of Michigan; plus the following shorts: I'll Fix That; A Panic in the Parlor; and Whispers. 1942 The Big Shop; Manila Calling; Just Off Broadway; Top Sergeant; Dear! Dear! (short); Bells of Capistrano (short). 1943 He Hired the Boss; Secrets of the Underworld; Gildersleeve's Bad Day; Hit the Ice. 1944 Wilson; Say Uncle (short); The Big Noise. 1948 Scudda Hoo! Scudda Hay! 1949 The Devil's Henchman; Trapped. 1950 No Way Out; Cheaper by the Dozen. 1951 Call Me Mister. 1952 The Model and the Marriage Broker. 1955 My Sister Eileen; Inside Detroit. 1956 Blackjack Ketchum, Desperado; The Werewolf. 1957 Fury at Showdown; Outlaw's Son; Utah Blaine; Escape from San Quentin.

CHURCH, ESME
Born: Feb. 10, 1893, England. Died: May 31, 1972, Quenington, England. Screen, stage actress and stage director.

Appeared in: 1934 Autumn Crocus; Mister Cinders. 1935 Old Roses. 1951 Men of the Sea.

CHURCHILL, BERTON
Born: 1876, Toronto, Canada. Died: Oct. 10, 1940, New York, N.Y. (uremic poisoning). Stage and screen actor.

Appeared in: 1923 Six Cylinder Love. 1924 Tongues of Flame. 1929 Nothing But the Truth. 1930 Five Minutes from the Station (short). 1931 Secrets of a Secretary; Air Eagles; A Husband's Holiday. 1932 The Rich Are Always with Us; Cabin in the Cotton; The Dark Horse; Taxi!; Impatient Maiden; Two Seconds; Week Ends Only; Crooked Circle; Silver Dollar; Big Stampede; Okay America; Laughter in Hell; Washington Parade; Fast Companions; Afraid to Talk; It's Tough to Be Famous; The Mouthpiece; The Wet Parade; The Information Kid; Faith; If I Had a Million; Common Ground; Forgotten Million; American Madness; False Faces; Scandal for Sale; I Am a Fugitive from a Chain Gang; Madame Butterfly. 1933 Ladies Must Love; From Hell to Heaven; Employees' Entrance; The Mysterious Rider; Billion Dollar Scandal; Elmer the Great; Private Jones; Her First Mate; Only Yesterday; The Little Giant; Heroes for Sale; The Big Brain; Golden Harvest; Master of Men; The

Avenger; Doctor Bull; College Coach; So This Is Africa. 1934 The Girl Is Mine; King of the Ritz; Dizzy Dames; Life Is Worth Living; Men of Steel; Men in White; If I was Rich; Alias the Deacon; Bachelor of Arts; Dames; Take the Stand; Kid Millions; Lillies of Broadway; Friends of Mr. Sweeney; Hi, Nellie; Babbitt; The Menace; Half a Sinner; Let's Be Ritzy; Judge Priest; Frontier Marshall; Helldorado; Sing Sing Nights; Red Head; Strictly Dynamite; Bachelor Bait; Murder in the Private Car. 1935 The County Chairman; $10 Raise; Steamboat 'Round the Bend; A Night at the Ritz; Page Miss Glory; I Live for Love; Vagabond Lady; The Rainmakers; Colorado; Speed Devils; The Spanish Cape Mystery. 1936 Colleen; You May Be Next; Three of a Kind; Dimples; Under Your Spell; Bunker Bean; Racing Lady; Parole; The Dark Hour. 1937 You Can't Beat Love; Quick Money; Parnell; The Singing Marine; He Couldn't Say No; Wild and Wooly; Racing Lady; Public Wedding; Sing and Be Happy. 1938 Wide Open Faces; Meet the Mayor; In Old Chicago; Four Men and a Prayer; Kentucky Moonshine; The Cowboy and the Lady; Ladies in Distress; Down in "Arkansaw"; Danger on the Air; Sweethearts. 1939 Daughters Courageous; Should Husbands Work?; Angels Wash Their Faces; Hero for a Day; On Your Toes; Stagecoach. 1940 Brother Rat and a Baby; I'm Nobody's Sweetheart Now; Saturday's Children; Twenty-Mule Team; Turnabout; Cross-Country Romance; The Way of All Flesh; Public Deb. No. 1.

CIANELLI, ALMA
Born: 1892. Died: June 23, 1968, Villa San Pietro, Italy (stroke). Stage and screen actress. Married to actor Eduardo Cianelli (dec. 1969).

CIANELLI, EDUARDO
Born: 1887, Naples, Italy. Died: Oct. 8, 1969, Rome, Italy (cancer). Screen, stage, opera, television actor and playwright. Married to actress Alma Cianelli (dec. 1968).

Appeared in: 1933 Reunion in Vienna. 1935 The Scoundrel. 1936 Winterset (stage and film versions). 1937 Criminal Lawyer; The Marked Woman; Super Sleuth; Hitting a New High; The League of Frightened Men; On Such a Night; Girl from Scotland Yard. 1938 Law of the Underworld; Blind Alibi. 1939 Angels Wash Their Faces; Society Lawyer; Risky Business; Bulldog Drummond's Bride; Gunga Din. 1940 Forgotten Girls; Outside the Three-Mile Limit; Strange Cargo; Zanzibar; Foreign Correspondent; Kitty Foyle; The Mummy's Hand; Mysterious Dr. Satan (serial). 1941 Ellery Queen's Penthouse Mystery; They Met in Bombay; I Was a Prisoner on Devil's Island; Paris Calling; Sky Raiders (serial). 1942 Dr. Broadway; You Can't Escape Me Forever; Cairo. 1943 Flight from Freedom; The Constant Nymph; They Got Me Covered; For Whom the Bell Tolls. 1944 The Mask of Dimitrios; Storm over Lisbon; The Conspirators; Passage to Marseille. 1945 A Bell for Adano; The Crime Doctor's Warning; Incendiary Blonde; Dillinger. 1946 The Wife of Monte Cristo; Joe Palooka, Champ; Heartbeat; Perilous Holiday. 1947 Seven Keys to Baldpate; The Lost Moment; Crime Doctor's Gamble; Miracles Can Happen; I Love Trouble; California. 1948 On Our Merry Way; To the Victor; Rose of Santa Rosa; The Creeper. 1950 Rapture. 1951 The People against O'Hara; Fugitive Lady. 1953 Volcano. 1954 The City Stands Trial; Voice of Silence. 1955 The Stranger's Hand; Mambo; Helen of Troy. 1957 Love Slaves of the Amazon. 1958 Houseboat; Attila; The Monster from Green Hell. 1962 Forty Pounds of Trouble. 1963 Ship of Condemned Women. 1964 The Visit. 1966 Dr. Satan's Robot; The Chase. 1968 The Brotherhood. 1969 Mackenna's Gold; The Secret of Santa Vittoria; Boot Hill.

CIOLLI, AUGUSTA
Born: 1901. Died: Feb. 3, 1967, New York, N.Y. Screen and stage actress.

Appeared in: 1955 Marty. 1960 Fast and Sexy. 1963 Love with the Proper Stranger.

CIRILLO, MICHAEL (Michael Anthony Cirillo)
Born: Apr. 20, 1903, Mass. Died: Aug. 29, 1968, South Pasadena, Calif. (heart attack). Screen and vaudeville actor. Brother of actor Tony Cirillo (dec. 1968).

Appeared in: 1956 Around the World in 80 Days.

CIRILLO, TONY (Anthony John Cirillo)
Born: Nov. 14, 1910, Mass. Died: Nov. 16, 1968, Los Angeles, Calif. (perontonitis). Screen, vaudeville actor and film extra. Brother of actor Michael Cirillo (dec. 1968).

CLAIRE, GERTRUDE
Born: 1852. Died: Apr. 28, 1928, Los Angeles, Calif. Screen and stage actress.

Appeared in: 1919 Stepping Out; Widow by Proxy. 1920 The Cradle of Courage. 1921 The Fox; Hail the Woman; Greater Than Love; Things Men Do; The Sin of Martha Queed; The Invisible Power; Society Secrets. 1922 The Crusader; Human Hearts; Forget-Me-Not; The Adventures of Robinson Crusoe (serial); Environment; The Super-Sex; Ridin' Wild; Oliver Twist. 1923 Itching Palms; Double Dealing. 1924 Daughters of Today; The Heart Bandit; Wine of Youth; Ladies to Board. 1925 The Wedding Song; Romance Road; The Goose Hangs High; Her Sister from Paris; His Majesty, Bunker Bean; The Storm Breaker; Tumbleweeds. 1926 The Little Irish Girl; Out of the West. 1927 We're all Gamblers; Married Alive. 1928 Red Head.

CLAIRE, HELEN
Born: 1906, Union Springs, Ala. Died: Jan. 13, 1974, Birmingham, Ala. Screen, stage, radio and television actress. She was a commentator for Fox Movietone Newsreels 1937-1949.

CLARANCE, ARTHUR
Born: 1883. Died: Oct. 26, 1956, Newcastle, England. Screen, stage, vaudeville and television actor.

CLARE, MADELYN
Born: 1894, Cleveland, Ohio. Died: Sept. 20, 1975, Raleigh, N.C. Screen actress. Married to Thomas Dixon (dec.) who wrote "The Klansman," the source for the film Birth of a Nation.

Appeared in: 1920 The Discarded Woman. 1921 If Women Only Knew; The Misleading Widow. 1922 False Fronts; Young America. 1923 Mark of the Beast; The Supreme Passion.

CLARE, MARY
Born: July 17, 1894, London, England. Died: Aug. 30, 1970, London, England. Stage and screen actress.

Appeared in: 1920 The Black Spider; The Skin Game. 1922 A Prince of Lovers (US 1927 aka The Life of Lord Byron); A Gipsy Cavalier (aka My Lady April). 1923 Becket; Lights of London. 1927 Packing Up. 1928 The Constant Nymph; The Princess in the Tower. 1929 The Feather. 1931 Hindle Wakes; Many Waters; Bill's Legacy; Keepers of Youth; Gipsy Blood (aka Carmen–US 1932); Shadows; The Outsider. 1933 The Constant Nymph (and 1928 version). 1934 Say It With Flowers; Jew Suess (aka Power–US); Night Club Queen. 1935 Lorna Doone; A Real Bloke; The Gov'nor (aka Mister Hobo–US 1936); Line Engaged; The Clairvoyant; The Passing of the Third Floor Back. 1937 The Mill On the Floss (US 1939); Young and Innocent (aka A Girl Was Young–US 1938); The Rat. 1938 The Challenge (US 1939); The Citadel; Climbing High (US 1939); The Lady Vanishes. 1939 A Girl Must Live (US 1941); There Ain't No Justice; Mrs. Pym of Scotland Yard; On the Night of the Fire (aka The Fugitive–US 1940). 1940 Old Bill and Son; The Briggs Family; Miss Grant Goes to the Door. 1941 The Patient Vanishes (US 1947 aka This Man Is Dangerous). 1942 The Next of Kin; The Night Has Eyes (aka Terror House–US 1943). 1943 The Hundred Pound Window. 1944 One Exciting Night (aka You Can't Do Without Love–US 1946); Fiddler's Three. 1946 London Town (aka My Heart Goes Crazy–US 1953). 1947 Mrs. Fitzherbert (US 1950). 1948 Oliver Twist (US 1951); The Three Weird Sisters; My Brother Jonathan (US 1949); Esther Waters. 1949 Cardboard Cavalier. 1950 Portrait of Clare; The Black Rose. 1952 Penny Princess (US 1953); Hindle Wakes (aka Holiday Week–US). 1953 Moulin Rouge; The Beggar's Opera. 1955 Mambo. 1960 The Price of Silence.

CLARE, PHYLLIS
Born: Sept. 12, 1908, London, England. Died: Nov. 1, 1947, England? Stage and screen actress.

Appeared in: 1931 The Gangbuster. 1932 Roadhouse Murder. 1933 Just My Luck; The Love Nest; The Flaw; Aunt Sally (aka Along Came Sally–US 1934). 1934 Romance in Rhythm; Clive of India. 1935 The Stoker. 1936 His Brother's Wife; Hot News. 1938 Convicted; Women are Like That. 1939 Manhattan Shakedown.

CLARENCE
Born: 1960. Died: July 12, 1969, California. Screen and television animal performer. Known as "Clarence the Cross-Eyed Lion."

Appeared in: 1965 Clarence the Cross-Eyed Lion.

CLARENCE, O. B. (Oliver B. Clarence)
Born: Mar. 25, 1870, London, England. Died: Oct. 2, 1955. Screen and stage actor.

Appeared in: 1914 Liberty Hall. 1920 London Pride; The Little Hour of Peter Wells. 1930 The Man from Chicago (US 1931). 1931 Keepers of Youth; The Bells. 1932 Where Is This Lady?; The Barton Mystery; The Flag Lieutenant; Goodnight Vienna (aka Magic Night–US). 1933 Perfect Understanding; Discord; The Only Girl (aka Heart Song–US 1934); A Shot in the Dark (US 1935); I Adore You; Eyes of Fate; His Grace Gives Notice; Soldiers of the King (aka The Woman in Command–US 1934); Falling For You; Excess Baggage. 1934 The Feathered Serpent; Song at Eventide; The Great Defender; Father and Son; The King of Paris; The Silver Spoon; The Double Event; Lady in Danger. 1935 The Scarlet Pimpernel; Barnacle Bill; Squibs; The Private Secretary; Captain Bill; No Monkey Business. 1936 Seven Sinners (aka Doomed Cargo–US); East Meets West; All In; King of Hearts; The Cardinal. 1937 The Return of the Scarlet Pimpernel (US 1938); The Mill on the Floss (US 1939). 1938 It's In the Air (aka George Takes the Air–US 1940); Pygmalion; Old Iron. 1939 Me and My Pal; Black Eyes. 1940 Return to Yesterday; Spy For a Day; Saloon Bar (US 1944); Old Mother Riley in Business. 1941 Quiet Wedding; Inspector Hornleigh Goes To It (aka Mail Train–US); Turned Out Nice Again; Penn of Pennsylvania (aka The Courageous Mr. Penn–US 1944); Old Mother Riley's Circus. 1942 Front Line Kids. 1944 On Approval (US 1945). 1945 A Place of One's Own (US 1949). 1946 Great Expectations (US 1947).

1947 While the Sun Shines; Uncle Silas (aka The Inheritance–US 1951). 1948 Meet Me at Dawn.

CLARENS, HENRY F.
Born: 1860. Died: Dec. 19, 1928, New York, N.Y. Screen and stage actor.

CLARGES, VERNER
Born: 1848. Died: Aug. 11, 1911, New York, N.Y. Screen and stage actor. Entered films with Biograph.

Appeared in: 1909 The Better Way; 1776, or the Hessian Renegades; In Old Kentucky; The Face at the Window. 1910 A Flash of Light; As the Bells Rang Out!; Little Angels of Luck. 1911 His Trust Fulfilled; Swords and Hearts.

CLARIOND, AIME
Born: 1894, France. Died: Jan. 1, 1960, France? Screen actor.

Appeared in: 1935 Sans Famille. 1936 Le Prince Jean. 1937 Lucrezia Borgia. 1938 The Lie of Nina Petrovna. 1939 Boys' School; Katia; Entente Cordiale. 1940 Mayerling to Sarajevo. 1942 32 Rue de Montmartre. 1947 Colonel Chabert; The Blue Veil; Midnight in Paris. 1948 Mlle. Desiree; Monsieur Vincent. 1949 The Wicked Duchess; The Eternal Husband. 1951 My First Love. 1957 Deadlier than the Male. 1958 Nathalie (aka Foxiest Girl in Paris). 1959 The Possessors. 1960 Une Fille Pour L'ete (A Mistress for the Summer–US 1964).

CLARK, ANDREW J. "ANDY"
Born: Mar. 1903, New York, N.Y. Died: Nov. 16, 1960, New Rochelle, N.Y. Screen, stage and vaudeville actor. Entered films with Edison in 1913 and starred in "Andy" series.

Appeared in: 1913 It Wasn't Poison After All; Greedy George; Mr. Newcomb's Necktie. 1914 The Adventures of Andy Clark; Andy Goes on the Stage; Andy the Actor; Andy Plays Cupid; One Touch of Nature; The New Partner; Andy and the Red; Andy Gets A Job; Getting Andy's Goat; Andy Plays Hero; Making A Convert. 1925 The Sporting Chance. 1926 The Shamrock Handicap. 1927 One Round Hogan; Wings. 1928 Beggars of Life. 1929 Rio Rita; The Man I Love. 1930 Hit the Deck.

CLARK, BILL
Died: June 6, 1973 (injuries received in plane crash). Screen actor and stuntman.

Appeared in: 1954 The Wild One; The Robe. 1955 The Tall Men. 1958 The Young Lions. 1959 Day of the Outlaw. 1965 Young Fury.

CLARK, BOBBY (Robert Edwin Clark)
Born: June 16, 1888, Springfield, Ohio. Died: Feb. 12, 1960, New York, N.Y. (heart attack). Screen, stage, vaudeville, minstrel, circus and burlesque actor. Was partner with Paul McCullough (dec. 1936) in comedy team of "Clark and McCullough."

Together they appeared in the following shorts: 1928 Clark and McCullough in the Interview; Clark and McCullough in the Honor System. 1929 The Bath Between; The Diplomats; Waltzing Around; In Holland; Belle of Samoa; Beneath the Law; The Medicine Men; Music Fiends; Knights Out; All Steamed Up; Hired and Fired; Detectives Wanted. 1931 False Roomers; Chesterfield Celebrities; A Melon-Drama; Scratch as Catch Can. 1932 The Iceman's Ball; The Millionaire Cat; Jitters the Butler. 1933 Hokus Focus; The Druggist's Dilemma; The Gay Nighties; Fits in a Fiddle; Kickin' the Crown Around; Snug in the Jug. 1934 Hey, Nanny Nanny; In the Devil's Doghouse; Bedlam of Beards; Love and Hisses; Odor in the Court; Everything's Ducky; In a Pig's Eye. 1935 Flying Down to Zero; Alibi Bye Bye. 1938 Clark appeared without McCullough in The Goldwyn Follies (feature).

CLARK, BUDDY
Died: Oct. 1, 1949, Beverly Hills, Calif. (plane crash). Screen, radio actor and singer. Married to model Nedra Clark. Do not confuse with other actors-entertainers with same name.

Appeared in: 1942 Seven Days' Leave.

CLARK, CHARLES DOW
Born: 1870. Died: Mar. 26, 1959, N.Y. Stage and screen actor.

Appeared in: 1924 The Confidence Man. 1925 Old Home Week. 1930 The Bat Whispers. 1932 Ladies of the Jury; The Half-Naked Truth. 1933 Quiet, Please (short).

CLARK, CLIFF
Born: 1893. Died: Feb. 8, 1953, Hollywood, Calif. (heart attack). Screen, vaudeville and television actor.

Appeared in: 1937 Mountain Music. 1938 Mr. Moto's Gamble; Time Out for Murder; The Patient in Room 18; While New York Sleeps; Inside Story; Kentucky; Cocoanut Grove. 1939 They Made Me a Criminal; Within the Law; Honolulu; It's A Wonderful World; Miracles for Sale; Fast and Furious; Joe and Ethel Turp Call on the President; Young Mr. Lincoln; Missing Evidence; Dust Be My Destiny; Help Wanted (short). 1940 Jack Pot (short); Slightly Honorable; Grapes of Wrath; Double Alibi; Black Diamonds; Honeymoon

Deferred; Three Cheers for the Irish; Cross Country Romance; Stranger on the Third Floor; Wagon Train. **1941** Law of the Tropics; Nine Loves Are Not Enough; Strange Alibi; Washington Melodrama; Manpower; Golden Hoofs; The Wagons Roll at Night. **1942** Kid Glove Killer; Tennessee Johnson; Babes on Broadway; Jail House Blues; Fingers at the Window; Monkey; Who Is Hope Schuyler?; Secret Enemies; Henry Aldrich, Editor; The Falcon's Brother; Army Surgeon; The Mummy's Tomb; Taxi, Mister? **1943** Ladies' Day; The Falcon Strikes Back; The Falcon in Danger; The Falcon and the Co-Eds. **1944** Barbary Coast Gent; The Falcon Out West; In the Meantime, Darling; The Missing Juror. **1947** Bury Me Dead; Buck Private Come Home. **1948** Deep Waters; Trouble Makers; Borrowed Trouble; False Paradise. **1949** Flaming Fury; Home of the Brave; Homicide; Powder River Rustlers; The Stratton Story; Post Office Investigator; Crime Doctor's Diary. **1950** Try and Get It; Vigilante Hideout; The Man; The Cariboo Trail; Gunfighter. **1951** Joe Palooka in the Triple Cross; Operation Pacific; Saddle Legion; The Second Woman; Cavalry Scout; Warpath. **1952** High Noon; The Pride of St. Louis; The Sniper.

CLARK, EDDIE (Edward Clark)
Born: 1879. Died: Nov. 18, 1954, Hollywood, Calif. (heart attack). Screen, stage, television actor and playwright.

Appeared in: **1926** Millionaires; Broken Hearts of Hollywood; Private Izzy Murphy. **1927** Finger Prints; The Gay Old Bird; Sally in Our Alley; Hills of Kentucky. **1928** Marriage by Contract. **1929** Unmasked; Silks and Saddles. **1930** Bitter Friends (short); Carnival Revue (short). **1949** Abandoned; Amazon Quest; Oh, You Beautiful Doll. **1950** Dancing in the Dark; Pretty Girl; A Ticket to Tomahawk. **1951** Little Egypt; Bedtime for Bonzo; Branded; Million Dollar Pursuit; Mr. Belvedere Rings the Bell; Savage Drums; Rhubarb. **1952** Thundering Caravans. **1953** Flame of Calcutta; It Happens Every Thursday; Topeka; Money from Home. **1954** Hell's Outpost. **1955** Crashout.

CLARK, ETHEL (Ethel Schneider)
Born: 1916. Died: Feb. 18, 1964, Hollywood, Calif. Screen, vaudeville and television actress.

Appeared in: **1938** The Headleys at Home.

CLARK, FRANK
Died: Apr. 10, 1945, Woodland Hills, Calif. Stage and screen actor. Do not confuse with actors Frank M. or Frank H. Clark.

CLARK, FRED (Frederic Leonard Clark)
Born: Mar. 9, 1914, Lincoln, Calif. Died: Dec. 5, 1968, Santa Monica, Calif. (liver ailment). Screen, stage, television and radio actor. Married to Gloria Glaser. Divorced from actress Benay Venuta.

Appeared in: **1947** Ride the Pink Horse; The Unsuspected. **1948** Fury at Furnace Creek; Mr. Peabody and the Mermaid; Cry of the Night; Hazard; Two Guys from Texas. **1949** The Younger Brothers; Task Force; Alias Nick Beal; The Lady Takes a Sailor; White Heat; Flamingo Road. **1950** The Eagle and the Hawk; Return of the Frontiersman; The Jackpot; Mrs. O'Malley and Mr. Malone; Sunset Boulevard; Dynamite Pass; Treasure Island. **1951** The Lemon Drop Kid; Hollywood Story; Meet Me after the Show; A Place in the Sun. **1952** Three for Bedroom C; Dreamboat. **1953** The Stars Are Singing; How to Marry a Millionaire; Here Come the Girls; The Caddy. **1954** Living It Up. **1955** How to Be Very, Very Popular; The Court-Martial of Billy Mitchell; Daddy Long Legs; Abbott and Costello Meet the Keystone Kops. **1956** The Solid Gold Cadillac; Miracle in the Rain; The Birds and the Bees; Back from Eternity. **1957** The Fuzzy Pink Nightgown; Joe Butterfly; Don't Go Near the Water. **1958** Mardi Gras; Auntie Mame. **1959** The Mating Game; It Started with a Kiss. **1960** Risate di Gioia (aka The Passionate Thief–US 1963); Bells are Ringing; Visit to a Small Planet. **1962** Hemingway's Adventures of a Young Man; Boys' Night Out; Zotz! **1963** Move Over, Darling. **1964** John Goldfarb, Please Come Home. **1965** Sergeant Deadhead; When the Boys Meet the Girls; Dr. Goldfoot and the Bikini Machine; The Curse of the Mummy's Tomb. **1967** War Italian Style. **1968** The Horse in the Gray Flannel Suit; Skidoo; Eve. **1969** I Sailed to Tahiti with an All Girl Crew.

CLARK, HARRY
Born: 1911. Died: Feb. 28, 1956, New York, N.Y. Screen and stage actor.

Appeared in: **1941** Ice Capades. **1953** Taxi.

CLARK, HARVEY (aka HARVEY CLARKE)
Born: 1886, Boston, Mass. Died: July 19, 1938, Hollywood, Calif. (heart attack). Screen, stage and vaudeville actor. Entered films with New York Motion Picture Co. in 1916.

Appeared in: **1916** The Innocence of Lizette; The Gentle Intruder; The Frame-Up; The Voice of Love; Periwinkle. **1917** New York Luck; Snap Judgment. **1918-20** American Film Mfg. Co. films. **1921** The Kiss; High Gear Jeffrey; Payment Guaranteed; The Servant in the House; Her Face Value. **1922** Don't Shoot; Alias Julius Caesar; The Gray Dawn; Mixed Faces; Money to Burn; Elope If You Must; The Men of Zanzibar; Thelma; The Woman He Loved; Shattered Idols. **1923** In the Palace of the King; The Man Who Won; Brass; Second Hand Love. **1924** Secrets; He Who Gets Slapped; The Man Who Came Back; The Roughnecks. **1925** Havoc; The Arizona Romeo; Blue Blood; The

Man Without a Country; Marriage in Transit. **1926** Black Paradise; The Frontier Trail; The Flying Horseman; The Dixie Merchant; Midnight Lovers; The Cowboy and the Countess; The Silver Treasure; The Palace of Pleasure. **1927** Rose of the Golden West; Get Your Man; Putting Pants on Phillip (short); The Magic Flame; Camille; In Old Kentucky; McFadden's Flats; The Understanding Heart. **1928** A Woman Against the World; Tragedy of Youth; Ladies Night in a Turkish Bath; Floating College; The Toilers; Beautiful But Dumb; The Head Man; The Night Bird; The Olympic Hero. **1929** His Lucky Day; The Rainbow; Seven Keys to Baldpate. **1930** Man Trouble; Going Wild; Anybody's Woman; Up the River; What a Man. **1931** Millie; The Deceiver; Cracked Nuts. **1932** The Big Shot; Red Headed Woman; Down to Earth. **1933** Strictly Personal; West of Singapore; I Love that Man; A Shriek in the Night; Alice in Wonderland; Picture Brides. **1934** Charlie Chan's Courage; Peck's Bad Boy; Countess of Monte Cristo. **1936** Three Godfathers; Grand Jury; Sitting on the Moon; The Singing Cowboy; Empty Saddles. **1937** History Is Made at Night; Dance, Charlie Dance; Dangerous Holiday; It's Love I'm After; Blonde Trouble; Partners of the Plains. **1938** Mother Carey's Chickens; Spawn of the North; What Price Safety (short).

CLARK, HELEN
Born: 1895, New York. Died: Jan. 9, 1974, Los Gatos, Calif. Screen, stage actress and dancer. Married to composer-conductor Frank E. Tours (dec.)

CLARK, IVAN-JOHN
Died: 1967. Screen actor.

CLARK, JOHN J. (aka JACK CLARK)
Born: 1877. Died: Apr. 12, 1947, Hollywood, Calif. Screen, stage actor, film director and stage producer. Entered films with Kalem in 1907.

Appeared in: **1913** In the Power of a Hypnotist; The Wives of Jamestown; Lady Peggy's Escape; When Men Hate; A Daughter of the Confederacy; In the Clutches of the Ku Klux Klan. **1914** Come Back to Erin; Rory O'More; His Brother's Wife. **1915** The Smuggler's Class; The Woman-Hater's Baby. **1927** Pajamas. **1928** Love and Learn. **1929** Howdy, Broadway.

CLARK, JOHNNY
Born: Aug. 10, 1916, Hampton, Iowa. Died: July 3, 1967, Hollywood, Calif. (heart attack). Screen, stage, television actor and composer.

Appeared in: **1941** Las Vegas Nights. **1943** Jive Junction. **1944** Hey Rookie; Weekend Pass; The Sultan's Daughter; Irish Eyes Are Smiling. **1947** The Locket.

CLARK, LES
Born: 1907. Died: Mar. 24, 1959, London, England (heart attack). Screen and vaudeville actor.

Appeared in: **1950** When Willie Comes Marching Home. **1954** The Country Girl; White Christmas.

CLARK, MARGUERITE
Born: Feb. 22, 1887, Avondale, Ohio. Died: Sept. 25, 1940, New York, N.Y. (pneumonia as a result of a cerebral hemorrhage). Stage and screen actress. Entered films with Famous Players.

Appeared in: **1914** Wildflower (film debut); The Crucible; The Pretty Sister of Jose; Gretna Green. **1915** Still Waters; The Prince and the Pauper; The Goose Girl; Morals of Marcus. **1916** Molly Make-Believe; Little Lady Eileen; Miss George Washington; Silks and Satins; Out of the Drifts. **1917** The Seven Sisters; The Amazons; The Seven Swans; Snow White. **1918** Out of a Clear Sky; Rich Man, Poor Man; Uncle Tom's Cabin. **1919** Mrs. Wiggs of the Cabbage Patch; Girls, Come Out of the Kitchen; Widow by Proxy; Luck in Pawn; Three Men and a Girl; Prunella. **1920** All-of-a-Sudden Peggy. **1921** Scrambled Wives.

CLARK, PAUL
Born: 1927. Died: May 20, 1960, Santa Barbara, Calif. (auto accident). Screen, stage and television actor.

Appeared in: **1938** Boy Meets Girl; How to Raise a Baby (short).

CLARK, WALLIS
Born: Mar. 2, 1889, Essex, England. Died: Feb. 14, 1961. Screen actor.

Appeared in: **1932** Hell's House; The Final Edition; Alias the Doctor; Shopworn; Attorney for the Defense; Okay America; My Pal the King; The Night Mayor. **1933** Double Harness; The World Gone Mad; Bureau of Missing Persons; Ever in My Heart; Police Car 17, Lady for a Day; Luxury Liner; They Just Had to Get Married; The Working Man; The Kiss before the Mirror; The World Changes. **1934** Beloved; Massacre; A Woman's Man; I've Got Your Number; It Happened One Night; The Life of Vergie Winters; I'll Fix It. **1935** It Happened in New York; Chinatown Squad; Mutiny on the Bounty. **1936** The Unguarded Hour; Parole; Missing Girls; Come Closer Folks; Great Guy; Easy Money. **1937** The Last of Mrs. Cheyney; I Promise to Pay; Big Business; She Had to Eat; Woman in Distress; River of Missing Men. **1938** The Higgins Family. **1939** Blondie Meets the Boss; Main Street Lawyer; Allegheny Uprising; I Stole a Million; Smuggled Cargo. **1940** The Big Guy. **1941** Penny Serenade; Murder by Invitation. **1942** The Remarkable Andrew; Yankee Doodle Dandy; Gentleman Jim. **1944** Uncertain Glory. **1949** Free for All. **1951** Criminal Lawyer.

CLARKE, BETTY ROSS. *See* BETTY ROSS

CLARKE, DOWNING GEORGE
Born: Birmingham, England. Died: Aug. 1930, New Haven, Conn. Stage and screen actor.

Appeared in: **1921** The Ghost in the Garret; Know Your Men. **1922** When Knighthood Was in Flower. **1923** Human Wreckage. **1924** Sandra; America; Monsieur Beaucaire. **1925** The Fool. **1932** Okay America; Here's George.

CLARKE, GAGE (aka GAGE CLARK)
Born: Mar. 3, 1900, Michigan. Died: Oct. 23, 1964, Woodland Hills, Calif. (lung cancer). Screen, stage and television actor.

Appeared in: **1956** The Bad Seed (film debut); Nightmare. **1957** The Invisible Boy; Fury at Showdown; Valerie. **1958** The Return of Dracula; I Want to Live; The Brothers Karamazov. **1960** Pollyanna; Midnight Lace. **1961** The Great Imposter; The Absent Minded Professor. **1965** The Monkey's Uncle.

CLARKE, GORDON B.
Born: 1907. Died: Jan. 11, 1972, New York, N.Y. (coronary). Screen, stage and television actor.

Appeared in: **1950** Under My Skin. **1954** Paris Playboys. **1956** The Wrong Man. **1960** From the Terrace. **1961** The Hustler; The Last Gunfighter.

CLARKE-SMITH, D. A. (Douglas A. Clarke-Smith)
Born: 1888, Montrose, Scotland. Died: Mar. 12, 1959, Withyham, Sussex, England. Screen, stage and television actor.

Appeared in: **1929** Atlantic. **1931** Peace and Quiet; Bracelets; Shadows; Michael and Mary (US 1932); The Old Man. **1932** Help Yourself; A Voice Said Goodnight; The Frightened Lady (aka Criminal at Large–US 1933); Illegal; White Face; A Letter of Warning. **1933** I'm an Explosive; The Thirteenth Candle; The Good Companions; Sleeping Car; Waltz Time; Follow the Lady; Head of the Family; The Ghoul; Mayfair Girl; The Laughter of Fools; Skipper of the Osprey (short); Friday the Thirteenth; Turkey Time; Criminal at Large; Smithy. **1934** Flat No. 3; A Cup of Kindness; Warn London; Passing Shadows; The Perfect Flaw; Money Mad; Sabotage (aka Menace and When London Sleeps–US); The Man Who Knew Too Much; The Feathered Serpent; Keep It Quiet; Designing Women. **1935** Lorna Doone; Key to Harmony; Royal Cavalcade (aka Regal Cavalcade–US–narration). **1936** Murder by Rope; The Happy Family; Southern Roses. **1937** Cafe Colette (aka Danger in Paris–US); Little Miss Somebody; Splinters in the Air; Dangerous Fingers (aka Wanted by Scotland Yard–US). **1938** Weddings are Wonderful; I've Got a Horse. **1939** Flying Fifty Five. **1951** Quo Vadis. **1952** The Pickwick Papers (US 1953); Something Money Can't Buy. **1953** The Sword and the Rose. **1956** The Man Who Never Was; The Baby and the Battleship.

CLARY, CHARLES
Born: Mar. 24, 1873, St. Charles, Ill. Died: Mar. 24, 1931, Los Angeles, Calif. Stage and screen actor.

Appeared in: **1910** The Englishman and the Girl. **1911** Two Orphans; Maud Muller; How They Stopped the Run on the Bank; Lost in the Jungle; Back to the Primitive. **1912** The Other Woman; The Law of the North; The Last Dance; The Adopted Son; Officer Murray; The Girl at the Cupola; The Coming of Columbus; Sons of the Northwoods; An Unexpected Fortune; When the Heart Rules; The Devil, the Servant and the Man; The Fire-Fighter's Love; The Three Valises; A Detective's Strategy. **1913** The Lesson; The Adventures of Kathlyn (serial). **1914** The Tragedy that Lived; The Woman of It; Her Sacrifice; The Story of the Blood Red Rose; The Carpet of Bagdad. **1915** The Way of a Woman's Heart; The Fortunes of Marian; At the Stroke of the Angelus; His Guiding Angel; A Day that is Dead; Children of the Sea. **1916** Joan the Woman. **1917** DuBarry. **1920** Street Called Straight; Woman in Room 13. **1921** A Connecticut Yankee at King Arthur's Court; Don't Neglect Your Wife; The Hole in the Wall; Opened Shutters; The Sea Lion; Sunset Jones. **1922** The Rosary; The Flaming Hour; Hate; Heroes and Husbands; Rich Men's Wives; Skin Deep; Two Kinds of Women; Very Truly Yours. **1923** The Last Hour; Michael O'Halloran; Money! Money! Money!; Nobody's Money; Prodigal Daughters; Thundering Dawn; Six Days; Cause for Divorce; In the Palace of the King. **1924** Behind the Curtain; The Breath of Scandal; Empty Hands; Flames of Desire; In Fast Company; On Time; The Whispered Name. **1925** An Enemy of Men; The Golden Bed; Jimmie's Millions; The Kiss Barrier; Seven Days; Speed Wild; Super Speed; She Wolves; Three Keys; The Unwritten Law. **1926** Beverly of Graustark; The Auction Block; The Blind Goddess; The Blue Streak; Modern Youth; Red Dice; Satan Town; Thrilling Youth; Whispering Wires. **1927** The Magic Garden; Man Power; Pretty Clothes; See You in Jail; Smile, Brother, Smile; What Price Love; When a Man Loves; His Foreign Wife; King of Kings; Land of the Lawless. **1928** The Big Hop; Jazz Mad; Nameless Men; The Power of the Press; A Woman Against the World. **1929** The Exalted Flapper; Eyes of the Underworld; Sailor's

Holiday; Prisoners; Wolves of the City; Trial Marriage. **1930** Kismet; Lucky Larkin; Night Work.

CLAUDIUS, DANE
Born: 1874. Died: Apr. 26, 1946, Los Angeles, Calif. Screen, stage and vaudeville actor. Entered films approx. 1930.

CLAYTON, DONALD
Born: 1890. Died: Jan. 18, 1964. Screen actor.

CLAYTON, ETHEL
Born: 1884, Champaign, Ill. Died: June 11, 1966, Oxnard, Calif. Stage and screen actress. Entered films in 1909. Divorced from actor Ian Keith (dec. 1969).

Appeared in: **1912** Her Own Money. **1914** Mazie Puts One Over; The Fortune Hunter. **1915** The College Widow; The Great Divide. **1916** A Woman's Way; Oliver Twist. **1919** Pettigrew's Girl; The Woman Next Door; Men, Women and Money; A Sporting Chance; Maggie Pepper. **1921** Sham; City Sparrow; Price of Possession; Sins of Rosanne; Wealth; Beyond. **1922** The Cradle; Exit the Vamp; For the Defense; Her Own Money (and 1912); If I Were Queen. **1923** Can A Woman Love Twice; The Remittance Woman. **1925** Lightnin'; The Mansion of Aching Hearts; Wings of Youth. **1926** The Bar-C Mystery (serial and feature film); His New York Wife; Risky Business; Sunny Side Up. **1927** The Princess on Broadway; The Princess from Hoboken. **1928** Mother Machree. **1930** The Call of the Circus; Hit the Deck. **1932** Thrill of Youth; The All-American; Hotel Continental; Crooked Circle. **1933** Private Jones; Secrets. **1937** Artists and Models; Easy Living; Hold 'Em Navy. **1938** The Buccaneer; Cocoanut Grove; Tom Sawyer, Detective; If I Were King. **1939** Ambush; The Sap Takes a Rap (short).

CLAYTON, GILBERT
Born: Dec. 18, 1860, Polo, Ill. Died: Mar. 1, 1950. Screen and stage actor. Entered films in 1920.

Appeared in: **1920** The Mark of Zorro. **1921** Across the Divide; Habit; The Three Musketeers. **1923** Blood and Sand; When Love Comes. **1924** Main Street; Trilby. **1925** Below the Line. **1926** Partners Again; The Silver Treasure; Ben Hur.

CLAYTON, HAZEL. *See* MRS. MACK HILLIARD

CLAYTON, LOU (Louis Finkelstein)
Born: 1887, Brooklyn, N.Y. Died: Sept. 12, 1950, Santa Monica, Calif. (cancer). Screen and vaudeville actor. Was part of "Clayton and Durante" vaudeville team.

Appeared in: **1930** Roadhouse Nights.

CLAYTON, MARGUERITE
Born: 1894 or 1896 (?), Salt Lake City, Utah. Died: Dec. 20, 1968. Stage and screen actress.

Appeared in: **1912** When Love and Honor Called; Last Round-Up; The Cowboy Coward. **1913** The Doctor's Duty; The Three Gamblers; Why Broncho Billy Left Bear Country; Bonnie of the Hills; The Struggle. **1914** The Promise Land; The Warning; Snakeville's New Doctor; Broncho Billy and the Sheriff; Broncho Billy Puts One Over; Broncho Billy and the Guesser; Broncho Billy— Favorite; A Snakeville Romance. **1915** A Daughter of the City; An Unexpected Romance; The Convict's Threat; Broncho Billy Misled; Suppressed Evidence; A Christmas Revenge. **1916** Is Marriage Sacred?; The Promise Land; Putting It Over; Prince of Graustark. **1917** The Dream Doll; The Clock Struck One; Two-Bit Seats; Star Dust; The Long Green Trail. **1918** Hit-the-Trail Holliday. **1919** The New Moon. **1920** Bride 13 (serial); Pleasure Seekers. **1921** Dangerous Toys; Forbidden Love; The Inside of the Cup. **1922** The Curse of Drink. **1923** Canyon of the Fools; Desert Driven; Men in the Raw; What Love Will Do. **1924** Idle Tongues; The Circus Cowboy; The Dawn of a Tomorrow; Flashing Spurs; The Street of Tears; Tiger Thompson. **1925** Barriers of the Law; Wolf Blood; Straight Through. **1926** The Palm Beach Girl; Sky High Corral; The Power of the Weak. **1927** Twin Flappers. **1928** Inspiration.

CLEARY, LEO THOMAS
Born: 1895. Died: Apr. 11, 1955, Hollywood, Calif. (uremic poisoning). Screen and stage actor.

Appeared in: **1940** You Can't Fool Your Wife. **1949** The Red Menace. **1950** Bells of Coronado; State Penitentiary; Johnny Holiday. **1952** The Price of St. Louis. **1954** The Human Jungle.

CLEARY, PEGGY
Born: 1892. Died: Jan. 10, 1972, Los Angeles, Calif. Screen actress and writer. Appeared in D. W. Griffith films.

CLEGG, VALCE V.
Born: 1888. Died: July 29, 1947, Hollywood, Calif. Screen and stage actor.

Appeared in: **1926** Lucky Spurs.

CLEMENT, CLAY
Born: 1888, Greentree, Ky. Died: Oct. 20, 1956, Watertown, N.Y. Screen, stage and television actor. Entered films approx. 1914.

Appeared in: 1930 Curses (short); Keeping Company (short). 1932 Washington Merry-Go-Round; False Faces; Evenings for Sale. 1933 Tonight Is Ours; Past of Mary Holmes; Second Hand Wife; Hold Me Tight; Bureau of Missing Persons; Son of a Sailor; The World Changes. 1934 I've Got Your Number; Wonder Bar; Journal of a Crime; I Sell Anything; Let's Be Ritzy; The Personality Kid. 1935 Sweet Music; Murder in the Clouds; Don't Bet on Blondes; Dinky; Chinatown Squad; Streamline Express; Confidential; Whipsaw. 1936 The Leavenworth Case; The Leathernecks Have Landed; Heart in Bondage; It Had to Happen; Let's Sing Again; Two Against the World; Nobody's Fool. 1937 Bad Guy; Give Till it Hurts (short); Rosalie. 1938 A Trip to Paris; Arson Gang Busters; Numbered Woman. 1939 Each Dawn I Die; Disbarred; Off the Record. 1940 Passport to Alcatraz; I'm Still Alive.

CLEMENT, DONALD
Born: 1941, Wantagh, N.Y. Died: July 28, 1970, New York, N.Y. (electrocuted). Stage and screen actor.

Appeared in: 1970 Tell Me That You Love Me, Junie Moon.

CLEMENTS, DUDLEY
Born: Mar. 31, 1889, New York, N.Y. Died: Nov. 4, 1947, New York, N.Y. (heart ailment). Stage and screen actor.

Appeared in: 1937 The Outcasts of Poker Flat; You Can't Buy Luck; New Faces of 1937; The Toast of New York; The Big Shot; Hideaway; Too Many Wives; Night Club Scandal; The Woman I Love; Man Who Found Himself; Take the Heir.

CLEMONS, JAMES K.
Born: 1883. Died: June 5, 1950, Hollywood, Calif. Screen and stage actor.

CLERGET, PAUL
Born: 1867, France. Died: Dec. 4, 1935, Paris, France. Screen and stage actor.

Appeared in: 1918 Woman. 1920 My Lady's Garter.

CLEVELAND, ANNA
Born: 1880. Died: Jan. 7, 1954, Manhasset, N.Y. Screen and stage actress.

CLEVELAND, GEORGE
Born: 1883, Sydney, Nova Scotia. Died: July 15, 1957, Burbank, Calif. (heart attack). Screen, stage, vaudeville, television actor, film producer and film director.

Appeared in: 1934 Mystery Line; Blue Steel; City Limits; Monte Carlo Nights; The Man from Utah; Star Packer; School for Girls. 1935 Make a Million; His Night Out; The Keeper of the Bees; The Spanish Cape Mystery; Forced Landing. 1936 I Conquer the Sea; Foolproof (short); Revolt of the Zombies; North of Nome; Don't Get Personal; Rio Grande Romance; Brilliant Marriage; Put on the Spot. 1937 Paradise Express; The River of Missing Men; Boy of the Streets; Swing It, Professor; The Adventure's End. 1938 Rose of the Rio Grande; Romance of the Limberlost; Under the Big Top; Ghost Town Riders; The Port of Missing Girls. 1939 The Sap Takes a Rap (short); Home on the Prairie; Streets of New York; Wolf Call; Stunt Pilot; Mutiny in the Big House; Overland Mail. 1940 Midnight Limited; Tomboy; The Haunted House; Queen of the Yukon; The Ol' Swimmin' Hole; Pioneers of the West; Hi-Yo Silver!; One Man's Law; Blazing Six Shooters; West of Abilene; Chasing Trouble; Konga; The Wild Stallion; The Ape. 1941 A Girl, a Guy and a Gob; Sucker List (short); All That Money Can Buy; Nevada City; Sunset in Wyoming; Two in a Taxi; Obliging Young Lady; Here Is a Man; Man at Large; Look Who's Laughing; Playmates. 1942 The Big Street; Call Out the Marines; Seven Miles from Alcatraz; Valley of the Sun; The Spoilers; Hold 'Em Jail (short); Mail Trouble (short); My Favorite Spy; The Falcon Takes Over; The Mexican Spitfire's Elephant; Army Surgeon; The Traitor Within; Valley of the Giants; Powder Town; Highway by Night. 1943 Cowboy in Manhattan; Woman of the Town; Johnny Come Lately; Ladies Day; The Man from Music Mountain; Drums of Fu Manchu. 1944 It Happened Tomorrow; Abroad with Two Yanks; Alaska; Yellow Rose of Texas; Home in Indiana; Can't Help Singing; My Best Gal; When the Lights Go on Again; My Pal Wolf. 1945 Song of the Sarong; It's in the Bag; Dakota; Senorita from the West; She Wouldn't Say Yes; Pillow of Death; Sunbonnet Sue; Her Highness and the Bellboy. 1946 Little Giant; Wake up and Dream; The Runaround; Angel on My Shoulder; Step by Step; Wild Beauty; Courage of Lassie; The Show-off. 1947 Mother Wore Tights; I Wonder Who's Kissing Her Now; The Wistful Widow of Wagon Gap; Easy Come, Easy Go; My Wild Irish Rose. 1948 Alburquerque; Fury at Furnace Creek; Miraculous Journey; The Plunderers; A Date with Judy. 1949 Kazan; Miss Grant Takes Richmond; Home in San Antone; Rimfire. 1950 Boy from Indiana; Please Believe Me; Trigger, Jr.; Frenchie. 1951 Flaming Feather; Fort Defiance. 1952 Cripple Creek; Carson City; Wac from Walla Walla; The Devil and Daniel Webster (reissue and retitle of All That Money Can Buy, 1941). 1953 San Antone; Affair with a Stranger; Walking My Baby Back Home. 1954 Outlaw's Daughter; Fireman Save My Child; Racing Blood; Untamed Heiress.

CLIFF, LADDIE (Laddie Perry)
Born: Sept. 3, 1891, Bristol, England. Died: Dec. 8, 1937, London, England. Screen, stage actor and stage producer.

Appeared in: 1922 The Card. 1927 On with the Dance Series. 1929 The Co-Optimists (US 1930). 1933 Sleeping Car. 1934 Happy. 1936 Sporting Love. 1937 Over She Goes.

CLIFFE, H. COOPER
Born: 1862, Oxford, England. Died: May 1, 1939, New York, N.Y. (pneumonia). Screen, stage and radio actor.

Appeared in: 1921 The Woman God Changed; Love's Redemption. 1922 Missing Millions. 1923 His Children's Children. 1924 Monsieur Beaucaire.

CLIFFORD, JACK (Virgil James Montani)
Born: 1880. Died: Nov. 10, 1956, New York, N.Y. Screen, stage actor and boxer. Divorced from actress Evelyn Nesbit Thaw (dec. 1967).

Appeared in: 1926 Sweet Adeline. 1931 Skippy. 1933 One Sunday Afternoon; One Track Minds (short). 1934 The Poor Rich. 1935 One Way Ticket. 1936 King of the Pecos; The Gallant Defender; Dimples; Timothy's Quest. 1937 Racketeers in Exile; High, Wide and Handsome; Midnight Madonna. 1938 Colorado Trail. 1940 Murder on the Yukon Flight. 1941 Beyond the Sacramento; Sky Raiders (serial); The Bandit Trail. 1944 The Old Texas Trail. 1945 Honeymoon Ahead; Rockin' in the Rockies. 1946 Canyon Passage. 1947 Ladies' Man.

CLIFFORD, KATHLEEN
Born: Charlottesville, Va. Died: Jan. 11, 1962, Hollywood, Calif. Screen, stage and vaudeville actress.

Appeared in: 1917 Who Is "Number One"? (serial). 1920 When the Clouds Roll By. 1921 Cold Steel. 1922 Kick In. 1923 Richard, the Lion-Hearted. 1924 No More Women. 1925 The Love Gamble; Sporting Life. 1928 Excess Baggage.

CLIFFORD, LARRY
Died: Feb. 9, 1955. Screen actor.

CLIFFORD, WILLIAM
Born: 1878, New Orleans, La. Died: Dec. 23, 1941, Los Angeles, Calif. Stage and screen actor. Do not confuse with producer William H. Clifford.

Appeared in: 1913 Sheridan's Ride. 1914 Cast Adrift in the South Seas; A Romance of Hawaii; Olana of the South Seas; Rescued by Wireless; The Vagabond Soldier; The Lure of the Geisha. 1915 Rosemary. 1916 The Hidden Law; The Bait; Highlights and Shadows; A Siren of the Jungle; The Lion Nemesis; Clouds in Sunshine Valley; The Ostrich Tip; Destiny's Boomerang; Fate's Decision; After the Battle; The Star of India; The Good for Nothing Brat; The Trap; The Jungle Flashlight. 1917 Snow White; The Square Deceiver. 1918 Broadway Bill; The Landlopers. 1919 Gambling in Souls; A Man of Honor. 1921 The Mask; Sowing the Wind; Parted Curtains. 1923 Ashes of Vengeance. 1924 Stepping Lively. 1927 Out of the Past; Three Miles Up.

CLIFT, MONTGOMERY
Born: Oct. 17, 1920, Omaha, Neb. Died: July 23, 1966, New York, N.Y. (heart attack). Stage and screen actor. Nominated for Academy Award for Best Actor in The Search (1948) and A Place in the Sun (1951). Nominated for Academy Award for Best Supporting Actor in From Here to Eternity (1953) and Judgment at Nuremberg (1961).

Appeared in: 1948 Red River; The Search. 1949 The Heiress. 1950 The Big Lift. 1951 A Place in the Sun. 1953 I Confess; From Here to Eternity. 1954 Indiscretion of an American Wife. 1957 Raintree County. 1958 The Young Lions; Lonelyhearts. 1959 Suddenly Last Summer. 1960 Wild River. 1961 The Misfits; Judgment at Nuremberg. 1962 Freud. 1966 The Defector.

CLIFTON, ELMER
Born: 1893, Chicago, Ill. Died: Oct. 15, 1949, Los Angeles, Calif. (cerebral hemorrhage). Screen, stage actor, film producer, film director and screenwriter.

Appeared in: 1915 Birth of a Nation. 1916 Intolerance. 1919 The Fall of Babylon.

CLIFTON, HERBERT
Born: 1884, London, England. Died: Sept. 26, 1947, Hollywood, Calif. (after major operation). Stage and screen actor.

Appeared in: 1935 False Pretenses. 1937 High Flyers; She's Got Everything. 1942 Mrs. Miniver. 1947 Ivy.

CLIFTON-JAMES, M.E.
Born: 1898. Died: May 8, 1963, Worthing, England. Screen, stage actor, screenwriter and author. He impersonated Field Marshal Montgomery so well he was used by British Intelligence to confuse the Germans during W.W.II.

Appeared in: 1948 Blanche Fury. 1959 I Was Monty's Double (which he also wrote).

CLINE, EDDIE (Edward Francis Cline)

Born: Nov. 7, 1892, Kenosha, Wisc. Died: May 22, 1961, Hollywood, Calif. Screen actor, film director and screenwriter. Entered films as an actor with Keystone in 1913.

Appeared in: **1921** The Haunted House.

CLITHEROE, JIMMY

Born: 1923, England Died: June 6, 1973, England (?). Screen actor.

Appeared in: **1967** Jules Verne's Rocket to the Moon (aka Those Fantastic Flying Fools and Blast-Off–US).

CLIVE, COLIN (Clive Greig)

Born: Jan. 9, 1898, St. Malo, France. Died: June 25, 1937, Los Angeles, Calif. (pulmonary and intestinal ailment). Stage and screen actor. Married to actress Jeanne de Casalis (dec. 1966).

Appeared in: **1930** Journey's End. **1931** The Stronger Sex; Frankenstein. **1932** Lily Christine. **1933** Christopher Strong; Looking Forward. **1934** Jane Eyre; The Key; One More River. **1935** Bride of Frankenstein; Clive of India; The Hands of Orlac; The Right to Live; The Widow from Monte Carlo; The Girl from 10th Avenue; Mad Love; The Man Who Broke the Bank at Monte Carlo. **1937** History is Made at Night; The Woman I Love.

CLIVE, E. E. (Edward E. Clive)

Born: 1898, Monmouthshire, Wales. Died: June 6, 1940, North Hollywood, Calif. (heart attack). Screen, stage actor, film producer and film director. Appeared as "Tenny" in the Bulldog Drummond series, 1937-1939.

Appeared in: **1933** The Invisible Man. **1934** The Poor Rich; Tin Pants; Bulldog Drummond Strikes Back; Charlie Chan in London; One More River; Long Lost Father; Riptide; Service; Bulldog Drummond. **1935** Atlantic Adventure; Father Brown, Detective; Sylivia Scarlett; The Widow from Monte Carlo; The Mystery of Edwin Drood; The Bride of Frankenstein; Remember Last Night?; We're in the Money; Stars over Broadway; A Tale of Two Cities; Captain Blood. **1936** Little Lord Fauntleroy; Love before Breakfast; Dracula's Daughter; The Unguarded Hour; Trouble for Two; Piccadilly Jim; All American Chump; Libeled Lady; Tarzan Escapes; Camille; The Golden Arrow; Isle of Fury; Charge of the Light Brigade; Cain and Mabel; Palm Springs; Ticket to Paradise; Lloyds of London; The Dark Hour. **1937** They Wanted to Marry; Maid of Salem; Bulldog Drummond Escapes; Bulldog Drummond Comes Back; Bulldog Drummond's Revenge; Ready, Willing and Able; On the Avenue; Love under Fire; Danger—Love at Work; Personal Property; Night Must Fall; The Emperor's Candlesticks; Live, Love and Learn; Beg, Borrow or Steal. **1938** Bulldog Drummond's Peril; Bulldog Drummond in Africa; Arsene Lupin Returns; The First Hundred Years; The Last Warning; Kidnapped; Gateway; Submarine Patrol. **1939** Mr. Moto's Last Warning; Arrest Bulldog Drummond; The Little Princess; I'm from Missouri; Bulldog Drummond's Secret Police; Bulldog Drummond's Bride; Man about Town; The Hound of the Baskervilles; Rose of Washington Square; The Adventures of Sherlock Holmes; The Honeymoon's Over; Bachelor Mother; Mr. and Mrs. Bulldog Drummond; Raffles. **1940** Foreign Correspondent; Pride and Prejudice; Earl of Chicago; Congo Maisie.

CLIVE, HENRY (Henry Clive O'Hara)

Born: Oct. 3, 1883, Melbourne, Australia. Died: Dec. 12, 1960, Hollywood, Calif. (lung cancer). Screen, stage, vaudeville actor, commercial artist and magician.

Appeared in: **1917** The Fighting Odds. **1921** Heedless Moths; The Oath. **1923** Obey the Law.

CLOSE, IVY

Born: 1890. Died: Dec. 4, 1968, Goring, England. Screen actress. Entered films with Britain's Hepworth Co. Mother of British film director Ronald Neame.

Appeared in: **1912** Sleeping Beauty; Dream Paintings; The Lady of Shallot; Pygmalion and Galatea. **1913** Mifanwy—A Tragedy; La Cigale. **1914** The Lure of London; Ghosts; The Hon. William's Donah; The Terrible Twins; Ivy's Elopement; Two Elderly Cupids; The Girl from the Sky. **1915** The Haunting of Silas P. Gould; Darkest London: Or, the Dancer's Romance. **1916** The Girl and the Terror; Peaches and Ponies; Doing the Demonstrator; He Wrote Poetry; Meter in the Kitchen; The Stolen Jail; That Pesky Parrot; The Mysterious Double; The Battered Bridegroom; Rival Artists. **1917** The Ware Case; The House Opposite; The Adventures of Dick Dolan; The Women's Land Army. **1918** Adam Bede; A Peep Behind the Scenes; Nelson; Missing the Tide. **1919** Darby and Joan; The Irresistible Flapper; The Flag Lieutenant; Her Cross. **1920** The Worldlings; La Roue. **1922** Expiation; Was She Justified? **1929** The Jolly Peasant.

CLOSE, JOHN

Died: Dec. 18, 1964. Screen actor.

Appeared in: **1950** Where the Sidewalk Ends. **1951** Korea Patrol; The Girl on the Bridge. **1952** Red Skies of Montana. **1953** Torpedo Alley; Gentlemen Prefer Blondes; Fangs of the Arctic. **1954** Francis Joins the WACS; Finger Man; Sudden Danger. **1957** Chain of Evidence; The Storm Rider; Beginning of the

End. **1958** Outcasts of the City; Street of Darkness. **1959** The Purple Gang. **1960** Pay or Die. **1962** Convicts 4. **1963** The Slime People.

CLOUZOUT, VERA

Died: Dec. 15, 1960, Paris, France (possible heart attack). Screen actress. Married to film director Henri Georges Clouzout (dec. 1977).

Appeared in: **1955** Diabolique. **1956** Wages of Fear. **1957** Les Espions.

CLOVELLY, CECIL

Born: 1891, England. Died: Apr. 25, 1965, New York, N.Y. Screen, stage actor and film director.

Appeared in: **1930** The Forest Ring. **1950** So Young, So Bad. **1951** Two Gals and a Guy.

CLUNES, ALEC S.

Born: May 17, 1912, Brixton, London, England. Died: Mar. 13, 1970, London, England (lung ailment). Screen, stage actor, stage producer and stage director. Son of stage actor Alexander Sheriff Sydney Clunes and stage actress Georgina Sumner Clunes.

Appeared in: **1940** Convoy; Sailors Three (aka Three Cockeyed Sailors–US 1941). **1941** Saloon Bar (US 1944). **1942** One of Our Aircraft is Missing. **1949** Now Barabbas. **1953** Melba. **1955** Quentin Durward; Richard III (US 1956). **1956** Tiger in the Smoke. **1962** Tomorrow at Ten (US 1964).

CLUTE, CHESTER L.

Born: 1891. Died: Apr. 5, 1956, Woodland Hills, Calif. (heart attack). Screen actor.

Appeared in: **1930** The Jay Walker (short). **1931** The Antique Shop (short). **1932** The Babbling Book (short). **1933** Walking the Baby (short). **1937** Dance, Charlie, Dance; The Great Garrick; He Couldn't Say No; Navy Blues; The Wrong Road; Exclusive; There Goes My Girl; Living on Love. **1938** Change of Heart; Touchdown Army; Rascals; Pardon Our Nerve; Comet over Broadway; Annabel Takes a Tour; Service DeLuxe; Mr. Chump. **1939** I Was a Convict; Dancing Coed; Laugh It Off; Too Busy to Work; East Side of Heaven. **1940** The Doctor Takes a Wife; Hired Wife; Millionaires in Prison; Dance, Girl, Dance; Too Many Girls; Love Thy Neighbor. **1941** Footlight Fever; Wedding Worries (short); She Couldn't Say No; Hold Back the Dawn; Sun Valley Serenade; Scattergood Meets Broadway; Niagara Falls; The Perfect Snob; The Man Who Came to Dinner. **1942** Larceny, Inc.; The Wife Takes a Flyer; Yankee Doodle Dandy; Just Off Broadway; The Forest Rangers; My Favorite Spy; George Washington Slept Here; Star Spangled Rhythm. **1943** Chatterbox; The Desperadoes; Someone to Remember; The Good Fellows; So's Your Uncle; Here Comes Elmer; Crazy House. **1944** Arsenic and Old Lace; Radio Bugs (short); Nothing but the Truth; Bermuda Mystery; Hat Check Honey; Rationing; San Diego, I Love You; The Reckless Age; Johnny Doesn't Live Here Anymore. **1945** She Gets Her Man; She Went to the Races; Saratoga Trunk; Let's Go Steady (short); Guest Wife; The Man Who Walked Alone; Anchors Aweigh; Arson Squad; Blonde Ransom; Mildred Pierce; Earl Carroll Vanities. **1946** Angel on My Shoulder; Cinderella Jones; One Exciting Week; Social Terrors (short); Spook Busters. **1947** Hit Parade of 1947; Web of Danger; Joe Palooka in the Knockout; The Crimson Key; Host to a Ghost (short); Something in the Wind. **1948** Mary Lou; Winner Take All; The Strange Mrs. Crane; Train to Alcatraz; Jiggs and Maggie in Court; Blondie's Reward. **1949** Master Minds; Square Dance Jubilee; Ringside; Blondie's Big Deal. **1950** Lucky Losers; Joe Palooka in Humphrey Takes a Chance; Mary Ryan, Detective. **1951** Kentucky Jubilee; Punchy Pancho (short); So You Want to be a Bachelor (short); Stop That Cab. **1952** Colorado Sundown.

CLYDE, ANDY

Born: Mar. 25, 1892, Blairgowrie, Scotland. Died: May 18, 1967, Los Angeles, Calif. Screen and television actor. Brother of actor David Clyde (dec. 1945) and actress Jean Clyde (dec. 1962). Married to actress Elsie Maud Tarron, Mack Sennett bathing beauty. Appeared in numerous westerns including several Hopalong Cassidy series films.

Appeared in: **1926** A Sea Dog's Tale (short). **1928** Branded Man; The Goodbye Kiss; Blindfold (short). **1929** Should a Girl Marry?; Ships of the Night; Midnight Daddies; plus the following shorts: The Lunkhead; The Golfers; A Hollywood Star; Clancy at the Bat; The New Halfback; Uppercut O'Brien; The Bride's Relations; The Old Barn; Whirls and Girls; The Bee's Buzz; The Big Palooka; Girl Crazy; The Barber's Daughter; The Constable. **1930** The following shorts: Scotch; Sugar Plum Papa; Match Play; Fat Wives for Thin; Campus Crushes; The Chumps; Goodbye Legs; Hello Television; Average Husband; Vacation Loves; Radio Kisses; The Bluffer; Grandma's Girl; Take Your Medicine; Don't Bite Your Dentist; Racket Cheers; Bulls and Bears. **1931** The following shorts: Speed; Taxi Troubles; Half Holiday; No, No, Lady; The College Vamp; The Dog Doctor; Just a Bear; In Conference; The Cow-Catcher's Daughter; Ghost Parade; Monkey Business in Africa; Fainting Lover; Too Many Husbands; The Cannonball; All-American Kickback; Great Pie Mystery. **1932** Million Dollar Legs; plus the following shorts: Shopping With Wifie; Heavens! My Husband; Speed in the Gay Nineties; The Boudoir Butler; Alaska Love; Her Royal Shyness; The Giddy Age; Sunkissed Sweeties; For the Love of Ludwig; A Fool About Women; Boy Oh Boy. **1933** The following shorts: Artist's Muddles; Feeling Rosy; Loose Relations; Big Squeal; Dora's Dunkin' Donuts; His Weak Moment; Frozen Assets. **1934** The Little Minister; plus the following shorts: Super Snooper; Hello Prosperity; Half-Baked Relations; An Old Gypsy Custom; It's the Cat's in the Dog House. **1935** McFadden's Flats; The Village Tale; Annie Oakley; plus the following shorts: I'm A Father; Old Sawbones; Tramp, Tramp, Tramp; Alimony Aches; It Always Happens; Hot Paprika. **1936** Yellow Dust; Straight From the Shoulder; Two In a Crowd; Red Lights Ahead; plus the following shorts: Caught in the Act; Share the Wealth; Peppery Salt; Mister Smarty; Am I Having Fun; Love Comes to Mooneyville. **1937** The Barrier; plus the following shorts: Knee Action; Stuck in the Sticks; My Little Feller; Lodge Night; Gracie at the Bat; He Done His Duty. **1938** The following shorts: The Old Raid Mule; Jump, Chum, Jump; Ankles Away; Soul of a Heel; Not Guilty Enough; Home on the Rage. **1939** It's a Wonderful World; Bad Lands; plus the following shorts: Swing, You Swingers; Boom Goes the Groom; Now It Can Be Sold; Trouble Finds Andy Clyde; All-American Blondes; Andy Clyde Gets Spring Chicken. **1940** Cherokee Strip; Three Men From Texas; Abe Lincoln in Illinois; Hopalong Cassidy; plus the following shorts: Mr. Clyde Goes to Broadway; Money Squawks; Boobs in the Woods; Fireman, Save My Choo Choo; A Bundle of Bliss. **1941** Doomed Caravan; In Old Colorado; Pirates on Horseback; Men of Action; Wide Open Town; Riders of the Timberline; Twilight on the Trail; Stick to Your Guns; Secret of the Wastelands; Outlaws of the Desert; Border Vigilantes; plus the following shorts: The Watchman Takes a Wife; Ring and the Belle; Yankee Doodle Andy; Host to a Ghost; Lovable Trouble. **1942** Undercover Man; This Above All; plus the following shorts: Sappy Birthday; How Spry I Am; All Work and No Pay; Sappy Pappy. **1943** Lost Canyon; Border Patrol; The Leather Burners; Hoppy Serves a Writ; Missing Men; False Colors; Bar 20; Sunset Riders; Colt Comrades; plus the following shorts: Wolf in Thief's Clothing; A Maid Made Mad; Farmer for a Day; He Was Only Feudin'. **1944** Texas Masquerade; Riders of the Deadline; Lumberjack; Forty Thieves; Mystery Man; plus the following shorts: His Tale Is Told; You Were Never Uglier; Gold Is Where You Lose It; Heather and Yon'. **1945** Roughly Speaking; Son of the Prairie; plus the following shorts: A Miner Affair; Spook to Me; Two Local Yokels. **1946** The Devil's Playground; Fool's Gold; The Green Years; That Texas Jamboree; Throw a Saddle on a Star; The Plainsman and the Lady; Unexpected Guest; plus the following shorts: The Blonde Stayed On; Andy Plays Hooky. **1947** The Marauders; Hoppy's Holiday; Dangerous Venture; plus the following shorts: Two Jills and a Jack; Wife to Spare. **1948** Strange Gamble; The Dead Don't Dream; Silent Conflict; False Paradise; plus the following shorts: Eight-Ball Andy; Go Chase Yourself; Sinister Journey; Borrowed Trouble. **1949** Crashing Thru; Riders of the Dusk; Shadows of the West; Haunted Trails; Range Land; Sunk in the Sink (short). **1950** Gunslingers; Silver Raiders; Fence Riders; Arizona Territory; Outlaws of Texas; Cherokee Uprising; plus the following shorts: Marinated Mariner; A Blunderful Time. **1951** Abilene Trail; Blonde Atom Bomb (short). **1952** A Blissful Blunder (short); Hooked and Rooked (short). **1953** The following shorts: Fresh Painter; Pardon My Wrench; Love's A-Poppin'; Oh, Say, Can You Sue. **1954** Two April Fools (short). **1955** Caroline Cannonball; The Road to Denver; plus the following shorts: Scratch, Scratch, Scratch; One Spooky Night. **1956** Andy Goes Wild (short); Pardon My Nightshirt (short). **1960** When Comedy Was King (documentary). **1963** Thirty Years of Fun (documentary); The Sound of Laughter (documentary).

CLYDE, DAVID

Born: 1855. Died: May 17, 1945, San Fernando Valley, Calif. Screen actor. Married to actress Fay Holden (dec. 1973). Brother of actor Andy Clyde (dec. 1967) and actress Jean Clyde (dec. 1962).

Appeared in: **1935** Cardinal Richelieu; Hard Rock Harrigan; The Man on the Flying Trapeze; Bonnie Scotland. **1936** Suzy. **1937** Fury and the Woman; Another Dawn; Love under Fire. **1938** If I Were King; Bulldog Drummond's Peril; Kidnapped. **1939** Arrest Bulldog Drummond; Bulldog Drummond's Secret Police; Death of a Champion; Captain Fury; Ruler of the Sea. **1941** Smilin' Through; The Feminine Touch; H. M. Pulham, Esq. **1942** Nightmare; Random Harvest; Mrs. Miniver; The Gay Sisters; Now, Voyager; Eagle Squadron. **1944** The Lodger; The Scarlet Claw. **1945** The Lost Weekend; Molly and Me; Love Letters; Molly, Bless Her; The House of Fear.

CLYDE, JEAN

Born: 1889. Died: July, 1962, Helensburgh, Scotland. Screen actress. Sister of actors Andy (dec. 1967) and David Clyde (dec. 1945).

CLYMER, BETH

Born: 1887. Died: Jan. 14, 1952, Woodland Hills, Calif. (heart attack). Screen actress.

COATES, PAUL

Born: 1921. Died: Nov. 17, 1968, West Hollywood, Calif. (heart attack). Columnist, television commentator and screen actor. Do not confuse with singer Richard Paul Coates (dec. 1972).

Appeared in: **1957** The Tijuana Story.

COBB, EDMUND F.

Born: 1892, Albuquerque, New Mexico. Died: Aug. 15, 1974, Woodland Hills, Calif. (heart attack). Stage and screen actor. Entered films in 1910.

Appeared in: **1915** Fifty-Fifty; The Destroyer; The Second Son; The Papered Door; Ties that Meet; Mind Over Motor; Brought Home; Tish's Spy; The Circular Path. **1916** Once a Thief; Captain Jinks of the Horse Marines; The Face in the Mirror; The War Bride of Plumville; The Condemnation; A Little Volunteer; The Promise Land; Money to Burn. **1917** Moral Courage. **1918** Social Briars. **1920** Wolves of the Street; Desert Scorpion. **1921** Finders Keepers; Out of the Depths. **1923** The Law Rustlers; Battling Bates; At Devil's Gorge; The Miracle Baby; Riders of the Range; Playing It Wild; The Sting of the Scorpion. **1924** A Rodeo Mix-up; Western Yesterdays; Blasted Hopes; Days of '49 (serial); Cupid's Rustler; California in '49 (feature made of Days of '49 serial); Midnight Shadows; Range Blood; Western Feuds. **1925** The Burning Trail. **1926** General Custer at Little Big Horn; The Galloping Cowboy; The Terror; Looking for Trouble; The Scrappin' Kid; Fighting with Buffalo Bill (serial). **1927** Fangs of Destiny; Wolf's Trail. **1928** Call of the Heart; The Fighting Redhead; The Hound of Silver Creek; The Four-Footed Ranger; Young Whirlwind. **1929** A Final Reckoning (serial). **1930** Beyond the Rio Grande; The Indians Are Coming (serial). **1931** Law of the Rio Grande. **1932** Human Targets; Lone Trail; Tangled Fortunes; Rider of Death Valley. **1933** Fourth Horseman; Deadwood Pass; Rusty Rides Alone. **1934** Mystery Mountain (serial); Tracy Rides; Racketeer Roundup; Tailspin Tommy (serial). **1935** Rustler's Paradise; The Miracle Rider; The Westerner; Gunners and Guns. **1936** The Fugitive Sheriff; Darkest Africa. **1937** The Mighty Treve; Springtime in the Rockies; Sergeant Murphy; Cherokee Strip. **1938** Wild Horse Rodeo; I'm from the City; Outlaws of the Prairie; Cattle Raiders; West of Cheyenne; Law of the Plains; Colorado Trail; Call of the Rockies; South of Arizona. **1939** Twelve Crowded Hours; Blue Montana Skies; West of Santa Fe; Spoilers of the Range; Western Caravans; Riders of Black River; Outpost of the Mounties; Stranger from Texas. **1940** West of Carson City; One Man's Law; Prairie Schooners; Melody Ranch; How High Is Up? (short); Deadwood Dick; Blazing Six Shooters. **1941** Prairie Stranger; The Son of Davy Crockett; The Medico of Painted Springs; Wyoming Wildcat; Back in the Saddle; I Was a Prisoner on Devil's Island; Texas; North from the Lone Star; So You Won't Squawk (short); The Wildcat of Tuscon; The Return of Daniel Boone; The Lone Star Vigilantes; Man from Montana. **1942** Two Yanks in Trinidad; Down Rio Grande Way; Heart of the Rio Grande; Stardust on the Sage; Westward Ho; Deep in the Heart of Texas. **1943** Silver City Raiders; Fighting Devil Dogs; The Old Chisholm Trail; Riding Through Nevada; Mission to Moscow; The Ghost Rider; The Stranger from Pecos; Frontier Fury; Jack London. **1944** Law Men; House of Frankenstein; Outlaws of Santa Fe; West of the Rio Grande; Raiders of the Border; Call of the Rockies; Song of the Range; The Old Texas Trail; Cyclone Prairie Rangers; The Missing Juror. **1945** The Man from Oklahoma; The Falcon in San Francisco; Law of the Valley. **1946** The Falcon's Alibi; Song of Arizona; Days of Buffalo Bill; Galloping Thunder; Roaring Rangers; The El Paso Kid; Sun Valley Cyclone; Last Frontier Uprising; Red River Renegades; Rustler's Round-up; Santa Fe Uprising; Rio Grande Raiders. **1947** Robin Hood of Texas; Stage Coach to Denver; Oregon Trail Scouts; The Wistful Widow of Wagon Gap; Flashing Guns; Law of the Canyon; Riders of the Lone Star; Land of the Lawless; Buffalo Bill Rides Again; Son of Zorro (serial). **1948** Pride of Virginia; The Bold Frontiersman; River Lady; Feudin', Fussin' and A-Fightin'; Carson City Raiders; The Far Frontier; Hidden Danger; The Mystery of the Golden Eye. **1949** The Daring Caballero; Sheriff of Wichita; The Wyoming Bandit; Gun Law Justice; San Antone Ambush. **1950** The Girl from San Lorenzo; Arizona Cowboy; Comanche Territory; The Vanishing Westerner; Bells of Coronado; Hills of Oklahoma; Frisco Tornado. **1951** Blazing Bullets; Montana Desperado. **1954** Broken Lance; River of No Return. **1955** The Girl in the Red Velvet Swing; Lucy Gallant. **1956** Hidden Guns; The Oklahoma Woman. **1957** The Amazing Colossal Man; Dragstrip Girl; Motorcycle Gang. **1962** Tales of Terror; The Underwater City. **1965** The Bounty Killer; Requiem for a Gunfighter. **1966** Johnny Reno.

COBB, IRVIN S.

Born: June 23, 1876, Paducah, Ky. Died: Mar. 11, 1944, New York, N.Y. Screen, radio actor, humorist, playwright, novelist, screenwriter and newspaperman.

Appeared in: **1914** Our Mutual Girl # 33. **1921** Pardon My French; Peck's Bad Boy. **1922** The Five Dollar Baby. **1924** The Great White Way. **1927** Turkish Delight. **1934** Judge Priest; a series of MGM shorts. **1935** Steamboat 'Round the Bend; La Fiesta de Santa Barbara (short). **1936** Everybody's Old Man; Pepper. **1938** Hawaii Calls; The Arkansas Traveler; The Young in Heart.

COBB, TY (Tyrus Raymond Cobb)

Born: Dec. 18, 1886, Narrows, Georgia. Died: July 17, 1961, Atlanta, Ga. Professional baseball player and screen actor.

Appeared in: **1942** The Ninth Inning.

COBORN, CHARLES (Colin Whitton McCallum)

Born: 1852, England. Died: Nov. 23, 1945, London, England. Screen, revue, stage actor and songwriter. Do not confuse with U.S. actor Charles Coburn.

Appeared in: **1934** Say it with Flowers. **1936** Pictorial Revue; Old Timers. **1943** Variety Jubilee.

COBURN, CHARLES DOUVILLE
Born: June 19, 1877, Savannah, Ga. Died: Aug. 30, 1961, N.Y. (heart ailment). Screen, stage, radio, television actor, stage producer and stage director. Won 1943 Academy Award for Best Supporting Actor in The More the Merrier and was nominated for 1941 Best Supporting Actor in The Devil and Miss Jones and in 1946 for The Green Years. Married to stage actress Ivah Wills (dec. 1937) and later to Winifred Natzka.

Appeared in: **1933** Boss Tweed. **1935** The People's Enemy. **1938** Idiot's Delight; Bachelor Mother; The Story of Alexander Graham Bell; Stanley and Livingstone; Made for Each Other; In Name Only. **1940** Road to Singapore; Edison the Man; The Captain Is a Lady; Three Faces West; Florian; Refugee. **1941** The Devil and Miss Jones; H.M. Pulham, Esq; The Lady Eve; Our Wife; Unexpected Uncle; King's Row. **1942** In This Our Life; George Washington Slept Here. **1943** The More the Merrier; The Constant Nymph; Heaven Can Wait; Princess O'Rourke; My Kingdom for a Cook. **1944** Since You Went Away; Knickerbocker Holiday; Wilson; The Impatient Years; Together Again. **1945** A Royal Scandal; Colonel Effingham's Raid; Shady Lady; Over 21; Rhapsody in Blue. **1946** The Green Years; Man of the Hour. **1947** Lured; Personal Column. **1948** B.F.'s Daughter; Green Grass of Wyoming; Rose of Singapore; The Paradine Case. **1949** The Doctor and the Girl; Everybody Does It; The Gal Who Took the West; Impact; Yes Sir, That's My Baby. **1950** Louisa; Mr. Music; Peggy. **1951** The Highwayman; Oh Money, Money. **1952** Monkey Business; Has Anybody Seen My Gal?; Alma Mater. **1953** Gentlemen Prefer Blondes; Trouble along the Way. **1954** The Rocket Man; The Long Wait. **1955** How to Be Very, Very Popular. **1956** Around the World in 80 Days; The Power and the Prize. **1957** How to Murder a Rich Uncle; Town on Trial; The Story of Mankind; Uncle George. **1959** The Remarkable Mr. Pennypacker; Stranger in My Arms; John Paul Jones. **1960** Pepe. **1974** That's Entertainment (film clips).

COCAINE
Died: c. 1973 (euthanasia). Screen and television animal performer (horse).

Appeared in: **1949** Three Godfathers; The Fighting Kentuckian; She Wore a Yellow Ribbon. **1950** Rio Grande. **1953** Hondo. **1959** Rio Bravo; The Horse Soldiers. **1960** The Alamo. **1961** The Comancheros. **1962** The Man Who Shot Liberty Valance. **1963** McClintock; How the West was Won. **1965** The Sons of Katie Elder. **1967** El Dorado; The War Wagon.

COCHRAN, EDDIE
Born: 1929, England? Died: Apr. 17, 1960, Bath, England (auto accident). Screen, stage actor and singer.

Appeared in: **1956** The Girl Can't Help It. **1957** Untamed Youth. **1959** Go, Johnny, Go! **1970** Woodstock.

COCHRAN, STEVE (Robert Alexander Cochran)
Born: May 25, 1917, Eureka, Calif. Died: June 15, 1965, Pacific Ocean, off coast of Guatemala (acute infectious edema which caused swelling in a lung). Stage and screen actor. Divorced from singer Fay McKenzie and artist Florence Lockwood. Married to actress Jonna Jensen.

Appeared in: **1945** Boston Blackie Booked on Suspicion; Boston Blackie's Rendezvous; The Gay Senorita; Wonder Man. **1946** The Kid from Brooklyn; The Best Years of Our Lives; The Chase. **1947** Copacabana. **1948** A Song Is Born. **1949** White Heat. **1950** The Big Stickup; The West Point Story; The Damned Don't Cry; Storm Warning; Dallas; Highway 301. **1951** Raton Pass; The Tanks Are Coming; Jim Thorpe—All American; Inside the Walls of Folsom Prison; Tomorrow Is Another Day; Operation Secret. **1953** The Desert Song; She's Back on Broadway; Back To God's Country; Shark River. **1954** Private Hell 36; Rummelplatz Der Liebe (The Carnival Story). **1956** Come Next Spring; Slander. **1957** The Weapon; Il Grido (aka The Outcry–US 1962). **1958** I, Mobster; Quantrill's Raiders. **1959** The Big Operator; The Beat Generation (aka This Rebel Age). **1961** The Deadly Companions. **1963** Of Love and Desire. **1966** Mozambique. **1967** Tell Me in Sunlight.

COCHRANE, FRANK
Born: Oct. 28, 1882, Durham, England. Died: 1962, London, England. Screen, stage and radio actor.

Appeared in: **1930** The Yellow Mast. **1934** Chu-Chin-Chow. **1935** McClusky the Sea Rover (aka Hell's Cargo–US 1938). **1936** The Tenth Man (US 1937). **1937** Bulldog Drummond at Bay; Jericho (aka Dark Sands–US 1938). **1938** Queer Cargo (aka Pirates of the Seven Seas–US). **1953** Ali Baba Nights.

COCKELBERG, LOUIS J.
Born: 1880. Died: July 7, 1962, Hollywood, Calif. Screen actor.

COCTEAU, JEAN (Clement Eugene Jean Maurice Cocteau)
Born: July 5, 1889, Maisons-Laffitte, France. Died: Oct. 11, 1963, Milly, France (heart attack). Screen, stage actor, film director, producer, screenwriter, playwright, musician and poet.

Appeared in: **1952** The Strange Ones. **1957** 8 x 8. **1960** Le Testament D'Orphee (The Testament of Orpheus–US 1962). **1963** Egypte O Egypte (narration). **1976** Singing Under the Occupation (documentary).

CODE, GRANT HYDE
Born: 1896. Died: June 28, 1974, New York, N.Y. Screen, stage, television actor and dancer.

Appeared in: **1961** The Young Doctors. **1962** The Miracle Worker.

CODEE, ANN
Born: 1890, Belgium. Died: May 18, 1961, Hollywood, Calif. (heart attack). Screen, television and vaudeville actress. Married to actor Frank Orth (dec. 1962). Appeared in vaudeville with her husband in an act billed "Codee and Orth."

Appeared with Orth as a team in the following shorts: **1929** A Bird in the Hand; Zwei Und Fierzigste Strasse; Stranded in Paris; Music Hath Charms; Meine Frau (Meet the Wife). **1930** Taking Ways; Imagine My Embarrassment. **1931** On the Job; Sleepy Head; Dumb Luck; The Bitter Half.

Appeared without Orth in: **1935** Under the Pampas Moon. **1936** Hi, Gaucho; Brilliant Marriage. **1937** Expensive Husbands. **1940** Drums of the Desert; Captain Caution; Arise My Love. **1941** Come Live with Me; Charlie Chan in Rio. **1942** Army Surgeon. **1943** Paris after Dark; Tonight We Raid Calais; Old Acquaintance. **1944** The Mummy's Curse; Bathing Beauty. **1945** Hangover Square; This Love of Ours; Tonight and Every Night; The Clock; Her Highness and the Bellboy. **1946** Holiday in Mexico; Kitty; It's Great to Be Young; So Dark the Night. **1947** Unfinished Dance; The Other Love. **1948** Rose of Santa Rosa. **1949** That Midnight Kiss. **1950** Under My Skin; When Willie Comes Marching Home. **1951** Mr. Imperium; The Lady Pays Off; On the Riviera. **1952** What Price Glory. **1953** Kiss Me, Kate; Dangerous When Wet; War of the Worlds. **1954** So This Is Paris. **1955** Daddy Long Legs; Interrupted Melody. **1958** Kings Go Forth. **1960** Can-Can.

CODY, BILL, SR. (William Frederick Cody, Sr.)
Born: 1891. Died: Jan, 24, 1948, Santa Monica, Calif. Screen actor and rodeo performer. Father of actor Bill Cody, Jr.

Appeared in: **1924** Border Justice. **1925** Cold Nerve; Dangerous Odds; Riders of Mystery; The Fighting Sheriff; The Fighting Smile; Love on the Rio Grande; Moccasins. **1926** The Galloping Cowboy; King of the Saddle. **1927** Laddie Be Good; The Arizona Whirlwind; Born to Battle; Gold from Weepah. **1928** Price of Fear. **1929** Wolves of the City; Slim Fingers; Eyes of the Underworld; Tip Off. **1931** Under Texas Skies; Dugan of the Bad Lands; The Montana Kid; Oklahoma Jim. **1932** Texas Pioneers; Ghost City; Law of the North; Mason of the Mounted; Land of Wanted Men. **1934** Frontier Days. **1935** The Cyclone Ranger; The Texas Rambler; The Vanishing Riders; Six-Gun Justice; Lawless Border. **1936** Outlaws of the Range; Blazing Justice. **1938** Girl of the Golden West. **1939** The Fighting Cowboy; The Fighting Gringo. **1948** Joan of Arc.

CODY, EMMETT F. (Emmett Francis Cody)
Born: 1920. Died: 1960. Screen actor.

Appeared in: **1944** Keys to the Kingdom; Our Hearts Were Young and Gay. **1945** Lady on the Train; State Fair. **1946** The Harvey Girls.

CODY, HARRY (Van Doak Covington)
Born: 1896. Died: Oct. 22, 1956, Hollywood, Calif. Screen and stage actor.

Appeared in: **1951** Callaway Went Thataway; People against O'Hara. **1952** Singin' in the Rain. **1954** The Vanquished.

CODY, LEW (Louis Code)
Born: Feb. 22, 1887, Waterville, Me. Died: May 31, 1934, Beverly Hills, Calif. (heart disease). Screen, stage, vaudeville actor and film producer. Married to actress Mabel Norman (dec. 1930) and divorced from actress Dorothy Dalton (dec. 1972).

Appeared in: **1915** A Branded Soul; Comrade John. **1917** Treasure of the Sea. **1918** The Demon; For Husbands Only; The Mating. **1919** Don't Change Your Husband; The Life Line; Our Better Selves. **1920** The Beloved Chester. **1921** Sign of the Door. **1922** Dangerous Pastime; The Secrets of Paris; The Valley of Silent Men. **1923** Within the Law; Rupert of Hentzau; Jacqueline of Blazing Barriers; Lawful Larceny; Souls for Sale. **1924** Reno; Husbands and Lovers; Defying the Law; Nellie, the Beautiful Cloak Model; Revelation; The Woman on the Jury; The Shooting of Dan McGrew; Three Women. **1925** The Tower of Lies; Man and Maid; Exchange of Wives; His Secretary; Slave of Fashion; So This Is Marriage?; Time, the Comedian. **1926** The Gay Deceiver; Monte Carlo. **1927** On Ze Boulevard; Adam and Evil; The Demi-Bride; Tea for Three. **1928** Beau Broadway; Wickedness Preferred; The Baby Cyclone. **1929** A Single Man. **1930** What a Widow. **1931** Dishonored; Stout Hearts and Willing Hands; Not Exactly Gentlemen; Common Law; Three Girls Lost; X Marks the Spot; Beyond Victory; Sweepstakes; Woman of Experience; Meet the Wife; Sporting Blood; Divorce among Friends. **1932** The Tenderfoot; 70,000 Witnesses; The Crusader; Madison Square Garden; Unwritten Law; Undercover Man; File 113; A Parisian Romance. **1933** I Love That Man; Wine, Women and Song;

By Appointment Only; Sitting Pretty. **1934** Private Scandal; Shoot the Works.

CODY, COLONEL WILLIAM FREDERICK (aka BUFFALO BILL)
Born: Feb. 26, 1846, Scott County, Iowa. Died: Jan. 10, 1917, Denver, Colo. Circus, rodeo performer and screen actor.

Appeared in: **1902** Parade of Buffalo Bill's West. **1911** Buffalo Bill Wild West and Pawnee Bill Far East. **1912** The Life of Buffalo Bill. **1914** The Indian Wars. **1915** Patsy of the Circus.

COEDEL, LUCIEN
Born: 1905. Died: Oct. 1947, France (fell from train). Screen actor.

Appeared in: **1946** Resistance: Releton d'Execution; Carmen. **1947** The Bellman. **1948** The Idiot; Portrait of Innocence. **1949** Strangers in the House; Counter Investigation.

COFFER, JACK
Born: 1939. Died: Feb. 18, 1967, Encino, Calif. (results of auto accident). Screen actor and stuntman.

Appeared in: **1967** The Way West.

COFFEY, JOHN
Born: 1909. Died: Mar. 25, 1944, Hollywood, Calif. Screen actor.

COFFIN, HANK
Born: 1904, Lakeport, Calif. Died: Sept. 17, 1966, Los Angeles, Calif. Screen, television actor and stunt flyer.

Appeared in: **1930** Dawn Patrol; Hell's Angels.

COGAN, ALMA
Born: 1933. Died: Oct. 26, 1966. Screen actress.

COGAN, FANNY HAY
Born: 1866, Philadelphia, Pa. Died: May 18, 1929, N.Y. (heart disease). Screen, stage actress and opera performer. Often called "the mother of the movies."

COGDELL, JOSEPHINE
Born: 1901. Died: May 2, 1969, N.Y. Screen actress and ballet dancer. Appeared as a Mack Sennett bathing beauty.

COGHLAN, CHARLES F.
Died: Mar. 18, 1972, Hershey, Pa. Screen, stage, vaudeville actor, stage producer and director.

Appeared in: **1921** Jim the Penman.

COGHLAN, KATHERINE
Born: 1889. Died: Sept. 21, 1965, Hollywood, Calif. (cancer). Screen actress (film extra 1919-20). Mother of actor Junior Coghlan.

COGHLAN, ROSE
Born: 1850, Peterborough, England. Died: Apr. 2, 1932, Harrison, N.Y. (cerebral hemorrhage). Stage and screen actress.

Appeared in: **1912** As You Like It. **1915** The Sporting Duchess. **1922** The Secrets of Paris; Beyond the Rainbow. **1923** Under the Red Rose. **1932** Hot Saturday. **1933** Jennie Gerhardt.

COGLEY, NICHOLAS "NICK" (Nicholas P.J. Cogley)
Born: 1869, N.Y. Died: May 20, 1936, Santa Monica, Calif. (following operation). Screen, stage actor and film director. Entered films with Selig.

Appeared in: **1913** Mabel's Heroes; Mother's Boy. **1915** Peanuts and Bullets; A Lucky Leap; Saved by the Wireless. **1916** Dizzy Heights and Daring Hearts; Hearts and Sparks; A La Cabaret; Dollars and Sense (sometimes referred to as The Twins). **1917** Her Circus Knight (sometimes referred to as The Circus Girl); Oriental Love. **1919** Toby's Bow. **1920** Jes' Call Me Jim. **1921** Beating the Game; Boys Will Be Boys; Guile of Women; The Old Nest; An Unwilling Hero. **1922** The Marriage Chance; One Clear Call; Restless Souls. **1923** Crinoline and Romance; Desire. **1924** Abraham Lincoln. **1927** The Missing Link; The Heart of Maryland; In Old Kentucky; Hey! Hey! Cowboy. **1928** Abie's Irish Rose. **1930** Ranch House Blues; The Cohens and the Kellys in Africa. **1933** Cross Fire.

COHAN, GEORGE M.
Born: July 4, 1878, Providence, R.I. Died: Nov. 3, 1942, New York, N.Y. (cancer). Screen, stage, vaudeville, radio actor, songwriter, stage producer, screenwriter and playwright. Appeared in vaudeville as "The Cohan Mirthmakers."

Appeared in: **1917** Seven Keys to Baldpate; Broadway Jones. **1918** Hit-the-Trail-Haliday. **1932** The Phantom President. **1934** Gambling.

COHN, JULIA
Born: Apr. 9, 1902, New York, N.Y. Died: Apr. 10, 1975, New York, N.Y. (heart attack). Screen, stage actress and attorney.

Appeared in: **1967** The Producers.

COLBURN, CARRIE
Born: 1859. Died: May 23, 1932, New York, N.Y. Screen and stage actress.

COLBY, BARBARA
Born: July 2, 1940, New York, N.Y. Died: July 24, 1975, Palms, Calif. (murdered—shot). Screen, stage and television actress.

Appeared in: **1968** Petulia. **1974** California Split; The Memory of Us. **1975** Rafferty and the Gold Dust Twins.

COLBY, HERBERT
Born: 1839. Died: Feb. 6, 1911, Brooklyn, N.Y. Screen actor.

COLCORD, MABEL
Born: 1872, San Francisco, Calif. Died: June 6, 1952, Los Angeles, Calif. Stage and screen actress.

Appeared in: **1933** Little Women. **1934** Sadie McKee. **1935** David Copperfield; Reckless. **1936** The Law in Her Hands; Three Married Men. **1937** The Great O'Malley. **1938** Out West with the Hardys; The Cowboy and the Lady. **1939** The Women.

COLE, BRIAN
Born: 1944, Portland, Ore. Died: Aug. 2, 1972, Hollywood, Calif. Screen actor, writer and singer. He was a member of the "Association" rock group.

COLE, BUDDY (Edwin LeMar Cole)
Born: Dec. 15, 1916, Irving, Ill. Died: Nov. 5, 1964, Hollywood, Calif. (heart attack). Screen, radio actor, pianist, composer and musical arranger.

Appeared in: **1949** Johnny Holiday. **1954** A Star is Born.

COLE, FRED
Born: 1901. Died: Sept. 20, 1964, Hollywood, Calif. Screen actor.

Appeared in: **1924** The Dangerous Blonde. **1925** Daring Days; Secrets of the Night; Two-Fisted Jones.

COLE, JACK
Born: 1914. Died: Feb. 17, 1974, Los Angeles, Calif. Screen, stage actor, dancer and choreographer.

Appeared in: **1941** Moon over Miami. **1944** Kismet. **1957** Designing Woman. **1966** The Case of the Stripping Wives.

COLE, JOHNNY
Died: Mar. 25, 1974. Screen actor.

COLE, LESTER
Born: 1900. Died: May 4, 1962, New York, N.Y. Screen, stage actor and singer.

Appeared in: **1929** Desert Song; Painted Faces. **1930** Love at First Sight.

COLE, MARY KEITH
Born: 1914. Died: Mar. 16, 1975, San Jose, Calif. Screen, stage, vaudeville actress and singer.

Appeared in: **1938** He Loved an Actress.

COLE, NAT "KING" (Nathaniel Adams Coles)
Born: Mar. 17, 1919, Montgomery, Ala. Died: Feb. 15, 1965, Santa Monica, Calif. (lung cancer). Black screen, television actor, singer and composer.

Appeared in: **1945** See My Lawyer. **1949** Make Believe Ballroom. **1953** The Blue Gardenia; Small Town Girl. **1955** Kiss Me Deadly. **1956** The Scarlet Hour. **1957** Istanbul; China Gate. **1958** St. Louis Blues. **1959** The Night of the Quarter Moon. **1965** Cat Ballou.

COLEAN, CHUCK
Born: 1908. Died: Jan. 8, 1971, Hollywood, Calif. (cancer). Screen actor, extra, stuntman and assistant film director.

COLEE, FOREST R.
Born: 1893. Died: Feb. 10, 1962, Calif. Screen actor.

COLEMAN, CHARLES
Born: Dec. 22, 1885, Sydney, Australia. Died: Mar. 8, 1951, Woodland Hills, Calif. (stroke). Screen, stage and television actor.

Appeared in: **1923** Big Dan; Second Hand Love. **1924** That French Lady; The Vagabond Trail. **1926** Sand. **1928** Good Morning, Judge; That's My Daddy. **1930** What a Man; Lawful Larceny; Once a Gentleman. **1931** Beyond Victory; Bachelor Apartment. **1932** The Heart of New York; Play Girl; Merrily We Go to Hell; Winner Take All; Jewel Robbery. **1933** Diplomaniacs; Midnight Club;

Gallant Lady; Sailor Be Good. **1934** Born to Be Bad; The Merry Frinks; Housewife; Million Dollar Ransom; Down to Their Last Yacht. **1935** Becky Sharp; The Goose and the Gander; His Family Tree. **1936** Colleen, Her Master's Voice; Don't Get Personal; Everybody's Old Man; The Poor Little Rich Girl; Mummy's Boys; Walking on Air; Lloyds of London. **1937** Love Is News; Too Many Wives; There Goes My Girl; Fight for Your Lady; Three Smart Girls. **1938** Alexander's Ragtime Band; Penrod and His Twin Brother; Little Miss Broadway; Gateway; The Rage of Paris; That Certain Age; Little Orphan Annie. **1939** Mexican Spitfire; You Can't Cheat an Honest Man; First Love. **1940** Mexican Spitfire Out West. **1941** Buck Privates; Free and Easy; It Started with Eve. **1942** Almost Married; Twin Beds; Miss Annie Rooney; Between Us Girls; Highways by Night; Arabian Nights; Design for Scandal. **1943** Air Raid Wardens; It Ain't Hay; It Comes up Love; Pittsburgh. **1944** Frenchman's Creek; In Society; The Whistler. **1945** The Picture of Dorian Gray; Missing Corpse; Stork Club; Diamond Horseshoe. **1946** Kitty; Cluny Brown; In High Gear; Oh, Professor, Behave (short); Magnificent Rogue; The Runaround; Never Say Goodbye; Ziegfeld Follies. **1947** Pilgrim Lady; The Impefect Lady; Ladies' Man. **1948** Trouble Makers. **1949** My Friend Irma; Oil's Well that Ends Well (short). **1950** Texas Tough Guy (short).

COLEMAN, CLAUDIA

Born: 1889, Atlanta, Ga. Died: Aug. 17, 1938, Hollywood, Calif. Screen, stage and vaudeville actress.

Appeared in: **1927** Putting It On (short). **1933** I Cover the Waterfront; Warrior's Husband; Son of the Border; Frisco Jenny; Let's Live Tonight. **1934** Big Hearted Herbert. **1935** Frisco Kid. **1936** King of Burlesque; Little Miss Nobody; The Country Beyond; Lady from Nowhere; Under Your Spell; Navy Born. **1938** Penrod and His Twin Brother; Test Pilot; Keep Smiling.

COLEMAN, EMIL

Born: 1893, Russia. Died: Jan. 26, 1965, New York, N.Y. (kidney infection). Bandleader and screen actor.

Appeared in: **1935** Melody Masters (short). **1945** Nob Hill.

COLEMAN, THOMAS

Born: 1897. Died: Jan. 28, 1959, Hollywood, Calif. Screen and television actor.

COLEMAN, WARREN R.

Born: 1901. Died: Jan. 13, 1968, Martha's Vineyard, Mass. Black screen, stage, television, radio actor, film director, stage director, film and stage producer. Played "Kingfish" on "Amos 'n Andy" radio show.

COLES, RUSSELL

Born: 1909. Died: Sept. 26, 1960, Hollywood, Calif. (heart attack). Screen actor.

COLL, OWEN G.

Born: 1879. Died: Feb. 7, 1960, L.I., N.Y. Screen, stage, and television actor.

COLLEANO, BONAR, JR. (Bonar Sullivan)

Born: Mar. 14, 1924, New York, N.Y. Died: Aug. 17, 1958, Birkenhead, England (auto accident). Screen, stage, vaudeville, radio actor and circus performer. Member of the Colleano circus family. Married to actress Susan Shaw.

Appeared in: **1944** Starlight Serenade. **1945** The Way to the Stars (aka Johnny in the Clouds–US). **1946** Wanted For Murder; A Matter of Life and Death (aka Stairway to Heaven–US). **1947** While the Sun Shines (US 1950). **1948** One Night With You; Good Time Girl (US 1950); Merry-Go-Round; Sleeping Car to Trieste (US 1949); Once a Jolly Swagman (aka Maniacs on Wheels–US 1951). **1949** Give Us This Day (aka Salt to the Devil–US). **1950** Dance Hall. **1951** Pool of London; A Tale of Five Cities (aka A Tale of Five Women–US 1952). **1952** Eight Iron Men. **1953** Is Your Honeymoon Really Necessary? **1954** Escape by Night; Flame and the Flesh; The Sea Shall Not Have Them (US 1955); Time Is My Enemy (US 1957). **1955** Joe Macbeth (US 1956). **1956** Stars In Your Eyes. **1957** Zarak; Interpol (aka Pickup Alley–US); Fire Down Below. **1958** No Time to Die (aka Tank Force–US); Them Nice Americans; The Man Inside.

COLLIER, CONSTANCE (Laura Constance Hardie)

Born: Jan. 22, 1878, Windsor, England. Died: Apr. 25, 1955, New York, N.Y. Screen, stage, radio actress, stage producer, director, playwright and screenwriter. Married to actor Julian L'Estrange (dec. 1918).

Appeared in: **1915** Intolerance (film debut). **1916** The Code of Marcia Gray; Macbeth. **1919** The Impossible Woman. **1920** Bleak House. **1922** The Bohemian Girl. **1933** Our Betters; Dinner at Eight. **1935** Peter Ibbetson; Shadow of Doubt. **1936** The Bohemian Girl; Professional Soldier; Girls' Dormitory; Little Lord Fauntleroy. **1937** Thunder in the City; Wee Willie Winkie; She Got What She Wanted; Stage Door; Clothes and the Woman; A Damsel in Distress. **1939** Zaza. **1940** Susan and God; Half a Sinner. **1945** Weekend at the Waldorf. **1946** Kitty; Monsieur Beaucaire; Dark Corner. **1947** The Perils of Pauline. **1948** An Ideal Husband; Rope; The Girl from Manhattan. **1950** Whirlpool.

COLLIER, WILLIAM, SR.

Born: Nov. 12, 1866, New York, N.Y. Died: Jan. 13, 1944, Beverly Hills, Calif. (pneumonia). Screen, stage actor, film dialog director and playwright. Father of actor William Collier, Jr.

Appeared in: **1915** Fatty and the Broadway Stars. **1916** Better Late Than Never (working title Getting Married); Plain Jane; Wife and Auto Trouble. **1920** The Servant Question. **1930** Happy Days; High Society Blues; Free and Easy; She's My Weakness; Up the River; Harmony at Home. **1931** Mr. Lemon of Orange; The Seas Beneath; The Brat; Six Cylinder Love; Annabel's Affairs. **1932** After Tomorrow; Hot Saturday; Washington Masquerade; Madison Square Garden; Stepping Sisters. **1934** A Successful Failure; All of Me; The Crosby Case; Cheaters. **1935** The Murder Man; Annapolis Farewell; The Bride Comes Home. **1936** Love on a Bet; Give Us This Night; Valiant Is the Word for Carrie; Cain and Mabel. **1938** Josette; Thanks for the Memory; Say It in French. **1939** I'm from Missouri; Invitation to Happiness; Television Spy; Disputed Passage; Persons in Hiding. **1940** A Miracle on Main Street. **1941** The Hard-Boiled Canary; There's Magic in Music.

COLLINGE, PATRICIA

Born: Sept. 20, 1894, Dublin, Ireland. Died: Apr. 10, 1974, New York, N.Y. (heart attack). Screen, stage, television actress, playwright and author.

Appeared in: **1941** The Little Foxes (stage and film versions). **1943** Shadow of a Doubt; Tender Comrade. **1944** Casanova Brown. **1951** Teresa. **1952** Washington Story. **1959** The Nun's Story.

COLLINS, BLANCHE M.

Born: 1910. Died: Mar. 30, 1968, Los Angeles, Calif. Screen and stage actress. Appeared in films 1929-1938.

COLLINS, C.E.

Born: July 23, 1873, Missouri. Died: Apr. 15, 1951. Screen and stage actor. Entered films in 1917.

Appeared in: **1917** Flame of the Yukon. **1920** Kismet. **1921** Four Horsemen of the Apocalypse; Conquering Power. **1923** The Hunchback of Notre Dame.

COLLINS, EDDIE (Edward Bernard Collins)

Born: 1884. Died: Sept. 2, 1940, Arcadia, Calif. (heart attack). Stage and screen actor.

Appeared in: **1938** In Old Chicago (film debut); Penrod and His Twin Brother; Sally, Irene and Mary; Kentucky Moonshine; Alexander's Ragtime Band; Little Miss Broadway; Always in Trouble; Up the River; Charlie Chan in Honolulu. **1939** Charlie Chan in Reno; News Is Made at Night; Stop, Look and Love; Quick Millions; Drums along the Mohawk; Young Mr. Lincoln; Hollywood Cavalcade. **1940** The Blue Bird; The Return of Frank James.

COLLINS, EDDY (Edward Collins)

Born: 1866. Died: Dec. 17, 1916, Hollywood, Calif. (suicide—leap from building). Screen and vaudeville actor.

COLLINS, G. PAT (George Pat Collins)

Born: Dec. 16, 1895, Brooklyn, N.Y. Died: Aug. 5, 1959, Los Angeles, Calif. (cancer). Screen, stage and television actor.

Appeared in: **1928** The Racket. **1929** Half Marriage. **1930** All Quiet on the Western Front; Manslaughter; Be Yourself!; Big Money; Only Saps Work. **1931** The Vice Squad. **1932** Central Park; Hold 'Em Jail. **1933** 20,000 Years in Sing Sing; Parachute Jumper; Girl Missing; Picture Snatcher; The Silk Express; Heroes for Sale; Fog. **1934** Keep 'Em Rolling; The Crime Doctor; The Big Shakedown; A Very Honorable Guy; The Personality Kid. **1935** Black Fury; Alibi Ike; West Point of the Air; Baby Face Harrington; West of the Pecos; Mr. Dynamite. **1938** What Price Safety (short). **1948** Scudda Hoo! Scudda Hay! **1949** Flaming Fury; I Married a Communist; White Heat. **1950** Indian Territory; The Woman on Pier 13. **1955** Betrayed Women; The Big Tip-Off; The Naked Street; Night Freight. **1956** Yaqui Drums.

COLLINS, JOSE

Born: May 23, 1887, London, England. Died: Dec. 6, 1958, London, England. Screen, stage and vaudeville actress.

Appeared in: **1916** The Light That Failed. **1919** Nobody's Child. **1920** The Sword of Damocles.

COLLINS, MONTE F., JR. "MONTY" (Monte Francis Collins, Jr.)

Born: Dec. 3, 1898, New York, N.Y. Died: June 1, 1951, North Hollywood, Calif. (heart attack). Screen, stage, vaudeville actor, film producer, director and screenwriter.

Appeared in: **1920** Forty Five Minutes from Broadway (film debut as an extra). **1921** Old Swimmin' Hole; Nineteen and Phyllis; The Cup of Life; The Man from Lost River; Midnight Bell; My Best Girl. **1922** My Wife's Relations (short); At the Sign of the Jack O'Lantern; The Man with Two Mothers; Come on Over. **1923** Big Dan; Long Live the King; Our Hospitality; The Old Fool. **1924** Men; A Boy of Flanders; Pride of Sunshine Alley; Tiger Love. **1925** All around Frying Pan; That Man Jack!; Cold Nerve; The Desert Flower; Tumbleweeds; plus a series of Fox short comedies. **1926** The Loves of Ricardo; The Cowboy and the Countess. **1927** King of Kings; Painting the Town. **1928** Arizona Wildcat. **1929** Why Bring That Up?; The Talkies; Romance Deluxe; plus the two following shorts: The Madhouse; Ticklish Business. **1930** The following shorts: Hail the Princess; Peace and Harmony; How's My Baby; His Error; French Kisses. **1921** Peach O'Reno. **1932** Girl Crazy; plus the following shorts: Show Business; Anybody's Goat; It's a Cinch; Keep Laughing; Hollywood Handicap; Hollywood Runaround; and Sunkissed Sweeties. **1933** The Gay Nighties (short). **1934** The following shorts: Woman Haters; Love and Hisses; In a Pig's Eye; Hey Nanny Nanny. **1935** Gobs of Trouble (short); The Mystery Man; Flying Down to Zero (short). **1936** Rent Free (short). **1937** Hollywood Round-Up; Columbia shorts. **1938** Wild Bill Hickok (serial); See My Lawyer (short); The Missing Links (short). **1939** Moochin' through Georgia (short); Boom Goes the Groom (short); The Gracie Allen Murder Case. **1940** The Heckler (short); Cold Turkey (short); Benny Rides Again. **1941** She's Oil Mine (short); General Nuisance (short); Kathleen. **1942** Cactus Makes Perfect (short); What Makes Lizzy Dizzy? (short). **1943** My Tomato (short).

COLLINS, PAMELA (Pamela Ray Collins)
Born: Nov. 29, 1948, Virginia. Died: Sept. 20, 1974, Beverly Hills, Calif. (suicide—pills). Screen actress.

Appeared in: **1968** Finders Keepers, Lovers Weepers. **1970** Substitution. **1973** Sweet Sugar; So Long, Blue Boy.

COLLINS, RAY
Born: 1890, Sacramento, Calif. Died: July 11, 1965, Santa Monica, Calif. (emphysema). Screen, stage, television, radio, and vaudeville actor.

Appeared in: **1940** The Grapes of Wrath. **1941** Citizen Kane. **1942** The Magnificent Ambersons; Highways by Night; Commandos Strike at Dawn; The Big Street; The Navy Comes Through. **1943** The Crime Doctor; The Human Comedy; Slightly Dangerous; Salute to the Marines; Whistling in Brooklyn. **1944** Eve of St. Mark; See Here, Private Hargrove; Barbary Coast Gent; Shadows in the Night; The Seventh Cross; The Hitler Gang; Can't Help Singing. **1945** Roughly Speaking; The Hidden Eye; Leave Her to Heaven; Miss Susie Slagle's. **1946** Badman's Territory; Boys' Ranch; Crack-Up; Return of Monte Cristo; The Best Years of Our Lives; Two Years before the Mast; Night in Paradise; Up Goes Maisie; Three Wise Fools. **1947** The Red Stallion; The Bachelor and the Bobby-Soxer; The Senator Was Indiscreet; The Swordsman. **1948** Homecoming; Good Sam; For the Love of Mary; The Man from Colorado; A Double Life. **1949** Red Stallion in the Rockies; Hideout; Francis; The Fountainhead; The Heiress; It Happens Every Spring; Free for All; Command Decision. **1950** Kill the Umpire!; Paid in Full; The Reformer and the Redhead; Summer Stock. **1951** Ma and Pa Kettle Back on the Farm; I Want You; You're in the Navy Now (aka U.S.S. Teakettle); Reunion in Reno; The Racket; Vengeance Valley. **1952** The Invitation; Young Man with Ideas; Dreamboat. **1953** Ma and Pa Kettle at the Fair; Ma and Pa Kettle on Vacation; The Desert Song; Column South; The Kid from Left Field; Bad for Each Other. **1954** Rose Marie; Athena. **1955** The Desperate Hours; Texas Lady. **1956** Never Say Goodbye; The Solid Gold Cadillac. **1957** Spoilers of the Forest. **1958** Touch of Evil. **1961** I'll Give My Life.

COLLINS, RUSSELL
Born: Oct. 11, 1897. Died: Nov. 14, 1965, West Hollywood, Calif. (heart attack). Screen, stage and television actor.

Appeared in: **1948** Close-Up. **1949** The Walking Hills; Shockproof. **1953** Destination Gobi; Miss Sadie Thompson; Niagara. **1955** Canyon Crossroads; The Last Frontier; Bad Day at Black Rock; Soldier of Fortune. **1957** Raintree County; The Enemy Below. **1958** The Matchmaker; God's Little Acre. **1959** The Rabbit Trap. **1964** Fail Safe. **1965** Those Calloways; When the Boys Meet the Girls.

COLLINS, S.D.J.
Born: 1907. Died: Dec. 28, 1947, Leavenworth, Kan. (heart ailment). Screen actor and circus performer.

Appeared in: **1935** A Night at the Opera.

COLLINS, TOM
Died: June 17, 1973. Screen actor.

Appeared in: **1939** Fast and Loose; Tell No Tales; These Glamour Girls; Burn 'Em Up O'Connor; Money to Loan (short). **1940** Dr. Kildare's Strangest Case; Dr. Kildare Goes Home. **1941** Dancing on a Dime.

COLLUM, JOHN
Born: 1926. Died: Aug. 28, 1962, Hollywood, Calif. Screen actor.

Appeared in: **1940** Tom Brown's School Days.

COLLYER, JUNE (Dorothea Heermance)
Born: Aug. 19, 1907. Died: Mar. 16, 1968, Los Angeles, Calif. (bronchial pneumonia). Screen, stage and television actress. Married to actor Stuart Erwin (dec. 1967).

Appeared in: **1927** East Side, West Side (film debut). **1928** Me, Gangster; Four

Sons; Hangman's House; Woman Wise. **1929** Red Wine; Let's Make Whoopee; Not Quite Decent; Illusion; River of Romance; The Love Doctor; The Pleasant Sin. **1930** Extravagance; Charley's Aunt; A Man from Wyoming; Sweet Kitty Bellairs; Toast of the Legion; Three Sisters; Beyond Victory. **1931** Damaged Love; The Brat; Honeymoon Lane; Kiss Me Again; Drums of Jeopardy; Alexander Hamilton; Dude Ranch. **1933** Revenge at Monte Carlo; Before Midnight. **1934** Cheaters; Lost in the Stratosphere. **1935** The Ghost Walks; Murder by Television.

COLMAN, IRENE
Born: 1915, Nashua, N.H. Died: July 19, 1975, Santa Monica, Calif. (leukemia). Screen actress.

Appeared in: **1934** Bottoms Up; Stand Up and Cheer; Springtime for Henry; Change of Heart.

COLMAN, RONALD
Born: Feb. 9, 1891, Richmond-Surrey, England. Died: May 19, 1958, Santa Barbara, Calif. (lung infection). Screen, stage, television and radio actor. Divorced from actress Victoria Maud (aka Thelma Ray) and married to actress Benita Hume (dec. 1967). Won 1947 Academy Award for Best Actor in A Double Life.

Appeared in: **1919** The Toilers; Sheba; The Snow in the Desert. **1920** Anna the Adventuress; The Black Spider; A Son of David. **1921** Handcuffs or Kisses. **1923** The White Sister; The Eternal City. **1924** Romola; $20 a Week; Heart Trouble; Her Night of Romance; Tarnish. **1925** The Sporting Venus; Stella Dallas; The Dark Angel; His Supreme Moment; Her Sister from Paris; Lady Windermere's Fan; A Thief in Paradise. **1926** Beau Geste; Kiki; The Winning of Barbara Worth. **1927** The Magic Flame; The Night of Love. **1928** Two Lovers. **1929** The Rescue; Condemned; I Have Been Faithful; Bulldog Drummond. **1930** Raffles; The Devil to Pay. **1931** Arrowsmith; The Unholy Garden. **1932** Cynara. **1933** The Masquerader. **1934** Bulldog Drummond Strikes Back. **1935** Clive of India; The Man Who Broke the Bank at Monte Carlo; A Tale of Two Cities. **1936** Under Two Flags. **1937** Lost Horizon; The Prisoner of Zenda. **1938** If I Were King. **1939** The Light that Failed. **1940** Lucky Partners. **1941** My Life with Caroline. **1942** Random Harvest; Talk of the Town. **1944** Kismet. **1947** A Double Life; The Late George Apley. **1950** Champagne for Caesar. **1956** Around the World in 80 Days. **1957** The Story of Mankind.

COLUMBO, RUSS (Ruggerio de Rudolpho Columbo)
Born: Jan. 14, 1908, Philadelphia, Pa. Died: Sept. 2, 1934, Hollywood, Calif. (accidentally shot). Screen, radio actor, singer and songwriter.

Appeared in: **1929** Wolf Song; The Street Girl; Dynamite; The Wonders of Women. **1931** Hellbound. **1933** That Goes Double (short); Broadway Thru a Keyhole. **1934** Moulin Rouge; Wake Up and Dream.

COLVIG, VANCE D. "PINTO"
Born: 1892, Jacksonville, Ore. Died: Oct. 3, 1967, Woodland Hills, Calif. Screen, stage actor and songwriter. Known as the "Dean of Hollywood Voice Men." Entered films with Sennett in 1923. He created the voices for "Goofy," "Pluto," and "Grumpy" in Snow White and the Seven Dwarfs (1937) and was the voice of "Bozo the Clown" on Capitol Records.

COMANCHE, LAURENCE "TEX"
Born: 1908. Died: Oct. 10, 1932, Hollywood, Calif. (suicide or accident—gun shot wounds). Screen actor and Indian film extra.

COMANT, MATHILDA
Born: 1888, France. Died: June 22, 1938, Hollywood, Calif. Stage and screen actress.

Appeared in: **1931** The Lash. **1935** Ceiling Zero. **1936** Anthony Adverse.

COMBER, BOBBIE (Edmund Comber)
Born: Jan. 8, 1890, Bury St. Edmunds, England. Died: Apr. 1942, Wales (heart attack). Screen, stage and radio actor.

Appeared in: **1930** Elstree Calling. **1931** Hot Heir. **1932** Brother Alfred. **1933** Sleeping Car; The Fortunate Fool. **1934** There Goes Susie (aka Scandals of Paris–US 1935); Lilies of the Field. **1935** The Ace of Spades; Lazybones; Be Careful Mr. Smith. **1936** Don't Rush Me; Sporting Love; Excuse My Glove. **1938** The Singing Cop.

COMINGORE, DOROTHY (Linda Winters)
Born: 1918. Died: Dec. 30, 1971, Stonington, Conn. Screen and stage actress.

Appeared in: **1939** Blondie Meets the Boss; The Awful Goof; Trade Winds; Mr. Smith Goes to Washington. **1940** Rockin' Through the Rockies (short); The Hecklers (short); Street of Missing Women. **1941** Citizen Kane. **1944** The Hairy Ape. **1949** Any Number Can Play. **1952** The Big Night.

COMMERFORD, THOMAS (aka THOMAS COMBERFORD)
Born: 1855, New York. Died: Feb. 17, 1920. Screen actor.

Appeared in: **1911** Two Orphans. **1912** The Miller of Burgundy; A Heart in Rags; The Girl at the Cupola. **1913** The Boomerang; Broken Threads United;

A False Order; The Ex-Convict; A Lucky Mistake; What's the Matter with Father?; Homespun; A Midnight Bell. **1914** The Grip of Circumstance; One Wonderful Night; The Fable of the Family that Did too Much for Nellie; The Private Officer; The Great Game. **1915** The White Sister; Graustark; Countess Veschi's Jewels; Mr. Buttles; Thirteen Down; The Surprise of My Life; The Little Straw Wife; A Night Given Over to Revelry; The Longer Voyage; The Call of Yesterday; Caught; On the Little Mill Trace; The Little Deceiver; The Greater Courage. **1916** The Sting of Victory; Is Marriage Sacred (series); The Romance of Billy Goat Hill; Our People; The Three Scratch Clue; His Little Wife; It Never Could Happen; What I Said, Goes; A Failure at Fifty. **1917** The Fable of the Uplifter and His Dandy Little Opus.

COMPSON, BETTY
Born: Mar. 18, 1897, Beaver, Utah. Died: Apr. 18, 1974, Glendale, Calif. Screen, stage, television actress and film producer. Divorced from actor/director James Cruze (dec. 1942) and business manager Irving Weinberg. Married to Silvius Jack Gall (dec. 1962). Nominated for 1928-29 Academy Award as Best Actress in The Barker.

Appeared in: **1915-1916** Wanted—a Leading Lady (film debut); Their Quiet Honeymoon; Where the Heater Blooms; Love and a Savage; Some Chaperone; Jed's Trip to the Fair; Mingling Spirits; When the Losers Won; Her Steady Carfare; A Quiet Supper for Four; Her Friend; the Doctor; When Lizzie Disappeared; Cupid Trims His Lordship; The Deacon's Waterloo; Love and Vaccination; He Almost Eloped; The Janitor's Busy Day; A Leap Year Tangle; Eddie's Night Out; The Newlywed's Mix-up; Lem's College Career; Potts Bungles Again; He's a Devil; The Wooing of Aunt Jemima; Her Celluloid Hero; All Over a Stocking; Almost a Widow; Wanted—A Husband. **1916-1918** His Baby; The Making Over of Mother; A Brass-Buttoned Romance; Some Kid; Hist at 6 O'Clock; Cupid's Uppercut; Out for the Coin; Her Crooked Career; Her Friend the Chauffeur; Small Change; Hubby's Night Out; A Bold Bad Knight; As Luck Would Have It; Suspended Sentence; His Last Pill; Those Wedding Bells; Almost a Scandal; Down by the Sea; Won in a Cabaret; Crazy by Proxy; Betty's Big Idea; Love and the Locksmiths; Almost a Bigamist; Almost Divorced; Betty Wakes Up; Their Seaside Tangle; Nearly a Papa; Cupid's Camouflage; Many a Slip; Whose Wife?; Betty's Adventure; All Dressed Up; Somebody's Baby; A Seminary Scandal. **1918** The Sheriff; Border Raiders. **1919** The Terror of the Range (serial); The Prodigal Liar; Light of Victory; The Little Diplomat; The Devil's Trail; The Miracle Man. **1921** Prisoners of Love; At the End of the World; Ladies Must Live; For Those We Love. **1922** The Little Minister; The Law and the Woman; The Green Temptation; Over the Border; Always the Woman; The Bonded Woman; To Have and To Hold; Kick In. **1923** The White Flower; The Rustle of Silk; The Woman with Four Faces; Hollywood; The Royal Oak; The Prude's Fall; Woman to Woman (US 1924). **1924** The Stranger; Miami; The Enemy Sex; The White Shadow (aka White Shadows–US); Ramshackle House; The Female; The Garden of Weeds; The Fast Set. **1925** Locked Doors; New Lives for Old; Eve's Secret; Beggar on Horseback; Paths to Paradise; The Pony Express. **1926** The Palace of Pleasure; The Counsel for Defense; The Wise Guy; The Belle of Broadway. **1927** Twelve Miles Out; The Ladybird; Say It with Diamonds; Temptations of a Shop Girl; Cheating Cheaters. **1928** Love Me and the World is Mine; Big-City; The Masked Angel; The Desert Bride; Life's Mockery; The Docks of New York; Court Martial; The Barker; Scarlet Seas. **1929** Weary River; On With the Show; The Time, the Place and the Girl; Street Girl; The Great Gabbo; Skin Deep; Woman to Woman (and 1923 version); The Show ofBrot Shows. **1930** Blaze O'Glory; The Case of Sergeant Grischa; Isle of Escape; The Midnight Mystery; The Czar of Broadway; Inside the Lines; Those Who Dance; The Spoilers; She Got What She Wanted; The Boudoir Diplomat. **1931** The Lady Refuses; Virtuous Husband; Three Who Loved; The Gay Diplomat. **1932** The Silver Lining; Guilty or Not Guilty. **1933** West of Singapore; Destination Unknown; Notorious But Nice. **1935** False Pretenses. **1936** Laughing Irish Eyes; The Millionaire Kid; The Dragnet; August Weekend; Hollywood Boulevard; Bulldog Edition; Killer at Large. **1937** Circus Girl; Two Minutes to Play; Federal Bullets. **1938** Blondes at Work; A Slight Case of Murder; The Port of Missing Girls; Torchy Blane in Panama; Two Gun Justice; Under the Big Top. **1939** News is Made at Night; The Mystic Circle Murder; Cowboys from Texas. **1940** Strange Cargo; Mad Youth; Laughing at Danger. **1941** Mr. and Mrs. Smith; The Invisible Ghost; The Roar of the Press. **1943** Danger! Women at Work; Her Adventurous Night. **1946** Claudia and David. **1947** Hard Boiled Mahoney; Second Chance. **1948** Here Comes Trouble.

COMPTON, BETTY
Born: 1907, Isle of Wight. Died: July 12, 1944, N.Y. Screen, stage actress, singer and dancer. Divorced from James J. Walker, former Mayor of New York (dec. 1946).

Appeared in: **1930** The Legacy (short). **1934** A British International film.

COMPTON, FRANCIS
Born: 1885, San Francisco, Calif. Died: Sept. 17, 1964, Noroton, Conn. Screen actor.

Appeared in: **1958** Witness for the Prosecution.

COMPTON, VIOLA
Born: 1886, London, England. Died: Apr. 7, 1971, Birchington, England. Stage and screen actress. Sister of actress Fay Compton.

Appeared in: **1932** Looking on the Bright Side. **1933** The Good Companions; The Medicine Man; The Shadow; Excess Baggage. **1936** Under Proof; The Big Noise; Find the Lady; Happy Days are Here Again; Servants All; The Man in the Mirror (US 1937).

CONDE, JOHNNY
Born: 1895. Died: Dec. 5, 1960, Hollywood, Calif. (heart attack). Screen actor.

CONE, MIKE "ZETS"
Born: 1910. Died: Jan. 4, 1969, North Miami Beach, Fla. (cancer). Screen, television actor and musician.

CONKLIN, CHARLES "HEINIE"
Born: 1880. Died: July 30, 1959, Hollywood, Calif. Screen actor.

Appeared in: **1923** The Day of Faith. **1924** The Cyclone Rider; Find Your Man; George Washington, Jr.; Troubles of a Bride. **1925** Below the Line; A Fool and His Money; Hogan's Alley; Clash of the Wolves; Red Hot Tires; Seven Sinners. **1926** The Fighting Edge; Hardboiled; The Man Upstairs; More Pay—Less Work; Whispering Wires; Fig Leaves; Honesty—the Best Policy; The Night Cry; The Sap; Ruggles of Red Gap. **1927** Beware of Widows; Ham and Eggs at the Front; Cheaters; Drums of the Desert; Silk Stockings. **1928** The Air Circus; Beau Broadway; Feel My Pulse; A Horseman of the Plains; A Trick of Hearts. **1929** The Show of Shows; Side Street; Tiger Rose. **1930** Duckling Duty (short); All Quiet on the Western Front. **1932** Trailing the Killer; Young Ironsides (short). **1933** Riders of Destiny. **1934** Most Precious Thing in Life. **1935** Girl From 10th Avenue; Ruggles of Red Gap; plus the following shorts: Old Sawbones; Tramp, Tramp, Tramp. **1936** Wedding Present. **1938** Passport Husband; Little Miss Broadway. **1939** Hollywood Cavalcade. **1940** Dr. Christian Meets the Women; The Courageous Dr. Christian; The Heckler (short). **1942** Even as I.O.U. (short); Hold 'Em Jail (short). **1943** Three Little Twerps (short). **1944** Lost in a Harem; plus following shorts: His Tale Is Told; Movie Pests. **1945** Song of the Prairie. **1947** The Perils of Pauline; Wife to Spare (short). **1949** Loaded Pistols. **1950** Joe Palooka in Humphrey Takes a Chance; County Fair. **1954** Pals and Gals (short). **1955** Abbott and Costello Meet the Keystone Kops.

CONKLIN, CHESTER
Born: Jan. 11, 1888, Oskaloosa, Iowa. Died: Oct. 11, 1971, Woodland Hills, Calif. Screen, stage, vaudeville and circus actor. Entered films in 1913 with Majestic and later appeared in several Keystone Kop comedies.

Appeared in: **1913** Ambrose-Walrus Series. **1914** Making a Living (reissued as A Busted Johnny); Mabel's Strange Predicament; Between Showers; Tango Tangles; Mabel at the Wheel (reissued as His Daredevil); Twenty Minutes of Love; Caught in a Cabaret (reissued as The Jazz Waiter); Mabel's Busy Day; Mabel's New Job; The Face on the Barroom Floor (reissued as The Ham Artist); Those Love Pangs; The Love Thief; Dough and Dynamite (reissued as The Doughnut Designers); Gentlemen of Nerve (reissued as Some Nerve); Curses! They Remarked; How Heroes Are Made; His Taking Ways; A Colored Girl's Love; Wild West Love. **1915** Hushing the Scandal (reissued as Friendly Enemies); Hash House Mashers; Love, Speed and Thrills; The Home Breakers (reissued as Other People's Wives); Caught in a Park; A Bird's a Bird; A One Night Stand; Hearts and Planets; Ambrose's Sour Grapes; Droppington's Devilish Dream; Droppington's Family Tree; Do-Re-Me-Fa; A Hash House Fraud; The Cannon Ball (reissued as The Dynamiter); When Ambrose Dared Walrus; The Battle of Ambrose and Walrus; Saved By the Wireless; The Best of Enemies. **1916** Dizzy Heights and Daring Hearts; Cinders of Love; Bucking Society; His First False Step; A Tugboat Romeo. **1917** The Pullman Bride; Dodging His Doom; A Clever Dummy; The Pawnbroker's Heart. **1919** Uncle Tom's Cabin. **1920** "Sunshine" comedies; Chicken a la Cabaret. **1921** Skirts. **1923** Anna Christie; Desire; Souls for Sale; Tea with a Kick. **1924** Galloping Fish; Another Man's Wife; The Fire Patrol; North of Nevada; Greed. **1925-26** 12 "Blue Ribbon" comedies (shorts). **1925** A Woman of the World; Battling Bunyon; The Great Love; The Masked Bride; Where Was I?; The Winding Stair; The Great Jewel Robbery; My Neighbor's Wife; One Year to Live; The Phantom of the Opera; The Pleasure Buyers; Under the Rouge; The Gold Rush. **1926-27** Series of shorts for Tennek Film Corp. **1926** The Wilderness Woman; A Social Celebrity; Say It Again; We're in the Navy Now; Behind the Front; The Duchess of Buffalo; Fascinating Youth; The Lady of the Harem; The Nervous Wreck; Midnight Lovers. **1927** Cabaret; Rubber Heels; Kiss in a Taxi; Tell It to Sweeney; McFadden's Flats. **1928** Two Flaming Youths; Fools for Luck; Gentlemen Prefer Blondes; Tillie's Punctured Romance; Varsity; The Big Noise; Trick of Hearts; The Haunted House; Feel My Pulse; Horseman of the Plains; Beau Broadway. **1929** Marquis Preferred; The House of Horror; Stairs of Sand; The Studio Murder Mystery; Sunset Pass; The Virginian; Shanghai Rose; Show of Shows; Taxi Thirteen; Fast Company; plus several Hal Roach shorts. **1930** Swing High; The Master Sweeper (short); The Love Trader. **1930-31** Six shorts for Paramount. **1931** The New Yorker; Her Majesty, Love; Stout Hearts and Willing Hands. **1933** Hallelujah, I'm a Bum. **1935** A Vitaphone short. **1936** Call of the Prairie; Modern Times; The Preview Murder

Mystery. **1937** Hotel Haywire; Forlorn River. **1938** Flatfoot Stooges (short); Every Day's a Holiday. **1939** Zenobia; The Teacher's Pet (short); Hollywood Cavalcade. **1940** The Great Dictator; Li'l Abner. **1941** Goodnight Sweetheart; Harmon of Michigan; Dutiful But Dumb (short). **1942** Piano Mooner (short); Sons of the Pioneers. **1943** Three Little Twerps (short); Phony Express (short). **1944** Adventures of Mark Twain; Knickerbocker Holiday; Sunday Dinner for a Soldier; Hail the Conquering Hero. **1945** Micro Phonies (short); Abbott and Costello in Hollywood. **1946** The Best Years of Our Lives; Little Giant. **1947** Perils of Pauline; Springtime in the Sierras. **1949** Jiggs and Maggie in Jackpot Jitters; The Beautiful Blonde from Bashful Bend; The Golden Stallion. **1950** Joe Palooka in Humphrey Takes a Chance. **1953** So You Want To Be a Musician (short). **1955** Apache Woman; Beast with a Million Eyes. **1958** Rock-a-Bye Baby. **1960** When Comedy Was King (documentary). **1962** Paradise Alley. **1966** A Big Hand for the Little Lady.

CONKLIN, WILLIAM
Born: Brooklyn, N.Y. Died: Mar. 21, 1935, Hollywood, Calif. (paralytic stroke). Screen, stage actor and film producer. Entered films in 1915.

Appeared in: **1915** Neal of the Navy (serial). **1917** Law of the Land. **1919** Hay Foot, Straw Foot; Red Hot Dollars. **1920** The Woman in the Suitcase; Hairpins. **1921** Beau Revel; Blind Hearts; The Lure of Youth; The Other Woman. **1922** Iron to Gold; The Unfoldment; Up and Going; When Husbands Deceive; The Woman He Married. **1923** Daytime Wives; The Darlings of New York; The Lone Star Ranger; The Lonely Road; The Man Alone; The Meanest Man in the World; Three Who Paid. **1924** The Goldfish; Never Say Die; Stolen Secrets. **1925** Counsel for the Defense; Fifth Avenue Models; A Gentleman Roughneck; The Man without a Country; Ports of Call; The Rag Man; Winds of Chance. **1926** Faithful Wives; Old Ironsides; Sweet Rosie O'Grady. **1927** Outlaws of Red River; Rose of the Golden West; Tumbling River. **1928** Life's Crossroads. **1929** The Divine Lady; Shanghai Rose.

CONLEY, HARRY J.
Born: 1885. Died: June 23, 1975, Cleveland, Ohio (heart attack). Screen, stage and vaudeville actor.

Appeared in: **1928** The Bookworm (short). **1930** Slick as Ever (short).

CONLEY, LIGE
Born: 1899. Died: Dec. 11, 1937, Hollywood, Calif. (hit by auto). Screen actor. Entered films in silents with Sennett.

Appeared in: **1928** The Charge of the Gauchos.

CONLEY, WILLIAM "BING"
Died: July 23, 1962. Screen actor.

CONLIN, JIMMY (aka JIMMY CONLON)
Born: Oct. 14, 1884, Camden, N.J. Died: May 7, 1962, Encino, Calif. Screen, stage, vaudeville and television actor. Married to actress Myrtle Glass with whom he appeared in vaudeville as "Conlin and Glass."

Appeared in: **1928** Sharps and Flats (film debut); Lights of New York. **1933** 20,000 Years in Sing Sing; College Humor. **1934** Now I'll Tell; Cross Country Cruise; City Limits. **1935** The Bride Comes Home. **1936** And Sudden Death; Rose Bowl. **1937** Find the Witness; The Bad Man Who Found Himself; The Adventurous Blonde. **1938** Crashing Hollywood; Torchy Blane in Panama; Broadway Musketeers; Cocoanut Grove. **1939** $1000 a Touchdown; No Place to Go. **1940** Calling Philo Vance; Second Chorus; The Great McGinty. **1941** Ridin' on a Rainbow; Sullivan's Travels. **1942** The Remarkable Andrew; The Forest Rangers; The Palm Beach Story; The Man in the Trunk. **1943** Hitler's Madness; Petticoat Larceny; Jitterbugs; Taxi, Mister? **1944** Lost in a Harem; Town Went Wild; Hail the Conquering Hero; Summer Storm; Army Wives; Ali Baba and the Forty Thieves; Miracle of Morgan's Creek. **1945** Bring on the Girls; What, No Cigarettes? (short); Don Juan Quilligan; An Angel Comes to Brooklyn; Fallen Angel; Picture of Dorian Gray. **1946** Whistle Stop. **1947** Mad Wednesday; It's a Joke, Son; Dick Tracy's Dilemma; Rolling Home; Seven Keys to Baldpate; The Hucksters; Mourning Becomes Electra. **1949** Prejudice; Knock on Any Door; Tulsa. **1950** Operation Haylift; Sideshow; The Great Rupert. **1953** It Happens Every Thursday. **1959** Anatomy of a Murder; The 30 Foot Bride of Candy Rock.

CONNELLY, BOBBY (Robert J. Connelly)
Born: 1909. Died: July 5, 1922, Lynbrook, N.Y. (enlarged heart and bronchitis). Screen and vaudeville actor. Brother of actress Helen Connelly. Entered films at age of three for Kalem in 1912.

Appeared in: **1913** Love's Sunset. **1914** Bunny's Mistake; Street Singer; Goodness Gracious!; The Heart of Sonny Jim; Carpenter; The Circus and the Boy; The Cave Dwellers. **1915** The Professor's Romance; The Night Before Christmas; The Island of Regeneration; To Cherish and Protect; Sonny Jim at the Mardi Gras; The Faith of Sonny Jim; Sonny Jim and the Great American Game; One Plus One Equals One; Sonny Jim's First Love Affair; The Turn of the Road; Old Good-for-Nothin'; A Case of Eugenics; Sonny Jim and the Amusement Co., Ltd.; Bobby's Bargain; Jim and the Family Party; The Third Party; The Prince in Disguise. **1916** A Prince in a Pawnshop; Salvation Jane; The Suspect; Fathers of Men; From Out of the Past; The Writing on the Wall;

Her Bad Quarter of an Hour; The Rookie; The Law Decides. **1917** Intrigue; Her Right to Live; Just What Bobby Wanted; Bobby's Secret; When Bobby Broke His Arm; Bobby and the Helping Hand; Bobby of the Home Defenders; Bobby and the Fairy; Bobby and Company; Bobby Takes a Wife; Bobby's Country Adventure; Bobby the Magician; To the Rescue. **1918** Out of a Clear Sky; A Youthful Affair; The Seal of Silence. **1919** What Love Forgives; The Unpardonable Sin. **1920** Other Men's Shoes; Humoresque. **1921** The Old Oaken Bucket. **1922** A Wide-Open Town; Wildness of Youth.

CONNELLY, EDWARD J.
Born: 1855, New York. Died: Nov. 21, 1928, Hollywood, Calif. (influenza). Stage and screen actor.

Appeared in: **1914** The Good Little Devil (film debut). **1917** The Great Secret (serial). **1920** Shore Acres; The Willow Tree. **1921** The Four Horsemen of the Apocalypse; Camille; The Conquering Power; The Conflict. **1922** Quincy Adams Sawyer; Kisses; Love in the Dark; Seeing's Believing; Red Hot Romance; The Prisoner of Zenda; Turn to the Right; Trifling Women. **1923** Desire; Where the Pavement Ends; Slave of Desire; Her Fatal Millions; Scaramouche. **1924** The Beauty Prize; The Goldfish; Revelation; Sinners in Silk; So This Is Marriage; A Fool's Awakening. **1925** Sun-Up; The Only Thing; The Denial; The Unholy Three; The Merry Widow. **1926** The Gay Deceiver; Bardely's, the Magnificent; Brown of Harvard; The Torrent. **1927** Lovers?; Winners of the Wilderness; The Show; The Student Prince. **1928** Brotherly Love; Across to Singapore; Forbidden Hours; The Mysterious Lady. **1929** The Desert Rider.

CONNELLY, ERWIN
Born: 1873. Died: Feb. 12, 1931, Los Angeles, Calif. (auto accident injuries). Screen, stage and vaudeville actor. Married to actress Jane Connelly (dec. 1925) and together they appeared in vaudeville.

Appeared in: **1922** The Man from Beyond. **1924** Sherlock, Jr. **1925** Beggar on Horseback; Marry Me; Seven Chances; When Husbands Flirt. **1926** The Blind Goddess; The Crown of Lies; The Danger Girl; The Fire Brigade; Kiki; Shipwrecked; The Son of the Sheik; The Winning of Barbara Worth. **1927** Cheating Cheaters; Rubber Tires.

CONNELLY, JANE
Died: Oct. 25, 1925, Los Angeles, Calif. (result of a nervous breakdown). Screen and vaudeville actress. Married to actor Erwin Connelly (dec. 1931) and together they appeared in vaudeville.

Appeared in: **1922** The Man from Beyond. **1924** Sherlock, Jr.

CONNESS, ROBERT
Born: 1868, La Salle County, Ill. Died: Jan. 15, 1941, Portland, Maine. Stage and screen actor. Married to actress Helen Strickland (dec. 1938).

Appeared in: **1911** His Misjudgment. **1916** The Witching Hour; The Martyrdom of Philip Strong; A Message to Garcia. **1917** The Rainbow; The Master Passion; The Ghost of Old Morro.

CONNOLLY, WALTER
Born: Apr. 8, 1887, Cincinnati, Ohio. Died: May 28, 1940, Beverly Hills, Calif. (stroke). Stage and screen actor.

Appeared in: **1930** Many Happy Returns (short). **1932** Washington Merry-Go-Round; Plainsclothes Man; No More Orchids; Man against Woman. **1933** Lady for a Day; Master of Men; East of Fifth Avenue; A Man's Castle; Paddy the Next Best Thing; The Bitter Tea of General Yen. **1934** Eight Girls in a Boat; It Happened One Night; Twentieth Century; Whom the Gods Destroy; Broadway Bill; Lady by Choice; White Lies; Once to Every Woman; Servants' Entrance; Captain Hates the Sea; Many Happy Returns. **1935** So Red the Rose; She Couldn't Take It; Father Brown, Detective; One Way Ticket. **1936** Soak the Rich; The Music Goes 'Round; The King Steps Out; Libeled Lady. **1937** The Good Earth; Nancy Steele Is Missing; Let's Get Married; The League of Frightened Men; First Lady; Nothing Sacred. **1938** Start Cheering; Penitentiary; Four's a Crowd; Too Hot to Handle. **1939** The Girl Downstairs; Those High Gray Walls; Good Girls Go to Paris; Bridal Suite; Coast Guard; The Adventures of Huckleberry Finn; Fifth Avenue Girl; The Great Victor Herbert.

CONNOR, EDRIC
Born: 1915, Mayaro, Trinidad. Died: Oct. 16, 1968, London, England (stroke). Black screen, stage, radio, television actor, singer, author and film producer. Entered films in 1952.

Appeared in: **1952** Cry, The Beloved Country (aka African Fury–US). **1954** East of Zanzibar. **1956** Moby Dick. **1957** Fire Down Below; Seven Thunders (aka The Beasts of Marseilles–US 1959). **1958** Virgin Island (US 1960); The Vikings. **1961** King of Kings. **1963** Four for Texas. **1968** Nobody Runs Forever (aka The High Commissioner–US); Only When I Larf.

CONRAD, EDDIE
Born: 1891. Died: Apr. 1941, Los Angeles, Calif. Screen, stage and vaudeville actor.

Appeared in: **1927** Broadway's Favorite Comedian (short). **1929** Blaze O'Glory.

1934 Done in Oil (short). 1935 Every Night at Eight; I Live for Love; Stars over Broadway; The Melody Lingers On. 1936 Big Brown Eyes; Hot Money. 1938 Happy Landing; Romance in the Dark; Always Goodbye; I'll Give a Million; Gateway; Just Around the Corner; Topper Takes a Trip. 1940 Saps at Sea; I Was an Adventuress; Foreign Correspondent; Lucky Partners; Down Argentine Way; Chad Hanna; Behind the News. 1941 You're the One; That Night in Rio; West Point Widow; Hurry, Charlie, Hurry; Angels with Broken Wings.

CONROY, FRANK
Born: Oct. 14, 1890, Derby, England. Died: Feb. 24, 1964, Paramus, N.Y. (heart ailment). Screen, stage and television actor.

Appeared in: 1930 The Royal Family of Broadway. 1931 Bad Company; Possessed; Hell Divers. 1932 Manhattan Parade; West of Broadway; Grand Hotel; Disorderly Conduct. 1933 Midnight Mary; Night Flight; Ann Carver's Profession; Ace of Aces; The Kennel Murder Case. 1934 Little Miss Marker; Keep 'Em Rolling; The Crime Doctor; The White Parade; The Little Minister; Frontier Marshal; Such Women Are Dangerous; The Cat and the Fiddle. 1935 Call of the Wild; Last Days of Pompeii; Show Them No Mercy; Charlie Chan in Egypt; West Point of the Air; I Live My Life. 1936 The White Angel; Stolen Holiday; Meet Nero Wolfe; Nobody's Fool; The Gorgeous Hussy; Charlie Chan at the Opera. 1937 Love Is News; Wells Fargo; That I May Live; Nancy Steele Is Missing; Big Business; This Is My Affair; The Emperor's Candlesticks; The Last Gangster; Music for Madame. 1941 This Woman Is Mine. 1942 Adventures of Martin Eden; Crossroads; The Loves of Edgar Allen Poe. 1943 The Ox-Bow Incident; Crash Dive; Lady of Burlesque. 1947 That Hagen Girl. 1948 Sealed Verdict; Rogues' Regiment; Naked City; All My Sons; The Snake Pit; For the Love of Mary. 1949 The Threat. 1951 The Day the Earth Stood Still; Lightning Strikes Twice. 1959 The Last Mile; Compulsion; The Young Philadelphians. 1960 The Bramble Bush.

CONROY, THOM
Born: 1911. Died: Nov. 16, 1971, Hollywood, Calif. (heart attack). Stage and screen actor.

Appeared in: 1955 Man with the Gun. 1961 The Young Savages; The Manchurian Candidate. 1963 The Ugly American. 1964 Robin and the 7 Hoods; Seven Days in May. 1965 The Hallelujah Trail; Marriage on the Rocks; None But the Brave. 1966 Assault on a Queen; Seconds. 1968 Swimmer.

CONSTANT, MAX
Born: France. Died: May, 1943, Mojave Desert, Calif. (died during flying test for Air Force). Screen actor.

Appeared in: 1923 Trilby.

CONTE, RICHARD (Nicholas Conte)
Born: Mar. 24, 1914, Jersey City, N.J. Died: Apr. 15, 1975, Los Angeles, Calif. (heart attack and paralyzing stroke). Screen, stage and television actor. Divorced from actress Ruth Strome and later married to actress Shirley Garner (aka Colleen Conte).

Appeared in: 1939 Heaven with a Barbed Wire Fence. 1943 Guadalcanal Diary. 1944 The Purple Heart. 1945 A Bell for Adano; Captain Eddie; A Walk in the Sun; The Spider. 1946 Somewhere in the Night; 13 Rue Madeleine. 1947 The Other Love. 1948 Call Northside 777; Cry of the City; Appointment with Murder. 1949 Thieves' Highway; Big Jack; House of Strangers; Whirlpool. 1950 The Sleeping City; Under the Gun. 1951 Hollywood Story; The Raging Tide. 1952 Thief of Damascus; The Fighter; The Raiders; The First Time. 1953 Desert Legion; The Blue Gardenia; Slaves of Babylon. 1954 Highway Dragnet; A Race for Life. 1955 Target Zero; The Big Combo; Bengazi; New York Confidential; The Big Tip-Off; I'll Cry Tomorrow. 1956 Full of Life. 1957 The Brothers Rico; Little Red Monkey (aka The Case of the Red Monkey—US). 1958 This Angry Age. 1959 They Came to Cordura. 1960 Ocean's Eleven; Pepe. 1963 Who's Been Sleeping in My Bed? 1964 The Eyes of Annie Jones; Circus World. 1965 Synanon; Stay Tuned for Terror; The Greatest Story Ever Told. 1966 Assault on a Queen. 1967 Tony Rome; Hotel. 1968 Lady in Cement. 1969 Operation Cross Eagle. 1970 Explosion (aka The Blast). 1972 The Godfather.

CONTI, ALBERT (Albert De Conti Cadassamare)
Born: Jan. 29, 1887, Trieste, Austria. Died: Jan. 18, 1967, Hollywood, Calif. (stroke). Screen actor. Entered films in 1922.

Appeared in: 1923 Merry-Go-Round (film debut). 1925 The Merry Widow; Eagle. 1926 The Blonde Saint; Old Loves and New; Watch Your Wife. 1927 Slipping Wives (short); Camille; The Devil Dancer; South Sea Love. 1928 The Chinese Parrot; Love Me and the World Is Mine; Stocks and Blondes; Plastered in Paris; Legion of the Condemned; Magnificent Flirt; Dry Martini; Alex the Great; Show People; Tempest. 1929 Making the Grade; The Exalted Flapper; Jazz Heaven; Captain Lash; Lady of the Pavements; Saturday's Children; He Loved the Ladies. 1930 Such Men Are Dangerous; Oh, For a Man!; The Melody Man; One Romantic Night; Morocco; Sea Legs; Madame Satan; Average Husband (short); Monte Carlo; Our Blushing Brides. 1931 This Modern Age; Reputation; Gang Busters; Strangers May Kiss; Just a Gigolo; Heartbreak. 1932 Shopworn; Doomed Battalion; The Giddy Age (short); As You Desire Me; Night Club Lady; Freaks; Lady with a Past; Second Fiddle. 1933

Gigolettes of Paris; Topaze; Men Are Such Fools; Love Is Dangerous; Love Is Like That; Shanghai Madness; Torch Singer. 1934 Love Time; Beloved; Elmer and Elsie. 1935 The Night Is Young; Hands Across the Table; Mills of the Gods; Symphony of Living; Diamond Jim; The Crusades; Here's to Romance. 1936 Fatal Lady; Hollywood Boulevard; One in a Million; Collegiate. 1937 Dangerously Yours; Cafe Metropole. 1938 Always Goodbye; Gateway; Suez. 1942 My Gal Sal.

CONWAY, CURT
Born: 1915, Boston, Mass. Died: Apr. 11, 1974, Los Angeles, Calif. (heart attack). Screen, stage actor, film, stage and television director.

Appeared in: 1947 Gentleman's Agreement; Singapore. 1948 Casbah; Raw Deal. 1949 A Woman's Secret; The Lady Gambles. 1958 The Goddess; Wind Across the Everglades. 1961 Run Across the River. 1963 Hud. 1964 Invitation to a Gunfighter. 1970 Macho Callahan. 1972 The Man.

CONWAY, JACK
Born: Ireland. Died: May 1951, Forest Hills, N.Y. Screen and vaudeville actor. Appeared in early Paramount pictures.

CONWAY, JACK
Born: July 17, 1887, Graceville, Minn. Died: Oct. 11, 1952, Pacific Palisades, Calif. Screen, stage actor and film director.

Appeared in: 1909 Her Indian Hero. 1914 The Old Arm Chair. 1919 Restless Souls.

CONWAY, JOSEPH
Born: c. 1889, Philadelphia, Pa. Died: Feb. 28, 1959, Philadelphia, Pa. Screen actor and circus owner. Appeared in early silents made in Philadelphia.

CONWAY, TOM (Thomas Charles Sanders)
Born: 1904, St. Petersburg, Russia. Died: Apr. 22, 1967, Culver City, Calif. (liver ailment). Screen, television and radio actor. Brother of actor George Sanders (dec. 1972).

Appeared in: 1940 Sky Murder. 1941 The People vs. Dr. Kildare; Tarzan's Secret Treasure; Mr. and Mrs. North; The Trial of Mary Dugan; Free and Easy; The Bad Man; Lady Be Good. 1942 Mrs. Miniver; Grand Central Murder; Rio Rita; The Falcon's Brother; The Cat People. 1943 The Falcon in Danger; The Falcon and the Co-Eds; The Seventh Victim; The Falcon Strikes Back; I Walked with a Zombie; One Exciting Night. 1944 The Falcon in Mexico; The Falcon Out West; A Night of Adventure; The Falcon in Hollywood. 1945 Two O'Clock Courage; The Falcon in San Francisco; One Exciting Month. 1946 Criminal Court; The Falcon's Adventure; The Falcon's Alibi; Whistle Stop; Runaway Daughters. 1947 Repeat Performance; Fun on a Weekend; Lost Honeymoon. 1948 One Touch of Venus; 13 Lead Soldiers; The Challenge; Repeat Performance; Bungalow 13; Checkered Coat. 1949 I Cheated the Law. 1950 The Great Plane Robbery. 1951 Painting the Clouds with Sunshine; The Bride of the Gorilla; Triple Cross. 1952 Confidence Girl. 1953 Tarzan and the She-Devil; Peter Pan (voice); Park Plaza 505; Paris Model; Norman Conquest. 1954 Three Stops to Murder; Prince Valiant. 1955 Barbados Quest. 1956 The Last Man to Hang; Operation Murder; Breakaway; Death of a Scoundrel; The She-Creature; Murder on Approval. 1957 Voodoo Woman. 1959 The Atomic Submarine; Rocket to the Moon. 1960 12 to the Moon. 1961 One Hundred and One Dalmatians (voice). 1964 What a Way to Go.

COOGAN, GENE B.
Died: Jan. 21, 1972, Los Angeles, Calif. (results of a fire). Screen, television actor and stuntman. Married to actress Linda Landi.

Appeared in: 1939 The Story of Alfred Nobel (short). 1952 Plymouth Adventure. 1961 Gun Fight.

COOGAN, JACK, SR. (John Coogan)
Born: 1880, Syracuse, N.Y. Died: May 4, 1935, near San Diego, Calif. (auto accident). Screen, stage and vaudeville actor. Father of actor Jackie Coogan. Married to vaudeville actress Lillian Dolliver.

Appeared in: 1921 The Kid.

COOK, AL
Born: 1882. Died: July 6, 1935, Santa Monica, Calif. Screen actor.

Appeared in: 1916 Fighting Blood. 1927 The Telephone Girl. 1929 As You Like It; Meet the Quince; Love's Labor Found; They Shall Not Pass Out; Eventually, but Not Now; The Captain of the Roll. 1930 The Sleeping Cutie; Lost and Foundered; Old Vamps for New; The Setting Son; The Dear Slayer; Cash and Merry; Land of the Sky Blue Daughters.

COOK, DONALD
Born: Sept. 26, 1901, Portland, Ore. Died: Oct. 1, 1961, New Haven, Conn. (heart attack). Screen, stage, television, radio and vaudeville actor.

Appeared in: 1930 Roseland (short). 1931 Eastside; The Silent Voice; Mad Genius; The Unfaithful; Party Husband; Side Show; The Public Enemy. 1932

Heart of New York; New Morals of Old; The Conquerors; So Big; Washington Merry-Go-Round; The Man Who Played God; The Trial of Vivienne Ware; The Unfaithful; The Penguin Pool Murder; Safe in Hell. **1933** Frisco Jenny; Kiss before the Mirror; Jennie Gerhardt; The Circus Queen Murder; Private Jones; Baby Face; The World Changes; The Woman I Stole; Brief Moment. **1934** The Lost Lady; Fury of the Jungle; Fog; The Ninth Guest; Jealousy; The Most Precious Thing in Life; Whirlpool; Viva Villa. **1935** The Night Is Young; Ladies Love Danger; Behind the Evidence; Fugitive Lady; Gigolette; Confidential; The Casino Murder Case; Here Comes the Band; Motive for Revenge; Murder in the Fleet; The Spanish Cape Mystery. **1936** Ring around the Moon; Girl from Mandalay; Can This Be Dixie?; Ellis Island; The Calling of Dan Matthews; The Leavenworth Case; Showboat. **1937** Circus Girl; Two Wise Maids; Beware of Ladies. **1944** Bowery to Broadway; Murder in the Blue Room; Patrick the Great. **1945** Blonde Ransom; Here Come the Co-Eds. **1950** Our Very Own.

COOK, ETHYLE
Born: Aug. 4, 1880, Lynn, Mass. Died: Apr. 20, 1949, Waukesha, Wisc. Screen actress. Married to actor Harry Benham (dec. 1969) and mother of actress Dorothy (dec. 1956) and actor Leland Benham.

Appeared in: **1914** A Dog's Love. **1915** The Game; Their Last Performance; Mr. Meeson's Will; All Aboard; A Call from the Dead; The Necklace of Pearls; The Commuted Sentence; His Vocation. **1916** John Brewster's Wife. **1917** Her Life and His; When Love was Blind. **1918** Convict 993.

COOK, JOE (Joseph Lopez)
Born: 1890, Evansville, Ind. Died: May 16, 1959, Clinton Hollows, N.Y. Screen, stage and vaudeville actor. Do not confuse with film director Joe Cook.

Appeared in: **1930** Rain or Shine (stage and film versions–film debut). **1933** Hold Your Horses. **1935** An Educational short. **1964** The Sound of Laughter (documentary).

COOK, KEN
Born: 1914. Died: Dec. 28, 1963, Hollywood, Calif. (heart attack). Stage and screen actor.

COOK, LILLIAN
Born: 1898, Hot Springs, Ark. Died: Mar. 14, 1918, New York, N.Y. Stage and screen actress.

Appeared in: **1915** Their Last Performance; The Cotton King; Mother. **1916** A Woman's Power (aka Code of the Mountains); Camille; As in a Looking Glass; The Spirit of the Game; The Common Law. **1917** The Submarine Eye; Betsy Ross; Rasputin, the Black Monk; Darkest Russia; The Corner Grocer; Her Hour; The Honeymoon. **1918** The Blue Bird; The Devil's Playground.

COOK, LUCIUS (Lucius Moore Cook)
Born: July 23, 1891, New York. Died: June 2, 1952, Los Angeles, Calif. (arteriosclerosis). Screen actor, stage director and drama coach.

Appeared in: **1952** Lone Star.

COOK, MARY
Died: May 27, 1944, Hollywood, Calif. Screen actress, singer, and dancer. Divorced from actor Elisha Cook, Jr.

Appeared in: **1942** Ride 'Em Cowboy.

COOK, ROSS
Born: 1898. Died: Jan. 2, 1930. Screen pilot.

Appeared in: **1930** Hell's Angels.

COOK, WARREN
Born: 1879. Died: May 2, 1939, New York, N.Y. Screen and stage actor.

Appeared in: **1920** My Lady's Garter; Lady Rose's Daughter. **1921** Conceit; The Fighter; The Girl from Nowhere; Is Life Worth Living?; The Last Door; The Man of Stone; Suspicious Wives; Worlds Apart. **1922** John Smith; Slim Shoulders. **1923** The Broken Violin; Dark Secrets; Fog Bound; The Silent Command. **1924** His Darker Self; The Truth about Women. **1925** Shore Leave; The Knockout; Wild, Wild Susan. **1926** Lew Tyler's Wives. **1927** The Lunatic at Large.

COOKE, STEPHEN BEACH
Born: 1898. Died: Sept. 16, 1948, Cooperstown, N.Y. Screen and stage actor.

COOKSEY, CURTIS
Born: 1892. Died: Apr. 19, 1962, Hollywood, Calif. (cancer—suicide). Stage and screen actor.

Appeared in: **1915** The Dawn of Courage; The Old and the New. **1916** My Partner; The Coward's Code. **1920** The Silver Horde. **1922** A Virgin's Sacrifice. **1932** The Misleading Lady. **1952** Because You're Mine; The Girl in White; Young Man with Ideas; Scaramouche. **1953** Taxi. **1956** Storm Center; Death of a Scoundrel.

COOLEY, CHARLES (Charles Cali)
Born: 1903, Cleveland, Ohio. Died: Nov. 15, 1960, Hollywood, Calif. (rare blood disease). Screen, television and vaudeville actor.

Appeared in: **1951** The Lemon Drop Kid. **1952** Son of Paleface; Sound Off.

COOLEY, FRANK L.
Born: 1870, Natchez, Miss. Died: July 6, 1941, Hollywood, Calif. Screen, stage actor and film director. Entered films with Keystone Company in 1912.

Appeared in: **1926** First Year; More Pay—Less Work. **1927** Wanted—A Coward. **1928** Honor Bound.

COOLEY, JAMES R.
Born: 1880. Died: Nov. 15, 1948, Hollywood, Calif. Screen and stage actor.

Appeared in: **1917** A Tale of Two Nations. **1924** The Song of Love. **1934** The Mighty Barnum.

COOLEY, SPADE (Donnell C. Cooley)
Born: 1910, Grand, Okla. Died: Nov. 23, 1969, Oakland, Calif. (heart attack). Bandleader, screen and television actor.

Appeared in: **1943** Chatterbox; The Silent Bandit. **1944** The Singing Sheriff. **1945** Rockin' in the Rockies; Outlaws of the Rockies. **1946** Texas Panhandle. **1947** Vacation Days. **1949** Square Dance Jubilee; The Kid from Gower Gulch; Border Outlaw; I Shot Billy the Kid. **1951** Casa Manana.

COOLIDGE, PHILIP
Born: Aug. 25, 1908, Concord, Mass. Died: May 23, 1967, Hollywood, Calif. (cancer). Screen, stage and television actor.

Appeared in: **1947** Boomerang. **1956** The Shark Fighters. **1957** Slander. **1958** I Want to Live! **1959** The Tingler; It Happened to Jane; The Mating Game; North by Northwest. **1960** Because They're Young; The Bramble Bush; Inherit the Wind. **1962** Bon Voyage! **1964** Hamlet. **1965** The Greatest Story Ever Told. **1966** The Russians Are Coming, The Russians Are Coming. **1968** Never a Dull Moment.

COOMBE, CAROL (Gwendoline Alice Coombe)
Born: Sept. 20, 1911, Perth, Australia. Died: Oct. 4, 1966, London, England. Stage and screen actress.

Appeared in: **1931** The Ghost Train (US 1933); The Rasp. **1932** Help Yourself; The Strangler. **1933** Double Bluff; My Lucky Star. **1935** The Man Without a Face. **1946** Woman to Woman.

COOMBS, JACK "COLBY JACK"
Born: 1883, LeGrand, Iowa. Died: Apr. 15, 1957, Palestine, Texas (heart attack). Professional baseball player and screen actor.

Appeared in: **1911** The Baseball Bug.

COONS, JOHNNY
Born: 1917. Died: July 6, 1975. Screen and television actor.

Appeared in: **1969** Tell Them Willie Boy is Here.

COOPER, ASHLEY
Born: 1882, Australia. Died: Jan. 3, 1952, New York, N.Y. Screen, stage and vaudeville actor.

Appeared in: **1921** Partners of the Tide; Shadows of Conscience. **1922** Gay and Devilish; The Hands of Nara; The Son of the Wolf; Tillie. **1923** Desert Driven; Robin Hood, Jr. **1924** The Torrent. **1926** Paradise.

COOPER, CLANCY
Died: June 14, 1975, Hollywood, Calif. (heart attack). Screen, stage, television actor and stage director. Married to author Elizabeth Cooper.

Appeared in: **1942** Native Land; Flight Lieutenant; Unseen Enemy; The Man Who Returned to Life; West of Tombstone. **1943** Riding through Nevada; Girls in Chains; Dead Man's Gulch; Frontier Fury; Deerslayer. **1944** The Whistler; Timber Queen; Sundown Valley; Riding West; Cyclone Prairie Rangers. **1945** Abbott and Costello in Hollywood; Enchanted Forest; Without Love. **1946** Courage of Lassie; The Wife of Monte Cristo; Somewhere in the Night; Centennial Summer; It Shouldn't Happen to a Dog. **1947** A Really Important Person (short); Her Husband's Affair. **1948** The Sainted Sisters; Lulu Belle; The Man from Texas. **1949** Song of Surrender; Mr. Belvedere Goes to College; Prison Warden. **1950** Whirlpool; The Great Rupert; Mary Ryan, Detective; Where the Sidewalk Ends. **1951** Distant Drums. **1952** The Man Behind the Gun; The Wild North; Deadline U.S.A.; Lydia Bailey. **1953** All the Brothers Were Valiant; The Silver Whip. **1954** Living It Up. **1955** Artists and Models. **1957** The True Story of Jesse James. **1958** A Time to Love and a Time to Die. **1959** The Sheriff of Fractured Jaw. **1961** Wild Youth. **1962** Incident in an Alley; Saintly Sinners.

COOPER, CLAUDE

Born: 1881. Died: July 20, 1932, Laurelton, N.Y. (heart attack). Screen, stage actor and film director.

Appeared in: 1915 The Country Girl. 1921 A Heart to Let; The Plaything of Broadway. 1924 Daughters of the Night. 1931 The Struggle.

COOPER, EDWARD

Born: England. Died: July 1956, Surrey, England. Screen and stage actor. Married to actress Ethel Griffies (dec. 1975). Do not confuse with British entertainer Edward Cooper (dec. 1945).

Appeared in: 1933 Officer 13; The Working Man; Female; Diplomaniacs. 1935 Clive of India; The Perfect Gentleman. 1936 To Mary—With Love. 1937 On the Avenue. 1938 Rascals. 1939 Wife, Husband and Friend. 1941 Marry the Boss's Daughter. 1944 Bermuda Mystery; Enter Arsene Lupin. 1945 Kitty.

COOPER, GARY (Frank James Cooper)

Born: May 7, 1901, Helena, Mont. Died: May 13, 1961, Hollywood, Calif. (cancer). Screen, television actor and film producer. Made one television special. Married to actress Veronica Balfe who acted under the name of Sandra Shaw. Won 1941 Academy Award for Best Actor in Sergeant York, and in 1952 for High Noon. Nominated for 1943 Academy Award for Best Actor in For Whom the Bell Tolls.

Appeared in: 1925 The Lucky Horseshoe; The Vanishing American; The Eagle; The Enchanted Hill; Watch Your Wife; Tricks. 1926 Three Pals; Lightning Justice; The Winning of Barbara Worth. 1927 Arizona Bound; Nevada; The Last Outlaw; Wings; Children of Divorce; It.1928 Beau Sabreur; The Legion of the Condemned; Doomsday; The First Kiss; Lilac Time; Half a Bride. 1929 Shopworn Angel; The Wolf Song; The Betrayal; The Virginian. 1930 Only the Brave; Paramount on Parade; The Texan; Seven Days' Leave; A Man from Wyoming; The Spoilers; Morocco. 1931 Fighting Caravans; City Streets; I Take This Woman; His Woman. 1932 The Devil and the Deep; Make Me a Star; If I Had a Million; A Farewell to Arms. 1933 Today We Live; One Sunday Afternoon; Design for Living; Alice in Wonderland; The Eagle and the Hawk. 1934 Operator 13; Now and Forever. 1935 La Fiesta de Santa Barbara (short); The Wedding Night; Lives of a Bengal Lancer; Peter Ibbetson. 1936 Desire; Mr. Deeds Goes to Town; The General Died at Dawn; Hollywood Boulevard; The Plainsman. 1937 Souls at Sea. 1938 The Adventures of Marco Polo; Bluebeard's Eighth Wife; The Cowboy and the Lady. 1939 Beau Geste; The Real Glory. 1940 The Westerner; Northwest Mounted Police. 1941 Meet John Doe; Sergeant York; Ball of Fire. 1942 The Pride of the Yankees. 1943 For Whom the Bell Tolls. 1944 The Story of Dr. Wassell; Casanova Brown. 1945 Along Came Jones; Saratoga Trunk. 1946 Cloak and Dagger. 1947 Unconquered; Variety Girl. 1948 Good Sam. 1949 The Fountainhead; It's a Great Feeling; Task Force. 1950 Bright Leaf; Dallas. 1951 You're in the Navy Now (aka U.S.S. Teakettle); Starlift; It's a Big Country; Distant Drums. 1952 High Noon; Springfield Rifle. 1953 Return to Paradise; Blowing Wild. 1954 Garden of Evil; Vera Cruz. 1955 The Court-Martial of Billy Mitchell. 1956 Friendly Persuasion. 1957 Love in the Afternoon. 1958 Ten North Frederick; Man of the West. 1959 The Hanging Tree; They Came to Cordura; The Wreck of the Mary Deare; Alias Jesse James. 1961 The Naked Edge.

COOPER, GEORGE

Born: Dec. 18, 1892, Newark, N.J. Died: Dec. 9, 1943. Screen and stage actor. Entered films in 1908. Do not confuse with other actors George Cooper or George A. Cooper.

COOPER, GEORGIA (aka GEORGIE COOPER)

Born: 1882. Died: Sept. 3, 1968, Hollywood, Calif. Screen and stage actress. Married to actor Landers Stevens (dec. 1940) and mother of actor/director George Stevens (dec. 1975).

Appeared in: 1928 The Question of Today (short). 1937 Four Days' Wonder; Hollywood Hotel.

COOPER, DAME GLADYS

Born: Dec. 18, 1888, Lewisham; England. Died: Nov. 17, 1971, Henley-on-Thames, England (pneumonia). Screen, stage, television actress, stage producer and author. Was made a Dame Commander of the Order of the British Empire in 1967. Divorced from Herbert Buckmaster and Sir Neville Pearson and later married to actor Philip Merivale (dec. 1946). Mother of actors John Merivale and John Buckmaster, actress Sally Cooper and Joan Buckmaster. Nominated for 1942 Academy Award for Best Supporting Actress in Now Voyager and in 1943 for The Song of Bernadette.

Appeared in: 1913 The Eleventh Commandment (film debut). 1914 Dandy Donovan, the Gentleman Cracksman. 1916 The Real Thing At Last. 1917 The Sorrows of Satan; Masks and Faces; My Lady's Dress. 1920 Unmarried. 1922 Headin' North; The Bohemian Girl. 1923 Bonnie Prince Charlie. 1935 The Iron Duke. 1940 Kitty Foyle; Rebecca. 1941 That Hamilton Woman (aka Lady Hamilton); The Black Cat; The Gay Falcon. 1942 This Above All; Eagle Squadron; Now Voyager. 1943 The Song of Bernadette; Forever and a Day; Mr. Lucky; Princess O'Rourke. 1944 The White Cliffs of Dover; Mrs. Parkington. 1945 The Valley of Decision; Love Letters. 1946 The Green Years; The Cockeyed Miracle. 1947 Green Dolphin Street; Beware of Pity; The Bishop's

Wife. 1948 The Pirate; Homecoming. 1949 Madame Bovary; The Secret Garden. 1951 Thunder on the Hill. 1952 At Sword's Point (aka Sons of the Musketeers). 1955 The Man Who Loved Redheads. 1958 Separate Tables. 1963 The List of Adrian Messenger. 1964 My Fair Lady. 1967 The Happiest Millionaire. 1969 A Nice Girl Like Me.

COOPER, HARRY

Born: 1882. Died: Aug. 28, 1957, Hollywood, Calif. Screen, vaudeville actor, stuntman and double. Appeared in vaudeville with his wife in an act billed "Cooper and Valli." Entered films as a stunt man with Vitagraph.

Appeared in: 1937 Golf Mistakes (short). 1953 The Caddy.

COOPER, MELVILLE G.

Born: Oct. 15, 1896, Birmingham, England. Died: Mar. 29, 1973, Woodland Hills, Calif. (cancer). Stage and screen actor. Divorced from Gladys Grice and actress Rita Page and later married to Elizabeth Sutherland (dec.).

Appeared in: 1934 The Private Life of Don Juan (film debut). 1935 The Scarlet Pimpernel; The Bishop Misbehaves. 1936 The Gorgeous Hussy. 1937 The Last of Mrs. Cheyney; Thin Ice; The Great Garrick; Tovarich. 1938 Women are Like That; The Adventures of Robin Hood; Gold Diggers in Paris; Four's a Crowd; Garden of the Moon; Hard to Get; Dramatic School; Comet over Broadway; Dawn Patrol. 1939 I'm from Missouri; Blind Alley; The Sun Never Sets; Two Bright Boys. 1940 Too Many Husbands; Rebecca; Pride and Prejudice; Murder over New York. 1941 The Lady Eve; Submarine Zone; Scotland Yard; The Flame of New Orleans; You Belong to Me. 1942 Once Upon a Thursday (aka Affairs of Martha); This Above All; Life Begins at Eight-Thirty; Random Harvest. 1943 The Immortal Sergeant; Hit Parade of 1943; Holy Matrimony; My Kingdom for a Cook. 1946 Heartbeat; 13 Rue Madeleine. 1947 The Imperfect Lady. 1948 Enchantment. 1949 The Red Danube; And Baby Makes Three; Love Happy. 1950 Father of the Bride; Pretty Girl; Let's Dance; The Whipped (aka Underworld Story). 1952 Return of Gilbert and Sullivan. 1954 It Should Happen to You. 1955 Moonfleet; The King's Thief; Diane. 1956 Around the World in 80 Days; Bundle of Joy. 1957 The Story of Mankind. 1958 From the Earth to the Moon.

COOPER, MERIAN C.

Born: Oct. 24, 1893, Jacksonville, Fla. Died: Apr. 21, 1973, Coronado, Calif. (cancer). Film director, producer, screenwriter, cinematographer, author and screen actor. Married to actress Dorothy Jordan. In 1952 he received a Special Academy Award for his innovations in the film industry.

Appeared in: 1925 Grass.

COOPER, TEX

Born: 1877. Died: Mar. 29, 1951, Hollywood, Calif. Screen actor. Entered films in 1916.

Appeared in: 1921 The Man Worthwhile. 1945 Pistol Packin' Nitwits (short).

COOTE, BERT

Born: 1868, England. Died: Sept. 1, 1938, London, England. Stage and screen actor.

COPAS, COWBOY

Born: 1914, Muskogee, Okla. Died: Mar. 5, 1963, near Camden, Tenn. (plane crash). Screen actor and singer.

Appeared in: 1949 Square Dance Jubilee.

COPEAU, JACQUES

Born: 1879, Paris, France. Died: Oct. 20, 1949, Beaune, France. Screen, stage, stage producer, director and playwright.

Appeared in: 1937 Razumov. 1938 The Courier of Lyons. 1939 The Affair Laflont.

COPELAND, NICHOLAS W. "NICK"

Born: 1895. Died: Aug. 17, 1940, Los Angeles, Calif. Screen, stage, vaudeville actor and screenwriter.

Appeared in: 1934 Manhattan Love Song; The Hell Cat. 1935 Murder in the Clouds. 1936 Man Hunt; Neighborhood House; The Legion of Terror. 1937 Lodge Night (short); Midnight Madonna. 1938 The Main Event; Romance in the Dark.

COPPEN, HAZEL

Born: 1925. Died: Apr. 8, 1975, London, England. Screen, stage and radio actress.

CORBE, EDUARDO

Born: 1878, Cuba. Died: Aug. 29, 1967, Cuba. Screen and television actor.

CORBETT, BEN "BENNY"

Born: 1892, Hudson, Ill. Died: May 19, 1961, Hollywood, Calif. Screen actor. Entered films approx. 1915. Doubled for actors William Duncan and Antonio Moreno.

Appeared in: **1919** Lightning Bryce (serial). **1921** Black Sheep. **1922** The Heart of a Texan; The Kingfisher's Roost; Lure of Gold; Rangeland; South of Northern Lights; West of the Pecos. **1923** Don Quickshot of the Rio Grande; The Red Warning. **1924** The Man from Wyoming; The Phantom Horseman; The Riddle Rider (serial). **1925** The Circus Cyclone; Daring Days; The Outlaw's Daughter. **1926** Law of the Snow Country; Shadows of Chinatown; Without Orders. **1927** The Border Cavalier; The Man from Hardpan; Somewhere in Sonora; One Glorious Scrap. **1928** The Black Ace; The Boss of Rustler's Roost; The Bronc Stomper; The Fearless Rider; A Made-to-Order Hero; Put 'Em Up; Quick Triggers; Arizona Cyclone; The Mystery Rider (serial). **1929** Forty-Five Calibre War; The Royal Rider. **1930** Bar-L Ranch; Beau Bandit; The Lonesome Trail; Phantom of the Desert; Ridin' Law; Romance of the West; Westward Bound. **1934** The Last Round-Up; Girl Trouble. **1936** Empty Saddles. **1937** Texas Trail. **1938** Gold Mine in the Sky. **1939** Racketeers of the Range. **1943** Hoppy Serves a Writ. **1946** Fool's Gold. **1950** County Fair. **1953** The Charge at Feather River.

CORBETT, JAMES J.

Born: 1867. Died: Feb. 18, 1933, Bayside, N.Y. (cancer of liver). Heavyweight boxing champion, screen, stage and vaudeville actor. Divorced from actress Olive Lake.

Appeared in: **1894** Corbett and Peter Courteney made the first fight film for Edison. **1913** The Man from the Golden West. **1915** The Lady and the Burglars. **1919** The Midnight Man (serial). **1920** The Prince of Avenue A. **1922** The Beauty Shop. **1924** Broadway After Dark. **1929** Happy Days; James J. Corbett and Neil O'Brien (short). **1930** At the Round Table (short). **1942** Gentleman Jim (film clips). **1968** The Legendary Champions (doc.).

CORBETT, LEONORA

Born: June 28, 1908, London, England. Died: July 29, 1960, Vleuten, Holland. Screen, stage actress and film producer.

Appeared in: **1932** Love on Wheels. **1933** The Constant Nymph; Friday the 13th (US 1934). **1934** Lady in Danger; Warn London; Wild Boy. **1935** Royal Cavalcade (aka Regal Cavalcade—US); Heart's Desire. **1936** Living Dangerously; The Happy Family. **1937** Farewell Again (aka Troopship—US 1938); The Price of Folly. **1938** Night Alone; Anything to Declare? **1940** Under Your Hat; Fingers.

CORBETT, MARY

Born: 1926. Died: Apr. 28, 1974, New York, N.Y. Screen, stage and television actress.

Appeared in: **1948** Portrait of Jenny.

CORBIN, VIRGINIA LEE

Born: Dec. 5, 1910, Prescott, Ariz. Died: June 5, 1942, Winfield, Ill. (heart disease). Stage and screen actress.

Appeared in: **1917** Aladdin and the Wonderful Lamp; Jack and the Beanstalk. **1923** Enemies of Children. **1924** Broken Laws; The Chorus Lady; The City That Never Sleeps; Sinners in Silk; Wine of Youth. **1925** The Cloud Rider; The Handsome Brute; Headlines; Lillies of the Streets; North Star; Three Keys. **1926** The Honeymoon Express; Hands Up!; Ladies at Play; The Whole Town's Talking. **1927** Driven from Home; No Place to Go; The Perfect Sap; Play Safe. **1928** Bare Knees; The Head of the Family; Jazzland; The Little Snob. **1929** Footlights and Fools; Knee High. **1931** Morals for Women; X Marks the Spot.

CORDER, LEETA

Born: 1890. Died: Aug. 10, 1956, New York, N.Y. (cancer). Screen, stage, opera and radio actress.

CORDING, HARRY

Born: Apr. 29, 1891, England. Died: Sept. 1, 1954, Sun Valley, Calif. Screen actor. Entered films in 1921.

Appeared in: **1925** The Knockout. **1927** Black Jack. **1928** Daredevil's Reward; The Patriot; Sins of the Fathers. **1929** The Rescue; The Squall; The Isle of Lost Ships; Christina. **1930** Captain of the Guard; Rough Romance; Bride of the Regiment. **1931** The Right of Way; The Conquering Horde; Honor of the Family. **1932** File No. 113; The World and the Flesh; Forgotten Commandments; Cabin in the Cotton. **1933** Captured; To the Last Man. **1934** The Black Cat. **1935** The Crusades; Peter Ibbetson; Captain Blood. **1936** Road Gang; Sutter's Gold; The White Angel; Daniel Boone. **1937** The Prince and the Pauper. **1938** Crime School; The Adventures of Robin Hood; Valley of the Giants; Painted Desert. **1939** Each Dawn I Die; The Hound of the Baskervilles; The Adventures of Sherlock Holmes. **1940** Passport to Alcatraz; The Great Plane Robbery; Trail of the Vigilantes. **1941** The Lady from Cheyenne; Mutiny in the Arctic; The Wolf Man. **1942** Arabian Nights; Tennessee Johnson; Yukon Patrol; Ride 'Em Cowboy; Sherlock Holmes and the Secret Weapon. **1944** Ali Baba and the Forty Thieves; Gypsy Wildcat; Mrs. Parkington; Lost In a Harem. **1945** The House of Fear; Sudan; San Antonio. **1946** Dressed to Kill; Fool's Gold. **1947** The Marauders; Dangerous Venture. **1948** A Woman's Vengeance; That Lady in Ermine. **1949** The Fighting O'Flynn; Bad Men of Tombstone; Secret of St. Ives. **1950** Fortunes of Captain Blood; Last of the Buccaneers. **1951** Mask of the Avenger; Santa Fe. **1952** The Big Trees; Against All Flags; Brave

Warrior; Cripple Creek; Night Stage to Galveston. **1953** Treasure of the Golden Condor; Abbott and Costello Meet Dr. Jekyll and Mr. Hyde. **1954** Man in the Attic; Demetrius and the Gladiators; Killer Leopard; Jungle Gents.

CORDY, HENRY (Henry Korn)

Born: 1908. Died: Nov. 27, 1965, New York, N.Y. (heart ailment). Screen actor and opera performer.

Appeared in: **1941** The Great American Broadcast; Unfinished Business.

CORDY, RAYMOND (Raymond Cordiaux)

Born: 1898, France. Died: 1956. Screen actor.

Appeared in: **1931** Le Million; A Nous la Liberte. **1933** La Quatorze Juillet. **1934** Le Dernier Milliardaire. **1937** Ignace. **1938** The Slipper Episode; They Were Five. **1942** Les Inconnus dans la Maison. **1946** Le Silence Est d'Or. **1947** Retour a l'Aube (She Returned at Dawn); Man About Town. **1949** Le Beaute du Diable (Beauty and the Devil—US 1952). **1954** A Nous la Liberte (rerelease of 1931 film). **1955** Les Grandes Maneuvers (The Grand Maneuver—US 1956). **1958** The Girl in the Bikini. **1960** Sin and Desire (aka l'Epave—The Wreck).

COREY, JOSEPH (Joseph Martorano)

Born: 1927. Died: Aug. 30, 1972, Los Angeles, Calif. (heart attack). Screen and television actor.

Appeared in: **1956** Gaby. **1957** The Delicate Delinquent.

COREY, WENDELL

Born: Mar. 20, 1914, Dracut, Mass. Died: Nov. 9, 1968, Woodland Hills, Calif. (liver ailment). Screen, stage and television actor.

Appeared in: **1947** Desert Fury (film debut); I Walk Alone. **1948** Man-Eater of Kumaon; The Search; Sorry, Wrong Number; The Accused. **1949** Holiday Affair; Thelma Jordan; Any Number Can Play. **1950** No Sad Songs for Me; Harriet Craig; The Great Missouri Raid; The Furies; There's a Girl in My Heart. **1951** The Wild Blue Yonder; Rich, Young and Pretty. **1952** My Man and I; The Wild North; Carbine Williams. **1953** Laughing Anne (US 1954); Jamaica Run. **1954** Fireman Save My Child; Rear Window; Laughing Anne; Hell's Half Acre. **1955** The Big Knife. **1956** The Killer Is Loose; The Bold and the Brave; The Rack; The Rainmaker. **1957** Loving You. **1958** The Light in the Forest. **1959** Giant Leeches; Alias Jesse James. **1964** Blood on the Arrow. **1965** Broken Sabre. **1966** Women of the Prehistoric Planet; Waco; Picture Mommy Dead; Agent for H.A.R.M. **1967** Cyborg 2087; Red Tomahawk. **1968** The Astro Zombies; Buckskin. **1969** Young Billy Young.

CORLEY, ROBERT

Died: Nov. 18, 1971. Screen, radio and television actor.

Appeared in: **1965** Forty Acre Feud; The Legend of Blood Mountain.

CORNELL, KATHARINE

Born: Feb. 16, 1893, Berlin, Germany. Died: June 9, 1974, Vineyard Haven, Mass. Stage, radio, television, screen actress and stage producer. Married to stage director Guthrie McClintic (dec. 1961).

Appeared in: **1943** Stage Door Canteen. **1954** The Unconquered (narr.—aka Helen Keller in Her Story).

CORNER, JAMES W.

Born: 1919. Died: Dec. 2, 1944, Germany (killed in action). Stage and screen actor.

Appeared in: **1939** Winter Carnival; What a Life.

CORNER, SALLY

Born: 1894. Died: Mar. 5, 1959, Hollywood, Calif. (heart attack). Stage and screen actress.

Appeared in: **1949** Abandoned Woman; Once More, My Darling. **1950** Two Flags West. **1953** The Robe. **1954** A Man Called Peter. **1957** The True Story of Jesse James.

CORRELL, CHARLES J.

Born: Feb. 3, 1890, Peoria, Ill. Died: Sept. 26, 1972, Chicago, Ill. (heart attack). Screen, stage, radio actor and circus performer. Married to dancer Alyce Mercedes McLaughlin (dec. 1937). Was partner with Freeman Gosden in team of "Amos and Andy" on radio.

Appeared in: **1930** Check and Double Check (with Gosden). **1936** The Big Broadcast.

CORRIGAN, CHARLES

Born: 1894. Died: Apr. 4, 1966, New York, N.Y. Screen and stage actor.

Appeared in: **1939** The Roaring 20's.

CORRIGAN, EMMETT

Born: 1867, Amsterdam, Holland. Died: Oct. 29, 1932, Los Angeles, Calif. Stage and screen actor.

Appeared in: **1923** The Rendezvous. **1924** The Turmoil. **1928** The Lion and the Mouse. **1930** Soldiers and Women. **1931** An American Tragedy; Corsair. **1932** The Beast of the City; The World and the Flesh; The Night Mayor; Man against Woman; Silver Dollar. **1933** The Bitter Tea of General Yen.

CORRIGAN, JAMES
Born: 1871. Died: Feb. 28, 1929, Los Angeles, Calif. Screen and stage actor.

Appeared in: **1921** Brewster's Millions; Lavender and Old Lace; Peck's Bad Boy; The Sky Pilot. **1922** A Front Page Story. **1923** April Showers; Divorce; Her Reputation. **1924** The Law Forbids; The Man from Wyoming; The White Sin. **1925** Durand of the Bad Lands; A Slave of Fashion. **1926** The Auction Block. **1927** Johnny Get Your Hair Cut.

CORRIGAN, LLOYD
Born: Oct. 16, 1900, San Francisco, Calif. Died: Nov. 5, 1969, Woodland Hills, Calif. Screen, television actor, film director and screenwriter. Entered films as an actor approx. 1925 and then turned to writing and directing. Son of actress Lillian Elliott (dec. 1959).

Appeared in: **1925** The Splendid Crime. **1939** The Great Commandment. **1940** Queen of the Mob; Sporting Blood; Jack Pot (short); Captain Caution; Return of Frank James; Dark Streets of Cairo; Lady in Question; High School; Young Tom Edison; Two Girls on Broadway; Public Deb No. 1; The Ghost Breakers. **1941** Mexican Spitfire's Baby; Whistling in the Dark; Kathleen; Confessions of Boston Blackie; A Girl, a Guy and a Gob; Men of Boys Town. **1942** Tennessee Johnson; London Blackout Murders; Bombay Clipper; North of the Klondike; Treat 'Em Rough; The Great Man's Lady; The Wife Takes a Flyer; The Mystery of Marie Roget; Maisie Gets Her Man; Lucky Jordan; Man Trap. **1943** Captive Wild Woman; Stage Door Canteen; Nobody's Darling; Tarzan's Desert Mystery; Hitler's Children; Secrets of the Underworld; King of the Cowboys; Song of Nevada. **1944** Passport to Adventure; Rosie the Riveter; Gambler's Choice; Goodnight, Sweetheart; Reckless Age; Lights of Old Santa Fe; The Thin Man Goes Home; Since You Went Away. **1945** Bring on the Girls; Boston Blackie Booked on Suspicion; The Fighting Guardsman; Lake Placid Serenade; Crime Doctor's Courage. **1946** She-Wolf of London; The Bandit of Sherwood Forest; Two Smart People; Lady Luck; The Chase; Alias Mr. Twilight. **1947** Stallion Road; Blaze of Noon; Shadowed; Ghost Goes Wild. **1948** Adventures of Casanova; Mr. Reckless; The Bride Goes Wild; A Date with Judy; Strike It Rich; Homicide for Three; The Big Clock; Return of October. **1949** Home in San Antone; Blondie Hits the Jackpot; Dancing in the Dark; Girl from Jones Beach. **1950** Father Is a Bachelor; And Baby Makes Three; When Willie Comes Marching Home; My Friend Irma Goes West. **1951** Her First Romance; The Last Outpost; Sierra Passage; Ghost Chasers; New Mexico; Cyrano de Bergerac. **1952** Son of Paleface; Rainbow 'Round My Shoulder; Sound Off. **1953** The Stars Are Singing; Marry Me Again. **1954** Return from the Sea; The Bowery Boys Meet the Monsters. **1955** Paris Follies of 1956. **1956** Hidden Guns. **1962** The Manchurian Candidate. **1963** It's a Mad, Mad, Mad, Mad World.

CORRIGAN, THOMAS J. *See* THOMAS J. CARRIGAN

CORTES, ARMAND (aka ARMAND CORTEZ)
Born: Aug. 16, 1880, Nimes, France. Died: Nov. 1948, San Francisco, Calif. Stage and screen actor.

Appeared in: **1914** House of Bondage. **1915** How Molly Malone Made Good. **1916** Yellow Menace (serial). **1917** Seven Keys to Baldpate; Her Better Self. **1920** Taking the Count; Return of Tarzan; His Temporary Wife. **1921** The Matrimonial Web; The Scarab Ring. **1924** Wages of Virtue; Galloping Hoofs (serial). **1925** The Crowded Hour. **1926** The Palm Beach Girl. **1927** The Music Master; Rubber Heels. **1938** Bluebeard's Eighth Wife.

CORTEZ, LEON
Born: 1898, England. Died: Dec. 31, 1970, Brighton, England. Screen, television, radio and vaudeville actor.

Appeared in: **1944** Can't Help Singing. **1963** I Could Go on Singing.

CORTHELL, HERBERT
Born: 1875, Boston, Mass. Died: Jan. 23, 1947, Hollywood, Calif. Stage and screen actor.

Appeared in: **1924** Classmates; Second Youth. **1933** The Cohens and the Kellys in Trouble; Only Yesterday; Lone Cowboy. **1934** Bombay Mail; There Ain't No Justice; Let's Talk It Over; Uncertain Lady. **1935** The Fire Trap. **1936** The Story of Louis Pasteur; Dancing Feet. **1937** Renfrew of the Royal Mounted; Man in Blue; Blazing Barriers. **1938** Sing You Sinners. **1939** Fifth Avenue Girl; Career; House of Fear; Espionage. **1942** Duke of the Navy.

CORY, ROBERT
Born: 1883. Died: Nov. 9, 1955, Hollywood, Calif. (cancer). Stage and screen actor. Entered films approx. 1925.

COSGRAVE, LUKE
Born: Aug. 6, 1862, Ballaghdreen, County Mayo, Ireland. Died: June 28, 1949, Woodland Hills, Calif. Stage and screen actor. Entered films in 1923.

Appeared in: **1923** Hollywood; The Light That Failed. **1924** The Border Legion; Code of the Sea; Flaming Barriers; Merton of the Movies. **1925** Contraband; Durand of the Bad Lands; Welcome Home. **1926** Rocking Moon; Sir Lumberjack. **1927** Jewels of Desire. **1928** Gentlemen Prefer Blondes; The Mating Call; The Red Mark. **1929** The Duke Steps Out. **1930** Men on Call; Lightin'. **1931** Not Exactly Gentlemen; The Squaw Man. **1932** Sinners in the Sun. **1940** Comin' 'Round the Mountain.

COSGROVE, ROBERT
Born: 1900. Died: Sept. 1960, Saranac Lake, N.Y. (tuberculosis—heart attack). Screen actor.

COSSAEUS, SOPHIE
Born: 1893, Wiesbaden, Germany. Died: Sept. 23, 1965, Frankfurt-Main, Germany. Screen, stage, television, radio actress and dancer.

COSSAR, JOHN HAY
Born: 1865, London, England. Died: Apr. 28, 1935, Hollywood, Calif. Screen, stage and vaudeville actor.

Appeared in: **1921** Hearts and Masks; Made in Heaven; The Night Rose; The Poverty of Riches; That Something. **1922** Doubling for Romeo; Grand Larceny; Thorns and Orange Blossoms; Watch Your Step; When Husbands Deceive. **1923** The Steel Trail (serial); Fools and Riches; The Hunchback of Notre Dame. **1924** The Fast Express (serial); The Great Diamond Mystery. **1926** The Sap. **1927** Melting Millions (serial); Web of Fate; Woman's Law. **1929** The Fire Detective (serial).

COSSART, ERNEST
Born: Sept. 24, 1876, Cheltenham, England. Died: Jan. 21, 1951, New York, N.Y. Stage and screen actor.

Appeared in: **1916** The Strange Case of Mary Page (serial). **1935** The Scoundrel; Accent on Youth; Two for Tonight. **1936** Desire; Big Broadcast of 1937; Palm Springs; My American Wife; Murder with Pictures; Champagne Waltz; The Great Ziegfeld. **1937** Three Smart Girls; Top of the Town; As Good as Married; The Lady Fights Back; Angel. **1938** A Letter of Introduction. **1939** Zaza; Tower of London; The Light That Failed; Lady of the Tropics; The Magnificent Fraud; Three Smart Girls Grow Up; Never Say Die. **1940** A Bill of Divorcement; Kitty Foyle; Tom Brown's School Days. **1941** Kings Row; Charley's Aunt; One Foot in Heaven; Skylark. **1944** Knickerbocker Holiday; Casanova Brown. **1945** The Girl of the Limberlost; Love Letters; Tonight and Every Night; The Jolson Story. **1947** Love from a Stranger. **1949** John Loves Mary.

COSTA, SEBASTIANO
Born: 1876. Died: July 18, 1935, New Rochelle, N.Y. (heart attack). Screen actor.

COSTE, MAURICE R.
Born: 1875. Died: Mar. 22, 1963, Chatham, Ontario, Canada. Stage and screen actor.

COSTELLO, DELMAR
Born: 1906. Died: July 29, 1961. Screen actor.

Appeared in: **1934** Four Frightened People. **1954** Elephant Walk; Secret of the Incas. **1955** Hell's Island.

COSTELLO, DON
Born: 1901. Died: Oct. 24, 1945, Hollywood, Calif. Stage and screen actor.

Appeared in: **1939** Another Thin Man. **1940** Joe and Ethel Turp Call on the President; One Crowded Night. **1941** Sleepers West; Ride on Vaquero; I'll Wait for You; Here Comes Mr. Jordan; Unholy Partners; Whistling in the Dark. **1942** Johnny Eager; Joe Smith, American; A-Haunting We Will Go; Just Off Broadway. **1943** A Night to Remember; Truck Busters; Air Raid Wardens; Crime Doctor; A Lady Takes a Chance. **1944** Mystery Man; Texas Masquerade; The Whistler. **1945** Incendiary Blonde; The Red Dragon; Here Come the Co-Eds. **1946** The Blue Dahlia.

COSTELLO, HELENE
Born: June 21, 1903, New York, N.Y. Died: Jan. 26, 1957, Los Angeles, Calif. (pneumonia, tuberculosis and narcotics). Stage and screen actress. Entered films with Vitagraph in 1912. Was a Wampus Baby Star of the 1920s. Sister of actress Dolores Costello and daughter of actor Maurice Costello (dec. 1950). Divorced from actor Lovell Sherman (dec. 1934).

Appeared in: **1912** The Night Before Christmas; The First Violin; The Black Sheep; Wanted—A Grandmother; She Never Knew; Lulu's Doctor; In the Garden Fair; The Church Across the Way. **1913** The Mystery of the Stolen Child; The Other Woman; Heartbroken Shep. **1925** The Man on the Box; Bobbed Hair; Ranger of the Big Pines. **1926** Wet Paint; Don Juan; The Honeymoon Express; The Love Toy; Millionaires; While London Sleeps. **1927** In Old Kentucky; Good Time Charley; Heart of Maryland; The Broncho Twister; Finger Prints. **1928** Burning Up Broadway; Comrades; The Circus Kid; The Midnight Taxi; Fortune Hunter; Lights of New York; Husbands for Rent;

Phantom of the Turf. **1929** Broken Barriers; The Fatal Warning (serial); When Dreams Come True; Show of Shows. **1935** Riffraff.

COSTELLO, LOU (Louis Francis Cristillo)

Born: Mar. 6, 1906, Paterson, N.J. Died: Mar. 3, 1959, Los Angeles, Calif. (heart attack). Screen, stage, burlesque, vaudeville and radio actor. Was part of the comedy team "Abbott and Costello" with Bud Abbott (dec. 1974).

Together they appeared in: **1940** One Night in the Tropics. **1941** Buck Privates; In the Navy; Hold That Ghost; Keep 'Em Flying. **1942** Ride 'Em Cowboy; Rio Rita; Hold Your Horses; Who Done It?; Pardon My Sarong. **1943** It Ain't Hay; Hit the Ice. **1944** Lost in a Harem; In Society. **1945** Here Come the Co-Eds; The Naughty Nineties; Abbott and Costello in Hollywood. **1946** Little Giant; The Time of Their Lives. **1947** Buck Privates Come Home; The Wistful Widow of Wagon Gap. **1948** The Noose Hangs High; Abbott and Costello Meet Frankenstein; Mexican Hayride. **1949** Abbott and Costello Meet the Killer, Boris Karloff; Africa Screams. **1950** Abbott and Costello in the Foreign Legion. **1951** Abbott and Costello Meet the Invisible Man; Comin' 'Round the Mountain. **1952** Jack and the Beanstalk; Lost in Alaska; Abbott and Costello Meet Captain Kidd; News of the Day (MGM short [newsreel] for promotion of U.S. Bonds). **1953** Abbott and Costello Go to Mars; Abbott and Costello Meet Dr. Jekyll and Mr. Hyde. **1954** Hollywood Grows Up (short). **1955** Abbott and Costello Meet the Keystone Kops; Abbott and Costello Meet the Mummy. **1956** Dance with Me, Henry. **1959** The 30-Foot Bride of Candy Rock (without Abbott). **1964** Big Parade of Comedy (doc.). **1965** The World of Abbott and Costello (doc.).

COSTELLO, MAURICE

Born: 1877, Pittsburgh, Pa. Died: Oct. 30, 1950, Hollywood, Calif. (heart ailment). Screen, stage and vaudeville actor. Entered films with Edison in 1905. Divorced from stage actress Ruth Reeves. Father of actresses Dolores and Helene (dec. 1957) Costello.

Appeared in: **1910** The New Stenographer. **1911** A Tale of Two Cities. **1912** The Night before Christmas; As You Like It. **1914** Mr. Barnes of New York. **1915** The Man Who Couldn't Beat God; Tried for His Own Murder. **1916** The Crown Prince's Double; The Crimson Stain Mystery (serial). **1918** Cap'n Abe's Niece. **1919** The Cambric Mask. **1920** Deadline at Eleven; Human Collateral. **1921** Conceit. **1922** Determination. **1923** None So Blind; Glimpses of the Moon; Fog Bound; Man and Wife. **1924** Virtuous Liars; Love of Women; Let No Man Put Asunder; The Story without a Name; Week-End Husbands; The Law and the Lady; Heart of Alaska; Roulette. **1925** The Mad Marriage. **1926** Wives of the Prophet; The Last Alarm. **1927** Johnny Get Your Hair Cut; The Shamrock and the Rose; Camille; Spider Webs; Wolves of the Air. **1928** The Wagon Show; Eagle of the Night (serial); Black Feather. **1936** Hollywood Boulevard. **1939** Rovin' Tumbleweeds. **1940** A Little Bit of Heaven. **1941** Lady from Louisiana.

COSTELLO, WILLIAM A.

Born: 1898. Died: Oct. 9, 1971, San Jose, Calif. Screen, radio actor, musician and singer. Voice of "Popeye the Sailor Man."

Appeared in: **1927** King of Kings. **1930** Border Romance. **1935** Melody Trail. **1938** The Port of Missing Girls; Wanted by the Police. **1939** Balalaika.

COTTO DEL VALLE, LUIS

Born: 1913. Died: Mar. 1971, Mexico City, Mexico. Stage and screen actor.

COTTON, BILLY (William Edward Cotton)

Born: 1900, England. Died: Mar. 25, 1969, London, England (heart attack). Bandleader, screen, radio and television actor.

Appeared in: **1921** The Old Next.

COTTON, FRED AYRES

Born: 1907, Hastings, Neb. Died: Jan. 29, 1964, New York, N.Y. Stage and screen actor.

Appeared in: **1944** Winged Victory (stage and screen versions).

COTTON, GEORGE

Born: 1903, Grand Rapids, Mich. Died: May 26, 1975, Lisbon, Portugal. Screen, stage and television actor.

Appeared in: **1964** The Curse of the Living Corpse.

COTTON, LUCY (Lucy Cotton Magraw)

Born: 1891. Died: Dec. 12, 1948, Miami Beach, Fla. (suicide—overdose of sleeping pills). Stage and screen actress.

Appeared in: **1910** The Fugitive. **1921** The Devil; Whispering Shadows; The Man Who.

COTTON, RICHARDSON

Died: Sept. 24, 1916, Ephraim, Wisc. (hit by auto). Screen actor.

Appeared in: **1915** Hearts and Roses; A Mansion of Tragedy; The Lighthouse by the Sea. **1916** Pieces of the Game; Folly; A Man's Work; The Danger Line; Once a Thief; Our People; The Sting of Victory.

COTTS, CAMPBELL

Born: 1903, England? Died: Feb. 19, 1964, London, England. Stage and screen actor.

Appeared in: **1949** Stop Press; Dear Mr. Prohack (US 1950). **1950** Last Holiday; The Angel with the Trumpet. **1951** Encore (US 1952). **1952** The Hour of 13. **1955** Barbados Quest (aka Murder on Approval—US 1956). **1956** Three Men in a Boat (US 1958). **1957** Doctor at Large; The Good Companions; Just My Luck.

COULTER, FRAZER

Born: 1849, Smith Falls, Ont., Canada. Died: Jan. 26, 1937, East Islip, N.Y. Stage and screen actor.

Appeared in: **1921** His Brother's Keeper; Love's Redemption. **1923** The Heart Raider; The Governor's Lady. **1926** The Prince of Tempters.

COUNTESS DUCELLA

Born: Buffalo, N.Y. Died: Nov. 28, 1921, Los Angeles, Calif. Screen actress.

COURT, ALFRED C.

Born: 1886, Australia. Died: Dec. 31, 1953, Hollywood, Calif. Stage and screen actor.

COURTENAY, WILLIAM

Born: 1875, Worcester, Mass. Died: Apr. 20, 1933, Rye, N.Y. (severe cold and heart weakness). Stage and screen actor. Married to stage actress Virginia Harned (dec. 1946).

Appeared in: **1894** Miss Jerry. **1917** Kick In. **1929** Evidence; The Show of Shows; The Sacred Flame. **1930** The Way of All Men; Three Faces East.

COURTLEIGH, STEPHEN

Died: 1968. Screen actor.

Appeared in: **1955** Yellowneck. **1960** North to Alaska.

COURTLEIGH, WILLIAM, JR.

Born: 1869, Guelph, Ontario, Canada. Died: 1930. Screen actor.

Appeared in: **1915** Neal of the Navy. **1916** Out of the Drifts; Susie Snowflake; Eyes of Youth. **1920** Madame X. **1922** Handle with Care; Ashes; Any Night; Midnight.

COURTLEIGH, WILLIAM, SR.

Born: June 28, 1892, Buffalo, N.Y. Died: Mar. 14, 1918, Philadelphia, Pa. (pneumonia). Stage and screen actor. Married to actress Ethel Flemming.

Appeared in: **1914** The Nightingale; The Better Man. **1915** Neal of the Navy (serial); Souls in Pawn; Life's Crucible. **1916** The Innocent Lie; Out of the Drifts; Cinders; The Sheriff of Pine Mountain. **1917** Miss U.S.A.; The Heart of a Lion. **1918** By Right of Purchase. **1919** Eyes of Youth.

COURTNEY, INEZ

Born: March 12, 1908, New York. Died: Apr. 5, 1975, Neptune, N.J. Stage and screen actress.

Appeared in: **1930** Loose Ankles; Not Damaged; Song of the Flame; Spring is Here; Hold Your Man; Sonny. **1931** Hot Heiress; Bright Lights. **1932** Big City Blues. **1933** The World Gone Mad; Cheating Blondes; I Love that Man. **1934** Jealousy; The Captain Hates the Sea; It's the Cat's (short); Broadway Bill. **1935** The Girl Friend; Millions in the Air; I'm a Father (short); Sweepstake Annie; Break of Hearts; Another Face; The Raven; Ship Cafe; The Affair of Susan; Magnificent Obsession. **1936** Dizzy Dames; Let's Sing Again; Suzy; It Couldn't Have Happened; Wedding Present; Brilliant Marriage. **1937** The Hurricane; Time Out for Romance; The Hit Parade; an MGM short; Armored Car; Clarence; Partners in Crime; The Thirteenth Man; The Thirteenth Chair. **1938** Having a Wonderful Time; Crime Ring; Five of a Kind. **1939** Blondie Meets the Boss; Beauty for the Asking; Missing Evidence. **1940** The Shop Around the Corner; The Farmer's Daughter; Turnabout.

COURTNEY, OSCAR W.

Born: 1877. Died: June 13, 1962, Chicago, Ill. Screen and vaudeville actor. Entered films with Essanay in 1912.

COURTRIGHT, CLYDE

Born: 1885. Died: Oct. 6, 1967, Santa Cruz, Calif. Screen actor. Stand-in for Gary Cooper and Charles Bickford.

COURTRIGHT, WILLIAM "UNCLE BILLY"

Born: Mar. 10, 1848, New Milford, Ill. Died: Mar. 6, 1933, Ione, Calif. Screen, stage and minstrel actor. Entered films in 1910.

Appeared in: **1920** Peaceful Valley. **1921** The Rookie's Return; The Speed Girl; Extravagance; R.S.V.P.; The Lure of Youth; The Millionaire. **1922** At the Sign of the Jack O'Lantern; The Deuce of Spades; A Man of Action; The Sunset Trail; The Man under Cover. **1923** The Girl I Loved; Bell Boy 13. **1924** The Heart Buster; George Washington, Jr. **1925** Are Parents People?; Some Pun'kins; Thank You; The Trouble With Wives; All around Frying Pan. **1926**

For Wives Only; The Grand Duchess and the Waiter; Atta Boy; The Two Gun Man; A Regular Scout; The Tough Guy; Lone Hand Saunders; Hands Across the Border. **1927** Don Mike; Arizona Nights; Jesse James; My Best Girl; Silver Comes Thru; The Poor Nut. **1928** The Pioneer Scout; Kit Carson; Sunset Legion.

COWAN, JEROME (Jerome Palmer Cowan)
Born: Oct. 6, 1897, New York, N.Y. Died: Jan. 24, 1972, Encino, Calif. Screen, stage, vaudeville, burlesque and television actor.

Appeared in: **1936** Beloved Enemy. **1937** Vogues of 1938; You Only Live Once; Shall We Dance; New Faces of 1937; The Hurricane. **1938** The Goldwyn Follies; There's Always a Woman. **1939** The Old Maid; St. Louis Blues; The Gracie Allen Murder Case; Exile Express; The Great Victor Herbert; East Side of Heaven; The Saint Strikes Back; She Married a Cop. **1940** Torrid Zone; Wolf of New York; Ma, He's Making Eyes at Me; Meet the Wildcat; City for Conquest; Melody Ranch; Victory; The Quarterback; Street of Memories; Castle on the Hudson; Framed. **1941** High Sierra; Rags to Riches; The Round-up; Affectionately Yours; One Foot in Heaven; Kiss the Boys Goodbye; Kisses for Breakfast; The Maltese Falcon; Out of the Fog; Singapore Woman; The Great Lie; Mr. and Mrs. North; Too Many Blondes. **1942** The Girl from Alaska; Frisco Lil; Moontide; Through Different Eyes; Joan of Ozark; Who Done It?; A Gentleman at Heart; Street of Chance; The Bugle Sounds. **1943** The Song of Bernadette; Ladies' Day; Crime Doctor; No Place for a Lady; Mission to Moscow; Hi Ya, Sailor!; Silver Spurs; Find the Blackmailer; Crime Doctor's Strangest Case. **1944** Sing a Jingle; Minstrel Man; Guest in the House; Crime by Night; South of Dixie; Mr. Skeffington. **1945** Fog Island; Divorce; Getting Gertie's Garter; Behind City Lights; Crime Doctor's Courage; Blonde Ransom; Hitchhike to Happiness; G.I. Honeymoon; Jungle Captive. **1946** My Reputation; One Way to Love; Claudia and David; Murder in the Music Hall; One Exciting Week; Blondie Knows Best; Mr. Ace; Deadline at Dawn; Deadline for Murder; A Night in Paradise; The Kid from Brooklyn; The Perfect Marriage. **1947** Blondie's Holiday; Blondie's Anniversary; Blondie's Big Moment; Driftwood; Flight to Nowhere; Riffraff; The Unfaithful; Miracle on 34th Street; Cry Wolf; Blondie in the Dough. **1948** So This is New York; Blondie's Reward; Wallflower; Arthur Takes Over; June Bride; Night Has a Thousand Eyes; Dangerous Year. **1949** Blondie Hits the Jackpot; Blondie's Secret; Blondie's Big Deal; Scene of the Crime; Always Leave Them Laughing; The Girl from Jones Beach; The Fountainhead. **1950** The West Point Story; Young Man with a Horn; Dallas; Joe Palooka Meets Humphrey; The Fuller Brush Girl; Peggy; When You're Smiling. **1951** Disc Jockey; The Fat Man; Criminal Lawyer. **1953** The System. **1959** Have Rocket, Will Travel. **1960** Private Property; Visit to a Small Planet. **1961** All in a Night's Work; Pocketful of Miracles. **1963** Critic's Choice; Black Zoo. **1964** The Patsy; John Goldfarb, Please Come Home. **1966** Frankie and Johnny; Penelope. **1967** The Gnome-Mobile. **1969** The Comic (aka Billy Bright).

COWAN, LYNN F.
Died: Aug. 29, 1973, Pensacola, Fla. Pianist, singer, composer, vaudeville and screen actor.

Appeared in: **1925** The Compromise. **1926** The Social Highwayman.

COWARD, SIR NOEL (Noel Pierce Coward)
Born: Dec. 16, 1899, Teddington-on-the-Thames, England. Died: Mar. 26, 1973, Kingston, Jamaica (heart attack). Screen, stage, television actor, film director, producer, stage producer, composer, playwright, screenwriter and author. In 1942 received a Special Academy Award for outstanding production achievement for In Which We Serve.

Appeared in: **1918** Hearts of the World (film debut). **1935** The Scoundrel. **1942** In Which We Serve. **1950** The Astonished Heart. **1956** Around the World in 80 Days. **1960** Our Man in Havana; Surprise Package. **1964** Paris When It Sizzles. **1965** Bunny Lake is Missing. **1968** Boom! **1969** The Italian Job.

COWL, JANE
Born: 1887, Boston, Mass. Died: June 22, 1950, Santa Monica, Calif. (cancer). Screen, stage actress and playwright.

Appeared in: **1915** The Garden of Lies. **1917** The Spreading Dawn. **1943** Stage Door Canteen. **1949** Once More, My Darling, Come Be My Love. **1950** No Man of Her Own; The Secret Fury. **1951** Payment on Demand.

COWLES, JULES
Born: 1878, Farmington, Conn. Died: May 22, 1943, Hollywood, Calif. Screen actor.

Appeared in: **1921** The Idol of the North; Tangled Trails; God's Crucible. **1922** The Bootleggers. **1923** Lost in a Big City; The Ne'er-Do-Well. **1924** The Love Bandit; High Speed. **1925** Seven Chances; The Lost World; Lord Jim. **1926** Man Rustlin'; Money to Burn; The Scarlet Letter; The Ace of Clubs. **1927** The Road to Romance. **1928** Bringing up Father; Dog Law; Why Sailors Go Wrong; Terror; Isle of Lost Men; Thundergod. **1929** Sal of Singapore; The Leatherneck. **1930** His First Command; One Hysterical Night. **1931** Heaven on Earth. **1933** Cross Fire; The Fighting Parson. **1934** The Scarlet Letter (and 1926 version); The Pursuit of Happiness. **1935** Barbary Coast; Mississippi. **1943** Air Raid Wardens.

COWPER, WILL C. (William C. Cowper)
Born: 1853, Manchester, England. Died: June 13, 1918. Stage and screen actor.

Appeared in: **1913** Gold is Not All. **1915** Emmy of Stork's Nest; A Yellow Streak; An Enemy of Society. **1916** Dimples.

COX, ROBERT
Born: 1895. Died: Sept. 8, 1974, Phoenix, Ariz. Screen actor and assistant film director. Was one of the original Keystone Kops and appeared in nearly 300 one-reelers.

COX, TOM (Thomas Sinclair Cox)
Born: 1892. Died: Dec. 6, 1914, La Crescenta, Calif. Screen actor. Appeared in Kalem films.

COX, WALLY (Wallace Maynard Cox)
Born: Dec. 1924, Detroit, Mich. Died: Feb. 15, 1973, Los Angeles, Calif. (heart attack). Screen, stage, radio, television actor and author.

Appeared in: **1962** State Fair. **1963** Spencer's Mountain. **1964** Fate is the Hunter. **1965** The Bedford Incident; Morituri; The Yellow Rolls-Royce. **1967** A Guide for the Married Man. **1968** The One and Only, Genuine, Original Family Band. **1970** The Boatniks; The Cockeyed Cowboys of Calico County (aka A Woman for Charlie); Up Your Teddy Bear.

COXEN, EDWARD ALBERT
Born: 1884. Died: Nov. 21, 1954, Hollywood, Calif. Screen and stage actor.

Appeared in: **1912** Where the Road Forks; Hypnotized. **1913** The Spartan Girl of the West; A Divorce Scandal; The End of Black Bart. **1914** The Dream Child; Daylight; Her Fighting Chance; Sheltering an Ingrate; Jim; A Modern Freelance; The Ruin of Manley; Down by the Sea; The Little House in the Valley; Lodging for a Night; The Hermit; The Shriner's Daughter; In the Firelight; False Gods; This is the Life. **1915** The Resolve; The Guiding Light; The Forecast; Comrades Three; It Was Like This; On Secret Service; Out of the Ashes; The Clean-Up; The Water Carrier of San Juan; The Sting of It; A Broken Genius; Spider Barlow Cuts In. **1916** The Profligate; A Woman's Daring; The Voice of Love; The Franchise; Ruth Ridley's Return; The Key; Citizens All; The Happy Masquerader; Bonds of Deception; In the Shuffle; The Trail of the Thief; The Suppressed Order. **1917** Madam Who; A Man's Man. **1918** Carmen of the Klondike; Honor's Cross; A Law Unto Herself; Blindfolded. **1921** Desperate Trails; No Man's Woman. **1922** Nine Points of the Law; The Stranger of the Hills; The Veiled Woman. **1923** A Man's Man; Scaramouche; Temporary Marriage; Our Hospitality; The Flying Dutchman; Foolish Mothers. **1924** Flashing Spurs; Singer Jim McKee; One Glorious Night. **1925** Cold Nerve; The Man Without a Country. **1926** The Man in the Shadow. **1927** The Web of Fate; Galloping Fury; God's Great Wilderness. **1930** The Spoilers. **1933** Cross Fire; The Fighting Parson. **1934** The Scarlet Letter (and 1926 version); The Pursuit of Happiness. **1935** Barbary Coast; Mississippi. **1943** Air Raid Wardens.

COY, JOHNNIE
Born: 1921. Died: Nov. 4, 1973, Barbados. Screen and stage actor.

Appeared in: **1945** Bring on the Girls; Duffy's Tavern; That's the Spirit; On Stage Everybody. **1946** Earl Carroll Sketchbook. **1947** Ladies' Man. **1954** Top Banana.

COY, WALTER
Born: Jan. 31, 1906, Great Falls, Mont. Died: Dec. 11, 1974. Screen, stage and vaudeville actor.

Appeared in: **1935** Paradise Lost. **1936** Love Letters of a Star; Case of Clyde Griffith. **1950** Barricade; Tyrant of the Sea; Saddle Tramp; Under Mexicali Skies; Colt 45. **1951** FBI Girl. **1952** The Lusty Men; Flat Top. **1953** So Big. **1954** Sign of the Pagan. **1955** Cult of the Cobra; Wichita; Running Wild. **1956** The Searchers; On the Threshold of Space; Pillars of the Sky; The Young Guns. **1957** Johnny Tremaine. **1958** Juvenile Jungle. **1959** Gunmen from Laredo; The Gunfight at Dodge City. **1961** Five Guns to Tombstone; Gun Fight.

COYAN, BETTY
Born: 1901. Died: Feb. 10, 1935, Council Bluffs, Iowa. Screen actress. Entered films approx. 1921.

COYLE, WALTER V.
Born: 1888. Died: Aug. 3, 1948, Freeport, N.Y. Screen and stage actor.

COYNE, JEANNE
Born: 1923. Died: May 10, 1973, Los Angeles, Calif. Screen, stage actress and film production assistant. Married to actor Gene Kelly.

Appeared in: **1953** Kiss Me Kate.

CRADDOCK, CLAUDIA
Born: 1889. Died: Dec. 17, 1945, Hollywood, Calif. Screen actress.

Appeared in: **1933** A Lady's Profession.

CRAFT, LYNNE

Died: Mar. 20, 1975. Screen actress and film extra.

Appeared in: **1956** Around the World in 80 Days.

CRAFTS, GRIFFIN

Born: 1900. Died: Aug. 7, 1973, New York, N.Y. (cancer). Screen, stage and radio actor.

Appeared in: **1960** I Passed for White.

CRAIG, ALEC

Born: 1885, Scotland. Died: June 25, 1945, Glendale, Calif. Stage and screen actor.

Appeared in: **1934** The Little Minister. **1935** Old Homestead; Vanessa, Her Love Story; Sweepstakes Annie. **1936** Winterset; Mary of Scotland (stage and film versions). **1937** That Girl from Paris; Hideaway; The Man Who Found Himself; The Woman I Love; China Passage; There Goes My Girl; Super Sleuth; She's Got Everything. **1938** If I Were King; Crashing Hollywood; Wise Girl; Double Danger; Vivacious Lady. **1939** Confessions of a Nazi Spy; Ruler of the Seas; Night Work; They Made Her a Spy. **1940** Abe Lincoln in Illinois; Phantom Raiders; Tom Brown's School Days; Golden Gloves; Stranger on the Third Floor. **1941** All That Money Can Buy; Shining Victory; A Date with the Falcon. **1942** Random Harvest; Mrs. Miniver; The Night before the Divorce; Cat People; Tennessee Johnson; Wrecking Crew. **1943** Action in the North Atlantic; Appointment in Berlin; Holy Matrimony; Lassie Come Home; Northern Pursuit. **1944** Sherlock Holmes and the Spider Woman; Calling Dr. Death. **1945** Serenade for Murder. **1946** Three Strangers; Kitty. **1952** The Devil and Daniel Webster (reissue of 1941 All That Money Can Buy).

CRAIG, CAROLYN

Born: Oct. 29, 193 (?), Long Island, N.Y. Died: Dec. 11, 1970. Screen, stage and television actress.

Appeared in: **1956** Giant (film debut). **1957** Portland Expose; Fury at Sundown; Gunsight Ridge. **1958** Apache Territory; House on Haunted Hill. **1960** Studs Lonigan.

CRAIG, FRANCES B.

Born: c. 1869. Died: July 22, 1925, Los Angeles, Calif. Stage and screen actress.

CRAIG, GODFREY

Born: 1915. Died: May 26, 1941, Los Angeles, Calif. Screen actor. Appeared in "Our Gang" comedies.

CRAIG, MAY

Born: 1889, Ireland. Died: Feb. 1972, Dublin, Ireland. Stage and screen actress.

Appeared in: **1952** The Quiet Man. **1957** The Rising of the Moon (aka A Minute's Wait). **1961** Johnny Nobody (US 1965). **1964** Girl with Green Eyes. **1965** Young Cassidy.

CRAIG, NELL

Born: 1891. Died: Jan. 5, 1965, Hollywood, Calif. Screen and stage actress. Entered films in 1913. Appeared in Essanay films in 1914.

Appeared in: **1915** The Return of Richard Neal; In the Palace of the King; The Primitive Strain. **1921** The Queen of Sheba. **1922** The Flirt; Remembrance. **1923** The Abysmal Brute. **1924** A Boy of Flanders; Abraham Lincoln. **1931** Cimarron; Consolation Marriage. **1936** Palm Springs. **1939** The Women; Calling Dr. Kildare; The Secret of Dr. Kildare. **1940** Dr. Kildare Goes Home; Dr. Kildare's Strangest Case; Dr. Kildare's Crisis. **1941** Glamour Boy; Dr. Kildare's Wedding Day; Dr. Kildare's Victory; The People vs. Dr. Kildare. **1942** Calling Dr. Gillespie; Dr. Gillespie's New Assistant. **1944** Between Two Women; Three Men in White. **1945** Out of This World. **1946** Our Hearts Were Growing Up. **1947** Dark Delusion.

CRAIG, RICHY, JR.

Born: 1902. Died: Nov. 28, 1933, New York, N.Y. Screen, stage, vaudeville and radio actor.

Appeared in: **1932-33** "Vitaphone Big Star" comedies and "Big V" comedies.

CRAMER, EDD

Born: 1924. Died: Dec. 21, 1963, New York, N.Y. Screen, stage and television actor.

Appeared in: **1954** On the Waterfront.

CRAMER, RICHARD (Richard Earl Cramer aka RYCHARD CRAMER)

Born: July 3, 1889, Bryan, Ohio. Died: Aug. 9, 1960, Los Angeles, Calif. (Laennec's cirrhosis). Screen and stage actor.

Appeared in: **1929** Illusion; Kid Gloves. **1930** Those Who Dance; Captain of the Guard; Sweet Mama; Hell's Island; Murder on the Roof; Big Money. **1931** An American Tragedy; Painted Desert; Air Police; In Line of Duty; Night Boat; Dancing Dynamite; Neck and Neck; Lariats and Six Shooters; Pocatello Kid. **1932** The Strange Love of Molly Louvain; The Tenderfoot; 45 Calibre

Echo; Pack Up Your Troubles; Scram! (short); Unexpected Father; His Royal Shyness (short). **1933** Fourth Horseman; The Fatal Glass of Beer (short); Private Jones; Storm at Daybreak. **1934** Hollywood Party; Rawhide Mail. **1935** Danger Ahead; Judgment Book; Riddle Ranch. **1936** Frontier Justice; Just My Luck; O'Malley of the Mounted; The Speed Reporter; Three Godfathers; Sutter's Gold; The Red Rider; Vanishing Shadow; Spanish Cape Mystery; Cappy Ricks Returns; Speed Demon; Rio Grande Romance. **1937** Woman Chases Man; The Trusted Outlaw; Where Trails Divide; Night Club Scandal; Crusade Against the Rackets. **1938** Rangers Roundup; Clipped Wings; Thunder in the Desert; Song and Bullets; Phantom Ranger; Knight of the Plains. **1939** In Old Montana; The Flying Deuces. **1940** Saps at Sea; Arizona Frontier; Northwest Passage. **1941** Double Trouble. **1942** Broadway Big Shot; Rock River; Renegades; This Time for Keeps; Eagle Squadron; The Phantom Plainsman. **1945** Song of Old Wyoming.

CRAMER, SUSANNE

Born: 1938, Germany. Died: Jan. 7, 1969, Hollywood, Calif. (pneumonia). Screen and television actress. Appeared in U.S., German and French films.

Appeared in: **1956** Kleines Gelt und Grosse Liebe (aka Two in a Sleeping Bag—US 1964). **1957** Every Second Counts. **1958** Wie ein Sturmwind (Tempestuous Love); Schwarze Nylons—Heisse Nachate (aka All Bad and aka Indecent—US 1962). **1959** Vacanzie a Lzchia (Holiday Island). **1964** Bedtime Story. **1968** Waylaid Women (reissue of 1958 Schwarze Nylons).

CRANE, DIXIE

Born: 1888. Died: Nov. 18, 1936, Hollywood, Calif. Screen and vaudeville actress. Appeared with her husband Henry Johnson in a vaudeville act billed as "Johnson and Crane." She appeared in early Lasky films.

CRANE, ETHEL G.

Died: Oct. 1930, San Bernardino, Calif. (suicide—poison). Screen actress.

CRANE, MAE

Born: 1925. Died: Apr. 15, 1969, Port Washington, N.Y. (lung ailment). Screen, stage, radio and television actress.

Appeared in: **1967** The Producers. **1968** For Love of Ivy; No Way to Treat a Lady.

CRANE, NORMA (Norma Anna Bella Zuckerman)

Born: 1931, New York, N.Y. Died: Sept. 28, 1973, West Los Angeles, Calif. (cancer). Stage and screen actress. Divorced from writer Herb Sargent.

Appeared in: **1956** Tea and Sympathy. **1961** All in a Night's Work. **1966** Penelope. **1968** The Sweet Ride. **1970** They Call Me Mr. Tibbs. **1971** Fiddler on the Roof.

CRANE, RICHARD O.

Born: 1918. Died: Mar. 9, 1969, San Fernando Valley, Calif. (heart attack). Screen and television actor.

Appeared in: **1940** Susan and God. **1941** The Saint in Palm Springs; In the Navy; Keep 'Em Flying. **1942** The Phantom Plainsman; This Time for Keeps. **1943** Someone to Remember; Riders of the Deadline; Happy Land. **1944** Wing and a Prayer; None Shall Escape. **1945** Captain Eddie. **1946** Johnny Comes Flying Home; Behind Green Lights. **1948** Angel on the Amazon; Arthur Takes Over; Waterfront at Midnight; Campus Honeymoon; Triple Threat. **1949** Dynamite. **1950** A Lady without a Passport. **1951** The Last Outpost; Mysterious Island (serial); Man in the Saddle. **1952** Thundering Caravans; Leadville Gunslinger. **1953** Winning of the West; The Neanderthal Man; The Woman They Almost Lynched. **1955** No Man's Woman; The Eternal Sea. **1957** Bailout at 43,000. **1958** The Deep Six. **1959** Battle Flame; The Alligator People. **1960** Thirteen Fighting Men. **1961** The Boy Who Caught a Crook. **1962** The Devil's Partner. **1963** House of the Damned. **1964** Surf Party.

CRANE, WARD

Born: 1891, Albany, N.Y. Died: July 21, 1928, Saranac Lake, N.Y. (pneumonia). Screen actor.

Appeared in: **1921** Heedless Moths. **1922** Broadway Rose; French Heels; No Trespassing; Destiny's Isle. **1923** Enemies of Children; Pleasure Mad; The Famous Mrs. Fair; Within the Law; The Meanest Man in the World. **1924** Sherlock, Jr.; Empty Hands; Bread; Gambling Wives. **1925** How Baxter Butted In; The Crimson Runner; The Mad Whirl; The Million Dollar Handicap; Classified; Borrowed Finery; The Phantom of the Opera; Peacock Feathers. **1926** Boy Friend; Risky Business; Upstage; That Model from Paris; The Blind Goddess; The Flaming Frontier; The Sporting Lover; Under Western Skies. **1927** The Lady in Ermine; The Auctioneer; Beauty Shoppers; The Rush Hour; Down the Stretch. **1928** Honeymoon Flats.

CRANE, WILLIAM H.

Born: 1892. Died: Jan. 22, 1957, Scranton, Pa. Screen and stage actor.

CRANE, WILLIAM H.
Born: 1845, Leicester, Mass. Died: Mar. 7, 1928, Hollywood, Calif. (general breakdown). Stage and screen actor.

CRAVAT, NOEL
Born: 1910. Died: Feb. 20, 1960, Hollywood, Calif. (after surgery). Screen actor.

Appeared in: 1943 G-Men vs. the Black Dragon (serial). 1948 The Iron Curtain. 1953 South Sea Woman; The 5,000 Fingers of Dr. T.

CRAVEN, FRANK
Born: 1875, Boston, Mass. Died: Sept. 1, 1945, Beverly Hills, Calif. (heart ailment). Screen, stage actor, film director, playwright and screenwriter.

Appeared in: 1928 We Americans. 1929 The Very Idea. 1932 The Putter (short). 1933 State Fair. 1934 That's Gratitude; He Was Her Man; Let's Talk It Over; City Limits; Funny Thing Called Love. 1935 Barbary Coast; Car 99; Vagabond Lady. 1936 Small Town Girl; The Harvester. 1937 Penrod and Sam; Blossoms on Broadway. 1938 You're Only Young Once; Penrod and His Twin Brother. 1939 Our Neighbors, the Carters; Miracles for Sale. 1940 Dreaming Out Loud; City for Conquest; Our Town. 1941 The Lady from Cheyenne; The Richest Man in Town. 1942 In This Our Life; Pittsburgh; Girl Trouble; Through Different Eyes. 1943 Son of Dracula; Harrigan's Kid; Jack London; The Human Comedy; Keeper of the Flame. 1944 Destiny; My Best Gal; They Shall Have Faith. 1945 The Right to Live; Colonel Effingham's Raid.

CRAWFORD, ANNE (Imelda Crawford)
Born: Nov. 22, 1920, Haifa, Israel. Died: Oct. 17, 1956, London, England. Screen, stage and television actress.

Appeared in: 1942 They Flew Alone (film debut—aka Wings and the Woman—US); The Peterville Diamond. 1943 The Dark Tower; Millions Like Us; Headline; The Hundred Pound Window; The Night Invader. 1944 2,000 Women. 1945 They Were Sisters (US 1946). 1946 Caravan (US 1947); Bedelia (US 1947). 1947 Master of Bankdam. 1948 Daughter of Darkness; Night Beat; The Blind Goddess (US 1949). 1950 Tony Draws a Horse (US 1951); Trio. 1951 Thunder On the Hill. 1953 Street Corner (aka Both Sides of the Law—US 1954). 1954 Knights of the Round Table; Mad About Men.

CRAWFORD, BESSIE
Born: 1882. Died: Nov. 11, 1943, Hollywood, Calif. (heart attack). Screen, stage and vaudeville actress. Married to screen actor T. Roy Barnes (dec. 1937) and appeared with him in a vaudeville act billed as "Barnes and Crawford."

CRAWFORD, CLIFTON
Born: 1875. Died: June 3, 1920. Screen actor.

Appeared in: 1915 The Galloper.

CRAWFORD, HOWARD MARION
Born: 1914. Died: Nov. 24, 1969, London, England (overdose of sleeping pills). Screen, stage, radio and television actor.

Appeared in: 1935 Forever England (aka Brown on Resolution and Born for Glory—US). 1938 13 Men and a Gun. 1941 Freedom Radio (aka A Voice in the Night—US). 1945 The Rake's Progress (aka Notorious Gentleman—US 1946). 1949 The Hasty Heart. 1951 Mr. Drake's Duck; The Man in the White Suit (US 1952). 1952 His Excellency (US 1956); Where's Charley? 1953 Top of the Form. 1954 Don't Blame the Stork; West of Zanzibar; Five Days (aka Paid to Kill—US); The Rainbow Jacket. 1956 Reach for the Sky (US 1957); The Silken Affaire. 1957 The Birthday Present; Don Kikhot (Don Quixote—US 1961—dubbed English voice); The Man in the Sky (aka Decision against Time—US); The Tyburn Case. 1958 Gideon's Day (aka Gideon of Scotland Yard—US 1959); The Silent Enemy; Next to No Time (US 1960); Virgin Island (US 1960); Nowhere to Go (US 1959). 1959 Model for Murder; Life in Danger (US 1964). 1960 Foxhole in Cairo (US 1961). 1962 Lawrence of Arabia. 1963 Man in the Middle (US 1964); Tamahine (US 1964). 1965 The Face of Fu Manchu. 1966 The Brides of Fu Manchu. 1967 Vengeance of Fu Manchu (US 1968); The Singing Princess (voice); Smashing Time. 1968 The Charge of the Light Brigade; The Blood of Fu Manchu (aka Kiss and Kill—US 1969).

CRAWFORD, CAPTAIN JACK (John Wallace Crawford)
Born: Mar. 4, 1847, County Donegal, Ireland. Died: Feb. 27, 1917, Ireland? Screen actor, playwright and military officer.

Appeared in: 1914 The Poet Scout's Pledge.

CRAWFORD, NAN
Born: 1893, Richmond, Va. Died: July 4, 1975, Inglewood, Calif. Screen, stage, vaudeville and radio actress. Married to actor Henry Hollingsworth (dec. 1947) with whom she appeared in vaudeville in an act billed as "Hollingsworth and Crawford."

Appeared in: 1929 Bedtime (short).

CRAWLEY, CONSTANCE
Born: Mar. 30, 1879, England. Died: Mar. 18, 1919, Los Angeles, Calif. (asthma). Screen actress and screenwriter.

Appeared in: 1913 Pelleas and Melisande; Jedediah's Daughter. 1914 Thais. 1915 The Alternative; The Wrath of Haddon Towers. 1916 Revelations; Lord Loveland Visits America; Powder; Embers.

CRAWLEY, SAYRE
Born: England. Died: Mar. 7, 1948, New York, N.Y. Screen and stage actor.

CREAMER, CHARLES
Born: 1894. Died: July 22, 1971, Hollywood, Calif. (heart attack). Screen actor, extra and stand-in for Walter Brennan.

CREGAR, LAIRD
Born: 1913, Philadelphia, Pa. Died: Dec. 9, 1944, Los Angeles, Calif. (heart attack). Stage and screen actor.

Appeared in: 1940 Granny Get Your Gun; Oh Johnny, How You Can Love; Hudson's Bay. 1941 Blood and Sand; Charley's Aunt; I Wake up Screaming. 1942 Rings on Her Fingers; This Gun for Hire; Joan of Paris; Black Swan; Ten Gentlemen from West Point. 1943 Heaven Can Wait; Holy Matrimony; Hello, Frisco, Hello. 1944 The Lodger. 1945 Hangover Square.

CREHAN, JOSEPH
Born: July 12, 1886, Baltimore, Md. Died: Apr. 15, 1966, Hollywood, Calif. Screen, stage and television actor.

Appeared in: 1931 Stolen Heaven. 1933 Hold the Press. 1934 Against the Law; Jimmy the Gent; Identity Parade; Before Midnight; The Line-Up; The Hell Cat. 1935 Go into Your Dance; Black Fury; The Traveling Saleslady; Bright Lights; The Case of the Lucky Legs; Shipmates Forever; Man of Iron; The Payoff; Oil for the Lamps of China; Stranded; Page Miss Glory; Front Page Woman; Alibi Ike; Special Agent; Dinky; Frisco Kid. 1936 Brides Are Like That; The Singing Kid; Bengal Tiger; Murder of Dr. Harrigan; Road Gang; God's Country and the Woman; King of Hockey; Smart Blonde; Gold Diggers of 1937; Here Comes Carter; Murder by an Aristocrat; Boulder Dam; The Law in Her Hands; Jail Break; Anthony Adverse; Bullets or Ballots; Earthworm Tractors; China Clipper; Cain and Mabel; Down the Stretch; Trailin' West. 1937 Draegerman Courage; Don't Pull Your Punches; Kid Galahad; Her Husband's Secretary; Once a Doctor; Midnight Court; Talent Scout; The Go-Getter; This Is My Affair; Born Reckless; There Goes My Girl; Midnight Madonna; The Wrong Road; The Duke Comes Back; Mama Runs Wild; Here's Flash Casey; Guns of the Pecos; Girls Can Play; Outlaws of the Orient; The Case of the Stuttering Bishop. 1938 A Criminal Is Born (short); Midnight Intruder; The Goldwyn Follies; Happy Landing; Alexander's Ragtime Band; The Arkansas Traveler; Illegal Traffic; Billy the Kid Returns; Night Spot; Four's a Crowd; Crime Takes a Holiday; Woman against Woman; The Kid Comes Back. 1939 Navy Secrets; Star Maker; Society Lawyer; Tell No Tales; Maisie; Babes in Arms; Hollywood Cavalcade; Behind Prison Gates; Private Detective; Geronimo; The Roaring Twenties; The Return of Dr. X; Whispering Enemies; You Can't Get Away with Murder; Pride of the Navy; Stanley and Livingstone; Union Pacific. 1940 Jack Pot (short); Emergency Squad; Music in My Heart; The Secret Seven; The House across the Bay; City for Conquest; Gaucho Serenade; Brother Orchid. 1941 Andy Hardy's Private Secretary; Nine Lives Are Not Enough; Doctors Don't Tell; Texas; The Case of the Black Parrot; Washington Melodrama; Scattergood Baines; Manpower; Love Crazy; Here Comes Happiness; Nevada City. 1942 Treat 'Em Rough; The Courtship of Andy Hardy; Cadets on Parade; Larceny, Inc.; To the Shores of Tripoli; Murder in the Big House; Men of Texas; Hello, Annapolis; Girl Trouble; You Can't Escape Forever; Gentleman Jim. 1943 Old Acquaintance; Eyes of the Underworld; Mystery Broadcast; Hit the Ice; Mission to Moscow; Hands Across the Border; The Desert Song. 1944 When the Lights Go on Again; Roger Touhy, Gangster; Phantom Lady; The Navy Way; Shine on Harvest Moon; The Adventures of Mark Twain; Black Magic; One Mysterious Night. 1945 The Missing Juror; The Chicago Kid; I Love a Mystery; Brewster's Millions; Man Alive; Dick Tracy; Youth on Trial; Captain Tugboat Annie. 1946 The Brute Man; A Guy Could Change; Girl on the Spot; The Big Sleep; Deadline at Dawn; Dick Tracy vs. Cueball; The Shadow Returns; O.S.S.; Phantom Thief; Behind the Mask; Night Train to Memphis; The Falcon's Adventure; Dangerous Money; The Virginian. 1947 The Trespasser; Philo Vance's Gamble; The Foxes of Harrow; Louisiana; Dick Tracy Meets Gruesome; Night Time in Nevada. 1948 Triple Threat; The Enchanted Valley; The Hunted; April Showers; Silver River; Adventures in Silverado; Homicide for Three; The Countess of Monte Cristo; Street Corner; Bad Men of Tombstone; Sundown at Santa Fe; The Story of Life. 1949 Red Desert; The Last Bandit; The Duke of Chicago; Prejudice; Alias the Champ; Ringside; Alimony; State Department File 649; Amazon Quest. 1950 The Arizona Cowboy; Square Dance Katy; The Tougher They Come; Triple Trouble. 1951 Pride of Maryland; Roadblock; Hometown Story. 1952 Deadline U.S.A. 1953 Crazylegs. 1954 Highway Dragnet.

CREIGHTON, CLEVA. *See* FRANCES CHANEY

CREWS, KAY C.
Born: 1901. Died: Nov. 29, 1959, San Antonio, Texas. Screen, stage and vaudeville actress. Appeared in silent films.

CREWS, LAURA HOPE
Born: 1880, San Francisco, Calif. Died: Nov. 13, 1942, New York, N.Y. Stage and screen actress.

Appeared in: 1929 Charming Sinners. 1932 Rockabye; New Morals for Old. 1933 Out All Night; The Silver Cord; I Love You Wednesday; Blind Adventure; If I Were Free; Female; Ever in My Heart. 1934 Rafter Romance; Age of Innocence. 1935 Behold My Wife; The Flame Within; Lightning Strikes Twice; Escapade; The Melody Lingers On. 1936 Her Master's Voice (stage and film versions); Camille. 1937 The Road Back; Confession; Angel. 1938 Dr. Rhythm; The Sisters; Thanks for the Memory. 1939 Idiot's Delight; Gone with the Wind; Remember?; Reno; The Rains Came; Starmaker. 1940 The Lady with Red Hair; The Bluebird; I'm Nobody's Sweetheart Now; Girl from Avenue A. 1941 The Man Who Came to Dinner; The Flame of New Orleans. 1942 One Foot in Heaven.

CRIMMINS, DANIEL "DAN" (Alexander M. Lyons)
Born: 1863, Liverpool, England. Died: July 11, 1945, U.S. Screen, stage and vaudeville actor. Father of actor Dan Crimmins, Jr.

Appeared in: 1914 Officer Kate; Second Sight. 1915 The Commuters. 1916 Ambition. 1919 The Garage; Johnny Get Your Gun; Under the Top; You're Fired. 1920 Pink Tights. 1921 Colorado; Straight from the Shoulder. 1923 Desert Driven. 1924 The Midnight Express; Women First. 1925 Not so Long Ago; Pretty Ladies. 1926 Peril of the Rail. 1929 Smiling Irish Eyes. 1932 White Zombie. 1935 Vagabond Lady. 1936 The Jungle Princess.

CRINLEY, WILLIAM A.
Died: Jan. 1, 1927, Hollywood, Calif. (following operation). Screen actor and film director.

Appeared in: 1921 Big Town Round-Up.

CRIPPS, KERNAN (John Kernan Cripps)
Born: July 8, 1886, Connecticut. Died: Aug. 12, 1953, Calif. Screen actor.

Appeared in: 1929 Alibi. 1930 Those Who Dance. 1934 I Hate Women. 1935 Northern Frontier; Wilderness Mail; Stone of Silver Creek; Smart Girl; Mary Burns, Fugitive. 1937 Hit the Saddle; Swing It, Sailor. 1940 Gaucho Serenade. 1943 Henry Aldrich Haunts a House. 1947 The Last Round-Up; Blondie in the Dough. 1950 Mary Ryan, Detective.

CRISMAN, ARLINE C.
Died: May 10, 1956, Hollywood, Calif. Screen actress.

CRISP, DONALD
Born: 1880, Aberfeddy, Scotland. Died: May 25, 1974, Van Nuys, Calif. Screen, opera, stage actor, film director, producer, stage director and magazine writer. Married to screenwriter Jane Murfin (dec. 1957). Won 1941 Academy Award for Best Supporting Actor in How Green Was My Valley.

Appeared in: 1910 Fate's Turning; The Two Paths. 1911 The Battle. 1914 The Battle of the Sexes; The Escape; Home Sweet Home. 1915 Birth of a Nation. 1919 Broken Blossoms. 1921 Beside the Bonnie Briar Bush (aka The Bonnie Briar Bush—US). 1925 Don Q., Son of Zorro. 1926 The Black Pirate. 1928 The River Pirate; The Viking. 1929 The Pagan; Trent's Last Case; The Return of Sherlock Holmes. 1930 Scotland Yard. 1931 Svengali; Kick In. 1932 Red Dust; Passport to Hell. 1933 Broadway Bad. 1934 The Little Minister; The Crime Doctor; The Life of Vergie Winters; The Key; What Every Woman Knows. 1935 Vanessa, Her Love Story; Laddie; Oil for the Lamps of China; Mutiny on the Bounty. 1936 Mary of Scotland; Beloved Enemy; The White Angel; Charge of the Light Brigade; A Woman Rebels. 1937 The Great O'Malley; Parnell; The Life of Emile Zola; Confession; That Certain Woman. 1938 Sergeant Murphy; Dawn Patrol; Jezebel; The Sisters; The Beloved Brat; The Amazing Dr. Clitterhouse; Valley of the Giants; Comet Over Broadway. 1939 Juarez; The Old Maid; The Oklahoma Kid; Wuthering Heights; Daughters Courageous; The Private Lives of Elizabeth and Essex. 1940 The Story of Dr. Ehrlich's Magic Bullet (aka Dr. Ehrlich's Magic Bullet); Brother Orchid; City for Conquest; Knute Rockne—All American; The Sea Hawk. 1941 Dr. Jekyll and Mr. Hyde; How Green Was My Valley; Shining Victory. 1942 The Battle of Midway (narrator); The Gay Sisters. 1943 Lassie Come Home; Forever and a Day. 1944 National Velvet; The Adventures of Mark Twain; The Uninvited. 1945 The Valley of Decision; Son of Lassie. 1947 Ramrod. 1948 Whispering Smith; Hills of Home. 1949 Challenge to Lassie. 1950 Bright Leaf. 1951 Home Town Story. 1954 Prince Valiant. 1955 The Man from Laramie; The Long Gray Line. 1957 Drango. 1958 Saddle the Wind; The Last Hurrah. 1959 A Dog of Flanders. 1960 Pollyanna. 1961 Greyfriar's Bobby. 1963 Spencer's Mountain.

CROCKER, HARRY
Born: July 2, 1893, San Francisco, Calif. Died: May 23, 1958. Screen, stage actor and assistant film director.

Appeared in: 1927 Tillie the Toiler; Becky; Sally in our Alley; South Sea Love. 1928 The Circus. 1942 A Night for Crime; Gentleman Jim. 1944 A Song for Miss Julie. 1945 The Great John L. 1949 Dancing in the Dark.

CROCKETT, CHARLES B.
Born: 1872, Md. Died: June 12, 1934, Los Angeles, Calif. Stage and screen actor.

Appeared in: 1924 Sundown; The Millionaire Cowboy. 1925 The Dressmaker from Paris; The Vanishing American; Daddy's Gone A-Hunting; Winds of Chance. 1926 Into Her Kingdom. 1927 The Princess from Hoboken; Arizona Bound; The Gingham Girl. 1930 Abraham Lincoln; Ex-Flame. 1931 Guilty Hands.

CROMWELL, RICHARD (Roy Radabaugh)
Born: Jan. 8, 1910, Los Angeles, Calif. Died: Oct. 11, 1960, Hollywood, Calif. Stage and screen actor. Divorced from actress Angela Lansbury.

Appeared in: 1930 Tol'able David (film debut); King of Jazz. 1931 Fifty Fathoms Deep; Shanghaied Love; Are These Our Children?; Maker of Men. 1932 Strange Love of Molly Louvain; The Age of Consent; Emma; Tom Brown of Culver; That's My Boy. 1933 This Day and Age; Above the Clouds; Hoopla. 1934 Among the Missing; When Strangers Meet; The Most Precious Thing in Life; Name the Woman; Carolina. 1935 Lives of a Bengal Lancer; McFadden's Flats; Unknown Woman. 1936 Poppy. 1937 Our Fighting Navy (aka Torpedoed—US 1939); The Road Back; The Wrong Road. 1938 Jezebel; Come on, Leathernecks; Storm over Bengal. 1939 Young Mr. Lincoln; Torpedoed. 1940 Enemy Agent; The Villain Still Pursued Her; Village Barn Dance. 1941 Riot Squad; Parachute Battalion. 1942 Baby Face Morgan. 1943 The Crime Doctor. 1948 Bungalow 13.

CROSBY, MARSHAL
Born: 1883, Australia. Died: Jan. 3, 1954, Port Macquarie, N.S.W., Australia (heart attack). Screen, stage, radio and vaudeville actor.

Appeared in: 1946 The Overlanders. 1947 Pacific Adventure. 1952 Kangaroo. Other Australian film: Eureka Stockade.

CROSBY, WADE
Born: 1905, Cedar Rapids, Iowa. Died: Oct. 1, 1975, Newport Beach, Calif. (grand mal seizure). Screen, stage actor and art director.

Appeared in: 1938 Marie Antoinette (film debut); Ride a Crooked Mile. 1940 Arizona; Wagon Train. 1941 Citadel of Crime; Sign of the Wolf. 1942 Shepard of the Ozarks. 1943 The Sundown Kid; Headin' for God's Country; The Woman of the Town. 1946 Traffic in Crime. 1947 The Wistful Widow of Wagon Gap; Along the Oregon Trail. 1948 Under California Skies; The Timber Trail; Angel's Alley; The Paleface. 1949 The Black Book; Rose of the Yukon. 1950 Hit Parade of 1951; Tales of Robin Hood. 1951 Valley of Fire. 1952 Invasion USA. 1953 Old Overland Trail; Prisoners of the Casbah. 1973 Westworld. 1975 Airport; The Hindenberg.

CROSMAN, HENRIETTA
Born: 1861, Wheeling, W. Va. Died: Oct. 31, 1944, Pelham Manor, N.Y. Stage and screen actress.

Appeared in: 1915 How Molly Made Good. 1923 Broadway Broke. 1925 Wandering Fires. 1930 The Roy Family of Broadway. 1933 Pilgrimage. 1934 Among the Missing; Carolina; Three on a Honeymoon; Such Women Are Dangerous; Menace; The Curtain Falls. 1935 Elinor Norton; The Right to Live; The Dark Angel. 1936 Hitchhike to Heaven; Charlie Chan's Secret; The Moon's Our Home; Girl of the Ozarks; Follow Your Heart. 1937 Personal Property.

CROSS, ALFRED FRANCIS
Born: 1891. Died: Jan. 28, 1938, San Diego, Calif. (heart attack). Screen, stage actor and stage director. Entered films approx. 1920.

Appeared in: 1931 Smart Woman.

CROSS, MILTON J.
Born: Apr. 16, 1897, New York, N.Y. Died: Jan. 3, 1975, New York, N.Y. (heart attack). Radio commentator, singer and screen actor. Known as the "Voice of the Metropolitan."

Appeared in: 1937 a Warner Bros. short. 1950 Grounds for Marriage (narrator).

CROSSE, RUPERT
Born: 1928. Died: Mar. 5, 1973, Nevis, West Indies (cancer). Black screen and television actor. Nominated for 1968 Academy Award as Best Supporting Actor in The Reivers.

Appeared in: 1961 Shadows. 1962 Too Late Blues. 1963 Twilight of Honor. 1965 Wild Seed. 1966 To Trap a Spy. 1967 Waterhole #3. 1968 The Reivers.

CROSSLEY, SID (aka SYD CROSSLEY)
Born: Nov. 18, 1885, London, England. Died: Nov. 1960, Troon, England. Screen actor and music hall comedian.

Appeared in: **1925** Keep Smiling; North Star. **1926** The Golden Web; The Unknown Soldier; One Hour Married. **1927** Ain't Love Funny?; Jewels of Desire; Romantic Rogue; Play Safe; The Blood Ship; The Gorilla. **1928** A Perfect Gentleman; That Certain Thing; Fangs of the Wild; The Circus Kid; The Cowboy Kid; Into No Man's Land. **1929** The Younger Generation; Atlantic; Hate Ship; Just for a Song; The Fatal Warning (serial). **1930** Suspense; The Middle Watch; Man from Chicago; All of a Tremble; Flying Fool; Never Trouble Trouble. **1931** Men Like These; Tonight's the Night. **1932** For the Love of Mike; Letting in the Sunshine; Leave It to Me. **1933** The Medicine Man; Excess Baggage; The Umbrella; Meet My Sister; You Made Me Love You; The Bermondsey Kid. **1934** Those Were the Days; Over the Garden Wall; Night Club Queen; Give Me a Ring; Gay Love; It's a Bet; Eighteen Minutes; Dandy Dick; Radio Parade of 1935. **1935** Me and Marlborough; Royal Cavalcade; Jimmy Boy; Honeymoon for Three; The Deputy Drummer; Music Hath Charms; Another Spot of Bother; Cheer Up; The Ghost Goes West; One Good Turn; Public Nuisance No. 1; Queen of Hearts; Man Behind the Mask; Royal Romance. **1946** Two's Company; Everything Is Rhythm. **1937** Man in the Mirror; Silver Blaze; Sensation; The Gang Show; Old Mother Riley. **1938** Young and Innocent (aka The Girl Was Young); We're Going to Be Rich; The Return of Carol; Everything Happens to Me; His Lordship Goes to Press; Peter's Pence; Save a Little Sunshine; Penny Paradise. Other British films: Romantic Rhythm; Paybox Adventure; Boys Will Be Girls; Sporting Love; Keep Your Seats, Please; Cotton Queen; The Limping Man; Ghosts Alive; Full Steam Ahead; Feather Your Nest; Double Alibi; Lucky Jade; Pearls Bring Tears; Racketeer Rhythm; Dark Stairway; Sweet Devil; Little Dolly Daydream; Open House; He Was Her Man.

CROSTHWAITE, IVY (aka RICE BARRETT)
Born: 1898, San Diego, Calif. Died: Nov. 8, 1962, Los Angeles, Calif. Screen actress. Was a Sennett Bathing Beauty.

Appeared in: **1915** The Beauty Bunglers; Fickle Fatty's Fall; Fatty and the Broadway Stars. **1916** By Stork Delivery. **1917** Brainstorm; A Bath House Tangle.

CROUCH, WORTH
Born: 1917. Died: Feb. 6, 1943, Calabasas, Calif. Screen actor and stuntman.

Appeared in: **1943** We've Never Been Licked (died on location during filming).

CROWELL, BURT (Walter J. Crowley)
Born: 1873. Died: Mar. 26, 1946, Chicago, Ill. Screen, stage and vaudeville actor. Appeared in vaudeville with his wife Ann as "Crowell and Gardner."

CROY, HOMER
Born: Mar. 11, 1883, near Maryville, Missouri. Died: May 24, 1965, New York, N.Y. (heart attack). Novelist, screen actor and screenwriter.

Appeared in: **1915** In the Land of the Mikado with Homer Croy.

CRUME, CAMILLA
Born: 1874. Died: Mar. 20, 1952, Norwalk, Conn. Screen, stage and radio actress. Appeared in early films made at Vitaphone Studios, Brooklyn, N.Y.

CRUSTER, AUD (Cruster Aud Olsen)
Born: 1889. Died: May 18, 1938, Moline, Ill. Screen and vaudeville actor.

Appeared in: **1926** Kid Boots.

CRUTE, SALLY (Sally C. Kirby)
Born: 1886. Died: Aug. 12, 1971, Miami, Fla. Screen actress.

Appeared in: **1915** While the Tide Was Rising. **1916** Helen of the Chorus. **1921** It Isn't Being Done This Season; Perjury. **1923** Broadway Broke; His Children's Children; The Tents of Allah. **1925** The Half-Way Girl; A Little Girl in a Big City; Ermine and Rhinestones.

CRUZE, JAMES (Jens Cruz Bosen)
Born: Mar. 27, 1894, Ogden, Utah. Died: Aug. 3, 1942, Los Angeles, Calif. Screen, stage, vaudeville actor, film director, producer and screenwriter. Divorced from actresses Margarite Snow (dec. 1958) and Betty Compson (dec. 1974).

Appeared in: **1911** The Higher Law. **1912** Lucille; Dr. Jekyll and Mr. Hyde; On Probation; Cross Your Heart; For Sale—A Life; Rejuvenation; Miss Robinson Crusoe; The Thunderbolt; The Other Half; Whom God Hath Joined; But the Greatest of These is Charity; Love's Miracle; A Militant Suffragette; The Ring of a Spanish Grandee; Put Yourself in His Place; Miss Arabella Smith; Jess; Called Back. **1913** The Silver-Tongued Doctor; A Poor Relation; The Tiniest of Stars; The Ward of the King; The Plot Against the Governor; The Idol of the Hour; The Lost Combination; Her Sister's Secret; Tannhauser; The Marble Heart; A Girl Worth While; Cymbeline; The Snare of Fate; Good Morning, Judge. **1914** The Leak in the Foreign Office; From Wash to Washington; A Debut in the Secret Service; A Mohammedan Conspiracy; The Million

Dollar Mystery (serial); Joseph in the Land of Egypt; Zudora—The Twenty Million Dollar Mystery (serial).

CRUZE, MAE
Born: 1891. Died: Aug. 16, 1965, Hollywood, Calif. Screen actress. Entered films in silents.

Appeared in: **1964** Mary Poppins.

CULLINGTON, MARGARET
Born: 1891. Died: July 18, 1925, Hollywood, Calif. Screen actress. Appeared in early "Christie" comedies.

Appeared in: **1921** The Son of Wallingford; The Mad Marriage. **1923** Wolves of the Border. **1924** Excitement; The Breathless Moment; That Wild West.

CUMMING, RUTH
Born: 1904. Died: Aug. 11, 1967, New York, N.Y. Screen, stage actress and opera performer.

CUMMINGS, FRANCES
Died: Aug. 12, 1923, New York, N.Y. (cancer). Screen and stage actress. Appeared in early Lupin Film Company and Famous Players productions.

CUMMINGS, IRVING, SR.
Born: Oct. 9, 1888, New York, N.Y. Died: Apr. 18, 1959, Hollywood, Calif. (heart attack). Screen, stage actor and film director. Entered films as an actor in 1909.

Appeared in: **1913** Ashes; The Man from Outside; Duty and the Man; The Tangled Web; The Woman Who Knew; London Assurance; The Bells; The Open Road. **1914** The Million Dollar Mystery (serial); The Messenger of Death; Jane Eyre; Broken Paths; The Finger of Fate; The Varsity Race; The Sword of Damocles; The Resurrection. **1915** The Diamond From the Sky (serial); The Lure of the Mask; The Silent Witness (serial). **1916** The Hidden Scar; Pamela's Past. **1918** Merely Players; The Heart of a Girl. **1919** Her Code of Honor; Some Bride; The Unveiling Hand; Men, Women and Money; Everywoman. **1920** The Thirteenth Commandment. **1921** The Saphead. **1925** As Man Desires. **1936** Girl's Dormitory. **1941** The Devil and Mrs. Jones.

CUMMINGS, RICHARD H.
Born: 1858. Died: Dec. 25, 1938, Los Angeles, Calif. Screen, stage, vaudeville and minstrel actor. Entered films with Tannhauser Co. in 1912.

Appeared in: **1915** Birth of a Nation. **1921** Red Courage; The Bride's Play; Partners of Fate; No Woman Knows; The Tomboy. **1922** Great Alone; The Top O' the Morning; Wolf Law. **1923** Thundergate; Itching Palms. **1925** Thank You. **1926** The Galloping Cowboy. **1930** The Social Lion.

CUMMINGS, ROBERT
Born: Feb. 22, 1867, Richmond, Va. Died: July 22, 1949. Stage and screen actor. Do not confuse with actor Robert "Bob" Cummings.

Appeared in: **1916** Romeo and Juliet; Bought. **1917** The Awakening of Helena Richie; Betsy Ross; A Rich Man's Plaything.

CUMMINGS, VICKI
Born: 1919, Northampton, Mass. Died: Nov. 30, 1969, New York, N.Y. Screen, stage and television actress.

Appeared in: **1951** I Can Get It for You Wholesale. **1962** The Time and the Touch.

CUMPSON, JOHN R.
Born: 1868. Died: Mar. 15, 1913, New York, N.Y. (pneumonia—diabetes). Screen actor.

Appeared in: **1908** A Calamitous Elopement; Monday Morning in a Coney Island Police Court; A Smoked Husband; Mr. Jones at the Ball. **1909** Mrs. Jones Entertains; The Cord of Life; At the Altar; Mr. Jones has a Card Party; His Wife's Mother; Jones and the Lady Book Agent; Her First Biscuits. **1911** A Famous Duel; His First Trip; The Escaped Lunatic; The Daisy Cowboys; Maiden of the Piefaced Indians; The Summer Girl; Mae's Suitors; The Kid from Klondyke; John Brown's Heir; Ludwig from Germany; The Troubles of a Butler; An International Heartbreaker. **1912** The Flag of Distress; The Broken Lease; Mr. Smith, Barber; A Piece of Ambergris; A Millionaire for a Day; Breach of Promise; The Maid's Stratagem; How Shorty Won Out; Portugee Joe; A Case of Dynamite; Ferdie's Family Feud; Chappie the Chaperon; Her Diary; An Exciting Outing; Curing Hubby.

CUNARD, GRACE (Harriet Mildred Jefferies)
Born: 1893, Columbus, Ohio. Died: Jan. 19, 1967, Woodland Hills, Calif. (cancer). Stage and screen actress. Married to actor Joe Moore (dec. 1926) and later married to actor Jack Shannon (dec. 1968). Sister of actress Myna Seymour.

Appeared in: **1912** Custer's Last Fight; The Duke's Plan. **1913** The Favorite Son; Captain Billy's Mate; The She Wolf; From Dawn Till Dark. **1914** Be Neutral; The Bride of Mystery; In the Fall of '64; Lady Raffles; Lucille Love, Girl of Mystery (serial); The Madcap Queen of Gretzhoffen; The Mystery of the White Car; The Mysterious Hand; The Mysterious Leopard Lady; The Mysterious Rose; The Phantom of the Violin; Washington at Valley Forge; A Wartime Reformation; The Unsigned Agreement. **1915** And They Called Him Hero; The Broken Coin (serial); The Campbells Are Coming; The Doorway of Destruction; The Heart of Lincoln; The Hidden City; The Lumber Yard Gang; Nabbed; One Kind of a Friend; 3 Bad Men and a Girl; An Outlaw's Honor. **1916** The Bandit's Wager; Behind the Mask; Brennon O' the Moor; Born of the People; The Elusive Enemy; Her Better Self; Her Sister's Sin; The Heroine of San Juan; His Majesty Dick Turpin; Lady Raffles Returns; The Mad Hermit; The Madcap Queen of Crona; Phantom Island; The Adventures of Pet O' the Ring (serial); The Powder Trail; The Princely Bandit; The Purple Mask (serial); The Sham Reality. **1917** Circus Sarah; Her Western Adventure; In Treason's Grasp; The Puzzle Woman; Society's Driftwood; True to Their Colors; Unmasked. **1918** Hell's Crater; The Spawn. **1919** After the War; Elmo the Mighty (serial). **1920** A Daughter of the Law; Gasoline Buckaroo; The Man Hater; The Woman of Mystery. **1922** The Girl in the Taxi; A Dangerous Adventure (serial); The Heart of Lincoln (reissue of 1915 film). **1924** The Last Man on Earth; Emblems of Love. **1925** The Kiss Barrier; Outwitted. **1926** Exclusive Rights; Fighting With Buffalo Bill (serial); The Winking Idol (serial). **1927** Blake of Scotland Yard (serial); The Denver Dude; The Return of Riddle Rider (serial); The Rest Cure. **1928** The Haunted Island (serial): The Masked Angel; The Price of Fear; The Chinatown Mystery (serial). **1929** The Ace of Scotland Yard (serial); Untamed. **1930** A Lady Surrenders. **1931** Ex-Bad Boy; Resurrection. **1933** Ladies They Talk About. **1935** The Bride of Frankenstein.

CUNEO, LESTER

Born: 1888, Indian Territory, Okla. Died: Nov. 1, 1925. Stage and screen actor. Married to actress Francelia Billington.

Appeared in: **1915** Thirteen Down; Graustark; The Silent Voice. **1916** Mr. Forty-Four; Big Tremaine. **1917** Pidgin Island; The Haunted Pajamas; Under Handicap; Paradise Garden; The Square Deceiver. **1920** Are All Men Alike?; The Terror; Food for Scandal. **1921** The Ranger and the Law. **1922** Blazing Arrows; Blue Blazes; The Masked Avenger; Silver Spurs; Trapped in the Air. **1923** The Eagle's Feather; Fighting Jim Grant; The Vengeance of Pierre; The Zero Hour. **1924** Lone Hand Texas; Ridin' Fool; Western Grit. **1925** Hearts of the West; Range Vultures; Two Fisted Thompson; Western Promise.

CUNNINGHAM, ALOYSIUS

Died: July 27, 1936, Pottsville, Pa. (heart attack). Stage and screen actor.

CUNNINGHAM, CECIL

Born: Aug. 2, 1888, St. Louis, Mo. Died: Apr. 17, 1959, Woodland Hills, Calif. (arteriosclerosis). Screen, stage, vaudeville and radio actress.

Appeared in: **1930** Their Own Desire; Anybody's Woman; Playboy of Paris; Paramount on Parade. **1931** Susan Lenox, Her Fall and Rise; Age for Love; Monkey Business; Safe in Hell. **1932** Impatient Maiden; Those We Love; Love is a Racket; Love Me Tonight. **1933** From Hell to Heaven; Ladies They Talk About; The Druggist's Dilemma (short). **1934** Manhattan Love Song; The Life of Vergie Winters; Return of the Terror; We Live Again. **1935** People Will Talk. **1936** Come and Get It. **1937** Swing High—Swing Low; King of Gamblers; Artists and Models; This Way Please; The Awful Truth; Night Club Scandal; Daughter of Shanghai. **1938** College Swing; Scandal Street; Four Men and a Prayer; Kentucky Moonshine; You and Me; Wives Under Suspicion; Girls' School; Blonde Cheat. **1939** The Family Next Door; It's a Wonderful World; Winter Carnival; Lady of the Tropics; Laugh It Off. **1940** Lillian Russell; New Moon; The Great Profile; Kitty Foyle. **1941** Back Street; Repent at Leisure; Blossoms in the Dust; Hurry, Charlie, Hurry. **1942** Cowboy Serenade; The Wife Takes a Flyer; Cairo; The Hidden Hand. **1943** Above Suspicion; In Old Oklahoma. **1946** My Reputation.

CUNNINGHAM, GEORGE

Born: 1904. Died: May 1, 1962, Los Angeles, Calif. Screen actor and dancer.

Appeared in: **1929** Broadway Melody (film debut); The Hollywood Revue of 1929; Our Modern Maidens; Thunder.

CUNNINGHAM, JOE (Joseph A. Cunningham)

Born: June 22, 1890, Philadelphia, Pa. Died: Apr. 3, 1943, Los Angeles, Calif. (coronary occlusion). Screen, radio actor, screenwriter and cartoonist.

Appeared in: **1936** The Country Gentlemen; Hot Money. **1937** Kid Galahad; Sensation; Fugitive in the Sky. **1938** Torchy Blane in Panama; Torchy Gets Her Man; Going Places; Four's a Crowd; Blondes at Work. **1939** They Drive by Night; Torchy Runs for Mayor; Torchy Plays with Dynamite; Blackwell's Island; Secret Service of the Air. **1940** It's in the Air. **1941** Tom, Dick and Harry. **1942** The Affairs of Jimmy Valentine; Dudes are Pretty People; The Navy Comes Through; Broadway; Talk of the Town; I Live on Danger.

CUNNINGHAM, ZAMAH

Born: 1893. Died: June 2, 1967, New York, N.Y. Screen, stage, vaudeville and television actress. Entered films with Griffith.

Appeared in: **1948** Dream Girl. **1950** Key to the City. **1953** Here Come the Girls. **1965** Baby, the Rain Must Fall.

CURCI, GENNARO (Baron Gennaro Mario Curci)

Born: Sept. 19, 1888, Italy. Died: Apr. 13, 1955, Los Angeles, Calif. (cerebral thrombosis). Screen actor and opera performer. Married to actress Elvira Curci.

Appeared in: **1935** The Melody Lingers On. **1937** Manhattan Merry-Go-Round; I Met Him in Paris; I'll Take Romance. **1939** Juarez; Midnight.

CURLEY, LEO

Born: Apr. 12, 1878, New York, N.Y. Died: Apr. 11, 1960, Woodland Hills, Calif. (arteriosclerosis). Screen actor. Married to actress Lucille Husting (dec. 1972).

Appeared in: **1935** Speed Devils. **1949** Johnny Holiday. **1952** Something for the Birds. **1953** The Robe; The President's Lady; City of Bad Men.

CURRAN, THOMAS A.

Born: 1880. Died: Jan. 24, 1941, Hollywood, Calif. (pneumonia). Stage and screen actor.

Appeared in: **1928** The Black Pearl. **1929** Object Alimony; Anne against the World; Ships of the Night; Two Sisters; Must We Marry?; Trial of Mary Dugan; Wolf of Wall Street; The Phantom in the House. **1930** Morocco; The Kibitzer; Worldly Goods. **1931** Dishonored; Mother and Son; Forgotten Women; The Ghost City. **1932** Dance Team; Charlie Chan's Chance; Lost Squadron; Lady with a Past. **1935** The Cowboy Millionaire. **1940** Her First Romance.

CURRIE, FINLAY

Born: Jan. 20, 1878, Edinburgh, Scotland. Died: May 9, 1968, Gerrards Cross, England. Screen, stage, minstrel and television actor. Married to stage actress Maude Courtney (dec. 1959).

Appeared in: **1931** The Old Man. **1932** Rome Express; The Frightened Lady (aka Criminal at Large—US 1933). **1933** Excess; The Good Companions; Orders is Orders (US 1934). **1934** Princess Charming (US 1935); Little Friend; Gay Love; Mister Cinders; My Old Dutch. **1935** The Big Splash. **1936** The Improper Duchess; The Gay Adventure. **1937** Wanted; Glamorous Night; Command Performance; Catch as Catch Can; The Edge of the World (US 1938): Paradise for Two (aka The Gaiety Girls—US 1938). **1938** The Claydon Treasure Mystery; Around the Town; Follow Your Star. **1939** Hospital Hospitality. **1941** 49th Parallel (aka The Invaders—US 1942). **1942** Thunder Rock (US 1944); The Day Will Dawn (aka The Avengers—US). **1943** The Bells Go Down; Warn that Man; They Met in the Dark (US 1945); The Shipbuilders; Undercover (aka Undercover Guerillas—US 1944); Theatre Royal. **1945** Don Chicago; I Know Where I'm Going (US 1947). **1946** The Trojan Brothers; Great Expectations (US 1947); Woman to Woman; Spring Song (aka Springtime—US); School for Secrets. **1947** The Brothers; Atlantic Episode (rerelease of 1943 Catch as Catch Can). **1948** My Brother Jonathan (US 1949); So Evil My Love; Mr. Perrin and Mr. Traill; Bonnie Prince Charlie; Sleeping Car to Trieste (US 1949). **1949** The History of Mr. Polly (US 1951). **1950** Treasure Island; My Daughter Joy (aka Operation X—US 1951); Trio; The Black Rose; The Mudlark. **1951** Quo Vadis; People Will Talk. **1952** Kangaroo; Ivanhoe; Walk East on Beacon; Stars and Stripes Forever. **1953** Treasure of the Golden Condor; Rob Roy the Highland Rogue. **1954** The End of the Road (US 1957); Beau Brummel; Make Me an Offer (US 1956); Captain Lightfoot. **1955** Third Party Risk (aka The Deadly Game—US); Footsteps in the Fog; King's Rhapsody. **1956** Around the World in 80 Days. **1957** Zarak; Seven Waves Away (aka Abandon Ship!—US); Saint Joan; The Little Hut; Campbell's Kingdom (US 1958); Dangerous Exile (US 1958). **1958** The Naked Earth; 6.5 Special; Corridors of Blood (US 1963). **1959** Ben Hur; Solomon and Sheba; Tempest. **1960** The Angel Wore Red; The Adventures of Huckleberry Finn; Kidnapped; Hand in Hand; Giuseppe Vinduto dai Fratelli (Joseph Sold by His Brothers aka The Story of Joseph and His Brethren—US 1962). **1961** Five Golden Hours; Francis of Assisi. **1962** Calling All Cars (reissue of 6.5 Special—1958); The Inspector (aka Lisa—US); The Amorous Prawn (aka The Playgirl and the War Minister—US 1963); Go to Blazes. **1963** Billy Liar!; The Three Worlds of Thomasina; Cleopatra. **1964** Who was Maddox?; The Fall of the Roman Empire. **1965** The Battle of the Villa Fiorita; Bunny Lake is Missing.

CURRIER, FRANK

Born: 1857, Norwich, Conn. Died: Apr. 22, 1928, Hollywood, Calif. (blood poisoning). Stage and screen actor.

Appeared in: **1919** Her Kingdom of Dreams; Should Women Tell? **1921** Clay Dollars; The Rookie's Return; Smiling All the Way; The Lotus Eater; Man Who; A Message from Mars; Without Limit. **1922** The Woman Who Fooled Herself; Why Announce Your Marriage?; The Lights of New York; Reckless Youth; My Old Kentucky Home; The Snitching Hour. **1923** The Tents of Allah; Children of Jazz; The Fog; The Victor; The Go-Getter; The Darling of New York; Desire; Stephen Steps Out. **1924** The Red Lily; Being Respectable; The Family Secret; The Heart Buster; The Sea Hawk; The Rose of Paris; Revelation; The Story without a Name; The Trouble Shooter. **1925** Graustark; Lights of Old Broadway; The White Desert; The Great Love; Too Many Kisses. **1926** The Big Parade; Ben Hur; La Boheme; Men of Steel; The First Year; Tell It to the Marines; The Exquisite Sinner. **1927** Annie Laurie; The Callahans and the Murphys; Rookies; California; The Enemy; Winners of the Wilderness; Foreign Devils. **1928** Across to Singapore; Easy Come, Easy Go; Telling the World; Riders of the Dark.

CURRY, DORA DEAN
Born: 1911. Died: July 1, 1931, U.S. (pneumonia). Screen, stage actress and ballet dancer.

CURTIS, ALAN (Harry Ueberroth)
Born: July 24, 1909, Chicago, Ill. Died: Feb. 1, 1953, New York, N.Y. (kidney operation). Screen actor. Divorced from screen actresses Ilona Massey (dec. 1974) and Betty Sundmark (dec. 1959).

Appeared in: **1936** The Smartest Girl in Town; Winterset; Walking on Air. **1937** Between Two Women; Bad Gun; China Passage; Don't Tell the Wife. **1938** Mannequin; Yellow Jack; Shopworn Angel; Duke of West Point. **1939** Good Girls Go to Paris; Sergeant Madden; Burn 'Em up O'Connor; Hollywood Cavalcade. **1940** Four Sons. **1941** Come Live with Me; New Wine; High Sierra; We Go Fast; Buck Privates; The Great Awakening. **1942** Remember Pearl Harbor. **1943** Crazy House; Two Tickets to London; Hitler's Madman; Gung Ho! **1944** Destiny; Phantom Lady; The Invisible Man's Revenge; Follow the Boys. **1945** Frisco Sal; Shady Lady; The Naughty Nineties; See My Lawyer; The Daltons Ride Again. **1946** Inside Job. **1947** Flight to Nowhere; Renegade Girl; Philo Vance's Secret Mission; Philo Vance's Gamble. **1948** Enchanted Valley. **1949** Captain Sorocco; Pirates of Capri; Apache Chief. **1950** The Masked Pirate.

CURTIS, BEATRICE (Beatrice White)
Born: 1901. Died: Mar. 26, 1963, Los Angeles, Calif. Screen and vaudeville actress. Divorced from actor Harry Fox (dec. 1959) with whom she appeared in vaudeville; together they made the following two shorts: **1929** The Fox and the Bee. **1930** The Play Boy. She appeared without Fox in: **1934** Most Precious Thing in Life. **1937** Paid to Dance.

CURTIS, DICK
Born: May 11, 1902, Newport, Ky. Died: Jan. 3, 1952, Hollywood, Calif. Stage and screen actor.

Appeared in: **1918** The Unpardonable Sin (film debut as an extra). **1930** Shooting Straight. **1932** Girl Crazy. **1933** King Kong. **1934** Wilderness Mail; Racing Luck; Burning Gold; Silver Streak; Mutiny Ahead. **1935** Code of the Mounted; Fighting Trooper; Lion's Den; Northern Frontier. **1936** The Wildcat Trooper. **1937** Paid to Dance; The Shadow. **1938** Penitentiary; Women in Prison; The Main Event; Adventure in Sahara; Rawhide; Time Out For Trouble (short); Flat Foot Stooges (short). **1939** West of Santa Fe; Spoilers of the Range; Western Caravans; Taming of the West; Behind Prison Gates; Riders of Black River; The Man They Could Not Hang; Outpost of the Mounties; The Stranger From Texas; plus the following shorts: Three Little Sew and Sews; We Want Money; Oily to Bed—Oily to Rise; The Awful Goof; Boom Goes the Groom; Now It Can Be Sold; Trouble Finds Andy Clyde; All-American Blondes; We Want Our Mummy; Yes, We Have No Bonanza. **1940** Blazing Six-Shooters; Bullets for Rustlers; Pioneers of the Frontier; Two-Fisted Rangers; Texas Stagecoach; Three Men from Texas; Ragtime Cowboy Joe; Men Without Souls; My Son Is Guilty; You Nazty Spy (short). **1941** Stick to Your Guns; The Roundup; Billy the Kid; Across the Sierras; Mystery Ship; I Was A Prisoner on Devil's Island. **1942** Two Yanks in Trinidad; Arizona Cyclone; Men of San Quentin; City of Silent Men; The Power of God; Jackass Mail. **1943** Pardon My Gun; Jack London; Salute to the Marines; Cowboy in the Clouds; Higher Than a Kite (short). **1944** Spook Town; Crash Goes the Hash (short). **1945** Wagon Wheels Westward; Song of the Prairie; Singing Guns; Hidden Trails; Shotgun Rider; plus the following shorts: Snooper Service; Pistol Packin' Nitwits; The Last Installment. **1946** California Gold Rush; Traffic in Crime; Song of Arizona; Abilene Town; Santa Fe Uprising; Three Troubledoers (short). **1947** Wyoming. **1949** Navajo Trail Raiders. **1950** Wabash Avenue; Covered Wagon Raid; The Vanishing Westerner. **1951** Lorna Doone; Rawhide; Whirlwind; Government Agents vs. Phantom Legion (serial); Three Arabian Nuts (short); Don't Throw That Knife (short). **1952** Rose of Cimarron; My Six Convicts.

CURTIS, JACK
Born: May 28, 1880, Calif. Died: Mar. 16, 1956, Hollywood, Calif. Screen actor. Do not confuse with former child actor Jack Curtis or Jack B. Curtis (dec. 1970).

Appeared in: **1915** Graft (serial); The Case of the First Born. **1916** The Torrent of Vengeance; The Iron Rivals; The Yaqui; Two Men of Sandy Bar; The Iron Hand; Her Great Part; The Romance of Billy Goat Hill; The Girl of Lost Lake; The Way of the World; The Secret of the Swamp; The End of the Rainbow; It Happened in Honolulu. **1917** A Prairie Romeo; Broadway, Arizona; Until They Get Me; The Firefly of Tough Luck; Southern Justice; Up or Down; God's Crucible. **1918** The Hard Rock Breed; The Golden Fleece; My Husband's Friend; Wolves of the Border; The Last Rebel; Marked Cards; Little Red Decides. **1919** Treat 'Em Rough; Hell Roarin' Reform; The Coming of the Law; The Pest. **1920** The Hell-Ship. **1921** The Big Punch; Steelheart; The Torrent; Beach of Dreams; Flowers of the North; An Unwilling Hero; The Serpent in the House; The Sea Lion. **1922** Caught Bluffing; The Long Chance; The Silent Vow; Two Kinds of Women; Western Speed; His Back to the Wall; The Stranger's Banquet. **1923** Reno; The Spoilers; Quicksands; Times Have Changed; Canyon of the Fools; Dangerous Trails; The Day of Faith; Masters of Men; Soft Boiled. **1924** Captain Blood; Fighter's Paradise. **1925** Greed; Bar-

ee, Son of Kazan; The Shadow on the Wall; Free and Equal; The Wedding Song. **1926** The Texas Streak; Through Thick and Thin; Hearts and Fists. **1927** Brass Knuckles; Jaws of Steel; Wolf's Clothing. **1928** Scarlet Seas. **1929** The Phantom in the House; The Show of Shows. **1930** Moby Dick; Under a Texas Moon; Mammy; The Love Trader; The Love Racket; The Dawn Trail; Hold Everything. **1934** The Mighty Barnum. **1935** Westward Ho.

CURTIS, JACK B.
Born: 1926. Died: Sept. 25, 1970, New York, N.Y. Screen, radio actor, film producer and director. Son of agent Jack Curtis and vaudeville actress Mabel Ford. Frequently served as voice of Italian actor/director Vittorio de Sica in American release of Italian films. Do not confuse with actor Jack Curtis (dec. 1956).

CURTIS, SPENCER M.
Born: 1856. Died: July 13, 1921, Long Beach, Calif. Stage and screen actor.

CURTIS, WILLA PEARL
Born: Mar. 21, 1896, Texas. Died: Dec. 19, 1970, Los Angeles, Calif. (cerebral arteriosclerosis and diabetes). Black screen actress.

Appeared in: **1942** Unexpected Riches (short). **1944** Tale of a Dog (short). **1951** Native Son; Prince of Peace (aka The Lawton Story). **1955** Queen Bee.

CURTIZ, MICHAEL (Mihaly Kertesz)
Born: Dec. 24, 1888, Budapest, Hungary. Died: Apr. 11, 1962, Hollywood, Calif. Film director, screen, stage actor, film producer and screenwriter.

CUSCADEN, SARAH D.
Born: 1873. Died: Oct. 18, 1954, Hollywood, Calif. Screen actress.

CUSTER, BOB (aka RAYMOND GLENN)
Born: Oct. 18, 1898, Frankfort, Ky. Died: Dec. 27, 1974, Torrance, Calif. (natural causes). Screen actor.

Appeared in: **1924** Trigger Finger. **1925** The Bloodhound; A Man of Nerve; Galloping Vengeance; No Man's Law; That Man Jack!; The Texas Bearcat; The Ridin' Streak; The Range Terror; Flashing Spurs. **1926** The Fighting Boob; Hair Trigger Baxter; Beyond the Rockies; The Border Whirlwind; Man Rustlin'; Dead Line; The Dude Cowboy; The Devil's Gulch. **1927** The Terror of Bar X; Bulldog Pluck; Galloping Thunder; Cactus Trails; The Fighting Hombre; Ladies at Ease. **1928** The Manhattan Cowboy; On the Divide; The Silent Trail. **1929** Arizona Days; The Law of the Mounted; Headin' Westward; West of Santa Fe; Texas Tommy; The Oklahoma Kid; The Last Roundup; The Fighting Terror; Riders of the Rio Grande. **1930** Code of the West; O'Malley Rides Alone; Covered Wagon Trails; The Parting of the Trails. **1931** Quick Trigger Lee; Riders of the North; Son of the Plains; Law of the Rio Grande; Headin' for Trouble; Under Texas Skies. **1932** Mark of the Spur; Scarlet Band. **1934** The Law of the Wild (serial). **1936** Ambush Valley.

CUTELLI, COUNT GAETANO
Died: July 16, 1944, Seattle, Wash. Screen actor. Voice of many animal characters in cartoon comedy films.

CUTTING, RICHARD H. "DICK"
Born: Oct. 31, 1912, Mass. Died: Mar. 7, 1972, Woodland Hills, Calif. (kidney disease and uremia). Screen actor and newswriter. Married to actress Edwina Booth.

Appeared in: **1953** War Paint; City of Bad Men; The Great Jesse James Raid; Shotgun; Law and Order; The Man from the Alamo. **1954** Magnificent Obsession; Black Widow; Shield for Murder; The Law vs. Billy the Kid; Taza, Son of Cochise; Drive a Crooked Mile. **1955** Prince of Players; The Left Hand of God; Seminole Uprising; Chicago Syndicate; Good Morning, Miss Dove; The Vagabond King; The Private War of Major Benson; You're Never Too Young; The Gun that Won the West. **1956** The Eddy Duchin Story; The Mountain; You Can't Run Away from It; Showdown at Abilene; The Fastest Gun Alive; Outside the Law. **1957** House of Numbers; Top Secret Affair; The Story of Mankind; Attack of the Crab Monster; The Night Runner; Rock all Night; Teenage Doll; The Girl in Black Stockings; The Monolith Monsters; War Drums. **1958** The World Was His Jury; Ride a Crooked Trail; The Last of the Fast Guns; The Law and Jake Wade; Monster on the Campus; South Pacific. **1959** Rally Round the Flag, Boys; A Nice Little Bank that Should be Robbed. **1960** Gunfighters of Abilene. **1963** The Raiders. **1967** The Ride to Hangman's Tree.

CUTTS, PATRICIA (aka PATRICIA WAYNE)
Born: July 20, 1926, London, England. Died: Sept. 6, 1974, London, England (suicide-overdose of pills). Screen, stage and television actress. Daughter of film director Jack Graham Cutts (dec.)

Appeared in: **1932** Self Made Lady (film debut). **1947** Just William's Luck (US 1948). **1950** Your Witness (aka Eye Witness—US). **1951** The Long Dark Hall. **1953** Those People Next Door. **1954** The Happiness of 3 Women. **1955** The Man Who Loved Redheads. **1958** Merry Andrew. **1959** The Tingler; Battle of the Coral Sea. **1971** Private Road.

CYBULSKI, ZBIGNIEW
Born: 1927, Poland. Died: Jan. 8, 1967, Wroclaw, Breslau, Poland (accidental fall). Stage and screen actor.

Appeared in: **1954** A Generation. **1958** Popiol i Diament (Ashes and Diamonds—US 1961). **1959** The Eighth Day of the Week; Pociag (aka Baltic Express—US 1962). **1962** La Poupee (aka He, She or It—US 1963): L'amour a Vingt Ans (Love at Twenty—US 1963). **1963** Milczenie (Silence); Jak byc Kochanna (How to be Loved—US 1965). **1964** Att Alska (To Love). **1965** Salto (US 1966); Rekopis Znaleziony w Saragossie (aka Adventures of a Noble Man and Manuscript Found in Saragossa aka The Saragossa Manuscript—US 1966). **1967** Jowita (Jovita—US 1970).

DA CUNHA, JOSE
Born: 1889, Portugal. Died: Sept. 25, 1956, Lisbon, Portugal. Screen, stage actor and stage manager.

DADE, FRANCES
Born: Feb. 14, 1910, Philadelphia, Pa. Died: Jan. 21, 1968, Philadelphia, Pa. Stage and screen actress.

Appeared in: **1930** Grumpy; Raffles; He Knew Women. **1931** Dracula; Mother's Millions; Daughter of the Dragon; Range Law; Seed. **1932** Pleasure; Big Town.

DAGET, ROBERT (Robert True Daget)
Died: July 20, 1975, Westboro, Mass. Screen, stage, television actor and stage producer.

Appeared in: **1961** The Hustler.

DAI, LIN
Born: 1931, China. Died: July 17, 1964, Hong Kong, China ("accident?"). Screen actress. Entered films approximately 1950.

Appeared in: **1964** The Last Woman of Shang.

DAIX, DAISY (Denis Cariveac)
Born: 1930, Belgium. Died: Aug. 16, 1950, suburbs of Asnieres, France (auto accident). Stage and screen actress.

DALBERT, SUZANNE
Born: May 12, 1927. Died: Dec. 31, 1970. Screen actress.

Appeared in: **1948** The Accused. **1949** Trail of the Yukon. **1950** Mark of the Gorilla; Breakthrough. **1951** Target Unknown; The Lady and the Bandit. **1953** The 49th Man.

D'ALBROOK, SIDNEY (aka SIDNEY DALBROOK)
Born: May 3, 1886, Chicago, Ill. Died: May 30, 1948, Los Angeles, Calif. (heart attack). Screen, stage and vaudeville actor.

Appeared in: **1914** The Bond Sinister. **1915** A Mystery of the Mountains; County Twenty. **1916** His Little Story. **1917** Draft 258. **1918** Under Suspicion; Heart of the Wilds. **1919** The Fatal Fortune (serial); Three Men and a Girl; The Lost Battalion. **1920** Parlor, Bedroom and Bath; The Flaming Clue; Mutiny of the Elsinore. **1921** Big Game; A Motion to Adjourn; The Right of Way; The Son of Wallingford. **1922** Across the Continent; I Can Explain; The Fighting Guide; Little Miss Smiles; Over the Border; West of Chicago; Yankee Doodle, Jr. **1923** Bucking the Barrier; The Call of the Wild; Tea—With a Kick. **1924** The King of Wild Horses. **1925** Without Mercy. **1926** So This is Paris. **1927** Chicago; King of Kings; The Princess from Hoboken. **1928** The Matinee Idol. **1929** The Spirit of Youth. **1930** Party Girl; Renegades; Midnight Mystery. **1931** Bat Whispers; Chances. **1932** Arlene Lupin.

DALBY, AMY
Born: c. 1888, England. Died: 1969. Screen actress.

Appeared in: **1945** The Wicked Lady (US 1946). **1958** The Man Upstairs (US 1959). **1962** The Lamp in Assassin Mews. **1963** The Haunting. **1964** Topkapi. **1965** The Secret of My Success. **1966** Who Killed the Cat?; The Spy with a Cold Nose. **1967** Smashing Time.

DALE, CHARLES (Charles Marks)
Born: 1881, New York, N.Y. Died: Nov. 16, 1971, Teaneck, N.J. Screen, vaudeville and television actor. Partner of Joseph Smith in vaudeville team of "Smith and Dale." Was the "Dr. Kronkhite" of the team. The team was originally called "Charlie Marks (Dale) and Joe Seltzer (Smith)" but they changed it to just "Smith and Dale."

Appeared in: **1929** Knights in Venice (short). **1931** Manhattan Parade. **1932** The Heart of New York. **1939** Mutiny on the Body (short). **1951** Two Tickets to Broadway.

DALE, DOROTHY
Born: 1883. Died: May 13, 1957, Hollywood, Calif. (fire). Screen actress and stand in for Mabel Normand. Her husband, Dr. Jacob Hyman (dec. 1944), had at one time been a partner with Harry Houdini in an act billed the "Houdini Brothers."

Appeared in: **1923** The Ten Commandments. The makeup with which she painted herself bronze for role of an Egyptian girl caused severe facial scars and she then went into retirement.

DALE, DOROTHY
Born: 1925. Died: Aug. 1, 1937 (heart ailment). Child screen and stage actress. Appeared in shorts.

DALE, ESTHER
Born: 1886, Beaufort, S.C. Died: July 23, 1961, Hollywood, Calif. Stage and screen actress. Married to producer/writer Arthur Beckhard.

Appeared in: **1934** Crime without Passion (film debut). **1935** The Great Impersonation; I Dream Too Much; Curly Top; In Old Kentucky; Private Worlds; The Wedding Night. **1936** Lady of Secrets; Fury; The Magnificent Brute; The Case against Mrs. Ames; Timothy's Quest; Hollywood Boulevard; The Farmer in the Dell. **1937** Wild Money; On Such a Night; Of Human Hearts; The Awful Truth; Damaged Goods; Dead End; Easy Living; Outcast. **1938** Condemned Women; Girls on Probation; Prison Farm; Stolen Heaven; 6,000 Enemies. **1939** Made for Each Other; Broadway Serenade; Big Town Czar; Tell No Tales; Blackmail; Swanee River; The Women. **1940** Convicted Woman; Village Barn Dance; And One Was Beautiful; Opened by Mistake; Women without Names; Untamed; Laddie; Blondie Has Servant Trouble; A Child is Born; Love Thy Neighbor; Arise, My Love; The Mortal Storm. **1941** Mr. and Mrs. Smith; There's Magic in Music; Aloma of the South Seas; Unfinished Business; All-American Co-ed; Dangerously They Live; Back Street. **1942** Blondie Goes to College; Ten Gentlemen from West Point; Wrecking Crew. **1943** The Amazing Mrs. Holiday; Swing Your Partner; Murder in Times Square; North Star; Old Acquaintance. **1945** Behind City Lights; Bedside Manner; On Stage, Everybody. **1946** A Stolen Life; Margie; My Reputation; Smoky. **1947** The Egg and I; The Unfinished Dance. **1948** A Song Is Born. **1949** Holiday Affair; Ma and Pa Kettle. **1950** No Man of Her Own; Surrender; Walk Softly, Stranger. **1951** Too Young to Kiss. **1952** Ma and Pa Ketttle at the Fair; Monkey Business. **1955** Ma and Pa Kettle at Waikiki; Betrayed Women. **1957** The Oklahoman.

DALE, MARGARET
Born: Mar. 6, 1880, Philadelphia, Pa. Died: Mar. 23, 1972, New York, N.Y. Stage and screen actress. Do not confuse with English dancer, Margaret Dale.

Appeared in: **1921** Disraeli. **1922** One Exciting Night. **1924** Second Youth; Week End Husbands. **1934** The Man with Two Faces.

DALE, PEGGY (Margaret Dale Dudley).
Born: Dec. 25, 1903, New York, N.Y. Died: June 6, 1967, Hollywood, Calif. (suicide—pills). Screen actress.

Appeared in: **1929** Desert Song. **1934** The Mighty Barnum.

DALEY, CASS (Katherine Daley)
Born: July 17, 1915, Philadelphia, Pa. Died: Mar. 23, 1975, Hollywood, Calif. (results of an accidental fall). Screen, stage, vaudeville and radio actress.

Appeared in: **1941** The Fleet's In. **1942** Star Spangled Rhythm. **1943** Riding High; Crazy House. **1945** Out of This World; Duffy's Tavern. **1947** Ladies' Man. **1951** Here Comes the Groom. **1954** Red Garters. **1967** The Spirit is Willing. **1970** Norwood; The Phynx.

DALEY, JACK
Born: Aug. 29, 1882. Died: Aug. 28, 1967, El Cajon, Calif. Stage and screen actor. Do not confuse with actor Jack Daly (dec. 1968).

Appeared in: **1930** The Sap from Syracuse. **1935** O'Shaughnessy's Boy. **1937** Parole Racket; Artists and Models. **1938** Goodbye Broadway; Kathleen; Born to the West. **1939** Mutiny in the Big House. **1941** Arizona Bound. **1942** West of the Law; Down Texas Way. **1943** The Ghost Rider. **1945** Within These Walls.

DALL, JOHN (John Dall Thompson)
Born: 1918. Died: Jan. 15, 1971, Beverly Hills, Calif. (heart attack). Screen, stage and television actor. Nominated for 1946 Academy Award for Best Supporting Actor in The Corn Is Green.

Appeared in: **1939** For the Love of Mary. **1946** The Corn Is Green. **1947** Something in the Wind. **1948** The Rope; Another Part of the Forest. **1949** Deadly Is the Female. **1950** Gun Crazy; The Man Who Cheated Himself. **1960** Spartacus. **1961** Atlantis, the Lost Continent.

DALLIMORE, MAURICE
Born: June 23, 1912, England. Died: Feb. 20, 1973, Los Angeles, Calif. (Laennec's cirrhosis). Screen and television actor.

Appeared in: **1962** Tender Is the Night; Lad a Dog. **1963** The Three Stooges Go Around the World in a Daze. **1965** The Collector. **1966** Not With My Wife, You Don't.

DALROY, HARRY "RUBE"

Born: 1879. Died: Mar. 8, 1954, Hollywood, Calif. Western screen actor. Known as the "Mayor of Gower Gulch."

Appeared in: 1923 Stormy Seas.

DALTON, DOROTHY

Born: Sept. 22, 1893, Chicago, Ill. Died: Apr. 12, 1972, Scarsdale, N.Y. Screen, stage and vaudeville actress. Divorced from actor Lew Cody (dec. 1934). Married to stage producer Arthur Hammerstein (dec.)

Appeared in: 1915 The Disciple. 1916 The Captive God; The Vagabond Prince. 1917 The Flame of the Yukon; Wild Winship's Widow. 1918 Vive la France; Quicksand. 1919 The Home Breaker; Market of Souls; Other Men's Wives. 1920 Black is White; Dark Mirror; Half an Hour. 1921 Fool's Paradise; Behind Masks; The Idol of the North. 1922 Moran of the Lady Letty; The Crimson Challenge; The Woman Who Walked Alone; The Siren Call; On the High Seas. 1923 Fog Bound; The Law and the Lawless; Dark Secrets. 1924 The Moral Sinner; The Lone Wolf.

DALTON, EMMET

Died: July 13, 1937, Los Angeles, Calif. Onetime real "badman" of the Old West and member of the "Dalton Gang" with his brothers Robert (dec. 1892) and Grattan (dec. 1892) Dalton. He was a horse thief, train robber and screen actor.

Appeared in: 1916 The Dalton Boys. 1918 Beyond the Law.

DALTON, IRENE

Born: 1901. Died: Aug. 15, 1934, Chicago, Ill. Screen and stage actress. Divorced from screen actor Lloyd Hamilton (dec. 1935).

Appeared in: 1922 "Christie" comedies. 1923 Bluebeard's Eighth Wife; Children of Jazz.

DALY, ARNOLD

Born: Oct. 4, 1875, Brooklyn, N.Y. Died: Jan. 13, 1927, New York, N.Y. (burned to death). Screen, stage and vaudeville actor.

Appeared in: 1915 The Exploits of Elaine (serial); The Romance of Elaine (serial). 1916 The New Exploits of Elaine (serial). 1924 For Another Woman. 1926 In Borrowed Plumes.

DALY, HERBERT

Born: 1902. Died: Mar. 12, 1940, New York, N.Y. Screen and stage actor.

Appeared in: 1932 Air Mail.

DALY, JACK

Died: June 2, 1968. Screen actor. Do not confuse with actor Jack Daley (dec. 1967).

Appeared in: 1949 Search for Danger. 1950 Once a Thief; Champagne for Caesar; For Heaven's Sake. 1951 Pickup; Badman's Gold. 1953 Phantom from Space. 1954 The Big Chase; Killers from Space; The Snow Creature. 1955 The Big Bluff; I'll Cry Tomorrow. 1956 Meet Me in Las Vegas. 1957 The Young Stranger. 1959 The Return of the Fly; Inside the Mafia. 1962 Lad: A Dog.

DALY, JAMES L.

Born: 1852. Died: Nov. 10, 1933, Philadelphia, Pa. (heart trouble). Stage and screen actor. Married to screen actress Clara Lamber (dec. 1921). Appeared in silents.

DALY, MARK

Born: Aug. 23, 1887, Edinburgh, Scotland. Died: Sept. 27, 1957. Screen, stage, vaudeville and radio actor.

Appeared in: 1931 East Lynne on the Western Front; The Beggar-Student. 1932 The Third String. 1933 Up For the Derby; Doss House; The Private Life of Henry VIII; A Cuckoo in the Nest. 1934 The River Wolves; There Goes Susie (aka Where There's a Will—US 1935); Say It With Flowers; By-Pass to Happiness; Music Hall; Flood Tide. 1935 That's My Uncle; Jubilee Window; The Small Man; A Real Bloke. 1936 The Ghost Goes West; The Man Who Could Work Miracles (US 1937); The Captain's Table; Shipmates O' Mine. 1937 Wings of the Morning; Wanted; Knight Without Armour; Good Morning Boys (aka Where There's a Will—US); Captain's Orders; Command Performance. 1938 Break the News (US 1941); Lassie From Lancashire; Follow Your Star. 1939 Q Planes (aka Clouds Over Europe—US); Ten Days in Paris (aka Missing Ten Days—US); Hoots Mon! 1942 The Big Blockade; The Next of Kin (US 1943). 1946 The Voyage of Peter Joe series. 1947 Stage Frights. 1948 Bonnie Prince Charlie. 1949 Three Bags Full; The Romantic Age (aka Naughty Arlette—US 1951). 1953 Alf's Baby. 1954 Lease of Life; Don't Blame the Stork; The Delavine Affair. 1956 The Dynamiters; The Feminine Touch (aka The Gentle Touch—US 1957). 1957 You Pay Your Money; The Tommy Steele Story (aka Rock Around the World—US).

DALY, PAT (Gordon C. Munger)

Born: 1891. Died: Nov. 19, 1947, Detroit, Mich. Screen, stage, minstrel, vaudeville and radio actor. Appeared in vaudeville with his wife, Genevieve, in an act billed as "Pat and Genevieve Daly."

Appeared in: 1938 A Slight Case of Murder.

D'AMBRICOURT, ADRIENNE

Born: 1888, France. Died: Dec. 6, 1957, Hollywood, Calif. (heart attack). Stage and screen actress.

Appeared in: 1924 Wages of Virtue; The Humming Bird. 1926 God Gave Me Twenty Cents. 1929 Footlights and Fools; The Trial of Mary Dugan. 1930 L'Enigmatique Monsieur Parkes (Mysterious Mr. Parkes); The Bad One; What a Widow! 1931 Svengali; This Modern Age; Transgression; The Men in Her Life. 1933 Eagle and the Hawk; Disgraced!; Design for Living; Gallant Lady. 1934 Marie Galante; Caravan; The Cat and the Fiddle; The Way to Love. 1935 It Happened in New York; Goin' to Town; Peter Ibbetson. 1936 Valiant Is the Word for Carrie. 1937 Seventh Heaven; Mama Steps Out. 1938 Artists and Models Abroad. 1939 Bulldog Drummond's Bride; Pack up Your Troubles; Charlie Chan in City in Darkness; Nurse Edith Cavell; The Story of Vernon and Irene Castle. 1942 The Pied Piper. 1945 Paris Underground; Saratoga Trunk. 1952 Bal Tabarin.

DAMEREL, DONNA

Born: 1913. Died: Feb. 15, 1941, Englewood, N.J. (childbirth). Screen and radio actress. Married to international swimming champion Peter J. Fick. Was "Marge" on Radio's "Myrt and Marge."

Appeared in: 1933 Myrt and Marge.

DAMON, LES

Born: 1909. Died: July 20, 1962. Screen actor.

DAMPIER, CLAUDE (Claude Cowan)

Born: 1879, Clapham, England. Died: Jan. 1, 1955, London, England (pneumonia). English screen, stage and radio actor.

Appeared in: 1930 Claude Deputises (short). 1934 Radio Parade of 1935 (US 1935). 1935 So You Won't Talk; White Lilac; Boys Will Be Boys; No Monkey Business; She Shall Have Music (US 1942). 1936 King of the Castle; Public Nuisance No. 1; She Knew What She Wanted; Such is Life; All In; Valiant is the Word for Carrie. 1937 Wanted; Mr. Stringfellow Says No; Sing as You Swing; Riding High (aka Remember When). 1940 The Backyard Front (short). 1944 Don't Take it to Heart (US 1949). 1946 Wot! No Gangsters? 1948 Accidental Spy (reissue of Mr. Stringfellow Says No—1937). 1954 Meet Mr. Malcolm.

DAMROSCH, WALTER (Walter Johannes Damrosch)

Born: Jan. 30, 1862, Breslau, Prussia (now Wroclaw, Poland). Died: Dec. 22, 1950, New York, N.Y. Musician, conductor and screen, radio actor.

Appeared in: 1939 The Star Maker. 1947 Carnegie Hall.

DANDRIDGE, DOROTHY

Born: 1923, Cleveland, Ohio. Died: Sept. 8, 1965, West Hollywood, Calif. (drug overdose). Black screen and stage actress. Nominated for 1954 Academy Award for Best Actress in Carmen Jones.

Appeared in: 1937 A Day at the Races. 1941 Lady from Louisiana; Sundown; Sun Valley Serenade; Bahama Passage. 1942 Drums of the Congo. 1943 Hit Parade of 1943. 1944 Since You Went Away; Atlantic City. 1945 Pillow to Post. 1951 Tarzan's Peril; Jungle Queen; Harlem Globetrotters. 1953 Bright Road; Remains to Be Seen. 1954 Carmen Jones. 1957 The Happy Road; Island in the Sun. 1958 The Decks Ran Red. 1959 Porgy and Bess; Tamango. 1960 Moment of Danger (aka Malaga—US 1962).

DANDY, JESS (Jesse A. Danzig)

Born: 1871, Rochester, N.Y. Died: Apr. 15, 1923, Brookline, Mass. (septicemia). Stage and screen actor. Appeared in early Keystone films.

DANE, KARL

Born: Oct. 12, 1886, Copenhagen, Denmark. Died: Apr. 15, 1934, Los Angeles, Calif. (suicide—gun). Stage and screen actor.

Appeared in: 1925 The Big Parade; His Secretary; Lights of Old Broadway; The Everlasting Whisper. 1926 Bardely's, The Magnificent; The Son of the Sheik; The Scarlet Letter; Monte Carlo; War Paint. 1927 The Red Mill; Rookies; Slide, Kelly, Slide. 1928 The Trail of 98; Show People; The Enemy; Alias Jimmy Valentine; Circus Rookies; Detectives; Baby Mine; Brotherly Love. 1929 Speedway; The Hollywood Revue of 1929; All at Sea; China Bound; The Duke Steps Out; The Voice of the Storm. 1930 The Big House; Navy Blues; Montana Moon; Free and Easy; Numbered Men; Billy the Kid. 1933 A Paramount Short; Whispering Shadow. 1964 Big Parade of Comedy (documentary). 1967 Show People (reissue of 1928 film).

DANEGGER, THEODOR

Born: 1891. Died: Oct. 11, 1959, Vienna, Austria. Screen, stage actor and opera performer.

Appeared in: 1935 Ehestreik. 1936 The Royal Waltz; Weiberregiment. 1940 Drei Vater um Anna (Three Fathers for Anna).

DANERI, JULIE

Born: 1914, Mexico. Died: Aug. 28, 1957, Mexico City, Mexico. Mexican screen and stage actor.

D'ANGELO, CARLO

Born: 1919, Italy? Died: May 1973, Bologna, Italy. Screen, stage and television actor.

Appeared in: 1954 Fugitive in Trieste. 1957 I Vampiri (aka The Vampires—The Devil's Commandment—US). 1959 La Grande Guerra (The Great War—US 1961). 1960 Hercules Unchained. 1961 David and Goliath. 1962 Rosmunda e Alboino (aka Rosamund and Alboino—Sword of the Conqueror); Nefertite, Regina del Nilo (aka Queen of the Nile—US 1964). 1966 Secret Agent Super Dragon.

DANIEL, BILLY (William Baker)

Born: July 4, 1912, Fort Worth, Texas. Died: May 15, 1962, Beverly Hills, Calif. (coronary attack). Screen, stage actor and dancer. Do not confuse with singer Billy Daniels.

Appeared in: 1937 Hold 'Em, Navy (film debut). 1944 Lady in the Dark; Frenchman's Creek. 1950 My Blue Heaven. 1953 Scared Stiff.

DANIELL, HENRY (Charles Henry Daniell)

Born: Mar. 5, 1894, London, England. Died: Oct. 31, 1963, Santa Monica, Calif. Stage and screen actor.

Appeared in: 1929 Jealousy (film debut); The Awful Truth. 1930 Last of the Lone Wolf. 1934 The Path of Glory. 1936 The Unguarded Hour; Camille. 1937 Under Cover of Night; The Thirteenth Chair; The Firefly; Madame X. 1938 Holiday; Marie Antoinette. 1939 We Are Not Alone; Private Lives of Elizabeth and Essex. 1940 The Sea Hawk; The Great Dictator; The Philadelphia Story; All This and Heaven Too. 1941 A Woman's Face; Dressed to Kill; Four Jacks and a Jill; The Feminine Touch. 1942 Sherlock Holmes and the Voice of Terror; Reunion; Castle in the Desert; The Great Impersonation; Nightmare. 1943 Mission to Moscow; Sherlock Holmes in Washington; Watch on the Rhine. 1944 Jane Eyre; The Suspect. 1945 Captain Kidd; Hotel Berlin; The Woman in Green; The Body Snatcher. 1946 The Bandit of Sherwood Forest. 1947 Song of Love; The Exile. 1948 Siren of Atlantis; Wake of the Red Witch. 1949 Secret of St. Ives. 1950 Buccaneer's Girl. 1954 The Egyptian. 1955 The Prodigal; Diane. 1956 The Man in the Gray Flannel Suit; Lust for Life. 1957 The Story of Mankind; Les Girls; The Sun Also Rises; Mr. Cory; Witness for the Prosecution. 1958 From the Earth to the Moon. 1959 The Four Skulls of Jonathan Drake. 1961 The Comancheros; Voyage to the Bottom of the Sea. 1962 Five Weeks in a Balloon; The Notorious Landlady; Mutiny on the Bounty; The Chapman Report; Madison Avenue. 1964 My Fair Lady.

DANIELS, BEBE (Virginia Daniels)

Born: Jan. 14, 1901, Dallas, Tex. Died: Mar. 16, 1971, London, England (cerebral hemorrhage). Screen, stage, radio, television actress and stage producer. Entered films at age seven. Married to actor Ben Lyon.

Appeared in: 1908 A Common Enemy (film debut). 1916–1917 "Lonesome Luke" series. 1919 Everywoman; Male and Female; Captain Kidd's Kids. 1920 Sick Abed; Why Change Your Wife?; The Dancin' Fool; Feet of Clay. 1921 The Affairs of Anatol; Ducks and Drakes; Oh, Lady, Lady; She Couldn't Help It; You Never Can Tell; The March Hare; One Wild Week; Speed Girl; Two Weeks with Pay. 1922 Nice People; The Game Chicken; Nancy from Nowhere; North of the Rio Grande; Pink Gods; Singed Wings. 1923 The Exciters; Glimpses of the Moon; His Children's Children; The World's Applause. 1924 Sinners in Heaven; Dangerous Money; The Heritage of the Desert; Monsieur Beaucaire; Daring Youth; Argentine Love; Unguarded Women. 1925 Wild, Wild Susan; The Manicure Girl; Miss Bluebeard; The Crowded Hour; Lovers in Quarantine. 1926 The Splendid Crime; Stranded in Paris; The Campus Flirt; Mrs. Brewster's Millions; The Palm Beach Girl; Volcano. 1927 She's a Sheik; Swim, Girl, Swim; Senorita; A Kiss in a Taxi. 1928 Feel My Pulse; The Fifty-Fifty Girl; What a Night!; Hot News; Take Me Home. 1929 Rio Rita. 1930 Love Comes Along; Alias French Gertie; Dixiana; Lawful Larceny. 1931 Reaching for the Moon; My Past; The Maltese Falcon; Honor of the Family. 1932 Silver Dollar; The Slippery Pearls (short); Radio Girl (short). 1933 Hollywood on Parade (short); Forty-Second Street; Cocktail Hour; Counsellor-at-Law. 1934 The Song You Gave Me; Registered Nurse. 1935 Music Is Magic; The Return of Carol Deane (US 1939). 1936 A Southern Maid. 1938 Not Wanted on a Voyage. 1940 Hi, Gang! 1953 Life with the Lyons. 1955 The Lyons in Paris.

DANIELS, FRANK

Born: 1860, Dayton, Ohio. Died: Jan. 12, 1935, West Palm Beach, Fla. Stage and screen actor. Entered films with Vitagraph in 1915.

Appeared in: 1915 Crooky Scruggs. 1916 Mr. Jack's Hat and the Cat; Mr. Jack, a Doctor by Proxy; Mr. Jack Goes Into Business; Dear Percy; His Dukeship, Mr. Jack; Kernel Nutt the Janitor; Kernel Nutt's One Hundred Dollar Bill; Kernel Nutt Wins a Wife; Kernel Nutt, the Footman; Kernel Nutt in Mexico; Kernel Nutt's Musical Shirt; Kernel Nutt Flirts With Wifie; Kernel Nutt and Prince Tango; Kernel Nutt, the Piano Tuner.

DANIELS, HANK (Henry Hartog Daniels)

Born: Jan. 27, 1919, New Jersey. Died: Dec. 21, 1973, Los Angeles, Calif. (heart attack). Screen actor.

Appeared in: 1944 Meet Me in St. Louis. 1945 The Chicago Kid; Bewitched. 1946 The Green Years; In Old Sacramento. 1948 The Burning Cross.

DANIELS, HAROLD

Born: 1903, Buffalo, N.Y. Died: Dec. 27, 1971, Hollywood, Calif. (died during surgery). Screen actor, television, film producer, director, screenwriter and writer for television.

Appeared in: 1936 Hi, Gaucho; Trail Dust. 1937 Hollywood Cowboy. 1940 Oklahoma Renegades; Secret of a Model.

DANIELS, VICTOR. See CHIEF THUNDERCLOUD

DANIELS, WALTER

Born: 1875. Died: Mar. 30, 1928, Los Angeles, Calif. Screen and vaudeville actor. Appeared in vaudeville with his wife, Mina Daniels.

Appeared in: 1927 The Dove. 1928 Stolen Love; Rough Ridin' Red. 1929 The Jazz Age; The Vagabond Club.

DANILO, DON. See ELMER DEWEY

DANIS, IDA

Born: France. Died: Apr. 9, 1921, Nice, France (consumption). Screen actress.

Appeared in: 1921 La Roue.

DANSEY, HERBERT (Count Berte Danyell Tassinari)

Born: Mar. 6, 1870, Rome, Italy. Died: May 30, 1917, New York, N.Y. Stage and screen actor.

Appeared in: 1915 For Her People.

DANSON, LINDA

Died: Mar. 14, 1975. Screen actress.

Appeared in: 1954 The Adventures of Haji Baba.

DANTE (Harry A. Jansen)

Born: 1884. Died: June 15, 1955, near Northridge, Calif. (heart attack). Screen, stage, vaudeville, burlesque, circus, radio and television actor. Billed as "Dante, King of Magicians."

Appeared in: 1942 A-Haunting We Will Go. 1954 The Golden Coach.

DANTE, LIONEL

Born: 1907. Died: July 30, 1974, Hollywood Calif. (heart attack). Screen, stage and television actor.

DARBAUD, MONIQUE

Born: 1924, France. Died: Feb., 1971, France? Screen and stage actress.

D'ARCY, CAMILLE

Born: 1879. Died: Sept., 1916, Chicago, Ill. Screen actress.

Appeared in: 1915 The White Sister; A Daughter of the City; Third Hand High; The Strength of the Weak; The Snow Burner; The Cave on Thunder-Cloud; Tish's Spy; The Circular Path; The Reaping; The Fable of the Escape of Arthur and the Salvation of Herbert; The Fable of the Low Down Expert on the Subject of Babies. 1916 Captain Jinks of the Horse Marines; Putting It Over; The Grouch; The Prince Chap; The Pacifist.

D'ARCY, ROY (Roy F. Guisti)

Born: Feb. 10, 1894, San Francisco, Calif. Died: Nov. 15, 1969, Redlands, Calif. Screen, stage and vaudeville actor.

Appeared in: 1925 The Merry Widow; Graustark; The Masked Bride; Pretty Ladies. 1926 Beverly of Graustark; La Boheme; The Temptress; Bardely's, The Magnificent; The Gay Deceiver; Monte Carlo. 1927 On Ze Boulevard; Lovers?; Winners of the Wilderness; Buttons; Valencia; The Road to Romance; Adam and Evil; Frisco Sally Levy. 1928 Beyond the Sierras; Riders of the Dark; Beware of Blondes; Domestic Meddlers; The Actress; Forbidden Hours. 1929 A Woman of Affairs; Stolen Kisses; The Last Warning; Girls Gone Wild; Woman from Hell; The Black Watch. 1930 Romance. 1931 Masquerade (short). 1932 Gay Buckaroo; File 113; Discarded Lovers; From Broadway to Cheyenne; Sherlock Holmes; Lovebound. 1933 Flying Down to Rio. 1934 Orient Express. 1935 Outlawed Guns; Kentucky Blue Streak. 1936 Revolt of the Zombies; Hollywood Boulevard; Captain Calamity. 1939 Chasing Danger.

DARE, DORRIS (Dorris Prince)
Born: 1899. Died: Aug. 16, 1927, Los Angeles, Calif. Screen and stage actress.

Appeared in: **1919** The Mystery of 13 (serial). **1923** Tango Cavalier. **1925** Fightin' Odds.

DARE, PHYLLIS
Born: Aug. 15, 1890, London, England. Died: Apr. 27, 1975, Brighton, England. Screen, stage and television actress. Sister of actress Zena Dare (dec. 1975).

Appeared in: **1913** The Argentine Tango and Other Dances. **1916** Dr. Wake's Patient. **1923** The Common Law. **1933** Crime on the Hill. **1936** Debt of Honour. **1938** Marigold.

DARE, VIRGINIA
Died: July 8, 1962, Hollywood, Calif. Screen, stage and television actress. Entered films in early 1920s.

DARE, ZENA
Born: Feb. 4, 1887, London, England. Died: Mar. 11, 1975, London, England. Screen, stage and vaudeville actress. Sister of actress Phyllis Dare (dec. 1975).

Appeared in: **1921** No. 5, John Street. **1929** A Knight in London. **1937** Over the Moon (US 1940). **1938** The Return of Carol Deane.

DARIEN, FRANK, JR.
Born: New Orleans, La. Died: Oct. 20, 1955, Hollywood, Calif. Stage and screen actor. Entered films approx. 1912.

Appeared in: **1914** D. W. Griffith productions; **1915** "Mack Sennett" comedies; **1931** Cimarron; Bad Girl; Big Business Girl; June Moon. **1932** The Miracle Man; Prosperity; Now We'll Tell One (short); The Big Shot; Okay America. **1933** Hello, Everybody!; Professional Sweetheart; Big Executive; From Headquarters. **1934** Marie Galante; Service With a Smile (short); Fashions of 1934; Journal of a Crime. **1935** Behind the Evidence; The Perfect Clue; The Little Colonel; Nurse to You (short); Here Comes Cookie. **1936** Brides Are Like That. **1937** Jim Hanvey, Detective; The River of Missing Men; Trapped by G-Men. **1938** Cassidy of Bar 20; Western Jamboree; Love Finds Andy Hardy; Long Shot; Prison Break. **1939** At the Circus; Sabotage; Maisie. **1940** The Grapes of Wrath; Arizona. **1941** Under Fiesta Stars. **1942** The Gay Sisters; Hello, Frisco, Hello. **1943** Get Hep to Love. **1945** Abbott and Costello in Hollywood; The Last Installment (short); Kiss and Tell; The Clock; Counter-Attack. **1946** Claudia and David; The Fabulous Suzanne; Bad Bascomb. **1947** Woman on the Beach; Magic Town. **1948** Belle Starr's Daughter. **1950** The Flying Saucer.

DARIN, BOBBY (Robert Walden Cassotto)
Born: May 14, 1936, Bronx, N.Y. Died: Dec. 20, 1973, Hollywood, Calif. (following heart surgery). Screen, television actor, singer and songwriter. Divorced from actress Sandra Dee. Married to Andrea Joy Yeager. Nominated for 1963 Academy Award for Best Supporting Actor in Captain Newman, M.D.

Appeared in: **1960** Pepe. **1961** Come September. **1962** Pressure Point; If a Man Answers; Too Late Blues; State Fair; Hell is for Heroes. **1963** Captain Newman, M.D. **1965** That Funny Feeling. **1967** Gunfight in Abilene; Stranger in the House. **1968** Cop-Out. **1969** The Happy Ending.

DARK, CHRISTOPHER
Died: Oct. 8, 1971, Hollywood, Calif. (heart attack). Screen, stage and television actor.

Appeared in: **1953** Raiders of the Seven Seas; The Steel Lady. **1954** Suddenly. **1955** Diane. **1956** World without End; Johnny Concho. **1957** The Halliday Brand; Baby Face Nelson. **1958** Day of the Bad Man; Wild Heritage. **1959** The Rabbit Trap. **1960** Platinum High School. **1965** None But the Brave. **1968** The Private Navy of Sgt. O'Farrell.

DARKCLOUD, BEULAH (Beulah T. Filson)
Died: Jan. 2, 1946, Thermolite, Calif. Screen actress. Entered films with D. W. Griffith in 1912.

Appeared in: **1922** The Crimson Challenge.

DARLING, CANDY (James Slattery)
Born: 1948. Died: Mar. 21, 1974, New York (cancer/pneumonia). Screen, stage actor and female impersonator. Known as one of Andy Warhol's "Superstars."

Appeared in: **1968** Flesh. **1970** Brand X. **1971** Andy Warhol's Women (aka Women in Revolt). **1972** Lady Liberty.

DARLING, IDA
Born: 1875. Died: June 5, 1936, Hollywood, Calif. Screen and stage actress.

Appeared in: **1914** The Nightingale. **1921** Society Snobs; Nobody; Wedding Bells. **1922** Destiny's Isle; The Ruling Passion. **1923** The Exciters. **1924** Meddling Women. **1925** The Sky Raider; Heart of a Sire. **1926** Irene; Stranded in Paris. **1927** Singed. **1928** The House of Scandal; A Woman against the World. **1929** Love in the Desert. **1930** Lummox. **1934** The Mighty Barnum. **1935** The Girl Who Came Back.

DARLING, RUTH
Died: Sept. 11, 1918, San Francisco, Calif. (auto accident). Screen actress.

Appeared in: **1916** Manhattan Madness; Fifty-Fifty.

DARMOND, GRACE
Born: 1898, Toronto, Canada. Died: Oct. 8, 1963, Los Angeles, Calif. (lung ailment). Stage and screen actress.

Appeared in: **1916** The Shielding Shadow (serial). **1920** Below the Surface; The Hawk's Trail (serial). **1921** The Hope Diamond Mystery (serial); The Beautiful Gambler; See My Lawyer; White and Unmarried. **1922** A Dangerous Adventure (serial and feature film); Handle with Care; The Song of Life; I Can Explain. **1923** The Midnight Guest; Gold Madness; Daytime Wives. **1924** Alimony; The Gaiety Girl; Discontented Husbands. **1925** Flattery; Where the Worst Begins; The Great Jewel Robbery. **1926** Honesty—The Best Policy; Her Big Adventure; The Marriage Clause; The Night Patrol; Midnight Thieves; Her Man O'War. **1927** Wide Open; Hour of Reckoning; Wages of Conscience.

DARNELL, JEAN
Born: 1889, Sherman, Texas. Died: Jan. 19, 1961, Dallas, Texas. Screen actress. Entered films with Thannhouser Company.

Appeared in: **1912** The Truant's Doom; The Thunderbolt. **1914** Sisters. **1916** The Woman Who Did Not Care.

DARNELL, LINDA
Born: Oct. 16, 1921, Dallas, Tex. Died: Apr. 12, 1965, Chicago, Ill. (fire burns). Screen, stage and television actress. Divorced from film cameraman Pererell Marley, Philip Liebman and Merle Ray Robertson.

Appeared in: **1939** Hotel for Women; Daytime Wife. **1940** Star Dust; Mark of Zorro; Brigham Young—Frontiersman; Chad Hanna. **1941** Blood and Sand; Rise and Shine. **1942** The Loves of Edgar Allan Poe. **1943** City without Men; The Song of Bernadette. **1944** Buffalo Bill; It Happened Tomorrow; Summer Storm; Sweet and Low Down. **1945** Hangover Square; All-Star Bond Rally (short); Fallen Angel; The Great John L; Strange Confession. **1946** My Darling Clementine; Centennial Summer; Anna and the King of Siam. **1947** Forever Amber. **1948** Unfaithfully Yours; The Walls of Jericho; A Letter to Three Wives. **1949** Slattery's Hurricane; Everybody Does It. **1950** No Way Out; Two Flags West. **1951** The 13th Letter; The Guy Who Came Back; The Lady Pays Off. **1952** Blackbeard the Pirate; Saturday Island (aka Island of Desire—US); Night without Sleep. **1953** Second Chance. **1954** This Is My Love. **1956** Dakota Incident; Angels of Darkness. **1957** Zero Hour. **1963** El Valle de las Espados (Valley of the Swords). **1965** Boeing Boeing; Black Spurs.

DARNOLD, BLAINE A.
Born: 1886. Died: Mar. 11, 1926, Kansas City, Mo. (pneumonia). Screen, stage and vaudeville actor.

DARRELL, J. STEVAN
Born: 1905. Died: Aug. 14, 1970, Hollywood, Calif. Screen, stage, radio and television actor.

Appeared in: **1939** Code of the Secret Service. **1945** The Bull Fighters; Lightning Raiders; Nothing But Trouble. **1946** Gentlemen With Guns; Terrors on Horseback; Roll On, Harvest Moon; **1947** Helldorado; Valley of Fear; Riders of the Lone Star; Song of My Heart; Under Colorado Skies. **1948** I Wouldn't Be In Your Shoes; Carson City Raiders; The Timber Trail; West of Sonoma; Overland Trail; Cowboy Cavalier; Son of God's Country; Adventures of Frank and Jesse James (serial). **1949** Ghost of Zorro (serial); Crashing Thru; Challenge of the Range; Abandoned; Frontier Outpost; Riders of the Sky; The Blazing Trail. **1950** The Arizona Cowboy; Outcasts of the Trail; The Blazing Sun; David Harding, Counterspy; Cow Town; Under Mexicali Skies. **1951** Rough Riders of Durango; Pecos River. **1953** Thunder Over the Plains. **1954** Dangerous Mission; Cannibal Attack; The Law vs. Billy the Kid. **1955** Good Morning, Miss Dove; Prince of Players; Treasure of Ruby Hills; The Tall Men. **1956** Red Sundown; **1957** Utah Blaine; The Monolith Monsters; Joe Dakota. **1959** These Thousand Hills; Warlock; Timbuktu.

DARVAS, LILI
Born: Apr. 10, 1902, Budapest, Hungary. Died: July 22, 1974, New York, N.Y. Screen, stage, radio and television actress. Married to playwright Ferenc Molnar (dec. 1952).

Appeared in: **1935** Tagebuch der Geliebten. **1938** The Affairs of Maupassant. **1956** Meet Me in Las Vegas. **1960** Cimarron. **1973** Love.

DARVI, BELLA (Baýla Wegier)
Born: Oct. 23, 1928, Sosnowiec, Poland. Died: Sept. 1971, Monte Carlo, Monaco (suicide—gas). Screen and television actress.

Appeared in: **1954** Hell and High Water; The Egyptian. **1955** The Racers; Je Suis un Sentimental. **1959** Sinners of Paris. **1965** Lipstick.

DARWELL, JANE (Patti Woodward)
Born: Oct. 15, 1880, Palmyra, Mo. Died: Aug. 1967, Woodland Hills, Calif.

(heart attack). Screen, stage and television actress. Won 1940 Academy Award for Best Supporting Actress in The Grapes of Wrath.

Appeared in: **1914** Rose of the Rancho (film debut); The Only Son; Brewster Millions; The Master Mind. **1930** Tom Sawyer. **1931** Huckleberry Finn; Fighting Caravans. **1932** Ladies of the Big House; Hot Saturday; Back Street; No One Man. **1933** Good Housewrecking (short); Jennie Gerhardt; Air Hostess; Women Won't Tell; One Sunday Afternoon; Design for Living; Emergency Call; Before Dawn; Only Yesterday; He Couldn't Take It; Bondage; Child of Manhattan; Murders in the Zoo; Roman Scandals. **1934** Wonder Bar; Fashions of 1934; Jimmy the Gent; Embarrassing Moments; Heat Lightning; Gentlemen Are Born; Blind Date; Once to Every Woman; The Most Precious Thing in Life; Happiness Ahead; The Scarlet Empress; The White Parade; Bright Eyes; Change of Heart; Let's Talk It Over; Desirable; Wake up and Dream; The Firebird; David Harum; Journal of a Crime; Million Dollar Ransom; One Night of Love. **1935** Tomorrow's Youth; Beauty's Daughter; One More Spring; Life Begins at Forty; Curly Top; McFadden's Flats; Paddy O'Day; Navy Wife; Metropolitan. **1936** We're Only Human; Captain January; The Country Doctor; Little Miss Nobody; The First Baby; Private Number; The Poor Little Rich Girl; White Fang; Star for a Night; Ramona; Craig's Wife. **1937** The Great Hospital Mystery; Love Is News; Dead Yesterday; Nancy Steele Is Missing; Fifty Roads to Town; Slave Ship; Wife, Doctor and Nurse; Dangerously Yours; The Singing Marine; Laughing at Trouble. **1938** Five of a Kind; Change of Heart (and 1934 version); Battle of Broadway; Three Blind Mice; Time Out for Murder; Inside Story; Up the River; The Jury's Secret. **1939** Jesse James; Unexpected Father; The Zero Hour; Grand Jury Secrets; The Rains Came; Gone with the Wind; 20,000 Men a Year. **1940** The Grapes of Wrath; Brigham Young—Frontiersman; A Miracle on Main Street; Youth Will Be Served; Chad Hanna; Untamed. **1941** Here Is a Man; All That Money Can Buy; Private Nurse; Small Town Deb. **1942** On the Sunny Side; Highways by Night; The Great Gildersleeve; All Through the Night; Battle of Midway (documentary); The Loves of Edgar Allan Poe; It Happened in Flatbush; Young America; Men of Texas. **1943** Gildersleeve's Bad Day; The Ox-Bow Incident; Tender Comrade; Stagedoor Canteen; Government Girl. **1944** She's a Sweetheart; Music in Manhattan; Double Indemnity; The Impatient Years; Reckless Age; Sunday Dinner for a Soldier. **1945** Captain Tugboat Annie; I Live in Grosvenor Square (aka A Yank in London—US 1946). **1946** My Darling Clementine; Three Wise Fools; Dark Horse. **1947** The Red Stallion; Keeper of the Bees. **1948** The Time of Your Life; Train to Alcatraz; Three Godfathers. **1949** Red Canyon. **1950** Red-Wood Forest Trail; Surrender; Three Husbands; The Second Face; Father's Wild Game; Wagonmaster; Caged; The Daughter of Rosie O'Grady. **1951** Fourteen Hours; Excuse My Dust; Journey into Light; The Lemon Drop Kid. **1952** We're Not Married; The Devil and Daniel Webster (reissue and retitle of All That Money Can Buy, 1941). **1953** It Happens Every Thursday; The Sun Shines Bright; Affair with a Stranger; The Bigamist. **1955** Hit the Deck; A Life at Stake. **1956** There's Always Tomorrow; Girls in Prison. **1958** The Last Hurrah. **1959** Hound-Dog Man. **1964** Mary Poppins.

DASH, PAULY (Paul Walter Dashiff)

Born: 1918, Brooklyn, N.Y. Died: Feb. 2, 1974, Miami Beach, Fla. (cancer). Stage and screen actor.

Appeared in: **1964** It's Hot on Sin Island; Sextet. **1966** The Hot Pearl Snatch. **1968** Lady in Cement; I Am for Sale.

DASHIELL, WILLARD

Born: 1867. Died: Apr. 19, 1943, Holyoke, Mass. Screen, stage, vaudeville actor, playwright and lawyer. Entered films during silents.

Appeared in: **1931** The Cheat. **1934** War is a Racket.

DA SILVA, HENRY

Born: 1881, Lisbon, Portugal. Died: June 6, 1947, Los Angeles, Calif. Actor.

DASTAGIR, SABU. *See* SABU

DATE, KESHAVRAO

Born: 1939, India. Died: Sept. 13, 1971, Bombay, India. Stage and screen actor.

DAUBE, HARDA (Belle Daube)

Born: 1888, Northampton, England. Died: May 25, 1959, Hollywood, Calif. Stage and screen actress.

DAUFEL, ANDRE (David Van Offel)

Born: 1919, England. Died: Apr. 22, 1975, Brussels, Belgium. Screen, stage actor, stage director and playwright.

DAVENPORT, ALICE (Alice Shepard)

Born: 1853 or 1864 (?), New York, N.Y. Died: June 24, 1936, Los Angeles, Calif. Stage and screen actress. Divorced from actor Harry Davenport (dec. 1949) and mother of actress Dorothy Davenport.

Appeared in: **1911** The Best Man Wins. **1912** The Love Trail; Drummer's Vacation; Mabel's Lovers. **1913** The Telltale Light; Cohen's Outing; John Brown's Luck. **1914** Making a Living; Mabel's Strange Predicament; The Star

Boarder; Caught in a Cabaret; Caught in the Rain; Mabel's New Job. **1915** My Valet; The Home Breakers; Ambrose's Fury; Fickle Fatty's Fall; Stolen Magic. **1916** Perils of the Park; A Love Riot; Wife and Auto Trouble; The Snow Cure; The Worst of Friends; Fido's Fate. **1917** Secrets of a Beauty Parlour; A Maiden's Trust; Maggie's First False Step. **1918** Little Red Decides; Her Blighted Love. **1921** Skirts. **1924** The Legend of Hollywood. **1930** The Dude Wrangler.

DAVENPORT, ANN

Died: Jan. 28, 1968, Hollywood, Calif. Screen actress. See Harry Davenport for family information.

DAVENPORT, HARRY

Born: Jan. 19, 1866, New York, N.Y. Died: Aug. 9, 1949, Los Angeles, Calif. (heart attack). Screen, stage actor and film director. Divorced from actress Alice Davenport (dec. 1936). Married to actress Phyllis Rankin (dec. 1934) and father of actor Arthur Rankin (dec. 1947) and actresses Ann (dec. 1968), Kate (dec. 1954) and Dorothy Davenport. Entered films in 1912.

Appeared in: **1930** Her Unborn Child. **1931** My Sin. **1932** His Woman. **1933** Get That Venus. **1934** Three Cheers for Love. **1935** The Scoundrel. **1936** Three Men on a Horse; The Case of the Black Cat; King of Hockey. **1937** Fly-Away Baby; The Life of Emile Zola; Under Cover of Night; Her Husband's Secretary; White Bondage; They Won't Forget; Mr. Dodd Takes the Air; First Lady; The Perfect Specimen; Paradise Express; As Good as Married; Armored Car; Wells Fargo; Fit for a King. **1938** Gold Is Where You Find It; Saleslady; The Sisters; Long Shot; The First Hundred Years; The Cowboy and the Lady; Reckless Living; The Rage of Paris; Tailspin; Young Fugitives; You Can't Take It with You; The Higgins Family; Orphans of the Street. **1939** Made for Each Other; My Wife's Relatives; Should Husbands Work?; The Covered Trailer; Money to Burn; Exile Express; Death of a Champion; The Story of Alexander Graham Bell; Juarez; Gone with the Wind; The Hunchback of Notre Dame. **1940** The Story of Dr. Ehrlich's Magic Bullet; Granny Get Your Gun; Too Many Husbands; Grandpa Goes to Town; Earl of Puddlestone; Lucky Partners; I Want a Divorce; All This and Heaven Too; Foreign Correspondent. **1941** That Uncertain Feeling; I Wanted Wings; Hurricane Smith; The Bride Came C.O.D.; One Foot in Heaven; Kings Row. **1942** Son of Fury; Larceny, Inc.; Ten Gentlemen from West Point; Tales of Manhattan. **1943** Headin' for God's Country; We've Never Been Licked; Riding High; The Ox-Bow Incident; Shantytown; The Amazing Mrs. Holliday; Gangway for Tomorrow; Government Girl; Jack London; Princess O'Rourke. **1944** Meet Me in St. Louis; The Impatient Years; The Thin Man Goes Home; Kismet. **1945** Music for Millions; The Enchanted Forest; Too Young to Know; This Love of Ours; She Wouldn't Say Yes. **1946** Courage of Lassie; A Boy, a Girl and a Dog; Faithful in My Fashion; Three Wise Fools; GI War Brides; Lady Luck; Claudia and David; Pardon My Past; Adventure. **1947** The Farmer's Daughter; That Hagen Girl; Stallion Road; Keeper of the Bees; Sport of Kings; The Fabulous Texan; The Bachelor and the Bobbysoxer. **1948** Three Daring Daughters; The Man from Texas; For the Love of Mary; That Lady in Ermine; The Decision of Christopher Blake. **1949** Down to the Sea in Ships; Little Women; Tell It to the Judge; That Forsyte Woman. **1950** Riding High (and 1943 version).

DAVENPORT, HARRY J.

Born: 1858. Died: Feb. 20, 1929, Glendale, Calif. (complication of diseases). Screen actor. Married to actress Milla Davenport (dec. 1936).

DAVENPORT, HAVIS

Born: 1933. Died: July 23, 1975, Hollywood, Calif. Screen and television actress.

DAVENPORT, KATE

Born: 1896. Died: Dec. 7, 1954, Hollywood, Calif. Screen actress. Daughter of actor Harry Davenport (dec. 1949). See Harry Davenport for family information.

Appeared in: **1921** Sentimental Tommy.

DAVENPORT, KENNETH

Born: 1879. Died: Nov. 10, 1941, Los Angeles, Calif. (heart attack). Stage and screen actor.

Appeared in: **1921** The Nut.

DAVENPORT, MILLA

Born: 1871, Sicily, Italy. Died: May 17, 1936, Los Angeles, Calif. Screen, stage, vaudeville and burlesque actress. Married to screen actor Harry J. Davenport (dec. 1929). Entered films approx. 1911.

Appeared in: **1919** Daddy Long Legs; In Mizzoura. **1920** Stronger Than Death; The Forbidden Woman; You Never Can Tell. **1921** Rip Van Winkle; Why Trust Your Husband; The Girl from God's Country; The Man from Lost River; Patsy. **1922** The Worldly Madonna; The Man Who Waited. **1923** The Christian; Dulcy. **1924** Daddies; The Red Lily; The Shooting of Dan McGrew; The Right of the Strongest. **1925** Wild West (serial); Dangerous Innocence. **1926** Crossed Signals; The Road to Glory. **1927** Hey! Hey! Cowboy; King of

Kings. **1928** Sins of the Fathers; The Danger Rider. **1929** The Girl from Woolworth's. **1932** Merrily We Go To Hell. **1934** In Love with Life. **1935** The Wedding Night; Here Comes Cookie.

DAVID, WILLIAM
Born: 1882, Vicksburg, Miss. Died: Apr. 10, 1965, East Islip, N.Y. Stage and screen actor.

Appeared in: **1922** Outcast; Received Payment. **1923** Fog Bound.

DAVIDOFF, SERAFIN
Died: Apr., 1975. Screen extra.

Appeared in: **1956** Around the World in 80 Days.

DAVIDS, HEINTJE
Born: 1888. Died: Feb. 14, 1975. Dutch film actress.

DAVIDSON, BING (aka JAMES B. DAVIDSON)
Born: 1939. Died: July 18, 1965, San Francisco, Calif. (fall from hotel window). Screen actor. Also in films as James B. Davidson.

DAVIDSON, DORE
Born: 1850. Died: Mar. 7, 1930 (complication of diseases). Screen, stage actor, stage producer and playwright.

Appeared in: **1920** Humoresque. **1922** The Rosary; Your Best Friend; The Good Provider; The Light in the Dark. **1923** Broadway Broke; The Purple Highway; Success; None So Blind. **1924** The Great White Way; Welcome Stranger; Grit. **1925** The Royal Girl. **1927** The Music Master; East Side, West Side.

DAVIDSON, JAMES B. *See* BING DAVIDSON

DAVIDSON, JOHN
Born: Dec. 25, 1886, New York. Died: Jan. 15, 1968, Los Angeles, Calif. (heart failure). Stage and screen actor. Do not confuse with singer/actor John Davidson.

Appeared in: **1914** The Genius Pierre. **1915** Green Cloak; Sentimental Lady; Danger Signal. **1916** The Wall Between; A Million a Minute; Caravan; Pawn of Fate. **1919** Black Circle; Forest Rivals; Through the Toils. **1920** The Great Lover. **1921** The Bronze Bell; Cheated Love; Fool's Paradise; The Idle Rich; No Woman Knows. **1922** Saturday Night; The Woman Who Walked Alone; Under Two Flags. **1923** His Children's Children. **1924** Monsieur Beaucaire; Ramshackle House. **1929** Kid Gloves; The Rescue; Queen of the Night Clubs; Skin Deep; The Time, the Place and the Girl; The Thirteenth Chair. **1930** The Life of the Party. **1932** Arsene Lupin; Docks of San Francisco; Six Hours to Live. **1933** Behind Jury Doors; The Perils of Pauline (serial); Dinner at Eight; The Mad Game. **1934** Burn 'Em Up Barnes (serial and feature film); Lightning Strikes Twice; Tailspin Tommy (serial); Bombay Mail; Hold That Girl; Murder in Trinidad; Hollywood Hoodlum. **1935** A Tale of Two Cities; The Call of the Savage (serial); Behind the Green Lights; Last Days of Pompeii; A Shot in the Dark. **1938** Fighting Devil Dogs (serial); Mr. Moto Takes a Vacation. **1939** Mr. Moto's Last Warning; Duel Personalities (short); Arrest Bulldog Drummond. **1940** King of the Royal Mounted (serial). **1941** Adventures of Captain Marvel (serial); Dick Tracy vs. Crime, Inc. (serial); Devil Bat. **1942** Perils of Nyoka (serial); The Yukon Patrol. **1943** Secret Service in Darkest Africa (serial). **1944** Captain America (serial); The Chinese Cat; Call of the Jungle. **1945** The Purple Monster Strikes (serial); Where Do We Go from Here? **1946** Shock; Sentimental Journey. **1947** Daisy Kenyon. **1948** A Letter to Three Wives; Bungalow 13; That Wonderful Urge. **1949** Slattery's Hurricane; Oh, You Beautiful Doll. **1954** Prince Valiant.

DAVIDSON, MAX
Born: 1875, Berlin, Germany. Died: Sept. 4, 1950, Woodland Hills, Calif. Stage and screen actor. Entered films in 1913.

Appeared in: **1915** Love in Armor. **1916** The Village Vampire (working title The Great Leap). **1921** The Idle Rich; No Woman Knows. **1922** Remembrance; The Light That Failed; Second Hand Rose. **1923** The Extra Girl; The Rendezvous; The Ghost Patrol; The Darling of New York. **1924** Fool's Highway; Untamed Youth; Hold Your Breath. **1925** Old Clothes; Hogan's Alley; The Rag Man; Justice of the Far North. **1926** Into Her Kingdom; Sunshine of Paradise Alley; The Johnstown Flood. **1927** Hotel Imperial; Pleasure Before Business; Cheaters; Hats Off (short); The Call of the Cuckoo (short). **1929** Moan and Groan, Inc. (short); So This Is College; Hurdy Gurdy (short). Shorts prior to 1930: Pass the Gravy; Dumb Daddies; Blow by Blow; Should Women Drive. **1930** The Shrimp (short). **1931** Oh! Oh! Cleopatra (short). **1932** Docks of San Francisco; Daring Danger. **1933** The Cohens and the Kellys in Trouble; Hokus Focus (short); The World Gone Wrong. **1935** Southern Exposure (short). **1936** Roamin' Wild. **1937** The Girl Said No. **1940** No Census, No Feeling (short). **1942** The Great Commandment. **1965** Laurel and Hardy's Laughing 20's (documentary).

DAVIDSON, WILLIAM B.
Born: June 16, 1888, Dobbs Ferry, N.Y. Died: Sept. 28, 1947, Santa Monica, Calif. (following surgery). Stage and screen actor. Entered films with Vitagraph in 1914.

Appeared in: **1915** For the Honor of the Crew. **1916** The Price of Malice; Her Debt of Honor; Dorian's Divorce; The Child of Destiny; The Pretenders; In the Diplomatic Service. **1917** White Raven; The Call of Her People; Modern Cinderella; Her Second Husband; The Greatest Power; Lady Barnacle; A Magdalene of the Hills; Mary Lawson's Secret; More Truth than Poetry; American Maid. **1918** Friend Husband; In Pursuit of Polly; Persuasive Peggy; Our Little Wife. **1920** Partners of the Night. **1921** Nobody; Conceit; The Girl from Nowhere. **1922** Destiny's Isle. **1923** Salomy Jane; Adam and Eva. **1924** The Storm Daughter. **1925** Hearts and Spurs; Ports of Call; Women and Gold; Recompense. **1927** The Cradle Snatchers; The Lash (short); Gentlemen of Paris; The Last Trail; Love Makes 'Em Wild. **1928** Sharp Tools (short); Good Morning, Judge; The Gaucho. **1929** Queen of the Night Clubs; Ain't It the Truth (short); The Carnation Kid; Woman Trap; Painted Faces. **1930** Fat Wives for Thin (short); Sunny; A Man from Wyoming; Hell's Angels; Playboy of Paris; Captain Applejack; The Silver Horde; Hook, Line and Sinker; Oh, For a Man!; The Costello Case; Men Are Like That; For the Defense; How I Play Golf; The Feathered Serpent; Blaze O'Glory; Scarlet Face; Letters (short). **1931** Half Holiday (short); No Limit; The Secret Call; Vice Squad; Graft. **1932** The Menace; The 13th Guest; Her Mad Night; Guilty or Not Guilty; Sky Devils; Scarface. **1932** Guilty as Hell; The Animal Kingdom. **1933** Dangerously Yours; Hello Everybody!; The Intruder; I'm No Angel; Sitting Pretty; Meet the Baron; Lady Killer; Torch Singer; Billion Dollar Scandal. **1934** The Big Shakedown; Housewife; Circus Clown; Friends of Mr. Sweeney; Dragon Murder Case; The Lemon Drop Kid; St. Louis Kid; Massacre; Fog Over Frisco; Laughing Boy; The Secret Bride. **1935** Sweet Music; Bordertown; Devil Dogs of the Air; A Night at the Ritz; Oil for the Lamps of China; Special Agent; Dangerous; Go Into Your Dance; In Caliente; The Crusades; Woman Wanted; Show Them No Mercy; Bright Lights. **1936** Road Gang; The Singing Kid; Murder by an Aristocrat; The Big Noise; Earthworm Tractors; Gold Diggers of 1937; Mind Your Own Business. **1937** Easy Living; Behind the Mike; Marked Woman; Midnight Court; Ever Since Eve; Marry the Girl; Sergeant Murphy; Hollywood Hotel; Let Them Live; The Road Back; The Affairs of Cappy Ricks; Paradise Isle; Something to Sing About; It Happened in Hollywood. **1938** The Jury's Secret; Cocoanut Grove; Mr. Doodle Kicks Off; Blockade; Cowboy from Brooklyn; Illegal Traffic. **1939** On Trial; Indianapolis Speedway; Private Detectives; Hidden Power; Each Dawn I Die; Smashing the Money Ring; The Honeymoon's Over; They Made Me a Criminal; On the Record; Dust Be My Destiny; Honeymoon in Bali. **1940** Tin Pan Alley; Three Cheers for the Irish; Florian; Lillian Russell; Half a Sinner; My Love Came Back; The Girl in 313; Sailor's Lady; Maryland; Hired Wife; Seven Sinners; A Night at Earl Carroll's; Sandy Gets Her Man; My Little Chickadee. **1941** San Francisco Docks; In the Navy; The Lady from Cheyenne; Thieves Fall Out; Hold That Ghost; Highway West; Three Sons O' Guns; Keep 'Em Flying; Sun Valley Serenade. **1942** In This Our Life; Juke Girl; The Magnificent Dope; Over My Dead Body; The Male Animal; Larceny, Inc; Yankee Doodle Dandy; Tennessee Johnson; Gentleman Jim; Affairs of Jimmy Valentine; Careful, Soft Shoulders. **1943** Mission to Moscow; Calaboose; Truck Busters; Murder on the Waterfront; The Good Fellows; Slick Chick. **1944** Greenwich Village; The Imposter; In Society; Shine on Harvest Moon; Song of Nevada. **1945** Saratoga Trunk; Blonde Ransom; The Man Who Walked Alone; Tell It to the Judge; Circumstantial Evidence; See My Lawyer. **1946** The Cat Creeps; Ding Dong Williams; The Plainsman and the Lady; The Notorious Lone Wolf. **1947** Dick Tracey's Dilemma; That's My Man; That Hagen Girl; My Wild Irish Rose; The Farmer's Daughter.

DAVIDT, MICHAEL
Born: 1877. Died: Mar. 15, 1944, Hollywood, Calif. Screen actor.

DAVIES, BETTY ANN
Born: Dec. 24, 1910, London, England. Died: May 14, 1955, Manchester, England (following appendectomy). Screen and stage actress.

Appeared in: **1933** Oh What a Duchess! (aka My Old Duchess). **1934** The Wigan Express (aka Death at Broadcasting House); Youthful Folly. **1935** Joy Ride; Play Up the Band. **1936** Chick; Radio Lover; She Knew What She Wanted; Tropical Trouble; Excuse My Glove. **1937** Merry Comes to Town; Under a Cloud; Lucky Jade. **1938** Silver Top; Mountains of Mourne. **1941** Kipps (aka The Remarkable Mr. Kipps—US 1942); I Bet. **1947** It Always Rains on Sunday (US 1949). **1948** Escape; To the Public Danger. **1949** The Passionate Friends (aka One Woman's Story—US); The History of Mr. Polly (US 1951); Now Barabbas; Which Will You Have? (aka Barabbas the Robber—US). **1950** The Blue Lamp; Trio; The Man in Black; The Woman with No Name (aka Her Panelled Door—US 1951); Sanitarium. **1951** Outcast of the Islands. **1952** Meet Me Tonight. **1953** Cosh Boy (aka The Slasher—US); Grand National Night (aka Wicked Wife—US 1955); Tonight at 8:30. **1954** Children Galore; The Belles of St. Trinian's (US 1955). **1955** Murder by Proxy (aka Blackout—US). **1956** Alias John Preston.

DAVIES, DAVID
Died: May 1920, Chicago, Ill. Screeen, stage and vaudeville actor.

DAVIES, GEORGE
Born: 1891. Died: Mar. 1960, Edinburgh, Scotland. Screen, stage, radio and television actor.

DAVIES, MARION
Born: Jan. 3, 1898. Died: Sept. 22, 1961, Hollywood, Calif. (cancer). Screen actress.

Appeared in: 1917 Runaway Romany (film debut). 1918 Cecilia of the Pink Roses. 1919 The Cinema Murder; The Dark Star; The Belle of New York. 1920 The Restless Sex; April Folly. 1921 Enchantment; Buried Treasure. 1922 The Bride's Play; Beauty Worth; When Knighthood Was in Flower; The Young Diana; Daughter of Luxury. 1923 Little Old New York; Adam and Eva. 1924 Janice Meredith; Yolanda. 1925 Lights of Old Broadway; Zander the Great. 1926 Beverly of Graustark. 1927 Quality Street; The Fair Co-ed; The Red Mill; Tillie the Toiler. 1928 The Cardboard Lover; The Patsy; Show People. 1929 The Hollywood Revue of 1929; Marianne; The Gay Nineties. 1930 Not So Dumb; The Floradora Girl. 1931 It's a Wise Child; Five and Ten; Bachelor Father. 1932 Polly of the Circus; Blondie of the Follies; The Dark Horse. 1933 Peg O' My Heart. 1934 Operator Thirteen; Going Hollywood. 1935 Page Miss Glory. 1936 Hearts Divided; Cain and Mabel. 1937 Ever Since Eve. 1964 Big Parade of Comedy (documentary). 1967 Show People (reissue of 1928 film).

DAVIS, ALLAN
Born: Aug. 30, 1913, London, England. Died: Dec. 11, 1943, Los Angeles, Calif. Screen, stage actor and stage director.

Appeared in: 1932 All American. 1935 Magnificent Obsession. 1937 Marked Woman; Penrod and Sam; The Barrier. 1938 Over the Wall. 1939 Wings of the Navy; King of the Underworld. 1940 The Big Guy; Arise, My Love.

DAVIS, ANNA
Born: 1890. Died: May 5, 1945, Hollywood, Calif. Screen actress.

DAVIS, BOB "ALABAM"
Born: 1910. Died: Sept. 22, 1971, Hollywood, Calif. (heart attack). Screen actor and sometime stand-in for Franchot Tone.

DAVIS, BOYD
Born: June 19, 1885, Santa Rosa, Calif. Died: Jan. 25, 1963, Hollywood, Calif. Stage and screen actor. Entered films in 1925.

Appeared in: 1932 Smiling Faces. 1941 You'll Never Get Rich; Two Latins from Manhattan. 1942 Hello, Annapolis; Harvard Here I Come; Star Spangled Rhythm. 1943 The Ghost Ship. 1945 Saratoga Trunk; Captain Eddie; Youth on Trial; Col. Effingham's Raid. 1946 Terror by Night; The Unknown. 1947 The Senator Was Indiscreet. 1948 The Wreck of the Hesperus; They Live By Night (aka The Twisted Road, aka Your Red Wagon); A Foreign Affair. 1949 Samson and Delilah; Ma and Pa Kettle. 1950 Girl's School. 1952 At Sword's Point.

DAVIS, DANNY
Born: 1929. Died: Feb. 10, 1970, N.Y. (struck by a car). Stage and screen actor, comedian/comedy writer.

DAVIS, EDWARDS
Born: 1871, Santa Clara, Calif. Died: May 16, 1936, Hollywood, Calif. Screen, stage and vaudeville actor.

Appeared in: 1920 The Invisible Ray (serial). 1921 The Right Way; Shams of Society; The Plaything of Broadway; The Silver Lining. 1924 Tainted Money; The Sea Hawk; Good Bad Boy; Hook and Ladder; The Woman on the Jury; On the Stroke of Three; The Only Woman; The Price She Paid; Stolen Secrets. 1925 The Best People; Flattery; Joanna; The Splendid Road; Part Time Wife; Not So Long Ago; Her Husband's Secret; The Charmer; Contraband; A Fool and His Money; My Neighbor's Wife. 1926 The Amateur Gentleman; High Steppers; Tramp, Tramp, Tramp; Butterflies in the Rain. 1927 A Hero on Horseback; The Life of Riley; A Reno Divorce; Face Value; Marriage; Singed; Winds of the Pampas. 1928 The Sporting Age; Happiness Ahead; The Power of the Press. 1929 A Song of Kentucky. 1930 The Love Racket; Love in the Rough; Madam Satan; Madonna of the Streets. 1933 Hello, Everybody!

DAVIS, FREEMAN (aka BROTHER BONES)
Born: 1903. Died: June 14, 1974, Long Beach, Calif. Screen actor and whistler/entertainer.

Appeared in: 1941 Pot of Gold. 1951 Yes Sir, Mr. Bones.

DAVIS, REV. GARY
Born: 1896. Died: May 5, 1972, Hammonton, N.J. (heart attack). Black screen actor, gospel and blues singer.

Appeared in: 1970 Black Roots (documentary).

DAVIS, GEORGE
Born: 1889, Amsterdam, Holland. Died: Apr. 19, 1965, Woodland Hills, Calif. (cancer). Screen and vaudeville actor. Appeared in U.S., French, German, English and Italian films.

Appeared in: 1924 Sherlock, Jr.; He Who Gets Slapped. 1926 Into Her Kingdom. 1927 The Magic Flame. 1928 The Circus; The Wagon Show; The Awakening; the following shorts: Going Places; Leaping Luck; Who's Lyin'. 1929 4 Devils; Broadway; The Kiss; Devil May Care. 1930 Men of the North; A Lady to Love; Not So Dumb; Die Sennsucht Jeder Frau; Le Petit Cafe; Le Spectre Vert (The Unholy Night). 1931 Parlor, Bedroom and Bath; Laugh and Get Rich; Strangers May Kiss; Private Lives. 1932 Arsene Lupin; The Man from Yesterday; Broken Lullaby; Love Me Tonight; Under-cover Man. 1934 The Black Cat. 1935 The Good Fairy. 1937 History Is Made at Night; I Met Him in Paris; Thin Ice; Charlie Chan at Monte Carlo; Conquest; You Can't Have Everything. 1938 The Baroness and the Butler; Passport Husband; Always Goodbye; Hunted Men. 1939 Topper Takes a Trip; Bulldog Drummond's Bride; Everything Happens at Night; Charlie Chan in City in Darkness. 1940 Chad Hanna. 1945 See My Lawyer. 1946 The Kid from Brooklyn. 1947 Crime Doctor's Gamble. 1950 Wabash Avenue. 1951 On the Riviera; Secrets of Monte Carlo; The Lady Says No. 1953 Gentlemen Prefer Blondes. Other foreign films: Louis the Fox (English, French, German and Italian versions); The Little Cafe and The Queen's Husband (both French versions).

DAVIS, HARRY
Born: 1874. Died: Apr. 4, 1929, New York, N.Y. (heart disease). Stage and screen actor.

Appeared in: 1925 Old Clothes. 1926 Devil's Dice; Unknown Treasures; Whispering Canyon; Dangerous Friends; Lightning Reporter. 1927 The Blood Ship; Burning Gold. 1928 Runaway Girls; Crashing Through.

DAVIS, JACK
Died: 1968. Screen actor.

Appeared in: 1946 Up Goes Maisie; Behind Green Lights; Somewhere in the Night; Talk about a Lady; Strange Triangle; Night Editor; Gallant Bess; Secret of the Whistler; Shadowed. 1947 Blondie's Big Moment; The Millerson Case. 1956 Crowded Paradise. 1967 The Gnome-Mobile.

DAVIS, JAMES GUNNIS
Born: 1874, Sunderland, England. Died: Mar. 23, 1937, Los Angeles, Calif. Stage and screen actor. Entered films in 1912.

Appeared in: 1921 A Certain Rich Man; The Secret of the Hills. 1922 The Gray Dawn. 1923 The Midnight Alarm; Refuge; Chastity. 1924 Jealous Husbands; The Trouble Shooter. 1925 Lord Jim; Winds of Chance; His Lucky Horseshoe. 1927 Twinkle Toes; The Notorious Lady. 1928 Lilac Time. 1930 Headin' North. 1931 A Melon Drama (short); East Lynne; Charlie Chan Carries On. 1934 One More River. 1935 The Bride of Frankenstein.

DAVIS, JEFF (Jefferson Davis)
Born: 1884, Cincinnati, Ohio. Died: Apr. 5, 1968, Cincinnati, Ohio. Screen actor and self-proclaimed "Hobo King."

Appeared in: 1915 The Bridge of Sighs.

DAVIS, JOAN
Born: June 29, 1907, St. Paul, Minn. Died: May 23, 1961, Palm Springs, Calif. (heart attack). Screen, radio and television actress. Mother of actress Beverly Wills (dec. 1963).

Appeared in: 1935 Way Up Thar (short); Millions in the Air. 1937 The Holy Terror; On the Avenue; Time Out for Romance; The Great Hospital Mystery; Life Begins in College; Wake Up and Live; Thin Ice; Sing and Be Happy; Angel's Holiday; Love and Hisses; Nancy Steele Is Missing; You Can't Have Everything. 1938 Sally, Irene and Mary; Josette; My Lucky Star; Just around the Corner; Hold That Co-Ed. 1939 Day-Time Wife; Tail Spin; Too Busy to Work. 1940 Free, Blonde and 21; Manhattan Heartbeat; Sailor's Lady. 1941 Sun Valley Serenade; For Beauty's Sake; Two Latins from Manhattan; Hold That Ghost. 1942 Sweetheart of the Fleet; Yokel Boy. 1943 He's My Guy; Two Senoritas From Chicago; Around the World. 1944 Beautiful but Broke; Kansas City Kitty; Show Business. 1945 She Gets Her Man; George White's Scandals. 1946 She Wrote the Book. 1948 If You Knew Susie. 1949 Make Mine Laughs. 1950 Love That Brute; Traveling Saleswoman. 1951 The Groom Wore Spurs. 1952 Harem Girl. 1963 The Sound of Laughter (documentary).

DAVIS, MILDRED
Born: Jan. 1, 1900, Brooklyn, N.Y. Died: Aug. 18, 1969, Santa Monica, Calif. (heart attack). Screen actress. Married to actor Harold Lloyd (dec. 1971) and mother of actor Harold Lloyd, Jr. (dec. 1971).

Appeared in: 1916 Marriage a la Carte. 1919 His Royal Slyness; From Hand to Mouth. 1921 Among Those Present; Sailor-Made Man. 1922 Grandma's Boy; Doctor Jack. 1923 Condemned; Safety Last; Temporary Marriage. 1927 Too Many Crooks.

DAVIS, OWEN, JR.

Born: 1907, New York, N.Y. Died: May 21, 1949, Long Island South, N.Y. (drowned—accident). Screen, stage and radio actor. Son of writer Owen Davis.

Appeared in: **1929** They Had to See Paris. **1930** Good Intentions; All Quiet on the Western Front. **1936** Bunker Bean; Murder on the Bridle Path; Special Investigator; Grand Jury; The Plot Thickens. **1937** It Could Happen to You; The Woman I Love. **1938** Touchdown Army. **1939** These Glamour Girls. **1940** Thou Shalt Not Kill; Knute Rockne—All American; Henry Goes to Arizona.

DAVIS, RUFE (Rufus Davidson)

Born: 1908, Dinson, Okla. Died: Dec. 13, 1974, Torrance, Calif. Screen, stage, radio and television actor.

Appeared in: **1937** Vitaphone shorts; Mountain Music; This Way Please; Blossoms on Broadway. **1938** Big Broadcast of 1938; Dr. Rhythm; Cocoanut Grove. **1939** Ambush; Some Like it Hot. **1940** Under Texas Skies; The Trail Blazers; Lone Star Raiders; Barnyard Follies. **1941** Prairie Pioneers; Pals of the Pecos; Saddlemates; Gangs of Sonora; Outlaws of the Cherokee Trail; Gauchos of El Dorado; West of Cimarron; Prairie Schooners. **1942** Code of the Outlaw; Westward, Ho; The Phantom Plainsmen; Riders of the Range. **1944** Jamboree. **1945** Radio Stars on Parade. **1948** The Strawberry Roan. **1952** Joe Palooka in the Triple Cross. **1969** Angel in My Pocket.

DAW, EVELYN

Born: 1912, Geddes, S.D. Died: Nov. 29, 1970, San Diego, Calif. Screen, stage and opera actress.

Appeared in: **1937** Something to Sing About. **1938** Panamint's Bad Man.

DAWN, ISABEL

Born: Oct. 20, 1905, Evansville, Ind. Died: June 29, 1966, Woodland Hills, Calif. (pulmonary infection). Screen, stage actress and screenwriter.

DAWSON, FRANK

Born: 1870. Died: Oct. 11, 1953, Hollywood, Calif. Screen actor.

Appeared in: **1934** Double Door. **1935** My Marriage; The Last Outpost; Broadway Hostess. **1936** Private Number; Ladies in Love. **1937** A Day at the Races. **1938** Four Men and a Prayer; I'll Give a Million. **1939** The Adventures of Sherlock Holmes; Beau Geste; Cafe Society. **1940** The Blue Bird. **1941** Scotland Yard. **1942** They All Kissed the Bride. **1943** What A Woman; Crash Dive. **1944** Bermuda Mystery; Woman in the Window. **1945** Wilson.

DAY, DULCIE

Born: 1911. Died: Dec. 1, 1954, Woodland Hills, Calif. Screen actress and singer.

DAY, EDITH

Born: 1896, Minneapolis, Minn. Died: May 1, 1971, London, England. Stage and screen actress.

Appeared in: **1918** The Grain of Dust; A Romance of the Air.

DAY, MARIE L.

Born: 1855, Troy, N.Y. Died: Nov. 7, 1939, Cleveland, Ohio (pneumonia). Stage and screen actress.

Appeared in: **1922** Timothy's Quest. **1923** The Ragged Edge. **1938** Mother Cary's Chickens.

DAYTON, FRANK

Born: 1865, Boston, Mass. Died: Oct. 17, 1924, New York, N.Y. Stage and screen actor.

Appeared in: **1915** Graustark; The Strange Case of Mary Page.

DAZE, MERCEDES

Born: 1892. Died: Mar. 18, 1945, Los Angeles, Calif. Screen and stage actress.

DEAGAN, CHARLES

Born: 1880. Died: July 19, 1932, New York, N.Y. (heart failure). Screen, vaudeville and radio actor.

Appeared in vaudeville as part of "Charles and Madeline Dunbar" team.

DE ALBA, CARLOS

Born: 1925. Died: Oct. 1960, Mexico City, Mexico (after brain surgery). Screen and television actor.

DEAN, BARNEY

Born: 1904, Russia. Died: Aug. 31, 1954, Santa Monica, Calif. (cancer). Screen, vaudeville actor and screenwriter. Appeared in vaudeville with Sid Tarradasch as the "Dean Bros."

Appeared in: **1938** Thanks for the Memory.

DEAN, FABIAN (Gibilaro)

Born: 1930. Died: Jan. 15, 1971, Hollywood, Calif. Screen and television actor.

Appeared in: **1962** Fallguy. **1967** The Ride to Hangman's Tree; The Reluctant Astronaut. **1968** Candy; Single Room Furnished. **1970** The Computer Wore Tennis Shoes.

DEAN, IVOR

Born: 1917, England. Died: Aug. 10, 1974, Truro, Cornwall, England (heart failure). Screen and television actor. Married to actress Patricia Hamilton.

Appeared in: **1966** Theatre of Death (aka Blood Fiend—US 1967). **1967** The Sorcerers (US 1968); Stranger in the House (aka Cop-Out—US 1968). **1968** Decline and Fall of a Bird Watcher (US 1969); The File of the Golden Goose (US 1969); Where Eagles Dare (US 1969). **1969** The Oblong Box (aka Edgar Allan Poe's "The Oblong Box"); Crooks and Coronets (aka Sophie's Place—US 1970).

DEAN, JACK (John Wooster Dean)

Born: 1875, Washington. Died: June 23, 1950, New York, N.Y. Stage and screen actor. Married to actress Fannie Ward (dec. 1952).

Appeared in: **1916** Tennessee's Pardner; Witchcraft; The Years of the Locust. **1917** Betty to the Rescue; Her Strange Wedding; Unconquered; The Crystal Gazer; The Winning of Sally Temple; A School for Husbands. **1918** The Yellow Ticket. **1919** Sealed Hearts.

DEAN, JAMES (James Byron Dean)

Born: Feb. 8, 1931, Marion, Ind. Died: Sept. 30, 1955 near Paso Robles, Calif. (auto accident). Screen, stage and television actor.

Appeared in: **1951** Fixed Bayonets; Sailor Beware. **1952** Has Anybody Seen My Girl. **1954** East of Eden. **1955** Rebel Without a Cause. **1956** Giant.

DEAN, JULIA

Born: May 12, 1878, St. Paul, Minn. Died: Oct. 17, 1952, Hollywood, Calif. Stage and screen actress.

Appeared in: **1915** How Molly Made Good; Judge Not. **1916** Matrimony. **1917** Rasputin; The Black Monk. **1942** The Cat People. **1944** Experiment Perilous; The Curse of the Cat People. **1946** Do You Love Me?; O.S.S. **1947** Magic Town; Nightmare Alley; Out of the Blue. **1948** The Emperor Waltz. **1949** Easy Living; Rimfire; Red Desert; Ringside; Treasure of Monte Cristo; Grand Canyon. **1950** Girl's School. **1951** People Will Talk; Elopement. **1952** You for Me.

DEAN, MAN MOUNTAIN (Frank S. Leavitt)

Born: 1890. Died: May 29, 1953, Norcross, Ga. Screen actor and wrestler.

Appeared in: **1933** Private Life of Henry VIII (doubled for Charles Laughton). **1935** Reckless; We're in the Money. **1937** Three Legionaires; Big City. **1938** The Gladiator. **1960** Surprise Package.

DEAN, MAY

Died: Sept. 1, 1937, N.Y. Stage and screen actress.

Appeared in: **1923** Riders of the Range. **1935** Mississippi.

DEAN, NELSON (Nelson S. Whipple)

Born: 1882. Died: Dec. 19, 1923, Detroit, Mich. (apoplexy). Stage and screen actor.

DEAN, RALPH

Born: 1868. Died: Sept. 15, 1923, New York, N.Y. Screen, stage actor and film director.

DEAN, ROSE

Born: 1892. Died: Oct. 6, 1952, Hollywood, Calif. Screen actress.

DEAN, RUBY

Born: 1887. Died: Feb. 23, 1935, Cleveland, Ohio. Screen and vaudeville actress.

DE ANDA, AGUSTIN

Born: 1935, Mexico. Died: May 29, 1960, Mexico (murdered). Mexican screen actor. Son of actor/producer Raoul de Anda. Entered films in 1952 with his father in a series of "Charro Negro" pictures.

DEANE, DORIS (aka DORRIS DEANE)

Born: 1901. Died: Mar. 24, 1974, Los Angeles, Calif. Screen actress. Divorced from actor Fatty Arbuckle (dec. 1933).

Appeared in: **1921** The Shark Master. **1922** The Half Breed.

DeANGELIS, JEFFERSON

Born: Nov. 30, 1859, San Francisco, Calif. Died: Mar. 20, 1933, Orange, N.J. Stage and screen actor.

Appeared in: **1915** The Funny Side of Jealousy; Beware the Dog.

DEARING, EDGAR (aka EDGAR DEERING)
Born: May 4, 1893, Ceres, Calif. Died: Aug. 17, 1974, Woodland Hills, Calif. (lung cancer). Screen, stage and television actor.

Appeared in: **1927** The Second Hundred Years; Call of the Cuckoos. **1928** Leave 'Em Laughing; Their Purple Moment; Two Tars. **1929** The Jazz Age; The Locked Door. **1930** Free and Easy; Big Money; A Man from Wyoming; Abraham Lincoln; plus the following shorts: Live and Learn; Rich Uncles; Two Plus Fours. **1932** Horse Feathers. **1933** The Midnight Patrol. **1935** The Crusades; The Nitwits; The Rainmakers; Lightning Strikes Twice. **1936** The Sky Parade; The Bride Walks Out; Swing Time; The Count Takes the Count (short); Down the Ribber (short). **1937** It Happened in Hollywood; They Gave Him a Gun; Love is News; Married before Breakfast; Big City. **1938** Thanks for Everything; Border G-Man. **1939** Honolulu; The Gracie Allen Murder Case; Twelve Crowded Hours; Blondie Meets the Boss; Torchy Plays with Dynamite; Some Like It Hot; Nick Carter, Master Detective. **1940** Go West; One Night in the Tropics; Little Orvie; Cross Country Romance; When the Daltons Rode; No Time for Comedy; Sailor's Lady; A Little Bit of Heaven. **1941** The Big Store; Hold That Ghost; Caught in the Draft; Niagara Falls. **1942** Star Spangled Rhythm; Henry Aldrich, Editor; A Hunting We Will Go; Miss Annie Rooney; Wings for the Eagle. **1943** Henry Aldrich Haunts a House; Henry Aldrich Swings It; The Good Fellows. **1944** Ghost Catchers; The Big Noise; In Society; Strange Affair; Seven Doors to Death. **1945** Swing Out, Sister; Her Lucky Night; Don't Fence Me In; Scarlet Street. **1947** The Bishop's Wife. **1948** The Return of the Whistler; Out of the Storm; **1949** Boston Blackie's Chinese Venture; Prison Warden. **1950** Raiders of Tomahawk Creek; Lightning Guns. **1951** As You Were (aka Present Arms); Silver Canyon; Riding the Outlaw Trail. **1952** The Kid from Broken Gun; My Wife's Best Friend. **1953** It Came from Outer Space. **1960** Pollyanna.

DEARLY, MAX
Born: 1874, France. Died: June 2, 1943, Paris, France. Stage and screen actor.

Appeared in: **1934** Madame Bovary. **1935** Le Dernier Milliardaire. **1936** Les Miserables. **1940** Claudine. **1941** They Met on Skis. **1942** Nine Bachelors.

DEASE, BOBBY (Robert C. McCahan)
Born: 1899. Died: Feb. 22, 1958, Reading. Pa. Screen actor.

Appeared in: **1939** Some Like It Hot. **1940** Dancing Co-Ed.

DE AUBRY, DIANE (Diane Rubini)
Born: 1890, Sault St. Marie, Mich. Died: May 24, 1969, Los Angeles, Calif. (heart attack). Screen, stage and vaudeville actress. Entered films with Biograph and World Films.

DeBALZAC, JEANNE
Born: France. Died: May, 1930, Paris, France. Screen actress.

DE BECKER, HAROLD
Born: 1889, England. Died: July 23, 1947, Hollywood, Calif. Screen, stage and radio actor. Brother of actress Marie de Becker (dec. 1946).

Appeared in: **1942** Sherlock Holmes and the Secret Weapon; Eagle Squadron; This above All.

DE BECKER, MARIE
Born: 1881. Died: Mar. 23, 1946, Hollywood, Calif. (heart attack). Stage and screen actress. Sister of actor Harold De Becker (dec. 1947).

Appeared in: **1942** Mrs. Miniver; Random Harvest. **1944** None But the Lonely Heart. **1946** Devotion.

DeBLASIO, GENE (aka HOUSTON SAVOY and HOUSTON SAVAGE)
Born: 1940. Died: Nov. 3, 1971, Arkansas (auto accident). Screen, stage and television actor.

Appeared in: **1970** The Losers.

DeBOZOKY, BARBARA (Barbara Springer)
Born: Nov. 10, 1871, Hungary. Died: Nov. 29, 1937, Los Angeles, Calif. (cancer). Stage and screen actress.

DE BRAY, HAROLD
Born: 1874. Died: Oct. 31, 1932, Los Angeles, Calif. (heart disease). Screen actor.

DE BRAY, HENRI
Born: 1889. Died: Apr. 5, 1965, Nottingham, England. Screen, stage, television actor and dancer.

DE BRAY, YVONNE
Born: 1889, France. Died: Feb. 1, 1954, Paris, France (heart ailment). Stage and screen actress.

Appeared in: **1944** The Eternal Return. **1949** Gigi; Les Parents Terribles (aka The Storm Within—US 1950). **1950** Olivia. **1952** Nous Sommes Tous Les Assassins. **1954** Caroline Cherie.

DE BRULIER, NIGEL
Born: 1878, England. Died: Jan. 30, 1948. Screen actor.

Appeared in: **1915** Ghost. **1916** Intolerance. **1917** 'Twixt Death and Dawn (serial); The Mystery Ship (serial); A Prince for a Day. **1918** Me und Gott; Kulter. **1919** The Mystery of 13 (serial); Sahara. **1920** Virgin of Stamboul; Cold Steel; The Devil Within; The Four Horsemen of the Apocalypse; His Pajama Girl; That Something; The Three Musketeers; Without Benefit of Clergy. **1922** A Doll's House; Omar the Tentmaker. **1923** Salome; The Eleventh Hour; The Hunchback of Notre Dame; Rupert of Hentzau; St. Elmo. **1924** A Boy of Flanders; Mademoiselle Midnight; Three Weeks; Wild Oranges. **1925** The Ancient Mariner; A Regular Fellow. **1926** Ben-Hur; Don Juan; The Greater Glory; Yellow Fingers. **1927** The Beloved Rogue; Patent Leather Kid; Soft Cushions; Surrender; Wings. **1928** The Divine Sinner; The Gaucho; Loves of an Actress; Me, Gangster; Two Lovers. **1929** Noah's Ark; The Iron Mask; Thru Different Eyes; The Wheel of Life. **1930** Golden Dawn; The Green Goddess; Moby Dick; Redemption. **1931** Song of India. **1932** Miss Pinkerton; Rasputin and the Empress. **1933** I'm No Angel; Life in the Raw. **1935** Charlie Chan in Egypt; The Three Musketeers (and 1921 version). **1936** Half Angel; Down to the Sea; Mary of Scotland; The Garden of Allah; The White Legion. **1937** The Californians. **1939** The Hound of the Baskervilles; Mutiny in the Big House; The Man in the Iron Mask; The Mad Empress. **1940** Viva Cisco Kid; One Million B.C.; Heaven With a Barbed Wire Fence. **1941** For Beauty's Sake; Adventure of Captain Marvel (serial). **1943** Tonight We Raid Calais.

DEBUCOURT, JEAN
Born: 1894, France. Died: Mar. 1958, Paris, France. Screen and stage actor.

Appeared in: **1922** Le Petit Chose. **1933** Mistigri. **1934** L'Agonie des Aigles. **1936** Le Prince Jean. **1937** Mayerling; The Life and Loves of Beethoven. **1940** Mayerling to Sarajevo. **1943** Douce. **1946** Le Diable au Corps. **1948** The Eagle Has Two Heads; The Idiot; Not Guilty; Monsieur Vincent. **1949** Man to Men; Woman Who Dared; Devil in the Flesh; Love Story; Occupe-Toi D'Amelie. **1950** Tainted. **1951** The Secret of Mayerling; Nana (US 1957). **1953** Justice Is Done; Fanfan La Tulipe (Fanfan the Tulip); Seven Deadly Sins. **1954** Desperate Decision; The Golden Coach. **1956** The Doctors; La Lumiere d'en Face (The Light across the Street). **1958** Inspector Maigret. **1959** Miracle of Saint Therese.

DeCARLOS, PERLA GRANDA
Born: 1903, Nicaragua. Died: June 8, 1973, Woodhaven, N.Y. Screen, stage and vaudeville actress. Married to actor Jack DeCarlos (dec.) with whom she appeared in a vaudeville act billed as "The DeCarlos."

Appeared in: **1933** Flying Down to Rio.

DE CASALIS, JEANNE (De Casalis de Pury)
Born: May 22, 1897, Basutoland, South Africa. Died: Aug. 19, 1966, London, England. Screen, stage, radio actress and playwright. Divorced from actor Colin Clive (dec. 1937).

Appeared in: **1925** Settled Out of Court (aka Evidence Enclosed). **1927** The Glad Eye; The Arcadians. **1928** Zero. **1930** Infatuation; Knowing Men. **1932** Nine 'Till Six. **1933** Radio Parade; Mixed Doubles. **1934** Nell Gwyn. **1938** Just Like a Woman. **1939** Jamaica Inn; The Girl Who Forgot. **1940** Charley's (Big Hearted) Aunt; Sailors Three (aka The Cockeyed Sailors—US 1941). **1941** Cottage to Let (aka Bombsight Stolen—US); The Fine Feathers. **1942** Those Kids from Town. **1943** They Met in the Dark (US 1945). **1944** Medal for the General. **1946** This Man Is Mine. **1947** The Turners of Prospect Road. **1948** Woman Hater (US 1949). **1950** The Twenty Questions Murder Mystery.

DE CASTREJON, BLANCA
Born: 1916, Mexico. Died: Dec. 26, 1969, Mexico City, Mexico. Mexican and US screen and stage actress.

Appeared in: **1963** Signs of the Zodiac.

DECKER, JOHN
Born: 1895, San Francisco, Calif. Died: June 7, 1947, Hollywood, Calif. Artist/painter employed to do stand-in painting for actors playing role of artists. Was a pal of numerous famous Hollywood film personalities.

DECKER, KATHRYN BROWNE
Born: Richmond, Va. Died: 1919, Colombo, Ceylon. Screen and stage actress.

Appeared in: **1915** The Prima Donna's Husband; The Beloved Vagabond; The Fifth Commandment; The Closing Net. **1917** The Pride of the Clan.

DECOMBIE, GUY
Born: France? Died: Aug., 1964, France? Screen actor.

Appeared in: **1936** Le Crime de Monsieur Lange. **1950** Francois Villon. **1952** Jour de Fete. **1957** The Winner's Circle. **1958** Inspector Maigret. **1959** Les Quarte Cents Coups (The 400 Blows); Les Cousins (The Cousins). **1961** Fever Heat.

DE COPPETT, THEODOSIA. *See* THEDA BARA

DE CORDOBA, PEDRO
Born: Sept. 28, 1881, New York, N.Y. Died: Sept. 17, 1950, Sunland, Calif. (heart attack). Screen, stage and radio actor.

Appeared in: **1915** Carmen. **1916** Maria Rosa. **1917** Runaway Romany. **1919** The New Moon. **1920** The World and His Wife; Barbary Sheep. **1921** The Inner Chamber. **1922** The Young Diana; Just a Song at Twilight; When Knighthood Was in Flower. **1923** The Enemies of Women; The Purple Highway. **1924** The Bandolero; The Desert Sheik. **1925** The New Commandment. **1933** Through the Centuries. **1935** The Crusades; Captain Blood; Professional Soldier. **1936** Ramona; Rose of the Rancho; Moonlight Murder; Trouble for Two; The Devil Doll; His Brother's Wife; Anthony Adverse; The Garden of Allah. **1937** Maid of Salem; Damaged Goods; Girl Loves Boy. **1938** International Settlement; Keep Smiling; Heart of the North; Storm Over Bengal. **1939** Chasing Danger; The Light That Failed; Juarez; Winner Take All; Man of Conquest; Law of the Pampas; Range War; Charlie Chan in City in Darkness. **1940** My Favorite Wife; South of Pago-Pago; Earthbound; The Mark of Zorro; Devil's Island; Before I Hang; The Sea Hawk; The Ghost Breakers. **1941** Romance of the Rio Grande; Phantom Submarine; Blood and Sand; The Corsican Brothers; Aloma of the South Seas. **1942** Saboteur; The Son of Fury; Shut My Big Mouth. **1943** Tarzan Triumphs; The Song of Bernadette; Background to Danger; For Whom the Bell Tolls. **1944** The Falcon in Mexico; Uncertain Glory; Tahiti Nights. **1945** Club Havana; Keys of the Kingdom; San Antonio; The Cisco Kid; In Old New Mexico; Picture of Dorian Gray. **1946** Cuban Pete; A Scandal in Paris; Swamp Fire. **1947** The Beast with Five Fingers; Carnival in Costa Rica; Robin Hood of Monterey. **1948** Time of Your Life; Mexican Hayride. **1949** Omoo Omoo the Shark God; The Daring Caballero; Daughter of the West; Samson and Delilah. **1950** Comanche Territory; The Lawless; When the Redskins Rode. **1951** Crisis.

DE CORDOVA, ARTURO (Arturo Garcia)
Born: May 8, 1907, Merida, Yucatan, Mexico. Died: Nov. 3, 1973, Mexico City, Mexico. Screen actor. Won Mexico's 1938, 1939 and 1940 motion picture industry Actor's Award.

Appeared in: **1934** Jealousy (film debut); Cielito Lindo (US 1936); La Zundunga; La Noche de Los Amayas; The Son's Command; Refugiados en Madrid; Miracle of Main Street. **1936** Celos. **1937** Esos Hombres. **1938** Ave sin Rumbo (Wandering Bird); Hombres de Mar (Men of the Sea). **1939** La Casa del Orgro (The House of the Ogre). **1940** Alexandra; Mientras Mexico Duerme (While Mexico Sleeps); Odio (Hate); La Bestia Negra (The Black Beast); El Conde de Monte Cristo (The Count of Monte Cristo—US 1943). **1941** Night of the Mayas. **1943** For Whom the Bell Tolls; Hostages; Rurales. **1944** Frenchman's Creek. **1945** A Medal for Benny; Incendiary Blonde; Duffy's Tavern; Masquerade in Mexico; La Selva de Fuego. **1946** Cinco Rostras de Mujer. **1947** New Orleans; The Flame. **1948** Adventures of Casanova. **1951** El Stronghold; Reportaje. **1954** Kill Him for Me. **1955** This Strange Passion. **1962** Assassino (Assassins—aka The Violent and the Damned); The New Invisible Man.

DeCORDOVA, LEANDER
Born: 1878, Jamaica. Died: Sept. 19, 1936. Screen, stage actor and film director. Appeared in US and British films.

DE CORSIA, TED
Born: 1904. Died: Apr. 11, 1973, Encino, Calif. (natural causes). Screen, vaudeville, radio and television actor.

Appeared in: **1948** The Naked City; The Lady from Shanghai. **1949** The Life of Riley; Neptune's Daughter; It Happens Every Spring; Mr. Soft Touch. **1950** The Outriders; Cargo to Capetown; Three Secrets. **1951** The Enforcer (aka Murder, Inc.); Vengeance Valley; Inside the Walls of Folsom Prison; New Mexico; A Place in the Sun; Win, Place and Show. **1952** The Turning Point; Captain Pirate; The Savage. **1953** Man in the Dark; Ride, Vaquero!; Hot News. **1954** Crime Wave; 20,000 Leagues Under the Sea. **1955** The Big Combo; Kismet; Man With the Gun. **1956** The Steel Jungle; Slightly Scarlet; The Conqueror; The Killing; Dance With Me Henry; The Kettles in the Ozarks; Mohawk; Showdown at Abilene. **1957** Gunfight at the O.K. Corral; The Midnight Story; The Joker is Wild; Baby Face Nelson; The Lawless Eighties; Gun Battle at Monterey; Man on the Prowl. **1958** The Buccaneer; Enchanted Island; Handle With Care. **1959** Inside The Mafia. **1960** From the Terrace; Noose for a Gunman; Oklahoma Territory. **1962** It's Only Money. **1964** Blood on the Arrow; The Quick Gun. **1966** Nevada Smith. **1967** The King's Pirate. **1968** Five Card Stud. **1970** The Delta Factor.

DE COSTA, MORRIS (Morris Miller).
Born: 1890. Died: Oct. 6, 1957, Phoenixville, Pa. Screen and vaudeville actor and xylophonist. Appeared in silents.

DeCOY, ROBERT
Died: 1975. Black screen actor and writer.

Appeared in: **1964** Looking for Love.

DECTREAUX, EVELYN
Born: 1902. Died: Aug. 28, 1952, Santa Monica, Calif. Screen actress.

DEE, FREDDIE (Freddie De Piano)
Born: 1924. Died: Apr. 27, 1958, Hollywood, Calif. Screen actor.

DEED, ANDRE (Andre Chapuis aka CRETINETTI)
Born: 1884, France. Died: date unknown, France. Screen actor, singer and acrobat.

Appeared in: **1907** Boreau Demanage; Les Apprentisages de Boireau.

DEELEY, J. BERNARD "BEN"
Born: 1878. Died: Sept. 23, 1924, Hollywood, Calif. (pneumonia). Screen, stage and vaudeville actor. Divorced from actress Barbara La Marr (dec. 1925) with whom he had appeared in vaudeville.

Appeared in: **1919** Victory. **1921** Kazan; Molly O; Sowing the Wind. **1922** The Crossroads of New York. **1923** The Acquittal; Lights Out. **1924** Passions Pathway; Winner Take All; The Cycle Rider. **1925** Never the Twain Shall Meet.

DEEN, NEDRA (Elizabeth Ann Deen)
Born: Shreveport, La. Died: Dec. 29, 1975, Los Angeles, Calif. (cerebral hemorrhage). Screen, stage and television actress.

Appeared in: **1972** Conquest of the Planet of the Apes.

DEERING, JOHN
Born: 1905. Died: Jan. 28, 1959, Hollywood, Calif. (cerebral hemorrhage). Screen, radio and television actor.

Appeared in: **1932** Forgotten Commandments. **1934** Most Precious Thing in Life.

DEETER, JASPER
Born: 1895, Mechanicsburg, Pa. Died: May 31, 1972, Media, Pa. Screen, stage actor, stage director, producer and drama coach.

Appeared in: **1959** 4D Man.

DeFERAUDY, MAURICE
Born: 1859, France. Died: May 12, 1932, France. Screen and stage actor.

DeFOE, ANNETTE
Born: 1889. Died: Aug. 7, 1960, US. Screen actress.

Appeared in: **1917** Social Pirates (short). **1922** One Clear Call.

DE FOREST, HAL (Aloysius J. De Sylva)
Born: 1862. Died: Feb. 16, 1938, New York, N.Y. (heart attack). Screen, stage actor and stage director.

Appeared in: **1916** Daughter of the Gods (her only film).

DE GRASSE, JOSEPH
Born: 1873, Bathurst, New Brunswick, Canada. Died: May 25, 1940, Eagle Rock, Calif. (heart attack). Brother of actor Sam De Grasse (dec. 1953). Screen, stage actor, screenwriter, screen director and newspaperman. Entered films in 1910 as an actor.

Appeared in: **1924** So Big. **1928** The Cowboy Kid.

DE GRASSE, SAM
Born: 1875, Bathurst, New Brunswick, Canada. Died: Nov. 29, 1953, Hollywood, Calif. (heart attack). Screen actor. Brother of screen actor/director Joseph De Grasse (dec. 1940). Entered films in 1912.

Appeared in: **1916** Birth of a Nation. **1917** Wild and Wooly; Blind Husbands. **1920** The Devil's Pass Key. **1921** Courage; A Wife's Awakening; The Cheater Reformed. **1922** Robin Hood; Forsaking All Others. **1923** Circus Days; A Prince of a King; Slippy McGee; The Spoilers; Tiger Rose; The Courtship of Miles Standish; The Dancer of the Nile; In the Palace of the King. **1924** Painted People; The Virgin; Pagan Passions; A Self-Made Failure. **1925** One Year to Live; Sun-Up; Sally, Irene and Mary. **1926** Mike; Love's Blindness; The Black Pirate; Her Second Chance; Broken Hearts of Hollywood; The Eagle of the Sea. **1927** King of Kings; Captain Salvation; The Country Doctor; The Fighting Eagle; When a Man Loves; The Wreck of the Hesperus. **1928** Dog Law; The Racket; The Man Who Laughs; Honor Bound; Our Dancing Daughters; The Farmer's Daughter. **1929** Silks and Saddles; Last Performance; Wall Street. **1930** Captain of the Guard.

DeGUINGAND, PIERRE
Born: France. Died: June, 1964, France (?). Screen actor.

Appeared in: **1928** L'Equipage. **1929** The Last Flight. **1932** La Chance; Le Bal. **1938** The Call.

DeHAVEN, FLORA (Flora Parker aka MRS. CARTER DeHAVEN)

Born: 1883, Perth Amboy, N.J. Died: Sept. 9, 1950, Hollywood, Calif. Screen, stage and vaudeville actress. Divorced from actor Carter DeHaven with whom she appeared in "Mr. and Mrs. Carter DeHaven" comedy series. Mother of actress Gloria DeHaven and film director Carter DeHaven, Jr.

Appeared in: **1915** College Orphan. **1916** The Madcap; Youth of Fortune. **1919** Close to Nature; Why Divorce? **1920** Twin Beds; plus the following shorts: Beating Cheaters; Teasing the Soil; Excess Baggage; What Could be Sweeter; Hoodooed. **1921** The Girl in the Taxi; Marry the Poor Girl; My Lady Friends. **1923** A Ringer for Dad.

DeHAVEN, MRS. CARTER. *See* FLORA DeHAVEN

DEIGHTON, MARGA ANN

Died: Apr. 10, 1971. Screen actress.

Appeared in: **1960** Seven Thieves.

DE KEREKJARTO, DUCI

Born: 1901. Died: Jan. 3, 1962, Hollywood, Calif. (heart attack). Concert violinist and screen actor.

Appeared in prior to 1933: Metro Movietone short. **1951** Rich, Young, and Pretty.

DEKKER, ALBERT

Born: Dec. 20, 1904, Brooklyn, N.Y. Died: May 5, 1968, Hollywood, Calif. ("accidental death" per coroner). Screen, stage and television actor. Divorced from actress Esther Guerini. Served in California Legislature 1944 to 1946 as the Democratic Assemblyman of 57th District.

Appeared in: **1937** The Great Garrick. **1938** Marie Antoinette; The Last Warning; She Married an Artist; The Lone Wolf in Paris; Extortion. **1939** Paris Honeymoon; Never Say Die; Hotel Imperial; The Great Commandment; Beau Geste; The Man in the Iron Mask. **1940** Rangers of Fortune; Seven Sinners; Dr. Cyclops; Strange Cargo. **1941** You're the One; Blonde Inspiration; Reaching for the Sun; Buy Me That Town; Honky Tonk; Among the Living. **1942** The Lady Has Plans; Yokel Boy; The Forest Rangers; Night in New Orleans; Wake Island; Once upon a Honeymoon; Star Spangled Rhythm. **1943** The Woman of the Town; In Old Oklahoma; Buckskin Frontier; The Kansan. **1944** Experiment Perilous; The Hitler Gang (narr.). **1945** Incendiary Blonde; Salome, Where She Danced; Hold That Blonde. **1946** Suspense; The French Key; Two Years before the Mast; The Killers. **1947** California; Slave Girl; The Fabulous Texan; The Pretender; Gentleman's Agreement; Wyoming; Cass Timberlane. **1948** Fury at Furnace Creek; Lulu Belle. **1949** Bride of Vengeance; Tarzan's Magic Fountain; Search for Danger. **1950** Destination Murder; The Kid from Texas; The Furies. **1951** As Young as You Feel. **1952** Wait 'til the Sun Shines, Nellie. **1954** The Silver Chalice. **1955** East of Eden; Kiss Me Deadly; Illegal. **1957** She Devil. **1958** Machete. **1959** The Sound and the Fury; These Thousand Hills; Middle of the Night; The Wonderful Country; Suddenly, Last Summer. **1965** Daikaiju Gamera (Gammera the Invincible—US 1966). **1967** Come Spy with Me. **1969** The Wild Bunch.

DE KOCK, HUBERT

Born: 1863. Died: Nov. 25, 1941, Montrose, Calif. Screen, stage and vaudeville actor.

DE KOWA, VIKTOR (Viktor Kowarzik)

Born: Mar. 8, 1904, near Goerlitz, Germany. Died: Apr. 8, 1973, Berlin, Germany (cancer). Screen, stage actor, film, stage and television director. Married to actress Michi Tanaka. Entered films in 1931.

Appeared in: **1931** Der Wahre Jakob. **1932** Der Stolz der 3 Kompagnie. **1934** Tannenberg; Der Junge Baron Neuhaus. **1935** Lockvogel; Die Finanzen des Grossherzogs (The Grand Duke's Finances). **1936** Das Schloss im Suden; Madonna, Wo Bist Du?; Pappi; Ein Lieb Geht um die Welt. **1937** Zwei im Sonnenschein. **1938** Herzensclieb (Heart Thief); Mit Versiegelter Order (Under Sealed Orders). **1951** The Joseph Schmidt Story. **1957** Des Teufels General (The Devil's General). **1958** Ein Liebesgeschichte (A Love Story). **1959** Das Madchen Scampolo (The Girl Scampolo); Embezzled Heaven. **1964** The House in Montevideo (aka Montevideo).

DE LA CRUZ, JOE (Jose De La Cruz)

Born: 1892. Died: Dec. 14, 1961. Screen actor.

Appeared in: **1922** The Bearcat. **1924** Western Yesterdays. **1930** A Devil with Women; Call of the West; Hell's Heroes. **1932** Trailing the Killer. **1933** Law and the Lawless. **1934** Four Frightened People. **1935** Unconquered Bandit; Lawless Border. **1936** Magnificent Obsession. **1957** The Black Scorpion.

DELAMARE, GIL

Born: France. Died: June 1966, near Paris, France. Screen actor and stuntman.

Appeared in: **1955** One Step to Eternity. **1960** Amazing Mr. Callaghan. **1964** That Man from Rio. **1966** Man from Cocody; Up to His Ears.

DE LA MOTHE, LEON

Born: 1880. Died: June 12, 1943, Woodland Hills, Calif. Screen actor and film director.

Appeared in: **1919** The Red Glove (serial). **1924** The Desert Hawk. **1925** Ridin' Wild; Northern Code. **1926** Desperate Chance; Cyclone Bob. **1928** Trailin' Back; Painted Trail; Trail Riders.

DE LA MOTTE, MARGURIETE

Born: June 22, 1902, Duluth, Minn. Died: Mar. 10, 1950, San Francisco, Calif. (cerebral thrombosis). Screen actress. Entered films in 1919. Married to actor John Bowers (dec. 1936).

Appeared in: **1919** Arizona. **1920** Mark of Zorro. **1921** The Three Musketeers; The Nut; Ten Dollar Raise. **1922** The Jilt; Shadows; Shattered Idols; Fools of Fortune. **1923** Desire; The Famous Mrs. Fair; What a Wife Learned; Just Like a Woman; Richard the Lion-Hearted; Scars of Jealousy; A Man of Action; Wandering Daughters. **1924** The Beloved Brute; The Clean Heart; Behold This Woman; When a Man's a Man; Those Who Dare; East of Broadway; In Love with Love; Gerald Cranston's Lady. **1925** The People vs. Nancy Preston; Off the Highway; Cheaper to Marry; Flattery; Daughters Who Pay; Children of the Whirlwind; The Girl Who Wouldn't Work. **1926** The Unknown Soldier; Red Dice; Fifth Avenue; Hearts and Fists; The Last Frontier; Meet the Prince; Pals in Paradise. **1927** Broadway Madness; Held by the Law; Ragtime; The Kid Sister; His Final Extra. **1929** Montmartre Rose; The Iron Mask. **1930** Shadow Ranch. **1934** A Woman's Man. **1942** Reg'lar Fellers.

DE LANDA, JUAN

Born: 1894, Motrico, Spain. Died: Feb. 18, 1968, Motrico, Spain. Screen actor and opera performer.

Appeared in: **1935** Se ha Fugado un Preso. **1938** The Penitentiary. **1947** The King's Jester. **1952** Brief Rapture. **1953** Devotion. **1954** Beat the Devil.

DELANEY, CHARLES

Born: Aug. 1892, New York, N.Y. Died: Aug. 31, 1959, Hollywood, Calif. Screen, stage, vaudeville and television actor.

Appeared in: **1922** Solomon in Society. **1923** The Devil's Partner. **1924** Emblems of Love; Those Who Dance; Barbara Frietchie. **1925** Accused; Sporting Life; Enemies of Youth. **1926** College Days; The Jade Cup; The Night Watch; Flaming Fury; Satan Town; The Sky Pirate; The Silent Power. **1927** The Main Event; Frisco Sally Levy; The Thirteenth Hour; Husband Hunters; Mountains of Manhattan; Lovelorn; The Silent Avenger; The Tired Business Man. **1928** Women Who Dare; The Cohens and the Kellys in Paris; Branded Man; After the Storm; The Air Circus; Home, James; The Show Girl; Stool Pigeon; The Adventurer; Do Your Duty; The River Woman; Outcast Souls. **1929** The Faker; Hard to Get; Girl from Woolworth's; The Clean-Up; Broadway Babies. **1930** The Man Hunter; Lonesome Trail; Kathleen Mavourneen; Around the Corner; Millie; Air Police; Playthings of Hollywood; Hell Bent for Frisco. **1932** Big Timber; Hearts of Humanity; Midnight Morals. **1933** Officer 13; Elmer the Great; Corruption; The Important Witness. **1934** Fighting Trooper; Big Time or Bust. **1935** What Price Crime?; Captured in Chinatown; Trails of the Wild. **1936** The Millionaire Kid; Below the Deadline. **1937** Bank Alarm; The Gold Racket. **1941** I'll Fix That (short). **1945** Blonde Ransom. **1950** Kansas Raiders. **1952** The Half-Breed. **1953** Winning of the West. **1959** Running Target. **1960** The Beatniks.

DELANEY, JERE A.

Born: 1888. Died: Jan. 2, 1954, Forest Hills, N.Y. Screen and stage actor.

Appeared in: **1928** Lights of New York. **1929** Rubeville. **1954** On the Waterfront.

DELANEY, LEO

Born: 1885, Swanton, Vermont. Died: Feb. 4, 1920, New York, N.Y. Screen actor.

Appeared in: **1911** Vanity Fair; As You Like It; The Stumbling Block. **1912** The Awakening of Bianca; The Mills of the Gods; Old Love Letters; The Days of Terror; The Light of St. Bernard; The Unknown Violinist; None but the Brave Deserve the Fair; The Extension Table; At Scorgineses Corner; A Lively Affair; Fate's Awful Jest; Her Boy.

DELANEY, MAUREEN (aka MAUREEN DELANY)

Born: 1888, Kilkenny, Ireland. Died: Mar. 27, 1961, London, England. Stage and screen actress.

Appeared in: **1947** Odd Man Out; Captain Boycott; Under Capricorn. **1948** Another Shore. **1952** The Holly and the Ivy (US 1953). **1956** The Long Arm (aka The Third Key—US 1957); Jacqueline. **1957** The Rising of the Moon; The Story of Esther Costello (aka Golden Virgin—US); The Scamp. **1958** Tread Softly Stranger (US 1959). **1959** The Doctor's Dilemma.

DE LANGE, EDDIE

Born: 1904, Long Island City, N.Y. Died: July 16, 1949, Hollywood, Calif.

Orchestra leader, screen actor, stuntman, and composer. Stunted for Reginald Denny whom he resembled.

Appeared in: **1930** Half Shot at Sunrise

DELANO, GWEN
Born: 1882. Died: Nov. 20, 1954, Hollywood, Calif. Screen, stage, radio and television actress. Appeared in silents.

DE LA VEGA, ALFREDO GOMEZ
Born: 1897, Mexico. Died: Jan. 15, 1958, Mexico City, Mexico. Stage and screen actor.

DE LAY, MEL
Born: 1900. Died: May 3, 1947, Saugus, Calif. (heart attack—collapsed on location). Screen actor and film director. Entered films as an actor in 1923.

DE LEON, ARISTIDES
Born: 1904. Died: July 23, 1954, New York, N.Y. Screen, stage, radio and television actor.

DeLEON, RAOUL
Born: June 19, 1905, New York, N.Y. Died: Jan. 6, 1972, Los Angeles, Calif. (heart disease). Screen actor.

Appeared in: **1960** The Third Voice. **1962** Advise and Consent. **1964** The Pleasure Seekers.

DELEVANTI, CYRIL
Born: 1887, England. Died: Dec. 13, 1975, Hollywood, Calif. (lung cancer). Screen, stage and television actor.

Appeared in: **1931** Devotion. **1942** Smilin' Jack (serial); Night Monster. **1944** The Invisible Man's Revenge. **1945** Jade Mask; The Phantom of 42nd Street; Captain Tugboat Annie. **1946** The Shadow Returns; I'll Be Yours. **1951** David and Bathsheba. **1952** The Voice of Merrill. **1955** Land of the Pharaohs. **1963** Bye Bye Birdie. **1964** Mary Poppins; Dead Ringer; Night of the Iguana. **1965** The Greatest Story Ever Told. **1967** Counterpoint; Oh Dad, Poor Dad, Mamma's Hung You in the Closet and I'm Feelin' So Sad. **1968** The Killing of Sister George. **1971** Bedknobs and Broomsticks.

DELGADO, MARIA
Born: 1906. Died: June 24, 1969, Hollywood, Calif. Screen actress. Mother of actress Rosita Delva. Entered films approximately 1932.

Appeared in: **1956** Around the World in 80 Days.

DELGADO, ROGER
Born: 1920. Died: June 19, 1973, Turkey (auto accident). Screen, stage and television actor.

Appeared in: **1953** Star. **1955** Third Party Risk (aka Deadly Game—US). **1956** Storm over the Nile; Battle of the River Plate (aka Pursuit of the Graf Spee—US 1957). **1957** Stowaway Girl; Man in the Shadow; Manuela. **1959** First Man into Space; Sea Fury. **1960** The Stranglers of Bombay. **1961** The Terror of the Tongs; The Singer Not the Song (US 1962). **1962** The Road to Hong Kong; In Search of the Castaways. **1963** The Mind Benders; The Running Man. **1964** Hot Enough for June (aka Agent 8 3/4—US 1965). **1965** Masquerade. **1966** Khartoum. **1967** The Mummy's Shroud. **1969** The Assassination Bureau. **1970** Underground.

DELIGHT, JUNE
Born: 1898, Rochester, N.Y. Died: Oct. 3, 1975, Carmel, Calif. Screen, stage, vaudeville actress and dancer.

Appeared in: **1920** Huckleberry Finn. **1923** The Ten Commandments.

DE LIGUORO, RINA
Born: 1893, Italy. Died: Apr. 1966, Rome, Italy. Screen actress.

Appeared in: **1923** Messalina. **1928** The Mystic Mirror. **1929** Loves of Casanova. **1930** Romance. **1963** The Leopard.

DELINSKY, VICTOR A.
Born: 1883. Died: May 8, 1951, Hollywood, Calif. (injuries from auto accident). Screen actor and stand-in for Adolphe Menjou.

Appeared in: **1927** King of Kings

DELL, DOROTHY (Dorothy Goff)
Born: Jan. 30, 1915, Hattiesburg, Miss. Died: June 8, 1934, Pasadena, Calif. (auto accident). Screen and stage actress.

Appeared in: **1934** Wharf Angel; Little Miss Marker; Shoot the Works.

DEL MAR, CLAIRE (Clare Eloise Mohr)
Born: 1901. Died: Jan. 10, 1959, Carmel, Calif. (murdered). Screen actress.

Appeared in: **1921** The Four Horsemen of the Apocalypse. **1927** The Jazz Singer. **1928** The Wedding March.

DELMAR, EDDIE (Robert Frandsen)
Born: 1886. Died: Mar. 2, 1944, Hollywood, Calif. Screen actor.

DELMONTE, JACK
Born: 1889. Died: June 8, 1973, New York, N.Y. Screen, stage and television actor.

DELPHIN (Jules Sirveaux)
Born: 1882, France. Died: 1938, France. Dwarf screen and stage actor.

Appeared in: **1933** Zero de Conduite. **1935** La Kermesse Heroique.

DEL VAL, JEAN (Jean Gauthier)
Born: 1892, France. Died: Mar. 13, 1975, Pacific Palisades, Calif. (heart attack). Screen and television actor.

Appeared in: **1924** A Sainted Devil. **1925** Fifty-Fifty; The Iron Man; A Man of Iron. **1927** Back to Liberty. **1930** Sea Legs. **1931** Women Men Marry; The Magnificent Lie. **1932** The Passionate Plumber. **1938** Blockheads. **1939** The Flying Deuces. **1940** Mystery Sea Raider; Arise, My Love; Drums of the Desert. **1941** Outlaws of the Desert. **1942** Secret Agent of Japan; The Pied Piper. **1943** For Whom the Bell Tolls; Paris After Dark; Mission to Moscow; Wintertime; The Song of Bernadette. **1944** Tampico. **1945** The Spider; Molly and Me. **1946** So Dark the Night. **1947** The Crime Doctor's Gamble; The Return of Monte Cristo. **1949** The Secret of St. Ives. **1950** Last of the Buccaneers; Under My Skin. **1953** The Hitch-Hiker; Little Boy Lost; Gentlemen Prefer Blonds. **1955** Pirates of Tripoli; Duel on the Mississippi. **1957** Funny Face; The Sad Sack. **1960** Can-Can. **1961** The Devil at 4 O'Clock. **1966** Fantastic Voyage.

DEL VALLE, LUIS COTTO. *See* LUIS COTTO DEL VALLE

DeMAIN, GORDON (aka GORDON D. WOOD)
Born: 1897. Died: Mar. 5, 1967. Screen actor.

Appeared in: **1929** The Marriage Playground; Why Leave Home? **1930** Headin' North; Men are Like That; Young Eagles. **1931** Rider of the Plains; Ridin' Fool; Rose of the Rio Grande; Son of the Plains; Ships of Hate. **1932** No Living Witness; Heart Punch; Honor of the Mounted; Galloping Thru; Two-Fisted Justice; Single-Handed Sanders. **1933** Cowboy Counsellor; Western Code; Behind Jury Doors; High Gear; Dude Bandit; Fighting Texans; Devil's Mate; The Fugitive; Rainbow Ranch; Lucky Larrigan; Return of Casey Jones. **1934** Beggars in Ermine; Mystery Liner; Lucky Texan. **1935** Port of Lost Dreams; Behind the Evidence; Lawless Frontier. **1941** International Lady; Thundering Hoofs.

DE MARCO, TONY
Born: 1898, Buffalo, N.Y. Died: Nov. 14, 1965, Palm Beach, Fla. (cerebral hemorrhage). Screen actor and dancer.

Appeared in: **1938** The Shining Hour. **1943** The Gang's All Here. **1944** Greenwich Village.

DEMAREST, RUBIN
Born: 1886. Died: Sept. 20, 1962, Hollywood, Calif. (cerebral hemorrhage). Screen and television actor. Brother of screen actor William Demarest.

Appeared in: **1939** The Gracie Allen Murder Case. **1941** A Girl, a Guy and a Gob.

DE MARNEY, TERRENCE
Born: March 1, 1909. Died: May 25, 1971, London, England (accidental subway fall). Screen, stage, radio, television actor and stage director. Brother of actor Derrick DeMarney. Married to Diana Hope Dunbar and later to actress Beryl Measor.

Appeared in: **1935** Immortal Gentleman; The Mystery of the Mary Celeste (aka Phantom Ships—US 1937). **1936** Born that Way. **1937** The House of Silence. **1939** I Killed the Count (aka Who is Guilty?—US 1940). **1947** Duel Alibi. **1949** No Way Back. **1954** The Silver Chalice. **1955** Desert Sands; Target Zero. **1956** 23 Paces to Baker Street; Pharaoh's Curse. **1957** My Gun is Quick. **1959** The Wreck of the Mary Deare. **1960** The Secret of the Purple Reef. **1961** On the Double. **1962** Confessions of an Opium Eater. **1965** Monster of Terror (aka Die, Monster, Die—US). **1966** Death is a Woman (aka Love is a Woman—US 1967); The Hand of Night (US 1968). **1968** Separation; The Strange Affair; All Neat in Black Stockings.

DE MILLE, CECIL B.
Born: Aug. 12, 1881, Ashfield, Mass. Died: Jan. 21, 1959, Los Angeles, Calif. (heart disease). Film producer, director, screen, stage, radio actor and playwright. Brother of film director/producer William C. De Mille (dec. 1955). Married to actress Constance Adams (dec. 1960).

Appeared in: **1925** Hollywood. **1930** Free and Easy. **1931** The Squaw Man. **1942** Star Spangled Rhythm. **1947** Variety Girl. **1949** History Brought to Life (short—narrator). **1950** Sunset Boulevard.

DE MILLE, WILLIAM C.

Born: July 25, 1878, Washington, D.C. Died: Mar. 8, 1955, Playa Del Rey, Calif. Playwright, screenwriter, film producer, director and one-time screen actor. Brother of film director/producer Cecil B. De Mille (dec. 1959).

DeMOTT, JOHN A.

Born: 1912. Died: Mar. 19, 1975, San Diego, Calif. (heart failure). Screen actor and television producer. One of the original members of "Our Gang" comedies.

DEMPSEY, CLIFFORD

Born: 1865. Died: Sept. 4, 1938, Atlantic Highlands, N.J. Stage and screen actor.

Appeared in: **1929** Salute; The Ghost Talks; Knights Out (short); Happy Days; The Valiant. **1930** Only Saps Work; Soup to Nuts. **1931** Too Many Cooks; Everything's Rosie. **1932** Guilty as Hell.

DEMPSEY, THOMAS

Born: 1862. Died: Oct. 7, 1947, Hollywood, Calif. Screen, stage and vaudeville actor. Entered films during early 1920s and played for a number of years in Sennett comedies.

Appeared in: **1927** The Bush Leaguer. **1930** Goodbye Legs (short). **1932** A Fool About Women (short). **1934** Elmer and Elsie. **1936** Share the Wealth (short); Peppery Salt (short). **1937** Stuck in the Sticks (short). **1939** Maid to Order (short). **1940** Trailer Tragedy (short).

DENNIS, CRYSTAL

Born: 1893. Died: Dec. 16, 1973. Screen actress.

DENNIS, RUSSELL

Born: 1916. Died: May 29, 1964, N.Y. (heart attack). Screen actor and physician.

Appeared in: **1951** Bright Victory.

DENNISTON, REYNOLDS

Born: 1881, Dunedin, New Zealand. Died: 1943, New York, N.Y. Stage and screen actor.

Appeared in: **1936** Love Letters of a Star.

DENNY, REGINALD (Reginald Leigh Daymore)

Born: Nov. 20, 1891, Richmond, Surrey, England. Died: June 16, 1967, Surrey, England (stroke). Screen, stage actor and screenwriter. Entered films in England in 1914. Starred in 24 "Leather Pusher" series (shorts) from 1922 to 1924.

Appeared in: **1920** 49 East. **1921** Footlights; Disraeli; The Iron Trail; Tropical Love; Paying the Piper; The Prince of Possession. **1922** The Kentucky Derby; Sherlock Holmes; plus the following "Leather Pusher" shorts: Let's Go; Round Two; Payment Through the Nose; A Fool and His Money; The Taming of the Shrew; Whipsawed; plus the following "New Leather Pusher" series shorts: Young King Cole; He Raised Kane; Chichasha Bone Crusher; When Kane Met Abel. **1923** The Abysmal Brute; The Thrill Chaser; plus the following "New Leather Pusher" series shorts: Strike Father, Strike Son; Joan of Newark; The Wandering Two; The Widower's Mite; Don Coyote; Something for Nothing; Columbia the Gem and the Ocean; Barnaby's Grudge; That Kid from Madrid; He Loops to Conquer. **1924** Sporting Youth; Captain Fearless; The Fast Worker; The Reckless Age; Oh, Doctor!; plus the following "New Leather Pusher" series shorts: Girls Will be Girls; A Tough Tenderfoot; Swing Bad the Sailor; Big Boy Blue. **1925** Where Was I?; California Straight Ahead; I'll Show You the Town; Skinner's Dress Suit. **1926** Take It from Me; Rolling Home; What Happened to Jones? **1927** The Cheerful Fraud; On Your Toes; Out All Night; Fast and Furious; Jaws of Steel. **1928** The Night Bird; That's My Daddy; Good Morning, Judge. **1929** Clear the Decks; His Lucky Day; Red Hot Speed. **1930** Madam Satan; What a Man!; Embarrassing Moments; Those Three French Girls; Oh, for a Man!; One Hysterical Night; A Lady's Morals. **1931** Private Lives; Kiki; Parlor, Bedroom and Bath; Stepping Out. **1932** Strange Justice. **1933** The Iron Master; The Barbarian; Only Yesterday; The Big Bluff. **1934** Fog; Of Human Bondage; The Richest Girl in the World; The World Moves On; Dancing Man; One More River; We're Rich Again; The Lost Patrol; The Little Minister. **1935** Lottery Lover; No More Ladies; Vagabond Lady; Anna Karenina; Here's to Romance; Midnight Phantom; Remember Last Night?; The Lady in Scarlet. **1936** The Rest Cure; The Preview Murder Mystery; Romeo and Juliet; It Couldn't Have Happened; Two in a Crowd; More Than a Secretary; Penthouse Party. **1937** Join the Marines; Bulldog Drummond Escapes; The Great Gambini; Let's Get Married; Bulldog Drummond Comes Back; Bulldog Drummond's Revenge; Beg, Borrow or Steal; Women of Glamour; Jungle Menace (serial). **1938** Bulldog Drummond's Peril; Bulldog Drummond in Africa; Blockade; Four Men and a Prayer; Everybody's Baby. **1939** Bulldog Drummond's Bride; Bulldog Drummond's Secret Police; Arrest Bulldog Drummond. **1940** Spring Parade; Seven Sinners; Rebecca. **1941** One Night in Lisbon; Appointment for Love; International Squadron. **1942** Eyes in the Night; Sherlock Holmes and the Voice of Terror; Thunder Birds; Over My Dead Body; Captains of the Clouds. **1943** The Ghost Ship; The Crime Doctor's Strangest Case. **1944** Song of the Open Road. **1945** Love Letters. **1946** Tangier; The Locket. **1947** Escape Me Never; My Favorite Brunette;

The Macomber Affair; Christmas Eve; The Secret Life of Walter Mitty. **1948** Mr. Blandings Builds His Dream House. **1950** The Iroquois Trail. **1953** Abbott and Costello Meet Dr. Jekyll and Mr. Hyde; Fort Vengeance; Hindu (aka Sadaka—US 1955). **1954** Bengal Brigade; The Snow Creature; World for Ransom. **1955** Escape to Burma. **1956** Around the World in 80 Days. **1957** Street of Sinners. **1959** Fort Vengeance. **1964** Advance to the Rear. **1965** Cat Ballou. **1966** Assault on a Queen; Batman.

DENT, VERNON

Born: 1900, San Jose, Calif. Died: Nov. 5, 1963, Hollywood, Calif. Screen actor and screenwriter. Appeared in early Mann comedies, Mack Sennett and educational comedies.

Appeared in: **1921** Hail the Woman. **1923** The Extra Girl; Soul of the Beast. **1925** Remember When? **1926** A Dead Dog's Tale; Flirty Four-Flushers. **1927** His First Flame. **1928** Golf Widows. **1929** Ticklish Business; The Talkies; plus the following shorts: The Old Barn; Girl Crazy; The Barber's Daughter. **1930** Johnny's Week End; Midnight Daddies; and the following shorts: Goodbye Legs; Take Your Medicine. **1931** Passport to Paradise; Fainting Lover (short); The Cannonball (short). **1932** Million Dollar Legs; plus the following shorts: The Big Flash; The Iceman's Ball; Hollywood Handicap; For the Love of Ludwig; Sunkissed Sweeties; A Fool About Women. **1933** The following shorts: Tired Feet; The Hitch Hiker; Knight Duty; Tied for Life; Marriage Humor; Hooks and Jabs; Roaming Romeo; Artist's Muddles; Three Little Swigs; On Ice. **1934** You're Telling Me; plus the following shorts: Good Morning, Eve; Circus Hoodoo; Petting Preferred. **1935** I Don't Remember (short); Tars and Stripes (short). **1936** The following shorts: Slippery Silks; Share the Wealth; Half-Shot Shooters. **1937** The Awful Truth; Easy Living; The Shadow; plus the following shorts: Dizzy Doctors; Back to the Woods; Calling All Doctors; Gracie at the Bat. **1938** Thanks for the Memory; Reformatory; plus the following shorts: Sue My Lawyer; Wee Wee, Monsieur; Tassels in the Air; Mutts to You; Time Out For Trouble; The Mind Needer; Many Sappy Returns; A Doggone Mixup; The Old Raid Mule; Ankles Away; Home on the Rage. **1939** Beasts of Berlin; plus the following shorts: Teacher's Pest; Three Little Sew and Sews; A-Ducking They Did Go; Yes, We Have No Bonanza. **1940** The following shorts: From Nurse to Worse; Nutty But Nice; No Census, No Feeling; How High Is Up; The Heckler; His Bridal Fright; Cold Turkey; Mr. Clyde Goes to Broadway; A Bundle of Bliss; Pardon My Berth Marks. **1941** The following shorts: In the Sweet Pie and Pie; So Long, Mr. Chumps; Dutiful But Dumb; I'll Never Heil Again; An Ache in Every Stake; Ring and the Bell; Yankee Doodle Andy; Lovable Trouble; So You Won't Squawk. **1942** House of Errors; plus the following shorts: Loco Boy Makes Good; Cactus Makes Perfect; Even As I.O.U.; Tireman, Spare My Tires; Sappy Birthday; All Work and No Pay; Sappy Pappy; Matri-Phony. **1943** The following shorts: Blitz on the Fritz; Back from the Front; A Maid Made Mad; His Tale is Told; They Stooge to Conga; Higher Than a Kite. **1944** The following shorts: Crash Goes the Hash; Busy Buddies; Idle Roomers; No Dough, Boys; To Heir is Human; Defective Detectives; Snooper Service. **1945** Rockin' in the Rockies; plus the following shorts: Three Pests in a Mess; Booby Dupes; Idiots Deluxe. **1946** The following shorts: A Bird in the Head; Beer Barrel Polecats; The Blonde Stayed On. **1947** The following shorts: Two Jills and a Jack; Half-Wits Holiday; Out West. **1948** The following shorts: Squareheads of the Round Table; Heavenly Daze; Mummu's Dummies; Eight-Ball Andy; Fiddlers Three. **1949** Make Believe Ballroom; plus the following shorts: Malice in the Palace; Hocus Pocus; Fuelin' Around. **1950** Punchy Cowpunchers (short); Studio Stoops (short). **1951** Bonanza Town; plus the following shorts: The Tooth Will Out; Three Arabian Nuts; The Pest Man Wins; Scrambled Brains. **1952** The following shorts: A Missed Fortune; Listen Judge; Gents in a Jam. **1953** Booty and the Beast (short); Rip Sew and Stitch (short). **1954** Musty Musketeers (short); Pal and Gals (short). **1955** Bedlam in Paradise (short). **1956** Hot Stuff (short); Andy Goes Wild (short). **1957** Gun A-Poppin (short). **1960** When Comedy Was King (documentary). **1963** Thirty Years of Fun (documentary).

DENTON, CRAHAN

Born: 1914. Died: Dec. 4, 1966, Piedmont, Calif. (heart attack). Screen, stage and television actor.

Appeared in: **1959** Great St. Louis Robbery. **1961** The Parent Trap; The Young One. **1962** To Kill a Mockingbird; Birdman of Alcatraz. **1963** Captain Newman, M.D.; Hud. **1965** Bus Riley's Back in Town.

DENTON, GEORGE

Born: 1865. Died: Mar. 18, 1918, New York, N.Y. (accidental asphyxiation). Stage and screen actor.

DePARIS, WILBUR

Born: 1901, Indiana. Died: Jan. 3, 1973, New York, N.Y. Bandleader, trombonist, screen and television actor.

Appeared in: **1958** Windjammer (with his New Orleans Jazz Band).

DEPP, HARRY

Born: 1886. Died: Mar. 31, 1957, Hollywood, Calif. Screen actor.

Appeared in: **1916** Honest Thieves; A Male Governess; The Haunted House. **1917** Her Candy Kid; The Book Worm Turns; Her Birthday Knight; Skirt

Strategy; The Girl and the Ring; A Janitor's Vengeance; Her Widow's Might; Half and Half; A Dark Room Secret; A Love Case. **1922** Quincy Adams Sawyer. **1923** His Last Race; Nobody's Money. **1924** Inez from Hollywood. **1926** When the Wife's Away. **1937** Bill Cracks Down; Swing It, Professor. **1938** Pals of the Saddle. **1941** Blues in the Night. **1942** Priorities on Parade; The Magnificent Dope; Heart of the Rio Grande. **1944** Black Magic.

DEPPE, HANS
Born: 1898, Berlin, Germany. Died: Sept. 23, 1969, West Berlin, Germany (diabetes). Screen, stage, television actor and film director.

Appeared in: **1933** Ein Tuer geht Auf. **1934** Der Stern von Valencia. **1935** Der Schimmelreiter (The Rider of the White Horse). **1952** The Berliner.

DE PUTTI, LYA
Born: 1901, Budapest, Hungary. Died: Nov. 27, 1931, New York, N.Y. (pneumonia after operation). Screen, stage, and vaudeville actor. Entered films in 1921 and appeared in German, British and U.S. films.

Appeared in: **1921** The Hidden Tombstone. **1925** The Phantom; Variety. **1926** God Gave Me Twenty Cents; The Sorrows of Satan; The Prince of Tempters. **1927** The Heart Thief. **1928** Midnight Rose; Jealousy: Buck Privates; The Scarlet Lady. **1929** The Informer.

DER ABRAHAMIAN, AROUSIAK. *See* AROUSIAK ABRAHAMIAN

DeRAVENNE, CAROLINE MARIE
Born: 1883. Died: May 8, 1962. Screen actress.

DE RAVENNE, RAYMOND
Born: 1904. Died: Oct. 14, 1950, Hollywood, Calif. (heart attack). Screen actor.

Appeared in: **1938** Romance in the Dark.

DERBA, MIMI (Hermina Perez de Leon)
Born: 1894, Mexico. Died: July 1953, Mexico City, Mexico (lung trouble). Stage and screen actress.

Appeared in: **1935** Martin Garatuza. **1936** So Juana Ines de La Cruz. **1938** Abnegacion. **1945** Flor Sylvestre.

DEREN, MAYA
Born: 1908, Russia. Died: 1961. Screen actress, film director, dancer and author.

Appeared in: **1943** Meshes of the Afternoon. **1944** At Land. **1961** Maeva (narrator)

DE ROCHE, CHARLES
Born: 1880, France. Died: Feb. 2, 1952, Paris, France. Screen, stage actor and stage producer.

Appeared in: **1923** Hollywood; The Law of the Lawless; The Ten Commandments; The Cheat; The Marriage Maker. **1924** Love and Glory; Shadows of Paris; The White Moth. **1925** Madame Sans Gene.

DE ROSAS, ENRIQUE
Born: Argentina. Died: Jan. 20, 1948, near Buenos Aires, Argentina. Screen, stage, radio actor and circus performer.

Appeared in: **1937** Sandflow.

DERWENT, CLARENCE
Born: March 23, 1884, London, England. Died: Aug. 6, 1959, New York, N.Y. Screen, stage actor and film director.

Appeared in: **1918** Men Who Have Made Love to Me. **1931** The Night Angel. **1939** Stanley and Livingston; The Story of Vernon and Irene Castle. **1940** British Intelligence. **1958** Uncle Vanya (stage and film versions).

DeSAI, V. H.
Born: India. Died: c. 1950, India? Screen actor.

Appeared in: **1943** Gyandev of India.

DES AUTELS, VAN
Born: 1911. Died: Sept. 2, 1968, Los Angeles, Calif. Screen, radio and television actor.

Appeared in: **1953** The Robe; How to Marry a Millionaire. **1955** Inside Detroit; The Crooked Web.

DE SEGUROLA, ANDREAS (Count Andreas Perello de Segurola)
Born: 1875, Madrid, Spain. Died: Jan. 23, 1953, Barcelona, Spain. Screen, stage actor and opera performer.

Appeared in: **1927** The Love of Sunya. **1928** The Red Dance; Glorious Betsy; My Man; Bringing up Father; The Cardboard Lover. **1929** Behind Closed Doors; Careers; General Crack. **1930** Mamba; The Man from Blankleys; Son O' My Heart. **1933** Cascarrabia; Su Eltimo Amor; El Principe Gondolero. **1934**
La Ciudad de Carton; Granaderos del Amore; Dos Mas Uno Dos; One Night of Love; We're Rich Again. **1935** Public Opinion.

DESFIS, ANGELO
Born: 1888. Died: July 28, 1950, Hollywood, Calif. Screen and stage actor. Appeared in silents and talkies.

DESHON, FLORENCE
Born: 1894, Tacoma, Wash. Died: Feb. 4, 1922, New York, N.Y. (accidental gas asphyxiation). Stage and screen actress.

Appeared in: **1917** The Auction Block. **1918** Clutch of Circumstance; Love Watches; The Other Man; The Desired Woman; A Bachelor's Children; The Golden Goal; One Thousand Dollars; Love Watches. **1919** The Cambric Mask. **1920** Dangerous Days; Duds; Dollars and Sense; Deep Waters; Twins of Suffering Creek; The Loves of Letty; The Cup of Fury. **1921** The Roof Tree.

DE SICA, VITTORIO
Born: July 7, 1901, Sora, Italy. Died: Nov. 13, 1974, Paris, France. Screen, stage, television actor, film director, producer, screenwriter and singer. Divorced from actress Giuditta Rissoni. Married to actress Maria Mercader.

Appeared in: **1932** Gli Uomini che Mascalzoni! (What Rascals Men Are!—film debut); Due Cuori Felici (Two Happy Hearts). **1933** Passa L'Amore. **1935** Lohengrin; Non Ti Conosco Piu; Dario un Milione (I'll Give a Million). **1936** Ma Non e una Cosa Seria; L'Uomo Che Sorride; Questi Ragazzi; Amo Te Sola; Tempo Massimo; La Canzione del Sole. **1937** Il Signor Max; Napoli di Altri Tempi; Le Dame e i Cavalieri. **1938** Hamo Rapito un Uoma (They Have Kidnapped a Man); Orologio a Cucu (The Cuckoo Clock); Partire (Departure); Giochi di Societa (Society Games). **1940** Due Dozzine di Rose Scarlette (Two Dozen Red Roses); La Mazurka de Papa; Le Due Madri (The Two Mothers). **1941** Manon Lescaut; Grandi Magazzini. **1942** Un Garibaldino in Convento. **1948** Bicycle Thieves. **1949** Lost in the Dark. **1950** Peddlin' in Society; Escape into Dreams; Heart and Soul; My Widow and I. **1951** Doctor, Beware; Miracolo a Milano (Miracle in Milan); Altri Tempi (Times Gone By—US 1953). **1952** Tomorrow is Too Late. **1954** Pare, Amore e Gelosia (Bread, Love and Jealousy); The Earrings of Madame De; Hello Elephant; Pane, Amore e Fantasia (Bread, Love and Dreams). **1955** Gran Varieta; The Bed (aka The Divorce); Frisky; Too Bad She's Bad. **1957** Gold of Naples (aka The Gambler); The Miller's Beautiful Wife; Scandal in Sorrento; It Happened in the Park; A Farewell to Arms; The Monte Carlo Story; Les Week-ends de Neron (aka Nero's Mistress—US 1962 and Nero's Big Weekend); Toto; Vittorio de la Dottoressa (aka The Lady Doctor—US 1963). **1958** A Plea for Passion (aka The Bigamist). **1959** Il Moralista (The Moralist—US 1964); Patri e Figli (Fathers and Sons and aka The Tailor's Maid); Anatomy of Love; Souvenir D'Italie (Souvenir of Italy and aka It Happened in Rome); Il Generale Della Rovere (General Della Rovere); Ballerina e Buon Dio (aka Angel in a Taxi—US 1963); Il Nemico di Mia Moglie (My Wife's Enemy—US 1967). **1960** Always Victorious; It Started in Naples; The Angel Wore Red; Fast and Sexy; Vacanzie a Izchia (Holiday Island); The Millionairess (US 1961). **1961** The Wonders of Aladdin. **1962** La Fayette (Lafayette—US 1963); Eva (US 1963). **1965** The Amorous Adventures of Moll Flanders. **1966** After the Fox. **1968** The Biggest Bundle of Them All; The Shoes of the Fisherman. **1969** If It's Tuesday, This Must be Belgium. **1974** Dracula.

DE SILVA, FRANK
Born: 1890, India. Died: Mar. 20, 1968, New York, N.Y. (throat cancer). Screen, stage and television actor.

DESLYS, GABY
Born: 1884, Marseilles, France. Died: Feb. 11, 1920, Paris, France (cancer of the throat). Stage and screen actor.

Appeared in: Rosy Rapture **1915** Her Triumph. **1918** Infatuation.

DESMOND, ETHEL
Born: 1874. Died: Feb. 5, 1949, San Bernardino, Calif. Screen, stage and vaudeville actress.

DESMOND, LUCILLE
Born: 1894. Died: Nov. 20, 1936, Los Angeles, Calif. Screen actress.

DESMOND, WILLIAM
Born: Jan. 1878, Dublin, Ireland. Died: Nov. 3, 1949, Los Angeles, Calif. (heart attack). Screen, stage and vaudeville actor. Married to actress Mary McIvor (dec. 1941).

Appeared in: **1915** Peggy (film debut). **1916** Not My Sister; The Captive God. **1917** Paws of the Bear. **1918** An Honest Man; The Sudden Gentleman; Society for Sale; The Pretender; Deuce Duncan. **1920** The Prince and Betty; The Man from Make Believe; Twin Beds. **1921** The Child Thou Gavest Me; Dangerous Toys; Women Men Love; Don't Leave Your Husband; The Parish Priest; Fighting Mad. **1922** Perils of the Yukon; Night Life in Hollywood. **1923** The Extra Girl; McGuire of the Mounted; Shadows of the North; Beast of Paradise (serial); The Phantom Fortune (serial); Around the World in 18 Days (serial). **1924** The Breathless Moment; The Riddle Rider (serial); Big Timber; The

Sunset Trail; Measure of a Man. **1925** Barriers of the Law; Duped; Outwitted; Straight Through; The Meddler; Ace of Spades (serial); Blood and Steel; The Burning Trail; Ridin' Pretty. **1926** The Winking Idol (serial); Strings of Steel (serial). **1927** The Return of the Riddle Rider (serial); Red Clay; Tongues of Scandal. **1928** The Vanishing Rider (serial); The Mystery Rider (serial); The Devil's Trade-Mark. **1929** No Defense. **1931** Hell Bent for Frisco. **1932** Scarlet Week-End; Heroes of the West (serial). **1933** Flying Fury; Rustlers Round-Up; Laughing at Life; The Phantom of the Air (serial); Mr. Broadway; Fargo Express; Strawberry Roan. **1935** Rustlers of Red Gap; Roaring West (serial); Courage of the North; Powdersmoke Range. **1936** Arizona Days; Nevada; Song of the Saddle; Cavalry; Hollywood Boulevard; Song of the Gringo; Headin' for the Rio Grande. **1940** A Little Bit of Heaven. **1941** Shy Raiders (serial). **1945** The Naughty Nineties.

DESMONDE, JERRY
Born: July 20, 1908, Middlesbrough, England. Died: Feb. 11, 1967, London, England. Screen, stage and television actor.

Appeared in: **1946** London Town (aka My Heart Goes Crazy—US 1953). **1949** Cardboard Cavalier. **1953** Alf's Baby; Malta Story (US 1954); Trouble in Store. **1954** The Angel Who Pawned Her Harp. **1955** Man of the Moment. **1956** Ramsbottom Rides Again; Up in the World. **1957** A King in New York. **1959** Follow a Star (US 1961). **1961** Carry On Regardless (US 1963). **1962** A Kind of Loving. **1963** The Stolen Hours; A Stitch in Time (US 1967). **1964** The Beauty Jungle (aka Contest Girl—US 1966). **1965** The Early Bird.

DeSOTO, HENRY
Born: 1888. Died: Sept 9, 1963. Screen actor.

Appeared in: **1946** Somewhere in the Night; The Dark Horseman.

DE STAFINI, HELEN
Born: 1880. Died: Jan. 8, 1938, Hollywood, Calif. Screen and stage actress. Married to screen actor Joseph de Stafini.

DESTE, LULI (Luli Kollsman and Luli Hohenberg)
Born: 1902, Vienna, Austria. Died: July 7, 1951, New York, N.Y. Stage and screen actress and author.

Appeared in: **1937** Thunder over the City; Thank You, Madame. **1938** She Married an Artist. **1940** Ski Patrol; South to Karanga. **1941** The Case of the Black Parrot; Outlaws of the Desert.

DESTINN, EMMY
Born: Feb. 20, 1878, Prague, Czechoslovakia. Died: Jan. 28, 1930, Budweis, Czech. (stroke). Screen actress and opera performer.

Appeared in: **1914** The Lion's Bride.

DE TELLIER, MARIETTE
Born: 1891, France. Died: Dec. 11, 1957, Cincinnati, Ohio. Screen actress. Appeared in silents.

DEUTSCH, ERNST
Born: 1891, Germany. Died: Mar. 22, 1969, Berlin, Germany. Stage and screen actor.

Appeared in: **1939** Nurse Edith Cavell. **1940** The Man I Married. **1941** So Ends Our Night. **1950** The Third Man.

DEUTSCH, LOU
Born: 1898. Died: Oct. 11, 1968, Calif. Screen actor. Appeared mostly in westerns.

DE VALDEZ, CARLOS J.
Born: Mar. 19, 1894, Arica, Peru. Died: Oct. 30, 1939, Encino, Calif. Stage and screen actor.

Appeared in: **1934** Little Man, What Now? **1935** Bonnie Scotland; Robin Hood of Eldorado. **1936** Men in Exile; The Beloved Rogue; Littlest Diplomat. **1937** Conquest; Drums of Destiny; Lancer Spy. **1938** Blockade; Romance in the Dark; Girl from Mexico; Suez; The Girl and the Gambler; The Llano Kid. **1940** British Intelligence.

DEVAULL, WILLIAM P.
Born: 1871. Died: June 4, 1945, Hollywood, Calif. Screen and vaudeville actor.

Appeared in: **1915** Birth of a Nation. **1921** Hole in the Wall. **1922** White Shoulders. **1923** Around the World in 18 Days (serial); Kentucky Days; Tea with a Kick. **1925** Lights of Old Broadway. **1927** In the First Degree.

DE VERA, CRIS (Cristobal Masilongan)
Born: 1925. Died: June 25, 1974, Manilla, Philippines (kidney ailment). Screen, stage, radio and television actor. Known as the "Man With a Thousand Voices."

Appeared in: **1950** An American Guerrilla in the Philippines.

DEVERE, ARTHUR
Born: 1883. Died: Sept. 23, 1961, Brussels, Belgium. Screen, stage and vaudeville actor.

Appeared in: **1936** La Kermesse Heroique. **1939** The End of a Day. **1945** Goupi Mains-Rouges (It Happened at the Inn). Other French films: Un de la Legion; Midnight Circuit.

DEVERE, FRANCESCA "FRISCO"
Born: 1891. Died: Sept. 11, 1952, Port Townsend, Wash. (heart attack). Stage and screen actress. Appeared in Keystone comedies and Mack Sennett productions.

DEVERE, MARGARET
Born: 1889. Died: Oct. 24, 1918, New York, N.Y. (Spanish influenza). Screen actress.

DEVEREAUX, JACK
Born: 1882. Died: Jan. 19, 1958, New York, N.Y. Screen and stage actor. Married to stage actress Louise Drew (dec. 1954). Father of actor John Drew Devereaux.

Appeared in: **1916** The Sentimental Lady. **1917** Her Father's Keeper; America—That's All. **1920** Romero's Dad. **1922** Superstition.

DEVERELL, JOHN W.
Born: May 30, 1880, England. Died: Mar. 2, 1965, Haywards Heath, England. Stage and screen actor.

Appeared in: **1930** Children of Chance. **1931** Alibi. **1932** Monte Carlo Madness. **1934** The Path of Glory. **1935** Marry the Girl; The Divine Spark.

DE VERNON, FRANK
Born: 1845. Died: Oct. 19, 1923, New York, N.Y. Screen and stage actor.

Appeared in: **1921** The Black Panther's Cub; The Man Worth While. **1923** Under the Red Robe. **1924** Cain and Mabel; Yolande.

DeVESTEL, GUY
Died: Apr. 28, 1973. Screen actor.

Appeared in: **1949** Secret of St. Ives. **1955** To Catch a Thief. **1964** Wild and Wonderful.

DEVI, PROVA
Born: India. Died: Nov. 8, 1952, India. Screen actress.

DEVINE, GEORGE
Born: Nov. 20, 1910, London, England. Died: Jan. 20, 1966, England. Screen, stage actor, stage producer and director.

Appeared in: **1939** The Silent Battle (aka Continental Express—US 1942). **1952** The Card (aka The Promoter—US). **1953** The Beggar's Opera. **1954** The Million Pound Note (aka Man With a Million—US). **1957** Time Without Pity. **1959** Look Back in Anger. **1963** Tom Jones.

DEVLIN, JOE A.
Born: 1899. Died: Oct. 1, 1973, Burbank, Calif. Screen, stage and television actor.

Appeared in: **1939** The Oklahoma Kid; Torchy Runs for Mayor; King of the Underworld; No Place to Go. **1940** A Fugitive from Justice; Half a Sinner; The Green Hornet Strikes Again (serial). **1942** The Devil with Hitler; Shepherd of the Ozarks. **1943** They Got Me Covered; The Phantom (serial); Taxi, Mister; That Nazty Nuisance; Hi Diddle Diddle. **1944** Sensations of 1945; Dixie Jamboree; Delinquent Daughters; My Buddy. **1945** Bedside Manner; Captain Eddie; The Shanghai Cobra; Brenda Starr, Reporter (serial); Abbott and Costello in Hollywood. **1946** Criminal Court; Bringing Up Father; Trouble or Nothing (short); Oh, Professor, Behave (short); San Quentin. **1947** That Way With Women; Body and Soul; Shoot to Kill. **1951** Double Dynamite (aka It's Only Money); All That I Have. **1954** Bitter Creek. **1955** Abbott and Costello Meet the Keystone Kops. **1956** Shake, Rattle and Rock. **1957** Up In Smoke. **1967** Good Times.

DEVOE, BERT
Born: 1884. Died: Jan. 17, 1930, Steelton, Pa. (cancer). Screen and vaudeville actor. Toured in vaudeville with Lew Worth. Appeared in early Mack Sennett comedies.

Appeared in: **1924** Shackles of Fear.

DEWEY, EARL S.
Born: June 2, 1881, Manhattan, Kans. Died: Feb. 5, 1950, Hollywood, Calif. Screen, stage and vaudeville actor. Married to Billie Rogers with whom he appeared in vaudeville. Appeared in "Pathe Folly" comedies, first series.

Appeared in: **1929** Fancy That (short); So This Is Marriage (short). **1940** Howards of Virginia; Arizona. **1942** I Married an Angel; This Gun for Hire; Between Us Girls. **1943** Seeing Nellie Home (short); Shadow of a Doubt. **1944** Say

Uncle (short); Adventures of Mark Twain. **1945** Rogues Gallery; Captain Eddie; George White's Scandals; Blonde Ransom. **1950** All the King's Men.

DEWEY, ELMER (aka DON DANILO)
Born: 1884. Died: Oct. 28, 1954, Hollywood, Calif. (heart attack). Screen actor.

Appeared in: **1921** Bring Him In; Girls Don't Gamble. **1922** Taking Chances. **1926** Shadows of Chinatown; The Escape. **1927** Million Dollar Mystery.

DEWHURST, WILLIAM
Born: 1888. Died: Oct. 26, 1937, London, England (heart failure). Stage and screen actor.

Appeared in: **1937** A Woman Alone; Victoria the Great; Non-Stop New York; Dark Journey; Bulldog Drummond at Bay; Dinner at the Ritz. **1938** Sailing Along. **1939** Sabotage. **1940** 21 Days Together.

DE WILDE, BRANDON (Andre Brandon de Wilde)
Born: Apr. 9, 1942, Brooklyn, N.Y. Died: July 6, 1972, Denver, Colo. (auto accident). Screen, stage and television actor. Son of actor-stage manager Frederic and actress Eugenia de Wilde.

Appeared in: **1952** The Member of the Wedding (stage and film versions—film debut). **1953** Shane. **1956** The Day They Gave Babies Away; Goodbye, My Lady. **1957** Night Passage. **1958** The Missouri Traveler. **1959** Blue Denim. **1962** All Fall Down. **1963** Hud. **1964** Those Calloways. **1965** In Harm's Way. **1967** The Trip. **1969** God Bless You, Uncle Sam. **1970** The Deserter. **1972** Wild in the Sky.

DE WOLFE, BILLY (William Andrew Jones)
Born: 1907, Wollaston, Mass. Died: Mar. 5, 1974, Los Angeles, Calif. (cancer). Screen, stage, vaudeville, television actor and dancer.

Appeared in: **1943** Dixie (film debut). **1945** Miss Susie Slagle's; Duffy's Tavern. **1946** Blue Skies; Our Hearts Were Growing Up. **1947** Dear Ruth; The Perils of Pauline; Variety Girl. **1948** Isn't It Romantic. **1949** Dear Wife. **1950** Tea for Two. **1951** Dear Brat; The Lullaby of Broadway. **1953** Call Me Madam. **1965** Billie. **1973** The World's Greatest Athlete.

DEXTER, ELLIOTT
Born: 1870, Galveston, Tex. Died: June 23, 1941, Amityville, N.Y. Screen and vaudeville actor. Divorced from actress Marie Doro (dec. 1956).

Appeared in: **1915** The Masqueraders. **1916** The Heart of Nora Flynn; The Lash; Diplomacy. **1917** A Romance of the Redwoods; Castles for Two; The Rise of Jennie Cushing. **1918** Woman and Wife. **1919** Don't Change Your Husband; For Better, For Worse; The Squaw Man; Maggie Pepper; We Can't Have Everything. **1920** Behold My Wife; Something to Think About. **1921** The Witching Hour; Forever; The Affairs of Anatol; Don't Tell Everything. **1922** Grand Larceny; Enter Madam; The Hands of Nara. **1923** Adam's Rib; Mary of the Movies; Only 38; Souls for Sale; Broadway Gold; The Common Law; Flaming Youth; An Old Sweetheart of Mine. **1924** The Fast Set; Age of Innocence; By Divine Right; For Woman's Favor; The Triflers; The Spitfire. **1925** Capital Punishment; The Verdict; Wasted Lives. **1926** Stella Maris.

DHELIA, FRANCE
Born: France. Died: May, 1964, France? Screen actress.

Appeared in: **1931** Mephisto.

DICENTA, MANUEL
Born: 1904, Spain. Died: Nov. 19, 1974, Madrid, Spain (cardiac-respiratory insufficiency). Screen, stage and television actor. Son of actress Consuelo Badillo and playwright Joaquin Dicenta.

Appeared in: **1938** Morena Clara.

DICKERSON, HENRY (Dudley Henry Dickerson)
Born: Nov. 27, 1906, Oklahoma. Died: Sept. 23, 1968, Lynwood, Calif. (cerebral thrombosis). Black screen actor.

Appeared in: **1935** The Virginia Judge. **1936** The Green Pastures. **1939** Some Like It Hot. **1941** Borrowed Hero. **1944** The Adventures of Mark Twain; Allergic to Love; Ever Since Venus. **1959** The Alligator People.

DICKEY, PAUL
Born: May 12, 1885, Chicago, Ill. Died: Jan. 8, 1933, N.Y. (heart disease). Screen, stage actor, screenwriter, playwright and stage director.

Appeared in: **1922** Robin Hood.

DICKINSON, HAL
Born: 1914. Died: Nov. 18, 1970, Santa Barbara, Calif. Screen, stage and radio actor and vocalist. Married to vocalist Paula Kelly. Founder and leader of "The Modernaires" singing group.

Appeared in: **1949** Home in San Antone. **1954** The Glenn Miller Story.

DICKINSON, HOMER
Born: 1890. Died: June 6, 1959, Hollywood, Calif. Screen, stage and vaudeville actor. Appeared in vaudeville from 1914 to 1926 with his wife, Florence Tempest and her sister in an act billed as "Sunshine and Tempest."

Appeared in: **1928** Broadway's Smart Musical Comedy Star (short).

DICKSON, DONALD
Born: 1911, Pittsburgh, Pa. Died: Sept. 20, 1972, Brooklyn, N.Y. Screen, radio actor and opera baritone.

Appeared in: **1944** Up in Arms.

DICKSON, GLORIA (Thais Dickerson)
Born: Aug. 13, 1916, Pocatello, Idaho. Died: Apr. 10, 1945, Hollywood, Calif. (asphyxiation from fire). Stage and screen actress.

Appeared in: **1936** They Won't Forget (film debut). **1938** Gold Diggers in Paris; Secrets of an Actress; Racket Busters; Heart of the North. **1939** Private Detective; No Place to Go; Cowboy Quarterback; On Your Toes; Waterfront; They Made Me a Criminal. **1940** I Want a Divorce; King of the Lumberjacks; Tear Gas Squad; This Thing Called Love. **1941** The Big Boss; Mercy Island. **1942** Affairs of Jimmy Valentine. **1943** The Crime Doctor's Strangest Case; Power of the Press; Lady of Burlesque. **1944** Crime Doctor; Rationing.

DICKSON, LYDIA
Born: 1878. Died: Apr. 2, 1928, Hollywood, Calif. Screen and stage comedienne and actress.

Appeared in: **1928** Don't Marry; Square Crooks.

DIDRICKSON, BABE (Mildred Ella Didrickson)
Born: June 16, 1914, Port Arthur, Texas. Died: Sept. 27, 1956, Galveston, Texas (cancer). Professional athlete and screen actress. Married to professional wrestler George Zaharias.

Appeared in: **1952** Pat and Mike.

DIDWAY, ERNEST
Born: 1872. Died: Jan. 3, 1939, Los Angeles, Calif. Screen and stage actor. Entered films approx. 1932.

DIE ASTA. *See* ASTA NIELSEN

DIEHL, KARL LUDWIG
Born: 1897, Germany. Died: Mar. 1958, Oberbayern, West Germany. Stage and screen actor.

Appeared in: **1931** Rosenmontag; Liebeswalzer. **1932** Koenigin der Unterwelt; Zirkus Leben. **1933** Ein Maedel der Strasse. **1934** Die Freundin Eines Grossen Mannes; Schuss in Morgengrauen; Ein Mann Will Nach Deutschland. **1935** Aschermittwoch (Ash Wednesday). **1936** Spy 77; Der Hoehere Befehl; Ein Liebesroman im Hause Hasburg; Die Ganze Welt Dreht Sich um Liebe. **1937** Ein Idealer Gatte; Episode. **1938** Seine Tochter 1st der Peter (His Daughter Is Peter); Es geht um mein Leben (My Life Is at Stake). **1939** Der Schritt vom Wege (The False Step); Ein Hoffnungsloser Fall. **1957** Des Teufeis General (The Devil's General). **1958** The Story of Vickie.

DIERKES, JOHN
Born: Feb. 10, 1908. Died: Jan. 8, 1975, Hollywood, Calif. (emphysema). Screen and television actor.

Appeared in: **1948** Macbeth. **1951** The Red Badge of Courage. **1952** Les Miserables; Plymouth Adventure. **1953** Abbott and Costello Meet Dr. Jekyll and Mr. Hyde; Shane; The Moonlighter; The Vanquished. **1954** Hell's Outpost; The Naked Jungle; Prince Valiant; The Desperado; Passion; The Raid. **1955** Betrayed Women; The Vanishing American. **1956** Jubal. **1957** Valerie; The Buckskin Lady; Daughter of Dr. Jekyll; Duel at Apache Wells. **1958** The Buccaneer; The Left-Handed Gun; Blood Arrow; The Rawhide Trail. **1959** Hanging Tree; The Oregon Trail. **1960** The Alamo. **1961** The Comancheros; One-Eyed Jacks. **1962** The Premature Burial; Convicts 4. **1963** The Haunted Palace; Johnny Cool; "X" The Man with the X-Ray Eyes. **1973** Oklahoma Crude.

DIESEL, GUSTAV
Born: 1900, Austria. Died: Mar. 20, 1948, Vienna, Austria. Stage and screen actor.

Appeared in: **1929** That Murder in Berlin: Die Drein um Edith. **1930** Die Weisse Holle von Piz Palu (The White Hell of Piz Palu); Menschen hinter Gettern. **1931** The Living Corpse; Mother Love; Comrades of 1918. **1932** Leutnant Warst Du Einst bei den Husaren; Teilnehmer Antwortet Nicht. **1934** Roman Einer Nacht. **1935** Alles um Eine Frau. **1937** Gilgi Eine Von Uns. **1938** Der Tiger von Eschnapur (The Indian Tomb). **1939** Die Gruene Hoelle (The Green Hell); Die Wiesse Majestat (The White Majesty); Amore sulle Alpi. **1940** Schatten der Vergangeheit (Shadows of the Past).

DIETERLE, WILLIAM (Wilhelm Dieterle)
Born: July 15, 1893, Rheinpfalz, Germany. Died: Dec. 9, 1972, Ottobrunn,

West Germany. Screen actor, film director and producer. Married to stage actress Charlotte Hagenbruch (dec.). Directed German and U.S. films.

Appeared in: **1921** Die Geirerwally; Fraeulein Julie; Hintertreppe. **1922** Lucrezia Borgia. **1923** Boheme; Der Zweite Schuss; Die Pagode; Die Gruene Manuela; Die Ausstreibung. **1924** Carlos und Elisabeth; Mutter und Kind; Das Wachsfigurenkabinett (Waxworks); Moderne Ehen. **1925** Der Rosa Diamond; Wetterleuchten; Lena Warnstetten; Die Blumenfrau von Potsdam-Erplatz; Sumpf und Moral; Die vom Diederrhein; Der Hahn im Korb. **1926** Die Dame aus Berlin; Die Gesunkenen; Die Foersterchristel; Familie Schimeck; Qualen der Nacht; Zopf und Schwert; Faust; Hoelle der Liebe; Die Flucht in den Zirkus; Der Jaeger von Fall; Der Pfarrer von Kirchfeld. **1927** Wie Bleibe ich Jung und Schoen; Unter Ausschluss der Oeffentlichkeit; Der Zigeunerbaron; Die vom Schicksal Verfolgten; Die Weber; Ich Habe im Mai von der Liebe Getraeumt; Am Rande der Welt; Liebesreigen; Heimweh; Petronella. **1928** Violantha; Frau Sorge; Ritter der Nacht. **1930** Daemon des Meeres; Der Tanz Geht Weiter (Those Who Dance).

DiGAETANO, ADAM

Born: 1907. Died: Apr. 30, 1966, Hollywood, Calif. (coronary ailment). Screen actor and dancer. Married to actress Jayne DiGaetano with whom he appeared as part of "Jayne and Adam DiGaetano" dance team.

Appeared in: **1946** Night and Day.

DIGGES, DUDLEY

Born: 1879, Dublin, Ireland. Died: Oct. 24, 1947, New York, N.Y. (stroke). Screen, stage actor and screen dialogue director.

Appeared in: **1929** Condemned. **1930** Outward Bound. **1931** Upper Underworld; The Maltese Falcon; The Ruling Voice; Alexander Hamilton; Devotion; Honorable Mr. Wong. **1932** The Hatchet Man; The Strange Case of Clara Deane; Roar of the Dragon; The First Year; Tess of the Storm Country. **1933** The King's Vacation; The Mayor of Hell; Silk Express; The Narrow Corner; Emperor Jones; Before Dawn; The Invisible Man. **1934** Fury of the Jungle; Caravan; The World Moves On; Massacre; What Every Woman Knows. **1935** I Am a Thief; A Notorious Gentleman; Mutiny on the Bounty; China Seas; The Bishop Misbehaves. **1936** Three Live Ghosts; The Voice of Bugle Ann; The Unguarded Hour; The General Died at Dawn; Valiant Is the Word for Carrie. **1937** Love Is News. **1939** The Light That Failed. **1940** The Fight for Life; Raffles. **1942** Son of Fury. **1946** The Searching Wind.

DI GOLCONDA, LIGIA

Born: 1884, Mexico. Died: 1942, Mexico City, Mexico. Mexican screen actor.

DILL, MAX M.

Born: 1878. Died: Nov. 21, 1949, San Francisco, Calif. Screen, stage and vaudeville actor. Was partner with Clarence Kolb (dec. 1964) in vaudeville team billed as "Kolb and Dill."

The team appeared in: **1916** a series of comedies. **1917** Glory; Mutual Star; Beloved Rogues.

DILLARD, BURT

Born: 1909. Died: June 19, 1960, Ruidoso Downs, N.M. (heart attack). Screen actor, stuntman and horse trainer.

Appeared in: **1935** Rainbow Valley. **1951** Three Desperate Men (aka Three Outlaws).

DILLIGIL, AVNI

Born: 1909, Turkey. Died: June, 1971, Ankara, Turkey (heart attack). Stage and screen actor.

DILLON, DICK (Kenneth Bowstead)

Born: 1896. Died: 1961, Boston, Mass. Screen and vaudeville actor. Known in vaudeville as part of "Dean and Dillon" act with Bob Dean.

Appeared in: **1914** Perils of Pauline (serial).

DILLON, EDWARD "EDDIE"

Born: 1880, N.Y. Died: July 11, 1933, Hollywood, Calif. (heart attack). Screen, stage actor and film director.

Appeared in: **1908** The Feud and the Turkey; The Reckoning; After Many Years; The Welcome Burglar; The Salvation Army Lass; The Fight For Freedom; The Black Viper. **1909** As the Bells Rang Out; The Sorrows of the Unfaithful; Examination Day at School; Muggsy Becomes a Hero; The Fugitive; His Sister-in-Law; The Brahma Diamond; The Little Teacher. **1910** Fisher Folks; The Oath and the Man; A Lucky Toothache; Waiter No. 5; White Roses. **1911** The Miser's Heart; Sunshine Through the Dark; Through His Wife's Picture; Priscilla's Engagement Kiss; Priscilla's April Fool Joke; The Spanish Gypsy; Priscilla and the Umbrella; Misplaced Jealousy; The Crooked Road; Dave's Love Affair; The Delayed Proposal; A Convenient Burglar. **1912** The Spirit Awakened; With a Kodak; A Voice From the Deep; Blind Love; A Limited Divorce; At the Basket Picnic; His Auto's Maiden Trip; The Leading Man; An Interrupted Elopement. **1913** Love in an Apartment Hotel; An Indian's Loyalty; Judity of Bethulia. **1915** Faithful to the Finish. **1926** The

Skyrocket. **1928** Lilac Time. **1929** The Broadway Melody; Hot for Paris. **1930** Caught Short; Whispering Whoopee (short); Fifty Million Husbands (short). **1931** Sob Sister; Thundering Tenors (short). **1932** The Trial of Vivienne Ware; Sherlock Holmes; The Nickel Nurser (short); Young Ironsides (short).

DILLON, GEORGE "TIM"

Born: 1888. Died: Oct. 22, 1965, Burbank, Calif. Screen actor.

Appeared in: **1951** The Mudlark.

DILLON, JOHN FRANCIS

Born: Nov. 28, 1884, New York, N.Y. Died: Apr. 4, 1934, Beverly Hills, Calif. (heart attack). Screen, stage actor, and film director. Divorced from stage actress Maud Housley and later married to actress Edith Hallor (dec. 1971). Father of actor Anthony Dillon and film editor John Dillon II.

Appeared in: **1914** Dough and Dynamite; The Rajah's Vow; The Key to Yesterday; The Magnet; Bess the Detectress or, The Old Mill at Midnight; Willie Walrus, Detective; Willie Walrus and the Baby; A Dramatic Mistake; The New Janitor. **1915** The Comeback; His Guiding Angel; Molly's Malady; He Fell in a Cabareta; A Desert Honeymoon; Love in a Hospital; Henry's Little Kid; Where the Deacon Lives; When His Lordship Proposed; Wanted: A Chaperone; A Maid by Proxy (aka A Maid and A Man); Almost a King; It Might Have Been Serious; Down On the Farm; Taking Her Measure; It Happened On a Friday; Kids and Corsets; His Only Pants; A Mixed-Up Elopement; All in the Same Boat; When Cupid Crossed the Bay; With Father's Help; Too Many Crooks; It Happened While He Fished; Dan Cupid, Fixer; Getting in Wrong. **1916** Paddy's Political Dream; The Lion-Hearted Chief; More Truth Than Poetry; Love, Dynamite and Baseballs. **1917** A Bachelor's Finish; Hobbled Hearts; A Berth Scandal; Her Finishing Touch; A Dishonest Burglar; Twin Troubles; Wheels and Woe; Aired in Court; His Sudden Rival; A Warm Reception; His Taking Ways; A Hotel Disgrace. **1919** Green-Eyed Johnny; A Burglar by Proxy. **1921** Cappy Ricks; The Journey's End. **1922** Without Compromise. **1923** Double Dealing. **1926** The Test of Donald Norton. **1927** Smile, Brother, Smile; Temptations of a Shopgirl.

DILLON, JOHN T. (aka JACK DILLON)

Born: 1866. Died: Dec. 29, 1937, Los Angeles, Calif. (pneumonia). Stage and screen actor. Do not confuse with screen actor and film director John Francis Dillon (dec. 1934) who also appeared in films as Jack Dillon.

Appeared in: **1910** The Iconoclast; The Oath and the Man; Examination Day at School; Waiter No. 5; His Sister-in-law; White Roses; The Fugitive; A Lucky Toothache. **1911** Priscilla's Engagement; Her Wedding Ring; Priscilla's April Fool Joke; The Spanish Gypsy; Priscilla and the Umbrella; Misplaced Jealousy; The Crooked Road; Dave's Love Affair; The Delayed Proposal; A Convenient Burglar; A Decree of Destiny; The Chief's Daughter; A Dutch Gold Mine; The Jealous Husband; Out From the Shadow. **1912** The Musketeers of Pig Alley. **1913** Love in an Apartment Hotel; The Sheriff's Baby; Her Mother's Oath; Three Friends. **1914** Birth of a Nation. **1915** The Keeper of the Flock. **1916** Seven Days. **1921** The Family Closet. **1922** For His Sake. **1924** Stepping Lively; Tiger Thompson. **1925** Midnight Molly. **1928** Bitter Sweets. **1929** In Old Arizona. **1931** The Cisco Kid.

DILLON, JOHN WEBB

Born: 1877. Died: Dec. 20, 1949, Hollywood, Calif. Screen and stage actor.

Appeared in: **1916** Romeo and Juliet; One Day. **1917** The Phantom Call. **1918** The Queen of Hearts. **1919** The Darling of Paris. **1920** Trailed by Three (serial). **1921** Jane Eyre; The Inner Chamber; The Mountain Woman; Perjury. **1922** Speed (serial); Married People; The Mohican's Daughter. **1923** The Exiles; No Mother to Guide Her. **1924** Rip Roarin' Roberts. **1925** The Air Mail; The Vanishing American; The Devil's Cargo; The Phantom Express. **1926** The Seventh Bandit; House Without a Key (serial); Snowed in (serial). **1927** A Bowery Cinderella; Wolf's Clothing. **1928** Dry Martini. **1929** The Black Book (serial). **1930** Girl of the Port; In the Next Room. **1933** The Diamond Trail. **1934** Carolina.

DILLON, JOSEPHINE

Born: 1884. Died: Nov. 10, 1971, Verdugo City, Calif. Screen actress and drama coach. Divorced from actor Clark Gable (dec. 1960).

Appeared in: **1944** The Lady and the Monster.

DILLON, MRS. STELLA

Born: 1878. Died: Apr. 28, 1934, Los Angeles, Calif. Screen actress.

DILLON, THOMAS PATRICK "TOM"

Born: 1896. Died: Sept. 15, 1962, Hollywood, Calif. Screen, stage, circus and vaudeville actor.

Appeared in: **1944** Going My Way; Whistling in Brooklyn; Thin Man Goes Home. **1945** Captain Eddie. **1946** The Virginian; Dressed to Kill; The Kid from Brooklyn; Black Beauty. **1948** My Girl Lisa. **1949** Saints and Sinners. **1950** Woman on the Run. **1956** The Search for Bridey Murphy; The Oklahoma Woman. **1963** Night Tide.

DILLON, TIM

Born: 1888. Died: Oct. 22, 1965, Burbank, Calif. Screen actor. Member of the Keystone Kops.

DILLSON, CLYDE (aka CLYDE DILSON)

Born: 1900. Died: Jan. 25, 1957. Screen actor.

Appeared in: **1929** Unmasked. **1935** Let 'Em Have It; Men Without Names; King Solomon of Broadway. **1936** You May be Next; Thirteen Hours by Air; Florida Special. **1937** There Goes My Girl; Midnight Madonna; Under Suspicion; The Duke Comes Back. **1938** Secrets of a Nurse. **1940** Andy Hardy Meets Debutante. **1941** Up in the Air; Naval Academy.

DILSON, JOHN H.

Born: 1893. Died: June 1, 1944, Ventura, Calif. Screen and stage actor.

Appeared in: **1935** Twin Triplets (short); Cheers of the Crowd; Every Night at Eight; The Girl Who Came Back. **1936** The Case of the Velvet Claws; The Public Pays (short). **1937** Easy Living. **1938** A Clean Sweep (short); Major Difficulties (short). **1939** At the Circus; Lady of the Tropics; When Tomorrow Comes; Women in the Wind; Fixer Dugan; Forgotten Women; Racketeers of the Range; A Woman Is the Judge; The Man with Nine Lives; Ring Madness (short); Weather Wizards (short). **1940** Girls Under 21; Pioneers of the West. **1941** Father's Son; Man Made Monster; Naval Academy; I'll Fix That (short); Sunset in Wyoming; Andy Hardy's Private Secretary. **1942** They All Kissed the Bride; You Can't Escape Forever. **1943** Lady Bodyguard.

DIMBLEBY, RICHARD

Born: May 25, 1913, England. Died: Dec. 22, 1965, London, England (cancer). Screen, television, radio actor, news commentator, author and publisher.

Appeared in: **1936** Strange Cargo (US 1940). **1950** The Twenty Questions Murder Mystery. **1958** Rockets Galore. **1959** Libel.

DIMON, FLORENCE IRENE. *See* FLORENCE IRENE FITZGERALD

DINEHART, ALAN

Born: Oct 3, 1889, Missoula, Mont. Died: July 17, 1944, Hollywood, Calif. Screen, stage, vaudeville actor and playwright.

Appeared in: **1931** Sob Sister; Girls about Town; Good Sport; The Brat; Wicked. **1932** The Trial of Vivienne Ware; Disorderly Conduct; Street of Women; Bachelor's Affairs; Almost Married; Week Ends Only; Penalty of Fame; Silver Dollar; Washington Merry-Go-Round; Rackety Rax; Devil Is Driving; Okay America; Lawyer Man. **1933** Sweepings; As the Devil Commands; Supernatural; Her Bodyguard; The Sin of Nora Moran; A Study in Scarlet; No Marriage Ties; Bureau of Missing Persons; I Have Lived; Dance, Girl, Dance; The World Changes. **1934** Cross Country Cruise; The Crosby Case; The Love Captive; A Very Honorable Guy; Jimmy the Gent; Baby, Take a Bow; Fury of the Jungle; The Cat's Paw. **1935** Dante's Inferno; Lottery Lover; $10 Raise; In Old Kentucky; Redheads on Parade; Thanks a Million; Your Uncle Dudley; The Pay-Off. **1936** It Had to Happen; Everybody's Old Man; The Country Beyond; Human Cargo; The Crime of Dr. Forbes; Charlie Chan at the Race Track; Star for a Night; King of the Royal Mounted; Reunion; Parole; Born to Dance. **1937** Fifty Roads to Town; King of the Turf; Step Lively, Jeeves!; Woman Wise; Midnight Taxi; This Is My Affair; Dangerously Yours; Danger—Love at Work; Ali Baba Goes to Town; Big Town Girl. **1938** Love on a Budget; Rebecca of Sunnybrook Farm; Up the River; The First Hundred Years. **1939** Hotel for Women; Money to Loan (short); Fast and Loose; House of Fear; Two Bright Boys; Second Fiddle; Everything Happens at Night. **1940** Slightly Honorable. **1942** Girl Trouble. **1943** The Heat's On; Sweet Rosie O'Grady; It's a Great Life; Fired Wife; What a Woman. **1944** Johnny Doesn't Live Here Anymore; Moon over Las Vegas; The Whistler; Oh, What a Night; Seven Days Ashore; Minstrel Man; A Wave, a Wac and a Marine.

DINGLE, CHARLES W.

Born: Dec. 28, 1887, Wabash, Ind. Died: Jan. 19, 1956, Worcester, Mass. Screen, stage, radio and television actor.

Appeared in: **1939** One Third of a Nation. **1941** Unholy Partners; The Little Foxes; Johnny Eager. **1942** Calling Dr. Gillespie; Are Husbands Necessary?; Tennessee Johnson; Somewhere I'll Find You; George Washington Slept Here; The Talk of the Town. **1943** Someone to Remember; She's for Me; Edge of Darkness; Lady of Burlesque. **1944** Home in Indiana; National Barn Dance; Practically Yours; The Song of Bernadette; Together Again. **1945** A Medal for Benny; Guest Wife; Here Come the Co-Eds; Three's a Crowd; A Song to Remember. **1946** Cinderella Jones; Sister Kenny; Centennial Summer; Three Wise Fools; Wife of Monte Cristo. **1946** The Beast with Five Fingers; Duel in the Sun. **1947** My Favorite Brunette; Welcome Stranger; The Romance of Rosy Ridge. **1948** If You Knew Susie; State of the Union; A Southern Yankee; The World and His Wife. **1949** Big Jack. **1952** Never Wave at a Wac. **1953** Call Me Madam; President's Lady; Half a Hero. **1955** The Court-Martial of Billy Mitchell.

DIONNE, EMELIE

Born: May 28, 1934, Callander, Ontario, Canada. Died: Aug. 6, 1954 (epileptic seizure). One of Dionne quintuplets. Screen actress. Surviving quintuplets are: Annette Dionne Allard; Yvonne Dionne; Cecile Dionne Langlois.

Appeared in **1936** Reunion; The Country Doctor; Going on Two (short), Pathe shorts. **1938** Five of a Kind; Quintupland (short).

DIONNE, MARIE

Born: May 28, 1934, Callander, Ontario, Canada. Died: Feb. 27, 1970. One of Dionne quintuplets. Screen actress.

Appeared in: **1936** Reunion; The Country Doctor; Going on Two (short); Pathe shorts. **1938** Five of a Kind; Quintupland (short).

DIRKSEN, EVERETT (Everett McKinley Dirksen)

Born: Jan. 4, 1896, Pekin, Ill. Died: Sept. 7, 1969, Washington, D.C. (lung cancer). United States Senator, author and screen actor.

Appeared in: **1969** The Monitors.

DITT, JOSEPHINE

Born: Sept. 7, 1868, Chicago, Ill. Died: Oct. 18, 1939, Hollywood, Calif. Screen actress.

Appeared in: **1914** Her Fighting Chance; False Gods. **1915**

DIX, BILLY (William H. Dixon)

Born: Sept. 4, 1911, Miami, Okla. Died: Mar. 22, 1973. Screen actor and rodeo performer. Do not confuse with actor William Dix.

Appeared in: **1945** Sunset in El Dorado. **1946** West of the Alamo; Rainbow Over the Rockies; Raiders of the South; Silver Range. **1947** Song of the Sierras. **1950** Buckaroo Sheriff of Texas. **1956** The Lonely Man; The Wild Dakotas.

DIX, MAE

Born: 1895, Lake Ann, Mich. Died: Oct. 21, 1958, Los Angeles, Calif. (burns in apartment fire). Screen, stage, burlesque and vaudeville actress. Entered films as an extra with Biograph in 1913.

DIX, RICHARD (Ernest Carlton Brimmer)

Born: Aug. 8, 1894, St. Paul, Minn. Died: Sept. 20, 1949, Los Angeles, Calif. (heart trouble). Stage and screen actor. Father of actor Robert Dix. Nominated for 1931 Academy Award for Best Actor in Cimarron.

Appeared in: **1921** The Sin Flood; The Old Nest; All's Fair in Love; Not Guilty; The Poverty of Riches; Dangerous Curve Ahead. **1922** Yellow Men and Gold; The Glorious Fool; The Bonded Women; The Wallflower; Fools First. **1923** Quicksands; Racing Hearts; The Woman with Four Faces; The Christian; The Call of the Canyon; The Ten Commandments; Souls for Sale; To the Last Man. **1924** Manhattan; Sinners in Heaven; Icebound; Iron Horse; The Stranger; Unguarded Women. **1925** The Vanishing American; Too Many Kisses; The Shock Punch; The Lucky Devil; A Man Must Live; Men and Women; The Lady Who Lied. **1926** Woman-handled; The Quarterback; Let's Get Married; Fascinating Youth; Say It Again. **1927** Paradise for Two; Knock-Out Reilly; Manpower; Shanghai Bound; Quicksands (and 1923 version). **1928** The Gay Defender; Sporting Goods; Easy Come, Easy Go; Warming Up; Moran of the Marines. **1929** Nothing but the Truth; The Wheel of Life; The Love Doctor; Redskin; Seven Keys to Baldpate. **1930** Lovin' the Ladies; Shooting Straight. **1931** Cimarron; The Public Defender; Young Donovan's Kid; Secret Service. **1932** The Slippery Pearls (short); The Lost Squadron; Roar of the Dragon; Hell's Highway; The Conquerors; Liberty Road. **1933** No Marriage Ties; The Great Jasper; Day of Reckoning; The Ace of Aces. **1934** Stingaree; West of the Pecos; His Greatest Gamble; I Won a Medal. **1935** Trans-Atlantic Tunnel; The Arizonian. **1936** Yellow Dust; Special Investigator; Devil's Squadron. **1937** Once a Hero; The Devil's Playground; The Devil Is Driving; It Happened in Hollywood. **1938** Blind Alibi; Sky Giant. **1939** Man of Conquest; Reno; Twelve Crowded Hours; Here I Am a Stranger. **1940** The Marines Fly High; Men against the Sky; Cherokee Strip. **1941** The Roundup; Badlands of Dakota. **1942** American Empire; Tombstone, the Town Too Tough to Die. **1943** The Iron Road; Buckskin Frontier; Top Man; The Kansan; Eyes of the Underworld; The Ghost Ship. **1944** The Mark of the Whistler; The Whistler. **1945** The Power of the Whistler. **1946** The Voice of the Whistler; The Mysterious Intruder; The Secret of the Whistler. **1947** The 13th Hour. **1939** The Fountainhead.

DIXEY, HENRY E.

Born: 1859, Boston, Mass. Died: Feb. 25, 1943, Atlantic City, N.J. (struck by bus). Stage and screen actor. Entered films with Universal in 1915.

DIXIT

Born: India. Died: June 29, 1949, India. Screen actor.

DIXON, CHARLOTTE L.

Died: 1970, West Palm Beach, Fla. Screen actress.

Appeared in: **1915** Birth of a Nation.

DIXON, CONWAY

Born: 1874, England. Died: Jan. 17, 1943, London, England (heart attack). Stage and screen actor.

Appeared in: **1935** The Triumph of Sherlock Holmes. **1937** The Mutiny of Elsinore (US 1939). **1938** Sixty Glorious Years (aka Queen of Destiny—US).

DIXON, DENVER (Victor Adamson)

Born: 1890, Kansas City, Mo. Died: Nov. 9, 1972, Hollywood, Calif. (heart attack). Screen, vaudeville actor, film director and producer. Father of film producer-director Al Adamson.

Appeared in: **1915** Birth of a Nation. **1919** The Squaw Man. **1922** The Lone Rider. **1936** Guns and Guitars. **1937** Way Out West. **1938** The Old Barn Dance. **1949** Riders in the Sky. **1969** Five Bloody Graves.

DIXON, GLORIA

Died: Apr. 10, 1945, Hollywood, Calif. (fire). Screen actress.

Appeared in: **1937** They Won't Forget. **1938** Gold Diggers of Paris; Racket Busters; Secrets of an Actress; Heart of the North. **1939** They Made Me a Criminal; Waterfront; The Cowboy Quarterback; No Place to Go; On Your Toes; Private Detective. **1940** King of the Lumberjacks; Tear Gas Squad; I Want a Divorce. **1941** This Thing Called Love. **1942** Lady of Burlesque.

DIXON, HENRY

Born: 1871. Died: May 3, 1943, Hollywood, Calif. Screen, vaudeville actor and burlesque producer.

DIXON, JAMES "JIM"

Born: 1949. Died: Mar. 13, 1974, Inyo County, Calif. (plane crash). Screen and television actor.

Appeared in: **1968** Ice Station Zebra.

DIXON, LEE

Born: Jan. 22, 1914, Brooklyn, N.Y. Died: Jan. 8, 1953, New York, N.Y. Screen, stage and vaudeville actor.

Appeared in: **1936** Gold Diggers of 1937. **1937** Ready, Willing and Able; The Singing Marine; Variety Show. **1947** Angel and the Badman.

DIXON, PAUL (Gregory Schleier)

Born: 1918. Died: Dec. 28, 1974, Cincinnati, Ohio (ruptured heart artery). Screen and television actor. Known on television as "The Mayor of Kneesville."

Appeared in: **1951** Disc Jockey.

DOBBINS, EARL E.

Born: 1911. Died: Feb. 9, 1949, Los Angeles, Calif. (result of knife wound). Screen actor and stuntman.

DOBLE, BUDD

Born: Philadelphia, Pa. Died: Sept. 3, 1919, Los Angeles, Calif. Screen actor and harness race driver.

Appeared in: **1913** Budd Doble Comes Back.

DOBLE, FRANCES

Died: Dec. 1969, England. Stage and screen actress.

Appeared in: **1928** The Constant Nymph; The Vortex. **1929** Dark Red Roses.

DOBSON, EDWARD

Died: Feb. 7, 1925, San Jose, Calif. Screen actor.

DOCKSON, EVELYN

Born: 1888. Died: May 20, 1952, Burbank, Calif. (cancer). Screen and vaudeville actress.

Appeared in: **1943** Let's Face It.

DODD, CLAIRE

Born: 1909 (?), New York, N.Y. Died: Nov. 23, 1973, Beverly Hills, Calif. (cancer). Stage and screen actress.

Appeared in: **1930** Whoopee; Our Blushing Brides. **1931** An American Tragedy; The Secret Call; Working Girls; Girls About Town; Up Pops the Devil; The Lawyer's Secret; Road to Reno. **1932** Under Eighteen; Two Kinds of Women; Alias the Doctor; The Broken Wing; Man Wanted; This is the Night; Guilty as Hell; Crooner; The Match King; Lawyer Man; Dancers in the Dark. **1933** Parachute Jumper; Hard to Handle; Blondie Johnson; Ex-Lady; Elmer the Great; Ann Carver's Profession; Footlight Parade; My Woman. **1934** Massacre; Gambling Lady; Journal of a Crime; The Personality Kid; Babbitt; I Sell Anything; Smarty. **1935** Roberta; The Case of the Curious Bride; The Glass Key; Don't Bet on Blondes; The Goose and the Gander; The Pay-Off; Secret of the Chateau. **1936** The Singing Kid; Murder by an Aristocrat; The Case of the Velvet Claws; Navy Born; Two Against the World; A Vitaphone short. **1937** The Women Men Marry. **1938** Romance in the Dark; Fast Company; Three Loves has Nancy; Charlie Chan in Honolulu. **1939** Woman Doctor.

1940 If I Had My Way; Slightly Honorable. **1941** The Black Cat; In the Navy. **1942** The Mad Doctor of Market Street; Don Winslow of the Navy (serial); Mississippi Gambler.

DODD, MRS. ELAN E.

Born: 1868. Died: Mar. 12, 1935, Brooklyn, N.Y. Screen actress. Entered films with Vitaphone.

DODD, JIMMIE

Born: 1910, Cincinnati, Ohio. Died: Nov. 10, 1964, Honolulu, Hawaii. Screen, television actor and songwriter.

Appeared in: **1940** Those Were the Days; Law and Order. **1941** The Richest Man in Town. **1942** Snuffy Smith; Hillbilly Blitzkrieg; Yard Bird; Flying Tigers. **1943** Shadows on the Sage; Riders of the Rio Grande. **1944** Hi, Beautiful!; Moon over Las Vegas; Twilight on the Prairie. **1945** Penthouse Rhythm; The Crimson Canary; China's Little Devils; Men in Her Diary. **1947** Rolling Home; Buck Privates Come Home; The Tender Years; Song of My Heart. **1948** The Noose Hangs High; Daredevils of the Clouds; You Gotta Stay Happy. **1949** Flaming Fury; Post Office Investigator; Incident. **1950** Singing Guns. **1951** Al Jennings of Oklahoma; The Second Woman; G. I. Jane. **1952** The Winning Team; The Lusty Men.

DODD, REV. NEAL

Born: Sept. 6, 1878, Port Madison, Iowa. Died: May 26, 1966, Los Angeles, Calif. Screen actor, film director and religious advisor. Known as the "Padre of Hollywood." Entered films in 1920.

Appeared in: **1924** The Only Woman. **1926** Lost at Sea. **1932** Merrily We Go to Hell. **1934** It Happened One Night; You Belong to Me. **1935** Hold 'Em Yale. **1939** Mr. Smith Goes to Washington. **1947** The Secret Life of Walter Mitty. **1948** Sorry, Wrong Number. **1951** Here Comes the Groom.

DODDS, CHUCK

Born: 1936. Died: Oct. 1, 1967, Hollywood, Calif. (leukemia). Screen actor and night club singer.

DODDS, JACK

Born: 1927. Died: June 2, 1962, Hollywood, Calif. (cancer). Screen, stage, television actor and dancer.

Appeared in: **1962** State Fair.

DODGE, ROGER (Roger Pryor Dodge)

Born: 1898, Paris, France. Died: June 2, 1974, New York, N.Y. Screen actor, choreographer and stage producer.

Appeared in: **1935** a Universal short.

DODSWORTH, JOHN (John Cecil Dodsworth)

Born: Sept. 17, 1910, England. Died: Sept. 11, 1964, Los Angeles, Calif. (suicide—asphyxiation). Screen actor.

Appeared in: **1952** Storm over Tibet; The Snows of Kilimanjaro; Bwana Devil; Rogue's March. **1953** Loose in London; The Maze. **1954** Bengal Brigade. **1955** Untamed. **1958** In the Money.

DOLENZ, GEORGE

Born: Jan. 5, 1908, Trieste, Italy. Died: Feb. 8, 1963, Hollywood, Calif. (heart attack). Screen, stage and television actor.

Appeared in: **1941** The Unexpected Uncle (film debut); Faculty Row. **1943** Fired Wife; The Strange Death of Adolf Hitler; She's for Me; Moonlight in Vermont; Calling Dr. Death; Young Ideas. **1944** In Society; The Climax; Enter Arsene Lupin; Bowery to Broadway. **1945** Song of the Sarong; Easy to Look At. **1946** Idea Girl; A Night in Paradise; Girl on the Spot. **1947** Song of Scheherazade. **1950** Vendetta. **1952** My Cousin Rachel. **1953** Thunder Bay; Scared Stiff; Wings of the Hawk. **1954** The Last Time I Saw Paris; Sign of the Pagan. **1955** The Racers; A Bullet for Joey; The Purple Mask. **1957** Sad Sack. **1959** Timbuktu. **1961** Look in Any Window. **1962** The Four Horsemen of the Apocalypse.

DOLLY, JENNY (Janszieka Deutsch)

Born: Oct. 25, 1892, Hungary. Died: June 1, 1941, Hollywood, Calif. (suicide—hanging). Screen, stage and vaudeville actress. She and her twin sister Rosie Dolly (dec. 1970) were known as the famous dancing "Dolly Sisters." Divorced from actor Harry Fox (dec. 1959).

Appeared in: **1915** The Call of the Dance. **1918** The Million Dollar Dollies.

DOLLY, LADY

Born: 1876. Died: Sept. 5, 1953, Hollywood, Calif. Screen actress (midget performer). Was also a stand-in for child actors.

DOLLY, ROSIE (Roszicka Deutsch)

Born: Oct. 25, 1892, Hungary. Died: Feb. 1, 1970, New York, N.Y. (heart failure). Screen, stage and vaudeville actress. She and her twin sister Jenny Dolly (dec. 1941) were known as the famous dancing "Dolly Sisters."

Appeared in: **1915** Dance of Creations; The Lily and the Rose. **1918** The Million Dollar Dollies.

DOMBRE, BARBARA
Born: **1950**. Died: Jan. 3, 1973, U.S. Stage and screen actress.

Appeared in: **1969** Heaven with a Gun.

DOMINGUEZ, BEATRICE
Died: Mar. 1921, Los Angeles, Calif. (after operation complications). Screen actress.

Appeared in: **1920** The Moon Riders (serial). **1921** The White Horseman (serial); The Fire Cat; The Four Horsemen of the Apocalypse.

DOMINGUEZ, JOE (Jose J. Dominguez)
Born: Mar. 19, 1894, Mexico. Died: Apr. 11, 1970, Woodland Hills, Calif. Screen actor.

Appeared in: **1932** Riders of the Desert; Mason of the Mounted. **1939** Mexicali Rose. **1940** Geronimo; Gaucho Serenade. **1941** Outlaws of the Rio Grande. **1942** Undercover Man. **1945** The Bull Fighters. **1949** Streets of Loredo; The Big Sombrero. **1950** One Way Street; Dallas; Bandit Queen. **1952** Rancho Notorious. **1953** Ride, Vaquero; Son of Belle Starr; The Hitch-hiker. **1954** Gypsy Colt; Green Fire. **1956** The Broken Star. **1957** The Ride Back. **1958** Man of the West. **1961** One-Eyed Jacks. **1968** I Love You, Alice B. Toklas.

DOMINIQUE, IVAN
Born: **1928**, Antwerp, Belgium. Died: Apr. 3, 1973, Ghent, Belgium. Screen, stage actor and composer. Son of writer Evelyne Pollet.

Appeared in: The Princess of Cleves.

DON, DAVID L.
Born: **1867**, Utica, New York. Died: Oct. 27, 1949, New York, N.Y. Screen actor.

Appeared in: **1915** Love and Swords. **1916** Half a Million; Romance of a Beanery; Limberger's Victory; No Place Like Jail; The Butler; Otto the Bell Boy; Skirts and Cinders; Frilby Frilled; Otto the Artist; Otto the Reporter; Otto the Salesman; Otto the Sleuth; Otto the Hero; Otto the Cobbler; Otto the Gardener; Otto's Vacation; Otto's Legacy; Otto the Traffic Cop. **1918** The Hidden Truth.

DONAHUE, JACK (John J. Donahue)
Born: **1892**. Died: Oct. 1, 1930, New York, N.Y. (heart disease). Stage, burlesque, vaudeville actor, stage producer, and playwright. Appeared in vaudeville with his wife in a team billed "Donahue and Stewart."

DONALDSON, JACK
Born: **1910**. Died: June 20, 1975, Woodland Hills, Calif. (stroke). Screen, stage actor and theatrical agent.

DONAT, ROBERT
Born: Mar. 18, 1905, Manchester, England. Died: June 9, 1958, London, England (respiratory ailment, asthma). Screen, stage actor and film director. Won 1939 Academy Award for Best Actor in Goodbye, Mr. Chips. Divorced from Ella Annesley Voysey and later married to actress Renee Asherson.

Appeared in: **1932** Men of Tomorrow (film debut); That Night in London (aka Overnight—US 1934). **1933** Cash (aka For Love or Money—US 1934); The Private Life of Henry VIII. **1934** The Count of Monte Cristo. **1935** The 39 Steps. **1936** The Ghost Goes West. **1937** Knight Without Armour. **1938** The Citadel. **1939** Goodbye, Mr. Chips. **1942** The Young Mr. Pitt. **1943** Adventures of Tartu (aka Tartu—US). **1945** Perfect Strangers (aka Vacation from Marriage—US). **1947** Captain Boycott. **1948** The Winslow Boy (US 1950). **1950** The Cure for Love. **1951** The Magic Box (US 1952). **1954** Lease of Life. **1956** Stained Glass at Fairford (short—voice only). **1958** The Inn of the Sixth Happiness.

DONATH, LUDWIG
Born: **1900**, Vienna, Austria. Died: Sept. 29, 1967, New York, N.Y. (leukemia). Screen, stage and television actor.

Appeared in: **1942** Ellery Queen; Lady from Chungking. **1943** Hangmen Also Die; The Strange Death of Adolf Hitler; Hostages. **1944** The Seventh Cross; The Hitler Gang; Tampico. **1945** The Story of Dr. Wassell; The Master Race; Counter-Attack. **1946** Blondie Knows Best; Gilda; The Jolson Story; The Devil's Mask; Prison Ship; Renegades; Return of Monte Cristo. **1947** Cigarette Girl; Assignment to Treasury. **1948** Sealed Verdict; To the Ends of the Earth. **1949** The Fighting O'Flynn; The Great Sinner; There's a Girl in My Heart; The Lovable Cheat. **1950** The Killer That Stalked New York; Mystery Submarine; Jolson Sings Again. **1951** Journey into Light; Sirocco; The Great Caruso. **1952** My Pal Gus. **1953** Sins of Jezebel; The Veils of Bagdad. **1966** Torn Curtain; Death Trap.

DONATI, MARIA
Born: **1902**, Mexico. Died: Nov. 4, 1966, Mexico. Screen actress.

Appeared in: **1947** La Vita Ricominicia (Life Begins Anew). **1948** Angelina. **1952** Tears of Blood.

DONER, MAURICE
Born: **1905**. Died: Feb. 21, 1971, Hollywood, Calif. Screen, stage and television actor.

Appeared in: **1949** Flame of Youth. **1952** Assignment—Paris. **1956** Congo Crossing. **1966** Torn Curtain.

DONER, ROSE
Born: **1905**. Died: Aug. 15, 1926, New York, N.Y. (following operation for appendicitis). Screen, stage, vaudeville actress and dancer. Appeared in vaudeville with her brother and sister, Ted and Kitty Donner.

DONLAN, JAMES
Born: **1889**. Died: June 7, 1938, Hollywood, Calif. (heart attack). Stage and screen actor.

Appeared in: **1929** Wise Girls; Big News. **1930** Night Work; The Bishop Murder Case; Beau Bandit; Remote Control; Sins of the Children. **1931** Good Bad Girl. **1932** Back Street. **1933** They Just Had to Get Married; College Humor; Design for Living; The Avenger. **1934** A Very Honorable Guy; The Cat's Paw; Now I'll Tell; Hi, Nellie!; Belle of the Nineties. **1935** Under Pressure; The Daring Young Man; The Whole Town's Talking; Traveling Saleslady; The Case of the Curious Bride; We're Only Human. **1936** The Plot Thickens; Crash Donovan; Murder on the Bridle Path. **1937** This Is My Affair; It Happened in Hollywood. **1938** Professor Beware.

DONLEVY, BRIAN
Born: Feb. 9, 1899, Portadown County, Armagh, Ireland. Died: Apr. 5, 1972, Woodland Hills, Calif. (throat cancer). Screen, stage and television actor. Divorced from singer Marjorie Lane. Married to Lillian Lugosi. Nominated for 1939 Academy Award as Best Supporting Actor in Beau Geste.

Appeared in: **1923** Jamestown. **1924** Damaged Hearts; Monsieur Beaucaire. **1925** School for Wives. **1926** A Man of Quality. **1929** Mother's Boy; Gentlemen of the Press. **1932** A Modern Cinderella. **1934** The Milky Way. **1935** Barbary Coast; Mary Burns, Fugitive; Another Face. **1936** Strike Me Pink; Thirteen Hours by Air; High Tension; Crack-Up; Human Cargo; 36 Hours to Kill; Half Angel. **1937** Born Reckless; This is My Affair; Midnight Taxi. **1938** In Old Chicago; Sharpshooters; Battle of Broadway; We're Going to be Rich. **1939** Jesse James; Destry Rides Again; Beau Geste; Union Pacific; Behind Prison Gates; Alleghany Uprising. **1940** The Great McGinty; When the Daltons Rode; Brigham Young—Frontiersman. **1941** I Wanted Wings; South of Tahiti; Birth of the Blues; Billy the Kid; Hold Back the Dawn. **1942** Wake Island; The Great Man's Lady; A Gentleman after Dark; The Remarkable Andrew; The Glass Key; Two Yanks in Trinidad; Stand by for Action; Cargo of Innocents; Nightmare. **1943** Hangmen Also Die; The City That Stopped Hitler—Heroic Stalingrad (narrator). **1944** An American Romance; The Miracle of Morgan's Creek. **1945** Duffy's Tavern. **1946** Our Hearts Were Growing Up; The Virginian; Two Years Before the Mast; Canyon Passage. **1947** Song of Scheherazade; Killer McCoy; Kiss of Death; The Beginning or the End; The Trouble with Women; Heaven Only Knows. **1948** A Southern Yankee; Command Decision. **1949** Impact; The Lucky Stiff. **1950** Kansas Raiders; Shakedown. **1951** Slaughter Trail; Fighting Coast Guard. **1952** Hoodlum Empire; Ride the Man Down. **1953** The Woman They Almost Lynched. **1955** The Big Combo; The Quatermass Experiment. **1956** The Creeping Unknown; A Cry in the Night. **1957** Enemy from Space; The Quatermass II. **1958** Cowboy; Escape from Red Rock. **1959** Never so Few; Juke Box Rhythm. **1961** The Girl in Room 13. **1962** The Pigeon that Took Rome; The Errand Boy. **1965** Curse of the Fly; How to Stuff a Wild Bikini; The Fat Spy. **1966** Waco. **1967** Hostile Guns; Gammera the Invincible. **1968** Arizona Bushwackers; Five Golden Dragons. **1969** Pit Stop.

DONLIN, MIKE
Born: May 30, 1877, Peoria, Ill. Died: Sept. 2, 1933, Los Angeles, Calif. Screen, stage, vaudeville actor and baseball player.

Appeared in: **1923** Woman Proof; Railroaded; The Unknown Purple. **1924** Oh, Doctor; Flaming Barriers; Hit and Run; The Trouble Shooter. **1925** Raffles; Fifth Avenue Models; The Unnamed Woman. **1926** The Sea Beast; Her Second Chance; Ella Cinders; The Fighting Marine (serial and feature film). **1927** The General; Slide, Kelly, Slide. **1928** Riley the Cop; Beggars of Life; Warming Up. **1929** Below the Deadline; Thunderbolt; Noisy Neighbors. **1930** Born Reckless; Hot Curves. **1931** Arrowsmith; Iron Man; The Tip Off. **1933** Air Hostess; High Gear.

DONNELLY, JAMES
Born: **1865**, Boston, Mass. Died: Apr. 13, 1937, Hollywood, Calif. Stage and screen actor.

Appeared in: **1916** The Snow Cure; Bubbles of Trouble. **1917** She Needed a Doctor. **1921** Black Beauty. **1922** A Girl's Desire.

DONNELLY, LEO
Born: 1878. Died: Aug. 21, 1935, Atlantic City, N.J. Screen, stage and vaudeville actor.

Appeared in: **1923** Potash and Perlmutter. **1930** Roadhouse Nights; Stepping Out (short); The Music Racket (short).

•DONOHUE, JOSEPH
Born: 1884. Died: Oct. 25, 1921, Brooklyn, N.Y. Screen and vaudeville actor.

Appeared in: **1917** Within the Law. **1920** Over the Hill.

DOOLEY, BILLY
Born: Feb. 8, 1893, Chicago, Ill. Died: Aug. 4, 1938, Hollywood, Calif. (heart attack). Screen, stage and vaudeville actor. Entered films with Al Christie.

Appeared in: **1926–28** Christie shorts. Other shorts prior to 1933 include: The Dizzy Diver; Happy Heels and early "Goofy Gob" series. **1936** Anything Goes. **1938** Call of the Yukon; The Marines Are Here.

DOOLEY, JOHNNY (John D. Dool)
Born: 1887, Glasgow, Scotland. Died: June 7, 1928, Yonkers, N.Y. (intestinal trouble). Screen, stage and vaudeville actor.

Appeared in: **1921** Skinning Skinners. **1922** When Knighthood Was in Flower. **1924** Yolanda. **1927** East Side, West Side.

DOONAN, GEORGE
Born: 1897, England. Died: Apr. 17, 1973, London, England. Screen, stage and vaudeville actor. Father of actors Patrick (dec. 1958) and Tony Doonan.

DOONAN, PATRICK
Born: 1927. Died: Mar. 10, 1958, London, England (suicide—gas). Stage and screen actor. Son of actor George Doonan (dec. 1973) and brother of actor Anthony Doonan.

Appeared in: **1948** Once a Jolly Swagman (aka Maniacs on Wheels—US 1951). **1949** Train of Events (US 1952); A Run for Your Money (US 1950); All Over Town. **1950** The Blue Lamp; Blackout; Highly Dangerous (US 1951). **1951** The Lavender Hill Mob; Calling Bulldog Drummond; The Man in the White Suit (US 1952); High Treason (US 1952); Appointment with Venus (aka Island Rescue—US 1952). **1952** The Gift Horse (aka Glory at Sea—US 1953); I'm a Stranger; The Gentle Gunman (US 1953). **1953** The Net (aka Project M7—US); The Red Beret (aka Paratrooper—US 1954); Wheel of Fate. **1954** What Every Woman Wants; Seagulls over Sorrento (aka Crest of the Wave—US). **1955** John and Julie (US 1957); Cockleshell Heroes (US 1956).

DORALDINA
Born: 1888. Died: Feb. 13, 1936, Los Angeles, Calif. (heart attack). Screen actress and stage dancer.

Appeared in: **1918** The Naulahka. **1921** Passion Fruit; Woman Untamed.

DORETY, CHARLES R.
Born: May 20, 1898, San Francisco, Calif. Died: Apr. 2, 1957, Hollywood, Calif. Screen, circus, vaudeville actor, film director and film producer.

Appeared in: **1931** La Senorita de Chicago (short—Spanish version of The Pip from Pittsburgh). **1934** Men in Black (short); Three Little Pigskins (short). **1935** The following shorts: Uncivil Warriors; I'm a Father; and Sawbones. **1936** Ants in the Pantry (short); Movie Maniacs (short).

DORHAM, KENNY (McKinley Howard Dorham)
Born: Aug. 30, 1924, Fairfield, Texas. Died: Dec. 5, 1972, New York, N.Y. (kidney disorder). Composer, jazz trumpeter and screen actor.

Appeared in: **1959** Witness in the City; Les Liasons Dangereuses (Dangerous Liaisons).

DORIAN, CHARLES
Born: 1893. Died: Oct. 21, 1942, Aubuquerque, N.M. (heart attack). Screen, vaudeville actor and assistant film director. Entered films in 1917.

DORLEAC, FRANCOISE
Born: 1941, France. Died: June 26, 1967, Nice, France (auto accident). Screen actress. Sister of actress Catherine Deneuve.

Appeared in: **1957** Mensonges. **1958** The Door Slams. **1959** Les Loups Dans la Berbaries. **1960** Ce Soir ou Jamais; Les Portes Claquent. **1961** Le Jeu de la Verite; A D'Autres Amours; La Gamberge; Tout L'Or de Monde; Payroll; La Fille aux Yeux D'Or (The Girl with the Golden Eyes—US 1962). **1962** Arsene Lupin Contre Arsene Lupin (Arsene Lupin against Arsene Lupin). **1964** La Ronde (Circle of Love—US 1965); La Peau Douce (The Soft Skin); L'Homme de Rio (That Man from Rio). **1965** Genghis Khan. **1966** Cul-de-Sac; Where the Spies Are. **1967** Les Demoiselles de Rochefort (The Young Girls of Rochefort—US 1968); Billion Dollar Brain.

DORN, PHILIP (Fritz Van Dungen)
Born: 1902, Scheveningen, Holland. Died: May 9, 1975, Woodland Hills, Calif. (heart attack). Stage and screen actor.

Appeared in: **1940** Ski Patrol (film debut); Enemy Agent; Escape; Diamond Frontier. **1941** Tarzan's Secret Treasure; Ziegfeld Girl; Underground. **1942** Random Harvest; Calling Dr. Gillespie; Reunion. **1943** Chetniks; Paris after Dark. **1944** Passage to Marseilles; Blonde Fever. **1945** Escape in the Desert. **1946** I've Always Loved You; Concerto. **1948** I Remember Mama. **1949** The Fighting Kentuckian; Panther's Moon. **1950** Spy Hunt. **1951** Sealed Cargo. **1956** Salto Mortale.

DORO, MARIE (Marie K. Steward)
Born: 1882, Duncannon, Pa. Died: Oct. 9, 1956, New York, N.Y. (heart ailment). Stage and screen actress. Divorced from actor Elliott Dexter (dec. 1941).

Appeared in: **1915** The Morals of Marcus (film debut); The White Pearl. **1916** The Heart of Nora Flynn; Oliver Twist (stage and film versions); Diplomacy; The Wood Nymph. **1917** Lost and Won; Castles for Two. **1919** The Mysterious Princess; A Sinless Sinner (aka Midnight Gambols—US 1920); Twelve Ten. **1920** Maid of Mystery. **1922** The Stronger Passion. **1923** Sally Bishop.

DORREE, BABETTE "BOBBIE"
Born: 1906, Vienna, Austria. Died: Jan. 10, 1974, Woodland Hills, Calif. (cancer). Screen actress and professional skater.

DORSAY, EDMUND
Born: 1897. Died: June 12, 1959, New York, N.Y. Screen, stage, vaudeville and television actor. Appeared in silents.

D'ORSAY, LAWRENCE
Born: 1860, England. Died: Sept. 13, 1931, London, England. Stage and screen actor.

Appeared in: **1918** Ruggles of Red Gap. **1922** The Bond Boy. **1923** His Children's Children. **1924** The Side Show of Life. **1925** Miss Bluebeard. **1926** The Sorrows of Satan.

DORSCH, KAETHE
Born: Dec. 29, 1889, Nurenburg, Germany. Died: Dec. 1957, Vienna, Austria. Stage and screen actress.

Appeared in: **1931** Drei Tage Liebe (Three Days of Love); Die Lindenwirtin Vom Rhein. **1938** Eine Frau Ohne Bedeutung. **1940** Mutterliebe (Mother Love). **1952** Singende Engel (Singing Angel). Other German film: Yvette.

DORSEY, JIMMY (James Francis Dorsey)
Born: 1904, Shenandoah, Pa. Died: June 12, 1957, New York, N.Y. (cancer). Bandleader and screen actor. Brother of bandleader and actor Tommy Dorsey (dec. 1956).

Appeared in: **1940** Paramount short. **1942** The Fleet's In. **1943** I Dood It. **1944** Lost in a Harem; Four Jills in a Jeep; Hollywood Canteen. **1947** The Fabulous Dorseys. **1949** Make Believe Ballroom.

DORSEY, TOMMY (Thomas Francis Dorsey)
Born: 1905, Mahanoy Plane, Pa. Died: Nov. 26, 1956, Greenwich, Conn. (choked while asleep). Bandleader and screen actor. Brother of bandleader and actor Jimmy Dorsey (dec. 1957).

Appeared in: **1941** Las Vegas Nights. **1942** Ship Ahoy. **1943** Du Barry Was a Lady; Presenting Lily Mars; Girl Crazy; I Dood It. **1944** Broadway Rhythm. **1947** The Fabulous Dorseys. **1948** A Song Is Born.

DOTY, WESTON and WINSTON
Born: 1915. Died: Jan. 2, 1934, Calif. (both drowned in flood). Twin screen actors.

Appeared in: **1925** Peter Pan; and four "Our Gang" comedies.

DOUCET, CATHERINE
Born: 1875, Richmond, Va. Died: June 24, 1958, New York, N.Y. Stage and screen actress.

Appeared in: **1933** Rendezvous at Midnight. **1934** As Husbands Go; Wake Up and Dream; Little Man, What Now?; The Party's Over; Servant's Entrance. **1935** Age of Indiscretion; Accent on Youth; Millions in the Air. **1936** These Three; The Golden Arrow; Poppy; The Longest Night; The Luckiest Girl in the World. **1937** When You're in Love; Oh, Doctor; Jim Harvey—Detective; Man of the People. **1941** Nothing but the Truth; It Started with Eve. **1949** Family Honeymoon.

DOUCET, M. PAUL
Born: 1886, France. Died: Oct. 10, 1928, N.Y. (septic poisoning). Stage and screen actor.

Appeared in: **1921** Tropical Love. **1922** Polly of the Follies. **1923** The Leavenworth Case. **1924** America. **1925** Heart of a Siren; The Little French Girl. **1927** The Broadway Drifter.

DOUGHERTY, VIRGIL JACK

Born: 1895. Died: May 16, 1938, Hollywood, Calif. (suicide—carbon monoxide). Screen actor. Married to actress Barbara Lamar (dec. 1925).

Appeared in: **1921** The Greater Claim. **1922** Impulse; Second Hand Rose; Chain Lightning. **1923** Money! Money! Money! **1924** Girl of the Limberlost. **1925** The Burning Trail; The Meddler. **1926** The Runaway Express. **1927** Arizona Bound; Special Delivery; Down the Stretch; The Lure of the Night Club. **1928** Gypsy of the North; Into No Man's Land. **1929** The Body Punch. **1937** Yodelin' Kid from Pine Ridge.

DOUGLAS, BYRON

Born: 1865. Died: Apr. 21, 1935, New York, N.Y. Screen and stage actor.

Appeared in: **1920** Held by the Enemy. **1921** Dynamite Allan; Know Your Man; Beyond Price. **1923** Under the Red Robe; The Silent Command: The Net. **1924** It Is the Law. **1925** That Devil Quemado; Two-Fisted Jones; Marriage in Transit. **1927** The Perfect Sap; The Coward; Dead Man's Curve; Ladies Beware; Red Clay. **1928** Man, Woman and Wife. **1929** Born to the Saddle; The Drake Case. **1931** Secret Service.

DOUGLAS, DON (Douglas Kinleyside)

Born: 1905, New York or London, England. Died: Dec. 31, 1945, Los Angeles, Calif. (complications after emergency appendectomy). Screen, stage actor and opera performer.

Appeared in: **1929** Great Gabbo; Tonight at Twelve. **1930** Ranch House Blues. **1932** Love in High Gear. **1933** He Couldn't Take It. **1934** A Woman's Man; Tomorrow's Children; Men in White. **1937** Headin' East. **1938** Law of the Texan; Alexander's Ragtime Band; Orphans of the Street; Fast Company; Come Across (short); The Crowd Roars; The Gladiator; Convicted; Smashing the Rackets. **1939** Fast and Loose; Within the Law; Zero Hour; The House of Fear; Mr. Moto in Danger Island; Forgotten Victory (short); The Dead End Kids on Dress Parade (aka On Dress Parade); Fugitive at Large; Manhattan Shakedown; Sabotage; The Mysterious Miss X; Wings of the Navy. **1940** A Fugitive from Justice; Calling Philo Vance; Gallant Sons; Deadwood Dick (serial); Charlie Chan in Panama; I Love You Again. **1941** Flight Command; Sleepers West; Dead Men Tell; Murder among Friends; The Great Swindle; The Get-Away; Hold Back the Dawn; Night of January 16th; Mercy Island; Melody Lane; Cheers for Miss Bishop; Whistling in the Dark. **1942** On the Sunny Side; Tales of Manhattan; Now, Voyager; Little Tokyo, U.S.A.; Juke Box Jenny; A Daring Young Man. **1943** The Meanest Man in the World; He's My Guy; Wintertime; Appointment in Berlin; Action in the North Atlantic; Behind the Rising Sun; The More the Merrier; The Crystal Ball. **1944** The Falcon Out West; Heavenly Days; Murder, My Sweet; Show Business; Tall in the Saddle. **1945** Grissly's Millions; A Royal Scandal; Tarzan and the Amazons; Tokyo Rose; Club Havana. **1946** The Strange Mr. Gregory; The Truth about Women; Gilda.

DOUGLAS, DORIS

Born: 1918. Died: May 30, 1970. Screen actress.

DOUGLAS, KENT. *See* DOUGLAS MONTGOMERY

DOUGLAS, MILTON

Born: 1906. Died: Sept. 5, 1970. Screen actor, dancer and singer.

Appeared in: **1930** Viennese Nights. **1934** Three Little Pigskins (short).

DOUGLAS, PAUL

Born: Apr. 11, 1907, Philadelphia, Pa. Died: Sept. 11, 1959, Hollywood, Calif. (heart attack). Screen, stage, television and radio actor. Married to actress Jan Sterling; divorced from Elizabeth Farnesworth, Sussie Welles, Geraldine Higgins and actress Virginia Field.

Appeared in: **1948** A Letter to Three Wives (film debut). **1949** It Happens Every Spring; Everybody Does It; Twelve O'Clock High. **1950** Panic in the Streets; The Big Lift; Love That Brute. **1951** Angels in the Outfield; Fourteen Hours; The Guy Who Came Back; Rhubarb (unbilled). **1952** We're Not Married; When in Rome; Clash by Night; Never Wave at a WAC. **1953** Forever Female. **1954** The Maggie (aka High and Dry—US); Executive Suite; Green Fire. **1956** Joe Macbeth; Solid Gold Cadillac; The Gamma People; The Leather Saint. **1957** This Could Be the Night; Beau James. **1959** The Mating Game.

DOUGLAS, VALERIE

Born: 1938, England. Died: Mar. 2, 1969, England. Screen and stage actress.

DOUGLAS, WALLY. *See* WALTER J. FROES

DOVEY, ALICE

Born: 1885, England. Died: Jan. 11, 1969, Tarzana, Calif. Stage and screen actress. Entered films with Famous Players-Lasky in 1915. Married to stage actor and playwright Jack Hazzard.

DOVZHENKO, ALEXANDER (aka ALEXANDER DOVJHENKO)

Born: 1894. Died: 1956. Screen actor, film director, film producer and screenwriter.

Appeared in: **1929** Arsenal. **1930** Earth. **1932** Ivan. **1935** Aerograd. **1947** Life in Blossom.

DOWLING, JOAN

Born: Jan. 1928, England. Died: Mar. 31, 1954, London, England (found dead in gas-filled room). Screen and stage actress. Married to actor Harry Fowler.

Appeared in: **1947** Hue and Cry (film debut—US 1950). **1948** Bond Street (US 1950); No Room at the Inn. **1949** A Man's Affair; For Them that Trespass (US 1950); Train of Events (US 1952); Landfall. **1950** Murder Without Crime (US 1951). **1951** The Magic Box (US 1952); Pool of London. **1952** 24 Hours of a Woman's Life (aka Affair in Monte Carlo—US 1953); Women of Twilight (aka Twilight Women—US 1953).

DOWLING, JOSEPH J.

Born: 1848. Died: July 10, 1928, Hollywood, Calif. Screen actor. Achieved fame as the "Miracle Man."

Appeared in: **1915** The Coward. **1919** The Miracle Man. **1920** The Kentucky Colonel. **1921** Fightin' Mad; The Lure of Egypt; The Spenders; The Other Woman; The Beautiful Liar; Breaking Point; The Sin of Martha Queed; A Certain Rich Man; The Grim Comedian; His Nibs; Little Lord Fauntleroy. **1922** If You Believe It, It's So; The Infidel; Quincy Adams Sawyer; The Girl Who Ran Wild; Half Breed; The Pride of Palomar; One Clear Call; The Trail of the Axe; The Danger Point. **1923** The Christian; A Man's Man; The Spider and the Rose; Dollar Devils; Tiger Rose; The Courtship of Miles Standish; Enemies of Children; The Girl Who Came Back. **1924** Those Who Dare; One Night in Rome; The Gaiety Girl; Tess of the D'Urbervilles; Untamed Youth; Her Night of Romance; The Law Forbids; Unseen Hands; Women Who Give; Free and Equal (reissue and retitle of The Coward, 1915). **1925** Lorraine of the Lions; Confessions of a Queen; Lord Jim; The Golden Princess; Flower of Night; New Lives for Old. **1926** The Rainmaker; The Little Irish Girl; Why Girls Go Back Home; Two Gun Man.

DOWLINING, CONSTANCE

Born: 1920, New York, N.Y. Died: Oct. 28, 1969, Los Angeles, Calif. (cardiac arrest). Stage and screen actress.

Appeared in: **1944** Knickerbocker Holiday; Up in Arms. **1946** The Black Angel; Blackie and the Law; The Well-Groomed Bride. **1947** Blind Spot. **1948** The Flame. **1950** Her Wonderful Lie; Mad about Opera. **1951** Stormbound. **1952** A Voice in Your Heart; Miss Italy. **1953** Duel without Honor. **1954** Gog. **1955** Othello.

DOWNES, OLIN

Born: 1886. Died: Aug. 22, 1955, New York, N.Y. (heart attack). Screen actor and writer.

Appeared in: **1947** Carnegie Hall. **1948** First Opera Film Festival (narr.).

DOWNING, HARRY

Born: 1894. Died: Jan. 9, 1972, Boston, Mass. (cancer). Screen and vaudeville actor.

Appeared in: High Up and Low Down (short). **1928** Lights of New York.

DOWNING, JOSEPH

Born: 1903. Died: Oct. 16, 1975, Canoga Park, Calif. (heart attack). Stage and screen actor.

Appeared in: **1935** Case of the Lucky Legs. **1937** Borrowing Trouble. **1938** A Slight Case of Murder; Wide Open Faces; The Devil's Party; Lady in the Morgue; Danger on the Air; The Night Hawk; Angels with Dirty Faces; Racket Busters; What Price Safety (short). **1939** You Can't Get Away with Murder; The Forgotten Woman; Each Dawn I Die; Smashing the Money Ring; Missing Evidence; Torchy Runs for Mayor; Invisible Stripes. **1940** The Secret Seven (short); Oh Johnny, How You Can Love; Jack Pot (short); Sandy Is a Lady. **1941** San Francisco Docks; Strange Alibi; Belle Starr; Unholy Partners; Johnny Eager; Flight from Destiny. **1942** Larceny, Inc.; The Big Shot; You Can't Escape Forever; My Gal Sal. **1953** Las Vegas Shakedown. **1957** Slaughter on Tenth Avenue.

DOWNING, ROBERT

Born: 1915. Died: June 15, 1975, Denver, Colorado. Screen, stage, television actor and drama critic.

Appeared in: **1954** On the Waterfront. **1961** Splendor in the Grass. **1968** No More Excuses.

DOWNING, WALTER

Born: 1874. Died: Dec. 21, 1937, Hollywood, Calif. Screen actor. Entered films in 1915.

Appeared in: **1924** Pied Piper Malone.

DOWSEY, ROSE WALKER. *See* ROSE WALKER

DOYLE, BUDDY

Born: 1901. Died: Nov. 9, 1939, New York, N.Y. (appendix operation). Stage and screen actor.

Appeared in: **1927** Take in the Sun (short); Georginia (short). **1929** At a Talkie Studio (short). **1936** The Great Ziegfeld.

DOYLE, JOHN T.

Born: 1873. Died: Oct. 16, 1935, New York, N.Y. Screen, stage actor and playwright.

Appeared in: **1929** Mother's Boy. **1931** His Woman. **1934** Gambling.

DOYLE, LEN

Born: 1893. Died: Dec. 6, 1959, Port Jervis, N.Y. Screen, stage, radio and television actor, stage director and stage producer.

Appeared in: **1962** Dead to the World.

DOYLE, MAXINE

Born: Jan. 1, 1915, San Francisco, Calif. Died: May 8, 1973, Studio City, Calif. (cancer). Screen, stage and radio actress. Married to film director William Witney.

Appeared in: **1934** The Key; Student Tour; 6-Day Bike Rider; Babbitt; Service with a Smile (short); Good Morning, Eve (short). **1935** The Mystery Man; Born to Gamble. **1936** Rio Grande Romance; Put on the Spot. **1937** Round-Up Time in Texas; Come On, Cowboys; SOS Coast Guard (serial); Thanks for Listening. **1938** Fury Below. **1943** G-Men vs. the Black Dragon (serial). **1944** Sing, Neighbor, Sing.

DOYLE, PATRICIA

Born: 1915. Died: Sept. 22, 1975, Los Angeles, Calif. (cancer). Screen actress and dancer. Married to film producer-director Robert Wise.

Appeared in: **1940** Grapes of Wrath.

DOYLE, REGINA

Born: 1907. Died: Sept. 30, 1931, Hollywood, Calif. (auto accident). Screen actress.

DRAINIE, JOHN

Born: 1916. Died: Oct. 30, 1966, Toronto, Ontario, Canada (cancer). Screen, television and radio actor.

Appeared in: **1963** The Incredible Journey.

DRAKE, JOSEPHINE S.

Died: Jan. 7, 1929, New York, N.Y. (pneumonia). Screen and stage actress.

Appeared in: **1926** The Song and Dance Man; A Social Celebrity; The Palm Beach Girl.

DRAKE, STEVE (Dale Laurence Fink)

Born: 1923. Died: Dec. 19, 1948, Burbank, Calif. (auto accident). Screen actor.

DRANE, SAM DADE

Died: Aug. 15, 1916, New York, N.Y. Stage and screen actor.

Appeared in: **1916** The Crisis.

DRANEM

Born: 1869, France. Died: Oct. 13, 1935, Paris, France. Stage and screen actor.

Appeared in: **1932** Il est Charmant (He Is Coming); Miche. **1935** Soir de Reveillon.

DRAPER, "OLD COLONEL" (Col. T. Waln-Morgan Draper)

Born: c. 1855. Died: Nov. 8, 1915. Screen actor. Entered films with Thanhouser.

DRAYTON, ALFRED (Alfred Varick)

Born: Nov. 1, 1881, Brighton, England. Died: Apr. 25, 1949, London, England. Stage and screen actor.

Appeared in: **1915** Iron Justice. **1919** A Little Bit of Fluff. **1920** The Honeypot; A Temporary Gentleman; The Winning Goal; **1921** The Adventures of Sherlock Holmes series including: A Scandal in Bohemia; Love Song. **1930** The Squeaker; The "W" Plan (US 1931). **1931** The Calendar (aka Bachelor's Folly—US); The Happy Ending; Brown Sugar. **1932** Lord Babs. **1933** Friday the Thirteenth; The Little Damozel; Falling for You; It's a Boy (US 1934). **1934** Jack Ahoy!; Red Ensign (aka Strike!—US); Radio Parade of 1935 (US 1935); Lady in Danger. **1935** The Love Affair of the Dictator (aka The Dictator and The Loves of a Dictator—US); Oh Daddy!; First a Girl; Look Up and Laugh; Me and Marlborough. **1936** The Crimson Circle; Tropical Trouble. **1937** Aren't Men Beasts! **1939** So This Is London (US 1940); **1941** Banada Ridge. **1942** The Big Blockade; Women Aren't Angels. **1944** Don't Take It to Heart (US 1949); The Halfway House (US 1945). **1945** They Knew Mr. Knight. **1947** Nicholas Nickleby. **1948** Things Happen at Night.

DRESSER, LOUISE (Louise Kerlin)

Born: Oct. 5, 1882, Evansville, Ind. Died: Apr. 24, 1965, Woodland Hills, Calif. (intestinal obstruction). Screen, stage and vaudeville actress. Divorced from actor Jack Norworth (dec. 1959) and later married actor and singer Jack Gardner (dec. 1950). During the first presentation of the Academy Awards she received a "Citation of Merit."

Appeared in: **1922** Enter Madame; Burning Sands; The Glory of Clementina. **1923** The Fog; Prodigal Daughters; Ruggles of Red Gap; Salomy Jane; Woman Proof; To the Ladies; **1924** The City That Never Sleeps; Cheap Kisses; What Shall I Do?; The Next Corner. **1925** The Eagle; The Goose Woman; Enticement; Percy. **1926** The Blind Goddess; Padlocked; Everybody's Acting; Gigolo; Broken Hearts of Hollywood; Fifth Avenue. **1927** The Third Degree; The White Flannels; Mr. Wu. **1928** The Air Circus; A Ship Comes in; The Garden of Eden; Mother Knows Best. **1929** The Madonna of Avenue A; Not Quite Decent. **1930** This Mad World; Mammy; Lightnin'; The Three Sisters. **1931** Caught. **1932** Stepping Sisters. **1933** Doctor Bull; Song of the Eagle; Cradle Song; State Fair. **1934** Hollywood on Parade (short); Servants Entrance; Girl of the Limberlost; David Harum; The Scarlet Empress; The World Moves On. **1935** The County Chairman. **1937** Maid of Salem.

DRESSLER, MARIE (Leila Koerber)

Born: Nov. 9, 1869, Coburg, Canada. Died: July 28, 1934, Santa Barbara, Calif. (cancer). Screen, stage, vaudeville actress and circus performer. Won 1930 Academy Award for Best Actress in Min and Bill.

Appeared in: **1914** Tillie's Punctured Romance (film debut). **1915** Tillie's Tomato Surprise; Tillie's Nightmare. **1917** The Scrublady. **1918** The Red Cross Nurse; The Agonies of Agnes. **1927** The Callahans and the Murphys; Breakfast at Sunrise; The Joy Girl. **1928** Bringing up Father; The Patsy. **1929** The Divine Lady; The Vagabond Lovers; The Hollywood Revue of 1929; Road Show. **1930** Chasing Rainbows; One Romantic Night; Let Us Be Gay; Derelict; Voice of Hollywood (short); Anna Christie; Caught Short; The Swan; March of Time; Call of the Flesh; The Girl Said No; Min and Bill. **1931** Reducing; Politics. **1932** Emma; Prosperity. **1933** Tugboat Annie; Dinner at Eight; Singer of Seville; Christopher Bean. **1964** Big Parade of Comedy (documentary).

DREW, ANN

Born: 1891, New York, N.Y. Died: Feb. 6, 1974, Miami, Fla. Screen actress. Entered films with D.W. Griffith in 1909.

Appeared in: **1921** His Brother's Keeper. **1923** Riders of the Range. **1927** The Red Raiders; Winds of the Pampas.

DREW, GLADYS RANKIN

Died: Jan. 9, 1914, New York, N.Y. Screen, stage actress and playwright. Married to actor Sidney Drew (dec. 1919) with whom she appeared on stage as his comedy partner. Mother of actor S. Rankin Drew (dec. 1918). She was daughter of actor McKee Rankin (dec.) and actress Kitty Blanchard (dec.).

DREW, SIDNEY

Born: Aug. 28, 1864, New York, N.Y. Died: Apr. 9, 1919, New York, N.Y. (uremia, heart disease). Screen, stage, vaudeville actor, film director and producer. Married to actress Gladys Rankin Drew (dec. 1914) with whom he appeared on stage as part of a comedy team. Later married to actress Lucille McVey (dec. 1925) who appeared on film with him in a series of "Mr. and Mrs. Sidney Drew" comedies between 1915 and 1919. Father of actor S. Rankin Drew (dec. 1918). He was member of Drew-Barrymore theatrical family.

Appeared in: **1911** When Two Hearts Are Won. **1913** A Regiment of Two; Jerry's Mother-in-Law; Beauty Unadorned; A Lesson in Jealousy; Why I Am Here; Sweet Deception; The Late Mr. Jones; The Master Painter; The Feudists. **1914** Innocent but Awkward; A Horseshoe—For Luck; Auntie's Portrait; Jerry's Uncle's Namesake; Good Gracious; A Florida Enchantment; Too Many Husbands; A Model Young Man; The Royal Wild West; Who's Who in Hogg's Hollow; Never Again. **1915** Wanted—A Nurse; Story of a Glove; A Safe Investment; Following the Scent; Boobley's Baby; A Case of Eugenics; The Fox Trot Finesse; The Home Cure; Romantic Reggie; When Two Play a Game; The Honeymoon Baby; Miss Sticky—Moufie-Kiss; The Combination; The Hair of Her Head; The Professor's Romance; Unlucky Louey; Their Night Out; The Cub and the Daisy Chain; Playing Dead; The Professor's Painless Cure; Mr. and Mrs. Drew in Their Agreement; Back to the Primitive. **1916** Childhood's Happy Days; At the Count of Ten; At a Premium; Taking a Rest; A Telegraphic Tangle; Too Clever by Half. **1917** How John Came Home; Diplomatic Henry; Rooney's Sad Case; By Might of His Right; All for the Love of a Girl; His Wife Knew About It; Beautiful Thoughts; Is Christmas a Bore?; The Hypochondriac; Cave Man's Bluff; His Perfect Day; The Pest; Blackmail; Locked Out; High Cost of Living; Awakening of Helen Minor; Handy Henry; Putting It Over on Henry; One of the Family; Her Lesson; Nothing to Wear; Her Anniversaries; Wages No Object; Too Much Henry; The Spirit of Merry Christmas; The Unmarried Look; Shadowing Henry; Rubbing It In; Her Obsession; Reliable Henry; The Matchmakers; Lest We Forget; Mr. Parker—Hero; Henry's Ancestors; His Ear for Music; Her Economic Independence; Her First Game; The Patriot; Music Hath Charm; His Curiosity; The Joy of Freedom; Double Life; The Dentist; Hist . . . Spies!; Twelve Good Hens and True; As Others See Us; A Lady in the Library; Duplicity; Help; Number

One; Nobody Home; His Deadly Calm; The Rebellion of Mr. Minor; Borrowing Trouble; His Rival; Their First; A Close Resemblance. **1918** Before and After Taking; Gas Logic; His First Love; Special Today; Romance and Rings; Why Henry Left Home. **1919** Squared; Once a Man; A Sisterly Scheme.

DREW, MRS. SIDNEY (Lucille McVey)
Born: Apr. 18, 1890, Sedalia, Mo. Died: Nov. 3, 1925, Hollywood, Calif. Screen, stage actress, film producer, director and screenwriter. She also appeared under her real name, Lucille McVey and as Jane Morrow. Was second wife of film actor Sidney Drew (dec. 1919) and appeared with him in a series of comedies between 1915 and 1919.

Appeared in: **1915** The Story of a Glove; Miss Sticky—Moufie-Kiss; A Safe Investment. **1916** At the Count of Ten; Childhood's Happy Days. **1917** Cave Man's Buff; His Perfect Day; The Pest; Blackmail; Her Obsession; Reliable Henry; Locked Out; High Cost of Living; Awakening of Helen Minor; Putting It over on Henry; Handy Henry; One of the Family; Safety First; Her Lesson; Nothing to Wear; Her Anniversaries; Tootsie; The Hypochondriac; The Matchmakers; Lest We Forget; Mr. Parker, Hero; Henry's Ancestors; His Ear for Music; Her Economic Independence; Her First Game; The Patriot; Music Hath Charms; Rubbing It In; His Curiosity; The Joy of Friends!; His Double Life; The Dentist; Hist . . . Spies!; Twelve Good Hens and True; His Deadly Calm; Rebellion of Mr. Minor; A Close Resemblance; As Others See Us; Too Much Henry; Wages No Object; The Spirit of Merry Christmas; The Unmarried Look; Shadowing Henry. **1918** A Youthful Affair; Duplicity. **1919** Romance and Rings; Once a Mason; A Sisterly Scheme; Bunkered; The Amateur Liar; Harold and the Saxons.

DREW, S. RANKIN (Sidney Rankin Drew)
Born: 1892, New York, N.Y. Died: May 19, 1918, France (shot down in plane during combat). Screen, stage actor and film director. Son of actor Sidney Drew (dec. 1919) and actress Gladys Rankin Drew.

Appeared in: **1913** His Tired Uncle; The Penalties of Reputation; My Lady Idleness; The Glove; An Unwritten Chapter; A Game of Cards. **1914** Mr. Barnes of New York. **1917** The Girl Philippa.

DREYFUSS, MICHAEL
Born: 1928. Died: Mar. 30, 1960, New York, N.Y. Screen, stage, television, radio actor and television director.

Appeared in: **1956** Patterns.

DRIGGERS, DONALD CLAYTON
Born: 1893. Died: Nov. 19, 1972, Birmingham, Ala. Screen actor. Entered films as an extra in 1927.

Appeared in: **1941** Sergeant York; Love Crazy; The Badlands of Dakota. **1942** Reap the Wild Wind; Woman of the Year.

DRISCOLL, BOBBY (Robert Driscoll)
Born: Mar. 3, 1937, Cedar Rapids, Iowa. Died: Jan. 1968, New York, N.Y. (occlusive coronary arteriosclerosis—hardening of the arteries). Screen actor. Won 1947 juvenile Academy Award for So Dear to My Heart and in 1949 for The Window.

Appeared in: **1943** Lost Angel (film debut). **1944** The Sullivans; Sunday Dinner for a Soldier. **1945** Big Bonanza; From This Day Forward; Identity Unknown. **1946** Miss Susie Slagle's; O.S.S.; So Goes My Love. **1947** So Dear to My Heart. **1948** Song of the South; If You Knew Susie; Melody Time. **1949** The Window. **1950** Treasure Island. **1951** When I Grow Up. **1952** The Happy Time. **1953** Peter Pan (voice). **1955** Scarlet Coat. **1958** Party Chasers.

DRISCOLL, SAM W.
Born: 1868. Died: Dec. 13, 1956, Hollywood, Calif. Screen actor and musician.

Appeared in: **1935** Mutiny on the Bounty.

DROESHOUT, ADRIAN
Born: 1897, New York. Died: Dec. 26, 1965, Los Angeles, Calif. Screen actor and publicist. Divorced from actress Frances Woodward.

DROUET, ROBERT
Died: Aug. 17, 1914, New York, N.Y. Screen actor. Entered films with Biograph.

Appeared in: **1913** On the Dumb Waiter. **1914** The Inspector's Story; Cricket on the Hearth.

DRUCE, HUBERT
Born: 1870, Richmond, England. Died: Apr. 6, 1931, New York, N.Y. (pneumonia). Stage and screen actor and stage producer.

Appeared in: **1917** Please Help Emily. **1918** Dodging a Million. **1928** Return of Sherlock Holmes. **1930** Laughing Lady. **1931** The Night Angel.

DRUMIER, JACK
Born: 1869. Died: Apr. 22, 1929, Clearwater, Fla. (pneumonia). Screen, stage and vaudeville actor.

Appeared in: **1917** The Adventures of Carol; The Volunteer. **1921** You Find It Everywhere; The Girl from Porcupine. **1922** The Broken Silence; The Splendid Lie; Shadows of the Sea. **1924** Emblems of Love. **1925** The Pinch Hitter; Enemies of Youth.

DUANE, JACK. See JACK PADJAN

DUARTE, MARIA EVA "EVITA"
Born: May 7, 1919, Los Toldos, Argentina. Died: July 26, 1952, Buenos Aires, Argentina (cancer). Screen and radio actress. Married to Argentine president Juan Peron (dec.)

DU BOIS, JEAN
Born: 1888, Sumatra, West Indonesia. Died: Oct. 28, 1957, Denver, Colo. (cancer). Screen actor. Entered films as a cameraman in 1925.

DUCHAMPS, MARCEL (Henri Robert Marcel Duchamps)
Born: July 28, 1887, Blainsville, Normandy, France. Died: Oct. 2, 1968, Neuilly, France. Artist and screen actor.

Appeared in: **1957** 8 x 8. **1968** Grimaces.

DUCHESS OLGA (Eva Liminana)
Born: 1899, Mexico. Died: Oct. 1953, Mexico City, Mexico. Screen actress, film producer and screenwriter. Divorced from Argentinian actor Jose Bohr. Appeared in Spanish language films made in both U.S. and Mexico.

DUCHIN, EDDY
Born: Apr. 1, 1909, Cambridge, Mass. Died: Feb. 9, 1951, New York, N.Y. (leukemia). Pianist, bandleader and screen actor.

Appeared in: **1932** Mr. Broadway. **1935** Coronado. **1937** Hit Parade.

DUDGEON, ELSPETH
Born: Dec. 4, 1871. Died: Dec. 11, 1955. Screen actress.

Appeared in: **1934** The Moonstone. **1935** Vanessa, Her Love Story; Becky Sharp; The Last Outpost. **1936** Give Me Your Heart. **1937** The Prince and the Pauper; Sh! The Octopus. **1938** Movie House. **1939** Bulldog Drummond's Secret Police. **1942** Random Harvest; Now, Voyager; Nightmare. **1943** Family Troubles (short). **1947** Yankee Fakir; Bulldog Drummond Strikes Back. **1949** Lust for Gold.

DUDLAH, DAVID (David Wiliford Kelly)
Born: 1892. Died: Feb. 26, 1947, Memphis, Tenn. Screen and carnival actor.

DUDLEY, JOHN (John Stuart Dudley)
Born: 1894. Died: May 1, 1966, Wilmington, N.C. Screen actor, screenwriter, playwright and lawyer.

Appeared in: **1956** Baby Doll. **1957** A Face in the Crowd.

DUDLEY, ROBERT Y.
Born: Sept. 13, 1875, Cincinnati, Ohio. Died: Nov. 12, 1955, San Clemente, Calif. Stage and screen actor. Entered films in 1920. Founder of the "Troupers Club of Hollywood."

Appeared in: **1921** The Traveling Salesman. **1922** Making a Man; The Ninety and Nine. **1923** Sixty Cents an Hour; The Tiger's Claw; The Day of Faith; Nobody's Bride. **1924** Flapper Wives; On the Stroke of Three. **1926** The Marriage Clause. **1927** Broadway Madness; The Lure of the Night Club. **1928** Skinner's Big Idea; On Trial; Fools for Luck; Baby Cyclone; The Night Flyer. **1929** Mysterious Island; Big News; Shanghai Rose. **1930** Wide Open. **1932** Three Wise Girls. **1937** Springtime in the Rockies; The Toast of New York. **1941** All That Money Can Buy. **1942** Palm Beach Story; Tennessee Johnson. **1944** It Happened Tomorrow. **1945** Col. Effingham's Raid. **1947** Magic Town. **1949** Portrait of Jennie. **1952** The Devil and Daniel Webster (reissue and retitle of All That Money Can Buy, 1941).

DUEL, PETER (Peter Deuel)
Born: 1940, Rochester, N.Y. Died: Dec. 31, 1971, Hollywood, Calif. (gunshot—suicide?). Screen and television actor. Brother of actor Geoffrey Deuel.

Appeared in: **1961** W.I.A.—Wounded in Action. **1968** The Hell with Heroes. **1969** Generation; Cannon for Cordoba.

DUFF, WARREN
Born: May 17, 1904, San Francisco, Calif. Died: Aug. 5, 1973, Los Angeles, Calif. (cancer). Screen, stage actor, screenwriter, television writer, stage and screen producer.

DUFFY, HENRY
Born: 1890, Chicago, Ill. Died: Nov. 18, 1961, Hollywood, Calif. (cancer). Screen, stage actor and stage producer.

DUFFY, JACK

Born: Sept. 4, 1882, Pawtucket, R.I. Died: July 23, 1939, Hollywood, Calif. Screen, stage, vaudeville actor and make-up artist.

Appeared in: 1924 The Brass Bowl; Reckless Romance. 1925 Madame Behave; Stop Flirting. 1926 Ella Cinders. 1927 No Control. 1928 Harold Teen. 1929 Loose Change (short); Hot Scotch (short); Divorce Made Easy; Sally. 1930 The Skin Game (short). 1931 Heaven on Earth. 1933 Alice in Wonderland. 1935 Pop Goes the Easel (short); Restless Knights (short); Here Comes Cookie. 1936 Wild Brian.

DUFRAINE, ROSA

Born: 1901. Died: Apr. 29, 1935, Duarte, Calif. Screen actress.

DUGAN, MARIE. *See* MARIE ENGLE

DUGAN, TOM (Thomas J. Dugan)

Born: 1889, Dublin, Ireland. Died: Mar. 6, 1955, Redlands, Calif. (auto accident). Screen, stage and vaudeville actor.

Appeared in: 1926 Early to Wed. 1927 By Whose Hand?; Swell Head; My Friend from India; The Kid Sister; The Small Bachelor. 1928 Soft Living; Shadows of the Night; The Barker; Broadway Daddies; Sharp Shooters; Dressed to Kill; Melody of Love; Midnight Taxi; Lights of New York. 1929 Broadway Babies; Drag; The Drake Case; The Million Dollar Collar; Kid Gloves; Sonny Boy; Hearts in Exile. 1930 They Learned about Women; The Bad One; Night Work; The Medicine Man; She Who Gets Slapped; Surprise. 1931 Bright Lights; Woman Hungry; Star Witness; The Hot Heiress. 1932 Big Timber; Dr. X; Big City Blues; Pride of the Legion; Blessed Event. 1933 Grand Slam; Skyway; Trick for Trick; The Sweetheart of Sigma Chi; Don't Bet on Love. 1934 Palooka; A Woman's Man; No More Women; The Circus Clown; Let's Talk It Over; Girl O' My Dreams; The President Vanishes. 1935 The Gilded Lady; One New York Night; Poker at Eight (short); Chinatown Squad; The Case of the Missing Man; Affair of Susan; Princess O'Hara; Three Kids and a Queen; Murder in the Fleet. 1936 Divot Diggers (short); The Calling of Dan Matthews; Pennies from Heaven; Wife vs. Secretary; Neighborhood House; Mister Cinderella. 1937 Nobody's Baby; Pick a Star; True Confession; She Had to Eat. 1938 Sing You Sinners; There's That Woman Again; Four Daughters. 1939 The Lone Wolf Spy Hunt; I'm from Missouri; Mystery of the White Room; The Lady and the Mob; House of Fear; Missing Evidence; $1000 a Touchdown; Laugh It Off; The Housekeeper's Daughter. 1940 Too Many Husbands; The Farmer's Daughter; The Fighting 69th; Isle of Destiny; The Ghost Breakers; Cross Country Romance; Half a Sinner; So You Won't Talk; A Little Bit of Heaven; Star Dust. 1941 Where Did You Get That Girl?; Ellery Queen's Penthouse Mystery; The Monster and the Girl; You're the One; A Dangerous Game; Tight Shoes; The Richest Man in Town; We Go Fast; Ellery Queen and the Murder Ring; The Bugle Sounds; Texas. 1942 Yokel Boy; A Haunting We Will Go; To Be or Not to Be; Yankee Doodle Dandy; Moontide; Meet the Stewarts; Star Spangled Rhythm. 1943 Bataan; Johnny Come Lately. 1944 Bermuda Mystery; Gambler's Choice; In Society; Greenwich Village; Hi, Beautiful!; Home in Indiana; Moon over Las Vegas; Swingtime Johnny; Ghost Catchers; Up in Arms. 1945 Don Juan Quilligan; Eadie Was a Lady; Earl Carroll Vanities; See My Lawyer; The Kid Sister; The Man Who Walked Alone; Tell It to a Star; Trail of Kit Carson; Her Highness and the Bellboy. 1946 The Best Years of Our Lives; Bringing up Father; Hoodlum Saint; Johnny Comes Flying Home; The Shadow Returns; Accomplice; It Shouldn't Happen to a Dog. 1947 The Fabulous Dorseys; The Pilgrim Lady; Good News; Ladies' Man; The Senator Was Indiscreet. 1948 Half Past Midnight; Texas, Brooklyn and Heaven. 1949 Take Me Out to the Ball Game. 1951 Painting the Clouds with Sunshine; The Lemon Drop Kid. 1952 Belle of New York. 1955 Crashout. 1968 The Further Perils of Laurel and Hardy (documentary).

DUGGAN, TOM (Thomas Duggan Goss)

Born: 1915, Chicago, Ill. Died: May 29, 1969, Los Angeles, Calif. (auto accident injuries). Screen, radio, television actor and newscaster. Divorced from actress Ann Duggan Goss. Do not confuse with actors Tom Dugan (dec. 1955) or Thomas Duggan.

DULAC, ARTHUR

Born: 1910, France. Died: Sept. 18, 1962, Hollywood, Calif. (coronary thrombosis). Screen actor.

Appeared in: 1953 Little Boy Lost.

DULIEN, TOBE (Tobie Ella Dulien)

Born: July 2, 1893, Latvia. Died: Nov. 27, 1969, Los Angeles, Calif. (heart attack). Screen and television actress.

DULLIN, CHARLES

Born: 1885, Yennes, France. Died: 1949, Paris, France. Screen, stage actor and stage producer.

Appeared in: 1921 Le Miracle des Loups (The Miracle of the Wolves—US 1925). 1925 Joueur D'Echecs (The Chessplayer—US 1930). 1927 Maldone (Misdeal). 1933 Les Miserables. 1937 Mademoiselle Docteur. 1938 The Courier of Lyons. 1939 Volpone. 1947 Les Jeux sont Faits; Que des Orfevres. 1948 Jenny Lamour. 1949 Chips are Down.

DuMAURIER, SIR GERALD

Born: Mar. 26, 1873, Hampstead, London, England. Died: Apr. 11, 1934, London, England (following operation for internal disorder). Screen, stage actor, author and stage producer. Married to stage actress Muriel Beaumont.

Appeared in: 1917 Justice; Masks and Faces; Everybody's Business. 1920 Unmarried. 1930 Escape. 1932 Lord Camber's Ladies. 1933 I Was a Spy (US 1934). 1934 Jew Suess (aka Power—US); Catherine the Great; The Scotland Yard Mystery (aka The Living Dead—US).

DUMBRILLE, DOUGLASS

Born: 1890, Hamilton, Ont., Canada. Died: Apr. 2, 1974, Woodland Hills, Calif. (heart attack). Screen, stage and television actor. Divorced from Jessie Lawson. Married to actress Patricia Mowbray.

Appeared in: 1931 His Woman; Monkey Business. 1932 That's My Boy; The Wiser Sex; Blondie of the Follies; Laughter in Hell. 1933 King of the Jungle; Heroes for Sale; Convention City; Female; The World Changes; Silk Express; Voltaire; Smoke Lightning; Rustlers' Round-Up; Lady Killer; The Big Brain; The Man Who Dared; The Way to Love; Elmer the Great; Laughter in Hell. 1934 Massacre; Fog over Frisco; Herold Teen; Journal of a Crime; The Secret Bride; Operator 13; Broadway Bill; Hi, Nellie; Treasure Island. 1935 Love Me Forever; Cardinal Richelieu; Peter Ibbetson; Lives of a Bengal Lancer; Naughty Marietta; Crime and Punishment; Air Hawks; Secret Bride; Unknown Woman; Public Menace. 1936 Calling of Dan Matthews; The Lone Wolf Returns; The Music Goes 'Round; Mr. Deeds Goes to Town; You May Be Next; End of the Trail; The Witness Chair; M'Liss; The Princess Comes Across. 1937 A Woman in Distress; A Day at the Races; Ali Baba Goes to Town; The Firefly; The Emperor's Candlesticks; Counterfeit Lady. 1938 Stolen Heaven; The Buccaneer; Mysterious Rider; Storm Over Bengal; Crime Takes a Holiday; Fast Company; Sharpshooters; Kentucky. 1939 Thunder Afloat; Charlie Chan at Treasure Island; Mr. Moto in Danger Island; The Three Musketeers; Charlie Chan in City in Darkness; Rovin' Tumbleweeds; Captain Fury; Tell No Tales. 1940 Slightly Honorable; The Catman of Paris; South of Pago Pago; Michael Shayne, Private Detective. 1941 Murder Among Friends; The Big Store; The Roundup; Washington Melodrama; Ellery Queen and the Perfect Crime. 1942 Stand by for Action; King of the Mounties (serial); I Married an Angel; Ride 'Em Cowboy; Castle in the Desert; A Gentleman After Dark; Ten Gentlemen from West Point. 1943 False Colors; DuBarry Was a Lady. 1944 Jungle Woman; Lost in a Harem; Forty Thieves; Lumberjack; Uncertain Gory; Gypsy Wildcat. 1945 Road to Utopia; The Frozen Ghost; Jungle Queen (serial); The Daltons Ride Again; Flame of the West. 1946 The Cat Creeps; Pardon my Past; Spook Busters; Night in Paradise; Monsieur Beaucaire; The Catman of Paris; Under Nevada Skies. 1947 Christmas Eve; Dishonored Lady; Blonde Savage; The Fabulous Texan; It's a Joke; Dragnet. 1948 Last of the Wild Horses. 1949 Alimony; Tell it to the Judge; Riders of the Whistling Pines; Dynamite; Joe Palooka in the Counterpunch; The Lone Wolf and His Lady. 1950 Her Wonderful Lie; Riding High; Buccaneer's Girl; Abbott and Costello in the Foreign Legion; The Kangaroo Kid; Rapture; The Savage Horde. 1951 A Millionaire for Christy. 1952 Sky Full of Moon; Son of Paleface; Apache War Smoke; Sound Off. 1953 Julius Caesar; Captain John Smith and Pocahontas; Plunder of the Sun. 1954 World for Ransom; Lawless Rider. 1955 Jupiter's Darling; Sky Full of Moon. 1956 The Ten Commandments; Shake, Rattle and Roll. 1958 The Buccaneer. 1962 Air Patrol. 1963 Johnny Cool. 1964 Shock Treatment.

DUMKE, RALPH

Born: 1900. Died: Jan. 4, 1964, Sherman Oaks, Calif. Screen, stage, radio and vaudeville actor.

Appeared in: 1949 All the King's Men. 1950 Where Danger Lives; Mystery Street; The Breaking Point; The Fireball; 1951 When I Grow Up; The Mob; The Law and the Lady. 1952 The San Francisco Story; Boots Malone; Carbine Williams; We're Not Married; Holiday for Sinners; Hurricane Smith. 1953 Lili; Hannah Lee; Mississippi Gambler; Massacre Canyon; The President's Lady. 1954 She Couldn't Say No; Alaska Seas; They Rode West; Rails into Laramie. 1955 Daddy Long Legs; Artists and Models; Violent Saturday; Hell's Island; They Came from Another World. 1956 Francis in the Haunted House; Forever Darling; When Gangland Strikes; Invasion of the Body Snatchers; Solid Gold Cadillac. 1957 The Buster Keaton Story; Loving You. 1960 Wake Me When It's Over. 1961 All in a Night's Work.

DuMONT, GORDON

Born: 1894, Milwaukee, Wis. Died: Mar. 1966, Hollywood, Calif. Screen actor.

Appeared in: 1921 A Certain Rich Man. 1924 Phantom Justice.

DUMONT, MARGARET

Born: 1889. Died: Mar. 6, 1965, Los Angeles, Calif. (heart attack). Screen, stage and television actress. Won 1937 Screen Actor Guild award for A Day at the Races.

Appeared in: 1929 The Cocoanuts. 1930 Animal Crackers. 1931 Girl Habit. 1933 Duck Soup. 1934 Gridiron Flash; Fifteen Wives; Kentucky Kernals. 1935

A Night at the Opera; Orchids to You; Rendezvous. **1936** Song and Dance Man; Anything Goes. **1937** A Day at the Races; The Life of the Party; High Flyers; Youth on Parole; Wise Girl. **1938** Dramatic School. **1939** The Women; At the Circus. **1941** The Big Store; Never Give a Sucker an Even Break; For Beauty's Sake. **1942** Born to Sing; Sing Your Worries Away; Rhythm Parade; About Face. **1943** The Dancing Masters. **1944** Bathing Beauty; Seven Days Ashore; Up in Arms. **1945** The Horn Blows at Midnight; Diamond Horseshoe; Sunset in El Dorado. **1946** The Little Giant; Susie Steps Out. **1952** Three for Bedroom C. **1953** Stop, You're Killing Me. **1956** Shake, Rattle and Roll. **1958** Auntie Mame. **1962** Zotz! **1964** What a Way to Go.

DUNBAR, DAVID

Born: Sept. 14, 1893, West Maitland, N.S.W., Australia. Died: Nov. 7, 1953, Woodland Hills, Calif. Screen actor.

Appeared in: **1924** Trail Dust; The Fortieth Door (serial and feature); Leatherstocking (serial); North of 36. **1925** The Bloodhound; Fair Play; The Cowboy Musketeer; Ridin' the Wind; Galloping Vengeance: A Man of Nerve. **1926** The Galloping Cowboy; The Non-Stop Flight; Beyond the Rockies. **1927** King of Kings; The Boy Rider; The Broncho Buster; Gold from Weepah; The Arizona Whirlwind; The Fighting Hombre. **1929** Plunging Hoofs. **1930** The Return of Dr. Fu Manchu. **1938** Kidnapped. **1942** Mrs. Miniver.

DUNBAR, HELEN

Born: 1868. Died: Aug. 28, 1933, Los Angeles, Calif. Screen, stage and vaudeville actress.

Appeared in: **1915** Graustark. **1917** The Great Secret (serial). **1920** Behold My Wife. **1921** Her Winning Way; The House That Jazz Built; Sham; The Great Moment; Sacred and Profane Love; The Little Clown. **1922** Beyond the Rocks; The Impossible Mrs. Bellew; The World's Champion; A Homespun Vamp; The Law and the Woman; Man of Courage; Thirty Days. **1923** Hollywood; The Call of the Canyon; The Cheat. **1924** Changing Husbands; This Woman; The Fighting Coward; Three Weeks. **1925** Siege; The Reckless Sex; Rose of the World; Compromise; The Man without a Conscience; The Woman Hater; His Majesty, Bunker Bean; Lady Windermere's Fan; New Lives for Old; She Wolves. **1926** Meet the Prince; Stranded in Paris; His Jazz Bride; Fine Manners; The Man Upstairs.

DUNCAN, BOB

Born: Dec. 7, 1904, Topeka, Kans. Died: Mar. 13, 1967, North Hollywood, Calif. (suicide—gun). Screen actor and television director.

Appeared in: **1944** End of the Road. **1945** The Cisco Kid Returns; Weekend at the Waldorf. **1949** The Fighting Redhead. **1950** Law of the Panhandle. **1953** The Marshal's Daughter. **1957** The Parson and the Outlaw. **1963** Black Gold.

DUNCAN, BUD (Albert Edward Duncan)

Born: Oct. 31, 1883, New York, N.Y. Died: Nov. 25, 1960, Los Angeles, Calif. (circulatory failure). Screen, stage, vaudeville actor and author. Partner with Lloyd Hamilton (dec. 1935) in vaudeville and film team of "Ham and Bud."

Appeared in: **1913** His Nobs, the Plumber; Teddy Loosebelt from Africa; The Rube Boss. **1914** Dad's Terrible Match; The Winning Whiskers; Ham at the Garbageman's Ball; Ham, the Piano Mover. **1915** Cookey's Adventure; A Melodious Mix-Up; Ham in the Harem; Ham and the Jitney Bus; The Merry Moving Men; Ham at the Fair; The Phoney Cannibal; Ham's Easy Eats; Rushing the Lunch Counter; Ham, the Detective; The Liberty Party; Ham in the Nut Factory; Romance a la Carte; Double Crossing Marmaduke; Foiled; Queering Cupid; Adam's Ancestors; The Knaves and the Knight; Minnie the Tiger; Only a Country Girl; Hoodoo's Busy Day; A Bargain in Brides; Oh, Doctor; The Bandits of Macaroni Mountains; The Hypnotic Monkey; Whitewashing William; Diana of the Farm; The Missing Mummy; The Caretaker's Dilemma; Ham's Harrowing Duel; Ham Among the Redskins; The Pollywog's Picnic; Lotta Cain's Ghost; Ham at the Beach; Mixing It Up; Nearly a Bride; Raskey's Road Show; The Spook Raisers; The Toilers; In High Society. **1916** Guardian Angels; Snoop Hounds; The Tale of a Coat; Artful Artists; Wurr-Wurra; Ham takes a Chance; A Molar Mix-Up; Ham the Diver; Winning the Widow; Ham Agrees with Sherman; Ham and the Hermit's Daughter; Maybe Moonshine; For Sweet Charity; From Altar to Halter; Millionaires by Mistake; Ham and Preparedness; Ham's Waterloo; Ham's Busy Day; A Bunch of Flivvers; Ham the Explorer; The Beggar of His Child; Ham and the Masked Marvel; The Tank Town Troupe; Midnight at the Old Mill; The Alaskan Mouse Hount; The Peach Pickers; The Baggage Smashers; The Great Detective; Ham's Whirlwind Finish; Good Evening, Judge; Ham's Strategy; Star Boarders; Ham in the Drugstore; Ham the Fortune Teller; Patented by Ham; One Step Too Far; The Mud Cure; The Bogus Booking Agents; The Love Magnet; A Sauerkraut Symphony; Bumping the Bumps. **1917** Rival Romeos; Cupid's Caddies; The Blundering Blacksmiths; Safety Pin Smugglers; A Flyer in Flapjacks; Efficiency Experts; Bulls or Bullets?; The Bogus Bride; Hard Times in Hardscrapple; The Deadly Doughnut; A Misfit Millionaire; A Menagerie Mixup; A Day Out of Jail; Seaside Romeos; Doubles and Troubles. **1918** Rip Roaring Rivals; The Curse of the Make-Believes; Wooing of Coffee Cake Cate. **1919** Maggie Pepper. **1927** The Haunted Ship. **1942** Snuffy Smith, Yard Bird; Hillbilly Blitzkrieg.

DUNCAN, EDITH JOHNSON. *See* EDITH JOHNSON

DUNCAN, EVELYN

Born: Jan. 21, 1893, Los Angeles, Calif. Died: June 8, 1972, Bellflower, Calif. Screen, stage and vaudeville actress. Sister of actresses Rosetta (dec. 1959) and Vivian Duncan.

Appeared in: **1929** Imperfect Ladies.

DUNCAN, KEENE (Kenneth D. MacLachlan)

Born: Feb. 17, 1902, Chatham, Ont., Canada. Died: Feb. 5, 1972, Hollywood, Calif. (stroke). Screen, stage actor and stuntman.

Appeared in: **1930** The Man from Wyoming; Derelict. **1931** No Limit. **1933** Shadow River. **1935** Charing Cross Road. **1936** Racetrack Racketeer; Under Cover; Cross My Heart; Make Up. **1937** Colorado Kid. **1938** Frontier Scout; Mars Attacks the World; The Spider's Web (serial). **1939** Roll, Wagons, Roll; Fighting Thoroughbreds; Buck Rogers (serial). **1941** Buck Privates; King of the Texas Rangers (serial); Adventures of Captain Marvel (serial); The Spider Returns (serial). **1942** Perils of Nyoka (serial); Westward, Ho; Code of the Outlaw; Man With Two Lives; Isle of Missing Men; Law and Order; Texas to Bataan. **1943** The Batman (serial); The Avenging Rider; The Sundown Kid; Border Buckaroos; Fugitive from Sonora; Daredevils of the West (serial). **1944** Sheriff of Las Vegas; End of the Road; Haunted Harbor (serial); Storm over Lisbon; Trail of Terror; Beneath Western Skies; The Tiger Woman (serial); Wolves of the Range; Outlaws of Santa Fe; Pride of the Plains; Mojave Firebrand; Hidden Valley Outlaws; Vigilantes of Dodge City; Stagecoach to Monterey; Sheriff of Sundown; Cheyenne Wildcat. **1945** A Sporting Chance; Road to Alcatraz; The Chicago Kid; The Master Key (serial); Trail of Kit Carson; Manhunt of Mystery Island (serial); The Purple Monster Strikes (serial). **1946** Drifting Along; Sioux City Sue; The Crimson Ghost (serial); Home on the Range; Rainbow Over Texas; Sheriff of Redwood Valley; Sun Valley Serenade; California Gold Rush; My Pal Trigger; The Phantom Rider (serial); Man from Rainbow Valley; Night Train to Memphis; Roll on Texas Moon; Santa Fe Uprising; Rio Grande Raiders; Red River Renegades; The Mysterious Mr. Valentine; Conquest of Cheyenne; Code of the Saddle; The Scarlet Horseman (serial). **1947** Twilight on the Rio Grande. **1948** Hidden Danger. **1949** Riders of the Sky; Deputy Marshall; Across the Rio Grande; Crashing Thru; Gun Runner; Law of the West; Range Land; West of El Dorado; Roaring Westward (aka Boom Town Badmen); Shadow of the West; Stampede; Range Justice; Lawless Code. **1950** Davy Crockett, Indian Scout; The Blazing Sun (aka The Blazing Hills); Mule Train; Radar Secret Service; Sons of New Mexico; Indian Territory; Code of the Silver Sage. **1951** Hills of Utah; Badman's Gold; Nevada Badmen; Whirlwind; Silver Canyon; Pirate's Harbor (rerelease and retitle of 1944 serial, Haunted Harbor). **1953** On Top of Old Smoky; Pack Train. **1954** The Lawless Rider. **1955** Hell's Horizon. **1956** Flesh and the Spur. **1957** Revolt at Fort Laramie. **1958** The Astounding She Monster. **1959** A Date With Death; Night of the Ghouls (aka Revenge of the Dead). **1960** Natchez Trace. **1961** The Sinister Urge.

DUNCAN, ROSETTA

Born: 1900, Los Angeles, Calif. Died: Dec. 4, 1959, Acero, Ill. (auto accident injuries). Screen, stage and vaudeville actress. Sister of Vivian Duncan and Evelyn Duncan (dec. 1972). Entered films in 1926.

Appeared in: **1927** Two Flaming Youths; Topsy and Eva. **1929** It's a Great Life. **1935** Broadway Brevities (short).

DUNCAN, WILLIAM A.

Born: 1880. Died: Feb. 8, 1961, Hollywood, Calif. Screen, stage actor and film director. Entered films in 1910. Married to actress Edith Johnson with whom he appeared in film serials.

Appeared in: **1917** Vengeance and the Woman (serial); The Fight Trail (serial). **1918** A Fight for Millions (serial). **1919** Man of Might (serial); Smashing Barriers (serial); Perils of Thunder Mountain (serial). **1920** The Silent Avenger (serial). **1921** Fighting Fate (serial); Where Men Are Men; Steelheart. **1922** No Defense; The Silent Vow; When Danger Smiles; The Fighting Guide. **1923** The Steel Trail (serial); Smashing Barriers (1919 serial rereleased as feature film); Playing It Wild. **1924** The Fast Express (serial); Wolves of the North (serial).

DUNCAN, WILLIAM CARY

Born: Feb. 6, 1874, North Brookfield, Mass. Died: Nov. 12, 1945, North Brookfield, Mass. (heart ailment). Screen actor, playwright, author, screenwriter and lyricist. Entered films with Famous Players in 1929.

Appeared in: **1935** Nevada. **1936** Three on the Trail. **1937** Hopalong Rides Again; Thunder Trail. **1938** Bar 20 Justice; The Frontiersman. **1939** Law of the Pampas. **1940** The Farmer's Daughter. **1941** Texas Rangers Ride Again.

DUNDEE, JIMMY

Born: 1901. Died: Nov. 20, 1953, Woodland Hills, Calif. (leukemia). Screen actor, stuntman, boxer and auto racer.

Appeared in: **1934** The Mighty Barnum. **1938** The Buccaneer. **1940** Murder over New York. **1944** Hail the Conquering Hero. **1948** Whispering Smith. **1949** My Friend Irma. **1950** My Friend Irma Goes West; At War with the Army. **1951** Sailor Beware.

DUNHAM, PHILLIP "PHIL" (Phillip Gray Dunham)
Born: Apr. 23, 1885, London, England. Died: Sept. 5, 1972, Los Angeles, Calif. Screen, stage and vaudeville actor.

Appeared in: 1915 Flirtation a la Carte; Dad's Dollars and Dirty Doings; Gaby's Gasoline Glide; Spring Fever; Lizzie's Lingering Love; Shooting His 'Art Out. 1916 Limburger Cyclone; Phil's Busy Days. 1917 On the Trail of the Lonesome Pill; Faking Fakers; After the Balled-Up Ball; Even as Him and Her; The Joy Riders; Love and Blazes; A Good Little Bad Boy; Dry Goods and Damp Deeds; Chicken Chased and Henpecked; Nabbing a Noble; Defective Detectives; Summer Boarders. 1918 Playthings; Kidder and Co. 1919 In Bad All Around; Man Hunters. 1920 All for the Dough Bag. 1921 Two Minutes to Go; Punch of the Irish (short). 1922 Alias Julius Caesar; The Barnstormer; The Deuce of Spades. 1923 The Dangerous Maid; Robin Hood, Jr. 1931 Scratch as Catch Can (short). 1932 Jitters the Butler (short); Hurry Call. 1933 Fighting Parson; Fugitive; Rainbow Ranch. 1934 Perfectly Mismated (short); Everything Ducky (short); Search for Beauty; Down to Their Last Yacht. 1935 I'm a Father (short). 1936 Hair-Trigger Casey; Idaho Kid; Cavalcade of the West. 1937 Beware of Ladies; Aces Wild; Navy Spy; Bank Alarm. 1938 Fury Below. 1939 Our Leading Citizen. 1940 West of the Pinto Basin. 1942 Code of the Outlaw. 1953 Hold Your Temper (short).

DUNN, EDWARD F. "EDDIE"
Born: 1896. Died: May 5, 1951, Hollywood, Calif. Screen actor.

Appeared in: 1928 The Fleet's In. 1929 The Saturday Night Kid; plus the following shorts: Bouncing Babies; The Hoose Gow; Sky Boy. 1930 Headin' North; True to the Navy; The Land of Missing Men; plus the following shorts: Another Fine Mess; Whispering Whoopee; Looser Than Loose; The Head Guy; The Fighting Parson. 1931 The Gang Buster; plus the following shorts: A Melon-Drama; False Roomers; The Pajama Party; Skip the Maloo!; The Hasty Marriage; Love Fever. 1932 The Big Broadcast; In Walked Charley (short). 1933 The following shorts: Me and My Pal; The Midnight Patrol; Asleep in the Fleet; Fallen Arches; Sherman Said It. 1935 Car 99; Here Comes Cookie; The Bride Comes Home; Powder Smoke Range. 1936 The Big Broadcast of 1937; The Preview Murder Mystery; plus the following shorts: Locks and Bonds; Dumb's the Word; Tramp Trouble. 1938 The Sky Parade; The Bride Walks Out; Rascals; Give Me a Sailor; plus the following shorts: Kennedy's Castle; Beaux and Errors; A Clean Sweep; His Pest Friend. 1939 Let Freedom Ring; Hollywood Cavalcade; Three Smart Girls Grow Up; Tail Spin; Wrong Room (short). 1940 On Their Own; The Great Profile; Mexican Spitfire Out West; The Great Dictator; One Night in the Tropics. 1941 In the Navy; The Saint in Palm Springs; The Gay Falcon. 1942 Mississippi Gambler; The Falcon's Brother; Invisible Agent; Ride 'Em Cowboy; Mexican Spitfire at Sea. 1943 Hit the Ice; The Falcon in Danger; Hello, Frisco, Hello; Dixie Dugan. 1944 Bermuda Mystery; Dead Man's Eyes; Henry Aldrich's Little Secret; Army Wives; Nothing But Trouble; Lost in a Harem. 1945 Frontier Gal; Wonder Man; George White's Scandals; State Fair; See My Lawyer; Here Come the Co-Eds. 1946 Centennial Summer; Bowery Bombshell. 1947 Scareheads; Buck Privates Come Home; The Flame; Television Turmoil (short). 1948 Call Northside 777; Lightning in the Forest; Big Punch; Homicide for Three; Checkered Coat. 1949 Incident; I Shot Jesse James; Mother Is a Freshman. 1950 Mary Ryan, Detective; Lonely Hearts; Bandits; Whirlpool; Buckaroo Sheriff of Texas.

DUNN, EMMA
Born: 1875, Cheshire, England. Died: Dec. 14, 1966, Los Angeles, Calif. Stage and screen actress. Entered films in 1919.

Appeared in: 1920 Old Lady 31. 1924 Pied Piper Malone. 1929 Side Street. 1930 The Texan; Broken Dishes; Manslaughter. 1931 Too Young to Marry; Big Business Girl; The Prodigal; Compromised; Bad Company; Morals for Women; Bad Sister; This Modern Age; The Guilty Generation. 1932 We Three; Wet Parade; The Man I Killed; The Cohens and the Kellys in Hollywood; Hell's House; Letty Lynton; It's Tough to Be Famous; Blessed Event; Broken Lullaby; Under Eighteen. 1933 Grand Slam; Hard to Handle; Man of Sentiment; Elmer, the Great; Private Jones; It's Great to Be Alive; Walls of Gold. 1934 Dark Hazard; The Quitter; Doctor Monica. 1935 This Is the Life; George White's Scandals of 1935; The Glass Key; Keeper of the Bees; The Little Big Shop; Ladies Crave Excitement; Another Face; Seven Keys to Baldpate; The Crusades. 1936 The Harvester; Second Wife; Mr. Deeds Goes to Town. 1937 When You're in Love; The Emperor's Candlesticks; Madame X; The Hideaway; Varsity Show; Circus Girl. 1938 The Cowboy from Brooklyn; Thanks for the Memory; The Cowboy and the Lady; Lord Jeff; Three Loves Has Nancy; Duke of West Point; Young Dr. Kildare. 1939 Calling Dr. Kildare; The Secret of Dr. Kildare; Hero for a Day; The Llano Kid; Son of Frankenstein; Each Dawn I Die. 1940 High School; Little Orvie; Dr. Kildare's Strangest Case; Dr. Kildare Goes Home; You Can't Fool Your Wife; Half a Sinner; One Crowded Night; Dance, Girl, Dance; Yesterday's Heroes; The Great Dictator. 1941 The Penalty; Scattergood Baines; Scattergood Pulls the Strings; Scattergood Meets Broadway; Mr. and Mrs. Smith; Dr. Kildare's Wedding Day; Ladies in Retirement; Rise and Shine. 1942 The Postman Didn't Ring; The Talk of the Town; Babes on Broadway; When Johnny Comes Marching Home; I Married a Witch. 1943 Hoosier Holiday; Minesweeper; The Cross of Lorraine. 1944 The Bridge of San Luis Rey; It Happened Tomor-

row; Are These Our Parents?; My Buddy. 1945 The Horn Blows at Midnight. 1946 The Hoodlum Saint; Night Train from Memphis. 1947 Life with Father; Mourning Becomes Electra. 1948 Woman in White.

DUNN, HARVEY B.
Born: Aug. 19, 1894, South Dakota. Died: Feb. 21, 1968, Hollywood, Calif. (cirrhosis of liver). Screen actor.

Appeared in: 1956 Bride of the Monster. 1959 Teenagers from Outer Space; The Remarkable Mr. Pennypacker.

DUNN, J. MALCOLM
Born: England. Died: Oct. 10, 1946, Long Island, N.Y. Screen, stage and radio actor.

Appeared in: 1920 Dr. Jekyll and Mr. Hyde. 1921 The Magic Cup; Dawn of the East. 1926 Sandy. 1930 The Sap from Syracuse; Absent Minded (short).

DUNN, JACK (John Edward Powell Dunn)
Born: Mar. 28, 1917, Tunbridge Wells, England. Died: July 16, 1938, Los Angeles, Calif. (tularemia). Ice Skater and screen actor. Won male figure skating title at 1936 Olympic Games.

DUNN, JAMES (James Howard Dunn)
Born: Nov. 2, 1905, New York, N.Y. Died: Sept. 1967, Santa Monica, Calif. Screen, stage and television actor. Married to singer Edna Rush. Divorced from Edna O'Lier and actress Frances Gifford. Won 1945 Academy Award for Best Supporting Actor in A Tree Grows in Brooklyn.

Appeared in: 1931 Bad Girl; Over the Hill; Sob Sister. 1932 Society Girl; Handle with Care; Dance Team; Walking Down Broadway. 1933 Jimmy and Sally; Sailor's Luck (aka Hello Sister); Hold Me Tight; Arizona to Broadway; Take a Chance; The Girl in 419. 1934 Hold That Girl; Change of Heart; Baby Takes a Bow; Have a Heart; She Learned about Sailors; 365 Nights in Hollywood; Bright Eyes; Stand Up and Cheer. 1935 George White's Scandals of 1935; The Daring Young Man; Welcome Home; The Pay-Off; Bad Boy. 1936 Don't Get Personal; Hearts in Bondage; Come Closer Folks; Two-Fisted Gentlemen. 1937 Mysterious Crossing; We Have Our Moments; Living on Love; Venus Makes Trouble. 1938 Shadows over Shanghai. 1939 Pride of the Navy. 1940 Son of the Navy; Mercy Plane; A Fugitive from Justice; Hold That Woman. 1942 The Living Ghost. 1943 The Ghost and the Guest; Government Girl. 1944 Leave It to the Irish. 1945 The Caribbean Mystery; A Tree Grows in Brooklyn. 1946 That Brennan Girl. 1947 Killer McCoy. 1948 Texas, Brooklyn and Heaven. 1950 The Golden Gloves Story. 1951 A Wonderful Life. 1960 The Bramble Bush. 1962 Hemingway's Adventures of a Young Man. 1966 The Oscar.

DUNN, JOHN J.
Born: 1906, Binghamton, N.Y. Died: Apr. 2, 1938, Bluefield, W.Va. (pneumonia). Screen, stage and radio actor.

Appeared in: 1917 The Seven Pearls (serial).

DUNN, MICHAEL (Gary Neil Miller)
Born: Oct. 20, 1934, Shattuck, Okla. Died: Aug. 29, 1973, London, England. Screen, stage and television actor. Nominated for 1965 Academy Award as Best Supporting Actor in Ship of Fools.

Appeared in: 1965 Ship of Fools. 1967 You're a Big Boy Now; Without Each Other. 1968 Madigan; No Way to Treat a Lady; Boom! 1969 Justine; Fight for Rome (Pt. 1). 1971 Murders in the Rue Morgue. 1973 House of Freaks.

DUNN, RALPH
Born: 1902. Died: Feb. 19, 1968. Screen actor.

Appeared in: 1938 The Tenth Avenue Kid; Numbered Woman; Come On Leathernecks. 1939 Tail Spin; The Return of the Cisco Kid; The Lone Ranger Rides Again (serial); Scouts to the Rescue (serial); Desperate Trails. 1940 The Green Hornet (serial). 1941 The Lady from Cheyenne; Sun Valley Serenade. 1942 Moontide. 1943 He Hired the Boss. 1944 Laura; The Hairy Ape; Roger Touhy, Gangster; Wilson; Dark Mountain. 1945 Circumstantial Evidence; Within These Walls; Along Came Jones; Love, Honor and Goodbye; An Angel Comes to Brooklyn; Dick Tracy. 1946 Murder is My Business; Larceny in Her Heart; The Missing Lady; Genius at Work; Nobody Lives Forever; Gas House Kids; Lady Chasers. 1947 Three on a Ticket; Too Many Winners; News Hounds; Dragnet. 1948 The Babe Ruth Story; Jinx Money; The Mystery of the Golden Eye; King of the Gamblers; Lady at Midnight; Train to Alcatraz; Incident. 1949 The Lost Tribe. 1950 Mary Ryan, Detective; Singing Guns; The Great Plane Robbery. 1953 Taxi. 1956 Crowded Paradise. 1957 The Pajama Game. 1960 From the Terrace. 1964 Black Like Me.

DUNN, ROBERT "BOBBY"
Born: 1891, Milwaukee, Wis. Died: Mar. 24, 1939, Hollywood, Calif. (heart attack). Screen actor.

DUNN, REV. ROBERT H.
Born: 1896. Died: Feb. 11, 1960, Portsmouth, N.H. Screen actor and clergyman.

Appeared in: **1920** "Mirthquake" comedies. **1921** Skirts. **1926** The Thrill Hunter; When the Wife's Away. **1928** The Upland Rider. **1929** The Wagon Master; Captain Cowboy; 'Neath Western Skies; Code of the West; The Racketeer; Riders of the Storm; The Royal Rider. **1930** Half Pint Polly (short); Call of the Desert; Canyon Hawks; Trails of Peril; The Parting of the Trails; Parade of the West; The Canyon of Missing Men; The Cry Baby (short). **1933** Me and My Pal (short). **1934** Them Thar Hills (short). **1935** Tit for Tat (short); The Fixer-Uppers (short). **1936** The Bohemian Girl; Our Relations. **1949** Lost Boundaries. **1951** The Whistle at Eaton Falls. **1952** Walk East on Beacon.

DUNNE, CHARLES
Died: Sept. 16, 1951, "Heartbreak Ridge," Korea (killed in action). Screen actor.

DUNROBIN, LIONEL CLAUDE
Born: 1875. Died: Aug. 15, 1950, Hollywood, Calif. (suicide). Screen actor.

DUNSKUS, ERICH
Born: 1890, Germany. Died: Nov. 25, 1967, Hagen, West Germany. Screen, stage and television actor.

Appeared in: **1940** Gluck auf den Lande (Rural Happiness). **1950** Girls behind Bars. **1954** A Prize of Gold.

DUNSMUIR, ALEXANDER
Born: 1877, Scotland. Died: July 30, 1938, Los Angeles, Calif. (auto crash injuries). Screen actor.

DUNTON, HELEN
Died: Nov. 1920, San Francisco, Calif. (suicide). Screen actress.

DU PEA, TATZUMBIE
Born: July 26, 1849, California. Died: Feb. 28, 1970, Los Angeles, Calif. (heart failure). American Indian screen actress.

Appeared in: **1931** Cimarron. **1934** Laughing Boy. **1940** 20 Mule Team. **1942** Tortilla Flat. **1944** Buffalo Bill. **1950** Across the Wide Missouri.

DU PONT, PATRICIA (aka MISS DU PONT)
Born: 1894, Frankfort, Ky. Died: Feb. 5, 1973. Screen and stage actress.

Appeared in: **1921** The Rage of Paris. **1922** False Kisses; The Golden Gallows; Foolish Wives; Shattered Dreams: A Wonderful Wife. **1923** The Common Law; The Broken Wing; The Man from Brodney's; Brass. **1924** So This is Marriage; One Night in Rome; Sinners in Silk; What Three Men Wanted. **1925** Raffles, the Amateur Cracksman; Three Keys; Defend Yourself; Accused; A Slave of Fashion. **1926** Good and Naughty; Mantrap; That Model from Paris. **1928** Wheel of Destiny.

DUPREE, MINNIE
Born: 1873, San Francisco, Calif. Died: May 23, 1947, New York, N.Y. Stage and screen actress.

Appeared in: **1929** Night Club. **1938** The Young in Heart. **1940** Anne of Windy Poplars.

DUPREZ, FRED
Born: Sept. 6, 1884, Detroit, Mich. Died: Oct. 27, 1938, aboard ship bound for England (heart attack). Screen, stage, radio and vaudeville actor. Father of actress June Duprez.

Appeared in: **1933** Heads We Go (aka The Charming Deceiver—US); Oh What a Duchess! (aka My Old Duchess); Meet My Sister. **1934** Without You; Love, Life and Laughter; Danny Boy. **1935** Dance Band; No Monkey Business; Dark World. **1936** Ball at Savoy; A Wife or Two; Queen of Hearts; The Big Noise; Gypsy Melody; International Revue; Hearts of Humanity; You Must Get Married; Reasonable Doubt; All that Glitters. **1937** Cafe Colette (aka Danger in Paris—US); Head Over Heels (aka Head Over Heels in Love—US); Kathleen Mavourneen (aka Kathleen—US 1938); Knights for a Day; Okay for Sound. **1938** Hey! Hey! U.S.A.; Take Off that Hat.

DU PUIS, ARTHUR (Adolph Arthur Pierre Piete Du Puis)
Born: Mar. 29, 1901, Canada. Died: Apr. 18, 1952, Los Angeles, Calif. Screen actor, stuntman and makeup artist.

Appeared in: **1936** The Last of the Mohicans.

DURAN, VAL
Born: 1896. Died: Feb. 1, 1937, Los Angeles, Calif. (influenza). Screen actor.

Appeared in: **1936** The General Died at Dawn. **1937** Join the Marines; The Lost Horizon.

DURAND, EDOUARD
Born: 1871, France. Died: July 31, 1926, Port Chester, N.Y. (stroke). Stage and screen actor.

Appeared in: **1922** Anna Ascends. **1923** Potash and Perlmutter. **1924** The Lone Wolf. **1925** The King on Main Street; The Sky Raider.

DURAND, JEAN
Born: 1882, Paris, France. Died: 1946, Paris, France. Screen actor and film director.

DURFEE, MINTA
Born: 1890, Los Angeles, Calif. Died: Sept. 9, 1975, Woodland Hills Calif. (congestive heart failure). Screen, television and vaudeville actress. Divorced from actor Fatty Arbuckle (dec. 1933).

Appeared in: **1913** His Wife's Mistake. **1914** A Misplaced Foot; A Busted Johnny (aka Making a Living); A Film Johnnie; Twenty Minutes of Love; The Jazz Waiter (aka Caught in a Cabaret); Our Country Cousin; The Pugilist (aka The Knock-out); The Masquerader; The Rounders; Among the Mourners; Leading Lizzie Astray; Tillie's Punctured Romance; Fattie and Minnie-He-Haw; Cruel, Cruel Love. **1915** Love, Speed and Thrills; Colored Villainy; Fatty's Spooning Day (aka Mabel, Fatty and the Law); Other People's Wives (aka The Home Breakers); Hearts and Planets; Our Daredevil Chief; Court House Crooks; A Desperate Scoundrel (aka Dirty Work in a Laundry); Fickle Fatty's Fall. **1916** The Great Pearl Tangle; Ambrose's Cup of Woe; His Wife's Mistakes; The Other Man. **1918** Mickey; The Cabaret. **1925** Bright Lights. **1926** Skinner's Dress Suit. **1941** Rolling Home to Texas; How Green Was my Valley. **1942** The Miracle Kid. **1956** Hollywood or Bust. **1964** The Unsinkable Molly Brown.

DURIEUX, TILLA (Ottilie Godeffroy)
Born: 1881, Vienna, Austria. Died: Feb. 21, 1971, Berlin, Germany (after operation necessitated by fall). Screen, stage and television actress.

Appeared in: **1957** The Last Bridge.

DURKIN, ELEANOR
Died: prior to 1968. Screen and vaudeville actress. Married to actor James Burke (dec. 1968) and appeared with him in vaudeville in an act billed as "Burke and Durkin."

They appeared in: **1929** A Tete-A-Tete in Songs (short).

DURKIN, JAMES PETER
Born: 1879. Died: Mar. 12, 1934, Los Angeles, Calif. Stage and screen actor.

Appeared in: **1930** Derelict; Shadow of the Law. **1934** Uncertain Lady; Wild Girl; Nice Women; Alexander Hamilton; Vice Squad; Gun Smoke; Conquering Horde; Heat Lightning.

DURKIN, JUNIOR (Trent Junior Durkin)
Born: 1915, New York, N.Y. Died: May 4, 1935, near San Diego, Calif. (auto accident). Stage and screen actor.

Appeared in: **1930** Fame (film debut); Tom Sawyer; Santa Fe Trail; Recaptured Love; The Law Rides West. **1931** The Conquering Horde; Huckleberry Finn. **1932** Hell's House. **1933** Manhunt. **1934** Little Men; Big Hearted Herbert.

DURNING, BERNARD J.
Born: 1893. Died: Aug. 29, 1923, New York, N.Y. (typhoid). Screen actor and film director. Married to screen actress Shirley Mason.

Appeared in: **1919** Blackie's Redemption. **1921** Devil Within; Seeds of Vengeance.

DURST, EDWARD
Born: 1917. Died: Mar. 10, 1945, Hollywood, Calif. Screen and stage actor.

Appeared in: **1944** Days of Glory.

DURYEA, DAN
Born: Jan. 23, 1907, White Plains, N.Y. Died: June 7, 1968, Los Angeles, Calif. (cancer). Screen, stage and television actor. Father of actor Peter Duryea.

Appeared in: **1941** The Little Foxes; Ball of Fire. **1942** Pride of the Yankees; That Other Woman. **1943** Sahara. **1944** Woman in the Window; Ministry of Fear; Main Street after Dark; Mrs. Parkington; None but the Lonely Heart; The Man from Frisco. **1945** Scarlet Street; Lady on a Train; Along Came Jones; The Great Flamarion; Valley of Decision. **1946** White Tie and Tails; Black Angel. **1948** Larceny; Another Part of the Forest; Black Bart; River Lady. **1949** Criss Cross; Manhandled; Too Late for Tears; Johnny Stool-Pigeon. **1950** One Way Street; Winchester 73; The Underworld Story. **1951** Al Jennings of Oklahoma; Chicago Calling. **1953** Thunder Bay; Sky Commando. **1954** Ride Clear of Diablo; World for Ransom; Thirty Six Hours (aka Terror Street—US); Rails into Laramie; This Is My Love; Silver Lode. **1955** The Marauders; Foxfire. **1956** Battle Hymn; Storm Fear. **1957** The Burglar; Slaughter on Tenth Avenue; Night Passage. **1958** Kathy O'. **1960** Platinum High School; Rich, Young and Deadly. **1962** Six Black Horses. **1964** He Rides

Tall; Taggart; Walk a Tightrope. **1965** Flight of the Phoenix; The Faceless Men; The Bounty Killer. **1966** Incident at Phantom Hill. **1967** The Hills Run Red; A River of Dollars. **1968** Five Golden Dragons; The Bamboo Saucer.

DURYEA, GEORGE. *See* TOM KEENE

DUSE, ELEANORA

Born: 1858, Vigerano, Italy. Died: Apr. 23, 1924, Pittsburgh, Pa. Stage and screen actress.

Appeared in: **1916** Cenere. **1927** Madre.

DuVAL, JOE (Jose DuVal)

Born: 1907. Died: Apr. 22, 1966. Screen actor.

Appeared in: **1951** The Girl on the Bridge. **1963** The Cardinal.

DUVAL, JUAN

Died: 1954. Screen actor.

Appeared in: **1930** One Mad Kiss. **1933** California Trail. **1936** The Black Coin (serial). **1940** Rhythm of the Rio Grande; Arise, My Love. **1946** Trail to Mexico. **1948** The Feathered Serpent. **1949** Neptune's Daughter. **1950** The Palomino.

DUVALLES (Frederic Duvalles)

Born: 1895, France. Died: Feb. 1971, France. Screen and stage actor.

Appeared in: **1932** Paris-Mediterranee. **1933** On Demande un Compagnon. **1963** The Burning Court.

DUXBURY, ELSPETH

Born: 1912, India. Died: Mar. 10, 1967, London, England. Screen, stage and television actress.

Appeared in: **1960** Make Mine Mink. **1966** The Great St. Trinian's Train Robbery (US 1967)

DWIGGINS, JAY

Died: Sept. 8, 1919. Screen actor.

Appeared in: **1914** Bunny's Little Brother. **1915** A Mistake in Typesetting; Mr. Jarr and Gertrude's Beaux; A Disciple of Plato; The Smoking Out of Bella Butts; The Lady of Shalott; The Capitulation of the Major; They Loved Him So; Whose Husband?; Strictly Neutral; War; The Starring of Flora Finchurch; The Kidnapped Stockbroker; Sis; Old Good-for-Nothin'; A Queen for an Hour; The Reward; Brown's Summer Boarders; The Dust of Egypt; A Man's Sacrifice; Sonny Jim's First Love Affair; Heredity. **1916** By Love Redeemed; A Film Exposure. **1917** A Finished Product; His Uncle Dudley; Whose Baby? **1918** He Comes Up Smiling; Bound in Morocco. **1919** The Poor Boob; In for Thirty Days; Whitewashed Walls; The Man Who Turned White. **1920** Everywoman.

DWIRE, EARL

Born: 1884. Died: Jan. 16, 1940, Carmichael, Calif. Screen actor.

Appeared in: **1931** Dugan of the Bad Lands. **1932** Law of the West; Man from Hell's Edges; Son of Oklahoma. **1933** Galloping Romeo; Riders of Destiny; Sagebrush Trail. **1934** West of the Divide; The Lucky Texan; Randy Rides Alone; The Star Packer; Trail Beyond; Lawless Frontier. **1935** Unconquered Bandit; Wagon Trail; Fighting Pioneers; Smokey Smith; Rider of the Law; Saddle Acres; Between Men; Last of the Clintons; Toll of the Desert. **1936** Millionaire Kid; Caryl of the Mountains; Desert Justice; Roamin' Wild; The Last Assignment; The Speed Reporter; Cavalcade of the West; Sundown Saunders; Headin' for the Rio Grande; Stormy Trails; The Gun Ranger. **1937** The Mystery of the Hooded Horseman; Arizona Days; Trouble in Texas; The Trusted Outlaw; Riders of the Rockies; Hittin' the Trail; Riders of the Dawn; Galloping Dynamite; Atlantic Flight; Trouble at Midnight; Git Along, Little Dogies. **1938** Accidents Will Happen; Under Western Stars; Trouble at Midnight; The Purple Vigilantes; The Old Barn Dance; The Daredevil Drivers; Two-gun Justice; Man from Music Mountain; Six Shootin' Sheriff; Mysterious Rider; Angels with Dirty Faces; Gold Mine in the Sky. **1939** The Star Maker; The Arizona Kid; On Trial. **1940** King of the Lumberjacks.

DWYER, JOHN T.

Born: 1877. Died: Dec. 7, 1936, New York, N.Y. Screen, stage and radio actor.

Appeared in: **1920** Over the Hill to the Poor House. **1926** Jack O'Hearts; The Man in the Shadow.

DYALL, FRANKLIN

Born: Feb. 3, 1874, Liverpool, England. Died: May 8, 1950, Worthing, England. Screen, stage, radio actor and stage producer. Father of actor Valentine Dyall.

Appeared in: **1919** The Garden of Resurrection. **1927** Easy Virtue (US 1928). **1929** Atlantic. **1931** Alibi; The Ringer (US 1932); A Night in Montmartre; Creeping Shadows (aka The Limping Man—US 1932); A Safe Affair. **1932** Men of Steel. **1933** Called Back; The Private Life of Henry VIII. **1935** The

Iron Duke; The Case of Gabriel Perry. **1936** Conquest of the Air. **1939** All at Sea. **1943** Yellow Canary (US 1944). **1948** Bonnie Prince Charlie.

D'YD, JEAN

Born: France. Died: May 1964, France. Screen actress.

Appeared in: **1929** The Passion of Joan of Arc. **1938** Rothschild. **1939** Entente Cordiale. **1940** SOS Mediterranean. **1948** The Room Upstairs; L'Eternal Retour (The Eternal Return). **1955** Martin Roumagnac; Chiens Perdus Sans Collier.

DYER, BOB (James Robert Dyer).

Born: 1900. Died: Nov. 19, 1965, Hollywood, Calif. Entered films approx. 1930. Screen actor.

DYER, JOHN E.

Born: 1884. Died: Oct. 11, 1951, Detroit, Mich. Screen and vaudeville actor.

EAGAN, EVELYN

Born: 1908. Died: July 17, 1946, Hollywood, Calif. Screen actress.

EAGELS, JEANNE

Born: 1894, Kansas City, Mo. Died: Oct. 3, 1929, New York, N.Y. Stage and screen actress.

Appeared in: **1916** The World and the Woman. **1917** Fires of Youth; Under False Colors. **1918** The Cross Bearer. **1927** Man, Woman and Sin. **1929** The Letter; Jealousy.

EAGER, JOHNNEY (John Tanner)

Born: 1930. Died: Sept. 8, 1963, Hollywood, Calif. Screen, stage and television actor.

Appeared in: **1963** Four for Texas.

EAGLE, JAMES "JIMMY" (James Crump Eagle)

Born: Sept. 10, 1907, Virginia. Died: Dec. 15, 1959, Los Angeles, Calif. (cirrhosis of liver). Screen actor.

Appeared in: **1928** Crooks Can't Win; Hey Rube! **1929** Half Marriage. **1930** Abraham Lincoln; The Big Fight; Son of the Gods. **1932** Thirteenth Guest; Parisian Romance; You Said a Mouthful; Gambling Sex. **1933** The Penal Code; From Hell to Heaven; She Done Him Wrong; Story of Temple Drake; To the Last Man. **1934** Massacre; He Was Her Man; Opened by Mistake (short). **1935** Sunset Range; Rocky Mountain Mystery; Charlie Chan in Egypt. **1936** I'd Give My Life; Down the Stretch; Racing Blood. **1938** The Painted Trail; All-American Sweetheart; Heroes of the Hills. **1950** When Willie Comes Marching Home.

EAMES, CLARE

Born: 1896, Hartford, Conn. Died: Nov. 8, 1930, London, England. Stage and screen actress.

Appeared in: **1924** Dorothy Vernon of Haddon Hall. **1929** The Three Passions.

EARL, CATHERINE V.

Born: 1886. Died: Aug. 14, 1946, Hollywood, Calif. (heart attack). Stage and screen actress.

EARL, KATHLEEN

Born: 1913. Died: May 21, 1954, Hollywood, Calif. Screen and stage actress.

EARLCOTT, GLADYS

Died: May 18, 1939, Los Angeles, Calif. Stage and screen actress.

EARLE, BLANCHE "BONNIE"

Born: 1883. Died: Jan. 22, 1952, Woodland Hills, Calif. (heart attack). Screen actress. Married to silent film director William P. S. Earle.

Appeared in: **1915** Battle Cry of Peace. **1917** Within the Law.

EARLE, DOROTHY

Died: 1958. Screen actress. Married to screen actor Gabby Hayes (dec. 1969).

Appeared in: **1927** Out of the Night; Pioneers of the West.

EARLE, EDWARD

Born: July 16, 1882, Toronto, Canada. Died: Dec. 15, 1972, Woodland Hills, Calif. Screen, stage and vaudeville actor.

Appeared in: **1915** Greater than Art; The Working of a Miracle; The Bedouin's Sacrifice; Olive and the Heirloom; Olive is Dismissed; The Lesson of the Flames; Olive's Opportunities; Olive's Manufactured Mother; Olive's Other Self. **1916** Ranson's Folly. **1917** For France. **1918** The Blind Adventure; One Thousand Dollars; Transients in Arcadia. **1919** Buried Treasure; His Bridal Night; Miracle of Love. **1920** Law of the Yukon. **1921** East Lynne; Passion Fruit. **1922** False Fronts; The Man Who Played God; The Streets of New York. **1923** Broadway Broke; None So Blind; You are Guilty. **1924** The Dangerous Flirt; The Lure of Love; How to Educate a Wife; Gambling Wives; The Family

Secret. **1925** Her Market Value; The Lady Who Lied; The Splendid Road; Why Women Love. **1926** The Greater Glory; A Woman's Heart; Irene; Pals First. **1927** Twelve Miles Out; Spring Fever. **1928** Runaway Girls; The Wind. **1929** The Hottentot; Kid Gloves; Spite Marriage; Smiling Irish Eyes. **1930** In the Next Room; Phantom of the Desert. **1931** Woman of Experience; Second Honeymoon. **1932** Forgotten Women. **1933** Revenge at Monte Carlo; Alimony Madness. **1934** Ticket to a Crime; Little Miss Marker; Mystery Mountain (serial); He Was Her Man. **1935** Revenge Rider; Fighting Lady; Chinatown Squad; Mutiny Ahead; Magnificent Obsession. **1936** Life Hesitates at 40 (short); The Case Against Mrs. Ames; Dangerous Waters. **1937** Headline Crasher; Find the Witness; The Frame Up; Artists and Models; A Day at the Races; History is Made at Night. **1938** When G-Men Step In; Her Jungle Love; The Marines are Here; Riders of the Black Hills; The Headleys at Home; I Am a Criminal; The Duke of West Point; Start Cheering; Give Me a Sailor. **1939** In Old Monterey; The Green Hornet (serial); Honolulu; East Side of Heaven. **1940** Seventeen; Sued for Libel; On Their Own. **1941** Ride, Kelly, Ride; Scattergood Baines; Blue, White and Perfect; Border Vigilantes; Great Guns. **1943** Two Weeks to Live; Alaska Highway; Bordertown Gun Fighters; The Good Fellows; Jack London; The Dancing Masters. **1944** Black Magic; I Accuse My Parents; Nothing but Trouble; Ghost Catchers. **1945** Circumstantial Evidence; Captain Tugboat Annie; The Cisco Kid in Old Mexico. **1946** The Harvey Girls; Dark Alibi; The Devil's Mask; Accomplice. **1947** Ride the Pink Horse; Beginning or the End. **1948** Command Decision. **1949** That Midnight Kiss; The Gal Who Took the West. **1950** Blondie's Hero; When You're Smiling. **1951** The Texas Rangers; Flight to Mars. **1953** Stranger Wore a Gun. **1955** A Man Called Peter.

EARLE, JACK (Jacob Ehrlich)
Born: 1906, Denver, Colo. Died: July 18, 1952, El Paso, Texas. Screen actor and circus performer.

Appeared in: **1924** Jack and the Beanstalk.

EARLY, MARGOT
Born: 1915. Died: Jan. 1936, Hollywood, Calif. (auto crash). Screen actress.

Appeared in: **1934** Operator 13. **1935** Naughty Marietta.

EARLY, PEARL M.
Born: 1879, Wooster, Ohio. Died: June 17, 1960, Oceanside, Calif. Screen and vaudeville actress. Toured in vaudeville with her husband John Early in an act billed as "Early & Laight."

Appeared in: **1942** My Favorite Blonde.

EASON, REEVES B. "BREEZY"
Born: 1886, Fryors Point, Miss. Died: June 10, 1956, Sherman Oaks, Calif. (heart attack). Screen, stage, vaudeville actor, film producer, director and screenwriter. Divorced from actress Jimsy Maye (dec. 1968). Father of child actor Breezy Eason (dec. 1921).

Appeared in: **1912** The Law of the Wilds. **1915** The Echo; When Empty Hearts are Filled; In the Purple Hills. **1916** The Better Woman. **1928** The Danger Rider.

EASON, REEVES "BREEZY, JR."
Born: 1913. Died: Oct. 24, 1921, Hollywood, Calif. (struck by auto). Screen actor. Son of actor Eason Reeves (dec. 1956). Entered films with Universal.

Appeared in: **1920** Two Kinds of Love. **1921** The Big Adventure; The Fox; Sure Fire.

EAST, ED
Born: 1896, Bloomington, Ind. Died: Jan. 18, 1952, New York, N.Y. (heart attack). Screen, stage, vaudeville, radio actor, and pianist. Appeared in vaudeville with Ralph Dumke.

Appeared in: **1937** Educational short. **1938** Universal short. **1949** Jackpot Jitters. **1951** Stop That Cab.

EATON, EVELYN
Born: 1924. Died: June 17, 1964, Los Angeles, Calif. Screen, stage and television actress. Married to announcer, Eddie King.

EATON, JAMES (James Latessa)
Born: Oct. 2, 1934, Ohio. Died: May 8, 1964, West Hollywood, Calif. (suicide—barbiturate poisoning). Screen and television actor.

EATON, JAY
Born: 1900. Died: Feb. 5, 1970, Hollywood, Calif. (heart attack). Screen actor. Entered films in 1919.

Appeared in: **1921** Where Lights Are Low. **1928** Lady Be Good; Man-Made Woman; The Noose; Three-Ring Marriage. **1929** Synthetic Sin. **1933** The Cocktail Hour. **1934** The Affairs of Cellini. **1935** A Night at the Opera; Southern Exposure (short). **1946** The Kid from Brooklyn.

EATON, MABEL
Died: Jan. 10, 1916, Chicago, Ill. Screen actress. Divorced from actor William Farnum (dec. 1953).

Appeared in: **1914** The Fable of the Good Fairy.

EATON, MARY
Born: 1901, Norfolk, Va. Died: Oct. 10, 1948, Hollywood, Calif. (heart attack). Stage and screen actress. Married to screen actor Eddie Lawton.

Appeared in: **1923** His Children's Children. **1924** Broadway after Dark. **1929** The Cocoanuts; Glorifying the American Girl.

EBERG, VICTOR
Born: 1925, Mexico? Died: Feb. 26, 1972, Hollywood, Calif. (sclerosis of the liver). Screen and television actor.

Appeared in: **1969** Butch Cassidy and the Sundance Kid.

EBERT, BERNIE
Born: 1915. Died: Jan. 13, 1969, Hollywood, Calif. (heart attack). Screen, stage, television actor and television producer, director.

EBI, EARL
Born: June 25, 1903, Fresno, Calif. Died: Jan. 24, 1973, Encino, Calif. (heart attack). Screen, stage actor, film producer, director, television producer, radio producer and director.

Appeared in: **1936** The Singing Cowboy; Hearts in Bondage.

EBURNE, MAUDE
Born: 1875. Died: Oct. 15, 1960, Hollywood, Calif. Screen and stage actress.

Appeared in: **1931** Lonely Wives; Bought; The Man in Possession; Larceny Lane; Blonde Crazy; The Bat Whispers; The Guardsman; Her Majesty; Love; Indiscreet. **1932** Under Eighteen; Panama Flo; Polly of the Circus; The Passionate Plumber; Woman from Monte Carlo; The Trial of Vivienne Ware; First Year; Stranger in Town; This Reckless Age. **1933** Vampire Bat; Ladies They Talk About; Ladies Must Love; Robbers' Roost; Shanghai Madness; The Warrior's Husband; My Lips Betray; Big Executive; East of Fifth Avenue; Havana Widows. **1934** Fog; When Strangers Meet; Here Comes the Navy; Return of the Terror; Lazy River; Love Birds. **1935** Maybe It's Love; Happiness C.O.D.; Ruggles of Red Gap; Party Wire; Don't Bet on Blondes. **1936** Doughnuts and Society; Reunion; Man Hunt; The Leavenworth Case; Poppy; Valiant Is the Word for Carrie. **1937** Champagne Waltz; When's Your Birthday?; Hollywood Cowboy; Fight for Your Lady; Live, Love and Learn; Paradise Express. **1938** Riders of the Black Hills. **1939** Exile Empress; My Wife's Relatives; Mountain Rhythm; Meet Dr. Christian; Sabotage; The Covered Trailer. **1940** The Courageous Dr. Christian; Dr. Christian Meets the Women; Remedy for Riches; The Border Legion. **1941** Melody for Three; They Meet Again; Glamour Boy; West Point Widow; Among the Living; You Belong to Me. **1942** Henry and Dizzy; To Be or Not to Be; Almost Married; Henry Aldrich, Editor; The Boogie Men Will Get You. **1943** Lady Bodyguard. **1944** Henry Aldrich Plays Cupid; The Princess and the Pirate; Rosie the Riveter; The Suspect; Goodnight, Sweetheart; The Town Went Wild; Bowery to Broadway; I'm from Arkansas. **1945** Man from Oklahoma; Hitchhike to Happiness; Leave It to Blondie. **1947** Mother Wore Tights. **1948** The Plunderers. **1949** Arson, Inc. **1951** Prince of Peace (aka The Lawton Story).

ECCLES, JANE
Born: 1896. Died: July 1966, London, England. Screen, stage, and television actress.

Appeared in: **1959** Look Back in Anger.

ECKERLEIN, JOHN E.
Born: 1884, N.Y. Died: Sept. 9, 1926, New York, N.Y. Screen and vaudeville actor.

Appeared in: **1923** Little Old New York.

ECKHARDT, OLIVER J.
Born: 1873. Died: Sept. 15, 1952, Hollywood, Calif. Screen actor.

Appeared in: **1925** Sporting Life. **1927** The Last Trail. **1928** The Cavalier. **1930** The Lone Star Ranger.

ECKLES, LEWIS C. "LEW"
Born: 1888. Died: Mar. 26, 1950, Kansas City, Mo. (heart attack). Stage and screen actor. Married to actress Cara Louise Field.

Appeared in: **1945** The House on Ninety-Second Street.

ECKLUND, CAROL
Born: 1934. Died: Nov. 4, 1939 (burns). Five-year-old screen actress.

EDDY, MRS. AUGUSTA ROSSNER
Born: 1860. Died: Sept. 21, 1925, New York, N.Y. Screen and stage actress.

EDDY, DOROTHY
Born: 1907. Died: June 10, 1959, Brooklyn, N.Y. Screen and vaudeville actress. One of the "Four Eddy Sisters," of vaudeville and film fame.

EDDY, NELSON
Born: June 29, 1901, Providence, R.I. Died: Mar. 6, 1967, Miami, Fla. (stroke). Screen, radio, opera and television actor.

Appeared in: **1933** Broadway to Hollywood; Dancing Lady. **1934** Student Tour. **1935** Naughty Marietta. **1936** Rose Marie. **1937** Maytime; Rosalie. **1938** The Girl of the Golden West; Sweethearts. **1939** Let Freedom Ring; Balalaika. **1940** Bitter Sweet; New Moon. **1941** The Chocolate Soldier. **1942** I Married an Angel. **1943** The Phantom of the Opera. **1944** Knickerbocker Holiday. **1946** Never Say Goodbye; Nobody Lives Forever; Willy, The Operatic Whale (voice only); Make Mine Music (voice only). **1947** End of the Rainbow; Northwest Outpost. **1974** That's Entertainment (film clips).

EDESON, ROBERT
Born: 1868, New Orleans, La. Died: Mar. 24, 1931, Hollywood, Calif. (heart attack). Stage and screen actor. Divorced from actress Mary Newcomb (dec. 1967).

Appeared in: **1914** Where the Trail Divides. **1915** How Molly Made Good. **1916** The Light That Failed. **1921** Extravagance. **1922** Any Night; The Prisoner of Zenda; Sure-Fire Flint; **1923** The Spoilers; Has the World Gone Mad?; Luck; The Silent Partner; Souls for Sale; The Ten Commandments; The Tie That Binds; To the Last Man; You Are Guilty. **1924** Feet of Clay; The Bedroom Window; Don't Call It Love; Mademoiselle Midnight; Men; Missing Daughters; Thy Name Is Woman; Triumph; Welcome Stranger. **1925** Blood and Steel, Braveheart; The Danger Signal; Go Straight; The Golden Bed; Hell's Highroad; Keep Smiling; Locked Doors; Men and Women; The Prairie Pirate; The Rag Man; The Scarlet West. **1926** The Blue Eagle; The Clinging Vine; Eve's Leaves; Her Man O'War; The Volga Boatman; Whispering Smith. **1927** King of Kings; Altars of Desire; The Heart Thief; His Dog; The Night Bride; The Rejuvenation of Aunt Mary. **1928** Tenth Avenue; Marriage by Contract; The Home Towners; The Man Higher Up; The Power of the Press; Beware of Blondes; A Ship Comes In; Walking Back. **1929** George Washington Cohen; Marianne; The Little Wildcat; The Doctor's Secret; A Most Immoral Lady; Romance of the Rio Grande; Dynamite. **1930** Danger Lights; Big Money; Little Johnny Jones; Way of All Men; Cameo Kirby; Pardon My Gun; Swing High; A Devil with Women. **1931** Aloha; The Lash.

EDGAR-BRUCE, TONI
Born: June 4, 1892, London, England. Died: Mar. 28, 1966, Chertsey, England. Screen, stage and radio actress. Daughter of stage actor/manager Edgar Bruce (dec.).

Appeared in: **1920** Duke's Son (aka Squandered Lives—US). **1930** A Warm Corner. **1932** Brother Alfred; Diamond Cut Diamond (aka Blame the Woman—US); Mr. Bill the Conqueror (aka The Man Who Won—US 1933); Lucky Girl. **1933** Letting in the Sunshine; The Melody Maker; As Good as New; Leave It to Me; Falling for You; Heads We Go (aka The Charming Deceiver—US); The Private Life of Henry VIII. **1934** Whispering Tongues; The Broken Melody; Lilies of the Field. **1935** Handle with Care; Night Mail; Mr. What's-His-Name; Captain Bill. **1936** The Last Waltz. **1937** Behind Your Back; Boys Will be Girls. **1938** Scruffy; The Citadel. **1939** Too Dangerous to Live. **1942** Gert and Daisy Clean Up; The First of the Few (aka Spitfire—US 1943); Somewhere on Leave. **1944** Heaven is Round the Corner. **1945** Waltz Time. **1952** Derby Day (aka Four Against Fate—US 1955).

EDLER, CHARLES
Born: 1877. Died: Mar. 29, 1942, Santa Monica, Calif. Screen and stage actor.

Appeared in: **1921** The Magnificent Brute; That Girl Montana. **1922** The Sign of the Rose.

EDMUNDSEN, AL
Born: 1896, Pueblo, Colo. Died: May 11, 1954. Screen and stage actor.

Appeared in: **1915** The Butterfly; Just Jim. **1922** Foolish Wives. **1923** Merry Go Round.

EDSTROM, KATHERINE
Born: 1901. Died: June 2, 1973, Hollywood, Fla. Screen, stage and television actress. Once billed as "Queen of the Alligator Wrestlers." She appeared in early silents.

EDWARDS, ALAN
Born: June 3, 1900, New York, N.Y. Died: May 8, 1954, Los Angeles, Calif. Stage and screen actor. Entered films with Edison Co. in 1912. Married to actress Nita Pike (dec. 1954).

Appeared in: **1921** A Virgin Paradise. **1933** The White Sister; Clear All Wires; Looking Forward; Stage Mother; Life in the Raw. **1934** The Show Off; The Frontier Marshall; Hold That Girl. **1935** If You Could Only Cook; Women Must Dress. **1936** Ring around the Moon; Forgotten Faces; Make Way for a Lady. **1937** Forty Naughty Girls. **1938** Little Tough Guy. **1939** South of the Border. **1941** Mr. District Attorney. **1945** Thoroughbreds; Junior Miss. **1946** Mr. Ace.

EDWARDS, CLIFF "UKELELE IKE"
Born: June 14, 1895, Hannibal, Mo. Died: July 17, 1971, Hollywood, Calif. Screen, stage, vaudeville actor and singer. Divorced from singer Irene Wiley and actress Nancy Dover.

Appeared in: **1929** The Hollywood Revue of 1929; So This Is College?; Marianne; What Price Glory? **1930** Montana Moon; Dogway Melody (short); Way Out West; Romeo in Pajamas; Those Three French Girls; Good News; Forward March; The Lullaby; Dough Boys; Lord Byron of Broadway; War Babies. **1931** Parlor, Bedroom and Bath; The Great Lover; The Sin of Madelon Claudet; Dance, Fools, Dance!; Stepping Out; The Prodigal; Shipmates; Sidewalks of New York; Laughing Sinners; Hell Divers. **1932** The Big Shot; Fast Life; Love Starved. **1933** Flying Devils; Take a Chance; MGM short. **1934** George White's Scandals. **1935** George White's 1935 Scandals; Red Salute. **1936** The Man I Marry. **1937** They Gave Him a Gun; Between Two Women; Saratoga; Bad Guy; The Women Men Marry; MGM short. **1938** The Girl of the Golden West; The Bad Man of Brimstone; The Little Adventuress. **1939** Maisie; Smuggled Cargo; Royal Rodeo (short); Gone with the Wind. **1940** High School; His Girl Friday; Pinocchio (voice of Jiminy Cricket); Millionaires in Prison; Flowing Gold; Friendly Neighbors. **1941** The Monster and the Girl; She Couldn't Say No; Power Dive; Knockout; International Squadron; Thunder Over the Prairie; Prairie Stranger. **1942** West of Tombstone; Sundown Jim; Lawless Plainsmen; Riders of the Northland; Bad Men of the Hills; Seven Miles to Alcatraz; Pirates of the Prairie; Overland to Deadwood; American Empire; Bandit Ranger. **1943** Fighting Frontier; The Falcon Strikes Back; Salute for Three; The Avenging Rider. **1947** Fun and Fancy Free (voice). **1965** The Man from Button Willow (voice). **1974** That's Entertainment (film clips).

EDWARDS, EDNA PARK
Born: 1895, Pittsburgh, Pa. Died: June 5, 1967, Burbank, Calif. Screen, stage, vaudeville actress and radio writer.

EDWARDS, ELEANOR
Born: 1883, N.Y. Died: Oct. 22, 1968, Los Angeles, Calif. Stage and screen actress. Entered films in 1922. Married to actor Snitz Edwards (dec. 1937).

EDWARDS, GUS (Gus Simon)
Born: Aug. 18, 1881, Germany. Died: Nov. 7, 1945, Los Angeles, Calif. Screen, stage, vaudeville, radio actor, songwriter and film producer.

Appeared in: **1929** The Hollywood Revue of 1929. **1932** Screen Songs (short). **1933** Screen Songs (short); Mr. Broadway.

EDWARDS, HENRY
Born: Sept. 18, 1882, Weston-Supern-Mare, England. Died: Nov. 2, 1952, Chobham, England. Screen, stage actor, film director, screenwriter and stage producer.

Appeared in: **1914** Clancarty; A Bachelor's Love Story. **1915** Lost and Won (aka Odds Against); The Man Who Stayed at Home; A Welsh Singer; Far from the Madding Crowd; Alone in London; My Old Dutch. **1916** Doorsteps; Grim Justice; East is East. **1917** Merely Mrs. Stubbs; Dick Carson Wins Through (aka The Failure); The Cobweb; Broken Threads; Nearer My God to Thee. **1918** The Refugee; Tares; The Hanging Judge; The Touch of a Child; Towards the Light; "Film Tags" series including: A New Version, The Message, Against the Grain, Anna, Her Savings Saved, The Poet's Windfall and The Secret; Hepworth. **1919** Her Dearest Possession; The City of Beautiful Nonsense; The Kinsman; Possession; Broken in the Wars. **1920** Aylwin; John Forrest Finds Himself; A Temporary Vagabond; The Amazing Quest of Mr. Ernest Bliss (serial). **1921** The Lunatic at Large; The Bargain. **1922** Simple Simon; Tit for Tat. **1923** Lily of the Alley; Boden's Boy; The Naked Man. **1924** The World of Wonderful Reality. **1926** The Flag Lieutenant. **1927** The Fake; Further Adventures of the Flag Lieutenant; Fear. **1929** Ringing the Changes; The Three Kings. **1930** The Call of the Sea. **1931** The Girl in the Night. **1932** The Flag Lieutenant (and 1926 version). **1933** General John Regan. **1935** Scrooge. **1937** Captain's Orders; High Treason; Juggernaut. **1941** Spring Meeting; East of Piccadilly (aka The Strangler—US 1942). **1946** Green for Danger (US 1947); The Magic Bow (US 1947). **1947** Take My Life (US 1948). **1948** Quartet (US 1949); Woman Hater (US 1949); London Belongs to Me (aka Dulcimer Street—US); Lucky Mascot (aka The Brass Monkey—US 1951); Oliver Twist (US 1951). **1949** Dear Mr. Prohack (US 1950); All Over Town. **1950** Trio; Madeleine; Golden Salamander; Double Confession (US 1953); The Verger. **1951** The Lady with the Lamp; The Magic Box (US 1952); The Rossiter Case; White Corridors. **1952** Something Money Can't Buy; Never Look Back. **1953** The Long Memory.

EDWARDS, JAMES
Born: 1912, Ind. Died: Jan. 4, 1970, San Diego, Calif. (heart attack). Black screen, stage and television actor.

Appeared in: **1949** Man Handled; The Set-Up; Home of the Brave. **1951** The Steel Helmet; Bright Victory. **1952** The Member of the Wedding. **1953** The Joe

Louis Story. **1954** The Caine Mutiny. **1955** African Manhunt; Seven Angry Men; The Phoenix City Story. **1956** Battle Hymn. **1957** Men in War. **1958** Anna Lucasta; Fraulein; Tarzan's Fight for Life. **1959** Night of the Quarter Moon; Pork Chop Hill; Blood and Steel. **1962** The Manchurian Candidate. **1965** The Sandpiper. **1968** The Young Runaways; Coogan's Bluff. **1970** Patton.

EDWARDS, MATTIE
Born: 1886. Died: June 26, 1944, Los Angeles, Calif. Screen actress. Entered films approx. 1924.

Appeared in: **1936** Give Us This Night.

EDWARDS, NATE
Born: 1902. Died: Sept. 12, 1972, Hollywood, Calif. Screen actor, film extra, stuntman, casting director and production manager.

EDWARDS, NEELY (Cornelius Limbach)
Born: Sept. 16, 1889, Delphos, Ohio. Died: July 10, 1965, Woodland Hills, Calif. Screen, stage and vaudeville actor. Married to actress Marguerite Snow (dec. 1958). Was half of hoofer-comedy team known as "The Hall Room Boys."

Appeared in: **1921** Brewster's Millions; The Little Clown. **1922** The Green Temptation. **1925** I'll Show You the Town. **1926** Footloose Widows; Made for Love. **1927** The Princess on Broadway. **1928** Excess Baggage; Sunny California (short). **1929** Dynamite; Gold Diggers of Broadway; Show Boat. **1930** Scarlet Pages; plus the following shorts: Her Relatives; The Window Cleaners; The Milky Way. **1931** The Hangover (short). **1932** The following shorts: Junior; The Weekend. **1933** Diplomaniacs; Love, Honor and Oh, Baby! **1939** Mr. Moto in Danger Island.

EDWARDS, SARAH
Born: 1883. Died: Jan. 7, 1965, Hollywood, Calif. Screen, stage and vaudeville actress.

Appeared in: **1929** Glorifying the American Girl. **1934** Smarty. **1935** Ruggles of Red Gap; The World Accuses; Welcome Home; The Dark Angel; Two-Fisted. **1936** The Golden Arrow; Earthworm Tractors; Palm Springs; Early to Bed. **1937** We're on the Jury; It's Love I'm After; Hollywood Hotel. **1938** Touchdown Army; A Doggone Mixup (short); Women Are Like That. **1939** Boy Trouble; Meet Doctor Christian; The Shop around the Corner. **1940** Young People; Strike up the Band; Mr. District Attorney. **1941** Meet John Doe; Glamour Boy; Sunset in Wyoming; All That Money Can Buy. **1942** Rings on Her Fingers; Dudes are Pretty People; The Forest Rangers; Scattergood Survives a Murder. **1943** Dixie Dugan; Calaboose. **1944** Storm over Lisbon; The Little Cynic (short); Henry Aldrich's Little Secret; The Big Noise; Where Are Your Children? **1945** Abbott and Costello in Hollywood; Mother-in-Law's Day (short); Saratoga Trunk. **1946** It's a Wonderful Life. **1947** The Bishop's Wife. **1950** Petty Girl; The Fuller Brush Girl; The Glass Menagerie. **1951** Honeychile. **1952** The Devil and Daniel Webster (reissue and retitle of All That Money Can Buy, 1941).

EDWARDS, SNITZ
Born: 1862, Hungary. Died: May 1, 1937, Los Angeles, Calif. (arthritis). Stage and screen actor. Entered films in 1920. Married to actress Eleanor Edwards (dec. 1968).

Appeared in: **1920** The City of Masks. **1921** The Charm School; Cheated Love; Ladies Must Live; The Love Special; No Woman Knows. **1922** The Ghost Breaker; The Gray Dawn; Human Hearts; June Madness; Love Is an Awful Thing; Rags to Riches; Red Hot Romance. **1923** Children of Jazz; Hollywood; The Huntress; Modern Matrimony; Rosita; Souls for Sale; Tea with a Kick. **1924** The Thief of Bagdad; Hill Billy; In Fast Company; Inez from Hollywood; Passion's Pathway; Tarnish; Tiger Love; The Tornado; A Woman Who Sinned. **1925** Seven Chances; Heir-Looms; A Lover's Oath; Old Shoes; The Phantom of the Opera; The White Desert. **1926** Battling Butler; April Fool; The Clinging Vine; The Cruise of the Jasper B; The Lady of the Harem; The Sea Wolf; Volcano; The Wanderer. **1927** Red Mill; College; Night Life. **1929** A Dangerous Woman; The Mysterious Island; The Phantom of the Opera (and 1925 version). **1931** Right of Way; Sit Tight; Public Enemy.

EDWARDS, TED (M. E. Barrell)
Born: 1883. Died: Sept. 29, 1945, Los Angeles, Calif. Screen and vaudeville actor. In Mack Sennett comedies and an original Keystone Kop.

Appeared in: **1924** Fires of Youth.

EDWARDS, VIRGINIA
Died: Mar. 7, 1964, Hollywood, Calif. Screen, stage actor, playwright and drama coach.

Appeared in: **1932** Silver Dollar.

EGAN, MISHKA
Born: 1891. Died: Feb. 15, 1964, Hollywood, Calif. Screen and vaudeville actor.

EGGENTON, JOSEPH
Born: 1870. Died: June 3, 1946, Hollywood, Calif. Screen and stage actor.

Appeared in: **1940** The Doctor Takes a Wife; You'll Find Out.

EGLI, JOSEPH E.
Born: 1900. Died: Aug. 2, 1974, Calif. Film casting director and screen extra. Entered films as an extra with Carl Laemmle.

EHFE, WILLIAM (William Carl Ehfe)
Born: June 19, 1887, Payette, Idaho. Died: Aug. 1940, Los Angeles, Calif. (heart ailment). Screen actor.

Appeared in: **1915** The End of the Road; Scandals. **1917** The Best Man. **1919** Code of the Yukon.

EICHBERG, RICHARD
Born: 1888, Berlin, Germany. Died: 1952, Munich, Germany. Screen actor, film producer, director and screenwriter. Married to actress Lee Parry and later married to actress Kitty Jantzen. He appeared in numerous German films.

EINSTEIN, HARRY. *See* PARKYAKARKUS

EKBORG, LARS
Born: 1926, Upsala, Sweden. Died: 1969, Sweden. Screen and stage actor.

Appeared in: **1939** U-Boat. **1958** Blonde in Bondage. **1965** Wedding—Swedish Style. Other Swedish films: Backyard; Mrs. Anderson's Charlie; Poker; When Lilacs Blossom; Meeting Life; Wingbeats in the Night; Summer with Monika; The Lunchbreak Cafe; Yellow Squadron; In Smoke and Dancing; Dangerous Freedom; Blocked Rails; The Dance Hall; Violence; Private Entrance; Little Fridolf and I; Stage Entrance; The Flame; A Guest in One's Own Home; Never in Your Life; Lights at Night; Little Fridolf Becomes a Grandfather; No Tomorrow; Fridolf is Rebellious; The Love Game; A Thief in the Bedroom; Three Wishes; Ticket to Paradise; Siska; Swedish Portraits; To Go Ashore; Stimulantia; The Murderer—an Ordinary Person; Duet for Cannibals; Ansiket (The Face and aka The Magician).

EKMAN, GOESTA
Born: 1887, Sweden. Died: Jan. 12, 1938, Stockholm, Sweden. Stage and screen actress.

Appeared in: **1926** Faust. **1928** Heart of a Clown; Discord; A Husband by Proxy. **1930** The Last Night; For Her Sake. **1931** Brokiga Blad. **1933** Charles XII. **1934** Kaera Slaekten. **1935** Swedenhielms; The Noble Prize Winner. **1937** Intermezzo.

EKMAN, JOHN
Born: 1880, Stockholm, Sweden. Died: 1949, Sweden? Screen and stage actor.

Appeared in: **1919** The Song of the Scarlet Flower. **1928** Sin. **1938** Baldwin's Wedding. **1943** Lasse-Maja. Other Swedish films: The Death Ride Under the Big Top; The Black Masks; A Secret Marriage; Lady Marion's Summer Flirtation; The Voice of Blood; Love Stronger than Hate; The Brothers; People of the Border; Half-Breed; The Miracle; Do Not Judge; Children of the Street; Daughter of the High Mountain; Hearts that Meet; The Strike; His Wife's Past; The Ace of Thieves; The Fight for the Rembrandt Painting; His Father's Crime; Judas Money; Madame de Thebes; The Avenger; The Governor's Daughters; Sea Vultures; Old Age and Folly; The Lucky Brooch; The Hermit's Wife; At Eleventh Hour; Who Fired?; The Jungle Queen's Jewels; Slave to Yourself; The Living Mummy; The Outlaw and His Wife; The Executioner; Family Traditions; The Phantom Carriage (aka They Shall Bear Witness); For High Ends; The Suitor from Roads; Johan Ulfstjerna; The Norrtull Gang; The Young Count Takes the Girl and the Prize; Kalle Utter; A Merchant House in the Archipelago; The Ingmar Inheritance; The Girls at Slovik; What Woman Wants; Black Rudolf; The Secret of the Paradise Hotel; The Atlantic Adventure; Synnove Solbakken; The Song of the Scarlet Flower; Outlawed; 33.333; Bombi Bitt and I; Baldevin's Wedding; His Grace's Will; The Gentleman Gangster; The Fight Goes On; Scanian Guerilla; General von Dobeln; Count the Happy Moments Only; The Rose of Thistle Island; Black Roses; The Serious Game; Don't Try It With Me; The Evening of the Fair; Lars Hard; Janne Vangman's New Adventures; Tall Lasse from Delsbo; To Joy.

EKSTROM, MARTA
Born: 1899, Sweden. Died: Jan. 26, 1952, Stockholm, Sweden. Stage and screen actress.

Appeared in: **1938** John Ericsson Victor of Hampton Roads. **1949** Katrina.

ELBA, MARTA
Born: 1920, Cuba. Died: Apr. 19, 1954, Mexico City, Mexico (cancer). Screen, stage actress and newspaper columnist.

ELDER, DOTTIE
Born: 1929. Died: Nov. 28, 1965, Hollywood, Calif. (heart attack). Screen and television actress.

ELDER, RICHARD LT. COL.

Born: 1911. Died: Oct. 4, 1963, Fort Huachuca, Ariz. (heart attack). Screen and radio actor.

ELDRIDGE, ANNA MAE

Born: 1894. Died: Apr. 17, 1950, Van Nuys, Calif. Screen actress. Appeared in silents.

ELDRIDGE, CHARLES

Born: 1854, Saratoga Springs, N.Y. Died: Oct. 29, 1922, New York, N.Y. (cancer). Stage and screen actor.

Appeared in: 1912 The Old Kent Road; The Spider Web; The Picture Idol; Who's to Win; Half a Hero; The Professor and the Lady; The Crossroads; The Little Minister; She Cried; The Red Barrier; As You Like It; An Elephant on their Hands; Reincarnation of Komar; The Model for St. John. 1918 Sporting Life. 1921 Ashamed of Parents; Made in Heaven. 1922 No Trespassing. 1925 Hearts and Spurs.

ELDRIDGE, JOHN (John Eldredge)

Born: Aug. 30, 1904, San Francisco, Calif. Died: Sept. 23, 1961, Laguna Beach, Calif. (heart attack). Screen, stage and television actor.

Appeared in: 1934 Flirtation Walk; The Man with Two Faces. 1935 Dangerous; Dr. Socrates; The Goose and the Gander; The Girl from Tenth Avenue; Snowed Under; Man of Iron; Oil for the Lamps of China; The Woman in Red; The White Cockatoo. 1936 The Murder of Dr. Harrigan; Follow Your Heart; His Brother's Wife; Murder by an Aristocrat. 1937 Fair Warning; Charlie Chan at the Olympics; The Go-Getter; The Holy Terror; Mr. Dodd Takes the Air; Mysterious Crossing; One Mile from Heaven; Sh! the Octopus. 1938 Blind Alibi; Women Are Like That; They're Always Caught (short); Persons in Hiding. 1939 King of Underworld; Private Detective; Television Spy; Undercover Doctor. 1940 Always a Bride; The Devil's Pipeline; Dr. Kildare's Strangest Case; The Marines Fly High; Son of Roaring Dan. 1941 Flight from Destiny; The Black Cat; Blossoms in the Dust; High Sierra; Horror Island; Mr. District Attorney in the Carter Case. 1942 Madame Spy; The Mad Doctor of Market Street. 1944 Beautiful but Broke; Bermuda Mystery; Song of Nevada. 1945 Bad Men of the Border; Dangerous Passage; Eve Knew Her Apples; Dangerous Partners. 1946 Swing Parade of 1946; Dark Alibi; Passkey to Danger; Little Miss Big; Temptation; Circumstantial Evidence; The French Key; I Ring Doorbells; Live Wires; There Goes Maisie. 1947 Backlash; Seven Were Saved; Second Chance; The Fabulous Joe. 1948 Angels' Alley; California's Gold; Jinx Money; Whispering Smith. 1949 The Sickle or the Cross; Sky Dragon; Square Dance Jubilee; Stampede; Top of the Morning. 1950 Champagne for Caesar; Lonely Hearts Bandits; Rustlers on Horseback; Unmashed. 1951 All That I Have; Insurance Investigator; Rhythm Inn; Street Bandits. 1953 Loophole. 1955 Toughest Man Alive. 1956 The First Traveling Saleslady. 1958 I Married a Monster from Outer Space. 1960 Freckles. 1961 Five Guns to Tombstone.

ELINOR, CARLI D.

Born: Sept. 21, 1890, Bucharest, Rumania. Died: Oct. 20, 1958, Hollywood, Calif. (heart attack). Screen actor and musician. Appeared in silents.

ELISCU, FERNANDA

Died: 1968. Stage and screen actress.

Appeared in: 1936 Winterset. 1950 The Harbor of Missing Men.

ELIZONDO, JOAQUIN

Born: 1896. Died: June 15, 1952, Hollywood, Calif. Screen actor and dancer. Formerly Mae Murray's dancing partner.

Appeared in: 1947 Twilight on the Rio Grande.

ELLINGFORD, WILLIAM

Born: 1863. Died: May 20, 1936, Los Angeles, Calif. Screen and stage actor.

Appeared in: 1927 Hands Off.

ELLINGTON, "DUKE" (Edward Kennedy Ellington)

Born: Apr. 29, 1899, Washington, D.C. Died: May 24, 1974, New York, N.Y. (lung cancer-pneumonia). Black screen, radio actor, bandleader and composer. Married to dancer Evie Ellis Ellington (dec. 1976) and father of bandleader Mercer Ellington.

Appeared in: 1929 Black and Tan (short). 1930 Check and Double Check. 1934 Murder at the Vanities (short). 1937 The Hit Parade; New Faces of 1937. 1943 Reveille with Beverly; Cabin in the Sky. 1959 Anatomy of a Murder. 1961 Paris Blues; Twist all Night. 1966 Assault on a Queen. 1969 Adalen 31; Change of Mind.

ELLINGWOOD, HELMERT

Born: 1907. Died: Oct. 13, 1971. Screen actor.

Appeared in: 1945 Objective Burma.

ELLIOTT, BERT (Berton Rex Elliott)

Born: Mar. 15, 1929, Michigan. Died: July 3, 1972, Valinda, Calif. (suicide—hanging). Screen actor.

ELLIOTT, CASSANDRA (Ellen Naomi Cohen aka "MAMA" CASS ELLIOTT)

Born: 1941, Arlington, Va. Died: July 29, 1974, London, England (heart attack/obesity). Singer, screen and television actress. Divorced from singer James Hendricks and Baron Donald von Wiedenman.

Appeared in: 1969 Monterey Pop. 1970 Monte Walsh; Pufnstuf.

ELLIOTT, DICK

Born: 1886. Died: Dec. 22, 1961, Hollywood, Calif. Screen, stage and television actor.

Appeared in: 1934 Shivers (short); We're Rich Again. 1935 Sprucin' Up (short); Annie Oakley; It Happened in New York. 1936 Brilliant Marriage; Her Master's Voice; Neighborhood House (short). 1937 China Passage; Quick Money; The Outcasts of Poker Flat. 1938 Campus Confessions; Penitentiary; Under Western Stars. 1939 Frontiers of '49; Home Boner (short); Nancy Drew and the Hidden Staircase; Truth Aches (short); Let Us Live; The Story of Alexander Graham Bell; Boy Trouble; Mr. Smith Goes to Washington; Sudden Money. 1940 Behind the News; Flight Angels; Melody Ranch; Florian; L'il Abner; One Man's Law. 1941 The Pittsburgh Kid; Top Sgt. Mulligan; Up in the Air; Sunset in Wyoming. 1942 The Man from Headquarters; Scattergood Survives a Murder; Sweetheart of the Fleet. 1943 Wintertime; After Midnight with Boston Blackie; Laugh Your Eyes Away. 1944 Adventures of Mark Twain; Silent Partners; Girl in the Case; Henry Aldrich Plays Cupid; Hi Beautiful; Whispering Footsteps; Goin' to Town; When Strangers Marry. 1945 Adventures of Kitty O'Day; The Clock; Gangs of the Waterfront; Christmas in Connecticut; Saratoga Trunk; plus the following shorts: You Drive Me Crazy; Mother-in-Law's Day; and Purity Squad. 1946 Partners in Time; Rainbow over Texas; That Texas Jamboree; Hot Cargo; High School Hero; Dangerous Money; Ginger; The Kid from Brooklyn; Trouble or Nothing (short); Follow That Blonde (short); Her Sister's Secret. 1947 Television Turmoil (short); For the Love of Rusty; Heading for Heaven. 1948 Main Street Kid; The Dude Goes West; Homicide for Three; Slippy McGee. 1949 Feudin' Rhythm; Night Unto Night; Rose of the Yukon; Trail of the Yukon. 1950 Across the Badlands; A Modern Marriage; Rock Island Trail; Western Pacific Agent. 1951 Fort Defiance; Honeychile. 1952 High Noon; Montana Belle. 1954 Witness to Murder. 1957 Don't Knock the Rock; The Joker Is Wild; New Day at Sundown; Up in Smoke. 1958 In the Money.

ELLIOTT, GERTRUDE (Gertrude Dermott)

Born: 1874, Rockland, Me. Died: Dec. 24, 1950, Kent, England. Stage and screen actress. Married to actor Sir Johnston Forbes-Robertson (dec. 1937). Mother of actress Jean Forbes-Robertson (dec. 1962). Sister of actress Maxine Elliott (dec. 1940).

Appeared in: 1913 Hamlet (US 1915). 1917 Masks and Faces.

ELLIOTT, GORDON. See WILLIAM "WILD BILL" ELLIOTT

ELLIOTT, JOHN H.

Born: July 5, 1876, Keosauqua, Iowa. Died: Dec. 12, 1956, Los Angeles, Calif. (heart attack). Stage and screen actor.

Appeared in: 1920 Homer Comes Home; A Master Stroke; Held in Trust; Are All Men Alike? 1921 Her Winning Way. 1923 The Eagle's Feather; The Spoilers. 1926 Christine of the Big Tops; Racing Blood; What Happened to Jones. 1927 Horse Shoes; Million Dollar Mystery. 1929 Only the Brave; The Phantom in the House. 1930 For the Defense; The Rampant Age; The Widow from Chicago. 1931 Conquering Horde. 1932 Galloping Thru; Two-Fisted Justice; Single-Handed Sanders; Riders of the Desert; Week-ends Only; Texas Pioneers; From Broadway to Cheyenne; Call Her Savage. 1933 Lucky Larrigan; Gallant Fool. 1934 Murder in the Museum; Green Eyes; Cowboy Holiday; Ticket to a Crime; Carolina; Sons of the Desert. 1935 Danger Ahead; Sunset Range; Red Hot Tires; Make a Million; Unconquered Bandit; Fighting Pioneers; What Price Crime?; Captured in Chinatown; Saddle Aces; Rider of the Law; Trails of the Wild; Midnight Phantom; Lawless Border; Skull and Crown. 1936 Frontier Justice; Millionaire Kid; Roamin' Wild; Avenging Waters; Rogues Tavern; Kelly of the Secret Service; Roaring Guns; The Clutching Hand (serial); Prison Shadows; The Fugitive Sheriff; Ambush Valley. 1937 Death in the Air; Headin' East. 1938 Cassidy of Bar 20; Heart of Arizona; Hold that Co-Ed. 1939 Jesse James. 1940 The Tulsa Kid; Gun Code; Lone Star Raiders. 1941 Tumble Down Ranch in Arizona; Texas Marshal; Gentleman from Dixie; The Kid's Last Ride; The Apache Kid; Land of the Open Range; Come on Danger. 1942 The Mad Monster; Rock River Renegades; Pirates of the Prairie; Pearls of the Royal Mounted (serial). 1943 Tenting Tonight on the Old Camp Grounds; Two-Fisted Justice. 1944 Law of the Saddle; Oklahoma Raiders; Fuzzy Settles Down; Wild Horse Phantoms. 1945 Allotment Wives; Escape in the Fog; Hollywood and Vine; Jungle Raiders (serial). 1946 Frontier Gunlaw; The Devil's Mask. 1947 Law of the Lash; News Hounds; The Fighting Vigilantes. 1948 I Wouldn't Be in Your Shoes; Angels' Alley. 1950 The Arizona Cowboy. 1956 Pearls of the Wilderness (serial).

ELLIOTT, LESTER

Born: 1888. Died: Nov. 9, 1954, Van Nuys, Calif. (heart attack). Stage and screen actor.

ELLIOTT, LILLIAN

Born: 1875. Died: Jan. 15, 1959, Hollywood, Calif. (stroke). Stage and screen actress. Mother of actor Lloyd Corrigan (dec. 1969).

Appeared in: 1921 Lavender and Old Lace; Too Much Married. 1924 The Chorus Lady; One Glorious Night. 1925 Old Clothes; Proud Flesh; Sally, Irene and Mary. 1926 The City; The Family Upstairs; Partners Again. 1927 Ankles Preferred; King of Kings. 1930 Her Wedding Night; Liliom; The Swellhead. 1931 The Single Sin; Thundering Tenors (short); The Hasty Marriage (short). 1932 The Man I Killed; Free Eats (short); Now We'll Tell One (short); Polly of the Circus. 1934 Trumpet Blows; Palsie Walsie (short); 1935 I'm a Father (short). 1938 The Jury's Secret; Wanted by the Police. 1939 Tough Kid. 1942 Road to Happiness. 1965 Laurel and Hardy's Laughing 20's (documentary).

ELLIOTT, MAXINE (Jessica Dermott)

Born: Feb. 5, 1873, Rockland, Me. Died: Mar. 5, 1940, Juan Les Pins, France (heart ailment). Stage and screen actress. Sister of actress Gertrude Elliott (dec. 1950). Divorced from stage actor Nat Goodwin.

Appeared in: 1917 Fighting Odds. 1919 The Eternal Magdalene.

ELLIOTT, MILTON "SKEETS"

Born: 1896, Gadsden, Ala. Died: Aug. 2, 1920, Los Angeles, Calif. (airplane accident during filming of The Skywayman). Screen actor and stunt flier.

Appeared in: 1920 The Skywayman.

ELLIOTT, ROBERT

Born: Oct. 9, 1879, Ohio. Died: Nov. 15, 1951. Screen actor.

Appeared in: 1919 Checkers. 1921 Lonely Heart; Money Maniac; A Virgin Paradise. 1922 The Broken Silence; Fair Lady; A Pasteboard Crown; Without Fear. 1923 Man Wife. 1928 Happiness Ahead; Light of New York; Obey Your Husband; Romance of the Underworld. 1929 The Lone Wolf's Daughter; Protection; Thunderbolt. 1930 Captain Thunder; The Divorcee; The Doorway to Hell; Hide-out; Kathleen Mavoureen; Men of the North; Sweet Mama. 1931 The Finger Points; The Maltese Falcon; The Star Witness; Five Star Final; Murder at Midnight; The Midnight Patrol; White Eagle; Madison Square Garden; The Phantom of Crestwood; Rose of the Rio Grande; Conquering Horde; The Montana Kid; Secret Menace; Mother and Son; Oklahoma Jim. 1932 Galloping Thru; Riders of the Desert; Call Her Savage; Broadway to Cheyenne; Two-Fisted Justice; Single-Handed Sanders; Week Ends Only; Texas Pioneers. 1933 Self Defense; Crime of the Century; Return of Casey Jones; Heroes for Sale; Lady Killer. 1934 Girl of the Limberlost; Transatlantic Merry-Go-Round; Gambling Lady; Woman Who Dared; Twin Husbands. 1935 The World Accuses; Black Sheep; Times Square Lady; Port of Lost Dreams; Circumstantial Evidence. 1936 I'd Give My Life. 1938 Trade Winds. 1939 The Roaring Twenties; I Stole a Million; Mickey the Kid; Gone with the Wind; The Saint Strikes Back. 1940 Half a Sinner. 1945 Captain Tugboat Annie. 1946 The Devil's Playground.

ELLIOTT, WILLIAM

Born: 1880. Died: Feb. 5, 1932, New York, N.Y. Screen, stage actor and stage manager.

Appeared in: 1918 Hearts of the World.

ELLIOTT, WILLIAM "WILD BILL" (Gordon Elliott)

Born: 1904, Pattonsburg, Mo. Died: Nov. 26, 1965, Las Vegas, Nev. (cancer). Screen, stage and television actor.

Appeared in: 1927 The Private Life of Helen of Troy. 1928 Valley of Hunted Men; The Arizona Wildcat; Beyond London's Lights. 1929 Passion Song; Restless Youth; Broadway Scandals; Napoleon, Jr. 1930 The Great Divide. 1933 Gold Diggers of 1933. 1934 Registered Nurse; Wonder Bar. 1935 The Traveling Saleslady; Devil Dogs of the Air; The Woman in Red; G-Men; The Girl from 10th Avenue; The Goose and the Gander; Moonlight on the Prairie; Man of Iron; Gold Diggers of 1935. 1936 The Murder of Dr. Harrigan; Murder by an Aristocrat; Down the Stretch; The Case of the Velvet Claws; Trailin' West; Polo Joe; The Case of the Black Cat. 1937 Melody for Two; Midnight Court; Fugitive in the Sky; Guns of the Pecos; Speed to Spare; Love Takes Flight; Wife, Doctor and Nurse; Swing it, Professor; Boots and Saddles; Boy of the Streets. 1938 The Great Adventures of Wild Bill Hickok (serial); In Early Arizona; The Devil's Party; Tarzan's Revenge; Lady in the Morgue. 1939 The Taming of the West; Lone Star Pioneers; The Law Comes to Texas; Overland with Kit Carson (serial); Frontiers of '49. 1940 Man from Tumbleweed; Prairie Schooners; The Return of Wild Bill; Pioneers of the Frontier. 1941 Return of Daniel Boone; Where Did You Get That Girl?; Roaring Frontiers; Beyond the Sacramento; The Wildcat of Tucson; North from the Lone Star; Hands across the Rockies; Across the Sierras; The Lone Star Vigilantes; The Son of Davy Crockett; King of Dodge City. 1942 Valley of Vanishing Men (serial); Bullets for Bandits; Vengeance of the West; The Devil's Trail; North of the Rockies; Prairie Gunsmoke. 1943 Calling Wild Bill Elliott; Bordertown Gun Fighters;

The Man from Thunder River; Wagon Tracks West; Death Valley Manhunt. 1944 Marshall of Reno; Hidden Valley Outlaws; Cheyenne Wildcat; Vigilantes of Dodge City; Mojave Firebrand; Sheriff of Las Vegas; Tucson Raiders; Overland Mail Robbery; The San Antonio Kid. 1945 The Great Stagecoach Robbery; Lone Texas Ranger; Phantom of the Plains; Bells of Rosarita; Colorado Pioneers; Marshall of Laredo; Wagon Wheels Westward. 1946 Sun Valley Cyclone; Sheriff of Redwood Valley; Conquest of Cheyenne; California Gold Rush; In Old Sacramento; The Plainsman and the Lady. 1947 Wyoming; The Fabulous Texas. 1948 The Gallant Legion; In Old Los Angeles. 1949 The Last Bandit; Hellfire. 1950 The Savage Horde; The Showdown. 1952 The Maverick; The Longhorn; Waco; Vengeance Trail; Kansas Territory; Fargo. 1953 The Homesteaders; Revel City; Vigilante Terror; Topeka. 1954 Bitter Creek; The Forty-Niners. 1955 Dial Red O; Sudden Danger. 1956 Calling Homicide. 1957 Footsteps in the Night; Chain of Evidence.

ELLIS, DIANE

Born: Dec. 20, 1909, Los Angeles, Calif. Died: Dec. 16, 1930, Madras, India. Screen actress.

Appeared in: 1927 Paid to Love; The Cradle Snatchers; Chain Lightning; Is Zat So?; Hook and Ladder No. 9. 1928 Happiness Ahead. 1929 The Leatherneck; High Voltage. 1930 Laughter.

ELLIS, EDWARD

Born: 1871, Coldwater, Mich. Died: July 26, 1952, Hollywood, Calif. Stage and screen actor.

Appeared in: 1921 The Frontier of the Stars. 1932 I Am a Fugitive from a Chain Gang. 1933 Girl Missing; From Headquarters; Without Glory; After Tonight; Strictly Personal. 1934 Madame Spy; Hi, Nellie; The Ninth Guest; The Last Gentleman; Trumpet Blows; The President Vanishes; The Thin Man. 1935 The Return of Peter Grimm; Wanderer of the Wasteland; Village Tale; Transient Lady; The Black Sheep. 1936 Chatterbox; The Lady Consents; Winterset; Fury; The Texas Rangers. 1937 Maid of Salem; Midnight Madonna; Let Them Live; The Man in Blue. 1938 Little Miss Broadway; A Man to Remember. 1939 Man of Conquest; Main Street Lawyer; Career; Three Sons; Remember. 1942 A Man Betrayed; Steel against the Sky. 1942 The Omaha Trail.

ELLIS, EVELYN

Born: 1894. Died: June 5, 1958, Saranac Lake, N.Y. (heart ailment). Screen, stage and television actress.

Appeared in: 1948 The Lady from Shanghai. 1953 The Joe Louis Story. 1955 Interrupted Melody.

ELLIS, FRANK B.

Died: Feb. 24, 1969. Screen actor.

Appeared in: 1923 King's Creek Law. 1924 Bringin' Home the Bacon. 1925 The Desert Demon; The Fighting Sheriff; Tearin' Loose. 1926 Ace of Action; The Outlaw Express; Speedy Spurs; Vanishing Hoofs; Without Orders. 1927 Code of the Cow Country. 1928 Yellow Contraband; The Valley of Hunted Men. 1929 Law of the Mounted; Texas Tommy. 1930 Trails of Danger. 1933 Treason. 1934 In Old Santa Fe; Mystery Mountain. 1935 The Phantom Empire. 1936 Lawless Riders; Comin' Round the Mountain. 1937 Public Cowboy Number One; Git Along, Little Dogies; Springtime in the Rockies; Hopalong Rides Again; Riders of the Whistling Skull; Range Defenders; Gun Lords of Stirrup Basin; Boothill Brigade; Two Fisted Sheriff. 1938 Western Jamboree; Border Wolves. 1939 In Old Monterey; Roll, Wagons, Roll; Rovin' Tumbleweeds; Ride 'em Cowgirl. 1940 Westbound Stage; Marshal of Mesa City. 1941 Outlaws of the Rio Grande; Wranglers' Roost; The Bandit Trail; The Kid's Last Ride; Man from Montana; Thundering Hoofs; Land of the Open Range; Billy the Kid Wanted; The Loan Rider Fights Back. 1942 Stardust on the Sage; Billy the Kid's Smoking Guns; Phantom Killer; Texas to Bataan. 1943 Two-Fisted Justice; Fugitive of the Plains; Black Market Rustlers. 1944 Trail of Terror; Law of the Saddle; Arizona Whirlwind; Westward Bound; Outlaw Roundup; Oath of Vengeance; Wild Horse Phantom. 1946 Son of the Guardsman (serial); Ambush Trail; Gentlemen with Guns; Overland Riders; Prairie Badmen; The Fighting Frontiersman; Stage to Mesa City. 1947 Out West (short). 1948 The Westward Trail; Deadline. 1950 Beyond the Purple Hills; Indian Territory; Cowboy and the Prizefighter; Cody of the Pony Express (serial); 1951 Roar of the Iron Horse (serial). 1952 The Old West; Blackhawk (serial); King of the Congo (serial).

ELLIS, PATRICIA (Patricia Leftwich)

Born: May 20, 1916, Birmingham, Mich. Died: Mar. 26, 1970, Kansas City, Mo. Stage and screen actress. She was a Wampas Baby Star of 1932. Daughter of actor/film producer Alexander Leftwich (dec. 1947).

Appeared in: 1932 Three on a Match; Central Park. 1933 Forty-Second Street; Hollywood on Parade (short); Picture Snatcher; Elmer the Great; The King's Vacation; The Narrow Corner; Convention City; The World Changes. 1934 Harold Teen; Melody for Two; St. Louis Kid; Easy to Love; Big Hearted Herbert; The Circus Clown; Here Comes the Groom; Let's Be Ritzy; Affairs of a Gentleman. 1935 While the Patient Slept; Bright Lights; The Case of the Lucky Legs; The Pay Off; A Night at the Ritz; Stranded; Hold 'Em Yale. 1936

Sing Me a Love Song; Freshman Love; Snowed Under; Boulder Dam; Love Begins at Twenty; Down the Stretch; Postal Inspector. **1937** Venus Makes Trouble; Step Lively, Jeeves!; Rhythm in the Clouds; Paradise for Two; Melody for Two. **1938** The Lady in the Morgue; Blockheads; Romance on the Run; The Gaiety Girls. **1939** Back Door to Heaven; Fugitives at Large.

ELLIS, ROBERT

Born: June 27, 1892, Brooklyn, N.Y. Died: May 19, 1935, Hollywood, Calif. Screen, stage actor and film director. Married to actress Vera Reynolds (dec. 1962).

Appeared in: **1919** Louisiana; Upstairs and Down. **1921** Handcuffs or Kisses; Ladies Must Live. **1922** The Woman Who Fooled Herself; Anna Ascends; Hurricane's Gal; The Dangerous Little Demon; Wild Honey; The Infidel; Love's Masquerade. **1923** The Wild Party; The Wanters; Dark Secrets; The Flame of Life; Mark of the Beast. **1924** A Cafe in Cairo; For Sale; The Law Forbids; On Probation; Lover's Lane; Silk Stocking Gal. **1925** Forbidden Cargo; Lady Robinhood; Northern Code; Capital Punishment; Defend Yourself; The Part Time Wife; Speed. **1926** S.O.S. Perils of the Sea; Brooding Eyes; The Girl from Montmartre; Devil's Dice; Ladies of Leisure; Whispering Canyon. **1927** The Lure of the Night Club; Ragtime. **1928** Varsity; Freedom of the Press; Law and the Man; The Law's Lash; Marry the Girl. **1929** Restless Youth; Tonight at Twelve; The Love Trap; Broadway; Night Parade. **1930** The Squealer; Undertow; What Men Want. **1931** The Last Parade; The Good Bad Girl; Murder at Midnight; Aloha; Caught Cheating; The Fighting Sheriff; Dancing Dynamite; Is There Justice?; The Devil Plays; Mounted Fury. **1932** American Madness; The Last Man; White Eagle; The Deadline; One Man Law; Behind Stone Walls; Fighting Fools; Phantom Express; Daring Danger; Last Man; From Broadway to Cheyenne; White Eagle; All American; The Penal Code; Women Won't Tell; Come on Danger?; A Man's Land; Slightly Married. **1933** Officer 13; Speed Demon; Reform Girl; Constant Woman; Treason; Soldiers of the Storm; Thrill Hunter; The Sphinx; Police Call; The Important Witness; Only Yesterday; Notorious but Nice. **1934** I've Got Your Number; Dancing Man; Madame Spy; Girl of the Limberlost.

ELLIS, ROBERT "BOBBY"

Born: 1933. Died: Nov. 23, 1973, Los Angeles, Calif. (kidney failure). Screen, radio and television actor. Played "Henry Aldrich" on the radio and television series. Entered films in 1938.

Appeared in: **1948** The Babe Ruth Story; April Showers. **1949** A Kiss for Corliss; The Green Promise; Easy Living; El Paso. **1950** Walk Softly, Stranger. **1951** Call Me Mister. **1952** Retreat, Hell! **1955** The McConnell Story. **1956** Pillars of the Sky. **1958** Space Master X-7. **1959** Gidget.

ELLSLER, EFFIE

Born: 1855, Philadelphia, Pa. Died: Oct. 9, 1942, Hollywood, Calif. (heart attack). Stage and screen actress.

Appeared in: **1926** Old Ironsides. **1927** Honeymoon Hate. **1928** The Actress. **1929** Woman Trap. **1930** Song O' My Heart; The Lady of Scandal. **1931** The Front Page; Up Pops the Devil; Daddy Long Legs. **1933** Doctor Bull; Second Hand Wife; The Girl in 419; The Chief. **1934** Hold that Girl. **1935** The Whole Town's Talking; Black Fury; We're Only Human. **1936** Drift Fence.

ELLSWORTH, JACK HERSCHEL

Born: 1911. Died: Aug. 19, 1949, Hollywood, Calif. Screen actor.

ELMAN, HARRY "ZIGGY"

Born: May 26, 1914, Philadelphia, Pa. Died: June 25, 1968, Van Nuys, Calif. Bandleader, musician, screen actor and composer.

Appeared in: **1955** The Benny Goodman Story.

ELMER, BILLY (William E. Johns)

Born: 1870. Died: Feb. 24, 1945, Hollywood, Calif. Screen, stage and vaudeville actor.

Appeared in: **1913** The Squaw Man. **1914** The Virginian. **1921** The Foolish Age; The Road Demon. **1922** The Bootlegger's Daughter; Pawned. **1923** In Search of a Thrill. **1924** Battling Mason; The Whipping Boss.

ELMORE, BRUCE (Alfred G. Kennedy)

Born: 1885. Died: May 15, 1940, New York, N.Y. Screen and stage actor.

ELTINGE, JULIAN (Bill Dalton)

Born: 1883, Butte, Mont. Died: Mar. 7, 1941, New York, N.Y. (cerebral hemorrhage). Screen, stage and vaudeville actor.

Appeared in: **1915** How Molly Made Good. **1917** The Countess Charming; The Clever Mrs. Carfax. **1918** Over the Rhine; Widows Might; War Relief. **1922** The Isle of Love. **1925** Madame Behave. **1940** If I Had My Way.

ELVIDGE, JUNE C.

Born: 1893, St. Paul, Minn. Died: May 1, 1965, Eatontown, N.J. Screen, stage and vaudeville actress.

Appeared in: **1915** The Lure of a Woman. **1916** La Boheme; The Almighty

Dollar; The World Against Him. **1917** The Tenth Case; The Family Hour; Shall We Forgive Her?; The Page Mystery; The Price of Pride; The Crimson Dove; The Guardian; The Marriage Market; Rasputin, the Black Monk; A Girl's Folly; Youth; A Square Deal. **1918** The Strong Way; The Power and the Glory; Broken Ties; The Oldest Law; The Way Out; The Cabaret; A Woman of Redemption; The Beautiful Mrs. Reynolds; Joan of the Woods; Stolen Order. **1919** Love and the Woman; The Poison Pen. **1921** Fine Feathers. **1922** Beauty's Worth; Beyond the Rocks; Forsaking All Others; The Impossible Mrs. Bellew; The Man Who Saw Tomorrow; The Power of a Lie; Quincy Adams Sawyer; Thelma; The Woman Conquers. **1923** The Prisoner; Temptation. **1924** Chalk Marks; Pagan Passions; Painted People; The Right of the Strongest; The Torrent.

ELWELL, GEORGE (Edmund George Elwell)

Born: 1896. Died: Nov. 3, 1916, Los Angeles, Calif. (heart attack). Screen actor.

Appeared in: **1916** The Raiders.

ELY, HARRY R.

Born: 1883. Died: July 15, 1951, Hollywood, Calif. Silent screen actor.

EMERICK, BESSE

Born: 1875, Rochester, Ind. Died: Dec. 13, 1939, Boston, Mass. Screen actress.

Appeared in: **1917** The Black Stork. **1922** Welcome to Our City.

EMERICK, ROBERT

Born: 1916, Tacoma, Wash. Died: June 1, 1973, San Diego, Calif. (heart attack). Screen, radio, television actor and drama coach.

Appeared in: **1970** Guess What We Learned in School Today? (aka Guess What? and I Ain't no Buffalo); Joe.

EMERSON, EDWARD

Born: 1910. Died: Apr. 11, 1975, Bronx, N.Y. (cancer). Screen, stage and television actor.

Appeared in: **1936** I Cover Chinatown. **1937** Behind the Criminal (short). **1943** Dixie. **1945** There Goes Kelly.

EMERSON, ERIC

Born: 1945. Died: May 28, 1975. Stage and screen actor.

Appeared in: **1966** The Chelsea Girls. **1968** Lonesome Cowboys; The Mine Blowers. **1972** Heat.

EMERSON, HOPE

Born: Oct. 29, 1897, Hawarden, Iowa. Died: Apr. 25, 1960, Hollywood, Calif. (liver ailment). Screen, stage, television and radio actress. Nominated for 1950 Academy Award for Best Supporting Actress in Caged.

Appeared in: **1932** Smiling Faces. **1948** Cry of the City; That Wonderful Urge. **1949** House of Strangers; Adam's Rib; Dancing in the Dark; Roseanne McCoy; Thieves' Highway. **1950** Caged; Copper Canyon; Double Crossbones. **1951** Belle Le Grande. **1952** Westward the Women. **1953** Lady Wants Mink; Champ for a Day; A Perilous Journey. **1954** Casanova's Big Night. **1955** Untamed. **1956** The Day They Gave Babies Away. **1957** Guns of Fort Petticoat; All Mine to Give. **1958** Rock-A-Bye Baby.

EMERSON, JOHN (Clifton Paden)

Born: May 29, 1874, Sandusky, Ohio. Died: Mar. 7, 1956, Pasadena, Calif. Screen, stage actor, playwright, screenwriter, film, stage producer and film director. Married to authoress Anita Loos.

Appeared in: **1914** The Conspiracy; Bachelor's Romance. **1915** The Failure; Ghosts. **1916** The Flying Torpedo.

EMERTON, ROY

Born: 1892, Canada. Died: 1944. Screen actor.

Appeared in: **1932** The Sign of the Four. **1934** The Lash. **1935** The Triumph of Sherlock Holmes; Lorna Doone; Java Head. **1936** Everything Is Thunder; Nine Days a Queen. **1937** The Silent Barrier; Big Fella; The Last Adventurers. **1938** Doctor Syn; Drums; Convict 99; Q Planes; Home from Home. **1940** Haunted Honeymoon; The Thief of Bagdad; Busman's Honeymoon. **1941** Frightened Lady. **1943** The Young Mr. Pitt; The Man in Grey. **1944** Henry V (US 1946).

EMERY, MRS. EDWARD. See ISABEL WALDRON

EMERY, GILBERT

Born: 1882. Died: Dec. 31, 1934, Los Angeles, Calif. Screen and stage actor. Entered films in 1924.

EMERY, GILBERT (Arthur MacArthur)

Born: 1875, Naples, N.Y. Died: Oct. 26, 1945. Screen, stage actor and screenwriter. Entered films in 1920.

Appeared in: **1921** Cousin Kate. **1929** Behind That Curtain; Sky Hawk. **1930** Sarah and Son; Prince of Diamonds; Let Us Be Gay; A Lady's Morals; Soul

Kiss. **1931** A Royal Bed; Scandal Sheet; The Lady Refuses; Ladies' Man; Party Husband; Upper Underworld; Rich Man's Folly; The Ruling Voice. **1932** Man Called Back; A Farewell to Arms. **1933** Gallant Lady. **1934** Coming Out Party; All of Me; The House of Rothschild; Where Sinners Meet; One More River; Now and Forever; Grand Canary; I Believed in You; Whom the Gods Destroy. **1935** Clive of India; Man Who Reclaimed His Head; Night Life of the Gods; Let's Live Tonight; Cardinal Richelieu; Goin' to Town; Reckless Roads; Ladies Crave Excitement; Harmony Lane; Without Regret; Peter Ibbetson; Magnificent Obsession. **1936** Wife vs. Secretary; Dracula's Daughter; Bullets or Ballots; The Girl on the Front Page; Little Lord Fauntleroy. **1937** The Life of Emile Zola; Double or Nothing; Souls at Sea. **1938** Making the Headlines; The House of Mystery; The Buccaneer; Lord Jeff; A Man to Remember; Storm over Bengal; Always Goodbye. **1939** The Saint Strikes Back; Juarez; The Lady's from Kentucky; Nurse Edith Cavell. **1940** Raffles; The House of the Seven Gables; Anne of Windy Poplars; The Rivers End; South of Suez. **1941** That Hamilton Woman; Rage in Heaven; Adam Had Four Sons; Scotland Yard; A Woman's Face; Singapore Woman; New Wine; Sundown. **1942** The Remarkable Andrew; Escape from Hong Kong; The Loves of Edgar Allan Poe. **1944** The Return of the Vampire; Between Worlds. **1945** The Brighton Strangler.

EMERY, JOHN

Born: 1905, New York, N.Y. Died: Nov. 16, 1964, New York, N.Y. Screen, stage and television actor. Divorced from actress Tallulah Bankhead (dec. 1968).

Appeared in: **1937** The Road Back. **1941** Here Comes Mr. Jordan; The Corsican Brothers. **1942** Two Yanks in Trinidad; Ship Ahoy; Eyes in the Night; George Washington Slept Here. **1943** Assignment in Brittany. **1944** Mademoiselle Fifi. **1945** Spellbound; Blood on the Sun; The Spanish Main. **1947** The Voice of the Turtle. **1948** Joan of Arc; The Woman in White; The Gay Intruders; Let's Live Again. **1950** Dakota Lil; Rocket Ship X-M; Frenchie; Double Crossbones. **1951** Joe Palooka in the Triple Cross. **1954** The Mad Magician. **1955** A Lawless Street. **1956** Forever Darling; The Girl Can't Help It. **1957** Kronos. **1958** Ten North Frederick. **1964** Youngblood Hawke.

EMMET, KATHERINE

Died: June 6, 1960, N.Y. Screen, stage and radio actress.

Appeared in: **1921** Orphans of the Storm; Paying the Piper. **1929** Hole in the Wall.

EMMETT, FERN

Born: 1896. Died: Sept. 3, 1946, Hollywood, Calif. Screen and stage actress.

Appeared in: **1930** Bar L Ranch; Ridin' Law; The Land of Missing Men; Romance of the West; Second Honeymoon; Westbound; Skip the Maloo! (short). **1932** The following shorts: A Fool About Women; Boy, Oh, Boy; Anybody's Goat; Bridge Wives; Mother's Holiday. **1933** His Weak Moment (short); Frozen Assets (short); East of Fifth Avenue; The Vampire Bat; Hello Everybody; The Trail Drive. **1934** City Limits; An Old Gypsy Custom (short). **1935** Behind the Green Lights; Motive for Revenge; Smart Girl; Melody Trail; Southern Exposure (short); The E-Flat Man (short). **1936** The Trail of the Lonesome Pine; The Harvester; M'Liss; Three on a Limb (short). **1937** Paradise Express; Dangerous Holiday; Riders of the Whistling Skull; Come On Cowboys; Calling All Doctors (short); Hillbilly Goat (short). **1938** Scandal Sheet; Hunted Men; Overland Stage Raiders. **1939** Made for Each Other; The Rains Came; They Shall Have Music; Disputed Passage; In Love Only; Romance of the Potato (short). **1940** Star Dust. **1941** Glamour Boy; All That Money Can Buy; Scattergood Baines; Love Crazy. **1942** Broadway; In Old California; Careful, Soft Shoulders; Henry Aldrich, Editor. **1944** Together Again; Can't Help Singing; San Diego I Love You; Henry Aldrich's Little Secret. **1945** A Song to Remember. **1946** The Kid from Brooklyn; Pillow of Death. **1952** The Devil and Daniel Webster (reissue of All That Money Can Buy, 1941).

EMMONS, LOUISE

Born: 1852. Died: Mar. 6, 1935, Hollywood, Calif. Screen actress. Entered films in 1909.

Appeared in: **1931** Heaven on Earth.

EMPEY, ARTHUR GUY

Born: 1884. Died: Feb. 22, 1963, Wadsworth, Kan. Screen actor, author, screenwriter, film director and film producer (president of Guy Empey Pictures Corp.).

Appeared in: **1918** Over the Top. **1919** The Undercurrent. **1921** Millionaire for a Day.

ENFIELD, HUGH. See CRAIG REYNOLDS

ENGEL, ALEXANDER

Born: 1902. Died: Sept., 1968, Saarbruecken, Germany. Screen, stage and television actor.

Appeared in: **1934** Eines Prinzen Junge Liebe. **1936** Einer zu viel an Bord. **1952** The Merry Wives of Windsor. **1958** A Time to Love and a Time to Die. **1959**

Taiga. **1960** Hamlet (US 1968). **1961** Im Stahinetz des Dr. Mabuse (Return of Dr. Mabuse—US 1966). **1963** Der Henker von London (The Mad Executioners—US 1965).

ENGLAND, PAUL

Born: 1893. Died: Nov. 21, 1968, Devonshire, England. Screen, radio actor and singer.

Appeared in: **1934** Charlie Chan in London; Love Time. **1954** Knock on Wood.

ENGLE, BILLY

Born: 1889. Died: Nov. 28, 1966, Hollywood, Calif. (heart attack). Screen and burlesque actor. Entered films in 1919 and appeared in Christie comedies during the 1920s.

Appeared in: **1926** Red Hot Leather. **1927** The Cat and the Canary; The Western Whirlwind. **1933** Knight Duty (short). **1935** I'm a Father (short); Uncivil Warriors (short); Big Broadcast of 1936; It's a Gift. **1936** Wedding Present. **1938** Tom Sawyer, Detective. **1940** Our Neighbors—the Carters. **1941** Glamour Boy. **1942** Mrs. Miniver. **1946** The Best Years of Our Lives. **1947** The Wistful Widow of Wagon Gap.

ENGLE, MARIE

Born: 1902. Died: Mar. 23, 1971, Hollywood, Calif. (stroke). Screen and vaudeville actress. Married to actor Tom Dugan (dec. 1955) and they appeared in vaudeville in an act billed as "Dugan and Engle."

ENGLISCH, LUCIE

Born: 1897, Germany. Died: Oct. 1965, Erlangen, Germany (liver ailment). Screen actress.

Appeared in: **1931** Das Rheinlandmaedel; Zwei Menschen. **1932** Der Ungetreue Eckehart; Mein Leopold; Reserve Hat Ruh; Rendez-Vous; Die Graefin von Monte Christo (The Countess of Monte Cristo); Der Schrecken der Garnison; Dienst 1st Dienst; Hurra! Ein Junge!; Schubert's Fruehlingstraum; Keine Feier Ohne Meyer. **1933** Drei Tage Mittelarrest; Das Lockende Ziel. **1934** Annemarie, Die Braut der Kompanie; Heimat am Rhein. **1935** Meine Frau; Die Schuetzenkoenigin; Die Kalte Mamsell; Gretl Zieht das Grosse Los; Die Unschuld vom Lande; Der Unbekannte Gast (The Unknown Guest). **1936** Der Mutige Seefahrer. **1937** Ein Falscher Fuffziger; The Postillon of Lonjumeau. **1938** Der Lachende Dritte; Die Landstreicher (The Hoboes). **1939** Kleines Bezirksgericht (Little Country Court); Dingehort mein Herz (My Heart Belongs to Thee); Solo per Danne; Der Kampf mit dem Dralhen (The Fight with the Dragon). **1940** Our Little Wife; Walzerlange (Waltz Melodies).

ENNIS, SKINNAY

Born: 1907. Died: June 2, 1963, Los Angeles, Calif. (suffocation). Bandleader, radio and screen actor.

Appeared in: **1938** College Swing. **1939** Blondie Meets the Boss.

ENRIGHT, FLORENCE

Died: Apr. 3, 1961, Hollywood, Calif. Screen, stage actress, and drama coach. Entered films in 1931.

Appeared in: **1931** Women Love Once; Street Scene; Possessed. **1932** Nice Women. **1934** Six of a Kind; Gift of Gab.

ENTRATTER, JACK

Born: Feb. 28, 1913, New York, N.Y. Died: Mar. 11, 1971, Las Vegas, Nev. (cerebral hemorrhage). Veteran hotel man, showman and screen actor. Married to Dorothy Entratter (dec.) and later married and divorced actress Corinne Cole.

Appeared in: **1960** Pepe.

ENTWISTLE, HAROLD (Charles H. Entwistle)

Born: Sept. 5, 1865, London, England. Died: Apr. 1, 1944, Hollywood, Calif. Screen, stage actor and film director. Entered films in 1910.

Appeared in: **1917** One of Many. **1919** The Divorcee; The Woman under Oath. **1932** Two against the World. **1933** Our Betters; She Done Him Wrong. **1934** The Journal of a Crime. **1935** Vanessa, Her Love Story; Paris in Spring; Mutiny on the Bounty; The Perfect Gentleman; Two Sinners. **1936** The Suicide Club. **1937** Easy Living.

ENTWISTLE, PEG (Lillian Millicent Entwistle)

Born: 1908, London, England. Died: Sept. 18, 1932, Hollywood, Calif. (suicide—leap off "Hollywoodland" sign). Stage and screen actress.

Appeared in: **1932** Thirteen Women.

EPPERSON, DON

Born: 1938. Died: Mar. 17, 1973, Cottonwood, Ariz. (auto accident). Screen, television actor, singer and assistant film director.

Appeared in: **1969** Wild Wheels. **1970** Cain's Way. **1971** The Female Bunch; Big Jake. **1973** Oklahoma Crude.

ERASTOFF, EDITH
Born: 1887, Helsinki, Finland. Died: 1945, Finland (?). Screen actress.

Appeared in: **1919** The Song of the Scarlet Flower. Other Finish films: A People of the Border; A Hero in Spite of Himself; The First Prize; The Avenger; Old Age and Folly; Mrs. B's Lapse; Terje Vigen; The Architect of One's Own Fortune; The Secret of the Inn; Chanson Triste; The Outlaw and His Wife; For High Ends; Johan Ulfstjerna.

ERICKSON, CHRIS
Born: 1945. Died: Feb. 11, 1971 (auto accident). Screen actor. Son of actor Leif Erickson.

ERICKSON, KNUTE
Born: 1871, Norrkoping, Sweden. Died: Jan. 1, 1946, Los Angeles, Calif. Screen, stage, radio and television actor. Entered films in 1920.

Appeared in: **1921** The Conflict; Gasoline Gus. **1922** They Like 'Em Rough. **1924** Fair Week. **1925** The Commandment; Johnny Get Your Hair Cut. **1928** The Fourflusher; Scarlet Seas; Waterfront. **1929** The Squall; Twin Beds; Illusion. **1930** The Spoilers. **1932** His Royal Shyness (short). **1933** The Bitter Tea of General Yen.

ERMELLI, CLAUDIO (Ettore Foa)
Born: 1892, Turin, Italy. Died: Oct. 29, 1964, Rome, Italy. Stage and screen actor. Entered films in 1932.

Appeared in: **1949** The Golden Madonna. **1953** Roman Holiday. **1957** A Farewell to Arms. **1960** It Started in Naples.

ERROL, LEON
Born: July 3, 1881, Sydney, Australia. Died: Oct. 12, 1951, Los Angeles, Calif. (heart attack). Screen, stage and vaudeville actor. Entered films in 1924. Married to dancer Stella Chatelaine (dec. 1946). Was Lord Epping in the "Mexican Spitfire" features of the early 1940s.

Appeared in: **1924** Yolanda. **1925** Sally; Clothes Make the Pirate. **1927** The Lunatic at Large. **1930** Only Saps Work; Let's Merge (short); Paramount on Parade; Queen of Scandal; One Heavenly Night. **1931** Fin and Hattie; Her Majesty, Love. **1933** Alice in Wonderland; plus the following shorts: Poor Fish; Three Little Swigs; Hold Your Temper. **1934** We're Not Dressing; The Captain Hates the Sea; The Notorious Sophie Lang; plus the following shorts: Perfectly Mismated; No More Bridge; Autobuyography; Service with a Smile; Good Morning, Eve; Fixing a Stew; One Too Many. **1935** Princess O'Hara; Coronado; plus the following shorts: Hit and Rum; Salesmanship Ahoy; Home Work; Honeymoon Bridge; Counselitis; Vitaphone shorts. **1936** The following shorts: Down the Ribber; Wholesailing Along; One Live Ghost; Columbia shorts. **1937** Make a Wish; plus the following shorts: Wrong Romance; Should Wives Work?; A Rented Riot. **1938** The following shorts: Dummy Owner; His Pest Friend; Berth Quakes; The Jitters; Stage Fright; Major Difficulties. **1939** The Girl from Mexico; Career; Dancing Co-Ed; Mexican Spitfire; plus the following shorts: Crime Rave; Home Boner; Moving Vanities; Ring Madness; Wrong Room; Truth Aches. **1940** Pop Always Pays; Mexican Spitfire Out West; The Golden Fleecing; plus the following shorts: Scrappily Married; Bested by a Beard; He Asked for It; Tattle Television. **1941** Six Lessons from Madame La Zonga; Where Did You Get That Girl?; Hurry, Charlie, Hurry; Mexican Spitfire's Baby; Never Give a Sucker an Even Break; Melody Lane; plus the following shorts: The Fired Man; When Wifie's Away; A Polo Phony; A Panic in the Parlor; Man I Cured; Who's a Dummy? **1942** Moonlight in Hawaii; Mexican Spitfire at Sea; Mexican Spitfire Sees a Ghost; Mexican Spitfire's Elephant; plus the following shorts: Home Work (and 1935 version); Wedded Blitz; Framing Father; Hold 'em Jail; Mail Trouble; Deal! Deer!; Pretty Dolly. **1943** Strictly in the Groove; Follow the Band; Mexican Spitfire's Blessed Event; Gals, Inc.; Higher and Higher; Cross Your Fingers; Cowboy in Manhattan; Cocktails for Two; plus the following shorts: Double Up; Gem Jams; Radio Runaround; Seeing Nellie Home; Cutie on Duty; Wedtime Stories. **1944** Hat Check Honey; The Invisible Man's Revenge; Slightly Terrific; Babes on Swing Street; Twilight on the Prairie; plus the following shorts: Say Uncle; Poppa Knows Worst; Girls, Girls, Girls; He Forgot to Remember. **1945** She Gets Her Man; Panamericana; Under Western Skies; Mama Loves Papa; What a Blonde; plus the following shorts: Birthday Blues; Let's Go Stepping; Beware of Redheads; Double Honeymoon; It Shouldn't Happen to a Dog. **1946** Riverboat Rhythm; Joe Palooka, Champ; Gentleman Joe Palooka; plus the following shorts: Maid Trouble; Oh, Professor, Behave; Twin Husbands; I'll Take Milk; Follow That Blonde. **1947** Joe Palooka in the Knockout; plus the following shorts: Borrowed Blonde; Wife Tames Wolf; In Room 303; Hired Husband; Blondes Away; The Spook Speaks. **1948** Joe Palooka in the Big Fight; Joe Palooka in the Counterpunch; Make Mine Laughs; plus the following shorts: Bet Your Life; Don't Fool Your Wife; Secretary Trouble; Bachelor Blues; Uninvited Blonde; Backstage Follies. **1949** The following shorts: Dad Always Pays; Cactus Cut-Up; I Can't Remember; Oil's Well That Ends Well; Sweet Cheat; Shocking Affair. **1950** Joe Palooka in Humphrey Takes a Chance; Joe Palooka Meets Humphrey; plus the following shorts: High and Dizzy; Texas Tough Guy; Spooky Wooky. **1951** Footlight Varieties; plus the following shorts: Chinatown Chump; Punchy Pancho; One Wild Night; Deal Me In; Lord Epping Returns; Too Many Wives.

ERSKINE, WALLACE
Born: 1862, England. Died: Jan. 6, 1943, Massapequa, L.I., N.Y. Stage and screen actor.

Appeared in: **1921** Perjury. **1923** The Ragged Edge.

ERWIN, JUNE
Born: 1918. Died: Dec. 28, 1965, Carmichael, Calif. Screen actress. Appeared in "Our Gang" comedies.

ERWIN, ROY (LeRoy Franklin Erwin)
Born: 1925. Died: June 18, 1958, Rosarito Beach, Baja, Calif. (heart attack). Screen, television actor and television writer.

ERWIN, STUART
Born: Feb. 14, 1902, Squaw Valley, Calif. Died: Dec. 21, 1967, Beverly Hills, Calif. (heart attack). Screen, stage and television actor. Married to actress June Collyer (dec. 1968).

Appeared in: **1928** Mother Knows Best (film debut). **1929** Happy Days; The Exalted Flapper; New Year's Eve; Dangerous Curves; This Thing Called Love; Cockeyed World; Speakeasy; Hold Your Man; Sweetie; The Sophomore; The Trespasser; Thru Different Eyes. **1930** Men without Women; Young Eagles; Dangerous Nan McGrew; Love among the Millionaires; Playboy of Paris; Only Saps Work; Along Came Youth; Paramount on Parade; Maybe It's Love. **1931** No Limit; Up Pops the Devil; Dude Ranch; Working Girls; The Magnificent Lie. **1932** Two Kinds of Women; Make Me a Star; The Big Broadcast; Hollywood on Parade (short); The Misleading Lady; Strangers in Love. **1933** The Crime of the Century; He Learned about Women; Face in the Sky; International House; Under the Tonto Rim; Stranger's Return; Day of Reckoning; Going Hollywood; Before Dawn; Make Me a Star; Hold Your Man. **1934** Palooka; Viva Villa!; The Band Plays On; Chained; Bachelor Bait; The Party's Over; Have a Heart. **1935** Ceiling Zero; After Office Hours; Three Men on a Horse. **1936** Exclusive Story; Pigskin Parade; Absolute Quiet; Women Are Trouble; All American Chump. **1937** Dance, Charlie, Dance; Slim; Second Honeymoon; Checkers; Small Town Boy; I'll Take Romance. **1938** Three Blind Mice; Passport Husband; Mr. Boggs Steps Out. **1939** Hollywood Cavalcade; The Honeymoon's Over; Back Door to Heaven; It Could Happen to You. **1940** Our Town; When the Daltons Rode; A Little Bit of Heaven; Sandy Gets Her Man. **1941** The Bride Came C.O.D.; Cracked Nuts. **1942** Drums of the Congo; Adventures of Martin Eden; Blondie for Victory; Through Different Eyes. **1943** He Hired the Boss. **1944** The Great Mike. **1945** Pillow to Post. **1947** Killer Dill; Heaven Only Knows; Heading for Heaven. **1948** Strike It Rich. **1950** Father Is a Bachelor. **1953** Mainstreet to Broadway. **1960** For the Love of Mike; When Comedy was King (documentary). **1963** Son of Flubber. **1964** The Misadventures of Merlin Jones.

ESCANDE, MAURICE
Born: 1893, France (?). Died: Feb. 11, 1973, Paris, France. Screen and stage actor.

Appeared in: **1933** Les Trois Mousquetaires. **1937** Lucrezia Borgia. **1947** The Queen's Necklace. **1949** Man to Men. **1963** Les Animaux (The Animals—US 1965).

ESDALE, CHARLES
Born: 1873. Died: July 10, 1937, New York, N.Y. (complication of diseases). Stage and screen actor.

Appeared in: **1925** Soul Fire. **1926** Summer Bachelors.

ESSER, PETER
Born: 1896, Germany. Died: June 23, 1970, Dusseldorf, Germany. Stage and screen actor.

Appeared in: **1956** Die Trapp-Familie (The Trapp Family—US 1961). **1961** King in Shadow.

ESSLER, FRED
Born: 1896. Died: Jan. 17, 1973, Woodland Hills, Calif. Screen and television actor.

Appeared in: **1943** Mission to Moscow. **1945** Captain Eddie; Where Do We Go from Here?; Saratoga Trunk; What Next, Corporal Hargrove? **1946** Faithful In My Fashion. **1948** Every Girl Should Be Married. **1950** The White Tower; The Admiral Was a Lady; Messenger of Peace. **1953** Houdini. **1955** The Girl in the Red Velvet Swing. **1956** Hot Rod Girl; The First Traveling Saleslady. **1957** My Man Godfrey. **1964** The Unsinkable Molly Brown. **1966** The Money Trap.

ESTEE, ADELYN
Born: 1871. Died: June 3, 1941, Los Angeles, Calif. Screen, vaudeville actress and opera performer.

ESTUDILLO, LEO B.
Born: 1900, San Diego, Calif. Died: Sept. 21, 1957, San Francisco, Calif. Screen actor and trick rider.

ETHIER, ALPHONSE

Born: 1875, Springville, Utah. Died: Jan. 4, 1943, Hollywood, Calif. Stage and screen actor.

Appeared in: 1910 Thelma. 1921 A Message from Mars; The Frontier of the Stars. 1924 The Moral Sinner; The Alaskan; The Lone Wolf. 1925 Contraband; The Midnight Flyer; Gold and the Girl; The People vs. Nancy Preston. 1926 Breed of the Sea; The Lone Wolf Returns. 1927 Cheaters; Alias the Lone Wolf; The Fighting Eagle. 1928 Say It with Sables; Shadows of the Night. 1929 The Donovan Affair; In Old Arizona; Hardboiled; Smoke Bellew. 1930 The Storm; His First Command; Lightnin'; The Big Trail. 1931 Fair Warning; Transgression; Honor of the Family. 1932 Rebecca of Sunnybrook Farm; Law and Order; Wild Girl; The Match King. 1933 Men of America; Ex-Lady; Baby Face. 1934 Voice in the Night; British Agent; No More Women. 1935 Secret of the Chateau; Red Morning; The Crusades. 1936 Boss Rider of Gun Creek. 1938 The Baroness and the Butler; Sunset Trail.

EVANS, BOB (Robert D. Evans)

Born: 1904. Died: Mar. 21, 1961, Hollywood, Calif. (heart attack). Screen actor. Do not confuse with ventriloquist, screen actor nor film executive with same name.

Appeared in: 1937 Kid Galahad. 1938 Fisticuffs (short). 1941 The Flame of New Orleans. 1956 Around the World in 80 Days.

EVANS, CECILIA

Born: 1902. Died: Nov. 11, 1960, San Rafael, Calif. Screen and stage actress. Entered films with Sennett.

Appeared in: 1924 Worldly Goods. 1925 Blue Blood; The Goose Hangs High; Heir-Loons; The Talker. 1926 The Family Upstairs; Whispering Wires. 1927 Prince of Headwaiters.

EVANS, CHARLES EVAN

Born: 1857, Rochester, N.Y. Died: Apr. 16, 1945, Santa Monica, Calif. Screen, stage actor and stage producer. Married to actress Helena Phillips Evans (dec. 1955).

Appeared in: 1929 The Greene Murder Case; Disraeli; Happy Days. 1932 The Man Who Played God; The Expert. 1933 The King's Vacation; The Working Man. 1934 Peck's Bad Boy; The House of Rothschild. 1935 Clive of India; Cardinal Richelieu.

EVANS, DOUGLAS "DOUG"

Born: 1904, Va. Died: Mar. 25, 1968, Hollywood, Calif. Screen, stage and radio actor.

Appeared in: 1937 Public Cowboy No. 1. 1947 The Crimson Key; Dangerous Venture. 1949 Powder River Rustlers; The Golden Stallion; Hideout. 1950 No Sad Songs for Me; North of the Great Divide; At War with the Army; Rustlers on Horseback; Champagne for Caesar; Lucky Losers. 1951 Sky High; Horsie; Leave It to the Marines; Let's Go Navy. 1952 Actors and Sin. 1953 City of Bad Men. 1954 The Eddie Cantor Story. 1956 The Birds and the Bees. 1957 Short Cut to Hell; The Female Animal. 1965 The Family Jewels; I Saw What You Did. 1966 The Oscar. 1968 Panic in the City.

EVANS, EDITH

Born: 1894. Died: Oct. 12, 1962, Madison, N.J. Screen actress. Appeared in silents. Do not confuse with Dame Edith Evans, English actress.

EVANS, EVAN

Born: 1901, Birkenhead, England. Died: Jan. 3, 1954, New York, N.Y. (heart ailment). Opera singer and screen actor. Appeared during the 1930s in film/musical shorts.

Appeared in: 1941 How Green Was My Valley.

EVANS, HELENA PHILLIPS

Born: 1875. Died: July 24, 1955, Santa Monica, Calif. (heart attack). Stage and screen actress. She appeared as both Helena Phillips and Helena Evans. Married to actor Charles E. Evans (dec. 1945).

Appeared in: 1921 My Lady's Latchkey. 1929 The Greene Murder Case. 1932 Two Seconds; Life Begins. 1933 The King's Vacation; Voltaire; Design for Living. 1934 Elmer and Elsie; I'll Fix It; Kiss and Make Up. 1935 College Scandal. 1938 Nancy Drew, Detective; My Bill. 1939 6,000 Enemies.

EVANS, HERBERT

Born: Apr. 16, 1883, London, England. Died: Feb. 10, 1952, San Gabriel, Calif. Stage and screen actor. Entered films in 1914.

Appeared in: 1927 The Devil Dancer. 1928 Speedy; Beyond London Lights; The Naughty Duchess. 1930 Way for a Sailor. 1933 Reunion in Vienna; Secrets; One Year Later; Brief Moment. 1934 Service With a Smile (short). 1935 The Glass Key; Peter Ibbetson. 1936 And Sudden Death. 1937 High Flyers. 1938 Everybody's Doing It; Dawn Patrol; The Mysterious Mr. Moto; Gangster's Boy. 1939 Susannah of the Mounties; The Adventures of Sherlock Holmes; The Rains Came; The Kid from Kokomo; Man about Town. 1940 The Blue Bird. 1941 Man Hunt. 1942 Miss Minerver. 1944 Abroad with Two

Yanks; Her Primitive Man. 1945 The Corn Is Green. 1946 Pardon My Past; Bringing up Father; Kitty. 1948 Hot Scots (short). 1949 Sky Liner; The Great Sinner; Who Done It? (short); Vagabond Loafers (short).

EVANS, JACK

Born: 1893. Died: Mar. 14, 1950, Hollywood, Calif. (heart attack). Screen actor.

Appeared in: 1922 The Hidden Woman. 1936 Guns and Guitars. 1937 Stuck in the Sticks (short).

EVANS, JOE

Born: 1916. Died: Sept. 12, 1973, Woodland Hills, Calif. Screen and vaudeville actor. Appeared in vaudeville and films in a dance act with George Boyce.

Appeared in: 1954 Three Ring Circus (with Boyce). 1955 The Seven Little Foys (with Boyce).

EVANS, NANCY

Died: July 29, 1963, Los Angeles, Calif. (cancer). Screen and stage actress. Married to actor/agent Jack Stuart-Fife.

Appeared in: 1945 Weekend at the Waldorf. 1946 My Reputation. 1947 Life with Father. 1956 The Peacemaker.

EVANS, PAULINE

Born: 1917. Died: Jan. 22, 1952, Calexico, Calif. Screen actress.

EVANS, RENEE

Born: 1908. Died: Dec. 22, 1971, Hollywood, Calif. (heart condition). Screen, stage actress and dancer. Married to stage actor John Alban and mother of stage actress Diane Alban.

Appeared in: 1933 42nd Street.

EVANS, REX

Born: 1903, England. Died: Apr. 3, 1969, Glendale, Calif. Stage and screen actor.

Appeared in: 1933 Along Came Sally. 1936 Camille. 1937 The Prince and the Pauper; The Wrong Road. 1939 Zaza. 1940 The Philadelphia Story; Adventure in Diamonds. 1941 A Woman's Face; The Shanghai Gesture. 1943 Frankenstein Meets the Wolf Man. 1944 Higher and Higher; The Thin Man Goes Home. 1945 Pursuit to Algiers. 1946 Till the Clouds Roll By. 1947 Dangerous Millions. 1952 Captain Pirate. 1953 Loose in London; Jamaica Run. 1954 Knock on Wood; A Star Is Born; It Should Happen to You. 1956 The Birds and the Bees. 1957 Merry Andrew. 1958 The Matchmaker. 1961 On the Double; All in a Night's Work.

EVELYN, JUDITH (J. E. Allen)

Born: 1913. Died: May 7, 1967, New York, N.Y. (cancer). Screen, stage, television and radio actress.

Appeared in: 1951 The Thirteenth Letter. 1954 The Egyptian; Rear Window. 1955 Female on the Beach. 1956 Hilda Crane; Giant. 1958 The Brothers Karamazov; Twilight for the Gods. 1959 The Tingler.

EVELYNNE, MAY

Born: 1856. Died: Apr. 3, 1943, Los Angeles, Calif. Screen and stage actress.

EVEREST, BARBARA

Born: June 9, 1890, London, England. Died: Feb. 9, 1968, London, England. Screen, stage, television and radio actress.

Appeared in: 1916 The Man Without a Soul (aka I Believe—US 1917); The Morals of Weybury (aka The Hypocrites). 1919 Not Guilty; The Lady Clare; Whosoever Shall Offend; Till Our Ship Comes In (series). 1920 Calvary; The Joyous Adventures of Aristide Pujol. 1921 The Biganist. 1922 The Persistent Lovers; Fox Farm; A Romance of Old Bagdad. 1932 Lily Christine; When London Sleeps; The Lodger (aka The Phantom Fiend—US 1935); There Goes the Bride; The World, The Flesh and the Devil. 1933 The Umbrella; The Wandering Jew; Love's Old Sweet Song; She Was Only a Village Maiden; The Lost Chord; The Rood. 1934 Passing Shadows; The Warren Case. 1935 Scrooge; The Passing of the Third Floor Back; The Phantom Fiend. 1936 Love in Exile; Man Behind the Mask. 1937 Death Croons the Blues; Jump for Glory (aka When Thief Meets Thief—US); Old Mother Riley. 1939 Discoveries; Trunk Crime (aka Design for Murder—US 1940); Meet Maxwell Archer (aka Maxwell Archer, Detective—US 1942); Inquest. 1940 The Second Mr. Bush; Bringing It Home. 1941 He Found a Star; This Man is Dangerous (aka The Patient Vanishes—US 1947); Telefootlers; The Prime Minister. 1942 Commandoes Strike at Dawn; Mission to Moscow; Phantom of the Opera. 1944 Jane Eyre; The Uninvited; Gaslight. 1945 The Valley of Decision; The Fatal Witness. 1946 Wanted for Murder. 1947 Frieda. 1949 Children of Chance. 1950 Madeleine; Tony Draws a Horse (US 1951). 1954 An Inspector Calls. 1958 The Safecracker. 1959 Upstairs and Downstairs (US 1961). 1961 Dangerous Afternoon; El Cid. 1962 The Damned (aka These are the Damned—US 1964); The Man Who Finally Died (US 1967). 1963 Nurse on Wheels (US 1964). 1965 Rotten to the Core. 1969 Franchette—Les Intrigues.

EVERS, ERNEST P.

Born: 1874. Died: July 22, 1945, Hollywood, Calif. Screen and stage actor. Entered films approx. 1915.

EVERTON, PAUL

Born: 1869. Died: Feb. 26, 1948, Woodland Hills, Calif. (heart attack). Stage and screen actor.

Appeared in: 1918 The Eagle's Eye (serial). 1921 Cappy Ricks; City of Silent Men; The Conquest of Canaan; Proxies; The Silver Lining. 1923 The Little Red Schoolhouse. 1925 That Royle Girl. 1937 They Won't Forget; The Life of Emile Zola; The Great Garrick. 1938 Reformatory; Touchdown Army; Midnight Intruder; The Beloved Brat; Merrily We Live; Outside the Law; Orphans of the Street; Gun Law; Strange Case of Dr. Meade. 1939 Topper Takes a Trip; Stand up and Fight; Whispering Enemies; Trapped in the Sky; Maisie; Joe and Ethel Turp Call on the President; The Great Man Votes. 1940 Mexican Spitfire Out West; You the People (short); Pound Foolish (short); Prairie Law. 1942 Tennessee Johnson. 1945 Leave Her to Heaven.

EYSOLDT, GERTRUD

Born: 1871, Germany. Died: Jan. 6, 1955, Ohlstadt, West Germany. Screen, stage actress and stage director.

Appeared in: 1953 Keepers of the Night.

EYTHE, WILLIAM

Born: Apr. 7, 1918, Mars. Pa. Died: Jan. 26, 1957, Los Angeles, Calif. (acute hepatitis). Screen, stage, radio, television actor, stage producer and stage director.

Appeared in: 1943 The Ox-Bow Incident (film debut); The Song of Bernadette. 1944 The Eve of St. Mark; Wilson; A Wing and a Prayer. 1945 Czarina; The House on 92nd Street; A Royal Scandal; Colonel Effingham's Raid. 1946 Centennial Summer; Man of the Hour. 1948 Meet Me at Dawn; Mr. Reckless. 1949 Special Agent. 1950 Customs Agent.

FABRE, SATURNIN

Born: 1884, France. Died: Oct. 24, 1961, Paris, France. Stage and screen actor.

Appeared in: 1932 Paris-Beguin. 1936 Les Petits. 1937 Pepe le Moko (US 1941). 1938 Generals without Buttons. 1940 The Mayor's Dilemma. 1942 Nine Bachelors; The Pasha's Wives. 1948 Un Ami Viendra Ce Soir (A Friend Will Come Tonight). 1950 Gates of the Night; The Scandals of Clochemerle; Ignace. 1951 Miquette. 1952 The French Way (US 1959). 1953 L'ennemi Public No. 1 (aka The Most Wanted Man in the World—US 1962). 1955 Holiday for Henrietta.

FABREGAS, VIRGINIA

Born: 1870, Vautepec, Morelos, Mexico. Died: Nov. 17, 1950, Mexico City, Mexico. Stage and screen actress. Made Spanish language films in Hollywood in 1919 and 1937–38.

Appeared in: 1934 La Sangre Manda. 1938 Abnegacion.

FABRIZI, MARIO

Born: 1925. Died: Apr. 5, 1963, London, England. Screen, stage and television actor.

Appeared in: 1962 Postman's Knock; On the Beat; Operation Snatch; Ring-A-Ding Rhythm! 1963 The Punch and Judy Man.

FADDEN, GENEVIEVE

Born: Oakdale, Calif. Died: Mar. 28, 1959, Santa Monica, Calif. Screen, stage and vaudeville actress. Married to actor Tom Fadden.

FAHEY, MYRNA

Born: 1939. Died: May 6, 1973, Santa Monica, Calif. Screen and television actress.

Appeared in: 1959 Face of a Fugitive; The Story on Page One. 1960 The House of Usher.

FAHRNEY, MILTON H.

Born: 1871. Died: Mar. 27, 1941, Culver City, Calif. (heart attack). Screen, stage actor and film director. Entered films in 1907.

Appeared in: 1924 Not Built for Runnin'; Yankee Speed. 1926 Chasing Trouble. 1927 In the First Degree. 1929 Untamed.

FAIN, JOHN

Born: 1915, Jonesville, La. Died: Jan. 9, 1970, Malibu, Calif. (hit by car). Screen actor.

Appeared in: 1963 Beach Party. 1964 Pajama Party.

FAIR, ELINOR

Born: 1903, Richmond, Va. Died: 1957. Screen, stage and vaudeville actress. Divorced from actor William Boyd (dec. 1972). She was a Wampas Baby Star of 1924.

Appeared in: 1919 Miracle Man. 1920 Kismet; Broadway and Home. 1921 Cold Steel; It Can be Done; Through the Back Door. 1922 The Able-minded Lady; Big Stakes; Dangerous Pastime; White Hands. 1923 Driven; The Eagle's Feather; Has the World Gone Mad!; The Mysterious Witness; One Million in Jewels. 1924 The Law Forbids. 1925 Flyin' Thru; Gold and the Girl; Timber Wolf; Trapped; The Wife Who Wasn't Wanted. 1926 Bachelor Brides; The Volga Boatman. 1927 Jim the Conqueror; My Friend from India; The Yankee Clipper. 1928 Let 'er Go Gallegher. 1929 Sin Town. 1932 45 Caliber Echo; Night Rider. 1934 The Scarlet Empress.

FAIRBANKS, DOUGLAS, SR. (Douglas Elton Ullman)

Born: May 23, 1883, Denver, Colo. Died: Dec. 12, 1939, Santa Monica, Calif. (heart attack). Screen, stage actor and film director. Won Photoplay 1922 Medal of Honor for Robin Hood. Divorced from Beth Sully and actress Mary Pickford. Married to Lady Sylvia Ashley. Father of actor Douglas Fairbanks, Jr.

Appeared in: 1915 The Lamb (film debut); His Picture in the Papers; Double Trouble. 1916 Reggie Mixes In; The Americano; The Matrimaniac; Manhattan Madness; The Good Bad Man; Flirting with Fate; Half Breed; American Aristocracy; The Habit of Happiness. 1917 In Again, out Again; Wild and Wooly; Down to Earth; The Man from Painted Post; Reaching for the Moon. 1918 Headin' South; Mr. Fix-It; Say! Young Fellow; War Relief; Bound in Morocco; He Comes up Smiling; Arizona. 1919 Knickerbocker Buckaroo; His Majesty the American; Modern Musketeers. 1920 Where the Clouds Roll By; The Mollycoddle; The Mark of Zorro. 1921 The Nut; The Three Musketeers. 1922 Robin Hood. 1924 The Thief of Bagdad. 1925 Don Q. 1926 The Black Pirate. 1927 The Gaucho; Show People. 1929 The Iron Mask; Taming of the Shrew. 1931 Reaching for the Moon (and 1917 version); Around the World in Eighty Minutes. 1932 Mr. Robinson Crusoe. 1934 The Private Life of Don Juan. 1961 Days of Thrills and Laughter (documentary). 1963 The Great Chase (documentary). 1973 Sky High (documentary). 1974 That's Entertainment (film clips).

FAIRBANKS, WILLIAM

Born: May 24, 1894, St. Louis, Mo. Died: Apr. 1, 1945, Los Angeles, Calif. (lobar pneumonia). Stage and screen actor.

Appeared in: 1921 Broadway Buckaroo; Go Get Him; A Western Adventurer; Montana Bill. 1922 Fighting Hearts; Hell's Border; The Clean Up; Peaceful Peters; A Western Demon; The Sheriff of Sun-Dog. 1923 Sun Dog Trails; The Devil's Dooryard; The Law Rustlers; Spawn of the Desert. 1924 The Battling Fool; Border Women; Women First; The Beautiful Sinner; Call of the Mate; The Cowboy and the Flapper; Do It Now; Down by the Rio Grande; The Fatal Mistake; A Fight for Honor; Her Man; Man from God's Country; Marry in Haste; The Martyr Sex; The Other Kind of Love; Racing for Life; Tainted Money; That Wild West; The Torrent; The Sheriff of Sun Dog; Spawn of the Desert; Law Rustlers; Sun Dog Trail. 1925 The Fearless Lover; A Fight to the Finish; Fighting Youth; The Great Sensation; The Handsome Brute; New Champion; Speed Mad. 1926 Flying High; The Mile-a-Minute Man; The Winning Wallop; Vanishing Millions (serial). 1927 When Danger Calls; Catch-As-Catch-Can; The Down Grade; One Chance in a Million; Spoilers of the West; Through Thick and Thin. 1928 Wyoming; Under the Black Eagle; The Vanishing West (serial).

FAIRBROTHER, SYDNEY

Born: July 31, 1872, England. Died: Jan. 4, 1941, London, England. Stage and screen actress.

Appeared in: 1915 Iron Justice. 1916 The Mother of Dartmoor; A Mother's Influence; Frailty (aka Temptation's Hour); Me and Me Moke (aka Me and M'Pal—US). 1917 Auld Lang Syne. 1919 In Bondage (aka Faith). 1920 Laddie; The Children of Gibeon; A Temporary Gentleman. 1921 The Bachelor's Club; The Rotters; The Golden Dawn. 1923 Maisie's Marriage (aka Married Love and Married Life); Love, Life and Laughter (aka Tip Toes); Heartstrings; The Beloved Vagabond; The Rest Cure; Don Quixote; Sally Bishop. 1924 Reveille; Pett Ridge Stories (series). 1925 Mrs. May Comedies (series). 1926 Nell Gwynne. 1927 The Silver Lining; Confetti; My Lord the Chauffeur. 1931 The Other Mrs. Phipps. 1932 Murder on the Second Floor; The Third String; Postal Orders; A Letter of Warning; Double Dealing; Down Our Street; Insult; The Return of Raffles; Lucky Ladies; The Temperance Fete. 1933 Excess Baggage; Home Sweet Home. 1934 The Spotting Series including A Touching Story; The Crucifix; Chu Chin Chow; Gay Love. 1935 Brewster's Millions; The Private Secretary; The Last Journey (US 1936). 1936 All In; Fame. 1937 Dreaming Lips; King Solomon's Mines; Paradise for Two (aka The Gaiety Girls—US 1938); Rose of Tralee (US 1938). 1938 Make it Three; Little Dolly Daydream.

FAIRFAX, JAMES

Born: 1897, England. Died: May 8, 1961, Papeete, Tahiti (heart attack). Screen, television and vaudeville actor.

Appeared in: 1948 The Challenge. 1949 Mrs. Mike. 1950 Tyrant of the Sea; Customs Agent; Fortunes of Captain Blood. 1952 Last Train from Bombay. 1953 White Goddess; Abbott and Costello Meet Dr. Jekyll & Mr. Hyde. 1962 Mutiny on the Bounty (died while filming).

FAIRMAN, AUSTIN
Born: Mar. 4, 1892, London, England. Died: Mar. 26, 1964, Dedham, Mass. Screen, stage, radio actor and playwright. Married to actress Hilda Moore (dec. 1929).

Appeared in: **1930** Her Hired Husband. **1931** The Grand Dame (short). **1938** Bulldog Drummond's Peril. **1940** British Intelligence.

FALCONETTI, RENEE
Born: 1901, France. Died: Dec. 12, 1946, Buenos Aires, Argentina. Stage and screen actress.

FALLON, CHARLES (Charles von Der Belin)
Born: 1885, Antwerp, Belgium. Died: Mar. 11, 1936, Hollywood, Calif. (heart attack). Screen, stage actor, film producer, and film director.

Appeared in: **1935** Ruggles of Red Gap; The Man Who Broke the Bank at Monte Carlo. **1936** Next Time We Love.

FANNING, FRANK B.
Born: 1880. Died: Mar. 3, 1934, Los Angeles, Calif. Screen and stage actor.

Appeared in: **1922** The Masked Avenger. **1930** Guilty.

FAREBROTHER, VIOLET
Born: Aug. 22, 1888, Grimsby, Lincs, England. Died: Sept. 27, 1969, Eastbourne, Sussex, England. Stage and screen actress.

Appeared in: **1911** Richard III (stage and film versions). **1927** Downhill (aka When Boys Leave Home—US 1928); Easy Virtue (US 1928). **1930** At the Villa Rose (aka Mystery at the Villa Rose—US); Murder. **1933** Enemy of the Police; This Acting Business. **1934** Nine Forty-Five; The Official Wife. **1935** It's a Bet; Mr. Cohen Takes a Walk (US 1936). **1936** Where's Sally? **1937** It's not Cricket; Change for a Sovereign; Les Perles de la Couronne. **1945** The Voice Within. **1948** Cup-Tie Honeymoon; Look Before You Love. **1955** Man of the Moment; The Woman for Joe. **1957** Fortune is a Woman (aka She Played with Fire—US 1958). **1958** The Solitary Child.

FARFAN, MARIAN
Born: 1913. Died: Apr. 3, 1965, Hollywood, Calif. Screen actress.

FARFARIELLO (Edward Migliaccio)
Born: 1881, Salerno, Italy. Died: Mar. 28, 1946, N.Y. Screen, vaudeville and radio actor. Appeared in several Hollywood shorts.

FARINA, RICHARD
Born: 1937, New York, N.Y. Died: Apr. 30, 1966, Carmel, Calif. (motorcycle accident). Novelist, singer and screen actor. Married to actress Mimi Baez.

Appeared in: **1967** Festival.

FARLEY, DOT (Dorothea Farley)
Born: Feb. 6, 1881, Chicago, Ill. Died: May 2, 1971, South Pasadena, Calif. Screen, stage actress and screenwriter.

Appeared in: **1910** Romantic Redskins. **1912** At the Basket Picnic; A Wife Wanted; Perils of the Plains; Raiders on the Mexican Border. **1913** A Life in the Balance. **1914** Soul Mates; Her Bandit Sweetheart; The Toll of the Warpath; How Johanna Saved the Home. **1915** Buy, Buy Baby; Her New Job; Wheeled into Matrimony; Oh, You Female Cop; Married in Disguise; She Couldn't Get Away from It; When Quality Meets; Aunt Matilda Outwitted; The Poor Fixer; Sammy's Scandalous Schemes. **1917** The House of Terrible Scandals. **1918** Wooing of Coffee Cake Kate. **1921** Home Talent; A Small Town Idol. **1922** The Crossroads of New York. **1923** The Acquittal; Boy of Mine; Tea—With a Kick. **1924** The Enemy Sex; The Fatal Mistake; Listen Lester; So Big; The Signal Tower; Vanity's Pride. **1925** Border Intrigue; Lure of the Track; My Son; Rugged Water; A Woman of the World. **1926** Brooding Eyes; The Family Upstairs; The Grand Duchess and the Waiter; Honesty—The Best Policy; The Little Irish Girl; Memory Lane; Money Talks; The Still Alarm; Young April; Weak but Billing (short). **1927** All Aboard; The Climbers; His First Flame; The King of Kings; The Lost Limited; McFadden's Flats; Nobody's Widow; The Overland Stage; The Shamrock and the Rose; Yours to Command; The Tired Business Man. **1928** Black Feather; Celebrity; The Code of Scarlet; Lady Be Good; The Head Man; Should a Girl Marry? **1929** Divorce Made Easy; Why Leave Home?; Whirls and Girls (short); The Bee's Buzz (short). **1930** Harmony at Home; The Little Accident; Road to Paradise; The Third Alarm; Swell People (short). **1931** Dancing Dynamite; Law of the Tongs; plus the following shorts: The Dog Doctor; Lemon Meringue; Thanks Again; Camping Out. **1932** While Paris Sleeps; plus the following shorts: Bon Voyage; Mother-in-Law's Day; Giggle Water; The Golf Chump; Parlor, Bedroom and Wrath; Fish Feathers. **1933** The following shorts: Art in the Raw; The Merchant of Menace; Good Housewrecking; Quiet, Please; What Fur; Grin and Bear It. **1934** Love Past Thirty; Down to Their Last Yacht; Mr. Average Man series; plus the following shorts: Love on a Ladder; Wrong Direction; In-Laws Are Out; A Blasted Event; Poisoned Ivory; Fixing a Stew. **1935** Diamond Jim; False Pretenses; plus the following shorts: Tramp Tramp Tramp; South Seasickness; Bric-a-Brac; Sock Me to Sleep; Ed-

gar Hamlet; In Love at 40; Happy Tho Married. **1936** The following shorts: Will Power; Gasoloons; High Beer Pressure; Dummy Ache. **1937** Too Many Wives; A Rented Riot (short). **1938** Stranger from Arizona; Lawless Valley; Road to Reno. **1942** The following shorts: Heart Burn; Inferior Decorator; Cooks and Crooks; Two for the Money; Rough on Rents; Duck Soup. **1943** The following shorts: Hold your Tempter; Indian Signs; Hot Foot; Not on My Account; Unlucky Dog. **1944** The following shorts: Prunes and Politics; Radio Rampage; Feather your Nest. **1945** The following shorts: Sleepless Tuesday; What, No Cigarettes?; It's Your Move; The Big Beef; Mother-in-Law's Day (and 1932 version). **1946** The following shorts: Trouble or Nothing; Wall Street Blues; Motor Maniacs; Noisy Neighbors; I'll Build It Myself; Social Terrors. **1947** The following shorts: Do or Diet; Heading for Trouble; Host to a Ghost; Television Turmoil; Mind over Mouse. **1948** The following shorts: Brother Knows Best; No More Relatives; How to Clean House; Home Canning; Contest Crazy. **1948** Variety Time.

FARLEY, JAMES LEE "JIM"
Born: Jan. 8, 1882, Waldron, Ark. Died: Oct. 12, 1947, Pacoima, Calif. Stage and screen actor.

Appeared in: **1919** Nugget Nell. **1921** That Something; The Devil Within; Bar Nothin'; The One-Man Trail; Bucking the Line. **1922** Gleam O'Dawn; Travelin' On; When Danger Smiles; Boy Crazy; Little Wildcat; My Wild Irish Rose. **1923** Trifling with Honor; The Woman with Four Faces; Wild Bill Hickok. **1924** The City That Never Sleeps. **1925** A Son of His Father. **1926** The Lodge in the Wilderness. **1927** King of Kings; The Tired Business Man; The General. **1928** The Racket; Shady Lady; The Grip of the Yukon; Mad Hour; The Perfect Crime; A Woman against the World. **1929** Weary River; In Old Arizona; Hunted; The Voice of the City; The Dance of Life; The Godless Girl; Courtin' Wildcats; Dynamite; Danger Lights. **1930** Lucky Larkin; Danger Lights. **1931** Fighting Caravans; Three Rogues. **1932** Scandal for Sale. **1934** Here Comes the Groom. **1935** Hold 'Em Yale; Down to Their Last Yacht; Midnight Phantom; Westward Ho. **1936** High Treason; Captain January; Dancing Pirate; Song of the Saddle; The Bride Walks Out. **1937** Mannequin; City of Havens; The Californian. **1938** Quick Money. **1939** Dodge City; I Stole a Million; The Forgotten Woman. **1940** East Side Kids. **1941** World Premiere; Sky Raiders (serial); Glamour Boy; Badlands of Dakota; Among the Living; All That Money Can Buy. **1942** This Gun for Hire; Quiet Please, Murder; The Silver Bullet; You Can't Escape Forever. **1943** What a Man!; Hot Foot (short). **1944** Hail the Conquering Hero; San Fernando Valley; The Adventures of Mark Twain; Gambler's Choice. **1945** The Cisco Kid in Old New Mexico. **1946** The Kid from Brooklyn. **1947** Ladies' Man. **1952** The Devil and Daniel Webster (retitle and reissue of All that Money Can Buy, 1941).

FARMER, FRANCES
Born: Sept. 19, 1914, Seattle, Wash. Died: Aug. 1, 1970, Indianapolis, Ind. (cancer). Screen, stage and television actress. Divorced from actor Leif Erickson and Alfred Lobley. Married to Leland Mikesell.

Appeared in: **1936** Come and Get It (film debut); Too Many Parents; Border Flight; Rhythm on the Range. **1937** Ebb Tide; The Toast of New York; Exclusive. **1938** Ride a Crooked Mile. **1940** South of Pago Pago; Flowing Gold. **1941** Badlands of Dakota; World Premiere; Among the Living. **1942** Son of Fury. **1958** The Party Crashers.

FARNUM, DUSTIN
Born: 1874, Hampton Beach, Maine. Died: July 3, 1929, New York, N.Y. (kidney trouble). Screen, stage and vaudeville actor. Brother of actor William Farnum (dec. 1953).

Appeared in: **1913** The Squaw Man. **1915** Cameo Kirby; Captain Courtesy; The Gentlemen from Indiana. **1916** The Iron Strain; David Garrick; Davy Crockett. **1917** The Scarlet Pimpernell; The Spy; North of 53. **1918** Light of the Western Stars. **1919** A Man's Fight; A Man in the Open; The Corsican Brothers. **1920** Big Happiness. **1921** The Primal Law; The Devil Within; Call of the North. **1922** Strange Idols; Iron to Gold; The Yosemite Trail; While Justice Waits; The Trail of the Axe; Oathbound; Three Who Paid. **1923** The Virginian; Bucking the Barrier; The Buster; The Grail; The Man Who Won. **1924** Kentucky Days; My Man. **1926** The Flaming Frontier.

FARNUM, FRANKLYN
Born: 1876, Boston, Mass. Died: July 4, 1961, Hollywood, Calif. (cancer). Stage and screen actor.

Appeared in: **1916** A Stranger from Somewhere; Little Partner. **1917** The Devil's Pay Day; The Man Who Took a Chance; Bringing Home Father; Anything Once; The Winged Mystery; The Scarlet Car; The Car of Chance. **1918** The Fighting Grin; The Empty Cab; The Rough Lover; Fast Company; $5,000 Reward; In Judgment Of. **1919** Go Get 'Em Garringer. **1920** Vanishing Trails (serial). **1921** The Fighting Stranger; The Hunger of the Blood; The White Masks; The Struggle; The Last Chance; The Raiders. **1922** Cross Roads; Gold Grabbers; Angel Citizens; Gun Shy; Texas; Smiling Jim; So This Is Arizona; When East Comes West; Trail's End; The Firebrand. **1923** The Man Getter; It Happened out West; Wolves of the Border. **1924** A Desperate Adventure; Two Fisted Tenderfoot; Battling Brewster; Calibre 45; Baffled; Courage; Crossed Trails; Western Vengeance. **1925** Border Intrigue; The Drug

Store Cowboy; The Gambling Fool; The Bandit Tamer; Double-Barreled Justice; Rough Going; Two Gun Sap. **1930** Beyond the Rio Grande; Beyond the Law. **1931** Hell's Valley; Battling With Buffalo Bill (serial); Not Exactly Gentlemen; Three Rogues; Leftover Ladies; Oklahoma Jim. **1932** Human Targets; Mark of the Spur; Honor of the Bad Man. **1934** Frontier Days; Honor of the Range. **1935** Hopalong Cassidy; The Crusades; The Ghost Riders; Powdersmoke Range. **1936** Frontier Justice; Preview Murder Mystery. **1938** Prison Train. **1942** Stardust on the Sage. **1944** Saddle Leather Law. **1948** Assigned to Danger. **1950** Destination Murder; Sunset Boulevard. **1952** My Pal Gus. **1956** The Ten Commandments; Around the World in 80 Days. **1958** King Creole; Rock-a-Bye Baby.

FARNUM, WILLIAM
Born: July 4, 1876, Boston, Mass. Died: June 5, 1953, Los Angeles, Calif. (cancer). Stage and screen actor. Brother of actor Dustin Farnum (dec. 1929). Divorced from actress Mable Eaton (dec. 1916).

Appeared in: **1913** The Redemption of David Corson. **1914** The Spoilers (small part in 1942 remake); The Sign of the Cross. **1915** The Plunderer; The Nigger. **1916** A Man of Sorrow. **1917** A Tale of Two Cities; The Heart of a Lion; The Conqueror. **1918** Les Miserables; Rough and Ready. **1919** The Last of the Duanes; The Man Hunter; The Lone Star Ranger. **1920** The Adventurer; Drag Harlan; If I Were King. **1921** His Greatest Sacrifice; The Scuttlers; Perjury. **1922** A Stage Romance; Shackles of Gold; Without Compromise; Moonshine Valley. **1923** The Gun Fighter; Brass Commandments. **1924** The Man Who Fights Alone. **1927** Ben Hur. **1930** If I Were King (and 1920 version); Du Barry, Woman of Passion. **1931** The Painted Desert; Oh! Oh! Cleopatra (short); Ten Nights in a Bar Room; A Connecticut Yankee; Pagan Lady. **1932** The Drifter; Mr. Robinson Crusoe; Law of the Sea; Wide Open Spaces (short). **1933** Supernatural; Marriage on Approval; Another Language; Flaming Guns. **1934** Cleopatra; Brand of Hate; Happy Landing; The Count of Monte Cristo; School for Girls; Good Dame; The Scarlet Letter; Are We Civilized?; The Silver Streak. **1935** The Crusades; The Eagles' Brood; Powdersmoke Range; Custer's Last Stand (serial); Between Men. **1936** The Last Assignment; The Clutching Hand (serial). **1937** Git Along Little Dogies; Public Cowboy No. 1; Maid of Salem. **1938** Santa Fe Stampede; If I Were King (and 1920 and 1930 versions); Shine on Harvest Moon. **1939** Mexicali Rose; Colorado Sunset; Rovin' Tumbleweeds; South of the Border. **1940** Convicted Woman; Hi-Yo Silver; Kit Carson. **1941** Cheers for Miss Bishop; A Woman's Face; Gangs of Sonora; The Corsican Brothers; Last of the Duanes. **1942** The Lone Star Ranger; Today I Hang; The Silver Bullet; Deep in the Heart of Texas; The Boss of Hangtown Mesa; American Empire; The Spoilers (and 1914 version); Tennessee Johnson. **1943** Frontier Badmen; Hangmen Also Die. **1944** The Mummy's Curse. **1945** Captain Kidd. **1946** God's Country. **1947** Perils of Pauline; Rolling Home. **1948** My Dog Shep. **1949** Bride of Vengeance; Daughter of the West. **1950** The Undersea Kingdom (serial). **1951** Samson and Delilah. **1952** Jack and the Beanstalk; Lone Star.

FARQUHARSON, ROBERT
Born: 1878. Died: Jan. 11, 1966, Ticiono, Switzerland. Screen, stage and radio actor.

Appeared in: **1931** Captivation. **1933** The Man They Couldn't Arrest.

FARR, FRANKIE (Frankie Farinacci)
Born: 1903, Albany, N.Y. Died: Mar. 20, 1953, Tulsa, Okla. Screen actor.

Appeared in: **1936** The Great Ziegfeld. **1939** Gone with the Wind.

FARR, KARL
Died: Sept. 20, 1961. Screen actor.

Appeared in: **1946** My Pal Trigger.

FARR, PATRICIA
Born: 1915. Died: Feb. 23, 1948, Burbank, Calif. Screen actress.

Appeared in: **1931** The Secret Call; Silence. **1933** I Loved You Wednesday; My Weakness. **1934** I Am Suzanne; Stand up and Cheer; Tailspin Tommy (serial). **1935** Orchids to You; Helldorado. **1936** Three of a Kind; Speed to Spare. **1937** Criminals of the Air; All American Sweetheart. **1938** Lady Behave; Trade Winds. **1941** Mr. and Mrs. Smith; West Point Story.

FARRAR, GERALDINE
Born: 1882. Died: Mar. 11, 1967, Conn. Opera and screen actress. Divorced from actor Lou Tellegen (dec. 1934).

Appeared in: **1915** Carmen. **1916** Temptation; Maria Rosa. **1917** The Devil Stone; Joan, the Woman; The Woman God Forgot. **1918** The Hell Cat; The Turn of the Wheel. **1919** The World and Its Women; The Stranger Vow; Flame of the Desert; Shadows. **1920** The Woman and the Puppet. **1921** Riddle Woman.

FARRAR, MARGARET
Born: 1901. Died: Aug. 9, 1925, Los Angeles, Calif. (suicide—poison). Screen actress.

FARRAR, STANLEY
Born: 1911. Died: Apr. 5, 1974, Mendocino, Calif. (heart attack). Screen, stage, radio and television actor.

Appeared in: **1953** Perils of the Jungle. **1955** How to Be Very, Very Popular. **1957** Badlands of Montana; Portland Expose. **1959** Face of a Fugitive.

FARRELL, CHARLES "SKIP" (Charles Farrell Fielder)
Born: 1919. Died: May 8, 1962, Hollywood, Calif. (heart attack). Screen, radio, television actor and singer. Do not confuse with US actor born in 1902 nor Irish actor born in 1905.

Appeared in: **1950** Night and the City. **1957** Morning Call. **1958** The Strange Case of Dr. Manning. **1959** The Sheriff of Fractured Jaw. **1960** Hidden Homicide.

FARRELL, GLENDA
Born: June 30, 1904, Enid, Okla. Died: May 1, 1971, New York, N.Y. Screen, stage and television actress. Mother of actor Tommy Farrell. Starred in several "Torchy Blane" series films. Won 1963 Emmy Award for Best Supporting Actress in Ben Casey television show.

Appeared in: **1929** Lucky Boy. **1930** Little Caesar; The Lucky Break (short). **1932** Life Begins (film and stage versions); I Am a Fugitive from a Chain Gang; The Match King; Three on a Match; Scandal for Sale; Night Nurse. **1933** The Mayor of Hell; Central Airport; The Keyhold; Girl Missing; Mary Stevens, M.D.; Bureau of Missing Persons; Gambling Ship; Lady for a Day; Man's Castle; Havana Widows; Grand Slam; The Mystery of the Wax Museum. **1934** The Big Shakedown; Dark Hazard; The Personality Kid; Hi, Nellie!; Merry Wives of Reno; Kansas City Princess; I've Got Your Number; Heat Lightning. **1935** Go into Your Dance; In Caliente; Traveling Saleslady; Gold Diggers of 1935; We're in the Money; Little Big Shot; Miss Pacific Fleet; The Secret Bride. **1936** Snowed Under; The Law in Her Hands; Smart Blonde; Here Comes Carter!; Gold Diggers of 1937; High Tension; Nobody's Fool. **1937** Dance, Charlie, Dance; Fly Away Baby; The Adventurous Blonde; Hollywood Hotel; Breakfast for Two; You Live and Learn. **1938** Stolen Heaven; Prison Break; The Road to Reno; Exposed; Blondes at Work; Torchy Gets Her Man. **1939** Torchy Blane in Chinatown; Torchy Runs for Mayor. **1941** Johnny Eager. **1942** A Night for Crime; The Talk of the Town; Twin Beds. **1943** Klondike Kate; City without Men. **1944** Ever since Venus. **1947** Heading for Heaven. **1948** I Love Trouble; Mary Lou; Lulu Belle. **1952** Apache War Smoke. **1953** Girls in the Night. **1954** Secret of the Incas; Susan Slept Here. **1955** The Girl in the Red Velvet Swing. **1959** Middle of the Night. **1964** The Disorderly Orderly; Kissin' Cousins. **1968** Dead Heat. **1970** Tiger by the Tail.

FARRELL, JOHN W.
Born: 1885. Died: July 8, 1953, Brooklyn, N.Y. Screen, stage, vaudeville and television actor. Appeared in vaudeville with his wife Josephine Saxton in an act billed as "Saxton & Farrell."

Appeared in: **1949** Portrait of Jenny.

FARRELL, VESSIE
Born: 1890. Died: Sept. 30, 1935, Los Angeles, Calif. Screen and stage actress.

Appeared in: **1935** The Healer.

FARRINGTON, ADELE
Born: 1867, Brooklyn, N.Y. Died: Dec. 19, 1936, Los Angeles, Calif. Screen, stage and vaudeville actress. Divorced from actor Hobart Bosworth (dec. 1943).

Appeared in: **1914** The Country Mouse. **1917** American Film Mfg. Co. films. **1921** Black Beauty; The Charm School; The Child Thou Gavest Me; A Connecticut Yankee at King Arthur's Court; Her Mad Bargain; The Spenders. **1922** The Bachelor Daddy; Bobbed Hair; The Cradle; Little Wildcat; The Ordeal; A Question of Honor. **1923** Bag and Baggage; A Gentleman of Leisure; The Man Next Door; One Stolen Night; The Scarlet Lily. **1924** Along Came Ruth. **1926** The Shadow of the Law; The Traffic Cop.

FARRINGTON, BETTY
Died: 1968. Screen actress.

Appeared in: **1929** The Fall of Eve. **1930** Anybody's War. **1934** Down to Their Last Yacht. **1935** One Hour Late. **1940** Our Neighbors the Carters. **1943** True to Life. **1944** Henry Aldrich Plays Cupid.

FARRINGTON, FRANK
Born: 1874. Died: May 27, 1924, Los Angeles, Calif. Screen actor.

Appeared in: **1914** The Million Dollar Mystery (serial); Zudora—The Twenty Million Dollar Mystery (serial). **1923** The Clean Up; The Courtship of Miles Standish. **1924** The Man Who Fights Alone.

FATIMA, "LA BELLE"
Born: 1880, Syria. Died: Mar. 14, 1921, Venice, Calif. (heart attack). Screen, stage actress and dancer. Appeared in shorts made at the St. Louis World's Fair.

FAUST, HAZEL LEE
Born: 1910. Died: Dec. 11, 1973. Screen actress.

FAUST, MARTIN J.
Born: Jan. 16, 1886, Poughkeepsie, N.Y. Died: July 20, 1943, Los Angeles, Calif. Stage and screen actor. Entered films in 1908.

Appeared in: **1910** A Winter's Tale. **1921** Hell Bound. **1923** Big Brother; Under the Red Robe; The Silent Command; The Tents of Allah. **1924** I Am the Man; Yolanda. **1925** North Star. **1927** Chain Lightning; Spider Webs. **1928** Hello Cheyenne. **1929** Caress. **1934** Six of a Kind. **1938** If I Were King. **1941** Saddlemates. **1943** The North Star (and 1925 version); Hold Your Temper (short); This Is the Army. **1944** Ali Baba and the Forty Thieves.

FAUSTMAN, ERIK "HAMPE"
Born: 1919, Stockholm, Sweden. Died: 1961, Sweden? Screen actor, film director and screenwriter.

Appeared in: **1939** They Staked Their Lives. **1945** Crime and Punishment. **1946** When Meadows Bloom. **1949** Vagabond Blacksmiths; Katrina. **1960** Die Sista Stegen (A Matter of Morals—US 1961). Other Swedish films: We Need Each Other; Lars Hard; A Woman on Board; Ride Tonight; Women in Prison; A Spring in Arms; There Burned a Flame; Darling I Surrender; His Excellency; My People Are Not Yours; When the Door was Closed; Never in Your Life.

FAVERSHAM, WILLIAM
Born: Feb. 12, 1868, London, England. Died: Apr. 7, 1940, Bay Shore, N.Y. (coronary embolism). Stage and screen actor.

Appeared in: **1919** The Silver King. **1920** The Man Who Lost Himself; The Sin That Was His. **1924** The Sixth Commandment. **1934** Lady by Choice. **1935** Becky Sharp; Secret of the Chateau; Mystery Woman. **1937** Arizona Days.

FAWCETT, GEORGE D.
Born: Aug. 25, 1860, Alexandria, Va. Died: June 6, 1939, Nantucket Island, Mass. (heart ailment). Stage and screen actor. Married to actress Percy Haswell (dec. 1945) who also appeared in films as Mrs. George Fawcett.

Appeared in: **1915** The Majesty of the Law (film debut). **1917** Panthea; The Cinderella Man. **1918** The Great Love; Hearts of the World. **1919** The Girl Who Stayed at Home; The Hope Chest; A Romance of Happy Valley; I'll Get Him Yet; Nobody Home; Turning the Tables; Scarlet Days; The Greatest Question. **1920** Two Weeks; The Branded Women; Little Miss Rebellion. **1921** Burn 'Em up Barnes; Chivalrous Charley; Hush Money; Lessons in Love; Little Italy; Nobody; Paying the Piper; Sentimental Tommy; Such a Little Queen; The Way of a Maid. **1922** Beyond the Rainbow; The Curse of Drink; Destiny's Isle; Ebb Tide; His Wife's Husband; Isle of Doubt; John Smith; Manslaughter; The Old Homestead; Polly of the Follies. **1923** Salomy Jane; The Drums of Fate; His Children's Children; Hollywood; Java Head; Just Like a Woman; Mr. Billings Spends His Dime; Only 38; The Woman with Four Faces. **1924** West of the Water Tower; The Bedroom Window; The Breaking Point; Broken Barriers; Code of the Sea; Her Love Story; In Every Woman's Life; Pied Piper Malone; Tess of the D'Urbervilles; Triumph. **1925** A Lost Lady; The Merry Widow; The Circle; The Fighting Cub; Go Straight; The Home Maker; Joanna; The Mad Whirl; 9 3/5 Seconds; Peacock Feathers; The Price of Pleasure; Some Pun'kins; Souls for Sables; The Sporting Venus; Thank You; Up the Ladder; The Verdict; The Sporting Chance. **1926** The Flaming Frontier; Flesh and the Devil; Man of the Forest; Men of Steel; Out of the Storm; The Son of the Sheik; There You Are; Two Can Play; Under Western Skies. **1927** Captain Salvation; Duty's Reward; The Enemy; Hard-Boiled Haggerty; The Little Firebrand; Love; Painting the Town; The Private Life of Helen of Troy; Rich Men's Sons; Riding to Fame; See You in Jail; Snowbound; Spring Fever; Tillie the Toiler; The Valley of the Giants. **1928** Prowlers of the Sea; Tempest; The Wedding March. **1929** Little Wildcat; Fancy Baggage; His Captive Woman; Tide of Empire; Lady of the Pavements; Innocents of Paris; Four Feathers; Wonder of Women; Hot for Paris; Hearts in Exile; Men Are Like That; The Prince of Hearts. **1930** The Great Divide; Once a Gentleman; Ladies of Leisure; Wild Company; Swing High; Hello Sister; The Bad One. **1931** Drums of Jeopardy; Woman of Experience; Personal Maid.

FAWCETT, JAMES
Born: 1905. Died: June 9, 1942, San Fernando Valley, Calif. (auto accident). Film stuntman and vaudeville acrobat.

FAWCETT, WILLIAM
Died: Jan. 25, 1974. Screen actor.

Appeared in: **1946** Stars Over Texas; The Michigan Kid; Driftin' River; Tumbleweed Trail. **1947** Wild Country; Black Hills; Green Dolphin Street; The High Wall; Ghost Town Renegades; Justice. **1948** Live Today for Tomorrow; Words and Music; An Act of Murder; The Tioga Kid; Check Your Guns. **1949** Barbary Coast; The Kid from Texas; Ride, Ryder Ride!; Roll, Thunder, Roll; Barbary Pirate; Batman and Robin (serial); Adventures of Sir Galahad (serial). **1950** Tyrant of the Sea; State Penitentiary; Cody of the Pony Express (serial); Pirates of the High Seas (serial); Chain Gang; Ace in the Hole. **1951** Valley of

Five; Hollywood Story; Wanted—Dead or Alive; Honeychile; Oklahoma Annie; Hills of Utah; The Magic Carpet; The Mating Season; Captain Video (serial); Montana Incident (aka Gun Smoke Range). **1952** The Longhorn; Roar of the Iron Horse (serial); King of the Congo (serial); Springfield Rifle; The Lion and the Horse; Kansas Territory; Barbed Wire; Jungle Jim in the Forbidden Land; Montana Incident; Blackhawk (serial). **1953** The Star of Texas; The Homesteaders; The Marksman; Has Anybody Seen My Gal?; Sweetheart Time; The Raiders; A Man's Country; Canadian Mounties vs Atomic Invaders (serial). **1954** Dawn at Socorro; The Law vs Billy the Kid; Alaska Seas; Riding with Buffalo Bill (serial). **1955** Seminole Uprising; Pirates of Tripoli; Tall Man Riding; Lay that Rifle Down; Timberjack; The Spoilers; Gang-Busters. **1956** The Kettles in the Ozarks; Dakota Incident; Cattle King; The Proud Ones; Canyon River. **1957** The Storm Rider; The Tijuana Story; Band of Angels; Tension at Table Rock; The First Traveling Saleslady. **1958** No Time for Sergeants; Damn Yankees. **1959** The Wild and the Innocent; Good Day for a Hanging. **1960** The Walking Target. **1961** Claudelle Inglish; The Comancheros. **1962** The Interns; Saintly Sinners; Gypsy; Music Man. **1963** The Wheeler Dealers. **1964** Sex and the Single Girl; The Quick Gun. **1965** Dear Brigitte; King Rat. **1966** Jesse James Meets Frankenstein's Daughter. **1967** Hostile Guns; Adventures of Batman and Robin (rerelease of 1949 serial Batman and Robin); The Gnome-Mobile. **1968** Blackbeard's Ghost.

FAY, BRENDAN
Born: 1921. Died: Feb. 7, 1975, Brooklyn, N.Y. (heart attack). Stage and screen actor.

Appeared in: **1960** Juke Box Racket. **1961** The Hustler. **1974** Man on a Swing.

FAY, FRANK
Born: Nov. 17, 1894, San Francisco, Calif. Died: Sept. 25, 1961, Santa Monica, Calif. Screen, stage, vaudeville, radio actor and stage producer. Divorced from actress Barbara Stanwyck.

Appeared in: **1929** Show of Shows (film debut). **1930** The Matrimonial Bed; Under a Texas Moon. **1931** Bright Lights; God's Gift to Women; Stout Hearts and Willing Hands. **1932** The Slippery Pearls (short); Fool's Advice. **1935** Stars over Broadway. **1937** Nothing Sacred. **1938** Meet the Mayor. **1940** I Want a Divorce; They Knew What They Wanted; A WAC in His Life. **1943** Spotlight Scandals. **1951** Love Nest; When Worlds Collide; Stage from Blue River.

FAY, GABY. See FAY HOLDEN

FAY, JACK
Born: 1903. Died: Nov. 15, 1928, Los Angeles, Calif. (after effects of injuries from explosion at Fox Studios while filming What Price Glory, 1926). Screen actor.

FAY, WILLIAM GEORGE
Born: Nov. 12, 1872, Dublin, Ireland. Died: Oct. 27, 1947, London, England. Screen, stage actor, film producer and stage producer. Was co-founder of Abbey Theatre, Dublin.

Appeared in: **1918** Doing Her Bit (film debut). **1933** The Blarney Stone. **1934** General John Regan. **1935** Dark World. **1936** The Show Goes On; Storm in a Teacup. **1937** Kathleen Mavourneen; My Last Curtain. **1938** My Irish Molly. **1941** Spellbound. **1947** Odd Man Out; The Patient Vanishes.

FAYE, JULIA
Born: Sept. 24, 1896, Richmond, Va. Died: Apr. 6, 1966, Santa Monica, Calif. (cancer). Screen actress. Entered films in 1916.

Appeared in: **1916** His Auto Ruination; His Last Laugh; A Lover's Might. **1918** Sandy. **1919** Stepping Out; Male and Female; Don't Change Your Husband. **1920** The Life of the Party. **1921** Affairs of Anatol; Fool's Paradise; Forbidden Fruit; The Great Moment; The Snob. **1922** Manslaughter; Nice People; Saturday Night. **1923** The Ten Commandments; Adam's Rib; Hollywood; Nobody's Money. **1924** Feet of Clay; Changing Husbands; Don't Call It Love; Triumph. **1925** The Golden Bed; Hell's Highroad; The Road to Yesterday. **1926** Volga Boatman; Corporal Kate; Meet the Prince; Bachelor Brides. **1927** King of Kings; The Yankee Clipper; His Dog; The Main Event; The Fighting Eagle. **1928** Chicago; Turkish Delight. **1929** The Godless Girl; Dynamite. **1930** Not So Dumb. **1933** Only Yesterday. **1936** 'Til We Meet Again. **1938** You and Me. **1939** Union Pacific. **1940** North West Mounted Police. **1943** So Proudly We Hail! **1946** The Californian. **1949** Red, Hot and Blue; A Connecticut Yankee in King Arthur's Court. **1950** Copper Canyon. **1951** Samson and Delilah. **1952** The Greatest Show on Earth. **1956** The Ten Commandments (and 1923 version). **1958** Buccaneer.

FAYLAUER, ADOLPH
Born: 1884. Died: Jan. 11, 1961, Los Angeles, Calif. (heart attack). Screen actor.

Appeared in: **1929** The Dream Melody.

FAZENDA, LOUISE
Born: June 17, 1889, Lafayette, Ind. Died: Apr. 17, 1962, Beverly Hills, Calif.

(cerebral hemorrhage). Screen and vaudeville actress. Married to film producer Hal Wallis.

Appeared in: **1913** The Cheese Special; Mike and Jake at the Beach. **1915** The Great Vacuum Robbery; Wilful Ambrose; Ambrose's Fury; Ambrose's Lofty Perch; A Bear Affair; Crossed Love and Swords; A Versatile Villain; A Hash House Fraud; Fatty's Tin Type Tangle; A Game Old Knight. **1916** His Hereafter (working title Murray's Mix-Up); The Judge; A Love Riot; Her Marble Heart; The Feathered Nest; Maid Mad (working title The Fortune Teller); Bombs. **1917** The Summer Girls; Maggie's First False Step; Her Fame and Shame; Her Torpedoed Love; The Betrayal of Maggie; His Precious Life. **1920** Down on the Farm. **1922** Quincy Adams Sawyer; The Beauty Shop. **1923** Beautiful and Damned; Main Street; The Fog; The Gold Diggers; Mary of the Movies; The Old Fool; The Spider and the Rose; The Spoilers; Tea with a Kick; The Wanters. **1924** Abraham Lincoln; Being Respectable; Galloping Fish; Listen, Lester; This Woman; True As Steel. **1925** Bobbed Hair; The Lighthouse by the Sea; A Broadway Butterfly; Cheaper to Marry; Compromise; Declassee; Grounds for Divorce; Hogan's Alley; The Love Hour; The Night Club; The Price of Pleasure. **1926** The Bat; Footloose Widows; Loose Ankles; Ladies at Play; The Lady of the Harem; Millionaires; Miss Nobody; The Old Soak; The Passionate Quest. **1927** The Cradle Snatchers; Babs Comes Home; Finger Prints; The Gay Old Bird; The Red Mill; A Sailor's Sweetheart; Simple Sis; A Texas Steer. **1928** The Terror; Tillie's Punctured Romance; Domestic Troubles; Five and Ten-Cent Annie; Heart to Heart; Outcast; Pay As You Enter; Riley the Cop; Vamping Venus. **1929** The Desert Song; Hot Stuff; The House of Horror; On with the Show; Noah's Ark; Stark Mad; Hard to Get; The Show of Shows. **1930** No, No, Nanette; Rain or Shine; Gold Diggers of Broadway; Viennese Nights; Loose Ankles (and 1926 version); Leathernecking; Wide Open; Bride of the Regiment; Broadway Hoofer; High Society Blues; Spring Is Here. **1931** Gun Smoke; Cuban Love Song; Mad Parade; Newly Rich. **1932** The Slippery Pearls (short); Forbidden Adventure; Racing Youth; Unwritten Law; Once in a Lifetime. **1933** Alice in Wonderland; Universal shorts. **1934** Wonder Bar; Caravan; Mountain Music. **1935** Bad Boy; The Casino Murder Case; The Winning Ticket; Broadway Gondolier; The Widow from Monte Carlo. **1936** Doughnuts and Society; Colleen; I Married a Doctor. **1937** Ready, Willing and Able; Ever Since Eve; First Lady; The Road Back; Merry-Go-Round of 1938. **1938** Swing Your Lady. **1939** Down on the Farm (and 1920 version); The Old Maid.

FEALY, MAUDE

Born: 1881. Died: Nov. 9, 1971, Woodland Hills, Calif. Screen and stage actress. Reportedly appeared in roles in every DeMille film after the advent of sound movies, including the producer's last The Ten Commandments (1956).

Appeared in: **1916** Pamela's Past. **1931** Laugh and Get Rich. **1938** The Buccaneer. **1956** The Ten Commandments.

FEE, VICKIE (Astrid Victoria Fee)

Born: 1947. Died: Dec. 13, 1975, Santa Monica, Calif. Screen actress. Daughter of actress Astrid Allwyn and sister of actress Melinda Fee.

Appeared in: **1966** Out of Sight.

FEILER, HERTA

Born: 1916. Died: Nov. 4, 1970, Munich, Germany. Screen actress.

Appeared in: **1939** Manner Mussen so Sein (Men Are That Way).

FELDARY, ERIC

Born: 1920, Budapest, Hungary. Died: Feb. 25, 1968, Los Angeles, Calif. (fire burns). Stage and screen actor.

Appeared in: **1941** Hold Back the Dawn. **1943** Hostages; For Whom the Bell Tolls. **1944** The Master Race; U-Boat Prisoner. **1948** I, Jane Doe; 16 Fathoms Deep. **1951** Sealed Cargo. **1954** The Iron Glove. **1956** Magnificent Roughnecks.

FELDMAN, ANDREA (Andrea Whips)

Died: Aug. 8, 1972, New York, N.Y. (suicide—jumped from building). Screen actress.

Appeared in: **1963** Cleopatra. **1970** Imitation of Christ; Groupies; Trash.

FELDMAN, EDYTHE A.

Born: 1913. Died: Feb. 28, 1971, Miami Beach, Fla. Screen, stage and television actress.

Appeared in: **1969** Midnight Cowboy.

FELDMAN, GLADYS

Born: 1892. Died: Feb. 12, 1974, New York, N.Y. Screen, stage and radio actress. Married to actor Horace Braham (dec. 1955).

Appeared in: **1921** Shams of Society. **1924** West of the Water Tower.

FELIPE, ALFREDO

Born: 1931. Died: 1958, Lisbon, Portugal. Screen and radio actor. Known as the Portuguese "Fernandel."

FELIX, GEORGE

Born: 1866. Died: May 12, 1949, New York, N.Y. Screen, stage, and vaudeville actor. Married to actress Lydia Berry (dec.) with whom he appeared in vaudeville.

Appeared in: **1916** Haystacks and Steeples.

FELLOWES, ROCKLIFFE

Born: 1885, Ottawa, Canada. Died: Jan. 30, 1950, Los Angeles, Calif. (heart attack). Stage and screen actor.

Appeared in: **1917** The Easiest Way. **1918** Friendly Husbands. **1920** In Search of a Sinner; Yes or No. **1921** Bits of Life; The Price of Possession. **1922** Island Wives; The Stranger's Banquet. **1923** Boy of Mine; Penrod and Sam; The Remittance Woman; The Spoilers; Trifling with Honor. **1924** The Border Legion; The Signal Tower; The Garden of Weeds; Borrowed Husbands; Cornered; Flapper Wives; Missing Daughters. **1925** The Golden Princess; Rose of the World; East of Suez; Declassee; Without Mercy; Counsel for the Defense. **1926** Syncopating Sue; Honesty—the Best Policy; The Road to Glory; Rocking Moon; Silence. **1927** The Understanding Heart; Third Degree; The Crystal Cup; The Taxi Dancer; The Satan Woman. **1929** The Charlatan. **1930** Outside the Law. **1931** Vice Squad; Monkey Business. **1932** Hotel Continental; Huddle; Renegades of the West; All American; Lawyer Man; 20,000 Years in Sing Sing; Ladies of the Big House. **1933** Rusty Rides Again; The Phantom Broadcast. **1934** Back Page.

FELLS, GEORGE (George Flevitsky)

Born: 1902. Died: May 10, 1960, N.Y. Screen, stage, radio actor and screenwriter.

FELTON, HAPPY (Francis J. Felton, Jr.)

Born: 1908. Died: Oct. 21, 1964, New York, N.Y. Screen, stage, television, vaudeville and circus actor. Was part of "Adele Jason and The Boys" vaudeville act.

Appeared in: **1943** Swing Shift Maisie; Whistling in Brooklyn; A Guy Named Joe.

FELTON, VERNA

Born: July 20, 1890, Salinas, Calif. Died: Dec. 14, 1966, North Hollywood, Calif. (stroke). Screen, stage, television and radio actress. Married to actor Lee Millar (dec. 1941).

Appeared in: **1940** If I Had My Way. **1941** Dumbo (voice only). **1946** She Wrote the Book. **1949** Cinderella (voice only). **1950** Buccaneer's Girl; The Gunfighter. **1951** Alice in Wonderland; Little Egypt; New Mexico. **1952** Belles on Their Toes; Don't Bother to Knock. **1955** Picnic; The Lady and the Tramp (voice only). **1957** The Oklahoman; Taming Sutton's Gal. **1959** Sleeping Beauty (voice only). **1960** Guns of the Timberland. **1965** The Man from Button Willow. **1967** Jungle Book (voice only).

FENIMORE, FORD (Ford Fenimore Hoft)

Died: Apr. 20, 1941, El Paso, Tex. Stage and screen actor. Appeared in early Griffith films.

FENNER, WALTER S.

Born: 1882, Akron, Ohio. Died: Nov. 7, 1947, Los Angeles, Calif. (diabetes). Screen actor.

Appeared in: **1930** The Sap from Syracuse. **1935** Speed Devils. **1936** Mixed Magic. **1939** Juarez; Mountain Rhythm; A Woman is the Judge; Torchy Runs for Mayor. **1940** You Can't Fool Your Wife. **1942** Henry Aldrich—Editor. **1943** Guadalcanal Diary. **1944** Lost Angel. **1945** The Shanghai Cobra.

FENTON, FRANK (Frank Fenton-Morgan)

Born: Apr. 9, 1906, Hartford, Conn. Died: July 24, 1957, Los Angeles, Calif. Screen, stage, television actor and screenwriter.

Appeared in: **1942** The Navy Comes Through. **1943** Claudia; Lady of Burlesque. **1944** Buffalo Bill; The Big Noise; Secret Command. **1945** Destiny; Hold That Blonde; This Man's Navy. **1946** If I'm Lucky; It's a Wonderful Life; Magic Town. **1947** Hit Parade of 1947. **1948** Red River; Mexican Hayride; Hazard; Relentless. **1949** The Clay Pigeon; The Doolins of Oklahoma; The Golden Stallion; Joe Palooka in the Big Fight; Ranger of Cherokee Strip; Rustlers. **1950** Modern Marriage; Sideshow; Trigger, Jr.; Tripoli; Rogue River; Wyoming Mail; The Lawless. **1951** Texans Never Cry; The Man with a Cloak; Silver City. **1953** Eyes of the Jungle; Island in the Sky; Vicki. **1956** Emergency Hospital; Fury at Gunsight Pass; The Naked Hills. **1957** Hell Bound.

FENTON, LUCILLE

Born: c. 1916. Died: Oct. 17, 1966, London, England. Stage and screen actress.

Appeared in: **1948** Citizen Saint.

FENTON, MABEL

Born: 1868, Van Buren County, Mich. Died: Apr. 19, 1931, Hollywood, Calif. Screen, stage, vaudeville and burlesque actress.

Appeared in: 1915 How Molly Made Good.

FENTON, MARK

Born: 1870. Died: July 29, 1925, Los Angeles, Calif. (surgery complications after auto accident). Screen actor.

Appeared in: 1915 The Black Box (serial). 1916 The Adventures of Peg O' the Ring (serial). 1919 The Mystery of 13. 1920 Behold My Wife. 1921 The Conquering Power; The Four Horsemen of the Apocalypse; Life's Darn Funny; The Unknown; The Wallop. 1922 Headin' West; Little Eva Ascends; Too Much Business; The Village Blacksmith; The Yellow Stain. 1923 Alias the Night Wind; Speed King. 1924 American Manners; The Battling Fool; Black Lightning; A Fool's Awakening; Name the Man; The Passing of Wolf MacLean; The Spirit of the U.S.A. 1925 Brand of Cowardice; The Storm Breaker.

FENWICK, IRENE (Irene Frizzel)

Born: 1887, Chicago, Ill. Died: Dec. 24, 1936, Beverly Hills, Calif. Stage and screen actress. Married to actor Lionel Barrymore (dec. 1954).

Appeared in: 1915 The Spendthrift; The Commuters. 1916 A Coney Island Princess.

FEODOROFF, LEO

Born: 1867, Odessa, Russia. Died: Nov. 23, 1949, Long Beach, N.Y. (auto accident injuries). Screen, stage actor and opera performer.

Appeared in: 1926 God Gave Me Twenty Cents. 1927 The Music Master. 1928 Laugh, Clown, Laugh.

FERGUSON, AL

Born: Apr. 19, 1888, Rosslarre, Ireland. Died: Dec. 4, 1971, Calif. Screen actor. Entered films in 1910.

Appeared in: 1920 The Lost City. 1921 High Gear Jeffrey; Sunset Jones; Miracles of the Jungle (serial). 1922 Smiling Jim; The Timber Queen (serial). 1923 Flames of Passion; The Power Divine; The Range Patrol; The Way of the Transgressor. 1924 The Trail of Vengeance; Driftwood; Shackles of Fear; Harbor Patrol. 1925 The Fighting Romeo; Phantom Shadows; Scarlet and Gold. 1926 Baited Trap; A Captain's Courage; Hi-Jacking Rustlers; West of the Law; Tentacles of the North; The Wolf Hunters. 1927 Fangs of Destiny; The Range Riders; Straight Shootin'; Shooting Straight; Western Courage. 1928 The Scarlet Arrow (serial); The Avenging Rider; Guardians of the Wild; Headin' for Danger; Terror; The Little Buckaroo; Tarzan—the Mighty (serial); Haunted Island (serial). 1929 Grit Wins; Hoofbeats of Vengeance; The Man from Nevada; Outlaw; The Saddle King; The Smiling Terror; The Vagabond Cub; Thundering Thompson; The Wagon Master; Wolves of the City; Tarzan—the Tiger (serial). 1930 The Lightning Express (serial); Near the Rainbow's End. 1931 Red Fork Range; Pueblo Terror; Two Gun Caballero; One Way Trail. 1932 The Lost Special (serial); Hurricane Express (serial). 1933 The Three Musketeers (serial). 1934 Tailspin Tommy (serial); Pirate Treasure (serial); The Vanishing Shadow (serial). 1935 Desert Trail. 1936 Roamin' Wild. 1937 North of the Rio Grande; Rustlers' Valley. 1942 Captain Midnight (serial). 1946 Son of the Guardsman (serial). 1956 Perils of the Wilderness (serial).

FERGUSON, CASSON

Born: 1894. Died: Feb. 12, 1929, Culver City, Calif. (pneumonia). Stage and screen actor. Entered films with Selig.

Appeared in: 1919 Flame of the Desert. 1920 Madame X. 1921 At the End of the World; Bunty Pulls the Strings; The Unknown Wife; A Virginia Courtship; What's a Wife Worth? 1922 Manslaughter; Borderland; The Law and the Woman; Over the Border; The Truthful Liar. 1923 Grumpy; Drums of Fate; A Gentleman of Leisure; Her Reputation. 1925 Cobra; The Road to Yesterday; The Wedding Song. 1926 For Alimony Only; Forbidden Waters. 1927 King of Kings. 1928 Tenth Avenue.

FERGUSON, ELSIE

Born: 1883, N.Y. Died: Nov. 15, 1961, New London, Conn. Screen and stage actress. Divorced from actor Frederick Worlock (dec. 1973).

Appeared in: 1917 Barbary Sheep (film debut); The Rise of Jennie Cushing. 1918 Rose of the World; Song of Songs; The Lie; Heart of the Wilds; A Doll's House; The Danger Mark; Under the Greenwood Tree. 1919 A Society Exile; His Parisian Wife; The Marriage Price; Eyes of the Soul; The Witness for the Defense; The Avalanche. 1920 His House in Order. 1921 Forever; Lady Rose's Daughter; Sacred and Profane Love; Footlights. 1922 Outcast. 1924 Broadway after Dark. 1930 Scarlet Pages.

FERGUSON, GEORGE S.

Born: 1884. Died: Apr. 24, 1944, Hollywood, Calif. Screen and stage actor. Appeared in silents.

FERGUSON, HILDA (Hildegarde Gibbons)

Born: 1903. Died: Sept. 3, 1933, N.Y. (heart disease). Screen actress and show girl. Appeared in Sennett films.

FERGUSON, WILLIAM J.

Born: 1845. Died: May 4, 1930, Pikesville, Md. Screen and stage actor. He was last surviving member of cast that played in Our American Cousin the night President Lincoln was assassinated.

Appeared in: 1920 Passers By. 1921 Dream Street. 1922 John Smith; To Have and to Hold; Kindred of the Dust; Peacock Alley; The World's Champion; The Yosemite Trail.

FERN, FRITZIE

Born: Sept. 19, 1901, Akron, Ohio. Died: Sept. 10, 1932, Hollywood, Calif. Stage and screen actress.

Appeared in: 1929 It Can Be Done; Clear the Decks; The Charlatan.

FERNANDEL (Fernand Joseph Desire Contandin)

Born: May 8, 1903, Marseilles, France. Died: Feb. 26, 1971, Paris, France (lung cancer). Screen actor and singer.

Appeared in: 1930 Black and White (film debut). 1931 Le Rosier de Madame Husson. 1932 Angele (US 1934); Francois Her; Les Bois du Sport; Paris-Beguin. 1935 L'Ordonnance (The Orderly). 1936 Francois Premier; La Porteuse de Pain. 1937 Regain (aka Harvest—US 1939); Le Schountz; Un Carnet de Bal. 1939 Fric-Frac; Paris Honeymoon; Heartbeat. 1940 La Fille de Puisatier. 1946 The Well Digger's Daughter. 1947 Francis the First; Nais. 1950 Ignace; Hoboes in Paradise. 1951 L'Auberge Rouge (aka The Red Inn—US 1954). 1952 Little World of Don Camillo (US 1953, first of the Don Camillo series); Forbidden Fruit (US 1959); Three Sinners; Topaz; The Cupboard Was Bare. 1953 Ali Baba; L'Ennemi Public No. 1 (aka The Most Wanted Man in the World and The Most Wanted Man—US 1962). 1954 The French Touch. 1955 The Sheep Has Five Legs. 1956 The Return of Don Camillo; Around the World in 80 Days; The Wild Oat. 1957 Pantaloons; Fernandel the Dressmaker; Three Feet in a Bed. 1958 Paris Holiday; Senechal the Magnificent; The Man in the Raincoat. 1959 The Law Is the Law; The Virtuous Bigamist. 1959 La Vache et le Prisonnier (aka The Cow and I—US 1961). 1960 The Big Chief; The Easiest Profession; Croesus; Virgin Man. 1962 Le Diable et les dix Commands (The Devil and the Ten Commandments—US 1963); Le Voyage a Biarritz (The Trip to Biarritz). 1963 La Cuisine au Beurre (aka My Wife's Husband—US 1965). 1964 Cherchez L'Idole (Find the Idol). 1966 Your Money or My Life; Le Voyage du Pere. 1967 L'Homme a la Buick.

FERNANDES, BERTA LUISA

Born: 1935, Spain. Died: 1954, near Lisbon, Portugal (injuries from auto accident). Stage and screen actress. Appeared in Spanish and Portuguese films.

FERNANDES, NASCIMENTO

Born: c. 1880, Portugal. Died: Late 1955 or early 1956, Lisbon, Portugal. Screen, stage actor and film producer.

FERNANDEZ, BIJOU

Born: 1877. Died: Nov. 7, 1961, N.Y. Stage and screen actor.

Appeared in: 1925 New Toys. 1926 Just Suppose.

FERNANDEZ, RAMON S.

Born: 1922, Mexico. Died: Sept. 22, 1962, Mexico City, Mexico (heart attack). Screen actor. Appeared in approx. 200 Mexican films.

FERNANDEZ, SEVERO

Died: 1961, Argentina. Screen actor.

Appeared in: 1935 Noches de Buenos Aires (Buenos Aires Nights).

FERRAND, EULA PEARL

Died: July 17, 1970, Visalia, Calif. Screen actress.

FERRIS, DILLON J.

Born: 1914. Died: Apr. 25, 1951, Pittsburgh, Pa. Screen and stage actor.

FETHERSTON, EDDIE (aka EDDIE FEATHERSTONE)

Died: June 12, 1965, Yucca Valley, Calif. (heart attack). Screen, stage, vaudeville and television actor.

Appeared in: 1925 The Flame Fighter (serial). 1926 Remember; Old Ironsides. 1930 True to the Navy; Worldly Goods. 1932 Movie Crazy. 1933 Cheating Blondes. 1935 The Lost City (serial). 1936 Grand Slam Opera (short). 1937 The following shorts: The Shadow; The Big Squirt; Gracie at the Bat. 1938 The Lone Wolf in Paris; Women in Prison; Who Killed Gail Preston?; plus the following shorts: Time Out for Trouble; A Doggone Mixup; Violent is the Word for Curly. 1939 Homicide Bureau. 1941 So You Won't Squawk (short). 1947 Second Chance.

FEUSIER, NORMAN

Born: 1885. Died: Dec. 27, 1945, Hollywood, Calif. Screen and stage actor.

Appeared in: **1933** The Diamond Trail.

FIDLER, BEN

Born: 1867. Died: Oct. 19, 1932, Los Angeles, Calif. Screen actor.

FIELD, BETTY

Born: Feb. 8, 1918, Boston, Mass. Died: Sept. 13, 1973, Hyannis, Mass. (stroke). Screen, stage and television actress. Divorced from playwright Elmer Rice and from Edwin Lukas. Married to Raymond Olivere.

Appeared in: **1939** What a Life (film debut); Of Mice and Men. **1940** Seventeen; Victory. **1941** The Shepherd of the Hills; Blues in the Night; King's Row; The Little Foxes. **1942** Are Husbands Necessary?; Great Without Glory. **1943** Flesh and Fantasy. **1944** The Great Moment; Tomorrow the World. **1945** The Southerner. **1947** The Great Gatsby. **1955** Picnic. **1956** Bus Stop. **1957** Peyton Place. **1959** Hound-Dog Man; Middle of the Night. **1960** Butterfield 8. **1962** Birdman of Alcatraz. **1965** Never Too Late. **1966** Seven Women. **1968** How to Save a Marriage—And Ruin Your Life (aka Band of Gold); Coogan's Bluff; The Subject was Roses.

FIELD, GEORGE

Born: 1878, San Francisco, Calif. Died: Mar. 9, 1925, Calif. (tuberculosis). Screen, stage and vaudeville actor.

Appeared in: **1912** The Sheriff's Round-Up; Young Wild West Leading a Raid; The Flower of the Forest; The Miner's Widow; Home and Mother. **1913** The Spartan Girl of the West. **1914** The Shriner's Daughter; The Hermit; Calamity Ann's Love Affair; Sheltering an Ingrate; Jim; Down by the Sea; The Dream Child; The Little House in the Valley; False Gods. **1915** The Derelict; The Truth of Fiction; Ancestry; His Mysterious Neighbor; The Greater Strength; The Reprisal; The Guiding Light; The Water Carrier of San Juan; Spider Barlow Cuts In; On Secret Service; It Was Like This; Out of the Ashes; Alice of Hudson Bay; Bonds of Deception; In the Shuffle; Justified; The Trail of the Thief. **1916** The Franchise; A Woman's Daring; The Profligate; Ruth Ridley's Return; The Key; Citizens All. **1918** Beware of Strangers; The Testing of Mildred Vane. **1919** A Trick of Fate; A Sage Brush Hamlet; End of the Game; A White Man's Chance; The Tiger's Trail (serial). **1920** The Moon Riders. **1921** Diamonds Adrift. **1922** Blood and Sand; The Crimson Challenge; You Never Know; North of the Rio Grande; The Young Rajah. **1923** Adam's Rib; Mr. Billings Spends His Dime; Stephen Steps Out; The Tiger's Claw. **1924** Trigger Finger.

FIELD, GLADYS (Gladys O'Brien)

Born: San Francisco, Calif. Died: Aug. 1920, Mount Vernon, N.Y. (childbirth). Screen actress. Appeared in early Essanay films.

FIELD, NORMAN

Born: 1879. Died: Sept. 11, 1956, Hollywood, Calif. Screen and stage actor.

Appeared in: **1950** Destination Big House; Mister 880. **1951** Street Bandits. **1952** The Invitation; The Greatest Show on Earth. **1953** The Twonky; Crazylegs. **1954** Tobor the Great.

FIELD, ROBERT. *See* ROBERT ROUNESVILLE

FIELD, SID (Sidney Arthur Field)

Born: Apr. 1, 1904, Birmingham, England. Died: Feb. 3, 1950, Surrey, England (heart attack). Screen, stage and vaudeville actor.

Appeared in: **1940** That's the Ticket. **1946** London Town (aka My Heart Goes Crazy—US 1953). **1948** Cardboard Cavalier.

FIELDING, EDWARD

Born: 1880, N.Y. Died: Jan. 10, 1945, Beverly Hills, Calif. (heart attack). Stage and screen actor.

Appeared in: **1930** The following shorts: Grounds for Murder; Seeing Things; The Pest of Honor. **1939** Intermezzo, a Love Story. **1940** The House across the Bay; The Invisible Man Returns; All This and Heaven Too; Down Argentine Way; South of Suez; Kitty Foyle; Rebecca. **1941** So Ends Our Night; In the Navy; Hold Back the Dawn; Badlands of Dakota; Scotland Yard; Parachute Battalion; Belle Starr. **1942** In This Our Life; Beyond the Blue Horizon; Star-Spangled Rhythm; Pride of the Yankees; The Major and the Minor; Pacific Rendezvous; Ten Gentlemen from West Point. **1943** Three Smart Guys (short); Mr. Lucky; What a Woman; Song of Bernadette. **1944** See Here, Private Hargrove; My Pal Wolf; The Man in Half Moon Street; Belle of the Yukon; Lady in the Dark; Dead Man's Eyes; Wilson. **1945** A Medal for Benny; The Beautiful Cheat; Guest Wife; Saratoga Trunk.

FIELDING, MARJORIE

Born: 1892, Gloucester, England. Died: 1956. Stage and screen actress.

Appeared in: **1941** Quiet Wedding (stage and film versions); Jeannie. **1943** Yellow Canary (US 1944); The Demi-Paradise (aka Adventure for Two—US 1945). **1946** Quiet Weekend (US 1948). **1947** Fame Is the Spur (US 1949). **1948**

Easy Money (US 1949); Spring in Park Lane (US 1949). **1949** Conspirator (US 1950); The Chiltern Hundreds (aka The Amazing Mr. Beecham—US). **1950** Portrait of Clare; Trio; The Mudlark. **1951** The Franchise Affair (US 1952); Circle of Danger; The Lavender Hill Mob; The Magic Box (US 1952). **1952** The Woman's Angle (US 1954); Mandy (aka Crash of Silence—US 1953). **1953** The Net (aka Project M7—US); Rob Roy the Highland Rogue.

FIELDING, MINNIE (Minnie Flynn)

Born: 1871. Died: July 22, 1936. Screen, stage and vaudeville actress. Appeared in early Biograph pictures.

FIELDING, ROMAINE

Born: 1882. Died: Dec. 16, 1927, Hollywood, Calif. (clot on brain due to infected tooth). Screen, stage actor, film director and film producer.

Appeared in: **1921** The Man Worth While; The Rich Slave. **1927** Gun Gospel; Rose of the Golden West; Ten Modern Commandments. **1928** The Noose; The Shepherd of the Hills.

FIELDS, BENNY (Benjamin Geisenfeld)

Born: 1894, Milwaukee, Wisc. Died: Aug. 16, 1959, New York, N.Y. (heart attack). Screen, minstrel and vaudeville actor. Married to actress Blossom Seeley, his one time vaudeville partner (dec. 1974).

Appeared in: **1933** Mr. Broadway. **1936** The Big Broadcast of 1937. **1944** Minstrel Man.

FIELDS, DOROTHY

Born: 1904. Died: Mar. 28, 1974, New York, N.Y. (heart attack). Lyricist, screenwriter and screen actress. Daughter of comedian Lew Fields (dec. 1941).

Appeared in: **1943** Stagedoor Canteen.

FIELDS, JOHN

Born: 1876. Died: Nov. 8, 1938, Los Angeles, Calif. Screen and stage actor.

FIELDS, LEW (Lewis Maurice Fields)

Born: 1867, N.Y. Died: July 20, 1941, Beverly Hills, Calif. Screen, stage, vaudeville, burlesque and minstrel actor. Father of lyricist and actress Dorothy Fields (dec. 1974). Was partner with Joe Weber (dec. 1962) in comedy team of "Weber and Fields." See Joe Weber for films they appeared in.

He appeared in the following without Weber: **1917** The Corner Grocer. **1930** 23 Skidoo (short); The Duel (short). **1936** an RKO short.

FIELDS, SID

Born: 1898, Milwaukee, Wisc. Died: Sept. 28, 1975, Las Vegas, Nev. (lung cancer). Screen, stage, television, burlesque, vaudeville, radio actor, comedy writer and comedian. Appeared in vaudeville with Jack Greenman.

FIELDS, STANLEY (Walter L. Agnew)

Born: 1880, Allegheny, Pa. Died: Apr. 23, 1941, Los Angeles, Calif. (heart attack). Screen, stage and vaudeville actor.

Appeared in: **1930** See America Thirst; Hook, Line and Sinker; Mammy; The Border Legion; Ladies Love Brutes; The Street of Chance; Manslaughter; Cimarron; Little Caesar; City Streets; The Dove; Traveling Husbands; Her Man. **1931** A Holy Terror; Riders of the Purple Sage; Skyline; Cracked Nuts. **1932** Two Kinds of Women; Destry Rides Again; Girl of the Rio Grande; Painted Woman; Hell's Highway; Rackety Rax; The Mouthpiece; Sherlock Holmes; The Kid from Spain; Way Back Home; Girl Crazy. **1933** Constant Woman; Destination Unknown; Island of Lost Souls; Terror Abroad; He Couldn't Take It. **1934** Name the Woman; Rocky Rhodes; Palooka; Sing and Like It; Strictly Dynamite; Many Happy Returns; Kid Millions. **1935** Life Returns; Helldorado; Baby Face Harrington; Mutiny on the Bounty; The Daring Young Man. **1936** It Had to Happen; O'Malley of the Mounted; The Mine with the Iron Door; Showboat; The Gay Desperado; The Devil Is a Sissy; Ticket to Paradise. **1937** Way out West; Maid of Salem; Souls at Sea; Wells Fargo; Three Legionnaires; The Hit Parade; The Sheik Steps Out; All over Town; Counsel for Crime; The Toast of New York; Wife, Doctor and Nurse; Danger—Love at Work; Ali Baba Goes to Town; Midnight Court. **1938** Wide Open Faces; Panamint's Bad Men; The Adventures of Marco Polo; Algiers; Flirting With Fate; Painted Desert; Straight, Place and Show. **1939** Fugitive at Large; Pack up Your Troubles; Exile Express; Chasing Danger; Hell's Kitchen; Blackwell's Island; The Kid from Kokomo. **1940** Viva Cisco Kid; Ski Patrol; The Great Plane Robbery; New Moon; King of the Lumberjacks. **1941** Where Did You Get That Girl?; I'll Sell My Life; The Lady from Cheyenne.

FIELDS, W. C. (Claude William Dukenfield)

Born: Feb. 20, 1879, Philadelphia, Pa. Died: Dec. 25, 1946, Pasadena, Calif. (dropsy and other ailments). Screen, stage, circus, vaudeville actor and screenwriter. Sometimes wrote under name of Otis Criblecoblis.

Appeared in: **1915** Pool Sharks (film debut). **1924** Janice Meredith. **1925** Sally of the Sawdust. **1926** So's Your Old Man; That Royle Girl; It's the Old Army Game. **1927** Two Flaming Youths; The Potters; Running Wild. **1928** Tillie's Punctured Romance; Fools for Luck. **1930** The Golf Specialist (short). **1931**

Her Majesty Love. **1932** If I Had a Million; The Dentist (short); Million Dollar Legs. **1933** International House; Hollywood on Parade (short); Tillie and Gus; Alice in Wonderland; The Fatal Glass of Beer (short); The Pharmacist (short); The Barber Shop (short). **1934** Six of a Kind; You're Telling Me; Old-Fashioned Way; Mrs. Wiggs of the Cabbage Patch; It's a Gift. **1935** Mississippi; David Copperfield; The Man on the Flying Trapeze. **1936** Poppy. **1938** Big Broadcast of 1938. **1939** You Can't Cheat an Honest Man. **1940** My Little Chickadee; The Bank Dick. **1941** Never Give a Sucker an Even Break. **1942** Tales of Manhattan. **1944** Follow the Boys; Song of the Open Road; Sensations of 1945. **1964** Big Parade of Comedy (documentary). **1966** W.C. Fields Comedy Festival (documentary).

FIGMAN, MAX

Born: 1867. Died: Feb. 13, 1952, Queens, N.Y. Stage and screen actor. Brother of actor Oscar Figman (dec. 1930). Married to actress Lolita Robertson.

Appeared in: **1914** The Man on the Box. **1915** The Adventures of Wallingford; The Truth Wagon; The Hoosier Schoolmaster; Jack Chanty; The Master Stroke; Two Rings and a Goat; A Rheumatic Joint. **1925** The Old Home Week.

FIGMAN, OSCAR (Oscar Brimberton Figman)

Born: 1882. Died: July 18, 1930, Neponsit, N.Y. Screen and stage actor. Brother of actor Max Figman (dec. 1952).

Appeared in: **1924** Manhattan.

FILAURI, ANTONIO

Born: Mar. 9, 1889, Italy. Died: Jan. 18, 1964, San Gabriel, Calif. (emphysema). Screen actor.

Appeared in: **1939** Code of the Secret Service. **1942** Road to Happiness. **1944** Wilson. **1946** The Mask of Dijon. **1947** Mother Wore Tights; King of the Bandits. **1949** The Big Sombrero. **1951** Too Young to Kiss; On the Riviera. **1952** Five Fingers.

FILLMORE, CLYDE

Born: Oct. 25, 1874, McConnelsville, Ohio. Died: Dec. 19, 1946. Screen, stage and radio actor. Entered films in 1918.

Appeared in: **1919** Millionaire Pirate; Five Fingers; Sundown Trail. **1920** The Soul of Youth; The City Sparrow; The Devil's Pass Key; Nurse Marjorie. **1921** Sham; Moonlight Follies; The Outside Woman; The Sting of the Lash. **1923** The Real Adventure; The Midnight Guest. **1924** Alimony. **1941** The Shanghai Gesture; Unholy Partners. **1942** The Remarkable Andrew; Two Yanks in Trinidad; The Mystery of Marie Roget; The Talk of the Town; My Sister Eileen; When Johnny Comes Marching Home. **1943** Fall In; Margin for Error; Taxi, Mister?; The More the Merrier; Watch on the Rhine; City Without Men; What a Woman; Swing Fever. **1944** Laura; Three is a Family. **1945** I'll Remember April; Lady on a Train; Colonel Effingham's Raid; Strange Voyage; Hit the Hay.

FILLMORE, NELLIE

Born: 1864. Died: June 20, 1942, Winthrop, Mass. Screen, stage, vaudeville and radio actress.

FINA, JACK

Died: May 13, 1968. Pianist, composer, conductor and screen actor.

Appeared in: **1946** It's Great to be Young. **1951** Disc Jockey.

FINCH, FLORA

Born: 1869, England. Died: Jan. 4, 1940, Los Angeles, Calif. (streptococcus infection). Screen, stage, vaudeville actress and film producer. She made 260 shorts with actor John Bunny (dec. 1915) between 1910 and 1915. They appeared as Mr. and Mrs. Bunny and/or Mr. and Mrs. Brown and fans referred to these shorts as "Bunnygraphs," "Bunnyfinches," and "Bunnyfinchgraphs."

A few of these "Bunnygraphs," etc. shorts in which they appeared are as follows: **1910** The New Stenographer. **1911** The Subduing of Mrs. Nag; Her Crowning Glory; The Gossip; Selecting His Heiress; The Ventriloquist's Trunk; Two Overcoats; The Woes of a Wealthy Widow; Intrepid Davy; The Politician's Dream. **1912** A Cure for Pokeritis; Leap Year Proposals; Stenographer Wanted; Bunny and the Twins; Irene's Infatuation; The First Woman Jury in America; Pandora's Box; Her Old Sweetheart; The Awakening of Jones; Diamond Cut Diamond; Umbrellas to Mend; The Suit of Armor; How He Papered the Room; Thou Shalt Not Covet; Suing Susan; Martha's Rebellion; Red Ink Tragedy; Pseudo Sultan; A Persistent Lover; Bunny's Suicide; Doctor Bridget; Freckles. **1913** John Tobin's Sweetheart; There's Music in the Hair; And His Wife Came Back; Hubby Buys a Baby; His Honor, the Mayor; The Wonderful Statue; Bunny's Dilemma; He Answered the Ad; Cupid's Hired Man; Bunny's Birthday Surprise; Love's Quarantine; The Pickpocket; When the Press Speaks; Which Way Did He Go?; A Gentleman of Fashion; Those Troublesome Tresses; The Feudists; The Girl at the Lunch Counter; Mr. Bolter's Niece; The Three Black Bags; Stenographer Troubles; The Locket; Suspicious Henry; The Fortune; A Millinery Bomb; Hubby's Toothache; The Autocrat of Flapjack Junction; The Schemers. **1914** Bunny's Scheme; The Golf

Game and the Bonnet; A Change in Baggage Checks; Bunny Buys a Harem; Bunco Bill's Visit; Love's Old Dream; Polishing Up; The Vases of Hymen; Tangled Tangoists; The Old Fire House and the New Fire Chief; The Old Maid's Baby; Bunny Buys a Hat for His Bride; Hearts and Diamonds; Such a Hunter; Father's Flirtation; Bunny's Swell Affair; Bunny in Disguise; Private Bunny; The Locked House; Bunny's Birthday; A Train of Incidents; Bunny Backslides; Bunny's Little Brother. **1915** How Cissy Made Good.

Other films she appeared in: **1908** Mrs. Jones Entertains. **1909** Jones and the Lady Book Agent. **1912** The First Violin. **1914** Cutey's Vacation. **1915** The Starring of Flora Finchurch. **1916** Prudence the Pirate. **1917** War Prides. **1921** Lessons in Love; Orphans of the Storm. **1922** Man Wanted; Orphan Sally; When Knighthood Was in Flower. **1923** Luck. **1924** Monsieur Beaucaire; Roulette. **1925** The Adventurous Sex; The Early Bird; His Buddy's Wife; The Live Wire; Lover's Island; Men and Women; The Wrongdoers. **1926** The Brown Derby; Fifth Avenue; A Kiss for Cinderella; Oh, Baby. **1927** The Cat and the Canary; Captain Salvation; Quality Street; Rose of the Golden West. **1928** The Wife's Relations; The Haunted House; Five and Ten-Cent Annie. **1929** The Faker; Come Across. **1930** Sweet Kitty Bellairs. **1931** I Take This Woman. **1934** The Scarlet Letter. **1936** Showboat; Way out West; Postal Inspector. **1939** The Women.

FINDLAY, RUTH

Born: 1904, N.Y. Died: July 13, 1949, New York, N.Y. Screen and stage actress.

Appeared in: **1937** Heroes of the Alamo. **1939** The Women.

FINDLEY, THOMAS BRUCE

Born: 1874, Guelph, Ontario, Canada. Died: May 29, 1941, Aylmer, Quebec, Canada. Stage and screen actor.

Appeared in: **1920** Heliotrope. **1921** Buried Treasure. **1923** Little Old New York. **1924** Yolanda. **1925** Lucky Devil. **1926** Let's Get Married.

FINE, LARRY (Laurence Fineburg)

Born: 1911, Philadelphia, Pa. Died: Jan. 24, 1975, Woodland Hills, Calif. (stroke). Screen, stage and vaudeville actor. Married to actress Mabel Haney (dec. 1967) with whom he appeared in vaudeville. Appeared in vaudeville with Ted Healy in an act billed as "Ted Healy and His Stooges." Was member of the original Three Stooges comedy team which included Moe Howard (dec. 1975) and Jerome "Curly" Howard (dec. 1952).

Appeared in: **1930** Soup to Nuts; Hollywood on Parade (short). **1933** Dancing Lady; Meet the Baron; Turn Back the Clock; Beer and Pretzels (short). **1934** Hollywood Party; Fugitive Lovers; The Captain Hates the Sea; Gift of Gab; plus the following shorts: The Big Idea; Woman Haters; Punch Drunks; Men in Black; Three Little Pigskins. **1935** The following shorts: Screen Snapshot #6; Horses' Collars; Restless Knights; Pop Goes the Easel; Uncivil Warriors; Pardon My Scotch; Hoi Polloi; Three Little Beers. **1936** The following shorts: Slippery Silks; Ants in the Pantry; Movie Maniacs; Half-Shot Shooters; Disorder in the Court; A Pain in the Pullman; False Alarms; Whoops I'm an Indian. **1937** Start Cheering; plus the following shorts: Grips, Grunts and Groans; Dizzy Doctors; Three Dumb Clucks; Back to the Woods; Goofs and Saddles; Cash and Carry; Playing the Ponies; The Sitter-Downers. **1938** The following shorts: Termites of 1938; Wee, Wee Monsieur; Tassels in the Air; Flat Foot Stooges; Healthy, Wealthy and Dumb; Violent is the Word for Curly; Three Missing Links; Mutts to You; Three Little Sew and Sews; We Want our Mummy. **1939** The following shorts: A-Ducking They Did Go; Yes, We Have No Bonanza; Saved by the Belle; Calling All Curs; Oily to Bed, Oily to Rise; Three Sappy People. **1940** The following shorts: You Nazty Spy; Rockin' Through the Rockies; A-Plumbing We Will Go; Nutty But Nice; How High is Up?; From Nurse to Worse; No Census, No Feeling; Cuckoo Cavaliers. **1941** Time Out for Rhythm; plus the following shorts: Boobs in Arms; So Long, Mr. Chumps; Dutiful But Dumb; All the World's a Stooge; I'll Never Heil Again; An Ache in Every Stake; In the Sweet Pie and Pie; Some More of Samoa; Loco Boy Makes Good. **1942** My Sister Eileen; plus the following shorts: Cactus Makes Perfect; What's the Matador?; Matri-Phony; Three Smart Saps; Even as I.O. U.; Sock-a-Bye Baby. **1943** The following shorts: They Stooge to Conga; Dizzy Detectives; Spook Louder; Back from the Front; Three Little Twerps; Higher Than a Kite; I Can Hardly Wait; Dizzy Pilots; Phony Express; A Gem of a Jam. **1944** The following shorts: Crash Goes the Hash; Busy Buddies; The Yoke's on Me; Idle Roomers; Gents without Cents; No Dough, Boys. **1945** Rockin' in the Rockies; plus the following shorts: Three Pests in a Mess; Booby Dupes; Idiot's Deluxe; If a Body Meets a Body; Micro-Phonies. **1946** Swing Parade of 1946; plus the following shorts: Beer Barrel Polecats; A Bird in the Head; Uncivil War Birds; Three Troubledoers; Monkey Businessmen; Three Loan Wolves; G.I. Wanna Go Home; Rhythm and Weep; Three Little Pirates. **1947** The following shorts: Half-Wits Holiday; Fright Night; Out West; Hold That Lion; Brideless Groom; Sing a Song of Six Pants; All Gummed Up. **1948** The following shorts: Shivering Sherlocks; Pardon My Clutch; Squareheads of the Round Table; Fiddlers Three; Hot Scots; I'm a Monkey's Uncle; Mummy's Dummies; Crime on Their Hands. **1949** The following shorts: Heavenly Daze; The Ghost Talks; Who Done It?; Hocus Pocus; Fuelin' Around; Malice in the Palace; Vagabond Loafers; Dunked in the Deep. **1950** The following shorts: Punchy Cowpunchers; Hugs and Mugs; Dopey Dicks; Love at First Bite; Self-Made Maids; Three Hams on Rye; Studio Stoops; Slap-Happy Sleuths; A

Snitch in Time. **1951** Gold Raiders; plus the following shorts: Three Arabian Nuts; Baby Sitters' Jitters; Dont't Throw That Knife; Scrambled Brains; Merry Mavericks; The Tooth Will Out; Hula La-La; The Pest Man Wins; A Missed Fortune. **1952** The following shorts: Listen, Judge; Corny Casanovas; He Cooked His Goose; Gents in a Jam; Three Dark Horses; Cuckoo on a Choo Choo. **1953** The following shorts: Up in Daisy's Penthouse; Booty and the Beast; Loose Loot; Tricky Dicks; Spooks; Pardon My Backfire; Rip, Sew and Stitch; Bubble Trouble; Goof on the Roof. **1954** The following shorts: Income Tax Sappy; Musty Musketeers; Pal and Gals; Knutzy Knights; Shot in the Frontier; Scotched in Scotland. **1955** The following shorts: Fling in the Ring; Of Cash and Hash; Gypped in the Penthouse; Bedlam in Paradise; Stone Age Romeos; Wham-Bam-Slam; Hot Ice; Blunder Boys. **1956** The following shorts: Husbands Beware; Creeps; Flagpole Jitters; For Crimin' Out Loud; Rumpus in the Harem; Hot Stuff; Scheming Schemers; Commotion on the Ocean. **1957** The following shorts: Hoofs and Goofs; Muscle Up a Little Closer; A Merry Mix-Up; Space Ship Sappy; Guns A-Poppin'; Horsing Around; Rusty Romeos; Outer Space Jitters. **1958** The following shorts: Quiz Whiz; Fifi Blows Her Top; Pies and Guys; Sweet and Hot; Flying Saucer Daffy; Oil's Well That Ends Well. **1959** Have Rocket, Will Travel; Triple Crossed (short); Sappy Bullfighters (short). **1960** Three Stooges Scrapbook; Stop, Look and Laugh. **1961** Snow White and the Three Stooges. **1962** The Three Stooges Meet Hercules; The Three Stooges in Orbit. **1963** It's a Mad, Mad, Mad, Mad World; The Three Stooges Go Around the World in a Daze; Four for Texas. **1964** Big Parade of Comedy. **1965** The Outlaws is Coming.

FINK, EMMA
Born: 1910, Guanajuato, Mexico. Died: June 13, 1966, Mexico City, Mexico (cancer). Stage and screen actress.

FINLAY, ROBERT "BOB" (Robert Finlay Bush)
Born: 1888, New Haven, Conn. Died: Apr. 2, 1929, Prescott, Ariz. Screen and vaudeville actor.

Appeared in: **1917** The Winning Punch.

FINLAYSON, HENDERSON (James Henderson Finlayson)
Born: Aug. 27, 1887, Falkirk, Scotland. Died: Oct. 9, 1953, Los Angeles, Calif. (heart attack). Screen, stage and television actor. Was in early Keystone Kop comedies.

Appeared in: **1921** Home Talent; A Small Town Idol. **1922** The Crossroads of New York. **1923** Hollywood. **1925** Welcome Home. **1927** No Man's Law; plus the following shorts: With Love and Hisses; Love 'Em and Weep; Do Detectives Think?; Flying Elephants; Sugar Daddies; The Call of the Cuckoo; The Second Hundred Years. **1928** Show Girl; Lady Be Good; Ladies Night in a Turkish Bath; Bachelor's Paradise. **1929** Two Weeks Off; Hard to Get; Wall Street; plus the following shorts: Liberty Big Business; Men O' War; The Hoose Gow. **1930** Young Eagles; Flight Commander; For the Defense; The Dawn Patrol; plus the following shorts: Dollar Dizzy; Night Owls; Another Fine Mess. **1931** Pardon Us; Stout Hearts and Willing Hands; Big Business; plus the following shorts: One of the Smiths; The Hasty Marriage; Our Wife; Chickens Come Home; One Good Turn; A Melon-Drama; Catch as Catch Can; Oh! Oh! Cleopatra. **1932** Thunder Below; Pack Up Your Troubles; plus the following shorts: Boy, Oh, Boy; The Chimp; The Iceman's Ball; The Millionaire Cat; Jitters the Butler. **1933** Fra Diavola (The Devil's Brother); The Girl In Possession; Dick Turpin; plus the following shorts: Mush and Milk; His Silent Racket; Me and My Pal; Hokus Focus; The Druggist's Dilemma; The Gay Nighties. **1935** Treasure Blues (photo only); Thicker Than Water; Bonnie Scotland; Manhattan Monkey Business (short). **1936** The Bohemian Girl; Our Relations; Way Out West; Life Hesitates at 40 (short). **1937** All Over Town; Pick a Star. **1938** Blockheads; False Roomers (short). **1939** The Great Victor Herbert; Hollywood Cavalcade; The Flying Deuces. **1940** A Chump at Oxford; Saps at Sea. **1942** To Be or Not to Be. **1943** Yanks Ahoy. **1947** Perils of Pauline; Thunder in the Valley (aka Bob, Son of Battle). **1948** Grand Canyon Trail. **1949** Down Memory Lane. **1951** Royal Wedding. **1955** Soldier of Fortune. **1960** When Comedy Was King (documentary). **1964** Big Parade of Comedy (documentary). **1965** Laurel and Hardy's Laughing 20's (documentary). **1968** The Further Perils of Laurel and Hardy (documentary).

FINLEY, NED
Died: Sept. 27, 1920, New York, N.Y. Screen actor and film director.

Appeared in: **1912** The Curio Hunters. **1913** A Heart of the Forest; A Game of Cards; Brother Bill; A Fighting Chance; The Leading Lady; Homespun Tragedy; Dr. Cathern's Experiment; Fortune's Turn. **1914** Children of the Feud; The Tattoo Mark; Steve O'Grady's Chance; The Reward of Thrift; Local Color; Good Gracious!; The Moonshine Maid and the Man. **1915** The Goddess (serial); O'Garry of the Royal Mounted; Breaking In; Lifting the Ban of Controversy; West Wind; A Man's Sacrifice; Hearts and the Highway; The Making Over of Geoffrey Manning; His Bunkie; From the Dregs. **1916** Britton of the Seventh; The Hunted Woman; Out of the Quagmire; The Kid; Myrtle the Manicurist; The Rookie; A Strange Case. **1917** Little Terror; The Bottom of the Well; The Secret Kingdom (serial). **1918** The Menace; The Raiders of Sunset Gap.

FINN, SAM
Born: 1893. Died: Dec. 14, 1958, Hollywood, Calif. (undergoing brain surgery). Screen actor and extra for 30 years.

FINNEGAN, WALTER
Born: 1873. Died: May 30, 1943, Hollywood, Calif. Screen actor.

FINNERTY, LOUIS
Born: 1883, N.J. Died: Aug. 4, 1937, Los Angeles, Calif. (intestinal obstruction). Screen and vaudeville actor.

Appeared in: **1937** Saratoga.

FINNERTY, WARREN
Born: 1934. Died: Dec. 22, 1974, New York, N.Y. (heart attack). Screen, stage and television actor.

Appeared in: **1960** Murder, Inc. **1962** The Connection (stage and film versions). **1965** The Pawnbroker; The Brig; Andy. **1967** Cool Hand Luke. **1969** Easy Rider; Marlowe; Free Grass.

FIO RITO, TED (Ted Fiorito)
Born: Dec. 20, 1900, Newark, N.J. Died: July 22, 1971, Scottsdale, Ariz. (heart attack). Bandleader, screen, radio actor and songwriter.

Appeared in: **1934** Twenty Million Sweethearts (with his orchestra). **1943** Silver Skates.

FIORENZA, ALFREDO
Born: 1868, Italy. Died: Feb. 24, 1931, Hollywood, Calif. Stage and screen actor. Entered films approx. 1924.

FIRTH, THOMAS PRESTON
Born: 1883. Died: Jan. 9, 1945, North Hollywood, Calif. Screen actor. Entered films approx. 1918.

FISCHER, MARGARITA (aka MARGARITE FISHER)
Born: Feb. 11, 1886, Missouri Valley, Iowa. Died: Mar. 11, 1975, Encinitas, Calif. (cerebral thrombosis). Screen and stage actress. Married to actor Harry Pollard (dec. 1934).

Appeared in: **1911** A Lesson to Husbands. **1912** The Trinity; The Worth of a Man; Call of the Drum; Better than Gold; Winning the Latonia Derby; The Dove and the Serpent; On the Shore; Melodrama of Yesterday; Jim's Atonement; Love, War and a Bonnet; The Parson and the Medicine Man; Exchanging Labels; The Tribal Law; The Rights of a Savage. **1913** Uncle Tom's Cabin; His Old-Fashioned Dad; The Great Ganton Mystery; The Wayward Sister; The Shadow; The Stolen Idol; The Turn of the Tide; The Fight Against Evil; Slavery Days; The Wrong Road; The Power of Heredity; Sally Scraggs— Housemaid; The Diamond Makers; Shon the Piper; Like Darby and Joan; The Boob's Dream Girl. **1914** A Tale of a Lonely Coast; Bess the Outcast; The Wife; Nancy's Husband; The Professor's Awakening; Caught in a Tight Pinch; Closed at Ten; Jane—the Justice; A Joke on Jane; Susanna's New Suit; The Other Train; A Suspended Ceremony; The Silence of John Gordon; A Modern Othello; Susie's New Shoes; The Primeval Test. **1915** The Lonesome Heart; The Miracle of Life; The Dragon. **1916** Susie's New Shoes; Pearl of Paradise; The Quest; Miss Jackie of the Navy; Miss Jackie of the Army; The Devil's Assistant. **1918** Molly Go Get 'Em; Jilted Janet; Impossible Susan; A Square Deal; Ann's Finish; The Girl Who Couldn't Grow Up; Primitive Woman. **1919** Mantle of Charity; Tiger Lily; Money Isn't Everything; Trixie from Broadway; Fair Enough; Folly of the Follies; Charge it to Me; Put Up Your Hands! **1920** The Week-end; Dangerous Talent; The Thirtieth Piece of Silver; The Hellion. **1921** The Gamester; Payment Guaranteed; The Butterfly Girl; Their Mutual Child; Beach of Dreams. **1924** K—The Unknown. **1925** Any Woman. **1927** Uncle Tom's Cabin (and 1913 version).

FISCHMAN, DAVID
Born: 1910. Died: Jan. 24, 1958, Los Angeles, Calif. Screen actor.

FISHER, ALFRED
Born: 1849, England. Died: Aug. 26, 1933, Glendale, Calif. Screen, stage actor and stage director. Entered films in 1918.

Appeared in: **1919** Third Degree. **1923** Burning Words; Railroaded. **1924** The Breathless Moment; The Fighting American; The Storm Daughter. **1925** The Home Maker. **1926** Atta Boy; The Country Beyond. **1927** Broadway Madness; Driven from Home. **1928** Fangs of Fate; A Million for Love; Romance of a Rogue.

FISHER, FREDDIE "SCHNICKELFRITZ"
Born: 1904. Died: Mar. 28, 1967. Bandleader and screen actor.

Appeared in: **1930** The Song Writers Revue (short). **1938** Gold Diggers in Paris. **1943** The Sultan's Daughter. **1944** Seven Days Ashore; Jamboree; That's My Baby. **1949** Make Mine Laughs.

FISHER, GEORGE B.
Born: 1894, Republic, Mich. Died: Aug. 13, 1960, Los Angeles, Calif. Stage and screen actor.

Appeared in: **1913** The Man Who Went Out. **1915** His Affianced Wife; Her Easter Hat; Hearts and Swords; The Artist's Model. **1916** Civilization. **1917** Environment; Conscience; Annie-for-Spite. **1921** Bare Knuckles; Beach of Dreams; Colorado Pluck; Hearts of Youth; Moonlight Follies; A Parisian Scandal; Sure Fire. **1922** Domestic Relations; Don't Shoot; The Trail of the Axe. **1923** Divorce. **1924** The Bowery Bishop; Excitement. **1925** After Marriage; Justice of the Far North. **1929** Apartment Hunting (short). **1947** The Last Round-Up. **1949** Joe Palooka in the Big Fight. **1950** Champagne for Caesar. **1951** Hard, Fast and Beautiful.

FISHER, HARRY
Born: Sept. 13, 1885, New York, N.Y. Died: May 21, 1917, Los Angeles, Calif. (auto accident). Screen actor.

Appeared in: **1913** Gold is Not All. **1914** The Orange Bandit; The Man on the Box. **1915** Bertie's Stratagem; The Missing Clue; The Fire Escape; Getting Rid of Aunt Kate; Alone in the City of Sighs and Tears; Mr. Jarr and Gertrude's Beaux; The Morning After; Kidding the Goats; Fits and Chills; Itsky the Inventor; Hughey of the Circus; The Faith of Sonny Jim; The Pest Vamooser; The Patent Food Conveyor. **1916** The Cold Feet Getaway; The Wrong Mr. Wright; Myrtle the Manicurist; Love's Getaway; Poisoned Lips; The Rummy.

FISHER, MAGGIE (Maggie Holoway Fisher)
Born: 1854, England. Died: Nov. 3, 1938, Glendale, Calif. Stage and screen actress.

FISHER, MARGARITE. *See* MARGARITA FISCHER

FISHER, MAX
Born: 1909, Austria. Died: Oct. 11, 1974, New York, N.Y. Screen, stage, television actor, film, stage director and drama coach.

Appeared in: **1938** Grande Illusion.

FISHER, SALLY
Born: 1881. Died: June 8, 1950, Twenty-Nine Palms, Calif. (heart attack). Screen, stage and vaudeville actress.

FISHER, WILLIAM
Born: 1868. Died: July 4, 1933, Hollywood, Calif. (heart attack). Screen actor and acrobat.

Appeared in: **1922** The Broken Silence. **1925** The Keeper of the Bees.

FISHER, WILLIAM G.
Born: 1883. Died: Oct. 4, 1949, Hollywood, Calif. Screen actor.

FISKE, MINNIE (Maria Augusta Davey aka MRS. FISKE)
Born: Dec. 19, 1865, New Orleans, La. Died: Feb. 15, 1932, Hollis, N.Y. (heart failure). Screen, stage actress and stage director. Married to writer Harrison Grey Fiske.

Appeared in: **1913** Tess of the D'Urbervilles (stage and film versions). **1915** Vanity Fair.

FISKE, RICHARD (Thomas Richard Potts)
Born: Nov. 20, 1915, Shelton, Wash. Died: Aug., 1944 (killed in action). Screen actor.

Appeared in: **1938** The Little Adventuress; Blondie; The Spider's Web (serial). **1939** Homicide Bureau; Blondie Meets the Boss; Behind Prison Gates; Man from Sundown; Parents on Trial; The Stranger from Texas; plus the following shorts: Pest from the West; Rattling Romeo; Skinny the Moocher; Teacher's Pest; Andy Clyde Gets Spring Chicken; Oily to Bed, Oily to Rise; Three Sappy People. **1940** Pioneers of the Frontier; Konga—the Wild Stallion; Men Without Souls; The Man from Tumbleweed; Prairie Schooners; plus the following shorts: The Heckler; His Bridal Fright; Fireman—Save My Choo Choo; Boobs in Arms; Nothing but Pleasure; Pardon My Berth Marks; The Taming of the Snood. **1941** The Lone Wolf Takes a Chance; Outlaws of the Panhandle; The Devil Commands; The Medico of Painted Springs; North from the Lone Star; Across the Sierras; The Officer and the Lady; The Son of Davy Crockett; All the World's a Stooge (short). **1942** Valley of the Sun. **1943** Dizzy Pilots (short).

FISKE, ROBERT L.
Born: Oct. 20, 1889, Griggsville, Missouri. Died: Sept. 12, 1944, Sunland, Calif. (congestive heart failure). Screen actor.

Appeared in: **1936** The Sky Parade. **1937** Old Louisiana; Battle Greed; Drums of Destiny. **1938** The Purple Vigilantes; Cassidy of Bar 20; Religious Racketeers; Numbered Woman; Flight into Nowhere; South of Arizona; Colorado Trail; Sunset Trail; Adventure in Sahara; I Am a Criminal. **1939** West of Santa Fe; Racketeers of the Range; Mystic Circle Murder; Fools Who Made History (short). **1940** East Side Kids; Passport to Alcatraz; Carolina Moon; Before I Hang; Texas Terrors; Law and Order. **1941** The Big Boss; Along the Rio Grande; The Apache Kid; Borrowed Hero. **1942** Valley of the Sun; Black Dragons; Today I Hang. **1944** Cyclone Prairie Rangers.

FITZGERALD, BARRY (William Joseph Shields)
Born: Mar. 10, 1888, Dublin, Ireland. Died: Jan. 4, 1961, Dublin, Ireland. Stage and screen actor. Won 1944 Academy Award for Best Supporting Actor in Going My Way. Brother of actor Arthur Shields (dec. 1970).

Appeared in: **1930** Juno and the Paycock. **1937** Ebb Tide; Plough and the Stars. **1938** Bringing up Baby; Dawn Patrol; Four Men and a Prayer; Marie Antoinette. **1939** Pacific Liner; The Saint Strikes Back; Full Confessions. **1940** The Long Voyage Home. **1941** The Sea Wolf; San Francisco Docks; Tarzan's Secret Treasure; How Green Was My Valley. **1943** Amazing Mrs. Halliday; Corvette K-225; Two Tickets to London. **1944** None but the Lonely Heart; I Love a Soldier; Going My Way. **1945** Stork Club; Duffy's Tavern; Incendiary Blonde; And Then There Were None; Forever Yours; The Bells of St. Mary's. **1946** California; Two Years before the Mast. **1947** Welcome Stranger; Easy Come, Easy Go; Variety Girl. **1948** Naked City; The Sainted Sisters; Miss Tatlock's Millions. **1949** Top O' the Morning; Story of Seabiscuit. **1950** Union Station. **1951** Silver City. **1952** The Quiet Man. **1954** Happy Ever After; Tonight's the Night. **1956** The Catered Affair. **1958** Rooney. **1959** Broth of a Boy.

FITZGERALD, CISSY
Born: 1874, England. Died: May 5, 1941, Ovingdean, England. Stage and screen actress. Entered films in a 50-foot film taken at the studio where Edison was attempting to perfect a motion picture camera.

Appeared in: **1914** The Win(k)some Widow. **1915** Curing Cissy; Cissy's Innocent Wink; The Widow Wins; The Dust of Egypt; A Corner in Cats; Zablitsky's Waterloo. **1916** Leave it to Cissy. **1924** Babbitt; Cornered; Daring Love; Flowing Gold; Lilies of the Field; Vanity's Price; A Woman Who Sinned. **1925** If Marriage Fails; I'll Show You the Town; Steppin' Out. **1926** The Crown of Lies; The Danger Girl; Flames; Her Big Night; The High Flyer; The Love Thief; Redheads Preferred. **1927** The Arizona Wildcat; Beauty Shoppers; Fire and Steel; Matinee Ladies; McFadden's Flats; Two Flaming Youths; Women Love Diamonds; Women's Wares. **1928** No Babies Wanted; Ladies of the Night Club; Laugh, Clown, Laugh. **1929** Seven Footprints to Satan; The Diplomat (short); His Lucky Day; Social Sinners (short). **1930** The Painted Angel. **1931** Transgression. **1933** The Masquerade; Only Yesterday. **1935** Strictly Legal.

FITZGERALD, EDWARD P.
Born: 1883. Died: May 1, 1942, Buffalo, N.Y. Screen and vaudeville actor. In vaudeville he was part of an act known as "Fitzgerald and Quigley" and later as "Fitzgerald and Madison." Appeared in Mack Sennett comedies during 1920s.

FITZGERALD, FLORENCE IRENE
Born: 1890. Died: Jan. 31, 1962, Hartford, Conn. Screen actress.

FITZGERALD, JAMES M.
Born: 1897. Died: Jan. 21, 1919, Los Angeles, Calif. (influenza). Screen actor.

FITZGERALD, LILLIAN
Born: New York. Died: July 9, 1947, New York, N.Y. Screen, stage, vaudeville actress and singer. Daughter of vaudeville performers Patrick and Catherine Fitzgerald.

Appeared in: **1939** Some Like it Hot.

FITZHARRIS, EDWARD "FITZ"
Born: 1890, England. Died: Oct. 12, 1974, Woodland Hills, Calif. (pneumonia). Screen actor and costumer.

FITZMAURICE, GEORGE
Born: Feb. 13, 1895, Paris, France. Died: June 13, 1940, Los Angeles, Calif. (streptococcus). Screen actor, film director, and screenwriter.

Appeared in: **1919** The Avalanche.

FITZMAURICE, MICHAEL T. (Michael Fitzmaurice-Kelly)
Born: Apr. 28, 1908, Chicago, Ill. Died: Aug. 31, 1967, New York, N.Y. Screen, stage, radio and television actor.

Appeared in: **1936** The House of a Thousand Candles; The Plough and the Stars. **1937** Reported Missing. **1951** Fourteen Hours.

FITZROY, EMILY
Born: 1861, London, England. Died: Mar. 3, 1954, Gardena, Calif. (stroke). Stage and screen actress.

Appeared in: **1919** The Climbers. **1920** Deadline at Eleven; Way Down East. **1921** Straight Is the Way; Jane Eyre; Out of the Chorus; Wife against Wife. **1922** The Splendid Lie; Fascination; Find the Woman; No Trespassing. **1923** Fury; Driven; Strangers of the Night; The Purple Highway. **1924** Jealous Husbands; His Hour; Secrets; The Whispered Name; Girl of the Limberlost; Her

Night of Romance; Love's Wilderness; The Red Lily; The Man Who Came Back; Untamed Youth. **1925** Are Parents People?; Lazybones; Bobbee Hair; Outwitted; Zander the Great; Thunder Mountain; The Denial; The Lady; Learning to Love; The Winding Stair; Never the Twain Shall Meet; The Spaniard. **1926** The Bat; Bardley's, the Magnificent; Marriage License?; What Happened to Jones; Hard Boiled; Don Juan; High Steppers. **1927** Love; The Cheerful Fraud; Orchids and Ermine; Married Alive; Mockery; The Sea Tigers; Once and Forever; One Increasing Purpose. **1928** The Trail of '98; Foreign Devils; Gentlemen Prefer Blondes; Love Me and the World Is Mine; No Babies Wanted. **1929** The Bridge of San Luis Rey; The Case of Lena Smith; Show Boat; Flirting Widow; Man from Blankley's; She's My Weakness; Song O' My Heart; New Moon. **1931** Misbehaving Ladies; Aren't We All; The Green Spot Mystery; It's a Wise Child; Unfaithful. **1932** High Society; Lucky Ladies. **1933** Dick Turpin. **1934** Don Quixote; Man with Two Faces; Two Heads on a Pillow; The Captain Hates the Sea. **1935** China Seas. **1936** The Beloved Rogue; The Bold Caballero. **1938** The Frontiersman. **1940** Vigil in the Night. **1943** Forever and a Day.

FIX, RESS (Ressie Mae Fix)
Born: June 19, 1893, Indiana. Died: Jan. 5, 1975, Hollywood, Calif. (heart attack). Screen and television actress. Mother of actor Jay Stewart.

FLAGG, JAMES MONTGOMERY
Born: June 18, 1877, Pelham Manor, N.Y. Died: May 27, 1960, New York, N.Y. Illustrator, artist, screenwriter and screen actor.

Appeared in: **1913** Saved by Parcel Post. **1918** The Good Sport; Perfectly Fiendish Flanagan; The Spoiled Girl; Tell That to the Marines. **1919** One Every Minute; Beresford and the Baboons.

FLAGSTAD, KIRSTEN
Born: 1895. Died: Dec. 9, 1962, Oslo, Norway. Screen actress and opera performer.

Appeared in: **1938** The Big Broadcast of 1938.

FLAHERTY, PAT J., SR.
Born: Mar. 8, 1903, Washington, D.C. Died: Dec. 2, 1970, N.Y. (heart attack). Screen actor, film technician and professional baseball player.

Appeared in: **1934** Come on Marines; The Mighty Barnum; Twentieth Century; Baby, Take a Bow; Brand of Hate. **1935** Secret of the Chateau; Chinatown Squad; One Way Ticket. **1936** Mutiny on the Bounty; My Man Godfrey; Hearts in Bondage; Pigskin Parade; Flying Hostess. **1937** Woman Wise; Navy Blue and Gold; On Again, off Again; A Day at the Races; A Star Is Born; Hold 'Em Navy. **1938** Hollywood Stadium Mystery; Always in Trouble; She Loved a Fireman; Telephone Operator; The Main Event. **1939** Legion of Lost Flyers; Only Angels Have Wings. **1940** A Miracle on Main Street; My Son, My Son; Midnight Limited; Black Diamonds; Flight Command. **1941** Sergeant York; Meet John Doe; Affectionately Yours; Highway West. **1942** Gentleman Jim; Who Is Hope Schuyler?; It Happened in Flatbush; Yankee Doodle Dandy. **1943** Hit the Ice. **1946** It Shouldn't Happen to a Dog; Home Sweet Homicide; The Best Years of Our Lives. **1947** The Bachelor and the Bobby-Soxer. **1948** Give My Regards to Broadway; All My Sons; The Noose Hangs High; The Babe Ruth Story; The Cobra Strikes. **1950** The Jackie Robinson Story; The Good Humor Man; Blondie's Hero. **1952** Hoodlum Empire; The Winning Team; Blackbeard the Pirate. **1955** The Desperate Hours.

FLANAGAN, BUD. See DENNIS O'KEEFE

FLANAGAN, BUD (Robert Winthrop)
Born: 1896, England. Died: Oct. 20, 1968, London, England. Screen, music hall, stage actor and songwriter. Married to comedienne/dancer Ann "Curley" Flanagan (dec. 1975) and father of actor Buddy Flanagan. Appeared with Chesney Allen as part of comedy team "Flanagan and Allen" and also appeared in "Crazy Gang" films and stage presentations with "Nervo and Knox" and "Naughton and Gold."

The "Crazy Gang" films include: **1937** Okay for Sound. **1938** Alf's Button Afloat. **1939** The Frozen Limits. **1940** Gasbags. **1958** Life Is a Circus (US 1962).

"Flanagan and Allen" appeared in: **1932** The Balliffs (short). **1933** They're Off (short); The Dreamers (short). **1934** Wild Boy. **1935** A Fire Has Been Arranged. **1937** Underneath the Arches. **1942** We'll Smile Again. **1943** Theatre Royal. **1944** Dreaming. **1945** Here Comes the Sun. **1952** Judgement Deferred (Flanagan only). **1958** Dunkirk. **1963** The Wild Affair (Flanagan only).

FLANAGAN, EDWARD J.
Born: 1880, St. Louis, Mo. Died: Aug. 18, 1925, Los Angeles, Calif. (peritonitis). Screen, stage and vaudeville actor. Was on screen and in vaudeville as "Flanagan and Edwards" and also worked separately.

Appeared in: **1921** Don't Call Me Little Girl; Hunch.

FLANAGAN, REBECCA
Born: 1876. Died: Jan. 30, 1938, Hollywood, Calif. Screen and stage actress. Entered films approx. 1928. Married to actor D. J. Flanagan.

FLANDERS, MICHAEL (Michael Henry Flanders)
Born: Mar. 1, 1922, London, England. Died: Apr. 14, 1975, Wales. Screen, stage, radio, television actor, humorist and lyricist. Partner with Donald Swann in two-man show entitled "At the Drop of a Hat."

Appeared in: **1963** Doctor in Distress (US 1964). **1970** The Raging Moon.

FLATEAU, GEORGES
Born: 1882, France. Died: Feb. 13, 1953, Paris, France. Screen, stage, radio and televison actor.

Appeared in: **1939** Katia.

FLEISCHMANN, HARRY
Born: 1899. Died: Nov. 28, 1943, Bakersfield, Calif. (heart attack). Screen actor.

Appeared in: **1937** She Asked for It. **1939** Ambush. **1942** Crossroads. **1943** Stand by for Action.

FLEMING, ALICE
Born: 1882. Died: Dec. 6, 1952, New York, N.Y. Screen, stage, and radio actress.

Appeared in: **1921** The Conquest of Canaan; His Greatest Sacrifice. **1941** Playmates. **1942** Who Done It? **1944** Storm over Lisbon; Vigilantes of Dodge City; Marshal of Reno. **1945** Affairs of Susan; It's a Pleasure; Saratoga Trunk.

FLEMING, BOB (Robert Fleming)
Born: 1878, Ontario, Canada. Died: Oct. 4, 1933. Screen and vaudeville actor.

Appeared in: **1914** The Man from Home; Rose of the Rancho; The Virginian. **1916** To Have and to Hold; The Love Mask; The Selfish Woman; The House with the Golden Windows. **1919** Nugget Nell. **1922** The Fighting Streak; Daring Danger. **1924** Riff Bang Buddy; The Fighting Sap. **1925** Hurricane Horseman; Saddle Horseman. **1926** Davy Crockett at the Fall of the Alamo; Riding for Life; Trumpin' Trouble. **1927** The Love of Paguita; Gun Gospel; The Mojave Kid. **1928** King Cowboy; The Avenging Rider; The Bantam Cowboy; The Fighting Redhead; The Riding Renegade; Vanishing Pioneer. **1930** The Dawn Trail; The Lone Star Ranger. **1931** Desert Vengeance. **1932** Texas Gun-Fighter.

FLEMING, ERIC
Born: 1926, Santa Paula, Calif. Died: Sept. 28, 1966, Tingo Maria area, Peru (drowned). Screen, stage and television actor.

Appeared in: **1955** Conquest of Space. **1957** Fright. **1958** Queen of Outer Space. **1959** Curse of the Undead. **1966** The Glass Bottom Boat.

FLEMING, IAN
Born: Sept. 10, 1888, Melbourne, Australia. Died: Jan. 1, 1969, London, England. Screen, stage and television actor. Do not confuse with deceased writer. Was Dr. Watson in English version of Sherlock Holmes series of films in 1930s with Arthur Wonter as Holmes.

Appeared in: **1926** Second to None. **1928** The Ware Case (US 1929). **1929** The Devil's Maze. **1930** The School for Scandal. **1931** The Sleeping Cardinal (aka Sherlock Holmes' Fatal Hour—US). **1932** The Missing Rembrandt; Lucky Girl; After Dark. **1933** Called Back. **1934** The Third Clue. **1935** The Triumph of Sherlock Holmes; The Riverside Murder; School for Stars; The Crouching Beast; Sexton Blake and the Mademoiselle. **1936** Prison Breaker. **1937** Jump for Glory (aka When Thief Meets Thief—US); Silver Blaze (aka Murder at the Baskervilles—US 1941); Racing Romance; Darby and Joan. **1938** If I Were Boss; Dial 999; The Reverse Be My Lot; Quiet Please; Double or Quits; Almost a Honeymoon; Ghost Tales Retold (series). **1939** The Nursemaid Who Disappeared; Men Without Honour; Shadowed Eyes. **1943** The Butler's Dilemma; Up With the Lark. **1945** I Didn't Do It. **1946** George in Civvy Street; Appointment With Crime (US 1950). **1947** Captain Boycott. **1948** Quartet. **1949** A Matter of Murder. **1950** The Woman in Question (aka Five Angles on Murder—US 1953). **1952** The Voice of Merrill (aka Murder Will Out—1953). **1953** Recoil; It's a Grand Life; Park Plaza (aka Norman Conquest). **1954** The Seekers (aka Land of Fury US 1955). **1957** High Flight (US 1958). **1958** A Woman Possessed. **1959** Innocent Meeting; Web of Suspicion; Crash Dive; Man Accused. **1960** Bluebeard's Ten Honeymoons; Your Money or Your Wife (US 1965); The Trials of Oscar Wilde (aka The Man With the Green Carnation—US and The Green Carnation); Too Hot to Handle (aka Playgirl After Dark—US 1962). **1961** No, My Darling Daughter (US 1964); The Lamp in Assassin Mews; What Every Woman Wants; Return of a Stranger. **1963** The Boys; Tamahine (US 1964). **1964** Seventy Deadly Pills. **1965** The Return of Mr. Moto.

FLETCHER, LAWRENCE M.
Born: 1902. Died: Feb. 11, 1970, Bridgeport, Conn. Screen, stage and television actor.

Appeared in: **1956** The Search for Bridey Murphy.

FLEU, DORRIS BELL

Born: 1922. Died: Sept. 12, 1955, Bryn Mawr, Pa. Screen actress and singer with bands of Bunny Berrigan, Harry James and Woody Herman.

FLICK, PAT C.

Born: 1899. Died: Nov. 1, 1955, Hollywood, Calif. (cancer). Screen, stage, radio actor and screenwriter.

Appeared in: **1935** Stars over Broadway. **1937** The Black Legion. **1938** Little Tough Guy; The Missing Guest.

FLIEGEL, MRS. ERNIE

Born: Minneapolis, Minn. Died: June 25, 1966, Minneapolis, Minn. Screen and vaudeville actress. In vaudeville appeared as part of the "Albee Sisters" act.

Appeared in: **1937** Turn off the Moon.

FLINT, HAZEL

Born: 1893. Died: Aug. 18, 1959, Hollywood, Calif. Screen and stage actress.

Appeared in: **1922** The Bootleggers. **1927** Modern Daughters.

FLINT, HELEN

Born: 1898. Died: Sept. 9, 1967, Washington, D.C. (auto injuries). Stage and screen actress.

Appeared in: **1920** Uncle Sam of Freedom Ridge. **1930** Married (short). **1934** The Ninth Guest; Broadway Bill; Midnight; Manhattan Love Song; Handy Andy. **1935** While the Patient Slept; Doubting Thomas; Ah, Wilderness. **1936** Riff Raff; Fury; Give Me Your Heart; Early to Bed; Little Lord Fauntleroy. **1937** Step Lively, Jeeves!; Married before Breakfast; Blonde Trouble; Sea Devils; The Black Legion. **1942** Time to Kill.

FLINT, JOSEPH W.

Born: 1893. Died: May 5, 1933, Los Angeles, Calif. (suicide—gunshot wounds). Screen actor.

FLIPPEN, JAY C.

Born: 1898, Little Rock, Ark. Died: Feb. 3, 1971, Hollywood, Calif. (aneurysm). Screen, stage, minstrel, vaudeville, radio and television actor.

Appeared in: **1928** The Ham What Am (short). **1934** Marie Galante; Million Dollar Ransom. **1947** Brute Force; Intrigue. **1948** They Live By Night (aka The Twisted Road and aka Your Red Wagon). **1949** A Woman's Secret; Down to the Sea in Ships; Oh, You Beautiful Doll; They Live by Night. **1950** Buccaneer's Girl; The Yellow Cab Man; Love That Brute; Winchester "73"; Two Flags West. **1951** The Lemon Drop Kid; Flying Leathernecks; The People against O'Hara; The Lady from Texas; The Model and the Marriage Broker. **1952** The Las Vegas Story; Bend of the River; Woman of the North Country. **1953** Thunder Bay; Devil's Canyon; East of Sumatra. **1954** The Wild One; Carnival Story. **1955** Six Bridges to Cross; The Far Country; Man without a Star; It's Always Fair Weather; Kismet; Oklahoma!; Strategic Air Command. **1956** The Killing; The Seventh Cavalry; The King and Four Queens. **1957** The Restless Breed; The Halliday Brand; Hot Summer Night; Public Pigeon No. 1; Night Passage; Run of the Arrow; The Midnight Story; Jet Pilot; The Deerslayer; Lure of the Swamp. **1958** Escape from Red Rock; From Hell to Texas (aka Manhunt). **1960** Wild River; Studs Lonigan; The Plunderers. **1962** Six-Gun Law; How the West Was Won. **1964** Looking for Love. **1965** Cat Ballou. **1967** The Spirit Is Willing. **1968** Firecreek; The Hellfighters. **1969** Hello, Dolly!

FLIPPER (Mitzi, the Dolphin)

Died: June 25, 1971, Grassy Key, Fla. (heart attack). Approx. 22 years old. Screen and television dolphin.

Appeared in: **1963** Flipper.

FLORATH, ALBERT

Born: 1888, Bielefeld, Germany. Died: Mar. 10, 1957, Gailsdorf-Nordwuertemberg, West Germany. Screen, stage actor, and film producer. Entered films in 1920.

Appeared in: **1933** Berlin-Alexanderplatz. **1939** Speil in Sommerwind (Play in the Summer Breezes); Der Biberpelz (The Beaver Coat). **1940** Hurra! Ich bin Papa (Hurrah! I'm a Papa).

"FLORELLE" (Odette Rousseau)

Born: 1901, France. Died: Oct. 1, 1974, La Roche-Sur-Yon, France. Screen, stage actress and singer.

Appeared in: **1931** Beggar's Opera. **1933** La Femme Nue; L'Opera de Quat' Sous; La Dame de Chez Maxim (The Woman at Maxim's). **1935** Liliom. **1936** Les Miserables. **1937** Amphytryon. **1957** Gervaise.

FLORESCO, MICHEL

Born: Italy. Died: Nov. 1925, Venice, Italy. Screen actor.

FLOWERTON, CONSUELO

Born: 1900. Died: Dec. 21, 1965, New York, N.Y. Screen, stage, television actress and singer. Mother of actress Nina Foch.

Appeared in: **1921** Camille. **1924** The Sixth Commandment.

FLYNN, ELINOR (Elinor Golden Flynn)

Born: Mar. 17, 1910, Chicago, Ill. Died: July 4, 1938, near Glen Falls, N.Y. (auto accident). Screen, stage and radio actress. Entered films in 1927.

Appeared in: **1929** The Royal Pair (short). **1930** Ladies in Love; Let Us Be Gay. **1931** She Wolf; Mother's Millions.

FLYNN, ERROL

Born: June 20, 1909, Hobart, Tasmania. Died: Oct. 14, 1959, Vancouver, B.C., Canada (heart attack). Screen, stage, television actor, screenwriter and author. Married to screen actress Patrice Wymore. Divorced from actresses Lili Damita and Nora Eddington. Father of actor and correspondent Sean Flynn (dec.).

Appeared in: **1934** Murder at Monte Carlo; In the Wake of the Bounty (documentary). **1935** The Case of the Curious Bride; Don't Bet on Blondes; Captain Blood; I Found Stella Parish. **1936** Charge of the Light Brigade; Private Party on Catalina (short). **1937** Green Light; Prince and the Pauper; Another Dawn; The Perfect Specimen. **1938** Four's a Crowd; The Sisters; Dawn Patrol; Adventures of Robin Hood. **1939** Dodge City; The Private Lives of Elizabeth and Essex. **1940** Santa Fe Trail; The Sea Hawk; Virginia City. **1941** They Died with Their Boots On; Dive Bomber; Footsteps in the Dark. **1942** Desperate Journey; Gentleman Jim. **1943** Edge of Darkness; Northern Pursuit; Thank Your Lucky Stars. **1944** Uncertain Glory. **1945** Objective, Burma!; San Antonio. **1946** Never Say Goodbye. **1947** Cry Wolf; Escape Me Never. **1948** Silver River; The Adventures of Don Juan. **1949** That Forsythe Woman. **1950** Rocky Mountain; Montana; Hello, God (US 1958); Kim. **1951** The Adventures of Captain Fabian. **1952** Against All Flags; Mara Maru. **1953** The Master of Ballantrae. **1954** Crossed Swords; Lilacs in the Spring (aka Let's Make Up—US 1955). **1955** The Dark Avenger (aka The Warriors—US). **1956** King's Rhapsody. **1957** Istanbul; The Sun Also Rises; The Big Boodle. **1958** Too Much, Too Soon; Roots of Heaven. **1959** Cuban Rebel Girls. **1974** That's Entertainment (film clips).

FLYNN, HAZEL E.

Born: Mar. 31, 1899, Chicago, Ill. Died: May 15, 1964, Santa Monica, Calif. (heart ailment). Screen extra actress, drama editor and newspaper film columnist. Appeared in early Essanay films.

FLYNN, JOE

Born: Nov. 8, 1924, Youngstown, Ohio. Died: July 19, 1974, Beverly Hills, Calif. (accidental drowning). Screen, stage and television actor.

Appeared in: **1948** The Babe Ruth Story (film debut). **1954** The Big Chase. **1955** The Seven Little Foys. **1956** The Ten Commandments; The Boss. **1957** Portland Expose; Panama Sal. **1958** This Happy Feeling. **1959** Thirty. **1961** Cry for Happy; Police Dog Story; The Last Time I Saw Archie; Lover Come Back. **1964** McHale's Navy. **1965** McHale's Navy Joins the Air Force. **1967** Divorce American Style. **1968** Did You Hear the One About the Traveling Saleslady?; The Love Bug. **1970** The Computer Wore Tennis Shoes. **1971** Million Dollar Duck. **1974** Superdad.

FLYNN, MAURICE B. "LEFTY"

Born: 1893. Died: Mar. 4, 1959. Screen actor. Divorced from actress Viola Dana.

Appeared in: **1920** The Silver Horde; Going Some; The Great Accident; Officer 666. **1921** Children of the Night; Dangerous Curve Ahead; Bucking the Line; Just Out of College; The Last Trail; The Night Rose; The Old Nest; Roads of Destiny. **1922** Omar the Tentmaker; Oath-bound; Rough Shod; Smiles are Trumps; The Woman who Walked Alone. **1923** Salomy Jane; The Snow Bride; Drums of Fate; Hell's Hole. **1924** Open All Night; The Breed of the Border; The Millionaire Cowboy; The No-Gun Man; Code of the Sea; The Uninvited Guest. **1925** O.U. West; Speed Wild; Heads Up; High and Handsome; Smilin' at Trouble. **1926** The College Boob; Glenister of the Mounted; Mulhall's Great Catch; The Traffic Cop; Sir Lumberjack. **1927** The Golden Stallion (serial).

FOLEY, JOSEPH F.

Born: 1910, Alpena, Mich. Died: July 22, 1955, Holyoke, Mass. (heart attack). Screen, stage and television actor.

Appeared in: **1951** The Whistle at Eaton Falls.

FOLEY, RED (Clyde Julian Foley)

Born: 1910, Bluelick, Ky. Died: Sept. 19, 1968, Fort Wayne, Ind. (acute pulmonary edema). Singer, screen, television, and radio actor.

Appeared in: **1966** Sing a Song, for Heaven's Sake.

FOLWELL, DENIS

Born: 1905, England. Died: Apr. 26, 1971, England. Screen and stage actor.

FONSS, OLAF
Born: 1882, Denmark. Died: Nov. 4, 1949, Copenhagen, Denmark (heart ailment). Stage and screen actor. Appeared in German and Danish films from 1911 to 1929.

Appeared in: Ich Lebe fur Dich (I Live for You).

FONTAINE, LILIAN
Born: 1886, Reading, England. Died: Feb. 20, 1975, Santa Barbara, Calif. Screen actress and stage director. Mother of actresses Olivia DeHavilland and Joan Fontaine.

Appeared in: 1945 The Lost Weekend. 1947 Time Out of Mind; Suddenly It's Spring; The Locket; Ivy; The Imperfect Lady. 1953 The Bigamist.

FONTAINE, TONY
Born: 1927. Died: June 30, 1974, Canoga Park, Calif. (cancer). Screen actor and singer.

FOO, LEE TUNG
Died: May 1, 1966. Screen actor.

Appeared in: 1936 The General Died at Dawn. 1938 Mister Wong—Detective. 1939 Mister Wong in Chinatown. 1941 Secrets of the Wastelands. 1942 Across the Pacific. 1943 Behind the Rising Sun; Mission to Moscow. 1944 Laura. 1946 It Shouldn't Happen to a Dog. 1947 Chinese Ring; The Red Hornet. 1948 Strange Gamble. 1949 There's a Girl in My Heart. 1950 The Cariboo Trail; Short Grass. 1957 Badlands of Montana.

FOO, WING
Born: 1910. Died: Dec. 9, 1953, Los Angeles, Calif. (heart attack). Screen and television actor.

Appeared in: 1941 Out of the Fog. 1944 The Purple Heart. 1945 Hotel Berlin; God Is My Co-Pilot; Blood on the Sun; Wonder Man.

FOOK, MONTE (Yuk Mong)
Born: 1908. Died: Mar. 27, 1933, Los Angeles, Calif. (gunshot wound). Screen actor.

FOOTE, COURTENEY
Born: Harregate, Yorkshire, England. Died: Mar. 4, 1925, Italy. Stage and screen actor.

Appeared in: 1912 Captain Barnacle—Reformer; Reincarnation of Komar. 1915 Captain Courtesy; Cross Currents. 1916 An International Marriage. 1918 Love's Law. 1919 The Two Brides; His Parisian Wife. 1920 The Star Rover. 1921 The Passion Flower; The Bronze Bell. 1922 Fascination. 1923 Little Old New York; Ashes of Vengeance. 1924 Tess of the D'Urbervilles; Madonna of the Streets; Dorothy Vernon of Haddon Hall.

FORAN, ARTHUR F.
Born: 1912. Died: Jan. 30, 1967, Queens, N.Y. Stage and screen actor.

FORBES, MARY
Born: Jan. 1, 1880, Hornsey, England. Died: July 22, 1974, Beaumont, Calif. Stage and screen actress. Mother of actor Ralph (dec. 1951) and actress Brenda Forbes.

Appeared in: 1916 Ultus and the Secret of the Night (aka Ultus 5—The Secret of the Night—US). 1919 Women Who Win; The Lady Clare. 1920 Nance; Inheritance. 1929 The Thirteenth Chair; Sunny Side Up; Her Private Life; The Trespasser. 1930 Holiday; East Is West; So This Is London; Strictly Unconventional; The Devil to Pay. 1931 The Man Who Came Back; Born to Love; The Brat; Working Girls; Chances. 1932 Silent Witness; Vanity Fair; Stepping Sisters; A Farewell to Arms. 1933 Bombshell; Cavalcade. 1934 You Can't Buy Everything; Most Precious Thing in Life; Shock; Blind Date; We Live Again; Happiness Ahead; Two Heads on a Pillow; British Agent. 1935 McFadden's Flats; Dizzy Dames; Les Miserables; Anna Karenina; Stranded; The Perfect Gentleman; Captain Blood; The Widow from Monte Carlo; Laddie. 1937 Women of Glamour; Wee Willie Winkie; Stage Door; The Awful Truth; Another Dawn. 1938 Everybody Sing; Outside of Paradise; Always Goodbye; You Can't Take It With You; Three Loves of Nancy; Just Around the Corner. 1939 You Can't Cheat an Honest Man; Fast and Loose; Risky Business; The Sun Never Sets; The Adventures of Sherlock Holmes; Hollywood Cavalcade; Should Husbands Work?; Ninotchka. 1940 Private Affairs; South of Suez. 1941 Nothing but the Truth. 1942 Klondike Fury; The Great Impersonation; Almost Married; This Above All. 1943 Two Tickets to London; Women in Bondage; Dangerous Blondes; Tender Comrade; Hitler's Women. 1944 Jane Eyre; Guest Wife. 1945 Earl Carroll Vanities; A Guy, a Gal and a Pal; I'll Remember April; Lady on a Train; The Picture of Dorian Gray. 1946 Down to Earth; Terror by Night. 1947 It Had to Be You; Cigarette Girl; Ivy; The Other Love; The Exile; Love Story; Indian Summer; Black Arrow. 1948 You Gotta Stay Happy. 1950 The Vanishing Lady.

FORBES, MARY ELIZABETH
Born: 1880, Rochester, N.Y. Died: Aug. 20, 1964, Los Angeles, Calif. (heart attack). Stage and screen actress. She was one of the original models for artists Charles Dana Gibson and Harrison Fisher. Do not confuse with British born actress, Mary Forbes (dec. 1974).

Appeared in: 1913 Prisoner of Zenda. 1914 Zudora—The Twenty Million Dollar Mystery (serial). 1917 Cy Whittaker's Ward. 1921 The Child Thou Gavest Me. 1956 The Ten Commandments.

FORBES, RALPH (Ralph Taylor)
Born: Sept. 30, 1896, London, England. Died: Mar. 31, 1951, New York, N.Y. Stage and screen actor. Married to actress Dora Sayers and divorced from actresses Ruth Chatterton (dec. 1961) and Heather Angel. Son of actress Mary Forbes (dec. 1974) and brother of actress Brenda Forbes.

Appeared in: 1921 The Fifth Form at St. Dominic's. 1922 A Lowland Cinderella. 1923 Comin' Thro' The Rye. 1924 Owd Bob; Reveille. 1926 Beau Geste. 1927 The Enemy; Mr. Wu. 1928 The Actress; Dog of War; The Masks of the Devil; The Latest from Paris; The Trail of '98; Under the Black Eagle; The Whip. 1929 Restless Youth; The High Road. 1930 The Lady of Scandal; Mamba; The Green Goddess; Inside the Lines; Her Wedding Night; The Devil's Battalion; Lilies of the Field. 1931 Beau Ideal; Bachelor Father. 1932 Thunder Below; Christopher Strong; Smilin' Through. 1933 False Front; Pleasure Cruise; Phantom Broadcast; The Avenger; The Solitaire Man. 1934 The Barretts of Wimpole Street; Shock; Bombay Mail; Outcast Lady; The Mystery of Mr. X; Riptide; Twentieth Century; The Fountain. 1935 Strange Wives; Enchanted April; Rescue Squad; Age of Indiscretion; Streamline Express; The Goose and the Gander; The Three Musketeers. 1936 Romeo and Juliet; Piccadilly Jim; Mary of Scotland; Daniel Boone; Love Letters of a Star. 1937 The Last of Mrs. Cheyney; The Thirteenth Chair; Make a Wish; Stage Door. 1938 Women Are Like That; Annabel Takes a Tour; Kidnapped; If I Were King; Women Against the World; Convicts at Large. 1939 The Hound of the Baskervilles; The Magnificent Fraud; Private Lives of Elizabeth and Essex; Tower of London. 1940 Calling Philo Vance; Curtain Call. 1944 Frenchman's Creek; Adventure in Diamonds.

FORBES-ROBERTSON, JEAN
Born: Mar. 16, 1905, London, England. Died: Dec. 24, 1962, London, England. Stage, screen actress and stage director. Daughter of actor Sir Johnston Forbes-Robertson (dec. 1937) and actress Gertrude Elliott (dec. 1950). Divorced from James Hamilton and later married to actor-producer Andre Van Gyseghem.

FORBES-ROBERTSON, SIR JOHNSTON
Born: 1853, London, England. Died: Nov. 6, 1937, St. Margaret's Bay, England. Stage and screen actor. Married to actress Gertrude Elliott (dec. 1950). Father of actress Jean Forbes-Robertson (dec. 1962).

Appeared in: 1913 Hamlet (US 1915). 1917 The Passing of the Third Floor Back.

FORCE, FLOYD CHARLES
Born: 1876. Died: June 9, 1947, Hollywood, Calif. Screen actor. Was one of the original Keystone Kops.

Appeared in: 1921 Cupid's Brand. 1922 The Infidel; The Game Chicken; The Lone Rider. 1923 The Love Pirate. 1924 Turned Up; Surging Seas. 1926 Hearts and Spangles. 1927 The Heart of Maryland.

FORD, DAISY
Born: 1906. Died: Dec. 14, 1959, Hollywood, Calif. Screen, stage and vaudeville actress.

FORD, FRANCIS (Francis O'Fearna)
Born: Aug. 15, 1882, Portland, Maine. Died: Sept. 5, 1953, Los Angeles, Calif. Screen, stage actor, screenwriter, film director and producer. Father of actor and director Philip Ford (dec. 1976); brother of film director John Ford (Sean O'Fearna, dec. 1973). Entered films as an actor with Edison and then went to Vitagraph and directed and acted.

Appeared in: 1912 The Deserter; The Indian Massacre; The Invaders; Custer's Last Fight. 1913 The Favorite Son. 1914 Be Neutral; Bride of Mystery; In the Fall of '64; Lady Raffles; Lucille Love; Girl of Mystery (serial); The Madcap Queen of Gretzhoffen; The Mystery of the White Car; The Mysterious Leopard Lady; The Phantom of the Violin; Washington at Valley Forge. 1915 And They Called Him Hero; The Broken Coin (serial); The Campbells Are Coming; The Doorway of Destruction; The Hidden City; The Lumber Yard Gang; Nabbed; One Kind of a Friend; 3 Bad Men and a Girl; The Heart of Lincoln; A Study in Scarlet. 1916 The Bandit's Wager; Behind the Mask; Brennon O' the Moor; Chicken Hearted Jim; The Cry of Erin; The Dumb Bandit; The Elusive Enemy; Her Sister's Sin; The Heroine of San Juan; His Majesty Dick Turpin; Lady Raffles Returns; The Mad Hermit; The Madcap Queen of Crona; Phantom Island; The Adventures of Peg O' the Ring (serial); Poisoned Lips; The Powder Trail; The Princely Bandit; The Purple Mask (serial); The Sham Reality; The Strong Arm Squad; Mr. Vampire; Orders is Orders; The Unexpected. 1917 The Puzzle Woman; In Treason's Grasp; True to Their Colors; Unmasked; To Berlin Via America; The Little Rebel's Sacrifice. 1918

The Silent Mystery (serial); The Craving; The Mystery Ship (serial); Crimson Shoals (serial); Delirium. **1919** The Woman of Mystery (serial). **1920** The Mystery of 13. **1921** The Great Reward (serial); Action; The Lady from Longacre; The Stampede. **1922** The Heart of Lincoln (and 1915 version); Another Man's Boots; The Boss of Camp 4; So This is Arizona; Storm Girl; They're Off; The Village Blacksmith; Thundering Hoofs. **1923** Mine to Keep; Haunted Valley (serial); Three Jumps Ahead. **1924** Western Feuds; Lash of the Whip; The Measure of a Man; Rodeo Mixup; Hearts of Oak; In the Days of the Covered Wagon; The Diamond Bandit. **1925** "Scar" Hanan; The Fighting Heart; The Red Rider; The Four from Nowhere; Ridin' Thunder; The Taming of the West; Soft Shoes; The Sign of the Cactus; A Roaring Adventure. **1926** Speed Cop. **1927** The Devil's Saddle; Upstream; The Wreck of the Hesperus; The Cruise of the Hellion; The Heart of Maryland; Men of Daring; One Glorious Scrap; Uncle Tom's Cabin. **1928** The Branded Sombrero; Sisters of Eve; The Chinatown Mystery (serial); Four-Footed Ranger. **1929** The Black Watch; The Drake Case; The Lariat Kid. **1930** Mounted Stranger; Kathleen Mavourneen; Song of the Caballero; Sons of the Saddle; The Indians are Coming (serial silent and sound versions); The Jade Box (serial silent and sound versions). **1931** Frankenstein; The Sea Beneath. **1932** The Last Ride; Tangled Fortunes; Airmail. **1933** Pilgrimage; Charlie Chan's Greatest Case; Life in the Raw; Man from Monterey; Gun Justice. **1934** Cheaters; Charlie Chan's Courage; Murder in Trinidad; Judge Priest. **1935** Goin' to Town; This Is the Life; The Informer; The Arizonian; Steamboat 'Round the Bend; Charlie Chan's Secret; Paddy O'Day. **1936** The Prisoner of Shark Island; Gentle Julia; Charlie Chan at the Circus; Sins of Man; Educating Father. **1937** Slave Ship; Checkers. **1938** In Old Chicago; Kentucky Moonshine; The Texans. **1939** Stagecoach; Young Mr. Lincoln; Drums along the Mohawk; Bad Lands; Geronimo. **1940** Viva Cisco Kid; Lucky Cisco Kid; South of Pago Pago; Diamond Frontier. **1941** Tobacco Road; Last of the Duanes. **1942** The Loves of Edgar Allan Poe; Outlaws of Pine Ridge; The Man Who Wouldn't Die. **1943** Girls in Chains; The Ox-Bow Incident. **1944** The Climax; The Big Noise; Bowery Champs. **1945** Gilda; A Stolen Life; Gallant Journey; Hangover Square. **1946** Renegades; Accomplice; My Darling Clementine; Wake up and Dream. **1947** Bandits of Dark Canyon; Driftwood; High Tide. **1948** The Timber Trail; Eyes of Texas; The Plunderers. **1949** The Far Frontier; Frontier Investigator; San Antone Ambush. **1950** Father Makes Good; Wagonmaster. **1952** The Quiet Man; Toughest Man in Arizona. **1953** The Sun Shines Bright; The Marshal's Daughter.

FORD, HARRISON
Born: Mar. 16, 1894, Kansas City, Mo. Died: Dec. 2, 1957, Woodland Hills, Calif. Stage and screen actor.

Appeared in: **1916** The Mysterious Mrs. M. **1918** The Cruise of the Make-Believe; A Pair of Silk Stockings; Such a Little Pirate. **1919** The Lottery Man; The Veiled Adventure; Hawthorne of the U.S.A.; The Third Kiss. **1921** The Passion Flower; Wedding Bells; A Heart to Let; Love's Redemption; Wonderful Thing. **1922** Smilin' Through; Find the Woman; The Primitive Lover; When Love Comes; The Old Homestead; Foolish Wives; Her Gilded Cage; Shadows. **1923** Little Old New York; Vanity Fair; Bright Lights of Broadway; Maytime. **1924** Janice Meredith; The Average Woman; A Fool's Awakening; The Price of a Party; Three Miles Out. **1925** Proud Flesh; The Wheel; Lovers in Quarantine; The Mad Marriage; The Marriage Whirl; Zander the Great. **1926** Up in Mabel's Room; That Royal Girl; Almost a Lady; The Song and Dance Man; Hell's 400; Sandy; The Nervous Wreck. **1927** The Rejuvenation of Aunt Mary; No Control; The Girl in the Pullman; The Night Bride; Rubber Tires. **1928** Let 'Er Go Gallagher; A Woman against the World; Golf Widows; Just Married; The Rush Hour; Three Week Ends. **1929** Her Husband's Women; The Flattering Word (short). **1932** Love in High Gear. Prior to **1933** Advice to Husbands (short).

FORD, JOHN (Sean O'Fearna)
Born: Feb. 1, 1895, Portland, Maine. Died: Aug. 31, 1973, Palm Desert, Calif. (cancer). Screen director, producer, screenwriter, cinematographer, stand-in and screen actor. Brother of actor Francis Ford (dec. 1953). Won 1935 Academy Award for Best Director for "The Informer," in 1940 for "The Grapes of Wrath," in 1941 for "How Green Was My Valley," and in 1952 for "The Quiet Man."

Appeared in: **1915** The Broken Coin (serial). **1917** The Tornado; Trail of Hate; The Scrapper.

FORD, MARTY
Born: 1900. Died: Nov. 12, 1954, Hollywood, Calif. Screen and stage actor.

FORD, WALLACE
Born: Feb. 12, 1899, England. Died: June 11, 1966, Woodland Hills, Calif. (heart ailment). Stage and screen actor.

Appeared in: **1930** Swellhead; Absent Minded (short); Fore (short). **1931** Possessed; X Marks the Spot. **1932** Wet Parade; Hypnotized; Freaks; City Sentinel; Are You Listening?; Skyscraper Souls; Prosperity; Central Park; Beast of the City. **1933** Employees' Entrance; The Big Cage; She Had to Say Yes; Goodbye Again; Headline Shooter; Night of Terror; My Woman: East of Fifth Avenue; Three-Cornered Moon. **1934** A Woman's Man; Money Means Nothing; The Lost Patrol; Men in White; I Hate Women. **1935** The Nut Farm; The

Informer; Another Face; Swell Head (and 1930 version); The Whole Town's Talking; In Spite of Danger; Men of the Hour; She Couldn't Take It; The Mysterious Mr. Wong; One Frightened Night; Mary Burns, Fugitive; The Man Who Reclaimed His Head; Sanders of the River; Get That Man. **1936** Two in the Dark; Absolute Quiet; A Son Comes Home; The Rogues' Tavern; O.H.M.S. (You're in the Army Now—US 1937). **1937** Swing It, Sailor; Jericho; Exiled to Shanghai. **1938** Dark Sands; He Loves an Actress. **1939** Back Door to Heaven. **1940** The Mummy's Hand; Scatterbrain; Two Girls on Broadway; Isle of Destiny; Love, Honor and Oh Baby!; Give Us Wings. **1941** A Man Betrayed; The Roar of the Press; Murder by Invitation; Blues in the Night. **1942** All through the Night; Inside the Law; Scattergood Survives a Murder; Seven Days' Leave; The Mummy's Tomb. **1943** The Ape Man; Shadow of a Doubt; The Marines Come Through; The Cross of Lorraine. **1944** Secret Command; Machine Gun Mama. **1945** On Stage Everybody; Spellbound; Blood on the Sun; They Were Expendable; The Great John L. **1946** Lover Come Back; Crack-Up; Black Angel; Rendezvous with Annie; A Guy Could Change; The Green Years. **1947** Magic Town; T-Men; Dead Reckoning. **1948** Coroner Creek; The Man from Texas; Shed No Tears; Embraceable You; Belle Starr's Daughter. **1949** Red Stallion in the Rockies; The Set-Up. **1950** The Furies; Dakota Lil; The Breaking Point; Harvey. **1951** Warpath; Painting the Clouds with Sunshine; He Ran All the Way. **1952** Flesh and Fury; Rodeo. **1953** The Great Jesse James Raid; The Nebraskan. **1954** Destry; She Couldn't Say No; The Boy from Oklahoma; Three Ring Circus. **1955** The Man from Laramie; The Spoilers; Lucy Gallant; Wichita; A Lawless Street. **1956** The Maverick Queen; Johnny Concho; Thunder over Arizona; Stagecoach to Fury; The First Texan; The Rainmaker. **1958** The Last Hurrah; Twilight for the Gods; The Matchmaker. **1959** Warlock. **1961** Tess of the Storm County. **1965** A Patch of Blue.

FORDE, EUGENIE
Born: New York, N.Y. Died: Sept. 5, 1940, Van Nuys, Calif. Stage and screen actress. Mother of actress Victoria Forde (dec. 1964).

Appeared in: **1912** A Pair of Jacks. **1913** Sheridan's Ride; Jim's Atonement. **1915** The Doughnut Vendor; An Eye for an Eye; Across the Desert; Polishing Up Polly; Mother's Birthday; The Great Question; The Diamond from the Sky; Curly. **1916** The White Rosette; Lying Lips; So Shall Ye Reap; The Undertow; The Girl Detective; The Courtesan; Purity; Out of the Shadows; Power of the Cross; Hedge of Heart's Desire. **1917** The Gentle Intruder; Annie-for-Spite; Conscience. **1918** Fair Enough. **1919** Strictly Confidential; Sis Hopkins; The Man Who Turned White. **1920** The Road to Divorce; The Virgin of Stamboul. **1923** Blow Your Own Horn. **1926** Memory Lane; That's My Baby. **1927** Captain Salvation; Wilful Youth.

FORDE, STANLEY H.
Born: 1881. Died: Jan. 28, 1929, New York, N.Y. Screen and stage actor.

Appeared in: **1924** The Great White Way.

FORDE, VICTORIA
Born: 1897, New York, N.Y. Died: July 24, 1964, Beverly Hills, Calif. Screen actress. Daughter of actress Eugenie Forde (dec. 1940). Divorced from actor Tom Mix (dec. 1940).

Appeared in: **1912** Lottery Ticket No. 13; Young Wild West Leading a Raid; Uncle Bill; A Pair of Jacks; Settled Out of Court; The Everlasting Judy; At Rolling Forks; Her Indian Hero; The Love Trail; The Renegade. **1913** Sheridan's Ride; The Yaqui Cur; The Stars and Stripes Forever. **1914** Those Persistent Old Maids; Cupid Pulls a Tooth; He Never Said a Word; Could You Blame Her?; The Troublesome Wink; The Way of Life; His Strenuous Honeymoon; She Was a Working Girl; Such a Villain; Her Moonshine Lover; When the Girls Joined the Force; A Lucky Deception; Captain Bill's Warm Reception; What a Baby Did; Sophie of the Films; When Eddie Went to the Front. **1915** Her Rustic Hero; When the Spirit Moved; Lizzie's Dizzy Career; When the Mummy Cried for Help; All Aboard; How Doctor Cupid Won; When He Proposed; The Mixup at Maxim's; In a Jackpot; Eddie's Awful Predicament; Two Hearts and a Ship; The Range Girl and the Cowboy; The Foreman's Choice; On the Eagle Trail; The Race for a Gold Mine; The Downfall of Potts; A Peach and a Pair; Athletic Ambitions; Never Again; When Her Idol Fell; When they Were Co-eds; Lost—Three Teeth; Tony the Wop; Lizzie and the Beauty Contest; When Lizzie Went to Sea; His Egyptian Affinity; When Cupid Caught a Thief; Jed's Little Elopement; Lizzie Breaks into the Harem. **1916** An Angelic Attitude; A Western Masquerade; A Bear of a Story; The Girl of Gold Gulch; Crooked Trails; Going West to Make Good; Taking a Chance; Making Good; Trilby's Love Disaster; Along the Border; The Man Within; Roping a Sweetheart; Tom's Strategy; The Desert Calls Its Own; A Corner in Water; After the Battle; Canby Hill Outlaws; An Eventful Evening; The Country that God Forgot; A Mistake in Rustlers; A Close Call; Tom's Sacrifice; When Cupid Slipped; The Sheriff's Blunder; Mistakes Will Happen; The Golden Thought. **1917** Starring Western Stuff; Hearts and Saddles; Please Be My Wife.

FOREST, FRANK (Frank Hayek aka FRANCO FORESTO)
Born: 1896, St. Paul, Minn. Died: Dec. 23, 1976, Santa Monica, Calif. Opera singer and screen actor.

Appeared in: **1936** The Big Broadcast of 1937. **1937** I'll Take Romance; Champagne Waltz.

FORMAN, TOM

Born: Feb. 22, 1893, Mitchell County, Texas. Died: Nov. 7, 1926, Venice, Calif. (suicide—gun). Screen, stage actor and film director.

Appeared in: **1915** The Wild Goose Chase. **1916** Sweet Kitty Bellairs. **1917** The Evil Eye; Those Without Sin; The Tides of Barngate; Jaguar's Claws; Her Strange Wedding; The American Consul; Forbidden Paths; A Kiss for Susie; Hashamura Togo; The Trouble Buster. **1919** Told in the Hills; The Tree of Knowledge; For Better, For Worse; Louisiana; The Heart of Youth. **1920** Round-Up; The Sea Wolf; The Ladder of Lies; Sins of Rosanne. **1922** White Shoulders. **1926** Devil's Dice; Kosher Kitty Kelly.

FORMBY, GEORGE, JR. (aka GEORGE HOY)

Born: May 26, 1904, Wigan, Lancashire, England. Died: Mar. 6, 1961, Preston, Lancashire, England. Screen, vaudeville, television actor, screenwriter and song writer. Son of British Music Hall star George Forby (dec.); brother of actress Beryl Formby. Voted among first ten money making stars in British productions in Motion Picture Herald-Fame Poll, 1942 and 1945.

Appeared in: **1914** No Fool Like an Old Fool. **1915** By the Shortest of Heads. **1934** Boots! Boots! **1935** Off the Dole; No Limit. **1936** Keep Your Seats, Please. **1937** Feather Your Nest; Keep Fit. **1938** I See Ice; It's In the Air (aka George Takes the Air—US 1940). **1939** Trouble Brewing; Come on George. **1940** Let George Do It; Spare a Copper. **1941** Turned Out Nice Again; South American George. **1942** Much Too Shy. **1943** Get Cracking; Bell-Bottom George. **1944** He Stoops to Conquer. **1945** I Didn't Do It. **1946** George in Civvy Street.

FORREST, ALAN (Allan Forest Fisher)

Born: Sept. 1, 1889, Brooklyn, N.Y. Died: July 25, 1941, Detroit, Mich. Stage and screen actor.

Appeared in: **1916-18** American Film Mfg. Co. films. **1919** Rosemary Climbs the Heights. **1921** Cheated Love; Forgotten Woman; The Hole in the Wall; The Invisible Fear; The Man from Lost River; They Shall Pay; What Women Will Do. **1922** The Heart Specialist; Lights of the Desert; The New Teacher; Seeing's Believing; Tillie; Very Truly Yours. **1923** Long Live the King; Crinoline and Romance; Her Fatal Millions; The Man Between; A Noise in Newboro; Wandering Daughters. **1924** Don't Doubt Your Husband; In Love with Love; The Siren of Seville; Captain Blood; Dorothy Vernon of Haddon Hall. **1925** The Dressmaker from Paris; The Great Divide; Old Clothes; Pampered Youth; Rose of the World. **1926** The Carnival Girl; Fifth Avenue; Partners Again; The Phantom Bullet; The Prince of Pilsen; Summer Bachelors; Two Can Play. **1927** Ankles Preferred; The Lovelorn. **1928** Black Feather; The Desert Bride; Riding for Fame; Sally of the Scandals; The Wild West Show. **1929** The Winged Horseman. **1930** Dangerous Nan McGrew.

FORREST, BELFORD (Fenton Ford)

Born: 1878. Died: May 1, 1938, Hollywood, Calif. Screen actor and playwright. One of the first comics signed by Hal Roach in silent bathing beauty days.

FORSTER, RUDOLF (aka RUDOLPH FORSTER)

Born: 1884, Grobming, Germany. Died Oct. 25, 1968, Attersee, Germany. Stage and screen actor.

Appeared in: **1927** At the Grey House. **1931** Die Dreigroschenoper (The Beggar's Opera). **1932** Die Graefin von Monte Christo (The Countess of Monte Cristo); Yorck. **1933** Morgenrot. **1934** Der Traeumende Mund. **1939** Island of Lost Men; Hohe Schule (College). **1957** The White Horse Inn (US 1959). **1958** Lian, Das Madchen aus dem Urwald (Liane, Girl of the Jungle and Liane, Jungle Goddess—US 1959). **1960** Die Dreigroschenoper (The Threepenny Opera); Der Rest ist Schweigen (The Rest is Silence); Die Schachnovelle (Brainwashed—US 1961 aka The Royal); Das Glas Wasser (A Glass of Water—US 1962). **1961** Im Stahlnetz des Dr. Mabuse (The Return of Dr. Mabuse—US 1966). **1962** Lulu. **1963** The Cardinal; Der Henker von London (aka The Mad Executioners—US 1965). **1964** Tonio Kroger (US 1968).

FORSYTHE, MIMI (Marie G. Armstrong)

Born: 1922. Died: Aug. 17, 1952, Hollywood, Calif. Screen actress.

Appeared in: **1944** Sensations of 1945; Three Russian Girls.

FORTE, JOE (Josef Forte)

Born: 1896. Died: Feb. 22, 1967, Hollywood, Calif. (heart attack). Screen, radio and television actor.

Appeared in: **1938** Pals of the Saddle. **1941** A Panic in the Parlor (short). **1946** The Crimson Ghost (serial). **1949** Riders in the Sky. **1950** County Fair. **1952** Assignment Paris. **1953** Three Sailors and a Girl. **1955** Cell 2455, Death Row. **1956** Fury at Gunsight Pass; He Laughed Last; The Buster Keaton Story. **1957** Short Cut to Hell. **1958** Return to Warbow. **1961** Homicidal. **1963** The Nutty Professor. **1964** Law of the Lawless. **1965** Black Spurs.

FORTIER, HERBERT

Born: 1867, Toronto, Canada. Died: Feb. 16, 1949, Philadelphia, Pa. Stage and screen actor.

Appeared in: **1914** By Whose Hand. **1915** The Sacrifice. **1921** Beyond; Children of the Night; A Connecticut Yankee in King Arthur's Court; Garments of Truth; The Shark Master; Whatever She Wants. **1922** The Black Bag; Dusk to Dawn; Little Wildcat; Midnight. **1923** Clean-Up; Legally Dead; Railroaded; Slander the Woman. **1924** Ridgeway of Montana; The Western Wallop; The Whispered Name.

FORTUNE, EDMUND

Born: 1863, Monmouthshire, England. Died: Sept. 21, 1939. Stage and screen actor. Entered films in 1919.

Appeared in: **1925** Lost Lady; Never the Twain Shall Meet. **1927** Sorrell and Son. **1928** Blue Danube.

FORTUNE, WALLACE

Born: 1884. Died: Jan. 12, 1926, New York, N.Y. (typhoid, pneumonia). Screen actor and stage director.

FOSHAY, HAROLD A.

Born: 1884. Died: Feb. 23, 1953, Charleston, S.C. Screen actor, film producer and film director.

Appeared in: **1915** The Reward; The Lesson of the Narrow Street. **1916** Kennedy Square; Myrtle the Manicurist; The Tarantula; Winifred the Shop Girl. **1921** The Devil's Confession; The Shadow. **1922** Why Not Marry? **1923** The Fair Cheat. **1924** Youth for Sale. **1926** The Brown Derby. **1936** To Mary with Love.

FOSTER, DONALD

Born: 1889. Died: Dec. 22, 1969, Hollywood, Calif. Screen, stage and television actor.

Appeared in: **1959** The Al Capone Story; Horse Soldiers. **1960** Please Don't Eat the Daisies. **1961** All in a Night's Work. **1966** Lord Love a Duck.

FOSTER, DUDLEY

Born: 1925, England. Died: Jan. 8, 1973, London, England. Screen, stage and television actor. Married to actress Eileen Kenally.

Appeared in: **1959** The Two Headed Spy. **1962** Term of Trial (US 1963). **1963** Ricochet (US 1966). **1965** Study in Terror (US 1966); The Little Ones. **1969** Moon Zero Two (US 1970); Where's Jack? **1970** Wuthering Heights.

FOSTER, J. MORRIS

Born: 1882, Foxbert, Pa. Died: Apr. 24, 1966. Stage and screen actor. Married to actress Mignon Anderson.

Appeared in: **1914** Jean of the Wilderness; The Guiding Hand; His Reward. **1915** The Game; The Maker of Guns; The Final Reckoning; The Cycle of Hatred; The Adventures of Florence; The Bridal Banquet; Bianca Forgets; The Vagabonds; Monsieur Nikole Dupree; God's Witness; The Light of the Reef; Ambition; In the Hands of the Enemy; Out of the Sea; The Bowl Bearer; Beating Back; Her Menacing Past. **1917** It Makes a Difference; An Eight Cylinder Romance; The Storm Woman; Beloved Jim; The Secret Man. **1918** The Voice of Destiny; Winning Grandma; The Fighting Grin. **1919** Blind Man's Eyes; You Never Saw Such a Girl. **1920** Overland Red; What Happened to Jones; Sundown Slim.

FOSTER, PRESTON

Born: Aug. 24, 1900, Ocean City, N.J. Died: July 14, 1970, La Jolla, Calif. Screen, stage, opera and television actor. Divorced from Gertrude Warren. Married to actress Rebecca Heffner (aka Sheila D'Arcy).

Appeared in: **1929** Nothing but the Truth. **1930** Follow the Leader; Heads Up. **1932** The Last Mile; Life Begins; Doctor X; Two Seconds; I Am a Fugitive from a Chain Gang; The All-American; You Said a Mouthful. **1933** Elmer the Great; Danger Crossroads; Corruption; The Man Who Dared; Hoopla; Devil's Mate; Ladies They Talk About; Sensation Hunters. **1934** Wharf Angel; Sleepers East; Heat Lightning; The Band Plays On. **1935** A Night at the Biltmore Bowl (short); People's Enemy; The Arizonian; Strangers All; Annie Oakley; The Last Days of Pompeii; The Informer. **1936** Muss 'Em Up; We Who Are about to Die; Love before Breakfast; We're Only Human; The Plough and the Stars. **1937** Sea Devils; The Outcasts of Poker Flat; You Can't Beat Love; The Westland Case; First Lady. **1938** Everybody's Doing It; Double Danger; Submarine Patrol; Up the River; The Lady in the Morgue; The Storm; The Last Warning; Army Girl; White Banners. **1939** Geronimo; Street of Missing Men; Chasing Danger; 20,000 Men a Year; Society Smugglers; News Is Made at Night; Missing Evidence. **1940** Moon over Burma; Cafe Hostess; North West Mounted Police. **1941** The Roundup; Unfinished Business. **1942** Secret Agent of Japan; Night in New Orleans; Little Tokyo, USA; American Empire; A Gentleman after Dark; Thunder Birds. **1943** Guadalcanal Diary; My Friend Flicka. **1944** The Bermuda Mystery; Roger Touhy, Gangster. **1945** Valley of Decision; The Last Gangster; Twice Blessed; Thunderhead, Son of Flicka; Abbott and Costello in Hollywood. **1946** The Harvey Girls; Tangiers; Inside Job;

Strange Triangle; Blonde from Brooklyn. **1947** Ramrod; King of Wild Horses. **1948** Green Grass of Wyoming; The Hunted; Thunderhoof. **1949** I Shot Jesse James; The Big Cat. **1950** The Tougher They Come. **1951** The Big Gusher; Three Desperate Men (aka Three Outlaws); Tomahawk; The Big Night. **1952** Face to Face; Montana Territory; Kansas City Confidential. **1953** I, the Jury; Law and Order. **1957** Destination 60,000. **1964** The Man from Galveston; The Time Travelers; Advance to the Rear. **1967** You've Got to Be Smart. **1968** Chubasco.

FOUGERS, PIERRE
Born: France. Died: Nov. 28, 1922, Paris, France (accidentally shot himself). Screen actor.

FOUGEZ, ANNA
Born: 1895, Italy. Died: Sept. 1966, Santa Marinella, Italy. Italian screen, stage actress and singer. Entered films in 1920.

FOULGER, BYRON
Born: 1900. Died: Apr. 4, 1970, Hollywood, Calif. (heart condition). Screen and television actor.

Appeared in: **1937** The Prisoner of Zenda; The Awful Truth; Larceny on the Air; The Duke Comes Back; A Day at the Races. **1938** Born to Be Wild; Tenth Avenue Kid; Tarnished Angel; I Am a Criminal; It's All in Your Mind. **1939** At the Circus; Exile Express; The Man They Could Not Hang; Mutiny on the Blackhawk; Television Spy; The Girl from Rio; Fools of Desire; In Name Only; Union Pacific. **1940** Edison, the Man; Heroes of the Saddle; The Saint's Double Trouble; Dr. Kildare's Crisis; The Man with Nine Lives; Ellery Queen, Master Detective; Arizona; Sky Murder. **1941** Sullivan's Travels; Man-Made Monster; The Gay Vagabond; Ridin' on a Rainbow; Sweetheart of the Campus; Mystery Ship; Dude Cowboy. **1942** The Panther's Claw; The Tuttles of Tahiti; Harvard, Here I Come; Quiet Please, Murder; Stand by for Action; Man from Headquarters. **1943** The Human Comedy; The Falcon Strikes Back; So Proudly We Hail!; Sweet Rosie O'Grady; The Adventures of a Rookie; In Old Oklahoma; Hi Diddle Diddle; Hoppy Serves a Writ; Hangmen Also Die; Enemy of Women; The Power of God; Dixie Dugan; Coney Island; Silver Spurs; Black Raven. **1944** He Forgot to Remember (short); Since You Went Away; Summer Storm; The Whistler; Roger Touhy, Gangster; Dark Mountain; Henry Aldrich's Little Secret; Ministry of Fear; Marriage Is a Private Affair; Swing in the Saddle; Beautiful but Broke. **1945** The Hidden Eye; Let's Go Steady; Purity Squad (short); Circumstantial Evidence; The Adventures of Kitty O'Day; Brewster's Millions; Arson Squad; The Blonde from Brooklyn; It's in the Bag. **1946** Snafu; Sensation Hunters; Sentimental Journey; The French Key; Dick Tracy vs. Cueball; 'Til the Clouds Roll By; The Plainsman and the Lady. **1947** The Michigan Kid; Lady Be Good; Hard-Boiled Mahoney; Adventures of Don Coyote; The Bells of San Fernando; Too Many Winners; The Red Hornet; The Chinese Ring; Stallion Road. **1948** Arch of Triumph; The Hunted; They Live By Night (aka The Twisted Road and Your Red Wagon); Return of October; Out of the Storm; I Surrender Dear. **1949** Arson, Inc.; Dancing in the Dark; I Shot Jesse James; The Inspector General; The Dalton Gang; Red Desert; Satan's Cradle. **1950** Champagne for Caesar; The Girl from San Lorenzo; The Return of Jesse James; Experiment Alcatraz; Salt Lake Raiders. **1951** Footlight Varieties; A Millionaire for Christy; FBI Girl; Gasoline Alley; The Sea Hornet; Lightning Strikes Twice; Home Town Story. **1952** Cripple Creek; My Six Convicts; Apache Country; The Steel Fist. **1953** The Magnetic Monster; Bandits of the West; Cruisin' Down the River; Confidentially Connie; Paris Model. **1956** You Can't Run Away from It. **1957** The River's Edge; Dino; Sierra Stranger; Gun Battle at Monterey; Up in Smoke; The Buckskin Lady; New Day at Sundown. **1958** The Long, Hot Summer; Going Steady. **1959** King of the Wild Stallions. **1960** Ma Barker's Killer Brood; Twelve Hours to Kill. **1962** The Devil's Partner. **1967** The Gnome-Mobile. **1969** There Was a Crooked Man.

FOWLER, ART
Born: 1902. Died: Apr. 4, 1953, Suffern, N.Y. Screen, radio, and television actor.

FOWLER, BRENDA
Born: 1883, Los Angeles, Calif. Died: Oct. 27, 1942, Los Angeles, Calif. Screen, stage actress and playwright. Entered films with Kalem and Rex productions.

Appeared in: **1923** Money! Money! Money! **1934** The Mighty Barnum; The World Moves On; Judge Priest. **1935** Ruggles of Red Gap. **1936** The Case against Mrs. Ames; Second Wife. **1938** The Cowboy and the Lady. **1939** Stage Coach; Dust Be My Destiny. **1940** Comin' 'Round the Mountain.

FOWLER, JOHN C. (John Crawford Fowler)
Born: July 25, 1869, New York, N.Y. Died: June 27, 1952, Los Angeles, Calif. (arteriosclerosis). Stage and screen actor.

Appeared in: **1924** Flapper Wives. **1925** Reckless Courage; S.O.S. Perils of the Sea. **1926** One Punch O'Day. **1927** Burning Gold; Wolf's Clothing. **1929** Campus Knights; The Peacock Fan. **1930** Fighting Legion. **1933** Midnight Patrol. **1934** Are We Civilized?

FOX, FRANKLYN
Born: 1894, England. Died: Nov. 2, 1967, Wantagh, N.Y. (heart attack). Screen, stage, radio and television actor.

Appeared in: **1957** High Tide at Noon. **1959** First Man into Space.

FOX, FRED (Frederick Strachan Fox)
Born: Jan. 22, 1884, London, England. Died: Dec. 1, 1949, Los Angeles, Calif. (heart attack). Screen, stage, radio actor and assistant film director.

FOX, HARRY (Arthur Carringford)
Born: 1882, Pomona, Calif. Died: July 20, 1959, Woodland Hills, Calif. Screen, stage and vaudeville actor. Married to actress Evelyn Brent (dec. 1975). Divorced from actresses Yancsi (Jenny) Dolly, of the famed "Dolly Sisters" (dec. 1941) and Beatrice Curtis (dec. 1936). He appeared in vaudeville with his wife at the time, Beatrice Curtis, and together they made two film shorts.

He appeared in: **1916** Beatrice Fairfax (serial). **1928** The Lemon (short). **1929** Harry Fox and His Six American Beauties (short); The Fox and the Bee (short with Beatrice Curtis). **1930** The Play Boy (short with Beatrice Curtis); The Lucky Break. **1931** Fifty Million Frenchman. **1934** Love Time; 365 Nights in Hollywood.

FOX, JOSEPHINE
Born: 1877. Died: Aug. 2, 1953, Englewood, N.J. Stage, screen, vaudeville and radio actress. Sister of actress Elizabeth Malone. Appeared in early Edison Co. films.

FOX, ROSE
Born: 1899. Died: Feb. 2, 1966. Screen actress.

FOX, SIDNEY (aka SYDNEY FOX)
Born: Dec. 10, 1910, New York, N.Y. Died: Nov. 14, 1942, Beverly Hills, Calif. Stage and screen actress. Entered films in 1931 as a Wampas Baby.

Appeared in: **1931** Strictly Dishonorable; Bad Sister; Six Cylinder Love. **1932** Afraid to Talk; The Cohens and the Kellys in Hollywood; Mouthpiece; Once in a Lifetime; Nice Women; Murders in the Rue Morgue. **1933** Don Quixote. **1934** Down to Their Last Yacht; Midnight; School for Girls.

FOY, EDDIE (Edward Fitzgerald)
Born: 1854. Died: Feb. 16, 1928, Kansas City, Mo. Screen, stage and vaudeville actor. Head of vaudeville team "Seven Foys" which included actors Bryan (dec. 1977), Eddie Jr., Charlie, Mary, Richard (dec.—no film appearance), Madeleine and Irving Foy. Widower three times by stage actresses Rose Howland (of the Howland Sisters), Lola Sefton and Madeline Morondo (dec. 1918), who was the mother of his seven children. Later married to Maria Combs.

Appeared in: **1912** A Solax Celebration. **1915** A Favorite Fool. **1928** Foys for Joys (short).

FOYER, EDDIE
Born: 1883. Died: June 15, 1934, Los Angeles, Calif. Screen and vaudeville actor.

Appeared in: **1930** Big House.

FRALICK, FREDDIE
Born: June 4, 1888, Detroit, Mich. Died: May 13, 1958, Hollywood, Calif. Screen, stage and vaudeville actor. Entered films with Biograph in 1912 and remained in films until 1917.

FRANCE, CHARLES V.
Born: June 30, 1868, Bradford, England. Died: Apr. 13, 1949, Gerrards Cross, England. Stage and screen actor.

Appeared in: **1930** The Skin Game (film debut). **1931** These Charming People; Black Coffee; A Night Like This. **1934** Chu Chin Chow; Lord Edgware Dies. **1935** Scrooge; Tudor Rose. **1936** Secret Agent; Broken Blossoms; Crime over London. **1937** Victoria the Great. **1938** A Yank at Oxford; Strange Borders; If I Were King; The Ware Case. **1939** Ten Days in Paris. **1940** Night Train to Munich. **1941** Missing Ten Days; Breach of Promise. **1942** Went the Day Well? **1943** Queen Victoria; The Yellow Canary. **1944** The Half-Way House; 48 Hours.

FRANCIS, ALEC B.
Born: Suffolk, England. Died: July 6, 1934, Hollywood, Calif. (following an emergency operation). Stage and screen actor. Entered films in 1911.

Appeared in: **1911** Vanity Fair. **1912** Robin Hood; The Transgression of Deacon Jones; Their Children's Approval; Dick's Wife; Silent Jim. **1913** When Pierrot Met Pierrette; A Son's Devotion; When Light Came Back; A Tammany Boarder; For Better or Worse; The Witch; The Beaten Path; The Spectre Bridegroom. **1914** The Drug Traffic; Duty; The Man of the Hour; The Greatest of These. **1915** Lola. **1919** Flame of the Desert; Heartsease; Lord and Lady Algy. **1920** The Street Called Straight; The Man Who Had Everything; The Paliser Case. **1921** What's A Wife Worth?; Godless Men; A Voice in the Dark; The Great Moment; A Virginia Courtship; Courage. **1922** Smilin' Through;

The Man Who Saw Tomorrow; Beyond the Rocks; North of the Rio Grande; The Forgotten Law. **1923** Three Wise Fools; Hollywood; Little Church Around the Corner; Children of Jazz; Is Divorce a Failure?; The Last Hour; The Eternal Three; The Spider and the Rose; The Drivin' Fool; Lucretia Lombard; Mary of the Movies; A Gentleman of Leisure; The Gold Diggers; His Last Race. **1924** A Fool's Awakening; Do It Now; Soiled; Listen Lester; The Tenth Woman; The Human Terror; Half-a-Dollar Bill; Beau Brummell. **1925** The Bridge of Sighs; Charley's Aunt; Thank You; The Coast of Folly; Champion of Lost Causes; A Thief in Paradise; The Mad Whirl; Thunder Mountain; The Circle; Rose of the World; Capital Punishment; The Reckless Sex; Waking up the Town; Wandering Footsteps; Where the Worst Begins; Man and Maid; Outwitted. **1926** Tramp, Tramp, Tramp; The Return of Peter Grimm; Forever After; Pals First; Three Bad Men; High Steppers; Faithful Wives; The Yankee Senor; Transcontinental Limited. **1927** The Music Master; Camille; Sally in Our Alley; The Tender Hour. **1928** The Lion and the Mouse; The Terror; The Little Snob; Companionate Marriage; Broadway Daddies; Life's Mockery; The Shepherd of the Hills. **1929** Evidence; The Sacred Flame; Evangeline; Murder Will Out; The Mississippi Gambler. **1930** The Bishop Murder Case; Feet First; The Case of Sgt. Grischa; Captain Apple Jack; Outward Bound. **1931** Arrowsmith; Oh! Oh! Cleopatra (short). **1932** .45 Calibre Echo; No Greater Love; The Last Man; The Last Mile; Alias Mary Smith; Mata Hari. **1933** Oliver Twist; Looking Forward; His Private Secretary; Alice in Wonderland. **1934** Mystery of Mr. X; I'll Tell the World; Outcast Lady.

FRANCIS, COLEMAN

Born: Jan. 24, 1919, Oklahoma. Died: Jan. 15, 1973, Hollywood, Calif. (arteriosclerosis). Screen actor, screenwriter and film director.

Appeared in: **1937** Uncivilized. **1940** The Howards of Virginia. **1942** The Black Swan. **1947** Blondie's Night Out. **1952** The Girl in White; Scarlet Angel; Leadville Gunslinger. **1957** The Phantom Stagecoach. **1958** Stakeout on Dope Street. **1960** Cimarron; From the Terrace; Spring Affair. **1965** Motor Psycho. **1966** The Lemon Grove Kids Meet the Grasshopper and the Vampire Lady from Outer Space (short); Night Train to Mundo Fine. **1970** Beyond the Valley of the Dolls.

FRANCIS, KAY (Katherine Edwina Gibbs)

Born: Jan. 13, 1903, Oklahoma City, Okla. Died: Aug. 26, 1968, New York, N.Y. (cancer). Screen, stage actress and film producer. Divorced from James Francis, actor William Gaston, and Kenneth MacKenna.

Appeared in: **1929** Dangerous Curves; Honest Finder; The Marriage Playground; The Illusion; Gentlemen of the Press; The Cocoanuts. **1930** Behind the Makeup; The Children; Paramount on Parade; A Notorious Affair; Raffles; Let's Go Native; For the Defense; The Virtuous Sin; Passion Flower; The Street of Chance. **1931** The Vice Squad; Transgression; Guilty Hands; Scandal Sheet; Ladies' Man; Girls about Town; 24 Hours. **1932** The False Madonna; House of Scandal; Strangers in Love; Man Wanted; Jewel Robbery; Street of Women; One Way Passage; Trouble in Paradise; Cynara. **1933** The Keyhole; The House on 56th Street; Mary Stevens, M.D.; Storm at Daybreak; I Loved a Woman. **1934** Mandalay; Wonder Bar; Dr. Monica; British Agent. **1935** Living on Velvet; The Goose and the Gander; Stranded; I Found Stella Parish. **1936** The White Angel; Give Me Your Heart; Stolen Holiday; One Hour of Romance. **1937** Another Dawn; Confession; First Lady; Unlawful. **1938** Secrets of an Actress; My Bill; Women Are Like That; Comet over Broadway. **1939** In Name Only; King of the Underworld; Women in the Wind. **1940** It's a Date; Little Men; When the Daltons Rode. **1941** The Man Who Lost Himself; Charley's Aunt; The Feminine Touch; Play Girl. **1942** Always in My Heart; Between Us Girls. **1944** Four Jills in a Jeep; Hours Between. **1945** Divorce; Allotment Wives, Inc. **1946** Wife Wanted.

FRANCIS, OLIN

Born: Sept. 13, 1892, Mooreville, Miss. Died: June 30, 1952, Hollywood, Calif. Stage and screen actor.

Appeared in: **1921** A Knight of the West. **1922** Fighting Devil; The Jungle Goddess (serial). **1924** Rarin' to Go; Walloping Wallace. **1925** Let's Go Gallagher. **1926** Call of the Klondike; Sea Beast. **1927** Win That Girl; The Kid Brother; Cross Breed; Flying U Ranch. **1928** The Devil's Trademark; Stormy Waters; Free Lips. **1930** Kismet. **1931** Adios; Homicide Squad; Lariats and Sixshooters; Suicide Fleet. **1932** Tex Takes a Holiday; A Woman Commands; .45 Calibre Echo; The Drifter. **1935** Hard Rock Harrigan. **1936** I Conquer the Sea; O'Malley of the Mounted. **1938** Red River Range; Two-Gun Justice; Overland Stage Raiders. **1939** Captain Fury. **1940** Kit Carson.

FRANCIS, ROBERT (Robert Charles Francis)

Born: Feb. 26, 1930, Glendale, Calif. Died: July 31, 1955, Burbank, Calif. (plane crash). Screen actor.

Appeared in: **1954** The Caine Mutiny (film debut); They Rode West. **1955** The Long Gray Line; The Bamboo Prison.

FRANCISCO, BETTY

Born: 1900, Little Rock, Ark. Died: Nov. 25, 1950, El Cerito, Calif. (heart attack). Stage and screen actress.

Appeared in: **1921** Greater Than Love; A Guilty Conscience; Riding with

Death; Straight from Paris. **1922** Across the Continent; Her Night of Nights. **1923** Ashes of Vengeance; Crinoline and Romance; The Darling of New York; Double Dealing; Flaming Youth; The Love Piker; Maytime; Noise in Newboro; The Old Fool; Poor Men's Wives. **1924** Big Timber; East of Broadway; Gambling Wives; How to Educate a Wife; On Probation. **1925** Faint Perfume; Fair Play; Fifth Avenue Models; Jimmie's Millions; Private Affairs; Seven Keys to Baldpate; Wasted Lives. **1926** Don Juan's Three Nights; The Lily; Man Bait; The Phantom of the Forest. **1927** The Gingham Girl; A Boy of the Streets; The Gay Retreat; Uneasy Payments; Too Many Crooks. **1928** Broadway Daddies; You Can't Beat the Law; Queen of the Chorus. **1929** Smiling Irish Eyes; Broadway; The Spirit of Youth. **1930** The Lotus Lady; Street of Chance; Madam Satan; The Widow from Chicago. **1931** Charlie Chan Carries On; Good Sport. **1932** Mystery Ranch.

FRANEY, WILLIAM "BILLY"

Born: 1885, Chicago, Ill. Died: Dec. 9, 1940, Hollywood, Calif. (influenza). Screen actor and film producer. Entered films in 1915.

Appeared in: **1915** Hubby's Cure. **1917** One Damp Day. **1918** An Honest Man. **1921** A Knight of the West. **1922** Quincy Adams Sawyer; A Western Demon. **1923** The Town Scandal; Tea with a Kick. **1924** Mile-a-Minute Morgan; North of Alaska; Border Women. **1925** Manhattan Madness; S.O.S. Perils of the Sea; The Great Sensation; The Fear Fighter; Kit Carson over the Great Divide. **1926** Senor Daredevil; King of the Saddle; The King of the Turf; A Desperate Moment; Code of the Northwest; Danger Quest; Moran of the Mounted; The Deadline; The Dangerous Dude. **1927** Aflame in the Sky; The Royal American; The Racing Fool; She's a Sheik; King of the Herd; Out All Night; The Lost Limited; Red Signals. **1928** Five and Ten-Cent Annie; Under the Tonto Rim; The Glorious Trail; Romance of a Rogue; The Canyon of Adventure. **1929** The Broadway Hoofer; Anne against the World; The Royal Rider; Cheyenne. **1930** The Heroic Lover. **1932** The Millionaire Cat (short); The Iceman's Ball (short). **1933** Somewhere in Sonora; Kickin' the Crown Around (short); Luncheon at Twelve (short). **1934** No More Women. **1935** Restless Knights (short); Old Sawbones (short). **1936** Wholesailing Along (short). **1937** Quick Money; The Marriage Business; Maid's Night Out; Joy of Living; Having a Wonderful Time; plus the following shorts: Locks and Bonds; Dumb's the Word; Tramp Trouble; Morning, Judge; Edgar and Goliath. **1938** The following shorts: Ears of Experience; False Roomers; Kennedy's Castle; Fool Coverage; Beaux and Errors; A Clean Sweep; Dummy Owner. **1939** The following shorts: Maid to Order; Clock Wise; Baby Daze; Feathered Pests; Act Your Age; Kennedy the Great. **1940** The following shorts: Slightly at Sea; Mutiny in the County; 'Taint Legal; Sunk by the Census; Trailer Tragedy; Drafted in the Depot. **1941** Mad About Moonshine (short); It Happened All Night (short).

FRANK, CARL

Born: 1909. Died: Sept. 23, 1972, St. John, Virgin Islands. Screen, stage, radio and television actor.

Appeared in: **1948** Lady from Shanghai.

FRANK, CHRISTIAN J. (Christian Julius Frank)

Born: Mar. 13, 1890, New York. Died: Dec. 10, 1967, Los Angeles, Calif. (cancer). Screen actor.

Appeared in: **1920** Thunderbolt Jack (serial). **1922** The Guttersnipe; Out of the Silent North; Wild Honey. **1923** The Ragged Edge. **1924** The Love Bandit. **1925** The Ancient Highway; Black Cyclone; Manhattan Madness. **1926** Forlorn River; The Lady of the Harem. **1927** Nevada; Arizona Bound. **1928** The Cavalier; Chicago After Midnight; Easy Come, Easy Go. **1929** Sunset Pass. **1930** Under Montana Skies. **1931** Hard Hombre. **1932** My Pal the King. **1933** The Sunset Pass (and 1929 version). **1934** Embarrassing Moments.

FRANK, WILLIAM

Born: 1880. Died: Dec. 23, 1925, Hollywood, Calif. (Bright's disease). Stage and screen actor. Was in early Roach comedies.

Appeared in: **1925** The Last Edition.

FRANKAU, RONALD

Born: Feb. 22, 1894, London, England. Died: Sept. 11, 1951. Screen, stage and radio actor. Married to actress Cynthia Robins. Divorced from Hilda Priest and Renee Roberts.

Appeared in: **1931** The Skin Game; Potiphar's Wife (aka Her Strange Desire—US 1932); Let's Love and Laugh (aka Bridegroom for Two—US 1932); The Calendar (aka Bachelor's Folly—US 1932); The Other Mrs. Phipps. **1934** Radio Parade of 1935 (US 1935). **1936** Talking Hands; International Revue. **1939** His Brother's Keeper. **1947** The Ghosts of Berkeley Square.

FRANKEL, FRANCHON

Born: 1874. Died: Aug. 12, 1937, Hollywood, Calif. Screen and stage actress.

Appeared in: **1927** Jake the Plumber; Sensation Seekers. **1928** Desperate Courage. **1930** Pick 'Em Young (short).

FRANKEL, HARRY

Died: June 12, 1948. Screen and radio actor. Known on radio as "Singing Sam."

FRANKEUR, PAUL

Born: 1905, France. Died: 1974, France (?). Screen actor.

Appeared in: **1947** Les Enfants du Paradis. **1948** Le Pere Tranquille (aka Mr. Orchid). **1949** Devil's Daughter; Counter Investigation. **1951** Nana (US 1957). **1952** Jour de Fete (The Big Day); Under the Paris Sky. **1957** We are All Murderers; Every Second Counts; The Winner's Circle. **1959** Touchez Pas au Grisbi (Don't Touch the Loot) (aka Grisbi—US); Oeil pour Oeil (An Eye for an Eye); Le Rouge est Mis (The Red Light is On aka Speaking of Murder—US). **1960** Voulez-Vous Danser avec Moi (Come Dance with Me!); Rue de Paris; Marie Octobre. **1961** Le Desordre et la Nuit (Disorder and Night aka Night Affair—US 1962). **1962** Archimede le Clochard (Archimede the Tramp aka The Magnificent Tramp—US); La Viaccia. **1963** Monkey in Winter. **1969** La Voie Lactee (The Milky Way).

FRANKLIN, IRENE

Born: 1884 or 1876, St. Louis, Mo. Died: June 16, 1941, Englewood, N.J. (cerebral hemorrhage). Screen, stage, radio, vaudeville actress and singer.

Appeared in: **1929** The American Comedienne (short); Those Were the Days (short). **1934** Change of Heart; A Very Honorable Guy; Registered Nurse; The Woman in His Life; Lazy River; The President Vanishes; Strictly Dynamite; Down to Their Last Yacht. **1935** Ladies Crave Excitement; Affairs of Susan; Death Flies East. **1936** Whipsaw; The Song and Dance Man; Timothy's Quest; Fatal Lady; Wanted: Jane Turner; Along Came Love. **1937** Midnight Madonna; Married before Breakfast; Blazing Barriers; Saratoga. **1938** Rebellious Daughters; Flirting with Fate. **1939** Fixer Dugan.

FRANKLIN, MARTHA

Born: 1876. Died: Apr. 19, 1929. Screen actress.

Appeared in: **1922** Little Miss Smiles. **1923** Other Men's Daughters; Trilby. **1924** Racing Luck. **1925** Don Q, Son of Zorro; Keep Smiling. **1926** The Duchess of Buffalo. **1927** The Beloved Rogue; Perch of the Devil; The Climbers; Serenade; Uncle Tom's Cabin. **1928** Love and Learn; Wheel of Chance; The Woman from Moscow. **1929** Points West; The Younger Generation.

FRANKLIN, RUPERT

Born: 1862. Died: Jan. 14, 1939, Los Angeles, Calif. Screen actor.

Appeared in: **1925** The Prairie Wife.

FRANKLIN, SIDNEY

Born: 1870. Died: Mar. 18, 1931, Hollywood, Calif. Screen and stage actor.

Appeared in: **1921** Playing with Fire; The Three Musketeers. **1922** Welcome Children; The Vermillion Pencil; The Guttersnipe; Call of Home; Dusk to Dawn. **1923** The Love Trap; Fashion Row. **1924** A Boy of Flanders; In Hollywood with Potash and Perlmutter. **1925** One of the Bravest; The Texas Trail; His People. **1926** Block Signal; Rose of the Tenements; Somebody's Mother. **1927** Fighting Failure; King of Kings; Colleen. **1928** Wheel of Chance. **1930** Lummox; Puttin' on the Ritz. **1932** The Kid from Spain.

FRANKLYN, IRWIN R.

Born: Jan. 8, 1904, New York, N.Y. Died: Sept. 7, 1966, Hollywood, Calif. (heart attack). Screen, stage actor, screenwriter, film producer and publicist. Married to actress Katherine Green.

FRANKLYN, LEO

Born: Apr. 7, 1897, London, England. Died: Sept. 17, 1975, London, England (heart attack). Screen, stage and television actor. Father of actor William Franklyn.

Appeared in: **1959** The Night We Dropped a Clanger (aka Make Mine a Double—US 1961).

FRANKS, DENNIS

Born: 1902. Died: Oct. 1967, Dublin, Ireland (heart attack). Stage and screen actor.

Appeared in: **1965** Ballad in Blue (aka Blues for Lovers—US 1966).

FRANTZ, DALIES E.

Born: 1908, Colorado. Died: Dec. 1, 1965, Dallas, Tex. (heart attack). Screen actor, concert pianist and artist.

Appeared in: **1938** Sweethearts. **1939** Balalaika. **1940** I Take This Woman.

FRASER, CONSTANCE

Born: 1910, England. Died: May 1973, Worthing, England. Screen and television actress.

Appeared in: **1956** The Feminine Touch (aka The Gentle Touch—US 1957).

FRASER, HARRY

Born: 1889. Died: Apr. 8, 1974, Pomona, Calif. Screen actor, film producer, director and screenwriter.

Appeared in: **1916** The Iron Claw (serial). **1917** The Mystery of the Double Cross (serial). **1921** Burn 'Em Up Barnes; Oh Mary Be Careful. **1923** Luck. **1924** Westbound.

FRAWLEY, WILLIAM

Born: Feb. 26, 1887, Burlington, Iowa. Died: Mar. 3, 1966, Los Angeles, Calif. (heart attack). Screen, stage, vaudeville, and television actor. Divorced from Louise Frawley with whom he appeared in vaudeville.

Appeared in: **1916** Lord Loveland Discovers America. **1929** Turkey for Two (short); Fancy That (short). **1931** Surrender. **1933** Hell and High Water; Moonlight and Pretzels. **1934** Bolero; The Witching Hour; Shoot the Works; Here Is My Heart; The Lemon Drop Kid; The Crime Doctor; Miss Fane's Baby Is Stolen. **1935** Ship Cafe; Alibi Ike; Welcome Home; Harmony Lane; Car 99; Hold 'Em Yale; College Scandal. **1936** Strike Me Pink; Desire; The Princess Comes Along; F Man; Rose Bowl; Three Cheers for Love; Three Married Men; The General Died at Dawn. **1937** Blossoms on Broadway; Something to Sing About; High, Wide and Handsome; Double or Nothing. **1938** Mad about Music; Professor Beware; Sons of the Legion; Touchdown Army; Crime Takes a Holiday. **1939** Persons in Hiding; St. Louis Blues; Ambush; Huckleberry Finn; Rose of Washington Square; Ex-Champ; Grand Jury Secrets; Stop, Look and Love; Night Work. **1940** The Farmer's Daughter; Opened by Mistake; Those Were the Days; Untamed; Golden Gloves; Rhythm on the River; The Quarterback; Sandy Gets Her Man; One Night in the Tropics. **1941** The Bride Came C.O.D.; Public Enemies; Six Lessons from Madame La Zonga; Dancing on a Dime; Footsteps in the Dark; Cracked Nuts; Blondie in Society. **1942** Treat 'Em Rough; Roxie Hart; It Happened in Flatbush; Give Out, Sisters; Moonlight in Havana; Wildcat; Gentleman Jim. **1943** Larceny with Music; We've Never Been Licked; Whistling in Brooklyn. **1944** The Fighting Seabees; Going My Way; Minstrel Man; Lake Placid Serenade. **1945** Flame of Barbary Coast; Lady on a Train; Hitchhike to Happiness. **1946** The Ziegfeld Follies; Rendezvous with Annie; The Inner Circle; The Crime Doctor's Manhunt; The Virginian. **1947** Mother Wore Tights; Miracle on 34th Street; My Wild Irish Rose; I Wonder Who's Kissing Her Now; Monsieur Verdoux; Down to Earth; The Hit Parade of 1947; Blondie's Anniversary. **1948** The Babe Ruth Story; Good Sam; Texas, Brooklyn and Heaven; Joe Palooka in Winner Take All; Chicken Every Sunday; The Girl from Manhattan. **1949** Home in San Antone; The Lady Takes a Sailor; East Side, West Side; The Lone Wolf and His Lady. **1950** Kiss Tomorrow Goodbye; Pretty Baby; Blondie's Hero; Kill the Umpire. **1951** The Lemon Drop Kid (and 1934 version); Abbott and Costello Meet the Invisible Man; Rhubarb. **1952** Rancho Notorious. **1962** Safe at Home!

FRAZER, ALEX (Alex Fraser)

Born: 1900. Died: July 30, 1958, Hollywood, Calif. (heart attack). Screen, stage and radio actor.

Appeared in: **1949** The Blonde Bandit; The Cowboy and the Indians; Secret of St. Ives. **1953** Gentlemen Prefer Blondes; Loose in London; War of the Worlds. **1956** Bigger than Life; The Boss.

FRAZER, ROBERT W.

Born: June 29, 1891, Worcester, Mass. Died: Aug. 17, 1944, Los Angeles, Calif. Stage and screen actor.

Appeared in: **1912** Robin Hood. **1916** The Feast of Life. **1919** The Bramble Bush. **1921** Love, Hate and a Woman; Without Limit. **1922** The Faithless Sex; Fascination; How Women Love; My Friend the Devil; Partners of the Sunset; When the Desert Calls. **1923** As a Man Lives; A Chapter in Her Life; Jazzmania; The Love Piker. **1924** Women Who Give; Men; After the Ball; Bread; Broken Barriers; The Foolish Virgin; When a Man's a Man; The Mine with the Iron Door; Traffic in Hearts. **1925** Splendid Road; Keeper of the Bees; The Charmer; The Scarlet West; The Golden Strain; The Love Gamble; Miss Bluebeard; The Other Woman's Story; Why Women Love (aka Sea Woman and Barriers Aflame); The White Desert. **1926** The City; Dame Chance; Desert Gold; The Isle of Retribution; Secret Orders; Sin Cargo; The Speeding Venus. **1927** Back to God's Country; One Hour to Love; The Silent Hero; Wanted a Coward. **1928** Out of the Ruins; The Little Snob; The Scarlet Dove; Burning up Broadway; City of Purple Dreams; Black Butterflies. **1929** The Woman I Love; Frozen Justice; Sioux Blood; Careers; The Drake Case. **1930** Beyond the Law. **1931** Ten Nights in a Barroom; Mystery Trooper (serial); Two-Gun Caballero. **1932** Rainbow Trail; Saddle Buster; Discarded Lovers; Arm of the Law; King Murder; White Zombie. **1933** Vampire Bat; Justice Takes a Holiday; Notorious But Nice; The Fighting Parson; Found Alive. **1934** Guilty Parents; Monte Carlo Nights; Fifteen Wives; Love Past Thirty; The Trail Beyond; Counsel for the Defense; Fight Trooper; One in a Million. **1935** The Fighting Pilot; Death from a Distance; Ladies Crave Excitement; Never Too Late; The World Accuses; Circumstantial Evidence; Public Opinion. **1936** Garden of Allah; Murder at Glen Athol; Below the Deadline; Gambling Souls; The Rest Cure; It Couldn't Have Happened; Easy Money. **1937** Black Aces; Left Handed Law. **1938** On the Great White Trail; Religious Racketeer; Cipher Bureau. **1939** Navy Secrets; Six-Gun Rhythm; Juarez and

Maximilian; Mystic Circle Murder; Danger of the Tong; Crashing Thru. **1940** One Man's Law. **1941** Pals of the Pecos; Law of the Wilds; Roar of the Press; Gangs of Sonora; Gunman from Bodie. **1942** Black Dragons; Riders of the West; Dawn of the Great Divide; A Night for Crime. **1943** Daredevils of the West; The Stranger from Pecos; Wagon Tracks West. **1944** Lawmen; Partners of the Trail; Forty Thieves.

FRAZIER, H. C.
Born: 1894. Died: Aug. 2, 1949, Hollywood, Calif. Screen actor and stand-in.

FRAZIN, GLADYS
Born: 1901. Died: Mar. 9, 1939, New York, N.Y. (suicide—jumped from apartment window). Stage and screen actress. Divorced from actor Monte Banks (dec. 1950).

Appeared in: **1924** Let Not Man Put Asunder. **1927** The Winning Oar. **1928** Inspiration; Spangles; Blue Peter. **1929** Power Over Men; The Return of the Rat. **1930** The Compulsory Husband; Kiss Me Sergeant. **1931** The Other Woman.

FRECHETTE, MARK
Born: Dec. 4, 1947. Died: Sept. 27, 1975, Norfolk, Mass. (accident while an inmate in prison). Screen actor.

Appeared in: **1970** Zabriskie Point.

FREDERICI, BLANCHE (Blanche Friderici Campbell aka BLANCHE FRIDERICI)
Born: 1878, Brooklyn, N.Y. Died: Dec. 24, 1933, Visalia, Calif. (heart attack). Stage and screen actress. Entered films in 1920.

Appeared in: **1922** No Trespassing. **1928** Fleetwing; Gentlemen Prefer Blondes; Sadie Thompson (stage and film versions). **1929** Stolen Love; Wonder of Women; The Trespasser; Jazz Heaven; The Awful Truth. **1930** Soldiers and Women; Courage; The Office Wife; Personality; Last of the Duanes; Kismet; The Bad One; Billy the Kid; The Cat Creeps; Numbered Men. **1931** Ten Cents a Dance; Woman Hungry; A Dangerous Affair; Wicked; Night Nurse; Murder by the Clock; The Woman Between; Friends and Lovers; Honor of the Family. **1932** Mata Hari; Thirteen Women; A Farewell to Arms; Lady with a Past; Love Starved; The Hatchet Man; So Big; Miss Pinkerton; Love Me Tonight; The Night Club; Young Bride. **1933** The Barbarian; Adorable; Hold Your Man; Aggie Appleby—Maker of Men; The Way to Love; Alimony Madness; Secrets; Behind Jury Doors; Man of the Forest; Flying Down to Rio. **1934** Thundering Herd; All of Me; It Happened One Night.

FREDERICK, PAULINE (Pauline Libbey)
Born: Aug. 12, 1884, Boston, Mass. Died: Sept. 19, 1938, Los Angeles, Calif. (asthma). Stage and screen actress. Divorced from actor Willard Mack (dec. 1934).

Appeared in: **1915** The Eternal City (film debut); Bella Donna; Zaza; Sold; Lydia Gilmore. **1916** The Moment Before; The Woman in the Case; Her Honor, the Governor; Audrey. **1917** The Slave Island; Sleeping Fires. **1918** Her Final Reckoning; Fedora; La Tosca; Resurrection; Mrs. Dane's Defense. **1919** Out of the Shadow; One Week of Life; The Peace of the Roaring River; Bonds of Love; Paid in Full. **1920** Paliser Case; Madame X. **1921** Slave of Vanity; Roads of Destiny; Mistress of Shenstone; Salvage; The Sting of the Lash; The Lure of Jade. **1922** Two Kinds of Women; The Woman Breed; The Glory of Clementine. **1924** Three Women; Fast Set; Smouldering Fires; Let Not Man Put Asunder; Married Flirts. **1925** The Lady. **1926** Devil's Island; Her Honor, the Governor (and 1916 version); Josselyn's Wife. **1927** Mumsie; The Nest. **1928** Woman from Moscow; On Trial. **1929** The Sacred Flame; Evidence. **1931** This Modern Age. **1932** Wayward; The Phantom of Crestwood. **1933** Self-Defense. **1934** Social Register. **1935** My Marriage. **1936** Ramona. **1937** Thank You, Mr. Moto. **1938** The Buccaneer.

FREDERICKS, CHARLES
Born: 1920. Died: May 14, 1970, Sherman Oaks, Calif. (heart attack). Screen, stage, radio and television actor.

Appeared in: **1954** Thunder Pass; Port of Hell. **1955** Night Freight; Las Vegas Shakedown; Treasure of Ruby Hills; Tarzan's Hidden Jungle. **1957** Hell Canyon. **1961** Lad: A Dog. **1962** Hemingway's Adventures of a Young Man; Tender Is the Night; The Cabinet of Caligari. **1963** To Kill a Mockingbird. **1964** A House Is Not a Home; My Fair Lady. **1965** The Great Race.

FREED, ALAN
Born: Oct. 15, 1922. Died: Jan. 20, 1965, Palm Springs, Calif. (uremia). Radio disc jockey and screen actor.

Appeared in: **1956** Rock Around the Clock. **1957** Mister Rock 'N Roll; Don't Knock the Rock. **1959** Go Johnny Go.

FREEDLEY, VINTON
Born: 1892. Died: June 5, 1969, New York, N.Y. Stage producer and screen actor.

Appeared in: **1943** Stagedoor Canteen.

FREEMAN, AL
Born: 1884. Died: Mar. 22, 1956, Los Angeles, Calif. Screen actor. Father of screen actor Al Freeman, Jr.

FREEMAN, HOWARD
Born: Dec. 9, 1899, Helena, Mont. Died: Dec. 11, 1967, New York, N.Y. Screen, stage and television actor.

Appeared in: **1943** Pilot No. 5; Margin for Error; Girl Crazy; Whistling in Brooklyn; Lost Angel; Air Raid Wardens; Slightly Dangerous; Hitler's Hangman. **1944** Carolina Blues; Dancing in Manhattan; Meet Miss Bobby-Socks; Meet the People; Once upon a Time; Rationing; Secret Command; The Unwritten Code. **1945** I'll Tell the World; Mexicana; This Love of Ours; That Night with You; You Came Along; Where Do We Go from Here?; A Song to Remember. **1946** House of Horrors; Inside Job; Night and Day; So Goes My Love; Abilene Town; Susie Steps Out; Sweet Guy; Monsieur Beaucaire; The Blue Dahlia. **1947** California; Cigarette Girl; Cross My Heart; My Brother Talks to Horses; That Way with Women; Cass Timberland; Magic Town; Long Night; Perfect Marriage. **1948** Summer Holiday; The Time of Your Life; Cry of the City; Arthur Takes Over; Give My Regards to Broadway; Letter from an Unknown Woman; Up in Central Park; Girl from Manhattan; The Snake Pit; If You Knew Suzie. **1949** Take One False Step. **1950** Perfect Strangers. **1951** Double Dynamite. **1952** Scaramouche; The Turning Point; Million Dollar Mermaid. **1953** No Time for Sergeants; Remains to Be Seen; Raiders of the Seven Seas. **1965** Dear Brigitte. Foreign films: We Are All Gamblers; Carriage Trade; Monsieur Et Madame.

FREEMAN, MAURICE
Born: 1872. Died: Mar. 26, 1953, Bayshore, N.Y. Screen, stage and vaudeville actor. Was in vaudeville with his wife, Nadine Winston, in an act billed as "Tony and the Stork." Entered films in 1915.

Appeared in: **1923** Stephen Steps Out. **1937** Strangers on a Honeymoon.

FREEMAN, RAOUL (Reuel Silvan Freeman)
Born: Apr. 24, 1894, Georgia. Died: Feb. 17, 1971, Redondo Beach, Calif. (heart disease). Stage and screen actor.

Appeared in: **1956** Around the World in 80 Days.

FREEMAN, WILLIAM B.
Died: June 8, 1932, Brockton, Mass. Stage and screen actor.

Appeared in: **1918** Mirandy Smiles.

FREEMAN-MITFORD, RUPERT
Born: 1895. Died: Aug. 7, 1939, London, England. Screen actor.

Appeared in: **1939** Goodbye, Mr. Chips.

FREIL, EDWARD
Born: 1878. Died: July 30, 1938, Los Angeles, Calif. Screen, vaudeville, circus actor and film stuntman.

FRENCH, CHARLES K. (Charles E. Krauss)
Born: 1860, Columbus, Ohio. Died: Aug. 2, 1952, Hollywood, Calif. (heart attack). Screen, stage, minstrel actor and film director. Married to actress Helen French (dec. 1917). Entered films in 1908.

Appeared in: **1909** A True Indian's Heart. **1915** The Coward. **1920** Stronger Than Death. **1921** Bare Knuckles; Hands Off; The Last Trail; The Night Horsemen; The Road Demon; Beyond. **1922** The Bearcat; Her Own Money; If You Believe It, It's So; Mixed Faces; The Unfoldment; West of Chicago; The Woman He Loved; The Yosemite Trail; Moran of the Lady Letty; Smudge; The Truthful Liar; White Shoulders. **1923** The Extra Girl; The Abysmal Brute; Grumpy; The Lonely Road; A Woman of Paris; Alias the Night Wind; Blinky; Gentle Julia; Hell's Hole; Man's Size; The Ramblin' Kid. **1924** Abraham Lincoln; The Torrent; Free and Equal (reissue and retitle of The Coward—1915); Oh, You Tony; Pride of Sunshine Alley; The Sawdust Trail; Being Respectable. **1925** The Girl of Gold; The Saddle Hawk; Let 'Er Buck; Speed Mad; The Texas Trail; Too Much Youth; The Way of a Girl. **1926** War Paint; The Flaming Frontier; Frenzied Flames; Hands Up!; The Hollywood Reporter; The Rainmaker; Oh, What a Night!; The Runaway Express; Under Western Skies; The Winning Wallop. **1927** Good as Gold; The Adventurous Soul; Cross Breed; The Cruise of the Hellion; The Down Grade; Fast and Furious; Man, Woman and Sin; The Meddlin' Stranger; One Chance in a Million; Ride 'Em High. **1928** Big Hop; The Charge of the Gauchos; The Cowboy Cavalier; The Flying Buckaroo; Riding for Fame. **1929** King of the Rodeo; The Last Warning. **1930** Fast Work (short); Overland Bound. **1931** Chickens Come Home (short). **1932** Boy, Oh, Boy (short). **1933** Big Squeal (short); Crossfire. **1935** When a Man Sees Red; The Crimson Trail; The Phantom Empire (serial). **1939** Rovin' Tumbleweeds.

FRENCH, GEORGE B.
Born: Apr. 14, 1883, Storm Lake, Iowa. Died: June 9, 1961, Hollywood, Calif. (heart attack). Stage and screen actor.

Appeared in: **1917** Black Hands and Soap Suds; Her Friend the Chauffeur;

Small Change; Twice in the Same Place; Love and the Ice Man; His Last Pill; Those Wedding Bells; Father's Bright Idea; Father Was Right; The Milky Way; With the Mummie's Help. **1918** Tarzan of the Apes; Wanted—A Leading Lady. **1921** His Pajama Girl. **1924** Reckless Romance; Wandering Husbands. **1925** Bashful Buccaneer; Flying Thru; The Snob Buster. **1926** Cupid's Knockout. **1927** Grinning Guns; Horse Shoes; The Lost Limited; One Glorious Scrap. **1928** Sawdust Paradise; Won in the Clouds; The Black Pear. Prior to 1929 "Christie" comedies. **1930** Street of Chance. **1935** Hoi Polloi (short).

FRENCH, HELEN (Helen Krauss)

Born: Feb. 13, 1863, Ohio. Died: Mar. 12, 1917, Los Angeles, Calif. (endocarditis). Stage and screen actress. Married to actor Charles K. French (dec. 1952).

FRESNAY, PIERRE (Pierre-Jules Laudenbach)

Born: Apr. 2, 1897, Paris, France. Died: Jan. 9, 1975, Neuilly-sur-Seine, France (respiratory ailment). Screen and stage actor. Married to actress Yvonne Printemps (dec. 1977).

Appeared in: **1915** France D'Abord. **1922** Les Mysteres de Paris. **1924** Rocanbole. **1929** La Vierge Folle. **1931** Marius. **1932** Fanny. **1934** Caesar; The Man Who Knew Too Much. **1935** Le Roman d'un Jeune Homme Pauvre; Koenigsmark; La Dame aux Camelias. **1936** Sous Les Yeux D'Occident; Mademoiselle Docteur. **1937** La Grande Illusion (The Grand Illusion—US 1938); Razumov; Alibi. **1938** Adrienne Lecouvreur. **1939** Three Waltzes; La Charrette Fantome (The Phantom Chariotte aka The Phantom Wagon); Le Puritain (The Puritan). **1940** S.O.S. Mediterranean. **1941** Le Dernier des Six. **1943** L'Assassin Habite au 21 (The Murderer Lives at Number 21—US 1947); Le Voyageur Sans Barage; Le Corbeau (The Raven—US 1948). **1947** Le Visiteur; Carnival of Sinners. **1948** Barry; Les Condamnes; Vient de Paraitre; Street of Shadows. **1949** Monsieur Vincent; Devil's Daughter; Strangers in the House; La Valse de Paris. **1950** Tainted; The Paris Waltz; Dieu a Besoin des Hommes (God Needs Men—US 1951). **1951** Un Grand Patrol; Au Grand Balcon. **1952** Le Voyage en Amerique (Voyage to America); Il est Minuit Docteur Schweitzer; The Perfectionist; The Amazing Monsieur Fabre. **1953** La Rome Napoleon; La Defroque. **1955** Les Aristocrates; Les Evades. **1956** L'Homme aux Clefs D'Or. **1957** Les Oeufs de L'Autruche; Les Fanatiques (The Fanatics aka A Bomb for a Dictator—US 1963). **1958** Et ta Soeur; Tant D'Amour Perdu. **1959** Les Affreux. **1960** La Milliente Fenetre; Les Vieux de la Vielle; The Ostrich has Two Eggs.

FREY, ARNO

Born: Oct. 11, 1900, Munich, Germany. Died: June 26, 1961, Los Angeles, Calif. (heart attack). Screen, stage and radio actor.

Appeared in: **1933** Best of Enemies. **1934** Hell in the Heavens. **1935** Mystery Woman. **1941** Man Hunt. **1942** Jungle Siren; Valley of the Hunted Men. **1943** Appointment in Berlin; Chetniks; They Came to Blow Up America; Hangmen Also Die; Tiger Fangs. **1944** Tampico; U-Boat Prisoner. **1945** The Adventures of Rusty. **1946** Rendezvous 24. **1953** The Desert Rats.

FREY, NATHANIEL

Born: 1913, N.Y. Died: Nov. 7, 1970, New York, N.Y. (cancer). Screen, stage and television actor.

Appeared in: **1957** Kiss Them for Me. **1958** Damn Yankees (stage and film versions). **1968** What's So Bad about Feeling Good?

FRIEBUS, THEODORE

Born: 1879, Washington, D.C. Died: Dec. 26, 1917, New York, N.Y. (heart disease). Stage and screen actor.

Appeared in: **1916** Pearl of the Navy (serial). **1917** Pearl of the Army (serial); The Warfare of the Flesh; The Mystery of the Double Cross (serial); Transgressors.

FRIEDGEN, JOHN RAYMOND

Born: 1893, New York, N.Y. Died: Mar. 1, 1966, Beverly Hills, Calif. Screen, stage actor, film producer and director. Appeared in early films for Vitagraph and Biograph.

FRIEDKIN, JOEL

Born: May 15, 1885, Russia. Died: Sept. 19, 1954, Burbank, Calif. Screen actor.

Appeared in: **1940** The Last Alarm; Who Killed Aunt Maggie? **1941** Borrowed Hero; Outlaws of the Cherokee Trail; Richest Man in Town. **1942** Bad Men of the Hills; The Cyclone Kid; The Sombrero Kid. **1943** Frontier Fury. **1944** Uncertain Glory; Sundown Valley; Wyoming Hurricane; Sagebrush Heroes. **1945** Don Juan Quilligan; Murder, He Says; The Great John L. **1946** California Goldrush; Unexpected Guest. **1947** Saddle Pals. **1948** Feudin', Fussin' and A-Fightin'; Phantom Valley; Money Madness; False Paradise; Strange Gamble. **1950** Lightning Guns. **1951** Bedtime for Bonzo; Fury of the Congo.

FRIEDMANN, SHRAGA

Born: 1923, Warsaw, Poland. Died: July 1970, Tel Aviv, Israel (heart attack). Israeli screen and stage actor. Married to actress Shoshannah Ravid.

Appeared in: **1965** Sallah. **1966** Judith.

FRIGANZA, TRIXIE (Delia O'Callahan)

Born: Nov. 29, 1870, Grenola, Kans. Died: Feb. 27, 1955, Flintridge, Calif. (arthritis). Screen, stage and vaudeville actress. Sister of actress Therese Thompson (dec. 1936).

Appeared in: **1923** Mind over Motor. **1925** The Charmer; The Road to Yesterday; Proud Flesh; Borrowed Finery; The Coming of Amos. **1926** Almost a Lady; Monte Carlo; The Whole Town's Talking. **1927** A Racing Romeo. **1928** Thanks for the Buggy Ride; Gentlemen Prefer Blondes. **1929** My Bag O'Trix (short). **1930** Free and Easy; Strong and Willing (short). Other shorts prior to 1933: Motor Maniac; The March of Time. **1933** Myrt and Marge. **1935** Wanderer of the Wasteland. **1940** If I Had My Way.

FRINTON, FREDDIE (Freddie Hargate)

Born: 1912, England. Died: Oct. 16, 1968, Poole, England. Screen, vaudeville, television actor and comedian.

Appeared in: **1960** Make Mine Mink.

FRISCH, LORE

Born: 1925, Germany. Died: July 1962, East Berlin, Germany (suicide). German screen and television actress.

Appeared in: Csar and Carpenter; My Wife Makes Music.

FRISCO, JOE (Lewis Joseph)

Born: 1890, Rock Island, Ill. Died: Feb. 16, 1958, Hollywood, Calif. Screen, stage and vaudeville actor.

Appeared in: **1930** The following shorts: The Benefit; The Song Plugger; The Happy Hottentots; The Border Patrol. **1931** The Gorilla. **1938** Western Jamboree. **1940** Ride, Tenderfoot, Ride. **1944** Atlantic City. **1945** Shady Lady. **1947** That's My Man. **1950** Riding High. **1957** Sweet Smell of Success.

FRITSCH, WILLY

Born: Jan. 27, 1901, Kattowitz, Germany. Died: July 13, 1973, Hamburg, Germany (heart attack). Screen and stage actor. Entered films in 1921. Married to dancer Dinah Grace (dec. 1963). Father of actor Thomas Fritsch.

Appeared in: **1921** Razzia. **1923** Die Fahrt ins Gluck; Seine Frau, die Unbekannte. **1924** Guillotine; Mutter und Kind. **1925** Blitzzug der Liebe; Der Farmer aus Texas; Das Madchen mit der Protektion; Der Tanzer meiner Frau; Ein Walzertraum. **1926** Die Doxerbraut; Die Fahrt ins Abenteuer; Die Keusche Susanne; Der Prinz und die Tanzerin. **1927** Die Frau im Schrank; Der Letzte Walzer (The Last Waltz); Schuldig (Guilty); Die Selige Excellenz (His Late Excellency); Die Sieben Tochter der Frau Guyrkovics; Die Carmen von St. Pauli; Ihr Dunkler Punkt. **1928** Spione (Spies); Der Tanzstudent; Ungarische Rhapsodie (Hungarian Rhapsody). **1929** Die Frau im Mond; Melodie des Herzens (Melody of the Heart). **1930** Die Drei von der Tankstelle (Three from the Gasoline Station—US 1931); Liebeswalzer (Love Waltzes); Einbrecher; Hokuspokus (aka The Temporary Widow). **1931** Ronny; Im Geheimdienst (In the Employ of the Secret Service); Ihre Hoheit Beflehlt; Der Kongress Tanzt (The Congress Dances—US 1932); By Rocket to the Moon. **1932** Ich Bei Tag und du Bei Nacht; Ein Blonder Traum (A Blond Dream); Der Frechdachs; Ein Toller Einfall (A Mad Idea). **1933** Saison in Kairo; Des Jungen Dessauers Grosse Liebe; Walzerkrieg. **1934** Prinzessin Turandot; Die Tochter Ihrer Excellenz; Die Insel. **1935** Schwarze Rosen (aka Did I Betray?—US 1936); Amphitryon. **1936** Boccaccio; Gluckskinder. **1937** Streit um den Knaben Jo (Strife over the Boy Jo); Menschen ohne Vaterland; Gewitterflug zu Claudia; Sieben Ohrfeigen (Seven Slaps). **1938** Preussische Liebesgeschichte; Am Seidenen Faden; Zwischen den Eltern (Between the Parents); Das Madchen von Gestern Nacht (The Girl of Last Night). **1939** Frau am Steuer; Die Geliebte. **1940** Die Keusche Geliebte; Die Unvollkommene Liebe; Das Leichte Madchen. **1941** Leichte Muse; Dreimal Hochzeit; Frauen sind doch Bessere Diplomaten. **1942** Wiener Blut; Anschlag auf Baku; Geliebte Welt. **1943** Die Gattin; Der Kleine Grenzverkehr; Liebesgeschichten. **1944** Jung Adler. **1945** Die Tolle Susanne; Die Fledermaus (The Bat). **1948** Finale; Film ohne Titel (Film without a Name—US 1950). **1949** Hallo—Sie Haben Ihre Frau Vergessen; Derby; Katchen fur Alles; Zwolf Herzen fur Charly. **1950** Konig fur Eine Nacht; Die Wunderschone Galathee; Herrliche Zeiten; Schatten der Nacht; Madchen mit Beziehungen. **1951** Schon muss man Sein; Die Verschleierte Maja; Grun ist die Heide; Die Dubarry; Mikosch Rucht Ein. **1952** Von Liebe Reden wir Spater; Damenwahl; Wenn der Weisse Fliedder Wieder Bluht; Ungarische Rhapsodie (remake of 1928 version). **1953** Weg in die Vergangenheit; Maxie. **1954** Stern von Rio; Drei Tage Mittelarrest; Der Frohliche Wanderer; Liebe ist ja Nur Ein Marchen; Die Drei von der Tankstelle (and 1930 version). **1956** Solange Noch die Rosen Bluhn; Das Donkosakenlied; Schwarzwaldmelodie; Wo die Alten Walder Rauschen. **1957** Der Schrage Otto; Die Bein von Dolores. **1958** Zwei Herzen im Mai; Schwarzwalder Kirsch; Mit Eva fing die Sunde An (aka The Playgirls and the Bellboy—US 1962); Hubertusjagd. **1959** Liebling der Gotter. **1961** Was Macht Papa denn in Italien? **1964** Das Hab ich von Papa Gelernt (I Learned That from Pop); Verliebt in Heidelberg. Other German films include: Die Carmen von T. Pauli; Ferien vom Ich; Am Brunnen vor dem Tore.

FROES, WALTER J. (aka WALLY DOUGLAS)

Born: 1922. Died: May 10, 1958, Los Angeles, Calif. Screen and radio actor. Known on radio as "Froggie Froes." Worked with Fred Waring and appeared in numerous film shorts.

Appeared in: **1940** Spies of the Air. **1941** Break the News; Chinese Den.

FRYE, DWIGHT

Born: Feb. 22, 1899, Salina, Kans. Died: Nov. 9, 1943, Los Angeles, Calif. (heart attack). Stage and screen actor.

Appeared in: **1927** The Night Bird. **1930** The Doorway to Hell. **1931** Man to Man; The Maltese Falcon; Dracula; The Black Camel; Frankenstein. **1932** By Whose Hand?; Attorney for the Defense. **1933** The Invisible Man; Strange Adventure; Western Code; The Vampire Bat; The Circus Queen Murder. **1935** King Solomon of Broadway; The Crime of Dr. Crespi; The Great Impersonation; Atlantic Adventure; Bride of Frankenstein. **1936** Florida Special; Alibi for Murder. **1937** The Man Who Found Himself; Something to Sing About; Beware of Ladies; The Shadow; The Great Guy; Sea Devils; Renfrew of the Royal Mounted. **1938** Think it Over (short); The Invisible Enemy; The Night Hawk; Fast Company; Adventure in the Sahara; Who Killed Gail Preston?; Sinners in Paradise. **1939** Conspiracy; Son of Frankenstein; The Man in the Iron Mask; The Cat and the Canary; I Take This Woman. **1940** Gangs of Chicago; Phantom Raiders; Drums of Fu Manchu; Sky Bandits. **1941** Mystery Ship; Son of Monte Cristo; The People vs. Dr. Kildare; The Blonde from Singapore; The Devil Pays Off. **1942** Prisoner of Japan; The Ghost of Frankenstein; Sleepytime Gal; Danger in the Pacific. **1943** Frankenstein Meets the Wolf Man; Dead Men Walk; Drums of Fu Manchu; Submarine Alert; Hangmen Also Die; Dangerous Blondes.

FULLER, BOBBY (Robert Gaston Fuller)

Born: Oct. 22, 1942, Texas. Died: July 18, 1966, Hollywood, Calif. Screen actor and singer.

Appeared in: **1966** The Ghost in the Invisible Bikini.

FULLER, CLEM

Born: 1909. Died: May 24, 1961, Hollywood, Calif. (cancer). Screen, television actor and stuntman. Entered films approx. 1931.

Appeared in: **1941** Twilight on the Trail. **1949** Gun Runner; Shadows of the West. **1950** The Sundowners; High Lonesome. **1951** The Cave of the Outlaws. **1953** Gunsmoke; The Great Sioux Uprising. **1959** They Came to Cordura.

FULLER, IRENE. See MARY LYGO

Do not confuse with actress listed below.

FULLER, IRENE

Born: 1898. Died: Mar. 20, 1945, Hollywood, Calif. Screen actress. Appeared in silents.

FULLER, LESLIE

Born: 1889, Margate, England. Died: Apr. 24, 1948, Margate, England. Screen, stage and radio actress and screenwriter.

Appeared in: **1930** Not So Quiet on the Western Front; Kiss Me Sergeant; Why Sailors Leave Home. **1931** Old Soldiers Never Die; Poor Old Bill; What a Night! **1932** The Last Coupon; Old Spanish Customers; Tonight's the Night. **1933** Hawleys of High Street; The Pride of the Force. **1934** A Political Party; The Outcast; Lost in the Legion; Doctor's Orders. **1935** Strictly Illegal; Captain Bill; The Stoker. **1936** One Good Turn. **1937** Boys Will be Girls. **1939** The Middle Watch. **1940** Here Comes a Policeman (reissue of Strictly Illegal—1935); Two Smart Men. **1941** My Wife's Family. **1942** Front Line Kids. **1945** What Do We Do Now?

FULLER, MARGARET

Born: 1905. Died: Jan. 6, 1952, Whittier, Calif. Screen, stage and radio actress. Married to actor Robert Griffin.

FULTON, MAUDE

Born: May 14, 1881, Eldorado, Kans. Died: Nov. 9, 1950, Los Angeles, Calif. Screen, stage, vaudeville actress, playwright, screenwriter and author.

Appeared in: **1927** The Gingham Girl; Silk Legs. **1928** Bare Knees. **1929** Nix on Dames. **1933** The Cohens and the Kellys in Trouble.

FUNG, WILLIE

Born: Mar. 3, 1896, Canton, China. Died: Apr. 16, 1945, Los Angeles, Calif. (coronary occlusion). Screen actor.

Appeared in: **1926** The Two-Gun Man; The Yellow Back. **1929** The Far Call; The Blackbook (serial). **1930** Dangerous Paradise; The Sea God. **1931** Gun Smoke. **1932** West of Broadway; Hatchet Man; Red Dust. **1933** The Cocktail Hour; Narrow Corner. **1934** Crime Doctor; A Lost Lady; Sequoia. **1935** Ruggles of Red Gap; Rocky Mountain Mystery; Red Morning; Oil for the Lamps of China; Shanghai; Hop-along Cassidy (aka Hopalong Cassidy Enters); One Way Ticket; China Seas. **1936** Call of the Prairie; Small Town Girl; We Who are About to Die; Happy Go Lucky; White Hunter; Secret Valley; Pan Han-

dlers; The General Died at Dawn; Stowaway. **1937** Lost Horizon; Git Along, Little Dogies; Come On Cowboys!; Wells Fargo; Wee Willie Winkie; The Trigger Trio; Jungle Menace (serial). **1938** Border Wolves; Sinners in Paradise; Too Hot to Handle; Pride of the West. **1939** Honolulu; The Gracie Allen Murder Case; Maisie; 6,000 Enemies; Hollywood Cavalcade; Barricade. **1940** The Great Profile; The Letter. **1941** Badlands of Dakota; Burma Convoy; The Gay Falcon; Public Enemies. **1942** North to the Klondike; Destination Unknown; The Black Swan. **1943** Halfway to Shanghai. **1944** The Adventures of Mark Twain.

FUQUA, CHARLES

Born: 1911. Died: Dec. 21, 1971, New Haven, Conn. Black screen actor and singer. A member of the original "Ink Spots" quartet.

FURBISH, RALPH E.

Born: 1914. Died: Oct. 8, 1974, Wilmington, Del. (heart attack). Screen, television actor and harmonica player. Was member of the "Harmonica Rascals" and once had his own band, the "Harmonica Ramblers."

FUREY, BARNEY

Born: Sept. 7, 1888, Boise, Idaho. Died: Jan. 18, 1938, Los Angeles, Calif. (liver ailment). Screen actor.

Appeared in: **1914** Algie's Sister. **1915** The Canceled Mortgage; The Queen of Hearts; The Fair God of Sun Island; Her Prey; The Shadows Fall; In Search of a Wife; The Gambler's IOU. **1916** The Family Secret; The Dupe; The Millionaire Plunger; Darcy of the Northwest Mounted; The Master Swindlers; Sauce for the Gander; The Fangs of the Tatler; A Stranger from Somewhere; The Golden Thought. **1917** Feet of Clay; A Branded Soul. **1918** True Blue. **1921** Experience; Headin' North; The Man Trackers; Terror Trail (serial). **1922** Four Hearts. **1923** The Sunshine Trail. **1924** The Loser's End; Riding Double. **1925** Ranchers and Rascals; The Trouble Buster; Winds of Chance. **1926** The Mile-a-Minute Man; Out of the West; Red Hot Hoofs; Stick to Your Story. **1927** The Sonora Kid; The Flying U Ranch; Splitting the Breeze; Tom's Gang. **1928** King Cowboy; Lightning Speed; Captain Careless; Red Riders of Canada; Tyrant of Red Gulch; When the Law Rides. **1929** Outlaw; The Pride of Pawnee; The Trail of the Horse Thieves; The Big Diamond Robbery; The Drifter; Gun Law; Idaho Red; 'Neath Western Skies; Night Parade. **1930** Beau Bandit. **1933** When a Man Rides Alone; The Penal Code. **1934** Meanest Gal in Town. **1935** Powdersmoke Range. **1936** Nevada. **1937** Don't Tell the Wife.

FURNISS, HARRY

Born: 1854, Wexford, Ireland. Died: Jan. 15, 1925, Hastings, England. Caricaturist and screen actor.

Appeared in: **1912** The Artist and the Brain Specialist; The Foundling; The Shadow on the Blind; Master and Pupil; The Artist's Joke; The Sketch with the Thumb Print.

FYFFE, WILL

Born: 1911, Dundee, Scotland. Died: Dec. 14, 1947, St. Andrews, Scotland (fall from hotel window). Screen, stage and vaudeville actor.

Appeared in: **1930** Elstree Calling. **1934** Happy. **1935** Rolling Home. **1936** King of Hearts; Debt of Honour; Love in Exile; Men of Yesterday; Annie Laurie. **1937** Well Done, Henry; Spring Handicap; Cotton Queen; Said O'Reilly to McNab (aka Sez O'Reilly to McNab—US). **1938** Owd Bob (aka To the Victor—US). **1939** Rulers of the Sea; The Mind of Mr. Reeder (aka The Mysterious Mr. Reeder—US 1940); The Missing People (US 1940). **1940** They Came by Night; For Freedom; Neutral Port. **1941** The Prime Minister. **1944** Heaven is Round the Corner; Give Me the Stars. **1947** The Brothers.

GABLE, CLARK (Clark William Gable)

Born: Feb. 1, 1901, Cadiz, Ohio. Died: Nov. 16, 1960, Los Angeles, Calif. (heart attack). Stage and screen actor. Divorced from actress Josephine Dillon (dec. 1971), Rhea Langham and Sylvia Hawkes. Married to actress Carole Lombard (dec. 1942) and later married to actress Kay (Williams) Spreckels. Won 1934 Academy Award for Best Actor in It Happened One Night. Nominated for 1935 Academy Award as Best Actor in Mutiny on the Bounty and in 1939 for Gone With the Wind.

Appeared in: **1924** White Man; Forbidden Paradise. **1925** The Merry Widow; Declassee; The Plastic Age; North Star. **1930** The Painted Desert. **1931** Night Nurse; The Easiest Way; The Secret Six; The Finger Points; Laughing Sinners; A Free Soul; Sporting Blood; Dance, Fools, Dance; Possessed; Hell Divers; Susan Lennox, Her Rise and Fall. **1932** Polly of the Circus; Strange Interlude; Red Dust; No Man of Her Own. **1933** The White Sister; Hold Your Man; Night Flight; Dancing Lady. **1934** It Happened One Night; Men in White; Manhattan Melodrama; Chained; Forsaking All Others; Hollywood on Parade (short). **1935** After Office Hours; Call of the Wild; China Seas; Mutiny on the Bounty; Riffraff. **1936** Wife vs. Secretary; San Francisco; Cain and Mabel; Love on the Run. **1937** Parnell; Saratoga. **1938** Test Pilot; Too Hot to Handle. **1939** Idiot's Delight; Gone With the Wind. **1940** Strange Cargo; Boom Town; Comrade X. **1941** They Met in Bombay; Honky Tonk. **1942** Somewhere I'll Find You. **1943** Aerial Gunner; Wings Up (narr.); Hollywood in Uniform (short). **1944** Combat America (documentary). **1945** Adventure. **1947** The

Hucksters. **1948** Command Decision; Homecoming. **1949** Any Number Can Play. **1950** Key to the City; To Please a Lady; Pygmy Island. **1951** Across the Wide Missouri; Callaway Went Thataway. **1952** Lone Star. **1953** Never Let Me Go; Mogambo. **1954** Betrayed. **1955** Soldier of Fortune; The Tall Men. **1957** Band of Angels; The King and Four Queens. **1958** Run Silent, Run Deep; Teacher's Pet. **1959** But Not for Me. **1960** It Started in Naples. **1961** The Misfits. **1964** The Big Parade of Comedy (documentary). **1974** That's Entertainment (film clips).

GABY, FRANK

Born: 1896. Died: Feb. 12, 1945, St. Louis, Mo. (suicide—hanging). Screen, stage and vaudeville actor.

Appeared in: **1927** The Tout (short). **1941** Mr. Dynamite.

GAGE, ERFORD

Born: 1913. Died: Mar. 1945. Screen actor.

Appeared in: **1942** Seven Miles from Alcatraz. **1943** Hitler's Children; The Falcon Strikes Back; Mr. Lucky; The Falcon in Danger; The Seventh Victim; The Adventures of a Rookie; Gangway for Tomorrow; Rookies in Burma. **1944** Days of Glory; The Curse of the Cat People.

GAIGE, RUSSELL

Died: 1974. Stage and screen actor.

Appeared in: **1944** Wilson. **1952** Something for the Birds. **1953** Sangaree; The Vanquished; Forever Female. **1954** Them. **1955** To Catch a Thief. **1956** The Court Jester.

GAILING, GRETCHEN

Born: 1918. Died: June 17, 1961, Hollywood, Calif. Screen actress.

GAINES, RICHARD H.

Born: July 23, 1904, Oklahoma City, Okla. Died: July 20, 1975, North Hollywood, Calif. (heart attack). Screen actor.

Appeared in: **1940** The Howards of Virginia. **1943** A Night to Remember; Tender Comrade; The More the Merrier. **1944** Double Indemnity; Mr Winkle Goes to War; Double Exposure. **1945** A Gun in His Hand (short); Don Juan Quilligan; The Enchanted Cottage; Twice Blessed. **1946** So Goes My Love; Do You Love Me?; White Tie and Tails; Humoresque; Nobody Lives Forever. **1947** Brute Force; The Invisible Wall; Cass Timberlane; Ride a Pink Horse; The Hucksters; Unconquered; Dangerous Years. **1948** Every Girl Should be Married; That Wonderful Urge. **1949** The Lucky Stiff; Strange Bargain; A Kiss for Corliss. **1951** Flight to Mars; Ace in the Hole. **1953** Marry Me Again. **1954** Drum Beat. **1955** Love Me or Leave Me. **1956** Ransom; Francis and the Haunted House. **1957** Five Steps to Danger.

GALE, MARGUERITE H.

Born: 1885. Died: Aug. 20, 1948, Amsterdam, N.Y. Screen and stage actress. Entered films in 1914.

Appeared in: **1915** The Missing Link; How Molly Made Good. **1916** The Yellow Menace (serial).

GALEEN, HENRIK

Born: 1882, Holland. Died: 1949, Germany? Screen actor, film director and screenwriter. Entered films as an actor in 1910.

Appeared in: **1914** Der Golem. **1915** Peter Schlemihl.

GALINDO, NACHO

Born: Mexico? Died: June 23, 1973. Screen actor.

Appeared in: **1946** The Gay Cavalier; Rose of Santa Rosa. **1947** Twilight on the Rio Grande. **1949** South of St. Louis; Holiday in Havana. **1950** Borderline; Surrender; Belle of Old Mexico; Killer Shark; Montana; The Showdown. **1951** Lightning Strikes Twice; Flaming Feather; Havana Rose; Yellow Fin. **1952** Lone Star. **1953** The Hitch-Hiker. **1954** Street Corner (aka Both Sides of the Law—US); Green Fire; Broken Lance; Gypsy Colt; The Outcast. **1955** Headline Hunters; Hell's Island. **1956** Wetbacks; Jaguar; Thunder Over Arizona. **1958** Buchanan Rides Again. **1959** Born Reckless. **1961** One-Eyed Jacks. **1968** The Pink Jungle.

GALLAGHER, GLEN B.

Born: 1909. Died: Mar. 31, 1960, Hollywood, Calif. (heart attack). Screen actor and cameraman.

Appeared in: **1946** Fool's Gold.

GALLAGHER, "SKEETS" (Richard Gallagher)

Born: July 28, 1891, Terre Haute, Ind. Died: May 22, 1955, Santa Monica, Calif. (heart attack). Screen, stage and vaudeville actor.

Appeared in: **1923** The Daring Years. **1927** The Potters; For the Love of Mike; New York. **1928** The Racket; Three Ring Marriage; Alex the Great; Stocks and Blondes. **1929** Close Harmony; Fast Company; Dance of Life; Pointed Heels. **1930** Paramount on Parade; Honey; The Social Lion; Let's Go Native; Her Wedding Night; Love among Millionaires. **1931** It Pays to Advertise; Possessed; Up Pops the Devil; Road to Reno. **1932** The Night Club Lady; The Unwritten Law; Merrily We Go to Hell; Trial of Vivienne Ware; Bird of Paradise; The Phantom of Crestwood; The Conquerors; The Sport Parade; Universal shorts; Hollywood on Parade (short). **1933** Easy Millions; The Past of Mary Holmes; Too Much Harmony; Reform Girl; Alice in Wonderland; Universal shorts. **1934** Riptide; The Meanest Girl in Town; Bachelor Bait; In the Money; Women Unafraid; The Crosby Case. **1935** Lightning Strikes Twice; The Perfect Clue. **1936** Polo Joe; Yours for the Asking; The Man I Marry; Hats Off. **1937** Espionage. **1938** Danger in the Air. **1939** Idiot's Delight. **1941** Zis Boom Bah; Citadel of Crime. **1942** Brother Orchid. **1949** The Duke of Chicago. **1952** Three for Bedroom C.

GALLARDO, LUIS ROJAS

Born: Chile. Died: Mar. 5, 1957, Santiago, Chile. Screen, stage, radio actor and writer.

GALLIAN, KETTI

Born: Dec. 25, (?), Nice, France. Died: Dec. 1972. Screen actress.

Appeared in: **1934** Marie Galante. **1935** Under the Pampas Moon. **1937** Espionage; Shall We Dance?

GALVANI, DINO (aka DINO GALVANONI)

Born: Oct. 27, 1890, Milan, Italy. Died: Sept. 14, 1960, London, England. Screen, stage, radio and television actor.

Appeared in: **1927** Blighty (aka Apres La Guerre). **1928** Adam's Apple (aka Honeymoon Ahead—US); Paradise; Adventurous Youth. **1929** Atlantic; Life's a Stage; The Vagabond Queen; The Flying Scotsman; Those Who Love. **1930** The Dizzy Limit; The Price of Things. **1931** The Chance of a Night Time; Black Coffee; Chin Chin Chinaman (aka Boat From Shanghai—US 1932). **1932** The Missing Rembrandt; In a Monastery Garden; Once Bitten; The Silver Greyhound. **1934** Princess Charming (US 1935); The Broken Rosary. **1936** Don't Rush Me; Ball at Savoy; Cafe Colette (aka Danger in Paris—US). **1937** Midnight Menace (aka Bombs Over London—US 1939). **1938** Mr. Satan; The Viper; The Last Barricade; Special Edition; George Bizet, Composer of Carmen. **1943** It's That Man Again. **1948** The Clouded Crystal; Sleeping Car to Trieste (US 1949). **1950** Paul Temple's Triumph (US 1951). **1951** Fugitive Lady; Three Steps North. **1953** Always a Bride (US 1954). **1954** Father Brown (aka The Detective—US). **1955** The Lyons in Paris. **1956** Fun at St. Fanny's; Checkpoint (US 1957). **1957** Second Fiddle. **1959** Breakout (US 1960—aka Danger Within). **1960** Bluebeard's Ten Honeymoons.

GAMBLE, FRED (Frederick Alvin Gambold)

Born: Oct. 26, 1868. Died: Feb. 17, 1939, Hollywood, Calif. Screen, stage and vaudeville actor. Billed in vaudeville as part of "Queen City Four" team. Entered films in 1906.

Appeared in: **1912-13** American Film Mfg. Co. films. **1915** Oh, Daddy. **1920** The Screaming Shadow (serial). **1921** Love Never Dies; Passing Thru. **1922** Boy Crazy; The Firebrand. **1923** The Virginian. **1924** The Tornado; Black Oxen. **1925** Tumbleweeds. **1926** Chasing Trouble; Born to Battle. **1927** Laddie Be Good; The Red Mill. **1928** Painted Post.

GAMBLE, RALPH

Born: 1902. Died: Mar. 11, 1966, Hollywood, Calif. Screen and vaudeville actor.

Appeared in: **1953** Mister Scoutmaster. **1955** Sudden Danger. **1958** In the Money; Unwed Mother.

GAN, CHESTER

Born: 1909. Died: June 30, 1959, San Francisco, Calif. Screen and television actor.

Appeared in: **1936** Klondike Annie; Drift Fence; Sea Spoilers. **1937** West of Shanghai; The Good Earth. **1938** Shadows of Shanghai. **1939** Mystery of Mr. Wong; Blackwell's Island; King of Chinatown. **1940** 'Til We Meet Again; Victory. **1941** The Maltese Falcon; Man Made Monster; The Get-Away; Burma Convoy. **1942** Flying Tigers; Moontide; China Girl; Across the Pacific. **1943** Crash Dive. **1955** Blood Alley.

GANE, NOLAN

Died: Feb. 12, 1915. Screen actor, film director and screenwriter. Entered films with Thanhouser.

Appeared in: **1914** Politeness Pays; The Varsity Race. **1915** Shep the Sentinel; The Master's Model.

GANNON, JOHN "JACK"

Born: 1903. Died: Nov. 8, 1969, Hollywood, Calif. (respiratory failure). Screen actor and stuntman.

GANTVOORT, HERMAN L.

Born: 1887. Died: Sept. 17, 1937, N.Y. Screen, stage actor and screenwriter.

GANZHORN, JOHN W. (aka JACK GANSHORN)
Born: 1881. Died: Sept. 19, 1956, Hollywood, Calif. Screen actor.

Appeared in: **1922** Thorobred. **1924** The Iron Horse. **1925** Fightin' Odds. **1927** Hawk of the Hills (serial). **1928** The Apache Raider; The Valley of Hunted Men. **1929** Hawk of tthe Hills (feature of 1927 serial).

GARAT, HENRI
Born: Apr. 3, 1902, Paris, France. Died: Aug. 13, 1959, Toulon, France. Stage and screen actor.

Appeared in: **1932** Congress Dances; Il est Charmant (He Is Charming); La Fille et le Garcon (The Girl and the Boy); Le Roi des Resquilleurs. **1933** Adorable. **1935** Soir de Revillon. **1937** Amphytryon. **1938** Advocate D'Amour. Other French films: The Fair Dream; The Charm School; Her Highness' Command.

GARCIA, ALLEN
Born: 1887. Died: Sept. 4, 1938, Los Angeles, Calif. Screen actor and screenwriter.

Appeared in: **1921** Reputation. **1922** The Three Buckaroos. **1928** The Circus. **1929** Morgan's Last Raid. **1931** City Lights; The Deceiver. **1933** Under the Tonto Rim; California Trail. **1936** Modern Times; The Gay Desperado. **1938** Blockade; In Old Mexico.

GARCIA, HENRY
Born: 1904. Died: Nov. 3, 1970, San Antonio, Tex. Screen, stage actor, musician, screenwriter and film technician.

Appeared in: **1964** No Man's Land.

GARCIA, HUMBERTO RODRIGUEZ
Born: 1915, Mexico. Died: June 21, 1960, Mexico City, Mexico. Stage and screen actor.

GARDEL, CARLOS (Charles Romuald Gardes)
Born: Dec. 11, 1887 or 1890 (?), Toulouse, France. Died: June 24, 1935, Colombia, South America (plane crash). Screen, stage actor and singer. Appeared in a series of pictures made by Paramount for Spanish Market.

Appeared in: **1931** Luces De Buenos Aires. **1932** La Casa es Seria. **1933** Esperame; Melodia de Arrabal. **1934** Cuesta Abajo; El Tango en Broadway. **1935** Tango-Bar; El Dia que me Quieras (The Day You Love Me); Cazadores de Estrellas (aka Big Broadcast of 1936).

GARDEN, MARY
Born: Feb. 20, 1874, Aberdeen, Scotland. Died: Jan. 3, 1967, Aberdeen, Scotland. Screen actress and opera performer.

Appeared in: **1918** The Splendid Sinner; Thais.

GARDIN, VLADIMIR
Born: 1877, Russia. Died: 1965, Russia. Screen actor and film director. Entered films in 1913.

Appeared in: **1932** Vstrechnyi (Counterplan). **1934** Dom Zhadnosti; Miracles. **1935** Pesnya o Stchasti; Peasants. **1936** Dubrovsky. **1937** Beethoven Concerto; Young Pushkin. **1938** Pugachev. **1939** The Conquest of Peter the Great. **1942** Spring Song. **1947** Russian Ballerina. **1950** Sekretnaya Missiya (Secret Mission).

GARDINER, PATRICK
Born: 1926. Died: Sept. 30, 1970, Dublin, Ireland (heart attack). Screen, stage and radio actor.

Appeared in: **1967** The Viking Queen. **1970** Country Dance (aka Brotherly Love—US).

GARDNER, CYRIL
Born: May 30, 1898, Paris, France. Died: Dec. 30, 1942, Hollywood, Calif. (heart attack). Screen actor, film director and film editor. Appeared in films at the age of 13.

GARDNER, DON (aka DON GARNER)
Born: 1932. Died: Sept. 21, 1958, Malibu, Calif. (auto accident). Screen actor.

Appeared in: **1946** My Darling Clementine. **1950** A Lady Without Passport.

GARDNER, ED
Born: 1901, Astoria, N.Y. Died: Aug. 17, 1963, Los Angeles, Calif. (liver ailment). Screen, stage, radio actor, stage director, stage producer, film producer and writer for radio. Divorced from actress Shirley Booth.

Appeared in: **1945** Duffy's Tavern, a film take-off of his famous radio program of the same name.

GARDNER, GEORGE
Born: 1868. Died: May 12, 1929, East Islip, N.Y. Screen and stage actor.

GARDNER, HELEN LOUISE
Died: Nov. 20, 1968, Orlando, Fla. Screen actress and film producer. She was the first film star to form her own film company, Helen Gardner Picture Corporation (1912).

Appeared in: **1911** Vanity Fair; Ups and Downs; The Girl and the Sheriff; Regeneration; Madge of the Mountains; Arbutus. **1912** Cleopatra; A Princess of Bagdad; Where the Money Went; A Problem in Reduction; An Innocent Theft; The Heart of Esmeralda; The Party Dress; The Miracle. **1913** A Sister to Carmen; Eureka; A Vampire of the Desert; The Wife of Cain. **1922** Devil's Angel. **1925** Sandra. **1930** Monte Carlo.

GARDNER, HUNTER
Born: 1899. Died: Jan. 16, 1952, Hollywood, Calif. (suicide—slashed wrists). Stage and screen actor.

Appeared in: **1934** Gambling.

GARDNER, JACK
Born: 1876. Died: Dec. 29, 1929, Glendale, Calif. (heart disease). Screen, stage and vaudeville actor. In vaudeville he had several partners: Jeanette Lowery, Al Lloyd, Marie Hartman and Edna Leedom.

Appeared in: **1917** Gift O' Gab. **1922** Wonders of the Sea; Youth to Youth. **1923** Hollywood; Wild Bill Hickok; To the Ladies. **1924** Bluff. **1927** Wild Geese; Blondes by Choice. **1929** Scarlet Seas; The Girl from Woolworth's.

GARDNER, JACK
Born: 1915. Died: Oct. 20, 1955, near Camarillo, Calif. Screen, television, radio actor and newscaster.

Appeared in: **1938** Bringing Up Baby; Cocoanut Grove. **1942** The Glass Key; Gentleman Jim; The Pride of the Yankees. **1943** Henry Aldrich Haunts a House; Adventures of Smilin' Jack (serial). **1944** Three Russian Girls; It Happened Tomorrow.

GARDNER, PETER
Born: 1898. Died: Nov. 13, 1953, Studio City, Calif. Screen and stage actor. Entered films approx. 1918.

GARFIELD, JOHN (Jules Garfinkle)
Born: Mar. 4, 1913, New York, N.Y. Died: May 21, 1952, New York, N.Y. (heart attack). Stage and screen actor. Father of actor John Garfield, Jr.

Appeared in: **1933** Footlight Parade. **1938** Four Daughters. **1939** Blackwell's Island; They Made Me a Criminal; Dust Be My Destiny; Daughters Courageous; Juarez; Four Wives. **1940** Saturday's Children; Castle on the Hudson; East of the River; Flowing Gold. **1941** The Sea Wolf; Out of the Fog; Dangerously They Live. **1942** Tortilla Flat. **1943** The Fallen Sparrow; Air Force; Thank Your Lucky Stars. **1944** Between Two Worlds; Destination Tokyo; Hollywood Canteen. **1945** Pride of the Marines. **1946** Nobody Lives Forever; Humoresque; The Postman Always Rings Twice. **1947** Body and Soul; Gentleman's Agreement. **1948** Force of Evil. **1949** We Were Strangers. **1950** The Breaking Point; Under My Skin; Difficult Years (narr.). **1952** He Ran All the Way.

GARGAN, EDWARD
Born: 1902. Died: Feb. 19, 1964, New York, N.Y. Screen and stage actor. Brother of actor William Gargan.

Appeared in: **1933** The Girl in 419; Gambling Ship; Three-Cornered Moon. **1934** Behold My Wife; Registered Nurse; Belle of the Nineties; The Lemon Drop Kid; Wild Gold; David Harum; Twentieth Century. **1935** Port of Lost Dreams; Hold 'Em Yale; The Gilded Lily; Here Comes Cookie; Hands across the Table; The Bride Comes Home; Behind the Green Lights; We're in the Money; False Pretenses. **1936** Anything Goes; Roaming Lady; Ceiling Zero; Stage Struck; Dangerous Waters; My Man Godfrey; Nobody's Fool; Two in a Crowd; Hearts in Bondage; Grand Jury; Wives Never Know; Great Guy. **1937** You Can't Buy Luck; We're on the Jury; High, Wide and Handsome; Jim Hanvey, Detective; Wake up and Live; The Go-Getter; A Girl with Ideas; Danger Patrol. **1938** That's My Story; Bringing Up Baby; The Devil's Party; The Texans; While New York Sleeps; Straight, Place and Show; Up the River; Thanks for the Memory; Annabel Takes a Tour; Crime School. **1939** Honolulu; The Saint Strikes Back; Blondie Meets the Boss; Yes, My Darling Daughter; For Love or Money; Lucky Night; Fixer Dugan; Night Work; They All Come Out; Pack up Your Troubles; 20,000 Men a Year. **1940** Three Cheers for the Irish; Road to Singapore; Wolf of New York; Brother Rat and a Baby; Spring Parade; Girl from God's Country; Queen of the Mob; Street of Memories; We're in the Army Now; Go West. **1941** Meet the Chump; San Francisco Docks; The Lone Wolf Keeps a Date; Bowery Boys; Tight Shoes; Tillie the Toiler; Here Comes Happiness; Thieves Fall Out; A Date with the Falcon; Dr. Kildare's Victory; Niagara Falls. **1942** Fly by Night; Blondie for Victory; The Falcon's Brother; Over My Dead Body; The Falcon Takes Over; Meet the Stewarts; They All Kissed the Bride; A-Haunting We Will Go; Miss Annie

Rooney; Between Us Girls. **1943** The Falcon Strikes Back; The Falcon in Danger; The Falcon and the Co-eds; Prairie Chickens; Princess O'Rourke; My Kingdom for a Cook; Taxi, Mister; Hit the Ice. **1944** The Falcon Out West; Detective Kitty Kelly; San Fernando Valley. **1945** Follow That Woman; Her Highness and the Bellboy; Sporting Chance; The Bullfighters; Diamond Horseshoe; High Powered; Wonder Man; The Beautiful Cheat; Earl Carroll Vanities; Sing Your Way Home; Life with Blondie; See My Lawyer; The Naughty Nineties. **1946** Life with Blondie; Behind the Mask; Cinderella Jones; The Dark Horse; The Inner Circle; Gay Blades; Little Giant. **1947** Linda Be Good; That's My Girl; Saddle Pals; Web of Danger; Little Miss Broadway; Exposed. **1948** Scudda Hoo! Scudda Hay!; The Dude Goes West; Strike It Rich; Campus Honeymoon; Miss Annie Rooney (reissue of 1942 film); Argyle Secrets; Waterfront at Midnight. **1949** Hold That Baby; Red Light; Dynamite; Love Happy. **1950** Belle of Old Mexico; Spooky Wooky (short); Triple Trouble; Square Dance Katy; Gallant Bess; Hit Parade of 1951. **1951** Bedtime for Bonzo; Abbott and Costello Meet the Invisible Man; Cuban Fireball.

GARIBAY, EMILIO
Born: 1927, Mexico? Died: Aug. 31, 1965, Mexico City, Mexico. Screen actor.

Appeared in: **1953** Adventures of Robinson Crusoe.

GARLAND, JUDY (Frances Gumm)
Born: June 10, 1922, Grand Rapids, Mich. Died: June 22, 1969, London, England (accidental overdose of drugs). Screen, stage, vaudeville and television actress. She and her sisters appeared in vaudeville in an act billed as the "Gumm Sisters." Won Academy's "Special" Award in 1939 for The Wizard of Oz. Nominated for 1961 Academy Award for Best Supporting Actress in Judgement at Nuremberg. Divorced from composer David Rose, film director Vincent Minnelli, producer Sid Luft. Married to Mickey Deans. Mother of Joseph Luft, actress–singer Liza Minnelli and singer Lorna Luft.

Appeared in: **1935** Every Sunday (short). **1936** Pigskin Parade. **1937** Thoroughbreds Don't Cry; Broadway Melody of 1938. **1938** Everybody Sing; Listen, Darling; Love Finds Andy Hardy. **1939** Babes in Arms; The Wizard of Oz. **1940** Strike Up the Band; Little Nellie Kelly; Andy Hardy Meets Debutante. **1941** Life Begins for Andy Hardy; Ziegfeld Girl; Babes on Broadway. **1942** For Me and My Gal. **1943** Girl Crazy; Presenting Lily Mars; Thousands Cheer. **1944** Meet Me in St. Louis. **1945** The Clock. **1946** Ziegfeld Follies; The Harvey Girls; Till the Clouds Roll By. **1948** The Pirate; Words and Music; Easter Parade. **1949** In the Good Old Summertime. **1950** Summer Stock. **1954** A Star is Born. **1960** Pepe (voice only). **1961** Judgement at Nuremberg. **1962** Gay Purr-ee (voice only). **1963** A Child Is Waiting; I Could Go on Singing. **1974** That's Entertainment (film clips).

GARLAND, RICHARD
Died: May 24, 1969. Screen actor. Divorced from actress Beverly Garland.

Appeared in: **1951** The Cimarron Kid. **1952** The Battle of Apache Pass; Red Ball Express; Untamed Frontier; The Lawless Breed. **1953** Vicki; Column South; Torpedo Alley. **1954** Jesse James vs. the Daltons; Dawn at Socorro; Forever Female. **1955** The Man from Bitter Ridge. **1957** Attack of the Crab Monster; My Gun is Quick; The Undead. **1960** 13 Fighting Men. **1962** Panic in Year Zero. **1965** Mutiny in Outer Space.

GARLY, EDWARD H.
Died: Nov. 25, 1938, Hollywood, Calif. Screen, vaudeville and minstrel actor.

GARON, NORM
Born: 1934. Died: Apr. 13, 1975, New York, N.Y. (auto accident). Screen, stage and television actor.

GARON, PAULINE (Marie Pauline Garon)
Born: Sept. 9, 1901, Montreal, Canada. Died: Aug. 30, 1965. Stage and screen actress. Divorced from actor Lowell Sherman (dec. 1934).

Appeared in: **1921** The Power Within. **1922** Sonny; Reported Missing. **1923** Adam's Rib; The Marriage Market; The Man from Glengary; You Can't Fool Your Wife; Children of Dust; Forgive and Forget. **1924** The Average Woman; The Turmoil; What the Butler Saw; Wine of Youth; Pal O'Mine; The Painted Flapper; The Spitfire. **1925** Satan in Sables; Compromise; Fighting Youth; Flaming Waters; The Love Gamble; Speed; The Great Sensation; Passionate Youth; Rose of the World; Where Was I?; The Splendid Road. **1926** Christine of the Big Tops. **1927** The Princess on Broadway; The College Hero; Eager Lips; Temptations of a Shop Girl; Love of Sunya; Naughty; Driven from Home; Ladies at Ease. **1928** The Candy Kid; Girl He Didn't Buy; The Heart of Broadway; The Devil's Cage; Dugan of the Dugouts; Riley of the Rainbow Division. **1929** The Gamblers; Must We Marry?; In the Headlines; Show of Shows. **1930** The Thoroughbred; Le Spectre Vert; plus the following shorts: Lovers Delight; Jack White Talking Pictures; Letters. **1933** One Year Later; Phantom Broadcast; By Appointment Only; Lost in the Stratosphere. **1934** Wonder Bar. **1935** The White Cockatoo; Becky Sharp. **1937** Her Husband's Secretary.

GARR, EDDIE
Born: 1900. Died: Sept. 3, 1956, Burbank, Calif. (heart ailment). Stage and screen actor.

Appeared in: **1933** Obey the Law; a Universal short. **1949** Ladies of the Chorus. **1951** Varieties on Parade.

GARRICK, RICHARD T.
Born: 1879. Died: Aug. 21, 1962, Hollywood, Calif. Screen actor.

Appeared in: **1947** Boomerang. **1948** Green Grass of Wyoming. **1951** A Streetcar Named Desire. **1952** Viva Zapata; Dream Boat; O. Henry's Full House; Something for the Birds; Stars and Stripes Forever. **1953** Call Me Madam; Law and Order. **1954** Desiree; Riding Shotgun. **1955** High Society; A Man Called Peter; Violent Saturday. **1956** Hilda Crane; The Mountain.

GARRISON, MICHAEL
Born: 1923. Died: Aug. 17, 1966, Bel Air, Calif. (skull fracture—fall). Screen, stage actor, film producer and television executive producer. Entered films approx. 1947.

Appeared in: **1968** Girl in Gold Boots.

GARTH, OTIS
Born: 1901. Died: Dec. 21, 1955, Hollywood, Calif. Screen and television actor.

Appeared in: **1953** Mister Scoutmaster.

GARVIE, ED (Edward Garvie aka ED GARVEY)
Born: 1865. Died: Feb. 17, 1939, New York, N.Y. Screen and stage actor.

Appeared in: **1926** Love 'Em and Leave 'Em. **1927** East Side, West Side. **1932** Smiling Faces. **1934** Social Register. **1936** Soak the Rich. **1937** An educational short.

GARWOOD, WILLIAM
Born: Apr. 28, 1884, Mississippi. Died: Dec. 28, 1950, Los Angeles, Calif. (coronary occlusion). Screen actor.

Appeared in: **1911** Pasha's Daughter; Cally's Comet; For Her Sake; Baseball in Bloomers; Adrift; Checkmate; The Honeymooners; Courting Across the Court. **1912** Under Two Flags; Vengeance is Mine; Lucille; Put Yourself in His Place; The Thunderbolt. **1913** Carmen; Rick's Redemption; A Caged Bird; Beautiful Bismark; Dora; The Heart of a Fool; The Shoemaker and the Doll; The Van Warden Rubies; Through the Sluice Gates; The Oats of Tsuru San. **1914** Their Worldly Goods; The Hunchback; The Trap; The Taming of Sunnybrook Nell; His Faith in Humanity; The Lost Sermon; The Painted Lady's Child; A Ticket to Red Horse Gulch. **1915** Uncle's New Blazer; The Alibi; Larry O'Neill—Gentleman; Getting His Goat; A Man's Way; Lord John's Journal (series); The Wolf of Debt; The Legend Beautiful; On Dangerous Ground; The Supreme Impulse; Wild Blood. **1916** His Picture; Billy's War Brides; Broken Fetters; Two Seats at the Opera; The Gentle Art of Burglary; A Society Sherlock; He Wrote a Book; The Decoy; Arthur's Desperate Resolve; A Soul at Stake. **1917** The Little Brother; A Magdalene of the Hills. **1918** Her Moment.

GARY, SID
Born: 1901. Died: Apr. 3, 1973, New York, N.Y. Screen, vaudeville, radio actor and singer. Appeared in vaudeville with George Burns and later teamed with Freddy Bernard. Brother of actor Harold Gary.

Appeared in: **1937** A Columbia short.

GARZA, EVA
Born: 1917, Mexico. Died: Nov. 1, 1966, Tucson, Ariz. (pneumonia). Screen actress and singer.

GATES, BERT
Born: 1883. Died: Dec. 18, 1952, Aberdeen, Scotland. Screen actor. He gave "talking films" to audiences, standing behind the screen with his wife and speaking the various parts.

GAUGE, ALEXANDER
Born: 1914, England. Died: Sept. 1960, Woking, Surrey, England. Screen, stage and television actor.

Appeared in: **1949** The Interrupted Journey (film debut—US 1951). **1952** Murder in the Cathedral; The Pickwick Papers (US 1953); Penny Princess (US 1953). **1953** Counterspy (aka Undercover Agent—US); House of Blackmail; Will Any Gentleman? (US 1955); The Square Ring; Martin Luther; The Great Game. **1954** The Blazing Caravan; Double Exposure; The Golden Link; Mystery on Bird Island; Fast and Loose; Dance Little Lady (US 1955). **1955** Before I Wake (aka Shadow of Fear—US); Tiger By the Tail (aka Crossup—US 1958); The Reluctant Bride (aka Two Grooms For a Bride—US 1957); The Hornet's Nest. **1956** The Iron Petticoat; Port of Escape; Breakaway. **1957** The Passionate Stranger (aka A Novel Affair—US). **1961** Nothing Barred. **1963** Les Canailles (The Ruffians).

GAUGUIN, LORRAINE
Born: 1924. Died: Dec. 22, 1974, Los Angeles, Calif. (fire). Screen actress, author and columnist.

Appeared in: **1940** One Million B.C.

GAULT, MILDRED
Born: 1905. Died: Sept. 15, 1938, Los Angeles, Calif. Screen actress and film dancer.

GAUNTIER, GENE (Genevieve Gauntier Liggett)
Born: c. 1880. Died: Dec. 18, 1966, Cuernavaca, Mexico. Screen actress, screenwriter and film producer.

Appeared in: **1906** The Paymaster; The Skyscraper. **1908** Days of 61 (aka The Blue and the Gray). **1910** The Kalem Girl; The Little Spreewald Maiden. **1911** The Romance of a Dixie Belle; The Colleen Bawn. **1912** From the Manger to the Cross. **1913** In the Power of a Hypnotist; The Wives of Jamestown; Lady Peggy's Escape; A Daughter of the Confederacy; When Men Hate; In the Clutches of the Ku Klux Klan. **1914** Come Back to Erin; Rory O'More; His Brother's Wife.

GAWTHORNE, PETER
Born: Sept. 1, 1884, Queen's County, Ireland. Died: Mar. 17, 1962, London, England. Screen, stage actor, stage producer and playwright.

Appeared One in: **1929** Behind That Curtain; Sunny Side Up; His Glorious Night. **1930** One Hysterical Night; Those Three French Girls; Temple Tower. **1931** Charlie Chan Carries On; The Man Who Came Back. **1932** The Flag Lieutenant; Jack's the Boy (aka Night and Day—US 1933); The Lodger (aka The Phantom Fiend—US 1935); C.O.D.; His Lordship. **1933** Perfect Understanding; The Blarney Stone (aka The Blarney Kiss—US); Prince of Arcadia; Just Smith; The House of Trent. **1934** Two Hearts in Waltztime; Grand Prix; Something Always Happens; Money Mad; My Old Dutch; The Camels Are Coming; Dirty Work; Girls, Please! **1935** The Iron Duke; Murder at Monte Carlo; Who's Your Father?; Me and Marlborough; Crime Unlimited; The Crouching Beast; Man of the Moment; No Limit; Stormy Weather (US 1936). **1936** Wolf's Clothing; The Man Behind the Mask; Potluck; A Woman Alone (aka Two Who Dared—US 1937); Everybody Dance. **1937** Good Morning, Boys (aka Where There's a Will—US); Mr. Stringfellow Says No; Brief Ecstasy; Gangway; Under a Cloud; The Ticket of Leave Man; The Last Adventurers; Riding High (aka Remember When); Father Steps Out. **1938** Easy Riches; George Bizet, Composer of Carmen; Convict 99; Scruffy; Alf's Button Afloat; Hey! Hey! U.S.A. **1939** Dead Men Are Dangerous; Home from Home; Ask a Policeman; Sword of Honour; Secret Journey (aka Among Human Wolves—US 1940); Where's the Fire?; What Would You Do Chums?; Traitor Spy (aka The Torso Murder Mystery—US 1940); Flying Fifty-Five. **1940** Laugh It Off; Band Wagon; Two For Danger; Three Silent Men; Gasbags; They Came By Night. **1941** Inspector Hornleigh Goes to It (aka Mail Train—US); Old Mother Riley's Ghosts; Pimpernel Smith (aka Mister V—US 1942); Love on the Dole. **1942** Let the People Sing; Much Too Shy. **1943** The Hundred Pound Window; Bell-Bottom George. **1946** This Man Is Mine. **1948** Nothing Venture; Accidental Spy (reissue of Mr. Stringfellow Says No—1937). **1949** The Case of Charles Peace; High Jinks in Society. **1950** Soho Conspiracy. **1951** Death Is a Number. **1952** Paul Temple Returns. **1954** Five Days (aka Paid to Kill—US).

GAXTON, WILLIAM (Arturo Gaxiola)
Born: Dec. 2, 1893, San Francisco, Calif. Died: Feb. 2, 1963, New York, N.Y. Screen, stage and vaudeville actor.

Appeared in: **1926** Stepping Along; It's the Old Army Game. **1931** Fifty Million Frenchmen. **1932** Silent Partners (short). **1934** Their Big Moment. **1942** Something to Shout About. **1943** The Heat's On; Best Foot Forward. **1944** Tropicana. **1945** Diamond Horseshoe.

GAY, FRED
Born: 1882. Died: June 11, 1955, Long Beach, Calif. Screen actor.

GAY, MAISIE
Born: 1883, England. Died: Sept. 14, 1945, London, England. British screen and stage actress.

GAY, RAMON (Ramon Gaytan)
Born: 1917. Died: June 1960, Mexico City, Mexico. Screen and stage actor.

Appeared in: **1953** Eugenia Grandet. **1956** Yambao (aka Young and Evil—US 1962). **1959** La Maldicion de la Momia Azteca (The Curse of the Aztec Mummy—US 1965); El Robot Humano (aka La Momia Azteca Contra el Robot Humano—The Robot vs. The Aztec Mummy—US 1965). **1960** Munecos Infernales (aka The Curse of the Doll People—US 1968); La Estrella Vacia (The Empty Star—US 1962).

GAY, YNEX
Died: Oct. 3, 1975. Screen actress.

GAYE, ALBIE
Died: Nov. 26, 1965, Chicago, Ill. Screen, stage, television actress and singer.

Appeared in: **1953** The Miami Story. **1956** The Vagabond King.

GAYER, ECHLIN
Born: 1878. Died: Feb. 14, 1926, New York, N.Y. (pneumonia). Stage and screen actor.

Appeared in: **1924** Her Love Story. **1925** The Mad Dancer.

GAYNOR, RUTH
Died: May 28, 1919, Seattle, Wash. (auto accident). Screen actress.

GEARY, BUD (S. Maine Geary)
Born: 1899. Died: Feb. 22, 1946, Hollywood, Calif. (injuries sustained in motor crash). Screen actor.

Appeared in: **1921** Everyman's Price. **1922** Four Hearts. **1932** High Flyers. **1936** The Trail of the Lonesome Pine. **1940** Murder Over New York; Adventures of Red Ryder; Saps at Sea. **1941** Great Guns; King of the Texas Rangers. **1942** Cowboy Serenade; Home in Wyomin'; A-Haunting We Will Go. **1943** Thundering Trails. **1944** Sheriff of Las Vegas; Haunted Harbor; Song of the Open Road. **1946** Smoky.

GEBHARDT, GEORGE M.
Born: 1879, Basle, Switzerland. Died: May 2, 1919 (tuberculosis). Stage and screen actor. Married to stage actress Mrs. George Gebhardt (dec.).

Appeared in: **1908** Balked at the Altar; A Calamitous Elopement. **1911** Getting His Man; The Sheriff and His Brother. **1912** The Everlasting Judy; At Rolling Forks; The Fighting Chance; A Pair of Jacks; Across the Sierras; The Love Trail; Two Men and the Law; Her Indian Hero; The Renegade; The Miner's Claim; The Gambler; The Penalty Paid; A Race for Liberty; A Redman's Loyalty; A Redskin's Appeal; The Cactus County Lawyer; Misleading Evidence. **1913** The Frame Up; Her Faithful Yuma Servant; The Blind Gypsy; The Bear Hunter; The Poisoned Stream; The Pioneer's Recompense; A Faithful Servitor; An Accidental Shot; Lillian's Nightmare; The Thwarted Plot; A Bear Escape. **1914** By the Two Oak Trees; Against Heavy Odds; The Dishonored Medal. **1915** The Fighting Hope; The Cost; The Voice in the Fog; Ready for Reno; Blackbirds. **1916** A Modern Knight; The Power of Mind; The Dyspeptic; Professor Jeremy's Experiment; The Penalty of Treason; The Sign of the Spade. **1917** Eternal Love; Jerry in Yodel Land. **1918** Madame Spy.

GEBUEHR, OTTO
Born: 1877, Germany. Died: Mar. 13, 1954, Wiesbaden, West Germany. Stage and screen actor who greatly resembled Frederick the Great. Entered films in 1920.

Appeared in: **1922** Fredericus Rex. **1929** Waterloo. **1931** Das Floetenkonzert von Sans-Souci (A Flute Concert at Sans-Souci). **1932** Barberina; Die Taenzerin Von Sans-Souci. **1935** Der Choral von Leuthen. **1937** Pretty Miss Schragg. **1938** Nanon. **1939** Fredericus. **1940** Leidenschaft (Passion). **1950** City of Torment. **1952** The Devil Makes Three. **1954** Angelika. **1956** Circus Girl. Other German films: Dr. Holl; Die Luege; Fritz and Friederike; Das Ewige Spiel.

GEE, GEORGE
Born: 1895, England. Died: Oct. 17, 1959, Coventry, England. Stage and screen actor.

Appeared in **1928** Weekend Wives (US 1929). **1931** Let's Love and Laugh (aka Bridegroom for Two—US 1922). **1933** Leave It To Me; Cleaning Up; Strike It Rich.

GEE, GEORGE D.
Died: Dec. 1917, Brooklyn, N.Y. Screen actor.

Appeared in: **1917** Queen X.

GEHRIG, LOU (Henry Louis Gehrig)
Born: June 19, 1903, New York, N.Y. Died: June 2, 1941, New York (spinal paralysis). Professional baseball player and screen actor.

Appeared in: **1938** Rawhide. **1942** The Ninth Inning.

GEHRMAN, MRS. LUCY
Died: May 8, 1954, New York, N.Y. Yiddish screen and stage actress.

Appeared in: **1950** God, Man and Devil.

GEIGER, HERMANN
Born: 1913. Died: Aug. 25, 1966, near Sitten, West Germany (plane crash). Screen actor and pilot.

GELDERT, CLARENCE
Born: June 9, 1867, St. John, B.C., Canada. Died: May 13, 1935, Calabasas, Calif. (heart attack). Screen, stage actor and film director. Entered films with D. W. Griffith in 1915.

Appeared in: **1917** Joan the Woman. **1921** All Souls Eve; The Great Moment;

The Hell Diggers; The House That Jazz Built; The Lost Romance; The Witching Hour. **1922** Rent Free. **1923** A Woman of Paris; Adam's Rib; Richard the Lion-Hearted; Wasted Lives. **1924** Behind the Curtain; The Fighting American; Love's Whirlpool; North of 36; The Whipping Boss; Oh, Doctor. **1925** The Bandit's Baby; My Neighbor's Wife. **1926** The Flaming Forest; Boy Friend; Hands Across the Border; Racing Blood; Young April. **1927** Dress Parade; One Man Game. **1929** Overland Telegraph; Square Shoulders; Sioux Blood; The Ghost Talks; Unholy Night; Thirteenth Chair. **1930** The Bishop Murder Case. **1931** Guilty Hands; Cuban Love Song; Daddy Long Legs. **1932** The Stoker; White Eagle; Emma. **1933** Jungle Bride; Lucky Dog; Telephone Trail; Revenge at Monte Carlo; Dance Hall Hostess; Rusty Rides Alone; Marriage on Approval; Lone Adventure. **1934** In Love with Life; Man Trailer. **1935** Mississippi. **1936** Go Get-'Em Haines.

GEMIER, FIRMIN

Born: 1886, France. Died: Nov. 26, 1933, Paris, France (heart failure). Screen, stage actor, stage director and screenwriter.

Appeared in: **1926** The Magician. **1937** Grandeur et Decadence.

GEMORA, CHARLIE

Born: 1903, Philippine Islands. Died: Aug. 19, 1961, Hollywood, Calif. (heart attack). Screen actor.

Appeared in: **1928** The Circus Kid. **1933** King Kong (was the gorilla). **1938** Swiss Miss. **1939** At the Circus; The Gorilla. **1948** Beauty and the Beast. **1953** War of the Worlds; White Witch Doctor. **1961** One-Eyed Jacks.

GENDRON, PIERRE

Born: Mar. 4, 1896, Toledo, Ohio. Died: Nov. 27, 1956, Hollywood, Calif. Screen, stage actor and screenwriter.

Appeared in: **1921** The Bashful Suitor. **1922** The Man Who Played God; The Young Painter. **1923** Broadway Broke; Does It Pay?; Outlaws of the Sea. **1924** The Dangerous Flirt; The City That Never Sleeps; Just Off Broadway; The Lover of Camille; Three Women. **1925** The Scarlet Honeymoon. **1927** The Enchanted Island. **1928** What Price Beauty.

GENTLE, ALICE

Born: 1889, Chatsworth, Ill. Died: Feb. 28, 1958, Oakland, Calif. Screen, stage actress and opera performer.

Appeared in: **1930** The Golden Dawn (film debut); Song of the Flame; A Scene from Carmen (short).

GEORGE, GLADYS (Gladys Clare)

Born: Sept. 13, 1900, Hatton, Maine. Died: Dec. 8, 1954, Los Angeles, Calif. (brain hemorrhage). Stage and screen actress. Daughter of actor Sir Arthur Clair. Divorced from actors Arthur Erway, Leonard Penn (dec. 1975), Edward Fowler and Kenneth Bradley.

Appeared in: **1920** Red Hot Dollars; Home Spun Folks. **1921** The Easy Road; Chickens; The House That Jazz Built. **1934** Straight Is the Way. **1936** Valiant Is the Word for Carrie. **1937** They Gave Him a Gun; Madame X. **1938** Love Is a Headache; Marie Antoinette. **1939** The Roaring Twenties; Here I Am a Stranger; I'm from Missouri. **1940** A Child Is Born; The Way of All Flesh; The House across the Bay. **1941** The Lady from Cheyenne; The Maltese Falcon; Hit the Road. **1942** The Hard Way. **1943** Nobody's Darling; The Crystal Ball. **1944** Minstrel Man; Christmas Holiday. **1945** Steppin' in Society. **1946** The Best Years of Our Lives. **1947** Millie's Daughter. **1948** Alias a Gentleman. **1949** Flamingo Road. **1950** The Undercover Girl; Bright Leaf. **1951** Detective Story; He Ran All the Way; Lullaby of Broadway; Silver City. **1953** It Happens Every Thursday.

GEORGE, GRACE

Born: Dec. 25, 1879, New York, N.Y. Died: May 19, 1961, New York, N.Y. Screen, stage actress and stage director.

Appeared in one film only: **1943** Johnny Come Lately.

GEORGE, HEINRICH

Born: 1893, Germany. Died: Sept. 27, 1946, Russia (Soviet internment camp). German screen and stage actor.

Appeared in: **1927** Metropolis. **1928** Bondage; Armored Vault. **1929** The Whirl of Life; The Wrath of the Seas; Theatre; Wasted Love. **1931** Der Mann der den Mord Beging (The Man Who Committed the Murder); Berlin-Alexanderplatz (US 1933). **1932** Der Andere; 1914: The Last Days before the War. **1934** Unsere Fahne Flattert Uns Voran. **1935** Hermine und die Sieben Aufrechten; Das Maedchen Johanna. **1936** Reifende Jugend; Stuetzen der Gesellschaft; Wenn der Hahn Kraeht. **1937** Promise Me Nothing. **1938** Ball in Metropol; Unternehmen Michael (The Private's Job); Magda. **1939** Der Biberpelz (The Beaver Coat); Frau Sylvelin. **1940** The Dreyfus Case.

GEORGE, JOHN

Born: Jan. 21, 1898, Syria. Died: Aug. 25, 1968, Los Angeles, Calif. (emphysema). Screen actor.

Appeared in: **1921** Miracles of the Jungle (serial). **1922** Trifling Women. **1923**
Where the Pavement Ends; Scaramouche. **1924** When a Girl Loves. **1926** The Road to Mandalay; Don Juan. **1927** The Night of Love; The Unknown. **1928** The Big City. **1930** Outside the Law. **1932** Island of Lost Souls. **1933** Trick for Trick. **1934** Babes in Toyland. **1946** The Devil's Playground. **1956** Around the World in 80 Days.

GEORGE, MURIEL

Born: Aug. 29, 1883, London, England. Died: Oct. 22, 1965, England. Screen, stage, vaudeville and television actress. Divorced from actor Ernest Butcher (dec. 1965).

Appeared in: **1932** His Lordship. **1933** Cleaning Up; Yes, Mr. Brown. **1934** Wedding Eve; Old Faithful; Key to Harmony. **1936** The Happy Family; Limelight (aka Backstage—US); Whom the Gods Love (aka Mozart—US 1940); Not So Dusty; Busman's Holiday; Merry Comes to Town. **1937** Overcoat Sam; 21 Days (aka The First and the Last; aka 21 Days Together—US 1940); Who's Your Lady Friend?; Song of the Road; Talking Feet; Dr. Syn; Lancashire Luck. **1938** Darts Are Trumps; A Sister to Assist 'Er; Crackerjack (aka The Man With a Hundred Faces—US). **1940** The Briggs Family; Pack Up Your Troubles; Food for Thought. **1941** Telefootlers; Freedom Radio (aka A Voice in the Night—US); Quiet Wedding; Lady Be Kind (short); Rush Hour; Love on the Dole; Cottage to Let (aka Bombsight Stolen—US). **1942** They Flew Alone (aka Wings and the Woman—US); Unpublished Story; Alibi; Went the Day Well? (aka 48 Hours—US 1944). **1943** The Bells Go Down; Dear Octopus (aka The Randolph Family—US 1945). **1944** The Man from Scotland Yard; Kiss the Bride Goodbye. **1945** For You Alone; Perfect Strangers (aka Vacation from Marriage—US); I'll Be Your Sweetheart. **1946** The Years Between (US 1947). **1947** When the Bough Breaks. **1950** The Dancing Years; Last Holiday. **1955** Simon and Laura (US 1956).

GEORGE, VOYA (Voya George Djordjevich)

Born: 1895. Died: May 8, 1951, New York, N.Y. Screen actor.

Appeared in: **1928** The Legion of the Condemned.

GEORGES, KATERINE

Born: France. Died: June 1973, Mexico City, Mexico. Stage and screen actress.

GERAGHTY, CARMELITA

Born: 1901, Rushville, Ind. Died: June 7, 1966, New York, N.Y. Screen actress.

Appeared in: **1923** Bag and Baggage. **1924** Jealous Husbands; Black Oxen; Discontented Husbands; Geared to Go; High Speed; Through the Dark. **1925** Passionate Youth; Brand of Cowardice; Cyclone Cavalier; The Mysterious Stranger; Under the Rouge. **1926** My Lady of Whims; The Great Gatsby; The Canyon of Light; Pleasure Garden; The Flying Mail; Josselyn's Wife; The Lily. **1927** The Last Trail; My Best Girl; The Slaver; The Small Bachelor; Venus of Venice; What Every Girl Should Know. **1928** The Goodbye Kiss. **1929** Object Alimony; Paris Bound; South of Panama; The Mississippi Gambler; This Thing Called Love. **1930** After the Fog; What Men Want; Men Without Law; Rogue of the Rio Grande; Fighting Through. **1931** Fifty Million Frenchmen; The Devil Plays; Millie; Texas Ranger; Night Life in Reno. **1932** Prestige; Forgotten Women; Escapade. **1933** Malay Nights; Flaming Signal. **1935** Manhattan Butterfly.

GERALD, JIM (Jacques Guenod)

Born: 1889, France. Died: 1958. Stage and screen actor. Entered films approx. 1911.

Appeared in: **1927** An Italian Straw Hat. **1931** La Chant au Marin; La Nuit est a Nous (The Night Is Ours); The Horse Ate the Hat. **1934** The Constant Nymph. **1936** The Robber Symphony. **1937** Bulldog Drummond at Bay. **1939** French without Tears. **1943** The Last Will of Dr. Mabuse. **1945** Boule de Suif. **1951** The Lady from Boston; Pardon My French; Adventures of Captain Fabian. **1952** L'Ile aux Femmes Nues (aka Naked in the Wind—US 1962); The Crimson Curtain. **1953** Moulin Rouge. **1954** Father Brown (aka The Detective); The Barefoot Contessa; The Moment of Truth. **1956** Foreign Intrigue. **1957** Eric Frac en Dentelles. **1959** Le Vente se Leve (The Wind Rises aka Time Bomb—US 1961).

GERARD, JOSEPH SMITH

Born: 1871. Died: Aug. 20, 1949, Woodland Hills, Calif. Screen actor.

GERARD, TEDDIE (Teresa Cabre)

Born: 1890, Buenos Aires, Argentina. Died: Aug. 31, 1942, London, England. Screen, stage actress, and dancer.

Appeared in: **1915** Billy's Spanish Love Spasm. **1922** Cave Girl; Seventh Day.

GERAY, STEVEN

Born: Nov. 10, 1898, Uzhored, Czechoslovakia. Died: Dec. 26, 1973. Stage and screen actor.

Appeared in: **1935** Dance Band; The Student's Romance. **1936** A Star Fell from Heaven. **1937** Let's Make a Night of It (US 1938). **1939** Inspector Hornleigh. **1941** Man at Large; Blue, White and Perfect. **1942** Secret Agent of Japan; A Gentleman at Heart; Castle in the Desert; The Moon and Sixpence;

Eyes in the Night. **1943** Pilot No. 5; Hostages; Night Plane from Chungking; Henry Aldrich Swings It; Appointment in Berlin; The Phantom of the Opera; Whistling in Brooklyn; To My Unborn Son. **1944** Meet the People; The Mask of Dimitrios; The Seventh Cross; In Society; The Conspirators; Easy Life. **1945** Tarzan and the Amazons; Hotel Berlin; Crimson Canary; Spellbound; Cornered; Mexicana. **1946** Gilda; Deadline at Dawn; So Dark the Night; Blondie Knows Best; The Return of Monte Cristo. **1947** Mr. District Attorney; Blind Spot; The Unfaithful; Gunfighters; When a Girl's Beautiful; The Crime Doctor's Gamble. **1948** I Love Trouble; Port Said. **1949** The Dark Past; El Paso; Ladies of the Chorus; Sky Liner; Once More My Darling; The Lone Wolf and His Lady; Holiday in Havana. **1950** Woman on the Run; The Harbor of Missing Men; Under My Skin; In a Lonely Place; A Lady Without a Passport; All About Eve; Pygmy Island. **1951** Target Unknown; I Can Get It For You Wholesale; The Second Woman; House on Telegraph Hill; Savage Drums; Little Egypt. **1952** Lady Possessed; Bal Tabarin; The Big Sky; Night Without Sleep; Affair in Trinidad; O'Henry's Full House. **1953** Tonight We Sing; Gentlemen Prefer Blondes; The Royal African Rifles; The Great Diamond Robbery; The Golden Blade; Call Me Madam; The Story of Three Loves. **1954** Knock on Wood; The French Line; Tobor, The Great; Paris Playboys. **1955** New York Confidential; A Bullet for Joey; Daddy Long Legs; Artists and Models. **1956** Attack!; Stagecoach to Fury; The Birds and the Bees. **1958** A Certain Smile. **1959** Verboten!; Count Your Blessings. **1963** Dame with a Halo. **1964** The Evil of Frankenstein; Wild and Wonderful. **1965** Ship of Fools. **1966** The Swinger; Jesse James Meets Frankenstein's Daughter.

GERMI, PIETRO
Born: Sept. 14, 1904, Genoa, Italy. Died: Dec. 5, 1974, Rome, Italy (hepatitis). Screen actor, film director, producer, screenwriter and author.

Appeared in: **1949** Flight into France. **1957** L'Uomo di Paglia. **1959** Un Maledetto Imbroglio (aka The Facts of Murder—US 1965). **1961** La Viaccia (US 1962 and aka The Love Makers). **1965** Il Ferroviere (Man of Iron aka The Railroad Man—US).

GERRARD, DOUGLAS (Douglas Gerrard McMurrogh-Kavanagh aka DOUGLAS GERARD)
Born: Aug. 12, 1888, Dublin, Ireland. Died: June 5, 1950, Hollywood, Calif. Screen, stage actor and film director. Entered films in 1913.

Appeared in: **1913** A Bear Escape. **1914** The Potter and the Clay; The Merchant of Venice. **1916** The Human Cactus; The Fur Trimmed Coat; Naked Hearts; Bettina Loved a Soldier; The Penalty of Treason; The Price of Victory; Under the Spell; The Evil Women Do; Through Baby's Voice; In the Dead O'Night; Her Wedding Day; The False Genius. **1919** Lord and Lady Algy. **1921** The Lady from Longacre. **1922** The Golden Gallows; Impulse; Omar the Tentmaker; A Tailor Made Man. **1924** On Time; In Fast Company; The Lighthouse by the Sea. **1925** My Neighbor's Wife; Wings of Youth. **1926** Doubling with Danger; Private Izzy Murphy; Footloose Widows. **1927** The College Widow; Dearie; The First Auto; The Desired Woman; Ginsberg the Great; Wolf's Clothing; A Million Bid. **1928** Five and Ten Cent Annie; Ladies of the Night Club. **1929** The Hottentot; The Glad Rag Doll; The Argyle Case; The Madonna of Avenue A; Painted Angel. **1930** General Crack; Sweet Kitty Bellairs; Lilies of the Field. **1931** Road to Singapore. **1932** The Tenderfoot; One Way Passage; Manhattan Parade. **1933** King's Vacation. **1934** Bombay Mail; Bulldog Drummond Strikes Back. **1935** The Ghost Walks. **1936** Under Two Flags; Ants in the Pantry. **1951** The Dumb Girl of Portici.

GERRARD, GENE (Eugene O'Sullivan)
Born: Aug. 31, 1892, Clapham, London, England. Died: June 1971, Sidmouth, Devon, England. Screen, stage actor, film director and playwright. Entered films with Hepworth Co. in 1912.

Appeared in: **1930** Let's Love and Laugh. **1932** Out of the Blue; My Wife's Family; Lucky Girl; Bridegroom for Two; Her Radio Romeo. **1933** Leave It to Me; Let Me Explain, Dear. **1935** No Monkey Business; It's a Bet. **1936** Mister Hobo. **1937** Wake Up Famous.

GERRON, KURT (Kurt Gerson)
Born: Berlin, Germany. Died: 1944, Auschwitz, Germany. Screen and stage actor and film director.

Appeared in: **1928** Manage; The Strange Case of Captain Ramper. **1929** Berlin After Dark; Der Blaue Engel (The Blue Angel). **1930** Survival; Liebe im Ring. **1931** Die Drei von der Tankstelle; Dolly Macht Karriere; Man Braucht Kein Geld (You Don't Need Any Money—US 1932). **1932** Trapeze. **1933** Ihre Majestaet die Liebe. **1936** Die Marquise von Pompadour.

GERSON, EVA
Born: 1903. Died: Sept. 5, 1959, New York, N.Y. Screen, stage, and television actress.

Appeared in: **1957** Street of Sinners. **1959** North by Northwest; Middle of the Night; The Last Angry Man.

GERSON, PAUL
Born: 1871. Died: June 5, 1957, Hollywood, Calif. Screen, stage actor and film director.

Appeared in: **1923** The Cricket on the Hearth.

GERSTEN, BERTA
Born: 1894, Poland. Died: Sept. 10, 1972, New York. Yiddish screen, stage and television actress.

Appeared in: **1939** Mirele Efros. **1950** God, Man and Devil. **1955** The Benny Goodman Story.

GERSTLE, FRANK "FRANKIE" (Frank Morris Gerstle)
Born: Sept. 27, 1915, New York, N.Y. Died: Feb. 23, 1970, Santa Monica, Calif. (cancer). Screen and television actor.

Appeared in: **1951** I Was a Communist for the FBI; Blue Veil; You Never Can Tell; Strictly Dishonorable. **1953** The Glory Brigade; Killers from Space; The Magnetic Monster; Vicki. **1955** I Cover the Underworld; Slightly Scarlet; Tight Spot. **1956** Autumn Leaves; Between Heaven and Hell; The Proud Ones. **1957** Top Secret Affair; The River's Edge; Under Fire. **1958** Ambush at Cimarron Pass. **1959** Vice Raid; The Wasp Woman; The Four Skulls of Jonathan Drake; Inside the Mafia; I, Mobster; Submarine Seahawk. **1962** 13 West Street. **1963** Shock Corridor. **1964** The Atomic Brain (aka Monstrosity); The Quick Gun. **1965** Young Dillinger. **1966** The Wild Angels; The Silencers. **1967** Hell on Wheels.

GEST, INNA
Born: 1922. Died: Jan. 1, 1965, San Francisco, Calif. (hepatitis). Screen actress.

Appeared in: **1940** The Ghost Creeps.

GETTINGER, WILLIAM. See WILLIAM "BILL" STEELE

GHIO, NINO
Born: 1887. Died: Jan. 15, 1956, Culver City, Calif. Screen actor and opera singer.

GIACHETTI, FOSCO
Born: 1904, Italy. Died: Dec. 22, 1974, Rome, Italy (heart ailment). Stage and screen actor.

Appeared in: **1936** Luci Sommerse; Scipione L'Africano (Scipio Africanus—US 1939); Tredici Uomini e Un Cannone (Thirteen Men and a Cannon). **1937** Sentinelli di Bronzo (Bronze Sentinels); L'Ultima Nemica (The Last Enemy—US 1940); Il Ponto di Vetro (The Glass Bridge). **1938** Alba di Domani (Tomorrow at Dawn). **1939** Lo Squadrone Bianco (The White Squadron). **1940** Napoli che non Muore (Naples That Never Dies); Life of Giuseppe Verdi. **1941** The Dream of Butterfly. **1947** La Vita Ricomincia (Life Begins Anew). **1948** Les Maudits (The Damned). **1949** Fear No Evil. **1956** House of Ricordi. **1959** The Virtuous Bigamist. **1960** Il Mattatore (aka Love and Larceny—US 1963). **1961** El Relitto (The Wastrel aka To Be a Man—US 1963).

GIACOMINO (Giuseppe Cireni)
Born: 1884. Died: 1956, Milan, Italy. Screen actor and circus clown. Was a stand-in for Charles Chaplin in several films.

GIBBONS, ROSE
Born: 1886. Died: Aug. 13, 1964, Oakland, Calif. Screen and stage actress.

GIBSON, CHARLES DANA
Born: Sept. 14, 1867, Roxbury, Mass. Died: Dec. 23, 1944, New York, N.Y. (heart failure). Artist, illustrator and screen actor. Creator of "The Gibson Girl."

Appeared in: **1913** Saved by Parcel Post.

GIBSON, EDWARD "HOOT"
Born: Aug. 6, 1892, Tememah, Neb. Died: Aug. 23, 1962, Woodland Hills, Calif. (cancer). Screen, vaudeville actor and circus, rodeo performer. Married to singer Dorothy Dunstan and divorced from actresses Helen Johnson and Sally Eilers.

Appeared in: **1915** The Hazards of Helen. **1917** Straight Shooting. **1919** The Cactus Kid. **1921** Action; Red Courage; The Fire Eater; Sure Fire. **1922** Step on It; Headin' West; Trimmed; Ridin' Wild; The Galloping Kid; The Loaded Door; The Lone Hand; The Bearcat; The Denver Dude. **1923** Dead Game; Double Dealing; The Gentleman from Arizona; Out of Luck; Kindled Courage; The Ramblin' Kid; Shootin' for Love; Single Handed; The Thrill Chaser; Blinky. **1924** Hit and Run; Ride for Your Life; The Sawdust Trail; Hook and Ladder; Broadway or Bust; Forty Horse Hawkins; The Ridin' Kid from Powder River. **1925** Taming the West; Spook Ranch; The Saddle Hawk; The Hurricane Kid; Let 'Er Buck; The Calgary Stampede; Arizona Sweepstake. **1926** The Buckaroo Kid; Chip of the Flying U; The Flaming Frontier; The Man in the Saddle; The Phantom Bullet; The Texas Streak. **1927** Rawhide Kid; Galloping Fury; Straight Shootin'; A Hero on Horseback; Hey, Hey, Cowboy; Painted Ponies; The Prairie King; The Hawaiian Serenaders (short);

The Silent Rider. **1928** Clearing The Trail; The Danger Rider; The Flying Cowboy; Ridin' for Fame; A Trick of Heart; The Wild West Show. **1929** Smilin' Guns; King of the Rodeo; The Lariat Kid; Burning the Wind; Winged Horseman; Courtin' Wildcats; Points West; The Long, Long Trail. **1930** Roaring Ranch; Spurs; Trigger Tricks; Trailin' Trouble; The Mounted Stranger; The Concentratin' Kid. **1931** Clearing the Range; Wild Horse; Hard Hombre. **1932** The Boiling Point; Spirit of the West; Gay Buckaroo; Local Bad Man; A Man's Land. **1933** Cowboy Counsellor; The Dude Bandit; The Fighting Parson; Boots of Destiny. **1935** Sunset Range; Powdersmoke Range; Rainbow's End. **1936** The Last Outlaw; The Riding Avenger; Swifty; Frontier Justice; Feud of the West; Cavalcade of the West. **1937** The Painted Stallion (serial). **1940** The Trail Blazers. **1943** The Law Rides Again; Death Valley Rangers; Blazing Guns; Wild Horse Stampede. **1944** Marked Trails; The Outlaw Trail; Sonora Stagecoach; Trigger Law; Arizona Whirlwind; The Utah Kid; Westward Bound. **1948** Flight to Nowhere. **1953** The Marshal's Daughter. **1959** The Horse Soldiers. **1961** Ocean's Eleven.

GIBSON, JAMES
Born: 1866. Died: Oct. 13, 1938, Los Angeles, Calif. Screen and vaudeville actor.

Appeared in: **1924** The Right of the Strongest. **1925** Greed. **1926** Glenister of the Mounted. **1930** The Social Lion; Arizona Kid.

GIBSON, MARGARET. *See* PATRICIA PALMER

GIEHSE, THERESE
Born: 1899, U.S. Died: Mar. 3, 1975, Munich, West Germany. Stage and screen actress. Married to writer John Hampson.

Appeared in: **1931** Acht Tage Glueck. **1934** Der Meisterdetektiv. **1945** The Last Chance. **1948** Anna Karenina. **1958** Madchen in Uniform (Maedchen in Uniform—US 1965).

GIGLI, BENIAMINO
Born: 1890, Italy. Died: Nov. 30, 1957, Rome, Italy. Opera singer and screen actor. Was in US and Italian films.

Appeared in: **1927** The following shorts: Scenes from "Cavalleria Rusticana"; Quartet from "Rigoletto"; Bergere Legere; Scenes from "Lucia Di Lammermoor"; Scenes from "La Gioconda." **1928** The Pearl Fishers (short). **1937** Forever Yours; Ave Maria. **1938** Solo per Te (Only for You). **1939** Dein Gehort Mein Herz (My Heart Belongs to Thee). **1940** Du Bist mein Gluck (Thou Art My Joy); Legittima Difesa (Self Defense). **1942** Pagliacci. **1950** Night Taxi. **1951** Soho Conspiracy. **1953** Singing Taxi Driver.

GILBERT, BILLY (William V. Campbell)
Born: 1891. Died: Apr. 29, 1961, Hollywood, Calif. Do not confuse with "sneezing" comedian Billy Gilbert (dec. 1971). Screen, stage and vaudeville actor. Entered films in 1928.

GILBERT, BILLY
Born: Sept. 12, 1894, Louisville, Ky. Died: Sept. 23, 1971, North Hollywood, Calif. (stroke). Screen, stage, vaudeville, minstrel, television actor and stage producer. Married to actress Lolly McKenzie.

Appeared in: **1916** Bubbles of Trouble. **1929** Noisy Neighbors; The Woman Tamer (short). **1930** The Beauties (short); The Doctor's Wife (short). **1931** Chinatown After Dark; plus the following shorts: Shiver My Timbers; Dogs Is Dogs; The Panic Is On; The Hasty Marriage; One Good Turn; A Melon-Drama; Catch As Catch Can; The Pajama Party. **1932** Pack Up Your Troubles; Million Dollar Legs; "The Taxi Boys" series; plus the following shorts: Free Eats; Spanky; The Tabasco Kid; The Nickel Nurser; In Walked Charley; First in War; Young Ironsides; You're Telling Me; County Hospital; Their First Mistake; The Music Box; The Chimp; Strictly Unreliable; Seal Skins; On the Loose; Red Noses; Sneak Easily; Towed in a Hole. **1933** This Day and Age; plus the following shorts: Fallen Arches; Luncheon at Twelve; Asleep In the Fleet; Maids a la Mode; The Bargain of the Century; One Track Minds. **1934** Happy Landing; Peck's Bad Boy; Sons of the Desert (voice); Cockeyed Cavalier; plus the following shorts: The Cracked Iceman; Another Wild Idea (voice); Them Thar Hills; Men in Black; Soup and Fish. **1935** A Night at the Opera; plus the following shorts: Nurse to You; His Bridal Sweet; Pardon My Scotch; Just Another Murder; Hail Brother. **1936** Dangerous Waters; Sutter's Gold; Three of a Kind; The Bride Walks Out; Grand Jury; The Big Game; Night Waitress; Early to Bed; Kelly the Second; The Brain Busters (short). **1937** We're on the Jury; Sea Devils; The Man Who Found Himself; The Outcasts of Poker Flat; China Passage; Music for Madame; The Toast of New York; The Life of the Party; On the Avenue; Espionage; Broadway Melody of 1938; Rosalie; One Hundred Men and a Girl; Captains Courageous; The Firefly; Maytime; Fight for Your Lady. **1938** She's Got Everything; My Lucky Star; The Girl Downstairs; Maid's Night Out; The Joy of Living; Breaking the Ice; Mr. Doodle Kicks Off; Peck's Bad Boy with the Circus; Army Girl; Block Heads; Snow White and the Seven Dwarfs (voice of Sneezy); Angels with Dirty Faces; Happy Landing. **1939** Forged Passport; The Under-Pup; Rio; Destry Rides Again; The Star Maker. **1940** His Girl Friday; Women in War; Scatterbrain; Sing, Dance, Plenty Hot; Safari; A Night at Earl Carroll's; Sandy Is a

Lady; A Little Bit of Heaven; Seven Sinners; Queen of the Mob; Cross Country Romance; The Villain Still Pursued Her; No, No, Nanette; The Great Dictator; Tin Pan Alley. **1941** Reaching for the Sun; One Night in Lisbon; Angels with Broken Wings; Model Wife; New Wine; Week-End in Havana; Our City. **1942** Sleepytime Gal; Arabian Nights; Valley of the Sun; Song of the Islands; Mr. Wise Guy. **1943** Shantytown; Crazy House; Spotlight Scandals; Stage Door Canteen; Always a Bride's Maid. **1944** Three of a Kind; Crazy Knights; Ghost Crazy; Three's a Family; Ever Since Venus. **1945** Anchors Aweigh; Trouble Chasers. **1947** Fun and Fancy Free (voice). **1948** The Kissing Bandit. **1949** Bride of Vengeance; Mickey and the Giant Killer (voice). **1953** Down Among the Sheltering Palms. **1962** Paradise Valley; Five Weeks in a Balloon. **1963** The Sound of Laughter (documentary).

GILBERT, BOBBY
Born: 1898. Died: Sept. 19, 1973, Hollywood, Calif. (hepatitis). Screen and vaudeville actor.

Appeared in: **1931** Never the Twain Shall Meet. **1937** A Vitaphone short.

GILBERT, JOE
Born: 1903. Died: May 26, 1959, Hollywood, Calif. Screen actor. Entered films in 1923.

GILBERT, JOHN (John Pringle)
Born: July 10, 1897, Logan, Utah. Died: Jan. 9, 1936, Los Angeles, Calif. (heart attack). Screen, stage actor, screenwriter, film producer and film director. Divorced from actresses Olivia Burwell, Leatrice Joy, Ina Claire and Virginia Bruce. Son of actor and extra John Pringle (dec. 1929).

Appeared in: **1915** The Mother Instinct. **1916** Hell's Hinges. **1917** Princess of the Dark; The Devil Dodger; Apostle of Vengeance; Golden Rule Kate. **1919** Heart of the Hills; Should a Woman Tell; Busher; Widow by Proxy. **1920** White Circle; The Great Redeemer. **1921** Ladies in Love; Ladies Must Live; The Servant in the House; The Bait; Love's Penalty; Shame. **1922** The Love Gambler; Arabian Love; The Yellow Stain; Gleam O'Dawn; The Count of Monte Cristo; Calvert's Valley; Honor First. **1923** Madness of Youth; California Romance; Truxton King; Cameo Kirby; The Exiles; St. Elmo; While Paris Sleeps. **1924** Romance Ranch; The Wolf Man; Just Off Broadway; The Lone Chance; The Snob; His Hour; Married Flirts; A Man's Mate; He Who Gets Slapped. **1925** The Big Parade; The Merry Widow; The Wife of the Centaur. **1926** La Boheme; Bardely's, The Magnificent. **1927** Flesh and the Devil; Twelve Miles Out; Love; The Show; Man, Woman and Sin. **1928** The Cossacks; Show People; Four Walls; Masks of the Devil. **1929** A Woman of Affairs; Desert Nights; His Glorious Night; Hollywood Revue of 1929; A Man's Mate. **1930** Redemption; Way for a Sailor. **1931** Phantom of Paris; Gentleman's Fate. **1932** Big Parade; West of Broadway; Downstairs. **1933** Queen Christina; Fast Workers. **1934** The Captain Hates the Sea. **1967** Show People (reissue of 1928 film).

GILBERT, MAUDE
Died: July 7, 1953, Laguna Beach, Calif. Stage and screen actress.

GILBERT, WALTER
Born: 1887. Died: Jan. 12, 1947, Brooklyn, N.Y. (heart attack). Stage and screen actor.

Appeared in: **1925** The Pearl of Love. **1930** She's My Weakness. **1934** Gambling. **1938** Dynamite Delaney.

GILES, ANNA
Born: 1874. Died: Feb. 2, 1973, Los Angeles, Calif. Screen actress.

GILFETHER, DANIEL
Born: 1854, Boston, Mass. Died: May 3, 1919, Long Beach, Calif. (kidney disease). Stage and screen actor. Entered films in 1913.

Appeared in: **1914** The Higher Law. **1915** Who Pays? (serial); The Fruit of Folly; The Red Circle (serial). **1916** Mismates; The Homebreakers; Shadows and Sunshine; The Broken Promise; An Old Man's Folly; Pay Dirt; The Better Instinct; From the Deep. **1917** Twin Kiddies; Told at the Twilight; Zollenstein; The Girl Angle; The Checkmate; The Wildcat; Brand's Daughter; His Old Fashioned Dad. **1918** No Children Wanted; The Locked Heart; Marylee Mixes In; Little Miss Grown-Up; Wanted—A Brother.

GILL, BASIL
Born: 1877, Birkenhead, England. Died: Apr. 23, 1955, Hove, England. Stage and screen actor.

Appeared in: **1911** Henry VIII (film debut). **1916** Chains of Bondage; On the Banks of Allan Water. **1917** The Adventures of Dick Dolan (short); The Ragged Messenger. **1918** The Admirable Crichton; Missing the Tide; Spinner O'Dreams; Film Tags series including What's the Use of Grumbling (short). **1919** God's Good Man; The Home Maker; The Irresistible Flapper; Keeper of the Door; The Rocks of Valpre; A Soul's Crucifixion (aka Crucifixion or The Soul of Gilda Lois). **1920** The Worldlings. **1926** Julius Caesar (short); Santa

Claus. **1929** High Treason. **1930** Should a Doctor Tell? (US 1931); The School for Scandal. **1931** Glamour. **1933** The Wandering Jew (US 1935); Mrs. Dane's Defence. **1935** The Immortal Gentleman; The Divine Spark; Royal Cavalcade (aka Regal Cavalcade—US). **1936** Rembrandt; His Lordship (aka Man of Affaires—US 1937); Gaol Break; The Crimson Circle. **1937** Knight Without Armour. **1938** St. Martin's Lane (aka Sidewalks of London—US 1940); The Citadel; Dangerous Medicine.

GILL, FLORENCE
Born: July 27, 1877, London, England. Died: Feb. 19, 1965, Woodland Hills, Calif. (arteriosclerosis). Stage and screen actress. Was the voice of numerous Disney characters.

Appeared in: **1933** Dora's Dunkin' Donuts. **1935** Every Night at Eight. **1937** Larceny in the Air. **1941** The Reluctant Dragon (voice).

GILLETT, ELMA
Born: 1874. Died: July 23, 1941, Hollywood, Calif. Screen and stage actress.

GILLETTE, WILLIAM
Born: 1856, Hartford, Conn. Died: Apr. 29, 1937, Hartford, Conn. (pulmonary hemorrhage). Stage, screen actor and playwright.

Appeared in: **1916** Sherlock Holmes.

GILLIE, JEAN
Born: 1915, Kensington, England. Died: Feb. 19, 1949, London, England. Screen, stage actress and dancer. Divorced from film producer/writer Jack Bernhard.

Appeared in: **1935** His Majesty and Co.; Smith's Wives; Brewster's Millions; School for Stars; It Happened in Paris; While Parents Sleep. **1936** This'll Make You Whistle (screen and stage versions—US 1938). **1937** The Girl in the Taxi; The Live Wire. **1938** Sweet Devil. **1939** The Middle Watch; What Would You Do Chums?; The Spider. **1940** A Call to Arms (short); Tilly of Bloomsbury; Sailors Don't Cry. **1941** The Saint Meets the Tiger (US 1943). **1943** The Gentle Sex. **1944** Tawny Pipit (US 1947). **1945** Flight from Folly. **1947** The Macomber Affair; Decoy.

GILLINGWATER, CLAUDE
Born: Aug. 2, 1870, Lauseanna, Mo. Died: Oct. 31, 1939, Beverly Hills, Calif. (suicide—gunshot). Stage and screen actor.

Appeared in: **1921** Little Lord Fauntleroy (film debut). **1922** My Boy; The Dust Flower; Fools First; Remembrance; The Stranger's Banquet. **1923** Alice Adams; Three Wise Fools; Dulcy; A Chapter in Her Life; The Christian; Crinoline and Romance; Souls for Sale; Tiger Rose. **1924** Daddies; How to Educate a Wife; Idle Tongues; Madonna of the Streets. **1925** Cheaper to Marry; Seven Sinners; A Thief in Paradise; Wages for Wives; We Moderns; Winds of Chance. **1926** For Wives Only; Into Her Kingdom; That's My Baby. **1927** Barbed Wire; Fast and Furious; The Gorilla; Naughty but Nice. **1928** Little Shepherd of Kingdom Come; Husbands for Rent; Oh, Kay; Women They Talk About; Remember. **1929** Stark Mad; Stolen Kisses; A Dangerous Woman; Smiling Irish Eyes; Glad Rag Doll. **1930** The Flirting Widow; The Great Divide; Toast of the Legion; Dumbbells in Ermine; So Long Letty. **1931** Illicit; The Conquering Horde; Kiss Me Again; Gold Dust Gertie; Daddy Long Legs; Compromised; Oh! Oh! Cleopatra (short). **1932** Tess of the Storm Country; **1933** Skyway; Ace of Aces; Ann Carver's Profession; Before Midnight; The Avenger. **1934** In Love with Life; Back Page; Green Eyes; Broadway Bill; The Captain Hates the Sea; You Can't Buy Everything; The Show-Off; The Unknown Blonde; City Limits. **1935** Mississippi; Baby Face Harrington; Calm Yourself; A Tale of Two Cities; The Woman in Red. **1936** Florida Special; Counterfeit; The Prisoner of Shark Island; The Poor Little Rich Girl; Can This Be Dixie?; Ticket to Paradise; Wives Never Know. **1937** Top of the Town; Conquest. **1938** Little Miss Broadway; Just Around the Corner; There Goes My Heart; A Yank at Oxford. **1939** Cafe Society.

GILLIS, WILLIAM S.
Died: Apr. 24, 1946, Los Angeles, Calif. Screen actor. Entered films approx. 1906.

Appeared in: **1920** Ruth of the Rockies (serial).

GILMORE, HELEN
Born: 1900, Chicago, Ill. Died: Oct. 8, 1947, New York, N.Y. (leukemia). Screen actress and magazine editor. Do not confuse with stage actress Helen Gilmore (dec. 1936).

Appeared in: **1921** The Blazing Trail; Dangerous Paths. **1922** Good Men and True; Impulse; Too Much Business. **1927** Sensation Seekers.

GILMORE, LOWELL
Died: Feb. 1, 1960, Hollywood, Calif. Screen actor.

Appeared in: **1944** Days of Glory. **1945** Johnny Angel; The Picture of Dorian Gray. **1946** Step by Step; Strange Conquest. **1947** The Arnelo Affair; Calcutta. **1948** The Prince of Thieves; Black Arrow; Walk a Crooked Mile; Dream Girl. **1949** The Secret Garden; Sword in the Desert. **1950** Fortunes of Captain Blood;

Tripoli; King Solomon's Mines; Rogues of Sherwood Forest. **1951** Roadblock; Hong Kong; Darling, How Could You?; The Highwayman. **1952** The Plymouth Adventure; Androcles and the Lion; Lone Star. **1953** Francis Covers the Big Town. **1954** Day of Triumph; Saskatchewan. **1955** The Sea Chase; Ma and Pa Kettle at Waikiki. **1956** Comanche.

GILPIN, CHARLES S.
Born: 1879. Died: May 6, 1930, Eldredge Park, N.J. Screen, stage actor and playwright.

Appeared in: **1926** Ten Nights in a Barroom.

GILSON, TOM (Thomas Peter Gilson)
Born: Jan. 6, 1934, New York, N.Y. Died: Oct. 6, 1962, Van Nuys, Calif. (shot). Screen and television actor.

Appeared in: **1958** Young and Wild; Rally Round the Flag, Boys! **1959** Home from the Hill. **1960** This Rebel Breed; The Threat; The Crowded Sky. **1962** Convicts Four.

GIM, H. W. (Hom Wing Gim)
Born: Jan, 22, 1908, China. Died: Mar. 15, 1973, Los Angeles, Calif. Screen and television actor.

Appeared in **1951** Peking Express. **1962** Gypsy. **1963** McLintock! **1966** Seven Women. **1969** True Grit; Paint Your Wagon.

GINIVA, JOHN "ALASKA JACK"
Born: 1868. Died: Feb. 22, 1936, Hollywood, Calif. Screen and vaudeville actor.

GINN, WELLS WATSON
Born: 1891, Bellefontaine, Ohio. Died: Apr. 15, 1959, Cincinnati, Ohio. Screen, stage, radio, vaudeville actor, and film director.

Appeared in and directed early Cosmopolitan Co. films in New York.

GIOI, VIVI
Born: 1917, Italy? Died: July 12, 1975, Fregene, Italy (heart attack). Stage and screen actress.

Appeared in: **1956** La Risaia (aka Rice Girl—US 1963).

GIRADOT, ETIENNE
Born: 1856, London, England. Died: Nov. 10, 1939, Hollywood, Calif. Stage and screen actor. Entered films with Vitagraph Co. in 1912.

Appeared in: **1912** The Violin of Monsieur. **1933** The Kennel Murder Case; Blood Money; Advice to the Lovelorn. **1934** Twentieth Century (stage and film versions); Fashions of 1934; Mandalay; Return of the Terror; Little Man, What Now?; The Dragon Murder Case; The Fire Brand. **1935** Grand Old Girl; The Whole Town's Talking; Clive of India; Chasing Yesterday; Hooray for Love; In Old Kentucky; Curly Top; The Bishop Misbehaves; I Live My Life; Metropolitan. **1936** The Garden Murder Case; The Devil Is a Sissy; The Longest Night; Go West, Young Man; College Holiday; The Music Goes 'Round; Half Angel; Hearts Divided. **1937** Wake up and Live; Danger—Love at Work; The Road Back; The Great Garrick; Breakfast for Two. **1938** Port of Seven Seas; Arizona Wildcat; Professor Beware; There Goes My Heart. **1939** Little Accident; The Hunchback of Notre Dame; The Story of Vernon and Irene Castle; Fast and Loose; Exile Express; For Love or Money; Hawaiian Nights. **1940** Isle of Destiny.

GIRARD, JOE (Joseph W. Girard)
Born: Apr. 2, 1871, Williamsport, Pa. Died: Aug. 12, 1949. Stage and screen actor.

Appeared in: **1911** Back to the Primitive. **1914** Shotgun Jones; Sheep's Clothing; The Birth of the Star Spangled Banner. **1915** The Trail of the Upper Yukon; The Last Act; The Parson of Pine Mountain; The Meddler. **1916** 20,000 Leagues Under the Sea; Aschenbroedel; The Laugh of Scorn; The Broken Spur; The Narrow Path; The Sheriff of Pine Mountain. **1917** The Voice on the Wire (serial); Treason; Hell Morgan's Girl; The Storm Woman; Fear Not. **1918** The Beast of Berlin; The Bride's Awakening; Danger, Go Slow; The Risky Road; Her Body in Bond; The Marriage Life; The Two-Soul Woman; The Brass Bullet (serial). **1919** What Am I Bid?; Bare Fists; Two Soiled Women; Kaiser—the Beast of Berlin; Loot; Paid in Advance; The Midnight Man (serial); Sign of the Rat. **1920** The Figurehead; The Branded Mystery; The Branded H (serial); The Screaming Shadow (serial); The Fatal Sign (serial); The Branded Four (serial). **1921** Dangerous Paths; Dead or Alive; Red Courage; The Sheriff of Hope Eternal; Her Social Value; A Yankee Go-Getter; The Blue Fox (serial). **1922** Step On It!; Chain Lightning; The Man Who Married His Own Wife; The Price of Youth; One Wonderful Night; Nan of the North (serial). **1923** Three Jumps Ahead; The Wild Party; The Devil's Dooryard; The Law Rustlers; Soft Boiled; Legally Dead; Lovebound; Where Is This West?; The Sting of the Scorpion. **1924** After a Million; Gambling Wives; Jack O'Clubs; The Night Hawk; Reckless Speed; In Hollywood with Potash and Perlmutter; Laughing at Danger; Leave It to Gerry; The Night Message; Wolves of the North (serial); Stolen Secrets; The Western Wallop. **1925** The Gambling Fool; Romance and Rustlers; Three Keys; The Fugitive; Ten Days;

Speed Madness; The Pride of the Force; Vic Dyson Pays; Youth and Adventure. **1926** The Dangerous Dub; Doubling with Danger; Driftin' Thru; Forlorn River; The High Flyer; Lightning Reporter; Modern Youth; Tentacles of the North; The Warning Signal; Flying High; The Flying Mail; The Night Owl; Ladies of Leisure; Out of the Storm; Speed Crazed; We're in the Navy Now. **1927** The Final Extra; Fireman—Save My Child; In the First Degree; The Ladybird; The Silent Hero; The Shield of Honor; When Seconds Count; Whispering Sage. **1928** The Fleet's In; Hello Cheyenne; The Bullet Mark; Marlie the Miller; Partners in Crime; Stop that Man; The Terror; Heart Trouble. **1929** Broken Barriers; Courtin' Wildcats; From Headquarters; The Girl from Havana; The Leatherneck; Redskin; The One Woman Idea; King of the Rodeo. **1930** The Girl of the Golden West; Just Imagine; Back from Shanghai; Sons of the Saddle; Troopers Three; Third Alarm. **1931** Strictly Dishonorable; Gang Busters; Defenders of the Law; Mystery Train; Sky Spider; Is There Justice? **1932** Scareheads; Radio Patrol; The Crusader; The Texas Bad Man; The Hurricane Express (serial). **1933** Officer 13; Racetrack; Renegades of the West; The World Gone Mad; The Whirlwind; Silent Men; Fiddlin' Buckaroo. **1934** Murder in the Museum; Woman Who Dared; Fighting Trouper. **1935** Kentucky Blue Streak; His Fighting Blood; Outlawed Guns; Ivory-Handled Gun; Outlaw Deputy. **1936** Frontier Justice; The Dragnet; The Oregon Trail; Ride 'Em Cowboy; The Clutching Hand (serial); Aces and Eights. **1937** Mystery of the Hooded Horseman. **1938** Unashamed; Held for Ransom. **1939** Ride 'Em Cowgirl; Tough Kid; Crashing Thru. **1940** The Green Archer (serial). **1942** Captain Midnight (serial); The Spider Returns (serial).

GIROUX, LEE
Born: 1911. Died: Jan. 26, 1973, North Hollywood, Calif. (natural causes). Television newscaster, author and screen actor.

Appeared in: **1961** X-15. **1963** Son of Flubber.

GISH, DOROTHY (Dorothy de Guiche)
Born: Mar. 11, 1898, Dayton, Ohio. Died: June 4, 1968, Rapallo, Italy (bronchial pneumonia). Stage and screen actress. Entered films in 1912. Sister of actress Lillian Gish. Divorced from actor James Rennie (dec. 1965).

Appeared in: **1912** An Unseen Enemy; The New York Hat; The Burglar's Dilemma; The Musketeers of Pig Alley; Gold and Glitter; The Informer; My Hero; A Cry for Help. **1913** The Perfidy of Mary; Her Mother's Oath; Oil and Water; The Lady and the Mouse; Just Gold; Almost a Wild Man; Pa Says; The Vengeance of Galora; Those Little Flowers; The Widow's Kids; The Adopted Brother; The Lady in Black; The House of Discord. **1914** Her Old Teacher; Judith of Bethulia; Her Father's Silent Partner; The Mysterious Shot; The Floor Above; The Old Man; Liberty Belles; The Mountain Rat; Silent Sandy; The Newer Woman; Their First Acquaintance; Arms and the Gringo; The Suffragette's Battle in Nuttyville; The City Beautiful; The Painted Lady; Home Sweet Home; The Tavern of Tragedy; Her Mother's Necklace; A Lesson in Mechanics; Granny; A Fair Rebel; Down the Road to Creditville; The Wife; Sands of Fate; The Warning; Back to the Kitchen; The Availing Prayer; The Saving Grace; The Sisters; The Better Way. **1915** Out of Bondage; Jordan Is a Hard Road; In Old Heidelberg; An Old Fashioned Girl; How Hazel Got Even; The Lost Lord Lowell; Minerva's Mission; Her Grandparents; Her Mother's Daughter; The Mountain Girl; The Little Catamount; Victorine; Bred in the Bone. **1916** Little Meena's Romance; Betty of Graystone; Susan Rocks the Boat; The Little School Ma'rm; Gretchen, the Greenhorn; Atta Boy's Last Race; Children of the Feud. **1917** The Little Yank; Stage Struck; Her Official Fathers. **1918** Battling Jane; The Hun Within; Hearts of the World. **1919** Out of Luck; The Hope Chest; Boots; Peppy Polly; Nobody Home; Turning the Tables; I'll Get Him Yet; Nugget Nell. **1920** Remodeling Her Husband; Mary Ellen Comes to Town; Little Miss Rebellion; Flying Pat. **1921** The Ghost in the Garret; Oh, Jo! **1922** The Country Flapper; Orphans of the Storm. **1923** Fury; The Bright Shawl. **1924** Romola. **1925** Night Life in New York; Clothes Make the Pirate; The Beautiful City. **1926** Nell Gwyn. **1927** London; Madame Pompadour; Tip Toes. **1930** Wolves. **1936** Wanted Men. **1944** Our Hearts Were Young and Gay. **1946** Centennial Summer. **1951** The Whistle at Eaton Falls; Mornings at Seven. **1964** The Cardinal; The Chalk Garden.

GLADMAN, ANNABELLE
Born: 1899. Died: Jan. 15, 1948, Hollywood, Calif. Screen actress.

GLAGOLIN, BORIS S.
Born: 1878, Russia. Died: Dec. 12, 1948, Hollywood, Calif. Screen, stage actor and stage director.

GLASER, VAUGHAN
Born: 1872. Died: Nov. 23, 1958, Van Nuys, Calif. Screen and stage actor.

Appeared in: **1939** What A Life; Rulers of the Sea. **1940** Those Were the Days. **1941** Adventure in Washington; Henry Aldrich for President. **1942** Henry Aldrich, Editor; Saboteur; Henry and Dizzy; My Favorite Spy. **1943** Henry Aldrich Gets Glamour; Henry Aldrich Swings It; Henry Aldrich Haunts a House. **1944** Arsenic and Old Lace; Henry Aldrich Plays Cupid.

GLASS, EVERETT
Born: 1891. Died: Mar. 22, 1966, Los Angeles, Calif. Screen actor.

Appeared in: **1949** The Undercover Man; Easy Living. **1950** Mother Didn't Tell Me; Father Makes Good; Two Flags West; The Petty Girl; Counter Spy Meets Scotland Yard. **1952** Deadline U.S.A.; Dreamboat. **1953** Inferno; Three Sailors and a Girl. **1954** Demetrius and the Gladiators; Day of Triumph. **1955** They Came from Another World. **1956** World Without End; Friendly Persuasion; Invasion of the Body Snatchers. **1957** The Quiet Gun. **1958** Gunman's Walk. **1960** Elmer Gantry; The Marriage-Go-Round.

GLASS, GASTON
Born: Dec. 31, 1898, Paris, France. Died: Nov. 11, 1965, Santa Monica, Calif. Screen, stage actor, assistant film director and television production manager. Married to actress "Bo-Peep" Karlin (dec. 1969).

Appeared in: **1919** Open Your Eyes. **1920** Humoresque; The World and His Wife. **1921** God's Crucible; Her Winning Way; The Lost Battalion; There are No Villains. **1922** I Am the Law; Glass Houses; The Kingdom Within; Little Miss Smiles; Monte Cristo; Rich Men's Wives; The Song of Life. **1923** The Hero; Gimme; The Spider and the Rose; Mothers-in-Law; Daughters of the Rich. **1924** I Am the Man; After the Ball. **1925** The Bad Lands; The Danger Signal; Fair Play; Flying Fool; The Mad Marriage; Parisian Nights; The Prince of Success; Pursued; The Scarlet West; Three Keys; The Verdict. **1926** Broken Homes; The Call of the Klondike; Exclusive Rights; Her Sacrifice; The Jazz Girl; Midnight Limited; The Road to Broadway; The Romance of a Million Dollars; Subway Sadie; Sweet Sadie; Sweet Daddies; Tentacles of the North; Wives at Auction. **1927** Better Days; Compassion; False Morals; The Gorilla; The Love Wager; The Show Girl; Sinews of Steel. **1928** The Red Mark; Name the Woman; A Gentleman Preferred; Innocent Love; My Home Town; Obey Your Husband; The Wife's Relations. **1929** Broken Barriers; Untamed Justice; Behind Closed Doors; Geraldine; The Faker; Tiger Rose. **1930** Just Like Heaven; She Got What She Wanted; The South Sea Pearl (short). **1931** The Bad Man; The Big Trail (both French versions). **1934** LeGong (narr.). **1935** Sylvia Scarlett. **1936** The Princess Comes Across; Desire; Gambling with Souls; Sutter's Gold; Mary of Scotland. **1937** Death in the Air; Espionage.

GLASSMIRE, AUGUSTIN J. "GUS"
Born: 1879. Died: July 23, 1946, Hollywood, Calif. Screen and stage actor. Entered films in 1932.

Appeared in: **1939** Our Leading Citizen. **1942** My Gal Sal; Saboteur; The Big Shot; Syncopation. **1944** Wilson. **1945** Fallen Angel; Scarlet Street; Enchanted Cottage; Col. Effingham's Raid; The Bullfighters.

GLAUM, LOUISE
Born: 1900, Baltimore, Md. Died: Nov. 25, 1970, Los Angeles, Calif. (pneumonia). Stage and screen actress. Appeared in Mack Sennett comedies.

Appeared in: **1915** The Lure of Woman; The Iron Strain. **1916** The Aryan; Honor Thy Name; Return of Draw Egan; Home; Hell's Hinges. **1919** The Poppy Girl's Husband; Sahara; The Lone Wolf's Daughter. **1920** Sex. **1921** I Am Guilty; The Leopard Woman; Love; Greater Than Love. **1925** Fifty-Fifty.

GLAZER, EVE F.
Born: 1903. Died: June 29, 1960, Hollywood, Calif. (cancer). Screen actress.

GLEASON, FRED
Born: 1854. Died: June 9, 1933, New York, N.Y. Screen and stage actor.

GLEASON, JAMES "JIMMY"
Born: May 23, 1886, New York, N.Y. Died: Apr. 12, 1959, Woodland Hills, Calif. (asthma). Screen, stage actor and screenwriter. Son of stage actress Mina Crolius Gleason (dec. 1931). Married to actress Lucille Gleason (dec. 1947). Father of actor Russell Gleason (dec. 1945). Nominated for 1941 Academy Award as Best Supporting Actor in Here Comes Mr. Jordan.

Appeared in: **1922** Polly of the Follies. **1928** The Count of Ten. **1929** Garden of Eatin'; Fairways and Foul; The Shannons of Broadway; The Broadway Melody; The Flying Fool; High Voltage; His First Command. **1930** Oh, Yeah!; Free Soul; Puttin' on the Ritz; Dumbbells in Ermine; The Matrimonial Bed; Big Money; Don't Believe It; No Brakes; The Swellhead; What a Widow!; Her Man. **1931** The Big Gamble; Sweepstakes; It's a Wise Child; Beyond Victory; Suicide Fleet. **1932** Information Kid; Blondie of the Follies; Lady and Gent; The Crooked Circle; The Penguin Pool Murder; The All American; The Devil Is Driving; Fast Companions. **1933** Hoopla; Billion Dollar Scandal; Clear All Wires. **1934** Pie for Two; Murder on the Blackboard; The Meanest Gal in Town; Search for Beauty; Orders Is Orders. **1935** Murder on a Honeymoon; Hot Tip; West Point of the Air; Helldorado. **1936** Murder on the Bridle Path; The Ex-Mrs. Bradford; Don't Turn 'Em Loose; The Big Game; The Plot Thickens; Yours for the Asking; We're Only Human. **1937** Forty Naughty Girls; Manhattan Merry-Go-Round. **1938** Army Girl; The Higgins Family; Dawn over Ireland; Goodbye Broadway. **1939** On Your Toes; My Wife's Relatives; Should Husbands Work?; The Covered Trailer. **1940** Money to Burn; Grandpa Goes to Town; Earl of Paddlestone. **1941** Meet John Doe; Here Comes Mr. Jordan; Tanks a Million; Nine Lives Are Not Enough; Affectionately Yours; A Date with the Falcon; Babes on Broadway. **1942** Tramp, Tramp, Tramp; Hay Foot; My Gal Sal; The Falcon Takes Over; Footlight Serenade; Tales of Manhattan; Manila Calling; All through the Night. **1943** A Guy Named Joe; Crash Dive. **1944** Keys of the Kingdom; Arsenic and Old Lace; Once Upon a Time; This Man's Navy. **1945** A Tree Grows in Brooklyn; Captain Eddie; The Clock. **1946** Lady Luck; Home Sweet Homicide; The Well-Groomed Bride; The Hoodlum Saint. **1947** Down to Earth; Tycoon; The Homestretch; The Tenderfoot; The Bishop's Wife. **1948** When My Baby Smiles at Me; The Return of October; Smart Woman; The Dude Goes West. **1949** The Life of Riley; Bad Boy; Take One False Step; Miss Grant Takes Richmond. **1950** The Jackpot; Joe Palooka in the Squared Circle; Key to the City; Riding High; Two Flags West; The Yellow Cab Man. **1951** Two Gals and a Guy; Come Fill the Cup; Joe Palooka in the Triple Cross; I'll See You in My Dreams. **1952** The Story of Will Rogers; What Price Glory; We're Not Married. **1953** Forever Female. **1954** Hollywood Thrillmakers; Suddenly. **1955** The Night of the Hunter; The Girl Rush. **1956** Star in the Dust. **1957** Spring Reunion; The Female Animal; Loving You; Money, Women and Guns; Man in the Shadow. **1958** Once Upon a Horse; Man or Gun; Rock-a-Bye Baby; The Last Hurrah.

GLEASON, LUCILLE (Lucille Webster)
Born: Feb. 6, 1888, Pasadena, Calif. Died: May 13, 1947, Brentwood, Calif. (heart attack). Stage and screen actress. Ran for California Assembly in 1944 but was defeated. Wife of actor James Gleason (dec. 1959) and mother of actor Russell Gleason (dec. 1945).

Appeared in: **1929** Garden of Eatin'; Fairways and Foul; The Shannons of Broadway; Pathe "Golden Rooster" comedies. **1930** Don't Believe It. **1931** Pagan Lady; Girls About Town. **1932** A Hockey Hick (short); Girl of the Rio; Nice Women. **1933** Don't Bet on Love; The Solitaire Man; Love, Honor and Oh, Baby! **1934** Woman Afraid; Successful Failure; Beloved; I Like It That Way. **1936** Klondike Annie; Rhythm on the Range; The Ex-Mrs. Bradford. **1937** Red Light Ahead; Navy Blues; First Lady. **1938** The Beloved Brat; The Nurse from Brooklyn; The Higgins Family. **1939** My Wife's Relatives; Should Husbands Work?; The Covered Trailer. **1940** Money to Burn; Grandpa Goes to Town; Earl of Puddlestone; Lucky Partners. **1941** The Gay Falcon. **1943** Stage Door Canteen. **1945** The Clock; Don't Fence Me In.

GLEASON, RUSSELL
Born: Feb. 6, 1908, Portland, Ore. Died: Dec. 26, 1945, New York, N.Y. (fall from hotel window). Screen actor. Son of actor James Gleason (dec. 1959) and actress Lucille Gleason (dec. 1947).

Appeared in: **1929** The Flying Fool; The Shady Lady; The Sophomore; Strange Cargo; Seven Faces. **1930** Officer O'Brien; All Quiet on the Western Front; Sisters. **1931** Beyond Victory; Laugh and Get Rich; Homicide Squad. **1932** Always Kickin' (sports short); The Strange Case of Clara Deane; Nice Women; Off His Base (sports short); A Hockey Hick (sports short). **1933** Private Jones. **1934** I Can't Escape. **1935** Hot Tip. **1936** Hitchhike to Heaven. **1937** Off to the Races; Big Business; Hot Water; Borrowing Trouble. **1938** Fury Below; The Higgins Family; Down on the Farm; Love on a Budget; A Trip to Paris; Safety in Numbers. **1939** My Wife's Relatives; News Is Made at Night; Should Husbands Work; The Covered Trailer; Here I Am a Stranger. **1940** Money to Burn; Young as You Feel; Grandpa Goes to Town; Earl of Puddlestone; Yesterday's Heroes. **1941** Unexpected Uncle. **1942** Dudes Are Pretty People; Fingers at the Window. **1943** Salute to the Marines. **1944** Adventures of Mark Twain.

GLECKLER, ROBERT P.
Born: Jan. 11, 1890, Pierre, S.D. Died: Feb. 26, 1939, Los Angeles, Calif. (uremic poisoning). Stage and screen actor. Entered films in 1928.

Appeared in: **1928** The Dove. **1929** Mother's Boy. **1930** The Sea God; Big Money. **1931** Night Nurse; Defenders of the Law; She Went for a Tramp; Finger Points. **1933** Take a Chance. **1934** Now I'll Tell; The Defense Rests; Million Dollar Ransom; The Personality Kid. **1935** Great Hotel Murder; The Perfect Clue; The Daring Young Man; The Farmer Takes a Wife; Dante's Inferno; Mr. Dynamite; It Happened in New York; The Case of the Curious Bride; The Glass Key; Headline Woman; Here Comes the Band; Whipsaw; Show Them No Mercy. **1936** Absolute Quiet; Sworn Enemy; Love Begins at Twenty; Forgotten Faces; Yours for the Asking; I'd Give My Life; The Girl on the Front Page; North of Nome; Great Guy. **1937** Pick a Star; King of Gamblers; Bulldog Drummond's Revenge; Hot Water; The Man Who Cried Wolf. **1938** Rascals; Alexander's Ragtime Band; Gangs of New York; Gun Law; Little Miss Broadway. **1939** They Made Me a Criminal; Stand up and Fight.

GLENDINNING, ERNEST
Born: 1884, Ulverston, England. Died: May 17, 1936, South Coventry, Conn. Stage and screen actor.

Appeared in: **1922** When Knighthood Was in Flower. **1930** Grounds for Murder (short).

GLENDON, JONATHAN FRANK
Born: 1887. Died: Mar. 17, 1937, Hollywood, Calif. Screen and stage actor.

Appeared in: **1917** The Third Judgement. **1918** The Wooing of Princess Pat; A

Woman in the Web (serial). **1920** Mid-Channel. **1921** Forgotten Woman; Hush; A Tale of Two Worlds; What Do Men Want? **1922** Belle of Alaska; Kissed; More to Be Pitied Than Scorned; Night Life in Hollywood; Yankee Doodle, Jr. **1923** Just Like a Woman; Rip Tide; Shattered Faith; South Sea Love. **1925** Lights of Old Broadway; Private Affairs; Tricks. **1926** Upstage. **1927** Cross Breed; Compassion. **1930** Border Romance. **1933** Sucker Money; Strange People; Gun Law; Her Splendid Folly. **1935** The Phantom Empire (serial); The Sagebrush Troubadour. **1936** King of the Pecos; Border Caballero.

GLENN, RAYMOND. *See* BOB CUSTER

GLENN, ROY E., SR.
Born: 1915, Pittsburg, Kan. Died: Mar. 12, 1971, Los Angeles, Calif. (heart attack). Black screen, stage and television actor.

Appeared in: **1952** Lydia Bailey; Chicago Calling. **1958** Tarzan's Fight for Life. **1961** A Raisin in the Sun. **1962** Sweet Bird of Youth. **1966** Dead Heat On a Merry-Go-Round; A Man Called Adam. **1967** Guess Who's Coming to Dinner; The Way West. **1968** Finian's Rainbow; Hang 'Em High; I Love You, Alice B. Toklas! **1970** The Great White Hope; Tick...Tick...Tick... **1971** Escape From the Planet of the Apes.

GLOECKNER-KRAMER, PEPI
Born: 1874, Austria. Died: 1954, Vienna, Austria. Screen and stage actress.

Appeared in: **1939** Verliebte Herzen (Hearts in Love).

GLORI, ENRICO
Born: 1901, Naples, Italy. Died: Apr. 22, 1966, Rome, Italy. Stage and screen actor.

Appeared in: **1936** Il Fu Mattia Pascal. **1937** Les Perles de la Couronne (Pearls of the Crown). **1948** Man of the Sea; The Spirit and the Flesh. **1949** Lost in the Dark. **1953** Stranger on the Prowl. **1960** La Giornata Balorda (aka A Crazy Day; Love Is a Day's Work; Pickup in Rome and From a Roman Balcony—US 1961); Les Nuits de Raspoutine (The Night They Killed Rasputin—US 1962). **1961** La Dolce Vita; Barabba (aka Barabbas—US 1962); Costantino il Grande (Constantine and the Cross—US 1962); Romolo e Remo (Romulus and Remus aka Duel of the Titans—US 1963); Il Mattatore (aka L'Homme aux Cent Visages—Love and Larceny—US 1963). **1962** Il Tiranno di Siracusa (aka Damone e Pitias—Damon and Pythias—US).

GLYN, NEVA CARR
Born: Australia. Died: Aug. 10, 1975, Mona Vale, Australia. Screen, stage, radio and television actress. Mother of actor Nick Tate.

Appeared in: **1974** Ride a Wild Pony.

GLYNNE, MARY
Born: Jan. 25, 1898, Penarth, Wales. Died: Sept. 22, 1954, London, England. Screen, stage and television actress. Married to actor Dennis Neilsen-Terry (dec. 1932).

Appeared in: **1919** The Cry for Justice; His Last Defence. **1920** The Hundredth Chance; Unmarried; The Call of Youth (US 1921). **1921** Appearances; The Mystery Road; Dangerous Lies; The Princess of New York; Beside the Bonnie Briar Bush (aka The Bonnie Briar Bush—US); Candytuft, I Mean Veronica. **1931** Inquest. **1933** The Good Companions; The Lost Chord. **1934** The Outcast; Flat No. 3. **1935** Emil and the Detectives (aka Emil—US 1938); Royal Cavalcade (aka Regal Cavalcade—US); Scrooge. **1936** The Heirloom Mystery; Grand Finale. **1937** The Angelus. **1938** Cavalcade of the Stars.

GNASS, FRIEDRICH (aka FRITZ GNASS)
Born: 1892, Bochum, Germany. Died: 1958, Berlin, Germany. Stage and screen actor.

Appeared in: **1929** Jenseits der Strasse (Harbour Drift); Mutter Krausens Fahrt ins Gluck (Mother Krausen's Journey to Happiness). **1931** Fra Diavolo; M (aka Morder unter Uns); Luise, Konigin von Preussen (Luise, Queen of Prussia). **1939** Aufruhr in Damaskus (Tumult in Damascus). Other German films include: Troika; Danton, F.P.; 1 Antwortet Nicht; Rasputin; Ich bei Tag und Du bei Nacht; Razzia in St. Pauli; Morgenrot; Fluchtlinge; Stern von Valancia; Achtung!; Wer kennt Diese Frau; Abenteuer eines Jungen Herrn in Polen; Hundert Tage; Blutsbruder; Pour le Merite; Nordlicht; Cappriccio; Kautschuk; Sergeant Barry; Geheimzeichen LB 17; Fahrendes Volk; Legion Condor; Wozzek; Der Biberpelz; Die Buntkarierten; Unser Taglich Brot; Familie Benthin; Der Untertan; Roman einer Jungen Ehe; Das Verurteile Dorf; Schatten uber den Inseln; Frauenschicksale; Die Geschichte vom Kleinen Muck; Anna Susanna; Leuchtfeuer; Einmal ist Keinmal; Wer Seine Frau Lieb Hat; Tinko; Gejagt bis sum Morgen; Madeleine und der Legionair.

GOBBLE, HARRY A. "HANK"
Born: 1923. Died: May 19, 1961, Hollywood, Calif. Screen actor and stuntman.

Appeared in: **1961** The Deadly Companions.

GODDERIS, ALBERT
Born: 1882. Died: Feb. 2, 1971. Screen actor.

Appeared in: **1958** Me and the Colonel.

GODFREY, PETER
Born: Oct. 16, 1899, London, England. Died: Mar. 4, 1970, Hollywood, Calif. Screen, stage, vaudeville actor; screen, stage director and playwright. Married to actress Renee Haal (dec. 1966) with whom he appeared briefly in vaudeville.

Appeared in **1938** Blockade. **1940** Raffles; The Earl of Chicago; Edison the Man. **1941** Dr. Jekyll and Mr. Hyde. **1947** The Two Mrs. Carrolls.

GODFREY, RENEE HAAL
Born: 1920. Died: May 2, 1964 (cancer). Screen and vaudeville actress. Married to actor and director Peter Godfrey (dec. 1970) with whom she appeared briefly in vaudeville. She was "Miss New York" in the 1937 Miss America contest. Entered films in 1941.

Appeared in: **1942** Wedded Blitz (short). **1945** Bedside Manner. **1946** Terror by Night. **1960** Inherit the Wind. **1965** Those Calloways.

GODFREY, SAMUEL T.
Born: Oct. 5, 1891, Brooklyn, N.Y. Died: Apr. 18, 1935, Los Angeles, Calif. (brain tumor). Screen, stage actor, playwright, dialog screenwriter and stage director.

Appeared in: **1932** Washington Merry-Go-Round. **1933** Frisco Jenny; I Loved a Woman; Parole Girl; After Tonight; Blondie Johnson. **1934** Beggars in Ermine; The Mighty Barnum; The Love Captive. **1935** Love in Bloom; Private Worlds.

GODOWSKY, DAGMAR
Born: 1897. Died: Feb. 13, 1975, New York, N.Y. Screen, television actress and author. Divorced (annulled) from actor Frank Mayo (dec. 1963).

Appeared in: **1920** The Forged Bride; The Path She Chose; Hitchin' Posts; The Marriage Pit; Honor Bound. **1922** The Altar Stairs; The Stranger's Banquet; The Trap. **1923** The Common Law; Red Lights; Souls for Sale. **1924** Greater Than Marriage; Meddling Women; Playthings of Desire; The Price of a Party; Roulette; A Sainted Devil; The Story Without a Name; Virtuous Liars. **1925** The Lost Chord; Camille of the Barbary Coast. **1926** In Borrowed Plumes.

GOETZKE, BERNHARD
Born: 1884, Danzig, Germany. Died: 1964, Berlin, Germany. Stage and screen actor.

Appeared in: **1921** Der Mude Tod (Between Worlds—US 1924 aka Destiny). **1922** Peter der Grosse (Peter the Great—US 1923). **1924** Die Nibelungen (aka Kriemhild's Revenge—US 1928 and Siegfried); Decameron Nights (US 1928). **1925** Die Verrufenen (aka Slums of Berlin—US 1927 and Funfte Stand); Blackguard. **1926** Der Bergadler (The Mountain Eagle aka Fear O'God—US). **1927** Schuldig (US 1928). **1928** Children of No Importance; Guilty. **1929** The Wrath of the Seas. **1930** Alraune (US 1934). **1931** Cities and Years; Luise, Konigin von Preussen (Luise, Queen of Prussia); Arme, Kleine Eva. **1934** Jud Suss (Jew Suess). Other German films include: Veritas Vincit; Madame Dubarry; Die Bruder Karamasoff; Das Geheimnis von Bombay; Mord ohne Toter; Opfer der Keuschheit; Der Schadel der Pharaoentochter; Die Toteninsel; Tschetschensen-Rache; Aus dem Schwarzbuch eines Polizeikommissars; Die Jagd nach dem Tode; Das Indische Grabmal; Das Weib des Pharao; Dr. Mabuse der Spieler; Vanina oder die Galgenhochzeit; Briefe; Die ihn Nicht Erreichten; Die Prinzessin und der Geiger; Zapfenstreich; Zwei und die Dame; Die Unehelichen; Die Versunkene Flotte; Feme; Das Gefahrliche Alter; Der Gefangenen von Shanghai; Die Sache mit Schorrsiegel; Der Schopfer; Der Staatsanwalt Klagt An; Die Tragodie im Zirkus Royal; Fruhlings Erwachen; Die Todesfahrt im Weltrekord; Sturmisch die Nacht; Zwischen Nacht und Morgen; Die Letzten Tage vom Weltbrand; Die Koffer des Herrn O.F.; Nachtkolonne; Geheimnis des Blauden Zimmers; Theodor Korner; Kampf um die Frau; Teilnehmer Antwortet Nicht; Rasputin; Der Schwarze Husar; Einmal Mocht ich Keine Sorgen Haben; Die Tanzerin von Sanssouci; Der Tolle Bomberg; Der Verliebte Blaskopf; Schusse an der Grenze; Moral und Liebe; Polizeiakte 909; Das Alte Recht; Abenteuer eines Jungen Herrn in Polen; Viktoria; Eskapade; Der Kurier des Zaren; Fridericus; Robert Koch; Bauhaus Goldener Engel; Salonwagen E 417; Die Gute Sieben; Die 3 Codonas; Zwischen Hamburg und Hatti; Der Fuchs von Glenarvon; Bismarck; Ich Klage An; Tanz mit dem Kaiser; Die Schwedische Nachtigall; Der Grosse Konig; Paracelsus; Munchhausen; Der Majoratsherr; Das War Mein Leben; Das Kalte Herz.

GOING, FREDERICA
Born: 1895. Died: Apr. 11, 1959, New York, N.Y. Stage, screen and television actress. Daughter of stage performers Frederick Going and Iola Munro Going. Appeared in early films for Edison Co., Pathe and Biograph.

GOLD, JIMMY
Born: 1886, Glasgow, Scotland. Died: Oct. 7, 1967, London, England. Screen, music hall and stage actor. Appeared with Charlie Naughton (dec. 1976) as part of comedy team "'Naughton and Gold," and also appeared in "Crazy Gang" films and stage presentations with "Flanagan and Allen" and "Nervo and Knox."

The "Crazy Gang" films include: **1937** Okay for Sound. **1938** Alf's Button Afloat. **1939** The Frozen Limits. **1940** Gasbags. **1958** Life Is a Circus (US 1962).

"'Naughton and Gold" appeared in: **1933** Sign Please (short); My Lucky Star. **1935** Cock O'the North. **1936** Highland Fling. **1937** Wise Guys. **1943** Down Melody Lane.

GOLDBERG, RUBE (Reuben Lucius Goldberg)
Born: July 4, 1883, San Francisco, Calif. Died: Dec. 7, 1970, New York, N.Y. Cartoonist, artist, writer and screen actor.

Appeared in: **1914** He Danced Himself to Death.

GOLDENBERG, SAMUEL
Born: 1886. Died: Oct. 31, 1945, Brooklyn, N.Y. (heart attack). Stage and screen actor.

Appeared in: **1935** Shir Hashirim. **1943** Mission to Moscow; Fallen Sparrow.

GOLDIN, PAT (aka PAT GOLDEN)
Born: Dec. 5, 1902, Russia. Died: Apr. 24, 1971, Los Angeles, Calif. (heart attack). Screen actor.

Appeared in: **1946** Bringing Up Father. **1947** Sarge Goes to College; Kilroy Was Here; King of the Bandits. **1948** Jiggs and Maggie in Society; Jiggs and Maggie in Court. **1949** Jiggs and Maggie in Jackpot Jitters; Master Minds. **1950** Jiggs and Maggie Out West. **1952** Glory Alley. **1953** Fast Company. **1955** Hold Back Tomorrow. **1956** The Kettles in the Ozarks; Edge of Hell. **1957** Lizzie; Hit and Run. **1959** Born to Be Loved. **1962** Paradise Alley (aka Stars in the Backyard).

GOLDNER, CHARLES
Born: 1900, Austria. Died: Apr. 15, 1955, London, England. Stage and screen actor.

Appeared in: **1940** Room For Two (US 1944). **1946** The Laughing Lady (US 1950). **1947** Brighton Rock. **1948** One Night With You; Bond Street (US 1950); No Orchids for Miss Blandish (US 1951); Bonnie Prince Charlie. **1949** Dear Mr. Prohack (US 1950); Give Us This Day (aka Salt to the Devil—US); The Rocking Horse Winner (US 1950); Third Time Lucky (US 1950); Black Magic. **1950** Shadow of the Eagle (US 1955). **1951** I'll Get You For This (aka Lucky Nick Cain—US); Encore. **1952** Secret People; Top Secret (aka Mr. Potts Goes to Moscow—US 1954); South of Algiers (aka The Golden Mask—US 1954). **1953** The Captain's Paradise; The Master of Ballantrae; Always a Bride (US 1954). **1954** Duel in the Jungle; Flame and the Flesh. **1955** The End of the Affair; The Racers.

GOLDSTEIN, BECKY
Born: 1887. Died: May 1971, London, England. Screen and stage actress.

GOLM, ERNEST
Born: 1886. Died: May 29, 1962. Screen actor.

Appeared in: **1943** Mission to Moscow.

GOLM, LISA (aka LIZA GOLM)
Died: Jan. 6, 1964. Screen actress.

Appeared in: **1941** Underground. **1942** Journey for Margaret. **1943** They Came to Blow Up America; Mission to Moscow. **1949** Anna Lucasta; The Doctor and the Girl; East Side, West Side. **1951** Payment on Demand; The Hoodlum. **1952** The Invitation; Come Back, Little Sheba; My Pal Gus. **1956** Ride the High Iron. **1957** Monkey on My Back.

GOLUBEFF, GREGORY
Died: Feb. 11, 1958, Hollywood, Calif. Screen actor and musician.

Appeared in: **1934** Bolero. **1945** The Seesaw and the Shoes (short).

GOLZ, ROSEMARY (aka MARIE GLOSZ)
Born: 1880. Died: Apr. 14, 1963, Rome, Italy. Screen actress and opera performer.

Appeared in: **1934** One Night of Love.

GOMBELL, MINNA
Born: 1892, Baltimore, Md. Died: Apr. 14, 1973, Santa Monica, Calif. Stage and screen actress.

Appeared in: **1929** Great Power. **1931** Good Sport; Skyline; Doctors' Wives; Bad Girl; Sob Sister. **1932** Stepping Sisters; The Rainbow Trail; Bachelors' Affairs; The First Year; Dance Team; Careless Lady; Walking Down Broadway; After Tomorrow; Wild Girl. **1933** What Price Innocence?; The Big Brain; Wild Boys of the Road; The Way to Love; Hoopla; Pleasure Cruise. **1934** Marrying Widows; Cross Country Cruise; No More Women; Strictly Dynamite; The Hell Cat; The Merry Widow; Keep 'Em

Rolling; Registered Nurse; The Lemon Drop Kid; Babbitt; The Thin Man; Cheating Cheaters. **1935** The White Cockatoo; Two Sinners; Women Must Dress; Miss Pacific Fleet. **1936** Champagne Charlie; Banjo on My Knee. **1937** Slave Ship; Wife, Doctor and Nurse; Make Way for Tomorrow. **1938** Block-Heads; Comet over Broadway; The Great Waltz; Going Places. **1939** Second Fiddle; Stop, Look and Love; The Hunchback of Notre Dame. **1940** Boom Town. **1941** High Sierra; Doomed Caravan; Thieves Fall Out. **1942** Mexican Spitfire Sees a Ghost; Cadets on Parade. **1943** Salute for Three. **1944** A Chip Off the Old Block; Johnny Doesn't Live Here Anymore; The Town Went Wild; Destiny. **1945** Night Club Girl; Man Alive; Swingin' on a Rainbow; Penthouse Rhythm; Sunbonnet Sue. **1946** Perilous Holiday; The Best Years of Our Lives. **1947** Wyoming. **1948** The Snake Pit; Mr. Reckless; Return of the Bad Men. **1949** The Last Bandit. **1950** Pagan Love Song. **1951** Here Comes the Groom; I'll See You in My Dreams.

GOMEZ, AUGUSTINE "AUGIE" WHITECLOUD

Born: 1891. Died: Jan. 1, 1966, Hollywood, Calif. Screen, stage and vaudeville actor.

Appeared in: **1939** Blue Mountain Skies. **1948** Old Los Angeles.

GOMEZ, RALPH

Born: 1897. Died: Apr. 18, 1954, Hollywood, Calif. (cancer). Screen actor and stuntman. Entered films approx. 1924.

GOMEZ, THOMAS

Born: July 10, 1905, Long Island, N.Y. Died: June 18, 1971, Santa Monica, Calif. Screen, stage and television actor.

Appeared in: **1942** Sherlock Holmes and the Voice of Terror (film debut); Arabian Nights; Pittsburgh; Who Done It? **1943** White Savage; Corvette K-225; Frontier Badman; Crazy House. **1944** The Climax; Phantom Lady; Dead Man's Eyes; Follow the Boys; In Society; Bowery to Broadway; Can't Help Singing. **1945** Patrick the Great; I'll Tell the World; The Daltons Ride Again; Frisco Sal. **1946** A Night in Paradise; Swell Guy; The Dark Mirror. **1947** Singapore; Ride the Pink Hourse; Captain from Castile; Johnny O'Clock. **1948** Casbah; Angel in Exile; Key Largo; Force of Evil. **1949** Come to the Stable; Sorrowful Jones; That Midnight Kiss; I Married a Communist. **1950** Kim; The Woman on Pier 13; Toast of New Orleans; The Eagle and the Hawk; The Furies; Dynamite Pass. **1951** Anne of the Indies; The Harlem Globetrotters; The Sellout. **1952** The Merry Widow; Pony Soldier; Macao. **1953** Sombrero. **1954** The Gambler from Natchez; The Adventures of Haji Baba. **1955** The Looters; The Magnificent Matador; Las Vegas Shakedown; Night Freight. **1956** Trapeze; The Conqueror. **1959** John Paul Jones; But Not for Me. **1961** Summer and Smoke. **1968** Stay Away, Joe! **1970** Beneath the Planet of the Apes.

GONDI, HARRY

Born: 1900, Germany. Died: Nov. 1968, Hamburg, Germany. Screen, stage and radio actor.

GONZALEZ, GILBERTO

Born: 1906, Mexico. Died: Mar. 21, 1954, Palenque, Chiapas, Mexico (heart attack). Screen actor.

Appeared in **1933** Viva Villa. **1940** Amor con Amor (Love for Love). **1948** The Pearl. **1952** Stronghold. **1955** The Littlest Outlaw.

GONZALEZ, MARIO TECERO

Born: 1919, Mexico. Died: Aug. 28, 1957, Mexico City, Mexico. Stage and screen actor.

GONZALEZ, MYRTLE

Born: Sept. 28, 1891, Los Angeles, Calif. Died: Oct. 22, 1918, Los Angeles, Calif. (heart disease and pneumonia). Screen and stage actress.

Appeared in: **1913** The Spell; The White Feather. **1914** Tony the Greaser; Anne of the Mines; Her Husband's Friend; The Masked Dancer; Millions for Defense; Ward's Claim. **1915** The Man from the Desert; A Natural Man; The Legend of the Lone Tree; The Chalice of Courage; Through Troubled Waters; The Repentance of Dr. Blimm; The Ebony Casket; The Quarrel; The Offending Kiss; The Bride of the Nancy Lee; The Terrible Truth; Her Last Flirtation; Does It End Right?; Inside Facts; His Golden Grain. **1916** Missy; Her Dream Man; The Gambler; The Wise Man and the Fool; The Secret Foe; Bill's Wife; Miss Blossom; The Windward Anchor; Her Great Part; It Happened in Honolulu; The Secret of the Swamp; The Pinnacle; The Girl of the Lost Lake; The End of the Rainbow; A Romance of Billy Goat Hill. **1917** Captain Alverez; God's Crucible; Mutiny; Southern Justice.

GONZALO, MARIA EDUARDA

Born: 1929, Portugal. Died: Jan. 24, 1955, Lisbon, Portugal (tuberculosis). Stage and screen actress.

GOOD, KIP

Born: 1919. Died, May 1, 1964, Gadsden, Ala. Screen, stage actor and stage director.

Appeared in: **1943** Stage Door Canteen.

GOODE, JACK (Irwin Thomas Whittridge)

Born: 1908, Columbus, Ohio. Died: June 24, 1971, New York, N.Y. (acute infectious hepatitis). Screen, stage and television actor. Married to stage dancer and actress Renalda Green.

Appeared in: **1933** Flying Down to Rio. **1935** Top Hat. **1936** Swing Time.

GOODRICH, AMY

Born: 1889. Died: July 1939, Hollywood, Calif. Screen actress. Married to actor Hal Price.

GOODRICH, CHARLES W.

Born: 1861. Died: Mar. 20, 1931, Norwalk, Conn. Screen and stage actor.

Appeared in: **1926** Show Off (stage and film versions).

GOODRICH, EDNA

Born: Dec. 22, 1883, Logansport, Ind. Died: May 26, 1971, New York, N.Y. Screen actress.

Appeared in: **1915** Armstrong's Wife. **1917** Her Second Husband; Queen X; A Daughter of Maryland; American Maid. **1918** Treason; Who Loved Him Best?; Her Husband's Honor.

GOODRICH, LOUIS (L. G. Abbott Anderson)

Born: 1865, Sandhurst, England. Died: Jan. 31, 1945, London, England. Screen, stage actor and playwright.

Appeared in: **1931** The Sleeping Cardinal (aka Sherlock Holmes' Fatal Hour—US). **1932** The Flag Lieutenant. **1933** The Thirteenth Candle. **1934** The Crimson Candle. **1935** Mr. What's His Name. **1936** Fair Exchange; The Captain's Table.

GOODWIN, BILL

Born: July 28, 1910, San Francisco, Calif. Died: May 9, 1958, Palm Springs, Calif. (heart attack). Screen, radio and television actor. Married to actress Phillippa Hilber.

Appeared in: **1940** Let's Make Music. **1941** Blondie in Society. **1942** Wake Island. **1943** Riding High; So Proudly We Hail; Henry Aldrich Gets Glamour; No Time for Love. **1944** Bathing Beauty. **1945** River Gang; Incendiary Blonde; Spellbound; The Stork Club. **1946** House of Horrors; Earl Carroll Sketchbook; To Each His Own; The Jolson Story. **1947** Hit Parade of 1947; Heaven Only Knows. **1948** Mickey; So This Is New York. **1949** It's a Great Feeling; The Life of Riley. **1950** Tea for Two; Jolson Sings Again. **1952** The First Time. **1954** The Atomic Kid; Lucky Me. **1956** The Opposite Sex; Bundle of Joy. **1958** The Big Beat; Going Steady.

GOODWIN, NAT C.

Born: 1857, Boston, Mass. Died: Jan. 31, 1919, New York. Screen actor.

Appeared in: **1912** Oliver Twist; Nathan Hale. **1915** The Master Hand; Business Is Business. **1916** Wall Street Tragedy; The Marriage Bond.

GOODWIN, RUBY BERKLEY

Died: May 31, 1961, Hollywood, Calif. Screen, television actress and author.

Appeared in: **1955** The View from Pompey's Head. **1956** Strange Intruder. **1959** The Alligator People. **1961** Wild in the Country.

GOODWINS, ERCELL WOODS. *See* ERCELL WOODS

GOODWINS, LESLIE

Born: Sept. 17, 1899, London, England. Died: Jan. 8, 1969, Hollywood, Calif. (pneumonia). Screen actor, film director and screenwriter. Appeared in early Christie Comedies.

GORCEY, BERNARD

Born: 1888, Switzerland. Died: Sept. 11, 1955, Hollywood, Calif. (auto accident). Stage and screen actor. Father of actors Leo (dec. 1969) and David Gorcey.

Appeared in: **1928** Abie's Irish Rose. **1940** The Great Dictator. **1941** Out of the Fog. **1942** Joan of Paris. **1943** The Unknown Guest. **1946** Mr. Hex; In High Gear; Spook Busters; Scareheads; Bowery Bombshell; The French Key; In Fast Company. **1947** Bowery Buckaroos; Hard Boiled Mahoney; News Hounds. **1948** Angels' Alley; No Minor Vices; Jinx Money; Trouble Makers. **1949** Fighting Fools; Angels in Disguise; Hold That Baby; Master Minds. **1950** Blonde Dynamite; Lucky Losers; Blues Busters; Triple Trouble. **1951** Ghost Chasers; Crazy over Horses; Bowery Battalion; Let's Go Navy; Pickup; Win, Place and Show. **1952** Here Come the Marines; Feudin' Fools; No Holds Barred; Hold That Line; Tell It to the Marines. **1953** Jalopy; Loose in London; Clipped Wings; Private Eyes. **1954** Paris Playboys; Jungle Gents; The Bowery

Boys Meet the Monsters. **1955** Bowery to Bagdad; High Society; Jail Busters; Spy Chasers. **1956** Dig That Uranium.

GORCEY, LEO B.

Born: June 3, 1915, New York, N.Y. Died: June 2, 1969, Oakland, Calif. Stage and screen actor. Son of actor Bernard Gorcey (dec. 1955) and brother of actor David Gorcey. One of the original "Dead End Kids."

Appeared in: **1937** Dead End (stage and film versions); Portia on Trial. **1938** Mannequin; Crime School; Angels with Dirty Faces. **1939** Hell's Kitchen; Angels Wash Their Faces; Battle of City Hall; They Made Me a Criminal; The Dead End Kids on Dress Parade (aka Dress Parade). **1940** That Gang of Mine; Boys of the City; Gallant Sons; Junior G-Men (serial); Angels with Broken Wings; Invisible Stripes. **1941** Flying Wild; Pride of the Bowery; Road to Zanzibar; Out of the Fog; Spooks Run Wild; Bowery Blitzkrieg; Down in San Diego; Sea Raiders (serial). **1942** Mr. Wise Guy; Sunday Punch; Let's Get Tough; Smart Alecks; 'Neath Brooklyn Bridge; Maisie Gets Her Man; Born to Sing; Jr. G-Men of the Air (serial). **1943** Clancy Street Boys; Destroyer; Mr. Muggs Steps Out. **1944** Block Busters; Follow the Leader; Million Dollar Kid; Bowery Champs. **1945** One Exciting Night; Docks of New York; Mr. Muggs Rides Again; Come Out Fighting; Midnight Manhunt. **1946** In Fast Company; Mr. Hex; Bowery Bombshell; Spook Busters; Live Wires. **1947** Hard-Boiled Mahoney; News Hounds; Pride of Broadway; Bowery Buckaroos. **1948** So This Is New York; Jinx Money; Trouble Makers; Angel's Alley; Smugglers Cove. **1949** Hold That Baby; Angels in Disguise; Master Minds; Fighting Fools. **1950** Blonde Dynamite; Blues Busters; Triple Trouble; Lucky Losers. **1951** Win, Place and Show; Ghost Chasers; Bowery Battalion; Crazy over Horses; Let's Go Navy. **1952** Hold That Line; Here Come the Marines; Feudin' Fools; No Holds Barred; Tell It to the Marines. **1953** Jalopy; Loose in London; Clipped Wings; Private Eyes. **1954** The Bowery Boys Meet the Monsters; Paris Playboys; Jungle Gents. **1955** Bowery to Bagdad; High Society; Spy Chasers; Jail Busters. **1956** Crashing Las Vegas; Dig That Uranium. **1957** Spook Chasers; Hold That Hypnotist; Looking for Danger; Up in Smoke. **1958** In the Money. **1963** It's a Mad, Mad, Mad, Mad World. **1965** Second Fiddle to a String Guitar. **1969** The Phynx.

GORDON, A. GEORGE

Born: 1882. Died: Dec. 27, 1953, Chicago, Ill. (heart ailment). Screen, stage actor and stage producer. Appeared in silents with Selig Poliscop Corp.

GORDON, BERT (aka THE MAD RUSSIAN)

Born: 1898, New York, N.Y. Died: Nov. 30, 1974, Duarte, Calif. (cancer). Screen, stage, vaudeville and radio actor. Appeared with his brother Harry Gordon in an act billed as "Stage Struck Kids" and later in an act billed as "Bert and Harry Gordon."

Appeared in: **1935** She Gets Her Man. **1937** New Faces of 1937. **1938** Outside of Paradise. **1939** Laugh Your Blues Away; Let's Have Fun. **1941** Sing for Your Supper. **1945** How Do You Do?

GORDON, BOBBY

Born: 1904. Died: Feb. 17, 1973, New York. Screen, vaudeville actor, comedian and comedy writer. Appeared in vaudeville as part of "Gordon, Reed and King" team. Do not confuse with other Gordons with similar first names.

GORDON, C. HENRY (Henry Racke)

Born: June 17, 1883, New York, N.Y. Died: Dec. 3, 1940, Los Angeles, Calif. (result of leg amputation). Stage and screen actor. Entered films in 1911.

Appeared in: **1930** A Devil with Women; Renegades. **1931** The Black Camel; Honor of the Family; Young As You Feel; Woman of Experience; Charlie Chan Carries On; Once a Sinner; Hush Money. **1932** State's Attorney; The Strange Love of Molly Louvain; Washington Masquerade; Miss Pinkerton; Jewel Robbery; Roar of the Dragon; Kongo; Hell's Highway; Thirteen Women; Scarlet Dawn; Rasputin and the Empress; Doomed Battalion; Scarface; Mata Hari; Gay Caballero; The Crooked Circle. **1933** Whistling in the Dark; Secret of Madame Blanche; Clear All Wires; Made on Broadway; Gabriel over the White House; Storm at Daybreak; Night Flight; Turn Back the Clock; Penthouse; Stage Mother; The Chief; The Devil's in Love; Broadway Thru a Keyhole; Advice to the Lovelorn; The Women in His Life. **1934** Straight Is the Way; Fugitive Lovers; This Side of Heaven; Hide-Out; Stamboul Quest; Death on a Diamond; Men in White; Lazy River. **1935** Lives of a Bengal Lancer; The Great Hotel Murder; Pursuit; The Crusades; The Big Broadcast of 1936. **1936** Professional Soldier; Under Two Flags; Hollywood Boulevard; The Big Game; Love Letters of a Star; Charge of the Light Brigade. **1937** Charlie Chan at the Olympics; Trouble in Morocco; The River of Missing Men; Trapped by G-Men; Sophie Lang Goes West; Stand-In; Conquest. **1938** Yellow Jack; Tarzan's Revenge; The Black Doll; Sharpshooters; The Long Shot; Adventure in Sahara; Invisible Enemy. **1939** Heritage of the Desert; Man of Conquest; Charlie Chan in City in Darkness; The Return of the Cisco Kid; Trapped in the Sky. **1940** Passport to Alcatraz; Kit Carson; Charlie Chan at the Wax Museum; Women in Hiding (short); You the People (short).

GORDON, COLIN

Born: Apr. 27, 1911, Ceylon. Died: Oct. 4, 1972, Haslemere, England. Screen, stage, radio and television actor.

Appeared in: **1948** Bond Street (US 1950); The Winslow Boy (US 1950). **1949** Traveller's Joy (US 1951); Edward My Son. **1950** The Happiest Days of Your Life. **1951** The Man in the White Suit (US 1952); Circle of Danger; The Third Visitor; Green Grow the Rushes. **1952** Folly to Be Wise; The Hour of 13. **1953** The Heart of the Matter (US 1954); Grand National Night (aka Wicked Wife—US 1955); Innocents in Paris (US 1955). **1955** Escapade (US 1957); Little Red Monkey (aka The Case of the Red Monkey—US). **1956** The Green Man (US 1957); The Key. **1958** Virgin Island (US 1960); The One that Got Away; Twelve Desperate Hours; The Safecracker. **1959** Alive and Kicking (US 1964); Please Turn Over (US 1960); Bobbikins (US 1960); The Mouse that Roared; The Doctor's Dilemma. **1960** The Day They Robbed the Bank of England. **1961** Don't Bother to Knock (aka Why Bother to Knock—US 1964); Very Important Person (aka A Coming Out Party—US 1962); In the Doghouse (US 1964); Three on a Spree. **1962** The Boys (US 1963); Night of the Eagle (aka Burn, Witch, Burn—US); Crooks Anonymous (US 1963); Strongroom. **1963** Bitter Harvest; The Running Man. **1964** Alley France! (aka The Counterfeit Constable—US 1966); The Pink Panther. **1965** The Liquidator (US 1966). **1966** The Great St. Trinian's Train Robbery (US 1967); The Family Way (US 1967); The Psychopath. **1967** Trygon Factor (US 1969); Casino Royale. **1968** Don't Raise the Bridge, Lower the River; Subterfuge. **1970** Body Beneath.

GORDON, CONSTANCE "KITTY"

Born: 1888, England. Died: May 26, 1974, Brentwood, N.Y. Screen, stage, vaudeville and television actress.

Appeared in: **1917** No Man's Land; Her Own; Diamonds and Pearls. **1918** The Divine Sacrifice; The Interloper; Merely Players; Stolen Orders; The Purple Lily; Tinsel. **1919** Playthings of Passion; The Scar; Adele; The Unveiling Hand.

GORDON, EDWARD R.

Born: 1886. Died: Nov. 10, 1938, Hollywood, Calif. Screen actor and film director. Appeared in: **1927** Gun-Hand Garrison; Ridin' Luck; Wild Born.

GORDON, G. SWAYNE

Born: 1880. Died: June 23, 1949, New York, N.Y. Screen, stage, radio and vaudeville actor. Appeared in vaudeville with his wife, Spain Thorne.

GORDON, GAVIN

Born: 1901, Chicora, Miss. Died: Nov. 18, 1970, London, England (coronary thrombosis). Screen, stage actor, vocalist, and composer.

Appeared in: **1929** Chasing Through Europe; All Steamed Up (short); Knights Out (short). **1930** His First Command; Romance; The Silver Horde; The Great Meadow; The Medicine Man. **1931** Secret Service; Shipmates. **1932** Two Against the World; The Phantom of Crestwood; American Madness; Man Against Woman. **1933** The Bitter Tea of General Yen; Black Beauty; Female; Hard to Handle; Mystery of the Wax Museum. **1934** Lone Cowboy; The Scarlet Empress; Happiness Ahead; Wake up and Dream. **1935** Red Hot Tires; Grand Old Girl; Women Must Dress; Bordertown; Stranded; Page Miss Glory; The Bride of Frankenstein; Love Me Forever. **1936** The Leavenworth Case; Ticket to Paradise; As You Like It. **1937** The Toast of New York; Windjammer; They Gave Him a Gun. **1938** I See Ice. **1941** I Killed That Man; Gangs, Inc.; The Lone Star Vigilantes; Paper Bullets; Murder by Invitation; Mr. Celebrity. **1946** Centennial Summer. **1947** Philo Vance's Gamble; Three on a Ticket. **1954** Knock on Wood; There's No Business Like Show Business; White Christmas. **1956** The Vagabond King; The Ten Commandments; Pardners. **1957** Johnny Tremain; Chicago Confidential. **1958** The Matchmaker. **1959** The Bat. **1961** Pocketful of Miracles. **1962** Girls! Girls! Girls! **1963** The Nutty Professor. **1964** The Patsy.

GORDON, GLORIA

Died: Nov. 23, 1962, Hollywood, Calif. Screen and television actress. Mother of actor Gale Gordon.

Appeared in: **1926** Dancing Days; Exclusive Rights. **1949** My Friend Irma. **1953** Beneath the 12 Mile Reef; Titanic. **1955** A Man Called Peter.

GORDON, HAROLD

Born: 1919. Died: Jan. 19, 1959, New York, N.Y. Screen, stage, opera and television actor.

Appeared in: **1952** Viva Zapata; The Jazz Singer; The Iron Mistress. **1954** Bengal Brigade. **1955** East of Eden; Yellowneck.

GORDON, HARRIS

Born: 1887. Died: Apr. 2, 1947, Burbank, Calif. (heart attack). Stage and screen actor.

Appeared in: **1921** Live and Let Live. **1922** Burning Sands; Out of the Silent North; The Woman Who Walked Alone; A Wonderful Wife. **1923** Hollywood.

1924 The Dawn of a Tomorrow. 1925 Easy Going Gordon; Let Women Alone; Romance and Rustlers; Too Much Youth. 1934 Our Daily Bread.

GORDON, HUNTLY

Born: 1897, Montreal, Quebec, Canada. Died: Dec. 7, 1956, Hollywood, Calif. (heart attack). Screen and radio actor.

Appeared in: 1918 Our Mrs. McChesney. 1921 Chivalrous Charley; Enchantment; The Girl from Nowhere; Society Snobs; Tropical Love; At the Stage Door. 1922 Beyond the Rainbow; His Wife's Husband; Man Wanted; Reckless Youth; What Fools Men Are; What's Wrong with the Women?; When the Desert Calls; Why Announce Your Marriage? 1923 Bluebeard's Eighth Wife; The Famous Mrs. Fair; Chastity; Cordelia the Magnificent; Male Wanted; Pleasure Mad; The Wanters; Her Fatal Millions; The Social Code; Your Friend and Mine. 1924 The Enemy Sex; Shadows of Paris; True as Steel; Wine; Darling Love; Married Flirts. 1925 Golden Cocoon; The Love Hour; The Great Divide; Never the Twain Shall Meet; My Wife and I; The Wife Who Wasn't Wanted. 1926 Gilded Butterfly; Her Second Chance; Silken Shackles; Lost at Sea; Other Women's Husbands; The Golden Web. 1927 The Sensation Seekers; The Truthful Sex; One Increasing Purpose; Don't Tell the Wife. 1928 Outcast; Sinners in Love; A Certain Young Man; Name the Women; Their Hour; Our Dancing Daughters; Sally's Shoulder; Gypsy of the North. 1929 The Marriage Playground; Melody Lane; Scandal. 1930 Anybody's Woman; Fox Movietone Follies of 1930. 1932 Phantom Express; Night World; From Broadway to Cheyenne; The King Murder; Red Haired Alibi; Speed Madness; The All American; Race Track; Sally of the Subway. 1933 Midnight Warning; Sailor Be Good; Secrets; Justice Takes a Holiday; The World Gone Mad; Corruption; Only Yesterday. 1934 The Dancing Man; Their Big Moment; Embarrassing Moments; Bombay Mail. 1935 The Spanish Cape Mystery; It Happened in New York; Front Page Woman; Circumstantial Evidence. 1936 Daniel Boone; Yours for the Asking. 1937 China Passage; Stage Door; Idol of the Crowds; Portia on Trial. 1938 Gangster's Boy. 1939 Mr. Wong in Chinatown. 1940 Phantom of Chinatown.

GORDON, JAMES

Born: 1881, Pittsburgh, Pa. Died: May 12, 1941, Hollywood, Calif. (operation complications). Stage and screen actor. Married to actress Mabel Van Buren (dec. 1947).

Appeared in: 1921 The Bait; The Man from Lost River; The Old Swimmin' Hole; Sunset Jones; Trailin'. 1922 Man's Size; The Game Chicken; The Love Gambler; Nancy from Nowhere; On the High Seas; Self-Made Man. 1923 Defying Destiny; Grail. 1924 The Courageous Coward; Hearts of Oak; The Iron Horse; The Man Who Came Back; Wanderer of the Wasteland; The White Sin. 1925 Beauty and the Bad Man; Tumbleweeds. 1926 The Buckaroo Kid; Devil's Dice; Flying High; The Ice Flood; Miss Nobody; Rose of the Tenements; The Social Highwayman. 1927 Babe Comes Home; Publicity Madness; Tongues of Scandal; The War Horse; The Wolf's Fangs; Cancelled Debts; Wanted—a Coward. 1928 The Escape. 1929 Masked Emotions. 1931 The Bachelor Father; The Front Page.

GORDON, JULIA SWAYNE

Born: 1879, Hollywood, Calif. Died: May 28, 1933, Los Angeles, Calif. Stage and screen actress.

Appeared in: 1910 Twelfth Night. 1911 Lady Godiva; Tale of Two Cities. 1912 The Troublesome Stepdaughters; Cardinal Wolsey; Stenographers' Wanted. 1913 Beau Brummel. 1914 Two Women. 1921 Behind the Masks; Burn 'Em up Barnes; Handcuffs or Kisses; Love, Hate and a Woman; The Passionate Pilgrim; Shams of Society; The Silver Lining; Why Girls Leave Home. 1922 The Darling of the Rich; How Women Love; My Old Kentucky Home; The Road to Arcady; Till We Meet Again; What's Wrong with the Women?; When Desert Calls; Wildness of Youth; Women Men Marry. 1923 Scaramouche; Dark Secrets; The Tie That Binds; You Can't Fool Your Wife. 1925 Lights of Old Broadway; Not So Long Ago; The Wheel. 1926 Bride of the Storm; Diplomacy; Early to Wed; The Far Cry. 1927 Children of Divorce; Heaven on Earth; Wings; It; King of Kings. 1928 Hearts of Men; Road House; The Scarlet Dove; The Smart Set; 13 Washington Square; Three Week Ends. 1929 The Eternal Woman; The Younger Generation; The Divine Lady; The Girl in the Glass Cage; The Viking; Is Everybody Happy?; Gold Diggers of Broadway; Scandal. 1930 The Dude Wrangler; Today; Dumbbells in Ermine; For the Love O' Lil. 1931 Misbehaving Ladies; Primrose Path; Drums of Jeopardy; Captain Applejack. 1932 Secrets of the French Police; The Golden West; Broken Lullaby; False Madonna. 1933 Hello, Everybody!

GORDON, MARY

Born: 1882, Scotland. Died: Aug. 23, 1963, Pasadena, Calif. Screen and radio actress. Played housekeeper for Sherlock Holmes in films and radio, 1939–1946.

Appeared in: 1925 The People vs. Nancy Preston; Tessie; The Home Maker. 1926 Black Paradise. 1927 Clancy's Kosher Wedding; Naughty Nanette. 1928 The Old Code. 1929 Dynamite; The Saturday Night Kid. 1930 When the Wind Blows (short); Dance With Me. 1931 Subway Express; The Black Camel. 1932 The Texas Cyclone; Almost Married; Pack Up Your Troubles. 1933 Nature in the Wrong (short). 1934 Beloved; The Little Minister. 1935 I'm a Father (short); Mutiny on the Bounty; Vanessa, Her Love Story; Bonnie Scotland;

The Bride of Frankenstein; The Irish in Us; Waterfront Lady. 1936 Share the Wealth (short); Yellowstone; Way Out West; Laughing Irish Eyes; Forgotten Faces; Mary of Scotland; Stage Struck; Great Guy. 1937 The Great O'Malley; The Plough and the Stars; Meet the Boy Friend; Double Wedding; Pick a Star; A Damsel in Distress. 1938 City Streets; Lady Behave; Kidnapped. 1939 Tail Spin; She Married a Cop; Parents on Trial; Rulers of the Sea; The Hound of the Baskervilles; Captain Fury; The Adventures of Sherlock Holmes. 1940 Tear Gas Squad; Joe and Ethel Turp Call on the President; The Last Alarm; I Take This Oath; Queen of the Mob; When the Daltons Rode; No, No, Nanette; Nobody's Children; My Son, My Son; Marshal of Mesa City. 1941 Pot O'Gold; Flight from Destiny; Appointment for Love; Riot Squad; The Invisible Woman; Borrowed Hero. 1942 Gentleman Jim; The Mummy's Tomb; Sherlock Holmes and the Voice of Terror; Sherlock Holmes and the Secret Weapon; Bombay Clipper; Meet the Stewarts; Dr. Broadway; Fly by Night; It Happened in Flatbush; Boss of Big Town. 1943 Half Way to Shanghai; Sarong Girl; Sherlock Holmes Faces Death; Keep 'Em Sluggin'; Two Tickets to London; Here Comes Kelly. 1944 Sherlock Holmes and the Spider Woman; Follow the Leader; Hat Check Honey; Hollywood Canteen; Whispering Footsteps; The Racket Man; Smart Guy; The Hour Before the Dawn; The Pearl of Death; The Last Ride. 1945 Divorce; See My Lawyer; Captain Eddie; The Woman in Green; Strange Confession; The Body Snatcher; Kitty. 1946 Dressed to Kill; Shadows Over Chinatown; The Dark Horse; In Fast Company; Sing While You Dance; The Hoodlum Saint; Little Giant; Sentimental Journey. 1947 Exposed; The Invisible Wall. 1948 Highway 13; The Strange Mrs. Crane; Angel's Alley. 1949 Deputy Marshal; Shamrock Hill; Haunted Trails. 1950 West of Wyoming.

GORDON, MAUD TURNER

Born: May 10, 1868, Franklin, Ind. Died: Jan. 12, 1940, Los Angeles, Calif. (pneumonia). Stage and screen actress.

Appeared in: 1921 Beyond Price; Enchantment; The Price of Possession. 1922 Back Home and Broke; Women Men Marry. 1923 Homeward Bound. 1924 Born Rich. 1925 The Early Bird; The Little French Girl. 1926 Mismates; The Palm Beach Girl. 1927 Home Made; Cheating Cheaters; The Wizard. 1928 Just Married; Hot News; The Naughty Duchess; Sporting Goods. 1929 The Glad Rag Doll; Illusion; The Hottentot; The Last of Mrs. Cheyney; Sally; The Marriage Playground; Kid Gloves. 1930 Lawful Larceny; The Florodora Girl. 1931 Ladies' Man; High Stakes. 1932 Mata Hari; Shopworn; Back Street. 1934 She Loves Me Not. 1935 Living on Velvet; Black Sheep; Personal Maid's Secret.

GORDON, NORA

Born: 1894, England. Died: May 11, 1970, London, England. Screen and television actress. Married to actor Leonard Sharp (dec. 1958).

Appeared in: 1949 The Fallen Idol. 1950 Woman in Question (aka Five Angles on Murder—US 1953). 1951 Blackmailed; Night Was Our Friend. 1952 A Woman's Angle (US 1954). 1955 The Glass Cage (aka The Glass Tomb—US). 1959 Horrors of the Black Museum. 1964 Carry on Spying. 1965 The Nanny.

GORDON, PAUL (Thomas Achelis)

Born: 1886, Brooklyn, N.Y. Died: May 3, 1929, Florence, Italy. Screen actor. Married to actress Ann Mason (dec. 1948).

GORDON, PETER

Born: 1888. Died: May 25, 1943, Los Angeles, Calif. Screen, vaudeville actor and acrobat. Entered films in 1916. Appeared in Vitagraph shorts with Larry Lemon.

Appeared in: 1934 The Live Ghost (short). 1935 Tit for Tat (short).

GORDON, RICHARD H.

Born: 1893, Philadelphia, Pa. Died: Sept. 20, 1956, Hollywood, Calif. (after operation). Screen and television actor. Entered films in 1918. Was president of Screen Actors Guild from 1948 to 1956.

Appeared in: 1925 Romance Road; The Flame Fighter (serial). 1929 Synthetic Sin; Words and Music. 1945 The Cisco Kid in Old New Mexico. 1946 The Best Years of Our Lives. 1947 13 Rue Madeleine. 1951 St. Benny the Dip. 1956 The Birds and the Bees.

GORDON, ROBERT (Robert Gordon Duncan)

Born: 1895, Kan. Died: Oct. 26, 1971, Victorville, Calif. Screen actor. Entered films in 1917.

Appeared in: 1917 Tom Sawyer. 1918 Huck and Tom; Missing. 1921 If Women Only Knew. 1922 The Super Sex; The Rosary. 1923 The Greatest Menace; The Mysterious Witness; Main Street. 1924 The Night Message; The Wildcat; Borrowed Husbands. 1925 Danger Signal; Night Ship; On the Threshold; Shattered Lives. 1926 Hearts and Spangles; King of the Pack.

GORDON, VERA

Born: June 11, 1886, Russia. Died: May 8, 1948, Beverly Hills, Calif. Screen, stage and vaudeville actress. Entered films in 1919.

Appeared in: 1920 Humoresque; North Wind's Malice. 1921 The Greatest

Love. **1922** The Good Provider; Your Best Friend. **1923** Potash and Perlmutter. **1924** In Hollywood with Potash and Perlmutter. **1926** Cohens and Kellys; Millionaires; Sweet Daddies; Private Izzy Murphy; Kosher Kitty Kelly. **1928** The Cohens and the Kellys in Paris; Four Walls. **1929** The Cohens and the Kellys in Atlantic City. **1930** Madam Satan; The Cohens and Kellys in Scotland; The Cohens and the Kellys in Africa. **1931** Fifty Million Frenchmen. **1934** When Strangers Meet. **1937** Michael O'Halloran. **1938** You and Me. **1942** The Living Ghost; The Big Street. **1946** Abie's Irish Rose.

GORE, ROSA

Born: 1867. Died: Feb. 4, 1941, Hollywood, Calif. Screen, stage and vaudeville actress. Appeared in vaudeville with her husband, Alexander Lyon, in an act billed as "Crimmins and Gore." Entered films with Pathe in 1912.

Appeared in: **1921** Colorado; The Mistress of Shenstone. **1922** A Dangerous Game. **1923** The Town Scandal; Vanity Fair. **1924** Half-A-Dollar Bill; Hold Your Breath; Madonna of the Streets. **1925** The Million Dollar Handicap; Seven Days. **1926** The Adorable Deceiver; Three Weeks in Paris; Lovey Mary. **1927** The Man from Hardpan; Play Safe; The Prairie King; The Royal American; Stranded. **1928** Anybody Here Seen Kelly?; The Head Man; That's My Daddy. **1929** Blue Skies; Shrimps for a Day (short).

GORGEOUS GEORGE (George Raymond Wagner)

Born: 1915. Died: Dec. 25, 1963, Los Angeles, Calif. (heart attack). Wrestler and television, screen actor.

Appeared in **1949** Alias the Champ.

GORMAN, ERIC

Born: 1886. Died: Nov. 24, 1971, Dublin, Ireland. Screen, stage and television actor.

Appeared in **1949** Saints and Sinners. **1952** The Quiet Man. **1957** The Rising Moon (aka The Majesty of the Law).

GORMAN, STEPHANIE

Born: June 11, 1949. Died: Aug. 5, 1965, Los Angeles, Calif. (murdered). Screen actress and dancer.

Appeared in: **1963** Bye Bye Birdie.

GORMAN, TOM

Born: 1908. Died: Oct. 2, 1971, Flushing, N.Y. (pulmonary embolism). Screen, stage, television actor and gag writer.

Appeared in: **1957** Edge of the City; 12 Angry Men. **1968** The Detective; Pretty Poison.

GORSS, SAUL M.

Born: 1908. Died: Sept. 10, 1966, Los Angeles, Calif. (heart attack). Screen actor and stuntman. Entered films in 1933.

Appeared in: **1940** Flowing Gold. **1955** Unchained. **1956** Yaqui Drums. **1958** Legion of the Doomed; Bullwhip. **1966** Murderer's Row. **1967** Red Tomahawk.

GOSFIELD, MAURICE

Born: 1913. Died: Oct. 19, 1964, Saranac Lake, N.Y. Screen, stage, television and radio actor.

Appeared in: **1947** Kiss of Death. **1948** The Naked City. **1961** Teenage Millionaire. **1963** The Thrill of It All.

GOSFORD, ALICE PECKHAM

Born: 1886. Died: Jan. 23, 1919, New York, N.Y. Screen actress.

GOSNELL, EVELYN

Born: 1896, Ill. Died: Nov. 11, 1947, New York, N.Y. (injuries from a fall). Stage and screen actress.

Appeared in: **1923** Under the Red Robe.

GOTTSCHALK, FERDINAND

Born: 1869, London, England. Died: Nov. 10, 1944, London, England. Screen, stage actor and author.

Appeared in: **1923** Zaza. **1930** Many Happy Returns (short). **1931** Tonight or Never. **1932** Without Honor; Land of the Wanted Men; Doomed Battalion; The Sign of the Cross; Grand Hotel. **1933** Parole Girl; Ex-Lady; Ann Vickers; Gold Diggers of 1933; Berkeley Square; Grand Slam; Goodbye Again; Girl Missing; Warrior's Husband; She Had to Say Yes; Female; Midnight Club. **1934** Madame Du Barry; The Notorious Sophie Lang; King Kelly of the U.S.A.; I Sell Anything; One Exciting Adventure; Nana; Bombay Mail; Horse Play; The Witching Hours; Long Lost Father; Gambling Lady; Upper World; Sing Sing Nights. **1935** Secret of the Chateau; I Am a Thief; The Man Who Reclaimed His Head; Folies Bergere; Night Life of the Gods; Clive of India; Les Miserables; Break of Hearts; Vagabond Lady; Here Comes the Band; The Gay Deception; The Man Who Broke the Bank at Monte Carlo; The Melody Lingers On; Peter Ibbetson. **1936** Bunker Bean; The White Legion; The Garden of Allah; The Man I Marry; That Girl from Paris; Along Came Love. **1937**

The Crime Nobody Saw; Cafe Metropole; Ali Baba Goes to Town; I'll Take Romance. **1938** The Adventures of Marco Polo; Romance in the Dark; Stolen Heaven; Josette. **1944** The Sign of the Cross (revised version of 1932 film).

GOTTSCHALK, JOACHIM

Born: 1904, Calau/Niederlausitz. Died: 1941, Berlin, Germany. Stage and screen actor.

Appeared in: **1938** Du und Ich. **1939** Flucht ins Dunkel; Aufruhr in Damaskus (Tumult in Damascus); Eine Frau wie Du. **1940** Das Madchen von Fano; Ein Leben Lang. **1941** Die Schwedische Nachtigall (The Swedish Nightingale).

GOUGH, JOHN

Born: Sept. 22, 1897, Boston, Mass. Died: June 30, 1968, Hollywood, Calif. (cancer). Stage and screen actor. Entered films in 1916.

Appeared in: **1916** A Studio Satire; In the Land of the Tortilla; The Dreamer; A Dream or Two Ago. **1918** Ann's Finish. **1921** The Girl in the Taxi. **1922** Gleam O'Dawn; Up and at 'Em. **1924** Silk Stocking Sal. **1925** Alias Mary Flynn; Border Justice; High and Handsome; Three Wise Crooks; Midnight Molly; When Love Grows Cold; Broadway Lady; Smooth as Satin. **1926** Secret Orders; A Poor Girl's Romance; Flaming Waters. **1927** The Gorilla; Ain't Love Funny? Hook and Ladder No. 9; Judgement of the Hills. **1928** The Street of Sin; The Circus Kid; The Haunted House; Air Legion. **1930** Sarah and Son. **1935** Two for Tonight.

GOULD, BILLY (William Gould)

Born: 1869, New York, N.Y. Died: Feb. 1, 1950, New York, N.Y. (cancer). Screen, stage, minstrel and vaudeville actor. Appeared in vaudeville with Valeska Suratt. Do not confuse with actor William Gould (dec. 1960).

Appeared in: **1924** The Great White Way.

GOULD, MYRTLE

Born: 1880. Died: Feb. 25, 1941, Los Angeles, Calif. Screen and stage actress. Appeared in silents until 1918.

GOULD, VIOLET

Born: 1884. Died: Mar. 29, 1962, England. Screen and television actress.

GOULD, WILLIAM A.

Born: 1915. Died: Mar. 20, 1960, Long Beach, Calif. (fire). Screen actor. Do not confuse with actor Billy Gould (dec. 1950).

GOULDING, ALFRED "ALF"

Born: 1896, Melbourne, Australia. Died: Apr. 25, 1972, Hollywood, Calif. (pneumonia). Screen, vaudeville, stage actor, film director and screenwriter. Married to actress Suzanne Raphael.

Appeared in: **1925** The Lady; Learning to Love.

GOULDING, EDMUND

Born: Mar. 20, 1891, London, England. Died: Dec. 24, 1959, Hollywood, Calif. Screen, stage, vaudeville actor, screenwriter, playwright, film, stage director-producer and composer.

Appeared in: **1911** Henry VIII. **1914** The Life of a London Shopgirl. **1922** Three Live Ghosts.

GOULDING, IVIS. See IVIS GOULDING PROCTER

GOVI, GILBERTO

Born: 1885, Italy. Died: 1966, Genoa, Italy (following pheumonia). Stage, screen and television actor.

GOWERS, SULKY

Died: Mar. 1970, London, England. Screen, television and cabaret actor.

GOWLAND, GIBSON

Born: Jan. 4, 1872, Spennymoor, England. Died: Sept. 9, 1951, London, England. Screen actor.

Appeared in: **1915** Birth of a Nation. **1919** Blind Husbands; The Fighting Shepherdess. **1921** Ladies Must Live. **1922** With Father's Help. **1923** Hutch Stirs 'Em Up (aka The Hawk); The Harbour Lights; Shifting Sands. **1924** Greed; The Border Legion; Love and Glory; The Red Lily. **1925** The Phantom of the Opera; The Prairie Wife. **1926** College Days; Don Juan; The Outsider. **1927** The Broken Gate; The Land Beyond the Law; The First Auto; Topsy and Eva; Isle of Forgotten Women; The Night of Love; The Tired Business Man. **1928** Rose Marie. **1929** The Mysterious Island. **1930** The Sea Bat; Hell Harbor; Phantom of the Opera (and 1925 version). **1932** Land of the Wanted Men; Without Honor; Doomed Battalion. **1933** S.O.S. Iceberg. **1934** The Private Life of Don Juan; The Secret of the Loch. **1935** The Mystery of the Mary Celeste (aka Phantom Ships—US 1937); The Stoken. **1936** Highland Fling. **1937** Cotton Queen; Wife of General Ling (US 1938); Ships Concert. **1938** Ten Leaves in the Wind.

GOWMAN, MILTON J.
Born: 1907. Died: Aug. 17, 1952, Los Angeles, Calif. Screen actor.

GRABLE, BETTY (Elizabeth Grable)
Born: Dec. 18, 1916, St. Louis, Mo. Died: July 2, 1973, Santa Monica, Calif. (cancer). Screen, stage, television actress, dancer and singer. Divorced from actor Jackie Coogan and bandleader Harry James.

Appeared in: **1930** Whoopee; New Movietone Follies of 1930; Let's Go Places. **1931** Kiki; Palmy Days. **1932** Hold 'Em Jail; RKO shorts; The Greeks Had a Word for Them; The Kid from Spain; Probation. **1933** Child of Manhattan; What Price Innocence?; Cavalcade. **1934** Student Tour; The Gay Divorcee. **1935** A Quiet Fourth (short); Old Man Rhythm; A Night at the Hollywood Bowl (short); The Nitwits. **1936** Collegiate; Don't Turn 'Em Loose; Pigskin Parade; Follow the Fleet. **1937** Thrill of a Lifetime; This Way, Please. **1938** Give Me a Sailor; Campus Confessions; College Swing. **1939** Man About Town; The Day the Bookies Wept; Million Dollar Legs. **1940** Tin Pan Alley; Down Argentine Way. **1941** A Yank in the RAF; Moon over Miami; I Wake Up Screaming (aka Hot Spot). **1942** Song of the Islands; Footlight Serenade; Springtime in the Rockies. **1943** Coney Island; Sweet Rosie O'Grady. **1944** Pin Up Girl; Four Jills in a Jeep. **1945** Billy Rose's Diamond Horseshoe; All-Star Band Rally (short); The Dolly Sisters. **1946** Do You Love Me? (cameo appearance). **1947** The Shocking Miss Pilgrim; Mother Wore Tights. **1948** That Lady in Ermine; When My Baby Smiles at Me. **1949** The Beautiful Blonde from Bashful Bend. **1950** My Blue Heaven; Wabash Avenue. **1951** Call Me Mister; Meet Me After the Show. **1953** The Farmer Takes a Wife; How to Marry a Millionaire. **1955** Three for the Show; How to be Very, Very Popular.

GRACE, CHARITY
Born: 1879. Died; Nov. 28, 1965, St. Louis, Mo. (cancer). Screen, stage, opera and television actress.

GRACE, DICK
Born: 1915. Died: June 1965 (cancer). Screen actor, stuntman, flier and author.

Appeared in: **1925** Flying Fool. **1927** Wide Open. **1928** Lilac Time. **1929** Wings; Hell's Angels. **1932** The Lost Squadron.

GRACE, DINAH (Ilse Schmidt)
Born: Germany. Died: May 12, 1963, Hamburg, Germany (cancer). Screen actress and dancer. Married to actor Willy Fritsch (dec. 1973).

GRAETZ, PAUL
Born: 1890. Died: Feb. 17, 1937, Hollywood, Calif. Screen actor.

Appeared in: **1923** Monna Vanna. **1931** Wien Du Stadt der Lieder (Vienna City of Song). **1934** Jew Suess; Blossom Time. **1935** Alias Bulldog Drummond; Mimi; Car of Dreams; 18 Minutes; Bulldog Jack. **1936** Mr. Cohen Takes a Walk; Red Wagon; Hot Money; Bengal Tiger; Isle of Fury. **1937** Heart's Desire; April Romance. **1939** The Fight for Matterhorn.

GRAF, PETER
Born: 1872. Died: Oct. 20, 1951, New York, N.Y. Screen, stage, and radio actor. Appeared in Yiddish films.

GRAF, ROBERT
Born: 1923, Witten, Germany. Died: 1966, Munich, Germany. Screen, stage, radio and television actor.

Appeared in: **1958** Wir Wunderkinder (Aren't We Wonderful—US 1959). **1959** Jonas; Buddenbrooks (US 1962). **1963** The Great Escape. **1965** Young Cassidy.

GRAFF, WILTON
Born: 1903. Died: Jan. 13, 1969, Pacific Palisades, Calif. Stage and screen actor.

Appeared in: **1945** Pillow of Death; Strange Confession; An Angel Comes to Brooklyn; Earl Carroll Vanities; Gangs of the Waterfront; A Royal Scandal. **1946** Avalanche; Just before Dawn. The Unknown; The Phantom Thief; Traffic in Crime; Valley of the Zombies. **1947** High Conquest; Shadowed; The Corpse Came C.O.D.; Bulldog Drummond Strikes Back; A Double Life; Gentleman's Agreement; Key Witness; The Web. **1948** The Wreck of the Hesperus; Return of the Whistler; Gallant Blade; Another Part of the Forest. **1949** Take Me out to the Ball Game; Once More, My Darling; Caught; Blondie's Big Deal; And Baby Makes Three; Reign of Terror; The Dark Past. **1950** Rogues of Sherwood Forest; Fortunes of Captain Blood; The West Point Story; Mother Didn't Tell Me; Girls' School. **1951** Mark of the Avenger; My True Story. **1952** Fearless Fagan; Springfield Rifle; Operation Secret; Million Dollar Mermaid; Something for the Birds; Young Man with Ideas. **1953** Lili; The I Don't Care Girl; Scandal at Scourie; Miss Sadie Thompson; So This Is Love. **1954** King Richard and the Crusaders; A Star Is Born. **1955** The Sea Chase; The Benny Goodman Story. **1956** Lust for Life. **1959** Compulsion. **1961** Return to Peyton Place; Sail a Crooked Ship; Bloodlust. **1963** Lonnie.

GRAHAM, CHARLIE
Born: 1897. Died: Oct. 9, 1943, Los Angeles, Calif. Screen actor.

Appeared in: **1919** The Master Mystery (serial). **1921** The Mountain Woman; On the High Card. **1922** Cardigan; Dawn of Revenge; The Headless Horseman; The Love Nest; White Hell. **1925** The Making of O'Malley. **1926** The Untamed Lady. **1929** Frozen Justice.

GRAHAM, FRANK
Born: 1915. Died: Sept. 2, 1950, Hollywood, Calif. (possible suicide). Radio announcer and narrator of many films. Known as "the man with a thousand voices."

Appeared in: **1945** The Three Caballeros.

GRAHAM, JULIA ANN
Born: 1915. Died: July 15, 1935, Los Angeles, Calif. (suicide—gunshot). Screen actress.

Appeared in: **1935** Love in Bloom.

GRAHAM, MORLAND (aka MORELAND GRAHAM)
Born: Aug. 8, 1891, Glasgow, Scotland. Died: Apr. 8, 1949, London, England (heart attack). Stage and screen actor.

Appeared in: **1934** What Happened to Harkness? **1935** The Scarlet Pimpernel; Moscow Nights (aka I Stand Condemned—US 1936); Get Off My Feet. **1936** Fair Exchange; Twelve Good Men; Where's Sally? **1939** Jamaica Inn; Full Speed Ahead. **1940** Night Train to Munich (aka Gestapo and Night Train—US); Old Bill and Son. **1941** Freedom Radio (aka A Voice in the Night—US); The Ghost Train; This England (aka Our Heritage—US); Ships With Wings (US 1942); The Tower of Terror (US 1942). **1942** The Big Blockade. **1943** The Shipbuilders. **1944** Medal for the General. **1945** Henry V (US 1946). **1946** Gaiety George (aka Showtime—US 1948). **1947** The Brothers; The Upturned Glass. **1948** Bonnie Prince Charlie. **1949** Whisky Galore! (aka Mad Little Island and Tight Little Island—US).

GRAHAM, RONALD
Born: 1912, Hamilton, Scotland. Died: July 4, 1950, New York, N.Y. Screen, stage, radio and television actor.

Appeared in: **1935** Old Man Rhythm. **1944** Ladies of Washington.

GRAHAME, BERT (R.A.S. Stanford)
Born: 1892. Died: Mar. 23, 1971, England. Screen, stage and vaudeville actor. Appeared in silents.

GRAINGER, WILLIAM F. See WILLIAM F. GRANGER

GRAMATICA, EMMA
Born: 1875, Fidenza, Parma, Italy. Died: Nov. 1965, Ostia, Italy. Screen, stage and television actress. Entered films in 1931.

Appeared in: **1932** La Vecchia Signora. **1935** Il Delitto di Mastrovanni. **1936** La Damigela di Bard; Il Fu Mattia Pascal. **1937** Marcella; Napoli d'Altri Tempi. **1938** Jeanne d'Ore; Il Destino; Quella (That One); La Vedova (The Widow). **1951** Miracle in Milan. Other Italian film: La Fortuna Di Zanze.

GRAN, ALBERT
Born: 1862. Died: Dec. 16, 1932, Los Angeles, Calif. (auto accident injuries). Screen actor.

Appeared in: **1916** Out of the Drifts. **1924** Her Night of Romance; Tarnish. **1925** Graustark. **1926** Beverly of Graustark; Early to Wed; Honesty—the Best Policy; More Pay—Less Work. **1927** Seventh Heaven; Breakfast at Sunrise; Children of Divorce; Hula; Love Makes 'Em Wild; Soft Cushions. **1928** We Americans; The Blue Danube; Dry Martini; Four Sons; Mother Knows Best; The Whip. **1929** The Gold Diggers of Broadway; Geraldine; The Glad Rag Doll; Our Modern Maidens; Show of Shows; Tanned Legs. **1930** Little Accident; Follow Thru; The Kibitzer; The Man from Blankley's; Sweethearts and Wives. **1931** Kiss Me Again; The Brat. **1932** Fast Life. **1933** Employees' Entrance.

GRANACH, ALEXANDER
Born: 1891, Poland. Died: Mar. 14, 1945, New York, N.Y. Stage and screen actor.

Appeared in: **1925** Lazybones. **1928** Warning Shadows. **1929** Nosferatu the Vampire. **1931** Danton. **1932** Der Raub der Mona Lisa. **1934** The Last Days before the War; Kameradschaft (Comradship). **1936** Der Kampf; Gypsies. **1939** Ninotchka. **1941** So Ends Our Night; A Man Betrayed. **1942** Joan of Paris; Wrecking Crew; Half Way to Shanghai. **1943** For Whom the Bell Tolls; Hangmen Also Die; Three Russian Girls. **1944** The Hitler Gang; Seventh Cross. **1945** Voice in the Wind.

GRANBY, JOSEPH

Born: 1885. Died: Sept. 22, 1965, Hollywood, Calif. (cerebral hemorrhage). Screen, stage, radio and television actor.

Appeared in: **1916** Jealousy; The Haunted Bell; The Capital Prize; The Man From Nowhere; The Crystal's Warning; Temptation and the Man; Aschen Broedel; The Lie Sublime; Ashes; It Didn't Work Out Right. **1917** The Awakening. **1918** Peck's Bad Girl. **1920** The Imp. **1944** Kismet. **1945** The Great Flamarion; The Phantom Speaks. **1949** Amazon Quest. **1950** Redwood Forest Trail; Where the Sidewalk Ends. **1952** Viva Zapata. **1956** Written on the Wind.

GRANDAIS, SUSANNE

Born: France. Died: Aug. 1920 (auto accident). French screen actress. Was called the "Mary Pickford of France."

GRANGER, ELSA G.

Born: 1904, Australia. Died: Feb. 8, 1955, New York, N.Y. Stage and screen actress. Appeared in Australian silent films; later appeared in US films.

GRANGER, WILLIAM F.

Born: 1854. Died: Dec. 23, 1938, Hollywood, Calif. Screen and stage actor.

Appeared in: **1930** The Other Tomorrow. **1933** Footlight Parade. **1934** Six-Day Bike Ride.

GRANT, EARL

Born: 1931. Died: June 10, 1970, near Lordsburg, N.M. (auto accident). Black screen, television actor and musician.

Appeared in: **1959** Imitation of Life; Juke Box Rhythm. **1962** Tender Is the Night.

GRANT, LAWRENCE

Born: 1870, England. Died: Feb. 19, 1952, Santa Barbara, Calif. Stage and screen actor.

Appeared in: **1918** To Hell with the Kaiser (film debut). **1921** Extravagance; The Great Impersonation. **1924** His Hour; Abraham Lincoln; Happiness. **1926** The Duchess of Buffalo; The Grand Duchess and the Waiter. **1927** A Gentleman of Paris; Service for Ladies; Serenade. **1928** Doomsday; Hold 'Em Yale; Red Hair; The Woman from Moscow; Something Always Happens. **1929** The Canary Murder Case; The Case of Lena Smith; The Rainbow; The Exalted Flapper; Is Everybody Happy?; Bulldog Drummond. **1930** Safety in Numbers; Boudoir Diplomat; The Cat Creeps; Oh, Sailor, Behave! **1931** Daughter of the Dragon; Command Performance; The Squaw Man; Their Mad Moment; The Unholy Garden. **1932** Man about Town; Speak Easily; Divorce in the Family; Jewel Robbery; Faithless; The Mask of Fu Manchu; Grand Hotel; Shanghai Express. **1933** Clear All Wires; Queen Christina; Looking Forward. **1934** The Count of Monte Cristo; By Candlelight; Nana; I'll Tell the World. **1935** The Man Who Reclaimed His Head; Werewolf of London; A Feather in Her Hat; Vanessa, Her Love Story; The Devil Is a Woman; The Dark Angel; Three Kids and a Queen; A Tale of Two Cities. **1936** Little Lord Fauntleroy; The House of a Thousand Candles; Mary of Scotland. **1937** Under the Red Robe; The Prisoner of Zenda. **1938** Service de Luxe; Bluebeard's Eighth Wife; The Young in Heart. **1939** Son of Frankenstein; Wife, Husband and Friend; Rulers of the Sea. **1940** The Son of Monte Cristo; Women in War. **1941** Dr. Jekyll and Mr. Hyde. **1942** S.O.S. Coast Guard; The Ghost of Frankenstein; The Living Ghost. **1945** Confidential Agent.

GRANT, SYDNEY

Born: 1873. Died: July 12, 1953, Santa Monica, Calif. Screen and stage actor.

Appeared in: **1915** Jane.

GRANT, VALENTINE

Born: 1894, Indiana. Died: Mar. 12, 1948, Hollywood, Calif. Screen actress. Married to actor–director Sidney Olcott (dec. 1949).

Appeared in: **1915** The Melting Pot; The Brute.

GRANVILLE, AUDREY

Born: 1910. Died: Oct. 20, 1972, Encino, Calif. (cancer). Screen, television actress and music editor. Child screen actress.

GRANVILLE, CHARLOTTE

Born: May 9, 1863, England. Died: July 8, 1942. Screen and stage actress.

Appeared in: **1931** Just a Gigolo; Twenty Four Hours. **1934** Now and Forever. **1935** Behold My Wife; Werewolf of London. **1936** Rose of the Rancho.

GRANVILLE, LOUISE

Born: 1896. Died: Dec. 22, 1969, Hollywood, Calif. (Hong Kong flu). Screen actress.

Appeared in: **1915** The Scrapper. **1918** Vitagraph shorts.

GRAPEWIN, CHARLES "CHARLIE"

Born: Dec. 20, 1875, Xenia, Ohio. Died: Feb. 2, 1956, Corona, Calif. Screen, stage, vaudeville actor, playwright, composer and author. Married to actress Anna Chance (dec. 1943).

Appeared in: **1902** Above the Limit. **1929** The Shannons of Broadway. Starred in comedy series for Christie which included the following shorts: Jed's Vacation; Ladies' Choice; That Red Headed Hussy. **1930** Only Saps Work. **1931** Millionaire; Gold Dust Gertie. **1932** Hell's House; Big Timer; Disorderly Conduct; The Woman in Room 13; Lady and Gent; Wild Horse Mesa; The Night of June 13th. **1933** Hello, Everybody!; Kiss before the Mirror; Lady of the Night; Heroes for Sale; Wild Boys of the Road; Midnight Mary; Beauty for Sale; Pilgrimage; Don't Bet on Love; Torch Singer; Hell and High Water. **1934** Return of the Terror; Caravan; Two Alone; Anne of Green Gables; Judge Priest; She Made Her Bed; The President Vanishes; The Quitter; The Loud Speaker. **1935** Superspeed; One Frightened Night; In Spite of Danger; Party Wire; Shanghai; Alice Adams; King Solomon of Broadway; Rendezvous; Ah, Wilderness; Eight Bells. **1936** The Petrified Forest; The Voice of Bugle Ann; Small Town Girl; Libeled Lady; Sinner Take All; Without Orders. **1937** The Good Earth; A Family Affair; Captains Courageous; Between Two Women; Bad Guy; Big City; Broadway Melody of 1938. **1938** Bad Man of Brimstone; Of Human Hearts; Girl of the Golden West; Three Comrades; Three Loves Has Nancy; Listen, Darling; Artists and Models Abroad. **1939** Sudden Money; I Am Not Afraid; The Man Who Dared; Hero for a Day; Sabotage; Dust Be My Destiny; Stand up and Fight; Burn 'Em up O'Connor; The Wizard of Oz. **1940** The Grapes of Wrath; Johnny Apollo; Earthbound; Rhythm on the River; Ellery Queen, Master Detective. **1941** Ellery Queen's Penthouse Mystery; Ellery Queen and the Perfect Crime; Ellery Queen and the Murder Ring; Texas Rangers Ride Again; Tobacco Road. **1942** Enemy Agents Meet Ellery Queen; They Died with Their Boots On. **1943** Crash Dive. **1944** Follow the Boys; The Impatient Years; Atlantic City. **1947** The Gunfighter. **1948** The Enchanted Valley. **1949** Sand. **1951** When I Grow Up.

GRASSBY, BERTRAM

Born: Dec. 23, 1880, Lincolnshire, England. Died: Dec. 7, 1953, Scottsdale, Arizona. Stage and screen actor.

Appeared in: **1916** Liberty—A Daughter of the U.S.A. (serial). **1918** Battling Jane. **1919** Romance of Happy Valley; The Lone Wolf's Daughter; The Hope Chest. **1920** For the Soul of Rafael; The Fighting Chance; The Week End. **1921** Fifty Candles; Her Social Value; Hush; A Parisian Scandal; Hold your Horses; Serenade; Straight from Paris. **1922** Borderland; Golden Dreams; For the Defense; The Sleepwalker; Shattered Dreams; The Young Rajah. **1923** Drums of Fate; The Dancer of the Nile; The Man from Brodney's; Pioneer Trails; The Tiger's Claw; The Prisoner. **1924** The Shadow of the East; One Law for the Woman; The Midnight Express; His Hour; The Heart Bandit; The Girl on the Stairs; Captain Blood; Fools in the Dark. **1925** Havoc; She Wolves. **1926** The Beautiful Cheat; The Taxi Mystery; Made for Love. **1927** The Beloved Rogue; When a Man Loves.

GRASSBY, MRS. GERARD A.

Born: 1877. Died: Apr. 6, 1962, Hollywood, Calif. Screen actress.

GRAVES, GEORGE

Born: 1876, England. Died: Apr. 2, 1949, London, England. Stage and screen actor.

Appeared in: **1936** The Robber Symphony (US 1937); The Tenth Man (US 1937).

GRAVET, FERNAND (Fernand Mertens aka FERNAND GRAVEY)

Born: Dec. 25, 1904, Belgium. Died: Nov. 2, 1970, Paris, France. Stage and screen actor. Son of actor Georges Mertens and actress Fernande Depernay.

Appeared in: **1913** Monsieur Beulemeester, Garde Civique; Ans Ou La Vie D'un Joueur; La Fille De Delft. **1930** L'Amour Chante; Cherie. **1931** Marions-Nous; Un Homme en Habit; Tu Seras Duchesse (US 1932); Coiffeur Pour Dames (US 1932). **1932** Passionnement; Le Fils Improvise; A Moi le Jour, A Toi la Nuit. **1933** Early to Bed; Le Pere Prematuré; La Guerre des Valses (The Court Waltzes); Bitter Sweet. **1934** The Queen's Affair (aka Runaway Queen—US 1935); C'Etait un Musicien; Si J'etais le Patron; Nuit de Mai. **1935** Antonio, Romance Hongroise; Monsieur Sans-Gene; Fanfare D'Amour; Varietes; Touche a Tout. **1936** Sept Hommes, Une Femme (aka Sept Hommes); Mister Flow (aka Compliments of Mr. Flow—US 1941); Le Grand Refrain. **1937** Le Mensonge de Nina Petrovna (aka Nina Petrovna and The Life of Nina Petrovna—US 1938); The King and the Chorus Girl (aka Romance is Sacred). **1938** Fools for Scandal; The Great Waltz. **1939** Paradis Perdu; Le Dernier Tournant. **1941** Histoire de Rire. **1942** Romance a Trois; La Nuit Fantastique (Fantastic Night); Le Capitaine Fracasse. **1943** Domino; La Rabouilleuse. **1944** Pamela. **1946** Il Suffit D'une Fois; **1947** Le Capitaine Blomet. **1949** Du Guesclin. **1950** Le Traque (Gunman in the Streets aka Time Running Out); La Ronde. **1951** Mademoiselle Josette Ma Femme; Ma Femme est Formidable. **1952** Le Plus Heureux des Hommes; Mon Mari est Merveilleux (My Husband Is Marvelous). **1953** L'Eta del' Amore (Age of Indiscretion aka Too Young For Love—US 1955); Si Versailles M'etait Conte (aka Versailles). **1956** Treize a Table; Courte Tete (Short Head); Mitsou (US 1958); La Garconne.

1958 Le Temps des Oeufs Durs (Time Running Out—US 1959); L'Ecole des Cocottes; Toto a Parigi. **1961** Les Croulants se Portent Bien; Les Petits Matins (Girl on the Road). **1965** La Dama de Beirut; **1966** How To Steal A Million; **1967** La Bataille de San Sebastian (The Guns for San Sebastian—US 1968). **1969** The Madwoman of Chaillot; Les Caprices de Marie (aka Give Her the Moon—US). **1970** La Promesse de L'aube (Promise at Dawn). **1971** L'Explosion (aka Sex Explosion).

GRAY, ALEXANDER

Born: Jan. 8, 1902, Wrightsville, Pa. Died: Oct. 4, 1975. Screen, stage and radio actor.

Appeared in: **1929** Sally (film debut); The Show of Shows. **1930** No, No, Nanette; Song of the Flame; Spring is Here; Viennese Nights. **1933** Moonlight and Pretzels.

GRAY, BETTY (Lily Pederson aka BEATA GRAY)

Born: Pasaic, N.J. Died: June 1919, New York, N.Y. (influenza). Screen, stage and vaudeville actress.

Appeared in: **1912** The Lass of Gloucester; His Little Indian Model; The Country Boy. **1913** The Beach Combers; The Cheapest Way; The Parting Eternal; $1,000 Reward. **1914** The Cricket on the Hearth. **1915** The Timid Mr. Troodles; The Girl Who Might have Been; The Mystery of Mary (aka Mystery Mary); Blood Heritage; Who Killed Joe Merrion?; The Park Honeymooners. **1916** Pique; Sunlight and Shadow; His Wife's Mistake; Madeleine Morel; Scorched Wings; The Power of the Press; The Light that Failed.

GRAY, BILLY JOE

Born: Feb. 19, 1941, New Mexico. Died: Mar. 3, 1966, Canoga Park, Calif. (murdered—shot). Screen stuntman and horse trainer. Do not confuse with actor Billy Gray.

GRAY, DON (Leo Don Gray)

Born: 1901. Died: July 24, 1966, Woodland Hills, Calif. (cancer). Screen actor. Do not confuse with English actor Donald Gray.

GRAY, EDDIE

Born: 1898, England. Died: Sept. 15, 1969, England. Screen and stage actor.

Appeared in: **1935** First a Girl. **1938** Keep Smiling (aka Smiling Along—US 1939). **1958** Life is a Circus (US 1962). **1962** The Fast Lady (US 1965).

GRAY, GENE

Born: 1899. Died: Feb. 10, 1950, Hollywood, Calif. Screen actor. Known as "Silver King of the Cowboys" because of the rich silver trappings on his horse.

GRAY, GEORGE G.

Born: 1894. Died: Sept. 1967, Asheville, N.C. (stroke). Screen actor, stuntman and film director. Appeared in early Sennett films and was a Keystone Kop.

Appeared in: **1934** Woman Haters (short). **1935** Old Sawbones (short); Uncivil Warriors (short). **1937** Goofs and Saddles (short).

GRAY, GILDA

Born: Oct. 24, 1901, Krakow, Poland. Died: Dec. 22, 1959, Hollywood, Calif. (heart attack). Screen, stage and vaudeville actress.

Appeared in: **1923** Lawful Larceny. **1926** Aloma of the South Seas. **1927** The Devil Dancer; Cabaret. **1929** Piccadilly. **1936** Rose Marie.

GRAY, GLEN

Born: 1900, Roanoke, Ill. Died: Aug. 23, 1963, Plymouth, Mass. Orchestra leader, musician and screen actor. Leader of the "Casa Loma Orchestra."

Appeared in: **1941** Time Out for Rhythm. **1943** Gals, Inc. **1944** Jam Session.

GRAY, JACK

Born: 1880. Died: Apr. 13, 1956, Woodland Hills, Calif. Screen actor.

Appeared in: **1933** Fugitive Lovers.

GRAY, JEAN

Born: 1902. Died: Sept. 23, 1953, Beverly Hills, Calif. Screen actress.

GRAY, JOE

Died: Mar. 15, 1971, Mexico. Screen actor and stuntman.

Appeared in: **1938** You and Me. **1942** The Miracle Kid. **1946** Mr. Hex. **1952** Flesh and Fury. **1964** Robin and the 7 Hoods. **1971** Something Big.

GRAY, LAWRENCE

Born: July 27, 1898, San Francisco, Calif. Died: Feb. 2, 1970, Mexico City, Mexico. Stage and screen actor.

Appeared in: **1925** Are Parents People?; Coast of Folly; The Dressmaker from Paris; Stage Struck. **1926** The American Venus; Eerybody's Acting; Kid Boots; Love 'Em and Leave 'Em; The Palm Beach Girl; The Untamed Lady. **1927** After Midnight; Ankles Preferred; The Callahans and the Murphys; Convoy;

Ladies Must Dress; Pajamas; The Telephone Girl. **1928** Diamond Handcuffs; Domestic Meddlers; Love Hungry; Marriage by Contract; Oh, Kay; The Patsy; Shadows of the Night. **1929** It's a Great Life; Marianne; The Rainbow; The Sin Sister; Trent's Last Case. **1930** Children of Pleasure; The Floradora Girl; Spring Is Here; Sunny; Temptation. **1931** Going Wild; Man of the World; Mother's Millions. **1933** Golden Harvest. **1934** Here Comes the Groom. **1935** Dizzy Dames Danger Ahead; The Old Homestead. **1936** Timber War; In Paris A.W.O.L.

GRAY, LINDA

Born: 1913. Died: Sept. 4, 1963, Hollywood, Calif. Screen actress.

Appeared in: **1938** Shadow over Shanghai. **1952** The Pickwick Papers (US 1953). **1958** In Between Age.

GRAYBILL, JOSEPH

Born: 1887, Milwaukee, Wisc. Died: Aug. 3, 1913, New York, N.Y. (spinal meningitis). Screen actor.

Appeared in: **1909** The Light That Came. **1910** A Victim of Jealousy; The Face at the Window; The Marked Time-Table; The Purgation; Turning the Tables; The Lesson; WHite Roses. **1911** The Last Drop of Water; A Decree of Destiny; The Italian Barber; How She Triumphed; Priscilla and the Umbrella; A Romany Tragedy; Bobby the Coward; The Baron; Italian Blood; Saved from Himself; Love in the Hills; The Voice of the Child; The Diving Girl. **1912** The Painted Lady; On Probation. **1913** Love in an Apartment Hotel; The Wizard of The Jungle.

GREAZA, WALTER

Born: Jan. 1, 1897, St. Paul, Minn. Died: June 1, 1973, New York. Screen, stage, radio and television actor.

Appeared in: **1947** Boomerang. **1948** Call Northside 777; Larceny; The Street With No Name. **1949** The Great Gatsby. **1959** It Happened to Jane (aka Twinkle and Shine).

GREEN, ABEL

Born: June 3, 1900. Died: May 10, 1973, New York. Newspaperman (editor of *Variety*), author and screen actor.

Appeared in: **1947** Copacabana.

GREEN, DENIS

Born: Apr. 11, 1905, London, England. Died: Nov. 6, 1954, New York, N.Y. (heart ailment). Screen, stage actor, screenwriter, television and radio writer.

Appeared in: **1939** The Witness Vanishes; The Hound of the Baskervilles. **1940** Northwest Passage; Men against the Sky. **1941** They Met in Bombay; Yank in the RAF; Scotland Yard; Dr. Jekyll and Mr. Hyde. **1942** This above All. **1944** Frenchman's Creek. **1947** Lone Wolf in London. **1949** Mighty Joe Young.

GREEN, DOROTHY

Born: 1892. Died: Nov. 16, 1963, New York, N.Y. Screen actress.

Appeared in: **1916** A Parisian Romance. **1917** Patria (serial). **1918** The Grouch. **1919** The American Way; Forest Rivals; Her Mother's Secret; The Dark Star. **1920** The Good Bad Wife.

GREEN, FRED E.

Born: 1890. Died: Aug. 1940, near San Mateo, Calif. (auto accident injuries). Screen actor.

Appeared in: **1927** Topsy and Eva.

GREEN, HARRY (Harry Blitzer)

Born: Apr. 1, 1892, New York, N.Y. Died: May 31, 1958, London, England. Screen, stage, vaudeville, television actor and magician.

Appeared in: **1929** Close Harmony; Why Bring That Up?; The Man I Love. **1930** The Kibitzer; Paramount on Parade; Be Yourself; Honey; True to the Navy; Light of Western Stars; The Spoilers; Sea Legs; No Limit. **1932** Marry Me. **1933** This Day and Age; Too Much Harmony; Hollywood on Parade (short). **1934** Coming out Party; Wild Gold; Love Time; Bottoms Up; She Learned About Sailors; A Woman's Man; Born to Be Bad. **1940** The Cisco Kid and the Lady; Star Dust. **1955** Joe Macbeth (US 1956). **1957** A King in New York. **1958** Next to No Time (US 1960).

GREEN, KENNETH

Born: 1908. Died: Feb. 24, 1969, Hollywood, Calif. (heart attack). Screen actor. Appeared in "Our Gang" series.

Appeared in: **1922** Penrod.

GREEN, MARTYN (William Martyn Green)

Born: Apr. 22, 1899, London, England. Died: Feb. 8, 1975, Hollywood, Calif. (blood infection). Screen, stage actor, stage director, author and screenwriter. Married to opera singer Yvonne Chaveau.

Appeared in: **1939** The Mikado (stage and film versions). **1953** The Story of

Gilbert and Sullivan (aka The Great Gilbert and Sullivan—US). **1968** A Lovely Way to Die. **1973** The Iceman Cometh.

GREEN, MITZI

Born: Oct. 22, 1920, New York, N.Y. Died: May 24, 1969, Huntington Harbour, Calif. (cancer). Stage and screen actress.

Appeared in: **1929** Marriage Playground. **1930** Honey; Paramount on Parade; Love among the Millionaires; Santa Fe Trail; Tom Sawyer. **1931** Finn and Hattie; Skippy; Dude Ranch; Forbidden Adventure; Newly Rich; Huckleberry Finn. **1932** Girl Crazy; Little Orphan Annie; The Slippery Pearls (short). **1934** Transatlantic Merry-Go-Round. **1940** Walk with Music. **1952** Lost in Alaska; Bloodhounds of Broadway.

GREEN, NIGEL

Born: 1924, Pretoria, So. Africa. Died: May 15, 1972, Brighton, England. Screen, stage and television actor.

Appeared in: **1954** The Sea Shall Not Have Them (US 1955). **1955** As Long as They're Happy (US 1957). **1956** Reach for the Sky (US 1957). **1957** Bitter Victory (US 1958). **1958** Corridors of Blood (US 1963); The Gypsy and the Gentleman. **1960** The Criminal (aka The Concrete Jungle—US 1962); Sword of Sherwood Forest (US 1961); Mysterious Island. **1961** The Queen's Guards (US 1963). **1962** The Man Who Finally Died (US 1967); The Durant Affair; Wild for Kicks. **1963** Jason and the Argonauts; Zulu (US 1964); Mystery Submarine. **1964** The Masque of the Red Death; Saturday Night Out. **1965** The Skull; The Face of Fu Manchu. **1966** Khartoum; Deadlier than the Male (US 1967); Let's Kill Uncle. **1967** Tobruk; Africa—Texas Style. **1968** Play Dirty (US 1969); The Pink Jungle. **1969** The Kremlin Letter (US 1970); The Wrecking Crew (aka House of 7 Joys); Fraulein Doktor (aka The Betrayal). **1970** Countess Dracula. **1971** The Ruling Class (US 1972).

GREEN, ROBERT

Born: 1940. Died: July 11, 1965, Oroville, Calif. (killed when parachute failed to open during filming). Screen actor and stuntman.

GREEN, SUE

Born: 1902. Died: Aug. 12, 1939, Hollywood, Calif. Screen actress.

Appeared in: **1931–1939** Hal Roach shorts.

GREENE, BILLY M.

Born: Jan. 6, 1897. Died: Aug. 24, 1973, Los Angeles, Calif. (heart attack). Screen, vaudeville, radio and television actor. Do not confuse with actor William Green (dec. 1970).

Appeared in: **1930** His Birthday Suit (short). **1945** Frisco Sal; Shady Lady; Sunbonnet Sue. **1946** Tangier. **1947** Violence. **1955** The Shrike. **1957** Slaughter on Tenth Avenue. **1959** The Cape Canaveral Monsters; The Legend of Tom Dooley; Never Steal Anything Small. **1968** Single Room—Furnished. **1973** Papillion.

GREENE, HARRISON

Born: 1884. Died: Sept. 28, 1945, Hollywood, Calif. Screen, stage and television actor.

Appeared in: **1933** International House; The Vampire Bat; Riot Squad; Murder on the Campus. **1934** Manhattan Love Song; Attention Suckers (short); Kentucky Kernels. **1935** Alibi Bye Bye (short). **1936** Ants in the Pantry (short); The Singing Cowboy; Will Power (short); Guns and Guitars; Ticket to Paradise; The Gentleman from Louisiana; The Sea Spoilers. **1937** Grips, Grunts and Groans (short); Midnight Court; Range Defenders; A Bride for Henry; Mr. Boggs Steps Out. **1938** Passport Husband; Born to Be Wild. **1939** Career; Dust Be My Destiny; New Frontier; The Honeymoon's Over. **1940** You Can't Fool Your Wife. **1941** Arkansas Judge. **1942** Tennnessee Johnson; Blondie for Victory. **1943** Unlucky Dog (short). **1944** Between Two Women; Prunes and Politics (short). **1946** Studio Visit (short).

GREENE, WILLIAM

Born: 1927, Ga. Died: Mar. 12, 1970, Cleveland Heights, Ohio (heart attack). Screen, stage, television actor, and stage director.

Appeared in: **1958** Orders to Kill. **1962** Lolita.

GREENLEAF, MACE

Born: Maine. Died; Mar. 24, 1912, Philadelphia, Pa. (typhoid/ pneumonia). Screen actor.

Appeared in: **1911** Grandfather. **1912** God Disposes; Falling Leaves; The Child of the Tenements; Blighted Lives.

GREENLEAF, RAYMOND

Born: 1892. Died: 1963. Screen actor.

Appeared in: **1948** Deep Waters; For the Love of Mary. **1949** Pinky; Slattery's Hurricane; A Kiss in the Dark; East Side, West Side; All the King's Men. **1950** A Ticket to Tomahawk; David Harding, Counterspy; Harriet Craig; On the Isle of Samoa; Storm Warning; No Sad Songs for Me. **1951** The Family Secret; FBI Girl; Pier 23; Al Jennings of Oklomana; Secret of Convict Lake; A Mil-

lionaire for Christy; Ten Tall Men. **1952** Paula; She's Working Her Way through College; Deadline U.S.A.; Washington Story. **1953** Powder River; The Last Posse; Three Sailors and a Girl; The Bandits of Corsica; South Sea Woman; Angel Face. **1954** Living It Up. **1955** Violent Saturday; Son of Sinbad; Headline Hunters; Texas Lady. **1956** When Gangland Strikes; Never Say Goodbye; Over-Exposed; You Can't Run Away from It; Three Violent People. **1957** Monkey on My Back; The Vampire; The Night the World Exploded. **1958** The Buccaneer. **1959** The Story on Page One. **1960** From the Terrace. **1961** Wild in the Country. **1962** Bird Man of Alcatraz.

GREENSTREET, SYDNEY

Born: Dec. 27, 1879, Sandwich, Kent, England. Died: Jan. 19, 1954, Los Angeles, Calif. (natural causes). Stage and screen actor. Nominated for 1941 Academy Award as Best Supporting Actor in The Maltese Falcon.

Appeared in: **1941** The Maltese Falcon (film debut); They Died with Their Boots On. **1942** Across the Pacific; Casablanca. **1943** Background to Danger. **1944** Hollywood Canteen; Passage to Marseille; Between Two Worlds; The Conspirators; The Mask of Dimitrios; One Man's Secret. **1945** Conflict; Christmas in Connecticut; Pillow to Post. **1946** Devotion; The Verdict; Three Strangers. **1947** That Way with Women; The Hucksters. **1948** Ruthless; The Velvet Touch; The Woman in White. **1949** Flamingo Road; East of the Rising Sun; It's a Great Feeling. **1950** Malaya.

GREENWOOD, ETHEL

Born: 1898. Died: Dec. 8, 1970, Hollywood, Calif. (heart attack). Screen and television actress.

GREENWOOD, WINIFRED L.

Born: 1892, Oswego, N.Y. Died: Nov. 23, 1961, Los Angeles, Calif. Screen, stage and vaudeville actress. Entered films in 1911 with Selig.

Appeared in: **1911** Two Orphans; A Tennessee Love Story; His Better Self. **1912** Where the Road Forks; The Slip; Murray the Masher; Under Suspicion; Hypnotized; The Adopted Son; The Last Dance; The Other Woman; An International Romance; Tempted by Necessity; A Detective's Strategy; A Citizen in the Making. **1913** A Divorce Scandal; The Spartan Girl of the West; A False Order; The Lesson; A Husband Won by Election; Pauline Cushman—the Federal Spy; The End of Black Bart; The Understudy; Dixieland; Love—the Winner; Belle Boyd—a Confederate Spy; The Post-Impressionists; Put to the Test. **1914** Like Father Like Son; The Shriner's Daughter; The Hermit; The Ruin of Manley; False Gods; The Little House in the Valley; Her Fighting Chance; The Dream Child; Down by the Sea; A Modern Free-Lance; Daylight; Sheltering an Ingrate; The Tin Can Shack; When a Woman Waits. **1915** The High Cost of Flirting; The Profligate; His Mysterious Neighbor; The Crucifixion of Al Brady; Justified; The Derelict; The Truth of Fiction; His Brother's Debt; Captain Courtesy; The Problem; The Water Carrier of San Juan; Imitations; Spider Barlow Cuts In; It Was Like This; Out of the Ashes; Alice of Hudson Bay; The Silver Lining; The Key to the Past; On Secret Service; The Clean-Up; The Sting of It; The Jilt; Comrades Three; Mixed Wires; The Greater Strength; His Obligation; Detective Blinn; The Reprisal; The Word; The Broken Window; The Resolve; The Guiding Light. **1916** A Woman's Daring; The Voice of Love; The Franchise; The Reclamation; Lying Lips; A Modern Sphinx; The Suppressed Order; The Happy Masquerader; Bonds of Deception; The Shuffle; Dust; The Trail of the Thief. **1917** The Crystal Gazer. **1918** Danger Within; M'Liss; Believe Me—Zantippe; The Deciding Kiss. **1919** Maggie Pepper; Men, Women and Money; Come Again Smith; The Lottery Man. **1920** The Life of the Party; An Adventure in Hearts; Sick-a-Bed. **1921** The Faith Healer; The Dollar-a-Year Man; Don't Call Me Little Girl; Love Never Dies; Sacred and Profane Love. **1923** To the Last Man. **1926** The Flame of the Yukon. **1927** King of Kings.

GREER, JULIAN

Born: 1871, London, England. Died: Apr. 15, 1928, N.Y. Screen, stage and vaudeville actor.

Appeared in: **1921** The Passion Flower. **1922** Sunshine Harbor.

GREET, CLARE

Born: June 14, 1871, England. Died: Feb. 14, 1939, London, England. Stage and screen actress.

Appeared in: **1921** Love at the Wheel; The Rotters. **1922** Three Live Ghosts. **1927** The Ring. **1928** The Rising Generation. **1929** The Manxman. **1930** Should A Doctor Tell? (US 1931). **1931** Third Time Lucky. **1932** The Sign of the Four; White Face; Lord Camber's Ladies; Lord Babs. **1933** Mrs. Dane's Defence; The Pointing Finger. **1934** Little Friend. **1935** Emil and the Detectives (aka Emil—US 1938); Maria Marten; or, The Murder in the Red Barn. **1938** St. Martin's Lane (aka Sidewalks of London—US 1940). **1939** Jamaica Inn.

GREGG, EVERLY

Died: June 9, 1959, Beaconfield, England. Screen, stage and television actress.

Appeared in: **1933** The Private Life of Henry VIII (film debut). **1936** The Ghost Goes West. **1937** Thunder in the City. **1938** Blondes for Danger; Pygmalion. **1939** Spies of the Air (US 1940). **1941** Major Barbara. **1942** Uncensored

(US 1944); In Which We Serve; The First of the Few (aka Spitfire—US 1943). **1943** The Gentle Sex; The Demi-Paradise (aka Adventure for Two—US 1945). **1944** The Two Fathers; This Happy Breed (US 1947). **1945** Brief Encounter (US 1946). **1946** Gaiety George (aka Showtime—US 1948); Great Expectations (US 1947); Piccadilly Incident. **1950** The Astonished Heart; The Woman in Question (aka Five Angles on Murder—US 1953). **1951** Worm's Eye View; The Franchise Affair (US 1952). **1952** Stolen Face. **1954** The Night of the Full Moon; Father Brown (aka The Detective—US). **1956** Lost (aka Tears for Simon—US 1957); The Man Who Never Was. **1957** Brothers in Law; Carry on Admiral (aka The Ship Was Loaded—US 1959). **1959** Room at the Top; Deadly Record.

GREGOR, NORA
Born: Gorizia, Italy. Died: Jan. 20, 1949, Santiago, Chile. Stage and screen actress.

Appeared in: **1930** Olympia. **1931** Und das ist die Hauptsache (That's All That Matters). **1932** But the Flesh Is Weak. **1933** Was Frauen Traeumen (What Women Dream). **1950** The Rules of the Game.

GREGORY, BOBBY
Born: 1900. Died: May 13, 1971, Nashville, Tenn. Screen actor, bandleader, song writer and rodeo performer. His band was called "The Cactus Cowboys."

GREGORY, DORA
Born: 1873, England. Died: Mar. 5, 1954, London, England. Screen, stage, radio and vaudeville actress.

Appeared in: **1931** The Skin Game. **1937** The Dominant Sex. **1938** Star of the Circus (aka Hidden Menace—US 1940). **1942** In Which We Serve.

GREGORY, EDNA (Edna Steinberg)
Born: Jan. 25, 1905, Winnipeg, Canada. Died: July 3, 1965, Los Angeles, Calif. Stage and screen actress. Appeared in early educational comedies and in Cristie films.

Appeared in: **1921** Short Skirts. **1922** Defying the Law. **1923** Devil's Door Yard; In the Palace of the King; The Law Rustlers; Prepared to Die. **1924** The Folly of Vanity. **1925** The Calgary Stampede; Cold Nerve; Sporting Life; The Desert Flower. **1926** The Better Man; Doubling with Danger; One Man Trail; Red Hot Leather. **1927** Blazing Days; Down the Stretch; Grinning Guns; Men of Daring; Romantic Rogue; The Rose of Kildare; Rough and Ready; The Western Rover. **1929** The Great Garbo.

GREGORY, WILLIAM H.
Died: Dec. 24, 1926, Los Angeles, Calif. Stage and screen actor.

Appeared in: **1927** Sensation Seekers.

GREGSON, JOHN
Born: Mar. 15, 1919, Liverpool, England. Died: Jan. 8, 1975, Porlock Weir, England (heart attack). Screen, stage and television actor. Entered films in 1948.

Appeared in: **1948** Saraband for Dead Lovers; Scott of the Antarctic. **1949** Train of Events (US 1952); Whiskey Galore (aka Tight Little Island—US and Mad Little Island). **1950** Treasure Island; Cairo Road. **1951** The Lavender Hill Mob. **1952** The Holly and the Ivy (US 1953); Angels One Five (US 1954); The Venetian Bird (aka The Assassin—US 1953); The Brave Don't Cry. **1953** The Titfield Thunderbolt; The Assassin; Genevieve (US 1954). **1954** To Dorothy, A Son (aka Cash on Delivery—US 1956); Conflict of Wings; The Crowded Day; The Weak and the Wicked. **1955** Three Cases of Murder (aka You Killed Elizabeth); Above Us the Waves (US 1956); Value for Money (US 1957). **1956** Jacqueline; Battle of the River Plate (aka Pursuit of the Graf Spee—US 1957); Cash on Delivery. **1957** True As a Turtle; Miracle in Soho. **1958** Rooney; Sea of Sand. **1959** The Captain's Table (US 1960); S.O.S. Pacific (US 1960). **1960** Faces in the Dark (US 1964); Hand in Hand (US 1961). **1961** The Frightened City (US 1962); The Treasure of Monte Cristo (aka The Secret of Monte Cristo—US). **1962** Live Now, Pay Later; Tomorrow at Ten (US 1964); The Longest Day; Desert Patrol. **1964** Tomorrow at Ten. **1966** The Night of the Generals (US 1967). **1971** Fright.

GREIG, ROBERT
Born: Dec. 27, 1880, Melbourne, Australia. Died: June 27, 1958, Hollywood, Calif. Stage and screen actor.

Appeared in: **1930** Animal Crackers; Paramount on Parade. **1931** Tonight or Never. **1932** Trouble in Paradise; Jitters the Butler (short); Stepping Sisters; Beauty and the Boss; Man Wanted; The Cohens and the Kellys in Hollywood; The Tenderfoot; Merrily We Go to Hell; Jewel Robbery; Horse Feathers; Love Me Tonight. **1933** Pleasure Cruise; It's Great to Be Alive; Peg O' My Heart; They Just Had to Get Married; Dangerously Yours; Men Must Fight; The Mind Reader. **1934** Easy to Love; Upperworld; One More River; The Love Captive; Cockeyed Cavaliers. **1935** Clive of India; Follies Bergere; Woman Wanted; The Bishop Misbehaves; The Gay Deception; I Live for Love. **1936** Three Live Ghosts; Rose Marie; The Unguarded Hour; Small Town Girl; Trouble for Two; The Devil Doll; Witch of Timbuctu; Suicide Club; Right in

Your Lap; Theodora Goes Wild; Lloyds of London; Stowaway; Easy to Take; Michael O'Halloran. **1937** Easy Living; My Dear Miss Aldrich. **1938** Lady Behave; Midnight Intruder; The Adventures of Marco Polo; Algiers. **1939** Drums along the Mohawk; It Could Happen to You; Way Down South. **1940** Hudson Bay; No Time for Comedy. **1941** The Lady Eve; Moon Over Miami; Sullivan's Travels. **1942** The Moon and Sixpence; I Married a Witch; Palm Beach Story. **1944** The Great Moment; Summer Storm. **1945** Hollywood and Vine; The Cheaters; Earl Carroll Vanities; Nob Hill; The Picture of Dorian Gray; Love, Honor and Goodbye. **1948** Unfaithfully Yours. **1949** Bride of Vengeance.

GREVILLE, EDMOND T.
Born: 1906, Nice, France. Died: 1966, France (?). Screen actor, film producer, director and screenwriter.

Appeared in: **1930** Sous les Toits de Paris (Under the Roofs of Paris).

GREY, GLORIA
Born: 1909. Died: Nov. 22, 1947, Hollywood, Calif. Screen, stage and vaudeville actress. Was a 1924 Wampas Baby Star.

Appeared in: **1922** The Great Alone (film debut). **1923** Bag and Baggage; The Supreme Test. **1924** Girl of the Limberlost; Dante's Inferno; The House of Youth; Little Robinson Crusoe; The Millionaire Cowboy; No Gun Man; The Spirit of the U.S.A. **1925** Heartless Husbands; The Snob Buster. **1926** The Boaster; The Ghetto Shamrock; The Hidden Way; The Night Watch; Officer Jim; Thrilling Youth; Unknown Dangers. **1927** The Broncho Buster; Range Courage; Blake of Scotland Yard (serial). **1928** The Thrill Seekers; The Cloud Dodger; The Hound of Silver Creek; Put 'Em Up. **1929** Married in Hollywood.

GREY, JANE
Born: 1883, Middleburg, Vt. Died: Nov. 9, 1944, N.Y. Screen and stage actress. Entered films with Triangle in 1914.

Appeared in: **1914** The Little Gray Lady. **1923** The Governor's Lady. **1927** The Love Wager.

GREY, JERRY (Gerald J. Grey)
Born: 1910. Died: June 7, 1954, San Antonio, Tex. (heart attack). Screen, stage and television dancer.

GREY, KATHERINE
Born: 1873, San Francisco, Calif. Died: Mar. 21, 1950, Orleans, Mass. Stage and screen actress. Married to stage actor Paul Arthor (dec.) and later married to stage actor John Mason. She appeared in early Kulee Co. films.

GREY, LEONARD
Died: Aug. 4, 1918, New York, N.Y. Screen actor.

GREY, LYNDA
Born: 1913. Died: Sept. 4, 1963. Screen actress.

Appeared in: **1938** Shadows over Shanghai. **1942** Holiday Inn. **1943** Happy Go Lucky.

GREY, MADELINE
Born: 1887. Died: Aug. 16, 1950, Los Angeles, Calif. Stage and screen actress.

Appeared in: **1929** Nothing but the Truth.

GREY, OLGA (Anna Zachak)
Born: 1897, Budapest, Hungary. Died: Apr. 25, 1973, Los Angeles, Calif. Screen actress.

Appeared in: **1915** His Lesson; A Day that is Dead; The Forged Testament; The Absentee; The Failure; A Bold Impersonation; A Woman of Nerve; Double Trouble; A Breath of Summer; Father Love. **1916** The Law of Success; A Wild Girl of the Sierras; Pillars of Society; Intolerance; The Little Liar. **1917** Jim Bludso; The Girl at Home; Fanatics; The Ghost House. **1918** When a Man Rides Alone. **1919** Trixie from Broadway; The Mayor of Filbert; Modern Husbands.

GRIBBON, EDWARD T. "EDDIE"
Born: Jan. 3, 1890, New York, N.Y. Died: Sept. 29, 1965, North Hollywood, Calif. Screen, stage and vaudeville actor. Brother of actor Harry Gribbon (dec. 1961). Entered films with Mack Sennett in 1916.

Appeared in: **1921** Home Talent; Molly O; Playing with Fire; A Small Town Idol. **1922** Alias Julius Caesar; The Crossroads of New York; Tailor-Made Man; The Village Blacksmith; Captain Fly-by-Night. **1923** The Victor; Crossed Wires; Double Dealing; The Fourth Musketeer. **1924** Hoodman Blind; After the Ball; East of Broadway; Jack O'Clubs; The Border Legion. **1925** Seven Days; Code of the West; Just a Woman; Limited Mail; Mansion of Aching Hearts. **1926** Bachelor Brides; The Bat; Desert Gold; The Flaming Frontier; The Flying Mail; Man Bait; There You Are; Under Western Skies. **1927** Tell It to the Marines; The Callahans and the Murphys; Cheating Cheaters; Convoy; Night Life; Streets of Shanghai. **1928** United States Smith; Bachelor's Paradise; Buck Privates; Gang War; Nameless Men; Stop That

Man. **1929** Two Weeks Off; Twin Beds; Honeymoon; Two Men and a Maid; Fancy Baggage; From Headquarters. **1930** Good Intentions; Lottery Bride; They Learned about Women; Born Reckless; Dames Ahoy; Song of the West. **1931** Mr. Lemon of Orange; Not Exactly Gentlemen. **1933** Hidden Gold. **1934** Search for Beauty; I Can't Escape; Everything's Ducky (short). **1935** The Cyclone Ranger; Rip Roaring Riley; Flying Down to Zero (short). **1936** Love on a Bet; The Millionaire Kid; I Cover Chinatown. **1937** The Big Shot; You Can't Buy Luck; Gangway. **1938** Anesthesia (short); Maid's Night Out. **1939** Moving Vanities (short). **1940** The Great Dictator; The Leather Pushers. **1943** Radio Runaround (short). **1944** To Heir is Human (short). **1946** Joe Palooka, Champ; Mr. Hex; Gentlemen Joe Palooka. **1947** Joe Palooka in the Knockout. **1948** Fighting Mad; Winner Take All. **1949** Joe Palooka in the Big Fight; Fighting Fools; Joe Palooka in the Counterpunch. **1950** Joe Palooka Meets Humphrey; Joe Palooka in Humphrey Takes a Chance; Triple Trouble; Joe Palooka in Triple Cross; Joe Palooka in the Squared Circle.

GRIBBON, HARRY

Born: 1886, New York, N.Y. Died: July 28, 1961, Los Angeles, Calif. Screen, stage and vaudeville actor. Brother of actor Eddie Gribbon (dec. 1965). Entered films with Sennett.

Appeared in: **1915** Colored Villainy; Mabel, Fatty and the Law; Ye Olden Grafter; Ambrose's Sour Grapes; A Janitor's Wife's Temptation; The Idle Rich; Does Flirting Pay? **1916** The Worst of Enemies; Perils of the Park; Love Will Conquer; His Auto Ruination; A Dash of Courage; His Wild Oats; A Lover's Might (working title The Fire Chief); The Great Pearl Tangle. **1917** Stars and Bars; Pinched in the Finish; Two Crooks (working title A Noble Crook). **1918** A Pullman Blunder. **1922** Self-Made Man. **1923** The Extra Girl. **1924** The Tomboy. **1927** Knockout Reilly. **1928** The Cameraman; Shakedown; Rose Marie; Smart Set; Show People; Chinatown. **1929** Tide of Empire; Honeymoon; On With the Show; The Mysterious Island; Midnight Daddies; plus the following shorts: The Bride's Relations; Whirls and Girls; The Bee's Buzz; The Big Palooka; The Constable; The Golfers; The Lunkhead; A Hollywood Star; Clancy at the Bat; The New Halfback; Uppercut O'Brien. **1930** So Long Letty; Song of the West; Swell People; Big Hearted; The Lottery Bride; Sugar Plum Papa (short). **1931** The Gorilla; plus the following shorts: Just A Bear; In Conference; The Cow-Catcher's Daughter; Ghost Parade; All-American Kickback. **1932** Ride Him, Cowboy; You Said a Mouthful; Ladies They Talk About. **1932-33** "Whoopee" comedies and Mack Sennett "Featurettes." **1933** Baby Face; Snug in the Jug (short). **1936** Sleepless Hollow (short). **1944** Arsenic and Old Lace (stage and film versions). **1963** The Sound of Laughter (documentary).

GRIER, JIMMY

Born: 1902, Pittsburgh, Pa. Died: June 4, 1959. Orchestra leader and screen actor.

Appeared in: **1934** Transatlantic Merry-Go-Round. **1937** Nobody's Baby.

GRIFFELL, JOSE MARTINEZ

Born: 1905, Mexico. Died: Nov. 14, 1955, Mexico City, Mexico. Stage and screen actor.

GRIFFIES, ETHEL (Ethel Woods)

Born: Apr. 26, 1878, England. Died: Sept. 9, 1975, London, England (stroke). Screen, stage and television actress. Daughter of actor-manager Samuel Rupert Woods and actress Lillie Roberts Woods. Married to stage actor Walter Beaumont (dec. 1910) and later married to actor Edward Cooper (dec. 1956).

Appeared in: **1930** Old English. **1931** Chances; Waterloo Bridge; The Road to Singapore; Once a Lady; Millionaire; Stepdaughters. **1932** Manhattan Parade; The Impatient Maiden; Westward Passage; Love Me Tonight; Are you Listening?; Union Depot; Lovers Courageous; Devil's Lottery; Payment Deferred. **1933** Tonight is Ours; A Lady's Profession; Alice in Wonderland; Midnight Club; Torch Singer; White Woman; Good Companions; Doctor Bull; Bombshell; Looking Forward. **1934** Bulldog Drummond Strikes Back; The House of Rothschild; We Live Again; Of Human Bondage; Jane Eyre; Olsen's Big Moment; Fog; Four Frightened People; Sadie McGee; Call It Luck; Painted Veil. **1935** Enchanted April; The Mystery of Edwin Drood; Vanessa—Her Love Story; Hold 'Em Yale; Anna Karenina; Werewolf of London; The Return of Peter Grimm. **1936** Twice Branded; Guilty Melody; Not so Dusty. **1937** Kathleen Mavourneen (aka Kathleen—US 1938). **1938** Crackerjack (aka The Man With 100 Faces—US). **1939** I'm from Missouri; We Are Not Alone; The Star Maker. **1940** Over the Moon; Vigil the Night; Irene; Anne of Windy Poplars; Stranger on the Third Floor; Waterloo Bridge. **1941** Dead Men Tell; A Yank in the RAF; Great Guns; How Green Was My Valley; Billy the Kid; Remember the Day; Man at Large. **1942** Mrs. Wiggs of the Cabbage Patch; Between us Girls; Time to Kill; Castle in the Desert; Right to the Heart; Son of Fury; The Postman Didn't Ring. **1943** Holy Matrimony; Forever and a Day; First Comes Courage. **1944** Jane Eyre; Music for Millions; Pardon My Rhythm; White Cliffs of Dover. **1945** The Horn Blows at Midnight; Thrill of a Romance; Molly and Me; Saratoga Trunk; Keys of the Kingdom; The Strange Affair of Uncle Harry. **1946** Devotion; Sing While you Dance. **1947** The Homestretch; Millie's Daughter; Forever Amber; Brasher Doubloon. **1963** Billy Liar (stage and film versions); The Birds. **1965** Bus Riley's Back in Town.

GRIFFIN, CARLTON ELLIOTT

Born: 1893. Died: July 23, 1940, Hollywood, Calif. (heart attack). Screen and vaudeville actor. Appeared in vaudeville with Grace Gordon in an act billed as "Magic Glasses." Divorced from actress Pauline Saxon. Entered films with Lubin Co.

Appeared in: **1921** At The Stage Door. **1922** Shackles of Gold. **1924** Girl Shy; The Painted Flapper. **1925** The Great Jewel Robbery. **1926** Her Big Adventure; The Imposter; Tramp, Tramp, Tramp. **1930** Shivering Shakespeare (short); High C's (short). **1931** The Pip From Pittsburgh (short); Rough Seas (short). **1932** First in War (short). **1933** Nature in the Wrong (short); Arabian Tights (short). **1934** Maid in Hollywood (short); Another Wild Idea (short). **1935** The following shorts: Southern Exposure; Nurse to You; Slightly Static.

GRIFFIN, CHARLES

Born: 1888. Died: Aug. 17, 1956, Hollywood, Calif. Screen actor.

GRIFFIN, FRANK L.

Born: 1889. Died: Mar. 17, 1953, Hollywood, Calif. (heart attack). Screen actor, screenwriter, film director, and film producer. Entered films as an actor with Lubin Co. in 1906.

GRIFFIN, GERALD

Born: 1892. Died: Jan. 11, 1962, Rhinebeck, N.Y. (complications after surgery). Vaudeville, stage and screen actor.

GRIFFIN, GERALD

Born: 1854, Pittsburgh, Pa. Died: Mar. 16, 1919, Venice, Calif. Screen actor. Do not confuse with vaudeville actor Gerald Griffin (dec. 1962).

Appeared in: **1916** The Yellow Menace (serial); Feathertop; The Sunbeam. **1918** A Pair of Cupids.

GRIFFIN, MARGARET FULLER. *See* MARGARET FULLER

GRIFFITH, DAVID WARK

Born: Jan. 22, 1875, La Grange, Ky. Died: July 23, 1948, Los Angeles, Calif. (stroke). Screen, stage actor, screenwriter, playwright and film director. Divorced from actresses Evelyn Marjorie Baldwin and Linda Arvidson (dec. 1948).

Appeared in: **1907** Rescued from an Eagle's Nest. **1908** At the Crossroads of Life. **1922** When Knighthood Was in Flower.

GRIFFITH, GORDON

Born: July 4, 1907, Chicago, Ill. Died: Oct. 12, 1958, Hollywood, Calif. (heart attack). Entered films as a child actor in 1913 and later became a film director.

Appeared in: **1914** Chicken Chaser; Caught in a Cabaret (reissued as The Jazz Waiter). **1918** Tarzan of the Apes. **1920** Huckleberry Finn; The Son of Tarzan (serial). **1921** That Something. **1922** Catch My Smoke; More to Be Pitied Than Scorned; Penrod; The Village Blacksmith. **1923** Jungle Trail of the Son of Tarzan (reduced version of 1920 serial Son of Tarzan); Main Street. **1924** The Street of Tears. **1925** Little Annie Rooney. **1926** The Cat's Pajamas. **1928** The Branded Man. **1935** The Crusades.

GRIFFITH, LINDA. *See* LINDA ARVIDSON

GRIFFITH, RAYMOND

Born: Jan. 23, 1890, Boston, Mass. Died: Nov. 25, 1957, Hollywood, Calif. Screen actor, film director, producer, and screenwriter. Entered films with Vitagraph in 1914.

Appeared in: **1917** The Surf Girl; The Scoundrel's Tale; A Royal Rogue. **1922** Crossroads of New York; Minnie; Fools First. **1923** Eternal Three; The Day of Faith; Going Up; Red Lights; Souls for Sale; White Tiger. **1924** Poisoned Paradise; Changing Husbands; The Dawn of a Tomorrow; Lily of the Dust; Nellie, the Beautiful Cloak Model; Never Say Die; Open All Night; The Yankee Consul. **1925** The Night Club; Forty Winks; Paths to Paradise; A Regular Fellow; Fine Clothes; Miss Bluebeard; When Winter Went. **1926** Hands Up; Wet Paint; You'd Be Surprised. **1927** Wedding Bill$; Time to Love. **1929** Trent's Last Case; The Sleeping Porch. **1930** All Quiet on the Western Front.

GRIFFITH, WILLIAM M.

Born: 1897. Died: July 21, 1960, Hollywood, Calif. (heart attack). Stage and screen actor.

Appeared in: **1937** Time out for Romance. **1949** Everybody Does It; Range Land. **1955** Devil Goddess.

GRIFFITHS, JANE

Born: Oct. 16, 1929, Peacehaven, Sussex, England. Died: June 1975, England. Screen, stage and television actress.

Appeared in: **1950** Double Confession (US 1953). **1952** The Gambler and the Lady. **1954** The Million Pound Note (aka Man With a Million—US); The Green Scarf (US 1955). **1957** The Traitor (aka The Accursed—US 1958); Three Sundays to Live. **1958** Tread Softly Stranger (US 1959). **1961** The Impersonator. **1962** Dead Man's Evidence. **1963** The Double (US 1967).

GRIGGS, JOHN

Born: 1909. Died: Feb. 25, 1967, Englewood, N.J. Screen, stage and radio actor.

Appeared in: **1937** Annapolis Salute.

GRIMES, THOMAS

Born: 1887. Died: Aug. 19, 1934, Tujunga, Calif. Screen actor and stuntman.

Appeared in: **1923** The Secret of the Pueblo.

GRISEL, LOUIS R.

Born: 1848, New Castle, Del. Died: Nov. 19, 1928, Fort Lee, N.J. Stage and screen actor.

Appeared in: **1921** The Black Panther's Cub; Jane Eyre.

GROCK (Adrien Wettach)

Born: 1880, Switzerland? Died: 1959. Screen actor and clown. Appeared in British and German films.

GROENEVELD, BEN

Born: 1899, Netherlands. Died: Feb. 14, 1962, Amsterdam, Netherlands. Stage and screen actor.

Appeared in: **1949** Man to Men.

GRONBERG, AKE

Born: 1914, Stockholm, Sweden. Died: 1969, Sweden? Screen actor.

Appeared in: **1943** Sonja. **1954** Sir Arne's Treasure. **1956** Sawdust and Tinsel (aka The Naked Night). **1960** Private 91 Karlsson is Demobbed or So He Thinks. **1964** 491 (US 1967). Other Swedish films: Toward New Times; The Melody from the Old Town; We from Sunny Glade; Brave Boys in Uniform; The Merry-Go-Round in Full Swing; Everybody at His Station; Our Boys in Uniform; Boys from the South of Stockholm; Our Gang; A Sailor in a Dress-coat; Tomorrow's Melody; The Yellow Ward; A Singing Girl; People of Roslagen; Take Care of Ulla; Nothing Will be Forgotten; Woman Takes Command; Lack of Evidence; The Halta Lotta Tavern; Captivated by a Voice; Anna Lans; Young Blood; Watch Out for Spies!; Count the Happy Moments Only; Marie in the Windmill; Girls in the Harbour; In the Beautiful Province of Roslagen; The Girls from Smaland; The Six Karlssons; Brita in the Wholesaler's House; Between Brothers; A Woman on Board; Handsome Augusta; The Song About Stockholm; Woman Without a Face; Navvies; The Night Watchman's Wife; Each Goes His Own Way; Life Begins Now; Dangerous Spring; The Intimate Restaurant; The Kiss on the Cruise; The Beef and the Banana; Ingenious Johansson; Skipper in Storm Weather; She Came Like a Wind; Summer with Monika; People on Manoeuvres; Barabbas; We Three Are Making our Debut; Merry Boys of the Navy; Seven Black Brassieres; Never With My Jemmy; A Storm Over Tjuro; A Lesson in Love; Simon the Sinner; Dolls and Balls; Beat It; Dangerous Freedom; The Merry-Go-Round in the Mountains; Paradise; Rasmus and the Tramp; The Matrimonial Advertisement; The Tough Game; Encounters and Dusk; Dlarar Bananen Biffen?; Line Six; Pirates on Lake Malar; Adam and Eve; My Love is a Rose; Loving Couples; Sailors and Sextants; A Summer Adventure.

GROONEY, ERNEST G.

Died: Jan. 20, 1946, Hollywood, Calif. Screen actor and film music director.

GROSS, WILLIAM J.

Born: 1837. Died: Apr. 12, 1924, Brooklyn, N.Y. Screen, stage, and vaudeville actor.

Appeared in: **1918** Prunella. **1921** Rainbow; Ashamed of Parents.

GROSSKURTH, KURT

Born: 1909, Rhineland, Germany. Died: May 29, 1975, Bad Aibling, Germany (auto accident). Screen, television actor and singer.

Appeared in: **1956** Magic Fire. **1967** Liebesspiele Im Schnee (aka Ski Fever—US 1969). **1971** Willy Wonka and the Chocolate Factory.

GROSSMITH, GEORGE

Born: May 11, 1875, London, England. Died: June 6, 1935, London, England. Screen, stage actor, stage producer and playwright. Son of stage actor George Grossmith, Sr. (dec.) and brother of actor Lawrence Grossmith (dec. 1944). Father of actress Ena Grossmith. Entered films in 1913.

Appeared in: **1913** The Argentine Tango and Other Dances. **1930** Women Everywhere; Are You There?; Those Three French Girls. **1932** Wedding Rehearsal; Service for Ladies (aka Reserved for Ladies—US); The Girl from Maxim's (US 1936). **1933** L'Homme a l'Hispano (The Man in the Hispano-Suiza). **1934** Princess Charming (US 1935). **1940** Les Amoureux.

GROSSMITH, LAWRENCE

Born: Mar. 29, 1877, London, England. Died: Feb. 21, 1944, Woodland Hills, Calif. Stage and screen actor. Son of stage actor George Grossmith, Sr. (dec.) and brother of actor George Grossmith, Jr. (dec. 1935).

Appeared in: **1914** The Brass Bottle. **1933** Counsel's Opinion; Cash (aka For

Love or Money—US 1934); Tiger Bay. **1934** Rolling in Money; The Luck Of a Sailor; The Private Life of Don Juan; Sing As We Go. **1935** It Happened in Paris. **1936** Everything in Life; Men are Not Gods (US 1937). **1937** Song of the Forge; Make Up; Silver Blaze (aka Murder at the Baskervilles—US 1941); The Girl in the Taxi; Smash and Grab. **1939** Captain Fury; I'm From Missouri. **1941** Larceny.

GROWER, RUSSELL GORDON

Died: Feb. 21, 1958, Ontario, Calif. (shot by bandit). Screen actor.

GRUENDGENS, GUSTAF (aka GUSTAF GRUNDGENS)

Born: 1900, Dusseldorf, Germany. Died: Oct. 7, 1963, Manila, Philippine Islands (internal hemorrhage). Screen, stage actor and film director.

Appeared in: **1930** Hocuspocus; Brand in der Opera (Fire in the Opera House—US 1932). **1931** Danton. **1932** Der Raub der Mona Lisa; Luise, Koenigin von Preussen; Yorck; Teilnehmer Antwortet Nicht; Die Graefin von Monte Cristo (The Countess of Monte Cristo). **1933** La Voce del Sangue; M; Die Schonen Tage van Aranjuez. **1934** Die Finanzen des Grossherzogs; Schwarzer Jager Johanna; Terra; So Endete Eine Liebe; Das Erbe in Pretoria (US 1936). **1935** Hundred Days; Das Madchen Johanna; Pygmalion. **1936** Ein Glas Wasser; Liebelei. **1938** Ein Frau Ohne Bedeutung; Liebe im Gleitflug (Love in Stunt Flying). **1960** Das Glas Wasser (A Glass of Water—US 1962). **1963** Faust.

GUARD, KIT (Christen Klitgaard)

Born: May 5, 1894, Hals, Denmark. Died: July 18, 1961, Hollywood, Calif. Stage and screen actor. Entered films in 1922.

Appeared in: **1925** The "Go-Getters" series of shorts including: The Sleeping Cutie; Ain't Love Grand; The Way of a Maid. The "Pacemaker" series of shorts including: Welcome Granger; He Who Gets Rapped; Merton of the Goofies; The Great Decide; The Fast Male; The Covered Flagon; Madame Sans Gin; Three Bases East; The Merry Kiddo; What Price Gloria?; Don CooCoo; Miss Me Again. **1926** One Minute to Play; plus the "Bill Grimm's Progress" series of shorts including: The Lady of Lyons, N.Y.; The Fight That Failed; Where There's a Bill; The Last of His Face; When a Man's a Fan; The Midnight Son; Bruisers and Losers; Little Miss Bluffit; Ladies Prefer Brunettes; Assorted Nuts; Blisters Under the Skin; The Knight before Christmas. **1927** Her Father Said No; In a Moment of Temptation; plus the "Beauty Parlor" series of shorts including: Beloved Rouge; Boys Will be Girls; Chin He Lived to Lift; Fresh Hair Fiends; Helene of Troy, N.Y.; New Faces of Old; Last Nose of Summers; Peter's Pan; She Troupes to Conquer; Toupay or Not Toupay. **1928** Lingerie; Legionnaires in Paris; Beau Braodway; Dead Man's Curve; Shamrock Alley (short). **1930** Big Money; Night Work; The Racketeer. **1931** Defenders of the Law; The Unholy Garden; Sky Raiders. **1932** Two-Fisted Justice; County Fair; Flames; The Last Man; The Fighting Champ; Tom Brown of Culver; The Racing Strain. **1933** Carnival Lady; Corruption; One Year Later; Riot Squad; Sucker Money. **1934** The Mighty Barnum. **1935** Kid Courageous; Reckless Roads; Rip Roaring Riley. **1937** Shadows of the Orient. **1938** Code of the Rangers; You and Me; Frontier Scout; Heroes of the Hills; Prison Train. **1939** Six-Gun Rhythm; El Diablo Rides; The Flying Deuces. **1943** Blitz on the Fritz (short); It Ain't Hay. **1947** Johnny O'Clock; The Perils of Pauline. **1948** So You Want to Be a Detective (short). **1951** Fort Defiance; Abbott and Costello Meet the Invisible Man. **1956** Around the World in 80 Days.

GUARD, SULLY

Died: Mar. 21, 1916, Jacksonville, Florida (auto accident). Screen actor.

Appeared in: **1915** The Necklace of Pearls.

GUDGEON, BERTRAND C.

Died: Oct. 22, 1948, North Bergen, N.J. Screen actor and stuntman. Entered films in 1908.

Appeared in: **1914** The Exploits of Elaine (serial); The Perils of Pauline (serial). **1916** The Iron Claw (serial).

GUELSTORFF, MAX

Born: 1882, Germany. Died: Feb. 9, 1947, Berlin, Germany. Stage and screen actor.

Appeared in: **1929** His Late Excellency; Meistersingers. **1930** Hurrah I'm Alive. **1931** Der Grosse Tenor. **1932** Der Raub der Mona Lisa; Ich Geh aus und Du Bleibst Da. **1933** Der Hauptmann von Koepenick. **1934** Liebe Muss Verstanden Sein. **1935** Die Sonne Geht auf; Ich Sing Mich in Dein Herz Hinein; Frischer Wind aus Kanada; So ein Maedel Vergisst Man Nicht; Ich Kenn Dich Nicht und Liebe Dich (I Don't Know You, but I Love You). **1936** Das Schloss Im Sueden; Annette in Paradise; Heisses Blut. **1937** Der Raub der Sabinerinnen; Ein Falscher Fuffziger; Kirschen in Nachbars Garten; Schabernack; Susanne im Bade (Susanna in the Bath). **1938** Der Zerbroechene Krug (The Broken Jug); Herzensdieb (Heart Thief). **1939** Der Schritt vom Wege (The False Step).

GUENSTEQ, F.F.

Born: 1862. Died: Mar. 28, 1936, Glendale, Calif. Screen and stage actor. Entered films approx. 1916.

GUENTHER, RUTH (aka RUTH JEW BABY)

Born: 1910. Died: June 25, 1974, Culver City, Calif. (lung cancer). Screen actress and psychic. Married to actor Irwin Guenther.

GUHL, GEORGE

Died: June 27, 1943, Los Angeles, Calif. Screen, vaudeville, and burlesque actor. Was in vaudeville in an act billed as "The Guhl Bros." and later, with another partner, in an act billed as "Adams and Guhl."

Appeared in: **1936** The Case against Mrs. Ames; Arbor Day (short); Sing Me a Love Song. **1937** The Adventurous Blonde; Fly-Away Baby; Night Club Scandal. **1938** Torchy Gets Her Man; Blondes at Work; Torchy Blane in Panama; Gold Mine in the Sky. **1939** Torchy Runs for Mayor; I Am Not Afraid; What a Life; Torchy Blane in Chinatown; Dust Be My Destiny; Nancy Drew and the Hidden Staircase. **1940** Buck Benny Rides Again; She Couldn't Say No. **1941** The Great Train Robbery; Glamour Boy; Murder by Invitation. **1942** Hidden Hand; Scattergood Survives a Murder. **1944** Crime by Night.

GUILBERT, YVETTE

Born: 1868, Paris, France. Died: Feb. 3, 1944, France. Screen, stage actress and singer.

Appeared in: **1926** Faust. **1929** L'Argent. **1934** La Frochard et les Deux Orphelienes. **1935** Pecheurs D'Islande.

GUILFOYLE, JAMES (James Ancel Guilfoyle)

Born: Apr. 18, 1892, Michigan. Died: Nov. 13, 1964, Woodland Hills, Calif. (heart disease). Screen actor.

Appeared in: **1929** Speakeasy. **1930** She Went for a Tramp; The Criminal Code; Dirigible; Officer O'Brien. **1931** Daybreak; Inspiration; A Free Soul; Graft. **1932** Get That Girl. **1949** Alimony.

GUILFOYLE, PAUL

Born: July l4, 1902, Jersey City, N.J. Died: 196l. Stage and screen actor.

Appeared in: **1935** The Crime of Dr. Crespi; Special Agent. **1936** Roaming Lady; Two-Fisted Gentleman; Wanted; Jane Turner; Winterset. **1937** Behind the Headlines; Danger Patrol; Fight for Your Lady; Flight from Glory; Hideaway; Soldier and the Lady; Super Sleuth; You Can't Buy Luck; The Woman I Love; You Can't Beat Love. **1938** Crashing Hollywood; Stage Fright (short); The Mad Miss Manton; Law of the Underworld; Double Danger; Blind Alibi; Fugitives for a Night; I'm from the City; The Law West of Tombstone; The Marriage Business; Quick Money; The Saint in New York; Sky Giant; Tarnished Angel. **1939** Heritage of the Desert; Money to Loan (short); The Story of Alfred Nobel (short); News Is Made at Night; Pacific Liner; Boy Slaves; One Hour to Live; Our Leading Citizen; Sabotage; Society Lawyer. **1940** Remember the Night; The Saint Takes Over; Brother Orchid; Millionaires in Prison; One Crowded Night; Thou Shalt Not Kill; East of the River; Wildcat Bus; Grapes of Wrath. **1941** The Saint in Palm Springs. **1942** The Man Who Returned to Life; Time to Kill; The Incredible Stranger (short); Madero of Mexico (short); Who is Hope Schuyler? **1943** Petticoat Larceny; The North Star; Three Russian Girls; White Savage; It Happened Tomorrow; Mark of the Whistler; The Seventh Cross. **1944** The Master Race; Dark Shadows (short); Thou Shalt Not Kill. **1945** The Missing Corpse; Why Girls Leave Home. **1946** Sweetheart of Sigma Chi; The Virginian. **1947** Second Chance; The Millerson Case; Roses are Red. **1948** The Hunted. **1949** There's A Girl in My Heart; Trouble Preferred; Follow me Quietly; Mighty Joe Young; The Judge; I Married A Communist; Miss Mink of 1949; White Heat. **1950** Bomba and the Hidden City; Davy Crockett, Indian Scout; The Woman on Pier 13; Messenger of Peace. **1951** When I Grow Up. **1952** Actors and Sin; Confidence Girl; Japanese War Bride. **1953** Julius Caesar; Torch Song. **1954** Apache; Golden Idol. **1955** Chief Crazy Horse; Valley of Fury; A Life at Stake. **1960** The Boy and the Pirates.

GUINAN, TEXAS (Mary Louise Cecelle Guinan)

Died: Nov. 5, 1933, Vancouver, B.C., Canada (infection of intestines). Screen, stage, vaudeville actress and club hostess.

Appeared in: **1917** Fuel of Life. **1918** The Gun Woman; The Love Broker. **1919** Little Miss Deputy; The Girl of Hell's Agony. **1921** I Am the Woman; The Stampede. **1929** Queen of the Night Clubs; Glorifying the American Girl. **1933** Broadway Thru a Keyhole.

GUITRY, SACHA

Born: Feb. 21, 1885, St. Petersburg, Russia. Died: July 24, 1957, Paris, France. Screen, stage actor, playwright, film producer, director and screenwriter. Divorced from actress Yvonne Printemps (dec. 1977).

Appeared in: **1915** Ceux de Chez Nous. **1932** Les Deux Couverts. **1936** Pasteur. **1937** Les Perles de la Couronne (Pearls of the Crown). **1938** Quadrille; The Story of a Cheat. **1939** Champs Elysees; Indiscretions. **1942** Nine Bachelors. **1943** Donne-Moi tes Yeux. **1948** En Scene (Private Life of an Actor); Mlle Desire. **1949** Le Comedien. **1951** Deburau. **1954** Versailles (aka Royal Affairs in Versailles—US 1957).

GUITTY, MADELEINE

Born: 1871. Died: Apr. 12, 1936, Paris, France. Screen, stage actress and songwriter.

Appeared in: **1925** Madame Sans-Gene. **1931** Il est Charmant. **1934** Le Roi des Champs Elysees. **1935** Les As Du Turf; Avec l'Assurance; Cette Veille Canaille; Sans Famille. **1936** La Porteuse de Pain; Ciboulette. Other French film: Barcarolle.

GUNN, CHARLES E.

Born: July 31, 1883, Wis. Died: Dec. 6, 1918, Los Angeles, Calif. (Spanish influenza). Screen actor.

Appeared in: **1916** The Cry of Conscience; The Eye of God; The Eagle's Wings; They Wouldn't Take Him; Priscilla's Prisoner; Along the Malibu; Weapons of Love; The Girl in Lower 9; The Eternal Way; Song of the Woods; Three of Many. **1917** Chicken Casey; Sweetheart of the Doomed; The Snarl; Love or Justice; A Phantom Husband; The Firefly of Tough Luck; Framing Framers. **1918** Betty Takes a Hand; Unfaithful; Captain of His Soul; Patriotism. **1919** The Midnight Stage.

GUNN, EARL

Born: 1902. Died: Apr. 14, 1963, San Francisco, Calif. Screen actor.

Appeared in: **1926** We Are from Kronstadt. **1937** The Missing Witness. **1939** Romance of the Redwoods; The Great Commandment; Devil's Island. **1940** Island of Doomed Men. **1941** Swamp Woman; Secret of the Wastelands.

GURIE, SIGRID (Sigrid Gurie Haukelid)

Born: 1911, Brooklyn, N.Y. Died: Aug. 14, 1969, Mexico City, Mexico (embolism). Screen actress.

Appeared in: **1938** The Adventures of Marco Polo (film debut); Algiers. **1939** Forgotten Woman. **1940** Rio; Three Faces West; The Refugee; Dark Streets of Cairo. **1943** The Private Life of Dr. Joseph Goebbels (apparently never released). **1944** Enemy of Women; A Voice in the Wind. **1946** Singing Under the Occupation (documentary). **1948** Sofia; Sword of the Avenger.

GURIN, ELLEN

Born: 1948, New York, N.Y. Died: June 5, 1972, New York, N.Y. (suicide). Stage and screen actress. Married to actor Richard Dow.

Appeared in: **1971** Who Killed Mary What's-Er-Name?

GURNEY, EDMUND

Born: 1852. Died: Jan. 14, 1925, N.Y. Stage and screen actor.

Appeared in: **1921** Tol'able David.

GUSTINE, PAUL (Paul Valentine Gustine)

Born: Dec. 8, 1893, Michigan. Died: July 16, 1974, Los Angeles, Calif. (cancer). Screen actor and aviator.

Appeared in: **1937** Hills of Old Wyoming. **1956** Around the World in 80 Days.

GUTHRIE, CHARLES W.

Born: 1871. Died: June 30, 1939, Washington, D.C. Screen and stage actor.

GUTIERREZ, ALICIA

Born: 1928, Mexico. Died: Jan. 17, 1967, Mexico. Screen actress.

GUY, EULA

Born: Corapolis, Pa. Died: Dec. 19, 1960. Stage and screen actress.

Appeared in: **1931** Over the Hill. **1932** The Rich Are Always with Us; Rebecca of Sunnybrook Farm. **1937** Expensive Husbands. **1941** Moon Over Her Shoulder. **1943** The Woman of the Town. **1946** The Spider Woman Srikes Back; The Glass Alibi. **1947** Yankee Fakir; The Pretender. **1949** That Wonderful Urge; Call of the Forest. **1950** My Blue Heaven. **1952** Paula.

GWENN, EDMUND

Born: Sept. 26, 1875, Glamorgan, Wales. Died: Sept. 6, 1959, Woodland Hills, Calif. Stage and screen actor. Won 1947 Academy Award for Best Supporting Actor in The Miracle on 34th Street.

Appeared in: **1916** The Real Thing at Last. **1920** Unmarried; The Skin Game. **1931** How He Lied to Her Husband; Hindle Wakes; The Skin Game (and 1920 version). **1932** Money for Nothing; Frail Women; Condemned to Death; Tell Me Tonight (aka Be Mine Tonight—US 1933); Love on Wheels. **1933** Smithy; The Good Companions; Cash (aka For Love or Money—US 1934); I Was a Spy (US 1934); Channel Crossing (US 1934); Marooned; Friday the Thirteenth (US 1934); Early to Bed. **1934** Passing Shadows; Warn London; Waltzes From Vienna (aka Strauss's Great Waltz—US 1935); Father and Son; Spring in the Air; The Admiral's Secret; Java Head (US 1935). **1935** Sylvia Scarlet; The Bishop Misbehaves. **1936** Laburnum Grove (stage and film versions—US 1931); The Walking Dead; Anthony Adverse; Country Bumpkin (aka All American Chump); Mad Holiday. **1937** Parnell. **1938** A Yank at Oxford; Penny Paradise; South Riding; **1939** Cheer Boys Cheer; An Englishman's Home (aka Madmen of Europe—US). **1940** The Earl of Chicago; Mad Men of Europe; The Doctor Takes a Wife; Pride and Prejudice; Foreign Correspondent. **1941** Scotland Yard; Cheers for Miss Bishop; The Devil and Miss Jones; Charley's Aunt; One Night in Lisbon. **1942** A Yank at Eton. **1943** The Meanest Man in the World; Forever and a Day; Lassie Come Home. **1944** Between Two Worlds. **1945** Keys to the Kingdom; Bewitched; Dangerous Partners; She Went to the Races. **1946** Of Human Bondage; Undercurrent. **1947** The Miracle on 34th Street; Thunder in the Valley; Life with Father; Green Dolphin Street. **1948** Apartment for Peggy; Hills of Home. **1949** Challenge to Lassie. **1950** A Woman of Distinction; Louisa; Pretty Baby; Mister 880; For Heaven's Sake. **1951** Peking Express. **1952** Sally and St. Anne; Bonzo Goes to College; Les Miserables; Something for the Birds. **1953** Mr. Scoutmaster; The Bigamist. **1954** Them; The Student Prince. **1955** The Trouble with Harry; It's a Dog's Life. **1958** Calabuch.

GYPSY GOULD. *See* VIVIAN VAUGHN

HAADE, WILLIAM
Born: 1903. Died: Nov. 15, 1966. Screen actor.

Appeared in: **1937** Kid Galahad; Without Warning; The Missing Witness; He Couldn't Say No. **1938** The Invisible Menace; Stadium Murders; The Texans; If I Were King; Shadows over Shanghai. **1939** Union Pacific; Full Confession; Kid Nightingale; Reno; Forty Invisible Stripes; The Man from Dakota; One Crowded Night; Cherokee Strip. **1941** The Roundup; The Penalty; Dance Hall; Rise and Shine; You're in the Army Now; Pirates on Horseback. **1942** Juke Girl; The Jackass Mail; Just Off Broadway; Star Spangled Rhythm; Heart of the Rio Grande. **1943** Pittsburgh; The Dancing Masters (short); Daredevils of the West (serial). **1944** Sheriff of Las Vegas. **1945** Phantom of the Plains. **1947** Down to Earth; Buck Privates Come Home. **1948** Lulu Belle. **1949** The Scene of the Crime; The Wyoming Bandit. **1950** Trial Without Jury; Outcast of Black Mesa; The Old Frontier; Buckaroo Sheriff of Texas; Joe Palooka in the Squared Circle. **1951** Leave It to the Marines; Oh! Susanna; Rawhide; The Sea Hornet; Stop that Cab; Three Desperate Men (aka Three Outlaws); A Yank in Korea. **1952** Carson City. **1953** Red River Shore. **1954** Untamed Heiress. **1955** Abbot and Costello Meet the Keystone Cops.

HAAGEN, AL H.
Born: 1871. Died: Mar. 8, 1953, Los Angeles, Calif. Screen, stage, vaudeville and minstrel actor.

HAAL, RENEE. *See* RENEE HAAL GODFREY

HAAS, HUGO
Born: Feb. 19, 1902, Brno, Czechoslovakia. Died: Dec. 1968, Vienna, Austria. Screen actor, stage and film director, film producer and screenwriter.

Appeared in: **1940** Skeleton on Horseback. **1944** Summer Storm; Days of Glory; Mrs. Parkington; The Princess and the Pirate; Strange Affair. **1945** Jealousy; A Bell for Adano; Dakota; What Next, Corporal Hargrove? **1946** Holiday in Mexico; Two Smart People. **1947** Northwest Outpost; The Foxes of Harrow; Fiesta; The Private Affairs of Bel Ami; Merton of the Movies. **1948** My Girl Tisa; Casbah; For the Love of Mary. **1949** The Fighting Kentuckian. **1950** King Solomon's Mines; Vendetta. **1951** Pickup; Girl on the Bridge. **1952** Strange Fascination. **1953** One Girl's Confession; The Neighbor's Wife. **1954** Bait; The Other Woman. **1955** Hold Back Tomorrow; Tender Trap. **1956** Edge of Hell. **1957** Hit and Run; Lizzie. **1959** Born to Be Loved. **1962** Paradise Alley.

HABERFIELD, GRAHAM
Born: 1941. Died: Oct. 17, 1975, Knutsford, Cheshire, England. Screen, stage and television actor.

HACK, HERMAN
Born: 1899. Died: Oct. 19, 1967, Hollywood, Calif. (heart attack). Screen actor.

Appeared in: **1940** Melody Ranch. **1941** The Singing Hill; Stick to Your Guns. **1950** Cow Town; Beyond the Purple Hills. **1953** Pack Train. **1956** Around the World in 80 Days.

HACK, SIGNE
Born: 1899. Died: Jan. 6, 1973, Hollywood, Calif. (leukemia). Screen actress and film extra. Mother of actress Dorothy Hack.

HACKATHORNE, GEORGE
Born: Feb. 13, 1896, Pendleton, Ore. Died: June 25, 1940, Los Angeles, Calif. Screen, stage and vaudeville actor.

Appeared in: **1916** Oliver Twist. **1918** The Heart of Humanity. **1920** To Please One Woman; The Last of the Mohicans. **1921** What Do Men Want?; The Little Minister; The Light in the Clearing; High Heels; The Sin of Martha Queed. **1922** Human Hearts; The Village Blacksmith; The Gray Dawn; Notoriety; The Worldly Madonna. **1923** Merry-Go-Round; The Human Wreckage. **1924** The Turmoil; When a Man's a Man; Judgment of the Storm; Surging Seas. **1925** Night Life in New York; Capital Punishment; Wandering Fires; The Lady; His Master's Voice. **1926** The Sea Urchin; The Highbinders. **1927** Cheaters; The Cabaret Kid; Paying the Price. **1928** Shepherd of the Hills; Sally Shoulders. **1929** Tip Off; The Squall. **1930** Lonesome Trail; Beyond the Law;

Hideout. **1933** Self Defense; Flaming Guns. **1936** I Cover Chinatown; The Magnificent Obsession. **1939** Gone with the Wind.

HACKER, MARIA
Born: 1904, Germany. Died: Feb. 20, 1963, Sherman Oaks, Calif. Screen actress. Wife of actor/tenor Lauritz Melchior (dec. 1973).

HACKETT, FLORENCE
Born: 1882. Died: August 21, 1954, New York, N.Y. Screen and stage actress. Mother of actors Raymond (dec. 1958) and Albert Hackett. Married to actor Arthur Johnson (dec. 1916).

Appeared in: **1914** The Beloved Adventurer (serial). **1915** Siren of Corsica.

HACKETT, HAL
Born: 1923. Died: Dec. 4, 1967, New York, N.Y. Screen, sstage, radio and television actor.

Appeared in: **1946** The Show Off; Love Laughs at Andy Hardy. **1948** Campus Honeymoon; Summer Holiday.

HACKETT, JAMES K.
Born: Sept. 6, 1869, Wolf Island, Ontario, Canada. Died: Nov. 8, 1926, Paris, France (cirrhosis of the liver). Screen and stage actor. Entered films with Famous Players in 1912.

Appeared in: **1913** The Prisoner of Zenda.

HACKETT, KARL
Born: 1893. Died: Oct. 24, 1948, Los Angeles, Calif. Screen actor.

Appeared in: **1936** Down to the Sea; The Public Pays (short); Happy Go Lucky. **1937** The Gold Racket; Sing, Cowboy, Sing; Tex Rides with the Boy Scouts; Texas Trail; Colorado Kid. **1938** Paroled to Die; Phantom Ranger; Down in Arkansaw; The Rangers Roundup; Starlight over Texas; Where the Buffalo Roam; Frontier Town. **1940** Yukon Flight; Take Me Back to Oklahoma; Chip of the Flying U. **1941** Outlaws of the Rio Grande. **1942** Sons of the Pioneers; Pirates of the Prairie; Jesse James, Jr.; Billy the Kid's Smoking Guns; Phantom Killer; Outlaws of Boulder Pass. **1943** The Avenging Rider; Fugitive of the Plains; Bordertown Gunfighters; Thundering Trails; The Renegade; Lost Canyon. **1944** Tucson Raiders; Wolves of the Range; Sonora Stagecoach; Westward Bound; Mojave Firebrand; Arizona Whirlwind; Oath of Vengeance; Thundering Gunslinger; The Pinto Bandit; Brand of the Devil. **1945** Lightning Raiders; His Brother's Ghost; Rustlers of the Badlands; Prairie Rustlers. **1946** Ghost of Hidden Valley; Gentlemen with Guns; Terrors on Horseback; Outlaw of the Plains; Gunman's Code. **1947** The Michigan Kid; Frontier Fighters; Raiders of Red Rock; Code of the Plains.

HACKETT, LILLIAN
Born: Oct. 11, 1899, Chicago, Illinois. Died: Feb. 28, 1973, Hollywood, Calif. Stage and screen actress.

Appeared in: **1920** Don't Tickle. **1921** Once a Plumber; Blue Sunday. **1922** Hired and Fired. **1923** Danger. **1924** In Hollywood with Potash and Perlmutter. **1927** Ladies at Ease.

HACKETT, RAYMOND
Born: July 15, 1902, New York, N.Y. Died: June 9, 1958, Hollywood, Calif. Stage and screen actor. Divorced from actress Myra Hampton (dec. 1945). Married to actress Blanche Sweet. Son of actress Florence Hackett (dec. 1954) and brother of actor Albert Hackett.

Appeared in: **1912** A Matter of Business; A Child's Devotion. **1913** Longing for a Mother. **1914** The Price of a Ruby; The Shadow of Tragedy. **1918** The Cruise of the Make-Believe. **1922** The Country Flapper. **1927** The Love of Sunya. **1928** Faithless Lover. **1929** Girl in the Show; The Trial of Mary Dugan; Madame X; Footlights and Fools. **1930** Let Us Be Gay; Our Blushing Brides; The Sea Wolf; Numbered Men; On Your Back; The Cat Creeps; Not So Dumb. **1931** Seed.

HADDON, PETER (Peter Tildsley)
Born: 1898, England. Died: Sept. 7, 1962, England. Screen, stage actor and author. Married to stage actress Rosaline Courtneidge (dec. 1926).

Appeared in: **1934** The Wigan Express (aka Death at Broadcasting House—US). **1935** Who's Your Father?; The Silent Passenger; No Monkey Business. **1936** Don't Rush Me!; Public Nuisance No. 1; The Beloved Vagabond; The House of the Spaniard; The Secret of Stamboul. **1937** Over the Moon (US 1940). **1938** Kate Plus Ten. **1949** Helter Skelter. **1952** The Second Mrs. Tanqueray (US 1954).

HADLEY, REED (Reed Herring)
Born: 1911, Petrolia, Tex. Died: Dec. 11, 1974, Los Angeles, Calif. (heart attack). Screen, stage, radio and television actor.

Appeared in: **1938** Hollywood Stadium Mystery; Female Fugitive; Orphans of the Street. **1939** Calling Dr. Kildare; Zorro's Fighting Legion (serial). **1940** I Take This Woman; Ski Patrol; The Bank Dick; Jack Pot (short); The Man from Montreal. **1941** I'll Wait for You; Whistling in the Dark; Adventures of

Captain Marvel (serial); Road Agent. **1942** Jail House Blues; Juke Box Jenny; Arizona Terrors; Mystery of Marie Roget. **1943** Guadalcanal Diary. **1946** Roger Touhy, Gangster; Wing and a Prayer; Rainbow Island; In the Meantime, Darling. **1945** The House on 92nd Street; Circumstantial Evidence; Caribbean Mystery; Doll Face; Diamond Horseshoe; A Bell for Adano; Leave Her to Heaven. **1946** It Shouldn't Happen to a Dog; The Dark Corner; If I'm Lucky; Shock. **1947** Captain from Castile; The Fabulous Texan. **1948** The Iron Curtain; Walk a Crooked Mile; A Southern Yankee; Panhandle; The Man from Texas; The Return of Wildfire (serial); Last of the Wild Horses. **1949** I Shot Jesse James; Grand Canyon; Riders of the Range; Rimfire. **1950** Dallas; The Baron of Arizona; A Modern Marriage; Motor Patrol. **1951** Little Big Horn; Rhythm Inn; Insurance Investigator. **1952** The Half-Breed. **1953** Woman They Almost Lynched; Kansas Pacific. **1954** Highway Dragnet. **1955** Big House, USA. **1962** Frigid Marriage (rerelease of A Modern Marriage—1950). **1964** Moro Witch Doctor (aka Amok). **1965** Young Dillinger. **1967** The St. Valentines Day Massacre. **1969** The Fabulous Bastard from Chicago (aka The Fabulous Kid from Chicago; The Chicago Kid and The Bastard Wench from Chicago). **1971** Brain of Blood (aka The Creature's Revenge).

HAEFELI, CHARLES "JOCKEY"
Born: 1889. Died: Feb. 12, 1955, Hollywood, Calif. Screen actor.

Appeared in: **1921** Four Horsemen of the Apocalypse. **1923** The Hunchback of Notre Dame. **1935** Les Miserables.

HAFTER, ROBERT (Robert Mark Hafter)
Born: Jan. 7, 1897, London, England. Died: Aug. 9, 1955, North Hollywood, Calif. (heart attack). Screen, television actor and television director.

HAGEMAN, RICHARD
Born: July 9, 1882, Leeuwarden, Holland. Died: Mar. 6, 1966, Beverly Hills, Calif. Screen actor, musician and composer.

Appeared in: **1941** The Hard-Boiled Canary. **1943** Hi Diddle Diddle. **1944** Sensations of 1945. **1946** The Bachelor's Daughter. **1947** New Orleans; Fun on a Week-End. **1950** The Toast of New Orleans; Grounds for Marriage. **1951** The Great Caruso; Grounds for Marriage. **1954** Rhapsody.

HAGEN, CHARLES F.
Born: 1872. Died: June 13, 1958, Hollywood, Calif. Screen and stage actor. Entered films with Griffith.

Appeared in: **1950** All about Eve.

HAGEN, MARGARETHE
Born: 1890, Germany. Died: Dec. 14, 1966, Gruenwald, Germany. Stage and screen actress.

Appeared in: Uncle Filsner; Kohlhiesel's Daughter; In Those Days; Beloved Liar; Fireworks; Her 106th Birthday.

HAGER, CLYDE
Born: 1887. Died: May 21, 1944, Harrisburg, Pa. (heart attack). Screen, stage, vaudeville actor and song writer.

Appeared in: **1930** Railroad Follies (short). **1936** Strike Me Pink.

HAGGARD, STEPHEN
Born: 1912, England. Died: Feb, 1943, Middle East (during war). Screen, stage actor and author.

Appeared in: **1939** Jamaica Inn. **1940** Fear and Peter Brown. **1942** The Young Mr. Pitt.

HAGNEY, FRANK S. (aka FRANK HAGNY)
Born: 1884, Sydney, Australia. Died: June 25, 1973, Los Angeles, Calif. Screen, stage, vaudeville, television actor and stuntman.

Appeared in: **1920** Gauntlet. **1921** Anne of Little Smoky; The Ghost in the Garret. **1923** The Backbone. **1924** The Martyr Sex; Poison; The Silent Stranger; Roaring Rails; The Breed of the Border; The Dangerous Coward; The Fighting Sap; Lightning Romance; Galloping Gallagher; The Mask of Lopez. **1925** New Champion; Wild Justice; Fighting Youth; Braveheart; Hogan's Alley; The Wild Bull's Lair. **1926** Fangs of Justice; The Ice Flood; The Fighting Marine (serial); The Sea Beast; Lone Hand Saunders; The Winning Wallop; The Two-Gun Man. **1927** All Aboard; One-Round Hogan; The Frontiersman; The Last Trail. **1928** On Your Toes; The Fight Pest (short); The Glorious Trail; Through the Breakers; Free Lips; The Rawhide Kid; Midnight Madness; Burning Daylight; The Charge of the Gauchos; Go Get 'Em Hutch (serial); Vultures of the Sea (serial). **1929** Broken Barriers; Masked Emotions; Captain Lash; Oh, Dear! **1931** Fighting Caravans; Sit Tight; The Squaw Man; I Like Your Nerve; No Limit; Reckless Living; City Sentinel; The Champ. **1932** A House Divided; You Said a Mouthful; The All American; Ride Him Cowboy!; The Golden West. **1934** Honor of the Range. **1935** Western Frontier. **1936** Wildcat Trooper; Heroes of the Range; The Plough and the Stars; Secret Valley; Conflict; Here Comes Trouble. **1937** Hollywood Cowboy; Ghost Town Gold; Riders of the Dawn; Windjammer; Valley of the Lawless; Night Key; Missing Men. **1938** The Mysterious Mr. Moto. **1939** Captain Fury. **1940** Misbehaving Husbands. **1941** The Lone Rider Ambushed; The Lone Rider in Ghost Town; The Lone Rider Fights Back; Mr. Celebrity; Blazing Frontier. **1942** The Glass Key; Tomorrow We Live; The Broadway Big Shot. **1943** The Renegade. **1944** Lost in a Harem; Louisiana Hayride. **1945** Abbott and Costello in Hollywood; Spook to Me (short). **1946** It's a Wonderful Life. **1947** The Wistful Widow of Wagon Gap; Code of the Plains. **1948** Where the North Begins; The Paleface. **1949** Grand Canyon. **1951** Man in the Saddle. **1952** The San Francisco Story. **1954** Riot in Cell Block 11; Demetrius and the Gladiators. **1955** Abbott and Costello Meet the Keystone Kops; A Bullet for Joey; A Lawless Street; Lucy Gallant; They Came from Another World. **1957** Zombies of Mora-Tau. **1958** The Buccaneer.

HAHN, SALLY
Born: 1908. Died: June 2, 1933, Los Angeles, Calif. Screen actress.

HAID, GRIT
Born: Germany. Died: Date unknown, Germany. Screen actress. Sister of actress Liana Haid.

Appeared in: **1934** Die Mutter der Kompagnie. **1935** Drei Kaiserjaeger. **1937** Fuerst Sepp'l.

HAIG, RAYMOND V.
Born: 1917. Died: Sept. 17, 1963, Chicago, Ill. (auto accident). Screen and vaudeville actor. Appeared in vaudeville in an act billed as "Haig and Haig" and the team made Paramount shorts.

HAINE, HORACE J.
Born: 1868, Detroit, Mich. Died: Sept. 26, 1940, New York, N.Y. Screen, stage actor, opera performer and stage producer.

Appeared in: **1916** The Other Man; The Moonshiners. **1924** The Fifth Horseman.

HAINES, DONALD
Died: c. 1942. Screen actor.

Appeared in: **1930** The following shorts: Shivering Shakespeare; The First Seven Years; Teacher's Pet; School's Out; Helping Grandma. **1931** Skippy; plus the following shorts: Readin' and Writin'; Little Daddy; Bargain Days; Big Ears; Love Business. **1932** When a Feller Needs a Friend; plus the following shorts: Spanky; Hook and Ladder; Free Eats; Choo Choo; Birthday Blues; A Lad an' a Lamp. **1933** Fish Hooky (short). **1934** No Greater Glory; Little Man, What Now? **1935** A Tale of Two Cities; Straight from the Heart. **1936** Little Miss Nobody; Woman Trap; The Invisible Ray. **1938** Kidnapped. **1939** Sergeant Madden. **1940** Prison Camp; The Ghost Creeps; East Side Kids; Seventeen; That Gang of Mine; Fugitive from a Prison Camp. **1941** Pride of the Bowery; Flying Wild; Spooks Run Wild; Bowery Blitzkrieg.

HAINES, RHEA
Born: 1895. Died: Mar 12, 1964, Los Angeles, Calif. Screen actress.

Appeared in: **1916** The Chalice of Sorrow. **1917** Nina the Flower Girl; Hands Up. **1919** Scarlet Days. **1920** Mary Ellen Comes to Town; Always Audacious; Master Stroke; Girls Don't Gamble. **1921** Smiling All the Way; Uncharted Seas.

HAINES, ROBERT T.
Born: 1870, Muncie, Ind. Died: May 6, 1943, N.Y. Screen, stage, vaudeville, radio actor, stage producer, director, and playwright.

Appeared in: **1912** The Capitol. **1921** The Victim; God's Crucible. **1923** Does It Pay?; The Governor's Lady. **1924** The Lone Wolf. **1926** Lew Tyler's Wives. **1928** How to Handle Women; The First Kiss; Ladies of the Mob; The Noose. **1928** Ten Minutes (short). **1929** Careers; Dynamite; The Girl in the Glass Cage; The Shannons of Broadway. **1930** Guilty? **1934** These Thirty Years. **1935** Gigolette.

HAINES, WILLIAM
Born: 1900. Died: Nov. 26, 1973, Santa Monica, Calif. (cancer). Screen actor and interior decorator.

Appeared in: **1922** Brothers Under the Skin (film debut). **1923** Three Wise Fools; Souls for Sale; Lost and Found. **1924** The Desert Outlaw; The Gaiety Girl Circe the Enchantress (aka Circe); Three Weeks; Wine of Youth; The Midnight Express; True as Steel; Wife of the Centaur. **1925** The Denial; Fighting the Flames; The Tower of Lies; Who Cares; A Fool and His Money; Little Annie Rooney; Sally, Irene and Mary; A Slave of Fashion. **1926** Brown of Harvard; Mike; Lovey Mary; Memory Lane; The Thrill Hunter. **1927** Spring Fever; Slide, Kelly, Slide; West Point; A Little Journey; Tell It to the Marines. **1928** Alias Jimmy Valentine; Excess Baggage; The Smart Set; Show People; Telling the World. **1929** A Man's Man; Speedway; The Duke Steps Out; The Hollywood Revue of 1929; Free and Easy; Remote Control; Way Out West; Navy Blues. **1931** A Tailor Made Man; Just a Gigolo; Get-Rich-Quick Wallingford (aka New Adventure of Get-Rich-Quick Wallingford). **1932** Are You Listening?; The Fast Life; The Slippery Pearls (short). **1934** Young and Beautiful; Marines are Coming.

HALE, ALAN, SR. (Rufas Alan McKanan)

Born: Feb. 10, 1892, Washington, D.C. Died Jan. 22, 1950, Hollywood, Calif. (liver ailment—virus infection). Screen, stage actor, film director, writer and singer. Father of actor Alan Jr., Karen and Jeanne Hale. Married to actress Gretchen Hartman.

Appeared in: **1911** The Cowboy and the Lady (film debut). **1914** Cricket on the Hearth. **1915** Jane Eyre; Under Two Flags; Dora; an untitled short. **1916** Pudd'n Head Wilson. **1917** The Price She Paid. **1921** A Voice in the Dark; A Wise Fool; The Four Horsemen of the Apocalypse; Shirley of the Circus; The Barbarian; The Fox; The Great Impersonation; Over the Wire. **1922** One Glorious Day; Robin Hood; A Doll's House; Dictator; The Trap. **1923** The Covered Wagon; Hollywood; Cameo Kirby; The Eleventh Hour; Long Live the King; Main Street; Quicksands. **1924** Troubles of a Bride; Black Oxen; Code of the Wilderness; For Another Woman; Girls Men Forget; One Night in Rome. **1925** Rolling Stones; Braveheart; The Crimson Runner; Dick Turpin; Flattery; The Scarlet Honeymoon; The Wedding Song. **1926** Forbidden Waters; Hearts and Fists; Risky Business; The Sporting Lover. **1927** Rubber Tires; Vanity; The Wreck of the Hesperus. **1928** The Leopard Lady; Skyscraper; The Cop; Power; Oh, Kay! **1929** Sal of Singapore; The Spieler; The Leatherneck; A Bachelor's Secret; Red Hot Rhythm; The Sap; Sailor's Holiday. **1930** She Got What She Wanted. **1931** Up and At 'Em; Aloha; The Night Angel; Susan Lennox, Her Rise and Fall; Sea Ghost; The Sin of Madelon Claudet; Rebound; So Big; Union Depot; Rebecca of Sunnybrook Farm; Gentlemen for a Day. **1932** The Match King. **1933** Picture Brides; What Price Decency?; Eleventh Commandment; Destination Unknown. **1934** It Happened One Night; Imitation of Life; Of Human Bondage; Little Man, What Now?; Great Expectations; The Lost Patrol; Miss Fane's Baby is Stolen; The Little Minister; Fog over Frisco; The Scarlet Letter; Babbitt; There's Always Tomorrow; Broadway Bill. **1935** Grand Old Girl; Last Days of Pompeii; Another Face; The Good Fairy; The Crusades. **1936** Jump for Glory; Two in the Dark; A Message to Garcia; The Country Beyond; Parole!; Yellowstone; Our Relations; God's Country and the Woman. **1937** When Thief Meets Thief; High, Wide and Handsome; Thin Ice; Music for Madame; The Prince and the Pauper; Stella Dallas. **1938** Valley of the Giants; The Adventures of Marco Polo; The Adventures of Robin Hood; Algiers; Four Men and a Prayer; Listen, Darling; The Sisters. **1939** Pacific Liner; (Dust Be My Destiny;) On Your Toes; The Private Lives of Elizabeth and Essex; Dodge City; Man in the Iron Mask. **1940** The Sea Hawk; Three Cheers for the Irish; Green Hell; Virginia City; The Fighting 69th; They Drive by Night; Santa Fe Trail; Tugboat Annie Sails Again. **1941** The Great Mr. Nobody; (Strawberry Blonde;) Manpower; The Smiling Ghost; Thieves Fall Out; Footsteps in the Dark. **1942** Desperate Journey; (Captains of the Clouds;) Juke Girl; Gentlemen Jim. **1943** Action in the North Atlantic; This Is the Army; Thank Your Lucky Stars; (Destination Tokyo.) **1944** The Adventures of Mark Twain; Make Your Own Bed; Janie; (Hollywood Canteen;) Strangers in Our Midst. **1945** Roughly Speaking; Hotel Berlin; God Is My Co-Pilot; Escape in the Desert. **1946** Perilous Holiday; The Time, the Place and the Girl; The Man I Love; Night and Day. **1947** My Wild Irish Rose; Cheyenne; That Way with Women; Pursued. **1948** The Adventures of Don Juan; My Girl Tisa; Whiplash. **1949** South of St. Louis; The Younger Brothers; The House Across the Street; Always Leave Them Laughing; The Inspector General. **1940** Rogues of Sherwood Forest; Stars in My Crown; Colt .45.

HALE, BARNABY

Born: 1927. Died: Nov. 5, 1964, Los Angeles, Calif. (following surgery). Screen, stage and television actor.

HALE, CREIGHTON (Patrick Fitzgerald)

Born: May 1882, Cork, Ireland. Died: Aug. 9, 1965, South Pasadena, Calif. Screen actor.

Appeared in: **1915** The New Exploits of Elaine (serial); The Romance of Elaine (serial). **1916** The Iron Claw (serial). **1917** The Seven Pearls (serial). **1919** The Thirteenth Chair. **1920** The Idol Dancer; Way Down East. **1921** Forbidden Love. **1922** Orphans of the Storm; Fascination; Her Majesty. **1923** Broken Hearts of Broadway; Mary of the Movies; Tea with a Kick; Three Wise Fools; Trilby. **1924** How to Educate a Wife; The Mine with the Iron Door; Name the Man; Riders Up; This Woman; Wine of Youth; The Marriage Circle. **1925** The Bridge of Sighs; The Circle; Exchange of Wives; Seven Days; The Shadow on the Wall; Time, the Comedian; Wages for Wives. **1926** Beverly of Graustark; The Midnight Message; Oh, Baby; A Poor Girl's Romance; Speeding Through. **1927** Annie Laurie; The Cat and The Canary; Thumbs Down. **1928** The House of Shame; Sisters of Eve; Rose Marie. **1929** Seven Footprints to Satan; Reilly of the Rainbow Division. **1930** Holiday; School's Out (short); The Great Divide. **1931** Grief Street; Big Ears (short). **1932** Prestige; Shop Angel; Free Wheeling (short); Stage Whispers. **1933** The Masquerader. **1934** Sensation Hunters; What's Your Racket? **1935** Death from a Distance. **1936** The Millionaire Kid; Hollywood Boulevard. **1939** Nancy Drew and the Hidden Staircase; Return of Dr. X. **1940** Calling Philo Vance. **1941** The Bride Came C.O.D. **1942** Bullet Scars; Larceny, Inc; Yankee Doodle Dandy; Murder in the Big House; Gorilla Man. **1943** Watch on the Rhine; The Mysterious Doctor; Action in the North Atlantic. **1944** The Adventures of Mark Twain; Crime by Night. **1947** That Way with Women; The Two Mrs. Carrolls; Perils of Pauline. **1949** Beyond the Forest.

HALE, DOROTHY

Born: 1905, Pittsburgh, Pa. Died: Oct. 21, 1938, New York, N.Y. Stage and screen actress.

Appeared in: **1934** Catherine the Great.

HALE, JONATHAN

Born: 1891. Died: Feb. 28, 1966, Woodland Halls, Calif. (suicide—gun). Screen actor.

Appeared in: **1934** Lightning Strikes Twice (film debut). **1935** Navy Wife; Alice Adams; The Voice of Bugle Ann; Hit and Run Driver (short); A Night at the Opera. **1936** Charlie Chan's Secret; Fury; The Devil Is a Sissy; Too Many Parents; The Case against Mrs. Ames; Educating Father; Charlie Chan at the Race Track; 36 Hours to Kill; Flying Hostess; Happy Go Lucky; Three Live Ghosts. **1937** She's Dangerous; Charlie Chan at the Olympics; League of the Frightened Men; Big Time Girl; You Only Live Once; Man of the People; Saratoga; Midnight Madonna; Outcast; John Meade's Woman; Madame X; This Is My Affair; Mysterious Crossing; Racketeers in Exile; Danger—Love at Work; Exiled to Shanghai. **1938** Blondie; The First Hundred Years; Bringing up Baby; Arsene Lupin Returns; Judge Hardy's Children; Yellow Jack; Boys Town; Road Demon; There's That Woman Again; Her Jungle Love; Duke of West Point; Wives under Suspicion; A Letter of Introduction; Over the Wall; The Saint in New York; Fugitives for a Night; Breaking the Ice; Tarnished Angel; Gangs of New York; Scandal Sheet. **1939** Thunder Afloat; The Saint Strikes Back; In Name Only; One Against the World (short); Blondie Meets the Boss; Fugitive at Large; Blondie Brings up Baby; The Amazing Mr. Williams; The Story of Alexander Graham Bell; Barricade; In Old Monterey; Stand up and Fight; Wings of the Navy; Tail Spin. **1940** The Big Guy; The Saint's Double Trouble; The Saint Takes Over; Private Affairs; We Who Are Young; Blondie Has Servant Trouble; Dulcy; Melody and Moonlight; Blondie Plays Cupid; Johnny Apollo. **1941** Blondie Goes Latin; Flight from Destiny; Ringside Maisie; The Pittsburgh Kid; Blondie in Society; The Saint in Palm Springs; The Great Swindle; Strange Alibi; The Bugle Sounds. **1942** Joe Smith, American; Blondie Goes to College; Lone Star Ranger; Miss Annie Rooney; Calling Dr. Gillespie; Flight Lieutenant; Blondie's Blessed Event; Blondie for Victory. **1943** Hangmen Also Die; It's a Great Life; Footlight Glamour; Jack London; Mission 36; The Amazing Mrs. Holliday; Sweet Rosie O'Grady. **1944** This Is the Life; The Black Parachute; Since You Went Away; Hollywood Canteen; Dead Man's Eyes; My Buddy; And Now Tomorrow; The End of the Road. **1945** Leave It to Blondie; The Phantom Speaks; Dakota; Man Alive; G.I. Honeymoon; Allotment Wives. **1946** Angel on My Shoulder; Life with Blondie; Blondie Knows Best; Blondie's Lucky Day; The Cat Creeps; Easy to Wed; Riverboat Rhythm; The Walls Came Tumbling Down; The Strange Mr. Gregory; Gay Blades; Wife Wanted. **1947** The Beginning or the End; The Ghost Goes Wild; Rolling Home; The Vigilantes Return; Her Husband's Affair; High Wall. **1948** Michael O'Halloran; King of the Gamblers; Silver River; Johnny Belinda; Call Northside 777; Rocky. **1949** Rose of the Yukon; Stampede; The Judge; State Department File 649. **1950** Federal Agent at Large; Three Husbands; Short Grass; Triple Trouble. **1951** Insurance Investigator; On the Sunny Side of the Street; Strangers on a Train; Let's Go Navy!; Rodeo King and the Senorita; Rhythm Inn. **1952** Steel Trap; My Pal Gus; Son of Paleface; Scandal Sheet. **1953** A Blueprint for Murder; Kansas Pacific; Taxi. **1954** Duffy of San Quentin; Riot in Cell Block 11. **1955** The Night Holds Terror; A Man Called Peter. **1956** Jaguar; The Opposite Sex.

HALE, LOUISE CLOSSER

Born: Oct. 13, 1872, Chicago, Ill. Died: July 26, 1933, Los Angeles, Calif. (following an accident). Screen, stage actress and playwright.

Appeared in: **1929** The Hole in the Wall; Paris. **1930** Dangerous Nan McGrew; Big Boy; The Princess and the Plumber. **1931** Captain Applejack; Born to Love; Rebound; Devotion; Daddy Long Legs; Platinum Blonde. **1932** Sky Bride; Faithless; No More Orchids; The Son-Daughter; Rebecca of Sunnybrook Farm; Movie Crazy; Rasputin and the Empress; The Shanghai Express; The Man Who Played God; New Morals for Old; Letty Lynton. **1933** The White Sister; Today We Live; The Barbarian; Storm at Daybreak; Another Language; Dinner at Eight.

HALE, ROBERT

Born: 1874, Devonshire, England. Died: Apr. 18, 1940, Maidenhead, Berkshire, England. Stage and screen actor. Father of music hall actress Binnie and actor Sonnie Hale (dec. 1959).

Appeared in: **1934** What Happened to Harkness?; Waltzes from Vienna (aka Strauss' Great Waltz—US 1935). **1935** Royal Cavalcade (aka Regal Cavalcade—US). **1936** It's Love Again. **1937** Storm in a Teacup.

HALE, ROBERTSON

Born: 1891, England. Died: 1967. Stage and screen actor.

HALE, SONNIE (John Robert Hale-Munro)

Born: May 1, 1902, London, England. Died: June 9, 1959, London, England. Screen, stage actor, film director and playwright. Wrote under name of Robert Munro. Son of actor Robert Hale (dec. 1940) and brother of actress Binnie

Hale. Divorced from actresses Evelyn Laye and Jessie Matthews; and later married to Mary Kelsey.

Appeared in: **1927** The Book of Psalms series including The Parting of the Ways—Psalm 57; On With the Dance series. **1932** Happy Ever After; Tell Me Tonight (aka Be Mine Tonight—US 1933). **1933** Early to Bed; Friday the Thirteenth (US 1934). **1934** Evergreen (US 1935); Wild Boy; Are You a Mason?; My Song for You; My Heart is Calling (US 1935). **1935** Marry the Girl; First a Girl. **1936** It's Love Again. **1938** The Gaunt Stranger (aka The Phantom Strikes—US 1939). **1939** Let's Be Famous. **1944** Fiddlers Three. **1946** London Town (aka My Heart Goes Crazy—US 1953).

HALL, ALEXANDER
Born: 1894, Boston, Mass. Died: July 30, 1968, San Francisco, Calif. (stroke). Screen, stage actor and film director.

Appeared in: **1927** Million Dollar Mystery (serial—film debut).

HALL, ALFRED HENRY
Born: 1880. Died: Apr. 21, 1943, Hollywood, Calif. (heart attack). Stage and screen actor.

Appeared in: **1942** Scattergood Survives a Murder; The Old Homestead; Pretty Dolly (short).

HALL, CHARLES D. "CHARLIE"
Born: Aug. 18, 1899, Birmingham, England. Died: Dec. 7, 1959, North Hollywood, Calif. Screen, stage actor and film art director. Entered films as an actor in 1923.

Appeared in: **1927** Battle of the Century; Love 'Em and Weep (short). **1928** Must We Marry?; Crooks Can't Win; plus the following shorts: You're Darn Tootin'; Two Tars; Leave 'Em Laughing. **1929** Why Bring That Up?; plus the following shorts: Boxing Gloves; The Hoose Gow; Skirt Shy; They Go Boom; Wrong Again; That's My Wife; Double Whoopee; Berth Marks; Men O'War; Bacon Grabbers; Angora Love. **1930** The following shorts: Bear Shooters; Pups Is Pups; The Real McCoy; Fifty Million Husbands; Dollar Dizzy; The Fighting Parson; Below Zero. **1931** Pardon Us; plus the following shorts: Be Big; Bear Hunks; The Pip From Pittsburgh; Rough Seas!; The Panic Is On; What a Bozo!; Air Tight; The Kickoff; Mama Loves Papa; Let's Do Things; The Pajama Party; Laughing Gravy; Scratch As Catch Can; Come Clean; War Mamas. **1932** The following shorts: Young Ironsides; Mr. Bride; Too Many Women; Wild Babies; Seal Skins; Sneak Easily; Any Old Port; The Music Box; Strictly Unreliable; Show Business; The Soilers; Bon Voyage. **1933** The following shorts: The Midnight Patrol; Fallen Arches; His Silent Racket; Luncheon at Twelve; Hold Your Temper; Maids A La Mode; One Tract Minds; Beauty and the Bus; Backs to Nature; Air Fright; Twice Two; Me and My Pal; Busy Bodies; Kickin' The Crown Around; Fits in a Fiddle; What Fur. **1934** Cockeyed Cavaliers; Sons of the Desert; Kentucky Kernels; plus the following shorts: Mike Fright; Hi Neighbor; I'll Take Vanilla; It Happened One Day; Something Simple; The Chases of Pimple Street; Them Thar Hills; The Live Ghost; Babes in the Goods; Soup and Fish; One Horse Farmers; Opened by Mistake; Maid in Hollywood. **1935** The following shorts: Beginner's Luck; Teacher's Beau; Okay Toots!; Poker at Eight; Southern Exposure; Treasure Blues; Sing, Sister, Sing; Twin Triplets; Hot Money; Tit for Tat; Thicker Than Water. **1936** Pick a Star; plus the following shorts: Pinch Singer; All-American Toothache; Neighborhood House. **1940** One Night in the Tropics; A Chump at Oxford; Saps at Sea; You Can't Fool Your Wife; Slightly at Sea (short); Trailer Tragedy (short). **1941** Top Sergeant Mulligan; plus the following shorts: An Apple in His Eye; I'll Fix That; A Quiet Fourth; A Polo Phony. **1942** The following shorts: Two For the Money; Rough on Rents; Framing Father. **1943** Gem Jams (short). **1944** In Society; Radio Rampage (short); Girls, Girls, Girls (short). **1945** Hangover Square; Mama Loves Papa. **1946** Wall Street Blues (short). **1948** How to Clean House (short); Home Canning (short). **1950** Spooky Wooky (short). **1951** The Vicious Years. **1956** So You Want to Play the Piano (short). **1958** The Further Perils of Laurel and Hardy (documentary).

HALL, DONALD
Born: Aug. 14, 1878, Murree, East India. Died: July 25, 1948, Hollywood, Calif. Screen, stage actor and singer.

Appeared in: **1914** The Christian; Mr. Barnes of New York; The Crucible of Fate. **1915** Mortmain; Anselo Lee. **1916** The Law Decides; The Man Who Went Sane; The Scarlet Runner (serial). **1917** The On-the-Square Girl; The Awakening of Ruth; Alias Mrs. Jessop; The Raggedy Queen. **1919** The Broken Melody; The Carter Case (Craig Kennedy serial). **1920** A Woman's Business; The Greatest Love. **1922** A Woman's Woman. **1923** The Last Moment. **1924** Her Love Story; Unguarded Women. **1929** The Spirit of Youth; The Younger Generation. **1930** Oh, For a Man!

HALL, DOROTHY
Born: 1906. Died: Feb. 3, 1953, New York, N.Y. Screen and stage actress.

Appeared in: **1927** Back to Liberty; The Broadway Drifter; The Winning Oar. **1929** Nothing but the Truth; The Laughing Lady. **1930** Home Made (short).

HALL, GABRIELLE
Died: Jan. 1, 1967, El Cajon, Calif. Screen and television actress. Entered films during silents.

HALL, GEORGE M.
Born: 1890, Sweden. Died: Apr. 24, 1930, Saranac Lake, N.Y. Stage and screen actor.

Appeared in: **1926** West of Broadway.

HALL, GERALDINE
Born: 1905. Died: Sept. 18, 1970, Woodland Hills, Calif. Stage and screen actress. Married to actor Porter Hall (dec. 1953).

Appeared in: **1936** More Than a Secretary. **1938** Bringing Up Baby. **1951** The Big Carnival. **1952** The Captive City. **1954** Secret of the Incas. **1955** Five Against the House. **1956** Over-Exposed; The Proud and the Profane.

HALL, HENRY LEONARD
Died: Dec. 11, 1954, Woodland Hills, Calif. Screen and stage actor.

Appeared in: **1933** Story of Temple Drake (film debut); Sagebrush Trail. **1934** Our Daily Bread; The Dude Ranger. **1935** The Phantom Empire (serial); Mary Burns, Fugitive. **1936** Jailbreak. **1937** County Fair; Yodelin' Kid from Pine Ridge. **1938** Block-Heads. **1940** Blazing Six Shooter; Prairie Law; The Haunted House; The Ape; Chip of the Flying U. **1941** Pirates on Horseback; Stick to Your Guns; The Lone Star Vigilantes. **1942** Murder in the Big House; Stagecoach Buckaroo; Boss of Hangtown Mesa; The Old Homestead; Butch Minds the Baby; Queen of Broadway. **1943** Girls in Chains. **1945** San Antonio; Jade Mask. **1946** Flying Serpent. **1947** The Beginning of the End. **1948** Panhandle. **1949** Cover Up.

HALL, JAMES (James Brown)
Born: Oct. 22, 1900, Dallas, Tex. Died: June 7, 1940, Jersey City, N.J. (liver ailment). Stage and screen actor.

Appeared in: **1923** The Man Alone. **1926** The Campus Flirt; Stranded in Paris. **1927** Hotel Imperial; Love's Greatest Mistake; Ritzy; Swim, Girl, Swim; Senorita; Silk Legs; Rolled Stockings. **1928** Just Married; The Fifty-Fifty Girl; The Fleet's In; Four Sons. **1929** The Saturday Night Kid; The Canary Murder Case; Smiling Irish Eyes; The Case of Lena Smith; This Is Heaven. **1930** Hell's Angels; Dangerous Nan McGrew; Maybe It's Love; Let's Go Native; Paramount on Parade; The Third Alarm. **1931** Mother's Millions; Sporting Chance; Millie; Man to Man; Lightning Flyer; The Good Bad Girl; Divorce Among Friends. **1932** Manhattan Tower.

HALL, JANE
Born: 1880, Winona, Minnesota. Died: Oct. 13, 1975, St. Paul, Minn. Stage and screen actress.

Appeared in: **1915** Madame Butterfly. **1916** Less than Dust.

HALL, JOHN (Michael Braughal)
Born: 1878. Died: Apr. 25, 1936, Los Angeles, Calif. Screen actor.

Appeared in: **1927** Men of Daring. **1928** The Wild West Show.

HALL, JUANITA
Born: 1902. Died: Feb. 28, 1968, Keyport, N.J. (diabetes). Stage and screen actress.

Appeared in: **1949** Miracle in Harlem. **1958** South Pacific. **1961** Flower Drum Song.

HALL, NELSON L.
Born: 1881. Died: July 28, 1944, Philadelphia, Pa. Screen actor and acrobat stuntman.

HALL, PORTER
Born: 1888, Cincinnati, Ohio. Died: Oct. 6, 1953, Los Angeles, Calif. (heart attack). Stage and screen actor. Won 1936 Screen Actors Guild Award for Best Supporting Actor in The Plainsman. Married to actress Geraldine Hall (dec. 1970).

Appeared in: **1934** The Thin Man (film debut); Murder in the Private Car. **1935** The Case of the Lucky Legs. **1936** The Story of Louis Pasteur; The Petrified Forest; The General Died at Dawn; Satan Met a Lady; Too Many Parents; Princess Comes Across; And Sudden Death; Snowed Under; The Plainsman. **1937** Let's Make a Million; Bulldog Drummond Escapes; Souls at Sea; Wells Fargo; Wild Money; Hotel Haywire; Make Way for Tomorrow; King of Gamblers; This Way, Please; True Confession. **1938** Scandal Street; Stolen Heaven; Dangerous to Know; Prison Farm; King of Alcatraz; The Arkansas Traveler; Men with Wings; Tom Sawyer, Detective; Bulldog Drummond's Peril. **1939** Grand Jury Secrets; They Shall Have Music; Mr. Smith Goes to Washington. **1940** Arizona; The Dark Command; Trail of the Vigilantes; His Girl Friday. **1941** The Parson of Panamint; Sullivan's Travels; Mr. and Mrs. North. **1942** The Remarkable Andrew; Tennessee Johnson; Butch Minds the Baby.

1943 A Stranger in Town; The Desperadoes; Woman of the Town. 1944 Standing Room Only; Double Indemnity; The Miracle of Morgan's Creek; Mark of the Whistler; Going My Way; The Great Moment. 1945 Murder, He Says; Kiss and Tell; Blood on the Sun; Weekend at the Waldorf; Bring on the Girls. 1947 Singapore; Miracle on 34th Street; Mad Wednesday. 1948 Unconquered; That Wonderful Urge. 1949 You Gotta Stay Happy; Beautiful Blonde From Bashful Bend; Chicken Every Sunday; Intruder in the Dust. 1951 The Big Carnival. 1952 The Half Breed; Carbine Williams; Holiday for Sinners. 1953 Pony Express; Vice Squad. 1954 Return to Treasure Island.

HALL, THURSTON

Born: 1883, Boston, Mass. Died: Feb. 20, 1958, Beverly Hills, Calif. (heart attack). Screen, stage, television, vaudeville actor and stage producer. Entered films in 1915.

Appeared in: 1917 Cleopatra. 1918 We Can't Have Everything; The Kaiser's Shadow; Brazen Beauty. 1921 Idle Hands; The Iron Trail; Mother Eternal. 1922 Fair Lady; Wildness of Youth. 1923 The Royal Oak. 1924 The Great Well (aka Neglected Women—US) 1930 Absent Minded (short). 1935 Hooray for Love; Metropolitan; Guard That Girl; Crime and Punishment; The Girl Friend; Too Tough to Live; Black Room; After the Dance; Love Me Forever; Public Menace; One Way Ticket; Case of the Missing Man; A Feather in Her Hat. 1936 Pride of the Marines; Roaming Lady; Two-Fisted Gentleman; Lady from Nowhere; The Lone Wolf Returns; Don't Gamble with Love; The Man Who Lived Twice; Killer at Large; Theodora Goes Wild; Devil's Squadron; The King Steps Out; Trapped by Television; Shakedown; Three Wise Guys. 1937 I Promise to Pay; Women of Glamour; Parole Racket; It Can't Last Forever; Counsel for Crime; Murder in Greenwich Village; We Have Our Moments; Oh, Doctor; Don't Tell the Wife. 1938 No Time to Marry; There's Always a Woman; Little Miss Roughneck; Campus Confessions; The Affairs of Annabel; Professor Beware; Women Are Like That; The Amazing Dr. Clitterhouse; Hard to Get; Fast Company; Going Places; Extortion; Squadron of Honor; Main Event. 1939 You Can't Cheat an Honest Man; First Love; Stagecoach; Ex-Champ; Our Neighbors, the Carters; Mutiny on the Blackhawk; Hawaiian Nights; Million Dollar Legs; The Star Maker; Each Dawn I Die; Jeepers Creepers; Money to Burn; The Day the Bookies Wept; Dancing Coed. 1940 The Great McGinty; Sued for Libel; The Blue Bird; Kiddie Cure (short); Blondie on a Budget; In Old Missouri; Alias the Deacon; Millionaires in Prison; The Lone Wolf Meets a Lady; City for Conquest; Friendly Neighbors; The Golden Fleecing. 1941 The Great Lie; Life with Henry; The Lone Wolf Takes a Chance; Repent at Leisure; Tuxedo Junction; The Invisible Woman; Flight from Destiny; The Lone Wolf Keeps a Date; Where Did You Get That Girl?; Washington Melodrama; She Knew All the Answers; Accent on Love; Design for Scandal; Midnight Angel; Remember That Day; In the Navy; Hold that Ghost. 1942 The Night Before the Divorce; Sleepytime Gal; Rings on her Fingers; The Great Man's Lady; Shepherd of the Ozarks; Call of the Canyon; Hello, Annapolis; Counter Espionage; The Hard Way; The Great Gildersleeve; Pacific Blackout. 1943 Sherlock Holmes in Washington; Hoosier Holiday; Footlight Glamour; Here Comes Elmer; He Hired the Boss; The Youngest Profession; This Land is Mine; I Dood It. 1944 Adventures of Mark Twain; Good Night, Sweetheart; Something for the Boys; Song of Nevada; Wilson; Cover Girl; The Great Moment; In Society; Ever since Venus. 1945 Brewster's Millions; Bring on the Girls; The Blonde from Brooklyn; Don Juan Quilligan; Col. Effingham's Raid; Saratoga Trunk; Lady on a Train; The Gay Senorita; Thrill of a Romance; Song of the Prairie; West of the Pecos. 1946 Dangerous Business; One More Tomorrow; She Wrote the Book; Three Little Girls in Blue; Two Sisters from Boston; Without Reservations. 1947 The Secret Life of Walter Mitty; Black Gold; The Unfinished Dance; It Had to Be You; The Farmer's Daughter; Welcome Stranger; Mourning Becomes Electra; Son of Rusty. 1948 King of Gamblers; Up in Central Park; Miraculous Journey. 1949 Stagecoach Kid; Manhattan Angel; Rim of the Canyon; Rusty Saves a Life; Square Dance Jubilee; Tell It to the Judge; Blondie's Secret. 1950 Bright Leaf; Bandit Queen; Belle of Old Mexico; Chain Gang; Federal Agent at Large; Girls' School; One Too Many. 1951 Belle Le Grand; Texas Carnival; Whirlwind. 1952 Carson City; One Big Affair; Night Stage to Galveston; Skirts Ahoy!; The Wac from Walla Walla. 1957 Affair in Reno.

HALL, WINTER

Born: June 21, 1878, New Zealand. Died: Feb. 10, 1947. Stage and screen actor. Entered films in 1916 at Lasky Studio.

Appeared in: 1919 The Turn in the Road; The Money Corporal; Why Smith Left Home. 1920 The Forbidden Woman; Behold my Wife. 1921 The Affairs of Anatol; The Breaking Point; Cheated Hearts; The Child Thou Gavest Me; Her Social Value; The Great Impersonation; The Little Clown; What Every Woman Knows; The Witching Hour. 1922 East Is West; On the High Seas; Burning Sands; Saturday Night; Skin Deep. 1923 Thundering Dawn; The Voice from the Minaret; Wasted Lives; Ashes of Vengeance; The Day of Faith; Little Church Around the Corner; Her Reputation. 1924 Husbands and Lovers; The Only Woman; Name the Man; The Right of the Strongest; The Turmoil; Secrets. 1925 Ben Hur; Free to Love; The Boomerang; Compromise; The Girl Who Wouldn't Work; The Pleasure Buyers; Graustark; Raffles—the Amateur Cracksman. 1928 Paradise; Balaclara (aka Jaws of Hell—US 1931); The Forger; The Wrecker (US 1929). 1929 The Lost Zeppelin; The Racketeer; The Love Parade; Kitty; After the Verdict (US 1930); Woman to Woman.

1930 Passion Flower; Road to Paradise. 1931 Girls Demand Excitement; Confessions of a Co-Ed. 1932 Tomorrow and Tomorrow. 1934 The Pursuit of Happiness. 1935 The Crusades. 1936 The Invisible Ray. 1937 Slave Ship. 1938 Four Men and a Prayer; If I Were King.

HALLARD, C. M.

Born: 1866, England. Died: Apr. 1942, Surrey, England. Stage and screen actor. Entered films in 1917.

Appeared in: 1918 The Man Who Won; The Elder Mrs. Blossom (aka Wanted—a Wife—US). 1919 Convict 99; The Bridal Chair; In Bondage (aka Faith); Edge O'Beyond; Gamblers All; Mrs. Thompson. 1920 The Husband Hunter; Her Story (US 1922); The Case of Lady Camber; Love in the Wilderness; In the Night. 1922 The Pauper Millionaire. 1927 Carry On! 1928 A Light Woman. 1930 Knowing Men; The "W" Plan (US 1931); Two Worlds; Almost a Honeymoon (US 1931); Compromising Daphne (aka Compromised—US 1931). 1931 The Woman Between (aka The Woman Decides—US 1932); Tell England (aka The Battle of Gallipoli—US); The Rasp. 1932 Strictly Business; The Chinese Puzzle. 1933 On Secret Service (aka Secret Agent—US 1935). 1934 The Third Clue; Rolling in Money. 1935 Royal Cavalcade (aka Regal Cavalcade—US); Moscow Nights (aka I Stand Condemned—US 1936); Night Mail. 1936 King of the Damned; Jack of All Trades (aka The Two of Us—US 1937). 1937 The Sky's the Limit; The Live Wire.

HALL-DAVIS, LILIAN

Born: 1901, Hampstead, England. Died: Oct. 25, 1933, London, England (suicide—gas). Screen actress.

Appeared in: 1918 The Admirable Crichton; The Better 'Ole (aka The Romance of Old Bill and Carry On—US). 1920 The Honeypot; Ernest Maltravers. 1921 Love Maggie. 1922 Stable Companions; The Wonderful Story; Brown Sugar; The Faithful Heart; The Game of Life; If Four Walls Told; Castles in the Air (aka Let's Pretend). 1923 The Right to Strike; Afterglow; Should a Doctor Tell?; The Hotel Mouse; I Pagliacci; Maisie's Marriage (aka Married Love and Life); The Knockout; A Royal Divorce. 1924 The Unwanted; The Eleventh Commandment; The Passionate Adventure. 1926 If Youth But Knew; Boadicea. 1927 Blighty (aka Apres la Guerre); The Ring; Roses of Picardy; Lost One (aka As We Lie). 1928 The White Sheik (aka King's Mate); The Farmer's Wife (US 1930); Tommy Atkins. 1930 Just for a Song. 1931 Her Reputation; Many Waters. 1933 Volga Volga.

HALLET, AGNES

Born: 1880. Died: Nov. 19, 1954, Hollywood, Calif. Screen actress.

HALLETT, ALBERT

Born: 1870. Died: Apr. 3, 1935, Hollywood, Calif. Screen and stage actor.

Appeared in: 1924 The Passing of Wolf McLean. 1925 The Gold Hunters. 1926 The Haunted Range; Midnight Faces.

HALLIDAY, GARDNER

Born: 1910. Died: Sept. 6, 1966, Hollywood, Calif. (suicide due to cancer). Stage and screen actor. Entered films in 1946.

HALLIDAY, JOHN

Born: Sept. 14, 1880, Brooklyn, N.Y. Died: Oct. 17, 1947, Honolulu, Hawaii (heart ailment). Stage and screen actor.

Appeared in: 1920 The Woman Gives. 1929 East Side Sadie. 1930 Father's Sons; Recaptured Love; Scarlet Pages. 1931 Smart Woman; Consolation Marriage; The Ruling Voice; Millie; Once a Sinner; Captain Applejack; Fifty Million Frenchmen; The Spy; Transatlantic. 1932 Men of Chance; Man Called Back; The Impatient Maiden; The Age of Consent; Weekends Only; Bird of Paradise. 1933 Perfect Understanding; Terror Abroad; Bed of Roses; The House on 56th Street; The Woman Accused. 1934 Return of the Terror; Housewife; A Woman's Man; Happiness Ahead; Registered Nurse; The Witching Hour; Desirable; Finishing School. 1935 Mystery Woman; The Dark Angel; The Melody Lingers On: Peter Ibbetson. 1936 Desire; Fatal Lady; Three Cheers for Love; Hollywood Boulevard. 1938 Arsene Lupin Returns; Blockade; That Certain Age. 1939 The Light That Failed; Hotel for Women; Intermezzo; A Love Story. 1940 The Philadelphia Story. 1941 Lydia; Escape to Glory.

HALLIGAN, WILLIAM

Born: Mar. 29, 1884. Died: Jan. 28, 1957, Woodland Hills, Calif. Screen, stage actor and screen writer.

Appeared in: 1919 The Wonder Man (film debut). 1929 Somewhere in Jersey (short). 1930 Follow the Leader; At Your Service (short); The Darling Brute (short). 1931 The Public Defender. 1932 Lady and Gent; The Crooner; Blessed Event; Babykins (short). 1940 You Can't Fool Your Wife; Hired Wife; 'Til We Meet Again; Boom Town; Third Finger, Left Hand. 1941 Gangs Incorporated. 1942 Life Begins at Eight-Thirty; Moontide; Lucky Jordan; The Powers Girl. 1943 He's My Guy; Rider of the Deadline; Coney Island; Dixie; The Leopard Man; Mission to Moscow. 1944 Show Business; Minstrel Man; Great Mike; The Hairy Ape. 1945 Within These Walls; The Spider; Dick Tracy. 1946 If I'm Lucky; 'Til The Clouds Roll By. 1947 The Shocking Miss Pilgrim.

HALLOR, EDITH

Born: 1896, Washington, D.C. Died: May 21, 1971, Newport Beach, Calif. Stage and screen actress. Married to actor and film director John Francis Dillon (dec. 1934) and sister of actor Ray Hallor (dec. 1944) and actress Ethel Hallor.

Appeared in: **1915** Dr. Rameau. **1917** Seven Deadly Sins. **1920** The Blue Pearl; Children of Destiny. **1921** The Inside of the Cup; Just Outside the Door. **1922** Human Hearts. **1937** Maid of Salem. **1944** Wilson. **1945** A Tree Grows in Brooklyn.

HALLOR, RAY

Born: Jan. 14, 1900, Washington, D.C. Died: Apr. 16, 1944, near Palm Springs, Calif. (auto crash). Stage and screen actor. Brother of actresses Edith (dec. 1971) and Ethel Hallor.

Appeared in: **1917** An Amateur Orphan; Kidnapped. **1921** Dream Street. **1923** The Courtship of Miles Standish; The Dangerous Maid. **1924** The Circus Cowboy; Inez from Hollywood. **1925** The Last Edition; Learning to Love; Sally; The Storm Breaker. **1926** The High Flyer; It Must Be Love; Red Dice. **1927** Driven from Home; Quarantined Rivals; Tongues of Scandal. **1928** Man Crazy; The Haunted Ship; The Avenging Shadow; The Trail of '98; Black Butterflies; The Black Pearl; Green Grass Widows; Manhattan Knights; Nameless Men; Tropical Nights. **1929** Thundergod; Circumstantial Evidence; Fast Life; In Old California; Noisy Neighbors. **1930** The Truth about Youth.

HALLS, ETHEL MAY

Born: 1882. Died: Sept. 16, 1967, Hollywood, Calif. Screen, stage and television actress. Entered films with Biograph.

Appeared in: **1939** Our Leading Citizen. **1940** Heroes of the Saddle; Thou Shalt Not Kill. **1951** Katie Did It.

HALTINER, FRED

Born: 1936, Switzerland. Died: Dec. 7, 1973, Zurich, Switzerland (suicide). Screen, stage and television actor.

Appeared in: **1969** Hannibal Brooks.

HALTON, CHARLES

Born: 1876. Died: Apr. 16, 1959, Los Angeles, Calif. (hepatitis). Stage and screen actor.

Appeared in: **1931** The Strange Case (short). **1936** Sing Me a Love Song; Dodsworth; Golddiggers of 1937; Stolen Holiday; Come and Get It; More Than a Secretary. **1937** The Black Legion; Penrod and Sam; Ready, Willing and Able; Talent Scout; Pick a Star; The Prisoner of Zenda; Woman Chases Man; Dead End; Blossoms on Broadway; Partners in Crime. **1938** Trouble at Midnight; Penitentiary; Bluebeard's Eighth Wife; Penrod and His Twin Brother; Penrod's Double Trouble; Stolen Heaven; The Saint in New York; Room Service; I'll Give a Million; I Am the Law; A Man to Remember. **1939** News Is Made at Night; Swanee River; Nancy Drew—Reporter; They Made Her a Spy; Reno; Indianapolis Speedway; Charlie Chan at Treasure Island; I'm from Missouri; Juarez; Ex-Champ; They Asked For It; Young Mr. Lincoln; Dodge City; Jesse James; Federal Manhunt. **1940** They Drive by Night; The Shop Across the Corner; The Story of Dr. Ehrlich's Magic Bullet; Gangs of Chicago; Young People; Stranger on the Third Floor; The Doctor Takes a Wife; Tugboat Annie Sails Again; Calling All Husbands; Behind the News; Dr. Cyclops; 20 Mule Team; Lillian Russell; The Westerner. **1941** Mr. District Attorney; Mr. and Mrs. Smith; Meet the Chump; A Very Young Lady; Million Dollar Baby; I Was a Prisoner on Devil's Island; Dance Hall; The Smiling Ghost; Three Sons O' Guns; Look Who's Laughing; Unholy Partners; H.M. Pulham, Esq.; Tobacco Road; The Body Disappears. **1942** To Be or Not to Be; Juke Box Jenny; Whispering Ghosts; Priorities on Parade; Across the Pacific; You Can't Escape Forever; Henry Aldrich, Editor; That Other Woman; The Spoilers; In Old California; My Sister Eileen; Captains of the Clouds. **1943** My Kingdom for a Cook; Jitterbugs; Lady Bodyguard; The Private Life of Dr. Paul Joseph Goebbels. **1944** Rationing; Address Unknown; Enemy of Women; The Town Went Wild; Shadows in the Night; Wilson; Up in Arms. **1945** One Exciting Night; She Went to the Races; A Tree Grows in Brooklyn; The Fighting Guardsman; Rhapsody in Blue; Midnight Manhunt; Mama Loves Papa. **1946** Singin' in the Corn; Because of Him; Three Little Girls in Blue; The Best Years of Our Lives. **1947** The Ghost Goes Wild. **1948** Three Godfathers. **1949** The Sickle or the Cross; The Daring Caballero; Hideout. **1950** Stella; Traveling Saleswoman; When Willie Comes Marching Home; Sabotage. **1951** Gasoline Alley. **1952** Carrie. **1953** The Moonlighter; A Slight Case of Larceny. **1956** Friendly Persuasion.

HAM, HARRY (aka HARRY HAMM)

Born: 1891, Napanee, Ont., Canada. Died: July 27, 1943. Screen actor.

Appeared in: **1916** A Seminary Scandal. **1917** Tramp, Tramp, Tramp; A Gay Deceiver; His Wedded Wife; Kidding Sister; He Fell on the Beach; Down by the Sea; Crazy by Proxy; The Honeymooners; Skirts. **1921** His Pajama Girl; Blood Money; The Broken Road; The Four Feathers. **1922** A Spanish Jade.

HAMER, FRED B.

Born: 1873. Died: Dec. 30, 1953, Los Angeles, Calif. Screen, stage actor and film director. Appeared in silents approx. 1910.

HAMER, GERALD

Born: 1886, South Wales. Died: July 6, 1972, Hollywood, Calif. (heart attack). Stage and screen actor.

Appeared in: **1936** Swing Time. **1937** Angel. **1938** Blond Cheat. **1939** Bulldog Drummond's Bride. **1942** Pretty Dolly (short). **1943** Sherlock Holmes Faces Death. **1944** The Scarlet Claw; Enter Arsene Lupin. **1945** Pursuit to Algiers. **1946** Terror by Night. **1948** The Sign of the Ram.

HAMID, SWEENEY

Born: c. 1898, Morocco. Died: Mar. 25, 1968, Baltimore, Md. (lung cancer). Screen, vaudeville actor, circus performer and acrobat.

HAMILTON, GEORGE W. "SPIKE"

Born: 1901. Died: Mar. 31, 1957, New York, N.Y. Orchestra leader, songwriter and screen actor.

HAMILTON, GORDON GEORGE

Born: Coytesville, N.J. Died: Jan. 16, 1939, Fort Lee, N.J. (heart attack). Stage and screen actor.

Appeared in: **1914** The Perils of Pauline (serial).

HAMILTON, HALE

Born: Feb. 28, 1880, Ft. Madison, Iowa. Died: May 19, 1942, Los Angeles, Calif. (cerebral hemorrhage). Stage and screen actor. Married to actress Grace LaRue (dec. 1956).

Appeared in: **1915** Her Painted Hero. **1918** The Winning of Beatrice. **1919** That's Good. **1923** His Children's Children. **1925** The Manicure Girl. **1926** The Great Gatsby; The Greater Glory; Summer Bachelors; Tin Gods. **1929** Listen, Lady. **1927** Girl in the Rain; The Telephone Girl. **1930** Common Clay; Good Intentions. **1931** Never the Twain Shall Meet; A Tailor-Made Man; Beau Ideal; Dance, Fools, Dance; Drums of Jeopardy; Rebound; The Great Lover; Strangers May Kiss; New Adventures of Get-Rich-Quick Wallingford; Cuban Love Song; The Champ; Paid; Susan Lennox, Her Rise and Fall; Murder at Midnight; Oh! Oh! Cleopatra (short). **1932** A Fool's Advice; Love Affair; Life Begins; Two against the World; Those We Love; Call Her Savage; Most Dangerous Game; Three on a Match; Manhattan Tower; Grand Hotel; The Woman in Room 13; A Successful Calamity. **1933** Employees' Entrance; Billion Dollar Scandal; Reform Girl; Parole Girl; Black Beauty; Strange People; One Man's Journey; Sitting Pretty. **1934** City Park; Big-Hearted Herbert; When Strangers Meet; The Marines Are Coming; Curtain at Eight; The Quitter; Twin Husbands; Heartburn (short); Doctor Monica; The Girl from Missouri. **1935** I Live My Life; After Office Hours; Grand Old Girl; The Nitwits; Hold 'Em Yale; The Woman in Red; Let 'Em Have It; Calm Yourself; Three Kids and a Queen. **1938** The Adventures of Marco Polo; Meet the Mayor.

HAMILTON, JACK "SHORTY" (John H. Hamilton)

Born: Nov. 9, 1879 or 1888 (?), Chicago, Ill. Died: Mar. 7, 1925, Hollywood, Calif. (auto accident). Screen actor.

Appeared in: **1915** Shorty in the Clutches of the Cannibals; Shorty's Troubled Sleep; Shorty Turns Actor. **1916** Bucking Society; Gypsy Joe; She Loved a Sailor; His Busted Trust. **1917** Adventures of Shorty Hamilton. **1918** Denny from Ireland.

HAMILTON, JOHN

Born: 1887. Died: Oct. 15, 1958, Hollywood, Calif. (heart condition). Screen, stage, vaudeville and television actor.

Appeared in: **1926** Rainbow Riley. **1930** White Cargo; Dangerous Nan McGrew; Heads Up. **1936** Two in a Crowd; The Legion of Terror; A Man Betrayed. **1937** Two Wise Maids; Seventh Heaven; This Is My Affair; Night Club Scandal; Bad Guy; Criminals of the Air. **1938** I Stand Accused; Mr. Moto's Gamble; Over the Wall; Dr. Rhythm; Mr. Wong, Detective. **1939** Angels Wash Their Faces; Rose of Washington Square. **1940** Johnny Apollo; Pound Foolish (short); The Great Plane Robbery. **1942** Yankee Doodle Dandy; Always in My Heart; To the Shores of Tripoli; In This Our Life; The Big Shot. **1944** The Girl Who Dared; Sheriff of Las Vegas; Meet Miss Bobby Socks; I'm from Arkansas; Crazy Knights. **1945** The Great Flamarion; Army Wives; Circumstantial Evidence. **1946** Wife Wanted; Johnny Comes Flying Home; The Brute Man; Home on the Range; Dangerous Business. **1947** Violence; Scareheads; The Beginning or the End. **1948** Song of My Heart. **1949** Law of the Golden West; The Wyoming Bandit; Sheriff of Wichita; Alias the Champ; Bandit King of Texas; Canadian Pacific; The Judge; Pioneer Marshal. **1950** Her Wonderful Lie; Bells of Coronado; Davy Crockett, Indian Scout; The Missourians. **1951** Million Dollar Pursuit. **1952** The Pace That Thrills. **1953** Donovan's Brain; Iron Mountain Trail; Marshal of Cedar Rock. **1954** On the Waterfront; Sitting Bull. **1957** Chicago Confidential. **1958** Outcasts of the City.

HAMILTON, JOHN F.

Born: 1894. Died: July 11, 1967, Paramus, N.J. Screen, stage, vaudeville and television actor.

Appeared in: **1927** The Masked Menace (serial). **1939** Allegheny Uprising. **1940** The Saint's Double Trouble; Gold Rush Maisie. **1949** The Undercover Man; Prison Warden. **1950** Body Hold; Military Academy.

HAMILTON, JOSEPH H. "JOE"

Born: 1898. Died: Feb. 20, 1965. Screen actor.

Appeared in: **1957** The Abductors. **1958** Jet Attack; Teenage Caveman; Cole Younger, Gunfighter. **1960** Cage of Evil; The Plunderers. **1961** The Hoodlum Priest. **1964** One Man's Way. **1965** Cat Ballou; Git.

HAMILTON, KAREN SUE

Born: 1946. Died: Sept. 3, 1969, Hollywood, Calif. (suicide). Screen and television actress.

HAMILTON, LAUREL L.

Died: Dec. 15, 1955, Hollywood, Calif. Screen, stage and vaudeville actress. Appeared in Sennett comedies.

HAMILTON, LLOYD

Born: Aug. 19, 1891, Oakland, Calif. Died: Jan. 19, 1935, Hollywood, Calif. (following surgery for stomach disorder). Screen, stage actor, screenwriter and film director. Was "Ham" in "Ham and Bud" comedy series (1914-1917) with Bud Duncan (dec. 1960). Appeared in "Sunshine" comedies (1918) and in "Mermaid" comedies (1921-1922). Divorced from actresses Ethel Floyd and Irene Dalton (dec. 1934). Entered films with Lubin Co. in 1914.

Appeared in: **1914** Ham at the Garbageman's Ball. **1915** Ham in the Harem; Ham and the Jitney Bus; Ham at the Fair; Ham's Easy Eats; Ham the Detective; Ham in the Nut Factory; Ham's Harrowing Duel; Ham Among the Redskins; Ham at the Beach. **1916** Ham Takes a Chance; Ham the Diver; Ham Agrees with Sherman; Ham and the Hermit's Daughter; Ham and Preparedness; Ham's Waterloo; Ham's Busy Day; Ham the Explorer; Ham and the Masked Marvel; Ham's Whirlwind Finish; Ham's Strategy; Ham in the Drugstore; Ham the Fortune Teller; Patented by Ham. **1923** Hollywood. **1924** His Darker Self; A Self-Made Failure. **1925** The following shorts: Hooked; Half a Hero; King Cotton; Waiting; The Movies; Framed. **1929** The Show of Shows; Tanned Legs; Black Waters. **1931** Are You There? **1932-33** Universal shorts. **1934** An Old Gypsy Custom (short).

HAMILTON, MAHLON

Born: 1883. Died: June 20, 1960, Woodland Hills, Calif. (cancer). Stage and screen actor.

Appeared in: **1916** Molly Make-Believe; The Eternal Question; The Black Butterfly; Extravagance. **1917** Exile; Bridges Burned; The Red Woman; The Hidden Hand (serial); The Waiting Soul; More Truth than Poetry; The Undying Flame; The Silence Sellers; The Soul of a Magdalen. **1918** The Danger Mark; The Death Dance. **1919** Adele; Daddy Long Legs; Her Kingdom of Dreams. **1920** The Third Generation; Earthbound; In Old Kentucky; The Deadlier Sex; Half a Chance. **1921** The Truant Husband; Under the Lash; I Am Guilty; Greater than Love; Ladies Must Live; That Girl Montana. **1922** The Green Temptation; A Fool There Was; The Lane that had no Turning; Paid Back; Peg O'My Heart; Under Oath. **1923** The Christian; The Heart Raider; Little Old New York; Her Children's Children. The Midnight Guest. **1924** The Recoil; Playthings of Desire. **1925** The Wheel; Enemies of Youth; The Other Woman's Story; The Winding Star; Idaho (serial). **1926** Morganson's Finish. **1927** Her Indiscretions; What Price Love. **1928** Life's Crossroads; White Flame. **1929** Honky Tonk; The Single Standard. **1930** Rich People; Code of Honor. **1931** Sporting Chance. **1932** Strangers of the Evening; Western Limited; Back Street. **1935** High School Girl; Mississippi. **1936** Boss Rider of Gun Creek.

HAMLER, JOHN E.

Born: 1891. Died: Dec. 2, 1969, N.Y. Screen actor and song and dance man.

HAMLIN, WILLIAM H.

Born: 1885. Died: Sept. 27, 1951, Los Angeles, Calif. Screen actor and stage director. Appeared in silents with Vitagraph.

HAMMERSTEIN, ELAINE

Born: 1897, Philadelphia, Pa. Died: Aug. 13, 1948, near Tijuana, Mexico (auto crash). Stage and screen actress. Daughter of producer Arthur Hammerstein.

Appeared in: **1917** The Argyle Case; The Mad Lover. **1920** Greater Than Fame. **1921** The Daughter Pays; The Miracle of Manhattan; Pleasure Seekers; Poor, Dear Margaret Kirby; The Girl from Nowhere; Remorseless Love; Way of a Maid; Handcuffs and Kisses. **1922** Evidence; Reckless Youth; Why Announce Your Marriage?; Under Oath; One Week of Love. **1923** Souls for Sale; Broadway Gold; Rupert of Hentzau. **1924** Daring Love; The Drums of Jeopardy; The Foolish Virgin; The Midnight Express; One Glorious Night. **1925** The Unwritten Law; After Business Hours; Every Man's Wife; Paint and Powder;

Parisian Nights; S.O.S. Perils of the Sea. **1926** The Checkered Flag; Ladies of Leisure.

HAMMERSTEIN, OSCAR, II

Born: July 12, 1895, New York, N.Y. Died: Aug. 23, 1960, Doylestown, Pa. (cancer). Composer, screen writer and screen actor. Married to actress Dorothy Blanchard.

Appeared in: **1953** Main Street to Broadway.

HAMMOND, DOROTHY

Died: Nov. 23, 1950, London, England. Stage and screen actress. Married to actor Sir Guy Standing (dec. 1937).

Appeared in: **1935** Jubilee Window. **1936** Nothing Like Publicity.

HAMMOND, VIRGINIA

Born: 1894, Virginia. Died: Apr. 6, 1972, Washington, D.C. Stage and screen actress. Entered films with Essanay in 1916.

Appeared in: **1916** The Discard. **1919** The Hand Invisible; Miss Crusoe; The World to Live In. **1920** A Manhattan Knight. **1930** Anybody's Woman; A Lady Surrenders. **1931** Newly Rich. **1932** The Crash; The Rich Are Always With Us; No One Man; Cabin in the Cotton; Chandu the Magician; Rockabye. **1933** Eagle and the Hawk; Torch Singer; Chance at Heaven. **1934** Search for Beauty; Come on Marines; Doctor Monica; Desirable; Great Expectations. **1935** Rumba; The Virginia Judge; Lady Tubbs. **1936** Romeo and Juliet.

HAMPDEN, WALTER (Walter Hempden Daugherty)

Born: June 30, 1879, Brooklyn, N.Y. Died: June 11, 1955, Hollywood, Calif. (stroke). Screen, stage and television actor.

Appeared in: **1915** The Dragon's Claw. **1940** Northwest Mounted Police; The Hunchback of Notre Dame; All This, and Heaven Too. **1941** They Died with Their Boots On. **1942** Reap the Wild Wind. **1944** The Adventures of Mark Twain. **1950** All about Eve. **1951** The First Legion. **1952** Five Fingers. **1953** Treasure of the Golden Condor; Sombrero. **1954** Sabrina. **1955** The Prodigal; Strange Lady in Town; The Silver Chalice. **1956** The Vagabond King.

HAMPER, GENEVIEVE

Born: 1889. Died: Feb. 13, 1971, N.Y. Stage and screen actress. Married to actor John Alexander and widow of stage actor Robert Mantell.

Appeared in: **1916** A Wife's Sacrifice. **1923** Under the Red Robe.

HAMPTON, FAITH

Born: 1909. Died: Apr. 1, 1949, Hollywood, Calif. (suffocation due to fire). Screen actress. Entered films during silents.

HAMPTON, GRAYCE (aka GRACE HAMPTON)

Born: 1876, England. Died: Dec. 20, 1963, Woodland Hills, Calif. Stage and screen actress.

Appeared in: **1916** The Pursuing Vengeance. **1931** The Bat Whispers; Broadminded; Ex-Bad Boy. **1932** Unexpected Father; Almost Married. **1935** Gigolette. **1936** Piccadilly Jim. **1941** Shanghai Gesture. **1946** Johnny Comes Flying Home. **1947** The Exile. **1948** Sitting Pretty; The Snake Pit. **1950** Love that Brute. **1951** The Mating Season. **1954** Forever Female.

HAMPTON, LOUISE

Born: 1881, Stockport, England. Died: Feb. 11, 1954, London, England (bronchial trouble). Stage and screen actress. Married to actor Edward Thane (dec. 1954).

Appeared in: **1932** Nine Till Six (film debut). **1939** Goodbye, Mr. Chips; Hell's Cargo (aka Dangerous Cargo—US 1940); The Middle Watch. **1940** The House of the Arrow (aka Castle of Crimes—US 1945); Busman's Honeymoon (aka Haunted Honeymoon—US). **1941** The Saint Meets the Tiger. **1946** Bedelia (US 1947). **1952** The Story of Robin Hood and His Merrie Men. **1953** The Oracle (aka The Horse's Mouth—US); Background (aka Edge of Divorce).

HAMPTON, MYRA

Born: 1901. Died: July 19, 1945, New York, N.Y. Screen, stage actress, author and stage casting director. Divorced from actor Raymond Hackett (dec. 1958).

Appeared in: **1929** The Trial of Mary Dugan. **1931** Once a Sinner.

HAMRICK, BURWELL F.

Born: 1906. Died: Sept. 21, 1970, Hollywood, Calif. Screen actor and film set designer.

Appeared in: **1916** The Pursuing Vengeance. **1917** The Devil Stone; John Ermine of the Yellowstone. **1918** A Law Unto Herself. **1922** The Face Between; Through A Glass Window. **1923** Rouged Lips.

HANCOCK, TONY (Anthony Hancock)

Born: May 12, 1924, Birmingham, England. Died: June 25, 1968, Sydney, Australia (overdose of sleeping tablets). Screen actor, author and screenwriter.

Appeared in: Orders Are Orders. **1961** The Rebel. **1962** The Punch and Judy

Man (US 1963). **1965** Those Magnificent Men in Their Flying Machines, or, How I Flew from London to Paris in 25 Hours and 11 Minutes. **1966** The Wrong Box.

HANDLEY, TOMMY

Born: 1902, England. Died: Jan. 9, 1949, London, England (cerebral hemorrhage). Screen, radio and vaudeville actor.

Appeared in: **1930** Elstree Calling. **1938** Two Men in a Box; **1943** It's That Man Again. **1944** Time Flies. **1946** Tom Tom Topia (short).

HANDWORTH, HARRY

Died: Mar. 22, 1916, Brooklyn, N.Y. Screen actor, film producer and director.

Appeared in: **1915** Gone to the Dogs.

HANEY, CAROL

Born: 1934. Died: May 5, 1964, Saddle River, N.J. (pneumonia—diabetes). Screen, television actress and dancer/choreographer. Divorced from actor Larry Blyden (dec. 1975).

Appeared in: **1953** Kiss Me, Kate. **1956** Invitation to the Dance. **1957** Pajama Game (stage and film versions).

HANFORD, CHARLES B.

Born: May 5, 1859, Sutter Creek, Calif. Died: Oct. 16, 1926, Washington. Stage and screen actor.

HANLEY, JIMMY

Born: Oct. 22, 1918, Norwich, Norfolk, England. Died: Jan. 13, 1970, England. Screen, circus, radio, television actor and writer. Divorced from actress Dinah Sheridan

Appeared in: **1934** Red Wagon (film debut—US 1935); Those Were the Days; Little Friend. **1935** Royal Cavalcade (aka Regal Cavalcade—US); Forever England (aka Brown on Resolution and Born For Glory—US 1935); Boys Will be Boys; The Tunnel (aka Transatlantic Tunnel—US). **1937** Landslide; Cotton Queen; Night Ride. **1938** Housemaster (US 1939); Coming of Age. **1939** Beyond Our Horizon; There Ain't No Justice. **1940** Gaslight (aka Angel Street—US). **1942** Salute John Citizen. **1943** The Gentle Sex. **1944** The Way Ahead; Kiss the Bride Goodbye. **1945** For You Alone; Henry V (US 1946); 29 Acacia Avenue (aka The Facts of Love—US 1949); Murder in Reverse (US 1946). **1946** The Captive Heart (US 1947). **1947** Holiday Camp (US 1948); Master of Bankdam (US 1949); It Always Rains on Sunday (US 1949). **1948** Here Come the Huggetts; It's Hard to be Good (US 1950). **1949** The Huggetts Abroad; Don't Ever Leave Me; Boys in Brown. **1950** The Blue Lamp; Room to Let. **1951** The Galloping Major. **1954** Radio Car Murder; The Black Rider. **1955** The Deep Blue Sea. **1956** Satellite in the Sky. **1968** The Lost Continent.

HANLEY, MICHAEL E.

Born: 1858. Died: June 18, 1942, Fort Wayne, Ind. (suicide—gun). Screen actor, film director and film producer.

HANLEY, WILLIAM B., JR.

Born: 1900. Died: Oct. 2, 1959, Hollywood, Calif. (heart attack). Stage and screen actor. Married to actress Madge Kennedy.

HANLON, BERT

Born: Aug. 19, 1895, New York, N.Y. Died: Jan 1, 1972, New York, N.Y. Screen, stage, vaudeville actor, film director, author, songwriter and screenwriter. Married to actress Doris Canfield.

Appeared in: **1931** Surrender. **1932** The Trial of Vivienne Ware; Society Girl; Me and My Gal; The Golden West. **1935** Wings in the Dark. **1936** Straight from the Shoulder. **1937** Park Avenue Logger; Double or Nothing. **1938** A Slight Case of Murder; The Amazing Dr. Clitterhouse; Boy Meets Girl. **1939** Sweepstakes Winner. **1943** Coney Island; Lady of Burlesque. **1948** Decision of Christopher Blake. **1949** Fighting Fools.

HANLON, TOM (Thomas Anthony Hanlon)

Born: Nov. 7, 1907, Kansas. Died: Sept. 29, 1970, Northridge, Calif. Screen actor and radio announcer.

Appeared in: **1934** Gift O'Gab; Night Alarm. **1935** The Big Broadcast of 1936. **1938** Kentucky Moonshine. **1941** Harmon of Michigan. **1942** Home in Wyomin'. **1945** It's a Pleasure. **1949** Father Was a Fullback. **1950** I'll Get By. **1951** The Guy Who Came Back. **1952** Hold That Line; The Pride of St. Louis. **1953** Jalopy; White Lightning.

HANNEFORD, EDWIN POODLES

Born: 1892, Barnsby, Yorkshire, England. Died: Dec. 9, 1967, Kattskill Bay, N.Y. Screen, circus and television actor, and trick horseback rider. Member of circus family known as "The Hannefords".

Appeared in: **1928** The Circus Kid. **1935** Our Little Girl; educational short. **1951** The Golden Horde; When I Grow Up. **1952** Springfield Rifle. **1962** Jumbo.

HANNEN, NICHOLAS (Nicholas James Hannen)

Born: May 1, 1881, London, England. Died: July 1972, London, England. Screen, stage actor and film director.

Appeared in: **1931** The Man They Couldn't Arrest (US 1933). **1933** F.P.1. **1934** Murder at the Inn. **1935** The Love Affair of the Dictator (aka The Dictator and The Loves of a Dictator—US). **1936** Hail and Farewell; Who Killed Doc Savage? **1938** Marigold; Secrets of F.P.1 (reissue of 1933 film). **1940** Spy for a Day; Fear and Peter Brown. **1941** The Prime Minister. **1945** Henry V (US 1946). **1948** The Winslow Boy (US 1950). **1951** Quo Vadis; Hell is Sold Out. **1953** Three Steps in the Dark. **1955** The Adventures of Quentin Durward; Richard III (US 1956). **1957** Seawife. **1958** Dunkirk; Family Doctor (aka Rx Murder—US and Prescription for Murder). **1961** Francis of Assisi. **1962** Term of Trial (US 1963).

HANOFER, FRANK

Born: 1897, Hungary. Died: Dec. 16, 1955, Newhall, Calif. Screen actor and stuntman.

HANSEN, HANS

Born: 1886, Germany. Died: June 18, 1962, New York, N.Y. Stage and screen actor.

Appeared in: **1945** The House on 92nd Street.

HANSEN, JUANITA

Born: 1897, Des Moines, Iowa. Died: Sept. 26, 1961, Hollywood, Calif. (heart attack). Stage and screen actress. Was a Mack Sennett bathing beauty.

Appeared in: **1915** The Failure; Betty in Search of a Thrill; The Martyrs of the Alamo. **1916** His Pride and Shame; Secret of the Submarine (serial). **1917** Glory; A Royal Rogue; Dangers of a Bride; Whose Baby?; A Clever Dummy. **1918** The Brass Bullet (serial); The Risky Road; Broadway Love; The Rough Lover; Fast Company; **1919** A Midnight Romance. **1920** The Lost City (serial); The Phantom Foe (serial). **1921** The Yellow Arm (serial). **1922** The Broadway Madonna. **1923** Girl From the West; The Jungle Princess.

HANSEN, WILLIAM

Born: 1911. Died: June 23, 1975, Woodland Hills, Calif. Screen, stage and television actor.

Appeared in: **1949** Pinky. **1952** A Member of the Wedding. **1960** The Bramble Bush. **1961** The Young Doctors. **1962** Bird Man of Alcatraz. **1964** Fail Safe. **1969** The Arrangement. **1971** Willard. **1974** The Terminal Man.

HANSON, EINER (aka EINER HANSEN)

Born: June 15, 1899, Stockholm, Sweden. Died: June 3, 1927, Santa Monica, Calif. (auto accident). Screen actor.

Appeared in: **1926** Her Big Night; Into Her Kingdom. **1927** The Lady in Ermine; The Masked Woman; Barbed Wire; Children of Divorce; Fashions for Women; Woman on Trial.

HANSON, GLADYS

Born: 1884, Atlanta, Ga. Died: Feb. 24, 1973, Atlanta, Ga. Stage and screen actress.

Appeared in: **1914** The Straight Road. **1915** The Climbers; The Primrose Path. **1916** The Havoc.

HANSON, LARS

Born: 1887, Sweden. Died: Apr. 8, 1965, Stockholm, Sweden. Stage and screen actor who appeared in U.S. and Swedish films.

Appeared in: **1913** Ingeborg Holm. **1916** Dolken. **1919** Erotikon. **1924** The Atonement of Gosta Berling. **1926** The Scarlet Letter. **1927** The Flesh and the Devil; Captain Salvation; Buttons. **1928** The Divine Woman; The Wind; The Legend of Gosta Berling. **1929** The Informer; In Dalarna and Jerusalem; Homecoming. **1936** Paa Solsidan. **1964** One Minute to Hell (aka Gates of Hell). **1967** 491.

HARBAUGH, CARL

Born: 1886. Died: Feb. 26, 1960, Hollywood, Calif. Screen actor, screenwriter and film director.

Appeared in: **1912** What the Milk Did. **1915** The Regeneration; Carmen. **1923** Jazzmania; Lost and Found on a South Sea Island; The Silent Command. **1927** College. **1933** The Devil's Brother. **1938** If I Were King. **1955** The Tall Men. **1956** The Revolt of Mamie Stover.

HARBEN, HUBERT

Born: July 12, 1878, London, England. Died: Aug. 24, 1941, London, England. Stage and screen actor.

Appeared in: **1915** The Great Adventure; **1916** Milestones. **1921** Mr. Pim Passes By. **1926** Every Mother's Son. **1931** Tell England (aka The Battle of Gallipoli—US); Uneasy Virtue; The Shadow Between. **1932** Fires of Fate (US 1933). **1933** Timbuctoo. **1934** The Secret of the Loch; Lady in Danger; Lilies of the Field. **1935** Fighting Stock; The City of Beautiful Nonsense. **1936** Whom the Gods Love (aka Mozart—US 1940); Dishonour Bright. **1937** For Valour; Sunset in Vienna (aka Suicide Legion—US 1940); Victoria the Great.

HARBOROUGH, WILLIAM
Born: 1899. Died: Oct. 1924, Yuma, Ariz. (drowned during filming of a Western movie). Screen actor and stuntman.

HARCOURT, PEGGIE
Died: Aug. 2, 1916, Hewletts, N.Y. (auto accident). Screen actress.

HARDIE, RUSSELL
Born: 1904, Buffalo, N.Y. Died: July 21, 1973, Clarence, N.Y. Screen, stage and television actor.

Appeared in: **1930** The Costello Case; The No-Account (short). **1933** Broadway to Hollywood; Stage Mother; Her Sweetheart—Christopher Bean. **1934** As the Earth Turns; Men in White; Operator 13; Hell in the Heavens; The Band Plays On; Murder in the Private Car; Sequoia; Pursued. **1935** West Point of the Air; In Old Kentucky; Speed Devils. **1936** The Harvester; Meet Nero Wolfe; Down to the Sea; Killer at Large; Camille. **1951** The Frogmen; The Whistle at Eaton Falls. **1958** Cop Hater. **1964** Fail Safe. **1966** The Group.

HARDING, GILBERT
Born: June 5, 1907, Hereford, England. Died: Nov. 16, 1960, London, England. Screen and television actor.

Appeared in: **1955** Simon and Laura (US 1956); An Alligator Named Daisy (US 1957); As Long as They're Happy (US 1957). **1959** Expresso Bongo (US 1960).

HARDING, LYN (David Llewellyn Harding)
Born: Oct. 12, 1867, Newport, Wales. Died: Dec. 26, 1952, London, England. Stage and screen actor.

Appeared in: **1920** A Bachelor Husband; The Barton Mystery. **1922** When Knighthood Was in Flower; Tense Moments With Great Authors series including: Les Miserables. **1924** Yolanda. **1927** Further Adventures of the Flag Lieutenant; Land of Hope and Glory. **1930** Sleeping Partners. **1931** The Speckled Band. **1932** The Barton Mystery (and 1920 version). **1933** The Constant Nymph. **1934** The Man Who Changed His Name; Wild Boy; The Lash. **1935** The Triumph of Sherlock Holmes; Escape Me Never. **1936** The Invader (aka An Old Spanish Custom—US); The Man Who Changed His Mind (aka The Man Who Lived Again—US); Spy of Napoleon (US 1939). **1937** Fire Over England; Underneath the Arches; Knight Without Armour; Silver Blaze (aka Murder at the Baskervilles—US 1941); The Mutiny of the Elsinore (US 1939); Les Perles de la Couronne (Pearls of the Crown); Please Teacher. **1939** The Missing People (US 1940); Goodbye Mr. Chips. **1941** The Prime Minister.

HARDTMUTH, PAUL
Born: 1889, Germany. Died: Feb. 5, 1962, London, England (fall from apartment building). Screen and television actor.

Appeared in: **1949** The Lost People; The Third Man. **1950** Highly Dangerous (US 1951). **1951** The Wonder Kid. **1953** Desperate Moment; Street of Shadows (aka Shadow Man—US). **1954** The Diamond (aka The Diamond Wizard—US). **1955** Timeslip (aka The Atomic Man—US); All for Mary. **1956** The Gamma People; Assignment Readhead (aka Million Dollar Manhunt—US 1962). **1957** The Curse of Frankenstein. **1961** Doctor Blood's Coffin (aka Face of Evil); Guns of Navarone.

HARDWICKE, SIR CEDRIC (Cecil Webster Hardwicke)
Born: Feb. 19, 1893, Stourbridge, England. Died: Aug. 6, 1964, New York, N.Y. (lung ailment). Screen, stage, television actor, film director and producer. Father of actor Edward Hardwicke. Divorced from actresses Helena Pickard and Mary Scott.

Appeared in: **1913** Riches and Rogues. **1926** Nelson. **1931** Dreyfus (aka The Dreyfus Case—US). **1932** Rome Express. **1933** Orders Is Orders (US 1934); The Ghoul. **1934** The Lady Is Willing; Nell Gwyn; Jew Suess (aka Power—US); The King of Paris; Bella Donna (US 1935). **1935** Les Miserables; Becky Sharp; Peg of Old Drury (US 1936). **1936** Things to Come; Tudor Rose (aka Nine Days a Queen—US); Laburnum Grove (US 1941); Calling the Truth. **1937** The Green Light; King Solomon's Mines. **1939** On Borrowed Time; Stanley and Livingstone; The Hunchback of Notre Dame. **1940** The Invisible Man Returns; Tom Brown's School Days; The Howards of Virginia; Victory. **1941** Suspicion; Sundown. **1942** Valley of the Sun; The Ghost of Frankenstein; Invisible Agent; Commandos Strike at Dawn. **1943** The Moon Is Down; Forever and a Day; The Cross of Lorraine. **1944** The Lodger; Wilson; The Keys of the Kingdom; Wing and a Prayer. **1945** The Picture of Dorian Gray and a Prayer. **1946** Beware of Pity (US 1947); Sentimental Journey. **1947** Song of My Heart (aka Tragic Symphony); The Imperfect Lady; Ivy; Lured; Nicholas Nickleby; Tycoon; A Woman's Vengeance. **1948** The Winslow Boy (US 1950); I Remember Mama; Rope. **1949** Now Barabbas Was a Robber; A Connecticut Yankee in King Arthur's Court. **1950** The White Tower. **1951** Mr. Imperium; The Desert Fox. **1952** The Green Glove; Caribbean. **1953** Salome; Botany Bay; The War of the Worlds (narr.). **1954** Bait (prologue). **1955** Richard III (US 1956); Diane; Helen of Troy. **1956** The Vagabond King; The Power and the Prize;

The Ten Commandments; Around the World in 80 Days; Gaby. **1957** The Story of Mankind; Baby Face Nelson. **1962** Five Weeks in a Balloon. **1964** The Pumpkin Eater; The Magic Fountain.

HARDY, OLIVER (Oliver Norvell Hardy)
Born: Jan. 18, 1892, Atlanta, Ga. Died: Aug. 7, 1957, North Hollywood, Calif. (paralytic stroke). Screen, stage, minstrel actor and film director. Was partner in comedy team of "Laurel and Hardy" with Stan Laurel (dec. 1965). See Stan Laurel for films they appeared in together.

Appeared in the following films without Laurel: **1913** Outwitting Dad (film debut). **1914** The Rise of the Johnsons; Back to the Farm. **1914-1915** "Pokes and Jabbs" series; "Harry Meyers and Rosemary Theby" series. **1915** The Twin Sister; Who Stole the Doggies?; A Lucky Strike; Matilda's Legacy; Babe's School Days; Ethel's Romeos; The Paperhanger's Helper; "Kate Price" series including: Spaghetti a la Mode; Charley's Aunt; Artists and Models; The Tramps and Mother's Child. **1916** What's Sauce for the Goose; The Brave Ones; Edison Bugg's Invention; The Water Cure; A Terrible Tragedy; Never Again; Thirty Days; Hungry Hearts; It Happened in Pikesville; Their Honeymoon; The Candy Trail; The Heroes; Life Savers; Stranded; An Aerial Joyride; Love and Duty; Royal Blood; Better Halves; Spaghetti; A Day at School; The Precious Parcel; Dreamy Knights; A Maid to Order; Pipe Dreams; "Billy West" series including: Back Stage; The Hero; The Millionaire; Dough Nuts; The Scholar; "Pokes and Jabbs" series including: The Try Out; Ups and Downs; This Way Out; Chickens; Frenzied Finance; Busted Hearts. **1916-1918** "Plump and Runt" series. **1917** The Slave; The Prospector; He Winked and Won; "Jimmy Aubrey" series. **1918** Hello Trouble; Lucky Dog; "Billy West" comedies; "King Bee Studios" series including: The Villain; The Artist; King Solomon; The Chief Cook. **1919-1921** "Jimmy Aubrey" comedy series. **1921-25** "Larry Semon" series including: The Fly Cop; The Sawmill; Scars and Stripes; The Wizard of Oz; The Girl in the Limousine and Kid Speed. **1922** Fortune's Mask; Little Wildcat. **1923** The Three Ages; Be Your Age; One Stolen Night. **1924** The Girl in the Limousine. **1925** The Wizard of Oz. **1926** Stop, Look and Listen; The Gentle Cyclone. **1927** No Man's Law. **1939** Zenobia; Elephants Never Forget. **1949** The Fighting Kentuckian; Riding High.

HARDY, SAM
Born: 1883, New Haven, Conn. Died: Oct. 16, 1935, Los Angeles, Calif. (intestinal problems). Screen, stage actor, and screenwriter. Entered films in 1917.

Appeared in: **1917** The Savage. **1918** A Woman's Experience. **1921** Get-Rich-Quick Wallingford. **1923** Little Old New York; Mighty Lak a Rose. **1925** The Half-Way Girl; When Love Grows Cold. **1926** Bluebeard's Seven Wives; The Great Deception; The Prince of Tempters; The Savage. **1927** High Hat; The Perfect Sap; Orchids and Ermine; Broadway Nights; The Life of Riley; A Texas Steer. **1928** Burning up Broadway; Turn Back the Hours; The Big Noise; Diamond Handcuffs; The Butter and Egg Man; The Night Bird; Outcast; Give and Take. **1929** The Rainbow Man; On with the Show; Big News; Acquitted; Mexicali Rose; A Man's Man; Fast Company. **1930** Burning Up; True to the Navy; Reno; Song of the West; The Floradora Girl; Borrowed Wives. **1931** The Millionaire; June Moon; Annabelle's Affairs; The Magnificent Lie; The Miracle Woman; Peach O'Reno. **1932** The Dark Horse; Make Me a Star; The Phantom of Crestwood. **1933** Face in the Sky; King Kong; Goldie Gets Along; Three-Cornered Moon; The Big Brain; One Sunday Afternoon; Ann Vickers. **1934** Curtain at Eight; Little Miss Marker; I Give My Love; The Gay Bride; Transatlantic Merry-Go-Round; Night Alarm; Along Came Sally. **1935** Hooray for Love; Break of Hearts; Powdersmoke Range.

HARDY, SAM (Samuel Stewart Hayes)
Born: 1905, Cookesville, Ill. Died: July 28, 1958, San Diego, Calif. (heart attack). Screen actor and radio announcer. Do not confuse with actor Sam Hardy (dec. 1935).

Appeared in: **1938** Rebecca of Sunnybrook Farm. **1953** The Hitch-Hiker.

HARE, F. LUMSDEN
Born: Oct. 17, 1874, Cashel, Ireland. Died: Aug. 28, 1964, Hollywood, Calif. Screen, stage actor and stage director. Entered films in 1916.

Appeared in: **1919** The Avalanche. **1921** The Education of Elizabeth. **1922** Sherlock Holmes. **1923** On the Banks of the Wabash. **1924** Second Youth. **1925** One Way Street. **1929** Fugitives; Masquerade; The Black Watch; Girls Gone Wild; Salute; The Sky Hawk. **1930** Crazy That Way; So This Is London; Scotland Yard. **1931** Under Suspicion; Always Goodbye; Svengali; Charlie Chan Carries On; The Road to Singapore; Arrowsmith. **1932** The Silent Witness; The Crusader. **1933** International House; College Humor. **1934** The World Moves On; Outcast Lady; His Double Life; Man of Two Worlds; The Little Minister; The House of Rothschild; Black Moon. **1935** Lady Tubbs; The Great Impersonation; Professional Soldier; Clive of India; Folies Bergere; Lives of a Bengal Lancer; The Crusades; Cardinal Richelieu; She; Freckles; The Three Musketeers; The Bishop Misbehaves. **1936** The Charge of the Light Brigade; Under Two Flags; Lloyds of London; The Princess Comes Across; The Last of the Mohicans. **1937** The Last of Mrs. Cheyney; The Life of Emile Zola; Life Begins with Love. **1939** The Giant of Norway (short). **1940** Northwest Passage; Rebecca; A Dispatch from Reuters. **1941** Shadows on the Stairs; Dr. Jekyll and Mr. Hyde; More Trifles of Importance (short); The Blonde from

Singapore; Suspicion; Passage from Hong Kong; Hudson's Bay. **1942** London Blackout Murders; The Gorilla Man. **1943** Mission to Moscow; Holy Matrimony; Jack London; Forever and a Day. **1944** Passport to Destiny; The Canterville Ghost; The Lodger. **1945** The Keys of the Kingdom; Love Letters; Valley of Decision. **1946** Three Strangers. **1947** Private Affairs of Bel Ami; The Swordsman; The Exile. **1948** Mr. Peabody and the Mermaid; Hills of Home. **1949** That Forsythe Woman; Fighting O'Flynn; Challenge to Lassie. **1950** Fortunes of Captain Blood. **1951** David and Bathsheba; The Lady and the Bandit; The Desert Fox. **1952** And Now Tomorrow; Diplomatic Courier; My Cousin Rachel. **1953** Julius Caesar; Young Bess. **1957** Johnny Tremain. **1959** Count Your Blessings; The Oregon Trail; The Four Skulls of Jonathan Drake.

HARE, SIR JOHN (John Fairs)

Born: 1844, Giggleswick, Yorkshire, England. Died: Dec. 28, 1921, London, England. Stage and screen actor.

Appeared in: **1916** A Pair of Spectacles; The Vicar of Wakefield (US 1917).

HARKER, GORDON

Born: Aug. 7, 1885, London, England. Died: Mar. 2, 1967, London, England. Screen, stage and radio actor.

Appeared in: **1927** The Ring (film debut). **1928** The Farmer's Wife (US 1930); Champagne; The Wrecker (US 1929). **1929** The Crooked Billet; Taxi For Two; The Return of the Rat. **1930** The W Plan (US 1931); The Squeaker; Escape; Elstree Calling; The Cockney Spirit in War series including: All Riot on the Western Front. **1931** Third Time Lucky; The Sport of Kings; The Stronger Sex; The Ringer (US 1932); The Calendar (aka Bachelor's Folly—US 1932); The Professional Guest; The Man They Could Not Arrest (US 1933); Shadows. **1932** Condemned to Death; The Frightened Lady (aka Criminal at Large—US 1933); White Face; Love on Wheels; Rome Express. **1933** The Lucky Number; Britannia of Billingsgate; This Is the Life (US 1935); Friday the Thirteenth (US 1934). **1934** My Old Dutch; Road House; Dirty Work. **1935** The Phantom Light; The Lad; Admirals All; Squibs; Boys Will Be Boys; Hyde Park Corner. **1936** The Amateur Gentleman; Wolf's Clothing; Two's Company; Millions; The Story of Papworth (short). **1937** Beauty and the Barge; The Frog (US 1939). **1938** Blondes for Danger; No Parking; Lightning Conductor; The Return of the Frog. **1939** Inspector Hornleigh; Inspector Hornleigh on Holiday. **1940** Saloon Bar (US 1944); Chanel Incident (short). **1941** Inspector Hornleigh Goes to It (aka Mail Train—US); Once a Crook. **1943** Warn That Man. **1945** 29 Acacia Avenue (aka The Facts of Love—US 1949). **1948** Things Happen at Night. **1950** Her Favorite Husband (aka The Taming of Dorothy—US). **1951** The Second Mate. **1952** Derby Day (aka Four Against Fate—US 1955). **1954** Bang! You're Dead (aka Game of Danger—US 1955). **1955** Out of the Clouds (US 1957). **1956** A Touch of the Sun. **1957** Small Hotel. **1959** Left, Right and Center (US 1961).

HARKINS, DIXIE

Born: 1906. Died: Sept. 1, 1963, Jacksonville, Fla. Screen actress.

Appeared in: **1925** Sally, Irene and Mary. **1926** The Temptress. **1927** Resurrection.

HARLAN, KENNETH

Born: July 26, 1895, Boston, Mass. Died: Mar. 6, 1967, Sacramento, Calif. (aneurysm). Screen, stage and vaudeville actor.

Appeared in: **1915** A Black Sheep. **1917** Betsy's Burglar; The Flame of the Yukon; The Lash of Power; Cheerful Givers. **1918** Midnight Madness; The Marriage Life; The Model's Confession. **1919** The Hoodlum. **1920** The Penalty; Dangerous Business. **1921** The Barricade; Dawn of the East; Finders Keepers; Mama's Affair; Lessons in Love; Nobody; Woman's Place. **1922** The Toll of the Sea; I Am the Law; Polly of the Follies; The Married Flapper; Received Payment; The Primitive Lover; Thorns and Orange Blossoms. **1923** The Virginian; The Beautiful and Damned; The Broken Wing; The World's a Stage; April Showers; East Side, West Side; The Girl Who Came Back; Little Church Around the Corner; A Man's Man; Temporary Marriage. **1924** Butterfly; For Another Woman; White Man; Soiled; Two Shall Be Born; The Virgin; The Man without a Heart; On the Stroke of Three; Poisoned Paradise. **1925** Bobbed Hair; The Marriage Whirl; Learning to Love; The Crowded Hour; Drusilla with a Million; The Golden Strain; Ranger of the Big Pines; Re-Creation of Brian Kent. **1926** The Sap; King of the Turf; The Ice Flood; The Fighting Edge; Twinkletoes. **1927** Easy Pickings; Cheating Cheaters; Streets of Shanghai. **1928** Stage Kisses; Willful Youth; United States Smith; Midnight Rose; Code of the Air; Man, Woman and Wife. **1930** Under Montana Skies; Paradise Island. **1931** Air Police; Danger Island (serial); Finger Prints (serial); Women Men Marry. **1932** Widow in Scarlet. **1935** Cappy Ricks Returns; Wanderer of the Wasteland. **1936** Man Hunt; The Walking Dead; Song of the Saddle; The Case of the Velvet Claws; Public Enemy's Wife; China Clipper; Movie Maniacs (short); San Francisco; They Met in a Taxi; Trail Dust; Flying Hostess. **1937** Hideaway Girl; Marked Woman; Wine, Women and Horses; The Shadow Strikes; Renfrew of the Royal Mounted; Paradise Isle; The Mysterious Pilot (serial); Penrod and Sam; Gunsmoke Ranch; Something to Shout About. **1938** Duke of West Point; The Saleslady; Under Western Stars; Blondes at Work; The Little Adventuress; Accidents Will Happen; Pride of the West; Law of the Texan; Sunset Trail; The Headleys at Home; Held for Ransom. **1939** Range

War; On Trial; Port of Hate. **1940** Slightly Honorable; Santa Fe Marshal; Murder in the Air; A Little Bit of Heaven; Prairie Schooners. **1941** Pride of the Bowery; Sky Raiders (serial); Paper Bullets; Dangerous Lady; Secret Evidence; Desperate Cargo; Wide Open Town. **1942** Black Dragon; Fighting Bill Fargo; Klondike Fury; Foreign Agent; The Corpse Vanishes; The Phantom Killer; Deep in the Heart of Texas. **1943** You Can't Beat the Law; Hitler—Dead or Alive; Wild Horse Stampede; The Law Rides Again; Melody Parade; The Underdog.

HARLAN, MACEY

Born: New York, N.Y. Died: June 17, 1923, Saranac Lake, N.Y. Stage and screen actor.

Appeared in: **1920** The Woman and the Puppet. **1921** The Conquest of Canaan; The Plaything of Broadway; Shams of Society; You Find It Everywhere. **1922** Always the Woman; Beyond the Rainbow; The Face in the Fog; Fair Lady; When Knighthood Was in Flower; Without Fear. **1923** Broadway Broke; The Tents of Allah; Bella Donna.

HARLAN, OTIS

Born: Dec. 29, 1865, Zanesville, Ohio. Died: Jan. 20, 1940, Martinsville, Ind. (stroke). Screen, stage and vaudeville actor.

Appeared in: **1921** Diamonds Adrift; The Foolish Age; Keeping up with Lizzie. **1922** The Girl in the Taxi; The Eternal Flame; Gay and Devilish; Is Matrimony a Failure?; The Ladder Jinx; Right That Failed; Two Kinds of Women; The Understudy; Up and at 'Em; Without Compromise; The World's a Stage. **1923** The Barefoot Boy; The Brass Bottle; Main Street; The Near Lady; Pioneer Trails; The Spider and the Rose; Truxton King; The Victor. **1924** Abraham Lincoln; Captain Blood; The Clean Heart; The Code of the Wilderness; George Washington, Jr.; The Lullaby; Mademoiselle Midnight; One Law for the Woman; Welcome Stranger; The White Sin; Oh, Doctor! **1925** The Redeeming Sin; Lightnin'; What Happened to Jones?; The Dixie Handicap; Dollar Down; Fine Clothes; How Baxter Butted In; The Limited Mail; 9⅗ Seconds; The Perfect Clown; Thunder Mountain; Where Was I? **1926** The Cheerful Fraud; The Midnight Message; The Prince of Pilsen; Three Bad Men; The Unknown Cavalier; Winning the Futurity; The Whole Town's Talking. **1927** Don't Tell the Wife; Down the Stretch; Galloping Fury; The Silent Rider; Silk Stockings; The Student Prince. **1928** Shepherd of the Hills; The Speed Classic; Grip of the Yukon; Good Morning Judge. **1929** Silks and Saddles; Show Boat; Clear the Decks; Broadway; Girl Overboard; His Lucky Day; Barnum Was Right; The Mississippi Gambler. **1930** Take the Heir; Parade of the West; Captain of the Guard; The King of Jazz; Loose Ankles; Dames Ahoy; Embarrassing Moments; Mountain Justice; Parade of the West. **1931** Man to Man; The Grand Parade; Ex-Rooster; Air Eagles. **1932** Racing Youth; The Big Shot; No Living Witness; Ride Him, Cowboy; That's My Boy; Rider of Death Valley; Pardners; The Hawk. **1933** Women Won't Tell; Telegraph Trail; Laughing at Life; The Sin of Nora Morgan; Marriage on Approval. **1934** I Can't Escape; King Kelly of the U.S.A.; The Old-Fashioned Way; Let's Talk It Over; Married in Haste. **1935** Life Returns; Chinatown Squad; Western Frontier; Hitchhike Lady; Diamond Jim; A Midsummer Night's Dream; The Hoosier Schoolmaster. **1936** Can This Be Dixie? **1937** Western Gold; Snow White and the Seven Dwarfs (voice of "Happy"). **1938** Mr. Boggs Steps Out; Outlaws of Sonora; The Texans.

HARLAN, RUSSELL B.

Born: Sept. 16, 1903. Died: Feb. 28, 1974, Newport Beach, Calif. Screen actor, stuntman and cinematographer. Entered films as a stuntman.

Appeared in: **1937** Hopalong Rides Again; North of the Rio Grande; Rustler's Valley; Texas Trail; Partners of the Plains. **1938** Cassidy of Bar 20. **1940** Stagecoach War. **1943** The Kansan. **1945** Walk in the Sun. **1948** Red River. **1952** The Big Sky. **1954** Riot in Cell Block 11. **1955** The Blackboard Jungle. **1957** This Could Be the Night; Witness for the Prosecution. **1958** Run Silent, Run Deep; King Creole. **1962** The Spiral Road; Hatari!; To Kill a Mockingbird. **1963** A Gathering of Eagles. **1964** Quick Before It Melts; Dear Heart; Man's Favorite Sport? **1965** The Great Race. **1966** Hawaii; Tobruk. **1967** Thoroughly Modern Millie. **1970** Darling Lili.

HARLAN, VEIT

Born: 1899, Berlin, Germany. Died: Apr. 13, 1964, Capri, Italy (cancer). Screen, stage actor, screenwriter, film director and writer. Married to Hilde Korber and later married to actress Kristina Soderbaum.

Appeared in: **1929** Meistersingers. **1930** Hungarian Nights.

HARLOW, JEAN (Harlean Carpenter)

Born: Mar. 3, 1911, Kansas City, Mo. Died: June 7, 1937, Los Angeles, Calif. (uremic poisoning). Screen actress. Divorced from producer/actor Paul Bern (dec. 1932), Charles McGrew and cinematographer Hal Rosson.

Appeared in: **1928** Moran of the Marines; a Hal Roach short. **1929** The Saturday Night Kid; The Love Parade; Close Harmony; Double Whoopee (short); Bacon Grabbers (short); Liberty (short); The Unkissed Man (short); Weak but Willing (short). **1939** Hell's Angels; New York Nights. **1931** The Secret Six; The Iron Man; The Public Enemy; Goldie; Platinum Blonde; City Lights. **1932** Three Wise Girls; The Beast of the City; Red Headed Woman; City

Sentinel; Red Dust. **1933** Hold Your Man; Dinner at Eight; Bombshell. **1934** The Girl from Missouri; Reckless. **1935** China Seas; Riffraff. **1936** Wife vs. Secretary; Libeled Lady; The Man in Possession; Suzy. **1937** Personal Property; Saratoga. **1964** Big Parade of Comedy (documentary). **1968** The Further Perils of Laurel and Hardy (documentary); The Queen (documentary). **1974** That's Entertainment (film clips).

HARMER, LILLIAN

Born: 1886. Died: May 15, 1946, Hollywood, Calif. Screen and stage actress.

Appeared in: **1931** She-Wolf; Huckleberry Finn; Smart Woman. **1932** New Morals for Old; Guilty as Hell; No Man of Her Own. **1933** Alice in Wonderland; Jennie Gerhardt; A Shriek in the Night. **1934** Forsaking All Others; Lady by Choice. **1935** Three Kids and a Queen; Romance in Manhattan; Public Hero No. 1; Riffraff. **1936** Don't Get Personal; Little Miss Nobody; Dancing Feet; Fugitive in the Sky; The Great O'Malley; Rainbow on the River.

HARMON, PAT

Born: 1888. Died: Nov. 26, 1958, Riverside, Calif. Screen actor and double for actor Wallace Beery.

Appeared in: **1922** The Firebrand; The Kentucky Derby. **1923** Ruth of the Range (serial); The Eternal Struggle; The Midnight Guest. **1924** American Manners; The Back Trail; The Battling Fool; Behind the Curtain; The Martyr Sex; The Midnight Express; Ridgeway of Montana; The Sawdust Trail; Surging Seas. **1925** Barriers Burned Away; A Fight to the Finish; Fighting Youth; The Freshman; The Lure of the Wild; S.O.S. Perils of the Sea. **1926** The Barrier; Breed of the Sea; College Days; The Cowboy Cop; The Dixie Flyer; The Fighting Edge; Josselyn's Wife; The Phantom Bullet; Sin Cargo; The Unknown Cavalier; Winning the Futurity. **1927** The Bachelor's Baby; The Haunted Ship; Hazardous Valley; Lightning; Snowbound; The Warning. **1928** The Broken Mask; Court-Martial; Waterfront. **1929** Small Talk (short); Dark Streets; Sal of Singapore; Homesick; The Sideshow; Sunset Pass; Berth Marks (short). **1930** Fast Work (short); Hell's Angels. **1931** The Gang Buster. **1933** Fallen Arches (short). **1934** Another Wild Idea (short). **1944** Teen Age. **1953** The Freshman.

HAROLDE, RALF (Ralf H. Wigger)

Born: 1899, Pa. Died: Nov. 1, 1974, Santa Monica, Calif. Stage and screen actor.

Appeared in: **1922** Sunshine Harbor. **1927** Babe Comes Home. **1930** Dixiana; Officer O'Brien; Check and Double Check; Framed; Young Desire; Hook, Line and Sinker. **1931** Night Nurse; Smart Money; Alexander Hamilton; The Tip Off; Safe in Hell; The Secret Witness; Terror by Night; Are These Our Children? **1932** The Expert; Winner Take All; Hollywood Speaks. **1933** Her Resale Value; The Billion Dollar Scandal; Picture Snatcher; The Deluge; Cheating Blondes; Night Flight; I'm No Angel. **1934** Fifteen Wives; Jimmy the Gent; He Was Her Man; The Witching Hour; She Loves Me Not; Once to Every Bachelor; Baby, Take a Bow. **1935** Great God Gold; Stolen Harmony; Silk Hat Kid; My Marriage; A Tale of Two Cities; The Perfect Clue; Million Dollar Baby; If You Could Only Cook; This Is the Life; Forced Landing. **1936** Our Relations; Song and Dance Man; Human Cargo; 15 Maiden Lane; The Accusing Finger; Little Red School House. **1937** A Man Betrayed; Her Husband Lies; One Mile from Heaven; Conquest. **1939** The Rookie Cop. **1941** Horror Island; Ridin' on a Rainbow; Rags to Riches; The Sea Wolf; No Greater Sin; Lucky Devils; Bad Man of Deadwood; The Stork Pays Off; I Killed That Man. **1942** Baby Face Morgan; Broadway; Sin Town; Gang Busters (serial). **1943** Farewell, My Lovely (aka Murder My Sweet); Secret Service in Darkest Africa (serial). **1945** The Phantom Speaks. **1947** Jewels of Brandenburg. **1948** Assigned to Danger; Behind Locked Doors. **1949** Alaska Patrol. **1950** Killer Shark. **1965** The Greatest Story Ever Told.

HAROUT, YEGHISHE

Born: Armenia. Died: June 7, 1974, Hollywood, Calif. Screen, stage, television actor and restaurateur. Father of actress Magda Harout.

Appeared in: **1954** The Egyptian.

HARPER, JAMES. *See* JAMES "JIM" TIROFF

HARRIGAN, WILLIAM

Born: Mar. 27, 1894, New York, N.Y. Died: Feb. 1, 1966, New York, N.Y. (following surgery). Stage and screen actor. Son of playwright Edward Harrigan (dec.). Divorced from actress Louise Groody and later married to Grace Culbert.

Appeared in: **1927** Cabaret. **1929** Nix on Dames. **1930** On the Level; Born Reckless. **1933** Pick Up; The Girl in 419; Disgraced; The Invisible Man. **1935** G-Men; Stranded; Silk Hat Kid; His Family Tree; The Melody Lingers On; Whipsaw. **1936** Frankie and Johnnie. **1937** Over the Goal; Federal Bullets; Exiled to Shanghai. **1938** Hawaii Calls. **1939** Back Door to Heaven. **1947** Desert Fury. **1948** Citizen Saint. **1951** Flying Leathernecks. **1952** Steel Town. **1953** Francis Covers the Big Town. **1954** Roogie's Bump. **1957** Street of Sinners.

HARRINGTON, BUCK

Died: Feb. 2, 1971. Screen actor.

Appeared in: **1944** Shake Hands with Murder.

HARRIS, ASA "ACE"

Born: 1910. Died: June 11, 1964, Chicago, Ill. Black singer and screen actor. Was member of the original "Inkspots" singing group.

Appeared in: **1941** The Great American Broadcast. **1942** Pardon My Sarong.

HARRIS, AVERELL

Died: Sept. 25, 1966, New York, N.Y. Stage and screen actor.

Appeared in: **1929** Her New Chauffeur (short). **1931** Secrets of a Secretary; His Woman.

HARRIS, ELSIE

Born: 1892. Died: May 17, 1953, Hollywood, Calif. Screen actress.

HARRIS, JOSEPH

Born: 1870. Died: June 11, 1953, Hollywood, Calif. Screen and stage actor.

Appeared in: **1915** Oh, Daddy. **1921** Freeze-Out; Red Courage; Sure Fire; The Wallop. **1922** The Bearcat; For Big Stakes; Pardon My Nerve; The Loaded Door. **1923** Canyon of the Fools; Crashin' Thru.

HARRIS, KAY

Born: 1920, Elkhorn, Wisc. Died: Oct. 23, 1971, Calif. Screen, stage and radio actress.

Appeared in: **1941** Tillie the Toiler. **1942** Sabotage Squad; Parachute Nurse; The Spirit of Stanford; Smith of Minnesota. **1943** Fighting Buckaroo; Robin Hood of the Range; Lucky Legs.

HARRIS, LEONORE

Born: 1879, New York, N.Y. Died: Sept. 27, 1953, New York, N.Y. Screen actress.

Appeared in: **1916** Betty of Graystone. **1917** Today. **1922** The Faithless Sex.

HARRIS, MILDRED

Born: Nov. 29, 1901, Cheyenne, Wyo. Died: July 20, 1944, Los Angeles, Calif. (pneumonia after surgery). Screen, stage, burlesque and vaudeville actress. Entered films at the age of nine. Divorced from actor Charles Chaplin.

Appeared in: **1917** Price of a Good Time. **1918** For Husbands Only; Borrowed Clothes. **1921** Old Dad; Habit; A Prince There Was; Fool's Paradise. **1922** The First Woman. **1923** The Fog; The Daring Years. **1924** One Law for the Women; Unmarried Wives; By Divine Right; The Desert Hawk; In Fast Company; The Shadow of the East; Soiled; Stepping Lively; Traffic in Hearts. **1925** Flaming Love; My Neighbor's Wife; Beyond the Border; The Dressmaker from Paris; Easy Money; Super Speed; The Unknown Lover; The Fighting Cub; Frivolous Sal; Iron Man; A Man of Iron; Private Affairs. **1926** The Cruise of the Jasper B; Dangerous Traffic; The Isle of Retribution; The Mystery Club; The Self Starter; The Wolf Hunters. **1927** The Adventurous Soul; Burning Gold; The Girl from Rio; Husband Hunters; One Hour of Love; Out of the Past; Rose of the Bowery; She's My Baby; The Show Girl; The Swell-Head; Wandering Girls; Wolves of the Air. **1928** Lingerie; Melody of Love; Heart of a Follies Girl; Power of the Press; Hearts of Men; Last Lap; The Speed Classic. **1929** Side Street; Sea Fury. **1930** No, No, Nanette; Ranch House Blues; The Melody Man. **1931** Night Nurse. **1935** Lady Tubbs; Never Too Late. **1936** Movie Maniacs (short). **1944** Here Come the Waves.

HARRIS, MITCHELL

Born: 1883, New York. Died: Nov. 16, 1948, New York, N.Y. Stage and screen actor. Son of stage actor William Harris (dec.)

Appeared in: **1930** The Sea Wolf; Fair Warning. **1931** A Connecticut Yankee; Peach O'Reno; Freighters of Destiny. **1932** Ghost Valley; Scandal for Sale. **1933** Hypnotized; Victims of Persecution. **1936** A Connecticut Yankee in King Arthur's Court.

HARRIS, STACY B.

Born: 1918, Big Timber, Que., Canada. Died: Mar. 13, 1973, Los Angeles, Calif. (heart attack). Screen, stage, radio, television actor, journalist and cartoonist.

Appeared in: **1951** Appointment with Danger; His Kind of Woman. **1952** The Redhead from Wyoming. **1953** The Great Sioux Uprising. **1954** Dragnet. **1955** New Orleans Uncensored. **1956** The Brass Legend; Comanche; The Mountain. **1958** The Hunters; New Orleans After Dark; Good Day for a Hanging. **1959** Cast a Long Shadow. **1962** Four for the Morgue. **1965** Brainstorm; The Great Sioux Massacre. **1966** An American Dream. **1967** A Covenant with Death; First to Fight. **1968** Countdown (aka Moon Shot). **1970** Bloody Mama; The Swappers.

HARRIS, WADSWORTH
Born: 1865, Calais, Maine. Died: Dec. 1942, Los Angeles, Calif. Stage and screen actor.

Appeared in: **1920** The Dragon's Net (serial). **1921** Rich Girl, Poor Girl. **1922** The Call of Home.

HARRISON, CAREY (Capt. Carey Harrison Reppeteau)
Born: 1890. Died: Mar. 25, 1957, Los Angeles, Calif. Screen actor.

Appeared in: **1929** Married in Hollywood. **1936** Pepper. **1938** The Buccaneer. **1942** Call of the Canyon. **1945** House of Dracula.

HARRISON, JUNE
Born: 1926. Died: Mar. 10, 1974, Hollywood, Calif. (cirrhosis of liver). Screen and radio actress. Entered films in 1937. Do not confuse with silent film actress June Harrison.

Appeared in: **1938** Girl of the Golden West. **1941** Sun Valley Serenade. **1947** Land of the Lawless. **1948** Bringing Up Father; Citizen Saint; Jiggs and Maggie in Society; Jiggs and Maggie in Court. **1949** Jiggs and Maggie in Jackpot Jitters. **1950** Jiggs and Maggie Out West.

HARRON, BOBBY (Robert Harron)
Died: Sept. 6, 1920, New York, N.Y. (gunshot—accident). Screen actor. Brother of actress Tessie Harron (dec. 1918) and actor John Harron (dec. 1939).

Appeared in: **1907** Dr. Skinum. **1908** At the Crossroads of Life; Bobby's Kodak. **1909** The Lonely Villa; The Drive for Life; Sweet Revenge. **1910** Ramona; In the Season of Buds. **1911** The Battle; Fighting Blood; Enoch Arden, Part I; The White Rose of the Wilds; The Last Drop of Water; Bobby, the Coward; The Unveiling; Billy's Strategem. **1912** Man's Lust for Gold; Fate's Interception; A Pueblo Legend; The Sands of Dee; An Unseen Enemy; Home Folks; Friends; So Near, Yet So Far; The Musketeers of Pig Alley; Brutality; The New York Hat; The Massacre; My Hero; Oil and Water; The Burglar's Dilemma; A Cry for Help; Fate; The Tender Hearted Boy; Man's Genesis. **1913** Love in an Apartment Hotel; Broken Ways; The Sheriff's Baby; A Misunderstood Boy; The Little Tease; His Mother's Son; The Yaqui Cur; A Timely Interception; Death's Marathon; Her Mother's Oath; The Reformers; The Battle of Elderberry Gulch; In Prehistoric Days. **1914** Judith of Bethulia; The Battle of the Sexes; The Great Leap; The Avenging Conscience; The Rebellion of Kitty Belle; The Outcast; The Victim; A Lesson in Mechanics; Her Shattered Idol; Paid with Interest; Home Sweet Home. **1915** Birth of a Nation; The Escape. **1916** Hoodoo Ann; The Missing Links; The Little Liar; A Child of the Paris Streets; The Wild Girl of the Sierras; The Wharf Rat; Intolerance; The Marriage of Molly O. **1917** An Old Fashioned Young Man; Sunshine Alley; The Bad Boy. **1918** Hearts of the World; The Great Love. **1919** The Greatest Thing in Life; A Romance of Happy Valley; The Mother and the Law; The Girl Who Stayed at Home; True Heart Susie. **1920** Everybody's Sweetheart; The Greatest Question. **1921** Coincidence; Darling Mine; The Rebel of Kitty Beale.

HARRON, JOHN
Born: Mar. 31, 1903, N.Y. Died: Nov. 24, 1939, Seattle, Wash. Screen actor. Married to actress Betty Egan. Brother of actor Bobby Harron (dec. 1920) and actress Tessie Harron (dec. 1918).

Appeared in: **1918** Hearts of the World. **1921** Through the Back Door (film debut); The Grim Comedian; The Fox. **1922** The Five Dollar Baby; Love in the Dark; Penrod; The Ragged Heiress. **1923** Dulcy; The Gold Diggers; The Supreme Test; The Westbound Limited. **1924** Behind the Curtain; The Fire Patrol; The Painted Flapper; What Shall I Do? **1925** Learning to Love; Old Shoes; Below the Line; My Wife and I; Satan in Sables; The Wife Who Wasn't Wanted; The Woman Hater. **1926** Bride of the Storm; The Boy Friend; The False Alarm; The Gilded Highway; Hell-Bent for Heaven; The Little Irish Girl; The Night Cry; Rose of the Tenements. **1927** Once and Forever; Silk Stockings; Closed Gates; Love Makes 'Em Wild; Naughty; Night Life. **1928** Finders Keepers; Green Grass Widows; Their Hour. **1929** Man in Hobbles; Street Girl. **1930** The Czar of Broadway; Big Boy. **1931** Laugh and Get Rich; The Last of the Tongs. **1932** White Zombie; Beauty Parlor. **1933** Sister to Judas; Midnight Warning. **1934** Stolen Sweets; City Park; Murder in the Private Car. **1935** Symphony of Living. **1937** That Girl from Paris; Without Warning; The Missing Witness; Talent Scout. **1938** Torchy Gets Her Man; Penrod's Double Trouble; A Slight Case of Murder; Torchy Blane in Panama; The Invisible Menace. **1939** Secret Service of the Air; The Cowboy Quarterback; Indianapolis Speedway; Nancy Drew—Trouble Shooter; Torchy Runs for Mayor; Torchy Plays with Dynamite; Angels Wash Their Faces.

HARRON, TESSIE (Anna Theresa Harron)
Born: Feb. 16, 1896, N.Y. Died: Nov. 9, 1918, Los Angeles, Calif. (Spanish influenza). Screen actress. Sister of actors Bobby (dec. 1920) and John Harron (dec. 1939).

HART, ALBERT
Born: 1874, Liverpool, England. Died: Jan. 10, 1940, Hollywood, Calif. Stage and screen actor.

Appeared in: **1921** Cotton and Cattle; A Cowboy Ace; Diane of Star Hollow;

Flowing Gold; Out of the Clouds; Doubling for Romeo; The Range Pirate; Rustlers of the Night; The Trail to Red Dog; The White Masks. **1922** Angel Citizens; Cross Roads; The Girl Who Ran Wild; Gold Grabbers; So This Is Arizona; Trail's End; The Hidden Woman. **1923** Can a Woman Love Twice; Spawn of the Desert; Crooked Alley; Kindled Courage; Shadows of the North; The Sunshine Trail. **1924** The Breathless Moment; Excitement. **1925** The Pony Express; The Man without a Country. **1926** Blind Trail; Forlorn River; The Outlaw Express. **1927** The Fire Fighters (serial); The Ridin' Rowdy; The Devil's Twin; Blake of Scotland Yard (serial); The Long Loop of the Pecos; The Man from Hardpan; The Mysterious Rider. **1928** The Ballyhoo Buster; The Boss of Rustler's Roost; Mother Knows Best; Honor Bound. **1929** Making the Grade; .45 Calibre War; The Diamond Master (serial). **1931** An American Tragedy. **1933** Big Executive. **1934** Home on the Range. **1938** Tom Sawyer, Detective.

HART, BILLY (William Lenhart)
Born: 1864. Died: June 18, 1942, Los Angeles, Calif. Screen, stage, burlesque and vaudeville actor. Appeared in vaudeville as part of "Billy and Marie Hart" team.

HART, JACK "INDIAN JACK"
Born: 1872. Died: Sept. 23, 1974, Las Vegas, Nevada. Screen actor and rodeo performer.

Appeared in: **1968** Born to Buck.

HART, JAMES T.
Born: 1868. Died: Aug. 12, 1926, Los Angeles, Calif. (stroke). Screen actor.

HART, MABEL
Born: Apr. 29, 1886, Illinois. Died: June 9, 1960, Los Angeles, Calif. (heart attack). Screen actress.

Appeared in: **1938** Over the Wall.

HART, NEAL (Cornelius A. Hart, Jr.)
Born: 1879, Richmond, N.Y. Died: Apr. 2, 1949, Woodland Hills, Calif. Screen actor and film director. Entered films in 1914.

Appeared in: **1916** Liberty, a Daughter of the USA (serial); The Committee on Credentials; For the Love of a Girl; Love's Lariat. **1917** The Raid; The Man from Montana; The Ninth Day; Roped In; Bill Brennan's Claim; Casey's Border Raid; Swede-Hearts; The Getaway. **1918** Beating the Limited; Roped and Tied; When Pan's Green Saw Red. **1919** The Wolf and His Mate (serial). **1921** South of Northern Lights; Danger Valley; Tangled Trails; Black Sheep; God's Gold. **1922** The Kingfisher's Roost; Rangeland; Lure of Gold; The Heart of a Texan; Butterfly Range; Table Top Ranch; West of the Pecos. **1923** The Secret of the Pueblo; Below the Rio Grande; The Devil's Bowl; Salty Saunders; The Fighting Strain; The Forbidden Range. **1924** The Left Hand Brand; Tucker's Top Hand; Branded a Thief; Lawless Men; Safe Guarded; The Valley of Vanishing Men. **1925** The Verdict of the Desert. **1927** Scarlet Brand (serial). **1930** Trigger Tricks. **1931** Wild Horse. **1932** Law and Order. **1939** The Renegade Ranger. **1947** Saddle Pals.

HART, RICHARD
Born: 1916, Providence, R.I. Died: Jan. 2, 1951, New York, N.Y. (heart attack). Screen, stage and television actor.

Appeared in: **1947** Desire Me; Green Dolphin Street. **1948** B. F.'s Daughter. **1949** The Black Book; Reign of Terror.

HART, TEDDY
Born: 1897. Died: Feb. 17, 1971, Los Angeles, Calif. Screen, stage and television actor. Brother of lyricist Lorenz Hart (dec.). Won 1936 Screen Actors Guild Award for Best Supporting Actor for Three Men on a Horse.

Appeared in: **1932** Million Dollar Legs. **1933** Diplomaniacs. **1936** Three Men on a Horse (stage and film versions); After the Thin Man. **1937** Ready, Willing and Able; That Man's Here Again; Hotel Haywire; Marry the Girl; Talent Scout; The Footloose Heiress. **1941** You're the One. **1942** My Favorite Spy. **1946** Lady Luck. **1951** Ma and Pa Kettle Back on the Farm; The Fat Man. **1952** Ma and Pa Kettle at the Fair; A Girl in Every Port. **1953** Ma and Pa Kettle on Vacation. **1955** Ma and Pa Kettle at Waikiki. **1965** Mickey One.

HART, WILLIAM S. (William Surrey Hart)
Born: Dec. 6, 1862, Newburgh, N.Y. Died: June 23, 1946, Los Angeles, Calif. (stroke). Screen, stage actor, writer, and film director.

Appeared in: **1913** The Fugitive. **1914** His Hour of Manhood; The Bargain; Jim Cameron's Wife; The Passing of Two-Gun Hicks; The Scourge of the Desert. **1915** On the Night Stage; Pinto Ben; The Grudge; In the Sagebrush Country; The Man from Nowhere; Bad Buck of Santa Ynez; The Sheriff's Streak of Yellow; Mr. Silent Haskins; The Taking of Luke McVane; The Ruse; Cash Parrish's Pal; The Conversion of Frosty Blake; The Rough Neck; Keno Bates; Liar; The Disciple; The Darkening Trail; A Knight of the Trail; The Tool of Providence; Grit; The Golden Claw; Between Men. **1916** The Last Act; Hell's Hinges; The Primal Lure; The Aryan; The Sheriff; The Captive God;

The Apostle of Vengeance; The Patriot; The Dawn Maker; The Return of Draw Egan; The Devil's Double; Truthful Tolliver. **1917** The Gun Fighter; Square Deal Man; The Desert Man; Wolf Diary; The Cold Deck; The Narrow Trail; The Silent Man; The Last Ace. **1918** Wolves of the Trail; Blue Blazes Rawden; Tiger Man; Shark Monroe; Riddle Gawne; The Border Wireless; Branding Broadway; The Toll Gate; Selfish Yates; War Relief; John Petticoats. **1919** Breed of Men; The Poppy Girl's Husband; The Money Corral; Square Deal Sanderson; Wagon Tracks. **1920** Sand!; The Toll Gate; The Cradle of Courage; The Testing Block. **1921** O'Malley of the Mounted; The Whistle; Three Word Brand; White Oak. **1922** The Covered Wagon; Travelin' On. **1923** Wild Bill Hickock; Hollywood; The Spoilers. **1924** Singer Jim McKee; Grit (and 1915 version). **1925** Tumbleweeds. **1928** Show People. **1939** Tumbleweeds (also appeared in 1925 version and did the prologue for the 1939 version). **1943** One Foot in Heaven; The Silent Man (1917 footage). **1963** The Great Chase (documentary). That's Entertainment (film clips).

HART, WILLIAM V. "POP"
Born: 1867. Died: Oct. 1925, New York, N.Y. Screen and vaudeville actor.

HARTE, BETTY (Daisy Mae Light)
Born: 1883, Philadelphia, Pa. Died: Jan. 3, 1965, Sunland, Calif. Screen actress.

Appeared in: **1908** The Roman. **1911** The Blacksmith's Son; In the Days of Gold; The Heart of John Barlow; Making a Man of Him; The Little Widow; The Profligate; Through Fire and Smoke; The Coquette. **1912** The Vow of Ysobel; Her Education; The Girl of the Lighthouse; The Pirate's Daughter; How the Cause was Won; The Shrinking Rawhide; The Substitute Mode; The Junior Officer; An Assisted Elopement; Getting Atmosphere; The Ace of Spades; The Epidemic in Paradise Gulch; Making a Man of Her; Kings of the Forest. **1913** The Good in the Worst of Us; An Innocent Informer. **1914** The Pride of Jennico. **1915** The Buzzard's Shadow. **1916** The Bait. **1922** Eternal Peace.

HARTFORD, DAVID
Born: Jan. 11, 1876, Ontonian, Mich. Died: Oct. 29, 1932, Hollywood, Calif. (heart attack). Screen, stage actor, film, stage director, stage and film producer.

Appeared in: **1926** Dame Chance. **1930** Rough Romance.

HARTLEY, CHARLES
Born: 1852. Died: Oct. 13, 1930, Fort Lee, N.J. (complication of diseases). Stage and screen actor.

Appeared in: **1919** Prunella. **1921** The Conquest of Canaan.

HARTMAN, AGNES A.
Born: 1860, Sweden. Died: Dec. 22, 1932, Los Angeles, Calif. Screen actress. Mother of actress Gretchen Hartman.

HARTMAN, GRACE (Grace Barrett)
Born: 1907. Died: Aug. 8, 1955, Van Nuys, Calif. (cancer). Screen, stage and television actress. Divorced from actor Paul Hartman (dec. 1973) with whom she appeared in vaudeville as part of "The Hartmans."

Appeared in: **1937** 45 Fathers. **1941** Sunny. **1944** Higher and Higher.

HARTMAN, JONATHAN WILLIAM "POP"
Born: 1872, Louisville, Ky. Died: Oct. 19, 1965, Tampa, Fla. Screen, stage and vaudeville actor.

HARTMAN, PAUL
Born: 1904. Died: Oct. 2, 1973, Los Angeles, Calif. (heart attack). Screen, stage, vaudeville, television actor and dancer. Son of stage actor and producer Ferris Hartman (dec.). Married to actress Grace Hartman (dec. 1955) with whom he appeared in vaudeville as part of "The Dancing Hartmans." He later married actress Francis Miggins. Do not confuse with German actor Paul Hartmann.

Appeared in: **1937** Forty Five Fathers (film debut). **1941** Sunny. **1943** Higher and Higher. **1953** Man on a Tightrope. **1960** Inherit the Wind. **1963** Soldier in the Rain; The Thrill of it All. **1964** Those Calloways. **1965** Inside Daisy Clover. **1967** Luv; How to Succeed in Business Without Really Trying; The Reluctant Astronaut.

HARTMANN, SADAKICHI
Born: c. 1864. Died: Nov. 21, 1944, St. Petersburgh, Fla. Author, dancer and screen actor.

Appeared in: **1924** The Thief of Baghdad.

HARTNELL, WILLIAM "BILLY"
Born: Jan. 8, 1908, Devon, England. Died: Apr. 24, 1975, London, England. Screen, stage and television actor. Married to actress and playwright Heather McIntyre.

Appeared in: **1933** I'm an Explosive; Follow the Lady; The Lure. **1934** Seeing is Believing; The Perfect Flaw. **1935** Swinging the Lead; While Parents Sleep. **1936** Nothing Like Publicity; Midnight at Madame Tussaud's (aka Midnight

at the Wax Museum—US). **1937** Farewell Again (aka Troopship—US 1938). **1938** They Drive by Night. **1939** Murder Will Out; Too Dangerous to Live. **1940** They Came by Night. **1942** Flying Fortress; Sabotage at Sea; Suspected Person; The Peterville Diamond. **1943** Bells go Down; The Dark Tower; Headline. **1944** Way Ahead. **1945** Strawberry Roan (US 1948); The Agitator; Murder in Reverse (US 1946). **1946** Appointment with Crime (US 1950). **1947** Odd Man Out; Temptation Harbour (US 1949); Brighton Rock (aka Young Scarface). **1948** Escape. **1949** Now Barrabas; The Lost People. **1950** Double Confession (US 1953). **1951** The Dark Man; The Magic Box (US 1952). **1952** Pickwick Papers (US 1953); The Ringer (US 1953); The Holly and the Ivy (US 1953). **1953** Will Any Gentleman? (US 1955). **1955** Footsteps in the Fog; Josephine and the Men. **1956** Doublecross; Private's Progress; Tons of Trouble. **1957** Yangtse Incident (aka Battle Hell—US); The Hypnotist (aka Scotland Yard Dragnet—US 1958); Hell Drivers (US 1958). **1958** On the Run; Carry on Sergeant (US 1959); Date with Disaster. **1959** Shake Hands with the Devil; The Mouse that Roared; The Night we Dropped a Clanger (aka Make Mine a Double—US 1961); The Desperate Man. **1960** And the Same to You; Jackpot; Piccadilly Third Stop (US 1968). **1962** Tomorrow at Ten (US 1964). **1963** This Sporting Life; The World Ten Times Over (aka Pussycat Alley—US 1965); Heavens Above.

HARVEY, DON C. (Don Carlos Harvey)
Born: Dec. 12, 1911, Kansas. Died: Apr. 24, 1963, Studio City, Calif. (heart attack). Screen, stage, radio and television actor. Married to actress Jean Harvey (dec. 1966).

Appeared in: **1949** Angels in Disguise; The Mutineers; Rimfire; Son of a Badman. **1950** Chain Gang; Forbidden Jungle; The Fighting Stallion; Trail of the Rustlers; The Girl from San Lorenzo; Gunmen of Abilene; Hoedown; Joe Palooka in the Triple Cross; The Lost Volcano. **1951** Night Riders of Montana; Teams Never Cry; Fort Worth; Northwest Territory; According to Mrs. Hoyle; Hurricane Island. **1952** The Old West; Prince of Pirates; A Yank in Indo-China. **1954** Golden Idol; Pushover; Violent Men. **1955** Apache Ambush; Wyoming Renegades; Creature with the Atom Brain; Women's Prison. **1956** Flagpole Sitters (short); Blackjack Ketchum, Desperado; Blazing the Overland Trail (serial); Jubal; Picnic; The Werewolf. **1957** Beginning of the End; No Time to Be Young; Dino. **1958** Buchanan Rides Alone. **1959** Gunmen from Laredo. **1962** The Wild Westerners. **1963** It's a Mad, Mad, Mad, Mad World.

HARVEY, EDWARD
Born: 1893. Died: Aug. 5, 1975, Ventor, Isle of Wight, England (heart attack). Screen, stage and television actor.

Appeared in: **1960** The Unstoppable Man (US 1961). **1962** The Damned (aka These are the Damned—US 1964). **1965** The Spy Who Came in from the Cold.

HARVEY, FORRESTER
Born: 1880, County Cork, Ireland. Died: Dec. 14, 1945, Laguna Beach, Calif. (stroke). Stage and screen actor.

Appeared in: **1922** The Lilac Sunbonnet. **1923** The Man Who Liked Lemons. **1925** Somebody's Darling. **1926** Nell Gwynne; If Youth But Knew; The Flag Lieutenant; Street Playlets Series including: Cash on Delivery. **1927** The Ring. **1928** The White Sheik (aka King's Mate); Toni; Glorious Youth (aka Eileen of the Trees); Spangles; That Brute Simmons. **1929** Ringing the Changes (aka The Crooked Staircase). **1931** Devotion; A Tailor-Made Man; The Man in Possession; Guilty Hands. **1932** Smilin' Through; Red Dust; Kongo; Young Onion (short); Tarzan the Ape Man; Shanghai Express; Sky Devils; But the Flesh is Weak; The Wet Parade; Mystery Ranch. **1933** Destination Unknown; The Eagle and the Hawk; Midnight Club; The Invisible Man. **1934** The Painted Veil; Menace; Limelight Blues; Great Expectations; Forsaking All Others; The Mystery of Mr. X; Tarzan and His Mate; Man of Two Worlds; Broadway Bill. **1935** The Best Man Wins; The Woman In Red; Captain Blood; Vagabond Lady; The Perfect Gentleman; Jalna; Gilded Lily; Right to Live; Mystery of Edwin Drood. **1936** Love Before Breakfast; Petticoat Fever; Lloyds of London; White Hunter. **1937** Personal Property; Thoroughbreds Don't Cry; The Prince and the Pauper; The Man Who Cried Wolf. **1938** Bulldog Drummond in Africa; The Mysterious Mr. Moto. **1939** Bulldog Drummond's Secret Police; The Lady's from Kentucky; The Witness Vanishes. **1940** The Invisible Man Returns; A Chump at Oxford; Tom Brown's School Days. **1941** Free and Easy; The Wolf Man; Dr. Jekyll and Mr. Hyde. **1942** Mrs. Miniver; This above All. **1944** The Lodger; None but the Lonely Heart; Secrets of Scotland Yard. **1945** Scotland Yard Investigator; Devotion (and 1931 version).

HARVEY, HANK (Herman Heacker)
Died: Dec. 4, 1929, Culver City, Calif. Screen actor.

HARVEY, JEAN (Jean Guy)
Born: Nov. 17, 1900, Ohio. Died: Dec. 14, 1966, Studio City, Calif. (arteriosclerosis). Screen actress. Married to actor Don C. Harvey (dec. 1963).

Appeared in: **1951** Chicago Calling. **1956** The Werewolf. **1959** City of Fear. **1961** Circle of Deception. **1963** It's all Happening (aka The Dream Maker—US 1964).

HARVEY, JOHN

Born: June 28, 1917, New Rockford, N.D. Died: Dec. 25, 1970. Screen actor. Married to actress Judith Parrish. Do not confuse with British actor John Harvey nor U.S. actor (dec. 1954).

HARVEY, JOHN "JACK"

Born: 1881. Died: Nov. 10, 1954, Hollywood, Calif. (natural causes). Screen cowboy actor.

HARVEY, LAURENCE (Larushka Mischa Skikne)

Born: Oct. 1, 1928, Yomishkis, Lithuania. Died: Nov. 25, 1973, London, England (cancer). Screen, stage and television actor, film producer and director. Married to model Paulene Stone. Divorced from actress Margaret Leighton (dec. 1976) and Joan Cohn. Nominated for 1959 Academy Award as Best Actor in Room at the Top.

Appeared in: **1948** House of Darkness; The Man from Yesterday. **1949** Man on the Run (US 1951); Landfall. **1950** Cairo Road; The Black Rose; A Killer Walks. **1951** There is Another Sun (aka Wall of Death—US 1952); Scarlet Thread. **1952** Women of Twilight (aka Twilight Women—US 1953); A Killer Walks; I Believe in You (US 1953). **1953** Ali Baba Nights; Innocents in Paris (US 1955). **1954** Dial M for Murder; The Good Die Young (US 1955); King Richard and the Crusaders; Romeo and Juliet. **1955** I am a Camera; None but the Brave; Storm over the Nile (US 1956). **1956** Three Men in a Boat (US 1958). **1957** After the Ball. **1958** The Truth about Women; The Silent Enemy. **1959** Room at the Top; Power among Men (narrator); Expresso Bongo (US 1960). **1960** Butterfield 8; The Alamo. **1961** Two Loves; Summer and Smoke; The Spinster; The Long and the Short and the Tall. **1962** Jungle Fighters; The Wonderful World of the Brothers Grimm; A Walk on the Wild Side; A Girl Named Tamiko; The Manchurian Candidate. **1963** The Running Man; The Ceremony. **1964** The Outrage; Of Human Bondage. **1965** Darling; Life at the Top. **1966** The Spy with a Cold Nose. **1967** Ice Station Zebra. **1968** The Winter's Tale; A Dandy in Aspic; H-Bomb Beach Party; A Flea in Her Ear. **1969** He and She; Fight for Rome; Charge of the Light Brigade. **1970** Hall of Mirrors; WUSA; L'Absolute Naturale; The Magic Christian. **1973** Night Watch.

HARVEY, LILIAN (Lilian Muriel Helen Harvey)

Born: Jan. 19, 1907, Horsey, England. Died: July 27, 1968, Antibes, France. Screen actress. Entered films in Germany c. 1920.

Appeared in: **1925** Die Liebschaften der Hella von Gilsa (The Love Story from the Hella von Gilsa aka Leidenschaft); Der Fluch; Liebe und Trompetenblasen; Die Kleine von Bummel. **1926** Prinzessin Trulala (Princess Trulala); Die Keusche Susanne; Vater Werden ist Nicht Schwer (It's Easy to Become a Father—US 1929). **1927** Die Tolle Lola; Eheferien. **1928** Du Solst Nicht Stehlen (You Should Not Steal); The Love Commandment. **1929** A Knight in London; Adieu Mascotte; Ihr Dunkler Punkt. **1930** Wenn du Einmal Dein Herz Verschenkst; Liebeswalzer (The Love Waltz); Hokuspokus (aka The Temporary Widow); Die Drei von der Tankstelle (Three from the Gasoline Station); Einbrecher; Murder for Sale. **1931** Nie Wieder Liebe (No More Love); Ihre Holeit Befiehlt; Der Kongress Tanzt (Congress Dances—US 1932). **1932** Zwei Herzen und ein Schlag (Two Hearts Beat as One); Quick; Ein Blonder Traum (A Blonde Dream); Happy Ever After. **1933** Ich und Die Kaiserin (The Only Girl aka Heart Song—US 1934); My Weakness; My Lips Betray; Koenig der Clows. **1934** I am Suzanne. **1935** Let's Live Tonight; Schwarze Rosen (aka Did I Betray?—US 1936); Invitation to the Waltz; Mein ist die Rache. **1936** Glueckskinder (Lucky Children). **1937** Sieben Ohrfeigen (Seven Slaps); Fanny Elssler; Untitled Dance. **1938** Capriccio; Black Roses (reissue of Schwarze Rosen, 1935). **1939** Castelli in Aria; Frau am Steuer. **1940** Serenade; Miquette. **1950** Herrliche Zeiten (Wonderful Times). **1951** Miquette and Her Mother. **1958** Das Gag's Nur Einmal (It Only Happened Once). **1960** Das Kommt Nicht Wieder (It Won't Happen Again).

HARVEY, LOTTIE

Born: 1890. Died: Aug. 2, 1948, Hollywood, Calif. Screen actress.

HARVEY, MARILYN

Born: 1929. Died: Mar. 29, 1973, Hollywood, Calif. Screen, stage and television actress. Married to film director Gene Narum.

Appeared in: **1958** The Astounding She-Monster. **1963** A Child is Waiting. **1968** Rosemary's Baby.

HARVEY, PAUL

Born: 1884, Ill. Died: Dec. 14, 1955, Hollywood, Calif. (coronary thrombosis). Stage and screen actor. Entered films with Selig Film Co. in 1917.

Appeared in: **1929** The Awful Truth. **1930** Strong Arm (short). **1932** The Wiser Sex. **1933** Advice to the Lovelorn. **1934** Hat, Coat and Glove; Handy Andy; Kid Millions; She Was a Lady; A Wicked Woman; The President Vanishes; Looking for Trouble; The House of Rothschild; The Affairs of Cellini; Born to Be Bad; Broadway Bill; Charlie Chan's Courage. **1935** Alibi Ike; Thanks a Million; The Whole Town's Talking; I'll Love You Always; Four Hours to Kill; Goin' to Town. **1936** August Week-End; Postal Inspector; Rose of the Rancho; The Return of Sophie Lang; The Plainsman; Mind Your Own Busi-

ness; The Petrified Forest; The Walking Dead; Three Men on a Horse; The Witness Chair; Private Number; Yellowstone. **1937** The Black Legion; Michael Strogoff; On Again—Off Again; High Flyers; The Devil Is Driving; Big City; My Dear Miss Aldrich; 23—1/2 Hours' Leave; The Soldier and the Lady. **1938** A Slight Case of Murder; If I Were King; Love on a Budget; Rebecca of Sunnybrook Farm; I'll Give a Million; Charlie Chan in Honolulu; There's That Woman Again; Algiers; The Higgins Family; The Sisters. **1939** Never Say Die; The Gorilla; News Is Made at Night; Stanley and Livingstone; Mr. Moto in Danger Island; High School; The Forgotten Woman; They Shall Have Music; Meet Dr. Christian. **1940** Brother Rat and a Baby; The Marines Fly High; Typhoon; Manhattan Heartbeat; Maryland; Behind the News; Arizona. **1941** Ride on, Vaquero; Out of the Fog; Puddin' Head; Law of the Tropics; Great Guns; You Belong to Me; Three Girls about Town; Remember the Night; Mr. District Attorney in the Carter Case; High Sierra; You're in the Army Now. **1942** A Tragedy at Midnight; The Man Who Wouldn't Die; Moonlight Masquerade; Heart of the Golden West; You Can't Escape Forever. **1943** The Man from Music Mountain; Mystery Broadcast. **1944** Four Jills in a Jeep; Henry Aldrich Plays Cupid; The Thoroughbreds; Jamboree; In the Meantime, Darling. **1945** Don't Fence Me In; Spellbound; Mama Loves Papa; The Chicago Kid; The Horn Blows at Midnight; Swingin' on a Rainbow; The Southerner; Swingin' on Broadway; State Fair; Pillow to Post. **1946** Gay Blades; They Made Me a Killer; Up Goes Maisie; In Fast Company; Blondie's Lucky Day; I've Always Loved You; The Bamboo Blonde; Helldorado; Early to Wed. **1947** The Beginning of the End; Out of the Blue; High Barbaree; Danger Street; When a Girl's Beautiful; The Late George Apley; Wyoming. **1948** Waterfront at Midnight; Lightnin' in the Forest; Give My Regards to Broadway; Blondie's Reward; Family Honeymoon; Smuggler's Cove; Speed to Spare; Call Northside 777. **1949** Take One False Step; The Fountainhead; The Girl from Jones Beach; Down to the Sea in Ships; The Duke of Chicago; Family Honeymoon; John Loves Mary; Make Believe Ballroom; Mr. Belvedere Goes to College. **1950** The Lawless; Father of the Bride; The Milkman; Side Street; The Skipper Surprised His Wife; Three Little Words; A Ticket to Tomahawk; Unmasked; Riding High; The Yellow Cab Man; Stella. **1951** The Tall Target; Let's Go, Navy!; Father's Little Dividend; Excuse My Dust; The Flying Missile; Thunder in God's Country; Up Front. **1952** The First Time; Has Anybody Seen My Gal?; Dreamboat; April in Paris; Here Come the Nelsons. **1953** Calamity Jane; Remains to Be Seen. **1954** Sabrina. **1955** Three for the Show; High Society. **1956** The Ten Commandments.

HASHASHIAN, AROUSIAK. *See* AROUSIAK DER ABRAHAMIAN

HASHIM, EDMUND "ED"

Born: 1932. Died: July 2, 1974, New York, N.Y. Screen and television actor.

Appeared in: **1955** Ghost Town. **1956** Quincannon—Frontier Scout. **1961** The Outsider. **1966** . . . and Now Miguel. **1968** Hellfighters.

HASKELL, AL

Died: Jan. 6, 1969. Screen actor.

Appeared in: **1939** Mexicali Rose. **1941** Border Vigilantes. **1956** Around the World in 80 Days.

HASKIN, CHARLES W.

Born: 1868. Died: June 10, 1927, New York, N.Y. Screen, stage actor and stage manager.

HASKINS, DOUGLAS (Douglas Neville Haskins)

Born: 1928, Canada. Died: June 8, 1973, Vancouver, B.C., Canada (cancer). Screen, radio actor, film director, television writer, producer, director and screenwriter.

HASSELL, GEORGE

Born: May 4, 1881, Birmingham, England. Died: Feb. 17, 1937, Chatsworth, Calif. (heart attack). Screen and stage actor.

Appeared in: **1915** Old Dutch. **1926** La Boheme. **1930** Where There's A Will (short). **1935** Night Life of the Gods; The Flame Within; Becky Sharp; Dressed to Thrill; Captain Blood. **1936** Petticoat Fever; The King Steps Out; Girl's Dormitory; White Hunter. **1937** Woman Wise.

HASTINGS, VICTORIA

Died: May 24, 1934, Hollywood, Calif. (heart ailment). Screen actress. Married to actor Trevor Bland-Addinsell.

HASWELL, PERCY

Born: 1871. Died: June 14, 1945, Nantucket, Mass. Screen and stage actress. She appeared as Mrs. George Fawcett and as Percy Haswell. Married to actor George Fawcett (dec. 1939).

Appeared in: **1929** Innocents of Paris; River of Romance.

HATCH, RILEY (William Riley Hatch)

Born: Sept. 2, 1865, Cleveland, Ohio. Died: Sept. 6, 1925, Bayshore, New York. Screen, stage actor and opera singer.

Appeared in: **1916** Hazel Kirke. **1919** Teeth of the Tiger. **1920** The Inner

Voice; Little Miss Rebellion. **1921** Something Different; The Matrimonial Web; The Conquest of Canaan; The Idol of the North; Sheltered Daughters; Nobody; What Women Will Do; You Find It Everywhere. **1922** Missing Millions. **1923** If Winter Comes; You are Guilty; Zaza; Little Old New York. **1924** America; Trouping with Ellen; West of the Water Tower. **1925** The Street of Forgotten Men; Night Life of New York.

HATHAWAY, JEAN

Born: 1876. Died: Aug. 23, 1938, Los Angeles, Calif. Screen actress.

Appeared in: **1914** The Master Key (serial). **1916** The Purple Mask (serial). **1921** Short Skirts. **1922** Boy Crazy.

HATHAWAY, LILIAN

Born: 1876, Liverpool, England. Died: Jan. 12, 1954, Englewood Cliffs, N.J. Stage and screen actress.

HATHAWAY, RHODY

Born: 1869. Died: Feb. 18, 1944, Hollywood, Calif. Screen actor.

Appeared in: **1908** American Film Co. films. **1924** Not a Drum Was Heard. **1925** A Daughter of the Sioux. **1926** Bigger Than Barnum's; The Phantom of the Forest. **1928** Into the Night; The Old Code.

HATTON, BRADFORD

Born: 1906. Died: Aug. 11, 1969, Denver, Colo. Screen and stage actor.

Appeared in: **1932** Smiling Faces. **1952** Walk East on Beacon. **1954** Top Banana.

HATTON, FRANCES

Born: 1888. Died: Oct. 1971, Palmdale, Calif. Screen and stage actress. Married to actor Raymond Hatton (dec. Oct. 1971).

Appeared in: **1921** The Mother Heart; Straight from the Shoulder; The Rowdy. **1922** At the Sign of the Jack O'Lantern. **1923** Java Head; The Grail; The Day of Faith. **1925** Confessions of a Queen.

HATTON, RAYMOND (Raymond William Hatton)

Born: July 7, 1892, Red Oak, Iowa. Died: Oct. 21, 1971, Palmdale, Calif. (heart attack). Screen, stage and television actor. Entered films with Kalem in 1911. Married to actress Frances Hatton (dec. Oct. 1971).

Appeared in: **1916** Oliver Twist. **1917** Woman God Forgot; Joan the Woman; The Little American. **1918** The Whispering Chorus; We Can't Have Everything; Sandy; The Source. **1919** You're Fired; The Love Burglar; Male and Female; Everywoman. **1920** The Dancin' Fool; Jes' Call Me Jim. **1921** The Ace of Hearts; The Affairs of Anatol; Bunty Pulls the Strings; The Concert; Peck's Bad Boy; Salvage; All's Fair in Love; Pilgrims of the Night; Doubling for Romeo. **1922** Ebb Tide; Head over Heels; Pink Gods; To Have and to Hold; Manslaughter; The Hottentot; His Back against the Wall; At Bay. **1923** The Barefoot Boy; Java Head; The Virginian; Trimmed in Scarlet; The Tie That Binds; Three Wise Fools; A Man of Action; Big Brother; Enemies of Children; The Hunchback of Notre Dame. **1924** True As Steel; Triumph; The Mine with the Iron Door; Cornered; The Fighting American; Half-a-Dollar Bill. **1925** Adventure; Contraband; In the Name of Love; The Devil's Cargo; A Son of His Father; The Thundering Herd; The Top of the World; Tomorrow's Love; Lord Jim. **1926** Behind the Front; Born to the West; Silence; Forlorn River; We're in the Navy Now. **1927** Fashions for Women; Fireman Save My Child; Now We're in the Air. **1928** The Big Killing; Wife Savers; Partners in Crime. **1929** The Office Scandal; Trent's Last Case; When Caesar Ran a Newspaper (short); Dear Vivien; Christie talking plays; Hell's Heroes; Christie shorts. **1930** The Silver Horde; Rogue of the Rio Grande; Murder on the Roof; Her Unborn Child; Midnight Mystery; The Road to Paradise; Pineapples; The Mighty. **1931** The Squaw Man; Honeymoon Lane; The Lion and the Lamb; Arrowsmith; The Challenge; Woman Hungry. **1932** Law and Order; Polly of the Circus; The Fourth Horseman; Uptown New York; Exposed; The Crooked Circle; Vanity Street; Malay Nights; Stranger in Town; Drifting Souls; Vanishing Frontier; Alias Mary Smith; Long Loop Laramie; Divorce a la Mode (short). **1933** State Trooper; Under the Tonto Rim; Alice in Wonderland; Lady Killer; Penthouse; Day of Reckoning; Tom's in Town; Terror Trail; Cornered; Hidden Gold; The Big Cage. **1934** The Defense Rests; Women in His Life; Lazy River; Once to Every Bachelor; Fifteen Wives; The Thundering Herd; Straight Is the Way; Wagon Wheels. **1935** Times Square Lady; Desert Death (short); Murder in the Fleet; Calm Yourself; Rustlers of Red Gap (serial); Nevada; Wanderer of the Wasteland; Red Morning; G-Men; The Daring Young Man; Steamboat 'Round the Bend; Stormy. **1936** Exclusive Story; Women Are Trouble; Mad Holiday; Laughing Irish Eyes; Desert Gold; Timothy's Quest; The Vigilantes Are Coming (serial); The Arizona Raiders; Yellowstone; Jungle Jim (serial). **1937** Marked Woman; Fly-Away Baby; The Adventurous Blonde; Love Is on the Air; The Missing Witness; Roaring Timber; Public Wedding; Over the Goal. **1938** He Couldn't Say No; Come Rangers; Love Finds Andy Hardy; The Texans; Touchdown Army; Tom Sawyer, Detective; Over the Wall. **1939** I'm from Missouri; Ambush; Undercover Doctor; Rough Riders' Roundup; Frontier Pony Express; Paris Honeymoon; New Frontier; Wyoming Outlaw; Wall Street Cowboy; The Kansas Terrors; The

Cowboys from Texas; Six Thousand Enemies; Career. **1940** Heroes of the Saddle; Pioneers of the West; Covered Wagon Days; Rocky Mountain Rangers; Oklahoma Renegades; Queen of the Mob; Kit Carson. **1941** Arizona Bound; Gunman from Bodie; Forbidden Trails. **1942** Ghost Town Law; Cadets on Parade; Girl from Alaska; Down Texas Way; Riders of the West; Dawn on the Great Divide; Below the Border; West of the Law. **1943** The Texas Kid; Outlaws of Stampede Pass; Six-Gun Gospel; Stranger from Pecos; The Ghost Rider. **1944** Raiders of the Border; Rough Riders; Partners of the Trail; West of the Rio Grande; Land of the Outlaws; Tall in the Saddle; Range Law; Ghost Guns; The Law Men. **1945** Law of the Valley; Flame of the West; Sunbonnet Sue; Frontier Feud; Gun Smoke; The Lost Trail; Northwest Trail; Rhythm Roundup; Stranger from Santa Fe. **1946** Fool's Gold; Drifting Along; Under Arizona Skies; The Haunted Mine; Border Bandits; Shadows on the Range; Raiders of the South; The Gentleman from Texas; Silver Range; Trigger Fingers. **1947** Trailing Danger; Land of the Lawless; Rolling Home; Valley of Fear; Black Gold; The Law Comes to Gunsight; Code of the Saddle; Prairie Express; Gun Talk; Unconquered. **1948** Crossed Trails; Triggerman; Overland Trails; Frontier Agent; Back Trail. **1949** Sheriff of Medicine Bow; Gunning for Trouble; Hidden Danger; The Fighting Ranger. **1950** Operation Haylift; County Fair; West of the Brazos; Marshal of Heldorado; Crooked River; Colorado Ranger; Fast on the Draw; Hostile Country. **1951** Skipalong Rosenbloom; Kentucky Jubilee. **1952** The Golden Hawk. **1953** Cow Country. **1954** Thunder Pass. **1955** The Twinkle in God's Eye; Treasure of Ruby Hills. **1956** Dig That Uranium; Shake, Rattle and Rock; Flesh and the Spur; Girls in Prison. **1957** Pawnee; Invasion of the Saucer Men; Motorcycle Gang. **1959** Alaska Passage. **1964** The Quick Gun. **1965** Requiem for a Gunfighter. **1967** In Cold Blood.

HATTON, RICHARD "DICK"

Born: 1891. Died: July 9, 1931, Los Angeles, Calif. (traffic accident). Screen actor and film director.

Appeared in: **1922** Four Hearts; Fearless Dick; Hellhounds of the West. **1923** In the West; The Seventh Sheriff; Unblazed Trail; Blood Test; The Golden Flame; Playing Double; Ridin' Thru. **1924** Come on, Cowboys; Western Fate; The Whirlwind Ranger; Rip Snorter; Horse Sense; Sagebrush Gospel; Trouble Trail; Two-Fisted Justice. **1925** Sell 'Em Cowboy; "Scar" Hanan; The Cactus Cure; My Pal; Range Justice; Ridin' Easy; The Secret of Black Canyon; Warrior Gap; A Western Engagement; Where Romance Rides. **1926** He-Man's Country; In Broncho Land; Roaring Bill Atwood; Temporary Sheriff. **1927** The Action Graver; Saddle Jumpers; Speeding Hoofs; Western Courage. **1928** The Boss of Rustler's Roost. **1930** Romance of the Week.

HATTON, RONDO

Born: Apr. 29, 1894, Hagerstown, Md. Died: Feb. 2, 1946, Beverly Hills, Calif. (heart attack). Screen actor.

Appeared in: **1930** Hell Harbor. **1938** In Old Chicago; Alexander's Ragtime Band. **1939** The Hunchback of Notre Dame; Captain's Fury. **1940** Chad Hanna; Moon over Burma; The Big Guy. **1942** The Cyclone Kid; The Moon and Sixpence. **1943** The Sleepy Lagoon; The Ox-Bow Incident. **1944** The Pearl of Death; Raiders of Ghost City (serial); The Princess and the Pirate; Johnny Doesn't Live Here Anymore. **1945** The Royal Mounted Rides Again (serial); Jungle Captive. **1946** Spider Woman Strikes Back; House of Horrors (aka Joan Medford Is Missing); The Brute Man.

HAUPT, ULLRICH

Born: Aug. 8, 1887, Prussia. Died: Aug. 5, 1931, near Santa Maria, Calif. (hunting accident). Screen, stage actor, stage director, stage producer and screenwriter. Entered films with Essanay Studios in Chicago.

Appeared in: **1917** The Fable of Prince Fortunatus, Who Moved Away from Easy Street and Silas, the Saver, Who Moved In; The Killjoy. **1928** Captain Swagger; The Tempest. **1929** Wonder of Women; The Far Call; Frozen Justice; The Iron Mask; Madame X; The Greene Murder Case. **1930** A Royal Romance; The Bad One; DuBarry, Woman of Passion; Morocco; The Rogue Song. **1931** The Man Who Came Back; The Unholy Garden.

HAVEL, JOE

Born: 1869. Died: Jan. 27, 1932, Los Angeles, Calif. Screen and vaudeville actor. Entered films in 1920.

HAVEN, CHARNA (Charna E. Kichaven)

Born: 1925. Died: Feb. 16, 1971, Hollywood, Calif. Screen actress, cellist and pianist. Entered films in 1941.

HAVER, PHYLLIS

Born: Jan. 16, 1899, Douglas, Kans. Died: Nov. 19, 1960, Falls Village, Conn. (suicide). Screen actress. Was a Mack Sennett bathing beauty and appeared in many Keystone comedies.

Appeared in: **1917** The Sultan's Wife; A Bedroom Blunder; The Pullman Bride; That Night. **1918** Ladies First; His Wife's Friend; Whose Little Wife Are You?; The Village Chestnut. **1919** Never Too Old; The Foolish Age; When Love is Blind; Hearts and Flowers; Trying to Get Along; Among Those Present; Yankee Doodle in Berlin; Why Beaches are Popular; A Lady's Tailor; Up in Alf's Place; Salome vs. Shenandoah; His Last False Step; The Speak Easy.

1920 Ten Dollars or Ten Days (short); Married Life; Love, Honor and Behave. 1921 A Small Town Idol; Home Talent; plus the following shorts: On a Summer's Day; An Unhappy Finish; She Sighed by the Seaside. 1922 The following shorts: Bright Eyes; Step Forward; Home-Made Movies. 1923 The Temple of Venus; The Bolted Door; The Christian; The Common Law. 1924 The Hollywood Kid (short); The Perfect Flapper; The Breath of Scandal; The Fighting Coward; The Foolish Virgin; Lilies of the Field; The Midnight Express; One Glorious Night; Singer Jim McKee; Single Wives; The Snob. 1925 So Big; After Business Hours; A Fight to the Finish; The Golden Princess; Her Husband's Secret; I Want My Man; New Brooms; Rugged Water. 1926 What Price Glory; Up in Mabel's Room; The Nervous Wreck; The Caveman; Don Juan; Fig Leaves; Hard Boiled; Other Women's Husbands; Three Bad Men. 1927 The Way of All Flesh; No Control; The Little Adventuress; The Rejuvenation of Aunt Mary; The Wise Wife; The Fighting Eagle; Your Wife and Mine; Nobody's Widow. 1928 Chicago; Tenth Avenue; The Battle of the Sexes. 1929 Sal of Singapore; The Shady Lady; The Office Scandal; Thunder; Hell's Kitchen. 1963 30 Years of Fun (documentary).

HAVIER, JOSE ALEX
Born: 1909. Died: Dec. 18, 1945, Hollywood, Calif. (suicide—gun). Screen actor.

Appeared in: 1943 Bataan. 1945 Back to Bataan; They Were Expendable.

HAVILAND, RENA
Born: 1878. Died: Feb. 20, 1954, Woodland Hills, Calif. Screen, stage and vaudeville actress. Entered films in 1911.

HAWKE, ROHN OLIN
Born: 1924. Died: Feb. 15, 1967, Albuquerque, N.M. (suicide—gun). Screen actor, disc jocky and writer. Appeared in films during late 1940s.

HAWKINS, COLEMAN "BEAN"
Born: Nov. 21, 1904, St. Joseph, Mo. Died: May 19, 1969, New York, N.Y. (liver ailment). Jazz musician and screen actor.

Appeared in: 1945 The Crimson Canary.

HAWKINS, JACK
Born: Sept. 14, 1910, London, England. Died: July 18, 1973, London, England (cancer). Screen, stage, television actor, screenwriter and film producer. Married to actress Doreen Lawrence and divorced from actress Jessica Tandy.

Appeared in: 1930 Birds of Prey (aka The Perfect Alibi—US 1931). 1932 The Lodger (aka The Phantom Fiend—US 1935). 1933 The Good Companions; The Lost Chord; I Lived with You; The Jewel; A Shot in the Dark (US 1935). 1934 Autumn Crocus; Death at Broadcasting House (aka The Wigan Express). 1935 Peg of Old Drury (US 1936). 1937 The Frog (US 1939); Beauty and the Barge. 1938 Who Goes Next?; A Royal Divorce (US 1939). 1939 Beau Geste; Murder Will Out. 1940 The Flying Squad. 1942 Next of Kin (US 1943). 1948 Bonnie Prince Charlie; The Fallen Idol (US 1949). 1949 Caught; The Small Back Room (US 1952). 1950 The Elusive Pimpernel; The Black Rose; State Secret (aka The Great Manhunt—US 1951). 1951 No Highway (aka No Highway in the Sky—US); The Adventurers (aka The Great Adventure—US). 1952 Home at Seven (aka Murder on Monday—US 1953); Mandy (aka Crash of Silence—US 1953); The Planter's Wife (aka Outpost in Malaya—US); Angels One Five (US 1954). 1953 The Cruel Sea; Twice Upon a Time; Malta Story (US 1954); The Intruder (US 1955). 1954 The Fighting Pimpernel; The Seekers (aka Land of Fury—US 1955); Front Page Story (US 1955). 1955 Land of the Pharaohs; The Prisoner; Touch and Go (aka The Light Touch—US 1956). 1956 The Long Arm (aka The Third Key—US 1957). 1957 The Man in the Sky (aka Decision Against Time—US); The Bridge on the River Kwai; Fortune is a Woman (aka She Played with Fire—US 1958); The Battle for Britain (short). 1958 The Two-Headed Spy (US 1959); Gideon's Day (aka Gideon of Scotland Yard—US 1959). 1959 Ben Hur. 1960 The League of Gentlemen (US 1961). 1961 Two Loves. 1962 Five Finger Exercise; Lawrence of Arabia. 1963 Lafayette; Rampage; Zulu (US 1964). 1964 The Third Secret; Guns at Batasi; Masquerade (US 1965). 1965 Lord Jim. 1966 Judith; The Poppy is Also a Flower (aka Danger Grows Wild). 1967 The Great Catherine (US 1968). 1968 Shalako. 1969 Monte Carlo or Bust; Oh, What a Lovely War!; Twinky (aka Lola—US); Those Daring Young Men in Their Jaunty Jalopies. 1970 Jane Eyre; The Adventures of Gerard. 1971 Waterloo; Kidnapped; Nicholas and Alexandra; Beloved (aka Sin); The Last Lion. 1972 Young Winston; Escape to the Sun. 1973 Theatre of Blood; Tales That Witness Madness.

HAWKINS, "PUNY"
Died: Mar. 30, 1947, Wichita, Kans. (heart attack). Screen, stage and radio actor. Appeared in silent films.

HAWKS, CHARLES MONROE
Born: 1874. Died: Dec. 15, 1951, Los Angeles, Calif. Screen actor. Appeared in silents.

HAWLEY, ALLEN BURTON
Born: 1895. Died: Sept. 1925, Troy, N.Y. Screen actor. Entered films approx. 1915. Divorced from screen actress Wanda Hawley.

HAWLEY, DUDLEY
Born: 1879, England. Died: Mar. 29, 1941, New York, N.Y. (coronary thrombosis). Stage and screen actor.

Appeared in: 1917 An American Widow. 1930 Young Man of Manhattan.

HAWLEY, ORMI
Born: 1890. Died: June 3, 1942, Rome, N.Y. Screen actor.

Appeared in: 1912 The Price of a Silver Fox; The Social Secretary; The Reformation of Kid Hogan; A New Beginning; Honor and the Sword; The Puppet's Hour; Fire and Straw; The Choir at Densmere; Together; The Crooked Path; Satin and Gingham; The Good-for-Nothing; 'Twixt Love and Ambition; The Players; His Life; When Love Leads; The Shepherd's Flute; The Montebank's Daughter. 1913 A Miracle of Love; A Mother's Strategy; Literature and Love; The House in the Woods; Her Only Son; The Soul of a Rose; Dolores' Decision; Women of the Desert; Tamandra, the Gypsy; A Moonshiner's Wife; The Call of the Heart; Into the Light; Fashion's Toy. 1914 The Two Roses; Through Fire to Fortune; Codes of Honor; The Price; Strength of Family Ties; The Ragged Earl; His Brother's Blood; A Love of '64. 1915 The Insurrection; The Path of the Rainbow; Destiny's Skein; The Intriguers; The Friendship of Lamond; The Shanghaied Baby; The Rainy Day; The Thief in the Night; Such Things Really Happen; Just Retribution; The Phantom Happiness; The Telegrapher's Peril; The Last Rebel; The Man of God; The Second Shot; A Heart Awakened. 1916 The Last Shot; Temptation; The Social Highwayman; The Weakness of Strength. 1917 The Antics of Anne; Runaway Romany. 1918 The Splendid Romance; Mrs. Dane's Defense. 1919 The Road Called Straight; The Unwritten Code.

HAWN, JOHN "HAPPY JACK"
Born: 1883. Died: Feb. 12, 1964, Fresno, Calif. Screen actor and stuntman.

HAWTREY, ANTHONY
Born: Jan. 22, 1909, Claygate, Surrey, England. Died: Oct. 18, 1954, London, England (heart attack). Stage and screen actor. Son of actor Sir Charles Hawtrey (dec. 1923).

Appeared in: 1943 Warn that Man; Headline. 1945 The World Owes Me a Living; The Hundred Pound Window; Latin Quarter. 1948 The First Gentleman (aka Affairs of a Rogue—US 1949).

HAWTREY, SIR CHARLES
Born: 1858, England. Died: July 30, 1923, London, England. Screen, stage actor and stage producer. Father of actor Anthony Hawtrey (dec. 1954). Do not confuse with British actor Charles Hawtrey born in 1914.

Appeared in: 1913 A Message from Mars. 1915 A Honeymoon for Three. 1917 Masks and Faces.

HAY, MARY
Born: Aug. 22, 1901, Fort Bliss, Tex. Died: June 4, 1957, Inverness, Calif. Stage and screen actress. Former Ziegfeld Follies star. Divorced from actor Richard Barthelmess (dec. 1963).

Appeared in: 1920 Way Down East. 1925 New Toys.

HAY, WILLIAM "WILL"
Born: 1888, Stockton-on-Tees, England. Died: Apr. 18, 1949, London, England. Screen, stage, vaudeville, radio actor, screenwriter, screen director and author. Father of actor Will Hay, Jr.

Appeared in: 1933 Know Your Apples (short). 1934 Those Were the Days; Radio Parade of 1935 (US 1935). 1935 Dandy Dick; Boys Will be Boys. 1936 Windbag the Sailor; Where There's a Way. 1937 Good Morning, Boys (aka Where There's a Will—US); Oh, Mr. Porter! 1938 Convict 99; Hey! Hey! USA; Old Bones of the River. 1939 Ask a Policeman; Where's That Fire? 1941 The Ghost of St. Michael's; The Black Sheep of Whitehall. 1942 The Big Blockade; The Goose Steps Out; Go to Blazes! (short). 1943 My Learned Friend.

HAYAKAWA, SESSUE (Kintaro Hayakawa)
Born: June 10, 1889, Chiba, Japan. Died: Nov. 23, 1973, Tokyo, Japan (cerebral thrombosis complicated by pneumonia). Screen, stage actor, film producer and author. Married to actress Tsuru Aoki (dec. 1961). Father of actress Yoshiko and dancer Fujiko Hayakawa. Nominated for 1957 Academy Award as Best Supporting Actor in Bridge on the River Kwai.

Appeared in: 1914 The Typhoon (film debut); The Last of the Line (aka Pride of Race); The Wrath of the Gods (aka The Destruction of Sakura Jima); The Ambassador's Envoy; The Vigil. 1915 The Secret Sin; After Five; The Clue; The Cheat. 1916 Alien Souls; Temptation; The Honorable Friend; The Soul of Kura-San. 1917 The Jaguar's Claw; Forbidden Paths; Each to His Kind; The Debt; The Victoria Cross (aka Honour Redeemed); The Bottle Imp; Hashimura Togo; The Call of the East; The Secret Game. 1918 The Temple of Dusk;

Hidden Pearls; The Honor of His House; The City of Dim Faces; The White Man's Law; The Bravest Way; His Birth Right. **1919** The Tong Man; The Dragon Painter; Bonds of Honor; Heart in Pawn; Courageous Coward; Gray Horizon (aka A Dead Line); Man Beneath; The Rajah's Amulet (reissue of Each to His Kind—1917); His Debt (aka The Debt). **1920** The Beggar Prince; The Brand of Lopez; The Devil's Claim; Liting Lang; An Arabian Knight. **1921** Black Roses; The First Born; The Swamp; Where Lights are Low. **1922** Five Days to Live; The Vermilion Pencil. **1923** La Bataille (aka The Danger Line—US 1924). **1924** The Great Prince Shan; J'ai Tue!; Sen Yan's Devotion. **1929** Sessue Hayakawa in The Man Who Laughed Last (short). **1931** Daughter of the Dragon. **1933** Tohjin Okichi. **1937** Yoshiwara; Fofaiture; Die Tochter des Samurai. **1938** Tempete sur L'Asie. **1939** Macao; L'Enfer du Jeu (Gambling Hall). **1941** Patrouille Blanche. **1946** Le Cabaret du Grand. **1947** Quartier Chinois. **1949** Tokyo Joe. **1950** Three Came Home; Les Miserables. **1953** Higego No Shogun Yamashita Yasubumi (The Tragic General, Yamashita Yasubumi). **1955** House of Bamboo. **1957** The Bridge on the River Kwai. **1958** The Geisha Boy. **1959** Green Mansions. **1960** Hell to Eternity; The Swiss Family Robinson. **1962** The Big Wave. **1966** The Daydreamer.

HAYDEL, RICHARD (aka RICKY JORDAN)
Born: May 31, 1927, Helena, Ark. Died: Sept. 1949, St. Louis, Mo. Screen actor.

Appeared in: **1944** Henry Aldrich, Boy Scout.

HAYDEN, HARRY
Born: 1882. Died: July 24, 1955, Los Angeles, Calif. Screen, stage and television actor.

Appeared in: **1936** I Married a Doctor; Fool Proof (short); Two against the World; Public Enemy's Wife; The Case of the Black Cat; God's Country and the Woman; The Man I Marry; Killer at Large; College Holiday. **1937** The Black Legion; Melody for Two; John Meade's Woman; Ever since Eve; Love Is on the Air. **1938** Little Tough Guy; Double Danger; Saleslady; Four Men and a Prayer; I'll Give a Million; Hold That Co-ed; Kentucky. **1939** Mr. Smith Goes to Washington; Wife, Husband and Friend; Rose of Washington Square; Frontier Marshal; The Rains Came; Here I Am a Stranger; The Honeymoon's Over; Barricade; Swanee River; Hidden Power; Flight at Midnight; At the Circus. **1940** The Cisco Kid and the Lady; He Married His Wife; Lillian Russell; Yesterday's Heroes; You're Not So Tough; Christmas in July; Saps at Sea. **1941** Sleepers West; Hold That Ghost; A Man Betrayed; The Parson of Panamint; The Night of January 16th; Remember the Day. **1942** Rings on Her Fingers; Whispering Ghost; Mississippi Gambler; Tales of Manhattan; Yankee Doodle Dandy; The Palm Beach Story; War against Mrs. Hadley; Joan of Ozark; Springtime in the Rockies; Get Hep to Love. **1943** Hello, Frisco, Hello; Meanest Man in the World; Submarine Alert. **1944** Barbary Coast Gent; Hail the Conquering Hero; The Big Noise; Weird Woman; Up in Mabel's Room; The Great Moment. **1945** Colonel Effingham's Raid; Boston Blackie's Rendezvous; Where Do We Go from Here; Guest Wife. **1946** The Blue Dahlia; Maid Trouble (short); The Virginian; If I'm Lucky; Two Sisters from Boston; The Killers; 'Til the Clouds Roll By. **1947** The Unfinished Dance; Key Witness; My Brother Talks to Horses; Merton of the Movies. **1948** Docks of New Orleans; Every Girl Should Be Married; Good Sam. **1949** The Judge Steps Out; Beautiful Blonde from Bashful Bend; Bad Men of Tombstone; Deadly Is the Female; Joe Palooka in the Big Fight; Mr. Whitney Had a Notion; The Lone Wolf and His Lady; Prison Warden; Abbott and Costello Meet the Killer, Boris Karloff. **1950** Intruder in the Dust; Traveling Saleswoman; Union Station. **1951** Double Dynamite; Pier 23; Street Bandits; Deal Me In (short); Angels in the Outfield. **1952** Army Bound; Carrie; O'Henry's Full House; When in Rome. **1953** The Last Posse; Money from Home.

HAYDEN, MARGARET. See MARGARET HAYDEN RORKE

HAYDOCK, JOHN
Died: Jan. 19, 1918, New York, N.Y. Screen actor.

HAYE, HELEN
Born: Aug. 28, 1874, Assam, India. Died: Sept. 1, 1957, London, England. Stage and screen actress.

Appeared in: **1916** Honour in Pawn. **1917** Masks and Faces. **1918** Not Negotiable. **1919** His Last Defense. **1920** Bleak House; The Skin Game. **1921** Tilly of Bloomsbury. **1929** Atlantic. **1930** Knowing Men; Beyond the Cities; The Brat (aka The Nipper); The Officer's Mess. **1931** The Skin Game (and 1920 version); Brown Sugar; Der Kongress Tanzt (Congress Dances—US 1932). **1932** Monte Carlo Madness; Her First Affair. **1933** It's a Boy! (US 1934); This Week of Grace. **1934** Crazy People; Money Mad. **1935** The Love Affair of the Dictator (aka The Dictator and The Loves of a Dictator—US); Drake of England (aka Drake the Pirate—US); The 39 Steps. **1936** The Interrupted Honeymoon; Everybody Dance; Wolf's Clothing. **1937** Wings of the Morning; The Girl in the Taxi; Remember When; Cotton Queen. **1938** St. Martin's Lane (aka Sidewalks of London—US 1940). **1939** The Spy in Black (aka U-Boat 29—US); A Girl Must Live (US 1941). **1940** The Case of the Frightened Lady (aka The Frightened Lady—US 1941). **1941** Kipps (aka The Remarkable Mr. Kipps—US 1942). **1943** The Man in Grey; Dear Octopus (aka The Randolph Family—US 1945). **1944** Fanny by Gaslight (aka Man of Evil—US 1948). **1945** A

Place of One's Own (US 1949). **1947** Mine Own Executioner; Mrs. Fitzherbert (US 1950). **1948** Anna Karenina. **1949** Third Time Lucky (US 1950); Conspirator (US 1950). **1954** Front Page Story (US 1955); Hobson's Choice; Lilacs in the Spring (aka Let's Make Up—US). **1955** Richard III (US 1956). **1956** My Teenage Daughter (aka Teenage Bad Girl—US 1957). **1957** Action of the Tiger. **1958** The Gypsy and the Gentleman.

HAYES, CARRIE
Born: 1878. Died: Dec. 22, 1954, Philadelphia, Pa. Screen and stage actress. Appeared in silent films.

HAYES, CATHERINE
Born: 1886. Died: Jan. 4, 1941, Los Angeles, Calif. Screen, stage and vaudeville actress.

Appeared in: **1933** Zoo in Budapest; Warrior's Husband.

HAYES, FRANK
Born: 1875. Died: Dec. 28, 1923, Hollywood, Calif. (pneumonia). Screen, stage and vaudeville actor.

Appeared in: **1915** Colored Villainy; Mabel, Fatty and the Law (reissue of Fatty's Spooning Day); Stolen Magic. **1916** Fatty and Mabel Adrift; Fido's Fate; A Bath House Blunder; Her Marble Heart; Madcap Ambrose. **1917** His Uncle Dudley. **1918** A Hoosier Romance. **1921** The Killer; The Lure of Egypt; The Man of the Forest; Mysterious Rider. **1922** Golden Dreams; Heart's Haven; The Old Homestead; When Romance Rides. **1923** Double Dealing; Souls in Bondage; Vanity Fair. **1924** Greed.

HAYES, GEORGE
Born: Nov. 13, 1888, London, England. Died: July 13, 1967, England? Stage and screen actor. Do not confuse with American actor George "Gabby" Hayes (dec. 1969).

Appeared in: **1935** Inside the Room; Old Roses; Emil and the Detectives (aka Emil—US 1938); The Guv'nor (aka Mister Hobo—US 1938). **1936** Land Without Music (aka Forbidden Music—US 1938); Wolf's Clothing; Everything Is Thunder. **1937** Death Croons the Blues. **1938** Break the News (US 1941); No Parking; The Return of the Frog. **1939** The Mind of Mr. Reeder (aka The Mysterious Mr. Reeder—US 1940); Secret Journey (aka Among Human Wolves—US 1940); Come on George. **1940** Spy for a Day. **1941** East of Piccadilly (aka The Strangler—US 1942). **1946** Great Expectations (US 1947). **1948** Esther Waters.

HAYES, GEORGE "GABBY"
Born: May 7, 1885, Wellesville, N.Y. Died: Feb. 9, 1969, Burbank, Calif. (heart ailment). Screen, stage and television actor. Married to actress Dorothy Earle (dec. 1958). Appeared in both Hopalong Cassidy film series and Roy Rogers film series.

Appeared in: **1929** The Rainbow Man (film debut); Smiling Irish Eyes. **1930** For the Defense. **1931** Rose of the Rio Grande; God's Country and the Man; Cavalier of the West; Nevada Buckaroo; Big Business Girl. **1932** Dragnet Patrol; Border Devils; Night Rider; Riders of the Desert; The Man from Hell's Edges; From Broadway to Cheyenne; Klondike; Texas Buddies; The Boiling Point; The Fighting Champ; Without Honor; Love Me Tonight; The Slippery Pearls (short). **1933** Wild Horse Mesa; Sagebrush Trail; Self Defense; Trailing North; Return of Casey Jones; Skyway; Gallant Fool; The Ranger's Code; Galloping Romeo; The Fugitive; The Phantom Broadcast; The Sphinx; Crashing Broadway; Breed of the Border; Fighting Texans; Devil's Mate; Riders of Destiny. **1934** In Old Santa Fe; Brand of Hate; Monte Carlo Nights; The Man from Utah; The Star Packer; West of the Divide; The Lucky Texan; Beggars in Ermine; Mystery Liner; Blue Steel; Randy Rides Alone; City Limits; The Lost Jungle (serial). **1935** Justice of the Range; Smokey Smith; The Throwback; $1,000 a Minute; Tumbling Tumbleweeds; Texas Terror; Lawless Frontier; Death Flies East; Rainbow Valley; The Hoosier School-Master; Honeymoon Limited; Headline Woman; Ladies Crave Excitement; Thunder Mountain; Hopalong Cassidy; The Eagle's Brood; Bar 20 Rides Again; Mister Hobo; Hitch Hike Lady; The Lost City (serial); Welcome Home. **1936** Call of the Prairie; Three on a Trail; The Lawless Nineties; Glory Parade; Hearts in Bondage; I Married a Doctor; Mr. Deeds Goes to Town; Heart of the West; Swiftly; The Texas Rangers; Valiant Is the Word for Carrie; Hopalong Cassidy Returns; The Plainsman; Trail Dust. **1937** Borderland; Hills of Old Wyoming; Mountain Music; North of the Rio Grande; Rustler's Valley; Hopalong Rides Again; Texas Trail. **1938** Forbidden Music; Gold Is Where You Find It; Bar 20 Justice; Pride of the West; In Old Mexico; Sunset Trail; The Frontiersman; Emil. **1939** Man of Conquest; Let Freedom Ring; Southward Ho!; In Old Caliente; In Old Monterey; Wall Street Cowboy; The Arizona Kid; Saga of Death Valley; Silver on the Sage; Days of Jesse James; The Renegade Trail; Fighting Thoroughbreds. **1940** Wagons Westward; The Dark Command; Young Buffalo Bill; The Carson City Kid; The Ranger and the Lady; Colorado; Young Bill Hickok; Melody Ranch; The Border Legion. **1941** Robin Hood of the Pecos; In Old Cheyenne; Sheriff of Tombstone; Nevada City; Jesse James at Bay; Bad Man of Deadwood; Red River Valley; The Voice in the Night; Frightened Lady. **1942** South of Santa Fe; Sunset on the Desert; Romance of the Range; Man of Cheyenne; Sons of the Pioneers; Sunset Serenade; Heart of the Golden West; Ridin' Down the Canyon. **1943** Calling Wild Bill Elliott; Bordertown Gunfighters; Wagon Tracks West; The Man from Thunder River; Death Valley Manhunt; In Old Oklahoma. **1944** Tucson Raiders; Leave It to the Irish; Mojave Firebrand; Tall in the Saddle; Lights of Old Santa Fe; Hidden Valley Outlaws; Marshal of Reno. **1945** Utah; The Big Bonanza; The Man from Oklahoma; Sunset in Eldorado; Don't Fence Me In; Out California Way; Bells of Rosarita; Along the Navajo Trail. **1946** My Pal Trigger; Home in Oklahoma; Badman's Territory; Song of Arizona; Rainbow over Texas; Roll on Texas Moon; Under Nevada Skies. **1947** Helldorado; Trail Street; Bells of San Angelo; Wyoming; The Trespasser; Great Expectations. **1948** Albuquerque; Slippy McGee; The Untamed Breed; Return of the Bad Men. **1949** Susanna Pass; Golden Stallion; Bells of Coronado; Trigger, Jr.; El Paso. **1950** The Cariboo Trail; Twilight in the Sierras. **1951** Pals of the Golden West.

HAYES, LAURENCE C.
Born: 1903. Died: Nov. 17, 1974, New York, N.Y. (heart complications). Screen, stage and television actor. Married to actress Anita Webb.

HAYES, SAM (Samuel Stewart Hayes)
Born: 1905, Cookesville, Ill. Died: July 28, 1958, San Diego, Calif. (heart attack). Screen actor and radio announcer.

Appeared in: **1937** Ali Baba Goes to Town. **1938** Rebecca of Sunnybrook Farm. **1939** They Made Me a Criminal; Tail Spin. **1941** High Sierra. **1946** Joe Palooka—Champ. **1947** Joe Palooka in the Knockout; The Checkered Coat. **1949** Fighting Fools; Maggie and Jiggs in Jackpot Jitters; Joe Palooka in the Counterpunch.

HAYES, SIDNEY
Born: 1865. Died: May 2, 1940, Beverly Hills, Calif. Screen, stage and vaudeville actor. Appeared in vaudeville in an act billed as "Hayes and Hayes."

HAYES, WILLIAM
Born: 1887. Died: July 13, 1937, Hollywood, Calif. (heart attack). Screen actor.

Appeared in: **1921** Get-Rich-Quick Wallingford. **1924** Flashing Spurs. **1925** A Gentleman Roughneck; Lena Rivers. **1926** Ace of Action; Cupid's Knockout; Hollywood Reporter. **1930** Terry of the Times (serial).

HAYLE, GRACE
Born: 1889. Died: Mar. 20, 1963, Los Angeles, Calif. Screen actress.

Appeared in: **1934** Wonder Bar; Twenty Million Sweethearts. **1937** Tovarich. **1939** Death of a Champion; Forgotten Woman; The Women; Mr. Moto in Danger Island; The Starmaker; Lady of the Tropics. **1940** Our Neighbors, the Carters; The Great Dictator. **1942** Madame Spy; Just Off Broadway; Crossroads; I Married an Angel. **1943** Footlight Glamour; Let's Face It. **1952** Don't Bother to Knock. **1953** Houdini; Money from Home.

HAYNES, ARTHUR
Born: 1914. Died: Nov. 19, 1966, London, England (heart attack). Screen, vaudeville, radio and television actor.

Appeared in: **1964** Strange Bedfellows. **1965** Doctor in Clover (aka Carnaby, M.D.—US 1967).

HAYNES, DANIEL L.
Died: July 23, 1954, Kingston, N.Y. Black screen and stage actor and clergyman.

Appeared in: **1929** Hallelujah (first all black film). **1932** The Last Mile. **1935** So Red the Rose; Escape from Devil's Island. **1936** The Invisible Ray.

HAYWARD, SUSAN (Edythe Marrener)
Born: June 30, 1918, Brooklyn, N.Y. Died: Mar. 14, 1975, Beverly Hills, Calif. (brain tumor). Screen and television actress. Divorced from actor Jess Barker. Married to Floyd Eaton Chalkley (dec. 1966). Won 1958 Academy Award for Best Actress in I Want to Live. Nominated for 1947 Academy Award as Best Actress in Smash Up; in 1949 for My Foolish Heart; in 1952 for With a Song in My Heart; and in 1955 for I'll Cry Tomorrow.

Appeared in: **1937** Hollywood Hotel. **1938** Comet Over Broadway; The Sisters; Girls on Probation. **1939** Beau Geste; $1,000 a Touchdown; Our Leading Citizen. **1941** Among the Living; Sis Hopkins; Adam Had Four Sons. **1942** Reap the Wild Wind; The Forest Rangers; Star Spangled Rhythm; I Married a Witch. **1943** Young and Willing; Hit Parade of 1943. **1944** And Now Tomorrow; The Fighting Seabees; The Hairy Ape. **1945** Murder—He Says. **1946** Canyon Passage; Deadline at Dawn. **1947** The Lost Moment; They Won't Believe Me; Smash-Up—The Story of a Woman (aka A Woman Destroyed). **1948** The Saxon Charm; Tap Roots. **1949** Change of Heart (reissue of Hit Parade of 1943); House of Strangers; Tulsa; My Foolish Heart. **1951** I Can Get It for you Wholesale; I'd Climb the Highest Mountain; Rawhide; David and Bathsheba. **1952** The Lusty Men; The Snows of Kilimanjaro; With a Song in My Heart. **1953** The President's Lady; White Witch Doctor. **1954** Garden of Evil; Demetrius and the Gladiators. **1955** Untamed; Soldier of Fortune; I'll Cry Tomorrow. **1956** The Conqueror. **1957** Top Secret Affair. **1958** I Want to Live.

1959 Thunder in the Sun; Woman Obsessed. **1960** The Marriage-Go-Round. **1961** Back Street; Ada. **1962** I Thank a Fool. **1963** Stolen Hours. **1954** Where Love Has Gone. **1967** The Honey Pot; Valley of the Dolls. **1972** The Revengers.

HAYWORTH, VINTON J.
Born: 1906. Died: May 21, 1970, Van Nuys, Calif. (heart attack). Screen, stage, radio and television actor.

Appeared in: **1956** The Girl He Left Behind; The Great Man. **1961** Police Dog Story. **1966** Chamber of Horrors.

HAZEL, HY (Hyacinth Hazel O'Higgins)
Born: 1920. Died: May 10, 1970, London, England. Screen and stage actress.

Appeared in: **1946** Meet Me at Dawn (US 1948). **1947** Just Williams' Luck (US 1948). **1949** Paper Orchid; Celia. **1950** The Body Said No; The Lady Craved Excitement; The Gay Duellist (reissue of Meet Me at Dawn—1947). **1951** Franchise Affair (US 1952). **1952** The Yellow Balloon (US 1954); The Night Won't Talk. **1953** Forces' Sweetheart. **1955** Stolen Assignment. **1956** Up in the World; Anastasia. **1957** The Mail Van Murder; Light Fingers; The Key Man. **1958** The Whole Truth. **1960** Trouble with Eve (aka In Trouble with Eve—US 1964). **1961** Five Golden Hours. **1962** What Every Woman Wants.

HAZELTON, JOSEPH
Born: 1853. Died: Oct. 8, 1936, Hollywood, Calif. Screen and stage actor.

Appeared in: **1921** False Kisses; "If Only" Jim; The Little Minister. **1922** Oliver Twist. **1937** Mountain Justice.

HAZLETT, WILLIAM. *See* CHIEF MANY TREATIES

HEALY, DAN
Born: 1889. Died: Sept. 1, 1969, Jackson Heights, N.Y. Stage and screen actor, song and dance man. Married to singer and actress Helen Kane (dec. 1966).

Appeared in: **1929** The Laughing Lady; Glorifying the American Girl. **1931** The Unfair Sex (short).

HEALY, TED
Born: Oct. 1, 1896, Houston, Tex. Died: Dec. 21, 1937, Los Angeles, Calif. (heart attack). Screen, stage, radio and vaudeville actor. Billed in vaudeville as "Ted Healy and His Racketeers" and "Ted Healy and His Stooges."

Appeared in: **1930** Soup to Nuts; Hollywood on Parade (short). **1932** Meet the Baron. **1933** Stage Mother; Bombshell; Dancing Lady; Turn Back the Clock; plus the following shorts: Beer and Pretzels; Hello Pop; Plane Nuts. **1934** Myrt and Marge; Fugitive Lovers; Hollywood Party; Death on the Diamond; The Band Plays On; Lazy River; Operation 13; Paris Interlude (short). **1935** The Winning Ticket; The Casino Murder Case; La Fiesta de Santa Barbara (short); Reckless; Murder in the Fleet; Mad Love; Here Comes the Band; It's in the Air. **1936** Speed; San Francisco; The Longest Night; Mad Holiday; Sing, Baby, Sing. **1937** Man of the People; Varsity Show (short); Hollywood Hotel; Good Old Soak. **1938** Love Is a Headache.

HEARN, EDWARD "EDDIE" (Guy Edward Hearn)
Born: Sept. 6, 1888, Dayton, Wash. Died: Apr. 15, 1963. Stage and screen actor.

Appeared in: **1915** The White Scar. **1916** The Lost Lode; Should She Have Told?; Idle Wives; Her Bitter Cup; The Seekers; **1917** Patsy; The Lost Express (serial); The Trapping of Two-Bit Tuttle; The American Girl series; Sage Brush Law. **1918** Lure of Luxury. **1919** The Undercurrent; The Last of His People. **1920** The Coast of Opportunity; Down Home. **1921** The Avenging Arrow (serial); All Dolled Up; Face of the World; Keeping Up with Lizzie; Things Men Do. **1922** The Fire Bride; Colleen of the Pines; The Flirt; The Glory of Clementina; Her Night of Nights; A Question of Honor; The Truthful Liar. **1923** The Love Letter; Mind over Motor; The Town Scandal; Daytime Wives; The Miracle Baby. **1924** When a Man's a Man; The Dangerous Blonde; Daughters of Today; Excitement; The Turmoil; Winner Take All. **1925** Lawful Cheaters; The Man Without a Country; One of the Bravest; Daring Days; The Outlaw's Daughter. **1926** Peril of the Rail; The Sign of the Claw; The Still Alarm. **1927** The Harvester; The Heart of the Yukon; Hero on Horseback; Hook and Ladder No. 9; Pals in Peril; Spuds; Winners of the Wilderness; The Desert Pirate. **1928** The Big Hop; Dog Justice; The Fightin' Readhead; The Yellow Cameo (serial). **1929** The One Man Dog; The Bachelor Girl; The Donovan Affair; The Drake Case; Ned McCobb's Daughter; Dare Devil Jack. **1930** Hide-Out; Reno; The Spoilers. **1931** The Vanishing Legion (serial); The Galloping Ghost (serial); The Avenger; Ex-Bad Boy; Son of the Plains. **1932** Cheyenne Cyclone; Rainbow Trail; Local Bad Man. **1933** Fighting with Kit Carson. **1934** Burn 'Em Up Barnes (serial and feature film); Texas Tornado; Fighting Hero; Young and Beautiful; Fighting Through; In Old Santa Fe; Mystery Mountain (serial). **1935** Behind the Green Lights; Tumbling Tumbleweeds; Hot Off the Press; The Miracle Rider (serial); Confidential; Headline Woman. **1936** King of the Pecos; Boss Rider of Gun Creek; Red River Valley. **1937** Anything for a Thrill; Springtime in the Rockies; Trouble at Midnight. **1939** West of Santa Fe. **1940** Remedy for Riches. **1941** Holt of the Secret Service (serial). **1943** Air Raid Wardens. **1951** Pistol Harvest.

HEARN, SAM

Born: 1889, New York, N.Y. Died: Oct. 28, 1964, Los Angeles, Calif. (heart attack). Screen, stage, radio and television actor. Best known for his role of "Schlepperman" on Jack Benny's radio and television programs.

Appeared in: **1936** Florida Special; The Big Broadcast for 1937. **1942** The Man in the Trunk. **1949** Inspector General. **1953** The I Don't Care Girl. **1958** Once upon a Horse.

HEATH, TED

Born: 1902, Wadsworth, London, England. Died: Nov. 18, 1969, Virginia Water, England. Band leader, screen and radio actor.

Appeared in: **1956** It's a Wonderful World (US 1961). **1960** Jazz Boat. **1961** Ted Heath and His Music (short).

HEATHERLEY, CLIFFORD (Clifford Lamb)

Born: Oct. 8, 1888, Preston, Lancashire, England. Died: Sept. 15, 1937, London, England. Stage and screen actor.

Appeared in: **1911** Henry VIII. **1920** Bleak House; The Tavern Knight. **1921** The Autumn of Pride; The Mystery of Mr. Bernard Brown. **1922** The Adventures of Sherlock Holmes (series). **1926** The Sea Urchin; The Steve Donoghue (series) including: Beating the Book; Mademoiselle from Armentieres; Boadicea. **1927** The King's Highway; Roses of Picardy; The Rolling Road. **1928** The Constant Nymph; The Passing of Mr. Quin; Tesha; Champagne. **1929** High Treason. **1930** The Compulsory Husband; The "W" Plan (US 1931); Symphony in Two Flats. **1931** The Love Habit; Glamour; Who Killed Doc Robin?; My Old China. **1932** Goodnight Vienna (aka Magic Night—US); Help Yourself; Brother Alfred; Indiscretions of Eve; Fires of Fate (US 1933); Happy Ever After; After the Ball; A Letter of Warning. **1933** Discord; The Little Damozel; Forging Ahead; Cash (aka For Love or Money—US 1934); Bitter Sweet; Yes, Mr. Brown; Beware of Women; I Adore You. **1934** Trouble in the Store; Catherine the Great; The Church Mouse (US 1935); Get Your Man; The Private Life of Don Juan; Adventure Limited; The Queen's Affair (aka Runaway Queen—US 1935). **1935** Abdul the Damned; A Little Bit of Bluff; No Monkey Business; Our Husband. **1936** Cafe Mascot; The Invader (aka An Old Spanish Custom—US); Show Flat; Reasonable Doubt; If I Were Rich. **1937** Feather Your Nest; It's Not Cricket; Don't Get Me Wrong; There Was a Young Man.

HEATTER, GABRIEL

Born: 1890, New York, N.Y. Died: Mar. 30, 1972, Miami Beach, Fla. (pneumonia). Radio newscaster, journalist, television producer and screen actor.

Appeared in: **1950** Champagne for Caesar. **1951** The Day the Earth Stood Still.

HECHT, BEN

Born: Feb. 1894, New York, N.Y. Died: Apr. 18, 1964, New York, N.Y. (heart attack). Newspaperman, novelist, screenwriter, screen director, producer and screen actor. Father of actress Jenny Hecht (dec. 1971).

Appeared in: **1935** The Scoundrel.

HECHT, JENNY

Born: July 30, 1943, New York, N.Y. Died: Mar. 25, 1971, North Hollywood, Calif. Stage and screen actress. Daughter of screenwriter Ben Hecht (dec. 1964).

Appeared in: **1952** Actors and Sin (aka Woman of Sin) (short). **1971** The Jesus Trip.

HECHT, TED (Theodore Hekt)

Born: 1908, New York, N.Y. Died: June 24, 1969, Los Angeles, Calif. Screen, stage and television actor.

Appeared in: **1942** Time to Kill (film debut); Manila Calling. **1943** So Proudly We Hail; Corregidor; Rookies in Burma. **1944** Dragon Seed; End of the Road. **1945** Three's a Crowd; Counterattack; The Lost Weekend. **1946** The Fighting Guardsman; Just Before Dawn. **1947** Tarzan and the Huntress; Spoilers of the North; The Gangster; Riding the California Trail. **1948** Man Eater of Kumaon. **1949** Apache Chief; Bad Men of Tombstone; Song of India; Tarzan's Magic Fountain. **1950** Tall Timber; Blue Grass of Kentucky; Killer Shark; Sideshow; Abbott and Costello in the Foreign Legion. **1953** Desert Legion. **1955** Abbott and Costello Meet the Mummy.

HEDLUND, GUY E.

Born: Aug. 21, 1884, Connecticut. Died: Dec. 29, 1964, Culver City, Calif. (injuries from being hit by auto). Screen actor.

Appeared in: **1909** Pippa Passes. **1910** Wilful Peggy; The Broken Doll; The Modern Prodigal. **1911** The Squaw's Love; The Revenue Man and the Girl; Bobby the Coward; A Country Cupid; The Ruling Passion; The Rose of Kentucky; The Sorrowful Example; Swords and Hearts; The Stuff Heroes Are Made Of; The Old Confectioner's Mistake; The Eternal Mother; Dan the Dandy.

HEFLIN, VAN (Emmet Evan Heflin)

Born: Dec. 13, 1910, Walters, Okla. Died: July 23, 1971, Hollywood, Calif. (heart attack). Screen, stage and television actor. Divorced from actress Frances Neal. Won 1941 Academy Award for Best Supporting Actor in Johnny Eager.

Appeared in: **1936** A Woman Rebels (film debut). **1937** The Outcasts of Poker Flat; Flight from Glory; Annapolis Salute; Saturday's Heroes; Salute to Romance. **1939** Back Door to Heaven. **1940** Santa Fe Trail. **1941** The Feminine Touch; H. M. Pulham, Esq.; Johnny Eager. **1942** Kid Glove Killer; Grand Central Murder; Seven Sweethearts; Tennessee Johnson. **1943** Presenting Lily Mars. **1946** The Strange Love of Martha Ivers; 'Til the Clouds Roll By. **1947** Green Dolphin Street; Possessed. **1948** B. F.'s Daughter; Act of Violence; The Three Musketeers; Tap Roots; Secret Land (narr.). **1949** East Side, West Side; Madame Bovary. **1951** The Prowler; Weekend with Father; Tomahawk. **1952** South of Algiers (aka The Golden Mask—US 1954); My Son, John. **1953** Shane; Wings of the Hawk. **1954** Tanganyika; The Raid; Woman's World; Black Widow. **1955** Battle Cry; Count Three and Pray. **1956** Patterns. **1957** 3:10 to Yuma. **1958** Gunman's Walk. **1959** Tempest; They Came to Cordura. **1960** Five Branded Women; Under Ten Flags. **1961** Il Relitto (The Wastrel, aka To Be a Man—US 1963). **1963** Cry of Battle. **1965** The Greatest Story Ever Told; Once a Thief. **1966** Stagecoach. **1968** The Man Outside; Das Gold von Sam Cooper (Sam Cooper's Gold aka Each Man for Himself and The Ruthless Four—US 1969). **1969** The Trackers; The Big Bounce. **1970** Airport. **1972** Revengers.

HEGGIE, O. P.

Born: Sept. 17, 1879, Angaston, South Australia. Died: Feb. 7, 1936, Los Angeles, Calif. (pneumonia). Screen and stage actor.

Appeared in: **1928** The Actress. **1929** The Letter; The Mysterious Dr. Fu Manchu; The Wheel of Life. **1930** Broken Dishes; Playboy of Paris; Sunny; The Mighty; The Vagabond King; The Return of Dr. Fu Manchu; The Bad Man; One Romantic Night. **1931** The Women Between; Too Young to Marry; Devotion; East Lynne. **1932** Smilin' Through. **1933** The King's Vacation; Zoo in Budapest. **1934** Anne of Green Gables; Count of Monte Cristo; Peck's Bad Boy; Midnight. **1935** Chasing Yesterday; Dog of Flanders; Return of Frankenstein; Ginger; Bride of Frankenstein. **1936** Prisoner of Shark Island.

HEGIRA, ANNE

Died: c. 1971. Screen actress. Divorced from actor and director Elia Kazan.

Appeared in: **1954** On the Waterfront. **1963** Love With the Proper Stranger. **1969** The Arrangement.

HEIDEMANN, PAUL "PAULCHEN"

Born: 1886, Cologne, Germany. Died: June 20, 1968, Berlin, Germany. Stage and screen actor.

Appeared in: **1931** Der Hampelmann (The Jumping Jack); Ihre Hoheit Befiehlt. **1932** Kyritz-Pyritz; Schoen 1st die Manoeverzeit; Pension Schoeller; Wenn die Soldaten. **1934** Die Mutter der Kompagnie; Ja, Treu 1st die Soldatenliebel; Wie Man Maenner Fesselt; Abel Mit der Mundharmonika; Liebe in Uniform. **1935** Drie von der Kavallerie; Der Schuechterne Felix; Der Tolle Bomberg. **1936** Der Vetter aus Dingsda; Die Ganze Welt Dreht Sich um Liebe; 1st Mein Mann Nich Fabelhaft; Der Junge Graf. **1937** Freuhling im Wien; Hilde Petersen; Postlagernd; Der Unwiderst Ehliche (The Irresistable Man). **1938** Der Lachdoktor (The Laugh Doctor). **1940** Peter, Paul and Nanette.

HELD, ANNA

Born: Mar. 8, 1873, Paris, France. Died: Aug. 12, 1918, New York, N.Y. (pneumonia, pernicious anemia). Screen and stage actress. Married to stage producer Florenz Ziegfeld (dec. 1932).

Appeared in: **1902** Anna Held. **1916** Madame La Presidente.

HELLINGER, MARK

Born: Mar. 21, 1903, New York, N.Y. Died: Dec. 21, 1947, Hollywood, Calif. (heart attack). Journalist, playwright, film producer and screen actor. Married to actress Gladys Glad.

Appeared in: **1943** Thank Your Lucky Stars.

HELMS, RUTH

Died: Oct. 27, 1960. Screen actress. Divorced from actor Conrad Nagel (dec. 1970) and film director Sidney Franklyn.

HELTON, PERCY

Born: 1894, N.Y. Died: Sept. 11, 1971, Hollywood, Calif. Screen, stage and television actor.

Appeared in: **1916** The Flower of Faith. **1922** Silver Wings. **1947** Miracle on 34th Street. **1948** Hazard; Call Northside 777; Let's Live Again; Chicken Every Sunday; That Wonderful Urge; Larceny, Inc. **1949** Thieves' Highway; The Crooked Way; Criss Cross; The Set-Up; My Friend Irma; Abbott and Costello Meet the Killer, Boris Karloff. **1950** Harbor of Missing Men; Copper Canyon; Wabash Avenue; The Sun Sets at Dawn; Cyrano de Bergerac; Under Mexicali Skies; Fancy Pants; Tyrant of the Sea. **1951** Chain of Circumstance; The Barefoot Mailman. **1952** A Girl in Every Port; The Belle of New York; I Dream of Jeanie. **1953** Down Laredo Way; Call Me Madam; The Robe; How to Marry a Millionaire; Wicked Woman; The Stooge; Scared Stiff; Ambush at Tomahawk Gap. **1954** 20,000 Leagues under the Sea; A Star Is Born; About Mrs.

Leslie; White Christmas. **1955** Kiss Me Deadly; Crashout; No Man's Woman; Jail Busters. **1956** Fury at Gunsight Pass; Terror at Midnight; Shake, Rattle and Rock. **1957** The Phantom Stagecoach; Spook Chasers; Looking for Danger. **1958** Rally 'Round the Flag, Boys! **1962** The Music Man; Ride the High Country. **1963** Four for Texas; The Wheeler Dealers. **1965** Hush, Hush, Sweet Charlotte; Zebra in the Kitchen; The Sons of Katie Elder. **1966** Don't Worry, We'll Think of a Title. **1968** Head; Funny Girl. **1969** Butch Cassidy and the Sundance Kid.

HEMINGWAY, RICHARD C.
Died: Date unknown. Screen actor. Divorced from actress Irene Bentley (dec. 1965).

Appeared in: **1934** Woman Condemned; Hell Cat. **1935** Society Fever.

HEMSLEY, ESTELLE
Born: May 5, 1887, Boston, Mass. Died: Nov. 4, 1968, Los Angeles, Calif. Screen, stage, radio and television actress.

Appeared in: **1950** Harvey (stage and film versions). **1957** Edge of the City. **1959** Green Mansions. **1960** Take a Giant Step; The Leech Woman. **1963** America, America. **1965** Baby, The Rain Must Fall.

HENCKLES, PAUL
Born: 1885, Hurth, Germany. Died: 1967, near Kettwich, Dusseldorf, Germany. Stage and screen actor.

Appeared in: **1928** Shadows of Fear. **1930** Last Company; Hungarian Nights. **1931** Mother Love; Skandal um Eva; Der Wahre Jakob; Die Lindenwirtin vom Rhein. **1932** Der Ungetreue Eckehart; Man Braucht Kein Geld. **1934** Die-oder Keine. **1935** Die Finanzen des Grossherzogs (The Grand Duke's Finances); Hermine und die Sieben Aufrechten; Pantoffelhelden; Der Tolle Bomberg. **1936** Glueckliche Reise; Zwischen Zwei Herzen (Between Two Hearts); Das Erbe in Pretoria; Alte Kameraden; Der Wackere Schustermeister; Alle Tage ist Kein Sonntag. **1937** Das Einmaleins der Liebe; Ein Idealer Gatte; Schabernack. **1938** Eine Seefahrt die ist Lustig (A Merry Sea Trip); Der Florentiner Hut (The Leghorn Hat); Die Glaserne Kugel (The Glass Ball). **1940** Peter, Paul and Nanette. **1949** Palace Scandal. **1958** The Confessions of Felix Krull; Das Tanzende Herz (The Dancing Heart); Griff Nach den Sternen (Reaching for the Stars). **1959** Das Unsterbliche Herz (The Immortal Heart). **1960** Liebe Kann Wie Gift Sein (Love Can be Like Poison aka Magdalena—US).

HENDEE, HAROLD F.
Born: 1879. Died: June 24, 1966, New York, N.Y. Screen and stage actor. Appeared in films during the 1920s.

HENDERSON, DEL (George Delbert Henderson)
Born: July 5, 1883, St. Thomas, Ontario, Canada. Died: Dec. 2, 1956, Hollywood, Calif. Screen, stage actor and film director. Entered films as a director with D. W. Griffith in 1909 and later turned to acting. Also directed several Mack Sennett films. Married to actress Florence Lee (dec. 1962).

Appeared in: **1909** Lines of White on a Sullen Sea. **1910** The Purgation; That Chink at Golden Gulch; When a Man Loves. **1911** Teaching Dad to Like Her; The Two Sides; The Poor Sick Men; Conscience; The Crooked Road; In the Days of '49; The Last Drop of Water; The Jealous Husband; The Ghost; The Baron; The Making of a Man; A Victim of Circumstances; A String of Pearls; Comrades. **1912** Who Got the Reward?; The Fatal Chocolate; A Message From the Moon. **1913** The Battle of Elderberry Gulch. **1916** Intolerance. **1926** The Clinging Vine. **1927** Getting Gertie's Garter. **1928** Wrong Again (short); Riley the Cop; The Patsy; The Crowd; Power of the Press; Three-Ring Marriage; Show People. **1930** The Richest Man in the World; Hit the Deck; Sins of the Children; plus the following shorts: Whispering Whoopee; All Teed Up; Fast Work; Looser Than Loose; Bigger and Better; The Laurel and Hardy Murder Case. **1931** The Champ; Playthings of Hollywood; Newly Rich; plus the following shorts: Helping Grandma; Thundering Tenors; Skip the Maloo! **1932** The following shorts: Choo Choo; In Walked Charley; Mr. Bride. **1933** Too Much Harmony; I Have Lived; From Hell to Heaven; The Big Brain; Rainbow Over Broadway. **1934** Lone Cowboy; The Notorious Sophie Lang; The Lemon Drop Kid; The Marines Are Coming; Mrs. Wiggs of the Cabbage Patch; It's A Gift; Search for Beauty; Bolero; You're Telling Me; The Old Fashioned Way; Bottoms Up; Something Simple (short); Men in Black (short). **1935** Ruggles of Red Gap; Slightly Static (short); Here Comes Cookie; Diamond Jim; The Mystery Man; Fighting Youth; Hot Tip; Hitch Hike Lady; The Daring Young Man; Black Sheep; This Is the Life. **1936** Our Relations; Poppy. **1937** Artists and Models; Make Way for Tomorrow. **1938** Rebellious Daughters; Goodbye Broadway. **1939** Frontier Marshal. **1940** Little Orvie; You Can't Fool Your Wife; If I Had My Way. **1944** Nothing But Trouble. **1945** Wilson. **1965** Laurel and Hardy's Laughing 20's (documentary).

HENDERSON, GEORGE A.
Born: New York, N.Y. Died: Nov. 28, 1923, San Francisco, Calif. (stroke). Screen, stage and vaudeville actor.

Appeared in: **1923** The Fog.

HENDERSON, GRACE
Born: 1860, Ann Arbor, Mich. Died: Oct. 30, 1944, New York, N.Y. Screen, stage actress and screenwriter.

Appeared in: **1909** Lucky Jim; A Corner in Wheat. **1910** The Marker Time-Table; The Purgation; A Midnight Cupid; The Usurer; His Trust Fulfilled. **1911** The Barren; The Diving Girl; A Convenient Burglar; The Old Confectioner's Mistake; Sunshine Through the Dark; A String of Pearls; Enoch Arden Part I; Her Sacrifice; The Unveiling. **1912** An Unseen Enemy.

HENDERSON, IVO
Born: England. Died: Apr. 12, 1968. Stage and screen actor.

Appeared in: **1936** Rogue's Tavern. **1937** Bulldog Drummond Comes Back. **1938** Adventures of Robin Hood.

HENDERSON, LUCIUS
Born: 1848. Died: Feb. 18, 1947, N.Y. Screen, stage, vaudeville actor, film director and film producer.

Appeared in: **1923** Toilers of the Sea. **1925** A Man Must Live; The New Commandment. **1926** The Great Deception; White Mice.

HENDERSON, STEFFI (Stephanie Le Beau)
Died: June 5, 1967, New York. Screen and television actress. Married to composer and arranger Luther Henderson.

Appeared in: **1966** Picture Mommy Dead.

HENDERSON, TALBOT V.
Born: 1879. Died: May 24, 1946, Los Angeles, Calif. Screen and stage actor.

Appeared in: **1929** The Bachelors' Club.

HENDERSON-BLAND, ROBERT
Born: England. Died: Aug. 18, 1941, London, England. Screen and stage actor.

Appeared in: From Manger to Cross.

HENDRICKS, BEN, SR.
Born: 1862, Buffalo, N.Y. Died: Apr. 30, 1930, Hollywood, Calif. Screen, stage and vaudeville actor. Father of actor Ben Hendricks, Jr. (dec. 1938).

Appeared in: **1923** Big Dan. **1924** The City That Never Sleeps. **1925** Greater Than a Crown; Tides of Passion; Welcome Home. **1926** Satan Town. **1930** Black Waters.

HENDRICKS, BEN, JR.
Born: Nov. 2, 1893, New York, N.Y. Died: Aug. 15, 1938, Los Angeles, Calif. Screen actor. Son of actor Ben Hendricks, Sr. (dec. 1930). Entered films in 1911.

Appeared in: **1921** The Land of Hope; Room and Board. **1922** The Headless Horseman; Free Air. **1923** The Broad Road; The Old Fool; Marriage Morals. **1924** Cyclone Rider; Just off Broadway; Against All Odds; The Man Who Played Square. **1926** Take It from Me; The Fighting Buckaroo; One Minute to Play; Rolling Home; Skinner's Dress Suit; What Happened to Jones? **1927** Barbed Wire; Birds of Prey; A Racing Romeo. **1928** My Friend from India; Waterfront. **1929** Footlights and Fools; The Great Divide; Twin Beds; Synthetic Sin; The Wild Party. **1930** Men without Women; The Furies; The Girl of the Golden West; Ladies Love Brutes; Road to Paradise; Sunny. **1931** The Public Enemy. **1932** Rain; Pack up Your Troubles; Fireman Save My Child; The Kid from Spain; Fast Life; The Woman from Monte Carlo. **1933** Out All Night; The Important Witness; After Tonight. **1934** The Big Shakedown; We're Not Dressing; Blind Date. **1935** Northern Frontier; O'Shaughnessy's Boy. **1936** Draegerman Courage; North of Nome. **1937** Slim; Roaring Timber. **1938** Sergeant Murphy; Born to Be Wild.

HENDRICKS, LOUIS
Born: Buffalo, N.Y. Died: Dec. 18, 1923 (long illness). Stage and screen actor.

Appeared in: **1921** The Conquest of Canaan; The Sign on the Door. **1923** The Custard Cup.

HENDRIKSON, ANDERS
Born: 1896, Stockholm, Sweden. Died: 1965, Sweden. Screen actor, film director and writer.

Appeared in: **1921** Sir Arne's Treasure. **1934** The Song of the Scarlet Flower. **1937** Oh What a Night. **1938** John Ericsson—The Victor at Hampton Roads; Frun Tillhanda (Servant Girls). **1939** They Staked Their Lives. **1940** Everybody at His Station; Hennes Lilla Majestat (Her Little Majesty). **1941** Life Goes On. **1942** Youth in Chains. **1943** Mr. Collin's Adventures. **1944** I Am Fire and Air; Henlaspelet. **1945** Tired Teodor. **1946** Asa-Hanna. **1947** The Key and the Ring. **1949** Fangelse (aka The Devil's Wanton—US 1962). **1950** Blood and Fire. **1952** Miss Julie. **1956** The Girl in the Dress-Coat; Giftas (Married Life aka Of Love and Lust—US 1959). **1962** Pojken I Tradet (The Boy in the Tree). **1965** Morianerna (aka I, the Body aka Morianna—US 1967). Other Swedish films: It Pays to Advertise; The Great Love; Only a Trumpeter; A Crime; Only a Woman; Dangerous Roads; The Ingegerd Bremssen Case; Train 56; Nothing

But Old Nobility; Blood and Fire; The Most Beautiful Thing on Earth; Alfred Loved by the Girls; Walpurgis Night; 33.333; Intermezzo; Conflict; A Cold in the Head; Let's Have Success; With the People for the Country; Mr. Karlsson Mate and His Sweethearts; A Woman's Face; Rejoice While You are Young; At the Lady's Service; Home from Babylon; The Road to Heaven; I Killed; Defiance; Love; The Journey to You; The Road to Klockrike; Barabbas; The Clergyman of Uddarbo.

HENDRIX, JIMI

Born: 1947. Died: Sept. 18, 1970, London, England (drug overdose). Guitarist, screen actor and singer.

Appeared in: 1969 Monterey Pop; Popcorn—An Audio/Visual Rock Thing. 1970 Woodstock. 1972 Superstars in Film Concert. 1973 Free; Jimi Plays Berkeley; Keep on Rockin' Jimi Hendrix; Rainbow Bridge.

HENDRIX, N. E. "SHORTY"

Died: Mar. 4, 1973. Screen actor.

Appeared in: 1924 Walloping Wallace; Battling Buddy; Cyclone Buddy; Galloping Gallagher. 1925 Double Action Daniels; Reckless Courage. 1926 Double Daring. 1930 Oklahoma Cyclone.

HENIE, SONJA

Born: Apr. 8, 1912, Oslo, Norway. Died: Oct. 12, 1969, in air near Oslo (leukemia). Screen, television actress and Olympic skating star.

Appeared in: 1936 One in a Million (film debut). 1937 Thin Ice. 1938 Happy Landing; My Lucky Star. 1939 Second Fiddle; Everything Happens at Night. 1941 Sun Valley Serenade. 1942 Iceland. 1943 Wintertime. 1945 It's a Pleasure. 1948 The Countess of Monte Cristo. 1961 Hello, London.

HENLEY, HOBART

Born: Nov. 23, 1891, Louisville, Ky. Died: May 22, 1964, Los Angeles, Calif. Screen, stage actor, film director and producer. Appeared in one-reelers produced in New York during early days of film.

Appeared in: 1914 Forgetting; When There's A Will, There's A Way; His Land Chance. 1915 Graft; The House of Fear; The Black Pearl; The Bombay Buddha; Court Martialed; Agnes Kempler's Sacrifice; The Eagle; A Little Brother of the Rich; The Silent Battle; The Phantom Fortune; The Measure of Leon Dubray; The Man in the Chair; The Terror. 1916 The Rogue With a Heart; A Dead Yesterday; The Crystal's Warning; Somewhere on the Battlefield; Temptation and the Man; A Child of Mystery; Partners; A Knight of the Night; The Sign of the Poppy; The Evil Women Do. 1917 A Woman of Clay. 1918 Parentage.

HENNEBERGER, BARBARA-MARIE "BARBI"

Born: 1941. Died: Apr. 12, 1964, St. Moritz, Switzerland (avalanche). West German ski champion and screen actress. Killed while making a sports documentary.

HENNECKE, CLARENCE R.

Born: Sept. 16, 1894, Omaha, Nebr. Died: Aug. 28, 1969, Santa Monica, Calif. Screen, vaudeville, television actor, film director and screenwriter. Entered films as a stuntman with Vitagraph. Appeared in Keystone Kop comedies.

Appeared in: 1950 Joe Palooka in Humphrey Takes a Chance.

HENNESSEY, DAVID

Born: 1852. Died: Mar. 24, 1926, Chicago, Ill. Screen and stage actor.

HENNING, PAT

Born: 1911. Died: Apr. 28, 1973, Miami, Fla. Screen, vaudeville, television actor, and circus performer.

Appeared in: 1938 Shine on Harvest Moon. 1953 Man on a Tightrope. 1954 On the Waterfront. 1958 Wind Across the Everglades. 1963 The Cardinal. 1969 Hello Down There.

HENNINGS, JOHN

Died: Nov. 8, 1933, St. Joseph, Mo. (suicide—gun shot). Stage and screen actor.

Appeared in: 1930 The Poor Millionaire.

HENRY, FRANK THOMAS PATRICK

Born: 1894. Died: Oct. 3, 1963, Hollywood, Calif. Screen and vaudeville actor.

HENRY, JAY

Born: July 14, 1910, New York, N.Y. Died: Dec. 23, 1951, White Plains, N.Y. Screen actor.

Appeared in: 1934 We're Not Dressing.

HENRY, JOHN

Born: 1882. Died: Aug. 12, 1958, Winthrop, Mass. Screen and vaudeville actor.

Appeared in: 1924 Poison; Those Who Judge; Yankee Speed.

HENRY, JOHN, JR.

Died: May 2, 1974. Screen actor.

HENRY, ROBERT "BUZZ"

Born: Sept. 4, 1931, Colorado. Died: Sept. 30, 1971, Los Angeles, Calif. (motorcycle accident). Screen actor, stuntman and rodeo performer.

Appeared in: 1936 The Unknown Ranger. 1940 Buzzy Rides the Range. 1941 Phantom Pinto (aka Buzzy and the Phantom Pinto); Mr. Celebrity. 1944 Trigger Trail; Three of a Kind; The Great Mike; Trail to Gunsight. 1945 The Virginian. 1946 Hop Harrigan (serial); Danny Boy; Wild Beauty; Son of the Guardsman (serial); Wild West. 1947 Last of the Redmen; Law of the Canyon; King of the Wild Horses. 1948 Tex Granger (serial); Moonrise; Prairie Outlaws. 1950 Blue Grass of Kentucky; Rocky Mountain. 1951 Heart of the Rockies. 1952 Against All Flags. 1953 The Homesteaders; Jubilee Trail; Last of the Pony Riders. 1954 The Outcast; Bamboo Prison; Hell's Outpost; Man With the Steel Whip. 1955 The Indian Fighters; The Road to Denver. 1956 Jubal; Duel at Apache Wells; 54 Washington Street. 1957 The Lawless Eighties; 3:10 to Yuma. 1958 Cowboy; The Sheepman; Tonka; Imitation General. 1959 Face of a Fugitive. 1960 The Rise and Fall of Legs Diamond. 1962 The Manchurian Candidate. 1963 Captain Newman, MD; Spencer's Mountain. 1964 Seven Days in May. 1965 The Rounders; Von Ryan's Express. 1966 Major Dundee; Our Man Flint; Texas Across the River. 1967 Tony Rome; In Like Flint; Waterhole #3. 1969 The Wild Bunch; Mackenna's Gold. 1970 Scullduggery; Macho Callahan.

HENSON, LESLIE

Born: Aug. 3, 1891, London, England. Died: Dec. 2, 1957, England. Stage and screen actor.

Appeared in: 1916 The Lifeguardsman; Wanted a Widow; The Real Thing. 1920 Broken Bottles; Alf's Button. 1924 Tons of Money. 1927 On With the Dance series. 1930 A Warm Corner. 1931 The Sport of Kings. 1933 It's a Boy! (US 1934); The Girl from Maxim's. 1935 Oh Daddy! 1943 The Demi-Paradise (aka Adventure for Two—US 1945). 1956 Home and Away.

HEPBURN, BARTON

Born: Feb. 28, 1906, Minneapolis, Minn. Died: Oct. 10, 1955, Hollywood, Calif. Stage and screen actor. Entered films in 1928.

Appeared in: 1929 Dynamite. 1930 Painted Faces. 1943 Hi Diddle Diddle. 1944 The Bridge of San Luis Rey. 1945 A Song for Miss Julie.

HEPWORTH, CECIL M.

Born: 1874, England. Died: Feb. 9, 1953, Greenford, Middlesex, England. Film producer, director, actor and screen writer. Married to actress Mrs. Cecil Hepworth.

Appeared in: 1900 The Bathers; Topsy-Turvy Villa. 1901 Interior of a Railway Carriage—Bank Holiday. 1902 The Call to Arms; How to Stop a Motor Car; Peace with Honour. 1903 Alice in Wonderland; The Tragical Tale of a Belated Letter; The Unclean World—The Suburban Bunkum Microbe-Guyoscope. 1904 The Joke that Failed; The Great Servant Question; The Honeymoon—First, Second and Third Class. 1905 Rescued by Rover; Bathers Will be Prosecuted.

HERBERT, HANS

Born: 1875. Died: June 21, 1957, Hollywood, Calif. Screen, stage and television actor.

Appeared in: 1943 The Phantom of the Opera. 1944 Mr. Skeffington. 1945 House of Frankenstein. 1950 Under My Skin.

HERBERT, HELEN

Born: 1873. Died: Oct. 27, 1946, Hollywood, Calif. Screen and stage actress. Entered films approx. 1924.

HERBERT, HENRY J.

Born: England. Died: Feb. 20, 1947, Flushing, N.Y. Screen and stage actor.

Appeared in: 1921 Suspicious Wives. 1923 The Day of Faith. 1924 Daughters of Today; Week-End Husbands; So Big; Stolen Secrets; Captain Blood. 1925 The Range Terror. 1926 The Blue Streak; The Mystery Club. 1927 The Girl from Rio; Whispering Smith Rides (serial); One Chance in a Million. 1928 Laddie Be Good; Look-Out Girl. 1930 Their Own Desire.

HERBERT, HOLMES E. (Edward Sanger)

Born: July 3, 1882, Mansfield Notts, England. Died: Dec. 26, 1956, Hollywood, Calif. Screen, stage, circus and minstrel actor.

Appeared in: 1918 The Doll's House. 1919 The White Heather. 1920 Black Is White; His House in Order; My Lady's Garter; The Right to Love; Lady Rose's Daughter. 1921 The Inner Chamber; The Family Closet; The Wild Goose; Heedless Moths; Her Lord and Master. 1922 Any Wife; A Woman's Woman; Divorce Coupons; Evidence; A Stage Romance; Moonshine Valley. 1923 Toilers of the Sea. 1924 Love's Wilderness; The Enchanted Cottage; Another Scandal; Sinners in Heaven; Her Own Free Will. 1925 Daddy's Gone A'Hunting; A Woman of the World; Wreckage; Up the Ladder; Wildfire. 1926

The Honeymoon Express; The Wanderer; The Passionate Quest; Josselyn's Wife. **1927** The Fire Brigade; East Side, West Side; Lovers?; Mr. Wu; The Heart of Salome; One Increasing Purpose; The Silver Slave; When a Man Loves; Slaves of Beauty; The Gay Retreat; The Nest. **1928** The Terror; On Trial; Gentlemen Prefer Blondes; The Sporting Age; Their Hour; Through the Breakers. **1929** Madame X; The Charlatan; Careers; The Careless Age; Her Private Life; The Kiss; The Thirteenth Chair; Untamed; Say It with Songs. **1930** The Ship from Shanghai. **1931** Chances; Broadminded; Daughter of Fu Manchu; The Hot Heiress; The Single Sin; Daughter of the Dragon. **1932** Dr. Jekyll and Mr. Hyde; Shop Angel; Central Park; Miss Pinkerton. **1933** Mystery of the Wax Museum; Sister of Judas; The Invisible Man. **1934** Beloved; The House of Rothschild; Count of Monte Cristo; The Curtain Falls; One in a Million; Pursuit of Happiness. **1935** Captain Blood; Cardinal Richelieu; Mark of the Vampire; Sons of Steel; Accent on Youth. **1936** The Country Beyond; 15 Maiden Lane; Lloyds of London; Brilliant Marriage; The Gentleman from Louisiana. **1937** Slave Ship; The Girl Said No; Here's Flash Casey; The Prince and the Pauper; Love under Fire; Lancer Spy; The Thirteenth Chair (and 1929 version); House of Secrets. **1938** The Adventures of Robin Hood; The Buccaneer; Mystery of Mr. Wong; Say It in French; The Black Doll. **1939** Juarez; Trapped in the Sky; Mr. Moto's Last Warning; The Little Princess; Hidden Power; Stanley and Livingstone; The Adventures of Sherlock Holmes; Everything Happens at Night; We Are Not Alone; Wolf Call; Bad Boy. **1940** South of Suez; British Intelligence. **1941** Man Hunt; International Squadron. **1942** This above All; Invisible Agent; The Undying Monster; The Ghost of Frankenstein; Sherlock Holmes and the Secret Weapon. **1943** Corvette K-225; Two Tickets to London; Sherlock Holmes in Washington. **1944** The Uninvited; Our Hearts Were Young and Gay; The Pearl of Death; The Bermuda Mystery; Enter Arsene Lupin; The Mummy's Curse; Calling Dr. Death. **1945** Jealousy; The House of Fear; Confidential Agent. **1946** Three Strangers; The Verdict; Sherlock Holmes and the Secret Code (aka Dressed to Kill). **1947** This Time for Keeps; Over the Santa Fe Trail; Singapore; Bulldog Drummond Strikes Back; Bulldog Drummond at Bay; The Swordsman. **1948** Johnny Belinda; Wreck of the Hesperus; Jungle Jim. **1949** Barbary Pirate; Post Office Investigator. **1950** The Iroquois Trail. **1951** David and Bathsheba; Anne of the Indies; Law and the Lady. **1952** At Sword's Point; The Brigand.

HERBERT, HUGH
Born: Aug. 10, 1887, Binghamton, N.Y. Died: Mar. 13, 1952, North Hollywood, Calif. (heart attack). Screen, stage, vaudeville, television actor, playwright and screenwriter. Brother of actor Thomas Herbert (dec. 1946). Married to actress Anita Pam (dec. 1974).

Appeared in: **1927** Realization (short); Solomon's Children (short) **1928** The Lemon (short); On the Air (short); The Prediction (short); Husbands for Rent; Caught in the Fog. **1930** Danger Lights; Hook, Line and Sinker; Mind Your Own Business; Sin Ship. **1931** Laugh and Get Rich; Traveling Husbands; Friends and Lovers. **1932** The Lost Squadron; Faithless; Million Dollar Legs. **1933** Strictly Personal; Diplomaniacs; Goodbye Again; Bureau of Missing Persons; Footlight Parade; College Coach; From Headquarters; She Had to Say Yes; Convention City; Goldie Gets Along. **1934** Fashions of 1934; Easy to Love; Dames; Kansas City Princess; Wonder Bar; Harold Teen. Merry Wives of Reno; Fog over Frisco; The Merry Frinks. **1935** The Traveling Saleslady; Gold Diggers of 1935; A Midsummer Night's Dream; We're in the Money; Miss Pacific Fleet; To Beat the Band; Sweet Adeline. **1936** Colleen; Love Begins at 20; Sing Me a Love Song; One Rainy Afternoon; We Went to College. **1937** That Man's Here Again; The Singing Marine; Marry the Girl; The Perfect Specimen; Sh! The Octopus; Hollywood Hotel; Top of the Town. **1938** Men Are Such Fools; Gold Diggers in Paris; Four's a Crowd; The Great Waltz. **1939** Eternally Yours; Dad for a Day (short); The Little Accident; The Family Next Door; The Lady's from Kentucky. **1940** La Conga Nights; Private Affairs; Slightly Tempted; A Little Bit of Heaven; The Villain Still Pursued Her; The Hit Parade of 1941. **1941** Hellzapoppin!; Cracked Nuts; Meet the Chump; The Black Cat; Hello Sucker; Badlands of Dakota; Nobody's Fool. **1942** Mrs. Wiggs of the Cabbage Patch; There's One Born Every Minute; Don't Get Personal; You're Killing Me. **1943** It's a Great Life; Stage Door Canteen. **1944** Kismet; Beauty for Sale; Ever since Venus; Music for Millions. **1946** One Way to Love; Carnegie Hall; The Mayor's Husband (short); When the Wife's Away (short). **1947** Blondie in the Dough. **1948** A Miracle Can Happen; So This is New York; A Song Is Born; Girl from Manhattan; On Our Merry Way. **1949** Beautiful Blonde from Bashful Bend. **1951** Havana Rose.

HERBERT, LEW
Born: 1903. Died: July 30, 1968, Pittsburgh, Pa. Screen, stage and television actor.

Appeared in: **1950** Young Man with a Horn. **1963** Love with a Proper Stranger.

HERBERT, THOMAS F.
Born: Nov. 25, 1888, New York, N.Y. Died: Apr. 3, 1946, Los Angeles, Calif. Screen, stage and vaudeville actor. Brother of actor Hugh Herbert (dec. 1952).

Appeared in: **1931** Traveling Husbands. **1933** Bed of Roses. **1934** Belle of the Nineties. **1937** Topper; Banjo on My Knee; Think Fast; Mr. Moto; Stars over Arizona. **1938** Professor Beware. **1940** Remedy for Riches. **1942** Tennessee Johnson.

HERIAT, PHILIPPE
Born: 1898, France. Died: Oct. 1971, France. Screen actor, author and screenwriter.

Appeared in: **1925** Les Miracles des Loups (The Miracle of the Wolves). **1929** Sea-Fever. **1938** Rothschild.

HERLEIN, LILLIAN
Born: c. 1895. Died: Apr. 13, 1971, New York, N.Y. Screen, stage, vaudeville, radio and television actress.

Appeared in: **1922** Solomon in Society.

HERMAN, AL
Born: 1886. Died: July 2, 1967, Los Angeles, Calif. Screen actor.

Appeared in: **1924** Captain Blood. **1926** Beyond the Trail. **1928** The Assassin of Grief (short). **1931** Bad Company. **1935** Harmony Lane. **1937** Hollywood Cowboy; Talent Scout; Paid to Dance; Torchy Blane, the Adventurous Blonde; Manhattan-Merry-Go-Round; Headin' East. **1939** Conspiracy; Swanee River. **1940** Oklahoma Renegades. **1952** Dream Boat.

HERMAN, JILL KRAFT
Born: 1931, N.Y. Died: June 25, 1970, Chicago, Ill. (cancer). Screen, stage and television actress.

Appeared in: **1951** Goodbye, My Fancy.

HERMAN, MILTON C.
Born: 1896. Died: Jan. 21, 1951, Astoria, N.Y. (coronary thrombosis). Screen, radio and television actor.

HERMAN, TOM
Born: 1909. Died: Mar. 26, 1972, Hollywood, Calif. Screen actor and professional prizefighter.

Appeared in: **1956** The Harder They Fall.

HERMINE, HILDA
Died: June 15, 1975. Screen actress.

HERNANDEZ, ALBERT
Born: 1899, Mexico. Died: Jan. 2, 1948, Los Angeles, alif. (after a fall). Screen actor. Appeared in silent films.

HERNANDEZ, ANNA (Anna Dodge)
Born: Oct. 19, 1867, River Falls, Wis. Died: May 4, 1945, Los Angeles, Calif. (pneumonia). Stage and screen actress. Married to actor George Hernandez (dec. 1922).

Appeared in: **1915** The Rosary; The Heritage. **1918** Battling Jane. **1919** Hearts Asleep; Leave it to Susan. **1920** The Gift Supreme; The Jack Knife; Darling Mine; Burglar Proof; An Amateur Devil (aka Wanted—A Blemish). **1921** Molly O'; The Rowdy. **1922** The Kentucky Derby. **1923** The Town Scandal; The Extra Girl. **1924** Name the Man; The Law Forbids. **1931** Fainting Lover (short); The Cannonball (short). **1932** Speed in the Gay Nineties.

HERNANDEZ, GEORGE F.
Born: June 6, 1863, Placerville, Calif. Died: Dec. 1922, Los Angeles, Calif. Stage and screen actor. Married to actress Anna Hernandez (dec. 1945).

Appeared in: **1912** When Helen was Elected; How the Cause Was Won; The Great Drought; Her Education; The Count of Monte Cristo. **1914** Footprints; Who Killed George Graves?; One Traveler Returns. **1915** The Lady of Cyclamen. **1917** The Greater Law; Broadway Arizona. **1918** Betty Takes a Hand. **1919** Mary Regan; The Silver Girl; Be a Little Sport; Courageous Coward. **1920** Village Sleuth; Seeds of Vengeance. **1921** After Your Own Heart; First Love; Just Out of College; The Innocent Cheat; The Lure of Egypt; The Road Demon. **1922** Arabia; Billy Jim; Bluebird, Jr.; The Man Under Cover; Flaming Hearts.

HERNANDEZ, JUAN G. "JUANO"
Born: 1896, San Juan, Puerto Rico. Died: July 17, 1970, San Juan, Puerto Rico (cerebral hemorrhage). Black screen, stage and circus actor.

Appeared in: **1949** Intruder in the Dust; The Accused. **1950** Stars in My Crown; The Breaking Point; Young Man with a Horn. **1955** Kiss Me Deadly; The Trial. **1956** Ransom. **1957** Something of Value. **1958** The Roots; St. Louis Blues; Machete; The Mark of the Hawk. **1960** Sergeant Rutledge. **1961** The Sins of Rachel Cade; Two Loves. **1962** Hemingway's Adventures of a Young Man. **1965** The Pawnbroker. **1969** The Reivers; The Extraordinary Seaman. **1970** They Call Me Mr. Tibbs.

HERRNFELD, ANTON
Born: 1865. Died: Oct. 1929, Berlin, Germany. Yiddish screen and stage actor.

HERSHFIELD, HARRY (Abe Kabible)
Born: 1885. Died: Dec. 15, 1974, New York, N.Y. Cartoonist, journalist, humorist and screen actor.

Appeared in: **1942** The Great White Way.

HERSHOLT, JEAN
Born: July 12, 1886, Copenhagen, Denmark. Died: June 2, 1956, Beverly Hills, Calif. (cancer). Screen, stage and radio actor. Won 1939 Special Academy Award for his work for the Motion Picture Relief Fund and won 1949 Special Award for Dancing in the Dark.

Appeared in: **1915** Don Quixote. **1916** Princess Virtue. **1921** The Four Horsemen of the Apocalypse; A Certain Rich Man; The Man of the Forest; The Servant in the House. **1922** Tess of the Storm Country; Golden Dreams; The Gray Dawn; Heart's Haven; When Romance Rides. **1923** Jazzmania; Quicksands; The Stranger's Banquet; Red Lights. **1924** Cheap Kisses; The Goldfish; Her Night of Romance; Sinners in Silk; Torment; The Woman on the Jury; Greed. **1925** Dangerous Innocence; Don Q; Fifth Avenue Models; So Big; If Marriage Fails; Stella Dallas; A Woman's Faith. **1926** Flames; The Greater Glory; It Must Be Love; My Old Dutch; The Old Soak. **1927** The Student Prince in Old Heidelberg; The Wrong Mr. Wright. **1928** Alias the Deacon; The Battle of the Sexes; Give and Take; Jazz Mad; The Secret Hour; 13 Washington Square; Abie's Irish Rose. **1929** The Girl on the Barge; Modern Love; The Younger Generation; You Can't Buy Love. **1930** The Case of Sergeant Grischa; The Cat Creeps; The Climax; Hell Harbor; Mamba; The Third Alarm; Viennese Nights; The Rise of Helga. **1931** Transatlantic; Susan Lennox, Her Rise and Fall; Sin of Madelon Claudet; Daybreak; Soldier's Plaything; Phantom of Paris; Private Lives; Lullaby. **1932** Emma; Grand Hotel; Hearts of Humanity; The Mask of Fu Manchu; Beast of the City; Are You Listening?; Night Court; New Morals for Old; Skyscraper Souls; Unashamed; Justice for Sale; Flesh. **1933** The Crime of the Century; Song of the Eagle; Dinner at Eight; Christopher Bean. **1934** Men in White; The Painted Veil; The Cat and the Fiddle; The Fountain. **1935** Mark of the Vampire; Murder in the Fleet; Break of Hearts. **1936** Tough Guy; His Brother's Wife; The Country Doctor; Sins of Man; Reunion; One in a Million; The Old Soak. **1937** Seventh Heaven; Heidi. **1938** Happy Landing; Alexander's Ragtime Band; I'll Give a Million; Five of a Kind. **1939** Mr. Moto in Danger Island; Meet Dr. Christian. **1940** The Courageous Dr. Christian; Dr. Christian Meets the Women; Remedy for Riches. **1941** They Meet Again; Melody for Three. **1943** Stage Door Canteen. **1949** Dancing in the Dark. **1955** Run for Cover.

HERTEL, ADOLPH R.
Born: 1878. Died: Mar. 16, 1958, Hollywood, Calif. Screen actor and film director.

HESLOP, CHARLES
Born: June 8, 1883, Thames Ditton, Surrey, England. Died: Apr. 13, 1966, London, England. Screen, stage and vaudeville actor.

Appeared in: **1920** Hobson's Choice. **1931** Sunshine Susie (aka The Office Girl—US 1932). **1933** This Is the Life (US 1935). **1934** Waltzes from Vienna (aka Strauss's Great Waltz—US 1935). **1935** Charing Cross Road. **1938** Crackerjack (aka The Man With a Hundred Faces—US). **1939** The Lambeth Walk (aka Me and My Girl—US 1940). **1942** Flying Fortress; The Peterville Diamond. **1950** Don't Say Die (aka Never Say Die). **1951** The Second Mate; The Late Edwina Black (aka Obsessed—US). **1959** Follow a Star (US 1961). **1962** A Pair of Briefs (US 1963).

HESSE, BARON WILLIAM
Born: 1885, Russia. Died: Apr. 4, 1936, West Coast, U.S. (following amputation of leg; also diabetes). Screen actor.

Appeared in: **1929** Prisoners.

HESTER, HARVEY
Died: 1967. Screen actor.

Appeared in: **1956** The Great Locomotive Chase.

HESTERBERG, TRUDE
Born: 1897, Berlin, Germany. Died: 1967, Munich, Germany. Stage and screen actress.

Appeared in: **1926** Manon Lescaut. **1927** Madame Wants No Children. **1929** Strauss—The Waltz King; Forbidden Love. **1932** Stuerm der Leidenschaft. **1934** In Wien Hab'Ich Einmal ein Maedel Geliebt. **1935** Der Page vom Dalmasse—Hotel; Die Grosse Chance. **1936** Alles Weg'n Dem Hund; Ist Mein Mann Nicht Fabelhaft. **1937** Der Unwiderst Ehliche (The Irresistable Man).

HEUSTON, ALFRED. See ALFRED H. HEWSTON

HEWITT, HENRY
Born: Dec. 28, 1885, London, England. Died: Aug. 1968, Newbury, England. Stage and screen actor.

Appeared in: **1931** Stamboul. **1932** Betrayal; The First Mrs. Fraser. **1934** Jew Suess (aka Power—US). **1935** Department Store (aka Bargain Basement). **1936** Rembrandt. **1937** The High Command. **1938** Just Like a Woman; Black Limelight (US 1939); Old Iron. **1940** Sailors Three (aka Three Cockeyed Sailors—US 1941). **1941** The Black Sheep of Whitehall. **1942** The Young Mr. Pitt; The Day Will Dawn (aka The Avengers—US). **1944** Give Us the Moon. **1951** Happy-Go-Lovely. **1952** Emergency Call (aka The Hundred Hour Hunt—US 1953); Top Secret (aka Mr. Potts Goes to Moscow—US 1954); Where's Charley? **1957** The Naked Truth (aka Your Past is Showing—US 1958).

HEWSTON, ALFRED H. (aka ALFRED HEUSTON)
Born: Sept. 12, 1880, San Francisco, Calif. Died: Sept. 6, 1947. Stage and screen actor. Son of stage actress Lillian O'Dell and actor Clarence King (dec.). Entered films in 1911.

Appeared in: **1915** Just Jim. **1920** The following shorts: Prince of Daffydill; Rocked to Sleep; Hay Fever; Henpecked and Pecked Hens; Sweet Dynamite. **1922** Blind Circumstances; The Hate Trail; Diamond Carlisle. **1923** The Web of the Law. **1924** Cyclone Buddy; Horse Fly Wiggins; Trail Dust. **1925** Let's Go Gallagher; The Wyoming Wildcat; Fightin' Odds; On the Go; Flashing Steeds; Tearin' Loose; Warrior Gap. **1926** Beyond All Odds; Masquerade Bandit; The Arizona Streak; Out of the West; Lure of the West. **1927** Spliting the Breeze. **1928** The Sky Rider. **1929** 'Neath Western Skies; The Cowboy and the Outlaw; Silent Sentinel; The Man from Nevada; West of the Rockies. **1930** Breezy Bill; Near the Rainbow's End; Firebrand Jordan. **1931** Rainbow Trail.

HEYBURN, WELDON
Born: Sept. 19, 1904, Selma, Ala. Died: May 18, 1951, Los Angeles, Calif. Stage and screen actor. His film career was hampered due to his resemblance to actor Clark Gable. Divorced from actress Greta Nissen.

Appeared in: **1932** Careless Lady; Chandu the Magician; Call Her Savage; The Gay Caballero; The Silent Witness. **1933** West of Singapore. **1934** Hired Wife. **1935** Convention Girl. **1936** Speed. **1937** Git Along Little Dogies; Sea Racketeers; Atlantic Flight; The Thirteenth Man. **1938** Saleslady; Crime School; The Mysterious Rider; Dynamite Delaney. **1939** Fugitive at Large; Panama Patrol; Should a Girl Marry? **1940** The Trail Blazers. **1941** Flight from Destiny; Redhead; Criminals Within; In Old Chicago; Stick to Your Guns; Jungle Man. **1942** Code of the Outlaw; Rock River Renegades; Murder in the Fun House. **1943** Death Valley Manhunt; Bordertown Trails; Code of the Prairie; Westward Bound; Yellow Rose of Texas. **1944** The Chinese Cat. **1946** Frontier Gun Law.

HEYDT, LOUIS JEAN
Born: Apr. 17, 1905, Montclair, N.J. Died: Jan. 29, 1960, Boston, Mass. Screen, stage and television actor. Entered films in 1937.

Appeared in: **1937** Make Way for Tomorrow. **1938** They're Always Caught (short); Test Pilot; I Am the Law. **1939** Charlie Chan at Treasure Island; Dad for a Day (short); Let Freedom Ring; They Made Her a Spy; Reno; Gone with the Wind; They Made Me a Criminal; Each Dawn I Die. **1940** A Child Is Born; The Man Who Talked Too Much; Pier 13; Let's Make Music; Abe Lincoln in Illinois; Dr. Ehrlich's Magic Bullet; All About Hash (short); The Hidden Master (short); The Great McGinty; Joe and Ethel Turp Call on the President. **1941** Sleepers West; Dive Bomber; Power Dive; Midnight Angel. **1942** Ten Gentlemen from West Point; Manila Calling; Tortilla Flat; Triumph over Pain; Commandos Strike at Dawn; Pacific Blackout; Captains of the Clouds. **1943** Mission to Moscow; Stage Door Canteen; Gung Ho. **1944** The Great Moment; See Here, Private Hargrove; Her Primitive Man; Thirty Seconds over Tokyo. **1945** Betrayal from the East; Our Vines Have Tender Grapes; Zombies on Broadway; They Were Expendable. **1946** The Big Sleep; The Hoodlum Saint; Gentleman Joe Palooka. **1947** I Cover Big Town; Spoilers of the North. **1948** California's Golden Beginning; Bad Men of Tombstone. **1949** Make Believe Ballroom; Come to the Stable; The Kid from Cleveland. **1950** The Great Missouri Raid; The Furies; Paid in Full. **1951** Raton Pass; Rawhide; Criminal Lawyer; Roadblock; Drums in the Deep South; Warpath; Two of a Kind; Sailor Beware. **1952** The Old West; Models, Inc. **1953** The Vanquished; Island in the Sky. **1954** Boy from Oklahoma. **1955** The Eternal Sea; Ten Wanted Men; No Man's Woman. **1956** Stranger at My Door; Wetbacks. **1957** Badge of Marshal Brennan; Raiders of Old California; The Wings of Eagles. **1958** The Man Who Died Twice. **1959** Inside the Mafia.

HEYES, HERBERT
Born: Aug. 3, 1889, Vaner, Wash. Died: May 30, 1958, North Hollywood, Calif. Stage and screen actor.

Appeared in: **1915** A Man Afraid; The Whirlpool. **1916** Under Two Flags; The Vixen; The Final Curtain; Wild Oats; Straight Way. **1917** The Outsider; The Tiger Woman; The Slave. **1918** The Heart of the Sunset; Salome; The Lesson; The Fallen Angel; Her Inspiration?; The Darling of Paris; Gambling in Souls. **1919** The Adventures of Ruth (serial). **1920** Ruth of the Rockies (serial). **1921** The Queen of Sheba; The Blushing Bride; The Dangerous Moment; Dr. Jim; Wolves of the North; Ever since Eve. **1922** Shattered Dreams. **1923** One Stolen

Night. **1924** It Is the Law. **1942** Destination Unknown; Tennessee Johnson. **1943** Calling Wild Bill Elliott; Campus Rhythm; Death Valley Manhunt; Mission to Moscow; It Ain't Hay. **1944** Detective Kitty O'Day; Outlaws of Santa Fe; Million Dollar Kid; Mr. Winkle Goes to War. **1945** Wilson. **1947** Miracle on 34th Street. **1948** T-Men; The Cobra Strikes; Behind Locked Doors. **1950** Kiss Tomorrow Goodbye; Tripoli; Union Station. **1951** Bedtime for Bonzo; Only the Valiant; A Place in the Sun; Three Guys Named Mike. **1952** Park Row; Carbine Williams; Ruby Gentry; Something to Live For. **1953** Man of Conflict; Let's Do It Again. **1955** The Court-Martial of Billy Mitchell; The Far Horizons; Love Is a Many Splendored Thing; New York Confidential; The Seven Little Foys; Sincerely Yours. **1956** The Ten Commandments.

HEYWOOD, HERBERT

Born: Feb, 1, 1881, Illinois. Died: Sept. 15, 1964, Van Nuys, Calif. (coronary thrombosis). Stage and screen actor.

Appeared in: **1934** Music in the Air; Gentlemen Are Born; Marie Galante; Caravan. **1935** Go Into Your Dance; Black Fury; Moonlight on the Prairie; Escape from Devil's Island; Ladies Crave Excitement. **1936** Road Gang; Draegerman Courage; King of the Pecos. **1937** Slave Ship. **1938** Born to be Wild; Three Blind Mice; Swing, Sister, Swing; King of the Lumberjacks; Blockade. **1940** No Time for Comedy; Legion of the Lawless; Little Old New York. **1941** Strawberry Blonde; Blues in the Night; The Great American Broadcast. **1942** Almost Married. **1943** Swingtime Johnny. **1946** Smoky. **1948** Green Grass of Wyoming; Scudda Hoo! Scudda Hay! **1950** Ticket to Tomahawk (aka The Sheriff's Daughter).

HIBBARD, EDNA

Born: 1895, Calif. Died: Dec. 26, 1942, New York, N.Y. Screen, stage and vaudeville actress.

Appeared in: **1922** Island Wives. **1930** An Ill Wind (short).

HIBBERT, GEOFFREY

Born: June 2, 1922, Hull, Yorkshire, England. Died: Feb. 3, 1969, Epsom, England (heart attack). Screen, stage and television actor.

Appeared in: **1941** Love on the Dole (stage and film versions); The Common Touch. **1942** The Next of Kin (US 1943); In Which We Serve. **1943** The Shipbuilders. **1952** Secret People; Emergency Call (aka The Hundred Hour Hunt—US 1955). **1953** Albert RN (aka Break to Freedom—US 1955). **1954** For Better, for Worse (aka Cocktails in the Kitchen—US 1955). **1957** The End of the Line. **1958** Orders to Kill. **1959** The Great Van Robbery (US 1963); Crash Dive. **1962** Live Now—Pay Later. **1963** Heavens Above!

HICKEY, HOWARD L.

Born: 1897. Died: Mar. 25, 1942, San Fernando, Calif. Screen actor and horse trainer.

HICKMAN, ALFRED D.

Born: Feb. 25, 1873, England. Died: Apr. 9, 1931, Hollywood, Calif. (cerebral hemorrhage). Stage and screen actor.

Appeared in: **1914** The Master Key (serial). **1917** Fall of The Romanoffs. **1919** The Mad Woman; Here Comes the Bride. **1924** The Enchanted Cottage. **1929** The Rescue. **1930** The Last of the Lone Wolf. **1931** Phantom of Paris; A Woman of Experience.

HICKMAN, HOWARD C.

Born: Feb. 9, 1880, Columbia, Mo. Died: Dec. 31, 1949, Los Angeles, Calif. (heart attack). Screen, stage actor and film director. Married to actress Bessie Barriscale (dec. 1965).

Appeared in: **1913** Rancho (film debut). **1916** Matrimony; Civilization. **1928** Alias Jimmy Valentine. **1930** Hello Sister; Brothers; The Broadway Hoofer; His First Command. **1931** Civilization (reissue of 1916 version). **1933** The Right to Romance. **1934** Madame DuBarry; Jimmy the Gent; Mystery Liner; Sisters under the Skin; Here Comes the Navy. **1935** Bright Lights; Rendezvous; It's in the Air. **1936** Too Many Parents; Hell-Ship Morgan; Fury; We Who Are about to Die; Wild Brian Kent; Career Woman; Happy Go Lucky; Two against the World; Crack-Up; August Weekend; Fifteen Maiden Lane. **1937** Charlie Chan at the Olympics; Give Till it Hurts (short); Artists and Models; The Lady Escapes; One Mile from Heaven; Western Gold; Borrowing Trouble; Join the Marines; Jim Hanvey, Detective; The Crime Nobody Saw; One Hundred Men and a Girl. **1938** Start Cheering; Flight into Nowhere; Juvenile Court; Rascals; Everybody's Baby; Numbered Woman; Come on, Leathernecks; I Stand Accused; Young Dr. Kildare. **1939** Convicts Code; Angels Wash Their Faces; Wife, Husband and Friend; The Kansas Terrors; Good Girls Go to Paris; Espionage Agent; Little Accident; Gone with the Wind; The Return of Dr. X; Kid from Texas. **1940** The Man from Dakota; Strike up the Band; Gangs of Chicago; Girls of the Road; The Secret Seven; Slightly Honorable; It All Came True; Bullet Code. **1941** Cheers for Miss Bishop; Washington Melodrama; Scattergood Pulls the Strings; Hurricane Smith; Sign of the Wolf; Nine Lives Are Not Enough; Belle Starr; Doctors Don't Tell; Tuxedo Junction; Bowery Boy; Golden Hoofs; Robbers of the Range; Blossoms in the Dust; Hold That Ghost. **1942** I Was Framed; Bells of Capistrano; Tarzan's New York Adventure. **1943** Watch on the Rhine; Three Hearts for Julie. **1944** Follow the Boys.

HICKOK, RODNEY

Born: 1892. Died: Mar. 9, 1942, Los Angeles, Calif. Stage and screen actor.

Appeared in: **1921** Father Tom. **1924** The Bandolero. **1928** The Rawhide Kid.

HICKS, BERT

Born: 1920. Died: Jan. 8, 1965, Pacoima, Calif. Screen actor. Father of actress Dolores Hart.

Appeared in: **1952** O'Henry's Full House.

HICKS, LEONARD M.

Born: 1918. Died: Aug. 8, 1971, New York, N.Y. (cancer). Stage and screen actor.

Appeared in: **1961** Guns of the Trees. **1964** Santa Claus Conquers the Martians.

HICKS, RUSSELL (Edward Russell Hicks)

Born: June 4, 1895, Baltimore, Md. Died: June 1, 1957, Hollywood, Calif. (heart attack). Screen, stage, television actor and film director.

Appeared in: **1928** Happiness Ahead. **1933** Enlighten Thy Daughter; Before Morning. **1934** Happiness Ahead (and 1928 version); The Firebird; The St. Louis Kid; Murder in the Clouds; Gentlemen Are Born; The Case of the Howling Dog; Babbitt. **1935** Sweet Music; While the Patient Slept; Living on Velvet; The Woman in Red; Lady Tubbs; Thunder in the Night; $1,000 a Minute; Devil Dogs of the Air; Cardinal Richelieu; Honeymoon Limited; Charlie Chan in Shanghai; Ladies Love Danger. **1936** Two in the Dark; Follow the Fleet; Special Investigator; Grand Jury; We Who are about to Die; Ticket to Paradise; Bunker Bean; Woman Trap; Laughing Irish Eyes; Hearts in Bondage; 15 Maiden Lane; The Sea Spoilers. **1937** Secret Valley; Midnight Taxi; Espionage; Pick a Star; 23½ Hours' Leave; Girl Overboard; The Westland Case; On Again, Off Again; The Toast of New York; The Big Shot; Fit for a King; Criminals of the Air. **1938** In Old Chicago; Kidnapped; Little Miss Broadway; Gateway; Hold That Co-Ed; Kentucky; Fugitives for a Night; Big Broadcast of 1938. **1939** The Real Glory; Hollywood Cavalcade; Our Leading Citizen; Hotel for Women; Boy Trouble; The Three Musketeers; The Story of Alexander Graham Bell; The Honeymoon's Over; Swanee River; Stanley and Livingstone; I Was a Convict; Joe and Ethel Turp Call on the President; Honolulu; East Side of Heaven. **1940** The Mortal Storm; Earthbound; The Big Guy; The Blue Bird; Virginia City; Johnny Apollo; Enemy Agent; Sporting Blood; The Return of Frank James; East of the River; Seven Sinners; A Night at Earl Carroll's; The Bank Dick; No, No, Nanette; Love Thy Neighbor. **1941** The Big Store; Western Union; The Great Lie; The Arkansas Judge; A Man Betrayed; Man-Made Monster; Ellery Queen's Penthouse Mystery; Here Comes Happiness; Blood and Sand; The Parson of Panamint; Buy Me That Town; Hold That Ghost; The Little Foxes; Doctors Don't Tell; Public Enemies; Midnight Angel; Dangerous Game; Great Guns. **1942** We Were Dancing; To the Shores of Tripoli; Butch Minds the Baby; Joe Smith, American; Fingers at the Window; Tarzan's New York Adventure; Tennessee Johnson; Pacific Rendezvous; Blondie for Victory; Wings for the Eagle; Ride 'Em Cowboy. **1943** Follow the Band; Strictly in the Groove; Harrigan's Kid; King of the Cowboys; Air Raid Wardens; The Woman of the Town; His Butler's Sister; Hitler—Dead or Alive. **1944** Hat Check Honey; Janie; Louisiana Hayride; Port of Forty Thieves; Blind Fools. **1945** Apology for Murder; The Valley of Decision; Flame of the Barbary Coast; A Game of Death; A Guy, a Gal and a Pal; The Hidden Eye; Scarlet Street; She Gets Her Man. **1946** Swing Parade of 1946; The Bandit of Sherwood Forest; Gay Blades; A Close Call for Boston Blackie; Dark Alibi; GI War Brides; The Plainsman and the Lady; The Bachelor's Daughters. **1947** The Pilgrim Lady; Exposed; Fun on a Weekend; Sea of Grass; Louisiana; Web of Danger; Buck Privates Come Home. **1948** The Hunted; Assigned to Danger; The Black Arrow; The Gallant Legion; Race Street; The Velvet Touch; The Shanghai Chest; My Dear Secretary; The Plunderers; The Return of October; Maggie and Jiggs in Court; The Noose Hangs High. **1949** Samson and Delilah; I Cheated the Law; Shocking Affair (short); Barbary Pirate; Manhattan Angel. **1950** Blue Grass of Kentucky; The Flying Saucer; Unmasked; Square Dance Katy; Halls of Montezuma; The Big Hangover. **1951** Bowery Battalion; As You Were; Overland Telegraph; Kentucky Jubilee; All That I Have. **1952** The Maverick; Old Oklahoma Plains; Mr. Walkie Talkie. **1953** Man of Conflict. **1956** Seventh Cavalry.

HICKS, SIR SEYMOUR

Born: Jan. 30, 1871, St. Heliers, Jersey, England. Died: Apr. 6, 1949, Hampshire, England. Screen, stage actor, playwright, stage manager, film producer, screenwriter and film director. Married to actress Ellaline Terriss (Lady Hicks) (dec. 1971).

Appeared in: **1907** Seymour Hicks Edits "The Tatler." **1913** David Garrick; Seymour Hicks and Ellaline Terris (short); Scrooge. **1914** Always Tell Your Wife. **1915** A Prehistoric Love Story. **1923** Always Tell Your Wife (and 1914 version). **1927** Blighty (aka Apres la Guerre). **1930** Sleeping Partners; Tell Tales (short). **1931** The Love Habit; Glamour. **1932** Money for Nothing. **1934** The Secret of the Loch. **1935** Royal Cavalcade (aka Regal Cavalcade); Mr. What's His Name; Vintage Wine; Scrooge (and 1913 version). **1936** Eliza

Comes to Stay; It's You I Want. **1937** Change for a Sovereign. **1939** The Lambeth Walk (US 1940 and aka Me and My Girl); Young Man's Fancy (US 1943). **1940** Pastor Hall; Busman's Honeymoon (aka Haunted Honeymoon—US). **1947** Fame Is the Spur (US 1949). **1949** Silent Dust.

HIERS, WALTER
Born: July 18, 1893, Cordele, Ga. Died; Feb. 27, 1933, Los Angeles, Calif. (pneumonia). Stage and screen actor. Entered films as an extra in 1915 with Griffith at Biograph. Married to actress Gloria Williams.

Appeared in: **1915** Jimmy. **1919** It Pays to Advertise; Leave It to Susan; Why Smith Left Home. **1920** Hunting Trouble. **1921** Sham; A Kiss in Time; Her Sturdy Oak; The Speed Girl; The Snob; Two Weeks with Pay. **1922** The Ghost Breaker; Bought and Paid For; Her Gilded Cage; Is Matrimony a Failure? **1923** Mr. Billing Spends His Dime; Sixty Cents an Hour; Hollywood. **1924** Fair Week; Along Came Ruth; Christine of the Hungry Heart; The Triflers; Hold Your Breath; The Virgin; Flaming Barriers; plus educational shorts. **1925** Excuse Me; plus the following shorts: Good Spirits; A Rarin' Romeo; Tender Feet; Oh, Bridget; Off His Beat; Hot Doggies. **1926** Hold That Lion. **1927** Beware of Widows; A Racing Romeo; Naughty; Hot Lemonade (short); Blondes by Choice; The Girl from Gay Paree; The Wrong Mr. Wright; The First Night; Husband Hunters; Night Life. **1928** A Woman against the World. **1931** Private Scandal; Oh! Oh! Cleopatra (short); 70,000 Witnesses. **1932** Dancers in the Dark.

HIGBY, WILBUR
Born: 1866. Died: Dec. 1, 1934, Hollywood, Calif. (heart attack). Stage and screen actor. Entered films in 1913. Married to stage actress Carolyn Higby.

Appeared in: **1919** Nugget Nell. **1921** Miracles of the Jungle (serial); Desert Blossoms; Live Wires; Play Square; Girls Don't Gamble. **1922** Do and Dare; My Dad; The Ladder Jinx. **1923** The Love Trap; Richard the Lion-Hearted. **1924** The Flaming Forties. **1925** Lights of Old Broadway; Confessions of a Queen. **1926** The Border Whirlwind. **1927** God's Great Wilderness. **1934** Hat, Coat and Glove; The Mighty Barnum.

HIGGINS, DAVID
Born: 1858. Died: June 30, 1936, Brooklyn, N.Y. Screen, stage actor and playwright.

Appeared in: **1924** The Confidence Man.

HILDEBRAND, RODNEY W.
Born: 1893. Died: Feb. 22, 1962. Screen actor.

Appeared in: **1926** Early to Wed; Hell's 400. **1927** The Bush Leaguer. **1928** Mother Machree.

HILDERBRAND, LO
Born: 1894. Died: Sept. 11, 1936, Los Angeles, Calif. (heart attack). Screen actor. Appeared in westerns.

HILFORDE, MARY (Mary Griggs)
Born: 1853, Carbondale, Pa. Died: Dec. 12, 1927, Amityville, N.Y. Stage and screen actress.

HILL, ARTHUR
Born: 1875. Died: Apr. 9, 1932, Hollywood, Calif. (heart attack). Stage and screen actor.

HILL, BEN A.
Born: 1894. Died: Nov. 30, 1969, Dallas, Tex. Screen actor.

Appeared in: **1921** On the High Card; The Border Raiders.

HILL, DUDLEY S.
Born: 1881. Died: Jan. 7, 1960, Wilkesboro, N.C. Screen and stage actor. Entered films in 1913.

HILL, CAPT. GEORGE
Born: 1872. Died: Mar. 2, 1945, Hollywood, Calif. Screen actor and stand-in for Nigel Bruce and Harry Lauder.

HILL, HALLENE (Hallene Christian Hill)
Born: Sept. 12, 1876, Missouri. Died: Jan. 6, 1966, Los Angeles, Calif. (cerebral thrombosis—arteriosclerosis). Screen actress.

Appeared in: **1935** One Hour Late. **1940** Remedy for Riches. **1942** Tramp, Tramp, Tramp; Wedded Blitz (short). **1956** The Search for Bridey Murphy. **1957** The Great Man; The Vampire. **1960** Spartacus. **1963** Forty Pounds of Trouble. **1965** Cat Ballou.

HILL, HOWARD
Born: 1899. Died: Feb. 4, 1975, Birmingham, Ala. Screen actor and professional archer.

Appeared in: **1929** Sal of Singapore. **1935** The Last Wildermess (short). **1938**

The Adventures of Robin Hood; Follow the Arrow (short). **1945** San Antonio. **1952** Cruise of the Zaca (short).

HILL, JACK. *See* CORNELIUS KEEFE

HILL, KATHRYN. *See* KATHRYN CARVER

HILL, RAYMOND
Born: 1891. Died: Apr. 16, 1941, Hollywood, Calif. Screen and radio actor.

HILL, THELMA (Thelma Hillerman)
Born: Dec. 12, 1906, Emporia, Kans. Died: May 11, 1938, Culver City, Calif. Screen actress. Entered films with Sennett in 1927 and was a Mack Sennett bathing beauty.

Appeared in: **1927** The Fair Co-ed. **1928** The Chorus Kid; Hearts of Men; Crooks Can't Win; The Play Girl. **1929** The following shorts: The Old Barn; The Bee's Buzz; The Big Palooka; Girl Crazy; The Barber's Daughter; The Constable; The Bride's Relations; The Lunkhead; and The Golfers. **1930** Two Plus Fours (short). **1931** The Miracle Woman. **1932** Sunkissed Sweeties (short).

HILL, VIRGINIA
Born: 1917. Died: Mar. 22, 1966, Koppl, Austria. Screen, vaudeville, television actress and dancer.

HILLIARD, ERNEST
Born: Feb. 1, 1890, New York, N.Y. Died: Sept. 3, 1947, Santa Monica, Calif. (heart attack). Stage and screen actor. Entered films in 1912.

Appeared in: **1921** Annabel Lee; Tropical Love; The Matrimonial Web. **1922** Evidence; The Ruling Passion; Married People; Who Are My Parents?; Silver Wings. **1923** Love's Old Sweet Song; Man and Wife; Modern Marriage. **1924** Galloping Hoofs (serial); The Recoil; Trouping with Ellen. **1925** Broadway Lady. **1926** Forest Havoc; White Mice; The Frontier Trail; The High Flyer. **1927** Broadway after Midnight; The Wheel of Destiny; Wide Open; The Fighting Failure; A Bowery Cinderella; Let It Rain; Compassion; The Scorcher; The Racing Fool; The Silent Hero; Smile, Brother, Smile; The Midnight Watch; Modern Daughters. **1928** Divine Sinners; The Matinee Idol; Dugan of the Dugouts; Lady Raffles; Out with the Tide; The Big Hop; A Midnight Adventure; Burning Up Broadway; Devil Dogs; The Noose; Sinners in Love. **1929** Red Wine; When Dreams Come True; The Big Diamond Robbery; Red Hot Rhythm; Dynamite; Say It with Songs; Weary River; Wall Street; Awful Truth. **1930** Broadway Hoofer. **1931** Second Honeymoon; Drums of Jeopardy; Mother and Son; Good Sport; Millie. **1934** The Witching Hour; Flirting with Danger. **1935** Smart Girl; Racing Luck. **1936** Boss Rider of Gun Creek; The Sea Spoilers. **1937** Life of the Party. **1942** The Magnificent Dope; Random Harvest. **1944** The Soul of a Monster. **1946** Deadline for Murder.

HILLIARD, HARRY S.
Died: Apr. 21, 1966, St. Petersburg, Fla. (complications after fall). Stage and screen actor.

Appeared in: **1916** Romeo and Juliet; The Little Fraud. **1917** The New York Peacock. **1918** A Successful Adventure. **1919** The Little White Savage; The Little Rowdy; The Sneak.

HILLIARD, MRS. MACK (Hazel Clayton)
Born: 1886. Died: Mar. 8, 1963, Forest Hills, N.Y. Stage and screen actress. Entered films during silents with original Fox Films Co. in Fort Lee, N.J. Appeared professionally as Mrs. Mack Hilliard.

HILLIAS, MARGARET "PEG"
Died: Mar. 18, 1960, Kansas City, Mo. Screen, stage, television and radio actress.

Appeared in: **1951** A Streetcar Named Desire. **1957** Peyton Place; The Wayward Girl.

HILTON, VIOLET and DAISY
Born: Feb. 5, 1908, Brighton, England. Died: Jan 4, 1969, Charlotte, North Carolina (complications after flu). Siamese twins and vaudeville screen actresses. Violet was married to dancer James Moore (later annulled) and Daisy was married to actor Harold Estep (aka Buddy Sawyer).

Appeared in: **1932** Freaks. Chained for Life (date unknown).

HINCKLEY, WILLIAM
Born: 1894. Died: May, 1918, New York, N.Y. Screen and stage actor.

Appeared in: **1915** Out of Bondage; The Primitive Spirit; The Light in the Window; Bred in the Bone; The Wolf Man; The Feud; The Lily and the Rose; The Stab; The Wayward Son. **1916** Martha's Vindication; The Children in the House. **1917** Bab's Burglar; The Amazons; Reputation; The Secret of Eve.

HINDS, SAMUEL S.
Born: Apr. 4, 1875, Brooklyn, N.Y. Died: Oct. 13, 1948, Pasadena, Calif. Screen, stage actor and attorney.

Appeared in: **1932** If I Had a Million. **1933** The World Changes; The House on 56th Street; Convention City; Women in His Life; The Crime of the Century; Gabriel over the White House; The Nuisance; Day of Reckoning; Lady for a Day; Bed of Roses; Berkeley Square; The Deluge; Little Women; One Man's Journey; Penthouse; Hold the Press; This Day and Age; Son of a Sailor. **1934** The Big Shakedown; Manhattan Melodrama; Operator 13; A Wicked Woman; Most Precious Thing in Life; Evelyn Prentice; He Was Her Man; Massacre; Crime Doctor; Straightaway; The Defense Rests; Have a Heart; A Lost Lady; Men in White; The Ninth Guest; No Greater Glory; West of the Pecos; Sisters under the Skin; Hat, Coat and Glove; Fog. **1935** Bordertown; Devil Dogs of the Air; Black Fury; Wings in the Dark; Sequoia; Strangers All; She; In Person; Man of the Gods; Behind the Evidence; Dr. Socrates; Rhumba; Private Worlds; College Scandal; Accent on Youth; Annapolis Farewell; The Big Broadcast of 1936; Two Fisted; Millions in the Air; Shadow of Doubt; Rendezvous; The Raven; Living on Velvet. **1936** I Loved a Soldier; The Longest Night; Timothy's Quest; Woman Trap; The Trail of the Lonesome Pine; Border Flight; Fatal Lady; Rhythm on the Range; Sworn Enemy; His Brother's Wife; Love Letters of a Star. **1937** She's Dangerous; The Black Legion; Top of the Town; The Mighty Treve; Night Key; Wings over Honolulu; The Road Back; A Girl with Ideas; Prescription for Romance; Double or Nothing; Navy Blue and Gold; Stage Door. **1938** Forbidden Valley; Young Dr. Kildare; Personal Secretary; The Jury's Secret; The Devil's Party; Wives under Suspicion; The Rage of Paris; The Road to Reno; Swing That Cheer; Secrets of a Nurse; Test Pilot; You Can't Take It with You; Double Danger. **1939** Calling Dr. Kildare; Ex-Champ; Hawaiian Night; The Under-Pup; Newsboys' Home; Within the Law; Charlie McCarthy, Detective; Career; Tropic Fury; Rio; First Love; Hero for a Day; You're a Sweetheart; Pirates of the Skies; Destry Rides Again; No Greater Glory; One Hour to Live; The Secret of Dr. Kildare. **1940** It's a Date; Dr. Kildare's Strangest Case; Ski Patrol; Boys from Syracuse; I'm Nobody's Sweetheart Now; Dr. Kildare Goes Home; Spring Parade; Seven Sinners; Trail of the Vigilantes; Zanzibar. **1941** Man-Made Monster; Buck Privates; Tight Shoes; Dr. Kildare's Wedding Day; Unfinished Business; Badlands of Dakota; Mob Town; Road Agent; Back Street; The Lady from Cheyenne; Adventure in Washington; The Shepherd of the Hills; Blossoms in the Dust. **1942** Frisco Lil; Ride 'Em Cowboy; Jail House Blues; Pittsburgh; Don Winslow of the Navy (serial); The Strange Case of Dr. Rx; The Spoilers; Kid Glove Killer; Grand Central Murder; Lady in a Jam; Pardon My Sarong. **1943** Mr. Big; Top Man; Fired Wife; Larceny with Music; Great Alaskan Mystery (serial); Weird Woman; Murder in the Blue Room; Son of Dracula; Strangers in Our Midst; It Ain't Hay; Good Morning Judge; Follow the Band; Hi, Buddy; We've Never Been Licked; Hers to Hold; Keep 'Em Slugging; He's My Guy. **1944** Sing a Jingle; Follow the Boys; Ladies Courageous; South of Dixie; The Singing Sheriff; Cobra Woman; A Chip off the Old Block; Jungle Woman. **1945** Frisco Sal; Swing out, Sister; I'll Remember April; Secret Agent X-9 (serial); Men in Her Diary; Lady on a Train; The Strange Affair of Uncle Harry; Weekend at the Waldorf; Scarlet Street; Escape in the Desert. **1946** It's a Wonderful Life; White Tie and Tails; Blonde Alibi; Strange Conquest; Little Miss Big; Danger Woman; Inside Job; Notorious Gentlemen; The Runaround. **1947** The Egg and I; Time out of Mind; In Self Defense; Slave Girl. **1948** Perilous Waters; The Return of October; Call Northside 777; The Boy with the Green Hair. **1949** The Bribe.

HINES, ADRIAN R.

Born: 1903. Died: Mar. 6, 1946, San Antonio, Tex. Screen actor, extra and circus animal trainer.

HINES, HARRY

Born: 1889. Died: May 3, 1967, Hollywood, Calif. (emphysema). Screen, burlesque and vaudeville actor.

Appeared in: **1950** One Too Many. **1951** Mr. Belvedere Rings the Bell. **1952** Boots Malone; Talk about a Stranger. **1953** Last of the Pony Riders; City of Bad Men; Houdini. **1954** The Raid. **1956** The Kettles in the Ozarks. **1965** The Cincinnati Kid. **1966** Texas across the River.

HINES, JOHNNY

Born: July 25, 1897, Golden, Colo. Died: Oct. 24, 1970, Los Angeles, Calif. (heart attack). Stage and screen actor. Entered films in 1915. Brother of actor Samuel E. Hines (dec. 1939).

Appeared in: **1920** "Torchy" series of shorts. **1921** Burn 'Em Up Barnes. **1922** Sure-Fire Flint. **1923** Little Johnny Jones; Luck. **1924** The Speed Spook; Conductor 1492. **1925** The Crackerjack; The Early Bird; The Live Wire. **1926** The Brown Derby; Stepping Along; Rainbow Riley. **1927** All Aboard; Home Made; White Pants Willie. **1928** Chinatown Charlie; The Wright Idea. **1929** Alias Jimmy Valentine. **1930** Johnny's Week End (short). **1931** Runaround. **1932** Whistling in the Dark. **1933** The Girl in 419; Her Bodyguard. **1935** Society Doctor. **1938** Too Hot to Handle. **1940** The Domineering Male (short).

HINES, SAMUEL E.

Born: 1881. Died: Nov. 17, 1939, Los Angeles, Calif. Stage and screen actor. Brother of actor Johnny Hines (dec. 1970).

Appeared in: **1925** The Lost Chord; Shore Leave. **1933** The Road Is Open (short). **1934** He Was Her Man.

HINTON, ED

Born: 1928. Died: Oct. 12, 1958, Catalina Island, Calif. (airplane accident). Screen actor. Father of actor Darby Hinton.

Appeared in: **1948** Harpoon. **1952** The Lion and the Horse; Hellgate; Leadville Slinger. **1953** Three Sailors and a Girl. **1954** Alaska Seas; River of No Return. **1955** Devil Goddess; Jungle Moon Men; Seminole Uprising. **1956** Julie; The Ten Commandments; Walk the Proud Land. **1957** The 27th Day; Under Fire; The Dalton Girls. **1958** Cry Terror; The Decks Ran Red; Escape from Red Rock; Fort Bowie. **1959** Gidget.

HIPPE, LEW

Born: 1880. Died: July 19, 1952, Hollywood, Calif. (following operation for lung ailment). Screen actor. Appeared in Mack Sennett films.

HIROSE, GEORGE

Born: 1899. Died: Aug. 9, 1974, New York, N.Y. Screen, stage, radio, television actor and singer. Married to actress Naoe Kondo.

Appeared in: **1965** Daikaiju Gamera (Gammera, the Invincible—US 1966).

HIRST, ALAN

Born: 1931. Died: Jan. 16, 1937, Hollywood, Calif. Six-year-old screen actor.

HITCHCOCK, KEITH. *See* KEITH KENNETH

HITCHCOCK, RAYMOND

Born: 1870, Auburn, N.Y. Died: Nov. 24, 1929, Beverly Hills, Calif. (heart trouble). Screen, stage and vaudeville actor. Married to actress Flora Zabelle (dec. 1968).

Appeared in: **1915** My Valet; Stolen Magic; The Village Scandal. **1922** The Beauty Shop. **1924** Broadway after Dark. **1926** Redheads Preferred; Everybody's Acting. **1927** The Money Talks; Upstream; The Tired Business Man. **1929** An Evening at Home with Hitchy (short).

HITCHCOCK, WALTER

Died: June 23, 1917, New York, N.Y. (heart failure). Screen actor.

Appeared in: **1915** The Idler; The House of Tears; The Great Ruby Mystery. **1916** The Blindness of Love; The Snowbird. **1917** The Moral Code.

HIX, DON (Don T. Hicks)

Died: Dec. 31, 1964, Hollywood, Calif. Screen, stage and radio actor. Entered films with Universal in 1914.

Appeared in: **1959** Diary of a High School Bride.

HOAGLAND, HARLAND

Born: 1896. Died: Jan. 9, 1971, Hollywood, Calif. (cancer). Stage and screen actor. Entered films in 1921.

HOBBES, HALLIWELL

Born: Nov. 16, 1877, Stratford-on-Avon, England. Died: Feb. 20, 1962, Santa Monica, Calif. (heart attack). Screen and stage actor.

Appeared in: **1929** Lucky in Love; Jealousy. **1930** Grumpy; Charley's Aunt; Scotland Yard. **1931** The Right of Way; The Bachelor Father; Five and Ten; Platinum Blonde; The Sins of Madelon Claudet; The Woman Between. **1932** The Menace; The Devil's Lottery; Man about Town; Week Ends Only; Love Affair; Six Hours to Live; Dr. Jekyll and Mr. Hyde; Lovers Courageous; Forbidden; Payment Deferred. **1933** Lady of the Night; Looking Forward; Midnight Mary; Should Ladies Behave?; A Study in Scarlet; Captured; Lady for a Day; The Masquerader. **1934** I Am Suzanne; All Men Are Enemies; Mandalay; The Key; Riptide; Double Door; Bulldog Drummond Strikes Back; Madame DuBarry; British Agent. **1935** Follies Bergere; Cardinal Richelieu; The Right to Live; Millions in the Air; Jalna; Charlie Chan in Shanghai; Father Brown, Detective. **1936** The Story of Louis Pasteur; Here Comes Trouble; Dracula's Daughter; Love Letters of a Star; The White Angel; Hearts Divided; Give Me Your Heart; Spendthrift; Whipsaw. **1937** Maid of Salem; The Prince and the Pauper; Varsity Show; Fit for a King. **1938** You Can't Take It with You; The Jury's Secret; Service DeLuxe; Bulldog Drummond's Peril; Storm over Bengal; Kidnapped. **1939** The Light That Failed; Pacific Liner; The Hardy's Ride High; Naughty but Nice; Nurse Edith Cavell; Tell No Tales; Remember? **1940** The Sea Hawk; The Earl of Chicago; Third Finger, Left Hand. **1941** That Hamilton Woman; Here Comes Mr. Jordan. **1942** To Be or Not to Be; The War against Mrs. Hadley; Journey for Margaret; The Undying Monster; Son of Fury. **1943** Sherlock Holmes Faces Death; Forever and a Day. **1944** The Invisible Man's Revenge; Gaslight; Mr. Skeffington; Casanova Brown. **1946** Canyon Passage. **1947** If Winter Comes. **1948** You Gotta Stay Happy; Black Arrow. **1949** That Forsyte Woman. **1956** Miracle in the Rain.

HOBBS, JACK

Born: 1893, London, England. Died: June 4, 1968, Brighton, England. Stage and screen actor.

Appeared in: **1915** Love's Legacy (aka The Yoke). **1919** The Lady Clare. **1920** The Face at the Window; Inheritance (aka Bred in the Bone); The Call of

Youth (US 1921); The Shuttle of Life; The Skin Game. **1922** The Lonely Lady of Grosvenor Square; The Crimson Circle; The Naval Treaty (short). **1923** The Last Adventures of Sherlock Holmes series including: The Crooked Man. **1924** The Eleventh Commandment. **1925** The Happy Ending. **1931** Never Trouble Trouble; Love Lies; Dr. Josser KC; Mischief; The Love Race. **1932** Josser Joins the Navy; The Last Coupon; His Wife's Mother; Josser in the Army; A Honeymoon in Devon. **1933** Double Wedding; Too Many Wives; Beware of Women. **1934** Trouble in Store; Oh No Doctor! **1935** Handle with Care; Car of Dreams; No Limit. **1936** Millions; The Interrupted Honeymoon; All That Glitters. **1937** Why Pick on Me?; The Show Goes On; Leave It to Me; Intimate Relations; Fine Feathers; When the Devil Was Well. **1938** Make It Three; It's in the Air (aka George Takes the Air—US 1940); Miracles Do Happen.

HOCH, EMIL H.

Born: Oct. 27, 1866, Pforzheim, Germany. Died: Oct. 13, 1944, Hollywood, Calif. (heart attack). Screen actor.

Appeared in: **1919** The Dark Star. **1921** The Girl with a Jazz Heart. **1924** America. **1925** Stage Struck.

HOCK, RICHARD

Born: 1933. Died: July 13, 1961, Santa Monica, Calif. (burned in auto accident). Screen actor and stuntman. Married to stunt woman Margo Hock.

HODD, JOSEPH B., SR.

Born: 1896. Died: June 26, 1965, Philadelphia, Pa. Screen actor and stuntman. Entered films in 1927.

HODGEMAN, THOMAS

Born: 1875. Died: Apr. 24, 1931, Los Angeles, Calif. Screen, stage actor and stage manager.

HODGES, WILLIAM CULLEN

Born: 1876, Newbury Township, Ohio. Died: July 28, 1961, Chardon, Ohio. Stage and screen actor.

HODGINS, EARL

Born: 1899. Died: Apr. 14, 1964, Hollywood, Calif. (heart attack). Screen, stage and television actor.

Appeared in: **1934** The Circus Clown. **1935** The Cyclone Ranger; The Texas Rambler; Paradise Canyon; Harmony Lane. **1936** The Singing Cowboy; Guns and Guitars; Ticket to Paradise; Oh, Susannah!; Border Caballero; Aces and Eights. **1937** Borderland; Hills of Old Wyoming; Partners of the Plains; I Cover the War; Range Defenders; All over Town; A Law Man Is Born; Round-up Time in Texas; Heroes of the Alamo; Headin' East; Nation Aflame. **1938** The Old Barn Dance; The Purple Vigilantes; Call the Mesquiteers; The Rangers Roundup; Long Shot; Pride of the West; Lawless Valley; Barefoot Boy. **1939** Home on the Prairie; Almost a Gentleman; Panama Lady; The Day the Bookies Wept. **1940** Santa Fe Marshal; Men against the Sky; The Range Busters; Under Texas Skies; Law and Order; The Bad Man from Red Butte. **1941** Scattergood Pulls the Strings; Riding the Wind; Sierra Sue; Keep 'em Flying. **1942** The Bashful Bachelor; Call of the Canyon; Undercover Man; Deep in the Heart of Texas; Scattergood Survives a Murder; The Power of God; Inside the Law. **1943** Riders of the Deadline; False Colors; Tenting Tonight on the Old Camp Ground; The Old Chisholm Trail; The Avenging Rider; Hi! Ya, Chum; Colt Comrades; Lone Star Trail; Hoppy Serves a Writ. **1944** Hidden Valley Outlaws; Firebrands of Arizona; San Antonio Kid; Sensations of 1945. **1945** The Southerner; Bedside Manner; GI Honeymoon; The Topeka Terror; Under Western Skies. **1946** The Bachelor's Daughters; Crime of the Century; The Devil's Playground; The Best Years of Our Lives; Live Wires; Fool's Gold; Unexpected Guest; Accomplice; Valley of the Zombies. **1947** The Marauders; Oregon Trail Scouts; Vigilantes of Boomtown; Rustler's Roundup; The Return of Rin-Tin-Tin. **1948** The Main Street Kid; Silent Conflict; Borrowed Trouble; Old Los Angeles; Let's Live Again. **1949** Henry, the Rainmaker; Sheriff of Wichita; Jiggs and Maggie in Jackpot Jitters; Slightly French. **1950** The Savage Horde; Square Dance Katy. **1953** Thunder over the Plains; The Great Jesse James Raid. **1954** Bitter Creek; The Forty-Niners. **1957** The D.I.; Up in Smoke. **1958** The Missouri Traveler. **1962** Saintly Sinners; The Man Who Shot Liberty Valance.

HODGINS, LESLIE

Born: 1885. Died: Sept. 1927, St. Louis, Mo. Screen actor and singer.

HODGSON, LELAND (aka LEYLAND HODGSON)

Born: England. Died: Mar. 16, 1949, Hollywood, Calif. (heart attack). Stage and screen actor.

Appeared in: **1930** The Case of Sergeant Grisha. **1932** Under Cover Man; Ladies of the Jury. **1933** The Eagle and the Hawk. **1935** Perfect Gentleman; Feather in Her Hat. **1936** Beloved Enemy; Trouble for Two. **1937** The Adventurous Blonde. **1938** The Buccaneer. **1939** Susannah of the Mounties; Eternally Yours; The Witness Vanishes; Mr. Moto's Last Warning. **1940** He Married His Wife; My Son, My Son; Murder over New York. **1941** The Adventures of Captain Marvel (serial); The Wolf Man; The Case of the Black Parrot; Scot-

land Yard; International Lady. **1942** To Be or Not to Be; The Ghost of Frankenstein; Secret Agent of Japan; The Strange Case of Dr. Rx; Escape from Hong Kong; Sherlock Holmes and the Voice of Terror; Just off Broadway. **1944** The Invisible Man's Revenge; Enter Arsene Lupin. **1945** Hangover Square; The Frozen Ghost; Molly and Me. **1946** Three Strangers; Terror by Night; Rendezvous 24; Black Beauty; Bedlam. **1947** Thunder in the Valley. **1948** Kiss the Blood off My Hands; A Woman's Vengeance. **1949** That Forsyte Woman.

HODIAK, JOHN

Born: Apr. 16, 1914, Pittsburgh, Pa. Died: Oct. 19, 1955, Tarzana, Calif. (coronary thrombosis). Screen, stage, radio and television actor. Divorced from actress-writer Anne Baxter.

Appeared in: **1943** A Stranger in Town (film debut); I Dood It; Song of Russia; Swing Shift Maisie. **1944** Lifeboat; Marriage Is a Private Affair; Maisie Goes to Reno; Sunday Dinner for a Soldier; You Can't Do That to Me. **1945** A Bell for Adano; Ziegfeld Follies; The Harvey Girls; Somewhere in the Night; Two Smart People. **1947** The Arnelo Affair; Love from a Stranger; Desert Fury. **1948** Homecoming; Command Decision. **1949** Ambush; The Bribe. **1950** A Lady without a Passport; Malaya; Battleground; The Miniver Story. **1951** Night into Morning; People against O'Hara; Across the Wide Missouri. **1952** Battle Zone; The Sellout. **1953** Conquest of Cochise; Ambush at Tomahawk; Mission over Korea. **1954** Dragonfly Squadron. **1955** Trial. **1956** On the Threshold of Space.

HOEFLICH, LUCIE

Born: 1883, Germany. Died: Oct. 9, 1956, Berlin, Germany (heart attack). Stage and screen actress.

Appeared in: **1936** 1914: The Last Days before the War. **1959** Himmel Ohne Sterne (Sky without Stars).

HOEY, DENNIS (Samuel David Hyams)

Born: Mar. 30, 1893, England. Died: July 25, 1960, Palm Beach, Fla. Stage and screen actor. Played character of "Inspector Lestrade" in Basil Rathbone's Sherlock Holmes series from 1939 to 1945.

Appeared in: **1927** Tiptoes. **1930** The Man from Chicago (US 1931). **1931** Tell England (aka The Battle of Gallipoli—US); Never Trouble Trouble; Love Lies. **1932** Life Goes On (aka Sorry You've Been Troubled); The Maid of the Mountains; Baroud (aka Love in Morocco—US 1933). **1933** The Good Companions; Facing the Music (US 1934); Maid Happy; Oh What a Duchess! (aka My Old Duchess); I Spy; The Wandering Jew (US 1935). **1934** Lily of Killarney (aka Bride of the Lake—US); Jew Suess (aka Power—US); Chu Chin Chow. **1935** Brewster's Millions; Immortal Gentleman; Maria Marten, or, The Murder in the Red Barn; Honeymoon for Three; The Mystery of the Mary Celeste (aka Phantom Ship—US 1937). **1936** Faust; Did I Betray? **1937** Uncivilized. **1941** How Green Was My Valley. **1942** Son of Fury; This above All; Cairo; Sherlock Holmes and the Secret Weapon. **1943** Frankenstein Meets the Wolf Man; They Came to Blow Up America; Forever and a Day; Sherlock Holmes Faces Death; Bomber's Moon. **1944** National Velvet; Keys of the Kingdom; Uncertain Glory; The Pearl of Death; Sherlock Holmes and the Spider Woman. **1945** House of Fear; A Thousand and One Nights. **1946** Roll on Texas Moon; She-Wolf of London; Tarzan and the Leopard Woman; The Strange Woman; Kitty; Terror by Night; Anna and the King of Siam. **1947** The Crimson Key; Second Chance; Golden Earrings; The Foxes of Harrow; Christmas Eve; Where There's Life; If Winter Comes. **1948** Ruthless; Badmen of Tombstone; Wake of the Red Witch. **1949** The Secret Garden. **1950** Joan of Arc; The Kid from Texas. **1951** David and Bathsheba. **1952** Caribbean. **1953** Ali Baba Nights.

HOEY, GEORGE J.

Born: 1885. Died: Feb. 17, 1955, Hollywood, Calif. Screen actor.

HOFER, CHRIS (Martin Christopher Hofer)

Born: 1920, N.Y. Died: Feb. 11, 1964, Rome, Italy (auto accident). Screen, stage and television actor.

Appeared in: **1959** Londra Chiama Polo Nord (London Calling North Pole aka The House of Intrigue).

HOFFE, MONCKTON

Born: Dec. 26, 1880, Connemara, Ireland. Died: Nov. 4, 1951, London, England. Screen, stage actor, playwright and screenwriter.

Appeared in: **1951** Lady with a Lamp.

HOFFMAN, DAVID

Born: Feb. 2, 1904, Russia. Died: June 19, 1961, Seattle, Wash. Screen, stage and radio actor.

Appeared in: **1940** Underground (film debut). **1943** Mission to Moscow; Flesh and Fantasy. **1944** The Mask of Dimitrios; The Conspirators. **1946** A Night in Casablanca; Beast with Five Fingers. **1947** Desire Me. **1948** Inner Sanctum. **1949** Backfire (aka Somewhere in the City); Trouble Makers. **1954** Woman's World. **1962** The Best of Everything.

HOFFMAN, EBERHARD
Born: 1883. Died: June 16, 1957, Denville, N.Y. Screen actor. Appeared in silents.

HOFFMAN, GERTRUDE (Gertrude Anderson)
Born: 1898, Montreal, Canada. Died: June 3, 1955, Washington, D.C. Stage and screen actress.

HOFFMAN, GERTRUDE W.
Born: May 17, 1871, Heidelberg, Germany. Died: Oct. 21, 1966, Hollywood, Calif. (heart attack). Screen, vaudeville actress and dancer. Mother of actor Max Hoffman, Jr. (dec. 1945).

Appeared in: **1933** Hell and High Water; Before Dawn. **1935** Les Miserables. **1936** A Son Comes Home; The Gentleman from Louisiana. **1938** Cassidy of Bar 20. **1940** The Ape; Untamed; Foreign Correspondent. **1941** Lydia. **1942** I Married an Angel; Tish; Commandos Strike at Dawn; A Wife Takes a Flier. **1943** The Moon Is Down; A Guy Named Joe; The Heavenly Body; What a Woman. **1949** Thelma Jordan.

HOFFMAN, HERMINE H.
Born: 1921. Died: Dec. 7, 1971, Broomall, Pa. Screen, stage and circus actress.

Appeared in: **1945** See My Lawyer.

HOFFMAN, HOWARD R. (Howard Ralph Hoffman)
Born: Nov. 4, 1893, Ohio. Died: June 27, 1969, Hollywood, Calif. (heart attack). Screen, stage, vaudeville, radio and television actor.

Appeared in: **1958** Macabre; The Littlest Hobo. **1959** House on Haunted Hill.

HOFFMAN, MAX, JR.
Born: Dec. 13, 1902, Norfolk, Va. Died: Mar. 31, 1945, New York, N.Y. Screen, stage and vaudeville actor. Son of dancer and actress Gertrude W. Hoffman (dec. 1966). Divorced from actress Helen Kane (dec. 1966).

Appeared in: **1936** Draegerman's Courage (film debut); King of Hockey. **1937** Counterfeit Lady; Rootin' Tootin' Rhythm; Swing It, Sailor; Sergeant Murphy; San Quentin. **1938** Sky Giant; Accidents Will Happen; The Great Waltz; Kidnapped; Little Orphan Annie. **1939** Ambush; Wings of Victory; Topper Takes a Trip; Hell's Kitchen; Confessions of a Nazi Spy; Kid Nightingale; Dust Be My Destiny. **1940** Brother Orchid; Lady from Hell; Virginia City; It All Came True; Castle on the Hudson. **1942** Man from Headquarters; Black Dragons.

HOFFMAN, OTTO (Otto Frederick Hoffman)
Born: May 2, 1879, New York, N.Y. Died: June 23, 1944, Woodland Hills, Calif. (lung cancer). Entered films in 1917 with Thomas Ince.

Appeared in: **1916** Behind Closed Doors. **1918** String Beans; Nine O'Clock. **1919** The Sheriff's Son; The Busher; The City of Comrades; The Egg Crate Wallop; 23½ Hours' Leave; Paris Green. **1920** The Great Accident; It's a Great Life; The Jail Bird; Homer Comes Home. **1921** The Bronze Bell; Just Out of College; Bunty Pulls the Strings; The Devil Within; Passing Thru; Whatever She Wants; Who Am I? **1922** The Bootlegger's Daughter; Boy Crazy; Confidence; A Dangerous Game; The Five Dollar Baby; Gas, Oil and Water; The Glorious Fool; Mr. Barnes of New York; The New Teacher; Pardon My Nerve!; Ridin' Wild; The Sin Flood; Trimmed; Very Truly Yours. **1923** One Stolen Night; Strangers of the Night; Double Dealing; Human Wreckage; Lucretia Lombard. **1924** Broadway After Dark; Daddies; The Gaiety Girl; High Speed; The Price She Paid; This Woman. **1925** The Circle; Satan in Sables; Secrets of the Night; Bobbed Hair; Confessions of a Queen; The Dixie Handicap; The Eagle. **1926** The Boy Friend; Millionaires; More Pay—Less Work. **1927** Beware of Widows; Painted Ponies; The Siren; The Stolen Bride. **1928** The Fourflusher; The Grain of Dust; Noah's Ark; The Terror; Rinty of the Desert. **1929** Acquitted; The Desert Song; The Hottentot; Hardboiled Rose; Is Everybody Happy?; The Madonna of Avenue A; On with the Show. **1930** Moby Dick; Kismet; Abraham Lincoln; The Other Tomorrow; Sinner's Holiday. **1931** The Criminal Code; Captain Applejack; Cimarron; Son of India; Side Show; The Avenger. **1932** Two Seconds; Downstairs; County Fair; Hello Trouble. **1933** The Iron Master; Haunted Gold; Cheyenne Kid; Man of Sentiment. **1934** Beloved; Death Takes a Holiday; Murder at the Vanities; Kid Millions. **1935** Barbary Coast; Behold My Wife; Captain Hurricane; Flying Shadows; Smart Girl. **1936** The Case Against Mrs. Ames; Career Woman. **1937** Living on Love; Hideaway; Girl Loves Boy; All Over Town. **1938** Romance in the Dark; Mr. Boggs Steps Out. **1939** Our Leading Citizen. **1940** Lucky Cisco Kid; Stranger on the Third Floor. **1944** This Is the Life.

HOGAN, EARL "HAP" (Earl Richard Traynor)
Died: Oct. 14, 1944, Los Angeles, Calif. Screen actor.

Appeared in: **1928** The Haunted Ship.

HOGAN, PAT
Born: 1931. Died: Nov. 22, 1966, Hollywood, Calif. (cancer). Screen actor.

Appeared in: **1951** Fixed Bayonets. **1952** Luke of the Wilderness; Return of Gilbert and Sullivan. **1953** Arrowhead; Back to God's Country; Gun Fury; Overland Pacific; Pony Express. **1954** Sign of the Pagan. **1955** Davy Crockett, King of the Wild Frontier; Kiss of Fire; Smoke Signal. **1956** The Last Frontier; Pillars of the Sky; Secret of Treasure Mountain; 7th Cavalry. **1962** Hemingway's Adventures of a Young Man. **1963** Savage Sam. **1965** Indian Paint.

HOGAN, "SOCIETY KID" (Salvatore de Lorenzo)
Born: 1899. Died: Apr. 10, 1962, Chicago, Ill. Screen actor.

Appeared in: **1951** Lemon Drop Kid. **1953** Money from Home.

HOGG, JACK "CURLY"
Born: 1917. Died: Sept. 1974, San Diego, Calif. (heart attack). Screen, television actor and musician. Was one of the original "Sons of the Pioneers" and was often called "King of the Banjoes."

HOHL, ARTHUR
Born: May 21, 1889, Pittsburgh, Pa. Died: Mar. 10, 1964, Calif. Stage and screen actor.

Appeared in: **1924** It Is the Law. **1931** The Cheat. **1932** The Sign of the Cross. **1933** Island of Lost Souls; Captured; Baby Face; Silk Express; The Life of Jimmy Dolan; Private Detective 62; The Narrow Corner; Footlight Parade; The Kennel Murder Case; College Coach; Infernal Machine; Wild Boys of the Road; The World Changes; Brief Moment; A Man's Castle; Jealousy. **1934** The Defense Rests; Cleopatra; Lady by Choice; Massacre; A Modern Hero; As the Earth Turns; Jimmy the Gent; Romance in Manhattan; Bulldog Drummond Strikes Back. **1935** Case of the Missing Man; The Whole Town's Talking; Eight Bells; In Spite of Danger; The Unknown Woman; I'll Love You Always; Guard That Girl; Village Tale; One Frightened Night. **1936** We're Only Human; It Had to Happen; Lloyds of London; Superspeed; The Lone Wolf Returns; Forgotten Faces; Showboat; The Devil Doll. **1937** Slave Ship; Hot Water; The Road Back; The River of Missing Men; Trapped by G-Men; Mountain Music. **1938** The Bad Man of Brimstone; Penitentiary; Kidnapped; Crime Takes a Holiday; Stablemates. **1939** Boy Slaves; You Can't Cheat an Honest Man; They Shall Have Music; Blackmail; Fugitive at Large; The Adventures of Sherlock Holmes; The Hunchback of Notre Dame. **1940** 20 Mule Team; Blondie Has Servant Trouble. **1941** Men of Boys Town; Ride On, Vaquero; We Go Fast. **1942** Son of Fury; Whispering Ghosts; Moontide. **1943** Idaho; The Woman of the Town. **1944** Sherlock Holmes and the Spider Woman; The Eve of St. Mark; The Scarlet Claw; Crime Doctor. **1945** Salome Where She Danced; The Frozen Ghost; Love Letters. **1947** It Happened on 5th Avenue; Monsieur Verdoux; The Vigilantes Return; The Yearling. **1949** Down to the Sea in Ships.

HOLDEN, FAY (Dorothy Hammerton aka GABY FAY)
Born: Sept. 26, 1895, Birmingham, England. Died: June 23, 1973, Woodland Hills, Calif. (cancer). Stage and screen actress. Married to actor David Clyde (dec. 1945). Appeared as Andy Hardy's mother in the "Andy Hardy" films.

Appeared in: **1936** Polo Joe (film debut); I Married a Doctor; Wives Never Know; The White Angel. **1937** Guns of the Pecos; A Family Affair; Souls at Sea; Exclusive; Double or Nothing; Bulldog Drummond Escapes; Internes Can't Take Money; King of Gamblers; Nothing Sacred. **1938** Test Pilot; You're Only Young Once; Love Is a Headache; Judge Hardy's Children; Hold that Kiss; Love Finds Andy Hardy; Out West with the Hardy's; Sweethearts; The Battle of Broadway. **1939** Sergeant Madden; The Hardys Ride High; Andy Hardy Gets Spring Fever; Judge Hardy and Son. **1940** Andy Hardy Meets a Debutante; Bitter Sweet. **1941** Andy Hardy's Private Secretary; Ziegfeld Girl; Washington Melodrama; I'll Wait for You; Blossoms in the Dust; Life Begins for Andy Hardy; H. M. Pulham, Esq. **1942** The Courtship of Andy Hardy; Andy Hardy's Double Life. **1944** Andy Hardy's Blonde Trouble. **1946** Canyon Passage; The Baxter Millions; Little Miss Big; Love Laughs at Andy Hardy. **1948** Whispering Smith. **1949** Samson and Delilah. **1950** The Big Hangover. **1958** Andy Hardy Comes Home.

HOLDEN, HARRY MOORE
Born: 1868. Died: Feb. 4, 1944, Woodland Hills, Calif. Stage and screen actor.

Appeared in: **1927** The Gay Defender; The Yankee Clipper; Winds of the Pampas; Show Boat. **1930** Code of Honor. **1938** What Price Glory? (short).

HOLDEN, VIOLA (Viola Martinelli)
Died: Aug. 23, 1967, Saratoga, N.Y. (heart attack). Screen and stage actress.

Appeared in: **1948** Mexican Hayride. **1952** Sailor Beware.

HOLDEN, WILLIAM
Born: May 22, 1872, Rochester, N.Y. Died: Mar. 2, 1932, Hollywood, Calif. (heart attack). Stage and screen actor. Do not confuse with actor born in 1918.

Appeared in: **1928** Roadhouse (film debut); The First Kiss; Three Week Ends. **1929** Weary River; The Trespasser; Dynamite; His Captive Woman; Fast Life. **1930** Not So Dumb; Numbered Men; Framed; Holiday; What a Widow; Three Faces East. **1931** The Man Who Came Back; Charlie Chan Carries On; Six Cylinder Love; Dance, Fool, Dance.

HOLDING, THOMAS

Born: Jan. 25, 1880, Blackheath, Kent, England. Died: May 4, 1929, New York, N.Y. (heart disease). Screen, stage actor and film director.

Appeared in: **1915** The Eternal City; The White Pearl; The Moment Before. **1917** Redeeming Love; Magda. **1918** Daughter of Destiny; Vanity Pool. **1919** The Peace of Roaring River; The Lone Wolf's Daughter; The Danger Zone; The Lady of Red Butte; Tangled Threads; Beckoning Roads. **1920** The Honey Bee; In Folly's Trail; Woman in His House. **1921** The Lure of Jade; The Three Musketeers; Sacred and Profane Love; Without the Benefit of Clergy. **1922** Rose O' the Sea; The Trouper. **1923** Stranger's Banquet; The Courtship of Miles Standish; Ruggles of Red Gap. **1925** The Necessary Evil; One Way Street; The White Monkey; The Pace that Thrills.

HOLDREN, JUDD (Judd Clifton Holdren)

Born: Oct. 16, 1915, Iowa. Died: Mar. 11, 1974, West Los Angeles, Calif. (suicide—gun). Screen actor.

Appeared in: **1951** Purple Heart Diary; Captain Video (serial). **1952** Zombies of the Stratosphere (serial); Lady in the Iron Mask; Gold Fever. **1953** The Lost Planet (serial). **1954** This Is My Love. **1957** The Amazing Colossal Man. **1958** Satan's Satellites; The Buccaneer.

HOLLAND, C. MAURICE

Died: Nov. 14, 1974, Greenwich, Conn. Stage, vaudeville, screen actor, television director and producer. Married to actress Frances Seaton.

Appeared in: **1929** Day of a Man of Affairs.

HOLLAND, MILDRED

Born: Apr. 9, 1869, Chicago, Ill. Died: Jan. 27, 1944, New York, N.Y. Screen actress. Appeared in silents.

HOLLAND, MIRIAM

Born: 1917. Died: Sept. 24, 1948, Hollywood, Calif. Screen actress.

HOLLAND, RALPH

Born: 1888. Died: Dec. 7, 1939, Los Angeles, Calif. Stage and screen actor. Entered films approx. 1927.

HOLLES, ANTONY (aka ANTHONY HOLLES)

Born: Jan. 17, 1901, London, England. Died: 1950. Screen and stage actor.

Appeared in: **1921** The Will. **1931** The Star Reporter. **1932** Hotel Splendide; Reunion; The Missing Rembrandt; Once Bitten; Life Goes On (aka Sorry You've Been Troubled); The Lodger (aka The Phantom Fiend—US 1935); Watch Beverly; The Midshipmaid. **1933** She Was Only a Village Maiden; Forging Ahead; Cash (aka For Love or Money—US 1934); Britannia of Billingsgate; That's a Good Girl. **1934** Borrowed Clothes; The Green Pack. **1935** Brewster's Millions; Gentleman's Agreement. **1936** Limelight (aka Backstage—US); Public Nuisance No. 1; Things to Come; Seven Sinners (aka Doomed Cargo—US); The Tenth Man (US 1937); Millions; This'll Make You Whistle (US 1938); The Gay Adventure. **1937** Glamorous Night; Smash and Grab; Paradise for Two (aka The Gaiety Girls—US 1938); The Sky's the Limit; Mademoiselle Docteur; Action for Slander (US 1938). **1938** Romance a la Carte; His Lordship Regrets; Dangerous Medicine; They Drive by Night; Miracles Do Happen; Weddings Are Wonderful. **1939** Down Our Alley; Ten Days in Paris (aka Missing Ten Days—US); The Spider; Blind Folly; The Missing People (US 1940). **1940** Neutral Port. **1942** Front Line Kids; Talk about Jacqueline; Lady from Lisbon; Tomorrow We Live (aka At Dawn We Die—US 1943). **1943** Warn that Man; Up with the Lark; It's in the Bag; Battle for Music; Old Mother Riley Overseas. **1944** A Canterbury Tale; Give Me the Stars. **1946** Caesar and Cleopatra; The Magic Bow (US 1947); Carnival; Gaiety George (aka Showtime—US 1948). **1947** Fortune Lane. **1948** The Dark Road. **1949** The Rocking Horse Winner (US 1950).

HOLLIDAY, BILLIE (Eleanor Gough McKay)

Born: Apr. 7, 1915, Baltimore, Maryland. Died: July 17, 1959, New York, N.Y. Black singer and screen actress.

Appeared in: **1935** Symphony in Black (short). **1947** New Orleans.

HOLLIDAY, FRANK, JR.

Born: 1913. Died: Aug. 3, 1948, Hollywood, Calif. (suicide—hanging). Screen and radio actor.

HOLLIDAY, JUDY (Judith Turin)

Born: June 21, 1923, New York, N.Y. Died: June 7, 1965, New York, N.Y. (cancer). Stage and screen actress. Divorced from musician David Oppenheim. Won 1951 Academy Award for Best Actress in Born Yesterday.

Appeared in: **1944** Greenwich Village; Something for the Boys; Winged Victory. **1949** Adam's Rib. **1951** Born Yesterday. **1952** The Marrying Kind. **1954** Phffft; It Should Happen to You. **1956** The Solid Gold Cadillac; Full of Life. **1960** Bells Are Ringing.

HOLLIDAY, MARJORIE (Marjorie St. Angel)

Born: 1920. Died: June 16, 1969, Hollywood, Calif. (brain hemorrhage). Screen actress.

HOLLINGSHEAD, GORDON

Born: Jan. 8, 1892, Garfield, N.J. Died: July 8, 1952, Balboa, Calif. Screen actor and film director. Entered films as an actor in 1914.

HOLLINGSWORTH, ALFRED

Born: 1874, Nebraska. Died: June 20, 1926, Glendale, Calif. Stage and screen actor.

Appeared in: **1915** American Film Mfg. Co. films. **1916** Hell's Hinges; The Sable Blessing; The Stampede; Purity; The Right Direction. **1917** The Girl and the Crisis; The Sudden Gentleman. **1919** Leave It to Susan. **1921** The Infamous Miss Revell. **1922** The Bearcat; Trimmed. **1924** Marry in Haste. **1925** The Mystery Box (serial).

HOLLINGSWORTH, HARRY

Born: Sept. 3, 1888, Los Angeles, Calif. Died: Nov. 5, 1947, Los Angeles, Calif. Screen, stage, vaudeville and radio actor. Married to Nan Crawford (dec. 1975) with whom he appeared in vaudeville in act billed as "Hollingsworth and Crawford."

Appeared in: **1916** The Tarantula. **1919** Bedtime (short with "Hollingsworth and Crawford"). **1936** Sing Me a Love Song. **1942** My Favorite Blonde.

HOLLISTER, ALICE

Born: Sept. 1886, Worcester, Mass. Died: Feb. 24, 1973, Costa Mesa, Calif. Screen actress.

Appeared in: **1911** The Colleen Bawn. **1912** An Arab Tragedy; Tragedy of the Desert; Ireland the Oppressed; The Kerry Gow. **1913** Shenandoah; The Bribe; A Saw Mill Hazard; The Prosecuting Attorney; The Peril of the Dance Hall; A War-Time Siren; The Scimitar of the Prophet; The Alien; A Victim of Heredity; The Terror of Conscience; A Virginia Feud; The Lost Diamond; The Blind Basket Weaver; Primitive Man; The Smuggler; The Vampire. **1914** The Brand. **1915** The Destroyer; The Haunting Fear; The Stolen Ruby; The Siren's Religion; A Sister's Burden; The Net of Deceit; The Man in Hiding; The Siren's Reign (aka The Reign of the Siren); The Sign of the Broken Shackles; The Mysterious Case of Meredith Stanhope; The Money Gulf. **1917** Her Better Self. **1918** The Knife. **1920** From the Manger to the Cross or Jesus of Nazareth; Milestones; The Great Lover. **1921** A Voice in the Dark; A Wise Fool. **1922** The Forgotten Law. **1924** Married Flirts. **1925** The Dancers.

HOLLYWOOD, JIMMY

Died: July 2, 1955. Screen and radio actor.

Appeared in: **1935** Every Night at Eight. **1943** Spotlight Scandals.

HOLM, SONIA

Born: Feb. 24, 1922, England? Died: July 2, 1974, England. Stage and screen actress.

Appeared in: **1948** Miranda (US 1949); Broken Journey (US 1949). **1949** Warning to Wantons; The Bad Lord Byron (US 1952).

HOLMAN, HARRY

Born: 1874. Died: May 2, 1947, Hollywood, Calif. (heart attack). Screen, stage and vaudeville actor.

Appeared in: **1929** Hard Boiled Hampton (short). **1930** Give Me Action (short). The Big Deal (short). **1933** Lucky Dog; Devil's Mate; One Year Later; My Woman; East of Fifth Avenue; Circus Queen Murder; Roman Scandals. **1934** It Happened One Night. **1935** Calling All Cars; Traveling Saleslady; In Caliente; Welcome Home; Cheers of the Crowd; Here Comes Cookie. **1936** Gentle Julia; The Count Takes the Count (short); The Criminal Within; Hitch Hike to Heaven. **1937** Nation Aflame. **1938** Western Jamboree. **1939** I Was a Convict. **1940** Slightly Tempted. **1941** Meet John Doe. **1942** Inside the Law; Tennessee Johnson; Mexican Spitfire; Seven Days' Leave. **1943** Shadows on the Sage. **1944** Swing Hostess.

HOLMAN, LIBBY

Born: 1906. Died: June 18, 1971, North Stamford, Conn. Screen, stage actress and singer.

Appeared in: **1943** The Russian Story (narrator).

HOLMES, BEN

Born: 1890, Richmond, Va. Died: Dec. 2, 1943, Hollywood, Calif. Screen, stage actor, stage and film director.

Appeared in: **1932** The Expert.

HOLMES, BURTON

Born: Jan. 8, 1870, Chicago, Ill. Died: July 22, 1958, Hollywood, Calif. Screen actor and film producer. Pioneer of travel films and shorts. Made first travel films in Italy (1897) and first travel films in Hawaii (1898).

Appeared in: **1922** Around the World with Burton Holmes. **1924** Glorious Switzerland. **1925** Teak Logging with Elephants; Tyrolean Perspectives; Under Cuban Skies; The Salt of Amping; A Cabaret of Old Japan; The Garden of the East. **1926** So This Is Florida. **1927** Closeups of China. **1928** Happy Hawaii. **1929** Motoring Thru Spain; Siam, the Land of Chang. **1930** France; Germany; London; Mediterranean Cruise; Venice.

HOLMES, HELEN

Born: 1892, Chicago, Ill. Died: July 8, 1950, Burbank, Calif. (heart attack). Screen actress. Entered films with Sennett in 1912.

Appeared in: **1914** The Hazards of Helen (serial). **1915** The Girl and the Game (serial). **1916** A Lass of the Lumberlands (serial). **1917** The Lost Express (serial); The Railroad Raiders (serial). **1919** The Fatal Fortune (serial). **1920** The Tiger Band (serial). **1921** A Crook's Romance. **1922** Ghost City; Hills of Missing Men; The Lone Hand. **1923** Stormy Seas; One Million in Jewels. **1924** Battling Brewster (serial); The Riddle Rider (serial); Fighting Fury; Forty Horse Hawkins. **1925** Blood and Steel; Barriers of the Law; The Sign of the Cactus; Webs of Steel; Duped; Outwitted; The Train Wreckers. **1926** Mistaken Orders; Crossed Signals; Peril of the Rail; The Lost Express; The Open Switch. **1936** Poppy. **1937** The Californian. **1941** Dude Cowboy.

HOLMES, J. MERRILL (Jack Merrill Holmes)

Born: July 21, 1889, Pennsylvania. Died: Feb. 27, 1950, Los Angeles, Calif. (heart failure). Screen actor.

Appeared in: **1941** The Bandit Trail; Land of the Open Range.

HOLMES, PHILLIPS

Born: July 22, 1909, Grand Rapids, Mich. Died: Aug. 12, 1942, near Armstrong, Ontario, Canada (air collision of two RCAF planes). Stage and screen actor. Son of actor Taylor Holmes (dec. 1959) and brother of actor Ralph Holmes (dec. 1945).

Appeared in: **1928** Varsity (film debut); His Private Life; The Return of Sherlock Holmes. **1929** The Wild Party; Stairs of Sand; Pointed Heels. **1930** The Dancers; Grumpy; Her Man; The Devil's Holiday; Only the Brave; Paramount on Parade. **1931** An American Tragedy; Stolen Heaven; Man to Man; Confessions of a Co-ed; The Criminal Code. **1932** Justice for Sale; Rockabye; The Man I Killed; Broken Lullaby; Two Kinds of Women; 70,000 Witnesses; Night Court. **1933** Dinner at Eight; Penthouse; Storm at Daybreak; Beauty for Sale; The Secret of Madame Blanche; Men Must Fight; Looking Forward; Stage Mother; The Big Brain; State Fair. **1934** Great Expectations; Nana; Million Dollar Ransom; Caravan; Private Scandal. **1935** No Ransom; Ten Minute Alibi; The Divine Spark. **1936** The House of a Thousand Candles; Chatterbox; General Spanky. **1937** The Dominant Sex. **1939** Housemaster.

HOLMES, RALPH

Born: May 20, 1889, Detroit, Mich. Died: Nov. 1945, New York, N.Y. (natural causes). Screen, stage actor and editor. Son of actor Taylor Holmes (dec. 1959) and brother of actor Phillips Holmes (dec. 1942).

HOLMES, RAPLEY

Born: 1868, Canada. Died: Jan. 11, 1928, Strathrey, Ont., Canada. Screen actor. Married to stage actress Gerda Holmes (dec.).

Appeared in: **1914** In the Moon's Ray; Seeds of Chaos; One Wonderful Night; Night Hawks; Through Eyes of Love. **1915** The Creed of the Clan; The Fable of the Cold Gray Dawn of the Morning After; The Victory of Virtue. **1916** Gloria's Romance.

HOLMES, STUART

Born: Mar. 10, 1887, Chicago, Ill. Died: Dec. 29, 1971, Hollywood, Calif. (ruptured abdominal aortic aneurism). Screen, stage and vaudeville actor.

Appeared in: **1914** Life's Shop Window. **1916** A Daughter of the Gods. **1917** The Scarlet Letter. **1919** The New Moon; The Other Man's Wife. **1920** The Evil Eye (serial); Trailed by Three (serial). **1921** The Four Horsemen of the Apocalypse; No Woman Knows; All's Fair in Love; Passion Fruit. **1922** The Prisoner of Zenda; Her Husband's Trademark; Paid Back; Under Two Flags. **1923** Daughters of the Rich; The Stranger's Banquet; The Rip-Tide; Tea with a Kick; Hollywood; The Scarlet Lily; Tipped Off; Temporary Marriage; The Unknown Purple. **1924** Tess of the D'Urbervilles; The Age of Innocence; Between Friends; Vanity's Price; The Beloved Brute; Three Weeks; In Every Woman's Life; On Time; The Siren of Seville. **1925** Fighting Cub; Three Keys; Friendly Enemies; Heir-Loons; The Primrose Path; The Salvation Hunters; Steele of the Royal Mounted; A Fool and His Money; Paint and Powder. **1926** North Star; Devil's Island; Good and Naughty; The Hurricane; The Midnight Message; Broken Hearts of Hollywood; Beyond the Trail; The Shadow of the Law; Everybody's Acting; My Official Wife. **1927** When a Man Loves; Your Wife and Mine; Polly of the Movies. **1928** The Man Who Laughs; Beware of Married Men; Burning Daylight; Danger Trail; Devil Dogs; The Cavalier; The Hawk's Nest; The Heroic Lover; Captain of the Guard. **1931** War Mamas (short). **1932** My Pal the King; The Millionaire Cat (short); Jitters the Butler (short). **1934** Are We Civilized?; Belle of the Nineties. **1936** Murder by an Aristocrat; Earthworm Tractors; The Case of the Velvet Claws; Trailin' West. **1937** Her Husband's Secretary. **1939** On Trial. **1940** British Intelligence;

Devil's Island. **1944** Last Ride; The Adventures of Mark Twain. **1945** Shady Lady. **1947** Moss Rose. **1948** A Letter to Three Wives. **1953** Remains to Be Seen. **1955** The Cobweb. **1956** The Birds and the Bees. **1962** The Man Who Shot Liberty Valance.

HOLMES, TAYLOR

Born: 1872, Newark, N.J. Died: Sept. 30, 1959, Hollywood, Calif. Screen, stage, vaudeville and television actor. Married to actress Edna Phillips (dec. 1952). Father of actors Phillips (dec. 1942) and Ralph Holmes (dec. 1945).

Appeared in: **1917** Efficiency Edgar's Courtship; Fools for Luck; Two-Bit Seats; Small Town Guy; Uneasy Money. **1918** Ruggles of Red Gap. **1919** It's a Bear; A Regular Fellow; Taxi; Upside Down. **1920** Nothing but the Truth. **1924** Twenty Dollars a Week. **1925** The Crimson Runner; The Verdict; Borrowed Finery; Her Market Value. **1927** One Hour of Love. **1929** The following shorts: He Did His Best; He Loved the Ladies. **1930** Dad Knows Best (short). **1931** An American Tragedy. **1933** Before Morning; Dinner at Eight. **1934** Nana. **1936** The Crime of Dr. Forbes; The First Baby; Make Way for a Lady. **1947** Kiss of Death; Nightmare Alley; The Egg and I; Time out of Mind; In Self Defense; Boomerang; Great Expectations. **1948** Smart Woman; Let's Love Again; The Plunderers; Act of Violence; That Wonderful Urge; Joan of Arc. **1949** Woman in Hiding; Joe Palooka in the Big Fight; Mr. Belvedere Goes to College; Once More My Darling. **1950** Bright Leaf; Caged; Copper Canyon; Double Deal; Father of the Bride; Quicksand. **1951** Drums in the Deep South; The First Legion; Rhubarb; Two Tickets to Broadway. **1952** Woman in the North Country; Beware My Lovely; Hold that Line; Hoodlum Empire; Ride the Man Down. **1953** Gentlemen Prefer Blondes. **1954** The Outcast; Tobor the Great; Untamed Heiress. **1955** The Fighting Chance; Hell's Outpost. **1956** The Maverick Queen; The Peace Maker. **1958** Wink of an Eye.

HOLMES, WENDELL

Born: 1915. Died: Apr. 26, 1962, Paris, France. Screen, stage and television actor.

Appeared in: **1949** Lost Boundaries. **1958** Young and Wild. **1959** Edge of Eternity; Good Day for a Hanging. **1960** Because They're Young; Elmer Gantry. **1961** The Absent-Minded Professor.

HOLMES, WILLIAM J.

Born: 1877. Died: Dec. 1, 1946, Hollywood, Calif. Screen, stage, vaudeville actor, playwright and stage producer.

Appeared in: **1930** Once a Gentleman.

HOLT, JACK (Charles John Holt)

Born: May 31, 1888, New York, N.Y. Died: Jan. 18, 1951, Los Angeles, Calif. (heart attack). Army officer. Father of actor Tim Holt (dec. 1973) and actress Jennifer Holt. Entered films in 1914 as a stuntman.

Appeared in: **1914** Salomy Jane. **1915** The Broken Coin (serial); A Cigarette—That's All; The Master Key (serial); Mother Ashton; The Power of Fascination; The Campbells Are Coming; The Lumber Yard Gang. **1916** The Better Man; The Black Sheep of the Family; Born of the People; Brennon O' the Moor; The Chalice of Sorrow; The Desperado; The Dumb Girl of Portici; The False Part; Her Better Self; His Majesty Dick Turpin; Liberty (serial); The Madcap Queen of Crona; Naked Hearts; The Princely Bandit; The Strong Arm Squad. **1917** The Call of the East; The Cost of Hatred; Giving Becky a Chance; The Inner Shrine; The Little American; Sacrifice; The Secret Game. **1918** The Claw; A Desert Wooing; Green Eyes; Headin' South; Love Me; The Marriage Ring; One More American; The Road through the Dark; The White Man's Law; The Squaw Man. **1919** Cheating Cheaters; For Better, for Worse; The Life Line; A Midnight Romance; A Sporting Chance; The Squaw Man; Victory; The Woman Thou Gavest Me. **1920** The Best of Luck; Crooked Streets; Held by the Enemy; Kitty Kelly, M.D.; Midsummer's Madness; The Sins of Rosanne. **1921** After the Show; All Soul's Eve; The Call of the North; Ducks and Drakes; The Grim Comedian; The Lost Romance; The Mask. **1922** Bought and Paid For; Making a Man; The Man Unconquerable; North of the Rio Grande; On the High Seas; While Satan Sleeps. **1923** The Cheat; A Gentleman of Leisure; Hollywood; The Marriage Maker; Nobody's Money; The Tiger's Claw. **1924** Don't Call It Love; Empty Hands; The Lone Wolf; North of 36; Wanderer of the Wasteland. **1925** The Ancient Highway; Eve's Secret; The Light of the Western Stars; The Thundering Herd; Wild Horse Mesa. **1926** The Blind Goddess; Born to the West; The Enchanted Hill; Forlorn River; Man of the Forest; Sea Horses. **1927** The Mysterious Rider; The Tigress; The Warning. **1928** Avalanche; Court-Martial; The Smart Set; Submarine; The Vanishing Pioneer; The Water Hole. **1929** The Donovan Affair; Father and Son; Flight; Sunset Pass. **1930** The Border Legion; Hell's Island; The Squealer; Vengeance. **1931** A Dangerous Affair; Dirigible; Fifty Fathoms Deep; The Last Parade; Maker of Men; Subway Express; White Shoulders. **1932** Behind the Mask; Man Against Woman; This Sporting Age; War Correspondent. **1933** Master of Men; When Strangers Marry; The Whirlpool (aka The Forgotten Man); The Woman I Stole; The Wrecker. **1934** Black Moon; The Defense Rests; I'll Fix It. **1935** The Awakening of Jim Burke; The Best Man Wins; The Littlest Rebel; Storm over the Andes; Unwelcome Stranger. **1936** Crash Donovan; Dangerous Waters; End of the Trail; North of Nome; San Francisco. **1937** Outlaws of the Orient; Roaring Timber; Trapped by G-

Men; Trouble in Morocco; Under Suspicion. **1938** Crime Takes a Holiday; Flight into Nowhere; Making the Headlines; Outside the Law; Reformatory. **1939** Fugitive at Large; Hidden Power; Trapped in the Sky; Whispering Enemies. **1940** The Great Plane Robbery; Outside the Three Mile Limit; Passport to Alcatraz; Prison Camp. **1941** The Great Swindle; Holt of the Secret Service (serial). **1942** Northwest Rangers; Thunder Birds. **1943** Customs of the Service (Army training film). **1944** The Articles of War (Army training film). **1945** They Were Expendable. **1946** The Chase; My Pal Trigger; Renegade Girl. **1947** The Wild Frontier. **1948** Arizona Rangers; Flight into Nowhere; The Gallant Legion; Strawberry Roan; The Treasure of Sierra Madre. **1949** Brimstone; The Last Bandit; Loaded Pistols; Red Desert; Task Force. **1950** Return of the Frontiersman; Trail of Robin Hood; King of the Bullwhip; The Daltons' Women. **1951** Across the Wide Missouri.

HOLT, TIM (John Charles Holt, III)
Born: Feb. 5, 1919, Beverly Hills, Calif. Died: Feb. 15, 1973, Shawnee, Okla. (cancer). Film, stage and television actor. Son of actor Jack Holt (dec. 1951), brother of actress Jennifer Holt. Divorced from Virginia Ashcroft and Alice Harrison. Married to Birdie Stephens Holt.

Appeared in: **1928** The Vanishing Pioneer (film debut). **1937** Stella Dallas; History Is Made at Night. **1938** I Met My Love Again; Gold Is Where You Find It; Sons of the Legion; The Law West of Tombstone. **1939** The Renegade Ranger; Stagecoach; Spirit of Culver; The Girl and the Gambler; Fifth Avenue Girl; The Rookie Cop. **1940** Swiss Family Robinson; Laddie; The Fargo Kid; Wagon Train. **1941** Back Street; Dude Cowboy; Along the Rio Grande; Robbers of the Range; Riding the Wind; Six-Gun Gold; Cyclone on Horseback; Land of the Open Range; Come On, Danger!; Thundering Hoofs; The Bandit Trail. **1942** The Magnificent Ambersons; Pirates of the Prairie; Bandit Ranger; **1943** Hitler's Children; The Avenging Rider; Red River Robin Hood; Sagebrush Law; Pirates of the Prairie; Fighting Frontier. **1946** My Darling Clementine; **1947** Thunder Mountain; Wild Horse Mesa; Under the Tonto Rim; The Treasure of Sierra Madre. **1948** His Kind of Woman; The Arizona Ranger; Guns of Hate; Western Heritage; Indian Agent; Gun Smugglers. **1949** The Mysterious Desperado; Rustlers; The Stagecoach Kid; Brothers in the Saddle; Gun Smugglers; Masked Raiders; Riders of the Range. **1950** Border Treasure; Rider from Tucson; Rio Grande Patrol; Storm over Wyoming; Dynamite Pass; Law of the Badlands. **1951** His Kind of Woman; Saddle Legion; Gunplay; Pistol Harvest; Overland Telegraph; Hot Lead. **1952** Trail Guide; Target; Road Agent; Desert Passage. **1957** The Monster that Challenged the World.

HOLUBAR, ALLEN
Born: 1889. Died: 1925. Screen, stage actor, playwright, film director, producer and screenwriter.

Appeared in: **1913** A Wolf among Lambs; The Prophecy. **1915** The White Terror. **1916** Twenty Thousand Leagues under the Sea; Any Youth; The Phone Message; The Shadow; The Taint of Fear; Stronger than Steel; The Prodigal Daughter. **1917** Heart Strings; The Old Toymaker; The War Waif; Where the Glory Waits; Treason; The Double Topped Trunk; The Grip of Love.

HOLZWORTH, FRED
Died: Feb. 1, 1970, Cleveland, Ohio. Stage and screen actor.

HOMANS, ROBERT E.
Born: 1875, Malden, Mass. Died: July 28, 1947, Los Angeles, Calif. (heart attack). Stage and screen actor.

Appeared in: **1923** Legally Dead. **1924** The Breathless Moment; Dark Stairways. **1925** Border Justice. **1926** Fighting with Buffalo Bill (serial); The Silent Power; College Days. **1927** The Fightin' Comeback; The Bandit Buster (serial); Ride 'em High; Fast and Furious; Range Courage; The Galloping Gobs; The Princess from Hoboken; Heroes of the Night; Mountains of Manhattan; The Silent Avenger. **1928** The Masked Angel; Pals in Peril; Obey Your Husband; Blindfold. **1929** Burning the Wind; The Isle of Lost Ships; Smiling Irish Eyes; Fury of the Wild. **1930** The Concentratin' Kid; Son of the Gods; Spurs; Trigger Tricks; The Thoroughbred. **1931** The Black Camel; Silence. **1932** Pack up Your Troubles; Young America; Madame Racketeer. **1933** From Headquarters; She Done Him Wrong. **1936** Ride, Ranger, Ride; Here Comes Trouble; Laughing Irish Eyes; The President's Mystery; Easy Money; It Couldn't Have Happened; Bridge of Sighs; Below the Deadline. **1937** The Plough and the Stars; Easy Living; Penrod and Sam; Don't Pull Your Punches; Dance, Charlie, Dance; Forlorn River; Jim Hanvey, Detective. **1938** The Kid Comes Back; Little Tough Guy; Penrod and His Twin Brother; Over the Wall; Little Miss Thoroughbred; The Amazing Dr. Clitterhouse; Heart of the North; Tom Sawyer, Detective; Gold Is Where You Find It; Hollywood Stadium Mystery; Gold Mine in the Sky; The Night Hawk; Hunted Men. **1939** Hell's Kitchen; Young Mr. Lincoln; Inside Information; Smuggled Cargo; The Old Maid; Ruler of the Sea; Five Came Back; King of the Turf. **1940** Goin' Fishin' (short); West of Carson City; East of the River; The Grapes of Wrath; Lillian Russell. **1941** Glamour Boy; Sierra Sue; Out of the Fog. **1942** Fingers at the Window; For Me and My Gal; It Happened in Flatbush; Lady in a Jam; The Sombrero Kid; X Marks the Spot; Night Monster. **1943** Happy Go Lucky; You Can't Beat the Law; Shantytown; Frontier Badmen; It Ain't Hay. **1944** Pin Up Girl; It Hap-

pened Tomorrow; Say Uncle (short); Nothing but Trouble; Jack London; The Whistler; The Merry Monahans; Cover Girl. **1945** Rogues' Gallery; River Gang; Beyond the Pecos; A Medal for Benny; Come Out Fighting; Captain Eddie; The Scarlet Clue. **1946** Earl Carroll Sketchbook.

HONDA, FRANK
Born: 1884, Japan. Died: Feb. 3, 1924, N.Y. Screen actor.

Appeared in: **1921** Dawn of the East; Wedding Bells. **1923** Lawful Larceny.

HONN, ELDON
Born: 1890. Died: Aug. 11, 1927, San Diego, Calif. (died in parachute fall). Screen actor and motorcycle stuntman.

HOOD, TOM
Born: 1919. Died: Dec. 8, 1950, Hollywood, Calif. (murdered). Screen actor.

HOOPE, AAF BOUBER-TEN
Died: May 23, 1974. Dutch screen actor.

HOOPII, SOL (Sol Hoopii Kaaiai)
Born: 1905, Hawaii. Died: Nov. 16, 1953, Seattle, Wash. Screen actor and musician.

HOOPS, ARTHUR
Born: 1870. Died: Sept. 17, 1916. Screen actor.

Appeared in: **1914** The Better Man; The Straight Road; Such a Little Queen. **1915** Gretna Green; A Woman's Resurrection; Should a Mother Tell?; The Song of Hate; Mistress Nell; Esmeralda; The Mummy and the Humming Bird; The Danger Signal. **1916** The Lure of Heart's Desire; The Devil's Prayer-Book; The Final Curtain; The Soul Market; The Scarlet Woman; The Eternal Question; Extravagance. **1917** Bridges Burned; The Secret of Eve.

HOOSMAN, AL
Born: 1918, U.S. Died: Oct. 26, 1968, Munich, Germany. American professional boxer turned screen actor.

Appeared in: **1962** Toller Hecht auf Krummer Tour (aka The Phoney American—US 1964). **1967** Jack of Diamonds.

HOOVER, J. EDGAR (John Edgar Hoover)
Born: Jan. 1, 1895, Washington, D.C. Died: May 2, 1972, Washington, D.C. (heart disease). Director of F.B.I., author and screen actor.

Appeared in: **1960** The FBI Story.

HOPE, DIANA
Born: 1872, England. Died: Nov. 20, 1942, Hollywood, Calif. (heart attack). Screen, stage and vaudeville actress.

Appeared in: **1930** The Man from Blankley's.

HOPE, MAIDIE
Born: 1881, England (?). Died: Apr. 20, 1937, London, England (following a fall). Screen, stage actress and singer.

Appeared in: **1920** The Honeypot; All the Winners. **1921** Love Maggy.

HOPE, VIDA
Born: 1918, England. Died: Dec. 23, 1963, Chelmsford, England (auto accident). Screen, stage actress and stage director. Married to film director Derek Twist.

Appeared in: **1944** English without Tears (aka Her Man Gilbey—US 1949). **1945** The Way to the Stars (aka Johnny in the Clouds—US). **1947** While the Sun Shines (US 1950); Nicholas Nickleby; It always Rains on Sunday (US 1949); They Made Me a Fugitive (aka I Became a Criminal—US 1948). **1949** For Them That Trespass (US 1950); Paper Orchid; The Interrupted Journey (US 1951). **1950** Double Confession (US 1953); The Woman in Question (aka Five Angles on Murder—US 1953). **1951** The Man in the White Suit (US 1952); Cheer the Brave; Green Grow the Rushes. **1952** Angels One Five (US 1954); Emergency Call (aka The Hundred Hour Hunt—US 1953); Women of Twilight (aka Twilight Women—US 1953). **1953** The Broken Horseshoe; The Long Memory; Marilyn (aka Roadhouse Girl—US 1955). **1954** Fast and Loose; Lease of Life. **1958** Family Doctor (aka Prescription for Murder and Rx Murder—US). **1961** In the Doghouse (US 1964).

HOPKINS, BOB
Born: 1918. Died: Oct. 5, 1962, Hollywood, Calif. (acute leukemia). Screen, stage and television actor.

Appeared in: **1945** On Stage Everybody. **1949** The Lucky Stiff. **1953** The Kid from Left Field. **1956** Autumn Leaves; Flight to Hong Kong. **1962** The Errand Boy; Saintly Sinners. **1963** Papa's Delicate Condition.

HOPKINS, MIRIAM (Ellen Miriam Hopkins)
Born: Oct. 18, 1902, Bainbridge, Ga. Died: Oct. 1972, New York, N.Y. (heart attack). Stage and screen actress. Divorced from actor Brandon Peters; playwright Austin Parker; and film producer Anatol Litvak (dec. 1974).

Appeared in: **1930** Holiday; Fast and Loose. **1931** Honest Finder; 24 Hours; The Smiling Lieutenant; Hours Between. **1932** The Best People; Dancers in the Dark; Two Kinds of Women; The World and the Flesh; Trouble in Paradise; Dr. Jekyll and Mr. Hyde. **1933** Strangers Return; Design for Living; The Story of Temple Drake. **1934** All of Me; She Loves Me Not; The Richest Girl in the World. **1935** Becky Sharp; Barbary Coast; Splendor. **1936** These Three. **1937** Men Are Not Gods; The Woman I Love; Wise Girl; Woman Chases Man. **1939** The Old Maid. **1940** Lady with Red Hair; Virginia City. **1942** A Gentleman After Dark. **1943** Old Acquaintance. **1949** The Heiress. **1951** The Mating Season. **1952** Carrie; The Outcasts of Poker Flat. **1962** The Children's Hour. **1965** Fanny Hill: Memoirs of a Woman of Pleasure. **1966** The Chase.

HOPPER, DE WOLF (William DeWolf Hopper)
Born: Mar. 30, 1858, New York, N.Y. Died: Sept. 23, 1935, Kansas City, Mo. Stage and screen actor. Married to stage actress Lillian Glaser (dec. 1969) and divorced from actresses Edna Wallace (dec. 1959) and Elda Furry (known professionally as Hedda Hopper) (dec. 1966) and father of actor William Hopper (dec. 1970).

Appeared in: **1914** The Newsboy's Friend. **1915** Don Quixote. **1916** Casey at the Bat; Macbeth; A Rough Knight; Wings and Wheels; The Girl and the Mummy; Puppets; Sunshine Dad. **1930** For Two Cents (short); At the Round Table (short). **1935** The Return of Dr. X.

HOPPER, EDNA WALLACE
Born: 1874, San Francisco, Calif. Died: Dec. 14, 1959, N.Y. Stage and screen actress. Filmed her own face-lifting operation. Divorced from actor DeWolf Hopper (dec. 1935).

HOPPER, HAL (Harold Stevens Hopper)
Born: Nov. 11, 1912, Oklahoma. Died: Nov. 2, 1970, Sylmar, Calif. (emphysema). Screen actor, composer and screenwriter.

Appeared in: **1964** Kitten with a Whip; Lorna. **1966** Beau Geste. **1969** Mud Honey (aka Rope of Flesh).

HOPPER, HEDDA (Elda Furry)
Born: June 2, 1890, Hallisdaysburg, Pa. Died: Feb. 1, 1966, Los Angeles, Calif. (pneumonia). Screen, stage, radio, television actress and columnist. Divorced from actor DeWolf Hopper (dec. 1935) and mother of actor William Hopper (dec. 1970).

Appeared in: **1916** Battle of Hearts (film debut). **1917** Seven Keys to Baldpate; Her Excellency, the Governor; The Food Gamblers; Nearly Married. **1918** By Right of Purchase. **1919** Virtuous Wives. **1920** The New York Idea; The Man Who Lost Himself; Conceit. **1922** Women Men Marry; What's Wrong with Women?; Sherlock Holmes. **1923** Has the World Gone Mad?; Reno. **1924** Happiness; Free Love; Miami; Another Scandal; Gambling Wives; The Snob; Sinners in Silk; Why Men Leave Home. **1925** Declassee; Raffles, the Amateur Cracksman; Zander the Great; Borrowed Finery; Dangerous Innocence; Her Market Value; The Teaser. **1926** Mona Lisa (short); Don Juan; The Caveman; Obey the Law; The Silver Treasure; Pleasures of the Rich; Dance Madness; Fools of Fashion; Lew Tyler's Wives; Skinner's Dress Suit. **1927** Wings; Children of Divorce; Adam and Evil; Black Tears; One Woman to Another; Matinee Ladies; The Cruel Truth; Orchids and Ermine; Venus of Venice; The Drop Kick; A Reno Divorce. **1928** Diamond Handcuffs; Companionate Marriage; The Chorus Kid; The Whip Woman; Giving In (short); Runaway Girls; Green Grass Widows; Harold Teen; The Port of Missing Girls; Undressed; Love and Learn. **1929** The Racketeer; Girls Gone Wild; Hurricane; His Glorious Night; The Last of Mrs. Cheyney; Half Marriage; A Song of Kentucky. **1930** Our Blushing Brides; High Society Blues; Divorcee; Such Men Are Dangerous; Holiday; War Nurse; Let Us Be Gay; Murder Will Out. **1931** Shipmates; The Easiest Way; Up for Murder; The Prodigal; Men Call It Love; Strangers May Kiss; A Tailor-Made Man; Rebound; Mystery Train; Flying High; Good Sport; Common Law. **1932** West of Broadway; Happy Landing; Night World; Speak Easily; Skyscraper Souls; The Unwritten Law; Downstairs; As You Desire Me; The Man Who Played God; The Slippery Pearls (short). **1933** The Barbarian; Pilgrimage; Beauty for Sale; Men Must Fight. **1934** Bombay Mail; Let's Be Ritzy; Little Man, What Now?; No Ransom. **1935** I Live My Life; Society Fever; One Frightened Night; Lady Tubbs; Three Kids and a Queen; Alice Adams. **1936** Dracula's Daughter; Doughnuts and Society; Bunker Bean; Dark Hour. **1937** You Can't Buy Luck; Topper; Dangerous Holiday; Artists and Models; Nothing Sacred; Vogues of 1938. **1938** Tarzan's Revenge; Dangerous to Know; Thanks for the Memory; Maid's Night Out. **1939** The Women; What a Life; Laugh It Off; Midnight; That's Right—You're Wrong. **1940** Queen of the Mob; Cross Country Romance. **1941** Life with Henry; I Wanted Wings. **1942** Reap the Wild Wind. **1946** Breakfast in Hollywood. **1950** Sunset Boulevard. **1960** Pepe. **1964** The Patsy. **1966** The Oscar.

HOPPER, WILLIAM (William DeWolf Hopper, Jr.)
Born: Jan. 26, 1915, New York, N.Y. Died: Mar. 6, 1970, Palm Springs, Calif. (pneumonia). Screen, stage and television actor. Entered films in 1937. Son of actress Hedda Hopper (dec. 1966) and actor DeWolf Hopper (dec. 1935).

Appeared in: **1937** The Adventurous Blonde; Footloose Heiress; Over the Goal; Love Is on the Air; Public Wedding; Women Are Like That. **1938** Mystery House; Daredevil Drivers. **1939** The Return of Dr. X; Angels Wash Their Faces; The Old Maid; Pride of the Bluegrass; Nancy Drew and the Hidden Staircase; The Cowboy Quarterback. **1940** Knute Rockne—All American; The Fighting Sixty-Ninth; Tear Gas Squad; Flight Angels; Ladies Must Live. **1941** The Maltese Falcon; The Bride Came C.O.D.; Flight from Destiny; Bullets for O'Hara; They Died with Their Boots On; Here Comes Happiness. **1942** Yankee Doodle Dandy; Lady Gangster. **1943** The Mysterious Doctor; Murder on the Waterfront. **1954** The High and the Mighty; Track of the Cat; Sitting Bull; This Is My Love. **1955** Conquest of Space; Rebel without a Cause; Robber's Roost; One Desire. **1956** The Bad Seed; Goodbye, My Lady; The First Texan. **1957** The Deadly Mantis; Slim Carter; 20,000,000 Miles to Earth. **1970** Myra Breckenridge.

HOPTON, RUSSELL "RUSS"
Born: Feb. 18, 1900, New York, N.Y. Died: Apr. 7, 1945, North Hollywood, Calif. Screen, stage actor and film director.

Appeared in: **1926** Ella Cinders. **1930** College Lovers; The Pay Off (short); Call of the Flesh; Min and Bill; Remote Control. **1931** Dance, Fools, Dance; Street Scene; Miracle Woman; Reckless Living; Arrowsmith; Twenty Grand; Blonde Crazy; Dance Team; The Criminal Code; Star Witness; Falling Star; Law and Order. **1932** Man Who Played God; The Drifter; Discarded Lovers; Big Timber; Night World; The Famous Ferguson Case; Radio Patrol; Back Street; Fast Companions; Air Mail; Tom Brown of Culver; Once in a Life Time. **1933** Successful Failure; I Sell Anything; Take the Stand; Destination Unknown; Desirable; Elmer the Great; The Little Giant; Lady Killer; One Year Later; Secret of the Blue Room; I'm No Angel. **1934** Good Dame; Men in White; Curtain at Eight; Half a Sinner; He Was Her Man; Born to Be Bad; School for Girls. **1935** Circus Shadows; Valley of Wanted Men; Time Square Lady; Northern Frontier; G-Men; Wings in the Dark; The World Accuses; Death from a Distance; False Pretenses; Star of Midnight; Headline Woman; Cheers of the Crowd; Frisco Waterfront; Car 99. **1936** The Last Outlaw; We Who Are about to Die; Below the Deadline; Rose of the Rancho. **1937** Beware of Ladies; Angel's Holiday; One Mile from Heaven; Idol of the Crowds. **1938** Crime Takes a Holiday. **1939** Made for Each Other; The Saint Strikes Back; Torture Ship; Mutiny in the Big House; The Renegade Trail. **1944** A Night of Adventure; plus the following shorts: Love Your Landlord; Radio Rampage; Girls! Girls! Girls! **1945** Birthday Blues (short); Zombies on Broadway; West of the Pecos.

HORAN, JAMES
Born: 1908. Died: May 4, 1967, Hollywood, Calif. (cancer). Screen and television actor.

Appeared in: **1964** The Unsinkable Molly Brown; My Fair Lady.

HORNBROOK, CHARLES "GUS"
Born: 1874. Died: May 8, 1937, Los Angeles, Calif. (pneumonia). Screen and vaudeville actor.

HORNE, DAVID
Born: July 14, 1898, Blacome, Sussex, England. Died: Mar. 15, 1970, London, England. Screen, stage actor and playwright.

Appeared in: **1933** General John Regan; Lord of the Manor. **1934** Badger's Queen; The Case for the Crown. **1935** Late Extra; That's My Uncle; The Village Squire; Gentleman's Agreement. **1936** Under Proof; Seven Sinners (aka Doomed Cargo—US); It's Love Again; The Interrupted Honeymoon; The House of the Spaniard; Debt of Honour; A Touch of the Moon. **1937** The Mill on the Floss (US 1939); Farewell Again (aka Troopship—US 1938); Four Dark Hours; 21 Days (aka The First and the Last and 21 Days Together—US 1940). **1939** Blind Folly. **1940** The Door with Seven Locks (aka Chamber of Horrors—US 1940); Crimes at the Dark House. **1941** Inspector Hornleigh Goes to It (aka Mail Train—US); Breach of Promise (aka Adventure in Blackmail—US 1943). **1942** The First of the Few (aka Spitfire—US 1943); The Day Will Dawn (aka The Avengers—US); They Flew Alone (aka Wings and the Woman—US). **1943** San Demetrio—London; Yellow Canary (US 1944). **1945** They Were Sisters (US 1946); The Seventh Veil (US 1946); The Rake's Progress (aka Notorious Gentleman—US 1946); The Man from Morocco; The Wicked Lady (US 1946). **1946** Gaiety George (aka Showtime—US 1948); Caravan (US 1947); Spring Song (aka Springtime—US); The Magic Bow (US 1947); Men of Two Worlds. **1947** The Green Cockatoo (rerelease of Four Dark Hours—1937); The Man Within (aka The Smugglers—US 1948). **1948** Saraband for Dead Lovers (aka Saraband—US 1949); It's Hard to Be Good (US 1950). **1949** Once Upon a Dream; History of Mr. Polly (US 1951). **1950** Madeleine. **1951** Appointment with Venus (aka Island Rescue—US 1952). **1953** Spaceways; Street Corner (aka Both Sides of the Law—US 1954). **1954** Beau Brummel. **1955** Three Cases of Murder. **1956** The Last Man to Hang; Lust for Life. **1957** The Prince and the Showgirl. **1958** The Safecracker; The Sheriff of Fractured Jaw.

1959 The Devil's Disciple. 1961 The Clue at New Pin; Goodbye Again; Dentist on the Job (aka Get on with It!—US 1963). 1963 Nurse on Wheels (US 1964). 1968 A Flea in Her Ear; Diamonds for Breakfast.

HORNE, JAMES W.

Born: Dec. 14, 1881, San Francisco, Calif. Died: June 29, 1942, Los Angeles, Calif. (cerebral hemorrhage). Screen, stage actor and film director. Married to actress Cleo Ridgely (dec. 1962).

Appeared in: 1915 The False Clue; The Pitfall; The Mysteries of the Grand Hotel.

HORTON, BENJAMIN

Born: 1872. Died: Aug. 9, 1952, Hollywood, Calif. Screen actor.

HORTON, EDWARD EVERETT

Born: Mar. 18, 1886, Brooklyn, N.Y. Died: Sept. 29, 1970, Encino, Calif. (cancer). Screen, stage, vaudeville, radio, television actor, stage producer and stage director.

Appeared in: 1922 A Front Page Story; The Lady Jinx; Two Much Business. 1923 Ruggles of Red Gap; To the Ladies. 1924 Try and Get It; Flapper Wives; Helen's Babies; The Man Who Fights Alone. 1925 Marry Me; Beggar on Horseback; The Nut-Cracker (aka You Can't Fool Your Wife). 1926 The Whole Town's Talking; The Business of Love; La Boheme; Poker Faces; plus six Harold Lloyd shorts. 1927 Taxi! Taxi!; Edward Everett Horton Comedy (short). 1928 Miss Information (short); The Terror. 1929 Sonny Boy; The Hottentot; The Sap; The Aviator; plus the following shorts: Ask Dad; Trusting Wives; Prince Gabby; The Eligible Mr. Bangs; Good Medicine; The Right Bed. 1930 Take the Heir; Wide Open; Holiday; Once a Gentleman. 1931 Kiss Me Again (aka The Toast of the Legion); Reaching for the Moon; Lonely Wives; Smart Woman; Six Cylinder Love; The Front Page; The Age for Love. 1932 But the Flesh Is Weak; Roar of the Dragon; Trouble in Paradise. 1933 Soldiers of the King (aka The Woman in Command—US 1934); The Way to Love; Design for Living; Alice in Wonderland; It's a Boy (US 1934); A Bedtime Story. 1934 Easy to Live; Sing and Like It; Uncertain Lady; Success at Any Price; The Merry Widow; Kiss and Make Up; Ladies Should Listen; The Poor Rich; The Gay Divorcee (aka The Gay Divorce); Smarty (aka Hit Me Again). 1935 Biography of a Bachelor Girl; The Night Is Young; All the King's Horses; The Devil Is a Woman (aka Caprice Espagnol); In Caliente; $10 Raise (aka Mr. Faintheart); Going Highbrow; Little Big Shot; Top Hat; The Private Secretary; His Night Out; Your Uncle Dudley. 1936 The Man in the Mirror (US 1937); Her Master's Voice; The Singing Kid; Hearts Divided (aka Glorious Betsy); Nobody's Fool (aka Unconscious). 1937 Lost Horizon; Let's Make a Million; Angel; Wild Money; The King and the Chorus Girl; The Perfect Specimen; The Great Garrick; Oh, Doctor; Shall We Dance?; Hitting a New High; Danger—Love at Work. 1938 Bluebeard's Eighth Wife; College Swing (aka Swing, Teacher, Swing); Holiday (aka Free to Live); Little Tough Guys in Society. 1939 Paris Honeymoon; The Gang's All Here (aka The Amazing Mr. Forrest); That's Right—You're Wrong. 1941 You're the One; Ziegfeld Girl; Sunny; Bachelor Daddy (aka Sandy Steps Out); Here Comes Mr. Jordan; Weekend for Three; The Body Disappears. 1942 I Married an Angel; The Magnificent Dope; Springtime in the Rockies. 1943 Forever and a Day; Thank Your Lucky Stars; The Gang's All Here (aka The Girls He Left Behind). 1944 Her Primitive Man; Summer Storm; San Diego I Love You; Arsenic and Old Lace; Brazil; The Town Went Wild. 1945 Steppin' in Society; Lady on a Train. 1946 Cinderella Jones; Faithful in My Fashion; Earl Carroll Sketchbook (aka Hats Off to Rhythm). 1947 The Ghost Goes Wild; Down to Earth; Her Husband's Affairs. 1952 Elstree Story (doc. with film clips of 1939 movie The Gangs All Here). 1957 The Story of Mankind. 1961 Pocketful of Miracles. 1963 It's a Mad, Mad, Mad, Mad World. 1964 Sex and the Single Girl. 1967 The Perils of Pauline. 1969 2,000 Years Later. 1970 Cold Turkey.

HORWITZ, JOSEPH

Born: 1858. Died: Oct. 26, 1922, Mt. Clemens, Mich. (uremic poisoning). Screen actor.

HOSTETTER, ROY

Born: 1885. Died: Sept. 22, 1951, near Carlsbad, Calif. (auto accident). Screen actor.

HOTALING, ARTHUR D. (Arthur Douglas Hotaling)

Born: 1872. Died: July 13, 1938, enroute to San Pedro from Palm Springs, Calif. (heart attack). Screen actor and film director. Married to actress Mae Hotely (dec. 1954).

Appeared in: 1925 Kit Carson over the Great Divide. 1927 Better Days; King of the Herd. 1928 The Little Wild Girl; Old Age Handicap.

HOTELY, MAE

Born: Oct. 7, 1872, Maryland. Died: Apr. 6, 1954, Coronado, Calif. Screen actress. Married to actor Arthur D. Hotaling (dec. 1938).

Appeared in: 1911 A Question of Modesty; The Wise Detective; A Stage Door Flirtation; Business and Love. 1912 The New Constable; Nora—the Cook. 1913 The Gay Time series; Fixing Aunty Up; A Masked Mix-Up; Kate, the Cop;

Building a Trust; The Widow's Wiles; Her Wooden Leg; The Engaging Kid; The Actress and Her Jewels; Giving Bill a Rest; An Interrupted Courtship; She Must Elope; The Missing Jewels; Training a Tightwad; The Fake Soldiers; His Widow; Minnie the Widow. 1915 The Twin Sister; A Lucky Strike; An Artful Artist; The Telegrapher's Peril; Price of Pies; Think of the Money; The Golden Oysters; The Cellar Spy; Playing Horse; His Bodyguard; His Suicide; Clothes Count; Si and Sue—Acrobats; The New Butler. 1929 Girls Who Dare.

HOUDINI, HARRY (Erik aka Ehrich Weisz and Henry Weiss)

Born: Mar. 24, 1874, Hungary. (Numerous publications indicate date of birth as Feb. 29, 1876, however, correct date explained as follows: "Perhaps to give Ehrich the security of American citizenship, she (his mother) told him that he, like his younger brother Theo, had been born in Appleton. The date she said was Apr. 6, 1874. That became his 'adopted birthday.' ")* Died: Oct. 31, 1926, Detroit, Mich. (following appendectomy). Magician, screen, stage, vaudeville actor and film producer. Entered films in 1918. Married to vaudeville performer Bess Rahner.

Appeared in: 1918 The Master Mystery (serial). 1919 The Grim Game. 1920 Terror Island. 1921 The Soul of Bronze. 1922 The Man from Beyond. 1923 Haldane of the Secret Service. 1961 Days of Thrills and Laughter (documentary).

HOUGHTON, ALICE

Born: 1888. Died: May 12, 1944, Los Angeles, Calif. Screen actress.

HOUSE, BILLY

Born: 1890. Died: Sept. 23, 1961, Hollywood, Calif. (heart attack). Screen, stage and vaudeville actor.

Appeared in: 1930 Resolution (short). 1931 Smart Money; God's Gift to Women. 1932–33 Paramount shorts. 1937 Merry-Go-Round of 1938. 1945 Thrill of a Romance. 1946 Bedlam; The Strangers. 1947 The Egg and I; Trail Street. 1950 Rogues of Sherwood Forest; Where Danger Lives. 1951 People Will Talk; Santa Fe. 1952 Aladdin and His Lamp; Outlaw Women. 1955 Imitation of Life.

HOUSE, JACK

Born: 1887. Died: Nov. 20, 1963, Hollywood, Calif. Screen actor and stuntman. Doubled for Rudolf Valentino and Fred Thomas.

Appeared in: 1924 The Smoking Trail. 1925 Fightin' Odds.

HOUSEMAN, ARTHUR (aka ARTHUR HOUSMAN)

Born: 1890, New York, N.Y. Died: Apr. 7, 1942, Los Angeles, Calif. (pneumonia). Stage and screen actor.

Appeared in: 1921 The Fighter; The Way of a Maid; Clay Dollars; Room and Board; Worlds Apart; Is Life Worth Living? 1922 The Snitching Hour; Man Wanted; Destiny's Isle; Love's Masquerade; Shadows of the Sea; Why Announce Your Marriage?; The Prophet's Paradise. 1923 Male Wanted; Under the Red Robe; Wife in Name Only. 1924 Manhandled; Nellie, the Beautiful Cloak Model. 1925 A Man Must Live; The Necessary Evil; Thunder Mountain; The Coast of Folly; The Desert's Price; Night Life of New York. 1926 The Bat; Braveheart; Early to Wed; Whispering Wires; The Midnight Kiss. 1927 Bertha, the Sewing Machine Girl; Publicity Madness; The Spotlight; Sunrise; Rough House Rosie; Love Makes 'Em Wild. 1928 The Singing Fool; Partners in Crime; Fools For Luck. 1929 Sins of the Fathers; Side Street; Queen of the Night Clubs; Fast Company; Times Square; Broadway; The Song of Love. 1930 Girl of the Golden West; The Squealer; Officer O'Brien; Feet First. 1931 Bachelor Girl; Five and Ten; Night Life in Reno; Anybody's Blonde; Caught Plastered. 1932 Movie Crazy; No More Orchids; Afraid to Talk; plus the following shorts: Parlor, Bedroom and Wrath; Scram!; Any Old Port. 1933 She Done Him Wrong; The Intruder; Her Bodyguard; The Way to Love; Sing, Sinner, Sing; Good Housewrecking (short). 1934 Mrs. Wiggs of the Cabbage Patch; Here Is My Heart; plus the following shorts: Something Simple; The Chases of Pimple Street; The Live Ghost; Babes in the Goods; Done in Oil; Punch Drunks. 1935 Hold 'Em Yale; Riffraff; Paris in the Spring; Here Comes Cookie; Diamond Jim; The Fire Trap; plus the following shorts: It Always Happens; The Fixer-Uppers; Treasure Blues; Sing, Sister, Sing. 1936 Our Relations; Wives Never Know; Racing Blood; With Love and Kisses; Am I Having Fun (short). 1937 Step Lively; Jeeves! 1939 Navy Secrets. 1940 Go West.

HOUSTON, CISCO

Born: 1919. Died: Apr. 23, 1961, San Bernardino, Calif. Screen actor, folk singer and song writer. Appeared in western films.

HOUSTON, GEORGE

Born: 1900, Hampton, N.J. Died: Nov. 12, 1944, Los Angeles, Calif. (heart ailment). Screen, stage actor and opera performer.

Appeared in: 1935 The Melody Lingers On (film debut). 1936 Let's Sing Again; Captain Calamity. 1937 Hurricane; Conquest; Wallaby Jim of the Islands. 1938 Frontier Scout; The Great Waltz. 1940 Laughing at Danger; The

*From Houdini: The Untold Story by Milbourne Christopher, c1969 by Milbourne Christopher. With permission of the publisher, Thomas Y. Crowell Company, Inc.

Howards of Virginia. **1941** The Lone Rider in Ghost Town; The Lone Rider Ambushed; The Lone Rider Fights Back. **1942** The Lone Rider in Border Roundup; The Lone Rider in Cheyenne.

HOUSTON, JEAN

Died: Jan. 1965, Paisley, Scotland. Screen, stage, radio actress and singer.

HOVICK, ROSE LOUISE. *See* GYPSY ROSE LEE

HOWARD, ART

Born: 1892. Died: May 28, 1963, Hollywood, Calif. (coronary thrombosis). Stage and screen actor.

HOWARD, BERT

Born: 1873. Died: Oct. 27, 1958, Hollywood, Calif. Stage and screen actor.

HOWARD, BOOTH (Boothe Howard)

Born: 1889. Died: Oct. 4, 1936, Los Angeles, Calif. (hit by auto). Stage and screen actor.

Appeared in: **1933** My Woman; Hot Pepper; Trick for Treat; The Avenger. **1934** Mystery Liner; Midnight Alibi. **1935** Smart Girl; Every Night at Eight; Mary Burns, Fugitive; Show Them No Mercy. **1936** The Robin Hood of El Dorado; Charlie Chan at the Circus; Undersea Kingdom (serial); Red River Valley; Oh, Susannah!

HOWARD, CHARLES (Charles Ray Howard)

Born: 1882, San Diego, Calif. Died: June 28, 1947, New York, N.Y. (heart attack). Screen, stage, burlesque and vaudeville actor.

Appeared in: **1917** Eternal Sin. **1918** Every Mother's Son; Neighbors. **1927** Home Struck. **1930** All Stuck Up (short). **1931** The Night Angel.

HOWARD, DAVID H.

Born: 1860, N.Y. Died: Dec. 9, 1944, Woodland Hills, Calif. Stage and screen actor.

HOWARD, EDDY

Born: 1909, Ill. Died: May 23, 1963, Palm Desert, Calif. (cerebral hemorrhage). Bandleader, song writer and screen actor.

HOWARD, ERNEST (Ernest Ladd)

Born: 1875. Died: Nov. 8, 1940, Brooklyn, N.Y. Screen and stage actor. Appeared in silent films.

HOWARD, ESTHER

Born: 1893. Died: Mar. 8, 1965, Hollywood, Calif. (heart attack). Stage and screen actress. Married to actor Arthur Albertson (dec. 1926).

Appeared in: **1930** The following shorts: Twixt Love and Duty; Ship Ahoy; The Woman Tamer; Who's the Boss; The Victim. **1931** Wicked; The Vice Squad. **1932** Ladies of the Big House; The Cohens and the Kellys in Hollywood; Merrily We Go to Hell; Winner Take All; Rackerty Rax. **1933** Below the Sea; Second Hand Wife; The Iron Master. **1935** Straight from the Heart; Ready for Love; The Misses Stooge (short); It Always Happens (short). **1936** Klondike Annie; M'Liss; Love Comes to Mooneyville (short); Foolproof (short). **1937** Rhythm in the Clouds; Stuck in the Sticks (short). **1938** Scandal Street; Swing, Sister, Swing. **1939** Broadway Serenade. **1940** The Great McGinty; plus the following shorts: Boobs in the Woods; Fireman, Save My Choo Choo; A Bundle of Bliss. **1941** Sullivan's Travels; Lovable Trouble (short). **1942** The Palm Beach Story; Sappy Birthday (short). **1944** Murder My Sweet; Hail the Conquering Hero; The Big Noise; The Miracle of Morgan's Creek. **1945** The Great Flamarion; Detour; A Letter for Evie; The Falcon in San Francisco. **1946** The Falcon's Alibi; Dick Tracy vs. Cueball. **1947** Born to Kill. **1949** Champion; The Lady Gambles; The Beautiful Blonde from Bashful Bend; Hellfire; Homicide. **1951** All that I Have. **1952** A Blissful Blunder (short—stock footage).

HOWARD, EUGENE (Eugene Levkowitz)

Born: 1881, Germany. Died: Aug. 1, 1965, New York, N.Y. Screen, stage, vaudeville and radio actor. Brother of screen actor Willie Howard (dec. 1949); together they appeared in vaudeville as "Eugene and Willie Howard."

The team appeared in: **1927** The following shorts: A Theatrical Manager's Office; Between the Acts of the Opera; Pal. **1929** The Music Makers (short); My People (short).

HOWARD, FLORENCE

Born: 1888. Died: Aug. 11, 1954, Hollywood, Calif. (heart attack). Stage and screen actress.

HOWARD, GERTRUDE

Born: Oct. 13, 1892, Hot Springs, Ark. Died: Sept. 30, 1934, Los Angeles, Calif. Black screen and stage actress. Entered films in 1914.

Appeared in: **1925** The Circus Cyclone. **1927** River of Romance; Easy Pickings; South Sea Love; Uncle Tom's Cabin. **1928** On Your Toes. **1929** Hearts in

Dixie; His Captive Woman; Synthetic Sin; Mississippi Gambler; Show Boat. **1930** Guilty; Conspiracy. **1931** Father's Son; The Prodigal. **1932** Strangers in Love; The Wet Parade. **1933** I'm No Angel. **1934** Peck's Bad Boy. **1959** Uncle Tom's Cabin (rerelease of 1927 film).

HOWARD, HELEN

Born: 1899. Died: Oct. 31, 1975, West Los Angeles, Calif. (cancer). Screen actress. Married to actor Moe Howard (dec. 1975).

Appeared in: **1919** Brass Buttons. **1922** Deserted at the Altar; My Wild Irish Rose; When Romance Rides. **1924** Captain Blood.

HOWARD, JEROME "CURLY"

Born: 1906, Brooklyn, N.Y. Died: Jan. 19, 1952, San Gabriel, Calif. Screen, stage and vaudeville actor. One of the original "Three Stooges" of stage and screen. Brother of actors Samuel "Shemp" (dec. 1955) and Moe Howard (dec. 1975).

Appeared in: **1933** Turn Back the Clock; Meet the Baron; Dancing Lady; plus the following shorts: Beer and Pretzels; Hello Pop; Plane Nuts. **1934** Fugitive Lovers; Hollywood Party; Gift of Gab; The Captain Hates the Sea; plus the following shorts: Woman Haters; Men in Black; Punch Drunks and Three Little Pigskins. **1935** The following shorts: Horse Collars; Restless Knights; Pop Goes the Easel; Uncivil Warriors; Pardon My Scotch; Hoi Polloi; Three Little Beers; Screen Snapshot #6. **1936** The following shorts: Ants in the Pantry; Movie Maniacs; Half-Shot Shooters; Disorder in the Court; A Pain in the Pullman; False Alarms; Whoops I'm an Indian; Slippery Silks. **1937** The following shorts: Grips, Grunts and Groans; Dizzy Doctors; Three Dumb Clucks; Goofs and Saddles; Back to the Woods; Cash and Carry; Playing the Ponies; The Sitter-Downers. **1938** Start Cheering; plus the following shorts: Termites of 1938; Wee Wee Monsieur; Tassels in the Air; Healthy, Wealthy and Dumb; Three Missing Links; Violent Is the Word for Curly; Mutts to You; Flat Foot Stooges. **1939** The following shorts: Three Little Sew and Sews; We Want Our Mummy; A-Ducking They Did Go; Yes We Have no Bonanza; Saved by the Belle; Calling All Curs; Oily to Bed and Oily to Rise; Three Sappy People. **1940** The following shorts: You Natzy Spy; Rockin' Through the Rockies; A-Plumbing We Will Go; From Nurse to Worse; Nutty But Nice; How High Is Up; No Census No Feeling; Cuckoo Cavaliers; Boobs in Arms. **1941** Time Out for Rhythm; plus the following shorts: So Long, Mr. Chumps; Dutiful But Dumb; All the World's a Stooge; I'll Never Heil Again; An Ache in Every Stake; In the Sweet Pie and Pie; Some More of Samoa. **1942** My Sister Eileen; plus the following shorts: Loco Boy Makes Good; Cactus Makes Perfect; What's the Matador; Matri-Phony; Three Smart Saps; Even as I.O.U.; Sock-a-Bye Baby. **1943** the following shorts: They Stooge to Conga; Dizzy Detectives; Spook Louder; Back from the Front; Three Little Twerps; Higher Than a Kite; I Can Hardly Wait; Dizzy Pilots; Phony Express; A Gem of a Jam. **1944** Ghost Crazy; plus the following shorts: Crash Goes the Hash; Busy Buddies; The Yoke's on Me; Idle Roomers; Gents without Cents; No Dough, Boys. **1945** Rockin' in the Rockies; plus the following shorts: Three Pests in a Mess; Booby Dupes; Idiots Deluxe; If a Body Meets a Body; Micro Phonies. **1946** The following shorts: Beer Barrel Polecats; A Bird in the Head; Uncivil Warbirds; Three Troubleeders; Monkey Businessmen; Three Loan Wolves; G.I. Wanna Go Home; Rhythm and Weep; Three Little Pirates. **1947** Hold That Lion (short); Half-Wits Holiday (short).

HOWARD, KATHLEEN

Born: 1879, Canada. Died: Apr. 15, 1956, Hollywood, Calif. Screen actress, opera performer and magazine editor.

Appeared in: **1934** Once to Every Bachelor; Death Takes a Holiday; It's a Gift; You're Telling Me; One More River. **1935** The Man on the Flying Trapeze. **1936** Stolen Holiday. **1939** Little Accident; First Love. **1940** Young People; Mystery Sea Raider; One Night in the Tropics; Five Little Peppers in Trouble. **1941** Miss Polly; Blossoms in the Dust; A Girl, a Guy and a Gob; Sweetheart of the Campus; Ball of Fire. **1942** The Mad Marindales; You Were Never Lovelier; Lady in a Jam. **1943** Crash Dive; My Kingdom for a Cook; Swing Out the Blues. **1944** Laura; Reckless Age. **1945** Sadie Was a Lady; Shady Lady; Snafu. **1946** Centennial Summer; Miss Susie Slagle's; Dangerous Woman; The Mysterious Intruder. **1947** The Late George Apley; Take a Letter, Darling; Cynthia; Curley. **1948** The Bride Goes Wild; Cry of the City. **1950** Born to Be Bad; Petty Girl.

HOWARD, LESLIE (Leslie Howard Stainer)

Born: Apr. 3, 1893, London, England. Died: June 2, 1943, Bay of Biscay (air crash). Screen, stage actor, film director and film producer. Nominated for 1933 Academy Award for Best Actor in Berkeley Square and in 1938 for Pygmalion. Father of actor Ronald Howard.

Appeared in: **1917** The Happy Warrior. **1919** The Lackey and the Lady. **1920** Bookworms (short); Five Pounds Reward (short). **1930** Outward Bound. **1931** Devotion; Five and Ten (aka A Daughter of Luxury); Never the Twain Shall Meet; A Free Soul. **1932** Service for Ladies (aka Reserved for Ladies—US); Smilin' Through; The Animal Kingdom (aka Woman in the House). **1933** Secrets; Berkeley Square; Captured. **1934** British Agent; The Lady is Willing; Of Human Bondage; Hollywood on Parade (short). **1935** The Scarlet Pimpernel. **1936** The Petrified Forest; Romeo and Juliet. **1937** It's Love I'm After;

Stand-In. **1938** Pygmalion. **1939** Intermezzo (aka Escape to Happiness); Gone With the Wind. **1941** Pimpernel Smith (aka Mister V—US 1942); 49th Parallel (aka The Invaders—US 1942); From the Four Corners (short). **1942** The First of the Few (aka Spitfire—US 1943).

HOWARD, LEWIS

Born: Jan. 16, 1919, New York, N.Y. Died: Sept. 29, 1951. Screen actor.

Appeared in: **1939** First Love. **1940** It's a Date; I'm Nobody's Sweetheart Now. **1941** Hellzapoppin; Horror Island; Meet the Chump; Hello Sucker; San Francisco Docks. **1942** Seven Sweethearts. **1946** Up Goes Maisie; I've Always Loved You. **1948** Song of My Heart. **1950** In a Lonely Place.

HOWARD, LISA K.

Born: Apr. 24, 1930. Died: July 4, 1963, East Hampton, N.Y. Screen actress and newscaster. Married to film producer Felix Feist (dec. 1965).

Appeared in: **1950** The Man Who Cheated Himself. **1953** Donovan's Brain; The Hindu (aka Sabaka—US 1955).

HOWARD, MAY

Born: 1870. Died: Feb. 1, 1935, Hollywood, Calif. (heart attack). Screen, stage, burlesque and vaudeville actress.

HOWARD, MOE

Born: June 19, 1897, Brooklyn, N.Y. Died: May 4, 1975, Hollywood, Calif. (cancer). Screen, stage, television and vaudeville actor. Married to actress Helen Howard (dec. 1975). Brother of actors Jerome "Curly" (dec. 1952) and Samuel "Shemp" Howard (dec. 1955). Appeared in vaudeville with Ted Healy in an act billed as "Ted Healy and His Stooges" and that same act (also referred to as "Ted Healy and His Racketeers") appeared in 1930 Soup to Nuts (film debut).

Appeared in: **1930** Soup to Nuts. **1933** Meet the Baron; Dancing Lady; Fugitive Lovers; Turn Back the Clock; Beer and Pretzels (short); Plane Nuts (short). **1934** The Captain Hates the Sea; Hollywood Party; Gift of Gab; plus the following shorts: Woman Haters; The Big Idea; Punch Drunks; Men in Black; Three Little Pigskins. **1935** The following shorts: Horses' Collars; Pop Goes the Easel; Uncivil Warriors; Pardon My Scotch; Hoi Polloi; Three Little Beers; Screen Snapshot #6. **1936** The following shorts: Ants in the Pantry; Movie Maniacs; Half Shot Shooters; Disorder in the Court; A Pain in the Pullman; False Alarms; Whoops I'm an Indian; Slippery Silks. **1937** Start Cheering; plus the following shorts: Grips, Grunts and Groans; Dizzy Doctors; Three Dumb Clucks; Back to the Woods; Goofs and Saddles; Cash and Carry; Playing the Ponies; The Sitter Downers. **1938** The following shorts: Termites of 1938; Wee Wee Monsieur; Tassels in the Air; Healthy, Wealthy and Dumb; Three Missing Links; Violent is the Word for Curly; Mutts to You; Flat Foot Stooges; Three Little Sew and Sews; We Want our Mummy. **1939** The following shorts: Yes, We Have No Bonanza; A Ducking They Did Go; Saved by the Belle; Calling All Curs; Oily to Bed and Oily to Rise; Three Sappy People. **1940** The following shorts: You Natzy Spy!; Rockin' Through the Rockies; A Plumbing We Will Go; Nutty But Nice; How High is Up?; From Nurse to Worse; No Census, No Feeling; Cuckoo Cavaliers. **1941** Time Out for Rhythm; plus the following shorts: Boobs in Arms; So Long Mr. Chumps; Dutiful But Dumb; All the World's a Stooge; I'll Never Heil Again; An Ache in Every Stake; In the Sweet Pie and Pie; Some More of Samoa; Loco Boy Makes Good. **1942** My Sister Eileen; plus the following shorts: Cactus Makes Perfect; What's the Matador; Matri-Phony; Three Smart Saps; Even as I.O.U.; Sock-a-Bye Baby. **1943** The following shorts: They Stooge to Conga; Dizzy Detectives; Back from the Front; Three Little Twerps; Higher Than a Kite; Spook Louder; I Can Hardly Wait; Dizzy Pilots; Phony Express; A Gem of a Jam. **1944** The following shorts: Crash Goes the Hash; Busy Buddies; The Yoke's on Me; Idle Roomers; Gents without Cents; No Dough, Boys. **1945** Rockin' in the Rockies; plus the following shorts: Three Pests in a Mess; Booby Dupes; Idiots Deluxe; If a Body Meets a Body; Micro-Phonies. **1946** Swing Parade of 1946; plus the following shorts: Beer Barrel Polecats; A Bird in the Head; Uncivil War Birds; Three Troubledoers; Monkey Businessmen; Three Loan Wolves; G.I. Wanna Go Home; Rhythm and Weep; Three Little Pirates. **1947** The following shorts: Half-Wits Holiday; Fright Night; Out West; Hold That Lion; Brideless Groom; Sing a Song of Six Pants; All Gummed Up. **1948** The following shorts: Shivering Sherlocks; Pardon My Clutch; Squareheads of the Round Table; Fiddlers Three; Hot Scots; I'm a Monkey's Uncle; Mummy's Dummies; Crime on Their Hands. **1949** The following shorts: The Ghost Talks; Who Done It?; Hocus Pocus; Feulin' Around; Heavenly Daze; Malice in the Palace; Vagabond Loafers; Dunked in the Deep. **1950** The following shorts: Punchy Cowpunchers; Dopey Dicks; Self-Made Maids; Hugs and Mugs; Love at First Bite; Three Hams on Rye; Studio Stoops; Slap-Happy Sleuths; A Snitch in Time. **1951** Gold Raiders; plus the following shorts: Three Arabian Nuts; Baby Sitters' Jitters; Don't Throw That Knife; Scrambled Brains; Merry Mavericks; The Tooth Will Out; Hula La-La; The Pest Man Wins; A Missed Fortune. **1952** The following shorts: Listen Judge; Corny Casanovas; He Cooked His Goose; Gents in a Jam; Three Dark Horses; Cuckoo in a Choo Choo. **1953** The following shorts: Booty and the Beast; Up in Daisy's Penthouse; Loose Loot; Tricky Dicks; Spooks; Pardon My Backfire; Rip, Sew and Stitch; Bubble Trouble; Goof on the Roof. **1954** The following shorts: Income Tax Sappy; Musty

Musketeers; Pals and Gals; Knutzy Knights; Shot in the Frontier; Scotched in Scotland. **1955** The following shorts: Fling in the Ring; Of Cash and Hash; Gypped in the Penthouse; Bedlam in Paradise; Stone Age Romeos; Wham-Bam-Slam; Hot Ice; Blunder Boys. **1956** The following shorts: Husbands Beware; Creeps; Flagpole Jitters; For Crimin' Out Loud; Rumpus in the Harem; Hot Stuff; Scheming Schemers; Commotion on the Ocean. **1957** The following shorts: Hoofs and Goofs; Muscle Up a Little Closer; A Merry Mix-Up; Space Ship Sappy; Guns a-Poppin; Horsing Around; Rusty Romeos; Outer Space Jitters. **1958** Space Master X-7; plus the following shorts: Quiz Whiz; Fifi Blows Her Top; Flying Saucer Daffy; Pies and Guys; Sweet and Hot; Oil's Well That Ends Well. **1959** Have Rocket, Will Travel; plus the following shorts: Triple Crossing; Sappy Bull Fighters. **1960** Stop, Look and Laugh; Three Stooges Scrapbook. **1961** Snow White and the Three Stooges. **1962** The Three Stooges Meet Hercules; The Three Stooges in Orbit. **1963** The Three Stooges Go Around the World in a Daze; It's a Mad, Mad, Mad, Mad World. **1964** Four for Texas; Big Parade of Comedy. **1965** The Outlaws is Coming. **1966** Don't Worry, We'll Think of a Title.

HOWARD, PETER

Born: Dec. 20, 1908, Maidenhead, England. Died: Mar. 25, 1965, Lima, Peru (heart failure). Playwright, screenwriter, author and screen actor. Do not confuse with actor Peter Howard (dec. 1968).

Appeared in: **1940** Man of the Hour.

HOWARD, PETER

Born: 1934. Died: Sept. 12, 1968. Screen actor. Do not confuse with actor Peter Howard (dec. 1965).

HOWARD, PETER "PETE THE HERMIT"

Born: June 26, 1878, Knocklong, Ireland. Died: Mar. 14, 1969, Los Angeles, Calif. (brain hemorrhage). Screen actor.

Appeared in: **1923** Souls in Bondage.

HOWARD, RUTH

Born: 1894. Died: Dec. 28, 1944, Los Angeles, Calif. Screen and vaudeville actress. Member of the "Ross and Howard" vaudeville team.

Appeared in: **1933** My Woman.

HOWARD, SAMUEL "SHEMP"

Born: Mar. 17, 1900, New York, N.Y. Died: Nov. 22, 1955, Hollywood, Calif. (coronary occlusion). Screen, stage and vaudeville actor. Brother of screen actors Jerome "Curly" (dec. 1952) and Moe Howard (dec. 1975). Appeared in vaudeville with Ted Healy in an act billed as "Ted Healy and His Stooges" and that same act (also referred to as "Ted Healy and His Racketeers") appeared in 1930 Soup to Nuts (film debut). He became a member of the "Three Stooges" team of screen fame upon the retirement of his brother "Curly" in 1947.

Appeared in: **1930** Soup to Nuts; Hollywood on Parade (short). **1934–1936** numerous Vitaphone shorts. **1937** Hollywood Round-Up; Headin' East. **1938** Home on the Range. **1940** Millionaires in Prison; The Leather Pushers; Give Us Wings; The Bank Dick; Money Squawks (short); Boobs in the Woods (short). **1941** Meet the Chump; Buck Privates; The Invisible Woman; Six Lessons from Madame La Zonga; Mr. Dynamite; In the Navy; Tight Shoes; San Antonio Rose; Hold That Ghost; Too Many Blondes; Hellzapoppin. **1942** The Strange Case of Dr. Rx; Butch Minds the Baby; Mississippi Gambler; Private Buckaroo; Pittsburgh; Arabian Nights. **1943** It Ain't Hay; Keep 'Em Sluggin; How's About It?; Strictly in the Groove; Crazy House; Farmer for a Day (short). **1944** Three of a Kind; Moonlight and Cactus; Strange Affair. **1945** Rockin' in the Rockies. **1946** Blondie Knows Best; Dangerous Business; The Gentleman Misbehaves; One Exciting Week; Swing Parade of 1946, plus the following shorts: Beer Barrel Polecats; A Bird in the Head; Uncivil Warbirds; Monkey Businessmen; The Three Troubledoers; Three Loan Wolves; G.I. Wanna Go Home; Rhythm and Weep; Three Little Pirates. **1947** The following shorts: Half-Wits Holiday; Fright Night; Out West; Hold That Lion; Brideless Groom; Sing a Song of Six Pants; All Gummed Up. **1948** The following shorts: Shivering Sherlocks; Pardon My Clutch; Squareheads of the Round Table; Fiddlers Three; Heavenly Daze; Hot Scots; I'm a Monkey's Uncle; Mummy's Dummies; Crime on Their Hands. **1949** Africa Screams; plus the following shorts: The Ghost Talks; Who Done It?; Hocus Pokus; Fuelin' Around; Malice in the Palace; Vagabond Loafers; Dunked in the Deep. **1950** Punch Cowpunchers; Hugs and Mugs; Dopey Dicks; Love at First Bite; Self Made Maids; Three Hams on Rye; Studio Stoops; Slap Happy Sleuths; A Snitch in Time. **1951** Gold Raiders; plus the following shorts: Three Arabian Nuts; Baby Sisters' Jitters; Don't Throw that Knife; Scrambled Brains; Merry Mavericks; The Tooth Will Out; Hula La-La; The Pest Man Wins. **1952** The following shorts: A Missed Fortune; Listen Judge; Corny Casanovas; He Cooked His Goose; Gents in a Jam; Three Dark Horses; Cuckoo in a Choo Choo. **1953** The following shorts: Loose Loot; Spooks; Up in Daisy's Penthouse; Booty and the Beast; Tricky Dicks; Pardon My Backfire; Rip, Sew and Stitch; Goof on the Roof; Bubble Trouble. **1954** The following shorts: Income Tax Snappy; Musty Musketeers; Pals and Gals; Knutzy Knights; Shot in the Frontier; Scotched in Scotland. **1955** The following shorts: Fling in the Ring; Of Cash and Hash; Gypped in the Penthouse; Bedlam in Paradise; Stone Age

Romeos; Wham Bam Slam; Hot Ice; Blunder Boys. **1956** The following shorts: Husbands Beware; Creeps; Flagpole Jitters; For Crimin' Out Loud; Rumpus in the Harem; Hot Stuff; Scheming Schemers; Commotion on the Ocean.

HOWARD, SYDNEY

Born: 1885, Yeadon, England. Died: June 12, 1946, London, England. Stage and screen actor.

Appeared in: **1929** Splinters (film debut). **1930** French Leave. **1931** Tilly of Bloomsbury; Almost a Divorce; Up for the Cup; Splinters in the Navy. **1932** The Mayor's Nest; It's a King. **1933** Up for the Derby; Night of the Garter; Trouble. **1934** It's a Cop; Girls Please! **1935** The Hope of His Side (aka Where's George?) **1936** Fame; Chick. **1937** Splinters in the Air; What a Man! **1939** Shipyard Sally. **1940** Tilly of Bloomsbury (and 1931 version). **1941** Once a Crook; Mr. Proudfoot Shows a Light (short). **1943** When We Are Married. **1945** Flight from Folly.

HOWARD, TOM

Born: 1886, County Tyrone, Ireland. Died: Feb. 27, 1955, Long Branch, N.J. Screen, stage, vaudeville, burlesque, radio and television actor.

Appeared in: **1930** Rain or Shine. **1932** The following shorts: The Mouse Trapper; The Acid Test; The Vest With a Tale; plus several Paramount shorts. **1933** The following shorts: A Drug on the Market; The Great Hokum Mystery; plus several Paramount shorts. **1934** The following shorts: Static; The Big Meow; A Good Scout. **1935** The following shorts: Easy Money; An Ear for Music; Grooms in Gloom; Time Out; The Magic Word; Stylish Stouts; He's a Prince. **1936** Where Is Wall Street?

HOWARD, WENDY (Wendy Black)

Born: 1925. Died: Feb. 21, 1972, North Hollywood, Calif. Screen actress.

Appeared in: **1955** That Lady. **1970** Airport.

HOWARD, WILLIAM

Born: 1884. Died: Jan. 23, 1944, Hollywood, Calif. Screen and stage actor.

Appeared in: **1935** Diamond Jim. **1936** Come and Get It.

HOWARD, WILLIE (William Levkowitz)

Born: 1887, Germany. Died: Jan. 14, 1949, New York, N.Y. Screen, stage, vaudeville and radio actor. Brother of actor Eugene Howard (dec. 1965) and together they appeared in vaudeville as "Eugene and Willie Howard" and in 1927–29 they made shorts as a team. He later appeared in vaudeville with Al Kelly.

Appeared in: **1927** The following shorts: A Theatrical Manager's Office; Between the Acts of the Opera; Pals. **1929** The following shorts: The Music Makers; My People. **1930** The Thirteenth Prisoner (aka The Thirteenth Hour). **1935** Millions in the Air. **1936** Rose of the Rancho. **1937** Broadway Melody of 1938. **1937–38** starred in a series of Educational shorts.

HOWDY, CLYDE

Born: 1920. Died: Oct. 3, 1969, Calif. Screen actor and stuntman.

Appeared in: **1959** Yellowstone Kelly. **1963** PT 109.

HOWERTON, CLARENCY "MAJOR MITE"

Born: 1913. Died: Nov. 18, 1975, Salem, Ore. Screen actor and circus performer.

Appeared in: **1939** The Wizard of Oz; various "Our Gang" comedies.

HOWES, BOBBY

Born: Aug. 4, 1895, Chelsea, London, England. Died: Apr. 27, 1972, London, England. Screen, stage, radio and vaudeville actor. Father of actress Sally Ann Howes and actor Peter Howes.

Appeared in: **1927** On with the Dance series. **1928** The Guns of Loos. **1931** Third Time Lucky. **1932** Lord Babs; For the Love of Mike. **1934** Over the Garden Wall. **1937** Please Teacher. **1938** Sweet Devil; Yes, Madam? **1946** The Trojan Brothers. **1951** Happy-Go-Lovely. **1957** The Good Companions. **1961** Watch it Sailor!

HOWES, REED (Herman Reed Howes)

Born: July 5, 1900, Washington, D.C. Died: Aug. 6, 1964, Woodland Hills, Calif. Stage and screen actor.

Appeared in: **1923** High Speed Lee; The Broken Violin. **1924** Geared to Go; Lightning Romance. **1925** Courageous Fool; The Cyclone Rider; Bobbed Hair; Crack O'Dawn; Youth's Gamble; The Snob Buster; Cyclone Cavalier; Bashful Buccaneer; Super Speed. **1926** The Night Owl; The High Flyer; The Gentle Cyclone; The Self-Starter; Wings of the Storm; Kentucky Handicap; Danger Quest; The Dangerous Dude; Moran of the Mounted; Racing Romance. **1927** Rough House Rosie; The Lost Limited; The Racing Fool; The Royal American; The Scorcher; Romantic Rogue; Catch as Catch Can. **1928** Ladies' Night in a Turkish Bath; Hellship Bronson; Fashion Madness; Sawdust Paradise; A Million for Love; Russ Farrell, Aviator (series). **1929** The Singing Fool; Stolen Kisses; Come Across. **1930** Clancy in Wall Street; Terry of the Times (serial).

1931 Sheer Luck; Hell Divers; Anybody's Blond. **1932** Devil on Deck; 70,000 Witnesses; Gorilla Ship. **1935** Paradise Canyon; Confidential; The Dawn Rider; Queen of the Jungle. **1936** The Last Assignment; Custer's Last Stand; Feud of the West; The Clutching Hand. **1937** Sweetheart of the Navy; Death in the Air; Zorro Rides Again (serial). **1938** Flight to Fame; Fighting Devil Dogs; Dick Tracy Returns (serial); The Lone Ranger (serial). **1939** South of the Border; Texas Wildcats; Fighting Renegade; Flaming Lead; Six-Gun Rhythm; Roll, Wagons, Roll; Buck Rogers; Daredevil of the Red Circle (serial). **1940** Westbound Stage; Riders of the Sage; Heroes of the Saddle; Straight Shooter; Texas Terrors; Mystery Sea Raider; Covered Wagon Days. **1941** Fugitive Valley; The Lone Rider in Ghost Town. **1943** Wild Horse Stampede; Thundering Trails. **1944** Outlaw Roundup; Law of the Saddle; Brand of the Devil; Saddle Leather Law. **1946** Til the Clouds Roll By; Under Arizona Skies. **1947** Black Bart; The Spirit of West Point. **1948** The Untamed Breed; Mexican Hayride. **1949** Loaded Pistols; The Walking Hills; Task Force; The Doolins of Oklahoma; Range Land. **1950** Stage to Tucson; Captain China; Gunslingers; The Savage Horde; Ambush; Santa Fe; Silver Raiders; Fortunes of Captain Blood. **1951** Man in the Saddle; Rich, Young and Pretty; Saddle Legion; Indian Uprising. **1952** The Iron Mistress; Hangman's Knot. **1953** The Stranger Wore a Gun; Calamity Jane; The Last Posse; The Man Behind the Gun. **1954** The Boy from Oklahoma; Three Hours to Kill; Violent Men. **1955** A Lawless Street. **1957** Decision at Sundown; The Guns of Fort Petticoat; Runaway Daughters. **1958** Sierra Baron; Seven Guns to Mesa; Screaming Mimi. **1959** Arson for Hire; Zorro Rides Again. **1960** Gunfighters of Abilene. **1961** The Sinister Urge (aka The Young and Immoral).

HOWLAND, JOBYNA

Born: 1881, Indianapolis, Ind. Died: June 7, 1936, Los Angeles, Calif. (heart attack). Stage and screen actress. Sister of actor Olin Howlin (Howland) (dec. 1959).

Appeared in: **1919** The Way of a Woman. **1924** Second Youth. **1930** A Lady's Morals; Soul Kiss; Honey; Dixiana; Hook, Line and Sinker; The Cuckoos; The Virtuous Sin. **1932** Big City Blues; Silver Dollar; Once in a Lifetime; Rockabye; Stepping Sisters. **1933** Topaze; Story of Temple Drake; Cohens and Kellys in Trouble. **1935** Ye Old Saw Mill (short).

HOWLIN, OLIN (aka OLIN HOWLAND)

Born: Feb. 10, 1896, Denver, Colo. Died: Sept. 20, 1959, Hollywood, Calif. Screen, stage and vaudeville actor. Brother of actress Jobyna Howland (dec. 1936).

Appeared in: **1918** Independence B'Gosh. **1924** The Great White Way; Janice Meredith. **1925** Zander the Great. **1931** Over the Hill. **1932** Cheaters at Play; So Big. **1933** Blondie Johnson. **1934** Treasure Island; Wagon Wheels. **1935** Behold My Wife; The Case of the Curious Bride; The Case of the Lucky Legs; Follies Bergere. **1936** The Widow from Monte Carlo; Man Hunt; Satan Met a Lady; Road Gang; I Married a Doctor; Boulder Dam; The Big Noise; The Case of the Velvet Claws; Earthworm Tractors; Country Gentlemen; Love Letters of a Star; The Longest Night; Gold Diggers of 1937. **1937** Mountain Music; Marry the Girl; Wife, Doctor and Nurse; Nothing Sacred; Men in Exile. **1938** Mad Miss Manton; Swing Your Lady; The Adventures of Tom Sawyer; The Old Raid Mule (short); Girl of the Golden West; Sweethearts; Kentucky Moonshine; Little Tough Guy; Brother Rat. **1939** Nancy Drew—Detective; Blondie Brings Up Baby; Return of Dr. X; Days of Jesse James; Zenobia; Gone With the Wind; Disbarred; Boy Slaves; Made for Each Other; One Hour to Live. **1940** Comin' Round the Mountain; Young People; Chad Hanna. **1941** Shepherd of the Hills; Buy Me That Town; One Foot in Heaven; Ellery Queen and the Murder Ring; The Great Lie; Belle Starr. **1942** Almost Married; Henry and Dizzy; Sappy Birthday (short); Dr. Broadway; When Johnny Comes Marching Home; The Man Who Wouldn't Die; Home in Wyomin'; This Gun for Hire; Blondie's Blessed Event; You Can't Escape Forever; Orchestra Wives. **1943** Lady Bodyguard; Young and Willing; Secrets of the Underground; A Stranger in Town; The Good Fellows; Jack London; The Falcon and the Co-eds. **1944** A Strange Lady in Town; Sing, Neighbor, Sing; Bermuda Mystery; Can't Help Singing; I'll Be Seeing You; The Man from Frisco; The Town Went Wild; Twilight on the Prairie; Goodnight, Sweetheart; Bermuda; In the Meantime, Darling; Nothing but Trouble. **1945** Sheriff of Cimarron Gap; Captain Eddie; Her Lucky Night; Colonel Effingham's Raid; Dakota; Fallen Angel; Senorita from the West; Santa Fe Saddlemates. **1946** Home Sweet Homicide; Crime Doctor's Man Hunt; Secrets of the Underworld. **1947** The Angel and the Badman; The Wistful Widow of Wagon Gap; Apache Rose; For the Love of Rusty; The Tenderfoot. **1948** The Dude Goes West; Return of the Whistler; My Dog Rusty; The Paleface; The Last of the Wild Horses; Station West; Bad Men of Tombstone. **1949** Massacre River; Grand Canyon; Leave It to Henry; Little Women. **1950** Father Makes Good; Rock Island Trail; A Ticket to Tomahawk; Stage to Tucson. **1951** Fighting Coast Guard; Santa Fe. **1952** The Fabulous Senorita; Gobs and Gals. **1954** Them. **1958** The Blob.

HOXIE, JACK

Born: Jan. 24, 1890, Okla. Died: Mar. 28, 1965, Keyes, Okla. Screen actor. Entered films in 1918.

Appeared in: **1919** Lightning Bryce (serial). **1920** Thunderbolt Jack (serial).

1921 The Broken Spur; Sparks of Flint; Hills of Hate; Cupid's Brand; Dead or Alive; Cyclone Bliss; Devil Dog Dawson; The Sheriff of Hope Eternal; Man from Nowhere. 1922 The Marshal of Moneymind; Two Fisted Jefferson; Barb-Wire; The Crow's Nest; Back Fire; The Desert's Crucible; Riders of the Law; A Desert Bridegroom. 1923 The Double O; Desert Rider; The Forbidden Trail; Don Quickshot of the Rio Grande; Wolf's Tracks; Men in the Raw; Where Is the West?; Galloping Thru; The Red Warning. 1924 Ridgeway of Montana; Fighting Fury; The Western Wallop; The Back Trail; Daring Chances; The Man from Wyoming; The Phantom Horseman; The Galloping Ace. 1925 The White Outlaw; A Roaring Adventure; Bustin' Thru; Don Daredevil; The Sign of the Cactus; Flying Hoofs; Hidden Loot; Two Fisted Jones; The Red Rider; Ridin' Thunder. 1926 The Last Frontier; The Border Sheriff; The Fighting Peacemaker; Red Hot Leather; The Wild Horse Stampede; The Demon; Looking for Trouble; Six Shootin' Romance. 1927 Men of Daring; The Fighting Three; Rough and Ready; The Western Whirlwind; Grinning Guns; The Rambling Ranger; Heroes of the Wild (serial). 1929 Forbidden Trail. 1932 The Phantom Express; Gold. 1933 Law and Lawless; Via Pony Express; Gun Law; Trouble Buster; Outlaw Justice.

HOYT, ARTHUR
Born: 1874, Georgetown, Colo. Died: Jan. 4, 1953, Woodland Hills, Calif. Screen, stage actor and stage director. Entered films in 1916.

Appeared in: 1920 Nurse Marjorie. 1921 The Foolish Age; The Four Horsemen of the Apocalypse; Camille; Don't Neglect Your Wife; Red Courage. 1922 Restless Souls; The Top of New York; Is Matrimony a Failure?; Kissed; Love Is an Awful Thing; The Understudy; Little Wildcat; Too Much Wife. 1923 The Love Piker; The Stranger's Banquet; An Old Sweetheart of Mine; To the Ladies; The White Flower; Souls for Sale. 1924 Bluff; Do It Now; Sundown; When a Man's a Man; Her Marriage Vow; The Dangerous Blonde; Daring Youth. 1925 The Lost World; Any Woman; Eve's Lover; The Sporting Venus; The Coming of Amos; Head Winds; Private Affairs. 1926 For Wives Only; The Crown of Lies; The Danger Girl; Monte Carlo; Eve's Leaves; Dangerous Friends; Up in Mabel's Room; Footloose Widows; The Gilded Butterfly; The Midnight Sun. 1927 An Affair of the Follies; The Rejuvenation of Aunt Mary; A Texas Steer; The Love Thrill; The Mysterious Rider; Shanghai Bound; Ten Modern Commandments; Tillie the Toiler. 1928 Just Married; My Man; Husband for Rent; Home James. 1929 The Wheel of Life; Stolen Kisses; Protection; Her Private Affair. 1930 Peacock Alley; Extravagance; The Life of the Party; Dumbbells in Ermine; Night Work; On Your Back; Going Wild; The Boss's Orders (short); Seven Days' Leave. 1931 The Criminal Code; Inspiration; The Flood; Gold Dust Gertie; Young Sinners; Side Show; Palmy Days; Peach O'Reno; Bought. 1932 Impatient Maiden; Love in High Gear; American Madness; The Devil and the Deep; Dynamite Ranch; Madame Racketeer; Make Me a Star; The Crusader; Washington Merry-Go-Round; Red Haired Alibi; Vanity Street; Call Her Savage; All American. 1933 Dangerously Yours; The Eleventh Commandment; Hold Your Temper (short); Shriek in the Night; Pleasure Cruise; Shanghai Madness; Darling Daughters; Cohens and Kellys in Trouble; Only Yesterday; Laughing at Life; Goldie Gets Along; Emergency Call; His Private Secretary; Sing, Sinner, Sing; 20,000 Years in Sing Sing. 1934 Super Snooper (short); The Meanest Girl in Town; In the Money; The Notorious Sophie Lang; Kansas City Princess; Wake up and Dream; When Strangers Meet; Babbitt; It Happened One Night; The Crosby Case; Uncertain Lady; Springtime for Henry; Unknown Blonde; Let's Try Again. 1935 Men of Action; No Ransom; A Night at the Ritz; Chinatown Squad; The Raven; Welcome Home; $1,000 a Minute; One Hour Late; Murder on a Honeymoon. 1936 Lady Luck; Magnificent Obsession; Mr. Deeds Goes to Town; The Poor Little Rich Girl; M'Liss; Walking on Air; Early to Bed. 1937 Four Days' Wonder; Easy Living; Join the Marines; Paradise Express; The Westland Case; The Wrong Road; A Star Is Born; It's All Yours; Ever since Eve; Love Takes Flight; She's No Lady. 1938 The Black Doll; The Devil's Party; Start Cheering; The Cowboy and the Lady; The Sisters; You and Me; Girls on Probation. 1939 It Could Happen to You; Should Husbands Work?; Made for Each Other; East Side of Heaven. 1940 I Take This Oath; Goin' Fishin' (short); The Great McGinty. 1941 1-2-3 Go! (short). 1944 Hail the Conquering Hero. 1947 Mad Wednesday; My Favorite Brunette; Brute Force.

HOYT, CLEGG
Born: 1911. Died: Oct. 6, 1967, Hollywood, Calif. (complications following stroke). Screen and television actor.

Appeared in: 1956 Fighting Trouble; Santiago. 1957 Damn Citizen; The Restless Breed; The True Story of Jesse James. 1958 Gun Fever. 1961 The Young Savages. 1962 Incident in an Alley; Pressure Point; 13 West Street; Paradise Alley. 1964 Seven Days in May. 1965 The Great Race. 1967 In the Heat of the Night.

HOYT, JULIA
Born: 1897. Died: Oct. 31, 1955, New York, N.Y. Screen and stage actress. Entered films in 1921.

Appeared in: 1921 The Wonderful Thing. 1925 The Man Who Found Himself.

HUBBARD, TOM (Thomas G. Hubbard)
Died: June 4, 1974, Rochester, Mich. (cancer). Screen actor and screenwriter.

Appeared in: 1951 The Hoodlum; Two Lost Worlds. 1952 Buffalo Bill in Tomahawk Territory. 1953 Murder without Tears. 1954 Highway Dragnet; Thunder Pass; Port of Hell. 1956 Hidden Guns; Secret of Treasure Mountain. 1957 Hell Canyon (aka Hell Canyon Outlaws); Raiders of Old California. 1958 Legion of the Doomed. 1959 Arson for Hire. 1960 Lust to Kill.

HUBER, HAROLD
Born: 1910. Died: Sept. 29, 1959, New York, N.Y. Screen, stage, radio, television actor and radio and television writer.

Appeared in: 1932 Central Park; The Match King. 1933 Central Airport; Girl Missing; Mary Stevens, M.D.; Mayor of Hell; Midnight Mary; The Silk Express; The Life of Jimmy Dolan; The Bowery; Police Car; Frisco Jenny; 20,000 Years in Sing Sing; Parachute Jumper; Ladies They Talk About. 1934 Hi, Nellie; He Was Her Man; The Merry Frinks; No More Women; A Very Honorable Guy; The Crosby Case; The Line-Up; The Thin Man; The Defense Rests; Hide-Out. 1935 Naughty Marietta; Mad Love; Pursuit; G-Men. 1936 We're Only Human; The Gay Desperado; Muss 'Em Up; Klondike Annie; Women Are Trouble; San Francisco; The Devil Is a Sissy; Kelly the Second. 1937 Trouble in Morocco; Midnight Taxi; Angel's Holiday; Charlie Chan on Broadway; Love under Fire; Charlie Chan at Monte Carlo; You Can't Beat Love; Outlaws of the Orient. 1938 International Settlement; Mr. Moto's Gamble; A Trip to Paris; The Mysterious Mr. Moto; Passport Husband; While New York Sleeps; The Adventures of Marco Polo; A Slight Case of Murder; Going Places; Gangs of New York; Little Tough Guys in Society. 1939 Charlie Chan in City in Darkness; King of the Turf; Chasing Danger; Main Street Lawyer; You Can't Get Away with Murder; Charlie McCarthy, Detective; Beau Geste; 6,000 Enemies; The Lady and the Mob. 1940 The Ghost Comes Home; Kit Carson; Dance, Girls, Dance. 1941 A Man Betrayed; Country Fair; Down Mexico Way; Charlie Chan in Rio. 1942 Pardon My Stripes; Sleepytime Gal; A Gentleman After Dark; Little Tokyo, U.S.A.; Lady from Chungking; Manila Calling. 1943 Crime Doctor. 1950 My Friend Irma Goes West; Let's Dance.

HUBER, MRS. JUANITA "BILLIE"
Born: 1905. Died: May 22, 1965, Camden, N.J. Screen actress and dancer. Entered films in early 1930s.

HUBERT, GEORGE
Born: 1881. Died: May 8, 1963, Hollywood, Calif. Screen, stage and vaudeville actor. Entered films in 1917.

Appeared in: 1956 Foreign Intrigue.

HUDD, WALTER
Born: Feb. 20, 1898, London, England. Died: Jan. 20, 1963, London, England. Screen, stage, television actor and playwright.

Appeared in: 1935 Moscow Nights (aka I Stand Condemned—US 1936) (film debut). 1936 Rembrandt. 1937 Elephant Boy. 1938 Housemaster (US 1939); Black Limelight (US 1939). 1939 Two Minutes (aka The Silence—US); Dead Man's Shoes; The Outsider (US 1940). 1940 Dr. O'Dowd. 1941 Major Barbara. 1942 Uncensored (US 1944). 1944 Love Story (aka A Lady Surrenders—US 1947). 1945 I Live in Grosvenor Square (aka A Yank in London—US 1946); I Know Where I'm Going (US 1947). 1948 Escape. 1949 Paper Orchid; Landfall. 1952 The Importance of Being Earnest. 1953 Cosh Boy (aka The Slasher—US); All Hallow'en. 1954 The Good Die Young (US 1955). 1955 Cast a Dark Shadow (US 1957). 1956 Reach for the Sky (US 1957); The Last Man to Hang?; Satellite in the Sky; Loser Takes All (US 1957). 1958 The Man Upstairs (US 1959); Further Up the Creek; The Two-Headed Spy (US 1959). 1959 Look Back in Anger. 1960 Two-Way Stretch (US 1961); Sink the Bismarck! 1962 Life for Ruth (aka Walk in the Shadow—US 1966); The Punch and Judy Man. 1963 It's All Happening (aka The Dream Maker—US 1964).

HUDMAN, WESLEY
Born: 1916. Died: Feb. 29, 1964, Williams, Ariz. (murdered). Screen and television actor.

Appeared in: 1949 Satan's Cradle. 1950 Indian Territory; Battle of Rogue River; The Girl from San Lorenzo. 1951 Fort Defiance. 1952 Leadville Gunslinger; Barbed Wire; Black Hills Ambush. 1953 Pack Train. 1954 Masterson of Kansas. 1956 The Lonely Man; Blackjack Ketchum, Desperado. 1958 The Sheepman.

HUDSON, LARRY
Born: 1920. Died: Jan. 8, 1961, Hollywood, Calif. (suicide). Screen and television actor.

Appeared in: 1952 Smoky Canyon. 1953 The Redhead from Wyoming. 1956 Jubal; Solid Gold Cadillac. 1959 Tank Commandos.

HUDSON, ROCHELLE
Born: Mar. 6, 1914, Claremore, Okla. Died: Jan. 17, 1972, Palm Desert, Calif. Screen, stage and television actress. Divorced from film editor Hal Thompson,

sportswriter Dick Hyland and Robert L. Mindell. Entered films in 1930. Was a 1931 Wampas Baby Star.

Appeared in: **1930** Laugh and Get Rich. **1931** Fanny Foley Herself; Are These Our Children? **1932** Beyond the Rockies; Liberty Road; Hell's Highway; Top of the Bill; Mysteries of the French Police; The Penguin Pool Murder. **1933** Love is Like That; She Done Him Wrong; Wild Boys of the Road; Walls of Gold; Doctor Bull; Notorious but Nice; Mr. Skitch; Love is Dangerous; The Savage Girl. **1934** Harold Teen; Judge Priest; Imitation of Life; The Mighty Barnum; Bachelor Bait; Such Women are Dangerous. **1935** I've Been Around; Show Them No Mercy; Life Begins at Forty; Les Miserables; Curly Top; Way Down East. **1936** Everybody's Old Man; The Music Goes Round; The Country Beyond; Poppy; Reunion. **1937** That I May Live; Born Reckless; Woman Wise; She Had to Eat. **1938** Mr. Moto Takes a Chance; Rascals; Storm over Bengal. **1939** Pride of the Navy; Smuggled Cargo; A Woman is the Judge; Missing Daughters; Pirates of the Skies. **1940** Babies for Sale; Convicted Woman; Girls Under Twenty-One; Men without Souls; Island of Doomed Men; Konga, the Wild Stallion. **1941** Meet Boston Blackie; The Stork Pays Off; The Officer and the Lady. **1942** Queen of Broadway; Rubber Racketeers. **1947** Bush Pilot. **1948** The Devil's Cargo. **1949** Sky Liner. **1955** Rebel Without a Cause. **1964** Strait-Jacket; The Night Walker. **1965** Broken Sabre. **1967** Dr. Terror's Gallery of Horrors (aka Return from the Past).

HUDSON, WiLLIAM (William Woodson Hudson, Jr.)
Born: Jan. 24, 1925, Calif. Died: Apr. 5, 1974, Woodland Hills, Calif. (Laennec's cirrhosis). Stage and screen actor. Brother of actor John Hudson.

Appeared in: **1943** Destination Tokyo (film debut). **1945** Objective Burma. **1950** Father Makes Good. **1951** Hard, Fast and Beautiful. **1955** Mister Roberts; Strategic Air Command. **1956** Battle Hymn. **1957** The Man Who Turned to Stone; The Amazing Colossal Man; My Man Godfrey. **1958** Attack of the 50 Ft. Woman. **1962** Moon Pilot. **1970** Airport.

HUESTIS, RUSSELL
Born: 1894. Died: Dec. 1, 1964, Seattle, Wash. (heart attack). Screen actor.

HUFF, FORREST
Born: 1876. Died: Aug. 21, 1947, New York, N.Y. Screen, stage actor and opera performer.

Appeared in: **1927** The Love of Sunya.

HUFF, JACK. *See* JACK KIRK

HUFF, LOUISE
Born: 1896, Columbus, Ga. Died: Aug. 22, 1973, New York. Stage and screen actress.

Appeared in: **1916** The Reward of Patience; Seventeen; Great Expectations. **1917** What Money Can't Buy; Tom Sawyer; Freckles; The Varmint; The Ghost House; Jack and Jill. **1918** T 'Other Dear Charmer; Sea Waif. **1919** Oh, You Woman; Crook of Dreams. **1920** What Women Want; Dangerous Paradise. **1922** The Seventh Day.

HUGHES, CHARISSA
Died: June 13, 1963, Hollywood, Calif. Screen actress.

HUGHES, DAVID (David Hughes Blees)
Born: 1924. Died: June 8, 1945, Hollywood, Calif. (heart attack). Screen and radio actor. Do not confuse with actor David Hillary Hughes (dec. 1974).

HUGHES, DAVID HILLARY
Died: Feb. 5, 1974. Screen actor.

Appeared in: **1954** Shield for Murder. **1958** The Brain Eaters.

HUGHES, GARETH
Born: Aug. 23, 1894, Llanelly, Wales. Died: Oct. 1, 1965, Woodland Hills, Calif. Stage and screen actor. Entered films in 1919.

Appeared in: **1919** Mrs. Wiggs and the Cabbage Patch; Eyes of Youth. **1921** Sentimental Tommy; The Hunch; Garments of Truth; Indiscretion; Life's Darn Funny; The Lure of Youth. **1922** Don't Write Letters; Little Eva Ascends; Forget-Me-Not. **1923** The Christian; The Spanish Dancer; The Enemies of Women; Kick In; Penrod and Sam. **1924** The Sunset Trail; Shadows of Paris. **1925** The Midnight Girl. **1926** Men of the Night. **1927** The Whirlwind of Youth; The Auctioneer; Broadway after Midnight; Eyes of the Totem; In the First Degree. **1928** The Sky Rider; Old Age Handicap; Better Days; Comrades; Top Sergeant Mulligan. **1929** Silent Sentinel; Mister Antonio; Broken Hearted. **1931** Scareheads.

HUGHES, JOSEPH ANTHONY
Born: May 2, 1904, New York, N.Y. Died: Feb. 11, 1970, Pasadena, Calif. (undetermined—suicide or accident—acute alcohol and barbituate mixture). Screen actor.

Appeared in: **1936** Whipsaw; The Country Doctor; Educating Father. **1939** Tail Spin. **1940** The Cisco Kid and the Lady; Beyond Tomorrow; Diamond

Frontier. **1942** Men of San Quentin. **1945** Keys of the Kingdom. **1951** The People Against O'Hara. **1955** Daddy Long Legs. **1959** Warlock.

HUGHES, LLOYD
Born: Oct. 21, 1897, Bisbee, Ariz. Died: June 6, 1958, Los Angeles, Calif. Screen actor.

Appeared in: **1915** Turn of a Road. **1919** The Haunted Bedroom. **1920** Below the Surface; Dangerous Hours; Home Spun Folks. **1921** Love Never Dies; Beau Revel; Mother O'Mine. **1922** Hail the Woman; Tess of the Storm Country. **1923** Scars of Jealousy; The Old Fool; Are You a Failure?; Her Reputation; Children of Dust; The Huntress. **1924** The Sea Hawk; The Heritage of the Desert; Untamed Youth; Judgment of the Storm; Welcome Stranger; In Every Woman's Life; The Whipping Boss. **1925** Declassee; The Dixie Handicap; The Desert Flower; The Half-Way Girl; If I Marry Again; The Lost World; Sally; Scarlet Saint. **1926** Pals First; Valencia; Ella Cinders; Irene; Loose Angles; Forever After; High Steppers; Ladies at Play. **1927** No Place to Go; American Beauty; The Stolen Bride; An Affair of the Follies; Too Many Crooks. **1928** Heart to Heart; Sailors' Wives; Three-Ring Marriage. **1929** Where East Is East; Acquitted; The Mysterious Island. **1930** The Runaway Bride; Sweethearts on Parade; Love Comes Along; Hello Sister; Big Boy; Moby Dick; Hell Bound; Extravagance. **1931** Drums of Jeopardy; Sky Raiders; Unwanted; Air Eagles; The Deceiver; Private Scandal. **1932** The Miracle Man; Heart Punch. **1935** Reckless Roads; Midnight Phantom; Skybound; Society Fever; Rip Roaring Riley; Honeymoon Limited; Harmony Lane. **1936** Night Cargo; Little Red School House; Kelly of the Secret Service. **1937** A Man Betrayed. **1938** Numbered Woman; Clipped Wings; I Demand Payment. **1939** Romance of the Redwoods. **1940** Vengeance of the Deep.

HUGHES, RUPERT
Born: Jan. 31, 1872, Lancaster, Missouri. Died: Sept. 9, 1956, Los Angeles, Calif. (heart failure). Author, historian, composer, poet, film director, screenwriter and screen actor.

Appeared in: **1913** Saved by Parcel Post.

HUGHES, RUSH (Russell Sheldon Hughes)
Born: Jan. 15, 1910, Ohio. Died: Apr. 16, 1958, Studio City, Calif. (heart attack). Screen actor, television writer and screenwriter.

Appeared in: **1922** The Wall Flower. **1923** Ashes of Vengeance; Reno; Souls for Sale. **1928** Beware of Married Men. **1938** Love and Hisses.

HUGHES, THOMAS ARTHUR
Born: 1887. Died: Nov. 25, 1953, Los Angeles, Calif. Screen actor. Resemblance to Sir Winston Churchill brought historical roles. Also played in many westerns.

HUGHES, YVONNE EVELYN
Born: 1900. Died: Dec. 26, 1950, New York, N.Y. (murdered—strangled). Stage and screen actress

Appeared in: **1923** Zaza; Big Brother; Lawful Larceny. **1924** A Society Scandal; Monsieur Beaucaire.

HUGO, MAURITZ
Born: 1909. Died: June 16, 1974, Woodland Hills, Calif. (heart ailment). Screen, stage and radio actor.

Appeared in: **1938** Wanted by the Police. **1943** Mission to Moscow; Revenge of the Zombies. **1944** The Utah Kid; Marked Trails. **1945** Jealousy. **1946** The Mask of Dijon; Secrets of a Sorority Girl; Blonde for a Day; Rustler's Round-Up. **1947** Homesteaders of Paradise Valley. **1948** When My Baby Smiles at Me; Renegades of Sonora; The Iron Curtain. **1949** Search for Danger; Death Valley Gunfighter. **1950** Frisco Tornado; Love that Brute; Ticket to Tomahawk (aka The Sheriff's Daughter); Whirlpool. **1951** Saddle Legion; The Dakota Kid; Gun Play; No Questions Asked; Pistol Harvest. **1952** Blue Canadian Rockies; The Kid from Broken Gun; Yukon Gold; Road Agent; Captive of Billy the Kid. **1954** Man with the Steel Whip. **1956** Crime Against Joe. **1957** Gun Battle at Monterey; The Vampire; War Drums. **1958** Seven Guns to Mesa. **1959** The Gunfighter at Dodge City. **1960** The Purple Gang; Thirteen Fighting Men. **1962** Stagecoach to Dancer's Rock. **1966** Alvarez Kelly. **1969** Marooned.

HULBERT, CLAUDE (Claude Noel Hulbert)
Born: Dec. 25, 1900, London, England. Died: Jan. 22, 1964, Sydney, Australia. Screen, stage, radio actor, screenwriter and composer. Brother of actor Jack Hulbert.

Appeared in: **1928** Champagne. **1930** Naughty Husbands. **1932** A Night Like This; The Mayor's Nest; Thark; The Face at the Window; Let Me Explain Dear. **1933** Their Night Out; Radio Parade; Heads We Go (aka The Charming Deceiver—US); The Song You Gave Me (US 1934). **1934** A Cup of Kindness; Love at Second Sight (aka The Girl Thief—US 1938). Lilies of the Field; Big Business. **1935** Bulldog Jack (aka Alias Bulldog Drummond—US); Hello Sweetheart; Man of the Moment. **1936** Wolf's Clothing; Where's Sally?; The Interrupted Honeymoon; Hail and Farewell; Honeymoon Merry-Go-Round (aka Olympic Honeymoon). **1937** Take a Chance; The Vulture; It's Not Cricket; Ship's Concert; You Live and Learn. **1938** Simply Terrific; The Viper; It's in the Blood; His Lordship Regrets; Many Tanks Mr. Atkins. **1940** Sailors Three (aka Three Cockeyed Sailors—US 1941). **1941** The Ghost of St. Michael's. **1943** The Dummy Talks; My Learned Friend. **1946** London Town (aka My Heart Goes Crazy—US 1953). **1947** The Ghosts of Berkeley Square. **1948** Under the Frozen Falls. **1949** Cardboard Cavalier. **1956** Fun at St. Fanny's. **1960** Not a Hope in Hell.

HULBURD, H. L. "BUD"
Died: Feb. 10, 1973, Burbank, Calif. Screen actor, stuntman and special effects technician.

Appeared in: **1915** Birth of a Nation.

HULEY, PETE (aka KLONDIKE PETE)
Born: 1893, Austria. Died: Feb. 6, 1973, Vancouver, B.C., Canada. Screen actor and gold prospector.

HULL, JOSEPHINE (Josephine Sherwood)
Born: 1884, Newton, Mass. Died: Mar. 12, 1957, New York, N.Y. (cerebral hemorrhage). Screen, stage, radio, television actress and stage director. Won 1950 Academy Award for Best Supporting Actress in Harvey.

Appeared in: **1929** The Bishop's Candlestick (short). **1932** After Tomorrow; Careless Lady. **1944** Arsenic and Old Lace (stage and film versions). **1950** Harvey (stage and film versions). **1951** The Lady from Texas.

HULL, SHELLY
Died: Jan. 14, 1919. Stage and screen actress.

HULL, WARREN (John Warren Hull)
Born: Jan. 17, 1903, Gasport, N.Y. Died: Sept. 21, 1974, Waterbury, Conn. (heart failure). Screen, stage, radio, television actor and singer.

Appeared in: **1935** Personal Maid's Secret (film debut); Miss Pacific Fleet; an Educational short. **1936** The Law in Her Hands; Love Begins at Twenty; The Big Noise; Bengal Tiger; Freshman Love; The Walking Dead. **1937** Fugitive in the Sky; Her Husband's Secretary; Big Business; Night Key; Michael O'Halloran; Rhythm in the Clouds; Paradise Isle; A Bride for Henry. **1938** Hawaii Calls; The Spider's Web (serial). **1939** Star Reporter; Mandrake the Magician (serial); Smashing the Spy Ring; Should a Girl Marry?; The Girl from Rio; Crashing Thru. **1940** The Green Hornet Strikes Again (serial); The Lone Wolf Meets a Lady; Wagons Westward; Remedy for Riches; The Last Alarm; Ride, Tenderfoot, Ride; Yukon Flight; Marked Men. **1941** Bowery Blitzkrieg; The Spider Returns (serial).

HUME, BENITA
Born: Oct. 14, 1906, London, England. Died: Nov. 1, 1967, Egerton, England. Screen, stage, radio and television actress. Married to actor Ronald Coleman (dec. 1958) and later married to actor George Sanders (dec. 1972).

Appeared in: **1925** Milestone Melodies series including: They Wouldn't Believe Me and Her Golden Hair Was Hanging Down Her Back. **1926** Second to None. **1927** Easy Virtue (US 1928). **1928** The Constant Nymph; A South Sea Bubble; A Light Woman; The Lady of the Lake (US 1930); The Wrecker (US 1929); Balaclava (aka Jaws of Hell—US 1931). **1929** The Clue of the New Pin; High Treason. **1930** The House of the Arrow; Symphony in Two Flats. **1931** The Flying Fool; A Honeymoon Adventure (aka Footsteps in the Night—US 1933); The Happy Ending. **1932** Service for Ladies (aka Reserved for Ladies—US); Women Who Play; Men of Steel; Diamond Cut Diamond (aka Blame the Woman—US); Sally Bishop; Lord Camber's Ladies; Help Yourself. **1933** Discord; The Little Damozel; Gambling Ship; Worst Woman in Paris?; Only Yesterday; Looking Forward; Clear All Wires. **1934** The Private Life of Don Juan; Jew Suess (aka Power—US). **1935** The Divine Spark; 18 Minutes; The Gay Deception. **1936** The Garden Murder Case; Moonlight Murder; Suzy; Tarzan Escapes; Rainbow on the River. **1937** The Last of Mrs. Cheyney. **1939** Peck's Bad Boy With the Circus.

HUMMELL, MARY ROCKWELL
Born: 1889. Died: Feb. 16, 1946, Hollywood, Calif. Screen actress. Entered films approx. 1916.

HUMPHREY, BESSIE
Born: Boston, Mass. Died: Mar. 8, 1933, Hollywood, Calif. Stage and screen actress.

HUMPHREY, WILLIAM (William Jonathan Humphrey)
Born: Jan. 2, 1874, Chicopee Falls, Mass. Died: Oct. 4, 1942, Woodland Hills, Calif. (coronary thrombosis). Screen, stage actor, film director and screenwriter.

Appeared in: **1911** Forgotten. **1912** The Bogus Napoleon; The King's Jester. **1913** The Penalties of Reputation; The Flirt; My Land Idleness; An Unwritten Chapter; Mixed Identities. **1914** The Man Who Knew; The Barnes of New York; The Awakening of Barbara Dare; The Upper Hand; His Wedded Wife; Fine Feathers Make Fine Birds; His Dominant Passion; Uncle Bill; The Spirit of Christmas; Hearts of Women. **1915** Heredity. **1916** From Out of the Past; Father of Men. **1917** In and Out (aka In Again Out Again). **1921** The Sky

Pilot. **1922** Foolish Monte Carlo; The Stranger's Banquet. **1923** Vanity Fair; Haldane of the Secret Service; The Man Life Passed By; The Social Code; Rouged Lips; Scaramouche. **1924** Beau Brummell; Abraham Lincoln; The Arizona Express; One Night in Rome. **1925** Dangerous Innocence; The Gold Hunters; Lady Robin Hood; Three Wise Crooks; Drusilla with a Million; The Unholy Three; Stella Dallas; Phantom of the Opera. **1925** Midnight Limited; The Silent Lover; The Danger Girl; The Volga Boatman. **1927** The Dice Woman; Aflame in the Sky; Yours to Command; Temptations of a Shop Girl. **1928** The Actress; Life's Crossroads. **1929** Devil May-Care; The Godless Girl. **1930** Not so Dumb. **1931** Subway Express; Murder at Midnight. **1932** Tangled Destinies; Manhattan Parade. **1933** One Year Later; Cheating Blondes; Secret Sinners; Strange Adventure; Cowboy Councellor; Vampire Bat; Sing, Sinner, Sing. **1934** Are We Civilized? **1935** False Pretenses.

HUMPHREYS, CECIL
Born: July 21, 1883, Cheltenham, England. Died: Nov. 6, 1947, New York, N.Y. Stage and screen actor. Entered films in 1916.

Appeared in: **1916** The Lifeguardsman; The Pleydell Mystery. **1917** The Sorrows of Satan; The Veiled Woman; The Profligate. **1919** The Romance of Lady Hamilton; The Swindler; The Elusive Pimpernel. **1920** The Pride of the North; The Hour of Trial; The House on the Marsh; The Amateur Gentleman; The Tavern Knight; The Winding Road. **1921** The White Hen; Greatheart; The Four Just Men; Shadow of Evil; The Adventures of Sherlock Holmes series including: The Dying Detective. **1922** The Glorious Adventure; Dick Turpin's Ride to York; False Evidence. **1924** The Gayest of the Gay (aka Her Redemption). **1925** Irish Luck. **1929** The Woman in White; The Broken Melody. **1931** 77 Park Lane; The Old Man. **1932** It's a King. **1933** Strictly in Confidence; Dick Turpin. **1934** The Silver Spoon; Oh, No, Doctor!; The Unfinished Symphony; Adventure Limited; Guest of Honour. **1935** Koenigsmark. **1936** Fair Exchange; Accused; Chick; Reasonable Doubt. **1939** Wuthering Heights. **1946** The Razor's Edge. **1947** Desire Me. **1948** A Woman's Vengeance.

HUN, HADI
Born: 1900, Turkey. Died: Dec. 1969, Istanbul, Turkey (heart attack). Stage and screen actor.

HUNT, GOVERNOR W. P. (George Wylie Paul Hunt)
Born: Nov. 1, 1859, Huntsville, Missouri. Died: Dec. 24, 1934. Former governor of Arizona and screen actor.

Appeared in: **1915** A Western Governor's Humanity.

HUNT, JAY
Born: 1857, Pa. Died: Nov. 18, 1932, Los Angeles, Calif. Stage and screen actor.

Appeared in: **1923** Hunchback of Notre Dame. **1924** After a Million; Yankee Speed. **1925** Counsel for the Defense; Lightnin'. **1926** A Man Four-Square; Three Bad Men; The Gentle Cyclone; The Golden Web; Men of the Night; My Own Pal; Out of the Storm; One Minute to Play. **1927** The Harvester; The Overland Stage; Captain Salvation; Better Days. **1930** The Poor Millionaire. **1931** The Sky Spider.

HUNT, MADGE
Born: 1875, New York, N.Y. Died: Aug. 2, 1935. Screen, stage and vaudeville actress. Married to stage actor and director William Hunt (dec.). Entered films with Reliance approximately 1915.

Appeared in: **1921** False Kisses; The Lamplighter; The Blazing Trail; Reputation. **1923** Can a Woman Love Twice?; Lorna Doone. **1924** Abraham Lincoln. **1926** The Runaway Express; Fiddlesticks. **1927** The Heart of Maryland; The Texas Steer. **1928** Heart Trouble; Sins of the Fathers. **1929** Show Boat.

HUNT, MARTITA
Born: 1900, Argentina. Died: June 13, 1969, London, England. Stage and screen actress.

Appeared in: **1932** Service For Ladies (aka Reserved for Ladies—US); Love on Wheels. **1933** I Was a Spy (US 1934); Friday the Thirteenth. **1934** Too Many Millions. **1935** Mr. What's-His-Name; The Case of Gabriel Perry; First a Girl. **1936** When Knights Were Bold (US 1942); Pot Luck; Tudor Rose (aka Nine Days a Queen—US); The Interrupted Honeymoon. **1937** The Mill on the Floss (US 1939); Good Morning, Boys (aka Where There's a Will—US); Farewell Again (aka Troopship—US 1938). **1938** Second Best Bed; Strange Boarders; Prison Without Bars (US 1939). **1939** Trouble Brewing; A Girl Must Live (US 1941); The Good Old Days; Young Man's Fancy (US 1943); At the Villa Rose (aka House of Mystery—US 1941); Old Mother Riley Joins Up; The Middle Watch; The Nursemaid Who Disappeared. **1940** Tilly of Bloomsbury; Miss Grant Goes to the Door. **1941** East of Piccadilly (aka The Strangler—US 1942); Freedom Radio (aka A Voice in the Night—US); Quiet Wedding; The Seventh Survivor. **1942** They Flew Alone (aka Wings and the Woman—US); Sabotage at Sea; Lady from Lisbon. **1943** The Man in Grey (US 1945). **1944** Welcome Mr. Washington. **1945** The Wicked Lady (US 1946). **1946** Great Expectations (US 1947). **1947** The Little Ballerina (US 1951); The Ghosts of Berkeley Square. **1948** So Evil My Love; Anna Karenina; My Sister and I. **1952** Treasure Hunt; Folly to be Wise; The Story of Robin Hood and His

Merrie Men; It Started in Paradise (US 1953); Meet Me Tonight. **1953** Melba; Tonight at 8:30. **1955** King's Rhapsody. **1956** Anastasia; Three Men in a Boat (US 1958). **1957** The Admirable Crichton (aka Paradise Lagoon—US); Dangerous Exile (US 1958). **1958** Bonjour Tristesse; Me and the Colonel. **1960** Bottoms Up; The Brides of Dracula; Song Without End. **1961** Mr. Topaze (aka I Like Money—US 1962). **1962** The Wonderful World of the Brothers Grimm. **1964** Becket; The Unsinkable Molly Brown. **1965** Bunny Lake is Missing. **1968** The Long Day's Dying. **1969** The Best House in London.

HUNT, REA M.

Born: 1893. Died: June 21, 1961. Screen actor. Was one of the original Keystone Kops.

HUNTER, GLENN

Born: 1897, Highland, N.Y. Died: Dec. 30, 1945, New York, N.Y. Screen, stage and vaudeville actor.

Appeared in: **1921** The Case of Becky. **1922** The Country Flapper; The Cradle Buster; Smilin' Through. **1923** Puritan Passions; Second Fiddle; Youthful Cheaters; The Scarecrow. **1924** Grit; The Silent Watcher; Merton of the Movies; West of the Water Tower. **1925** The Little Giant; His Buddy's Wife. **1926** The Pinch Hitter; The Broadway Boob; The Romance of a Million Dollars; The Little Giant.

HUNTER, IAN

Born: June 13, 1900, Cape Town, South Africa. Died: Sept. 24, 1975, England. Screen, stage, television actor and screenwriter.

Appeared in: **1922** Mr. Oddy. **1924** Not for Sale. **1925** Confessions; A Girl of London. **1927** Downhill (aka When Boys Leave Home—US 1928); Easy Virtue (US 1928); The Ring. **1928** His House in Order; The Physician (US 1929); The Thoroughbred; The Valley of the Ghosts. **1929** Syncopation. **1930** Escape. **1931** Cape Forlorn (aka The Love Storm—US); Sally in Our Alley. **1932** The Water Gypsies; The Sign of Four; Marry Me. **1933** The Man from Toronto; Orders is Orders (US 1934); Skipper of the Osprey (short). **1934** Something Always Happens; The Silver Spoon; The Night of the Party; The Church Mouse (US 1935); No Escape; The Wigan Express (aka Death at Broadcasting House). **1935** The Phantom Light; Lazybones; The Morals of Marcus (US 1936); The Girl from Tenth Avenue; Jalna; A Midsummer Night's Dream; I Found Stella Parrish; Dinky. **1936** The White Angel; To Mary—With Love; The Devil is a Sissy; Stolen Holiday. **1937** Call It a Day; Another Dawn; That Certain Woman; Confession; 52nd Street. **1938** Comet over Broadway; The Sisters; The Adventures of Robin Hood; Always Goodbye; Secrets of an Actress. **1939** Tower of London; Tarzan Finds a Son; Yes, My Darling Daughter; The Little Princess; Broadway Serenade; Maisie; Bad Little Angel. **1940** Strange Cargo; Bitter Sweet; Broadway Melody of 1940; Dulcy; The Long Voyage Home; Gallant Sons. **1941** Billy the Kid; Dr. Jekyll and Mr. Hyde; Andy Hardy's Private Secretary; Come Live with Me; Ziegfeld Girl; Smilin' Through. **1942** A Yank at Eton. **1943** Forever and a Day; It Comes Up Love. **1946** Bedelia (US 1947). **1947** White Cradle Inn (aka High Fury—US 1948); The White Unicorn (aka Bad Sisters—US 1948). **1949** Edward, My Son. **1952** It Started in Paradise (US 1953). **1953** Appointment in London (US 1955). **1954** Eight O'Clock Walk (US 1955); Don't Blame the Stork. **1956** The Battle of the River Plate (aka Pursuit of the Graf Spee—US 1957); The Door in the Wall (short). **1957** Fortune is a Woman (aka She Played With Fire—US 1958). **1958** Rockets Galore; Mad Little Island. **1959** Northwest Frontier (aka Flame over India—US 1960). **1960** The Bulldog Breed. **1961** The Queen's Guards (US 1963); Dr. Blood's Coffin (aka Face of Evil); The Treasure of Monte Cristo (aka The Secret of Monte Cristo—US). **1962** Guns of Darkness (aka Act of Mercy).

HUNTER, JACKIE

Born: 1901, Canada. Died: Nov. 21, 1951, London, England. Screen, stage, vaudeville and radio actor.

HUNTER, JEFFREY (Henry Herman McKinnies)

Born: Nov. 23, 1926, New Orleans, La. Died: May 27, 1969, Van Nuys, Calif. (injuries from fall). Screen, stage, radio and television actor. Married to actress Emily McLaughlin and divorced from actress Barbara Rush, and Dusty Bartlett.

Appeared in: **1951** Call Me Mister; The Frogman; Take Care of My Little Girl; Fourteen Hours. **1952** Red Skies of Montana (aka Smoke Jumpers); Belles on Their Toes; Lure of the Wilderness; Dreamboat. **1953** Single Handed (aka Sailor of the King—US). **1954** Three Young Texans; Princess of the Nile. **1955** Seven Angry Men; White Feather; Seven Cities of Gold. **1956** The Proud Ones; A Kiss Before Dying; The Great Locomotive Chase; Four Girls in Town; The Searchers. **1957** The True Story of Jesse James; The Way to the Gold; No Down Payment; Gun for a Coward. **1958** The Last Hurrah; In Love and War; Count Five and Die; Mardi Gras. **1960** Key Witness; Hell to Eternity; Sergeant Rutledge. **1961** Man-Trap; King of Kings. **1962** The Longest Day; No Man is an Island. **1964** The Man from Galveston; Gold for the Caesars. **1965** Vendetta; Brainstorm; The Woman Who Wouldn't Die. **1966** Dimension 5. **1967** A Witch without a Broom; The Christmas Kid; A Guide for the Married Man. **1968** The Private Navy of Sgt. O'Farrell; Custer of the West; Sexy Susan at the

King's Court; Joe, Find a Place to Die. **1969** The Hostess Also Has a County.

HUNTER, RICHARD

Born: 1875. Died: Dec. 22, 1962, Santa Monica, Calif. Cowboy screen actor.

HUNTLEY, CHET (Chester Robert Huntley)

Born: 1912, Cardwell, Montana. Died: Mar. 20, 1974, Bozeman, Montana (lung cancer). Television, radio news commentator and screen actor.

Appeared in: **1949** I Cheated the Law; Arctic Manhunt. **1952** The Pride of St. Louis. **1955** Mau Mau (narrator). **1958** Cry Terror. **1959** Behind the Great Wall (narrator).

HUNTLEY, FRED (aka FRED HUNTLY)

Born: 1862. Died: Nov. 1, 1931, Hollywood, Calif. (heart attack). Stage and screen actor.

Appeared in: **1918** Heart of Wetona. **1919** Heart o' the Hills; Everywoman. **1921** Brewster's Millions; Bronze Bell; Face of the World; Gasoline Gus; A Prince There Was; A Wise Fool; Little Minister; What Every Woman Knows. **1922** Crimson Challenge; Man with Two Mothers; Borderland; North of the Rio Grande; To Have and to Hold; While the City Sleeps; **1923** Peg O' My Heart; Law of the Lawless; Where the North Begins; To the Last Man; Call of the Canyon; Go Getter. **1924** The Age of Innocence; Thundering Hoofs. **1927** King of Kings.

HURLEY, JULIA

Born: 1847, New York, N.Y. Died: June 4, 1927, New York, N.Y. Stage and screen actress.

Appeared in: **1913** Blood and Water; A Child's Intuition. **1914** The Jungle. **1915** The Price He Paid. **1918** Love's Conquest. **1919** Little Women; Poison Pen. **1920** Easy to Get; The Cost; Guilty of Love; New York Idea. **1921** The Bride's Play; Jane Eyre. **1924** Argentine Love. **1925** The Little French Girl; The Making of O'Malley. **1926** Married?

HURN, DOUGLAS

Born: 1925, England. Died: Oct. 22, 1974, London, England. Screen, stage actor and television producer.

HURST, BRANDON

Born: Nov. 30, 1866, London, England. Died: July 15, 1947, Burbank, Calif. (arteriosclerosis). Stage and screen actor.

Appeared in: **1923** The Hunchback of Notre Dame; World's Applause; Legally Dead. **1924** He Who Gets Slapped; Thief of Bagdad; Silent Watcher; Cytherea; Lover of Camille; One Night in Rome. **1925** Lightnin' Lady. **1926** Amateur Gentleman; Grand Duchess and the Waiter; Secret Orders; Lady of the Harem; Volcano; Enchanted Hill; Made for Love; Paris at Midnight; Rainmaker; Shamrock Handicap. **1927** Seventh Heaven; High School Hero; Love; King of Kings; Annie Laurie. **1928** Man Who Laughs; Interference; News Parade. **1929** Voice of the Storm; Her Private Life; Greene Murder Case; Wolf of Wall Street. **1930** High Society Blues; Eyes of the World. **1931** A Connecticut Yankee; Right of Way; Young as You Feel; Murder at Midnight. **1932** Down to Earth; White Zombies; Sherlock Holmes; Murders in the Rue Morgue; Scarface; Midnight Lady. **1934** Sequoia; Bombay Mail; Lost Patrol; Little Minister; House of Rothschild. **1935** The Great Impersonation; While the Patient Slept; Bright Eyes; Red Morning; Bonnie Scotland; Woman in Red. **1936** Gasoloons (short); The Plough and the Stars; The Moon's Our Home; Mary of Scotland. **1937** Maid of Salem; Wee Willie Winkle. **1938** If I Were King; Four Men and a Prayer; Suez. **1939** The Adventures of Sherlock Holmes; Stanley and Livingstone. **1940** The Blue Bird; If I Had My Way; Rhythm on the River. **1941** Sign of the Wolf. **1942** Mad Martindales; The Remarkable Andrew; Tennessee Johnson; The Ghost of Frankenstein; The Pied Piper; Road to Happiness. **1943** Dixie; Frankenstein Meets the Wolf Man. **1944** The Princess and the Pirate; The Man in Half Moon Street. **1945** The Corn is Green; House of Frankenstein.

HURST, PAUL C.

Born: 1888, Tulare County, Calif. Died: Feb. 27, 1953, Hollywood, Calif. (suicide). Screen, stage actor, film director and screenwriter.

Appeared in: **1912** The Stolen Invention; When Youth Meets Youth; Red Wing and the Paleface; Driver of the Deadwood Coach; The Mayor's Crusade. **1913** The Big Horn Massacre; Daughter of the Underworld; The Struggle; On the Brink of Ruin; The Last Blockhouse; The Redemption. **1914** The Barrister of Ignorance; The Rajah's Vow; The Smugglers of Lone Isle. **1915** The Pitfall. **1916** The Social Pirates; The Missing Millionaire; Whispering Smith; Medicine Bend; Judith of the Cumberlands; The Manager of the B & A; The Moth and the Star; A Voice in the Wilderness; The Taking of Stingaree; To the Vile Dust; The Black Hole of Glenranald; The Millionaire Plunger. **1917** A Race for a Fortune (serial); The Railroad Raiders (serial); The Further Adventures of Stingaree (series) including: The Jackaroo and The Tracking of Stingaree. **1918** Smashing Through. **1926** The High Hand; The Outlaw Express. **1927** Buttons; The Valley of Giants; The Red Raiders; The Devil's Saddle; The Man from Hardpan; The Overland Stage. **1928** The Cossacks. **1929** Tide of Empire; The California Mail; The Lawless Legion; The Rainbow; Sailor's

Holiday. **1930** The Swellhead; Mountain Justice; The Runaway Bride; Hot Curves; Shadow of the Law; Paradise Island; Borrowed Wives; The Third Alarm; Oh, Yeah?; The Racketeer; His First Command; Officer O'Brien; Lucky Larkin. **1931** The Single Sin; The Secret Six; The Kick In; The Public Defender; Sweepstakes; Bad Company; Terror by Night; The Secret Witness. **1932** Panama Flow; The 13th Guest; Hold 'Em Jail; The Big Stampede; My Pal the King. **1933** Island of Lost Souls; Men are Such Fools; Hold Your Man; Saturday's Millions; Women in His Life; Scarlet River; Terror Abroad; The Sphinx; Tugboat Annie; Day of Reckoning. **1934** The Big Race; Among the Missing; Take the Stand; Sequoia; The Line-Up; Midnight Alibi; There Ain't No Justice (short). **1935** Tomorrow's Youth; Star of Midnight; The Case of the Curious Bride; Mississippi; Shadow of Doubt; Public Hero No. 1; Calm Yourself; Wilderness Mail; The Gay Deception; Riffraff. **1936** The Blackmailer; It Had to Happen; To Mary with Love; I'd Give My Life; The Gay Desperado; We Who Are about to Die; North of Nome; Robin Hood of El Dorado. **1937** Trouble in Morocco; You Can't Beat Love; Super Sleuth; Fifty Roads to Town; Wake Up and Live; Angel's Holiday; This is My Affair; Slave Ship; Wife, Doctor and Nurse; Danger—Love at Work; Ali Baba Goes to Town; Second Honeymoon; Small Town Boy; She's No Lady; The Lady Fights Back. **1938** In Old Chicago; Rebecca of Sunnybrook Farm; Island in the Sky; Alexander's Ragtime Band; Josette; My Lucky Star; Hold That Co-ed; Thanks for Everything; No Time to Marry; Prison Break; The Last Express; Secrets of a Nurse. **1939** Broadway Serenade; Cafe Society; Topper Takes a Trip; It Could Happen to You; Each Dawn I Die; Remember?; The Kid from Kokomo; Quick Millions; Bad Lands; On Your Toes; Gone With the Wind. **1940** Edison the Man; Torrid Zone; Goin' Fishing (short); They Drive by Night; South of Karango; The Westerner; Heaven with a Barbed Wire Fence; Tugboat Annie Sails Again; Star Dust; Men against the Sky. **1941** The Parson of Panamint; This Woman is Mine; Tall, Dark and Handsome; The Great Mr. Nobody; Ellery Queen and the Murder Ring; Bowery Boy; Petticoat Politics; Virginia; Caught in a Draft. **1942** Pardon My Stripes; Sundown Jim; Night in New Orleans; Dudes are Pretty People. **1943** The Ox-Bow Incident; Hi'Ya, Chum; Young and Willing; Jack London; The Sky's the Limit; Coney Island; Calaboose. **1944** The Ghost that Walks Alone; Greenwich Village; Barbary Coast Gent; Something for the Boys; Girl Rush; Summer Storm. **1945** One Exciting Night; Nob Hill; The Big Show-Off; Dakota; The Dolly Sisters; Penthouse Rhythm; Midnight Manhunt; Scared Stiff; Steppin' in Society. **1946** In Old Sacramento; The Virginian; The Plainsman and the Lady; Murder in the Music Hall. **1947** The Angel and the Badman; Death Valley; Under Colorado Skies. **1948** The Arizona Ranger; California Firebrand; Heart of Virginia; Son of God's Country; Gun Smugglers; Yellow Sky; A Miracle Can Happen; Old Los Angeles, Madonna of the Desert. **1949** Law of the Golden West; Outcasts of the Trail; Prince of the Plains; Ranger of Cherokee Strip; San Antone Ambush; South of Rio. **1950** The Missourians; The Old Frontier; Pioneer Marshal; The Vanishing Westerner. **1951** Million Dollar Pursuit. **1952** Big Jim McLain; Toughest Man in Arizona. **1953** The Sun Shines Bright; Pine Bluff.

HUSING, TED (Edward Husing)
Born: Nov. 27, 1901, Bronx, N.Y. Died: Aug. 10, 1962, Pasadena, Calif. (brain tumor). Screen actor, radio announcer, screenwriter and sportswriter.

Appeared in: **1932–33** Sport Thrills series. **1933** Mr. Broadway. **1934–37** Grantland Rice Sportlights (narrator). **1935–37** Broadway Highlights. **1936–37** Hollywood Star Reporter. **1937–38** Paramount shorts. **1940** Broadway Highlights (narrator). **1948** The Olympic Games (narrator). **1950** To Please a Lady.

HUSSY, JIMMY
Born: 1891. Died: Nov. 20, 1930, Woodcliff, N.Y. (stomach trouble and tuberculosis). Screen, stage and vaudeville actor. Appeared in early Vitaphone shorts.

HUSTING, LUCILLE
Born: c. 1900. Died: June 30, 1972, Hollywood, Calif. (stroke). Screen, radio and television actress. Married to actor Leo Curley (dec. 1960).

HUSTON, WALTER
Born: Apr. 6, 1884, Toronto, Canada. Died: Apr, 7, 1950, Beverly Hills, Calif. (aneurism). Screen, stage and vaudeville actor. Divorced from Bayonne Whipple. Married to actress Nan Sutherland (dec. 1973). Nominated for 1936 Academy Award for Best Actor in Dodsworth and in 1948 nominated for Best Supporting Actor in The Treasure of Sierra Madre.

Appeared in: **1929** Gentlemen of the Press (film debut); The Lady Lies; The Bishop's Candlesticks (short); The Carnival Man (short); Two Americans (short); The Virginian. **1930** The Bad Man; Abraham Lincoln; The Virtuous Sin. **1931** The Criminal Code; The Star Witness; The Ruling Voice; Upper Underworld. **1932** A Woman from Monte Carlo; A House Divided; Law and Order; The Beast of the City; The Wet Parade; American Madness; Rain; Night Court; Kongo. **1933** The Prizefighter and the Lady; Hell Below; Gabriel over the White House; Ann Vickers; Storm at Daybreak. **1934** Keep 'Em Rolling. **1935** The Tunnel (aka Transatlantic Tunnel); Rhodes. **1936** Dodsworth. **1938** Of Human Hearts. **1939** The Light That Failed. **1941** All That Money Can Buy; Swamp Water; Maltese Falcon; The Shanghai Gesture. **1942** Our Russian Front (narr. Russian war relief documentary); Always in My Heart; Yankee Doodle Dandy; Prelude to War (narr. U.S. War Dept. documentary);

In This Our Life. **1943** Armored Attack (documentary); Edge of Darkness; The Outlaw (released nationally 1950); Mission to Moscow; The North Star; Safeguarding Military Information (Army training film documentary). **1944** Dragon Seed. **1945** And Then There Were None. **1946** Dragonwyck; Duel in the Sun. **1947** Let There Be Light (Signal Corps film). **1948** Summer Holiday; The Treasure of the Sierra Madre. **1949** The Great Sinner. **1950** The Furies. **1952** The Devil and Daniel Webster (reissue and retitle of All That Money Can Buy, 1941).

HUTCHINSON, CANON CHARLES
Born: 1887, England. Died: Apr. 22, 1969, Brighton, England. Actor Canon Charles Hutchinson is not to be confused with American actor and director "Lightning Hutch" (Charles Hutchinson). Canon Charles Hutchinson was former president of the Actors Church Union.

HUTCHINSON, MURIEL
Born: 1915, New York. Died: Mar. 24, 1975, New York, N.Y. (cancer). Stage and screen actress.

Appeared in: **1939** The Women; Another Thin Man; One Third of a Nation.

HUTCHINSON, WILLIAM
Born: May 16, 1869, Edinburgh, Scotland. Died: Sept. 7, 1918, Los Angeles, Calif. Stage and screen actor.

Appeared in: **1912** Her Education; The Count of Monte Cristo. **1913** The Governor's Daughter; The Three Wise Men; Yankee Doodle Dixie; The Old Clerk; An Old Actor; The Beaded Buckskin Bag; The Flight of the Crow. **1914** The Rummage Sale. **1915** Landing the Hose Reel; Sho Fly; The Comeback of Percy; A Thing or Two in Movies; The Run on Percy; The Chronicles of Bloom Center; The Manicure Girl; Perkins' Pep Producer. **1916** Diamonds are Trumps; Apple Butter; No Sir-ee Bob; Small Town Stuff; Regeneration of Jim Halsey. **1917** The Happiness of Three Women; Everybody was Satisfied; Baseball at Mudville; The Fair Barbarian. **1918** Captain Kidd, Jr.

HUTH, HAROLD
Born: 1892, Huddersfield, Yorkshire, England. Died: Oct. 26, 1967, London, England. Screen, stage actor, film director, film producer and screenwriter.

Appeared in: **1927** One of the Best. **1928** A South Sea Bubble; The Triumph of the Scarlet Pimpernel (aka The Scarlet Daredevil—US 1929); Balaclava (aka Jaws of Hell—US 1931); Sir or Madam. **1929** When Knights were Bold; The Silver King; City of Play; Downstream. **1930** Hours of Loneliness (aka An Obvious Situation); Leave it to Me. **1931** Guilt; Bracelets; The Outsider; Down River; A Honeymoon Adventure (aka Footsteps in the Night—US 1933). **1932** Aren't We All?; The First Mrs. Fraser; Sally Bishop; Rome Express; The Flying Squad; The World, The Flesh and the Devil. **1933** My Lucky Star; The Ghoul; Discord. **1934** The Camels Are Coming. **1937** Take My Tip. **1942** This was Paris. **1951** Blackmailed.

HUTTON, LEONA
Born: 1892. Died: Apr. 1, 1949, Toledo, Ohio (overdose of sleeping pills). Stage and screen actress. Appeared in films from 1913 to 1924.

HUXHAM, KENDRICK
Born: 1892. Died: July 24, 1967, Hollywood, Calif. (heart attack). Stage and screen actor.

Appeared in: **1961** Pirates of Tortuga. **1967** Games.

HYAMS, JOHN
Born: 1877, Syracuse, N.Y. Died: Dec. 9, 1940, Hollywood, Calif. Screen, stage, vaudeville and minstrel actor. Appeared in vaudeville with his wife actress Leila McIntyre (dec. 1953). Father of actress Leila Hyams.

Appeared in: **1927** Life of an Actress; All in Fun (short). **1929** Broadway Scandals. **1930** Cameo Kirby; Swell People; Mind Your Business; Give Me Action; Some Babies. **1934** The Mighty Barnum. **1935** Murder in the Fleet; In Caliente; The Virginia Judge. **1936** And Sudden Death. **1937** Pick a Star; A Day at the Races. **1939** The Housekeeper's Daughter.

HYATT, CLAYTON
Died: July 1932, Windsor, Ontario, Canada (suicide—hanging). Screen actor.

HYATT, HERMAN
Born: 1906, Russia. Died: Jan. 24, 1968, Baltimore, Md. Screen and burlesque actor.

HYLAN, DONALD
Born: 1899. Died: June 20, 1968, New York, N.Y. (heart attack). Screen, stage and television actor. Appeared in silent films.

HYLAND, AUGUSTIN ALLEN
Born: 1905. Died: Feb. 8, 1963, Hollywood, Calif. Screen actor and stand-in for James Cagney.

HYLTON, RICHARD

Born: 1921. Died: May 12, 1962, San Francisco, Calif. (heart attack). Screen, stage and television actor.

Appeared in: **1949** Lost Boundaries. **1950** Halls of Montezuma. **1951** Secret of Convict Lake; Fixed Bayonets! **1952** The Pride of St. Louis.

HYMACK, MR. See QUINTON McPHERSON

HYMER, WARREN

Born: Feb. 25, 1906, New York, N.Y. Died: Mar. 25, 1948, Los Angeles, Calif. Stage and screen actor. Son of actress Elinor Kent (dec. 1957). Divorced from actress Virginia Meyer.

Appeared in: **1929** The Far Call; The Girl from Havana; Speak-easy; Frozen Justice; Fox Movietone Follies of 1929. **1930** Born Reckless; Lone Star Ranger; Oh, For a Man!; Men without Women; Sinner's Holiday; Up the River; Men on Call. **1931** The Spider; Seas Beneath; Goldie; The Unholy Garden; Charlie Chan Carries On. **1932** Hold 'Em Jail; One Way Passage; The Night Mayor; Madison Square Garden; Love is a Racket. **1933** 20,000 Years in Sing Sing; I Love that Man; Midnight Mary; Her First Mate; King for a Night; My Woman; In the Money; The Billion Dollar Scandal; Mysterious Rider; A Lady's Profession. **1934** The Gold Ghost (short); George White's Scandals; The Crosby Case; Belle of the Nineties; Little Miss Marker; The Cat's Paw; She Loves Me Not; Young and Beautiful; One is Guilty; Woman Unafraid; Kid Millions. **1935** Hold 'Em Yale; The Gilded Lily; The Case of the Curious Bride; The Daring Young Man; Silk Hat Kid; She Gets Her Man; Confidential; Show Them No Mercy; Navy Wife; Hitch Hike Lady; Straight from the Heart; Our Little Girl; Beauty's Daughter; Hong Kong Nights. **1936** Tango; Desert Justice; The Widow from Monte Carlo; The Leavenworth Case; Laughing Irish Eyes; Everybody's Old Man; 36 Hours to Kill; Mr. Deeds Goes to Town; San Francisco; Rhythm on the Range; Nobody's Fool; Love Letters of a Star. **1937** You Only Live Once; Join the Marines; Navy Blues; Meet the Boy Friend; Sea Racketeers; We Have Our Moments; Wake Up and Live; Ali Baba Goes to Town; Married before Breakfast; Bad Guy; Tainted Money; She's Dangerous. **1938** Lady Behave; Arson Gang Busters; Joy of Living; Gateway; Submarine Patrol; Thanks for Everything; Bluebeard's Eighth Wife; You and Me. **1939** The Lady and the Mob; Coast Guard; Destry Rides Again; Boy Friend; Calling All Marines; Charlie McCarthy, Detective; Mr. Moto in Danger Island. **1940** I Can't Give You Anything but Love, Baby; Love, Honor and Oh-Baby! **1941** Meet John Doe; Buy Me That Town; Birth of the Blues; Skylark. **1942** Mr. Wise Guy; So's Your Aunt Emma; Henry and Dizzy; Dr. Broadway; Girl's Town; Baby Face Morgan; She's in the Army; One Thrilling Night; Phantom Killer; Police Bullets; Jail House Blues; Meet the Mob; Lure of the Islands. **1943** Danger! Women at Work; Hitler—Dead or Alive; Gangway for Tomorrow. **1944** Since You Went Away; Three is a Family. **1946** Gentleman Joe Palooka; Joe Palooka, Champ.

HYNES, JOHN E.

Born: 1853. Died: Apr. 12, 1931, Long Island, N.Y. Stage and screen actor.

HYTTEN, OLAF

Born: 1888, Scotland. Died: Mar. 11, 1955, Los Angeles, Calif. (heart attack). Screen actor.

Appeared in: **1921** The Knave of Diamonds; Demos (aka Why Men Forget—US); Money; Sonia (aka The Woman Who Came Back—US 1922); The Leaves From My Life series including: The Girl Who Came Back. **1922** The Knight Errant; Trapped by the Mormons; The Wonderful Story; Tense Moments from Opera series including: The Bride of Lammermoor; The Crimson Circle; The Missioner; His Wife's Husband; "Famous Poems by George" series including: Sir Rupert's Wife. **1923** Out to Win; The Little Door into the World (aka The Evil That Men Do); Chu Chin Chow (US 1925); A Gamble with Hearts; The Reverse of the Medal; The Cause of all the Trouble. **1924** The White Shadow (aka White Shadows—US); It is the Law. **1925** The Salvation Hunters. **1928** Old Age Handicap. **1929** Kitty; Master and Man; City of Play. **1930** Grumpy; Playboy of Paris. **1931** Daughter of the Dragon. **1933** Berkeley Square. **1934** Mystery Liner; Jane Eyre; Money Means Nothing; Glamour. **1935** Becky Sharp; The Dark Angel; Two Sinners; The Last Outpost; Bonnie Scotland; Les Miserables. **1936** The House of a Thousand Candles; The Last of the Mohicans; White Hunter. **1937** Easy Living; The Good Earth; California Straight Ahead; I Cover the War; Dangerous Holiday; First Lady. **1938** The Lone Wolf in Paris; Adventures of Robin Hood; Blonde Cheat; Youth Takes a Fling. **1939** Andy Hardy Gets Spring Fever; Rulers of the Sea; Allegheny Uprising; Our Leading Citizen. **1940** Our Neighbors, the Carters; Gaucho Serenade; Drums of Fu Manchu. **1941** Washington Melodrama; All the World's a Stooge (short); That Hamilton Woman. **1942** The Black Swan; Sherlock Holmes; Spy Ship; Sherlock Holmes and the Voice of Terror; The Ghost of Frankenstein; To Be or Not to Be; Bedtime Story; Destination Unknown; The Great Commandment. **1943** Sherlock Holmes Faces Death. **1944** The Lodger; The Return of the Vampire. **1945** My Name is Julia Ross; The Brighton Strangler; Christmas in Connecticut; House of Frankenstein. **1946** The Notorious Lone Wolf; Three Strangers; Black Beauty. **1947** That Way with Women. **1948** Shanghai Chest. **1953** Perils of the Jungle.

IHNAT, STEVE

Born: 1935, Hungary or Czechoslovakia? Died: May 12, 1972, Cannes, France (heart attack). Screen, television actor, film director and screenwriter. Married to actress Sally Carter.

Appeared in: **1958** Dragstrip Riot (film debut). **1962** Passion Street (aka Bourbon Street). **1966** The Chase. **1967** Hour of the Gun; In Like Flint. **1968** Madigan; Kona Coast; Countdown (aka Moon Shot). **1970** Zig Zag. **1972** Fuzz.

ILLING, PETER

Born: 1899, Vienna, Austria. Died: Oct. 29, 1966, London, England. Screen, stage, television and radio actor. Was the voice of Winston Churchill on BBC European radio programs.

Appeared in: **1947** The End of the River. **1948** Against the Wind (US 1949). **1949** Eureka Stockade; Floodtide; Madness of the Heart (US 1950); Children of Chance; Traveller's Joy (US 1951). **1950** State Secret (aka The Great Manhunt—US 1951); My Daughter Joy (aka Operation X—US 1951). **1951** I'll Get You for This (aka Lucky Nick Cain—US); Outcast of the Islands. **1952** The Woman's Angle (US 1954); 24 Hours of a Woman's Life (aka Affair in Monte Carlo—US 1953). **1953** Never Let Me Go; Innocents in Paris (US 1955). **1954** Flame and the Flesh; The House Across the Lake (aka Heatwave—US); West of Zanzibar; The Young Lovers (aka Chance Meeting—US 1955); Mask of Dust (aka Race for Life—US); Svengali. **1955** That Lady; As Long as They're Happy (US 1957). **1956** Bhowani Junction; Loser Takes All; The Battle of the River Plate (aka Pursuit of the Graf Spee—US 1957); Passport to Treason. **1957** Zarak; Interpol (aka Pickup Alley—US); Fire Down Below; A Farewell to Arms; Manuela (aka Stowaway Girl—US); Miracle in Soho; Campbell's Kingdom; Man in the Shadow. **1958** I Accuse!; Escapement (aka The Electric Monster—US 1960). **1959** Whirlpool; The Angry Hills; The Wreck of the Mary Deare; Jet Storm (US 1961); Friends and Neighbors (US 1963). **1960** Moment of Danger (aka Malaga—US 1962); Bluebeard's Ten Honeymoons; Sands of the Desert. **1961** The Secret Partner; The Happy Thieves; Das Geheimnis der Gelben Narzissen (aka Daffodil Killer and The Devil's Daffodil—US 1967). **1962** Village of Daughters; The Middle Course. **1963** Nine Hours to Rama; The V.I.P.'s; Echo of Diana. **1964** The Secret Door (aka Now It Can Be Told). **1965** Devils of Darkness. **1966** A Man Could Get Killed.

ILLINGTON, MARGARET

Born: 1881, Bloomington, Ill. Died: Mar. 11, 1934, Miami Beach, Fla. Stage and screen actress. Married to radio and screen actor Major Bowes (dec. 1946).

Appeared in: **1917** The Inner Shrine (film debut); Sacrifice.

IMBODEN, DAVID C.

Born: Mar. 6, 1887, Kansas City, Mo. Died: Mar. 19, 1974, Kansas City, Mo. Screen actor, stage director and muralist. Married to actress Hazel Bourne (dec. 1956).

Appeared in: **1923** Gimme; Souls for Sale. **1927** King of Kings.

IMBODEN, HAZEL (Hazel Bourne)

Born: Washburn, Ill. Died: Oct. 8, 1956, Kansas City, Mo. Stage and screen actress. Married to actor David Imboden (dec. 1974). Entered films in 1914.

IMHOF, ROGER

Born: Apr. 15, 1875, Rock Island, Ill. Died: Apr. 15, 1958, Hollywood, Calif. Screen, stage, circus and vaudeville actor. Was in vaudeville with his wife Marcelle Coreine (dec. 1977). Appeared in most of Will Rogers' pictures.

Appeared in: **1930** Rural Hospital (short). **1933** Paddy, The Next Best Thing; Charlie Chan's Greatest Case; Hoopla. **1934** David Harum; Wild Gold; Judge Priest; Handy Andy; Ever since Eve; Grand Canary; Music in the Air; Under Pressure. **1935** One More Spring; Life Begins at Forty; The Farmer Takes a Wife; George White's 1935 Scandals; Steamboat 'Round the Bend. **1936** Riff Raff; Three Godfathers; San Francisco; A Son Comes Home; In His Steps; North of Nome. **1937** There Goes the Groom; Every Day's a Holiday. **1939** Young Mr. Lincoln; Nancy Drew—Trouble Shooter; They Shall Have Music; Everything Happens at Night; Drums along the Mohawk. **1940** Abe Lincoln in Illinois; The Grapes of Wrath; Little Old New York; The Way of All Flesh; I was an Adventuress. **1941** Mystery Ship; Man Hunt. **1942** It Happened in Flatbush; Tennessee Johnson; This Gun for Hire. **1944** Casanova in Burlesque; Home in Indiana; Adventures of Mark Twain. **1945** Wilson.

IMPOLITO, JOHN

Born: 1887. Died: May 1, 1962, Los Angeles, Calif. Screen actor.

Appeared in: **1956** Around the World in 80 Days.

INCE, ETHEL. See ETHEL KENT

INCE, JOHN E. (John Edward Ince)

Born: 1877, New York, N.Y. Died: Apr. 10, 1947, Hollywood, Calif. (pneumonia). Screen, stage actor, film director and film producer. Brother of actors Thomas (dec. 1924) and Ralph Ince (dec. 1937). Entered films in 1913 in various capacities.

Appeared in: **1918** Madame Sphinx. **1921** The Hole in the Wall. **1922** Hate. **1927** The Hour of Reckoning. **1930** Alias French Gertie; Hot Curves; Little Caesar; Moby Dick. **1931** Children of Dreams. **1932** Human Targets; Passport to Paradise; No Living Witness; Afraid to Talk. **1933** The Penal Code; One Year Later; Thrill Hunter. **1935** Circle of Death; Circus Shadows; Men of Action; Behind the Green Lights; In Old Kentucky. **1936** Peppery Salt (short); Comin' Round the Mountain; Grand Slam Opera (short); Three on a Limb (short); Night Cargo; Way Out West; The Speed Reporter; Don't Turn 'em Loose. **1939** Mr. Smith Goes to Washington. **1940** The Heckler (short). **1941** Mr. Celebrity. **1942** Code of the Outlaw; The Miracle Kid; The Panther's Claw; Tennessee Johnson; Prison Girls; Broadway Big Shot; Pride of the Yankees. **1943** Man of Courage; What a Man! **1944** Wilson. **1945** The Lost Trail. **1946** The Best Years of Our Lives. **1947** The Last Frontier Uprising. **1948** The Paradine Case.

INCE, RALPH WALDO

Born: 1887, Boston, Mass. Died: Apr. 10, 1937, London, England (auto accident). Screen, stage actor, film director and screenwriter. Brother of actors Thomas (dec. 1924) and John Ince (dec. 1947). Entered films in 1905 as a director. Married to Helen Trigges and divorced from actresses Lucille Stewart and Lucille Mendez.

Appeared in: **1906** "Historical" series on Lincoln for Vitagraph. **1920** Land of Opportunity. **1921** The Highest Law; Wet Gold. **1926** The Sea Wolf; Yellow Fingers. **1927** Not for Publication; Shanghaied. **1928** Chicago after Midnight; The Singapore Mutiny. **1929** Wall Street. **1930** Numbered Men; The Big Fight; Little Caesar. **1931** A Gentleman's Fate; Hell Bound; The Star Witness; Big Gamble; Law and Order; The Dove; Exposed. **1932** The Lost Squadron; Men of Chance; Girl of the Rio; The Mouthpiece; State's Attorney; The Tenderfoot; Guilty as Hell; The Pride of the Legion; Law of the Sea; Gorilla Ship; Maylay Nights; Men of America; Lucky Devils; The Hatchet Man; County Fair. **1933** Havana Widows; No Escape; The Big Payoff. **1934** Love at Second Sight (aka The Girl Thief—US 1938). **1935** Blue Smoke; Rolling Home; So You Won't Talk? **1936** Gaol Break. **1937** The Perfect Crime.

INCE, THOMAS H.

Born: 1882. Died: Nov. 20, 1924, Beverly Hills, Calif. (heart failure). Screen, stage actor, film director, producer and screenwriter. Entered films in 1911. Brother of actors John (dec. 1947) and Ralph Ince (dec. 1937).

Appeared in: **1910** His New Lid.

INCLAN, MIGUEL

Born: 1900, Mexico. Died: July 25, 1956, Tijuana, Mexico. Screen actor.

Appeared in: **1943** Creo en Dios. **1947** The Fugitive. **1948** Fort Apache. **1952** Indian Uprising; The Young and the Damned. **1955** Seven Cities of Gold. **1956** Bandido.

INDRISANO, JOHN "JOHNNY"

Born: 1906, Boston, Mass. Died: July 9, 1968, San Fernando Valley, Calif. (apparent suicide—hanging). Screen actor and boxer.

Appeared in: **1935** The Winning Ticket; She gets her Man; Two Fisted. **1936** Laughing Irish Eyes. **1937** Every Day's a Holiday. **1941** Ringside Maisie. **1944** Lost in a Harem. **1945** Live Wires; Johnny Angel; Duffy's Tavern; The Naughty Nineties. **1946** The Kid From Brooklyn; Criminal Court; Crack-Up. **1947** Killer McCoy; Christmas Eve; A Palooka Named Joe. **1948** In This Corner; Lulu Belle; Trouble Makers; The Numbers Racket; Knock on Any Door; The Accused; Bodyguard; Fighting Fools. **1949** Bride for Sale; Tension; Shadow On the Wall; Joe Palooka In the Counterpunch; The Lady Gambles. **1950** The Yellow Cab Man. **1951** Pier 23; Callaway Went Thataway. **1952** Glory Alley; No Holds Barred. **1953** Shane. **1956** The Cruel Tower. **1957** Chicago Confidential. **1958** Hot Spell. **1959** Some Like It Hot; Career. **1960** The Purple Gang; Ocean's Eleven. **1961** Blueprint for Robbery. **1962** Who's got the Action? **1963** Hud; Four For Texas; Under the Yum Yum Tree. **1964** Where Love has Gone; The Best Man; A House Is Not a Home. **1965** The Human Duplicator. **1967** The Ambushers; Barefoot in the Park. **1968** The Legend of Lylah Clare.

INFANTE, PEDRO

Born: 1918, Mexico. Died: Apr. 15, 1957, Merida, Yucatan (airplane crash). Mexican screen, radio actor and singer.

INGE, WILLIAM (aka WALTER GAGE)

Born: 1913, Independence, Kansas. Died: June 10, 1973, Hollywood, Calif. (suicide). Playwright, screenwriter and screen actor.

Appeared in: **1961** Splendor in the Grass.

INGERSOLL, WILLIAM

Born: 1860. Died: May 7, 1936, Los Angeles, Calif. (acute indigestion). Stage and screen actor. Married to actress Mab Ingersoll.

Appeared in: **1920** Partners of the Night. **1931** The Cheat. **1935** Mary Burns, Fugitive; Whipsaw. **1936** Half Angel.

INGLE, RED

Born: 1907. Died: Sept. 7, 1965, Santa Barbara, Calif. Screen actor and musician.

INGRAHAM, LLOYD

Born: Rochelle, Ill. Died: Apr. 4, 1956, Woodland Hills, Calif. (pneumonia). Screen, stage actor and stage and film director. Entered films in 1912.

Appeared in: **1914** A Law Unto Himself; Aurora of the North. **1922** A Front Page Story. **1923** Scaramouche. **1924** The Chorus Lady. **1929** Untamed; Night Parade; The Rainbow Man. **1930** So Long Letty; Montana Moon; The Spoilers; Last of the Duanes; A Lady to Love; Wide Open. **1931** The Lady Who Dared. **1932** Texas Gun Fighter; The Crusader; Get That Girl; Sinister Hands; The Widow in Scarlet. **1933** I Love That Man; The World Gone Mad; Midnight Warning; Officer 13; Cornered; Revenge at Monte Carlo; Silent Men. **1934** Sixteen Fathoms Deep; In Love With Life; Lost Jungle; The Dude Rancher; The Curtain Falls; The Gold Ghost (short). **1935** The World Accuses; Northern Frontier; Rainbow Valley; Circumstantial Evidence; The Cowboy Millionaire; Headline Woman; Sons of Steel; On Probation; Rider of the Law; Between Men. **1936** Ghost Patrol; Empty Saddles; The Lonely Trail; Timber Way; Frontier Justice; Captain Calamity; Rogue of the Range; Burning Gold; Hearts in Bondage; Too Much Beef; Everyman's Law; Go Get 'em Haines!; Conflict; Stormy Trails; Red River Valley. **1937** Tennessee Johnson; Park Avenue Logger; Battle of Greed; Riders of the Dawn; Tramp Trouble (short). **1938** Painted Desert; Man From Music Mountain; Reformatory; Gun Packer. **1939** Home Boner (short); Truth Aches (short). **1940** Melody Ranch; Marshal of Mesa City; 20 Mule Team; Bad Man From Red Butte; Colorado; My Little Chicadee. **1941** Dude Cowboy; Never Give a Sucker an Even Break. **1942** Tennessee Johnson; Stagecoach Buckaroo; Boss of Big Town. **1943** Blazing Guns; The Mystery of the 13th Guest. **1944** Partners of the Trail; Range Law; West of the Rio Grande; The Merry Monahans; Love Your Landlord (short). **1945** Frontier Gal; Frontier Feud; Lawless Empire; The Man Who Walked Alone; Springtime in Texas. **1946** The Caravan Trail. **1950** The Savage Horde.

INGRAM, JACK

Born: 1903. Died: Feb. 20, 1969, Canoga Park, Calif. (heart attack). Screen actor.

Appeared in: **1936** Rebellion; The Lonely Trail; With Love and Kisses. **1937** Public Cowboy No. 1; Zorro Rides Again (serial); Headline Crasher; Yodelin' Kid from Pine Ridge; Wild Horse Rodeo. **1938** Code of the Rangers; Outlaws of Sonora; Riders of the Black Hills; Dick Tracy Returns (serial); Frontier Scout; Western Jamboree. **1939** The Night Riders; Home on the Prairie; Blue Montana Skies; Wyoming Outlaw; Colorado Sunset; New Frontier; Wall Street Cowboy; Sage of Death Valley; Rovin' Tumbleweeds; Down the Wyoming Trail; Mexicali Rose; Mountain Rhythm. **1940** Ghost Valley Raiders; Under Texas Skies; Young Bill Hickock; The Green Archer (serial); Melody Ranch. **1941** South of Panama; King of the Texas Rangers (serial); Sheriff of Tombstone; Nevada City; The Gang's All Here; Prairie Pioneers; Law of the Wolf; The Lone Rider Ambushed. **1942** The Man from Cheyenne; Tomorrow We Live; Billy the Kid Trapped. **1943** The Mysterious Rider; Fugitive of the Plains; Lone Star Trail; Border Buckaroos; Riders of the Rio Grande; Silver Raiders; Santa Fe Scouts. **1945** Bandits of the Badlands; Devil Riders; Enemy of the Law; Flame of the West; The Jade Mask; Out of Vengeance; Outlaw Roundup; Saddle Serenade; Sheriff of Cimarron; Stranger from Santa Fe; Frontier Gal. **1946** Frontier Fugitives; Moon Over Montana; West of the Alamo. **1947** Pioneer Justice; Slave Girl; South of the Chisholm Trail; Ghost Town Renegades. **1948** The Strawberry Roan; Whirlwind Raiders; Racing Luck. **1949** Son of a Badman; Law of the West; Roaring Westward; Desert Vigilante. **1950** The Texan Meets Calamity Jane; Short Grass; Bandit Queen; Sierra; Sideshow; Streets of Ghost Town. **1951** Fort Dodge Stampede. **1952** The Battle of Apache Pass; Fargo. **1953** Cow Country; Son of the Renegade. **1955** Man Without a Star; Five Guns West. **1957** Utah Blaine. **1959** Zorro Rides Again.

INGRAM, REX (Reginald Ingram Montgomery Hitchcock, and aka REX HITCHCOCK)

Born: Jan. 15, 1893, Dublin, Ireland. Died: July 21, 1950, North Hollywood, Calif. (cerebral hemorrhage). Do not confuse with black actor who died Sept. 19, 1969. Screen, stage actor, film director, producer and screenwriter. Divorced from actress Doris Pawn. Married to actress Alice Terry.

Appeared in: **1914** The Necklace of Rameses; The Spirit and the Clay; Her Biggest Scoop; Eve's Daughter (aka Artist's Madonna); The Crime of Lust; The Evil Men Do; The Circus and the Boy; His Wedded Wife; The Upper Hand; Fine Feathers Make Fine Birds; The Moonshine Maid and the Man; Snatched from Burning Death. **1923** Mary of the Movies. **1933** Baroud (aka Love in Morocco; Passion in the Desert and Les Hommes Blus).

INGRAM, REX

Born: Oct. 20, 1895, Cairo, Ill. Died: Sept. 19, 1969, Los Angeles, Calif. (heart attack). Black screen, stage and television actor.

Appeared in: **1915** Snatched from a Burning Death. **1918** Tarzan of the Apes; Salome. **1923** Scaramouche; The Ten Commandments. **1926** The Big Parade. **1927** King of Kings. **1929** Hearts in Dixie; The Four Feathers. **1932** Sign of the Cross. **1933** King Kong; The Emperor Jones; Love in Morocco. **1935** Captain

Blood. **1936** Green Pastures. **1939** Adventures of Huckleberry Finn. **1940** The Thief of Bagdad. **1942** The Talk of the Town. **1943** Fired Wife; Sahara; Cabin in the Sky. **1944** Dark Waters. **1945** A Thousand and One Nights. **1948** Moonrise. **1950** King Solomon's Mines. **1955** Tarzan's Hidden Jungle; Desire in the Dust. **1956** The Ten Commandments (and 1923 version); Congo Crossing. **1957** Hell on Devil's Island. **1958** God's Little Acre; Anna Lucasta. **1959** Escort West; Watusi. **1960** Elmer Gantry. **1964** Your Cheatin' Heart. **1967** Hurry Sundown; Journey to Shiloh; How to Succeed in Business Without Really Trying.

INGRAM, WILLIAM D.
Born: 1857. Died: Feb. 2, 1926, New York, N.Y. Screen and stage actor.

IRELAND, ANTHONY
Born: Feb. 5, 1902, Peru. Died: Dec. 4, 1957, London, England. Screen, stage and television actor.

Appeared in: **1931** These Charming People. **1932** The Water Gypsies. **1933** Called Back. **1936** The Three Maxims; Juggernaut. **1937** When Thief Meets Thief; Twin Faces; Sweet Devil; Sweet Racket. **1942** The Prime Minister. **1952** Gambler and the Lady. **1953** Spaceways. **1958** I Accuse!

IRGAT, CAHIT
Born: 1916, Luleburgaz, Turkey. Died: June 1971, Sisli, Turkey (lung cancer). Screen, stage actor, poet and writer.

Appeared in: Yil maz Ali (film debut).

IRVIN, LESLIE
Born: 1895. Died: Oct. 9, 1966. Screen actor and stuntman.

IRVING, GEORGE
Born: 1874, New York. Died: Sept. 11, 1961, Hollywood, Calif. (heart attack). Screen, stage actor and film director. Entered films in 1913.

Appeared in: **1924** Wanderer of the Wasteland; The Man Who Fights Alone; North of 36; For Sale; Madonna of the Streets. **1925** The Goose Hangs High; The Air Mail; The Golden Princess; Wild Horse Mesa; Her Market Value. **1926** Desert Gold; The City; His Jazz Bride; The Midnight Kiss; The Eagle of the Sea; Fangs of Justice; Three Bad Men; Risky Business; The King of the Turf. **1927** The Broncho Twister; Home Struck; Two Flaming Youths; Man Power; Drums of the Desert; One Increasing Purpose; Shanghai Bound; Wings. **1928** Modern Mothers; The Port of Missing Girls; Craig's Wife; Feel My Pulse; Honor Bound; Partners in Crime; The Wright Idea; Runaway Girls. **1929** The Godless Girl; The Dance of Life; Thunderbolt; Paris Bound; Coquette; The Last Performance. **1930** Son of the Gods; The Divorcee; Puttin' on the Ritz; Shadow of the Law; The Poor Millionaires; Conspiracy; Maybe It's Love; Only Saps Work; Free Love; Young Eagles; Young Desire. **1931** Dishonored; Hush Money; The Naughty Flirt; The American Tragedy; Cisco Kid; Hot Heiress; Five and Ten; A Free Soul; Resurrection; Graft; Confessions of a Co-Ed; The Runaround; Shipmates; Girls Demand Excitement; The Star Witness; Touchdown; Wicked. **1932** Merrily We Go to Hell; Vanishing Frontier; Thrill of Youth; Guilty or Not Guilty; All-American; Broken Lullaby; Lady with a Past; Ladies of the Big House. **1933** Island of Lost Souls; The Worst Woman in Paris; Humanity; One Year Later; Son of a Sailor. **1934** The Moves On; Bright Eyes; Wonder Bar; Here Comes the Navy; George White's Scandals; Manhattan Love Song; Once to Every Bachelor; You're Telling Me. **1935** Buried Loot (short); Beauty's Daughter; Society Fever; Dangerous; Death Flies East; Age of Indiscretion; A Notorious Gentleman; Navy Wife; Under the Pampas Moon; A Night at the Opera. **1936** Captain January; Charlie Chan at the Race Track; Hearts Divided; Hearts in Bondage; Hats Off; It Had to Happen; Nobody's Fool; Private Number; Sutter's Gold; The Sea Spoilers; Navy Born. **1937** Border Cafe; China Passage; Morning Judge (short); The Mandarin Mystery; Don't Tell the Wife; The Big Shot; High Flyers; The Life of the Party; The Man Who Found Himself; Meet the Missus; Saturday's Heroes; She's Got Everything; There Goes the Groom; The Toast of New York; Too Many Wives; We're on the Jury; You Can't Buy Luck. **1938** Blind Alibi; Condemned Women; Crashing Hollywood; Crime Ring; Bringing up Baby; Go Chase Yourself; The Law West of Tombstone; Maid's Night Out; Mother Carey's Chickens; Mr. Doodle Kicks Off; Smashing the Rackets; This Marriage Business. **1939** Wife, Husband and Friend; The Hardy's Ride High; Dust Be My Destiny; Hotel for Women; Streets of New York. **1940** Knute Rockne— All American; A Child Is Born; Florian; Johnny Apollo; New Moon; Yesterday's Heroes. **1941** Bullets for O'Hara; Golden Hoofs; She Couldn't Say No; Out of the Fog; The Vanishing Virginian. **1942** The Great Man's Lady; Spy Ship. **1943** Hangmen Also Die; Son of Dracula. **1944** The Impostor; Christmas Holiday; Lady in the Death House. **1947** Magic Town.

IRVING, H. B. (Henry Broadribb Irving)
Born: 1870, London, England. Died: Oct. 17, 1919, London, England. Stage and screen actor. Son of stage actor Henry Irving (dec. 1905). Married to actress Dorothea Baird (aka Dorothy Vernon) (dec. 1972).

Appeared in: **1911** Princess Clementina. **1918** Masks and Faces.

IRVING, PAUL
Born: 1877, Boston, Mass. Died: May 8, 1959, Hollywood, Calif. Stage and screen actor.

Appeared in: **1932** Bill of Divorcement. **1933** The Silver Cord. **1934** Count of Monte Cristo. **1936** The Great Ziegfeld; Gold Diggers of 1937. **1937** On the Avenue; Hollywood Hotel. **1938** Battle of Broadway; Gold Diggers of 1939. **1939** Balalaika.

IRVING, WILLIAM J.
Born: 1893. Died: Dec. 25, 1943, Los Angeles, Calif. Screen and vaudeville actor.

Appeared in: **1923** Gentle Julia; The Love Trap. **1924** Love Letters. **1925** Pampered Youth. **1927** She's My Baby; Ham and Eggs at the Front. **1928** Coney Island; Beautiful but Dumb; The Singapore Mutiny; Nothing to Wear; Red Hair. **1929** From Headquarters; Hearts in Exile. **1930** All Quiet on the Western Front; Song of the Caballero; On the Border; Rough Waters; plus the following shorts: The Body Slam; Won to Lose; Surprise; Ginsberg of Newberg; Skin Game. **1931** Her Majesty, Love; Manhattan Parade. **1933** Diplomaniacs; plus the following shorts: The Hitch Hiker; Tired Feet; Hooks and Jabs; On Ice. **1934** Orient Express; Melody in Spring; plus the following shorts: Mike Fright; Washee Ironee; It's the Cat's; One Too Many; Punch Drunks; Three Little Pigskins. **1935** Air Hawks; The Big Broadcast of 1936. **1936** The following shorts: Caught in the Act; Restless Knights; Hoi Polloi. **1937** The Shadow; plus the following shorts: Calling All Doctors; Gracie at the Bat; Grips, Grunts, and Groans; Playing the Ponies. **1938** Convicted. **1941** Wedding Worries (short).

IRWIN, BOYD
Born: Mar. 12, 1880, Brighton, England. Died: Jan. 22, 1957, Woodland Hills, Calif. Stage and screen actor.

Appeared in: **1921** The Three Musketeers. **1922** The Long Chance. **1923** Ashes of Vengeance; Enemies of Children. **1924** Captain Blood. **1932** The Man from Yesterday. **1934** What Every Woman Knows; Pursuit of Happiness. **1935** Cardinal Richelieu; The Crusades; The Werewolf of London. **1936** Dangerous Intrigue; The Blackmailer; Killer at Large; Devil's Squadron; Meet Nero Wolfe. **1937** Prisoner of Zenda. **1939** Man in the Iron Mask; Sky Patrol. **1940** The Invisible Killer; Drums of the Desert. **1941** Mr. and Mrs. North; Secret Evidence; City of Missing Girls; The Great Swindle; Passage from Hong Kong. **1942** Joe Smith, American; True to the Army; The Major and the Minor; Random Harvest; Foreign Agent. **1943** Thank Your Lucky Stars; Chatterbox. **1944** Frenchman's Creek; The Lodger; Double Indemnity; Our Hearts Were Young and Gay; The Story of Dr. Wassell. **1945** Molly and Me. **1946** Rendezvous 29; Dragonwyck; Tomorrow Is Forever; Devotion; The Time of Their Lives. **1947** A Double Life; King of the Bandits. **1948** Docks of New Orleans; Campus Honeymoon.

IRWIN, CHARLES W.
Born: 1888, Ireland. Died: Jan. 12, 1969, Woodland Hills, Calif. (cancer). Screen, stage actor and screenwriter.

Appeared in: **1928** The Debonair Humorist (short). **1930** The King of Jazz; Blind Adventure. **1933** Looking Forward; Racket Cheers (short); Hell Below; Kickin' the Crown Around (short). **1934** The Mystery of Mr. X. **1935** The Gilded Lily; Whipsaw. **1936** The White Angel. **1937** Another Dawn; The League of Frightened Men. **1938** Kidnapped; Lord Jeff. **1939** Susannah of the Mounties; The Light That Failed; Man about Town. **1940** The Man I Married. **1941** International Squadron. **1942** To Be or Not To Be; Desperate Journey; Great Impersonation; Mrs. Miniver; Yankee Doodle Dandy; The Black Swan. **1943** No Time for Love; The Gorilla Man. **1944** Sing, Neighbor, Sing; Nothing but Trouble. **1945** Hangover Square. **1947** The Foxes of Harrow; Thunder in the Valley; My Wild Irish Rose. **1949** Bomba on Panther Island; Challenge to Lassie. **1950** Montana. **1951** Mystery Junction. **1952** Captain Pirate; A Tale of Five Women. **1953** Charge of the Lancers; Fort Vengeance; The Caddy; Son of the Renegade. **1954** The Iron Glove. **1956** The King and I; The Court Jester. **1959** The Sheriff of Fractured Jaw. **1964** He Rides Tall.

IRWIN, MAY
Born: 1862, Whitby, Ontario, Canada. Died: Oct. 22, 1958, New York, N.Y. Stage and screen actress.

Appeared in: **1896** The Kiss (Edison—One of the most famous of the early films showing the kissing scene from the stage play The Widow Jones.) **1914** Mrs. Black is Back.

IRWIN, WALLACE
Born: Mar. 15, 1875, Oneida, N.Y. Died: Feb. 14, 1959, Southern Pines, N.C. Humorist, screenwriter and screen actor. Brother of journalist and actor Will Irwin (dec. 1948).

Appeared in: **1913** Saved by Parcel Post.

IRWIN, WILL (William Henry Irwin)
Born: 1874, Oneida, N.Y. Died: Feb. 24, 1948, New York, N.Y. (cerebral occlu-

sion). Journalist, playwright, novelist and screen actor. Brother of humorist and actor Wallace Irwin (dec. 1959).

Appeared in: **1913** Saved by Parcel Post. **1914** Our Mutural Girl No. 33.

ISAACS, ISADORE "IKE"

Born: 1901. Died: Mar. 18, 1957, Culver City, Calif. Screen actor and stand-in. Entered films approx. 1932.

ISBERT, JOSE

Born: 1884, Spain. Died: Nov. 28, 1966, Madrid, Spain (heart ailment). Stage and screen actor.

Appeared in Spanish films: Ramon and Dalila; Broken Lives; The Whole Truth; The Dancer and the Laborer; Welcome, Mr. Marshall; Manolo the Policeman; Calabuch; An Afternoon of Bulls; El Verdugo. **1961** Un Angel Paso Sobre Brooklyn (The Man Who Wagged His Tail). **1965** El Ver (The Executioner, aka Not on Your Life). **1967** Operacion Dalila (Operation Delilah).

ISHII, KAN

Born: 1901, Japan. Died: Apr. 29, 1972, Tokyo, Japan (cancer). Screen, stage, television actor and composer. Entered films in 1922 with Shochiku Motion Picture Co.

ITURBI, AMPARO

Born: 1899. Died: Apr. 21, 1969. Screen actor. Brother of actor and pianist Jose Iturbi.

Appeared in: **1946** Holiday in Mexico. **1949** That Midnight Kiss.

IVAN, ROSALIND

Born: 1884, England. Died: Apr. 6, 1959, New York, N.Y. Stage and screen actress.

Appeared in: **1944** The Suspect. **1945** The Corn is Green; Scarlet Street; Pillow of Death; Pursuit to Algiers. **1946** The Verdict; Three Strangers; That Brennan Girl; Alias Mr. Twilight. **1947** Ivy. **1948** Johnny Belinda. **1953** The Robe. **1954** Elephant Walk.

IVES, DOUGLAS

Died: Mar. 6, 1969, London, England. Stage and screen actor.

Appeared in: **1953** Innocents in Paris (US 1955). **1954** Doctor in the House (US 1955). **1955** Room in the House. **1957** Miracle in Soho; The Big Chance; Man in the Shadow. **1961** Raising the Wind (aka Roommates—US 1962). **1962** The Iron Maiden (aka The Swingin' Maiden—US 1963). **1963** Live it Up (aka Sing and Swing—US 1964); Just for Fun.

IVINS, PERRY (Carrell Perry Ivins)

Born: Nov. 21, 1895, Trenton, N.J. Died: Aug. 22, 1963, Los Angeles, Calif. (arteriosclerosis). Screen actor, assistant film director and dialogue director.

Appeared in: **1931** Reckless Living. **1934** Charlie Chan in London; Orient Express; Notorious Sophie Lang. **1935** Charlie Chan in Paris; Les Miserables; Hooray for Love; Lady Tubbs; Smart Girl. **1938** Red River Range; Fighting Devil Dogs (serial). **1948** That Wonderful Urge. **1949** Streets of Laredo. **1950** The Sun Sets at Dawn; The Missourians; The Redhead and the Cowboy. **1959** The Big Fisherman.

IZVITZKAYA, ISOLDA

Born: 1933, Russia. Died: 1971, Russia. Screen actress.

Appeared in: **1957** The Forty-First. **1960** Fathers and Sons. **1961** Mir Vkhodyashchemu (aka Peace to Him and aka Peace to Him that Enters—US 1963).

JACK, T. C.

Born: 1882. Died: Oct. 4, 1954, Hollywood, Calif. (heart attack). Screen actor. Entered films approx. 1914.

Appeared in: **1925** Daring Days.

JACKIE, WILLIAM "BILL"

Born: 1890. Died: Sept. 19, 1954, San Francisco, Calif. (heart attack). Screen actor. Entered films during silents.

Appeared in: **1937** Don't Tell the Wife.

JACKSON, ANDREW, IV

Born: 1887. Died: May 23, 1953, Los Angeles, Calif. Screen actor. Great grandson of President Andrew Jackson.

Appeared in: **1953** The President's Lady.

JACKSON, COLLETTE

Died: May 15, 1969. Screen and television actress.

Appeared in: **1957** Teenage Doll. **1958** Unwed Mother; The Beast of Budapest. **1962** House of Women; All Fall Down. **1964** Seven Days in May.

JACKSON, ETHEL. *See* ETHEL KENT

JACKSON, ETHEL SHANNON. *See* ETHEL SHANNON

JACKSON, HENRY (Henry Conrad Jackson)

Born: 1927. Died: July 30, 1973, New York, N.Y. Screen, stage, television actor and film producer.

Appeared in: **1957** The Night Runner; Panama Sal; The Monolith Monsters. **1958** The True Story of Lynn Stuart. **1960** Strangers When We Meet. **1962** Bird Man of Alcatraz.

JACKSON, MAHALIA

Born: Oct. 25, 1911, New Orleans, La. Died: Jan. 27, 1972, Evergreen Park, Ill. (heart disease). Black gospel singer and screen actress.

Appeared in: **1958** St. Louis Blues. **1959** Imitation of Life. **1960** Jazz on a Summer's Day. **1964** The Best Man.

JACKSON, SELMER (Selmer Adolph Jackson)

Born: May 7, 1888, Iowa. Died: Mar. 30, 1971, Burbank, Calif. (heart disease). Screen actor.

Appeared in: **1921** The Supreme Passion. **1929** Thru Different Eyes; Why Bring that Up? **1930** Lovin' the Ladies. **1931** Subway Express; Dirigible; Secret Call; Left Over Ladies. **1932** You Said a Mouthful. **1933** Forgotten; Hell and High Water. **1934** I've Got Your Number; Let's Fall in Love; Sisters Under the Skin; The Witching Hour; Defense Rests; I'll Fix It. **1935** Black Fury; Traveling Saleslady; Public Hero Number One; Front Page Woman; This is the Life; Grand Exit; A Night at the Opera. **1936** Bridge of Sighs; Public Enemy's Wife; Ace Drummond (serial); My Man Godfrey; Parole; Easy Money; The Magnificent Brute; Robinson Crusoe of Clipper Island (serial). **1937** Two Wise Maids; A Family Affair; The Case of the Stuttering Bishop; The Man in Blue; The Thirteenth Man; Meet the Boy Friend; The Westland Case; The Wrong Road; Federal Bullets; Manhattan Merry-Go-Round; Hot Water; The Duke Comes Back; West of Shanghai; Jungle Jim (serial). **1938** You're Only Young Once; Prison Nurse; Midnight Intruder; Arson Gang Busters; Alexander's Ragtime Band; The Missing Guest; Gambling Ship; Flight to Fame; Gangster's Boy; Personal Secretary; Rhythm of the Saddle; Secrets of an Actress; Down in "Arkansaw". **1939** Off the Record; Stand up and Fight; Inside Information; The Star Maker; On Dress Parade; Calling All Marines; South of the Border. **1940** Scandal Sheet; The Grapes of Wrath; Son of the Navy; Johnny Apollo; Wagons Westward; Millionaires in Prison; Babies for Sale; Sailor's Lady; Men Against the Sky; Hired Wife; City for Conquest; Brigham Young; Public Deb. No. 1; The Ape; Lady With Red Hair. **1941** Bowery Boy; International Squadron; The Man Who Lost Himself; Tight Shoes; Paper Bullets; Parachute Battalion; Navy Blues; Remember the Day; Buck Privates; Play Girl; They Died With Their Boots On. **1942** Road to Happiness; Secret Agent of Japan; Ten Gentlemen from West Point; Miss Annie Rooney; Thru Different Eyes; The Falcon takes Over. **1943** It Ain't Hay; Adventures of the Flying Cadets (serial); You Can't Beat the Law; Harrigan's Kid; Margin for Error; Guadalcanal Diary. **1944** The Sullivans; Roger Touhy—Gangster; Hey, Rookie; Stars on Parade; The Big Noise. **1945** They Shall Have Faith; Circumstantial Evidence; The Caribbean Mystery; A Sporting Chance; Dakota; This Love of Ours; The Royal Mounted Rides Again (serial); Allotment Wives; Black Market Babies. **1946** Johnny Comes Flying Home; The Glass Alibi; The French Key; Child of Divorce; Wife Wanted; Boston Blackie and the Law; Dangerous Money; The Time of Their Lives; Shock. **1947** Magic Town; Sarge Goes to College; Stepchild; Her Husband's Affair; The Pretender; Key Witness. **1948** King of the Gamblers; The Fuller Brush Man; Pitfall; The Girl from Manhattan; Stage Struck. **1949** Alaska Patrol; Forgotten Women; Renegades of the Sage; The Crime Doctor's Diary. **1950** Gunmen of Abilene; Mark of the Gorilla; Buckaroo Sheriff of Texas; Lucky Losers. **1951** Elopement; That's My Boy; Bowery Battalion; Purple Heart Diary. **1952** We're Not Married; Deadline USA. **1953** The President's Lady; Sky Commando; Rebel City; Jack McCall; Desperado. **1954** Demetrius and the Gladiators. **1955** Devil Goddess. **1956** Autumn Leaves. **1957** Hellcats of the Navy. **1958** The Lost Missile. **1959** The Atomic Submarine. **1960** The Gallant Hours.

JACKSON, THOMAS (Thomas E. Jackson)

Born: 1886, New York, N.Y. Died: Sept. 8, 1967, Hollywood, Calif. (heart attack). Screen, stage and television actor.

Appeared in: **1929** Broadway (stage and film versions). **1930** Little Caesar; Good News; The Fall Guy; Double Cross Roads; For the Defense. **1931** Lawless Woman; Sweepstakes; Twenty-four Hours; Women Go on Forever; Reckless Living. **1932** Afraid to Talk; Big City Blues; Escapade; Unashamed; Doctor X; Strange Justice. **1933** Terror Abroad; The Avenger; Parachute Jumper; The Mystery of the Wax Museum; From Hell to Heaven; Strictly Personal. **1934** Myrt and Marge; Manhattan Melodrama; The Personality Kid; Melody in Spring. **1935** Carnival; Call of the Wild; Gold Diggers of 1935; The Case of the Curious Bride; The Irish in Us; George White's 1935 Scandals. **1936** Preview Murder Mystery; A Son Comes Home; Hollywood Boulevard; It Had to Happen; Little Miss Nobody; Grand Jury; A Man Betrayed; The Magnificent Brute. **1937** Beware of Ladies; Dangerous Holiday; Outcast; The Westland Case; Fugitive in the Sky; She's No Lady. **1938** Blondes at Work; International Crime; I Stand Accused; Crime Takes a Holiday; The Lady in the Morgue;

Torchy Gets Her Man. **1939** Nancy Drew—Reporter. **1940** Free, Blonde and 21; A Fugitive from Justice; Millionaires in Prison; Golden Gloves; Girl from God's Country. **1941** Law of the Tropics. **1943** Crime Doctor's Strangest Case. **1944** Woman in the Window; "Thin Man" series. **1945** Circumstantial Evidence; Why Girls Leave Home; How Do You Do; Shady Lady; The Hidden Eye. **1946** Valley of the Zombies; The Face of Marble; Just Before Dawn; The Big Sleep. **1947** The Guilty; Dead Reckoning; The Guilt of Janet Ames. **1948** Here Comes Trouble. **1949** The Great John L. **1952** Stars and Stripes Forever; Phone Call from a Stranger. **1953** Meet Me at the Fair. **1958** Attack of the 50 Foot Woman. **1965** Synanon.

JACKSON, WARREN

Born: 1893. Died: May 10, 1950, Hollywood, Calif. (auto accident). Screen and television actor.

Appeared in: **1937** Hollywood Round-Up. **1938** Call the Mesquiteers. **1940** Drafted in the Depot (short). **1941** A Polo Phony (short). **1945** Under Western Skies. **1946** The Brute Man. **1949** Oh, You Beautiful Doll. **1950** Montana; Square Dance Katy.

JACOBS, ANGELA

Born: 1893, Sioux City, Iowa. Died: Feb. 7, 1951, Detroit, Mich. (heart attack). Screen, stage and vaudeville actress.

Appeared in: **1933** Counsellor-at-Law (stage and film versions).

JAFFE, CARL

Born: 1902, Germany. Died: May 12, 1974, London, England. Screen, stage actor and stage producer.

Appeared in: **1937** Over the Moon (US 1940). **1938** Second Best Bed. **1939** An Englishman's Home (aka Madmen of Europe—US); The Silent Battle (aka Continental Express—US 1942); The Lion Has Wings (US 1940); The Saint in London. **1940** All Hands; Law and Disorder; Gasbags. **1942** Uncensored (US 1944). **1943** The Night Invader; The Life and Death of Colonel Blimp (aka Colonel Blimp—US 1945); Warn that Man. **1944** 2,000 Women. **1945** I Didn't Do It. **1946** Gaiety George (aka Showtime—US 1948). **1948** The Blind Goddess (US 1949); Counterblast. **1950** Lilli Marlene (US 1951); State Secret (aka The Great Manhunt—US 1951). **1951** A Tale of Five Cities (aka A Tale of Five Women—US 1952). **1952** Ivanhoe. **1953** Appointment in London (US 1955); Park Plaza (aka Norman Conquest—US); Desperate Moment. **1954** Child's Play. **1955** Cross Channel; Timeslip (aka The Atomic Man—US). **1956** Satellite in the Sky; House of Secrets (aka Triple Deception—US); The Hostage. **1957** The Traitors (aka The Accused—US 1958). **1959** Subway in the Sky; First Man into Space. **1958** Battle of the VI (aka Unseen Heroes—US); I Accuse; Mad Little Island; Escapement (aka The Electric Monster—US 1960); Rockets Galore. **1961** The Roman Spring of Mrs. Stone. **1965** Operation Crossbow (aka The Great Spy Mission—US). **1967** The Double Man (US 1968); Battle Beneath the Earth.

JAHR, ADOLF

Born: 1894. Died: Apr. 19, 1964, Stockholm, Sweden. Screen, stage actor and opera performer. Known as the "Swedish Douglas Fairbanks."

Appeared in: **1924** Den Gamia Herrgarden (The Old Manor). **1934** Petterson and Bendel. **1937** Adolf Armstrong. **1940** Kryss med Albertin (Cruise in the Albertina). **1944** Homsoborna.

JAMES, ALF P. (Alfred Peter James)

Born: 1865, Australia. Died: Oct. 9, 1946, Hollywood, Calif. Screen, stage and vaudeville actor. Was in vaudeville with his wife in an act billed as "James and Pryor."

Appeared in: **1931** Everything's Rosie; Heaven on Earth. **1933** Thrill Hunter; Hokus Focas (short). **1934** Six of a Kind; Wondar Bar; Most Precious Things in Life; Elmer and Elsie; Cockeyed Cavaliers. **1936** The Singing Cowboy.

JAMES, BEN (James B. Solomon)

Born: 1921. Died: Mar. 29, 1966, Hollywood, Calif. (natural causes). Screen and television actor.

JAMES, EDDIE

Born: 1880. Died: Dec. 22, 1944, New York. Screen, stage actor and assistant film director.

Appeared in: **1925** Lucky Devil. **1926** Wild Oaks Lane.

JAMES, GLADDEN

Born: 1892, Zanesville, Ohio. Died: Aug. 28, 1948, Hollywood, Calif. (leukemia). Stage and screen actor.

Appeared in: **1917** The Mystery of the Double Cross (serial). **1919** The Heart of the Wetona. **1920** Yes or No. **1921** His Brother's Keeper; Bucking the Tiger; Wise Husbands; The Silver Lining; Footfalls. **1922** Channing of the Northwest; The Faithless Sex. **1923** The Broken Violin; The Woman with Four Faces; A Clouded Name. **1924** Marry in Haste. **1925** Alias Mary Flynn; The Wedding Song. **1926** Tex. **1927** The Temptations of a Shop Girl. **1928** Sweet Sixteen; Adorable Cheat; Driftin' Sands; The Hound of Silver Creek; The Look Out

Girl; The Girl He Didn't Buy. **1929** The Peacock Fan; His Captive Woman; The Girl from Woolworth's; Weary River. **1930** Paradise Island. **1931** Bad Company. **1933** Lucky Devils. **1936** The Case against Mrs. Ames; The Princess Comes Across. **1942** For Me and My Gal; The Postman Didn't Ring; Tennessee Johnson. **1944** Henry Aldrich Plays Cupid.

JAMES, HORACE D.

Born: 1853, Baltimore, Md. Died: Oct. 16, 1925, Orange, N.J. Stage and screen actor.

Appeared in: **1921** Get-Rich-Quick Wallingford (stage and film versions). **1922** A Woman's Woman. **1923** Adam and Eve.

JAMES, JOHN

Died: May 20, 1960, New York. Stage and screen actor.

Appeared in: **1942** Westward Ho; Flying Tigers. **1943** Thundering Trails; Santa Fe Scouts; Gung Ho! **1944** Sign of the Cross. **1945** Bedside Manner; This Man's Navy; Saddle Pals. **1946** Our Hearts Were Growing Up. **1949** Gun Law Justice; The Valiant Hombre. **1953** Topeka.

JAMES, RUTH

Died: May 11, 1970. Screen actress.

JAMES, WALTER

Born: 1886, Tenn. Died: June 27, 1946, Gardena, Calif. (heart attack). Stage and screen actor.

Appeared in: **1922** Fair Lady; The Secrets of Paris. **1924** Two Shall Be Born. **1925** Little Annie Rooney; The Everlasting Whisper; The Monster. **1926** The Seventh Bandit; Battling Butler; Glenister of the Mounted. **1927** The Blood Ship; Patent Leather Kid; The Irresistible Lover; The Kid Brother. **1928** The Wright Idea; The Big Killing; Me, Gangster. **1930** Shadow of the Law. **1931** Street Scene.

JAMESON, HOUSE

Born: 1903. Died: Apr. 23, 1971, Danbury, Conn. Screen, stage, radio and television actor. Noted for his radio and television portrayals as the father in "The Aldrich Family" series.

Appeared in: **1948** The Naked City. **1961** Parrish. **1965** Mirage. **1968** The Swimmer.

JAMIN, GEORGES

Born: 1907. Died: Feb. 23, 1971, Hemptinne, Belgium. Screen, stage and television actor.

Appeared in: **1931** Occupe-toi d'Amelia (film debut). **1939** Bouquets from Nicholas.

JAMISON, ANNE

Born: 1910. Died: Apr. 16, 1961, Hollywood, Calif. Screen actress and radio opera performer.

Appeared in: **1938** Hollywood Hotel.

JAMISON, WILLIAM "BUD"

Born: 1894, Vallejo, Calif. Died: Sept. 30, 1944, Hollywood, Calif. Screen, stage and vaudeville actor.

Appeared in: **1917** Lonesome Luke. **1924** Troubles of a Bride; Dante's Inferno; Darwin Was Right; The Cyclone Rider. **1927** Jake the Plumber; Closed Gates; Ladies Beware; His First Flame; Play Safe; Texas Steer; Wolves of the Air. **1928** Buck Privates; The Chaser; Heart Trouble. **1930** The Grand Parade; Traffic; plus the following shorts: Sugar Plum Papa; Bulls and Bears; Match Play; The Chumps. **1931** Folly Comedies: second series of shorts including: Help Wanted Female; Gossipy Plumber; Parents Wanted; No, No, Lady. **1932** Hurry Call; Make Me a Star; plus the following shorts: The Dentist; Strictly Unreliable; All-American Toothache; Heavens! My Husband; The Giddy Age; In the Devil's Doghouse; In a Pigs Eye. **1933** The following shorts: Loose Relations; Big Squeal; Dora's Dunkin' Donuts; His Weak Moment; Good Housewrecking; Quiet, Please; Hold Your Temper. **1934** The following shorts: Wrong Direction; One Too Many; Woman Haters; Men in Black; Three Little Pigskins. **1935** The following shorts: Old Sawbones; Alimony Aches; It Always Happens; Home Work; Honeymoon Bridge; Flying Down to Zero; Alibi Bye Bye; Uncivil Warriors; Hoi Polloi; Three Little Beers. **1936** Ticket to Paradise; plus the following shorts: Caught in the Act; Disorder in the Court; Grand Slam Opera; Movie Maniacs; On the Wrong Trek; A Pain in the Pullman; Ants in the Pantry; Whoops I'm an Indian. **1937** Melody of the Plains; plus the following shorts: The Grand Hooter; The Wrong Miss Wright; The Big Squirt; Man Bites Lovebug; Gracie at the Bat; Morning, Judge; Jail Bait; Love Nest on Wheels; Back to the Woods; Dizzy Doctors. **1938** The following shorts: Time Out For Trouble; A Doggone Mixup; Sue My Lawyer; The Old Raid Mule; Jump, Chump, Jump; Soul of a Heel; Kennedy's Castle; Stage Fright; Termites of 1938; Wee Wee, Monsieur; Tassels in the Air; Healthy, Wealthy and Dumb; Violent is the Word for Curly; Mutts to You. **1939** Topper Takes a Trip; plus the following shorts: The Sap Takes a Wrap; Rattling Romeo; Teacher's Pest; The Awful Good; Crime Rave; Moving Vanities; Ring Madness; Pest from the West; Mooching Through Georgia; Three Little Sew and Sews; A-Ducking They Did Go; We Want Our Mummy; Three Sappy People. **1940** Li'l Abner; Slightly Honorable; Captain Caution; plus the following shorts: The Heckler; His Bridal Fright; Cold Turkey; Boobs in the Woods; Nothing But Pleasure; A-Plumbing We Will Go. **1941** Wild Bill Hickock Rides; plus the following shorts: A Polo Phony; So You Won't Squawk; She's Oil Mine; General Nuisance; I'll Never Heil Again; Dutiful But Dumb; All the World's a Stooge; An Ache in Every Stake. **1942** You Can't Escape Forever; Her Cardboard Lover; plus the following shorts: Stardust on the Sage; What Makes Lizzy Dizzy?; Tireman, Spare My Tires; All Work and No Pay; Rough on Rents; Dear! Deer!; Three Smart Saps; Sock-a-Bye Baby; Loco Boy Makes Good; Even as I.O.U. **1943** True to Life; plus the following shorts: Farmer for a Day; Hot Foot; Double Up; Seeing Nellie Home; Dizzy Detectives; Back from the Front; Three Little Twerps; I Can Hardly Wait; Phony Express; A Gem of a Jam; Blitz on the Fritz. **1944** Lost in a Harem; plus the following shorts: His Tale is Told; Gold is Where You Lose It; Love Your Landlord; Say Uncle; Crash Goes the Hash. **1945** Nob Hill.

JAMOIS, MARGUERITE
Born: 1901, France. Died: Nov. 20, 1964, Paris, France (cancer). Screen, stage actress and stage director.

Appeared in: **1951** The Secret of Mayerling.

JANNEY, WILLIAM "BILL" (William Preston Janney)
Born: Feb. 15, 1908, New York, N.Y. Died: June, 1938, New York, N.Y. Stage and screen actor. Entered films in 1928.

Appeared in: **1929** Conquette; Mexicali Rose; Salute. **1930** The Dawn Patrol; The Girl Said No; The Pay Off; Shooting Straight; Those Who Dance; Young Desire. **1931** Girls Demand Excitement; The Right of Way; Meet the Wife. **1932** The Man Who Played God; The Mouthpiece; Two Seconds; A Successful Calamity; Under-Cover Man; Crooner. **1933** The Iron Master; The Crime of the Century; The Secret of the Blue Room; The World Changes; Should Ladies Behave? **1934** As the Earth Turns; King of the Wild Horses; A Modern Hero; A Successful Failure. **1935** The Great Hotel Murder; Sweepstake Annie; Bonnie Scotland; Born to Gamble. **1936** Sutter's Gold; Penthouse Party; Sitting on the Moon; Hopalong Cassidy Returns. **1938** Clipped Wings.

JANIS, ELSIE (Elsie Bierbower)
Born: Mar. 16, 1889, Ohio. Died: Feb. 26, 1956, Beverly Hills, Calif. Screen, stage, vaudeville actor, composer, author and screenwriter. Married to actor Gilbert Wilson.

Appeared in: **1915** The Caprices of Kitty; Betty in Search of a Thrill; Nearly a Lady. **1919** A Regular Girl. **1920** Everybody's Sweetheart. **1927** Behind the Lines (short). **1940** Women in War; also several short subjects.

JANNINGS, EMIL
Born: July 26, 1886, Brooklyn, N.Y. Died: Jan. 3, 1950, Austria (cancer). Stage and screen actor. Entered films in 1915. Won Academy Award for Best Actor in 1927–28 for his two roles in The Way of All Flesh and The Last Command. Was the first actor ever to receive an Academy Award.

Appeared in: **1917** Passion. **1918** Madame DuBarry. **1920** Passion (and 1917 version). **1921** Deception; All for a Woman; Vendetta. **1922** The Loves of Pharaoh. **1923** Othello; Peter the Great. **1925** Quo Vadis; The Last Laugh; Variety. **1926** Faust; The Three Way Works. **1927** Tartuffe; Husband or Lovers; The Way of All Flesh. **1928** The Street of Sin; The Patriot; Fortune's Fool; The Last Command; Power; Sins of the Fathers. **1929** Betrayal; Fighting the White Slave Traffic. **1930** The Blue Angel; Liebling der Gotter (Darling of the Gods). **1932** Stuerme der Leidenschaft (Storms of Passion); The Tempest. **1933** Der Grosse Tenor (The Great Tenor). **1934** Der Schwarze Walfisch. **1935** Der Alte und der Junge Konig. **1936** Traumulus. **1937** The Ruler. **1938** Der Zerbrochene Krug (The Broken Jug). **1941** Ohm Kruger (German propaganda film).

JANS, HARRY
Born: 1900. Died: Feb. 4, 1962, Hollywood, Calif. (heart attack). Screen, stage and vaudeville actor. Was in vaudeville team of "Jans and Whalen."

Appeared in: **1929** Two Good Boys Gone Wrong (short). **1936** Special Investigator; Two in Revolt; The Last Outlaw; Grand Jury; Don't Turn 'Em Loose; Smartest Girl in Town; Racing Lady; Charlie Chan at the Race Track; Murder on a Bridal Path. **1937** Don't Tell the Wife; That Girl from Paris.

JANSEN, HARRY A. See DANTE

JANSON, VICTOR
Born: 1885, Germany. Died: July, 1960, Berlin. Screen actor and film director.

Appeared in: **1929** At the Edge of the World. **1932** 1914: The Last Days Before the War. **1939** Nanu; Sie Kennen Korff noch Nicht (So You Don't Know Korff Yet?). **1950** Marriage of Figaro. **1952** Prince of Pappenheim. **1953** Hit Parade. **1954** Anne of Tharau.

JAQUET, FRANK (Frank Garnier Jaquet)
Born: Mar. 16, 1885, Wis. Died: May 11, 1958, Los Angeles, Calif. (heart attack). Screen actor.

Appeared in: **1934** War is a Racket. **1938** Crime School; When Were You Born?; My Lucky Star; Shine on Harvest Moon; Hold that Co-ed; Party Fever. **1939** Stanley and Livingstone; Dust Be My Destiny; Eternally Yours. **1941** No Greater Sin. **1942** Call of the Canyon; Raiders of the Range. **1944** None Shall Escape; Beneath Western Skies; Black Magic; Call of the South Seas; Call of the Rockies; Bowery Champs; Silver City Kid. **1945** Federal Operator 99 (serial); The Vampire's Ghost; Grissly's Millions; A Bell for Adano; Mr. Muggs Rides Again; The Cisco Kid in Old New Mexico. **1949** Shockproof; The Mutineers; Barbary Pirate; Riders in the Sky; The Daring Caballero. **1950** Over the Border; Mule Train. **1951** The Big Carnival (aka Ace in the Hole); The Scarf. **1952** O'Henry's Full House. **1953** Winning of the West.

JARRETT, ARTHUR L. "ART"
Born: Feb. 5, 1888, Marysville, Calif. Died: June 12, 1960, New York, N.Y. Screen, stage, television actor and songwriter. Father of Art Jarrett, singer and orchestra leader and brother of actor Dan Jarrett (dec. 1938).

Appeared in: **1932–33** Universal "Radio Star Reels." **1933** Ace of Aces; Dancing Lady; Sitting Pretty; Let's Fall in Love. **1934** Riptide; Hollywood Party. **1936** Blue Blazes (short). **1937** an Educational short. **1939** Trigger Pals. **1950** The Tattooed Stranger.

JARRETT, DAN
Born: 1894. Died: Mar. 13, 1938, Hollywood, Calif. (heart ailment). Screen, stage actor, screenwriter and playwright. Brother of actor Arthur Jarrett (dec. 1960).

Appeared in: **1922** Sunshine Harbor. **1935** The Cowboy Millionaire.

JARVIS, AL
Born: 1910, Winnipeg, Canada. Died: May 6, 1970, Newport Beach, Calif. (heart attack). Screen, radio and television actor.

Appeared in: **1953** The Twonky. **1962** The Phantom Planet.

JARVIS, JEAN
Born: 1903. Died: Mar. 16, 1933, Hollywood, Calif. Screen actress and showgirl.

Appeared in: **1925** Fear-bound. **1926** The Little Giant.

JARVIS, LAURA E.
Born: 1866. Died: Mar. 9, 1933, near Downey, Calif. (injuries received from hit and run driver). Screen actress.

JARVIS, ROBERT C.
Born: 1892. Died: Nov. 13, 1971, Bloomsbury, N.J. Screen, stage actor and stage director.

Appeared in: **1930** Putting It On (short). **1933** Gold Diggers of 1933. **1938** Torchy Gets Her Man. **1939** Torchy Blane Runs for Mayor; Torchy Blane in Chinatown.

JARVIS, SYDNEY (aka SIDNEY JARVIS)
Born: 1881, New York, N.Y. Died: June 6, 1939, Hollywood, Calif. Screen, stage and vaudeville actor. Entered films in 1914.

Appeared in: **1927** Casey at the Bat; The Prairie King. **1928** Circus Rookies; The Upland Rider; The Wagon Show. **1929** The Unholy Night; Footlights and Fools. **1930** Kismet. **1932** Movie Crazy. **1934** The Count of Monte Cristo; The Mighty Barnum; Hey Nanny Nanny (short).

JAUDENES, JOSE ALVARES "LEPE"
Born: 1891, Spain. Died: July 1967, Madrid, Spain. Screen actor. Entered films in 1935.

Appeared in: Nine Letters to Bertha.

JAVOR, PAL (Paul Javor)
Born: Jan. 31, 1902, Arad, Hungary. Died: Aug. 14, 1959, Budapest, Hungary. Stage and screen actor.

Appeared in: **1933** A Key Balvany. **1934** Iza Neni (Aunt Isa); My Wife; The Miss; Rakoczi Indulo. **1935** Huszarszerelem; Koeszoenoem Hogy Elgazolt; Igloi Diakok; Elnoek Kisasszony; A Csunya Lany. **1936** The New Squire; Nem Elhetek Muzsikaszo Nelkuel; Az uj Foeldesur. **1937** Salary, 200 a Month; Naszut Felaron; Fizessen Nagysag; Viki; A Ferfi Mind Oeruelt (All Men Are Crazy); Toprini Nasz (Wedding in Toprin). **1938** Pusztai Szel (Beauty of the Pusta); Torockoi Menyasszony (Torockoi Bride); Ill-es Szobaban (In Room 111); Mother Love; Noszty Flue Este Toth Marival; Maga Lesz a Ferjem (You Will Be My Husband); Marika; Ket Fogoly (Two Prisoners). **1939** Fekete Gyemantok (Black Diamonds). **1940** Uz Bence. **1949** Carmela. **1951** The Great Caruso; Assignment—Paris.

JAY, ERNEST

Born: Sept. 18, 1893, London, England. Died: 1957. Stage and screen actor.

Appeared in: **1933** Tiger Bay. **1935** The Iron Duke. **1936** Broken Blossoms. **1937** O.H.M.S. (aka You're in the Army Now—US). **1938** I See Ice. **1944** Don't Take it to Heart (US 1949). **1946** School for Secrets. **1948** Vice Versa; Death in the Hand; Blanche Fury. **1949** The History of Mr. Polly (US 1951); Edward My Son; Golden Arrow (aka Three Men and a Girl). **1951** The Franchise Affair (US 1952). **1952** I Believe in You (US 1953); Top Secret (aka Mr. Potts Goes to Moscow—US 1954). **1953** The Sword and the Rose. **1955** The Reluctant Bride (aka Two Grooms for a Bride—US 1957). **1956** Who Done It? **1957** The Curse of Frankenstein; Doctor at Large.

JEANS, URSULA (Ursula McMinn)

Born: May 5, 1906, Simla, India. Died: Apr. 21, 1973, near London, England. Stage and screen actress. Married to stage actor Robin Irvine (dec. 1933) and later married to actor Roger Livesey (dec. 1976).

Appeared in: **1922** A Gypsy Cavalier (film debut). **1923** The Virgin Queen. **1924** My Lady April (rerelease of A Gypsy Cavalier—1922). **1927** Quinneys; The Fake; False Colours. **1928** The Passing of Mr. Quin; S.O.S. **1931** The Love Habit; The Flying Fool. **1932** The Crooked Lady; Once Bitten; The Barton Mystery. **1933** Cavalcade; I Lived With You; Friday, the Thirteenth (US 1934); On Thin Ice. **1936** The Man in the Mirror (US 1937). **1937** Dark Journey; Over the Moon (US 1940); Storm in a Teacup. **1943** The Life and Death of Colonel Blimp (aka Colonel Blimp—US 1945). **1944** Mr. Emmanuel (US 1945). **1946** Gaiety George (aka Showtime—US 1948). **1947** The Woman in the Hall (US 1949). **1948** The Weaker Sex (US 1949). **1955** The Night My Number Came Up; The Dam Busters. **1959** Northwest Frontier (aka Flame Over India—US 1960). **1961** The Green Helmet; The Queen's Guards (US 1963). **1964** Boy With a Flute. **1965** The Battle of the Villa Fiorita.

JEAYES, ALLAN

Born: Jan. 19, 1885, London, England. Died: Sept. 20, 1963, London, England (heart attack). Screen, stage actor, playwright and author.

Appeared in: **1918** Nelson; A Gentleman of France; The Hound of the Baskervilles. **1921** The Adventures of Sherlock Holmes series including: The Solitary Cyclist. **1922** The Missioner. **1925** Bulldog Drummond's Third Round (aka The Third Round). **1929** The Hate Ship. **1931** The Ghost Train (US 1933); Stranglehold. **1932** Above Rubies; The Impassive Footman (aka Woman in Bondage—US). **1933** Anne One Hundred; Purse Strings; Little Napoleon; Paris Plane; Song of the Plough; Eyes of Fate; Ask Beccles. **1934** Colonel Blood; Catherine the Great; Red Ensign (aka Strike!—US); The Camels Are Coming. **1935** Koenigsmark; Drake of England (aka Drake the Pirate—US); The Scarlet Pimpernel; Sanders of the River. **1936** King of the Damned; Things to Come; Crown V Stevens; Forget-Me-Not (aka Forever Yours—US 1937); Seven Sinners (aka Doomed Cargo—US); The House of the Spaniard; Rembrandt; His Lordship (aka Man of Affaires—US 1937). **1937** The High Command; Elephant Boy; The Squeaker (aka Murder on Diamond Row—US); The Return of the Scarlet Pimpernel (US 1938); The Green Cockatoo (aka Four Dark Hours). **1938** Dangerous Medicine; 13 Men and a Gun; They Drive By Night; A Royal Divorce. **1939** The Good Old Days; The Four Feathers; The Stars Look Down (US 1941); The Spider. **1940** You Will Remember; The Proud Valley; Spy For a Day; Convoy; The Thief of Bagdad; Sailors Three (aka Three Cockeyed Sailors—US 1941). **1941** Pimpernel Smith (aka Mister V—US 1942). **1942** Tomorrow We Live (aka At Dawn We Die—US 1943); Talk About Jacqueline. **1943** The Shipbuilders. **1945** Perfect Strangers (aka Vacation from Marriage—US). **1946** Lisbon Story. **1947** The Man Within (aka The Smugglers—US 1948). **1948** An Ideal Husband; Blanche Fury; Saraband for Dead Lovers (aka Saraband—US 1949). **1949** Obsession (aka The Hidden Room—US 1950). **1950** Waterfront (aka Waterfront Women—US 1952); The Reluctant Widow (US 1951). **1962** Reach For Glory (US 1963).

JEFFERS, JOHN S.

Born: 1874. Died: Jan. 3, 1939, Long Beach, N.Y. Screen and stage actor. Entered films with Bison Company.

JEFFERS, WILLIAM L.

Born: 1898. Died: Apr. 18, 1959, Hollywood, Calif. Screen and stage actor. Appeared in silents.

JEFFERSON, DAISY

Born: 1889. Died: June 3, 1967, California. Screen actress. Appeared in silents.

JEFFERSON, HILTON W.

Born: 1902. Died: Nov. 14, 1968, Sydenham, N.Y. Black screen actor and musician.

Appeared in: **1943** Stormy Weather.

JEFFERSON, JOSEPH, III

Born: Feb. 20, 1829, Philadelphia, Pa. Died: Apr. 23, 1905, West Palm Beach, Fla. (pneumonia). Joseph Jefferson was a fourth generation member of the Jefferson theatrical family. He was the father of stage actor Charles Burke (dec.?) and William Winter (dec. 1946) and Thomas Jefferson (dec. 1932).

Married to stage actress Margaret Clements Lockyer (dec.) and later married to Sarah Warren.

Appeared in: **1903** Rip Van Winkle (stage and film versions).

JEFFERSON, THOMAS

Born: 1859. Died: Apr. 2, 1932, Hollywood, Calif. Screen and stage actor. Entered films with D.W. Griffith in 1909. Regarding family, see Joseph Jefferson III.

Appeared in: **1913** Judith of Bethulia. **1915** Sable Lorcha; The Fortune Hunter; The Old Chemist; The Fencing Master; The Old Clothes Shop. **1916** The Beloved Liar; Corporal Billy's Comeback; The Attic Princess; The Sea Lily; Betty's Hobo; A Child of Mystery; The Grip of Crime; Little Eve Edgarton; Under the Gaslight; Classmates; Through Solid Walls. **1918** The Romance of Tarzan; A Hoosier Romance; Tarzan of the Apes. **1919** Sis Hopkins; The Spenders. **1921** Rip Van Winkle; The Idle Rich; My Lady's Latchkey; Straight from Paris. **1922** Beauty's Worth; A Tailor Made Man; The Son of the Wolf; Good Men and True; Vermillion Pencil. **1925** Thoroughbred. **1927** Paid to Love. **1928** The Fortune Hunter (and 1915 version); Soft Living. **1929** On with the Show. **1930** Double Cross Roads; Just Like Heaven; Lightnin'. **1931** Ten Nights in a Bar Room. **1932** Forbidden.

JEFFERSON, WILLIAM WINTER

Died: Feb. 10, 1946, Honolulu, Hawaii. Stage and screen actor. Divorced from stage actress Christie MacDonald (dec. 1962) and married to stage actress Vivian Martin. Regarding family, see Joseph Jefferson III.

Appeared in: **1913** The Rivals. **1915** Marrying Money. **1917** Her Own People.

JEFFREY, MICHAEL

Born: 1895. Died: Sept. 30, 1960, Hollywood, Calif. (heart attack). Screen, stage and television actor.

Appeared in: **1937** Dangerous Holiday; Mr. Boggs Steps Out. **1956** Man in the Gray Flannel Suit.

JEFFREYS, ELLIS

Born: May 17, 1877, Ceylon. Died: Jan. 21, 1943, Surrey, England. Stage and screen actress.

Appeared in: **1930** Birds of Prey (aka The Perfect Alibi—US 1931). **1934** Lilies of the Field. **1935** While Parents Sleep; Limelight (aka Backstage—US). **1936** Eliza Comes to Stay.

JEFFRIES, JAMES J. (James Jackson Jeffries)

Born: Apr. 15, 1875, Carroll, Iowa. Died: Mar. 3, 1953, Burbank, Calif. (stroke). Screen actor and professional boxer.

Appeared in: **1924** Jeffries, Jr. (short); Kid Speed (short). **1926** Prince of Broadway. **1927** One Round Hogan. **1928** Beau Broadway. **1932** Midnight Patrol; They Never Come Back; The Fighting Gentleman. **1937** Big City. **1940** Barnyard Follies. **1941** Mr. Celebrity. **1968** The Legendary Champions (documentary).

JENKINS, ALLEN (Alfred McGonegal)

Born: Apr. 9, 1890 or 1900 (?), New York, N.Y. Died: July 20, 1974, Santa Monica, Calif. (complications following surgery). Screen, stage and television actor.

Appeared in: **1931** The Girl Habit. **1932** Blessed Event; Three on a Match; I Am a Fugitive from a Chain Gang; Lawyer Man. **1933** The Mind Reader; Silk Express; Hard to Handle; Bureau of Missing Persons; The Keyhole; The Mayor of Hell; Tomorrow at Seven; Professional Sweetheart; Havana Widows; 42nd Street; Blondie Johnson; Employees' Entrance; Ladies They Talk About; a Vitaphone short. **1934** I've Got Your Number; Jimmy the Gent; The Merry Frinks; Twenty Million Sweethearts; Happiness Ahead; Bedside; Whirlpool; St. Louis Kid; The Big Shakedown; The Case of the Howling Dog. **1935** Sweet Music; While the Patient Slept; A Night at the Ritz; I Live for Love; Miss Pacific Fleet; Case of the Curious Bride; Page Miss Glory; The Irish in Us; The Case of the Lucky Legs; Broadway Hostess. **1936** The Singing Kid; Three Men on a Horse; Sins of Man; Cain and Mabel; Sing Me a Love Song. **1937** Ever Since Eve; The Perfect Specimen; Dead End; Ready, Willing and Able; Marked Woman; Dance, Charlie, Dance; There Goes My Girl; The Singing Marine; Marry the Girl; Sh! The Octopus. **1938** Swing Your Lady; Going Places; A Slight Case of Murder; The Amazing Dr. Clitterhouse; Golddiggers in Paris; Racket Busters; Hard to Get; Fools for Scandal; Heart of the North. **1939** Five Came Back; Destry Rides Again; Torchy Plays with Dynamite; Naughty But Nice; Sweepstakes Winner. **1940** Tin Pan Alley; Brother Orchid; Meet the Wildcat; Oh Johnny—How You Can Love; Margie. **1941** Go West, Young Lady; Footsteps in the Dark; Ball of Fire; A Date with the Falcon; The Gay Falcon; Time Out for Rhythm; Dive Bomber. **1942** Maisie Gets Her Man; The Falcon Takes Over; Tortilla Flat; Eyes in the Night; They All Kissed the Bride. **1943** Stage Door Canteen. **1945** Wonder Man; Lady on a Train. **1946** Meet Me on Broadway; The Dark Horse; Singin' in the Corn. **1947** Wild Harvest; The Hat Box Mystery; The Senator Was Indiscreet; Fun on a Weekend; Easy Come, Easy Go. **1948** The Inside Story. **1949** The Big Wheel. **1950** Bodyhold. **1951** Behave Yourself; Let's Go Navy; Win, Place and Show; Crazy

Over Horses. **1952** Oklahoma Annie; Wac from Walla Walla. **1959** Pillow Talk. **1963** It's a Mad, Mad, Mad, Mad World. **1964** Robin and the 7 Hoods; I'd Rather be Rich; For Those Who Think Young. **1967** Doctor—You've Got to be Kidding! **1974** Front Page.

JENKINS, ELIZABETH

Born: 1879. Died: Jan. 18, 1965, Caldwell, N.Y. Screen and stage actress. Appeared in silent films.

JENKS, FRANK

Born: 1902, Des Moines, Iowa. Died: May 13, 1962, Hollywood, Calif. (cancer). Screen and television actor.

Appeared in: **1933** College Humor. **1936** Farmer in the Dell; The Smartest Girl in Town; Follow the Fleet; The Witness Chair; The Last Outlaw; Walking on Air; Don't Turn 'Em Loose; We Who are about to Die; That Girl from Paris; The Big Broadcast of 1937. **1937** When's Your Birthday?; There Goes My Girl; Saturday's Heroes; Angel's Holiday; One Hundred Men and a Girl; The Westland Case; You're a Sweetheart; Prescription for Romance. **1938** Love is a Headache; Goodbye Broadway; Reckless Living; The Lady in the Morgue; The Devil's Party; A Letter of Introduction; Youth Takes a Fling; The Storm; Strange Faces; The Last Warning. **1939** Society Smugglers; Big Town Czar; S.O.S. Tidal Wave; First Love; You Can't Cheat an Honest Man; The Under-Pup. **1940** Melody and Moonlight; Three Cheers for the Irish; A Little Bit of Heaven; His Girl Friday. **1941** Tall, Dark and Handsome; Dancing on a Dime; Scattergood Meets Broadway; Back Street; Flame of New Orleans. **1942** Maisie Gets Her Man; The Navy Comes Through; Manhattan Maisie; Syncopation; Two Yanks in Trinidad; Seven Miles from Alcatraz. **1943** Hi Ya, Sailor; Shantytown; Corregidor; Thousands Cheer; His Butler's Sister; Gildersleeve's Bad Day; So's Your Uncle. **1944** Take It or Leave It; Dixie Jamboree; This Is the Life; Shake Hands with Murder; Ladies Courageous; Rosie the Riveter; Follow the Boys; Two Girls and a Sailor; Three Little Sisters; The Falcon in Hollywood; The Impatient Years; Strange Affair; Rogue's Gallery; Roger Touhy—Gangster. **1945** The Kid Sister; The Missing Corpse; Zombies on Broadway; The Phantom of 42nd Street; Christmas in Connecticut; Bedside Manner; G. I. Honeymoon; Steppin' in Society. **1946** Blondie's Lucky Day; That Brennan Girl; White Tie and Tails; One Way to Love. **1947** Philo Vance's Gamble; That's My Girl; Kilroy Was Here; Philo Vance's Secret Mission. **1948** Blonde Savage; Family Honeymoon; Mary Lou; Winner Take All; Blondie's Reward. **1949** Shep Comes Home. **1950** Motor Patrol; Blondie's Hero; To Please a Lady; Woman on the Run; The Petty Girl; The Dungeon; Mother Didn't Tell Me; Joe Palooka in the Squared Circle. **1951** Silver City Bonanza; The Scarf; Let's Go Navy; Bowery Battalion; Utah Wagon Train; Pecos River. **1952** Mr. Walkie-Talkie **1953** White Lightning. **1954** Highway Dragnet. **1955** Artists and Models; Sudden Danger. **1956** The She-Creature; The Houston Story; Shake, Rattle and Rock. **1957** The Amazing Colossal Man.

JENKS, LULU BURNS

Born: 1870. Died: Apr. 15, 1939, Los Angeles, Calif. Screen actress.

JENKS, SI (Howard Jenkins)

Born: Sept. 23, 1876, Pennsylvania. Died: Jan. 6, 1970, Woodland Hills, Calif. (heart disease). Screen, stage, vaudeville actor and circus performer. Entered films in 1920.

Appeared in: **1931** Man from Death Valley; Oklahoma Jim. **1932** Galloping Through. **1933** Self Defense; Dr. Bull and Mr. Skitch. **1934** Stand Up and Cheer; Charlie Chan's Courage; Sixteen Fathoms Deep. **1935** Law Beyond the Range; Fighting Shadows; Rider of the Law; Outlaw Deputy; Another Face; plus the following shorts: Old Sawbones; Uncivil Warriors; The E-Flat Man. **1936** Pigskin Parade; Captain January; Special Investigator; Follow Your Heart; The President's Mystery; All American Toothache (short). **1937** The Outcasts of Poker Flat; Don't Tell the Wife; Topper; Hillbilly Goat (short); Pick a Star; A Day at the Races; The Lady Fights Back. **1938** Rawhide; Kentucky Moonshine; Tom Sawyer—Detective. **1939** Gone With the Wind; Drums Along the Mohawk; Frontier Marshal; Union Pacific. **1940** The Ranger and the Lady; Girl from God's Country; Ride, Tenderfoot, Ride; The Trail Blazers; The Old Swimmin' Hole; Chad Hanna. **1941** The Great Train Robbery; Buy Me That Town. **1942** Ice Capades Revue; Cowboy Serenade. **1943** Wild Horse Stampede. **1945** The Man from Oklahoma. **1946** The Dark Horse. **1948** The Dude Goes West. **1951** Kentucky Jubilee. **1952** Oklahoma Annie.

JENNINGS, AL

Born: 1864, Va. Died: Dec. 26, 1961, Tarzana, Calif. Screen actor and author. Onetime real "badman" of the Old West—convicted train robber, cattle thief and gunman.

Appeared in: **1908** The Bank Robbery. **1915** When Outlaws Meet; Beating Back; The Lady of the Dugout. **1916** The Dalton Boys. **1918** The Captain of the Gray Horse Troop; Beyond the Law; The Fighting Trail (serial). **1924** Fighting Fury; The Sea Hawk. **1926** The Demon; The Ridin' Rascal. **1927** Loco Luck. **1930** The Land of Missing Men.

JENNINGS, DE WITT

Born: June 21, 1879, Cameron, Mo. Died: Mar. 1, 1937, Hollywood, Calif. Stage and screen actor. Entered films in 1920.

Appeared in: **1921** Lady Fingers; The Invisible Power; Alias Lady Fingers; Beating the Game; There Are No Villains; Three Sevens; The Poverty of Riches; The Greater Claim; The Golden Snare; From the Ground Up. **1922** The Face Between; Mixed Faces; Flesh and Blood; Sherlock Brown; The Right That Failed. **1923** Circus Days; Out of Luck; Within the Law; Blinky. **1924** Name the Man; Hit and Run; Along Came Ruth; By Divine Right; The Silent Watcher; The Heart Bandit; The Deadwood Coach; The Desert Outlaw; The Enemy Sex; The Gaiety Girl; Merton of the Movies. **1925** Go Straight; Don't; The Mystic; The Splendid Road; The Re-Creation of Brian Kent. **1926** Chip of the Flying U; The Passionate Quest; The Ice Flood; Exit Smiling; While London Sleeps; The Fire Brigade. **1927** McFadden's Flats; The Great Mail Robbery; Home Made; Two Arabian Knights. **1928** The Night Flyer; Marry the Girl; The Air Mail Pilot; The Crash. **1929** Through Different Eyes; Fox Movietown Follies of 1929; Seven Keys to Baldpate; Alibi; The Trial of Mary Dugan; The Valiant; Seven Footprints to Satan; Red Hot Speed. **1930** The New Racket (short); The Big House; Scarlet Pages; Outside the Law; The Bat Whispers; Min and Bill; In the Next Room; Captain of the Guard; Those Who Dance; Night Ride; The Big Trail. **1931** The Criminal Code; Primrose Path; Secret Six; The Squaw Man; Full of Notions; Salvation Nell; Caught Plastered; A Dangerous Affair; The Deceiver; Arrowsmith. **1932** Dancers in the Dark; Midnight Morals; Movie Crazy; Tess of the Storm Country; Central Park; The Match King; Silver Dollar. **1933** Mystery of the Wax Museum; Strictly Personal; Ladies They Talk About; A Lady's Profession; Reform Girl; One Year Later; Police Car 17. **1934** Death on the Diamond; The Fighting Rookie; Charlie Chan's Courage; A Man's Game; Take the Stand; A Wicked Woman; The President Vanishes; Massacre; Little Man, What Now? **1935** Secret of the Chateau; The Daring Young Man; A Dog of Flanders; Murder on a Honeymoon; The Village Tale; Mary Jane's Pa; Mutiny on the Bounty. **1936** Sins of Man; The Crime of Dr. Forbes; Kelly the Second; We Who are About to Die; The Accusing Finger. **1937** That I May Live; Nancy Steele is Missing; This is My Affair; Slave Ship; Fifty Roads to Town.

JEROME, EDWIN

Born: 1884. Died: Sept. 10, 1959, Pasadena, Calif. (following surgery). Screen, stage, radio and television actor.

Appeared in: **1930** Grounds for Murder (short). **1945** The House on Ninety-Second Street. **1957** The Three Faces of Eve; The Tattered Dress. **1959** The Man Who Understood Women.

JEROME, ELMER

Born: 1872. Died: Aug. 10, 1947. Screen actor.

Appeared in: **1943** This Land is Mine; False Colors; Heavenly Music (short).

JEROME, PETER

Born: 1893. Died: July 9, 1967, Tucson, Ariz. Screen, stage, television actor, playwright and novelist.

JERROLD, MARY (Mary Allen)

Born: Dec. 4, 1877. Died: Mar. 3, 1955, London, England. Screen, stage and television actress. Mother of actor Philip Harben.

Appeared in: **1916** Disraeli. **1919** A Sinless Sinner (aka Midnight Gambols—US 1920). **1921** "Candytuft, I Mean Veronica." **1925** Twisted Tales series including: Parted. **1930** The "W" Plan (US 1931). **1931** Alibi; The Sport of Kings; The Shadow Between. **1932** The Last Coupon; Blind Spot. **1933** Perfect Understanding; Friday the Thirteenth (US 1934). **1934** The Lash; The Great Defender; Doctor's Orders; Spring in the Air. **1935** The Price of Wisdom; Fighting Stock; The Tunnel (aka Transatlantic Tunnel—US). **1936** Jack of all Trades (aka The Two of Us—US 1937). **1937** Saturday Night Revue. **1941** The Man at the Gate (aka Men of the Sea—US). **1943** The Gentle Sex; The Flemish Farm. **1946** The Way Ahead. **1946** The Magic Bow (US 1947). **1947** The Ghosts of Berkeley Square. **1948** Bond Street (US 1950); Mr. Perrin and Mr. Traill; Woman Hater (US 1949); Colonel Bogey. **1949** Marry Me (US 1951); The Queen of Spades. **1950** She Shall Have Murder. **1952** Meet Me Tonight. **1953** Top of the Form; Tonight at 8:30.

JESKE, GEORGE

Born: 1891. Died: Oct. 28, 1951, Hollywood, Calif. Screen actor and film director. One of the original seven Keystone Kops.

Appeared in: **1927** Heart of the Yukon.

JESSEL, PATRICIA

Born: 1920, Hong Kong, British Crown Colony. Died: June 10, 1968, London, England (heart attack). Screen, stage and television actress.

Appeared in: **1951** Quo Vadis. **1957** The Flesh is Weak. **1958** The Man Upstairs (US 1959). **1959** Model for Murder. **1960** No Kidding (aka Beware of Children—US 1961); The City of the Dead (aka Horror Hotel—US 1962). **1963** A Jolly Bad Fellow (aka They All Died Laughing—US 1964). **1966** A Funny Thing Happened on the Way to the Forum.

JESSUP, STANLEY

Born: 1878. Died: Oct. 26, 1945, Bronx, N.Y. Screen actor.

Appeared in: **1930** Heads Up.

JETT, SHELDON

Born: 1901. Died: Feb. 1, 1960, New York. Screen and television actor.

Appeared in: **1935** Crime and Punishment. **1942** The Pride of the Yankees. **1944** Hollywood Canteen. **1945** Yolanda and the Thief. **1947** Body and Soul. **1951** The Lady and the Bandit. **1953** The Robe. **1961** King of Kings.

JEW BABY. *See* RUTH GUENTHER

JEWELL, ISABEL

Born: July 19, 1910, Shoshoni, Wyo. Died: Apr. 5, 1972, Hollywood, Calif. (natural causes). Screen, stage and television actress. Divorced from actor Paul Marion.

Appeared in: **1933** Bondage; Beauty for Sale; Bombshell; Day of Reckoning; Counsellor at Law; Design for Living; Advice to the Lovelorn; The Women in His Life. **1934** Manhattan Melodrama; Evelyn Prentice; Here Comes the Groom; Let's be Ritzy; She Had to Choose. **1935** Times Square Lady; The Casino Murder Case; Shadow of Doubt; Mad Love; A Tale of Two Cities; I've Been Around; Ceiling Zero. **1936** The Leathernecks Have Landed; Dancing Feet; Small Town Girl; Big Brown Eyes; Valiant Is the Word for Carrie; Go West, Young Man; Career Woman; The Man Who Lived Twice; Thirty-Six Hours to Kill. **1937** Lost Horizon; Marked Woman; Swing it, Sailor. **1938** Love on Toast; The Crowd Roars. **1939** Gone With the Wind; They Asked for It; Missing Daughters. **1940** Northwest Passage; Babies for Sale; Little Men; Scatterbrain; Oh, Johnny—How You Can Love; Irene; Marked Men. **1941** High Sierra; For Beauty's Sake. **1943** Danger—Women at Work!; The Falcon and the Co-eds; The Leopard Man; The Seventh Victim; Calling Doctor Death. **1944** The Merry Monahans. **1945** Steppin' in Society. **1946** Sensation Hunters; Badman's Territory. **1947** Born to Kill; The Bishop's Wife. **1948** Michael O'Halloran; Belle Starr's Daughter; The Snake Pit; Unfaithfully Yours. **1949** The Story of Molly X. **1954** Drum Beat; The Man in the Attic. **1957** Bernadine.

"JIGGS"

Died: June, 1932 (paralytic stroke). Screen animal performer—Boston Bulldog.

Appeared in: **1922** The Leather Pushers series (film debut). **1931** Skippy.

JIMINEZ, SOLEDAD

Born: Feb. 28, 1874, Santander, Spain. Died: Oct. 17, 1966, Hollywood, Calif. (stroke). Screen actress.

Appeared in: **1929** In Old Arizona; The Cock-Eyed World; Romance of the Rio Grande. **1930** The Texan; Billy the Kid; A Devil with Women; The Arizona Kid. **1931** Captain Thunder. **1932** Broken Wing. Spanish versions of films prior to 1933: Resurrection; Cat and the Canary; Ten Cents a Dance. **1935** Bordertown; Rumba; The Cyclone Ranger; Under the Pampas Moon; In Caliente. **1936** Robin Hood of El Dorado; The Traitor. **1937** Man of the People; Kid Galahad. **1938** Forbidden Valley; California Frontier. **1939** The Return of the Cisco Kid; The Kid from Rio. **1945** South of the Rio Grande. **1946** Bad Men of the Border. **1947** Carnival in Costa Rica. **1948** Black Bart. **1949** Red Light.

JINGU, MIYOSHI

Born: 1894. Died: Jan. 19, 1969, Los Angeles, Calif. Screen actress.

Appeared in: **1962** The Machurian Candidate. **1966** Walk Don't Run. **1970** Dreams of Glass.

JOBY, HANS

Born: 1884. Died: Apr. 30, 1943, Los Angeles, Calif. Screen, stage actor and opera performer.

Appeared in: **1929** The Prince of Hearts. **1930** Hell's Angels. **1931** Suicide Fleet. **1936** Sons O' Guns. **1937** I Met Him in Paris. **1939** Thunder Afloat; Beasts of Berlin.

JOHANNSEN, CARY

Born: 1939. Died: Aug. 28, 1966, San Quentin Prison, Calif. (suicide). Screen, stage actor and writer. Appeared in a documentary film dealing with the Farm Labor Program for the Department of Corrections while in prison.

JOHNSON, A. EMORY

Born: 1894. Died: Apr. 18, 1960, San Mateo, Calif. (burns from fire). Screen actor, film director, producer and screenwriter.

Appeared in: **1914** The Calling of Jim Barton. **1916** Her Husband's Honor; Heartaches; Two Mothers; Her Soul's Song; The Way of the World; No. 16 Martin Place; A Yoke of Gold; The Unattainable; The Devil's Bondwoman; The Human Gamble; Barriers of Society; The Right to Be Happy. **1917** The Gray Ghost (serial); A Kentucky Cinderella; The Gift Girl; My Little Boy; The Circus of Life. **1918** The Ghost Flower; New Love for Old; Beauty in Chains; A Mother's Secret. **1919** Put Up Your Hands; Trixie from Broadway; Alias

Mike Moran; Charge It to Me; The Girl Next Door. **1920** Prisoners of Love; The Walk-Offs. **1921** The Sea Lion. **1922** Don't Doubt Your Wife; In the Name of the Law; Always the Woman.

JOHNSON, ARTHUR V.

Born: Feb. 2, 1876, Cincinnati, Ohio. Died: Jan. 17, 1916, Philadelphia, Pa. Screen, stage actor, film director and producer. Married to actress Florence Hackett (dec. 1954).

Appeared in: **1908** The Bandit's Waterloo; The Adventures of Dollie; The Fight for Freedom; Balked at the Altar; After Many Years; The Planter's Wife; Concealing a Burglar; Where Bankers Roar; The Vaquero's Vow; The Taming of the Shrew; The Valet's Wife; The Test of Friendship; The Helping Hand. **1909** The Song of the Shirt; Resurrection; The Gibson Goddess; The Light That Came; The Little Teacher; Pippa Passes; A Drunkard's Reformation; The Way of a Man; The Girls and Daddy; A Sound Sleeper; Two Memories; Pranks; Confidence; The Little Darling; At the Altar; The Politician's Love Story; The Converts; The Mills of the Gods; The Mountaineers' Honor; The Trick That Failed; A Corner in Wheat; To Save Her Soul. **1910** All on Account of the Milk; The Cloister's Touch; Taming a Husband; The Final Settlement; The Newlyweds; The Thread of Destiny; Faithful; Unexpected Help; Rose O' Salem-Town; In Old California; The Unchanging Seat; A Rich Revenge; The Day After; A Romance of the Western Hills; Her Two Sons. **1911** Her Awakening; The Lily of the Tenants; Through Jealous Eyes; A Rebellious Blossom; The Maniac; The Slave's Affinity; The Life Saver; The Match Maker; The Actress and the Singer; His Chorus Girl Wife; A Girlish Impulse; Higgins vs. Judsons; One on Reno; A Head for Business; A Rural Conqueror. **1912** An Antique Ring; A Cure for Jealousy; A Matter of Business; My Princess; The Physician's Honor; The Preacher and the Gossips; A College Girl; A Leap Year Lottery Prize; In After Years; The Violin's Message; Her Gift; The Wooden Bowl; The New Physician; The Spoiled Child; The Stolen Ring; A Child's Devotion; A Little Family Affair; An Amateur Iceman; The Substitute Heiress; The Sporting Editor; The Heavenly Voice; The Country School Teacher; The Samaritan of Coogan's Tenement. **1913** Two Boys; John Arthur's Trust; The Artist's Romance; The Insurance Agent; A Timely Rescue; Annie Rowley's Fortune; A Counterfeit Courtship; Dr. Maxwell's Experiment; When John Brought Home His Wife; Friend John; The Gift of the Storm; The Burden Bearer; The Pawned Bracelet; The Power of the Cross; The District Attorney's Conscience; His Niece from Ireland; Her Husband's Wife; The School Principal; His Better Self; The Stolen Melody; A Jealous Husband; The Benefactor; The Sea Eternal; Just Cissy's Little Way; The Road to the Dawn. **1914** The Parasite; The Blinded Heart; The Question and Answer Man; Lord Algy; An American Heiress; The Beloved Adventurer (series); The Holdup; The Girl from the West; A Partner to Providence; A Man's Faith; The Untarnished Shield; The Shadow of Tragedy. **1915** An Hour of Freedom; Country Blood; Comrade Kitty; When Father Interfered; Socially Ambitious; Her Martyrdom; Poet and Peasant; Winning Winsome Winnie; Who Violates the Law; On the Road to Reno; The Cornet; The Last Rose.

JOHNSON, BILL

Died: Mar. 16, 1957. Stage and screen actor.

Appeared in: **1945** It's a Pleasure; Keep Your Powder Dry.

JOHNSON, BURGES

Born: 1878. Died: Feb. 23, 1963, Schenectady, N.Y. Author, humorist and screen actor.

Appeared in: **1913** Saved by Parcel Post.

JOHNSON, CHIC (Harold Ogden Johnson)

Born: Mar. 5, 1891 or 1895, Chicago, Ill. Died: Feb. 1962, Las Vegas, Nev. (kidney ailment). Screen, stage, vaudeville and television actor. Was partner in comedy team of "Olsen and Johnson" with Ole Olsen (dec. 1963). For films they appeared in, see Ole Olsen.

JOHNSON, CHUBBY (Charles Randolph Johnson)

Born: 1903, Terre Haute, Ind. Died: Oct. 31, 1974, Hollywood, Calif. Screen, radio, television actor and columnist.

Appeared in: **1950** Rocky Mountain. **1951** The Scarf; Fort Dodge Stampede; Night Riders of Montana; Wells Fargo Gunmaster; The Raging Tide. **1952** Bend of the River; Here Come the Nelsons (aka Meet the Nelsons); Last of the Comanches; The Treasure of Lost Canyon. **1953** Calamity Jane; Gunsmoke; Back to God's Country. **1954** The Human Jungle; Overland Pacific; Cattle Queen of Montana. **1955** The Far Country; Tennessee's Partner; Headline Hunters. **1956** Tribute to a Bad Man; The Rawhide Years; The First Texan; The Fastest Gun Alive; The Young Guns. **1957** The True Story of Jesse James; The River's Edge; Drango. **1958** Gunfire at Indian Gap. **1962** The Firebrand. **1964** Seven Faces of Dr. Lao. **1966** Cyborg 2087. **1969** Sam Whiskey.

JOHNSON, EDITH

Died: Sept. 6, 1969, Los Angeles, Calif. (injuries from fall). Screen actress. Married to actor William Duncan (dec. 1961). She appeared with him in silent serials.

Appeared in: **1918** A Fight for Millions (serial). **1919** Man of Might (serial);

Smashing Barriers (serial). **1920** The Silent Avenger (serial). **1921** No Defense; Where Men Are Men; Steelheart; Fighting Fate (serial). **1922** The Fighting Guide; When Danger Smiles; The Silent Vow. **1923** The Steel Trail (serial); Smashing Barriers (rerelease of 1919 serial as a feature film); Playing It Wild. **1924** The Fast Express (serial); Wolves of the North (serial).

JOHNSON, EDWARD

Born: 1862. Died: Feb. 7, 1925, San Jose, Calif. Screen actor.

Appeared in: **1919** The Egg Crate Wallop. **1923** The Hunchback of Notre Dame.

JOHNSON, HALL

Born: 1888, Athens, Ga. Died: Apr. 30, 1970, New York, N.Y. (apartment fire). Black screen actor, musician and playwright. Founder of the Hall Johnson Choir.

Appeared in: **1936** Hearts Divided; The Green Pastures. **1939** Swanee River; St. Louis Blues; Zenobia; Way Down South. **1941** Lady for a Night; Meet John Doe. **1942** Syncopation; Tales of Manhattan; Heart of the Golden West. **1943** Cabin in the Sky.

JOHNSON, JACK

Born: Mar. 31, 1878, Galveston, Texas. Died: June 10, 1946, Raleigh, N.C. Black professional boxer and screen actor.

Appeared in: **1919** Strength. **1921** As the World Rolls On. **1922** The Black Thunderbolt; For His Mother's Sake.

JOHNSON, JAY

Born: 1928. Died: June 13, 1954, San Fernando Valley, Calif. (motorcycle accident). Screen actor and vocalist with Stan Kenton orchestra.

Appeared in: **1955** A Star Is Born.

JOHNSON, KATIE (Katherine Johnson)

Born: 1878, England. Died: May 4, 1957, Elham, England. Stage and screen actress. Voted the best British actress in 1955 for her performance in The Lady Killers.

Appeared in: **1936** Dusty Ermine (aka Hideout in the Alps—US 1938); Laburnum Grove (US 1941). **1937** Farewell Again (aka Troopship—US 1938); Sunset in Vienna (aka Suicide Legion—US 1940); The Last Adventure; The Rat. **1941** Jeannie; Hellzapoppin. **1942** Talk About Jacqueline. **1946** The Years Between (US 1947). **1947** Meet Me at Dawn (US 1948). **1952** I Believe in You (US 1953). **1953** The Gay Duellist (reissue of Meet Me at Dawn—1947). **1957** The Lady Killers (US 1956); How to Murder a Rich Uncle.

JOHNSON, LORIMER GEORGE

Born: 1859. Died: Feb. 20, 1941, Hollywood, Calif. Screen, stage actor and film director.

Appeared in: **1922** The Stranger's Banquet. **1923** Scaramouche; The Cricket on the Hearth; Ruth of the Range (serial). **1924** A Fool's Awakening; The Shadow of the East; Dante's Inferno. **1925** Enticement; The Top of the World; Never Too Late. **1926** Modern Youth. **1928** Midnight Rose; Tarzan, The Mighty (serial). **1930** Madam Satan; Ex-Flame. **1935** Crime and Punishment.

JOHNSON, MARTIN

Born: Oct. 9, 1884, Rockford, Ill. Died: Jan. 13, 1937, Los Angeles, Calif. (plane crash). Explorer, writer, film producer, director and screen actor. Married to actress Osa Johnson (dec. 1953) with whom he produced and appeared in numerous travelogues, etc.

Appeared in: **1912** Cannibals of the South Seas. **1921** Jungle Adventure. **1922** Head Hunters of the South Seas. **1923** Trailing African Wild Animals. **1928** Simba, the King of Beasts—a Saga of the African Veldt. **1930** Across the World with Mr. and Mrs. Johnson. **1932** Congorilla.

JOHNSON, MOFFAT

Born: 1886, England? Died: Nov. 3, 1935, Norwalk, Conn. (following appendectomy). Stage and screen actor. Father of actor Peter Johnson.

Appeared in: **1934** Midnight.

JOHNSON, ORRIN

Born: 1865, Louisville, Ky. Died: Nov. 24, 1943, Neenah, Wis. Stage and screen actor. Appeared in films for Triangle.

JOHNSON, OSA (Osa Leighty)

Born: Mar. 14, 1894, Chanute, Kan. Died: Jan. 7, 1953, New York, N.Y. (heart attack). Explorer, writer, film producer and screen actress. Married to explorer and actor Martin Johnson (dec. 1937) with whom she produced and appeared in numerous travelogues, etc. See Martin Johnson for the films they made together.

JOHNSON, RITA

Born: Aug. 13, 1913, Worcester, Mass. Died: Oct. 31, 1965, Los Angeles, Calif. (brain hemorrhage). Screen actress.

Appeared in: **1931** The Spy. **1937** London by Night; My Dear Miss Aldrich. **1938** Man Proof; A Letter of Introduction; Rich Man, Poor Girl; Smashing the Rackets. **1939** Stronger Than Desire; Honolulu; Within the Law; 6,000 Enemies; They All Come Out; Nick Carter, Master Detective; The Girl Downstairs; Broadway Serenade. **1940** Congo Maisie; The Golden Fleecing; Forty Little Mothers; Edison the Man. **1941** Here Comes Mr. Jordan; Appointment for Love. **1942** The Major and the Minor. **1943** My Friend Flicka. **1944** Thunderhead, Son of Flicka. **1945** The Affairs of Susan; The Naughty Nineties. **1946** The Perfect Marriage; Pardon My Past. **1947** They Won't Believe Me; The Michigan Kid. **1948** Sleep My Love; The Big Clock; The Innocent Affair; Family Honeymoon. **1950** The Second Face. **1954** Susan Slept Here. **1956** Emergency Hospital. **1957** The Day They Gave Babies Away; All Mine to Give.

JOHNSON, S. KENNETH 2nd

Born: 1912. Died: Nov. 1, 1974, Los Angeles, Calif. Screen actor. Was one of the early "Our Gang" members.

JOHNSON, TEFFT

Born: Sept. 23, 1887, Washington. Died: Oct. 1956. Screen actor.

Appeared in: **1911** Vanity Fair; Foraging. **1912** Cardinal Wolsey; The Light of St. Bernard; The Cave Man; Old Love Letters; As You Like It; The Mills of the Gods; The Lady of the Lake; Yellow Bird; The Light That Failed; Fate's Awful Jest; The Miracle; An Official Apartment; Wild Pat; A Leap Year Proposal. **1915** The Knight Before Christmas. **1926** The New Klondike; Striving for Fortune.

JOHNSON, TOR (Tor Johansson)

Born: Oct. 19, 1903, Sweden. Died: May 12, 1971, San Fernando, Calif. (heart condition). Screen actor and wrestler.

Appeared in: **1935** The Man on the Flying Trapeze. **1943** Swing Out the Blues. **1944** The Canterville Ghost; Lost in a Harem; The Ghost Catchers. **1945** Sudan. **1947** Road to Rio. **1948** State of the Union; Behind Locked Doors. **1949** Alias the Champ. **1950** Abbott and Costello in the Foreign Legion; The Reformer and the Redhead. **1951** Dear Brat; The Lemon Drop Kid. **1952** The San Francisco Story; The Lady in the Iron Mask. **1953** Houdini. **1956** Carousel; The Black Sheep; Bride of the Monster. **1957** The Unearthly; Journey to Freedom. **1959** Plan 9 from Outer Space; Night of the Ghouls (aka Revenge of the Dead). **1961** The Beast of Yucca Flats.

JOHNSON, WILLIAM

Born: 1916. Died: Mar. 6, 1957, Flemington, N.J. (heart attack). Screen, stage, television actor and singer.

Appeared in: **1945** Keep Your Powder Dry; It's a Pleasure.

JOHNSTON, JOHN W.

Born: 1876, Ireland. Died: Aug. 1, 1946, Hollywood, Calif. Stage and screen actor.

Appeared in: **1914** The Virginian; Where the Trail Divides. **1915** Runaway June (serial). **1921** The Kentuckians; Mother Eternal. **1922** The Ruling Passion; The Valley of Silent Men; Channing of the Northwest; Partners of the Sunset. **1923** Backbone; Unseeing Eyes. **1925** The Greatest Love of All; Winds of Chance. **1926** Desert Valley; The New Klondike. **1927** Flying Luck; The Black Diamond Express. **1928** Driftwood; Take Me Home; The Sawdust Paradise.

JOHNSTON, JOHNNY

Born: 1869. Died: Jan. 4, 1931, Hollywood, Calif. (heart disease). Screen and vaudeville actor. Was partner in vaudeville team of "Hardy and Johnston."

JOHNSTON, OLIVER

Born: 1888. Died: Dec. 22, 1966, London, England. Screen, stage and television actor.

Appeared in: **1955** Room in the House. **1957** The Hypnotist (aka Scotland Yard Dragnet—US 1958); A King in New York. **1958** Indiscreet. **1959** Beyond This Place (aka Web of Evidence—US); A Touch of Larceny; The Night We Dropped a Clanger (aka Make Mine a Double—US 1961). **1960** Kidnapped. **1961** Francis of Assisi; Raising the Wind (aka Roommates—US 1962). **1962** Dr. Crippin (US 1964); The Fast Lady (US 1965); Backfire. **1963** Cleopatra; The Three Lives of Thomasina; Island of Love (aka Not on Your Life). **1964** The Tomb of Ligeia. **1965** You Must be Joking. **1966** It (US 1967—aka The Curse of the Golem). **1967** A Countess from Hong Kong.

JOHNSTONE, LAMAR

Born: 1886, Fairfax, Virginia. Died: May 21, 1919, Palm Springs, Calif. Screen actor.

Appeared in: **1912** Robin Hood; Because of Bobby; Filial Love; Caprices of Fortune; Silent Jim; Their Children's Approval; Foiling a Fortune Hunter;

Dick's Wife. **1913** His Sister; Grease Paint Indians; A Trade Secret; A Perilous Ride. **1914** One Traveler Returns; Fate and Ryan; Mollie and the Old King; Helen's Stratagem; The Tie that Binds; The Portrait of Anita; The Reformed Candidate. **1915** The Face in the Mirror; Jimmy; The Unfinished Portrait; The Lady or the Tiger; The Face at the Window; The Blood Yoke; W'llie Goes to Sea; The Van Thornton Diamonds. **1916** The Return of James Jerome; The Secret of the Submarine (serial); The Tongues of Man. **1918** That Devil— Bateese. **1919** A Man in the Open; The Sheriff's Son; Diane of the Green Van.

JOLSON, AL (Asa Yoelson)
Born: May 26, 1886, St. Petersburg, Russia. Died: Oct. 23, 1950, San Francisco, Calif. (heart attack). Screen, stage, vaudeville, radio actor and singer. Married to actress Erle Galbraith. Divorced from Henrietta Keller, actresses Ruby Keeler and Alma Osborne (aka Ethel Delmar).

Appeared in: **1926** Vitaphone short. **1927** The Jazz Singer. **1928** The Singing Fool. **1929** Say It with Songs; New York Nights; Sonny Boy; Lucky Boy. **1930** Mammy; Big Boy. **1933** Hallelujah, I'm a Bum. **1934** Wonder Bar. **1935** Go into Your Dance. **1936** The Singing Kid; Sons O' Guns; The New Yorker. **1938** Alexander's Ragtime Band. **1939** Rose of Washington Square; Swanee River; Hollywood Cavalcade. **1945** Rhapsody in Blue; Burlesque. **1946** The Jolson Story (voice). **1949** Jolson Sings Again (voice).

JONES, BRIAN
Born: 1943, England? Died: July 3, 1969, London, England (drowned). Musician and screen actor. Member of the Rolling Stones rock group.

Appeared in: **1964** Rolling Stones Gather Moss (short). **1967** The T.A.M.I. Show (Teenage Awards Music International). **1968** Tonight Let's All Make Love in London; Sympathy for the Devil (US 1969).

JONES, BUCK (Charles Frederick Gebhart)
Born: Dec. 4, 1889, Vincennes, Ind. Died: Nov. 30, 1942, Boston, Mass. (burned in fire). Screen actor, film director and circus performer.

Appeared in: **1917** Blood Will Tell. **1918** Western Blood; True Blue; Riders of the Purple Sage; The Rainbow Trail; Pitfalls of a Big City. **1919** Speed Maniac. **1920** Brother Bill; Uphill Climb; Desert Rat; The Two Doyles; The Last Straw; Forbidden Trails; Square Shooter; Firebrand Trevision; Sunset Sprague; Just Pals; Two Moons. **1921** The Big Punch; One Man Trail; Get Your Man; Straight from the Shoulder; To a Finish; Riding with Death. **1922** Pardon My Nerve; Western Speed; Trooper O'Neil; West of Chicago; Fast Mail; Bells of San Juan; The Boss of Camp Four; Bar Nothin'. **1923** Footlight Ranger; The Eleventh Hour; Hell's Hole; Second Hand Love; Skid Proof; Snowdrift; Big Dan; Cupid's Fireman. **1924** Western Luck; Against All Odds; The Vagabond Trail; Not a Drum Was Heard; The Circus Cowboy; The Desert Outlaw; Winner Take All. **1925** Arizona Romeo; Gold and the Girl; The Trail Rider; Hearts and Spurs; The Man Who Played Square; The Timber Wolf; Lazybones; Durand of the Bad Lands; The Desert's Price; Good as Gold. **1926** The Fighting Buckaroo; 30 Below Zero; The Cowboy and the Countess; The Gentle Cyclone; A Man Four Square. **1927** The Flying Horseman; War Horse; Hills of Peril; Chain Lightning; Whispering Sage. **1928** The Branded Sombrero; The Big Hop; Blood Will Tell (and 1917 version). **1930** Stranger from Arizona; The Lone Rider; Shadow Ranch; Men without Law. **1931** Border Law; Branded; Range Feud; Ridin' for Justice; Desert Vengeance; The Avenger; The Texas Ranger; Fugitive Sheriff; South of the Rio Grande; Sundown Trail. **1932** Deadline; Born to Trouble; High Speed; One Man Law; Hello Trouble; McKenna of the Mounted; White Eagle; Riders of Death Valley; Reckless Romance. **1933** California Trail; Unknown Valley; Treason; The Forbidden Trail; Thrill Hunter; Gordon of Ghost City (serial); The Sundown Rider; Child of Manhattan; Fighting Sheriff. **1934** Dawn Trail; The Fighting Code; The Fighting Rangers; The Man Trailer; Rocky Rhodes; When a Man Sees Red; The Red Rider (serial); Texas Ranger. **1935** The Crimson Trail; Stone of Silver Creek; The Roaring West (serial); Border Brigands; Outlawed Guns; The Throwback; the Ivory-Handled Gun; Square Shooter. **1936** The Boss of Gun Creek; The Phantom Rider (serial); Sunset of Power; Silver Spurs; For the Service; The Cowboy and the Kid; Empty Saddles; Ride 'em, Cowboy! **1937** Sandflow; Law for Tombstone; The Left-Handed Law; Smoke Tree Range; Black Aces; Hollywood Round-Up; Headin' East; Boss of Lonely Valley; Pony Express. **1938** The Overland Express; Sudden Bill Dorn; California Frontier; Law of the Texan; Stranger from Arizona. **1939** Unmarried. **1940** Wagons Westward. **1941** Riders of Death Valley (serial); White Eagle (serial); Arizona Bound; The Gunman from Bodie; Forbidden Trails. **1942** Ghost Town Law; Down Texas Way; Riders of the West; West of the Law; Below the Border; Down on the Great Divide.

JONES, CHESTER
Died: June 27, 1975. Screen actor.

Appeared in: **1949** You're My Everything. **1958** The Buccaneer. **1965** Clarence the Cross-Eyed Lion. **1966** Dark Intruder; The Bubble.

JONES, CURTIS ASHY "CURT"
Born: 1873. Died: Dec. 1956, Winchester, Ill. Screen, vaudeville actor and stuntman.

JONES, ELIZABETH "TINY"
Died: Mar. 22, 1952, Hollywood, Calif. Screen actress. Entered films during silents.

Appeared in: **1930** The Man from Blankley's. **1939** Drums along the Mohawk.

JONES, EMRYS
Born: Sept. 22, 1915, Manchester, England. Died: July 10, 1972, Johannesburg, South Africa (heart attack). Screen, stage and television actor.

Appeared in: **1942** One of Our Aircraft is Missing (film debut). **1944** Give Me the Stars. **1945** The Wicked Lady (US 1946); The Rake's Progress (aka Notorious Gentleman—US 1946). **1947** Holiday Camp (US 1948); Nicholas Nickleby. **1948** This Was a Woman (US 1949). **1949** The Small Back Room (US 1952); Blue Scar. **1953** Deadly Nightshade. **1955** Three Cases of Murder. **1960** The Trials of Oscar Wilde (aka The Green Carnation and The Man with the Green Carnation—US). **1961** Ticket to Paradise. **1963** On the Run (US 1967).

JONES, FUZZY Q. *See* AL "FUZZY" ST. JOHN

JONES, GORDON
Born: Apr. 5, 1911, Alden, Iowa. Died: June 20, 1963, Tarzana, Calif. (heart attack). Screen and television actor.

Appeared in: **1930** Beau Bandit. **1935** Let 'Em Have It; Red Salute. **1936** Strike Me Pink; The Devil's Squadron; Walking on Air; Don't Turn 'Em Loose; We Who Are About to Die; Night Waitress. **1937** They Wanted to Marry; Sea Devils; China Passage; There Goes My Girl; The Big Shot; Fight for Your Lady. **1938** Quick Money; Long Shot; Night Spot; Rich Man, Poor Girl; I Stand Accused; Out West with the Hardys. **1939** Disputed Passage; Pride of the Navy; Big Town Czar. **1940** The Green Hornet (serial); I Take This Oath; The Doctor Takes a Wife; Girl from Havana. **1941** Up in the Air; Among the Living; The Blonde from Singapore; You Belong to Me; The Feminine Touch. **1942** To the Shores of Tripoli; True to the Army; They All Kissed the Bride; My Sister Eileen; Flying Tigers; Highways by Night. **1947** The Secret Life of Walter Mitty; The Wistful Widow of Wagon Gap. **1948** A Foreign Affair; The Untamed Breed; The Black Eagle; Sons of Adventure. **1949** Easy Living; Dear Wife; Mr. Soft Touch; Black Midnight; Tokyo Joe. **1950** Belle of Old Mexico; Sunset in the West; Trigger, Jr.; Bodyhold; The Palomino; North of the Great Divide; Arizona Cowboy. **1951** Spoilers of the Plains; Corky of Gasoline Alley; Heart of the Rockies; Yellow Fin. **1952** Sound Off; The Winning Team; Wagon Team; Gobs and Gals. **1953** Island in the Sky; The Woman They almost Lynched. **1954** The Outlaw Stallion. **1955** Treasure of Ruby Hills; Smoke Signals. **1957** The Monster That Challenged the World; Spring Reunion; Shoot-Out at Medicine Bend. **1958** Live Fast, Die Young; The Perfect Furlough. **1959** Battle of the Coral Sea; Battle Flame. **1960** The Rise and Fall of Legs Diamond. **1961** Everything's Ducky. **1963** McLintock!; Son of Flubber.

JONES, HAZEL
Born: 1895, England? Died: Nov. 13, 1974, New York, N.Y. Stage and screen actress.

Appeared in: **1916** The Merchant of Venice. **1927** Is Your Daughter Safe? **1930** Mamba. **1933** Strictly Personal.

JONES, JOAN GRANVILLE
Died: Jan. 3, 1974, Hollywood, Calif. (cancer). Screen and television actress.

Appeared in: **1959** The Young Captives.

JONES, JOHNNY (Charles Edward Peil, Jr.)
Born: 1908. Died: Nov. 7, 1962, San Andreas, Calif. Screen actor. Appeared as a child actor during silents as Johnny Jones and later as Edward Peil, Jr. See Edward Peil, Jr. for later films.

Appeared in: **1920** Edgar and the Teacher's Pet; Edgar's Little Saw. **1921** The Old Nest. **1922** Night Life in Hollywood.

JONES, MARK
Born: 1890. Died: Apr. 1965, Hollywood, Calif. Screen actor. Appeared in silents and early Hal Roach shorts.

JONES, MORGAN
Born: 1879. Died: Sept. 21, 1951, New York, N.Y. Screen actor.

Appeared in: **1903** The Great Train Robbery. **1928** Mark of the Frog (serial).

JONES, NORMAN
Born: 1928. Died: Mar. 26, 1963, London, England. Screen and television actor.

JONES, PAUL MEREDITH
Born: 1897, Bristol, Tenn. Died: Dec. 30, 1966, North Hollywood, Calif. (heart attack). Screen actor, extra, film producer and screenwriter.

Appeared in: **1916** Intolerance.

JONES, R. D.
Died: 1925 (drowned while shooting rapids in canoe for the film Ancient Highway). Screen actor and stuntman.

JONES, ROZENE K.
Born: 1890. Died: July 8, 1964, Hollywood, Calif. (heart attack). Stage and screen actor. Entered films approx. 1940.

JONES, SPIKE (Lindley Armstrong Jones)
Born: Dec. 14, 1911, Long Beach, Calif. Died: May 1, 1965, Beverly Hills, Calif. (emphysema). Screen, radio actor and bandleader.

Appeared in: 1943 Thank Your Lucky Stars. 1944 Meet the People. 1945 Bring on the Girls. 1946 Breakfast in Hollywood. 1947 Variety Girl; Ladies' Man. 1954 Fireman Save My Child.

JONES, STANLEY "STAN D."
Born: 1914. Died: Dec. 13, 1963, Los Angeles, Calif. Screen, television actor and songwriter.

Appeared in: 1950 Rio Grande. 1951 Whirlwind. 1952 The Last Musketeer. 1956 The Great Locomotive Chase; The Rainmaker. 1959 The Horse Soldiers. 1960 Ten Who Dared. 1964 Invitation to a Gunfighter.

JONES, T. C. (Thomas Craig Jones)
Born: 1921. Died: Sept. 25, 1971, Duarte, Calif. (cancer). Femme impersonator, screen, stage, television and night club actor.

Appeared in: 1963 Promises, Promises. 1964 Three Nuts in Search of a Bolt. 1966 Movie Star American Style or: LSD, I Hate You. 1967 The President's Analyst. 1968 Head; The Name of the Game Is Kill!

JONES, WALLACE
Born: 1883, London, England. Died: Oct. 7, 1936, Los Angeles, Calif. Screen actor.

Appeared in: 1925 Red Love.

JOPLIN, JANIS
Born: 1943, Port Arthur, Tex. Died: Oct. 4, 1970, Hollywood, Calif. (drug overdose). Singer and screen actress.

Appeared in: 1968 Petulia; Big Brother. 1969 Monterey Pop. 1970 Woodstock (documentary).

JORDAN, MARIAN (Marian Driscoll)
Born: Apr. 15, 1897, Peoria, Ill. Died: Apr. 7, 1961, Encino, Calif. (cancer). Screen, stage, radio and vaudeville actress. Married to Jim Jordan and the two of them teamed as "Fibber McGee and Molly"—famous radio program.

They appeared in the following films: 1938 This Way, Please (their film debut). 1941 Look Who's Laughing. 1942 Here We Go Again. 1944 Heavenly Days.

JORDAN, RHODA
Died: Feb. 8, 1962. Screen actress.

JORDAN, RICKY. See RICHARD HAYDEL

JORDAN, ROBERT "BOBBY"
Born: 1923. Died: Sept. 10, 1965, Los Angeles, Calif. (liver ailment). Stage and screen actor.

Appeared in: 1933 a Universal short. 1937 Dead End (stage and film versions). 1938 A Slight Case of Murder; My Bill; Crime School; Angels with Dirty Faces; Reformatory. 1939 Dust Be My Destiny; The Dead End Kids on Dress Parade (aka Dress Parade); They Made Me a Criminal; Off the Record; Hell's Kitchen; Angels Wash Their Faces. 1940 Young Tom Edison; Boys of the City; That Gang of Mine; You're Not So Tough; Give Us Wings; Military Academy. 1941 Bride of the Bowery; Flying Wild; Bowery Blitzkrieg; Spooks Run Wild. 1942 Mr. Wise Guy; Let's Get Tough; Smart Alecks; 'Neath Brooklyn Bridge. 1943 Clancy Street Boys; Keep 'Em Slugging; Adventures of the Flying Cadets (serial); Kid Dynamite; Ghosts on the Loose. 1944 Bowery Champs. 1946 Bowery Bombshell; In Fast Company; Mr. Hex; Spook Busters; Live Wires. 1947 Scareheads; Hard-Boiled Mahoney; News Hounds; Bowery Buckaroos. 1949 Treasure of Monte Cristo. 1956 The Man Is Armed.

JORGE, PAUL
Born: 1849, France. Died: Jan. 1929, France. Screen actor.

Appeared in: 1926 Les Miserables. 1929 La Passion de Jeanne d'Arc.

JOSEPH, LARRY (Lawrence A. Joseph)
Born: Oct. 13, 1911, New York, N.Y. Died: Mar. 12, 1974, Los Angeles, Calif. (heart attack). Screen actor.

JOSLIN, HOWARD
Born: 1908. Died: Aug. 1, 1975, Woodland Hills, Calif. (heart attack). Screen actor and assistant film director.

Appeared in: 1951 Quebec. 1953 Pony Express. 1954 The Country Girl. 1958 The Space Children. 1965 Black Spurs.

JOUVET, LOUIS
Born: 1888, France. Died: Aug. 16, 1951, Paris, France (heart attack). Screen, stage actor, film and stage producer.

Appeared in: 1932 Topaze. 1933 Dr. Knock. 1936 Carnival in Flanders; La Kermesse Heroique. 1937 Un Carpet de Bal; The Lower Depths; Mademoiselle Docteur; Life Dances On. 1938 Hotel de Nord; La Fin du Jour; L'Alibi. 1939 Bizarre, Bizarre; The Curtain Rises; The End of a Day; Marseillaise. 1940 La Charrette Fantome; Schubert's Serenade. 1941 Compliments of Mr. Iflow. 1943 The Heart of a Nation. 1945 De Drame Shanghai (The Shanghai Drama); The Barge-Keeper's Daughter. 1946 Sirocco; Le Revenant (A Lover's Return). 1947 Quai des Orfeures; Volpone. 1948 Jenny Lamour; Return to Life; Confessions of a Rogue; Street of Shadows. 1949 Retour a la Vie. 1950 Between Eleven and Midnight; Dr. Knock (and 1933 version). 1951 Miquette; Lady Paname; Un Histoire d'Amour. 1952 Ramuntcho.

JOY, NICHOLAS
Born: 1884, Paris, France. Died: Mar. 16, 1964, Philadelphia, Pa. Screen, stage and television actor.

Appeared in: 1947 Daisy Kenyon; Dishonored Lady; A Gentleman's Agreement; If Winter Comes. 1948 The Fuller Brush Man; Joan of Arc; Larceny; The Iron Curtain. 1949 The Great Gatsby; Bride of Vengeance; The Sun Comes Up; Abbott and Costello Meet the Killer, Boris Karloff; Song of Surrender. 1950 And Baby Makes Three. 1951 Native Son; Here Comes the Groom; The Man with a Cloak. 1953 Affair with a Stranger. 1957 Desk Set.

JOYCE, ALICE
Born: Oct. 1, 1890, Kansas City, Mo. Died: Oct. 9, 1955, Hollywood, Calif. (heart ailment). Screen actress. Divorced from actor Tom Moore (dec. 1955). Entered films with Kalem in 1909.

Appeared in: 1910 Engineer's Sweetheart. 1912 A Bell of Penance. 1913 Nina of the Theatre. 1914 The Brand; The Dance of Death; Fate's Midnight Hour; The Cabaret Dancer; A Celebrated Case; The Green Rose; The Old Army Coat; The Beast; The Vampire's Trail; The School for Scandal; The Mystery of the Sleeping Death. 1915 Battle Cry of Peace. 1917 Womanhood; Within the Law; The Courage of Silence. 1918 A Woman between Friends; Cap'n Abe's Niece; Captains' Captain. 1919 The Cambric Mask; The Third Degree; The Lion and the Mouse. 1920 The Sporting Duchess. 1921 Vice of Fools; The Scarab Ring; Cousin Kate; Her Lord and Master; The Inner Chamber. 1923 The Green Goddess. 1924 Passionate Adventurer; White Man. 1925 Stella Dallas; The Little French Girl; Headlines; Daddy's Gone A-Hunting; The Home Maker. 1926 Beau Geste; So's Your Old Man; Dancing Mothers; The Ace of Cads; Mannequin. 1927 Sorrell and Son. 1928 13 Washington Square; The Rising Generation; The Noose. 1929 The Squall. 1930 The Green Goddess (and 1923 version); Song O' My Heart; He Knew Women; The Midnight Mystery. 1931-32 Paramount Screen Songs (shorts).

JOYCE, MARTIN
Born: 1915. Died: Jan. 2, 1937, Los Angeles, Calif. (injuries received in auto accident). Screen actor.

JOYCE, PEGGY HOPKINS (Margaret Upton)
Born: 1893, Norfolk, Va. Died: June 12, 1957, New York, N.Y. Stage and screen actress.

Appeared in: 1926 Skyrocket. 1933 International House.

JUANO. See JUAN G. HERNANDEZ

JUDEL, CHARLES
Born: Aug. 17, 1882, Amsterdam, Netherlands. Died: Feb. 14, 1969. Screen, stage actor, stage and film director.

Appeared in: 1915 The Commuter; Old Dutch. 1923 Little Old New York; Under the Red Robe. 1928 The Air Circus; Mother Knows Best. 1929 Frozen Justice; Hot for Paris. 1930 The Big Party; Cheer Up and Smile; College Lovers; The Doorway to Hell; Let's Go Places; The Life of the Party. 1931 Captain Thunder; Fifty Million Frenchmen; Gold Dust Gertie; War Mamas (short); Oh, Sailor, Behave!; God's Gift to Women; Women of All Nations. 1932 One Hour with You; Hurry Call; High Pressure. 1934 The Good Bad Man. 1935 The Night is Young; Enchanted April; Florentine Dagger; Symphony of Living. 1936 Love on the Run; The Great Ziegfeld; San Francisco; Suzie; I'd Give My Life; Along Came Love; Give Us This Night; The Plainsman. 1937 It Can't Last Forever; The Big Show; Maytime; Swing High, Swing Low; When's Your Birthday?; Song of the City; Rhythm in the Clouds; Life of the Party; Wife, Doctor and Nurse; Marry the Girl; Ebb Tide; Fight for Your Lady; Live, Love and Learn; High Flyers; Love and Hisses. 1938 Swing Miss; Reckless Living; You're Only Young Once; Mad about Music; Stolen Heaven; Flirting with Fate. 1940 Florian; Viva Cisco Kid; It All Came True; On Their Own; Gold Rush Mazie; Down Argentine Way; Public Deb No. 1; Bitter Sweet. 1941 Cheers for Miss Bishop; Sweetheart of the Campus; Law of the Tropics; The Chocolate Soldier; Kathleen; This Woman is Mine. 1942 Baby

Face Morgan; The Hard Way. **1943** Something to Shout About; I Dood It; Kid Dynamite; Swing Your Partner; Career Girl. **1945** A Bell for Adano; Sunbonnet Sue; Two Local Yokels (short). **1946** Whistle Stop; Tangier; In Old Sacramento; Her Adventurous Night; Plainsman and the Lady; The Mighty McGurk.

JUDGE, ARLENE
Born: Feb. 1912, Bridgeport, Conn. Died: Feb. 7, 1974, West Hollywood, Calif. (natural causes). Screen, stage and television actress. Divorced from actor-director Wesley Ruggles (dec. 1972); Dan Topping; Capt. James R. Addams; Vincent Morgan Ryan; Henry J. (Bob) Topping; George Ross, Jr.; and Edward Cooper Heard. Entered films in 1931.

Appeared in: **1931** Bachelor Apartment; An American Tragedy; Are These Our Children? **1932** Love Starved; Girl Crazy; The Roadhouse Murder; Roar of the Dragon; The Age of Consent; Young Bride; Is My Face Red? **1933** Flying Devils; Party's Over; Sensation Hunters; Bachelor of Arts; When Strangers Meet; Looking for Trouble; Shoot the Works; Name the Woman. **1935** College Scandal; The Mysterious Mr. Wong; One Hour Late; George White's 1935 Scandals; Million Dollar Baby; Ship Cafe; Welcome Home; King of Burlesque. **1936** Here Comes Trouble; Pigskin Parade; Valiant is the Word for Carrie; It Had to Happen; One in a Million; Star for a Night. **1942** The Lady is Willing; Wildcat; Harvard—Here I Come; Smith of Minnesota; Law of the Jungle. **1943** Girls in Chains; Song of Texas. **1944** Take It Big; The Contender. **1945** G.I. Honeymoon. **1946** From this Day Forward. **1947** Mad Wednesday (aka Sin of Harold Diddlebock). **1963** A Swingin' Affair. **1964** The Crawling Hand.

JULIAN, ALEXANDER
Born: 1893. Died: May 18, 1945, Hollywood, Calif. Screen actor.

JULIAN, RUPERT
Born: Jan. 25, 1889, Auckland, New Zealand. Died: Dec. 27, 1943, Hollywood, Calif. (stroke). Screen, stage actor, film director and screenwriter.

Appeared in: **1914** The Merchant of Venice. **1915** The Dumb Girl of Portici. **1916** The Bugler of Algiers. **1917** A Kentucky Cinderella. **1918** Kaiser, The Beast of Berlin.

JUNE, MILDRED
Born: 1906. Died: June 19, 1940, Hollywood, Calif. Screen actress. Entered films in 1920.

Appeared in: **1922** Ma and Pa; The Crossroads of New York; The Rosary; Rich Men's Wives. **1923** Crinoline and Romance; Fashionable Fakers; The Greatest Menace. **1924** Troubles of a Bride; Hook and Ladder. **1927** The Snarl of Hate; When Seconds Count.

JUNKERMANN, HANS
Born: 1872 or 1876 (?), Stuttgart, Germany. Died: 1943, Berlin, Germany. Stage and screen actor. Son of stage actor August Junkermann. Entered films in 1912.

Appeared in: **1929** His Late Excellency; Beautiful Blue Danube. **1930** Liebeswalzer (The Love Waltz—US 1931); Anna Christie (US 1931); Olympia. **1932** Ein Walzer vom Strauss; Ein Prinz Verliebt Sich; Der Storch Streikt; Barberina, Die Taenzerin von Sans-Souci; Man Braucht Kein Geld. **1933** Zapfenstreich am Rhein; Traum von Schoenbrunn. **1934** In Wien Hab' Ich Einmal ein Maedel Geliebt; Liebe in Uniform; Hochzeit am Wolfgangsee; Heimat am Rhein. **1935** Aschermittwoch (Ash Wednesday); Der Page vom Dalmasse-Hotel; Rosen`aus dem Sueden (Roses from the South); Pantoffelhelden. **1936** Ist Mein Mann Nicht Fabelhaft; Der Junge Graf. **1939** Ueber Alles die Treue; Hummel-Hummel; Der Lustige Witwenball (The Merry Widows' Ball); Das Ekel (The Grouch). **1940** Peter, Paul and Nanette; Leidenschaft (Passion).

JUSTICE, JAMES ROBERTSON
Born: 1905, Scotland. Died: July 2, 1975, Winchester, Hampshire, England. Screen actor, journalist and naturalist. Married to actress Baroness Irena von Meyerndoff.

Appeared in: **1944** Fiddlers Three (film debut). **1948** Scott of the Antarctic (US 1949); Vice Versa; My Brother Jonathan (US 1949); Against the Wind (US 1949); The Facts of Life. **1949** Poets Pub; Christopher Columbus; Whisky Galore! (aka Tight Little Island and Mad Little Island); Stop Press Girl; Private Angelo. **1950** The Black Rose; My Daughter Joy (aka Operation X—US 1951); Prelude to Fame. **1951** Blackmailed; Pool of London; Captain Horatio Hornblower; David and Bathsheba; Anne of the Indies; The Lady Says No. **1952** The Story of Robin Hood and His Merrie Men; The Voice of Merrill (aka Murder Will Out—US 1953); Miss Robin Hood; Les Miserables. **1953** The Sword and the Rose; Rob Roy the Highland Rogue. **1954** Doctor in the House (US 1955). **1955** Out of the Clouds (US 1957); Above Us the Waves (US 1956); An Alligator Named Daisy (US 1957); Storm Over the Nile (US 1956); Doctor at Sea (US 1956); Land of the Pharaohs. **1956** Checkpoint (US 1957); The Iron Petticoat; Moby Dick. **1957** Campbell's Kingdom (US 1958); Seven Thunders (aka The Beasts of Marseilles—US 1959); Doctor at Large. **1958** Orders to Kill. **1959** Upstairs and Downstairs (US 1961). **1960** Doctor in Love (US 1962); Foxhole in Cairo (US 1961); A French Mistress. **1961** Very Important Person

(aka A Coming Out Party—US 1962); Raising the Wind (aka Roommates—US 1962); Murder She Said (US 1962); The Guns of Navarone. **1962** A Pair of Briefs (US 1963); Crooks Anonymous (US 1963); Dr. Crippen (US 1964); The Fast Lady (US 1965); Guns of Darkness. **1963** Doctor in Distress (US 1964); Le Repos du Guerrier (Love on a Pillow and aka Warrior's Rest); Father Came Too (US 1966 and aka We Want to Live Alone); Mystery Submarine. **1965** Doctor in Clover (aka Carnaby, M.D.—US 1967); The Face of Fu Manchu; You Must be Joking; Up from the Beach; Those Magnificent Men in Their Flying Machine. **1967** The Trygon Factor (US 1969); Two Weeks in September; Hell is Empty. **1968** Mayerling (US 1969); Histories Extraordinaires (aka Spirits of the Dead—US 1969); Chitty Chitty Bang Bang. **1970** Some Will—Some Won't; Doctor in Trouble.

JUSTIN, MORGAN (Claude Olin Wurman)
Born: 1927, Wichita Falls, Texas. Died: July 7, 1974, Tarzana, Calif. (cancer). Screen and television actor.

Appeared in: **1953** The Kid from Left Field (film debut). **1956** The Court Jester. **1970** Dirty Dingus Magee.

JUUL, RALPH
Born: 1888. Died: Nov. 5, 1955, Chicago, Ill. Screen, stage and radio actor.

KAART, HANS
Born: 1924. Died: June 1963, Amsterdam, Holland (following ear surgery). Screen actor and operatic singer. Appeared in German and Dutch films.

KAHANAMOKU, DUKE P.
Born: Aug. 24, 1890, Honolulu, Hawaii. Died: Jan. 22, 1968, Honolulu, Hawaii (heart attack). Screen actor and Olympic swimming champion.

Appeared in: **1925** Adventure; Lord Jim. **1926** Old Ironsides. **1927** Isle of Sunken Gold. **1928** Woman Wise. **1929** The Rescue. **1930** Girl of the Port; Isle of Escape. **1948** Wake of the Red Witch. **1955** Mr. Roberts. **1969** I Sailed to Tahiti With an All Girl Crew.

KAHN, RICHARD C.
Born: 1897. Died: Jan. 28, 1960, Hollywood, Calif. (heart attack). Screen actor, film director and film producer. Entered films as an actor in silents.

KAHN, WILLIAM "SMITTY"
Born: 1882. Died: May 14, 1959, Hollywood, Calif. Screen and television actor.

Appeared in: **1951** Girl on the Bridge. **1956** Edge of Hell.

KALICH, BERTHA
Born: 1875, Lemberg, Poland. Died: Apr. 18, 1939, New York, N.Y. Stage and screen actress.

Appeared in: **1914** Marta of the Lowlands. **1916** Slander; Ambition.

KALICH, JACOB
Born: 1892, Rymanov, Poland. Died: Mar. 16, 1975, Lake Mahopac, N.Y. (cancer). Yiddish screen, stage, television actor, stage director and playwright. Married to actress Molly Picon.

Appeared in: **1924** Mazel Tov. **1971** Fiddler on the Roof.

KALIONZES, JANET (Janet Manson)
Born: 1922. Died: Aug. 10, 1961, New York, N.Y. Screen and television actress.

Appeared in: **1948** A Double Life.

KALIZ, ARMAND
Born: Oct. 23, 1892, Paris, France. Died: Feb. 1, 1941, Beverly Hills, Calif. (heart attack). Screen, stage, vaudeville actor and screenwriter.

Appeared in: **1919** A Temperamental Wife. **1926** Josselyn's Wife; The Temptress; Yellow Fingers; The Belle of Broadway; The Better Way. **1927** The Stolen Bride; Fast and Furious; Say It with Diamonds; Temptations of a Shop Girl; Wandering Girls. **1928** The Love Mart; The Devil's Cage; Lingerie; That's My Daddy; The Wife's Relations; A Woman's Way. **1929** The Marriage Playground; Twin Beds; The Aviator; Gold Diggers of Broadway; Noah's Ark. **1930** L'Enigmatique Monsieur Parkes (The Mysterious Mr. Parkes); Little Caesar; The Eternal Triangle (short). **1931** Honeymoon Lane. **1932** Three Wise Girls. **1933** Secret Sinners; Design for Living; Flying Down to Rio. **1934** Caravan; George White's Scandals. **1935** Diamond Jim; Ruggles of Red Gap; Here's to Romance. **1936** Desire. **1937** Cafe Metropole; The King and the Chorus Girl. **1938** Algiers; A Trip to Paris; Josette; I'll Give a Million; Gold Diggers in Paris; Vacation from Love. **1939** Off the Record; Topper Takes a Trip; Midnight. **1940** Down Argentine Way. **1941** Skylark.

KALKHURST, ERIC
Born: 1902. Died: Oct. 13, 1957, Washington, D.C. Screen and stage actor. Entered films in 1922.

Appeared in: **1930** The Virtuous Sin. **1931** Unfaithful.

KALSER, ERWIN
Born: 1883, Germany. Died: Mar. 26, 1958, Berlin, Germany. Stage and screen actor.

Appeared in: **1930** Rasputin: The Holy Devil. **1931** The Last Company; Thirteen Men and a Girl. **1933** Hertha's Erwachen. **1941** Kings Row; Escape to Glory (aka Submarine Zone); Dressed to Kill. **1942** Berlin Correspondent. **1943** Watch on the Rhine; Underground. **1944** Address Unknown; America's Children; Strange Affair; U-Boat Prisoner. **1945** Hotel Berlin. **1952** The Girl in White. **1953** Stalag 17.

KALTHOUM, UM
Born: 1898, Tamay al-Zahirah, Egypt. Died: Feb. 3, 1975, Cairo, Egypt (cerebral hemorrhage). Screen, radio actress and singer. Known as "Daughter of the Nile."

KAMENZKY, ELIEZER
Born: 1889, Russia. Died: 1957, Lisbon, Portugal. Screen and stage actor.

KAMIYAMA, SOJIN. *See* SOJIN

KAMMER, KLAUS
Born: 1929, Hannover, Germany. Died: May 9, 1964, Berlin, Germany (suicide—carbon monoxide). Screen, stage and television actor.

Appeared in: **1959** Kriegsgericht (Court Martial—US 1962).

KAMPERS, FRITZ
Born: 1891. Died: 1950, Garmisch-Partenkirchen, Germany. Screen and stage actor and film director.

Appeared in: **1929** Berlin After Dark; His Late Excellency. **1931** Gretel and Liesel (Kohlhiesel's Daughters); Comrades of 1918; Lumpenball; Die Drei von ver Tankstelle. **1932** Reserve Hat Ruh; Der Stolz der 3 Kompagnie; Pension Schoeller; Gloria; Kameradschaft. **1933** Der Korvettenkapitaen; Die Lustigen Musikanten; Frau Lehmann's Toechter; Zwei Gute Kameraden. **1934** Der Meisterdetektiv; Strich Durch die Rechnung; Das Blaue vom Himmel; Liebe in Uniform; Eine Frau wie Du; Kaiserwalzer. **1935** Die Sonne Geht auf; Die Liebe und die Erste Eisenbahn (Love and the First Railroad); Drei Kaiserjaeger; Drei von der Kavallerie; Der Judas von Tirol; Die vom Niederrhein (Lower Rhine Folks); Zigeunerbaron; Gruen ist die Heide; Die Vier Musketiere (The Four Musketeers). **1936** Leichte Kavallerie; Die Fahrt ins Gruene; Ein Lied Gaht um die Welt; Letzte Rose; La Paloma; Der Bettelstudent; Drei Blaune Jungs—Ein Blondes Maedel. **1937** Weisse Sklaven; Drama on the Threshing Floor. **1938** Urlaub auf Ehrenwort (Furlough on Word of Honor). **1939** Konzert in Tirol; La Veilchen vom Potsdamer Platz (Violet of Potsdam Square); Pour le Merite; Das Ekel (The Grouch). **1940** Die Drei um Christine (The Three After Christine). **1951** The Joseph Schmidt Story.

KANE, BLANCHE
Born: 1889. Died: Aug. 24, 1937, Hollywood, Calif. Screen and stage actress.

KANE, EDDIE
Born: Aug. 12, 1889, Missouri. Died: Apr. 30, 1969, Hollywood, Calif. (heart attack). Screen, stage, vaudeville and television actor. Was part of "Kane and Herman" vaudeville team.

Appeared in: **1928** Lights of New York. **1929** Why Bring That Up?; The Broadway Melody; Street Girl; Times Square; Illusion. **1930** The Cohens and the Kellys in Africa; The Doorway to Hell; The Squealer; Puttin' On the Ritz; Framed; The Kibitzer. **1931** My Past; Stolen Jools (short); Dirigible; Public Enemy; Smart Money; Goldie; Son of Rajah; Ex Bad Boy; Bought; Susan Lennox, Her Rise and Fall; Forbidden; Peach O' Reno; Forgotten Women. **1932** Stepping Sisters; Once In a Lifetime; Love Is a Racket; The Slippery Pearls (short); The Mummy. **1933** Dangerous Crossroads; Thrill Hunter. **1934** Autobuyography (short); Fixing a Stew (short); Wonder Bar. **1935** Million Dollar Baby; Hooray for Love; Hit and Run (short); Counselitis (short). **1936** An RKO short. **1937** Melody For Two; All Over Town; Manhattan Merry-Go-Round; Hollywood Round-up; Mr. Boggs Steps Out; Small Town Boy; Pick a Star. **1938** Swiss Miss; The Gladiator; You Can't Take It With You; Give Me a Sailor; Dummy Owner (short). **1939** Some Like It Hot; Missing Daughters; Crime Rave (short); Home Boner (short); Rovin' Tumbleweeds. **1940** Music In My Heart. **1942** Yankee Doodle Dandy; Inferior Decorator (short); Tarzan's New York Adventure. **1943** Mission to Moscow. **1944** Jam Session; Two Girls and a Sailor; Up In Arms; Minstrel Man; The Hairy Ape; Dark Mountains. **1945** Man From Oklahoma; You Drive Me Crazy (short); The Big Beef (short). **1947** Ladies' Man; Wife Tames Wolf (short). **1948** Mexican Hayride. **1949** Jiggs and Maggie in Jackpot Jitters. **1956** The Ten Commandments.

KANE, GAIL (Abigail Kane)
Born: 1885. Died: Feb. 17, 1966, Augusta, Maine. Screen and stage actress.

Appeared in: **1916** Paying the Price. **1917** Southern Pride; A Game of Wits; Souls in Pawn. **1918** Love's Law. **1921** A Good Woman; Idle Hands; Wise Husbands. **1923** The White Sisters. **1927** Convoy.

KANE, HELEN "BABE"
Born: Aug. 4, 1908, New York, N.Y. Died: Sept. 26, 1966, Jackson Heights, N.Y. (chest cancer). Screen, stage, vaudeville and television actress. Divorced from businessman Joseph Kane; actor Max Hoffman, Jr. (dec. 1945) and later married to emcee and singer Dan Healey.

Appeared in: **1929** Nothing But the Truth; Sweetie; Pointed Hills. **1930** Dangerous Nan McGrew; Paramount on Parade; Heads Up. **1932** The Dentist (short); The Spot on the Rug (short). **1933** The Pharmacist (short). **1934** Counsel on the Fence. **1950** Three Little Words (voice only).

KANE, JOHN J. "JOHNNY"
Died: Mar. 15, 1969, N.Y. Screen, stage, radio and television actor.

Appeared in: **1951** Man with My Face. **1959** The FBI Story. **1964** Fail Safe.

KANE, LIDA
Died: Oct. 7, 1955, New York, N.Y. Screen, stage, radio, and television actress.

Appeared in: **1930** Follow the Leader. **1931** Secrets of a Secretary.

KANE, WHITFORD
Born: 1881, Ireland. Died: Dec. 17, 1956, New York, N.Y. Stage and screen actor.

Appeared in: **1934** Hideout. **1944** The Adventures of Mark Twain. **1947** The Ghost and Mrs. Muir. **1948** The Walls of Jericho. **1949** The Judge Steps Out.

KANNON, JACKIE
Born: 1919, Windsor, Ont., Canada. Died: Feb. 1, 1974, New York, N.Y. (heart attack). Nightclub comedian, television and screen actor.

Appeared in: **1964** Diary of a Bachelor.

KAPOOR, PRITHVI RAJ
Born: 1906, India. Died: May 29, 1972, Bombay, India. Screen, stage actor, film producer, director and member of the Upper House of the Indian Parliament. Father of actors Raj Kapoor, Shammi Kapoor and Shasi Kapoor. In 1972 he received the Dadasaheb Phalke film award.

Appeared in: Alam Ara (first Indian film). **1956** The Vagabond. **1958** Boot Polish. **1960** Khozhdenie Za Tri Morya (Journey Beyond Three Seas).

KARELS, HARVEY
Died: Nov. 17, 1975. Screen actor.

Appeared in: **1925** The Merry Widow.

KARLIN, BO-PEEP
Died: Feb. 25, 1969, Hollywood, Calif. Screen and television actress. Married to actor Gaston Glass (dec. 1965).

Appeared in: **1929** Happy Days. **1930** Just Imagine. **1963** Bye Bye Birdie.

KARLOFF, BORIS (William Henry Pratt)
Born: Nov. 23, 1887, London, England. Died: Feb. 2, 1969, London, England (respiratory ailment). Screen, stage, radio and television actor.

Appeared in: **1919** His Majesty the American; Prince and Betty. **1920** The Deadlier Sex; The Courage of Marge O'Doone; The Last of the Mohicans. **1921** Without Benefit of Clergy; The Hope Diamond Mystery; Cheated Hearts; The Cave Girl. **1922** The Man from Downing Street; The Infidel; The Altar Stairs; Omar the Tentmaker. **1923** Woman Conquers; The Prisoner. **1924** Dynamite Dan. **1925** Parisian Nights; Forbidden Cargo; The Prairie Wife; Lady Robinhood; Never the Twain Shall Meet. **1926** The Bells; The Greater Glory; Her Honor, the Governor; The Nicklehopper; Eagle of the Sea; Old Ironsides; Flames; The Golden Web; Flaming Fury; Man in the Saddle. **1927** The Meddlin' Stranger; The Phantom Buster; Tarzan and the Golden Lion; Soft Cushions; Two Arabian Knights; Let It Rain; The Princess from Hoboken. **1928** The Love Mart; Vultures of the Sea (serial). **1929** The Fatal Warning (serial); Little Wild Girl; The Phantom of the North; Two Sisters; Devil's Chaplain; King of the Kongo (serial); The Unholy Night; Behind That Curtain; Burning the Wind. **1930** The Sea Bat; The Bad One; The Utah Kid; Mother's Cry; The Scar on the Nation; Assorted Nuts (short). **1931** King of the Wild (serial); The Criminal Code; Cracked Nuts (short); Smart Money; The Public Defender; I Like Your Nerve; Five Star Final; The Mad Genius; Frankenstein; Young Donovan's Kid; The Guilty Generation; The Yellow Ticket; Graft; Tonight or Never. **1932** Business and Pleasure; Behind the Mask; The Cohens and the Kellys in Hollywood; The Mummy; Night World; The Old Dark House; The Mask of Fu Manchu; Alias The Doctor; The Miracle Man; Scarface. **1933** The Man Who Dared; The Ghoul. **1934** The House of Rothschild; The Lost Patrol; The Black Cat; Gift of Gab. **1935** The Raven; The Black Room; Mysterious Mr. Wong; The Bride of Frankenstein. **1936** The Walking Dead; The Invisible Ray; Charlie Chan at the Opera; The Man Who Changed His Mind (US—The Man Who Lived Again). **1937** Juggernaut; Night Key; Without Warning; West of Shanghai; War Lord. **1938** Mr. Wong, Detective; The Invisible Menace. **1939** The Man They Could Not Hang; Mr. Wong in Chinatown; Son of Frankenstein; Tower of London; The Mystery of Mr. Wong. **1940** British Intelligence; The Man with Nine Lives; Devil's Island;

Doomed to Die; The Ape; You'll Find Out; Before I Hang; The Fatal Hour; Black Friday. **1941** Behind the Door; The Devil Commands. **1942** The Boogie Man Will Get You. **1944** The Climax. **1945** House of Dracula; House of Frankenstein; Isle of the Dead; The Body Snatchers. **1946** Bedlam. **1947** The Secret Life of Walter Mitty; Lured; Dick Tracy Meets Gruesome; Unconquered. **1948** Tap Roots. **1949** Abbott and Costello Meet the Killer, Boris Karloff. **1951** The Strange Door; Emperor's Nightingale (narr.). **1952** The Black Castle. **1953** Abbott and Costello Meet Dr. Jekyll and Mr. Hyde; The Monster of the Island; The Hindu (aka Sabaka—US 1955). **1957** Voodoo Island; The Juggler of Our Lady. **1958** Corridor of Blood (US 1963); Grip of the Strangler (aka The Haunted Strangler—US); Frankenstein—1970. **1961** Days of Thrills and Laughter (documentary). **1963** The Raven (and 1935 version); The Terror. **1964** A Comedy of Terrors; Black Sabbath; Bikini Beach; Today's Teen (short—narr.); Scarlet Friday. **1965** Die, Monster, Die! **1966** The Daydreamer (narr.); Ghost in the Invisible Bikini; The Venetian Affair; Monster of Terror; The House at the End of the World. **1967** The Corpse Collector; Mondo Balordo (narr.); The Sorcerers. **1968** The Curse of the Crimson Altar (aka The Crimson Cult—US 1970); Targets. **1969** Mad Monster Party (narr.)

KARLSTADT, LIESL

Born: 1893, Germany. Died: Aug. 1, 1960, Garmisch-Partenkirchen, Germany (stroke). Screen, stage actress, singer and dancer.

Appeared in: **1934** Mit dir Durch Dick und Duenn. **1937** Kirschen in Nachbars Garten. **1956** Die Trapp Familie (The Trapp Family—US 1961). **1958** Wir Wunderkinder (We Amazing Children, aka Aren't We Wonderful—US 1959). Other German film: Feuerwerk.

KARLWEISS, OSCAR

Born: 1895, Vienna, Austria. Died: Jan. 24, 1956, New York, N.Y. (heart attack). Stage and screen actor.

Appeared in: **1930** Zwei Hertzen in Drei-Viertel Takt. **1931** Die Foresterchristl; Die Drei von ver Tankstelle; Dolly Macht Karriere; Sein Liebeslied. **1933** Der Tanzhusar. **1951** St. Benny the Dip. **1952** Anything Can Happen; Five Fingers. **1953** The Juggler; Tonight We Sing. **1956** Meet Me in Las Vegas.

KARNS, ROSCOE

Born: Sept. 7, 1893, San Bernardino, Calif. Died: Feb. 6, 1970, Los Angeles, Calif. Screen, stage and television actor.

Appeared in: A Western Governor's Humanity. **1921** The Man Turner; Too Much Married. **1922** Afraid to Fight; Conquering the Woman; Her Own Money; The Trouper. **1923** Other Man's Daughters. **1924** Bluff; The Foolish Virgin; The Midnight Express. **1925** Headlines; The Overland Limited; Dollar Down. **1927** The Jazz Singer; Ritzy; Ten Modern Commandments. **1928** Win That Girl; Warming Up; The Desert Bride; Object—Alimony; Moran of the Marines; Beggars of Life; Something Always Happens; Jazz Mad; Beau Sabreau. **1929** This Thing Called Love; New York Nights. **1930** Safety in Numbers; Troopers Three; New York Lights; Man Trouble; The Costello Case; Little Accident. **1931** The Gorilla; Dirigible; Laughing Sinners; Leftover Ladies; Many a Slip. **1932** Ladies of the Big House; Lawyer Man; Night after Night; Roadhouse Murder; Week-End Marriage; Two against the World; The Crooked Circle; I Am a Fugitive from a Chain Gang; One Way Passage; If I Had a Million; Under Cover Man; The Stowaway; Pleasure; Rockabye. **1933** Gambling Ship; One Sunday Afternoon; Alice in Wonderland; Today We Live; A Lady's Profession; 20,000 Years in Sing Sing. **1934** Twentieth Century; Search for Beauty; The Women in His Life; Shoot the Works; Come on Marines; Elmer and Elsie; It Happened One Night; I Sell Anything. **1935** Red Hot Tires; Stolen Harmony; Four Hours to Kill; Wings in the Dark; Two-Fisted; Alibi Ike; Front Page Woman. **1936** Woman Trap; Border Flight; Three Cheers for Love; Three Married Men; Cain and Mabel. **1937** Murder Goes to College; A Night of Mystery; On Such a Night; Clarence; Partners in Crime. **1938** Scandal Sheet; Dangerous to Know; Tip-Off Girls; You and Me; Thanks for the Memory. **1939** King of Chinatown; Everything's on Ice; That's Right—You're Wrong; Dancing Co-ed. **1940** Double Alibi; His Girl Friday; Saturday's Children; They Drive by Night; Ladies Must Live; Meet the Missus. **1941** Petticoat Politics; Footsteps in the Dark; The Gay Vagabond. **1942** The Road to Happiness; A Tragedy at Midnight; Yokel Boy; You Can't Escape Forever; Woman of the Year. **1943** Stage Door Canteen; My Son, the Hero; His Butler's Sister; Old Acquaintance. **1944** The Navy Way; Hi, Good Lookin'; Minstrel Man. **1946** Ring Doorbells; One Way to Love; The Kid from Brooklyn; Avalanche; It's a Wonderful Life; Down Missouri Way. **1947** That's My Man; Vigilantes of Boomtown; Will Tomorrow Ever Come? **1948** The Devil's Cargo; The Inside Story; Speed to Spare; Texas, Brooklyn and Heaven. **1958** Onionhead. **1964** Man's Favorite Sport?

KARR, DARWIN

Born: July 25, 1875, Almond, N.Y. Died: Dec. 31, 1945, Calif. Stage and screen actor. Married to actress Florence Bindley. Entered films in 1911 with Edison Co.

Appeared in: **1911** That Winsome Winnie Smile; Eugene Wraygrun; The Girl and the Motor Boat; A Modern Cinderella; Willie Wise and his Motor Boat; The Ghost's Warning; The Story of the Indian Ledge. **1912** Falling Leaves; The Boarding House Heiress; The Detective Dog; Billy's Shoes; The Child of

the Tenements; The Fugitive; The Idol Worshipper; Saved by a Cat; Phantom Paradise; Father and the Boys; Canned Harmony; The Equine Spy; The Wooing of Alice; Souls in the Shadow; Mickey's Pal; For the Love of the Flag; Auto Suggestion. **1914** Her Husband; The Tangle. **1915** His Bunky. **1921** Our Mutual Friend. **1922** The Sin Flood; Mr. Barnes of New York.

KARRINGTON, FRANK

Born: Mar. 9, 1858. Died: Mar. 5, 1936, Cornwall, N.Y. Stage and screen actor.

KASHEY, ABE

Born: Nov. 28, 1903, Syria. Died: Sept. 24, 1965, Lynwood, Calif. (congestive heart failure). Screen actor.

Appeared in: **1943** That Nazty Nuisance. **1945** Crime Doctor's Courage.

KASTNER, BRUNO

Born: Germany. Died: Prior to 1958. Screen actor. Married to actress Ida Wuest (dec. 1958).

Appeared in: **1929** Thou Shalt Not Steal; Carnival of Crime; Luther.

KATCH, KURT (Isser Kac)

Born: Jan. 28, 1896, Grodno, Poland. Died: Aug. 14, 1958, Los Angeles, Calif. (during cancer surgery). Screen and stage actor.

Appeared in: **1938** Tkies Khaf (The Vow). **1941** Men at Large. **1942** The Wife Takes a Flyer; Berlin Correspondent; Counter Espionage; They Came to Blow up America; Edge of Darkness; Quiet Please, Murder; Secret Agent of Japan. **1943** Background to Danger; Mission to Moscow; Watch on the Rhine. **1944** Ali Baba and the Forty Thieves; The Purple Heart; The Mask of Dimitrios; Make Your Own Bed; The Conspirators; The Seventh Cross. **1945** The Mummy's Curse; Salome, Where She Danced. **1946** Angel on My Shoulder; Rendezvous 24. **1947** Song of Love; Strange Journey. **1954** The Secret of the Incas; The Adventures of Hajji Baba. **1955** Abbott and Costello Meet the Mummy. **1956** Hot Cars. **1957** The Girl in the Kremlin; The Pharaoh's Curse. **1958** The Young Lions; The Beast of Budapest.

KAUFMAN, JOSEPH

Born: 1882, Washington, D.C. Died: Feb. 1, 1918, New York, N.Y. (pneumonia). Screen actor, film producer and director.

Appeared in: **1914** Madam Cigarette; A Daughter of Eve. **1915** When the Light Came In; Money! Money! Money!; His Soul Mate; The Little Detective; The Millinery Man; A Woman went Forth; The Blessed Miracle; Monkey Business; The Stroke of Fate; Just Look at Jake; The Darkness Before Dawn; In the Dark; The Silent Accuser.

KAUFMAN, WILLIAM "WILLY"

Died: 1967. Screen actor.

Appeared in: **1939** Confessions of a Nazi Spy; Beasts of Berlin; Nurse Edith Cavell. **1940** The Man I Married; Mystery Sea Raider; British Intelligence. **1962** Hitler (aka Women of Nazi Germany).

KAY, HENRY

Born: 1911. Died: Dec. 9, 1968, London, England. Screen and television actor.

Appeared in: **1962** The Dock Brief (aka Trial and Error—US). **1968** Oliver.

KAYE, PHIL

Born: 1912. Died: Nov. 28, 1959, New York, N.Y. Screen, stage, vaudeville actor and singer.

Appeared in: **1950** The Asphalt Jungle. **1951** The Red Badge of Courage.

KAYE, SPARKY (Philip Kaplan)

Born: 1906, New York, N.Y. Died: Aug. 23, 1971, Las Vegas, Nev. (heart attack). Screen, stage, burlesque and night club actor.

Appeared in: **1937** Firefly. **1960** Ocean's 11.

KAYSSLER, CHRISTIAN

Born: 1898, Germany. Died: 1944, Germany? Screen and stage actor. Son of actor Friedrich Kayssler (dec. 1945). Married to actress Mila Kopp (dec. 1973).

Appeared in: **1940** Die Neue Deutsche Luftwaffe Greift An (The New German Airforce Attacks).

KAYSSLER, FRIEDRICH

Born: 1874, Neurode-Grafschaft Glatz, Germany. Died: 1945, Leinmachnow, Germany. Stage and screen actor. Father of actor Christian Kayssler (dec. 1944).

Appeared in: **1928** A Modern DuBarry. **1930** The Burning Heart. **1931** Das Floetenkonzert von Sanssouci. **1932** Avalanche; Luise, Loenigin von Preussen (Luise, Queen of Prussia); Yorck. **1933** Der Hauptmann von Koepenick. **1935** Der Alte und der Jung Koenig. **1936** Friesennot. **1938** Der Zerbrochene Krug (The Broken Jug); Zwischen den Eltern (Between the Parents); Winter Stuerme (Winter Storms). **1939** Verwehte Spuren (Covered Tracks).

KEAN, RICHARD

Born: 1892. Died: Dec. 30, 1959, Laguna Beach, Calif. (heart attack). Stage and screen actor.

Appeared in: 1949 The Beautiful Blonde from Bashful Bend. 1950 Storm over Wyoming. 1952 The Story of Will Rogers. 1956 The Court Jester; The Ten Commandments.

KEANE, CONSTANCE. *See* VERONICA LAKE

KEANE, DORIS

Born: 1885, Mich. Died: Nov. 25, 1945, New York, N.Y. Stage and screen actress. Divorced from actor Basil Sydney (dec. 1968).

Appeared in: 1920 Romance (stage and film versions); Kismit.

KEANE, EDWARD

Born: May 28, 1884, New York, N.Y. Died: Oct. 12, 1959. Screen actor.

Appeared in: 1921 The Supreme Passion. 1931 Stolen Heaven; His Woman. 1933 Ann Carver's Profession; I Have Lived. 1934 The Count of Monte Cristo; I Am Suzanne; Man of Iron; Green Eyes; One Exciting Adventure; Girl in Danger. 1935 Mills of the Gods; Circumstantial Evidence; Public Opinion; Whispering Smith Speaks; Hard Rock Harrigan; Behind the Evidence; Border Brigands; Manhattan Butterfly; A Night at the Opera. 1936 The Singing Kid; Princess Comes Across; The Dragnet; Parole; Down the Stretch; Gambling with Souls; Mummy's Boys; an RKO Radio short. 1937 I Promise to Pay; Seventh Heaven; The Californian; Hollywood Round-Up. 1938 Alcatraz Island; Shadows over Shanghai; Nancy Drew—Detective; I Demand Payment; Slander House; Torchy Gets Her Man; Border G-Man. 1939 Frontier Pony Express; Heroes in Blue; The Roaring Twenties; My Wife's Relatives. 1940 Winners of the West (serial); Charlie Chan in Panama; Midnight Limited; Devil's Island; City for Conquest; Money and the Woman; The Son of Monte Cristo; A Fugitive from Justice. 1941 Sea Raiders (serial); Ride, Kelly, Ride; Riders of the Timberline. 1942 The Man with Two Lives; Wildcat; The Traitor Within; Who Done It?; Who is Hope Schulyer? 1943 Let's Have Fun; Truck Busters; The Good Fellows; Mission to Moscow; I Escaped from the Gestapo. 1944 Haunted Harbor (serial); Captain America (serial); Bermuda Mystery; Nothing but Trouble. 1945 Rogue's Gallery; Fashion Model. 1946 Night Editor; Roll on Texas Moon; Out California Way. 1947 Trail to San Antone; The Invisible Wall; Roses are Red; Saddle Pals. 1948 Chicken Every Sunday. 1949 It Happens Every Spring. 1950 A Modern Marriage; Twilight in the Sierras; The Baron of Arizona. 1952 Deadline USA.

KEANREY, JOHN L.

Born: 1871, New York, N.Y. Died: Aug. 3, 1945, New York, N.Y. Screen, stage actor and circus performer.

Appeared in: 1927 East Side, West Side. 1931 Honor Among Lovers.

KEARNS, ALLEN B.

Born: 1895. Died: Apr. 20, 1956, Albany, N.Y. Screen, stage and television actor.

Appeared in: 1929 Tanned Legs; The Very Idea. 1930 Lovin' the Ladies; Purely an Accident (short).

KEARNS, JOSEPH

Born: 1907, Salt Lake City, Utah. Died: Feb. 17, 1962, Los Angeles, Calif. Screen, television and radio actor. Played Mr. Wilson on "Dennis the Menace" television show.

Appeared in: 1951 Hard, Fast and Beautiful. 1955 Daddy-Long-Legs. 1956 Our Miss Brooks; Storm Center. 1958 The Gift of Love. 1959 Anatomy of Murder.

KEATAN, A. HARRY

Born: 1896. Died: June 18, 1966, Hollywood, Calif. (heart attack). Screen actor, film producer, director and screenwriter. A comic in two-reelers during silents.

KEATING, FRED

Born: Mar. 27, 1902, New York, N.Y. Died: June 29, 1961, N.Y. (heart attack). Screen, stage, vaudeville actor, circus performer and writer.

Appeared in: 1929 Illusions (short). 1934 The Captain Hates the Sea. 1935 The Nitwit; To Beat the Band; Shanghai; I Live My Life. 1936 13 Hours by Air; The Devil on Horseback. 1937 Melody for Two; When's Your Birthday? 1938 Dr. Rhythm; Prison Train. 1939 Eternally Yours; Society Smugglers. 1940 Tin Pan Alley.

KEATING, KATHERINE. *See* FRANCES SAGE

KEATING, LARRY

Born: 1896, St. Paul, Minn. Died: Aug. 26, 1963, Hollywood, Calif. (leukemia). Screen, radio and television actor.

Appeared in: 1945 Song of the Sarong. 1949 Whirlpool. 1950 Mister 880; Right Cross; I Was a Shoplifter; My Blue Heaven; Three Secrets; Mother Didn't Tell Me; Stella. 1951 The Mating Season; Francis Goes to the Races; Follow the

Sun; Bright Victory; Too Young to Kiss; Bannerline; The Light Touch; Come Fill the Cup; When Worlds Collide. 1952 Carson City; About Face; Monkey Business; Something for the Birds; Above and Beyond. 1953 Inferno; She's Back on Broadway; Give a Girl a Break; A Lion Is in the Streets. 1954 Gypsy Colt. 1955 Daddy Long Legs. 1956 The Eddie Duchin Story; The Best Things in Life Are Free. 1957 The Wayward Bus; The Buster Keaton Story; Stopover Tokyo. 1960 Who Was That Lady? 1962 Boys' Night Out; Be Careful How You Wish (aka The Incredible Mr. Limpet—US 1964).

KEATON, BUSTER, JR. (Joseph Keaton, Jr.)

Born: Oct. 4, 1895, Piqua, Kan. Died: Feb. 1, 1966, Woodland Hills, Calif. (lung cancer). Screen, stage, vaudeville, television actor, screenwriter and film director. Son of actor Joseph Keaton, Sr. (dec. 1946) and actress Myra Keaton (dec. 1955). Divorced from actress Natalie Talmadge (dec. 1969) and Mae Scribbens. Later married to Eleanor Norris. Father of actor Robert Talmadge. After his divorce from Miss Talmadge, she had their son's name legally changed from Keaton to Talmadge. Appeared in vaudeville with his parents in an act billed as "The Three Keatons."

Appeared in: 1917 The Butcher Boy (film debut); The Rough House; His Wedding Night; Fatty at Coney Island; Oh, Doctor!; A Country Hero; A Reckless Romeo. 1918 The Bell Boy; Goodnight Nurse; Moonshine; The Cook; Out West. 1919 A Desert Hero; The Hayseed; Back Stage. 1920 The Saphead; plus the following shorts: The Garage, One Week; Convict 13; The Scarecrow; Neighbors. 1921 The following shorts: The Haunted House; Hard Luck; The Goat; The Electric House (incomplete first version, destroyed); The Playhouse; The Boat; The Paleface; The High Sign. 1922 The following shorts: Cops; My Wife's Relations; The Blacksmith; The Frozen North; Daydreams; The Electric House (second version). 1923 The Three Ages; Our Hospitality; plus the following shorts: Balloonatics; The Love Nest. 1924 Sherlock, Jr.; Navigator. 1925 Seven Chances; Go West. 1926 Battling Butler; The General. 1927 College. 1928 Steamboat Bill, Jr.; The Cameraman. 1929 Spite Marriage; Hollywood Review of 1929. 1930 Free and Easy; The Big Shot; Dough Boys. 1931 Sidewalks of New York. 1932 Speak Easily; Parlor, Bedroom and Bath; The Passionate Plumber; The Slippery Pearls (short). 1933 What, No Beer? 1934 Le Roi Des Champs-Elysees (The Champ of the Champs Elysees); The Gold Ghost (short); Allez Ooop (short). 1935 The following shorts: La Fiesta de Santa Barbara; Palooka from Paducah; Tars and Stripes; Hayseed Romance; The E-Flat Man; The Timid Young Man; One Run Elmer. 1936 Three Men on a Horse; The Invader (aka An Old Spanish Custom—US); plus the following shorts: The Chemist; Three on a Limb; Grand Slam Opera; Blue Blazes; Mixed Magic. 1937 The following shorts: Ditto; Jail Bait; Love Nest on Wheels. 1938 Hollywood Handicap; Streamlined Swing; Life in Sometown U.S.A. 1939 Hollywood Cavalcade; The Jones Family in Hollywood; The Jones Family in Quick Millions; Mooching Through Georgia (short); The Pest from the West (short). 1940 L'il Abner; The Villain Still Pursued Her; plus the following shorts: Nothing But Pleasure; His Ex Marks the Spot; Pardon My Berth Marks; The Spook Speaks; The Taming of the Snood. 1941 The following shorts: So You Won't Squawk; She's Oil Mine; General Nuisance. 1943 Forever and a Day. 1944 San Diego, I Love You; Two Girls and a Sailor; Bathing Beauty. 1945 That's the Spirit; That Night with You. 1946 El Moderno Barba Azul; God's Country. 1948 Un Duel a Mort. 1949 A Southern Yankee; You're My Everything; In the Good Old Summertime; The Cheat; Neptune's Daughter. 1950 Sunset Boulevard. 1952 Limelight. 1953 The Awakening; Paradise for Buster (never released commercially). 1956 Around the World in 80 Days. 1960 The Adventures of Huckleberry Finn; When Comedy Was King (documentary). 1962 Ten Girls Ago. 1963 Pajama Party; It's a Mad, Mad, Mad, Mad World; The Triumph of Lester Snapwell; The Great Chase (documentary); 30 Years of Fun (documentary); The Sound of Laughter (documentary). 1965 Sergeant Deadhead; Beach Blanket Bingo; The Railrodder; How to Stuff a Wild Bikini; Marines e un General. 1966 A Funny Thing Happened on the Way to the Forum; The Scribee. 1967 War Italian Style. 1974 That's Entertainment (film clips).

KEATON, JOSEPH, SR.

Born: 1867. Died: Jan. 13, 1946, Hollywood, Calif. Screen, vaudeville and burlesque actor. Appeared in vaudeville as "The Three Keatons" and also with magician Harry Houdini. Married to actress Myra Keaton (dec. 1955) and father of actor Buster Keaton (dec. 1966).

Appeared in: 1918 Out West; The Bell Boy. 1920 Convict 13. 1921 The Electric House (incomplete first version, destroyed). 1922 The Electric House (second version). 1923 Our Hospitality. 1924 Sherlock, Jr. 1927 The General. 1935 Palooka from Paducah (short).

KEATON, MYRA

Died: 1955. Screen and vaudeville actress. Married to screen actor Joseph Keaton, Sr. (dec. 1946) and mother of actor Buster Keaton, Jr. (dec. 1966). Appeared in vaudeville with husband and son in act billed as "The Three Keatons."

Appeared in: 1920 Convict 13. 1921 The Electric House (incomplete first version, destroyed). 1922 The Electric House (second version). 1935 Palooka from Paducah (short). 1937 Love on Wheels (short).

KEDROV, MIKHAIL N.

Born: 1894, Russia. Died: Mar. 22, 1972, Moscow, Russia. Stage actor, director, drama coach and screen actor.

Appeared in: 1932 Sibirsky Patrul.

KEEFE, CORNELIUS (aka JACK HILL)

Born: July 13, 1900, Boston, Mass. Died: Dec. 11, 1972, Los Angeles, Calif. (heart attack). Stage and screen actor. Do not confuse with actor–comedian Jack Hill or film producer–director Jack Hill.

Appeared in: 1924 The Fifth Horseman; The Law and the Lady; A Society Scandal; Those Who Judge. 1925 The Fighting Demon; The Unguarded Hour. 1927 Come to My House; Hook and Ladder No. 9; In a Moment of Temptation; A Light in the Window; The Poor Nut (stage and film versions); Three's a Crowd. 1928 Thanksgiving Day (short); Hearts of Men; The Adorable Cheat; Man from Headquarters; Satan and the Woman; Thundergod; You Can't Beat the Law. 1929 Brothers; Circumstantial Evidence; The Cohens and Kellys in Atlantic City; Devil's Chaplin. 1930 Ex-Flame; Those Who Dance; Hearts and Hoofs (short). 1932 A Lady with a Past; Disorderly Conduct; The Silver Lining. 1933 Tomorrow at Seven; Charlie Chan's Greatest Case; Man of Sentiment; Grand Slam. 1934 Mystery Liner; Three on a Honeymoon; The Chase of Pimple Street (short). 1935 Kentucky Blue Streak; Thunder in the Night; Death from a Distance; Tumbling Tumbleweeds; Hong Kong Nights; Harmony Lane. 1937 The Old Corral; The Trigger Trio. 1938 Telephone Operator; My Old Kentucky Home. 1939 Fifth Avenue Girl; Stagecoach; Mooching Through Georgia (short). 1941 Saddlemates. 1951 Gunplay. 1953 The Vanquished. 1956 Female Jungle. 1958 The Brain Eaters.

KEEN, MALCOLM

Born: Aug. 8, 1887, Bristol, England. Died: Jan. 30, 1970, England. Stage and screen actor.

Appeared in: 1916 Jimmy. 1917 A Master of Men; The Lost Chord. 1920 The Skin Game. 1922 A Bill for Divorcement. 1925 Settled Out of Court (aka Evidence Enclosed). 1926 The Lodger (aka The Case of Jonathan Drew—US 1928); The Mountain Eagle (aka Fear O' God—US); Julius Caesar (short). 1927 Packing Up. 1929 The Manxman. 1930 Wolves (aka Wanted Men—US 1936). 1931 77 Park Lane; Jealousy; The House of Unrest. 1934 The Night of the Party; Whispering Tongues; Dangerous Ground. 1936 The Lonely Road (aka Scotland Yard Commands—US 1937). 1938 Sixty Glorious Years (aka Queen of Destiny—US); Mr. Reeder in Room 13 (aka Mystery of Room 13—US 1941). 1942 The Great Mr. Handel (US 1943). 1951 The Lady and the Bandit; Lorna Doone; The Mating Season; 14 Hours; Queen for a Day. 1953 Rob Roy the Highland Rogue. 1957 Fortune is a Woman (aka She Played with Fire—US 1958). 1959 Operation Amsterdam (US 1960). 1961 Macbeth (US 1963); Francis of Assisi. 1962 Life for Ruth (aka Walk in the Shadow—US 1966); Two and Two Make Six (aka A Change of Heart and The Girl Swappers).

KEENAN, FRANCES

Born: 1886, Boston, Mass. Died: Feb. 28, 1950, Los Angeles, Calif. Screen actress. Daughter of actor Frank Keenan (dec. 1929).

KEENAN, FRANK

Born: 1859, Dubuque, Iowa. Died: Feb. 24, 1929, Hollywood, Calif. (pneumonia). Screen, stage and vaudeville actor. Father of actress Frances Keenan (dec. 1950).

Appeared in: 1915 The Coward. 1916 Honor Thy Name; The Thoroughbred. 1918 More Trouble; The Bells. 1922 Hearts Aflame; Lorna Doone. 1923 Brass; Scars of Jealousy. 1924 Women Who Give. 1925 The Dixie Handicap; My Lady's Lips; When the Door Opened; East Lynne. 1926 The Gilded Butterfly.

KEENE, ELSIE

Died: Dec. 29, 1973, Ft. Lauderdale, Fla. Stage and screen actress.

KEENE, RICHARD

Born: Sept. 16, 1890, Philadelphia, Pa. Died: Mar. 11, 1971. Screen, stage and vaudeville actor. Entered films in 1929.

Appeared in: 1929 Why Leave Her?; Words and Music. 1930 Happy Days; The Big Party; The Golden Calf; Up the River; Wild Company; The Middle Watch. 1933 Moonlight and Pretzels. 1939 The Mutiny of the Elsinore; She Married a Cop. 1940 Charlie Chan's Murder Cruise. 1946 Murder is My Business. 1954 The Country Girl. 1956 That Certain Feeling.

KEENE, TOM (George Duryea aka RICHARD POWERS)

Born: Dec. 20, 1898, Rochester, N.Y. Died: Aug. 4, 1963, Woodland Hills, Calif. Screen, stage actor and cowboy.

Appeared in: 1928 Marked Money. 1929 The Godless Girl; Honky Tonk; Thunder; Tide of Empire; In Old California. 1930 Night Work; Radio Kisses (short); The Dude Wrangler; Tol'able David; Beau Bandit; Pardon My Gun. 1931 Freighters of Destiny; Sundown Trail. 1932 Partners; Ghost Valley; Saddle Buster; Beyond the Rockies. 1933 Renegades of the West; Come on Danger; Scarlet River; Cheyenne Kid; Strictly Business; Crossfire; Son of the Border;

Sunset Pass. 1934 Our Daily Bread. 1935 Hong Kong Nights. 1936 Timothy's Quest; Drift Fence; Desert Gold; The Glory Trail; Rebellion. 1937 The Law Commands; Where Trails Divide; Battle of Greed; Old Louisiana; Drums of Destiny. 1938 Under Strange Flags; The Painted Trail. 1941 Wanderers of the West; Riding the Sunset Trail; The Driftin' Kid; Dynamite Cargo. 1942 Arizona Roundup; Where the Trail Ends. 1944 Up in Arms. 1945 The Enchanted Cottage; Girls of the Big House. 1946 San Quentin. 1948 If You Knew Susie. 1950 Desperadoes of the West (serial); Trail of Robin Hood. 1951 Texans Never Cry. 1952 Red Planet Mars. 1958 Once upon a Horse. 1959 Plan 9 from Outer Space.

KEFAUVER, ESTES (Carey Estes Kefauver)

Born: July 26, 1903, near Madisonville, Tenn. Died: Aug. 10, 1963, Bethesda, Maryland (heart attack). Former United States Senator, author and screen actor.

Appeared in: 1952 The Captive City.

KEIM, BUSTER C.

Born: 1906. Died: July 23, 1974, Hollywood, Calif. (cardiac condition). Screen, vaudeville actor and choreographer. Married to actress Dorothy Keim.

KEITH, IAN (Keith Ross)

Born: Feb. 27, 1899, Boston, Mass. Died: Mar. 26, 1960, New York, N.Y. Stage and screen actor. Married to actress Ethel Clayton (dec. 1966) and divorced from actress Blanche Yurka (dec. 1974).

Appeared in: 1924 Christine of the Hungry Heart; Love's Wilderness; Manhandled; Her Love Story. 1925 Enticement; My Son; The Tower of Lies; The Talker. 1926 The Lily; The Prince of Tempters; The Truthful Sex; Greater Glory. 1927 Convoy; Two Arabian Knights; A Man's Past; The Love of Sunya; What Every Girl Should Know. 1928 The Street of Illusion; Look-Out Girl. 1929 Prisoners; Light Fingers; The Divine Lady. 1930 Abraham Lincoln; The Great Divide; The Big Trail; Prince of Diamonds; The Boudoir Diplomat. 1931 A Tailor Made Man; The Phantom of Paris; The Deceiver; Sin Ship; Susan Lennox, Her Rise and Fall. 1932 The Sign of the Cross. 1933 Queen Christina. 1934 Dangerous Corner; Cleopatra. 1935 The Crusades; The Three Musketeers. 1936 Preview Murder Mystery; Don't Gamble with Love; Mary of Scotland; The Wife Legion. 1938 The Buccaneer; Comet over Broadway. 1940 All This and Heaven Too; The Sea Hawk. 1942 Remember Pearl Harbor; The Pay-Off. 1943 Five Graves to Cairo; The Sundown Kid; Wild Horse Stampede; That Nazty Nuisance; Bordertown Gun Fighters; Corregidor; I Escaped from the Gestapo; Here Comes Kelly. 1944 Casanova in Burlesque; Arizona Whirlwind; The Cowboy from Lonesome River; The Chinese Cat; Bowery Champs; The Sign of the Cross (revised version of 1932 film). 1945 The Spanish Main; Identity Unknown; Under Western Skies; Phantom of the Plains; Captain Kidd; China's Little Devils. 1946 Fog Island; Northwest Trail; She Gets Her Man; Song of Old Wyoming; Valley of the Zombies; Mr. Hex; Dick Tracy vs. Cueball. 1947 Dick Tracy's Dilemma; Border Feud; Nightmare Alley; The Strange Woman. 1948 The Three Musketeers (and 1935 version). 1954 The Black Shield of Falworth. 1955 Prince of Players; New York Confidential; It Came from beneath the Sea; Duel on the Mississippi. 1956 The Ten Commandments.

KEITH, JAMES

Born: 1902. Died: Dec. 27, 1970, Pasadena, Calif. (heart attack). Stage and screen actor.

KEITH, ROBERT

Born: Feb. 10, 1898, Fowler, Ind. Died: Dec. 22, 1966, Los Angeles, Calif. Screen, stage and television actor. Father of actor Brian Keith.

Appeared in: 1924 The Other Kind of Love. 1930 Just Imagine. 1931 Bad Company. 1939 Spirit of Culver. 1947 Boomerang; Kiss of Death. 1949 My Foolish Heart. 1950 Branded; Woman on the Run; The Reformer and the Redhead; Edge of Doom. 1951 Fourteen Hours; Here Comes the Groom; I Want You. 1952 Just across the Street; Somebody Loves Me. 1953 Small Town Girl; Battle Circus; Devil's Canyon. 1954 The Wild One; Drum Beat; Young at Heart. 1955 Underwater!; Guys and Dolls; Love Me or Leave Me. 1956 Ransom; Written on the Wind; Between Heaven and Hell. 1957 Men in War; My Man Godfrey. 1958 The Lineup; The Tempest. 1959 They Came to Cordura; Orazi et Curiazzi (Duel of Champions—US 1964). 1960 Cimarron. 1961 Posse from Hell.

KEITH, SHERWOOD (Sherwood Keith LaCount)

Born: 1912. Died: Feb. 21, 1972, Hollywood, Calif. (cancer). Screen, stage and television actor. Married to radio actress Louise Winter.

Appeared in: 1961 The Case of Patty Smith (aka The Shame of Patty Smith); The Silent Call. 1963 Terrified. 1964 The Best Man. 1965 Dear Brigitte. 1968 Funny Girl. 1969 Pendulum.

KELCEY, HERBERT

Born: 1856, England. Died: July 10, 1917, Bayport, N.Y. Stage and screen actor.

Appeared in: 1914 After the Ball. 1916 The Sphinx.

KELLARD, RALPH

Born: June 16, 1882, New York, N.Y. Died: Feb. 5, 1955. Stage and screen actor.

Appeared in: 1915 Her Mother's Secret. 1916 The Precious Racket; Pearl of the Army (serial); The Shielding Shadow (serial). 1918 The Hillcrest Mystery. 1919 Scream in the Night. 1920 The Cost; The Restless Sex; The Master Mind. 1921 Love, Hate and a Woman. 1924 Virtuous Liars. 1930 Women Everywhere. 1931 Upper Underworld; The Ruling Voice.

KELLAWAY, CECIL

Born: Aug. 22, 1893, Capetown, So. Africa. Died: Feb. 28, 1973, West Los Angeles, Calif. Screen, stage, radio, television actor, film director, stage producer and screenwriter. Father of actor Bryan Kellaway. Nominated for 1948 Academy Award as Best Supporting Actor in Luck of the Irish and in 1967 for Guess Who's Coming to Dinner?

Appeared in: 1937 It Isn't Done. 1938 Double Danger; Everybody's Doing It; Law of the Underworld; Tarnished Angel; This Marriage Business; Maid's Night Out; Night Spot; Wise Girl; Blonde Cheat. 1939 Wuthering Heights; Intermezzo—A Love Story; We are Not Alone; Mexican Spitfire; The Sun Never Sets; The Under-Pup. 1940 The Invisible Man Returns; The House of the Seven Gables; Brother Orchid; Phantom Raiders; The Mummy's Hand; Diamond Frontier; Mexican Spitfire Out West; The Letter; Lady with Red Hair; South of Suez. 1941 West Point Widow; Burma Convoy; Appointment for Love; New York Town; The Night of January 16th; A Very Young Lady; Small Town Deb; Bahama Passage. 1942 The Lady Has Plans; Take a Letter Darling; Are Husbands Necessary?; I Married a Witch; My Heart Belongs to Daddy; Night in New Orleans; Star-Spangled Rhythm. 1943 The Crystal Ball; It Ain't Hay; The Good Fellows; Forever and a Day. 1944 Frenchman's Creek; Mrs. Parkington; And Now Tomorrow; Practically Yours. 1945 Love Letters; Bring on the Girls; Kitty. 1946 The Postman Always Rings Twice; Easy to Wed; Monsieur Beaucaire; The Cockeyed Miracle. 1947 Unconquered; Always Together; Variety Girl. 1948 The Luck of the Irish; Joan of Arc; The Decision of Christopher Blake; Portrait of Jennie. 1949 Down to the Sea in Ships. 1950 Kim; The Reformer and the Redhead; Harvey. 1951 Half Angel; Francis Goes to the Races; Katie Did It; The Highwayman. 1952 Just Across the Street; My Wife's Best Friend. 1953 Thunder in the East; Young Bess; The Beast from 20,000 Fathoms; Cruisin' Down the River; Paris Model; Hurricane at Pilgrim Hill. 1955 Interrupted Melody; The Prodigal; The Female on the Beach. 1956 Toy Tiger. 1957 Johnny Trouble. 1958 The Proud Rebel. 1959 The Shaggy Dog. 1960 The Private Lives of Adam and Eve; The Cage of Evil; The Walking Target. 1961 Tammy Tell Me True; Francis of Assisi. 1962 Zotz! 1963 The Cardinal. 1965 Hush . . . Hush, Sweet Charlotte. 1966 Spinout. 1967 Guess Who's Coming to Dinner?; Fitzwilly; The Adventures of Bullwhip Griffin; A Garden of Cucumbers. 1970 Getting Straight.

KELLER, GERTRUDE

Born: 1881. Died: July 12, 1951, Hollywood, Calif. Screen and stage actress. Appeared in silent films.

KELLER, NAN

Died: Dec. 10, 1975, Oklahoma City, Okla. Vaudeville, radio and screen actress. Appeared in vaudeville with her sister and brother in an act billed as "Keller Sisters and Lynch."

Appeared in: 1930 Metro Movietone Act #88.

KELLER, NELL CLARK

Born: 1876. Died: Sept. 2, 1965, Tacoma, Wash. Screen and stage actress.

Appeared in: 1922 Ten Nights in a Bar Room. 1924 The Virgin. 1925 Lightnin'.

KELLERMAN, ANNETTE

Born: July 6, 1887, Sydney, N.S.W., Australia. Died: Oct. 30, 1975, Southport, Australia. Screen, stage, vaudeville actress, champion swimmer and dancer. Known as Australia's "Million Dollar Mermaid."

Appeared in: 1909 "Miss Annette Kellerman." 1914 Neptune's Daughter. 1916 A Daughter of the Gods. 1917 The Honor System. 1918 Queen of the Sea. 1920 What Women Love; The Art of Diving. 1924 Venus of the South Seas.

KELLEY, BOB

Born: 1917. Died: Sept. 9, 1966. Screen, radio and television actor.

Appeared in: 1957 The Fuzzy Pink Nightgown.

KELLOGG, CONELIA

Born: 1877. Died: Feb. 21, 1934, Los Angeles, Calif. Screen actress and fashion model.

Appeared in: 1928 Lingerie.

KELLY, DON (Donald Patrick Kelly aka DON O'KELLY)

Born: Mar. 17, 1924, New York, N.Y. Died: Oct. 2, 1966, Culver City, Calif. (pneumonia, etc.). Screen, stage and television actor.

Appeared in: 1957 The Big Land; Bombers B-52; The Crooked Circle. 1958 The Notorious Mr. Monks; Suicide Battalion; Tank Battalion. 1961 Frontier Uprising. 1962 Shoot Out at Big Sag. 1966 The Hostage.

KELLY, DOROTHY "DOT"

Born: Feb. 12, 1894, Philadelphia, Pa. Died: May 31, 1966, Minneapolis, Minn. (cerebral hemorrhage). Screen actress. Do not confuse with actress Dorothy H. Kelly (dec. 1969).

Appeared in: 1912 All for a Girl; Rip Van Winkle; Suing Susan; O'Hare—Squatter and Philosopher; Popular Betty; The Counts; None But the Brave Deserve the Fair. 1913 The Penalties of Reputation; Playing the Pipers; M's Apron Strings; O'Hara's Godchild; Bunny's Honeymoon; Disciplining Daisy; Tricks of the Trade; The Flirt; A Modern Psyche; The Glove; An Unwritten Chapter; My Lady Idleness; The Tables Turned. 1914 The Wheat and the Tares; Two Stepchildren; The Toll; The Love of Pierre LaRosse; The First Indorsement; In the Old Attic; The Vanity Case; Regan's Daughter; A Double Error; The Greater Motive. 1915 Four Grains of Rice; The Kidnapped Stockbroker; In the Days of Famine; The Wheels of Justice; From Out of the Big Snows; The Sultan of Zulon; Pawns of Mars; Stage Money; The Law Decides; A Wireless Rescue; The Man, the Mission and the Maid; Mother's Roses; A Madcap Adventure. 1917 The Money Mill; The Awakening; The Secret Kingdom (serial).

KELLY, DOROTHY HELEN

Born: 1918. Died: Nov. 28, 1969, La Jolla, Calif. (burned to death). Screen actress. Entered films during the 1940s.

KELLY, MRS. FANNIE

Born: 1876. Died: Jan. 27, 1925, Hollywood, Calif. Screen and vaudeville actress. Appeared in vaudeville with her husband Pat Kelly (dec. 1938) in an act billed as "Pat and Fannie Kelly." Entered films with Sennett approx. 1922.

KELLY, GREGORY

Born: 1891. Died: July 9, 1927, New York, N.Y. (heart attack). Screen, stage and vaudeville actor. Married to screen actress Ruth Gordon.

Appeared in: 1924 Manhattan. 1926 The Show-Off.

KELLY, JAMES

Born: 1915. Died: May 5, 1964, Hollywood, Calif. (heart ailment). Screen and vaudeville actor. Appeared in vaudeville as "Tiny" (340 lbs).

KELLY, JOE

Died: May 26, 1959. Screen and radio actor.

Appeared in: 1944 National Barn Dance.

KELLY, JOHN

Born: June 29, 1901, Boston, Mass. Died: Dec 9, 1947. Screen actor.

Appeared in: 1927 After Midnight. 1928 Blindfold; Dressed to Kill. 1929 From Headquarters. 1930 The Man Hunter. 1931 Subway Express. 1932 The Devil is Driving; Hold 'Em Jail. 1933 Three-Cornered Moon; The Bowery. 1934 Goodbye Love; Little Miss Marker; Many Happy Returns; Fifteen Wives; Old-Fashioned Way; Kid Millions. 1935 Navy Wife; Men of the Night; Police Hero Number One; Motive for Revenge; Doctor Socrates. 1936 Timothy's Quest; In Paris—AWOL; Bridge of Sighs; Poor Little Rich Girl; Easy Money; The Gentleman from Louisiana; Polo Joe; Lady Luck; After the Thin Man. 1937 Fugitive in the Sky; 23½ Hours Leave; Angel's Holiday; You Can't Buy Luck; Armored Car; The Big Shot; Portia on Trial. 1938 Bringing Up Baby; Female Fugitive; Convicts at Large; Exposed. 1939 Sergeant Madden; Wolf Call; Meet Dr. Christian. 1940 Young Tom Edison; Road to Singapore; Black Friday; The Green Hornet (serial). 1941 Bowery Boy; The Pittsburgh Kid; Three Sons' O' Guns. 1942 Jailhouse Blues; My Gal Sal; Moontide; Dr. Broadway; Girl Trouble. 1943 No Time for Love; Jack London. 1944 Summer Storm; Wing and a Prayer. 1945 Blonde from Brooklyn; The Tiger Woman. 1946 Joe Palooka—Champ; The Tiger Woman. 1948 Sofia.

KELLY, JOHN T.

Born: 1852, South Boston, Mass. Died: Jan. 16, 1922, New York, N.Y. (Bright's disease). Screen, stage, vaudeville actor, song and dance man and songwriter. Divorced from actress Florence Moore Eques with whom he appeared in a vaudeville sketch billed as "A Game of Con." He also appeared in vaudeville with Thomas J. Ryan in an act billed as "Kelly and Ryan" and later appeared with Dan Mason in an act billed as "Kelly and Mason."

KELLY, KITTY

Born: 1902, New York, N.Y. Died: June 29, 1968, Hollywood, Calif. (cancer). Stage and screen actress.

Appeared in: 1925 A Kiss in the Dark. 1930 The Head Man (short). 1931 Behind Office Doors; White Shoulders; Bachelor Apartment; La Nuit est a Nous (The Night Is Ours). 1932 Men of Chance; Ladies of the Jury; Girl Crazy. 1933 The Girl in 419; Too Much Harmony. 1934 All of Me; A Woman's Man; The Lemon Drop Kid. 1935 Beginner's Luck (short); The Farmer Takes a Wife. 1937 Blossoms on Broadway; Heart's Desire. 1938 Men with Wings. 1939 Grand Jury Secrets; All Women Have Secrets; The Mutiny of the Elsinore; Geronimo. **1940** Women without Names. **1941** The Mad Doctor. **1942** The Lady Is Willing. **1943** So Proudly We Hail. **1958** The Lost Missile.

KELLY, LEW

Born: 1879, St. Louis, Mo. Died: June 10, 1944, Los Angeles, Calif. Screen, stage, vaudeville and burlesque actor.

Appeared in: **1929** Barnum Was Right. **1930** The Woman Racket; The Chumps (short). **1931** Heaven on Earth. **1932** Scandal for Sale; The Miracle Man; Pack Up Your Troubles. **1933** State Trooper; Strange People; Laughter in Hell. **1934** What's Your Racket?; Six of a Kind; Old Fashioned Way; Something Simple (short); Fixing a Stew (short). **1935** The Nitwits; Diamond Jim; The Man on the Flying Trapeze; Circumstantial Evidence; Death from a Distance; Public Opinion; Hit and Rum (short); Salesmanship Ahoy (short). **1936** Three of a Kind; Wild Brian Kent; Rainbow on the River; The Man I Marry. **1937** Paradise Express; All Over Town; Forlorn River; Western Gold; Some Blondes Are Dangerous. **1938** Born to Be Wild; Man from Music Mountain; The Overland Express; Lawless Valley; Flirting with Fate; Painted Desert; Gold Mine in the Sky. **1939** Tough Kid; Home Boner (short); Three Texas Steers. **1940** Shooting High. **1942** Cooks and Crooks (short). **1943** Lady of Burlesque; Taxi, Mister. **1944** To Heir Is Human (short).

KELLY, MARY "BUBBLES"

Born: 1895, Chicago, Ill. Died: June 7, 1941, Hollywood, Calif. Screen, stage, radio and vaudeville actress.

Appeared in: **1937** Universal short. **1940** Love Thy Neighbor. **1941** Model Wife.

KELLY, MAURICE

Born: Mar. 6, 1928, Maidstone, England. Died: Aug. 28, 1974, Hollywood, Calif. (heart attack). Screen, stage, vaudeville actor and dancer.

Appeared in: **1940** You Will Remember; Old Mother Riley in Business. **1942** Went the Day Well? (aka 48 Hours—US 1944). **1943** My Learned Friend; It's That Man Again. **1946** 'Till the Clouds Roll By. **1965** The Family Jewels.

KELLY, NELL

Born: 1910, Memphis, Tenn. Died: Dec. 16, 1939, New York, N.Y. (diabetes). Screen, stage and vaudeville actress.

Appeared in: **1928** College Swing. **1935** The following shorts: Rhythm of Paree; Sorority Blues; Perfect Thirty-Sixes. **1936** Thanks, Mr. Cupid (short).

KELLY, PAT (Patrick J. Kelly)

Born: July 18, 1891, Philadelphia, Pa. Died: Mar. 19, 1938. Screen and vaudeville actor. Married to actress Fannie Kelly (dec. 1925) with whom he appeared in vaudeville in an act billed as "Pat and Fannie Kelly."

Appeared in: **1916** Love Under Cover; Heart Strategy; A Mail Governess; Done in Oil!; His Hereafter. **1917** His Rise and Tumble; Her Birthday Knight; Skirt Strategy; His Marriage Failure; His Perfect Day; A Warm Reception; Half and Half.

KELLY, PAUL (Paul Michael Kelly)

Born: Aug. 9, 1899, Brooklyn, N.Y. Died: Nov. 6, 1956, Los Angeles, Calif. (heart attack). Screen, stage and television actor. Married to actress Dorothy MacKaye (dec. 1940) and later married to actress Claire Owen (Zona Mardell). Served two years for manslaughter of Miss MacKaye's first husband, stage actor Ray Raymond.

Appeared in: **1911** How Milly Became an Actress. **1912** A Juvenile Love Affair; An Expensive Shine; Captain Barnacle's Waif. **1913** The Mouse and the Lion; Counselor Bobby. **1914** Lillian's Dilemma; Heartease. **1915** The Shabbies; A Family Picnic. **1916** Myrtle the Manicurist; Claudia. **1918** Fit to Fight (U.S. government information film). **1919** Ann of Green Gables. **1920** Uncle Sam of Freedom Ridge. **1921** The Old Oaken Bucket; The Great Adventure. **1926** The New Klondike. **1927** Special Delivery; Slide, Kelly, Slide. **1932** Girl from Calgary. **1933** Broadway thru a Keyhole. **1934** The Love Captive; The President Vanishes; Blind Date; Death on the Diamond; Side Streets; School for Girls. **1935** When a Man's a Man; Star of Midnight; Public Hero No. 1; Silk Hat Kid; My Marriage; Speed Devils. **1936** Here Comes Trouble; Song and Dance Man; The Country Beyond; Women Are Trouble; Murder with Pictures; The Accusing Finger; It's a Great Life. **1937** Join the Marines; Fit for a King; Parole Racket; Navy Blue and Gold; The Frame Up; It Happened Out West. **1938** Island in the Sky; Nurse from Brooklyn; The Devil's Party; The Missing Guest; Torchy Blane in Panama; Juvenile Court; Adventure in Sahara. **1939** Forged Passport; The Flying Irishman; 6,000 Enemies; Within the Law; The Roaring Twenties. **1940** Girls under 21; Invisible Stripes; Queen of the Mob; The Howards of Virginia; Flight Command; Wyoming. **1941** Ziegfeld Girl; I'll Wait for You; Parachute Battalion; Mystery Ship; Mr. and Mrs. North. **1942** Call Out the Marines; Tarzan's New York Adventure; Tough As They Come; Not a Ladies' Man; Flying Tigers; The Secret Code (serial); Gang Busters (serial). **1943** The Man from Music Mountain. **1944** The Story of Dr. Wassell; That's My Baby; Dead Man's Eyes; Faces in the Fog. **1945** Grissly's Millions; China's Little Devils; San Antonio; Allotment Wives. **1946** The Cat Creeps;

Strange Impersonation; Strange Journey; Deadline for Murder; The Glass Alibi. **1947** Fear in the Night; Wyoming; Adventures of the North; Crossfire. **1949** Thelma Jordan; Guilty of Treason. **1950** Side Street; There's a Girl in My Heart; The Secret Fury; Frenchie; Treason. **1951** The Painted Hills. **1952** Springfield Rifle. **1953** Split Second; Gunsmoke. **1954** Duffy of San Quentin; The High and the Mighty; Johnny Dark; Steel Cage. **1955** Narcotic Squad; The Square Jungle. **1956** Storm Center. **1957** Bailout at 43,000.

KELLY, WALTER C.

Born: Oct. 29, 1873, Mineville, N.Y. Died: Jan. 6, 1939, Philadelphia, Pa. (result of head injury). Screen, stage, vaudeville actor and screenwriter.

Appeared in: **1931** Seas Beneath. **1935** McFadden's Flats; The Virginia Judge. **1936** Laughing Irish Eyes.

KELLY, WILLIAM J.

Born: c. 1875, Boston, Mass. Died: May 17, 1949, New York, N.Y. (heart attack). Stage and screen actor.

Appeared in: **1924** Lily of the Dust. **1925** Parisian Nights; Proud Flesh. **1926** Her Second Chance. **1933** Below the Sea; The Woman Accused. **1934** Six of a Kind. **1943** Spook Louder (short).

KELSEY, FRED A.

Born: Aug. 20, 1884, Sandusky, Ohio. Died: Sept. 2, 1961, Hollywood, Calif. Screen actor. Entered films in 1909.

Appeared in: **1921** Four Horsemen of the Apocalypse (played four roles); The Match-Breaker; There Are No Villains; Puppets of Fate. **1922** The Song of Life; Captain Fly-by-Night; Manslaughter; One Clear Call; South of Suva; Deserted at the Altar; Don't Shoot. **1923** The Eleventh Hour; Lovebound; Bag and Baggage; The Bishop of the Ozarks; Souls for Sale; Lights Out. **1924** Stepping Lively; The Yankee Consul; Madonna On the Streets. **1925** Excuse Me; Seven Sinners; Smooth As Satin; Seven Keys to Baldpate; Paths to Paradise; Friendly Enemies; Youth and Adventure. **1926** Atta Boy; The Social Highwayman; That's My Baby; Doubling with Danger. **1927** The Third Degree; Held by the Law; Thirteenth Juror; Thirteenth Hour; The Gorilla; Soft Cushions. **1928** Ladies Night in a Turkish Bath; Harold Teen; A Midnight Adventure; Tenderloin; The Wright Idea; On Trial. **1929** The Donovan Affair; The Faker; The Fall of Eve; The Last Warning; Naughty Baby; Smiling Irish Eyes. **1930** Murder on the Roof; She Got What She Wanted; Men without Law; The Laurel and Hardy Murder Case (short); Only Saps Work; The Big Jewel Case; Going Wild; Wide Open; Scarlet Pages. **1931** The Falling Star; Subway Express; Young Donovan's Kid. **1932** Discarded Lovers; Love in High Gear; Guilty As Hell; Red Haired Alibi; The Iceman's Ball (short); Shopping with Wifie (short). **1933** Girl Missing; School for Girls; Quiet, Please (short); Grin and Bear It (short). **1934** Young and Beautiful; Shadows of Sing Sing; Beloved; The Crime Doctor; I'll Be Suing You (short). **1935** One Frightened Night; Danger Ahead; Public Menace; Hot Off the Press; The Sagebrush Troubadour; Carnival; Death Flies East; Diamond Jim; Lightning Strikes Twice; plus the following shorts: Nurse to You; Horses Collars; Hot Money. **1936** At Sea Ashore (short). **1937** All Over Town; Super Sleuth; That I May Live; Time Out for Romance; A Damsel in Distress. **1938** Many Sappy Returns (short); Berth Quakes (short); Mr. Moto's Gamble. **1939** Rough Riders' Round-Up; Too Busy to Work; plus the following shorts: Tiny Troubles; Clock Wise; Moving Vanities. **1940** The Lone Wolf Keeps a Date; A Bundle of Bliss (short); Mutiny in the County (short). **1942** Counter Espionage; Yankee Doodle Dandy; Gentleman Jim; Murder in the Big House; X Marks the Spot; Dear! Dear! **1943** Murder on the Waterfront; True to Life; One Dangerous Night. **1944** Adventures of Mark Twain; Crime by Night; The Great Mystic; Busy Buddies (short). **1945** Come Out Fighting; How Do You Do?; plus the following shorts: Snooper Service; Micro-Phonies; If a Body Meets a Body. **1946** Bringing Up Father; Strange Mr. Gregory; Monkey Businessmen (short); So You Want to Play the Horses (short). **1948** Jiggs and Maggie in Court; The Noose Hangs High. **1951** So You Want to Buy a Used Car (short); So You Want to Be a Bachelor (short). **1952** Hans Christian Andersen; O. Henry's Full House; A Blissful Blunder (short). **1953** Murder without Tears; plus the following shorts: Pardon My Backfire; So You Want to Be a Musician; So You Want a Television Set; So You Think You Can't Sleep. **1954** Racing Blood; plus the following shorts: So You Want to Be Your Own Boss; So You Want to Be a Banker; So You're Taking in a Roomer. **1955** So You Don't Trust Your Wife (short).

KELSO, MAYME

Born: Feb. 28, 1867, Dayton, Ohio. Died: June 5, 1946, South Pasadena, Calif. (heart attack). Screen, stage and vaudeville actress.

Appeared in: **1912** Human Hearts. **1915** The Bigger Man; One Million Dollars; The Warning; The Little Singer; Man and His Angel. **1917** Castles for Two; The Cost of Hatred; The Silver Partner; The Secret Game. **1918** The Widow's Might; The Thing We Love; The White Man's Law; The Honor of His House; Old Wives for New; His Birthright; The Cruise of the Make-Believers; Mirandy Smiles. **1919** In for Thirty Days; You Never Saw Such a Girl; Johnny Get Your Gun; Experimental Marriage; Men, Women and Money; Daughter of the Wolf; Male and Female; Peg O' My Heart; Don't Change Your Husband; Cheating Cheaters; Why Smith Left Home. **1920** Jack Straw;

The Week-end; Simple Souls; The Hope; Never Get Married; Help Wanted—Male; The Furnace; Why Change Your Wife?; Conrad in Quest of His Youth; The Brand of Lopez. **1921** Ducks and Drakes; Her Sturdy Oak; The Lost Romance; The March Hare; One Wild Week. **1922** For the Defense; Glass Houses; Kick In; The Woman Who Walked Alone; Clarence; Penrod. **1923** Hollywood; The Love Piker; The Marriage Market; Modern Matrimony; Slander the Woman; The World's Applause. **1924** Girls Men Forget; Nellie—The Beautiful Cloak Model. **1925** The Danger Signal; Flaming Waters; The Unchastened Woman; Dollar Down; Seven Keys to Baldpate. **1926** Lightning Reporter; Whispering Wires. **1927** Vanity; The Drop Kick.

KELTON, PERT

Born: 1907, Great Falls, Mont. Died: Oct. 30, 1968, Westwood, N.Y. (stroke). Screen, stage, vaudeville, television and radio actress. Married to actor Ralph Bell.

Appeared in: **1929** Sally. **1930** Hot Curves. **1933** Wine, Women and Song; Bed of Roses; The Bowery. **1934** Pursued; The Meanest Gal in Town; Sing and Like It; Bachelor Bait. **1935** Lightning Strikes Twice; Hooray for Love; Annie Oakley; Mary Burns, Fugitive. **1936** Sitting on the Moon; Kelly the Second; Cain and Mabel; Pan Handlers (short). **1937** Women of Glamour; The Hit Parade; Meet the Boy Friend; Laughing at Trouble. **1938** Slander House; Whispering Enemies; Rhythm of the Saddle. **1962** The Music Man (stage and film versions). **1965** Love and Kisses. **1969** The Comic (aka Billy Bright).

KEMBLE-COOPER, VIOLET

Born: 1886, London, England. Died: Aug. 17, 1961, Hollywood, Calif. (Parkinson's disease—stroke). Stage and screen actress. Daughter of stage actor Frank Kemble-Cooper (dec. 1918). Sister of actress Lillian (dec. 1977) and actor Anthony Kemble-Cooper.

Appeared in: **1933** Our Betters. **1934** The Fountain. **1935** David Copperfield; Vanessa, Her Love Story; Cardinal Richelieu. **1936** Romeo and Juliet; The Invisible Ray.

KEMP, EVERETT

Born: 1874, Shelbyville, Ill. Died: Oct. 1, 1958, Kansas City, Mo. (heart attack). Screen, stage, radio and television actor. Appeared in shorts with Mr. and Mrs. Sidney Drew (1915–1919).

KEMP, HAL

Born: 1904. Died: Dec. 21, 1940, Madera, Calif. (pneumonia after auto injuries). Orchestra leader and screen actor.

Appeared in: **1938** Radio City Revels.

KEMP, PAUL

Born: May 20, 1899, Godesburg, Germany. Died: Aug. 13, 1953, Godesberg, West Germany. Stage and screen actor.

Appeared in: **1931** Die Blonde Nachtigall; Die Grosse Sehnsucht; Lumpenball; Dolly Macht Karriere. **1932** Gitta Entdeckt Ihr Herz; Sehnsucht 202 (Longing 202); Mein Herz Ruft Nach Dir (A Song for You); Der Fluchtling aus Chikago (US 1936). **1934** Die Verkaufte Braut; Roman Einer Nacht; Mit dir Durch Dink und Duenn; Czardasfuerstin (The Czardas Duchess—US 1935); Charley's Tante (Charlie's Aunt, stage and film versions); Prinzessin Turandot. **1935** Amphytrion; Les Dieux s'Amusent; Das Lied vom Glueck (The Song of Happiness). **1936** Das Schloss im Sueden; Der Schuechterne Casanova; Heisses Blut; Der Mutige Seefahrer; Boccaccio. **1937** Glueckskinder; Die Schwebende Jungfrau. **1938** Capriccio; Ihr Leibhusar; The Charm of la Boheme; Aus den Wolken Kommt das Glueck (Luck Comes from the Clouds). **1939** Dingehort Mein Herz (My Heart Belongs to Thee); Blumen aus Nizza (Flowers from Nice); Solo per Danne. **1940** Das Leichte Madchen. **1941** Immer nur Du. **1942** Ein Windstoss. **1944** Fahrt ins Abenteurer. **1947** Triumph der Liebe; Das Singende Haus. **1948** Das Himmlische Walzer; Lysistrata. **1949** Lambert Fuhlt Sich Bedroht. **1950** Kein Engel; Der Mann der Sich Selber Sucht; Madchen mit Beztehunger; Die Nacht Ohne Sunde; Die Dritte von Rechts. **1951** Die Mitternachtsvenus; Engel im Abendlkleid; Mutter sein Dagegen Sehr. **1952** In Muchen Steht ein Hofbrauhaus; Die Diebin von Bagdad; Konigin der Arena. **1953** Salto Mortale; Liebeskrieg nach Noten; Gluk Muss Man Haben. **1960** The Threepenny Opera.

KEMPER, CHARLES

Born: 1901. Died: May 12, 1950, Burbank, Calif. (auto crash injuries). Screen, stage, minstrel, vaudeville and radio actor.

Appeared in: **1929** Beach Babies; Haunted; His Operation; Wednesday at the Ritz. **1945** The Southerner. **1946** Gallant Journey; Scarlet Street; Sister Kenny. **1947** The Shocking Miss Pilgrim; Gunfighters; That Hagen Girl. **1948** Fighting Father Dunne; Fury at Furnace Creek; Yellow Sky. **1949** Adventure in Baltimore; The Doolins of Oklahoma; Belle Starr's Daughter; Intruder in the Dust. **1950** A Ticket to Tomahawk; Mr. Music; Stars in My Crown; Mad with Much Heart; California Passage; The Nevadan; Wagonmaster; Where Danger Lives. **1951** On Dangerous Ground.

KENDALL, CY (Cyrus W. Kendall)

Born: Mar. 10, 1898, St. Louis, Mo. Died: July 22, 1953, Woodland Hills, Calif. Screen, stage and radio actor.

Appeared in: **1936** Man Hunt; Hot Money; Dancing Feet; The Public Pays (short); King of the Pecos; Bulldog Edition; The Lonely Trail; Women Are Trouble; Sworn Enemy; Sea Spoilers; Dancing Pirate. **1937** Once a Doctor; White Bondage; They Won't Forget; Without Warning; Angel's Holiday; Borrowing Trouble; Meet the Boy Friend; The Shadow Strikes. **1938** Rawhide; Crime School; Valley of the Giants; The Night Hawks; Hollywood Hotel; The Invisible Menace; Hawaii Calls. **1939** Stand up and Fight; Twelve Crowded Hours; Fugitive at Large; Angels Wash Their Faces; Calling All Marines; Pacific Liner. **1940** The House across the Bay; The Saint Takes Over; Prairie Law; The Fargo Kid; Men without Souls; Andy Hardy Meets Debutante; Youth Will Be Served; 'Til We Meet Again. **1941** Billy the Kid; Midnight Angel; Johnny Eager; Coffins on Wheels (short); Robin Hood of the Pecos; Ride, Kelly, Ride; Mystery Ship. **1942** Fly by Night; Road to Morocco; Tarzan's New York Adventure; The Wife Takes a Flyer; Silver Queen. **1943** A Lady Takes a Chance; After Midnight with Boston Blackie. **1944** The Chinese Cat; Laura; Outlaw Trail; Roger Touhy, Gangster; A Wave, a Wac and a Marine; Whispering Footsteps; Crime by Night; Girl Rush; The Last Ride; Dancing in Manhattan; Lady in the Death House; The Whistler. **1945** Scarlet Street; She Gets Her Man; Docks of New York; The Cisco Kid Returns; Wilson; Tahiti Nights; The Tiger Woman; Shadow of Terror; Power of the Whistler; A Thousand and One Nights. **1946** Blonde for a Day; The Glass Alibi; The Invisible Informer. **1947** The Farmer's Daughter; Sinbad the Sailor; In Self Defense. **1948** In This Corner; Fighting Mad; Sword of the Avenger; Perilous Waters. **1949** Secret Agent X-9 (serial).

KENDALL, HENRY

Born: May 28, 1898, London, England. Died: June 9, 1962, France (heart attack). Screen, stage actor, stage producer, screenwriter and songwriter.

Appeared in: **1921** Mr. Pim Passes By; Tilly of Bloomsbury. **1930** French Leave. **1931** The House Opposite; The Flying Fool; Rich and Strange (aka East of Shanghai—US 1932). **1932** The Innocents of Chicago (aka Why Saps Leave Home—US); Watch Beverly; Mr. Bill the Conqueror (aka The Man Who Won—US 1933). **1933** The Shadow; The Iron Stair; Counsel's Opinion; Timbuctoo; King of the Ritz; The Man Outside; Great Stuff; The Stickpin; This Week of Grace; The Ghost Camera; The Flaw. **1934** The Girl in Possession; Guest of Honour; Without You; The Man I Want; Sometimes Good; Leave It to Blanche; The Wigan Express (aka Death at Broadcasting House—US); Crazy People. **1935** Death on the Set (aka Murder on the Set—US 1936); Three Witnesses; Lend Me Your Wife. **1936** A Wife or Two; Twelve Good Men; The Amazing Quest of Ernest Bliss (aka Romance and Riches—US 1937); The Mysterious Mr. Davis (aka My Partner Mr. Davis). **1937** Take a Chance; The Compulsory Wife; Side Street Angel; It's Not Cricket; Ship's Concert; School for Husbands (US 1939). **1943** The Butler's Dilemma. **1945** 29 Acacia Avenue (aka The Facts of Love—US 1949); Dumb Dora Discovers Tobacco. **1947** Fag End (reissue of Dumb Dora Discovers—1945). **1949** Helter Skelter; **1952** The Voice of Merrill (aka Murder Will Out—US). **1955** An Alligator Named Daisy (US 1957). **1961** The Shadow of the Cat.

KENDALL, KAY (Justine McCarthy)

Born: 1926, Hull, Yorkshire, England. Died: Sept. 6, 1959, London, England (leukemia). Stage and screen actress. Married to actor Rex Harrison.

Appeared in: **1945** Waltz Time. **1946** Caesar and Cleopatra; London Town (aka My Heart Goes Crazy—US 1953). **1950** Dance Hall. **1951** Happy-Go-Lovely; Lady Godiva Rides Again (US 1954). **1952** Wings of Danger (aka Dead on Course—US); Curtain Up (US 1953); It Started in Paradise (US 1953). **1953** Street of Shadows (aka Shadow Man—US); Mantrap (aka Woman in Hiding—US); Genevieve (US 1954); The Square Ring (US 1955); Meet Mr. Lucifer. **1954** Doctor in the House (US 1955); Fast and Loose. **1955** The Constant Husband; Simon and Laura (US 1956). **1956** The Adventures of Quentin Durward; Abdullah's Harem. **1957** Les Girls. **1958** The Reluctant Debutant. **1960** Once More, with Feeling.

KENDRICK, BRIAN

Born: 1930. Died: Mar. 11, 1970, Ruislip, England (heart attack). Screen, television and radio actor.

KENNEDY, CHARLES RANN

Born: 1871, England. Died: Feb. 16, 1950, Westwood, Calif. Screen, stage actor and playwright. Married to actress Edith Wynne Matthison (dec. 1955).

Appeared in: **1923** Little Old New York. **1934** Crime without Passion.

KENNEDY, DOUGLAS (Douglas Richards Kennedy)

Born: Sept. 14, 1915, New York, N.Y. Died: Aug. 10, 1973, Kailua, Hawaii (cancer). Screen and television actor.

Appeared in: **1940** Opened by Mistake (film debut); The Way of All Flesh; Northwest Mounted Police; Women without Names. **1941** The Roundup; The Great Mr. Nobody. **1947** Possessed; The Unfaithful; Dark Passage; That Hagen Girl; Always Together; Deep Valley; Nora Prentiss. **1948** To the Victor; The Decision of Christopher Blake; Adventures of Don Juan; Whiplash; Embraceable You; Johnny Belinda. **1949** South of St. Louis; Look for the Silver Lining; One Last Fling; Fighting Man of the Plains; East Side, West Side; Ranger of Cherokee Strip; The Strawberry Blonde; Flaxy Martin; South of Rio; Whirlpool. **1950** Montana; The Caribou Trail; Convicted; Chain Gang. **1951** Oh Susanna; I Was an American Spy; The Texas Rangers; Callaway Went Thataway; The Lion Hunters; China Corsair. **1952** The Next Voice You Hear; For Men Only; Ride the Man Down; Fort Osage; Indian Uprising; Last Train from Bombay. **1953** War Paint; Gun Belt; Torpedo Alley; Safari Drums; San Antone; Sea of Lost Ships; Mexican Manhunt; Jack McCall—Desperado. **1954** Massacre Canyon; Sitting Bull; The Big Chase; Lone Gun; Ketchikan; Cry Vengeance. **1955** The Eternal Sea; Wyoming Renegades; Strange Lady in Town. **1956** The Last Wagon; Wiretappers; Strange Intruder. **1957** Chicago Confidential; Rockabilly Baby; The Land Unknown; Last of the Badmen; Hell's Crossroads. **1958** The Lone Ranger and the Lost City of Gold; The Bonnie Parker Story. **1959** The Lone Texan; The Alligator People. **1961** Flight of the Lost Baloon. **1967** The Fastest Guitar Alive; Valley of Mystery. **1968** The Destructors.

KENNEDY, EDGAR

Born: Apr. 26, 1890, Monterey, Calif. Died: Nov. 9, 1948, Woodland Hills, Calif. (throat cancer). Screen, stage and vaudeville actor. Married to actress Patricia Allwyn, with whom he appeared in vaudeville. Was one of the original Keystone Kops. Was star of "Mr. Average Man" series from 1929 to 1934.

Appeared in: **1912** Hoffmeyer's Legacy. **1914** The Star Boarder; Twenty Minutes of Love; Caught in a Cabaret (reissued as The Jazz Waiter); The Knockout (reissued as The Pugilist); Our Country Cousin; The Noise of Bombs; Getting Acquainted; Tillie's Punctured Romance. **1915** Fatty's Tin Type Tangle; A Game Old Knight; The Great Vacuum Robbery. **1916** His Hereafter (working title Murry's Mix-up); His Bitter Pill; Madcap Ambrose; Bombs; The Scoundrel's Tale; Ambrose's Cup of Woe; Bucking Society. **1917** Her Fame and Shame; Oriental Love; Her Torpedoed Love. **1918** She Loved Him Plenty. **1922** The Leather Pushers. **1924** The Night Message. **1925** Golden Princess; His People; Proud Heart. **1926** Better 'Ole; My Old Dutch; Oh! What a Nurse! **1927** Wedding Bill$; The Wrong Mr. Wright. **1928** The Chinese Parrot; plus the following shorts: The Finishing Touch; Leave 'Em Laughing; Should Married Men Go Home?; Two Tars. **1929** The Gay Old Bird; Going Crooked; They Had to See Paris; Trent's Last Case; plus the following shorts: Moan and Groan, Inc.; Great Gobs; Hotter Than Hot; Bacon Grabbers; Unaccustomed as We Are; Hurdy-Gurdy; Dad's Day; Perfect Day; Angora Love. **1930** The following shorts: Night Owls; Shivering Shakespeare; The First Seven Years; When the Wind Blows; The Real McCoy; All Teed Up; Fifty Million Husbands; Girl Shock; Dollar Dizzy; Looser Than Loose; The Head Guy; The Big Kick; Doctor's Orders; Bigger and Better; Ladies Last. **1931** Midnight Patrol; Bad Company; High Gear (short); Love Fever (short); "Mr. Average Man" series including: Rough House Rhythm; Lemon Meringue; Thanks Again; Camping Out. **1932** Carnival Boat; The Penguin Pool Murder; Little Orphan Annie; "Mr. Average Man" series including: Bon Voyage; Mother-In-Law's Day; Giggle Water; The Golf Chump; Parlor, Bedroom and Wrath; Fish Feathers. **1933** Scarlet River; Crossfire; Professional Sweetheart; Son of the Border; Duck Soup; Tillie and Gus; Kickin' the Crown Around (short—seen in stock footage); "Mr. Average Man" series including: Art in the Raw; The Merchant of Menace; Good Housewrecking; Quiet, Please; What Fur; Grin and Bear It. **1934** Flirting with Danger; All of Me; Heat Lightning; Murder on the Blackboard; The Silver Streak; We're Rich Again; Kid Millions; Twentieth Century; Money Means Nothing; Gridiron Flash; King Kelly of the USA; The Marines Are Coming; "Mr. Average Man" series including: Love on a Ladder; Wrong Direction; In-Laws Are Out; A Blasted Event; Poisoned Ivory. **1935** Living on Velvet; Woman Wanted; The Cowboy Millionaire; Little Big Shot; In Person; A Thousand Dollars a Minute; The Bride Comes Home; Rendezvous at Midnight; A Night at the Biltmore Bowl (short); "Mr. Average Man" series including: Bric-A-Brac; South Seasickness; Sock Me to Sleep; Edgar Hamlet; In Love at 40; Happy Tho Married; Gobs of Trouble (short). **1936** San Francisco; The Return of Jimmy Valentine; Small Town Girl; Mad Holiday; Fatal Lady; Yours for the Asking; Three Men on a Horse; Robin Hood of El Dorado; "Mr. Average Man" series including: Gasoloons; Will Power; High Beer Pressure; Dummy Ache; Vocalizing. **1937** When's Your Birthday?; Super Sleuth; A Star is Born; Double Wedding; True Confession; Hollywood Hotel; "Mr. Average Man" series including: Hillbilly Goat; Bad Housekeeping; Locks and Bonds; Dumb's the Word; Morning, Judge; Edgar and Goliath. **1938** The Black Doll; Scandal Street; Hey! Hey! U.S.A.; Peck's Bad Boy with the Circus; "Mr. Average Man" series including: Ears of Experience; False Roomers; Kennedy's Castle; Fool Coverage; Beaux and Errors; A Clean Sweep. **1939** It's a Wonderful World; Little Accident; Everything's on Ice; Charlie McCarthy, Detective; Laugh It Off; "Mr. Average Man" series including: Maid to Order; Clock Wise; Baby Daze; Feathered Pests; Act Your Age; Kennedy the Great; **1940** Sandy Is a Lady; Dr. Christian Meets the Women; The Quarterback; Margie; Who Killed Aunt Maggie?; Remedy for Riches; Sandy Gets Her Man; Li'l Abner; "Mr. Average Man" series including: Slightly at Sea; Mutiny in the County; 'Taint Legal; Sunk by the Census; Trailer Tragedy; Drafted in the Depot. **1941** The Bride Wore Crutches; Public Enemies; Blondie in Society; "Mr. Average Man" series including: Mad about Moonshine; It Happened All Night; An Apple in His Eye; Westward Ho-Hum; I'll Fix That; A Quiet Fourth. **1942** Snuffy Smith, Yard Bird; Pardon

My Stripes; In Old California; Hillbilly Blitzkrieg; "Mr. Average Man" series including: Heart Burn; Inferior Decorator; Cooks and Crooks; Two for the Money; Rough on Rents; Duck Soup. **1943** The Falcon Strikes Back; Cosmo Jones—Crime Smasher; Air Raid Wardens; Hitler's Madman; The Girl from Monterey; Crazy House; "Mr. Average Man" series including: Hold Your Temper; Indian Signs; Hot Foot; Not on My Account; Unlucky Dog. **1944** It Happened Tomorrow; The Great Alaskan Mystery (serial); "Mr. Average Man" series including: Prunes and Politics; Love Your Landlord; Radio Rampage; The Kitchen Cynic; Feather Your Nest. **1945** Anchors Aweigh; Captain Tugboat Annie; "Mr. Average Man" series including: Alibi Baby; Sleepless Tuesday; What, No Cigarettes?; It's Your Move; You Drive Me Crazy; The Big Beef; Mother-In-Law's Day (and 1932 version). **1946** "Mr. Average Man" series including: Trouble or Nothing; Wall Street Blues; Motor Maniacs; Noisy Neighbors; I'll Build It Myself; Social Terrors. **1947** Heaven Only Knows; Sin of Harold Diddlebock (aka Mad Wednesday—US 1951); "Mr. Average Man" series including: Do or Diet; Heading for Trouble; Host of a Ghost; Television Turmoil; Mind over Mouse. **1948** Variety Time; Unfaithfully Yours; "Mr. Average Man" series including: Brother Knows Best; No More Relatives; How to Clean House; Dig That Gold; Home Canning; Contest Crazy. **1949** My Dream Is Yours. **1960** When Comedy Was King (documentary). **1963** The Sound of Laughter (documentary). **1965** Laurel and Hardy's Laughing '20's (documentary). **1968** The Further Perils of Laurel and Hardy (documentary).

KENNEDY, FREDERICK O.

Born: 1910. Died: Dec. 5, 1958, Natchitoches, La. (killed while filming The Horse Soldiers). Screen actor and stuntman.

Appeared in: **1949** She Wore a Yellow Ribbon. **1950** Rio Grande. **1953** The Charge at Feather River. **1959** The Horse Soldiers.

KENNEDY, HELEN

Died: Oct. 21, 1973, Hollywood, Calif. Screen and vaudeville actress. Mother of actor George Kennedy. Appeared in vaudeville as star of "Le Ballet Classique."

KENNEDY, JOHN F.

Died: Nov. 6, 1960, Hollywood, Calif. Screen actor. Appeared in "Keystone Kop" comedies.

KENNEDY, JOSEPH C.

Born: 1890, Canada. Died: May 4, 1949, Halifax, Canada. Stage and screen actor. Appeared in Canadian Bioscope Co. films.

KENNEDY, JOYCE

Born: 1898, London, England. Died: Mar. 12, 1943, London, England (pneumonia). Stage and screen actress.

Appeared in: **1930** The Man from Chicago (US 1931). **1931** Bracelets. **1932** Say It with Music. **1934** Dangerous Ground; The Return of Bulldog Drummond. **1935** Black Mask. **1936** Debt of Honour; Twelve Good Men; Hail and Farewell; Seven Sinners (aka Doomed Cargo—US). **1937** Big Fella.

KENNEDY, KING

Born: 1904, Kokomo, Ind. Died: Nov. 1974, Los Angeles, Calif. (heart attack). Screen, stage actor, playwright, journalist and public relations executive. Divorced from film producer Harriet Parsons.

Appeared in: **1935** On Probation. **1942** Seven Days' Leave. **1943** Higher and Higher.

KENNEDY, MERNA (Maude Kahler)

Born: Sept. 7, 1908, Kankakee, Ill. Died: Dec. 20, 1944, Los Angeles, Calif. (heart attack). Stage and screen actress. Divorced from dance director Busby Berkeley (dec. 1976).

Appeared in: **1928** The Circus. **1929** Broadway; Barnum Was Right; Skinner Steps Out. **1930** The Rampant Age; Worldly Goods; Midnight Special; Embarrassing Moments; The King of Jazz. **1931** Stepping Out. **1932** The Gay Buckaroo; Ghost Valley; The All American; Laughter in Hell; Red Haired Alibi; Reputation; Lady with a Past. **1933** Come on Tarzan; Big Chance; Easy Millions; Emergency Call; Don't Bet on Love; Arizona to Broadway; Police Call; Son of a Sailor. **1934** Wonder Bar; I Like It That Way.

KENNEDY, TOM

Born: 1884, New York, N.Y. Died: Oct. 6, 1965, Woodland Hills, Calif. (bone cancer). Screen and television actor. Entered films in 1915. (Do not confuse with television host Tom Kennedy.)

Appeared in: **1916** The Village Blacksmith; Hearts and Sparks; Ambrose's Rapid Rise. **1917** Nick of Time Baby. **1921** Serenade; Skirts. **1922** The Flirt; If You Believe It, It's So; Afraid to Fight; The Flaming Hour; Our Leading Citizen. **1923** Scaramouche; With Naked Fists. **1924** Loving Lies; Madonna of the Streets. **1925** The Knockout; As Man Desires; The Best Bad Man; High and Handsome; The Fearless Lover. **1926** Behind the Front; Mantrap; Better 'Ole; Sir Lumberjack; We're in the Navy Now; The Yankee Senor; Born to the West; Man of the Forest. **1927** Fireman Save My Child; Silver Valley; The Mysterious Rider; One Round Hogan; Alias the Deacon. **1928** Hold 'Em Yale; The Cop; Tillie's Punctured Romahce; Love over Night; Marked Money;

None but the Brave; Wife Savers. **1929** The Glad Rag Doll; Post Mortems; Big News; The Cohens and the Kellys in Atlantic City; The Shannons of Broadway; Liberty (short). **1930** See America Thirst; The Big House; Fall Guy. **1931** It Pays to Advertise; Caught; The Gang Busters; Monkey Business. **1932** Pack Up Your Troubles; The Devil Is Driving; The Boudoir Butler (short); Fish Feathers (short). **1933** Blondie Johnson; Man of the Forest; She Done Him Wrong (short). **1934** Hollywood Party; Strictly Dynamite; Down to Their Last Yacht; plus the following shorts: Circus Hoodoo; In the Devil's Doghouse; Odor in the Court. **1935** Bright Lights; Alibi Bye Bye (short); Sock Me to Sleep (short). **1936** Poppy; Hollywood Boulevard; Smart Blonde (short); Free Rent (short). **1937** Fly-Away Baby; Marry the Girl; The Adventurous Blonde; He Couldn't Say No; Behind the Headlines; The Big Shot; Forty Naughty Girls; Living on Love; Married before Breakfast; Armored Car; Swing It, Sailor; She Had to Eat; The Case of the Stuttering Blonde (short). **1938** Making the Headlines; Torchy Blane in Panama; Pardon Our Nerve; Long Shot; Crime Ring; Go Chase Yourself; Wise Girl; Crashing Hollywood; House of Mystery; Blondes at Work; Torchy Gets Her Man; A Criminal Is Born (short). **1939** Torchy Blane in Chinatown; Torchy Runs for Mayor; Covered Trailer; Society Lawyer; Torchy Plays with Dynamite; The Day the Bookies Wept; Mexican Spitfire. **1940** Flowing Gold; Remember the Night; Millionaire Playboy; Curtain Call; Pop Always Pays; Mexican Spitfire Out West; An Angel from Texas; Sporting Blood. **1941** The Great Swindle; Angels with Broken Wings; The Officer and the Lady; Sailors on Leave; Yankee Doodle Andy (short); Man I Cured (short); Mexican Spitfire's Baby. **1942** Pardon My Stripes; Wildcat; plus the following shorts: Home Work; Hold 'em Jail; Pretty Dolly. **1943** Ladies' Day; Dixie; Here Comes Elmer; My Darling Clementine; Petticoat Larceny; Hit Parade of 1943; Stage Door Canteen; Cutie on Duty (short); Wedtime Stories (short). **1944** Rosie the Riveter; Princess and the Pirate; And the Angels Sing; Moonlight and Cactus; plus the following shorts: Love Your Landlord; Radio Rampage; Girls, Girls, Girls. **1945** The Man Who Walked Alone; It Shouldn't Happen to a Dog (short). **1946** The Kid from Brooklyn; Voice of the Whistler; Bringing Up Father; Motor Maniacs (short). **1947** The Burning Cross; The Case of the Baby Sister; The Pretender. **1948** They Live by Night (aka The Twisted Road and Your Red Wagon); The Devil's Cargo; Jinx Money; The Paleface; Thunder in the Pines. **1949** Jackpot Jitters; Square Dance Jubilee; The Mutineers. **1950** Border Rangers. **1951** Havana Rose; Let's Go Navy. **1952** Invasion U.S.A.; Gold Fever; **1953** Loose Loot (short); Spooks (short). **1963** It's a Mad, Mad, Mad, Mad World. **1968** The Further Perils of Laurel and Hardy (documentary).

KENNETH, HARRY D.

Born: 1854. Died: Jan. 18, 1929, Newark, N.J. (brain hemorrhage). Screen, stage and vaudeville actor. Appeared in early Essanay films.

KENNETH, KEITH (aka KEITH HITCHCOCK)

Born: 1887, England. Died: Apr. 11, 1966, California. Screen, stage, television actor and author. Married to talent agent Betty Fairfax (dec. 1962).

Appeared in: **1934** Limehouse Blues. **1935** Clive of India; Cardinal Richelieu; Uncivil Warriors (short). **1936** Daniel Boone. **1937** I Cover the War. **1938** Paris Honeymoon. **1939** The Little Princess; Adventures of Sherlock Holmes; Kennedy the Great (short). **1940** Raffles; The Blue Bird. **1941** Man Hunt; A Polo Phony (short). **1942** The Black Swan; London Blackout Murders; Interior Decorator (short). **1946** Three Strangers; Dragonwyck.

KENNEY, JACK

Born: 1888. Died: May 26, 1964, Hollywood, Calif. Screen actor.

Appeared in: **1929** Not Quite Decent; Beauty and Bullets. **1935** I'm a Father (short). **1936** Movie Maniacs (short). **1938** a Columbia short. **1944** Atlantic City. **1952** Cattle Town. **1953** Up in Daisy's Penthouse (short). **1954** The Country Girl. **1957** The Tin Star; Chicago Confidential. **1958** Hong Kong Confidential; Toughest Gun in Tombstone. **1959** Inside the Mafia; Invisible Invaders. **1960** Vice Raid; When the Clock Strikes; Cage of Evil; Three Came to Kill; Walking Target. **1961** The Gambler Wore a Gun; Gun Fight.

KENNY, COLIN

Born: Dublin, Ireland. Died: Dec. 2, 1968. Screen and stage actor.

Appeared in: **1917** Price of a Good Time. **1918** Unexpected Places; Tarzan of the Apes. **1919** Girl from Outside; Toby's Bow. **1920** Return of Tarzan; Blind Youth; The Triflers; 813. **1921** Black Beauty; The Fighting Lover; Heart of Youth; Little Lord Fauntleroy. **1922** The Ladder Jinx; Seeing's Believing; They Like 'Em Rough; Watch Him Step. **1924** Dorothy Vernon of Haddon Hall. **1925** Silent Pal. **1928** Adam's Apple (aka Honeymoon Abroad—US). **1930** Grumpy. **1933** Alice in Wonderland. **1934** Limehouse Blues. **1935** Captain Blood; Bonnie Scotland; The Four-Star Boarder (short). **1936** The Charge of the Light Brigade; 'Til We Meet Again. **1938** Adventures of Robin Hood; Booloo. **1939** We Are Not Alone. **1940** My Son, My Son. **1943** Two Tickets to London. **1945** Kitty. **1946** Three Strangers. **1954** Desiree.

KENNY, LEOLA (aka LEE KENNY)

Born: 1892. Died: Oct. 17, 1956, Hollywood, Calif. Screen and stage actress.

Appeared in: **1930** Just Imagine.

KENNY, NICK

Born: 1895. Died: Dec. 1, 1975, Sarasota, Fla. Songwriter, sports columnist, professional football player, author and screen actor.

Appeared in: **1933** Universal shorts. **1934** Radio Star series of shorts.

KENT, ARNOLD (Lido Manetti)

Born: Jan. 21, 1899, Florence, Italy. Died: Sept. 29, 1928, Los Angeles, Calif. (auto accident). Screen actor.

Appeared in: **1927** The Woman on Trial; Hula; The World at Her Feet. **1928** Beau Sabreur; Easy Come, Easy Go; The Woman Disputed; The Showdown.

KENT, CHARLES

Born: 1852, London, England. Died: May 21, 1923, Brooklyn, N.Y. Stage and screen actor. Entered films with Vitagraph in 1905.

Appeared in: **1910** Uncle Tom's Cabin; Twelfth Night. **1911** The Death of Edward III; Vanity Fair; The Ninety and Nine; Suffer Little Children; Madge of the Mountains. **1912** The Party Dress; The Awakening of Bianca; She Never Knew; The Unknown Violinist; The Days of Terror. **1913** Daniel; The Last Millionaire; The Tiger; A Window on Washington Park; The Diamond Mystery; The Treasure of Desert Isle; The Carpenter; The Only Veteran in Town. **1914** His Last Call; Mrs. Maloney's Fortune; In the Old Attic; The First Indorsement; The Barnes of New York. **1915** A Price for Folly; Hearts and the Highway; Heights of Hazard. **1916** The Enemy; Kennedy Square; The Supreme Temptation; The Blue Envelope Mystery; The Tarantula; Carew and Son; The Chattel; The Scarlet Runner; Whom the Gods Destroy. **1917** The Marriage Speculation; The Money Mill; Soldiers of Chance; Duplicity of Hargraves. **1919** Miss Dulcie from Dixie; The Gamblers. **1920** The Dream; Body and Soul; Forbidden Valley. **1921** Rainbow; The Single Track; The Charming Deceiver. **1922** The Prodigal Judge. **1923** The Ragged Edge; The Leopardess; The Purple Highway.

KENT, CRAUFORD

Born: 1881, London, England. Died: May 14, 1953, Los Angeles, Calif. Screen actor. Entered films in 1915.

Appeared in: **1917** Thais. **1918** The Song of Songs. **1919** Good Gracious Annabelle. **1920** Other Men's Shoes. **1921** Silas Marner; Jane Eyre; The Plaything of Broadway. **1922** Shadows of the Sea; The Hidden Woman; Shirley of the Circus; Other Women's Clothes. **1923** The Eagle's Feather; Mothers-in-Law; Self Made Wife; The Abysmal Brute. **1924** Daddies; Flowing Gold; Lover's Lane; Virtue's Revolt; The Painted Flapper; The Guilty One; Lilies of the Field; Turned Up. **1925** Easy Money; The Pride of the Force; The Midshipman; Seven Keys to Baldpate; Man and Maid. **1926** Fifth Avenue; Out of the Storm; College Days; Morganson's Finish; The Outsider; The Winning Wallop; That Model from Paris. **1927** The Missing Link; Pirates of the Sky; His Dog; Little Mickey Grogan; See You in Jail; Mother. **1928** The Foreign Legion; Blindfold; Man, Woman and Wife; Into No Man's Land; Bitter Sweets; Manhattan Knights; Out with the Tide; Wallflowers; The Olympic Hero; Queen of the Chorus; Show Folks. **1929** The Charlatan; Seven Keys to Baldpate (and 1925 version); The Wolf of Wall Street; Come Across; The Ace of Scotland Yard (serial); Careers. **1930** Ladies Love Brutes; In the Next Room; Sweethearts and Wives; The Second Floor Mystery; The Devil to Pay; Three Faces East; The Unholy Three. **1931** Grief Street; Body and Soul; Transatlantic; Delicious; The Feathered Serpent; Women Men Marry; His Last Performance; Goldberg; Oh! Oh! Cleopatra (short). **1932** Sinister Hands; The 13th Guest; File 113; The Menace; Murder at Dawn; The Fighting Gentleman; Western Limited; Sally of the Subway; The Purchase Price. **1933** Sailor Be Good; The Eagle and the Hawk; Only Yesterday; Humanity. **1934** The Lost Jungle; The House of Rothschild; Little Miss Marker. **1935** Vanessa, Her Love Story; Mutiny on the Bounty. **1936** Hitchhike to Heaven; Down the Stretch; Magnificent Obsession; Daniel Boone; O'Malley of the Mounted; It Couldn't Have Happened. **1937** Navy Spy. **1938** Love, Honor and Behave; Service de Luxe. **1939** I Was A Convict; Rovin' Tumbleweeds; We Are Not Alone. **1940** Foreign Correspondent; South of Suez. **1941** Shining Victory; International Squadron. **1943** The Constant Nymph; Mysterious Doctor. **1944** The Black Parachute. **1945** The Fatal Witness. **1946** Kitty. **1950** Tea for Two.

KENT, DOUGLAS. See DOUGLAS MONTGOMERY

KENT, ELINOR

Died: Sept. 15, 1957, Hollywood, Calif. Screen actress. Mother of actor Warren Hymer (dec. 1948). Married to stage actor and playwright John B. Hymer (dec.).

KENT, ETHEL (Ethel Jackson aka ETHEL INCE)

Born: 1884, New York, N.Y. Died: July 27, 1952, Hollywood, Calif. (cerebral hemorrhage). Screen actress. Entered films in 1911. Married to actor and director John Ince (dec. 1947).

Appeared in: **1950** Buccaneer's Girl.

KENT, GERALD (Gerald MacIntosh Johnston)
Born: Canada. Died: Nov. 5, 1944, Germany (German prison camp). Stage and screen actor.

Appeared in British film: Four Corners.

KENT, KATE
Born: 1864. Died: Dec. 1934, Hollywood, Calif. (hit by auto). Screen actress.

KENT, KENETH
Born: 1892. Died: Nov. 17, 1963, London, England. Screen, stage, opera, television actor and playwright.

Appeared in: 1940 Night Train to Munich (aka Gestapo and Night Train—US). 1941 Dangerous Moonlight (aka Suicide Squadron—US 1942).

KENT, MARSHA (Marjorie Kent)
Born: 1919. Died: Mar. 1971, Huntington, N.Y. Screen actress and ballerina.

Appeared in: 1936 The Great Ziegfeld. 1937 Prisoner of Zenda; The Bride Wore Red. 1938 The Great Waltz. 1939 The Wizard of Oz; Gone with the Wind.

KENT, RAY
Born: 1886. Died: 1948. Screen actor. Entered films during the silents.

KENT, ROBERT (Douglas Blackley)
Born: Dec. 3, 1908, Hartford, Conn. Died: May 4, 1955. Screen and stage actor. Divorced from actress Astrid Allwyn.

Appeared in: 1935 Car 99; Love in Bloom. 1936 The Country Beyond; The Crime of Dr. Forbes; King of the Royal Mounted; Dimples; Reunion; Love Before Breakfast. 1937 That I May Live; Nancy Steele is Missing; Angel's Holiday; Born Reckless; Charlie Chan at Monte Carlo; Step Lively, Jeeves! 1938 The Gladiator; Mr. Moto Takes a Chance; Wanted by the Police; Little Orphan Annie; Gang Bullets. 1939 The Phantom Creeps (serial); East Side of Heaven; For Love or Money; Andy Hardy Gets Spring Fever; Calling All Marines; Secret of Dr. Kildare; Almost a Gentleman. 1941 Sunset in Wyoming; Twilight on the Trail; The Blonde Comet. 1942 Stagecoach Express. 1943 Yanks Ahoy; Find the Blackmailer; What a Man! 1944 Hot Rhythm. 1945 Who's Guilty? (serial); What Next, Corporal Hargrove? 1946 Joe Palooka—Champ; The Phantom Rider (serial). 1947 Shoot to Kill; Jungle Flight; Dragnet; Big Town After Dark. 1948 The Counterfeiters. 1950 Federal Agent at Large; Radar Secret Service; For Heaven's Sake. 1953 Rebel City. 1954 The Country Girl.

KENT, WILLARD
Born: 1883. Died: Sept. 5, 1968, Woodland Hills, Calif. Screen actor. Entered films during the silents.

Appeared in: 1936 Prison Shadows. 1937 Death in the Air.

KENT, WILLIAM T.
Born: 1886. Died: Oct. 5, 1945, N.Y. Screen, stage, vaudeville, burlesque actor and circus performer.

Appeared in: 1922 When Knighthood Was in Flower. 1930 The King of Jazz. 1933 Saturday's Millions. 1934 The Scarlet Letter.

KEPPENS, EMILE (aka EMILE KOPPENS)
Born: France. Died: Oct. 1926, France. Screen actor.

KERN, JAMES V.
Born: Sept. 22, 1909, New York, N.Y. Died: Nov. 9, 1966, Encino, Calif. (pneumonia). Screen actor, film and television director, screenwriter, composer and member of "Yacht Club Boys" singers on stage, radio and screen.

KERR, FREDERICK (Frederick Keen)
Born: Oct. 11, 1858, London, England. Died: May 3, 1933, London, England. Stage and screen actor.

Appeared in: 1916 The Lifeguardsman. 1927 The Honour of the Family (US 1931). 1929 Raffles. 1930 The Devil to Pay; The Lady of Scandal. 1931 Born to Love; Frankenstein; Waterloo Bridge; Always Good-Bye. 1932 The Midshipmaid; Lovers Courageous; Beauty and the Boss; But the Flesh Is Weak. 1933 The Man from Toronto.

KERR, JANE
Born: 1871 or 1891. Died: Nov. 19, 1954, Compton, Calif. Screen, stage, vaudeville and television actress.

Appeared in: 1934 Broadway Bill. 1935 Les Miserables. 1936 The Garden of Allah.

KERR, LORENCE "LARRY"
Died: 1968. Screen actor.

Appeared in: 1956 The Best Things in Life are Free. 1958 The Lost Missile.

KERRICK, THOMAS
Died: Apr. 27, 1927. Screen actor.

Appeared in: 1923 Men in the Raw.

KERRIGAN, J. WARREN (George Warren Kerrigan)
Born: July 25, 1889, Louisville, Ky. Died: June 9, 1947, Balboa, Calif. (bronchial pneumonia). Screen, stage actor and film producer. Brother of actress Kathleen Kerrigan (dec. 1957).

Appeared in: 1909 Hand of Uncle Sam. 1910–11 American Film Mfg. Co. films. 1912 Strangers at Coyote; For the Flag. 1913 The Wishing Seat. 1914 Samson. 1915 The Adventures of Terrence O'Rourke. 1916 Landon's Legacy. 1918 A Man's Man. 1919 A White Man's Chance. 1920 Thirty Thousand Dollars. 1921 Coast of Opportunity; House of Whispers. 1923 The Man from Brodney's; The Girl of the Golden West; Hollywood; Mary of the Movies; Thundering Dawn; The Covered Wagon. 1924 Captain Blood.

KERRIGAN, JOSEPH M.
Born: Dec. 16, 1887, Dublin, Ireland. Died: Apr. 29, 1964, Hollywood, Calif. Stage and screen actor.

Appeared in: 1916 O'Neil of Glen. 1923 Little Old New York. 1924 Captain Blood. 1929 Lucky in Love. 1930 Song O' My Heart; New Movietone Follies of 1930; Under Suspicion; Lightnin'. 1931 Don't Bet on Women; Merely Mary Ann; The Black Camel. 1932 The Rainbow Trail; Careless Lady; Rockabye. 1933 Air Hostess; Lone Cowboy; A Study in Scarlet; Paddy, the Next Best Thing. 1934 The Fountain; Happiness Ahead; The Lost Patrol; A Modern Hero; The Key; Gentlemen Are Born; Treasure Island. 1935 A Feather in Her Hat; Mystery of Edwin Drood; Werewolf of London; The Informer; Hot Tip; Barbary Coast. 1936 Timothy's Quest; Spendthrift; The General Died at Dawn; Colleen; The Prisoner of Shark Island; Lloyds of London; Laughing Irish Eyes; Hearts in Bondage; Special Investigator. 1937 The Plough and the Stars; Lets Make a Million; The Barrier; London by Night. 1938 Vacation from Love; Ride a Crooked Mile; Little Orphan Annie; The Great Man Votes; Boy Slaves. 1939 The Flying Irishman; Sorority House; The Kid from Texas; Two Thoroughbreds; Two Bright Boys; 6,000 Enemies; Gone with the Wind; The Zero Hour; Sabotage; Union Pacific; The Witness Vanishes. 1940 Congo Maisie; Young Tom Edison; The Long Voyage Home; Three Cheers for the Irish; The Sea Hawk; No Time for Comedy; Curtain Call; One Crowded Night; Untamed. 1941 Adventure in Washington; Appointment for Love; The Wolf Man. 1942 Captains of the Clouds; The Vanishing Virginian. 1943 None but the Lonely Heart; Mr. Lucky; Action in the North Atlantic; The American Romance. 1944 The Fighting Seabees; Wilson. 1945 The Great John L; Big Bonanza; Tarzan and the Amazons; The Crime Doctor's Warning; The Spanish Main. 1946 Abie's Irish Rose; Black Beauty; She Went to the Races. 1948 Call Northside 777; The Luck of the Irish. 1949 Mrs. Mike; Fighting O'Flynn. 1951 Sealed Cargo; Two of a Kind. 1952 The Wild North; Park Row; My Cousin Rachel. 1953 The Silver Whip. 1954 20,000 Leagues under the Sea. 1955 It's a Dog's Life. 1956 The Fastest Gun Alive.

KERRIGAN, KATHLEEN
Born: 1869. Died: Feb. 1957. Screen actress. Sister of actor J. Warren Kerrigan (dec. 1947).

Appeared in: 1914 Samson. 1923 None so Blind. 1927 The Music Master. 1929 Sinner Steps Out. 1931 Wicked.

KERRY, NORMAN (Arnold Kaiser)
Born: June 16, 1889, Rochester, N.Y. Died: Jan. 12, 1956, Hollywood, Calif. Stage and screen actor.

Appeared in: 1916 Manhattan Madness (film debut); The Black Butterfly. 1918 The Rose of Paradise. 1919 The Dark Star; Soldiers of Fortune. 1921 Get-Rich-Quick Wallingford; Buried Treasure; The Wild Goose; Little Italy; Proxies. 1922 Brothers under the Skin; Three Live Ghosts; Find the Woman; The Man from Home; 'Til We Meet Again. 1923 Merry-Go-Round; The Hunchback of Notre Dame; The Spoilers; The Acquittal; Is Money Everything?; The Satin Girl; The Thrill Chaser. 1924 Cytherea; Butterfly; Between Friends; Daring Youth; The Shadow of the East; True As Steel; Tarnish. 1925 Fifth Avenue Models; The Price of Pleasure; Lorraine of the Lions; The Phantom of the Opera. 1926 The Love Thief; Mlle. Modiste; The Barrier; Under Western Skies. 1927 The Unknown; Annie Laurie; Body and Soul; The Claw; The Irresistible Lover. 1928 Man, Woman and Wife; The Foreign Legion; Love Me and the World Is Mine; The Woman from Moscow; Affairs of Hannerl. 1929 The Bondsman; Trial Marriage; The Prince of Hearts; The Woman I Love. 1930 Phantom of the Opera (and 1925 version). 1931 Ex-Flame; Bachelor Apartments; Air Eagles. 1941 Tanks a Million.

KERSHAW, WILLETTE
Born: 1882. Died: May 6, 1960. Screen actress.

Appeared in: 1918 Men; Cecilia of the Pink Rose; Sporting Life. 1928 The Vortex.

KERWOOD, DICK
Died: Oct. 16, 1924, Pico Canyon, Calif. (fall from plane while doing a film stunt). Screen stuntman. Appeared in Franklyn Farnum Film Company films.

KETCHUM, ROBYNA NEILSON
Died: Nov. 9, 1972, Greenwich, Conn. Screen, stage and radio actress.

KEY, KATHLEEN
Born: 1906, Buffalo, N.Y. Died: Dec. 22, 1954, Woodland Hills, Calif. Screen actress.

Appeared in: 1921 The Four Horsemen of the Apocalypse; The Rookie's Return. 1922 Bells of San Juan; Where Is My Wandering Boy Tonight?; West of Chicago. 1923 Beautiful and Damned; Hell's Hole; The Rendezvous; Reno; The Man from Brodney's; North of Hudson Bay. 1924 The Sea Hawk; The Trouble Shooter; Revelation. 1925 A Lover's Oath; The Midshipman. 1926 Ben Hur; College Days; Money Talks; The Desert's Toll; Under Western Skies; The Flaming Frontier. 1927 Hey! Hey! Cowboy; Irish Hearts. 1928 Golf Widows. 1929 The Phantom of the North. 1931 Ben Hur (sound version).

KEYES, JOHN
Born: 1892. Died: Aug. 28, 1966. Screen actor.

Appeared in: Rackety Rax.

KEYS, NELSON
Born: 1887. Died: Apr. 26, 1939, London, England (heart attack). Stage and screen actor.

Appeared in: 1910 Drowsy Dick Dreams He's a Burglar; Drowsy Dick's Dream. 1914 Alone I Did It. 1916 Judged by Appearances; The Real Thing at Last. 1918 Once Upon a Time. 1922 Castles in the Air (aka Let's Pretend). 1927 Tip Toes; Mumsie; Madame Pompadour. 1928 The Triumph of the Scarlet Pimpernel (aka The Scarlet Daredevil—US 1929). 1929 When Knights Were Bold; Splinters. 1931 Almost a Divorce. 1933 Send 'Em Back Half Dead. 1935 We've Got to Have Love; The Last Journey (US 1936). 1936 Eliza Comes to Stay; In the Soup; Dreams Come True. 1937 Knights for a Day; Wake Up Famous.

KHAN, MAZHAR
Born: India. Died: Sept. 24, 1950, India? Screen actor, film producer and director.

KHMELOF, N. P. *See* NIKOLAI KHMELYOV

KHMELYOV, NIKOLAI (aka N. P. KHMELOF)
Born: 1901, Russia. Died: Nov. 1945, Russia. Screen, stage actor and stage director.

Appeared in: 1932 House of Death. 1936 Revolutionists.

KHOURY, EDITH LESLIE
Died: Apr. 9, 1973, Los Angeles, Calif. (cancer). Screen and stage actress.

Appeared in: 1969 Hello Dolly. 1971 Bedknobs and Broomsticks.

KIBBEE, GUY (Guy Bridges Kibbee)
Born: Mar. 6, 1886, El Paso, Tex. Died: May 24, 1956, East Islip, N.Y. (Parkinson's disease). Stage and screen actor. Married to stage actress Lois Kibbee. Brother of actor Milton Kibbee (dec. 1970).

Appeared in: 1931 Man of the World; Stolen Heaven; Laughing Sinners; Happy Landing; Side Show; New Adventures of Get-Rich-Quick Wallingford; Flying High; Blonde Crazy; Larceny Lane; City Streets. 1932 Crooner; Scarlet Dawn; Taxi; Fireman Save My Child; Mouthpiece; Weekend Marriage; Union Depot; High Pressure; Play Girl; Central Park; The Conquerors; The Crowd Roars; Rain; Gentleman for a Day; Two Seconds; Big City Blues; Man Wanted; The Dark Horse; Strange Love of Molly Louvain; So Big; Winner Take All. 1933 They Just Had to Get Married; 42nd Street; Lilly Turner; The Silk Express; Girl Missing; The Life of Jimmy Dolan; Gold Diggers of 1933; Footlight Parade; Lady for a Day; The World Changes; Havana Widows; Convention City. 1934 Easy to Love; Dames; Harold Teen; Big Hearted Herbert; Merry Wives of Reno; The Merry Frinks; Wonder Bar; Babbitt. 1935 While the Patient Slept; Mary Jane's Pa; Don't Bet on Blondes; Crashing Society; Going Highbrow; I Live for Love; Captain Blood. 1936 Three Men on a Horse; Little Lord Fauntleroy; Captain January; I Married a Doctor; The Big Noise; Earthworm Tractors; M'Liss; The Captain's Kid. 1937 Mamma Steps Out; Don't Tell the Wife; Riding on Air; The Big Shot; Jim Hanvey, Detective; Mountain Justice. 1938 Bad Man of Brimstone; Of Human Hearts; Three Comrades; Rich Man, Poor Girl; Three Loves Has Nancy; Joy of Living. 1939 It's a Wonderful World; Bad Little Angel; Let Freedom Ring; Mr. Smith Goes to Washington; Babes in Arms. 1940 Our Town; Henry Goes Arizona; Street of Memories; Chad Hanna. 1941 Scattergood Baines; Scattergood Pulls the Strings; Scattergood Meets Broadway; It Started with Eve; Design for Scandal. 1942 Scattergood Rides High; This Time for Keeps; Sunday Punch; Miss Annie Rooney; Tish; Whistling in Dixie; Scattergood Survives a Murder. 1943 Cinderella Swings It; Girl Crazy; White Savage; The Power of the Press. 1944 Dixie Jamboree. 1945 The Horn Blows at Midnight; White Pongo. 1946

Singing on the Trail; Cowboy Blues; Gentleman Joe Palooka; Lone Star Moonlight. 1947 Over the Santa Fe Trail; The Red Stallion; The Romance of Rosy Ridge. 1948 Fort Apache; Three Godfathers. 1974 That's Entertainment (film clips).

KIBBEE, MILTON
Died: 1970. Screen actor. Brother of actor Guy Kibbee (dec. 1956).

Appeared in: 1934 Registered Nurse. 1935 Mary Jane's Pa; Bright Lights. 1936 Man Hunt; Treachery Rides the Range; Murder by an Aristocrat; The Law in Her Hands; Love Begins at 20; The Case of the Black Cat; Polo Joe; Trailin' West. 1937 White Bondage; Guns of the Pecos. 1939 The Cat and the Canary. 1940 That Gang of Mine; Strike Up the Band. 1941 Kansas Cyclone; Two-Gun Sheriff; Across the Sierras. 1942 Billy the Kid—Trapped; Billy the Kid's Smoking Guns; Jungle Siren; In Old California; My Heart Belongs to Daddy; The Mad Doctor of Market Street; Heart of the Rio Grande; Queen of Broadway. 1943 Air Raid Wardens; Dixie Dugan; Happy Land. 1944 The Contender; When Strangers Marry; Three Little Sisters; In the Meantime, Darling; Rogues' Gallery. 1945 Who's Guilty? (serial); The Scarlet Clue; Muggs Rides Again; Come Out Fighting; Strange Holiday; White Pongo. 1946 Junior Prom; The Flying Serpent; Freddie Steps Out; High School Hero; Homesteaders of Paradise Valley; Conquests of Cheyenne; Strange Holiday. 1947 Body and Soul; The Sea Hound (serial); Vacation Days; Little Miss Broadway; Frontier Fighters; Luckiest Guy in the World (short). 1948 River Lady; An Old Fashioned Girl. 1949 State Department File 649; Daughter of the West. 1950 County Fair. 1951 Blue Blood; Three Desperate Men (aka Three Outlaws); When the Redskins Rode. 1952 Rodeo.

KIDD, JIM
Born: 1846, Texas. Died: Dec. 9, 1916, Los Angeles, Calif. Screen cowboy actor. Appeared in Kay-Bee films.

KIDD, KATHLEEN
Born: 1899, England. Died: Feb. 23, 1961, Toronto, Canada. Screen, stage, radio and television actress.

Appeared in: 1926 What Price Glory?

KIDDER, HUGH
Born: 1880. Died: June 3, 1952, Hollywood, Calif. Screen, stage and radio actor.

Appeared in: 1933 His Private Secretary.

KIEPURA, JAN
Born: May 16, 1902, Warsaw, Poland. Died: Aug. 15, 1966, Harrison, N.Y. (heart ailment). Screen, opera and stage actor.

Appeared in: 1931 Ein Lied fur Dich (A Song for You—US 1933). 1932 Die Singende Stadt (US 1935). 1933 Das Lied Ein Nach; Mein Herz Ruft Nach Dir; Farewell to Love; Be Mine Tonight. 1934 Ich Liebe Alles Frauen; My Song Goes Round the World. 1935 My Heart Is Calling; My Song for You. 1936 Zauber der Boheme (The Charm of La Boheme—US 1938); Give Us This Night. 1937 Thank You Madame. 1949 La Vie de Boheme. 1950 Her Wonderful Lie.

KIERNAN, JAMES
Born: 1939. Died: July 24, 1975, Palms, Calif. (murdered—shot). Stage and screen actor.

KIKUME, AL
Born: 1894, Hawaii? Died: Mar. 27, 1972, Hollywood, Calif. (heart ailment). Screen actor. Father of actor Bernie Gozier.

Appeared in: 1937 The Hurricane. 1938 Air Devils; Mr. Moto Takes a Chance. 1939 Mandrake the Magician (serial). 1940 Typhoon. 1941 Jungle Girl (serial). 1942 The Mad Doctor of Market Street. 1947 Green Dolphin Street. 1949 Daughter of the Jungle. 1950 On the Isle of Samoa.

KILBRIDE, PERCY
Born: July 16, 1888, San Francisco, Calif. Died: Dec. 11, 1964, Los Angeles, Calif. (brain injury due to auto accident). Screen and stage actor.

Appeared in: 1933 White Woman. 1936 Soak the Rich. 1942 Keeper of the Flame. 1943 George Washington Slept Here; Crazy House; The Woman of the Town. 1944 The Adventures of Mark Twain; Guest in the House; Knickerbocker Holiday. 1945 She Wouldn't Say Yes; State Fair; Fallen Angel. 1946 The Well-Groomed Bride. 1947 The Egg and I; Riffraff; Welcome Stranger. 1948 Black Bart; Feudin', Fussin' and A-Fightin'; You Were Meant for Me; You Gotta Stay Happy. 1949 Mr. Soft Touch; The Sun Comes Up; Free for All; Ma and Pa Kettle. 1950 Ma and Pa Kettle Go to Town; Riding High. 1951 Ma and Pa Kettle Back on the Farm. 1952 Ma and Pa Kettle at the Fair. 1953 Ma and Pa Kettle on Vacation; Ma and Pa Kettle Hit the Road. 1954 Ma and Pa Kettle at Home. 1955 Ma and Pa Kettle at Waikiki.

KILBRIDE, RICHARD D.

Born: 1919. Died: June 20, 1967, Cambridge, Mass. Screen, stage and television actor.

Appeared in: **1965** The Playground.

KILDUFF, HELEN. *See* LITTLE HELEN ALLERTON

KILGALLEN, DOROTHY

Born: July 3, 1913, Chicago, Ill. Died: Nov. 8, 1965, N.Y. Radio, television, screen actress and columnist.

Appeared in: **1936** Sinner Take All. **1964** Pajama Party.

KILGOUR, JOSEPH

Born: 1864, Ayr, Ont., Canada. Died: Apr. 21, 1933, Bay Shore, N.Y. Stage and screen actor. Entered films in 1915.

Appeared in: **1915** The Battle Cry for Peach; My Lady's Slipper. **1917** The Easiest Way; The Secret Kingdom (serial). **1919** The Divorcee. **1920** Thou Art the Man; Hearts are Trumps; The Leopard Woman; Love. **1921** At the End of the World; I Am Guilty; Lying Lips; Mother O' Mine. **1923** Within the Law; The Woman with Four Faces; Ponjola; The Midnight Alarm. **1924** Try and Get It; Janice Meredith; On Probation; Torment; The Torrent. **1925** Percy; Capital Punishment; The Top of the World; One Year to Live; The King on Main Street. **1926** Let's Get Married.

KILPACK, BENNETT

Born: 1883, England. Died: Aug. 17, 1962, Santa Monica, Calif. Screen, stage and radio actor. Star of radio's Mr. Keen, Tracer of Lost Persons.

Appeared in: **1932** Way Back Home.

KIMBALL, EDWARD M.

Born: June 26, 1859, Keokuk, Iowa. Died: Jan. 4, 1938, Hollywood, Calif. Stage and screen actor. Father of actress Clara Kimball Young (dec. 1960). Entered films with Solax Studio in 1910.

Appeared in: **1911–14** Vitagraph films. **1914–16** World films. **1915** Lola. **1917** Magda; The Marionettes. **1920** Mid-Channel. **1921** An Unwilling Hero; Charge It; Boys Will Be Boys. **1922** The Masquerader; Yankee Doodle, Jr.; Omar the Tentmaker. **1923** The Woman of Bronze; The Cheat; Trilby; The Remittance Woman. **1924** Passion's Pathway. **1925** I'll Show You the Town.

KIMBALL, PAULINE (Pauline Garrett)

Born: Mar. 15, 1860, Chicago, Ill. Died: Dec. 11, 1919. Screen, stage actress and opera performer. Mother of actress Clara Kimball Young (dec. 1960).

Appeared in: **1913** Memories that Haunt. **1916** The Feast of Life; The Deep Purple.

KIMURA, MASSA KICHI

Born: 1890. Died: Nov. 21, 1918, New York, N.Y. (Spanish influenza). Screen actor.

KING, ALLYN

Born: 1901. Died: Mar. 30, 1930, New York, N.Y. (suicide—leap from building). Stage and screen actress.

Appeared in: **1923** The Fighting Blade.

KING, ANITA

Born: 1889. Died: June 10, 1963, Hollywood, Calif. (heart attack). Stage and screen actress.

Appeared in: **1914** The Virginian. **1915** Snobs.

KING, CHARLES

Born: Oct. 31, 1889, New York, N.Y. Died: Jan. 11, 1944, London, England (pneumonia). Screen, stage and vaudeville actor.

Appeared in: **1929** Broadway Melody (film debut); Road Show; Hollywood Revue of 1929; Orange Blossom Time; Climbing the Golden Stairs. **1930** The Girl in the Show; Chasing Rainbows; Remote Control. **1934** Perfectly Mismated (short); Men in Black (short). **1935** The Miracle Rider (serial); The Singing Vagabond; Tumbling Tumbleweeds. **1936** The Lawless Nineties; Guns and Guitars; Red River Valley. **1937** Rootin' Tootin' Rhythm; The Trusted Outlaw; A Lawman is Born; Ridin' the Lone Trail. **1938** Thunder in the Desert; Gold Mine in the Sky. **1939** South of the Border. **1943** Riders of the Rio Grande.

KING, CHARLES L., SR.

Born: 1899. Died: May 7, 1957, Hollywood, Calif. Screen actor. Father of actor Charles L. King, Jr.

Appeared in: **1921** A Motion to Adjourn; Singing River. **1922** The Black Bag; Price of Youth. **1923** Merry-Go-Round. **1925** Hearts of the West; Triple Action. **1926** What Happened to Jane (serial). **1927** Range Courage. **1928** You Can't Beat the Law; Sisters of Eve. **1929** Slim Fingers. **1930** Dawn Trail; Fighting Through; Oklahoma Cyclone; Beyond the Law. **1931** Oh, Sailor, Behave!;

Branded Men; Range Law. **1932** Gay Buckaroo; A Man's Land; The Fighting Champ; Ghost City; Honor of the Mounted. **1933** The Fighting Parson; Crashing Broadway; Son of the Border; The Lone Avenger; Strawberry Roan; Young Blood; Outlaw Justice. **1934** Mystery Ranch; Men in Black. **1935** Northern Frontier; Outlawed Guns; The Ivory-Handled Gun; His Fighting Blood; Mississippi; Red Blood of Courage. **1936** Just My Luck; O'Malley of the Mounted; Headin' for the Rio Grande; Sunset of Power; Desert Phantom; Sundown Saunders; Men of the Plains; Last of the Warrens; Idaho Kid. **1937** Trouble in Texas; Sing, Cowboy, Sing; Tex Rides with the Boy Scouts; Headline Crasher; Island Captives; Black Aces; Riders of the Rockies; The Red Rope; The Mystery of the Hooded Horsemen; Hittin' the Trail. **1938** Starlight over Texas; Where the Buffalo Roam; Gun Packer; Frontier Town; Song and Bullets; Phantom Ranger; Man's Country. **1939** Wild Horse Canyon; Song of the Buckaroo; Zorro's Fighting Legion (serial); Rollin' Westward; Mutiny in the Big House; Down the Wyoming Trail; Oklahoma Frontier. **1940** Son of the Navy; West of Carson City; Wild Horse Range. **1941** Billy the Kid's Fighting Pals; Outlaws of the Rio Grande; The Roar of the Press; The Lone Ranger in Ghost Town; Texas Marshal; Gunman from Bodie; Borrowed Hero; Billy the Kid Wanted; Billy the Kid's Roundup; The Lone Ranger Fights Back. **1942** Riders of the West; Law and Order; Pirates of the Prairie. **1943** Ghost Rider; Two-Fisted Justice; The Rangers Take Over; The Stranger from Pecos; Border Buckaroos; Riders of the Rio Grande. **1946** The Caravan Trail.

KING, CLAUDE (Claude Ewart King)

Born: Jan. 15, 1879, Northhampton, England. Died: Sept. 18, 1941, Los Angeles, Calif. Screen, stage actor and stage director.

Appeared in: **1920** Judy of Rogue's Harbor. **1921** The Scarab Ring; Why Girls Leave Home. **1923** Bella Donna; Six Days. **1925** The Making of O'Malley; Irish Luck; The Unguarded Hour; The Knockout. **1926** Paradise; The Silent Lover. **1927** Mr. Wu; Becky; Singed; London after Midnight. **1928** Red Hair; A Night of Mystery; Love and Learn; Outcast; Oh, Kay!; Warming Up; Sporting Goods. **1929** Strange Cargo; Nobody's Children; Madame X; Behind That Curtain; The Black Watch; Blue Skies; The Mysterious Dr. Fu Manchu. **1930** Son of the Gods; In Gay Madrid; Second Floor Mystery; Love among the Millionaires; Prince of Diamonds; One Night at Susie's; Follow Thru. **1931** Rango; The Reckless Hour; Women Love Once; Transatlantic; Devotion; Once a Lady; Heartbreak; Arrowsmith; Born to Love. **1932** Behind the Mask; He Learned about Women; Sherlock Holmes; Shanghai Express. **1933** The Big Brain; Charlie Chan's Greatest Case; White Woman. **1934** The Moonstone; Stolen Sweets; The World Moves On; Two Heads on a Pillow; Long Lost Father; Murder in Trinidad. **1935** The Great Impersonation; The Right to Live; The Gilded Lily; Smart Girl; The Last Outpost; Circumstantial Evidence; A Thousand Dollars a Minute; Bonnie Scotland. **1936** The Leathernecks Have Landed; Shanghai Gesture; Three on the Trail; The Last of the Mohicans; Beloved Enemy; It Couldn't Have Happened; Happy Go Lucky. **1937** Lover under Fire; Lancer Spy. **1938** If I Were King; Four Men and a Prayer; Booloo. **1939** Within the Law. **1940** New Moon.

KING, DENNIS (aka DENNIS PRATT and DENNY PRATT)

Born: Nov. 2, 1897, Warwickshire, Coventry, England. Died: May 21, 1971, New York, N.Y. (heart condition). Screen and stage actor. Married to stage actress Edith Wright (dec.).

Appeared in: **1919** Monsieur Beaucaire (film debut). **1930** The Vagabond King; Paramount on Parade. **1931** Fra Diavolo (The Devil's Brother). **1937** Between Two Worlds. **1959** The Miracle. **1969** The One with the Fuzz; Some Kind of a Nut.

KING, EMMETT C.

Born: 1866, Griffin, Ga. Died: Apr. 21, 1953, Woodland Hills, Calif. Screen, stage and radio actor.

Appeared in: **1921** Fightin' Mad; Flower of the North; Lying Lips; Three Sevens; Eden and Return; The Mistress of Shenstone; Little Lord Fauntleroy; The Silver Car. **1922** The Adventures of Robinson Crusoe (serial); The Beautiful and Damned; The Call of Home; The Kentucky Derby; Human Hearts; Manslaughter. **1923** Don Quickshot of the Rio Grande; The Flame of Life; The Acquittal; Trifling with Honor; The Near Lady; The Day of Faith. **1924** Barbara Fritchie; Captain January; T.N.T.; the Air Hawk; Dark Stairways; The Fighting American. **1925** The Man without a Country; The Devil's Cargo; Counsel for the Defense; Peacock Feathers; Pampered Youth; The Overland Limited. **1926** The Arizona Sweepstakes; The Man in the Saddle. **1928** Laugh, Clown, Laugh; God of Mankind; Midnight Madness. **1929** When Dreams Come True; On Trial; Noisy Neighbors; Shopworn Angel. **1930** Reno; Africa Speaks; The Right of Way. **1931** Three Who Loved; Public Defender. **1932** Mata Hari; Westward Passage. **1937** The Prisoner of Zenda.

KING, EUGENE W.

Died: Nov. 1950, Hollywood, Calif. Screen actor.

Appeared in: **1937** Bill Cracks Down. **1951** The Great Caruso.

KING, JACK

Born: 1883. Died: Oct. 8, 1943, New York, N.Y. (stroke). Screen, vaudeville actor and songwriter. Married to actress Rhea King who appeared with him in vaudeville in a song-dance-patter act.

Appeared in: **1930** Madam Satan; Harmonizing Songs (short).

KING, JOE (Joseph King)
Born: Feb. 9, 1883, Austin, Tex. Died: Apr. 11, 1951, Woodland Hills, Calif. Stage and screen actor. Entered films in 1913.

Appeared in: **1913** The Missionary and the Actress; Mounted Officer Flynn; The Mysterious Way; The Battle of Gettysburg. **1914** Suspended Sentence. **1915** The Face in the Mirror; The Dancer; A Girl of the Pines; The Faith of Her Father; Haunted Hearts; The Mother Instinct. **1919** Love's Prisoner. **1920** Humoresque; Children Not Wanted; The North Wind's Malice; The Broadway Bubble. **1921** Salvation Nell; Anne of Little Smoky; The Girl With a Jazz Heart; The Idol of the North; Man and Woman; Moral Fibre; The Scarab Ring. **1922** The Face in the Fog; Sisters; The Valley of Silent Men. **1923** Big Brother; The Daring Years; Counterfeit Love; Twenty-One. **1924** The Masked Dancer; Unguarded Women. **1926** Tin Gods. **1929** The Laughing Lady. **1930** Roadhouse Nights; Battle of Paris. **1934** Woman in the Dark. **1935** Front Page Woman; Alibi Ike; Special Agent; Moonlight on the Prairie; Frisco Kid; Shipmates Forever; Man of Iron; Broadway Hostess; Let 'Em Have It. **1936** The Case of the Velvet Claw; Polo Joe; Bengal Tiger; Road Gang; The Walking Dead; The Singing Kid; Jail Break; Sons O'Guns; Bullets or Ballots; Public Enemy's Wife; China Clipper; God's Country and the Woman. **1937** Once a Doctor; Slim; That Man's Here Again; Armored Car; San Quentin; White Bondage; Fly Away Baby; Hot Water. **1938** In Old Chicago; City Streets; Alexander's Ragtime Band; Heart of the North. **1939** My Son is a Criminal; Off the Record; You Can't Get Away with Murder; Code of the Secret Service; Smashing the Money Ring; Destry Rides Again. **1940** Three Cheers for the Irish; Black Friday; It's a Date; You're Not so Tough; Charlie Chan at the Wax Museum; Always a Bride. **1941** Blondie Goes Latin; Bullets for O'Hara; Strange Alibi. **1942** The Big Shot; The Glass Key; Butch Minds the Baby.

KING, LESLIE
Born: 1876, Baltimore, Md. Died: Oct. 10, 1947, Amityville, N.Y. Stage and screen actor.

Appeared in: **1916** Temperance Town; Milk White Flag. **1919** The Fatal Fortune (serial). **1921** Experience; Orphans of the Storm. **1922** The Bond Boy; The Streets of New York. **1923** If Winter Comes; Broadway Broke. **1924** The New School Teacher. **1931** Alice in Wonderland.

KING, WILL
Born: 1886. Died: Jan. 22, 1958, San Francisco, Calif. Screen, stage, vaudeville actor, playwright and stage producer. Married to actress Claire Starr who appeared in vaudeville with him.

Appeared in: **1929** The Fatal Forceps; Weak but Willing.

KINGDON, DOROTHY
Born: 1894. Died: Mar. 31, 1939, Los Angeles, Calif. Screen and stage actress.

Appeared in: **1925** The Iron Man; A Man of Iron; The Lost Chord.

KINGSFORD, ALISON
Born: 1899. Died: June 10, 1950, North Hollywood, Calif. Screen actress. Married to actor Walter Kingsford (dec. 1958).

KINGSFORD, WALTER
Born: Sept. 20, 1882, Redhill, England. Died: Feb. 7, 1958, North Hollywood, Calif. (heart attack). Stage and screen actor. Married to actress Alison Kingsford (dec. 1950).

Appeared in: **1934** Pursuit of Happiness; The President Vanishes. **1935** The Mystery of Edwin Drood; The White Cockatoo; Naughty Marietta; Shanghai; I Found Stella Parish; The Melody Lingers On; Frankie and Johnnie. **1936** The Story of Louis Pasteur; Hearts Divided; Stolen Holiday; Professional Soldier; The Invisible Ray; Little Lord Fauntleroy; Trouble for Two; Mad Holiday; Meet Nero Wolfe; The Music Goes 'Round. **1937** Maytime; Behind the Criminal (short); Captains Courageous; My Dear Miss Aldrich; Bulldog Drummond Escapes; Double or Nothing; The Life of Emile Zola; The League of Frightened Men; The Devil Is Driving; I'll Take Romance; It Could Happen to You. **1938** Paradise for Three; A Yank at Oxford; The Toy Wife; Lord Jeff; There's Always a Woman; Algiers; The Young in Heart; Carefree; If I Were King; Say It in French; The Lone Wolf in Paris; Young Dr. Kildare. **1939** Juarez; Smashing the Spy Ring; Calling Dr. Kildare; Man in the Iron Mask; Miracles for Sale; The Witness Vanishes; The Secret of Dr. Kildare; Dancing Co-ed. **1940** Star Dust; Lucky Partners; A Dispatch from Reuters; Kitty Foyle; Dr. Kildare Goes Home; Dr. Kildare's Crisis; Adventure in Diamonds; Dr. Kildare's Strangest Case. **1941** The Devil and Miss Jones; The Lone Wolf Takes a Chance; The People vs. Dr. Kildare; Hit the Road; Ellery Queen and the Perfect Crime; Dr. Kildare's Wedding Day; Unholy Partners; Dr. Kildare's Victory; The Corsican Brothers. **1942** Fly by Night; Fingers at the Window; My Favorite Blonde; Calling Dr. Gillespie; Dr. Gillespie's New Assistant; The Loves of Edgar Allan Poe. **1943** Flight for Freedom; Forever and a Day; Bomber's Moon; Dr. Gillespie's Criminal Case; Hi Diddle Diddle; Mr.

Lucky. **1944** Secrets of Scotland Yard; Three Men in White; The Hitler Gang; Mr. Skeffington; Ghost Catchers; Between Two Women. **1948** The Black Arrow; The Velvet Touch. **1949** Slattery's Hurricane. **1950** Experiment Alcatraz. **1951** My Forbidden Past; The Desert Fox; Tarzan's Peril; Two Dollar Bettor. **1952** The Brigand; Confidence Girl. **1953** Loose in London; Walking My Baby Back Home; The Pathfinder. **1956** The Search for Bridey Murphy; Around the World in 80 Days. **1958** Merry Andrew.

KINGSTON, THOMAS
Born: 1902. Died: Jan. 27, 1959, Hollywood, Calif. (heart attack). Screen and television stand-in.

KINGSTON, WINIFRED
Born: 1895. Died: Feb. 3, 1967, La Jolla, Calif. Screen actress. Married to actor Dustin Farnum (dec. 1929).

Appeared in: **1913** The Squaw Man. **1914** Son of Erin; Where the Trail Divides. **1915** The Light of the Reef. **1916** David Garrick. **1917** The Scarlet Pimpernel. **1919** The Corsican Brothers. **1921** Beyond. **1922** The Trail of the Axe. **1929** The Virginian.

KINNELL, MURRAY
Born: 1889, London, England. Died: Aug. 11, 1954, Santa Barbara, Calif. Stage and screen actor.

Appeared in: **1930** Old English (film debut); The Princess and the Plumber. **1931** Reckless Living; The Secret Six; The Public Enemy; The Black Camel; The Guilty Generation; Honor of the Family; The Deceiver. **1932** Grand Hotel; Under Eighteen; The Beast of the City; The Man Who Played God; The Menace; The Mouthpiece; The Purchase Price; The Painted Woman; Secrets of the French Police; The Match King. **1933** Zoo in Budapest; Voltaire; From Headquarters; I Loved a Woman; Ann Vickers; The Avenger. **1934** I Am Suzanne; Such Women Are Dangerous; The House of Rothschild; Affairs of a Gentleman; Hat, Coat and Glove; Murder in Trinidad; Charlie Chan's Courage; Charlie Chan in London; Anne of Green Gables. **1935** Charlie Chan in Paris; Cardinal Richelieu; Mad Love; Kind Lady; The Silver Streak; The Great Impersonation; The Last Days of Pompeii; The Three Musketeers; Fighting Youth. **1936** The Witness Chair; Mary of Scotland; The Big Game; Make Way for a Lady; One Rainy Afternoon; Lloyds of London; Fifteen Maiden Lane. **1937** Four Days' Wonder; Outcast; Think Fast, Mr. Moto; Damaged Lives.

KINSELLA, KATHLEEN (Kathleen Freeland)
Born: 1878, Liverpool, England. Died: Mar. 25, 1961, Washington. Stage and screen actress. Appeared in silents for Biograph.

KINSELLA, WALTER A.
Born: Aug. 16, 1900, New York, N.Y. Died: May 11, 1975, Englewood, N.J. Screen, stage, television, radio actor and amateur track star.

Appeared in: **1950** The Tattooed Stranger.

KINSOLVING, LEE (Arthur Lee Kinsolving, Jr.)
Born: 1938. Died: Dec. 4, 1974, Palm Beach, Fla. Screen, stage and television actor.

Appeared in: **1960** All the Young Men; Khovanschina; The Dark at the Top of the Stairs. **1961** The Explosive Generation.

KIPPEN, MANART
Died: Oct. 12, 1947, Claremore, Okla. (auto accident injuries). Screen, stage and radio actor.

Appeared in: **1941** Flight from Destiny. **1942** The Wife Takes a Flyer; Jungle Siren. **1943** Mission to Moscow; The Song of Bernadette. **1944** Three Russian Girls. **1945** Mildred Pierce; Roughly Speaking; Flame of Barbary Coast.

KIRBY, DAVID D.
Born: 1880. Died: Apr. 4, 1954, Hollywood, Calif. Screen actor.

Appeared in: **1921** The Ranger and the Law. **1923** Danger Ahead; The Mailman; In the Palace of the King. **1924** Darwin Was Right; Spirit of the U.S.A.; The Man Who Came Back; Nellie, the Beautiful Cloak Model; The Dangerous Coward; Life's Greatest Game; The Man Who Played Square; Lightning Romance; The Mask of Lopez. **1925** Easy Money; Ridin' the Wind; Youth's Gamble; The Last Edition; Lawful Cheaters; The Snob Buster. **1926** Danger Quest; The King of the Turf; The Fighting Edge; The Dangerous Dude; The Night Owl. **1927** The Royal American; The Shield of Honor; The Sunset Derby; The Silent Avenger. **1928** Burning Bridges; The Upland Rider.

KIRBY, JOHN
Born: 1932, Australia. Died: July 3, 1973, Madrid, Spain (apparent heart attack). Screen, stage and television actor.

Appeared in: **1947** Sepia Cinderella. **1955** An Annapolis Story; Air Strike.

KIRBY, WILLIAM WARNER
Born: Apr. 4, 1876, Germany. Died: Apr. 17, 1914, Los Angeles, Calif. (blood poisoning following lacerations inflicted by lion during filming). Screen actor.

KIRK, FAY B. (Fay Baker)
Born: 1894. Died: Nov. 13, 1954, New York, N.Y. (heart attack). Screen, stage and vaudeville actress.

Appeared in: **1946** Notorious. **1950** Chain Lightning. **1951** The House on Telegraph Hill.

KIRK, JACK "PAPPY" (aka JOHN KIRKHUFF and aka JACK HUFF)
Born: 1895. Died: Sept. 3, 1948, Alaska. Screen actor. Was one of the first singing cowboys.

Appeared in: **1925** Sackcloth and Scarlet; Limited Mail; Zander the Great. **1926** The Stolen Ranch. **1934** In Old Santa Fe. **1936** The Singing Cowboy; Guns and Guitars; The Lonely Trail. **1937** Hit the Saddle; Git Along, Little Dogies; Yodelin' Kid from Pine Ridge; Springtime in the Rockies. **1938** Gold Mine in the Sky; Pals of the Saddle; Rhythm of the Saddle; The Last Stand. **1939** Rovin' Tumbleweeds; Rough Riders' Round-Up. **1940** Gaucho Serenade; Melody Ranch; Lone Star Raiders; Rocky Mountain Rangers; The Tulsa Kid. **1941** Under Fiesta Stars; Sierra Sue; Prairie Pioneers; In Old Cheyenne; Bad Man of Deadwood; Jesse James at Bay; Death Valley Outlaws; Prairie Schooners; The Shining Hill; Kansas Cyclone. **1942** Home in Wyomin'; Westward Ho; The Phantom Plainsmen; West of Tombstone; Jesse James, Jr.; South of Santa Fe; Sunset Serenade. **1943** Hail to the Rangers; Carson City Cyclone; Death Valley Manhunt. **1944** The Cowboy and the Senorita; Beneath Western Skies; The Vigilantes Ride; Call of the Rockies; The San Antonio Kid; Pride of the Plains; Mojave Firebrand; Silver City Kid; Stagecoach to Monterey; Sheriff of Sundown; Firebrands of Arizona; Cheyenne Wildcat; Code of the Prairie; Bordertown Trail; Zorro's Black Whip (serial). **1945** Sheriff of Cimarron; Trail of Kit Carson. **1946** King of the Forest Rangers (serial); Home on the Range; Gunning for Vengeance; California Gold Rush; Texas Panhandle; Desert Horseman; Conquest of Cheyenne; The Phantom Rider (serial). **1947** Oregon Trail Scouts; Law of the Canyon; Son of Zorro (serial). **1948** Adventures of Frank and Jesse James (serial). **1949** Oklahoma Badlands; The Bold Frontiersman.

KIRKE, DONALD (William H. F. Kirk)
Born: May 17, 1902, Jersey City, N.J. Died: May 18, 1971. Screen actor.

Appeared in: **1930** Follow the Leader. **1933** Women Won't Tell; Blondie Johnson; Hidden Gold. **1935** Let 'Em Have It; The Ghost Walks. **1936** Country Gentlemen; Border Flight; In His Steps; Sunset of Power; Ride 'Em Cowboy; Oh, Susanna! **1937** Venus Makes Trouble; The Shadow; The Emperor's Candlesticks; Midnight Madonna; Take the Heir; The Big Shot; Paradise Express. **1938** Hawaii Calls; I Demand Payment. **1940** The Showdown. **1942** A Night for Crime; Outlaws of Pine Ridge. **1943** G-Men vs. the Black Dragon (serial). **1947** Hoppy's Holiday. **1956** Scandal, Inc.

KIRKHUFF, JOHN. See JACK KIRK

KIRKLAND, DAVID
Born: 1878, San Francisco, Calif. Died: Oct. 27, 1964. Screen, stage actor, film director, producer, stage director and screenwriter. Entered films as an extra in 1911 with Melies Company.

Appeared in: **1914–15** Snakeville Comedies.

KIRKLAND, HARDEE
Born: c. 1864, England. Died: Feb. 20, 1929, Calif. Screen, stage and vaudeville actor.

Appeared in: **1918** Sporting Life. **1919** The Peace of Roaring River. **1921** The Ace of Hearts; Ladies Must Live; From the Ground Up; A Perfect Crime; Roads of Destiny; The Lure of Jade. **1922** Sherlock Brown; Honor First; Youth to Youth; Without Compromise; They Like 'Em Rough; The Face Between; Very Truly Yours. **1923** Woman-Proof; Are You a Failure?; The Mailman; Quicksands; Hell's Hole; While Paris Sleeps. **1924** The Great Diamond Mystery. **1925** The Shadow on the Wall; Private Affairs; The Arizona Romeo.

KIRKLAND, MURIEL
Born: Aug. 19, 1903, Yonkers, N.Y. Died: Sept. 25, 1971, New York, N.Y. (emphysema and complications). Screen, stage, radio and television actress. Married to actor Staats Cotsworth.

Appeared in: **1933** Fast Workers; Hold Your Man; Cocktail Hour; To the Last Man; Secret of the Blue Room. **1934** Nana; Little Man, What Now?; The White Parade.

KIRKWOOD, GERTRUDE. See GERTRUDE R. ROBINSON

KIRKWOOD, JACK
Born: 1895, Scotland. Died: Aug. 2, 1964, Las Vegas, Nev. (heart attack). Screen, stage, vaudeville, burlesque, radio and television actor.

Appeared in: **1949** Chicken Every Sunday. **1950** Father Makes Good; Joe Pa-

looka in Humphrey Takes a Chance; Never a Dull Moment; Fancy Pants. **1951** One Wild Night (short).

KIRKWOOD, JAMES
Born: Feb. 22, 1883, Grand Rapids, Mich. Died: Aug. 21, 1963, Woodland Hills, Calif. Stage and screen actor. Divorced from actresses Gertrude Robinson (dec. 1962), Beatrice Power and Lila Lee (dec. 1973).

Appeared in: **1909** The Road to the Heart; The Message; Was Justice Served?; The Rununciation; The Seventh Day; A Convict's Sacrifice; The Indian Runner's Romance; The Better Way; Pippa Passes; The Death Disc; 1776, or the Hessian Renegades; Through the Breakers; A Corner in Wheat; The Redman's View; The Rocky Road; The Honor of His Family; The Last Deal; The Renovations; The Mended Lute; Comato the Sioux. **1910** The Final Settlement; A Victim of Jealousy; The Modern Prodigal; Winning Back His Love. **1914** The Eagle's Mate; Home Sweet Home. **1920** Luck of the Irish; Heart of a Fool; Man, Woman and Marriage; The Branding Iron. **1921** The Sin Flood; The Great Impersonation; Bob Hampton of Placer; A Wise Fool. **1922** The Man from Home; Ebb Tide; Pink Gods; Under Two Flags. **1923** The Eagle's Feather; Ponjola; Human Wreckage; You Are Guilty. **1924** Wandering Husbands; Another Man's Wife; Broken Barriers; Circe, the Enchantress; The Painted Flapper; Discontented Husbands; Gerald Cranston's Lady; Love's Whirlpool. **1925** Lover's Island; Secrets of the Night; The Top of the World; The Police Patrol. **1926** That Royle Girl; Butterflies in the Rain; The Reckless Lady; The Wise Guy. **1927** Million Dollar Mystery. **1928** Someone to Love. **1929** Hearts in Exile; Black Waters; The Time, the Place and the Girl. **1930** Devil's Holiday; Worldly Goods; The Spoilers. **1931** A Holy Terror; Over the Hill; Young Sinners. **1932** Cheaters at Play; Charlie Chan's Chance; Lena Rivers; Careless Lady; She Wanted a Millionaire; The Rainbow Trail; My Pal, the King. **1934** Hired Wife. **1941** The Lady from Cheyenne; No Hands on the Clock. **1947** Driftwood. **1948** The Untamed Breed. **1949** The Doolins of Oklahoma; Red Stallion in the Rockies. **1950** The Nevadan; Fancy Pants; Stage to Tucson. **1951** Man in the Saddle. **1952** I Dream of Jeanie. **1953** Winning of the West; The Last Posse. **1954** Passion. **1956** The Search for Bridey Murphy. **1963** The Ugly American.

KIRKWOOD-HACKETT, EVA
Born: 1877, England. Died: Feb. 8, 1968, Dublin, Ireland. Screen actress and singer.

KITZMILLER, JOHN
Born: 1913, Battlecreek, Mich. Died: Feb. 23, 1965, Rome, Italy (cirrhosis of the liver). Black screen actor. Received Cannes Film Festival Best Acting Award in 1957 for Dolina Mira.

Appeared in: **1946** Paisa; To Live in Peace. **1948** Senza Pieta (Without Pity—US 1950). **1951** Lieutenant Craig—Missing; Luci del Varieta (Variety Lights—US 1965). **1956** Dolina Mira (aka Sergeant Jim—US 1962 and Mr. Jim—American). **1957** The Naked Earth. **1958** Vite Perdute (Lost Souls—US 1961). **1960** The Island Sinner. **1962** La Rivolta dei Mercenari (Revolt of the Mercenaries—US 1964); El Hijo del Captain Blood (The Son of Captain Blood—US 1964). **1963** Dr. No; La Tigre dei Sette Mari (Tiger of the Seven Seas—US 1964). **1964** Der Fluch der Grunen Augen (Cave of the Living Dead—US 1966). **1965** Onkel Toms Hutte (Uncle Tom's Cabin—US 1969).

KLEIN, AL
Born: 1885, New York, N.Y. Died: Sept. 5, 1951, Los Angeles, Calif. (cancer). Screen, stage and vaudeville actor. Part of vaudeville team of "The Klein Bros."

Appeared in: **1928** Jest Moments (short). **1932** Opportunity Night (short); Gold Digging Gentlemen (short). **1933** Broadway Bad; One Year Later. **1934** That's Gratitude; Million Dollar Ransom; 365 Nights in Hollywood. **1949** Oh, You Beautiful Doll.

KLEINAU, WILLY A.
Born: Germany. Died: Oct. 23, 1957, Berlin-Nuernberg Hwy.; Germany (auto accident). Stage and screen actor.

Appeared in: **1958** Der Hauptmann von Koepenick (The Captain from Koepenick); Wie Ein Sturmwind (Tempestuous Love). Other German film: Mein Bruder Josua.

KLEIN-ROGGE, RUDOLF
Born: 1889, Germany. Died: 1955. Screen actor.

Appeared in: **1921** Der Mude Tod. **1922** Dr. Mabuse (US 1927). **1924** Siegfried; Between Worlds. **1926** Metropolis. **1927** Peter the Pirate. **1928** Kriemhild's Revenge; Spione (Spies). **1929** Loves of Casanova; Forbidden Love. **1932** The Testament of Dr. Mabuse. **1935** Zwischen Himmel und Erde (Between Heaven and Earth). **1936** Die Frauen vom Tannhof; Grenzfeuer. **1937** Truxa. **1943** The Last Will of Dr. Mabuse.

KLERCKER, GEORG A. F.
Born: 1877, Kristianstad, Sweden. Died: 1951, Sweden? Screen actor, film director and screenwriter.

Appeared in: **1913** For Your Country. **1916** Love Will Conquer. Other Swedish films: This is Too Much for Me; The Power of Music; Arms in Your Hands; The Scandal; Tied to One's Memories; The First Prize; In the Spring of Life; When Love Kills; The Virago of the Osterman Brothers; The Secret of the Paradise Hotel; South of the Main Road.

KLOEPFER, EUGEN

Born: 1886, Thalheim, Germany. Died: 1950, Wiesbaden, Germany. Stage and screen actor. Entered films in 1918.

Appeared in: **1927** The Street; Explosion. **1929** Luther. **1932** 1914: The Last Day Before the War. **1934** Gehetzte Menschen; Fluechtlinge. **1936** The Private Life of Louis XIV. **1939** Jugend (Youth). **1940** The Living Dead.

KLONDIKE, PETE. *See* PETE HULEY

KNABB, HARRY G.

Born: 1891. Died: Dec. 17, 1955, Cincinnati, Ohio (heart attack). Stage and screen actor. Appeared in silent films.

KNAGGS, SKELTON (Skelton Barnaby Knaggs)

Born: June 27, 1911, England. Died: Apr. 30, 1955, Los Angeles, Calif. (cirrhosis of the liver). Screen actor.

Appeared in: 1943 The Ghost Ship. **1945** None but the Lonely Heart; Island of the Dead; House of Dracula. **1946** Terror by Night; A Scandal in Paris; Dick Tracy vs. Cueball. **1947** Dick Tracy and Gruesome. **1949** Master Minds. **1952** Blackbeard the Pirate. **1953** Rogue's March. **1955** Moonfleet.

KNIGHT, PERCIVAL

Born: c. 1873. Died: Nov. 27, 1923, Switzerland (tuberculosis). Stage and screen actor.

Appeared in: **1922** Sherlock Holmes.

KNOTT, ADELBERT (Adelbert del Knott)

Born: 1859. Died: May 3, 1933, Los Angeles, Calif. (injuries from fall). Stage and screen actor.

Appeared in: **1920** Flame of Youth. **1921** Serenade; The Lamplighter; Straight from the Shoulder. **1924** Dynamite Smith. **1925** Percy.

KNOTT, CLARA

Born: 1882. Died: Nov. 11, 1926, Hollywood, Calif. Screen and stage actress.

Appeared in: **1920** Old Lady 31.

KNOTT, ELSE

Born: 1912, Germany. Died: Aug. 10, 1975, Frankfurt-Main, West Germany (cancer). Screen, stage and television actress.

Appeared in: **1932** Morgenrot.

KNOTT, LYDIA

Born: Oct. 1, 1866, Tyner, Ind. Died: Mar. 30, 1955, Woodland Hills, Calif. Screen, stage and vaudeville actress.

Appeared in: **1917** Sudden Jim; The Clodhopper; Crime and Punishment. **1918** His Mother's Boy. **1919** Home; The Pointing Finger; Heart of Youth; What Every Woman Learns; In Wrong; Should a Woman Tell. **1920** Blackmail; Dwelling Place of Light; Homespun Folks; Peaceful Valley. **1921** Beating the Game; The Breaking Point; A Certain Rich Man; The Infamous Miss Revell; The Lure of Youth; Playing with Fire; Scrap Iron. **1922** Across the Dead-Line; Afraid to Fight; The Broadway Madonna; The Dangerous Little Demon; Dusk to Dawn; The Flirt; The Isle of Love; The Super Sex; Turn to the Right; The Unfoldment. **1923** Dollar Devils; Garrison's Finish; Held to Answer; The Man Life Passed By; St. Elmo; A Woman of Paris. **1924** Chalk Marks; Dynamite Smith; Gerald Cranston's Lady; The Perfect Flapper; Racing for Life; Those who Dance; The Whipping Boss; Women First. **1925** East Lynne; The Fearless Lover; High and Handsome; The Primrose Path; Rose of the World. **1926** Going Crooked; Kentucky Handicap. **1927** The King of Kings; Pretty Clothes; Life of an Actress. **1928** The House of Scandal; Two Lovers; Our Dancing Daughters; Guilty. **1930** Overland Bound; Men Without Law. **1931** The Conquering Horde; Skippy. **1932** Valley of Lawless Men; Final Edition. **1933** If I Had a Million; Hit the Deck. **1934** I'll Fix It; Men Without Law; Rocky Rhodes. **1937** Fair Warning.

KNOX, HUGH (Hugo B. Koch)

Died: Sept. 9, 1926, Seattle, Wash. Screen, stage actor, film and stage director.

KOBS, ALFRED

Born: 1881. Died: Oct. 20, 1929, Los Angeles, Calif. (tuberculosis). Screen actor.

KOERBER, HILDE

Born: 1906, Germany. Died: June 1, 1969, Berlin, Germany. Stage and screen actress.

Appeared in: **1936** Maria Die Magd (Maria, the Maiden). **1938** The Kreutzer

Sonata. **1948** Morituri. **1956** Hot Harvest. **1958** Das Madchen vom Moorhof (The Girl of the Moors—US 1961). **1959** The Third Sex. Other German films: The Ruler; The Great King.

KOHLER, FRED, SR.

Born: Apr. 20, 1889, Kansas City, Mo. Died: Oct. 28, 1938, Los Angeles, Calif. (heart attack). Screen, stage and vaudeville actor. Father of actor Fred Kohler, Jr.

Appeared in: **1911** Code of Honor (film debut). **1919** The Tiger's Trail (serial); Soldiers of Fortune. **1921** Cyclone Bliss; The Stampede; Thunder Island; A Daughter of the Law; Partners of the Tide. **1922** The Son of the Wolf; His Back against the Wall; Trimmed; The Scrapper; Without Compromise; Yellow Men and Gold. **1923** Anna Christie; Three Who Paid; The Eleventh Hour; The Flame of Life; Thru the Flames; Hell's Hole; The Red Warning; Shadows of the North. **1924** North of Hudson Bay; The Iron Horse; Abraham Lincoln; Fighting Fury. **1925** Dick Turpin; Winds of Chance; The Prairie Pirate; The Thundering Herd; Riders of the Purple Sage. **1926** The Country Beyond; The Ice Flood; Old Ironsides; Danger Quest. **1927** Shootin' Irons; The Way of All Flesh; The City Gone Wild; Underworld; The Blood Ship; The Gay Defender; Open Range; Loves of Carmen; The Devil's Masterpiece; The Rough Riders. **1928** The Spieler; Chinatown Charlie; The Vanishing Pioneer; The Dragnet; The Showdown; Forgotten Faces. **1929** Tide of Empire; Sal of Singapore; Say It with Songs; The Leatherneck; The Quitter; Broadway Babies; The Case of Lena Smith; The Dummy; River of Romance; Stairs of Sand; Thunderbolt. **1930** The Light of Western Stars; Nuits de Chicago (French release of Underworld—1927); Roadhouse Nights; Hell's Heroes; Under a Texas Moon; The Steel Highway. **1931** The Lash; Fighting Caravans; Right of Way; Woman Hungry; Other Men's Women; Soldiers' Plaything; Corsair; X Marks the Spot. **1932** Carnival Boat; Call Her Savage; Wild Horse Mesa; Rider of Death Valley; The Texas Bad Man. **1933** Constant Woman; The Fiddlin' Buckaroo; Under the Tonto Rim; The Deluge; Ship of Wanted Men; The Fourth Horseman. **1934** The Man from Hell; Last Round Up; Honor of the Range; Little Man; What Now? **1935** The Pecos Kid; Outlawed Guns; Border Brigand; Men of Action; The Trail's End; Toll of the Desert; Mississippi; Times Square Lady; West of the Pecos; Wilderness Mail; Goin' to Town; Hard Rock Harrigan; Stormy; The Frisco Kid; Horses Collars (short). **1936** Dangerous Intrigue; I Loved a Soldier; For the Service; Heart of the West; The Accusing Finger; Texas Ranger; The Plainsman. **1937** Arizona Mahoney; Daughter of Shanghai. **1938** Forbidden Valley; Gangs of New York; Painted Desert; Billy the Kid Returns; The Buccaneer; Blockade; Pure in Mind; Lawless Valley.

KOHLMAR, LEE

Born: 1878, Nuremberg, Germany. Died: May 15, 1946, Hollywood, Calif. (heart attack). Stage and screen actor.

Appeared in: **1920** The Flaming Disc (serial). **1921** High Heels; Orphans of the Storm. **1922** Breaking Home Ties. **1923** Potash and Perlmutter. **1930** Caught Short; Children of Pleasure; The Thirteenth Prisoner (short); The Richest Man in the World; Sins of the Children; The Kibitzer; The Melody Man; Personality. **1932** Jewel Robbery; Scarlet Dawn; The Strange Case of Clara Deane; The Tenderfoot; Silver Dollar. **1933** She Done Him Wrong; I Love That Man; Forgotten; Roman Scandals; Son of Kong. **1934** When Strangers Meet; The House of Rothschild; Twentieth Century; Shoot the Works. **1935** One More Spring; Ruggles of Red Gap; The Girl Friend; McFadden's Flats; Love in Bloom; Four Hours to Kill; Here Comes Cookie; Break of Hearts; Death from a Distance. **1936** A Son Comes Home. **1941** The Big Store.

KOKO

Born: 1940, Mexico, Mo. Died: 1968, Calif. Screen animal performer. Rex Allen's movie horse.

Appeared in: **1950** Under Mexicali Stars; Redwood Forest Trail; Hills of Oklahoma. **1951** Silver City Bonanza; Thunder in God's Country; Rodeo King and the Senorita; Utah Wagon Trail. **1952** The Last Musketeer; Colorado Sundown; Border Saddlemates; Old Oklahoma Plains. **1953** Old Overland Trail; Iron Mountain Trail; Down Laredo Way; Shadows of Tombstone. **1954** Red River Shore; Phantom Stallion.

KOLB, CLARENCE

Born: 1875. Died: Nov. 25, 1964, Los Angeles, Calif. (stroke). Screen, vaudeville and television actor. Partner with Max Dill (dec. 1949) in vaudeville team billed as "Kolb and Dill." The team appeared in film comedies 1916–1917.

Appeared in: **1917** Beloved Rogue; Mutual Star; Glory (Kolb and Dill). **1937** The Toast of New York; Portia on Trial; Wells Fargo. **1938** Gold Is Where You Find It; Merrily We Live; Give Me a Sailor; Carefree; The Law West of Tombstone. **1939** The Great Man Votes; It Could Happen to You; Honolulu; Society Lawyer; Five Little Peppers; I Was a Convict; Good Girls Go to Paris; Beware, Spooks!; Amazing Mr. Williams; Our Leading Citizen. **1940** The Five Little Peppers at Home; His Girl Friday; The Man Who Talked Too Much; No Time for Comedy; Tugboat Annie Sails Again; Michael Shayne, Private Detective. **1941** You're in the Army Now; Caught in the Draft; Nothing but the Truth; Bedtime Story; Night of January 16th; Hellzapoppin; Blossoms in the Dust. **1942** True to Life; The Ship's the Limit. **1943** The Falcon in Danger. **1944** Standing Room Only; Irish Eyes Are Smiling; Something for the Boys;

Three Is a Family. 1945 Road to Alcatraz; What a Blonde. 1946 The Kid from Brooklyn; White Tie and Tails. 1947 The Pilgrim Lady; Fun on a Weekend; Christmas Eve; The Lost Honeymoon; The Fabulous Joe; Shadowed; The High Cost of Living; Blondie in the Dough. 1949 Impact; Adam's Rib. 1952 The Rose Bowl Story. 1956 Glory; Shake, Rattle and Rock. 1957 Man of a Thousand Faces.

KOLB, THERESE
Born: 1856, Alsace, France. Died: Aug. 19, 1935, Levallois-Perret, France. Stage and screen actress.

Appeared in: 1929 Appasionata.

KOLKER, HENRY
Born: 1874, Germany. Died: July 15, 1947, Los Angeles, Calif. (injured in fall). Screen, stage actor, stage, film director and writer.

Appeared in: 1915 How Molly Made Good. 1916 Gloria's Romance. 1921 Disraeli; Bucking the Tiger; The Fighter; Who Am I? 1923 The Leopardess; The Snow Bride; The Purple Highway. 1925 Any Woman; Sally, Irene and Mary. 1926 Hell's 400; The Palace of Pleasure; Winning the Futurity; Wet Paint. 1927 Kiss in a Taxi; Rough House Rosie. 1928 Don't Marry; The Charge of the Gauchos; Midnight Rose; Soft Living. 1929 The Valiant; Pleasure Crazed; Coquette; Love, Live and Laugh. 1930 The Bad One; East is West; Way of All Men; Good Intentions; DuBarry, Woman of Passion. 1931 Don't Bet on Women; The Spy; Indiscreet; I Like Your Nerve. 1932 Washington Masquerade; The Devil and the Deep; The First Year; The Crash; Faithless; Jewel Robbery; Invincible. 1933 Gigolettes of Paris; Baby Face; The Keyhole; The Narrow Corner; Bureau of Missing Persons; A Bedtime Story; Golden Harvest; The Power and the Glory; Blood Money; I Loved a Woman; Meet the Baron; Notorious but Nice; Love, Honor and Oh, Baby! 1934 Name the Woman; Madame DuBarry; Blind Date; Imitation of Life; Exciting Adventure; The Band Plays On; A Lost Lady; Love Time; Million Dollar Ransom; Lady by Choice; Sing Sing Nights; Massacre; Wonder Bar; Sisters under the Skin; The Hell Cat; Whom the Gods Destroy; Journal of a Crime; Success at Any Price; She Loves Me Not; The Girl from Missouri; Now and Forever. 1935 One New York Night; Only Eight Hours; The Black Room Mystery; Ladies Love Danger; Times Square Lady; Red Hot Tires; The Case of the Curious Bride; Shipmates Forever; Charlie Chan in Paris; Diamond Jim; Three Kids and a Queen; Society Doctor; Mad Love; Here Comes the Band; Red Salute; The Mystery Man; Honeymoon Limited; My Marriage; The Ghost Walks; The Florentine Dagger; Last Days of Pompeii; Frisco Waterfront. 1936 Collegiate; Bullets or Ballots; Romeo and Juliet; Sitting on the Moon; In His Steps; Great Guy; The Man Who Lived Twice; Theodora Goes Wild. 1937 They Wanted to Marry; Under Cover of Night; Conquest; Thoroughbreds Don't Cry; Green Light; Once a Doctor; Without Warning; Maid of Salem; Let Them Live; The Devil Is Driving. 1938 The Invisible Menace; The Adventures of Marco Polo; The Cowboy and the Lady; Holiday; Safety in Numbers; Too Hot to Handle. 1939 Let Us Live; Hidden Power; Parents on Trial; Should Husbands Work?; Main Street Lawyer; The Real Glory; Here I Am a Stranger; Union Pacific. 1940 Grand Ole Opry; Money and the Woman. 1941 The Parson of Panamint; The Man Who Lost Himself; The Great Swindle; A Woman's Face; Sing for Your Supper; Las Vegas Nights. 1942 Reunion. 1943 Sarong Girl. 1944 Bluebeard. 1947 Monsieur Verdoux.

KOLLMAR, RICHARD
Born: 1910. Died: Jan. 7, 1971. Screen actor.

Appeared in: 1948 Close-Up.

KOLOSSY, ERIKA
Born: Hungary. Died: Aug. 14, 1963, New York, N.Y. (leukemia). Screen actress, opera performer and singer.

KOMAI, TETSU (Tetsuo Komai)
Born: Apr. 23, 1894, Kumamoto, Japan. Died: Aug. 10, 1970, Gardena, Calif. (congestive heart failure). Screen actor. Entered films in 1923.

Appeared in 1926 Old Ironsides. 1927 Shanghai Bound; Streets of Shanghai. 1928 Detectives; Moran of the Marines; The Woman from Moscow. 1929 Bulldog Drummond; Chinatown Nights (aka Tong War). 1930 East is West; The Return of Dr. Fu Manchu. 1931 Daughter of the Dragon. 1932 She Wanted a Millionaire; War Correspondent. 1933 Island of Lost Souls; Secrets of Wu Sin; A Study in Scarlet. 1934 Four Frightened People; Now and Forever. 1935 Oil for the Lamps of China; Without Regret. 1936 Klondike Annie; Roaming Lady; Princess Comes Across; Isle of Fury. 1937 China Passage; That Man's Here Again; West of Shanghai. 1939 The Real Glory. 1940 The Letter. 1941 Sundown; Adventures of Captain Marvel (serial). 1949 Tokyo Joe. 1952 Japanese War Bride. 1958 Tank Battalion. 1964 The Night Walker.

KOMISSAROV, ALEKSANDR
Born: 1904, Russia. Died: Aug. 4, 1975, Moscow, Russia. Stage and screen actor.

Appeared in: 1968 War and Peace.

KONSTANTIN, LEOPOLDINE
Born: c. 1890. Died: 1950s, Vienna, Austria? Stage and screen actress.

Appeared in: 1933 Saison in Kairo. 1935 Prinzessin, Turandot; Liebe Dumme Mama (Stupid Mamma); Frischer Wind aus Kanada; Der Alte und der Junge Koenig. 1946 Notorious.

KOOY, PETE
Died: Apr. 20, 1963, Hollywood, Calif. Screen actor.

Appeared in: 1957 Death in Small Doses; Dino.

KOPP, MILA
Born: 1905, Vienna, Austria. Died: Jan. 15, 1973, Stuttgart, Germany (circulatory ailment). Screen, stage and television actress. Married to actor Christian Kayssler (dec. 1944).

KOPPENS, EMILE. See EMILE KEPPENS

KORAYIM, MOHAMED
Born: 1898, Egypt. Died: May 28, 1972, Cairo, Egypt. Screen actor, film producer and director. Appeared in films during the silents.

KORFF, ARNOLD
Born: 1871. Died: June 2, 1944, New York, N.Y. (heart ailment). Screen, stage and radio actor.

Appeared in: 1929 Dancing Vienna. 1930 Doughboys; Monsieur Le Fox; The Royal Family at Broadway; Men of the North; Olympia; The Jazz King. 1931 An American Tragedy; Ambassador Bill; The Unholy Garden. 1932 Scarlet Dawn; Evenings for Sale; Secrets of the French Police. 1934 Black Moon. 1935 Shanghai; All the Kings Horses; Wings in the Dark; Paris in Spring. 1936 Magnificent Obsession.

KORNMAN, MARY
Born: 1917, Idaho Falls, Idaho. Died: June 1, 1973, Glendale, Calif. (cancer). Screen and vaudeville actress. Divorced from cameraman Leo Tovar and later married to screen extra and animal trainer Ralph McCutcheon (dec. 1975). Was first leading lady in the "Our Gang" comedies.

Appeared in: 1930 The following shorts: Doctor's Orders; Bigger and Better; Ladies Last. 1931 Are These Our Children?; plus the following shorts: Blood and Thunder; High Gear; Love Fever; Air Tight; Call a Cop; Mama Loves Papa; The Kickoff. 1932 The following shorts: Love Pains; The Knockout; You're Telling Me; Too Many Women; Wild Babies. 1933 Flying Down to Rio; Bondage (aka The House of Refuge); Neighbors' Wives; College Humor; Fish Hooky (short); Please (short). 1934 The Quitter; Strictly Dynamite; Picture Brides; Just an Echo (short). 1935 Roaring Roads; Desert Trail; Adventurous Knights; Smoky Smith. 1936 The Calling of Dan Matthews. 1937 Youth on Parole; Swing It, Professor; Reunion in Rhythm (short). 1938 King of the Newsboys; I Am a Criminal; Outside of Paradise. 1940 On the Spot.

KORTMAN, ROBERT F.
Born: Dec. 24, 1887, Philadelphia, Pa. Died: Mar. 13, 1967, Long Beach, Calif. (cancer). Screen actor.

Appeared in: 1916 Lieut. Denny, U.S.A.; Ambrose's Rapid Rise; Safety First Ambrose; The Waifs; The No-Good Guy; Captive God. 1917 Cactus Nell; His Naughty Thought. 1918 The Narrow Trail. 1919 The Great Radium Mystery; Square Deal Sanderson. 1921 Godless Men; Montana Bill. 1922 Another Man's Boots; Arabian Love; Gun Shy; The Lone Hand; Travelin' On; Wolf Pack. 1923 Fleetwing; All the Brothers Were Valiant. 1924 The White Sheep. 1926 The Devil Horse. 1927 Blood Will Tell; Hills of Peril; Sunrise—A Song of Two Humans. 1928 The Big Killing. 1930 The Lone Defender (serial); Bear Shooters (short); The Big Kick (short). 1931 The Lightning Warrior (serial); The Vanishing Legion (serial); Pardon Us; Beau Hunks (short); The Conquering Horde; 24 Hours; Branded. 1932 Fighting Fool; Night Rider; White Eagle; Gold; Island of Lost Souls; Come on Danger; The Forty-Niners. 1933 Rainbow Ranch; Whispering Shadows (serial); The Midnight Patrol (short); Phantom Thunderbolt; Terror Trail; Island of Lost Souls; Come on Danger; Sunset Pass; The Fugitive; King of the Arena; Trail Drive. 1934 Sixteen Fathoms Deep; Fighting Code; Smoking Guns; A Man's Game; Burn 'Em Up Barnes (serial and feature); Mystery Mountain; The Trail Drive. 1935 When a Man Sees Red; The Miracle Rider (serial); Crimson Trail; The Ivory-Handled Gun; Wild Mustang. 1936 Swifty; Heroes of the Range; Feud of the West; Winds of the Wasteland; Romance Rides the Range; The Lonely Trail; Robinson Crusoe of Clipper Island (serial); The Vigilantes are Coming (serial); On the Wrong Trek (short); Trail of the Lonesome Pine; Ghost Town Gold. 1937 Sandflow; Black Aces; Texas Trail; Zorro Rides Again (serial); Wild West Days (serial). 1938 Law of the Texan. 1939 The Renegade Trail; The Renegade Ranger; Oklahoma Frontier. 1940 Adventures of Red Ryder (serial). 1941 Fugitive Valley. 1943 Avenging Rider; The Sundown Kid; The Black Hills Express. 1944 Forty Thieves; Wyoming Hurricane; The Vigilantes Ride; Call of the Rockies; The Pinto Bandit; Guns of the Law; The Whispering Skull; Saddle Leather Law. 1946 Frontier Gun Law; Gunning for Vengeance; Landrush; Wild Harvest. 1948 Whispering Smith. 1949 Copper Canyon. 1951 Flaming Feather.

KORTNER, FRITZ

Born: May 12, 1892, Vienna, Austria. Died: July 22, 1970, Munich, Germany (leukemia). Screen actor, stage director and writer.

Appeared in: 1926 Backstairs. 1927 Beethoven; Warning Shadows. 1928 Maria Stuart; Primanerliebe; Dame Care; The Hands of Orlac; Mata Hari; The Red Dancer; Pandora's Box. 1929 The Life of Beethoven; A Scandal in Paris; Three Loves; The Spy of Madame de Pompadour. 1930 Caught in Berlin's Underworld; The Last Night; Murderer Dimitri Karamasoff; Danton. 1931 The Dreyfus Case. 1932 Der Andere. 1934 Chu Chin Chow; Evensong. 1935 Abdul the Damned. 1936 The Crouching Beast. 1940 The Dreyfus Case (and 1931 version). 1943 The Strange Death of Adolf Hitler. 1945 The Hitler Gang. 1946 Somewhere in the Night; The Wife of Monte Cristo. 1947 The Brasher Doubloon; The High Window; The Razor's Edge. 1945 The Vicious Circle; Berlin Express. 1951 The Last Illusion. 1953 Ali Baba Nights. 1955 Die Stadt ist Voller Geheinnisse (aka City of Secrets—US 1963).

KOSHETZ, NINA

Born: 1892, Russia. Died: May 14, 1965, Santa Ana, Calif. Screen actress and singer. Mother of actress Marina Koshetz.

Appeared in: 1938 Algiers. 1944 Our Hearts Were Young and Gay. 1946 The Chase. 1950 It's a Small World. 1952 Captain Pirate. 1956 Hot Blood.

KOSLOFF, THEODORE

Born: Russia. Died: Nov. 22, 1956, Los Angeles, Calif. Screen actor and ballet dancer.

Appeared in: 1917 The Woman God Forgot. 1920 Why Change Your Wife?; The City of Masks. 1921 The Affairs of Anatol; Fool's Paradise; Forbidden Fruit. 1922 The Green Temptation; Manslaughter; To Have and to Hold; The Dictator; The Lane That Had No Turning; The Law of the Lawless. 1923 Adam's Rib; Children of Jazz; Hollywood. 1924 Triumph; Don't Call It Love; Feet of Clay. 1925 Beggar on Horseback; The Golden Bed; New Lives for Old. 1926 The Volga Boatman. 1927 King of Kings; The Little Adventuress. 1928 Woman Wise. 1930 Sunny; Madam Satan.

KOTSONAROS, GEORGE

Born: Nauplie, Greece. Died: July 13, 1933. Screen actor.

Appeared in: 1926 Cupid's Knockout; While London Sleeps. 1927 Catch-As-Catch-Can; The Private Life of Helen of Troy; The Wizard; The Tender Hour; King of the Jungle (serial). 1928 Beggars of Life; The Fifty-Fifty Girl; The Street of Sin. 1929 The Shakedown; The Body Punch. 1930 Dangerous Paradise. 1931 Honeymoon Lane.

KOVACS, ERNIE

Born: Jan. 23, 1919, Trenton, N.J. Died: Jan. 12, 1962, Beverly Hills, Calif. (auto accident). Screen, stage and television actor. Married to actress Edie Adams.

Appeared in: 1957 Operation Mad Ball (film debut). 1958 Bell, Book and Candle; Showdown at Ulcer Gulch (a commercial short for Saturday Evening Post). 1959 It Happened to Jane. 1960 Our Man in Havana; Strangers When We Meet; Wake Me When It's Over; North to Alaska; Pepe. 1961 Sail a Crooked Ship; Five Golden Hours.

KOWAL, MITCHELL (aka MITCHELL KOWAL)

Born: 1916. Died: May 2, 1971, near Fuernitz, Austria (train wreck). Screen actor. Appeared in U.S., Italian and Polish films.

Appeared in: 1953 Violated 1954 Francis Joins the WACS. 1955 The Big Bluff; Abbott and Costello Meet the Mummy. 1959 John Paul Jones. 1962 Jada Goscie Jada (Guests Are Coming—US 1965). 1963 55 Days at Peking. 1969 Francesco Bertazzoli; Investigator.

KOZINTSEV, GRIGORY

Born: 1905, Russia. Died: May 11, 1973, Leningrad, Russia. Screen actor, film director, producer, screenwriter and author. Entered film as an actor and then turned director.

KRAH, MARC (Max Krahmalkov)

Born: Jan. 24, 1906. Died: Sept. 25, 1973 (nephrosclerosis). Screen actor.

Appeared in: 1947 Riff-raff; Devilship; Intrigue. 1948 Alias a Gentleman. 1949 Criss Cross. 1950 Black Hand; Call of the Klondike. 1951 Sky High. 1952 Strange Fascination. 1953 Beneath the 12 Mile Reef.

KRAHLY, HANNS (aka HANS KRALY)

Born: 1885. Died: 1950, Los Angeles, Calif. Screen actor, film director and screenwriter.

KRAMER, IDA

Born: 1878. Died: Oct. 15, 1930, Brooklyn, N.Y. (heart attack). Stage and screen actress.

Appeared in: 1928 Abie's Irish Rose (stage and film versions).

KRAMER, PHIL

Born: 1900. Died: Mar. 31, 1972, North Hudson, N.J. (heart attack). Screen, radio and television actor.

Appeared in: 1935 Hands Across the Table. 1942 Suicide Squadron.

KRAMER, WRIGHT

Born: 1870. Died: Nov. 14, 1941, Hollywood, Calif. Screen, stage and vaudeville actor.

Appeared in: 1938 The Gladiator; Professor Beware. 1939 Mr. Smith Goes to Washington; Good Girls Go to Paris; It Could Happen to You. 1940 Anne of Windy Poplars; Before I Hang; Dark Streets of Cairo; The Showdown.

KRAUSS, CHARLES

Born: France. Died: Oct. 1926. Screen actor and film producer.

KRAUSS, WERNER

Born: 1884, Gestungshausen, Germany. Died: Oct. 20, 1959, Vienna, Austria. Screen actor.

Appeared in: 1919 The Cabinet of Dr. Caligari. 1921 All for a Woman; Shattered. 1923 Othello. 1924 Waxworks. 1925 The Student of Prague. 1926 Secrets of a Soul; The Three Way Works; Shattered (and 1921 version). 1927 Streets of Sorrow; Tartuffe. 1928 Jealousy; Unwelcome Children; The Man Who Cheated Life; Midsummer Night's Dream; Decameron Nights. 1929 Three Wax Men; The Jolly Peasant; Nana; Royal Scandal; The Treasure; Looping the Loop; Fighting the White Slave Traffic. 1932 Mensch Ohne Namen (The Man without a Name); Yorck. 1934 Crown of Thorns. 1937 Vienna Burgtheater. 1939 Robert Koch. 1940 Jew Suess (German propaganda film).

KRIEGER, LEE

Born: 1919. Died: Dec. 22, 1967, Van Nuys, Calif. Screen, stage and television actor.

Appeared in: 1961 Bachelor in Paradise. 1962 Period of Adjustment; Convicts Four; The Horizontal Lieutenant. 1967 The Reluctant Astronaut.

KROELL, ADRIENNE

Born: 1892. Died: Oct. 2, 1949, Evanston, Ill. (arthritis). Screen actress.

Appeared in: 1911 Two Orphans; Strategy. 1912 The Law of the North; An Unexpected Fortune; Into the Genuine; The Fire-Fighter's Love; The Miller of Burgundy; Her Bitter Lesson; The Adopted Son; Under Suspicion; Murray the Masher. 1913 Nobody's Boy; Don't Let Mother Know or, The Bliss of Ignorance; Tommy's Atonement; A Change of Administration; The Water Rat; The Ex-Convict's Plunge; The Pink Opera Cloak.

KROHNER, SARAH

Born: 1883. Died: June 9, 1959, Brooklyn, N.Y. Screen, stage and radio actress. Appeared in Yiddish films.

Appeared in: 1939 Molly. 1951 Mirele Efros.

KRUEGER, BUM (Willy Krueger)

Born: 1906, Germany. Died: Mar. 15, 1971, West Berlin, Germany (heart attack). Screen, stage and television actor.

Appeared in: 1956 Du Bist Musik (US 1962). 1959 The Eighth Day of the Week; Verbrechen nach Schulschluss (The Young Go Wild—US 1962). Other German films: Film without Title; The Gentleman from the Other Star; The Devil's General.

KRUGER, ALMA

Born: 1868, Pittsburgh, Pa. Died: Apr. 5, 1960, Seattle, Wash. Screen, stage and radio actress. Her best known role was as Mollie Bird, head nurse, in "Dr. Kildare" film series.

Appeared in: 1936 These Three; Craig's Wife; Love Letters of a Star. 1937 Breezing Home; The Mighty Treve; The Man in Blue; One Hundred Men and a Girl; Vogues of 1938. 1938 The Toy Wife; Marie Antoinette; The Great Waltz; Mother Carey's Chickens; Tarnished Angel; Four's a Crowd. 1939 The Secret of Dr. Kildare; Made for Each Other; Balalaika; Calling Dr. Kildare. 1940 His Girl Friday; Dr. Kildare's Strangest Case; Dr. Kildare's Crisis; Dr. Kildare Goes Home; Anne of Windy Poplars; You'll Find Out. 1941 Blonde Inspiration; Trial of Mary Dugan; Puddin' Head; The People vs. Dr. Kildare; Dr. Kildare's Wedding Day; Dr. Kildare's Victory. 1942 Saboteur; Calling Dr. Gillespie; Dr. Gillespie's New Assistant; That Other Woman. 1943 Dr. Gillespie's Criminal Case. 1944 Three Men in White; Our Hearts Were Young and Gay; Babes on Swing Street; Between Two Women. 1945 The Crime Doctor's Warning; A Royal Scandal. 1946 Do You Love Me? 1947 Forever Amber; Dark Delusion; Fun On a Weekend.

KRUGER, FRED H.

Born: 1913. Died: Dec. 5, 1961, Hollywood, Calif. (cerebral hemorrhage). Screen and television actor.

Appeared in: 1958 Girls on the Loose.

KRUGER, HAROLD "STUBBY"

Born: 1897, Honolulu, Hawaii. Died: Oct. 7, 1965, Hollywood, Calif. (heart attack). Screen stuntman and swimmer. Doubled for Douglas Fairbanks in the Black Pirate (1926) and Spencer Tracy in The Old Man and the Sea (1958).

Appeared in: Paramount shorts: Grantland Rice Sportlight for Pathe. **1926** Black Pirate; Beloved Rogue. **1955** Mister Roberts. **1958** The Old Man and the Sea.

KRUGER, OTTO

Born: Sept. 6, 1885, Toledo, Ohio. Died: Sept. 6, 1974, Woodland Hills, Calif. (stroke and cerebral vascular complications). Screen, stage, radio, vaudeville and television actor. Married to actress Sue MacManamy (dec. 1976).

Appeared in: **1915** When the Call Came. **1923** Under the Red Robe. **1929** Mr. Intruder (short). **1933** Turn Back the Clock; Beauty for Sale; Ever in My Heart; Gallant Lady; The Prizefighter and the Lady; The Women in His Life. **1934** The Crime Doctor; Men in White; Springtime for Henry; Paris Interlude; Chained; Treasure Island. **1935** Vanessa—Her Love Story; Two Sinners. **1936** Lady of Secrets; Dracula's Daughter; Living Dangerously. **1937** They Won't Forget; Glamorous Nights; Counsel for Crime; The Barrier. **1938** Thanks for the Memory; I Am the Law; The Housemaster (US 1939); Exposed; Star of the Circus (aka Hidden Menace—US 1940). **1939** Disbarred; Another Thin Man; Zero Hour; A Woman Is the Judge; The Gang's All Here (aka The Amazing Mr. Forrest—US); Black Eyes. **1940** Seventeen; Scandal Sheet; The Story of Dr. Ehrlich's Magic Bullet (aka Dr. Ehrlich's Magic Bullet); A Dispatch from Reuters; The Man I Married. **1941** The Big Boss; The Men in Her Life; Mercy Island. **1942** Saboteur; Friendly Enemies; Secrets of a Co-Ed. **1943** Corregidor; Night Plane from Chungking; Stage Door Canteen; Tarzan's Desert Mystery; Hitler's Children. **1944** Cover Girl; Knickerbocker Holiday; Storm Over Lisbon; Farewell, My Lovely (aka Murder My Sweet); They Live in Fear; American's Children; The Amazing Mr. Forrest. **1945** Wonder Man; The Chicago Kid; Earl Carroll's Vanities; Jungle Captive; On Stage Everybody; The Woman Who Came Back; Allotment Wives; Escape in the Fog. **1946** Duel in the Sun; The Fabulous Suzanne. **1947** Love and Learn. **1948** Smart Woman; Lulu Belle. **1950** 711 Ocean Drive. **1951** Payment on Demand (aka Story of Divorce); Valentino. **1952** High Noon. **1954** Magnificent Obsession; Black Widow. **1955** The Last Command. **1958** The Colossus of New York. **1959** The Young Philadelphians; Cash McCall. **1962** The Wonderful World of the Brothers Grimm. **1964** Sex and the Single Girl.

KRUMSCHMIDT, EBERHARD

Born: 1905. Died: June 3, 1956, New York, N.Y. Screen, stage, radio, television actor and stage director.

Appeared in: **1946** Notorious.

KRUPA, GENE

Born: Jan. 15, 1909, Chicago, Ill. Died: Oct. 16, 1973, Yonkers, N.Y. (leukemia). Musician, drummer, band leader and screen actor.

Appeared in: **1939** Some Like It Hot. **1942** Ball of Fire. **1945** George White's Scandals. **1947** Beat the Band. **1948** Glamour Girl. **1949** Make Believe Ballroom. **1954** The Glenn Miller Story. **1955** The Benny Goodman Story.

KRUPP, VERA (Vera Hosenfeldt)

Born: 1910, Germany. Died: Oct. 16, 1967, Los Angeles, Calif. Screen actress.

KULKAVICH, BOMBER. See HENRY KULKY

KULKY, HENRY "HANK" (aka BOMBER KULKAVICH)

Born: Aug. 11, 1911, Hastings-on-the-Hudson, N.Y. Died: Feb. 12, 1965, Oceanside, Calif. (heart attack). Screen, television actor and professional wrestler known as "Bomber Kulkavich."

Appeared in: **1947** A Likely Story. **1948** Call Northside 777. **1949** Tarzan's Magic Fountain; Bandits of El Dorado. **1950** Wabash Avenue; South Sea Sinner; Bodyhold; Jiggs and Maggie Out West. **1951** The Guy Who Came Back; The Love Nest; Chinatown Chump (short); The Kid from Amarillo; Fixed Bayonets. **1952** The World in His Arms; Gobs and Gals; No Holds Barred; Target Hong Kong; My Wife's Best Friend; Red Skies of Montana; What Price Glory? **1953** The Robe; The 5,000 Fingers of Dr. T.; Down Among the Sheltering Palms; The Glory Brigade; The Charge at Feather River. **1954** A Star Is Born; Fireman Save My Child; Yukon Vengeance; Hell and High Water; Tobor the Great; The Steel Cage. **1955** Prince of Players; New York Confidential; Abbott and Costello Meet the Keystone Kops; Illegal. **1957** Sierra Stranger. **1959** Up Periscope; The Gunfight at Dodge City. **1960** Guns of the Timberland. **1964** A Global Affair.

KUMARI, MEENA (Mehzabeenara Begum)

Born: 1932, India. Died: Mar. 31, 1972, Bombay, India (liver ailment). Screen actress and screenwriter.

Appeared in: Baiju Bawra; Parineeta; Bandish; Sahib Bibi Aur Ghulam; Ek Hi Bhool.

KUN, MAGDA

Born: 1911, Hungary. Died: Nov. 7, 1945, London, England. Stage and screen actress.

Appeared in: **1933** Filleres Gyoers. **1934** Und Es Leuchtet die Puszta. **1935** Dance Band. **1938** Busuini Nem Jo (Don't Worry); Majd a Zsuzsi.

KUNDE, AL

Born: 1888. Died: Aug. 10, 1952, Los Angeles, Calif. (cancer). Screen actor and professional boxer known as "Al Krieger."

KUNDE, ANNE

Born: 1896. Died: June 14, 1960, Hollywood, Calif. Screen actress.

Appeared in: **1959** Li'l Abner. **1961** One-Eye Jacks.

KUNKEL, GEORGE

Born: 1867. Died: Nov. 8, 1937, Hollywood, Calif. (heart attack). Screen actor.

Appeared in: **1919** Leave It to Susan. **1921** An Unwilling Hero; Where Men Are Men.

KUPCINET, KARYN

Born: Mar. 6, 1941. Died: Nov. 28, 1963, West Los Angeles, Calif. (murdered). Screen, stage and television actress.

Appeared in: **1961** The Ladies' Man.

KUWA, GEORGE K.

Born: Apr. 7, 1885, Japan. Died: Oct. 13, 1931. Screen and stage actor.

Appeared in: **1919** Toby's Bow. **1921** Invisible Fear; Nobody's Fool. **1922** The Beautiful and Damned; Bought and Paid For; Enter Madame; Five Days to Live; The Half Breed; Moran of the Lady Letty; Sherlock Brown. **1923** Daddy; The Eternal Struggle; The World's Applause. **1924** Broken Barriers; Curlytop; The Storm Daughter; The Man from Wyoming. **1925** Head Winds; Oh, Doctor!; The Wife Who Wasn't Wanted; A Son of His Father. **1926** A Trip to Chinatown; The Enchanted Hill; That Model from Paris; The Nut-Cracker; Money Talks; The Silver Treasure; The House Without a Key (serial). **1927** The Chinese Parrot; The Dice Woman; Perch of the Devil; The Night Bride; White Pants Willie; The Warning; Melting Millions (serial). **1928** After the Storm; Chinatown Charlie; The Showdown; The Secret Hour.

KUZNETZOFF, ADIA

Born: 1890, Russia. Died: Aug. 10, 1954, Port Washington, N.Y. Screen, television actor and gypsy singer.

Appeared in: **1930** A Russian Rhapsody. **1935** A Universal short. **1937** Easy Living; Madame X. **1938** Spawn of the North; The Mysterious Mr. Moto; Swiss Miss. **1939** Devil's Island. **1941** Second Chorus; The Wolf Man. **1942** My Sister Eileen. **1944** Lost in a Harem.

KYLE, AUSTIN C.

Born: 1893. Died: Nov. 10, 1916, France (killed in action). Screen actor.

LaBADIE, FLORENCE

Born: 1893, Canada. Died: Oct. 13, 1917, Ossining, N.Y. (auto accident). Screen actress and model.

Appeared in: **1911** The Broken Cross; Enoch Arden; How She Triumphed; Cinderella; Blind Princess and the Poet; The Primal Call. **1912** The Merchant of Venice; Lucile; Undine; Star of Bethlehem; East Lynne; Aurora Floyd; Flying to Fortune; My Baby's Voice; A Love of Long Ago; Rejuvenation; The Saleslady; Jess; Under Two Flags; The Ring of a Spanish Grandee; Dottie's New Doll; The Troublemaker; Arab's Bride; Whom God Hath Joined; Extravagance; Dr. Jekyll and Mr. Hyde; The Case of the Lady Anne; The Baseball Bug; A Star Re-born; Miss Robinson Crusoe; When Mercy Tempers Justice; Through the Flames; Mme. Rex; The Thief and the Girl; As It Was in the Beginning; Blossom Time. **1913** Little Brother; The Junior Partner; A Poor Relation; The Marble Heart; A Twentieth Century Farmer; Some Fools There Were; Louie the Life Saver; Life's Pathway; The Snare of Fate; Cymbeline; When the Worm Turned; Oh! Such a Beautiful Ocean; The Ward of the King; Tannhauser; Curfew Shall Not Ring Tonight; A Peaceful Victory. **1914** The Million Dollar Mystery (serial); Under False Colors; The Somnambulist; The Success of Selfishness; A Mohammedan Conspiracy. **1915** The Country Girl; Crossed Wires; God's Witness; The Cycle of Hatred; Bianca Forgets; The Final Reckoning; Graft Versus Love; The Adventures of Florence; A Smuggled Diamond; Monsieur Nikola Dupree; When the Fleet Sailed In; The Price of Her Silence; A Freight Car Honeymoon; A Disciple of Nietzsche; Mr. Meeson's Will; All Aboard; Her Confession. **1916** Master Shakespeare; Her Sacrifice; Divorce and the Daughter; The Five Faults of Flo. **1917** Her Life and His; When Love was Blind.

LaBRAKE, HARRISON

Born: 1891. Died: Dec. 2, 1936, Malone, N.Y. Circus performer and screen actor. Appeared in silents.

LACKAYE, JAMES

Born: 1867, Washington, D.C. Died: June 8, 1919, New York, N.Y. (pneumonia). Stage and screen actor. Brother of actor Wilton Lackaye (dec. 1932).

Appeared in: 1913 That Suit at Ten; If Dreams Came True; Bingles Mends the Clock; Counselor Bobby; Three to One; Two Hearts that Beat as One; Two's Company—Three's a Crowd; The Forgotten Latch Key; The Coming of Gretchen; Bingles and the Cabaret; Troublesome Daughters; An Old Man's Love Story. 1914 Good Gracious; Mr. Bingle's Melodrama. 1915 The Battle Cry of Peace; York State Folks. 1916 The Upstart.

LACKAYE, WILTON

Born: 1862, Loudoun County, Va. Died: Aug. 22, 1932, New York, N.Y. (heart attack). Stage and screen actor. Brother of actor James Lackaye (dec. 1919). Appeared in "World" productions in 1915.

Appeared in: 1921 God's Crucible. 1922 What's Wrong with Women? 1924 For Woman's Favor; The Lone Wolf. 1925 The Sky Raider.

LACKTEEN, FRANK

Born: Aug. 29, 1894, Kubber-Ilias, Asia Minor. Died: July 8, 1968, Woodland Hills, Calif. (cerebral and respiratory illness). Screen actor.

Appeared in: 1916 Less Than Dust; The Yellow Menace (serial). 1921 The Avenging Arrow (serial). 1922 White Eagle (serial). 1924 The Virgin; The Fortieth Door (serial). 1925 The Pony Express; plus the following serials: The Green Archer; Idaho; Sunken Silver. 1926 Desert Gold; The Last Frontier; The Unknown Cavalier; House without a Key (serial). 1927 Melting Millions (serial); Hawk of the Hills (serial). 1928 The Warning; Court Martial; Prowlers of the Sea; Mark of the Frog (serial). 1929 The Black Book (serial); The Fire Detective (serial); Hawk of the Hills (feature of 1927 serial). 1931 Law of the Tong; Hell's Valley; Cracked Nuts. 1932 Texas Pioneer; Jungle Mystery (serial). 1933 Nagana; Rustler's Roundup; Tarzan the Fearless (serial and feature film). 1934 The Perils of Pauline (serial). 1935 Escape from Devil's Island. 1936 Under Two Flags; Mummy's Boys; Isle of Fury; Comin' Round the Mountain. 1937 I Cover the War; The Mysterious Pilot (serial); Man Bites Lovebug (short). 1939 The Girl and the Gambler; Juarez; The Kansas Terrors. 1940 Stagecoach War; The Girl from Havana; Moon over Burma; The Mummy's Hand. 1941 The Sea Wolf; South of Tahiti; Jungle Girl (serial). 1942 Bombs over Burma; All Work and No Pay (short). 1943 Chetniks; Frontier Badmen. 1944 Moonlight and Cactus. 1945 Frontier Gal; Under Western Skies. 1946 A Bird in the Head (short). 1947 Oregon Trail Scouts; Singin' in the Corn; 1948 Man-Eater of Kumoan. 1949 The Cowboy and the Indians; Amazon Quest; Daughter of the Jungle; Son of the Badman; The Mysterious Desperado; Malice in the Palace (short). 1950 Indian Territory. 1951 Flaming Feather. 1953 King of the Khyber Rifles; Northern Patrol. 1955 Devil Goddess; Of Cash and Hash (short). 1956 Flesh and the Spur; The Ten Commandments. 1959 The Atomic Submarine. 1960 Three Came to Kill. 1962 The Underwater City. 1965 Requiem of a Gunfighter; The Bounty Killer.

LADD, ALAN

Born: Sept. 3, 1913, Hot Springs, Ark. Died: Jan. 29, 1964, Palm Springs, Calif. (accidental death). Screen, television and radio actor. Married to actress Sue Carol and father of actor David Ladd.

Appeared in: 1932 Once in a Lifetime. 1936 Pigskin Parade. 1937 Last Train from Madrid; Souls at Sea; Hold 'Em Navy. 1938 Born to the West; The Goldwyn Follies; Freshman Year; Come on Leathernecks. 1939 Green Hornet; Rulers of the Sea; Beasts of Berlin. 1940 Light of Western Stars; In Old Missouri; Meet the Missus; Captain Caution; Her First Romance; Gangs of Chicago; Howards of Virginia; Those Were the Days; Wildcat Bus. 1941 The Reluctant Dragon; Paper Bullets; Citizen Kane; Great Guns; Cadet Girl; Petticoat Politics; The Black Cat. 1942 This Gun for Hire; Joan of Paris; The Glass Key; Star Spangled Rhythm; Lucky Jordan. 1943 China; Hollywood Uniform (short). 1944 And Now Tomorrow; Skirmish on the Home Front (short); Salty O'Rourke. 1945 Duffy's Tavern; Hollywood Victory; Caravan. 1946 Two Years before the Mast; Blue Dahlia; O.S.S. 1947 Wild Harvest; Variety Girl; Calcutta; My Favorite Brunette. 1948 Saigon; Beyond Glory; Whispering Smith. 1949 Great Gatsby; Chicago Deadline; Eyes of Hollywood (short); Variety Club Hospital (trailer). 1950 Captain Carey, U.S.A.; Branded; Quantrell's Raiders. 1951 Appointment with Danger; Red Mountain. 1952 The Iron Mistress. 1953 Shane; Thunder in the East; Botany Bay; Desert Legion; The Red Beret (aka Paratrooper—US 1954). 1954 Hell below Zero; Saskatchewan; The Black Knight; Drum Beat. 1955 The McConnell Story; The Long Gray Line; Hell on Frisco Bay. 1956 Santiago. 1957 The Big Land; Boy on a Dolphin. 1958 The Deep Six; The Proud Rebel; The Badlanders. 1959 The Man in the Net. 1960 Guns of the Timberland; One Foot in Hell; All the Young Men. 1961 Orazio Orazi E Curiazi (aka Duel of Champions—US 1964). 1963 13 West Street. 1964 The Carpetbaggers.

LADMIRAL, NICOLE

Born: 1931, France. Died: Apr. 1958, Paris, France (fell or jumped under subway train?). Stage and screen actress.

Appeared in: 1954 The Diary of a Country Priest.

LAEMMLE, CARL, SR.

Born: Jan. 17, 1867, Laupheim,Wurtemberg, Germany. Died: Sept. 24, 1939, Beverly Hills, Calif. (heart attack). Film producer and screen actor.

Appeared in: 1914 Love and Vengeance. 1915 The Broken Coin; Cy Perkins in the City of Delusions. 1929 Show Boat (gave a short speech in an 18-minute prologue).

LAFAYETTE, RUBY

Born: 1845. Died: Apr. 3, 1935, Bell, Calif. Stage and screen actress. Married to stage actor John Curran (dec. 1918). Entered films approx. 1917.

Appeared in: 1918 My Mother. 1919 The Miracle Man; Toby's Bow. 1922 Borderland; Catch My Smoke; The Power of a Lie. 1923 The Day of Faith; Hollywood. 1924 Idle Tongues; The Phantom Horseman. 1925 The Coming of Amos; The Wedding Song; Tomorrow's Love. 1926 Butterflies in the Rain. 1928 Mother O' Mine; Marriage By Contract. 1930 Not So Dumb.

LA FLEUR, JOY

Born: 1914, Canada. Died: Nov. 6, 1957, Los Angeles, Calif. Screen, stage, radio and television actress.

Appeared in: 1948 Whispering City. 1956 D-Day the Sixth of June.

LAHR, BERT (Irving Lahrheim)

Born: Aug. 13, 1895, New York, N.Y. Died: Dec. 4, 1967, New York, N.Y. (internal hemorrhage). Screen, stage, television, vaudeville and burlesque actor.

Appeared in: 1929 Faint Heart (short). 1931 Flying High. 1933 Mr. Broadway. 1934 Hizzoner (short). 1936 Gold Bricks (short). 1937 Merry-Go-Round of 1938; Love and Hisses. 1938 Josette; Just around the Corner. 1939 Wizard of Oz; Zaza. 1940 DuBarry Was a Lady. 1942 Sing Your Worries Away; Ship Ahoy. 1944 Meet the People. 1949 Always Leave Them Laughing. 1951 Mr. Universe. 1954 Rose Marie. 1955 The Second Greatest Sex. 1962 Ten Girls Ago. 1963 The Sound of Laughter (documentary). 1964 Big Parade of Comedy (documentary). 1965 The Fantasticks. 1968 The Night They Raided Minskey's. 1974 That's Entertainment (film clips).

LAHTINEN, WARNER H. "DUKE"

Born: 1910. Died: Dec. 12, 1968, Minneapolis, Minn. Screen and stage actor.

LAIDLAW, ETHAN

Born: Nov. 25, 1899, Butte, Mont. Died: May 25, 1963. Screen actor. Entered films in 1923.

Appeared in: 1925 The Wyoming Wildcat; No Man's Law; Crack O'Dawn; Makers of Men. 1926 Born to Battle; Is That Nice?; Racing Romance; Out of the West; Dangerous Traffic; The Masquerade Bandit; Wild to Go. 1927 The Sonora Kid; Wolf's Clothing; When Danger Calls; Breed of Courage; The Silent Rider; Thunderbolt's Tracks. 1928 The Big Killing; Bitter Sweets; Rough Ridin' Red; Danger Patrol; The Riding Renegade. 1929 Big Diamond Robbery; Laughing at Death; The Little Savage; Outlawed; Bride of the Desert. 1930 Pardon My Gun. 1931 A Melon Drama (short); Monkey Business. 1934 The Mighty Barnum. 1935 Powdersmoke Range. 1936 Silly Billies; Yellow Dust; Special Investigator; Two in Revolt; The Sea Spoilers; Mummy's Boys. 1937 Goofs and Saddles (short). 1938 Rhythm of the Saddle; I'm From the City; Border G-Man. 1939 Home on the Prairie; The Night Riders; Cowboys from Texas; Western Caravans; Three Texas Steers. 1940 The Marines Fly High; Son of Roaring Dan; The Tulsa Kid; Wagon Train; Stage to Chino; Law and Order. 1941 Westward Ho-Hum (short); Law of the Range; The Lone Star Vigilantes. 1942 Stagecoach Express; Cowboy Serenade. 1943 Riding Through Nevada; Border Buckaroos; The Desperados; Fugitive from Sonora. 1944 Marshal of Gunsmoke; Oklahoma Raiders. 1945 Lawless Empire; Blazing the Western Trail. 1946 Three Troubledoers (short). 1947 Rustler's Round-Up; Singin' in the Corn. 1948 Six-Gun Law; Buckaroo from Powder River; Joan of Arc. 1950 The Great Missouri Raid; Traveling Saleswoman. 1951 Flaming Feather. 1952 Montana Territory. 1953 Powder River. 1956 The Ten Commandments.

LAIR, GRACE (Grace Gaylor)

Died: Jan. 5, 1955, Cleveland, Ohio. Screen, stage actress and singer. Was the original "Coca-Cola Girl" in Coca Cola's advertising.

LAIT, JACK (Jacquin Leonard Lait)

Born: Mar. 13, 1883, New York, N.Y. Died: Apr. 1, 1954, Beverly Hills, Calif. (circulatory ailment). Newspaperman, screenwriter, author and screen actor.

Appeared in: 1932 Madison Square Garden.

LA JANA (Henriette Margarethe Hiebel)

Born: 1905, Berlin, Germany. Died: 1940, Berlin, Germany. Screen actress and dancer. Appeared in German and Swedish films.

Appeared in: 1928 Shadows of Fear. 1934 Der Schlemihl. 1937 Truxa.

LAKE, ALICE

Born: Brooklyn, N.Y. Died: Nov. 15, 1967, Paradise. Calif. (heart attack). Screen actress.

Appeared in: **1912** Her Picture Idol. **1916** The Moonshiners; The Waiter's Ball; A Creampuff Romance (sometimes referred to as His Alibi). **1917** Her Nature Dance; The Butcher Boy; His Wedding Night; Oh, Doctor; Come Through. **1918** Out West; Coney Island; Goodnight, Nurse; Moonshine; The Cook. **1919** A Desert Hero; Backstage; A Country Hero; The Garage. **1920** Shore Acres; Should a Woman Talk? **1921** Body and Soul; The Greater Claim; Uncharted Seas; A Hole in the Wall; Over the Wire; The Infamous Miss Revell. **1922** The Golden Gift; Hate; Kisses; Environment; I Am the Law; More to Be Pitied Than Scorned. **1923** The Spider and the Rose; Red Lights; Broken Hearts of Broadway; The Unknown Purple; The Marriage Market; Modern Matrimony; Souls for Sale; Nobody's Bride. **1924** The Dancing Cheat; The Law and the Lady; The Virgin. **1925** Broken Homes; The Hurricane; The Wives of the Prophet. **1927** The Angel of Broadway; Roaring Fires; The Haunted Ship; Spider Webs. **1928** Obey Your Husband; Women Men Like; Runaway Girls. **1929** Untamed Justice; Circumstantial Evidence; Twin Beds; Frozen Justice. **1930** Dining Out (short); I'll Fix It (short); Young Desire. **1931** Wicked. **1933** Skyward. **1934** Wharf Angel; Glamour; The Mighty Barnum.

LAKE, FRANK
Born: 1849. Died: Apr. 19, 1936, Los Angeles, Calif. Screen actor.

Appeared in: **1930** The Rogue Song.

LAKE, HARRY
Born: 1885. Died: Mar. 4, 1947, Chicago, Ill. Screen actor.

LAKE, JOHN (John W. Laycock)
Born: 1904, Leesburg, Va. Died: June 28, 1960, Saranac Lake, N.Y. (tuberculosis). Screen and radio actor.

LAKE, VERONICA (Constance Ockelman aka CONSTANCE KEANE)
Born: Nov. 15, 1921, Brooklyn, N.Y. Died: July 7, 1973, Burlington, Vt. (acute hepatitis). Screen, stage actress and author. Divorced from film director Andre De Toth, art film director John Detlie, music publisher Joseph A. McCarthy and Robert Carleton Munro.

Appeared in: **1939** All Women Have Secrets; Wrong Room (short); Sorority House. **1940** Forty Little Mothers. **1941** I Wanted Wings; Sullivan's Travels; Hold Back the Dawn. **1942** This Gun for Hire; I Married a Witch; The Glass Key; Star Spangled Rhythm. **1943** So Proudly We Hail. **1944** The Hour Before the Dawn. **1945** Bring on the Girls; Leave It to Blondie; Hold that Blonde; Duffy's Tavern; Out of This World; Miss Susie Slagle's. **1946** The Blue Dahlia. **1947** Ramrod; Variety Girl. **1948** Saigon; The Sainted Sisters; Isn't It Romantic. **1949** Slattery's Hurricane. **1952** Stronghold. **1966** Footsteps in the Snow. **1970** Flesh Feast.

LALOR, FRANK
Born: 1869. Died: Oct. 15, 1932, New York, N.Y. (acute indigestion). Screen, stage and vaudeville actor.

Appeared in: **1922** Red Hot Romance; Polly of the Follies.

LaMARR, BARBARA (Reatha Watson)
Born: July 28, 1896. Died: Jan. 30, 1926, Altadena, Calif. (overdieting). Screen, stage actress and cabaret artist. Married then divorced Jack Lytell, Lawrence Converse, Phil Ainsworth, Ben Deely and Jack Daugherty.

Appeared in: **1921** Desperate Trails; The Nut; Cinderella of the Hills; The Three Musketeers. **1922** Trifling Women; The Prisoner of Zenda; Quincy Adams Sawyer; Arabian Love; Domestic Relations. **1923** The Eternal Struggle; Strangers of the Night; The Eternal City; The Brass Bottle; The Hero; St. Elmo; Mary of the Movies; Poor Men's Wives. **1924** The Name Is Woman; The White Moth; The Shooting of Dan McGrew; My Husband's Wives; The White Monkey. **1925** Sandra.

LaMARR, RICHARD
Died: Apr. 24, 1975. Screen actor, stuntman and stand-in.

LAMB, FLORENCE
Born: 1884. Died: May 9, 1966. Screen actress.

LAMBERT, CLARA
Died: 1921. Screen actress. Married to actor James L. Daly (dec. 1933).

LAMBERTI, PROFESSOR (Michael Lamberti)
Died: Mar. 13, 1950, Hollywood, Calif. Screen, stage and vaudeville actor.

Appeared in: **1945** Tonight and Every Night. **1946** The Gay Intruders. **1947** Linda Be Good.

LA MONT, HARRY (Alfred Gilbert)
Born: June 17, 1887, New York, N.Y. Died: May 8, 1957, Venice, Calif. Screen, stage, vaudeville and radio actor.

Appeared in: **1915** A Tale of Two Cities (film debut). **1920** Fazil. **1922** Blood and Sand; Peaceful Peters. **1923** Robin Hood, Jr. **1928** Two Lovers; Mysterious

Lady. **1938** Romance in the Dark. **1942** The Black Swan; China Girl. **1947** San Antonio.

LAMONT, JACK (Jack Capitola)
Born: 1893. Died: Feb. 28, 1956, Cleveland, Ohio (heart attack). Screen, stage and burlesque actor. Appeared in silents and was in several "Keystone Kop" comedies.

LAMOURET, ROBERT
Died: Mar. 16, 1959. Screen actor and ventriloquist.

Appeared in: **1949** Make Mine Laughs.

LAMPTON, DEE
Born: 1898, Ft. Worth, Tex. Died: Sept. 2, 1919, New York, N.Y. (appendicitis). Stage and screen actress.

Appeared in: **1915** A Night in a Show. **1917** Them Were the Happy Days; Lonesome Luke series.

LAMY, DOUGLAS N. *See* JOHN MITCHELL

LANCASTER, ANN
Born: 1920. Died: Oct. 31, 1970, London, England. Screen, stage, television and radio actress.

Appeared in: **1952** Angels One Five (US 1954). **1965** The Secret of My Success. **1967** Fathom; Three Bites of the Apple. **1968** Hot Millions; Inadmissible Evidence; Decline and Fall . . . of a Birdwatcher! (US 1969). **1969** A Nice Girl Like Me.

LANCASTER, JOHN
Born: 1857, Richmond, Va. Died: Oct. 11, 1935, Washington, D.C. Screen actor and circus performer.

Appeared in: **1912** The Katzenjammer Kids. **1913** Sweeney and the Million; Alas! Poor Yorick.

LANDAU, DAVID
Born: 1878. Died: Sept. 20, 1935, Hollywood, Calif. Stage and screen actor.

Appeared in: **1931** Street Scene; Arrowsmith. **1932** I Am a Fugitive from a Chain Gang; Union Depot; Taxi; This Reckless Age; 70,000 Witnesses; Under Cover Man; Polly of the Circus; It's Tough to Be Famous; Amateur Daddy; Roadhouse Murder; The Purchase Price; Horse Feathers; Air Mail; False Faces; Lawyer Man. **1933** Heritage of the Desert; She Done Him Wrong; The Crime of the Century; One Man's Journey; Gabriel over the White House; The Nuisance; No Marriage Ties; They Just Had to Get Married. **1934** As the Earth Turns; Bedside; Wharf Angel; The Man with Two Faces; Death on the Diamond.

LANDI, ELISSA (Elizabeth Marie Zanardi-Landi)
Born: Dec. 6, 1904, Venice, Italy. Died: Oct. 31, 1948, Kingston, N.Y. (cancer). Screen, stage, radio actress, and novelist.

Appeared in: **1926** London. **1928** Bolibar (aka The Marquis of Bolibar); Underground. **1929** The Inseparables; The Betrayal. **1930** Knowing Men; The Price of Things; Children of Chance. **1931** Body and Soul; Sin; Always Goodbye; Wicked; The Yellow Ticket; She Parisian. **1932** Devil's Lottery; Woman in Room 13; A Passport to Hell; Sign of the Cross. **1933** The Masquerader; The Warrior's Husband; I Loved You Wednesday. **1934** Man of Two Worlds; By Candlelight; The Count of Monte Cristo; The Great Flirtation; Sisters Under the Skin. **1935** Koenigsmark; Enter Madame; Without Regrets. **1936** The Amateur Gentleman; Mad Holiday; After the Thin Man. **1937** The Thirteenth Chair. **1943** Corregidor. **1944** The Sign of the Cross (revised version of 1932 film).

LANDICK, OLIN
Born: 1895. Died: Mar. 26, 1972, New York, N.Y. Screen, radio and television actor.

Appeared in: **1930** All Stuck Up (short).

LANDIN, HOPE
Born: 1893, Minneapolis, Minn. Died: Feb. 28, 1973, Hollywood, Calif. Stage and screen actress.

Appeared in: **1942** Reap the Wild Wind. **1944** Bridge of San Luis Rey. **1945** The Great John L. **1946** The Mask of Dijon; The Dark Corner; Gas House Kids. **1947** Unconquered. **1948** I Remember Mama (stage and film versions); The Walls of Jericho. **1949** The Sun Comes Up. **1951** Sugarfoot. **1952** Scaramouche. **1953** How to Marry a Millionaire. **1954** She Couldn't Say No (aka She Had to Say Yes). **1965** The Greatest Story Ever Told.

LANDIS, CAROLE (Frances Ridste)
Born: Jan. 1, 1919, Fairchild, Wis. Died: July 5, 1948, Brentwood Heights, Calif. (suicide). Stage and screen actress. The screen's original "Sweater Girl."

Appeared in: **1937** A Day at the Races; The Emperor's Candlesticks; Broadway Melody of 1938; Varsity Show; Adventurous Blonde; Hollywood Hotel; A

Star is Born. **1938** Golddiggers in Paris; Four's a Crowd; Blondes at Work; Boy Meets Girl; Men are Such Fools; Over the Wall; When Were You Born? **1939** Daredevils of the Red Circle (serial); Three Texas Steers; Cowboys from Texas. **1940** Mystery Sea Raider; One Million, B.C.; Turnabout. **1941** I Wake up Screaming; Topper Returns; Dance Hall; Hot Spot; Cadet Girl; Road Show; Moon over Miami. **1942** A Gentleman at Heart; The Power's Girl; My Gal Sal; Orchestra Wives; It Happened in Flatbush; Manila Calling. **1943** Screen Snapshot #2 (short); Wintertime. **1944** Secret Command; Four Jills in a Jeep. **1945** Having a Wonderful Crime; Behind Green Lights. **1946** It Shouldn't Happen to a Dog; A Scandal in Paris. **1947** Out of the Blue. **1948** The Brass Monkey (aka The Lucky Mascot—US 1951); Noose (aka The Silk Noose—US 1950).

LANDIS, CULLEN

Born: July 19, 1898, Nashville, Tenn. Died: Aug. 26, 1975, Bloomfield Hills, Mich. Screen, stage actor, film director and later became director-producer of industrial films and war documentaries. Divorced from actress Minon LeBrun (dec. 1941).

Appeared in: **1916** Joy and the Dragon. **1917** The Checkmate; Who is Number One (serial). **1918** What Will Father Say?; Her Friend—the Enemy; All Kinds of a Girl; Beware of Blondes. **1919** The Outcasts of Poker Flat; The Girl from Outside; Almost a Husband; Where the West Begins; Upstairs; Jinx. **1920** It's a Great Life; Pinto; Going Some. **1921** Bunty Pulls the Strings; Snowblind; The Infamous Miss Revell; The Night Rose; The Old Nest. **1922** Remembrance; Watch Your Step; Where Is My Wandering Boy Tonight?; Forsaking all Others; Gay and Devilish; Love in the Dark; The Man With Two Mothers; Youth to Youth. **1923** The Famous Mrs. Fair; Masters of Men; Pioneer Trails; Soul of the Beast; Dollar Devils; Crashin' Thru; The Fog; The Man Life Passed By; The Midnight Alarm. **1924** The Fighting Coward; Born Rich; Cheap Kisses; A Girl of the Limberlost; One Law for the Woman. **1925** A Broadway Butterfly; Easy Money; The Mansion of Aching Hearts; The Midnight Flyer; Pampered Youth; Peacock Feathers; Wasted Lives; Sealed Lips. **1926** Buffalo Bill on the U.P. Trail; Christine of the Big Tops; Davy Crockett at the Fall of the Alamo; The Dixie Flyer; Frenzied Flames; Jack O'Hearts; My Old Dutch; Perils of the Coast Guard; The Smoke Eaters; Sweet Rosie O'Grady; Then Came the Woman; Winning the Futurity. **1927** The Fighting Failure; Broadway after Midnight; Finnegan's Ball; Heroes of the Night; We're All Gamblers; The Crimson Flash (serial); On Guard (serial). **1928** The Broken Mask; Lights of New York; The Devil's Skipper; The Little Wild Girl; A Midnight Adventure; On to Reno; Out with the Tide. **1930** The Convict's Code.

LANDIS, JESSIE ROYCE (Jessie Royce Medbury)

Born: Nov. 25, 1904, Chicago, Ill. Died: Feb. 2, 1972, Danbury, Conn. (cancer). Screen, stage and television actress.

Appeared in: **1930** Derelict. **1937** Oh Doctor! **1949** It Happens Every Spring; Mr. Belvedere Goes to College; My Foolish Heart. **1950** Mother Didn't Tell Me. **1951** Meet Me Tonight. **1953** Tonight at Eight-Thirty. **1954** She Couldn't Say No. **1955** To Catch a Thief. **1956** The Girl He Left Behind; The Swan. **1957** My Man Godfrey. **1958** I Married a Woman. **1959** A Private Affair; North by Northwest. **1961** Goodbye Again. **1962** Boys' Night Out; Bon Voyage! **1963** Critic's Choice; Gidget Goes to Rome. **1970** Airport.

LANDRETH, GERTRUDE GRIFFITH

Born: 1897, New York, N.Y. Died: Nov. 25, 1969, Palo Alto, Calif. Screen and vaudeville actress. Appeared in silent films and was in several "Keystone" comedies. She founded the Hollywood Studio Club, a home for aspiring actresses.

LANE, ALLAN "ROCKY" (Harry Albershart)

Born: c. 1901 or 1904? Mishawaka, Ind. Died: Oct. 27, 1973, Woodland Hills, Calif. (bone marrow disorder). Screen, stage, television actor and professional football player. Was the voice of "Mr. Ed" in the television series of same name.

Appeared in: **1929** Not Quite Decent; The Forward Pass; Knights Out (short); Detectives Wanted (short). **1930** Madam Satan; Love in the Rough. **1931** Night Nurse; Honor of the Family; Expensive Women; War Mamas (short). **1932** Winner Take All; Miss Pinkerton; The Tenderfoot; Heavens! My Husband (short). **1936** Stowaway. **1937** Charlie Chan at the Olympics; Big Business; Fifty Roads to Town; Sign and Be Happy; Laughing at Trouble; The Duke Comes Back. **1938** Crime Ring; Fugitives for a Night; The Law West of Tombstone; Night Spot; Maid's Night Out; This Marriage Business; Having a Wonderful Time. **1939** Pacific Liner; Twelve Crowded Hours; They Made Her a Spy; Conspiracy; The Spellbinder; Panama Lady. **1940** Grande Ole Opry; King of the Royal Mounted (serial). **1941** All-American Coed. **1942** King of the Mounties (serial); Yukon Patrol. **1943** Daredevils of the West (serial); The Dancing Masters. **1944** Tiger Woman (serial); Call of the South Seas; Stagecoach to Monterey; Sheriff of Sundown; The Silver City Kid. **1945** Bells of Rosarita; Corpus Christi Bandits; The Topeka Terror; Trail of Kit Carson. **1946** Gay Blades; A Guy Could Change; Night Train to Memphis; Out California Way; Santa Fe Uprising; Stagecoach to Denver. **1947** Homesteaders of Paradise Valley; Vigilantes of Boomtown; Oregon Trail Scouts; Marshal of Cripple Creek; Rustlers of Devil's Canyon; Bandits of Dark Canyon; The Wild Frontier. **1948** Bold Frontiersman; Oklahoma Badlands; Carson City Raiders;

Desperadoes of Dodge City; Marshal of Amarillo; The Denver Kid; Sundown at Santa Fe; Renegades of Sonora. **1949** Bandit King of Texas; Death Valley Gunfighter; Frontier Investigator; Navajo Trail Raiders; Powder River Rustlers; Sheriff of Wichita; The Wyoming Bandit. **1950** Covered Wagon Raiders; Frisco Tornado; Gunmen of Abilene; Rustlers on Horseback; Salt Lake Raiders; Vigilante Hideout; Trail of Robin Hood; Code of the Silver Sage. **1951** Desert of Lost Men; Fort Dodge Stampede; Night Riders of Montana; Night Riders of Durango; Wells Fargo Gunmaster. **1952** Black Hills Ambush; Desperadoes' Outpost; Leadville Gunslinger; Thundering Caravans; Captive of Billy the Kid. **1953** Savage Frontier; Marshal of Cedar Rock; Bandits of the West; El Paso Stampede. **1958** The Saga of Hemp Brown. **1960** Hell Bent for Leather. **1961** Posse from Hell.

LANE, CHARLES (Charles Willis Lane)

Born: Jan. 25, 1869, Madison, Ill. Died: Oct. 17, 1945, Van Nuys, Calif. (cancer). Stage and screen actor. Do not confuse with actor Charles Lane who was born approximately 1905.

Appeared in: **1921** If Women Only Knew; Without Limit; Love's Penalty. **1922** Fascination; How Women Love; Broadway Rose. **1923** The Tents of Allah; The White Sister. **1924** Second Youth. **1925** The Dark Angel; I Want My Man; The Marriage Whirl; Romola; The Pearl of Love. **1926** Padlocked; The Winning of Barbara Worth; The Blind Goddess; The Outsider; Marriage License?; The Mystery Club. **1927** Barbed Wire; Married Alive; Service for Ladies; The Whirlwind of Youth; The Music Master. **1928** Sadie Thompson. **1929** Saturday's Children; The Canary Murder Case.

LANE, DOROTHY

Born: 1905. Died: Oct. 7, 1923, New York, N.Y. (heart disease). Screen actress and dancer.

LANE, HARRY

Born: 1910. Died: July 1960, London, England. Screen, stage and television actor.

Appeared in: **1946** Appointment With Crime (US 1950). **1950** My Daughter Jay (aka Operation X—US 1951). **1951** Old Mother Riley's Jungle Treasure. **1953** Watch Out! **1954** Malaga (aka Fire Over Africa—US). **1959** The Night We Dropped a Clanger (aka Make Mine a Double—US 1961). **1960** Too Hot to Handle (aka Playgirl After Dark—US 1962).

LANE, LUPINO "NIPPER" (Henry George Lupino)

Born: June 16, 1892, London, England. Died: Nov. 10, 1959, London, England. Screen, stage actor, playwright and director. Brother of actor Wallace Lupino (dec. 1961).

Appeared in: **1915** The Man in Possession; Nipper and the Curate; His Cooling Courtship; Nipper's Busy Holiday. **1916** The Dummy; Nipper's Busy Bee Time; A Wife in a Hurry. **1917** The Missing Link; Splash Me Nicely; Hullo! Who's Your Lady Friend? **1918** "Kinekature Comedies" series including: The Blunders of Mr. Butterbun; Unexpected Treasure; Trips and Tribunals; His Busy Day; His Salad Days; and Love and Lobster. **1919** Clarence, Crooks and Chivalry; A Dreamland Frolic. **1920** A Night Out and a Day In; A Lot About Lottery. **1922** The Reporter. **1923** A Friendly Husband. **1924** Isn't Life Wonderful? **1925** The Fighting Dude (short). **1927** Monty of the Mounted. **1929** Show of Shows; The Love Parade; "Educational—Lupino Lane" comedies including: Ship Mates; Buying a Gun; Fireproof; Purely Circumstantial; Only Me; Evolution of the Dance. **1930** Bride of the Regiment; Golden Dawn; Yellow Mask. **1931** Never Trouble Trouble; No Lady. **1933** A Southern Maid. **1935** The Deputy Drummer; Who's Your Father?; Trust the Navy. **1936** Hot News. **1939** Me and My Gal (aka The Lambeth Walk—US 1940).

LANE, PAT

Born: 1900. Died: July 4, 1953, Beverly Hills, Calif. (heart attack). Screen and vaudeville actress.

Appeared in: **1948** Appointment with Murder.

LANE, ROSEMARY (Rosemary Mullican)

Born: Apr. 4, 1914, Indianola, Iowa. Died: Nov. 25, 1974, Woodland Hills, Calif. (diabetes and pulmonary obstruction). Screen, stage, radio actress and singer. Sister of actresses Priscilla and Lola Lane and singer Leota Lane (dec. 1960). Divorced from makeup artist Bud Westmore.

Appeared in: **1937** Hollywood Hotel; Varsity Show. **1938** Four Daughters; Gold Diggers in Paris. **1939** Blackwell's Island; Daughters Courageous; Four Wives; The Oklahoma Kid; The Return of Dr. X. **1940** The Boys from Syracuse; Ladies Must Live; An Angel from Texas; Always a Bride. **1941** Time Out for Rhythm; Four Mothers. **1943** Chatterbox; Harvest Melody; All by Myself. **1944** Trocadero.

LANE, WALLACE. See WALLACE LUPINO

LANG, HAROLD

Born: 1923, England. Died: Nov. 16, 1970, Cairo, Egypt. Screen, stage and television actor.

Appeared in: **1949** Floodtide; The Spider and the Fly (US 1952). **1950** Cairo

Road. **1951** The Franchise Affair (US 1952); Cloudburst (US 1952); Calling Bulldog Drummond. **1952** It Started in Paradise (US 1953); Wings of Danger (aka Dead on Course—US); So Little Time. **1953** The Long Memory; Laughing Anne (US 1954); The Saint's Return (aka The Saint's Girl Friday—US). **1954** Dance Little Lady (US 1955); The Passing Stranger; Thirty-Six Hours (aka Terror Street—US); Star of My Night; Men of Sherwood Forest. **1955** Murder by Proxy (aka Blackout—US); The Quatermass Experiment (aka The Creeping Unknown—US 1956). **1956** It's a Wonderful World. **1957** The Flesh Is Weak. **1958** The Betrayal; Carve Her Name With Pride; Man With a Gun; Chain of Events. **1963** West 11; Paranoiac. **1964** Dr. Terror's House of Horrors (US 1965). **1965** The Nanny. **1966** The Psychopath. **1969** Two Gentlemen Sharing.

LANG, HARRY
Born: 1895. Died: Aug. 3, 1953, Hollywood, Calif. (heart attack). Screen, radio, television and vaudeville actor. Part of vaudeville teams "Lang and Haley" and "Lang and O'Neill."

Appeared in: **1929** Who's Who (short). **1951** Soldiers Three.

LANG, HOWARD
Born: 1876. Died: Jan. 26, 1941, Hollywood, Calif. Screen and stage actor.

Appeared in: **1922** Peacock Alley. **1933** This Day and Age; Cradle Song. **1934** The Witching Hour; Born to Be Bad. **1935** Bar 20 Rides Again; Mystery Woman. **1936** Call of the Prairie. **1937** Navy Spy; Here's Flash Casey; The Prisoner of Zenda.

LANG, MATHESON
Born: May 15, 1879, Montreal, Canada. Died: Apr. 11, 1948, Bridgeton, Barbados. Screen, stage actor and playwright. Entered films in 1916.

Appeared in: **1916** The Merchant of Venice. **1917** Everybody's Business; The House Opposite; Masks and Faces; The Ware Case. **1918** Victory and Peace. **1919** Mr. Wu. **1921** The Carnival. **1922** Dick Turpin's Ride to York; A Romance of Old Baghdad. **1923** The Wandering Jew; Guy Fawkes. **1924** White Slippers; Henry, King of Navarre; Slaves of Destiny (aka Miranda of the Balcony). **1925** The Qualified Adventurer; The Secret Kingdom. **1926** The Chinese Bungalow; Island of Despair. **1927** The King's Highway. **1928** The Triumph of the Scarlet Pimpernel (aka The Scarlet Daredevil—US 1929); The Blue Peter. **1929** Beyond the Veil (rerelease of The Secret Kingdom—1925). **1930** The Chinese Bungalow (and 1926 version). **1931** Carnival (aka Venetian Nights—US and 1921 version). **1933** Channel Crossing (US 1934). **1934** Little Friend; The Great Defender. **1935** Royal Cavalcade (aka Regal Cavalcade—US); Drake of England (aka Drake The Pirate—US). **1936** The Cardinal.

LANG, PETER
Born: 1867. Died: Aug. 20, 1932, New York (heart attack). Stage and screen actor.

Appeared in: **1913** Peter's Pledge (serial). **1924** Dangerous Money.

LANG, WALTER
Born: Aug. 10, 1898, Memphis, Tenn. Died: Feb. 7, 1972, Palm Springs, Calif. (kidney failure). Film director, screenwriter, screen and stage actor.

Appeared in: **1935** Lady Tubbs.

LANGDON, HARRY
Born: June 15, 1884, Council Bluffs, Iowa. Died: Dec. 22, 1944, Los Angeles, Calif. (cerebral hemorrhage). Screen, stage, vaudeville actor, film director, producer and screenwriter.

Appeared in: **1918** The Mastery Mystery. **1924** Picking Peaches; plus the following shorts: The Luck O' the Foolish; Smile Please; Feet of Mud; All Night Long; Shanghaied Lovers; Flickering Youth; The Cat's Meow; His New Mamma; The First Hundred Years; The Hanson Cabman. **1925** The following shorts: The Sea Squawk; Boobs in the Woods; His Marriage Vow; Plain Clothes; Remember When?; Lucky Stars; Horace Greeley, Jr.; There He Goes; The White Wing's Bride. **1926** Ella Cinders; The Strong Man; Tramp Tramp Tramp; plus the following shorts: Saturday Afternoon; Fiddlesticks; The Soldier Man. **1927** Long Pants; Three's a Crowd; His First Flame. **1928** The Chaser; Heart Trouble; There He Goes. **1929** The following shorts: Hotter Than Hot; The Fighting Parson; Sky Boy; Skirt Shy. **1930** See America Thirst; plus the following shorts: The Fighting Parson; The Head Guy; The Shrimp; The King; The Big Kick. **1931** Soldier's Plaything. **1932** The Big Flash (short). **1933** My Weakness; Hallelujah, I'm A Bum; plus the following shorts: Tired Feet; The Hitch Hiker; Knight Duty; Tied for Life; Hooks and Jabs; Marriage Humor; The Stage Hand; Leave It to Dad; On Ice; Pop's Pal; A Roaming Romeo. **1934** No Sleep on the Deep; plus the following shorts: Trimmed in Furs; Circus Hoodoo; Petting Preferred; Counsel on de Fence; Shivers. **1935** Atlantic Adventure; plus the following shorts: His Bridal Sweet; The Leather Necker; His Marriage Mixup; I Don't Remember. **1938** Block Heads; There Goes My Heart; He Loved an Actress; A Doggone Mixup (short); Sue My Lawyer (short). **1939** Zenobia; Elephants Never Forget. **1940** A Chump at Oxford; Saps at Sea; Misbehaving Husbands; Goodness, a Ghost (short); Cold Turkey (short). **1941** Road Show; All-American Coed; Double Trouble. **1942**

House of Errors, plus the following shorts: What Makes Lizzie Dizzy?; Tireman, Spare My Tires; Carry Harry; Piano Mooner. **1943** Spotlights Scandals; plus the following shorts: Blitz on the Fritz; Here Comes Mr. Zerk; Blonde and Groom. **1944** The following shorts: Hot Rhythm; To Heir Is Human; Defective Detectives; Block Busters Mopey Dope. **1945** Swingin' On a Rainbow; Snooper Service (short); Pistol Packin' Nitwits (short). **1961** Days of Thrills and Laughter (documentary). **1963** Thirty Years of Fun (documentary); The Sound of Laughter (documentary).

LANGDON, LILLIAN
Born: New Jersey. Died: Feb. 8, 1943, Santa Monica, Calif. Stage and screen actress.

Appeared in: **1921** The Swamp; What's a Wife Worth?; The Mother Heart. **1922** Another Man's Shoes; Kissed; Lights of the Desert; The Glorious Fool; The Stranger's Banquet; Fools of Fortune; Too Much Wife. **1923** The Prisoner; Going Up; Nobody's Bride; Crossed Wires; The Footlight Ranger; The Wanters. **1924** Daring Youth; Circe the Enchantress. **1925** Cobra; Raffles; The Amateur Cracksman; After Business Hours; The Wall Street Whiz; The Thoroughbred; Joanna; Enticement. **1926** The Millionaire Policeman; The Blonde Saint; Pleasures of the Rich; Fifth Avenue. **1927** What Every Girl Should Know; Compassion. **1928** The Cheer Leader.

LANGE, MARY
Born: 1913. Died: Apr. 20, 1973, Coral Gables, Fla. Screen and stage actress. Entered films in 1933.

Appeared in: **1933** Roman Scandals; Moonlight and Pretzels. **1934** Bottoms Up. **1936** The Great Ziegfeld.

LANGFORD, MARTHA
Died: Apr. 21, 1935, Syracuse, N.Y. Stage and screen actress.

LANGFORD, WILLIAM
Born: 1920, Montreal, Canada. Died: July 20, 1955, New York, N.Y. Screen, stage and television actor.

Appeared in Swedish film: The True and the False.

LANGLEY, FAITH
Born: 1929. Died: 1972, New York, N.Y. Stage and screen actress.

Appeared in: **1953** Donovan's Brain.

LANGLEY, HERBERT
Born: 1888. Died: Oct. 1967. Screen actor and opera baritone.

Appeared in: **1922** The Wonderful Story; Flames of Passion. **1923** Chu Chin Chow (US 1925). **1924** Southern Love (aka Spanish Passion).

LANGTRY, LILLIE (Emilie Charlotte Le Breton)
Born: Oct. 13, 1853, Isle of Jersey, Great Britain. Died: Feb. 12, 1929, Monaco (heart attack). Screen, stage actress and author. Entered films with Famous Players in 1913.

Appeared in: **1913** His Neighbor's Wife.

LANI, MARIA
Born: 1906, Warsaw, Poland. Died: Mar. 11, 1954, Paris, France. Screen, stage actress and writer. Appeared in French silents.

LANPHIER, FAYE
Born: 1906. Died: June 21, 1959, Oakland, Calif. (pneumonia). Screen actress. She was "Miss America" of 1925.

LANPHIER, JAMES F.
Born: 1921. Died: Feb. 11, 1969, Los Angeles, Calif. (stroke). Screen, stage and television actor.

Appeared in: **1957** Operation Mad Ball. **1958** Bell, Book and Candle; The Perfect Furlough. **1961** Flight of the Lost Balloon; Breakfast at Tiffany's. **1962** Experiment in Terror; Days of Wine and Roses. **1964** The Pink Panther. **1966** What Did you do in the War, Daddy? **1968** The Party; The Legend of Lylah Clare. **1970** Darling Lili.

LANSING, JOI (Joi Loveland)
Born: 1930, Salt Lake City, Utah. Died: Aug. 7, 1972, Santa Monica, Calif. (cancer). Screen, stage, television actress and singer.

Appeared in: **1948** The Counterfeiters. **1949** Super Cue Men (short). **1951** On the Riviera. **1954** So You Want to go to a Nightclub (short); So You've Taken in a Roomer (short). **1955** So You Want to be a V.P. (short); So You Want to be a Policeman (short). **1956** So You Think the Grass is Greener (short); The Brave One; Hot Cars; Hot Shots; The Fountain of Youth (short). **1959** Hole in the Head; The Atomic Submarine. **1960** Who Was that Lady? **1965** Marriage on the Rocks. **1967** Hillbillys in a Haunted House. **1970** Bigfoot.

LANSING, RUTH DOUGLAS

Born: 1881. Died: Aug. 19, 1931, Hollywood, Calif. (toxic poisoning). Stage and screen actress.

LANZA, MARIO (Alfred Arnold Cocozza)

Born: Jan. 31, 1921 or 1925, Philadelphia, Pa. Died: Oct. 7, 1959, Rome, Italy (heart attack). Screen, television actor and opera performer.

Appeared in: **1944** Winged Victory (appeared as an extra while in the service). **1949** That Midnight Kiss. **1950** Toast of New Orleans. **1951** The Great Caruso. **1952** Because You're Mine. **1954** The Student Prince (voice). **1956** Serenade. **1958** Seven Hills of Rome. **1959** For the First Time. **1974** That's Entertainment (film clips).

LAPAURI, ALEKSANDR

Born: 1926, Russia. Died: Aug. 5, 1975, Russia (auto accident). Screen actor and ballet dancer. Married to dancer Raissa Struchkova.

Appeared in: **1956** The Ballet of Romeo and Juliet. **1961** Khrustalnyy Bashmachok (aka Cinderella—US).

LAPID, JESS

Born: Philippines. Died: July 13, 1968, Manila, Philippines (murdered—shot). Screen actor.

LA RENO, RICHARD "DICK"

Born: Oct. 31, 1873, County Limerick, Ireland. Died: July 26, 1945, Hollywood, Calif. Stage and screen actor.

Appeared in: **1913** The Squaw Man. **1915** Cameo Kirby. **1917** The Gray Ghost (serial). **1921** A Daughter of the Law. **1922** One-Eighth Apache; Out of the Silent North; Trimmed. **1923** Playing It Wild; Times Have Changed; Single Handed. **1924** Oh, You Tony!; Crashin' Through; Ridin' Mad; Waterfront Wolves; Three Days to Live. **1925** Flashing Steeds; Drug Store Cowboy. **1926** The High Hand; Buffalo Bill on the U.P. Trail; Sea Horses. **1927** The Long Loop on the Pecos; The Border Cavalier; Gold from Weepah; The Silent Rider. **1928** The Apache Raider.

LARGAY, RAYMOND J. "RAY"

Born: 1886. Died: Sept. 28, 1974, Woodland Hills, Calif. (stroke). Screen, stage, vaudeville and radio actor. Married to vaudeville actress Sue Snee.

Appeared in: **1930** Soldiers and Women; Lilies of the Field. **1931** Grief Street; Rebound. **1938** Holiday. **1945** The Hidden Eye. **1946** The Dark Horse; She Wrote the Book. **1947** Louisiana; The Shocking Miss Pilgrim; Gentleman's Agreement. **1948** Are You With It?; Four Faces West; Force of Evil; Slippy McGee; The Girl from Manhattan. **1949** Rusty's Birthday; The Lawton Story (aka Prince of Peace). **1950** The Petty Girl; Johnny One-Eye; Experiment Alcatraz. **1951** The Second Woman; Katie Did It. **1952** April in Paris. **1954** Jesse James vs. the Daltons.

LARIMORE, EARLE

Born: 1899, Portland, Ore. Died: Oct. 22, 1947, New York, N.Y. Screen, stage and radio actor.

Appeared in: **1922** Inspection. **1926** The Kickoff.

LARKIN, GEORGE

Born: Nov. 11, 1888, New York, N.Y. Died: Mar. 27, 1946. Screen, stage, vaudeville actor and circus performer.

Appeared in: **1912** The Return of Lady Linda; The Transgression of Deacon Jones; The Letter with the Black Seals; Robin Hood; A Choice by Accident; Making Uncle Jealous. **1913** While Father Telephoned. **1916** Unto Those Who Sin. **1918** Zongar; Hands Up (serial); Border Raiders. **1919** The Tiger's Trail (serial); The Terror of the Ranger (serial); The Man Trackers; The Lurking Peril (serial); Terror Trail (serial). **1920** The Unfortunate Sex. **1921** The Man Trackers; Terror Trail (serial). **1922** Boomerang Justice; Saved by the Radio; Barriers of Folly; Bulldog Courage. **1923** The Apache Dancer; Flames of Passion; The Flash; Gentleman Unafraid; Mysterious Goods; Her Reputation; Tango Cavalier; The Way of the Transgressor. **1924** Deeds of Daring; Stop at Nothing; Midnight Secrets; The Pell Street Mystery; Yankee Madness. **1925** Getting 'Em Right; Quick Change; The Right Man; Rough Stuff. **1926** Silver Fingers. **1928** Midnight Rose. **1931** Alexander Hamilton.

LARKIN, JOHN

Born: 1874. Died: Mar. 19, 1936, Los Angeles, Calif. (pneumonia). Black screen actor.

Appeared in: **1931** Smart Money; Man to Man; The Prodigal; Sporting Blood. **1932** Wet Parade; The Tenderfoot; Stranger in Town. **1933** Black Beauty; Day of Reckoning; The Great Jasper. **1934** The Witching Hour. **1935** Mississippi; A Notorious Gentleman. **1936** Frankie and Johnnie; Hearts Divided; Green Pastures.

LARKIN, JOHN

Born: 1912, Oakland, Calif. Died: Jan. 29, 1965, Studio City, Calif. (heart attack). Screen, radio and television actor. Do not confuse with John Larkin, black actor (dec. 1936) nor stage actor (dec. 1929).

Appeared in: **1950** Farewell to Yesterday. **1964** Seven Days in May; Those Calloways. **1965** The Satan Bug.

LA ROCQUE, ROD (Roderick la Rocque de la Rour)

Born: Nov. 29, 1898, Chicago, Ill. Died: Oct. 15, 1969, Beverly Hills, Calif. Screen, stage actor and radio producer. Married to actress Vilma Banky.

Appeared in: **1917** Efficiency Edgar's Courtship; Much Obliged; Sundaying in Fairview Filling His Own Shoes; The Girl Who Took Notes and Got Wise and Then Fell Down; The Rainbow Box; The Fable of the Back Tracker from the Hot Sidewalks; The Fable of the Speedy Sprite; The Fable of What Transpires After the Wind-Up; The Fable of the Uplifter and His Dandy Little Opus; The Dream Doll; Sadie Goes to Heaven. **1918** The Venus Model. **1919** Love and The Woman. **1920** Stolen Kiss. **1921** Paying the Piper; Suspicious Wives. **1922** What's Wrong with the Women?; Notoriety; The Challenge; Slim Shoulders; A Woman's Woman. **1923** The Ten Commandments; Zaza; Jazzmania; The French Doll. **1924** Triumph; Feet of Clay; Forbidden Paradise; A Society Scandal; Code of the Sea; Don't Call it Love; Phantom Justice. **1925** The Coming of Amos; Braveheart; The Golden Bed; Night Life of New York; Wild, Wild Susan. **1926** Hold "Em Yale; Stand and Deliver; Captain Swagger; Love Pirate; Love over Night. **1929** The Man and the Moment; The One Woman Idea; Our Modern Maidens; The Locked Door; Our Dancing Daughter; The Delightful Rogue; Forbidden Paradise. **1930** One Romantic Night; Let Us Be Gay; Beau Bandit. **1931** The Yellow Ticket. **1933** S.O.S. Iceberg. **1935** Mystery Woman; Frisco Waterfront. **1936** The Preview Murder Mystery; Till We Meet Again; Hi, Gaucho!; The Dragnet. **1937** The Shadow Strikes; Clothes and the Woman. **1938** International Crime; Taming the Wild. **1939** The Hunchback of Notre Dame. **1940** Beyond Tomorrow; Dr. Christian Meets the Women; Dark Streets of Cairo. **1941** Meet John Doe.

LARQUEY, PIERRE

Born: 1884, France. Died: Apr. 17, 1962, Paris, France. Screen actor.

Appeared in: **1935** Topaze. **1936** Second Bureau. **1937** Dr. Knock. **1939** A Man and His Wife; Mademoiselle ma Mere; The Citadel of Silence. **1940** The Mayor's Dilemma; Two Women. **1944** Moulin Rouge. **1945** Des Dames aux Chapeaux Verts (The Ladies in the Great Hats). **1946** Jericho. **1947** The Murderer Lives at Number 21; The Blue Veil. **1948** Le Corbeau (The Raven); Jenny Lamour; Portrait of Innocence. **1950** Sylvie and the Phantom. **1951** Face to the Wind. **1952** A Simple Case of Money; Topaze (and 1935 version). **1955** Diabolique. **1958** Witches of Salem.

LARRIMORE, FRANCINE

Born: 1898, France. Died: Mar. 7, 1975, New York, N.Y. (pneumonia). Stage and screen actress.

Appeared in: **1915** The Devil's Darling. **1916** The Princess from the Poorhouse. **1917** Max Wants a Divorce; Somewhere in America; Royal Pauper. **1918** Resurrection. **1937** John Meade's Woman.

LARSON, LORLEE

Born: 1935. Died: Oct. 4, 1954, Los Angeles, Calif. Screen and radio actress.

LA RUE, FRANK H. (Frank Herman La Rue)

Born: Dec. 5, 1878, Ohio. Died: Sept. 26, 1960, Woodland Hills, Calif. Screen, stage and vaudeville actor.

Appeared in: **1931** Sidewalks of New York. **1932** Once in a Life Time. **1933** Strange People; Flying Devils; Thrill Hunter. **1934** Mike Fright (short); The Fighting Ranger. **1935** When a Man Sees Red; Motive for Revenge; The Girl Who Came Back; The Singing Vagabond; Red River Valley. **1937** Bar-Z Bad Men; Gun Lords of Stirrup Basin; A Lawman Is Born; It Happened Out West; Boothill Brigade; Public Cowboy No. 1; Colorado Kid. **1938** Song and Bullets; Lightning Carson Rides Again; I Demand Payment; Outlaws of Sonora; Overland Stage Raiders; Knight of the Plains; Frontier Scout. **1939** In Old Montana; Down the Wyoming Trail; Port of Hate; Roll Wagons Roll; Code of the Fearless; Song of the Buckaroo; Trigger Pals. **1940** Frontier Crusader; The Durango Kid; Arizona Frontier; Westbound Stage; Land of the Six Guns; The Range Busters; Riders of Pasco Basin; Return of Wild Bill; Fugitive from a Prison Camp; The Courageous Dr. Christian; The Shadow (serial). **1941** Beyond the Sacramento; Gunman from Bodie; Robbers of the Range; Prairie Stranger; Hands across the Rockies; A Missouri Outlaw. **1942** Stardust on the Sage. **1943** Robin Hood of the Range; Saddles and Sagebrush. **1944** Ghost Guns; The Last Horseman; Saddle Leather Law; West of the Rio Grande. **1945** Blazing the Western Trail; Devil Riders; Frontier Feud; The Lost Trail. **1946** Border Bandits; The Fighting Frontiersman; Frontier Gun Law; The Gentleman from Texas; Gunning for Vengeance; The Haunted Mine; Silver Range; Under Arizona Skies. **1947** Prairie Raiders; South of Chisholm Trail; Cheyenne Takes Over; Gun Talk. **1948** Song of the Drifter; Frontier Agent. **1949** Sheriff of Medicine Bow.

LA RUE, GRACE

Born: 1881. Died: Mar. 12, 1956, Burlingame, Calif. Screen, stage and vaudeville actress. Married to actor Hale Hamilton (dec. 1942).

Appeared in: **1919** That's Good (she used the name of Stella Gray and received no billing for that film). **1929** The International Star of Songs (short). **1933** She Done Him Wrong. **1940** If I Had My Way.

LA RUE, JEAN (Eugene Marcus Bailey)

Born: 1901. Died: June 1956, San Antonio, Tex. Screen actor.

Appeared in: **1923** Where the Pavement Ends. **1928** Tracy, the Outlaw.

LASCOE, HENRY

Born: 1914. Died: Sept. 1, 1964, Hollywood, Calif. (heart attack). Screen, stage and television actor.

Appeared in: **1951** The Man with My Face.

LASSIE

Born: 1941. Died: 1959. Screen animal performer (collie).

Appeared in: **1943** Lassie Come Home. **1945** Son of Lassie. **1946** Courage of Lassie.

LATELL, LYLE (Lyle Zeiem)

Born: Apr. 9, 1905, Elma, Iowa. Died: Oct. 24, 1967, Hollywood, Calif. (heart attack). Married to actress Mary Foy (one of the Seven Little Foys). Screen and television actor. Appeared in the "Boston Blackie" series during the 1940s.

Appeared in: **1941** Texas; Great Guns; In the Navy; Sky Raiders (serial). **1942** The Wife Takes a Flyer; The Night before the Divorce. **1944** One Mysterious Night. **1945** Hold That Blonde; Dick Tracy vs. Cueball. **1947** Dick Tracy's Dilemma; Dick Tracy and Gruesome; Buck Privates Come Home. **1948** The Noose Hangs High. **1949** Sky Dragon. **1951** Deal Me In (short). **1953** Pardon My Wrench (short). **1955** The Girl Rush.

LATHROP, DONALD

Born: 1888, England. Died: July 15, 1940, London, England (heart ailment). Stage and screen actor.

LAUDER, SIR HARRY

Born: Aug. 4, 1870, Portobello, Scotland. Died: Feb. 25, 1950, Lenarkshire, Scotland (kidney ailment). Screen and stage actor.

Appeared in: **1927** Huntingtower. **1929** Happy Days; Auld Lang Syne. **1936** The End of the Road. **1940** Song of the Road.

LAUGHLIN, BILLY (William Laughlin)

Born: July 5, 1932, San Gabriel, Calif. Died: Aug. 31, 1948, Covina, Calif. (motor scooter-truck accident). Screen actor. Was the "Froggy" character in the Our Gang Comedies.

Appeared in: **1940** The following shorts: The New Pupil; Waldo's Last Stand; Kiddie Cure. **1941** The following shorts: Fightin' Fools; Baby Blues; Ye Olde Minstrels; Go; Robot Wrecks; Helping Hands; Come Back, Miss Pipps; Wedding Worries. **1942** The following shorts: Melodies Old and New; Going to Press; Don't Lie; Surprised Parties; Doin' Their Bit; Rover's Big Chance; Mighty Lak a Goat; Unexpected Riches. **1943** The following shorts: Benjamin Franklin, Jr.; Family Troubles; Calling All Kids; Farm Hands; Election Daze; Little Miss Pinkerton; Three Smart Guys. **1944** The following shorts: Radio Bugs; Tale of a Dog; Dancing Romeo.

LAUGHTON, CHARLES

Born: July 1, 1899, Scarborough, England. Died: Dec. 15, 1962, Los Angeles, Calif. (cancer). Screen, stage actor, film and stage director. Married to actress Elsa Lanchester. Won 1933 Academy Award for Best Actor for Private Life of Henry VIII.

Appeared in: **1928** H. G. Wells Comedic Series including: Bluebottles; Daydreams. **1929** Piccadilly. **1930** Wolves (aka Wanted Men—US 1936); Comets. **1931** Down River. **1932** Devil and the Deep; Payment Deferred (stage and film versions); The Old Dark House; The Sign of the Cross; If I had a Million. **1933** Island of Lost Souls; White Woman; The Private Life of Henry VIII. **1934** The Barretts of Wimpole Street. **1935** Les Miserables; Ruggles of Red Gap; Mutiny on the Bounty; Frankie and Johnny (short). **1936** I Claudius (never released); Rembrandt. **1938** Vessel of Wrath (aka The Beachcomber—US); St. Martin's Lane. **1939** A Miracle Can Happen; Jamaica Inn; The Hunchback of Notre Dame. **1940** They Knew What They Wanted. **1941** It Started with Eve. **1942** The Tuttles of Tahiti; Tales of Manhattan; Stand by for Action. **1943** Forever and A Day; This Land is Mine; The Man from Down Under. **1944** The Canterville Ghost; The Suspect; The Sign of the Cross (revised version of 1932 film). **1945** Captain Kidd. **1946** Because of Him. **1947** The Queen's Necklace. **1948** The Paradine Case; Arch of Triumph; Girl from Manhattan; The Big Clock; On our Merry Way (aka A Miracle Can Happen). **1949** The Bribe; Man on the Eiffel Tower. **1951** The Strange Door; The Blue Veil. **1952** O'Henry's Full House; Abbott and Costello meet Captain Kidd; "News of the Day" (newsreel). **1953** Young Bess; Salome. **1954** Hobson's Choice. **1957** Wit-

ness for the Prosecution. **1960** Spartacus; Under Ten Flags. **1962** Advise and Consent. **1968** Head (film clips).

LAUGHTON, EDWARD "EDDIE"

Born: 1903, Sheffield, England. Died: Mar. 21, 1952, Hollywood, Calif. (pneumonia). Screen and vaudeville actor.

Appeared in: **1939** The Lone Wolf Spy Hunt; My Son is a Criminal; Flying G-Men (serial); North of Shanghai; Romance of the Redwood; Scandal Sheet; Outside These Walls; Mandrake the Magician; Beware Spooks; Those High Grey Walls; The Amazing Mr. Williams; Cafe Hostell; Bullets for Rustlers; Oily to Bed, Oily to Rise (short); Pest from the West (short). **1940** Blazing Six Shooters; Texas Stagecoach; Men without Souls; The Doctor Takes a Wife; Girls of the Road; Cold Turkey (short); A-Plumbing We Will Go (short). **1941** Outlaws of the Panhandle; I was a Prisoner on Devil's Island; Mystery Ship; In the Sweet Pie and Pie (short); She's Oil Mine (short). **1942** Canal Zone; Lawless Plainsmen; Submarine Raider; Honolulu Lu; Sabotage Squad; The Boogie Man Will Get You; Atlantic Convoy; All Work and No Pay (short); What's the Matador? (short). **1944** The Girl in the Case; Defective Detectives (short). **1945** The Lost Weekend; Idiot's Deluxe (short). **1947** The Shocking Miss Pilgrim. **1949** Chicken Every Sunday.

LAUHER, BOB

Born: 1931. Died: Aug. 22, 1973, Tarzana, Calif. Screen, television, radio actor, radio and television writer.

Appeared in: **1970** Which Way to the Front?

LAUNDERS, PERC

Born: 1905. Died: Oct. 2, 1952, Hollywood, Calif. Screen actor and studio musician.

Appeared in: **1944** The Falcon Out West. **1945** Under Western Skies; The Stork Club. **1946** The Brute Man. **1949** Abandoned Woman. **1950** For Heaven's Sake.

LAUREL, KAY

Born: 1890, Newcastle, Pa. Died: Jan. 31, 1927, London, England (pneumonia). Stage and screen actress.

Appeared in: **1919** The Brand. **1921** Lonely Heart.

LAUREL, STAN (Arthur Stanley Jefferson)

Born: June 16, 1890, Ulverston, England. Died: Feb. 23, 1965, Santa Monica, Calif. (heart attack). Screen, stage, vaudeville actor, film producer, director and screenwriter. Was partner in comedy team of "Laurel and Hardy" with Oliver Hardy (dec. 1957). The pair won Academy Award in 1933 for Best Short Subject for The Music Box. Married to singer Ida Kitaeva. Divorced from Lois Nielson and Virginia Ruth.

Appeared in: **1917** Nuts in May; The Evolution of Fashion. **1918** Hoot Mon; Hickory Hiram; Whose Zoo; Huns and Hyphens; Just Rambling Along; No Place Like Jail; Bears and Bad Men; Frauds and Frenzies; Do You Love Your Wife?; Lucky Dog. **1919** Mixed Nuts; Scars and Stripes; When Knights were Cold. **1920** The following shorts: Under Two Jags; Wild Bill Hiccup; Rupert of Hee-Haw (aka Coleslaw); The Spilers; Oranges and Lemons. **1921** The Rent Collector (short). **1922** The following shorts: The Pest; The Egg; Mud and Sand. **1923** The following shorts: The Noon Whistle; White Wings; Pick and Shovel; Kill and Cure; Gas and Air; Mud and Sand; The Handy Man; Short Orders; A Man about Town; The Whole Truth; Scorching Sands; Save the Ship; Roughest Africa; Frozen Hearts; Mother's Joy. **1924** The following shorts: Smithy; Zeb vs. Paprika; Postage Due; Near Dublin; Brothers under the Chin; Short Kilts; Monsieur Don't Care; West of Hot Dog. **1925** The following shorts: Somewhere in Wrong; Dr. Pycle and Mr. Pryde; Pie-Eyed; Mandarin Mix-Up; The Snow Hawk; Navy Blues Days; Twins; The Sleuth; Half a Man; Cowboys Cry for It. **1926** The following shorts: Atta Boy; Slipping Wives (with Oliver Hardy); On the Front Page; Get 'Em Young. The following film listings include both Laurel and Hardy. **1927** The following shorts: With Love and Hisses; Sailors Beware; Forty-Five Minutes from Hollywood; Do Detectives Think?; Flying Elephants; Sugar Daddies; Call of the Cuckoo; The Rap; Duck Soup; Eve's Love Letters; Love 'Em and Weep; Why Girls Love Sailors; Should Tall Men Marry?; Hats Off; The Battle of the Century; The Second Hundred Years; Let George Do It; Putting Pants on Philip (the first "Laurel and Hardy" film). **1928** The following shorts: Leave 'Em Laughing; From Soup to Nuts; You're Darn Tootin'; Their Purple Moment; Should Married Men Go Home?; Habeas Corpus; Two Tars; We Faw Down; The Finishing Touch; Early to Bed. **1929** Hollywood Revue of 1929; plus the following shorts: Liberty; Unaccustomed as We Are; Double Whoopee; Big Business; Men O'War; A Perfect Day; Angora Love; Bacon Grabbers; They Go Boom; The Hoose Gow; Berth Marks; Wrong Again; That's My Wife. **1930** The Rogue Song; plus the following shorts: Night Owls; Blotto; Hay Wire; Brats; Below Zero; The Laurel and Hardy Murder Case; Another Fine Mess; Hog Wild (aka Aerial Antics). **1931** Pardon Us; plus the following shorts: Chickens Come Home; Our Wife; Laughing Gravy; Come Clean; One Good Turn; Beau Hunks (aka Beau Chumps); Slippery Pearls; Be Big; On the Loose (short). **1932** Pack up Your Troubles; plus following shorts: Any Old Port; The Music Box; The Chimp; County Hospital; Scram; Their First Mistake; Helpmates; Towed in a Hole. **1933** Fra

Diavolo (The Devil's Brother); plus following shorts: Busy Bodies; Twice Two; Me and My Pal; The Midnight Patrol; Wild Poses; Dirty Work. **1934** Sons of the Desert; Babes in Toyland; Hollywood Party of 1934; plus following shorts: Going Bye-Bye; Oliver the Eighth; Them Thar Hills; The Live Ghost. **1935** Bonnie Scotland; plus following shorts: Tit for Tat; The Fixer-Uppers; Thicker Than Water. **1936** The Bohemian Girl; Our Relations; On the Wrong Trek (short). **1937** Way Out West; Pick a Star. **1938** Swiss Miss; Blockheads. **1939** The Flying Deuces. **1940** A Chump at Oxford; Saps at Sea. **1941** Great Guns. **1942** A-Haunting We Will Go. **1943** Air Raid Wardens; Jitterbugs; The Dancing Masters; Tree in a Test Tube (Government short). **1944** The Big Noise; Nothing but Trouble. **1945** The Bullfighters. **1951** Atoll K (aka Escapade—England 1952; aka Utopia 1954; aka Robincrusoeland—France 1952). **1957** Big Parade of Comedy (documentary). **1960** When Comedy Was King (documentary). **1961** Days of Thrills and Laughter (documentary). **1963** 30 Years of Fun (documentary). **1964** Big Parade of Comedy (documentary). **1967** The Crazy World of Laurel and Hardy (documentary); Further Peril's of Laurel and Hardy (documentary).

LAURENZ, JOHN

Born: 1909. Died: Nov. 7, 1958, Brooklyn, N.Y. Screen actor and singer.

Appeared in: **1946** A Walk in the Sun. **1947** Apache Rose. **1948** Tarzan and the Mermaids. **1950** Border Outlaws; Federal Agent at Large.

LAURIER, JAY (Jay Chapman)

Born: May 31, 1879, Birmingham, England. Died: Apr. 1969, Durban, South Africa. Screen, stage and vaudeville actor.

Appeared in: **1931** Hobson's Choice. **1932** Pajamas Preferred. **1933** Waltz Time; I'll Stick to You. **1937** Black Tulip.

LaVELLE, KAY

Born: 1889. Died: Nov. 18, 1965, Tujunga, Calif. Screen actress.

Appeared in: **1928** Don't Handle the Goods (short). **1934** Cross Country Cruise. **1951** People Will Talk.

LA VERNE, LUCILLE

Born: Nov. 8, 1872, Nashville, Tenn. Died: May 4, 1945, Culver City, Calif. Stage and screen actress. Her voice was that of the Queen and the Wicked Witch in Walt Disney's Snow White (1937).

Appeared in: **1917** Polly of the Circus. **1922** Orphans of the Storm. **1923** The White Rose; Zaza. **1924** America; His Darker Self. **1925** Sun Up. **1928** The Last Moment. **1930** Abraham Lincoln; Sinner's Holiday; Little Caesar. **1931** The Great Meadow; Union Depot; An American Tragedy; Twenty-four Hours; The Unholy Garden. **1932** Hearts of Humanity; Breach of Promise; Alias the Doctor; She Wanted a Millionaire; When Paris Sleeps. **1933** Wild Horse Mesa; The Last Trail; Strange Adventure; Pilgrimage. **1934** Kentucky Kernels; The Mighty Barnum; Beloved; School for Girls. **1935** A Tale of Two Cities. **1937** Snow White (voice).

LA VERNIE, LAURA (Laura Anderson)

Born: Mar. 2, 1853, Jefferson City, Mo. Died: Sept. 18, 1939, Los Angeles, Calif. Stage and screen actress. Entered films in 1909.

Appeared in: **1925** Who's Your Friend? **1930** Devil's Holiday; Lummox. **1931** Kiki.

LAW, BURTON

Born: 1880. Died: Nov. 2, 1963. Screen, stage, burlesque actor and screenwriter.

Appeared in: **1915** Broken Coin; Graft. **1916** The Sea Lily; A Mountain Tragedy. **1917** Treason; Like Wildfire. **1921** Winners of the West (serial). **1922** They Like 'Em Rough; Under Two Flags. **1923** The Oregon Trail (serial).

LAW, DONALD

Born: 1920. Died: Feb. 26, 1959, Meadville, Pa. Screen actor.

Appeared in: "Our Gang" comedies.

LAW, RODMAN

Born: 1885, Massachusetts. Died: Oct. 14, 1919, Greenville, S.C. (tuberculosis). Aviator, parachute jumper and screen actor.

Appeared in: **1913** Death's Short Cut.

LAW, WALTER

Born: 1876. Died: Aug. 8, 1940, Hollywood, Calif. Screen, stage and vaudeville actor.

Appeared in: **1918** A Perfect Lady. **1920** If I Were King. **1922** Forgotten Law; Great Alone. **1923** Flying Dutchman. **1924** Janice Meredith. **1925** Clothes Make the Pirate. **1930** Whoopee.

LAWES, LEWIS E.

Born: 1884. Died: Apr. 23, 1947, Garrison, N.Y. (cerebral hemorrhage). Had been warden of Sing Sing prison for 20 years. Film, radio actor and writer.

Appeared in: **1946** Prologue of San Quentin.

LAWFORD, BETTY

Born: 1910, England. Died: Nov. 20, 1960, N.Y. Screen, stage and television actress. Daughter of stage actor Ernest Lawford (dec.) and actress Janet Seeter Lawford.

Appeared in: **1925** The Night Club. **1928** Return of Sherlock Holmes. **1929** Gentlemen of the Press; Lucky in Love. **1930** Old English. **1931** Secrets of a Secretary. **1933** Berkeley Square; Gallant Lady. **1934** Let's Be Ritzy; The Human Side. **1936** Love before Breakfast; Stolen Holiday. **1937** Criminal Lawyer. **1943** Stage Door Canteen. **1947** The Devil Thumbs a Ride.

LAWFORD, LT. GEN. SIR SYDNEY

Born: 1866. Died: Feb. 15, 1953, Hollywood, Calif. Screen actor. Father of actor Peter Lawford.

LAWRENCE, CHARLIE. See LIVIO LORENZON

LAWRENCE, EDDY

Born: San Francisco, Calif. Died: Dec. 5, 1931, San Diego, Calif. (suicide—gas). Stage and screen actor.

Appeared in: **1925** The Knockout.

LAWRENCE, FLORENCE

Born: 1888. Died: Dec. 27, 1938, Beverly Hills, Calif. (suicide—ant paste). Screen actress. Was known as the "Biograph Girl" and the "Imp Girl." Entered films with Vitagraph in 1907.

Appeared in: **1908** A Calamitous Elopement; The Girl and the Outlaw; Betrayed by a Hand Print; Behind the Scenes; Where the Breakers Roar; The Heart of Oyama; A Smoked Husband; The Devil; The Barbarian, Ingomar; The Vaquero's Vow; The Planter's Wife; The Zulu's Heart; Romance of a Jewess; The Call of the Wild; Mr. Jones at the Ball; Concealing a Burglar; Taming of the Shrew; The Ingrate; A Woman's Way; The Song of the Shirt; Mr. Jones Entertains; An Awful Moment; The Christmas Burglars; Mr. Jones Has a Card Party; The Salvation Army Lass; Romeo and Juliet. **1909** Redemption; "Jonesy Picture" series: Mrs. Jones Entertains; The Mended Lute; The Slave; The Brahma Diamond; Resurrection; The Jones Have Amateur Theatricals; His Wife's Mother; The Deception; The Lure of the Gown; Lady Helen's Escapade; Jones and His New Neighbor; The Winning Coat; The Road to the Heart; Confidence; The Note in the Shoe; Eloping with Auntie; Her First Biscuits; The Peach Basket Hat; The Necklace; The Way of Man; Mrs. Jones' Lover; The Cardinal's Conspiracy; Mr. Jones' Burglar. **1910** The Angel of the Studio. **1911** Flo's Discipline; Her Two Sons; A Good Turn; Through Jealous Eyes; A Rebellious Blossom; The Slave's Affinity; The Wife Saver; The Match Maker; One on Reno; The Professor's Ward; A Rural Conqueror; His Chorus Girl Wife; A Girlish Impulse. **1912** In Swift Waters. **1914** A Singular Cynic. **1922** The Unfoldment. **1923** Satin Girl. **1924** Gambling Wives.

LAWRENCE, GERTRUDE (Gertrude Klasen and Alexandre Dagmar Lawrence Klasen)

Born: July 4, 1898 or 1902, London, England. Died: Sept. 6, 1952, New York, N.Y. (cancer of the liver). Screen, stage actress and dancer.

Appeared in: **1929** The Battle of Paris (film debut). **1932** Aren't We All; Lord Camber's Ladies. **1933** No Funny Business. **1935** Mimi. **1936** Rembrandt; Men Are Not Gods (US 1937). **1950** The Glass Menagerie.

LAWRENCE, JOHN (John Darms Lawrence)

Born: July 1910, Utah. Died: June 26, 1974, Los Angeles, Calif. (heart attack). Screen actor, film producer and screenwriter.

Appeared in: **1951** Where No Vultures Fly (aka The Ivory Hunters—US 1952). **1958** The Goddess. **1962** The Manchurian Candidate. **1964** The Great American Can Swindle. **1965** The Family Jewels; Tales of a Salesman. **1966** Seconds; Out of Sight; Nevada Smith. **1967** The Glory Stompers. **1968** The Destructors. **1969** Free Grass. **1971** The Seven Minutes. **1974** Busting.

LAWRENCE, LILLIAN

Born: 1870, Alexander, W. Va. Died: May 7, 1926, Beverly Hills, Calif. Stage and screen actress.

Appeared in: **1921** Making the Grade; A Parisian Scandal. **1922** A Girl's Desire; The Eternal Flame; East Is West; White Shoulders. **1923** The Common Law; Fashionable Fakers; Three Ages; Crinoline and Romance; The Voice from the Minaret. **1924** Christine of the Hungry Heart. **1925** Graustark. **1926** Stella Maris. **1927** Sensation Seekers.

LAWRENCE, WILLIAM E. "BABE"

Born: 1896, Los Angeles, Calif. Died: Nov. 28, 1947, Hollywood, Calif. Stage and screen actor.

Appeared in: **1915** Birth of a Nation. **1920** Bride 13 (serial). **1921** Get Your Man; The Kiss; The Snob; Fightin' Mad; Morals; Ducks and Drakes. **1922** They Like 'Em Rough; Blood and Sand; Forget-Me-Not; A Front Page Story; The Love Gambler. **1923** Blinky; Cameo Kirby; The Thrill Chaser. **1924** The Law Forbids; The Reckless Age; The Whispered Name. **1926** A Man Four-Square; Hard Boiled. **1930** The Costello Case. **1931** Hell Bound.

LAWSON, ELEANOR (Eleanor Smith)

Born: Dec. 23, 1875, Illinois. Died: Mar. 22, 1966, Pasadena, Calif. (heart attack). Screen actress.

Appeared in: 1923 Hollywood. 1924 Merton of the Movies. 1925 Lights of Broadway. 1927 It. 1933 Pick Up. 1942 The Man with Two Lives. 1944 Ladies Courageous.

LAWSON, HELEN MITCHELL MOROSCO. *See* HELEN MITCHELL

LAWSON, WILFRID (Wilfred Worsnop)

Born: Jan. 14, 1900, Bradford, Yorkshire, England. Died: Oct. 10, 1966, London, England (heart attack). Screen, stage and television actor.

Appeared in: 1931 East Lynn on the Western Front. 1933 Strike it Rich. 1935 Turn of the Tide. 1936 Ladies in Love; White Hunter. 1937 The Man Who Made Diamonds. 1938 Bank Holiday (aka Three on a Weekend—US); Yellow Sands; The Terror; Pygmalion; The Gaunt Stranger (aka The Phantom Strikes—US 1939). 1939 Stolen Life; Allegheny Uprising; Dead Man's Shoes. 1940 Pastor Hall; Gentleman of Venture (aka It Happened to One Man—US 1941); The Long Voyage Home. 1941 The Farmer's Wife; Danny Boy (US 1941); The Tower of Terror (US 1942); Jeannie; The Man at the Gate (aka Men of the Sea—US). 1942 Hard Steel; The Night Has Eyes (aka Terror House—US 1943); The Great Mr. Handel (US—1943). 1943 Thursday's Child. 1944 Fanny by Gaslight (aka Man of Evil—US 1948). 1945 Macbeth (short). 1947 The Turners of Prospect Road. 1954 Make Me an Offer (US 1956). 1955 The Prisoner; An Alligator Named Daisy (US 1957). 1956 War and Peace. 1957 Miracle in Soho; Hell Drivers (US 1958). 1958 Tread Softly Stranger (US 1959). 1959 Room at the Top; Expresso Bongo (US 1960). 1961 The Naked Edge; Nothing Barred; Over the Odds. 1962 Postman's Knock; Go to Blazes. 1963 Tom Jones. 1964 Becket. 1966 The Wrong Box. 1967 The Viking Queen.

LAWTON, FRANK

Born: Sept. 30, 1904, London, England. Died: June 10, 1969, London, England. Stage and screen actor. Married to actress Evelyn Laye, son of actor Frank Mokeley and actress Daisy May Collier.

Appeared in: 1930 Young Woodley (stage and film versions); Birds of Prey (aka The Perfect Alibi—US 1931). 1931 The Skin Game; The Outsider; Michael and Mary (US 1953). 1932 After Office Hours. 1933 Heads We Go (aka The Charming Deceiver—US); Friday the Thirteenth; Cavalcade. 1934 One More River. 1935 David Copperfield; Bar-20 Rides Again. 1936 The Invisible Ray; Devil Doll. 1937 The Mill on the Floss (US 1939). 1939 The Four Just Men (aka The Secret Four—US 1940). 1942 Went the Day Well? (aka 48 Hours—US 1944). 1948 The Winslow Boy (US 1950). 1953 Rough Shoot (aka Shoot First—US). 1956 Doublecross. 1957 The Rising of the Moon. 1958 Gideon's Day (aka Gideon of Scotland Yard—US 1959); A Night to Remember. 1961 The Queen's Guards (US 1963).

LAWTON, THAIS

Born: 1881, Louisville, Ky. Died: Dec. 18, 1956, N.Y. Stage and screen actress.

Appeared in: 1915 The Battle Cry for Peace.

LAX, FRANCES

Born: Oct. 5, 1895, New York, N.Y. Died: May 6, 1975, Santa Monica, Calif. (heart disease). Screen and television actress.

Appeared in: 1960 The Apartment. 1961 The Errand Boy. 1965 The Family Jewels.

LAY, IRVING T.

Died: Mar. 1932, Seneca Falls, N.Y. (suicide—gas poisoning). Screen actor.

LEAHY, EUGENE

Born: Mar. 14, 1883, Newcastle West Co., Limerick, Ireland. Died: Mar. 1967, London, England. Stage and screen actor.

Appeared in: 1922 A Prince of Lovers (US 1927 and aka Life of Lord Byron). 1937 Love from a Stranger. 1957 The Curse of Frankenstein.

LEAHY, MARGARET

Died: Feb. 17, 1967. Screen actress.

Appeared in: 1923 The Three Ages.

LEAL, MILAGROS

Born: 1902. Died: Mar. 1, 1975, Madrid, Spain (cancer). Stage and screen actress. Married to actor Salvador Soler Marti. Mother of actress Amparo Soler Leal.

Appeared in: 1949 The Nail.

LEASE, REX

Born: Feb. 11, 1901, Central City, W. Va. Died: Jan. 3, 1966, Hollywood, Calif. Screen actor. Entered films as an extra.

Appeared in: 1924 A Woman Who Sinned; Chalk Marks. 1925 Before Midnight; The Last Edition; Easy Money. 1926 The Timid Terror; Mystery Pilot (serial); The Last Alarm; Race Wild; Somebody's Mother. 1927 Clancy's Kosher Wedding; Moulders of Men; Heroes of the Night; The Cancelled Debt; The College Hero; Not for Publication; The Outlaw Dog. 1928 The Law of the Range; Last Lap; Riders of the Dark; Broadway Daddies; The Candy Kid; Red Riders of Canada; The Speed Classic; Phantom of the Turf; Making the Varsity; Queen of the Chorus. 1929 Stolen Love; The Younger Generation; Two Sisters; When Dreams Come True; Girls Who Dare. 1930 Borrowed Wives; The Utah Kid; Wings of Adventure; Troopers 3; Sunny Skies; Hot Curves; So This Is Mexico. 1931 In Old Cheyenne; Why Marry; Chinatown after Dark; Monster Walks; Is There Justice; Sign of the Wolf (serial). 1932 The Lone Trail; Midnight Morals; Cannonball Express. 1934 Inside Information. 1935 Fighting Caballero; The Ghost Rider; The Man from Gun Town; Cowboy and the Bandit; Pals of the Range; Rough Riding Ranger; Cyclone of the Saddle. 1936 Fast Bullets; Lightnin' Bill Carson; Roarin' Guns; Cavalcade of the West; Aces and Eight; The Clutching Hand (serial); The Man from Gun Town; Gentleman Jim McGee. 1937 The Silver Trail; Heroes of the Alamo; The Freedom; Swing it Sailor; The Mysterious Pilot (serial). 1938 Fury Below; Code of the Rangers; Desert Patrol; A Criminal Is Born (short). 1939 South of the Border; In Old Monterey. 1940 Rancho Grande; Under Texas Skies; Lone Star Raiders; A Chump at Oxford; The Trail Blazers. 1941 Outlaws of the Rio Grande; The Phantom Cowboy; Death Valley Outlaws; Pals of the Range; Sierra Sue; Outlaws of the Cherokee Trail. 1942 Arizona Terrors; The Silver Bullet; The Cyclone Kid; Tomorrow We Live; The Boss of Hangtown Mesa; Home in Wyomin'; Stardust on the Sage. 1943 Haunted Ranch; Tenting on the Old Camp Ground; Dead Man's Gulch. 1944 Firebrands of Arizona; Bordertown Trail; The Cowboy and the Senorita. 1945 Texas Ranger; The Naughty Nineties; Santa Fe Saddlemates; Frontier Gal; Flame of Barbary Coast. 1946 Days of Buffalo Bill; Sun Valley Cyclone; The Time of Their Lives. 1947 Helldorado; Slave Girl; The Wistful Widow of Wagon Gap; Buck Privates Come Home. 1948 Out of the Storm. 1949 Ma and Pa Kettle. 1950 Singing Guns; Bells of Coronado; Code of the Silver Sage; Curtain Call at Cactus Creek; Covered Wagon Raiders; Hills of Oklahoma; Frisco Tornado. 1952 Ma and Pa Kettle at the Fair; Lone Star; Abbott and Costello Meet Captain Kidd. 1953 Ride, Vaquero!; Money from Home; Abbott and Costello Go to Mars. 1956 On the Threshold of Space.

LEAVITT, DOUGLAS "ABE"

Born: 1883. Died: Mar. 3, 1960, Levittown, Pa. Screen, burlesque and vaudeville actor. Was part of vaudeville team of "Leavitt and Lockwood."

Appeared in: 1942 You Were Never Lovelier; Smith of Minnesota. 1943 Reveille with Beverly; Murder in Times Square; Two Senoritas from Chicago; Blitz on the Fritz (short); Farmer for a Day (short); It's a Great Life.

LE BEAU, STEPHANIE

Died: June 5, 1967, New York, N.Y. Screen, stage and television actress.

LEBEDEFF, IVAN

Born: June 18, 1899, Uspoliai, Lithuania. Died: Mar. 31, 1953, Hollywood, Calif. (heart attack). Screen actor, screenwriter and author. Appeared in French, German, U.S. films, etc. Married to actress Vera Engels.

Appeared in: 1922 King Frederick (German film debut). 1924 The Lucky Death; The Soul of an Artist; 600,000 Francs per Month; The Charming Prince. 1925 Burned Fingers. 1926 The Sorrows of Satan. 1927 The Loves of Sunya; The Angel of Broadway; The Forbidden Woman. 1928 Let 'er Go Gallagher; Walking Back. 1929 Sin Town; The Veiled Woman; The Cuckoos; The Midnight Mystery; The Conspiracy; Half-Shot at Sunrise. 1931 The Bachelor Apartment; The Lady Refuses; Deceit; Woman Pursued; The Gay Diplomat. 1932 Unholy Love; Hollywood Handicap (short); Hollywood on Parade (short). 1933 Bombshell; Made on Broadway; Laughing at Life; Sweepings. 1934 Kansas City Princess; Merry Widow; The Merry Frinks; Moulin Rouge. 1935 China Seas; Sweepstakes Annie; Goin' to Town. 1936 Pepper; The Golden Arrow; Love on the Run. 1937 Fair Warning; History is Made at Night; Atlantic Flight; Mama Steps Out; Conquest; Angel. 1938 Straight, Place and Show; Wise Girl. 1939 Trapped in the Sky; The Mystery of Mr. Wong; Hotel for Women; You Can't Cheat an Honest Man. 1940 Passport to Alcatraz; Public Enemy No. 1. 1941 The Shanghai Gesture; Blue, White, and Perfect. 1942 Lure of the Islands; Foreign Agent. 1943 Mission to Moscow; Around the World. 1944 Oh, What a Night!; Are These Our Parents? 1945 Rhapsody in Blue; They Are Guilty. 1952 The Snows of Kilimanjaro; California Conquest.

LE BRANDT, GERTRUDE N.

Born: 1863. Died: Aug. 28, 1955, Hollywood, Calif. Stage and screen actress.

Appeared in: 1921 Mama's Affair.

LE BRUN, MINON

Born: 1888. Died: Sept. 20, 1941, Los Angeles, Calif. Screen actress. Divorced from actor Cullen Landis (dec. 1975).

LeCLERCY, REGINA

Born: Brazil. Died: 1973, France (plane crash). Screen actress.

LEDERER, GRETCHEN

Born: 1891. Died: Dec. 20, 1955, Anaheim, Calif. Screen actress. Divorced from screen actor Otto Lederer. Entered films in 1910.

Appeared in: **1914** An Eleventh Hour Reformation. **1917** A Kentucky Cinderella; The Spotted Lily; Polly Redhead; Bondage; The Double Topped Trunk; The Cricket; My Little Boy; The Pointed Finger; The Townsend Divorce Case; Bartered Youth. **1918** Beauty in Chains; Hungry Eyes; The Red, Red Heart; Riddle Gawne. **1919** Wife or Country.

LEDERER, OTTO

Born: Apr. 17, 1886, Prague, Czech. Died: Sept. 3, 1965. Entered films with Vitagraph.

Appeared in: **1913** Why Tightwad Tips. **1914** The Love of Tokiwa; The Face of Fear. **1915** The Legend of the Lone Tree; The Chalice of Courage; What Did He Whisper?; Ghosts and Flypaper; The Offending Kiss; The Quarrel; Cal Marvin's Wife; The Wanderers; Her Last Flirtation; His Golden Grain; Willie Stayed Single. **1916** La Paloma; Pansy's Poppas; Sin's Penalty; When it Rains it Pours; A Squared Account; The Waters of Lethe; Some Chicken; Curfew at Simpton Center; Miss Adventure; A Race for Life. **1917** The Captain of the Gray Horse Troop; The Fighting Trail (serial); Dead Shot Baker; When Men are Tempted; The Flaming Omen. **1918** The Woman in the Web; The Wild Strain; Cavanaugh of the Forest Rangers; The Changing Woman; By the World Forgot. **1919** Cupid Forecloses. **1920** The Dragon's Net (serial). **1921** Making the Grade; The Struggle; Without Benefit of Clergy; The Spenders; The Avenging Arrow (serial). **1922** Forget-Me-Not; Hungry Hearts; White Eagle (serial). **1923** Souls in Bondage; Vanity Fair; Your Friend and Mine. **1924** Behind Two Guns; A Fighting Heart; Black Oxen; Poison; The Sword of Valor; What Three Men Wanted; Worldly Goods; Turned Up. **1925** Bowery Finery. **1926** Sweet Rosie O'Grady; That Model from Paris; The Cruise of the Jasper B. **1927** Chicago; The Jazz Singer; King of Kings; Sailor Izzy Murphy; The Shamrock and the Rose; The Trunk Mystery; Music Master. **1928** A Bit of Heaven; Celebrity; The Prediction (short); You're Darn Tootin'! (short). **1929** From Headquarters; Smiling Irish Eyes; One Stolen Night. **1933** Forgotten.

LEDERMAN, D. ROSS

Born: Dec. 11, 1895, Lancaster, Pa. Died: Aug. 24, 1972, Hollywood, Calif. (heart condition). Screen actor, prop man, film director and screenwriter. Entered films as an extra in 1913 in Mack Sennett Comedies.

LEDNER, DAVID

Born: 1900. Died: Dec. 17, 1957, Hollywood, Calif. (heart attack). Screen actor and stand-in. Entered films in 1941.

Appeared in: **1958** The Buccaneer (stand-in).

LEDUC, CLAUDINE (Sadi Lindsay)

Born: Paris, France. Died: Feb. 15, 1969, New York, N.Y. Screen, stage, television, radio actress and writer.

Appeared in: **1943** Once Upon a Honeymoon; The Song of Bernadette.

LEE, ALLEN

Born: 1875. Died: Feb. 5, 1951, New York, N.Y. Screen and stage actor.

LEE, AURIOL

Born: London, England. Died: July 2, 1941, Hutchinson, Kans. (auto accident). Screen, stage actress, stage producer and stage director.

Appeared in: **1941** Suspicion (only film).

LEE, BELINDA

Born: June 15, 1935, Devon, England. Died: Mar. 13, 1961, San Bernardino, Calif. (auto accident). Screen, stage and television actress.

Appeared in: **1954** The Runaway Bus; Life With the Lyons (aka Family Affair—US); Meet Mr. Gallaghan; The Belles of St. Trinian's (US—1955). **1955** Murder by Proxy (aka Blackout—US); Footsteps in the Fog; Man of the Moment; No Smoking. **1956** Who Done It?; The Feminine Touch (aka The Gentle Touch—US 1957); Eyewitness; The Big Money. **1957** The Secret Place (US—1958); Miracle in Soho; Dangerous Exile (US 1958). **1958** Nor the Moon by Night (aka Elephant Gun—US 1959); Big Money (US 1962). **1960** Giuseppe Venduto dai Fratelli (The Story of Joseph and His Brethren—US 1962); Femmine de Lusso (Love the Italian Way—US 1964); Goddess of Love; Le Notti De Lucrezia Borgia (The Nights of Lucretia Borgia); The Chasers (aka Les Dragueurs—The Dredgers). **1961** She Walks by Night; Aphrodite; Die Warheit Uber Rosemarie (The Truth About Rosemarie); Constantino il Grande (Constantine and the Cross—US 1962). **1962** Messalina. **1963** Long Night at 43 (aka It Happened In '43); The Devil's Choice. Other foreign films: Marie des Iles; Visa Pour Caracas; Ce Corps Tant Desire; I Magliari; Katja.

LEE, BESSIE

Born: 1904. Died: Nov. 1931, Hollywood, Calif. (cerebral hemorrhage). Screen actress.

LEE, BESSIE

Born: 1906. Died: June 28, 1972, Pittsburgh, Pa. Screen and stage actress.

Appeared in: **1928** The Night Bird. **1939** Mr. Wong in Chinatown.

LEE, BRUCE (Lee Yuen Kam aka LEE SIU LOONG)

Born: Nov. 27, 1940, San Francisco, Calif. Died: July 30, 1973, Hong Kong (acute cerebral edema). Screen and television actor and martial arts expert. Son of a Cantonese opera and vaudeville performer. Made 20 films as child actor in Hong Kong under the name, Lee Siu Loong (The Little Dragon).

Appeared in: **1969** Marlowe. **1973** Fists of Fury (aka The Chinese Connection—US and aka The Big Boss); Five Fingers of Death; Way of the Dragon (aka Return of the Dragon—US); Enter the Dragon.

LEE, CANADA

Born: 1907. Died: May 9, 1952, New York, N.Y. (heart attack). Screen, stage, radio, television actor and orchestra leader.

Appeared in: **1944** Lifeboat. **1947** Body and Soul; The Roosevelt Story (narr.). **1949** Lost Boundaries. **1952** Cry, the Beloved Country. **1955** Othello.

LEE, CHARLES T.

Born: 1882. Died: Mar. 14, 1927, Los Angeles,Calif. (heart trouble). Screen actor.

LEE, DIXIE (Wilma Wyatt)

Born: Nov. 4, 1911, Harriman, Tenn. Died: Nov. 1, 1952, Holmby Hills, Calif. (cancer). Stage and screen actress. Married to actor and singer Bing Crosby. Mother of actors Gary, Phillip, Dennis and Lindsay Crosby.

Appeared in: **1924** Not for Sale. **1929** Fox Movietone Follies of 1929; Knights Out (short); Why Leave Home? **1930** Happy Days; Cheer Up and Smile; The Big Party; Let's Go Places; Harmony at Home. **1931** No Limit; Night Life in Reno. **1934** Manhattan Love Song. **1935** Love in Bloom; Redheads on Parade.

LEE, DUKE R.

Born: 1881, Va. Died: Apr. 1, 1959, Los Angeles, Calif. Screen, stage and vaudeville actor. Entered films in 1918.

Appeared in: **1918** Lure of the Circus. **1921** Trailin'; "If Only" Jim. **1922** In the Days of Buffalo Bill (serial); Don't Shoot; Just Tony; Tracked to Earth. **1923** Mile-a-Minute Romeo; In the Days of Daniel Boone (serial). **1924** The Gaiety Girl; Fighting Fury; The Western Wallop. **1925** The Red Rider; Don Dare Devil; Flying Hoofs; The Call of Courage; The White Outlaw. **1926** Tony Runs Wild; The Canyon of Light; Sky High Corral; The Man in the Saddle; Man of the Forest; Rustlers' Ranch. **1927** Galloping Fury; The Terror of Bar X; The Circus Ace; Lands of the Lawless; Outlaws of Red River. **1928** Crashing Through; Clearing the Trail; Son of the Golden West; The Big Hop; The Heart of Broadway. **1929** .45 Calibre War. **1930** The Concentratin' Kid. **1948** Fort Apache.

LEE, EARL

Born: 1886. Died: June 2, 1955, Redwood City, Calif. Screen and stage actor.

Appeared in: **1951** Five. **1952** Assignment—Paris; The Story of Will Rogers; Tropical Heat Wave. **1954** Geraldine.

LEE, ETTA

Born: 1906. Died: Oct. 27, 1956, Eureka, Calif. Screen actress.

Appeared in: **1921** The Sheik; A Tale of Two Worlds. **1922** The Toll of the Sea. **1923** The Untameable; The Remittance Woman. **1924** The Thief of Bagdad. **1925** A Thief in Paradise; The Trouble with Wives; Recompense. **1927** Camille; The Chinese Parrot. **1928** Out with the Tide. **1933** International House.

LEE, FLORENCE

Born: 1888. Died: Sept. 1, 1962, Hollywood, Calif. Screen and stage actress. Married to actor Del Henderson (dec. 1956).

Appeared in: **1922** The Top O' the Morning; The Trouper. **1923** Blood Test; Mary of the Movies. **1924** Jack O' Clubs; Virtue's Revolt; Way of a Man (serial and feature). **1925** Luck and Sand; Across the Deadline; Speed Mad. **1926** The High Hand; Man Rustlin'. **1928** The Bronc Stomper; The Little Buckaroo. **1929** Illusion of Love. **1931** City Lights.

LEE, GWEN (Gwendolyn LePinski)

Born: Nov. 12, 1904, Hastings, Nebr. Died: Aug. 20, 1961. Stage and screen actress.

Appeared in: **1924** His Hour. **1925** His Secretary; Pretty Ladies. **1926** The Boy Friend; There You Are!; The Lone Wolf Returns; Upstage. **1927** Adam and Evil; After Midnight; Heaven on Earth; Her Wild Oats; Twelve Miles Out; Orchids and Ermine; Women Love Diamonds. **1928** The Actress; A Thief in the Dark; The Baby Cyclone; Diamond Handcuffs; A Lady of Chance; Laugh, Clown, Laugh; Sharp Shooters; Show Girl. **1929** Lucky Boy; Fast Company; The Hollywood Revue of 1929; Untamed; The Man and the Moment; The Duke Steps Out; The Road Show. **1930** Caught Short; Chasing Rainbows; Extravagance; Free and Easy; Lord Byron of Broadway; Paid; Our Blushing

Brides. **1931** Inspiration; The Lawless Woman; Pagan Lady; Traveling Husbands. **1932** Alias Mary Smith; Midnight Morals; West of Broadway; From Broadway to Cheyenne; Boy, Oh, Boy (short). **1933** The Intruder; Corruption. **1934** City Park; One in a Million. **1937** Candid Cameramaniacs (short); A Night at the Movies (short). **1938** Paroled from the Big House; Penny's Party (short).

LEE, GYPSY ROSE (Rose Louise Hovick)
Born: Jan. 9, 1914, Seattle, Wash. Died: Apr. 26, 1970, Los Angeles, Calif. (cancer). Screen, stage, burlesque, radio, vaudeville actress and author. Sister of actress June Havoc.

Appeared in: **1936** The Ziegfeld Follies of 1936. **1937** You Can't Have Everything; Ali Baba Goes to Town. **1938** Sally, Irene and Mary; The Battle of Broadway. **1939** My Lucky Star. **1943** Stage Door Canteen. **1944** Belle of the Yukon. **1945** Doll Face. **1952** Babes in Bagdad. **1958** Wind across the Everglades; The Screaming Mimi. **1963** The Stripper. **1966** The Trouble with Angels.

LEE, HARRY (William Henry Lee)
Born: June 1, 1872, Richmond, Va. Died: Dec. 8, 1932, Hollywood, Calif. (suicide—jump). Stage and screen actor.

Appeared in: **1921** Bucking the Tiger. **1922** Channing of the Northwest; Boomerang Bill; The Man She Brought Back. **1924** Monsieur Beaucaire. **1925** The Wrongdoers. **1926** Men of Steel. **1929** Gentlemen of the Press; Sunny Skies.

LEE, JANE
Born: 1912. Died: Mar. 17, 1957, New York, N.Y. Screen and vaudeville actress. Sister of actress Katherine Lee and actor Davey Lee. Was member of vaudeville team, "Katherine and Jane Lee."

Appeared in: **1914** Neptune's Daughter; Two Little Imps. **1915** Soul of Broadway; His Prior Claim. **1916** Daredevil Kate; Love and Hate; The Unwelcome Mother. **1917** Troublemakers. **1918** American Buds; We Should Marry?; Swat the Spy; Doing Their Bit. **1919** Smiles. **1927** Jane and Katherine Lee (short).

LEE, JENNIE
Born: 1850. Died: Aug. 4, 1925, Hollywood, Calif. Screen, stage and vaudeville actress.

Appeared in: **1913** His Mother's Son; Her Mother's Oath. **1915** Birth of a Nation. **1921** The Big Punch; One Man in a Million. **1923** North of Hudson Bay. **1924** Young Ideas; Hearts of Oak.

LEE, JOHNNY (John Dotson Lee, Jr.)
Born: July 4, 1898, Missouri. Died: Dec. 12, 1965, Los Angeles, Calif. (heart attack). Black screen, television and radio actor. Played "Calhoun" in both the radio and television "Amos n' Andy" shows. Do not confuse with British actor John Lee.

Appeared in: **1943** Stormy Weather. **1947** Mantan Runs for Mayor. **1956** The Bottom of the Bottle. **1957** The Cat Girl. **1958** Hot Spell.

LEE, LEONA
Died: Aug. 1975, Los Angeles, Calif. Screen actress.

LEE, LILA (Augusta Appel)
Born: July 25, 1902, Union Hill, N.J. Died: Nov. 13, 1973, Saranac Lake, N.Y. (stroke). Screen, stage and vaudeville actress. Divorced from actor Jack Kirkwood (dec. 1963), Jack R. Paine and John E. Murphy. Mother of playwright James Kirkwood. Entered films at age 13 with Jesse Lasky.

Appeared in: **1918** The Cruise of the Makebelieve; Such a Little Pirate. **1919** Puppy Love; Secret Garden; Rustling a Bride; Rose of the River; Heart of Youth; Male and Female; Hawthorne of the U.S.A.; Daughter of the Wolf; Lottery Man. **1920** Terror Island; The Prince Chap; The Soul of Youth; Midsummer Madness. **1921** After the Show; The Charm School; Crazy to Marry; The Dollar-a-Year Man; The Easy Road; Gasoline Gus; If Women Only Knew. **1922** Back Home and Broke; Blood and Sand; The Dictator; Ebb Tide; The Ghost Breaker; Is Matrimony a Failure?; One Glorious Day; Rent Free; The Road to Arcady. **1923** Hollywood; Homeward Bound; The Ne'er-Do-Well; Woman Proof. **1924** Another Man's Wife; Love's Whirlpool; Wandering Husbands. **1925** Coming Through; The Midnight Girl; Old Home Week; The Unholy Three. **1926** Broken Hearts; Fascinating Youth; The New Klondike. **1927** Million Dollar Mystery; One Increasing Purpose. **1928** The Adorable Cheat; A Bit of Heaven; Black Butterflies; The Black Pearl; Just Married; The Little Wild Girl; The Man in Hobbies; Thundergod; Top Sergeant Mulligan; United States Smith; You Can't Beat the Law. **1929** The Argyle Case; Dark Streets; Drag; Fight; Honky Tonk; Love, Live and Laugh; Queen of the Night Clubs; The Sacred Flame; The Show of Shows. **1930** Double Cross Roads; The Gorilla; Murder Will Out; Second Wife; Those Who Dance; The Unholy Three (and in 1925 version). **1931** Misbehaving Ladies; Woman Hungry. **1932** War Correspondent; Radio Patrol; Exposure; Unholy Love; Night of June 13; False Faces. **1933** Officer 13; Face in the Sky; Iron Master; The Intruder; Lone Cowboy. **1934** Whirlpool; In Love with Life; I Can't Escape. **1935** Champagne

for Breakfast; Marriage Bargain; People's Enemy. **1936** The Ex-Mrs. Bradford; Country Gentlemen. **1937** Two Wise Maids; Nation Aflame.

LEE, LILA DEAN
Born: 1890. Died: Nov. 3, 1959, West Covina, Calif. Screen actress. Do not confuse with actress Lila Lee (dec. 1973).

LEE, MARGO
Died: Oct. 8, 1951, Los Angeles, Calif. Screen, radio and television actress.

Appeared in: **1950** So Young, So Bad.

LEE, RAYMOND
Born: 1910. Died: June 26, 1974, Canoga Park, Calif. (cancer). Screen actor and author.

Appeared in: **1921** No Woman Knows. **1923** Long Live the King; The Pilgrim. **1924** Abraham Lincoln; Bread.

LEE, ROSE. *See* ROSE LEE McQUOID

LEE, ROWLAND
Born: 1891, Findlay, Ohio. Died: Dec. 21, 1975, Palm Desert, Calif. (heart attack). Screen actor, screenwriter and film director. Son of stage actress Marie (dec.) and stage actor C. W. Lee (dec.).

Appeared in: **1917** The Stainless Barrier; The Maternal Spark; Wild Winship's Widow. **1920** Woman in the Staircase; Water, Water, Everywhere; Her Husband's Friend. **1921** His Own Law.

LEE, RUTH (Ruth Rhodes)
Born: 1896. Died: Aug. 3, 1975, Woodland Hills, Calif. Screen actress. Married to actor Grandon Rhodes.

Appeared in: **1939** How to Eat (short). **1940** The Trouble with Husbands (short). **1941** Crime Control (short); The Forgotten Man (short). **1942** The Witness (short); The Man's Angle (short). **1943** Mexican Spitfire's Blessed Event; Silver Skates; The Adventures of a Rookie; My Tomato (short). **1944** Tucson Raiders; Sensations of 1945; Goin' to Town; The Town Went Wild; Important Business (short); Why, Daddy? (short). **1945** The Man Who Walked Alone; Honeymoon; Divorce; Mama Loves Papa; The Daltons Ride Again; The Naughty Nineties; Here Come the Co-eds. **1946** Partners in Time; Ding Dong Williams; The Dark Horse; The Magnificent Rogue. **1949** Cover Up; It Happens Every Spring; Henry, the Rainmaker; Whirlpool; Annie was a Wonder (short). **1950** Eye Witness. **1951** When I Grow Up; Insurance Investigator; As You Were. **1955** Hell's Outpost. **1961** Three on a Spree.

LEE, SAMMY
Born: 1890, New York City. Died: Mar. 20, 1968, Woodland Hills, Calif. Screen, stage actor and dance director.

Appeared in: **1933** I Loved You Wednesday. **1939** The Gracie Allen Murder Case.

LEE, WENDIE
Born: 1923. Died: Aug. 23, 1968, Los Angeles, Calif. Television model and screen actress.

Appeared in: **1950** Everybody's Dancing.

LEFAUR, ANDRE (Andre Lefaurichon)
Born: 1879, France. Died: Dec. 4, 1952, Paris, France. Screen and stage actor.

Appeared in: **1932** Le Bal. **1939** With a Smile. **1941** The King. **1942** Nine Bachelors. **1944** 32 Rue de Montmartre.

LE FEUVRE, PHILIP
Born: 1871. Died: Aug. 23, 1939, Arcadia, Calif. Screen and stage actor.

LeFEVRE, NED (Roy Ned LeFevre)
Born: Mar. 9, 1912, Indiana. Died: June 10, 1966, Sun Valley, Calif. (cancer). Radio announcer, screen and television actor.

Appeared in: **1954** Creature from the Black Lagoon. **1957** The Joker is Wild.

LEFTWICH, ALEXANDER
Born: 1884, Philadelphia, Pa. Died: Jan. 13, 1947, Los Angeles, Calif. (heart attack). Screen, radio actor, stage director–producer and television director–producer. Father of actress Patricia Ellis (dec. 1970).

Appeared in: **1937** Swing It Sailor. **1938** Prison Train. **1939** Juarez; Zaza. **1941** Melody for Three.

LEGAL, ERNEST
Born: 1881, Germany. Died: June 29, 1955, Berlin, Germany. Screen, stage actor, playwright and stage director.

Appeared in: **1938** Kater Lampe. **1939** Das Unsterbliche Herz (The Immortal Heart). **1950** Marriage of Figaro. Other German film: Heaven is Never Brought Out.

LEGNEUR, CHARLES
Born: 1892. Died: Feb. 14, 1956, Hollywood, Calif. (heart attack). Screen actor.

LeGUERE, GEORGE
Born: 1871. Died: Nov. 21, 1947, New York, N.Y. Screen and stage actor.

Appeared in: **1918** Cecilia of the Pink Roses. **1919** The Way of a Woman; The Hand Invisible. **1921** Mama's Affair. **1922** Missing Millions. **1930** Men without Women. **1933** Three-Cornered Moon.

LEHR, LEW
Born: May 14, 1895, Philadelphia, Pa. Died: Mar. 6, 1950, Brookline, Mass. Screen, stage, vaudeville, radio actor, screenwriter and film producer. Married to actress Anna Leonhardt, professionally known as Nancy Belle, with whom he toured in vaudeville. Well known for his comedy newsreel commentary, "Monkeys is the Angriest People."

Appeared in prior to 1936: Looking Back (voice); Tintypes (comm.); Adventures of a Newsreel Cameraman (comm.); Magic Carpet; Newsettes; Lew Lehr's Unnatural History. **1937** Borneo (narr.).

LEHRER, GEORGE J.
Born: 1889. Died: Aug. 25, 1966, Cleveland, Ohio. Screen, stage actor and stage director. Known for his Abraham Lincoln impersonations.

LEHRMAN, HENRY
Born: Mar. 30, 1886, Vienna, Austria. Died: Nov. 7, 1946, Hollywood, Calif. (heart attack). Screen actor, film producer, film director and screenwriter. Entered films with Griffith in 1910. Founded L-KO productions ("Lehrman-Knockout" comedies) in 1914.

Appeared in: **1910** As the Bells Rang Out; The Iconoclast; Her Sacrifice. **1912** A Beast at Bay. **1914** Making a Living (later reissued as A Bustled Johnny); Kid Auto Races at Venice.

LEIBER, FRITZ
Born: Jan. 31, 1882, Chicago, Ill. Died: Oct. 14, 1949, Pacific Palisades, Calif. (heart attack). Stage and screen actor.

Appeared in: **1917** Cleopatra. **1920** If I Were King. **1921** Queen of Sheba. **1935** A Tale of Two Cities. **1936** Sins of Man; Under Two Flags; Down to the Sea; Camille; The Story of Louis Pasteur; Anthony Adverse; Hearts in Bondage. **1937** Champagne Waltz; The Prince and the Pauper; The Great Garrick. **1938** The Jury's Secret; Flight into Nowhere; Gateway; If I Were King (and 1920 version). **1939** Nurse Edith Cavell; They Made Her a Spy; Pack up Your Troubles; The Hunchback of Notre Dame. **1940** Lady with Red Hair; The Way of All Flesh; All This and Heaven Too; The Sea Hawk. **1941** Aloma of the South Seas. **1942** Crossroads. **1943** The Desert Song; First Comes Courage; Phantom of the Opera. **1944** The Imposter; Cry of the Werewolf; Bride of the Vampire. **1945** The Cisco Kid Returns; This Love of Ours; The Spanish Main; Son of Lassie. **1946** A Scandal in Paris; Strange Journey; Humoresque; Angel on my Shoulder. **1947** High Conquest; Bells of San Angelo; The Web; Monsieur Verdoux; Dangerous Venture. **1948** Adventures of Casanova; To the Ends of the Earth; Inner Sanctum; Another Part of the Forest. **1949** Bagdad; Bride of Vengeance; Samson and Delilah; Song of India; Devil's Doorway.

LEICESTER, WILLIAM (William Francis Leichester)
Born: 1915. Died: Jan. 9, 1969, Van Nuys, Calif. Screen actor and television writer.

Appeared in: **1948** Strange Gamble. **1952** Operation Secret. **1955** Finger Man. **1956** Beyond a Reasonable Doubt.

LEIGH, FRANK
Born: London, England. Died: May 9, 1948, Hollywood, Calif. Stage and screen actor. Entered films in England in 1912.

Appeared in: **1918** Fedora. **1919** Lord and Lady Algy. **1920** Nurse Marjorie; Cup of Fury; Dangerous Days; One Hour Before Dawn. **1921** Bob Hampton of Placer; The Light in the Clearing; Pilgrims of the Night. **1922** Golden Dreams; Domestic Relations; Out of the Silent North. **1923** Ashes of Vengeance; Truxton King; The Gentleman from America; North of Hudson Bay; Rosita; The Lonely Road. **1924** The Hill Billy; The Breath of Scandal; The Reckless Age; Flames of Desire; Hutch of the U.S.A.; Honor among Men. **1925** Contraband; The Winding Stair; His Majesty Bunker Bean; American Pluck; As Man Desires. **1926** The Adorable Deceiver; Flame of the Argentine; The Flaming Forest; The Lady of the Harem; The Imposter; Secret Orders. **1927** Soft Cushions; The Tigress; Somewhere in Sonora. **1928** A Night of Mystery; King Cowboy; Prowlers of the Sea. **1929** Below the Deadline; Love in the Desert; Montmartre Rose; Thirteenth Chair; Captain's Wife. **1930** The Lotus Lady. **1931** The Woman from Monte Carlo; Ten Nights in a Barroom.

LEIGH, VIVIEN (Vivian Mary Hartley)
Born: Nov. 5, 1913, Darjeeling, India. Died: July 8, 1967, London, England (natural causes). Stage and screen actress. Divorced from actor Sir Laurence Olivier and from Herbert Leigh Holman. Won 1939 Academy Award for Best Actress in Gone with the Wind and in 1951 for A Streetcar Named Desire.

Appeared in: **1934** Things Are Looking Up (film debut). **1935** Village Squire; Gentleman's Agreement; Look up and Laugh. **1937** Fire over England; Dark Journey; Storm in a Teacup; 21 Days (aka 21 Days Together—US 1940 and aka The First and the Last). **1938** St. Martin's Lane (aka Sidewalks of London—US 1940); A Yank at Oxford. **1939** Gone with the Wind. **1940** Waterloo Bridge. **1941** That Hamilton Woman. **1946** Caesar and Cleopatra. **1948** Anna Karenina. **1951** A Streetcar Named Desire. **1955** The Deep Blue Sea. **1961** The Roman Spring of Mrs. Stone. **1965** Ship of Fools. **1974** That's Entertainment (film clips).

LEIGHTON, DANIEL
Born: 1880. Died: June 20, 1917, Los Angeles, Calif. Screen actor.

Appeared in: **1915** A Question of Right or Wrong; The Patent Food Conveyor. **1916** The Crown Prince's Double; The Supreme Temptation; Oh! Oh! Oh! Henry!; A Man's Sin; When She Played Broadway; The Answer. **1917** The Girl Who Lost; The Startling Climax; Chubby Takes a Hand; The Phantom's Secret; The Thief Maker; A Blissful Calamity.

LEIGHTON, LILLIAN (aka LYLLIAN BROWN LEIGHTON)
Born: 1874, Auroville, Wis. Died: Mar. 19, 1956, Woodland Hills, Calif. Screen, stage and vaudeville actress.

Appeared in: **1911** The Two Orphans; Cinderella. **1912** Katzenjammer Kids; My Wife's Bonnet; The Three Valises; Bread Upon the Waters; The Other Woman. **1913** Sweeney and the Million; Turn Him Out; The Fugitive; Sweeney and the Fairy; Sweeney's Dream; Two Artists and One Suit of Clothes; Henrietta's Hair; The College Chaperone; The Clue. **1914** King Baby's Birthday; Castles in the Air. **1915** Shoo-Fly; Apple Butter; The Tides of Barnegat. **1916** Small Town Stuff; The Plowgirl. **1917** Bill and the Bearded Lady; Everybody was Satisfied; Betty to the Rescue; Castles for Two; Romance and Roses; Freckles; The Ghost House. **1918** Old Wives for New. **1919** Men, Women and Money. **1920** All-of-a-Sudden Peggy; A Girl Named Mary. **1921** Crazy to Marry; The Lost Romance; Peck's Bad Boy; Love Never Dies; The Barbarian; The Girl from God's Country; Under the Lash. **1922** Is Matrimony a Failure?; The Lane That Had No Turning; Rent Free; Red Hot Romance; Saturday Night; Tillie. **1923** The Call of the Canyon; Hollywood; Only 38; Crinoline and Romance; Ruggles of Red Gap; Wasted Lives; The Eternal Three. **1924** The Bedroom Window; $50,000 Reward; Code of the Sea; Phantom Justice. **1925** Code of the West; Go Straight; In the Name of Love; Parisian Love; Tumbleweeds; The Thundering Herd; Contraband. **1926** The False Alarm; Sandy; The Torrent. **1927** California; The Fair Co-Ed; The Frontiersman; By Whose Hand?; The Golden Yukon; Lovers? **1930** Feet First; The Grand Parade; The Last Dance. **1931** Subway Express; Sweepstakes. **1933** The Sphinx. **1935** Whipsaw.

LEISEN, J. MITCHELL
Born: Oct. 1898, Menomie, Mich. Died: Oct. 27, 1972, Woodland Hills, Calif. (coronary complications). Film producer, director and screen actor. Divorced from actress and singer Sandra Gahle.

Appeared in: **1941** Hold Back the Dawn. **1947** Variety Girl. **1948** Miss Tatlock's Millions.

LE MAIRE, GEORGE
Born: 1884, Fort Worth, Tex. Died: Jan. 20, 1930, New York, N.Y. (heart attack). Screen, stage, vaudeville actor and film producer. Appeared in vaudeville with his brother William and later as partner in "Conroy and Le Maire" vaudeville team. Brother of screen actor William Le Maire (dec. 1933).

Appeared in: **1928** The Circus Kid. **1929** seventeen "George Le Maire" shorts.

LE MAIRE, WILLIAM
Born: Dec. 21, 1892, Fort Worth, Tex. Died: Nov. 11, 1933, Los Angeles, Calif. (heart ailment). Screen, vaudeville and radio actor. Brother of actor George Le Maire (dec. 1930). Appeared in vaudeville with his brother George and later with Ed Gallagher. Entered films in 1928.

Appeared in: **1928** The Circus Kid. **1930** The Light of Western Stars; Only the Brave; Whoopee; Common Clay. **1931** The Painted Desert. **1932** Cabin in the Cotton; I Am a Fugitive from a Chain Gang. **1933** 20,000 Years in Sing Sing; Captured.

LE MANS, MARCEL
Born: 1897, Antwerp, Belgium. Died: Jan. 9, 1946, Lyons, N.J. Stage and screen actor. Flying ace of Lafayette Escadrille in W.W. I. Entered films with Pathe in 1924.

LE MOYNE, CHARLES (Charles J. Lemon)
Born: 1880. Died: Sept. 13, 1956, Hollywood, Calif. Screen and stage actor.

Appeared in: **1921** Colorado; The Fox; The Freeze Out; The Wallop. **1922** Headin' West; The Kick Back; Rough Shod; Good Men and True; Man to Man. **1923** Canyon of the Fools; Desert Driven; Brass Commandments; Crashin' Thru. **1925** Riders of the Purple Sage.

LEMUELS, WILLIAM E.
Born: 1891. Died: Feb. 21, 1953, Los Angeles, Calif. Screen, stage and vaudeville actor. Appeared in vaudeville with James Barton and they made several short subjects.

Appeared in: **1935** His Family Tree.

LENGLEN, SUZANNE
Born: 1899, France. Died: July 4, 1938, Paris, France (pernicious anemia). Screen actress and tennis champion. Appeared in film shorts.

LENI, PAUL
Born: July 8, 1885, Stuttgart, Germany. Died: 1929, Hollywood, Calif. Screen, stage actor and film director.

LENIHAN, WINIFRED
Born: 1899, Brooklyn, N.Y. Died: July 27, 1964, Sea Cliff, N.Y. Screen, stage, radio actress and radio director.

Appeared in: **1949** Jigsaw.

LENOIR, PASS
Born: 1874. Died: June 12, 1946, Hollywood, Calif. (heart attack). Screen, stage actor, circus and minstrel gymnast.

Appeared in: **1936** Mixed Magic (short).

LENROW, BERNARD "BERNIE"
Born: 1903. Died: Oct. 9, 1963, Englewood, N.J. Screen, stage, television and radio actor.

Appeared in: **1957** The Violators.

LEON, CONNIE
Born: 1880. Died: May 10, 1955, Hollywood, Calif. Screen actress.

Appeared in: **1935** Clive of India. **1939** The Little Princess. **1941** Singapore Woman. **1942** Bombs over Burma; Mrs. Miniver; This Above All; Thunder Birds. **1944** And Now Tomorrow. **1945** Love Letters; Hangover Square. **1946** Anna and the King of Siam; That Brennan Girl; Of Human Bondage; Three Strangers.

LEON, VALERIANO
Born: 1892, Spain. Died: Dec. 1955 or Jan. 1956 in Madrid, Spain. Stage and screen actor.

LEONARD, ARCHIE
Born: 1917. Died: Feb. 7, 1959, Des Moines, Iowa (heart attack). Screen, stage, radio actor, television director and writer.

Appeared in: **1949** Mrs. Mike.

LEONARD, DAVID A.
Born: 1892. Died: Apr. 2, 1967, Encino, Calif. Screen, stage, radio, television actor and screenwriter.

Appeared in: **1933** Victims of Persecution. **1948** Song of My Heart; Sword of the Avenger. **1949** The Daring Caballero; Adventures of Don Juan. **1950** Captain Carey, U.S.A. **1953** Fighter Attack; The Robe. **1954** Desiree; Forever Female. **1955** The Prodigal. **1956** Lust for Life. **1959** Say One for Me.

LEONARD, EDDIE
Born: 1870, Richmond, Va. Died: July 29, 1941, New York, N.Y. Minstrel and screen actor.

Appeared in: **1929** Melody Lane. **1940** If I Had My Way.

LEONARD, GUS (Gustav Lerond)
Born: 1856, Marseilles, France. Died: Mar. 27, 1939, Los Angeles, Calif. Screen, stage and vaudeville actor. Entered films in 1915.

Appeared in: **1917** The Lonesome Luke. **1921** Two Minutes to Go. **1922** The Deuce of Spades; The Barnstormer; Watch Your Step. **1923** The Girl I Loved; Second Hand Love; Her Reputation; Times Have Changed. **1928** Coney Island. **1932** Babes in Toyland; When a Feller Needs a Friend. **1933** Mush and Milk (short). **1934** The Mighty Barnum. **1935** Teacher's Beau (short). **1936** The Lucky Corner (short); Life Hesitates at 40 (short). **1937** Maytime. **1950** Revenge is Sweet (reissue of 1932 version of Babes in Toyland).

LEONARD, JACK E. (Leonard Lebitsky)
Born: Apr. 24, 1911, Chicago, Ill. Died: May 9, 1973, New York, N.Y. (diabetic complications). Screen, vaudeville, television actor and night club performer.

Appeared in: **1964** The Disorderly Orderly. **1965** The World of Abbott and Costello. **1966** The Fat Spy.

LEONARD, JAMES
Born: 1868. Died: July 4, 1930, Glendale, Calif. Screen, vaudeville and burlesque actor. Was partner in vaudeville team of "Jim and Sadie Leonard."

Appeared in: **1927** All Aboard. **1928** The Cheer Leader.

LEONARD, MARION
Born: 1880. Died: Jan 9, 1956, Woodland Hills, Calif. Screen actress.

Appeared in: **1908** At the Crossroads of Life; The Test of Friendship; An Awful Moment; Father Gets in the Game; The Fatal Hour; The Christmas Burglars; A Calamitous Elopement; A Wreath in Time; The Welcome Burglar; The Criminal Hypnotist. **1909** Comato the Sioux; The Gibson Goddess; The Welcome Burglar; The Maniac Cook; A Burglar's Mistake; The Hindu Dagger; Pranks; The Cord of Life; Shadows of Doubt; Two Memories; The Roue's Heart; The Lovely Villa; At the Altar; Fools of Fate; The Convert; The Voice of the Violin; A Rude Hostess; The Eavesdropper; The Jilt; With her Card; The Mills of the Gods; His Lost Love; Nursing a Viper; The Sealed Room; The Expiation; The Restoration; Through the Breakers; In Little Italy; A Trap for Santa Claus; Pippa Passes. **1910** On the Reef; Gold is Not All; Love Among the Roses; In Old California; The Two Brothers; Over Silent Paths; The Day After; His Wife's Sweethearts; A Salutary Lesson; The Sorrows of the Unfaithful; The Two Paths. **1912** The Defender of the Name; So Speaks the Heart; Taming Mrs. Shrew; Under Her Wing; The End of the Circle; The Final Pardon; Through Flaming Gates; Songs of Childhood Days; Eyes That See Not; In Payment Full; What Avails the Crown; The Tears O'Peggy; Through Memory Blank; Thus Many Souls; The Leader of the Band; In Honor Bound; Lost—A Husband; What's in an Aim? **1913** Carmen; As In a Looking Glass; The Dead Secret; A Leaf in the Storm; In the Watches of the Night. **1914** A Sight Unseen. **1915** Dragon's Claw.

LEONARD, MURRAY
Born: 1898. Died: Nov. 6, 1970, Sherman Oaks, Calif. (heart attack). Screen, stage, burlesque and vaudeville actor.

Appeared in: **1944** Lost in a Harem; In Society. **1945** Thousand and One Nights. **1955** Bring Your Smile Along.

LEONARD, ROBERT Z.
Born: Oct. 7, 1889, Chicago, Ill. Died: Aug. 27, 1968, Beverly Hills, Calif. (aneurysm). Screen, stage actor, opera performer, film producer, film director and screenwriter. Married to actress Gertrude Olmstead (dec. 1975). Divorced from actress Mae Murray (dec. 1965). Entered films as an actor with Selig in 1907.

Appeared in: **1910** The Courtship of Miles Standish; The Roman. **1913** Robinson Crusoe; His Old-Fashioned Dad; Shon the Piper; The Turn of the Tide; The Stolen Idol; The Power of Heredity; Sally Scraggs, Housemaid; Like Darby and Joan; The Boob's Dream Girl; The Wayward Sister; The Shadow; The Diamond Makers; By Fate's Decree. **1914** The Primeval Test; The Master Key (serial); The Mistress of Deadwood Basin; The Senator's Bill; The Boob Incognito; The House Discordant; The Fox; The Boob Detective; The Boob's Legacy; For the Secret Service; Little Sister; Olaf Erickson, Boss; At the Foot of the Stairs; Aurora of the North; The Boob's Nemesis; The Little Blond Lady; Out of the Darkness; An Awkward Cinderella. **1945** Abbott and Costello in Hollywood.

LEONARDO, HARRY (H. L. Gottsacker)
Born: 1903. Died: Nov. 23, 1964, New York, N.Y. (heart ailment). Screen and vaudeville actor. Was partner in vaudeville team of "Ward Hall and Leonardo."

LEONE, HENRY
Born: Mar. 30, 1958, Vienna, Austria. Died: June 9, 1922, Mount Vernon, N.Y. (apoplexy). Screen, stage actor, film director and screenwriter. Entered films in 1909.

Appeared in: **1918** My Cousin. **1921** His Greatest Sacrifice; Such a Little Queen. **1922** Fair Lady.

LE PAUL, PAUL (Paul Braden)
Born: 1901. Died: June 8, 1958, St. Louis, Mo. Screen, stage actor, magician and author.

Appeared in: **1939** Eternally Yours.

LePEARL, HARRY
Born: 1885, Danville, Ill. Died: Jan. 13, 1946, Hollywood, Calif. Circus clown and screen actor.

Appeared in: **1915** Still Waters; Once is Enough; Bunks Bunked; Where's Oliver?; The Trouble Maker.

LE SAINT, EDWARD J.
Born: 1871. Died: Sept. 10, 1940, Hollywood, Calif. Screen, stage actor, film director and screenwriter. Entered films in 1912.

Appeared in: **1923** Mary of the Movies. **1929** The Talk of Hollywood. **1930** The Dawn Trail; For the Defense. **1931** The Last Parade. **1932** The Night of June

13th; The Last Man; Central Park; The Cohens and the Kellys in Trouble; Tomorrow at Seven; The Wrecker; Horse Feathers; Boy, Oh, Boy (short). **1933** No More Orchids; Thrill Hunter; Torch Singer; Broken Dreams; Feeling Rosy (short). **1934** George White's Scandals; The Lemon Drop Kid; The Frontier Marshal; Once to Every Woman; The Old Fashioned Way; Half-Baked Relations (short). **1935** In Spite of Danger; Fighting Shadows; Public Opinion; Thunder Mountain; Ruggles of Red Gap. **1936** The Trail of the Lonesome Pine; The Witness Chair; We Who Are about to Die; The Case against Mrs. Ames; The Cowboy Star; The Gallant Defender; The Legion of Terror; End of the Trail; Bulldog Edition; College Holiday; Disorder in the Court (short); Too Many Parents. **1937** Counterfeit Lady; The Gold Racket; A Day at the Races. **1938** College Swing; My Lucky Star. **1939** Jesse James; Arizona Legion; The Stranger from Texas.

LE SAINT, STELLA R.
Born: 1881. Died: Sept. 21, 1948, Malibu, Calif. Screen actress.

Appeared in: **1926** The Three Bad Men. **1936** Ants in the Pantry (short).

LESLEY, CAROLE (Maureen Rippingale)
Born: 1935, Chelmsford, England. Died: Feb. 28, 1974, New Barnet, England. Screen, television actress and dancer.

Appeared in: **1957** Good Companions (US 1958); Those Dangerous Years (aka Dangerous Youth—US 1958); Woman in a Dressing Gown. **1959** No Trees in the Street (US 1964); Operation Bullshine (US 1962). **1960** Doctor in Love (US 1962). **1961** What A Whooper (US 1962); Three on a Spree. **1962** The Pot Carriers.

LESLIE, ARTHUR
Born: 1902, England. Died: June 30, 1970, England. Screen and stage actor.

LESLIE, EDITH
Died: Apr. 9, 1973. Screen, stage and television actress.

Appeared in: **1947** Green Dolphin Street. **1948** Jiggs and Maggie in Society. **1949** Red Hot and Blue. **1953** Private Eye. **1954** Casanova's Big Night. **1957** Just for You; Will Success Spoil Rock Hunter? **1965** The Greatest Story Ever Told. **1969** Hello Dolly.

LESLIE, FRED
Born: 1884. Died: Aug. 1, 1945. Screen actor.

LESLIE, GENE (Leslie Eugene Halverson)
Born: 1904. Died: Feb. 20, 1953, Los Angeles, Calif. Screen actor, dancer and ice skater.

Appeared in: **1945** The Bells of St. Mary's; The Spanish Main; Ten Cents a Dance; Twice Blessed. **1946** The Gay Senorita; Holiday in Mexico; People Are Funny. **1948** Duel in the Sun.

LESLIE, NOEL
Born: 1889, England. Died: Mar. 10, 1974, New York, N.Y. Screen, stage and television actor.

Appeared in: **1956** The Search for Bridey Murphy.

L'ESTELLE, ELEANOR SCOTT
Born: 1880. Died: Apr. 25, 1962, Los Angeles, Calif. Screen actress.

LESNEVITCH, GUS
Born: 1915. Died: Feb. 28, 1964, Cliffside Park, N.J. (heart attack). Professional boxer and screen actor.

Appeared in: **1962** Requiem for a Heavyweight.

LESSEY, GEORGE A.
Born: Amherst, Mass. Died: Aug. 17, 1947. Screen, stage actor and film director.

Appeared in: **1911** Romeo and Juliet. **1912** A Romance of the Rails; The Governor; The Corsican Brothers; Mother and Daughter; A Fresh Air Romance; The Little Artist from the Market; The Dam Builder; The Harbinger of Peace; The Boss of Lumber Camp No. 4; Rowdy and His New Pal; Their Hero; The Man Who Made Good. **1913** The Governess; The Ambassador's Daughter; Sally's Romance; Leonie. **1914** The Witness to the Will. **1915** The Parson's Horse Race. **1918** To Him that Hath. **1919** Twilight. **1920** The $1,000,000 Reward. **1921** A Divorce of Convenience; Handcuffs or Kisses; Is Life Worth Living?; Rainbow; School Days; Why Girls Leave Home. **1922** The Snitching Hour. **1923** The Silent Command. **1924** It is the Law. **1925** Durand of the Bad Lands; The Fool; Scar Hanan; White Thunder. **1940** Edison the Man; Sporting Blood; Boom Town; Strike Up the Band; The Golden Fleecing; Sky Murder; Gallant Sons; Go West; Dr. Kildare's Strangest Case; Andy Hardy Meets Debutante; Good Bad Guys (short); Soak the Old (short). **1941** Blonde Inspiration; The Big Boss; Moon Over Miami; Blossoms in the Dust; Sweetheart of the Campus; We Go Fast; Men of Boys Town. **1942** Rings on Her Fingers; The Gay Sisters; The Pride of the Yankees; Girl Trouble. **1943** Dixie Dugan; Old Acquaintance; Pistol Packin' Mama. **1944** None Shall Escape; Buffalo Bill; Charlie Chan in the Secret Service; The Adventures of Mark Twain; Roger Touhy—Gangster; Sweet and Lowdown.

LESTER, KATE
Born: Thorpe, England. Died: Oct. 12, 1924 (burns suffered in fire). Stage and screen actress.

Appeared in: **1916** A Coney Island Princess. **1918** Little Women; The Unbeliever. **1919** A Man and His Money; Bonds of Love. **1920** The Paliser Case; Cup of Fury; Scratch My Back; Earthbound; Simple Souls. **1921** The Beautiful Liar; Dangerous Curve Ahead; The Hole in the Wall; Don't Neglect your Wife; Made in Heaven. **1922** The Eternal Flame; The Fourteenth Lover; The Glorious Fool; One Week of Love; Rose O' the Sea; Remembrance; Quincy Adams Sawyer; A Tailor Made Man. **1923** Can a Woman Love Twice?; Gimmie; The Fourth Musketeer; Her Accidental Husband; The Love Trap; The Hunchback of Notre Dame; The Marriage Market; The Rendezvous; Modern Matrimony; The Satin Girl; The Wild Party. **1924** The Goldfish; Beau Brummell; the Beautiful Sinner; Black Oxen; Leave it to Gerry; Wife of the Centaur. **1925** The Meddler; Raffles—the Amateur Cracksman; The Price of Pleasure.

LESTER, LOUISE
Born: 1867. Died: Nov. 18, 1952, Hollywood, Calif. Screen and stage actress. Married to actor and director Frank Beal (dec. 1934) and mother of actress Dolly and actor Scott Beal (dec. 1973). Entered films in 1910 with the Flying A Co. in Santa Barbara.

Appeared in: "Calamity Ann" series beginning in 1912. **1923** Her Reputation. **1924** The Desert Hawk. **1925** Galloping On.

L'ESTRANGE, DICK (Gunther von Strensch)
Born: Dec. 27, 1889, Asheville, N.C. Died: Nov. 19, 1963, Burbank, Calif. Screen, vaudeville actor, opera performer and film director. Appeared in early Sennett films and was one of the original Keystone Kops.

Appeared in: **1913** The Squaw Man. **1927** Blazing Days; The Border Cavalier; The Silent Rider; Desert Dust; One Glorious Scrap. **1928** Arizona Cyclone; Made-to-Order Hero; Thunder Riders; Quick Triggers.

L'ESTRANGE, JULIAN
Born: 1880, England. Died: Oct. 22, 1918, New York, N.Y. (Spanish influenza). Stage and screen actor. Married to actress Constance Collier (dec. 1955).

Appeared in: **1915** Bella Donna; Zaza. **1916** The Girl with the Green Eyes; The Quest of Life. **1918** Daybreak.

LE SUEUR, HAL
Born: 1904. Died: May 3, 1963, Los Angeles, Calif. (ruptured appendix). Screen actor. Brother of actress Joan Crawford (dec. 1977).

LETONDAL, HENRI
Born: 1902, France. Died: Feb. 14, 1955, Burbank, Calif. (heart attack). Screen actor.

Appeared in: **1946** The Razor's Edge. **1947** Crime Doctor's Gamble. **1948** Apartment for Peggy. **1949** Come to the Stable; Madame Bovary; Mother Is a Freshman. **1950** Please Believe Me. **1951** Across the Wide Missouri; Kind Lady; On the Riviera; Royal Wedding; Ten Tall Men. **1952** The Big Sky; Monkey Business; What Price Glory? **1953** Dangerous When Wet; Desert Legion; South Sea Woman; Gentlemen Prefer Blondes; Little Boy Lost. **1954** The Gambler from Natchez. **1955** A Bullet for Joey.

LETTIERI, ALFREDO "AL"
Born: Feb. 24, 1928, New York, N.Y. Died: Oct. 18, 1975, New York, N.Y. Screen, stage actor and screenwriter.

Appeared in: **1967** The Bobo. **1969** The Night of the Following Day. **1972** The Godfather; The Getaway. **1973** The Don is Dead; Deadly Trackers. **1974** Mr. Majestyk; McQ.

LEVANCE, CAL (Charles Waite)
Died: Sept. 6, 1951, Toronto, Canada. Screen, stage and vaudeville actor.

LEVANT, OSCAR
Born: Dec. 27, 1906, Pittsburgh, Pa. Died: Aug. 14, 1972, Beverly Hills, Calif. (heart attack). Screen, radio, television actor, composer, author, pianist and screenwriter. Divorced from dancer Barbara Smith. Married to actress June Gale.

Appeared in: **1929** The Dance of Life. **1940** Rhythm on the River. **1941** Kiss the Boys Good-bye. **1945** Rhapsody in Blue. **1946** Humoresque. **1948** Romance on the High Seas; You Were Meant for Me. **1949** The Barkleys of Broadway. **1951** An American in Paris. **1952** O Henry's Full House. **1953** The Band Wagon; The I Don't Care Girl. **1955** The Cobweb.

LEVELLE, ESTELLE
Born: 1896. Died: Jan. 6, 1960, Chicago, Ill. Screen, stage actress, dancer and singer.

LEVIN, LUCY

Born: 1907, Russia. Died: Sept. 4, 1939, New York, N.Y. Screen and stage actor. Appeared in Yiddish films.

LE VINESS, CARL

Born: 1885. Died: Oct. 15, 1964, Hollywood, Calif. (pneumonia). Screen actor and film director.

Appeared in: **1915** A Bag of Diamonds; Terror. **1929** Twin Beds. **1935** Slightly Static (short). **1946** The Kid from Brooklyn. **1956** Around the World in 80 Days. **1958** In Love and War.

LEVY, SYLVAN

Born: 1906. Died: Oct. 30, 1962, New York. Screen, stage and vaudeville actor.

Appeared in: **1929** The Cocoanuts.

LEWIS, CATHY

Born: 1918. Died: Nov. 20, 1968, Hollywood Hills, Calif. (cancer). Screen, stage, television, radio actress and singer.

Appeared in: **1941** Double Trouble. **1942** The Kid Glove Killer. **1949** My Friend Irma; The Story of Molly X. **1950** My Friend Irma Goes West. **1958** Party Crashers. **1961** The Devil at 4 O'Clock.

LEWIS, DOROTHY W.

Born: 1871. Died: June 16, 1952, Hollywood, Calif. Screen actress.

LEWIS, ED "STRANGLER" (Robert H. Friedrich)

Born: 1890. Died: Aug. 7, 1966, Muskogee, Okla. Professional wrestler and screen actor.

Appeared in: **1943** The Nazty Nuisance. **1950** Bodyhold.

LEWIS, EDGAR

Born: June 22, 1872, Holden, Missouri. Died: May 21, 1938, Los Angeles, Calif. Screen, stage actor, film producer, director and screenwriter.

Appeared in: **1911** The Violin Maker of Nuremberg. **1912** Magnon. **1915** The Plunderer. **1921** The Sage Hen. **1932** Human Targets; Texas Gunfighter.

LEWIS, ELLIOTT. *See* FRANK REMLEY

LEWIS, FREDERICK G.

Born: 1874, Oswego, N.Y. Died: Mar. 19, 1947, Amityville, N.Y. Stage and screen actor.

Appeared in: **1924** The Moral Sinner.

LEWIS, GORDON

Died: Mar. 17, 1933, Tucson, Ariz. (suicide—gun). Screen actor.

LEWIS, HARRY

Born: 1886. Died: Nov. 18, 1950, Hollywood, Calif. Screen and stage actor.

Appeared in: **1926** God Save Me Twenty Cents. **1942** Always in My Heart; Busses Roar. **1944** The Last Ride; Winged Victory. **1946** Her Kind of Man. **1947** The Unsuspected. **1948** Key Largo. **1949** Bomba on Panther Island; Deadly is the Female; Joe Palooka in the Counterpunch. **1950** Gun Crazy. **1951** The Fat Man.

LEWIS, IDA

Born: 1871, New York. Died: Apr. 21, 1935, Hollywood, Calif. Screen, stage and vaudeville actress. Entered films with Horsley Co.

Appeared in: **1918** The Bells. **1923** A Man's Man. **1925** Some Pun'kins. **1926** Sweet Adeline. **1928** Law of Fear. **1932** Sinners in the Sun.

LEWIS, JAMES H. "DADDY"

Died: Nov. 3, 1928, Pawtucket, R.I. Stage and screen actor.

Appeared in: **1923** The Broken Violin.

LEWIS, JOE

Born: 1898. Died: Oct. 9, 1938, Corning, Calif. Screen actor and stunt flyer. Do not confuse with world champion prize-fighter Joe Lewis.

LEWIS, JOE E.

Born: 1902, New York, N.Y. Died: June 4, 1971, New York, N.Y. (liver and kidney ailments). Screen actor, burlesque and vaudeville comedian. Divorced from singer Martha Stewart.

Appeared in: **1931** Too Many Husbands. **1942** Private Buckaroo. **1969** Lady in Cement.

LEWIS, MARTIN

Born: Sept. 8, 1888, Blackheath, England. Died: Apr. 1970, Farnborough, Kent, England. Screen, stage and radio actor.

Appeared in: **1916** The Vicar of Wakefield.

LEWIS, MARY (Mary Kidd)

Born: 1900, Hot Springs, Ark. Died: Dec. 31, 1941, New York. Screen, stage actress and opera performer. Entered films in 1920 and appeared in early Christie comedies.

Appeared in: **1927** Way Down South (short).

LEWIS, MEADE LUX

Born: 1906. Died: June 6, 1964, Minneapolis, Minn. (auto accident). Screen actor and jazz pianist.

Appeared in: **1947** New Orleans.

LEWIS, MICHAEL

Born: 1931. Died: Mar. 6, 1975, Summit, N.J. Stage and screen actor. Son of author Sinclair Lewis and journalist Dorothy Thompson (dec.)

Appeared in: **1961** The Curse of the Werewolf. **1969** Baby Love.

LEWIS, MITCHELL J.

Born: June 26, 1880, Syracuse, New York. Died: Aug. 24, 1956, Woodland Hills, Calif. Stage and screen actor. Entered films in 1914 with Thanhauser.

Appeared in: **1914** The Million Dollar Mystery (serial). **1917** The Barrier; The Bar Sinister. **1918** The Sign Invisible; Safe for Democracy. **1921** At the End of the World. **1922** The Siren Call; Salome; The Marriage Chance; On the High Seas; The Woman Conquers. **1923** The Destroying Angel; The Little Girl Next Door; The Miracle Makers; The Spoilers; Gold Madness; Her Accidental Husband; A Prince of a King; Rupert of Hentzau. **1924** The Mine with the Iron Door; Half-a-Dollar Bill; The Red Lily; Three Weeks. **1925** Frivolous Sal; The Crimson Runner; The Mystic; Tracked in the Snow Country; Flaming Love. **1926** The Eagle of the Sea; Ben Hur; The Last Frontier; Miss Nobody; Old Ironsides; The Sea Wolf; Tell It to the Marines; Wild Oats Lane; Typhoon Love. **1927** Hard-Boiled Hagerty; Back to God's Country. **1928** Tenderloin; The Way of the Strong; Beau Sabreur; The Docks of New York; The Hawk's Nest; Out with the Tide; The Speed Classic; The Death Ship (short). **1929** The Bridge of San Luis Rey; Madame X; The Leatherneck; Linda; The Black Watch; One Stolen Night. **1930** The Cuckoos; Beau Bandit; See America Thirst; The Bad One; Girl of the Port; Mammy. **1931** Never the Twain Shall Meet; The Squaw Man; Oh! Oh! Cleopatra (short); Song of India; Ben Hur (sound of 1926 version). **1932** World and the Flesh; New Morals for Old; McKenna of the Mounted; Kongo. **1933** Secret of Madame Blanche; Ann Vickers. **1934** Count of Monte Cristo. **1935** Red Morning; The Best Man Wins; A Tale of Two Cities. **1936** Sutter's Gold; The Dancing Pirate; Mummy's Boys; The Bohemian Girl. **1937** Mama Steps Out; Espionage; Waikiki Wedding. **1938** The Mysterious Mr. Moto; Anesthesia (short); What Price Safety? (short). **1940** Go West. **1941** Meet John Doe; The Big Store; I'll Wait for You; Billy the Kid. **1942** Cairo; Rio Rita. **1944** Lost in a Harem. **1946** Courage of Lassie. **1949** Mr. Whitney Had a Notion (short). **1951** Man with a Cloak. **1952** Talk about a Stranger. **1953** All the Brothers Were Valiant; The Sun Shines Bright.

LEWIS, RALPH

Born: 1872, Englewood, Ill. Died: Dec. 1937, Los Angeles, Calif. Stage and screen actor. Entered films with Reliance-Majestic in 1912.

Appeared in: **1915** The Birth of a Nation. **1919** Eyes of Youth. **1921** The Conquering Power; Man-Woman-Marriage; A Private Scandal; Salvage; Outside the Law; Prisoners of Love; Sowing the Wind. **1922** Broad Daylight; Environment; The Five Dollar Baby; Flesh and Blood; The Third Alarm; In the Name of the Law; The Sin Flood. **1923** Blow Your Own Horn; Desire; The Fog; Manhattan; Vengeance of the Deep; The Westbound Limited; Tea With a Kick. **1924** Dante's Inferno; East of Broadway; The Man Who Came Back; In Every Woman's Life; Untamed Youth. **1925** Heir-Loons; The Last Edition; The Million Dollar Handicap; The Bridge of Sighs; Who Cares; The Recreation of Brian Kent; The Overland Limited; One of the Bravest. **1926** Bigger Than Barnum's; The Lady from Hell; The Silent Power; The Block Signal; The False Alarm; Fascinating Youth; The Shadow of the Law. **1927** Casey Jones; Held by the Law; Outcast Souls. **1929** The Girl in the Glass Cage. **1930** Abraham Lincoln; The Bad One; The Fourth Alarm. **1933** Sucker Money; Riot Squad. **1934** Mystery Liner. **1935** The Lost City; Behind the Green Light.

LEWIS, RICHARD

Born: 1869. Died: Apr. 30, 1935, Los Angeles, Calif. Screen actor.

Appeared in: **1924** Yankee Speed. **1926** Stick to Your Story.

LEWIS, SAM

Born: 1878. Died: Apr. 28, 1963, Hollywood, Calif. (heart ailment). Screen actor and extra.

LEWIS, SHELDON

Born: 1869, Philadelphia, Pa. Died: May 7, 1958, San Gabriel, Calif. Stage and screen actor. Married to actress Virginia Pearson (dec. 1958).

Appeared in: **1914** The Exploits of Elaine (serial). **1916** The Iron Claw (serial); Dr. Jekyll and Mr. Hyde. **1917** The Hidden Hand (serial). **1918** Wolves of Kultur (serial). **1919** The Bishop's Emeralds. **1922** Orphans of the Storm; When the Desert Calls. **1923** The Darling of New York; The Little Red Schoolhouse; Jacqueline of Blazing Barriers. **1924** The Enemy Sex; Honor among Men; In Fast Company; Missing Daughters; Those Who Dare; The Dangerous Flirt. **1925** Top of the World; Bashful Buccaneer; Fighting the Flames; Kit Carson over the Great Divide; Super Speed; Lure of the Track; Accused; Defend Yourself; The Mysterious Stranger; New Lives for Old; Silent Sanderson; The Sporting Chance. **1926** Bride of the Storm; Lightning Hutch (serial); Vanishing Millions (serial); Beyond the Trail; Buffalo Bill on the U.P. Trail; Exclusive Rights; A Desperate Moment; The Sky Pirate; Senor Daredevil; The Self Starter; The Gilded Highway; Moran of the Mounted; Don Juan; The Two-Gun Man; The Red Kimono. **1927** Burning Gold; Hazardous Valley; Life of an Actress; The Cruise of the Hellion; Driven from Home; The Ladybird; The Love Wager; The Overland Stage. **1928** The Sky Rider; The Chorus Kid; The Code of the Scarlet; Marlie the Killer; The Little Wild Girl; The River Woman; Turn Back the Hours; Top Sergeant Mulligan. **1929** Untamed Justice; Seven Footprints to Satan; Black Magic. **1930** Firebrand Jordan; Terry of the Times (serial released in two versions; silent and sound); Danger Man. **1932** The Monster Walks; Tex Takes a Holiday. **1933** Tombstone Canyon. **1934** Gun Justice. **1936** The Cattle Thief.

LEWIS, TED (Theodore Leopold Friedman)

Born: June 6, 1891, Circleville, Ohio. Died: Aug. 25, 1971, New York, N.Y. (heart attack). Screen, stage, vaudeville actor and bandleader. Entered films in 1929.

Appeared in: **1929** Is Everybody Happy?; Show of Shows. **1935** Here Comes the Band. **1937** Manhattan Merry-Go-Round. **1941** Hold That Ghost. **1943** Follow the Boys; Is Everybody Happy? (and 1929 version).

LEWIS, TOM

Born: 1864, St. John, New Brunswick, Canada. Died: Oct. 19, 1927, New York (cancer). Screen, stage, minstrel actor and circus performer.

Appeared in: **1920** Passers By. **1921** Enchantment. **1923** Adam and Eva; The Go-Getter; Marriage Morals. **1924** The Great White Way. **1927** The Callahans and the Murphys. **1928** Steamboat Bill, Jr.

LEWIS, WALTER P.

Born: June 1871, Albany, N.Y. Died: Jan. 30, 1932. Screen, stage and vaudeville actor.

Appeared in: **1912** My Hero; Gold and Glitter; The God Within; Musketeers of Pig Alley. **1914** Cinderella. **1915** Gambler of the West. **1916** Big Jim Garrity. **1921** The Family Closet; The Ghost in the Garret; Tol'able David. **1922** Lonesome Corners. **1923** The Steadfast Heart. **1924** Three Miles Out. **1925** Down Upon the Swannee River. **1927** The Crimson Flash (serial). **1928** The Little Shepherd of Kingdom Come; Beware of Blondes. **1930** The Arizona Kid; A Royal Romance.

LEWIS, VERA

Born: New York, N.Y. Died: Feb. 8, 1956, Los Angeles, Calif. Stage and screen actress. Entered films in 1914.

Appeared in: **1916** Intolerance. **1919** The Mother and the Law. **1920** Nurse Marjorie. **1922** The Glorious Fool; Nancy from Nowhere. **1923** Peg O' My Heart; Long Live the King; Brass; Desire; The Marriage Market. **1924** Broadway after Dark; The Dark Swan; How to Educate a Wife; Cornered; In Every Woman's Life. **1925** Enticement; Eve's Secret; Stella Dallas; The Only Thing; Who Cares. **1926** Ella Cinders; The Gilded Butterfly; King of the Pack; Take it from Me; The Lily; The Passionate Quest. **1927** Thumbs Down; Resurrection; The Broken Gate; The Small Bachelor; What Happened to Father. **1928** The Home Towners; Ramona; Satan and the Woman. **1929** The Iron Mask. **1930** Wide Open. **1931** Command Performance; Night Nurse. **1933** Hold Your Man. **1935** Never Too Late; The Man on the Flying Trapeze; Way Down East; Paddy O'Day. **1936** Missing Girls; Dancing Pirate. **1938** Four Daughters; Nancy Drew, Detective; Comet over Broadway. **1939** Naughty but Nice; Sweepstakes Winner; Nancy Drew and the Hidden Staircase; Mr. Smith Goes to Washington; Women in the Wind; On Trial; Hell's Kitchen; Roaring Twenties; Four Wives; Return of Dr. X. **1940** Granny Get Your Gun; A Night at Earl Carroll's; The Courageous Dr. Christian. **1941** Nine Lives Are Not Enough; She Couldn't Say No; Four Mothers; Here Comes Happiness. **1942** Lady Gangster; Busses Roar; Moon Tide; The Hard Way; Yankee Doodle Dandy. **1945** Hollywood and Vine; Rhythm on the Range; The Suspect. **1946** The Cat Creeps; Spook Busters; The Time, the Place and the Girl. **1947** It's a Joke, Son; Wife to Spare (short).

LEXA, JAKE

Died: Jan. 21, 1973. Screen actor.

Appeared in: **1972** Fuzz.

LEYSSAC, PAUL

Born: Denmark. Died: Aug. 20, 1946, Copenhagen, Denmark. Screen, stage and radio actor.

Appeared in: **1937** Victoria the Great; Head over Heels. **1941** Paris Calling.

LIBBEY, J. ALDRICH

Born: 1872. Died: Apr. 1925, San Francisco, Calif. (heart failure). Stage and screen actor.

Appeared in: **1924** Greed.

LICHINE, DAVID (David Lichtenstein)

Born: 1910, Russia? Died: June 28, 1972, Los Angeles, Calif. (kidney failure). Screen actor, choreographer and ballet dancer.

Appeared in: **1943** The Heat's On. **1944** Sensations of 1945.

LICHO, EDGAR ADOLPH

Born: 1876, Russia. Died: Oct. 11, 1944, Hollywood, Calif. Stage and screen actor.

Appeared in: **1930** Menschen hinter Gettern. **1944** White Cliffs of Dover; Seventh Cross; Days of Glory.

LIEB, HERMAN

Born: 1873, Chicago, Ill. Died: Mar. 9, 1966, Tucson, Ariz. Screen, stage and vaudeville actor.

Appeared in: **1918** Daybreak. **1936** The Chemist (short).

LIEBERMAN, JACOB

Born: 1879. Died: Feb. 16, 1956, Philadelphia, Pa. Screen and stage actor.

LIEBMANN, HANS H.

Born: 1895. Died: Jan. 24, 1960, Hannacroix, N.Y. Screen, vaudeville, television actor and dancer. With his wife Lois, was known in vaudeville as the team of "Harold and Lola."

Appeared in: **1945** Pan-Americana. **1948** Variety Time.

LIEDTKE, HARRY

Born: 1881, Konigsberg, Germany. Died: 1945, Bad Saarow-Pieskow, Germany. Stage and screen actor.

Appeared in: **1921** Gypsy Blood. **1927** The Queen was in the Parlor; Madame Wants No Children. **1928** Love is a Lie. **1929** Bohemian Dancer; Beautiful Blue Danube; Forbidden Love. **1931** Nie Wieder Liebe (No More Love). **1932** I Kiss Your Hand Madame. **1933** Der Korvettenkapitaen; Eine Liebesnacht. **1934** Liebe in Uniform. **1935** Der Page vom Dalmasse-Hotel; Wenn am Sonntagabend die Dorfmusik Spielt. **1936** Zwichen Zwei Herzen (Between Two Hearts); Liebesleute.

LIEVEN, ALBERT

Born: June 23, 1906, Hohenstein, Prussia. Died: Dec. 22, 1971, near London, England. Screen, stage, television actor and opera performer. Divorced from actresses Tatiana Lieven, Petra Peters, Valerie White and Susan Shaw.

Appeared in: **1935** Krach um Iolanthe; Die Vom Niederrhein (Lower Rhine Folks); Fraeulein Liselott; Hermine und Die Sieben Aufrechten. **1936** Reifende Jugend; Glueckspilze. **1938** Ein Frau Ohne Bedeutung; Kater Lampe. **1940** Jeannie; Night Train to Munich. **1941** Convoy. **1942** The Young Mr. Pitt; Big Blockade (war documentary). **1943** The Yellow Canary. **1944** English without Tears. **1945** The Life and Death of Colonel Blimp. **1946** The Seventh Veil; Beware of Pity. **1947** Frieda. **1949** Sleeping Car to Trieste; Her Man Gilbey. **1951** Hotel Sahara. **1953** Desperate Moment. **1956** Die Halbstarken (Wolf Pack); Loser Takes All (US 1957). **1957** Des Teufels General (The Devil's General); **1958** Der Fischer Von Heiligensee (The Fisherman from Heiligensee, aka The Big Barrier). **1959** Subway in the Sky; The House of Intrigue; Londra Chiama Polo Nord (London Calling North Pole). **1960** Conspiracy of Hearts. **1961** Foxhole in Cairo; The Guns of Navarone; Brainwashed. **1963** The Victors; Mystery Submarine. **1965** City of Terror; Coast of Skeletons. **1966** Traitor's Gate. Other German films: Yellow Daffodils; Secret City; Ride the High Wind.

LIGERO, MIGUEL

Born: 1898, Spain. Died: Feb. 20, 1968, Madrid, Spain. Screen, stage and television actor.

Appeared in: **1927** Frivolina (film debut). **1938** Nobleza Baturra (Rustic Chivalry); La Verbena de la Paloma; Morena Clara; Hamelin. **1939** La Vida Bohemia. **1940** Rumbo al Cairo (Bound for Cairo).

LIGETY, LOUIS

Born: 1881, Hungary. Died: Nov. 27, 1928, Los Angeles, Calif. (results of auto accident). Screen actor.

LIGHTNER, WINNIE

Born: Sept. 17, 1901, Greenport, N.Y. Died: Mar. 5, 1971, Sherman Oaks, Calif. (heart attack). Screen, stage and vaudeville actress.

Appeared in: **1928** The Song-a-Minute Girl (short); Broadway Favorite (short). **1929** Show of Shows; Gold Diggers of Broadway. **1930** She Couldn't Say No; Hold Everything; Life of the Party. **1931** Sit Tight; Why Change Your Husband?; Side Show; Gold Dust Gertie. **1932** Play Girl; Eight to Five; Manhattan

Parade; The Slippery Pearls (short). **1933** She Had to Say Yes; Dancing Lady. **1934** I'll Fix It.

LIGON, GROVER (aka GROVER LIGGON)

Born: 1885. Died: Mar. 4, 1965, Hollywood, Calif. Screen actor and stuntman. Entered films with Biograph.

Appeared in: **1913** Sennett films and was one of the first Keystone Kops. **1917** A Maiden's Trust. **1929** The Million Dollar Collar. **1931** Father's Son.

LILLARD, CHARLOTTE

Born: 1844. Died: Mar. 4, 1946, Hollywood, Calif. Screen and stage actress. Entered films with Edison and Vitagraph Companies.

Appeared in: **1935** Mary Burns, Fugitive; The Great Impersonation. **1936** The Garden of Allah. **1938** Kentucky; Marie Antoinette.

LINCOLN, E. K. (Edward Kline Lincoln)

Born: Johnstown, Pa. Died: Jan. 9, 1958, Los Angeles, Calif. Stage and screen actor. Do not confuse with Elmo Lincoln (dec. 1952).

Appeared in: **1913** The Call. **1914** The Littlest Rebel. **1916** Heart's Tribute; Expiation; World Against Him. **1917** Jimmy Dale Alias the Grey Seal (serial); For the Freedom of the World. **1921** Devotion; The Woman God Changed. **1922** The Light in the Dark; Man of Courage; Women Men Marry. **1923** The Little Red Schoolhouse; The Woman in Chains. **1924** The Right of the Strongest. **1925** My Neighbor's Wife.

LINCOLN, ELMO (Otto Elmo Linkenhelt)

Born: 1889. Died: June 27, 1952, Hollywood, Calif. (heart attack). Screen actor and circus performer. He was the original "Tarzan" of silent films.

Appeared in: **1915** Birth of a Nation. **1916** Intolerance. **1918** Tarzan of the Apes; The Romance of Tarzan. **1919** Elmo the Mighty (serial); The Greatest Thing in Life; Lafayette, We Come. **1920** Elmo, the Fearless (serial); The Flaming Disc (serial); Under Crimson Skies. **1921** The Adventures of Tarzan (serial—recut and rereleased with sound effects in 1928). **1922** Quincy Adams Sawyer. **1923** Fashion Row; Rupert of Hentzau; The Rendezvous. **1925** All around Frying Pan. **1926** Whom Shall I Marry? **1934** The Hunchback of Notre Dame. **1939** Blue Montana Skies; Colorado Sunset; Wyoming Outlaw. **1942** Tarzan's New York Adventure. **1949** Tarzan's Magic Fountain. **1951** The Hollywood Story; The Iron Man. **1952** Carrie.

LINDENBURN, HENRY

Born: 1874. Died: Mar. 28, 1952, Cincinnati, Ohio. Riverboat captain and screen actor.

Appeared in: **1939** Gone with the Wind (piloted steamer in the film).

LINDER, ALFRED

Died: July 6, 1957, Hollywood, Calif. Screen, stage actor, and stage director.

Appeared in: **1945** The House on 92nd Street. **1947** 13 Rue Madeline; The Brasher Doubloon. **1948** Canon City. **1949** I Was a Male War Bride. **1950** Guilty of Treason. **1952** Diplomatic Courier. **1957** The Invisible Boy; The Girl in the Kremlin.

LINDER, MAX (Gabriel Leviell)

Born: 1883, France. Died: 1925. Screen, stage actor, screenwriter and film director.

Appeared in: **1917** Max Wants a Divorce; Max Comes Across. **1921** Be My Wife; Seven Years Bad Luck. **1922** The Three Must-Get-Theres; Au Secours! (never released).

LINDO, OLGA

Born: July 13, 1899, London, England. Died: May 7, 1968, London, England. Screen, stage and television actress.

Appeared in: **1931** The Shadow Between. **1935** The Case of Gabriel Perry; The Last Journey (US 1936). **1939** The Stars Look Down (US 1941). **1943** When We are Married. **1946** Bedelia (US 1947). **1949** Obsession (aka The Hidden Room—US 1950); Train of Events (US 1952). **1954** An Inspector Calls. **1955** Raising a Riot (US 1957). **1956** Yield to the Night (aka Blond Sinner—US). **1957** Woman in a Dressing Gown. **1958** Twelve Desperate Hours. **1959** Sapphire. **1962** Dr. Crippen (US 1964).

LINDSAY, HOWARD

Born: Mar. 29, 1889, Waterford, N.Y. Died: Feb. 11, 1968, New York, N.Y. Screen, stage, vaudeville and burlesque actor, playwright, stage director and stage producer. Appeared in silent films.

LINDSAY, KEVIN

Born: 1924, Australia. Died: May 1975, London, England (heart attack). Screen, stage and television actor.

LINDSAY, LEX

Born: 1901. Died: Apr. 24, 1971, Pa. (stroke). Stage and screen actor.

Appeared in: **1931** Sob Sister.

LINDSAY, MARQUERITA

Born: 1883. Died: Dec. 26, 1955, Calif. (heart attack). Screen actress. Married to actor Noah Beery (dec. 1946) and mother of actor Noah Beery, Jr. She appeared in silent films.

LINDSEY, EMILY

Born: 1887. Died: Mar. 3, 1944, Los Angeles, Calif. Screen, stage, opera, vaudeville actress and singer.

LINGHAM, THOMAS J.

Born: Apr. 7, 1874, Indianapolis, Ind. Died: Feb. 19, 1950, Woodland Hills, Calif. Stage and screen actor. Entered films in 1913.

Appeared in: **1916** Lass of the Lumberlands (serial). **1917** The Railroad Raiders (serial); The Lost Express (serial). **1918** The Lion's Claw (serial). **1919** The Adventures of Ruth (serial); The Red Glove (serial). **1920** Ruth of the Rockies (serial); The Vanishing Dagger (serial). **1921** My Lady Friends; The Fire Eater. **1922** The Crow's Nest. **1923** The Forbidden Trail; Desert Driven; Desert Rider; Eyes of the Forest; The Lone Star Ranger; Itching Palms. **1924** The Lightning Rider; Western Luck. **1925** Don Dare Devil; Riders of Mystery; Where Was I?; Heartless Husbands; Across the Deadline. **1926** The Set-Up; The Border Sheriff; Sky High Corral; Davy Crockett at the Alamo. **1927** The Bandit's Son; Tom's Gang; Splitting the Breeze; The Desert Pirate; Daring Dude; Sitting Bull at the Spirit Lake Massacre. **1928** The Bandit Cowboy; Fangs of the Wild; Orphan of the Sage; The Trail of Courage; Young Whirlwind; The Rawhide Kid; The Bantam Cowboy; Into the Night; Man in the Rough; Son of the Golden West. **1929** The Cowboy and the Outlaw; The Fatal Warning; The Amazing Vagabond; The Freckles Rascal; Pals of the Prairie; Two Sisters; The Invaders.

LINK, WILLIAM

Born: 1867. Died: Apr. 17, 1937, Hollywood, Calif. Screen and stage actor.

LINK, WILLIAM E.

Born: 1897. Died: Dec. 13, 1949, Hollywood, Calif. Screen and stage actor.

LINLEY, BETTY

Born: 1890, Malmesbury, England. Died: May 9, 1951, New York, N.Y. Stage and screen actress.

Appeared in: **1949** The Heiress (stage and film versions).

LINN, BUD (Grafton E. Linn)

Born: 1909. Died: July 31, 1968, Conejo Valley, Calif. (heart attack). Screen, radio actor and singer. Founder of the "King's Men Quarter." Father of daughters Penelope, Kathy and Susan who sang as the "Linn Sisters."

Appeared in: **1942** Call Out the Marines. **1944** Heavenly Days.

LINN, MARGARET

Born: 1934, Richmond, Ind. Died: Sept. 12, 1973, Hollywood, Calif. (brain hemorrhage). Screen, stage and television actress.

Appeared in: **1970** Puzzle of a Downfall Child. **1971** Klute.

LION, LEON M.

Born: 1879, England. Died: Mar. 28, 1947, Sussex, England. Screen, stage actor, stage producer and playwright.

Appeared in: **1915** Hard Times; Grip. **1917** The Woman Who Was Nothing. **1919** The Chinese Puzzle. **1931** The Chinese Puzzle (and 1919 version). **1932** Number Seventeen. **1934** Lady in Danger. **1936** The Amazing Quest of Ernest Bliss (aka Romance and Riches—US 1937). **1938** Strange Boarders; Crackerjack (aka The Man With a Hundred Faces—US).

LIPSON, MELBA

Born: 1901. Died: July 1, 1953, Hollywood, Calif. Screen actress.

LIPTON, LAWRENCE

Born: 1898. Died: July 9, 1975, San Francisco, Calif. Poet and screen actor.

Appeared in: **1960** The Hypnotic Eye. **1968** You Are What You Eat.

LISTER, FRANCIS

Born: Apr. 2, 1899, London, England. Died: Oct. 28, 1951, London, England. Stage and screen actor.

Appeared in: **1920** Branded. **1921** The Fortune of Christina McNab (US 1923). **1923** Should a Doctor Tell?; Boden's Boy; Comin' Through the Rye. **1924** The Unwanted; Chappy—That's All. **1929** Atlantic. **1930** At the Villa Rose (aka Mystery at the Villa Rose—US). **1931** Uneasy Virtue; Brown Sugar. **1932** Jack's the Boy (aka Night and Day—US 1933). **1933** Counsel's Opinion; Hawley's of High Street. **1935** Mutiny on the Bounty. **1936** Living Dangerously. **1937** Sensation; The Return of the Scarlet Pimpernel (US 1938). **1939** Murder in Soho (aka Murder in the Night—US 1940). **1944** Henry V (US 1946). **1945** The Wicked Lady (US 1946). **1949** Christopher Columbus. **1951** Home to Danger. **1958** Henry V (reissue of 1944 film).

LISTON, SONNY (Charles Liston)
Born: May 8, 1932, near Little Rock, Ark. Died: Dec. 1971, Las Vegas. Black professional boxer and screen actor.

Appeared in: **1965** Harlow. **1968** Head.

LITEL, JOHN (John Beach Litel)
Born: Dec. 30, 1894, Albany, Wis. Died: Feb. 3, 1972, Woodland Hills, Calif. Screen, stage and television actor.

Appeared in: **1929** The Sleeping Porch (short). **1930** Don't Believe It; On the Border. **1932** Wayward. **1936** Black Legion. **1937** Fugitive in the Sky; The Life of Emile Zola; Marked Woman; Midnight Court; Slim; The Missing Witness; Back in Circulation. **1938** Alcatraz Island; Nancy Drew—Detective; Gold Is Where You Find It; A Slight Case of Murder; My Bill; Broadway Musketeers; Love, Honor and Behave; Jezebel Over the Wall; Little Miss Thoroughbred; The Amazing Dr. Clitterhouse; Valley of the Giants; Comet over Broadway. **1939** Secret Service of the Air; On Trial; Dust Be my Destiny; Dodge City; Dead End Kids on Dress Parade (aka On Dress Parade); The Return of Dr. X; Nancy Drew—Trouble Shooter; Nancy Drew and the Hidden Staircase; One Hour to Live; Wings of the Navy; You Can't Get Away with Murder; Nancy Drew—Reporter. **1940** A Child is Born; The Fighting Sixty-Ninth; Castle on the Hudson; Flight Nurse; They Drive by Night; Knute Rockne—All American; Virginia City; It All Came True; An Angel from Texas; The Man Who Talked too Much; Murder in the Air; Money and the Woman; Lady with Red Hair; Santa Fe Trail; Flight Angels; Men Without Souls; Father Is a Prince; Gambling on the High Seas. **1941** The Trial of Mary Dugan; Father's Son; Thieves Fall Out; The Big Boss; Henry Aldrich for President; Sealed Lips; The Great Mr. Nobody; They Died With Their Boots On. **1942** Kid Glove Killer; Henry and Dizzy; The Mystery of Marie Roget; Men of Texas; Mississippi Gambler; Invisible Agent; A Desperate Chance for Ellery Queen; Henry Aldrich—Editor; Boss of Big Town; Madame Spy; Don Winslow of the Navy (serial). **1943** Henry Aldrich Gets Glamour; Submarine Base; Dangerous Age; Murder in Times Square; Henry Aldrich Swings It; Henry Aldrich Haunts a House; Crime Doctor; Where Are Your Children? **1944** Henry Aldrich Plays Cupid; Henry Aldrich's Little Secret; Henry Aldrich—Boy Scout; Murder in the Blue Room; Faces in the Fog; Lake Placid Serenade; My Buddy. **1945** The Crime Doctor's Warning; Brewster's Millions; The Daltons Ride Again; Northwest Trail; The Enchanted Forest; Salome, Where She Danced; San Antonio; Crimson Canary. **1946** A Night in Paradise; The Return of Rusty; Sister Kenny; She Wrote the Book; Smooth as Silk; Swell Guy; Lighthouse; The Madonna's Secret; Notorious Gentleman. **1947** The Beginning of the End; Christmas Eve; The Guilty; Cass Timberlane; Heaven Only Knows; Easy Come, Easy Go. **1948** Rusty Leads the Way; My Dog Rusty; I, Jane Doe; Pitfall; The Valiant Hombre; Triple Threat; Smart Woman. **1949** Rusty Saves a Life; Rusty's Birthday; The Gal Who Took the West; Outpost in Morocco; Shamrock Hill; Woman in Hiding. **1950** Mary Ryan—Detective; The Sundowners; Fuller Brush Girl; Kiss Tomorrow Goodbye. **1951** Texas Rangers; The Groom Wore Spurs; Cuban Fireball; Little Egypt; Two Dollar Better; Flight to Mars; Take Care of My Little Girl. **1952** Jet Job; Montana Belle; Scaramouche. **1953** Jack Slade. **1954** Sitting Bull. **1955** Texas Lady; The Kentuckian; Double Jeopardy. **1956** The Wild Dakotas; Comanche. **1957** The Hired Gun; Decision at Sundown. **1958** Houseboat. **1961** A Pocketful of Miracles; Lover Come Back; Voyage to the Bottom of the Sea. **1963** The Gun Hawk. **1965** The Sons of Katie Elder. **1966** Nevada Smith.

LITTLE, BILLY (Billy Rhodes)
Born: 1895. Died: July 24, 1967, Hollywood, Calif. (stroke). Midget screen and stage actor.

Appeared in: **1926** Oh Baby. **1929** The Flaming Youth (short); The Head of the Family (short); The Side Show. **1930** Swing High; No Questions Asked (short); prior to 1933: Some Babies (short); The Bigger They Are (short). **1934** Men in Black (short). **1938** The Terror of Tiny Town. **1939** The Wizard of Oz. **1961** Not Tonight, Henry. **1967** Mondo Hollywood.

LITTLE BOZO (John F. Pizzo)
Born: 1907. Died: May 9, 1952, Los Angeles, Calif. (heart ailment). Screen actor and circus performer.

Appeared in: **1927** White Pants Willie. **1932** Sign of the Cross; Freaks. **1939** At the Circus.

LITTLE, JAMES F.
Born: 1907. Died: Oct. 12, 1969, Miami, Fla. (cancer). Screen, stage and television actor.

Appeared in: **1953** Taxi.

LITTLE, LITTLE JACK (John Leonard)
Born: 1901, England. Died: Apr. 9, 1956, Hollywood, Calif. (possible suicide). Screen, radio, vaudeville actor, bandleader, songwriter and singer.

Appeared in: **1932–33** Universal's "Radio Star Reels." **1934** A Vitaphone short; a Paramount short. **1936** A Vitaphone short.

LITTLE, MAJOR GORDON W. "PAWNEE BILL"
Born: Feb. 14, 1860, Bloomington, Ill. Died: Feb. 3, 1942, Pawnee, Okla. Screen actor and circus performer. Married to circus performer May Little (dec. 1936).

Appeared in: **1911** Buffalo Bill Wild West and Pawnee Bill Far East. **1915** Pawnee Bill. **1935** Two Hearts in Harmony.

LITTLEFIELD, LUCIEN
Born: Aug. 16, 1895, San Antonio, Tex. Died: June 4, 1960, Hollywood, Calif. Screen actor and screenwriter. Entered films in 1913.

Appeared in: **1921** The Little Clown; The Hell Diggers; The Sheik; Too Much Speed; Crazy to Marry. **1922** Her Husband's Trademark; Rent Free; Tillie; To Have and to Hold; Across the Continent; Our Leading Citizen; Manslaughter; The Siren Call. **1923** The French Doll; The Tiger's Claw; Three Wise Fools; In the Palace of the King; The Rendezvous; Mr. Billings Spends His Dime. **1924** Babbitt; The Deadwood Coach; Gold Heels; True as Steel; Gerald Cranston's Lady; Name the Man; The Painted Lady; Teeth; A Woman Who Sinned; Never Say Die. **1925** Tumbleweeds; Charley's Aunt; Gold and the Girl; The Rainbow Trail; Soul Mates. **1926** The Torrent; Bachelor Brides; Brooding Eyes; Take It from Me; Tony Runs Wild; Twinkletoes. **1927** The Small Bachelor; My Best Girl; The Cat and the Canary; Cheating Cheaters. Taxi!, Taxi!; Uncle Tom's Cabin; A Texas Steer. **1928** Heart to Heart; The Head Man; Do Your Duty; Mother Knows Best; Harold Teen; A Ship Comes In. **1929** Seven Keys to Baldpate; Drag; The Girl in the Glass Cage; Saturday's Children; Making the Grade; This is Heaven; Clear the Decks; The Man in Hobble's; Dark Streets. **1930** Tom Sawyer; Clancy in Wall Street; She's My Weakness; No, No, Nanette; Captain of the Guard; The Great Divide; High Society Blues; also starred in "The Potter" series of shorts, including the following: Getting a Raise; At Home; Done in Oil; Pa Gets a Vacation; Big Money; Out for Game; His Big Ambition. **1931** Misbehaving Ladies; It Pays to Advertise; Reducing; Scandal Sheet; Young as You Feel. **1932** High Pressure; Broken Lullaby; Strangers in Love; Shopworn; Strangers of the Evening; Miss Pinkerton; Downstairs; Speed Demon; Pride of the Legion; That's My Boy; Evenings for Sale; If I Had a Million, a Paramount short. **1933** The Bitter Tea of General Yen; Dirty Work (short); Sailor's Luck; Sweepings; Skyway; Rainbow over Broadway; Alice in Wonderland; The Big Brain; Professional Sweetheart; Chance at Heaven; East of Fifth Avenue, a Paramount short. **1934** When Strangers Meet; Love Time; Sons of the Desert; Thirty Day Princess; Kiss and Make Up; Mandalay; Gridiron Flash. **1935** Ruggles of Red Gap; Sweepstake Annie; The Man on the Flying Trapeze; One Frightened Night; The Murder Man; She Gets Her Man; The Return of Peter Grimm; I Dream Too Much; Cappy Ricks Returns; Magnificent Obsession. **1936** Rose Marie; Early to Bed; The Moon's Our Home; Let's Sing Again. **1937** Hotel Haywire; Wild Money; Partners in Crime; High, Wide and Handsome; Souls at Sea; Bulldog Drummond's Revenge; Wells Fargo. **1938** Wide Open Faces; Born to the West; Scandal Street; Hollywood Stadium Mystery; The Night Hawk; The Gladiator. **1939** Mystery Plane; Sky Pirate; Tumbleweeds; Unmarried; What a Life!; Sabotage; Jeepers Creepers. **1940** Money to Burn; Those Were the Days; The Great American Broadcast. **1941** Murder among Friends; Henry Aldrich for President; Man at Large; The Little Foxes; Mr. and Mrs. North; Life with Henry. **1942** Hillbilly Blitzkrieg; Castle in the Desert; The Great Man's Lady; Bells of Capistrano; Whistling in Dixie. **1943** Henry Aldrich Haunts a House; Johnny Come Lately. **1944** Lady, Let's Dance; When the Lights Go on Again; Lights of Old Santa Fe; Casanova in Burlesque; Goodnight, Sweetheart; Cowboy and the Senorita; One Body Too Many. **1945** The Caribbean Mystery; Detour; Scared Stiff. **1946** Rendezvous with Annie; That Brennan Girl. **1947** The Hal Roach Comedy; The Fabulous Joe; Sweet Genevieve. **1948** Lightnin' in the Forest; Jinx Money; Badmen of Tombstone. **1949** Susanna Pass. **1952** At Sword's Point. **1953** Roar of the Crowd. **1954** Casanova's Big Night. **1955** Sudden Danger. **1957** Bop Girl. **1958** Wink of an Eye.

LITVAK, ANATOLE (Michael Anatole Litvak)
Born: May 21, 1902, Kiev, Russia. Died: Dec. 15, 1974, Paris, France. Film director, producer, screenwriter, stage and screen actor. Divorced from actress Miriam Hopkins (dec. 1972). Married to fashion designer Sophie Steur Litvak.

LIVANOV, BORIS
Born: 1904, Russia. Died: Sept. 23, 1972, Moscow, Russia. Screen, stage actor and stage director.

Appeared in: **1934** Deserter. **1935** Peter Vinogradov. **1936** Dubrovsky. **1937** Baltic Deputy. **1938** Men of the Sea. **1947** The Great Glinka. **1949** The First Front. **1954** Admiral Ushakov. **1959** Poem of the Sea. **1961** Slepoy Muzykant (Sound of Life—US 1962).

LIVESEY, JACK
Born: 1901, England. Died: Oct. 12, 1961, Burbank, Calif. Screen, stage and television actor. Son of actor Sam Livesey (dec. 1936) and brother of actor Roger Livesey (dec. 1976).

Appeared in: **1933** The Wandering Jew (US 1935). **1935** The Passing of the

Third Floor Back; Variety. **1936** The Howard Case. **1937** Behind Your Back; When the Poppies Bloom Again; It's Never Too Late to Mend; First Night. **1938** Murder Tomorrow; Penny Paradise; Old Bones of the River; Bedtime Story. **1940** Old Bill and Son. **1945** The World Owes Me a Living. **1948** The First Gentleman (aka Affairs of a Rogue—US 1949). **1949** Murder at the Windmill (aka Murder at the Burlesque—US). **1950** Paul Temple's Triumph (US 1951). **1962** The Notorious Landlady; That Touch of Mink.

LIVESEY, SAM

Born: Oct. 14, 1873, Flintshire, England. Died: Nov. 7, 1936, London, England (following surgery). Stage and screen actor. Father of actors Jack (dec. 1961) and Roger Livesey (dec. 1976).

Appeared in: **1916** The Lifeguardsman. **1918** Spinner O' Dreams; Victory and Peace. **1919** A Chinese Puzzle; The Sins of Youth; A Sinless Sinner (aka Midnight Gambols—US 1920). **1920** All the Winners; The Black Spider; Burnt In. **1921** The Marriage Lines. **1923** Married Life (aka Married Love or Maisie's Marriage). **1928** Wait and See; The Forger; Zero. **1929** Young Woodley (US 1930); Blackmail (silent version). **1930** One Family; Raise the Roof. **1931** The Hound of the Baskervilles; Jealousy; Dreyfus (aka The Dreyfus Case—US); The Girl in the Night; Up for the Cup; The Wickham Mystery; Many Waters. **1932** Insult; The Flag Lieutenant; Mr. Bill the Conqueror (aka The Man Who Won—US 1933); The Wonderful Story. **1933** The Private Life of Henry VIII; The Shadow; Commissionaire. **1934** Tangled Evidence; Jew Suess (aka Power—US); The Great Defender. **1935** Royal Cavalcade (aka Regal Cavalcade—US); Turn of the Tide; Variety; Drake of England (aka Drake the Pirate—US); The Hope of His Side (aka Where's George?). **1936** Rembrandt; Men of Yesterday; Calling the Tune. **1937** Wings of the Morning; Dark Journey; The Mill on the Floss (US 1939).

LLOYD, AL (Albert Lloyd)

Born: 1884. Died: July 10, 1964, Hollywood, Calif. (heart attack). Screen and vaudeville actor. Appeared as partner in vaudeville team of "Aveling and Lloyd."

Appeared in: **1938** Penrod's Double Trouble.

LLOYD, ALICE

Born: 1873, England. Died: Nov. 17, 1949, Banstead, England. Screen, stage, vaudeville actress and singer. Appeared in early Kinemacolor shorts.

LLOYD, CHARLES M.

Born: 1870, Died: Dec. 4, 1948, Hollywood, Calif. (heart attack). Screen, stage and vaudeville actor. Entered films with Mack Sennett.

LLOYD, DORIS

Born: 1900, Liverpool, England. Died: May 21, 1968, Santa Barbara, Calif. ("strained" heart). Stage and screen actress.

Appeared in: **1920** The Shadow Between. **1925** The Lady; The Man from Red Gulch. **1926** The Black Bird; Exit Smiling; The Midnight Kiss; Black Paradise. **1927** Is Zat So?; The Auctioneer; Two Girls Wanted; Lonesome Ladies; The Bronco Twister; Rich but Honest. **1928** Come to My House; Trail of '98. **1929** The Careless Age; The Drake Case. **1930** Disraeli; Sarah and Son; Reno; Old English; Way for a Sailor; Charley's Aunt. **1931** The Bachelor Father; Once a Lady; Waterloo Bridge; Bought; Transgression; Devotion. **1932** Back Street; Tarzan the Ape Man. **1933** Oliver Twist; Always a Lady; Robbers' Roost; Looking Forward; Peg O' My Heart; A Study in Scarlet; Voltaire; Secrets. **1934** Glamour; Sisters under the Skin; She Was a Lady; One Exciting Adventure; Tarzan and His Mate; Dangerous Corner; Kiss and Make Up; British Agent. **1935** Clive of India; Straight from the Heart; Kind Lady; The Perfect Gentlemen; The Woman in Red; Motive for Revenge; Chasing Yesterday; Becky Sharp; A Shot in the Dark; Peter Ibbetson; A Feather in Her Hat. **1936** Don't Get Personal; Too Many Parents; Mary of Scotland; Brilliant Marriage. **1937** The Plough and the Stars; Tovarich. **1938** The Black Doll; Alcatraz Island. **1939** I'm from Missouri; The Under-Pup; Barricade; First Love; The Private Lives of Elizabeth and Essex; The Old Maid; The Spellbinder. **1940** The Great Plane Robbery; Till We Meet Again; The Letter; Vigil in the Night. **1941** Keep 'Em Flying; The Great Lie; Shining Victory; The Wolf Man; Life with Henry. **1942** Night Monster; This above All; Journey for Margaret; The Ghost of Frankenstein. **1943** Mission to Moscow; Forever and a Day; The Constant Nymph; Eyes of the Underworld. **1944** The Invisible Man's Revenge; Frenchman's Creek; Follow the Boys; The Conspirators; Phantom Lady; The Lodger. **1945** Allotment Wives; Molly and Me; Scotland Yard Investigates; My Name is Julia Ross. **1946** Devotion (and 1931 version); G.I. War Brides; Holiday in Mexico; Of Human Bondage; Tarzan and the Leopard Woman; To Each His Own; Three Strangers. **1947** The Secret Life of Walter Mitty. **1948** Sign of the Ram. **1950** Tyrant of the Sea. **1951** The Son of Dr. Jekyll; Kind Lady. **1953** Young Bess. **1955** A Man Called Peter. **1956** The Swan. **1960** Midnight Lace; The Time Machine. **1962** The Notorious Landlady. **1964** Mary Poppins. **1965** Sound of Music. **1967** Rosie.

LLOYD, FRANK

Born: Feb. 1889, Glasgow, Scotland. Died: Aug. 10, 1960, Santa Monica, Calif. Screen, stage actor, film director, producer and screenwriter. Won Academy Awards for Best Director for his The Divine Lady 1928–29 and Cavalcade, 1932–33. Entered films as an actor in 1910 and then a writer and director.

Appeared in: **1914** The Test. **1915** The Black Box (serial); Damon and Pythias; To Redeem an Oath; The Bay of the Seven Isles; A Prophet of the Hills. **1916** The Stronger Love.

LLOYD, FREDERICK W.

Born: Jan. 15, 1880, London, England. Died: Nov. 24, 1949, Hove, England. Screen, stage and radio actor.

Appeared in: **1911** Princess Clementina. **1928** Balaclava (aka Jaws of Hell—US 1931). **1930** The "W" Plan (US 1931); The Temporary Widow. **1931** Tell England (aka The Battle of Gallipoli—US); The Perfect Lady; The Great Gay Road; The Hound of the Baskervilles; The Beggar Student; A Gentleman of Paris. **1932** Arms and the Man; Sleepless Nights. **1933** The Crime at Blossoms; Up for the Derby; The Song You Gave Me (US 1934); Mixed Doubles. **1934** Blossom Time (aka April Romance—US 1937). **1935** Radio Pirates; Royal Cavalcade (aka Regal Cavalcade—US); Lieutenant Daring, RN. **1936** Everything is Thunder. **1937** Mademoiselle Docteur; 21 Days (aka The First and the Last and aka 21 Days Together—US 1940); Secret Lives (aka I Married a Spy—US 1938). **1938** Weddings are Wonderful. **1948** Oliver Twist (US 1951).

LLOYD, GLADYS

Born: 1896, Yonkers, N.Y. Died: June 6, 1971, Culver City, Calif. (stroke). Stage and screen actress. Divorced from actor Edward G. Robinson (dec. 1973). Mother of actor Edward G. Robinson, Jr. (dec. 1974). Played roles as an extra in many films with Robinson.

Appeared in: **1931** Smart Money; Five Star Final. **1932** The Hatchet Man; Two Seconds.

LLOYD, HAROLD (Harold Clayton Lloyd)

Born: Apr. 20, 1893, Burchard, Nebr. Died: Mar. 8, 1971, Beverly Hills, Calif. (cancer). Screen, stage actor, film producer, director and screenwriter. Married to actress Mildred Davis (dec. 1969). Father of actor Harold Lloyd, Jr. (dec. 1971). Appeared in "Lonesome Luke" series. In 1952 received Special Academy Award as "Master Comedian and Good Citizen." Entered films in 1912.

Appeared in: **1914** From Italy's Shore; Curses! They Remarked. **1915** Once Every Ten Minutes; Spit Ball Sadie; Soaking the Clothes; Pressing the Suit; Terribly Stuck Up; A Mixup for Mazie; Some Baby; Fresh from the Farm; Giving Them Fits; Bughouse Bell Hops; Tinkering with Trouble; Great While It Lasted; Ragtime Snap Shots; A Fozzle at a Tea Party; Ruses, Rhymes, Roughnecks; Peculiar Patients Pranks; Social Gangster; Just Nuts; A One Night Stand; "Phunphilms" series. **1916** Luke Leans to the Literary; Luke Lugs Luggage; Luke Rolls in Luxury; Luke the Candy Cut-Up; Luke Foils the Villain; Luke and Rural Roughnecks; Luke Pipes the Pippins; Lonesome Luke; Circus King; Skylight Sleep; Luke's Double; Them Was the Happy Days; Trouble Enough; Luke and the Bomb Throwers; Reckless Wrestlers; Luke's Late Lunches; Ice; Luke Laughs Out; An Awful Romance; Luke's Fatal Fliver; Luke's Washful Waiting; Luke Rides Roughshod; Unfriendly Fruit; Luke, Crystal Gazer; A Matrimonial Mixup; Luke's Lost Lamb; Braver Than the Bravest; Luke Does the Midway; Caught in a Jam; Luke Joins the Navy; Busting the Beanery; Luke and the Mermaids; Jailed; Luke's Speedy Club Life; Luke and the Bang-Tails; Luke Laughs Last; Luke's Society Mix-Up. **1916** Luke, the Chauffeur; Luke's Preparedness Preparation; Luke's Newsie Knockout; Luke, Gladiator; Luke, Patient Provider; Luke's Movie Muddle; Luke's Fireworks Fizzle; Luke Locates the Loot; Luke's Shattered Sleep; Marriage a la Carte. **1917** Luke's Last Liberty; Luke's Busy Days; Drama's Dreadful Deal; Luke's Trolley Trouble; Lonesome Luke, Lawyer; Luke Wins Ye Ladye Faire; Lonesome Luke's Lively Rifle; Lonesome Luke on Tin Can Alley; Lonesome Luke's Lively Life; Lonesome Luke's Honeymoon; Lonesome Luke, Plumber; Stop! Luke! Listen!; Lonesome Luke, Messenger; Lonesome Luke, Mechanic; Lonesome Luke's Wild Women; Over the Fence; Lonesome Luke Loses Patients; Pinched; By the Sad Sea Waves; Birds of a Feather; Bliss; Lonesome Luke from London to Laramie; Rainbow Island; Love, Laughs and Lather; The Flirt; Clubs Are Trump; All Aboard; We Never Sleep; Bashful; The Tip; Step Lively; Move On. **1918** The Big Idea; The Lamb; Hit Him Again; Beat It; A Gasoline Wedding; Look Pleasant Please; Here Comes the Girls; Let's Go; On the Jump; Follow the Crowd; Pipe the Whiskers; It's a Wild Life; Hey There; Kicked Out; The Non-Stop Kid; Two-Gun Gussie; Fireman Save My Child; The City Slicker; Sic 'Em Towser; Somewhere in Turkey; Are Crooks Dishonest?; An Ozark Romance; Kicking the Germ Out of Germany; That's Him; Too Scrambled; Swing Your Partner; Why Pick on Me?; Nothing but Trouble; Hear 'Em Rave; Take a Chance; She Loses Me; Bride and Groom; Bees in His Bonnet; She Loves Me Not. **1919** Wanted—$5,000; Going! Going! Going!; Ask Father; On the Fire; I'm on My Way; Look Out Below; The Dutiful Dub; Next Aisle Over; A Sammy in Siberia; Just Dropped In; Crack Your Heels; Ring up the Curtain; Young Mr. Jazz; Si, Senor; Before Breakfast; The Marathon; Back to the Woods; Pistols for Breakfast; The Rajah; Swat the Crook; Off the Trolley; Spring Fever; Billy Blazes, Esq.; Just Neighbors; At the Stage Door; Never Touched Me; A Jazzed Honeymoon; Count Your Change; Chop Suey and Co.; Heap Big Chief; Don't Shove; Be My Wife; He Leads, Others Follow; Soft Money; Count the Votes; Pay Your Dues; Bumping into Broadway; Captain Kidd's Kids; From Hand to

Mouth; His Royal Slyness. **1920** The following shorts: Haunted Spooks; An Eastern Westerner; High and Dizzy; Get out and Get Under; Number, Please. **1921** Among Those Present; I Do; A Sailor-Made Man; plus the following shorts: Now or Never; Never Weaken. **1922** Grandma's Boy; Doctor Jack. **1923** Safety Last; Why Worry? **1924** Girl Shy; Hot Water. **1925** The Freshman. **1926** For Heaven's Sake. **1927** The Kid Brother. **1928** Speedy. **1929** Welcome Danger. **1930** Feet First. **1931** Stout Hearts and Willing Hands. **1932** Movie Crazy. **1934** The Cat's Paw. **1936** The Milky Way. **1938** Professor Beware. **1947** Mad Wednesday (aka The Sin of Harold Diddlebock). **1957** The Golden Age of Comedy (documentary). **1962** Harold Lloyd's World of Comedy (documentary). **1964** Funny Side of Life.

LLOYD, HAROLD, JR. "DUKE" (Harold Clayton Lloyd, Jr.)
Born: Jan. 25, 1931, Calif. Died: June 9, 1971, North Hollywood, Calif. Screen, television actor and singer. Son of actor Harold Lloyd, Sr. (dec. 1971) and actress Mildred Davis (dec. 1969).

Appeared in: **1949** Our Very Own (film debut). **1955** Yank in Ermine. **1958** Frankenstein's Daughter. **1959** Girls Town. **1960** Platinum High School. **1962** Married Too Young. **1965** Mutiny in Outer Space.

LLOYD, ROLLO
Born: Mar. 22, 1883, Akron, Ohio. Died: July 24, 1938, Los Angeles, Calif. Screen, stage actor, screenwriter, stage and film director.

Appeared in: **1932** Okay America; Laughter in Hell; Prestige. **1933** Destination Unknown; Today We Live; Carnival Lady; Strictly Personal; Out All Night. **1934** Private Scandal; Madame Spy; The Party's Over; Whom the Gods Destroy. **1935** Lives of a Bengal Lancer; His Night Out; Mad Love; Barbary Coast; Hot Tip; The Mystery Man; Murder on a Honeymoon; The Man Who Reclaimed His Head. **1936** Come and Get It; Professional Soldier; Magnificent Obsession; Yellowstone; The Man I Marry; Love Letters of a Star; I Conquer the Sea; The White Legion; Hell-Ship Morgan; Anthony Adverse; The Devil Doll; Straight from the Shoulder. **1937** Four Days Wonder; Armored Car; The Westland Case; Seventh Heaven; Women Men Marry. **1938** Arsene Lupin Returns; The Lady in the Morgue; Goodbye Broadway; Spawn of the North.

LOBACK, MARVIN (aka MARVIN LOBACH)
Born: 1898. Died: Aug. 18, 1938, Hollywood, Calif. Screen and stage actor.

Appeared in: **1921** Hands Off. **1932** Shopping with Wifie (short); Speed in the Gay 90's (short). **1935** Uncivil Warriors (short); Old Sawbones (short).

LOCHER, FELIX (Felix Maurice Locher)
Born: July 16, 1882, Switzerland. Died: Mar. 13, 1969, Sherman Oaks, Calif. Screen and television actor. Father of actor Jon Hall.

Appeared in: **1957** Hell Ship Mutiny; Don Mike. **1958** Curse of the Faceless Man; Desert Hell; Frankenstein's Daughter; Kings Go Forth. **1959** Thunder in the Sun; The Man Who Understood Women; Beloved Infidel. **1960** Walk Tall. **1962** The Firebrand. **1963** California; House of the Damned. **1965** The Greatest Story Ever Told.

LOCKHART, GENE (Eugene Lockhart)
Born: July 18, 1891, London, Ontario, Canada. Died: Apr. 1, 1957, Santa Monica, Calif. (coronary thrombosis). Screen, stage, television, vaudeville, radio actor, songwriter, stage director, stage producer and radio writer. Father of actress June Lockhart. Married to actress Kathleen Arthur (aka Kathleen Lockhart). Wrote the song "The World is Waiting for the Sunrise."

Appeared in: **1934** By Your Leave. **1935** I've Been Around; Captain Hurricane; Star of Midnight; Thunder in the Night; Storm over the Andes; Crime and Punishment. **1936** Brides Are Like That; Times Square Playboy; Earthworm Tractors; The First Baby; Career Woman; The Garden Murder Case; The Gorgeous Hussy; The Devil Is a Sissy; Wedding Present; Mind Your Own Business; Come Closer, Folks! **1937** Mama Steps Out; Too Many Wives; The Sheik Steps Out; Something to Sing About; Make Way for Tomorrow. **1938** Of Human Hearts; Listen, Darling; A Christmas Carol; Sweethearts; Penrod's Double Trouble; Men Are Such Fools; Blondie; Sinners in Paradise; Algiers; Meet the Girls. **1939** Blackmail; I'm from Missouri; Hotel Imperial; Our Leading Citizen; Geronimo; Tell No Tales; Bridal Suite; The Story of Alexander Graham Bell. **1940** Edison the Man; Dr. Kildare Goes Home; We Who Are Young; South of Pago Pago; A Dispatch from Reuter's; His Girl Friday; Abe Lincoln in Illinois. **1941** Keeping Company; Meet John Doe; The Sea Wolf; Billy the Kid; All That Money Can Buy; One Foot in Heaven; They Died with Their Boots On; Steel against the Sky; International Lady. **1942** Juke Girl; The Gay Sisters; You Can't Escape Forever. **1943** Forever and a Day; Hangmen Also Die; Mission to Moscow; The Desert Song; Madame Curie; Find the Blackmailer; Northern Pursuit. **1944** Going My Way; The White Cliffs of Dover; Action in Arabia; The Man from Frisco. **1945** The House on 92nd Street; That's the Spirit; Leave Her to Heaven. **1946** A Scandal in Paris; Meet Me on Broadway; She-Wolf of London; The Strange Woman. **1947** Miracle on 34th Street; The Shocking Miss Pilgrim; The Foxes of Harrow; Cynthia; Honeymoon; Her Husband's Affairs. **1948** Joan of Arc; Inside Story; That Wonderful Urge; Apartment for Peggy; I, Jane Doe. **1949** The Inspector General; Down to the Sea in Ships; Madame Bovary; Red Light. **1950** The Big Hangover; Riding High. **1951** Rhubarb; I'd Climb the Highest Mountain; Seeds of

Destruction; The Lady from Texas. **1952** Face to Face; Hoodlum Empire; Bonzo Goes to College; Androcles and the Lion; Apache War Smoke; A Girl in Every Port; The Devil and Daniel Webster (reissue of All That Money Can Buy, 1941). **1953** Francis Covers the Big Town; Down among the Sheltering Palms; Confidentially Connie; The Lady Wants Mink. **1954** World for Ransom. **1955** The Vanishing American. **1956** The Man in the Gray Flannel Suit; Carousel. **1957** Jeanne Eagles.

LOCKHART, TIM
Born: 1930, Columbus, Ga. Died: Mar. 26, 1963, Louisville, Ky. (heart attack). Screen, stage, radio and television actor.

LOCKLEAR, OMAR
Born: Oct. 28, 1891, Fort Worth, Tex. Died: Aug. 2, 1920, Los Angeles, Calif. (airplane accident). Screen actor and stunt flyer in films. Died during filming of The Skywayman.

Appeared in: **1919** Cassidy of the Air Lanes. **1920** The Great Air Robbery; The Skywayman.

LOCKWOOD, HAROLD A.
Born: 1887, Brooklyn, N.Y. Died: Oct. 19, 1918, New York, N.Y. (Spanish influenza). Screen, stage and vaudeville actor.

Appeared in: **1908** Harbor Island. **1912** The Lost Address; The Torn Letter; Over a Cracked Bowl; The Bachelor and the Baby. **1913** Northern Hearts; A Mansion of Misery; The Spanish Parrot-Girl; Phantoms; The Burglar Who Robbed Death; The Lipton Cup; With Love's Eyes; Two Men and a Woman; Lieutenant Jones; A Little Child Shall Lead Them; The Stolen Melody; Her Only Son; Woman—Past and Present; Diverging Paths; Love Before Ten; The Tie of the Blood; Margarita and the Mission Funds; Child of the Sea. **1914** The Unwelcome Mrs. Hatch; Wildflower; Tess of the Storm Country; Hearts Adrift; Through the Centuries; The Attic Above; The County Chairman; Elizabeth's Prayer; A Message from Across the Sea; When Thieves Fall Out; Such a Little Queen; The Conspiracy. **1915** The Turn of the Road; Shopgirls; Secretary of Frivolous Affairs; The Lure of the Mask; Jim the Penman; The Great Question; The House of a Thousand Scandals; Pardoned; The Buzzard's Shadow; The Tragic Circle. **1916** The Secret Wire; Big Temaine; The River of Romance; Life's Blind Alley; The Other Side of the Door; The Gamble; The Man in the Sombrero; The Broken Cross; Lillo of the Sulu Seas; The Comeback; Pidgin Island; The Masked Rider. **1917** The Promise; The Haunted Pajamas; The Avenging Trail; The Hidden Children; The Square Deceiver; Paradise Garden. **1918** Broadway Bill; Under the Handicap; The Landloper; Lend Me Your Name. **1919** The Great Romance; Shadows of Suspicion; The Crucible; A Man of Honor; Yankee Doodle in Berlin; Pals First.

LOCKWOOD, KING
Born: 1898. Died: Feb. 23, 1971, Hollywood, Calif. (stroke). Screen and television actor.

Appeared in: **1956** The Man in the Gray Flannel Suit.

LOEB, PHILIP
Born: 1894. Died: Sept. 1, 1955, New York, N.Y. Screen, stage and television actor.

Appeared in: **1938** Room Service. **1948** A Double Life. **1951** Molly.

LOEDEL, ADI
Born: 1937, Germany. Died: June 2, 1955, Hamburg, Germany (suicide—hanging). Screen, stage, radio and television actor.

Appeared in: **1950** Lockende Gefahr. **1955** Kinder, Mutter und ein General.

LOESSER, FRANK
Born: June 29, 1910, New York, N.Y. Died: July 28, 1969, New York, N.Y. (lung cancer). Composer, screenwriter and screen actor.

Appeared in: **1949** Red, Hot and Blue.

LOFF, JEANETTE (Jeanette Lov)
Born: Oct. 9, 1906, Orofino, Idaho. Died: Aug. 4, 1942, Los Angeles, Calif. (ammonia poisoning). Stage and screen actress.

Appeared in: **1927** My Friend from India. **1928** The Black Ace; Man-Made Woman; Hold 'Em Yale; Love over Night; Annapolis; Geraldine; The Man without a Face (serial). **1929** The Racketeer; .45 Calibre War; The Sophomore. **1930** The Boudoir Diplomat; Fighting Through; Party Girl; The King of Jazz. **1935** Million Dollar Baby; St. Louis Woman.

LOFGREN, MARIANNE
Born: 1910, Stockholm, Sweden. Died: 1957, Sweden. Screen actress.

Appeared in: **1934** The Song of the Scarlet Flower. **1942** En Enda Natt. **1943** Elvira Madigan. **1949** Incorrigible; Fangelse (The Devil's Wanton—US 1962). **1952** Affairs of a Model. **1956** Flamman (The Flame aka Girls Without Rooms—US 1963); Children of the Night. **1958** The Time for Desire. Other Swedish films: The Dangerous Game; What Do Men Know?; On the Sunny Side; A Lady Becomes a Maid; The Great Love; With the People for the

Country; Mr. Karlsson Mate and His Sweethearts; The Old is Coming; One Single Night; Nothing But the Truth; The Little WRAC of the Veteran Reserves; Charmers at Sea; My Little Brother and I; Night in June; A Big Hug; The Little Shrew of the Veteran Reserves; The Gentleman Gangster; Fransson the Terrible; A Poor Millionaire; Only a Woman; Talk of the Town; A Singing Lesson; Scanian Guerilla; The Ingegerd Bremssen Case; Sailor in a Dresscoat; Nothing Will be Forgotten; Jacob's Ladder; Woman Takes Command; Women in Prison; As You Like Me; Mr. Collin's Adventures; King's Street; Life Is There to be Lived; Kajan Goes to Sea; I Killed; Darling I Surrender; The Halta Lotta Tavern; Little Napoleon; She Thought It Was Him; Dangerous Roads; The Awakening of Youth; A Girl for Me; His Official Fiancee; I Am Fire and Air; And All These Women; The Emperor of Portugal; The Holy Lie; Watch Out for Spies!; Stop! Think of Something Else; Wandering with the Moon; The Suffering and Happiness of Motherhood; Hunted; The New Affairs of Pettersson and Bendel; The Rose of Thistle Island; Good Morning Bill; Asa-Hanna; The Gay Party; It's My Model; Bad Eggs; A Lovely Young Lady; Crisis; When the Door Was Closed; The Balloon; Dynamite; A Father Wanted; The Most Beautiful Thing on Earth; The Sixth Commandment; The Women; Woman Without a Face; Life at Forsbyholm; On These Shoulders; A Swedish Tiger; Miss Sunbeam; Gentlemen of the Navy; Woman in White; The Street; Boman Gets Crazy; Girl With Hyacinths; Knockout at the "Breakfast Club"; The Quartet that Split Up; The Kiss on the Cruise; A Gentleman Maybe; My Name is Puck; Divorced; Bom the Customs Officer; A Fiancee for Hire; Defiance; Salka Valka; Simon the Sinner; Hoppsan!; The Merry Boys of the Fleet; Matrimonial Announcement; Love Chastised; Little Fridolf and I; Private Entrance.

LOFT, ARTHUR
Born: May 25, 1897, Colorado. Died: Jan. 1, 1947, Los Angeles, Calif. Stage and screen actor.

Appeared in: 1933 Behind Jury Doors; Alimony Madness. 1935 On Probation; What Price Crime?; Danger Ahead; Kid Courageous. 1936 M'Liss; Postal Inspector; King of the Royal Mounted; Without Orders; Legion of Terror; Night Waitress; The Prisoner of Shark Island; Ace Drummond (serial). 1937 Woman in Distress; Paradise Express; Motor Madness; The Game that Kills; It Happened in Hollywood; Public Cowboy No. 1; The Shadow; Paid to Dance. 1938 Start Cheering; No Time to Marry; Women in Prison; All-American Sweetheart; Rawhide; Extortion; Who Killed Gale Preston?; City Streets; The Main Event; I Am the Law; Highway Patrol; Squadron of Honor; Down in Arkansaw; The Lady Objects; Gang Bullets; Rhythm of the Saddle. 1939 Risky Business; Hell's Kitchen; Street of Missing Men; Southward Ho; A Woman is the Judge; Pride of Blue Grass; Smuggled Cargo; Everybody's Baby; Days of Jesse James; Help Wanted (short). 1940 The Green Hornet (serial); Cafe Hostess; The Crooked Road; Riders of Pasco Basin; The Carson City Kid; Colorado; Texas Terrors; Glamour for Sale. 1941 Back in the Saddle; Caught in the Draft; Hold Back the Dawn; North from the Lone Star; We Go Fast; Down Mexico Way; The Stork Pays Off; Blue, White and Perfect; Henry Aldrich for President. 1942 Fly by Night; South of Santa Fe; The Lady Has Plans; The Magnificent Dope; Priorities on Parade; The Glass Key; The Man in the Trunk; Girl Trouble; Street of Chance; Dr. Broadway. 1943 My Friend Flicka; Hangmen Also Die; Happy Go Lucky; The Meanest Man in the World; Mission to Moscow; Let's Face It; Frontier Badmen; Wintertime; Jack London. 1944 Charlie Chan in the Secret Service; Rosie the Riveter; The Hitler Gang; Louisiana Hayride; Wilson; Leave It to the Irish; The Woman in the Window; Lights of Old Santa Fe. 1945 Beware of Redheads (short); Blood on the Sun; Nob Hill; Along Came Jones; The Shanghai Cobra; The Man from Oklahoma; Arson Squad; The Strange Affair of Uncle Harry; Men in Her Diary; Scarlet Street; The Naughty Nineties; Blonde from Brooklyn; Honeymoon Ahead; It's a Pleasure! 1946 To Each His Own; The Cat Creeps; Sheriff of Redwood Valley; One Exciting Week; Blondie Knows Best; Traffic in Crime; Lone Star Moonlight. 1947 Cigarette Girl.

LOFTUS, CECILIA "CISSIE"
Born: Oct. 22, 1876, Glasgow, Scotland. Died: July 12, 1943, New York, N.Y. (heart attack). Screen, stage and vaudeville actress.

Appeared in: 1913 Lady of Quality. 1917 Diana of Dobson's. 1929 Famous Impersonations (short). 1931 Doctor's Wives; Young Sinners; East Lynn. 1935 Once in a Blue Moon. 1939 The Old Maid; The Dead End Kids on Dress Parade (aka On Dress Parade). 1940 It's a Date; The Bluebird; Lucky Partners. 1941 The Black Cat.

LOFTUS, WILLIAM C.
Born: 1862. Died: Mar. 11, 1931, Hollywood, Calif. (hit by auto). Screen actor.

LOGAN, ELLA
Born: Mar. 6, 1913, Glasgow, Scotland. Died: May 1, 1969, San Mateo, Calif. Screen, stage, vaudeville actress and vocalist.

Appeared in: 1936 Flying Hostess. 1937 Top of the Town; Woman Chases Man; 52nd Street. 1938 The Goldwyn Follies.

LOGAN, JANET
Born: 1919. Died: Oct. 23, 1965, Glendale, Calif. Screen, radio and television actress.

LOGAN, JOHN
Born: 1924. Died: Dec. 7, 1972, San Pedro, Calif. (auto accident). Screen actor.

Appeared in: 1970 Beyond the Valley of the Dolls.

LOGAN, STANLEY
Born: June 12, 1885, Earlsfield, England. Died: Jan. 30, 1953, New York. Screen, stage actor, stage producer, film producer, director and screenwriter.

Appeared in: 1918 What Would a Gentleman Do? 1919 As He was Born. 1939 We Are Not Alone. 1940 My Son, My Son; Women in War; South of Suez. 1941 Submarine Zone (aka Escape to Glory); Singapore Woman; Wedding Worries (short). 1942 Counter Espionage; Nightmare; Unexpected Riches (short). 1943 Two Tickets to London. 1944 The Return of the Vampire. 1945 Wilson. 1946 Three Strangers; Home Sweet Homicide. 1949 Double Crossbones; Sword in the Desert. 1950 Young Daniel Boone. 1951 Pride of Maryland. 1952 The Prisoner of Zenda; Five Fingers; With a Song in My Heart.

LOHMAN, ZALLA
Born: 1906, Yugoslavia. Died: July 17, 1967, Hollywood, Calif. Screen actress. Appeared in silent films.

LOHR, MARIE
Born: July 28, 1890, Sydney, Australia. Died: Jan. 21, 1975, London, England. Screen, stage and television actress.

Appeared in: 1932 Aren't We All? (film debut). 1934 My Heart is Calling You (US 1935); Road House. 1935 Oh Daddy! 1936 Whom the Gods Love (aka Mozart—US 1940); It's You I Want. 1938 South Riding; Pygmalion. 1940 George and Margaret. 1941 Major Barbara. 1942 Went the Day Well? (aka 48 Hours—US 1944). 1945 The Rake's Progress (aka Notorious Gentleman—US 1946). 1946 The Magic Bow (US 1947). 1947 The Ghosts of Berkeley Square. 1948 Counterblast; The Winslow Boy (US 1950); Anna Karenina. 1949 Silent Dust. 1952 Little Big Shot. 1953 Always a Bride (US 1954). 1955 Escapade (US 1957); Out of the Clouds (US 1957). 1956 A Town Like Alice (US 1957). 1957 Seven Waves Away (aka Abandon Ship—US); Small Hotel. 1959 Carlton-Browne of the F.O. (aka Man in a Cocked Hat—US 1960). 1967 Great Catherine (US 1968).

LOMAS, HERBERT
Born: 1887, Burnley, England. Died: Apr. 11, 1961, Devonshire, England. Screen, stage and television actor.

Appeared in: 1931 Hobson's Choice (film debut); Many Waters. 1932 The Missing Rembrandt; When London Sleeps; The Sign of the Four; Frail Women. 1933 Daughters of Today; The Man from Toronto. 1934 Java Head (US 1935). 1935 The Phantom; Black Mask; Fighting Stock; Lorna Doone. 1936 Rembrandt; The Ghost Goes West; Fame. 1937 Knight Without Armour. 1938 South Riding. 1939 Inquest; Jamaica Inn; Ask a Policeman; The Lion Has Wings (US 1940). 1940 Mr. Borland Thinks Again. 1941 The Ghost Train; South American George; Penn of Pennsylvania (aka The Courageous Mr. Penn—US 1944). 1943 They Met in the Dark (US 1945). 1945 I Know Where I'm Going (US 1947). 1947 The Man Within (aka The Smugglers—US 1948); Master of Bankdam (US 1949). 1948 The Guinea Pig (US 1949); Bonnie Prince Charlie. 1951 The Magic Box (US 1952). 1953 The Net (aka Project M7—US).

LOMAS, JACK M.
Born: 1911. Died: May 13, 1959, Hollywood, Calif. Screen actor.

Appeared in: 1952 April in Paris. 1957 Copper Sky; The Night Runner; The Shadow on the Window. 1955 Seven Angry Men. 1956 That Certain Feeling. 1958 Cattle Empire.

LOMAX, LOUIS
Born: Aug. 16, 1922, Valdosta, Ga. Died: July 31, 1970, Santa Rosa, New Mexico (auto accident). Black television commentator, screen actor and writer.

Appeared in: 1968 Wild in the Streets.

LOMBARD, CAROLE (Jane Peters)
Born: Oct. 6, 1909, Fort Wayne, Ind. Died: Jan. 16, 1942, near Las Vegas (air crash). Screen actress. Divorced from actor William Powell. Married to actor Clark Gable (dec. 1960).

Appeared in: 1921 The Perfect Crime. 1925 Marriage in Transit; Hearts and Spurs; Durand of the Bad Lands. 1928 Power; Me, Gangster; Show Folks; Ned McCobb's Daughter; Divine Sinner. 1929 Big News; The Racketeer; Dynamite; High Voltage; Parachute. 1930 Fast and Loose; Safety in Numbers; The Arizona Kid; It Pays to Advertise. 1931 Man of the World; 1932 Ladies' Man; No Man of Her Own; Up Pops the Devil; I Take This Woman; Sinners in the Sun; No More Orchids; Virtue; No One Man. 1933 White Woman; The Match King; Supernatural; From Hell to Heaven; Brief Moment; Billion Dollar Scandal; The Eagle and the Hawk. 1934 Bolero; The Gay Bride; Now and

Forever; 20th Century; We're Not Dressing; Lady by Choice. **1935** Hands across the Table; Rumba. **1936** My Man Godfrey; Love before Breakfast; The Princess Comes Across. **1937** Swing High, Swing Low; Nothing Sacred; True Confession. **1938** Fools for Scandal. **1939** Made for Each Other; In Name Only; Vigil in the Night. **1940** They Knew What They Wanted. **1941** Mr. and Mrs. Smith; To Be or Not To Be. **1964** Big Parade of Comedy (documentary).

LOMBARDO, CARMEN
Born: 1904. Died: Apr. 17, 1971, North Miami, Fla. (cancer). Musician (saxophonist), songwriter and screen actor. Brother of bandleader Guy Lombardo.

Appeared in: **1934** Many Happy Returns.

LONDON, JACK
Born: 1905, British Guiana. Died: May 31, 1966, London, England. Screen actor and pianist.

LONDON, TOM (Leonard Clapham)
Born: Aug. 24, 1893, Louisville, Ky. Died: Dec. 5, 1963, North Hollywood, Calif. Screen and television actor.

Appeared in: **1903** The Great Train Robbery. **1917** Lone Larry. **1924** The Loser's End. **1925** The Demon Rider; Ranchers and Rascals; Three in Exile; Winds of Chance. **1926** Snowed In (serial); Chasing Trouble; Code of the Northwest; The Grey Devil; West of the Rainbow's End; Dangerous Traffic. **1927** Return of the Riddle Rider (serial); King of Kings; Border Blackbirds; The Devil's Twin; The Long Loop of the Pecos. **1928** The Mystery Rider (serial); The Yellow Cameo (serial); The Apache Raider; The Boss of Rustler's Roost; The Bronc Stomper; Put 'Em Up; Yellow Contraband; The Price of Fear. **1929** Lawless Region; The Devil's Twin; Hell's Heroes; The Harvest of Hate; Untamed Justice; The Border Wildcat. **1930** Troopers Three; The Third Alarm; Romance of the West; Firebrand Jordan; The Woman Racket; The Storm; All Quiet on the Western Front; Borrowed Wives. **1931** Under Texas Skies; Westbound; Air Police; Two Gun Man; Trails of the Golden West; Range Law; The Arizona Terror; Lightnin' Smith Returns; Secret Six; Hell Divers; River's End; East of Borneo; The Men in Her Life; Dishonored. **1932** Night Rider; Gold; Beyond the Rockies; The Boiling Point; Trailing the Killer; Without Honors; Freaks; Dr. Jekyll and Mr. Hyde. **1933** Iron Master; Outlaw Justice; The Fugitive; Sunset Pass; One Year Later. **1934** Mystery Ranch; Outlaw's Highway; Fighting Hero; Mystery Mountains (serial); Burn 'Em up Barnes. **1935** Tumbling Tumbleweeds; The Miracle Rider (serial); Toll of the Desert; Courage of the North; The Sagebrush Troubadour; Just My Luck; The Last of the Clintons; Hong Kong Nights; Skull and Crown; Gun Play. **1936** The Lawless Nineties; Guns and Guitars; O'Malley of the Mounted; The Border Patrolman; Heroes of the Range. **1937** Bar-Z Bad Men; Law of the Range; Roaring Timber; Springtime in the Rockies; Western Gold. **1938** Prairie Moon; Pioneer Trail; Six Shootin' Sheriff; Phantom Ranger; Outlaws of Sonora; Riders of the Black Hills; Santa Fe Stampede; Sunset Trail. **1939** Rollin' Westward; Mexicali Rose; The Renegade Ranger; Southward Ho!; The Night Riders; Mountain Rhythm; Roll, Wagons, Roll; Song of the Buckaroo. **1940** Westbound Stage; Gaucho Serenade; Shooting High; Ghost Valley Raiders; Hi-Yo, Silver; Covered Wagon Days; Wild Horse Range; Stage to Chino; Trailing Double Trouble; Melody Ranch; The Kid from Santa Fe; Lone Star Raiders. **1941** Dude Cowboy; Robbers of the Range; Land of the Open Range; Romance of the Rio Grande; Pals of the Pecos; Twilight on the Trail; Ridin' On a Rainbow; Stick to Your Guns; Fugitive Valley. **1942** West of Tombstone; Stardust on the Sage; Down Texas Way; Arizona Terrors; Ghost Town Law; Cowboy Serenade; Sons of the Pioneers; American Empire. **1943** Tenting Tonight on the Old Camp Ground; The Renegade; Wild Horse Stampede; False Colors; Daredevils of the West; Hail to the Rangers; Shadows on the Sage; Wagon Tracks West; Fighting Frontier. **1944** Yellow Rose of Texas; Sheriff of Sundown; Code of the Prairie; The Cheyenne; Beneath Western Skies; The San Antonio Kid; Hidden Valley Outlaws; Vigilantes of Dodge City; Stagecoach to Monterey; Firebrands of Arizona; The Cheyenne Wildcat; Faces in the Fog; Three Little Sisters; Thoroughbreds. **1945** Colorado Pioneers; Three's a Crowd; Don't Fence Me In; Sunset in Eldorado; Corpus Christi Bandits; Wagon Wheels Westward; Marshal of Laredo; The Cherokee Flash; Oregon Trail; Trail of Kit Carson; Rough Riders of Cheyenne; The Topeka Terror; Sheriff of Cimarron; Grissly's Millions; Earl Carroll Vanities; Behind City Lights. **1946** Sheriff of Redwood Valley; Days of Buffalo Bill; Crime of the Century; Out California Way; California Gold Rush; The Undercover Woman; Alias Billy the Kid; Roll on Texas Moon; Rio Grande Raiders; The Invisible Informer; Man from Rainbow Valley; Red River Renegades; Murder in the Music Hall; Passkey to Danger. **1947** Last Frontier Uprising; Homesteaders of Paradise Valley; Twilight on the Rio Grande; Santa Fe Uprising; Saddle Pals; Wyoming; Marshal of Cripple Creek; Rustlers of Devil's Canyon; Thunder Gap Outlaws; Along the Oregon Trail; The Wind Frontier; Shootin' Irons; Under Colorado Skies; Code of the Plains. **1948** Mark of the Lash; Marshal of Amarillo. **1949** Brand of Fear; Sand; Red Desert; Riders in the Sky; Frontier Investigator; South of Rio; San Antone Ambush. **1950** The Old Frontier; Code of the Pony Express; The Blazing Hills (aka The Blazing Sun). **1951** The Secret of Convict Lake; Hills of Utah; Rough Riders of Durango. **1952** The Old West; High Noon; Trail Guide; Blue Canadian Rockies; Apache Country. **1953** Pack Train; The Marshal's Daughter. **1958** The Lone Texan; The Saga of Hemp Brown. **1961** Underworld. **1962** 13 West Street.

LONERGAN, LESTER
Born: 1869. Died: Aug. 13, 1931, Lynn, Mass. Screen, stage actor, film director and stage producer. Father of actor Lester Lonergan, Jr. (dec. 1959). Entered films with Thanhauser Co.

Appeared in: **1929** Seven Faces.

LONERGAN, LESTER, JR.
Born: 1894. Died: Dec. 23, 1959, New York, N.Y. Screen, stage, vaudeville, television actor and stage director. Son of actor Lester Lonergan (dec. 1931).

Appeared in: **1947** Boomerang.

LONG, FREDERIC
Born: 1857. Died: Oct. 18, 1941, Hollywood, Calif. Screen, stage and vaudeville actor.

Appeared in: **1929** The Lost Patrol.

LONG, JACK
Died: Aug. 7, 1938, Los Angeles, Calif. (motorcycle accident). Screen actor and stuntman.

Appeared in: **1933** Police Car. **1934** Speed Wings. **1937** The Sitter-Downers (short).

LONG, LURAY (Luray Roble)
Born: Dec. 3, 1890, Wis. Died: Jan. 2, 1919, Los Angeles, Calif. (Spanish influenza). Screen actress. Married to actor Walter Long (dec. 1952).

LONG, MELVYN HARRY
Born: 1895. Died: Nov. 14, 1940, Los Angeles, Calif. (stroke). Screen, stage and vaudeville actor.

Appeared in: **1940** Queen of the Yukon. **1941** Meet John Doe.

LONG, NICK, JR.
Born: 1906, Greenlawn, N.Y. Died: Aug. 31, 1949, New York, N.Y. (results of an auto accident). Screen, stage and vaudeville actor. Son of actor Nick Long.

Appeared in: **1935** Broadway Melody of 1936. **1936** King of Burlesque.

LONG, RICHARD
Born: Dec. 17, 1927, Chicago, Ill. Died: Dec. 22, 1974, Los Angeles, Calif. (heart ailment). Screen and television actor. Married to actress Suzan Ball (dec. 1955) and later married to actress Mara Corday.

Appeared in: **1946** Tomorrow is Forever (film debut); The Stranger; The Dark Mirror. **1947** The Egg and I. **1948** Tap Roots. **1949** Ma and Pa Kettle; Criss Cross; The Life of Riley. **1950** Kansas Raiders; Ma and Pa Kettle Go to Town. **1951** Ma and Pa Kettle Back on the Farm; Air Cadet. **1952** Back at the Front. **1953** The All-American; All I Desire. **1954** Saskatchewan; Playgirl; Return to Treasure Island. **1955** Cult of the Cobra. **1956** Fury at Gunsight Pass; He Laughed Last. **1958** House on Haunted Hill. **1959** Tokyo After Dark. **1960** Home from the Hill. **1963** Follow the Boys. **1964** Tenderfoot. **1967** Make Like a Thief.

LONG, WALTER
Born: Mar. 5, 1879, Milford, N.H. Died: July 4, 1952, Los Angeles, Calif. (heart attack). Screen, stage actor and film director. Married to actress Luray Long (dec. 1919). Entered films in 1909.

Appeared in: **1915** The Birth of a Nation. **1916** Intolerance. **1917** The Evil Eye; The Little America. **1918** The Queen of the Sea. **1919** The Mother and the Law; Scarlet Days. **1920** What Women Love; The Fighting Shepherdess; Go and Get It. **1921** The Fire Cat; The Sheik; Tiger True; A Giant of His Race; White and Unmarried. **1922** Moran of the Lady Letty; The Dictator; Blood and Sand; Across the Continent; The Beautiful and Damned; My American Wife; Omar the Tentmaker; To Have and to Hold; South of Suva; Shadows. **1923** Kick In; The Broken Wing; Desire; The Call of the Wild; His Great Chance; Little Church around the Corner; The Isle of Lost Ships; Quicksands; The Shock; A Shot in the Night; The Huntress; The Last Hour. **1924** Daring Love; The Ridin' Kid from Powder River; Yankee Madness; Wine; White Man; Missing Daughters. **1925** Soul-Fire; Raffles; The Amateur Cracksman; The Verdict; Bobbed Hair; The Lady; The Reckless Sex; The Road to Yesterday; The Shock Punch. **1926** Eve's Leaves; Red Dice; Steel Preferred; The Highbinders; West of Broadway. **1927** White Pants Willie; Back to God's Country; The Yankee Clipper; Jewels of Desire; Jim the Conqueror. **1928** Gang War; Me, Gangster; Forbidden Grass; Thundergod. **1929** Black Cargoes of the South Seas; The Black Watch. **1930** Beau Bandit; Conspiracy; Moby Dick; The Steel Highway. **1931** Sea Devils; Taxi Troubles (short); The Maltese Falcon; Other Men's Women; Souls of the Slums; Pardon Us. **1932** Dragnet Patrol; Escapade; Any Old Port (short). **1933** Women Won't Tell. **1934** Three Little Bigskin's (short); The Live Ghost (short); Going Bye Bye (short); Six of a Kind; Operator 13; Lightning Strikes Twice. **1935** Naughty Marietta. **1936** Drift Fence; The Glory Trail; The Beloved Rogue; The Bold Caballero. **1937** Pick a Star; North of the Rio Grande. **1938** The Painted Trail; Bar 20 Justice; Six-Shootin' Sheriff; Man's Country. **1939** Wild Horse Canyon. **1941** Silver

Stallion; Ridin' On a Rainbow; City of Missing Girls. **1948** No More Relatives (short). **1950** Wabash Avenue.

LONSDALE, HARRY G.
Born: Dec. 6 (?), Worcester, England. Died: June 12, 1923. Screen, stage actor and opera performer.

Appeared in: **1912** The Devil, the Servant and the Man; An Unexpected Fortune; When Women Rule. **1913** Master of the Garden. **1915** Ebbtide. **1916** The Ne-er-Do-Well; The Brand of Cain. **1917** Conscience; The Garden of Allah. **1918** Beware of Strangers. **1919** The Illustrious Prince; The Last of His People; Shepherd of the Hills. **1920** The Week-end. **1921** The Mask; The Night Horsemen; Payment Guaranteed; Where Men are Men. **1922** Thelma; The Call of Home; The Fighting Guide; A Fool There Was; The Great Night; Monte Cristo; The Rosary. **1924** The Last of the Duanes; The Vagabond Trail. **1925** Her Husband's Secret; Brand of Cowardice.

LONTOC, LEON
Born: 1909. Died: Jan. 22, 1974, Los Angeles, Calif. Screen and television actor.

Appeared in: **1950** On the Isle of Samoa. **1951** I Was an American Spy; Peking Express. **1953** City Beneath the Sea. **1954** The Naked Jungle. **1955** Jump Into Hell; The Left Hand of God. **1956** The Revolt of Mamie Stover. **1960** Gallant Hours. **1962** The Spiral Road. **1963** The Ugly American. **1966** One Spy Too Many. **1968** Panic in the City.

LOONG, LEE SIU. *See* BRUCE LEE

LOOP, PHIL
Died: June 11, 1975. Screen actor.

LOOS, THEODOR
Born: 1883, Germany. Died: June 27, 1954, Stuttgart, West Germany. Stage and screen actor.

Appeared in: **1925** Siegfried. **1926** Manon Lescaut. **1927** Mr. Metropolis. **1928** Kriemhild's Revenge. **1929** The Weavers. **1931** Die Grosse Sehnsucht; In Geheimdienst (In the Employ of the Secret Service). **1932** Der Fall des Oberst Redl; 1914: The Last Days before the War; Ich Geh' aus und Du Bleibst da; Yorck. **1933** Halzapfel Weiss Alles; Tod Ueber Schanghai. **1934** Die Blonde Christl; Trenck. **1956** Circus Girl (US).

LOPER, DON
Born: 1906, Toledo, Ohio. Died: Nov. 22, 1972, Santa Monica, Calif. (complications following a lung puncture). Fashion designer, screen actor and dancer.

Appeared in: **1943** Thousands Cheer. **1944** Lady in the Dark. **1945** It's a Pleasure.

LOPEZ, CARLOS (Carlos Chaflan Lopez y Valles)
Born: Nov. 4, 1887, Durango, Mexico. Died: Feb. 13, 1942, Tapachula, Mexico (drowned). Stage and screen actor.

Appeared in: **1925** El Aguila y el Nopal. **1933** Sobre las Olas; Una Vida por Otra. **1934** El Compadre Mendoza; El Escandalo; Clemencia; La Sangre Manda; Quien mato a Eva. **1935** Hu Hijo; Chucho El Roto; Oro y Plata; Silencio Subline; Mujeres sin Alma; Martin Garatuza; Corazon Bandolero; Cruz Diablo; Juarez y Maximiliano; El Tesora de Pancho Villa; Monja u Casada; Virgen y Martir; Payada de la vida. **1936** Vamanos Con Pancho Villa; El Baul Macabro (The Big Trunk); Alla en el Rancho Grande (Three on the Big Ranch); Cielito Lindo. **1938** Ave sin Rumbo (Wandering Bird); Rancho Grande. **1939** El Inio.

LOPEZ, TONY
Born: 1902, Mexico. Died: Sept. 23, 1949, Hollywood, Calif. Screen actor.

LOPEZ, VINCENT (Vincent Joseph Lopez)
Born: Dec. 10, 1898, Brooklyn, N.Y. Died: Sept. 20, 1975, Miami Beach, Florida (liver and pancreas failure). Orchestra leader, radio performer and screen actor.

Appeared in: **1932** The Big Broadcast. **1933** Universal, Warner Bros., Metro and Paramount shorts. **1940** Vitaphone shorts.

LORCH, THEODORE A.
Born: 1873, Springfield, Ill. Died: Nov. 12, 1947, Hollywood, Calif. Screen, stage and vaudeville actor.

Appeared in: **1921** Gasoline Gus. **1923** Shell Shocked Sammy. **1924** The Sea Hawk; Westbound. **1925** Heir-Loons; Once in a Lifetime; Where the Worst Begins; Manhattan Madness; The Man on the Box. **1926** Across the Pacific; Unknown Dangers; The Better 'Ole. **1927** Black Jack; King of Kings; Sailor Izzy Murphy; Tracked by the Police. **1928** Ginsberg the Great; The Canyon of Adventure; Grip of the Yukon. **1929** Show Boat; The Royal Rider; Wild Blood; Spite Marriage. **1930** The Runaway Bride; plus the following shorts: An Ill Wind; The Border Patrol; More Sinned against Than Usual. **1933** Black Beauty; The Whirlwind. **1934** The Mighty Barnum. **1935** Rustler's Paradise; Unciv-

il Warriors (short); Hold 'Em Yale. **1936** Romance Rides the Range; Rebellion. **1937** The Big Squirt (short); Goofs and Saddles (short). **1945** If a Body Meets a Body (short). **1946** Uncivil Warbirds (short). **1947** Half-Wits Holiday (short). **1948** Hot Scots (short).

LORD, MARION
Born: 1883. Died: May 25, 1942, Hollywood, Calif. Screen and stage actress.

Appeared in: **1929** Broadway. **1930** Queen of Scandal. **1931** One Heavenly Night. **1935** Salesmanship Ahoy (short).

LORD, PAULINE
Born: 1890, Hanford, Calif. Died: Oct. 11, 1950, Alamogordo, N.M. (heart trouble). Stage and screen actress.

Appeared in: **1934** Mrs. Wiggs of the Cabbage Patch. **1935** A Feather in Her Hat.

LORD, PHILIP F. (Philip Francis Lord)
Born: 1879. Died: Nov. 25, 1968, Chicago, Ill. (heart ailment). Screen, stage, television and radio actor.

LORD, PHILLIPS H. (Phillips Haynes Lord aka SETH PARKER)
Born: July 13, 1902, Hartford, Vt. Died: Oct. 19, 1975, Ellsworth, Maine. Radio, television writer, radio actor, producer and screen actor.

Appeared in: **1929** Silver King. **1932** Way Back Home. **1935** Obeah.

LORDE, ATHENA
Born: 1915. Died: May 23, 1973, Van Nuys, Calif. (cancer). Screen, radio and television actress. Married to actor Jim Boles. Mother of actress Barbara and actor Eric Boles.

Appeared in: **1958** Marjorie Morningstar. **1965** Hush, Hush, Sweet Charlotte. **1968** Firecreek. **1969** Angel in My Pocket; Fuzz. **1971** How to Frame a Figg. **1973** Dr. Death—Seeker of Souls.

LORENZON, LIVIO (aka CHARLIE LAWRENCE)
Born: May 6, 1926, Trieste, Italy. Died: Dec. 23, 1971, Latisana, Italy. Screen actor.

Appeared in: **1953** Ombre Su Trieste. **1957** El Amamei; L'Inferno Trema. **1958** Captain Fuoco; Il Cavaliere del Castello Maledetto; Il Figlio del Corsaro Rosso. **1959** L'Arcierre Nero; El Terrore della Maschera Rossa; Il Vedovo; Il Terrore dell' Oklahoma; I Reali di Francia; La Sceriffa; La Grande Guerra (The Great War—US 1961). **1960** Cavalcata Selvaggia; Le Signore; La Venere dei Pirati; La Furia dei Barbari (Fury of the Barbarians aka Fury of the Pagans—US 1963); Il Pirati della Costa. **1961** La Rivolta dei Mercenari; Una Spada Nell 'Ombra; I Masnadieri; Il Segreto dello Sparviero; La Vendetta di Ursus; Ponzio Pilato; Il Terrore del Mare (Terror of the Sea, aka Guns of the Black Witch—US); El Gladiatore Invincible (The Invincible Gladiator—US 1963). **1962** Zorro alla Corte di Spagna; Tharus Figlio di Attila; Un 'Ora per Vivere; I Sette Gladiatori; L'Ultimo Czar (The Last Czar aka The Night They Killed Rasputin). **1963** Maciste L'Eroe Piu 'Grande del Mondo (aka Goliath and the Sins of Babylon—US); Frenesia dell 'Estate; Zorro E I Tre Moschettiert. **1964** Ercole Contro I Tiranni di Babilonia; Ercole Contro Roma; Il Figlio di Cleopatra; Jim Il Primo; La Vendetta dei Gladiatori. **1965** Colorado Charlie; Ercole, Sansome, Maciste e Ursus gli Invincibili; Il Gladiatore che Sfido L'Impero. **1966** The Secret Seven; Il Buono, Il Brutto, Il Cattivo (The Good, the Bad and the Ugly—US 1967). **1967** Colpo Maestro di Sua Maestra' Britannica; Texas Addio; Cjamango. **1969** Ace High.

LORNE, CONSTANCE (Constance MacLaurin)
Born: Apr. 26, 1914, Peebles, Scotland. Died: Dec. 21, 1969, London, England. Stage and screen actress. Entered films in 1948.

Appeared in: **1951** One Wild Oat. **1952** Curtain Up (US 1953).

LORNE, MARION (M. L. MacDougal)
Born: 1888, Pa. Died: May 9, 1968, New York, N.Y. (heart attack). Screen, stage and television actress.

Appeared in: **1951** Strangers on a Train. **1955** The Girl Rush. **1967** The Graduate.

LORRAINE, BETTY
Born: June 30, 1908, Louisville, Ky. Died: Sept. 1, 1944. Stage and screen actress.

Appeared in: **1929** Red Wine; When Caesar Ran a Newspaper (short). **1933** A Bedtime Story.

LORRAINE, LEOTA
Born: 1893, Kansas City, Mo. Died: July 9, 1975. Screen actress.

Appeared in: **1915** Rule Sixty Three. **1917** Feet of Clay; The Promise. **1918** Playing the Game; The Kaiser's Shadow; A Daughter of the West; The Finger of Justice. **1919** The Pest; The Gay Lord Quex; Be a Little Sport; Luck in Pawn; The Girl Dodger. **1920** The Turning Point; Her Five Foot Highness;

The Misfit Wife; The Loves of Letty. 1924 The Bowery Bishop. 1925 Infatuation. 1929 The Woman I Love. 1935 Ruggles of Red Gap; Sprucin' Up (short). 1938 His Pest Friend (short).

LORRAINE, OSCAR
Born: 1878. Died: May 10, 1955, Hollywood, Calif. Screen and vaudeville actor. Was partner in vaudeville team of "Lorraine and Starr."

LORRE, PETER
Born: June 26, 1904, Rosenberg, Hungary. Died: Mar. 23, 1964, Hollywood, Calif. (stroke). Screen, stage and television actor. Divorced from actress Karen Verne (dec. 1967) and later married to Anna Brenning; father of actor Peter Lorre, Jr.

Appeared in: 1928 Pioniere in Inoplastadt; Springs Awakening. 1931 Thirteen Trunks of Mr. O.F.; White Demon; De Haute A Bas; The Man Who Knew Too Much. 1932 F.P.I. Antwortet Nicht. 1933 "M"; What Women Dream. 1934 The Man Who Knew Too Much. 1935 Mad Love (aka The Hands of Orlac); Crime and Punishment. 1936 The Hidden Power; The Secret Agent; Crack-Up. 1937 Nancy Steele is Missing; Think Fast, Mr. Moto; Lancer Spy; Thank You, Mr. Moto. 1938 Mr. Moto Takes a Chance; Mr. Moto's Gamble; The Mysterious Mr. Moto; I'll Give a Million. 1939 Mr. Moto Takes a Vacation; Mr. Moto's Last Warning; Mr. Moto in Danger Island; Confessions of a Nazi Spy. 1940 Strange Cargo; I Was an Adventuress; Island of Doomed Men; The Stranger on the Third Floor; You'll Find Out. 1941 The Face Behind the Mask; Mr. District Attorney; They Met in Bombay; The Maltese Falcon. 1942 All through the Night; Invisible Agent; The Boogie Man Will Get You; Casablanca; In This Our Life. 1943 The Constant Nymph; Background to Danger; The Cross of Lorraine. 1944 Passage to Marseilles; The Mask of Dimitrios; The Conspirators; Arsenic and Old Lace; Hollywood Canteen. 1945 Hotel Berlin; Confidential Agent. 1946 Three Strangers; The Verdict; The Black Angel; The Chase; The Beast with Five Fingers. 1947 My Favorite Brunette. 1948 Casbah. 1949 Rope of Sand. 1950 Quicksand; Double Confession (US 1953). 1951 Die Verlorne (German). 1954 Beat the Devil; 20,000 Leagues under the Sea. 1956 Congo Crossing; Meet Me in Las Vegas; Around the World in 80 Days. 1957 The Buster Keaton Story; The Story of Mankind; The Sad Sack; Silk Stockings. 1958 Hell Ship Mutiny. 1959 The Big Circus. 1960 Scene of Mystery. 1961 Voyage to the Bottom of the Sea. 1962 Five Weeks in a Balloon; Tales of Terror. 1963 The Raven; The Comedy of Terrors. 1964 Muscle Beach Party; The Patsy.

LOSCH, TILLY (Ottilie Ethel Losch)
Born: Nov. 15, 1902, Vienna, Austria. Died: Dec. 24, 1975, New York, N.Y. (cancer). Screen, stage actress, dancer and painter.

Appeared in: 1936 The Garden of Allah. 1937 The Good Earth. 1946 Duel in the Sun.

LOSEE, FRANK
Born: 1856. Died: Nov. 14, 1937, Yonkers, N.Y. (pulmonary embolism). Stage and screen actor.

Appeared in: 1915 The Masqueraders; The Old Homestead. 1916 Ashes of Embers; Hulda from Holland. 1917 The Valentine Girl. 1918 La Tosca; Uncle Tom's Cabin; The Song of Songs; In Pursuit of Polly. 1919 His Parisian Wife; Here Comes the Bride. 1920 Lady Rose's Daughter. 1921 Dangerous Toys; Orphans of the Storm; Such a Little Queen; Disraeli. 1922 False Fronts; The Man She Brought Back; Man Wanted; The Seventh Day; Missing Millions. 1923 As a Man Lives. 1924 The Speed Spook; Unguarded Women. 1935 Four Hours to Kill; Annapolis Farewell.

LOTHAR, HANNS
Born: Hanover, Germany. Died: Mar. 11, 1967, Hamburg, Germany (heart attack). Screen, stage and television actor.

Appeared in: 1959 Menschen im Netz (Unwilling Agent—US 1968); Buddenbrooks (US 1962). 1961 One, Two, Three; Bis zum Ende Aller Tage (Girl from Hong Kong—US 1966). 1964 Polizeirevier Davidswache (Seven Consenting Adults—US 1970); Schloss Gripholm (The Gripholm Castle).

LOTINGA, ERNEST (aka DAN ROY)
Born: 1876, Sunderland, England. Died: Oct. 28, 1951. Screen, stage, vaudeville actor, screenwriter and stage producer.

Appeared in: 1928 The Raw Recruit (short); The Orderly Room (short); Nap (short); Joining Up (short). 1929 Josser, KC (short); Doing his Duty (short); Acci-dental Treatment (short); Spirits (short). 1931 P.C. Josser; Dr. Josser, KC. 1932 Josser Joins the Navy; Josser on the River; Josser in the Army. 1934 Josser on the Farm. 1935 Smith's Wives. 1936 Love Up the Pole.

LOUDEN, THOMAS
Born: 1874. Died: Mar. 15, 1948, Hollywood, Calif. (stroke). Stage and screen actor.

Appeared in: 1938 Kidnapped; Prison Break. 1939 Our Leading Citizen. 1940 Safari. 1942 Mrs. Miniver; Are Husbands Necessary. 1945 The Corn Is Green; Dangerous Partners. 1946 Tomorrow Is Forever.

LOUGHRAN, LEWIS
Born: 1950. Died: Feb. 24, 1975. Screen actor.

LOUIS, WILLARD
Born: 1886. Died: July 22, 1926, Glendale, Calif. (typhoid fever and pneumonia). Stage and screen actor.

Appeared in: 1920 Going Some; Madame X. 1921 Moonlight and Honeysuckle; Roads of Destiny. 1922 The Man Unconquerable; Robin Hood; Too Much Wife; Only a Shop Girl. 1923 Vanity Fair; McGuire of the Mounted; Daddies; The French Doll; The Marriage Market. 1924 Beau Brummell; Babbitt; The Lover of Camille; Three Women; Pal O' Mine; A Lady of Quality; The Age of Innocence; Broadway after Dark; Don't Doubt Your Husband; Her Marriage Vow. 1925 A Broadway Butterfly; Eve's Lover; Kiss Me Again; Three Weeks in Paris; The Man without a Conscience; His Secretary; Hogan's Alley; The Limited Mail; The Love Hour. 1926 Mlle. Modiste; Don Juan; The Honeymoon Express; The Love Toy; The Shamrock Handicap; The Passionate Quest. 1928 A Certain Young Man.

LOUISE, ANITA (Anita Louise Fremault)
Born: Jan. 9, 1915, New York, N.Y. Died: Apr. 25, 1970, West Los Angeles, Calif. (massive stroke). Screen, stage and television actress. Married to producer Buddy Adler (dec.) and later to importer Henry Berger.

Appeared in: 1920 The Sixth Commandment (film debut at age 5). 1927 The Music Master; The Life of Franz Schubert (short). 1929 Wonder of Women; Square Shoulders; The Marriage Playground. 1930 The Floradora Girl; What a Man!; Just Like Heaven; The Third Alarm. 1931 The Great Meadow; Heaven on Earth; Everything's Rosie; Millie; Madame Julie; Marriage Interlude; Fraternity House; Are These Our Children?; The Woman Between. 1932 Pack up Your Troubles; Phantom of Crestwood; Duck Soup. 1933 Little Women; Our Betters. 1934 The Most Precious Thing in Life; Are We Civilized?; Madame du Barry; The Firebrand; Cross Streets; Bachelor of Arts; I Give My Love; Judge Priest. 1935 Here's to Romance; Personal Maid's Secret; Midsummer Night's Dream; Lady Tubbs; The Story of Louis Pasteur. 1936 Anthony Adverse; Brides Are Like That. 1937 The Go Getter; That Certain Woman; Green Light; Call It a Day; First Lady; Tovarich. 1938 Going Places; Marie Antoinette; My Bill; The Sisters. 1939 These Glamour Girls; Reno; The Little Princess; The Gorilla; Main Street Lawyer; Hero for a Day; The Personality Kid. 1940 Glamour for Sale; Wagons Westward; The Villain Still Pursued Her. 1941 Harmon of Michigan; Two in a Taxi; The Phantom Submarine. 1943 Dangerous Blondes. 1944 Nine Girls; Casanova Brown. 1945 Love Letters; The Fighting Guardsman. 1946 The Bandit of Sherwood Forest; The Devil's Mask; The Swan Song; Shadowed; Personality Kid. 1947 Bulldog Drummond at Bay; Blondie's Holiday; Blondie's Big Moment. 1952 Retreat, Hell!

LOVE, LAURA
Died: Date unknown. Screen actress. Married to actor Henry Belmar (dec. 1931).

LOVE, MONTAGU (aka MONTAGUE LOVE)
Born: 1877, Portsmouth, England. Died: May 17, 1943, Beverly Hills, Calif. Screen, stage and vaudeville actor.

Appeared in: 1914 The Suicide Club. 1916 A Woman's Way; Bought and Paid For. 1917 Rasputin; The Black Monk. 1919 The Gilded Cage. 1920 The World and His Wife. 1921 The Case of Becky; The Wrong Woman; Forever; Love's Redemption; Shams of Society. 1922 What's Wrong with the Woman?; The Beauty Shop; The Darling of the Rich; The Secrets of Paris. 1923 The Eternal City; The Leopardess. 1924 Restless Wives; Week End Husbands; Roulette; Who's Cheating?; Love of Women; A Son of the Sahara; Sinners in Heaven. 1925 The Mad Marriage; The Ancient Highway; The Desert's Price. 1926 Hands Up!; Don Juan; Brooding Eyes; The Son of the Sheik; The Social Highwayman; The Silent Lover; Out of the Storm. 1927 The Night of Love; Good Time Charley; The Haunted Ship; King of Kings; Jesse James; One Hour of Love; Rose of the Golden West; The Tender Hour. 1928 The Haunted House; The Devil's Skipper; The Hawk's Nest; The Wind; The Noose; Character Studies (short). 1929 The Divine Lady; Her Private Life; A Most Immoral Lady; Synthetic Sin; The Mysterious Island; Charming Sinners; Midstream; Bulldog Drummond; The Last Warning; Silks and Saddles; The Voice Within. 1930 Back Pay; A Notorious Affair; Double Cross Roads; Reno; Inside the Lines; Outward Bound; Love Comes Along; The Cat Creeps; Kismit; The Furies. 1931 Alexander Hamilton; Lion and the Lamb. 1932 Stowaway; The Fighting Tornado; Vanity Fair; The Silver Lining; Midnight Lady; The Broadway Tornado; Love Bond; Dream Mother; The Engineer's Daughter; Out of Singapore. 1933 His Double Life. 1934 The Menace; Limehouse Blues. 1935 Clive of India; The Crusades; The Man Who Broke the Bank at Monte Carlo. 1936 The Country Doctor; Sing, Baby, Sing; Reunion; Lloyds of London; One in a Million; Sutter's Gold; The White Angel; Hi Gaucho; Champagne Charlie. 1937 The Prince and the Pauper; The Life of Emile Zola; Tovarich; Parnell; London by Night; The Prisoner of Zenda; Adventure's End; A Damsel in Distress. 1938 The Buccaneer; The Adventures of Robin Hood; Professor Beware; If I Were King; Kidnapped. 1939 Gunga Din; Ruler of the Seas; Man in the Iron Mask; Juarez; We Are Not Alone. 1940 Son of Monte Cristo; Northwest Passage; A Dispatch from Reuter's; The Lone Wolf Strikes;

Private Affairs; Hudson's Bay; Dr. Ehrlich's Magic Bullet; Northwest Mounted Police; All This and Heaven Too; The Mark of Zorro; The Sea Hawk. **1941** The Devil and Miss Jones; Shining Victory; Lady for a Night. **1942** Devotion; Tennessee Johnson; The Remarkable Andrew; Sherlock Holmes and the Voice of Terror. **1943** Forever and a Day; Constant Nymph; Holy Matrimony.

LOVE, ROBERT
Born: 1914. Died: July 8, 1948, Hollywood, Calif. (suicide—leap). Screen actor.

Appeared in: **1945** Counterattack; Blonde from Brooklyn.

LOVEJOY, FRANK
Born: Mar. 28, 1914, New York, N.Y. Died: Oct. 2, 1962, New York, N.Y. (heart attack). Screen, stage, radio and television actor. Married to actress Joan Banks.

Appeared in: **1948** Black Bart. **1949** Home of the Brave. **1950** Three Secrets; Breakthrough; South Sea Sinner; In a Lonely Place. **1951** Force of Arms; I Was a Communist for the FBI; Goodbye, My Fancy; Starlift; I'll See You in My Dreams; Try and Get Me. **1952** Retreat, Hell!; The Winning Team. **1953** The Hitch Hiker; House of Wax; The System; She's Back on Broadway; The Charge at Feather River. **1954** Beachhead; Men of the Fighting Lady. **1955** The Americano; Strategic Air Command; Mad at the World; Top of the World; Finger Man; The Crooked Web; Shack Out on 101. **1956** Julie; Country Husband. **1957** Three Brave Men. **1958** Cole Younger, Gunfighter.

LOVELL, RAYMOND
Born: Apr. 13, 1900, Montreal, Canada. Died: Oct. 2, 1953, London, England. Screen, stage actor and stage director.

Appeared in: **1934** Love, Life and Laughter; The Third Clue; Warn London. **1935** The Case of Gabriel Perry; Some Day; Crime Unlimited; Sexton Blake and the Mademoiselle. **1936** King of the Damned; Not So Dusty; Gypsy Melody; Fair Exchange; Gaol Break; Troubled Waters. **1937** Secret Lives (aka I Married a Spy—US 1938); Midnight Menace (aka Bombs Over London—US 1939); Glamorous Night; Mademoiselle Docteur; Behind Your Back. **1938** Murder Tomorrow. **1939** Q Planes (aka Clouds Over Europe—US). **1940** Contraband (aka Blackout—US). **1941** I Found a Star; The Common Touch; 49th Parallel (aka The Invaders—US 1942). **1942** Alibi; The Young Mr. Pitt; The Goose Steps Out; Uncensored (US 1944). **1943** Candlelight in Algeria (US 1944); Warn That Man; The Man In Grey (US 1945). **1944** The Way Ahead; Hotel Reserve (US 1946). **1946** Caesar and Cleopatra; Night Boat to Dublin; Appointment With Crime (US 1950). **1947** End of the River. **1948** Easy Money; Who Killed Van Loon?; The Three Weird Sisters; So Evil My Love; My Brother's Keeper (US 1949); The Blind Goddess (US 1949); Quartet; The Calendar; But Not in Vain. **1949** Once Upon a Dream; Fools Rush In; The Bad Lord Byron (US 1952); Madness of the Heart (US 1950); The Romantic Age (aka Naughty Arlette—US 1951). **1950** The Mudlark. **1952** Time Gentlemen Please!; The Pickwick Papers. **1953** The Steel Key.

LOVERIDGE, MARGUERITE. *See* MARGUERITE MARSH

LOW, JACK
Born: 1898. Died: Feb. 21, 1958, Hollywood, Calif. Screen and television actor. Entered films approx. 1930.

Appeared in: **1956** The Proud Ones.

LOWE, EDMUND
Born: Mar. 3, 1892, San Jose, Calif. Died: Apr. 21, 1971, Woodland Hills, Calif. (lung ailment). Screen, stage and television actor. Married to actress Lilyan Tashman (dec. 1934) and later married and divorced actresses Rita Kaufman and Ester Miller.

Appeared in: **1917** The Spreading Dawn. **1918** Vive La France. **1919** Eyes of Youth. **1921** The Devil; My Lady's Latchkey. **1922** Living Lies; Peacock Alley. **1923** The Silent Command; The White Flower; In the Palace of the King; Wife in Name Only. **1924** Barbara Frietchie; Honor among Men; The Brass Bowl; Nellie, The Beautiful Cloak Model. **1925** The Winding Stair; Soul Mates; The Kiss Barrier; Marriage in Transit; Greater Than a Crown; East Lynne; Ports of Call; The Fool; Champion of Lost Causes; East of Suez. **1926** What Price Glory?; Black Paradise; Soul Mates; The Palace of Pleasure; Siberia. **1927** Is Zat So?; Publicity Madness; Baloo; One Increasing Purpose; The Wizard. **1928** Happiness Ahead; Dressed to Kill; Outcast. **1929** Cock Eyed World; Making the Grade; In Old Arizona; This Thing Called Love; Thru Different Eyes. **1930** Good Intentions; Born Reckless; The Painted Angel; The Bad One; Happy Days; Men on Call; More Than a Kiss; Scotland Yard; Part Time Wife; The Squealer; The Shepper—Newfounder. **1931** Women of All Nations; The Spider; The Cisco Kid; Don't Bet on Women; Transatlantic. **1932** Attorney for the Defense; Guilty As Hell; The Misleading Lady; American Madness; Chandu, the Magician; The Devil Is Driving; The Slippery Pearls (short). **1933** Hot Pepper; I Love That Man; Her Bodyguard; Dinner at Eight. **1934** Let's Fall in Love; No More Women; Bombay Mail; Gift of Gab. **1935** Under Pressure; La Fiesta de Santa Barbara (short); The Great Hotel Murder; Black Sheep; Mr. Dynamite; The Best Man Wins; Thunder in the Night; King Solomon of Broadway; The Great Impersonation. **1936** The Grand Exit; The Wrecker; The Garden Murder Case; Mad Holiday; Doomed

Cargo; The Girl on the Front Page; Seven Sinners. **1937** Under Cover of Night; Espionage; The Squeakers (aka Murder on Diamond Row—US); Every Day's a Holiday. **1938** Secrets of a Nurse. **1939** The Witness Vanishes; Our Neighbors, the Carters; Newsboys' Home. **1940** The Crooked Road; Honeymoon Deferred; I Love You Again; Men against the Sky; Wolf of New York. **1941** Double Date; Flying Cadets. **1942** Call Out the Marines; Klondike Fury. **1943** Dangerous Blonde; Oh, What a Night!; Murder in Times Square. **1944** The Girl in the Case. **1945** Dillinger; The Enchanted Forest; The Great Mystic. **1946** The Strange Mr. Gregory. **1948** Good Sam. **1956** Around the World in 80 Days. **1957** The Wings of Eagles. **1958** The Last Hurrah. **1959** Plunderers of Painted Flats. **1960** Heller in Pink Tights.

LOWE, JAMES B.
Born: 1880. Died: May 18, 1963, Hollywood, Calif. Screen and stage actor.

Appeared in: **1925** The Demon Rider. **1926** Blue Blazes. **1927** Uncle Tom's Cabin.

LOWE, K. ELMO
Born: 1900. Died: Jan. 26, 1971, Cleveland, Ohio (stroke). Screen, stage actor and stage director. Married to actress Dorothy Paxton.

Appeared in: **1949** The Kid from Cleveland. **1950** Trial Without Jury; Woman from Headquarters.

LOWELL, DOROTHY
Born: 1916. Died: July 1, 1944, New York. Screen and radio actress. Entered films approx. 1936.

LOWELL, HELEN (Helen Lowell Robb)
Born: June 2, 1866, New York, N.Y. Died: June 28, 1937, Hollywood, Calif. Stage and screen actress.

Appeared in: **1923** Love's Old Sweet Song. **1924** Three Days to Live; Isn't Life Wonderful? **1934** Midnight Alibi; Side Street; The Dragon Murder Case; Madame du Barry; The Merry Frinks; Big Hearted Herbert; The Case of the Howling Dog. **1935** Maybe It's Love; Transient Lady; Devil Dogs of the Air; Page Miss Glory; The Goose and the Gander; Dr. Socrates; Living on Velvet; Party Wire. **1936** Strike Me Pink; Snowed Under; I'd Give My Life; Valiant is the Word for Carrie; Wild Brian Kent. **1937** Four Days Wonder; Racketeers in Exile; The Party Getter; High, Wide and Handsome.

LOWELL, JOAN (aka HELEN TRASK)
Born: 1900. Died: Nov. 7, 1967, Brasilia, Brazil. Screen, stage actress and author.

Appeared in: **1924** Loving Lies. **1925** Cold Nerve. **1934** Adventure Girl.

LOWELL, JOHN (John L. Russell)
Died: Sept. 19, 1937, Los Angeles, Calif. Screen actor and film director.

Appeared in: **1922** Ten Nights in a Barroom. **1923** Lost in a Big City. **1924** Floodgates. **1925** Red Love. **1926** The Big Show. **1928** Silent Trail; Headin' Westward. **1929** Bad Men's Money; Captain Cowboy; Fighters of the Saddle.

LOWERY, ROBERT (Robert Lowery Hanks)
Born: 1914, Kansas City, Mo. Died: Dec. 26, 1971, Hollywood, Calif. (heart attack). Screen, stage, television actor and singer. Divorced from actresses Vivian Wilcox, Rusty Farrell and Jean Parker.

Appeared in: **1937** Wake up and Live; Life Begins in College. **1938** Passport Husband; Submarine Patrol. **1939** Young Mr. Lincoln; Charlie Chan in Reno; Hollywood Cavalcade; Drums along the Mohawk; Mr. Moto in Danger Island; Tail Spin. **1940** City of Chance; Free, Blonde and Twenty-One; Shooting High; Star Dust; Charlie Chan's Murder Cruise; Four Sons; Maryland; The Mark of Zorro; Murder over New York. **1941** Private Nurse; Ride On, Vaquero!; Cadet Girls; Great Guns. **1942** Who Is Hope Schuyler?; She's in the Army; Criminal Investigator; Lure of the Islands; Rhythm Parade; Dawn on the Great Divide. **1943** The Immortal Sergeant; Tarzan's Desert Mystery; So's Your Uncle; The North Star; Campus Rhythm; Revenge of the Zombies. **1944** The Navy Way; Hot Rhythm; Dark Mountain; Dangerous Passage; The Mummy's Ghost; Mystery of the River Boat (serial); A Scream in the Dark. **1945** Thunderbolt; Homesick Angel; Road to Alcatraz; Fashion Model; High Powered; Prison Ship; The Monster and the Ape. **1946** Sensation Hunters; They Made Me a Killer; House of Horrors; God's Country; Lady Chaser; The Gas House Kids. **1947** Big Town; Danger Street; I Cover Big Town; Killer at Large; Queen of the Amazons; Jungle Flight. **1948** Death Valley; Mary Lou; Heart of Virginia; Highway 13. **1949** Shep Comes Home; Arson, Inc.; The Dalton Gang; Batman and Robin (serial); New Adventures of Batman (serial); Call of the Forest. **1950** Gunfire; Border Rangers; Western Pacific Agent; Train to Tombstone; Everybody's Dancing. **1951** Crosswinds. **1953** Jalopy; Cow Country; The Homesteaders. **1955** Lay That Rifle Down. **1956** Two Gun Lady. **1957** The Parson and the Outlaw. **1960** The Rise and Fall of Legs Diamond. **1962** When the Girls Take Over; Deadly Duo; Young Guns of Texas. **1963** McLintock! **1964** Stage to Thunder Rock. **1965** A Zebra in the Kitchen. **1966** Johnny Reno; Waco; Pride of Virginia. **1967** The Adventures of Batman and Robin; The Undertaker and His Pals; The Ballad of Josie.

LOWRY, RUDD
Born: 1892. Died: Dec. 15, 1965, New York, N.Y. Screen, stage and television actor. Married to actress Judith Rudd (dec. 1976).

LUBITSCH, ERNST
Born: Jan. 28, 1892, Berlin, Germany. Died: Nov. 30, 1947, Los Angeles, Calif. (heart attack). Screen, stage actor, film producer, film director and screenwriter. Entered films in 1913.

Appeared in: **1921** One Arabian Night. **1922** The Loves of Pharaoh. **1923** Souls for Sale. **1933** Mr. Broadway.

LUCAN, ARTHUR (Arthur Towle)
Born: 1887, England. Died: May 17, 1954, Hull, England. Screen, stage and vaudeville actor. Married to actress Kitty McShane (dec. 1964) with whom he appeared in vaudeville and films in an act billed as "Lucan and McShane." The two played in "Old Mother Riley" series of films, Lucan playing the mother and his wife playing the daughter.

They appeared in: **1936** Kathleen Mavourneen (aka Kathleen—US 1938). **1936** Stars on Parade. **1937** Old Mother Riley. **1938** Old Mother Riley in Paris. **1939** Old Mother Riley MP; Old Mother Riley Joins Up. **1940** Old Mother Riley in Business; Old Mother Riley in Society. **1941** Old Mother Riley's Circus; Old Mother Riley's Ghosts. **1942** Old Mother Riley Catches a Quisling (reissue of Old Mother Riley in Paris—1938). **1943** Old Mother Riley Overseas. **1945** Old Mother Riley at Home. **1949** Old Mother Riley's New Venture. **1950** Old Mother Riley, Headmistress. **1951** Old Mother Riley's Jungle Treasure. **1952** Mother Riley Meets the Vampire (aka Vampire Over London—US) (without McShane).

LUCAS, JIMMY
Born: 1888. Died: Feb. 21, 1949, Hollywood, Calif. (heart attack). Screen, vaudeville actor and song writer.

Appeared in: **1942** My Heart Belongs to Daddy; Call of the Canyon; Saboteur. **1943** Strictly in the Groove.

LUCAS, SAM
Born: 1841. Died: Jan. 10, 1916, New York, N.Y. Black screen actor.

Appeared in: **1914** Uncle Tom's Cabin.

LUCAS, WILFRED
Born: 1871, Ontario, Canada. Died: Dec. 13, 1940, Los Angeles, Calif. Screen, stage actor, film director and screenwriter. Entered films with Biograph Co. in 1907.

Appeared in: **1908** The Barbarian; Ingomar. **1909** 1776, or the Hessian Renegades. **1910** Fisher Folks; The Lonedale Operator; Winning Back His Love; His Trust; His Trust Fulfilled; Heart Beats of Long Ago; The Diamond Star. **1911** Was He a Coward?; The Spanish Gypsy; His Mother's Scarf; The New Dress; Enoch Arden, Part I and Part II; The Primal Call; The White Rose of the Wild; The Indian Brother; The Thief and the Girl; The Rose of Kentucky; The Sorrowful Example; Swords and Hearts; The Old Confectioner's Mistake; Dan and Dandy; Italian Blood; A Woman Scorned; The Miser's Heart; The Failure; As in a Looking Glass; A Terrible Discovery; The Transformation of Mike; Billy's Stratagem. **1912** Under Burning Skies; Fate's Interception; Just Like a Woman; When Kings Were the Law; Man's Genesis; A Pueblo Legend; The Massacre; The Girl and Her Trust. **1913** Cohen's Outing. **1916** Acquitted; The Wild Girl of the Sierras; Hell-to-Pay Austin. **1919** The Westerners. **1921** The Beautiful Liar; The Breaking Point; The Fighting Breed; The Better Man; Through the Back Door; The Shadow of Lightning Ridge. **1922** The Kentucky Derby; Barriers of Folly; Flesh and Blood; Across the Dead-Line; Paid Back; The Barnstormer; Heroes of the Street. **1923** Can a Woman Love Twice?; Jazzmania; Trilby; The Girl of the Golden West; The Greatest Menace; Innocence; Why Women Remarry. **1924** The Fatal Mistake; Daughters of Pleasure; Racing for Life; Women First; Cornered; The Valley of Hate; The Price She Paid; Dorothy Vernon of Haddon Hall; A Fight for Honor; Lightning Romance; The Fighting Sap; Girls Men Forget; North of Nevada; Passion's Pathway; On Probation; The Mask of Lopez. **1925** Easy Money; How Baxter Butted In; The Snob Buster; The Bad Lands; Youth's Gamble; Cyclone Cavalier; A Broadway Butterfly; The Wife Who Wasn't Wanted; Was It Bigamy?; Riders of the Purple Sage; The Man without a Country. **1926** Her Sacrifice. **1927** The Nest; Burnt Fingers. **1930** One Good Deed (short); Hello Sister; Madame Satan; Looser Than Loose (short); The Arizona Kid; Those Who Dance; Cock of the Walk; Just Imagine. **1931** Big Ears (short); The Age for Love; House of Mystery ("Shadow" detective series); The Phantom; Convicted; Homicide Squad; His Woman; Caught; Politics; Pardon Us; Le Petit Cafe; Dishonored; Young Donovan's Kid; Are These Our Children?; Thirty Days; Men Call It Love; Rich Man's Folly; Millie. **1932** Cross Examination; Midnight Patrol; The Tenderfoot; The Unwritten Law; plus the following shorts: Free Wheeling; The Tabasco Kid; and Red Noses. **1933** Sister to Judas; Lucky Larrigan; The Intruder; Fra Diavolo (The Devil's Brother); Phantom Thunderbolt; The Big Cage; The Sphinx; Day of Reckoning; I Cover the Waterfront; Notorious but Nice; Breed of the Border; Racetrack; Strange People. **1934** Count of Monte Cristo; Shrimps for a Day (short); The Chases of Pimple Street (short); The Moth; Sweden, Land of Vikings (narr.). **1936** Modern Times; Chatterbox;

Mary of Scotland; We Who Are about to Die. **1937** Mile a Minute Love; Dizzy Doctors (short); Criminal Lawyer. **1938** Crime Afloat; The Baroness and the Butler. **1939** Zenobia. **1940** A Chump at Oxford; Ragtime Cowboy Joe; Triple Justice; Brother Orchid. **1941** The Sea Wolf.

LUCHAIRE, CORINNE
Born: 1921, France. Died: Jan. 22, 1950, Paris, France. Stage and screen actress.

Appeared in English and French versions of: **1939** Prison with Bars; The Affair Lafont (Conflict). **1944** Three Hours.

LUCY, ARNOLD
Born: 1865, Tottenham, England. Died: Dec. 15, 1945. Screen and stage actor. Entered films in 1915.

Appeared in: **1916** Devil's Toy; Merely Mary Ann. **1920** In Search of a Sinner; Love Expert. **1921** School Days; You Find It Everywhere. **1922** Fair Lady. **1923** Modern Marriage; Little Old New York. **1929** The Ghost Talks; Masquerade; The One Woman Idea. **1930** All Quiet on the Western Front; City Girl; Manslaughter; Scotland Yard; The Princess and the Plumber. **1931** Merely Mary Ann (and 1916 version). **1932** Dr. Jekyll and Mr. Hyde; Lady With a Past; Alias the Doctor; Guilty as Hell; Sherlock Holmes. **1933** The Wandering Jew (US 1935). **1935** Midshipman Easy (aka Men of the Sea—US). **1937** Victoria the Great.

LUEDERS, GUENTHER
Born: 1905, Germany. Died: Mar. 1, 1975, Duesseldorf, Germany (cancer). Screen, stage, television actor and stage director.

Appeared in: **1935** Fraeulein Liselott. **1938** Dell Etappenhase; Musketier Meir III. **1958** Das Wirtshaus in Spessart (The Spessart Inn—US 1961). **1960** Eternal Love.

LUFKIN, SAM (Samuel William Lufkin)
Born: May 8, 1892, Utah. Died: Feb. 19, 1952, Los Angeles, Calif. (uremia). Stage and screen actor.

Appeared in: **1924** The Battling Orioles. **1926** The Fighting Boob. **1927** Sugar Daddies; Hats Off; The Battle of the Century. **1928** Leave 'Em Laughing; The Finishing Touch; From Soup to Nuts; Their Purple Moment; Should Married Men Go Home?; Two Tars. **1929** Confessions of a Wife; Liberty; Wrong Again; That's My Wife; Double Whoopee; They Go Boom; Bacon Grabbers; The Hoose-Gow (short). **1930** The Shepper-Newfounder; Part Time Wife; The Big Kick (short). **1931** Pardon Us; Beau Hunks; Call a Cop (short). **1932** The following shorts: Any Old Port; The Music Box; County Hospital; Scram. **1933** Sons of the Beast. **1934** Going Bye-Bye (short); Them Thar Hills; Babes in Toyland; The Live Ghost (short). **1935** Bonnie Scotland; It Always Happens (short); The Mystery Man. **1936** The Bohemian Girl; Our Relations; plus the following shorts: The Lucky Corner; Am I Having Fun; Life Hesitates at 40. **1937** Way Out West; Pick a Star; Grips, Grunts and Groans (short); Boots and Saddles (short). **1938** Swiss Miss; Blockheads. **1939** The Flying Deuces. **1940** A Chump at Oxford; Saps at Sea.

LUGOSI, BELA (Bela Lugosi Blasko aka ARISZTID OLT)
Born: Oct. 20, 1882, Lugos, Hungary. Died: Aug. 16, 1956, Hollywood, Calif. (heart attack). Stage and screen actor. Entered films in Budapest in 1915.

Appeared in: **1917** Lulu; A Leopard; Az Elet Kiralya; Tavaszi; Alarcosbal; Az Ezredes. **1918** Casanova; Kuzdelem a Letert; 99. **1919** Nachenschnur des Tot (Necklace of Death); Der Tanz Auf Dem Vulken (Daughters of the Night); Sklaven Fremder Willens; Hamlet. **1920** Szineszno; Die Frau in Delphin; Der Januskopf (Dr. Jekyll and Mr. Hyde); Le Dernier des Mohicans (Last of the Mohicans); Hohan Hopkins der Dritte. **1923** Diadalmas; Elet; The Silent Command. **1924** The Rejected Woman; The Daughters Who Pay. **1925** The Midnight Girl; Prisoners. **1928** How to Handle Women; Wild Strawberries. **1929** The Thirteenth Chair; Veiled Woman; Prisoners (and 1925 version). **1930** Renegades; Wild Company; Such Men Are Dangerous; Oh, for a Man!; Viennese Nights. **1931** 50 Million Frenchmen; Women of All Nations; Dracula; The Black Camel; Broadminded. **1932** Murders in the Rue Morgue; White Zombie; Chandu the Magician; The Phantom Creeps (serial); The Yellow Phantom (serial). **1933** The Whispering Shadow (serial); Island of Lost Souls; The Death Kiss; International House; Night of Terror. **1934** Return of Chandu (serial); The Black Cat; The Gift of Gab. **1935** Best Man Wins; Mysterious Mr. Wong; The Mystery of the Mary Celeste (aka Phantom Ship—US 1937); Mandrake the Magician (serial). **1936** Shadow of Chinatown (serial); The Invisible Ray; Dracula's Daughter; Postal Inspector. **1937** Blake of Scotland Yard (serial). **1938** Killer Rats. **1939** The Phantom Creeps (serial); Son of Frankenstein; Dark Eyes of London (aka The Human Monster—US 1940); Ninotchka; The Gorilla. **1940** The Saint's Double Trouble; Black Friday; You'll Find Out; Fantasia (voice only). **1941** Devil Bat; The Wolf Man; The Invisible Ghost; Spooks Run Wild. **1942** Black Dragons; The Corpse Vanishes; Night Monster; The Ghost of Frankenstein; Bowery at Midnight; Phantom Killer. **1943** The Ape Man; Ghosts on the Loose; Eyes of the Underworld; Frankenstein Meets the Wolf Man. **1944** Return of the Vampire; Voodoo Man; Return of the Ape Man; One Body Too Many. **1945** Zombies on Broadway; The Body Snatcher. **1946** Genius at Work; My Son, the Vampire. **1947** Scared to Death. **1948**

Abbott and Costello Meet Frankenstein. **1949** Master Minds. **1952** Bela Lugosi Meets the Brooklyn Gorilla; Old Mother Riley Meets the Vampire (aka Vampire over London). **1956** He Lived to Kill; Bride of the Monster; The Black Sheep; The Shadow Creeps. **1959** Plan 9 from Outer Space. **1965** The World of Abbott and Costello (film clips).

LUKAS, PAUL (Paul Lukacs)
Born: May 26, 1895, Budapest, Hungary. Died: Aug. 15, 1971, Tangier, Morocco (heart attack). Screen, stage and television actor. Appeared in both stage and screen versions of Watch on the Rhine, receiving New York Drama League award for stage role and the 1943 Academy Award for Best Actor in the film version.

Appeared in: **1922** Samson and Delilah (German film debut). **1928** Loves of an Actress; Three Sinners; The Woman from Moscow; Hot News; Two Lovers; Manhattan Cocktail; The Night Watch. **1929** Illusion; The Wolf of Wall Street; Half Way to Heaven; The Shopworn Angel. **1930** Behind the Make Up; The Benson Murder Case; The Devil's Holiday; Slightly Scarlet; Young Eagles; Grumpy; Anybody's Woman; The Right to Love. **1931** Beloved Bachelor; Women Love Once; Unfaithful; City Streets; Working Girls; Strictly Dishonorable; The Vice Squad. **1932** No One Man; Tomorrow and Tomorrow; Downstairs; Burnt Offering; Rockabye; A Passport to Hell; Thunder Below. **1933** Grand Slam; The Kiss Before the Mirror; Captured!; Sing, Sinner, Sing; The Secret of the Blue Room; Little Women. **1934** By Candlelight; Nagana; The Countess of Monte Cristo; Glamour; Affairs of a Gentleman; I Give My Love; Gift of Gab; The Fountain. **1935** The Casino Murder Case; Father Brown, Detective; The Three Musketeers; I Found Stella Parrish; Age of Indiscretion. **1936** Dodsworth; Ladies in Love. **1937** Espionage; Dinner at the Ritz; Mutiny on the Elsinore (US 1939). **1938** The Lady Vanishes; Dangerous Secrets; Rebellious Daughters. **1939** Confessions of a Nazi Spy; Captain Fury. **1940** The Ghost Breakers; Strange Cargo; A Window in London. **1941** The Monster and the Girl; The Chinese Den; They Dare Not Love. **1942** Lady in Distress. **1943** Watch on the Rhine; Hostage. **1944** Uncertain Glory; Address Unknown; One Man's Secret; Experiment Perilous. **1946** Deadline at Dawn; Temptation. **1947** Whispering City. **1948** Berlin Express. **1950** Kim. **1954** 20,000 Leagues Under the Sea. **1956** The Chinese Bungalow. **1957** Under Fire. **1958** The Roots of Heaven. **1960** Scent of Mystery. **1962** The Four Horsemen of the Apocalypse; Tender Is the Night. **1963** 55 Days at Peking; Fun in Acapulco. **1965** Lord Jim. **1968** Sol Madrid.

LUKIN, MRS. CECIL E. SCHULTZ. See MRS. CECIL E. SCHULTZ

LULLI, FOLCO
Born: 1912, Italy. Died: May 24, 1970, Rome, Italy (heart attack). Screen actor.

Appeared in: **1948** Tragic Hunt. **1949** The Bandit; Flight into France. **1950** Senza Pieta (Without Pity). **1951** No Peace Among the Olive Trees; Altri Tempi (Times Gone By—US 1953); Luci del Varieta (Variety Lights—US 1965). **1954** Carosello Napoletano (Neapolitan Carousel—US 1961). **1955** Maddalena. **1956** Wages of Fear; Air of Paris; La Risaia (aka La Fille de la Riziere and aka Rice Girl—US 1963). **1959** La Grande Guerra (The Great War—US 1961); Oeil Pour Oeil (An Eye for an Eye); Companions; Sign of the Gladiator; Londra Chiama Polo Nord (London Calling North Pole aka The House of Intrigue); La Grande Speranza (The Great Hope aka Torpedo Zone). **1960** Esther and the King; Under Ten Flags; Always Victorious; The Island Sinner. **1961** La Reine des Barbares (The Huns—US 1962); I Tartari (The Tartars—US 1962); Gli Invasori (Erik the Conqueror—US 1963 aka The Invaders). **1962** La Guerra Continua (Warriors 5—US and aka The War Continues); La Fayette (Lafayette—US 1963); Dulcinea. **1963** I Compagni (The Organizer—US 1964 aka The Strikers). **1964** Parias de la Gloire (Pariahs of Glory). **1965** Oltraggio al Pudore (aka Cheating Italian Style and All the Other Girls Do—US 1966); La Fabuleuse Aventure de Marco Polo (Marco the Magnificent—US 1966). **1966** Operazione Goldman (Lightning Bolt—US 1967). **1967** Le Vicomte Regle ses Comptes (The Viscount).

LUNCEFORD, JIMMY (James Melvin Lunceford)
Born: June 6, 1902, Fulton, Mississippi. Died: July 13, 1947, Seaside, Oregon. Orchestra leader, musician, composer and screen actor.

Appeared in: **1941** Blues in the Night.

LUND, GUS A.
Born: 1896. Died: June 5, 1951, Los Angeles, Calif. Screen, stage and television actor.

LUND, RICHARD
Born: 1885, Goteborg, Sweden. Died: 1960, Sweden. Screen and stage actor.

Appeared in: **1928** The Three Who Were Doomed. Other Swedish films: A Secret Marriage; Smiles and Tears; Lady Marion's Summer Flirtation; The Voice of Blood; On the Fateful Roads of Life; Ingeborg Holm; Life's Conflicts; The Modern Suffragette; The Clergyman Love Stronger than Hate; People of the Border; Because of Her Love; Do Not Judge; Stormy Petrel; A Good Girl Should Solve Her Own Problems; Hearts That Meet; The Strike; The Playmates; It Was in May; His Wife's Past; To Each His Calling; His Father's

Crime; The Avenger; The Governor's Daughters; Sea Vultures; His Wedding Night; At the Moment of Trial; The Lucky Brooch; Love and Journalism; The Struggle for His Heart; The Ballet Primadonna; The Architect of One's Own Fortune; Who Fired?; The Jungle Queen's Jewel; The Living Mummy; Sir Arne's Treasure; The Monastery of Sendomir; The Executioner; Family Traditions; The Girls from Are; Carolina Rediviva; The Surrounded House; Life in the Country; A Million Dollars; Uncle Frans; False Svensson; Voice of the Heart; What Do Men Know?; Under False Colours; Walpurgis Night; Conscientious Adolf; Johan Ulfstjerna; He, She and the Money; The "Paradise" Boarding House; A Cold in the Head; Adolf Armstrong; A Rich Man's Son; With the People for the Country; Great Friends and Faithful Neighbours; Nothing But the Truth; Rejoice While You Are Young; The Little WRAC of the Veteran Reserves; Whalers; Steel; Night in June; Kiss Her; A Big Hug; We Are All Errand Boys; The Gentleman Gangster; A Schoolmistress on the Spree; Sextuplets; Life on a Perch; The Knockout Clergyman; Katrina; There Burned a Flame; Frenzy (aka Torment).

LUNDIGAN, WILLIAM "BILL"
Born: June 12, 1914, Syracuse, N.Y. Died: Dec. 20, 1975, Duarte, Calif. (lung and heart congestion). Screen, radio and television actor.

Appeared in: **1937** Armored Car (film debut); The Lady Fights Back. **1938** State Police; The Black Doll; Reckless Living; That's My Story; Wives Under Suspicion; Danger on the Air; The Missing Guest; Freshman Year. **1939** Dodge City; They Asked for It; Legion of the Lost Flyers; Three Smart Girls Grow Up; The Old Maid; Forgotten Woman. **1940** The Fighting 69th; Three Cheers for the Irish; The Man Who Talked Too Much; The Sea Hawk; East of the River; Santa Fe Trail; a Vitaphone short. **1941** The Case of the Black Parrot; A Shot in the Dark; The Great Mr. Nobody; Highway West; International Squadron; Sailors on Leave; The Bugle Sounds. **1942** Sunday Punch; The Courtship of Andy Hardy; Apache Trail; Andy Hardy's Double Life; Northwest Rangers. **1943** Dr. Gillespie's Criminal Case; Salute to the Marines; Headin' for God's Country. **1945** What Next, Corporal Hargrove? **1947** The Fabulous Dorseys; Dishonored Lady. **1948** Inside Story; Mystery in Mexico. **1949** Follow Me Quietly; State Department—File 649; Pinky. **1950** I'll Get By; Mother Didn't Tell Me. **1951** I'd Climb the Highest Mountain; Love Nest; House on Telegraph Hill; Elopement. **1953** Down Among the Sheltering Palms; Inferno; Serpent of the Nile. **1954** Riders to the Stars; The White Orchid; Terror Ship. **1962** The Underwater City. **1967** The Way West. **1968** Where Angels Go . . . Trouble Follows!

LUNG, CHARLES "CHARLIE"
Died: June 22, 1974. Screen actor.

Appeared in: **1942** Destination Unknown. **1943** Flight for Freedom; Headin' for God's Country; Jack London. **1944** Dragon Seed. **1951** Secrets of Monte Carlo. **1953** Thunder in the East; Siren of Bagdad. **1954** Jivaro. **1955** Ma and Pa Kettle at Waikiki.

LUPINO, MARK
Born: 1894. Died: Apr. 4, 1930, London, England. Screen and stage actor. Brother of actor Stanley Lupino (dec. 1942).

Appeared in: **1927** The King's Highway.

LUPINO, STANLEY
Born: June 17, 1893, London, England. Died: June 10, 1942, London, England. Screen, stage actor, screenwriter, playwright, screen and stage producer. Married to stage actress Connie Emerald. Father of actress Ida Lupino and brother of actor Mark Lupino (dec. 1930). Entered films in 1931.

Appeared in: **1931** Love Lies; The Love Race. **1932** Sleepless Nights. **1933** King of the Ritz; Facing the Music (US 1934); You Made Me Love You. **1934** Happy. **1935** Honeymoon for Three. **1936** Cheer Up!; Sporting Love. **1937** Over She Goes (stage and film versions). **1938** Hold My Hand. **1939** Lucky to Me.

LUPINO, WALLACE (aka WALLACE LANE)
Born: Jan. 23, 1898, Edinburgh, Scotland. Died: Oct. 11, 1961, Ashford, England. Stage and screen actor. Brother of actor Lupino Lane (dec. 1959).

Appeared in: **1918** "Kinekature Comedies" Series including: The Blunders of Mr. Butterbun: Unexpected Treasure. **1922–33** Educational shorts including: Buying a Gun. **1930** The Yellow Mask; Children of Chance. **1931** The Love Race; Love Lies; Aroma of the South Seas; No Lady; Never Trouble Trouble; Bull Rushes. **1932** The Maid of the Mountains; Josser on the River; Old Spanish Customers; The Innocents of Chicago (aka Why Saps Leave Home—US); The Bad Companions. **1933** The Melody Maker; The Stolen Necklace; Forging Ahead; Song Birds. **1934** Master and Man; Bagged; Wishes; Lyde Park. **1935** The Student's Romance; The Deputy Drummer; Trust the Navy. **1936** The Man Who Could Work Miracles (US 1937); Hot News; Shipmates o'Mine; Love Up the Pole. **1937** The First and the Last (aka 21 Days—US 1940). **1939** Me and My Gal (aka The Lambeth Walk—US 1940). **1945** Waterloo Road.

LUPO, GEORGE G.
Born: 1924. Died: Aug. 8, 1973, Long Beach, Calif. (massive stroke). Screen and television actor.

LUSK, FREEMAN
Born: 1906. Died: Aug. 25, 1970, Orange, Calif. Screen, radio and television actor.

Appeared in: **1951** Little Egypt; Half Angel; The Day the Earth Stood Still. **1952** Phone Call from a Stranger; The Pride of St. Louis. **1953** The Caddy. **1955** The Girl Rush. **1966** To the Shores of Hell.

LUTHER, ANN (aka ANNA LUTHER)
Born: 1893, Newark, N.J. Died: Dec. 16, 1960, Hollywood, Calif. Screen actress. Married to actor Edward Gallagher.

Appeared in: **1915** I'm Glad My Boy Grew Up to Be a Soldier; The Manicure Girl; Crooked to the End. **1916** The Village Vampire. **1917** Her Father's Station; Neglected Wife (serial). **1918** Moral Suicide; Her Moment. **1919** The Great Gamble (serial); The Lurking Peril (serial). **1921** Soul and Body. **1922** The Woman Who Believed. **1923** The Governor's Lady; The Truth About Wives. **1924** The Fatal Plunge; Sinners in Silk.

LUTHER, JOHNNY
Born: 1909. Died: July 31, 1960, San Pedro, Calif. (drowned in boating accident). Screen actor.

LUTHER, LESTER
Born: 1888. Died: Jan. 19, 1962, Hollywood, Calif. (stroke). Screen, stage and radio actor.

Appeared in: **1949** The Red Menace.

LUTTRINGER, ALFONSE "AL"
Born: 1879, San Francisco, Calif. Died: June 9, 1953, Hollywood, Calif. Stage and screen actor.

LYGO, MARY (Irene Goodall aka IRENE "RENE" FULLER)
Died: June 1, 1927, Los Angeles, Calif. (suicide—poison). Screen and vaudeville actress. Appeared professionally under both names.

LYMAN, ABE
Born: 1897. Died: Oct. 23, 1957, Los Angeles, Calif. Screen, radio actor, bandleader and song writer.

Appeared in: **1933** a Vitaphone short; Mr. Broadway; Broadway; Thru a Keyhole.

LYMON, FRANKIE
Born: 1942. Died: Feb. 27, 1968, New York, N.Y. Screen actor and singer.

Appeared in: **1957** Mister Rock and Roll.

LYNCH, BRID (Brid Ni Loinsigh)
Born: 1913, County Kerry, Ireland. Died: Oct. 27, 1968, Dublin, Ireland (heart ailment). Stage and screen actress.

Appeared in: **1957** Professor Tim (US 1959). **1960** The Poacher's Daughter.

LYNCH, FRANK J.
Died: Dec. 4, 1932, Springfield, Mass. (air crash burns). Screen actor, stunt flyer and exhibitionist.

LYNCH, FRANK T.
Born: 1869. Died: Dec. 18, 1933, New York, N.Y. (heart attack). Screen, stage actor, professional baseball player and stage manager.

LYNCH, HELEN
Born: Apr. 6, 1904, Billings, Mont. Died: 1965. Screen and stage actress. Married to actor Carroll Nye (dec. 1974). She was a Wampas Baby Star of 1923.

Appeared in: **1917** Showdown. **1920** Honor Bound. **1921** The House that Jazz Built; My Lady Friends; Live and Let Live; What's a Wife Worth? **1922** The Dangerous Age; The Other Side; Midnight; Fools First; Glass Houses. **1923** Cause for Divorce; The Eternal Three; The Meanest Man in the World. **1924** The Village of Hate; On Probation; The Tomboy; American Manners; In High Gear. **1925** After Marriage; Bustin' Thru; Smilin' at Trouble; Fifth Avenue Models; Three Weeks in Paris; Smouldering Fires; Oh, Doctor! **1926** My Own Pal; The Arizona Sweepstakes; General Custer at Little Big Horn; Tom and His Pals; Speeding Through. **1927** Avenging Fangs; Cheaters; Husbands for Rent; Underworld. **1928** Ladies of the Mob; Love and Learn; Romance of the Underworld; The Singing Fool; Thundergod. **1929** Stolen Love; In Old Arizona; Speedeasy; Why Bring That Up? **1930** Behind the Make-Up; City Girl. **1933** Emergency Call. **1934** Elmer and Elsie. **1940** Women Without Names.

LYNCH, JIM
Died: Apr. 20, 1916, Chicago, Ill. (pneumonia). Screen and stage actor.

LYNCH, RUTH SPROULE. *See* RUTH SPROULE

LYNDON, ALICE
Born: 1874. Died: July 9, 1949, Woodland Hills, Calif. Screen and vaudeville actress. Entered films with Sennett in 1914.

LYNN, DIANA (Dolores Loehr aka DOLLY LOEHR)
Born: Oct. 7, 1926, Los Angeles, Calif. Died: Dec. 18, 1971, Los Angeles, Calif. (brain hemorrhage). Screen, stage actress and pianist.

Appeared in: **1939** They Shall Have Music. **1941** There's Magic in Music. **1942** The Major and the Minor; Star-Spangled Rhythm. **1943** Henry Aldrich Gets Glamour. **1944** The Miracle of Morgan's Creek; Henry Aldrich Plays Cupid; And the Angels Sing; Our Hearts Were Young and Gay. **1945** Out of This World; Duffy's Tavern. **1946** Our Hearts Were Growing Up; The Bride Wore Boots. **1947** Variety Girl; Easy Come, Easy Go. **1948** Ruthless; Texas, Brooklyn and Heaven; Every Girl Should Be Married. **1949** My Friend Irma. **1950** Paid in Full; Rogues of Sherwood Forest; My Friend Irma Goes West; Peggy. **1951** Bedtime for Bonzo; Take Care of My Little Girl; The People against O'Hara. **1952** Meet Me at the Fair. **1953** Plunder of the Sun. **1954** Track of the Cat. **1955** An Annapolis Story; You're Never Too Young; The Kentuckian. **1970** Company of Killers.

LYNN, EDDIE (Edward Lynn Meminger)
Born: 1905, Toledo, Ohio. Apr. 18, 1975, New York, N.Y. Screen, stage actor and stage producer.

Appeared in: **1939** Reform School.

LYNN, EMMETT
Born: Feb. 14, 1897, Muscatine, Iowa. Died: Oct. 20, 1958, Hollywood, Calif. (heart attack). Screen, stage, vaudeville, radio and burlesque actor. Entered films with Biograph in 1913.

Appeared in: **1913** The Imp. **1940** Grandpa Goes to Town; Scatterbrain; Wagon Train; The Fargo Kid. **1941** Along the Rio Grande; Robbers of the Range; Thunder over the Ozarks; Puddin' Head. **1942** Frisco Lil; Baby Face Morgan; Tireman, Spare My Tires (short); Stagecoach Express; In Old California; Road Agent; The Spoilers; City of Silent Men; Tomorrow We Live; Outlaws of Pine Ridge; Westward Ho! **1943** Carson City Cyclone; The Law Rides Again; Girls in Chains; Sundown Kid; Dead Man's Gulch. **1944** You Were Never Uglier (short); Gold is Where You Lose It (short); Good Night, Sweetheart; Outlaws of Santa Fe; Frontier Outlaws; Return of the Rangers; Cowboy Canteen; When the Lights Go on Again; The Laramie Trail; Johnny Doesn't Live Here Any More; The Town Went Wild; Swing Hostess; Bluebeard. **1945** Song of Old Wyoming; Shadow of Terror; Hollywood and Vine; The Big Show-Off; The Cisco Kid Returns. **1946** The Caravan Trail; Romance of the West; Throw a Saddle on a Star; Man from Rainbow Valley; The Fighting Frontiersmen; Stagecoach to Denver; Conquest of Cheyenne; Landrush; Santa Fe Uprising. **1947** Code of the West; Oregon Trail Scouts; Rustlers of Devil's Canyon. **1948** Relentless; West of Sonora; Grand Canyon Trail; Here Comes Trouble. **1949** Roll, Thunder, Roll; Cowboy and the Prizefighter; Ride, Ryder, Ride; The Fighting Redhead. **1950** The Dungeon. **1951** Badman's Gold; Best of the Badmen; The Scarf. **1952** Hooked and Rooked (short); Desert Pursuit; Lone Star; Monkey Business; Oklahoma Annie; Skirts Ahoy!; Apache War Smoke; Sky Full of Moon. **1953** Pickup on South Street; The Robe; The Homesteaders; Northern Patrol. **1954** Ring of Fear; Living It Up; Bait. **1955** A Man Called Peter. **1956** The Ten Commandments.

LYNN, GEORGE M.
Died: 1967. Screen actor.

Appeared in: **1936** Sinner Take All. **1937** Charlie Chan at Monte Carlo; The Duke Comes Back; City Girl. **1942** To Be or Not to Be; Grand Central Murder; A Haunting We Will Go. **1943** Crime Doctor's Strangest Case; Tonight We Raid Calais. **1944** Two-Man Submarine. **1945** Sudan; House of Frankenstein. **1946** Tangier; The Last Installment (short); Under Nevada Skies. **1947** Killer at Large. **1948** Best Man Wins; Homicide for Three. **1951** The Day the Earth Stood Still. **1952** The Atomic City; The Bushwackers. **1954** Magnificent Obsession. **1956** The Werewolf; The Boss. **1957** The Man Who Turned to Stone; I Was a Teenage Frankenstein. **1958** Girl in the Woods.

LYNN, HASTINGS
Born: 1879. Died: June 30, 1932, Elstree, England (liver ailment). Screen actor.

LYNN, NATALIE
Died: Dec. 3, 1964, Isleworth, England. Screen, stage, radio and television actress.

Appeared in: **1960** For Members Only (aka The Nudist Story).

LYNN, RALPH
Born: 1881, Manchester, England. Died: Aug. 8, 1962, London, England. Screen, stage actor and film director. Father of film director Robert Lynn.

Appeared in: **1929** Peace and Quiet (short). **1930** Rookery Nook (aka One Embarrassing Night—US). **1931** Plunder; Tons of Money; The Chance of a Night Time; Mischief. **1932** A Night Like This; Thark. **1933** Just My Luck; Summer Lightning; Up to the Neck; Turkey Time; A Cuckoo in the Nest. **1934** A Cup of Kindness; Dirty Work. **1935** Fighting Stock; Stormy Weather (US 1936); Foreign Affaires. **1936** In the Soup; Pot Luck; All In. **1937** For Valour.

LYNN, ROBERT

Born: 1897. Died: Dec. 18, 1969, Los Angeles, Calif. Screen actor.

Appeared in: **1951** The Barefoot Mailman. **1958** The Return of Dracula; Good Morning Miss Dove.

LYNN, SHARON E. (D'Auvergne Sharon Lindsay)

Born: 1904, Weatherford, Tex. Died: May 26, 1963, Hollywood, Calif. Screen, stage actress and songwriter. Entered films as an extra.

Appeared in: **1927** Aflame in the Sky; Clancy's Kosher Wedding; Jake the Plumber; The Cherokee Kid; Tom's Gang; The Coward. **1928** Red Wine; Give and Take; None but the Brave; Son of the Golden West. **1929** Fox Movietone Follies of 1929; Speakeasy; Sunny Side Up; Hollywood Night; The One Woman Idea; Trail of the Horse Thieves; Dad's Choice. **1930** Crazy That Way; Lightnin'; Up the River; Happy Days; Let's Go Places; Wild Company; Man Trouble. **1931** Men on Call; Too Many Cooks; Fallen Star. **1932** Discarded Lovers; The Big Broadcast. **1933** Big Executive. **1935** Enter Madame; Go into Your Dance. **1937** Way Out West. **1941** West Point Widow.

LYNN, WILLIAM H.

Born: 1889. Died: Jan. 5, 1952, New York, N.Y. Screen, stage, vaudeville, radio and television actor.

Appeared in: **1951** Mr. Belvedere Rings the Bell; Harvey; Katie Did It. **1952** Outcasts of Poker Flat. **1953** The Twonky.

LYON, FRANK

Born: 1901, Bridgeport, Conn. Died: Jan. 6, 1961, Gardner, Mass. Stage and screen actor.

Appeared in: **1930** The Big Pond. **1932** Lovers Courageous. **1936** After the Thin Man. **1937** Parnell; Night Must Fall; Conquest. **1938** I Met My Love Again; Dramatic School; Invisible Enemy; The Road to Reno. **1943** Paris after Dark.

LYON, THERESE

Died: Apr. 15, 1975. Stage and screen actress.

Appeared in: **1945** Love, Honor and Goodbye; A Letter for Evie; Strangler of the Swamp. **1946** The Green Years. **1947** The Late George Apley. **1948** Apartment for Peggy. **1951** Half Angel. **1962** The Music Man.

LYONS, CANDY

Born: 1945. Died: June 19, 1966, aboard an Atlantic liner. Screen actress.

Appeared in: **1963** Palm Springs Holiday.

LYONS, CLIFF "TEX" (Clifford William Lyons)

Born: 1902. Died: Jan. 6, 1974, Los Angeles, Calif. Screen actor, film director and stuntman.

Appeared in: **1926** West of the Law. **1928** Flashing Hoofs; Master of the Range; The Riddle Trail; Across the Plains; Headin' Westward; Manhattan Cowboy; The Old Code. **1929** The Arizona Kid; Captain Cowboy; The Cowboy and the Outlaw; Fighters of the Saddle; The Fighting Terror; The Last Roundup; West of the Rockies; The Sheriff's Lash; The Galloping Lover; The Saddle King; Law of the Mounted. **1930** Code of the West; Crusaders of the West; Red Gold; Breezy Bill; Call of the Desert; Canyon Hawks; The Canyon of Missing Men; Firebrand Jordan; O'Malley Rides Alone; The Oklahoma Sheriff; Western Honor. **1931** Painted Desert; Red Fork Range. **1932** Night Rider. **1935** The Miracle Rider (serial); Tumbling Tumbleweeds; Outlawed Guns. **1936** The Lawless Nineties. **1943** Wagon Tracks West. **1944** The Tiger Woman (serial). **1949** She Wore a Yellow Ribbon. **1950** Wagonmaster. **1952** Bend of the River. **1957** The Abductors; Apache Warrior. **1959** The Young Land. **1960** Spartacus; The Alamo. **1961** Two Rode Together; The Comancheros. **1962** Taras Bulba. **1963** The Great Train Robbery; Donovan's Reef; McLintock! **1964** The Long Ships. **1965** Genghis Khan; Major Dundee. **1966** Marco the Magnificent. **1967** The War Wagon. **1968** The Green Berets. **1970** Chisum.

LYONS, EDDIE

Born: Nov. 25, 1886, Beardstown, Ill. Died: Aug. 30, 1926, Pasadena, Calif. Screen, stage actor and stage director. Married to actress Virginia Kirtley, and brother of actor Harry M. Lyons (dec. 1919).

Appeared in: **1912** The Dove and the Serpent; Melodrama of Yesterday; Making a Man of Her; Jim's Atonement; Henpecked Ike; Love, War and a Bonnet; The Parson and the Medicine Man; Big Sin; Almost a Suicide. **1913** Some Runner. **1914** She Was a Working Girl; What a Baby Did; Such a Villain; When Eddie Went to the Front. **1915** Love in a Hospital; Wanted—A Chaperone; Eddie's Awful Predicament; Mrs. Plumb's Pudding. **1917** The Rushin'

Dancers; A Fire Escape Finish; A Hasty Hazing; His Wife's Relatives. **1918** There and Back. **1920** Fixed by George; Everything but the Truth; La, La, Lucille. **1921** Once a Plumber; Roman Romeos; A Shocking Night. **1925** Declasse. **1926** The Lodge in the Wilderness; The Shadow of the Law.

LYONS, FRANKIE

Died: Jan. 26, 1937 (auto accident). Screen stuntman.

Appeared in: **1937** Racing Luck.

LYONS, FRECKLES (Francis Lunakiaki Lyons)

Born: 1909. Died: Sept. 1, 1960, Honolulu, Hawaii. Screen, stage actor, musician and singer.

LYONS, FRED (Fred F. Leyva)

Died: Mar. 16, 1921 (auto accident). Screen actor.

LYONS, GENE

Born: 1921. Died: July 8, 1974, Hollywood, Calif. Screen and stage actor.

Appeared in: **1957** The Young Don't Cry. **1965** Sylvia. **1969** Daddy's Gone A-Hunting.

LYONS, HARRY M.

Born: Nov. 12, 1879, Ill. Died: Mar. 12, 1919, Los Angeles, Calif. (aneurism of aorta). Screen actor. Brother of actor Eddie Lyons (dec. 1926).

LYTELL, BERT

Born: Feb. 24, 1885, New York, N.Y. Died: Sept. 28, 1954, New York, N.Y. (following surgery). Screen, stage, radio, television, vaudeville actor and film director. Married to stage actress Grace Mencken; divorced from actress Claire Windsor (dec. 1972); and brother of actor Wilfred Lytell (dec. 1954). Entered films in 1917.

Appeared in: **1917** The Lone Wolf. **1918** The Trail to Yesterday. **1919** Easy to Make Money. **1920** Alias Jimmy Valentine. **1921** A Message from Mars; Misleading Lady; Price of Redemption; The Man Who; A Trip to Paradise; The Idle Rich; Ladyfingers; Alias Ladyfingers. **1922** The Face Between; The Right That Failed; Sherlock Brown; To Have and to Hold. **1923** Kick In; Rupert of Hentzau; The Eternal City; The Meanest Man in the World. **1924** Born Rich; A Son of the Sahara. **1925** Sandra; Lady Windermere's Fan; Steele of the Royal Mounted; The Boomerang; Eve's Lover; Never the Twain Shall Meet; Ship of Souls; Sporting Life. **1926** That Model from Paris; The Lone Wolf Returns; The Gilded Butterfly; Obey the Law. **1927** Alias the Lone Wolf; The First Night; Women's Wares. **1928** On Trial. **1929** The Lone Wolf's Daughter. **1930** The Last of the Lone Wolf; Brothers (stage and film versions). **1931** The Single Sin; Stolen Jools (short). **1943** Stage Door Canteen.

LYTELL, WILFRED

Born: 1892. Died: Sept. 10, 1954, Salem, N.Y. Screen, stage, radio and television actor. Brother of actor Bert Lytell (dec. 1954).

Appeared in: **1916** The Combat. **1918** Our Mrs. McChesney. **1920** Heliotrope. **1921** Know Your Men; The Kentuckians. **1922** The Man Who Paid; The Wolf's Fangs. **1923** The Fair Cheat; The Leavenworth Case. **1924** Trail of the Law; The Wardens of Virginia. **1926** Bluebeard's Seven Wives.

LYTTON, L. ROGERS

Born: 1867, New Orleans, La. Died: Aug. 9, 1924. Screen actor.

Appeared in: **1912** Off the Road; Checkmated; The Final Justice; Papa Puts One Over. **1913** The Model for St. John; Three Girls and a Man. **1914** Heartease; Jerry's Uncle's Namesake; The Shadow of the Past; The Win(k)some Widow. **1915** Battle Cry of Peace. **1916** The Tarantula; The Scarlet Runner; My Official Wife; The Price of Fame. **1917** Panthea; The Vengeance of Durand (aka Two Portraits); Lest We Forget. **1918** Burden of Proof; The Forbidden City. **1919** A Regular Girl; The Third Degree. **1920** High Speed; Love or Money. **1921** His Brother's Keeper. **1922** The Road to Arcady; Silver Wings; Who are my Parents? **1923** Zaza. **1924** A Sainted Devil.

MABLEY, JACKIE "MOMS" (Loretta Mary Aiken)

Born: 1897, North Carolina. Died: May 23, 1975, White Plains, N.Y. Black screen, stage, vaudeville, radio and television actress.

Appeared in: **1933** Emperor Jones. **1970** It's Your Thing.

MacARTHUR, CHARLES

Born: Nov. 5, 1895, Scranton, Pa. Died: Apr. 21, 1956, New York, N.Y. (internal hemorrhage). Screenwriter, film director, film producer, playwright and screen actor. Married to actress Helen Hayes and father of actor James MacArthur.

Appeared in: **1934** Crime without Passion. **1935** The Scoundrel.

MacBRIDE, DONALD. See DONALD McBRIDE

MACCHIA, JOHN

Born: 1932. Died: July 30, 1967, Los Angeles, Calif. (stroke). Screen actor.

Appeared in: **1963** Beach Party; The Nutty Professor. **1964** The Disorderly Orderly. **1965** Beach Blanket Bingo; Family Jewels; How to Stuff a Wild Bikini; Sergeant Deadhead. **1966** Three on a Couch; The Ghost in the Invisible Bikini.

MacCOLL, JAMES A.

Born: 1912. Died: Apr. 18, 1956, New York, N.Y. Screen, stage, television actor and playwright.

Appeared in: **1954** This Is the Army (stage and film versions).

MacCORMACK, FRANKLYN

Born: 1908. Died: June 12, 1971. Screen actor.

Appeared in: **1921** The Case of Becky; Experience. **1929** The Phantom of the Opera. **1930** Brothers; The Case of Sergeant Grischa.

MacDERMOTT, JOHN W. "JACK"

Born: Sept. 9, 1892, Green River, Wyo. Died: July 22, 1946, Los Angeles, Calif. Screen, stage actor, screenwriter and film director. Entered films in 1913.

Appeared in: **1923** Mary of the Movies.

MacDERMOTT, MARC. *See* MARC McDERMOTT

MacDONALD, DONALD

Born: Mar. 13, 1898, Denison, Tex. Died: Dec. 9, 1959, New York, N.Y. Screen, stage, television and radio actor. Married to stage actress Ruth Hammond.

Appeared in: **1955** The Kentuckian. **1956** The Brass Legend; Great Day in the Morning.

MacDONALD, EDMUND

Born: 1911. Died: Sept. 1951, Los Angeles, Calif. Screen and radio actor.

Appeared in: **1933** Enlighten Thy Daughter. **1938** Prison Break. **1939** I Stole a Million. **1940** Sailor's Lady; Black Friday; The Gay Caballero. **1941** Great Guns; The Bride Wore Crutches; Texas. **1942** Whispering Ghosts; To the Shores of Tripoli; Call of the Canyon; Castle in the Desert; The Strange Case of Dr. Rx; Flying Tigers; Heart of the Golden West; Madame Spy; Who Done It? **1943** Hangmen Also Die; Sherlock Holmes in Washington; Hi Ya Chum; Corvette K-225. **1944** Sailor's Holiday. **1945** The Lady Confesses; Detour; Hold That Blonde. **1946** They Made Me a Killer. **1947** Shoot to Kill; Blondie's Anniversary. **1948** That Lady in Ermine; Black Eagle. **1949** Red Canyon.

MacDONALD, J. FARRELL

Born: June 6, 1875, Waterbury, Conn. Died: Aug. 2, 1952, Hollywood, Calif. Screen, stage actor, film director and opera performer.

Appeared in: **1911** Imp Productions films. **1915** The Heart of Maryland. **1921** Little Miss Hawkshaw; Bucking the Line; Riding with Death; Trailin'; Sky High; Action; Desperate Youth; The Freeze Out; The Wallop. **1922** The Ghost Breaker; The Bachelor Daddy; The Bonded Woman; Manslaughter; Tracks; Come On Over; The Young Rajah; Over the Border. **1923** Drifting; Quicksands; The Age of Desire; Fashionable Fakers; Racing Hearts; While Paris Sleeps. **1924** Western Luck; The Brass Bowl; The Iron Horse; Fair Week; Mademoiselle Midnight; The Signal Tower; The Storm Daughter. **1925** Gerald Cranston's Lady; The Scarlet Honeymoon; The Fighting Heart; Lightnin'; Thank You; The Lucky Horseshoe; Kentucky Pride; Let Women Alone. **1926** The First Year; A Trip to Chinatown; The Dixie Merchant; The Shamrock Handicap; The Family Upstairs; The Country Beyond; Three Bad Men. **1927** Bertha the Sewing Machine Girl; Love Makes 'Em Wild; Ankles Preferred; The Cradle Snatchers; Rich but Honest; Colleen; Paid to Love; Sunrise; East Side, West Side. **1928** The Cohens and the Kellys in Paris; Bringing Up Father; Abie's Irish Rose; Riley the Cop; None But the Brave. **1929** In Old Arizona; Masked Emotion; Masquerade; Strong Boy; Four Devils; South Sea Rose. **1930** Broken Dishes; The Truth about Youth; Song O' My Heart; Born Reckless; The Painted Angel; The Steel Highway; Men without Women; Happy Days; The Girl of the Golden West. **1931** The Easiest Way; The Millionaire; Woman Hungry; The Maltese Falcon; Other Men's Women; The Squaw Man; Too Young to Marry; The Brat; Sporting Blood; The Spirit of Notre Dame; Touchdown; The Painted Desert; River's End. **1932** Under Eighteen; Discarded Lovers; Hotel Continental; Probation; The Phantom Express; Week-End Marriage; The 13th Guest; 70,000 Witnesses; The Vanishing Frontier; Hearts of Humanity; This Sporting Age; The Pride of the Legion; No Man of Her Own; Me and My Gal; Steady Company; The Racing Strain; Scandal for Sale. **1933** The Iron Master; Heritage of the Desert; Under Secret Orders; The Working Man; Peg O' My Heart; Laughing at Life; The Power and the Glory; I Loved a Woman; Murder on the Campus. **1934** Myrt and Marge; Man of Two Worlds; The Crime Doctor; Romance in Manhattan; Once to Every Woman; The Cat's Paw; The Crosby Case; Beggar's Holiday. **1935** Swell Head; Maybe It's Love; Danger Ahead; Square Shooter; The Whole Town's Talking; Northern Frontier; Star of Midnight; The Best Man Wins; The Healer; Let 'Em Have It; Our Little Girl; The Irish in Us; Front Page Woman; Stormy; Fight-

ing Youth; Waterfront Lady. **1936** Hitchhike Lady; Florida Special; Riff Raff; Exclusive Story; Showboat. **1937** The Game That Kills; Courage of the West; Shadows of the Orient; Maid of Salem; Mysterious Crossing; The Silent Barrier; Roaring Timber; The Hit Parade; Slave Ship; County Fair; Slim; Topper; My Dear Miss Aldrich. **1938** My Old Kentucky Home; Numbered Woman; Gang Bullets; State Police; Little Orphan Annie; White Banners; Come on Rangers; The Crowd Roars; Submarine Patrol; Flying Fists; There Goes My Heart. **1939** Susannah of the Mounties; Mickey the Kid; Conspiracy; The Gentleman from Arizona; Zenobia; Coast Guard; East Side of Heaven. **1940** Knights of the Range; The Dark Command; Light of the Western Stars; Prairie Law; I Take This Oath; The Last Alarm; Untamed; Stagecoach War; Friendly Neighbors. **1941** Meet John Doe; The Great Lie; In Old Cheyenne; Riders of the Timberline; Law of the Timber; Broadway Limited. **1942** One Thrilling Night; Phantom Killer; Bowery at Midnight; Little Tokyo, U.S.A.; Snuffy Smith, Yardbird; The Living Ghost; Captains of the Clouds. **1943** The Ape Man; Clancy Street Boys; True to Life; Tiger Fangs. **1944** The Miracle of Morgan's Creek; Texas Masquerade; The Great Moment; Follow the Boys; Shadow of Suspicion. **1945** The Woman Who Came Back; A Tree Grows in Brooklyn; Nob Hill; Johnny Angel; Pillow of Death. **1946** Smoky; My Darling Clementine; Joe Palooka; Champ. **1947** Thunder in the Valley; Web of Danger; Keeper of the Bees. **1948** Whispering Smith; Panhandle; Fury at Furnace Creek; Walls of Jericho; Belle Starr's Daughter. **1949** She Comes Home; Streets of San Francisco; Beautiful Blonde from Bashful Bend; Fighting Man of the Plains; The Dalton Gang; Law of the Barbary Coast. **1950** Dakota Lil; Hostile Country; Woman on the Run. **1951** Elopement; Mr. Belvedere Rings the Bell.

MacDONALD, JAMES W.

Born: 1899. Died: Aug. 31, 1962, Santa Cruz, Calif. Screen and stage actor.

Appeared in: **1949** Cinderella (voice only).

MacDONALD, JEANETTE

Born: June 18, 1906, Philadelphia, Pa. Died: Jan. 14, 1965, Houston, Tex. (heart attack). Screen, stage, television, radio actress and opera performer. Married to actor Gene Raymond.

Appeared in: **1929** The Love Parade (film debut). **1930** The Vagabond King; The Lottery Bride; Let's Go Native; Monte Carlo; Oh, for a Man! **1931** Don't Bet on Women; Annabelle's Affairs (aka The Affairs of Annabelle). **1932** One Hour with You; Love Me Tonight. **1934** The Merry Widow (US and French version); The Cat and the Fiddle. **1935** Naughty Marietta. **1936** Rose Marie; San Francisco. **1937** Maytime; The Firefly. **1938** The Girl of the Golden West; Sweethearts. **1939** Broadway Serenade. **1940** New Moon; Bitter Sweet. **1941** Smilin' Through. **1942** I Married an Angel; Cairo. **1944** Follow the Boys. **1948** Three Daring Daughters; The Birds and the Bees. **1949** The Sun Comes Up. **1974** That's Entertainment (film clips).

MacDONALD, KATHERINE

Born: 1894. Died: June 4, 1956, Santa Barbara, Calif. Screen actress and film producer.

Appeared in: **1918** Headin' South; Riddle Gawne. **1919** The Woman Thou Gavest Me; The Squaw Man. **1920** Curtain; The Beauty Market. **1921** The Beautiful Liar; My Lady's Latchkey; Passion's Playground; Stranger Than Fiction; Trust Your Wife. **1922** Domestic Relations; Her Social Value; Heroes and Husbands; The Infidel; The Woman Conquers; The Woman's Side; White Shoulders. **1923** The Lonely Road; Money, Money, Money; Refuge; Chastity; The Scarlet Lily. **1925** The Unnamed Woman. **1926** Old Loves and New.

MacDONALD, RAY. *See* RAY McDONALD

MacDOUGALL, ALLAN R.

Born: 1894, Scotland. Died: July 19, 1956, Paris, France. Screen, stage actor, author and editor.

Appeared in: **1936** Soak the Rich.

MacDOWELL, MELBOURNE

Born: 1857, South River, N.J. Died: Feb. 18, 1941, Decoto, Calif. (blood clot on the brain). Stage and screen actor.

Appeared in: **1920** Nomads of the North. **1921** Diamonds Adrift; The March Hare; The Golden Snare; Outside the Law. **1922** Beyond the Crossroads; The Bootlegger's Daughter; Confidence; The Infidel; The Flaming Hour; Forsaking All Others. **1923** The Ghost Patrol; The Love Pirate; A Million to Burn; Richard the Lion-Hearted. **1924** Virtue's Revolt; Geared to Go. **1925** Bandits of the Air; Savages of the Sea; Sky's the Limit; The Cloud Rider; Fighting Courage; Speed Mad. **1926** The Outlaw Express; Behind the Front; The Rainmaker; The Winning Wallop; Stick to Your Story; What Happened to Jones; The City. **1927** Code of the Cow Country; Driven from Home. **1928** Feel My Pulse; The Old Code.

MACE, FRED

Born: 1879, Philadelphia, Pa. Died: Feb. 21, 1917, New York, N.Y. (apoplexy). Screen, stage actor, film producer and director.

Appeared in: **1911** The Village Hero; A Convenient Burglar; Too Many Burglars; Trailing the Counterfeiters; Through His Wife's Picture; A Victim of

Circumstances; Dooley's Scheme; Why He Gave Up; Caught with the Goods; $500.00 Reward. **1912** Brave and Bold; A Near-Tragedy; A Spanish Dilemma; Their First Kidnapping Case; The Leading Man; One Round O'Brien; The Speed Demon; A Dash Through the Clouds; Cohen Collects a Debt; The Water Nymph; Riley and Schultz; Lie Not to Your Wife; The New Neighbor; Pedro's Dilemma; Stolen Glory; Ambitious Butler; A Desperate Lover; Mr. Fixer; The Deacon's Trouble; A Bear Escape; Hoffmeyer's Legacy. **1913** Mabel's Adventures; Mabel's Strategem; Drummer's Vacation; The Elite Ball; Just Brown's Luck; The Battle of Who Run; The Stolen Purse; His Nobs—The Plumber; Teddy Loosebelt from Africa; At Twelve O'Clock; A Widow's Wiles; The Turkish Bath; Her New Beau; Algy on the Force; The Tale of a Black Eye; Mimosa's Sweetheart; The Gangsters; One Round O'Brien Comes Back; Gaffney's Gladiator; A Horse on Fred; The Doctor's Ruse; A Would-Be Detective; The Speed Bear; Fred's Trained Nurse; The Rube Boss; Catchem and Killem; The Mexican Sleep Producer. **1914** Heinze's Resurrection; Mabel's Heroes; The Professor's Daughter; A Red Hot Romance; The Sleuth's Last Stand; The Rural Third Degree; Her New Beau; Love and Pain; The Man Next Door; A Deaf Burglar; The Sleuth at the Floral Parade; The Rube and the Baron; Jenny's Pearls; Cupid in a Dental Parlour; Black Hand Conspiracy; Rafferty's Raffle; Up in the Air over Sadie; The Bangville Police; The Darktown Belle; Village School Days; Some Bull's Daughter; The Firebugs; The Tale of a Shirt; Hubby's Job; The Foreman of the Jury; Dad's Terrible Match; The Battle of Chili and Beans; A Parcel's Post Auto; Apollo Fred Sees the Point; Up and Down; The Cheese of Police; Apollo Fred Becomes a Homeseeker; Very Much Alive. **1915** What Happened to Jones?; My Valet; A Janitor's Wife's Temptation; Crooked to the End. **1916** Love Will Conquer; The Village Vampire; Bath Tub Perils; A Lover's Might; An Old Scoundrel; His Last Scent.

MacFADDEN, BERNARR (Bernard A. MacFadden)
Born: Aug. 16, 1868, near Mill Springs, Missouri. Died: Oct. 12, 1955, Jersey City, N.J. (jaundice). Health culturist, publisher and screen actor.

Appeared in: **1915-16** Building of the Health of a Nation series; **1925** The Wrongdoers.

MacFADDEN, GERTRUDE "MICKEY"
Born: 1900. Died: June 3, 1967, Hollywood, Calif. Screen, stage and vaudeville actress. Appeared with her sister, Florence, in vaudeville and films as the "Mac-Fadden Sisters."

MacFARLANE, BRUCE
Born: 1910. Died: Nov. 25, 1967, Hollywood, Calif. Screen, stage and television actor. Son of opera singer Alice Gentle.

Appeared in: **1938** Come On, Leathernecks; Come On, Rangers. **1939** Torchy Plays with Dynamite.

MacFARLANE, GEORGE
Born: 1877. Died: Feb. 22, 1932, Hollywood, Calif. (auto accident). Screen, stage and vaudeville actor.

Appeared in: **1929** Frozen Justice; Nix on Dames; South Sea Rose; Wall Street; Happy Days. **1930** Cameo Kirby; Double Cross Roads; The Painted Angel; Half Shot at Sunrise; Up the River. **1931** Rich Man's Folly. **1932** Union Depot; Taxi; Fireman, Save My Child; The Heart of New York.

MacGILL, MOYNA (Moyna McIldowie)
Born: Dec. 10, 1895, Belfast, Ireland. Died: Nov. 25, 1975, Santa Monica, Calif. Stage and screen actress. Mother of actress Angela Lansbury, film producers Edgar and Bruce Denham and Isolde Denham. Divorced from film director Reginald Denham and later married Edgar Lansbury (dec. 1935).

Appeared in: **1920** Garry Owen; Nothing Else Matters. **1924** Miriam Rozella. **1940** Gaslight (aka Angel Street—US 1944). **1944** Frenchman's Creek. **1945** Uncle Harry; Picture of Dorian Gray. **1946** Black Beauty. **1947** Green Dolphin Street. **1948** Three Daring Daughters. **1951** Kind Lady. **1964** My Fair Lady; The Unsinkable Molly Brown.

MacGOWRAN, JACK
Born: Oct. 13, 1918, Dublin, Ireland. Died: Jan. 31, 1973, New York, N.Y. (London flu). Screen, stage and television actor.

Appeared in: **1951** No Resting Place (US 1952). **1952** The Quiet Man; The Gentle Gunman (US 1953). **1953** The Titfield Thunderbolt. **1954** The Young Lovers (aka Chance Meeting—US 1955). **1956** Jacqueline. **1957** The Rising of the Moon (aka The Majesty of the Law); Manuela (aka Stowaway Girl—US). **1958** Rooney; She Didn't Say No (US 1962). **1959** Darby O'Gill and the Little People; Behemoth the Sea Monster (aka The Giant Behemoth—US). **1962** Mix Me a Person; Captain Clegg (aka Night Creatures—US); Two and Two Make Six; Vengeance (aka The Brian—US 1964). **1963** Tom Jones; The Ceremony. **1965** Lord Jim; Young Cassidy; Doctor Zhivago. **1966** Cul-de-Sac. **1967** How I Won the War; Dance of the Vampires (aka The Fearless Vampire Killers or Pardon Me, but Your Teeth are in My Neck—US). **1968** Wonderwall. **1969** Age of Consent (US 1970). **1970** King Lear. **1973** The Exorcist.

MacGREGOR, HARMAN
Born: 1878, New York, N.Y. Died: Dec. 5, 1948, Marblehead, Mass. Stage and screen actor.

Appeared in: **1923** Cause for Divorce; Slave of Desire; Vengeance of the Deep. **1924** The Dancing Cheat.

MacGREGOR, LEE (aka LEE McGREGOR)
Died: June 1964. Screen actor.

Appeared in: **1947** Gentleman's Agreement; Moss Rose; Mother Wore Tights. **1948** You Were Meant for Me; Sitting Pretty; The Luck of the Irish; Road House; Scudda Hoo! Scudda Hay!; When My Baby Smiles at Me. **1949** Mother is a Freshman; You're My Everything; Slattery's Hurricane; Mr. Belvedere Goes to College; It Happens Every Spring; Father was a Fullback; Twelve O'Clock High. **1950** Where the Sidewalk Ends; A Ticket to Tomahawk; Two Flags West; When Willie Comes Marching Home; My Blue Heaven; Three Came Home; Under My Skin. **1951** Sealed Cargo; Best of the Badmen; Hot Lead. **1952** The Half-Breed; Above and Beyond; Toughest Man in Arizona; What Price Glory?

MacGREGOR, MALCOLM. *See* MALCOLM McGREGOR

MacINTOSH, LOUISE
Born: 1865. Died: Nov. 1, 1933, Beverly Hills, Calif. Screen and stage actress.

Appeared in: **1930** Up the River.

MACK, ANDREW
Born: Boston, Mass. Died: May 21, 1931, Bayside, N.Y. Screen, stage actor and singer.

Appeared in: **1914** The Ragged Earl. **1926** Bluebeard's Seven Wives.

MACK, ARTHUR
Born: 1877. Died: June 19, 1942, Jamaica Plain, Mass. (gas poisoning suffered in Flanders during W.W.I). Screen and stage actor.

Appeared in: **1928** The Return of Sherlock Holmes.

MACK, BILL "BILLY"
Died: Jan. 27, 1961, New York, N.Y. (stroke). Screen and vaudeville actor. Was part of vaudeville acts of "Reigel and Mack" and later as "Rickard and Mack."

Appeared in: **1926** The Black Bird. **1944** A Wave, a Wac and a Marine.

MACK, CHARLES (Charles McGaughey)
Born: 1878. Died: Nov. 29, 1956, Hollywood, Calif. Screen, stage actor and film producer. Entered films in 1919.

Appeared in: **1925** The Lost Chord; Silent Pal; The White Monkey. **1927** The Trunk Mystery.

MACK, CHARLES E. (Charles E. Sellers)
Born: Nov. 22, 1887, White Cloud, Kans. Died: Jan. 11, 1934, near Mesa, Ariz. (auto accident). Screen, stage, vaudeville, radio minstrel and actor. He was the Mack in "Moran and Mack" comedy team, usually referred to as the "Two Black Crows."

Films he appeared in as part of team are: **1927** Two Flaming Youths. **1929** Why Bring That Up. **1930** Anybody's War (previous title was Two Black Crows in the A.E.F.). **1932** Hypnotized. **1932-33** Appeared in "Moran and Mack" shorts for Educational: Two Black Crows in Africa; As the Crows Fly. Note: Anybody's War. A few other shorts were without George Moran who left the team after Why Bring That Up, but returned to do Hypnotized and a few shorts.

MACK, CHARLES EMMETT
Born: 1900, Scranton, Pa. Died: Mar. 17, 1927, Riverside, Calif. (auto accident). Screen and vaudeville actor. Entered films as a property man with Griffith in 1917.

Appeared in: **1921** Dream Street. **1922** One Exciting Night. **1923** Driven; The Daring Years; The White Rose. **1924** America; The Sixth Commandment; Youth for Sale. **1925** Down upon the Swanee River; Bad Company; A Woman of the World; The White Monkey. **1926** The Devil's Circus; The Unknown Soldier. **1927** The First Auto; The Rough Riders; Old San Francisco.

MACK, DICK
Born: 1854. Died: Feb. 4, 1920, San Francisco, Calif. Screen, stage and vaudeville actor.

MACK, FRANCES
Born: 1907. Died: Sept. 26, 1967, Hollywood, Calif. Screen and stage actress. Entered films approx. 1945. Married to screen actor and costumer Alexis Davidoff.

MACK, HUGHIE (Hugh McGowan)
Born: Nov. 26, 1884, Brooklyn, N.Y. Died: Oct. 13, 1927, Santa Monica, Calif. (heart disease). Screen actor.

Appeared in: **1913** John Tobin's Sweetheart; Roughing the Cub. **1914** The Win(k)some Widow; The New Secretary. **1922** Trifling Women. **1923** Going Up; Reno. **1924** The Riddle Rider (serial); Greed. **1925** A Woman's Faith; The Merry Widow. **1926** Mare Nostrum. **1927** The Arizona Whirlwind; Where Trails Begin. **1928** Four Sons; The Wedding March.

MACK, JAMES "BUCK"
Died: Sept. 19, 1959, Los Angeles, Calif. Screen, stage and vaudeville actor. Do not confuse with actor James T. Mack. Was member of vaudeville dance team of "Miller and Mack."

MACK, JAMES T.
Born: 1871, Chicago, Ill. Died: Aug. 12, 1948, Hollywood, Calif. Stage and screen actor.

Appeared in: **1926** The Cruise of the Jasper B; Sin Cargo; Fools of Fashion. **1927** Wild Geese; The First Night; Husband Hunters; Women's Wares; Swim, Girl, Swim. **1928** The Home Towners. **1929** Ain't It the Truth (short); Queen of the Night Clubs. **1930** Anna Christie; Hello Sister. **1932** Arsene Lupin. **1933** One Year Later. **1934** I Hate Women; In Love with Life. **1935** Mary Burns, Fugitive; G-Men.

MACK, JOSEPH P. "JOE"
Born: May 4, 1878, Rome, Italy. Died: Apr. 8, 1946, Hollywood, Calif. Screen and vaudeville actor.

Appeared in: **1903** Great Train Robbery. **1918** Wild Honey. **1920** Wonder Man. **1927** Cross Breed. **1928** Finders Keepers; Man from Headquarters; Driftwood. **1936** A Woman Rebels.

MACK, LESTER
Born: 1906. Died: Oct. 11, 1972, New York, N.Y. Screen, stage and television actor.

Appeared in: **1968** Funny Girl; Star; The Night They Raided Minsky's; For Love of Ivy.

MACK, MAX
Born: 1885, Germany. Died: Mar. 1973, London, England. Film producer, director, author and screen actor.

Appeared in: **1934** You Belong to Me.

MACK, ROBERT
Born: 1877. Died: May 2, 1949, Jamaica, N.Y. Screen, stage, vaudeville actor and songwriter. Do not confuse with actor Bobby Mack.

Appeared in: **1922** Under Two Flags; The Cowboy and the Lady. **1923** Vanity Fair. **1925** Smouldering Fires; Timber Wolf.

MACK, ROSE
Born: 1866. Died: Oct. 1927, New York, N.Y. Screen, stage and vaudeville actor.

MACK, WILBUR
Born: Binghamton, N.Y. Died: Mar. 13, 1964, Hollywood, Calif. Screen, stage, vaudeville actor and long time film extra. Married to actress Gertrude Purdy with whom he appeared in vaudeville in the team of "Mack and Purdy." Divorced from actress Nella Walker with whom he appeared in vaudeville in the team of "Mack and Walker."

Appeared in: **1925** Gold and Grit. **1926** The Hidden Way. **1927** The Love of Paquita; Shooting Straight; Straight Shootin'. **1928** The Avenging Shadow; Quick Triggers; The Crimson Canyon; The Body Punch. **1929** Honky Tonk; The Argyle Case; Slim Fingers; Beauty and Bullets; and "Mack and Purdy" appeared in An Everyday Occurance (short). **1930** Remote Control; The Girl Said No; Up the River; Woman Racket; Sweethearts on Parade; The Czar of Broadway; Scarlet Pages; The Stand Up (short). **1931** Annabelle's Affairs. **1934** The Loud Speaker. **1935** Redheads on Parade; Million Dollar Baby; A Night at the Opera. **1936** The Crime Patrol. **1937** Larceny on the Air; Atlantic Flight; A Day at the Races. **1938** Law of the Texan. **1939** Tough Kid. **1940** Doomed to Die; That Gang of Mine; Half a Sinner. **1943** Dixie. **1944** Atlantic City. **1947** Ladies' Man. **1948** Stage Struck. **1951** According to Mrs. Hoyle. **1957** Up in Smoke.

MACK, WILLARD
Born: 1873, Morrisburg, Ontario, Canada. Died: Nov. 18, 1934, Los Angeles, Calif. Screen, stage actor, film director, screenwriter and playwright. Divorced from actresses Pauline Fredericks (dec. 1938) and Marjorie Rambeau (dec. 1970).

Appeared in: 1916 Aloha Oe. **1923** Your Friend and Mine. **1929** The Voice of the City. **1933** What Price Innocence; Broadway to Hollywood.

MACK, WILLIAM B.
Born: 1872. Died: Sept. 13, 1955, Islip, N.Y. Screen and stage actor.

Appeared in: **1920** Heliotrope. **1922** Missing Millions. **1923** Backbone; The Steadfast Heart. **1926** The Song and Dance Man; The American Venus.

MACKAY, CHARLES
Born: 1867. Died: Nov. 19, 1935, Englewood, N.J. Screen and stage actor. Entered films with Edison.

Appeared in: **1921** Diane of Star Hollow; Ten Nights in a Barroom; Peggy Puts It Over; The Matrimonial Web. **1922** The Inner Man; The Man She Brought Back; Without Fear. **1923** Lost in a Big City.

MACKAY, EDWARD J.
Born: 1874. Died: Dec. 26, 1948, Elizabeth, N.J. Screen, stage actor, film producer and film director. Appeared in early silents.

MACKAYE, DOROTHY
Born: 1898. Died: Jan. 5, 1940, San Fernando Valley, Calif. (injuries sustained in an auto accident). Stage and screen actress. Married to stage actor Ray Raymond (dec. 1927) and later married to actor Paul Kelly (dec. 1956).

Appeared in: **1917** Jack and the Beanstalk.

MacKAYE, NORMAN. *See* NORMAN McKAY

MACKEN, WALTER
Born: 1915, Ireland. Died: Apr. 22, 1967, Galway, Ireland (heart attack). Playwright, novelist, screenwriter, stage and screen actor.

Appeared in: **1959** Home is the Hero (US 1961). **1962** The Quare Fellow.

MacKENNA, KATE
Born: 1877. Died: June 14, 1957, Hollywood, Calif. (lung cancer). Screen and television actress.

Appeared in: **1935** The Bride Comes Home. **1941** So Ends Our Night. **1942** The Wife Takes a Flyer; Fly by Night. **1951** Lemon Drop Kid. **1956** Bus Stop.

MacKENNA, KENNETH (Leo Mielziner)
Born: Aug. 19, 1899, Canterbury, N.H. Died: Jan. 15, 1962, Hollywood, Calif. (cancer). Screen, stage actor, film director, story editor, stage director and stage producer. Married to actress Mary Phillips (dec. 1975). Entered films with Paramount Astoria Studios in 1925.

Appeared in: **1925** A Kiss in the Dark; Miss Bluebeard. **1926** The American Venus. **1927** The Lunatic at Large. **1929** Pleasure Crazed; South Sea Rose. **1930** Crazy That Way; Men without Women; Temple Tower; The Three Sisters; Man Trouble; Sin Takes a Holiday; Virtuous Sin. **1931** The Man Who Came Back. **1932** Those We Love. **1960** High Time. **1961** Judgement at Nuremberg. **1962** 13 West Street.

MacKENZIE, ALEXANDER (aka ALEX McKENZIE)
Born: 1886, Scotland. Died: Jan. 1966, Scotland. Screen and stage actor.

Appeared in: **1954** The Maggie (aka High and Dry—US). **1955** Geordie (aka Wee Geordie—US 1956). **1958** Mad Little Island. **1959** The Bridal Path; The Battle of the Sexes (US 1960).**1960** Kidnapped. **1961** Greyfriars' Bobby. **1963** The Three Lives of Thomasina.

MacKENZIE, DONALD (aka DONALD McKENZIE)
Born: 1880, Edinburgh, Scotland. Died: July 21, 1972, Jersey City, N.J. Screen actor and film producer.

Appeared in: **1914** Perils of Pauline (serial). **1929** The Studio Murder Mystery; The Mysterous Dr. Fu Manchu; True Heaven. **1930** Conspiracy; Scarlet Pages; Girl of the Port. **1931** Fighting Caravans; Unfaithful; Kick In.

MacKENZIE, GEORGE
Born: 1901, England. Died: Sept. 4, 1975, England? Screen actor and magician.

MACKENZIE, MARY
Born: 1922. Died: Sept. 20, 1966, London, England (auto accident). Screen, stage and television actress.

Appeared in: **1952** Stolen Face; Lady in the Fog (aka Scotland Yard Inspector—US). **1953** The Long Memory; The Man Who Watched Trains Go By. **1954** Duel in the Jungle; The Master Plan; Trouble in the Glen. **1955** Track the Man Down. **1956** Cloak Without Dagger (aka Operation Conspiracy—US 1957); Yield to the Night (aka Blonde Sinner—US). **1958** A Question of Adultery (US 1959).

MACKIE, BERT (Robert James Mackie)
Born: 1893. Died: July 23, 1967, Hollywood, Calif. Screen actor.

MACKIN, WILLIAM
Born: 1883. Died: Sept. 9, 1928, Los Angeles, Calif. Screen actor.

MACKRIS, ORESTES
Born: 1900, Chalkis, Eubea. Died: Jan. 30, 1975, Athens, Greece. Stage and screen actor.

MacLANE, BARTON
Born: Dec. 25, 1900, Columbia, S.C. Died: Jan. 1, 1969, Santa Monica, Calif. (double pneumonia). Screen, stage and television actor.

Appeared in: **1926** The Quarterback (film debut). **1929** The Cocoanuts. **1933** Men of the Forest; Big Executive; The Torch Singer; To the Last Man; Tillie and Gus; Hell and High Water; Let's Dance (short). **1934** The Last Round-Up; The Thundering Herd; Lone Cowboy. **1935** Black Fury; Go into Your Dance; The G-Men; Case of the Curious Bride; Stranded; Page Miss Glory; Dr. Socrates; I Found Stella Parish; Frisco Kid; The Case of the Lucky Legs; Man of Iron; Ceiling Zero. **1936** The Walking Dead; Times Square Playboy; Jail Break; Bullets or Ballots; Bengal Tiger; Smart Blonde; God's Country and the Woman. **1937** Draegerman Courage; You Only Live Once; Don't Pull Your Punches; San Quentin; The Prince and the Pauper; Fly-Away Baby; Ever Since Eve; Wine, Woman and Horses; The Adventurous Blonde; Born Reckless. **1938** The Kid Comes Back; Blondes at Work; Torchy Gets Her Man; Gold Is Where You Find It; You and Me; Prison Break; The Storm. **1939** Big Town Czar; Torchy Blane in Chinatown; I Was a Convict; Stand Up and Fight; Torchy Runs for Mayor; Mutiny in the Big House. **1940** Men Without Souls; The Secret Seven; Gangs of Chicago; Melody Ranch. **1941** Manpower; Barnacle Bill; Wild Geese Calling; Hit the Road; Come Live with Me; Western Union; Dr. Jekyll and Mr. Hyde; The Maltese Falcon; High Sierra. **1942** The Big Street; Highways by Night; All through the Night. **1943** The Underdog; The Crime Doctor's Strangest Case; Man of Courage; Bombardier; Song of Texas. **1944** The Cry of the Werewolf; The Mummy's Ghost; Nobonga; Marine Raiders; Secret Command; Gentle Annie. **1945** Treasure of Fear; The Spanish Main; Scared Stiff; Tarzan and the Amazons. **1946** Santa Fe Uprising; Mysterious Intruder; San Quentin. **1947** Tarzan and the Huntress; Jungle Flight; Cheyenne. **1948** Silver River; The Dude Goes West; The Walls of Jericho; Angel in Exile; Relentless; Unknown Island; The Treasure of the Sierra Madre. **1949** Red Light. **1950** Kiss Tomorrow Goodbye; Rookie Fireman; The Bandit Queen; Let's Dance. **1951** Best of the Badmen; Drums in the Deep South. **1952** The Half Breed; Thunderbirds; Bugles in the Afternoon. **1953** Kansas Pacific; Cow Country; Jack Slade; Sea of Lost Ships; Captain Scarface. **1954** Rails into Laramie; Jubilee Trail; The Glenn Miller Story. **1955** The Last of the Desperadoes; Hell's Outpost; Treasure of Ruby Hills; The Silver Star; Foxfire; Jail Busters. **1956** The Man Is Armed; Three Violent People; The Naked Gun; Jaguar; Backlash; Wetbacks. **1957** Sierra Stranger; Naked in the Sun; The Storm Rider; Hell's Crossroads. **1958** Girl in the Woods; Frontier Gun; The Geisha Boy. **1960** Noose for a Gunman; Gunfighters of Abilene. **1961** Pocketful of Miracles. **1964** Law of the Lawless. **1965** The Rounders; Town Tamer. **1968** Arizona Bushwackers; Buckskin.

MacLANE, MARY (aka MARY McLANE)
Born: Butte, Mont. Died: Aug. 1929. Screen actress and novelist.

Appeared in: **1918** Men Who Have Made Love to Me. **1924** Which Shall It Be? **1925** The Night Ship. **1926** Sparrows.

MACLAREN, IVOR
Born: 1904, Wimbledon, England. Died: Oct. 30, 1962, London, England. Screen, television actor and film director.

Appeared in: **1933** Aunt Sally. **1934** Evergreen; Princess Charming; Friday the 13th; The Woman in Command; Along Came Sally. **1935** Radio Parade of 1935.

MacLEAN, DOUGLAS
Born: Jan. 14, 1890 or 1897 (?), Philadelphia, Pa. Died: July 9, 1967, Beverly Hills, Calif. (stroke). Screen, stage actor, film producer and screenwriter.

Appeared in: **1916** Amer. Film Mfg. Co. films. **1917** Souls in Pawn. **1918** Johanna Enlists; The Hun Within; Fuss and Feathers; Mirandy Smiles. **1919** Captain Kidd, Jr.; As Ye Sow; The Home Breaker; Twenty-Three and a Half Hour's Leave. **1920** Let's Be Fashionable; Mark's Ankle; The Jailbird. **1921** Chickens; The Home Stretch; One a Minute; Passing Thru; The Rookie's Return. **1922** The Hottentot. **1923** The Sunshine Trail; Going Up; Bell Boy 13; A Man of Action; Mary of the Movies. **1924** Never Say Die; The Yankee Consul. **1925** Introduce Me; Seven Keys to Baldpate. **1926** That's My Baby; Hold That Lion. **1927** Soft Cushions; Let It Rain. **1929** The Carnation Kid; Divorce Made Easy.

MacLEAN, R. D. (Rezin Donald MacLean)
Born: 1859, New Orleans, La. Died: June 27, 1948. Screen, stage actor and stage director.

Appeared in: **1920** The Silver Horde; Little Shepard of Kingdom Come. **1921** Don't Neglect Your Wife. **1933** Cradle Song.

MacLEOD, KENNETH
Born: 1895. Died: Dec. 6, 1963, Hollywood, Calif. Screen actor.

MacMILLIAN, VIOLET
Born: 1887. Died: Dec. 28, 1953, Grand Rapids, Mich. Screen and stage actress.

Appeared in: **1915** Mrs. Plumb's Pudding. **1920** The Mystery Mind (serial).

MacNEAL, F. A. (Frank Ashby MacNeal)
Born: Nov. 18, 1867, Missouri. Died: Feb. 27, 1918, Los Angeles, Calif. (coronary occlusion). Screen actor.

MACOLLUM, BARRY
Born: Apr. 6, 1889 or 1894(?), Ireland. Died: Feb. 22, 1971, West Los Angeles, Calif. (peritonitis). Stage and screen actor.

Appeared in: **1923** Fury. **1929** The Hole in the Wall. **1937** Interns Can't Take Money; Parnell; Murder in Greenwich Village. **1938** If I Were King. **1939** Beau Geste; Rulers of the Sea. **1943** Hi Diddle Diddle. **1944** Jayne Eyre; Make Your Own Bed; Kismet; Marine Raiders; National Velvet. **1954** On the Waterfront. **1955** The Trouble with Harry.

MACOWAN, NORMAN
Born: Jan. 2, 1877, St. Andrews, Scotland. Died: Dec. 29, 1961. Screen actor.

Appeared in: **1951** Valley of the Eagles. **1953** Laxdale Hall. **1955** Footsteps in the Fog. **1956** X the Unknown. **1957** Action of the Tiger. **1958** Tread Softly Stranger (US 1959). **1959** The Boy and the Bridge; Battle of the Sexes (US 1960). **1960** Kidnapped. **1961** Horror Hotel (US 1963 aka City of the Dead).

MacPHERSON, JEANIE
Born: Boston, Mass. Died: Aug. 26, 1946, Hollywood, Calif. Screen, stage actress, screenwriter and film director.

Appeared in: **1908** The Vaquero's Vow; Mr. Jones at the Ball; Mrs. Jones Entertains. **1909** The Death Disc; A Corner in Wheat. **1910** Winning Back His Love; Heart Beats of Long Ago; The Last Drop of Water; Enoch Arden, Part I; Fisher Folks. **1911** The Blind Princess and the Poet; Out From the Shadow; The Village Hero; A Man For All That; Home; The Two Flats. **1912** The Butler and the Maid; Partners For Live; A Man; The Wreckers. **1913** The Tarantula; The Violet Bride; The Awakening; The Sea Urchin; Carmen. **1914** The Undertow. **1923** Hollywood. **1939** Land of Liberty (narr.).

MacQUARRIE, MURDOCK
Born: Aug. 26, 1878, San Francisco, Calif. Died: Aug. 22, 1942, Los Angeles, Calif. Screen, stage actor and film director. Entered films with Biograph in 1902.

Appeared in: **1913** The Embezzler; The Lamb, the Woman, the Wolf; The End of the Feud; Red Margaret—Moonshiner; The Lie. **1914** The Honor of the Mounted; Remember Mary Magdalen; Discord and Harmony; The Menace of Charlotte (aka Carlotta, the Bead Stringer); The Tragedy of Whispering Creek; The Unlawful Trade; The Forbidden Room; The Old Cobbler; A Ranch Romance; Her Grave Mistake; By the Sun's Ray; The Oubliette; A Miner's Romance; The Higher Law; Richelieu; Discord and Harmony; The Wall of Flame; The Star Gazer; The Old Bellringer; Monsieur Bluebeard; The Embezzler; The End of the Feud; The Hopes of Blind Alley. **1915** The Stranger Mind; The Trap. **1917** Bloodhounds of the North. **1921** Cheated Hearts; Sure Fire. **1922** If I Were Queen; The Unfoldment; The Hidden Woman. **1923** Ashes of Vengeance; Canyon of the Fools. **1924** The Only Woman. **1925** A Gentleman Roughneck. **1926** Going the Limit; Hair Trigger Baxter; The High Hand; The Jazz Girl. **1927** Black Jack; The Long Loop on the Pecos. **1928** The Man From Hardpan; The Apache Raider. **1929** A .45 Calibre War. **1930** Captain of the Guard. **1932** Wild Girls; Dr. Jekyll and Mr. Hyde. **1933** Cross Fire. **1934** Return of Chandu; The Mighty Barnum. **1935** Stone of Silver Creek. **1937** Git Along, Little Dogies. **1938** Tom Sawyer, Detective; Blockage. **1940** The Mummy's Hand. **1942** Tennessee Johnson.

MACRAE, DUNCAN (aka JOHN DUNCAN GRAHAM MACRAE)
Born: 1905, Glasgow, Scotland. Died: Mar. 23, 1967, Glasgow, Scotland. Screen, stage and television actor. Married to actress Gertrude McCoy (dec. 1967).

Appeared in: **1947** The Brothers. **1949** Whisky Galore (aka Tight Little Island—US and Mad Little Island). **1950** The Woman in Question (aka Five Angles on Murder—US 1953). **1952** You're Only Young Twice! **1953** The Kidnappers (aka The Little Kidnappers—US 1954). **1955** Geordie (aka Wee Geordie—US 1956). **1959** The Bridal Path. **1960** Kidnapped; Our Man in Havana; Tunes of Glory. **1961** Greyfriars Bobby. **1962** The Best of Enemies. **1963** Girl in the Headlines (aka The Model Murder Case—US 1964); A Jolly Bad Fellow (US 1964 aka They All Died Laughing). **1967** Casino Royale; 30 Is a Dangerous Age; Cynthia (US 1968).

MACREADY, GEORGE
Born: Aug. 29, 1909, Providence, R.I. Died: July 2, 1973, Los Angeles, Calif.

(emphysema). Screen, stage and television actor. Divorced from actress Elizabeth Dana.

Appeared in: **1942** Commandos Strike at Dawn (film debut). **1944** Wilson; The Seventh Cross; Story of Dr. Wassell; The Conspirators; Follow the Boys; Soul of a Monster. **1945** Counter-Attack; Don Juan Quilligan; The Fighting Guardsman; My Name is Julia Ross; I Love a Mystery; A Song to Remember; The Missing Juror; The Monster and the Ape (serial). **1946** Gilda; The Bandit of Sherwood Forest; The Walls Came Tumbling Down; The Man Who Dared; The Return of Monte Cristo. **1947** Down to Earth; The Swordsman. **1948** The Big Clock; Beyond Glory; Gallant Blade; The Black Arrow; Coroner Creek. **1949** Knock on Any Door; Alias Nick Beal (aka The Contact Man); The Doolins of Oklahoma; Johnny Allegro. **1950** The Nevadan; A Lady Without Passport; The Desert Hawk; Fortunes of Captain Blood; Rogues of Sherwood Forest. **1951** The Desert Fox; Detective Story; The Golden Horde; Tarzan's Peril. **1952** The Green Glove. **1953** Treasure of the Golden Condor; The Stranger Wore a Gun; The Golden Blade; Julius Caesar. **1954** Duffy of San Quentin; Vera Cruz. **1956** Thunder Over Arizona; A Kiss Before Dying. **1957** Paths of Glory; The Abductors. **1958** Gunfire at Indian Gap; Jet Over the Atlantic (US 1960). **1959** Plunderers of Painted Flats; The Alligator People. **1962** Two Weeks in Another Town; Taras Bulba. **1964** Dead Ringer; Seven Days in May; Where Love Has Gone. **1965** The Great Race; The Human Duplicators. **1970** Tora! Tora! Tora!; Count Yorga. **1971** Return of Count Yorga.

MacSARIN, KENNETH (Max Kenneth Sarin)
Born: 1912. Died: Jan. 17, 1967, New York, N.Y. (cancer). Stage and screen actor.

MacTAGGART, JAMES
Born: 1928. Died: May 29, 1974, London, England. Screen, stage actor, film producer, television director and screen writer.

MACY, CARLETON
Born: 1861. Died: Oct. 18, 1946, Bay Shore, N.Y. Screen, stage and vaudeville actor. Was in vaudeville with his wife Maude Hall in an act billed as "Magpie and the Jay" and later was with Al Lydell in an act billed as "Two Old Cronies."

Appeared in: **1929** Seven Keys to Baldpate.

MACY, JACK
Born: 1886. Died: July 2, 1956, Wyo. (heart attack). Screen, stage and television actor.

Appeared in: **1955** Untamed.

MADEIRA, HUMBERTO
Born: 1921, Portugal. Died: July 15, 1971, Lisbon, Portugal (cancer). Stage and screen actor.

Appeared in: **1956** Lisbon.

MADISON, C. J.
Died: Jan. 20, 1975. Animal trainer and screen actor.

Appeared in: **1962** Jumbo.

MADISON, CLEO
Born: 1883. Died: Mar. 11, 1964, Burbank, Calif. (heart attack). Screen actress.

Appeared in: **1913** The Heart of a Cracksman. **1914** The Trey of Hearts (serial); The Pine's Revenge; The Fascination of the Fleur de Lis; Alas and Alack; A Mother's Atonement. **1915** Damon and Pythias; Liquid Dynamite; The Power of Fascination; The Ring of Destiny. **1916** Alias Jane Jones; The Chalice of Sorrow; Cross Purposes; Eleanor's Catch; The Girl in Lower 4; The Guilty One; Her Bitter Cup; Her Defiance; His Return; The Severed Hand; To Another Woman; Virginia; When the Wolf Howls; The Crimson Yoke; Priscilla's Prisoner; The Triumph of Truth. **1917** Black Orchids; The Daring Change. **1918** The Romance of Tarzan. **1919** The Great Radium Mystery (serial). **1920** The Girl From Nowhere. **1921** Ladies Must Live; The Lure of Youth. **1922** The Dangerous Age; A Woman's Woman. **1923** Gold Madness; Souls in Bondage. **1924** The Roughneck; The Lullaby; True as Steel; Discontented Husbands; Unseen Hands.

MADISON, HARRY
Born: 1877. Died: July 8, 1936, Los Angeles, Calif. (throat ailment). Screen, stage and vaudeville actor. Was part of vaudeville team of "Bailey and Madison" and later "Thurber and Madison."

Appeared in: **1920** King of the Circus (serial).

MADISON, NOEL N. (Noel Moscovitch)
Born: c. 1905, New York, N.Y. Died: Jan. 6, 1975, Fort Lauderdale, Fla. Screen, stage actor and stage director. Son of actor Maurice Moscovitch (dec. 1940).

Appeared in: **1930** The Doorway to Hell; Sinners Holiday; Little Caesar; The Honorable Mr. Wong. **1931** The Star Witness. **1932** Me and My Gal; Hat

Check Girl; The Last Mile; The Trial of Vivienne Ware; Man About Town; The Hatchet Man; Play Girl; Symphony of Six Million. **1933** The Important Witness; West of Singapore; Laughter in Hell; Destination Unknown; Humanity. **1934** Manhattan Melodrama; I Like It That Way; Journal of a Crime; The House of Rothschild. **1935** Four Hours to Kill; The Morals of Marcus (US 1936); G-Men; Woman Wanted; The Girl Who Came Back; Three Kids and a Queen; My Marriage. **1936** Our Relations; Muss 'Em Up; The Criminal Within; Missing Girls; Easy Money; Straight from the Shoulder; Champagne Charlie; Murder at Glen Athol. **1937** Man of the People; Gangway; The Man Who Made Diamonds; Kate Plus Ten; Nation Aflame; House of Secrets. **1938** Sailing Along; Anything to Declare; Crackerjack (aka The Man With a Hundred Faces—US). **1939** Climbing High; Charlie Chan in City in Darkness; Missing Evidence. **1940** Know Your Money (short); The Great Plane Robbery. **1941** Sucker List; Queen of Crime; Ellery Queen's Penthouse Mystery; Footsteps in the Dark; Highway West; A Shot in the Dark. **1942** Secret Agent of Japan; Bombs over Burma; Joe Smith—American. **1943** Miss V. from Moscow; Jitterbugs; Shantytown; Black Raven. **1949** Gentleman from Nowhere.

MADRIGUERA, ENRIC
Born: 1902. Died: Sept. 7, 1973. Screen actor, composer, musician and orchestra leader.

Appeared in: **1946** The Thrill of Brazil (with his orchestra).

MAE, JIMSEY (Charlotte Rawley)
Born: 1894. Died: Apr. 10, 1968, Jackson, Ore. Screen actress.

Appeared in: **1915** Damaged Goods.

MAERTENS, WILLY
Born: 1893, Germany. Died: Nov. 28, 1967, Hamburg, Germany. Screen, stage, television actor and stage director.

MAGEE, HARRIETT
Born: 1878. Died: Apr. 19, 1954, Los Angeles, Calif. Screen actress. Appeared in silent films.

MAGNANI, ANNA
Born: 1909, Alexandria, Egypt. Died: Sept. 26, 1973, Rome, Italy (cancer). Screen, stage, vaudeville, television actress and screenwriter. Married to film director Goffredo Alessandrini. Entered films in 1934. Won National Board of Review Award in 1946 as Best Foreign Actress for Open City; in 1947 won Venice Festival Award for Best International Actress and the Italian Silver Ribbon Award for Love; and won 1955 Academy Award for Best Actress in The Rose Tattoo.

Appeared in: **1934** The Blind Woman of Sorrento; Calvary; Down with Misery. **1936** Tempo Massimo; La Cieca di Sorrento. **1946** Woman Trouble (US 1949); Dreams in the Streets; Citta Aperta (Open City); The Bandit (US 1949); Unknown Men of San Marino. **1947** Before Him All Rome Trembled; Revenge; Love. **1948** Angelina. **1949** The Peddler and the Lady (US 1952); Peddlin' in Society (US 1950). **1950** The Miracle (aka The Ways of Love—US 1951). **1951** Doctor, Beware; Scarred. **1953** Volcano; Bellissima (US 1954); Anita Garibaldi. **1954** The Golden Coach; We Women. **1955** The Rose Tattoo. **1957** Wild is the Wind. **1958** The Awakening; Of Life and Love; Nella Citta L'Inferno (aka Hell in the City and The Wild Wild Women—US 1961). **1959** Woman Obsessed. **1960** The Fugitive Kind; Risate di Gioia (aka The Passionate Thief—US 1963). **1962** Hell in the City; Mamma Roma. **1965** Made in Italy (US 1967). **1969** The Secret of Santa Vittoria; Year of the Lord.

MAGRI, COUNT PRIMO
Born: 1849. Died: Oct. 31, 1920, Middleboro, Mass. Circus midget and screen actor. Married to circus performer and actress Mrs. General Tom Thumb (dec. 1919).

Appeared in: **1915** The Lilliputian's Courtship.

MAGRILL, GEORGE
Born: Jan. 5, 1900, New York, N.Y. Died: May 31, 1952, Los Angeles, Calif. Screen, stage actor and stuntman. Entered films in 1921.

Appeared in: **1922** Rose of the Sea. **1924** Fast and Fearless; North of Nevada; The Mask of Lopez; Stolen Secrets. **1925** Lord Jim; Vanishing American; Wild Horse Mesa; Duped; The Fighting Smile. **1926** The Enchanted Hill. **1927** The Desert of the Lost; The Ballyhoo Buster; Roarin' Broncs; Hawk of the Hills (serial); Ride 'Em High; The Cyclone Cowboy. **1928** Blockage; Vultures of the Sea (serial); The Count of Ten. **1929** Hawk of the Hills (feature of 1927 serial). **1934** Charlie Chan's Courage. **1935** The Phantom Empire (serial). **1936** Too Many Parents. **1937** Outcast; Midnight Madonna. **1938** Born to Be Wild; Passport Husbands; Romance in the Dark; Give Me a Sailor. **1939** The Flying Irishman. **1941** Meet Boston Blackie. **1947** Pirates of Monterey; G-Men Never Forget (serial); Twilight on the Rio Grande. **1948** So You Want to Be a Detective (short). **1950** When Willie Comes Marching Home. **1952** At Sword's Point.

MAGUIRE, CHARLES J.

Born: 1882. Died: July 22, 1939, North Hollywood, Calif. Screen, stage and circus actor. Married to actress Janet Sully.

MAGUIRE, EDWARD

Born: 1867. Died: Apr. 10, 1925, New York, N.Y. (heart disease). Screen extra.

MAGUIRE, TOM "LITTLE TOM MAGUIRE"

Born: Sept. 7, 1869, Milford, Conn. Died: June 21, 1934, North Hollywood, Calif. (blood clot on the heart). Stage and screen actor.

Appeared in: 1921 Star Dust. 1922 The Bond Boy. 1926 The Savage; Then Came the Woman. 1927 One Increasing Purpose; Shanghai Bound; Colleen. 1928 Cameraman; The Sawdust Paradise. 1930 City Girl.

MAGYARI, IMRE

Born: 1894, Hungary. Died: June 1940. Hungarian screen, stage actor and gypsy band leader.

MAHAN, VIVIAN L.

Born: 1902. Died: Oct. 13, 1933, Los Angeles, Calif. (suicide). Screen actress and film extra. Married to actor Harry Bayfield.

MAHER, WALTER "WALLY"

Born: 1908. Died: Dec. 27, 1951, Los Angeles, Calif. Screen, radio and television actor.

Appeared in: 1935 Murder in the Fleet. 1937 23½ Hours' Leave; Submarine D-1; Hollywood Hotel. 1938 Miracle Money (short). 1940 Pound Foolish (short). 1945 Strange Holiday. 1949 Johnny Stool Pigeon. 1950 Mystery Street; The Reformer and the Redhead; Right Cross; The Story of Molly X.

MAHONEY, WILL

Born: 1894, U.S. Died: Feb. 8, 1966 or 1967 (?), Melbourne, Australia. Screen actor.

Appeared in: 1928 Lost in the Arctic; Gang War. 1933 A Columbia short. 1937 Said O'Reilly to McNab (aka Sez O'Reilly to McNab—US 1938). 1939 Come Up Smiling (aka Ants in His Pants). 1963 The Sound of Laughter.

MAIGNE, CHARLES M.

Born: 1879, Va. Died: Nov. 23, 1929, San Francisco, Calif. (pneumonia). Screen actor, film director and screenwriter.

MAILES, CHARLES HILL

Born: May 25, 1870, Halifax, Nova Scotia, Canada. Died: Feb. 17, 1937, Los Angeles, Calif. Stage and screen actor. Married to actress Claire McDowell (dec. 1966).

Appeared in: 1909 At the Altar. 1911 A Woman Scorned; The Miser's Heart; A Terrible Discovery; A Tale of the Wilderness; A Blot on the 'Scutcheon. 1912 The Girl and Her Trust; Just Like a Woman; A Beast at Bay; Home Folks; Lena and the Geese; Man's Genesis; The Sands of Dee; The Narrow Road; Iola's Promise; A Change of Spirit; Friends; So Near, Yet So Far; The Painted Lady; The Unwelcome Guest; The New York Hat; An Adventure in the Autumn Woods. 1913 A Welcome Intruder; The Hero of Little Italy; A Misunderstood Boy; The House of Darkness; Olaf—an Atom; Her Mother's Oath; The Coming of Angelo; The Reformers; The Battle of Elderberry Gulch; Judith of Bethulia. 1918 The Brass Bullet (serial). 1919 Red Hot Dollars. 1920 Treasure Island; Go and Get It. 1921 Chickens; The Home Stretch; Courage; The Ten Dollar Raise; Uncharted Seas. 1922 The Bond Boy; The Man from Downing Street; The Lying Truth. 1923 Held to Answer; East Side—West Side; Soft Boiled; Crashin' Thru; The Town Scandal; Michael O'Halloran. 1924 Thundering Hoofs; Find Your Man; Name the Man; When a Man's a Man. 1925 The Lighthouse by the Sea; The Midnight Flyer; The Fighting Demon; The Crimson Runner; The Overland Limited; Free to Love; Playing with Souls. 1926 Old Ironsides; The Combat; The Blue Streak; The Social Highwayman; Exclusive Rights; The Man in the Saddle; The Frontier Trail; Hearts and Fists; The Better Man. 1927 Bitter Apples; Play Safe; Man Power; Ain't Love Funny?; The City Gone Wild; The College Widow; Somewhere in Sonora. 1928 What a Night!; Give and Take; The Charge of the Gauchos; Drums of Love; Queen of the Chorus. 1929 The Bellamy Trial; The Faker; The Carnation Kid; One Stolen Night; Phantom City. 1930 Mother's Cry; Lilies of the Field. 1931 The Unholy Garden. 1932 No More Orchids. 1933 Women Won't Tell.

MAIN, MARJORIE

Born: Feb. 24, 1890, Acton, Ind. Died: Apr. 10, 1975, Los Angeles, Calif. (cancer). Screen, stage, vaudeville, radio and television actress. Married to psychologist-lecturer Dr. Stanley L. Krebs (dec. 1935). Nominated for 1947 Academy Award as Best Supporting Actress in The Egg and I.

Appeared in: 1932 A House Divided. 1933 Take a Chance. 1934 Music in the Air (stage and film versions); Crime Without Passion; New Deal Rhythm (short). 1935 Naughty Marietta. 1937 Love in Bungalow; The Man Who Cried Wolf; The Wrong Road; The Shadow; Boy of the Streets; Stella Dallas; Dead End (stage and film versions). 1938 City Girl; Three Comrades; Penitentiary;

Girl's School; Romance of the Limberlost; Under the Big Top; King of the Newsboys; Test Pilot; Too Hot To Handle; Prison Farm; Little Tough Guy; There Goes My Heart. 1939 Two Thoroughbreds; Another Thin Man; Angels Wash Their Faces; Lucky Night; The Women; They Shall Have Music. 1940 Women Without Names; The Dark Command; Turnabout; Susan and God; The Captain is a Lady; I Take This Woman; Wyoming; Bad Man of Wyoming. 1941 The Trial of Mary Dugan; The Wild Man of Borneo; Barnacle Bill; The Bugle Sounds; The Shepherd of the Hills; Honky Tonk; A Woman's Face. 1942 Jackass Mail; Once Upon a Thursday; Tish; Tennessee Johnson; The Affairs of Martha; We Were Dancing. 1943 Johnny Come Lately; Woman of the Town; Heaven Can Wait. 1944 Meet Me in St. Louis; Rationing. 1945 Gentle Annie; Murder, He Says. 1946 Undercurrent; Bad Bascomb; The Harvey Girls; The Show-Off. 1947 The Egg and I; The Wistful Widow of Wagon Gap. 1948 Feudin' and Fussin' and A-Fightin'. 1949 Ma and Pa Kettle; Big Jack. 1950 Mrs. O'Malley and Mr. Malone; Ma and Pa Kettle Go to Town; Summer Stock. 1951 Ma and Pa Kettle Back on the Farm; Mr. Imperium; The Law and the Lady; It's a Big Country. 1952 The Belle of New York; Ma and Pa Kettle at the Fair; Fast Company. 1953 Ma and Pa Kettle on Vacation; Fast Company. 1954 Ricochet Romance; The Long, Long Trailer; Rose Marie; Ma and Pa Kettle at Home. 1955 Ma and Pa Kettle at Waikiki. 1956 The Kettles in the Ozarks; Friendly Persuasion. 1957 The Kettles on Old MacDonald's Farm.

MAINES, DON

Born: 1869. Died: Jan. 2, 1934, Los Angeles, Calif. (heart trouble). Screen actor.

Appeared in: 1922 The Man Who Waited.

MAISON, EDNA

Born: 1893. Died: Jan. 11, 1946, Hollywood, Calif. Screen actress and opera singer. Entered films in 1911.

MAJERONI, MARIO

Born: 1870. Died: Nov. 18, 1931, New York, N.Y. Screen and stage actor.

Appeared in: 1917 Heart's Desire; The Broadway Sport; A Sleeping Memory. 1920 Partners of the Night. 1921 The Face in the Fog; The Valley of Silent Men; Destiny's Isle. 1923 The Enemies of Women; The Snow Bride; The Steadfast Heart. 1924 Argentine Love; The Humming Bird; Her Love Story. 1925 Share and Share Alike; The Little French Girl; The Substitute Wife; The King on Main Street. 1927 Rubber Heels.

MAJOR, SAM COLLIER

Died: July 31, 1955, Houston, Tex. Screen, stage actor and stage director. Father of actress Colleen Moore.

MAKEHAM, ELIOT

Born: Dec. 22, 1882, London, England. Died: Feb. 8, 1956, London, England. Stage and screen actor.

Appeared in: 1932 Rome Express. 1933 The Lost Chord; I Lived With You; Orders Is Orders (US 1934); Little Napoleon; I Was A Spy (US 1934); Friday the Thirteenth; The Laughter of Fools; Home Sweet Home; The Roof; I'm An Explosive; Forging Ahead. 1934 The Unfinished Symphony; By-Pass to Happiness; The Crimson Candle. 1935 Lorna Doone; The Clairvoyant; Peg of Old Drury (US 1936); The Last Journey (US 1936); Once in a Blue Moon; His Last Affaire; Two Hearts in Harmony. 1936 The Brown Wallet; A Star Fell From Heaven; To Catch A Thief; Born That Way; East Meets West; Calling the Tune; Tomorrow We Live. 1937 Head Over Heels (aka Head Over Heels in Love—US); The Mill on the Floss (US 1939); Dark Journey; Farewell Again (aka Troopship—US 1938); Storm In a Teacup; Racing Romance; East of Ludgate Hill; Take My Tip. 1938 Darts Are Trumps; Coming of Age; Bedtime Story; Vessel of Wrath (aka The Beachcomber—US); It's In the Air (aka George Takes the Air—US 1940); The Citadel; Merely Mr. Hawkins; You're the Doctor; Anything to Declare? 1939 The Nursemaid Who Disappeared; Me and My Pal; Inspector Hornleigh; The Four Just Men (aka The Secret Four—US 1940); What Men Live By. 1940 Spy For A Day; Pastor Hall; Night Train to Munich (aka Night Train—US and Gestapo); Busman's Honeymoon (aka Haunted Honeymoon—US); Food For Thought; John Smith Wakes Up; Spare a Copper; All Hands. 1941 The Common Touch; Facing the Music. 1942 They Flew Alone (aka Wings and the Woman—US); Suspected Person; Uncensored (US 1944). 1943 Bell-Bottom George. 1944 The Halfway House (US 1945); A Canterbury Tale; Candles at Nine; Give Us the Moon. 1945 I'll Be Your Sweetheart; Perfect Strangers (aka Vacation from Marriage—US). 1946 Daybreak; The Magic Bow (US 1947). 1947 Frieda; The Little Ballerina (US 1951); Jassy (US 1948). 1948 Call of the Blood. 1949 Murder at the Windmill (aka Murder at the Burlesque—US); Children of Chance; Forbidden. 1950 The Miniver Story; Trio. 1951 Green Grow the Rushes; Scarlet Thread; Scrooge. 1952 Decameron Nights; The Crimson Pirate; The Yellow Balloon. 1953 The Fake; Always a Bride. 1954 The Million Pound Note (aka Man With a Million—US); Doctor in the House (US 1955). 1956 Sailor Beware! (aka Panic in the Parlour—US 1957).

MALA, RAY "MALA"

Born: 1906, near Candle, Alaska. Died: Sept. 23, 1952, Hollywood, Calif. (heart attack). Screen actor.

Appeared in: 1932 Igloo. 1933 Eskimo. 1935 The Last of the Pagans. 1936 Jungle Princess; Robinson Crusoe of Clipper Island. 1938 Call of the Yukon; Hawk of the Wilderness (serial). 1939 Mutiny on the Blackhawk; Coast Guard; Desperate Trails. 1940 Zanzibar; Green Hell; Girl from God's Country; The Devil's Pipeline. 1942 The Tuttles of Tahiti. 1952 Red Snow.

MALAN, WILLIAM

Born: 1868. Died: Feb. 13, 1941, Hollywood, Calif. Screen and stage actor. Appeared in early Sennett films.

Appeared in: 1923 Slow as Lightning. 1924 Flashing Spurs. 1926 The College Boob; Red Hot Leather; One Punch O'Day. 1927 The Broncho Buster; Men of Daring; The Fighting Three; A One Man Game; The Overland Stage; Three Miles Up. 1929 The Border Wildcat.

MALATESTA, FRED

Born: Apr. 18, 1889, Naples, Italy. Died: Apr. 8, 1952, Burbank, Calif. (following surgery). Screen actor and film director. Entered films in 1915.

Appeared in: 1919 The Terror of the Range (serial). 1921 The Mask; All Dolled Up; Little Lord Fauntleroy. 1922 White Shoulders; The Woman He Loved. 1923 The Girl Who Came Back; Refuge; The Man Between. 1924 The Lullaby; Broadway or Bust; Honor among Men; The Reckless Age; Forbidden Paradise; The Night Hawk. 1925 Without Mercy. 1926 Bardely's the Magnificent. 1928 The Gate Crasher; The Wagon Show. 1929 The Peacock Fan. 1930 Wings of Adventure. 1932 A Farewell to Arms. 1933 Picture Brides; What's Your Racket? 1934 Perfectly Mismated (short). 1935 The Crusades; A Night at the Opera. 1938 The Black Doll.

MALCOLM, REGINALD

Born: 1884, Nottingham, England. Died: Jan. 20, 1966, Ottawa, Canada. Screen, stage and radio actor.

MALIPIERO, LUIGI

Born: 1901, Germany. Died: Feb. 24, 1975, Sommerhausen, W. Germany (heart attack). Screen, stage, television actor, playwright and screenwriter. Married to actress Ingelborg Matly.

MALLESON, MILES

Born: May 25, 1888, Croydon, England. Died: Mar. 15, 1969, London, England. Screen, stage, television actor, playwright and screenwriter. Divorced from actress Colette O'Neil (dec. 1975).

Appeared in: 1921 The Headmaster. 1931 City of Song (aka Farewell to Love—US 1933). 1932 The Sign of Four; The Mayor's Nest; Love on Wheels; Money Means Nothing (US 1934); The Love Contract. 1933 Summer Lightning. 1934 The Queen's Affair (aka Runaway Queen—US 1935); Nell Gwyn. 1935 Lazybones; Vintage Wine. 1936 Tudor Rose (aka Nine Days a Queen—US). 1937 Knight Without Armour; Victoria the Great. 1940 The Thief of Bagdad. 1941 Major Barbara. 1942 Unpublished Story; They Flew Alone (aka Wings and the Woman—US). 1943 Thunder Rock (US 1944); This Was Paris; The Gentle Sex. 1945 Dead of Night. 1947 While the Sun Shines (US 1950). 1948 Saraband for Dead Lovers (aka Saraband—US 1949); One Night With You; Woman Hater (US 1949); The Mark of Cain; Idol of Paris. 1949 The Queen of Spades; The Perfect Woman (US 1950); Kind Hearts and Coronets (US 1950); Train of Events (US 1952); The History of Mr. Polly (US 1951); Cardboard Lover. 1950 Stage Fright; Golden Salamander. 1951 The Man in the White Suit (US 1952); The Magic Box (US 1952); Scrooge. 1952 The Happy Family (aka Mr. Lord Says No—US); Treasure Hunt; The Importance of Being Earnest (stage and film versions); Venetian Bird (aka The Assassin—US 1953); Trent's Last Case (US 1953); The Woman's Angle (US 1954); Folly to be Wise. 1953 The Captain's Paradise. 1955 King's Rhapsody; Geordie (aka Wee Geordie—US 1956). 1956 The Silken Affair (US 1957); The Man Who Never Was; Private's Progress; Three Men in a Boat (US 1958); Dry Rot. 1957 Brothers-in-Law; The Admirable Crichton (aka Paradise Lagoon); Barnacle Bill (aka All at Sea—US 1958); The Naked Truth (aka Your Past Is Showing—US 1958). 1958 Dracula (aka Horror of Dracula—US); Bachelor of Hearts (US 1962); Gideon's Day (aka Gideon of Scotland Yard—US 1959); Happy Is the Bride (US 1959); Behind the Mask. 1959 I'm All Right, Jack (US 1960); The Captain's Table (US 1960); Carlton-Browne of the F.O. (aka Man in a Cocked Hat—US 1960); The Hound of the Baskervilles. 1960 Kidnapped; Peeping Tom (US 1962); The Day They Robbed the Bank of England; The Brides of Dracula; And the Same to You. 1961 Double Bunk; The Hellfire Club (US 1963); Fury at Smugglers Bay (US 1963). 1962 Postman's Knock; Go to Blazes; The Phantom of the Opera; Vengeance (aka The Brain—US 1964). 1963 Heavens Above; A Jolly Bad Fellow (US 1964 aka They All Died Laughing). 1964 First Men in the Moon; Murder Ahoy; Circus World. 1965 You Must Be Joking.

MALLORY, PATRICIA "BOOTS"

Born: 1913, New Orleans, La. Died: Dec. 1, 1958, Santa Monica, Calif. (chronic throat ailment). Stage and screen actress. Divorced from actor Charles Bennett (dec. 1943) and William Cagney. Married to actor Herbert Marshall (dec. 1966). Was a 1932 Wampas Baby star.

Appeared in: 1932 Handle with Care. 1933 Humanity; Walking Down Broadway (aka Hello Sister); Carnival Lady; Hollywood on Parade (short). 1935 Sing Sing Nights; Powdersmoke Range. 1937 Here's Flash Casey.

MALLOY, JOHN J. (aka JOHN J. MALLOR)

Born: 1898, Dover, Del. Died: Feb. 9, 1968, Los Angeles, Calif. (heart attack). Screen actor, singer and artist. Appeared in silents.

MALO, GINA (Janet Flynn)

Born: June 1, 1909, Cincinnati, Ohio. Died: Nov. 30, 1963, New York, N.Y. Stage and screen actress. Married to actor Romney Brent (dec. 1976).

Appeared in: 1932 In a Monastery Garden; Good-Night Vienna; One Magic Night; King of the Ritz. 1933 Waltz Time; Strike It Rich; Lily of Killarney. 1934 The Private Life of Don Juan. 1936 My Song for You; Where There's a Will; Jack of All Trades. 1937 The Gang Show. 1938 Over She Goes. 1939 The Gentle People. 1940 Door with Seven Locks. 1941 Chamber of Horrors.

MALONE, DUDLEY FIELD

Born: 1882. Died: Oct. 5, 1950, Culver City, Calif. (heart attack). Screen actor. He was Asst. Secretary of State for Woodrow Wilson.

Appeared in: 1943 Mission to Moscow (played role of Churchill, whom he resembled).

MALONE, FLORENCE

Died: Mar. 4, 1956, Lyons, N.Y. Screen, stage, radio and television actress.

Appeared in: 1916 The Yellow Menace (serial).

MALONE, MOLLY

Born: Denver, Colo. Died: Feb. 15, 1952, Hollywood, Calif. Screen, vaudeville and radio actress.

Appeared in: 1917 The Pulse of Life; The Telltale Clue; The Phantom's Secret; The Thief Maker; To Be or Not to Be Remarried; A Marked Man; Bucking Broadway. 1918 The Phantom Rides; The Scarlet Drops; Wild Women; A Woman's Fool. 1919 Sally's Blighted Career. 1920 It's a Great Life. 1921 Just out of College; Bucking the Line; Made in Heaven; Not Guilty; A Poor Relation; An Unwilling Hero; They Flew Alone; Sure Fire; Red Courage. 1922 Blaze Away; Trail of Hate; Across the Dead-Line; The Freshie. 1923 Little Johnny Jones. 1924 Westbound. 1925 Battling Bunyon; The Knockout Kid. 1926 The Bandit Buster; Bad Man's Bluff; Rawhide. 1927 Daring Deeds; The Golden Stallion (serial).

MALONE, PAT

Died: Oct. 5, 1963, New York, N.Y. Screen, stage and television actor. Appeared in films prior to 1941.

MALONE, PICK

Died: Jan. 22, 1962. Screen and radio actor. Was "Pick" on radio's "Pick and Pat" program.

Appeared in: 1937 The Hit Parade.

MALONE, RAY

Died: Apr. 18, 1970. Screen actor.

Appeared in: 1943 Moonlight in Vermont. 1944 Slightly Terrific.

MALONEY, LEO D.

Born: 1888, San Jose, Calif. Died: Nov. 2, 1929, New York, N.Y. (heart disease). Screen actor, film director and producer.

Appeared in: 1914 Hazards of Helen (serial). 1915 The Girl and the Game. 1916 The Lumberlands (serial). 1920 The Fatal Sign (serial). 1921 No Man's Woman; The Wolverine. 1922 Ghost City; Nine Points of the Law; The Western Musketeer. 1923 King's Creek Law; The Rum Runners. 1924 Built for Running; Headin' Through; Payable on Demand; Riding Double; Huntin' Trouble; The Perfect Alibi; Not Built for Runnin'; The Loser's End. 1925 Across the Deadline; The Blood Bond; Flash O' Lightning; Ranchers and Rascals; Luck and Sand; The Shield of Silence; Win, Lose or Draw; The Trouble Buster.

MALTBY, HENRY F.

Born: Nov. 25, 1880, Ceres, South Africa. Died: Oct. 25, 1963, London, England. Screen, stage actor, playwright, screenwriter and author.

Appeared in: 1933 I Spy. 1934 A Political Party; Those Were the Days; The Luck Of a Sailor; Freedom of the Seas; Lost in the Legion; Falling in Love (aka Trouble Ahead—US); Girls Will be Boys (US 1935); Josser On the Farm. 1935 The Morals of Marcus (US 1936); A Little Bit of Bluff; The Right to Marry; Vanity. 1936 King of the Castle; Queen of Hearts; Jack of All Trades (aka The Two of Us—US 1937); Not So Dusty; Two's Company; To Catch A Thief; Where There's a Will; Fame; Calling the Tune; Everything Is Thunder; Head Office; Busman's Holiday; The Heirloom Mystery; Everything in Life; Reasonable Doubt. **1937** Wake Up Famous; Pearls Bring Tears; Okay For Sound; Take My Tip; Mr. Smith Carries On; The Live Wire; Paradise For Two (aka The Gaiety Girls—US 1938); Young and Innocent (aka A Girl Was Young—US 1938); What a Man!; The Sky's the Limit; Captain's Orders; Song of the Road. **1938** Owd Bob (aka To the Victor—US); Darts Are Trumps; A Yank at Oxford; His Lordship Goes to Press; Pygmalion; Everything Happens to Me. **1939** The Good Old Days; The Gang's All Here (aka The Amazing Mr. Forrest—US); Old Mother Riley Joins Up. **1940** Garrison Follies; Under Your Hat. **1941** Facing the Music. **1942** The Great Mr. Handel (US 1943). **1943** Old Mother Riley, Detective; Somewhere in Civvies. **1944** A Canterbury Tale; Medal For the General. **1945** Home Sweet Home. **1946** The Trojan Brothers; Caesar and Cleopatra.

MALYON, EILY (Eily Sophie Lees-Craston)
Born: Oct. 30, 1879, London, England. Died: Sept. 26, 1961, South Pasadena, Calif. Stage and screen actress. Daughter of actress Agnes Thomas and Harry Lees-Craston.

Appeared in: **1932** Lovers Courageous; Wet Parade; Night Court. **1933** Looking Forward; Today We Live. **1934** Forsaking All Others; Romance in Manhattan; The Little Minister; His Greatest Gamble; Great Expectations; Limehouse Blues. **1935** The Widow from Monte Carlo; The Florentine Dagger; Stranded; Nina; Clive of India; Les Miserables; The Flame Within; A Tale of Two Cities; Kind Lady; The Melody Lingers On. **1936** Little Lord Fauntleroy; One Rainy Afternoon; Angel of Mercy; Anthony Adverse; Cain and Mabel; Three Men on a Horse; God's Country and the Woman; Dracula's Daughter; The White Angel; A Woman Rebels; Career Woman. **1937** Night Must Fall; Another Dawn. **1938** Rebecca of Sunnybrook Farm; Kidnapped; The Young in Heart. **1939** The Hound of The Baskervilles; The Little Princess; Confessions of a Nazi Spy; On Borrowed Time; We Are Not Alone; Barricade. **1940** Young Tom Edison; Untamed; Foreign Correspondent. **1941** Arkansas Judge; Man Hunt; Hit the Road. **1942** The Man in the Trunk; The Undying Monster; Scattergood Survives a Murder; I Married a Witch. **1944** Jane Eyre; Going My Way; The Seventh Cross. **1945** Roughly Speaking; Scared Stiff; Grissly's Millions; Paris Underground; Son of Lassie. **1946** She Wolf of London; Devotion; The Secret Heart. **1948** The Challenger.

MANDEL, FRANCES WAKEFIELD
Born: 1891. Died: Mar. 26, 1943, Batavia, N.Y. Screen actress. Posed for a number of James Montgomery Flagg's W.W.I posters.

MANDER, MILES (Lionel Mander aka LUTHER MANDER)
Born: Nov. 14, 1888, Wolverhampton, England. Died: Feb. 8, 1946, Hollywood, Calif. (heart attack). Screen actor, film director, film producer and screenwriter.

Appeared in: **1918** Once Upon a Time. **1920** The Children of Gideon; Testimony; The Old Arm Chair; A Rank Outsider. **1921** A Temporary Lady; The Road to London; The Place of Honour. **1922** Open Country; Half a Truth. **1924** Lovers in Araby; The Prude's Fall. **1925** The Art of Love series including: Red Lips (aka The Painted Lady) and Sables of Death (aka The Lady in Furs); Racing Dramas (shorts). **1926** The Steve Donoghue series including: Riding for a King; The Pleasure Garden; London Love; Castles in the Air (short). **1927** Lost One Wife (aka As We Lie); Tiptoes; The Fake. **1928** The Physician (US 1929); The First Born; Balaclava (aka Jaws of Hell—US 1931). **1929** The Crooked Billet. **1930** Loose Ends; Murder. **1932** Frail Women; The Missing Rembrandt; Lily Christine; That Night in London (aka Overnight—US 1934). **1933** Matinee Idol; Loyalties; Don Quixote; Bitter Sweet; The Private Life of Henry VIII. **1934** Four Masked Men; The Queen's Affair (aka Runaway Queen—US 1935); The Battle (aka Thunder in the East); The Case for the Crown. **1935** Death Drives Through; Here's to Romance; The Three Musketeers. **1936** Lloyd's of London. **1937** Slave Ship; Wake up and Live; Youth on Parole. **1938** Kidnapped; Suez; The Mad Miss Manton. **1939** Stanley and Livingstone; Man in the Iron Mask; Little Princess; The Three Musketeers (and 1935 version); Wuthering Heights; Tower of London. **1940** Road to Singapore; Primrose Path; The House of Seven Gables; Babies for Sale; Captain Caution; Laddie; South of Suez. **1941** Shadows on the Stairs; Dr. Kildare's Wedding Day; That Hamilton Woman. **1942** Fingers at the Window; Mrs. Miniver (voice); Fly by Night; A Tragedy at Midnight; To Be or Not to Be; Tarzan's New York Adventure; Journey for Margaret; The War against Mrs. Hadley; Apache Trail; This above All. **1943** Assignment in Britany; Secrets of the Underground; Guadalcanal Diary; Five Graves to Cairo; The Phantom of the Opera. **1944** Enter Arsene Lupin; Four Jills in a Jeep; The Pearl of Death; The Return of the Vampire; The Scarlet Claw. **1945** Confidential Agent; The Picture of Dorian Gray; Brighton Strangler; Weekend at the Waldorf; The Crime Doctor's Warnings. **1946** The Bandit of Sherwood Forest; The Walls Came Tumbling Down. **1947** The Imperfect Lady.

MANDVILLE, WILLIAM C.
Born: 1867, Louisville, Ky. Died: Apr. 19, 1917, New York, N.Y. (heart disease). Screen actor.

MANDY, JERRY
Born: 1893. Died: May 1, 1945, Hollywood, Calif. (heart attack). Screen, stage and vaudeville actor.

Appeared in: **1925** North Star. **1927** The Gay Defender; Underworld. **1928** Hold 'Em Yale!; Love and Learn. **1929** The Sap; Love, Live and Laugh. **1930** Girl Shock (short); Nuits de Chicago (French release of Underworld—1927); The Doorway to Hell. **1931** Girls Demand Excitement; plus the following shorts: Rough Seas; Skip the Maloo!; Let's Do Things. **1932** Bon Voyage (short). **1933** Strange People; Sailor's Luck. **1935** It's a Gift; The Bride Who Comes Home; McFadden's Flats. **1936** King of Burlesque; Spendthrift. **1938** Hawaii Calls. **1939** Naughty but Nice. **1940** The Ghost Creeps.

MANJEAN, TEDDY
Born: 1901. Died: Sept. 9, 1964, Hollywood, Calif. Screen actor and stuntman.

Appeared in: **1934** The Mighty Barnum.

MANLEY, CHARLES "DADDY"
Born: Sept. 25, 1830, Ireland. Died: Feb. 26, 1916, Los Angeles, Calif. (arteriosclerosis). Stage and screen actor. Married to actress Marie Manley.

Appeared in: **1913** The Calling of Louis Mona. **1915** The Master Key (serial); The Golden Wedding; Learning to Be a Father; His Last Thirty; The Last Word; The Fair God of Sun Island. **1916** The Cry of Erin; Brennan O' the Moor. **1917** Her Wayward Parents.

MANLEY, DAVE
Born: 1883. Died: May 1943, Calif. Screen and vaudeville actor.

Appeared in: **1931** The Struggle.

MANN, BILLY (William B. Mann)
Died: Apr. 14, 1974, New York, N.Y. Screen actor and singer.

Appeared in: **1935** Thanks a Million; Hoi Polloi (short). **1936** Stage Struck; Pigskin Parade; The Singing Kid. **1937** Artists and Models; Thrill of a Lifetime.

MANN, HANK (David W. Lieberman)
Born: 1887, New York, N.Y. Died: Nov. 25, 1971, South Pasadena, Calif. Screen actor and film director. Entered films in 1912.

Appeared in: **1914** In the Clutches of a Gang; Tillie's Punctured Romance; Mabel's Strange Predicament; Caught in a Cabaret (reissued as The Jazz Waiter); The Knock-Out (reissued as The Pugilist); Mabel's Married Life (reissued as The Squarehead). **1915** L-KO comedies. **1916** Fox Film Co. productions: A Modern Enoch Arden; The Village Blacksmith; His Bread and Butter; Hearts and Sparks. **1920** Arrow Film shorts. **1922** Quincy Adams Sawyer. **1923** Hollywood; Lights Out; Tea with a Kick; Don't Marry for Money; The Near Lady; A Noise in Newboro; The Wanters. **1924** The Man Who Played Square; A Woman Who Sinned; Empty Hands; Rivers Up. **1925** The Arizona Romeo; The Sporting Venus. **1926-27** Tennek Film Corp. shorts. **1926** Wings of the Storm; The Skyrocket; The Boob; The Flying Horseman. **1927** The Patent Leather Kid; Broadway after Midnight; When Danger Calls; Paid to Love; Smile, Brother, Smile; The Scorcher; Lady Bird. **1928** Fazil; The Garden of Eden. **1929** Morgan's Last Raid; The Donovan Affair; Fall of Eve; Spite Marriage. **1930** The Arizona Kid; Sinners' Holiday; The Dawn Trail. **1931** City Lights; Annabelle's Affairs; Stout Hearts and Willing Hands. **1932** Ridin' for Justice; Strange Love of Molly Louvain; Million Dollar Legs. **1933** The Big Chance; Smoky. **1934** Fugitive Road; Men in Black (short). **1935** A Vitaphone short; The Devil Is a Woman; The Big Broadcast of 1936. **1936** Call of the Prairie; Modern Times; Reunion; Preview Murder Mystery. **1937** Goofs and Saddles (short). **1938** Stranger from Arizona. **1939** Hollywood Cavalcade. **1940** Alfalfa's Double (short); Bubbling Trouble (short); The Great Dictator. **1941** Bullets for O'Hara. **1942** Yankee Doodle Dandy; Bullet Scars. **1943** The Mysterious Doctor; The Dancing Masters. **1944** Gold is Where You Lose It (short); Crime by Night. **1947** The Perils of Pauline. **1949** Jackpot Jitters. **1950** Joe Palooka in Humphrey Takes a Chance. **1953** The Caddy. **1954** Living It Up. **1955** Abbott and Costello Meet the Keystone Kops; Abbott and Costello Meet the Mummy. **1956** Pardners. **1957** Man of a Thousand Faces. **1958** Rock-a-Bye Baby. **1959** Daddy-O.

MANN, LOUIS
Born: Apr. 20, 1865, New York, N.Y. Died: Feb. 15, 1931, New York, N.Y. Screen, stage actor and playwright.

Appeared in: **1929** Father's Day. **1930** The March of Time; The Richest Man in the World; Sins of the Children.

MANN, MARGARET
Born: Apr. 4, 1868, Aberdeen, Scotland. Died: Feb. 4, 1941, Los Angeles, Calif. (cancer). Screen actress.

Appeared in: **1918** The Heart of Humanity. **1919** The Right to Happiness. **1921** Black Beauty; Desert Blossoms; Man-Woman-Marriage; The Millionaire; The Smart Sex; The New Disciple. **1922** The Call of Home; Don't Write Letters; Love in the Dark. **1925** Her Sister from Paris. **1928** Four Sons. **1929** The River; Disraeli. **1931** The following shorts: Helping Grandma; Fly My

Kite; The Panic Is On. **1932** Bachelor Mother. **1934** I Hate Women; Little Men; Beloved. **1935** Bonnie Scotland; Kentucky Blue Streak. **1936** The Bohemian. **1937** Conflict. **1939** Federal Man-Hunt.

MANN, NED H.
Born: 1893, Redkey, Ind. Died: July 1, 1967, La Jolla, Calif. Screen actor and special effects director. Entered films as an actor in 1920 and then became technical director, etc.

MANN, STANLEY
Born: 1884. Died: Aug. 10, 1953, Los Angeles, Calif. Screen actor. Entered films during silents.

Appeared in: **1938** If I Were King. **1942** Mrs. Miniver. **1953** The Robe.

MANNERING, LEWIN
Born: 1879, Poland. Died: June 7, 1932, London, England. Screen and stage actor.

MANNES, FLORENCE V.
Born: 1896. Died: Oct. 30, 1964, Hollywood, Calif. (heart attack). Screen actress. Entered films as a bit player and extra approx. 1924.

MANNING, AILEEN
Born: 1886, Denver, Colo. Died: Mar. 25, 1946, Hollywood, Calif. Screen actress.

Appeared in: **1921** Home Stuff. **1922** The Power of Love; A Tailor Made Man; Rags to Riches; Mixed Faces; Beauty's Worth. **1923** Main Street; Nobody's Money. **1924** The House of Youth; Lovers' Lane; The Snob; Her Marriage Vow. **1925** The Bridge of Sighs; Enticement; Under the Rouge; Thank You. **1926** Stella Maris; The Whole Town's Talking; The Boy Friend. **1927** Uncle Tom's Cabin; Man, Woman and Sin. **1928** Heart to Heart; The Olympic Hero; Home James. **1929** "Great Events" series. **1930** Wedding Rings; The Third Alarm. **1931** Huckleberry Finn.

MANNING, JOSEPH
Died: July 31, 1946, Hollywood, Calif. (heart attack). Screen and stage actor.

Appeared in: **1920** The Screaming Shadow (serial).

MANNING, MARY LEE
Died: Dec. 7, 1937, Hollywood, Calif. Screen actress.

MANNING, TOM
Born: 1880. Died: Oct. 10, 1936, Hollywood, Calif. Screen and stage actor.

Appeared in: **1936** The Singing Kid.

MANSFIELD, JAYNE (Jayne Palmer)
Born: Apr. 19, 1932, Bryn Mawr, Pa. Died: June 29, 1967, New Orleans, La. (auto accident). Screen, stage and television actress. Divorced from Paul Mansfield, actor and former Mr. Universe Mickey Hargitay, and actor and director Matteo Ottaviano aka Matt Cimber. Mother of actress Jayne Marie Hargitay.

Appeared in: **1955** Underwater; Pete Kelly's Blues; Illegal. **1956** Hell on Frisco Bay (aka The Darkest Hour); Female Jungle (aka Hangover). **1957** The Girl Can't Help It; Will Success Spoil Rock Hunter? (aka Oh, For a Man); The Burglar; The Wayward Bus; Kiss Them for Me. **1958** The Sheriff of Fractured Jaw. **1960** The Challenger (aka It Takes a Thief—US 1962); The Loves of Hercules (aka The Life of Hercules); Playgirl After Dark (aka Spin of a Coin). **1962** It Happened in Athens. **1963** Promises! Promises! **1964** Panic Button; Heimweh Nach St. Pauli (Homesick for St. Paul); L'amore Primitivo (Primitive Love—US 1966); Einer Frisst deN A.r9en (aka Dog Eat Dog—US 1966). **1966** The Fat Spy; Las Vegas Hillbillys (aka Country Music U.S.A.). **1967** A Guide for the Married Man; Spree (aka Las Vegas by Night). **1968** Single Room Furnished; The Wild, Wild World op Jayne Mansfield (doc.).

MANSFIELD, JOHN
Born: 1919. Died: Sept. 18, 1956, Hollywood, Calif. (heart attack). Screen actor.

Appeared in: **1948** Man-Eater of Kumaon. **1951** F.B.I. Girl; Savage Drums; Silver City; Warpath. **1952** Denver and Rio Grande. **1953** Pony Express; Prisoners of the Casbah. **1954** The Naked Jungle. **1956** The Boss.

MANSFIELD, MARTHA (Martha Ehrlich)
Born: 1900, Mansfield, Ohio. Died: Nov. 20, 1923, San Antonio, Tex. (burns). Stage and screen actress. Died while filming The Warrens of Virginia, when her dress was accidentally ignited.

Appeared in: **1918** Broadway Bill. **1920** Civilian Clothes; Dr. Jekyll and Mr. Hyde. **1921** The Man of Stone; Gilded Lies; The Last Door; Women Men Love; His Brother's Keeper. **1922** Queen of the Moulin Rouge; Till We Meet Again. **1923** Youthful Cheaters; Fog Bound; Is Money Everything?; The Leavenworth Case; Potash and Perlmutter; The Little Red Schoolhouse; The Silent Command; The Woman in Chains. **1924** The Warrens of Virginia.

MANSFIELD, RANKIN
Died: Jan. 22, 1969. Screen actor.

Appeared in: **1953** How to Marry a Millionaire. **1954** The Human Jungle. **1955** Dial Red O. **1956** World Without End. **1957** Badlands of Montana. **1959** Face of a Fugitive.

MANSO, JUANITA
Born: 1873, Spain. Died: Feb. 25, 1957, Madrid, Spain. Stage and screen actress.

MANSON, ISABEL MERSON
Born: 1884. Died: May 19, 1952, New York, N.Y. Screen and stage actress.

MANTELL, ROBERT BRUCE
Born: 1854, Ayrshire, Scotland. Died: June 27, 1928, Atlantic Highlands, N.J. (effects of a breakdown). Stage and screen actor.

Appeared in: **1915** The Blindness of Devotion. **1916** The Green Eyed Monster; A Wife's Sacrifice. **1923** Under the Red Robe.

MANTZ, PAUL (Albert Paul Mantz)
Born: 1904, Redwood City, Calif. Died: July 8, 1965, Buttercup Valley, Calif. (Ariz. border plane crash). Screen actor and aerial stuntman. Died in plane crash while filming The Flight of the Phoenix.

Appeared in: **1930** Airmail; Hell's Angels. **1938** Men with Wings; Test Pilot. **1949** Twelve O'Clock High. **1951** Flying Leathernecks. **1957** The Spirit of St. Louis. **1963** A Gathering of Eagles; It's a Mad, Mad, Mad, Mad World. **1965** The Flight of the Phoenix.

MANX, KATE
Born: 1930. Died: Nov. 15, 1964, Torrance, Calif. (suicide—pills). Screen and television actress.

Appeared in: **1960** Private Property. **1962** Hero's Island.

MAPLE, AUDREY
Born: 1899. Died: Apr. 18, 1971, N.Y. Screen, stage and vaudeville actress.

Appeared in: **1934** Enlighten Thy Daughter.

MARBLE, JOHN
Born: 1844. Died: June 23, 1919, New York, N.Y. Screen actor.

MARBURGH, BERTRAM
Born: May 17, 1875. Died: Aug. 22, 1956, Woodland Hills, Calif. Stage and screen actor.

Appeared in: **1919** Checkers; The Social Pirate; You Never Know Your Luck. **1920** Whispers. **1921** The Greatest Love. **1922** Timothy's Quest. **1925** His People; A Streak of Luck; Proud Heart. **1926** The Outsider; Unknown Treasures; Silken Shackles. **1927** An Affair of the Follies; King of Kings; The Woman on Trial. **1930** For the Defense; The Melody Man. **1933** They Just Had to Get Married. **1940** Before I Hang. **1942** Crossroads; A Gentleman at Heart. **1943** The Human Comedy; Two Weeks to Live.

MARCH, EVE
Died: Sept. 19, 1974, Hollywood, Calif. (cancer). Screen, stage and television actress.

Appeared in: **1941** How Green Was My Valley. **1943** Calling Wild Bill Elliott; Song of Texas. **1944** Curse of the Cat People. **1946** Danny Boy. **1947** Killer McCoy. **1949** Adam's Rib; Streets of San Francisco. **1951** The Model and the Marriage Broker. **1953** The Sun Shines Bright.

MARCH, FREDRIC (Ernest Frederick McIntyre Bickel)
Born: Aug. 31, 1897, Racine, Wisc. Died: Apr. 14, 1975, Los Angeles, Calif. (cancer). Screen, stage and television actor. Married to actress Florence Eldridge. Won 1932 Academy Award for Best Actor in Dr. Jekyll and Mr. Hyde and in 1946 for The Best Years of Our Lives. Entered films as an extra.

Appeared in: **1921** Paying the Piper (film debut). **1929** The Dummy; Footlights and Fools; Jealousy; The Marriage Playground; Paris Bound; The Studio Murder Mystery. **1930** Ladies Love Brutes; Laughter; Manslaughter; Paramount on Parade; Sarah and Son; True to the Navy; The Royal Family of Broadway. **1931** Honor Among Lovers; The Night Angel; My Sin. **1932** Strangers in Love; Merrily We Go to Hell; Make Me a Star; Smilin' Through; The Sign of the Cross; Dr. Jekyll and Mr. Hyde. **1933** Tonight is Ours; The Eagle and the Hawk; Design for Living. **1934** The Affairs of Cellini; We Live Again; All of Me; Good Dame; The Barretts of Wimpole Street; Death Takes a Holiday. **1935** Lives of a Bengal Lancer; The Dark Angel; Anna Karenina; Les Miserables. **1936** Mary of Scotland; The Road to Glory; Anthony Adverse. **1937** Nothing Sacred; A Star is Born. **1938** There Goes My Heart; Trade Winds; The Buccaneer. **1940** Victory; Susan and God. **1941** So Ends Our Night; One Foot in Heaven; Bedtime Story. **1942** I Married a Witch. **1944** The Adventures of Mark Twain; Tomorrow the World. **1946** The Best Years of Our Lives. **1948** Live Today for Tomorrow; Another Part of the Forest; An Act of Murder. **1949** Christopher Columbus. **1950** The Titan—Story of Michelangelo. **1951** Death of a Salesman; It's a Big Country. **1953** Man on a Tightrope. **1954** Executive Suite; The Bridges at Toko-Ri. **1955** The Desperate Hours. **1956** The Man in the Gray Flannel Suit; Alexander the Great. **1957** Albert Schweitzer (narrator). **1959** Middle of the Night. **1960** Inherit the Wind. **1961** The Young Doctors. **1962** I Sequestrati di Altona (The Condemned of Altona—US 1963). **1964** Seven Days in May. **1967** Hombre. **1970** Tick . . . Tick . . . Tick. . . . **1973** The Iceman Cometh.

MARCH, HAL
Born: 1920, San Francisco, Calif. Died: Jan. 19, 1970, Los Angeles, Calif. (pneumonia—lung cancer). Screen, stage, radio, television, burlesque and vaudeville actor.

Appeared in: **1939** The Gracie Allen Murder Case. **1950** Ma and Pa Kettle Go to Town; Outrage. **1953** Combat; The Eddie Cantor Story. **1954** Yankee Pasha; The Atomic Kid. **1955** It's Always Fair Weather; My Sister Eileen. **1957** Hear Me Good. **1964** Send Me No Flowers. **1967** A Guide for the Married Man.

MARCH, IRIS
Died: Feb. 23, 1966, Hollywood, Calif. (heart attack). Screen, stage actress and drama coach. Mother of puppeteer Marilyn March.

MARCHAT, JEAN
Born: 1902, France. Died: Oct. 1966, Paris, France (following surgery). Screen, stage actor and stage director.

Appeared in: **1946** Stormy Waters. **1953** L'ennemi Public No. 1 (aka The Most Wanted Man—US 1962). **1960** Le Passage du Rhin (aka Tomorrow Is My Turn—US 1962). **1964** Les Dames du Bois de Boulogne. **1963** La Glaive et la Balance (aka Two Are Guilty—US 1964).

MARCIANO, ROCKY (Rocco Marchegiano)
Born: Sept. 1, 1923, Brockton, Mass. Died: Aug. 31, 1969, near Des Moines, Iowa (plane crash). Professional fighter and screen actor.

Appeared in: **1957** The Delicate Delinquent. **1960** College Confidential. **1970** The Super Fight (documentary).

MARCUS, JAMES A.
Born: Jan. 21, 1868, New York, N.Y. Died: Oct. 15, 1937, Hollywood, Calif. (heart attack). Stage and screen actor. Entered films in 1915.

Appeared in: **1921** Little Lord Fauntleroy; Serenade. **1922** Broken Chains; Oliver Twist; Come on Over; The Stranger's Banquet. **1923** Scaramouche; Vanity Fair; Quicksands. **1924** The Iron Horse; Beau Brummell. **1925** The Eagle; The Goose Hangs High; All around Frying Pan; Lightnin'; Dick Turpin; The Fighting Heart; The Isle of Hope. **1926** The Lily; The Scarlet Letter; The Eagle of the Sea; Hell-Bent for Heaven; Siberia; The Traffic Cop; The Texas Streak. **1927** Captain Salvation; The Bachelor's Baby; The Meddlin' Stranger; Beauty Shoppers; King of Kings; Life of an Actress; Marriage. **1928** Revenge; Sadie Thompson; The Border Patrol; Isle of Lost Men; The Broken Mask; Buck Privates. **1929** Evangeline; In Old Arizona; Whispering Winds; In Holland (short). **1930** Back Pay; Captain of the Guard; Billy the Kid; Liliom; The Texan. **1931** Fighting Caravans; Arrowsmith. **1932** Hell's House. **1933** The Lone Avenger; Strawberry Roan. **1934** Wagon Wheels; Honor of the Range. **1936** The Lonely Trail.

MARCUSE, THEODORE "THEO"
Born: 1920. Died: Nov. 29, 1967, Los Angeles, Calif. (auto accident). Screen, stage and television actor.

Appeared in: **1961** Operation Eichmann; The Two Little Bears. **1962** For Love or Money; Hitler. **1964** A Tiger Walks. **1965** Mara of the Wilderness; Harem Skarum; The Cincinnati Kid. **1966** The Glass Bottom Boat; Sands of Beersheba; Last of the Secret Agents. **1967** Picasso Summer. **1968** The Wicked Dreams of Paula Schultz.

MARGETSON, ARTHUR
Born: 1897, England. Died: Aug. 12, 1951, London, England. Stage and screen actor.

Appeared in: **1931** Other People's Sins. **1933** His Grace Gives Notice. **1934** The Great Defender; Little Friend. **1935** The Divine Spark; Music Hath Charms; I Give My Heart. **1936** Wanted Men. **1937** Broken Blossoms; Juggernaut; Pagliacci (aka A Clown Must Laugh); Action for Slander. **1938** The Loves of Madame DuBarry. **1940** Return to Yesterday. **1941** Larceny Street. **1942** Commandos Strike at Dawn. **1943** Random Harvest; Sherlock Holmes Faces Death.

MARGOLIS, CHARLES "DOC"
Born: 1874. Died: Sept. 22, 1926, Glendale, Calif. Screen actor.

Appeared in: **1925** The Merry Widow.

MARGULIES, VIRGINIA M.
Born: 1916. Died: Feb. 16, 1969, Hollywood, Calif. Screen actress. Daughter of actor Edward Peil (dec. 1958).

MARGULIS, CHARLES "CHARLIE"
Born: 1903. Died: Apr. 24, 1967, Little Falls, Minn. Musician, screen and television actor.

Appeared in: **1930** King of Jazz.

MARIAN, FERDINAND
Born: 1902, Vienna, Austria. Died: 1946, near Durneck, Germany (auto accident). Stage and screen actor.

Appeared in: **1938** Die Heimat Ruft (Home Is Calling).

MARIANO, LUIS (Luis Gonzalez)
Born: 1920, Irun, Spain. Died: July 14, 1970, Paris, France (cerebral hemorrhage). Screen actor and singer.

Appeared in: **1954** Zarewitsch (US 1961). **1960** Candide, Ou L'Optimisme au XXe Siecle (aka Candide—US 1962).

MARINOFF, FANIA
Born: 1890, Russia. Died: Nov. 17, 1971, Englewood, N.J. Stage and screen actress.

Appeared in: **1915** The Money Master; Nedra; McTeague. **1917** The Rise of Jennie Cushing.

MARION, EDNA (Edna Hannam)
Born: Dec. 12, 1908, Chicago, Ill. Died: Dec. 2, 1957, Hollywood, Calif. Screen, stage and vaudeville actress. Appeared in Charlie Chase and Edna Marion comedies.

Appeared in: **1925** The Desert's Price; plus the following shorts: Her Daily Dozen; My Baby Doll; Powdered Chickens; Putting on Airs; Puzzled by Crosswords; Dangerous Peach. **1926** The Call of the Wilderness; Readin' Ritin' Rithmetic; The Still Alarm. **1927** For Ladies Only; Flying Elephants (short); Sugar Daddies (short). **1928** From Soup to Nuts (short); Should Married Men Go Home? **1929** Skinner Steps Out. **1930** Romance of the West; Today.

MARION, FRANCES
Born: 1888, San Francisco, Calif. Died: May 12, 1973, Los Angeles, Calif. Screen actress, screenwriter, film director, author and commercial artist. Married to actor Fred Thomson (dec. 1928) and later married to film director George Hill (dec.). Do not confuse with actor Francis Marion.

Appeared in: **1915** A Girl of Yesterday; The Jest of Jealousy. **1921** Little Lord Fauntleroy. **1941** New York Town.

MARION, GEORGE F., SR.
Born: July 16, 1860, San Francisco, Calif. Died: Nov. 30, 1945, Carmel, Calif. (heart attack). Screen, stage actor and stage director. Father of screenwriter George F. Marion, Jr. Entered films in 1914.

Appeared in: **1921** Go Straight. **1922** Gun Shy. **1923** Anna Christie; The Girl I Loved; A Million to Burn. **1924** Bringin' Home the Bacon. **1925** On the Go; Clothes Make the Pirate; Straight Through; Tumbleweeds; The White Monkey. **1926** The Highbinders; Rolling Home; The Wise Guy. **1927** King of Kings; A Texas Steer; Loco Luck; Skedaddle Gold. **1929** Evangeline. **1930** Anna Christie (and 1923 version); The Bishop Murder Case; The Pay Off; The Sea Bat; A Lady's Morals; Hook, Line and Sinker; The Big House. **1931** Man to Man; Laughing Sinners; Safe in Hell. **1932** Six Hours to Live. **1933** Her First Mate. **1935** Port of Lost Dreams; Rocky Mountain Mystery; Death from a Distance; Metropolitan.

MARION, SID
Born: 1900. Died: June 29, 1965, Hollywood, Calif. (heart attack). Stage and screen actor.

Appeared in: **1934** The Mighty Barnum. **1936** Magnificent Obsession. **1937** An RKO-Radio short. **1943** Lady of Burlesque. **1949** Oh, You Beautiful Doll; Jiggs and Maggie In Jackpot Jitters. **1950** Love That Brute; Trial without Jury; Woman from Headquarters. **1953** Call Me Madam. **1965** The Outlaws is Coming.

MARION, WILLIAM
Born: 1878. Died: Jan. 3, 1957. Stage and screen actor.

Appeared in: **1915** The Boss; The Heart of Blue Ridge. **1917** The Streets of Illusion; One Hour. **1921** The Hope Diamond Mystery (serial). **1922** Across the Dead-Line; One Clear Call; The Worldly Madonna. **1923** The Huntress. **1928** Sally's Shoulders.

MARION-CRAWFORD, HOWARD. See HOWARD MARION CRAWFORD

MARK, MICHAEL
Born: Mar. 15, 1889, Russia. Died: Feb. 3, 1975, Woodland Hills, Calif. Screen, stage, vaudeville actor, stage director and producer.

Appeared in: **1924** Four Sons. **1931** Frankenstein; Resurrection. **1935** All the King's Horses. **1936** The Dark Hour; Sons O'Guns. **1937** Missing Witness. **1938** Ride a Crooked Mile. **1940** Flash Gordon Conquers the Universe (serial); The

Mummy's Hand. **1942** The Ghost of Frankenstein; Men of San Quentin. **1943** Mission to Moscow. **1945** House of Frankenstein; The Great Glamarion. **1946** Joe Palooka—Champ. **1947** The Trespasser; Joe Palooka in the Knockout. **1948** Appointment with Murder; Fighting Mad; The Vicious Circle. **1949** Search for Danger. **1950** Once a Thief. **1955** The Big Combo. **1956** Rock Around the Clock; Edge of Hell. **1957** Lizzie. **1959** Attack of the Puppet People; The Big Fisherman; The Return of the Fly.

MARKS, JOE E.

Born: June 15, 1891. Died: June 14, 1973, New York, N.Y. (pneumonia). Screen, stage, burlesque and vaudeville actor. Appeared in vaudeville in an act billed as "Joe Marks and Co."

Appeared in: **1938** Outside of Paradise. **1941** So Ends Our Night. **1959** Li'l Abner (stage and film versions). **1968** The Night They Raided Minsky's. **1970** Diary of a Mad Housewife.

MARLE, ARNOLD (aka A. MARLE)

Born: 1888, England. Died: Feb. 21, 1970, London, England. Screen, stage and television actor. Married to actress Lilly Frued Marle.

Appeared in: **1942** One of Our Aircraft Is Missing. **1944** Mr. Emmanuel (US 1945). **1946** Men of Two Worlds. **1948** Portrait From Life (aka The Girl In the Painting—US 1949). **1949** The Glass Mountain. **1954** The Green Buddha (US 1955). **1955** Little Red Monkey (aka The Case of the Red Monkey—US); Cross Channel; The Glass Cage (aka The Glass Tomb—US); Break In the Circle (US 1957). **1957** The Abominable Snowman. **1959** The Man Who Could Cheat Death. **1961** The Snake Woman.

MARLO, MARY

Born: 1898. Died: Feb. 25, 1960, Hollywood, Calif. (heart attack). Screen, stage, radio and television actress.

Appeared in: **1955** The Second Greatest Sex.

MARLOWE, ALAN

Born: 1935. Died: Jan. 5, 1975, near Seward, Neb. (plane crash). Jazz musician, screen, stage and television actor.

Appeared in: **1970** Sweet Vengeance.

MARLOWE, ANTHONY

Born: 1910. Died: June 29, 1962, Detroit, Mich. Screen actor and opera tenor.

Appeared in: **1941** Flame of New Orleans. **1942** The Great Commandment. **1944** Mrs. Parkington. **1953** Saadia. **1954** Doctor in the House (US 1955). **1955** Room in the House.

MARLOWE, FRANK

Born: 1904. Died: Mar. 30, 1964, Hollywood, Calif. (heart attack). Screen and television actor.

Appeared in: **1934** Now I'll Tell. **1935** The Glass Key. **1938** Bringing up Baby. **1944** Murder in the Blue Room. **1946** Sioux City Sue. **1947** Riding the California Trail. **1948** They Live by Night (aka The Twisted Road and Your Red Wagon). **1950** Barricade; Triple Trouble. **1952** The Winning Team; My Pal Gus. **1954** The Long Wait. **1955** The Square Jungle; Lucy Gallant; The Americano. **1956** The Man with the Golden Arm. **1957** Rockabilly Baby; Chicago Confidential. **1958** Escape from Red Rock; The Lone Texan.

MARLOWE, MARILYN

Born: 1927. Died: Sept. l, 1975, Hollywood, Calif. (heart attack). Screen actress and stand-in. Married to actor Rock Marlowe.

MARMER, LEA

Born: Aug. 16, 1918, Michigan. Died: May 11, 1974, Los Angeles, Calif. (brain tumor). Stage and screen actress.

Appeared in: **1961** Walk the Angry Beach. **1967** What Am I Bid? **1968** The War Between Men and Women. **1969** Easy Rider.

MARR, WILLIAM (William Dobie)

Born: 1897. Died: May 15, 1960, N.Y. Stage and screen actor.

Appeared in: **1926** Men of Steel.

MARRIOTT, CHARLES

Born: 1859, England. Died: Dec. 8, 1917, Los Angeles, Calif. (tuberculosis). Stage and screen actor.

Appeared in: **1915** Sunshine Molly; The Wild Olive; False Colors; It's No Laughing Matter. **1916** The Tongues of Men; Wanted—A Home. **1917** Betty and the Buccaneers.

MARRIOTT, MOORE (George Thomas Moore-Marriott)

Born: 1885, West Drayton, England. Died: 1949. Screen and stage actor.

Appeared in: **1914** His Sister's Honour. **1915** By the Shortest of Heads. **1920** The Flying Scotsman; The Grip of Iron; Mary Latimer, Nun; The Winding Road. **1921** Four Men in a Van. **1922** The Head of the Family; The Skipper's Wooing. **1923** Monkey's Paw; An Odd Freak. **1924** The Mating of Marcus; Not For Sale; Lawyer Quince; Dixon's Return; The Clicking of Cuthbert series including: The Clicking of Cuthbert; The Long Hole; Ordeal by Golf; The Old Man in The Corner series including: The Affair at the Novelty Theatre. **1925** King of the Castle; The Gold Cure; Afraid of Love; The Qualified Adventurer; There's Many a Slip; The Only Man (aka The Leading Man); Thrilling Stories from the Strand Magazine Series including: A Madonna of the Cells. **1926** The Conspirators; Every Mother's Son; London Love; Second to None; The Happy Rascals Series; Screen Playlet Series including: Cash on Delivery and The Greater War. **1927** Carry On; Huntingtower; Passion Island; The Silver Lining. **1928** Widecombe Fair; Sweeney Todd; Toni; Victory; The Burglar and the Girl; When We Were Very Young Series including: The King's Breakfast. **1929** Kitty; Mr. Smith Wakes Up. **1930** The Barnes Murder (rerelease of The Conspirators—1926); The Lady From the Sea (aka The Goodwin Sands); Kissing Cup's Race. **1931** Aroma of the South Seas; Up for the Cup; The Lyons Mail. **1932** Mr. Bill the Conqueror (aka The Man Who Won—US 1933); The Wonderful Story; Little Waitress; The Water Gypsies; Dance Pretty Lady; The Crooked Lady; Nine Till Six; Heroes of the Mine. **1933** A Moorland Tragedy; Money for Speed; Hawleys of High Street; Love's Old Sweet Song; The House of Trent; The Crime at Blossoms; Dora; Lucky Blaze. **1934** A Political Scoop; Not for Publication Series including: The Black Skull. **1935** His Apologies; Turn of the Tide; Gay Old Dog; Dandy Dick; Drake of England (aka Drake the Pirate—US); The Man Without a Face; The Half-Day Excursion. **1936** When Knights Were Bold (US 1942); Strange Cargo; Wednesday's Luck; Accused; Windbag the Sailor; What the Puppy Said; The Amazing Quest of Ernest Bliss (aka Romance and Riches—US 1937); Luck of the Turf; Talk of the Devil. **1937** O, Mr. Porter; The Fatal Hour; Feather Your Nest; Fifty-Shilling Boxer; Night Ride; Intimate Relations. **1938** Owd Bob (aka To the Victor—US); Old Bones of the River; Convict 99. **1939** Cheer Boys Cheer; Ask A Policeman; Where's That Fire?; A Girl Must Live (US 1941); The Frozen Limits. **1940** Gasbags; Band Wagon; Charley's (Big Hearted) Aunt. **1941** I Thank You; Hi Gang! **1942** Back Room Boy. **1943** Millions Like Us. **1944** Time Flies; Don't Take It to Heart (US 1949); It Happened One Sunday. **1945** A Place of One's Own (US 1949); The Agitator; I'll Be Your Sweetheart. **1946** Green For Danger (US 1947). **1947** Green Fingers; The Hills of Donegal; The Root of All Evil. **1949** The History of Mr. Polly (US 1951); High Jinks in Society.

MARRIOTT, SANDEE

Born: 1899. Died: June 7, 1962, Hollywood, Calif. (heart attack). Screen actor and stuntman. Entered films in 1927.

Appeared in: **1956** Hilda Crane; Around the World in 80 Days.

MARSDEN, MARY. *See* MARY MARSDEN YOUNG

MARSH, CHARLES L. "CHARLEY"

Died: Mar. 7, 1953, Hollywood, Calif. Screen and vaudeville actor.

Appeared in: **1942** Gentleman Jim. **1944** Atlantic City. **1945** Christmas in Connecticut; Out of This World; Too Young to Know. **1947** My Wild Irish Rose.

MARSH, DELLA

Died: May 6, 1973, Ithaca, N.Y. Screen and vaudeville actress. Married to vaudeville actor Walter Fischter (dec.).

MARSH, MAE (Mary Warne Marsh)

Born: Nov. 9, 1895, Madrid, N.M. Died: Feb. 13, 1968, Hermosa Beach, Calif. (heart attack). Screen actress. Mother of prominent Beverly Hills attorney Brewster Arms and sister of screen actress Marguerite Marsh (dec. 1925). She won the George Eastman Award in 1957 naming her one of five leading actresses of the silent era. Was known as Samuel Goldwyn's original "Goldwyn Girl."

Appeared in: **1912** Man's Genesis; The Lesser Evil; The New York Hats; One Is Business, the Other Crime; Lena and the Geese; The Sands of Dee; Brutality; An Adventure in the Autumn Woods. **1913** Judith of Bethulia; The Telephone Girl and the Lady; Love in an Apartment Hotel; The Perfidy of Mary; The Little Tease; The Wanderer; His Mother's Son; The Reformers; The Battle of Elderberry Gulch; In Prehistoric Days. **1914** Home Sweet Home; The Avenging Conscience. **1915** The Birth of a Nation. **1916** Intolerance; The Wild Girl; A Child of the Paris Street; The Wharf Rat; Hoodoo Ann; The Marriage of Molly-O. **1917** Cinderella Man; Polly and the Circus; Brute Force. **1918** The Beloved Traitor; All Woman; The Face in the Dark. **1919** Spotlight Sadie; The Mother and the Law. **1921** Little 'Fraid Lady; Nobody's Kid. **1922** Flames of Passion; Till We Meet Again. **1923** The White Rose; Paddy-the-Next-Best-Thing. **1924** A Woman's Secret; Daddies. **1925** The Rat; Rides of Passion. **1928** Racing Through. **1931** Over the Hill. **1932** That's My Boy; Rebecca of Sunnybrook Farm. **1933** Alice in Wonderland. **1934** Little Man, What Now?; Bachelor of Arts. **1935** Black Fury. **1936** Hollywood Boulevard; The Man Who Wouldn't Talk; Young People. **1941** Great Guns; Blue, White and Perfect. **1942** Tales of Manhattan. **1943** Dixie Dugan. **1944** In the Meantime, Darling; Jane Eyre. **1945** A Tree Grows in Brooklyn. **1948** Apartment for Peggy; Three Godfathers; Deep Waters. **1949** The Fighting Kentuckian; Impact. **1950** When Willie Comes Marching Home; The Gunfighter. **1952** Night without Sleep; The Sun Shines Bright. **1953** The Robe; Blueprint for Murder. **1955** The Tall Men; Hell on Frisco Bay; Prince of Players. **1956** Julie; While the City Sleeps. **1957** The Wings of Eagles. **1958** Cry Terror. **1960** Sergeant Rutledge; From the Terrace. **1961** Two Rode Together. **1963** Donovan's Reef. **1968** Arabella.

MARSH, MARGUERITE (Margaret Marsh aka MARGUERITE LOVERIDGE)

Born: 1892. Died: Dec. 8, 1925, New York, N.Y. (bronchial pneumonia). Sister of screen actress Mae Marsh (dec. 1968). Married to film production manager and assistant director George Bertholon (dec.).

Appeared in: **1912** The Mender of the Nets. **1913** Buck Richard's Bride; His Nobs, the Plumber; The Woodman's Daughter; Dora; A Trade Secret; Seeds of Silver. **1914** Blue Blood and Red. **1915** The Old High Chair; The Housemaid; The Turning Point; The Doll-House Mystery; The Queen of the Band; A Romance of the Alps. **1916** The Price of Power; Casey at the Bat; The Devil's Needle; Little Meena's Romance; Mr. Goode, the Samaritan. **1918** A Voice From the Deep; Our Little Wife; Conquered Hearts; Fields of Honor. **1919** Royal Democrat; Fair Enough; Eternal Magdalene; The Master Mystery (serial). **1920** Phantom Honeymoon; Wits vs. Wits. **1921** The Idol of the North; Oh Mary Be Careful; Women Men Love. **1922** Boomerang Bill; Face to Face; Iron to Gold; The Lion's Mouse.

MARSH, MYRA

Born: Oct. 29, 1894. Died: 1964. Screen actress.

Appeared in: **1936** Gentle Julia; Navy Born. **1938** Rascals. **1939** Boy Friend; The Kansas Terrors. **1940** Glamour for Sale. **1941** Father's Son; Private Nurse. **1942** Young America. **1943** Hitler—Dead or Alive. **1952** Ruby Gentry. **1953** The Man from the Alamo; The Moonlighter. **1955** The Cobweb.

MARSH, RISLEY HALSEY

Born: 1927. Died: Jan. 14, 1965, Newark, N.J. Screen and stage actor.

MARSHAL, ALAN

Born: Jan. 29, 1909, Sydney, Australia. Died: July 9, 1961, Chicago, Ill. Stage and screen actor.

Appeared in: **1936** After the Thin Man; The Garden of Allah. **1937** Conquest; Night Must Fall; Parnell; The Robbery Symphony. **1938** Dramatic School; I Met My Love Again; Invisible Enemy; The Road to Reno. **1939** The Adventures of Sherlock Holmes; Exile Express; Four Girls in White; The Hunchback of Notre Dame. **1940** He Stayed for Breakfast; The Howards of Virginia; Irene; Married and in Love. **1941** Lydia; Tom, Dick and Harry. **1944** Bride by Mistake; The White Cliffs of Dover. **1949** The Barkeleys of Broadway. **1956** The Opposite Sex. **1958** House on Haunted Hill. **1959** Day of the Outlaw.

MARSHALL, BOYD

Born: 1885, Ohio. Died: Nov. 9, 1950, Jackson Heights, N.Y. Stage and screen actor.

Appeared in: **1913** Bread Upon the Waters; Her Right to Happiness; His Imaginary Family. **1914** The Tangled Cat; The Keeper of the Light. **1915** A Call From the Dead; The Mill on the Floss; At the Patrician's Club; Hannah's Henpecked Husband; Their Last Performance; The Baby and the Boss. **1916** King Lear; Lucky Larry's Lady Love; The Optimistic Oriental Occults; The World and the Woman. **1917** A Modern Monte Cristo; When Love Was Blind.

MARSHALL, CHARLES E. "RED"

Born: 1899. Died: Apr. 15, 1975, Jersey City, N.J. (pneumonia). Screen, stage, burlesque and vaudeville actor.

Appeared in: **1944** A Wave, A Wac and a Marine. **1946** Specter of the Rose.

MARSHALL, CHET

Born: 1932. Died: June 22, 1974. Screen actor. Divorced from actress Karen Sharpe.

Appeared in: **1952** The Las Vegas Story. **1956** D-Day the Sixth of June.

MARSHALL, GEORGE E.

Born: Dec. 29, 1891, Chicago, Ill. Died: Feb. 17, 1975, Los Angeles, Calif. Screen, television actor, film director, television director and screenwriter. Entered films as an extra and stuntman in 1912.

Appeared in: **1914** Universal shorts. **1932** Pack Up Your Troubles; Their First Mistake; The Soilers (short). **1947** Variety Girl. **1974** The Crazy World of Julius Vrooder.

MARSHALL, HERBERT

Born: May 23, 1890, London, England. Died: Jan. 22, 1966, Beverly Hills, Calif. (heart attack). Screen, stage, radio, television actor and writer. Married to actress Boots Mallory (dec. 1958) and later married Dee Anne Kahmann. Divorced from model Lee Russell, actress Edna Best (dec. 1974), and model Molly Maitland. Father of actress Sarah Best Marshall.

Appeared in: **1927** Mumsie. **1929** The Letter. **1930** Murder. **1931** Michael and Mary (US 1932); The Calendar (aka Bachelor's Folly—US 1932); Secrets of a Secretary. **1932** The Faithful Heart (aka Faithful Hearts—US 1933); Evenings for Sale; Blonde Venus; Trouble in Paris. **1933** I Was a Spy (US 1934); White Woman; Clear All Wires; The Solitaire Man. **1934** Four Frightened People; Outcast Lady; The Painted Veil; Riptide. **1935** If You Could Only Cook; The Good Fairy; The Flame Within; Accent on Youth; The Dark Angel. **1936** Crack-Up; The Lady Consents; A Woman Rebels; Make Way for a Lady; Till We Meet Again; Forgotten Faces; Girls' Dormitory. **1937** Fight for Your Lady; Angel; Breakfast for Two. **1938** Marie Antoinette; Mad About Music; Always Goodbye; Woman Against Woman. **1939** Zaza. **1940** A Bill of Divorcement; Foreign Correspondent; The Letter (and 1929 version). **1941** The Little Foxes; Adventure in Washington; When Ladies Meet; Kathleen. **1942** The Moon and Sixpence; Portrait of a Rebel. **1943** Flight for Freedom; Forever and a Day; Young Ideas. **1944** Andy Hardy's Blonde Trouble. **1945** The Unseen; The Enchanted Cottage. **1946** The Razor's Edge; Duel in the Sun; Crack-Up. **1947** High Wall; Ivy. **1949** The Secret Garden. **1950** Underworld Story. **1951** Anne of the Indies. **1952** Captain Black Jack. **1953** Angel Face. **1954** Riders to the Stars; Gog; The Black Shield of Falworth. **1955** The Virgin Queen. **1956** Portrait in Smoke; Wicked As They Come (US 1957); The Weapon (US 1957). **1958** Stage Struck; The Fly; **1960** Midnight Lace; College Confidential. **1961** Fever in the Blood. **1962** Five Weeks in a Balloon. **1963** The List of Adrian Messenger; The Caretakers. **1965** The Third Day.

MARSHALL, OSWALD

Born: 1875, Newcastle-on-Tyne, England. Died: Apr. 19, 1954, New York, N.Y. Stage and screen actor.

MARSHALL, TULLY (William Phillips)

Born: Apr. 13, 1864, Nevada City, Calif. Died: Mar. 10, 1943, Encino, Calif. (heart and lung ailment). Stage and screen actor. Entered films in 1915.

Appeared in: **1916** Oliver Twist; Intolerance; Joan the Woman. **1917** Countess Charming. **1918** We Can't Have Everything; Too Many Millions. **1919** Cheating Cheaters; The Girl Who Stayed Home; The Crimson Gardenia; The Fall of Babylon; Her Kingdom of Dreams; The Life Line; The Lottery Man; Hawthorne of the U.S.A; Everywoman. **1920** The Slim Princess; Double Speed; The Dancin' Fool. **1921** The Cup of Life; Hail the Woman; Silent Years; What Happened to Rosa? **1922** Any Night; Good Men and True; Is Matrimony a Failure?; The Super-Sex; Without Compromise; The Village Blacksmith; The Beautiful and Damned; Deserted at the Altar; Fools of Fortune; The Ladder Jinx; The Lying Truth; Only a Shop Girl; Penrod; The Marriage Chance; Too Much Business. **1923** The Hunchback of Notre Dame; Let's Go; The Barefoot Boy; Broken Hearts of Broadway; Temporary Marriage; Thundergate; The Covered Wagon; The Brass Bottle; The Dangerous Maid; Dangerous Trails; Defying Destiny; Fools and Riches; His Last Race; The Law and the Lawless; Ponjola; Richard, the Lion-Hearted; Her Temporary Husband. **1924** He Who Gets Slapped; Hold Your Breath; Pagan Passions; Passion's Pathway; Along Came Ruth; For Sale; The Stranger; The Right of the Strongest; The Ridin' Kid from Powder River; Reckless Romance. **1925** The Merry Widow; Clothes Make the Pirate; Anything Once; The Half-Way Girl; The Pace That Thrills; Smouldering Fires; The Talker. **1926** Her Big Night; Torrent; Twinkletoes; Old Loves and New. **1927** Beware of Widows; The Gorilla; The Cat and the Canary; Jim the Conqueror. **1928** Drums of Love; The Mad Hour; The Perfect Crime; Queen Kelly; Trail of '98; Alias Jimmy Valentine. **1929** Redskin; The Show of Shows; Thunderbolt; Tiger Rose; Conquest; The Bridge of San Luis Rey; The Mysterious Dr. Fu Manchu; Skin Deep. **1930** Murder Will Out; The Big Trail; Numbered Men; One Night at Susie's; Burning Up; Mammy; She Couldn't Say No; Under a Texas Moon; Common Clay; Redemption; Dancing Sweeties; Tom Sawyer. **1931** Fighting Caravans; The Unholy Garden; The Millionaire; The Virtuous Husband; Mr. Wong; City Sentinels. **1932** Broken Lullaby; The Beast of the City; Night Court; Scandal for Sale; Strangers of the Evening; Two-Fisted Law; Exposure; Klondike; Cabin in the Cotton; Afraid to Talk; Hurricane Express (serial); Arsene Lupin; The Hatchet Man; Scarface; Red Dust; Grand Hotel; The Man I Killed. **1933** Laughing at Life; Corruption; Night of Terror. **1934** Massacre; Murder on the Blackboard. **1935** Black Fury; A Tale of Two Cities; Diamond Jim. **1937** California Straight Ahead; Souls at Sea; She Asked for It; Hold 'Em Navy; Stand In; Behind Prison Bars. **1938** Mr. Boggs Steps Out; Making the Headlines; A Yank at Oxford; Arsene Lupin Returns; College Swing; Hold That Kiss; House of Mystery. **1939** Blue Montana Skies; The Kid from Texas. **1940** Invisible Stripes; Brigham Young, Frontiersman; Youth Will Be Served; Go West; Chad Hanna. **1941** Ball of Fire; For Beauty's Sake. **1942** This Gun for Hire; Moontide; Ten Gentlemen from West Point. **1943** Behind Prison Walls; Hitler's Madman.

MARSHALOV, BORIS

Born: 1902, Russia. Died: Oct. 16, 1967, New York, N.Y. Stage and screen actor.

Appeared in: **1964** Pie in the Sky (aka Terror in the City—1966).

MARSON, AILEEN (Aileen Pitt Marson)

Born: 1913, England. Died: May 5, 1939, London, England (child-birth). Stage and screen actress.

Appeared in: **1932** Watch Beverly. **1934** Lucky Loser; Way of Youth; My Song for You; Roadhouse; Passing Shadows; The Green Pack; Ten Minute Alibi. **1935** Honeymoon for Three; The Black Mask. **1936** Living Dangerously; The

Tenth Man (US 1937); Someone at the Door. **1937** The Green Cockatoo (aka Four Dark Hours); Spring Handicap.

MARSTINI, ROSITA
Born: 1894. Died: Apr. 24, 1948, Hollywood, Calif. Screen actress.

Appeared in: **1917** Tale of Two Cities. **1921** The Outside Woman; The Primal Law; Serenade. **1922** Enter Madame. **1924** Shadows of Paris; The Lover of Camille. **1925** The Big Parade; The Redeeming Sin; Proud Flesh. **1926** Flame of the Argentine. **1928** We Americans; No Other Woman. **1929** Hot for Paris. **1933** I Cover the Water. **1934** In Love with Life.

MARSTON, ANN
Born: 1939. Died: Mar. 6, 1971, Detroit, Mich. (stroke caused by vascular complications of diabetes). Screen actress (starlet at age 9). Was "Miss Michigan" of the 1960 Miss America Pageant.

MARSTON, JOHN
Born: 1890. Died: Sept. 2, 1962, New York, N.Y. Screen and stage actor.

Appeared in: **1932** Cabin in the Cotton; Three on a Match; Silver Dollar; Love Is a Racket; Skyscraper Souls; Scarlet Dawn. **1933** Son of a Sailor; Good Dame; All of Me; Hell and High Water; Heroes for Sale; Lady Killer; Mary Stevens, M.D.; Mayor of Hell; Son of Kong. **1934** The Pursuit of Happiness. **1937** History Is Made at Night. **1939** Union Pacific. **1950** Broken Arrow.

MARTIN, CHRIS-PIN
Born: 1894, Tucson, Ariz. Died: June 1953, Montebello, Calif. (heart attack). Screen actor.

Appeared in: **1929** In Old Arizona. **1931** The Squaw Man; The Cisco Kid. **1932** South of Santa Fe; Girl Crazy; The Stoker; The Painted Woman. **1933** Outlaw Justice; California Trail. **1934** Four Frightened People. **1935** Bordertown; Under the Pampas Moon. **1936** The Gay Desperado; The Beloved Rogue; The Bold Caballero. **1937** Boots and Saddles. **1938** Flirting with Fate; Tropic Holiday; The Texans. **1939** Stagecoach; The Return of the Cisco Kid; The Girl and the Gambler; Fighting Gringo; Frontier Marshal; The Llano Kid. **1940** Down Argentine Way; The Cisco Kid and the Lady; Charlie Chan in Panama; Viva Cisco Kid; Lucky Cisco Kid; The Gay Caballero; The Mark of Zorro. **1941** Romance of the Rio Grande; Ride On, Vaquero; The Bad Man; Week-End in Havana. **1942** Undercover Man; Tombstone, the Town Too Tough to Die; American Empire. **1943** The Sultan's Daughter; The Ox-Bow Incident. **1944** Ali Baba and the Forty Thieves; Tampico. **1945** Along Came Jones; San Antonio. **1946** Suspense; Gallant Journey. **1947** King of the Bandits; Robin Hood of Monterey; The Fugitive. **1948** Belle Starr's Daughter; The Return of Wildfire; Mexican Hayride. **1949** Rimfire; The Beautiful Blonde from Bashful Bend. **1950** Arizona Cowboy. **1951** The Lady from Texas; A Millionaire for Christy. **1952** Ride the Man Down. **1953** Mesa of Lost Women.

MARTIN, CYE (Seymore Martin)
Born: 1914. Died: Mar. 28, 1972, New York, N.Y. (heart attack). Screen actor and theatrical clothier.

Appeared in: **1948** Naked City. **1961** The Hustler. **1966** A Man Called Adam.

MARTIN, EDIE
Born: 1880. Died: Feb. 23, 1964, London, England. Screen, stage and vaudeville actress. Entered films in 1932.

Appeared in: **1937** Farewell Again (aka Troopship—US 1938); Under the Red Robe. **1943** The Demi-Paradise (aka Adventure for Two—US 1945). **1945** A Place of One's Own. **1948** Oliver Twist (US 1951). **1949** The History of Mr. Polly (US 1951). **1951** The Lavender Hill Mob; The Man in the White Suit (US 1952). **1952** Time Gentlemen Please! **1953** The Titfield Thunderbolt. **1954** The End of the Road (US 1957); Lease of Life. **1955** As Long as They're Happy; The Lady Killers (US 1956). **1956** My Teenage Daughter (aka Teenage Bad Girl—US 1957). **1959** Too Many Crooks. **1961** A Weekend with Lulu. **1963** Sparrows Can't Sing.

MARTIN, FRANK WELLS
Born: 1880. Died: Aug. 9, 1941, Los Angeles, Calif. Screen actor and film director.

MARTIN, JOHN E.
Born: 1865. Died: Nov. 22, 1933, New York. Screen and stage actor.

MARTIN, LEWIS H.
Died: Feb. 21, 1969, Los Angeles, Calif. (heart attack). Screen, stage and television actor.

Appeared in: **1950** Experiment Alcatraz. **1951** The Big Carnival; Drums in the Deep South; Operation Pacific; Three Guys Named Mike. **1952** Red Planet Mars; The Wild North. **1953** Arrowhead; The Caddy; Houdini; No Escape; Pony Express; The War of the Worlds. **1954** Cry Vengeance; Knock on Wood; Men of the Fighting Lady; Witness to Murder. **1955** Las Vegas Shakedown; Night Freight; Night Nurse. **1956** The Man Who Knew Too Much; The Court

Jester; These Wilder Years. **1957** The Quiet Gun; Rockabilly Baby; Slander. **1958** Crash Landing. **1963** Diary of a Madman.

MARTIN, LOCK
Died: c. 1959. Screen actor.

Appeared in: **1951** The Day the Earth Stood Still.

MARTIN, OWEN
Born: 1889. Died: May 4, 1960, Saranac Lake, N.Y. Screen and stage actor.

Appeared in: **1957** The Pajama Game.

MARTIN, PETE (Peter Halfpenny)
Born: 1899. Died: May 1973, Glasgow, Scotland. Stage, vaudeville and screen actor. Married to vaude performer Edith Thomson. He appeared in vaude as part of "Martin and Holbein" team.

MARTIN, TONY
Died: Feb. 1932, N.Y. Screen actor. Do not confuse with singer and actor. Appeared in shorts as half of "Nick and Tony" comedy team.

MARTINDEL, EDWARD B.
Born: July 8, 1876, Hamilton, Ohio. Died: May 4, 1955, Woodland Hills, Calif. (heart attack). Screen, stage and vaudeville actor. Entered films in 1917.

Appeared in: **1921** The Call of the North; Ducks and Drakes; Greater Than Love; Short Skirts; Hail the Woman. **1922** The Dangerous Little Demon; Nice People; Clarence; Little Eva Ascends; The Ordeal; A Daughter of Luxury; The Glory of Clementina; Manslaughter; Midnight. **1923** The White Flower; Lovebound; The Day of Faith. **1924** Love's Whirlpool. **1925** The Dixie Handicap; The Sporting Venus; Compromise; Lady Windermere's Fan; Scandal Proof; The Man without a Country. **1926** The Duchess of Buffalo; The Dixie; You'd Be Surprised; Everybody's Acting; Tony Runs Wild; Somebody's Mother. **1927** Lovers?; In Old Kentucky; Children of Divorce; Fashions for Women; Lonesome Ladies; Taxi! Taxi!; Venus of Venice. **1928** The Singing Fool; On Trial; Companionate Marriage; We Americans; The Desert Bride; The Garden of Eden. **1929** The Devil's Apple Tree; Footlights and Fools; Why Be Good?; The Desert Song; Modern Love; Hardboiled Rose; The Phantom of the Opera; The Aviator. **1930** Second Choice; Mamba; Song of the West; Golden Dawn; Rain or Shine; Check and Double Check; Song O' My Heart. **1931** Divorce among Friends; High Stakes; Woman Pursued; The Gay Diplomat. **1932** American Madness; False Faces; Afraid to Talk. **1933** By Appointment Only. **1934** Two Heads on a Pillow. **1935** Champagne for Breakfast; The Girl Who Came Back.

MARTINEZ, CONCHITA
Born: 1912, Mexico. Died: May 1960, Mexico City, Mexico (heart attack). Screen, stage, radio actress and singer.

MARTINEZ, EDUARDO L.
Born: 1900, Mexico. Died: Oct. 31, 1968, San Antonio, Tex. Screen actor and orchestra leader.

MARTYN, MARTY
Died: Dec. 25, 1964, Beverly Hills, Calif. Screen, stage actor and dance director.

Appeared in: **1932** Night after Night.

MARTYN, PETER
Born: 1928, England. Died: Feb. 16, 1955, London, England. Screen, stage and television actor.

Appeared in: **1952** Folly to Be Wise. **1954** Orders Are Orders; You Know What Sailors Are.

MARUM, MARILYN (Marilyn Harvey)
Born: 1929. Died: Mar. 29, 1973, Hollywood, Calif. Screen, stage and television actress. Married to assistant director Gene Marum.

Appeared in: **1963** A Child Is Waiting. **1968** Rosemary's Baby.

MARVIN, JACK
Died: Oct. 17, 1956. Screen actor.

MARX, ALBERT A.
Born: 1892. Died: Feb. 18, 1960, Houston, Tex. Screen, radio actor and clown. Known professionally as "Almar the Clown." Appeared in film shorts.

MARX, "CHICO" (Leonard Marx)
Born: Mar. 22, 1891, New York, N.Y. Died: Oct. 11, 1961, Hollywood, Calif. (heart attack). Screen, stage, vaudeville and television actor. Member of Marx Bros. comedy team. For films the Marx Bros. appeared in see Harpo Marx listing.

Appeared in: **1933** Hollywood on Parade (Chico only—short).

MARX, "HARPO" (Adolph—later changed to Arthur Marx)
Born: Nov. 23, 1893, New York, N.Y. Died: Sept. 28, 1964, Los Angeles, Calif. (heart surgery). Screen, stage, vaudeville, television actor and author. Was member of Marx Bros. comedy team with Chico (dec. 1961), Groucho, Gummo (dec. 1977) and Zeppo. Unless otherwise stated, all films shown were for the Marx Bros. team.

Appeared in: **1925** Too Many Kisses (Harpo only). **1929** The Cocoanuts. **1930** Animal Crackers. **1931** Monkey Business. **1932** Horse Feathers; Hollywood on Parade (short). **1933** Duck Soup. **1935** A Night at the Opera; La Fiesta de Santa Barbara (short). **1937** A Day at the Races. **1938** Room Service. **1939** At the Circus. **1940** Go West. **1941** The Big Store. **1943** Screen Snapshots (short); Stage Door Canteen. **1944** Hollywood Canteen (Harpo only). **1945** All-Star Bond Rally (Harpo only—short). **1946** A Night in Casablanca. **1949** Love Happy. **1957** The Story of Mankind. **1958** Showdown at Ulcer Gulch. **1964** Big Parade of Comedy (documentary).

MARX, MARVIN
Born: 1925. Died: Dec. 23, 1975, Miami Beach, Fla. (heart failure). Screen, stage actor, television writer and producer.

MARX, MAX
Died: 1925, Universal City, Calif. (killed when rope snapped during shooting of Strings of Steel). Screen actor and stuntman.

Appeared in: **1926** Strings of Steel (serial).

MASKELL, VIRGINIA
Born: Feb. 27, 1936, Shepherd's Bush, London, England. Died: Jan. 25, 1968, Stoke Mandeville, England (exposure and overdose of drugs). Screen, stage and television actress. Married to stage director Geoffrey Shakerley.

Appeared in: **1958** Virgin Island (film debut—US 1960); Happy Is the Bride (US 1959); The Man Upstairs. **1959** Jet Storm (US 1961). **1960** Suspect (aka The Risk—US 1961); Doctor in Love (US 1962). **1962** Only Two Can Play; The Wild and the Willing (aka Young and Willing—US 1964). **1967** Interlude (US 1968).

MASON, ANN
Born: 1889. Died: Feb. 6, 1948, New York, N.Y. (burns sustained in fire). Stage and screen actress. Married to actor Paul Gordon (dec. 1929) and later married and divorced actor Philip Pepper.

Appeared in: **1919** Deliverance.

MASON, BUDDY
Born: 1903. Died: Apr. 15, 1975, Woodland Hills, Calif. Screen stuntman and stand-in.

Appeared in: **1927** College. **1963** The Comedy of Terrors.

MASON, DAN (Dan Grassman)
Born: 1853. Died: July 6, 1929, Baersville, N.Y. Screen and stage actor. Created the role of Skipper in the "Toonerville Trolley" series. Entered films approx. 1912.

Appeared in: **1913** The Horrible Example; A Pair of Foils; Porgy's Bouquet; The Comedian's Downfall; The Awakening of a Man; How Did It Finish?; Professor William Nutt; As the Tooth Came Out; The Thrifty Janitor; The Janitor's Flirtation. **1914** Dinkelspiel's Baby; Lena; A Night Out; Tango in Tuckerville; A Tight Squeeze; The Janitor's Quiet Life. **1915** Joey and His Trombones; That Heavenly Cook; Where Can I Get a Wife? **1917** The Broadway Sport; Unknown 274. **1918** Over the Hill; Bonnie Annie Laurie; Brave and Bold; Jack Spurlock, Prodigal; Sherman Was Right; The Yellow Ticket. **1921** Why Girls Leave Home; "Toonerville Trolley" series of shorts including: Boos-Em-Friends; Skipper's Scheme; Skipper's Treasure Garden; Toonerville Tactics; Skipper Has His Fling. **1922** Iron to Gold; Is Matrimony a Failure? **1924** A Self-Made Failure; Conductor 1492; Darwin Was Right; The Plunderer; Idle Tongues. **1925** Sally; Seven Sinners; The Wall Street Whiz; American Pluck; Thunder Mountain; Wages for Wives. **1926** A Desperate Moment; The Fire Brigade; Stepping Along; Hearts and Fists; Forbidden Waters; Rainbow Riley; Hard Boiled. **1927** The Chinese Parrot; A Hero on Horseback; The Price of Honor; Out All Night.

MASON, ELLIOTT
Born: 1897. Died: 1949. Stage and screen actress.

Appeared in: **1936** The Ghost Goes West; Jailbreak; Born That Way; First and the Last; Owd Bob; Break the News. **1938** The Ware Case; Marigold; The Citadel. **1939** Black Limelight. **1940** 21 Days Together. **1941** The Ghost of St. Michael's; Turned Out Nice Again. **1943** The Gentler Sex. **1944** On Approval. **1945** Vacation from Marriage. **1946** The Captive Heart. **1949** The Agitator.

MASON, EVELYN M.
Born: 1892. Died: Oct. 29, 1926, Los Angeles, Calif. (following surgery for ptomaine poisoning). Black screen actress.

MASON, GREGORY
Born: 1889. Died: Nov. 29, 1968, Greenwich, Conn. Journalist and screen actor.

Appeared in: **1914** Our Mutual Girl No. 33.

MASON, JAMES
Born: 1890, Paris, France. Died: Nov. 7, 1959, Hollywood, Calif. (heart attack). Screen actor. Do not confuse with British actor James Mason.

Appeared in: **1914** The Squaw Man. **1918** Knickerbocker Buckaroo. **1921** The Silent Call; Godless Men; The Sage Hen; Two Weeks with Pay; Mysterious Rider. **1922** The Fast Mail; Lights of the Desert; The Old Homestead. **1923** Why Worry?; Scars of Jealousy; Mile-a-Minute Romeo; The Footlight Ranger. **1924** The Flaming Forties; The Heritage of the Desert; Wanderer of the Wasteland; The Plunderer. **1925** Beggar on Horseback; Rugged Water; Barriers Burned Away; Dashing Thru; Old Clothes; Under the Rouge. **1926** Bred in Old Kentucky; For Heaven's Sake; Ladies of Leisure; The Phantom of the Forest; Whispering Smith; Whispering Canyon; The Unknown Cavalier; The Night Owl. **1927** King of Kings; Let It Rain; Alias the Lone Wolf; Back to God's Country; Dead Man's Curve. **1928** Chicago after Midnight; Race for Life; The Big Killing; Across to Singapore; A Thief in the Dark; The Singapore Mutiny; The Speed Classic. **1929** The Phantom City; The Long Long Trail. **1930** The Concentratin' Kid; The Shrimp (short); Last of the Duanes. **1931** The Painted Desert; Caught; Fly My Kite (short); Border Love. **1932** Texas Gun Fighter. **1933** Renegades of the West; Drum Taps; The Story of Temple Drake; Sunset Pass. **1934** The Dude Ranger; The Last Round-Up. **1935** Hopalong Cassidy. **1936** Call of the Prairie; The Plainsman. **1937** Public Cowboy No. 1. **1938** Rhythm of the Saddle. **1939** The Renegade Stranger; I Met a Murderer; In Old Monterey.

MASON, JOHN
Born: 1859, Orange, N.J. Died: Jan. 12, 1919, Stamford, Conn. Stage and screen actor. Do not confuse with stage actor John Mason born c. 1875.

Appeared in: **1915** Jim the Penman; The Fatal Card. **1916** The Libertine. **1918** Moral Suicide.

MASON, LeROY
Born: 1903, Larimore, N. Dak. Died: Oct. 13, 1947, Los Angeles, Calif. (heart attack). Screen actor. Entered films with the old William Fox studios.

Appeared in: **1926** The Arizona Streak; Born to Battle; Flying High; Tom and His Pals. **1927** Closed Gates. **1928** The Law's Lash; Hit of the Show; Revenge; The Viking; The Avenging Shadow; Golden Shackles. **1929** Bride of the Desert. **1930** The Climax; See America Thirst; The Danger Man; The Woman Who Was Forgotten. **1933** The Phantom of the Air (serial); Smoky. **1934** Redhead; Are We Civilized?; The Dude Ranger; When a Man Sees Red. **1935** The Mystery Man; Rainbow Valley. **1936** Comin' Round the Mountain; Ghost Town Gold; The Border Patrolman. **1937** California Straight Ahead; Yodelin' Kid from Pine Ridge; Round Up Time in Texas; Western Gold; The Painted Stallion (serial); It Happened Out West; Jungle Menace (serial). **1938** The Spy Ring; The Painted Trail; Gold Mine in the Sky; Heroes of the Hills; Rhythm of the Saddle; Santa Fe Stampede; Topa Topa. **1939** West of Santa Fe; Wyoming Outlaw; Mexicali Rose; New Frontier; Fighting Gringo; Sky Patrol; Saved by the Belle (short). **1940** Shooting High; Rocky Mountain Rangers; The Range Busters; Triple Justice; Ghost Valley Raiders; Killers of the Wild. **1941** Silver Stallion; Across the Sierras; Robbers of the Range; The Apache Kid; The Perfect Snob; Great Guns. **1942** Time to Kill; It Happened in Flatbush; Six-Gun Gold; Sundown Jim; The Man Who Wouldn't Die; The Silver Bullet. **1943** Chetniks; Blazing Guns; Hands across the Border. **1944** Beneath Western Skies; Firebrands of Arizona; Hidden Valley Outlaws; The Rockies; Call of the South Seas; None Shall Escape; The Silver City Kid; Marshal of Reno; The Mojave Firebrand; Outlaws of Santa Fe; The San Antonio Kid; Song of Nevada; Stagecoach of Monterey; Tucson Raiders; Vigilantes of Dodge City. **1945** Home on the Range. **1946** Heldorado; My Pal Trigger; Sioux City Sue; Daughter of Don Q. (serial); Night Train to Memphis; Red River Renegades; Under Nevada Skies; Valley of the Zombies; Murder in the Music Hall; The Tiger Woman (serial). **1947** Apache Rose; Along the Oregon Trail; Under Colorado Skies; Saddle Pals; Bandits of Dark Canyon. **1948** California Firebrand; The Gay Ranchero.

MASON, LOUIS
Born: 1888, Danville, Ky. Died: Nov. 12, 1959, Hollywood, Calif. Screen, stage and radio actor. Entered films in 1933.

Appeared in: **1934** Kentucky Kernals; Spitfire; This Man Is Mine; Judge Priest. **1935** Mary Jane's Pa; In Person. **1936** Girl of the Ozarks; M'Liss; Banjo on My Knee. **1937** Marry the Girl; Trouble at Midnight. **1939** Stagecoach. **1940** Gold Rush Maisie; The Return of Frank James. **1941** The Sea Wolf. **1942** Tennessee Johnson; Yankee Doodle Dandy; Whistling in Dixie. **1943** What's Buzzin' Cousin. **1944** Broadway Rhythm. **1945** Grissly's Millions; Hit the Hay. **1946** Somewhere in the Night; Decoy. **1947** Sport of Kings. **1949** I Cheated the Law.

MASON, MARJORIE
Died: Nov. 21, 1968. Screen actress. Appeared in silents.

MASON, REGINALD
Born: 1882, San Francisco, Calif. Died: July 10, 1962, Hermosa Beach, Calif. Stage and screen actor.

Appeared in: **1920** Two Weeks. **1921** The Highest Bidder. **1932** Life Begins. **1933** A Bedtime Story; Emergency Call; Topaze; Shanghai Madness; Brief Moment; The Big Brain; Baby Face; Mary Stevens, M.D.; Kiss before the Mirror. **1934** Call It Luck; Charlie Chan's Courage; You Can't Buy Everything. **1936** Suzy.

MASON, SULLY P.
Born: 1906. Died: Nov. 27, 1970, Los Angeles, Calif. (cerebral hemorrhage). Screen, television actor, saxophonist and vocalist.

Appeared in: **1939** That's Right, You're Wrong. **1940** You'll Find Out. **1941** Playmates. **1943** Around the World.

MASON, WILLIAM C. "SMILING BILLY"
Born: 1888. Died: Jan. 24, 1941, Orange, N.J. Screen, stage and vaudeville actor. He aided Thomas Edison in early film experimentation.

Appeared in: **1912** Cupid's Quartet; Hearts of Men; A Corner in Whiskers; The Snare; Miss Simkins' Summer Boarder; The Stain; Almost a Man; A Money? **1913** Essanay films. **1916** Dizzy Heights and Daring Hearts; Cinders of Love; A Dash of Courage. **1922** A series of short comedies.

MASSEY, ILONA (Ilona Hajmassy)
Born: 1910, Budapest, Hungary. Died: Aug. 10, 1974, Bethesda, Md. Screen, stage, radio, television actress and opera performer. Divorced from actor Alan Curtis (dec. 1953), Nicholas Szarozd, and Charles Walker. Married to Air Force General Donald Dawson.

Appeared in: **1937** Rosalie. **1939** Balalaika; Honeymoon in Bali. **1941** International Lady; New Wine. **1942** Invisible Agent. **1943** Frankenstein Meets the Wolf Man. **1945** Tokyo Rose. **1946** The Gentleman Misbehaves; Holiday in Mexico. **1947** Northwest Outpost. **1948** The Plunderers. **1949** Love Happy. **1957** Sabu and the Magic Ring. **1958** Jet Over the Atlantic (US 1960).

MASSINGHAM, RICHARD
Born: 1898, England. Died: 1953. Screen actor, film director, producer, screenwriter and physician. He produced, directed, wrote and acted in numerous short subjects 1935-1953.

MASSON, TOM (Thomas L. Masson)
Born: July 21, 1866, Essex, Conn. Died: June 18, 1934, Glen Ridge, N.J. Humorist, magazine editor and screen actor.

Appeared in: **1913** Saved by Parcel Post.

MASTERS, DARYL
Born: 1913. Died: May 24, 1961, Toronto, Canada. Screen and television actor.

Appeared in: **1958** Wolf Dog; Flaming Frontier. **1961** 1 + 1 (Exploring the Kinsey Reports).

MASTERS, HARRY
Born: 1885. Died: May 12, 1974, Los Angeles, Calif. Screen and vaudeville actor.

Appeared in: **1930** The Beauties (short).

MASTERS, RUTH
Born: 1899. Died: Sept. 22, 1969, Stamford, Conn. Screen, stage and television actress.

Appeared in: **1961** Bridge to the Sun.

MATA, MIGUEL P.
Born: 1914, Spain. Died: Feb. 1956, Madrid, Spain (auto accident). Screen, stage and radio actor.

MATEOS, HECTOR
Born: 1901, Mexico. Died: Feb. 13, 1957, Mexico City, Mexico. Screen actor.

MATHER, AUBREY
Born: Dec. 17, 1885, Minchinhampton, England. Died: Jan. 16, 1958, London, England. Stage and screen actor.

Appeared in: **1930** Young Woodley. **1932** The Impassive Footman (aka Woman in Bondage—US); Love on the Spot; Aren't We All?; Tell Me Tonight (aka Be Mine Tonight—US 1933). **1934** Red Wagon (US 1935); The Admiral's Secret; The Man Who Changed His Name; The Lash; Anything Might Happen. **1935** The Silent Passenger. **1936** Ball at Savoy; When Knights Were Bold (US 1942); As You Like It; Chick; The Man in the Mirror (US 1937); Sabotage (aka The Woman Alone—US 1937). **1937** Underneath the Arches; Night Must Fall; Life Begins with Love. **1939** Jamaica Inn; Just William. **1940** No,

No, Nanette. **1941** Rage in Heaven. **1942** The Wife Takes a Flyer; Mrs. Miniver; Careful, Soft Shoulders; The Undying Monster; The Great Impersonation; Random Harvest; Ball of Fire. **1943** Hello, Frisco, Hello; Forever and a Day; Heaven Can Wait. **1944** Jane Eyre; The Lodger; The Song of Bernadette. **1945** Wilson; National Velvet; Keys of the Kingdom; The House of Fear. **1947** The Mighty McGurk; Temptation; It Happened in Brooklyn; For the Love of Rusty; The Hucksters. **1948** Julia Misbehaves. **1949** That Forsyte Woman; Adventures of Don Juan; Everybody Does It; The Secret Garden; Secret of St. Ives. **1950** Joan of Arc. **1952** The Importance of Being Earnest; South of Algiers (aka The Golden Mask—US 1954). **1954** To Dorothy a Son (aka Cash on Delivery—US 1956); Fast and Loose.

MATHER, JACK
Born: 1908. Died: Aug. 15, 1966, Wauconda, Ill. (heart attack). Screen, radio and television actor.

Appeared in: **1952** Dream Boat. **1954** River of No Return; Broken Lance. **1955** How to Be Very, Very Popular; The View from Pompey's Head (aka Secret Interlude). **1956** The Man in the Gray Flannel Suit; The Revolt of Mamie Stover. **1957** My Man Godfrey. **1958** The Bravados. **1959** This Earth Is Mine.

MATHEWS, GEORGE H.
Born: 1877. Died: June 7, 1952, Woodland Hills, Calif. Stage and screen actor.

MATHEWSON, CHRISTY (Christopher Mathewson)
Born: Aug. 12, 1880, Factorville, Pa. Died: Oct. 7, 1925, Saranac Lake, N.Y. (tuberculosis). Professional baseball player and screen actor.

Appeared in: **1914** Love and Baseball.

MATHIESON, MUIR
Born: Jan. 24, 1911, Stirling, Scotland. Died: Aug. 2, 1975, Oxford, England. Screen actor, musical director and conductor.

Appeared in: **1936** Things to Come. **1941** Dangerous Moonlight (aka Suicide Squadron—US 1942). **1942** In Which We Serve. **1945** The Seventh Veil (US 1946); Brief Encounter (US 1946). **1951** The Magic Box (US 1952). **1952** Sound Barrier (aka Breaking the Sound Barrier—US). **1960** Swiss Family Robinson.

MATHOT, LEON
Born: 1896, France. Died: Mar. 6, 1968, Paris, France. Screen actor and film director. Entered films in 1914.

Appeared in: **1928** A Daughter of Israel. **1929** Apassionata.

MATIESEN, OTTO
Born: 1873, Copenhagen, Denmark. Died: Feb. 20, 1932, Safford, Ariz. Stage and screen actor.

Appeared in: **1922** Bells of San Juan; Money to Burn. **1923** Scaramouche; Alias the Night Wind; Boston Blackie; Vanity Fair; The Dangerous Maid. **1924** The Dawn of Tomorrow; Captain Blood; The Folly of Vanity; Revelation. **1925** The Happy Warrior; Morals for Men; Parisian Love; Sackcloth and Scarlet; The Salvation Hunters. **1926** Bride of the Storm; The Silver Treasure; Christine of the Big Tops; While London Sleeps; Whispering Wires; Yellow Fingers. **1927** The Beloved Rogue; The Road to Romance; Too Many Crooks; Surrender. **1928** The Desert Bride; The Last Moment; The Woman from Moscow; The Scarlet Lady. **1929** Strange Cargo; Prisoners; General Crack; Behind Closed Doors; The Show of Shows; Golden Dawn; Last of the Lone Wolf; Conspiracy. **1931** Beau Ideal; Man of the Sky; Soldier's Plaything; The Maltese Falcon.

MATSUI, SUISEI
Born: 1900, Japan. Died: Aug. 1, 1973, Kamakura City, Japan (cancer). Screen, radio and vaudeville actor. Narrated films during the silents.

Appeared in: **1951** Tokyo File 212.

MATTERSTOCK, ALBERT
Born: 1912. Died: June 30, 1960, Hamburg, West Germany. Screen actor.

Appeared in: **1937** Stimme des Blutes (Blood Bond). **1939** Ziel den Wolken (Goal in the Clouds); Solo per Danne. **1940** Our Little Wife.

MATTESON, RUTH
Born: 1910. Died: Feb. 5, 1975, Westport, Conn. Screen, stage and radio actress. Divorced from actor and director Arthur Pierson (dec. 1975).

MATTHEWS, A. E. "MATTY" (Alfred Edward Matthews)
Born: Nov. 22, 1869, Bridlington, England. Died: July 25, 1960, Bushey Heath, England. Screen, stage and television actor.

Appeared in: **1914** A Highwayman's Honour. **1916** The Real Thing at Last; The Lifeguardsman; Wanted—a Widow. **1918** Once Upon a Time. **1919** The Lackey and the Lady; Castles of Dreams. **1935** Men Are Not Gods (US 1937). **1941** Quiet Wedding; Pimpernel Smith (aka Mister V—US 1942); Surprise Broadcast (short). **1942** The Great Mr. Handel (US 1943); Thunder Rock (US 1944). **1943** The Life and Death of Colonel Blimp (aka

Colonel Blimp—US 1945). Escape to Danger; The Man in Grey (US 1945). **1944** The Way Ahead; They Came to a City; Love Story (aka A Lady Surrenders—US 1947); Twilight Hour. **1945** Flight from Folly. **1946** Piccadilly Incident. **1947** The Ghosts of Berkeley Square; Just William's Luck (US 1948). **1948** William Comes to Town; Britannia Mews (aka Forbidden Str·et—US 1949). **1949** The Chiltern Hundreds (stage and film versions—aka The Amazing Mr. Beecham—US); Landfall; Whisky Galore (aka Tight Little Island—US and Mad Little Island). **1951** Mr. Drake's Duck; The Galloping Major; Laughter in Paradise; The Magic Box (US 1952). **1952** Castle in the Air; Something Money Can't Buy; Penny Princess (US 1953); Made in Heaven; Who Goes There! (aka The Passionate Sentry—US 1953). **1953** Skid Kids. **1954** The Million Pound Note (aka Man with a Million—US); The Weak and the Wicked; Happy Ever After (aka Tonight's the Night—US); Aunt Clara. **1955** Miss Tulip Stays the Night. **1956** Jumping for Joy; Loser Takes All (US 1957); Three Men in a Boat (US 1958); Around the World in 80 Days. **1957** Doctor at Large; Carry on Admiral (aka The Ship Was Loaded—US 1959). **1960** Inn for Trouble.

MATTHEWS, BEATRICE

Born: 1890. Died: Nov. 10, 1942, Hollywood, Calif. Screen actress.

MATTHEWS, FORREST

Born: 1908. Died: Nov. 22, 1951, Dallas, Texas (heart attack). Screen and television actor.

Appeared in: **1948** Docks of New Orleans; Triggerman; Joe Palooka in Winner Take All; Fighting Mustang; Sunset Carson Rides Again.

MATTHEWS, JEAN D.

Died: Jan. 20, 1961, Dallas, Tex. Stage and screen actress. Appeared in films prior to 1918.

MATTHEWS, LESTER (aka LESTER MATHEWS)

Born: Dec. 3, 1900, Nottingham, England. Died: June 6, 1975. Screen, stage and television actor.

Appeared in: **1931** The Lame Duck; Creeping Shadows (aka The Limping Man—US 1932); The Man at Six (aka The Gables Mystery—US 1932); The Wickham Mystery; Gipsy Blood (aka Carmen—US 1932); The Old Man. **1932** Indiscretions of Eve; Fires of Fate (US 1933); Her Night Out. **1933** On Secret Service (aka Secret Agent—US 1935); The Stolen Necklace; Out of the Past; Called Back; She Was Only a Village Maiden; The Melody Maker; Facing the Music (US 1934); The Song You Gave Me (US 1934); House of Dreams. **1934** Borrowed Clothes; Boomerang; Song at Eventide; Blossom Time (aka April Romance—US 1937); Irish Hearts (aka Norah O'Neale—US); The Poisoned Diamond. **1935** The Werewolf of London; The Raven. **1936** Thank You, Jeeves; Professional Soldier; Song and Dance Man; Spy 77; Too Many Parents; Lloyd's of London; 15 Maiden Lane; Crack Up; Tugboat Princess. **1937** The Prince and the Pauper; Lancer Spy. **1938** There's Always a Woman; The Adventures of Robin Hood; Three Loves Has Nancy; Mysterious Mr. Moto; I Am a Criminal; If I Were King; Time Out for Murder; Think It Over (short). **1939** The Three Musketeers; Susannah of the Mounties; Should a Girl Marry; Conspiracy; Rulers of the Sea; Everything Happens at Night. **1940** Northwest Passage; British Intelligence; The Biscuit Eater; Women in War; Sing, Dance, Plenty Hot. **1941** The Lone Wolf Keeps a Date; Man Hunt; A Yank in the RAF. **1942** The Pied Piper; Desperate Journey; Across the Pacific; London Blackout Murders; Son of Fury; Manila Calling. **1943** Mysterious Doctor; Tonight We Raid Calais. **1944** Nine Girls; The Invisible Man's Revenge; Gaslight; Wing and a Prayer; Four Jills in a Jeep; Between Two Worlds; The Story of Dr. Wassell; Ministry of Fear; Shadows in the Night. **1945** Objective, Burma; I Love a Mystery; The Beautiful Cheat; Salty O'Rourke; Two O'Clock Courage. **1947** Dark Delusion; Bulldog Drummond at Bay; The Exile. **1948** Fighting Father Dunne. **1950** Tyrant of the Sea; Montana; Rogues of Sherwood Forest; Her Wonderful Lie. **1951** The Son of Dr. Jekyll; Lorna Doone; Corky of Gasoline Alley; Tales of Robin Hood. **1952** Lady in the Iron Mask; Les Miserables; Operation Secret; Stars and Stripes Forever; Jungle Jim and the Forbidden Land; Brigand; Captain Pirate. **1953** Niagara; Trouble Along the Way; Young Bess; Fort Ti; Bad for Each Other; Savage Mutiny; Jamaica Run; Sangaree. **1954** Charge of the Lancers; King Richard and the Crusaders; Desiree; Jungle Man-Eaters. **1956** Flame of the Island. **1960** Song without End. **1964** Mary Poppins. **1966** Assault on a Queen. **1968** Star!

MATTHISON, EDITH WYNNE

Born: 1875, England. Died: Sept. 23, 1955, Los Angeles, Calif. Stage and screen actress. Married to actor Charles Rann Kennedy (dec. 1950). Entered films with Lasky Co. in 1915.

Appeared in: **1915** The Governor's Lady.

MATTIOLI, RAF

Born: 1936, Naples, Italy. Died: Oct. 12, 1960, Rome, Italy (heart attack). Screen actor.

Appeared in: **1958** Guendalina. **1959** Estate Violenta (Violent Summer); Vacanzie a Izchia (Holiday Island). **1960** Where the Hot Wind Blows (aka La

Legge—The Law). **1961** Le Baccanti (US 1963). Other Italian films: First Love; Young Husbands; Tunisi Top Secret.

MATTOX, MARTHA

Born: 1879, Natchez, Miss. Died: May 2, 1933, Sidney, N.Y. (heart ailment). Stage and screen actress. Entered films in 1913.

Appeared in: **1920** Huckleberry Finn. **1921** The Conflict; The Son of Wallingford. **1922** Restless Souls; Rich Men's Wives; The Top O' the Morning; Beauty's Worth; The Angel of Crooked Street; The Game Chicken; The Hands of Nara; The Married Flapper. **1923** The Hero; Three Wise Fools; Bavu; Hearts Aflame; Look Your Best; Penrod and Sam; Maytime; Times Have Changed; Woman-Proof. **1924** The Family Secret. **1925** Dangerous Innocence; East Lynne; Heir-Loons; I'll Show You the Town; The Keeper of the Bees; The Home Maker; Oh, Doctor!; The Man in Blue; With This Ring. **1926** Lonely Mary; Torrent; Infatuation; Christine of the Big Tops; Forest Havoc; The Nut-Cracker; The Rainmaker; Shameful Behavior?; The Waning Sex; The Warning Signal; The Yankee Senor. **1927** The Cat and the Canary; The Devil Dancer; Finger Prints; Snowbound; The 13th Juror. **1928** Love Me and the World Is Mine; Her Wild Oat; A Bit of Heaven; Fools for Luck; The Little Shepherd of Kingdom Come; The Naughty Duchess; The Singapore Mutiny; Kentucky Courage. **1929** The Big Diamond Robbery; Montmartre Rose. **1930** Night Work; Extravagance; The Love Racket. **1931** Misbehaving Ladies; Born to Love; Dangerous Affair; Thirty Days; Murder by the Clock. **1932** Murder at Dawn; The Silver Lining; The Monster Walks; Careless Lady; So Big; No Greater Love; Heroes of the West (serial); Dynamite Ranch; Torchy Raises the Auntie (short). **1933** Haunted Gold; Bitter Tea of General Yen.

MATTRAW, SCOTT

Born: Oct. 19, 1885, Evans Mills, N.Y. Died: Nov. 9, 1946, Hollywood, Calif. Screen, stage and minstrel actor.

Appeared in: **1924** The Thief of Bagdad (film debut). **1927** The Return of the Riddle Rider (serial); One Glorious Scrap. **1928** Haunted Island (serial); A Made-to-Order Hero; Quick Triggers; Two Lovers. **1929** Captain Cowboy. **1934** Babes in Toyland. **1935** Okay Toots! (short). **1938** In Old Chicago. **1950** Revenge Is Sweet (reissue of 1934 version of Babes in Toyland).

MATZENAUER, MARGUERITE

Born: June 1, 1881, Temesvar, Hungary. Died: Mar. 19, 1963, Van Nuys, Calif. Opera singer and screen actress.

Appeared in: **1936** Mr. Deeds Goes to Town.

MAUDE, CYRIL

Born: Apr. 24, 1862, London, England. Died: Feb. 20, 1951, Torquay, England. Stage and screen actor. Married to stage actress Winifred Emery (dec. 1924) and later married to Mrs. P. H. Trew.

Appeared in: **1913** The House of Temperley. **1914** Beauty and the Barge. **1915** Peer Gynt. **1921** The Headmaster. **1930** Grumpy (stage and film versions). **1931** These Charming People. **1933** Counsel's Opinion; Orders Is Orders (US 1934). **1935** Heat Wave. **1947** While the Sun Shines (US 1950),

MAUGHAM, W. SOMERSET (William Somerset Maugham)

Born: Jan. 25, 1874, Paris, France. Died: Dec. 16, 1965, Nice, France. Playwright, author, screenwriter and screen actor.

Appeared in: **1950** Trio.

MAUPAIN, ERNEST

Born: 1881, Paris, France. Died: 1949, France. Screen and stage actor.

Appeared in: **1915** Graustark. **1930** Le Miracle des Loups.

MAURICE

Died: May 18, 1927, Lausanne, Switzerland (consumption). Screen, stage, vaudeville actor and ballroom dancer. Appeared in vaude as part of dance team "Valentino, Muris and Maurice," with Rudolph Valentino.

Appeared in: **1916** The Quest of Life.

MAURICE, MARY "MOTHER" (Mary Birch)

Born: Nov. 15, 1844, Morristown, Ohio. Died: May 1918, Pennsylvania. Stage and screen actress. Entered films with Vitagraph in 1910.

Appeared in: **1911** Saving an Audience; My Old Dutch; Wisteria. **1912** The Seventh Son; The Firing of the Patchwork Quilt; Her Choice; Her Boy; The Diamond Brooch; His Mother's Shroud; Mrs. Lirriper's Lodgers; Their Golden Anniversary; The Picture Idol; Martha's Rebellion; The Church Across the Way; Her Grandchild; Aunty's Romance; Captain Barnacle, Reformer; The Crossroads. **1913** The Wings of a Moth; In the Shadow; Troublesome Daughters; O'Hara Helps Cupid; The Locket; Luella's Love Story; O'Hara and the Youthful Prodigal; One Can't Always Tell; An Unwritten Chapter; O'Hara as Guardian Angel. **1914** The Sins of the Mothers; The Portrait; The Memories that Haunt. **1915** The Battle Cry of Peace; Twice Rescued; A Keyboard Strategy; The Scar; The Return of Maurice Donnelly; The Barrier of Faith; The Man Who Couldn't Beat God; The Gods Redeem; The Lesson of the Narrow Street; On with the Dance; Rags and the Girl; Sam's Sweetheart; Is Christmas a Bore?; Dorothy. **1916** The Chattel; Rose of the South; The Man He Used to Be; The Supreme Temptation; Carew and Son; Phantom Fortunes; The Dollar and the Law; The Redemption of Dave Darcey; The Price of Fame; Whom the Gods Destroy. **1917** For France; I Will Repay (aka The Courage of Fidelity); Who Goes There? Her Secret; Transgression. **1918** Over the Top; The Little Runaway.

MAURUS, GERDA

Born: 1909, Germany. Died: Aug. 1968, Dusseldorf, Germany. Stage and screen actress.

Appeared in: **1928** Spione (Spies). **1931** By Rocket to the Moon. **1933** Tod Ueber Schanghai. **1939** Prinzessin Sissy.

MAWSON, EDWARD

Born: 1861. Died: May 20, 1917, New York, N.Y. Screen and stage actor.

Appeared in: **1916** Return of Eve.

MAX, JEAN

Born: 1897, France. Died: Jan. 1971, France. Screen and stage actor.

Appeared in: **1932** Paris Beguin. **1936** Pension Mimosas. **1938** Dark Eyes. **1939** That They May Live.

MAXAM, LOUELLA MODIE

Born: 1896. Died: Sept. 4, 1970, Burbank, Calif. Screen actress.

Appeared in: **1916** A Movie Star; An Oily Scoundrel; Bucking Society; His Bitter Pill; His Lying Heart; Ambrose's Rapid Rise.

MAXEY, PAUL

Born: 1908, Wheaton, Ill. Died: June 3, 1963, Pasadena, Calif. (heart attack). Screen, stage and television actor.

Appeared in: **1941** Father Steps Out; I'll Sell My Life; City Limits; Let's Go Collegiate. **1946** Social Terrors (short); Oil's Well That Ends Well (short); Till the Clouds Roll By; Below the Deadline; Personality Kid. **1947** Borrowed Blonde (short); In Room 303 (short); Millie's Daughter. **1948** Contest Crazy (short); Winter Meeting; Brother Knows Best (short); The Noose Hangs High. **1949** Mississippi Rhythm; Bride for Sale; Sky Dragon; Fighting Fools; South of St. Louis. **1950** The Reformer and the Redhead; The Return of Jesse James. **1951** Casa Manana; Abbott and Costello Meet the Invisible Man; Too Many Wives (short). **1952** The Narrow Margin; Kid Monk Baroni; Here Come the Marines; Singin' in the Rain; With a Song in My Heart; Stars and Stripes Forever; Dream Boat. **1953** So You Want to Be a Musician (short); The Stranger Wore a Gun. **1954** Black Tuesday. **1957** High Tide at Noon. **1958** Showdown at Boot Hill. **1961** 20,000 Eyes. **1962** Walk on the Wild Side.

MAXTED, STANLEY

Born: 1900, England. Died: May 10, 1963, London, England. Screen, stage, television and radio actor.

Appeared in: **1953** Never Let Me Go; The Final Test (US 1954). **1955** I Am a Camera. **1956** The Weapon (US 1957). **1957** Campbell's Kingdom (US 1958); Fiend without a Face. **1958** Across the Bridge; The Strange Awakening (aka Female Friends—US 1960).

MAXWELL, EDWIN

Born: 1886, Dublin, Ireland. Died: Aug. 1948, Falmouth, Mass. (cerebral hemorrhage). Screen, stage actor, stage director and associate film director.

Appeared in: **1929** The Taming of the Shrew. **1930** All Quiet on the Western Front; Top Speed; Du Barry, Woman of Passion. **1931** Kiki; Inspiration; Daybreak; The Gorilla; Daddy Long Legs; Men of the Sky; Yellow Ticket; Ambassador Bill. **1932** Two Kinds of Women; Shopworn; Scarface; American Madness; Those We Love; Six Hours to Live; You Said a Mouthful; The Girl from Calgary; Grand Hotel; The Cohens and the Kellys in Hollywood; Blessed Event. **1933** The Mystery of the Wax Museum; Tonight Is Ours; State Trooper; Fog; The Mayor of Hell; Heroes for Sale; Dinner at Eight; Gambling Ship; Duck Soup; Emergency Call; The Woman I Stole; Night of Terror; Police Car 17; Big Time or Bust. **1934** The Dancing Man; Cleopatra; Gift of Gab; Happiness C.O.D.; Miss Fane's Baby Is Stolen; The Ninth Guest; Mystery Liner; Burn 'Em up Barnes (feature and serial); The Cat's Paw. **1935** Public Ghost No. 1 (short); Men of Action; The Devil Is a Woman; All the King's Horses; Great God Gold; Motive for Revenge; The Crusades; Thanks a Million; G-Men. **1936** The Plainsman; Dangerous Waters; Big Brown Eyes; Panic on the Air; Fury; Come and Get It. **1937** Love Is News; Night Key; The Road Back; Slave Ship; Love Takes Flight; A Man Betrayed. **1938** Romance on the Run. **1939** Young Mr. Lincoln; Drums along the Mohawk; Way Down South; Ninotchka. **1940** The Shop around the Corner; Pound Foolish (short); The Blue Bird; New Moon; His Girl Friday; Know Your Money (short); Kit Carson; Brigham Young—Frontiersman. **1941** The Devil and Miss Jones; Ride On, Vaquero!; Midnight Angel. **1942** I Live on Danger; Ten Gentlemen from West Point. **1943** Holy Matrimony; Behind Prison Walls; Mr. Big; The Great Moment; Since You Went Away; Waterfront; Wilson. **1945** Mama Loves Papa. **1946** Swamp Fire; The Jolson Story. **1947** Second Chance; The Gangster. **1948**

The Vicious Circle. **1949** Ride, Ryder, Ride!; The Set Up; Follow Me Quietly; Thieves' Highway; Law of the Barbary Coast; Side Street.

MAXWELL, ELSA

Born: May 24, 1883, Keokuk, Iowa. Died: Nov. 1, 1963, New York, N.Y. Columnist, songwriter, professional party giver and screen actress.

Appeared in: **1939** Hotel for Women. **1940** Public Deb. No. 1. **1943** Stagedoor Canteen.

MAXWELL, MARILYN (Marvel Marilyn Maxwell)

Born: Aug. 3, 1922, Clarinda, Iowa. Died: Mar. 20, 1972, Beverly Hills, Calif. (high blood pressure and a pulmonary ailment). Screen, radio, television actress and singer. Divorced from actor John Conte, restauranteur Andy McIntyre and producer Andy Davis.

Appeared in: **1942** Cargo of Innocents (film debut); Stand By for Action. **1943** Swing Fever; Thousands Cheer; Presenting Lily Mars; DuBarry Was a Lady; Dr. Gillespie's Criminal Case; Salute to the Marines; Right about Face; Crazy to Kill; Pilot No. 5; Best Foot Forward. **1944** Lost in a Harem; Ziegfeld Follies; Music for Millions; Three Men in White; Between Two Women. **1946** The Show-Off. **1947** High Barbaree. **1948** Summer Holiday; Race Street. **1949** The Champion. **1950** Key to the City; Outside the Wall. **1951** The Lemon Drop Kid; New Mexico. **1953** Off Limits; East of Sumatra; Paris Model. **1955** New York Confidential. **1956** Forever Darling. **1958** Rock-A-Bye Baby. **1963** Critic's Choice. **1964** The Lively Set; Stage to Thunder Rock. **1968** Arizona Bushwhackers. **1969** From Nashville with Music. **1970** The Phynx.

MAY, EDNA

Born: 1879, Syracuse, N.Y. Died: Jan. 1, 1948, Lausanne, Switzerland (heart attack). Stage and screen actress.

Appeared in: **1913** David Copperfield. **1916** Salvation Joan.

MAY, HAROLD R.

Born: 1903. Died: Sept. 16, 1973, Hollywood, Calif. Screen actor. Appeared in Mack Sennett comedies.

MAY, JAMES

Born: 1857, England. Died: Aug. 25, 1941, Los Angeles, Calif. Screen actor and double for W. C. Fields.

MAY, MARTY

Born: 1898, New York, N.Y. Died: Nov. 11, 1975, Las Vegas, Nev. (heart ailment). Stage, vaudeville, radio, television and screen actor. Appeared in vaudeville with Olsen and Johnson. Married to vaude actress June Johnson.

Appeared in: **1943** Salute for Three.

MAY, SAMUEL RODERICK

Born: 1910, Lamont, Iowa. Died: Aug. 9, 1963, Lebanon, Mo. Screen, stage and radio actor.

MAYALL, HERSHELL

Born: 1863. Died: June 10, 1941, Detroit, Mich. (cerebral hemorrhage). Screen, stage and radio actor.

Appeared in: **1917** Cleopatra. **1919** The Money Corporal. **1920** Daredevil Jack (serial). **1921** The Beautiful Gambler; The Blushing Bride; Three Word Brand; To a Finish; The Queen of Sheba; Straight from the Shoulder. **1922** Arabian Love; The Yellow Stain; Thirty Days; Smiles are Trumps; Extra! Extra!; Calvert's Valley; Oath-Bound. **1923** The Isle of Lost Ships; Itching Palms; Money! Money! Money!; Wild Bill Hickok. **1924** Alimony. **1925** After Marriage. **1929** Great Power. **1930** Fast and Loose; The Royal Family of Broadway. **1931** His Women; plus the following shorts: The Antique Shop; Second Childhood; Revenge Is Sweet. **1934** War Is a Racket.

MAYE, JIMSY

Born: 1894. Died: Apr. 10, 1968. Screen actress. Divorced from actor and director B. Reeves Eason (dec. 1956). Appeared in silents.

MAYER, PAUL M.

Born: 1914. Died: June 1968, Tucson, Ariz. (traffic accident). Screen and television actor and commentator.

MAYFIELD, CLEO

Born: 1897. Died: Nov. 8, 1954, New York, N.Y. Screen, stage and vaudeville actress.

Appeared in: **1930** MGM shorts.

MAYHEW, KATE

Born: 1853. Died: June 16, 1944, New York, N.Y. Screen and stage actress.

Appeared in: **1916** Hazel Kirke. **1924** Tongues of Flame.

MAYNARD, CLAIRE (Marie McCarthy)

Born: 1912, Brooklyn, N.Y. Died: July 1941, New York, N.Y. (suicide—gas). Stage and screen actress.

Appeared in: **1931** Over the Hill; Good Sport.

MAYNARD, KEN

Born: July 21, 1895, Vevey, Ind. Died: Mar. 23, 1973, Woodland Hills, Calif. Brother of actor Kermit Maynard (dec. 1971). Screen actor, rodeo and circus performer.

Appeared in: **1923** The Man Who Won. **1924** Janice Meredith; $50,000 Reward. **1925** The Haunted Ranch; The Demon Rider; Fighting Courage. **1926** North Star; Unknown Cavalier; Senor Daredevil. **1927** Overland Stage; Somewhere in Sonora; Land Beyond the Law; Devil's Saddle; The Red Raiders; Gun Gospel. **1928** The Canyon of Adventure; The Wagon Show; The Upland Rider; The Code of the Scarlet; The Glorious Trail. **1929** Senor Americano; The Phantom City; Cheyenne; The Lawless Legion; The California Mail; The Royal Rider; Wagon Master; The Voice of Hollywood (short). **1930** Parade of the West; The Fighting Legion; Lucky Larkin; Mountain Justice; Song of the Caballero; Sons of the Saddle; Fighting Thru (aka California in 1878). **1931** Two Gun Man; Alias—The Bad Man; Arizona Terror; Range Law; Branded Men; Pocatello Kid. **1932** Texas Gun-Fighter; Sunset Trail; Whistlin' Dan; Hell Fire Austin; Dynamite Ranch; Trail Blazers (serial). **1933** The Lone Avenger; Drum Taps; Phantom Thunderbolt; King of the Arena; Strawberry Roan; The Fiddlin' Buckaroo; Between Fighting Men; Tombstone Canyon; Come On Tarzan; Fargo Express. **1934** Gun Justice; Trail Drive; Wheels of Destiny; Smoking Guns; In Old Santa Fe; Mystery Mountain (serial); Honor of the Range; Doomed to Die. **1935** Western Frontier; Heir to Trouble; Lawless Riders; Northern Frontier. **1936** Heroes of the Range; Avenging Waters; The Cattle Thief; The Fugitive Sheriff. **1937** Boots of Destiny; Trailing Trouble. **1938** Whirlwind Horseman; Six Shootin' Trouble. **1943** Wild Horse Stampede; The Law Rides Again; Blazing Guns; Death Valley Rangers. **1944** Westward Bound; Arizona Whirlwind. **1945** Blazing Frontier. **1961** Frontier Uprising; Gun Fight; You Have to Run Fast. **1970** Bigfoot.

MAYNARD, KERMIT

Born: Sept. 20, 1902, Mission, Tex. or Vevey, Ind. Died: Jan. 16, 1971, Hollywood, Calif. (heart attack). Screen and circus actor. Once doubled for actors George O'Brien, Victor McLaglen, Warner Baxter and Edmund Lowe. Brother of actor Ken Maynard (dec. 1973) for whom he doubled in early films. Entered films in 1926 with F.B.O. Studio.

Appeared in: **1933** Drum Taps; Outlaw Justice. **1934** The Fighting Trooper; Sandy of the Mounted. **1935** Northern Frontier; Code of the Mounted; The Red Blood of Courage; Wilderness Mail; His Fighting Blood; Trails of the Wild. **1936** Timber War; Song of the Trail; Phantom Patrol; Wildcat Trooper; Wild Horse Roundup; Whistling Bullets. **1937** The Fighting Texan; Valley of Terror; Galloping Dynamite; Roaring Six-Guns. **1938** Wild Bill Hickok (serial); Western Jamboree. **1939** The Night Riders; Colorado Sunset. **1940** The Showdown; The Range Busters; Pony Post. **1941** Billy the Kid; The Man from Montana; Sierra Sue; Stick to Your Guns; Blazing Frontier. **1942** Men in Wyomin'; Rock River Renegades. **1943** The Blocked Trail; The Mysterious Rider; Fugitive of the Plains; Beyond the Last Frontier. **1944** The Drifter; Gunsmoke Mesa; Frontier Outlaws; Thundering Gunslingers; Brand of the Devil. **1945** Devil Riders; Enemy of the Law; Fighting Bill Carson; Gangsters; Stagecoach Outlaws; Wild Horse Phantom. **1946** Oath of Vengeance; Ambush Trail; Galloping Thunder; Prairie Badmen; Prairie Rustlers; Under Arizona Skies; Stars over Texas; Terror on Horseback. **1947** Buckaroo from Powder River; Ridin' Down the Trail; Raiders of Red Rock; Frontier Fighters; Panhandle Trail. **1948** Tumbleweed Trail; 'Neath Canadian Skies. **1949** Massacre River; Riders in the Sky; Range Land. **1950** Law of the Panhandle; Silver Raiders. **1951** Three Desperate Men (aka Three Outlaws); Fort Dodge Stampede; Golden Girl. **1953** Pack Train. **1956** Flesh and the Spur. **1958** Once upon a Horse. **1960** Noose for a Gunman.

MAYNE, CLARICE

Born: 1890. Died: Jan. 17, 1966, London, England. Screen, stage and vaudeville actress. Divorced from actor James Tate. Married to actor Teddy Knox.

Appeared in: **1916** Nursie! Nursie!

MAYNE, ERIC

Born: 1866, Dublin, Ireland. Died: Feb. 10, 1947, Hollywood, Calif. Stage and screen actor.

Appeared in: **1921** Garments of Truth; Little Miss Hawkshaw; The Silver Car; The Conquering Power. **1922** Suzanne; Doctor Jack; My American Wife; Turn to the Right; Pawned; Shattered Dreams. **1923** The Last Hour; Prodigal Daughters; Refuge; A Prince of a King; Cameo Kirby; The Christian; Human Wreckage; Her Reputation; Drums of Jeopardy. **1924** Behind the Curtain; Black Oxen; His Forgotten Wife; The Goldfish; Gerald Cranston's Lady; Never Say Die; The Yankee Consul; The Extra Girl. **1926** The Black Bird; Money to Burn; Beyond the Trail; Hearts and Spangles; Midnight Limited; Transcontinental Limited; Barriers Burned Away. **1927** Married Alive; Driven from Home. **1928** The Canyon of Adventure; Hangman's House. **1931** The Easiest

Way; East Lynne. **1932** Rackety Rax. **1933** Duck Soup. **1935** All the King's Horses. **1936** Ticket to Paradise.

MAYO, ALBERT

Born: 1887. Died: May 20, 1933, Los Angeles, Calif. (heart attack). Stage and screen actor.

MAYO, ARCHIE

Born: 1898, New York, N.Y. Died: Dec. 4, 1968, Guadalajara, Mexico. Screen actor, film director and screenwriter. Entered films as an extra.

MAYO, EDNA

Born: 1893, Philadelphia, Pa. Died: May 5, 1970, San Francisco, Calif. Stage and screen actress.

Appeared in: **1914** The Key to Yesterday. **1915** The Blindness of Virtue; Frauds; The Greater Courage; Means and Morals; The Little Deceiver; Vengeance; A Bit of Lace; The Edge of Things; The Woman Eater; The Little Straw Wife. **1916** The Misleading Lady; The Retun of Eve; The Chaperone; The Strange Case of Mary Page (serial).

MAYO, FRANK

Born: 1886, New York. Died: July 9, 1963, Laguna Beach, Calif. (heart attack). Screen, stage, vaudeville actor and film director. Marriage to actress Dagmar Godowsky (dec. 1975) annulled in 1928. Entered films with World Film Co. of New Jersey approx. 1913.

Appeared in: **1915** The Red Circle (serial). **1918** The Interloper. **1919** The Brute Breaker; Mary Regan. **1921** The Blazing Trail; Colorado; Honor Bound; Magnificent Brute; The Marriage Pit; Tiger True; Dr. Jim; Go Straight; The Fighting Lover; The Shark Master. **1922** Afraid to Fight; Across the Dead-Line; Man Who Married His Own Wife; Out of the Silent North; Tracked to Earth; Wolf Law; The Flaming Hour; The Altar Stairs; Caught Bluffing. **1923** The Bolted Door; The First Degree; Souls for Sale; Six Days. **1924** Is Love Everything?; The Perfect Flapper; The Price She Paid; The Shadow of the East; The Plunderer; The Triflers; The Woman on the Jury; Wild Oranges. **1925** If I Marry Again; Passionate Youth; Barriers Burned Away; The Necessary Evil; The Unknown Lover; Women and Gold. **1926** Lew Tyler's Wives; Then Came the Woman. **1930** Doughboys; Big Shot. **1931** Alias the Bad Man; Range Law; Chinatown after Dark. **1932** The Last Ride; Hell's Headquarters. **1934** The Mighty Barnum. **1935** One Hour Late. **1936** Hollywood Boulevard; Desert Gold; Burning Gold; Too Many Parents; Magnificent Obsession. **1939** Confessions of a Nazi Spy; Nancy Drew and the Hidden Staircase. **1940** British Intelligence; Torrid Zone; Flowing Gold. **1941** The Gorilla Man; She Couldn't Say No; The Wagons Roll at Night. **1942** Lady Gangster; The Male Animal; Yankee Doodle Dandy; Gentleman Jim. **1943** Murder on the Waterfront; Mysterious Doctor. **1944** Adventures of Mark Twain; The Last Ride (and 1932 version). **1945** The Great Mystic. **1946** The Devil's Mask; The Strange Mr. Gregory. **1947** Her Husband's Affair; Buck Privates Come Home.

MAYO, GEORGE

Born: 1891. Died: Dec. 21, 1950, Hollywood, Calif. (heart ailment). Screen, stage and vaudeville actor.

Appeared in: **1930** A Perfect Match (short). **1934** A Woman's Man.

MAYO, HARRY A. (Ray Sampson)

Born: Mar. 11, 1898, Helena, Mont. Died: Jan. 6, 1964, Woodland Hills, Calif. (heart illness). Screen actor.

Appeared in: **1912** A Juvenile Love Affair. **1915** The Birth of a Nation. **1916** His Lucky Day; Harold the Nurse Girl; A Lucky Tumble; Wrong Beds. **1956** Around the World in 80 Days.

MAYO, JOSEPH ANTHONY

Born: 1930. Died: Nov. 12, 1966, Hollywood, Calif. (heart attack). Stage and screen actor.

MAYOR, AGUSTIN G.

Born: 1935. Died: Nov. 19, 1968, Woodside, N.Y. Screen, stage, television actor, dancer and at one time a matador in Spain.

Appeared in: **1962** Requiem for a Heavyweight. **1964** The Horror of Party Beach.

McALLISTER, PAUL

Born: 1875, New York, N.Y. Died: July 8, 1955. Screen and stage actor. Married to actress Margaret McKinney.

Appeared in: **1914** Scales of Justice. **1921** Forever; The Sign on the Door. **1922** A Stage Romance; What's Wrong with the Women? **1923** Trilby; Columbus; Jamestown; You Can't Fool Your Wife. **1924** The Lone Wolf; For Woman's Favor; The Moral Sinner; Manhandled; Yolanda. **1926** Beau Geste; The Winning of Barbara Worth. **1927** She's a Sheik; Sorrell and Son. **1928** The Big Killing; Noah's Ark; The Yellow Ticket. **1929** Hearts in Exile; Evangeline. **1930** The Case of Sergeant Grischa. **1931** Beau Ideal; Inspiration. **1933** Pilgrimage. **1934** Judge Priest. **1936** Mary of Scotland. **1940** The Doctor Takes a Wife.

McATEE, BEN

Born: 1903. Died: Dec. 3, 1961, Hollywood, Calif. Screen, stage, vaudeville, television and minstrel actor.

McATEE, CLYDE

Born: 1880. Died: Feb. 20, 1947, Woodland Hills, Calif. Screen actor.

Appeared in: **1925** Percy. **1926** Crossed Signals.

McAVOY, CHARLES (aka CHARLIE McAVOY)

Born: 1885. Died: Apr. 20, 1953. Screen actor.

Appeared in: **1930** Those Who Dance; Night Owls (short). **1934** I'll Be Suing You (short); Murder at the Vanities; Shoot the Works. **1936** The Singing Cowboy; Strike Me Pink. **1939** King of the Turf. **1945** Strange Holiday.

McBRIDE, CARL

Born: 1894, Sioux City, Iowa. Died: Dec. 17, 1937, Los Angeles, Calif. Screen, vaudeville actor and film director. Appeared in Charles B. Dillingham productions on screen.

McBRIDE, DONALD (aka DONALD MACBRIDE)

Born: 1889, Brooklyn, N.Y. Died: June 21, 1957, Los Angeles, Calif. Screen, stage, television and vaudeville actor. Appeared in films at old Vitagraph studio in Brooklyn approx. 1913.

Appeared in: **1932** Misleading Lady. **1933** Get That Venus. **1936** The Chemist (short). **1938** Room Service (stage and film versions); Annabel Takes a Tour. **1939** The Great Man Votes; Twelve Crowded Hours; The Girl and the Gambler; The Flying Irishman; The Story of Vernon and Irene Castle; The Girl from Mexico; The Gracie Allen Murder Case; Blondie Takes a Vacation; The Amazing Mr. Williams; Charlie Chan at Treasure Island. **1940** The Saint's Double Trouble; Northwest Passage; Murder over New York; Michael Shayne, Private Detective; My Favorite Wife; Hit Parade of 1941. **1941** The Invisible Woman; Footlight Fever; Topper Returns; High Sierra; Love Crazy; Here Comes Mr. Jordan; You'll Never Get Rich; Rise and Shine; You're in the Navy Now; Louisiana Purchase. **1942** Two Yanks in Trinidad; Juke Girl; The Mexican Spitfire Sees a Ghost; The Glass Key; My Sister Eileen. **1943** A Night to Remember; They Got Me Covered; Best Foot Forward; Lady Bodyguard; A Stranger in Town. **1944** The Doughgirls; The Thin Man Goes Home. **1945** Penthouse Rhythm; Hold That Blonde; Out of This World; Girl on the Spot; She Gets Her Man; Abbott and Costello in Hollywood; Doll Face. **1946** Blonde Alibi; Little Giant; The Killers; The Time of Their Lives; The Dark Horse; The Brute Man. **1947** Beat the Band; The Old Gray Mayor; Joe Palooka in the Knockout; Hal Roach Comedy Carnival; Good News; Buck Privates Come Home; The Egg and I; The Fabulous Joe. **1948** Campus Sleuth; Jinx Money; Smart Politics. **1949** The Story of Seabiscuit; Challenge to Lassie. **1950** Joe Palooka Meets Humphrey; Holiday Rhythm. **1951** Cuban Fireball; Bowery Battalion; Texas Carnival; Sailor Beware. **1952** Gobs and Gals. **1953** The Stooge. **1955** the Seven Year Itch.

McCABE, GEORGE

Born: Chicago, Ill. Died: Dec. 17, 1917, Bellevue, N.Y. Screen actor.

McCABE, HARRY

Born: 1881. Died: Feb. 11, 1925, Los Angeles, Calif. Screen actor.

Appeared in: **1916** American Film Mfg. Co. films. **1922** A Western Thoroughbred. **1924** The No-Gun Man.

McCABE, MAY

Born: 1873. Died: June 22, 1949, New York, N.Y. Screen and stage actor. Married to stage actor Jack McCabe (dec. 1967) and mother of stage actor Clyde North. Appeared in silents.

McCALL, WILLIAM

Born: May 19, 1879, Delavan, Ill. Died: Jan. 10, 1938, Hollywood, Calif. Screen, stage and television actor. Was billed in vaudeville as part of "McCall Trio."

Appeared in: **1919** Smashing Barriers (serial). **1921** Fighting Fate (serial); Flower of the North; Where Men Are Men; It Can Be Done. **1922** Across the Border; The Angel of Crooked Street; Fortune's Mask; The Fighting Guide; The Little Minister; Rounding up the Law; When Danger Smiles. **1923** Smashing Barriers. **1924** Sell 'Em Cowboy; The Back Trail; Daring Chances; The Phantom Horseman. **1925** His Marriage Vow; The Red Rider; Ridin' Thunder. **1930** The Lonesome Trail; Under Texas Skies; Trailin' Trouble. **1937** Lodge Night (short).

McCANN, CHARLES ANDREW

Died: Sept. 1927, Paris, France. Screen actor and musician.

Appeared in: **1917** The Tiger Woman (film debut).

McCANN, FRANCES

Born: 1922. Died: Mar. 14, 1963. Opera singer and screen actress.

Appeared in: **1962** The Creation of the Humanoids.

McCARROLL, FRANK

Died: Mar. 9, 1954, Burbank, Calif. (accidental fall at home). Screen actor, stuntman and rodeo performer.

Appeared in: **1949** Brand of Fear; Lawless Code; Renegades of the Sage. **1950** Fence Riders; Gunslingers; Over the Border.

McCARTHY, MYLES (aka MILES McCARTHY)

Born: Toronto, Canada. Died: Sept. 27, 1928, Hollywood, Calif. (heart attack). Screen, stage and vaudeville actor.

Appeared in: **1922** Smiles Are Trumps. **1923** Dollar Devils; The Day of Faith. **1924** Captain Blood; Abraham Lincoln; Oh, You Tony! **1925** Tricks; The Lady. **1926** The Heart of a Coward. **1927** The Racing Fool.

McCARTHY, PAT (Patricia Cook)

Born: 1911. Died: Jan. 25, 1943, New York. Screen, stage actress and dancer.

McCAULEY, EDNA

Born: Detroit, Michigan. Died: Jan. 28, 1919, Rome, Italy (typhoid fever). Screen actress. Appeared in Famous Players films.

McCLAIN, BILLY (William C. McClain)

Born: 1857. Died: Jan. 28, 1950, near Los Angeles, Calif. (trailer fire). Screen, and minstrel actor.

Appeared in: **1934** The Mighty Barnum. **1935** The Virginia Judge. **1936** Dimples.

McCLAY, CLYDE

Born: 1895. Died: June 30, 1939, Hollywood, Calif. (accident on location filming In Old Monterey—crushed by army tank). Screen actor and extra.

Appeared in: **1939** In Old Monterey.

McCLELLAN, HURD

Died: Apr. 20, 1933, Los Angeles, Calif. (accidental gunshot while filming). Screen actor and stuntman.

McCLELLAND, DONALD

Born: Sept. 29, 1903, New York, N.Y. Died: Nov. 15, 1955. Screen actor.

McCLOSKEY, ELIZABETH H.

Born: 1870. Died: Jan. 8, 1942, Hollywood, Calif. Screen and stage actress. Entered films approx. 1920.

McCLUNG, BOBBY

Born: 1921. Died: Jan. 27, 1945, Columbia, S.C. (pneumonia). Screen, stage and vaudeville actor. Appeared in "Dead End Kids" series.

Appeared in: **1937** Two Wise Maids; Paradise Express; The Toast of New York.

McCLURE, BUD

Born: 1886. Died: Nov. 2, 1942, North Hollywood, Calif. Screen actor and cowboy.

McCLURE, FRANK

Born: 1895. Died: Jan. 23, 1960. Stage and screen actor.

McCLURE, IRENE

Died: Sept. 4, 1928, Bakersfield, Calif. (injuries from auto accident). Screen actress.

McCOMAS, CARROLL

Born: 1886, Albuquerque, N. Mex. Died: Nov. 9, 1962, New York. Screen, stage, vaudeville, television actress, singer and dancer.

Appeared in: **1916** When Love is King. **1953** Jamaica Run. **1955** Chicago Syndicate.

McCOMAS, GLENN

Born: 1900. Died: June 10, 1959, Los Angeles, Calif. Screen actor.

McCOMAS, LILA

Born: 1906. Died: June 13, 1936, Los Angeles, Calif. (auto accident). Screen actress.

McCONNELL, LULU

Born: 1882, Kansas City, Mo. Died: Oct. 9, 1962, Hollywood, Calif. (cancer). Screen, stage, vaudeville and radio actress. Married to actor Grant Simpson (dec. 1932).

Appeared in: **1936** Stage Struck.

McCONNELL, MOLLY

Born: 1870, Chicago, Ill. Died: Dec. 10, 1920. Screen and stage actress. Married to stage manager William McConnell (dec.) and later married stage actor Sherwood McDonald (dec.).

Appeared in: 1915 Who Pays? (serial). 1916 Joy and the Dragon. 1917 The Checkmate; The Wildcat; Bab the Fixer; The Best Man; The Girl Angle. 1921 Black Beauty; Hearts and Masks; The Home Stretch.

McCORD, MRS. LEWIS

Born: Philadelphia, Pa. Died: Dec. 24, 1917, New York, N.Y. (pneumonia, diabetes). Screen, stage, opera and vaudeville actress. Married to stage actor Lewis McCord (dec. 1911).

Appeared in: 1914 The Virginian. 1915 The Marriage of Kitty; The Chorus Lady; Chimmie Fadden; Kindling; Chimmie Fadden Out West; The Wild Goose Chase; The Secret Orchard. 1916 Common Ground; The Dream Girl; The Race; Unprotected. 1917 The Golden Fetter; The Ghost House.

McCORMACK, BILLIE (Blanche E. Burke)

Died: Feb. 1, 1935, Santa Monica, Calif. Screen actress.

McCORMACK, JOHN

Born: June 14, 1884, Athlone, Ireland. Died: Sept. 16, 1945, Dublin, Ireland. Screen actor, radio and opera tenor.

Appeared in: 1930 Song O' My Heart. 1937 Wings of the Morning.

McCORMACK, WILLIAM M.

Born: 1891. Died: Aug. 19, 1953, Hollywood, Calif. (heart attack). Screen actor.

Appeared in: 1921 Red Courage; The Robe. 1922 Robin Hood. 1923 Danger; Good Men and Bad. 1924 Abraham Lincoln. 1925 Fangs of Fate; Reckless Courage; The Secret of Black Canyon; Flashing Steeds; Vic Dyson Pays. 1926 The Desperate Game. 1927 The Long Loop on the Pecos; Arizona Nights; Whispering Smith Rides (serial). 1928 The Apache Raider; A Son of the Desert. 1929 Romance of the Rio Grande; Born to the Saddle; Riders of the Rio Grande. 1936 Trail of the Lonesome Pine; Tundra. 1953 Salome; The Robe (and 1921 version).

McCORMICK, ALYCE (aka JOY AUBURN)

Born: Jan. 13, 1904, Chicago, Ill. Died: Jan. 7, 1932, Hollywood, Calif. (pneumonia). Stage and screen actress.

Appeared in: 1928 Mother Knows Best. 1930 Reno. 1931 Spirit of Notre Dame; Frankenstein; Bad Girl. 1939 The Mysterious Mr. X.

McCORMICK, F. J. (Peter Judge)

Born: 1891. Died: Apr. 24, 1947, Dublin, Ireland. Screen and stage actor.

Appeared in: 1937 The Plough and the Stars. 1947 Odd Man Out; Hungry Hill.

McCORMICK, MYRON

Born: Feb. 8, 1908, Albany, Ind. Died: July 30, 1962, New York, N.Y. (cancer). Screen, stage, radio and television actor.

Appeared in: 1937 Winterset. 1939 One Third of a Nation. 1940 The Fight for Life. 1943 China Girl. 1949 Jigsaw; Jolson Sings Again; Gun Moll. 1955 Three for the Show; Not As a Stranger. 1958 No Time for Sergeants. 1959 The Man Who Understood Women. 1961 The Hustler. 1962 The Haircut (short); A Public Affair.

McCOY, GERTRUDE

Died: July 17, 1967, Atlanta, Ga. Screen actress. Entered films as an extra and appeared in early Edison Co. films. Made films in U.S., England, Germany and South America. Married to actor Duncan Macrae (dec. 1967).

Appeared in: 1911 That Winsome Winnie Smile. 1912 Cynthia's Agreement; Every Rose Has its Stem; The Stranger and the Taxi Cab; The Usurer's Grip; Under False Colors; A Baby's Shoe; The Sketch with the Thumb Print; A Dangerous Lesson; The Little Girl Next Door; Annie Crawls Upstairs; Kitty's Holdup; Her Face. 1913 The Mountaineers; The Manicure Girl; Peg O' the Movies; A Serenade by Proxy; How They Outwitted Father; Kathleen Mavourneen; The Road of Transgression; Aunt Elsa's Visit; His Enemy; A Letter to Uncle Sam. 1914 The Birth of the Star Spangled Banner; When the Cartridges Failed; The Man in the Street; A Real Help-Mate; The Mystery of the Silver Snare; The Shattered Tree; Sheep's Clothing; The Stuff that Dreams Are Made Of; The New Partner. 1918 The Blue Bird. 1919 Angle, Esquire; The Usurper. 1920 The Auction Mart; Burnt In; Tangled Hearts (aka The Wife Whom God Forgot). 1921 Christie Johnston; The Golden Dawn; Out of the Darkness. 1922 Tell Your Children; Was She Guilty? (aka Thou Shalt Not Kill). 1923 Heartstrings; A Royal Divorce; The Temptation of Carlton Earle; Always Tell Your Wife. 1924 Chappy—That's All; The Diamond Man; Nets of Destiny; Miriam Rozella. 1928 On the Stroke of 12. 1931 The Working Girl. 1932 The Silent Witness.

McCOY, HARRY

Born: 1894. Died: Sept. 1, 1937, Hollywood, Calif. (heart attack). Screen, radio actor, film director and song writer. Was a Keystone Kop and appeared in "Joker" comedies.

Also appeared in: 1913 Mike and Jake at the Beach; The Cheese Special (short). 1914 Mabel's Strange Predicament; Caught in a Cabaret; Mabel at the Wheel; Mabel's Busy Day; Mabel's Married Life; The Masquerader; Getting Acquainted. 1915 One Night Stand; For Better—But Worse; A Human Hound's Triumph; Those Bitter Sweets; Merely a Married Man; Saved by Wireless; The Village Scandal. 1916 His Last Laugh; The Great Pear Tangle; Love Will Conquer; Perils of the Park; A Movie Star; Cinders of Love; His Auto Ruination; Bubbles of Trouble; She Loved a Sailor. 1921 Skirts; plus "Hallroom Boys" comedies. 1924 The Fatal Mistake. 1925 Dashing Thru; Heads Up; Heir-Loons. 1938 Hearts of Men.

McCOY, KID. See NORMAN "KID McCOY" SELBY

McCRACKEN, JOAN

Born: 1923. Died: Nov. 1, 1961, New York, N.Y. (heart condition). Screen, stage actress and dancer.

Appeared in: 1944 Hollywood Canteen. 1947 Good News.

McCULLOUGH, PAUL

Born: 1884, Springfield, Ohio. Died: Mar. 25, 1936, Boston, Mass. (suicide). Screen, stage, vaudeville, minstrel actor, and circus performer. Was partner with Bobby Clark (dec. 1960) in comedy team of "Clark and McCullough." For films he appeared in see Bobby Clark.

McCULLUM, BARTLEY

Died: Mar. 25, 1916, Philadelphia, Pa. Screen actor.

Appeared in: 1913 The Village Blacksmith; The Old Oaken Bucket; The Heart Brokers; Granny; Home, Sweet Home. 1915 The Comedienne's Strategy; The Mirror; Think Mothers; Playing the Same Game; The Silent Accuser; Sorrows of Happiness. 1916 Dollars and the Woman.

McCUTCHEON, GEORGE BARR

Born: July 26, 1866, Tippecanoe County, Ind. Died: Oct. 23, 1928, New York, N.Y. (heart disease). Novelist and screen actor.

Appeared in: 1913 Saved by Parcel Post.

McCUTCHEON, RALPH

Born: 1899. Died: Apr. 16, 1975, North Hollywood, Calif. (pneumonia). Film extra and animal trainer. Married to actress Mary Kornman (dec. 1973).

McCUTCHEON, WALLACE

Born: 1881. Died: Jan. 27, 1928, Los Angeles, Calif. (shot himself). Screen, stage actor and film director. Divorced from actress Pearl White (dec. 1938).

Appeared in: 1904 The Moonshiner. 1919 A Virtuous Vamp; The Black Secret (serial). 1920 The Phantom Foe (serial).

McDANIEL, ETTA

Born: Dec. 1, 1890, Wichita, Kans. Died: Jan. 13, 1946. Black screen, stage, vaudeville and radio actress. Sister of actor Sam (dec. 1962), actress Hattie (dec. 1952) and Otis McDaniel.

Appeared in: 1934 Smoking Guns. 1935 So Red the Rose; The Virginia Judge. 1936 The Invisible Ray; The Magnificent Brute; The Prisoner of Shark Island; The Lawless Nineties; The Lonely Trail; Palm Spring; The Glory Trail; The Devil Is a Sissy; Hearts in Bondage. 1937 Man Bites Lovebug; Living On Love; Mile a Minute Love; Sweetheart of the Navy; On Such a Night. 1938 Keep Smiling; Crime Afloat; Tom Sawyer—Detective. 1939 Sergeant Madden. 1940 The House Across the Bay; Carolina Moon; Charter Pilot. 1941 Thieves Fall Out; The Pittsburgh Kid; Life With Henry; The Big Store. 1942 The Great Man's Lady; Mokey; American Empire. 1943 They Came to Blow Up America; What a Man!

McDANIEL, GEORGE

Born: 1886. Died: Aug. 20, 1944, Hollywood, Calif. Screen and stage actor.

Appeared in: 1915 The Girl and the Game (serial). 1921 Silent Years. 1922 The Scrapper. 1923 The Barefoot Boy. 1926 Burning Words. 1927 The Iron Hearts.

McDANIEL, HATTIE

Born: June 10, 1895, Wichita, Kans. Died: Oct. 26, 1952, San Fernando Valley, Calif. Black screen, radio, vaudeville and television actress and singer. Sister of actor Sam McDaniel (dec. 1962), actress Etta (dec. 1946) and Otis McDaniel. Won 1939 Academy Award for Best Supporting Actress in Gone with the Wind.

Appeared in: 1932 The Golden West; Blonde Venus; Hypnotized; Washington Masquerade. 1933 I'm No Angel; The Story of Temple Drake. 1934 Operator 13; Little Men; Judge Priest; Fate's Fathead (short); Lost in the Stratosphere; The Chases of Pimple Street (short); Babbitt; Imitation of Life. 1935 Music Is Magic; China Seas; Another Face; Alice Adams; The Little Colonel; The Travelling Saleslady; plus the following shorts: Anniversary Trouble; Okay Toots!; and The Four-Star Boarder. **1936** Gentle Julia; The First Baby; High Tension; Star for a Night; Can This Be Dixie?; Reunion; Showboat; Postal Inspector; Hearts Divided; The Bride Walks Out; Big Time Vaudeville Reels (shorts); Valiant Is the Word for Carrie; Next Time We Love; Libeled Lady; High Treason; Arbor Day (short); The Singing Kid. **1937** Don't Tell the Wife; Racing Lady; The Crime Nobody Saw; True Confession; Saratoga; Over the Goal; 45 Fathers; Nothing Sacred; Merry-Go-Round of 1938; The Wildcatter. **1938** Battle of Broadway; Everybody's Baby; Shopworn Angel; The Shining Hour; The Mad Miss Manton. **1939** Gone with the Wind; Zenobia. **1940** Maryland. **1941** Affectionately Yours; The Great Lie; They Died with Their Boots On. **1942** The Male Animal; In This Our Life; George Washington Slept Here; Reap the Wild Wind. **1943** Thank Your Lucky Stars; Johnny Come Lately. **1944** Since You Went Away; Janie; Three Is a Family. **1945** Hi, Beautiful. **1946** Margie; Never Say Goodbye; Janie Gets Married. **1947** Song of the South; The Flame. **1948** Mr. Blandings Builds His Dream House; Mickey. **1949** Family Honeymoon; The Big Wheel.

McDANIEL, SAM "DEACON" (Samuel Rufus McDaniel)

Born: Jan. 28, 1886, Columbus, Kans. Died: Sept. 24, 1962, Woodland Hills, Calif. (throat cancer). Black screen actor. Brother of Otis and actresses Hattie (dec. 1952) and Etta McDaniel (dec. 1946).

Appeared in: **1932** Once in a Lifetime. **1934** Lemon Drop Kid. **1935** George White's 1935 Scandals; Unwelcome Stranger; Lady Tubbs; The Virginia Judge. **1936** Hearts Divided. **1937** Captains Courageous. **1938** Sergeant Murphy; Gambling Ship; Stablemates. **1939** Pride of Bluegrass. **1940** Calling All Husbands. **1941** The Great Lie; South of Panama; Broadway Limited; New York Town; Bad Men of Missouri; Mr. and Mrs. North; Louisiana Purchase. **1942** All Through the Night; I Was Framed; Mokey; Johnny Doughboy; The Traitor Within. **1943** Dixie Dugan; The Ghost and the Guest; Gangway for Tomorrow. **1944** Three Men in White; Sweet and Low Down; The Adventures of Mark Twain; Home in Indiana; Three Little Sisters; Andy Hardy's Blonde Trouble. **1945** The Naughty Nineties; A Guy, a Gal and a Pal. **1946** Joe Palooka—Champ; Gentleman Joe Palooka. **1947** The Foxes of Harrow. **1948** Pride of Virginia; Secret Service Investigator; Heavenly Daze (short). **1949** Flamingo Road. **1950** Girl's School. **1951** Too Many Wives (short). **1952** Something for the Birds. **1955** A Man Called Peter.

McDERMOTT, HUGH

Born: Mar. 20, 1908, Edinburgh, Scotland. Died: Jan. 30, 1972, London, England. Screen, stage, television actor and author.

Appeared in: **1936** David Livingstone (film debut); The Captain's Table. **1937** Wife of General Ling (US 1938); Well Done, Henry. **1939** Where's that Fire? **1940** For Freedom; Neutral Port. **1941** Pimpernel Smith (aka Mister V—US 1942); Spring Meeting. **1942** Young Mr. Pitt. **1945** The Seventh Veil (US 1946). **1946** This Man is Mine. **1948** Good Time Girl (US 1950); No Orchids for Miss Blandish (US 1951). **1949** The Huggetts Aboard. **1950** Lilli Marlene (US 1951). **1951** Two on the Tiles; Four Days. **1952** Trent's Last Case (US 1953). **1953** The Wedding of Lilli Marlene. **1954** The Love Lottery; Johnny on the Spot; Night People; Malaga (aka Fire Over Africa); Devil Girl from Mars. **1955** As Long as They're Happy (US 1957). **1957** You Pay Your Money; A King in New York. **1958** The Man Who Wouldn't Talk (US 1960). **1960** Moment of Danger (aka Malaga—US 1962). **1964** First Men in the Moon. **1968** The File of the Gold Goose (US 1969). **1969** The Adding Machine; Guns in the Heather; The Games (US 1970). **1971** Captain Apache. **1972** Chato's Land.

McDERMOTT, MARC (aka MARC MacDERMOTT)

Born: 1881, London, England. Died: Jan. 5, 1929, Glendale, Calif. (gall bladder surgery). Stage and screen actor.

Appeared in: **1911** Aida; Papa's Sweetheart; Eleanore Cuyler; Please Remit; Two Officers; The Declaration of Independence; At the Threshold of Life; The Girl and the Motor Boat; An Old Sweetheart of Mine; An Island Comedy; The Ghost's Warning; The Death of Nathan Hale; The Story of the Indian Ledge; The Heart of Nichette; How Sir Andrew Lost His Vote. **1912** What Happened to Mary (serial); His Daughter; The Heir Apparent; Politics and Love; Her Face; The Maid of Honor; When She Was About Sixteen; The Little Girl Next Door; The Dumb Wooing; Billie; Their Hero; The Sunset Gun; The Little Wooden Show; The Convict's Parole; The Passer-By; The Angel and the Stranded Troupe; After Many Days; The Close of the American Revolution; An Unsullied Shield; A Suffragette in Spite of Himself; A Dangerous Lesson; The Foundling; Nerves and the Man; Jack and the Beanstalk; The Little Organist; Lady Clare; Fog; An Old Appointment; A Letter to the Princess; The Corsican Brothers. **1913** The Stolen Plans; While John Bolt Slept; A Clue to Her Parentage; Barry's Breaking In; The Gauntlets of Washington; Kathleen Mavourneen; With the Eyes of the Blind; The Dear Daughters; The Portrait; The Duke's Dilemma; The Heart of Valeska; A Splendid Scapegrace; A Daughter of Romany; A Concerto for the Violin; Flood Tide; Keepers of the Flock. **1914** The Man Who Disappeared (serial); With His Hands; Sophia's Imaginary Visitors; A Princess of the Desert; All for His Sake; When East Meets West in Boston; The Hunted Animal; The Living Dead; Comedy and Tragedy; The Man in the Street; A Question of Hats and Gowns; Face to Face;

A Matter of Minutes; The Necklace of Rameses; By the Aid of a Film. **1915** Sallie Castleton, Southerner; The Man Who Could Not Sleep; Theft in the Dark. **1916** Ranson's Folly; The Price of Fame; Whom the Gods Destroy. **1917** The Blind Adventure; Intrigue; The Last Sentence; Mary Jane's Pa; The Sixteenth Wife. **1918** The Green God. **1919** Buchanan's Wife; New Moon. **1920** While New York Sleeps. **1921** Blind Wives; Amazing Lovers; Footlights. **1922** The Lights of New York; The Spanish Jade. **1923** Hoodman Blind; Lucretia Lombard; The Satin Girl. **1924** Dorothy Vernon of Haddon Hall; In Every Woman's Life; The Sea Hawk; This Woman; Three Miles Out; He Who Gets Slapped. **1925** The Lady; The Goose Woman; Siege; Graustark. **1926** Flesh and the Devil; Kiki; The Temptress; The Love Thief; The Lucky Lady. **1927** California; Man, Woman and Sin; The Taxi Driver; The Road to Romance; Resurrection. **1928** The Whip; The Yellow Lily; Under the Black Eagle; Glorious Betsy.

McDONALD, CHARLES B.

Born: May 26, 1886, Springfield, Mass. Died: Dec. 29, 1964, Hollywood, Fla. Screen, stage, vaudeville actor, journalist and film executive. Entered films with Essanay in the early 1900s.

Appeared in: **1914** Michael Strogoff. **1921** Salvation Nell. **1925** Irish Luck.

McDONALD, FRANCIS J.

Born: Aug. 22, 1891, Bowling Green, Ky. Died: Sept. 18, 1968, Hollywood, Calif. Stage and screen actor.

Appeared in: **1918** The Gun Woman. **1920** Nomads of the North. **1921** The Call of the North; The Golden Snare; Puppets of Fate; Hearts and Masks. **1922** Captain Fly-by-Night; The Man Who Married His Own Wife; The Woman Conquers; Trooper O'Neil; Monte Cristo. **1923** Mary of the Movies; South Sea Love; Going Up; Trilby; The Buster; Look Your Best. **1924** The Arizona Express; East of Broadway; Racing Luck; So This Is Marriage. **1925** Anything Once; Bobbed Hair; Go Straight; The Hunted Woman; My Lady of Whims; Satin in Sables; Northern Code. **1926** Battling Butler; The Yankee Senor; The Desert's Toll; Puppets; The Temptress; The Palace of Pleasure. **1927** The Notorious Lady; The Valley of Hell; Outlaws of Red River; The Wreck. **1928** The Dragnet; Legion of the Condemned; A Girl in Every Port. **1929** The Carnation Kid; Girl Overboard. **1930** Brothers; Dangerous Paradise; Safety in Numbers; The Runaway Bride; Burning Up; Morocco. **1931** The Lawyer's Secret; In Line of Duty; The Gang Buster. **1932** Honor of the Mounted; Texas Buddies; The Devil Is Driving; Trailing the Killer; Woman from Monte Carlo. **1933** Broadway Bad; Terror Trail; Kickin' the Crown Around. **1934** Voice in the Night; Girl in Danger; Straightaway; No More Bridge (short); The Trumpet Blows; The Line-Up; Burn 'Em up Barnes (feature film and serial). **1935** Mississippi; Marriage Bargain; Star of Midnight; Red Morning; Ladies Crave Excitement. **1936** Robin Hood of El Dorado; The Prisoner of Shark Island; Under Two Flags; Big Brown Eyes; The Plainsman; Mummy's Boys. **1937** The Devil's Playground; Parole Racket; Born Reckless; Love under Fire; Every Day's a Holiday. **1938** Gun Law; If I Were King. **1939** Range War; Union Pacific; The Bad Lands; The Light That Failed. **1940** One Night in the Tropics; The Carson City Kid; The Sea Hawk; Northwest Mounted Police; Green Hell; The Devil's Pipeline. **1941** The Sea Wolf; Men of Timberland; The Kid from Kansas. **1942** The Girl from Alaska. **1943** Buckskin Frontier; Bar 20; The Kansan. **1944** Texas Masquerade; Cheyenne Wildcat; Lumberjack; Mystery Man; Border Town; Zorro's Black Whip (serial). **1945** The Great Stagecoach Robbery; South of the Rio Grande; Strange Confessions; Corpus Christi Bandits. **1946** Bad Men of the Border; Canyon Passage; The Catman of Paris; The Devil's Playground; Invisible Informer; Tangier; My Pal Trigger; Roll on Texas Moon; Night Train to Memphis; The Magnificent Doll. **1947** Duel in the Sun; Saddle Pals; Dangerous Venture; Spoilers of the North; The Perils of Pauline. **1948** Bold Frontiersman; The Paleface; The Dead Don't Dream; Panhandle; Desert Passage; Bandits of Corsica. **1949** Son of God's Country; Brothers in the Saddle; Daughter of the Jungle; Rose of the Yukon; Son of the Badman; Apache Chief; Samson and Delilah; Strange Gamble; Rim of the Canyon; Abandoned; Powder River Rustlers. **1950** California Passage. **1951** Gene Autry and the Mounties. **1952** The Raiders; Rancho Notorious; Red Mountain; Fort Osage. **1954** Three Hours to Kill; The Bandits of Corsica. **1955** Ten Wanted Men. **1956** Thunder over Arizona; The Ten Commandments. **1957** Last Stagecoach West; Duel at Apache Wells; Pawnee. **1958** Saga of Hemp Brown; Fort Massacre. **1959** The Big Fisherman.

McDONALD, JAMES

Born: 1886. Died: Dec. 26, 1952, Los Angeles, Calif. Screen actor and trick rider.

McDONALD, JOSEPH

Born: 1861. Died: Oct. 24, 1935, Redondo Beach, Calif. (drowned). Screen actor.

McDONALD, MARIE (Marie Frye)

Born: 1923, Burgin, Ky. Died: Oct. 21, 1965, Hidden Hills, Calif. (accidental drug overdose). Screen, stage actress and singer. Known as "The Body." Entered films in 1941.

Appeared in: **1941** It Started with Eve; You're Telling Me. **1942** Pardon My

Sarong; Lucky Jordan. **1943** Tornado; Riding High. **1944** I Love a Soldier; Standing Room Only; Guest in the House; A Scream in the Dark. **1945** It's a Pleasure; Getting Gertie's Garter. **1946** Swell Guy. **1947** Living in a Big Way. **1949** Tell It to the Judge. **1950** Once a Thief; Hit Parade of 1951. **1958** The Geisha Boy. **1963** Promises, Promises.

McDONALD, RAY
Born: 1924, Boston, Mass. Died: Feb. 20, 1959, New York, N.Y. Screen, stage and vaudeville actor. Brother of actress Grace McDonald. Divorced from actress Elizabeth Fraser.

Appeared in: **1941** Down in San Diego; Life Begins for Andy Hardy; Babes on Broadway. **1942** Born to Sing. **1943** Presenting Lily Mars. **1946** Till the Clouds Roll By. **1947** Good News. **1949** Shamrock Hill. **1950** There's a Girl in My Heart. **1953** All Ashore.

McDONOUGH, MICHAEL
Born: 1876. Died: Aug. 8, 1956, Hollywood, Calif. Screen actor.

McDOWELL, CLAIRE (aka CLAIRE MacDOWELL)
Born: Nov. 2, 1877, New York, N.Y. Died: Oct. 23, 1966, Woodland Hills, Calif. Stage and screen actress. Entered films with American Biograph Co. in 1910. Married to actor Charles Hill Mailes (dec. 1937).

Appeared in: **1910** His Last Burglary; Wilful Peggy; A Mohawk's Way; The Golden Supper; His Trust Fulfilled; In the Days of '49; A Romany Tragedy; The Primal Call; The Sorrowful Example. **1911** Swords and Hearts; A Woman Scorned; As in a Looking Glass; A Blot on the 'Scutcheon; Billy's Strategem; The Sunbeam. **1912** The Female of the Species; Lena and the Geese; The Sands of Dee; The Daughters of Eve; In the Aisles of the Wild; The Unwelcome Guest; The Massacre. **1913** A Welcome Intruder; The Wanderer; The House of Darkness; Olaf—An Atom; The Ranchero's Revenge. **1919** Heart O' the Hills. **1920** Something to Think About; Midsummer Madness; The Woman in the Suitcase. **1921** Love Never Dies; Prisoners of Love; Wealth; Chickens; What Every Woman Knows; Mother O'Mine. **1922** The Gray Dawn; Heart's Haven; In the Name of the Law; The Lying Truth; Penrod; Quincy Adams Sawyer; Nice People; Rent Free; The Ragged Heiress. **1923** The Westbound Limited; Ponjola; Michael O'Halloran; Ashes of Vengeance; Enemies of Children; Human Wreckage; Circus Days. **1924** Black Oxen; A Fight for Honor; Judgement of the Storm; Leave It to Gerry; Secrets; Thy Name is Woman; Those Who Date. **1925** The Big Parade; One of the Bravest; The Reckless Sex; Walking up the Town; The Town of Lies; Dollar Down; The Midnight Flyer. **1926** Ben Hur; The Show-Off; The Devil's Circus; The Dixie Merchant; The Flaming Forest; The Shamrock Handicap; The Unknown Soldier. **1927** Almost Human; The Auctioneer; The Black Diamond Express; The Taxi Dancer; Winds of the Pampas; Cheaters; A Little Journey; The Shield of Honor; Tillie the Toiler. **1928** The Viking; Don't Marry; Marriage by Contract; The Tragedy of Youth. **1929** Silks and Saddles; Whispering Winds; The Quitter; When Dreams Come True; Four Devils. **1930** The Big House; Mothers Cry; Redemption; Wild Company; Young Desire; The Second Floor Mystery; Brothers. **1931** An American Tragedy. **1932** Manhattan Parade; It's Tough to Be Famous; Strange Love of Molly Louvain; Phantom Express; Rebecca of Sunnybrook Farm. **1933** Cornered; Two Heads on a Pillow; Central Airport; The Working Man; Paddy, the Next Best Thing; Wild Boys of the Road; By Appointment Only. **1936** August Weekend. **1937** Two-Fisted Sheriff; High, Wide and Handsome. **1939** Honolulu; One Against the World (short). **1944** Are These Our Parents?; Men on Her Mind; Teen Age.

McDOWELL, NELSON
Born: Aug. 18, 1875, Greenville, Mo. Died: Nov. 3, 1947, Hollywood, Calif. (suicide—gun). Screen actor. Entered films with American Biograph in 1910.

Appeared in: **1916** Wheels of Destiny. **1921** The Silent Call; Home Stuff; Shadows of Conscience; The Last of the Mohicans. **1922** The Phantom Bullet; Whispering Smith; Blind Trail; Crossed Signals; Lightning Reporter; The Outlaw Express; The Frontier Trail; The Valley of Bravery. **1927** Uncle Tom's Cabin; The Claw; Code of the Range; Hands Off; Border Blackbirds; The Bugle Call; The Great Mail Robbery. **1928** Heart Trouble; The Vanishing Rider (serial); The Little Shepherd of Kingdom Come; Kit Carson; Kentucky Courage. **1929** Wild Blood; Born to the Saddle; Grit Wins. **1930** The Real McCoy (short); All Tied Up (short); Billy the Kid. **1933** Oliver Twist. **1934** Wheels of Destiny (and 1916 version). **1935** Wilderness Mail. **1936** The Desert Phantom; Feud of the West; Girl of the Ozarks; Ride, Ranger, Ride. **1938** College Swing.

McELROY, JACK
Born: 1914. Died: Mar. 2, 1959, Santa Monica, Calif. (lung cancer). Screen, radio and television actor.

Appeared in: **1956** Hollywood or Bust.

McEVOY, ERNEST SIMON
Born: 1894. Died: Apr. 14, 1953, Hollywood, Calif. Screen and stage actor.

McEWAN, ISABELLE
Born: 1897, Scotland. Died: Feb. 19, 1963, Vancouver, B.C., Canada. Screen, stage and radio actress.

McFADDEN, IVOR (Charles Ivor McFadden)
Born: Aug. 6, 1887, San Francisco, Calif. Died: Aug. 14, 1942, Los Angeles, Calif. (cerebral hemorrhage). Screen actor and film producer.

Appeared in: **1916** The Measure of a Man; Giant Powder. **1919** Elmo, the Mighty (serial); The Delicious Little Devil. **1921** The Heart Line; Three Word Brand; The Wolverine. **1924** Big Timer. **1925** Fangs of Fate; Tides of Passion. **1926** Two-Gun Man.

McGAUGH, WILBUR
Born: 1895. Died: Jan. 31, 1965, Hollywood, Calif. (heart attack). Screen actor and film director. Entered films in 1911.

Appeared in: **1921** The Broken Spur; Dead or Alive; Devil Dog Dawson; Cupid's Brand; The Sheriff of Hope Eternal. **1922** One Eighth Apache; Peaceful Peters. **1923** At Devil's Gorge; The Law Rustlers; The Devil's Dooryard. **1924** Days of '49 (serial); California in '49 (feature of Days of '49 serial); Bringin' Home the Bacon; Ridin' Mad; Cupid's Rustler. **1925** The Cactus Cure; Whistling Jim; The Fugitive. **1926** Bad Man's Bluff. **1929** The Sky Skidder.

McGHEE, GLORIA (Gloria McGehee)
Born: 1922. Died: May 4, 1964, Meadville, Miss. (heart attack). Screen, stage and television actress.

Appeared in: **1956** The Boss. **1957** Sierra Stranger. **1963** A Child is Waiting.

McGIVENEY, OWEN
Born: 1884. Died: July 31, 1967, Woodland Hills, Calif. Screen, stage and vaudeville actor.

Appeared in: **1948** If Winter Comes. **1951** Show Boat. **1952** Scaramouche; Pat and Mike; Plymouth Adventure. **1953** The Maze. **1954** Brigadoon. **1955** The King's Thief. **1958** Hong Kong Confidential; In the Money. **1961** Snow White and the Three Stooges. **1964** My Fair Lady.

McGIVER, JOHN (George Morris)
Born: 1913. Died: Sept. 9, 1975, West Fulton, N.Y. (heart attack). Screen, stage and television actor. Married to designer Ruth Shmigelsky.

Appeared in: **1957** Love in the Afternoon. **1958** Once Upon a Horse; I Married a Woman; The Man in the Raincoat. **1959** The Gazebo. **1961** Love in a Goldfish Bowl; Bachelor in Paradise; Breakfast at Tiffany's. **1962** The Manchurian Candidate; Mr. Hobbs Takes a Vacation; Period of Adjustment; Who's Got the Action? **1963** Take Her, She's Mine; Who's Minding the Store?; Johnny Cool; Hot Horse (reissue of Once Upon a Horse—1958); My Six Loves. **1964** A Global Affair; Man's Favorite Sport. **1965** Marriage on the Rocks. **1966** The Glass Bottom Boat; Made in Paris. **1967** The Spirit is Willing; Fitzwilly. **1969** Midnight Cowboy.

McGLYNN, FRANK
Born: 1867, San Francisco, Calif. Died: May 17, 1951, Newburgh, N.Y. Stage and screen actor. Played Abraham Lincoln in many films. Appeared in Edison Stock Company films in 1907.

Appeared in: **1916** Gloria's Romance (serial). **1924** America. **1927** Judgement of the Hills. **1930** Min and Bill; Good News; Jazz Cinderella. **1931** The Secret Six; Huckleberry Finn; Riders of the Purple Sage. **1932** The Silent Partners (short); No Man of Her Own. **1933** Unknown Valley; Charlie Chan's Greatest Case; Frisco Jenny; Face in the Sky. **1934** Massacre; Little Miss Marker; The Mighty Barnum; Kentucky Kernels; Search for Beauty; Are We Civilized?; Lost in the Stratosphere. **1935** Folies Bergere; It's a Small World; Roaring West (serial); Outlawed Guns; The Littlest Rebel; Custer's Last Stand (serial); Captain Blood; Hopalong Cassidy. **1936** The Prisoner of Shark Island; King of the Royal Mounted; Career Woman; Hearts in Bondage; Parole; The Last of the Mohicans; North of Nome; The Plainsman; For the Service; The Trail of the Lonesome Pine. **1937** Wild West Days (serial); Western Gold; Wells Fargo; Silent Barriers; Sing and Be Happy. **1938** Sudden Bill Dorn; Kentucky Moonshine. **1939** The Honeymoon's Over; Union Pacific; The Mad Empress. **1940** Hi-Yo Silver; Boom Town. **1941** A Girl, a Guy and a Gob; Marry the Boss's Daughter; Three Girls in Town. **1944** Delinquent Daughters. **1945** Rogues' Gallery. **1947** Hollywood Barn Dance.

McGOWAN, JOHN P.
Born: Feb. 1880, Terowie, South Australia. Died: Mar. 26, 1952, Hollywood, Calif. Screen, stage actor, film director, film producer and screenwriter. Entered films as an actor with Kalem in 1909.

Appeared in: **1912** From the Manger to the Cross. **1915** Hazards of Helen (serial). **1917** The Railroad Raiders (serial). **1921** Do or Die (serial); Discontented Wives; Cold Steel; A Crook's Romance; The White Horseman (serial); King of the Circus (serial). **1922** Hills of Missing Men; Reckless Chances; The Ruse of the Rattler. **1923** The Whipping Boss; One Million in Jewels; Stormy Seas. **1924** Crossed Trails; A Two Fisted Tenderfoot. **1925** Barriers of the Law; Border Intrigue; Crack O'Dawn; Duped; The Fear Fighter; Makers of Men; Outwitted; Blood and Steel; The Fighting Sheriff. **1926** Danger Quest; Moran of the Mounted; The Patent Leather Kid; Red Blood; Senor Daredevil; The Ace of Clubs; The Lost Express. **1927** Arizona Nights; Gun Gospel; The Lost

Limited; Red Signals; The Red Raiders; The Slaver; Whispering Smith Rides (serial); The Royal American; Tarzan and the Golden Lion. **1928** The Black Ace; Arizona Days; The Code of the Scarlet; Devil Dogs; Devil's Tower; Dugan of the Dugouts; Headin' Westward; Law of the Mounted; Lighting Shot; The Old Code; On the Divide; Ships of the Night; Silent Trail; Texas Tommy; The Two Outlaws; West of Santa Fe; Painted Trail; Chinatown Mystery (serial); Senor Americano. **1929** The Phantom Raider; The Invaders; Fighting Terror; Arizona Days; Bad Man's Money; The Clean Up; Below the Deadline; The Lawless Legion; Captain Cowboy; On the Divide; The Silent Trail; The Last Roundup; West of Santa Fe; The Lone Horseman; Oklahoma Kid; The Golden Bridle; Ships of the Night; Plunging Hoofs; Riders of the Rio Grande; 'Neath Western Skies. **1930** Cowboy and the Outlaw; Pioneers of the West; Canyon of Missing Men; Covered Wagon Trails; O'Malley Rides Alone; Breezy Bill; Near the Rainbow's End. **1931** Riders of the North. **1932** Hurricane Express. **1933** Somewhere in Arizona; When a Man Rides Alone. **1934** No More Women; Wagon Wheels; Fighting Hero. **1935** Mississippi; Border Brigands; Bar 20 Rides Again. **1936** Stampede; Guns and Guitars; The Three Mesquiteers; Secret Patrol; Ride 'Em Cowboy. **1937** Fury and the Woman; Hit the Saddle; Heart of the Rockies; Slave Ship. **1938** The Buccaneer; Kennedy's Castle (short); Hunted Men. **1939** In Old Montana; Code of the Fearless; Calling All Marines; Stagecoach.

McGOWAN, OLIVER F.

Born: 1907. Died: Aug. 23, 1971, Hollywood, Calif. Screen, stage, radio and television actor.

Appeared in: **1958** Screaming Mimi. **1966** Stagecoach. **1967** Banning.

McGRAIL, WALTER B.

Born: 1899, Brooklyn, N.Y. Died: Mar. 19, 1970. Screen and stage actor.

Appeared in: **1916** The Scarlet Runner (serial). **1917** Within the Law. **1918** Miss Ambition. **1919** The Black Secret (serial); The Adventure Shop; The Girl Problem. **1921** Playthings of Destiny; The Invisible Fear; The Breaking Point; Her Mad Bargain; Pilgrims of the Night. **1922** The Cradle; The Kentucky Derby; Suzanna; The Top of New York; The Yosemite Trail. **1923** The Bad Man; The Eleventh Hour; Flaming Youth; Is Divorce a Failure?; Nobody's Money; Lights Out; Where the North Begins. **1924** A Son of the Sahara; Gerald Cranston's Lady; Is Love Everything?; Unguarded Women. **1925** Havoc; The Dancers; The Mad Marriage; Champion of Lost Causes; Adventure; A Son of His Father; When the Door Opened; The Teaser; Her Husband's Secret; The Scarlet West. **1926** Across the Pacific; The City; The Combat; Forbidden Waters; Marriage License?; Prisoners of the Storm. **1927** The Secret Studio; American Beauty. **1928** Man Crazy; The Play Girl; Stop That Man; Midnight Madness; Blockade; The Old Code. **1929** One Splendid Hour; Confessions of a Wife; Hey Rube!; The Veiled Woman; River of Romance. **1930** Soldiers and Women; The Lone Star Ranger; Men without Women; Women Everywhere; Last of the Duanes; Anybody's War; The Pay-Off; Part Time Wife. **1931** River's End; The Seas Beneath; Murder by the Clock; Night Nurse. **1932** Night Beat; Under Eighteen; McKenna of the Mounted; Exposed. **1933** State Trooper; Robbers' Roost; Sing, Sinner, Sing!; Police Call. **1935** All the King's Horses; Sunset Range; Men of the Night. **1937** The Shadow Strikes. **1938** Held for Ransom. **1939** Stagecoach; Calling All Marines; The Sun Never Sets. **1940** My Little Chickadee. **1942** Billy the Kid Trapped; Riders of the West.

McGRANARY, AL (Aloysius Cornelius McGranary)

Born: Sept. 3, 1902, Pa. Died: May 15, 1971, Los Angeles, Calif. (uremia, arteriosclerosis). Screen actor.

Appeared in: **1959** Riot in Juvenile Prison. **1960** Sunrise at Campobello. **1952** Advise and Consent.

McGRATH, DENNIS

Born: c. 1875. Died: 1955, New York, N.Y. Stage and screen actor. Appeared in silent films.

McGRATH, FRANK

Born: 1903. Died: May 13, 1967, Beverly Hills, Calif. (heart attack). Screen and television actor. Entered films as a stuntman.

Appeared in: **1942** Sundown Jim. **1945** They Were Expendable. **1949** She Wore a Yellow Ribbon. **1953** Ride, Vaquero. **1957** Hell Bound; The Tin Star. **1965** The Sword of Ali Baba. **1967** The Last Challenge; Tammy and the Millionaire; Gunfight in Abilene; The War Wagon; The Reluctant Astronaut. **1968** The Shakiest Gun in the West.

McGRATH, LARRY (Lawrence Joseph McGrath)

Born: Aug. 28, 1888, N.Y. Died: July 6, 1960, Los Angeles, Calif. (heart attack). Screen actor.

Appeared in: **1927** Knockout Reilly. **1930** The Arizona Kid; The Big Fight. **1934** Picture Brides. **1936** The Milky Way. **1942** The Miracle Kid. **1944** Wilson. **1950** The Jackie Robinson Story. **1951** Flaming Feather.

McGRAW, JOHN

Born: Apr. 7, 1873, Truxton, N.Y. Died: Feb. 25, 1934, New Rochelle, N.Y. Professional baseball player and screen actor.

Appeared in: **1914** The Universay Boy.

McGREGOR, MALCOLM (aka MALCOLM MacGREGOR)

Born: Oct. 13, 1892, Newark, N.J. Died: Apr. 29, 1945, Los Angeles, Calif. (burns). Screen actor.

Appeared in: **1922** The Prisoner of Zenda; Broken Chains. **1923** The Untamable; All the Brothers Were Valiant; The Dancer of the Nile; Can a Woman Love Twice?; A Noise in Newboro; The Social Code; You Can't Get Away With It. **1924** Smouldering Fires; The House of Youth; The Bedroom Window; Idle Tongues. **1925** Headlines; Alias Mary Flynn; The Circle; The Happy Warrior; Flaming Waters; The Girl of Gold; Lady of the Night; The Overland Limited; The Vanishing American. **1926** Infatuation; The Silent Flyer (serial); Don Juan's Three Nights; It Must Be Love; The Gay Deceiver; Money to Burn. **1927** A Million Bid; The Girl from Gay Paree; The Kid Sister; The Ladybird; Matinee Ladies; The Wreck; The Price of Honor. **1928** Buck Privates; Freedom of the Press; Lingerie; The Port of Missing Girls; Tropical Nights; Stormy Waters. **1929** The Girl on the Barge; Whispering Winds. **1930** Murder Will Out. **1935** Happiness C.O.D.

McGREGOR, PARKE (Parke Cushnie)

Born: 1907. Died: Dec. 5, 1962, Hollywood, Calif. (heart attack). Screen actor and singer.

McGUINN, JOSEPH FORD "JOE"

Born: Jan. 21, 1904, Brooklyn, N.Y. Died: Sept. 22, 1971, Hollywood, Calif. (heart attack). Stage and screen actor.

Appeared in: **1940** Ride, Tenderfoot, Ride; Pioneers of the West. **1941** Back in the Saddle. **1942** The Glass Key; Flight Lieutenant; Bells of Capistrano; In Old California; Two Yanks in Trinidad; The Cyclone Kid. **1945** Three's a Crowd. **1953** Prince of Pirates. **1957** Chicago Confidential; Three Brave Men. **1958** Ten North Frederick; Showdown at Boot Hill. **1959** The Story on Page One. **1961** The Gambler Wore a Gun. **1962** The Wild Westerners.

McGUIRE, BENJAMIN

Born: 1875. Died: Apr. 10, 1925, New York, N.Y. (heart failure). Screen actor. Appeared in Famous Players' films.

McGUIRE, HARP (Henry Herbert McGuire)

Born: Nov. 1, 1921, Tennessee. Died: Oct. 21, 1966, Los Angeles, Calif. (coronary sclerosis). Screen actor.

Appeared in: **1959** On the Beach. **1960** The Cage of Evil; The Walking Target. **1962** Incident in an Alley.

McGUIRE, TOM

Born: 1874. Died: May 6, 1954, Hollywood, Calif. Screen and stage actor.

Appeared in: **1921** The Girl in the Taxi; R.S.V.P.; See My Lawyer; Stranger Than Fiction. **1922** Afraid to Fight; The Five Dollar Baby; A Front Page Story; The Ladder Jinx; The Married Flapper. **1923** April Showers; A Million to Burn; The Scarlet Car; The Self-Made Wife; Single Handed; The Spoilers; The Victor. **1924** Captain Blood; Dark Stairways; Her Man; The Reckless Age. **1925** Fighting Fate; Red Hot Tires; We Moderns. **1926** The Better 'Ole; My Own Pal. **1927** Babe Comes Home; Colleen; The Missing Link; Pleasure before Business; Shanghai Bound. **1928** Lights of New York; A Thief in the Dark; The Sawdust Paradise; Steamboat Bill, Jr. **1930** Voice of the City. **1931** Politics; Oh! Oh! Cleopatra (short). **1932** No Greater Love. **1933** She Done Him Wrong. **1936** Charlie Chan at the Opera.

McGUIRK, HARRIET (Harriet Nawrot)

Born: 1903, Chicago, Ill. Died: Dec. 19, 1975, Wilmington, Del. Professional roller skater, screen, stage and television actress.

Appeared in: **1935** Transient Lady.

McGURK, BOB

Born: 1907. Died: May 30, 1959, Los Angeles, Calif. Screen actor.

McHALE, JAMES

Died: Feb. 4, 1973. Screen actor.

Appeared in: **1970** Kelly's Heroes.

McHUGH, CATHERINE

Born: 1869. Died: June 28, 1944, Hollywood, Calif. Screen actress. Mother of actors Matt (dec. 1971) and Frank McHugh.

McHUGH, CHARLES PATRICK

Born: Philadelphia, Pa. Died: Oct. 22, 1931, Los Angeles, Calif. (heart attack). Stage and screen actor.

Appeared in: **1921** Be My Wife; A Shocking Night; Smiling All the Way. **1922** The Beautiful and Damned. **1923** Cupid's Fireman; The Eagle's Feather; The

Girl of the Golden West. 1924 The Trouble Shooter. 1925 Brand of Cowardice; The Golden Cocoon; Lights of Old Broadway; Smilin' at Trouble. 1926 Her Honor the Governor; The Prince of Broadway; The Sporting Lover; The Waning Sex. 1927 Finnegan's Ball; The Princess from Hoboken. 1928 Phantom of the Range. 1929 Smiling Irish Eyes; The Quitter.

McHUGH, JIMMY

Born: July 10, 1894, Boston, Mass. Died: May 23, 1969, Beverly Hills, Calif. (heart attack). Songwriter and screen actor.

Appeared in: 1957 The Helen Morgan Story.

McHUGH, MATT (Mathew O. McHugh)

Born: 1894, Connellsville, Pa. Died: Feb. 22, 1971, Northridge, Calif. (heart attack). Screen, stage and vaudeville actor. Entered films with Mack Sennett. Brother of actor Frank McHugh. Son of actress Catherine McHugh (dec. 1944).

Appeared in: 1931 Street Scene (screen and stage versions); Reckless Living. 1932 Alaska Love (short); Freaks; The Wet Parade; Afraid to Talk. 1933 Paramount shorts; The Last Trail; The Man Who Dared; Jimmy and Sally; Devil's Brother; Night of Terror. 1934 She Loves Me Not; Sandy McKee; Judge Priest; Wake up and Dream. 1935 Wings in the Dark; Lost in the Stratosphere; Murder on a Honeymoon; The Good Fairy; Enter Madame; Mr. Dynamite; Diamond Jim; The Glass Key; Ladies Crave Excitement; Barbary Coast. 1936 Two in a Crowd; The Big Broadcast of 1937. 1937 Navy Blue and Gold. 1938 No Time to Marry; Tropic Holiday. 1939 Federal Man Hunt; Jones Family in Hollywood; The Escape; At the Circus. 1940 His Ex Marks the Spot (short); You the People (short); Yesterday's Heroes. 1941 So You Won't Squawk (short). 1942 Sappy Birthday (short); It Happened in Flatbush; The Man in the Trunk; Girl Trouble. 1943 Henry Aldrich Swings It; Flight for Freedom; The West Side Kid. 1944 My Buddy; Home in Indiana. 1945 Salome, Where She Danced; The Bells of St. Mary's; How Do You Do? 1946 Deadline for Murder; Dark Corner; Vacation in Reno. 1947 The Trouble with Women. 1948 Scudda Hoo! Scudda Hay!; Pardon My Clutch (short). 1949 Duke of Chicago. 1950 Bodyhold; Return of the Frontiersman. 1955 Wham-Bam-Slam (short).

McILLWAIN, WILLIAM A.

Born: 1863. Died: May 27, 1933, Los Angeles, Calif. (heart attack). Stage and screen actor.

Appeared in: 1924 Abraham Lincoln. 1925 Passionate Youth; Reckless Courage.

McINTOSH, BURR

Born: Aug. 21, 1862, Wellsville, Ohio. Died: Apr. 28, 1942, Hollywood, Calif. (heart attack). Screen, stage, radio actor, screenwriter and writer for radio. Entered films in 1913.

Appeared in: 1915 Adventures of Wallingford. 1920 Way Down East. 1923 Driven; The Exciters; On the Banks of the Wabash. 1924 The Average Woman; Lend Me Your Husband; Reckless Wives; The Spitfire; Virtuous Liars. 1925 Camille of the Barbary Coast; Enemies of Youth; The Pearl of Love; The Green Archer (serial). 1926 The Buckaroo Kid; Dangerous Friends; Lightning Reporter; The Wilderness Woman. 1927 The Golden Stallion (serial); A Hero for the Night; Breakfast at Sunrise; Fire and Steel; Framed; Hazardous Valley; Naughty but Nice; Once and Forever; See You in Jail; Silk Stockings; Taxi! Taxi!; The Yankee Clipper; Non Support (short). 1928 Across the Atlantic; The Adorable Cheat; The Grip of the Yukon; Me, Gangster; The Racket; That Certain Thing; Lilac Time; The Four Flusher; Sailor's Wives. 1929 The Last Warning; Fancy Baggage; Skinner Steps Out. 1930 The Rogue Song. 1933 The Sweetheart of Sigma Chi. 1934 The Richest Girl in the World.

McINTYRE, DUNCAN

Born: 1907, Scotland (?). Died: Dec. 1973, London, England. Screen, radio, stage and television actor.

Appeared in: 1954 The Maggie (aka High and Dry—US). 1962 Strongroom.

McINTYRE, FRANK

Born: 1878. Died: June 8, 1949, Ann Arbor, Mich. Screen, stage and radio actor.

Appeared in: 1917 The Traveling Salesman. 1918 Too Fat to Fight.

McINTYRE, LEILA

Born: 1882. Died: Jan. 9, 1953, Los Angeles, Calif. Screen, stage and vaudeville actress. She appeared in vaudeville with her husband, actor John Hyams (dec. 1940), in an act called "Hyams and McIntyre." Mother of actress Leila Hyams. Her married name was Leila Hyams, but do not confuse her with her daughter by the same name (Leila Hyams) who was born on May 1, 1905.

Appeared in: 1927 All in Fun (Hyams and McIntyre short). 1929 Hurricane. 1930 On the Level; Swell People; All for Mabel. 1933 Marriage on Approval. 1935 Murder in the Fleet. 1936 The Prisoner of Shark Island. 1937 Pick a Star; Live, Love and Learn; Topper. 1939 The Housekeeper's Daughter; Three Smart Girls Grow Up; The Women; Zenobia. 1942 Tennessee Johnson.

McINTYRE, MARION (Marion Gray)

Born: 1885. Died: Nov. 19, 1975, Woodland Hills, Calif. Screen, radio and television actress.

McIVOR, MARY

Born: 1901. Died: Feb. 28, 1941, Hollywood, Calif. (heart attack). Screen and vaudeville actress. Married to actor William Desmond (dec. 1949).

Appeared in: 1925 The Burning Trail.

McKAY, GEORGE W. (George Reuben)

Born: 1880, Minsk, Russia. Died: Dec. 3, 1945, Hollywood, Calif. Screen, stage and vaudeville actor. Married to actress Ottie Ardine with whom he appeared in vaudeville; prior to that he teamed with Johnny Cantwell in vaudeville acts.

Appeared in: 1929 Back from Abroad (McKay and Ardine short). 1930 Sixteen Sweeties. 1935 The Case of the Missing Man. 1936 Don't Gamble with Love; You May Be Next; Superspeed; Shakedown; Killer at Large; End of the Trail; One Way Ticket; Crime and Punishment; Pride of the Marines; Counterfeit; The Final Hour; Two Fisted Gentleman; Come Closer, Folks. 1937 A Fight to the Finish; Frame-Up; Right Guy; Counterfeit Lady; Woman in Distress; The Devil's Playground; It's All Yours; Murder in Greenwich Village; Racketeers in Exile. 1938 There's Always a Woman; Highway Patrol; Convicted; Duke of West Point; Illegal Traffic. 1939 King of the Turf; Babes in Arms. 1940 The Big Guy. 1941 The Face behind the Mask. 1942 Canal Zone; Sabotage Zone; The Boogie Man Will Get You. 1943 Murder in Times Square. 1944 Going My Way.

McKAY, NORMAN

Born: 1906. Died: Apr. 24, 1968, New York, N.Y. Screen, stage, radio and television actor.

Appeared in: 1947 Untamed Fury; Kiss of Death. 1948 Call Northside 777. 1951 The Frogmen; USS Teakettle (aka You're in the Navy Now). 1953 Niagara. 1961 The Hoodlum Priest.

McKEE, BUCK

Born: 1865, Claremore, Okla. Died: Mar. 1, 1944, Roseville, Calif. Screen actor.

McKEE, DONALD M.

Born: 1899. Died: June 27, 1968, Chebeague Island, Maine. Screen, stage and television actor.

Appeared in: 1951 The Whistle at Eaton Falls. 1958 The Goddess.

McKEE, LAFE (Lafayette Stocking McKee)

Born: Jan. 23, 1872, Morrison, Ill. Died: Aug. 10, 1959, Temple City, Calif. (arteriosclerosis). Stage and screen actor. Entered films in 1912.

Appeared in: 1913 The Adventures of Kathlyn (serial). 1915 The Jaguar Trap; The Two Natures Within Him; How Callahan Cleaned Up Little Hell. 1922 Blazing Arrows. 1923 Blood Test; The Lone Wagon. 1924 Mile a Minute Morgan; Western Girl; Hard Hittin' Hamilton; Bringin' Home the Bacon; Rainbow Rangers; Thundering Romance; Battling Brewster (serial). 1925 Double Action Daniels; Triple Action; The Human Tornado; On the Go; Pursued; Saddle Cyclone; Warrior Gap; The Mystery Box (serial). 1926 Baited Trap; The Bandit Buster; The Bonanza Buckaroo; A Captain's Courage; Fort Frayne; Rawhide; Twin Triggers; West of the Law. 1927 Roarin' Broncs; Daring Deeds; The Ridin' Rowdy; Riding to Fame; The Fire Fighters (serial). 1928 The Ballyhoo Buster; Reilly of the Rainbow Division; The Upland Rider; Desperate Courage; Freckles; Manhattan Cowboy; On the Divide; Painted Trail; The Riding Renegade; Saddle Mates; Trail Riders; Trailin' Back. 1929 The California Mail; The Amazing Vagabond. 1930 Code of Honor; The Lonesome Trail; The Utah Kid; The Lone Defender (serial); Under Montana Skies; The Rainbow's End. 1931 Red Fork Range; The Vanishing Legion (serial); The Lightning Warrior (serial); Two Gun Man; Alias—The Bad Man; Partners of the Trail; Grief Street; Hurricane Horseman; Range Law; Neck and Neck; Lariats and Six Shooters; Cyclone. 1932 Fighting Marshal; Without Honors; Gay Buckaroo; Mark of the Spur; Spirit of the West; Hell Fire Austin; Riding Tornado; Man from New Mexico; Klondike; Gold; Hello Trouble; The Boiling Point; The Fighting Champ; Tombstone Canyon. 1933 Terror Trail; End of the Cross Fire; Fighting Texans; Self Defense; Young Blood; Fighting for Justice; Mystery Squadron (serial); Deadwood Pass; Dude Bandit; Man from Monterey; Crossfire; Galloping Romeo; War of the Range; Whispering Shadows (serial); Riders of Destiny; Under Secret Orders; Tombstone Canyon. 1934 The Quitter; Mystery Mountain (serial); The Trail Drive; Gun Justice; West of the Divide; Riding Thru; Straightaway; Tracy Rides; Hellbent for Love; Man from Utah; City Park; Rawhide Mail; Demon for Trouble; Outlaws' Highway; Frontier Days. 1935 The Keeper of the Bees; Rustlers of Red Dog (serial); Port of Lost Dreams; What Price Crime?; Kid Courageous; The Hawk; Desert Trail; The Ivory-Handled Gun. 1936 Swifty; Frontier Justice; Silly Billies; Roamin' Wild; Bridge of Sighs; The Cowboy and the Kid; The Last of the Warrens; Idaho Kid; Men of the Plains. 1937 The Mystery of the Hooded Horseman; North of the Rio Grande; Melody of the Plains; Law of the Ranger. 1938 Rawhide; I'm from the City; Knight of the Plains. 1940 Pioneers of the Frontier; Covered Wagon Trails; Riders of Pasco Basin; The Bad Man from Red Butte; Son of Roaring Dan. **1942** Inside the Law.

McKEE, PAT

Born: 1897. Died: Jan. 9, 1950, El Monte, Calif. Screen actor.

Appeared in: **1938** Straight, Place and Show. **1943** Coney Island; Behind Prison Walls. **1944** Voodoo Man.

McKEE, TOM

Born: 1917. Died: June 20, 1960, Burbank, Calif. (accidental fall). Screen, radio and television actor.

Appeared in: **1955** The Court Martial of Billy Mitchell. **1956** The Search for Bridey Murphy. **1957** Fury at Showdown; The River's Edge; Under Fire; Valerie. **1960** Three Came to Kill; Vice Raid.

McKEEN, LAWRENCE D., JR. "SNOOKUMS"

Born: 1925. Died: Apr. 2, 1933, Los Angeles, Calif. (blood poisoning). Screen actor. Made his film debut as "Baby Snookums" at age of 18 months. By the time he was four he had his own series.

Appeared in: **1926** The Newlyweds and Their Baby (series).

McKEEVER, MIKE

Born: Jan. 1, 1940. Died: Aug. 24, 1967, Hollywood, Calif. (brain injuries resulting from an auto accident). All-American football player and screen actor. Brother of actor and football player Marlin McKeever.

Appeared in: **1961** Love in a Goldfish Bowl. **1962** The Three Stooges Meet Hercules.

McKELVIE, HAROLD

Born: 1910. Died: June 1937, Los Angeles, Calif. Screen actor and stuntman.

McKENNA, HENRY T.

Born: 1894, Brooklyn, N.Y. Died: June 17, 1958, Hollywood, Calif. (heart attack). Screen actor.

McKENZIE, EVA B.

Born: 1889. Died: Sept. 15, 1967, Hollywood, Calif. Screen actress. Entered films in 1915. Married to actor Robert McKenzie (dec. 1949) and mother of actresses Ida Mae, Lally and Fay McKenzie.

Appeared in: **1931** Virtuous Husband. **1937** The following shorts: The Wrong Miss Wright; Stuck in the Sticks; Lodge Night. **1938** The following shorts: The Nightshirt Bandit; Soul of a Heel; Beaux and Errors; Stage Fright. **1939** The following shorts: Andy Clyde Gets Spring Chicken; Oily to Bed, Oily to Rise; Feathered Pests. **1944** Gold is Where You Lose It (short).

McKENZIE, ROBERT B.

Born: Sept. 22, 1883, Bellymania, Ireland. Died: July 8, 1949, R.I. (heart attack). Stage and screen actor. Entered films in 1915. Married to actress Eva McKenzie (dec. 1967) and father of actresses Ida Mae, Lally and Fay McKenzie.

Appeared in: **1921** A Knight of the West. **1922** Fightin' Devil; The Sheriff of Sun-Dog; A Western Demon. **1923** The Devil's Dooryard; Don Quickshort of the Rio Grande; The Gentleman from America; Single Handed; Where Is This West?; In the West. **1924** The Covered Trail; The Desert Hawk; The Whirlwind Ranger. **1925** Fifth Avenue Models. **1926** A Six Shootin' Romance; Bad Man's Bluff; The Fighting Peacemaker. **1927** One Glorious Scrap; Red Signals; Set Free. **1929** The White Outlaw. **1930** Shadow Ranch. **1931** Cimarron. **1933** Tillie and Gus; Beauty and the Bus (short). **1934** You're Telling Me; Opened by Mistake (short); Little Minister. **1935** Stone of Silver Creek; A Shot in the Dark; The Bride Comes Home; plus the following shorts: Beginner's Luck; Teacher's Beau; It Always Happens; Hoi Polloi. **1936** Love before Breakfast; Comin' Round the Mountain; Rebellion; Heart of the West; Love Comes to Mooneyville (short). **1937** Sing Cowboy Sing; Hideaway; Stars over Arizona; plus the following shorts: The Wrong Miss Wright; Stuck in the Sticks; He Done His Duty; The Sitter-Downers. **1938** The Old Raid Mule (short). **1939** They Asked for It; Blondie Takes a Vacation; Death of a Champion. **1940** Dreaming Out Loud; Buried Alive; Triple Justice. **1941** Citadel of Crime; Death Valley Outlaws; Sierra Sue. **1942** In Old California; The Sombrero Kid. **1943** Jive Junction. **1944** Texas Masquerade; Three of a Kind; Tall in the Saddle; The Yoke's on Me (short). **1946** Duel in the Sun; Romance of the West; Colorado Serenade.

McKIM, ROBERT

Born: 1887, San Francisco, Calif. Died: June 2, 1927, Hollywood, Calif. (cerebral hemorrhage). Screen and vaudeville actor.

Appeared in: **1915** The Edge of the Abyss; The Disciple. **1916** The Primal Lure; The Stepping Stone; The Return of Draw Egan. **1919** Wagon Tracks; Her Kingdom of Dreams. **1920** The Mark of Zorro; Riders of the Dawn; The Silver Horde. **1921** A Certain Rich Man; The Lure of Egypt; The Man of the Forest; Mysterious Rider; The Spenders. **1922** The Gray Dawn; Heart's Haven; Monte Cristo; White Hands; Without Compromise. **1923** All the Brothers

Were Valiant; Dead Game; His Last Race; Hollywood; Human Wreckage; Maytime; Mr. Billings Spends His Dime; The Spider and the Rose; The Spoilers; Strangers of the Night; Thundergate. **1924** Flaming Barriers; The Galloping Ace; Mademoiselle Midnight; Ride for Your Life; The Torrent; When a Girl Loves. **1925** North of Nome; The Police Patrol; Spook Ranch. **1926** The Bat; The Dead Line; Kentucky Handicap; The Pay Off; A Regular Scout; The Strong Man; Tex; The Tough Guy; The Wolf Hunters. **1927** A Flame in the Sky; The Denver Dude; The Show Girl; The Thrill Seekers.

McKINNELL, NORMAN

Born: 1870, England. Died: Mar. 29, 1932, London, England (heart disease). Screen, stage actor and stage director.

Appeared in: **1915** The Shulamite. **1917** Everybody's Business; Dombey and Son; Mary Girl. **1918** Hindle Wakes. **1920** Pillars of Society; A Gamble in Lives. **1927** Hindle Wakes (aka Fanny Hawthorne—US 1929); Downhill (aka When Boys Leave Home—US 1928); The Fake. **1931** Potiphar's Wife (aka Her Strange Desire—US 1932); The Sleeping Cardinal (aka Sherlock Holmes' Fatal Hour—US); The Outsider; Hindle Wakes (also 1918 and 1927 versions). **1932** The Frightened Lady (aka Criminal at Large—US 1933); White Face.

McKINNEY, NINA MAE

Born: 1909, New York, N.Y. Died: 1968. Black screen actress.

Appeared in: **1929** Hallelujah. **1931** Safe in Hell. **1935** Sanders of the River; Reckless. **1939** Pocomania. **1944** Dark Waters; Together Again. **1946** Night Train to Memphis. **1947** Danger Street. **1949** Pinky.

McLAGLEN, VICTOR

Born: Dec. 11, 1886, Tunbridge Wells, Kent, England. Died: Nov. 7, 1959, Newport Beach, Calif. (heart attack). Screen, stage and vaudeville actor. Won 1935 Academy Award for Best Actor in The Informer. Nominated for 1952 Academy Award for Best Supporting Actor in The Quiet Man. Brother of actors Leopold, Arthur, Clifford, Kenneth and Cyril McLaglen.

Appeared in: **1920** The Call of the Road. **1921** Corinthian Jack; The Prey of the Dragon; Carnival; The Sport of Kings. **1922** The Glorious Adventure; A Romance of Old Bagdad; Little Brother of God; A Sailor Tramp; The Crimson Circle. **1923** The Romany; Heartstrings; M'Lord of the White Road; In the Blood. **1924** The Beloved Brute; The Boatswain's Mate; Women and Diamonds (aka Conscripts of Misfortune or It Happened in Africa); The Gay Corinthian; The Passionate Adventure. **1925** The Hunted Woman; Percy; The Fighting Heart; The Unholy Three; Winds of Chance. **1926** Beau Geste; What Price Glory; Men of Steel; The Isle of Retribution. **1927** Loves of Carmen. **1928** Mother Machree; A Girl in Every Port; Hangman's House; The River Pirate. **1929** Captain Lash; Strong Boy; King of the Khyber Rifles; The Cock Eyed World; The Black Watch; Sez You—Sez Me; Hot for Paris. **1930** Happy Days; On the Level; A Devil with Women; Wings of Adventures. **1931** Not Exactly Gentlemen; Dishonored; Women of All Nations; Wicked; Annabelle's Affairs. **1932** Guilty as Hell; Devil's Lottery; While Paris Sleeps; The Slippery Pearls (short); The Gay Caballero; Rackety Rax. **1933** Hot Pepper; Laughing at Life; Dick Turpin. **1934** The Lost Patrol; No More Women; Wharf Angel; Murder at the Vanities; The Captain Hates the Sea. **1935** Under Pressure; Great Hotel Murder; The Informer; Professional Soldier. **1936** Under Two Flags; Mary of Scotland; Klondike Annie; The Magnificent Brute. **1937** Sea Devils; Nancy Steele Is Missing; Wee Willie Winkie; This Is My Affair. **1938** We're Going to Be Rich; The Devil's Party; Battle of Broadway. **1939** Gunga Din; Pacific Liner; Rio; Let Freedom Ring; Black Watch; Captain Fury; Ex-Champ; Full Confession. **1940** The Big Guy; Diamond Frontier; South of Pago Pago. **1941** Broadway Limited. **1942** Call Out the Marines; Powder Town; China Girl. **1943** Forever and a Day. **1944** Tampico; The Princess and the Pirate. **1945** Rough, Tough and Ready; Roger Touhy, Gangster; Love, Honor and Goodbye. **1946** Whistle Stop. **1947** Michigan Kid; Foxes of Harrow; Calendar Girl. **1948** Fort Apache. **1949** She Wore a Yellow Ribbon. **1950** Rio Grande. **1952** The Quiet Man. **1953** Fair Wind to Java. **1954** Prince Valiant; Trouble in the Glen. **1955** Many Rivers to Cross; Bengazi; Lady Godiva; City of Shadows. **1956** Around the World in 80 Days. **1957** The Abductors. **1959** Sea Fury.

McLEOD, BARBARA (Barbara Fielding)

Born: 1908. Died: May 26, 1940, Van Nuys, Calif. (suicide—gun). Screen actress.

McLEOD, HELEN

Born: 1924. Died: Apr. 20, 1964, Bakersfield, Calif. (cancer). Screen actress.

McLEOD, TEX (Alexander D'Avila McLeod)

Born: Nov. 11, 1896, Gonzales, Tex. Died: Feb. 12, 1973, Brighton, England (heart attack). Screen, stage, vaudeville actor, circus and rodeo performer.

Appeared in: **1915** Broncho Billy (serial). **1928** A Rope and a Story (short). **1933** Radio Parade.

McMAHON, DAVID

Born: 1909. Died: Jan. 27, 1972, Pasadena, Calif. (heart attack). Screen actor.

Appeared in: **1949** I Was a Male War Bride. **1950** Where the Sidewalk Ends; When Willie Comes Marching Home. **1951** The Scarf. **1952** Eight Iron Men;

Glory Alley. **1955** Top of the World. **1956** The Peacemaker; Dance With Me, Henry; The Creature Walks Among Us. **1957** Operation Mad Ball. **1962** The Case of Patty Smith (aka The Shame of Patty Smith).

McMAHON, HORACE (aka HORACE MacMAHON)

Born: 1907, South Norwalk, Conn. Died: Aug. 17, 1971, Norwalk, Conn. (heart ailment). Screen, stage, vaudeville, radio and television actor. Married to actress Louise Campbell.

Appeared in: **1937** Navy Blues; The Wrong Road; Exclusive; A Girl with Ideas; They Gave Him a Gun; Double Wedding; Kid Galahad. **1938** King of the Newsboys; When G-Men Step In; Fast Company; Ladies in Distress; Tenth Avenue Kid; Secrets of a Nurse; Broadway Musketeers; Pride of the Navy; Alexander's Ragtime Band; Gangs of New York. **1939** Sergeant Madden; The Gracie Allen Murder Case; Rose of Washington Square; I Was a Convict; Federal Man-Hunt; Laugh It Off; Big Town Czar; For Love or Money; She Married a Cop; Quick Millions; Sabotage. **1940** The Marines Fly High; Dr. Kildare's Strangest Case; Dr. Kildare Goes Home; I Can't Give You Anything but Love, Baby; Gangs of Chicago; Millionaires in Prison; Oh Johnny, How You Can Love!; We Who Are Young; The Leather Pushers; Melody Ranch; Dr. Kildare's Crisis. **1941** Come Live with Me; Rookies on Parade; The Bride Wore Crutches; Lady Scarface; Buy Me That Town; Birth of the Blues; The Stork Pays Off. **1942** Jail House Blues. **1944** Roger Touhy, Gangster; Timber Queen. **1945** Lady Gangster. **1948** Smart Woman; Fighting Mad; Waterfront at Midnight; The Return of October. **1951** Detective Story (stage and film versions). **1953** Abbott and Costello Go to Mars; Man in the Dark; Fast Company; Champ for a Day. **1954** Duffy of San Quentin; Susan Slept Here. **1955** The Blackboard Jungle; My Sister Eileen; Texas Lady. **1957** The Delicate Delinquent; Beau James. **1959** Never Steal Anything Small. **1966** The Swinger. **1968** The Detective.

McMAHON, JOHN G.

Died: Aug. 18, 1968. Screen actor.

McMANUS, GEORGE

Died: Oct. 22, 1954. Cartoonist and screen actor. Creator of comic strip "Bringing Up Father".

Appeared in: **1924** The Great White Way. **1946** Bringing Up Father. **1948** Jiggs and Maggie In Court. **1949** Maggie and Jiggs in Jackpot Jitters. **1950** Jiggs and Maggie Out West.

McMILLAN, WALTER KENNETH

Born: 1917. Died: Jan., 1945 (killed in action in Philippine invasion, W.W. II). Stage and screen actor. Was a member of Hal Roach's "Our Gang."

McNAMAR, JOHN

Died: Oct. 27, 1968. Screen actor.

Appeared in: **1957** Slaughter on Tenth Avenue; From Hell it Came. **1958** Suicide Battalion; The Return of Dracula; War of the Colossal Beast; Crash Landing. **1960** Ma Barker's Killer Brood; Portrait in Black.

McNAMARA, EDWARD C.

Born: 1884, Paterson, N.J. Died: Nov. 9, 1944, on train near Boston, Mass. (heart attack). Screen, stage actor and opera tenor.

Appeared in: **1929** Lucky in Love. **1932** I Am a Fugitive from a Chain Gang. **1933** 20,000 Years in Sing Sing. **1937** Great Guy; Girl Overboard; The League of Frightened Men. **1941** Strawberry Blonde; The Devil and Miss Jones. **1943** Johnny Come Lately; Margin of Error. **1944** Arsenic and Old Lace.

McNAMARA, TED

Born: Australia. Died: Feb. 3, 1928, Ventura, Calif. (pneumonia). Screen and vaudeville actor.

Appeared in: **1925** Shore Leave. **1926** What Price Glory? **1927** Chain Lightning; Colleen; The Gay Retreat; The Monkey Talks; Rich but Honest; Upstream. **1928** The Gateway of the Moon; Mother Machree; Why Sailors Go Wrong.

McNAMARA, THOMAS J.

Died: May 21, 1953, Brooklyn, N.Y. Screen and vaudeville actor.

McNAMEE, DONALD

Born: 1897. Died: July 17, 1940, Hollywood, Calif. (skull fracture). Stage and screen actor.

Appeared in: **1928** Fashion Madness. **1929** The Great Garbo.

McNAUGHTON, GUS (August Le Clerq)

Born: 1884, London, England. Died: Dec., 1969, Castor, England. Stage and screen actor.

Appeared in: **1930** Murder; Children of Chance. **1932** Lucky Girl; The Maid of the Mountains; The Last Coupon; His Wife's Mother; Money Talks. **1933** Radio Parade; Leave It to Me; Their Night Out; Heads We Go (aka The Charming Deceiver—US); The Love Nest; Song Birds; Crime on the Hill. **1934**

Seeing is Believing; Bagged; Spring in the Air; Happy; Wishes; Master and Man; The Luck of a Sailor; There Goes Susie (aka Scandals of Paris—US 1935). **1935** Barnacle Bill; Royal Cavalcade (aka Regal Cavalcade—US); The 39 Steps; Joy Ride; The Crouching Beast; Invitation to the Waltz; Music Hath Charms. **1936** Not So Dusty; Southern Roses; Busman's Holiday; Keep Your Seats Please; The Heirloom Mystery; When We Get Married. **1937** The Strange Adventures of Mr. Smith; Action for Slander (US 1938); Storm in a Teacup; Keep Fit. **1938** You're the Doctor; South Riding; The Divorce of Lady X; Easy Riches; We're Going to Be Rich; St. Martin's Lane (aka Sidewalks of London—US 1940); Keep Smiling (aka Smiling Along—US 1939). **1939** Q Planes (aka Clouds Over Europe—US); Trouble Brewing; I Killed the Count (aka Who is Guilty?—US 1940); There Ain't No Justice; Blind Folly; What Would You Do Chums?; All at Sea. **1940** That's the Ticket; Old Bill and Son; George and Margaret; Two for Danger. **1941** Facing the Music; Penn of Pennsylvania (aka The Courageous Mr. Penn—US 1944); Jeannie; South American George. **1942** Let the People Sing; Much Too Shy; Rose of Tralee. **1943** The Shipbuilders. **1944** Demobbed. **1945** A Place of One's Own (US 1949); Here Comes the Sun. **1946** The Trojan Brothers. **1947** The Turners of Prospect Road.

McNAUGHTON, HARRY

Born: 1897, England. Died: Feb. 26, 1967, Amityville, N.Y. Screen, stage and radio actor.

Appeared in: **1921** Wet Gold (short). **1930** The following shorts: All Stuck Up; Sixteen Sweeties; The Fight; Office Steps; Her Hired Husband; Seeing Off Service; Tom Thumbs Down. **1956** The Vagabond King.

McNEAR, HOWARD

Born: 1905. Died: Jan. 3, 1969, San Fernando Valley, Calif. Screen, radio and television actor. Played Doc Adams on radio's Gunsmoke.

Appeared in: **1954** Drums across the River. **1956** You Can't Run Away from It; Bundle of Joy. **1957** Public Pigeon No. 1; Affair in Reno. **1958** Bell, Book and Candle; Good Day for a Hanging; The Big Circus. **1959** Anatomy of a Murder; The Big Circus. **1961** Bachelor Flat; Blue Hawaii; Voyage to the Bottom of the Sea. **1962** Follow That Dream; The Errand Boy. **1963** Irma La Douce; The Wheeler Dealers. **1964** Kiss Me, Stupid! **1965** My Blood Runs Cold; Love and Kisses. **1966** The Fortune Cookie.

McPETERS, TAYLOR

Born: 1900. Died: Apr. 16, 1962, Hollywood, Calif. (heart attack). Screen actor.

Appeared in: **1963** The Ugly American.

McPHAIL, DOUGLAS

Born: Apr. 16, 1910, Los Angeles, Calif. Died: Dec. 7, 1944, Los Angeles, Calif. (effects of poison). Screen, stage actor and singer. Divorced from actress Betty Jaynes.

Appeared in: **1936** Born to Dance. **1937** Maytime. **1938** Sweethearts; Toy Wife; Test Pilot. **1939** Babes in Arms; Honolulu. **1940** Little Nellie Kelly; Broadway Melody of 1940. **1942** Born to Sing.

McPHERSON, QUINTON (aka MR. HYMACK)

Born: 1871, England. Died: Jan., 1940, London, England. Screen, stage and vaudeville actor.

Appeared in: **1933** Mixed Doubles; Anne One Hundred. **1934** The Third Clue. **1935** Maria Marten: Or, The Murder in the Red Barn. **1936** The Ghost Goes West; If I Were Rich; Annie Laurie; The Beloved Vagabond; The Tenth Man (US 1937); Land Without Music (aka Forbidden Music—US 1938); Talk of the Devil (US 1937). **1937** Storm in a Teacup; 21 Days (aka The First and the Last and 21 Days Together—US 1940); Captain's Orders. **1938** Dangerous Medicine.

McQUARY, CHARLES S.

Born: 1908. Died: Feb. 9, 1970, Hollywood, Calif. (stroke). Screen, television actor, stand-in for Buddy Ebsen in television and double for Smiley Burnett in films.

McQUOID, ROSE LEE (aka ROSE LEE)

Born: 1887. Died: May 4, 1962, Hollywood, Calif. Screen actress. Entered films approx. 1912.

Appeared in: **1930** Just Imagine.

McRAE, BRUCE

Born: Jan. 18, 1867, India. Died: May 7, 1927, City Island, N.Y. (heart trouble). Stage and screen actor.

Appeared in: **1916** Hazel Kirke. **1919** A Star Overnight. **1922** The World's a Stage.

McRAE, DUNCAN. *See* DUNCAN MACRAE

McSHANE, KITTY

Born: 1898. Died: Mar. 24, 1964, London, England. Screen, stage and vaudeville actress. Married to actor Arthur Lucan (dec. 1954), with whom she appeared in vaudeville and films in an act billed as "Lucan and McShane." The two played in "Old Mother Riley" series of films, McShane playing the mother. For the films they appeared in, see Arthur Lucan.

McTAGGART, JAMES

Born: 1911. Died: May 29, 1949, Beverly Hills, Calif. (swimming pool accident). Screen actor.

McTURK, JOE

Born: 1899. Died: July 19, 1961, Hollywood, Calif. (heart attack). Screen, stage and television actor.

Appeared in: 1953 Money from Home. 1955 Guys and Dolls. 1956 Man with the Golden Arm. 1961 Pocketful of Miracles.

McVEY, LUCILLE. *See* MRS. SIDNEY DREW

McVEY, PATRICK "PAT"

Born: 1910. Died: July 6, 1973, New York, N.Y. Screen, stage and television actor.

Appeared in: 1942 Pierre of the Plains; The Mummy's Tomb. 1946 Two Guys from Milwaukee; Swell Guy. 1957 The Big Caper. 1958 Party Girl. 1959 North by Northwest. 1968 The Detective. 1972 The Visitors.

McVICKER, JULIUS

Born: 1876. Died: Mar. 11, 1940, Beverly Hills, Calif. Stage and screen actor.

Appeared in: 1932 The Phantom President.

McWADE, EDWARD

Died: May 1943, Hollywood, Calif. Married to actress Margaret McWade (dec. 1956). Screen actor.

Appeared in: 1921 Wing Toy. 1922 The Stranger's Banquet. 1923 The Town Scandal. 1925 The Monster. 1932 Big City Blues; The Big Shot; Two Seconds; Six Hours to Live; Lawyer Man. 1933 Murders in the Zoo. 1934 I'll Tell the World; Journal of a Crime; The Notorious Sophie Lang; A Lady Lost. 1935 Murder in the Clouds; Oil for the Lamps of China; Stranded; Frisco Kid; The Girl from Tenth Avenue; Red Salute; Dr. Socrates. 1936 The Calling of Dan Matthews; The Big Noise; The Man I Marry; Reunion. 1937 Let's Get Married; They Won't Forget; The Women Men Marry. 1938 White Banners; Garden of the Moon; Comet over Broadway; The Patient in Room 18. 1939 They Asked for It; Indianapolis Speedway; The Magnificent Fraud. 1940 Our Neighbors the Carters; Hot Steel; The Return of Frank James; Chad Hanna. 1941 The Big Store. 1942 The Hard Way; You Can't Escape Forever; Yankee Doodle Dandy; Famous Boners (short); Lady in a Jam. 1943 Crash Dive. 1944 Arsenic and Old Lace.

McWADE, MARGARET

Born: Sept 3, 1872. Died: Apr. 1, 1956. Screen, stage and vaudeville actress. Married to actor Edward McWade (dec. 1943). Appeared in vaudeville with Margaret Seddon (dec. 1968) in an act billed as the "Pixilated Sisters."

Appeared in: 1914 A Foolish Agreement; The Blind Fiddler. 1915 Taming a Grouch. 1917 Blue Jeans. 1918 Flower of the Dusk. 1919 Why Germany Must Pay; Broken Commandments. 1920 Alias Miss Dodd; Shore Acres; Food for Scandal; Her Beloved Villain; When a Man Loves; Stronger than Death. 1921 Blue Moon; The Blot; The Foolish Matrons; Her Mad Bargain; A Tale of Two Worlds; Garments of Truth. 1923 Alice Adams. 1924 Broken Barriers; The Cyclone Rider; Sundown; The Painted Lady. 1925 The Lost World; White Fang. 1926 High Steppers. 1928 Women Who Dare. 1936 Theodora Goes Wild; Mr. Deeds Goes to Town. 1937 Lost Horizon; Let's Make a Million; Wings Over Honolulu; Love in a Bungalow; Danger—Love at Work. 1938 Forbidden Valley. 1940 Remedy for Riches. 1942 Scattergood Survives a Murder; The Woman of the Year. 1943 The Meanest Man in the World. 1947 It's a Joke, Son; The Bishop's Wife.

McWADE, ROBERT, JR.

Born: 1882, Buffalo, N.Y. Died: Jan. 20, 1938, Culver City, Calif. (heart attack). Stage and screen actor. Son of actor Robert McWade, Sr. (dec. 1913).

Appeared in: 1924 Second Youth. 1925 New Brooms. 1928 The Home Towners. 1930 Night Work; Good Intentions; Feet First; The Pay Off; Sins of the Children. 1931 Cimarron; Too Many Cooks; Kept Husbands; Skyline; It's a Wise Child. 1932 Grand Hotel; The First Year; Ladies of the Jury; Madame Racketeer; Back Street; The Match King; Movie Crazy; The Phantom of Crestwood; Once in a Lifetime. 1933 I Loved a Woman; The Prizefighter and the Lady; Journal of a Crime; Heroes for Sale; The Solitaire Man; Fog; The Kennel Murder Case; A Lost Lady; Employees' Entrance; Big City Blues; High Spot; Two Seconds; Hard to Handle; Ladies They Talk About; 42nd Street; Pick Up; The Big Cage. 1934 Countess of Monte Cristo; Let's Be Ritzy; No Ransom; Operator 13; Cross Country Cruise; Hold That Girl; Thirty-Day Princess; Midnight Alibi; The Dragon Murder Case; The Lemon Drop Kid; College Rhythm; The President Vanishes. 1935 The County Chairman; Soci-

ety Doctor; Here Comes the Band; Straight from the Heart; Diamond Jim; His Night Out; Mary Jane's Pa; The Healer; Cappy Ricks Returns; Frisco Kid. 1936 Next Time We Love; The Big Noise; Anything Goes; Early to Bed; Moonlight Murder; Old Hutch; High Tension; 15 Maiden Lane; Bunker Bean. 1937 Benefits Forgot; We're on the Jury; California Straight Ahead; The Good Old Soak; This Is My Affair; Mountain Justice; On Such a Night; Under Cover of Night. 1938 Gold Is Where You Find It; Of Human Hearts.

McWADE, ROBERT, SR.

Born: 1835. Died: Mar. 5, 1913. Stage and screen actor. Father of actor Robert McWade, Jr. (dec. 1938).

Appeared in: 1912 Rip Van Winkle; As You Like It; The Curio Hunters; Captain Barnacle—Reformer. 1913 The Joke Wasn't on Ben Bolt; Papa Puts One Over; There's Music in the Air.

McWATTERS, ARTHUR J.

Born: 1871. Died: July 16, 1963, Freeport, N.Y. Screen, stage and vaudeville actor. Appeared in vaudeville with his wife, Grace Tyson, as "McWatters and Tyson." Appeared in early George Burns and Gracie Allen films.

MEADE, BILL

Died: 1941 (fell from horse onto his sword during filming of They Died with Their Boots On). Screen actor.

MEADE, CLAIRE (Marguerite Fields)

Born: Apr. 2, 1883, New Jersey. Died: Jan. 14, 1968, Encino, Calif. (pneumonia). Screen actress.

Appeared in: 1947 The Unfaithful. 1949 Mother is a Freshman; Miss Grant Takes Richmond. 1950 Belle of Old Mexico. 1953 Three Sisters and a Girl.

MEADER, GEORGE

Born: July 6, 1888, Minneapolis, Minn. Died: Dec. 1963. Screen actor. Entered films in 1940.

Appeared in: 1940 The Courageous Dr. Christian; Gambling on the High Seas. 1941 Life with Henry; Man-Mad Monster; Father Takes a Wife; The Smiling Ghost; The Monster and the Girl; Petticoat Politics; Dancing on a Dime; New York Town; Bachelor Daddy. 1942 The Glass Key. 1945 Roughly Speaking; A Tree Grows in Brooklyn; Boston Blackie Booked on Suspicion; Spellbound. 1947 Betty Co-Ed; Too Many Winners; For the Love of Rusty; Keeper of the Bees. 1949 That Midnight Kiss; On the Town. 1950 Champagne for Caesar. 1951 The Groom Wore Spurs. 1952 She's Working Her Way Through College.

MEAKIN, CHARLES

Born: 1880. Died: Jan. 17, 1961, Hollywood, Calif. Screen and stage actor.

Appeared in: 1921 Maid of the West. 1922 Penrod. 1926 Lightning Bill; The Marriage Clause; Upstage. 1927 Ladies at Ease.

MEAKIN, RUTH

Born: 1879. Died: Nov. 3, 1939, Los Angeles, Calif. Screen and stage actress.

MEARS, BENJAMIN S.

Born: 1872. Died: Jan. 27, 1952, Cliffside, N.J. Screen, stage and vaudeville actor.

MEARS, MARION

Born: 1899. Died: Jan. 26, 1970, Hollywood, Calif. Screen and stage actress. Stand-in for Margaret Lindsay, Hilary Brooks and Natalie Schaefer.

MEECH, EDWARD "MONTANA" (Edward Raymond Meech)

Died: Mar. 2, 1952, Findlay, Ohio. Screen, radio actor and circus performer. Appeared in silents riding horses and performed riding feats.

MEEHAN, JOHN

Born: May 8, 1890, Lindsay, Ontario, Canada. Died: Nov. 12, 1954, Woodland Hills, Calif. Screen, stage actor, playwright, stage director, screenwriter and film director.

MEEHAN, LEW (aka LEW MEAHAN)

Born: 1891. Died: Aug. 10, 1951. Screen actor.

Appeared in: 1921 Crossing Trails. 1922 Blazing Arrows; Daring Danger. 1923 The Greatest Menace. 1924 Ace of the Law; Lightnin' Jack; Man from God's Country; Rainbow Rangers; Ridgeway of Montana; Thundering Romance; Travelin' Fast; Walloping Wallace. 1925 Kit Carson over the Great Divide; Silent Sheldon; Thundering Through; White Thunder. 1926 Beyond All Odds; The Desert's Toll; The Desperate Game; Fighting Luck; Hair Trigger Baxter; Red Blood. 1927 Cactus Trails; The Code of the Range. 1928 King Cowboy; The Sky Rider. 1929 Gun Law; Idaho Red; The Pride of Pawnee; Silent Sentinel; The White Outlaw. 1930 Firebrand Jordan; Hunted Men; Pardon My Gun; South of Sonora; Those Who Dance; Trails of Peril. 1931 Pocatello Kid. 1934 The Lost Jungle (serial). 1935 The Unconquered Bandit. 1936 The Black Coin (serial); The Roarin' Guns. 1937 Melody of the Plains; Gun Lords of

Stirrup Basin; The Red Robe; Arizona Gunfighter; Ridin' the Lone Trail. **1938** Thunder in the Desert.

MEEK, DONALD

Born: July 14, 1880, Glasgow, Scotland. Died: Nov. 18, 1946, Los Angeles, Calif. Stage and screen actor.

Appeared in: **1923** Six Cylinder Love. **1929** The Hole in the Wall. **1930** The Love Kiss. **1931** The Girl Habit; Personal Maid. **1932–33** "S.S. Van Dine" series. **1932** The Babbling Brook (short). **1933** Love, Honor and Oh, Baby!; College Coach. **1934** Hi, Nellie; Bedside; Mrs. Wiggs of the Cabbage Patch; Murder at the Vanities; The Merry Widow; The Last Gentleman; The Defense Rests; The Captain Hates the Sea; Romance in Manhattan. **1935** Biography of a Bachelor Girl; Peter Ibbetson; Happiness C.O.D.; The Whole Town's Talking; The Informer; Only Eight Hours; Village Tale; The Return of Peter Grimm; Old Man Rhythm; The Gilded Lily; Accent on Youth; The Bride Comes Home; Society Doctor; Mark of the Vampire; Baby Face Harrington; Kind Lady; Barbary Coast; She Couldn't Take It; Captain Blood; China Seas; Top Hat. **1936** Everybody's Old Man; And So They Were Married; Pennies from Heaven; One Rainy Afternoon; Three Wise Guys; Old Hutch; Love on the Run; Three Married Men; Two in a Crowd. **1937** Double Wedding; Maid of Salem; Artists and Models; Parnell; Three Legionnaires; Behind the Headlines; The Toast of New York; Make a Wish; Breakfast for Two; You're a Sweetheart. **1938** Double Danger; Having a Wonderful Time; The Adventures of Tom Sawyer; Goodbye Broadway; Little Miss Broadway; Hold That Coed; You Can't Take It with You. **1939** Hollywood Cavalcade; Jesse James; Young Mr. Lincoln; The Housekeeper's Daughter; Blondie Takes a Vacation; Nick Carter—Master Detective; Stagecoach. **1940** Hullabaloo; Oh Johnny, How You Can Love; Dr. Ehrlich's Magic Bullet; The Man from Dakota; Turnabout; Star Dust; Phantom Raiders; The Return of Frank James; Third Finger, Left Hand; Sky Murder; The Ghost Comes Home; My Little Chickadee. **1941** Blonde Inspiration; Come Live with Me; Rise and Shine; Babes on Broadway; A Woman's Face; Wild Man of Borneo; Barnacle Bill; The Feminine Touch. **1942** Tortilla Flat; Maisie Gets Her Man; Seven Sweethearts; The Omaha Trail; Keeper of the Flame. **1943** Air Raid Wardens; They Got Me Covered; Du Barry Was a Lady; Lost Angel; The Honest Thief. **1944** Rationing; Two Girls and a Sailor; Bathing Beauty; Barbary Coast Gent; Maisie Goes to Reno; Thin Man Goes Home. **1945** Colonel Effingham's Raid; State Fair. **1946** Because of Him; Janie Gets Married; Affairs of Geraldine. **1947** The Hal Roach Comedy Carnival; The Fabulous Joe; Magic Town. **1974** That's Entertainment (film clips).

MEEKER, ALFRED

Born: 1901. Died: June 6, 1942, Los Angeles, Calif. (heart attack). Stage and screen actor.

MEHAFFEY, BLANCHE

Born: July 28, 1907, Cincinnati, Ohio. Died: 1968. Stage and screen actress. Married to film producer Ralph M. Like. Was a Wampas Baby Star of 1924.

Appeared in: **1924** The Battling Orioles; The White Sheep. **1925** His People; Proud Heart; A Woman of the World. **1926** The Runaway Express; Take It from Me; The Texas Street. **1927** The Denver Dude; The Princess from Hoboken; The Silent Rider; The Tired Business Man. **1928** The Air Mail Pilot; Marlie the Killer; Finnegan's Ball; Silks and Saddles. **1929** Smilin' Guns. **1930** Medicine Man. **1931** Soul of the Slums; Sunrise Trail; Riders of the North; Dugan of the Bad Lands; Dancing Dynamite; The Sky Spider; Is There Justice?; Mounted Fury. **1932** Sally of the Subway; Alias Mary Smith; Dynamite Denny; Passport to Paradise. **1938** Held for Ransom.

MEHRMANN, HELEN ALICE

Died: Sept. 25, 1934, Oakland, Calif. Stage and screen actress.

Appeared in: **1929** The Shannons on Broadway.

MEIGHAM, MARGARET

Died: Sept. 29, 1961, Chatsworth, Calif. Screen actress. Entered films approx. 1930.

MEIGHAN, THOMAS

Born: Apr. 9, 1879, Pittsburgh, Pa. Died: July 8, 1936, Great Neck, N.Y. Stage and screen actor.

Appeared in: **1914** Dandy Donovan, The Gentleman Cracksman. **1915** The Secret Sin; Kindling; The Fighting Hope; Out of Darkness; Blackbirds; Armstrong's Wife; The Immigrant. **1916** Pudd'nhead Wilson; The Sowers; The Trail of the Lonesome Pine; The Clown; The Dupe; Common Ground; The Storm; The Heir to the Hoorah. **1917** The Land of Promise; The Mysterious Miss Terry; The Slave Market; Sapho; Sleeping Fires; The Silent Partner; Her Better Self; Arms and the Girl. **1918** M'Liss; Out of a Clear Sky; Heart of the Wilds; Her Moment; Madame Jealousy; Eve's Daughter; Missing; In Pursuit of Polly; The Forbidden City; The Heart of Wetona. **1919** The Miracle Man; The Probation Wife; Peg O' My Heart; The Thunderbolt; Male and Female (aka The Admirable Crichton). **1920** Conrad in Quest of His Youth; Why Change Your Wife?; Civilian Clothes; The Prince Chap. **1921** The Easy Road; City of Silent Men; The Frontier of the Stars; White and Unmarried; A Prince

There Was; The Conquest of Canaan; Cappy Ricks. **1922** The Bachelor Daddy; Our Leading Citizen; Back Home and Broke; If You Believe It, It's So; The Man Who Saw Tomorrow; Manslaughter; Hollywood. **1923** The Ne'er-Do-Well; Homeward Bound; Woman Proof. **1924** Pied Piper Malone; Tongues of Flame; The Confidence Man; The Alaskan. **1925** Irish Luck; The Man Who Found Himself; Old Home Week; Coming Through. **1926** Tin Gods; The New Klondike; The Canadian; Fascinating Youth. **1927** We're All Gamblers; The City Gone Wild; Blind Alleys. **1928** The Racket; The Mating Call. **1929** The Argyle Case. **1931** Young Sinners; Skyline. **1932** Madison Square Garden; Cheaters at Play. **1934** Peck's Bad Boy.

MEISTER, OTTO L.

Born: 1869. Died: July 10, 1944, Milwaukee, Wis. Screen, stage and medicine show actor.

Appeared in: **1914** Droppington's Family Tree.

MELACHRINO, GEORGE

Born: 1909. Died: June 18, 1965, London, England. Orchestra leader, screen and television actor.

MELCHIOR, LAURITZ

Born: Mar. 20, 1890, Copenhagen, Denmark. Died: Mar. 18, 1973, Santa Monica, Calif. (following gall bladder operation). Opera tenor, screen, stage, radio and television actor. Married to actress Maria Hacker (dec. 1963) and later married and divorced Mary Markham.

Appeared in: **1945** Thrill of a Romance. **1946** Two Sisters from Boston. **1947** This Time for Keeps. **1948** Luxury Liner. **1953** The Stars are Singing.

MELESH, ALEX (Alexander Melesher)

Born: Oct. 21, 1890, Kiev, Russia. Died: Mar. 5, 1949, Hollywood, Calif. Stage and screen actor.

Appeared in: **1928** His Private Life; The Adventurer. **1929** Charming Sinners. **1932** The Big Broadcast. **1933** Girl without a Room. **1938** Golden Boy; Artists and Models Abroad. **1939** Paris Honeymoon; On Your Toes. **1940** Beyond Tomorrow. **1942** Once upon a Honeymoon. **1943** A Lady Takes a Chance. **1948** The Fuller Brush Man.

MELFORD, GEORGE

Born: Rochester, N.Y. Died: Apr. 25, 1961, Hollywood, Calif. (heart attack). Screen, stage actor and film director. Married to actress Louise Melford (dec. 1942). Entered films as an actor with Kalem.

Appeared in: **1933** The Cowboy Counselor; Officer 13. **1939** Ambush; Rulers of the Sea. **1940** My Little Chickadee; Safari; Brigham Young, Frontiersman. **1941** Robbers of the Range; Flying Cadets. **1942** That Other Woman; Lone Star Ranger. **1943** Dixie Dugan. **1944** The Miracle of Morgan's Creek; Hail the Conquering Hero. **1945** Col. Effingham's Raid; Diamond Horseshoe; A Tree Grows in Brooklyn. **1946** Strange Triangle. **1948** Call Northside 777. **1953** A Blueprint for Murder; City of Bad Men; President's Lady; The Robe. **1954** The Egyptian; There's No Business Like Show Business; Woman's World. **1955** Prince of Players. **1956** The Ten Commandments. **1960** Bluebeard's Ten Honeymoons.

MELFORD, LOUISE

Born: 1880. Died: Nov. 15, 1942, North Hollywood, Calif. Stage and screen actress. Married to actor and film director George Melford (dec. 1961).

MELGAREJO, JESUS

Born: 1876, Mexico. Died: Dec. 29, 1941, Mexico City, Mexico. Stage and screen actor.

MELIES, GEORGES

Born: Dec. 8, 1861, Paris, France. Died: Jan. 21, 1938, Paris, France. Film director, producer and screen actor. Was one of the pioneers of the French cinema.

Appeared in: **1902** A Trip to the Moon. **1905** Rip's Dream.

MELLER, HARRO

Born: 1907. Died: Dec. 26, 1963, New York, N.Y. Screen actor and playwright.

Appeared in: **1945** The House on 92nd Street; Counter-Attack. **1946** A Night in Casablanca. **1947** Jewels of Brandenburg.

MELLER, RAQUEL

Born: 1888, Madrid, Spain. Died: July 26, 1962, Barcelona, Spain. Screen actress and singer. Appeared in U.S. films during the 1920s.

Appeared in: **1928** Carmen; La Veneosa; Violette Imperiale (The Imperial Violet). **1929** The Oppressed. **1935** La Viletera. Other foreign films: The Promised Land; The White Gypsy.

MELLINGER, MAX (Maxon Mellinger)

Born: Mar. 18, 1906, Oregon. Died: Feb. 25, 1968, Burbank, Calif. (lung cancer). Screen actor.

Appeared in: **1960** I Passed for White. **1961** When the Clock Strikes; You Have to Run Fast; Return to Peyton Place; Secret of Deep Harbor. **1962** Incident in an Alley; Saintly Sinners.

MELLISH, FULLER, JR.

Born: 1895. Died: Feb. 8, 1930, Forest Hills, N.Y. (cerebral hemorrhage). Stage and screen actor. Son of stage actor Fuller Mellish, Sr. (dec. 1936) and stage actress Mrs. Fuller Mellish, Sr. (dec. 1950). Married to stage actress Olive Reeves-Smith (dec. 1972).

Appeared in: **1921** Diane of Star Hollow; The Land of Hope; The Scarab Ring; The Single Track. **1923** Sinner or Saint. **1924** Two Shall Be Born. **1929** Applause. **1930** Sarah and Son. **1934** Crime without Passion.

MELTON, FRANK

Born: Dec. 6, 1907, Pineapple, Ala. Died: Mar. 19, 1951, Hollywood, Calif. (heart attack). Screen actor.

Appeared in: **1933** Cavalcade; State Fair; Mr. Skitch; Ace of Aces. **1934** The White Parade; 365 Nights in Hollywood; Stand up and Cheer; David Harum; Handy Andy; Judge Priest; The World Moves On. **1935** The County Chairman; $10 Raise; The Daring Young Man; Welcome Home. **1936** The Return of Jimmy Valentine; The Glory Trail; They Met in a Taxi. **1937** Outcast; Too Many Wives; The Affairs of Cappy Ricks; Damaged Goods; Wild and Wooly; Trouble at Midnight. **1938** Riders of the Black Hills; Freshman Year; Marriage Forbidden. **1939** Big Town Czar; Cat and the Canary. **1940** Second Chorus. **1941** Pot O' Gold; They Meet Again; Tanks a Million. **1942** The Loves of Edgar Allan Poe; To the Shores of Tripoli; Wrecking Crew. **1945** It's a Pleasure. **1946** Do You Love Me?

MELTON, JAMES

Born: Jan. 2, 1905, Moultrie, Ga. Died: Apr. 21, 1961, New York, N.Y. (pneumonia). Screen, stage, radio actor and opera performer.

Appeared in: **1934** Song Hit Stories (short). **1935** Stars Over Broadway. **1936** Sing Me a Love Song. **1937** Melody for Two. **1946** Ziegfeld Follies.

MELVILLE, EMILIE

Born: 1852. Died: May 19, 1932, San Francisco, Calif. Stage and screen actress. Daughter of stage actress Julie Miles (dec.).

Appeared in: **1929** Illusion.

MELVILLE, ROSE

Born: Jan. 30, 1873, Terre Haute, Ind. Died: Oct. 8, 1946. Screen, stage and vaudeville actress. Married to actor Frank Minzey (dec. 1949). They appeared in early Biograph and Keystone films and later in shorts produced by Fox, Goldwyn, etc.

Appeared in: **1916** She Came, She Saw, She Conquered; Leap Year Wooing; A Flock of Skeletons; When Things Go Wrong; A Double Barreled Courtship; Almost a Heroine; Romance and Riot; A Lunch Room Legacy; An Innocent Vampire; A Baby Grand; The Dumb Heiress; Sis the Detective; Juggling Justice; Her Great Invention; A Lucky Mistake; Setting the Fashion; The Wishing Ring; The Psychic Phenomenon; A Double Elopement.

MENAHAN, JEAN

Died: 1963. Stage and screen actress. Mother of actress Eileen Brennan.

Appeared in: **1927** The Jazz Singer.

MENARD, MICHAEL M.

Born: 1898. Died: Apr. 27, 1949, Los Angeles, Calif. Screen actor.

MENDEL, JULES

Born: 1875. Died: Mar. 17, 1938, Los Angeles, Calif. Stage and screen actor.

MENDELSSOHN, ELEONORA

Born: 1900. Died: Jan. 24, 1951, New York, N.Y. (suicide—pills). Stage and screen actress.

Appeared in: **1950** The Black Hand.

MENDES, JOHN PRINCE

Born: 1919. Died: Sept. 30, 1955, New York, N.Y. Screen, stage, television actor and magician.

Appeared in: **1943** This Is Your Army (stage and film versions).

MENDES, LOTHAR

Born: May 19, 1894, Berlin, Germany. Died: Feb. 25, 1974, London, England. Film producer, director, author, stage and screen actor.

MENDOZA, HARRY

Born: 1905. Died: Feb. 15, 1970, Houston, Tex. (heart ailment). Screen actor and magician.

MENHART, ALFRED

Born: 1899, Germany. Died: Nov. 14, 1955, Munich, Germany (following surgery). Screen actor.

Appeared in: The Major and the Steers.

MENJOU, ADOLPHE

Born: Feb. 18, 1890, Pittsburgh, Pa. Died: Oct. 29, 1963, Beverly Hills, Calif. (chronic hepatitis). Screen, stage and television actor. Divorced from actress Kathryn Carver (dec. 1947). Married to actress Veree Tinsley.

Appeared in: **1916** Blue Envelope. **1917** The Amazons; The Valentine Girl; The Moth. **1921** The Sheik; Courage; The Three Musketeers; Queenie; Through the Back Door; Kiss; The Faith Healer. **1922** The Eternal Flame; The Fast Mail; Head over Heels; Is Matrimony a Failure?; Pink Gods; Singed Wings. **1923** A Woman of Paris; Rupert of Hentzau; The World's Applause; The Spanish Dancer; Bella Donna. **1924** Broadway after Dark; Broken Barriers; The Fast Set; The Marriage Circle; For Sale; Shadows of Paris; The Marriage Cheat; Open All Night; Sinners in Silk. **1925** Are Parents People?; The King on Main Street; A Kiss in the Dark; Lost—a Wife; The Swan. **1926** The Grand Duchess and the Waiter; The Sorrows of Satan; A Social Celebrity; The Ace of Cads; Fascinating Youth. **1927** Blonde or Brunette; Service for Ladies; Serenade; A Gentleman of Paris; Evening Clothes. **1928** His Private Life; The Tiger Lady; A Night of Mystery. **1929** Marquis Preferred; Fashions in Love; Bachelor Girl; The Kiss (and 1921 version). **1930** Morocco; New Moon; Mon Gosse de Pere; L'Enigmatique Monsieur Parkes. **1931** Easiest Way; Men Call It Love; The Great Lover; The Front Page; Friends and Lovers; The Marriage Interlude; The Parisian. **1932** Prestige; The Man from Yesterday; Two White Arms; Diamond Cut Diamond (aka Blame the Woman—US); Bachelor's Affair; Forbidden; A Farewell to Arms; The Night Club Lady. **1933** Convention City; Morning Glory; The Circus Queen Murder; The Worst Woman in Paris? **1934** The Trumpet Blows; Little Miss Marker; Journal of a Crime; Easy to Love; The Great Flirtation; The Human Side; The Mighty Barnum. **1935** Broadway Gondolier; Gold Diggers of 1935. **1936** The Milky Way; Wives Never Know; One in a Million; Sing, Baby, Sing! **1937** One Hundred Men and a Girl; A Star Is Born; Stage Door; Cafe Metropole. **1938** The Goldwyn Follies; Thanks for Everything; Letter of Introduction. **1939** Golden Boy; That's Right, You're Wrong; The Housekeeper's Daughter; King of the Turf. **1940** A Bill of Divorcement; Turnabout. **1941** Road Show; Father Takes a Wife. **1942** Roxie Hart; Syncopation; You Were Never Lovelier. **1943** Sweet Rosie O'Grady; Hi Diddle Diddle. **1944** Step Lively. **1945** Man Alive. **1946** The Bachelor's Daughter; Heartbeat. **1947** I'll Be Yours; Mr. District Attorney; The Hucksters. **1948** State of the Union. **1949** My Dream Is Yours; Dancing in the Dark. **1950** To Please a Lady. **1951** Across the Wide Missouri; The Tall Target. **1952** The Sniper. **1953** Man on a Tightrope. **1955** Timberjack. **1956** Bundle of Joy; Ambassador's Daughter. **1957** The Fuzzy Pink Nightgown; Paths of Glory. **1958** I Married a Woman. **1960** Pollyanna.

MENKEN, HELEN

Born: 1902, New York. Died: Mar. 27, 1966, New York, N.Y. (heart attack). Screen, stage and radio actress. Divorced from actor Humphrey Bogart (dec. 1957).

Appeared in: **1943** Stage Door Canteen.

MENKEN, MARIE

Born: 1909. Died: Dec. 1970, Brooklyn, N.Y. Screen actress.

Appeared in: **1965** The Life of Juanita Castro. **1966** The Chelsea Girls. **1969** Diaries, Notes and Sketches.

MERA, EDITH

Born: France. Died: Feb. 24, 1935, Paris, France (anthrax). Stage and screen actress. Had appeared in French and U.S. films.

Appeared in: **1931** Le Culte de Beaute; Un Soire de Rafle. **1932** Miche. **1933** Les Trois Mousquetaires (The Three Musketeers). **1935** Criez-Le Sur les Toits (Shout It from the Housetops). **1937** Grandeur et Decadence.

MERANDE, DORO (Dora Matthews)

Born: c. 1970, Columbia, Kans. Died: Nov. 1, 1975, Miami, Fla. (massive stroke). Screen, stage and television actress.

Appeared in: **1931** Front Page (stage and film versions). **1940** Our Town. **1949** Cover Up. **1951** The Whistle at Eaton Falls (stage and film versions). **1955** The Man with the Golden Arm; The Seven Year Itch. **1959** The Remarkable Mr. Pennypacker; The Gazebo. **1963** The Cardinal. **1964** Kiss Me Stupid. **1966** The Russians Are Coming, The Russians Are Coming. **1967** Hurry Sundown. **1968** Skidoo. **1969** Change of Habit.

MERCER, BERYL

Born: 1882, Seville, Spain. Died: July 28, 1939, Santa Monica, Calif. Stage and screen actress.

Appeared in: **1916** The Final Curtain. **1922** Broken Chains. **1923** Christian. **1928** We Americans. **1929** Mother's Boy; Three Live Ghosts. **1930** In Gay Madrid; All Quiet on the Western Front; Dumbells in Ermine; Common Clay;

The Matrimonial Bed; Outward Bound; Seven Days Leave. **1931** East Lynne; The Public Enemy; Inspiration; Always Goodbye; Merely Mary Ann; The Miracle Woman; The Man in Possession; Are These Our Children?; Sky Spider. **1932** The Devil's Lottery; Forgotten Women; Lovers Courageous; Lena Rivers; Young America; No Greater Love; Unholy Love; Smilin' Through; Six Hours to Live; Midnight Morals. **1933** Cavalcade; Berkeley Square; Her Splendid Folly; Broken Dreams; Blind Adventure; Supernatural. **1934** Change of Heart; The Little Minister; Jane Eyre; Richest Girl in the World. **1935** Age of Indiscretion; My Marriage; Hitch Hike Lady; Magnificent Obsession; Three Live Ghosts (and 1929 version). **1936** Forbidden Heaven. **1937** Call It a Day; Night Must Fall. **1939** The Hound of the Baskervilles; The Little Princess; A Woman Is the Judge.

MERCER, TONY
Born: 1922. Died: July 14, 1973, London, England (heart complaint). Screen actor and singer.

Appeared in: **1956** Davy Crockett and the River Pirates. **1963** It's All Happening (aka The Dream Maker—US 1964).

MEREDITH, CHARLES
Born: 1894, Knoxville, Pa. Died: Nov. 28, 1964, Los Angeles, Calif. Screen, stage and television actor.

Appeared in: **1919** Luck in Pawn. **1920** Simple Souls. **1921** The Beautiful Liar; Beyond; The Cave Girl; The Foolish Matrons; Hail The Woman; That Something. **1922** The Cradle; Woman, Wake Up! **1924** In Hollywood with Potash and Perlmutter. **1947** Daisy Kenyon. **1948** The Boy with the Green Hair; They Live By Night (aka The Twisted Road and Your Red Wagon); All My Sons; A Foreign Affair; The Miracle of the Bells; For the Love of Mary. **1949** Tokyo Joe; Francis; The Lady Takes a Sailor. **1950** Perfect Strangers; The Sun Sets at Dawn; Counterspy Meets Scotland Yard. **1951** Al Jennings of Oklahoma; Along the Great Divide; Submarine Command. **1952** The Big Trees; Cattle Town. **1953** So This Is Love. **1956** The Lone Ranger; The Birds and the Bees. **1957** Chicago Confidential. **1958** The Buccaneer. **1960** Twelve Hours to Kill. **1962** Be Careful How You Wish (U.S. 1964). **1964** The Incredible Mr. Limpet; The Quick Gun.

MEREDITH, CHEERIO
Born: 1890. Died: Dec. 25, 1964, Woodland Hills, Calif. Screen and television actress.

Appeared in: **1958** The Case against Brooklyn; I Married a Woman. **1959** The Legend of Tom Dooley. **1962** The Wonderful World of the Brothers Grimm; The Three Stooges in Orbit.

MEREDYTH, BESS (Helen MacGlashan)
Born: Buffalo, N.Y. Died: July 6, 1969, Woodland Hills, Calif. Screen actress and screenwriter. Entered films as an extra with Biograph in 1911.

Appeared in: **1914** The Magnet; Bess the Detectress, or the Old Mill at Midnight; When Bess Got in Wrong; Her Twin Brother; The Little Auto-Go-Mobile; Father's Bride; Willie Walrus and the Awful Confession. **1916** A Sailor's Heart.

MERIVALE, PHILIP
Born: Nov. 2, 1880, Rehutia, Manickpur, India. Died: Mar. 1946, Los Angeles, Calif. (heart ailment). Screen and stage actor. Married to actress Viva Birkett (dec. 1934) and later married to actress Gladys Cooper (dec. 1971). Entered films during silents.

Appeared in: **1933** I Loved You Wednesday. **1935** The Passing of the Third Floor Back. **1936** Give Us This Night. **1941** Midnight Angel; Rage in Heaven; Mr. and Mrs. Smith; Lady for a Night. **1942** Crossroads; This above All; Pacific Blackout. **1943** This Land Is Mine. **1944** Lost Angel; Nothing but Trouble; The Hour before Dawn. **1945** Adventure; Tonight and Every Night. **1946** Sister Kenny; The Stranger.

MERKYL, WILMUTH
Born: Jan. 2, 1885, Iowa. Died: May 1, 1954, Los Angeles, Calif. (coronary occlusion). Screen actor.

Appeared in: **1915** Gretna Green; Wife for Wife; The Price; The Victory of Virtue; The Fortunate Youth; The Soul Maker. **1916** Her Surrender. **1918** Fedora; Let's Get a Divorce.

MERRILL, FRANK
Born: 1894. Died: Feb. 12, 1966, Hollywood, Calif. Screen actor. Fifth actor to play Tarzan.

Appeared in: **1921** The Adventures of Tarzan (serial) **1924** Battling Mason; A Fighting Heart; Reckless Speed. **1925** Dashing Thru; A Gentleman Roughneck; Savages of the Sea; Shackled Lightning; Speed Madness. **1926** Cupid's Knockout; The Fighting Doctor; The Hollywood Reporter; Unknown Dangers. **1927** Perils of the Jungle (serial). **1928** Tarzan the Mighty (serial); The Little Wild Girl. **1929** Below the Deadline; Tarzan the Tiger (serial).

MERRILL, LOUIS "LOU"
Born: 1911. Died: Apr. 7, 1963, Hollywood, Calif. Screen and television actor.

Appeared in: **1939** Tropic Fury. **1940** Kit Carson. **1948** The Lady from Shanghai. **1953** Charge of the Lancers; The Hindu (aka Sabaka—US 1955). **1955** The Crooked Web. **1957** The Giant Claw. **1961** The Devil at 4 O'Clock.

MERTON, COLLETTE (Collette Helene Mazzoletti)
Born: Mar. 7, 1907, New Orleans, La. Died: July 24, 1968, Hollywood, Calif. Screen actress. Appeared in three of the "Collegians" series prior to 1929.

Appeared in: **1929** Clear the Decks; Walking Back; Why Be Good; King of the Campus; The Godless Girl.

MERTON, JOHN (John Merton La Varre)
Born: 1901. Died: Sept. 19, 1959, Los Angeles, Calif. (heart attack). Stage and screen actor. Father of actor Robert Lavarre and Lane Bradford (dec. 1973).

Appeared in: **1934** Sons of the Desert. **1935** The Eagle's Brood; Bar 20 Rides Again. **1936** Call of the Prairie; Aces and Eights; The Three Mesquiteers. **1937** Drums of Destiny; Range Defenders; Colorado Kid; Federal Bullets. **1938** Female Fugitive; Two Gun Justice; Where the Buffalo Roam; Gang Bullets; Knight of the Plains; Dick Tracy Returns (serial). **1939** The Renegade Trail; Code of the Fearless. **1940** Melody Ranch; Drums of Fu Manchu; Hi-Yo Silver; Covered Wagon Days; The Trail Blazers; Lone Star Raiders; Frontier Crusader; Queen of the Yukon. **1941** Under Fiesta Stars. **1942** Billy the Kid's Smoking Guns; Law and Order. **1943** Frontier Marshal in Prairie Pals; Mysterious Rider. **1944** Mystery Man; Texas Masquerade; Girl Rush. **1946** The Gay Cavalier. **1947** Cheyenne Takes Over; Jack Armstrong (serial); Brick Bradford (serial). **1949** Riders of the Dusk; Thieves Highway; Western Renegades. **1950** Marinated Mariner (short); Arizona Territory; Bandit Queen; Border Rangers; Fence Riders; West of Wyoming. **1951** Silver Canyon; Gold Raiders; Man from Sonora. **1952** The Old West; Blue Canadian Rockies. **1953** Up In Daisy's Penthouse (short); Saginaw Trail. **1956** The Ten Commandments.

MESKIN, AHARON
Born: 1897, Russia. Died: Nov. 11, 1974, Tel Aviv, Israel (heart attack). Stage and screen actor. Father of actor and director Amon Meskin.

Appeared in: **1934** Chalutzin. **1965** Shnei Kuni Lemel (The Flying Matchmaker—US 1970).

MESSENGER, BUDDY (Melvin Joe Messinger)
Born: Oct. 26, 1909, San Francisco, Calif. Died: Oct. 25, 1965, Hollywood, Calif. Stage and screen actor. Son of actress Josephine Messenger (dec. 1968) and brother of actress Gertrude Messenger.

Appeared in: **1917** Aladdin and His Wonderful Lamp; Treasure Island. **1919** The Hoodlum; Fighting Joe. **1921** The Old Nest. **1922** The Flirt; A Front Page Story; Shadows; When Love Comes. **1923** The Abysmal Brute; Penrod and Sam; Trifling with Honor. **1924** The Whispered Name; Young Ideas; Buddy Messenger Comedies (shorts) including: All for a Girl; Breaking into the Movies; The Homing Birds. **1928** Undressed. **1929** A Lady of Chance; Hot Stuff. **1930** Cheer up and Smile. **1934** Most Precious Thing in Life. **1936** All American Toothache (short); College Holiday; Our Relations.

MESSINGER, JOSEPHINE
Born: 1885. Died: Mar. 3, 1968, Calif. Screen actress. Mother of actress Gertrude and actor Buddy Messenger (dec. 1965). Appeared in silent films.

MESSITER, ERIC
Born: 1892. Died: Sept. 13, 1960, London, England (heart attack). Stage and screen actor.

Appeared in: **1949** Kind Hearts and Coronets (US 1950). **1951** The Mudlark.

MESTEL, JACOB
Born: 1884, Poland. Died: Aug. 5, 1958, New York, N.Y. Screen, stage, television actor, stage director and screenwriter.

Appeared in: **1933** The Wandering Jew. **1939** Mirele Efros. **1949** A Vilna Legend.

METAXA, GEORGES
Born: Sept. 11, 1899, Bucharest, Romania. Died: Dec. 8, 1950, Monroe, La. Stage and screen actor.

Appeared in: **1931** Secrets of a Secretary. **1936** Swing Time. **1940** Submarine Base; The Doctor Takes a Wife. **1942** Paris Calling. **1943** Hi Diddle Diddle. **1944** The Mask of Dimitrios. **1945** Scotland Yard Investigator.

METCALF, EARL
Born: 1889, Newport, Ky. Died: Jan. 1928, Burbank, Calif. (flying accident—fell from plane). Stage and screen actor. Entered films with Vitagraph.

Appeared in: **1915** The Insurrection. **1916** Perils of Our Girl Reporters (serial). **1920** Deadline at Eleven. **1921** Eden and Return; Mother Eternal; What Woman Will Do. **1922** White Eagle (serial); The New Teacher; While Justice Waits; Back to Yellow Jacket; The Great Night; Ignorance; The Power of a

Lie. **1923** The Lone Wagon; Skid Proof; Look Your Best. **1924** The Courageous Coward; Fair Week; The Valley of Hate; The Silent Accuser; Silk Stocking Sal; Surging Seas. **1925** The Man without a Country; Ship of Souls; Kit Carson over the Great Divide. **1926** Atta Boy; Love's Blindness; The Midnight Message; The Midnight Sun; The Mystery Club; Partners Again; Buffalo Bill on the U.P. Trail; The Call of the Klondike; The High Flyer; Remember; Sin Cargo. **1927** King of Kings; Night Life; Daring Deeds; The Devil's Saddle; The Notorious Lady. **1928** The Air Mail Pilot; Eagle of the Night (serial).

METCALFE, JAMES S.
Born: 1901. Died: Apr. 2, 1960, Northridge, Calif. (heart attack). Stage and screen actor.

Appeared in: **1942** The Hard Way; Who Is Hope Schuyler?; A Gentleman at Heart.

METHOT, MAYO
Born: 1904, Portland, Ore. Died: June 9, 1951, Portland, Ore. Stage and screen actress. Divorced from actor Humphrey Bogart (dec. 1957).

Appeared in: **1930** Taxi Talks (short). **1931** Corsair; Squaring the Triangle (short). **1932** The Night Club Lady; Virtue; Vanity Street; Afraid to Talk. **1933** The Mind Reader; Lilly Turner; Counsellor-at-Law. **1934** Jimmy the Gent; Goodbye Love; Harold Teen; Side Streets; Registered Nurse. **1935** Mills of the Gods; The Case of the Curious Bride; Dr. Socrates. **1936** Mr. Deeds Goes to Town; The Case against Mrs. Ames. **1937** Marked Woman. **1938** Women in Prison; The Sisters; Numbered Woman. **1939** Unexpected Father; A Woman Is the Judge; Should a Girl Marry? **1940** Brother Rat and a Baby.

METZ, ALBERT
Born: 1886. Died: Aug. 20, 1940, North Hollywood, Calif. Stage and screen actor.

METZ, OTTO
Born: 1891. Died: Feb. 1, 1949, Hollywood, Calif. Screen, vaudeville actor and stunt flyer.

METZETTI, VICTOR
Born: 1895. Died: Aug. 21, 1949, Los Angeles, Calif. (pneumonia). Screen actor, circus performer and stuntman.

Appeared in: **1922** Putting It Over. **1924** Stepping Lively. **1927** Bulldog Pluck. **1950** The Border Outlaws.

MEYER, FREDERIC
Born: 1910. Died: Sept. 16, 1973, en route from Mt. Gretna, Pa. to New York, N.Y. (heart attack). Screen, stage, vaudeville actor and stage director. Married to actress Catheleen Claypool.

MEYER, HYMAN "HY"
Born: 1875, San Francisco, Calif. Died: Oct. 7, 1945, Hollywood, Calif. Screen and vaudeville actor.

Appeared in: **1929** The Saturday Night Kid. **1934** Judge Priest.

MEYER, TORBEN
Born: Dec. 1, 1884, Copenhagen, Denmark. Died: May 22, 1975, Hollywood, Calif. (bronchial pneumonia). Screen and stage actor.

Appeared in: **1927** The Man Who Laughs. **1928** Jazz Mad; The Viking. **1929** Behind Closed Doors; The Last Warning. **1930** Just Like Heaven; Lummox; Mamba. **1933** The Crime of the Century. **1934** Pursued. **1935** Enter Madam; The Girl Who Came Back; Splendor; East of Java; Roberta; Black Room Mystery; The Man Who Broke the Bank at Monte Carlo. **1936** Till We Meet Again; Anything Goes. **1937** Thin Ice; The King and the Chorus Girl; The Prisoner of Zenda; Tovarich. **1938** Romance in the Dark; Bulldog Drummond's Peril; The First Hundred Years. **1939** Topper Takes a Trip. **1940** Four Sons; Christmas in July. **1941** Sunny. **1942** Sullivan's Travels; Berlin Correspondent; Palm Beach Story. **1943** Edge of Darkness; Jack London. **1944** The Purple Heart; Hail the Conquering Hero; The Miracle of Morgan's Creek; The Great Moment; Greenwich Village. **1945** Hotel Berlin. **1946** Mad Wednesday (aka Sin of Harold Diddlebock); The Mighty McGurk. **1947** Alias Mr. Twilight. **1948** Unfaithfully Yours. **1949** The Beautiful Blonde from Bashful Bend. **1952** What Price Glory? **1953** Call Me Madam. **1954** Living It Up. **1955** We're No Angels. **1956** Anything Goes (rerelease of 1936 film). **1958** The Matchmaker; The Fly. **1961** Judgment at Nuremberg.

MEYN, ROBERT
Born: 1896, Germany? Died: Mar. 3, 1972, Hamburg, Germany. Stage and screen actor.

Appeared in: **1954** Sunderin. **1956** Teufel in Seide (Devil in Silk—US 1968). **1957** The Last Bridge. **1959** Kriegsgericht (Court Martial—US 1962). **1960** Der Rest Ist Schweigen (The Rest is Silence).

MICHAEL, GERTRUDE
Born: June 1, 1911, Talladega, Ala. Died: Dec. 31, 1964, Beverly Hills, Calif. Screen, stage and television actress. She was heroine of "Sophie Lang" series.

Appeared in: **1932** Wayward; Unashamed. **1933** A Bedtime Story; Night of Terror; Ann Vickers; Sailor Be Good; Cradle Song; I'm No Angel. **1934** She Was a Lady; Murder on the Blackboard; Notorious Sophie Lang; Murder at the Vanities; Menace; George White's Scandals; I Believed in You; Search for Beauty; Hold That Girl; Bolero; Cleopatra; The Witching Hour. **1935** Father Brown, Detective; It Happened in New York; Four Hours to Kill; The Last Outpost; Protegees. **1936** Woman Trap; The Return of Sophie Lang; Make Way for a Lady; Second Wife; 'Til We Meet Again. **1937** Sins of the Fathers; Mr. Dodd Takes the Air; Sophie Lang Goes West; Just Like a Woman. **1939** Hidden Power. **1940** The Farmer's Daughter; The Hidden Menace; Pound Foolish (short); I Can't Give You Anything but Love, Baby; Parole Fixer; Slightly Tempted. **1942** Prisoner of Japan. **1943** Behind Prison Walls; Where Are Your Children?; Women in Bondage. **1944** Faces in the Fog. **1945** Three's a Crowd; Club Havana; Allotment Wives. **1948** That Wonderful Urge. **1949** Flamingo Road. **1950** Caged. **1951** Darling, How Could You? **1952** Bugles in the Afternoon. **1953** No Escape. **1955** Women's Prison. **1961** The Outsider. **1962** Twist All Night.

MICHAEL, MICKIE
Born: 1943. Died: Nov. 18, 1973, Hollywood, Calif. (auto accident). Stage and screen actress. Married to cinematographer Jim Childs.

MICHAELS, SULLY
Born: 1917. Died: Jan. 4, 1966, New York, N.Y. Screen, stage and television actor.

Appeared in: **1959** The Last Mile.

MICHEL, GASTON
Born: 1856, France? Died: Nov. 1921, Lisbon, Portugal. Screen actor.

Appeared in: **1922** L'Orpheline (The Orphan).

MICHELENA, BEATRICE (Beatriz Michelena)
Born: 1890. Died: Oct. 10, 1942, San Francisco, Calif. Stage and screen actress. Sister of actress Vera Michelena (dec. 1961). Entered films in 1913.

Appeared in: **1914** Salomy Jane. **1915** Mignon.

MICHELENA, VERA
Born: 1884. Died: Aug. 26, 1961, Bayside, N.Y. Screen, stage and vaudeville actress. Sister of actress Beatrice Michelena (dec. 1942).

MIDDLEMASS, ROBERT M.
Born: Sept. 3, 1885, New Britain, Conn. Died: Sept. 1949, Los Angeles, Calif. Screen, stage, vaudeville actor, playwright and author.

Appeared in: **1934** Hotel Anchovy (short). **1935** Air Hawks; Awakening of Jim Burke; After the Dance; Unknown Woman; Atlantic Adventure; Public Menace; Grand Exit; One Way Ticket; Superspeed; Too Tough to Kill; Air Fury. **1936** You May be Next; F-Man; The Lone Wolf Returns; Muss 'Em Up; Nobody's Fool; Two Against the World; A Son Comes Home; The Case of the Velvet Claws; Cain and Mabel; General Spanky; Hats Off; Grand Jury. **1937** Hideaway Girl; Guns of the Pecos; A Day at the Races; Meet the Boy Friend; Navy, Blue and Gold. **1938** When New York Sleeps; Miracle Money (short); Blondes at Work; Highway Patrol; Spawn of the North; I Am the Law; Kentucky; I Stand Accused. **1939** Stanley and Livingstone; Indianapolis Speedway; Blondie Brings Up Baby; Stand Up and Fight; The Magnificent Fraud; Coast Guard. **1940** The Saint Takes Over; Little Old New York; Slightly Dishonorable; Pop Always Pays. **1941** No Hands on the Clock; Road to Zanzibar. **1943** Truck Busters. **1944** Lady in the Death House; Wilson. **1945** A Sporting Chance; The Dolly Sisters.

MIDDLETON, CHARLES B.
Born: Oct. 3, 1879, Elizabethtown, Ky. Died: Apr. 22, 1949, Los Angeles, Calif. Screen, stage, circus and vaudeville actor. Entered films in 1927. Best remembered as "Ming the Merciless" in the "Flash Gordon" serials. Married to actress Leora Spellman (dec. 1945) with whom he appeared in vaudeville as "Middleton and Spellmeyer."

Appeared in: **1928** A Man of Peace (short); The Farmer's Daughter. **1929** Bellamy Trail; The Far Call; Welcome Danger. **1930** Beau Bandit; Way Out West; The Frame (short); Christmas Knight (short); East Is West; More Sinned against Than Usual (short). **1931** An American Tragedy; Beau Hunks (short); Full of Notions; Ships of Hate; Caught Plastered; Miracle Woman; Palmy Days; Alexander Hamilton. **1932** The Sign of the Cross; High Pressure; The Hatchet Man; Manhattan Parade; Strange Love of Molly Louvain; Pack Up Your Troubles; Hell's Highway; Silver Dollar; Rockabye; Breach of Promise; Mystery Ranch; Kongo. **1933** Pickup; Destination Unknown; Tomorrow at Seven; Sunset Pass; Disgraced; This Day and Age; Big Executive; White Woman; Duck Soup. **1934** When Strangers Meet; Lone Cowboy; Last Round Up; Murder at the Vanities; Behold My Wife; Massacre; David Harum; Mrs. Wiggs of the Cabbage Patch. **1935** Special Agent; The Fixer-Uppers (short);

Steamboat 'Round the Bend; The Miracle Rider (serial); County Chairman; Hopalong Cassidy; Square Shooter; In Spite of Danger; Red Morning; The Virginia Judge. **1936** Texas Rangers; Space Soldiers; Sunset of Power; Road Gang; The Trail of the Lonesome Pine; Flash Gordon (serial); Showboat; Empty Saddles; Song of the Saddle; Jail Break; A Son Comes Home; Career Woman. **1937** Two-Gun Law; We're on the Jury; Hollywood Cowboy; Yodelin' Kid from Pine Ridge. **1938** Flash Gordon's Trip to Mars (serial aka Mars Attacks the World); Flaming Frontiers (serial); Dick Tracy Returns (serial); Outside the Law; Kentucky. **1939** Captain Fury; Blackmail; Daredevils of the Red Circle (serial); Wyoming Outlaw; Slave Ship; Cowboys from Texas; Juarez; Way down South; $1,000 a Touchdown; One Against the World (short); Jesse James; The Flying Deuces; The Oklahoma Kid. **1940** Thou Shalt Not Kill; Charlie Chan's Murder Cruise; Virginia City; Flash Gordon Conquers the Universe (serial); Chad Hanna; Abe Lincoln in Illinois; The Grapes of Wrath; Shooting High; Santa Fe; Island of Doomed Men. **1941** Western Union; Wild Geese Calling; Belle Starr; Wild Bill Hickok Rides; Jungle Man. **1942** The Mystery of Marie Roget; Men of San Quentin. **1943** The Black Raven; Two Weeks to Live. **1944** The Sign of the Cross (revised version of 1932 film); The Town Went Wild. **1945** Our Vines Have Tender Grapes; Hollywood and Vine; Captain Kidd; How Do You Do. **1946** Spook Busters; Strangler of the Swamp. **1947** The Pretender. **1948** Station West; Jiggs and Maggie in Court. **1949** The Last Bandit; The Black Arrow.

MIDDLETON, GUY

Born: Dec. 14, 1908, Hove, England. Died: July 30, 1973, near London, England. Screen, stage and television actor.

Appeared in: **1935** Jimmy Boy; Two Hearts in Harmony; Trust the Navy. **1936** Under Proof; A Woman Alone (aka Two Who Dared—US 1937); The Mysterious Mr. Davis (aka My Partner Mr. Davis); Gay Adventure; Fame. **1937** Keep Fit; Take a Chance. **1938** Break the News (US 1941). **1939** French Without Tears (US 1940); Goodbye, Mr. Chips. **1940** For Freedom. **1941** Dangerous Moonlight (aka Suicide Squadron—US 1942). **1942** Talk About Jacqueline. **1943** The Demi-Paradise (aka Adventure for Two—US 1945). **1944** Halfway House (US 1945); Champagne Charlie; English Without Tears (aka Her Man Gilbey—US 1949). **1945** The Rake's Progress (aka Notorious Gentleman—US 1946); 29 Acacia Avenue (aka The Facts of Love—US 1949). **1946** The Captive Heart (US 1947); Night Boat to Dublin. **1947** The White Unicorn (aka Bad Sister—US 1948); A Man About the House (US 1949). **1948** Snowbound (US 1949); One Night With You. **1949** Marry Me (US 1951); Once Upon a Dream. **1950** No Place for Jennifer (US 1951); The Happiest Days of Your Life. **1951** Laughter in Paradise; Young Wives' Tale (US 1954); The Third Visitor. **1952** Never Look Back. **1953** Albert, RN (aka Break to Freedom—US 1955); The Fake. **1954** The Belles of St. Trinian's (US 1955); Malaga (aka Fire Over Africa—US); Make Me an Offer (US 1956); The Sea Shall Not Have Them (US 1955); The Harassed Hero; Conflict of Wings. **1955** Gentlemen Marry Brunettes; Break in the Circle (US 1957); A Yank in Ermine. **1957** Alive on Saturday; Let's Be Happy; Doctor at Large; Light Fingers; Now and Forever. **1958** The Passionate Summer. **1960** Escort for Hire. **1962** The Waltz of the Toreadors; What the Woman Wants. **1969** Oh! What a Lovely War; The Magic Christian (US 1970).

MIDDLETON, JOSEPHINE

Born: 1883. Died: Apr. 8, 1971, England. Screen, stage and vaudeville actress.

Appeared in: **1944** Love Story (aka A Lady Surrenders—US 1947). **1950** The Woman in Question (aka Five Angles on Murder—US 1953). **1951** The Browning Version. **1955** Before I Wake (aka Shadow of Fear—US 1956).

MIDDLETON, LEORA. *See* LEORA SPELLMAN

MIDGELY, FANNIE

Born: Nov. 26, 1877, Cincinnati, Ohio. Died: Jan. 4, 1932. Stage and screen actress. Entered films with Biograph.

Appeared in: **1915** Aloha Oe. **1916** The Waifs; The Apostle of Vengeance; Civilization; The Man from Oregon; Somewhere in France; The Criminal; Jim Grimsby's Boy. **1919** The Lottery Man. **1921** All Souls' Eve; First Love; Don't Call Me Little Girl; Patsy. **1922** Blue Blazes; When Love Comes; Through a Glass Window; The Young Rajah. **1923** Wasted Lives; Stephen Steps Out. **1925** Three Wise Crooks; Greed; Marry Me; The Bridge of Sighs; Some Pun'-kins. **1926** Hair Trigger Baxter; Ace of Action; The Fighting Cheat; The Dangerous Dub; Laddie. **1927** The Harvester. **1928** The Flying Buckaroo; The Cowboy Cavalier. **1929** Behind Closed Doors; Naughty Baby; Welcome Danger. **1930** The Poor Millionaire. **1931** An American Tragedy.

MIDGLEY, FLORENCE

Born: 1890. Died: Nov. 16, 1949, Hollywood, Calif. Screen and stage actress. Entered films in 1918.

Appeared in: **1921** The Great Impersonation; Partners of the Tide. **1926** Memory Lane. **1928** Sadie Thompson; Burning Bridges. **1929** The Three Outcasts; Painted Faces.

MIDGLEY, RICHARD A.

Born: 1910. Died: Nov. 30, 1956, New York, N.Y. Screen and stage actor.

MIHAIL, ALEXANDRA

Born: 1947, Belgium? Died: Dec. 17, 1975, Brussels, Belgium (asphyxiation). Stage and screen actress.

MILAM, PAULINE

Born: 1912. Died: May 2, 1965, Hollywood, Calif. Screen, vaudeville actress and dancer. Was a "Goldwyn Girl."

MILANI, JOSEPH L. *See* CHEF MILANI

MILASH, ROBERT E. (aka ROBERT E. MILASCH)

Born: 1885, New York, N.Y. Died: Nov. 14, 1954, Woodland Hills, Calif. (uremic poisoning). Stage and screen actor. Entered films with Edison Co.

Appeared in: **1903** The Great Train Robbery. **1921** Black Beauty. **1922** Confidence; The Prodigal Judge; Catch My Smoke. **1924** Abraham Lincoln; The Right of the Strongest; Captain Blood. **1925** Thank You. **1927** Grinning Guns; Men of Daring; A Hero for a Night. **1928** The Little Shepherd of Kingdom Come; The Upland Rider. **1930** Dangerous Nan McGrew. **1936** Give Us This Night.

MILCREST, HOWARD

Born: 1892. Died: Dec. 1920, Huachuca Mountains, Ariz. (fall from horse). Screen actor. Entered films with Griffith approx. 1910.

MILES, ARTHUR K.

Born: 1899. Died: Nov. 6, 1955, Hollywood, Calif. Screen actor.

Appeared in: **1939** The Gorilla. **1942** The Spoilers. **1944** Gentle Annie. **1945** Paris Underground. **1946** Night in Paradise.

MILES, DAVID

Born: Milford, Conn. Died: Oct. 28, 1915, New York, N.Y. (hemorrhage). Screen actor and film director. Married to stage actress Anita Hendrie (dec.). Entered films with Biograph in 1909.

Appeared in: **1909** The Violin Maker of Cremona.

MILES, LOTTA (Florence Court)

Born: 1899. Died: July 25, 1937, Los Angeles, Calif. (heart ailment). Stage and screen actress.

Appeared in: **1935** Waterfront Lady.

MILES, GENERAL NELSON APPLETON

Born: Aug. 8, 1839, Westminster, Mass. Died: May 15, 1925, Washington, D.C. (heart disease). Professional soldier, author and screen actor. He fought in the Civil War, various Indian campaigns, etc.

Appeared in: **1914** The Indian Wars.

MILHAUD, DARIUS

Born: 1893, Aix-en-Provence, France. Died: June 22, 1974, Geneva, Switzerland. Composer, conductor, writer and screen actor.

Appeared in: **1924** Entracte.

MILJAN, JOHN

Born: Nov. 9, 1893, Lead City, S.D. Died: Jan. 24, 1960, Hollywood, Calif. Stage and screen actor.

Appeared in: **1923** Love Letters (film debut). **1924** The Painted Lady; Romance Ranch; The Lone Wolf; On the Stroke of Three; Empty Hearts; The Lone Chance. **1925** The Unnamed Woman; Silent Sanderson; Sackcloth and Scarlet; Morals for Men; The Overland Limited; The Phantom of the Opera; Sealed Lips; Wreckage; The Unchastened Woman. **1926** The Devil's Circus; Flaming Waters; Almost a Lady; Footloose Widows; My Official Wife; The Amateur Gentleman; Brooding Eyes; Devil's Island; Race Wild; Unknown Treasures. **1927** The Yankee Clipper; Old San Francisco; Wolf's Clothing; The Ladybird; What Happened to Father?; A Sailor's Sweetheart; The Desired Woman; Sailor Izzy Murphy; The Silver Slave; The Clown; Stranded; The Final Extra; Framed; Lovers?; Paying the Price; Quarantined Rivals; Rough House Rosie; The Satin Woman; The Slaver. **1928** Lady Be Good; Husbands for Rent; The Beast (short); The Crimson City; The Little Snob; Glorious Betsy; Tenderloin; Land of the Silver Fox; Women They Talk About; The Terror; The Home Towners; His Night Out (short); Devil-May-Care. **1929** Untamed; The Desert Song; Hardboiled Rose; Hunted; Stark Mad; The Unholy Night; Queen of the Night Club; Speedway; Voice of the City; The Eternal Woman; Times Square; Fashions in Love; Innocents in Paris; Gossip (short). **1930** Lights and Shadows; Remote Control; Not So Dumb; Free and Easy; Our Blushing Brides; The Sea Bat; The Woman Racket; Showgirl in Hollywood; The Unholy Three. **1931** Inspiration; The Iron Man; The Secret Six; A Gentleman's Fate; Son of India; Rise of Helga; The Green Meadow; War Nurse; Politics; Hell Divers; Susan Lennox, Her Rise and Fall; Possessed; Paid. **1932** Emma; Sky Devils; West of Broadway; Beast of the City; Arsene

Lupin; The Wet Parade; Are You Listening?; Justice for Sale; Grand Hotel; The Rich Are Always with Us; Unashamed; Flesh; Night Court; Prosperity; The Kid from Spain. 1933 What! No Beer?; Whistling in the Dark; The Sin of Nora Moran; The Nuisance; King for a Night; Blind Adventure; The Way to Love; The Mad Game. 1934 Young and Beautiful; The Poor Rich; Madame Spy; Whirlpool; The Line-Up; The Belle of the Nineties; Unknown Blonde; Twin Husbands. 1935 Tomorrow's Youth; Mississippi; Charlie Chan in Paris; Under the Pampas Moon; The Ghost Walks; Three Kids and a Queen. 1936 Murder at Glen Athol; Sutter's Gold; The Criminal Within; Private Number; The Gentleman from Louisiana; North of Nome; The Plainsman. 1937 Arizona Mahoney. 1938 Man-Proof; If I Were King; Pardon Our Nerve; Miracle Money (short); Border G-Man; Ride a Crooked Mile. 1939 Juarez; The Oklahoma Kid; Torchy Runs for Mayor; Fast and Furious. 1940 Emergency Squad; Women without Names; Queen of the Mob; New Moon; Young Bill Hickok. 1941 Texas Rangers Ride Again; Forced Landing; The Cowboy and the Blonde; The Deadly Game; Riot Squad; Double Cross. 1942 The Big Street; True to the Army; Scattergood Survives a Murder; Boss of the Big Town; Criminal Investigator. 1943 Bombardier; Submarine Alert; The Fallen Sparrow. 1944 Bride by Mistake; I Accuse My Parents; The Merry Monahans. 1945 It's in the Bag. 1946 The Last Crooked Mile; The Killers; White Tie and Tails; Gallant Man. 1947 Unconquered; Sinbad, the Sailor; Queen of the Amazons; In Self Defense; The Flame; That's My Man; Quest of Willie Hunter. 1948 Perilous Waters. 1949 Adventure in Baltimore; Mrs. Mike; Stampede; Samson and Delilah. 1950 Mule Train. 1951 M. 1952 The Savage; Bonzo Goes to College. 1955 Pirates of Tripoli; Run for Cover. 1956 The Ten Commandments; The Wild Dakotas. 1957 Apache Warrior. 1958 The Lone Ranger and the Lost City of Gold.

MILLAR, LEE

Born: 1888. Died: Dec. 24, 1941, Glendale, Calif. (heart attack). Screen, stage and radio actor. Voice of Pluto in Walt Disney cartoons. Married to actress Verna Felton (dec. 1966).

MILLAR, MARJIE

Born: Tacoma, Wash. Died: 1966. Screen actress. Divorced from television director John Florea.

Appeared in: 1953 Money from Home. 1954 About Mrs. Leslie. 1956 When Gangland Strikes.

MILLARD, HARRY W. (Harry Millard Williams)

Born: 1928. Died: Sept. 2, 1969, New York, N.Y. (cancer). Screen, stage, television actor and film producer.

Appeared in: 1959 The Last Mile.

MILLARDE, HARRY

Died: Prior to 1936. Screen actor and film director. Married to actress June Caprice (dec. 1936).

Appeared in: 1913 The War Correspondent; The Woe of Battle; The Fire Fighting Zouaves; The Secret Marriage; The Mermaid. 1914 The Hand of Fate; The Vampire's Trail; The Storm at Sea; Into the Depths; The False Guardian; Seed and the Harvest. 1915 The Sign of the Broken Shackles; The Man in Hiding; The Money Gulf; The Mysterious Case of Meredith Stanhope; Don Caesar de Bazan. 1916 Elusive Isabel.

MILLER, ALICE MOORE. See ALICE MOORE

MILLER, ASHLEY

Born: 1867. Died: Nov. 19, 1949, New York, N.Y. Screen, stage actor and stage director. Appeared in early films.

MILLER, CHARLES B.

Born: 1891. Died: June 5, 1955, Hollywood, Calif. (shot). Screen actor.

Appeared in: 1939 The Night of Nights. 1940 Phantom of Chinatown. 1941 Caught in the Act. 1942 South of Santa Fe; Raiders of the Range; The Phantom Plainsman; Joan of Ozark; They All Kissed the Bride. 1943 Days of Old Cheyenne. 1944 Black Hills Express. 1945 Wilson; House of Frankenstein; Honeymoon Ahead; The Caribbean Mystery. 1946 Rendezvous 24-F; Rustler's Round-Up; Gunman's Code. 1947 I'll Be Yours. 1948 Mexican Hayride.

MILLER, E. G. (Edward George Miller)

Born: 1883. Died: Dec. 1, 1948, Los Angeles, Calif. Screen actor. Entered films with Biograph.

Appeared in: 1921 Without Benefit of Clergy.

MILLER, EDDIE

Born: 1891. Died: Mar. 9, 1971. Screen actor and singer. Headed musical group known as "Eddie Miller and His Bob Cats."

Appeared in: 1941 Safe at Home. 1943 Mister Big. 1955 Pete Kelly's Blues.

MILLER, FLOURNOY E.

Born: 1887, Nashville, Tenn. Died: June 6, 1971, Hollywood, Calif. (coronary failure). Black screen, stage, vaudeville actor, script writer for television, playwright and stage producer. Partner in vaudeville team of "Miller and Lyles."

Appeared in: 1939 Harlem Rides the Range. 1943 Stormy Weather. 1951 Yes Sir, Mr. Bones.

MILLER, GLENN (Alton Glenn Miller)

Born: Mar. 1, 1904, Clarinda, Iowa. Died: Dec. 15, 1944, Europe (plane crash). Bandleader, composer and screen actor.

Appeared in: 1942 Orchestra Wives; Sun Valley Serenade.

MILLER, HUGH J.

Born: 1902. Died: May 11, 1956, Los Angeles, Calif. Screen actor. Father of actress Barbara Heller.

Appeared in: 1927 Blind Alleys. 1935 The Divine Spark; I Give My Heart. 1937 The Dominant Sex; Victoria the Great; Bulldog Drummond at Bay. 1938 The Rat; The Return of the Scarlet Pimpernel; The Loves of Madame Du Barry.

MILLER, JACK

Born: 1888. Died: Sept. 25, 1928, San Diego, Calif. (intestinal trouble). Stage and screen actor.

Appeared in: 1930 Hell's Angels.

MILLER, JACK "SHORTY"

Born: 1895. Died: Feb. 28, 1941, Burbank, Calif. (heart attack). Screen cowboy actor.

MILLER, JUANITA

Born: 1880. Died: Apr. 1970, Oakland, Calif. Poet and screen actress. Appeared in films during early 1920s. Daughter of poet Joaquin Miller (dec. 1913). "Her second marriage in April, 1921, began with the bride in a corpselike state in a funeral setting. The groom kissed her and she awoke. There followed a naturalistic ritual involving the sacrifice of a goat and a demonstration of Miss Miller's cooking prowess."

MILLER, LOU (aka LU MILLER)

Born: 1906. Died: May 2, 1941, Hollywood, Calif. Screen actress. Married to actor William Ruhl.

Appeared in: 1937 Easy Living. 1938 Hunted Men.

MILLER, MARILYN (Marilyn or Mary Ellen Reynolds)

Born: Sept. 1, 1898, Evansville, Ind. Died: Apr. 7, 1936, New York, N.Y. (toxic poisoning). Stage and screen actress. Divorced from screen actor Jack Pickford (dec. 1933).

Appeared in: 1929 Sally. 1930 Sunny. 1931 Her Majesty, Love.

MILLER, MARTIN (Rudolph Muller)

Born: 1899, Czechoslovakia. Died: Aug. 26, 1969, Austria (heart attack). Screen, stage and television actor.

Appeared in: 1942 Squadron Leader X. 1943 Adventures of Tartu (aka Tartu—US). 1944 English Without Tears (aka Her Man Gilbey—US 1949). 1948 Counterblast; Bonnie Prince Charlie. 1949 The Huggets Abroad. 1951 Encore (US 1952). 1952 Where's Charley? 1954 Front Page Story (US 1955); You Know What Sailors Are; Mad about Men; To Dorothy a Son (aka Cash on Delivery—US 1956). 1955 An Alligator Named Daisy (US 1957). 1956 The Gamma People; The Baby and the Battleship. 1957 Seven Thunders (aka The Beasts of Marseilles—US 1959). 1959 Libel; Expresso Bongo (US 1960); Exodus; The Rough and the Smooth (aka Portrait of a Sinner—US 1961); Violent Moment (US 1966). 1960 Peeping Tom (US 1962). 1962 55 Days at Peking; The Phantom of the Opera. 1963 The VIPs; Children of the Damned (US 1964); The Yellow Rolls Royce (US 1965); Incident at Midnight (US 1966). 1964 The Pink Panther. 1965 Up Jumped a Swagman.

MILLER, MAX (Thomas Sargent)

Born: 1895, England. Died: May 7, 1963, Brighton, England. Screen, circus and vaudeville actor. Known as "The Cheeky Chappie."

Appeared in: 1933 The Good Companions; Channel Crossing (US 1934); Friday the Thirteenth (US 1934). 1934 Princess Charming (US 1935). 1935 Things are Looking Up; Get Off My Foot. 1936 Educated Evans. 1937 Don't Get Me Wrong; Take It from Me (aka Transatlantic Trouble). 1938 Thank Evans; Everything Happens to Me. 1939 The Good Old Days; Hoots Mon! 1942 Asking for Trouble.

MILLER, RANGER BILL

Born: 1878. Died: Nov. 12, 1939, Los Angeles, Calif. Screen actor. Adopted son of Buffalo Bill.

Appeared in: 1923 The Web of the Law. 1924 A Pair of Hellions. 1925 Heartbound.

MILLER, SETON I.
Born: May 3, 1902, Chehalis, Wash. Died: Mar. 29, 1974, Woodland Hills, Calif. (emphysema). Film, television producer, screenwriter, stage and screen actor. Married to stage actress Ann Evers. Entered films in 1926 as an actor.

Appeared in: **1926** Brown of Harvard.

MILLER, THOMAS
Born: 1872. Died: Dec. 6, 1942, Los Angeles, Calif. Stage and screen actor.

Appeared in: **1934** The Old Fashioned Way.

MILLER, W. CHRISTY (William Christy Miller)
Born: 1843. Died: Sept. 23, 1922, Staten Island, N.Y. Stage and screen actor.

Appeared in: **1909** The Redman's View; The Day After. **1910** The Rocky Road; The Newlyweds; In Old California; The Thread of Destiny; The Way of the World; The Tenderfoot; Triumph; Her Father's Pride; The Lesson; Examination Day at School; The Two Brothers; A Plain Song. **1911** What Shall We Do With Our Old?; Dooley's Scheme; In the Days of '49; The Last Drop of Water; Swords and Hearts; The Old Bookkeeper. **1912** The Unwelcome Guest; An Indian Summer; The Chief's Blanket; Man's Genesis; The Sands of Dee; The Old Actor; The Informer; My Baby. **1913** The Battle at Elderberry Gulch; His Mother's Son; A Timely Interception; The Reformers.

MILLER, WALTER C.
Born: Mar. 9, 1892, Dayton, Ohio. Died: Mar. 30, 1940, Los Angeles, Calif. Screen, stage and vaudeville actor.

Appeared in: **1912** The Musketeers of Pig Alley; Oil and Water; Two Daughters of Eve; So Near, Yet So Far; A Feud in the Kentucky Hills; Brutality; An Adventure in the Autumn Woods. **1913** Love in an Apartment Hotel; The Perfidy of Mary; His Mother's Son; Death's Marathon; The Wanderer; The Mothering Heart; The Coming of Angelo. **1916** The Marble Heart. **1917** Miss Robinson Crusoe; The Slacker. **1919** Thin Ice; A Girl at Bay. **1920** The Stealers. **1921** The Shadow; Luxury. **1922** Beyond the Rainbow; The Bootleggers; 'Till We Meet Again; The Woman Who Believed; Unconquered Woman. **1923** The Tie That Binds; Unseeing Eyes. **1924** Leatherstocking (serial); Men, Women and Money; Those Who Judge; Playthings of Desire. **1925** Sunken Silver (serial); Play Ball (serial); The Green Archer (serial); The Sky Raider. **1926** The House without a Key (serial and feature film); The Fighting Marine (serial and feature film); Snowed In (serial); The Unfair Sex. **1927** Hawk of the Hills (serial); Melting Millions (serial). **1928** Police Reporter (serial); The Man without a Face (serial); The Mysterious Airman (serial); The Terrible People (serial); Manhattan Knights. **1929** The Black Book (serial); King of the Kongo (serial released in silent and sound versions); Queen of the Northwoods (serial); Hawk of the Hills (feature of 1927 serial). **1930** Lone Defender (serial); On the Border; The Utah Kid; Rogue of the Rio Grande; King of the Wild (serial); Rough Waters. **1931** The Galloping Ghost (serial); Swanee River; Street Scene; Hell's Valley; Sky Raiders; Hurricane Horseman. **1932** Three Wise Girls; Manhattan Parade; The Famous Ferguson Case; Ridin' for Justice; Ghost City; Face on the Barroom Floor; Heart Punch. **1933** Sin of a Sailor; Parachute Jumper; Maisie; Behind Jury Doors; Gordon of Ghost City (serial). **1934** Rocky Rhodes; Fighting Trooper; Gun Justice; Pirate Treasure (serial); The Vanishing Shadow (serial); The Red Rider; Smoking Guns. **1935** Alias Mary Dow; Gun Valley; Valley of Wanted Men; Call Her Savage (serial); Rustlers of Red Dog (serial); The Roaring West (serial); Stormy. **1936** Heart of the West; Desert Gold; The Fugitive Sheriff; Ghost Patrol; Without Orders; Night Waitress. **1937** Draegerman Courage; Boss of Lonely Valley; Midnight Court; Slim; Border Cafe; Flight from Glory; Saturday's Heroes; Danger Patrol; Wild West Days (serial). **1938** Wild Horse Rodeo; The Secret of Treasure Island (serial); Blind Alibi; Crime Ring; Lawless Valley; Come on Leathernecks; Down in "Arkansaw"; Smashing the Rackets. **1939** Dick Tracy's G-Men (serial); Home on the Prairie. **1940** Bullet Code; Grandpa Goes to Town; Three Cheers for the Irish; Gaucho Serenade; The Saints' Double Trouble.

MILLICAN, JAMES
Born: 1910, Palisades, N.Y. Died: Nov. 24, 1955, Los Angeles, Calif. Screen actor.

Appeared in: **1932** The Sign of the Cross. **1933** Mills of the Gods. **1938** Who Killed Gail Preston? **1939** The Sap Takes a Wrap (short). **1942** The Remarkable Andrew; Star Spangled Rhythm. **1943** So Proudly We Hail! **1944** The Story of Dr. Wassell; The Sign of the Cross (revised version of 1932 film). **1945** Bring on the Girls; Tokyo Rose; The Affairs of Susan; Love Letters. **1946** The Tender Years; The Trouble with Women; Stepchild; Rendezvous with Annie. **1948** Mr. Reckless; Hazard; Let's Live Again; Disaster; Man from Colorado; Return of Wildfire; Last of the Wild Horses; Rogue's Regiment; In This Corner. **1949** Command Decision; The Dalton Gang; Fighting Man of the Plains; The Gal Who Took the West; Grand Canyon; Rimfire. **1950** Beyond the Purple Hills; The Devil's Doorway; Gunfighter; Military Academy with That 10th Ave. Gang; Mister 880; Winchester "73". **1951** Al Jennings of Oklahoma; Calvary Scout; Fourteen Hours; The Great Missouri Raid; I Was a Communist for the FBI; Missing Women; Rawhide; Warpath. **1952** Bugles in the Afternoon; Carson City; Diplomatic Courier; High Noon; Scandal Sheet; Springfield Rifle; The Winning Team. **1953** Cow Country; Gun Belt; Silver Whip; Torpedo Alley; A Lion in the Streets. **1954** Crazylegs; Dawn at Socorro; Jubilee Trail;

The Long Wait; The Outcast; Riding Shotgun. **1955** Las Vegas Shakedown; Top Gun; The Vanishing American; Strategic Air Command; The Man from Laramie; Big Tip Off; Chief Crazy Horse; I Died One Thousand Times. **1956** Red Sundown.

MILLIGAN, MARY "MIN"
Born: 1882, Ireland. Died: Mar. 10, 1966, Belfast, Ireland. Screen, stage and television actress.

MILLMAN, WILLIAM (William L'Estrange Millman)
Born: 1883. Died: July 19, 1937, Hollywood, Calif. Screen and stage actor.

Appeared in: **1935** The Lost City; Motive for Revenge. **1937** Silent Barriers.

MILLS, FRANK
Born: Jan. 26, 1891, Kalamazoo, Mich. Died: Aug. 18, 1973, Los Angeles, Calif. (arteriosclerosis). Screen and stage actor.

Appeared in: **1915** The Golden Claw; The Edge of the Abyss. **1916** The Moral Fabric; The Dollar and the Law; The Wheel of the Law. **1917** The Eternal Mother (aka The Red Horse Hill); A Sleeping Memory; The Price of Pride; To-Day. **1918** Wives of Men; The Unchastened Woman; The Silent Woman; De Luxe Annie; Wild Honey. **1919** Twilight; Let's Elope; The Bramble Bush; The Right to Lie. **1920** Women Men Forget. **1922** My Husband's Friend. **1928** Chicago After Midnight; Hit of the Show; Danger Street. **1930** Those Who Dance. **1932** Make Me a Star. **1935** Another Face. **1936** Hi, Gaucho; Parole; Way Out West; Follow the Fleet. **1937** Dizzy Doctors (short). **1938** The Goldwyn Follies. **1940** Father Was a Fullback. **1942** Heart of the Rio Grande. **1944** Gold Is Where You Lose It. **1956** Around the World in 80 Days. **1957** The Joker is Wild. **1970** The Golden Box.

MILLS, FREDDIE
Born: 1919. Died: July 22, 1965, London, England (suicide—shot). Former World's light heavyweight champion, restaurateur, screen and television actor.

Appeared in: **1952** Emergency Call (aka The Hundred Hour Hunt—US 1953). **1958** Kiss Me Tomorrow. **1960** Carry on Constable (US 1961). **1961** Carry on Regardless (US 1963). **1964** Saturday Night Out.

MILLS, GRANT
Died: Aug. 4, 1973, Skowhegan, Maine. Stage and screen actor. Divorced from actress Violet Heming.

Appeared in: **1938** Professor Beware.

MILLS, GUY (Louis Miller)
Born: 1898. Died: Oct. 15, 1962, Chichester, England. Stage and screen actor. Appeared in films mostly doubling for stars in riding sequences.

MILLS, JOHN, SR.
Born: Feb. 11, 1889, Bellefonte, Pa. Died: Dec. 8, 1967, Ohio. Black singer, screen, radio and vaudeville actor. Father of singers, Herbert, Harry and Donald Mills with whom he appeared as a member of the "Mills Brothers Quartet" and singer John Mills, Jr. (dec. 1936).

Appeared in: **1943** He's My Guy; Reveille with Beverly; Chatterbox.

MILLS, JOHN, JR.
Born: 1910, Piqua, Ohio. Died: Jan. 23, 1936, Bellefontaine, Ohio (tuberculosis). Black singer, screen, radio and vaudeville actor. Brother of singers Herbert, Harry and Donald Mills with whom he appeared as a member of the "Mills Brothers Quartet." Son of singer John Mills, Sr. (dec. 1967).

Appeared in: **1932** The Big Broadcast; Paramount Screen Songs (shorts). **1934** 20 Million Sweethearts; Operator 13; Stictly Dynamite. **1935** Broadway Gondolier.

MILLS, JOSEPH S. (Joseph Stapleton Mills)
Born: 1875. Died: Oct. 19, 1935 (heart attack). Screen and stage actor.

Appeared in: **1924** Abraham Lincoln; Love's Whirlpool. **1934** Men in Black (short).

MILLS, THOMAS R.
Born: 1878. Died: Nov. 29, 1953, Woodland Hills, Calif. Screen, stage and radio actor.

Appeared in: **1916** The Scarlet Runner (serial). **1924** The Guilty One; The Star Dust Trail; A Man's Mate; The Wolf Man. **1925** The Kiss Barrier; Tides of Passion; The Arizona Romeo. **1926** The Gilded Highway. **1934** Great Expectations. **1935** Les Miserables. **1937** It's Love I'm After. **1938** An MGM short.

MILLWARD, MIKE
Born: 1943, England. Died: Mar. 8, 1966, Bromoborough, England (throat cancer). Screen actor, singer and guitarist. Member of pop group "The Fourmost."

Appeared in: **1965** Go Go Mania.

MILOS, MILOS (Milos Milosevic)

Born: July 1, 1941, Yugoslavia. Died: Jan. 31, 1966, Los Angeles, Calif. (suicide—gun). Screen actor.

Appeared in: **1961** Lion of Sparta. **1962** The 300 Spartans. **1965** Incubus. **1966** The Russians Are Coming, The Russians Are Coming.

MILTERN, JOHN

Born: 1870. Died: Jan. 15, 1937, Los Angeles, Calif. (hit by auto). Stage and screen actor.

Appeared in: **1920** On with the Dance. **1921** Experience; The Kentuckians. **1922** Manslaughter; The Hands of Nara; Kick In; Love's Boomerang; The Man Who Saw Tomorrow; Three Live Ghosts; The Man from Home. **1923** The Ne'er-Do-Well. **1924** Tongues of Flame. **1925** Coming Through. **1926** Fine Manners. **1927** East Side, West Side; The Love of Sunya. **1935** Diamond Jim; The Dark Angel. **1936** Give Us This Night; Everybody's Old Man; Sins of Man; Ring around the Moon; Murder on the Bridle Path; Parole. **1937** The Lost Horizon.

MILTON, ERNEST

Born: Jan. 10, 1890, San Francisco. Died: July 27, 1974, London, England. Screen, stage, television actor, playwright and author. Married to playwright Naomi Royde Smith (dec. 1964).

Appeared in: **1935** The Scarlet Pimpernel. **1936** It's Love Again. **1944** Fiddlers Three. **1951** Alice in Wonderland. **1957** The Cat Girl.

MILTON, GEORGES (Georges Michaud)

Born: 1888, France. Died: Oct. 16, 1970, Nice, France. Stage and screen actor.

Appeared in: **1932** Le Roi des Resquilleurs (King of the Gate Crashers). **1933** Nu Comme un Ver (Naked As a Worm). **1944** The Queen and the Cardinal.

MILTON, HARRY

Born: June 26, 1900, London, England. Died: Mar. 8, 1965, London, England. Screen, stage actor and assistant director. Divorced from actress Chili Bouchier.

Appeared in: **1933** The King's Cup; To Brighton with Gladys; King of the Ritz. **1934** Adventure Limited. **1936** Pagliacci (aka A Clown Must Laugh—US 1938).

MILTON, LOUETTE

Born: 1907. Died: Oct. 29, 1930, Wyo. Stage and screen actress.

Appeared in: **1930** Bride of the Regiment.

MINCIOTTI, ESTHER

Born: 1888, Italy. Died: Apr. 15, 1962, New York, N.Y. Screen, stage and television actress. Married to actor Silvio Minciotti (dec. 1961).

Appeared in: **1949** House of Strangers; Shockproof; The Undercover Man. **1951** Strictly Dishonorable. **1955** Marty. **1956** Full of Life. **1957** The Wrong Man.

MINCIOTTI, SILVIO

Born: 1883, Italy. Died: May 2, 1961, Elmhurst, N.Y. Stage and screen actor. Married to actress Esther Minciotti (dec. 1962).

Appeared in: **1949** House of Strangers. **1950** Deported. **1951** Strictly Dishonorable; The Great Caruso; Up Front; Fourteen Hours. **1952** Clash by Night. **1953** Francis Covers the Big Town. **1955** Marty; Kiss Me Deadly. **1956** Serenade; Full of Life. **1957** The Wrong Man.

MINER, DANIEL

Born: 1880. Died: June 24, 1938, Hollywood, Calif. Screen and stage actor. Entered films approx. 1914.

MINEVITCH, BORRAH

Born: approx. 1904, Kiev, Russia. Died: June 25, 1955, Paris, France. Screen actor, television producer and musician.

Appeared in: **1934** A Vitaphone short (with his "Harmonica Rascals"). **1936** One in a Million. **1937** Love under Fire. **1938** Rascals. **1942** Always in My Heart. **1952** Jour de Fete.

MING, MOY LUKE

Born: 1863, Canton, China. Died: Aug. 16, 1964, Granada Hills, Calif. Screen actor.

Appeared in: **1933** The Bitter Tea of General Yen. **1937** Broken Blossoms; The Good Earth; China Passage. **1955** The Left Hand of God.

MINNER, KATHRYN

Born: 1892. Died: May 26, 1969, Van Nuys, Calif. (heart attack). Screen, stage and television actress.

Appeared in: **1968** The Love Bug; Blackbeard's Ghost.

MINOR, ROY

Born: 1905. Died: Mar. 28, 1935, Los Angeles, Calif. (heart attack). Screen actor and stunt flyer.

Appeared in: **1930** Hell's Angels.

MINTER, WILLIAM F.

Born: 1892. Died: July 13, 1937, Los Angeles, Calif. (bullet wound). Screen actor. Entered films approx. 1922.

MINZEY, FRANK

Born: 1879. Died: Nov. 12, 1949, Lake George, N.Y. Screen, stage and vaudeville actor. Married to actress Rose Melville (dec. 1946). Appeared in early Biograph and Keystone films. Later in shorts produced by Fox, Goldwyn, etc.

Appeared in: **1916** Leap Year Wooing.

MIRANDA, CARMEN (Maria Da Carmo Miranda da Cunha)

Born: Feb. 9, 1904, Marco Canavezes, Portugal. Died: Aug. 5, 1955, Beverly Hills, Calif. (heart attack). Screen and television actress. Married to film producer David Sebastian.

Appeared in: **1934-38** Alo, Alo, Brazil; Estudiantes; Alo, Alo, Carnaval; Banana La Terra. **1940** Down Argentine Way. **1941** That Night in Rio; Weekend in Havana. **1942** Springtime in the Rockies. **1943** The Gang's All Here. **1944** Four Jills in a Jeep; Greenwich Village; Something for the Boys. **1945** Doll Face; Hollywood on Parade (short). **1946** If I'm Lucky; Come Back to Me. **1947** Copacabana. **1948** A Date with Judy. **1950** Nancy Goes to Rio. **1953** Scared Stiff. **1974** That's Entertainment (film clips).

"MIRANDY" (Marjorie Bauersfield)

Died: July 21, 1974. Screen, stage and radio actress.

Appeared in: **1940** Comin' Round the Mountain.

MIROSLAVA (Miroslava Stern)

Born: 1930, Czechoslovakia. Died: Mar. 10, 1955, Mexico City, Mexico (suicide—poison). Stage and screen actress.

Appeared in: **1946** Cinco Nostras de Mujer. **1947** Nocturno de Amor; A Volar Joven; Juane Charrasqueado. **1948** Secreto Entre Mujeres; Adventures of Casanova. **1949** La Casa Chica; La Posesion. **1951** The Brave Bulls; Ella y Yo; Carcel de Mujeres; El de Los Siete Vicios; Trotocalles. **1952** Los Tres Perfectas Casadas; The Bullfighter and the Lady; La Bestia Magnifica. **1953** Reportaje. **1954** La Visita Que no Toco el Timbre; Escuella de Vagabundos. **1955** Stranger on Horseback; Ensayo de un Crimen.

MISENER, HELEN

Born: 1909. Died: Aug. 1, 1960, London, England. Screen actress. Entered films as a child actress.

Appeared in: **1958** A Night to Remember.

MISHIMA, MASAO

Born: 1906, Japan. Died: July 18, 1973, Tokyo, Japan (heart ailment). Screen, stage and television actor.

Appeared in: **1952** Saikaku Ichidai Onna (aka Life of Oharu—US 1964). **1959** Ningen No Joken (The Human Condition). **1961** Buta to Gunkan (The Flesh Is Hot—US 1963 aka The Dirty Girls). **1962** Seppuku (Harakiri—US 1963). **1965** Yotsuya Kaidan (aka Illusion of Blood—US 1966). **1967** Joi-Uchi (Rebellion). **1968** Fushin No Taki (The Time of Reckoning—US 1970). **1970** No Greater Love (reissue of Ningen No Joken—1959).

MISHIMA, YUKIO

Born: Japan. Died: Nov. 25, 1971, Tokyo, Japan (hara-kiri). Screen actor, film director, film producer, screenwriter and novelist. The film Yukoku (1966) was destroyed at widow's request because the movie and novel which he wrote, starred in and directed featured a hero who committed hara-kiri also.

MISTRAL, JORGE (aka GEORGE MISTRAL)

Born: 1923. Died: Apr. 20, 1972, Mexico City, Mexico (self-inflicted gunshot wound). Screen and television actor.

Appeared in: **1950** The Mad Queen. **1957** Boy on a Dolphin. **1958** El Vaquero and the Girl. **1960** Le Schiave de Cartegene (The Slaves of Carthage aka The Sword and the Cross). **1962** The Devil Made a Woman. **1963** A Girl Against Napoleon; Abismos de Pasion (Depths of Passion); Sheherazada (Scheherezade—US 1965). **1964** Love on the Riviera. **1965** Gunfighters of Casa Grande.

MITCHEL, LES

Born: 1905. Died: Jan. 12, 1975, Sacramento, Calif. Screen actor, film, radio director and stage producer.

Appeared in: **1957** Outlaw's Son.

MITCHELL, BRUCE (H. Bruce Mitchell)

Born: Nov. 16, 1883, Freeport, Ill. Died: Sept. 26, 1952, Hollywood, Calif.

(anemia). Screen actor, film director and screenwriter. Entered films as a director in 1912.

Appeared in: **1934** Burn 'Em up Barnes. **1935** The Phantom Empire (serial); G-Men; Four Hours to Kill. **1936** Half Angel. **1937** Paradise Express. **1938** Bar 20 Justice; Pride of the West. **1939** Silver on the Sage; Riders of the Frontier. **1941** Sky Raiders (serial).

MITCHELL, CAROLYN (Barbara Ann Thomason)
Born: Jan. 25, 1937, Arizona. Died: Jan. 31, 1966, Los Angeles, Calif. (murdered—shot). Screen actress. Married to actor Mickey Rooney.

Appeared in: **1958** Dragstrip Riot; The Cry Baby Killer.

MITCHELL, CHARLES
Born: 1884. Died: Dec. 14, 1929, Hollywood, Calif. (suicide). Screen actor.

MITCHELL, DOBSON (aka DODSON MITCHELL)
Born: Jan. 23, 1868. Died: June 2, 1939, New York, N.Y. Screen, stage actor and author.

Appeared in: **1914** The Conspiracy. **1920** Deadline at Eleven. **1926** The Little Giant.

MITCHELL, GEORGE
Born: 1905. Died: Jan. 18, 1972, Washington, D.C. Screen and stage actor.

Appeared in: **1955** The Phenix City Story. **1957** 3:10 to Yuma. **1959** The Wild and the Innocent. **1962** Kid Galahad; Bird Man of Alcatraz; Fallguy; Third of a Man. **1963** Twilight of Honor. **1964** The Unsinkable Molly Brown. **1966** Nevada Smith. **1967** The Flim Flam Man. **1969** The Learning Tree. **1971** The Andromeda Strain.

MITCHELL, GRANT
Born: June 17, 1874, Columbus, Ohio. Died: May 1, 1957, Los Angeles, Calif. Stage and screen actor.

Appeared in: **1923** Radio Mania. **1931** Man to Man; The Star Witness; a DeForest Phonofilm short. **1932** M.A.R.S.; Three on a Match; Big City Blues; The Famous Ferguson Case; Week-End Marriage; No Man of Her Own; 20,000 Years in Sing Sing; A Successful Calamity. **1933** Central Airport; Lily Turner; Heroes for Sale; I Love That Man; Tomorrow at Seven; Dinner at Eight; Stranger's Return; Dancing Lady; Saturday's Millions; King for a Night; Wild Boys of the Road; Convention City; Our Betters. **1934** The Poor Rich; The Show-Off; We're Rich Again; The Gridiron Flash; Twenty Million Sweethearts; The Secret Bride; Shadows of Sing Sing; The Cat's Paw; The Case of the Howling Dog; 365 Nights in Hollywood; One Exciting Adventure. **1935** One More Spring; Traveling Saleslady; Gold Diggers of 1935; Straight from the Heart; Broadway Gondolier; Men without Names; A Midsummer Night's Dream; In Person; Seven Keys to Baldpate; It's in the Air. **1936** Next Time We Love; The Garden Murder Case; Moonlight Murder; Picadilly Jim; The Devil is a Sissy; Her Master's Voice; My American Wife; The Ex-Mrs. Bradford; Parole! **1937** The Life of Emile Zola; Hollywood Hotel; Music for Madame; The Last Gangster; First Lady; Lady Behave. **1938** The Headleys at Home; Women Are Like That; Peck's Bad Boy at the Circus; Reformatory; Youth Takes a Fling; That Certain Age. **1939** 6,000 Enemies; On Borrowed Time; Mr. Smith Goes to Washington; Juarez; the Secret of Dr. Kildare; Hell's Kitchen. **1940** It All Came True; The Grapes of Wrath; My Love Came Back; Edison the Man; New Moon; We Who Are Young; Father Is a Prince. **1941** Tobacco Road; The Bride Wore Crutches; Nothing but the Truth; Skylark; One Foot in Heaven; Footsteps in the Dark; The Penalty; The Feminine Touch; The Man Who Came to Dinner; The Great Lie. **1942** Larceny, Inc.; Meet the Stewarts; My Sister Eileen; The Gay Sisters; Cairo; Orchestra Wives. **1943** The Amazing Mrs. Holiday; The Gold Tower; Dixie; All by Myself. **1944** Laura; See Here, Private Hargrove; The Impatient Years; And Now Tomorrow; When the Lights Go on Again; Arsenic and Old Lace; Step Lively. **1945** Crime, Inc.; A Medal for Benny; Bring on the Girls; Colonel Effingham's Raid; Bedside Manner; Guest Wife; Leave Her to Heaven; Conflict. **1946** Cinderella Jones; Easy to Wed. **1947** The Corpse Came C.O.D.; It Happened on Fifth Avenue; Blondie's Anniversary; Blondie's Holiday; Honeymoon. **1948** Who Killed "Doc" Robbin?

MITCHELL, HELEN (Helen McRuer)
Died: June 25, 1945, Los Angeles, Calif. Screen, stage actress and playwright. Divorced from producer Oliver Morosco and married to actor Robert Sterling Lawson.

Appeared in: **1929** Unmasked.

MITCHELL, HOWARD
Born: 1888. Died: Oct. 9, 1958, Hollywood, Calif. Screen actor and film director.

Appeared in: **1914** The Beloved Adventurer (serial). **1915** The Road of Strife (serial). **1927** A Bowery Cinderella. **1936** Too Many Parents. **1938** Hunted Men; Tom Sawyer, Detective; Prison Farm. **1940** Queen of the Mob. **1941** The Mad Doctor. **1942** Gentleman Jim; Heart of the Rio Grande. **1949** Abandoned.

MITCHELL, JAMES IRVING
Born: 1891. Died: Aug. 3, 1969, Hollywood, Calif. (heart attack). Screen, stage and television actor. Do not confuse with actor Irving Mitchell born in 1920.

MITCHELL, JOHN (Douglas N. Lamy)
Born: 1919. Died: Jan. 19, 1951, New York, N.Y. (suicide—gun). Screen and radio actor. Known in films as John Mitchell and on radio as Douglas Drake.

Appeared in: **1944** Mr. Skeffington. **1945** Pillow to Post. **1952** Navajo.

MITCHELL, JULIEN
Born: Nov. 13, 1888, Glossop, Derbyshire, England. Died: 1954. Stage and screen actor.

Appeared in: **1935** The Last Journey (film debut) (US 1936). **1937** Double Exposures; The Frog (US 1939); Mr. Smith Carries On. **1938** Quiet Please; The Drum (aka The Drums—US); It's in the Air (aka George Takes the Air—US 1940). **1940** Vigil in the Night; The Sea Hawk. **1942** The Goose Steps Out. **1943** Rhythm Serenade. **1944** Hotel Reserve (US 1946). **1945** The Echo Murders. **1946** Bedelia (US 1947). **1948** Bonnie Prince Charlie. **1949** A Boy, a Girl and a Bike. **1950** Chance of a Lifetime (US 1951); The Magnet (US 1951). **1951** The Galloping Major. **1954** Hobson's Choice.

MITCHELL, LESLIE "LES" (Leslie Harold Mitchell)
Born: 1885, Brandon, Manitoba, Canada. Died: Oct. 25, 1965, Vancouver, B.C. Screen actor. Entered films in 1911 with Keystone and was an early Keystone Kop and retired in 1920. Do not confuse with screen and radio actor Les Mitchell (dec. 1975).

MITCHELL, MARY RUTH
Born: 1906. Died: May 21, 1941, Los Angeles, Calif. Screen actress.

MITCHELL, MILLARD
Born: 1900, Havana, Cuba. Died: Oct. 12, 1953, Santa Monica, Calif. (lung cancer). Stage and screen actor.

Appeared in: **1941** Mr. and Mrs. North (film debut). **1942** The Mayor of 44th Street; Grand Central Murder; Get Hep to Love; Little Tokyo; Big Street. **1943** Slightly Dangerous. **1946** Swell Guy. **1947** Kiss of Death. **1948** A Double Life; A Foreign Affair. **1949** Twelve O'Clock High; Everybody Does It; Thieves' Highway. **1950** The Gunfighter; Mr. 880, Winchester "73"; Convicted. **1951** Strictly Dishonorable; You're in the Navy Now (aka U.S.S. Teakettle). **1952** My Six Convicts; Singin' in the Rain. **1953** The Naked Spur; Here Come the Girls.

MITCHELL, NORMA
Born: Boston, Mass. Died: May 29, 1967, Essex, Conn. Screen, stage actress and playwright.

Appeared in: **1933** The Woman Accused. **1934** Melody in Spring. **1940** Susan and God.

MITCHELL, RHEA "GINGER"
Born: 1905. Died: Sept. 16, 1957, Los Angeles, Calif. (found strangled). Screen actress.

Appeared in: **1915** On the Night Stage. **1916** The Sequel to the Diamond from the Sky (serial); The Overcoat; The Release of Dan Forbes. **1918** Honor's Cross; The Blindness of Divorce; Social Ambition; Satan's Pawn; Boston Blackie's Little Pal. **1919** The Money Corporal; The Sleeping Lion. **1920** The Hawk's Trail.

MITCHELL, THOMAS
Born: 1895, Elizabeth, N.J. Died: Dec. 17, 1962, Beverly Hills, Calif. (cancer). Screen, stage, television actor, stage producer, stage director, playwright and screenwriter. Won 1939 Academy Award for Best Supporting Actor in Stagecoach.

Appeared in: **1934** Cloudy with Showers. **1936** Craig's Wife; Theodora Goes Wild; Adventure in Manhattan. **1937** Man of the People; When You're in Love; Lost Horizon; I Promise to Pay; Make Way for Tomorrow; The Hurricane. **1938** Love, Honor and Behave; Trade Winds. **1939** Stagecoach; Only Angels Have Wings; Mr. Smith Goes to Washington; The Hunchback of Notre Dame; Gone With the Wind. **1940** Three Cheers for the Irish; Our Town; The Long Voyage Home; Angels over Broadway; Swiss Family Robinson. **1941** Flight from Destiny; Out of the Fog. **1942** Joan of Paris; Song of the Islands; This Above All; Moontide; Tales of Manhattan; The Black Swan. **1943** The Outlaw; Bataan; Flesh and Fantasy; The Immortal Sergeant. **1944** The Sullivans; Wilson; Buffalo Bill; The Keys of the Kingdom; Dark Waters. **1945** Within These Walls; Captain Eddie; Adventure. **1946** It's a Wonderful Life; Three Wise Fools; The Dark Mirror. **1947** High Barbaree; The Romance of Rosy Ridge; Silver River. **1949** Alias Nick Beal; The Big Wheel. **1951** Journey into Light. **1952** High Noon. **1953** Tumbleweed. **1954** Destry; Secret of the Incas. **1956** While the City Sleeps. **1958** Handle with Care. **1961** By Love Possessed; Pocketful of Miracles.

MITTELL, LYN DONALDSON
Born: 1892. Died: Mar. 2, 1966, Los Angeles, Calif. Screen and radio actress.

MIX, TOM (Thomas Hezikiah Mix)
Born: Jan. 6, 1880, Mix Run, Penn. Died: Oct. 12, 1940, Florence, Ariz. (auto accident). Screen actor, producer, screenwriter, vaudeville, circus and rodeo performer. Father of actress Ruth Mix. Marriage annulled from Grace Allin; divorced from Olive Stokes, Kitty Jewel Perrine and actress Victoria Forde (dec. 1964). Married to circus aerialist Mabel Ward.

Appeared in: 1910 Ranch Life in the Great Southwest; Up San Juan Hill; Briton and Boer; The Millionaire Cowboy; The Range Rider; An Indian Wife's Devotion. 1911-12 Back to the Primitive; The Wagon Trail; Single Shot Parker; Days of Daring; The Sheriff's Girl; My Haywood Producer; Weary Goes Wooing; Sagebrush Tom. 1913 Child of the Prairie; Escape of Jim Dolan; Law and the Outlaw; The Stage Coach Driver and the Girl. 1914 The Wilderness Mail; Moving Picture Cowboy; In the Days of the Thundering Herd; The Man from the East; Ranger's Romance; Saved by a Watch; The Scapegoat; The Sheriff's Reward; The Telltale Knife; The Way of the Redman; Why the Sheriff is a Bachelor; The Defiance of the Law; The Rival Stage Lines; Chip of the Flying U; Cactus Jake, Heartbreaker; The Mexican; The Real Thing in Cowboys. 1915 An Arizona Wooing; On the Eagle Trail; Cactus Jim's Shop Girl; Foreman of the Bar Z; The Outlaw's Bride; The Parson Who Fled West; Saved by Her Horse; Getting a Start in Life; Athletic Ambitions; The Brave Deserve the Fair; Child of the Prairie (and 1913 version); Heart of the Sheriff; Lucky Deal; The Man from Texas; Ma's Girls; Mrs. Murphy Cooks; Never Again; Pals in Blue; The Range Girl and the Cowboy; Sage Brush Tom; Slim Higgins; Stagecoach Guard; The Auction Sale of a Run-Down Ranch; Bad Man Bobbs; The Girl in the Mail Bag; The Chef at Circle G; The Child, The Dog and the Villain; The Conversion of Smiling Tom; The Foreman's Choice; Forked Trails; The Gold Dust and the Squaw; The Grizzly Gulch Chariot Race; Her Slight Mistake; The Impersonation of Tom; The Legal Light; A Matrimonial Boomerang; The Race for a Gold Mine; Roping a Bride; The Taking of Mustang Pete; The Tenderfoot's Triumph. 1916 Making an Impression; A $5,000 Elopement; Along the Border; A Bear of a Story; The Canby Hill Outlaws; A Close Call; Comer in Water; The Drifter; The Cowpuncher's Peril; Crooked Trails; Going West to Make Good; Legal Advice; Local Color; Making Good; Mistakes in Rustlers; Mix-up in Movies; The Passing of Pete; The Pony Express Rider; The Raiders; Roping a Sweetheart; The Sheriff's Blunder; The Sheriff's Duty; Shooting Up the Movies; Some Duel; Taking a Chance; The Taming of Grouchy Bill; Tom's Sacrifice; Tom's Strategy; Too Many Chefs; Trilby's Love Disaster; Western Masquerade; The Desert Circle Calls Its Own; An Eventful Evening; The Girl of Gold Gulch; The Golden Thought; The Man Within; Mistakes Will Happen; Starring In Western Stuff. 1917 Hearts and Saddles; Roman Cowboy; Six Cylinder Love; The Soft Tenderfoot; Tom and Jerry Mix; Twisted Trails; The Heart of Texas Ryan; Six Shooter Andy. 1918 Cupid's Roundup; Western Blood; Ace High; The Rainbow Trail; Durand of the Badlands. 1919 Fame and Fortune; The Wilderness Trail; Hell Roarin' Reform; Fighting for Gold; Coming of the Law. 1920 Desert Love; The Daredevil; The Cyclone; The Speed Maniac; The Terror; The Feud; Three Gold Coins; The Untamed; Mr. Logan, U.S.A.; Treat 'Em Rough; Rough Riding Romance. 1921 The Rough Diamond; Hands Off; Prairie Trails; The Queen of Sheba; A Ridin' Romeo; The Road Demon; The Texan; Big Town Round-Up; The Night Horsemen; After Your Own Heart; Trailin'! 1922 Up and Going; Sky High; For Big Stakes; The Fighting Streak; Chasing the Moon; Do and Dare; Just Tony; Tom Mix in Arabia; Arabia; Catch My Smoke. 1923 The Lone Star Ranger; Romance Land; Softboiled; Stepping Fast; Three Jumps Ahead; Mile-a-Minute Romeo. 1924 Oh, You Tony; North of Hudson Bay; A Golden Thought; The Last of the Duanes; Ladies to Board; Teeth; Eyes of the Forest; The Trouble Shooter; The Heart Buster; The Foreman of Bar Z Ranch. 1925 Everlasting Whisper; The Lucky Horseshoe; Law and the Outlaw; The Best Bad Man; Riders of the Purple Sage; The Rainbow Trail; Dick Turpin; The Deadwood Coach; A Child of the Prairie. 1926 The Great K and a Train Robbery; The Yankee Senor; No Man's Gold; Hardboiled; The Canyon of Light; My Own Pal; Tony Runs Wild. 1927 Tumbling River; The Circus Ace; The Last Trail; Silver Valley; Outlaws of Red River; The Broncho Twister. 1928 Painted Post; King Cowboy; Hello Cheyenne; A Horseman of the Plains; Arizona Wildcat; Son of the Golden West; Daredevil's Reward. 1929 Drifter; Outlawed; The Big Diamond Robbery. 1930 Under a Texas Moon. 1931 The Dude Ranch; Six Cylinder Love; The Galloping Ghost (serial). 1932 The Fourth Horseman; Destry Rides Again; My Pal, the King; Texas Bad Man; Rider of Death Valley. 1933 Flaming Guns; Hidden Gold; Terror Trail; Rustler's Roundup. 1935 The Miracle Rider (serial). 1943 Daredevils of the West (serial).

MIZOGHUCHI, KENJI
Born: 1898, Japan. Died: 1956. Screen actor and film director. Entered films as an actor during early silents.

M'KIN, ROBERT. See ROBERT McKIM

MOCK, ALICE
Died: Oct. 24, 1972. Screen actress.

Appeared in: 1945 Wonder Man.

MODIE, LOUELLA. See LOUELLA MODIE MAXAM

MODOT, GASTON
Born: 1887, Paris, France. Died: 1970, France? Screen actor and screenwriter. Appeared in the Onesime series beginning in 1908.

Appeared in: 1920 La Fete Espagnole; Fievre. 1925 Le Miracle des Loups (The Miracle of the Wolves). 1928 Carmen. 1930 Sous les Toits de Paris (Under the Roofs of Paris). 1931 Die Dreigroschenoper. 1932 Secrets of the Orient. 1934 Fantomas; Crainquebille. 1936 Pepe le Moko. 1938 Grand Illusion. 1939 Escape from Yesterday; The End of a Day; The Devil is an Empress; La Regle du Jeu (Rules of the Game—US 1950). 1947 Les Enfants du Paradis. 1948 Antoine and Antoinette. 1951 Passion for Life. 1952 Casque d'Or; Beauty and the Devil. 1956 French Can Can (aka Only the French Can). 1959 The Lovers; Le Testament de Dr. Cordelier (aka Experiment in Evil). 1961 Les Menteurs (The Liars—US 1964). 1962 Le Diable et les Dix Commandments (The Devil and the Ten Commandments—US 1963). 1964 L'Age d'Or (The Golden Age—originally released in 1930).

MOEHRING, KANSAS
Died: Oct. 2, 1968. Screen actor.

Appeared in: 1923 Out of Luck; Shootin' for Love. 1942 Down Texas Way. 1944 Land of the Outlaws. 1947 Trailing Danger. 1948 Frontier Agent. 1950 The Cariboo Trail.

MOFFAT, MARGARET
Born: 1892, England. Died: Feb. 19, 1942, Los Angeles, Calif. (pneumonia). Screen actress. Married to film producer Sewell Collins.

Appeared in: 1934 Just Smith. 1937 Farewell Again. 1938 Troopship. 1939 U-Boat 29. 1940 Song of the Road. 1941 Ringside Maisie. 1942 My Gal Sal.

MOFFATT, GRAHAM
Born: 1919, London, England. Died: July 2, 1965, Bath, England. Screen and television actor. Do not confuse with stage actor–playwright Graham Moffatt (dec. 1951).

Appeared in: 1933 Till the Bells Ring. 1934 A Cup of Kindness. 1935 Stormy Weather (US 1936). 1936 Windbag the Sailor. 1937 Good Morning, Boys (aka Where There's a Will—US); Okay For Sound; Gangway; Dr. Syn; Oh, Mr. Porter! 1938 Owd Bob (aka To the Victor—US); Convict 99; Old Bones of the River. 1939 Ask a Policeman; Where's the Fire?; Cheer Boys Cheer. 1940 Charley's (Big Hearted) Aunt. 1941 Hi Gang!; I Thank You. 1942 Back Room Boys. 1943 Dear Octopus (aka The Randolph Family—US 1945). 1944 Time Flies; Welcome Mr. Washington. 1945 I Know Where I'm Going (US 1947). 1946 The Voyage of Peter Joe series. 1947 Stage Frights. 1948 Woman Hater (US 1949). 1949 Three Bags Full. 1950 The Dragon of Pendragon Castle. 1951 The Second Mate. 1952 Mother Riley Meets the Vampire (aka Vampire Over London—US). 1960 Inn for Trouble.

MOHAN, CHANDRA
Born: India. Died: Apr. 2, 1949, India? Screen actor.

Appeared in: 1947 Shakuntala.

MOHAN, EARL
Died: Oct. 15, 1928, Los Angeles, Calif. Screen actor.

Appeared in: 1927 Love Makes 'Em Wild.

MOHR, GERALD
Born: June 11, 1914, New York, N.Y. Died: Nov. 10, 1968, Stockholm, Sweden. Screen, stage, radio and television actor. He was on the "Lone Wolf" series, both radio and screen, and was "Philip Marlowe, radio private eye."

Appeared in: 1941 We Go Fast; Jungle Girl (serial); The Monster and the Girl. 1942 The Lady Has Plans. 1943 Murder in Times Square; King of the Cowboys; Lady of Burlesque; One Dangerous Night; The Desert Song. 1946 The Notorious Lone Wolf; Gilda; A Guy Could Change; The Catman of Paris; Passkey to Danger; Invisible Informer; The Truth about Murder; Dangerous Business; The Magnificent Rogue. 1947 Lone Wolf in Mexico; Heaven Only Knows; The Lone Wolf in London. 1948 Two Guys from Texas. 1949 The Blonde Bandit. 1950 Undercover Girl; Hunt the Man Down. 1951 Sirocco; Ten Tall Men; Detective Story. 1952 The Sniper; The Ring; Son of Ali Baba; The Duel at Silver Creek; Invasion U.S.A. 1953 Raiders of the Seven Seas; Money from Home; The Eddie Cantor Story. 1954 Dragonfly Squadron. 1957 The Buckskin Lady. 1958 Terror in the Haunted House; Guns, Girls and Gangsters. 1959 A Date with Death. 1960 This Rebel Breed; The Angry Red Planet. 1968 Funny Girl.

MOISSI, ALEXANDER
Born: 1880, Trieste, Italy. Died: Apr. 1935, Vienna, Austria (pneumonia). Stage and screen actor.

Appeared in: 1929 The Royal Box. 1936 Lorenzino de Medici.

MOJA, HELLA

Born: 1898, Germany. Died: Feb. 1937, Berlin, Germany. Screen actress and screenwriter. Entered films approx. 1916.

Appeared in: 1929 U-Boat 9.

MOJAVE, KING

Died: Mar. 23, 1973. Screen actor.

Appeared in: 1937 Public Cowboy No. 1.

MOJICA, JOSE

Born: Sept. 14, 1899, San Gabriel, Jalisco, Mexico. Died: Sept. 20, 1974, Lima, Peru (heart ailment). Screen, stage actor, opera performer, writer and later an ordained priest.

Appeared in: 1925 Dick Turpin. 1930 One Mad Kiss. 1933 El Rey de los Gitanos; La Ley Del Haren; El Precio de un Beso; Su Ultimo Amor; La Melodia Prohibida (Forbidden Melody); Quando el Amor Rie. 1934 La Cruz y la Espada; Las Fronteras del Amor. 1939 El Capitan (Adventureous Captain). 1940 La Cancion del Milagro (The Miracle Song).

MOLANDER, OLAF

Born: 1892, Helsinki, Finland. Died: 1966, Finland? Screen actor and film director.

Appeared in: 1917 Thomas Graal's Ward. 1940 A Big Hug. 1945 Wandering With the Moon.

MOLONEY, JOHN

Born: 1911. Died: July 14, 1969, Los Angeles, Calif. Screen actor, emcee and singer.

Appeared in: 1962 Gypsy.

MOMO, ALESSANDRO

Born: Nov. 25, 1953, Italy. Died: Nov. 20, 1974, Rome, Italy (motorcycle accident). Screen and television actor.

Appeared in: 1974 Malizia. Other Italian films: Venial Sin; Honey and Darkness.

MONCRIES, EDWARD (aka EDWARD MONCRIEF)

Born: 1859. Died: Mar. 22, 1938, Hollywood, Calif. (heart attack). Screen, stage actor and stage manager. Was in many Charles Chaplin films.

Appeared in: 1921 Western Hearts. 1923 The Girl I Loved.

MONDOSE, ALEX (Alexandre Onsmonde)

Born: 1894, Liege, Belgium. Died: Feb. 8, 1972, Brussels, Belgium. Screen, stage actor and singer. Apparently appeared in only one film in 1955.

MONG, WILLIAM V.

Born: 1875, Clambersbury, Pa. Died: Dec. 10, 1940, Studio City, Calif. Screen, stage and vaudeville actor. Entered films in 1910.

Appeared in: 1910 The Connecticut Yankee. 1911 Lost in the Jungle. 1912 The Redemption of Greek Joe. 1915 Alias Holland Jimmy; The Word; Out of the Silence; Tainted Money. 1916 The Son of a Rebel Chief; To Another Woman; The Wrath of Cactus Moore; The Last of the Morgans; The Iron Hand; When the Wolf Howls; Shoes; Crimson Love; Husks of Love; A Son of Neptune; Tillie the Little Swede; The Girl in Lower 9; Along the Malibu; Two Men of Sandy Bar; The Good Woman; Her Bitter Cup; Fighting Joe; Birds of a Feather; The Severed Hand. 1917 An Old Soldier's Romance; Good-for-Nothing Gallagher; The Daring Chance; Bartered Youth; The Girl and the Crisis; The Grudge; Chubby Takes a Hand; Fanatics. 1918 The Hopper; The Painted Lily. 1919 Love's Prisoner; The Spender; Put Up Your Hands; The Follies Girl; After His Own Heart; The Amateur Adventurers; Fools and Their Money; The Master Man. 1921 Connecticut Yankee at King Arthur's Court; Sowing the Wind; Shame; The Ten Dollar Raise; The Winding Trail; Ladies Must Live; Pilgrims of the Night; Playthings of Destiny. 1922 Fool There Was; Shattered Idols; The Woman He Loved; Monte Cristo. 1923 All the Brothers Were Valiant; Drifting; In the Palace of the King; Lost and Found; Wandering Daughters; Penrod and Sam. 1924 Thy Name Is Woman; Flapper Wives; Why Men Leave Home; Welcome Stranger; What Shall I Do? 1925 Alias Mary Flynn; Excuse Me; Fine Clothes; Under the Rouge; The Unwritten Law; Barriers Burned Away; Off the Highway; Oh, Doctor!; The People vs. Nancy Preston; The Shadow on the Wall; Speed. 1926 The Old Soak; What Price Glory; Brooding Eyes; Fifth Avenue; The Shadow of the Law; The Silent Lover; Steel Preferred; The Strong Man. 1927 Alias the Lone Wolf; The Clown; The Magic Garden; Taxi! Taxi!; The Price of Honor; Too Many Crooks. 1928 The Broken Mask; The Haunted House; Code of the Air; The Devil's Trademark; No Babies Wanted; Ransom; Telling the World; White Flame. 1929 Should a Girl Marry?; Dark Skies; The House of Horror; Seven Footprints to Satan; Noah's Ark. 1930 The Girl Said No; In Gay Madrid; Murder on the Roof; Double Cross Roads; The Big Trail. 1931 The Flood; Gun Smoke; Bad Company; A Dangerous Affair. 1932 Cross Examination; By Whose Hands?; Fighting Fool; Widow in Scarlet; Dynamite Denny; The Sign of the Cross; No More Orchids. 1933 Women Won't Tell; Strange Adventure;

The Vampire Bat; The 11th Commandment; Fighting for Justice; Silent Men; Her Forgotten Past; The Mayor of Hell; The Narrow Corner; I Loved a Woman. 1934 Dark Hazard; Massacre; Treasure Island. 1935 The County Chairman; The Hoosier Schoolmaster; The Last Days of Pompeii; Whispering Smith Speaks. 1936 Dancing Pirate; The Last of the Mohicans; The Dark Hour. 1937 Stand-In. 1938 Painted Desert. 1944 The Sign of the Cross (revised version of 1932 film).

MONROE, MARILYN (Norma Jeane Baker)

Born: June 1, 1926, Los Angeles, Calif. Died: Aug. 5, 1962, Brentwood, Calif. (suicide?). Screen actress. Divorced from merchant seaman James Dougherty, professional baseball player Joe DiMaggio and playwright Arthur Miller.

Appeared in: 1948 Scudda Hoo! Scudda Hay!; Dangerous Years. 1949 Love Happy; Ladies of the Chorus. 1950 A Ticket to Tomahawk; All about Eve; Asphalt Jungle; Right Cross; The Fire Ball. 1951 Let's Make It Legal; Love Nest; As Young as You Feel; Hometown Story. 1952 Don't Bother to Knock; We're Not Married; Clash by Night; Monkey Business; O. Henry's Full House. 1953 Gentlemen Prefer Blondes; How to Marry a Millionaire; Niagara. 1954 River of No Return; There's No Business Like Show Business. 1955 The Seven Year Itch. 1956 Bus Stop. 1957 The Prince and the Showgirl. 1959 Some Like It Hot. 1960 Let's Make Love. 1961 The Misfits. 1963 Marilyn (film clips documentary).

MONROE, VAUGHN

Born: Oct. 7, 1911, Akron, Ohio. Died: May 21, 1973, Stuart, Fla. Radio, television singer, bandleader, author and screen actor.

Appeared in: 1944 Meet the People. 1947 Carnegie Hall. 1950 Singing Guns. 1952 Toughest Man in Arizona.

MONTAGUE, EDNA WOODRUFF. See EDNA WOODRUFF

MONTAGUE, FREDERICK

Born: 1864, London, England. Died: July 3, 1919, Los Angeles, Calif. (acute intestinal obstruction). Screen and stage actor. Married to actress Rita Montague (dec. 1962).

Appeared in: 1914 Where the Trail Divides; The Man on the Box; The Ghost Breaker; What's His Name; The Man from Home; The Circus Man; The Call of the North; Ready Money. 1915 Cameo Kirby. 1916 The Bait; The Hidden Law; The Leopard's Bride; Barriers of Society; Circumstantial Guilt; The Lawyer's Secret; The Lion Nemesis; The Haunted Symphony; For Her Good Name; Destiny's Boomerang; The Good for Nothing Brat; The Kaffir's Gratitude; Clouds in Sunshine Valley; The Star of India; A Siren of the Jungle. 1917 The Red Stain; God's Crucible; The Gift Girl; The Flame of Youth; A Prince for a Day; Little Marian's Triumph; The Winged Mystery; The Saintly Sinner; Good-for-Nothing Gallagher. 1918 Fast Company; The Fighting Grin; His Robe of Honor; The Rough Love. 1919 His Debt (aka The Debt); The Ghost Girl; The Best Man; All Wrong.

MONTAGUE, RITA

Born: 1884. Died: May 5, 1962, Hollywood, Calif. Screen, stage actress and playwright. Married to actor Frederick Montague (dec. 1919).

MONTALVAN, CELIA

Born: 1899, Mexico. Died: Jan. 10, 1958, Mexico City, Mexico (heart attack). Stage and screen actress.

Appeared in: 1936 Les Amours de Toni.

MONTANA, BULL (Lugia Montagna)

Born: May 16, 1887, Vogliera, Italy. Died: Jan. 24, 1950, Los Angeles, Calif. (coronary thrombosis). Screen actor and professional wrestler. Entered films in 1918.

Appeared in: 1919 Victory; Brass Buttons; The Unpardonable Sin. 1920 Treasure Island; Go and Get It. 1921 The Four Horsemen of the Apocalypse; Crazy to Marry; The Foolish Age; One Wild Week. 1922 Gay and Devilish; The Three Must-Get-There's; The Timber Queen (serial). 1923 Breaking into Society; Hollywood; Held to Answer. 1924 Jealous Husbands; The Fire Patrol; Painted People. 1925 Bashful Buccaneer; Dick Turpin; The Gold Hunters; Manhattan Madness; Secrets of the Night; The Lost World. 1926 Vanishing Millions (serial); The Skyrocket; The Son of the Sheik; Stop, Look and Listen. 1928 How to Handle Women; Good Morning Judge. 1929 The Show of Shows; Tiger Rose. 1935 Palooka from Paducah (short). 1937 Big City. 1943 Good Morning Judge.

MONTANO, A.

Born: Barbados, W.I. Died: Sept. 6, 1914, Long Island, N.Y. (heart failure after performing stunt in film). Screen actor and stuntman.

MONTEIRO, PILAR

Born: 1886, Portugal. Died: Dec. 1962, Lisbon, Portugal. Screen actress. Appeared in films during 1920s and 1930s.

MONTEREY, CARLOTTA (Hazel Neilson Taasinge)
Born: 1888. Died: Nov. 18, 1970, Westwood, N.J. Screen and stage actress. Married to playwright Eugene O'Neill (dec. 1953).

Appeared in: **1925** The King on Main Street; Soul Fire.

MONTEZ, MARIA (Maria de Santo Silas)
Born: June 6, 1918, Barahona, Dominican Republic. Died: Sept. 7, 1951, France (heart failure or drowning?). Stage and screen actress. Married to actor Jean Pierre Aumont.

Appeared in: **1941** Boss of Bullion City; The Invisible Woman; That Night in Rio; Raiders of the Desert; Moonlight in Hawaii; South of Tahiti; Lucky Devils. **1942** Bombay Clipper; The Mystery of Marie Roget; Arabian Nights. **1943** White Savage. **1944** Ali Baba and the Forty Thieves; Follow the Boys; Cobra Woman; Gypsy Wildcat; Bowery to Broadway. **1945** Sudan. **1946** Tangier. **1947** Pirates of Monterey; The Exile; Song of Scheherezade. **1948** The Siren of Atlantis. **1951** Wicked City; The Pirates Revenge. **1952** The Thief of Venice. Italian film: Sensuality.

MONTGOMERY, DOUGLAS (Robert Douglass Montgomery aka KENT DOUGLAS)
Born: Oct. 29, 1908, Los Angeles, Calif. Died: July 23, 1966, Ridgefield, Conn. Screen, stage and television actor. Appeared in films as Douglass Montgomery and Kent Douglas.

Appeared in: **1931** Waterloo Bridge; Five and Ten; Paid; Daybreak. **1932** A House Divided. **1933** Little Women. **1934** Music in the Air; Little Man, What Now?; Eight Girls in a Boat. **1935** The Mystery of Edwin Drood; Lady Tubbs; Harmony Lane; Tropical Trouble. **1936** Everything is Thunder. **1937** Life Begins with Love; Counsel for Crime. **1939** The Cat and the Canary. **1945** The Way to the Stars (aka Johnny in the Clouds—US). **1946** Woman to Woman. **1949** Forbidden. **1952** When in Rome.

MONTGOMERY, EARL (Earl Triplett Montgomery)
Born: 1893, Santa Cruz County, Calif. Died: Oct. 28, 1966. Stage and screen actor.

Appeared in: **1918** Bums and Boarders; Chumps and Cops; Farms and Fumbles. **1919** Love and Leather; Damsels and Dandies; Zip and Zest; Harems and Hokum; Caves and Croquettes; Vamps and Variety. **1923** Tea With a Kick. **1926** Stop, Look and Listen. **1936** Navy Born.

MONTGOMERY, FRANK
Born: 1870, Petrolia, Pa. Died: July 18, 1944, Hollywood, Calif. Screen, stage actor and film director. Married to actress Mary Darkfeather. Entered films in 1908.

Appeared in: **1922** Cardigan; The Man from Beyond; The Man Who Paid. **1924** Who's Cheating?; A Sainted Devil; Floodgates. **1925** The Mad Dancer; Children of the Whirlwind; Red Love. **1926** Aloma of the South Seas; So's Your Old Man.

MONTGOMERY, JACK
Born: 1892. Died: Jan. 21, 1962, Hollywood, Calif. (cancer). Screen actor and stuntman. Married to actress Marian Baxter (dec. 1977). Entered films during early silents. Father of "Baby Peggy," silent film moppet.

Appeared in: **1955** Run for Cover.

MONTIEL, NELLY
Born: Mexico. Died: Sept. 14, 1951, near Acapulco, Mexico (auto accident). Screen actress.

MONTOYA, ALEX P.
Born: Oct. 19, 1907, Texas. Died: Sept. 25, 1970, Los Angeles, Calif. (congestive heart failure). Screen and television actor. Brother of actress Julia Montoya.

Appeared in: **1946** Beauty and the Bandit; Trail to Mexico. **1947** Twilight on the Rio Grande; The Last Round-Up; Riding the California Trail; Robin Hood of Monterey. **1949** Square Dance Jubilee; Ghost of Zorro (serial); The Big Sombrero; Daughter of the Jungle. **1951** Hurricane Island. **1952** California Conquest; Wild Horse Ambush; The Golden Hawk; King of the Congo (serial); Voodoo Tiger. **1953** Son of Belle Starr; Conquest of Cochise. **1954** Passion; Three Young Texans. **1955** Hell's Island; Escape to Burma; Apache Ambush. **1956** Stagecoach to Fury. **1957** War Drums. **1958** The Toughest Gun in Tombstone. **1959** Ghost of Zorro (serial). **1962** Dangerous Charter. **1964** Island of the Blue Dolphins. **1965** The Flight of the Phoenix. **1966** The Appaloosa. **1967** King's Pirate. **1968** Daring Game.

MONTROSE, BELLE
Born: 1886. Died: Oct. 25, 1964, Hollywood, Calif. (heart attack). Screen, vaudeville and television actress. Mother of actor Steve Allen. Appeared in vaudeville as part of team "Allen and Montrose."

Appeared in: **1961** The Absent-Minded Professor.

MONTT, CHRISTINA
Born: 1897, Chile. Died: Apr. 22, 1969, Hollywood, Calif. (coronary failure). Screen actress.

Appeared in: **1924** The Sea Hawk. **1927** Rose of the Golden West. **1930** Alma de Gaucho.

MOODY, RALPH
Born: Nov. 5, 1887, St. Louis, Mo. Died: Sept. 16, 1971, Burbank, Calif. (heart attack). Screen, stage, radio, television actor and circus performer. Entered films in 1944.

Appeared in: **1948** Man-Eater of Kumaon. **1949** Square Dance Jubilee. **1951** Red Mountain. **1952** Affair in Trinidad; Road to Bali. **1953** Seminole; Column South; Tumbleweed. **1955** Many Rivers to Cross; Strange Lady in Town; Rage at Dawn; The Far Horizons; I Died a Thousand Times. **1956** The Last Hunt; The Steel Jungle; Toward the Unknown; Reprisal! **1957** The Monster That Challenged the World; Pawnee. **1958** Going Steady; The Lone Ranger and the Lost City of Gold. **1959** The Legend of Tom Dooley; The Big Fisherman. **1960** The Story of Ruth. **1961** Homicidal; The Outsider.

MOOERS, DE SACIA
Born: 1888, Allesandro, Mojave Desert, Calif. Died: Jan. 11, 1960, Hollywood, Calif. Stage and screen actress.

Appeared in: **1904** The Great Train Robbery. **1922** The Blonde Vampire; The Challenge. **1923** Potash and Perlmutter. **1924** The Average Woman; It Is the Law; Restless Wives. **1925** Any Woman. **1926** Forbidden Waters. **1927** Tongues of Scandal; Lonesome Ladies; By Whose Hand?; Back to Liberty. **1928** Broadway Daddies; Confessions of a Wife. **1929** Shanghai Rose; Just Off Broadway. **1930** The Arizona Kid.

MOON, DONNA
Died: Oct. 24, 1918, Helena, Montana (Spanish influenza). Screen actress. Married to actor Morse Moon (dec. 1918).

Appeared in: **1917** The Flame of Youth.

MOON, GEORGE
Born: 1886, Australia. Died: June 4, 1967, London, England. Stage and screen actor. Son of actor George Moon (dec.). Married to vaudeville actress Gertie McQueen.

Appeared in: **1938** Lightning Conductor. **1939** Me and My Pal. **1944** Time Flies. **1955** An Alligator Named Daisy (US 1957). **1957** Carry on Admiral (aka The Ship Was Loaded—US 1959); Davy. **1962** The Boys (US 1963). **1965** Monster of Terror (aka Die Monster Die—US). **1966** Promise Her Anything. **1967** Half a Sixpence (US 1968).

MOON, MORSE
Died: Oct. 1918, Helena, Montana (Spanish influenza). Screen actor. Married to actress Donna Moon (dec. 1918).

MOORE, ALICE (Alice Moore Miller)
Born: 1916. Died: May 7, 1960, Washington, D.C. Screen actress. Daughter of actor Tom Moore (dec. 1955) and actress Alice Joyce (dec. 1955). Niece of actors Matt (dec. 1960), Joe (dec. 1926), Owen (dec. 1939) and actress Mary Moore (dec. 1919).

Appeared in: **1934** Babes in Toyland. **1950** Revenge Is Sweet (reissue of 1934 film Babes in Toyland).

MOORE, CARLYLE, SR.
Born: 1875. Died: June 26, 1924. Stage and screen actor. Father of actor Carlyle Moore, Jr.

MOORE, CLEO
Born: Oct. 31, 1928, Baton Rouge, La. Died: Oct. 25, 1973, Inglewood, Calif. Screen actress.

Appeared in: **1948** Congo Bill (serial). **1950** Rio Grande Patrol; This Side of the Law; Dynamite Pass; Hunt the Man Down; Gambling House. **1951** On Dangerous Ground. **1952** Strange Fascination; The Pace that Thrills. **1953** One Girl's Confession; Thy Neighbor's Daughter. **1954** The Other Woman; Bait. **1955** Women's Prison; Hold Back Tomorrow. **1956** Over Exposed. **1957** Hit and Run.

MOORE, DEL
Born: 1917. Died: Aug. 30, 1970, Encino, Calif. (heart attack). Screen, stage and television actor.

Appeared in: **1952** So You Want to Enjoy Life (short). **1954** So You Want to Go to a Nightclub (short). **1955** So You Want to Be a Gladiator (short); So You Want to Be a V.P. (short). **1956** So You Think the Grass is Greener (short). **1961** The Last Time I Saw Archie. **1962** The Errand Boy; It's Only Money; Stagecoach to Dancer's Rock. **1963** The Nutty Professor. **1964** The Patsy; The Disorderly Orderly. **1966** Movie Star—American Style or: LSD I Hate You. **1967** The Big Mouth. **1968** The Catalina Caper.

MOORE, EULABELLE

Born: 1903. Died: Nov. 30, 1964, New York, N.Y. Screen, stage and television actress.

Appeared in: **1964** The Horror of Party Beach.

MOORE, EVA

Born: Feb. 9, 1870, Brighton, Sussex, England. Died: Apr. 27, 1955. Stage and screen actress.

Appeared in: **1920** The Law Divine. **1922** The Crimson Circle; Flames of Passion. **1923** Chu Chin Chow (US 1925). **1924** The Great Well (aka Neglected Women—US). **1927** Motherland. **1931** Brown Sugar; The Other Woman; Almost a Divorce. **1932** The Old Dark House; The Flesh is Weak. **1933** I was a Spy (US 1934); Just Smith; The Song You Gave Me; House of Dreams. **1934** Little Stranger; Blind Justice; Jew Suess (aka Power—US); A Cup of Kindness. **1935** Annie, Leave the Room; Vintage Wine. **1938** Old Iron. **1945** Scotland Yard Investigator. **1946** The Bandit of Sherwood Forest; Of Human Bondage.

MOORE, FLORENCE

Born: 1886, Philadelphia, Pa. Died: Mar. 9, 1935, Darby, Pa. (operation complications). Stage and screen actress. Sister of actor Frank F. Moore (dec. 1924).

Appeared in: **1924** Broadway after Dark. **1928** Broadway Comedienne (short); Soldier Composer (short).

MOORE, FRANK F.

Died: May 28, 1924, Los Angeles, Calif. Screen, stage and vaudeville actor. Brother of actress Florence Moore (dec. 1935).

MOORE, GRACE

Born: Dec. 5, 1901, Jellico, Tenn. Died: Jan. 26, 1947, Copenhagen, Denmark (plane crash). Screen, stage actress and opera performer.

Appeared in: **1930** A Lady's Morals; New Moon. **1934** One Night of Love. **1935** Love Me Forever. **1936** The King Steps Out. **1937** When You're in Love; I'll Take Romance. **1940** Louise.

MOORE, HARRY R. "TIM"

Born: 1888, Rock Island, Ill. Died: Dec. 13, 1958, Los Angeles, Calif. Screen, radio and television actor. Was Kingfish of "Amos 'n Andy" radio series.

MOORE, HILDA

Born: England. Died: May 18, 1929, New York, N.Y. (throat infection). Stage and screen actress. Married to actor Austin Fairman (dec. 1964).

Appeared in: **1916** The Broken Melody; The Second Mrs. Tangueray; Whoso is Without Sin. **1917** Justice. **1928** Palais de Danse. **1929** Jealousy.

MOORE, IDA

Born: 1883. Died: Sept. 1964. Screen actress.

Appeared in: **1925** The Merry Widow; Thank You. **1943** Cuty on Duty (short). **1944** Riders of the Santa Fe; The Ghost Walks Alone; She's a Soldier Too. **1945** Rough, Tough and Ready; Her Lucky Night; Girls of the Big House. **1946** To Each His Own; Cross My Heart. **1947** Host to a Ghost (short); The Egg and I; Easy Come, Easy Go; It's a Joke, Son. **1948** Good Sam; Johnny Belinda; Money Madness; Rusty Leads the Way. **1949** Manhattan Angel; Ma and Pa Kettle; Leave It to Henry; Hold That Baby; Paid in Full. **1950** Harvey; Backfire; Mr. Music; Mother Didn't Tell Me. **1951** The Lemon Drop Kid; Comin' 'Round the Mountain; Leave It to the Marines; Honeychile. **1952** Scandal Sheet; Rainbow 'Round My Shoulders. **1953** Scandal at Scourie. **1954** The Country Girl. **1955** Ma and Pa Kettle at Waikiki. **1957** The Desk Set. **1958** Rock-a-Bye Baby.

MOORE, JOE

Born: County Meath, Ireland. Died: Aug. 22, 1926, near Santa Monica, Calif. (heart attack). Screen actor. Married to actress Grace Cunard (dec. 1967). See Alice Moore for family information.

Appeared in: **1920** Love's Battle. **1921** Arrest Norma MacGregor. **1922** Judgement; False Brands; Wolf Pack; Up in the Air About Mary. **1924** Wages of Virtue. **1925** Goat Getter. **1926** The Golden Web.

MOORE, MARY

Died: Feb. 1919, France. Screen actress. See Alice Moore for family information.

Appeared in: **1915** Lola.

MOORE, MATT

Born: Jan. 1888, County Meath, Ireland. Died: Jan. 21, 1960, Hollywood, Calif. Screen actor. See Alice Moore for family information.

Appeared in: **1913** Traffic in Souls. **1914** A Singular Cynic. **1917** Pride of the Clan. **1919** The Unpardonable Sin; Sahara; A Regular Girl. **1920** Everybody's Sweetheart; Don't Ever Marry; Hairpins. **1921** A Man's Home; The Miracle of Manhattan; The Passionate Pilgrim; Straight Is the Way. **1922** Back Pay; Minnie; Sisters; The Storm; The Jilt. **1923** White Tiger; Strangers of the Night; Drifting. **1924** Fools in the Dark; Another Man's Wife; The Breaking Point; The Narrow Street; A Self-Made Failure; No More Women; The Wise Virgin. **1925** How Baxter Butted In; Grounds for Divorce; A Lost Lady; His Majesty, Bunker Bean; The Unholy Three; Where the Worst Begins; The Way of a Girl. **1926** His Jazz Bride; Three Weeks in Paris; The First Year; The Caveman; Early to Wed; The Mystery Club; Summer Bachelors; Diplomacy. **1927** Married Alive; Tillie the Toiler. **1928** Dry Martini; Beware of Blondes; Phyllis of the Follies. **1929** Coquette; Side Street. **1930** The Squealer; Call of the West. **1931** Penrod and Sam; The Front Page; Married in Haste; Consolation Marriage. **1932** Rain; Cock of the Air. **1933** The Deluge. **1934** All Men Are Enemies; Such Women Are Dangerous. **1936** Anything Goes; Absolute Quiet. **1939** Bad Boy; Range War. **1941** My Life with Caroline. **1942** Mokey. **1943** Happy Land. **1944** Wilson. **1945** Spellbound. **1946** The Hoodlum Saint. **1948** Good Sam. **1949** That Forsyte Woman. **1950** The Big Hangover. **1952** Plymouth Adventure; Invitation. **1954** Seven Brides for Seven Brothers. **1956** The Birds and the Bees; Pardners. **1957** An Affair to Remember. **1958** I Bury the Living.

MOORE, MONETTE

Born: 1912. Died: Oct. 21, 1962, Anaheim, Calif. (heart attack). Stage and screen actress.

Appeared in: **1951** Yes Sir, Mr. Bones.

MOORE, OWEN

Born: Dec. 12, 1886, County Meath, Ireland. Died: June 9, 1939, Beverly Hills, Calif. Screen, stage actor and film producer. Divorced from actress Mary Pickford. Married to actress Kathryn Perry. See Alice Moore for family information. Entered films in 1908 with Biograph.

Appeared in: **1908** In a Lonely Villa; In Old Kentucky; The Honor of Thieves; The Salvation Army Lass. **1909** The Cricket on the Hearth; The Winning Coat; A Baby's Shoe; The Violin Maker of Cremona; The Mended Lute; Pippa Passes; 1776, or the Hessian Renegades; Leather Stocking; A Change of Heart; His Lost Love; The Expiation; The Light That Came; The Open Gate; The Dancing Girl of Butte; Her Terrible Ordeal; The Last Deal; The Iconoclast. **1911** Flo's Discipline; The Courting of Mary. **1912** Swift Waters. **1913** Caprice. **1914** Battle of the Sexes. **1915** Mistress Nell; Pretty Mrs. Smith; Nearly a Lady; The Little Teacher (reissued as A Small Town Bully). **1916** A Coney Island Princess; Betty of Graystone; Little Meera's Romance; Under Cover. **1917** The Little Boy Scout; The Silent Partner; A Girl Like That. **1919** Crimson Gardenia. **1920** Piccadilly Jim; Poor Simp. **1921** A Divorce of Convenience; The Chicken in the Case. **1922** Oh, Mabel Behave; Reported Missing; Love Is an Awful Thing. **1923** Hollywood; Modern Matrimony; Her Temporary Husband; The Silent Partner. **1924** Thundergate; Torment; East of Broadway. **1925** The Parasite; Go Straight; Married?; Camille of the Barbary Coast; Code of the West. **1926** False Pride; The Skyrocket; The Black Bird; Money Talks; The Road to Mandalay. **1927** The Red Mill; The Taxi Dancer; Women Love Diamonds; Becky; Tea for Three. **1928** The Actress; Husbands for Rent. **1929** High Voltage; Stolen Love; Side Street. **1930** Outside the Law; What a Widow!; Extravagance. **1931** Hush Money. **1932** Cannonball Express; As You Desire Me. **1933** She Done Him Wrong; Man of Sentiment. **1937** A Star Is Born.

MOORE, PATTI

Born: 1901. Died: Nov. 26, 1972, Los Angeles, Calif. (cancer). Screen, stage and vaudeville actress.

Appeared in: **1964** When the Boys Meet the Girls.

MOORE, PERCY

Born: 1878. Died: Apr. 8, 1945, New York, N.Y. Screen and stage actor.

Appeared in: **1925** The Shock Punch.

MOORE, RUTH HART

Died: May 2, 1952, New York, N.Y. Screen, stage and vaudeville actress.

Appeared in: **1913** Judith of Bethulia. **1928** The Companionate Marriage.

MOORE, SCOTT

Born: 1889. Died: Dec. 18, 1967, Miami Beach, Fla. Screen actor.

Appeared in: **1931** The Struggle.

MOORE, SUE

Born: 1916. Died: Apr. 10, 1966, Calif. Stage and screen actress.

Appeared in: **1938** Swing Your Lady. **1939** Tiny Troubles (short). **1940** The Mortal Storm. **1941** Cheers for Miss Bishop. **1945** Pillow to Post.

MOORE, TOM

Born: 1885, County Meath, Ireland. Died: Feb. 12, 1955, Santa Monica, Calif. (cancer). Screen, stage, vaudeville and television actor. Married to actress Eleanor Merry. Divorced from actresses Alice Joyce (dec. 1955) and Renee Adoree (dec. 1933). See Alice Moore for family information. Entered films with the Kalem Company.

Appeared in: **1913** Nine of the Theatre. **1914** The Brand; Vampire's Trail; The

Mystery of the Sleeping Death. 1916 Who's Guilty. 1917 The Cinderella Man; The Primrose Ring. 1918 Thirty a Week; The Kingdom of Youth. 1919 Lord and Lady Algy; Toby's Bow; City of Comrades; Heartsease; Dub; A Man and His Money; One of the Finest. 1920 Great Accident; Officer 666; Stop Thief. 1921 Dangerous Money; Made in Heaven; Hold Your Horses; Beating the Game; From the Ground Up. 1922 Over the Border; Mr. Barnes of New York; The Cowboy and the Lady; Pawned. 1923 Rouged Lips; Big Brother; Marriage Morals; Harbor Lights; Mary of the Movies. 1924 One Night in Rome; Manhandled; The Isle of Vanishing Men; Dangerous Money. 1925 Adventure; The Trouble with Wives; On Thin Ice; Pretty Ladies; Under the Rough. 1926 Kiss for Cinderella; The Clinging Vine; Good and Naughty; Syncopating Sue; The Song and Dance Man. 1927 The Love Thrill; The Wise Wife; Cabaret; The Siren. 1928 Anybody Here Seen Kelly? 1929 The Yellowback; His Last Haul; Side Street. 1930 The Costello Case; The Woman Racket. 1931 The Last Parade. 1932 Cannonball Express; Vanishing Men. 1933 Men Are Such Fools; Neighbors' Wives; Mr. Broadway. 1934 Bombay Mail. 1936 Trouble for Two; Reunion. 1946 Behind Green Lights. 1947 Moss Rose; Forever Amber. 1948 Scudda Hoo! Scudda Hay! 1949 The Fighting O'Flynn. 1950 The Redhead and the Cowboy.

MOORE, VICTOR

Born: Feb. 24, 1876, Hammonton, N.J. Died: July 1962, Long Island, N.Y. (heart attack). Screen, stage and vaudeville actor. Entered films in 1915.

Appeared in: 1915 Chimmie Fadden; Chimmie Fadden Out West; Snobs. 1916 The Clown; The Race; The Best Man. 1917 Invited Out; Oh! U-Boat; Faint Heart and Fair Lady; Bungalowing; Commuting; Moving; Flivering; Home Defense. 1925 The Man Who Found Himself; prior to 1930 appeared in 41 Lever Co. shorts. 1930 Heads Up; Dangerous Nan McGrew. 1932-33 Appeared in Vitaphone shorts. 1934 Romance in the Rain; Gift of Gab. 1936 Swing Time; Gold Diggers of 1937. 1937 We're on the Jury; Meet the Missus; The Life of the Party; She's Got Everything; Make Way for Tomorrow. 1938 Radio City Revels; This Marriage Business. 1941 Louisiana Purchase. 1942 Star Spangled Rhythm. 1943 True to Life; Riding High; The Heat's On. 1944 Carolina Blues. 1945 Duffy's Tavern; It's in the Bag. 1946 Ziegfeld Follies. 1947 It Happened on Fifth Avenue. 1948 A Miracle Can Happen. 1949 A Kiss in the Dark. 1952 We're Not Married. 1955 The Seven Year Itch.

MOORE, VIN

Born: 1878, Mayville, N.Y. Died: Dec. 5, 1949, Hollywood, Calif. Screen, stage actor, film director and screenwriter.

Appeared in: 1916 By Stork Delivery. 1926 Lazy Lightning; The Man from the West.

MOOREHEAD, AGNES (Agnes Robertson Moorehead)

Born: Dec. 6, 1906, Clinton, Mass. Died: Apr. 30, 1974, Rochester, Minn. (lung cancer). Screen, stage, vaudeville, radio and television actress. Divorced from actors Jack G. Lee and Robert Gist. Nominated for 1942 Academy Award as Best Supporting Actress in The Magnificent Ambersons and in 1948 for Johnny Belinda.

Appeared in: 1941 Citizen Kane (film debut). 1942 The Magnificent Ambersons; The Big Street; Journey into Fear. 1943 The Youngest Profession; Government Girl. 1944 Mrs. Parkington; Since You Went Away; The Seventh Cross; Dragon Seed; Tomorrow the World. 1945 Her Highness and the Bell Boy; Keep Your Powder Dry; Our Vines Have Tender Grapes. 1947 Dark Passage; The Lost Moment. 1948 Johnny Belinda; Summer Holiday; The Woman in White; Station West. 1949 Without Honor; The Stratton Story; The Great Sinner. 1950 Caged. 1951 Adventures of Captain Fabian; Show Boat; Fourteen Hours; The Blue Veil. 1952 Captain Blackjack; The Blazing Forest. 1953 The Story of Three Loves (aka The Jealous Lover); Main Street to Broadway; Scandal at Scourie; Those Redheads from Seattle. 1954 Magnificent Obsession. 1955 The Left Hand of God; Untamed; All That Heaven Allows. 1956 Meet Me in Las Vegas; The Conqueror; The Revolt of Mamie Stover; The Swan; Pardners; The Opposite Sex. 1957 Raintree County; The True Story of Jesse James; Jeanne Eagels; The Story of Mankind. 1959 Night of the Quarter Moon; Tempest; The Bat. 1960 Pollyanna. 1961 Twenty Plus Two; Bachelor in Paradise. 1962 Jessica; How the West was Won. 1963 Who's Minding the Store? 1964 Hush, Hush, Sweet Charlotte. 1965 The Singing Nun. 1971 What's the Matter with Helen?; Dear Dead Delilah; Charlotte's Web (voice).

MOOREY, STEFA

Born: 1934, London. Died: Feb. 3, 1972, Birmingham, England (suicide—drowned). Screen actress. Married to actor Frank Moorey.

MOORHOUSE, BERT

Born: 1895. Died: Jan. 26, 1954, Hollywood, Calif. (suicide—gun). Screen actor.

Appeared in: 1928 Rough Ridin' Red. 1929 Hey Rube!; The Woman I Love; The Delightful Rogue; The Girl from Woolworths. 1930 Conspiracy; Pay Off. 1934 Smarty. 1944 Kitchen Cynic (short). 1950 Sunset Boulevard; The Big Hangover; Duchess of Idaho.

MORALES, ISHMAEL "ESY"

Born: 1917, Puerto Rico. Died: Nov. 2, 1950, New York, N.Y. (heart attack). Screen actor and orchestra leader.

Appeared in: 1945 Film Vodvil (short with his Copacabana Orchestra). 1949 Criss Cross.

MORAN, FRANK (Frank Charles Moran)

Born: Mar. 18, 1887, Ohio. Died: Dec. 14, 1967, Hollywood, Calif. (heart attack). Screen actor and professional heavyweight boxer.

Appeared in: 1928 Ships of the Night. 1933 Hooks and Jabs (short); Sailor's Luck; Gambling Ship. 1934 Three Chumps Ahead (short); No More Women; The World Moves On; By Your Leave. 1936 Mummy's Boys. 1937 Shall We Dance? 1938 Battle of Broadway. 1939 Captain Fury. 1940 The Great McGinty. 1941 Federal Fugitives; A Date with the Falcon; Sullivan's Troubles. 1942 Butch Minds the Baby; Sullivan's Travels; The Corpse Vanishes. 1943 Ghosts on the Loose. 1944 The Great Moment; Return of the Ape Man; Hail the Conquering Hero; The Miracle of Morgan's Creek. 1945 Yolanda and the Thief. 1946 Pardon My Past. 1947 Mad Wednesday. 1948 A Miracle Can Happen. 1949 The Lady Gambles.

MORAN, GEORGE (George Searcy)

Born: 1882, Elwood, Kan. Died: Aug. 1, 1949, Oakland, Calif. (stroke). Screen, stage, vaudeville, minstrel and radio actor. He was the Moran in "Moran and Mack" comedy team, usually referred to as the "Two Black Crows"; however, he did not appear in several shorts and films as he was replaced by Bert Swor, but did return to the team for Hypnotized and later shorts.

Appeared in, as part of team: 1927 Two Flaming Youths. 1929 Why Bring That Up. 1932 Hypnotized. 1932-33 "Moran and Mack" short comedies for Educational: Two Black Crows in Africa; As the Crows Fly. 1940 My Little Chickadee; The Bank Dick.

MORAN, LEE

Born: June 23, 1890, Chicago, Ill. Died: Apr. 24, 1961, Woodland Hills, Calif. (heart attack). Stage and screen actor. Part of comedy team of "Lyons and Moran" in Christie comedies from 1914 to 1920.

Appeared in: 1912 The Sheriff Outwitted; Making a Man of Her. 1913 Weighed in the Balance; Her Friend the Butler; Locked Out at Twelve. 1914 She Was a Working Girl; What a Baby Did; Such a Villain; Her Moonshine Lover; Captain Bill's Warm Reception; When the Girls Joined the Force; A Lucky Deception; Sophie of the Films; When Eddie Went to the Front; When Bess Gets in Wrong. 1915 When the Mummy Cried for Help; Wanted, a Leading Woman; Eddie's Little Love Affair; He Fell in a Cabaret; When His Lordship Proposed; When Cupid Caught a Thief; When the Deacon Swore; How Doctor Cupid Won; Jed's Little Elopement; The Mix-Up at Maxim's; The Baby's Fault; When He Proposed; A Coat's a Coat; Eddie's Awful Predicament; When Her Idol Fell; Too Many Crooks; When They Were Co-Eds; The Downfall of Potts; A Peach and a Pair; When the Spirit Moved; The Tale of His Pants; The Rise and Fall of Officer 13; Little Egypt Malone; Tony the Wop; Kids and Corsets; Their Happy Honeymoon; Too Many Smiths; When Lizzie Went to Sea; Their Quiet Honeymoon; Love and a Savage; Some Chaperone; It Almost Happened; Some Fixer; Almost a Knockout. 1916 Jed's Trip to the Fair; When Aunt Matilda Fell; Mingling Spirits. 1917 War Bridegrooms; A Hasty Hazing; Down Went the Key; A Million in Sight; A Bundle of Trouble; When the Cat's Away; Some Specimens; Shot in the West; Mixed Matrimony; The Home Wreckers; Under the Bed; Follow the Tracks; To Oblige a Vampire; The Lost Appetite; What a Clue Will Do; Moving Day; Tell Morgan's Girl; A Burglar by Request; Who's Looney Now?; Jilted in Jail; His Wife's Relations; Pete the Prowler; To Be or Not to Be Remarried; Hot Applications; A Fire Escape Finish; Why, Uncle!; The Other Stocking; One Thousand Miles an Hour; Treat 'Em Rough; A Macaroni Sleuth. 1918 Please Hit Me; The Extra Bridegroom; Hearts and Let'us; The Knockout; Almost Welcome; The Vamp Cure; Giver Her Gas; Damaged Goods; Housecleaning Horrors. 1919 The Wife Breakers; Skidding Thrones; Kitchen Police; How's Your Husband?; Three in a Closet; The Bullskeviki; Fun in a Flat; The Expert Eloper; Lay Off!; The Smell of the Yukon. 1920 Bungled Bungalows; Caught in the End. 1921 A Shocking Night; Fixed by George; Once a Plumber. 1924 The Fast Worker; Gambling Wives; Daring Youth; The Tomboy; Listen, Lester. 1925 After Business Hours; Fifth Avenue Models; Where Was I?; Tessie; My Lady of Whims; Jimmie's Millions. 1926 Her Big Night; Syncopating Sue; The Little Irish Girl; Take It from Me. 1927 Fast and Furious; The Rose of Kildare; The Irresistible Lover; Spring Fever; The Thrill Seekers; Wolf's Clothing. 1928 The Actress; Ladies of the Night Club; Outcast; Look-Out Girl; The Racket; Taxi 13; Thanks for the Buggy Ride; A Woman against the World; Show Girl. 1929 On with the Show; The Aviator; Children of the Ritz; Dance Hall; Glad Rag Doll; Gold Diggers of Broadway; Madonna of Avenue A; No Defense; The Show of Shows; Hearts in Exile. 1930 Golden Dawn; Hide Out; Mammy; Pardon My Gun; Sweet Mama. 1931 A Soldier's Plaything; Caught Plastered. 1932 Stowaway; Exposure; Racetrack; The Fighting Gentleman; Uptown New York; The Death Kiss. 1933 Sister of Judas; Grand Slam; The 11th Commandment; Goldie Gets Along; High Gear; Sitting Pretty. 1934 Circus Clown. 1935 Circumstantial Evidence; Honeymoon Limited. 1936 The Calling of Dan Matthews.

MORAN, MANOLO

Born: 1904, Madrid, Spain. Died: Apr. 27, 1967, Alicante, Spain. Screen actor. Won the Spanish Oscar in 1958 for his role in Viva la Imposible (Long Live the Impossible).

Appeared in: **1949** Don Quixote de la Mancha. **1958** Viva la Imposible (Long Live the Impossible). **1966** Operation Delilah. **1967** Flame Over Viet Nam. Other Spanish films: Angels of the Wheel; Manolo, Guardia Urbana (Manolo, Traffic Cop).

MORAN, PAT

Born: 1901. Died: Aug. 9, 1965, Woodland Hills, Calif. Screen, stage actor and stuntman. Married to actress Patsy Moran (dec. 1968).

Appeared in: **1949** Trouble Makers. **1956** The Ten Commandments. **1963** Move Over Darling. **1964** The Unsinkable Molly Brown.

MORAN, PATSY

Born: Dec. 10, 1968, Hollywood, Calif. Screen and stage actress. Married to actor and stuntman Pat Moran (dec. 1965).

Appeared in: **1938** Topa Topa; Blockheads. **1940** Cowboy from Sundown; The Golden Trail. **1942** Foreign Agent. **1945** Come Out Fighting; Trouble Chasers. **1949** Billie Gets Her Man (short).

MORAN, POLLY (Pauline Theresa Moran)

Born: June 28, 1883, Chicago, Ill. Died: Jan. 25, 1952, Los Angeles, Calif. (heart ailment). Screen, stage, vaudeville and radio actress. Entered films as a Mack Sennett bathing beauty in 1915.

Appeared in: **1915** Their Social Splash; Those College Girls (reissued as His Better Half); A Favorite Fool; Her Painted Hero; The Hunt. **1916** The Village Blacksmith; By Stork Alone; A Bath House Blunder; His Wild Oats; Madcap Ambrose; Pills of Peril; Vampire Ambrose; Love Will Conquer; Because He Loved Her. **1917** Her Fame and Shame; His Naughty Thought; Cactus Nell; She Needed a Doctor; His Uncle Dudley; Roping Her Romeo. **1921** The Affairs of Anatol; Two Weeks with Pay; Skirts. **1923** Luck. **1926** Scarlet Letter. **1927** The Callahans and the Murphys; London after Midnight; Buttons; The Thirteenth Hour. **1928** The Enemy; Rose Marie; The Divine Woman; Bringing up Father; Telling the World; Show People; Beyond the Sierras; Shadows of the Night; While the City Sleeps; Movie Chatterbox (short). **1929** The Unholy Night; Honeymoon; China Bound; Dangerous Females; Hollywood Revue of 1929; Hot for Paris; So This Is College; Speedway. **1930** Remote Control; Way for a Sailor; Way Out West; The Girl Said No; Chasing Rainbows; Caught Short; Paid. **1931** Guilty Hands; Reducing; Politics; It's a Wise Child. **1932** The Passionate Plumber; Prosperity; The Slippery Pearls (short). **1933** Alice in Wonderland. **1934** Hollywood Party; Down to Their Last Yacht. **1936** Columbia shorts. **1937** Two Wise Maids. **1938** Ladies in Distress. **1939** Ambush. **1940** Tom Brown's School Days; Meet the Missus. **1941** Petticoat Politics. **1949** Adam's Rib. **1950** The Yellow Cab Man. **1964** Big Parade of Comedy (documentary).

MORANTE, JOSEPH

Born: 1853. Died: Apr. 13, 1940, Hollywood, Calif. Screen actor.

MORANTE, MILBURN (Milburn Charles Morante aka MILBURN MORANTI)

Born: Apr. 6, 1887, San Francisco, Calif. Died: Jan. 28, 1964, Pacoima, Calif. (heart disease). Screen, stage actor, film director and producer.

Appeared in: **1915** A Millionaire for a Minute; No Babies Allowed; Pete's Awful Crime; Mysterious Lady Baffles and Detective Duck in the Lost Roll; Leomade Aids Cupid; The Ore Mystery; Freaks; The Way He Won the Widow. **1916** A Perfect Match; Wanted—A Piano Tuner; Leap and Look Thereafter; The Tale of a Telegram; The Jitney Driver's Romance; His Highness the Janitor; Hubby Puts One Over; Muchly Married; Some Vampire; I've Got Yer Number; Kate's Affinities; She Wrote a Play and Played It; A Marriage for Revenge; Soup to Nuts; In Onion There is Strength; The Elixir of Life; The Deacon Stops the Show; Father Gets in Wrong; Bears and Bullets; A Crooked Mix-Up; A Shadowed Shadow; In Love With a Fireman; Their First Arrest; A Janitor's Vendetta; Musical Madness; Scrappily Married; A Wife for a Ransom; A Dark Suspicion; Love Quarantined; Bashful Charley's Proposal; An All Around Cure; A Raffle for a Husband; A Stage Villain; The Fall of Deacon Stillwaters; The Harem Scarem Deacon; The Tramp Chef; Their Dark Secret; Jags and Jealousy; Mines and Matrimony. **1917** Love in Suspense; Love Me—Love My Biscuits; His Coming-Out Party; Out for the Dough; Mule Mates; Rosie's Rancho; Passing the Grip; Wanta Make a Dollar; 'Art Aches; Whose Baby?; What the—?; A Boob for Luck; The Careless Cop; The Leak; Left in the Soup; The Man With the Package; The Last Scent; The Boss of the Family; Uneasy Money; One Damp Day; His Fatal Beauty; Her Naughty Choice; The Shame of the Bullcon; Water on the Brain. **1919** Mixed Wives. **1921** Hearts O' the Range. **1922** Diamond Carlisle; The Hate Trail. **1924** Battling Mason; A Fighting Heart; Rainbow Rangers. **1925** Don X; Flying Fool; The Range Terror; The Rip Snorter; Triple Action; Wolf Blood. **1926** Buffalo Bill on the U.P. Trail; The Desperate Game; Lawless Trails; Modern Youth; West of the Rainbow's End. **1927** The Grey Devil; Cactus Trails; Daring Deeds; The Swift Shadow; Perils of the Jungle (serial). **1928** The Fightin' Redhead; The

Pinto Kid; The Little Buckaroo; Wizard of the Saddle. **1929** The Freckled Rascal; The Little Savage; The Vagabond Cub; Pals of the Prairie. **1935** The Lost City (serial); The Vanishing Riders; Wild Mustang. **1936** Blazing Justice; Sundown Saunders; plus the following serials: The Black Coin; The Clutching Hand; Custer's Last Stand. **1937** Public Cowboy No. 1; The Old Corral; Bar Z Bad Men. **1938** Gold Spur; Gold Mine in the Sky. **1941** Buzzy and the Phantom Pinto; Trail of the Silver Spur. **1942** West of the Law. **1943** Ghost Rider. **1946** Drifting Along. **1947** Ridin' Down the Trail. **1948** Oklahoma Blues; Range Renegades; Hidden Danger; The Rangers Ride; Cowboy Cavalier; The Fighting Ranger. **1949** Western Renegades; West of El Dorado; Haunted Trails. **1950** Six Gun Mesa; Over the Border; Law of the Panhandle; Outlaw Gold; West of Wyoming. **1951** Abilene Trail; Blazing Bullets.

MORDANT, EDWIN

Born: 1868, Baltimore, Md. Died: Feb. 15, 1942, Hollywood, Calif. Stage and screen actor. Married to actress Grace Atwell.

Appeared in: **1915** Seven Sisters; The Prince and the Pauper; The Royal Family. **1916** Molly-Make-Believe; Poor Little Peppina. **1917** The Undying Flame. **1920** The Cost. **1934** I'll Tell the World. **1938** Shadows over Shanghai; Outlaws of Sonora.

MORDANT, GRACE (Grace Atwell)

Born: 1872. Died: Nov. 2, 1952, Hollywood, Calif. Screen and stage actress. Married to actor Edwin Mordant (dec. 1942).

MORELAND, MANTAN

Born: Sept. 4, 1902, Monroe, La. Died: Sept. 28, 1973, Hollywood, Calif. Black screen, stage, vaudeville, television actor and circus performer. Appeared in the Charlie Chan films as "Birmingham Brown," Charlie's chauffeur.

Appeared in: **1936** Lucky Ghost. **1937** Spirit of Youth. **1938** Harlem on the Prairie; Frontier Scout; Next Time I Marry; There's That Woman Again. **1939** Irish Luck; One Dark Night; Tell No Tales; Riders of the Frontier. **1940** Laughing at Danger; Millionaire Playboy; Pier 13; Chasing Trouble; On the Spot; The City of Chance; Drums of the Desert; Mr. Washington Goes to Town; The Man Who Wouldn't Talk; Star Dust; Maryland; Viva Cisco Kid. **1941** Four Jacks and a Jill; Marry the Boss's Daughter; World Premiere; King of the Zombies; Ellery Queen's Penthouse Mystery; Up in the Air; The Gang's All Here; Hello Sucker; Dressed to Kill; You're Out of Luck; Sign of the Wolf; Let's Go Collegiate; Cracked Nuts; Footlight Fever; Sleepers West. **1942** Andy Hardy's Double Life; A-Haunting We Will Go; Professor Creeps; The Strange Case of Dr. Rx; Treat 'Em Rough; Mexican Spitfire Sees a Ghost; Footlight Serenade; Phantom Killer; Eyes in the Night; Girl Trouble; Tarzan's New York Adventure; The Palm Beach Story. **1943** Cabin in the Sky; The Crime Smasher; Sarong Girl; Revenge of the Zombies; Melody Parade; She's for Me; Hit the Ice; My Kingdom for a Cook; Slightly Dangerous; Swing Fever; You're a Lucky Fellow, Mr. Smith; We've Never Been Licked. **1944** Chip Off the Old Block; See Here, Private Hargrove; Charlie Chan in the Secret Service; The Chinese Cat; Moon Over Las Vegas; Pin-Up Girl; South of Dixie; Black Magic; Bowery to Broadway; This Is the Life; The Mystery of the River Boat (serial). **1945** The Scarlet Clue; The Jade Mask; The Shanghai Cobra; The Spider; Captain Tugboat Annie; She Wouldn't Say Yes. **1946** Dark Alibi; Shadows over Chinatown; Mantan Messes Up; Mantan Runs for Mayor; Professor Creeps. **1947** Murder at Malibu Ranch; The Trap; Chinese Ring. **1948** Docks of New Orleans; Shanghai Chest; The Feathered Serpent; The Mystery of the Golden Eye; The Best Man Wins. **1949** Sky Dragon. **1956** Rockin' the Blues. **1957** Rock n' Roll Revue. **1967** Enter Laughing. **1968** Spider Baby (aka Cannibal Orgy; The Maddest Story Ever Told; The Liver Eaters). **1970** Watermelon Man.

MORENCY, ROBERT "BUSTER"

Born: 1932. Died: Mar. 30, 1937, Regina, Saskatchewan, Canada (leukemia). Child screen actor.

MORENO, ANTONIO

Born: Sept. 26, 1888, Madrid, Spain. Died: Feb. 15, 1967, Beverly Hills, Calif. Screen actor.

Appeared in: **1912** Two Daughters of Eve; So Near, Yet So Far; Voice of the Million. **1913** Judith of Bethulia. **1914** In the Latin Quarter. **1915** The Island of Regeneration. **1916** The Tarantula; Kennedy Square. **1917** The Magnificent Meddler; Aladdin from Broadway. **1918** The House of Hate (serial); The Iron Test (serial); The House of a Thousand Candles. **1919** Perils of Thunder Mountain (serial). **1920** The Invisible Hand (serial); The Veiled Mystery (serial). **1921** Three Sevens; The Secret of the Hills. **1922** Guilty Conscience. **1923** The Exciters; The Trail of the Lonesome Pine; The Spanish Dancer; My American Wife; Look Your Best; Lost and Found. **1924** The Story without a Name; The Border Legion; Bluff; Flaming Barriers; Tiger Love. **1925** Learning to Love; Her Husband's Secret; One Year to Live. **1926** Mare Nostrum; The Temptress; Beverly of Graustark; Love's Blindness; The Flaming Forest. **1927** It; Venus of Venice; Madame Pompadour; Come to My House. **1928** The Midnight Taxi; Adoration; The Air Legion; The Whip Woman; Nameless Men. **1929** Careers; Synthetic Sin; Romance of the Rio Grande. **1930** One Mad Kiss; Rough Romance; The Benson Murder Case; The Cat Creeps; Those Who Dance. **1932**

Aguilas Frente al Sol (Eagles across the Sun); Wide Open Spaces. **1933** Primavera en Otono; El Precio de un Beso. **1934** La Cuidad de Carton. **1935** Senora Casada Necesita Marido (My Second Wife); Storm over the Andes; Rosa de Francia; Asegure a su Mujer (Insure Your Wife); He Trusted His Wife. **1936** The Bohemian Girl; Rose of the Rancho. **1938** Rose of the Rio Grande. **1939** Ambush. **1940** Seven Sinners. **1941** They Met in Argentina; Two Latins from Manhattan; The Kid from Kansas. **1942** Undercover Man; Valley of the Sun; Fiesta. **1944** Tampico. **1945** The Spanish Main. **1946** Notorious. **1947** Captain from Castile. **1949** Lust for Gold. **1950** Crisis; Dallas; Saddle Tramp. **1951** Mark of the Renegade. **1952** Untamed Frontier. **1953** Wings of the Hawk; Thunder Bay. **1954** Saskatchewan; Creature from the Black Lagoon. **1956** The Searchers. **1958** El Senore Faron y la Cleopatra (Mr. Pharoah and Cleopatra).

MORENO, DARIO

Born: Apr. 3, 1921, Smirne, Turkey. Died: Dec. 1968, Istanbul, Turkey. Screen, stage actor and singer.

Appeared in: **1951** Pas des Vacances pour Monsieur. **1952** Le Salire de la Peur; Rires de Paris; Deux de l'Escadrille; La Mome Vert-de-Gris. **1953** Les Femmes s'en Balancent; Quai des Blondes. **1954** Le Mouton a Cinq Pattes. **1956** Pardonnez-nous nos Offenses. **1957** Le feu aux Poudres. **1958** Incognito; Oh! Que Mambo. **1959** Oeil pour Oeil (Eye for an Eye); Wages of Fear; The Prisoner. **1960** Come Dance with Me; The Female (aka A Woman Like Satan); Toucher pas aux Blondes; Nathalie Agent Secrete. **1961** The Revolt of the Slaves. **1962** Candide. **1966** Hotel Paradiso. **1969** La Prisonniere.

MORENO, MARGUERITE

Born: 1871, France. Died: July 14, 1948, France. Screen and stage actress.

Appeared in: **1937** Amphytryon; Les Perles de la Couronne (Pearls of the Crown). **1949** Chips Are Down. Other French film: La Sexe Faible.

MORENO, PACO

Born: 1886. Died: Oct. 15, 1941, Beverly Hills, Calif. Stage and screen actor.

Appeared in: **1935** The Devil Is a Woman; Storm over the Andes. **1939** Papa Soltero (Bachelor Father).

MORENO, THOMAS "SKY BALL"

Born: 1895. Died: Oct. 25, 1938, West Los Angeles, Calif. Screen actor and stuntman.

MOREY, HARRY T.

Born: 1873, Mich. Died: Jan. 25, 1936, Brooklyn, N.Y. (abscessed lung). Screen, stage actor and opera performer. Entered films with Vitagraph.

Appeared in: **1911** The Deerslayer. **1914** My Official Wife. **1916** Salvation Joan. **1917** Within the Law; The Courage of Silence. **1918** Forgotten Faces. **1921** A Man's Home. **1922** Beyond the Rainbow; Wildness of Youth; The Curse of Drink. **1923** The Green Goddess; The Empty Cradle; Marriage Morals; Where the Pavement Ends. **1924** Captain January; The Painted Lady; The Roughneck. **1925** Camille of the Barbary Coast; The Adventurous Sex; Heart of a Siren; Headlines; Barriers Burned Away. **1926** Aloma of the South Seas. **1927** Twin Flappers. **1928** Return of Sherlock Holmes; Under the Tonto Rim.

MOREY, HENRY A.

Born: 1848. Died: Jan. 8, 1929, Astoria, N.Y. (heart trouble). Stage and screen actor.

Appeared in: **1921** Inside of the Cup.

MORGAN, CLAUDIA

Born: Nov. 12, 1911, Brooklyn, N.Y. Died: Sept. 17, 1974, New York, N.Y. Screen, stage and radio actress. Daughter of actor Ralph Morgan (dec. 1956).

Appeared in: **1932** Vanity Street; Once in a Lifetime. **1938** That's My Story. **1939** Stand Up and Fight. **1952** Venus Observed.

MORGAN, DAN

Died: Mar. 4, 1975. Screen actor.

Appeared in: **1968** Charly; Pretty Poison.

MORGAN, FRANK (Francis Philip Wupperman)

Born: July 1, 1890, New York, N.Y. Died: Sept. 18, 1949, Beverly Hills, Calif. Screen, stage, vaudeville and radio actor. Brother of actor Ralph Morgan (dec. 1956).

Appeared in: **1916** The Suspect. **1917** Raffles the Amateur Cracksman; Modern Cinderella; Baby Mine. **1918** At the Mercy of Men. **1924** Born Rich; Manhandled. **1925** The Crowded Hour; The Man Who Found Himself; Scarlet Saint. **1927** Love's Greatest Mistake. **1930** Dangerous Nan McGrew; Queen High; Fast and Loose; Laughter. **1932** Secrets of the French Police; The Half-Naked Truth. **1933** Luxury Liner; Reunion in Vienna; The Nuisance; Bombshell; Best of Enemies; When Ladies Meet; Broadway to Hollywood; The Billion Dollar Scandal; Sailor's Luck; Kiss before the Mirror; Hallelujah, I'm a Bum. **1934** The Cat and the Fiddle; The Affairs of Celini; There's Always Tomorrow; By Your Leave; Success at Any Price; The Mighty Barnum; Sisters under the Skin; Lost Lady. **1935** Naughty Marietta; The Good Fairy; Esca-

pade; I Live My Life; The Perfect Gentleman; Enchanted April. **1936** Dancing Pirate; Trouble for Two; Piccadilly Jim; Dimples; The Great Ziegfeld. **1937** The Last of Mrs. Cheyney; The Emperor's Candlesticks; Saratoga; Beg, Borrow or Steal; Rosalie. **1938** Paradise for Three; Port of Seven Seas; Sweethearts; The Crowd Roars. **1939** Broadway Serenade; The Wizard of Oz; Balalaika. **1940** The Shop around the Corner; Henry Goes Arizona; Broadway Melody of 1940; The Ghost Comes Home; The Mortal Storm; Boom Town; Hullabaloo. **1941** Keeping Company; Washington Melodrama; Wild Man of Borneo; Honky Tonk; The Vanishing Virginian. **1942** Tortilla Flat; White Cargo; Night Monster. **1943** A Stranger in Town; The Human Comedy; Thousands Cheer. **1944** The White Cliffs of Dover; Casanova Brown; Dear Barbara; The Miracle of Morgan's Creek; Hail the Conquering Hero. **1945** Yolanda and the Thief. **1946** Courage of Lassie; The Great Morgan; Mr. Griggs Returns; Pardon My Past; Lady Luck; The Cockeyed Miracle. **1947** Green Dolphin Street. **1948** The Three Musketeers; Summer Holiday. **1949** Any Number Can Play; The Stratton Story; The Great Sinner. **1950** Key to the City. **1974** That's Entertainment (film clips).

MORGAN, GENE (Eugene Schwartzkopf)

Born: 1892, Montgomery, Ala. Died: Aug. 13, 1940, Santa Monica, Calif. (heart attack). Screen, stage, vaudeville actor and orchestra leader. Appeared in Pathe "Folly" comedies and in early Hal Roach silent films.

Appeared in: **1926** Kid Boots. **1930** The Boss; Rogue of the Rio Grande; Orders; Railroad (shorts). **1932** Night World; Blonde Venus. **1933** Railroad (shorts); Elmer the Great; Song of the Eagle; Jennie Gerhardt. **1935** Men of the Hour; Crime and Punishment; Bright Lights; If You Could Only Cook. **1936** Lady from Nowhere; Come Closer, Folks; The Music Goes 'Round; You May Be Next; Mr. Deeds Goes to Town; Devil's Squadron; Meet Nero Wolfe; Shakedown; Alibi for Murder; End of the Trail; Panic on the Air; Counterfeit. **1937** Counterfeit Lady; Woman in Distress; Speed to Spare; Parole Racket; Counsel for Crime; Murder in Greenwich Village; All American Sweetheart; Make Way for Tomorrow. **1938** Home on the Rage (short); G-Men; Ankles Away (short); Start Cheering; There's Always a Woman; The Main Event; When G-Men Step In; Who Killed Gail Preston? **1939** Captain Fury; The Sap Takes a Wrap (short); Mr. Smith Goes to Washington; Federal Man-Hunt; Homicide Bureau; The Housekeeper's Daughter. **1940** Gaucho Serenade; Girl from God's Country; Saps at Sea. **1941** Meet John Doe.

MORGAN, HELEN

Born: 1922. Died: July 19, 1955, Burbank, Calif. (cancer). Screen actress and former Olympic diving champion. Do not confuse with actress and singer Helen Morgan (dec. 1941).

MORGAN, HELEN

Born: 1900, Danville, Ill. Died: Oct. 9, 1941, Chicago, Ill. (kidney and liver ailments). Screen, stage actress and club entertainer.

Appeared in: **1929** Applause (film debut); Glorifying the American Girl; Show Boat. **1930** Roadhouse Nights. **1932** Gigolo Racket (short). **1934** Marie Galante; The Lemon Drop Kid; You Belong to Me. **1935** Go into Your Dance; Sweet Music; Frankie and Johnnie. **1936** Showboat (and 1929 version).

MORGAN, JANE

Born: 1881, England. Died: Jan. 1, 1972, Burbank, Calif. (heart attack). Screen, radio, vaudeville and television actress. Do not confuse with singer Jane Morgan.

Appeared in: **1965** Our Miss Brooks (and television series).

MORGAN, LEE (Raymond Lee Morgan)

Born: June 12, 1902, Texas. Died: Jan. 30, 1967, Los Angeles, Calif. (heart disease). Screen actor. Entered films during the silents.

Appeared in: **1947** Return of the Lash; Black Hills; Shadow Valley; Cheyenne Takes Over; Stage to Mesa City; The Fighting Vigilantes. **1948** The Westward Trail. **1949** Roll, Thunder, Roll!; Rio Grande. **1950** Raiders of Tomahawk Creek. **1951** Hills of Utah; Riding the Outlaw Trail. **1956** Daniel Boone—Trailblazer. **1958** Sierra Baron; The Last of the Fast Guns; Villa. **1961** The Last Rebel. **1962** The Weird Ones. **1964** Dungeons of Terror; No Man's Land.

MORGAN, MARGO (Margaret Rockwood)

Born: 1897. Died: May 16, 1962, Hollywood, Calif. Screen actress and singer.

MORGAN, PAUL

Born: Germany. Died: Jan. 1939 (congestion of the lungs). Stage and screen actor.

Appeared in: **1930** Why Cry at Parting?; Menschen Hinter Geitern; Zwei Hertzen in Drei-Viertel Takt. **1931** Wien Du Stadt der Lieder (Vienna City of Song); Das Kabinett des Dr. Larifari. **1932** Theaternaechte von Bath; Liebeskommando. **1933** Holzapfel Weiss Alles.

MORGAN, RALPH (Raphael Kuhner Wupperman)

Born: July 6, 1883, New York, N.Y. Died: June 11, 1956, N.Y. Stage and screen actor. Married to actress Grace Arnold (dec. 1948). Father of actress Claudia

Morgan (dec. 1974) and brother of actor Frank Morgan (dec. 1949). One-time president of the Screen Actors Guild.

Appeared in: 1930 Excuse the Pardon (short). 1931 Honor among Lovers. 1932 Charlie Chan's Chance; Dance Team; Rasputin and the Empress; Strange Interlude; Cheaters at Play; Disorderly Conduct; The Devil's Lottery; The Son-Daughter. 1933 The Power and the Glory; Shanghai Madness; Humanity; Trick for Trick; The Mad Game; Walls of Gold; Doctor Bull; The Kennel Murder Case. 1934 Transatlantic Merry-Go-Round; Their Big Moment; Hell in the Heavens; Orient Express; She Was a Lady; Stand up and Cheer; No Greater Glory; Girl of the Limberlost; The Last Gentleman; Little Men; The Cat and the Fiddle. 1935 Condemned to Live; I've Been Around; Star of Midnight; Unwelcome Stranger; Calm Yourself. 1936 Anthony Adverse; Magnificent Obsession; Yellowstone; Muss 'Em Up; The Ex-Mrs. Bradford; Little Miss Nobody; Human Cargo; Speed; General Spanky; Crack Up. 1937 The Man in Blue; The Life of Emile Zola; Exclusive; Wells Fargo; Behind Prison Bars. 1938 Love Is a Headache; Out West with the Hardys; Wives under Suspicion; Army Girl; Orphans of the Street; Mother Carey's Chickens; Barefoot Boy; Shadow over Shanghai; Mannequin; That's My Story. 1939 Off the Record; Fast and Loose; Man of Conquest; Smuggled Cargo; Way Down South; Trapped in the Sky; The Lone Spy Hunt; Geronimo. 1940 Forty Little Mothers; I'm Still Alive; Soak the Old (short); Wagons Westward. 1941 The Mad Doctor; Adventure in Washington; Dick Tracy vs. Crime, Inc. (serial). 1942 Close Call for Ellery Queen; Klondike Fury; Night Monster; The Traitor Within; Gang Busters (serial). 1943 Stage Door Canteen; Jack London; Hitler's Madman. 1944 Trocadero; Double Furlough; I'll Be Seeing You; The Monster Maker; Weird Woman; The Imposter; The Great Alaskan Mystery (serial); Enemy of Women. 1945 Black Market Babies; This Love of Ours; Hollywood and Vine; Monster and the Ape (serial). 1947 The Last Round-Up; Song of the Thin Man; Mr. District Attorney. 1948 Sleep My Love; The Sword of the Avenger; The Creeper. 1950 Blue Grass of Kentucky. 1951 Heart of the Rockies. 1952 Dick Tracy vs. the Phantom Empire (serial); Gold Fever.

MORGAN, RAY (Raymond Storrs Morgan)
Died: Jan. 5, 1975, Englewood, N.J. (cancer). Screen, radio, television actor and announcer. Appeared mainly in industrial; educational and army films.

Appeared in: 1950 Congolaise (narrator). 1951 Two Gals and a Guy. 1952 The Old West. 1960 Wild Rapture.

MORGAN, RUSS
Born: 1904, Scranton, Pa. Died: Aug. 7, 1969, Las Vegas, Nev. (cerebral hemorrhage). Bandleader, songwriter and screen actor. Wrote hit songs "You're Nobody Till Somebody Loves You," "Somebody New Is Taking My Place" and "Does Your Heart Beat for Me?"

Appeared in: 1951 Disc Jockey. 1956 The Great Man; Mister Cory. 1958 The Big Beat.

MORGAN, SYDNEY
Born: c. 1875, Ireland. Died: Dec. 5, 1931, London, England. Stage and screen actor.

Appeared in: 1929 Dark Red Roses; Juno and the Paycock (aka The Shame of Mary Boyle—US).

MORIARTY, JOANNE
Born: 1939. Died: Mar. 2, 1964, Hollywood, Calif. (suicide—pills). Screen actress. Married to actor Michael Parks.

Appeared in: 1964 Bedtime Story.

MORIARTY, MARCUS
Died: June 21, 1916, New York, N.Y. Screen actor.

Appeared in: 1915 The Pretenders. 1916 The Flower of No Man's Land; The Little Fraud; Partners.

MORIYA, SHIZU
Born: 1911, Japan. Died: Mar. 12, 1961, N.Y. Screen, stage and television actress.

MORLAY, GABY (Blanche Fumoleau)
Born: 1897. Died: July 4, 1964, Nice, France. Screen and stage actress.

Appeared in: 1913 La Sandale Rouge. 1929 Les Nouveaux Messieurs (The New Gentlemen). 1934 Le Scandale. 1935 Jeanne. 1936 Le Bonheur. 1938 Derrière La Facade; The Kreutzer Sonata. 1939 Entente Cordiale. 1940 Life of Giuseppe Verdi; The Living Corpse. 1941 The King. 1942 La Voile Bleu (The Blue Veil—US 1947). 1944 32 Rue de Montmartre. 1948 Gigi (US 1950); Le Revenant (A Lover's Return); Mlle. Desiree. 1951 Le Plaisir (House of Pleasure—US 1953); Anna. 1952 Father's Dilemma; A Simple Case of Money. 1954 The Mask. 1955 Mitsou (US 1958). 1957 Royal Affairs in Versailles; Les Collegiennes (aka The Twilight Girls—US 1961). 1958 Ramuntcho. Other French films: The Most Dangerous Sin; Crime and Punishment; Accusee; Levez-Vous; Les Amants Terribles; Entente Cordiale; Sa Majeste M. Dupont; L'Amour d'Une Femme; Paris-New York.

MORLEY, ROBERT JAMES
Born: 1892. Died: Aug. 30, 1952, Hollywood, Calif. Screen actor.

MORNE, MARYLAND
Born: 1900. Died: July 28, 1935, Hollywood, Calif. Screen actress.

MORPHY, LEWIS H. (Lewis Harris Morphy)
Born: 1904. Died: Nov. 7, 1958, Hollywood, Calif. (suicide). Screen actor, stuntman and rodeo performer.

Appeared in: 1950 The Blazing Hills (aka The Blazing Sun).

MORRELL, GEORGE
Born: 1873. Died: Apr. 28, 1955, Hollywood, Calif. Screen and stage actor.

Appeared in: 1921 The Heart of the North. 1929 Silent Sentinel. 1936 Guns and Guitars. 1937 Yodelin' Kid from Pine Ridge; Git Along, Little Dogies; Hit the Saddle. 1938 Pride of the West. 1943 False Colors. 1944 Mystery Man; Texas Masquerade. 1950 Mule Train.

MORRIS, ? (married name: Mrs. Harold (Buddy) Kusell)
Born: 1903. Died: May 13, 1971, Buffalo, N.Y. Screen, stage, radio and vaudeville actress. See William Morris for family information.

MORRIS, ADRIAN
Born: 1903, Mt. Vernon, N.Y. Died: Nov. 30, 1941, Los Angeles, Calif. Screen, stage and vaudeville actor. See William Morris for family information.

Appeared in: 1929 Fast Life; The Jazz Age. 1931 The Age for Love. 1932 Me and My Gal. 1933 Trick for Trick; Bureau of Missing Persons; Wild Boys on the Road. 1934 The Big Shakedown; Let's Be Ritzy; The Pursuit of Happiness. 1935 Age of Indiscretion; One Frightened Night; Powdersmoke Range; Fighting Marines (serial); G-Men; Dr. Socrates. 1936 The Petrified Forest; Poppy; My American Wife; Rose Bowl. 1937 Her Husband Lies; The Woman I Love; There Goes the Groom; Every Day's a Holiday. 1938 You and Me; If I Were King; Angels with Dirty Faces. 1939 The Return of the Cisco Kid; 6,000 Enemies; Wall Street Cowboy; Gone With the Wind. 1940 Florian; The Grapes of Wrath; Know Your Money (short).

MORRIS, BARBOURA (aka BARBOUR O'NEIL)
Born: Oct. 22, 1932. Died: Oct. 23, 1975, Santa Monica, Calif. Stage and screen actress.

Appeared in: 1954 The Helen Keller Story (aka The Unconquered). 1957 Sorority Girl. 1959 The Wild and the Innocent; A Bucket of Blood. 1961 Atlas. 1963 The Haunted Palace. 1967 The Trip; St. Valentine's Day Massacre. 1970 The Dunwich Horror.

MORRIS, CHESTER (John Chester Brooks Morris)
Born: Feb. 16, 1901, New York, N.Y. Died: Sept. 11, 1970, New Hope, Pa. (overdose of barbiturates). Screen, stage, vaudeville, radio and television actor. Married to model Lillian Kenton Barker (the original "Chesterfield Girl") and divorced from actress Suzanne Kilbourne. Entered films at age of 9 in 1910. Best known as film and television's "Boston Blackie." See William Morris for family information.

Appeared in: 1929 Alibi; Fast Life; Woman Trap; The Show of Shows. 1930 Playing Around; The Big House; The Divorcee; The Case of Sergeant Grischa; She Couldn't Say No; Second Choice. 1931 Bat Whispers; Corsair. 1932 Cock of the Air; The Miracle Man; Breach of Promise; Sinners in the Sun; Red Headed Woman. 1933 Blondie Johnson; The Infernal Machine; Kid Gloves; Tomorrow at Seven; Golden Harvest; King for a Night. 1934 The Gay Bride; Let's Talk It Over; Embarrassing Moments; Gift of Gab. 1935 Princess O'Hara; Public Hero No. 1; Society Doctor; Pursuit; I've Been Around; Frankie and Johnnie. 1936 Three Godfathers; Moonlight Murder; They Met in a Taxi; Counterfeit. 1937 I Promise to Pay; The Devil's Playground; Flight to Glory. 1938 Law of the Underworld; Sky Giant; Smashing the Rackets. 1939 Blind Alley; Pacific Liner; Five Came Back; Thunder Afloat. 1940 The Marines Fly High; Wagons Westward; The Girl from God's Country. 1941 Meet Boston Blackie; Confessions of Boston Blackie; No Hands on the Clock; The Phantom Thief. 1942 Canal Zone; I Live on Danger; The Wrecking Crew; Boston Blackie Goes to Hollywood. 1943 High Explosive; Aerial Gunner; After Midnight with Boston Blackie; Tornado; Thunderbolt; The Chance of a Lifetime. 1944 Dark Mountain; One Mysterious Night; Gambler's Choice; Derelict Ship; Secret Command; The Awakening of Jim Burke; Double Exposure; Men of the Deep. 1945 The Blonde from Brooklyn; One Way to Love; Rough, Tough and Ready; Boston Blackie Booked on Suspicion; Boston Blackie's Rendezvous. 1946 Boston Blackie and the Law; A Close Call for Boston Blackie; Phantom Thief. 1947 Blind Spot. 1948 Trapped by Boston Blackie. 1949 Boston Blackie's Chinese Venture. 1955 Unchained. 1956 The She-Creature. 1964 Big Parade of Comedy (documentary). 1970 The Great White Hope.

MORRIS, CLARA
Born: 1897, Omaha, Neb. Died: 1925. Screen actress.

Appeared in: 1921 My Lady Friends. 1925 Where Romance Rides.

MORRIS, CORBET (Louis McClanahan Thompson)
Born: Dec. 31, 1881, Colorado. Died: Mar. 10, 1951, Los Angeles, Calif. (broncho-pneumonia). Screen actor.

Appeared in: **1936** I'd Give My Life. **1937** The Firefly. **1938** Tarzan's Revenge; The House of Mystery; Making the Headlines.

MORRIS, DENIESE
Died: Feb. 20, 1969. Screen actress.

MORRIS, DIANA
Born: 1907. Died: Feb. 19, 1961, Hollywood, Calif. (throat cancer). Stage and screen actress.

MORRIS, GLENN
Born: 1911. Died: Jan. 1, 1974, Palo Alto, Calif. Professional football player, Olympic gold medal winner and screen actor.

Appeared in: **1937** Decathlon Champion (short). **1938** Tarzan's Revenge; Hold That Co-Ed.

MORRIS, GORDON
Born: 1899. Died: Apr. 7, 1940, Hollywood, Calif. Screen, stage actor and screenwriter. See William Morris for family information.

MORRIS, JOHNNIE (John Morris Erickson)
Born: 1886, New York, N.Y. Died: Oct. 7, 1969, Hollywood, Calif. Screen, stage, burlesque and vaudeville actor.

Appeared in: **1928** Beggars of Life; The Fifty-Fifty Girl; The Street of Sin; Love and Learn. **1929** Innocents of Paris; Square Shoulders. **1930** Big Money; Dance With Me. **1932** Once in a Lifetime; Checker Comedies (shorts). **1938** Barefoot Boy; Sons of the Legion; Thanks for the Memory. **1939** The Star Maker; The Gentleman from Arizona. **1940** Golden Gloves.

MORRIS, MARGARET
Born: Nov. 7, 1903, Minneapolis, Minn. Died: June 7, 1968. Stage and screen actress. Was a Wampas Baby Star of 1924.

Appeared in: **1921** Hickville to Broadway. **1923** The Town Scandal. **1924** The Galloping Ace; Horseshoe Luck. **1925** The Best People; Welcome Home; Wild Horse Mesa; Womanhandled; Youth's Gamble. **1926** Born to the West; That's My Baby. **1927** The Magic Garden; Moulders of Men. **1928** The Avenging Shadow; Mark of the Frog (serial). **1929** The Woman I Love. **1932** Single-Handed Sanders. **1936** Desert Guns; The Bride Walks Out.

MORRIS, MARY
Born: 1896, Mass. Died: Jan. 16, 1970, N.Y. Screen and stage actress. Do not confuse with Mary Morris born in 1915.

Appeared in: **1934** Double Door. **1937** Victoria the Great.

MORRIS, PHILIP (Francis Charles Philip Morris)
Born: Jan. 20, 1893, Duluth, Minn. Died: Dec. 18, 1949, Los Angeles, Calif. Stage and screen actor.

Appeared in: **1934** Home on the Range. **1935** Seven Keys to Baldpate. **1936** Desert Gold. **1937** Super Sleuth. **1938** Passport Husband. **1946** Cluny Brown; Home Sweet Homicide. **1947** Buckaroo from Powder River. **1948** Whirlwind Raiders. **1949** The Flying Saucer.

MORRIS, REGGIE (James Reginald Morris)
Born: June 25, 1886, New Jersey. Died: Feb. 16, 1928, Los Angeles, Calif. (heart attack). Screen, stage actor, film producer, screenwriter and author.

Appeared in: **1916** A Male Governess; Madcap Ambrose; Haystacks and Steeples.

MORRIS, RICHARD (W. Richard Stuart Morris)
Born: 1861, Boston, Mass. Died: Oct. 11, 1924, Los Angeles, Calif. Screen, stage actor and opera performer. Entered films in 1909.

Appeared in: **1916** The Devil's Bondswoman; Morals of Hilda. **1921** The Sea Lion. **1922** In the Name of the Law. **1923** The Third Alarm; The Mailman; The Westbound Limited. **1924** The Spirit of the U.S.A.

MORRIS, WAYNE (Bert de Wayne Morris)
Born: Feb. 17, 1914, Los Angeles, Calif. Died: Sept. 14, 1959, Pacific Ocean, aboard aircraft carrier (heart attack). Screen, stage and television actor.

Appeared in: **1936** China Clipper (film debut); King of Hockey; Here Comes Carter; Polo Joe; Smart Blonde. **1937** Don't Pull Your Punches; Kid Galahad; Submarine D-1; Once a Doctor. **1938** Love, Honor and Behave; Men Are Such Fools; Valley of the Giants; The Kid Comes Back; Brother Rat. **1939** The Kid from Kokomo; Return of Dr. X. **1940** Brother Rat and a Baby; An Angel from Texas; Double Alibi; Ladies Must Live; The Quarterback; Gambling on the High Seas; Flight Angels. **1941** Three Sons O'Guns; I Wanted Wings; Bad Men of Missouri; The Smiling Ghost. **1947** Deep Valley; The Voice of the Turtle. **1948** The Big Punch; The Time of Your Life. **1949** A Kiss in the Dark;

The Younger Brothers; John Loves Mary; The House across the Street; Task Force. **1950** Johnny One Eye; The Tougher They Come; Stage to Tucson. **1951** Sierra Passage; The Big Gusher; Yellow Fin. **1952** The Bushwhackers; Desert Pursuit; Arctic Flight. **1953** The Fighting Lawman; The Marksman; The Star of Texas. **1954** Riding Shotgun; The Desperado; The Green Buddha (US 1955); Two Guns and a Badge; Port of Hell. **1955** Lord of the Jungle; The Master Plan; Cross Channel; The Lonesome Trail. **1956** The Dynamiters. **1957** Plunder Road. **1958** Paths of Glory.

MORRIS, WILLIAM
Born: 1861. Died: Jan. 11, 1936, Los Angeles, Calif. (heart attack). Stage and screen actor. Married to actress Etta Hawkins Morris (dec. 1945) and father of actors Chester (dec. 1970), Adrian (dec. 1941) and Gordon Morris (dec. 1940) and actress Mrs. Harold Kusell (Morris) (dec. 1971).

Appeared in: **1930** Brothers; The Convict's Code. **1931** The Gang Buster; Behind Office Doors. **1932** The Washington Masquerade.

MORRISON, ANNA MARIE
Born: 1874. Died: July 5, 1972, Hollywood, Calif. Screen actress. Married to actor Chick Morrison (dec.). Appeared in silents.

MORRISON, ARTHUR
Born: 1880, St. Louis, Mo. Died: Feb. 20, 1950, Los Angeles, Calif. Screen, stage and vaudeville actor. Entered films with World Films in 1917.

Appeared in: **1921** The Light in the Clearing; The Sage Hen; Singing River; The Roof Tree. **1922** The Men of Zanzibar; Strength of the Pines. **1923** The Gunfighter; In the West; The Sting of the Scorpion. **1925** Cold Nerve; Riders of the Purple Sage. **1926** Lazy Lightning; Riding Romance; Tony Runs Wild; Silver Fingers. **1927** The Silent Rider; Grinning Guns; King of the Jungle (serial). **1928** Willful Youth. **1929** Slim Fingers.

MORRISON, CHESTER A.
Born: 1922. Died: Mar. 28, 1975, Portland, Ore. Screen actor. Appeared in Our Gang Comedies.

MORRISON, CHICK
Died: prior to 1970 (fall from horse). Screen actor and animal trainer. Married to actress Anna Marie Morrison (dec. 1972).

Appeared in: **1921** The Duke of Chimney Butte. **1922** Hair Trigger Casey.

MORRISON, EFFIE
Born: 1917, Scotland. Died: Oct. 1974, Glasgow, Scotland. Screen, stage, radio and television actress.

MORRISON, GEORGE "PETE"
Born: Aug. 8, 1891, Denver, Colo. Died: Feb. 5, 1973, Los Angeles, Calif. Screen actor. Entered films in 1908.

Appeared in: **1918** His Buddy; By Indian Post; Even Money; Gun Law; Ace High; The Gun Packer. **1921** Headin' North; Crossing Trails. **1922** Duty First; Daring Danger; The Better Man Wins; West vs. East. **1923** Making Good; Smilin' On; Western Blood; Ghost City (serial). **1924** Black Gold; False Trails; Pioneer's Gold; Buckin' the West; Pot Luck Pards; Rainbow Rangers. **1925** One Shot Ranger; Range Buzzards; Always Ridin' to Win; Cowboy Grit; The Empty Saddle; The Ghost Rider; The Mystery of Lost Ranch; A Ropin' Ridin' Fool; Santa Fe Pete; Stampede Thunder; Triple Action; West of Arizona. **1926** Blue Blazes; Bucking the Truth; Chasing Trouble; The Desperate Game; The Escape. **1929** Chinatown Nights; Courtin' Wildcats; The Three Outcasts. **1930** The Big Trail; Beyond the Rio Grande; Phantom of the Desert; Spurs; Ridin' the Law; Trails of Peril; Trailin' Trouble; Westward Bound.

MORRISON, JAMES (James Woods Morrison)
Born: Nov. 15, 1888, Mattoon, Ill. Died: Nov. 15, 1974, New York, N.Y. Screen, stage actor, novelist and drama coach.

Appeared in: **1911** Saving an Audience; A Tale of Two Cities. **1912** As You Like It; Two Battles; The Foster Child; The Miracle; Willie's Sister; Dr. Lafleur's Theory; Beau Brummel; An Eventful Elopement. **1913** The Butler's Secret; The Glove; His Life for His Emperor; An Infernal Tangle; A Husband's Trick. **1914** The Vanity Case; A Double Error; The Love of Pierre Larosse; The Hero; He Never Knew; Regan's Daughter; The Greater Motive; The Toll; Fanny's Melodrama; The Portrait; The Honeymooners; The Wheat and the Tares; Two Stepchildren. **1915** From Out of the Big Snows; In the Days of Famine; Four Grains of Rice; The Wheels of Justice; The Battle Cry of Peace; A Wireless Rescue; The Man, the Mission and the Maid; Mother's Roses; A Madcap Adventure; The Ruling Power; For the Honor of the Crew; Pawns of Mars; Stage Money; A Fortune Hunter. **1916** The Hero of Submarine D2; The Redemption of Dave Darcey; The Enemy; Phantom Fortune; The Sex Lure. **1917** The Battle Hymn of the Republic; Babbling Tongues; Life Against Honor; One Law for Both; A Tale of Two Cities. **1918** Over the Top; Moral Suicide. **1919** Sacred Silence; Womanhood; Miss Dulcie from Dixie. **1920** Love Without Question; The Midnight Bride. **1921** Black Beauty; Danger Ahead; When We Were Twenty-One; A Yankee Go-Getter. **1922** The Little Minister; The Dangerous Age; Handle with Care; Shattered Idols; Only a Shop Girl.

1923 Held to Answer; The Little Girl Next Door; The Unknown Purple; The Nth Commandment; On the Banks of the Wabash. 1924 Captain Blood; Wine of Youth. 1925 Don't; Wreckage; The Pride of the Force. 1926 The Count of Luxembourg; The Imposter; The Seventh Bandit. 1927 Twin Flappers.

MORRISON, JIM
Born: 1944, France. Died: July 2, 1971, Paris, France (heart attack). Singer, lyricist and screen actor. Was leader of combo "The Doors."

Appeared in: 1970 Machine Gun McGain.

MORRISSEY, BETTY (aka BETTY MORRISEY)
Born: N.Y. Died: Apr. 20, 1944, New York, N.Y. Screen actress.

Appeared in: 1923 A Woman of Paris. 1924 What Shall I Do?; The Fast Worker; Virtue's Revolt; Traffic in Hearts; Turned Up. 1925 Lady of the Night; The Gold Rush; Skinner's Dress Suit; The Desert Demon. 1928 The Circus.

MORRISSEY, WILL
Born: 1885. Died: Dec. 16, 1957, Santa Barbara, Calif. Screen, vaudeville actor, stage producer, song writer and playwright. Was in vaudeville with Midgie Miller in an act billed as "Morrissey and Miller."

Together they appeared in the following shorts: 1927 The Morrissey and Miller Vitaphone Revue. 1928 The Morrissey and Miller Night Club.

MORROW, DORETTA (Doretta Marano)
Born: 1927, Brooklyn, N.Y. Died: Feb. 28, 1968, London, England (cancer). Screen, stage, television actress and singer.

Appeared in: 1952 Because You're Mine.

MORROW, JANE. See MRS. SIDNEY DREW

MORSE, LEE
Born: 1904. Died: Dec. 16, 1954, Rochester, N.Y. Screen, vaudeville, radio actress, singer and composer.

Appeared in: 1930 The Music Racket (short).

MORSE, ROBIN
Born: 1915. Died: Dec. 11, 1958, Hollywood, Calif. (heart attack). Screen and television actor.

Appeared in: 1953 The Great Jesse James Raid. 1955 Marty; Abbott and Costello Meet the Mummy. 1956 The Boss; He Laughed Last. 1957 Pal Joey; Sabu and the Magic Ring.

MORTIMER, CHARLES
Born: 1885. Died: May 1964, London, England. Screen and stage actor.

Appeared in: 1933 You Made Me Love You. 1934 The Return of Bulldog Drummond. 1935 The Guv'nor (aka Mister Hobo—US 1936); The Small Man; The Price of a Song; Old Roses; The Triumph of Sherlock Holmes. 1936 Rhodes of Africa (aka Rhodes—US); Living Dangerously; Someone at the Door. 1937 Aren't Men Beasts! 1939 Poison Pen (US 1941). 1955 Dial 999 (aka The Way Out—US 1956). 1957 The Counterfeit Plan.

MORTIMER, EDMUND
Born: 1875. Died: May 21, 1944, Hollywood, Calif. Screen actor, film director and screenwriter.

Appeared in: 1937 It's Love I'm After; The Awful Truth.

MORTIMER, HENRY (John O. D. Rennie)
Born: 1875. Died: Aug. 20, 1952, Whitby, Ontario, Canada. Stage and screen actor. Entered films during silents.

Appeared in: 1930 La Grande Mare.

MORTON, CHARLES S.
Born: Jan. 28, 1907, Vallejo, Calif. Died: Oct. 26, 1966, North Hollywood, Calif. (heart disease). Screen, stage and vaudeville actor. Son of actor Frank Morton.

Appeared in: 1927 Colleen; Rich But Honest; Wolf Fangs. 1928 Dressed to Kill; Four Sons; None But the Brave. 1929 Christina; The Far Call; Four Devils; New Year's Eve. 1930 Cameo Kirby; Caught Short; The Dawn Trail; Check and Double Check. 1932 Last Ride. 1933 Goldie Gets Along. 1934 Dawn Trail. 1936 Hollywood Boulevard. 1939 Stunt Pilot. 1944 Lumberjack; Outlaws of Santa Fe; Trail to Gunsight.

MORTON, CLIVE
Born: Mar. 16, 1904, London, England. Died: Sept. 24, 1975, London, England. Screen, stage and television actor. Married to actress Fanny Rowe.

Appeared in: 1932 Fires of Fate (US 1933). 1933 The Blarney Stone (aka The Blarney Kiss—US). 1934 The Great Defender; Evergreen. 1938 Dead Men Tell No Tales (US 1939). 1947 While the Sun Shines (US 1950); Jassy (US 1948); Mine Own Executioner (US 1949). 1948 Scott of the Antarctic (US

1949); The Blind Goddess (US 1949). 1949 Kind Hearts and Coronets (US 1950); A Run for Your Money (US 1950). 1950 The Blue Lamp; Trio. 1951 Night Without Stars (US 1953); The Lavender Hill Mob. 1952 His Excellency (US 1956); Castles in the Air. 1953 Turn the Key Softly (US 1954). 1954 Carrington VC (aka Court-Martial—US 1955). 1955 Richard III (US 1956). 1957 Seven Waves Away (aka Abandon Ship!—US); Lucky Jim. 1958 The Safecracker. 1959 Make Mine a Million (US 1965); Shake Hands with the Devil. 1960 The Pure Hell of St. Trinian's (US 1961). 1961 A Matter of Who (US 1962). 1962 I Thank a Fool; Lawrence of Arabia. 1965 The Alphabet Murders (US 1966). 1967 Stranger in the House (aka Cop-Out—US 1968). 1969 Lock Up Your Daughters!; Goodbye Mr. Chips. 1970 Jane Eyre.

MORTON, DREW
Born: 1855. Died: Sept. 4, 1916, New York, N.Y. Screen actor and film director.

MORTON, JAMES C.
Born: 1884, Helena, Mont. Died: Oct. 24, 1942, Reseda, Calif. Screen, stage and vaudeville actor.

Appeared in: 1930 Follow the Leader. 1932 Pack Up Your Troubles; plus the following shorts: A Lad an' a Lamp; Sneak Easily; Alum and Eve; The Spoilers. 1933 The Devil's Brother; plus the following shorts: Fallen Arches; His Silent Racket; Hold Your Temper; The Midnight Patrol; Me and My Sal; Hokus Focus; Snug in the Jug. 1934 The following shorts: Mike Fright; Washee Ironee; I'll Take Vanilla; Another Wild Idea; It Happened One Day; Something Simple; You Said a Hateful; Circus Hoodoo; One Horse Farmers; Maid in Hollywood. 1935 The following shorts: Beginner's Luck; Old Sawbones; Uncivil Warriors; Tit for Tat; The Fixer-Uppers; Pardon My Scotch; The Misses Stooge; Hoi Polloi; Poker at Eight. 1936 The Bohemian Girl; Our Relations; Way Out West, plus the following shorts: The Lucky Corner; Caught in the Act; Share the Wealth; Hill Tillies; Ants in the Pantry; Disorder in the Court; A Pain in the Pullman. 1937 Two Wise Maids; Rhythm in the Clouds; Public Cowboy #1; Mama Runs Wild, plus the following shorts: Calling All Doctors; Dizzy Doctors; The Sitter-Downers. 1938 Topper Takes a Trip, plus the following shorts: The Nightshirt Bandit; A Doggone Mixup; Soul of a Heel; Healthy, Wealthy and Dumb; Three Missing Links. 1939 The following shorts: Clock Wise; Moving Vanities; We Want Our Mummy; Three Little Sew and Sews. 1940 Earl of Puddlestone; My Little Chickadee; The Courageous Dr. Christian; Mutiny in the County (short). 1941 Never Give a Sucker an Even Break; Dutiful but Dumb (short); Lady from Louisiana; Wild Geese Calling; A Polo Phony (short). 1942 Yokel Boy; The Boogie Man Will Get You. 1944 Gold is Where You Lose It (short).

MORTON, MAXINE. See KATHERINE WEST

MOSCOVITCH, MAURICE
Born: Nov. 23, 1871, Odessa, Russia. Died: June 18, 1940, Los Angeles, Calif. (following operation). Screen and stage actor.

Appeared in: 1936 Winterset. 1937 Lancer Spy; Make Way for Tomorrow. 1938 Gateway; Suez. 1939 Everything Happens at Night; Susanna of the Mountains; Love Affair; In Name Only; Rio. 1940 Dance, Girl, Dance; South to Karanga; The Great Dictator. 1942 The Great Commandment.

MOSER, HANS (Jean Juliet)
Born: 1880, Austria. Died: June 19, 1964, Vienna, Austria (cancer). Screen actor.

Appeared in: 1930 Liebling der Gotter; (Darling of the Gods). 1931 Der Grosse Tenor. 1932 His Majesty; King Ballyhoo; Causa Kaiser (The Kaiser Case); Man Braucht Kein Geld. 1933 Madame Wuensch Keine Kinder. 1935 Polenblut (Polish Blood); Der Himmel auf Erden; Winternachtstraum. 1936 Frasquite; Karneval und Liebe; Die Fahrt in Die Jugend. 1937 The World's in Love; Masquerade in Vienna; Endstation; Schabernack; Das Gaesschen zum Paradies; Vienna Burgtheater. 1938 Eva, das Fabriksmaedel; Solo per To (Only for Thee); Die Gluecklichste Ehe von Wien (Happiest Married Couple in Vienna); Wir Sind von K u K Infantrie-Regiment. 1939 Alles Fuer Veronika; Kleines Bezirksgericht (Little Country Court); Fasching in Wien; Hohe Schule (College); Familie Schimek; Das Ekel (The Grouch). 1940 Walzerlange (Waltz Melodies); Wiener Geschichten (Vienna Tales); Opernball (Opera Ball). 1950 State Secret (aka The Great Manhunt—US 1951); Vienna Blood. 1953 Der Onkel aus Amerika (Uncle from America). 1955 Congress Dances. 1962 Der Flendermaus.

MOSICK, MARIAN
Born: 1906. Died: Feb. 2, 1973. Screen actress.

Appeared in: 1954 Jivaro.

MOSJOUKINE, IVAN
Born: 1889. Died: Jan. 18, 1939, Paris, France. Screen actor.

Appeared in: 1911 The Defense of Sevastopol. 1922 Satan Triumphant; Tempest. 1923 Shadows That Mass. 1926 Michael Strogoff. 1927 Surrender; The Living Dead Man; Edmund Kean; Prince among Lovers; The Loves of Casanova (US 1929); Surrender. **1929** The President; The White Devil (US 1931). **1936** Nitchevo. Other French film: Sergeant X.

MOSKVIN, IVAN M.

Born: 1874, Russia. Died: Feb. 16, 1946, Moscow, Russia. Stage and screen actor.

Appeared in: **1927** Polikushka. **1928** The Station Master. **1933** An Hour with Tchekhof. Other Russian film: Death of a Government Clerk.

MOSLEY, FRED (Frederick Charles Mosley)

Born: 1854. Died: Mar. 9, 1972, Staten Island, N.Y. Stage and screen actor.

MOULAN, FRANK

Born: 1876. Died: May 13, 1939, New York, N.Y. Screen actor and opera performer.

Appeared in: **1927** Oh, How I Love My Little Bed (short). **1937** The Girl Said No.

MOULDER, WALTER C.

Born: 1933. Died: July 1, 1967, New York, N.Y. (heart attack). Screen, stage and television actor.

Appeared in: **1959** North by Northwest; That Kind of Woman.

MOVAR, DUNJA

Born: 1940, Germany. Died: Mar. 30, 1963, Goettingen, Germany (suicide—sleeping pills). Screen, stage and television actress. Received Federal Youth Film Award in 1959 for The Angel That Pawned a Harp.

Appeared in: **1959** The Angel That Pawned a Harp. **1968** Hamlet.

MOWBRAY, ALAN

Born: Aug. 18, 1896, London, England. Died: Mar. 25, 1969, Hollywood, Calif. (heart attack). Screen, stage, television actor and playwright.

Appeared in: **1931** Guilty Hands; Honor of the Family; God's Gift to Women; Alexander Hamilton; The Man in Possession; Leftover Ladies. **1932** The Silent Witness; Lovers Courageous; Man about Town; Winner Take All; Jewel Robbery; Two against the World; The Man Called Back; Nice Women; Hotel Continental; The World and the Flesh; The Man from Yesterday; Sherlock Holmes. **1933** Our Betters; Her Secret; Peg O' My Heart; A Study in Scarlet; Voltaire; Berkeley Square; Midnight Club; The World Changes; Roman Scandals. **1934** One More River; Embarrassing Moments; Long Lost Father; Where Sinners Meet; The Girl from Missouri; Charlie Chan in London; The House of Rothschild; Cheaters; Little Man, What Now? **1935** Lady Tubbs; Night Life of the Gods; Becky Sharp; The Gay Deception; In Person; She Couldn't Take It. **1936** Rose Marie; Muss 'Em Up; Mary of Scotland; Rainbow on the River; Desire; Give Us This Night; The Case against Mrs. Ames; Fatal Lady; My Man Godfrey; Ladies in Love. **1937** Four Days' Wonder; As Good As Married; Topper; Stand-In; On Such a Night; Music for Madame; On the Avenue; The King and the Chorus Girl; Marry the Girl; Hollywood Hotel; Vogues of 1938. **1938** Merrily We Live; There Goes My Heart. **1939** Never Say Die; Way Down South; The Llano Kid; Topper Takes a Trip. **1940** Music in My Heart; Curtain Call; The Villain Still Pursued Her; The Boys from Syracuse; Scatterbrain; The Quarterback. **1941** Ice-Capades; The Perfect Snob; That Hamilton Woman; That Uncertain Feeling; Footlight Fever; The Cowboy and the Blonde; I Woke up Screaming; Moon over Her Shoulder. **1942** Yokel Boy; So This Is Washington; Panama Hattie; The Mad Martindales; A Yank at Eton; Isle of Missing Men; The Devil with Hitler; We Were Dancing; The Powers Girl. **1943** Stage Door Canteen; His Butler's Sister; Holy Matrimony; Slightly Dangerous; Screen Snapshots No. 8 (short). **1944** Ever since Venus; The Dough Girls; My Gal Loves Music. **1945** Tell It to a Star; The Phantom of 42nd Street; Earl Carroll Vanities; Men in Her Diary; Where Do We Go from Here?; Sunbonnet Sue; Bring on the Girls. **1946** Terror by Night; My Darling Clementine; Idea Girl. **1947** Captain from Castile; Lured; Merton of the Movies; Pilgrim Lady. **1948** My Dear Secretary; An Innocent Affair; Every Girl Should Be Married; Main Street Kid; Prince of Thieves. **1949** Abbott and Costello Meet the Killer, Boris Karloff; The Lone Wolf and His Lady; You're My Everything; The Lovable Cheat. **1950** The Jackpot; Wagonmaster. **1951** Crosswinds; The Lady and the Bandit; Dick Turpin's Ride. **1952** Just across the Street; Blackbeard the Pirate. **1953** Androcles and the Lion. **1954** Ma and Pa Kettle at Home; The Steel Cage. **1955** The King's Thief. **1956** Around the World in 80 Days; The Man Who Knew Too Much; The King and I. **1962** A Majority of One.

MOWBRAY, HENRY (Harry E. Sweeney)

Born: Sept. 5, 1882, Australia. Died: July 9, 1960, Woodland Hills, Calif. (arteriosclerosis). Screen actor.

Appeared in: **1931** Fifty Fathoms Deep. **1934** Pursuit of Happiness. **1936** The Leathernecks Have Landed.

MOWER, JACK

Born: 1890, Honolulu, Hawaii. Died: Jan. 6, 1965, Hollywood, Calif. Screen, stage and vaudeville actor.

Appeared in: **1915** The Wanderers. **1916** A Race for Life; Miss Jackie of the Navy. **1917** The Devil's Assistant; Miss Jackie of the Army. **1918** Molly Go Get 'Em; Jilted Janet; A Square Deal; Impossible Susan; Ann's Finish; The Primitive Woman. **1919** The Island of Intrigue; Fair Enough; Molly of the Follies. **1920** The Third Eye (serial); The Tiger Band (serial). **1921** The Beautiful Gambler; Cotton and Cattle; Danger Ahead; Silent Years; The Trail to Red Dog; A Cowboy Ace; Flowing Gold; Out of the Clouds; The Range Pirate; Riding with Death; The Rowdy; Rustlers of the Night; Short Skirts. **1922** Manslaughter; The Crimson Challenge; The Golden Gallows; Saturday Night; When Husbands Deceive. **1923** The Last Hour; Pure Grit; The Shock; In the Days of Daniel Boone (serial). **1924** Robes of Sin; Ten Scars Make a Man (serial). **1925** Cyclone Cavalier; Kit Carson over the Great Divide; Perils of the Wind (serial); The Rattler. **1926** False Friends; Her Own Story; Officer 444 (serial); The Ghetto Shamrock; The Radio Detective (serial); Sky High Corral; Melodies; The Lost Express. **1927** Trail of the Tiger (serial); Uncle Tom's Cabin; Pretty Clothes; Face Value. **1928** The Water Hole; Sailor's Wives; The Air Patrol; Sinners' Parade. **1929** Anne against the World; Ships of the Night. **1930** Ridin' Law; The Woman Who Was Forgotten. **1932** Midnight Patrol; Phantom Express; Lone Trail. **1933** Come on Tarzan; Law and the Lawless; King of the Arena; Fiddlin' Buckaroo. **1935** Revenge Rider. **1936** Hollywood Boulevard. **1937** White Bondage; Love Is on the Air; Without Warning; The Missing Witness. **1938** Penrod's Double Trouble; Penrod and His Twin Brother; Crime School; Hard to Get; Comet over Broadway; Tarzan and the Green Goddess; The Invisible Menace. **1939** Code of the Secret Service; Smashing the Money Ring; Everybody's Hobby; Confessions of a Nazi Spy; The Return of Dr. X; Private Detectives. **1940** Always a Bride; British Intelligence; King of the Lumberjacks; Torrid Zone; Tugboat Annie Sails Again. **1941** The Bride Came C.O.D.; Bullets for O'Hara; The Wagons Roll at Night. **1942** Gentleman Jim; Yankee Doodle Dandy; Murder in the Big House; Spy Ship. **1943** Mysterious Doctor. **1944** Adventures of Mark Twain; The Last Ride. **1946** Dangerous Business. **1947** That Way with Women; Shadows over Chinatown. **1948** Fighting Mad. **1949** Angels in Disguise. **1950** County Fair. **1952** So You Want to Get it Wholesale (short).

MOZART, GEORGE

Born: Feb. 15, 1864, Yarmouth, England. Died: Dec. 10, 1947, London, England. Screen, stage actor and music hall singer.

Appeared in: **1913** Coney as Peacemaker; Coney Gets the Glad Eye; Coney—Ragtimer. **1932** Indiscretions of Eve. **1933** The Medicine Man. **1935** The Private Life of Henry the Ninth; Breakers Ahead; The Mystery of the Mary Celeste (aka Phantom Ship—US 1939). **1936** Cafe Mascot; Full Speed Ahead; The Bank Messenger Mystery; Two on a Doorstep; Strange Cargo (US 1940); Song of Freedom; Polly's Two Fathers. **1947** Overcoat Sam; Dr. Sin Fang. **1938** Pygmalion.

MOZHUKIN, IVAN

Born: 1890, Russia. Died: 1939, Russia. Screen, stage actor and film director.

Appeared in: **1923** Kean, ou Desordre et Genie; Le Brasier Ardent.

MUDIE, LEONARD (Leonard Mudie Cheetham)

Born: Apr. 11, 1884, England. Died: Apr. 14, 1965, Hollywood, Calif. (heart ailment). Stage and screen actor.

Appeared in: **1921** A Message from Mars. **1922** Through the Storm. **1932** The Mummy. **1933** Voltaire. **1934** The Mystery of Mr. X; The House of Rothschild; Cleopatra. **1935** Clive of India; Cardinal Richelieu; Becky Sharp; Rendezvous; Captain Blood; The Great Impersonator. **1936** Magnificent Obsession; Anthony Adverse; Mary of Scotland; His Brother's Wife; Lloyds of London. **1937** The King and the Chorus Girl; They Won't Forget; The League of Frightened Men; London by Night; Lancer Spy. **1938** The Mysterious Mr. Moto; The Jury's Secret; Adventures of Robin Hood; Kidnapped; Suez; When Were You Born? **1939** Tropic Fury; Arrest Bulldog Drummond; Don't Gamble with Strangers; Dark Victory; Mutiny on the Black Hawk; Man about Town. **1940** Congo Maisie; Charlie Chan's Murder Cruise; South of Suez; Devil's Island; British Intelligence. **1941** Shining Victory; The Nurse's Secret. **1942** Berlin Correspondent; Random Harvest. **1943** Appointment in Berlin. **1944** Winged Victory; Dragon Seed. **1945** Divorce; My Name Is Julia Ross; The Corn Is Green. **1946** Don't Gamble with Strangers. **1947** Private Affairs of Bel Ami; Bulldog Drummond at Bay. **1948** The Checkered Coat; Song of My Heart. **1951** Bomba and the Elephant Stampede. **1952** Bomba and the Jungle Girl; African Treasure. **1953** Safari Drums; The Magnetic Monster; Perils of the Jungle. **1954** Killer Leopard; Golden Idol. **1955** Lord of the Jungle. **1956** Autumn Leaves. **1957** The Story of Mankind. **1959** Timbuktu; Rosen fur den Staatsanwalt (Roses for the Prosecutor—US 1961); The Big Fisherman. **1965** The Greatest Story Ever Told.

MUELLER, BARBARA

Born: 1909, Germany. Died: Jan. 3, 1967, Germany? Screen and stage actress.

MUELLER, WOLFGANG (aka WOLFGANG MULLER)

Born: 1923, Berlin, Germany. Died: Apr. 26, 1960, Lostallo, Switzerland (plane crash). Stage and screen actor.

Appeared in: **1958** Wir Wunderkinder (narr.) (We Amazing Children aka

Aren't We Wonderful—US 1959). **1958** Das Wirthaus im Spessart (Restaurant in the Spessart aka The Spessart Inn—US 1961).

MUIR, FLORABEL

Born: 1889, Laramie, Wyo. Died: Apr. 27, 1970, Los Angeles, Calif (heart attack). Columnist, screenwriter, author, stage and screen actress. Married to newspaperman Dennis "Denny" Morrison (dec. 1966).

MUIR, GAVIN

Born: Sept. 8, 1907, Chicago, Ill. Died: May 24, 1972, Fort Lauderdale, Fla. Stage and screen actor.

Appeared in: **1936** Mary of Scotland; Lloyds of London; Charlie Chan at the Racetrack; Half Angel. **1937** Wee Willie Winkie; The Holy Terror; Fair Warning. **1939** Tarzan Finds a Son. **1942** Nightmare; Eagle Squadron. **1943** Hitler's Children; Sherlock Holmes in Washington; Passport to Suez; Sherlock Holmes Faces Death. **1944** The Master Race; Passport to Adventure; The Merry Monahans. **1945** The House of Fear; Salome—Where She Danced; Patrick the Great; Tonight and Every Night. **1946** O.S.S.; Temptation; California. **1947** Unconquered; Ivy; Calcutta. **1948** The Prince of Thieves. **1949** Chicago Deadline. **1950** Rogues of Sherwood Forest. **1951** The Son of Dr. Jekyll; Thunder on the Hill; Abbott and Costello Meet the Invisible Man. **1953** King of the Khyber Rifles. **1955** Sea Chase. **1957** Johnny Trouble; The Abductors. **1959** Island of Lost Women. **1963** Night Tide.

MUIR, HELEN

Born: 1864. Died: Dec. 2, 1934, Los Angeles, Calif. Screen and stage actress. Entered films with Griffith in 1915.

Appeared in: **1919** Strictly Confidential. **1921** Live and Let Live; The Mistress of Shenstone.

MULCASTER, GEORGE H.

Born: 1891, London, England. Died: Jan. 19, 1964, England. Stage and screen actor.

Appeared in: **1918** God Bless Our Red, White and Blue. **1920** Tangled Hearts (aka The Wife Whom God Forgot). **1921** Wild Heather. **1923** The Pipes of Pan; Mist in the Valley. **1925** The Squire of Long Hadley; The Wonderful Wooing; A Girl of London. **1928** Ghosts of Yesterdays series including: The Princess in the Tower; The Man in the Iron Mask. **1929** Sacrifice. **1930** A Romance of Riches (rerelease of The Squire of Long Hadley—1925); The Way of a Woman (rerelease of The Wonderful Wooing—1925). **1931** Inquest. **1933** Purse Strings. **1935** The River House Mystery. **1936** Second Bureau. **1937** The Five Pound Man; The Gap; Old Mother Riley. **1938** Lily of Laguna; Little Dolly Daydream. **1939** The Lion Has Wings (US 1940); All Living Things. **1940** Pack Up Your Troubles; Sailors Don't Care. **1941** The Patient Vanishes (US 1947 aka This Man is Dangerous). **1942** Let the People Sing; Asking for Trouble; The Owner Goes Aloft (short). **1943** The Dummy Talks; My Learned Friend. **1945** For You Alone. **1946** Under New Management. **1948** Spring in Park Lane (US 1949). **1949** That Dangerous Age (aka If This Be Sin—US 1950); Under Capricorn. **1951** The Naked Heart. **1955** Contraband Spain (US 1958). **1957** Lady of Vengeance.

MULCAY, JIMMY

Born: 1900. Died: Dec. 31, 1968. Screen actor.

Appeared in: **1945** Night Club Girl. **1951** Varieties on Parade. **1966** The Girl from Tobacco Row.

MULGREW, THOMAS G.

Born: 1889. Died: Dec. 3, 1954, Providence, R.I. Screen, stage and vaudeville actor. Appeared in early films with Eastern Film Co.

MULHAUSER, JAMES

Born: Oct. 31, 1890, Brooklyn, N.Y. Died: June 15, 1939, Beverly Hills, Calif. Screen, stage actor and screenwriter. Entered films in 1918.

Appeared in: **1928** The Head Man. **1929** China Bound. **1932** Slim Summerville Comedies.

MULLE, IDA

Born: approx. 1864. Died: Aug. 9, 1934, New York, N.Y. (complications from fall). Stage and screen actress.

MULLER, RENATE (aka RENATE MUELLER)

Born: 1907, Germany. Died: Oct. 7, 1937, Berlin, Germany.

Appeared in: **1930** Liebe im Ring; Liebling der Gotter (Darling of the Gods). **1931** Der Grosse Tenor; Das Floetenkonzert von Sanssouci. **1932** Der Kleine Seitensprung; Office Girl; Die Blumenfrau von Lindenau (Flower Lady of Lindenau); Herzblut. **1933** Der Sohn der Weissen Berge; Wenn die Liebe Mode Macht; Saison in Kairo. **1934** Wie Sag' Ich's Meinem Mann?; Waltz Time in Vienna. **1935** Viktor und Viktoria. **1936** The Private Life of Louis XIV; Liebesleute. **1937** Togger; For Her Country's Sake.

MULOCK, AL

Born: England? Died: c. 1970, Rome, Italy. Screen actor.

Appeared in: **1955** Joe MacBeth (US 1956). **1957** Interpol (aka Pickup Alley—US); Kill Me Tomorrow (US 1958). **1958** High Hell. **1959** Tarzan's Greatest Adventure. **1960** Jazzboat; Tarzan the Magnificent. **1961** The Hellions (US 1962). **1962** Play it Cool (US 1963). **1963** Call Me Bwana; The Small World of Sammy Lee. **1964** Dr. Terror's House of Horrors (US 1965). **1966** Lost Command; Il Buono, Il Brutto, Il Cattiro (The Good, the Bad and the Ugly—US 1967). **1967** A Witch Without a Broom; The Treasure of Makuba; The Hellbenders; Reflections in a Golden Eye; Battle Beneath the Earth (US 1968).

MUMBY, DIANA

Born: July 1, 1922, Detroit, Mich. Died: May 19, 1974, Westlake, Calif. Stage and screen actress.

Appeared in: **1940** A Night at Earl Carroll's (film debut). **1944** Up in Arms. **1946** The Kid from Brooklyn. **1947** Winter Wonderland. **1948** A Song is Born. **1951** G.I. Jane.

MUNDIN, HERBERT

Born: Aug. 21, 1898, England. Died: Mar. 4, 1939, Van Nuys, Calif. (auto accident). Stage and screen actor.

Appeared in: **1932** Life Begins; One Way Passage; The Silent Witness; Almost Married; The Devil's Lottery; The Trial of Vivienne Ware; Bachelor's Affairs; Chandu, the Magician; Sherlock Holmes; Love Me Tonight. **1933** Dangerously Yours; Cavalcade; Pleasure Cruise; Adorable; It's Great to Be Alive; Arizona to Broadway; The Devil's in Love; Shanghai Madness; Hoopla. **1934** Bottoms Up; Call It Luck; Such Women Are Dangerous; Orient Express; Springtime for Harry; All Men Are Enemies; Hell in Heavens; Love Time; Ever since Eve. **1935** Mutiny on the Bounty; Black Sheep; The Perfect Gentlemen; The Widow from Monte Carlo; Ladies Love Danger; King of Burlesque; David Copperfield. **1936** Charlie Chan's Secret; A Message to Garcia; Under Two Flags; Tarzan Escapes; Champagne Charlie. **1937** Another Dawn; You Can't Beat Love; Angel. **1938** The Adventures of Robin Hood; Lord Jeff; Invisible Enemy; Exposed. **1939** Society Lawyer.

MUNI, PAUL (Muni Weisenfreund)

Born: Sept. 22, 1895, Austria or Poland. Died: Aug. 25, 1967, Montecito, Calif. (heart trouble). Screen, stage, vaudeville and burlesque actor. Son of stage actor Nathan Philip and actress Sally Weisenfreund. Won 1936 Academy Award for Best Actor in The Story of Louis Pasteur.

Appeared in: **1929** The Valiant (film debut); Seven Faces. **1932** I Am a Fugitive from a Chain Gang; Scarface. **1933** The World Changes. **1934** Hi, Nellie. **1935** Bordertown; Dr. Socrates; Black Fury. **1936** The Story of Louis Pasteur. **1937** The Good Earth; The Life of Emile Zola; The Woman I Love. **1938** For Auld Lang Syne (short); Rasputin. **1939** Juarez; We Are Not Alone. **1940** Hudson's Bay. **1942** The Commandos Strike at Dawn. **1943** Stage Door Canteen. **1945** A Song to Remember; Counter-Attack. **1946** Angel on My Shoulder. **1953** Stranger on the Prowl. **1959** The Last Angry Man.

MUNIER, FERDINAND

Born: Dec. 3, 1889, San Diego, Calif. or Boston, Mass.? Died: May 27, 1945, Hollywood, Calif. (heart attack). Screen, stage, radio and vaudeville actor.

Appeared in: **1923** The Broken Wing. **1931** Ambassador Bill. **1932** Stepping Sister; Wild Girl; After Tomorrow. **1933** The Woman I Stole; Queen Christina; The Bowery; Kickin' the Crown Around (short). **1934** The Barretts of Wimpole Street; Love and Hisses (short); Babes in Toyland; The Merry Widow; Count of Monte Cristo. **1935** I'm a Father (short); Okay Toots! (short); Roberta; Clive of India; The Gilded Lily; China Seas; His Family Tree; Follies Bergere; Page Miss Glory; Hands across the Table; Harmony Lane; Two Sinners; Top Flat (short). **1936** One Rainy Afternoon; The White Legion; Can This Be Dixie?; The Beloved Rogue; The Bold Caballero; The White Angel. **1937** Tovarich; Damaged Goods. **1938** Marriage Forbidden; The Great Waltz; Going Places. **1939** Midnight; Everything Happens at Night. **1941** Model Wife. **1942** Invisible Agent; Commandos Strike at Dawn; Tennessee Johnson. **1943** Claudia. **1945** Diamond Horseshoe. **1950** Revenge Is Sweet (reissue of Babes in Toyland, 1934 film).

MUNIZ, JUAN DE DIOS

Born: 1906. Died: Oct. 1951, Madrid, Spain. Screen and stage actor. Dubbed Spanish voice of Spencer Tracy.

MUNRO, JANET

Born: 1934, Blackpool, England. Died: Dec. 6, 1972, London, England. Screen, stage and television actress. Divorced from actors Tony Wright and Ian Hendry.

Appeared in: **1957** Small Hotel. **1958** The Trollenberg Terror (aka The Crawling Eye—US); The Young and the Guilty. **1959** Third Man on the Mountain; Tommy the Toreador; Darby O'Gill and the Little People. **1961** Swiss Family Robinson; The Day the Earth Caught Fire (US 1962); The Horsemasters. **1962** Life for Ruth (aka Walk in the Shadow—US 1966). **1963** Bitter Harvest; Hide and Seek (US 1964); A Jolly Bad Fellow (US 1964 aka They All Died Laughing). 1964 Daylight Robbery. 1967 Sebastian (US 1968).

MUNSHIN, JULES
Born: 1915, New York, N.Y. Died: Feb. 19, 1970, N.Y. (heart attack). Stage and screen actor.

Appeared in: 1948 Easter Parade. 1949 On the Town; Take Me Out to the Ball Game; That Midnight Kiss. 1954 Monte Carlo Baby. 1957 Silk Stockings; Ten Thousand Bedrooms. 1964 Wild and Wonderful. 1967 Monkeys, Go Home! 1974 That's Entertainment (film clips).

MUNSON, ONA (Ona Wolcott)
Born: June 16, 1903, Portland, Ore. Died: Feb. 11, 1955, New York, N.Y. (suicide—sleeping pills). Screen, stage, vaudeville and radio actress. Received 1939 Academy Award nomination for Best Supporting Actress in Gone with the Wind.

Appeared in: 1928 Head of the Family. 1931 Going Wild; The Hot Heiress; The Collegiate Model (short); Broadminded; Five Star Final. 1938 His Exciting Night. 1939 Gone with the Wind; Legion of Lost Flyers. 1940 The Big Guy; Wagons Westward; Scandal Sheet. 1941 Lady from Louisiana; Wild Geese Calling; The Shanghai Gesture. 1942 Drums of the Congo. 1943 Idaho. 1945 Dakota; The Cheaters. 1946 The Magnificent Rogue. 1947 The Red House.

MURA, CORRINE (Corinna Wall)
Born: 1910. Died: Aug. 1, 1965, Mexico City, Mexico (cancer). Screen, stage, radio actress and singer.

Appeared in: 1942 Call Out the Marines. 1943 Casablanca. 1944 Passage to Marseille. 1945 The Gay Senorita. 1947 Honeymoon.

MURAT, JEAN
Born: 1888, France. Died: Jan. 5, 1968, Aix-en-Provence, France (coronary thrombosis). Stage and screen actor. Divorced from actress Annabella. Entered films in 1922.

Appeared in: 1928 Carmen; The Legion of Honor; L'Eau du Nil. 1929 Venus; Escaped from Hell; The Soul of France; La Nuit est a Nous (The Night is Ours—US 1931—also a 1953 version). 1932 Paris-Mediterranee. 1936 Second Bureau; La Kermesse Heroique. 1938 Generals without Buttons; L'Equipage (aka Flight into Darkness). 1943 L'Eternel Retour (The Eternal Return). 1949 The Wench. 1951 On the Riviera; Rich, Young and Pretty. 1955 Il Mantello Rosso (The Red Cloak—US 1961). 1958 Paris Holiday. 1959 Lady Chatterley's Lover; The Possessors; Le Vent se Leve (The Wind Rises aka Time Bomb—US 1961). 1962 It Happened in Athens. Les Sept Peches Capitaux (Seven Capital Sins—US 1963).

MURATORE, LUCIEN
Born: 1878, Marseilles, France. Died: July 16, 1954, Paris, France. Opera singer and screen actor.

Appeared in: 1914 Manon Lescaut.

MURO, HENRI
Born: July 13, 1884, France. Died: Dec. 12, 1967, Hollywood, Calif. (heart attack). Screen actor.

MURPHY, ADA
Born: 1888. Died: Aug. 25, 1961, Encino, Calif. Screen actress. Entered films in 1915.

MURPHY, AUDIE
Born: June 20, 1924, Kingston, Tex. Died: May 31, 1971, near Roanoke, Va. (plane crash). Screen, television actor and author. Most decorated hero of W. W. II. Married to Pamela Archer. Divorced from actress Wanda Hendrix.

Appeared in: 1948 Beyond Glory (film debut); Texas, Brooklyn and Heaven. 1949 Bad Boy. 1950 Sierra; The Kid from Texas; Kansas Raiders. 1951 The Cimarron Kid; The Red Badge of Courage. 1952 Duel at Silver Creek. 1953 Gunsmoke; Column South; Tumbleweed. 1954 Ride Clear of Diablo; Drums across the River; Destry. 1955 To Hell and Back. 1956 World in My Corner; Walk the Proud Land. 1957 Guns of Fort Petticoat; Joe Butterfly; Night Passage. 1958 Ride a Crooked Trail; The Gun Runner; The Quiet American. 1959 No Name on the Bullet; Cast a Long Shadow; The Wild and the Innocent. 1960 Hell Bent for Leather; The Unforgiven; Seven Ways from Sundown. 1961 Posse from Hell; The Battle at Bloody Beach. 1962 Six Black Horses. 1963 Showdown; Gunfight at Comanche Creek. 1964 The Quick Gun; Bullet for a Badman; Apache Rifles; War Is Hell (narr.). 1965 Arizona Raiders. 1966 Gunpoint; The Texican. 1967 Forty Guns to Apache Pass; Trunk to Cairo. 1969 A Time for Dying (cameo).

MURPHY, CHARLES B.
Born: 1884. Died: June 11, 1942, Bakersfield, Calif. (accident on location of Lost Canyon). Screen actor.

Appeared in: 1921 The Man of the Forest; The Rowdy; The Man Tamer. 1922

Golden Dreams; The Gray Dawn. 1923 Single Handed; Red Lights. 1937 County Fair. 1938 The Road to Reno. 1942 Lost Canyon.

MURPHY, JOHN DALY
Born: 1873, Ireland. Died: Nov. 20, 1934, New York, N.Y. (heart attack). Stage and screen actor.

Appeared in: 1918 Our Mrs. McChesney. 1921 Thunderclap. 1922 Polly of the Follies. 1923 The Truth about Wives; You Can't Fool Your Wife. 1924 Icebound.

MURPHY, JOSEPH J.
Born: 1877. Died: July 31, 1961, San Jose, Calif. Screen actor. One of the original Keystone Kops. Also portrayed "Andy Gump" on the screen.

MURPHY, ROBERT "BOB" (Duke Foster Dunnell)
Born: 1889, Webster, N.Y. Died: Aug. 6, 1948, Santa Monica, Calif. (pneumonia). Screen and vaudeville actor.

Appeared in: 1935 Broadway Gondolier. 1936 The Case against Mrs. Ames; Hideaway Girl; Two in a Crowd. 1937 Nancy Steele Is Missing; Portia on Trial; You're a Sweetheart. 1938 Girl of the Golden West; In Old Chicago. 1944 Shine on Harvest Moon.

MURRAY, CHARLIE (Charles Murray)
Born: June 22, 1872, Laurel, Ind. Died: July 29, 1941, Hollywood, Calif. (pneumonia). Screen, stage and vaudeville actor. Entered films with Biograph Co. in 1912. He was Murray of the vaudeville team "Murray and Mack"; Mack was Oliver Trumbull (dec. 1934). In the Keystone comedies, Murray was the Hogan character, and in later years, he was the Kelly of "The Cohens and the Kellys" series.

Appeared in: 1914 The Passing of Izzy; A Fatal Flirtation; Her Friend the Bandit; Love and Bullets (reissued as The Trouble Mender); Soldiers of Misfortune; The Great Toe Mystery; She's a Cook (reissued as The Bungling Burglars); The Masquerader; The Anglers; Stout Heart but Weak Knees; Cursed by His Beauty; His Talented Wife; The Noise of Bombs; His Halted Career; The Plumber; Tillie's Punctured Romance; Hogan's Annual Spree; His Second Childhood; The Fatal Bumping; Mabel's Married Life; A Missing Bride; A Gambling Rube. 1915 Hogan's Wild Cats; Hogan's Mussy Job; Hogan the Porter; Hogan's Romance Upset; Hogan's Aristocratic Dream; Hogan Out West; From Patches to Plenty; The Beauty Bunglers; Their Social Splash; Those College Girls; A Game Old Knight; Her Painted Hero; The Great Vacuum Robbery; Only a Farmer's Daughter. 1916 His Hereafter; Fido's Fate; The Judge; A Love Riot; Her Marble Heart; Pills of Peril; The Feathered Nest (aka Girl Guardian); Maid Mad; Bombs. 1917 Maggie's First False Step; Her Fame and Shame; The Betrayal of Maggie; His Precious Life; A Bedroom Blunder. 1918 Watch Your Neighbor. 1921 A Small Town Idol; Home Talent. 1922 The Crossroads of New York. 1923 Luck; Bright Lights of Broadway. 1924 Empty Hearts; Lilies of the Field; The Girl in the Limousine; The Fire Patrol; The Mine with the Iron Door; Fool's Highway; Painted People; Sundown. 1925 My Son; Who Cares; Classified; Fighting the Flames; White Fang; Paint and Powder; Percy; Why Women Love (aka Sea Women and Barriers Aflame); The Wizard of Oz. 1926 The Cohens and the Kellys; Irene; The Boob; Mismates; Subway Sadie; Her Second Chance; Mike; Paradise; The Reckless Lady; Steel Preferred; The Silent Lover; Sweet Daddies. 1927 McFadden's Flats; The Gorilla; The Life of Riley; Lost at the Front; The Poor Nut; The Masked Woman. 1928 The Head Man; Flying Romeos; The Cohens and the Kellys in Paris; Do Your Duty; Vamping Venus. 1930 Clancy in Wall Street; Around the Corner; Cohens and the Kellys in Scotland; The King of Jazz; The Duke of Dublin; His Honor the Mayor; The Cohens and the Kellys in Africa; 10 Universal shorts. 1931 Caught Cheating. 1932 The Cohens and the Kellys in Hollywood; Hypnotized. 1933 The Cohens and the Kellys in Trouble. 1936 Dangerous Waters. 1937 Circus Girl. 1938 Breaking the Ice.

MURRAY, DAVID MITCHELL
Born: 1853. Died: Oct. 20, 1923, Long Island, N.Y. Stage and screen actor.

Appeared in: 1924 The Silent Watcher.

MURRAY, EDGAR
Born: 1865. Died: Oct. 31, 1932, Hollywood, Calif. (complication of diseases). Screen actor.

MURRAY, EDGAR
Born: 1892. Died: Oct. 16, 1959, Hollywood, Calif. (heart attack). Screen actor. Married to actress Nadia Popkova. Entered films with Vitagraph.

MURRAY, ELIZABETH M.
Born: 1871. Died: Mar. 27, 1946, Philadelphia, Pa. Screen, stage and vaudeville actress.

Appeared in: 1923 Little Old New York. 1929 Lucky in Love. 1931 The Bachelor Father.

MURRAY, J. HAROLD (Harry Roulon)

Born: Feb. 17, 1891, South Berwick, Maine. Died: Dec. 11, 1940, Killingworth, Conn. Screen, stage and vaudeville actor.

Appeared in: **1929** Married in Hollywood. **1930** Cameo Kirby; Happy Days; Women Everywhere. **1937** Universal and RKO shorts.

MURRAY, JACK (John W. B. Murray)

Died: May 1, 1941, Bronx, N.Y. Screen, stage, vaudeville, burlesque and radio actor.

MURRAY, JAMES

Born: Feb. 9, 1901, New York, N.Y. Died: July 11, 1936, New York, N.Y. (drowned in Hudson River). Screen and stage actor.

Appeared in: **1922** When Knighthood Was in Flower. **1923** The Pilgrims. **1927** In Old Kentucky; The Last Outlaw; The Lovelorn; Stark Love; Rough House Rosie. **1928** The Crowd; Rose Marie; The Big City. **1929** The Little Wildcat; The Shakedown; Thunder; Shanghai Lady. **1930** Hide-Out; The Rampant Age. **1931** Kick In; In Line of Duty; Bright Lights. **1932** The Reckoning; Alaska Love (short); Bachelor Mother. **1933** Air Hostess; Heroes for Sale; Frisco Jenny; High Gear; Central Airport; Baby Face; Peerless. **1935** $20 a Week; Skull and Crown; Ship Cafe.

MURRAY, JEAN

Born: Sydney, Nova Scotia, Canada. Died: Oct. 5, 1966, Winnipeg, Canada. Screen, stage and radio actress.

MURRAY, JOHN T.

Born: 1886, Australia. Died: Feb. 12, 1957, Woodland Hills, Calif. (stroke). Screen and vaudeville actor. Married to actress Vivian Oakland (dec. 1958) with whom he appeared in vaudeville as "John T. Murray and Vivian Oakland" and also made several shorts together during 1929–30.

Appeared in: **1924** Madonna of the Streets. **1925** Joanna; Sally; Stop Flirting; Winds of Chance. **1926** High Steppers; Bardely's the Magnificent. **1927** Finger Prints; The Gay Old Bird. **1928** Fazil. **1929** Sonny Boy; Honky Tonk; plus the following shorts billed as "John T. Murray and Vivian Oakland": Satires; The Hall of Injustice. **1930** Personality; Night Work; plus the following shorts with his wife: Who Pays; The Servant Problems. **1931** Charlie Chan Carries On; Young as You Feel; Alexander Hamilton. **1932** Man Called Back; Vanity Comedies shorts. **1933** Keyhole Katie (short). **1934** Air Maniacs (short); Love Birds. **1935** Great God Gold. **1936** Cain and Mabel; Here Comes Carter; Caught in the Act (short). **1937** The Lost Horizon; Ever Since Eve; True Confession; Girl Loves Boy; Sweetheart of the Navy; plus the following shorts: The Wrong Miss Wright; Calling All Doctors; Man Bites Lovebug. **1938** Gang Bullets; plus the following shorts: Violent is the Word for Curley; The Mind Needer; Many Sappy Returns; Ankles Away. **1939** The Hardys Ride High; Andy Hardy Gets Spring Fever; The Sap Takes a Wrap (short); Skinny the Moocher (short). **1940** Mr. Clyde Goes to Broadway (short).

MURRAY, JULIAN "BUD"

Born: Nov. 21, 1888, New York, N.Y. Died: Nov. 1, 1952, West Los Angeles, Calif. (cerebral hemorrhage). Screen actor, stage and film dance director.

MURRAY, LOLA

Born: 1914. Died: Nov. 11, 1961, Shrewsbury, N.J. Screen actress.

MURRAY, MAE (Marie Adrienne Koenig)

Born: May 10, 1886 or 1889 (?), Portsmouth, Va. Died: Mar. 23, 1965, North Hollywood, Calif. (heart condition). Screen, stage actress and dancer. Divorced from actor and film director Robert Z. Leonard (dec. 1968).

Appeared in: **1916** To Have and To Hold (film debut); Honor Thy Name; Sweet Kitty Bellairs; The Dream Girl; The Big Sister; The Plow Girl. **1917** The Morman Maid; On Record; First Sight; Princess Virtue. **1918** Modern Love; Her Body in Bond; Face Value; Danger—Go Slow; The Bride's Awakening. **1919** The Delicious Little Devil; Blind Husbands; The Scarlet Shadow; What Am I Bid (aka Girl for Sale); The Big Little Person; A.B.C. of Love; Twin Pawns (aka The Curse of Greed). **1920** On with the Dance; The Right to Love; Idols of Clay. **1921** The Gilded Lily. **1922** Fascination; Peacock Alley; Broadway Rose. **1923** The French Doll; Jazzmania; Fashion Row. **1924** Mademoiselle Midnight; Married Flirts; Circe, The Enchantress. **1925** The Masked Bride; The Merry Widow. **1927** Valencia; Altars of Desire. **1928** Show People. **1930** Peacock Alley (and 1922 version). **1931** Bachelor Apartment; High Stakes. **1951** Valentino.

MURRAY, MARION

Born: 1885. Died: Nov. 11, 1951, New York, N.Y. Screen actress. Entered films during silents. Married to actor Jed Prouty (dec. 1956).

Appeared in: **1942** Paris Calling. **1948** The Pirate.

MURRAY, THOMAS

Born: 1902. Died: Nov. 20, 1961, Hollywood, Calif. (heart attack). Screen actor.

MURRAY, TOM

Born: 1875. Died: Aug. 27, 1935, Hollywood, Calif. Screen, vaudeville and radio actor.

Appeared in: **1922** French Hells; The Ladder Jinx; Too Much Business. **1923** The Pilgrim; The Meanest Man in the World. **1925** The Business of Love; The Gold Rush. **1926** Private Izzy Murphy; Tramp, Tramp, Tramp; Into Her Kingdom.

MURRAY, "UNCLE." *See* MURRAY PARKER

MURRAY-HILL, PETER

Born: Apr. 20, 1908, Bushy Heath, England. Died: 1957. Stage and screen actor. Married to actress Phyllis Calvert.

Appeared in: **1938** Mr. Reeder in Room 13 (film debut—aka Mystery of Room 13—US 1941); A Yank at Oxford; Jane Steps Out (US 1940). **1939** The Outsider (US 1940); At the Villa Rose (aka House of Mystery—US 1941). **1940** The House of the Arrow (aka Castle of Crimes—US 1945). **1941** The Ghost Train. **1943** Rhythm Serenade; Bell-Bottom George. **1944** Madonna of the Seven Moons. **1945** They Were Sisters (US 1946).

MURROW, EDWARD R.

Born: Apr. 25, 1908, Greensboro, N.C. Died: Apr. 27, 1965, Pawling, N.Y. Radio, television commentator and screen actor.

Appeared in: **1943** Siege of Leningrad (narr.). **1956** Around the World in 80 Days. **1958** Satchmo the Great (narr.). **1960** Sink the Bismarck.

MURTH, FLORENCE

Born: 1902. Died: Mar. 29, 1934, Los Angeles, Calif. Screen actress. Appeared in early Sennett and Christie comedies.

Appeared in: **1922** Thundering Hoofs.

MUSIDORA (Jeanne Roques)

Born: 1889, France. Died: Dec. 1957, Paris, France. Screen, stage actress and film director. Became celebrated for her work in two 12-episode serials, Les Vampires and Judex.

MUSSELMAN, JOHNSON J.

Born: 1890. Died: Apr. 8, 1958, Louisville, Ky. Magician and screen and vaudeville actor. Known as "Aska the Magician."

MUSSEY, FRANCINE

Born: France. Died: Mar. 26, 1933, Paris, France (suicide—poison). Screen actress.

Appeared in: **1932** La ronde des Heures.

MUSSIERE, LUCIENE (Lucien Meurisse)

Born: 1890. Died: Dec. 23, 1972, Brussels, Belgium. Stage and screen actor.

Appeared in: **1956** Around the World in 80 Days.

MUSSON, BENNET

Born: 1866. Died: Feb. 17, 1946, Amityville, N.Y. Screen and stage actor.

Appeared in: **1921** White Oak.

MUTION, RICARDO

Born: 1884, Mexico. Died: Apr. 2, 1957, Mexico City, Mex. (heart attack). Stage and screen actor.

Appeared in: **1939** Nobleza Ranchero (Rural Chivalry).

MUZQUIZ, CARLOS

Born: 1906, Mexico. Died: Feb. 1960, Mexico City, Mexico. Screen actor. Known as "Compadre Muzquiz."

Appeared in: **1950** Hidden River. **1951** My Outlaw Brother. **1955** A Life in the Balance. **1957** The Sun Also Rises; The Black Scorpion.

MYERS, HARRY

Born: 1886, Philadelphia, Pa. or New Haven, Conn.? Died: Dec. 26, 1938, Los Angeles, Calif. (pneumonia). Stage and screen actor. Married to actress Rosemary Theby with whom he made a series of films as "Myers & Theby."

Appeared in: **1908** The Guerrilla. **1909** Her First Biscuits; The Jonesy Pictures. **1911** Her Two Sons. **1916** Housekeeping (first Myers and Theby film in series made from 1916 to April 1917). **1919** The Masked Rider (serial). **1920** Peaceful Valley. **1921** A Connecticut Yankee in King Arthur's Court; On the High Card; The March Hare; Nobody's Fool; Oh, Mary Be Careful; R.S.V.P. **1922** The Adventures of Robinson Crusoe (serial); Boy Crazy; Handle with Care; Kisses; Turn to the Right; Top O' the Morning; When the Lad Comes Home. **1923** The Bad Man; The Beautiful and Damned; Stephen Steps Out; Brass; Brass Bottle; Little Johnny Jones; The Printer's Devil; The Common Law; Main Street. **1924** Behold This Woman; Daddies; Listen, Lester; Reckless Romance; The Marriage Circle; Tarnish. **1925** Grounds for Divorce; She Wolves; Zander the Great. **1926** Exit Smiling; Up in Mabel's Room; The Beautiful

Cheat; Monte Carlo; Nut Cracker. 1927 Getting Gertie's Garter; The Girl in the Pullman; The Bachelor's Baby; The First Night. 1928 The Dove; The Street of Illusion; Dream of Love. 1929 The Clean Up; Montmartre Rose; Wonder of Women. 1931 City Lights; Meet the Wife. 1932 The Savage Girl. 1933 Police Call; The Important Witness; Strange Adventure. 1935 Mississippi. 1936 Hollywood Boulevard. 1937 Dangerous Lives.

MYERS, PETER

Born: 1928. Died: Oct. 4, 1968. Screen actor and screenwriter.

Appeared in: 1958 The Reluctant Debutante; Bachelor of Hearts (US 1962). 1959 Expresso Bongo (US 1960). 1961 Very Important Person (aka A Coming-Out Party—US 1962). 1963 Mystery Submarine; The Punch and Judy Man. 1969 The Magic Christian (US 1970). 1970 Hello-Goodbye.

MYERS, ROBERT FRANCIS

Born: 1925. Died: July 18, 1962, Hollywood, Calif. (murdered—stabbed). Screen, stage actor and cab driver.

MYLONG, JOHN

Born: 1893, Austria. Died: Sept. 8, 1975, Beverly Hills, Calif. Screen, stage and television actor. Appeared in Austrian and German films prior to going to Hollywood in 1937.

Appeared in: 1937 Conquest. 1940 Overture to Glory. 1942 Crossroads. 1943 The Moon is Down; For Whom the Bell Tolls; Hostages; The Strange Death of Adolph Hitler. 1945 The Falcon in San Francisco; Hotel Berlin. 1950 Young Daniel Boone. 1951 His Kind of Woman. 1955 The Crooked Web. 1956 The Eddy Duchin Story. 1958 The Beast of Budapest; I, Mobster. 1962 The Mermaids of Tiburon.

NADAJAN

Died: Sept. 20, 1974, Hollywood, Calif. (heart attack). Screen actor. Known in clubs in an act billed as "Beauty and the Beast."

Appeared in: 1969 Justine.

NADI, ALDO

Born: 1899, Leghorn, Italy. Died: Nov. 10, 1965, Los Angeles, Calif. Screen actor, champion foil expert and author.

Appeared in: 1929 Le Tournoi. 1943 Frenchman's Creek. 1945 To Have and Have Not.

NAGEL, ANNE (Ann Dolan)

Born: Sept. 30, 1912, Boston, Mass. Died: July 6, 1966, Los Angeles, Calif. (cancer). Stage and screen actress.

Appeared in: 1933 I Loved You Wednesday (film debut); College Humor. 1934 Stand up and Cheer. 1936 Hot Money; China Clipper; King of Hockey; Here Comes Carter; Love Begins at Twenty. 1937 Guns of the Pecos; The Case of the Stuttering Bishop; Footloose Heiress; Three Legionnaires; The Hoosier Schoolboy; A Bride for Henry; Escape by Night; The Adventurous Blonde; She Loved a Fireman. 1938 Saleslady; Under the Big Top; Gang Bullets; Mystery House. 1939 Convict's Code; Unexpected Father; Call a Messenger; Legion of Lost Flyers; Should a Girl Marry? 1940 Black Friday; Ma, He's Making Eyes at Me; Winners of the West (serial); Hot Steel; My Little Chickadee; Argentine Nights; Diamond Frontier; The Green Hornet (serial); The Green Hornet Strikes Again (serial). 1941 Road Agent; The Invisible Woman; Meet the Chump; Man-Made Monster; Mutiny in the Arctic; Don Winslow of the Navy (serial); Sealed Lips; Never Give a Sucker an Even Break. 1942 The Mad Doctor of Market St; Dawn Express; Nazi Spy Ring; Stagecoach Buckaroo; The Secret Code (serial). 1943 Women in Bondage. 1946 Murder in the Music Hall; Traffic in Crime. 1947 Blondie's Holiday; The Trap; The Spirit of West Point. 1948 Don't Trust Your Husband. 1949 Prejudice.

NAGEL, CONRAD

Born: Mar. 16, 1897, Keokuk, Iowa. Died: Feb. 24, 1970, New York, N.Y. Screen, stage, radio, television actor and film director. Divorced from actress Ruth Helms (dec. 1960). In 1940 he received a Special Academy Award for his work on the Motion Picture Relief Fund.

Appeared in: 1918 Little Women. 1920 The Fighting Chance; Midsummer Madness. 1921 What Every Woman Knows; The Lost Romance; A Fool's Paradise; Sacred and Profane Love. 1922 The Impossible Mrs. Bellew; Nice People; Hate; The Ordeal; Saturday Night; Singed Wings. 1923 The Rendezvous; Lawful Larceny; Bella Donna; Grumpy. 1924 Three Weeks; Tess of the D'Urbervilles; The Snob; Married Flirts; Name the Man; The Rejected Woman; Sinners in Silk; So This Is Marriage. 1925 Sun-Up; The Only Thing; Cheaper to Marry; Pretty Ladies; Lights of Old Broadway; Excuse Me. 1926 The Waning Sex; Tin Hats; The Exquisite Sinner; Memory Lane; Dance Madness; There You Are. 1927 Quality Street; The Hypnotist; Slightly Used; The Jazz Singer; Heaven on Earth; The Girl from Chicago; London after Midnight. 1928 The Mysterious Lady; If I Were Single; Glorious Betsy; Caught in the Fog; The Terror; Tenderloin; Diamond Handcuffs; The Michigan Kid; State Street Sadie; The Divine Woman. 1929 Dynamite; Red Wine; The Idle Rich; Kid Gloves; The Kiss; Thirteenth Chair; The Sacred Flame;

Hollywood Revue of 1929; The Redeeming Sin. 1930 Redemption; The Ship from Shanghai; Numbered Men; Second Wife; DuBarry, Woman of Passion; One Romantic Night; A Lady Surrenders; Free Love; The Divorcee; Today. 1931 The Right of Way; East Lynne; Bad Sister; The Reckless Hour; Son of India; Three Who Loved; Hell Divers; The Pagan Lady. 1932 The Man Called Back; Divorce in the Family; Kongo; Fast Life. 1933 The Constant Woman; Ann Vickers. 1934 Dangerous Corner; Marines Are Coming. 1935 One Hour Late; Death Flies East; One New York Night. 1936 Wedding Present; Yellow Cargo; Girl from Mandalay. 1937 Navy Spy; The Gold Racket. 1939 The Mad Express. 1940 I Want a Divorce; One Million B.C. (narr.). 1944 They Shall Have Faith; Dangerous Money (narr.). 1945 The Adventures of Rusty; Forever Yours. 1947 The Vicious Circle. 1948 Stage Struck; The Woman in Brown. 1949 Dynamite. 1955 All That Heaven Allows. 1957 Hidden Fear. 1959 Stranger in My Arms; The Man Who Understood Women. 1974 That's Entertainment (film clips).

NAGIAH, V.

Born: 1903, India. Died: Dec. 30, 1973, Madras. Screen actor, film director and singer.

Appeared in: 1930 Gruhalakshmi (film debut).

NAGY, BILL

Born: Canada. Died: Jan. 19, 1973, London, England. Screen, stage, radio and television actor.

Appeared in: 1955 The Brain Machine (US 1956); Joe MacBeth (US 1956). 1956 Assignment Redhead (aka Million Dollar Manhunt—US 1962). 1957 High Tide at Noon; Accused (aka Mark of the Hawk—US 1958); Across the Bridge. 1959 First Man Into Space; I Was Monty's Double (aka Hell, Heaven or Hoboken). 1960 Surprise Package. 1961 Never Take Candy from a Stranger; The Boy Who Stole a Million. 1962 The Road to Hong Kong. 1963 The Girl Hunters. 1964 Goldfinger. 1965 Those Magnificent Men in Their Flying Machines; Where the Spies Are (US 1966). 1967 Battle Beneath the Earth (US 1968); The Man Outside; A Countess from Hong Kong. 1968 Subterfuge. 1969 The Adding Machine. 1970 The Revolutionary.

NAIDOO, BOBBY

Born: 1927, South Africa. Died: July 6, 1967, London, England. Black screen, stage and television actor.

Appeared in: 1960 The Criminal (aka The Concrete Jungle—US 1962). 1963 Nine Hours to Rama.

NAISH, J. CARROL (Joseph Patrick Carrol Naish)

Born: Jan. 21, 1900, New York, N.Y. Died: Jan. 24, 1973, La Jolla, Calif. Screen, stage, radio, vaudeville and television actor. Married to actress Gladys Heaney. Nominated for 1945 Academy Award as Best Supporting Actor in A Medal for Benny.

Appeared in: 1930 Cheer Up and Smile; Good Intentions; Scotland Yard. 1931 Royal Bed; Gun Smoke; Kick In; Homicide Squad. 1932 The Hatchet Man; The Conquerors; Cabin in the Cotton; Famous Ferguson Case; Crooner; Tiger Shark; No Living Witness; The Kid from Spain; Two Seconds; It's Tough to be Famous; Beast of the City. 1933 Mystery Squadron (serial); Central Airport; World Gone Mad; The Past of Mary Holmes; The Avenger; Arizona to Broadway; The Devil's in Love; The Whirlwind; Captured; The Big Chance; Notorious But Nice; Last Trail; Mad Game; Silent Men; Elmer the Great; No Other Woman; Frisco Jenny; Infernal Machine. 1934 Defense Rests; Sleepers East; What's Your Racket; Murder in Trinidad; One Is Guilty; Upper World; Hell Cat; Girl in Danger; Hell in the Heavens; Return of the Terror; The President Vanishes; Marie Galante. 1935 The Crusades; The Lives of a Bengal Lancer; Captain Blood; Special Agent; Behind the Green Lights; Black Fury; Under the Pampas Flood; Little Big Shot; Front Page Woman; Confidential. 1936 Two in the Dark; Anthony Adverse; Absolute Quiet; We Who Are About to Die; Robin Hood of El Dorado; The Charge of the Light Brigade; The Leathernecks Have Landed; Moonlight Murder; The Return of Jimmy Valentine; Exclusive Story; Charlie Chan at the Circus; Special Investigator; Ramona; Crack-Up. 1937 Song of the City; Think Fast Mr. Moto; Hideaway; Border Cafe; Bulldog Drummond Comes Back; Sea Racketeers; Thunder Trail; Night Club Scandal; Daughter of Shanghai. 1938 Her Jungle Love; Tip-Off Girls; Hunted Men; Prison Farm; Bulldog Drummond in Africa; Illegal Traffic; King of Alcatraz. 1939 King of Chinatown; Persons in Hiding; Hotel Imperial; Undercover Doctor; Beau Geste; Island of Lost Men. 1940 Typhoon; Queen of the Mob; Golden Gloves; Down Argentine Way; A Night at Earl Carroll's. 1941 The Corsican Brothers; Birth of the Blues; Blood and Sand; The Pied Piper; That Night in Rio; Mr. Dynamite; Forced Landing; Accent on Love. 1942 Dr. Renault's Secret; A Gentleman at Heart; Sunday Punch; Dr. Broadway; Jackass Mail; Tales of Manhattan; The Man in the Trunk; The Secret Code (serial). 1943 Harrigan's Kid; Good Morning Judge; Behind the Rising Sun; Calling Mr. Death; Sahara; Gung Ho!; Batman (serial). 1944 Voice in the Wind; The Monster Maker; The Whistler; Two-Man Submarine; Waterfront; Jungle Woman; Enter Arsene Lupin; Dragon Seed. 1945 A Medal for Benny; House of Frankenstein; The Southerner; Getting Gertie's Garter; Strange Confession. 1946 The Beast with Five Fingers; Bad Bascomb; Humoresque. 1947 Carnival in Costa Rica; The Fugitive. 1948 Joan of Arc; The

Kissing Bandit. **1949** Canadian Pacific; The Midnight Kiss. **1950** Annie Get Your Gun; Black Hand; Please Believe Me; The Toast of New Orleans; Rio Grande. **1951** Across the Wide Missouri; Mark of the Renegade; Bannerline. **1952** The Denver and Rio Grande; Clash by Night; Woman of the North Country; Ride the Man Down. **1953** Beneath the 12 Mile Reef; Fighter Attack. **1954** Sitting Bull; Saskatchewan. **1955** Hit the Deck; Rage at Dawn; The Last Command; Desert Sands; Violent Saturday; New York Confidential. **1956** Rebel in Town; Yaqui Drums. **1957** The Young Don't Cry; This Could Be the Night. **1961** Force of Impulse. **1964** The Hanged Man. **1965** An Evening with Batman and Robin. **1971** Dracula vs. Frankenstein.

NALDI, NITA (Anita Donna Dooley)
Born: Apr. 1, 1899, New York, N.Y. Died: Feb. 17, 1961, New York, N.Y. Screen, stage and television actress.

Appeared in: **1920** Dr. Jekyll and Mr. Hyde. **1921** Experience; A Divorce of Convenience; The Last Door. **1922** Blood and Sand; Anna Ascends; Channing of the Northwest; The Man from Beyond; The Snitching Hour; Reported Missing. **1923** The Glimpses of the Moon; Lawful Larceny; The Ten Commandments; You Can't Fool Your Wife; Hollywood. **1924** A Sainted Devil; The Breaking Point; Don't Call It Love. **1925** Clothes Make the Pirate; Cobra; The Lady Who Lied; The Marriage Whirl. **1926** The Unfair Sex; The Pleasure Garden; The Mountain Eagle (aka Fear-o-God—US); The Miracle of Life. **1928** What Price Beauty?

NAMU
Died: July 1966, Seattle, Wash. (drowned). Animal screen performer (whale). The first killer whale to become a film star.

Appeared in: **1966** Namu, the Killer Whale.

NANSEN, BETTY
Born: 1876. Died: Mar. 15, 1943, Copenhagen, Denmark (pneumonia). Stage and screen actress.

Appeared in: **1915** Man Without a Country; A Woman of Impulse. **1916** For Her Son.

NAPIER, RUSSELL
Born: 1910, Australia. Died: 1975, England. Screen and stage actor.

Appeared in: **1954** Conflict of Wings; The Stranger Came Home (aka The Unholy Four—US). **1955** The Brain Machine (US 1956); Little Red Monkey (aka The Case of the Red Monkey—US); The Blue Peter (aka Navy Heroes—US 1959). **1956** The Last Man in Tang?; The Man in the Road (US 1957). **1957** The Shiralee; Robbery Under Arms (US 1958). **1958** A Night to Remember; Tread Softly Stranger (US 1959). **1960** The Angry Silence; Hell Is a City. **1961** Francis of Assisi; The Mark. **1962** Mix Me a Person; H.M.S. Defiant (Damn the Defiant—US). **1963** Man in the Middle (US 1964). **1967** It. **1968** Nobody Runs Forever (aka The High Commissioner—US); Twisted Nerve (US 1969); The Blood Beast Terror (aka The Vampire Beast Craves Blood—US 1969).

NARCISO, GRAZIA
Died: Dec. 10, 1967. Screen actress.

Appeared in: **1948** Madonna of the Desert; Music Man. **1950** Black Hand; Between Midnight and Dawn; September Affair. **1951** Up Front. **1954** Three Coins in the Fountain. **1957** Dragstrip Girl.

NARDELLI, GEORGE
Died: Sept. 15, 1973. Screen actor.

Appeared in: **1924** Galloping Hoofs (serial). **1933** Cocktail Hour. **1934** Another Wild Idea (short). **1956** Around the World in 80 Days. **1958** Lafayette Escadrille.

NARES, OWEN (Owen Ramsay)
Born: Aug. 11, 1888, Maiden Erlegh, England. Died: July 30, 1943, Brecon, Wales. Stage and screen actor. Entered films in 1913.

Appeared in: **1913** His Choice. **1914** Dandy Donovan, The Gentleman Cracksman. **1916** Just a Girl; Milestones; The Real Thing at Last. **1917** The Sorrows of Satan; The Labour Leader; One Summer's Day; Flames. **1918** God Bless Our Red, White and Blue; The Elder Miss Blossom (aka Wanted a Wife—US); Onward Christian Soldiers; The Man Who Won; Tinker, Tailor, Soldier, Sailor. **1919** Edge O'Beyond; Gamblers All. **1920** The Last Rose of Summer; All the Winners; A Temporary Gentleman. **1921** For Her Father's Sake. **1922** The Faithful Heart; Brown Sugar. **1923** The Indian Love Lyrics; Young Lochinvar. **1924** Miriam Rozella. **1927** This Marriage Business; His Great Moment (aka The Sentence of Death). **1930** Loose Ends; The Middle Watch. **1931** The Woman Between (aka The Woman Decides—US 1932); Sunshine Susie (aka The Office Girl—US 1932). **1932** Frail Women; Aren't We All?; The Impassive Footman (aka Woman in Bondage—US); The Love Contract; There Goes the Bride; Where Is This Lady? **1933** Discord; One Precious Night. **1934** The Private Life of Don Juan. **1935** Royal Cavalcade (aka Regal Cavalcade—US); I Give My Heart. **1936** Head Office. **1937** The Show Goes On. **1941** The Prime Minister.

NARVAEZ, SARA
Born: Nicaragua. Died: Dec. 1935, Mexico City, Mexico. Screen, stage, vaudeville and radio actress.

NASH, EUGENIA
Born: 1866. Died: Apr. 8, 1937, Culver City, Calif. Screen actress. Mother of actor Ted Healy (dec. 1937).

NASH, FLORENCE
Born: 1888, Troy, N.Y. Died: Apr. 2, 1950, Los Angeles, Calif. Screen, stage and vaudeville actress. Sister of actress Mary Nash (dec. 1966).

Appeared in: **1939** The Women.

NASH, GEORGE FREDERICK
Born: 1873. Died: Dec. 31, 1944, Amityville, N.Y. Stage and screen actor. Married to stage actress Julia Hay (dec. 1937).

Appeared in: **1922** The Face in the Fog; The Valley of Silent Men; When Knighthood Was in Flower. **1923** Under the Red Robe. **1924** The Confidence Man; Janice Meredith. **1925** A Man Must Live. **1926** The Great Gatsby; The Song and Dance Man. **1933** Oliver Twist; Fighting Texans; Phantom Broadcast. **1934** Sixteen Fathoms Deep; Mystery Liner; Blue Steel; City Limits.

NASH, MARY EVELYN
Died: June 28, 1965, Paramus, N.J. Stage and screen actress. Do not confuse with actress Mary Nash (dec. 1976).

NATHEAUX, LOUIS
Born: 1898, Pine Bluff, Ark. Died: Aug. 23, 1942, Los Angeles, Calif. Screen actor.

Appeared in: **1921** Passing Thru. **1922** The Super Sex. **1924** The Fast Set. **1926** Man Bait; Risky Business; Sunny Side Up. **1927** The Country Doctor; Dress Parade; Harp in Hock; Fighting Love; King of Kings; My Friend from India; Turkish Delight. **1928** Stand and Deliver; Midnight Madness; A Ship Comes In; Tenth Avenue; The Cop; Four Walls; Stool Pigeons; Ned McCobb's Daughter. **1929** Broadway Babies; Weary River; Why Be Good?; Girls Gone Wild; Mexicali Rose. **1930** Madame Satan; Big Money; The Big House; The Squealer; Lightnin'; This Mad World. **1931** Secret Six; Bad Girl; Transatlantic; Young as You Feel; Reckless Living; Street Scene. **1932** Behind the Mask. **1933** Gambling Ship. **1935** Freckles; Slightly Static (short); The Four-Star Boarder (voice only—short); Southern Exposure (short); Hot Money (short). **1936** Murder on the Roof; Modern Times; Captain Calamity; Yours for the Asking; Go Get 'Em Haines. **1937** Missing Witnesses.

NATRO, JIMMY
Born: 1908. Died: Jan. 31, 1946, Los Angeles, Calif. Screen actor.

NAVARRO, CARLOS
Born: Feb. 24, 1922, Mexico. Died: Feb. 13, 1969, Mexico City, Mexico. Screen and television actor.

Appeared in: **1956** The Brave One. **1962** La Estrella Vacia (The Empty Star). Other Mexican film: Dona Perfecta.

NAVARRO, JESUS GARCIA
Born: 1913, Mexico. Died: Sept. 1960, Mexico City, Mexico (heart attack). Stage and screen actor.

Appeared in: **1952** The Young and the Damned.

NAZARRO, CLIFF
Born: Jan. 31, 1904, New Haven, Conn. Died: Feb. 18, 1961. Screen, stage and vaudeville actor.

Appeared in: **1927** Cliff Nazarro and the Two Marjories (short). **1936** Romance Rides the Range. **1938** A Desperate Adventure; Outside of Paradise. **1939** King of the Turf; St. Louis Blues; Forged Passport. **1940** Arise, My Love. **1941** Mr. Dynamite; Rookies on Parade; World Premiere; Dive Bomber; You'll Never Get Rich; In Old Colorado; Artists and Models Abroad; Sailors on Leave; Night of January 16th; Melody for Three; Blondie Goes to College. **1942** Pardon My Stripes; Call of the Canyon; Hillbilly Blitzkrieg; Rhythm Parade. **1943** Shantytown. **1944** Swing Hostess; I'm from Arkansas; Trocadero. **1946** Ding Dong Williams; Gentleman Joe Palooka.

NAZIMOVA, ALLA
Born: May 22, 1879, Yalta, Crimea, Russia. Died: July 13, 1945, Los Angeles, Calif. (coronary thrombosis). Screen, stage actress, film producer and screenwriter. Divorced from actor Charles Bryant (dec. 1948).

Appeared in: **1916** War Brides (film debut). **1918** Revelation; Eye for Eye; Toys of Fate. **1919** The Red Lantern; The Brat; Out of the Fog. **1920** Stronger Than Death; Billions; Heart of a Child. **1921** Madame Peacock; Camille. **1922** A Doll's House. **1923** Salome. **1924** The Madonna of the Streets. **1925** My Son; The Redeeming Sin. **1940** Escape. **1941** Blood and Sand. **1943** Song of Bernadette. **1944** Since You Went Away; In Our Time; The Bridge of San Luis Rey.

NEAL, FRANK

Born: 1917. Died: May 8, 1955, Astoria, N.Y. (auto accident). Black screen actor and dancer.

Appeared in: **1943** Stormy Weather. **1955** Three in the Round (short).

NEAL, TOM

Born: Jan. 28, 1914, Evanston, Ill. Died: Aug. 7, 1972, North Hollywood, Calif. (natural causes). Divorced from non-professional Patricia Neal (dec. 1958) and actress Vicki Lane. Later married to Gail Evatt whom he was convicted of slaying in 1965.

Appeared in: **1938** Out West with the Hardys; The Great Heart (short—aka Father Damien the Leper Priest). **1939** Four Girls in White; Within the Law; Burn 'em Up O'Connor; Another Thin Man; 6000 Enemies; They All Come Out; Joe and Ethel Turp Call on the President; Honolulu; Stronger Than Desire; Money to Loan (short); Help Wanted (short). **1940** Sky Murder; The Courageous Dr. Christian; Jack Pot (short). **1941** Under Age; To Sergeant Mulligan; Jungle Girl (serial). **1942** Flying Tigers; Bowery at Midnight; The Miracle Kid; Ten Gentlemen from West Point; One Thrilling Night; Pride of the Yankees. **1943** China Girl; Behind the Rising Sun; Good Luck, Mr. Yates; Klondike Kate; There's Something about a Soldier; She Has What it Takes. **1944** Thoroughbreds; Unwritten Code; Two Man Submarine; The Racket Man. **1945** Crime, Inc.; First Yank into Tokyo; Detour. **1946** The Unknown; Club Havana; The Brute Man; Blonde Alibi; My Dog Shep. **1947** The Case of the Babysitter; The Hat Box Mystery. **1948** Beyond Glory. **1949** Red Desert; Apache Chief; Amazon Quest; Bruce Gentry (serial). **1950** Radar Secret Service; Joe Palooka in Humphrey Takes a Chance; King of the Bullwhip; Train to Tombstone; Everybody's Dancing; Call of the Klondike; I Shot Billy the Kid. **1951** G.I. Jane; Let's Go Navy!; Danger Zone; Navy Bound; Stop That Cab; Fingerprints Don't Lie; Varieties on Parade. **1952** The Dalton's Women; The Dupont Story. **1953** The Great Jesse James Raid.

NEASON, HAZEL

Died: Jan. 24, 1920. Screen actress. Married to film producer and actor Albert E. Smith (dec. 1958).

NEDD, STUART

Died: Mar. 5, 1971. Screen actor.

Appeared in: **1953** The Glory Brigade. **1955** Illegal.

NEDELL, ALICE BLAKENEY

Died: Oct. 21, 1959, Hollywood, Calif. Screen, stage and television actress. Married to actor Bernard Nedell (dec. 1972).

NEDELL, BERNARD (Bernard Jay Nedell)

Born: Oct. 14, 1898, New York, N.Y. Died: Nov. 23, 1972, Hollywood, Calif. Stage and screen actor. Married to actress Olive Blakeney (dec.).

Appeared in: **1916** The Serpent (film debut). **1929** The Silver King; The Return of the Rat; A Knight in London. **1930** The Call of the Sea (US 1935); The Man from Chicago (US 1931). **1931** Shadows (US 1936). **1932** Innocents of Chicago (aka Why Saps Leave Home—US). **1933** Her Imaginary Lover. **1934** Girl in Possession. **1935** Lazybones; Heat Wave (US 1936). **1936** Man Who Could Work Miracles (US 1937); First Offense. **1937** The Shadow Man; Plunder in the Air. **1938** Mr. Moto's Gamble; Exposed; Come Across (short). **1939** Lucky Night; They All Come Out; Secret Service of the Air; Some Like It Hot; Fast and Furious; Angels Wash Their Faces; Those High Grey Walls. **1940** Rangers of Fortune; Slightly Honorable; Strange Cargo; So You Won't Talk. **1941** Ziegfeld Girl. **1942** Ship Ahoy. **1943** The Desperadoes; Northern Pursuit. **1944** Maisie Goes to Reno; One Body Too Many. **1945** Allotment Wives. **1946** Crime Doctor's Man Hunt; Behind Green Lights. **1948** Albuquerque; The Loves of Carmen. **1972** Hickey and Boggs.

NEFF, RALPH

Died: Feb. 27, 1973. Screen actor.

Appeared in: **1955** The Man with the Golden Arm. **1958** The Last of the Fast Guns. **1960** Cage of Evil. **1961** The Case of Patty Smith (aka The Shame of Patty Smith).

NEGRETE, JORGE

Born: 1911, Mexico. Died: Dec. 5, 1953, Los Angeles, Calif. (cirrhosis of liver). Mexican screen, stage actor and singer.

Appeared in: **1938** La Madrina del Diablo (The Devil's Godmother). **1939** Perjura; El Cementario de las Aquilas (The Eagles' Cemetary); Juntos Pero No Revueltos (United but Not Mixed). **1943** Silk, Blood and Sun; Ay Jalisco No te Rajes; Asi Se Quiere En Jalisco. **1944** Tierra de Pasiones.

NEILAN, MARSHALL

Born: 1891, San Bernardino, Calif. Died: Oct. 26, 1958, Woodland Hills, Calif. (cancer). Screen actor, film director, film producer and screenwriter. Divorced from actress Blanche Sweet.

Appeared in: **1911** American Film Mfg. Co. films. **1912** The Reward of Valour; The Weaker Brother; The Stranger at Coyote. **1913** Judith of Bethulia; When Women are Police; The Rube and the Boob; The Tenderfoot's Luck; A Busy Day in the Jungle; Coupon Courtship; The Peace Offering; The Mission of a Bullet; A Mountain Tragedy; Fatty's Deception; Jones' Jonah Day; The Hash House Count; The Fired Cook; The Manicurist and the Mutt; Toothache. **1914** The Tattered Duke; The Deadly Battle at Hicksville; The Slavery of Foxicus; Only One Skirt. **1915** Rags; A Girl of Yesterday; Cupid Backs the Winners; Love, Oil and Grease; The Winning Whiskers; Madam Butterfly. **1916** Men and Women; The House of Discord; The Wedding Gown; Classmates; Calamity Anne; Guardian; The Crisis. **1919** Daddy Long Legs. **1923** Broadway Gold; Souls for Sale. **1957** A Face in the Crowd.

NEILL, JAMES

Born: Dec. 28, 1860, Savannah, Ga. Died: Mar. 16, 1931, Glendale, Calif. (heart trouble). Stage and screen actor. Married to actress Edythe Chapman (dec. 1948).

Appeared in: **1916** Oliver Twist. **1917** The Bottle Imp. **1918** Sandy. **1919** Men, Women and Money; Everywoman. **1920** The Paliser Case. **1921** Bits of Life; Dangerous Curve Ahead; A Voice in the Dark. **1922** Dusk to Dawn; The Heart Specialist; Her Husband's Trademark; Our Leading Citizen; Saturday Night; Manslaughter. **1923** The Thrill Chaser; Ten Commandments; The Lonely Road; Nobody's Money; Salomy Jane; Scars of Jealousy; The World's Applause. **1924** A Man's Mate. **1925** Any Woman; The Crimson Runner; New Brooms; Thank You. **1926** A Desperate Moment. **1927** King of Kings. **1928** The Border Patrol; Love Hungry; Three-Ring Marriage. **1929** Idle Rich. **1930** Shooting Straight; Only the Brave. **1931** Man to Man.

NEILL, RICHARD R.

Born: 1876, Philadelphia, Pa. Died: Apr. 8, 1970, Woodland Hills, Calif. Stage and screen actor.

Appeared in: **1914** The Active Life of Dolly of the Dailies (serial). **1919** The Great Gamble (serial). **1920** The Whirlwind (serial). **1922** Go Get 'Em Hutch (serial); Jan of the Big Snows. **1923** A Clouded Name; Sinner or Saint. **1924** Trail of the Law; The Heritage of the Desert; Wanderer of the Wasteland; The Fighting Coward. **1925** Tumbleweeds; Peggy of the Secret Service; Percy. **1926** Born to the West; Whispering Smith; Satan Town. **1927** Bulldog Pluck; Galloping Thunder; Code of the Cow Country; The Fightin' Comeback; King of Kings; Somewhere in Sonora; The Trunk Mystery. **1928** Beyond the Sierras; The Law's Lash; The Desert of the Lost; The Bushranger.

NEILSEN-TERRY, DENNIS

Born: 1895. Died: July 12, 1932, Bulawayo, South Africa (double pneumonia). Screen, stage actor, stage producer and stage manager. Son of actor Fred Terry (dec. 1933) and stage actress Julia Neilsen. Married to actress Mary Glynne (dec. 1954).

Appeared in: **1916** Her Greatest Performance. **1917** Masks and Faces. **1919** His Last Defence. **1920** The Hundredth Chance; The Magic Skin (aka Desire). **1922** The Romance of British History series including: The Flight of the King and A Story of Nell Gwynne. **1930** The House of the Arrow. **1931** 77 Park Lane. **1932** Murder at Covent Garden.

NELL, MRS. LOUISE M.

Born: 1884. Died: Nov. 1, 1944, Los Angeles, Calif. (killed—bus). Stage and screen actress.

NELSON, ANNE

Born: 1911. Died: July 6, 1948, Torrance, Calif. Screen actress.

NELSON, EDDIE "SUNKIST"

Born: 1894. Died: Dec. 5, 1940, Hollywood, Calif. (heart attack). Screen and vaudeville actor.

Appeared in: **1928** Stop and Go (short).

NELSON, HAROLD

Died: Jan. 26, 1937, Los Angeles, Calif. (pneumonia). Screen actor.

Appeared in: **1928** Sisters of Eve.

NELSON, LOTTIE

Born: 1875. Died: May 8, 1966, Hollywood, Calif. (stroke). Screen actress. Appeared in silents.

NELSON, OZZIE (Oswald George Nelson)

Born: Mar. 20, 1906, Jersey City, N.J. Died: June 3, 1975, Hollywood Hills, Calif. (cancer). Screen, stage, radio, television actor, film producer, director, bandleader, television producer, director and author. Married to actress Harriet Hilliard. Father of actors Rick and David Nelson.

Appeared in: **1940** A Vitaphone short. **1941** Sweetheart of the Campus. **1942** The Big Street. **1943** Strictly in the Groove; Honeymoon Lodge. **1944** Take It Big; Hi Good Lookin'. **1946** People are Funny. **1952** Here Come the Nelsons. **1965** Love and Kisses. **1968** The Impossible Years.

NELSON, VIRGINIA (Virginia Tallent)

Born: 1911. Died: Sept. 26, 1968, Escondido, Calif. Screen actress. Daughter of actress Jane Tallent.

NERVO, JIMMY (James Nervo)

Born: 1890, England. Died: Dec. 5, 1975, London, England. Screen, music hall and stage actor. Married to dancer Minna Nervo. Appeared with Teddy Knox as part of comedy team of "Nervo and Knox" and also appeared in "Crazy Gang" films and stage presentations with "Flanagan and Allen" and "Naughton and Gold."

The "Crazy Gang" films include: **1937** Okay for Sound. **1938** Alf's Button Afloat. **1939** The Frozen Limits. **1940** Gasbags. **1958** Life Is a Circus (US 1962).

"Nervo and Knox" appeared in: **1926** Phonofilm (short). **1928** The Rising Generation. **1930** Alf's Button. **1936** It's in the Bag; Skylarks. **1938** Cavalcade of the Stars.

NESBIT, EVELYN. *See* EVELYN NESBIT THAW

NESBITT, JOHN

Born: Aug. 23, 1910, Victoria, B.C., Canada. Died: Aug. 10, 1960. Screen, radio actor, screenwriter and film producer.

NESBITT, MIRIAM

Born: Sept. 11, 1873, Chicago, Ill. Died: Aug. 11, 1954, Hollywood, Calif. Stage and screen actress.

Appeared in: **1911** The Three Musketeers; Mary's Masquerade; An Old Sweetheart of Mine; An Island Comedy; The Reform Candidate; The Story of Indian Ledge; Home; A Man for all That; Eleanore Cuyler; The Awakening of John Bond; The Ghost's Warning; The Girl and the Motor Boat; The Minute Man; Bob and Rowdy; The New Church Carpet; The Unfinished Letter; A Suffragette in Spite of Himself; Friday the Thirteenth; The Winds of Fate; Then You'll Remember Me; Captain Barnacle's Baby; Betty's Buttons; Her Face; The Declaration of Independence; Aida. **1912** The Lord and the Peasant; Jack and the Beanstalk; The Bank President's Son; Mother and Daughter; The Jewels; The Sunset Gun; The Artist and the Brain Specialist; Nerves and the Man; The Foundling; Helping John; A Letter to the Princess; Fog; Lady Clare. **1913** The Foreman's Treachery; A Youthful Knight; The Two Merchants; A Clue to Her Parentage; The Portrait; He Swore off Smoking; The Princess and the Man; Leonie; The Ambassador's Daughter; The Heart of Valeska; A Daughter of Romany; Flood Tide; Keepers of the Flock; A Concerto for the Violin. **1914** Lena; The Living Dead; Sophia's Imaginary Visitor; A Question of Hats and Gowns; By the Aid of a Film; Face to Face; A Matter of Minutes; The Coward and the Man; Stanton's Last Flight; The Necklace of Rameses. **1915** The Glory of Clementina; A Theft in the Dark; The Portrait in the Attic; Killed Against Orders; Her Proper Place; A Woman's Revenge. **1917** The Last Sentence; Infidelity.

NESMITH, OTTOLA

Born: 1888. Died: Feb. 7, 1972, Hollywood, Calif. Screen, stage, radio and television actress.

Appeared in: **1915** Still Waters. **1921** Beyond Price; Wife Against Wife. **1928** The Girl-Shy Cowboy. **1935** Becky Sharp. **1936** Three Men on a Horse. **1937** Nobody's Baby. **1938** Fool's for Scandal. **1939** The Star Maker. **1940** Lillian Russell; Her First Romance. **1941** The Invisible Ghost; The Deadly Game. **1944** The Return of the Vampire. **1945** My Name is Julia Ross; Molly and Me. **1946** Cluny Brown. **1947** Buck Privates Come Home; The Late George Apley. **1954** Man Crazy. **1957** Witness for the Prosecution. **1960** From the Terrace. **1965** Inside Daisy Clover.

NESS, OLE M.

Born: 1888. Died: July 19, 1953, North Hollywood, Calif. Screen actor.

Appeared in: **1928** Chicago after Midnight; The Price of Fear; Skinner's Big Idea; Danger Street; Hit of the Show. **1929** Jazz Heaven; Hardboiled. **1931** The Sin of Madelon Claudet. **1933** Dawn to Dawn. **1935** The Last Days of Pompeii.

NESTELL, BILL

Born: 1895. Died: Oct. 18, 1966, Bishop, Calif. (stroke—heart attack). Screen actor.

Appeared in: **1926** Sir Lumberjack. **1928** Cheyenne Trails; Texas Flash; The Thrill Chaser; When the Law Rides. **1929** The Trail of the Horse Thieves. **1930** The Fighting Legion; The Man from Nowhere. **1939** The Night Riders. **1942** Stardust on the Sage. **1947** Dangerous Venture.

NEU, OSCAR F.

Born: June 22, 1886, Buffalo, N.Y. Died: Aug. 26, 1957, Crestwood, N.Y. Screen, vaudeville actor and film director. He toured in vaudeville with comedian Al Wilson. Appeared in films from 1911 to 1912.

NEUMANN, KURT

Born: Apr. 5, 1908, Nuremburg, Germany. Died: Aug. 21, 1958, Hollywood, Calif. Screen actor and film director.

Appeared in: **1943** Above Suspicion; Action in the North Atlantic; Hostages; Hangmen Also Die.

NEUSSER, ERIC

Born: 1902. Died: Aug. 30, 1957, Vienna, Austria (heart attack). Screen actor and film producer. Appeared in German films.

NEVARO (Otto Willkomm)

Born: 1887. Died: Nov. 13, 1941, Milwaukee, Wis. Screen actor and acrobat. Was part of acrobatic act billed as "Mareena, Nevaro and Mareena."

NEWALL, GUY

Born: 1885, England. Died: Feb. 25, 1937, London, England. Screen, stage actor, film director and screenwriter. Divorced from actress Ivy Duke with whom he appeared in films. Married to actress Dorothy Batley. Entered films with London Film Co. in 1912.

Appeared in: **1915** The Heart of Sister Ann. **1916** Trouble for Nothing; Money for Nothing; Motherlove; The Manxman; Driven (aka Desperation—US); Esther; Vice Versa. **1917** Smith. **1919** Comradeship (aka Comrades in Arms); Fancy Dress; I Will; The Garden of Resurrection. **1920** The Lure of Crooning Water; Duke's Son (aka Squandered Lives—US). **1921** The Bigamist. **1922** Beauty and the Beast (short); The Persistent Lovers; Boy Woodburn; Fox Farm; A Maid of the Silver Sea. **1923** The Starlit Garden. **1924** What the Butler Saw. **1927** The Ghost Train. **1928** Number Seventeen. **1930** The Road to Fortune. **1931** Potiphar's Wife (aka Her Strange Desire—US 1932); The Eternal Feminine. **1932** The Marriage Bond. **1936** Grand Finale. **1937** Merry Comes to Town.

NEWBERRY, HAZZARD P.

Born: 1907. Died: May 27, 1952, Chicago, Ill. Screen and stage actor. Entered films approx. 1935.

NEWBURG, FRANK

Born: 1886. Died: Nov. 11, 1969, Woodland Hills, Calif. Screen and vaudeville actor. Entered films approx. 1912.

Appeared in: **1916** The Windward Anchor; The Beloved Liar; The Iron Hand; The Grip of Crime; The Sea Lilly. **1917** Fuel of Life. **1924** Abraham Lincoln. **1925** The Sign of the Cactus; The Home Maker; Smouldering Fires; Lorraine of the Lions. **1927** Fire and Steel. **1928** The Singapore Mutiny.

NEWCOMB, MARY

Born: 1894, North Adams, Mass. Died: Jan. 1967, Dorchester, England. Stage and screen actress. Divorced from actor Robert Edeson (dec. 1931).

Appeared in: **1921** The Passionate Pilgrim. **1932** Frail Women; Women Who Play.

NEWCOMBE, JESSAMINE

Born: London, England. Died: Mar. 15, 1961, Hollywood, Calif. Screen, stage and radio actress.

NEWELL, WILLIAM "BILLY"

Born: 1894. Died: Feb. 21, 1967, Hollywood, Calif. Screen, stage, vaudeville and television actor.

Appeared in: **1935** Riffraff. **1936** The Voice of Bugle Ann; Libeled Lady; Navy Born; Bulldog Edition; Sitting on the Moon; The Mandarin Mystery; Happy Go Lucky; A Man Betrayed. **1937** Larceny on the Air; Beware of Ladies; Bill Cracks Down; Rhythm in the Clouds; Dangerous Holiday. **1938** Ride a Crooked Mile; Mr. Smith Goes to Washington. **1940** The Invisible Killer; Slightly Tempted; Mysterious Doctor Satan (serial); Fugitive from Justice; Hold That Woman. **1941** Caught in the Act; The Bride Came C.O.D.; Miss Polly. **1942** Keeper of the Flame; A Tragedy at Midnight; Who is Hope Schuyler?; Get Hep to Love; Orchestra Wives; Priorities on Parade. **1944** Sing a Jingle; Kansas City Kitty. **1945** Captain Eddie; Her Lucky Night; Out of the Depths; Stork Club; The Dolly Sisters. **1946** The Kid from Brooklyn; The Best Years of Our Lives; Girl on the Spot. **1947** Key Witness; The Second Chance. **1948** Song of My Heart. **1949** The Lone Wolf and His Lady. **1950** Traveling Saleswoman. **1955** Our Miss Brooks. **1957** Short Cut to Hell. **1958** Tank Force; The Missouri Traveler. **1959** High Flight; The Man Inside. **1960** Who Was That Lady?; The High-Powered Rifle.

NEWHALL, MAYO

Born: 1890. Died: Dec. 11, 1958, Burbank, Calif. Screen actor.

Appeared in: **1944** Meet Me in St. Louis. **1945** Yolanda and the Thief; Her Highness and the Bellboy. **1946** Of Human Bondage. **1948** That Lady in Ermine.

NEWLAND, ANNA DEWEY
Born: 1881. Died: June 24, 1967, Hollywood, Calif. Screen actress, model and author.

NEWLAND, PAUL (Paul Emory Newland)
Born: June 29, 1903, Nebraska. Died: Nov. 23, 1973, Studio City, Calif. (congestive failure). Screen actor.

Appeared in: **1938** Cocoanut Grove; You and Me. **1941** The Gay Vagabond. **1942** Down Rio Grande Way. **1943** True to Life. **1944** The Adventures of Mark Twain; I'm from Arkansas; Lost in a Harem. **1945** The Man Who Walked Alone; Within These Walls. **1946** Don Ricardo Returns. **1947** Bells of San Francisco; Dragnet. **1951** David and Bathsheba. **1952** Captive City; Against all Flags. **1953** Prisoners of the Casbah. **1955** Pirates of Tripoli. **1964** The Americanization of Emily. **1965** The Slender Thread. **1970** There Was a Crooked Man.

NEWMAN, ALFRED
Born: Mar. 17, 1901, New Haven, Conn. Died: Feb. 17, 1970, Los Angeles, Calif. (emphysema and complications). Composer, conductor and screen actor.

Appeared in: **1939** They Shall Have Music.

NEWMAN, CANDY
Born: 1945. Died: June 19, 1966. Screen actress.

Appeared in: **1963** Palm Springs Weekend.

NEWMAN, JOHN K.
Born: 1864. Died: Mar. 2, 1927, New York, N.Y. Screen and stage actor.

Appeared in: **1924** Greatest Love of All.

NEWMAN, LUR BARDEN
Died: Dec. 1, 1918. Screen actress. Appeared in Biograph films.

NEWMAN, NELL
Born: 1881. Died: Aug. 1931, Hollywood, Calif. (pneumonia). Screen actress.

NEWMARK, STEWART (Max Nathan)
Born: Jan. 23, 1916, California. Died: July 11, 1968, North Hollywood, Calif. (heart disease). Screen actor.

NEWSOME, CARMAN
Born: 1912. Died: July 18, 1974, Cleveland, Ohio. Bandleader, radio and screen actor.

NEWTON, CHARLES
Died: 1926. Stage and screen actor. Married to actress Dorrit Ashton (dec. 1936).

Appeared in: **1916-17** American Film Mfg. Co. films. **1920** The Moon Riders (serial). **1921** Red Courage; Sure Fire; Action; High Gear Jeffrey; Colorado. **1922** The Loaded Door; Western Speed. **1923** Danger; In the Palace of the King. **1924** The Iron Horse; $50,000 Reward; Vanity's Price. **1925** Riders of the Purple Sage. **1926** Yellow Fingers; Western Pluck.

NEWTON, ROBERT
Born: June 1, 1905, Shaftesbury, Dorset, England. Died: Mar. 25, 1956, Beverly Hills, Calif. (heart attack). Screen, stage and television actor. Voted one of top ten British moneymaking stars in Motion Picture Herald-Fame Poll, 1947-51.

Appeared in: **1932** Reunion. **1937** Fire Over England; Dark Journey; The Squeaker (aka Murder on Diamond Row—US); Farewell Again (aka Troopship—US 1938); The Green Cockatoo (US 1947 aka Four Dark Hours); 21 Days (aka 21 Days Together—US 1940 and The First and the Last). **1938** Vessel of Wrath (aka The Beachcomber—US); Yellow Sands. **1939** Jamaica Inn; Dead Men are Dangerous; Poison Pen (US 1941); Hell's Cargo (aka Dangerous Cargo—US 1940). **1940** Gaslight (aka Angel Street—US); Bulldog Sees It Through; Cannel Incident (short); Busman's Honeymoon (aka Haunted Honeymoon—US). **1941** Major Barbara; Hatter's Castle. **1942** They Flew Alone (aka Wings and the Woman—US). **1944** The Happy Breed (US 1947). **1945** Henry V (US 1946). **1946** Night Boat to Dublin. **1947** Odd Man Out; Temptation Harbour (US 1949). **1948** Snowbound (US 1949); Oliver Twist (US 1951); Kiss the Blood Off My Hands. **1949** Obsession (aka The Hidden Room—US 1950). **1950** Treasure Island; Waterfront (aka Waterfront Women—US 1952). **1951** Tom Brown's School Days; Soldiers Three. **1952** Blackbeard the Pirate; Les Miserables. **1953** The Desert Rats; Androcles and the Lion. **1954** The Beachcomber (US 1955); The High and the Mighty. **1955** Long John Silver. **1956** Around the World in 80 Days.

NEWTON, THEODORE
Born: 1905, Lawrenceville, N.Y. Died: Feb. 23, 1963, Hollywood, Calif. (cancer). Screen, stage and television actor.

Appeared in: **1933** The House on 56th Street; The Working Man; Voltaire; From Headquarters; Ace of Aces; The World Changes; The Sphinx. **1934** Gambling; Blind Date; Heat Lightning; Upperworld; Now I'll Tell; A Modern

Hero; Let's Try Again. **1935** Jalna. **1945** The Hidden Eye; What Next, Corporal Hargrove? **1946** Two Years before the Mast; Miss Susie Slagle's. **1956** The Come On; The Proud and the Profane; Friendly Persuasion; Somebody up There Likes Me. **1959** The Story on Page One (US 1960). **1963** Dime with a Halo.

NIBLO, FRED, SR. (Federico Nobile)
Born: Jan. 6, 1874, York, Nebr. Died: Nov. 11, 1948, New Orleans, La. (pneumonia). Screen, stage, vaudeville actor, film, stage director and stage producer. Father of screenwriter and actor Fred Niblo, Jr. (dec. 1973). Married to actress Enid Bennett (dec. 1969).

NIBLO, FRED, JR.
Born: Jan. 23, 1903, New York, N.Y. Died: Feb. 18, 1973, Encino, Calif. Screenwriter, author and screen actor. Son of film director and actor Fred Niblo, Sr. (dec. 1948).

Appeared in: **1930** Free and Easy. **1940** I'm Still Alive; Ellery Queen, Master Detective. **1941** Life With Henry.

NICHOLS, ERNEST LORING "RED"
Born: May 8, 1905, Ogden, Utah. Died: June 28, 1965, Las Vegas, Nev. (heart attack). Bandleader, screen, television and radio actor.

Appeared in: **1929** Red Nichols and His Five Pennies (short). **1935** Melody Masters (short). **1936** Red Nichols and His World Famous Pennies (short).

NICHOLS, GEORGE, SR.
Born: 1865. Died: Sept. 20, 1927, Hollywood, Calif. Screen actor and film director. Father of actor and director George Nichols, Jr. (dec. 1939).

Appeared in: **1910** The Usurer. **1919** The Turn in the Road. **1920** The Greatest Question. **1921** The Fox; Live and Let Live; Shame; The Queen of Sheba; Molly O.; Oliver Twist, Jr. **1922** The Barnstormer; Don't Get Personal; Suzanna; The Pride of Palomar; The Flirt; One Glorious Day. **1923** Children of Dust; The Country Kid; Let's Go; The Miracle Makers; The Ghost Patrol; The Extra Girl; Don't Marry for Money. **1924** The Midnight Express; Secrets; The Beautiful Sinner; Daughters of Today; Geared to Go; The Red Lily; The Slanderers; East of Broadway; The Silent Stranger; The Silent Watcher. **1925** The Goose Woman; Capital Punishment; The Eagle; Proud Flesh; His Majesty, Bunker Bean; The Light of Western Stars. **1926** Bachelor Brides; Broken Hearts of Hollywood; The Timid Terror; Sea Horses; Senor Daredevil; Flames; Gigolo; Miss Nobody; Rolling Home. **1927** Ritzy; White Gold; White Flannels; Finger Prints. **1928** The Wedding March.

NICHOLS, GEORGE, JR.
Born: May 5, 1897, San Francisco, Calif. Died: Nov. 13, 1939, Los Angeles, Calif. (auto accident). Screen actor and film director. Son of actor and director George Nichols, Sr. (dec. 1927).

Appeared as a child actor in early Biograph films.

NICHOLS, MARGARET
Born: 1900. Died: Mar. 17, 1941, Los Angeles, Calif. (pneumonia). Screen actress. Married to film producer Hal Roach.

NICHOLS, MARJORIE J.
Died: Sept. 26, 1970, N.Y. Screen, stage and television actress.

Appeared in: **1959** North by Northwest. **1961** Splendor in the Grass.

NICHOLS, NELLIE V.
Born: 1885. Died: July 16, 1971, Los Angeles, Calif. Screen and vaudeville actress.

Appeared in: **1930** Playing Around (film debut). **1931** Women Go on Forever. **1937** Manhattan Merry-Go-Round.

NICHOLSON, NORA
Born: Dec. 7, 1892, Leamington, Warwickshire, England. Died: Sept. 18, 1973, London, England. Screen, stage actress, novelist and playwright. Entered films in 1934.

Appeared in: **1949** The Blue Lagoon. **1952** Crow Hollow; Tread Softly. **1955** Raising a Riot (US 1957). **1956** A Town Like Alice (US 1957). **1957** Light Fingers; Seawife. **1958** Law and Disorder. **1959** The Captain's Table (US 1960); Upstairs and Downstairs (US 1961). **1963** The Devil Doll (US 1964); Three Lives of Thomasina. **1968** Diamonds for Breakfast.

NICHOLSON, PAUL
Born: 1877, Orange, N.J. Died: Feb. 2, 1935, Santa Monica, Calif. (influenza). Screen, stage and vaudeville actor. Appeared in vaudeville as part of the "Mimic Four" act. Entered films with American Motoscope and Biograph Co. in 1897.

Appeared in: **1921** The Woman God Changed. **1924** Married Flirts. **1925** As Man Desires; Chickie; I Want My Man; Joanna. **1926** Bachelor Brides; The Johnstown Flood; The Nervous Wreck; Up in Mabel's Room. **1927** The Broncho Twister; The Brute; Bertha the Sewing Machine Girl. **1928** The Smart Set;

Port of Missing Girls. **1929** Not Quite Decent. **1930** Fox Movietone Follies of 1930. **1931** Oh! Oh! Cleopatra (short); Man to Man; Silence. **1932** Scandal for Sale. **1934** Two Alone.

NICKOLS, WALTER
Born: 1853. Died: Dec. 25, 1927, New York, N.Y. (heart trouble). Stage and screen actor.

NICOL, JOSEPH E.
Born: 1856. Died: June 1, 1926, Bernardsville, N.J. Screen, stage actor and musicial director.

NICOLETTI, LOUIS
Born: 1907. Died: Oct. 16, 1969, Hollywood, Calif. (lung illness). Screen actor and assistant film director.

Appeared in: **1951** Across the Wide Missouri. **1953** Money from Home.

NIELSEN, ASTA (aka DIE ASTA)
Born: 1882, Copenhagen, Denmark. Died: May 24, 1972, Copenhagen, Denmark. Screen, stage actress and film producer.

Appeared in: **1910** The Abyss (film debut); Der Abgrund. **1913** Engelein. **1914** The Devil's Assistant; Lady Madcap's Way. **1921** Hamlet. **1923** Downfall; Erdgeist. **1924** Hedda Gabler. **1925** The Joyless Street. **1927** The Lusts of Mankind; Streets of Sorrow; The Tragedy of the Street. **1928** Pandora's Box; Women without Men; Small Town Sinners; Vanina. **1934** Crown of Thorns. Other films include: The Little Angel; Miss Julie; The Black Dream; Gypsy Blood; Woman without Country; Youthful Folly; Die Suffragette; Das Liebes A-B-C; Intoxication.

NIELSEN, GERTRUDE
Born: 1918, en route Europe to U.S. Died: Mar. 27, 1975, Hollywood, Calif. Screen, stage, vaudeville, radio actress and singer.

Appeared in: **1934** Keeps Rainin' All the Time (short). **1937** Top of the Town. **1938** Start Cheering. **1941** Rookies on Parade. **1943** He's My Guy; This is the Army. **1948** The Babe Ruth Story.

NIELSEN, HANS
Born: 1911, Hamburg, Germany. Died: 1967, Berlin, Germany. Stage and screen actor.

Appeared in: **1939** Rote Orchiden (Red Orchids); Aufruhr in Damaskus (Tumult in Damascus). **1949** Palace Scandal. **1953** Keepers of the Night. **1956** Teufel in Seide (Devil in Silk—US 1968); Vor Sonnenuntergang (US 1961); Kleines Gelt und Grosse Liebe (Two in a Sleeping Bag—US 1964). **1958** Das Madchen vom Moorhof (The Girl of the Moors—US 1961); International Counterfeiters. **1959** Verbrechen Nach Schulschluss (The Young Go Wild—US 1962); Bewildered Youth (aka The Third Sex—US); Kriegsgericht (Court Martial—US 1962). **1960** Der Jugendrichter (The Judge and the Sinner—US 1964). **1961** Town Without Pity; Gestehen Sie Dr. Corda! (Confess Dr. Corda!); Die Wahrheit uber Rosemarie (The Truth About Rosemarie aka She Walks by Night—US). **1962** Vengeance (aka The Brain—US 1964); Ich Bin Auch nur Eine Frau (I, Too, Am Only a Woman—US 1966). **1964** Das Ungeheur von London (The Monster of London City—US 1967); Das Phantom von Soho (The Phantom of Soho—US 1967). **1965** Die Holle von Manitoba (A Place Called Glory—US 1966).

NIEMEYER, JOSEPH H.
Born: 1887. Died: Sept. 27, 1965, Santa Monica, Calif. Screen, vaudeville actor and dancer.

NIGH, WILLIAM
Born: Oct. 12, 1881, Berlin, Wis. Died: Nov. 28, 1955, Burbank, Calif. Screen actor, film producer, director and screenwriter. Entered films in 1911 with Mack Sennett.

Appeared in: **1914** The Clerk; The Higher Law; A Yellow Streak; A Royal Family; Salome Jane. **1916** His Great Triumph; Life's Shadows. **1920** Democracy, the Vision Restored. **1925** Fear-Bound.

NIGHT, HARRY A. "HANK"
Born: 1847. Died: Apr. 24, 1930, Hollywood, Calif. Screen actor. Abraham Lincoln impersonator.

NILE, FLORIAN MARTINEZ
Born: 1936, Spain. Died: Jan. 8, 1959, Madrid, Spain. Screen actor.

NILSSON, ANNA Q. (Anna Querentia Nilsson)
Born: Mar. 30, 1888, Ystad, Sweden. Died: Feb. 11, 1974, Hemet, Calif. (natural causes). Stage and screen actress. Entered films in 1910.

Appeared in: **1911** Molly Pitcher. **1912** War's Havoc; "Fighting" Dan McCool; Under a Flag of Truce; The Siege of Petersburgh; The Prison Ship; Saved from Court Martial; The Darling of the C.S.A.; The Grit of the Girl Telegrapher; The Confederate Ironclad; His Mother's Picture; The Farm Bully; Toll Gate

Raiders. **1913** The Grim Tale of War; Prisoners of War; The Battle of Bloody Ford; A Mississippi Tragedy; John Burns of Gettysburg; Shenandoah; Shipwrecked; The Fatal Legacy; Retribution; The Breath of Scandal; The Counterfeiter's Confederate; Uncle Tom's Cabin. **1914** A Shot in the Dark; Tell-Tale Stains; Perils of the White Lights; The Secret of the Will; A Diamond in the Rough; The Man with the Glove; The Ex-Convict; The Man in the Vault. **1915** In the Hands of the Jury; Barriers Swept Aside; The Night Operator at Buxton; The Siren's Reign; The Second Commandment; The Haunted House of Wild Isle; The Destroyer; A Sister's Burden; Rivals; The Haunting Fear; Hiding from the Law; The Regeneration; Voices in the Dark; The Night of the Embassy Ball; Barbara Frietchie. **1916** The Scarlet Road; Puppets of Fate (serial); Her Surrender. **1917** Infidelity; The Moral Code; The Inevitable; Seven Keys to Baldpate; Over There; The Silent Master. **1918** Venus in the East; Heart of the Sunset; The Trail to Yesterday; No Man's Land; In Judgement Of; Vanity Pool. **1919** Cheating Cheaters; The Way of the Strong; The Love Burglar; Her Kingdom of Dreams; Soldiers of Fortune; A Very Good Young Man. **1920** The Thirteenth Commandment; The Luck of the Irish; The Toll Gate; The Figurehead; One Hour Before Dawn; The Fighting Chance; In the Heart of a Fool; The Brute Master. **1921** What Women Will Do; Without Limit; The Oath; Why Girls Leave Home; Varmlanningarna; The Lotus Eater; Ten Nights in a Bar-room. **1922** Three Live Ghosts; The Man from Home; Pink Gods; Innocence. **1923** Adam's Rib; The Isle of Lost Ships; Souls for Sale; The Rustle of Silk; The Spoilers; Hollywood; Ponjola; Thundering Dawn; Innocence; Enemies of Children; Judgement of the Storm. **1924** Half-a-Dollar Bill; Painted People; Flowing Gold; Between Friends; Broadway After Dark; The Side Show of Life; The Fire Patrol; Vanity's Price; Inez from Hollywood. **1925** The Top of the World; If I Marry Again; One Way Street; The Talker; Winds of Chance; The Splendid Road; The Breath of Scandal; The Viennese Medley. **1926** Too Much Money; Her Second Chance; The Greater Glory; Miss Nobody; Midnight Lovers. **1927** The Masked Woman; Easy Pickings; Babe Comes Home; Lonesome Ladies; Sorrell and Son; The Thirteenth Juror. **1928** Blockade; The Whip. **1933** The World Changes. **1934** School for Girls; The Little Minister. **1935** Wanderer of the Wasteland. **1937** Behind the Criminal (short). **1938** Prison Farm; Paradise for Three. **1941** The Trial of Mary Dugan; Riders of the Timberline; The People vs. Dr. Kildare. **1942** Girl's Town; The Great Man's Lady; I Live on Danger. **1943** Headin' for God's Country; Cry Havoc. **1945** The Sailor Takes a Wife; The Valley of Decision. **1946** The Secret Heart. **1947** The Farmer's Daughter; Cynthia; It Had to Be You. **1948** Fighting Father Dunne; Every Girl Should be Married; The Boy with Green Hair; In the Good Old Summertime. **1949** Malaya. **1950** Sunset Boulevard; The Big Hangover; Grounds for Marriage. **1951** Show Boat; An American in Paris; The Law and the Lady; The Unknown Man. **1953** The Great Diamond Robbery. **1954** Seven Brides for Seven Brothers.

NINCHI, CARLO
Born: 1896, Italy. Died: May 1, 1974, Italy. Screen, stage and television actor.

Appeared in: **1931** Terra Madre. **1939** La Wally; Scipio Africanus. **1947** The King's Jester; Marco Visconti; Cavalleria Rusticana. **1948** The Spirit and the Flesh. **1949** Il Grido della Terra (The Earth Cries Out). **1950** Woman; Bullet for Stefano. **1952** The Island of Procida; Beauty and the Devil. **1953** L'Ennemi Public No. 1 (aka The Most Wanted Man—US 1962). **1954** Anita Garibaldi; Side Street Story; Sins of Rome. **1956** Queen of Babylon. **1960** La Ciociara (aka Two Women—US 1961). **1961** Constantino il Grande (aka Constantine and the Cross—US 1962). **1963** La Tigre dei Sette Mari (Tiger of the Seven Seas—US 1964).

NIXON, ARUNDEL
Born: 1907, England. Died: Apr. 4, 1949, Brisbane, Australia (cerebral hemorrhage). Screen actor.

NIXON, CLINT (Clinton James Hecht)
Born: 1906. Died: Oct. 22, 1937, Hollywood, Calif. Screen actor.

NOA, JULIAN
Born: 1879. Died: Nov. 26, 1958, New York, N.Y. Screen, stage, radio and television actor.

Appeared in: **1956** Pacific Destiny.

NOAKOVA, JANA
Born: 1948, Czechoslovakia. Died: Dec. 4, 1968, Prague, Czechoslovakia. Screen actress.

NOBLES, MILTON
Born: 1844, Cincinnati, Ohio, or Almont, Mich.? Died: June 14, 1924, Brooklyn, N.Y. (heart trouble). Screen, stage and vaudeville actor. Father of stage actor Milton Nobles, Jr. (dec. 1925). Married to actress Dollie Woolwine and together they appeared in vaudeville in an act billed as "Dolly and Milton Nobles."

Appeared in: **1924** America.

NOEMI, LEA

Born: 1883. Died: Nov. 6, 1973, New York, N.Y. Yiddish screen and stage actress.

Appeared in: 1937 Green Fields. 1938 The Singing Blacksmith. 1939 Mirele Efros (stage and film versions).

NOLAN, MARY (Mary Imogene Robertson)

Born: Dec. 18, 1905, Louisville, Ky. Died: Oct. 31, 1948, Los Angeles, Calif. Stage and screen actress. She used numerous names: Imogene "Bubbles" Wilson while with Ziegfeld; Mary Robertson while film star in Germany; Imogene Robertson, also while in Germany; and Mary Nolan in American films.

Appeared in: 1927 Sorrell and Son. 1928 Armored Vault; Silks and Saddles; The Foreign Legion; Uneasy Money; Good Morning Judge. 1929 Charming Sinners; Desert Nights; Eleven Who Were Loyal; Shanghai Lady; West of Zanzibar. 1930 Outside the Law; Undertow; Young Desire. 1931 Enemies of the Law; X Marks the Spot. 1932 The Big Shot; File 113; Docks of San Francisco; Midnight Patrol. Foreign films prior to 1930: The Viennese Lover; The Woman God Forgot.

NOMIS, LEO

Born: Iowa. Died: Feb. 5, 1932, Los Angeles, Calif. (plane crash while filming Sky Bride). Film stunt flyer.

Appeared in: 1926 California Straight Ahead. 1930 Hell's Angels. 1932 The Lost Squadron; The Crowd Roars; Sky Bride.

NOON, PAISLEY

Born: 1897, Los Angeles, Calif. Died: Mar. 27, 1932, Hollywood, Calif. (appendicitis). Stage and screen actor. Entered films approx. 1927.

Appeared in: 1932 Night World.

NOONAN, PATRICK

Born: Jan. 9, 1887, Dublin, Ireland. Died: May 19, 1962, Wokinham, England. Stage and screen actor.

Appeared in: 1915 Do Unto Others; Royal Love. 1932 Arms and the Man. 1934 Lily of Killarney (aka Bride of the Lake—US). 1936 Ourselves Alone (aka River of Unrest—US). 1937 Kathleen Mavoureen (aka Kathleen—US 1938); The Mutiny of the Elsinore (US 1939); Over the Moon (US 1940). 1938 Mountains O' Mourne. 1940 Dr. O'Down. 1947 Captain Boycott. 1948 Anna Karenina.

NOONAN, TOMMY (Tommy Noon)

Born: Apr. 29, 1922, Bellingham, Wash. Died: Apr. 24, 1968, Woodland Hills, Calif. (brain tumor). Screen, stage, burlesque actor, film producer and screenwriter. Part of film comedy team "Noonan and Marshall." Half-brother of actor John Ireland.

Appeared in: 1945 George White's Scandals (film debut); What No Cigarettes? (short); The Big Beef (short); Beware of Redheads (short). 1946 Ding Dong Williams; The Truth about Murder; The Bamboo Blonde. 1947 The Big Fix. 1948 Jungle Patrol; Open Secret. 1949 Trapped; I Shot Jesse James; I Cheated the Law. 1950 The Return of Jesse James; Holiday Rhythm. 1951 Starlift (with Marshall); F.B.I. Girl. 1953 Gentlemen Prefer Blondes. 1954 A Star Is Born. 1955 How to Be Very, Very Popular; Violent Saturday. 1956 The Ambassador's Daughter; Bundle of Joy; The Best Things in Life Are Free. 1957 The Girl Most Likely. 1959 The Rookie (with Marshall). 1961 Double Trouble. 1962 Swingin' Along (with Marshall). 1963 Promises! Promises! 1964 Three Nuts in Search of a Bolt. 1967 Cotton Pickin' Chickenpickers.

NORCROSS, FRANK

Born: 1856. Died: Sept. 13, 1926, Glendale, Calif. Screen and stage actor.

Appeared in: 1921 All Dolled Up; Garments of Truth. 1922 The Challenge. 1924 The Flaming Forties. 1925 The Man from Red Gulch. 1926 The Escape; King of the Pack.

NORDEN, CLIFF

Born: 1923. Died: Sept. 23, 1949, Hollywood, Calif. (suicide—pills). Screen actor.

NORDSTROM, CLARENCE

Born: 1893. Died: Dec. 13, 1968, East Orange, N.J. Screen and stage actor.

Appeared in: 1922 The Lights of New York. 1930 Ship Ahoy (short). 1932 The Crooner. 1933 Gold Diggers of 1933; 42nd Street.

NORIEGA, MANOLO

Born: 1880, Mexico. Died: Aug. 1961, Mexico City, Mexico. Screen actor, film director and screenwriter.

Appeared in: 1935 Los Muertos Hablan (The Dead Speak). 1936 Malditas Sean las Mujeres; Asi es la Mujer. 1937 El Misterio del Rostro Palida; El Baul Macabro (The Macabre Trunk). 1938 Ave Sin Rumbo (Wandering Bird); El Traidor; Huapango; Rancho Grande. 1939 Ojos Tapatios; Estrellita (Starlet); Odio (Hate); Vivire Otra Vez (I Shall Live Again).

NORMAN, GERTRUDE

Born: 1848, London, England. Died: July 20, 1943, Hollywood, Calif. Stage and screen actress.

Appeared in: 1914 The Unwelcome Mrs. Hatch. 1919 Widow by Proxy; Strictly Confidential. 1921 Partners of the Tide; Little Italy; A Voice in the Dark; Beach of Dreams. 1922 The Game Chicken. 1924 The Age of Innocence; The Right of the Strongest. 1927 King of Kings. 1929 The Greene Murder Case. 1933 Cradle Song. 1934 The Trumpet Blows.

NORMAN, JOSEPHINE (Josephine Arrich)

Born: Nov. 12, 1904, Vienna, Austria. Died: Jan. 24, 1951, Roslyn, N.Y. Screen actress. Married to actor Herbert Rawlins (dec. 1947).

Appeared in: 1924 Ramshackle House. 1925 The Road to Yesterday. 1926 Fifth Avenue; Prince of Pilsen. 1927 King of Kings; Wreck of the Hesperus; The Forbidden Woman. 1928 Chicago; Into No Man's Land.

NORMAND, MABEL

Born: Nov. 10, 1894, Boston, Mass. Died: Feb. 23, 1930, Monrovia, Calif. (tuberculosis). Screen, stage actress and film director. Married to actor Lew Cody (dec. 1934).

Appeared in: 1911 The Unveiling; The Eternal Mother; The Squaw's Love; Her Awakening; Saved from Herself; The Subduing of Mrs. Nag. 1912 Race for a Life; The Mender of the Nets; The Water Nymph; Pedro's Dilemma; Ambitious Butler; The Grocery Clerk's Romance; Mabel's Lovers; The Deacon's Trouble; A Temperamental Husband; A Desperate Lover; A Family Mixup; Mabel's Adventures; Mabel's Stratagem; The New Neighbor; Stolen Glory; The Flirting Husband; Cohen at Coney Island; At It Again; The Rivals; Mr. Fix-It; Brown's Seance; A Midnight Elopement; The Duel. 1913 Teddy Telzlaff and Earl Cooper; Speed Kings; Love Sickness at Sea; Cohen Saves the Flag; Fatty's Flirtation; Zuzu, the Band Leader; The Cure That Failed; For Lizzie's Sake; The Battle of Who Run; Mabel's Heroes; A Tangled Affair; A Doctored Affair; The Rural Third Degree; Foiling Fickle Father; At Twelve O'Clock; Her New Beau; Hide and Seek; The Ragtime Band (reissued as The Jazz Band); Mabel's Awful Mistake (reissued as Her Deceitful Lover); The Foreman of the Jury; The Hansom Driver; The Waiter's Picnic; The Telltale Light; Love and Courage; A Muddy Romance (reissued as Muddled in Mud); The Gusher; Saving Mabel's Dad; The Champion; The Mistaken Masher; Just Brown's Luck; Heinze's Resurrection; The Professor's Daughter; A Red Hot Romance; The Sleuths at the Floral Parade; A Strong Revenge; The Rube and the Baron; The Chief's Predicament; Those Good Old Days; Father's Choice; A Little Hero; Hubby's Job; Barney Oldfield's Race for a Life; The Speed Queen; For the Love of Mabel; A Noise from the Deep; Professor Bean's Removal; The Riot; Mabel's New Hero; The Gypsy Queen; The Faithful Taxicab; Baby Day; Mabel's Dramatic Career (reissued as Her Dramatic Debut); The Bowling Match. 1914 A Misplaced Foot; Mabel's Stormy Love Affair; Mabel's Bare Escape; Love and Gasoline; Mabel at the Wheel; Mabel's Nerve; The Fatal Mallet; Mabel's Busy Day; Mabel's New Job; Those Country Kids; Mabel's Blunder; Hello, Mabel; Lovers Post Office; How Heroes Are Made; Fatty's Wine Party; Getting Acquainted; A Missing Bride; Between Showers; A Glimpse of Los Angeles; Won in a Closet; Mabel's Strange Predicament; Back at It Again; Caught in a Cabaret; The Alarm; Her Friend the Bandit; Mabel's Married Life (reissued as The Squarehead); Mabel's Latest Prank (reissued as Touch of Rheumatism); Gentlemen of Nerve (reissued as Some Nerve); His Trysting Place; Fatty's Jonah Day; The Sea Nymphs (reissued as His Diving Beauty); Tillie's Punctured Romance; A Gambling Rube. 1915 Rum and Wallpaper; Mabel and Fatty's Simple Life; Mabel, Fatty and the Law (reissued as Fatty's Spooning Day); That Little Band of Gold (reissued as For Better or Worse); Wished on Mabel; Mabel's Wilful Way; Mabel Lost and Won; My Valet; Stolen Magic; Mabel and Fatty's Wash Day; Fatty and Mabel at the San Diego Exposition; Fatty's and Mabel's Married Life; His Luckless Love; Their Social Splash; Mabel and Fatty Viewing the World's Fair at San Francisco; The Little Teacher (reissued as A Small Town Bully). 1916 Fatty and Mabel Adrift; The Bright Lights (aka The Lure of Broadway); He Did and He Didn't (aka Love and Lobsters). 1918 Back to the Woods; The Venus Model; The Floor Below; Mickey; Peck's Bad Girl. 1919 Sis Hopkins; Sis; Upstairs. 1920 The Slim Princess. 1921 Mooly O'; What Happened to Rose? 1922 Head over Heels; Oh, Mabel, Behave. 1923 Suzanna; The Extra Girl. 1960 When Comedy Was King (documentary). 1961 Days of Thrills and Laughter (documentary).

NORRIS, ALEXANDER. See MAX NOSSECK

NORRIS, WILLIAM

Born: 1872, New York, N.Y. Died: Mar. 20, 1929, West Bronxville, N.Y. Stage and screen actor.

Appeared in: 1922 When Knighthood Was in Flower. 1923 The GoGetter; The Love Piker; Maytime; Adam and Eve; The Eternal Three. 1924 My Man. 1925 Never the Twain Shall Meet. 1927 The Joy Girl.

NORTH, BOB (Harold Young)

Born: 1881. Died: Mar. 18, 1936, Hollywood, Calif. (suicide—gas inhalation). Screen actor.

NORTH, JOSEPH B.

Born: 1874, England. Died: Jan. 8, 1945, Woodland Hills, Calif. Stage and screen actor.

Appeared in: **1924** Stolen Secrets; The Whispered Name. **1930** Ex-Flame. **1934** Ladies Should Listen. **1935** Paris Spring; Without Regret.

NORTH, WILFRID

Born: 1853, London, England. Died: June 3, 1935, Hollywood, Calif. Screen actor and film director. Joined Vitagraph as a director in 1915.

Appeared in: **1921** A Millionaire for a Day; The Son of Wallingford. **1923** The Huntress; The Love Brand; The Drivin' Fool. **1924** The Beloved Brute; A Man's Mate. **1925** The Happy Warrior; On Thin Ice. **1926** The Belle of Broadway; Hell Bent for Heaven; Peril of the Rail. **1927** Tongues of Scandal; The Bush Leaguer; Tracked by the Police. **1928** The Terrible People (serial); The Four-Flusher; Captain Careless. **1929** Girl Overboard; The Trial of Mary Dugan. **1930** The Dude Wrangler. **1932** Unashamed.

NORTHRUP, HARRY S.

Born: July 31, 1877, Paris, France. Died: July 2, 1936, Los Angeles, Calif. Stage and screen actor. Entered films in 1911.

Appeared in: **1911** Vanity Fair; The Star Reporter; The Cave Man; The Lady of the Lake; At the Eleventh Hour; Rock of Ages; The Indian Mutiny; His Lordship the Valet; The Mills of the Gods. **1913** Roughing the Cub. **1920** The Blue Moon; The White Circle; Sowing the Wind; Polly of the Storm Country. **1921** Flower of the North; The Four Horsemen of the Apocalypse; Wing Toy. **1922** Winning with Wits; Hate; Saved by Radio. **1928** The Christian; The Greatest Menace; Jazzmania; Human Wreckage; A Woman of Paris. **1924** A Fool's Awakening. **1925** The Gambling Fool; He Who Laughs Last; The Unchastened Woman. **1926** Devil's Island; Wanted—a Coward. **1927** Shield of Honor; The Heart of Maryland. **1928** Burning Daylight; The Cheer Leader; Divine Sinner. **1929** The Last Warning; Prisoners. **1930** Party Girl. **1931** Men Call it Love; Squaw Man; Arizona (aka Men Are Like That).

NORTON, BARRY (Alfredo Biraben)

Born: June 16, 1905, Buenos Aires, Argentina. Died: Aug. 24, 1956, Hollywood, Calif. (heart attack). Screen actor.

Appeared in: **1926** The Lily; What Price Glory; The Canyon of Light. **1927** The Wizard; The Heart of Salome; Ankles Preferred; Sunrise. **1928** Fleetwing; Mother Knows Best; Legion of the Condemned; Sins of the Fathers. **1929** The Exalted Flapper; Four Devils. **1930** The Benson Murder Case (Spanish version); Slightly Scarlet (French and Spanish versions). **1931** Dishonored. **1933** Cascarrabias; The Cocktail Hour; Only Yesterday; Lady for a Day. **1934** Nana; Unknown Blonde; Grand Canary; The World Moves On. **1935** Storm over the Andes. **1936** The Criminal Within; Murder at Glen Athol; Captain Calamity; El Diablo Del Mar; Asi es la Mujer. **1937** History Is Made at Night; I'll Take Romance; Timberesque. **1938** The Buccaneer; El Trovador de la Radio (Radio Troubador); El Traidor; El Pasado Acusa (The Accusing Past). **1939** Should Husbands Work?; Papa Soltero (Bachelor Father). **1946** Devil Monster. **1947** Twilight on the Rio Grande. **1956** Around the World in 80 Days.

NORTON, CECIL A.

Born: 1895. Died: Nov. 30, 1955, Hollywood, Calif. Screen, stage actor and television writer. Entered films approx. 1915.

NORTON, ELDA

Born: 1891. Died: Apr. 22, 1947, Hollywood, Calif. Screen and stage actress.

NORTON, FLETCHER

Born: 1877. Died: Oct. 3, 1941, Los Angeles, Calif. Screen and stage actor.

Appeared in: **1926** The Cowboy and the Countess; Davy Crockett at the Fall of the Alamo; Exclusive Rights. **1928** Dream of Love. **1930** Sweethearts and Wives; The Big House; Let's Go Place; Men of the North. **1931** The Phantom of Paris; The Secret Six; The Star Witness. **1932** Is My Face Red. **1933** Sucker Money; The Bowery. **1934** Most Precious Thing in Life; The Private Scandal. **1935** Call of the Wild.

NORTON, HENRY FIELD

Born: 1899. Died: Aug. 10, 1945, Hollywood, Calif. (following operation). Screen actor and singer. One of the founders of the Screen Extras Guild.

NORTON, JACK (Mortimer J. Naughton)

Born: 1889, Brooklyn, N.Y. Died: Oct. 15, 1958, Saranac Lake, N.Y. (respiratory ailment). Screen, stage and vaudeville actor. Played the drunk in more than 200 films; in real life never took a drink. Married to actress Lucille Norton (dec. 1959) with whom he appeared in vaudeville.

Appeared in: **1934** Sweet Music; Cockeyed Cavaliers; plus the following shorts: Super Snooper; Fixing a Stew; One Too Many; Counsel on De Fence; Woman Haters. **1935** Bordertown; Ship Cafe; Calling All Cars; Stolen Harmony; Don't Bet on Blondes; His Night Out; Ruggles of Red Gap. **1936** Too Many Parents; Down the Ribber (short). **1937** Swing Fever (short); Marked Woman; Meet the

Missus; Pick a Star; A Day at the Races. **1938** The Awful Tooth (short); Meet the Girls; Thanks for the Memory. **1939** Grand Jury Secrets; Joe and Ethel Turp Call on the President. **1940** The Farmer's Daughter; Opened by Mistake; A Night at Earl Carroll's; The Bank Dick. **1941** Louisiana Purchase; Road Show. **1942** The Fleet's In; The Spoilers; The Palm Beach Story; Moonlight Havana; Dr. Renault's Secret; Brooklyn Orchid; Tennessee Johnson. **1943** Taxi, Mister; Lady Bodyguard; Prairie Chicken; It Ain't Hay; The Falcon Strikes Back. **1944** His Tale is Told (short); The Chinese Cat; Hail the Conquering Hero; The Big Noise; Ghost Catchers. **1945** Wonder Man; Fashion Model; Flame of the Barbary Coast; A Guy, A Gal, A Pal; Captain Tugboat Annie; Strange Confession; Man Alive; Hold That Blonde; Her Highness and the Bellboy; The Scarlet Clue; The Naughty Nineties; Double Honeymoon (short). **1946** Blue Skies; No Leave, No Love; The Kid from Brooklyn; The Sin of Harold Diddlebock (aka Mad Wednesday); Shadows over Chinatown; Corpus Delecti; The Strange Mr. Gregory; Bringing up Father; Rendezvous 24; Rhythm and Weep (short). **1947** Linda, Be Good; The Hired Husband (short). **1948** Variety Time.

NORTON, LUCILLE

Born: 1894. Died: June 17, 1959, Beverly Hills, Calif. Screen, stage and vaudeville actress. Was in vaudeville as one of the "Haley Sisters" and later teamed in vaudeville with husband, actor Jack Norton (dec. 1958).

NORWORTH, JACK

Born: Jan. 5, 1879, Philadelphia, Pa. Died: Sept. 1, 1959, Laguna Beach, Calif. Screen, stage, vaudeville, minstrel, radio, television actor and songwriter. Married to stage actress Amy Swor (dec. 1974). Divorced from stage actress Nora Bayes (dec. 1965); actresses Dorothy Norworth (with whom he appeared in "Nagger" film series) and Louise Dresser (dec. 1965). Entered films in 1928.

Appeared in: **1929** Queen of the Night Clubs, plus the following shorts: Song and Things; Odds and Ends. **1930** The following two shorts: Song and Things; Odds and Ends. **1930-32** The following "Nagger" series shorts: **1930** The Naggers; The Naggers at Breakfast; The Naggers Go South. **1931** The Naggers' Day of Rest; The Naggers Go Rooting; The Naggers Go Camping; The Naggers at the Dentist's; The Naggers in the Subway. **1932** The Naggers at the Ringside; The Naggers Go Shopping; The Naggers at the Races; The Naggers' Housewarming. **1942** Shine on Harvest Moon. **1945** The Southerner.

NORWORTH, NED

Born: 1889. Died: Feb. 12, 1940, New York, N.Y. (after fall and brain operation). Screen and vaudeville actor. Appeared in vaudeville with his first wife, actress Josephine Bennett, in an act billed as "Ned Norworth and Co."

NOSSECK, MAX (aka ALEXANDER M. NORRIS)

Born: Sept. 19, 1902, Nakel, Poland. Died: Sept. 29, 1972, Bad Wiesse, Germany. Screen, stage actor, film director, producer and screenwriter. Entered films as an actor.

Appeared in: **1927** Around the World Without Money.

NOTARI, GUIDO

Born: 1894, Italy. Died: Jan. 21, 1957, Rome, Italy. Screen and radio actor.

Appeared in: **1947** Before Him All Rome Trembled. **1956** Helen of Troy.

NOVARRO, RAMON (Ramon Samaniegoes)

Born: Feb. 6, 1899, Durango, Mexico. Died: Oct. 31, 1968, Hollywood, Calif. (murdered). Screen, television actor, screenwriter and film director.

Appeared in: **1919** The Goat (film debut). **1921** A Small Town Idol. **1922** The Prisoner of Zenda; Trifling Women; Mr. Barnes of New York. **1923** Scaramouche; Where the Pavement Ends. **1924** The Arab; The Red Lily; Thy Name Is Woman. **1925** The Midshipman; A Lover's Oath. **1926** Ben Hur. **1927** The Student Prince; The Road to Romance; Lovers? **1928** A Certain Young Man; Forbidden Hours; Across to Singapore. **1929** The Flying Fleet; The Pagan; Devil May Care. **1930** In Gay Madrid; The Singer of Seville; Call of the Flesh. **1931** Son of India; Ben Hur (rerelease of 1926 version in sound); Daybreak. **1932** Mata Hari; Son-Daughter; Huddle. **1933** The Barbarian. **1934** The Cat and the Fiddle; Laughing Boy. **1935** The Night Is Young. **1937** The Sheik Steps Out. **1938** La Comedie de Bonheur; A Desperate Adventure; As You Are. **1942** La Virgen Que Forjo una Patria. **1949** We Were Strangers; The Big Steal. **1950** The Outriders; Crisis. **1960** Heller in Pink Tights.

NOVELLO, IVOR (Ivor Novello Davies)

Born: Jan. 15, 1893, Cardiff, Wales. Died: Mar. 6, 1951, London, England (coronary thrombosis). Screen, stage actor, screenwriter, playwright and composer. Wrote song, "Keep the Home Fires Burning."

Appeared in: **1921** Carnival. **1922** The Bohemian Girl. **1923** The White Rose; Bonnie Prince Charlie; The Man without Desire. **1925** The Rat. **1926** The Triumph of the Rat; The Lodger (aka The Case of Jonathan Drew—US 1928). **1927** Downhill (aka When Boys Leave Home—US 1928); The Vortex. **1928** A South Sea Bubble; The Constant Nymph. **1929** The Return of the Rat. **1930** Symphony in Two Flats. **1931** Once a Lady. **1932** The Lodge (aka The Phantom Fiend—US 1935). **1933** I Lived with You; Sleeping Car. **1934** Autumn Crocus.

NOVINSKY, ALEXANDER "ALEX"
Born: July 2, 1878, St. Petersburg, Russia. Died: June 30, 1960. Screen actor.

Appeared in: 1928 Abie's Irish Rose; Red Dance; Night Watch. 1929 Leatherneck. 1930 The Princess and the Plumber. 1931 Transatlantic; Ambassador Bill. 1932 Union Depot; Love Me Tonight; Six Hours to Live. 1933 Cavalcade; Night of Terror. 1936 Give Us This Night; Suzy. 1937 Nothing Sacred.

NOVIS, DONALD
Born: Mar. 3, 1907, Hastings, England. Died: July 23, 1966, Norwalk, Calif. Screen, stage, radio actor and singer.

Appeared in: 1929 New York Nights; Irish Fantasy (short). 1930 Monte Carlo. 1931 The Pajama Party (short). 1932 The Singing Plumber (short); One Hour with You; The Big Broadcast; "Mack Sennett Star" series. 1933 The Singing Boxer (short); a Vitaphone short. 1934 An RKO short. 1935 Paramount shorts. 1944 Slightly Terrific. 1950 Mr. Universe.

NOWELL, WEDGEWOOD
Born: 1878, Portsmouth, N.H. Died: June 17, 1957, Philadelphia, Pa. Screen, stage actor and stage producer. Entered films in 1915.

Appeared in: 1916 The Deserter. 1921 813; Devotion; The Match-Breaker. 1922 The Eternal Flame; Enter Madame; Ashes; A Doll's House; The Song of Life; Thelma. 1923 The Westbound Limited; A Wife's Romance; Heroes of the Street; Adam's Rib; Don't Marry for Money. 1924 Jealous Husbands. 1936 To Mary, with Love; Stolen Holiday. 1937 The Big Show. 1940 Calling Philo Vance.

NOYES, JOSEPH
Born: 1869. Died: Apr. 17, 1936, Los Angeles, Calif. (hit by auto). Screen actor.

NUEMANN, CHARLES
Born: 1873. Died: July 16, 1927, Glendale, Calif. Screen actor.

NUGENT, J. C.
Born: Apr. 6, 1875, Niles, Ohio. Died: Apr. 21, 1947, New York, N.Y. (coronary thrombosis). Screen, stage actor, playwright, screenwriter and film director. Father of actor Elliott Nugent.

Appeared in: 1929 Wise Girls; Navy Blues. 1930 They Learned About Women; Love in the Rough; Remote Control; The Big House. 1931 The Millionaire; Many a Slip; Virtuous Husbands. 1935 Love in Bloom; Men without Names. 1937 A Star Is Born; Stand-In; This Is My Affair; Life Begins in College. 1938 It's All Yours; Midnight Intruder; Give Me a Sailor.

NUNEZ, JUAN MANUEL
Born: Cuba. Died: Jan. 24, 1966, Havana, Cuba. Screen actor.

NUNN, WAYNE (Shephard Wayne Nunn)
Born: 1881, Ind. Died: Dec. 17, 1947, New York, N.Y. Screen and stage actor. Divorced from actress Grace Valentine (dec. 1964). Married to actress Zoe Barnett.

Appeared in: 1939 One Third of a Nation.

NYE, CARROLL
Born: Oct. 4, 1901, Canton, Ohio. Died: Mar. 17, 1974, North Hollywood, Calif. (heart attack and kidney failure). Screen, stage actor, radio commentator and columnist. Married to actress Helen Lynch (dec. 1965) and later married to Dorothy Nye.

Appeared in: 1925 Classified; Three Wise Crooks. 1926 The Earth Woman; The Imposter; Kosher Kitty Kelly; Her Honor the Governor. 1927 The Black Diamond Express; Death Valley; The Silver Slave; The Brute; The Girl from Chicago; The Heart of Maryland; Little Mickey Grogan; The Rose of Kildare; What Every Girl Should Know. 1928 The Perfect Crime; Powder My Back; A Race for Life; Rinty of the Desert; The Sporting Age; While the City Sleeps; Craig's Wife; Jazzland; Land of the Silver Fox. 1929 Madame X; The Squall; The Flying Fleet; Light Fingers; The Girl in the Glass Cage. 1930 The Bishop Murder Case; The Lottery Bride; Sons of the Saddle. 1931 The Lawless Woman; Hell Bent for Frisco; Neck and Neck; One Way Trail. 1935 Traveling Saleslady. 1938 Rebecca of Sunnybrook Farm; Kentucky Moonshine. 1939 Gone with the Wind. 1940 The Trail Blazers. 1944 Dark Mountain.

OAKLAND, VIVIEN (Vivian Anderson)
Born: 1895. Died: Aug. 1, 1958, Hollywood, Calif. Screen, stage and vaudeville actress. Married to actor John T. Murray (dec. 1957). They appeared in vaudeville as "John T. Murray and Vivan Oakland," and also made several shorts together during 1929-30.

Appeared in: 1924 Madonna of the Streets. 1925 The Teaser; The Rainbow Trail. 1926 Tony Runs Wild; Redheads Preferred; Tell 'Em Nothing (short). 1927 Love 'Em and Weep (short); Wedding Bills; Uncle Tom's Cabin. 1929 The Man in Hobbles; The Time, the Place and the Girl; The Crazy Nut; In the Headlines; "Educational Mermaid" shorts; plus the following shorts billed as "John T. Murray and Vivian Oakland": Satires; The Hall of Injustice. 1930 The Floradora Girl; Personality; Back Pay; A Lady Surrenders; The Matrimo-

nial Bed; plus the following shorts: Oh, Sailor, Behave!; Below Zero; Big Hearted; Let Me Explain; Vanity; A Mother of Ethics; and the following two with her husband: Who Pays; The Servant Problems. 1931 The Age for Love; Gold Dust Gertie. 1932 A House Divided; Cock of the Air; The Tenderfoot; Scram! (short). 1933 They Just Had to Get Married; Neighbors' Wives; Only Yesterday. 1934 The Defense Rests; Money Means Nothing; plus the following shorts: In the Doghouse; Perfectly Mismated; One Too Many. 1935 Rendezvous at Midnight; Star of Midnight; Alimony Aches (short). 1936 Lady Luck; The Bride Walks Out; One Live Ghost (short). 1937 Way Out West; Mile a Minute Love; plus the following shorts: Knee Action; Bad Housekeeping; Dumb's the Word; Tramp Trouble; Wrong Romance; Should Wives Work? 1938 Double Danger; Crime Afloat; Slander House; Rebellious Daughters; plus the following shorts: Fool Coverage; Beaux and Errors; A Clean Sweep; The Pest Friend; Berth Quakes. 1939 The following shorts: Boom Goes the Groom; Maid to Order; Clock Wise; Baby Daze; Feathered Pests; Act Your Age; Kennedy the Great. 1940 On Their Own; plus the following shorts: Mr. Clyde Goes to Broadway; Slightly at Sea; Mutiny in the County; 'Taint Legal; Sunk by the Census; Trailer Tragedy; Drafted in the Depot. 1941 The following shorts: Ring and the Belle; Mad About Moonshine; It Happened All Night; An Apple in His Eye. 1942 The Man in the Trunk; Sappy Pappy (short). 1943 Laugh Your Blues Away. 1944 The Girl Who Dared. 1945 Utah; The Man Who Walked Alone. 1946 Social Terrors (short). 1947 Borrowed Blonde (short). 1948 Home Canning (short). 1950 Bunco Squad. 1951 Punchy Pancho (short). 1965 Laurel and Hardy's Laughing 20's (documentary).

OAKLAND, WILL
Born: 1883. Died: May 15, 1956, Bloomfield, N.J. Screen, radio, vaudeville, minstrel actor and singer.

Appeared in: 1927 While We Danced Till Dawn; Dreamy Melody (both shorts).

OAKLEY, ANNIE (Phoebe Anne Oakley Mozee)
Born: Aug. 13, 1860, Patterson Township, Darke County, Ohio. Died: Nov. 3, 1926, Greenville, Ohio. Rodeo, vaudeville, circus performer and screen actress. Married to marksman Frank E. Butler. Appeared in a pre-1900 film.

OAKLEY, FLORENCE
Born: 1891. Died: Sept. 25, 1956, Hollywood, Calif. Screen actress.

Appeared in: 1929 A Most Immoral Lady.

OAKLEY, LAURA
Born: July 10, 1879, Oakland, Calif. Died: Jan. 30, 1957, Altadena, Calif. (heart ailment). Screen actress.

Appeared in: 1915 Star of the Sea; Changed Lives; The Black Box (serial). 1920 The Vanishing Dagger (serial).

OAKMAN, WHEELER
Born: 1890, Va. Died: Mar. 19, 1949, Van Nuys, Calif. Screen and stage actor.

Appeared in: 1913 The Long Ago. 1914 The Spoilers. 1916 The Ne'er-Do-Well. 1920 The Virgin of Stamboul. 1921 Peck's Bad Boy; Outside the Law; Penny of Top Hill Trail. 1922 The Half Breed; The Son of the Wolf. 1923 Slippery McGee; The Love Trap; Mine to Keep; Other Men's Daughters. 1925 Lilies of the Street; The Pace That Thrills. 1926 In Borrowed Plumes; Fangs of Justice; Outside the Law (revised version of 1921 film). 1927 Out All Night; Hey! Hey! Cowboy; Heroes of the Night. 1928 Top Sergeant Mulligan; Lights of New York; The Broken Mask; Masked Angel; The Power of the Press; What a Night; While the City Sleeps; Black Feather; Danger Patrol; The Good-Bye Kiss; The Heart of Broadway. 1929 The Show of Shows; The Hurricane; The Girl from Woolworth's; On with the Show; Devil's Chaplain; Handcuffed; Morgan's Last Raid; The Donovan Affair; Father and Son; Shanghai Lady; The Shakedown. 1930 Little Johnny Jones; On Your Back; The Big Fight; The Costello Case; Roaring Ranch. 1931 The Good Bad Girl; The Lawless Woman; First Aid; Sky Raiders. 1932 Texas Cyclone; Two-Fisted Law; Riding Tornado; Gorilla Ship; Beauty Parlor; The Heart Punch; The Boiling Point; Guilty or Not Guilty; Devil on Deck. 1933 Revenge at Monte Carlo; Sundown Rider; Rusty Rides Alone; Silent Men; Hold the Press; Man of Action; Western Code; Speed Demon; End of the Trail; Soldiers of the Storm. 1934 Lost Jungle; Frontier Days; In Old Santa Fe; Murder in the Clouds; One Is Guilty. 1935 The Phantom Empire (serial); Code of the Mounted; Death from a Distance; Annapolis Farewell; Trails of the Wild; The Man from Guntown; Square Shooter; Motive for Revenge; Headline Woman. 1936 Timber War; Song of the Trail; Roarin' Guns; Gambling with Souls; Darkest Africa (serial); Aces and Eights; Ghost Patrol. 1937 Death in the Air; Bank Alarm. 1938 Code of the Rangers; Mars Attacks the World. 1939 In Old Montana; Torture Ship; Mutiny in the Big House. 1940 Men with Steel Faces. 1941 Meet the Mob. 1942 Double Trouble; Bowery at Midnight; So's Your Aunt Emma. 1943 Ghosts on the Loose; The Girl from Monterey; What a Man!; The Ape Man; Kid Dynamite; Fighting Buckaroo; Saddles and Sagebrush. 1944 Riding West; Sundown Valley; Three of a Kind; Bowery Champs. 1945 Rough Ridin' Justice; Trouble Chasers; Brenda Starr, Reporter (serial).

OATES, CICELY

Born: England. Died: 1935, England (?). Stage and screen actress.

Appeared in: **1933** I Lived with You. **1934** The Man Who Knew Too Much. **1935** The Price of Wisdom; Things are Looking Up.

OBECK, FRED

Born: 1881. Died: Jan. 31, 1929, Hollywood, Calif. (heart trouble). Screen actor.

Appeared in: **1927** The Patent Leather Kid; Wanted a Coward. **1928** Vamping Venus; Oh, Kay!

OBER, GEORGE

Died: Nov. 1912, New York, N.Y. Stage and screen actor. Married to stage actress Adelaide Ober (dec. 1922) and father of stage actor Frederic Powers (dec.).

Appeared in: **1912** The Curio Hunters; The Maid's Stratagem; The Little Minister; As You Like It; Blind Musician; The Widow's Might; The Indian Mutiny; The Staff of Age. **1913** It All Came Out in the Wash; Papa Puts One Over.

OBER, KIRT

Born: 1875. Died: June 1, 1939, Huntington Beach, Calif. (heart attack). Screen, stage, vaudeville actor and jockey.

OBER, ROBERT

Born: 1882, St. Louis, Mo. Died: Dec. 7, 1950, New York, N.Y. Screen, stage actor and film director. Married to actress Mabel Taliaferro.

Appeared in: **1922** The Young Rajah. **1925** Souls for Sables; Time, the Comedian; The Big Parade; Introduce Me; The Mystic; Morals for Man. **1926** Butterflies in the Rain; Fools of Fashion; The Whole Town's Talking; The Checkered Flag. **1927** King of Kings; A Reno Divorce; The Little Adventures; Held by the Law. **1928** Across the Atlantic; Black Butterflies; A Regular Business Man (short). **1929** The Idle Rich; In the Headlines; Four in a Flat (short). **1930** The Woman Racket.

OBERLE, FLORENCE

Born: 1870. Died: July 10, 1943, Hollywood, Calif. Screen and stage actress.

Appeared in: **1921** R.S.V.P. **1922** Smudge; The Barnstormer.

OBERLIN, JAMES "JIM"

Born: 1931. Died: Oct. 2, 1962, Los Angeles, Calif. (following heart surgery). Screen and television actor.

O'BRIEN, DAVID "DAVE" (David Barclay)

Born: May 13, 1912, Big Spring, Tex. Died: Nov. 8, 1969, Catalina Island, Calif. (heart attack). Screen actor, film director, television director, screenwriter and television writer.

Appeared in: **1933** College Humor; Jennie Gerhardt. **1934** Little Colonel. **1935** Welcome Home. **1936** The Black Coin (serial). **1937** Million Dollar Racket; Victory. **1938** Frontier Scout; Where the Buffalo Roam; Man's Country. **1939** Song of the Buckaroo; Driftin' Westward; Water Rustlers; Rollin' Westward; Mutiny in the Big House; New Frontier; Daughter of the Tong. Joined the "Renfrew of the Royal Mounted" series which included: Crashing Thru; Fighting Mad. **1940** Other "Renfrew" films include: Danger Ahead; Yukon Flight; Murder on the Yukon; Sky Bandits; other 1940 films are: The Cowboy from Sundown; Boys of the City; Queen of the Yukon; That Gang of Mine; A Fugitive from Justice; Gun Code; The Kid from Santa Fe; Hold That Woman!; East Side Kids; Son of the Navy; The Ghost Creeps. **1941** Flying Wild; Texas Marshal; Murder by Invitation; Buzzy and the Phantom Pinto; The Deadly Game; Gunman from Bodie; Spooks Run Wild; Double Trouble; Billy the Kid Wanted. **1942** Down Texas Way; Prisoner of Japan; Billy the Kid's Smoking Guns; King of the Stallions; Bowery at Midnight; The Yanks are Coming; Captain Midnight (serial); 'Neath Brooklyn Bridge; Devil Bat; plus the following shorts: Carry Harry; What About Daddy; Victory Quiz; Victory Vittles; Calling All Pas. **1943** Texas Ranger; The Rangers Take Over; Border Buckaroo; plus the following shorts: First Aid; Seventh Column; Tips on Trips; Fixin' Tricks; Who's Superstitious? **1944** Trail of Terror; Gunsmoke Mesa; Return of the Rangers; Boss of Rawhide; Outlaw Roundup; Guns of the Law; The Pinto Bandit; Spook Town; Dead or Alive; The Whispering Skull; Gangsters of the Frontier; Movie Pests (short); Safety Sleuth (short). **1945** The Man Who Walked Alone; Enemy of the Law; Flaming Bullets; Three in the Saddle; Marked for Murder; Tahiti Nights; The Phantom of 42nd St.; Bus Pests (short). **1946** Frontier Fugitives; plus the following shorts: Studio Visits; Equestrian Quiz; Treasures from Trash; Sure Cures; I Love My Husband. **1947** Thundercap Outlaws; Shootin' Irons; plus the following shorts: Early Sports Quiz; I Love My Wife, But!; Neighbor Pests; Pet Peeves; Have You Ever Wondered. **1948** The following shorts: I Love My Mother-in-Law, But!; You Can't Win; Just Suppose; Why Is It?; Let's Cogitate. **1949** The following shorts: What I Want Next; Those Good Old Days; How Come?; We Can Dream, Can't We? **1950** The following shorts: That's His Story?; A Wife's Life; Wrong Way Butch; Wanted: One Egg. **1951** The following shorts: Fixin' Fool; Band-

age Bait; That's What You Think. **1952** The following shorts: Reducing; It Could Happen to You; Pedestrian Safety; Sweet Memories; I Love Children, But! **1953** Kiss Me Kate; plus the following shorts: The Postman; Cash Stashers; It Would Serve 'em Right; Landlording It; Things We Can Do Without. **1954** Tennessee Champ; plus the following shorts: Ain't It Aggravatin'; Do Someone a Favor; Out for Fun; Safe at Home. **1955** The following shorts: The Man around the House; Keep Young; Just What I Needed; Fall Guy. **1956** The Desperadoes Are in Town. **1964** Big Parade of Comedy (documentary).

O'BRIEN, DONNELL

Died: July 27, 1970, New York, N.Y. Screen, stage, vaudeville, television singer and actor.

Appeared in: **1954** On the Waterfront. **1959** The Last Angry Man; That Kind of Woman. **1960** Butterfield 8. **1961** The Hustler. **1965** The Pawnbroker.

O'BRIEN, EUGENE

Born: Nov. 14, 1882, Boulder, Colo. Died: Apr. 29, 1966, Los Angeles, Calif. (bronchial pneumonia). Stage and screen actor.

Appeared in: **1916** The Chaperon; Return of Eve; Poor Little Peppina. **1917** Poppy; Brown of Harvard; Rebecca of Sunnybrook Farm. **1918** The Safety Curtain; A Romance of the Underworld; Under the Greenwood Tree. **1919** Come out of the Kitchen; The Perfect Lover; By Right of Purchase; Fires of Faith. **1920** The Thief. **1921** Worlds Apart; Gilded Lies; Wonderful Chance; Broadway and Home; The Last Door; Is Life Worth Living?; Clay Dollars. **1922** Chivalrous Charley; Channing of the Northwest; John Smith; The Prophet's Paradise. **1923** The Voice from a Minaret; Souls for Sale. **1924** The Only Woman; Secrets. **1925** Graustark; Siege; Dangerous Innocence; Flaming Love; Frivolous Sal; Simon the Jester; Souls for Sables. **1926** Fine Manners; Flames. **1927** The Romantic Age. **1928** Faithless Lover.

O'BRIEN, "SHOTS" (Charles Brennan)

Born: 1895. Died: Mar. 29, 1961, Los Angeles, Calif. (heart attack). Screen, stage, vaudeville actor and circus performer.

O'BRIEN, TOM (Thomas O'Brien)

Born: July 25, 1891, San Diego, Calif. Died: June 9, 1947, Los Angeles, Calif. Screen, stage and vaudeville actor. Entered films in 1913.

Appeared in: **1921** Scrap Iron; The Devil Within. **1925** The Big Parade; White Fang; Crack O'Dawn; So This Is Marriage. **1926** The Runaway Express; Tin Hats; The Flaming Forest; Poker Faces; The Winner; Take It from Me. **1927** The Bugle Call; The Fire Brigade; The Frontiersman; San Francisco Nights; The Private Life of Helen of Troy; Rookies; Twelve Miles Out; Winners of the Wilderness. **1928** That's My Daddy; Anybody Seen Kelly?; The Last Warning; The Chorus Kid; Outcast Souls. **1929** Dark Skies; Dance Hall; The Peacock Fan; Hurricane; Smiling Irish Eyes; The Flying Fool; His Lucky Day; It Can Be Done; Untamed; Broadway Scandals; Last Warning. **1930** Call of the West; Moby Dick; The Midnight Special. **1931** The Stowaway; Scared Stiff; Sailor Maid Love; Trapped; Hell Bent for Frisco; Yesterday in Santa Fe; The Hawk; Pudge. **1932** Unexpected Father; Phantom Express; The Night Mayor. **1933** Lucky Dog. **1934** Woman Condemned.

O'BYRNE, PATSY

Born: 1886, Kans. Died: Apr. 18, 1968, Woodland Hills, Calif. Screen actress. Entered films with Mack Sennett and appeared in "Charlie Chase" comedies.

Appeared in: **1920** Paris. **1926** My Old Dutch; A Sea Dog's Tale. **1928** Outcast. **1929** South Sea Rose; Condemned; Barnum Was Right. **1930** Loose Ankles. **1932** Nice Women. **1933** Doctor Bull; Alice in Wonderland. **1935** Ruggles of Red Gap; It's a Gift. **1940** You Can't Fool Your Wife; Saps at Sea. **1945** Under Western Skies.

O'CONNELL, HUGH

Born: Aug. 4, 1898, New York, N.Y. Died: Jan. 19, 1943, Hollywood, Calif. (heart attack). Stage and screen actor.

Appeared in: **1929** The following shorts: The Familiar Face; Dead or Alive; The Interview; The Ninety-Ninth Amendment. **1930** The Head Man (short); Find the Woman (short). **1931** The Smiling Lieutenant; Secrets of a Secretary; Personal Maid. **1933** Cheating Cheaters; Broadway Through a Keyhole. **1934** Gift of Gab. **1935** The Good Fairy; The Man Who Reclaimed His Head; It Happened in New York; Chinatown Squad; Diamond Jim; He Gets Her Man; Manhattan Moon. **1937** Ready, Willing and Able; Fly-Away Baby; That Certain Woman; Marry the Girl; The Perfect Specimen. **1938** Swing Your Lady; Accidents Will Happen; Penrod's Double Trouble; Torchy Blane in Panama; Women Are Like That; Mystery House. **1940** My Favorite Wife; Lucky Partners. **1941** The Mad Doctor; My Life with Caroline.

O'CONNER, EDWARD

Born: Feb. 20, 1862, Dublin, Ireland. Died: May 15, 1932, New York, N.Y. Screen, stage and vaudeville actor.

Appeared in: **1911** The Trapper's Five Dollar Bill; The Sign of the Three Labels; The Question Mark; Pat Clancy's Adventure; A Cure for Crime; At the Threshold of Life; The Bo'sun's Watch; That Winsome Winnie Smile;

Turning the Tables; The Rise and Fall of Weary Willie; Logan's Babies; An International Heartbreaker; The Daisy Cowboys. **1912** A Doctor for an Hour; Lazy Bill Hudson; The Stranger and the Taxi Cab; The Green-Eyed Monster; The Angel and the Stranded Troupe; The Totville Eye; Marjorie's Diamond Ring; Aladdin Up-to-Date; Bridget's Sudden Wealth. **1916** The Man Who Stood Still. **1917** One Touch of Nature. **1918** Cecilia of the Pink Roses. **1921** The Inside of the Cup; Get-Rich-Quick Wallingford; Anne of Little Smokey. **1924** Dangerous Money. **1929** Lucky in Love.

O'CONNOR, FRANK

Born: Apr. 11, 1888, N.Y. Died: Nov. 22, 1959, Hollywood, Calif. Screen, stage actor, screenwriter and film director.

Appeared in: **1932** Handle with Care. **1933** Son of Kong; Kickin' the Crown Around (short). **1934** The Mighty Barnum; As Husbands Go. **1935** Ruggles of Red Gap; False Pretenses. **1937** Night Club Scandal; Edgar and Goliath (short). **1938** The Purple Vigilantes; Riders of the Black Hills; Dummy Owner (short). **1939** Boy Slaves. **1940** Adventure in Diamonds; Our Neighbors, the Carters; Drafted in the Depot (short). **1941** Man-Made Monster; Mad about Moonshine (short); A Panic in the Parlor (short). **1942** Tennessee Johnson; Stardust on the Sage. **1947** Saddle Pals; Shoot to Kill; G-Men Never Forget (serial). **1949** Loaded Pistols. **1950** Mule Train; Cow Town; Beyond the Purple Hills; County Fair; The Tougher They Come. **1953** Pack Train.

O'CONNOR, HARRY M.

Born: 1873, Chicago, Ill. Died: July 10, 1971, Woodland Hills, Calif. (pneumonia). Screen, stage and vaudeville actor. Entered films approx. 1910.

Appeared in: **1921** Stranger Than Fiction. **1925** Flashing Steeds. **1926** Red Hot Hoofs. **1927** Cyclone of the Range. **1928** When the Law Rides. **1929** The Trail of the Horse Thieves; Come and Get It. **1930** Half Pint Polly (short).

O'CONNOR, JOHN

Born: 1874. Died: Sept. 10, 1941, Santa Monica, Calif. Screen and stage actor.

Appeared in: **1921** The Barricade.

O'CONNOR, KATHLEEN

Born: 1897. Died: June 25, 1957, Hollywood, Calif. Screen actress. Entered films with Mack Sennett.

Appeared in: **1919** The Lion Man (serial); The Midnight Man (serial). **1921** Life's Darn Funny; Sunset Jones. **1922** The Married Flapper; The Trouper; Come on Over; The Old Homestead. **1923** Wild Bill Hickok. **1924** Dark Stairways.

O'CONNOR, KATHRYN

Born: 1894, Cortland, N.Y. Died: Nov. 16, 1965, Albuquerque, N.M. Stage and screen actress.

O'CONNOR, LOUIS J.

Born: 1880, Providence, R.I. Died: Aug. 9, 1959, Los Angeles, Calif. Stage and screen actor.

Appeared in: **1921** Diane of Star Hollow. **1922** Watch Your Step; Don't Shoot. **1923** The Call of the Hills; Souls for Sale. **1924** Four Sons; Rarin' To Go; Sporting Youth. **1925** Gold and Grit; The Night Ship; Thundering Through; Heartless Husbands. **1926** The Silent Guardian; Out of the West; Midnight Limited. **1929** The Tip-Off.

O'CONNOR, ROBERT EMMETT

Born: 1885, Milwaukee, Wisc. Died: Sept. 4, 1962, Hollywood, Calif. (burns). Screen actor.

Appeared in: **1926** Tin Gods. **1928** The Noose; Dressed to Kill; Four Walls; Freedom of the Press; The Singing Fool. **1929** The Isle of Lost Ships; Smiling Irish Eyes. **1930** Up the River; Alias French Gertie; The Big House; Shooting Straight; Our Blushing Brides; In the Next Room; Framed. **1931** Man to Man; Paid; The Single Sin; The Public Enemy; Three Who Loved; Reckless Living; Fanny Foley Herself. **1932** Two Kinds of Women; Big Timber; Night World; The Dark Horse; Blonde Venus; The Kid from Spain; American Madness. **1933** Lady of the Night; Don't Bet on Love; Frisco Jenny; The Great Jasper; Picture Snatcher; The Big Brain; Midnight Mary; Lady for a Day; Penthouse. **1934** Return of the Terror; White Lies; The Big Shakedown; Bottoms Up. **1935** Waterfront Lady; The Whole Town's Talking; The Mysterious Mr. Wong; Star of Midnight; Stolen Harmony; Let 'Em Have It; Diamond Jim; A Night at the Opera. **1936** We Who Are about to Die; Desire; The Lone Wolf Returns; Little Lord Fauntleroy; Sing Me a Love Song; At Sea Ashore (short). **1937** The Frame Up; Super Sleuth; Park Avenue Logger; The Crime Nobody Saw; Girl Overboard; The River of Missing Men; Trapped by G-Men; Boy of the Streets; Wells Fargo. **1938** Trade Winds. **1939** Streets of New York; Joe and Ethel Turp Call on the President. **1940** Double Alibi; Hot Steel; A Fugitive from Justice; No Time for Comedy. **1941** Tight Shoes. **1942** Tennessee Johnson. **1943** Air Raid Wardens; Whistling in Brooklyn. **1944** Gentle Annie; Nothing but Trouble. **1946** Boys' Ranch.

O'CONNOR, UNA

Born: Oct. 23, 1880, Belfast, Ireland. Died: Feb. 4, 1959, New York, N.Y. Stage and screen actress.

Appeared in: **1929** Dark Red Roses (film debut). **1930** Murder; To Oblige a Lady; Timbuctoo. **1933** Cavalcade; The Invisible Man; Mary Stevens, M.D.; Pleasure Cruise. **1934** The Poor Rich; Horse Play; Orient Express; All Men Are Enemies; The Barretts of Wimpole Street; Stingaree; Chained. **1935** David Copperfield; The Informer; The Bride of Frankenstein; Thunder in the Night; The Perfect Gentleman; Father Brown, Detective. **1936** Rose Marie; The Plough and the Stars; Little Lord Fauntleroy; Lloyds of London; Suzy. **1937** Call It a Day; Personal Property. **1938** The Adventures of Robin Hood; The Return of the Frog. **1939** We Are Not Alone; All Women Have Secrets. **1940** It All Came True; Lillian Russell; The Sea Hawk; He Stayed for Breakfast. **1941** Kisses for Breakfast; Strawberry Blonde; Her First Beau; Three Girls about Town; How Green Was My Valley. **1942** Always in My Heart; My Favorite Spy; Random Harvest. **1943** This Land Is Mine; Forever and a Day; Holy Matrimony; Government Girl. **1944** The Canterville Ghost; My Pal Wolf. **1945** Christmas in Connecticut; The Bells of St. Mary's; Whispering Walls. **1946** Cluny Brown; Of Human Bondage; Child of Divorce; Unexpected Guest; The Return of Monte Cristo; Banjo. **1947** Lost Honeymoon; Ivy; The Corpse Came C.O.D. **1948** Fighting Father Dunne; Adventures of Don Juan. **1957** Witness for the Prosecution.

O'DAY, PEGGY (Peggy Reis)

Born: 1900. Died: Nov. 26, 1964, Santa Monica, Calif. Screen actress and stuntwoman.

Appeared in: **1922** Thundering Hoofs; The Storm Girl; Angel Citizens; They're Off; Trail's End. **1923** The Fighting Skipper (serial); The Man Getter. **1924** Ace of the Law; Battlin' Buckaroo; Crashin' Through; Shootin' Square; Travelin' Fast. **1925** Peggy of the Secret Service; The Four from Nowhere; Red Blood and Blue; Riders of the Sand Storm; Sporting West; Whistling Jim. **1927** Hoof Marks. **1928** The Clean-Up Man.

O'DEA, JIMMY

Born: 1899, England. Died: Jan. 7, 1965, Dublin, Ireland. Screen, vaudeville, radio and television actor.

Appeared in: **1935** Jimmy Boy. **1938** Blarney (aka Ireland's Border Line—US 1939). **1939** Cheer Boys Cheer; Let's Be Famous. **1957** The Rising of the Moon. **1959** Darby O'Gill and the Little People. **1961** Johnny Nobody (US 1965).

O'DEA, JOSEPH

Born: 1903, Ireland. Died: Mar. 1, 1968, Dublin, Ireland. Screen, stage and radio actor.

Appeared in: **1952** The Quiet Man. **1957** The Rising of the Moon.

O'DELL, DIGGER (John H. Brown)

Born: 1904. Died: May 16, 1957, Hollywood, Calif. (heart attack). Screen, stage, radio and television actor.

O'DELL, SEYMOUR H.

Born: 1863, Ireland. Died: Apr. 3, 1937, Los Angeles, Calif. Screen, stage and radio actor.

ODELL, "SHORTY" (Solomon Schwartz)

Born: c. 1874. Died: Nov. 11, 1924, New York, N.Y. Screen actor.

ODEMAR, FRITZ

Born: 1890, Germany. Died: June 3, 1955, Munich, Germany. Screen actor.

Appeared in: **1932** Das Lied ist Aus; Der Raub der Mona Lisa; Liebeskommando. **1941** The Last Days before the War. **1933** Ich Will Nicht Wissen Wer du Bist; Hertha's Erwachen; M; Eine Tur geht Auf; Salon Dora Green; Stern von Valencia; Ein gewisser herr Gran; Ein Unsichtbarer geht durch die Stadt; Schloss im Suden; Viktor und Viktoria (US 1935). **1934** Der Doppelganger; Fraulein; Frau; Heute abend bei mir; Ein Walzer for Dich; Charley's Tante; Furst Woronzeff; Englische Heirat; Peer Gynt; Ein Toller Einfall; Roman Einer Nacht; Schuss im Morgengrauen; Eine Frau wie Du. **1935** Der alte und der Junge Konig; Der Gefangene des Konigs; Lady Windemere's Fan; Ich Sing Mich in Dein Herz Hinein; Gruen ist die Heide; Herr Kobin Geht auf Abenteurer (Mr. Kobin Seeks Adventure). **1936** Der junge Graf; Familie Schimek; Zwischen Zwei Herzen (Between Two Hearts); Knock-Out. **1938** Gross Reinemachen (General Housecleaning); Ein Teufelskerl (A Devil of a Fellow); Der Arme Millionar (The Poor Millionaire).

ODIN, SUSAN (Susan Mary Odin)

Died: Oct. 17, 1975. Screen actress.

Appeared in: **1952** Wild Stallion. **1953** Girls in the Night. **1954** The Eddie Cantor Story. **1960** Because They're Young.

O'DONNELL, CATHY (Ann Steely)

Born: July 6, 1925, Siluria, Ala. Died: Apr. 11, 1970, Los Angeles, Calif. Stage and screen actress.

Appeared in: **1946** The Best Years of Our Lives (film debut). **1947** Bury Me Dead. **1948** They Live by Night (aka The Twisted Road and Your Red Wagon); The Amazing Mr. X. **1950** Side Street; The Miniver Story. **1951** Never Trust a Gambler; Detective Story. **1952** A Woman's Angle (US 1954). **1954** Eight O'Clock Walk (US 1955). **1955** The Man from Laramie; Mad at the World. **1957** The Deerslayer; The Story of Mankind. **1959** Ben Hur; Terror in the Haunted House (aka My World Dies Screaming).

O'DONNELL, CHARLES H.
Born: 1886. Died: Sept. 10, 1962, Pompano Beach, Fla. Screen and vaudeville actor. Appeared in vaudeville team of "Lane and O'Donnell" and later "O'Donnell and Blair."

O'DONOVAN, FRANK
Born: 1900, Ireland. Died: June 28, 1974, Majorca, Spain. Screen, stage, vaudeville, television actor and composer.

Appeared in: **1961** Murder in Eden. **1962** The Quare Fellow.

O'DUNN, IRVIN
Born: 1904. Died: Jan. 1, 1933, New York, N.Y. (accidental fall). Screen, vaudeville actor and magician. Appeared in vaudeville team as part of "O'Dunn and O'Day."

OFFENBACH, JOSEPH
Born: 1905, Germany. Died: Oct. 15, 1971, Darmstadt, West Germany (heart attack). Screen, stage and television actor.

Appeared in: **1957** Robinson soll Nicht Sterben (aka The Girl and the Legend—US 1966). **1958** Unruhige Nacht (The Restless Night—US 1964); Das Madchen vom Moorhof (The Girl of the Moors—US 1961). **1959** Mon Petit (aka Monpti); Buddenbrooks (US 1962); Verbrechen nach Schulschluss (aka The Young Go Wild—US 1962). **1963** Willy.

OFFERMAN, GEORGE, SR.
Born: 1880. Died: Mar. 5, 1938, Hollywood, Calif. Screen, stage and vaudeville actor. Father of screen actor George Offerman, Jr. (dec. 1963). Married to actress Marie Offerman (dec. 1950). Appeared in vaudeville in an act billed as "The Original Singing Nut" and later in an act with his wife.

Appeared in: **1929** Girl on the Barge. **1933** The Mayor of Hell.

OFFERMAN, GEORGE, JR.
Born: Mar. 14, 1917, Chicago, Ill. Died: Jan. 14, 1963, New York, N.Y. Stage and screen actor. Son of actor George Offerman, Sr. (dec. 1938) and actress Marie Offerman (dec. 1950).

Appeared in: **1927** The Broadway Drifter. **1929** The Girl on the Barge. **1933** Mayor of Hell. **1934** The House of Rothschild. **1935** Grand Old Girl; Jalna; Black Fury; Old Grey Mayor (short). **1936** Chatterbox; Wedding Present. **1937** Midnight Court; Night Club Scandal. **1938** Scandal Sheet; Crime School; Three Comrades. **1939** Dust Be My Destiny; They Asked for It; Calling Dr. Kildare. **1940** Prison Camp. **1942** Whispering Ghosts; War against Mrs. Hadley; Saboteur. **1943** Action in the North Atlantic. **1944** The Sullivans; See Here, Private Hargrove. **1945** Out of the Depths. **1946** A Walk in the Sun. **1949** A Letter to Three Wives. **1951** People Will Talk; Purple Heart Diary. **1952** With a Song in My Heart.

OFFERMAN, MARIE
Born: 1894. Died: May 14, 1950, Hollywood, Calif. Screen, stage and vaudeville actress. Wife of actor George Offerman, Sr. (dec. 1938), with whom she appeared in vaudeville, and mother of actor George Offerman, Jr. (dec. 1963).

O'GATTY, JIMMY "PACKY" (Pasquale O'Gatty)
Born: 1899. Died: Oct. 10, 1966, New York, N.Y. Professional boxer and screen actor.

Appeared in: **1936** Laughing Irish Eyes. **1940** East of the River. **1958** Missile Monster.

OGDEN, VIVIA (aka VIVA OGDEN)
Died: Dec. 22, 1953. Screen actress.

Appeared in: **1919** Mrs. Wiggs of the Cabbage Patch. **1921** At the Stage Door; Stardust; The Chicken in the Case. **1922** John Smith; Timothy's Quest. **1923** Way Down East. **1924** Idle Tongues. **1925** The Denial; Thank You; A Slave of Fashion; The Unguarded Hour. **1926** The Fire Brigade; Lovely Mary.

OGLE, CHARLES (Charles Stanton Ogle)
Born: June 5, 1865, Steubenville, Ohio. Died: Oct. 11, 1940, Long Beach, Calif. Screen actor. Entered films in 1907. Was the first actor to portray Frankenstein's monster.

Appeared in: **1910** Frankenstein. **1911** Uncle Hiram's List; The Reform Candidate; Love and Hatred; Home; A Man for all That; How Sir Andrew Lost His Vote; The Minute Man; The Doctor; The Battle of Bunker Hill; The Winds of Fate; The Modern Dianas; Captain Barnacle's Baby; The Surgeon's Temptation; That Winsome Winnie Smile; The Battle of Trafalgar; The Death of

Nathan Hale; A Cure for Crime; Foul Play; Her Wedding Ring; The Black Arrow; How Mrs. Murray Saved the American Army. **1912** The Third Thanksgiving; The Lord and the Peasant; What Happened to Mary? (serial); A Question of Seconds; To Save Her Brother; For the Cause of the South; His Secretary; At the Point of the Sword; For the Commonwealth; Politics and Love; The Dumb Wooing; The Convict's Parole; Blinks and Jinks—Attorneys-at-Law; The Sunset Gun; The Grandfather; The Angel and the Stranded Troupe; The Dam Builder; The Father; The Sketch with the Thumb Print; The Governor; Like Knights of Old; The Totville Eye; Sally Ann's Strategy; On Donovan's Division. **1913** When Greek Meets Greek; While John Bolt Slept; The Great Physician; Hard Cash; The Gunmaker of Moscow; A Clue to Her Parentage; The Doctor's Duty; Janet of the Dunes; The Mountaineers; The Ambassador's Daughter; False to Their Trust; The Princess and the Man; Barry's Breaking In; The Doctor's Photograph; The Ranch Owner's Love Making; Ann; The Gauntlets of Washington; Mother's Lazy Boy; With the Eyes of the Blind; The Duke's Dilemma; The High Tide of Misfortune; A Splendid Scapegrace. **1914** Molly the Drummer Boy; The Active Life of Dolly of the Dailies (serial); His Sob Story; Dolly at the Helm; The Coward and the Man; The President's Special; The Man in the Street; The Lonely Road; The Uncanny Mr. Gumble. **1915** My Lady High and Mighty; His Guardian Angel; The Bribe; Faces in the Night; The Memory Tree; Circus Mary; The Tale of the 'C'; Under Southern Skies; The Woman Who Lied; The Meddler. **1916** Aschenbroedel; The Laugh of Scorn; The Broken Spur; The Sheriff of Pine Mountain; Code of His Ancestors; The Heir to the Horrah; In the Heart of New York; The Girl Who Didn't Tell. **1917** The Case of Dr. Standing; Those Without Sin; The Secret Game; Nan of Music Mountain; The Cost of Hatred; At First Sight; On Record. **1918** The Things We Love; We Can't Have Everything; M'Liss; Wild Youth; The Source; The Squaw Man; Rimrock Jones; Xantippe; The Firefly of France; Less than Kin; Too Many Millions. **1919** Lottery Man; The Poor Boob; The Fires of Faith; Hawthorne of the U.S.A.; The Dud; Alias Mike Moran; The Valley of the Giants. **1920** Everywoman; What's Your Hurry?; Conrad in Quest of His Youth; Treasure Island. **1921** The Affairs of Anatol; After the Show; Crazy to Marry; Brewster's Millions; Miss Lulu Bett; A Wise Fool; What Every Woman Knows. **1922** Her Husband's Trademark; A Homespun Vamp; The Young Rajah; If You Believe It—It's So; Is Matrimony a Failure?; Kick In; Manslaughter; North of the Rio Grande; Our Leading Citizen; Thirty Days; The Woman Who Walked Alone. **1923** The Covered Wagon; Garrison's Finish; Grumpy; Hollywood; Ruggles of Red Gap; Salomy Jane; The Ten Commandments; Sixty Cents an Hour. **1924** The Alaskan; The Border Legion; The Bedroom Window; Flaming Barriers; Merton of the Movies; The Garden of Weeds; Secrets; Triumph. **1925** Code of the West; The Thundering Herd; Contraband; The Golden Bed. **1926** The Flaming Forest; One Minute to Play.

OH GRAN, GILBERT (Justo Masso)
Born: 1886, Spain. Died: Sept. 12, 1971, Barcelona, Spain. Stage and screen actor.

Appeared in: **1965** Broken Toys.

O'HARA, FISKE
Born: 1878. Died: Aug. 2, 1945, Hollywood, Calif. Screen, stage, radio and vaudeville actor.

Appeared in: **1933** Paddy the Next Best Thing. **1934** Change of Heart.

O'HARA, GEORGE
Born: Feb. 22, 1899, Idaho. Died: Oct. 16, 1966, Los Angeles, Calif. (cancer). Screen actor.

Appeared in: **1921** Love, Honor and Behave (short); Queenie; A Small Town Idol. **1922** The Crossroads of New York; Shirley of the Circus. **1924** Darwin Was Right; Listen Lester. **1926** Bigger than Barnum's; The False Alarm; Going the Limit; The Sea Beast; Is That Nice?; The Timid Terror; Why Girls Go Back Home; Casey of the Coast Guard (serial). **1927** Burnt Fingers; California or Bust; Yours to Command; Ladies Beware. **1928** Beau Broadway; Honeymoon; Pirates of the Pines (serial). **1929** A Single Man; Side Street; Night People.

OHARDIENO, ROGER
Born: 1919. Died: July 14, 1959, New York, N.Y. Black screen and stage dancer.

Appeared in: **1943** Stormy Weather.

OJEDA, JESUS "CHUCHO"
Born: 1892, Mexico. Died: Nov. 1943, Mexico City, Mexico (heart attack). Stage and screen actor.

O'KEEFE, ARTHUR J.
Born: 1874. Died: Mar. 29, 1959, Hollywood, Calif. Screen stuntman and vaudeville actor. Entered films approx. 1915.

O'KEEFE, DENNIS (Edward Vanes Flanagan, Jr.)
Born: Mar. 28, 1908, Fort Madison, Iowa. Died: Aug. 31, 1968, Santa Monica, Calif. (cancer). Screen, stage, vaudeville, television actor, film director and

screenwriter. Married to actress Steffi Duna. Divorced from Louise Stanley. Entered films as a stuntman and extra. Appeared as Bud Flanagan until approx. 1936 and then used the name of Dennis O'Keefe. Wrote screen scripts under his pen name, Jonathan Ricks.

Appeared in: **1931** Reaching for the Moon; Cimarron. **1932** I Am A Fugitive from a Chain Gang; Two against the World; Cabin in the Cotton; Central Park; Night after Night. **1933** Girl Missing; Hello, Everybody!; The Eagle and the Hawk; From Hell to Heaven; Gold Diggers of 1933; Too Much Harmony; Duck Soup; I'm No Angel; The House on 56th Street; Torch Singer; Lady Killer. **1934** Jimmy the Gent; Upperworld; Wonder Bar; Smarty; Registered Nurse; Fog over Frisco; Man with Two Faces; Lady by Choice; Madame Du Barry; College Rhythm; Imitation of Life; Transatlantic Merry-Go-Round; Everything's Ducky (short). **1935** Gold Diggers of 1935; Devil Dogs of the Air; Rumba; Mississippi; Let 'Em Have It; Doubting Thomas; Every Night at Eight; The Daring Young Man; Anna Karenina; Personal Maid's Secret; It's in the Air; Shipmates Forever; Broadway Hostess; A Night at the Biltmore Bowl (short). **1936** Born to Dance; Anything Goes; Hats Off; Mr. Deeds Goes to Town; 13 Hours by Air; Love before Breakfast; Great Guy; Libeled Lady; Theodora Goes Wild; The Accusing Finger; Sworn Enemy; And So They Were Married; Nobody's Fool; Rhythm on the Range; Yours for the Asking; The Plainsman; Burning Gold. **1937** When's Your Birthday?; Top of the Town; Married before Breakfast; Parole Racket; Swing High, Swing Low; Captains Courageous; A Star Is Born; Riding on Air; The Girl from Scotland Yard; Easy Living; Saratoga; The Firefly; Blazing Barriers. **1938** Bad Man of Brimstone; Hold That Kiss; The Chaser; Vacation from Love. **1939** Unexpected Father; Burn 'Em up O'Connor; The Kid from Texas; That's Right—You're Wrong. **1940** Alias the Deacon; La Conga Nights; I'm Nobody's Sweetheart Now; Pop Always Pays; You'll Find Out; The Girl from Havana; Arise, My Love. **1941** Topper Returns; Bowery Boy; Mr. District Attorney; Broadway Limited; Lady Scarface; Weekend for Three. **1942** Affairs of Jimmy Valentine; Moonlight Masquerade. **1943** Hangmen Also Die; Good Morning Judge; Tahiti Honey; The Leopard Man; Hi Diddle Diddle. **1944** The Fighting Seabees; Up in Mabel's Room; Abroad with Two Yanks; The Story of Dr. Wassell; Sensations of 1945. **1945** The Affairs of Susan; Doll Face; Brewster's Millions; Earl Carroll Vanities; Getting Gertie's Garter. **1946** Her Adventurous Night; Come Back to Me. **1947** T-Men; Dishonored Lady; Mister District Attorney (and 1941 version). **1948** Raw Deal; Siren of Atlantis; Walk a Crooked Mile. **1949** Cover Up; The Great Dan Patch; Abandoned. **1950** The Eagle and the Hawk; Woman on the Run; The Company She Keeps. **1951** Passage West; Follow the Sun. **1952** One Big Affair; Everything I Have Is Yours. **1953** The Lady Wants Mink; The Fake. **1954** The Diamond (aka The Diamond Wizard—US); Drums of Tahiti. **1955** Angela; Chicago Syndicate; Las Vegas Shakedown. **1956** Inside Detroit. **1957** Dragon Wells Massacre; Lady of Vengeance. **1958** Graft and Corruption. **1961** All Hands on Deck. **1963** The Flame (US 1970).

O'KELLY, DON. *See* DON KELLY

OLAND, WARNER
Born: Oct. 3, 1880, Umea, Sweden. Died: Aug. 5, 1938, Stockholm, Sweden (bronchial pneumonia). Screen, stage actor and stage producer. Appeared as Charlie Chan in "Charlie Chan" film series (1931–1938). Married to actress Edith Shearn (dec. 1968).

Appeared in: **1909** Jewels of the Madonna (film debut). **1916** The Rise of Susan; The Eternal Question. **1917** The Fatal Ring (serial); Patria (serial). **1918** The Niulahka; The Yellow Ticket. **1919** The Lightning Raider; The Avalanche; Witness for the Defense. **1920** The Phantom Foe; The Third Eye. **1921** Hurricane Hutch; The Yellow Arm. **1922** East Is West; The Pride of Palomar. **1923** His Children's Children. **1924** One Night in Rome; Curlytop; The Fighting American; So This Is Marriage. **1925** Don Q.; Flower of Night; Riders of the Purple Sage; The Winding Stair. **1926** Infatuation; The Mystery Club; Tell It to the Marines; Twinkletoes; Don Juan; Man of the Forest; The Marriage Clause. **1927** The Jazz Singer; Good Time Charley; A Million Bid; Old San Francisco; Sailor Izzy Murphy; What Happened to Father; When a Man Loves. **1928** Wheels of Chance; Stand and Deliver; The Scarlet Lady; Dream of Love. **1929** The Faker; Chinatown Nights; The Mysterious Dr. Fu Manchu; The Studio Murder Case. **1930** The Mighty; Dangerous Paradise; Paramount on Parade; The Return of Dr. Fu Manchu; The Vagabond King. **1931** Drums of Jeopardy; Dishonored; The Black Camel; Daughter of the Dragon; The Big Gamble; Charlie Chan Carries On. **1932** Charlie Chan's Chance; A Passport to Hell; The Son-Daughter; Shanghai Express. **1933** Charlie Chan's Greatest Case; As Husbands Go; Before Dawn. **1934** Mandalay; Bulldog Drummond Strikes Back; Charlie Chan's Courage; Charlie Chan in London; The Painted Veil. **1935** Charlie Chan in Paris; Charlie Chan in Egypt; Werewolf of London; Shanghai; Charlie Chan in Shanghai. **1936** Charlie Chan's Secret; Charlie Chan at the Circus; Charlie Chan at the Race Track; Charlie Chan at the Opera. **1937** Charlie Chan on Broadway; Charlie Chan at the Olympics; Charlie Chan at Monte Carlo. **1961** Days of Thrills and Laughter (documentary).

OLCOTT, SIDNEY (John S. Alcott)
Born: 1873, Toronto, Canada. Died: Dec. 16, 1949, Hollywood, Calif. Screen, stage actor, film and stage director. Married to actress Valentine Grant (dec.

1948). Entered films with Biograph and joined Kalen studios as an actor and director in 1907.

OLDAKER, MAX
Born: 1908, Davenport, Tasmania. Died: Feb. 2, 1972, Launceston, Tasmania. Screen, stage, opera, television actor, singer, stage producer, press and radio critic.

OLDFIELD, BARNEY (Berna Eli)
Born: Jan. 29, 1878, near York Township, Fulton County, Ohio. Died: Oct. 4, 1946 (cerebral hemorrhage). Screen actor, circus performer and sportsman (racer).

Appeared in: **1913** Barney Oldfield's Race for a Life. **1925** The Speed Demon. **1927** The First Auto. **1932** Speed in the Gay 90's (short).

OLDHAM, DEREK (John Stephens Oldham)
Born: 1893, Accrington Lanes, England. Died: Mar. 20, 1968, England. Screen, stage actor and opera performer.

Appeared in: **1934** The Broken Rosary. **1935** Charing Cross Road. **1957** Dangerous Exile (US 1958).

OLDRING, RUBE
Born: 1885. Died: Sept. 9, 1961, Bridgeton, N.J. Professional baseball player and screen actor.

Appeared in: **1911** The Baseball Bug.

OLGA, DUCHESS. *See* DUCHESS OLGA

OLIN, BOB
Born: 1908. Died: Dec. 16, 1956, New York, N.Y. Screen, radio actor and pro boxer.

OLIVER, EDNA MAY (Edna May Cox Nutter)
Born: 1883, Malden, Mass. Died: Nov. 9, 1942, Hollywood, Calif. (intestinal disorder). Screen, stage and radio actress. Entered films in 1923 with Famous Players.

Appeared in: **1923** Wife in Name Only. **1924** Three O'Clock in the Morning; Icebound; Manhattan; Restless Wives. **1925** Lucky Devil; Lovers in Quarantine; The Lady Who Lied. **1926** Let's Get Married; The American Venus. **1929** The Saturday Night Kid. **1930** Half Shot at Sunrise. **1931** Laugh and Get Rich; Cracked Nuts; Cimarron; Newly Rich (aka Forbidden Adventure); Fanny Foley Herself (aka Top of the Bill). **1932** Ladies of the Jury; The Penguin Pool Murder; The Conquerors; Hold 'Em Jail. **1933** The Great Jasper; Only Yesterday; Little Women; It's Great to Be Alive; Alice in Wonderland; Ann Vickers; Meet the Baron. **1934** The Last Gentleman; Murder on the Blackboard; The Poor Rich; We're Rich Again. **1935** David Copperfield; A Tale of Two Cities; No More Ladies; Murder on a Honeymoon. **1936** Romeo and Juliet. **1937** Parnell; My Dear Miss Aldrich. **1938** Paradise for Three (aka Romance for Three); Little Miss Broadway. **1939** The Story of Vernon and Irene Castle; Second Fiddle; Nurse Edith Cavell; Drums Along the Mohawk. **1940** Pride and Prejudice. **1941** Lydia.

OLIVER, GUY
Born: 1875, Chicago, Ill. Died: Sept. 1, 1932, Hollywood, Calif. Screen and vaudeville actor. Entered films in 1908.

Appeared in: **1912** Robin Hood. **1919** Secret Service; The Lottery Man; Hawthorne of the U.S.A. **1921** City of Silent Men; Fool's Paradise; The Little Minister; Moonlight and Honeysuckle; A Prince There Was; Too Much Speed; A Virginia Courtship; What Every Woman Knows. **1922** Across the Continent; The Cowboy and the Lady; A Homespun Vamp; Manslaughter; Our Leading Citizen; Pink Gods; The World's Champion. **1923** The Covered Wagon; To the Last Man; The Cheat; Hollywood; Mr. Billings Spends His Dime; Ruggles of Red Gap; Sixty Cents an Hour; The Woman with Four Faces. **1924** The Bedroom Window; The Dawn of a Tomorrow; North of '36. **1925** The Air Mail; The Vanishing American; A Woman of the World. **1926** The Eagle of the Sea; Man of the Forest; Old Ironsides. **1927** Arizona Bound; Drums of the Desert; The Mysterious Rider; Nevada; Open Range; Shootin' Irons. **1928** Avalanche; The Vanishing Pioneer; Three Week Ends; Beggars of Life; Hot News; The Docks of New York; Easy Come, Easy Go; Half a Bride; Love and Learn. **1929** Texas Tommy; Far Western Trails; Fighting Terror; Stairs of Sand; The Studio Murder Case; Sunset Pass; Woman Trap; Half Way to Heaven. **1930** Playboy of Paris; The Devil's Holiday; The Kibitzer; The Light of Western Stars; Only the Brave. **1931** Gun Smoke; Skippy; Dude Ranch; Up Pops the Devil; I Take This Woman; Caught; Huckleberry Finn; The Beloved Bachelor; Rich Man's Folly; Sooky.

OLIVER, LARRY
Born: 1880. Died: Jan. 22, 1973. Screen actor.

Appeared in: **1950** Born Yesterday.

OLIVER, TED

Born: 1895. Died: June 30, 1957, Los Angeles, Calif. Screen actor.

Appeared in: **1925** Daring Days; Triple Action. **1926** The Fighting Peacemaker. **1934** We're Not Dressing. **1936** Klondike Annie; The Return of Sophie Lang; Border Flight; Yellow Dust. **1937** The Frame-Up; Trapped. **1938** She Loved a Fireman. **1939** Geronimo.

OLIVER, VIC (Viktor Oliver Samek)

Born: July 8, 1898, Vienna, Austria. Died: Aug. 15, 1964, Johannesburg, South Africa. Stage and screen actor. Divorced from actress Sarah Churchill.

Appeared in: **1936** Rhythm in the Air. **1937** Who's Your Lady Friend? **1938** Around the Town; Meet Mr. Penny. **1940** Room for Two (US 1944). **1941** He Found a Star; Hi Gang! **1944** Give Us the Moon. **1945** I'll Be Your Sweetheart.

OLIVETTE, MARIE

Born: 1892. Died: Mar. 15, 1959, New York, N.Y. (burns from fire). Stage and screen actress.

OLIVETTE, NINA

Born: 1908. Died: Feb. 21, 1971, N.Y. (heart attack). Screen, stage and vaudeville actress. Married to actor Harry Stockwell and mother of actors Dean and Guy Stockwell.

Appeared in: **1930** Queen High.

OLMOS, PIO

Born: Mexico (?). Died: May 24, 1965, Guanajato, Mexico. Screen actor and stuntman.

OLMSTEAD, GERTRUDE

Born: Nov. 10, 1904, Chicago, Ill. Died: Jan. 18, 1975, Beverly Hills, Calif. Stage and screen actress. Married to actor and director Robert Z. Leonard (dec. 1968). Entered films with Universal in 1920.

Appeared in: **1921** The Big Adventure; Shadows of Conscience; The Fighting Lover; The Fox. **1922** The Loaded Door; The Scrapper; The Adventures of Robinson Crusoe (serial). **1923** Cameo Kirby; Trilby. **1924** Babbitt; Empty Hands; George Washington, Jr; A Girl of the Limberlost; Ladies to Board; Life's Greatest Game; Lover's Lane. **1925** California Straight Ahead; The Monster; Time, the Comedian; Cobra. **1926** Ben Hur; Puppets; Sweet Adeline; The Boob; Monte Carlo; Ibanez's Torrent (aka The Torrent); The Cheerful Fraud. **1927** Becky; Buttons; Mr. Wu; The Callahans and the Murphys. **1928** The Passion Song; Bringing Up Father; The Cheer Leader; Green Grass Widows; Hey Rube!; Hit of the Show; Midnight Life; Sporting Goods; Sweet Sixteen; A Woman Against the World. **1929** The Lone Wolf's Daughter; Show of Shows; Sonny Boy; The Time, the Place and the Girl.

OLSEN, GEORGE

Born: 1893. Died: Mar. 18, 1971, Paramus, N.J. Bandleader, screen, stage actor and recording artist.

Appeared with his orchestra in: **1930** Happy Days.

OLSEN, IRENE

Born: 1902. Died: Apr. 1931, Brooklyn, N.Y. Screen, stage and vaudeville actress.

OLSEN, MORONI

Born: 1889, Ogden, Utah. Died: Nov. 22, 1954, Los Angeles, Calif. (natural causes). Stage and screen actor.

Appeared in: **1935** The Three Musketeers (film debut); Annie Oakley; Seven Keys to Baldpate. **1936** The Farmer in the Dell; Air Force; Two in the Dark; We're Only Human; Yellow Dust; The Witness Chair; Two in Revolt; M'Liss; Mary of Scotland; Grand Jury; Mummy's Boys. **1937** The Plough and the Stars; Adventure's End; Manhattan Merry-Go-Round. **1938** Gold Is Where You Find It; Kidnapped; Submarine Patrol; Kentucky. **1939** Homicide Bureau; Code of the Secret Service; Susannah of the Mounties; Allegheny Uprising; Dust Be My Destiny; That's Right—You're Wrong; Barricade; Rose of Washington Square; The Three Musketeers (and 1935 version). **1940** Invisible Stripes; Brother Rat and a Baby; East of the River; Virginia City; Santa Fe Trail; If I Had My Way; Brigham Young, Frontiersman. **1941** Life with Henry; Dive Bomber; Three Sons O' Guns; One Foot in Heaven; Dangerously They Live. **1942** Mrs. Wiggs of the Cabbage Patch; Reunion; Sundown Jim; My Favorite Spy; The Glass Key; Nazi Spy. **1943** Mission to Moscow; The Song of Bernadette; Air Force; Reunion in France. **1944** Ali Baba and the Forty Thieves; Roger Touhy, Gangster; Cobra Woman; Buffalo Bill. **1945** Pride of the Marines; Weekend at the Waldorf; Mildred Pierce; Don't Fence Me In; Behind City Lights. **1946** A Night in Paradise; Boys' Ranch; Notorious; The Strange Woman; The Walls Came Tumbling Down. **1947** The Beginning or the End?; The Long Night; That Hagen Girl; Possessed; High Wall; Life with Father; Black Gold. **1948** Up in Central Park; Call Northside 777. **1949** The Fountainhead; Samson and Delilah; Command Decision; Task Force. **1950** Father of the Bride. **1951** Father's Little Dividend; Submarine Command; Payment on Demand; No Questions Asked. **1952** The Lone Star; Washington Story; At Sword's Point. **1953** Marry Me Again; So This Is Love. **1954** The Long, Long Trailer; Sign of the Pagan.

OLSEN, OLE (John Sigvard Olsen)

Born: 1892, Peru, Ind. Died: Jan. 26, 1963, Albuquerque, N.M. (kidney ailment). Screen, stage, vaudeville and television actor. Brother of screen actor Stephen Olsen (dec. 1946). Was partner with Chic Johnson (dec. 1962) in comedy team of "Olsen and Johnson" both in vaudeville and on screen.

The films they appeared in are: **1930** Oh, Sailor Behave! (film debut). **1931** Fifty Million Frenchmen; Gold Dust Gertie. **1932** Hollywood on Parade (short). **1934** Holly on Parade (short). **1937** Country Gentlemen; All over Town. **1941** Hellzapoppin (stage and film versions). **1943** Crazy House. **1944** Ghost Catchers. **1945** See My Lawyer.

OLSEN, STEPHEN

Born: 1900. Died: Dec. 14, 1946, Van Nuys, Calif. (sinus infection). Screen and vaudeville actor. Brother of Ole Olsen (dec. 1963). He was member of vaudeville team of "Olsen and Alexandria." Entered films approx. 1941.

OLT, ARISZTID. *See* BELA LUGOSI

OLVERA, ERNESTO HILL (Hermengildo Olvera Gonzalez)

Born: 1937, Mexico. Died: Mar. 1967, Guadalajara, Mexico (heart attack). Screen actor and organist.

Appeared in one film: Crimen en tus Manos.

O'MADIGAN, ISABEL

Born: 1872. Died: Jan. 23, 1951, Los Angeles, Calif. Screen and stage actress.

Appeared in: **1932** Smiling Faces. **1947** The Egg and I. **1949** Ma and Pa Kettle.

O'MALLEY, GRANIA

Born: 1898, Ireland. Died: June 14, 1973, New York. Screen, stage, vaudeville and television actress. Married to William Dunham with whom she appeared in vaude in an act billed as "Dunham and O'Malley."

Appeared in: **1972** The Hot Rock.

O'MALLEY, JOHN

Born: 1904. Died: Feb. 27, 1945, Malibu Beach, Calif. (auto crash). Stage and screen actor.

Appeared in: **1945** A Sporting Chance (film debut).

O'MALLEY, JOHN P.

Born: 1916, Australia. Died: Aug. 26, 1959, Hollywood, Calif. (heart attack). Screen and television actor.

Appeared in: **1951** Kind Lady. **1952** Julius Caesar. **1953** The Desert Rats. **1955** The Scarlet Coat. **1956** Diane; The Court Jester. **1957** The Invisible Boy.

O'MALLEY, PAT (Patrick H. O'Malley, Jr.)

Born: Sept. 3, 1892, Forest City, Pa. Died: May 21, 1966, Van Nuys, Calif. Screen, vaudeville and television actor. Married to actress Lillian O'Malley (dec. 1976). Do not confuse with actor J. Patrick O'Malley. Entered films with Edison.

Appeared in: **1911** The Papered Door. **1919** The Red Glove (serial). **1920** The Blooming Angel; Go and Get It. **1922** Brothers under the Skin. **1923** The Man from Brodney's; Wandering Daughters; The Eternal Struggle. **1924** Worldly Goods; Happiness; The Fighting American; Bread. **1925** The Teaser; Tomorrow's Love; Proud Flesh; The White Desert. **1926** Spangles; The Midnight Sun. **1929** Alibi; The Man I Love. **1930** The Fall Guy; Mothers Cry; Average Husband (short); The People Versus (short). **1931** Night Life in Reno; Sky Spider; Homicide Squad; Anybody's Blonde. **1932** The Reckoning; High Speed; American Madness; Exposure; Those We Love; Klondike; Speed Madness; The Penal Code. **1933** Frisco Jenny; Mystery of the Wax Museum; One Year Later; Sing, Sinner, Sing; Sundown Rider; Man of Sentiment; Parachute Jumper; I Love That Man; Laughing at Life; The Whirlwind; Riot Squad. **1934** Love Past Thirty; Crime Doctor; Girl in Danger. **1935** Man on the Flying Trapeze; The Perfect Clue; Heir to Trouble; Behind the Evidence; Men of the Hour; Lady Tubbs; Wanderer of the Wasteland. **1936** Hollywood Boulevard; Beloved Enemy. **1937** Mysterious Crossing. **1938** Bringing Up Baby; Little Tough Guy. **1939** Wolf Call; Stunt Pilot; Romance of the Redwoods; Frontier Marshal; Dust Be My Destiny. **1940** Shooting High; Rocky Mountain Rangers; The Night of Nights; A Little Bit of Heaven. **1941** Pals of the Pecos; Sky Raiders (serial); Law of the Range; Reg'lar Fellers; Double Dates; Meet Boston Blackie. **1942** Tennessee Johnson; Gentleman Jim; Hold 'Em Jail (short); Two Yanks in Trinidad; Cairo; The Glass Key. **1943** Double Up (short); Deep in the Heart of Texas; Through Different Eyes. **1944** Sailor's Holiday; Adventures of Mark Twain. **1948** Blazing across the Pecos. **1949** Boston Blackie's Chinese Venture; The Rugged O'Riordans. **1950** Mule Train. **1951** Kid from Broken Gun; Kind Lady. **1954** The Wild One. **1956** Invasion of the Body Snatchers; Black-Jack Ketchum, Desperado.

O'MALLEY, THOMAS E.

Born: 1856, Boston, Mass. Died: May 5, 1926, Brooklyn, N.Y. (complications of disease). Stage and screen actor.

Appeared in: **1921** Cappy Ricks; Rainbow. **1924** His Darker Self.

O'MOORE, BARRY. See HERBERT A. YOST

O'NEAL, WILLIAM J.

Born: 1898. Died: May 23, 1961, Hollywood, Calif. Screen, stage, television actor and singer.

O'NEIL, COLETTE

Born: 1895, Ireland. Died: Oct. 6, 1975, London, England. Screen, stage actress and novelist. Married to actor Miles Malleson (dec. 1969).

Appeared in: **1969** Frankenstein Must Be Destroyed (US 1970).

O'NEIL, NANCE

Born: 1875, Oakland, Calif. Died: Feb. 7, 1965, Englewood, N.J. Stage and screen actress.

Appeared in: **1915** The Kreutzer Sonata. **1917** The Fall of the Romanoffs; Hedda Gabler; Greed. **1919** The Mad Woman. **1929** His Glorious Night. **1930** The Rogue Song; The Floradora Girl; The Lady of Scandal; The Singer of Seville; Ladies of Leisure; The Eyes of the World; Call of the Flesh. **1931** The Good Bad Girl; Cimarron; Their Mad Moment; A Woman of Experience; Transgression; Secret Service; Resurrection; The Royal Bed. **1932** False Faces; Okay, America. **1935** Jack Ahoy; Brewster's Millions.

O'NEIL, SALLY (Virginia Louise Noonan aka SALLY O'NEILL)

Born: Oct. 23, 1910, Bayonne, N.J. Died: June 18, 1968, Galesburg, Ill. (internal bleeding). Stage and screen actress.

Appeared in: **1925** Sally, Irene and Mary. **1926** The Battling Butler; Mike; The Auction Block; Don't. **1927** Frisco Sally Levy; The Callahans and the Murphys; Slide, Kelly, Slide; Becky; The Lovelorn. **1928** The Mad Hour; The Battle of the Sexes; Bachelor's Paradise; The Floating College. **1929** Show of Shows; Mysterious Island; The Sophomore; Hardboiled; Broadway Fever; The Girl on the Barge; On with the Show; Broadway Scandals; Jazz Heaven. **1930** Hold Everything; Girl of the Port; Sisters; Kathleen Mavoureen. **1931** Salvation Nell; Murder by the Clock; The Brat. **1933** Ladies Must Love; By Appointment Only. **1934** Sixteen Fathoms Deep. **1935** Convention Girl. **1936** Too Tough to Kill. **1938** Kathleen.

O'NEILL, HENRY

Born: Aug. 10, 1891, Orange, N.J. Died: May 18, 1961, Hollywood, Calif. Stage and screen actor.

Appeared in: **1933** Strong Arm (film debut); I Loved a Woman; The World Changes; The Kennel Murder Case; Ever in My Heart; Footlight Parade; The House on 56th Street; From Headquarters; Lady Killer. **1934** The Key; Murder in the Clouds; Bedside; Wonder Bar; Twenty Million Sweethearts; Madame Du Barry; The Big Shakedown; Massacre; Fashions of 1934; Journal of a Crime; I've Got Your Number; Fog over Frisco; The Upperworld; Side Streets; The Personality Kid; The Man with Two Faces; Big-Hearted Herbert; Gentlemen Are Born; Flirtation Walk; Now I'll Tell; Midnight; Midnight Alibi. **1935** The Man Who Reclaimed His Head; The Secret Bride; While the Patient Slept; Great Hotel Murder; Bordertown; The Florentine Dagger; Oil for the Lamps of China; Stranded; We're in the Money; Dinky; Dr. Socrates; Special Agent; Bright Lights; The Case of the Lucky Legs; Alias Mary Dow; The Story of Louis Pasteur; Black Fury; Sweet Music; Living on Velvet. **1936** Anthony Adverse; Road Gang; The Golden Arrow; Bullets or Ballots; The White Angel; Freshman Love; The Walking Dead; Boulder Dam; The Big Noise; Two against the World; Rainbow on the River. **1937** Draegerman Courage; The Great O'Malley; Green Light; Marked Woman; The Go Getter; The Life of Emile Zola; The Singing Marine; Mr. Dodd Takes the Air; First Lady; The Great Garrick; Submarine D-1; Wells Fargo. **1938** Brother Rat; Jezebel; White Banners; The Amazing Dr. Clitterhouse; Racket Busters; Yellow Jack; The Chaser; Girls on Probation; Gold Is Where You Find It. **1939** Torchy Blane in Chinatown; Wings of the Navy; Confessions of a Nazi Spy; Juarez; Lucky Night; The Man Who Dared; Angels Wash Their Faces; Everybody's Hobby; Four Wives. **1940** Invisible Stripes; A Child Is Born; Calling Philo Vance; The Story of Dr. Ehrlich's Magic Bullet; Castle on the Hudson; The Fighting 69th; 'Til We Meet Again; Money and the Woman; Santa Fe Trail; They Drive by Night. **1941** Johnny Eager; The Bugle Sounds; Men of Boys Town; The Get-Away; Blossoms in the Dust; Whistling in the Dark; Down in San Diego; Honky Tonk; Shadow of the Thin Man; The Trial of Mary Dugan; Billy the Kid. **1942** Born to Sing; Stand by for Action; Tortilla Flat; White Cargo; This Time for Keeps. **1943** The Human Comedy; Air Raid Wardens; Dr. Gillespie's Criminal Case; Girl Crazy; Whistling in Brooklyn; Lost Angel; The Heavenly Body; A Guy Named Joe; Best Foot Forward. **1944** Dark Shadows (short); The Honest Thief; Airship Squadron No. 4; Rationing; Two Girls and a Sailor; Barbary Coast Gent; Nothing but Trouble. **1945** Keep Your Powder Dry; Anchors Aweigh; This Man's Navy; Dangerous Partners. **1946** The Hoodlum Saint; Bad Bascombe; The Virginian; The Green Years; Three Wise Fools; Little Mr. Jim. **1947** This Time for Keeps; The Beginning or

the End. **1948** Leather Gloves; Return of October. **1949** Alias Nick Beal; Holiday Affair; The Reckless Moment; You're My Everything; Strange Bargain. **1950** No Man of Her Own; The Milkman; Convicted; The Flying Missile. **1951** Family Secret; The Second Woman; People against O'Hara. **1952** Scandal Sheet; Scarlet Angel. **1953** The Sun Shines Bright. **1955** Untamed. **1957** The Wings of Eagles.

O'NEILL, JACK

Born: 1883. Died: Aug. 20, 1957, Hollywood, Calif. Screen actor and film director. Entered films with Lubin in 1905. Was a stand-in for Percy Kilbride.

O'NEILL, JAMES

Died: Oct. 8, 1938, Hollywood, Calif. Screen and vaudeville actor. Entered films approx. 1918. Do not confuse with other actors with same name.

O'NEILL, JAMES, SR.

Born: Oct. 14, 1847, County Kilkenny, Ireland. Died: Aug. 10, 1920, New London, Conn. (cancer). Stage and screen actor. Father of actor James, Jr. (dec. 1923) and playwright Eugene O'Neill (dec. 1953). Married to Ella Quinlan.

Appeared in: **1913** The Count of Monte Cristo.

O'NEILL, JAMES, JR.

Born: Sept. 10, 1878, San Francisco, Calif. Died: Nov. 8, 1923, Trenton, N.J. (pneumonia). Stage and screen actor. Son of actor James O'Neill (dec. 1920). Brother of playwright Eugene O'Neill (dec. 1953).

Appeared in: **1914** The Temptations of Satan. **1917** God's Little Children; The Boy Girl; Susan's Gentleman; The Raggedy Queen. **1918** The Grain of Dust. **1919** The Traveling Salesman.

O'NEILL, JAMES C.

Born: 1876. Died: Nov. 27, 1944, New York (heart ailment). Stage and screen actor.

O'NEILL, MARIE (Marie Allgood)

Born: 1885, Ireland. Died: 1952. Stage and screen actress. Sister of actress Sara Allgood (dec. 1950).

Appeared in: **1930** Juno and the Paycock. **1934** Sing As We Go. **1935** Peg of Old Drury; Come out of the Pantry. **1936** Ourselves Alone. **1937** Glamorous Night; Farewell Again; Bulldog Drummond at Bay; River of Unrest. **1938** St. Martin's Lane; Penny Paradise; Troopship. **1940** Dr. O'Dowd; Sidewalks of London. **1941** You Will Remember; Love on the Dole; Those Kids from Town. **1943** Courageous Mr. Penn. **1945** Love on the Dole (and 1941 version). **1946** Gaiety George. **1947** Murder in Reverse. **1948** Showtime; Piccadilly Incident. **1949** Saints and Sinners. **1950** Someone at the Door. **1952** Treasure Hunt. **1953** The Horse's Mouth.

O'NEILL, MICKEY (Clarence J. H. Dion)

Born: 1903. Died: May 14, 1932, Atascadero, Calif. (auto accident). Screen actor, film director and screenwriter.

O'NEILL, PEGGY

Born: 1924. Died: Apr. 13, 1945, Beverly Hills, Calif. (suicide—sleeping tablets). Screen actress.

Appeared in: **1944** Song of the Open Road. **1945** It's a Pleasure.

O'NEILL, ROBERT A.

Born: 1911. Died: Oct. 8, 1951, Hollywood, Calif. Screen actor.

Appeared in: **1951** The Raging Tide; Drums in the Deep South.

OPPENHEIM, MENASHA

Died: Oct. 23, 1973, New York. Yiddish screen, stage actor and singer.

Appeared in: **1938** Tkies Khaf (The Vow).

ORDE, BERYL

Born: 1912, England. Died: Sept. 10, 1966, London, England. Screen, stage and radio actress.

Appeared in: **1935** Radio Parade of 1935.

ORDUNA, JUAN

Born: 1908, Spain. Died: Feb. 3, 1974, Madrid, Spain (heart attack). Screen actor, film, stage, television director and film producer. Entered films as an actor.

Appeared in: **1928** Nobleza Baturra (Rustic Chivalry).

ORELLANA, CARLOS

Born: 1901, Mexico. Died: Feb. 1960, Mexico City, Mexico (heart attack). Screen actor.

Appeared in: **1935** La Llorona. **1937** Corazon No te Enganes (Don't Fool Thyself, Heart). **1938** No Basta Ser Madre (Motherhood Is Not Enough). **1939** El Hotel de Los Chiflados; El Capitan Adventurero (The Adventurous Captain).

1940 La Cancion del Milagro (The Miracle Song); En un Burro Tres Baturros (Three Rustics on One Donkey). **1943** The Life of Simon Bolivar. **1944** Tierra de Pasiones.

ORKIN, HARVEY
Born: 1918. Died: Nov. 3, 1975, New York, N.Y. Screen, television actor, talent agent and writer.

ORLAMOND, WILLIAM
Born: Aug. 1, 1867, Copenhagen, Denmark. Died: Apr. 23, 1957. Stage and screen actor. Entered films with Lubin Co. in 1912.

Appeared in: **1920** Vanishing Trails (serial). **1921** Beating the Game; Camille. **1922** Arabian Love; Broken Chains; Doubling for Romeo; The Sin Flood; Golden Dreams. **1923** All the Brothers Were Valiant; The Eagle's Feather; The Eternal Three; Look Your Best; Slander the Woman; Slave of Desire; Souls for Sale. **1924** Reno; Nellie, the Beautiful Cloak Model; Name the Man; When a Girl Loves; The White Moth; Wife of the Centaur; True as Steel. **1925** The Dixie Handicap; Seven Keys to Baldpate; The Great Divide; Smouldering Fires. **1926** Kiki; Flesh and the Devil; Mantrap; That's My Baby; Up in Mabel's Room. **1927** The Red Mill; Fashions for Women; Getting Gertie's Garter; See You in Jail; The Taxi Dancer; A Texas Steer. **1928** The Awakening; The Little Yellow House; Rose Marie; Skinner's Big Idea; The Wind; While the City Sleeps. **1929** Blue Skies; The Girl from Woolworth's; The House of Horror; Words and Music; Her Private Affair. **1930** The Way of All Men. **1931** Cimarron; Are These Our Children? **1932** The Roar of the Dragon.

ORLIK, IVAN A. "VANYA"
Born: 1898, Russia. Died: July 4, 1953, Alexandria, Va. Screen actor and dancer. Appeared in German and U.S. films.

ORLOVA, LYUBOV (aka LUBOV ORLOVA)
Born: 1903, Russia. Died: Jan. 26, 1975, Moscow, Russia. Stage and screen actress. Married to film director Grigori Alexandrov.

Appeared in: **1934** Petersburg Nights (film debut); The Jolly Fellows. **1935** Moscow Laughs. **1936** The Circus. **1941** Volga-Volga. **1942** Tanya. **1948** Spring. **1951** Mussorgsky. **1953** Man of Music.

ORMAN, FELIX (Gus Abraham)
Born: 1884. Died: Jan. 1933, Nashville, Tenn. Screen actor.

ORNELLAS, NORMAN
Born: 1939, Honolulu, Hawaii. Died: May 31, 1975, New York, N.Y. (cancer). Stage and screen actor.

Appeared in: **1974** Serpico.

ORONA, VICENTE, JR.
Born: 1931, Mexico. Died: Mar. 11, 1961, Mexico City, Mexico (heart attack). Screen and television actor.

Appeared in: **1934** A Cafe in Cairo. **1935** Cruz Diablo. **1936** Mater Nostra. **1938** Abnegacion; Guadalupe la Chinaca; A la Orilla de un Palmar (At the Edge of a Palm Grove). **1940** Luna Criolla (Creole Moon).

OROPEZA, ANDREW L. (aka ANDRE OROPEZA)
Born: Oct. 2, 1908, Tex. Died: May 5, 1971, Culver City, Calif. (cancer). Screen actor.

Appeared in: **1960** The Third Voice.

O'ROURKE, BREFNI (aka BREFNI O'RORKE)
Born: June 26, 1889, Dublin, Ireland. Died: Nov. 11, 1946. Stage and screen actor.

Appeared in: **1941** The Ghost of St. Michael's; Hatter's Castle; This Man Is Dangerous (aka The Patient Vanishes—US 1947). **1942** They Flew Alone (aka Wings and the Woman—US); Tomorrow We Live (aka At Dawn We Die—US 1943); Unpublished Story; The First of the Few (aka Spitfire—US 1943); Secret Mission; We'll Meet Again. **1943** The Lamp Still Burns; The Flemish Farm. **1944** Tawny Pipit (US 1947); Don't Take It to Heart (US 1949); Twilight Hour. **1945** They Were Sisters (US 1946); Murder in Reverse (US 1946); The Voice Within; Perfect Strangers (aka Vacation from Marriage—US); The Rake's Progress (aka Notorious Gentleman—US 1946); Waltz Time. **1946** I see a Dark Stranger (aka The Adventuress—US 1947).

O'ROURKE, THOMAS
Born: 1872. Died: Oct. 16, 1958, Queens, N.Y. Screen actor. Appeared in films between 1910-1940.

O'ROURKE, TIM
Born: 1933. Died: Nov. 17, 1962, Hollywood, Calif. (auto accident). Screen actor.

ORR, FORREST H.
Died: Apr. 20, 1963, Paterson, N.J. Stage and screen actor.

Appeared in: **1944** Rainbow Island.

ORRACA, JUAN
Born: 1911, Mexico. Died: Aug. 2, 1956, Mexico City, Mexico (heart attack). Stage and screen actor.

ORTH, FRANK
Born: Feb. 21, 1880, Philadelphia, Pa. Died: Mar. 17, 1962, Hollywood, Calif. Screen, stage, vaudeville and television actor. Married to actress Ann Codee (dec. 1961). Appeared in vaudeville with his wife in an act billed as "Codee and Orth." In 1928 he made first foreign language shorts in sound for Warner Bros.

Appeared in: **1929-31** The following shorts with his wife, billed as "Codee and Orth": **1929** A Bird in the Hand; Zwei Und Fierzigste Strasse; Stranded in Paris; Music Hath Charms; Meine Frau (Meet the Wife). **1930** Taking Ways; Imagine My Embarrassment. **1931** On the Job; Sleepy Head; Dumb Luck; The Bitter Half. Without Codee in the following shorts: **1930** The Salesman; The Victim. **1931** The Painter. Other films: **1935** Unwelcome Stranger. **1936** Hot Money; Polo Joe; Two against the World. **1937** The Footloose Heiress; The Patient in Room 18. **1938** Think it Over (short); Nancy Drew, Detective. **1939** Burn 'Em up O'Connor; Broadway Serenade; Fast and Furious; Nancy Drew, Reporter; Nancy Drew and the Hidden Staircase; The Secret of Dr. Kildare; At the Circus. **1940** Dr. Kildare's Strangest Case; La Conga Nights; Pier No. 13; Gold Rush Maisie; Let's Make Music; Dr. Kildare's Crisis; Michael Shayne, Private Detective; Dr. Kildare Goes Home; Father Is a Prince; His Girl Friday; Boom Town; 'Til We Meet Again. **1941** The Great American Broadcast; The People vs. Dr. Kildare; Dr. Kildare's Wedding Day; Dr. Kildare's Victory; Blue, White and Perfect; Come Live with Me; Strawberry Blonde. **1942** I Wake up Screaming; Right to the Heart; The Magnificent Dope; Footlight Serenade; Little Tokyo; Tales of Manhattan; Orchestra Wives; Springtime in the Rockies; Dr. Gillespie's New Assistant; Over My Dead Body; To the Shores of Tripoli; My Gal Sal; Rings on Her Fingers. **1943** Sweet Rosie O'Grady; Hello, Frisco, Hello; Coney Island; The Ox-Bow Incident. **1944** Caroline Blues; Storm over Lisbon; Greenwich Village; Buffalo Bill; Summer Storm; Wilson; The Impatient Years. **1945** She Went to the Races; Tell It to a Star; Pillow to Post; Colonel Effingham's Raid; The Lost Weekend; Doll Face; Nob Hill; The Dolly Sisters. **1944** Blondie's Lucky Day; It's Great to Be Young; The Strange Love of Martha Ivers; Murder in the Music Hall; The Well Groomed Bride. **1947** Born to Speed; The Guilt of Janet Ames; Heartaches; Gas House Kids in Hollywood; Mother Wore Tights; It Had to Be You. **1948** So This Is New York; Fury at Furnace Creek; The Girl from Manhattan. **1949** Red Light; Blondie's Secret; Make Believe Ballroom. **1950** The Great Rupert; Father of the Bride; Cheaper by the Dozen; Petty Girl. **1951** Double Dynamite. **1952** Something to Live For. **1953** Houdini; Here Come the Girls.

ORTIN, LEOPOLDO "CHATO"
Born: 1893, Mexico. Died: Aug. 1953, en route to Acapulco, Mexico (heart attack). Stage and screen actor.

Appeared in: **1939** Alla en el Rancho Chico (Out on the Little Ranch); El Muerto Murio (The Dead Man Died). **1940** Caballo a Caballo (Horse for Horse).

ORTIZ, THULA
Born: 1894. Died: July 30, 1961, New York, N.Y. Screen, stage and television actress.

ORY, EDWARD "KID"
Born: 1887. Died: Jan. 23, 1973, Honolulu, Hawaii (pneumonia and heart disease). Jazz musician and screen actor.

Appeared in: **1947** New Orleans. **1955** The Benny Goodman Story.

ORZAZEWSKI, KASIA
Born: Oct. 16, 1888, Pa. Died: July 17, 1956, Los Angeles, Calif. (rheumatic heart disease). Screen actress.

Appeared in: **1948** Call Northside 777. **1949** The Red Danube; Thieves' Highway. **1951** I Was a Communist for the FBI; Queen for a Day (aka Horsie). **1952** Deadline—USA.

OSBORN, LYN (Clair Lynn Osborn)
Born: Jan. 23, 1926, Wichita Falls, Tex. Died: Aug. 30, 1958, Los Angeles, Calif. (following brain surgery). Screen and television actor.

Appeared in: **1957** The Amazing Colossal Man; Invasion of the Saucer Men. **1958** Torpedo Run. **1959** Arson for Hire; The Cosmic Man.

OSBORNE, JEFFERSON (J. W. Schroeder)
Born: 1871, Bay City, Mich. Died: June 11, 1932, Hondo, Calif. (stroke). Stage and screen actor. Entered films in 1912.

Appeared in: **1915** Jerry's Revenge; Hearts and Clubs; Doctor Jerry; A Shotgun Romance. **1916** Jerry's Perfect Day; Preparedness; Jerry and the Moonshiners; Jerry's Elopement; Jerry's Big Haul; The Rookie; The Hero of Z Ranch;

Jerry's Strategem; The Masque Ball; Jerry's Collaboration; Jerry and the Counterfeiters; Jerry and the Bandits; Making Things Hum; The Girl of His Dreams; Around the World. **1917** Jerry and His Pal; Jerry's Big Mystery.

OSBORNE, LENNIE "BUD" (aka MILES OSBORNE)
Born: July 20, 1881, Knox County, Tex. Died: Feb. 2, 1964, Hollywood, Calif. Screen and television actor. Entered films with Thomas Ince Co. in 1915.

Appeared in: **1917** Roped In; Border Wolves; Swede-Hearts; The Getaway; Bill Brennan's Claim; Casey's Border Raid. **1921** The Raiders; The Struggle. **1922** White Eagle (serial); Barriers of Folly. **1923** The Prairie Mystery. **1924** Way of a Man (serial); Cyclone Buddy; The Loser's End; Not Built for Runnin'; The Silent Stranger. **1925** Fighting Ranger (serial); Across the Deadline; Flash O'Lightning; The Knockout Kid; Ranchers and Rascals; The Trouble Buster; Win, Lose or Draw. **1926** Blind Trail; Hi-Jacking Rustlers; Law of the Snow Country; Lawless Trails; Looking for Trouble; The Outlaw Express; Three Bad Men; Without Orders. **1927** The Long Loop on the Pecos; A One Man Game; Riders of the West; Don Desperado; Two-Gun of the Tumbleweed; Border Blackbirds; Sky High Saunders; Cactus Trails; The Devil's Twin; King of the Herd. **1928** The Bronc Stomper; The Mystery Rider (serial and feature film); The Vanishing Rider (serial); Cheyenne Trails; The Danger Rider; Forbidden Trails; On the Divide; Secrets of the Range; Texas Flash; Texas Tommy; The Thrill Chaser; Yellow Contraband. **1929** The Cowboy and the Outlaw; West of the Rockies; Bad Man's Money; Days of Daring; The Fighting Terror; The Lariat Kid; The Law of the Mounted; On the Divide; The Last Round-Up; West of Santa Fe; The Invaders. **1930** Half Pint Polly; The Indians Are Coming (serial); Canyon of Missing Men; O'Malley Rides Alone; Call of the Desert; Western Honor; Code of the West; Breezy Bill; The Utah Kid. **1931** Red Fork Range. **1932** Mark of the Spur. **1933** When a Man Rides Alone; The Diamond Trail; Flaming Guns; Deadwood Pass; Rustler's Roundup. **1934** Outlaw Justice. **1935** Outlaw Deputy; The Crimson Trail. **1936** Roamin' Wild; Treachery Rides the Range; Song of the Saddle; Heroes of the Range; Headin' for the Rio Grande. **1937** Guns of the Pecos; The Californian; Yodelin' Kid from Pine Ridge; Western Gold; Boots and Saddles. **1938** Man's Country; Prairie Moon; The Painted Trail; The Mexicali Kid; The Overland Express. **1939** Racketeers of the Range; Legion of the Lawless; Rovin' Tumbleweeds; New Frontier; Across the Plains. **1940** Pioneer Days; Land of Six-Guns; West of Abilene; Lone Star Raiders. **1941** The Phantom Cowboy; Outlaws of the Panhandle; The Medico of Painted Springs; Riding the Wind; Robbers of the Range; The Return of Daniel Boone; The Bandit Trail. **1942** 'Neath Brooklyn Bridge; The Spoilers; Riders of the West. **1943** Robin Hood of the Range; Stranger from Pecos; The Carson City Cyclone; Haunted Ranch; Rangers Take Over; The Avenging Rider; Cowboy Commandos; The Ghost Rider. **1944** Sonora Stagecoach; Song of the Range; Adventures of Mark Twain; Law Men; Range Law; Valley of Vengeance; Outlaw Trail; Marked Trails; Trigger Law; Laramie Trail; Outlaw Roundup; Dead or Alive. **1945** Prairie Rustlers; Three in the Saddle; The Cisco Kid Returns; Fighting Bill Carson; The Navajo Kid; Flaming Bullets; The Cherokee Flash; His Brother's Ghost. **1946** Thundertown; Six-Gun Man; Border Bandits; Overland Riders; Outlaw of the Plains; Landrush; Desert Horseman. **1947** Six-Gun Serenade; Thundergap Outlaws; Twilight on the Rio Grande; The Last Round-Up; Trailing Danger; Code of the Saddle; Bowery Buckaroos. **1948** Six-Gun Law; Song of the Drifter; Blood on the Moon; Indian Agent; Crossed Trails; Courtin' Trouble. **1949** Frontier Revenge; Riders in the Sky; Gunning for Justice; The Gay Amigo. **1950** Six-Gun Mesa; Cow Town; The Cowboy and the Prizefighter; Hostile Country; Arizona Territory; Border Rangers; Over the Border; West of the Brazos; Colorado Ranger; Fast on the Draw; Marshal of Heldorado; The Crooked River. **1951** Nevada Badmen; Valley of Fire; Whirlwind; Whistling Hills. **1952** Barbed Wire; Texas City. **1954** The Lawless Rider. **1958** Escape from Red Rock.

OSBORNE, VIVIENNE
Born: Dec. 10, 1896, Des Moines, Iowa. Died: June 10, 1961. Stage and screen actress.

Appeared in: **1920** In Walked Mary; Love's Flame; The Restless Sex; Over the Hill to the Poorhouse. **1921** Mother Eternal; The Right Way. **1922** The Good Provider. **1930** The Nightingale (short). **1931** Beloved Bachelor. **1932** Husband's Holiday; Two Kinds of Women; The Famous Ferguson Case; Two Seconds; Weekend Marriage; The Dark Horse; Life Begins. **1933** Phantom Broadcast; Supernatural; Tomorrow at Seven; The Devil's in Love; Luxury Liner; Sailor Be Good; Men are Such Fools. **1935** No More Ladies. **1936** Let's Sing Again; Follow Your Heart; Wives Never Know; Sinner Take All. **1937** Champagne Waltz; The Crime Nobody Saw; She Asked For It. **1940** Primrose Path; Captain Caution; So You Won't Talk. **1944** I Accuse My Parents. **1946** Dragonwyck.

OSCAR, HENRY (Henry Wale)
Born: July 14, 1891, London, England. Died: Dec. 28, 1969, London, England. Screen, stage and television actor.

Appeared in: **1932** After Dark (film debut). **1933** I Was a Spy. **1934** The Man Who Knew Too Much; Red Ensign (aka Strike 1—US); Brides to Be. **1935** The Case of Gabriel Perry; Night Mail; Sexton Blake and the Bearded Doctor; Me and Marlborough; Father O'Flynn (US 1938); The Tunnel (aka Transat-lantic Tunnel—US). **1936** Love in Exile; Seven Sinners (aka Doomed Cargo—US); No Escape; Spy of Napoleon (US 1939); Dishonour Bright; The Man Behind the Mask. **1937** Sensation; Fire Over England; Dark Journey; The Academy Decides; Who Killed John Savage?; The Return of the Scarlet Pimpernel (US 1938). **1938** Black Limelight (US 1939); The Terror; Luck of the Navy (aka North Sea Patrol—US 1940). **1939** Spies of the Air (US 1940); The Saint in London; Dead Man's Shoes; On the Night of the Fire (aka The Fugitive—US 1940); Hell's Cargo (aka Dangerous Cargo—US 1940); The Four Feathers. **1940** Two for Danger; The Flying Squad; Tilly of Bloomsbury. **1941** Atlantic Ferry (aka Sons of the Sea—US); Penn of Pennsylvania (aka The Courageous Mr. Penn—US 1944); The Seventh Survivor; Hatter's Castle. **1942** The Day Will Dawn (aka The Avengers—US); Squadron Leader X. **1947** The Upturned Glass; Mrs. Fitzherbert (US 1950). **1948** Idol of Paris; The Greed of William Hart; Bonnie Prince Charlie; House of Darkness; It Happened in Soho. **1949** The Man from Yesterday; Which Will You Have? (aka Barabbas the Robber—US); The Bad Lord Byron (US 1952). **1950** Prelude to Fame; Black Rose. **1954** Beau Brummell; Diplomatic Passport. **1955** Portrait of Alison (aka Postmark for Danger—US 1956). **1956** It's a Great Day. **1957** The Little Hut. **1958** The Spaniard's Curse; The Secret Man. **1959** Beyond This Place (aka Web of Evidence—US). **1960** Oscar Wilde; The Brides of Dracula; Foxhole in Cairo (US 1961). **1961** Mein Kampf. **1962** Lawrence of Arabia. **1965** The City Under the Sea (aka War-Gods of the Deep—US). **1964** Murder Ahoy; The Long Ships.

OSE, JAY
Born: Nov. 1911. Died: Nov. 5, 1967, Hollywood, Calif. Magician, screen and television actor.

Appeared in: **1967** Waterhole #3; The Flim-Flam Man.

O'SHEA, JACK "BLACKJACK" (Jack Rellaford)
Born: 1906, San Francisco, Calif. Died: Oct. 2, 1967, Paradise, Calif. (heart attack). Screen and television actor.

Appeared in: **1937** The Big Show. **1939** In Old Monterey; South of the Border. **1940** Cuckoo Cavaliers (short). **1942** Sons of the Pioneers. **1944** The San Antonio Kid. **1946** Rio Grande Raiders. **1947** G-Men Never Forget (serial); Law of the Lash; Twilight on the Rio Grande; King of the Bandits; Wyoming. **1949** Ride, Ryder, Ride. **1951** Silver Canyon.

O'SHEA, MICHAEL
Born: 1906, Conn. Died: Dec. 1973, Dallas, Tex. (heart attack). Screen, stage, radio, television actor and singer. Divorced from Grace Watts. Married to actress Virginia Mayo.

Appeared in: **1943** Lady of Burlesque (film debut); Jack London. **1944** The Eve of St. Mark; Something for the Boys; Man from Frisco. **1945** It's a Pleasure; Circumstantial Evidence. **1947** Mr. District Attorney; Violence; Last of the Redmen. **1949** The Big Wheel; Captain China; The Threat. **1950** Underworld Story (aka The Whipped). **1951** Fixed Bayonets. **1952** The Model and the Marriage Broker; Bloodhounds of Broadway. **1954** It Should Happen to You.

O'SHEA, OSCAR
Born: 1882. Died: Apr. 6, 1960, Hollywood, Calif. Screen actor.

Appeared in: **1937** Captains Courageous; Rosalie; Big City; Mannequin. **1938** Man Proof; The Main Event; King of the Newsboys; International Crime; Stablemates; The Shining Hour; Numbered Woman; Racket Busters; Youth Takes a Fling. **1939** Lucky Night; King of the Turf; Big Town Czar; Missing Evidence; Invitation to Happiness; The Star Maker; Tell No Tales; S.O.S, Tidal Wave; She Married a Cop; Those High Grey Walls; Of Mice and Men; The Night of Nights. **1940** Zanzibar; The Singing Dude; 20 Mule Team; You Can't Fool Your Wife; Wildcat Bus; Stranger on the Third Floor; Pier 13; Always a Bride. **1941** The Strawberry Blonde; Ringside Maisie; The Phantom Submarine; Sleepers West; The Officer and the Lady; Harmon of Michigan; Mutiny in the Arctic. **1942** The Bashful Bachelor; I Was Framed; The Postman Didn't Ring; Just Off Broadway; Halfway to Shanghai; Henry Aldrich, Editor. **1943** Two Weeks to Live; Good Morning Judge; Two Tickets to London; Corvette K-225. **1944** Her Primitive Man; The Mummy's Ghost. **1945** Bewitched. **1946** The Brute Man; Personality Kid. **1947** Sport of Kings; My Wild Irish Rose. **1948** The Senorita from the West; One Sunday Afternoon.

OSTERMAN, JACK (Jack Rosenthal)
Born: 1902, Toledo, Ohio. Died: June 8, 1939, Atlantic City, N.J. Screen, stage and vaudeville actor.

Appeared in: **1936** Wanted Men.

OSTERMAN, KATHRYN
Born: 1883, Toledo, Ohio. Died: Aug. 25, 1956, New York, N.Y. Stage and screen actress.

Appeared in: **1903** A Search for Evidence. **1904** The Lost Child.

O'SULLIVAN, ANTHONY "TONY"
Died: July 5, 1920, Bronx, N.Y. Screen actor. Entered films with Biograph and later with Mack Sennett. Appeared in several "Jonesy" comedies.

Appeared in: **1908** The Red Girl; The Pirate's Gold. **1909** 'Tis An Ill Wind That Blows No Good; What Drink Did; A Convict's Sacrifice; A Strange Meeting; Getting Even; In the Watches of the Night; Her Terrible Ordeal; Mrs. Jones Entertains; The Honor of His Family. **1910** The Newlyweds; The Final Settlement.

O'SULLIVAN, MICHAEL

Born: 1934, Phoenix, Ariz. Died: July 24, 1971, San Francisco, Calif. Stage and screen actor.

Appeared in: **1967** You're a Big Boy Now. **1968** Hang 'Em High.

OSWALDA, OSSI (Oswalda Staglich)

Born: 1899, Berlin, Germany. Died: 1948, Prague, Czechoslovakia. Stage and screen actress. Known as the "German Mary Pickford."

Appeared in: **1934** Der Stern von Valencia.

OTT, ALEXANDER

Born: 1888. Died: Dec. 13, 1970. Theatrical producer (mainly water shows) and screen actor.

OTT, FREDERICK P.

Born: 1860. Died: Oct. 24, 1936, West Orange, N.J. He was the first person to be photographed in the motion picture experiments of Thomas A. Edison; was a member of Edison's scientific staff and not an actor.

Appeared in: **1893** Sneeze.

OTTIANO, RAFAELA

Born: Mar. 4, 1894, Venice, Italy. Died: Aug. 18, 1942, Boston, Mass. Screen, stage and radio actress.

Appeared in: **1924** The Law and the Lady. **1932** As You Desire Me; Grand Hotel; Washington Masquerade. **1933** Her Man; She Done Him Wrong; Bondage; Ann Vickers; Female. **1934** Mandalay; A Lost Lady; The Last Gentleman; All Men Are Enemies; Great Expectations. **1935** The Florentine Dagger; Lottery Lover; Curly Top; One Frightened Night; Remember Last Night?; Enchanted April; Crime and Punishment. **1936** That Girl from Paris; Riffraff; Anthony Adverse; The Devil Doll; Mad Holiday; We're Only Human. **1937** Maytime; Seventh Heaven; The League of Frightened Men. **1938** I'll Give a Million; Suez. **1939** Paris Honeymoon. **1940** The Long Voyage Home; Victory. **1941** Topper Returns. **1942** The Adventures of Martin Eden.

OTTO, ARTHUR

Died: Jan. 1918, Tacoma, Wash. Screen actor.

OTTO, HENRY

Born: 1878. Died: Aug. 3, 1952, Hollywood, Calif. Screen actor and film director.

Appeared in: **1926** The Outlaw Express. **1929** The Quitter; The Iron Mask. **1930** A Matter of Ethics (short); One Hysterical Night. **1938** Fighting Devil Dogs (serial). **1939** The Lone Ranger Rides Again (serial).

OUSPENSKAYA, MARIA

Born: July 29, 1876, Tula, Russia. Died: Dec. 3, 1949, Los Angeles, Calif. (burns). Stage and screen actress.

Appeared in: **1936** Dodsworth (film debut—screen and stage versions). **1937** Conquest (aka Marie Walewska). **1939** Love Affair; The Rains Came; Judge Hardy and Son. **1940** Dr. Ehrlich's Magic Bullet; Waterloo Bridge; The Man I Married; Beyond Tomorrow; Dance, Girl, Dance; The Mortal Storm. **1941** The Wolf Man; King's Row; The Shanghai Gesture. **1942** The Mystery of Marie Roget. **1943** Frankenstein Meets the Wolf Man. **1945** Tarzan and the Amazons. **1946** I've Always Loved You. **1947** Wyoming. **1949** A Kiss in the Dark.

OVERMAN, JACK

Born: 1916. Died: Jan. 4, 1950, Hollywood, Calif. (heart attack). Screen actor.

Appeared in: **1941** GI Honeymoon. **1947** Johnny Angel; Honeymoon Ahead; The Naughty Nineties. **1946** The Runaround. **1947** Brute Force; The Brasher Doubloon. **1948** Force of Evil; T-Men; The Noose Hangs High. **1949** Flaxy Martin; The Lone Wolf and His Lady; I Can't Remember (short); Shocking Affair (short); Prison Warden. **1950** The Good Humor Man. **1957** Jet Pilot.

OVERMAN, LYNNE

Born: Sept. 19, 1887, Maryville, Mo. Died: Feb. 19, 1943, Santa Monica, Calif. (heart attack). Screen, stage, minstrel and vaudeville actor.

Appeared in: **1930** Horseshoes (short); Five Minutes from the Station (short). **1933** Poor Fish (short). **1934** Little Miss Marker; The Great Flirtation; She Loves Me Not; Midnight; Broadway Bill; You Belong to Me. **1935** Paris in Spring; Rhumba; Men without Names; Two for Tonight; Enter Madame. **1936** Collegiate; Poppy; Yours for the Asking; Three Married Men; Jungle Princess. **1937** Wild Money; Nobody's Baby; Don't Tell the Wife; Murder Goes to College; Hotel Haywire; Blonde Trouble; Night Club Scandal; True Confession; Partners in Crime. **1938** Big Broadcast of 1938; Her Jungle Love; Hunted

Man; Spawn of the North; Sons of the Legion; Men with Wings; Ride a Crooked Mile. **1939** Persons in Hiding; Death of a Champion; Union Pacific. **1940** Safari; Northwest Mounted Police; Typhoon; Edison the Man. **1941** Aloma of the South Seas; Caught in the Draft; There's Magic in Music; The Hard-Boiled Canary; New York Town. **1942** Reap the Wild Wind; The Forest Rangers; Star Spangled Rhythm; Roxie Hart; Silver Queen. **1943** Dixie; The Desert Song.

OVERTON, FRANK

Born: 1918. Died: Apr. 24, 1967, Pacific Palisades, Calif. (heart attack). Screen, stage and television actor.

Appeared in: **1950** No Way Out. **1957** The True Story of Jesse James. **1958** Desire under the Elms; Lonelyhearts. **1959** The Last Mile. **1960** Wild River; The Dark at the Top of the Stairs; Khovanschina. **1961** Posse from Hell; Claudelle Inglish. **1962** To Kill a Mockingbird. **1964** Fail Safe.

OVEY, GEORGE

Born: Dec. 13, 1870, Kansas City, Mo. Died: Sept. 13, 1951, Hollywood, Calif. Screen, stage and vaudeville actor. Married to actress Louise Horner.

Appeared in: **1915** Jerry and the Gunman; Father Forgot; The Treasure Box; An Oriental Spasm; The Stolen Case; Waking Up Father; Making Matters Worse; He's in Again; A Change of Luck; Hearts and Clubs; The Little Detective; Doctor Henry; Who's Who; Jerry to the Rescue; The Fighting Four; The Double Cross; Taking a Chance; The Hold-Up; A Shotgun Romance. **1916** Jerry's Perfect Day; Preparedness; Jerry's Big Lark; Jerry and the Moonshiners; Jerry's Elopement; Jerry's Big Haul; The Hero of Z Ranch; Jerry's Stratagem; Jerry and the Counterfeiters; The Bookie; A Merry Mix-Up; The Masque Ball; When Jerry Came to Town; Jerry's Celebration; On the Rampage; Jerry and the Smugglers; The Winning Punch; Jerry in the Movies; Jerry in Mexico; Around the World; The Girl of His Dreams; Jerry's Millions; Too Proud to Fight; Going Up; The Desperate Chance; Jerry's Big Game; The Conquering Hero; The Traitor; Jerry and the Bandits; Making Things Hum; Movie Struck; Jerry's Double Header; Jerry's Winning Way; Jerry's Big Doing. **1917** Jerry in Yodel Land; Jerry and the Outlaws; Jerry and His Pal; Jerry's Big Raid; Jerry's Big Mystery; Jerry's Brilliant Scheme; Jerry's Romance; The Flying Target; Jerry's Triple Alliance; Minding the Baby; Be Sure You're Right; The Lady Detective; The Gypsy Prince; The Ransom; Jerry's Picnic; There and Back; Jerry's Finishing Touch; Jerry Joins the Army; Jerry's Master Stroke; Jerry's Getaway; Jerry's Red Hot Trail; Jerry's Hopeless Tangle; Jerry's Soft Snap; Jerry and the Bully; Jerry's Lucky Day; Jerry and the Vampire; Jerry's Running Fight; Jerry's Victory; Jerry and the Burglars; Jerry Takes Gas; Jerry's Boarding House; Jerry's Best Friend. **1918** Jerry Tries Again. **1926** The Arizona Sweepstakes; The Sporting Lover; Transcontinental Limited; Strings of Steel (serial). **1927** Better Days; Desert Dust; Pals in Peril; The Yankee Clipper. **1928** My Friend from India. **1929** Broadway. **1930** Hit the Deck; Night Ride. **1933** Alice in Wonderland. **1935** Old Sawbones (short). **1938** Jump, Chump, Jump (short).

OWASSO

Died: Nov. 1962. Animal screen performer (turkey). Nominated for Patsy Award as Best Animal Performer.

Appeared in: **1961** All Hands on Deck.

OWEN, CATHERINE DALE

Born: July 28, 1903, Louisville, Ky. Died: Sept. 7, 1965, New York, N.Y. Stage and screen actress.

Appeared in: **1927** Forbidden Woman. **1929** His Glorious Night. **1930** The Rogue Song; Born Reckless; Today; Such Men Are Dangerous; Strictly Unconventional. **1931** The Circle; Behind Office Doors; In Defense of the Law.

OWEN, GARRY

Born: Dec. 18, 1902, Brookhaven, Miss. Died: June 1, 1951, Los Angeles, Calif. (heart attack). Screen, stage and vaudeville actor.

Appeared in: **1933** Son of a Sailor; Hold Your Man; Child of Manhattan; Stage Mother; The Prizefighter and the Lady; Havana Widows; Bombay Mail. **1934** Little Miss Marker; No Ransom; The Thin Man. **1935** Hold 'Em Yale; Top Flat (short). **1936** Ceiling Zero; The Case of the Black Cat; King of Hockey; The Return of Sophie Lang. **1937** Racketeers in Exile; San Quentin; True Confession. **1938** Call of the Yukon; Heart of the North. **1940** Grandpa Goes to Town. **1941** Meet John Doe; The Wagons Roll at Night. **1942** Yankee Doodle Dandy; Pride of the Yankees. **1944** Arsenic and Old Lace; Nothing but Trouble. **1945** The Last Installment (short); Abbott and Costello in Hollywood; Fallen Woman; Mildred Pierce; Anchors Aweigh. **1946** The Tiger Woman; Crime of the Century; The Killers; Dark Mirror; Swell Guy. **1947** The Flame. **1949** I Cheated the Law. **1950** The Admiral Was a Lady; The Flying Missile; The Milkman.

OWEN, REGINALD (John Reginald Owen)

Born: Aug. 5, 1887, Wheathampstead, England. Died: Nov. 5, 1972, Boise, Idaho (heart attack). Screen, stage actor, screenwriter and author. Divorced from Lydia Bilbrooke. Married stage actress Mrs. Harold Austin (dec. 1956) and later married Barbara Haveman.

Appeared in: **1911** Henry VIII. **1916** Sally in Our Alley; A Place in the Sun. **1923** Phroso. **1929** The Letter. **1931** Platinum Blonde; Man in Possession. **1932** A Woman Commands; Lovers Courageous; Downstairs; The Man Called Back; Sherlock Holmes; Bill of Divorcement. **1933** Robbers' Roost; A Study in Scarlet; The Big Brain; Double Harness; Voltaire; The Narrow Corner; Queen Christina. **1934** Fashions of 1934; Nana; The House of Rothschild; Madame Du Barry; Mandalay; The Countess of Monte Cristo; Where Sinners Meet; Of Human Bondage; Here Is My Heart; The Human Side; Stingaree; Music in the Air. **1935** The Good Fairy; Call of the Wild; Anna Karenina; Escapade; A Tale of Two Cities; The Bishop Misbehaves; Enchanted April. **1936** Rose Marie; Petticoat Fever; Trouble for Two; The Great Ziegfeld; Love on the Run; The Girl on the Front Page; Adventure in Manhattan; Yours for the Asking; Rich and Reckless; The Suicide Club. **1937** Dangerous Number; Personal Property; Madame X; The Bride Wore Red; Conquest; Rosalie. **1938** Paradise for Three; Everybody Sing!; Three Loves Has Nancy; Vacation with Love; A Christmas Carol; Kidnapped; Stablemates; Sweethearts. **1939** The Girl Downstairs; Balalaika; Fast and Loose; Bridal Suite; Bad Little Angel; Remember?; Hotel Imperial; The Real Glory. **1940** The Earl of Chicago; The Ghost Comes Home; Florian; Hullabaloo; Pride and Prejudice. **1941** Blonde Inspiration; Free and Easy; They Met in Bombay; Lady Be Good; Tarzan's Secret Treasure; A Woman's Face; Charley's Aunt. **1942** Mrs. Miniver; White Cargo; Random Harvest; We Were Dancing; Woman of the Year; I Married an Angel; Pierre of the Plains; Somewhere I'll Find You; Cairo; Reunion. **1943** Above Suspicion; Three Hearts for Julia; Forever and a Day; Salute to the Marines; Madame Curie; Assignment in Brittany; Lassie Come Home. **1944** National Velvet; The Canterville Ghost. **1945** The Diary of a Chambermaid; She Went to the Races; Monsieur Beaucaire; The Valley of Decision; Captain Kidd; The Sailor Takes a Wife; Kitty. **1946** Cluny Brown; Mrs. Loring's Secret. **1947** Thunder in the Valley; Green Dolphin Street; If Winter Comes; Imperfect Lady (aka They Met at Midnight); The Pirate; Julia Misbehaves. **1948** The Three Musketeers; Picadilly Incident; Hills of Home. **1949** Challenge to Lassie; The Secret Garden. **1950** Kim; Grounds for Marriage; The Miniver Story. **1953** The Great Diamond Robbery. **1954** Red Garters. **1958** Darby's Rangers. **1962** Five Weeks in a Balloon. **1963** The Thrill of it All; Tammy and the Doctor. **1964** Mary Poppins; Voice of the Hurricane. **1967** Rosie!

OWEN, SEENA (Signe Auen)

Born: 1896, Spokane, Wash. Died: Aug. 15, 1966, Hollywood, Calif. Screen, stage actress and screenwriter.

Appeared in: **1914** Out of the Air. **1915** The Lamb; A Day that is Dead. **1916** Intolerance. **1918** Branding Broadway. **1919** Victory; The Sheriff's Son; A Man and His Money; The Life Line. **1921** The Cheater Reformed; Lavender and Old Lace; The Woman God Changed. **1922** Back Pay; The Face in the Fog; Sisters; At the Cross Roads. **1923** The Go Getter; The Leavenworth Case; Unseeing Eyes. **1924** For Woman's Favor; I Am the Man; The Great Wall (aka Neglected Women—US). **1925** Faint Perfume; The Hunted Woman. **1926** Shipwrecked; The Flame of the Yukon. **1928** His Last Haul; Man-Made Woman; Queen Kelly; Sinners in Love; The Blue Danube; The Rush Hour. **1929** The Marriage Playground.

OWENS, PEGGY

Born: 1905. Died: May 27, 1931 (heart failure). Screen wild west rider.

OWENS, WILLIAM

Born: 1863, N.Y. Died: Aug. 20, 1926, Chicago, Ill. Screen and stage actor.

OWSLEY, MONROE

Born: 1901, Atlanta, Ga. Died: June 7, 1937, Belmont, Calif. (heart attack). Stage and screen actor.

Appeared in: **1928** The First Kiss. **1930** Free Love; Holiday (screen and stage versions). **1931** Ten Cents a Dance; Honor among Lovers; Indiscreet; This Modern Age. **1932** Hat Check Girl; Call Her Savage. **1933** The Keyhole; Ex-Lady; Brief Moment. **1934** She Was a Lady; Little Man, What Now?; Wild Gold; Twin Husbands. **1935** Goin' to Town; Behold My Wife; Rumba: Remember Last Night? **1936** Private Number; Yellowstone; Hideaway Girl. **1937** The Hit Parade.

OYA, ICHIJIRO

Born: 1894, Japan. Died: May 28, 1972, Tokyo, Japan (lung cancer). Stage and screen actor.

Appeared in: **1958** Byakuya no Yojo (The Temptress and the Monk—US 1963).

OYSHER, MOISHE

Born: 1907, Lipkon, Bessarabia, Russia. Died: Nov. 27, 1958, New Rochelle, N.Y. Screen, stage, radio actor, composer and cantor.

Appeared in: **1938** The Singing Blacksmith. **1940** Overture to Glory. **1956** Singing in the Dark (also composed words and music).

PABST, GEORG WILHELM

Born: 1885, Vienna, Austria. Died: May 29, 1967, Vienna, Austria. Film director, screenwriter and screen actor. Entered films as an actor in 1921.

Appeared in: **1922** Luise Millerin.

PACE, MAX

Born: 1906. Died: Aug. 3, 1942, Hollywood, Calif. (suicide—gun). Screen actor.

PACKARD, CLAYTON L.

Born: 1888. Died: Sept. 6, 1931, San Diego, Calif. (complications following surgery). Stage and screen actor.

Appeared in: **1927** King of Kings.

PACKER, NETTA

Born: 1897. Died: Nov. 7, 1962, Hollywood, Calif. Screen actor.

Appeared in: **1938** Condemned Woman. **1939** Crime Rave (short). **1942** Enemy Agents Meet Ellery Queen; Powder Town. **1948** Good Sam. **1959** It Started with a Kiss.

PADDEN, SARAH

Died: Dec. 4, 1967. Screen actress.

Appeared in: **1926** Obey the Law. **1927** The Bugle Call; Colleen; Heroes of the Night; The Woman Who Did Not Care; The Eternal Barrier (short). **1928** The Companionate Marriage; Souvenirs (short). **1929** The Sophomore; Wonder of Women. **1930** Today; Hide-Out. **1931** Sob Sisters; Yellow Ticket; Great Meadow. **1932** Rebecca of Sunnybrook Farm; Cross Examination; Young America; Midnight Lady; Blondie of the Follies; Tess of the Storm Country; Wild Girl. **1933** The Power and the Glory; The Important Witness; The Sin of Nora Moran; Women Won't Tell; Face in the Sky. **1934** Spitfire; Man of Two Worlds; The Defense Rests; Little Man, What Now?; As the Earth Turns; He Was Her Man; David Harum; Tomorrow's Children; Finishing School; Marrying Widow; Hat, Coat and Glove; The Fountain; When Strangers Meet. **1935** A Dog of Flanders; The Raven; Youth on Parole; Exiled to Shanghai. **1938** Women in Prison; Rich Man-Poor Girl; Romance of the Limberlost; Woman Against Woman; Little Orphan Annie. **1939** Angels Wash Their Faces; Let Freedom Ring; Zero Hour; Should a Girl Marry?; I Stole a Million. **1940** Forgotten Girls; Son of the Navy; Lone Star Raiders; Chad Hanna. **1941** City of Missing Girls; The Man Who Lost Himself; In Old Colorado; A Woman's Face; Tight Shoes; Murder by Invitation; Reg'lar Fellers; The Corsican Brothers. **1942** Snuffy Smith—Yard Bird; Heart of the Rio Grande; The Mad Monster; Riders of the West; Law and Order; The Power of God. **1943** Assignment in Brittany; Hangmen also Die; So This is Washington; Jack London; Family Troubles (short). **1944** Summer Storm; Range Law; Trail to Gunsight; Girl Rush; Ghost Guns. **1945** Identity Unknown; Song of Old Wyoming; The Master Key (serial); Dakota; Honeymoon Ahead. **1946** So Your My Love; Joe Palooka—Champ; Angel on My Shoulder; Gentleman Joe Palooka; That Brennan Girl; Wild West. **1947** Joe Palooka in the Knockout; The Millerson Case; Ramrod. **1948** Fighting Mad; The Dude Goes West; Prairie Outlaws; The Return of the Whistler. **1949** Homicide; Range Justice. **1950** House by the River; Gunslingers; The Missourians. **1951** Utah Wagon Train. **1952** Big Jim McLain. **1955** Prince of Players.

PADEREWSKI, IGNACE JAN

Born: 1860. Died: June 2, 1941. Former Polish prime minister and classical pianist.

Appeared in: **1937** Moonlight Sonata.

PADILLA, EMA

Born: 1900, Mexico City, Mexico. Died: July 2, 1966, Mexico City, Mexico (diabetes). Screen actress.

Appeared in: **1916** La Luz.

PADJAN, JACK (aka JACK DUANE)

Born: 1888. Died: Feb. 1, 1960. Screen actor.

Appeared in: **1924** The Iron Horse. **1926** Tony Runs Wild. **1927** Land of the Lawless; The King of Kings. **1928** Crashing Through; Forbidden Grass. **1929** Redskin. **1930** The Big Trail.

PADOVANO, JOHN

Born: 1916. Died: Nov. 27, 1973 (auto accident). Screen actor and film producer.

Appeared in: **1956** Foreign Intrigue.

PADULA, VINCENT (Vicente Padula)

Born: 1900, Argentina. Died: Jan. 16, 1967, Glendale, Calif. (peritonitis). Screen actor.

Appeared in: **1927** Winds of the Pampas. **1934** Cuesta Abajo; El Tango en Broadway. **1950** The Avengers. **1954** Three Coins in the Fountain. **1955** The Girl Rush. **1956** The Three Outlaws. **1957** Escape from Red Rock; Hell Canyon (aka Hell Canyon Outlaws). **1958** The Flame Barrier. **1959** Pier 5, Havana. **1960** Raymie.

PAGE, ARTHUR W. (Arthur Wellington)
Born: Aug. 2, 1885, Mass. Died: Feb. 8, 1968, Los Angeles, Calif. (heart attack). Stage and screen actor.

Appeared in: **1952** The Winning Team. **1953** The Robe.

PAGE, DON. *See* DON ALVARADO

PAGE, JAMES E.
Born: 1870, England. Died: Mar. 27, 1930, London, England. Stage and screen actor.

Appeared in: **1925** Charley's Aunt (stage and screen versions).

PAGE, LUCILLE (Lucille Berdell)
Born: 1871. Died: Dec. 31, 1964, Hollywood, Calif. Screen, stage and vaudeville actress. Married to actor Art Wellington and they appeared in vaudeville as "Berdell and Wellington."

Appeared in: **1935** and **1937** Educational shorts.

PAGE, PAUL (Campbell U. Hicks)
Born: May 13, 1903, Birmingham, Ala. Died: Apr. 28, 1974, Hermosa Beach, Calif. (heart attack). Screen and vaudeville actor. Entered films in 1929.

Appeared in: **1929** Speakeasy; Protection; Girl from Havana; Happy Days. **1930** Men Without Women; Born Reckless; The Golden Calf. **1931** The Naughty Flirt; Women Go on Forever; Palmy Days. **1932** Pleasure; 70,000 Witnesses; Bachelor Mother. **1933** Phantom Broadcast; Below the Sea. **1934** The Road to Ruin; Countess of Monte Carlo; The Month; Have a Heart. **1935** Kentucky Kernels.

PAGE, RITA
Born: Aug. 16, 1906, London, England. Died: Dec. 19, 1954. Screen actress.

Appeared in: **1932** Aren't We All? **1940** Vigil in the Night; Little Nellie Kelly.

PAGET, ALFRED
Died: 1925. Stage and screen actor. Entered films with Biograph in 1910.

Appeared in: **1910** A Romance of the Western Hills; The Banker's Daughter. **1911** Enoch Arden; Out of the Shadow. **1912** Goddess of Sagebrush Gulch; A Dash through the Clouds; Man's Genesis; A Temporary Truce; The Girl and Her Trust; The Lesser Evil; When Kings Were the Law; A Beast at Bay; The Spirit Awakened; The Inner Circle; Heredity; The Musketeers of Pig Alley. **1913** Oil and Water; A Timely Interception; Just Gold; The Primitive Man; A Girl's Stratagem; The Tenderfoot's Money; Fate; Broken Ways. **1914** The Battle of Firebush Gulch. **1915** The Lamb; The Martyrs of the Alamo; A Romance of the Alps; The Bankhurst Mystery; The Opal Pin; The Decoy; The Gambler of the West. **1916** The Swan's Love ; The Telephone Girl and the Lady; The Conscience of Hassan Bey; Intolerance; The Heiress at Coffee Dan's; Iola's Promise. **1917** Nina the Flower Girl; Big Timber; Aladdin and His Wonderful Lamp. **1918** When A Girl Loves. **1919** The Fall of Babylon.

PAIA, JOHN
Born: 1908, Hawaii. Died: Oct. 24, 1954, Los Angeles, Calif. Screen actor.

PAIGE, MABEL
Born: 1880, New York, N.Y. Died: Feb. 8, 1954, Van Nuys, Calif. Stage and screen actress.

Appeared in: **1915** Caught with the Goods; Flossie's Daring Loyalty; The Flesh Agent; Shoddy, The Tailor; He Couldn't Explain; Mixed Flats; Dog-Gone-Luck; The Wayville Slumber Party; That Brute. **1916** It Happened in Pikesville. **1942** Lucky Jordan, My Heart Belongs to Daddy; Girl's Town. **1943** Young and Willing; True to Life; Happy Go Lucky; Star Spangled Rhythm; The Crystal Ball; The Good Fellows; The Prodigal's Mother. **1944** Someone to Remember; National Barn Dance; Fun Time; Can't Help Singing; You Can't Return Love. **1945** Kitty; She Wouldn't Say Yes; Out of This World; Dangerous Partners; Murder, He Says. **1946** Behind Green Lights; Nocturne. **1947** Johnny O'Clock; Her Husband's Affairs; Beat the Band. **1948** If You Knew Susie; Johnny Belinda; Hollow Triumph; The Mating of Millie; Half Past Midnight; Canon City. **1949** Roseanna McCoy. **1950** The Petty Girl; Edge of Doom. **1952** The Sniper. **1953** Houdini.

PAIGE, PATSY. *See* PATTI BRILL

PAIGE, RAYMOND
Born: 1900, Wausau, Wis. Died: Aug. 7, 1965, Larchmont, N.Y. Screen, stage, radio actor and musical conductor.

Appeared in: **1937** Hollywood Hotel. **1938** Hawaii Calls.

PAIVA, NESTOR
Born: June 30, 1905, Fresno, Calif. Died: Sept. 9, 1966, Sherman Oaks, Calif. Screen, stage, television and radio actor. Entered films in 1937.

Appeared in: **1938** Ride a Crooked Mile; Prison Trail. **1939** Beau Geste; Bachelor Mother; The Magnificent Fraud. **1940** Dark Streets of Cairo; The Primrose Path; Northwest Mounted Police; Arise, My Love; The Marines Fly High. **1941** Hold Back the Dawn; The Kid from Kansas; Tall, Dark and Handsome; Johnny Eager; Hold That Ghost. **1942** Fly by Night; The Girl from Alaska; Broadway; Timber; Reap the Wild Wind; Road to Morocco; The Hard Way; Flying Tigers. **1943** Rhythm of the Islands; The Dancing Masters; The Desert Song; The Crystal Ball; Song of Bernadette; Pittsburgh. **1944** The Falcon in Mexico; The Purple Heart. **1945** Along the Navajo Trail; A Medal for Benny; The Southerner; Salome, Where She Danced; Nob Hill; Fear; A Thousand and One Nights. **1946** Badman's Territory; Sensation Hunters; The Last Crooked Mile; Road to Utopia; Humoresque. **1947** Ramrod; Carnival in Costa Rica; Shoot to Kill; A Likely Story; Robin Hood of Monterey; Lone Wolf in Mexico; Road to Rio. **1948** Mr. Reckless; Adventures of Casanova; Mr. Blandings Builds His Dream House; The Paleface; Angels' Alley. **1949** Bride of Vengeance; Alias Nick Beal; Oh, You Beautiful Doll; The Inspector General; Mighty Joe Young; Follow Me Quietly. **1950** Joan of Arc; Young Man with a Horn. **1951** Flame of Stamboul; The Great Caruso; Millionaire for Christy; The Lady Pays Off; Double Dynamite; Jim Thorpe—All American. **1952** The Fabulous Senorita; South Pacific Trail; Phone Call from a Stranger; Five Fingers; Mara Maru. **1953** The Bandits of Corsica; The Killer Cop; Call Me Madam; Prisoners of the Casbah; Killer Ape. **1954** The Cowboy; Jivaro; Casanova's Big Night; Thunder Pass; The Desperado; Four Guns to the Border; The Creature from the Black Lagoon. **1955** New York Confidential; Revenge of the Creature; Tarantula; Hell on Frisco Bay. **1956** The Mole People; Ride the High Iron; Scandal, Incorporated; Comanche. **1957** Guns of Fort Petticoat; 10,000 Bedrooms; Les Girls. **1958** The Deep Six; The Lady Takes a Flyer; Outcasts of the City; The Left-Handed Gun; The Case against Brooklyn. **1959** Pier 5, Havana; The Nine Lives of Elfego Baca. **1960** Vice Raid; The Purple Gang; Can-Can. **1961** Frontier Uprising. **1962** The Three Stooges in Orbit; Girls! Girls! Girls!; The Four Horsemen of the Apocalypse; The Martians; The Wild Westerners. **1963** Ballad of a Gunfighter; California. **1964** Madmen of Mandoras. **1966** Let's Kill Uncle; Jesse James Meets Frankenstein's Daughter. **1967** The Spirit is Willing.

PAL
Born: 1915. Died: Nov. 1929, Tujunga, Calif. Screen animal performer (bull terrier). Father of "Petey" (dec. 1930). Entered films in 1921 and appeared in "Pal Comedies" made by Century Film Company.

PALLANTE, ALADDIN. *See* ALADDIN

PALLENBERG, MAX
Born: 1877, Vienna, Austria. Died: 1934, near Karlovy Vary, Czechoslovakia. (plane crash). Stage and screen actor. Married to operetta star Fritzy Massary (dec. 1969).

Appeared in: **1931** Der Brave Suender (The Upright Sinners—US 1933).

PALLETTE, EUGENE
Born: July 8, 1889, Winfield, Kan. Died: Sept. 3, 1954, Los Angeles, Calif. Stage and screen actor.

Appeared in: **1912** American Film Mfg. Co. films. **1913** The Tattooed Arm. **1916** Intolerance. **1919** Fair and Warmer. **1920** Parlor, Bedroom and Bath; Alias Jimmy Valentine. **1921** Fine Feathers; The Three Musketeers. **1922** Two Kinds of Women; Without Compromise. **1923** Hell's Hole; A Man's Man; To the Last Man; North of Hudson Bay. **1924** The Cyclone Rider; The Wolf Man; Wandering Husbands. **1925** The Light of Western Stars; Without Mercy. **1926** Desert Valley; The Fighting Edge; Mantrap; Rocking Moon; Whispering Canyon; Whispering Smith. **1927** Chicago; Moulders of Men; plus 12 Roach shorts including: Sugar Daddies; The Second Hundred Years; Battle of the Century. **1928** Don't be Jealous (short); The Good-Bye Kiss; Lights of New York; His Private Life; How's Your Stock? (short); Out of the Ruins; The Red Mark. **1929** The Canary Murder Case; The Dummy; The Greene Murder Case; The Love Parade; The Studio Murder Mystery; The Virginian; Pointed Heels. **1930** The Benson Murder Case; The Border Legion; Men Are Like That; Slightly Scarlet; Let's Go Native; The Santa Fe Trail; Follow Thru; The Sea God; Paramount on Parade; The Kibitzer; Sea Legs; Playboy of Paris. **1931** Fighting Caravans; Gun Smoke; Dude Ranch; The Adventures of Huckleberry Finn; It Pays to Advertise; Girls about Town. **1932** Tom Brown of Culver; Shanghai Express; Off His Base (short); Thunder Below; Strangers of the Evening; The Night Mayor; Wild Girl; The Half-Naked Truth; A Hocky Hick (short); Dancers in the Dark; Phantom Fame; Pig Boat; Slippery Pearls (short). **1933** Made on Broadway; Hell Below; Storm at Daybreak; Shanghai Madness; Mr. Skitch; The Kennel Murder Case; From Headquarters. **1934** Cross Country Cruise; I've Got Your Number; Strictly Dynamite; Friends of Mr. Sweeney; The Dragon Murder Case; Caravan; One Exciting Adventure. **1935** Bordertown; All the King's Horses; Baby Face Harrington; Black Sheep; Steamboat 'Round the Bend. **1936** Dishonour Bright; Easy to Take; The Ghost Goes West; The Golden Arrow; My Man Godfrey; The Luckiest Girl in the World; Stowaway. **1937** Clarence; The Crime Nobody Saw; Topper; She Had to Eat; One Hundred Men and a Girl; Song of the City. **1938** The Adventures of Robin Hood; There Goes My Heart. **1939** Wife, Husband and Friend; First Love; Mr. Smith Goes to Washington. **1940** It's a Date; Sandy Is a Lady;

Young Tom Edison; A Little Bit of Heaven; He Stayed for Breakfast; The Mark of Zorro. **1941** Ride, Kelly, Ride; The Bride Came C.O.D.; World Premiere; The Lady Eve; Unfinished Business; Appointment for Love; Swamp Water. **1942** Are Husbands Necessary?; Almost Married; The Forest Rangers; Silver Queen; Lady in a Jam; The Big Street; Tales of Manhattan; The Male Animal. **1943** Slightly Dangerous; It Ain't Hay; The Kansan; Heaven Can Wait; The Gang's All Here. **1944** Laramie Trail; Pin-Up Girl; Sensations of 1945; Step Lively; In the Meantime, Darling; Lake Placid Serenade; Heavenly Days; Manhattan Serenade. **1945** The Cheaters. **1946** In Old Sacramento; Suspense. **1948** Silver River.

PALMER, DAWSON
Born: 1937. Died: Sept. 10, 1972, Los Angeles, Calif. (auto accident). Stage and screen actor.

PALMER, EFFIE
Died: Aug. 19, 1942, New York, N.Y. Screen, stage and radio actress.

Appeared in: **1931** Huckleberry Finn. **1932** Way Back Home (film and radio versions).

PALMER, PATRICIA (aka MARGARET GIBSON)
Born: Sept. 14, 1895, Colorado Springs, Colo. Died: Oct. 21, 1964, Hollywood, Calif. Stage and screen actress.

Appeared in: **1916** Island of Desire; Public Approval. **1917** Local Color. **1918** The Rose of Wolfville. **1919** The Canyon Hold-Up; The Money Corporal; Sand. **1920** The Fourteenth Man. **1921** Greater than Love; Things Men Do. **1922** Across the Border; The Cowboy King; The Cowboy and the Lady; Rounding Up the Law. **1923** To the Ladies; Mr. Billings Spends His Dime; The Web of the Law. **1924** Hold Your Breath; A Pair of Hellions. **1925** The Part Time Wife; Who's Your Friend?; Without Mercy. **1927** King of Kings; Naughty Nanette. **1929** The Little Savage.

PALMESE, ROSE MARIE
Born: 1871. Died: Mar. 21, 1953, Altadena, Calif. Screen actress.

PALTENGHI, DAVID
Born: 1919, Christchurch, England. Died: 1961, Windsor, England. Screen actor, film director, ballet dancer and choreographer.

Appeared in: **1949** The Queen of Spades. **1954** The Black Knight.

PAM, ANITA
Died: Apr. 15, 1973. Stage and screen actress. Married to actor Hugh Herbert (dec. 1952).

PANGBORN, FRANKLIN
Born: 1894, Newark, N.J. Died: July 20, 1958, Santa Monica, Calif. Screen, stage and television actor.

Appeared in: **1926** Exit Smiling. **1927** The Girl in the Pullman; The Cradle Snatchers; Finger Prints; Getting Gertie's Garter; The Night Bride; The Rejuvenation of Aunt Mary. **1928** On Trial; Blonde for a Night; My Friend from India. **1929** The Sap; The Crazy Nut; Watch Out; Lady of the Pavements. **1930** Cheer up and Smile; Her Man; A Lady Surrenders; Not So Dumb; plus the following shorts: The Doctor's Wife; Reno or Bust; Poor Aubrey; The Chumps; Who's the Boss? **1931** A Woman of Experience; Rough House Rhythm (short). **1932** A Fool's Advice; plus the following shorts: The Giddy Age; Torchy Turns the Trick; Torchy's Nightcap; Torchy's Vocation; What Price Taxi?; The Candid Camera; Torchy Rolls His Own. **1933** Design for Living; Flying Down to Rio; International House; Headline Shooters; The Important Witness; Only Yesterday; Professional Sweetheart; plus the following shorts: Art in the Raw; Torchy's Kitty Coup; Wild Poses. **1934** Imitation of Life; King Kelly of the U.S.A.; College Rhythm; Manhattan Love Song; Many Happy Returns; Strictly Dynamite; That's Gratitude; Tomorrow's Children; Unknown Blonde; Young and Beautiful; Cockeyed Cavaliers; Stand up and Cheer. **1935** Eight Bells; Headline Woman; A Thousand Dollars a Minute; She Couldn't Take It; Tomorrow's Youth; Ye Old Saw Mill (short). **1936** Don't Gamble with Love; Doughnuts and Society; Hats Off; The Luckiest Girl in the World; Mr. Deeds Goes to Town; The Mandarin Mystery; My Man Godfrey; Tango; To Mary with Love. **1937** Danger, Love at Work; Dangerous Number; High Hat; Easy Living; The Lady Escapes; Dangerous Holiday; The Life of the Party; Living on Love; She's Dangerous; She Had to Eat; Stage Door; A Star is Born; Step Lively, Jeeves; Swing High, Swing Low; Thrill of a Lifetime; Turn Off the Moon; Vivacious Lady; All over Town; When Love is Young; Hotel Haywire; It Happened in Hollywood; Bad Housekeeping (short). **1938** Love on Toast; Mad about Music; Rebecca of Sunnybrook Farm; She Married an Artist; Meet the Mayor; Four's a Crowd; Topper Takes a Trip; Three Blind Mice; Always Goodbye; Just around the Corner; The Joy of Living; Carefree; Bluebeard's Eighth Wife; Dr. Rhythm. **1939** Broadway Serenade; Fifth Avenue Girl; The Girl Downstairs. **1940** The Bank Dick; Public Deb No. 1; Spring Parade; Turnabout; The Villain Still Pursued Her; The Hit Parade of 1941; Christmas in July. **1941** Bachelor Daddy; A Girl, a Guy and a Gob; The Flame of New Orleans; Mr. District Attorney in the Carter Case; Never Give a Sucker an Even Break; Obliging Young Lady; Sandy Steps Out; Sullivan's Travels;

Tillie the Toiler; Week-End for Three; Where Did You Get That Girl? **1942** Call Out the Marines; George Washington Slept Here; Moonlight Masquerade; The Palm Beach Story; Now Voyager; What's Cooking? **1943** His Butler's Sister; Crazy House; Holy Matrimony; Reveille with Beverly; Two Weeks to Live; Stage Door Canteen; Strictly in the Groove; Honeymoon Lodge; Slick Chick. **1944** The Great Moment; My Best Gal; Reckless Age; Hail the Conquering Hero. **1945** Hollywood and Vine; The Horn Blows at Midnight; See My Lawyer; You Came Along; Tell It to a Star. **1946** Two Guys from Milwaukee; Lover Come Back. **1947** I'll Be Yours; Calendar Girl; Mad Wednesday. **1948** Romance on the High Seas. **1949** My Dream Is Yours; Down Memory Lane. **1950** Her Wonderful Lie. **1957** Oh, Men! Oh, Women!; The Story of Mankind.

PANNACI, CHARLES
Born: 1904. Died: Mar. 1927, Long Branch, N.J. (pneumonia). Screen actor.

PANTHULU, B. R.
Born: 1910, India. Died: Oct. 8, 1974, Bangalore, India. Screen, stage actor, film director and producer.

Appeared in: **1935** Samsara Nowka (film debut). **1960** Veerapandia Kattabomman.

PANZER, PAUL
Born: approx. 1867. Died: Apr. 11, 1937, New York, N.Y. (heart trouble). Screen, stage actor and circus performer. Do not confuse with actor Paul W. Panzer (dec. 1958).

PANZER, PAUL WOLFGANG (Paul Panzerbeiter)
Born: 1872, Wurtzberg, Bavaria. Died: Aug. 16, 1958, Hollywood, Calif. Stage and screen actor. Entered films with Vitagraph.

Appeared in: **1904** Stolen by Gypsies (film debut). **1908** Romeo and Juliet. **1913** The Cheapest Way. **1914** The Perils of Pauline (serial); Exploits of Elaine (serial). **1917** Jimmy Dale; Alias the Grey Seal (serial). **1918** The House of Hate (serial). **1919** The Masked Rider. **1920** The Mystery Mind (serial). **1922** The Bootleggers; The Mohican's Daughter; When Knighthood Was in Flower. **1923** The Enemies of Women; Big Brother; Unseeing Eyes; Jacqueline of Blazing Barriers; Mighty Lak' a Rose; Under the Red Robe. **1924** A Son of the Sahara; Wages of Virtue; Monsieur Beaucaire; Week-End Husbands. **1925** Thunder Mountain; Too Many Kisses; The Fool; The Shock Punch; The Best Bad Man; East Lynne; Greater Than a Crown; The Mad Marriage. **1926** The Ancient Mariner; Siberia; The Johnstown Flood; Black Paradise; The Dixie Merchant; The High Flyer; 30 Below Zero. **1927** Sally in Our Alley; Hawk of the Hills (serial); The Girl from Chicago; Wolf's Clothing; Brass Knuckles. **1928** Glorious Betsy; Rinty of the Desert; The Candy Kid; City of Purple Dreams; George Washington Cohen. **1929** Hawk of the Hills (feature of 1927 serial); Redskin; The Black Book (serial). **1930** Der Tanz Geht Weiter. **1931** The Montana Kid; First Aid; Cavalier of the West. **1933** A Bedtime Story. **1934** Bolera; The Mighty Barnum; **1936** Cain and Mabel; **1938** Penrod's Double Trouble; **1939** Beasts of Berlin; **1942** Casablanca; **1943** Action in the North Atlantic. **1944** The Adventures of Mark Twain. **1945** Hotel Berlin; Roughly Speaking. **1947** The Perils of Pauline.

PAPE, EDWARD LIONEL
Born: 1867. Died: Oct. 24, 1944, Woodland Hills, Calif. Stage and screen actor.

Appeared in: **1921** Nobody. **1935** The Man Who Broke the Bank at Monte Carlo. **1936** Mary of Scotland; The White Legion; Beloved Enemy. **1937** The King and the Chorus Girl; The Prince and the Pauper; Wee Willie Winkie; Angel. **1938** Big Broadcast of 1938; Outside of Paradise; Bluebeard's Eighth Wife; Booloo; The Young in Heart. **1939** Love Affair; Rulers of the Sea; Midnight; Fifth Avenue Girl; Drums along the Mohawk. **1940** Raffles; Tin Pan Alley; Zanzibar; The Philadelphia Story; Congo Maisie; The Long Voyage Home; Arise My Love. **1941** Hudson's Bay; Scotland Yard; Charley's Aunt; How Green Was My Valley. **1942** Almost Married.

PARAIN, BRICE
Born: 1897, France. Died: 1971, France. Philosopher, writer and screen actor.

Appeared in: **1963** Vivre sa Vie (To Live One's Life aka My Life to Live—US).

PARDAVE, JOAQUIN
Born: 1901, Guanajuato, Mexico. Died: July 10, 1955, Mexico City, Mexico. Screen actor, film director and composer.

Appeared in: **1938** La Zandunga; Los Millones de Chaflan; Cancion del Alma (Song of the Soul); Tierra Brava; Mi Candidato (My Candidate); Bajo el Cielo de Mexico (Beneath the Sky of Mexico); El Senor Alcade (The Mayor); **1939** La Tia de las Muchachas (The Girls' Aunt). **1940** Caballo a Caballo (Horse for Horse); Luna Criolla (Creole Moon); En un Burro Tres Gaturros (Three Rustics on One Donkey); Vivire Otra Vez (I Shall Live Again). **1943** Guadalajara.

PARDAVE, JOSE
Born: 1902, Mexico. Died: May 26, 1970, Mexico City, Mexico. Screen actor.

PARDEE, C. W. "DOC"

Born: 1885. Died: July 17, 1975, Glendale, Ariz. Screen actor, rodeo performer and trainer.

Appeared in: **1925** The Vanishing American. **1933** Wild Horse Mesa. **1939** The Gentleman from Arizona.

PARERA, GRACE MOORE. *See* GRACE MOORE

PARIS, MANUEL (Manuel R. Conesa)

Born: July 27, 1894, Spain. Died: Nov. 19, 1959, Woodland Hills, Calif. (congestive heart failure). Screen actor.

Appeared in: **1935** Odio. **1948** French Leave. **1951** Havana Rose.

PARK, CUSTER B.

Born: 1900. Died: Sept. 25, 1955, Hollywood, Calif. Screen actor and stuntman. Entered films approx. 1927.

Appeared in: **1939** Gone with the Wind. **1954** Vera Cruz.

PARK, FLORENCE OIE CHAN

Born: 1886. Died: Feb. 5, 1967, Calif. Screen actress. Married to technical director Ed Park (dec.) and mother of actresses Bo-Ling and Bo-Ching Park.

PARKE, MACDONALD

Born: 1892. Died: July 1960, London, England. Screen, stage and television actor.

Appeared in: **1939** Shipyard Sally. **1943** Candlelight in Algeria (US 1944). **1947** Teheran (aka The Plot to Kill Roosevelt—US). **1948** No Orchids for Miss Blandish; The Fool and the Princess. **1950** Dangerous Assignment. **1951** A Tale of Five Cities (aka A Tale of Five Women—US 1952). **1952** Penny Princess (US 1953); Babes in Bagdad; Saturday Island (aka Island of Desire—US). **1953** The Man Who Watched Trains Go By (aka Paris Express—US); Is Your Honeymoon Really Necessary? **1954** The Good Die Young (US 1955). **1955** Summertime. **1956** The March Hare. **1957** Beyond Mombasa. **1958** I Was Monty's Double (aka Hell, Heaven or Hoboken). **1959** The Mouse That Roared; A Touch of Larceny (US 1960); The Battle of the Sexes (US 1960). **1960** Never Take Sweets from a Stranger (aka Never Take Candy from a Stranger—US 1961).

PARKE, WILLIAM, SR.

Born: 1873. Died: July 28, 1941, New York, N.Y. (heart attack). Screen, stage actor and stage and film director.

Appeared in: **1922** Tailor-Made Man. **1923** The Hunchback of Notre Dame.

PARKER, ADELE (Adele Von Ohl)

Born: 1885, Plainsfield, N.J. Died: Jan. 20, 1966, Cleveland, Ohio. Screen, vaudeville actress, stuntwoman and rodeo, circus performer. Appeared in silent films.

PARKER, BARNETT (William Barnett Parker)

Born: Sept. 11, 1886, Batley, Yorkshire, England. Died: Aug. 5, 1941, Los Angeles, Calif. Stage and screen actor.

Appeared in: **1916** Prudence the Pirate. **1936** The President's Mystery; We Who Are about to Die; Born to Dance. **1937** Personal Property; Dangerous Number; The Last of Mrs. Cheyney; Espionage; Live, Love and Learn; Married before Breakfast; The Emperor's Candlesticks; Broadway Melody of 1938; Double Wedding; Navy Blue and Gold; Wake Up and Live. **1938** Love Is a Headache; Hold That Kiss; Marie Antoinette; Listen Darling; The Girl Downstairs; Sally, Irene and Mary; Ready, Willing and Able. **1939** Babes in Arms; At the Circus. **1940** He Married His Wife; La Conga Nights; Hit Parade of 1941; Love Thy Neighbor; One Night in the Tropics. **1941** Tall, Dark and Handsome; A Man Betrayed; The Reluctant Dragon. **1942** New Wine.

PARKER, CECIL

Born: Sept. 3, 1897, Hastings, Sussex, England. Died: Apr. 21, 1971, Brighton, England. Screen, stage and television actor.

Appeared in: **1929** The Woman in White. **1933** A Cuckoo in the Nest; The Golden Cage. **1934** Nine Forty-Five; The Blue Squadron; Flat No. 3; The Silver Spoon; Dirty Work; Little Friend; The Office Wife; Lady in Danger. **1935** Crime Unlimited; Me and Marlborough; Foreign Affaires; Her Last Affaire. **1936** Men of Yesterday; The Man Who Changed His Mind (aka The Man Who Lived Again—US); Jack of All Trades (aka The Two of Us—US 1937); Dishonour Bright. **1937** Dark Journey; Storm in a Teacup. **1938** Bank Holiday (aka Three on a Weekend—US); Housemaster (US 1939); The Lady Vanishes; The Citadel; Old Iron. **1939** The Stars Look Down (US 1941); Sons of the Sea; The Spider; She Couldn't Say No. **1940** Two for Danger; Under Your Hat. **1941** The Saint's Vacation; Dangerous Moonlight (aka Suicide Squadron—US 1942); Ships with Wings (US 1942). **1946** Caesar and Cleopatra; The Magic Bow (US 1947). **1947** Hungry Hill; The Woman in the Hall (US 1949); Captain Boycott. **1948** The First Gentleman (aka Affairs of a Rogue—US 1949); The Weaker Sex (US 1949); Quartet (US 1949). **1949** Dear Mr. Prohack (US 1950); Under Capricorn; The Chiltern Hundreds (aka The

Amazing Mr. Beecham—US). **1950** Tony Draws a Horse (US 1951). **1951** The Man in the White Suit (US 1952); The Magic Box (US 1952). **1952** His Excellency (US 1956); I Believe in You (US 1953). **1953** Isn't Life Wonderful! **1954** Father Brown (aka The Detective—US); For Better, For Worse (aka Cocktails in the Kitchen—US 1955). **1955** The Constant Husband; The Ladykillers. **1956** The Court Jester; It's Great to be Young (US 1958); 23 Paces to Baker Street. **1957** True as Turtle; The Admirable Crichton (aka Paradise Lagoon—US). **1958** A Tale of Two Cities; Happy is the Bride (US 1959); Indiscreet; I was Monty's Double (aka Hell, Heaven or Hoboken). **1959** The Wreck of the Mary Deare; The Night We Dropped a Clanger (aka Make Mine a Double—US 1961); The Navy Lark. **1960** A French Mistress; The Pure Hell of St. Trinian's (US 1961); Follow That Horse! (US 1961); Under Ten Flags. **1961** Swiss Family Robinson; Petticoat Pirates; On the Fiddle (aka Operation Snafu—US 1965; War Head; Operation Warhead). **1962** Vengeance (aka The Brain—US 1964); The Iron Maiden (aka The Swingin' Maiden—US 1963); The Amorous Prawn (aka The Playgirl and the War Minister—US 1963). **1963** Heavens Above!; The Comedy Man. **1964** Guns at Batasi; Carry On, Jack. **1965** The Amorous Adventures of Moll Flanders; A Study in Terror (aka Fog—US 1966). **1966** Circus of Fear (aka Psycho-Circus—US 1967); Lady L; A Man Could Get Killed. **1967** The Magnificent Two. **1969** Oh! What a Lovely War.

PARKER, EDWIN (aka ED PARKER and EDDIE PARKER)

Born: Dec. 12, 1900, Minn. Died: Jan. 20, 1960, Sherman Oaks, Calif. (heart attack). Screen, television actor and stuntman.

Appeared in: **1932** First in War. **1934** Lucky Texan; The Star Packer; Trail Beyond. **1935** Courageous Avenger. **1936** Flash Gordon (serial); Our Relations; On the Wrong Trek. **1937** Rhythm in the Clouds. **1938** Flash Gordon's Trip to Mars (serial). **1939** Son of Frankenstein; Buck Rogers (serial); The Lone Ranger Rides Again (serial); Danger Flight. **1940** Flash Gordon Conquers the Universe (serial). **1941** Hellzapoppin. **1942** The Spoilers; Ghost of Frankenstein; The Mummy's Tomb. **1943** The Masked Marvel (serial); Frankenstein Meets the Wolfman; Pistol Packin' Mamma. **1944** The Mummy's Ghost; The Tiger Woman (serial); Haunted Harbor (serial). **1945** The Mummy's Curse; The Phantom Rider; The Phantom Speaks; Ding Dong Williams; Escape in the Fog; The Enchanted Cottage; Manhunt of Mystery Island; The Monster and the Ape; The Body Snatcher; The Adventures of Rusty. **1946** King of the Forest Rangers (serial); My Pal Trigger; The Shadow Returns; The Return of Rusty; The Last Crooked Hill; Daughter of Don Q (serial); Chick Carter, Detective (serial); Days of Buffalo Bill; The Inner Circle; South of the Chisholm Trail; Raiders of the South; Trigger Fingers; Silver Range. **1947** Silver River; My Wild Irish Rose; Dangers of the Canadian Mounted; Son of Zorro (serial); Jack Armstrong (serial); Riders of the Lone Star; The Vigilante (serial); Jesse James Rides Again (serial); Trailing Danger; The Millerson Case; Shadow Valley; Adventures of Don Coyote. **1948** The Strawberry Roan; Whirlwind Raiders; Flaxy Martin; Knock on Any Door; The Fighting Ranger; An Act of Murder; One Touch of Venus; The Tioga Kid; The Hawk of Powder River. **1949** Ghost of Zorro (serial); Mighty Joe Young; Mule Train; Kong of the Rocketmen (serial); Law of the West; Bruce Gentry, Daredevil of the Skies (serial); Batman and Robin (serial); Range Justice. **1950** Louisa; Convicted; Texas Rangers; Daredevils of the West; Radar Patrol vs. Spy King (serial); The Invisible Monster; Abbott and Costello Meet the Mummy; The Good Humor Man; One Too Many. **1951** The Big Gusher; Al Jennings of Oklahoma; The Strange Door; The Barefoot Mailman; Government Agents vs. Phantom Legion (serial); Paula; My Six Convicts; Cripple Creek. **1952** The Raiders; The Racket; Barbed Wire; The Hawk of Wild River; The Texas Man; Winning of the West; Scarlet Angel. **1953** Law and Order; The Man from the Alamo; The Lone Hand; Abbott and Costello Meet Dr. Jekyll and Mr. Hyde; All Ashore. **1954** The Far Country; Naked Alibi; Rear Window; Yankee Pasha; Son of Sinbad. **1955** This Island Earth; Smoke Signal; The Vagabond King; Abbott and Costello Meet the Mummy. **1956** The Mole People; Around the World in 80 Days; Ransom; Bride of the Monster; Tarantula; Red Sundown; Over-Exposed; Reprisal; Storm Center. **1958** Monster on the Campus; Live Fast, Die Young. **1959** Curse of the Undead. **1960** Spartacus.

PARKER, FRANK "PINKY"

Born: 1891. Died: June 13, 1962, Hollywood, Calif. (heart attack). Screen, stage actor and singer.

Appeared in: **1934** Transatlantic Merry-Go-Round. **1935** Sweet Surrender; a Vitaphone short.

PARKER, LEW

Born: Oct. 28, 1907. Died: Oct. 27, 1972, New York, N.Y. (cancer). Screen, stage, vaudeville, radio and television actor. Married to actress Betty Kean who appeared with him in vaudeville.

Appeared in: **1937** A Universal short. **1948** Are You With It? **1958** Country Music Holiday.

PARKER, MARY

Born: 1915, Fort Worth, Tex. Died: June 1, 1966, Beverly Hills, Calif. Stage and screen actress.

Appeared in: **1938** Artists and Models. **1939** St. Louis Blues. **1944** Lady in the

Dark; Music for Millions. **1952** Lure of the Wilderness. **1955** Third Party Rich (aka Deadly Game—US).

PARKER, MURRAY
Born: 1896. Died: Oct. 18, 1965, Hollywood, Calif. (heart attack). Screen, television and vaudeville actor. He performed usually under name of "Uncle Murray."

PARKER, SETH. *See* PHILLIPS H. LORD

PARKER, VIVIEN
Born: 1897. Died: Feb. 2, 1974, Bronx, N.Y. (stroke). Screen actress. Married to musician Walter R. Thalin (dec.). Appeared in silent films.

PARKHURST, FRANCES
Died: Dec. 31, 1969, Caldwell, N.J. Screen actress.

Appeared in: **1926** Men of Steel.

PARKINGTON, BEULAH
Died: Nov. 7, 1958, Hollywood, Calif. (heart condition). Screen actress. Entered films approx. 1928. One of the founders of Screen Extra's Guild.

Appeared in: **1950** My Blue Heaven.

PARKS, LARRY (Samuel Klausman)
Born: Dec. 3, 1914, Olathe, Kans. Died: Apr. 13, 1975, Studio City, Calif. (heart attack). Screen, stage and television actor. Married to actress Betty Garrett. Nominated for 1956 Academy Award as Best Actor in The Jolson Story.

Appeared in: **1941** Mystery Ship; Harmon of Michigan. **1942** Blondie Goes to College; Harvard—Here I Come; The Boogie Man Will Get You; Atlantic Convoy; Canal Zone; Three Girls About Town; You Belong to Me; Sing for Your Supper; Flight Lieutenant; Submarine Raider; Honolulu Lu; Hello Annapolis; You Were Never Lovelier; A Man's World. **1943** Power of the Press; The Deerslayer; Destroyer; Reveille with Beverly. **1944** She's a Sweetheart; The Racket Man; The Black Parachute; Stars on Parade; Hey Rookie. **1945** Counter-Attack; Sergeant Mike; Jealousy. **1946** Renegades; The Jolson Story. **1947** Down to Earth; The Swordsman. **1948** Gallant Blade. **1949** Jolson Sings Again. **1950** Emergency Wedding. **1952** Love Is Better than Ever. **1955** Tiger by the Tail (aka Crossup—US 1958). **1962** Freud.

"PARKYAKARKUS" (Harry Einstein, aka HARRY PARKE)
Born: 1904, Boston, Mass. Died: Nov. 24, 1958, Los Angeles, Calif. (heart attack). Screen, stage, television and radio actor.

Appeared in: **1936** Strike Me Pink. **1937** New Faces of 1937; The Life of the Party. **1938** Night Spot; She's Got Everything. **1940** Glamour Boy. **1942** A Yank in Libya; The Yanks Are Coming. **1944** Sweethearts of the U.S.A.; Earl Carroll's Vanities; Out of This World; Movie Pests (short); Badminton (short).

PARLO, DITA (Gerthe Gerda Kornstaedt)
Born: 1907, Stettin, Germany. Died: Dec. 1971, Paris, France. Stage and screen actress.

Appeared in: **1928** Die Dame mit den Maske; Homecoming. **1929** Hungarian Rhapsody. **1930** Hearts Melody (aka Melody of Hearts); Menschen hinter Gettern. **1931** Honor of the Family. **1932** Secrets of the Orient. **1933** Mr. Broadway. **1934** L'Atalante (US 1947). **1936** The Mystic Mountain; Mademoiselle Docteur. **1937** La Grande Illusion (The Grand Illusion—US 1938); Realization d'art Cinematographique. **1938** The Courier of Lyons. **1940** Ultimatum. **1948** Street of Shadow. **1950** Justice est Faite (Justice is Done). **1956** Quand le Soleil Montera.

PARNELL, JAMES
Born: 1923. Died: Dec. 27, 1961, Hollywood, Calif. Screen, stage and television actor. Son of actor Emory Parnell.

Appeared in: **1951** G.I. Jane. **1952** Yankee Buccaneer; No Room for the Groom. **1953** War Paint. **1954** White Christmas; The Looters. **1955** Crime against Joe; You're Never Too Young. **1956** The Birds and the Bees; Running Target. **1957** War Drums; Outlaw's Son. **1960** Walking Target. **1961** Gun Fight. **1962** The Clown and the Kid; Incident in an Alley.

PARRAVICINI, FLORENCIO
Born: 1874, South America. Died: Mar. 25, 1941, Buenos Aires, Argentina (suicide following long illness). Screen, stage actor, stage producer and screenwriter.

Appeared in: **1937** Melgarejo. **1938** Que Tiempos Aquellos (Those Were the Days). **1939** La Vida es un Tango (Life Is a Tango).

PARRISH, HELEN
Born: Mar. 12, 1924, Columbus, Ga. Died: Feb. 22, 1959, Hollywood, Calif. Screen and television actress. Appeared in "Our Gang" series and "Smithy" comedies from 1927–1929.

Appeared in: **1927** Babe comes Home (film debut). **1929** Words and Music. **1930** His First Command; The Big Trail. **1931** Cimarron; Seed; X Marks the Spot. **1932** When a Feller Needs a Friend. **1934** There's Always Tomorrow. **1935** A Dog of Flanders; Straight from the Heart. **1936** Make Way for a Lady; Three Smart Girls. **1938** Mad about Music; Little Tough Guy; Little Tough Guy in Society. **1939** Three Smart Girls Grow Up; First Love; Winter Carnival. **1940** I'm Nobody's Sweetheart Now; You'll Find Out. **1941** Where Did You Get That Girl?; Six Lessons from Madame La Zonga; Too Many Blondes. **1942** They All Kissed the Bride; In Old California; X Marks the Spot (and 1931 version); Tough as They Come. **1943** Cinderella Swings It; The Mystery of the 13th Guest. **1944** They Live in Fear; Meet Miss Bobby-Socks. **1945** Let's Go Steady; A Thousand and One Nights. **1948** Trouble Makers. **1949** The Wolf Hunters; Quick on the Trigger.

PARROTT, CHARLES. *See* CHARLEY CHASE

PARROTT, JAMES (aka POLL PARROTT)
Born: 1892, Baltimore, Md. Died: May 10, 1939, Hollywood, Calif. (heart attack). Screen actor, film director, producer and screenwriter. Entered films for Pathe under name of Poll Parrott in 1918. Brother of actor Charlie Chase (dec. 1940).

Appeared in: **1921** Big Town Ideas.

PARRY, PAUL
Born: 1908. Died: Dec. 4, 1966, Calif. Screen actor, film producer and photographer.

Appeared in: **1934** Servants' Entrance.

PARSON, CAROL
Died: Dec. 18, 1958, New York, N.Y. Stage and screen actress.

PARSONS, GRAM
Born: 1946. Died: Sept. 19, 1973. Screen actor and musician. Member of "The Byrds" group.

PARSONS, LOUELLA O. (Louella Oettinger)
Born: Aug. 6, 1881 (?), Freeport, Ill. Died: Dec. 9, 1972, Santa Monica, Calif. (generalized arteriosclerosis). Newspaper columnist, novelist, screenwriter, radio and screen actress. Mother of film producer Harriet Parsons.

Appeared in: **1937** Hollywood Hotel. **1946** Without Reservations. **1951** Starlift.

PARSONS, PERCY
Born: June 12, 1878, Louisville, Kentucky. Died: Oct. 3, 1944, England? Screen, stage and radio actor.

Appeared in: **1930** The Brat (aka The Nipper); Suspense; Beyond the Cities. **1931** Creeping Shadows (aka The Limping Man—US 1932). **1932** Strictly Business; Love on Wheels; The Frightened Lady (aka Criminal at Large—US 1933); Sleepless Nights. **1933** The Good Companions; Orders is Orders (US 1934); The Man from Toronto. **1934** Red Wagon (US 1935); Jew Suess (aka Power—US). **1936** King of the Damned; Twelve Good Men. **1937** Victoria the Great. **1938** The Citadel. **1941** Dangerous Moonlight (aka Suicide Squadron—US 1942); Hi Gang! **1942** Flying Fortress.

PARSONS, "SMILING BILLY" (William Parsons)
Born: Aug. 14, 1878, New York. Died: Sept. 29, 1919, Los Angeles, Calif. (diabetic coma). Screen actor, film producer and former president of National Film Corporation. Married to actress Billie Rhodes. Do not confuse with actor William E. Parsons.

PASHA, KALLA
Born: 1877, New York, N.Y. Died: June 10, 1933, Talmage, Calif. Stage and screen actor. Entered films with Mack Sennett.

Appeared in: **1921** Home Talent; A Small Town Idol. **1922** The Dictator; Thirty Days. **1923** Breaking into Society; Hollywood; A Million to Burn; Racing Hearts; Scaramouche; Ruggles of Red Gap. **1924** Yukon Jake. **1925** Heads Up. **1926** Don Juan's Three Nights; Rose of the Tenements; Silken Shackles. **1927** Wolf's Clothing; The Devil Dancer; The Dove. **1928** Tillie's Punctured Romance; West of Zanzibar. **1929** Seven Footprints to Satan; The Show of Shows.

PASOLINI, PIER PAOLA
Born: 1922, Bologna, Italy. Died: Nov, 1975, near Ostia, Italy (murdered—beaten). Film director, poet, novelist, screenwriter and screen actor.

Appeared in: **1960** Il Gobbo (aka The Hunchback of Rome—US 1963). **1971** The Decameron.

PASQUIER, CHARLES "BACH"
Born: 1881, France. Died: Nov. 19, 1953, Paris, France (heart attack). Screen, stage, radio and circus actor.

PATCH, WALLY (Walter Vinicombe)
Born: Sept. 26, 1888, London, England. Died: Oct. 27, 1970, London, England. Screen actor.

Appeared in: **1927** The Luck of the Navy; The King's Highway; Blighty (aka Apres la Guerre); Carry On! **1928** Guns of Loos; Shooting Star; Balaclava (aka Jaws of Hell—US 1931); Dr. Sin Fang (series); The Man in the Saddle (aka A Reckless Gamble); You Know What Sailors Are; Warned Off. **1929** Dick Turpin (series); High Treason. **1930** Kissing Cup's Race; Thread O'Scarlet; The Great Game. **1931** Never Trouble Trouble; The Great Gay Road; The Sport of Kings; Shadows; Tell England (aka The Battle of Gallipoli—US). **1932** Castle Sinister; Heroes of the Mine; Here's George. **1933** The Crime at Blossoms; Britannia of Billingsgate; Orders is Orders (US 1934); Tiger Bay; Channel Crossing (US 1934): Don Quixote; Trouble; Sorrell and Son; The Good Companions; Marooned. **1934** The Old Curiosity Shop (US 1935); The Scoop; Music Hall; The Perfect Flaw; What Happened to Harkness; Virginia's Husband; Badger's Green; Crazy People; A Glimpse of Paradise; Borrow a Million; The Man I Want; Passing Shadows; The Scotland Yard Mystery (aka The Living Dead—US); Those Were the Days; Lost Over London. **1935** His Majesty and Co.; Dandy Dick; Death on the Set (aka Murder on the Set—US 1936); That's My Uncle; Street Song; Off the Dole; Marry the Girl; The Half-Day Excursion; Where's George? (aka The Hope of His Side—US); Old Faithful; What the Parrot Saw; While Parents Sleep; Get Off My Foot; Once in a Blue Moon; The Public Life of Henry the Ninth. **1936** Ticket of Leave; On Top of the World; King of the Castle; Excuse My Glove; What the Puppy Said; Prison Breaker; A Touch of the Moon; Apron Fools; Luck of the Turf; Hail and Farewell; Busman's Holiday; The Scarab Murder Case; Not So Dusty; The Interrupted Honeymoon; The Man Who Could Work Miracles (US 1937); Men Are Not Gods (US 1937); You Must Get Married; A Wife or Two. **1937** The Inspector; The Price of Folly; The High Command; The Street Singer; Night Ride; Missing, Believed Married; Captain's Orders; The Sky's the Limit; Farewell Again (aka Troopship—US 1938); Doctor Syn; Holiday's End. **1938** Quiet Please; On Velvet; Night Alone; The Ware Case (US 1939); Pygmalion; Bank Holiday (aka Three on a Weekend—US); Owd Bob (aka To the Victor—US); Alf's Button Afloat; 13 Men and a Gun; Break the News (US 1941); Almost a Honeymoon. **1939** What Would You Do Chums?; Inspector Hornleigh; Home from Home; The Mind of Mr. Reeder (aka The Mysterious Mr. Reeder—US 1940); Poison Pen (US 1941); Down Our Alley; Inspector Hornleigh on Holiday; Hospital Hospitality; Sword of Honour. **1940** Return to Yesterday; Laugh It Off; Band Waggon; They Came by Night; Charley's (Big Hearted) Aunt; Two Smart Men; Old Mother Riley in Business; Henry Steps Out; Everything Okay (rerelease of On Top of the World—1936); Gasbags; Neutral Port; Pack Up Your Troubles. **1941** I Thank You; The Seventh Survivor; Gert and Daisy's Weekend; Once a Crook. **1942** Let the People Sing; Sabotage at Sea; We'll Smile Again; In Which We Serve. **1943** Jeannie; Women in Bondage; Get Cracking; The Butler's Dilemma; Strange to Relate; Death by Design. **1944** Up in Mabel's Room. **1945** Old Mother Riley at Home; I Didn't Do It; Don Chicago; Dumb Dora Discovers Tobacco. **1946** Appointment with Crime (US 1950); George in Civvy Street; Gaiety George (US 1948). **1947** The Ghosts of Berkeley Square; Green Fingers; Dusty Bates; Fag End (rerelease of Dumb Dora Discovers Tobacco—1945). **1948** The Guinea Pig (US 1949); River Patrol; A Date with a Dream; Calling Paul Temple. **1949** The History of Mr. Polly (US 1951); The Adventures of Jane. **1950** The Twenty Questions Murder Mystery. **1952** Salute the Toff; Hammer the Toff. **1953** The Wedding of Lilli Marlene; Will Any Gentleman? **1956** Not So Dusty. **1957** Morning Call; Suspended Alibi; The Naked Truth (aka Your Past is Showing—US 1958). **1960** The Challenge (aka It Takes a Thief—US 1962); The Millionairess (US 1961); Operation Cupid. **1961** Nothing Barred. **1962** The Damned (aka They All Died Laughing—US 1964); Serena. **1963** Sparrows Can't Sing; A Jolly Bad Fellow. **1964** The Bargee. **1967** Poor Cow (US 1968).

PATON, STUART
Born: 1885, Glasgow, Scotland. Died: Dec. 16, 1944, Woodland Hills, Calif. Stage and screen actor, film director, producer and screenwriter. Married to actress Ethel Patrick (dec. 1944).

PATRICK, ETHEL
Born: 1887. Died: Sept. 18, 1944, Woodland Hills, Calif. Stage and screen actress. Married to actor and director Stuart Paton (dec. 1944).

PATRICK, JEROME
Born: 1883, New Zealand. Died: Sept. 26, 1923, N.Y. (heart disease). Stage and screen actor.

Appeared in: **1919** Three Men and a Girl. **1920** The Furnace; Officer 666. **1921** Don't Call Me Little Girl; School Days; The Other Woman; Forever; The Heart Line. **1924** Sinners in Silk.

PATRICOLA, TOM
Born: Jan. 27, 1894, New Orleans, La. Died: Jan. 1, 1950, Pasadena, Calif. (following brain surgery). Screen, stage and vaudeville actor. Entered films in 1929.

Appeared in: **1929** Happy Days; Words and Music; Frozen Justice; Married in Hollywood; Si-Si Senor (short); South Sea Rose. **1930** The Three Sisters; One Mad Kiss; Anybody's Woman. **1931** Children of Dreams. **1932** Moonlight and Cactus (short). **1933** El Precio de un Beso; La Melodia Prohibida; No Dejes la Puerta Abierta. **1935** The following shorts: Moonlight and Melody; Dame Shy; Kiss the Bride. **1936** Fresh from the Fleet (short). **1945** Rhapsody in Blue.

PATSTON, DORIS
Born: 1904, London, England. Died: June 12, 1957, Darien, Conn. Stage and screen actress.

Appeared in: **1932** Smiling Faces.

PATTEN, DOROTHY
Born: 1905. Died: Apr. 11, 1975, Westhampton, N.Y. Screen, stage and television actress.

Appeared in: **1953** Botany Bay. **1973** Ten from Your Show of Shows (television film clips).

PATTERSON, ALBERT
Died: July 10, 1975. Screen actor.

PATTERSON, ELIZABETH
Born: 1876, Savannah, Tenn. Died: Jan. 31, 1966, Los Angeles, Calif. Screen, stage, television and radio actress.

Appeared in: **1926** The Boy Friend; The Return of Peter Grimm. **1929** Words and Music; South Sea Rose. **1930** The Lone Star Ranger; Harmony at Home; The Big Party; The Cat Creeps. **1931** Tarnished Lady; The Smiling Lieutenant; Daddy Long Legs; Penrod and Sam; Heaven on Earth. **1932** Love Me Tonight; Miss Pinkerton; Husband's Holiday; A Bill of Divorcement; Dangerous Brunette; The Way of Life; Two against the World; The Expert; Play Girl; So Big; New Morals for Old; Life Begins; Guilty as Hell; They Call It Sin; Breach of Promise; No Man of Her Own; The Conquerors. **1933** They Just Had to Get Married; The Infernal Machine; Story of Temple Drake; Golden Harvest; Dinner at Eight; Hold Your Man; The Secret of the Blue Room; Doctor Bull. **1934** Hideout. **1935** Chasing Yesterday; Men without Names; So Red the Rose. **1936** The Return of Sophie Lang; Timothy's Quest; Her Master's Voice; Three Cheers for Love; Go West, Young Man; Small Town Girl; Old Hutch. **1937** A Night of Mystery; High, Wide and Handsome; Hold 'Em Navy; Night Club Scandal. **1938** Scandal Sheet; Bulldog Drummond's Peril; Bluebeard's Eighth Wife; Sing, You Sinners; The Adventures of Tom Sawyer; Sons of the Legion. **1939** The Story of Alexander Graham Bell; Bulldog Drummond's Bride; The Cat and the Canary; Our Leading Citizen; Bad Little Angel; Bulldog Drummond's Secret Police. **1940** Remember the Night; Adventure in Diamonds; Anne of Windy Poplars; Earthbound; Who Killed Aunt Maggie?; Michael Shayne, Private Detective. **1941** Kiss the Boys Goodbye; Tobacco Road; Belle Starr; The Vanishing Virginian. **1942** Almost Married; Beyond the Blue Horizon; Her Cardboard Lover; My Sister Eileen; I Married a Witch; Lucky Legs. **1943** The Sky's the Limit. **1944** Follow the Boys; Hail the Conquering Hero; Together Again. **1945** Colonel Effingham's Raid; Lady on a Train. **1946** I've Always Loved You; The Secret Heart. **1947** Welcome Stranger; The Shocking Miss Pilgrim; Out of the Blue. **1948** Miss Tatlock's Millions. **1949** Little Women; Intruder in the Dust; Song of Surrender. **1950** Bright Leaf. **1951** Katie Did It. **1952** Washington Story. **1955** Las Vegas Shakedown. **1957** Pal Joey. **1959** The Oregon Trail. **1960** Tall Story.

PATTERSON, HANK (Elmer Calvin Patterson)
Born: Oct. 9, 1888, Alabama. Died: Aug. 23, 1975, Woodland Hills, Calif. (bronchial pneumonia). Screen, stage, vaudeville and television actor.

Appeared in: **1946** Abilene Town; I Ring Doorbells; The El Paso Kid; Santa Fe Uprising. **1947** Robin Hood of Texas; Bells of San Angelo; Springtime in the Sierras; Under Colorado Skies. **1948** Relentless; Oklahoma Badlands; The Denver Kid. **1949** The Cowboy and the Indians; Riders in the Sky. **1950** The James Brothers of Missouri (serial); Code of the Silver Sage; Desperadoes of the West (serial). **1951** Silver City Bonanza; Don Daredevil Rides Again (serial). **1952** California Conquest. **1953** Canadian Mounties vs. Atomic Invaders (serial). **1956** Tarantula; Julie. **1957** The Amazing Colossal Man. **1958** The Spider; Attack of the Puppet People; Monster on the Campus; Escape from Red Rock; Terror in a Texas Town; The Decks Ran Red. **1960** Gunfighters of Abilene.

PATTERSON, JAMES
Born: 1932. Died: Aug. 19, 1972, New York, N.Y. (cancer). Screen, stage, radio and television actor. Married to actress Rochelle Oliver.

Appeared in: **1963** The Slave. **1964** Lilith. **1967** In the Heat of the Night. **1969** Castle Keep.

PATTERSON, JOY W.
Born: 1906. Died: Mar. 23, 1959, Santa Ana, Calif. Screen actress and dancer.

Appeared in: **1926–29** many of the "Collegians" series of shorts.

PATTERSON, TROY (Ettore Corvino)
Born: 1926, U.S. Died: Nov. 1, 1975, Rome, Italy (heart attack). Screen, stage actor and dancer.

Appeared in: **1959** Speed Crazy; Bloodlust (US 1961).

PATTON, PHIL
Born: 1911. Died: May 28, 1972, Hollywood, Calif. (heart attack). Documentary film director, musician, stage and screen actor.

PATWARDHAN, VINAYAKARAO
Born: 1897, India. Died: 1975, Poona, India. Screen, stage actor, musician and music director.

Appeared in: Madhuri.

PAUL, LOGAN
Born: 1849, Ayr, Scotland. Died: Jan. 15, 1932, Brooklyn, N.Y. Stage and screen actor.

Appeared in: 1922 Flesh and Spirit.

PAUL, WAUNA
Born: 1912, New York, N.Y. Died: Mar. 31, 1973, Ibiza, Spain (auto accident). Screen, stage actress and stage producer. Daughter of actress Josephine Brown.

PAULIG, ALBERT
Born: Germany. Died: Mar. 1933 (heart trouble). Screen and stage actor.

Appeared in: 1929 Dancing Vienna; It's Easy to Become a Father. 1931 Ein Burschenlied aus Heidelberg; Susanne Macht Ordnung. 1932 Ein Ausgekochter Junge; Der Schrecken der Garnison; Girsekorn Greift Ein; Shoen 1st die Manoeverzeit; Drunter und Drueber. 1933 Der Tanzhusar. 1934 Zu Befehl, Herr Unteroffizier; Es War Einmal ein Walzer; Annemarie, Die Braut der Kompanie. 1935 Drei von der Kavallerie.

PAULL, TOWNSEND D.
Born: 1898. Died: Oct. 8, 1933, Los Angeles, Calif. (murdered). Stage and screen actor.

PAULSEN, ARNO
Born: 1900, Stettin, Germany. Died: Sept. 17, 1969, Baden-Baden, West Germany. Stage and screen actor.

Appeared in: 1948 Razzia; Murderers among Us. 1949 The Affair Blum. 1962 Wozzeck.

PAULSEN, HARALD
Born: 1895, Elmshorn, Hollstein, Germany. Died: Aug. 5, 1954, Hamburg, Germany (heart attack). Screen, stage actor, opera performer and stage director.

Appeared in: 1932 Mein Leopold; Die Blumenfrau von Lindenau. 1934 Tausend Fuer Eine Nacht; Alraune. 1935 Ich Sing Mich in Dein Herz Hinein; Frischer Wind aus Kanada. 1936 Oberwachtmeister Schwenke; Traumulus; Der Mutige Seefahrer. 1937 Besuch am Abend; If We All Were Angels; For Her Country's Sake. 1938 Der Lachende Dritte; Krach und Blueckum Kuennemann (Row and Joy about Kuennemann); Sie und die Drei (She and the Three). 1939 1A in Oberbayern (1A in Upper Bavaria). 1940 The Living Dead. Other German films; Die Ledige Witwe; Stradivari; Kunstlerliebe.

PAUNCEFORT, GEORGE
Born: 1870. Died: Mar. 25, 1942, Los Angeles, Calif. Screen and stage actor. Entered films approx. 1932.

PAVLOVA, ANNA
Born: Jan. 3, 1885, St. Petersburg, Russia. Died: Jan. 23, 1931, The Hague, Netherlands. Ballerina and screen actress. Entered films in 1915.

Appeared in: 1916 The Dumb Girl of Portici.

PAVON, BLANCA ESTELA
Born: 1926, Mexico. Died: Sept. 26, 1949, near Mexico City, Mexico (plane crash). Screen and radio actress. Dubbed in Spanish voice of Vivien Leigh in 1939 Gone with the Wind and Ingrid Bergman in 1944 Gaslight (aka Angel Street).

PAWLE, LENNOX
Born: 1872, London, England. Died: Feb. 22, 1936, Los Angeles, Calif. (cerebral hemorrhage). Stage and screen actress.

Appeared in: 1918 The Admirable Crichton. 1919 All the Sad World Needs (aka Peep O' Day). 1920 The Temptress. 1922 The Glorious Adventure. 1929 Married in Hollywood; Hot for Paris; The Sky Hawk. 1931 The Sin of Madelon Claudet. 1935 David Copperfield; Sylvia Scarlet; The Gay Deception.

PAWLEY, WILLIAM
Born: 1905, Kansas City, Mo. Died: June 15, 1952, New York, N.Y. Stage and screen actor.

Appeared in: 1931 Bad Girl; The Spider; Over the Hill. 1932 Cheaters at Play; After Tomorrow; Careless Lady; Amateur Daddy; The Trial of Vivienne Ware; Letty Lynton; Speak Easily; Central Park. 1933 Robbers' Roost; Gabriel over the White House. 1935 The Daring Young Man; Stolen Harmony; Mary Burns, Fugitive; Kentucky Kernels. 1936 Boulder Dam; The Public Pays (short); The Big Noise; Bullets or Ballots; Public Enemy's Wife. 1937 San Quentin; Born Reckless; The River of Missing Men; Trapped by G-Men. 1938 International Crime; Crime Takes a Holiday; Pairie Moon; White Banners. 1939 Boy Slaves; Panama Lady; Rough Riders Round-Up; Union Pacific;

Disputed Passage. 1940 Grapes of Wrath; Johnny Apollo; The Great Profile; Double Alibi; Yukon Flight; West of Abilene; Mercy Plane; The Return of Frank James. 1941 The Great American Broadcast. 1942 Time to Kill.

PAXINOU, KATINA (Katina Konstantopoulou)
Born: Dec. 17, 1900, Piraeus, Greece. Died: Feb. 22, 1973, Athens, Greece (cancer). Stage and screen actress. Married to actor Alexis Minotis. Won 1943 Academy Award as Best Supporting Actress in For Whom the Bell Tolls.

Appeared in: 1943 For Whom the Bell Tolls (film debut); Hostages. 1945 Confidential Agent. 1946 California. 1947 Uncle Silas; Mourning Becomes Electra. 1949 Prince of Foxes. 1951 The Inheritance. 1955 Mr. Arkadin (US 1962 aka Confidential Report). 1959 The Miracle. 1960 Rocco e i Suoi Fratelli (Rocco and his Brothers—US 1961). 1962 Le Proces (The Trial—US 1963). 1968 Tante Zita (Zita).

PAXTON, GEORGE
Died: Feb. 19, 1914, near Fort Lee, N.J. Screen actor.

PAXTON, SIDNEY
Born: 1861. Died: Oct. 13, 1930, Montauk, N.Y. Screen and stage actor.

Appeared in: 1915 A Vagabond's Revenge. 1919 The Divine Gift. 1920 A Man's Shadow; The Shadow Between. 1921 Single Life; The Old Country; Money; The Bachelor's Club; Bluff; The Prince and the Beggarmaid; The Rotters. 1922 The Card. 1923 The School for Scandal; The Audacious Mr. Squire; Becket; The Hypocrites; Little Miss Nobody. 1924 The Crimson Circle; Miriam Rozella. 1925 The Midnight Girl; Old Home Week. 1928 Mark of the Frog (serial).

PAYNE, DOUGLAS
Born: 1875. Died: Aug. 1965, England. Stage and screen actor.

Appeared in: 1912 The Adventures of Dick Turpin—The Gunpowder Plot. 1913 Maria Marten—Or, the Murder in the Red Barn; The Fallen Idol; Fraudulent Spiritualism Exposed (aka Spiritualism Exposed and The Seer of Bond Street—US); The Great Gold Robbery; Ju-Jitsu to the Rescue. 1914 The Mystery of the Diamond Belt; The Finger of Destiny; The Cup Final Mystery; His Country's Honour (aka The Aviator Spy—US); The Houseboat Mystery; Captain Nighthawk; The Stolen Masterpiece; Guarding Britain's Secrets (aka The Fiends of Hell—US); The White Feather; Enoch Arden; Harbour Lights; In the Ranks. 1915 The Airman's Children; The Romany Rye; Flying from Justice; Royal Love; The Avenging Hand (aka The Wrath of the Tomb); The Coal King; The Great Cheque Fraud; The Devil's Bondsman (aka The Scorpion's Sting—US); The Little Minister; Married for Money; Master and Man; The Trumpet Call. 1916 The Devil's Bondman. 1919 Further Exploits of Sexton Blake; Heart of a Rose. 1920 Rodney Stone; Won by a Head. 1922 Potter's Clay. 1928 What Next?; The Trumph of the Scarlet Pimpernel (aka The Scarlet Daredevil—US 1929).

PAYNE, EDNA
Born: Dec. 5, 1891, New York, N.Y. Died: Jan. 31, 1953, Los Angeles, Calif. (liver ailment). Screen actress.

Appeared in: 1911 Higgenses vs. Judsons; The Story of Rosie's Rose. 1912 The Silent Signal; A Half Breed's Treachery; A Mexican Courtship; The Moonshiner's Daughter. 1913 The Bravery of Dora; Private Smith; The Engraver. 1914 The Squatter; The Return; The Price Paid. 1915 The Man and the Law; Colonel Steele—Master Gambler; Brand Blotters; The Little Band of Gold; The Sacrifice of Jonathan Gray; The Dawn Road; An Innocent Villain; The Trap that Failed; Babbling Tongues; In the Folds of the Flag; One Fifty Thousand Dollar Jewel Theft; The Sheriff of Red Rock Gulch; The Fool's Heart; Shadows of the Harbor; The Oath of Smoky Joe; Saved by the Telephone; The Thief and the Chief; The Lone Game; Within an Inch of His Life; The Flag of Fortune. 1916 John Osborne's Triumph; The Unpardonable Sin; The Bad Samaritan.

PAYNE, LOUIS "LOU" (Louis William Payne)
Born: Jan. 13, 1876, New York, N.Y. Died: Aug. 14, 1953, Woodland Hills, Calif. Stage and screen actor. Married to screen actress Mrs. Leslie Carter (dec. 1937). Entered films in 1920.

Appeared in: 1924 True as Steel; For Sale; In Hollywood with Potash and Perlmutter. 1925 Alias Mary Flynn; The Last Edition; The Fate of a Flirt; We Moderns; As Man Desires; The Only Thing; The Lady Who Lied. 1926 The Blind Goddess; The Shamrock Handicap; The Outsider; A Woman's Heart. 1927 King of Kings; Broadway Madness; Vanity; The Yankee Clipper. 1928 The Whip. 1929 Evangeline; Big News; Interference; Lawful Larceny; Part Time Wife; The Dude Wrangler. 1945 Saratoga Trunk.

PAYNE, WILLIAM
Died: Dec. 26, 1967. Screen actor.

PAYSON, BLANCHE
Born: 1881. Died: July 3, 1964, Hollywood, Calif. Screen actress. Entered films with Mack Sennett.

Appeared in: **1916** Wife and Auto Trouble; A Bath House Blunder; A la Cabaret; Dollars and Sense. **!917** Oriental Love. **1925** Oh, Doctor!; We Moderns. **1926** La Boheme. **1927** Figures Don't Lie; The Bachelor's Baby. **1930** Below Zero (short). **1931** Wicked; plus the following shorts: Dogs is Dogs; Our Wife; Taxi Troubles. **1932** The Impatient Maiden; plus the following shorts: Love Pains; Helpmates; Red Noses. **1933** Loose Relations (short). **1935** Hoi Polloi (short). **1937** All over Town. **1938** If I Were King. **1943** A Maid Made Mad (short).

PAYTON, BARBARA
Born: Nov. 16, 1927, Cloquet, Minn. Died: May 8, 1967, San Diego, Calif. (natural causes). Screen actress. Divorced from actor Franchot Tone (dec. 1968).

Appeared in many westerns during the 1940s and the following: **1940** Once More, My Darling; Trapped. **1949** Silver Butte (short). **1950** Dallas; Kiss Tomorrow Goodbye. **1951** Only the Valiant; Drums in the Deep South; Bride of the Gorilla. **1953** Run for the Hills; The Flanagan Boy (aka Bad Blonde—US); The Great Jesse James Raid; Four-Sided Triangle. **1955** Murder Is My Beat.

PAYTON, LEW
Born: 1875. Died: May 27, 1945. Black screen actor.

Appeared in: **1936** Valiant is the Word for Carrie. **1938** Jezebel. **1939** The Lady's from Kentucky. **1941** Lady for a Night.

PEABODY, EDDY
Born: Feb. 19, 1912, Reading, Mass. Died: Nov. 7, 1970, Covington, Ky. (stroke). Screen, television, radio actor and banjo player. Known as "King of the Banjo."

Appeared in: **1927** Banjomania (short). **1928** In a Music Shop (short); Banjoland (short). **1934** The Lemon Drop Kid. **1935** Shoestring Follies (short). **1936–1938** Vitaphone and Paramount shorts.

PEACOCK, KEITH
Born: 1931. Died: Nov. 1, 1966, Perivale, England (accident while filming a stunt for television). Screen and television stuntman.

Appeared in: **1964** The 7th Dawn. **1966** Our Man in Marrakesh (aka Bang, Bang You're Dead—US); Circus of Fear (aka Psycho-Circus—US 1967). **1967** Casino Royale.

PEACOCK, KIM
Born: 1901, Watford Herts, England. Died: Dec. 26, 1966, Emsworth, England (heart attack). Screen, stage, radio and television actor.

Appeared in: **1929** The Manxman; The Clue of the New Pin; The Crooked Billet. **1930** A Warm Corner. **1933** Waltz Time. **1935** The Mad Hatter; Expert's Opinion. **1936** Things to Come; Grand Finale; Midnight at Madame Tussaud's (aka Midnight at the Wax Museum—US). **1937** Sunset in Vienna (aka Suicide Legion—US 1940); Captain's Orders. **1938** Climbing High (US 1939); Night Alone; Alerte en Mediteranee (SOS Mediterranean—US 1940). **1939** Hell's Cargo (aka Dangerous Cargo—US 1940).

PEACOCK, LILLIAN
Born: Oct. 23, 1890 or 1894 (?), Pa. Died: Aug. 18, 1918, Los Angeles, Calif. (injuries sustained previously while filming). Screen actress.

Appeared in: **1915** Saved by a Shower; Hiram's Inheritance; How Billy Got His Raise; Their Bewitched Elopement; At the Beach Incognito; Slightly Mistaken; Twentieth Century Susie; The Last Roll; The Opera Singer's Romance; The Ore Mystery; When the Wets Went Dry; Dad's Awful Crime; A Millionaire for a Minute; Chills and Chickens; Leomade Aids Cupid. **1916** A Perfect Match; Mrs. Green's Mistake; Wanted—A Piano Tuner; Muchly Married; The Tale of a Telegram; His Highness the Janitor; Hubby Puts One Over; The Jitney Driver's Romance; A Wife for a Ransom; A Raffle for a Husband; A Stage Villain; A Dark Suspicion; Love Quarantined; The Fall of Deacon Stillwaters; The Harem Scarem Deacon; Bashful Charley's Proposal; An All Around Cure; Some Vampire; I've Got Yer Number; Kate's Affinities; She Wrote a Play and Played It; The Deacon Stops the Show; A Marriage for Revenge; In Onion There's Strength; The Elixir of Life; Soup and Nuts; Musical Madness; Father Gets in Wrong; Beans and Bullets; Their First Arrest; In Love with a Fireman; A Janitor's Vendetta; Scrappily Married; A Shadowed Shadow. **1917** Barred from the Bar; Why They Left Home; The Little Pirate; His Coming-Out Party; Out for the Dough; Mule Mates; Rosie's Rancho; Passing the Grip; Wanta Make a Dollar?; A Boob for Luck; 'Art Aches; Whose Baby?; The Leak; Left in the Soup? What the—?; The Carless Cop; The Man with the Package; The Last Scent; The Boss of the Family; Uneasy Money; His Fatal Beauty; One Damp Day. **1918** Who's to Blame?

PEARCE, ALICE
Born: 1919. Died: Mar. 3, 1966, Los Angeles, Calif. (cancer). Screen, stage and television actress.

Appeared in: **1949** On the Town. **1952** The Belle of New York. **1955** How to Be Very, Very Popular. **1956** The Opposite Sex. **1962** Lad: A Dog. **1963** The Thrill of It All; Tammy and the Doctor; Beach Party; My Six Loves. **1964** The

Disorderly Orderly; Dear Heart; Kiss Me, Stupid. **1965** Dear Brigitte; Darn That Cat; Bus Riley's Back in Town. **1966** The Glass Bottom Boat.

PEARCE, GEORGE C.
Born: 1865, New York, N.Y. Died: Aug. 12, 1940, Los Angeles, Calif. Screen, stage actor, opera performer and film director.

Appeared in: **1921** Black Beauty; The Traveling Salesman; Three Word Brand. **1922** The Primitive Lover; Watch Your Step. **1923** The Midnight Alarm; The Printer's Devil; The Country Kid. **1924** Cornered; Daring Youth; The Narrow Street; Wandering Husbands; Hold Your Breath. **1925** The Wife Who Wasn't Wanted. **1926** The Social Highwayman; Hold That Lion. **1927** The Irresistible Lover; Quarantined Rivals. **1928** Do Your Duty; Masquerade; Home James; Wild West Romance. **1929** The Valiant. **1930** The Lone Rider; Personality; Vengeance; The Right of Way. **1931** Men in Her Life; The Right to Love. **1932** This Reckless Age. **1933** Story of Temple Drake; Lone Cowboy. **1934** British Agent; Six of a Kind. **1936** The Singing Cowboy. **1937** When You're in Love; The Awful Truth.

PEARCE, VERA
Born: 1896, Australia. Died: Jan. 21, 1966, London, England. Screen, stage actress and singer.

Appeared in: **1933** Yes, Mr. Brown; Just My Luck; That's a Good Girl. **1935** So You Won't Talk. **1938** Yes, Madam? **1939** What's a Man. **1947** Nicholas Nickleby. **1951** One Wild Oat. **1954** Men of Sherwood Forest (US 1956). **1959** The Night We Dropped a Clanger (aka Make Mine a Double—US 1961).

PEARL, EULA (Eula Pearl Ferrand)
Died: July 17, 1970, Visalia, Calif. (heart attack). Screen actress and piano, voice instructor.

PEARSON, DREW (Andrew Russell Pearson)
Born: Dec. 13, 1897, Evanston, Ill. Died: Sept. 1, 1969, Washington, D.C. Newspaper columnist and screen actor.

Appeared in: **1951** The Day the Earth Stood Still. **1961** Death to the World (narrator).

PEARSON, LLOYD
Born: Dec. 13, 1897, Bradford, Yorkshire, England. Died: June 2, 1966, London, England. Screen, stage and television actor.

Appeared in: **1938** The Challenge (film debut—US 1939). **1940** Tilly of Bloomsbury. **1941** Kipps (aka The Remarkable Mr. Kipps—US 1942); Banana Ridge. **1942** Uncensored (US 1944). **1943** When We are Married; My Learned Friend; Schweik's New Adventures; Rhythm Serenade. **1948** The Three Weird Sisters; Mr. Perrin and Mr. Traill. **1950** Portrait of Clare. **1952** Private Information; Hindle Wakes (aka Holiday Week—US). **1955** Black in the Face. **1957** The Good Companions. **1960** The Angry Silence.

PEARSON, MOLLY
Born: 1876, Scotland. Died: Jan. 26, 1959, Newton, Conn. Stage and screen actress.

Appeared in: **1918** Passing of the Third Floor Back.

PEARSON, TED
Died: Oct. 5, 1961. Radio announcer and screen actor.

Appeared in: **1938** Test Pilot; You're Only Young Once. **1939** Dick Tracy's G-Men (serial); Boy Friend.

PEARSON, VIRGINIA
Born: 1888, Louisville, Ky. Died: June 6, 1958, Los Angeles, Calif. (uremic poisoning). Stage and screen actress. Married to actor Sheldon Lewis (dec. 1958).

Appeared in: **1916** The Vital Question; The Kiss of a Vampire; Blazing Love. **1917** A Royal Romance. **1919** The Bishop's Emeralds. **1923** Sister against Sister; A Prince of a King. **1925** The Phantom of the Opera; The Wizard of Oz; Red Kimona. **1926** Lightning Hutch (serial); Atta Boy; Silence; The Taxi Mystery. **1927** Driven from Home. **1928** What Price Beauty?; The Big City; The Actress; The Power of Films. **1929** Smilin' Guns. **1930** Danger Man. **1931** Primrose Path. **1932** Back Street.

PEARSON, W. BLAINE (William Blaine Pearson)
Born: Mar. 21, 1892, Kentucky. Died: Nov. 6, 1918, Los Angeles, Calif. (pneumonia). Screen actor and screenwriter.

PECHEUR, BRUCE
Born: 1942. Died: Aug. 16, 1973, New York, N.Y. (murdered—stabbed). Screen, stage actor and model.

Appeared in: **1970** Trash. **1971** Road to Salina.

PECKHAM, FRANCES MILES
Born: 1893. Died: June 7, 1959, New York, N.Y. Screen and stage actress.

PEER, HELEN
Born: 1898. Died: May 6, 1942, New Rochelle, N.Y. Screen, stage actress and singer. Appeared on screen for the Thomas A. Edison Co.

"PEERLESS ANNABELLE" (Annabelle Whitford Buchan)
Born: 1878. Died: Nov. 30, 1961, Chicago, Ill. Screen and stage actress. She was the original "Gibson Girl" as created by Charles Dana Gibson.

Appeared in: 1897 Annabelle's Butterfly Dance.

PEGLER, WESTBROOK
Born: Aug. 12, 1894, Minneapolis, Minn. Died: June 24, 1969, Tucson, Ariz. (cancer). Columnist, journalist and screen actor.

Appeared in: 1932 Madison Square Garden.

PEIL, EDWARD, SR. (Charles Edward Peil)
Born: 1888. Died: Dec. 29, 1958, Hollywood, Calif. Screen actor. Father of actor Edward Peil, Jr. (dec. 1962). Entered films in 1908.

Appeared in: 1919 Broken Blossoms. 1920 Isobel. 1921 Dream Street; That Girl Montana; The Killer; The Servant in the House. 1922 Arabia; Don't Doubt Your Wife; Broken Chains; The Dust Flower; The Song of Life. 1923 Purple Dawn; The Lone Star Ranger; Stepping Fast; Three Jumps Ahead. 1924 The Iron Horse; $50,000 Reward; The Man Who Came Back; Teeth. 1925 The Hunted Woman; Double Action Daniels; The Man without a Country; The Pleasure Buyers; The Wife Who Wasn't Wanted; The Fighting Heart. 1926 The Girl from Montmartre; Midnight Faces; Black Paradise; Yellow Fingers; The Great K&A Train Robbery. 1927 King of Kings; Framed; Tumbling River. 1929 Masked Emotions; In Old Arizona. 1930 Cock O' the Walk. 1931 Clearing the Range; The Texas Ranger; Wild Horse; Cracked Nuts. 1932 The Gay Buckaroo; Charlie Chan's Chance; Local Bad Man; The Hatchet Man. 1933 Tombstone Canyon; The Big Cage. 1934 Blue Steel; The Man from Utah; Pursuit of Happiness. 1935 The Phantom Empire (serial); Million Dollar Baby; Mysterious Mr. Wong; Ladies Crave Excitement. 1936 Oh Susannah!; Texas Rangers. 1937 Come on, Cowboys!; The Awful Truth; Two-Fisted Sheriff; Heroes of the Alamo. 1938 Colorado Trail. 1939 The Night Riders; Spoilers of the Range. 1940 One Man's Law. 1941 Billy the Kid's Fighting Pals; The Lone Rider in Ghost Town; Texas Marshal. 1942 Black Dragons; Pride of the Yankees; Foreign Agent. 1943 Robin Hood of the Range; Billy the Kid in the Kid Rides Again. 1947 Saddle Pals; The Last Round-Up.

PEIL, EDWARD, JR. (Charles Edward Peil)
Born: 1908. Died: Nov. 7, 1962. Screen actor. Appeared as a child actor during silents as Johnny Jones and later as Edward Peil, Jr. See Johnny Jones for early films. Son of actor Edward Peil (dec. 1958).

Appeared in: 1925 The Goose Hangs High; Rose of the World. 1926 The Family Upstairs. 1928 The Little Yellow House. 1929 The College Coquette.

PEIRCE, EVELYN. See EVELYN PIERCE

PELLICER, PINA (Josefina Pellicer Lopez Llergo)
Born: 1940, Mexico. Died: Dec. 10, 1964, Mexico City, Mexico (suicide). Screen, stage and television actress.

Appeared in: 1960 Macario. 1961 One Eyed Jacks. 1963 Dias de Otoro (Autumn Days)—received the PECIME (Mexican Film Writers) award for Best Actress. 1967 Los Bandidos. 1968 Days of the Evil Gun.

PELLY, FARRELL
Born: 1891. Died: Apr. 23, 1963, New York, N.Y. Screen, stage and television actor.

Appeared in: 1959 Darby O'Gill and the Little People.

PEMBERTON, HENRY W.
Born: 1875. Died: July 26, 1952, Orlando, Fla. Screen, stage and vaudeville actor.

Appeared in: 1921 Luxury.

PEMBROKE, GEORGE. See GEORGE PRUD'HOMME

PENA, JULIO
Born: 1912, Madrid, Spain. Died: July 22, 1972, Marbella, Spain (heart attack). Stage and screen actor.

Appeared in: 1929 Madame X; The Lady Lies (Spanish version). 1930 Min and Bill. 1933 Mama. 1935 Angelita; Rosa de Francia. 1939 Las Cinco Advertencias de Satanas (Satan's Five Warnings). 1956 Alexander the Great. 1958 Spanish Affair. 1959 Solomon and Sheba. 1961 La Rivolta degli Schiavi (The Revolt of the Slaves—US); Happy Thieves. 1963 El Valle de las Espadas (aka The Castilian—US). 1965 Tierra de Fuego (aka Sunscorch—US 1966). 1966 Tre Notti Violente (Web of Violence—US); Campanadas a Medianoche (Chimes at Midnight—US 1967 aka Falstaff); Kid Rodelo; Pampa Salvaje

(Savage Pampas—US 1967); L'Homme du Minnesota (aka Minnesota Clay—US). 1967 I Crudeli (aka The Hellbenders—US). 1968 Rey de Africa (aka One Step to Hell—US 1969); The Oldest Profession. 1970 El Condor. Other films include: Correo de Indias; Intriga; Mission Blanca; Fuenteovejuna; Confidencia; Alhucemas; Siempre Vuelvan de Madrugada; Manicomio; Horas de Panica; Simon Bolivar.

PENA, RALPH
Born: 1927. Died: May 20, 1969, Mexico City, Mexico (car accident injuries). Screen actor, screenwriter and musician.

PENBROOK, HARRY
Born: 1887. Died: Sept. 14, 1960, Hollywood, Calif. Screen actor and extra. Entered films approx. 1908.

PENDER, DORIS (Doris Lomas)
Born: 1900, England. Died: July 24, 1975, London, England (leukemia). Screen, stage and vaudeville actress. Appeared in vaude in an act billed as "Fun and Antics in Monkeyland" with her parents Bob and Margaret Loma. Divorced from vaudeville actor Jack Hartman with whom she appeared in vaudeville in an act billed as "Hart, Pender and O'Neill" (with Chuck O'Neill).

PENDLETON, NAT
Born: Aug. 9, 1899, Davenport, Iowa. Died: Oct. 11, 1967, San Diego, Calif. (heart attack). Screen, stage actor and professional wrestler. Entered films as a juvenile with Lubin.

Appeared in: 1924 The Hoosier Schoolmaster. 1926 Let's Get Married. 1929 The Laughing Lady. 1930 Fair Warning; The Sea Wolf; Last of the Duanes; The Big Pond; Liliom. 1931 Secret Witness; Larceny Lane; Vigor of Youth; The Seas Beneath; The Star Witness; Mr. Lemon of Orange; Blonde Crazy; Spirit of Notre Dame; Pottsville Paluka; Cauliflower Alley. 1932 Play Girl; The Sign of the Cross; Cardigan's Last Case; Taxi; Attorney for the Defense; Hell Fire Austin; Exposure; You Said a Mouthful; Night Club Lady; Horse Feathers; Manhattan Parade; Beast of the City; A Fool's Advice; By Whose Hands? 1933 Deception; Whistling in the Dark; Baby Face; College Coach; Goldie Gets Along; Lady for a Day; Penthouse; The Chief; I'm No Angel. 1934 Fugitive Lovers; The Defense Rests; The Cat's Paw; Girl from Missouri; Straight Is the Way; Lazy River; Manhattan Melodrama; Death on the Diamond; The Thin Man; The Gay Bride; Sing and Like It. 1935 Times Square Lady; Baby Face Harrington; Reckless; Murder in the Fleet; Calm Yourself; Here Comes the Band; It's in the Air. 1936 The Garden Murder Case; The Great Ziegfeld; Sworn Enemy; Trapped by Television; Two in a Crowd; The Luckiest Girl in the World; Sing Me a Love Song. 1937 Under Cover of Night; Song of the City; Gangway; Life Begins in College. 1938 Meet the Mayor; Young Dr. Kildare; Swing Your Lady; Arsene Lupin Returns; Fast Company; Shopworn Angel; The Chaser; The Crowd Roars. 1939 Burn 'em Up, O'Connor; Calling Dr. Kildare; It's a Wonderful World; 6,000 Enemies; On Borrowed Time; At the Circus; Another Thin Man; The Secret of Dr. Kildare. 1940 The Ghost Comes Home; Dr. Kildare's Strangest Case; Phantom Raiders; The Golden Fleecing; Flight Command; Dr. Kildare's Crisis; Dr. Kildare's Wedding Day; Dr. Kildare Goes Home; Northwest Passage. 1941 Death Valley; Buck Privates; Top Sergeant Mulligan; The Mad Doctor of Market Street. 1942 Jail House Blues; Calling Dr. Gillespie; Dr. Gillespie's New Assistant. 1943 Dr. Gillespie's Criminal Case. 1944 The Sign of the Cross (revised version of 1932 film); Swing Fever. 1945 Rookies Come Home. 1947 Buck Privates Come Home; Scared to Death. 1949 Death Valley. 1964 Big Parade of Comedy (documentary).

PENMAN, LEA
Born: 1895. Died: Oct. 12, 1962, Hollywood, Calif. Screen and stage actress.

Appeared in: 1926 The Romance of a Million Dollars. 1950 Stella; Fancy Pants. 1955 We're No Angels. 1957 Portland Expose.

PENN, LEONARD (Leonard Monson Penn)
Born: 1907, Mass. Died: May 20, 1975, Los Angeles, Calif. (heart attack). Screen actor. Divorced from actress Gladys George (dec. 1954). Do not confuse with actor Leo Penn.

Appeared in: 1937 Between Two Women; The Women Men Marry; The Firefly. 1938 Judge Hardy's Children; Man Proof; Girl of the Golden West; The Toy Wife; Ladies in Distress (short); Marie Antoinette; What Price Safety? (short). 1939 Bachelor Mother; Almost a Gentleman. 1940 The Way of All Flesh. 1946 Son of the Guardsman (serial); Chick Carter, Detective (serial). 1947 I Cover the Big Town; Hoppy's Holiday; Killer at Large; Brick Bradford (serial). 1948 Congo Bill (serial); Dead Don't Dream; Courtin' Trouble. 1949 Batman and Robin (serial). 1950 The Girl from San Lorenzo; Silver Raiders; Woman from Headquarters; Gunfire; Six Gun Mesa; Lonely Hearts Bandits; Law of the Badlands. 1951 Sirocco; South of Caliente; Mysterious Island (serial). 1952 King of the Congs (serial); Outlaw Woman; Barbed Wire; A Yank in Indochina; Thief of Damascus; And Now Tomorrow; Westminster; No Holds Barred. 1953 Eyes of the Jungle; Fangs of the Arctic; Flame of Calcutta; Savage Mutiny; Murder Without Tears; The Lost Planet (serial). 1954 The Saracen Blade. 1956 On the Threshold of Space. 1958 In the Money.

PENNELL, RICHARD O.

Born: 1861, Chester, England. Died: Mar. 22, 1934, Hollywood, Calif. Screen actor. Entered films in 1914.

Appeared in: **1927** The Masked Woman. **1928** The Olympic Hero; Dressed to Kill; Clothes Make the Woman. **1930** On the Level.

PENNER, JOE (Joseph Pinter)

Born: Nov. 11, 1905, Budapest, Hungary. Died: Jan. 10, 1941, Philadelphia, Pa. (heart attack). Screen, stage, radio, vaudeville and burlesque actor.

Appeared in: **1930** The following shorts: Seeing-Off-Service; Stepping Out; A Stuttering Romance; Surface Stripes. **1931** Making Good (short); Sax Appeal (short). **1932** The following shorts: Gangway; Moving In; Where Men Are Men. **1932–33** Big Star Comedies and Big "V" Comedies. **1934** College Rhythm. **1936** Collegiate. **1937** New Faces of 1937. **1938** I'm from the City; Mr. Doodle Kicks Off; Go Chase Yourself. **1939** The Day The Bookies Wept. **1940** Millionaire Playboy; Glamour Boy; The Boys from Syracuse.

PENNICK, JACK (Robert Jack Pennick)

Born: 1895, Portland, Oreg. Died: Aug. 16, 1964, Hollywood, Calif. Stage and screen actor.

Appeared in: **1927** The Broncho Twister; The Lone Eagle. **1928** Plastered in Paris; The Four Sons; Why Sailors Go Wrong. **1929** Strong Boy. **1930** The City Girl; Paramount on Parade; Way Out West; Born Reckless. **1931** Hell Divers. **1932** Strangers of the Evening; Phantom Express; Air Mail; If I Had a Million; Sky Bride. **1933** Strange People; Tugboat Annie; Renegades of the West; Hello Everybody!; Skyway, Man of Sentiment. **1934** Come on Marines!; The World Moves On. **1935** West Point of the Air; Steamboat 'Round the Bend; Waterfront Lady. **1936** Prisoner of Shark Island; The Music Goes 'Round; Under Two Flags; Private Number; Drift Fence. **1937** Wee Willie Winkie; The Big City; Live, Love and Learn; Navy Blue and Gold; Great Guy; Devil's Playground; Submarine. **1938** You and Me; The Buccaneer; Banjo on My Knee; Alexander's Ragtime Band; King of the Newsboys; Submarine Patrol; Cocoanut Grove. **1939** Union Pacific; Star Maker; Tail Spin; Young Mr. Lincoln; Stagecoach; Mountain Rhythm; Drums along the Mohawk. **1940** The Grapes of Wrath; The Long Voyage Home; The Westerner; Northwest Mounted Police. **1941** Tobacco Road; Sergeant York; Wild Geese Calling; Lady from Louisiana. **1945** They Were Expendable. **1946** My Darling Clementine. **1947** The Fugitive; Unconquered. **1948** Fort Apache; Three Godfathers. **1949** She Wore a Yellow Ribbon; Mighty Joe Young; The Fighting Kentuckian. **1950** When Willie Comes Marching Home; Rio Grande; Tripoli. **1951** Operation Pacific; The Fighting Coast Guard; The Sea Hornet. **1952** What Price Glory? **1953** The Sun Shines Bright; The Beast from 20,000 Fathoms. **1955** Mr. Roberts; The Long Gray Line. **1956** Searchers. **1957** The Wings of Eagles. **1958** The Last Hurrah; The Buccaneer (and 1938 version). **1959** The Horse Soldiers. **1960** The Alamo; Sergeant Rutledge. **1961** Two Rode Together. **1962** The Man Who Shot Liberty Valance. **1963** How the West Was Won.

PENNINGTON, ANN

Born: 1894, Camden, N.J. Died: Nov. 4, 1971, N.Y. Screen, stage actress and dancer. Credited with having popularized the dance craze "The Black Bottom."

Appeared in: **1916** Susie Snowflakes; The Rainbow Princess. **1917** The Antics of Ann; Sunshine Nan; Little Boy Scout. **1924** Manhandled. **1925** The Mad Dancer; The Lucky Horseshoe; A Kiss in the Dark; The Golden Strain; Madame Behave; Pretty Ladies. **1929** Tanned Legs; The Gold Diggers of Broadway; Is Everybody Happy?; Night Parade; Night Club. **1930** Happy Days; Hello Baby (short). **1943** China Girl.

PENNINGTON, EDITH MAE

Died: May 16, 1974, Shreveport, La. Screen actress. Voted the "Most Beautiful Girl in the World" in 1921. Appeared in silent films.

PENNY, FRANK

Born: 1895. Died: Apr. 20, 1946, New York. Screen, radio, vaudeville and burlesque actor. Was in vaudeville in an act billed as "Penny, Reed and Gold."

Appeared in: **1941** Hold That Ghost; Keep 'Em Flying. **1942** Pardon My Sarong; Eagle Squadron; Who Done It? **1943** It Ain't Hay. **1944** Lost in a Harem. **1945** Abbott and Costello in Hollywood; Dolly Sisters; Diamond Horseshoe.

PEPPER, BARBARA

Born: May 31, 1916, New York, N.Y. Died: July 18, 1969, Panorama City, Calif. (coronary). Screen, stage and television actress.

Appeared in: **1933** Roman Scandals. **1934** Our Daily Bread. **1935** Home Work (short); The Singing Vagabond; Let 'Em Have It; Waterfront Lady; Frisco Waterfront; Forced Landing; The Sagebrush Troubadour. **1936** Showboat; Rogues' Tavern; Wanted: Jane Turner; M'Liss; Mummy's Boys; The Big Game; Winterset. **1937** Sea Devils; Wrong Romance (short); Too Many Wives; You Can't Buy Luck; You Can't Beat Love; The Big Shot; Forty Naughty Girls; The Westland Case; Portia on Trial; Music for Madame. **1938** Hollywood Stadium Mystery; Army Girl; Outside the Law; The Lady in the Morgue; Wide Open Faces. **1939** They Made Me a Criminal; The Magnificent

Fraud; Colorado Sunset; Flight at Midnight; The Women; Three Sons. **1940** Forgotten Girls; Foreign Correspondent; The Castle on the Hudson; The Return of Frank James; Women in War. **1941** Manpower; Man at Large; Three Sons O'Guns; Birth of the Blues. **1942** Carry Harry (short); Sappy Pappy (short); One Thrilling Night. **1943** He Was Only Feudin' (short); So This is Washington; Girls in Chains; A Maid Made Mad (short); Let's Face It; Star Spangled Rhythm. **1944** Since You Went Away; Henry Aldrich Plays Cupid; Cover Girl; Once upon a Time. **1945** The Hidden Eye; Brewster's Millions; Murder, He Says; Trouble Chasers; The Naughty Nineties. **1946** Prison Ship. **1947** Terror Trail; The Millerson Case. **1950** Unmasked. **1952** Thunderbirds. **1953** Inferno. **1957** The D.I. **1962** It's Only Money; The Music Man. **1963** A Child is Waiting; It's a Mad, Mad, Mad, Mad World; Who's Minding the Store? **1964** Kiss Me, Stupid; My Fair Lady.

PEPPER, ROBERT C.

Born: 1916. Died: Oct. 27, 1964, Hollywood, Calif. Screen actor and stuntman. Stand-in for Broderick Crawford and Lon Chaney, Jr.

PERCIVAL, ARLENE. See ARLENE WALKER

PERCIVAL, WALTER C. (Charles David Lingenfelter)

Born: 1887, Chicago, Ill. Died: Jan. 28, 1934, Hollywood, Calif. Screen, stage and vaudeville actor. Was partner in vaudeville with his wife, Rennie Noel.

Appeared in: **1924** The Moral Sinner. **1926** The Flying Horseman. **1928** The Big City; Lights of New York. **1930** Twixt Love and Duty (short); The Leather Pushers (serial); Shooting Straight; Lightnin'. **1931** Blonde Crazy; The Avenger; Smart Money; Sweepstakes; Pagan Lady; Homicide Squad; Larceny Lane; The Champ. **1932** Carnival Boat; Cabin in the Cotton.

PERCY, EILEEN

Born: 1901, Belfast, Ireland. Died: July 29, 1973, Beverly Hills, Calif. Screen actress, stage actress and newspaper columnist. Married to composer Harry Ruby (dec. 1974).

Appeared in: **1917** Down to Earth. **1919** Brass Buttons; In Mizzoura; Some Liar; Where the West Begins; The Gray Horizon; The Beloved Cheater; Told in the Hills; Desert Gold. **1920** The Third Eye (serial); The Husband Hunter; Beware of the Bride; Man Who Dared; Her Honor, the Mayor. **1921** The Blushing Bride; Big Town Ideas; Hickville to Broadway; Maid of the West; Little Miss Hawkshaw; The Tomboy; Whatever She Wants; Why Trust Your Husband?; The Land of Jazz. **1922** The Flirt; Elope If You Must; The Fast Mail; Western Speed; Pardon My Nerve! **1923** Children of Jazz; East Side—West Side; Let's Go; The Prisoner; The Fourth Musketeer; Hollywood; Within the Law; Yesterday's Wife. **1924** Tongues of Flame; The Turmoil; Missing Daughters. **1925** Fine Clothes; Under the Rouge; Cobra; The Shadow on the Wall; Souls for Sables; The Unchastened Woman. **1926** Lovey Mary; Race Wild; The Model from Paris; The Phantom Bullet. **1927** Backstage; Spring Fever; Twelve Miles Out; Burnt Fingers. **1928** Telling the World. **1929** The Broadway Hoofer. **1930** Temptation. **1931** Wicked. **1932** The Cohens and Kellys in Hollywood. **1943** First Aid (short).

PERCY, ESME (Saville Esme Percy)

Born: Aug. 8, 1887, London, England. Died: June 17, 1957, Brighton, England. Screen, stage actor and stage producer.

Appeared in: **1930** Murder. **1933** The Lucky Number; On Secret Service (aka Secret Agent—US 1935); Bitter Sweet; Summer Lightning; The Unfinished Symphony. **1934** Lord Edgware Dies; Nell Gwyn. **1935** Royal Cavalcade (aka Regal Cavalcade—US); Abdul the Damned; Invitation to the Waltz; It Happened in Paris. **1936** The Invader (aka An Old Spanish Custom—US); The Amateur Gentleman; A Woman Alone (aka Two Who Dared—US 1937); Accused; Song of Freedom; Land without Music (aka Forbidden Music—US 1938). **1937** Jump for Glory (aka When Thief Meets Thief—US): Our Fighting Navy (aka Torpedoed—US 1939); The Return of the Scarlet Pimpernel (US 1938); 21 Days (aka 21 Days Together—US 1940 and aka The First and the Last); The Frog (US 1939). **1938** Pygmalion. **1945** Dead of Night. **1946** Caesar and Cleopatra; Lisbon Story. **1947** The Ghosts of Berkeley Square. **1948** Death in the Hand.

PEREZ, PEPITO

Born: 1896, Spain. Died: July 13, 1975, Santa Ana, Calif. (cancer). Screen, stage, vaudeville and television actor. Known as "Pepito the Spanish Clown."

Appeared in: **1938** Army Girl; Annabella Takes a Tour. **1944** Lady in the Dark. **1945** A Medal for Benny. **1951** The Raging Tide.

PERIOLAT, GEORGE

Born: 1876, Chicago, Ill. Died: Feb. 20, 1940, Los Angeles, Calif. (suicide—arsenic). Stage and screen actor. Entered films with Essanay in 1911.

Appeared in: **1915** The Adventures of Terence O'Rourke; The Diamond from the Sky (serial). **1916** Landon's Legacy. **1917** The Mate of the Sally Ann. **1920** The Mark of Zorro. **1921** Her Face Value; The Kiss; A Parisian Scandal; They Shall Pay; Wealth; Who Am I? **1922** Blood and Sand; The Dust Flower; Gay and Devilish; Shattered Idols; The Young Rajah. **1923** Rosita; The Barefoot Boy; Slave of Desire; The Tiger's Claw. **1924** The Red Lily; The Girl on the

Stairs; Lover's Lane; The Yankee Consul. 1925 Any Woman; Fighting Youth; The Phantom Express. 1926 Butterflies in the Rain; Atta Boy; The Nut-Cracker; The Mile-a-Minute Man. 1927 Fangs of Destiny; The Prairie King; Through Thick and Thin; Speedy Smith. 1928 The Secret Hour; The Night Watch; Black Butterflies. 1929 When Dreams Come True; One Splendid Hour; The Fatal Warning (serial).

PERIOT, ARTHUR

Born: 1899. Died: Feb. 24, 1929, Monterey, Calif. (auto accident). Screen actor and stuntman.

PERIQUIN (Armando Espinosa de los Monteros)

Born: 1912, Mexico. Died: Nov. 6, 1957, Mexico City, Mexico (cancer). Stage and screen actor.

PERKINS, JEAN EDWARD

Born: 1899. Died: 1923 (while filming The Eagle's Talons serial). Screen actor and stuntman.

Appeared in: 1921 Do or Die (serial). 1923 The Eagle's Talons (serial).

PERKINS, OSGOOD

Born: 1892, West Newton, Mass. Died: Sept. 23, 1937, Washington, D.C. (heart attack). Stage and screen actor. Father of actor Anthony Perkins.

Appeared in: 1922 The Cradle Buster. 1923 Puritan Passions; Second Fiddle. 1924 Grit. 1925 Wild, Wild Susan. 1926 Love 'Em and Leave 'Em. 1927 High Hat; Knockout Reilly. 1929 Mother's Boy; Syncopation. 1931 The Front Page (stage and film versions); Tarnished Lady; Loose Ankles. 1932 Scarface. 1934 Kansas City Princess; Madame Du Barry; The President Vanishes. 1935 I Dream Too Much; Secret of the Chateau. 1936 Gold Diggers of 1937.

PERKINS, WALTER

Born: 1870, Biddeford, Maine. Died: June 3, 1925, Brooklyn, N.Y. Screen, stage and vaudeville actor.

Appeared in: 1919 Bill Henry. 1920 Peaceful Valley. 1921 The New Disciple. 1922 Golden Dreams; When Romance Rides.

PERLEY, ANNA

Born: 1849. Died: Jan. 20, 1937, Los Angeles, Calif. Screen and stage actress.

PERLEY, CHARLES

Born: 1886. Died: Feb. 10, 1933, Santa Ana, Calif. (heart attack). Stage and screen actor. Appeared in early Biograph films.

PERREDOM, LUIS

Born: 1882, Spain. Died: Apr. 7, 1958, Madrid, Spain. Stage and screen actor.

PERRIN, JACK

Born: 1896, Three Rivers, Mich. Died: Dec. 17, 1967, Hollywood, Calif. (heart attack). Stage and screen actor.

Appeared in: 1917 His Speedy Finish; His Sudden Rival; A Love Case; His Unconscious Conscience; Ambrose's Icy Love. 1919 The Lion Man (serial); Two Men of Tinted Butte; Blind Husbands. 1920 Pink Tights. 1921 The Match-Breaker; Partners of the Tide; The Rage of Paris; The Torrent. 1922 The Dangerous Little Demon; The Trouper; The Guttersnipe. 1923 The Santa Fe Trail (serial); Golden Silence; The Lone Horseman; The Fighting Shippers (serial); Mary of the Movies. 1924 Coyote Fangs; Riders of the Plains (serial); Crashin' Through; Lightnin' Jack; Travelin' Fast; Virginian Outcast; Shootin' Square; Ridin' West; Those Who Dance. 1925 Border Vengeance; Winning a Woman; Double Fisted; Cactus Trails; Canyon Rustlers; Desert Madness; The Knockout Kid; Starlight; The Untamed; Dangerous Fists; Silent Sheldon. 1926 A Ridin' Gent; Mistaken Orders; Midnight Faces; Dangerous Traffic; The Grey Devil; Hi-Jacking Rustlers; The Thunderbolt Strikes; West of the Rainbow's End; Starlight's Revenge; The Man from Oklahoma. 1927 Code of the Range; Fire and Steel; The Laffin' Fool; Where the North Holds Sway; Thunderbolt's Tracks. 1928 Guardians of the Wild; The Vanishing West (serial); The Two Outlaws; The Water Hole. 1929 Wild Blood; The Harvest of Hate; Hoofbeats of Vengeance; Plunging Hoofs. 1930 The Apache Kid's Escape; Phantom of the Desert; Beyond the Rio Grande; Ridin' Law; Trails of Peril; Overland Bound; Romance of the West; The Jade Box (serial). 1931 Wild West Whoopee; The Kid from Arizona; The Sheriff's Secret; Lariats and Six-Shooters. 1932 Hell Fire Austin; .45 Calibre Echo; Dynamite Ranch. 1934 Rawhide Mail; Girl Trouble (short). 1936 Hair Trigger Casey; Desert Justice. 1937 The Painted Stallion (serial). 1938 Western Jamboree; Angels with Dirty Faces; The Purple Vigilantes. 1940 West of Pinto Basin. 1941 Sky Raiders (serial). 1942 Broadway Big Shot. 1943–1949 Numerous westerns. 1950 Bandit Queen. 1956 Around the World in 80 Days.

PERRINS, LESLIE

Born: 1902, Moseley, England. Died: Dec. 13, 1962, Esher, England. Screen, stage and radio actor.

Appeared in: 1928 Sexton Blake series including: The Clue of the Second Goblet; and Blake the Lawbreaker. 1931 Immediate Possession; The Rosary; The Sleeping Cardinal (aka Sherlock Holmes' Fatal Hour—US); The Calendar (aka Bachelor's Folly—US 1932); We Dine at Seven. 1932 Betrayal; White Face. 1933 The Lost Chord; Just Smith; The Roof; The Pointing Finger; Early to Bed. 1934 Lily of Killarney (aka Bride of the Lake—US); The Man Who Changed His Name; The Lash; Song at Eventide; Lord Edgware Dies; Open All Night; Gay Love; The Scotland Yard Mystery (aka The Living Dead—US); Womanhood. 1935 D'ye Ken John Peel? (aka Captain Moonlight—US); The Shadow of Mike Emerald; The Rocks of Valpre (aka High Treason—US 1937); White Lilac; The Triumph of Sherlock Holmes; Lucky Days; Expert's Opinion; Line Engaged; The Village Squire. 1936 Tudor Rose (aka Nine Days a Queen—US); Sunshine Ahead; Rhythm in the Air; Southern Roses; No Escape; The Limping Man; They Didn't Know. 1937 Secret Lives (aka I Married a Spy—US 1938); The High Command; Sensation; Dangerous Fingers (aka Wanted by Scotland Yard—US); Bulldog Drummond at Bay; The House of Unrest; The Price of Folly. 1938 Mr. Reeder in Room 13 (aka Mystery of Room 13—US 1941); Romance a la Carte; The Gables Mystery; No Parking; Calling All Crooks; His Lordship Goes to Press; Luck of the Navy (aka North Sea Patrol—US 1940); Old Iron. 1939 The Gang's All Here (aka The Amazing Mr. Forrest—US); All at Sea; Blind Folly; I Killed the Count (aka Who is Guilty?—US 1940). 1940 John Smith Wakes Up. 1941 The Prime Minister. 1942 Suspected Person; Women Aren't Angels. 1944 Heaven is Round the Corner. 1946 I'll Turn to You. 1947 The Turners of Prospect Road. 1948 Idols of Paris. 1949 A Run for Your Money (US 1950); Man on the Run (US 1951). 1950 Midnight Episode (US 1951). 1952 The Lost Hours (aka The Big Frame—US 1953). 1956 Guilty? 1958 Grip of the Strangler (aka The Haunted Strangler—US).

PERRY, ANTOINETTE (aka ANNETTE PERRY)

Born: 1888. Died: June 28, 1946, New York, N.Y. (heart attack). Screen, stage actress and stage director.

Appeared in: 1924 Yankee Madness. 1925 After Marriage.

PERRY, CHARLES EMMETT

Born: 1907. Died: Feb. 26, 1967, Hollywood, Calif. (heart ailment). Screen actor. Married to actress Naomi Perry. Entered films in 1923. Do not confuse with British actor Charles Perry.

PERRY, MARY

Born: 1888, Gainesville, Ga. Died: Mar. 6, 1971, N.Y. Screen, stage and television actress.

Appeared in: 1958 Uncle Vanya (stage and film versions). 1960 The Fugitive Kind. 1963 All the Way Home.

PERRY, ROBERT E. "BOB"

Born: 1879, New York, N.Y. Died: Jan. 8, 1962, Hollywood, Calif. Screen and television actor.

Appeared in: 1921 The Devil Within. 1922 Oath-Bound; Iron to Gold. 1925 The Light of Western Stars; The Thundering Herd. 1926 Volcano; Gigolo. 1927 Finger Prints; Jaws of Steel; White Gold; Brass Knuckles. 1928 The Fortune Hunter; Beggars of Life; Dressed to Kill; The River Pirate; Me, Gangster. 1929 The Man I Love; Noisy Neighbors; Sin Town; Skin Deep. 1930 Those Who Dance; Trailin' Trouble; The Sea God. 1932 Carnival Boat; Hell's Highway. 1933 The Chief. 1934 The Mighty Barnum. 1936 Riffraff; Cain and Mabel; My Man Godfrey. 1937 Manhattan Merry-Go-Round. 1941 The Big Store. 1946 The Kid from Brooklyn.

PERRY, SARA

Born: 1872. Died: Jan. 18, 1959, White Plains, N.Y. Screen and stage actress.

Appeared in: 1950 The Damned Don't Cry.

PERRY, VICTOR "VIC"

Born: 1920, England. Died: Aug. 14, 1974, Van Nuys, Calif. Screen, stage and television actor. Billed as "The World's Greatest Pickpocket."

Appeared in: 1953 Julius Caesar; Pickup on South Street. 1956 The Atomic Man. 1966 Mozambique.

PERSSE, THOMAS

Died: Apr. 1920, Venice, Calif. Screen actor and opera performer.

Appeared in: 1920 It's a Great Life.

PERSSON, EDVARD

Born: 1887, Sweden. Died: Sept. 26, 1957, Halsinborg, Sweden. Screen actor.

Appeared in: 1934 Flickorna Fran Gamla Stan. 1935 Tjocka Slaekten (Near Relatives); Larsson I Andra Giftet. 1936 Loerdagsvaellar; Vaaran Pojke; Soederkaakar. 1937 The Old Gods Still Live. 1938 Baldvins Brollop (Baldwin's Wedding). 1939 Skanor-Falsterbo. 1940 Kalle Paa Spaangen; Kvinnorna Kring Larsson (The Women around Larsson). 1944 Sun over Klara. 1953 Pimpernel Sversson; Each Heart Has It's Own Story.

PETERS, ANN

Born: 1920, Santa Monica, Calif. Died: Dec. 24, 1965, Paris, France (heart attack). Black screen, stage actress and singer. Member of the "Peters Sisters" singing group. Married to musician Willy Katz.

Appeared in: 1937 Ali Baba Goes to Town. 1938 Love and Hisses; Happy Landing; Rebecca of Sunnybrook Farm.

PETERS, DON (Donald Ambrose Peters)

Born: Jan. 15, 1921, Calif. Died: Sept. 28, 1953. Screen and stage actor.

Appeared in: 1942 Ten Gentlemen from West Point.

PETERS, FRED

Born: June 30, 1884, Waltham, Mass. Died: Apr. 23, 1963, Hollywood, Calif. Screen actor. Entered films in 1916.

Appeared in: 1921 Miracles of the Jungle (serial). 1923 Salome. 1924 The Millionaire Cowboy. 1927 "12" Miles Out; Tarzan and the Golden Lion. 1929 Spieler. 1936 I Conquer the Sea.

PETERS, GUNNAR

Died: Mar. 11, 1974, Fort Salonga, N.Y. (coronary). Screen and television actor.

Appeared in: 1964 Lilith.

PETERS, HOUSE, SR.

Born: 1880 or 1888, Bristol, England. Died: Dec. 1967, Woodland Hills, Calif. Screen actor. Father of actor House Peters, Jr. Brother of actor Page Peters (dec. 1916).

Appeared in: 1913 Leah-Kleshna; Lady of Quality. 1914 The Pride of Jennico; Salomy Jane. 1915 The Girl of the Golden West; The Great Divide; Mignon. 1920 The Great Redeemer; Isobel. 1921 The Invisible Power; Lying Lips. 1922 The Man from Lost River; Human Hearts; The Storm; Rich Men's Wives. 1923 Held to Answer; Counsel for the Defense; Lost and Found; Don't Marry for Money. 1924 The Tornado. 1925 Raffles; Head Winds; The Storm Breaker. 1926 The Combat; Prisoners of the Storm. 1928 Rose Marie. 1952 O'Henry's Full House; The Old West.

PETERS, CAPT. JOHN

Born: Germany. Died: Oct. 21, 1940, Santa Rosa, Calif. Screen actor and circus performer.

Appeared in: 1926 Ransom's Folly.

PETERS, JOHN S. (John Sylvester Peters)

Died: Nov. 7, 1963, Los Angeles, Calif. Screen actor.

Appeared in: 1926 The Amateur Gentleman; Under Western Skies; Ransom's Folly. 1927 A Dog of the Regiment; The Frontiersman; The Enemy; The Student Prince in Old Heidelberg. 1928 Divine Sinner; The Scarlet Lady. 1932 White Zombie. 1934 Beast of Borneo. 1939 Mystery Plane; Beast of Berlin; Sky Patrol. 1955 Chief Crazy Horse.

PETERS, PAGE E.

Died: June 22, 1916, Hermosa Beach, Calif. (drowned). Screen actor. Brother of actor House Peters (dec. 1967).

Appeared in: 1914 The Siren. 1915 The Clue; The Unexpected; The Unafraid; The Captive. 1916 Madame Le Presidente; Davy Crockett; An International Marriage.

PETERS, PETER

Born: 1926, Germany. Died: Oct. 1, 1955, Berlin, Germany (suicide—jump from building). Stage and screen actor.

PETERS, RALPH

Born: 1903. Died: June 5, 1959, Hollywood, Calif. Screen actor.

Appeared in: 1937 The Great Gambini; Swing It Professor. 1938 Outlaws of Sonora; Man's Country; Wanted by the Police. 1939 Tough Kid; Six-Gun Rhythm; Rovin' Tumbleweeds. 1940 Ghost Valley Raiders; Laughing at Danger; Margie. 1941 You Belong to Me; Outlaws of the Rio Grande; Across the Sierras; You're Out of Luck; Two in a Taxi. 1942 Ball of Fire; Shut My Big Mouth; Bells of Capistrano; Ride 'Em Cowboy; A Man's World. 1943 It Ain't Hay; One Dangerous Night; Good Morning, Judge; Find the Blackmailer; My Kingdom for a Cook. 1944 Take it Big; Roger Touhy—Gangster; Black Magic; Twilight on the Prairie; Ghost Catchers; Charlie Chan in Black Magic. 1945 Radio Stars on Parade; Hold that Blonde; Honeymoon Ahead; See My Lawyer. 1946 Nobody Lives Forever; Little Giant. 1947 Trail to San Antone. 1948 So You Want to Build a House (short). 1949 Fighting Fools; Sky Liner; Cactus Cut-Up (short). 1950 Beyond the Purple Hills; Experiment Alcatraz; Where the Sidewalk Ends. 1951 Gasoline Alley; A Millionaire for Christy; Slaughter Trail. 1952 The Sniper. 1953 Gentlemen Prefer Blondes. 1954 Three Ring Circus; Destry. 1956 While the City Sleeps. 1957 Badlands of Montana.

PETERS, SUSAN (Suzanne Carnahan)

Born: July 3, 1921, Spokane, Wash. Died: Oct. 23, 1952, Visalia, Calif. (chronic kidney infection, pneumonia and starvation). Screen, stage and television actress. Appeared in films originally as Suzanne Carnahan.

Appeared in: 1940 Money and the Woman; River's End; Young America Flies; Sockaroo; The Man Who Talked Too Much; Susan and God; Santa Fe Trail. 1941 Strawberry Blonde; Meet John Doe; Here Comes Happiness; Three Sons O'Guns; Scattergood Pulls the Strings. 1942 Escape from Crime; Dr. Gillespie's New Assistant; Random Harvest; The Big Shot; Tish; Andy Hardy's Double Life. 1943 Assignment in Brittany; Young Ideas. 1944 Song of Russia. 1945 Keep Your Powder Dry. 1948 The Sign of the Ram.

PETERS, WERNER

Born: 1919, Germany. Died: Mar. 31, 1971, Wiesbaden, West Germany. Screen, stage actor and film producer.

Appeared in: 1951 The Subject. 1958 Unruhige Nacht (The Restless Night—US 1964); Nachts Wenn der Teufel Kam (Nights When the Devil Came aka The Devil Strikes at Night—US 1959). 1959 Rosen fur den Staatsanwalt (Roses for the Prosecutor—US 1961); Kriegsgericht (Court Martial—US 1962). 1960 Liebe Kann Wie Gift Sein (Love Can Be Like Poison aka Magdalena); Rosemary. 1961 Im Stahlnetz des Dr. Mabuse (The Return of Dr. Mabuse—US 1966). 1962 The Counterfeit Traitor; Die Unsichtbaren Krallen des Dr. Mabuse (The Invisible Dr. Mabuse—US 1965). 1963 Das Feuerschiff (The Lightship); Nur Tote Zeugen Schweigen (aka Hypnosis—US 1966). 1964 Einer Frisst den Anderen (aka Dog Eat Dog—US 1966); Das Phantom von Soho (The Phantom of Soho—US 1967). 1965 The Battle of the Bulge; Thirty Six Hours. 1966 A Fine Madness; I Deal in Danger; Il Sigillo de Pechino (aka The Corrupt Ones—US 1967 and aka The Peking Medallion and Hell to Macao). 1967 Deux Billets pour Mexico (aka Dead Run—US 1969). 1968 Assignment K; The Secret War of Harry Frigg.

PETERSEN, PETER

Born: 1876, Hamburg, Germany. Died: Apr. 1, 1956, Vienna, Austria. Screen, stage, burlesque actor and stage director.

Appeared in: 1934 Masquerade. 1937 The Eternal Mask; Masquerade in Vienna; The Kreutzer Sonata. 1940 Der Spiegel des Lebens (Life's Mirror).

PETERSON, KAREN

Born: England. Died: Feb. 16, 1940, London, England. Screen and stage actress. Married to film producer Maurice Ostrer.

PETERSON, MARJORIE

Born: Houston, Texas. Died: Aug. 19, 1974, New York, N.Y. (heart attack). Stage and screen actress.

Appeared in: 1932 Panama Flo; Love Is a Racket; Tess of the Storm Country.

PETERSON, WILBUR "PETE"

Born: 1915, Hawaii. Died: Oct. 24, 1960, Miami, Fla. Screen, television and vaudeville actor.

PETEY

Born: 1923, Pasadena, Calif. Died: Apr. 1930, Los Angeles, Calif. (arsenic poisoning). Screen animal performer (dog). Son of "Pal" (dec. 1929). Appeared in Our Gang comedies—the dog with the ring around his eye—and also played "Tige" in Buster Brown Comedies.

PETIT, ALBERT

Born: 1887, Switzerland. Died: Feb. 28, 1963, Woodland Hills, Calif. Stage and screen actor.

Appeared in: 1934 Here is My Heart; Bum Voyage (short).

PETRIE, HAY (David Hay Petrie)

Born: July 16, 1895, Dundee, Scotland. Died: July 30, 1948. Stage and screen actor.

Appeared in: 1930 Suspense; Night Birds. 1931 Gipsy Blood (aka Carmen—US 1932); Many Waters. 1932 Help Yourself. 1933 Matinee Idol; The Lucky Number; Daughters of Today; Crime on the Hill; The Private Life of Henry VIII. 1934 Colonel Blood; The Queen's Affair (aka Runaway Queen—US 1935); The Private Life of Don Juan; Nell Gwyn; The Old Curiosity Shop (US 1935); Blind Justice. 1935 Invitation to the Waltz; Peg of Old Drury (US 1936); I Give My Heart; Moscow Nights (aka I Stand Condemned—US 1936); Koenigsmark; The Silent Passenger. 1936 Forget-Me-Not (aka Forever Yours—US 1937); The Ghost Goes West; The House of the Spaniard; Men of Yesterday; Hearts of Humanity; Rembrandt; No Escape; Conquest of the Air; Not Wanted on Voyage (aka Treachery on the High Seas—US). 1937 Secret Lives (aka I Married a Spy—US 1938); Knight Without Armour; 21 Days (aka 21 Days Together—US 1940 and aka The First and the Last). 1938 Keep Smiling (aka Smiling Along—US 1939); Consider Your Verdict; The Last Barricade. 1939 Ten Days in Paris (aka Missing Ten Days—US); Q Planes (aka Clouds over Europe—US); The Spy in Black (aka U-Boat 29—US); Jamaica Inn; Inquest; Four Feathers; Trunk Crime (aka Design for Murder—US 1940).

1940 Crimes at the Dark House; Spy for a Day; Convoy; The Thief of Bagdad; Contraband (aka Blackout—US); Pastor Hall. **1941** Freedom Radio (aka A Voice in the Night—US); Spellbound (aka The Spell of Amy Nugent—US); Cottage to Let (aka Bombsight Stolen—US); Turned Out Nice Again; The Ghost of St. Michaeli. **1942** Hard Steel; This Was Paris; One of Our Aircraft is Missing; They Flew Alone (aka Wings and the Woman—US); The Great Mr. Handel (US 1943). **1943** Battle for Music. **1944** On Approval (US 1945); Kiss the Bride Goodbye; A Canterbury Tale. **1945** Waltz Time; The Voice Within. **1946** The Laughing Lady (US 1950); Great Expectations (US 1947); Under New Management. **1948** The Monkey's Paw; The Red Shoes; The Guinea Pig (US 1949); The Fallen Idol (US 1949); Noose (aka The Silk Noose—US 1950). **1949** The Queen of Spades.

PETRIE, HOWARD A.

Born: 1907, Beverly, Mass. Died: Mar. 26, 1968, Keene, N.H. Screen, radio and television actor.

Appeared in: **1950** Walk Softly, Stranger; Rocky Mountain. **1951** No Questions Asked; Cattle Drive; The Golden Horde. **1952** The Wild North; Red Ball Express; Bend of the River; Carbine Williams; Woman in the North Country; Pony Soldier. **1953** Fort Ti; Fair Wind to Java; The Veils of Bagdad. **1954** Sign of the Pagan; The Bob Mathias Story; The Bounty Hunter; Seven Brides for Seven Brothers; Border River; Street Corner (aka Both Sides of the Law—US). **1955** Rage at Dawn; How to Be Very, Very Popular; The Return of Jack Slade; Timberjack. **1956** Johnny Concho; The Maverick Queen; A Kiss Before Dying. **1957** The Tin Star.

PETRUZZI, JULIAN (Julian Joseph Petruzzi)

Born: May 17, 1907, Ohio. Died: Mar. 1, 1967, Woodland Hills, Calif. (heart attack). Screen actor.

Appeared in: **1938** Tenth Avenue Kid.

PETTINGELL, FRANK

Born: Jan. 1, 1891, Liverpool, England. Died: Feb. 17, 1966, London, England. Screen, stage and television actor.

Appeared in: **1931** Hobson's Choice; Jealousy. **1932** Frail Women; The Crooked Lady; In a Monastery Garden; Once Bitten; Double Dealing; A Tight Corner. **1933** Yes, Madam; The Medicine Man; Excess Baggage; The Good Companions; That's My Wife; The Lucky Number; A Cuckoo in the Nest; This Week of Grace. **1934** Red Wagon; Keep it Quiet; Sing as We Go; My Old Dutch. **1935** The Big Splash; The Hope of His Side (aka Where's George?); Say It with Diamonds; The Last Journey (US 1936); The Right to Marry. **1936** The Amateur Gentleman; Millions; On Top of the World; Fame. **1937** It's a Grand Old World; Spring Handicap; Take My Tip. **1938** Sailing Along; Queer Cargo (aka Pirates of the Seven Seas—US). **1940** Busman's Honeymoon (aka Haunted Honeymoon—US); Return to Yesterday; Gaslight (aka Angel Street—US). **1941** Kipps (aka The Remarkable Mr. Kipps—US 1942); Once a Crook; Ships with Wings (US 1942); The Seventh Survivor; This England (aka Our Heritage). **1942** The Young Mr. Pitt; The Goose Steps Out. **1943** Get Cracking; When We Are Married. **1946** Gaiety George (aka Showtime—US 1948). **1948** Escape; No Room at the Inn. **1951** The Magic Box (US 1952). **1952** The Crimson Pirate; The Card (aka The Promoter—US); Meet Me Tonight. **1953** Tonight at 8:30. **1955** Value for Money (US 1957). **1958** Up the Creek; Corridors of Blood (US 1963). **1962** Term of Trial (US 1963); The Dock Brief (aka Trial and Error—US). **1964** Becket.

PEUKERT-IMPEKOVEN, SABINE

Born: 1890, Germany. Died: May 5, 1970, Frankfurt, Germany. Stage and screen actress. Pioneer actress of German silent films.

PEYTON, LAWRENCE R. "LARRY"

Born: Hartford, Kentucky. Died: 1918, France (killed in action). Stage and screen actor.

Appeared in: **1913** The Sea Wolf. **1914** Martin Eden. **1915** The Unexpected; A Gentleman of Leisure; The Unafraid; My Best Girl; The Americano; Man Afraid of His Wardrobe; Author! Author!; This Is the Life; Buck Parvin and the Movies. **1916** Water Stuff; The Extra Man and the Milkfed Lion; Now Stuff; Margy of the Foothills; The Return; A Man's Friend; The Gulf Between. **1917** The Red Ace (serial); Joan the Woman; The Golden Fetter; The Greater Law; The Pullman Mystery. **1918** Ace High; How Could You, Jean?

PHELPS, LEE

Born: 1894. Died: Mar. 19, 1953, Culver City, Calif. Screen, stage and vaudeville actor.

Appeared in: **1921** The Road Demon. **1922** The Freshie. **1927** Putting Pants on Philip (short). **1930** Annie Christie; The Criminal Code. **1932** Cross Examination; The Night Club Lady; Hold 'Em Jail. **1933** Parole Girl; Bedtime Stories (short); The Woman I Stole. **1934** Six of a Kind; Beggars in Ermine. **1935** $1,000 a Minute; Hot Money (short); Southern Exposure (short); Wings in the Dark. **1936** Palm Springs; Crash Donovan; Cain and Mabel; Life Hesitates at 40 (short); Boss Rider of Gun Creek; The Bohemian Girl; Our Relations. **1937** Tough to Handle; Easy Living; Under Suspicion; A Nation Aflame; Boss of Lonely Valley; Sandflow; Lefthanded Law. **1938** Long Shot; Trade Winds;

Female Fugitive; The Gladiator. **1939** The Flying Irishman; Kid Nightingale; Gone with the Wind. **1940** Murder Over New York; Hidden Gold. **1941** Andy Hardy's Private Secretary; A Shot in the Dark; The Big Store. **1942** Scattergood Rides High; Two Yanks in Trinidad; Tennessee Johnson; Gentleman Jim; Life Begins at 8:30; War Dogs. **1943** Air Raid Wardens. **1944** Nothing but Trouble. **1945** Don Juan Quilligan; The Hidden Eye. **1949** Angels in Disguise; Sky Dragon; The Lone Wolf and His Lady; Shadows of the West; Gun Law Justice. **1950** The Girl from San Lorenzo; Hills of Oklahoma; Square Dance Katy; Timber Fury; Western Pacific Agent. **1953** Man of Conflict; The Marshal's Daughter.

PHILIPE, GERARD

Born: France. Died: Nov. 27, 1959, Paris, France (heart attack). Screen, stage actor and film director.

Appeared in: **1943** The Land without Stars (film debut). **1946** Le Diable au Corps (The Devil in the Flesh—US 1949). **1947** L'Idiot (The Idiot). **1948** Une Si Folie Petite Plage. **1949** La Beautie du Diable (The Beauty of the Devil—US 1952). **1950** La Ronde (US 1954). **1951** Rip Tide. **1952** Fanfan La Tulipe (US 1953); Belles de Nuit (Beauties of the Night). **1953** Seven Deadly Sins; Les Orgeuilleux; Knave of Hearts. **1954** Le Rouge et le Noir (The Red and the Black—US 1958). **1955** Les Granes Manoeuvres (The Grand Maneuver—US 1956); Lovers Happy Lovers. **1956** The Proud and the Beautiful; Till Eulenspiegel. **1957** It Happened in the Park; Royal Affairs in Versailles. **1958** Pot-Bouville; Lovers of Paris. **1959** Les Liaisons Dangereuses (US 1961). **1961** Modigliani of Montparnasse. Other French films: The Fever Rises in El Pao; All Roads Lead to Rome.

PHILLIBER, JOHN

Born: 1872, Elkhart, Ind. Died: Nov. 6, 1944, Elkhart, Ind. Stage and screen actor.

Appeared in: **1943** A Lady Takes a Chance. **1944** The Imposter; It Happened Tomorrow; Ladies of Washington; Summer Storm; Double Indemnity. **1945** Gentle Annie.

PHILLIPS, ALBERT

Born: 1875. Died: Feb. 24, 1940, New York, N.Y. Screen actor.

Appeared in: **1923** Broadway Broke.

PHILLIPS, CHARLES

Born: 1904. Died: May 25, 1958, Hollywood, Calif. Screen actor and stuntman. Doubled for Charles Laughton and Oliver Hardy.

Appeared in: **1936** Peppery Salt (short).

PHILLIPS, CLEMENT K.

Died: Oct. 1928, Hayward, Calif. (airplane crash). Screen actor and stunt flier.

PHILLIPS, EDNA

Born: 1878. Died: Feb. 26, 1952, Los Angeles, Calif. Screen actress. Wife of actor Taylor Holmes (dec. 1959) and mother of actors Phillips (dec. 1942) and Ralph Holmes (dec. 1945).

PHILLIPS, EDWARD N.

Born: 1899. Died: Feb. 22, 1965, North Hollywood, Calif. (struck by auto). Screen actor and film editor.

Appeared in "The Collegians" series of shorts which began in 1926 with Benson at Calford and continued until 1929. The following are all "Collegians" series of shorts: **1926** Benson at Calford; Fighting to Win; Making Good; The Last Lap; Around the Bases; Fighting Spirit; The Relay. **1927** Cinder Path; Flashing Oars; Breaking Records; Crimson Colors; Winning Five; The Dazzling Coeds; A Fighting Finish; Samson at Calford; The Winning Punch; Running Wild; Splashing Through; The Winning Goal; Sliding Home. **1928** The Junior Year; Calford vs. Redskins; Kicking Through; Calford in the Movies; Radding Coeds; Fighting for Victory; Dear Old Calford; Calford on Horseback; The Bookworm Hero; Speeding Youth; Farewell; The Winning Point. **1929** King of the Campus; The Rivals; On Guard; Junior Luck; The Cross Country Run; Sporting Courage; Flying High; The Varsity Drag; On the Side Lines; Use Your Feet; Splash Mates; Graduation Daze.

PHILLIPS, EDWIN R.

Born: Providence, Rhode Island. Died: Aug. 30, 1915, Coney Island, N.Y. Screen actor. Entered films in 1908 with Vitagraph.

Appeared in: **1910** The New Stenographer. **1911** Carr's Regeneration; The Latent Spark. **1912** The Counts; Uncle Tom's Cabin; The Bogus Napoleon; A Bunch of Violets; The Black Sheep; An Expensive Shine.

PHILLIPS, FESTUS "DAD"

Born: 1872. Died: Sept. 5, 1955, Hollywood, Calif. Screen actor and makeup artist.

PHILLIPS, HELENA. *See* HELENA PHILLIPS EVANS

PHILLIPS, JEAN

Born: Sept. 22, ? Died: Dec. 15, 1970. Screen actress.

Appeared in: **1941** Among the Living; Outlaws of the Desert. **1942** Timber; Night in New Orleans; Dr. Broadway.

PHILLIPS, MARY

Born: 1901, New London, Conn. Died: Apr. 22, 1975, Santa Monica, Calif. (cancer). Stage and screen actress. Divorced from actor Humphrey Bogart (dec. 1957) and later married to actor Kenneth MacKenna (dec. 1962).

Appeared in: **1930** Stepping Out (short); Broadway's Like That (short). **1932** A Farewell to Arms; Life Begins. **1937** As Good as Married; Wings over Honolulu; That Certain Woman; The Bride Wore Red; Mannequin. **1944** Lady in the Dark. **1945** Incendiary Blonde; Captain Eddie; Kiss and Tell; Leave Her to Heaven. **1947** Dear Ruth. **1949** A Woman's Secret; Dear Wife. **1951** I Can Get it for You Wholesale. **1954** Prince Valiant.

PHILLIPS, MINNA

Born: June 1, 1885, Sydney, Australia. Died: Jan. 29, 1963, New Orleans, La. (heart ailment). Stage and screen actress.

Appeared in: **1942** The Male Animal; A Yank at Eaton; My Sister Eileen. **1943** Sherlock Holmes Faces Death; Girls, Inc. **1950** Bandit Queen. **1951** Queen for a Day.

PHILLIPS, NORMA

Born: 1893, Baltimore, Md. Died: Nov. 12, 1931, New York (cancer). Stage and screen actress. Known as "Our Mutual Girl" in series of silents in 1914.

Appeared in: **1915** Runaway June.

PHILLIPS, NORMAN, SR.

Born: 1892. Died: Feb. 11, 1931, Culver City, Calif. (heart attack). Screen and vaudeville actor. Father of actor Norman Phillips, Jr.

PHILLIPS, RICHARD

Born: 1826. Died: May 4, 1941, Los Angeles, Calif. Screen actor. Claimed to be 115 years old—oldest actor in the world!

PHILLIPS, WILLIAM "BILL"

Born: Washington, D.C. Died: June 27, 1957. Stage and screen actor.

Appeared in: **1940** City for Conquest. **1941** Sergeant York. **1942** Larceny, Inc.; The Lady Gangster. **1943** Johnny Come Lately; Action in the North Atlantic; Swingtime Johnny. **1944** See Here Private Hargrove; Music for Millions; Thirty Seconds over Tokyo. **1945** The Last Installment (short); Abbott and Costello in Hollywood. **1946** The Harvey Girls; Holiday in Mexico; 'Til the Clouds Roll By; What Next Corporal Hargrove?; The Hoodlum Saint. **1947** Sea of Grass; Living in a Big Way. **1949** Johnny Allegro; Easy Living; Big Jack; Blondie's Secret; Prison Warden; Man from Colorado. **1950** Customs Agent; Chain Gang; Mary Ryan, Detective; He's a Cockeyed Wonder; The Vanishing Westerner. **1951** Detective Story; Al Jennings of Oklahoma; Cavalry Scout; A Yank in Korea. **1952** High Noon; Because You're Mine; Bugles in the Afternoon. **1953** Devil's Canyon; Gun Belt; Private Eyes. **1954** Wicked Woman; The Law vs. Billy the Kid. **1955** New York Confidential; Fort Yuma; Ghost Town; Top Gun. **1956** The Broken Star; The Man in the Gray Flannel Suit; Stagecoach to Fury; The Fastest Gun Alive. **1957** Revolt at Fort Laramie; Hellcats of the Navy.

PIAF, EDITH (Edith Gassion)

Born: 1916, Paris, France. Died: Oct. 11, 1963, Paris, France (internal hemorrhage). Screen, stage actress and singer.

Appeared in: **1947** Etoile Sans Lumiere (Star without Light). **1956** French-Cancan. **1957** Royal Affairs in Versailles. **1962** I Love, You Love. **1976** Singing Under the Occupation (documentary).

PIAZZA, DARIO

Born: 1904. Died: Sept. 1, 1974, Glendale, Calif. (cancer). Costumer, film actor and extra.

PICA, TINA

Born: 1888, Italy. Died: Aug. 16, 1968, Naples, Italy. Stage and screen actress.

Appeared in: **1949** Guaglio. **1954** Bread, Love and Dreams. **1955** Frisky. **1957** Scandal in Sorrento. **1959** The Virtuous Bigamist. **1964** Leri, Oggi, Domani (Yesterday, Today and Tomorrow).

PICASSO, PABLO

Born: Oct. 25, 1881, Malaga, Spain. Died: Apr. 8, 1973, Mougins, France. Artist, sculptor and screen actor.

Appeared in: **1952** La Vie Commence Demain (Life Begins Tomorrow). **1962** Testament of Orpheus.

PICHEL, IRVING

Born: 1891, Pittsburgh, Pa. Died: July 13, 1954, Hollywood, Calif. (heart attack). Screen, stage actor, film director and screenwriter.

Appeared in: **1930** The Right to Love. **1931** Murder by the Clock; The Road to Reno; An American Tragedy; The Cheat. **1932** Westward Passage; The Painted Woman; Strange Justice; Wild Girl; The Miracle Man; Two Kinds of Women; Forgotten Commandments; Island of Lost Souls; Most Dangerous Game; Madame Butterfly. **1933** Mysterious Rider; The Woman Accused; King of the Jungle; Oliver Twist; The Story of Temple Drake; I'm No Angel; The Right to Romance; The Billion Dollar Scandal. **1934** British Agent; Return of the Terror; Silver Streak; She Was a Lady; Such Women Are Dangerous; Cleopatra; Fog over Frisco. **1935** I Am a Thief; Three Kids and a Queen; Special Agent. **1936** Hearts in Bondage; Down to the Sea; The House of a Thousand Candles; Don't Gamble with Love; General Spanky; Dracula's Daughter. **1937** High, Wide and Handsome; There Goes My Heart; Jezebel; Gambling Ship. **1939** Newsboys' Home; Torture Ship; Rio; Topper Takes a Trip; Dick Tracy's G-Men (serial); Juarez. **1943** The Moon is Down. **1951** Santa Fe. **1953** Martin Luther.

PICK, LUPE

Born: 1886, Germany. Died: Mar. 1931 (poison). Screen actor and film director.

Appeared in: **1928** Spione (Spies).

PICKARD, HELENA

Born: 1900. Died: Sept. 27, 1959, Oxfordshire, England. Screen and television actress. Divorced from actor Sir Cedric Hardwicke (dec. 1964).

Appeared in: **1934** Nell Gwyn. **1935** Limelight. **1940** Let George Do It. **1944** The Lodger.

PICKETT, INGRAM B.

Born: 1899. Died: Feb. 14, 1963, Santa Fe, N.M. Screen actor. Was early member of Mack Sennett's Keystone Kops.

PICKFORD, JACK (Jack Smith)

Born: Aug. 18, 1896, Toronto, Canada. Died: Jan. 3, 1933, Paris, France (multiple neuritis). Stage and screen actor. Son of actress Charlotte Smith (dec. 1928). Brother of actresses Mary Pickford and Lottie Pickford (dec. 1936). Married to actress Olive Thomas (dec. 1920) and divorced from actress Marilyn Miller (dec. 1936).

Appeared in: **1910** The Modern Prodigal; The Iconoclast; The Kid; Examination Day at School; A Child's Stratagem. **1912** Heredity; Mr. Grouch at the Seashore; The Unwelcome Guest; The New York Hat. **1914** Wildflower; Home Sweet Home. **1915** The Pretty Sister of Jose. **1916** Seventeen; The Dummy; Great Expectations; Tom Sawyer. **1918** Huck and Tom; Sandy; His Majesty, Bunker Bean; Mile-a-Minute Kendall. **1920** The Little Shepherd of Kingdom Come. **1921** Little Lord Fauntleroy; Just out of College; Man Who Had Everything; Through the Back Door. **1922** Valley of the Wolf. **1923** Hollywood; Garrison's Finish. **1924** The Hillbilly; The End of the World. **1925** Waking up the Town; My Son; The Goose Woman. **1926** The Bat; Brown of Harvard; Exit Smiling. **1928** Gang War.

PICKFORD, LOTTIE (Lottie Smith)

Died: Dec. 9, 1936, Brentwood, Calif. (heart attack). Screen actress. Sister of actress Mary Pickford and actor Jack Pickford (dec. 1933). Daughter of actress Charlotte Smith (dec. 1928). Entered films with Imp Company in 1910.

Appeared in: **1910** A Gold Necklace; White Roses. **1915** The Diamond from the Sky (serial). **1918** Mile-a-Minute Kendall. **1924** Dorothy Vernon from Haddon Hall. **1925** Don Q.

PIDAL, JOSE

Born: 1896, Spain. Died: Oct. 26, 1956, Mexico City, Mexico (cancer). Stage and screen actor.

PIEL, EDWARD, SR. and PIEL, EDWARD, JR. *See* "PEIL"

PIEL, HARRY

Born: 1892, Dusseldorf, Germany. Died: 1963, Munich, Germany. Screen actor and film director. Married to actress Dary Holm.

Appeared in: **1938** Sein Bester Freund (His Best Friend).

PIERCE, EVELYN

Born: Feb. 5, 1908, Del Rio, Tex. Died: Aug. 9, 1960, Oyster Bay, N.Y. Screen actress. Married to actor Theodore Baehr. Entered films in 1925.

Appeared in: **1925** Don't. **1927** The Border Cavalier. **1928** Sonia; Tenderloin. **1929** The Million Dollar Collar. **1930** Once a Gentleman. **1931** An American Tragedy; Monkey Business. **1935** I'm a Father (short).

PIERCE, GEORGE. *See* GEORGE C. PEARCE

PIERLOT, FRANCIS
Born: 1876. Died: May 11, 1955, Hollywood, Calif. (heart ailment). Screen, stage and television actor.

Appeared in: **1931** Night Angel. **1940** The Captain Is a Lady; Strike up the Band; Escape to Glory (aka Submarine Zone); Always a Bride. **1941** The Trial of Mary Dugan; International Lady; Rise and Shine; Remember the Day; A-Haunting We Will Go. **1942** Just Off Broadway; Henry Aldrich, Editor; Night Monster; Yankee Doodle Dandy; My Heart Belongs to Daddy; A Gentleman at Heart. **1943** Mission to Moscow; Mystery Broadcast. **1944** The Doughgirls; Uncertain Glory; Adventures of Mark Twain; Bathing Beauty; The Very Thought of You. **1945** Hit the Hay; Affairs of Susan; Fear; Grissly's Millions; The Hidden Eye; How Do You Do?; Our Vines Have Tender Grapes; Roughly Speaking; Yolanda and the Thief; A Tree Grows in Brooklyn; Bewitched. **1946** Life with Blondie; Dragonwyck; The Catman of Paris; The Crime Doctor's Manhunt; G.I. War Brides; Two Guys from Milwaukee; The Walls Came Tumbling Down. **1947** Cigarette Girl; The Late George Apley; Philo Vance's Gamble; Second Chance; The Senator Was Indiscreet; The Trespasser. **1948** The Dude Goes West; Chicken Every Sunday; The Accused; That Wonderful Urge; I, Jane Doe. **1949** Bad Boy; Take One False Step; My Friend Irma. **1950** Copper Canyon; Cyrano de Bergerac; The Flame and the Arrow. **1951** Anne of the Indies; The Lemon Drop Kid; Savage Drums; That's My Boy. **1952** Hold That Line; The Prisoner of Zenda. **1953** The Robe.

PIERPONT, LAURA
Born: 1881. Died: Dec. 11, 1972, New Canaan, Conn. Screen and stage actress. Married to vaudeville actor and film producer Taylor Granville (dec. 1923).

Appeared in: **1950** My Blue Heaven.

PIERRE, ANATOLE
Died: Feb. 1926, New Orleans, La. Black screen and minstrel actor.

PIERRE, ANDRE
Born: 1884, France. Died: Feb. 9, 1975, France. Screen actor and screenwriter.

PIERSON, ARTHUR
Born: June, 1891 or 1901 (?), Oslo, Norway. Died: Jan. 1, 1975, Santa Monica, Calif. Screen, stage actor, stage director, playwright, film, television director, television producer and screenwriter. Divorced from actress Ruth Matteson (dec. 1975).

Appeared in: **1932** Tomorrow and Tomorrow; The Golden West; No One Man; The Strange Case of Clara Deane; Bachelor's Affairs; Hat Check Girl; Rackety Rax. **1933** Air Hostess; Ann Carver's Profession; The Devil's Brother; The Way to Love; Before Midnight. **1934** You Belong to Me; Murder in the Clouds. **1935** Sweet Surrender.

PIGOTT, TEMPE
Born: 1884. Died: Oct. 13, 1962, Hollywood, Calif. Screen and stage actress.

Appeared in: **1921** The Great Impersonation. **1922** The Masked Avenger. **1923** The Rustle of Silk; Vanity Fair. **1924** The Dawn of a Tomorrow; The Narrow Street. **1925** Without Mercy; Greed. **1926** The Midnight Kiss; The Black Pirate. **1927** Silk Stockings; Wallflowers. **1928** Road House; Night Work; America or Bust; Seven Days Leave. **1931** Devotion. **1932** Dr. Jekyll and Mr. Hyde. **1933** A Study in Scarlet; Doctor Bull; If I Were Free; Cavalcade; Oliver Twist; Man of the Forest. **1934** Long Lost Father; One More River; Of Human Bondage; The Lemon Drop Kid; Limehouse Blues. **1935** The Devil Is a Woman; Becky Sharp; Calm Yourself; Bride of Frankenstein. **1936** Little Lord Fauntleroy; The White Angel. **1938** Fools for Scandal. **1939** Boys Reformatory.

PIKE, HARRY J.
Died: Dec. 18, 1919, New York, N.Y. Screen actor.

PIKE, NITA
Born: 1913. Died: May 10, 1954, Los Angeles, Calif. (suicide). Screen actress. Married to actor Alan Edwards (dec. 1954).

Appeared in: **1933** Sherman Said It (short). **1940** The Great Dictator.

PILA, MAXIMO
Born: 1886. Died: Aug. 2, 1939, Hollywood, Calif. Screen and stage actor.

PILCER, HARRY
Born: 1885, U.S. Died: Jan. 14, 1961, Cannes, France (heart attack). Screen, stage actor and dancer.

Appeared in: **1915** Her Triumph. **1946** The Razor's Edge.

PILOTTO, CAMILLO
Born: 1883 or 1890. Died: May 27, 1963. Italian screen actor.

Appeared in: **1933** Passa L'Amore. **1935** Il Delitto di Mastrovanni; Le Scarpe a Sole. **1936** Tempo Massimo; Lorenzino de Medici; Alpine Love; Anonima Roylott; Italia. **1937** Scipione l'Africanus (US 1939); I Due Misantropi; I Tre Desideri; Allegri Masnardi; Gil Ultimi Giorni di Pompeo; I Fratelli Castiglioni; Pietro Micca. **1938** Il Padre delle Patria (The Father of His Country);

Amore in Quarantena (Love in Quarantine). **1939** Il Grande Appello (The Last Roll-Call). **1940** Il Paraninfo (The Matchmaker); Tutta la Vita in una Notte (All of Life in One Night); The Life of Giuseppi Verdi; Abuna Messias. **1948** Foria; Furia; Rossini. **1952** The Thief of Venice. **1954** Mistress of the Mountains. **1960** Goddess of Love; Guiditta e Oloferne (Judith and Holophernes) (aka Head of a Tyrant—US). **1962** Marco Polo.

PILTZ, GEORGE
Died: 1968. Screen actor.

Appeared in: **1937** Ebb Tide. **1949** Daughter of the Jungle.

PIMLEY, JOHN
Born: 1919. Died: May 17, 1972, Hollywood, Calif. (heart attack). Screen, stage actor, film producer, director and playwright.

PINCHOT, ROSAMOND
Born: 1905, New York, N.Y. Died: Jan. 24, 1938, Old Brookfield, N.Y. Stage and screen actress.

Appeared in: **1930** South Seas. **1935** The Three Musketeers.

PINE, ED
Born: 1904. Died: May 9, 1950, Woodland Hills, Calif. Screen actor.

PINERO, ANTHONY
Born: 1887. Died: Jan. 5, 1958, Bridgeport, Conn. Screen actor and circus performer.

PINERO, ARTHUR WING
Born: May 24, 1855, London, England. Died: Nov. 23, 1934, London, England. Playwright, screen and stage actor.

Appeared in: **1918** Masks and Faces.

PINZA, EZIO (Fortunato Pinza)
Born: May 8, 1892, Rome, Italy. Died: May 9, 1957, Stamford, Conn. (stroke). Opera star, screen, stage and television actor.

Appeared in: **1947** Carnegie Hall. **1951** Mr. Imperium; Strictly Dishonorable. **1953** Tonight We Sing.

PIPEIRO, ROBERTO (aka ROBERTO PIPERIO)
Died: Jan. 28, 1963. Screen, stage actor and extra.

PIPO (Gustave Sofman)
Born: 1902, France. Died: Aug. 6, 1970, Paris, France. Screen actor and circus clown.

PITT, ARCHIE
Born: 1895, England. Died: Nov. 12, 1940, London, England. Screen, stage actor and screenwriter. Divorced from actress Gracie Fields.

Appeared in: **1934** Danny Boy. **1935** Barnacle Bill. **1936** Excuse My Glove.

PITTMAN, MONTE
Born: 1918. Died: June 26, 1962, Hollywood, Calif. (cancer). Screen, stage actor, film director and screenwriter. Entered films as an actor in early 1950s.

Appeared in: **1951** G.I. Jane.

PITTMAN, TOM
Born: 1933. Died: Oct. 31, 1958, Hollywood, Calif. (auto accident). Stage and screen actor.

Appeared in: **1957** Blackpatch; Bernardine; No Time to Be Young; The True Story of Jesse James; The Way to Gold; The Young Stranger. **1958** Apache Territory; Proud Rebels. **1959** The High School Big Shot; Verboten!

PITTS, ZASU
Born: Jan. 3, 1898, Parsons, Kans. Died: June 7, 1963, Hollywood, Calif. (cancer). Screen and television actress. She appeared as part of the comedy film team of "Todd and Pitts" with Thelma Todd (dec. 1935).

Appeared in: **1917** The Little Princess (film debut); Uneasy Money; His Fatal Beauty. **1918** A Society Sensation; As the Sun Went Down; How Could You, Jean?; Men, Women and Money. **1919** Better Times. **1922** A Daughter of Luxury; For the Defense; Is Matrimony a Failure?; Youth to Youth. **1923** Patsy; The Girl Who Came Back; Three Wise Fools; Mary of the Movies; Poor Men's Wives; Souls for Sale; Tea with a Kick. **1924** Changing Husbands; Daughters of Today; The Goldfish; Greed; The Fast Set; The Legend of Hollywood; West of the Water Tower; Triumph; Wine of Youth. **1925** What Happened to Jones?; The Business of Love; The Great Divide; The Great Love; Pretty Ladies; Lazybones; Old Shoes; The Recreation of Brian Kent; A Woman's Faith; Wages for Wives; Thunder Mountain; Secrets of the Night. **1926** Early to Wed; Her Big Night; Risky Business; Mannequin; Monte Carlo; Sunny Side Up. **1927** Casey at the Bat. **1928** Wife Savers; Sins of the Father; The Wedding March; Buck Privates; 13 Washington Square. **1929** The Dummy; The Squall; Twin Beds; The Argyle Case; This Thing Called Love; The Locked Door; Her Private Life; Paris. **1930** The Squealer; Monte Carlo (and 1926 version); The Little Accident; The Lottery Bride; No, No, Nanette; Oh, Yeah!; Honey; The Devil's Holiday; War Nurse; Passion Flower; Sin Takes a Holiday; Free Love; All Quiet on the Western Front (She was only in original European version and was replaced in cast by Beryl Mercer). **1931** Terror by Night; Finn and Hattie; Bad Sister; Beyond Victory; Seed; Woman of Experience; The Guardsman; Their Mad Moment; Big Gamble; On the Loose; Penrod and Sam; Secret Witness; River's End; plus the following shorts made with Thelma Todd: Let's Do Things; Catch As Catch Can; The Pajama Party; War Mamas. **1932** Unexpected Father; Strangers of the Evening; Broken Lullaby; Destry Rides Again; Steady Company; Shopworn; Sneak Easily; The Trial of Vivienne Ware; Westward Passage; Is My Face Red?; Blondie of the Follies; Roar of the Dragon; Make Me a Star; Vanishing Frontier; The Crooked Circle; Madison Square Garden; Back Street; Once in a Lifetime; Eternally Yours; The Man I Killed; plus the following shorts with Thelma Todd: Seal Skins; Red Noses; Strictly Unreliable; The Old Bull; Show Business; Alum and Eve; The Soilers. **1933** Out All Night; They Just Had to Get Married; Walking Down Broadway (aka Hello Sister!); Mr. Skitch; Her First Mate; Love, Honor and Oh, Baby; Professional Sweethearts; Aggie Appleby; Maker of Men; Meet the Baron; plus the following shorts with Thelma Todd: Asleep in the Fleet; Maids a la Mode; The Bargain of the Century; One Track Minds. **1934** Two Alone; Their Big Moment; The Meanest Gal in Town; Sing and Like It; Dames; Private Scandal; Mrs. Wiggs of the Cabbage Patch; The Gay Bride; Love Birds; Three on a Honeymoon. **1935** Ruggles of Red Gap; Spring Tonic; She Gets Her Man; Hot Tip; Going Highbrow; The Affairs of Susan. **1936** 13 Hours by Air; Sing Me a Love Song; Mad Holiday; The Plot Thickens. **1937** Merry Comes to Town; Forty Naughty Girls; 52nd Street; Wanted. **1939** The Lady's from Kentucky; Mickey the Kid; Naughty but Nice; Nurse Edith Cavell; Eternally Yours. **1940** No, No, Nanette (and 1930 version); It All Came True. **1941** The Mexican Spitfire's Baby; Broadway Limited; Niagara Falls; Miss Polly; Weekend for Three. **1942** Meet the Mob; Mexican Spitfire at Sea; The Bashful Bachelor; So's Your Aunt Emma; Tish. **1943** Let's Face It. **1946** Breakfast in Hollywood; The Perfect Marriage. **1947** A Film Goes to Market (short); Life with Father. **1949** Francis. **1952** The Denver and the Rio Grande. **1954** Francis Joins the WACS. **1957** This Could Be the Night. **1959** The Gazebo. **1961** Teen-Age Millionaire. **1963** The Thrill of It All; It's a Mad, Mad, Mad, Mad World. **1964** Big Parade of Comedy (documentary).

PITTSCHAU, WERNER

Born: 1903, Germany. Died: Oct. 1928, Spandau, Germany (auto accident). Screen actor.

Appeared in: **1928** Women without Men.

PIXLEY, GUS

Born: 1874. Died: June 2, 1923, Saranac Lake, N.Y. Screen and stage actor. Married to stage actress Mary Malatesta (dec.?).

Appeared in: **1913** The Cure; Those Little Flowers; Dyed, But Not Dead. **1915** His Last Wish; His Poor Little Girl; The Need of Money; The Little Scapegoat; The Little Slavey; Between Father and Son; The Reproach of Annesley; Blow by Blow; The Hungarian Nabob; Count 20. **1916** Lord Chumley. **1921** The Girl from Porcupine.

PLATT, ED (Edward C. Platt)

Born: 1916, Staten Island, N.Y. Died: Mar. 20, 1974, Santa Monica, Calif. (heart attack). Screen, stage, radio, television actor and singer.

Appeared in: **1953** Stalag 17. **1954** The Rebel Set. **1955** The Shrike; Rebel Without a Cause; Sincerely Yours; Illegal; The Private War of Major Benson. **1956** The Lieutenant Wore Skirts; Serenade; The Great Man; Rock, Pretty Baby; Written on the Wind; The Proud Ones; Backlash; Storm Center; The Unguarded Moment; Reprisal. **1957** Designing Woman; The Tattered Dress; Omar Khayyam; House of Numbers; The Helen Morgan Story. **1958** Damn Citizen; The Gift of Love; Summer Love; Oregon Passage; The Last of the Fast Guns; The High Cost of Loving; Gunman's Walk. **1959** North by Northwest; Cash McCall; They Came to Cordura; Inside the Mafia; The Rebel Set. **1960** Pollyanna. **1961** The Fiercest Heart; The Explosive Generation; Atlantis, the Lost Continent. **1962** Cape Fear. **1963** A Ticklish Affair; Black Zoo. **1964** Bullet for a Badman. **1965** Man from Button Willow.

PLAYFAIR, SIR NIGEL

Born: 1874, England. Died: Aug. 19, 1934, London, England. Stage and screen actor.

Appeared in: **1911** Princess Clementina. **1917** Masks and Faces (US 1918). **1933** The Perfect Understanding; Crime on the Hill (US 1934). **1934** The Lady is Willing.

PLAYTER, WELLINGTON

Born: Dec. 9, 1879, Rawcliffe, England. Died: July 15, 1937, Oakland, Calif. Screen, stage actor and film director.

Appeared in: **1914** The Pride of Jennico; Marta of the Lowlands; The Ring and the Man. **1915** Polly of the Circus; The Blood of His Brother; The Test of a Man; Chasing the Limited; Coral Queen of the Jungleland; Business is Business; The Torrent; Pennington's Choice. **1917** The Slave Market. **1919** In Search of Arcady; Back to God's Country; The Wicked Darling; Spotlight Sadie; Fool's Gold. **1921** The Golden Snare.

PLOWDEN, ROGER S.

Born: 1902. Died: Sept. 26, 1960, N.Y. Stage and screen actor.

Appeared in: **1952** Five Fingers.

PLUES, GEORGE L.

Born: 1895. Died: Aug. 16, 1953, Woodland Hills, Calif. Screen actor.

Appeared in: **1936** Guns and Guitars. **1937** Come on, Cowboys; Public Cowboy No. 1; Hit the Saddle.

PLUMB, E. HAY (Edward Hay Plumb)

Born: 1883, England. Died: 1960. Screen actor, film director, producer, screenwriter and opera performer.

Appeared in: **1910** Heart of Oak; The Heart of a Fishergirl. **1911** The Three Lovers; Children Mustn't Smoke; The Road to Ruin; Harry the Footballer; Mother's Boy; Faust; A Touch of Nature; PC Hawkeye's Busy Day; A Double Deception; Till Death Do Us Part; The Demon Dog; Twin Roses; PC Hawkeye Turns Detective; The Heat Wave; Love and a Sewing Machine; Hawkeye Learns to Punt; The Smuggler's Step-Daughter; A Seaside Introduction; The Greatest of These; Envy, Hatred and Malice; Rachel's Sin; Tilly and the Smugglers; All's Right with the World; The Stolen Letters; For a Baby's Sake; PC Hawkeye Leaves the Force. **1912** A Curate's Love Story; The Mermaid; The Lieutenant's Bride; Our Bessie; PC Hawkeye Falls in Love; PC Hawkeye, Sportsman; PC Hawkeye Goes Fishing; The Bishop's Bathe; Hawkeye, Coastguard; Hawkeye, Showman. **1913** Hawkeye Has to Hurry; Ragtime Mad; Drake's Love Story (aka The Love Romance of Admiral Sir Francis Drake—US); Hawkeye Rides in a Point-to-Point; Haunted by Hawkeye; Captain Jack VC; A Precious Cargo; The Cloister and the Hearth; David Garrick; Hawkeye Meets His Match. **1914** Hawkeye, Hall Porter; A Friend in Need; The Heart of Midlothian. **1915** Hawkeye, King of the Castle. **1931** The Professional Guest; Deadlock. **1933** Orders is Orders (US 1934); Channel Crossing (US 1934). **1934** Jew Suess (aka Power—US); The Blue Squadron; Guest of Honour. **1935** Widow's Might. **1937** Song of the Forge. **1939** Let's Be Famous.

PLUMER, LINCOLN

Born: 1876. Died: Feb. 14, 1928, Hollywood, Calif. (heart disease). Stage and screen actor.

Appeared in: **1921** The Girl in the Taxi; Her Face Value; See My Lawyer; The Ten Dollar Raise. **1922** The Barnstormer; The Glory of Clementina; The Deuce of Spades; Confidence. **1923** The Dangerous Maid; Within the Law. **1924** Hold Your Breath; Reckless Romance; Fool's Highway. **1925** A Regular Fellow. **1926** Atta Boy; When the Wife's Away. **1927** Backstage; The Tired Business Man; Down the Stretch. **1928** The Bullet Mark; Masked Angel; Alias the Deacon.

PLUMER, ROSE LINCOLN

Died: Mar. 3, 1955, Hollywood, Calif. Screen, stage and television actress.

Appeared in: **1934** Opened by Mistake (short). **1937** Git Along, Little Dogies. **1939** Rovin' Tumbleweeds. **1940** Her First Romance. **1941** Pacific Blackout; Scattergood Baines. **1942** Pacific Blackout (aka Midnight Angel). **1943** Jack London; The Desperadoes. **1944** The Girl in the Case. **1949** Knock on Any Door. **1950** Ma and Pa Kettle Go to Town.

POFF, LON (Alonzo M. Poff)

Born: Feb. 8, 1870, Bedford, Ind. Died: Aug. 8, 1952. Stage and screen actor. Entered films in 1914.

Appeared in: **1921** Big Town Ideas; The Night Horsemen; The Old Swimmin' Hole; The Three Musketeers. **1922** Suzanna; Tracked to Earth; The Village Blacksmith. **1923** The Girl I Loved; Brass Commandments; Main Street; The Man Who Won. **1924** The Man from Wyoming; Excitement; Dante's Inferno; Darwin was Right. **1925** A Fool and His Money; The Merry Widow; Greed; A Thief in Paradise; The Million Dollar Handicap. **1926** Marriage License? **1927** The Silent Rider; Silver Valley; The Tender Hour. **1928** Greased Lightning; Two Lovers; Wheels of Chance. **1929** The Faker; The Iron Mask; Lone Star Ranger. **1930** Tom Sawyer; The Laurel-Hardy Murder Case (short). **1931** Behind Office Doors; I Take This Woman; Caught; Ambassador Bill. **1932** Stepping Sisters. **1935** Teacher's Beau (short). **1937** Calling All Doctors (short). **1943** No News is Good News (short).

POGUE, TOM

Born: 1876. Died: Mar. 21, 1941, Hollywood, Calif. Screen, stage and television actor.

Appeared in: **1936** Divot Diggers (short); I Married a Doctor; Stage Struck. **1937** Once A Doctor; It's Love I'm After; Lloyds of London. **1940** Foreign Correspondent; The Letter. **1941** Citizen Kane; Back Street; Meet John Doe.

POL, TALITHA

Born: 1940, Holland. Died: July 1971, Rome, Italy (heroin overdose). Screen actress. Married to oil scion Paul Getty, Jr.

Appeared in: **1961** Village of Daughters. **1965** Return from the Ashes. **1966** The Girl Getters. **1968** Barbarella.

POLK, GORDON

Born: 1924. Died: June 9, 1960, Hollywood, Calif. (during heart surgery). Screen, stage and television actor.

Appeared in: **1960** Inherit the Wind.

POLLA, PAULINE M.

Born: 1868. Died: Apr. 19, 1940, Albany, N.Y. Screen actress and opera performer. Appeared in silents.

POLLACK, BEN

Born: 1904. Died: June 7, 1971, Palm Springs, Calif. (suicide—hanged). Bandleader, jazz drummer, screen actor and songwriter.

Appeared in: **1929** Ben Pollack and His Park Central Orchestra (short). **1934** Universal short. **1951** Disc Jockey. **1954** The Glenn Miller Story. **1955** The Benny Goodman Story.

POLLARD, BUD

Born: 1887. Died: Dec. 16, 1952, Hollywood, Calif. (heart attack). Screen actor, film director and screenwriter.

Appeared in: **1933** Victims of Persecution.

POLLARD, HARRY

Born: 1883. Died: July 6, 1934, Pasadena, Calif. Screen, stage, vaudeville actor and film director. Married to actress Margarita Fisher (dec. 1975). Entered films as an actor with Selig.

Appeared in: **1912** The Worth of a Man; Call of the Drum; Better Than Gold; The Dove and the Serpent; Melodrama of Yesterday; Love, War and a Bonnet; On the Shore; Jim's Atonement; The Parson and the Medicine Man; Exchanging Labels; Big Jim. **1913** Uncle Tom's Cabin. **1914** The Wife; Nancy's Husband; The Professor's Awakening; Caught in a Tight Pinch; Closed at Ten; Jane, the Justice; The Other Train; A Modern Othello; A Suspended Ceremony; The Silence of John Gordon; A Joke on Jane; Susanna's New Suit. **1915** The Peacock Feather Fan. **1916** Suzie's New Shoes.

POLLARD, HARRY "SNUB" (Harold Frazer)

Born: 1886, Melbourne, Australia. Died: Jan. 19, 1962, Burbank, Calif. Screen, stage, vaudeville, television actor and film producer. Do not confuse with Harry Pollard, film actor and director (dec. 1934). Entered films as a bit player with Broncho Billy Anderson at Essanay Studios. He was one of the original Keystone Kops.

Appeared in: **1915** Great While It Lasted. **1919** Start Something; All at Sea; Call for Mr. Cave Man; Giving the Bride Away; Order in Court; It's a Hard Life; How Dry I Am; Looking for Trouble; Tough Luck; The Floor Below; His Royal Slyness. **1920** The following shorts: Red Hot Hottentots; Why Go Home?; Slippery Slickers; The Dippy Dentist; All Lit Up; Getting His Goat; Waltz Me Around; Raise the Rent; Find the Girl; Fresh Paint; Flat Broke; Cut the Cards; The Dinner Hour; Cracked Wedding Bells; Speed to Spare; Shoot on Sight; Don't Weaken; Drink Hearty; Trotting through Turkey; All Dressed Up; Grab the Ghost; All in a Day; Any Old Port; Don't Rock the Boat; The Home Stretch; Call a Taxi; Live and Learn; Run 'Em Ragged; A London Bobby; Money to Burn; Go As You Please; Rock-a-bye-Baby; Doing Time; Fellow Citizens; When the Wind Blows; Insulting the Sultan; The Dearly Departed; Cash Customers; Park Your Car. **1921** The following shorts: The Morning After; Whirl O' the West; Open Another Bottle; His Best Girl; Make it Snappy; Fellow Romans; Rush Orders; Bubbling Over; No Children; Own Your Own Home; Big Game; Save Your Money; Blue Sunday; Where's the Fire; The High Rollers; You're Next; The Bike Bug; At the Ringside; No Stopover; What a Whopper; Teaching the Teacher; Spot Cash; Name the Day; The Jail Bird; Late Lodgers; Gone to the Country; Law and Order; Fifteen Minutes; On Location; Hocus-Pocus; Penny-in-the-Slot; The Joy Rider; The Hustler; Sink or Swim; Shake 'Em Up; Corner Pocket. **1922** The following shorts: Lose No Time; Call the Witness; Years to Come; Blow 'Em Up; Stage Struck; Down and Out; Pardon Me; The Bow Wows; Hot off the Press; The Anvil Chorus; Jump Your Job; Full o'Pep; Kill the Nerve; Days of Old; Light Showers; Do Me a Favor; In the Movies; Punch the Clock; Strictly Modern; Hale and Hearty; Some Baby; The Dumb Bell; Bed of Roses; The Stone Age; 365 Days; The Old Sea Dog; Hook, Line and Sinker; Nearly Rich; Our Gang. **1923** The following shorts: Dig Up; A Tough Winter; Before the Public; Where Am I?; California or Bust; Sold at Auction; The Courtship of Miles Sandwich; Jack Frost; The Mystery Man; The Walkout; It's a Gift; Dear Ol' Pal; Join the Circus; Fully Insured; It's a Boy. **1924** The following shorts:

The Big Idea; Why Marry?; Get Busy. **1925** Are Husbands Human? (short). **1926** The following shorts: Do Your Duty; The Old Warhorse; The Doughboy; The Yokel; The Fire; All Wet. **1927** The Bum's Rush. **1931** Ex-Flame; One Good Turn (short). **1932** Midnight Patrol; Make Me a Star; The Purchase Price. **1934** Stingaree; Cockeyed Cavaliers. **1936** Just My Luck; The Crime Patrol; The White Legion; The Gentleman from Louisiana; Headin' for the Rio Grande. **1937** Riders of the Rockies; Hittin' the Trail; Nation Aflame; Arizona Days; Tex Rides with the Boy Scouts. **1938** Frontier Town; Starlight over Texas; Where the Buffalo Roam. **1939** Song of the Buckaroo. **1940** Murder on the Yukon. **1943** Phony Express (short). **1944** Defective Detectives (short); His Tale is Told. **1945** Three Pests in a Mess (short). **1946** Monkey Businessmen (short). **1947** Perils of Pauline. **1948** Blackmail. **1949** Loaded Pistols; The Crooked Way. **1954** So You Want to Be a Barber (short). **1957** A Man of a Thousand Faces. **1958** Rock-a-bye Baby. **1960** Who Was That Lady?; Studs Lonigan; When Comedy Was King (documentary). **1961** The Errand Boy. **1962** Pocketful of Miracles; Days of Thrills and Laughter (documentary). **1963** Thirty Years of Fun (documentary). **1968** The Further Perils of Laurel and Hardy (documentary).

POLO, EDDIE (Edward P. Polo)

Born: 1875, Los Angeles, Calif. Died: June 14, 1961, Hollywood, Calif. (heart attack). Brother of actor Sam Polo (dec. 1966). Screen actor, film stuntman and circus performer. Do not confuse with Swedish circus performer Eddie Polo—Edward Kristensson—(dec. 1956).

Appeared in: **1915** Yellow Streak; The Broken Coin (serial). **1916** Heritage of Hate; The Adventures of Peg O' the Ring (serial); Liberty, a Daughter of the U.S.A. (serial). **1917** The Wolf and His Mate; The Gray Ghost (serial). **1918** Bull's Eye (serial); Lure of the Circus (serial). **1919** A Prisoner for Love; The Phantom Fugitive; The Wild Rider; A Pistol Point Proposal; "Cyclone Smith" series including: Cyclone Smith Plays Trumps; Cyclone Smith's Partner; Cyclone Smith's Comeback. **1920** The Vanishing Dagger (serial); King of the Circus (serial). **1921** The Secret Four (serial); Do or Die (serial); The White Horseman (serial). **1922** Captain Kidd (serial); With Stanley in Africa (serial). **1923** Knock on the Door; Dangerous Hour; Prepared to Die. **1940** Son of Roaring Dan. **1942** Between Us Girls. **1943** Hers to Hold. Other "Cyclone Smith" series films he appeared in are: Square Deal Cyclone, Cyclone Smith's Vow. **1956** Around the World in 80 Days.

POLO, ROBERT

Died: May 4, 1968, Hollywood, Calif. (brain tumor). Screen actor, extra and stand-in for Gilbert Roland.

POLO, SAM

Born: 1873. Died: Oct. 3, 1966, Hollywood, Calif. Screen actor, circus performer and make-up artist. Brother of actor Eddie Polo (dec. 1961).

Appeared in: **1919** The Midnight Man (serial). **1920** The Invisible Hand (serial). **1922** Captain Kidd (serial). **1925** Fighting Ranger (serial).

PONTO, ERICH

Born: Luebeck, Germany. Died: Feb. 4, 1957, Stuttgart, Germany. Screen, stage and radio actor.

Appeared in: **1935** Das Maedchen Johanna. **1949** Palace Scandal. **1950** The Third Man. **1958** Das Fliegende Klassen-Zimmer (The Flying Classroom); Rosen Fuer Bettina (Roses for Bettina—aka Ballgrina). **1959** Himmel ohne Sterne (Sky without Stars). Other German films: Tailor Wibbel; Film without Title; Love 47; If All of Us Were Angels; Robinson Shall Not Die.

POPE, UNOLA B.

Born: 1884. Died: Feb. 1, 1938, Fremont, Ohio. Screen and stage actress. Said to be a member of a cast of first motion pictures made in Corning, N.Y.

PORCASI, PAUL

Born: 1880, Palermo, Italy. Died: Aug. 8, 1946, Hollywood, Calif. Screen, stage actor and opera singer.

Appeared in: **1920** The Fall of the Romanoffs. **1926** Say It Again. **1929** Broadway. **1930** A Lady's Morals; Three Sisters; Murder on the Roof; Morocco; Born Reckless; Derelict. **1931** Children of Dreams; I Like Your Nerve; Doctor's Wives; Bought; Good Bad Girl; Svengali; Gentleman's Fate; Party Husbands; Under Eighteen; A Woman Commands; While Paris Sleeps; The Man Who Played God; Smart Money. **1932** The Devil and the Deep; Cynara. **1933** When Strangers Marry; Devil's Mate; I Loved a Woman; Footlight Parade; Flying Down to Rio; He Couldn't Take It; Grand Slam. **1934** British Agent; The Great Flirtation; Wake up and Dream; Tarzan and His Mate; Imitation of Life. **1935** Rumba; Enter Madame; The Florentine Dagger; A Night at the Ritz; Stars over Broadway; Under the Pampas Moon; Charlie Chan in Egypt; Waterfront Lady; I Dream Too Much; Million Dollar Baby. **1936** Muss 'Em Up; Down to the Sea; Crash Donovar.; The Leathernecks Have Landed. **1937** Maytime; The Emperor's Candlesticks; The Bride Wore Red; Seventh Heaven; Cafe Metropole. **1938** Crime School. **1939** Everything Happens at Night; Lady of the Tropics. **1940** Dr. Kildare's Strangest Case; I Was an Adventuress; Torrid Zone; The Border Region; Argentine Nights. **1942** Star Spangled Rhythm; Road to Happiness; Quiet Please Murder. **1943** Hi Diddle Diddle.

1944 Hail the Conquering Hero; Swing Hostess; Nothing but Trouble. 1945 I'll Remember April.

PORCELAIN, BESSIE PETTS
Died: June 14, 1968. Screen actress.

PORTEN, HENNY
Born: 1890, Germany. Died: Oct. 15, 1960, Berlin, Germany. Screen actress. One of Germany's first silent film stars.

Appeared in: 1921 Deception. 1926 Backstairs. 1930 Skandal Um Eva (Scandal about Eva). 1931 Gretel and Liesel (aka Kohlhiesel's Daughters); Mother Love. 1934 Crown of Thorns; Mutter und Kind (Mother and Child). 1937 Krach im Hinterhaus (Trouble Back Stairs). Other German films: The Marriage of Luis Rohrbach; Anne Boleyn; Rose Bernd; Queen Luis; Family Buchholz.

PORTER, EDWARD D.
Born: 1881. Died: July 29, 1939, Hollywood, Calif. (stroke). Stage and screen actor.

Appeared in: 1925 Friendly Enemies.

PORTER, HAROLD B.
Born: 1896. Died: July 30, 1939, Hollywood, Calif. (suicide). Screen actor, radio performer and cameraman.

PORTER, VIOLA ADELE
Born: 1879. Died: Dec. 29, 1942, Hollywood, Calif. Screen actress.

PORTERFIELD, ROBERT H.
Born: 1905, Austinville, Va. Died: Oct. 28, 1971, Abingdon, Va. (heart attack). Screen, stage actor and stage director.

Appeared in: 1941 Sergeant York. 1946 The Yearling. 1958 Thunder Road.

PORTMAN, ERIC
Born: July 13, 1903, Yorkshire, England. Died: Dec. 7, 1969, St. Veep, England. Screen, stage and television actor.

Appeared in: 1935 Maria Marten Or, The Murder in the Red Barn (film debut); Abdul the Damned; Old Roses; Hyde Park Corner. 1936 The Cardinal; The Crimes of Stephen Hawke; Hearts of Humanity. 1937 Moonlight Sonata; The Prince and the Pauper. 1941 The 49th Parallel (aka The Invaders—US 1942). 1942 One of Our Aircraft is Missing; Squadron Leader X; Uncensored (US 1944). 1943 The Carmer (rerelease of Moonlight Sonata 1937); We Dive at Dawn; Escape to Danger; Millions Like Us. 1944 A Canterbury Tale. 1945 Great Day. 1946 Wanted for Murder; Daybreak. 1947 Dear Murderer (US 1948). 1948 The Mark of Cain; Corridor of Mirrors; The Blind Goddess (US 1949). 1949 The Spider and the Fly (US 1952). 1950 Cairo Road. 1951 The Magic Box (US 1952). 1952 A Voice in the Night (rerelease of Wanted for Murder 1946); A Man of Two Worlds; South of Algiers (aka The Golden Mask—US 1954); His Excellency (US 1956). 1955 The Colditz Story (US 1957); The Deep Blue Sea. 1956 Child in the House. 1957 The Good Companions. 1961 The Naked Edge. 1962 Freud; The Man Who Finally Died (US 1967). 1963 West 11. 1965 The Bedford Incident. 1966 The Spy with a Cold Nose; The Whisperers. 1967 Deadfall (US 1968). 1969 Assignment to Kill.

POST, GUY BATES
Born: 1875, Seattle, Wash. Died: Jan. 16, 1968, Los Angeles, Calif. Stage and screen actor. Divorced from stage actress Adele Ritchie (dec. 1930). Married to actress Lillian Kemble-Cooper (dec. 1977).

Appeared in: 1922 The Masquerader; Omar the Tentmaker. 1923 Gold Madness. 1932 Prestige. 1936 Camille; Till We Meet Again; The Case against Mrs. Ames; Fatal Lady; Trouble for Two; Ace Drummond (serial). 1937 Champagne Waltz; Daughter of Shanghai; Maid of Salem; Maytime; Blazing Barriers; The Mysterious Pilot. 1940 The Mad Empress. 1942 Crossroads. 1947 A Double Life.

POST, WILEY
Born: Grand Plain, Tex. Died: Aug. 15, 1935, near Barrow, Alaska, (airplane crash). Aviator, screen actor and stunt flyer. Died in crash with Will Rogers.

Appeared in: 1935 Air Hawks.

POST, WILMARTH H.
Died: Aug. 25, 1930, Rutherford, N.J. (heart failure). Screen, stage actor, film director and author.

POTEL, VICTOR
Born: 1889, Lafayette, Ind. Died: Mar. 8, 1947, Los Angeles, Calif. Screen actor. Entered films in 1910. Was one of the original Keystone Kops.

Appeared in: 1910 Joyriding. 1911 "Snakeville" comedy series. 1916 His Last Scent. 1919 The Outcasts of Poker Flat; Captain Kidd, Jr. 1920 Mary's Ankle. 1921 Lavender and Old Lace; Bob Hampton of Placer. 1922 Step on It!; At the Sign of the Jack O'Lantern; Quincy Adams Sawyer; Don't Write Letters; A Tailor Made Man; The Loaded Door; I Can Explain. 1923 Anna Christie; Penrod and Sam; Itching Palms; The Meanest Man in the World; Refuge; Reno; Modern Matrimony; Tea with a Kick. 1924 Along Came Jones; The Law Forbids; A Self-Made Failure; Women Who Give. 1925 A Lost Lady; Below the Line; Ten Days; Contraband. 1926 The Bar-C Mystery (serial); The Carnival Girl; The Lodge in the Wilderness; Racing Romance; Morganson's Finish. 1927 Uneasy Payments; Special Delivery; The Craver. 1928 What Price Beauty?; Little Shepherd of Kingdom Come; Lingerie; Melody of Love; Captain Swagger. 1929 Marianne; The Virginian. 1930 The Bad One; The Big Shot; Paradise Island; Virtuous Sin; Call of the West; Border Romance; Dough Boys. 1931 10¢ a Dance; The Squaw Man. 1932 Partners; Make Me a Star; The Purchase Price. 1933 Hallelujah, I'm a Bum. 1934 Thunder over Texas; Inside Information; Frontier Days. 1935 Mississippi; The Girl Friend; Ruggles of Red Gap; The Trail's End; Last of the Clintons; Lady Tubbs; Hard Rock Harrigan; Waterfront Lady; Whispering Smith Speaks. 1936 Three Godfathers; O'Malley of the Mounted; Yellow Dust; Song of the Saddle; The Captain's Kid; God's Country and the Woman; Down to the Sea. 1937 Two-Gun Law; White Bondage; Western Gold; Small Town Boy. 1938 Outside the Law. 1939 Rovin' Tumbleweeds. 1940 Girl from God's Country; Christmas in July. 1941 Birth of the Blues; Sullivan's Travels; The Big Store. 1944 The Miracle of Morgan's Creek; The Great Moment; Going to Town; Hail the Conquering Hero. 1945 Strange Illusion; Captain Tugboat Annie; Medal for Benny; Rhythm Round-up. 1946 The Glass Alibi. 1947 The Millerson Case; Mad Wednesday (aka The Sin of Harold Diddlebock); Ramrod; The Egg and I.

POWELL, DAVID
Born: Wales. Died: Apr. 16, 1925, N.Y. (pneumonia). Screen actor.

Appeared in: 1916 Less Than the Dust; Gloria's Romance (serial). 1917 The Beautiful Adventure. 1918 A Romance of the Underworld; The Unforseen. 1919 The Firing Line; His Parisian Wife. 1920 The Right to Love; Idols of Clay; On with the Dance; Lady Rose's Daughter. 1921 Appearances; The Princess of New York; Dangerous Lies; The Mystery Road. 1922 Outcast; The Siren Call; Perpetua (aka Love's Boomerang—US); Anna Ascends; Her Gilded Cage; Missing Millions; The Spanish Jade. 1923 The Glimpses of the Moon; Fog Bound; The Green Goddess. 1924 The Average Woman; Lend Me Your Husband; The Truth about Women; The Man without a Heart; Virtuous Liars. 1925 Back to Life; The Lost Chord.

POWELL, DICK
Died: Sept. 26, 1948, Hales Corners, Wis. (accidental fall from plane). Screen actor and stunt flier. Do not confuse with actor dec. 1963.

Appeared in: 1920 The Great Air Robbery. 1925 The Cloud Rider; Air Hawks. 1930 Hell's Angels; Dawn Patrol. 1947 Blaze of Noon.

POWELL, DICK (Richard E. Powell)
Born: Nov. 24, 1904, Mt. View, Ark. Died: Jan. 2, 1963, Hollywood, Calif. (cancer). Screen, stage, radio, television actor, film director, producer, stage director and singer. Married to actress June Allyson. Divorced from actresses Joan Blondell and Mildred Maund. Father of actor Richard Powell, Jr. and Pamela Powell.

Appeared in: 1931 Street Scene; Gold Diggers of 1933; Footlight Parade; College Coach; Convention City; The King's Vacation. 1934 Wonder Bar; Twenty Million Sweethearts; Happiness Ahead; Flirtation Walk; Dames. 1935 Gold Diggers of 1935; If You Could Only Cook; A Midsummer Night's Dream; Page Miss Glory; Broadway Gondolier; Shipmates Forever; Thanks a Million; Ginger. 1936 Colleen; Hearts Divided; Stage Struck; Gold Diggers of 1937; For Auld Lang Syne (documentary). 1937 On the Avenue; The Singing Marine; Varsity Show; Hollywood Hotel. 1938 The College Coed. 1938 The Cowboy from Brooklyn; Hard to Get; Going Places. 1939 Naughty but Nice. 1940 Christmas in July; I Want a Divorce. 1941 Model Wife; In the Navy. 1942 Star Spangled Rhythm. 1943 Happy Go Lucky; True to Life; Riding High. 1944 Meet the People; It Happened Tomorrow; Farewell, My Lovely. 1945 Cornered. 1947 Johnny O'Clock. 1948 To the Ends of the Earth; Pitfall; Station West; Rogue's Regiment. 1949 Mrs. Mike. 1950 The Reformer and the Redhead; Right Cross. 1951 Cry Danger; Callaway Went Thataway; Tall Target; You Never Can Tell. 1952 The Bad and the Beautiful. 1954 Susan Slept Here.

POWELL, LEE (Alfred E. Lee)
Born: 1896. Died: Feb. 3, 1954, Hollywood, Calif. Screen and stage actor.

POWELL, LEE B.
Born: May 15, 1908, Long Beach, Calif. Died: Aug. 1944 (killed in action in Marines in the South Pacific). Screen and stage actor. The original "Lone Ranger" of the films.

Appeared in: 1938 The Lone Ranger (serial); The Fighting Devil Dogs (serial); Come on, Rangers. 1939 Trigger Pals.

POWELL, RICHARD
Born: 1897. Died: Jan. 1, 1937, Hollywood, Calif. (fractured skull, from auto accident). Screen actor and opera performer. Do not confuse with actors Dick Powell (dec. 1948 and 1963).

Appeared in: 1933 Feeling Rosy (short). 1935 The Wedding Night; Woman

Wanted; Every Night at Eight. **1936** Yours for the Asking; Hollywood Boulevard. **1937** Another Dawn.

POWELL, RUSS (Russell J. Powell)
Born: Sept. 16, 1875, Indianapolis, Ind. Died: Nov. 28, 1950, Woodland Hills, Calif. (arteriosclerosis). Screen, stage and vaudeville actor.

Appeared in: **1915** Alone in the City of Sighs and Tears; Kidding the Goats; The Morning After. **1921** The Concert. **1922** Head over Heels; Through a Glass Window. **1923** One Stolen Night. **1924** A Boy of Flanders; Dynamite Smith. **1925** The Re-creation of Brian Kent; The Wheel. **1927** Soft Cushions; No Place to Go; The Red Mill. **1928** Vamping Venus; The Gate Crasher; Riley the Cop. **1929** Fashions in Love; The Love Parade. **1930** The Big Trail; Check and Double Check; The Grand Parade. **1931** An American Tragedy; The Sin of Madelon Claudet. **1932** Mystery Ranch. **1933** Zoo in Budapest; Arabian Tights (short); Snug in the Jug (short); To the Last Man. **1934** The Count of Monte Cristo; Wharf Angel. **1935** Call of the Wild. **1936** Rose of the Rancho; Sutter's Gold. **1937** The Wrong Road; Hit the Saddle. **1940** The Night of Nights. **1941** Prairie Stranger.

POWER, HARTLEY
Born: Mar. 14, 1894, New York, N.Y. Died: Jan. 29, 1966, London, England. Stage and screen actor. Married to actress Betty Paul.

Appeared in: **1933** Yes Mr. Brown; Just Smith; Friday the Thirteenth (US 1934); Aunt Sally (aka Along Came Sally—US 1934). **1934** Evergreen (US 1935); The Camels are Coming; Road House. **1936** Jury's Evidence; Living Dangerously. **1938** Just Like a Woman; The Return of the Frog. **1939** A Window in London (aka Lady in Distress—US 1942); Murder Will Out. **1940** Return to Yesterday. **1941** Atlantic Ferry (aka Sons of the Sea—US). **1942** Alibi. **1945** The Man from Morocco; Dead of Night; The Way to the Stars (aka Johnny in the Clouds—US). **1946** A Girl in a Million (US 1950). **1952** The Armchair Detective. **1953** Roman Holiday. **1954** The Million Pound Note (aka Man with a Million—US); To Dorothy a Son (aka Cash on Delivery—US 1956). **1957** Island in the Sun.

POWER, JOHN
Born: 1874. Died: Sept. 25, 1951, Culver City, Calif. Stage and screen actor.

Appeared in: **1934** The Live Ghost (short). **1939** Dog Daze (short). **1942** Mrs. Miniver.

POWER, PAUL (Luther Vestergard)
Born: 1902, Chicago, Ill. Died: Apr. 5, 1968, Hollywood, Calif. Screen, stage and television actor. Entered films in 1925.

Appeared in: **1927** False Values. **1928** Trial Marriage; Hot Heels. **1929** Words and Music. **1934** Wonder Bar. **1935** I've Been Around. **1938** Adventures of Robin Hood. **1955** The Girl in the Red Velvet Swing. **1958** Jet Attack. **1960** Ma Barker's Killer Brood. **1962** The Underwater City; Advise and Consent.

POWER, TYRONE F., SR.
Born: 1869, London, England. Died: Dec. 30, 1931, Hollywood, Calif. (heart attack). Stage and screen actor. Father of actor Tyrone Power, Jr. (dec. 1958). Married to stage actress Patia Power (dec.).

Appeared in: **1915** A Texas Steer. **1916** John Needham's Double; Where Are My Children? **1919** The Miracle Man. **1921** The Black Panther's Cub; Dream Street; Footfalls. **1923** Bright Lights of Broadway; The Daring Years; Fury; The Truth about Wives; The Day of Faith; Wife in Name Only. **1924** Damaged Hearts; Janice Meredith; For Another Woman; The Law and the Lady; Trouping with Ellen; The Story without a Name; The Lone Wolf. **1925** Braveheart; Red Kimono; A Regular Fellow; Where Was I? **1926** Bride of the Storm; Hands Across the Border; The Wanderer; Out of the Storm; The Test of Donald Norton. **1930** The Big Trail.

POWER, TYRONE F., JR.
Born: May 5, 1914, Cincinnati, Ohio. Died: Nov. 15, 1958, Madrid, Spain (heart attack). Stage and screen actor. Son of actor Tyrone Power, Sr. (dec. 1931) and stage actress Patia Power. Divorced from actresses Annabella and Linda Christian. Married to actress Debbie Ann Minardos Power. Father of actress Taryn and Romina and Tyrone Power.

Appeared in: **1932** Tom Brown of Culver. **1934** Flirtation Walk. **1936** Girl's Dormitory; Ladies in Love; Lloyds of London. **1937** Love Is News; Cafe Metropole; Thin Ice; Second Honeymoon. **1938** In Old Chicago; Alexander's Ragtime Band; Marie Antoinette; Suez. **1939** Jesse James; Rose of Washington Square; Second Fiddle; Daytime Wife. **1940** Johnny Apollo; Brigham Young—Frontiersman; The Mark of Zorro; The Return of Frank James. **1941** Blood and Sand; A Yank in the R.A.F **1942** Son of Fury; This Above All; The Black Swan. **1943** Crash Dive. **1946** The Razor's Edge. **1947** Nightmare Alley; Captain from Castile. **1948** Luck of the Irish; That Wonderful Urge. **1949** Prince of Foxes. **1950** The Black Rose; American Guerrila in the Philippines. **1951** Rawhide; I'll Never Forget You (aka Man of Two Worlds and The House in the Square). **1952** Diplomatic Courier; Pony Soldier. **1953** Mississippi Gambler; King of the Khyber Rifles. **1955** The Long Gray Line; Untamed. **1956** The Eddy Duchin Story. **1957** Abandon Ship!; Seven Waves

Away; The Rising of the Moon (narr.); The Sun Also Rises; Witness for the Prosecution.

POWERS, JOHN H.
Born: 1885. Died: Jan. 17, 1941, New York, N.Y. Screen, stage, vaudeville actor and circus performer. Was partner in vaudeville in an act billed as "McAvoy and Powers."

Appeared in: **1923** Adam and Eva. **1937** Hills of Old Wyoming. **1939** Zaza. **1941** Twilight on the Trail.

POWERS, JULE
Died: Feb. 1932, Hollywood, Calif. Stage and screen actress.

POWERS, MARIE
Born: Pennsylvania. Died: Dec. 29, 1973, New York, N.Y. Screen, stage actress and opera performer.

Appeared in: **1951** The Medium.

POWERS, MARY GARE
Died: July 25, 1961. Screen actress. Appeared in silents.

POWERS, RICHARD. *See* TOM KEENE

POWERS, TOM
Born: 1890, Owensboro, Ky. Died: Nov. 9, 1955, Hollywood, Calif. (heart ailment). Screen, stage actor and author. Entered films in 1910.

Appeared in: **1911** Saving an Audience. **1914** Creatures of Habit; Flotilla the Flirt; Terror of the Air. **1915** As Ye Repent; Barnaby Rudge; The Canker of Jealousy. **1917** The Auction Block. **1944** Practically Yours; Double Indemnity. **1945** The Phantom Speaks; The Chicago Kid. **1946** Two Years before the Mast; The Blue Dahlia; The Last Crooked Mile; Her Adventurous Night. **1947** Son of Rusty; Angel and the Badman; The Farmer's Daughter; They Won't Believe Me. **1948** Angel in Exile; I Love Trouble; The Time of Your Life; Up in Central Park; Mexican Hayride; Station West. **1949** Special Agent; Scene of the Crime; Chicago Deadline; East Side, West Side. **1950** Destination Moon; Chinatown at Midnight; The Nevadan; Right Cross. **1951** Fighting Coast Guard; The Strip; The Tall Target; The Well. **1952** Denver and Rio Grande; Diplomatic Courier; We're Not Married; Steel Trap; Deadline—U.S.A.; Jet Job; Phone Call from a Stranger; Bal Tabarin; The Fabulous Senorita; Horizons West. **1953** The Last Posse; The Marksman; Hannah Lee; Julius Caesar; Scared Stiff; Donovan's Brain; Sea of Lost Ships. **1955** The Americano; New York Confidential; Ten Wanted Men. **1956** UFO.

POWLEY, BRYAN
Born: Sept. 16, 1871, Reading, England. Died: Dec. 1962, London, England. Stage and screen actor.

Appeared in: **1920** The Joyous Adventures of Aristide Pujol. **1921** The Old Curiosity Shop; Fortune of Christina McNab (US 1923). **1922** Open Country; The Wee MacGregor's Sweetheart. **1935** Forever England (aka Brown on Resolution and Born for Glory—US). **1936** Rhodes of Africa (aka Rhodes—US); All In; Conquest of the Air. **1937** Love from a Stranger; Fire over England; Thunder in the City; Moonlight Sonata; When the Devil was Well; Mademoiselle Docteur; What a Man! **1938** Mr. Satan; Darts are Trumps; Strange Boarders; You're the Doctor. **1939** Old Mother Riley Joins Up. **1943** The Charmer (reissue of Moonlight Sonata—1937); We Dive at Dawn.

PRAGER, STANLEY
Born: Jan. 8, 1917, New York, N.Y. Died: Jan. 18, 1972, Hollywood, Calif. Screen, stage actor, film and television director. Married to actress Georgiann Johnson.

Appeared in: **1944** The Eve of St. Mark; Take It or Leave It; In the Meantime, Darling; Wing and a Prayer. **1945** Doll Face; Junior Miss; A Bell for Adano. **1946** Do You Love Me?; Behind Green Lights; Gentleman Joe Palooka. **1947** The Shocking Miss Pilgrim; Stork Bites Man. **1948** Force of Evil; A Foreign Affair; Joe Palooka in Winner Take All; You Gotta Stay Happy. **1949** The Lady Takes a Sailor; Deadly as the Female. **1950** Joe Palooka in the Squared Circle; Gun Crazy.

PRAGER, WILLY
Born: 1877, Germany. Died: Mar. 4, 1956, West Germany. Stage and screen actor.

Appeared in: **1931** Der Grosse Tenor. **1948** Marriage in Shadows.

PRATA, JOAQUIM
Born: 1882. Died: Nov. 18, 1953, Lisbon, Portugal. Screen, stage actor and playwright.

PRATHER, LEE (Oscar Lee Prather)
Born: 1890. Died: Jan. 3, 1958, Los Angeles, Calif. (during surgery). Stage and screen actor.

Appeared in: **1935** Hot Money (short). **1938** The Buccaneer; Women in Prison. **1939** Homicide Bureau. **1942** Tennessee Johnson.

PRATT, LYNN

Born: 1863, Sylvan Center, Mich. Died: Jan. 1930, New York. Screen, stage and vaudeville actor.

Appeared in: **1921** A Virgin Paradise.

PRATT, NEIL

Born: 1890, San Diego, Calif. Died: Jan. 3, 1934, Hollywood, Calif. (heart attack). Stage and screen actor. Entered films approx. 1933.

Appeared in: **1934** Trimmed in Furs (short).

PRATT, PURNELL B.

Born: Oct. 20, 1886, Bethel, Ill. Died: July 25, 1941, Hollywood, Calif. Stage and screen actor.

Appeared in: **1925** The Lady Who Lied. **1926** Midnight Lovers. **1929** The Trespasser; Through Different Eyes; Fast Life; Is Everybody Happy?; Alibi; On with the Show. **1930** Painted Faces; The Furies; Common Clay; Sinner's Holiday; Lawful Larceny; The Silver Horde; The Locked Door; Puttin' on the Ritz. **1931** The Gorilla; The Road to Romance; Fires of Youth; Five Star Final; Woman Pursued; The Secret Witness; The Public Defender; The Spider; Terror by Night; The Gay Diplomat; Beyond Victory; Paid; The Prodigal; Dance, Fools, Dance; Up for Murder; Bachelor Apartments; Traveling Husbands. **1932** Hat Check Girl; Red Haired Alibi; False Faces; Unwritten Law; The Famous Ferguson Case; Roadhouse Murder; Grand Hotel; Scarface; Ladies of the Big House; Emma. **1933** The Billion Dollar Scandal; Pick Up; A Shriek in the Night; Headline Shooter; I Cover the Waterfront; Midshipman Jack; The Sweetheart of Sigma Chi; Love, Honor and Oh, Baby; The Chief; Son of a Sailor. **1934** Name the Woman; The Crimson Romance; School for Girls; The Witching Hour; Midnight Alibi; The Hell Cat. **1935** Death Flies East; Black Fury; The Winning Ticket; The Casino Murder Case; It's in the Air; Behind the Green Lights; Ladies Crave Excitement; Waterfront Lady; Diamond Jim; Red Salute; $1,000 a Minute; Frisco Waterfront; Rendezvous at Midnight; A Night at the Opera; Magnificent Obsession. **1936** Dancing Feet; The Return of Sophie Lang; Hollywood Boulevard; Straight from the Shoulder; Lady Be Careful; Murder with Pictures; Wives Never Know; Wedding Present; The Plainsman. **1937** Join the Marines; Let's Make a Million; Murder Goes to College; King of Gamblers; A Night of Mystery; Under Suspicion; High, Wide and Handsome. **1938** Come On, Rangers! **1939** My Wife's Relatives; Grand Ole Opry; Colorado Sunset. **1941** Doctors Don't Tell; Ringside Maisie.

PRAXY, RAOUL

Born: 1892. Died: June 28, 1967. Screen actor.

PRAY, ANNA M.

Born: 1891. Died: June 30, 1971, N.Y. Stage and screen actress. Married to stage actor Fleming Ward (dec.).

PREER, EVELYN

Born: July 26, 1896, Chicago, Ill. or Vicksburg, Miss. Died: Nov. 18, 1932, Los Angeles, Calif. (pneumonia). Black screen and stage actress.

Appeared in: **1921** The Gunsaulus Mystery. **1922** The Homesteader. **1923** Deceit. **1924** Birthright. **1925** The Brute. **1926** The Conjure Woman; The Devil's Disciple. **1927** The Spider's Web. **1929** Melancholy Dame. **1930** Georgia Rose. **1932** Blonde Venus.

PRENTIS, LEWIS R.

Born: 1905. Died: June 26, 1967, Chicago, Ill. Screen and stage actor.

PRESS, MARVIN

Born: Oct. 20, 1915, Conn. Died: March 17, 1968, Los Angeles, Calif. (suicide—gas asphyxiation and barbiturates). Screen actor.

Appeared in: **1952** Sea Tiger; The Treasure of Lost Canyon. **1955** Mexican Manhunt; Dragon's Gold.

PRESTON, EDNA

Born: 1892. Died: Aug. 18, 1960, New York. Screen, stage, radio and television actress.

PREVOST, FRANK G.

Born: 1894. Died: Apr. 17, 1946, Hollywood, Calif. Screen actor.

PREVOST, MARIE (Marie Bickford Gunn)

Born: Nov. 8, 1898, Sarnia, Canada. Died: Jan. 21, 1937, Los Angeles, Calif. Screen actress. Was an early Sennett bathing beauty. Divorced from H. B. "Sonny" Gerke and actor Kenneth Harlan (dec. 1967). Sister of actress Peggy Prevost.

Appeared in: **1917** Her Nature Dance; Secrets of a Beauty Parlor; Two Crooks (aka A Noble Crook). **1918** His Hidden Purpose; His Smothered Love; Sleuths;

Hide and Seek; Detectives; The Village Chestnut; She Loved Him Plenty. **1919** Never Too Old; Rip and Stitch, Tailors; East Lynne with Variations; Reilly's Wash Day; When Love is Blind; Love's False Faces; Yankee Doodle in Berlin; Why Beaches are Popular; Uncle Tom without the Cabin; The Dentist; Up in Alf's Place; Salome vs Shenandoah; The Speak Easy. **1920** Down on the Farm; His Youthful Fancy (short); Fickle Fancy (short); Love, Honor and Behave; Divorce Made Easy. **1921** Kissed; A Small Town Idol; Moonlight Follies; Nobody's Fool; A Parisian Scandal; plus the following shorts: On a Summer's Day; She Sighed by the Seaside; Call a Cop. **1922** The Beautiful and the Damned; Don't Get Personal; The Dangerous Little Demon; Her Night of Nights; The Married Flapper. **1923** Red Lights; Heroes of the Street; The Wanters. **1924** Tarnish; The Marriage Circle; Three Women; The Dark Swan; Being Respectable; Daughters of Pleasure; How to Educate Your Wife; Cornered; The Lover of Camille; The Hollywood Kid (short). **1925** Bobbed Hair; Kiss Me Again; Recompense; Seven Sinners. **1926** Up in Mabel's Room; Almost a Lady; The Caveman; His Jazz Bride; Other Women's Husbands. **1927** For Wives Only; Man Bait; Getting Gertie's Garter; The Night Bride; The Girl in the Pullman. **1928** The Rush Hour; On to Reno; A Blonde for a Night; The Racket. **1929** The Godless Girl; The Flying Fool; Side Show; Divorce Made Easy. **1930** Ladies of Leisure; Party Girl; War Nurse; Sweethearts on Parade; Paid (aka Within the Law). **1931** The Sin of Madelon Claudet (aka The Lullaby); The Easiest Way; The Good Bad Girl; Reckless Living; Sporting Blood; A Gentleman's Fate; It's a Wise Child; The Runaround; Hell Divers. **1932** Three Wise Girls; Carnival Boat; Slightly Married. **1933** Parole Girl; Only Yesterday; The 11th Commandment; Pick Me Up; Hesitating Love (short); a Universal short. **1935** Hands Across the Table; a Vitaphone short. **1936** Tango; Cain and Mabel; 13 Hours by Air.

PRICE, ALONZO

Born: 1888. Died: June 5, 1962. Screen actor.

Appeared in: **1936** Forgotten Faces; Foolproof (short). **1937** Black Legion; Slim. **1938** Forbidden Valley. **1939** Weather Wizards (short).

PRICE, DENNIS (Dennistoun Franklyn John Rose-Price)

Born: June 23, 1915, Twyford, England. Died: Oct. 7, 1973, Guernsey, Channel Islands. Screen, stage and television actor.

Appeared in: **1944** A Canterbury Tale (film debut); A Place of One's Own (US 1949). **1945** The Echo Murders. **1946** The Magic Bow (US 1947); Caravan (US 1947). **1947** Hungry Hill; Master of Bankdam (US 1949); The White Unicorn (aka Bad Sister—US 1948); Jassy (US 1948); Holiday Camp (US 1948); Dear Murderer (US 1948). **1948** Good Time Girl (US 1950); Easy Money (US 1949); Snowbound (US 1949). **1949** The Bad Lord Byron (US 1950); Kind Hearts and Coronets (US 1950); The Lost People; Helter Skelter. **1950** The Dancing Years; Murder without Crime (US 1951). **1951** The Adventurers (aka The Great Adventure—US); The House in the Square (aka I'll Never Forget You—US); The Magic Box (US 1952); Lady Godiva Rides Again (US 1964). **1952** Song of Paris (aka Bachelor in Paris—US 1953); Tall Headlines. **1953** The Intruder (US 1955); Noose for a Lady; Murder at 3 a.m. **1954** For Better, For Worse (aka Cocktails in the Kitchen—US 1955); Time is My Enemy (US 1957). **1955** Oh, Rosalinda; That Lady. **1956** Private's Progress; Port Afrique; Charley Moon; A Touch of the Sun. **1957** The Tommy Steele Story (aka Rock Around the World—US 1958); The Naked Truth (aka Your Past is Showing—US 1958); Fortune is a Woman (aka She Played with Fire—US 1958). **1958** Hello London. **1959** I'm All Right, Jack (US 1960); Breakout (aka Danger Within—US 1960); Don't Panic Chaps! **1960** Oscar Wilde; School for Scoundrels; Tunes of Glory; The Millionairess (US 1961); The Pure Hell of St. Trinian's (US 1961); Piccadilly Third Stop (US 1968). **1961** What a Carve Up! (US 1962 and aka No Place Like Homicide); Five Golden Hours; Double Bunk; No Love for Johnnie; Victim (US 1962); The Rebel (aka Call Me Genius—US); Watch It Sailor! **1962** Behave Yourself (short); Kill or Cure; Play It Cool (US 1963); The Wrong Arm of the Law (US 1963); The Amorous Prawn (aka The Playgirl and the War Minister—US 1963); Go to Blazes; The Pot Carriers. **1963** The V.I.P.'s; The Cracksman; A Jolly Bad Fellow (aka They All Died Laughing—US 1964); Doctor in Distress (US 1964); Tamahine (US 1964); The Comedy Man; The Cool Mikado. **1964** The Horror of It All; The Earth Dies Screaming. **1965** Murder Most Foul; A High Wind in Jamaica; Curse of Simba (aka Curse of the Voodoo—US). **1966** Ten Little Indians; Just Like a Woman. **1967** Jules Verne's Rocket to the Moon (aka Those Fantastic Flying Fools—US and aka Blast Off—US). **1969** The Magic Christian (US 1970); The Haunted House of Horror (aka Horror House—US 1970). **1970** The Horror of Frankenstein; Venus in Furs. **1971** Twins of Evil. **1972** Alice's Adventures in Wonderland; Theatre of Blood.

PRICE, GEORGIE (George E. Price)

Born: 1900. Died: May 10, 1964, New York, N.Y. (heart attack). Screen, vaudeville actor and singer.

Appeared in: **1929** Don't Get Nervous (short). **1930** Metro Movietone short.

PRICE, HAL

Born: June 14, 1886, Waukegon, Ohio. Died: Apr. 15, 1964. Screen actor.

Appeared in: **1930** Night Ride; Party Girl. **1932** Sin's Pay Day; Lady and Gent; The Last Man; Widow in Scarlet; This Sporting Age. **1933** The Girl in

419; Ranger's Code. **1934** Hell Bent for Love. **1936** Just My Luck; The Desert Phantom; Navy Born; The Fugitive Sheriff; Cavalry. **1937** Public Cowboy No. 1; Trouble in Texas; Melody of the Plains; Stars over Arizona. **1938** Code of the Rangers; Call the Mesquiteers; Pioneer Trail. **1939** South of the Border; In Old Monterey; Across the Plains; Home on the Prairie; Overland Mail; New Frontier. **1940** Mad Youth; Frontier Crusader; Out West with the Peppers; Arizona Frontier; Lone Star Raiders; Jack Pot (short). **1941** Billy the Kid's Fighting Pals; Devil Bat; Arizona Bound; Gangs of Sonora; Jungle Man; Secrets of the Wasteland; The Lone Rider Ambush; The Singing Hill; Sierra Sue. **1942** Raiders of the Range; Home in Wyomin'; Law and Order; War Dogs; Cowboy Serenade; Not a Ladies' Man. **1943** Two-Fisted Justice; My Son the Hero; Dead Men Walk; Fugitive of the Plains; Robin Hood of the Range; The Blocked Trail. **1944** Wyoming Hurricane; West of the Rio Grande; Outlaw Trail; Mohave Firebrand; Law of the Valley; Westward Bound; Rustler's Hideout; Fuzzy Settles Down; Oath of the Vengeance; Wild Horse Phantom. **1945** Law of the Valley. **1947** Raiders of Red Rock; Frontier Fighters. **1950** Tarnished; Father Makes Good; Frisco Tornado. **1952** Junction City. **1963** How the West Was Won.

PRICE, KATE (Kate Duffy)
Born: Feb. 13, 1872, Cork, Ireland. Died: Jan. 4, 1943, Woodland Hills, Calif. Screen, stage and vaudeville actress.

Appeared in: **1912** Stenographers Wanted. **1916** The Waiter's Ball. **1919** The Perils of Thunder Mountain (serial). **1920** Dinty. **1921** God's Crucible; The Girl Montana; Little Lord Fauntleroy; The Other Woman. **1922** My Wife's Relations (short); Come on Over; Flesh and Blood; A Dangerous Game; Paid Back; The New Teacher; The Guttersnipe. **1923** Broken Hearts of Broadway; Good-By Girls!; The Spoilers; Crossed Wires; The Dangerous Maid; Enemies of Children; Her Fatal Millions; The Near Lady. **1924** Fool's Highway; Riders Up; The Tornado; Wife of the Centaur; Passion's Pathway; The Sea Hawk. **1925** The Desert Flower; The Man without a Conscience; The Way of a Girl; The Sporting Venus; His People; The Perfect Clown; Sally, Irene and Mary; Proud Heart. **1926** Irene; The Cohens and the Kellys; The Arizona Sweepstakes; Faithful Wives; Paradise; Love's Blindness; Memory Lane. **1927** Frisco Sally Levy; The Third Degree; Casey Jones; Mountains of Manhattan; Orchids and Ermine; The Sea Tigers; Quality Street. **1937** Easy Living.

PRICE, MARK
Born: Ireland. Died: Mar. 31, 1917, New York, N.Y. Screen actor.

Appeared in: **1916** A Daughter of the Gods.

PRICE, NANCY (Lillian Nancy Maude)
Born: Feb. 3, 1880, Kinver, Staffs, England. Died: Mar. 31, 1970, Worthing, England. Screen, stage actress and author. Do not confuse with actress Nancy Price born in 1918.

Appeared in: **1916** The Lyons Mail. **1921** Belphegor the Mountebank. **1923** Bonnie Prince Charlie; Comin' Thro' the Rye; Love, Life and Laughter (aka Tip Toes); The Woman Who Obeyed. **1927** Huntingtower. **1928** His House in Order; The Price of Divorce. **1929** The American Prisoner. **1930** The Loves of Robert Burns. **1931** The Speckled Band. **1932** Down Our Street. **1934** The Crucifix. **1939** The Stars Look Down (US 1941); Dead Man's Shoes. **1942** Secret Mission. **1944** Madonna of the Seven Moons. **1945** I Live in Grosvenor Square (aka A Yank in London—US 1946); I Know Where I'm Going (US 1947). **1946** Carnival. **1947** Master of Bankdam (US 1949). **1948** The Three Weird Sisters. **1950** The Naked Earth. **1952** Mandy (aka Crash of Silence—US). **1955** The Naked Heart.

PRICE, STANLEY L.
Born: 1900. Died: July 13, 1955, Hollywood, Calif. (heart attack). Screen, stage actor and screenwriter.

Appeared in: **1922** Your Best Friend. **1934** It Happened One Day (short). **1935** Okay Toots! (short); The Miracle Rider (serial). **1938** Hunted Men; Tom Sawyer, Detective. **1939** Sudden Money; Undercover Doctor. **1940** Seventeen; The Way of All Flesh; Moon over Burma; The Golden Trail. **1941** Sky Raiders (serial); Adventures of Captain Marvel (serial). **1942** Outlaws of Pine Ridge; The Great Commandments; Tennessee Johnson. **1943** Lone Rider in Wild Horse Rustlers. **1944** Bride by Mistake; Zorro's Black Whip; Range Law. **1945** Phantom of 42nd Street; Lost Weekend; Crime, Inc.; Power of the Whistler. **1947** G-Men Never Forget (serial). **1950** Studio Stoops (short); The Sundowners; Dopey Dicks (short). **1951** Hills of Utah. **1956** The Ten Commandments.

PRIETO, ANTONIO
Born: 1915, Portugal. Died: Mar. 1965, Madrid, Spain (heart attack). Screen, stage and television actor.

Appeared in: **1964** Los Tarantos. **1967** A Fistful of Dollars.

PRINCE, JOHN T.
Born: Sept. 11, 1871, Boston, Mass. Died: Dec. 24, 1937, Los Angeles, Calif. Stage and screen actor.

Appeared in: **1913** Mission Bells. **1916** Phantom Island. **1917** Over There. **1922**

Doctor Jack; Little Eva Ascends. **1923** East Side, West Side. **1924** The Battling Orioles; Defying the Law. **1925** Capital Punishment; Heartless Husbands; The Call of Courage; Women and Gold; The Gold Hunters. **1926** Jack O'Hearts; Money to Burn; The Phantom Bullet; Dame Chance; Prowlers of the Night; The Radio Detective (serial). **1927** King of Kings; Hawk of the Hills (serial). **1928** Ramona; Haunted Island (serial). **1929** Hawk of the Hills (feature of 1927 serial). **1936** The Country Beyond.

PRINCE RANDIAN (Prince Randion)
Born: c. 1871, British Guiana. Died: c. 1934, New York, N.Y. Screen actor and circus performer.

Appeared in: **1932** Freaks.

PRINCESS KANZA OMAR
Born: 1912. Died: Mar. 6, 1958, Los Angeles, Calif. (cancer). Screen actress and dancer.

Appeared in: **1938** The Buccaneer.

PRINGLE, JOHN
Died: 1929. Stage and screen actor. Father of actor John Gilbert (dec. 1936).

Appeared in: **1924** Black Lightning; Travelin' Fast. **1925** His Greatest Battle.

PRIOR, HERBERT (aka HERBERT PRYOR)
Born: July 2, 1867, Oxford, England. Died: Oct. 3, 1954. Stage and screen actor. Married to actress Mabel Trunnelle.

Appeared in: **1909** The Cricket on the Hearth; Tis an Ill Wind that Blows No Good. **1911** Spare the Rod; At the Point of the Sword; His Stepmother; The Best Man Wins; The Unwilling Bigamist; Leap Year; The Eternal Masculine; Next!; Papa's Double; The Flat Upstairs; The Lost Messenger; The Butterfly; Mary's Chauffeur; Thorns of Success; The Disputed Claim; Willie's Dog; Little Music Teacher; All for Jim; The Winner and the Spoils; A Garrison Joke; The Call of the Blood; A Game of Chess; The Sign of the Three Labels; A Romance of the Cliff-Dwellers. **1912** The Risen Soul of Jim Grant; Captain Ben's Yarn; The Three Imps; Rough on Rats; The Capture of Fort Ticonderoga; The Younger Brother; Christian and Moor; The Switchman's Tower; The Spirit of the Gorge; The Venom of the Poppy; Al Jones' Ferry; Under the Tropical Sun; The Battle of Trafalgar; The Sailor's Love Letter; The Big Dam; Leaves of a Romance; Three of a Kind; The Doctor; A Perilous Ride; The Quarrel of the Cliff; Buckskin Jack, the Earl of Gilmore; The Actress; Keeping Mabel Home. **1913** How They Got the Vote; Othello in Jonesville; How Did it Finish?; Scenes from Other Days; Jones Goes Shopping; The Unprofitable Boarder; How They Outwitted Father; The Ranch Owner's Love Making; A Perilous Cargo; The Phantom Ship; Jan Vedder's Daughter; The Lost Deed. **1914** The Sultan and the Rollerskates; A Tale of Old Tucson; The Mexican's Gratitude; A Romance of the Everglades; The Two Vanrevels; Bootle's Baby; In the Shadow of Disgrace; In Lieu of Damages; Farmer Rodney's Daughter; The One Who Loved Him Best; Twins and Trouble; On the Lazy Line. **1915** An Unwilling Thief; Snap Shots; The Newly Rich; A Pipe Dream; Olive's Manufactured Mother; The Family Bible; Mr. Daly's Wedding Day; Olive and the Heirloom; Not Wanted; The Test; The Struggle Upward; Cartoons in the Kitchen; Breaking the Shackles; The Truth About Helen. **1916** A Message to Garcia; Helen of the Chorus; Miss George Washington; The Southerner. **1917** The Poor Little Rich Girl; Great Expectations; The Last Sentence. **1918** The Menace; Society for Sale; After the War; A Burglar for a Night; The Model's Confession. **1919** That's Good; After Your Own Heart; You're Fired; Creaking Stairs; The Love Hunger. **1920** The House of Whispers; Little 'Fraid Lady; Stronger than Death; Pollyanna. **1921** Garments of Truth; Not Guilty; Made in Heaven; Without Benefit of Clergy. **1922** The Dangerous Little Demon; The Man from Downing Street; The Snowshoe Trail; The Half Breed. **1923** Garrison's Finish; Slave of Desire; Little Johnny Jones. **1924** Madonna of the Streets. **1925** The Fighting Demon; The Taming of the West; Tearing Through; The Wild Bull's Lair; Waking Up the Town. **1926** Across the Pacific; Why Girls Go Back Home; The Better Man; Doubling with Danger; The Midnight Kiss; Rustling for Cupid. **1927** The Last Outlaw; The King of Kings. **1929** All at Sea; The Duke Steps Out; The Winged Horseman; The Ace of Scotland Yard (serial). **1930** Caught Short.

PROCTER, IVIS GOULDING
Born: 1906. Died: May 14, 1973, Hollywood, Calif. (heart attack). Screen actress. Sister of film director Edmund Goulding (dec. 1959).

Appeared in: **1952** Plymouth Adventure. **1953** Botany Bay; How to Marry a Millionaire. **1955** The Rains of Ranchipur.

PROCTER, JESSIE OLIVE
Born: 1874. Died: July 6, 1975, Woodland Hills, Calif. (heart failure). Screen actress. Entered films as an extra in the 1930s.

Appeared in: **1962** Music Man.

PROHASKA, JANOS
Born: 1921, Hungary. Died: Mar. 13, 1974, Inyo County, Calif. (plane crash).

Screen and television actor and stuntman. Father of actor Robert Prohaska (dec. 1974).

Appeared in: **1962** Jumbo. **1964** Bikini Beach. **1968** Planet of the Apes. **1970** Pussycat, Pussycat, I Love You. **1974** Zandy's Bride.

PROHASKA, ROBERT
Died: Mar. 13, 1974, Inyo County, Calif. (plane crash). Screen and television actor. Son of actor Janos Prohaska (dec. 1974 in same accident).

PROMIS, FLO
Born: 1884. Died: Apr. 23, 1956, Hollywood, Calif. Screen actress.

Appeared in: **1936** Ants in the Pantry (short).

PROSSER, HUGH
Born: 1906. Died: Nov. 8, 1952, near Gallup, N.Mex. (auto accident). Screen actor.

Appeared in: **1938** Blockade. **1941** Sierra Sue; West of Cimarron. **1942** The Boss of Hangtown Mesa; Sabotage Squad. **1943** Border Patrol; Riders of the Deadline; Lost Canyon. **1945** Flame of the Barbary Coast; Dillinger. **1946** People Are Funny. **1949** Western Renegades. **1950** Outlaw Gold; Across the Badlands. **1951** Montana Incident. **1952** Guns along the Border; The Greatest Show on Earth; Treasure of Lost Canyon; Bend of the River.

PROUTY, JED
Born: Apr. 6, 1879, Boston, Mass. Died: May 10, 1956, New York. Screen, stage, radio, television and vaudeville actor. At age sixteen he formed a vaudeville act known as "Maddux and Prouty."

Appeared in: **1921** The Conquest of Canaan; Experience; Room and Board; The Great Adventure. **1922** Kick In. **1923** The Girl of the Golden West; Souls for Sale; The Gold Diggers. **1925** The Coast of Folly; Scarlet Saint; The Knockout; The Unguarded Hour. **1926** Bred in Old Kentucky; Don Juan's Three Nights; Miss Nobody; Unknown Treasures; Ella Cinders; Everybody's Acting; Her Second Chance; The Mystery Club. **1927** Smile, Brother, Smile; Orchids and Ermine; The Gingham Girl; No Place to Go. **1928** Domestic Meddlers; Name the Woman; The Siren. **1929** Imperfect Ladies; The Fall of Eve; His Captive Woman; Two Weeks Off; It's a Great Life; Why Leave Home?; Sonny Boy; The Broadway Melody. **1930** True to the Navy; No Questions Asked (short); The Floradora Girl; Girl in the Show; The Devil's Holiday. **1931** Strangers May Kiss; Annabelle's Affairs; The Secret Call; The Age for Love. **1932** Business and Pleasure; Manhattan Tower. **1933** Skyway; The Big Bluff; Jimmy and Sally. **1934** I Believed in You; Music in the Air; Private Scandal; One Hour Late; Hollywood Party. **1935** George White's 1935 Scandals; Black Sheep; Navy Wife; One Hour Late; A Trip to Paris. **1936** Every Saturday Night; Little Miss Nobody; Educating Father; Back to Nature; Can This Be Dixie?; Under Your Spell; Special Investigator; His Brother's Wife; The Texas Rangers; College Holiday; Happy Go Lucky. **1937** Borrowing Trouble; Off to the Races; Big Business; Hot Water; Life Begins in College; The Crime Nobody Saw; Sophie Lang Goes West; Dangerous Holiday; One Hundred Men and a Girl; Small Town Boy; You Can't Have Everything. **1938** Love on a Budget; Walking down Broadway; A Trip to Paris; Keep Smiling; Safety in Numbers; Duke of West Point; Goodbye Broadway; Danger on the Air; Down on the Farm. **1939** Everybody's Baby; The Jones Family in Hollywood; Too Busy to Work; The Gracie Allen Murder Case; Second Fiddle; The Jones Family in Grand Canyon; Coat Tales (short); The Jones Family in Quick Millions; Hollywood Cavalcade; Exile Express. **1940** Young as You Feel; On Their Own; Barnyard Follies; Remedy for Riches. **1941** The Lone Wolf Keeps a Date; Pot O' Gold; Father Steps Out; Bachelor Daddy; Unexpected Uncle; City Limits; Look Who's Laughing; Go West Young Lady; Roar of the Press. **1942** The Affairs of Jimmy Valentine; Hold 'Em Jail (short); Scattergood Rides High; It Happened in Flatbush; Moonlight Masquerade; The Old Homestead; Mud Town. **1950** Guilty Bystander.

"PRUDENCE PENNY" (Norma Young)
Born: 1889. Died: Mar. 28, 1974. Screen and radio actress.

Appeared in: **1937** Penny Wisdon (short). **1938** Penny's Party (short); Penny's Picnic (short). **1941** Penny to the Rescue (short).

PRUD'HOMME, CAMERON
Born: 1892. Died: Nov. 27, 1967, Pompton Plains, N.J. Screen, stage and radio actor.

Appeared in: **1930** Abraham Lincoln; Doorway to Hell; Half Shot at Sunrise. **1931** Soldiers' Plaything; Honor of the Family; I Like Your Nerve. **1956** The Power and the Prize; Back from Eternity; The Rainmaker. **1963** The Cardinal.

PRUD'HOMME, GEORGE (aka GEORGE PEMBROKE)
Born: 1901. Died: June 11, 1972, Los Angeles, Calif. (brain tumor). Screen, stage actor and opera performer.

Appeared in: **1938** Irish and Proud of It. **1940** Cowboy from Sundown; The Last Alarm; Buried Alive; Paper Bullets. **1941** Flying Wild; Spooks Run Wild; I Killed That Man; The Invisible Ghost; Gangs Incorporated; The Adventures of Captain Marvel (serial); Miss Polly. **1942** Black Dragons. **1943** Drums of Fu

Manchu. **1944** Bluebeard. **1951** All That I Have. **1952** Red Snow; And Now Tomorrow. **1955** The Girl Rush. **1957** Fear Strikes Out; Hell Canyon (aka Hell Canyon Outlaws); Outlaw's Son. **1958** Showdown at Boot Hill.

PRYOR, AINSLIE
Born: 1921, Memphis, Tenn. Died: May 27, 1958, Hollywood, Calif. (brain cancer). Screen, stage and television actor.

Appeared in: **1955** The Girl in the Red Velvet Swing. **1956** Ransom!; The Last Hunt; Four Girls in Town; Walk the Proud Land. **1957** Guns at Fort Petticoat; The Shadow on the Window. **1958** Kathy-O; Cole Younger, Gunfighter; The Left Handed Gun; Onionhead.

PRYOR, HUGH
Born: 1925. Died: Nov. 11, 1963. Screen and television actor. Married to actress Jacqueline Pryor (dec. 1963).

Appeared in: **1958** Imitation General; Torpedo Run.

PRYOR, JACQUELINE (Connie Williamson)
Born: June 23, 1930, Calif. Died: Nov. 5, 1963, Pasadena, Calif. (murdered—shot). Married to actor Hugh Pryor (dec. 1963).

PRYOR, ROGER
Born: Aug. 27, 1901, Asbury Park, N.J. Died: Jan. 31, 1974, Puerta Vallarta, Mexico (heart attack). Stage, screen, radio actor, stage director and musician. Son of composer and conductor Arthur Pryor (dec. 1942). Divorced from Priscilla Mitchell and actress Ann Sothern.

Appeared in: **1931** The Collegiate Model (short). **1933** Moonlight and Pretzels. **1934** Romance in the Rain; I'll Tell the World; Wake Up and Dream; I Like It That Way; The Gift of Gab; Belle of the Nineties; Lady by Choice. **1935** Straight from the Heart; Headline Woman; Dinky; To Beat the Band; A Thousand Dollars a Minute; The Case of the Missing Man; The Girl Friend; Strange Wives. **1936** The Return of Jimmy Valentine; Missing Girls; Ticket to Paradise; Sitting on the Moon. **1939** The Man They Could Not Hang. **1940** Gambling on the High Seas; A Fugitive from Justice; Glamour for Sale; Sued for Libel; The Man with Nine Lives; The Lone Wolf Meets a Lady; Money and the Woman. **1941** She Couldn't Say No; Power Dive; Flying Blind; South of Panama; Richest Man in Town; Bullets for O'Hara; The Officer and the Lady; Bowery Boys; Gambling Daughters. **1942** I Live on Danger; So's Your Aunt Emma; Smart Alecks; A Man's World; Meet the Mob. **1943** Lady Bodyguard; Submarine Alert. **1944** Thoroughbreds. **1945** Identity Unknown; The Cisco Kid Returns; High Powered; The Man from Oklahoma; Scared Stiff; Kid Sister.

PUDDLES
Died: May, 1912, La Mesa, Calif. (poisoned). Screen dog performer. Appeared in films for American Manufacturing Company.

PUDOVKIN, VSEVOLOD
Born: 1893, Russia. Died: 1953, Russia. Screen actor, film producer, film director and author.

Appeared in: **1931** The Living Corpse. **1942** Ivan the Terrible—Part I (US 1947). **1948** Admiral Nakhimov.

PUGLIA, FRANK
Born: 1892, Sicily. Died: Oct. 25, 1975, South Pasadena, Calif. Screen, stage, television actor and opera performer.

Appeared in: **1921** Orphans of the Storm. **1922** Fascination. **1924** Isn't Life Wonderful? **1925** Romola; The Beautiful City. **1928** The Man Who Laughs. **1934** Men in White; Viva Villa! **1935** The Melody Lingers On. **1936** Fatal Lady; The Devil is a Sissy; Bulldog Edition; The Gay Desperado; The Garden of Allah; The Public Pays (short). **1937** A Doctor's Diary; You Can't Have Everything; Maytime; When You're in Love; Song of the City; Mama Steps Out; The Bride Wore Red; Bulldog Drummond's Revenge. **1938** Rascals; I'll Give a Million; Spawn of the North; Barefoot Boy; Dramatic School; Sharpshooters; Yellow Jack; Tropic Holiday. **1939** Forged Passport; Code of the Secret Service; In Old California; Zaza; Balalaika; The Girl and the Gambler. **1940** The Fatal Hour; Charlie Chan in Panama; Torrid Zone; Down Argentine Way; Arise, My Love; Meet the Wildcat; Te Mark of Zorro. **1941** That Night in Rio; Billy the Kid; The Parson of Panamint; Law of the Tropics. **1942** Escape from Hong Kong; Now Voyager; Always in My Heart; Who is Hope Schuyler?; Secret Agent of Japan; Jungle Book; Flight Lieutenant; Casablanca; The Boogie Man Will Get You. **1943** Action in the North Atlantic; The Phantom of the Opera; Pilot No. 5; Mission to Moscow; Background to Danger; For Whom the Bell Tolls; Princess O'Rourke; Tarzan's Desert Mystery. **1944** Tall in the Saddle; Together Again; Brazil; This is the Life; Ali Baba and the Forty Thieves. **1945** Blood on the Sun; A Song to Remember; Roughly Speaking. **1946** Without Reservations. **1947** Road to Rio; Brute Force; The Lost Moment; Escape Me Never; My Favorite Brunette; Fiesta. **1948** Joan of Arc; Dream Girl. **1949** Bagdad; Special Agent; Colorado Territory; Bride of Vengeance. **1950** Black Hand; Captain Carey, USA; Desert Hawk; Walk Softly, Stranger; Federal Agent at Large. **1953** The Caddy; Steel Lady; The Bandits of Corsica. **1954** Casanova's Big Night; The Shanghai Story. **1956**

Serenade; The Burning Hills; The First Texan. **1959** Cry Tough; The Black Orchid. **1962** Girls! Girls! Girls! **1965** The Sword of Ali Baba.

PUIG, EVA G.

Born: Feb. 3, 1894, Mexico. Died: Oct. 6, 1968, Panorama City, Calif. (diabetes and heart failure). Screen actress.

Appeared in: **1940** North West Mounted Police. **1941** Romance of the Rio Grande; Texas Rangers Ride Again; Singapore Woman; Hold Back the Dawn. **1942** Undercover Man; Rio Rita. **1945** The Cisco Kid Returns; A Medal for Benny. **1946** Snafu; Wild Beauty; Plainsman and the Lady.

PULLY, B. S.

Born: 1911. Died: Jan. 6, 1972, Philadelphia, Pa. (heart attack). Screen, stage and television actor.

Appeared in: **1944** Four Jills in a Jeep; Wing and a Prayer; Greenwich Village; In the Meantime, Darling. **1945** A Tree Grows in Brooklyn; Within These Walls; Nob Hill; Don Juan Quilligan. **1946** Do You Love Me? **1953** Taxi. **1955** Guys and Dolls. **1959** A Hole in the Head. **1969** The Love of God. **1970** Myra Breckenridge.

PURCELL, IRENE

Born: 1902, Hammond, Ind. Died: July 9, 1972, Racine, Wis. Stage and screen actress.

Appeared in: **1931** Just a Gigolo; The Man in Possession. **1932** The Passionate Plumber; Westward Passage; Bachelor's Affairs; The Crooked Circle.

PURCELL, RICHARD "DICK"

Born: Aug. 6, 1908, Greenwich, Conn. Died: Aug. 10, 1944, Los Angeles, Calif. (heart attack). Stage and screen actor.

Appeared in: **1935** Ceiling Zero. **1936** Brides Are Like That; Times Square Playboy; Law in Her Hands; Bullets or Ballots; Jail Break; The Captain's Kid; Men in Exile; King of Hockey; Melody for Two; The Case of the Velvet Claws; Public Enemy's Wife; Man Hunt; Broadway Playboy; Bengal Tiger. **1937** Public Wedding; Navy Blues; Slim; Wine, Women and Horses; The Missing Witness; Reported Missing. **1938** Mystery House; The Daredevil Drivers; Alcatraz Island; Accidents Will Happen; Over the Wall; Penrod's Double Trouble; Garden of the Moon; Valley of the Giants; Flight into Nowhere; Air Devils; Broadway Musketeers; Nancy Drew, Detective. **1939** Blackwell's Island; Drunk Driving (short); While America Sleeps (short); Irish Luck; Tough Kid; Heroes in Blue; Streets of New York. **1940** Private Affairs; Outside the Three-Mile Limit; New Moon; The Bank Dick; Flight Command; Arise My Love. **1941** The Pittsburgh Kid; Flying Blind; Two in a Taxi; No Hands on the Clock; Bullets for O'Hara; King of the Zombies. **1942** Torpedo Boat; In Old California; The Old Homestead; I Live on Danger; X Marks the Spot; Phantom Killer. **1943** Aerial Gunner; Idaho; High Explosives; Reveille with Beverly; The Mystery of the Thirteenth Guest. **1944** Trocadero; Leave It to the Irish; Farewell My Lovely; Captain America (serial); Timber Queen.

PURDELL, REGINALD (Reginald Grasdorf)

Born: Nov. 4, 1896, Clapham, London, England. Died: Apr. 22, 1953, London, England. Screen, stage, television actor and screenwriter.

Appeared in: **1930** The Middle Watch. **1931** A Night in Montmartre; Congress Dances (US 1932). **1933** Up to the Neck; Crime on the Hill; My Lucky Star; Strictly in Confidence. **1934** The Old Curiosity Shop; What's in a Name?; The Luck of a Sailor; The Queen's Affaire (aka Runaway Queen—US 1935); On the Air. **1935** Key to Harmony; Royal Cavalcade (aka Regal Cavalcade—US); Get Off My Foot. **1936** Hail and Farewell; Debt of Honour; Where's Sally?; Crown v. Stevens. **1937** Side Street Angel; Ship's Concert. **1938** Quiet Please; Many Tanks Mr. Atkins; The Viper; The Dark Stairway; Simply Terrific. **1939** Q Planes (aka Clouds over Europe—US); His Brother's Keeper; The Missing People (US 1940); The Middle Watch (and in 1930 version). **1940** Pack Up Your Troubles; Busman's Holiday (aka Haunted Honeymoon—US); Fingers. **1943** Variety Jubilee; We Dive at Dawn; Bell-Bottom George; It's in the Bag. **1944** Candles at Nine; Love Story (aka A Lady Surrenders—US 1947); 2,000 Women. **1946** London Town (aka My Heart Goes Crazy—US 1953). **1947** Holiday Camp (US 1948); Captain Boycott; The Root of All Evil; A Man About the House (US 1949); Brighton Rock. **1951** Files from Scotland Yard.

PURDY, CONSTANCE

Born: c. 1885, Kansas. Died: Apr. 1, 1960, Los Angeles, Calif. (arteriosclerosis). Screen actress.

Appeared in: **1943** White Savage; Air Raid Wardens; Double Up (short). **1947** The Shocking Miss Pilgrim. **1950** Blonde Dynamite.

PURVIANCE, EDNA

Born: 1894, Reno, Nev. Died: Jan. 13, 1958, Woodland Hills, Calif. Screen actress. She was Charlie Chaplin's leading lady for nine years in his early films.

Appeared in: **1915** A Night Out; The Champion; Work. **1916** The Vagabond; Carmen; The Count; The Bank. **1917** The Cure; The Adventurer; Easy Street. **1918** A Dog's Life; Shoulder Arms. **1919** Sunnyside. **1921** The Kid; The Idle

Class. **1922** The Pilgrim. **1923** A Woman of Paris. **1926** The Seagull; A Woman of the Sea. **1952** Limelight. **1963** 30 Years of Fun (documentary).

PUTMAN, GEORGE

Died: Apr. 8, 1974. Screen actor. Do not confuse with news commentator, George Putnam.

Appeared in: **1951** Fourteen Hours.

PYNE, JOE

Born: 1925, Chester, Pa. Died: Mar. 23, 1970, Los Angeles, Calif. (lung cancer). Screen, television and radio actor.

Appeared in: **1966** Mother Goose a Go-Go. **1967** The Love-Ins.

QUALTERS, TOT (Marguerite Qualters)

Born: 1895. Died: Mar. 27, 1974, New York, N.Y. Stage and screen actress.

Appeared in: **1931** Reaching for the Moon.

QUARANTA, LYDIA

Born: 1891, Italy. Died: 1928, Italy. Screen actress. Sister of actresses Letizia and Isabella Quaranta.

Appeared in: **1914** Cabiria. **1925** Voglio Tradire Mio Marito.

QUARTERMAINE, LEON

Born: Sept. 24, 1876, Richmond, Surrey, England. Died: June 28, 1967, Salisbury, England. Stage and screen actor. Married to actress Barbara Wilcox. Divorced from Aimee de Burgh and actress Fay Compton.

Appeared in: **1935** Dark World; Escape Me Never. **1936** As You Like It.

QUIGLEY, CHARLES

Born: Feb. 12, 1906, New Britain, Conn. Died: Aug. 5, 1964, Los Angeles, Calif. (cirrhosis of liver). Stage and screen actor.

Appeared in: **1932** Saddle Buster. **1935** King of Burlesque. **1936** Charlie Chan's Secret; And Sudden Death; Lady from Nowhere; Racing Luck. **1937** The Shadow; Criminals of the Air; Find the Witness; The Game That Kills; Girls Can Play; Speed to Spare. **1938** Convicted. **1939** Daredevils of the Red Circle (serial); Heroes in Blue; Special Inspector. **1940** Mexican Spitfire Out West; Men Against the Sky. **1941** A Woman's Face; The Iron Claw; Playgirl; Footlight Fever; Secret Evidence. **1942** A Yank at Eton. **1943** The Masked Marvel (serial). **1944** The National Barn Dance. **1945** Duffy's Tavern. **1946** Larceny in Her Heart; Affairs of Geraldine; The Crimson Ghost (serial). **1947** Brick Bradford (serial); Three on a Ticket; Danger Street. **1948** Superman (serial). **1949** The Cowboy and the Indians. **1950** Unmasked; David Harding, Counterspy.

QUILLAN, SARAH

Born: 1879. Died: Aug. 3, 1969. Screen actress. Mother of actor Eddie Quillan. Married to actor Joseph Quillan (dec. 1952).

Appeared in: **1929** Noisy Neighbors.

QUILLIAN, JOSEPH F.

Born: July 27, 1884, Glasgow, Scotland. Died: Nov. 16, 1952, Hollywood, Calif. (cancer). Screen and vaudeville actor. Married to actress Sara Quillan (dec. 1969). Father of actor Eddie Quillan.

Appeared in: **1928** A Little Bit of Everything (short). **1929** Noisy Neighbors.

QUIMBY, MARGARET

Died: Aug. 1965, Minneapolis, Minn. Screen actress.

Appeared in: **1925** The Teaser; Perils of the Wild (serial). **1926** What Happened to Jones; The Whole Town's Talking; The Radio Detective (serial). **1927** New York; The Western Whirlwind; The Tired Business Man; The World at Her Feet. **1928** Sally of the Scandals; The Tragedy of Youth. **1929** Lucky Boy; Two Men and a Maid. **1930** Ladies Love Brutes; The Rampant Age; Trailin' Trouble.

QUINCE, LOUIS VEDA

Born: 1900. Died: Sept. 24, 1954, Dallas, Tex. (heart attack). Screen, stage and radio actor.

Appeared in: **1945** Mildred Pierce.

QUINLIVAN, CHARLES

Born: 1924. Died: Nov. 12, 1974, Fountain Valley, Calif. (coronary). Screen, stage and television actor.

Appeared in: **1957** Zero Hour! **1958** Seven Guns to Mesa. **1960** All the Young Men. **1974** Airport 1975.

QUINN, ALAN J.

Born: 1889. Died: Jan. 1944, Philadelphia, Pa. Screen actor.

Appeared in: **1915** The Sporting Duchess.

QUINN, JAMES
Born: 1884. Died: Nov. 30, 1919, New York, N.Y. Screen actor.

QUINN, JAMES "JIMMIE"
Born: 1885, New Orleans, La. Died: Aug. 22, 1940, Hollywood, Calif. Stage and screen actor. Entered films in 1919. Was featured with Billie Sullivan in a series of racetrack shorts.

Appeared in: **1922** Afraid to Fight; Rags to Riches. **1923** Mile-a-Minute Romeo; Second Hand Love. **1924** Broadway after Dark. **1925** Red Hot Tires; The Dixie Handicap; Pretty Ladies; Speed Madness; The Wife Who Wasn't Wanted; On Thin Ice; Soft Shoes. **1926** The Imposter. **1927** Two Flaming Youths. **1928** The Spieler; Ginsberg the Great; Women Who Dare. **1929** Come and Get It; The Dance of Life; The Argyle Case. **1930** Hold Everything. **1934** I Hate Women. **1935** The Gilded Lily.

QUINN, JOE
Born: 1899. Died: May 20, 1974, Los Angeles, Calif. (emphysema). Screen, stage, television and vaudeville actor.

Appeared in: **1917** The Argyle Case. **1921** The Unknown Wife.

QUINN, JOE
Born: 1917. Died: Feb. 2, 1971, Hollywood, Calif. (heart attack). Screen, stage and television actor. Do not confuse with actor Joe Quinn (dec. 1974).

QUINN, JOHN (John Phillip Quinn)
Born: 1851, near St. Louis, Mo. Died: Apr. 18, 1916, Philadelphia, Pa. Screen actor and professional gambler.

Appeared in: **1915** Gambling Inside and Out.

QUINN, PAUL
Born: 1870. Died: Apr. 20, 1936, Los Angeles, Calif. Screen, stage, vaudeville and minstrel actor.

QUINN, TONY
Born: June 27, 1899, Naas, County Kildare, Ireland. Died: June 1, 1967, London, England. Screen, stage and television actor. Do not confuse with actor Anthony Quinn.

Appeared in: **1934** Lest We Forget. **1941** Danny Boy (US 1946). **1943** It's in the Bag. **1949** Saints and Sinners; The Strangers Came (aka You Can't Fool an Irishman—US). **1955** Shadow of a Man. **1956** Tons of Money. **1957** Booby Trap. **1959** The Great Van Robbery (US 1963). **1960** Trouble with Eve (aka In Trouble with Eve—US 1964). **1970** The Strawberry Statement.

QUIRK, WILLIAM "BILLY"
Born: 1881. Died: Apr. 20, 1926, Hollywood, Calif. Screen actor.

Appeared in: **1909** The Son's Return; The Renunciation; Sweet and Twenty; His Wife's Visitor; Oh, Uncle; Getting Even; The Little Teacher; A Midnight Adventure; A Corner in Wheat; The Mended Lute; They Would Elope; 1776, or The Hessian Renegades; The Gibson Goddess. **1910** The Woman from Mellon's; A Rich Revenge; The Two Brothers; Muggsy's First Sweetheart. **1912** Fra Diavolo; The Blood Stain; Hubby Does the Washing. **1913** Billy's Troubles. **1914** Bridal Attire. **1915** Billy, the Bear Tamer. **1921** At the Stage Door; The Man Worth While. **1922** My Old Kentucky Home. **1923** A Bride for a Knight; Broadway Broke; Success. **1925** The Dixie Handicap.

QUIROZ, SALVADOR
Born: 1881, Mexico, Died: Nov. 23, 1956, Mexico City, Mexico. Screen actor.

RABAGLIATI, ALBERTO (Alberto Rabagliati-Vinata)
Born: June 26, 1906, Milan, Italy. Died: Mar. 8, 1974, Rome, Italy (cerebral thrombosis). Screen, radio actor and singer. Went to Hollywood in 1927 as the winner of a "successor to Rudolph Valentino" contest.

Appeared in: **1928** Street Angel. **1930** Seu tu L'amore? **1940** Una Famiglia Impossibile. **1941** La Scuola dei Timidi. **1942** Lascia Cantare il Cuore. **1943** La Vita e Bella; In Cerca di Felicita. **1948** Partenza Ore 7. **1948** Natale al Campo. **1950** Escape into Dreams. **1951** La Avventura di Mandrin. **1952** Il Maestro di Don Giovanni. **1953** Crossed Swords. **1954** Scuola Elementare; The Barefoot Contessa. **1956** The Monte Carlo Story. **1957** Susanna Tutta Panna. **1959** La Cento Chilometri. **1961** Jessica. **1966** The Christmas That Almost Wasn't. **1967** The Birds, the Bees, the Italians.

RADCLIFFE, JACK (Charles Smith)
Born: Sept. 18, 1900, Cleland, Scotland. Died: Apr. 26, 1967, Glasgow, Scotland (cancer). Screen, stage, vaudeville and television actor.

Appeared in: **1955** Geordie (aka Wee Geordie—US 1956).

RADFORD, BASIL
Born: June 25, 1897, Chester, England. Died: Oct. 20, 1952, London, England (heart attack). Stage and screen actor.

Appeared in: **1929** Barnum Was Right (film debut). **1932** There Goes the Bride. **1933** Just Smith; A Southern Maid. **1936** Broken Blossoms; Dishonour

Bright. **1937** Captain's Orders; Jump for Glory (aka When Thief Meets Thief—US); Young and Innocent (aka A Girl was Young—US 1938). **1938** Convict 99; Climbing High (US 1939); The Lady Vanishes. **1939** The Girl Who Forgot; Let's Be Famous; Jamaica Inn; Secret Journey (aka Among Human Wolves—US 1940); Just William; She Couldn't Say No; Spies of the Air (US 1940); Trouble Brewing. **1940** Room for Two (US 1944); The Flying Squad; The Girl in the News (US 1941); Crook's Tour; Night Train to Munich (aka Gestapo and Night Train—US). **1942** Flying Fortress; Unpublished Story; Partners in Crime. **1943** Dear Octopus (aka The Randolph Family—US 1945); Millions Like Us. **1944** Twilight Hour. **1945** Dead of Night; The Way to the Stars (aka Johnny in the Clouds—US). **1946** A Girl in a Million (US 1950); The Captive Heart (US 1947). **1948** Quartet (US 1949); The Winslow Boy (US 1950). **1949** Passport to Pimlico; It's Not Cricket; Whiskey Galore (aka Tight Little Island—US and Mad Little Island); Stop Press Girl. **1950** Chance of a Lifetime (US 1951). **1951** The Galloping Major; White Corridors (US 1952).

RADILAK, CHARLES H.
Born: 1907, Czechoslovakia. Died: July 19, 1972, Inglewood, Calif. Screen, television, stage and radio actor.

Appeared in: **1963** Rampage. **1966** Torn Curtain.

RAE, CLAIRE
Born: 1889. Died: July 7, 1938, Canton, Ohio (leukemia). Stage and screen actress. Appeared in silents.

RAE, JACK (Alton Sampley)
Born: 1899. Died: May 3, 1957, Hollywood, Calif. (heart attack). Stage and screen actor.

RAE, MELBA
Born: 1922. Died: Dec. 29, 1971, N.Y. (cerebral hemorrhage). Screen, stage, radio and television actress. Did film short subject narration and foreign film dubbing.

RAEBURN, HENZIE
Born: 1901, England. Died: Oct. 27, 1973, London, England. Screen, stage actor and author.

Appeared in: **1958** Orders to Kill.

RAFFERTY, CHIPS (John Goffage)
Born: 1909, Australia. Died: May 27, 1971, Sydney, Australia (heart attack). Screen, stage and television actor.

Appeared in: **1938** Ants in His Pants (film debut). **1939** Dan Rudd, M.P. **1940** Forty Thousand Horsemen. **1945** The Rats of Tobruk (aka The Fighting Rats of Tobruk—US 1951). **1946** The Overlanders. **1947** The Loves of Joanna Godden; Bush Christmas. **1949** Eureka Stockade. **1950** Bitter Springs. **1951** Massacre Hill. **1952** Kangaroo. **1953** The Desert Rats. **1956** King of the Coral Sea; Walk into Paradise; Smiley (US 1957). **1958** Smiley Gets a Gun (US 1959). **1961** The Sundowners; The Wackiest Ship in the Army. **1962** Mutiny on the Bounty. **1966** Double Trouble; They're a Weird Mob. **1968** Kona Coast. **1970** Skullduggery.

"RAFFLES BILL" (Andreas Aglassinger)
Born: 1895, Braunau-on-the-Inn, Austria. Died: Feb. 21, 1940, Berlin, Germany (stomach ailment). Screen, vaudeville actor and circus performer. Appeared in German and U.S. films.

RAGAN, RUTH
Died: Sept 15, 1962, Hollywood, Calif. (auto accident). Screen actress and dancer.

RAGLAN, JAMES
Born: 1901. Died: Nov. 15, 1961, London, England. Screen, stage and television actor.

Appeared in: **1952** Whispering Smith vs. Scotland Yard.

RAGLAND, ESTHER
Born: 1912. Died: July 6, 1939, Los Angeles, Calif. Screen and vaudeville whistling actress. She did whistling numbers in 1937 Snow White and the Seven Dwarfs.

RAGLAND, RAGS (John Lee Morgan Beauregard Ragland)
Born: Aug. 23, 1905, Louisville, Ky. Died: Aug. 20, 1946, Los Angeles, Calif. (uremia). Screen, stage and burlesque actor.

Appeared in: **1941** Whistling in the Dark; Ringside Masie. **1942** Masie Gets Her Man; Somewhere I'll Find You; Panama Hattie; Whistling in Dixie; The War against Mrs. Hadley; Sunday Punch; Born to Sing. **1943** Whistling in Brooklyn; Du Barry Was a Lady; Girl Crazy. **1944** The Canterville Ghost; Meet the People; Three Men in White. **1945** Anchors Aweigh; Her Highness and the Bellboy; Abbott and Costello in Hollywood. **1946** The Hoodlum Saint; Ziegfeld Follies.

RAHM, KNUTE
Born: Mar. 20, 1876, Sweden. Died: July 23, 1957, Los Angeles, Calif. (heart disease). Screen actor.

Appeared in: **1912** The Bell of Penance; The Apache Renegade; The Power of a Hymn; Red Wing and the Paleface; The Indian Uprising at Santa Fe. **1913** The Last Blockhouse; The Redemption; The Missing Bonds; A Daughter of the Underworld. **1915** The Mystery of the Tea Dansant (serial). **1917** The Secret of the Lost Valley; Sage Brush Law; The Door In the Mountain.

RAIMU, JULES (Jules Muraire)
Born: 1883, France. Died: Sept. 20, 1946, Paris, France (heart attack). Stage and screen actor.

Appeared in: **1931** Marius (US 1933). **1932** Fanny. **1933** Theodore et Cie. (Theodore and Co.); Mam'zelle Nitouche. **1934** Caesar. **1935** Charlemagne. **1937** Un Carnet de Bal (US 1938); Les Perles de le Couronne. **1939** Le Famille Lefrancois (Heroes of the Marne); La Femme du Boulanger (The Baker's Wife); Heart of Paris; Last Desire. **1940** La Fille du Puisatier (The Well-Digger's Daughter—US 1946); Heart of a Nation (US 1943). **1941** The Man Who Seeks the Truth; The King. **1942** Les Inconnus dans la Maison (Strangers in the House—US 1949). **1944** Colonel Chabert (US 1947). **1945** Dawn Over France; L'Homme au Chapeau Rond. **1947** Midnight in Paris; Fanny (and 1932 version); The Eternal Husband (US 1949); Hoboes in Paradise (US 1950).

RAINEY, NORMAN (William Morrison)
Born: Apr. 28, 1888, Ireland. Died: Sept. 10, 1960, Los Angeles, Calif. (cancer). Screen actor. Do not confuse with screenwriter Norman Rainey (dec. 1971).

Appeared in: **1951** Lorna Doone.

RAINS, CLAUDE
Born: Nov. 10, 1889, London, England. Died: May 30, 1967, Laconia, N.H. (intestinal hemorrhage). Screen, stage and television actor. Divorced from actress Isabel Jeans, Marie Hemingway, Beatrix Thomson and Frances Propper. Married to Agi Jambor.

Appeared in: **1933** The Invisible Man (film debut). **1934** Crime without Passion. **1935** The Man Who Reclaimed His Head; The Mystery of Edwin Drood; The Clairvoyant; The Last Outpost. **1936** Anthony Adverse; Hearts Divided; Stolen Holiday. **1937** The Prince and the Pauper; They Won't Forget. **1938** White Banners; The Adventures of Robin Hood; Four Daughters; Gold Is Where You Find It. **1939** They Made Me a Criminal; Daughters Courageous; Juarez; Mr. Smith Goes to Washington; Four Wives; Sons of Liberty (short). **1940** Saturday's Children; The Sea Hawk; Lady with Red Hair. **1941** Four Mothers; Here Comes Mr. Jordan; Kings Row; The Wolf Man; Riot Squad. **1942** Moontide; Now, Voyager; Eyes of the Underworld; Casablanca. **1943** Forever and a Day; Phantom of the Opera. **1944** Passage to Marseilles; Mr. Skeffington. **1945** This Love of Ours. **1946** Caesar and Cleopatra; Angel on My Shoulder; Deception; Notorious; Strange Holiday. **1947** The Unsuspected. **1948** The Passionate Spring. **1949** Song of Surrender; Rope of Sand; One Woman's Story. **1950** The White Tower; Where Danger Lives. **1951** Sealed Cargo. **1952** The Man Who Watched Trains Go By. **1953** The Paris Express. **1961** The Pied Piper of Hamelin. **1962** Lawrence of Arabia. **1963** Battle of the Worlds; Twilight of Honor. **1965** The Greatest Story Ever Told.

RAISA, ROSE
Born: 1878. Died: Sept. 28, 1963. Stage and screen actress.

Appeared in: **1928** The Soprano of the Chicago Civic Opera Company (shorts). **1937** Men Are Not Gods.

RAJU (Raju Ahmed)
Born: 1937, India. Died: Dec. 12, 1972, Dacca, Bangladesh (murdered). Screen, television and radio actor.

RAKER, LORIN (aka LORRIN RAKER)
Born: May 8, 1891, Joplin, Mo. Died: Dec. 25, 1959, Woodland Hills, Calif. (cancer). Stage and screen actor.

Appeared in: **1928** Gang War. **1929** Mother's Boy. **1930** Kismet. **1931** Six Cylinder Love; Women Go on Forever. **1933** My Woman. **1934** Odor in the Court (short); The Loud Speaker. **1935** The Nut Farm; Honeymoon Limited; Les Miserables. **1937** California Straight Ahead; Mysterious Crossing. **1942** What Makes Lizzy Dizzy? (short). **1943** Cowboy in Manhattan. **1944** Sing a Jingle. **1945** Men in Her Diary. **1946** I'll Be Yours. **1948** Chicken Every Sunday. **1950** The Fuller Brush Girl; Tale of Robin Hood.

RALLI, PAUL
Born: Dec. 29, 1905, Cyprus. Died: Sept. 4, 1953, Van Nuys, Calif. Screen, stage actor, attorney and author.

Appeared in: **1928** The Waterhole; Show People. **1929** Montmartre Rose; Married in Hollywood.

RALPH, JESSIE (Jessie Ralph Chambers)
Born: Nov. 5, 1876, Gloucester, Mass. Died: May 30, 1944, Gloucester, Mass. Stage and screen actress. Married to stage actor William Patton (dec.).

Appeared in: **1916** New York. **1921** Such a Little Queen. **1933** Cocktail Hour; Child of Manhattan (stage and film versions); Elmer the Great; Ann Carver's Profession. **1934** One Night of Love; Evelyn Prentice; Nana (aka Lady of the Boulevard); We Live Again; Murder at the Vanities; The Affairs of Cellini; The Coming Out Party. **1935** David Copperfield; Les Miserables; Paris in Spring (aka Paris Love Song); Captain Blood; Enchanted April; Vanessa, Her Love Story; Mark of the Vampire; I Live My Life; Jalna; Metropolitan; I Found Stella Parish. **1936** Bunker Bean (aka His Majesty Bunker Bean); San Francisco; Walking on Air; The Garden Murder Case; The Unguarded Hour; After the Thin Man; Camille; Little Lord Fauntleroy; Yellow Dust. **1937** The Good Earth; The Last of Mrs. Cheyney; Double Wedding. **1938** Love Is a Headache; Port of Seven Seas; Hold That Kiss. **1939** Cafe Society; The Kid from Texas; Mickey the Kid; Drums along the Mohawk; Four Girls in White. **1940** Star Dust; Girl from Avenue A; I Can't Give You Anything but Love, Baby; I Want a Divorce; The Bank Dick (aka The Bank Detective); The Bluebird. **1941** The Lady from Cheyenne; They Met in Bombay.

RALSTON, JOBYNA
Born: Nov. 21, 1904, South Pittsburg, Tenn. Died: Jan. 22, 1967, Woodland Hills, Calif. Stage and screen actress. Divorced from actor Richard Arlen (dec. 1976).

Appeared in: **1922** Grandma's Boy; The Call of Home; Three Must-Get-Theres. **1923** Why Worry? **1924** Girl Shy; Hot Water. **1925** The Freshman. **1926** For Heaven's Sake; Gigolo; Sweet Daddies. **1927** A Racing Romeo; Special Delivery; Wings; The Kid Brother; Lightning; Pretty Clothes. **1928** The Power of the Press; Little Mickey Grogan; The Count of Ten; The Toilers; The Night Flyer; The Big Hop; Black Butterflies. **1929** Some Mother's Boy; The College Coquette. **1930** Rough Waters.

RAMBAL, ENRIQUE
Born: 1924, Mexico. Died: Dec. 15, 1971, Mexico City, Mexico (heart attack). Screen, stage and television actor.

Appeared in: **1958** El Hombre y el Monstruo (The Man and the Monster—US 1966). **1962** La Estrella Vacia (The Empty Star); El Angel Exterminador (The Exterminating Angel—US 1967).

RAMBEAU, MARJORIE
Born: July 15, 1889, San Francisco, Calif. Died: July 7, 1970, Palm Springs, Calif. Stage and screen actress. Nominated for 1940 Academy Award for Best Supporting Actress in Primrose Path.

Appeared in: **1916** The Dazzling Miss Davison (film debut). **1917** Mary Moreland; The Mirror; The Greater Woman. **1920** The Fortune Teller. **1926** Syncopating Sue. **1930** Her Man; Dark Star; Min and Bill. **1931** Leftover Ladies; Son of India; Inspiration; The Easiest Way; Silence; Hell Divers; Laughing Sinners; This Modern Age; The Secret Six; Strangers May Kiss; A Tailor-Made Man. **1933** Strictly Personal; The Warrior's Husband; A Man's Castle. **1934** Palooka; A Modern Hero; Grand Canary; Ready for Love. **1935** Under Pressure; Dizzy Dames. **1937** First Lady. **1938** Merrily We Live; Woman against Woman. **1939** Sudden Money; The Rains Came; Laugh It Off. **1940** 20 Mule Team; Tugboat Annie Sails Again; East of the River; Heaven with a Barbed Wire Fence; Santa Fe Marshal. **1941** Tobacco Road; Three Sons O'Guns; So Ends Our Night. **1942** Broadway. **1943** In Old Oklahoma. **1944** Oh What a Night; Army Wives. **1945** Salome, Where She Danced. **1948** The Walls of Jericho. **1949** Any Number Can Play; The Lucky Stiff; Abandoned. **1953** Torch Song; Forever Female; Bad for Each Other. **1955** A Man Called Peter; The View from Pompey's Head. **1956** Slander. **1957** Man of a Thousand Faces.

RAMBOVA, NATACHA (Winifred Shaunessy aka WINIFRED HUDNUT-adopted name)
Born: Jan. 19, 1897, Salt Lake City, Utah. Died: June 5, 1966, Pasadena, Calif. (dietary complications). Screen, stage actress, dancer and screenwriter. Divorced from actor Rudolph Valentino (dec. 1926).

Appeared in: **1925** When Love Grows Cold.

RAMIREZ, PEPITA
Born: 1902. Died: Dec. 1927, Hollywood, Calif. (auto crash). Screen, stage actress and dancer.

RAMOS, JESUS MAZA
Born: 1911. Died: Apr. 1955, Mexico. Screen, stage and radio actor. Appeared in an act known as "Los Fikaros."

RAMSEY, JOHN NELSON (aka NEILSON RAMSAYE)
Died: Apr. 5, 1929, London, England (heart disease). Stage and screen actor.

Appeared in: **1916** The Second Mrs. Tanqueray; The Broken Melody. **1917** The Lyons Mail; Her Greatest Performance. **1918** God and the Man; Tom Jones. **1920** The Breed of the Treshams; The Twelve Pound Look. **1922** Dicky

Monteith; The House of Peril. **1924** White Slippers; Young Lochinvar. **1925** The Qualified Adventurer. **1928** Thou Fool. **1929** The Burgomaster of Stilemonde; A Romance of Seville.

RANALDI, FRANK
Born: 1905. Died: May 2, 1933, Hollywood, Calif. (complications from operation). Screen child actor and later a film casting director.

RAND, JOHN F.
Born: 1872. Died: Jan. 25, 1940, Hollywood, Calif. Screen, vaudeville actor and circus performer.

Appeared in: **1928** The Circus. **1935** Old Sawbones (short).

RAND, LIONEL (Lionel Van Clouser)
Born: 1909, Shamokin, Pa. Died: Oct. 15, 1942, Queens, N.Y. Screen actor, song writer and orchestra leader.

RANDALL, ADDISON "JACK" (Addison Owen Randall)
Born: 1907. Died: July 16, 1945, Canoga Park, Calif. (fall from horse while filming). Screen actor. Brother of actor Robert Livingston. Married to actress Barbara Bennett (dec. 1958).

Appeared in: **1935** His Family Tree; Another Face. **1936** Two in the Dark; Love on a Bet; Follow the Fleet; Don't Turn 'Em Loose; Navy Born; Flying Hostess. **1937** Red Lights Ahead; Riders of the Dawn; Stars over Arizona; Blazing Barriers. **1938** The Mexicali Kid. **1939** Driftin' Westward. **1940** Wild Horse Range; Nothing but Pleasure.

RANDALL, BERNARD "BARNEY"
Born: 1884. Died: Dec. 17, 1954, New York, N.Y. Screen, stage, radio and television actor.

Appeared in: **1920** The Master Mind; The Evil Eye (serial); The $1,000,000 Reward (serial). **1921** Closed Doors. **1922** Determination; Polly of the Follies. **1923** The French Doll; Ponjola. **1924** Sundown; Unmarried Wives. **1925** Classified; Counsel for the Defense; Pretty Ladies; Share and Share Alike; Shattered Lives. **1926** Say It Again; The Skyrocket; Subway Sadie. **1928** Show Girl; Nothing but Pleasure (short).

RANDALL, LARRY
Born: 1920. Died: Oct. 17, 1951, near Port Hueneme, Calif. (auto accident). Screen actor.

RANDALL, RAE (Sigrum Salvason)
Born: 1909. Died: May 7, 1934, Hollywood, Calif. (suicide). Screen actress who doubled for Greta Garbo.

Appeared in: **1927** King of Kings. **1929** The Godless Girl.

RANDALL, WILLIAM
Born: 1877. Died: Apr. 22, 1939, Elizabeth, N.J. Screen, stage, radio actor, author and writer for radio. Appeared in silents.

RANDI, ERMANNO
Born: Italy. Died: Nov. 20, 1951. Screen actor.

Appeared in **1948** Tragic Hunt. **1952** Brief Rapture; The Cliff of Sin. **1953** The Young Caruso.

RANDLE, FRANK (Arthur McEvoy)
Born: 1901, Wigan, England. Died: July 7, 1957, Blackpool, England. Screen, stage, vaudeville, radio actor and screenwriter.

Appeared in: **1940** Somewhere in England. **1942** Somewhere in Camp; Somewhere on Leave. **1943** Somewhere in Civvies. **1945** Home Sweet Home. **1947** When You Come Home. **1948** Holidays with Pay. **1949** Somewhere in Politics; School for Randle. **1953** It's a Grand Life.

RANDOLPH, AMANDA
Born: 1902. Died: Aug. 24, 1967, Duarte, Calif. (stroke). Black screen, stage, radio and television actress.

Appeared in: **1939** At the Circus. **1950** No Way Out. **1952** She's Working Her Way through College. **1953** Mr. Scoutmaster. **1955** A Man Called Peter. **1967** The Last Challenge.

RANDOLPH, ANDERS (aka ANDERS RANDOLF)
Born: Dec. 18, 1876, Denmark. Died: July 3, 1930, Hollywood, Calif. (relapse after operation). Stage and screen actor. Entered films with Vitagraph.

Appeared in: **1916** Hero of Submarine D-2. **1917** Within the Law. **1918** The Splendid Sinner. **1919** The Lion and the Mouse; Erstwhile Susan. **1920** The Love Flower. **1921** Buried Treasure; Jim the Penman. **1922** Notoriety; The Referee; Sherlock Holmes; Peacock Alley; Slim Shoulders; The Streets of New York. **1923** The Bright Shawl; The Eternal Struggle; Mighty Lak' a Rose; None So Blind; The Man from Glengarry. **1924** Behold This Woman; In Hollywood with Potash and Perlmutter; By Divine Right; Madonna of the Streets; Dorothy Vernon of Haddon Hall. **1925** The Happy Warrior; Her Market Val-

ue; Seven Keys to Baldpate; Souls for Sables. **1926** The Black Pirate; Broken Hearts of Hollywood; The Johnstown Flood; Miss Nobody; Ranson's Folly; Womanpower. **1927** The Climbers; The College Widow; Dearie; The Jazz Singer; The Love of Sunya; Old San Francisco; A Reno Divorce; Sinews of Steel; Slightly Used; The Tender Hour. **1928** The Crimson City; The Gateway of the Moon; Powder My Back; The Power of Silence; The Big Killing; Three Sinners; Women They Talk About; Me, Gangster. **1929** Four Devils; The Kiss; Shanghai Lady; The Show of Shows; Snappy Sneeze (short); The Sin Sister; Young Nowheres; The Viking; Dangerous Curves; Noah's Ark; Last Performance. **1930** Maybe It's Love; Night Owls (short); Son of the Gods; The Way of All Men. **1931** Going Wild. **1965** Laurel and Hardy's Laughing 20's (documentary).

RANDOLPH, DOROTHY (Dorothy Cohen)
Died: Mar. 10, 1918, Atlanta, Ga. Screen actress. Appeared in films for Triangle.

RANDOLPH, ISABEL
Born: 1890. Died: Jan. 11, 1973, Burbank, Calif. Screen, stage, radio and television actress.

Appeared in: **1940** On Their Own; Yesterday's Heroes; Ride, Tenderfoot, Ride; Barnyard Follies; Sandy Gets Her Man. **1941** Look Who's Laughing; Small Town Deb. **1942** Here We Go Again; Ride 'Em Cowboy. **1943** Follow the Band; Hoosier Holiday; O My Darling Clementine. **1944** Standing Room Only; Jamboree; Wilson. **1945** Practically Yours; The Man Who Walked Alone; The Missing Corpse; Tell It To a Star. **1946** Our Hearts Were Growing Up. **1948** If You Knew Susie; The Noose Hangs High; That Wonderful Urge. **1949** Feudin' Rhythm. **1950** The Fuller Brush Girl; Mary Ryan, Detective. **1951** Secrets of Monte Carlo; A Wonderful Life; Two Dollar Bettor. **1952** Thundering Caravans. **1953** Border City Rustlers; The Lady Wants Mink. **1954** The Shanghai Story. **1955** You're Never Too Young. **1956** Hot Shots.

RANDOLPH, MAY
Born: 1873. Died: Apr. 13, 1956, Hollywood, Calif. Screen actress.

RANGA RAO, S. V.
Born: 1918, India. Died: July 19, 1974, Madras, India (heart attack). Screen actor.

Appeared in: Varudhini (film debut); Pathala Bhairavi; Pellichesi Choodu; Raju Peda; Bengarupapa; Brathukutheruvu; Dasi; Kanakatara; Charanadasi; Devadas; Missiamma; Anakali; Gunasunderi Katha; Sasirekha Parinayam.

RANGEL, ARTURO SOTO
Born: 1882, Mexico. Died: May 25, 1965, Mexico City, Mexico. Screen actor.

Appeared in: **1943** Silk, Blood and Sun; The Virgin of Guadalupe. **1944** Maria Candelaria. **1947** St. Francis of Assisi. **1948** The Treasure of Sierra Madre. **1953** Sombrero. **1954** Garden of Eden; other Mexican films: La Intrusa; La Mentira; La Plegaria a Dios; Los Orgullosas; El Cristo de mi Cabacera.

"RANGER BILL." See JOSEPH WILLIAM

RANIER, RICHARD ROBERT
Born: 1889. Died: Aug. 25, 1960, West Los Angeles, Calif. (arthritis). Screen, stage and vaudeville actor. Appeared in early Vitagraph and Reliance Co. films.

RANIN, HELGE
Born: 1897. Died: Apr. 15, 1952, Stockholm, Sweden. Screen and stage actor. Appeared in Finnish films.

RANKIN, ARTHUR (Arthur Rankin Davenport)
Born: Aug. 30, 1900, New York, N.Y. Died: Mar. 23, 1947, Hollywood, Calif. (cerebral hemorrhage). Screen actor. Son of actor Harry Davenport (dec. 1949). See Harry Davenport regarding family information.

Appeared in: **1921** Enchantment; The Great Adventure; Jim the Penman; The Lure of Jade. **1922** Enter Madame; The Five Dollar Baby; Little Miss Smiles; To Have and to Hold. **1923** The Call of the Canyon. **1924** The Dark Swan; Discontented Husbands; Vanity's Price. **1925** Fearless Lover; The Love Gamble; Pursued; Speed; Sun-Up; Tearing Through. **1926** The Hidden Way; The Man in the Shadow; The Millionaire Policeman; Old Loves and New; The Sporting Lover; Volga Boatman. **1927** The Adventurous Soul; Dearie; The Love Wager; Riding to Fame; Slightly Used; The Woman Who Did Not Care; The Blood Ship. **1928** Broken Laws; Say It with Sables; Walking Back; Making the Varsity; Finders Keepers; Companionate Marriage; Submarine; Code of the Air; Domestic Troubles; Runaway Girls; The Wife's Relations. **1929** Glad Rag Doll; The Fall of Eve; Below the Deadline; The Wild Party; Mexicali Rose; Ships of the Night; The Wolf of Wall Street. **1930** Brothers. **1933** Thrill Hunter; Terror Trail. **1934** Search for Beauty; Carnival; Most Precious Thing in Life; Perfectly Mismated (short); Men in Black (short). **1935** Death Flies East; Hoi Polloi (short); Eight Bells; Case of the Missing Man. **1936** Roaming Lady.

RANKIN, HERBERT
Born: 1876. Died: July 16, 1946, Hollywood, Calif. Screen actor.

RANOUS, WILLIAM V.
Born: 1847. Died: Apr. 1, 1915, Santa Monica, Calif. Screen actor and film producer.

Appeared in: **1911** Vanity Fair. **1912** The Little Minister. **1913** A Maid of Mandalay; Sue Simpkin's Ambition; Getting Up a Practice; The Lonely Princess; A Faithful Servant; The Taming of Betty; Jack's Chrysanthemum. **1914** The Upper Hand. **1915** An Intercepted Vengeance; The Chalice of Courage.

RAPHAEL, ENID
Died: Mar. 5, 1964, New York, N.Y. Stage and screen actress.

RAPPE, VIRGINIA
Died: Sept. 5, 1921, San Francisco, Calif. (ruptured bladder). Screen actress.

Appeared in: **1917** Paradise Green. **1920** A Twilight Baby.

RASCH, ALBERTINA
Born: 1891, Vienna, Austria. Died: Oct. 2, 1967, Woodland Hills, Calif. Screen actress, dancer, ballerina and choreographer. Married to composer Dmitri Tiomkin.

Appeared in: **1929** The Hollywood Revue of 1929; The Rogue Song; Devil May Care. **1930** Lord Byron of Broadway; Our Blushing Brides. **1933** Broadway to Hollywood.

RASUMNY, MIKHAIL
Born: 1890, Odessa, Russia. Died: Feb. 17, 1956, Los Angeles, Calif. Screen, stage and television actor.

Appeared in: **1940** Comrade X. **1941** Hold Back the Dawn; The Shanghai Gesture; Forced Landing. **1942** Wake Island; This Gun for Hire; Road to Morocco; Yokel Boy. **1943** Her Heart in Her Throat; Hostages; For Whom the Bell Tolls. **1944** And the Angels Sing; Practically Yours; Henry Aldrich Plays Cupid. **1945** A Royal Scandal; The Unseen; A Medal for Benny; The Stork Club; Bring on the Girls; Masquerade in Mexico. **1946** Kitty; Holiday in Mexico; Anna and the King of Siam; Heart Beat; Our Hearts Were Growing Up. **1947** Her Husband's Affairs; Song of My Heart; Pirates of Monterey. **1948** Saigon. **1949** The Kissing Bandit; Free for All; The Pirates of Capri. **1950** Hit Parade of 1951. **1952** Anything Can Happen. **1953** The Stars Are Singing; Tonight We Sing. **1956** Hot Blood.

RATHBONE, BASIL (Philip St. John Basil Rathbone)
Born: June 13, 1892, Johannesburg, South Africa. Died: July 21, 1967, New York, N.Y. (heart attack). Screen, stage, radio and television actor. Divorced from Ethel Marion Forman. Married to actress and screenwriter Ouida Bergere (dec. 1974). Star of "Sherlock Holmes" film series.

Appeared in: **1921** Innocent; The Fruitful Vine. **1924** Trouping with Ellen; The School of Scandal. **1925** The Masked Bride. **1926** The Great Deception. **1929** The Last of Mrs. Cheyney; Barnum Was Right. **1930** The High Road; This Mad World; The Flirting Widow; A Notorious Affair; Sin Takes a Holiday; A Lady Surrenders; The Bishop Murder Case; The Lady of Scandal. **1931** Once a Lady. **1932** A Woman Commands; After the Ball (US 1933). **1933** One Precious Year. **1934** Loyalties. **1935** David Copperfield; Anna Karenina; The Last Days of Pompeii; Captain Blood; Kind Lady; A Feather in Her Hat; A Tale of Two Cities. **1936** Romeo and Juliet; Private Number; The Garden of Allah. **1937** Love from a Stranger; Make a Wish; Confession; Tovarich. **1938** The Adventures of Robin Hood; The Adventures of Marco Polo; If I Were King; Dawn Patrol. **1939** The Adventures of Sherlock Holmes (16 in series); The Sun Never Sets; The Hound of the Baskervilles; Son of Frankenstein; Tower of London; Rio. **1940** Rhythm on the River; The Mark of Zorro; A Date with Destiny. **1941** Paris Calling; International Lady; The Mad Doctor; The Black Cat. **1942** Crossroads; Sherlock Holmes and the Voice of Terror; Fingers at the Window; Sherlock Holmes and the Secret Weapon. **1943** Sherlock Holmes in Washington; Above Suspicion; Sherlock Holmes Faces Death; Crazy House. **1944** The Scarlet Claw; The Pearl of Death; Frenchman's Creek; Sherlock Holmes and the Spider Woman; Bathing Beauty. **1945** The House of Fear; Pursuit to Algiers; The Woman in Green. **1946** Terror by Night; Dressed to Kill; Heartbeat. **1949** The Adventures of Ichabod and Mr. Toad (narrator). **1954** Casanova's Big Night. **1955** We're No Angels. **1956** The Black Sheep; The Court Jester. **1958** The Last Hurrah. **1962** The Magic Sword (voice only); Tales of Terror; Two before Zero. **1963** The Comedy of Terrors. **1965** The Adventures of Marco Polo (and 1938 version); Queen of Blood. **1966** Ghost in the Invisible Bikini; Prehistoric Planet Woman. **1967** Dr. Rock and Mr. Roll; Gill Women; Hillbillies in the Haunted House.

RATNAM, KALI N.
Died: Aug. 7, 1950. South Indian screen actor.

RATNER, ANNA
Born: 1892. Died: July 2, 1967, Chicago, Ill. Screen, stage actress and dancer. Appeared in films between 1912 and 1916 at Essanay Studio.

RATOFF, GREGORY
Born: Apr. 20, 1897, Petrograd, Russia. Died: Dec. 14, 1960, Solothurn, Switzerland. Screen, stage actor, screenwriter; film director, stage and film producer.

Appeared in: **1929** For Sale (short). **1932** Melody of Life; Roar of the Dragon; Deported; Skyscraper Souls; Once in a Lifetime; Secrets of the French Police; Undercover Man; Symphony of Six Million; What Price Hollywood; Thirteen Women. **1933** Sweepings; Professional Sweetheart; Headline Shooters; I'm No Angel; Sitting Pretty; Girl without a Room; Broadway Thru a Keyhole. **1934** The Great Flirtation; Let's Fall in Love; Forbidden Territory (US 1938); George White's Scandals. **1935** King of Burlesque; Hello Sweetheart (aka The Butter and Egg Man); Remember Last Night. **1936** Here Comes Trouble; Sins of Man; Under Two Flags; The Road to Glory; Sing, Baby, Sing; Under Your Spell; Falling in Love (aka Trouble Ahead—US). **1937** Top of the Town; Cafe Metropole; Seventh Heaven. **1938** Sally, Irene and Mary; Gateway. **1939** Rose of Washington Square; Barricade; Hotel for Women; Daytime Wife; Intermezzo. **1940** I Was an Adventuress; The Great Profile; Public Deb No. 1. **1941** Adam Had Four Sons; The Corsican Brothers. **1942** Two Yanks in Trinidad; Footlight Serenade. **1944** Irish Eyes Are Smiling. **1945** Where Do We Go from Here?; Paris Underground. **1946** Do You Love Me? **1947** Carnival in Costa Rica. **1950** If This Be Sin; All about Eve. **1951** Operation X. **1952** O. Henry's Full House. **1956** Abdullah's Harem. **1957** The Sun Also Rises. **1960** Once More, with Feeling; Exodus. **1961** The Big Gamble.

RATTENBERRY, HARRY (aka HARRY RATTENBURY)
Born: 1860. Died: Dec. 10, 1925, Hollywood, Calif. Screen actor and opera performer.

Appeared in: **1914** Lucille Love; Girl of Mystery (serial); When Eddie Went to the Front. **1915** He Fell in a Cabaret; The Frame Up on Dad; Some Chaperone; An Heiress for Two; Father's Boy; Father's Lucky Escape; A Looney Love Affair; When Father Had the Gout; Where the Deacon Lives; When Father was the Goat; Keeping It Dark; Some Fixer; Father's Helping Hand; A Mixed-Up Elopement; When Cupid Crossed the Bay. **1916** Oh! for a Cave Man; His Wedding Night; The Deacon's Widow; That Dog-Gone Baby; Oliver Twist; Won by a Foul; Innoculating Hubby; Tramp, Tramp, Tramp; Cupid's Undercut; Nearly a Hero; Lovers and Lunatics; Henry's Little Kid; The Boy, the Girl and the Auto; Her Steady Carfare. **1917** Black Hands and Soapsuds; Her Friend the Chauffeur; A Gay Deceiver; Oh, for a Wife; Suspended Sentence; Father was Right; A Lucky Slip; A Marked Man; Indiscreet Corinne; The Learnin' of Jim Benton. **1918** The Law's Outlaw; Playing the Game. **1919** Hearts of Men; Almost Married; The Delicious Little Devil. **1920** Huckleberry Finn. **1921** The Broken Spur; His Pajama Girl; A Motion to Adjourn. **1922** Watch Your Step. **1923** The Printer's Devil; Soul of the Beast. **1924** Abraham Lincoln. **1925** Daring Days.

RAUCOURT, JULES
Born: 1891, Brussels, Belgium. Died: Jan. 30, 1967. Screen, stage actor and author. Entered films in 1916.

Appeared in: **1917** At First Sight; The Hungry Heart (aka Frou Frou). **1918** La Tosca. **1919** Prunella. **1927** Ranger of the North. **1928** Glorious Betsy; His Tiger Lady. **1930** Le Spectre Vert. **1934** Caravan. **1938** Artists and Models Abroad.

RAVEL, SANDRA
Died: Aug. 13, 1954, Milan, Italy. Screen actress.

Appeared in: **1930** L'Enigmatique Monsieur Parkes; Those Three French Girls. **1931** The Single Sin. **1935** Une Etoile Disparait (A Star Disappears). **1937** Tre Anni Senza Donne; Al Buio Insieme. **1940** A Wife in Peril. Other Italian films: Two Million for a Smile; Ho Visto Brillare Una Stella.

RAVELLE, RAY. *See* OTTO FRANCIS WESS

RAVENEL, FLORENCE
Died: Dec. 18, 1975. Screen actress.

Appeared in: **1953** The Twonky. **1955** Violent Saturday. **1958** Going Steady.

RAVENEL, JOHN (Donald M. Upshur)
Born: 1912. Died: Sept. 14, 1950, Chicago, Ill. (heart attack). Screen actor, radio and television producer.

RAWLINS, HERBERT
Died: 1947. Screen actor. Married to actress Josephine Norman (dec. 1951).

RAWLINS, JUDITH "JUDY" (Judith Ellen Riedel)
Born: June 24, 1936, Wis. Died: Mar. 28, 1974, Los Angeles, Calif. (probably suicide—drug overdose). Screen actress. Divorced from singer and actor Vic Damone.

Appeared in: **1961** 20,000 Eyes.

RAWLINSON, HERBERT
Born: 1885, Brighton, England. Died: July 12, 1953, Woodland Hills, Calif. (lung cancer). Screen, stage, radio and vaudeville actor.

Appeared in: **1912** The God of Gold; The Count of Monte Cristo. **1913** The

Sea Wolf. **1914** Kid Regan's Hands; Flirting with Death. **1915** The Black Box; Damon and Pythias. **1917** Come Through. **1918** Back to the Woods; Turn of the Wheel. **1919** The Carter Case (serial); Good Gracious Annabelle. **1920** Passers By. **1921** Charge It; The Wakefield Case; The Conflict; Playthings of Destiny; Wealth; You Find It Everywhere; Cheated Hearts; The Millionaire. **1922** The Black Bag; The Man under Cover; The Scrapper; Another Man's Shoes; Confidence; Don't Shoot; One Wonderful Night. **1923** The Clean-Up; Fools and Riches; Nobody's Bride; The Prisoner; Railroaded; The Scarlet Car; Victor; His Mystery Girl; Million to Burn; Mary of the Movies. **1924** High Speed; Stolen Secrets; The Dancing Cheat; Dark Stairways; Jack O'Clubs; The Tomboy. **1925** The Man in Blue; My Neighbor's Wife; The Flame Fighter (serial); The Adventurous Sex; Every Man's Wife; The Great Jewel Robbery; The Prairie Wife; The Unnamed Woman. **1926** Phantom Police (serial); Trooper 77 (serial); The Belle of Broadway; The Gilded Butterfly; Her Big Adventure; Her Sacrifice; Men of the Night; Midnight Thieves; The Millionaire Policeman. **1927** The Bugle Call; The Hour of Reckoning; Wages of Conscience; Slipping Wives (short); Burning Gold. **1928** The Monologist of the Screen (short). **1933** Moonlight and Pretzels; Enlighten Thy Daughter. **1935** The People's Enemy; Show Them No Mercy; Men without Names; Confidential; Convention Girl. **1936** Hitchhike to Heaven; Ticket to Paradise; Dancing Feet; Bullets or Ballots; A Son Comes Home; Hollywood Boulevard; Mad Holiday; God's Country and the Woman. **1937** Don't Pull Your Punches; The Go Getter; That Certain Woman; Over the Goal; Love Is on the Air; Nobody's Baby; Mysterious Crossing; Back in Circulation; Make a Wish; Blake of Scotland Yard. **1938** Hawaii Calls; Orphans of the Street; Women Are Like That; Under the Big Top; The Kid Comes Back; Torchy Gets Her Man; Secrets of an Actress. **1939** You Can't Get Away with Murder; Dark Victory; Sudden Money. **1940** Money to Burn; The Five Little Peppers at Home; Free, Blonde and 21; Framed; Seven Sinners; Swiss Family Robinson. **1941** Scattergood Meets Broadway; A Gentleman from Dixie; Bad Man at Deadwood; I Killed That Man; Riot Squad; Flying Wild; I Wanted Wings; Arizona Cyclone. **1942** Smart Alecks; I Live on Danger; Tramp, Tramp, Tramp; Lady Gangster; The Broadway Big Shot; The Panther's Claw; SOS Coast Guard; The Yukon Patrol; Stagecoach Buckaroo; Hello, Annapolis; Foreign Agent; War Dogs. **1943** Colt Comrades; Where Are Your Children?; Border Patrol; Lost Canyon; Cosmo Jones in the Crime Smasher; Two Weeks to Live; The Woman of the Town; Riders of the Deadline. **1944** Sailor's Holiday; Shake Hands with Murder; Oklahoma Raiders; Marshal of Reno; Marshal of Gunsmoke; Nabonga; Goin' To Town; Sheriff of Sundown; Forty Thieves; Lumberjack. **1946** Accomplice. **1948** The Argyle Secrets; The Gallant Legion; Borrowed Trouble; The Counterfeiters; Silent Conflict; Sinister Journey; The Strange Gamble. **1949** Brimstone; Fighting Man of the Plains. **1951** Gene Autry and the Mounties.

RAY, BARBARA

Born: 1914. Died: May 19, 1955, Los Angeles, Calif. (leukemia). Screen actress. Married to actor Roscoe Ates (dec. 1962).

RAY, CHARLES

Born: Mar. 15, 1891, Jacksonville, Ill. Died: Nov. 23, 1943, Los Angeles, Calif. (throat and jaw infection). Screen, stage, vaudeville actor, film producer and director.

Appeared in: **1913** The Favorite Son; The Sharpshooter; The Lost Dispatch; The Sinews of War; Bread Cast upon the Waters; A Slave's Devotion; The Boomerang; The Transgressor; The Quakeress; The Bondsman; The Exoneration; The Witch of Salem; Soul of the South; The Open Door; Eileen of Erin. **1914** A Military Judas; The House of Bondage; Her Brother's Sake; In the Tennessee Hills; Repaid; Desert Gold; For the Wearing of the Green; The Paths of Genius; The Rightful Heir; Shorty's Sacrifice; The Card Sharps; In the Cow Country; The Latent Spark; The Curse of Humanity; The City; Red Mask; Joe Hibbard's Claim; One of the Discard; Word of His People; The Fortunes of War; The City of Darkness; The Friend; Not of the Flock. **1915** The Grudge; The Wells of Paradise; The Cup of Life; The Spirit of the Bell; The Renegade; The Shoal Light; The Conversion of Frosty Blake;The Ace of Hearts; City of the Dead; The Painted Soul; The Lure of Woman; The Coward. **1916** Peggy; The Dividend; A Corner in Colleens; The Wolf Woman; The Honorable Algy; The Weaker Sex; Honor Thy Name; Home; Plain Jane; The Deserter. **1917** Back of the Man; The Millionaire Vagrant; Sudden Jim; The Son of His Father; Clod Hopper; The Pinch Hitter. **1918** His Mother's Boy; The Hired Man; The Family Skeleton; Playing the Game; His Own Home Town; The Law of the North; The Claws of the Hun; Nine O'Clock Town; String Beans. **1919** Crooked Straight; Hayfoot, Strawfoot; The Sheriff's Son; Greased Lightning; The Girl Dodger; Bill Henry; The Busher; The Egg-Crate Wallop. **1920** Red Hot Dollars; Paris Green; Alarm Clock Andy; Homer Comes Home; Forty-five Minutes from Broadway; Village Sleuth; Old-Fashioned Boy; Peaceful Valley. **1921** Nineteen and Phyllis; The Old Swimmin' Hole; Scrap Iron; A Midnight Bell; R.S.V.P.; Two Minutes to Go. **1922** Gas, Oil and Water; The Deuce of Spades; Alias Julius Caesar; The Barnstormer; Smudge; Tailor-Made Man. **1923** The Girl I Loved; The Courtship of Miles Standish; Ponjola. **1924** Dynamite Smith. **1925** Some Pun'kins; Percy; Bright Lights. **1926** Sweet Adeline; Paris; The Auction Block. **1927** The Fire Brigade; The Flag Maker; Getting Gertie's Garter; Nobody's Widow; Vanity. **1928** The Garden of Eden; The Count of Ten. **1932** The Bride's Bereavement. **1934**

Ladies Should Listen; Ticket to a Crime; School for Girls. **1935** By Your Leave; Welcome Home. **1936** Hollywood Boulevard; Just My Luck. **1940** The Lady from Cheyenne; A Little Bit of Heaven. **1941** Wild Geese Calling; The Man Who Lost Himself; A Yank in the R.A.F. **1942** The Magnificent Dope; Tennessee Johnson.

RAY, EMMA (Emma Sherwood)

Born: 1871. Died: Jan. 3, 1935, Los Angeles, Calif. Screen, stage and vaudeville actress. Married to actor Johnny Ray (dec. 1927). They appeared in vaudeville together.

Appeared in: **1934** The Old Fashioned Way (short).

RAY, ESTELLE GOULDING

Born: 1888. Died: Aug. 1, 1970, Hollywood, Calif. (due to fall). Stage and screen actress. Appeared in early silents.

RAY, HELEN

Born: 1879, Fort Stockton, Tex. Died: Oct. 2, 1965, Wolfboro, N.H. Screen, stage, vaudeville and television actress. Married to vaudeville actor Homer Miles (dec.) and they appeared in an act billed as "Homer and Helen Miles."

Appeared in: **1921** Experience; Sheltered Daughters.

RAY, JACK

Born: 1917. Died: Oct. 31, 1975, Montclair, Calif. Screen and vaudeville actor. Married to Marion Ray. Appeared in "Our Gang" silents as "Freckles."

RAY, JOHNNY (John Matthews)

Born: 1859, Wales. Died: Sept. 4, 1927, Los Angeles, Calif. (paralytic stroke). Screen, stage and vaudeville actor. Married to actress Emma Sherwood Ray (dec. 1935). They appeared in vaudeville together.

Appeared in: **1928** Bringing up Father.

RAY, MARJORIE

Born: 1900. Died: July 21, 1924, San Diego, Calif. (tetanus). Stage and screen actress.

RAY, NAOMI

Born: 1893. Died: Mar. 13, 1966, New York, N.Y. Screen, stage and vaudeville actress. Appeared in vaudeville with her husband, Eddie Harrison, in an act billed as "Ray and Harrison."

Appeared in: **1932** The Riding Master (short); plus other early shorts.

RAYMOND, FORD

Born: 1900. Died: Apr. 25, 1960, Hollywood, Calif. Screen, stage and vaudeville actor.

Appeared in: **1960** One Foot in Hell.

RAYMOND, FRANCES "FRANKIE"

Born: 1869. Died: June 18, 1961, Hollywood, Calif. Screen and stage actress. Entered films in 1915.

Appeared in: **1921** Garments of Truth; The March Hare; One a Minute; One Wild Week; Smiling All the Way; Two Weeks with Pay. **1922** The Ghost Breaker; Hurricane's Gal; Shadows; Young America. **1923** A Chapter in Her Life; The Grail; The Meanest Man in the World; Money, Money, Money. **1924** Abraham Lincoln; Excitement; Flirting with Love; The Girl on the Stairs; Girls Men Forget. **1925** Seven Chances. **1926** Behind the Front; What Happened to Jones. **1927** The Cruel Truth; The Gay Defender; The Gay Old Bird; Get Your Man; Stage Kisses; Three's a Crowd; Wandering Girls; Web of Fate; The Wreck. **1928** Rich Men's Sons. **1929** The Illusion. **1934** The Mighty Barnum. **1935** Love in Bloom. **1937** The Awful Truth. **1943** Happy Go Lucky. **1947** Ladies' Man.

RAYMOND, HELEN

Born: c. 1885, Philadelphia, Pa. Died: Nov. 26, 1965, New York, N.Y. Stage and screen actress.

Appeared in: **1920** Twin Beds. **1921** Her Mad Bargain; My Lady Friends; Her Social Value; Through the Back Door. **1922** Very Truly Yours; Wild Honey; The Ableminded Lady. **1923** The Huntress.

RAYMOND, JACK (George Feder)

Born: Dec. 14, 1901, Minneapolis, Minn. Died: Dec. 5, 1951, Santa Monica, Calif. (heart attack). Screen, stage, vaudeville, television actor, cameraman and film director.

Appeared in: **1921** The Miracle of Manhattan. **1924** Roulette. **1925** Lover's Island; Scarlet Saint. **1927** The Lunatic at Large; Pleasure before Business. **1928** Sally of the Scandals; The Butter and Egg Man; Lonesome; Melody of Love; Three Week Ends; The Last Command; The Price of Fear; Riley of the Rainbow Division; Thanks for the Buggy Ride. **1929** The Wild Party; Synthetic Sin; The Younger Generation; Points West. **1933** His Silent Racket (short). **1935** Headline Woman; Poker at Eight (short); Paris in Spring. **1936** Preview

Murder Mystery; Night Club Scandal. **1937** Easy Living. **1949** Omoo Omoo. **1950** Abbott and Costello in the Foreign Legion.

RAYMOND, ROYAL (Royal Aaron Raymond)
Born: Sept. 29, 1916, New York, N.Y. Died: Dec. 20, 1949, Van Nuys, Calif. (cancer). Screen, stage and television actor.

Appeared in: **1949** The Red Menace.

RAYNAUD, FERNAND
Died: Sept. 28, 1973, Massif Central region, France (automobile accident). Screen, stage, television and radio actor.

RAZETTO, STELLA
Born: 1881, San Diego, Calif. Died: Sept. 21, 1948, Malibu, Calif. Screen actress. Married to film director E. J. Lee Saint.

Appeared in: **1913** Outwitted by Billy; Northern Hearts; His Sister; Lure of the Road. **1914** The Mistress of His House; The Girl Behind the Barrier; The Reporter On the Case; What Became of Jane?; Who Killed George Graves?; Ye Vengeful Vagabonds; A Typographical Error; Peggy of Primrose Lane; The Wasp; C.D.; Fate and Ryan; One Traveler Returns. **1915** The Richest Girl In the World; The Passer-By; The Spirit of the Violin; The Poetic Justice of Omar Khan; The Lady of Cyclamen; The Blood Yoke; The Fortunes of Marian; The Face in the Mirror; The Unfinished Portrait; The Circular Staircase; The Strange Case of Princess Khan. **1916** Selig films.

REA, MABEL LILLIAN
Born: 1932. Died: Dec. 24, 1968, Charlotte, N.C. (auto accident). Screen and television actress.

Appeared in: **1956** Bundle of Joy. **1957** Pal Joey; The Devil's Hairpin. **1958** I Married a Woman. **1959** Submarine Seahawk.

READ, BARBARA
Born: Dec. 29, 1917, Port Arthur, Canada. Died: Dec. 12, 1963. Stage and screen actress. Divorced from actor William Talman (dec. 1968).

Appeared in: **1937** Three Smart Girls; The Mighty Treve; The Road Back; The Man Who Cried Wolf; Merry-Go-Round of 1938; Make Way for Tomorrow. **1938** The Crime of Dr. Hallet; Midnight Intruder. **1939** The Spellbinder; Sorority House. **1940** Married and In Love; Curtain Call. **1942** Too Many Women; Rubber Racketeers. **1946** The Shadow Returns; Behind the Mask; The Missing Lady; Ginger. **1947** Key Witness. **1948** Coroner Creek.

READICK, FRANK M.
Born: 1861. Died: Aug. 26, 1924, New York, N.Y. (heart failure). Screen and vaudeville actor.

REAL, BETTY
Died: Sept. 9, 1969, Miami, Calif. Stage and screen actress.

Appeared in: **1934** Crime without Passion.

RED WING. *See* LILLIAN "RED WING" ST. CYR.

REDDING, OTIS
Born: 1941. Died: Dec. 10, 1967 (plane crash). Screen actor and singer.

Appeared in: **1969** Monterey Pop; Popcorn—An Audio Visio Rock Think.

REDWING, RODD (Rederick Redwing; aka ROD REDWING, RODRIC REDWING, ROD RED WING and RODERIC REDWING)
Born: 1905, N.Y. Died: May 30, 1971, Los Angeles, Calif. (heart attack). Screen, stage, television actor and gun coach. Full-blooded Chickasaw Indian.

Appeared in: **1931** The Squaw Man. **1939** Gunga Din!; Lives of a Bengal Lancer. **1945** Objective Burma! **1946** Out of the Depths. **1947** The Last Round-Up. **1949** Apache Chief; Song of India. **1951** Little Big Horn. **1952** Buffalo Bill in Tomahawk Territory; Rancho Notorious; The Pathfinder; Hellgate. **1953** Winning of the West; Conquest of Cochise; Saginaw Trail; Flight to Tangier. **1954** Creature from the Black Lagoon; Cattle Queen of Montana; The Naked Jungle; Elephant Walk; The Cowboy. **1956** Jaguar; The Ten Commandments; The Mole People. **1957** Copper Sky. **1958** The Flame Barrier. **1960** Flaming Star. **1961** One-Eyed Jacks; Watch it Sailor. **1962** Sergeants Three. **1964** Invitation to a Gunfighter. **1966** Apache Uprising; Johnny Reno. **1967** El Dorado. **1968** Shalako. **1969** Charro!; The McMasters. **1972** The Red Sun.

REECE, BRIAN
Born: 1914. Died: Apr. 12, 1962, London, England (bone disease). Screen, stage, radio and television actor.

Appeared in: **1951** A Case for P.C. 49. **1954** Orders Are Orders; Fast and Loose. **1955** Geordie (aka Wee Geordie—US 1956). **1957** Carry On Admiral (aka The Ship Was Loaded—US 1959).

REED, BILLY
Born: 1914. Died: Feb. 4, 1974, New York, N.Y. (heart attack). Screen, vaude-

ville and stage actor. Was member of dance team of "Gordon, Reed and King" and "Reed and Carruthers."

Appeared in: **1931** 50 Million Frenchmen (stage and film versions). **1937** A Universal short. **1943** Crazy Horse. **1963** The Cardinal.

REED, DAVE
Born: 1872, New York, N.Y. Died: Apr. 11, 1946, N.Y. Screen, stage, vaudeville, radio actor and song writer. Appeared in silents.

REED, DONALD
Born: 1907, Mexico City. Died: Feb. 27, 1973. Screen actor.

Appeared in: **1927** Convoy; Naughty But Nice. **1928** Mad Hour; Show Girl; The Night Watch; Mark of the Frog (serial). **1929** Little Johnny Jones; A Most Immoral Lady; Hardboiled; Evangeline. **1930** The Texan. **1931** Aloha; Playthings of Hollywood. **1932** The Racing Strain. Prior to **1933** There You Are; His Secretary; The Auction Block. **1933** Man From Monterey. **1934** Hollywood, Ciudad de Ensueno; Uncertain Lady; Happy Landing. **1935** The Devil Is a Woman; The Cyclone Ranger; The Vanishing Riders. **1936** Darkest Africa. **1937** Crusade Against Rackets; Renfrew of the Royal Mounted.

REED, FLORENCE
Born: Jan. 10, 1883, Philadelphia, Pa. Died: Nov. 21, 1967, East Islip, N.Y. Screen, stage, vaudeville and television actress.

Appeared in: **1915** The Dancing Girl. **1916** New York. **1917** Today; The Eternal Sin. **1918** Wives of Men. **1921** The Eternal Mother; Black Panther's Cub; Indiscretion. **1930** The Code of Honor. **1934** Great Expectations. **1936** Frankie and Johnnie. **1941** Shanghai Gesture.

REED, GEORGE E.
Died: June 11, 1952, Camden, N.J. Stage and screen actor. Married to actress Alice Lucey. They appeared as a song and dance team billed as "Reed and Lucey."

Appeared in: **1919** Checkers.

REED, GEORGE H. (George Henry Reed)
Born: Nov. 27, 1866, Macon, Ga. Died: Nov. 6, 1952, Woodland Hills, Calif. (arteriosclerosis). Black screen actor. Do not confuse with George E. Reed (dec. June 11, 1952).

Appeared in: **1920** Huckleberry Finn; The Veiled Mystery (serial). **1922** The Jungle Goddess (serial); Scars of Jealousy; Red Lights. **1924** Helen's Babies; The Vagabond Trail. **1925** The Golden Strain; The Isle of Hope. **1926** Danger Quest; Pals First. **1928** Absent; The Clean-Up Man; Three-Ring Marriage. **1929** River of Romance. **1930** Father's Son. **1931** Trails of the Golden West; Little Daddy. **1933** Hold Your Man; Last Trail. **1934** Mrs. Wiggs of the Cabbage Patch; Witching Hour. **1936** The Green Pastures. **1938** The Buccaneer; Kentucky; Going Places. **1939** Secret of Dr. Kildare; Swanee River. **1940** Dr. Kildare's Strangest Case; Sporting Blood; Dr. Kildare's Crisis; Dr. Kildare Goes Home. **1941** Kiss the Boys Goodbye; The People vs. Dr. Kildare; Dr. Kildare's Victory. **1942** Tales of Manhattan; Dr. Gillespie's New Assistant. **1943** Dixie. **1944** The Adventures of Mark Twain; Three Men in White; Home In Indiana. **1945** Strange Illusion. **1947** Dark Delusion (aka Cynthia's Secret).

REED, GUS (Harold Nelson)
Born: 1880. Died: July 17, 1965, Cherry Valley, Calif. Screen, vaudeville, minstrel actor and singer.

Appeared in: **1930** The Woman Tamer (short). **1934** Order in the Court (short).

REED, MAXWELL
Born: 1919, Larne, England. Died: Oct. 31, 1974, England. Screen, stage and television actor. Divorced from actress Joan Collins.

Appeared in: **1946** The Years Between (US 1947); Gaiety George (aka Showtime—US 1948); Daybreak. **1947** Dear Murderer (US 1948); The Brothers. **1948** Night Beat; Daughter of Darkness. **1949** Madness of the Heart (US 1950); The Lost People. **1950** Blackout; The Clouded Yellow (US 1952). **1951** There Is Another Sun (aka Wall of Death—US 1952); The Dark Man; Flame of Araby. **1953** Sea Devils; The Square Ring (US 1955); Marilyn (aka Roadhouse Girl—US 1955). **1955** The Brain Machine; Before I Wake (aka Shadow of Fear—US 1956); Helen of Troy. **1961** Pirates of Tortuga. **1962** The Notorious Landlady; Advise and Consent. **1966** Picture Mommy Dead.

REESE, W. JAMES
Born: 1898. Died: Feb. 17, 1960, N.Y. Screen, stage and television actor.

Appeared in: **1957** The Young Don't Cry.

REEVE, ADA
Born: Mar. 3, 1874, London, England. Died: Sept. 25, 1966, London, England. Stage and screen actress.

Appeared in: **1944** They Came to a City. **1947** Meet Me at Dawn (US 1948); When the Bough Breaks. **1949** Dear Mr. Prohack (US 1950). **1950** Night and the City. **1953** The Gay Duellist (rerelease of Meet Me at Dawn—1947). **1952** I Believe in You (US 1953). **1956** Eye Witness. **1957** The Passionate Stranger (aka A Novel Affair—US).

REEVES, BILLY
Born: 1864, England. Died: Dec. 29, 1943, Suffolk, England. Screen, stage, vaudeville actor and pantomimist.

Appeared in: **1915** The New Butler.

REEVES, GEORGE (George Basselo)
Born: 1914, Ashland, Ky. Died: June 16, 1959, Beverly Hills, Calif. (suicide—gun). Screen, stage and television actor.

Appeared in: **1939** Gone with the Wind. **1940** Torrid Zone; Tear Gas Squad; Calling All Husbands; Always a Bride; Argentine Nights; Gambling on the High Seas; Father Is a Prince; Knute Rockne—All American; The Fighting 69th; 'Til We Meet Again; Ladies Must Live. **1941** Blue, White and Perfect; Strawberry Blonde; Dead Men Tell; Man at Large; Blood and Sand; Lydia. **1942** The Mad Martindales. **1943** So Proudly We Hail; Border Patrol; Hoppy Serves a Writ; The Leather Burners; The Last Will and Testament of Tom Smith (short); Colt Comrades; Bar-20; Buckskin Frontier. **1944** Winged Victory. **1947** Variety Girl. **1948** Jungle Goddess; The Sainted Sisters; Thunder in the Pines. **1949** The Great Lover; The Mutineers; Special Agent; Pirate Ship; Jungle Jim. **1950** The Good Humor Man; Adventures of Sir Galahad (serial). **1951** Samson and Delilah; Superman and the Mole Men. **1952** Bugles in the Afternoon; Rancho Notorious. **1953** From Here to Eternity; The Blue Gardenia; Forever Female. **1956** Westward Ho the Wagons.

REEVES, JIM
Born: 1924. Died: July 31, 1964, near Nashville, Tenn. (airplane crash). Screen actor and country music singer.

Appeared in: **1964** Kimberly Jim; Country Music Caravan; Tennessee Jamboree.

REEVES, KYNASTON (Kynaston Philip Reeves)
Born: May 29, 1893, London, England. Died: Dec. 10, 1971, London, England. Screen, stage and television actor. Entered films in 1919.

Appeared in: **1932** The Sign of the Four; The Lodger (aka The Phantom Fiend—US 1935). **1933** Puppets of Fate (aka Wolves of the Underworld—US 1935). **1934** Jew Suess (aka Power—US); The Crimson Candle. **1935** Vintage Wine; Dark World. **1937** Take a Chance; A Romance in Flanders (aka Lost on the Western Front—US 1940). **1938** Housemaster (US 1939); Sixty Glorious Years (aka Queen of Destiny—US). **1939** The Outsider (US 1940); Inspector Hornleigh on Holiday; The Stars Look Down (US 1941); Sons of the Sea; Dead Men are Dangerous. **1940** Two for Danger; The Flying Squad. **1941** The Prime Minister. **1942** The Young Mr. Pitt. **1943** The Night Invader. **1945** Strawberry Road (US 1948); The Echo Murders; Murder in Reverse (US 1946); The Rake's Progress (aka Notorious Gentleman—US 1946). **1946** Bedelia (US 1947). **1947** Mrs. Fitzherbert (US 1950). **1948** Vice Versa; This Was a Woman (US 1949); The Weaker Sex (US 1949); The Winslow Boy (US 1950); The Guinea Pig (US 1949). **1949** Badger's Green; Madness of the Heart (US 1950). **1950** The Twenty Questions Murder Mystery; Madeleine; Tony Draws a Horse (aka Blackout. **1951** The Undefeated; Smart Alec; Captain Horatio Hornblower, RN. **1952** Penny Princess (US 1953); Top Secret (aka Mr. Potts Goes to Moscow—US 1954); Song of Paris (aka Bachelor in Paris—US 1953). **1953** Top of the Form; Laxdale Hall (aka Scotch on the Rocks—US 1954); Four Sided Triangle (US 1955); Burnt Evidence; The Crowded Day. **1956** Fun at St. Fanny's; Guilty? **1956** Brothers in Law; Light Fingers; High Flight (US 1958). **1958** Family Doctor (aka Prescription for Murder and Rx Murder—US); A Question of Adultery (US 1959); Fiend without a Face. **1959** Carlton-Browne of the F.O. (aka Man in a Cocked Hat—US 1960). **1960** School for Scoundrels; In the Nick; The Night We Got the Bird. **1961** The Shadow of the Cat; Carry on Regardless (US 1963); In the Doghouse (US 1964); Don't Bother to Knock (aka Why Bother to Knock—US 1964). **1962** Go to Blazes. **1963** Hide and Seek (US 1964). **1968** Hot Millions. **1969** Anne of the Thousand Days. **1970** The Private Life of Sherlock Holmes.

REEVES, RICHARD (Richard Jourdan Reeves)
Born: Aug. 10, 1912, New York, N.Y. Died: Mar. 17, 1967, Northridge, Calif. (cirrhosis of liver). Screen, stage, television actor and opera singer.

Appeared in: **1943** This Is the Army (stage and film versions). **1947** The Hunted; Unconquered. **1951** Tomorrow Is Another Day; Double Deal; Come Fill the Cup; The Blue Veil; Force of Arms. **1952** She's Working Her Way Through College; The Pride of St. Louis; Hoodlum Empire; A Girl in Every Port; Finders Keepers; Gobs and Gals; Androcles and the Lion; The Racket; Retreat, Hell!; Ma and Pa Kettle at Waikiki; I Dream of Jeannie; Carbine Williams; Fair Wind to Java; We're Not Married; Stop, You're Killing Me; Thunderbirds; Fargo. **1953** City of Bad Men; So You Want to Get it Wholesale (short); Devil's Canyon; A Perilous Journey; Jack Slade; Money From Home; The Glass Wall. **1954** Trader Tom of the China Seas (serial); Loophole; Target Earth; Destry. **1955** The Eternal Sea; I Died a Thousand Times; Top Gun; The Silver Chalice; City of Shadows; Tarzan's Hidden Jungle. **1956** The Man

is Armed; Running Target; Dance with Me, Henry; Dangerous Cargo. **1957** Gunfight at O.K. Corral; The Buckskin Lady. **1958** Gunsmoke in Tucson; Auntie Mame. **1959** Riot in Juvenile Prison; The Rookie. **1960** Twelve Hours to Kill. **1961** Blue Hawaii. **1963** Toys In the Attic. **1964** A House Is Not a Home. **1965** Harum Scarum. **1966** Billy the Kid vs. Dracula.

REEVES, ROBERT JASPER
Born: Jan. 28, 1892, Marlin, Tex. Died: Apr. 2, 1960, Hollywood, Calif. (heart attack). Stage and screen actor.

Appeared in: **1919** The Great Radium Mystery (serial). **1923** The Thrill Chaser. **1924** The Mask of Lopez; No Gun Man; The Silent Stranger. **1926** Ambushed; Cyclone Bob; Desperate Chance; Fighting Luck; Iron Fist; Ridin' Straight; Riding for Life. **1927** The Cherokee Kid. **1930** Canyon Hawks.

REEVES-SMITH, H.
Born: 1863. Died: Jan. 29, 1938, Elwell, Surrey, England (heart trouble). Stage and screen actor.

Appeared in: **1924** Three Weeks; No More Women. **1929** The Return of Sherlock Holmes (English version).

REGAN, BERRY
Born: 1914. Died: Jan. 16, 1956, Hollywood, Calif. (surgery for brain tumor). Screen actor.

Appeared in: **1955** A Bullet for Joey.

REGAN, EDGAR J.
Died: June 21, 1938, San Francisco, Calif. (heart attack). Stage and screen actor.

REGAN, JOSEPH
Born: 1896, Boston, Mass. Died: Nov. 9, 1931, New York, N.Y. (cerebral hemorrhage). Screen, stage, vaudeville, radio actor and concert performer. Married to actress Alberta Curlis and appeared with her in vaudeville.

Appeared in: **1928** America's Foremost Irish Tenor (short).

REGAS, GEORGE (aka GEORGE RIGAS)
Born: Nov. 9, 1890, Sparta, Greece. Died: Dec. 13, 1940, Los Angeles, Calif. Stage and screen actor. Brother of actor Pedro Regas (dec. 1974).

Appeared in: **1921** The Dangerous Moment; The Love Light. **1922** Omar the Tentmaker. **1923** Fashionable Fakers; The Rip Tide. **1925** Wanderer. **1926** That Royal Girl; Beau Geste; Desert Gold. **1929** Redskin; Wolf Song; The Rescue; Acquitted; Sea Fury; Hearts and Hoofs (short). **1930** The Lonesome Trail. **1931** Beau Ideal; Newly Rich. **1933** Destiny Unknown; The Way to Love; Blood Money. **1934** Kid Millions; Viva Villa; Sixteen Fathoms Deep; Bulldog Drummond Strikes Back; Grand Canary. **1935** Bordertown; Lives of a Bengal Lancer; The Marines Are Coming. **1936** Rose Marie; Hell-Ship Morgan; Under Two Flags; Isle of Fury; Daniel Boone; Robin Hood of El Dorado; The Charge of the Light Brigade. **1937** Waikiki Wedding; Another Dawn; Lefthanded Law; Love under Fire; The Californian. **1938** Mr. Moto Takes a Chance; Torchy Blane in Panama; Penrod's Double Trouble. **1939** Arrest Bulldog Drummond; The Adventures of Sherlock Holmes; The Light That Failed. **1940** Torrid Zone; The Mask of Zorro.

REGAS, PEDRO (Panagiotis Regas)
Born: Apr. 12, 1882, Sparta, Greece. Died: Aug. 10, 1974, Hollywood, Calif. Screen, stage and television actor. Brother of actor George Regas (dec. 1940).

Appeared in: **1932** Danger Island; Scarface; Tiger Shark. **1934** Viva Villa; West of the Pecos. **1935** Black Fury. **1936** Sutter's Gold; The Traitor. **1939** Only Angels Have Wings. **1940** Road to Singapore. **1943** Tiger Fangs. **1945** South of the Rio Grande. **1946** Perilous Holiday. **1948** French Leave. **1952** Viva Zapata. **1964** Madmen of Mandoras. **1968** The Hell With Heroes. **1970** Angel Unchained; Flap.

REHAN, MARY
Born: 1887. Died: Aug. 28, 1963, Rochester, Minn. Screen and stage actress.

Appeared in: **1922** Flesh and Spirit.

REICHER, FRANK
Born: Dec. 2, 1875, Munich, Germany. Died: Jan. 19, 1965, Playa del Rey, Calif. Screen, stage actor, film, director and screenwriter. Entered films in 1915.

Appeared in: **1921** Behind Masks; Idle Hands; Out of the Depths; Wise Husbands. **1926** Her Man O'War. **1928** Beau Sabreur; The Blue Danube; The Masks of the Devil; Four Sons; Sins of the Fathers; Someone to Love; Napoleon's Barber. **1929** His Captive Woman; Mister Antonio; Black Waters; Her Private Affair; The Changeling; Strange Cargo; Big News; Paris Bound. **1930** Girl of the Port; The Grand Parade; Die Sehnsucht Jeder Frau. **1931** Gentleman's Fate; Beyond Victory; Suicide Fleet. **1932** A Woman Commands; The Crooked Circle; Scarlet Dawn; Mata Hari. **1933** Topaze; Employees' Entrance; Jennie Gerhardt; Captured; Ever in My Heart; Before Dawn; Son of Kong; King Kong. **1934** I Am a Thief; Return of the Terror; The Case of the Howling Dog; The Fountain; Hi, Nellie; Journal of a Crime; Countess of

Monte Cristo; Little Man, What Now?; Let's Talk It Over; No Greater Glory. **1935** The Great Impersonation; Star of Midnight; The Florentine Dagger. **1936** A Dog of Flanders; Mills of the Gods; The Man Who Broke the Bank at Monte Carlo; Remember Last Night; Rendezvous; Kind Lady; The Story of Louis Pasteur; The Murder of Dr. Harrigan; Magnificent Obsession; The Invisible Ray; Sutter's Gold; The Country Doctor; Under Two Flags; Girl's Dormitory; Star for a·Night; 'Til We Meet Again; Murder on the Bridle Path; The Ex-Mrs. Bradford; Second Wife; Anthony Adverse; Stolen Holiday. **1937** Laughing at Trouble; Night Key; On Such a Night; The Great O'Malley; Under Cover of Night; Lancer Spy; Espionage; The Emperor's Candlesticks; The Road Back; Prescription for Romance; Fit for a King; Stage Door; Midnight Madonna. **1938** City Streets; Torchy Gets Her Man; Prison Nurse; Rascals; I'll Give a Million; Suez. **1939** Unexpected Father; Mystery of the White Room; Woman Doctor; Juarez; The Magnificent Fraud; Our Neighbors, the Carters; The Escape; South of the Border; Everything Happens at Night. **1940** Dr. Cyclops; The Man I Married; Devil's Island; Typhoon; The Lady in Question; South to Karanga; Sky Murder. **1941** Flight from Destiny; They Dare Not Love; Shining Victory; The Nurse's Secret; Underground; Dangerously They Live. **1942** Nazi Agent; Salute to Courage; To Be or Not to Be; The Mystery of Marie Roget; Beyond the Blue Horizon; The Gay Sisters; Secret Enemies; Scattergood Survives a Murder; The Mummy's Tomb; Night Monster. **1943** Mission to Moscow; Yanks Ahoy; Tornado; The Song of Bernadette; The Canterville Ghost. **1944** Adventures of Mark Twain; The Hitler Gang; The Conspirators; The Mummy's Ghost; Address Unknown; Gildersleeve's Ghost. **1945** The Big Bonanza; Jade Mask; Phantoms, Inc.; Hotel Berlin; The Tiger Woman; House of Frankenstein; Blonde Ransom; A Medal for Benny. **1946** The Strange Mr. Gregory; Voice of the Whistler; The Shadow Returns; My Pal Trigger; Home in Oklahoma. **1947** Escape Me Never; The Secret Life of Walter Mitty; Violence; Yankee Faker; Mr. District Attorney. **1948** Carson City Raiders; Fighting Mad. **1949** Samson and Delilah; Barbary Pirate. **1950** Cargo to Capetown; Kiss Tomorrow Goodbye. **1951** The Lady and the Bandit.

REICHOW, WERNER

Born: 1922. Died: Aug. 17, 1973, Santa Monica, Calif. (cancer).

REID, CARL BENTON

Born: 1894. Died: Mar. 16, 1973, Studio City, Calif. Screen, stage and television actor.

Appeared in: **1941** The Little Foxes. **1942** Tennessee Johnson. **1943** The North Star. **1950** In a Lonely Place; The Fuller Brush Girl; The Flying Missile; Convicted; Stage to Tucson; The Killer That Stalked New York. **1951** The Great Caruso; Criminal Lawyer; Lorna Doone; Family Secret; Smuggler's Gold. **1952** Boots Malone; Carbine Williams; The Story of Will Rogers; The Brigand; The First Time; Indian Uprising. **1953** Main Street to Broadway; Escape From Fort Bravo. **1954** The Command; Broken Lance; The Egyptian; Athena. **1955** One Desire; The Left Hand of God; The Spoilers; Wichita. **1956** The First Texan; The Last Wagon; A Day of Fury; Battle Hymn; Strange Intruder. **1957** Time Limit; Spoilers of the Forest. **1958** Tarzan's Fight for Life; The Last of the Fast Guns. **1959** The Trap. **1960** The Bramble Bush; The Gallant Hours. **1962** Pressure Point; The Underwater City. **1963** The Ugly American. **1966** Madame X.

REID, HAL

Died: May 22, 1920. Screen actor, film director, producer and screenwriter. Father of actor Wallace Reid (dec. 1923). Appeared in Vitagraph films in 1911.

Appeared in: **1911** The Deerslayer. **1912** Every Inch a Man; Indian Romeo and Juliet; Jean Intervenes; The Hobo's Redemption; Father Beaudaine; Cardinal Wolsey. **1915** Time Lock 1776.

REID, MAX (Maxwell Reid)

Born: Aug. 22, 1903, Apia, Western Samoa. Died: May 3, 1969, Los Angeles, Calif. (heart attack). Musician and screen actor.

Appeared in: **1956** Around the World in 80 Days; The Revolt of Mamie Stover. **1967** Lupe.

REID, TREVOR

Born: 1909. Died: Apr. 19, 1965, London, England. Screen, stage and television actor.

Appeared in: **1956** Satellite in the Sky; Murder Reporter (US 1960). **1957** How to Murder a Rich Uncle. **1958** A Question of Adultery (US 1959). **1960** Marriage of Convenience (US 1970). **1961** Mary Had a Little; Attempt to Kill (US 1966). **1962** The Fast Lady (US 1965); The Longest Day. **1963** Walk a Tightrope (US 1964). **1964** Night Train to Paris.

REID, WALLACE

Born: Apr. 15, 1891, St. Louis, Mo. Died: Jan. 18, 1923, Los Angeles, Calif. (drug addiction). Screen actor and film producer. Married to actress Dorothy Davenport (who also appeared under her married name "Reid") and father of actor Wallace Reid, Jr. Son of actor Hal Reid (dec. 1920).

Appeared in: **1910** The Phoenix. **1911** The Reporter; The Deerslayer; Leather Stocking Tales; The Leading Lady. **1912** Chumps; Indian Romeo and Juliet; The Telephone Girl; The Seventh Son; The Illumination; Brothers; The Victo-

ria Cross (aka The Charge of the Light Brigade); The Hieroglyphic; Diamond Cut Diamond; Curfew Shall Not Ring Tonight; Kaintuck; Before the White Man Came; A Man's Duty; At Cripple Creek; His Only Son; Making Good; The Secret Service Man; Indian Raiders; Every Inch a Man; The Tribal Law. **1913** The Heart of a Cracksman; Love and the Law; A Rose of Old Mexico; The Ways of Fate; The Picture of Dorian Grey; When Jim Returned; The Tattooed Arm; Youth and Jealousy; The Kiss; Her Innocent Marriage; His Mother's Son; A Modern Snare; When Luck Changes; Via Cabaret; The Spirit of the Flag; Hearts and Horses; In Love and War (aka Women and War); Dead Man's Shoes; Pride of Lonesome; The Powder Flash of Death; A Foreign Spy; The Picket Guard; Mental Suicide; The Animal; The Harvest of Flame; The Mystery of the Yellow Aster Mine; The Gratitude of Wanda; The Wall of Money; The Cracksman's Reformation; Cross Purposes; The Fires of Fate; Retribution; A Cracksman Santa Claus; The Lightning Bolt; A Hopi Legend (aka A Pueblo Romance). **1914** Who So Diggeth a Pit; The Intruder; The Countess Betty's Mine; The Wheel of Life; Fires of Conscience; The Greater Devotion; A Flash in the Dark; Breed of the Mountains; Regeneration; The Heart of the Hills; The Way of a Woman; The Voice of the Viola; The Spider and Her Web; The Mountaineer; Cupid Incognito; A Gypsy Romance; The Skeleton; The Fruit of Evil (aka The Sins of the Father); Women and Roses; The Quack; The Siren; The Man Within; Passing of the Beast; Love's Western Flight (aka Children of Fate); A Wife on a Wager; 'Cross the Mexican Line; The Den of Thieves; Arms and the Gringo; Down by the Sounding Sea; Moonshine Molly; The City Beautiful; The Second Mrs. Roebuck; Sierra Jim's Reformation; Down the Hill to Creditville; Her Awakening; For Her Father's Sins; A Mother's Influence (aka His Mother's Last Word); The Niggard; The Odalisque; The Little Country Mouse; Another Chance; Over the Ledge (aka On the Ledge); Baby's Ride; The Test; At Dawn. **1915** The Craven; The Three Brothers; The Lost House; Station Content; A Yankee from the West; The Golden Chance; The Chorus Lady; Birth of a Nation; Carmen; Enoch Arden; Old Heidelberg. **1916** The Selfish Woman; The House with the Golden Windows; The Yellow Pawn; Maria Rosa; To Have and to Hold; The Love Mask; Intolerance. **1917** Joan, the Woman; The Golden Fetter; The Prison without Walls; The World Apart; The Squaw Man's Son; The Hostage; The Devil Stone; The Woman God Forgot; Big Timber; Nan of Music Mountain. **1918** The Things We Love; The House of Silence; The Man from Funeral Range; The Firefly of France; The Source; Too Many Millions; Believe Me, Zantippe; Rimrock Jones; Less Than Kin; Ruggles of Red Gap. **1919** The Dub; Alias Mike Moran; Hawthorne of the U.S.A.; Valley of the Giants; The Roaring Road; You're Fired; The Love Burglar; The Lottery Man. **1920** Always Audacious; What's Your Hurry?; Double Speed; Sick Bed; The Dancin' Fool; Excuse My Dust. **1921** The Affairs of Anatol; Too Much Speed; Don't Tell Everything; Forever; The Call of the North; The Love Special; The Hell Diggers; The Charm School. **1922** Across the Continent; Night Life in Hollywood; Rent Free; Nice People; The World's Champion; The Ghost Breaker; Clarence; The Dictator; Thirty Days.

REILLY, MICHAEL

Born: 1933. Died: Jan. 10, 1962, Newhaven, England (parachute jump). Parachutist and double for Robert Wagner.

Appeared in: **1962** The War Lover.

REINER, FRITZ

Born: Dec. 19, 1888, Budapest, Hungary. Died: Nov. 15, 1963, New York, N.Y. Violinist and screen actor.

Appeared in: **1947** Carnegie Hall.

REINHARDT, JOHN

Born: 1901. Died: Aug. 6, 1953, Berlin, Germany (heart attack). Screen actor, film director, author and screenwriter.

Appeared in: **1929** The Prince of Hearts; Love, Live and Laugh; The Climax. **1931** Der Tanz Geht Weiter. **1936** The Rest Cure.

REINOLD, BERNARD (Major Bernard Adolph Reinold)

Died: Mar. 25, 1940, New York, N.Y. Stage and screen actor.

Appeared in: **1921** The Passionate Pilgrim.

REIS, ALBERTO

Born: 1902, Portugal. Died: Feb. 1953 (tropical disease). Stage and screen actor. Married to actress Branca Saldanha.

REISNER, CHARLES F. "CHUCK" (aka CHARLES F. RIESNER)

Born: Mar. 14, 1887, Minneapolis, Minn. Died: Sept. 24, 1962, La Jolla, Calif. Screen, stage, vaudeville actor, film director, producer, screenwriter and television writer.

Appeared in: **1916** His First False Step; His Lying Heart. **1918** A Dog's Life. **1921** The Kid. **1922** The Pilgrim. **1923** Her Temporary Husband; Breaking into Society; Hollywood. **1924** A Self-Made Failure; Universal comedies. **1925** Man on the Box; Justice of the Far North. **1936** Everybody Dance.

REITHE, ALOISE D.
Born: 1890, Los Angeles, Calif. Died: Sept. 5, 1943, Los Angeles, Calif. Screen actor and film director. Appeared in and directed silent films.

REJANE, GABRIELLA
Born: 1857, Paris, France. Died: June 14, 1920, Paris, France. Stage and screen actress.

Appeared in: **1912** Madame Sans-Gene; Miarka, the Daughter of the Bear. **1922** Gypsy Passion.

RELPH, GEORGE
Born: Jan. 27, 1888, Cullercoast, Northumberland, England. Died: Apr. 24, 1960, London, England. Stage and screen actor. Married to Deborah Nanson and later to actress Mercia Swinburne.

Appeared in: **1916** Paying the Price. **1921** Candytuft, I Mean Veronica; The Door That Has No Key (US 1922). **1944** Give Us the Moon. **1947** Nicholas Nickleby. **1952** I Believe in You (US 1953). **1953** The Titfield Thunderbolt; The Final Test (US 1954). **1957** Doctor at Large; Davy. **1960** Ben Hur.

REMARQUE, ERICH MARIA
Born: 1898, Germany. Died: Sept. 25, 1970, Locarno, Switzerland (heart collapse). Novelist, screen actor and screenwriter. Divorced from Ilsa Jeanne Zamboul. Married to actress Paulette Goddard.

Appeared in: **1958** A Time to Love and a Time to Die.

REMLEY, FRANK (aka ELLIOTT LEWIS)
Born: 1902. Died: Jan. 28, 1967, Newport Beach, Calif. Radio, screen guitarist and actor. Appeared in films as Elliott Lewis.

Appeared in: **1949** The Story of Molly X. **1950** Ma and Pa Kettle Go to Town. **1951** Saturday's Hero. **1953** Let's Do It Again.

REMLEY, RALPH McHUGH
Born: 1885. Died: May 26, 1939, Los Angeles, Calif. Screen and stage actor.

Appeared in: **1934** Keep 'Em Rolling; Double Door; Behold My Wife; One Is Guilty; Home on the Range. **1935** Princess O'Hara; Dr. Socrates. **1936** Poppy; Yours for the Asking; Bullets or Ballots; Robin Hood of El Dorado. **1937** Let Them Live; Make Way for Tomorrow. **1938** Outside of Paradise. **1939** King of the Underworld; The Story of Alexander Graham Bell.

REMY, ALBERT
Born: 1912, France. Died: Jan. 26, 1967, Paris, France. Screen actor.

Appeared in: **1944** Les Enfants du Paradis (Children of Paradise—US 1946). **1945** Groupi Mains Rouge (It Happened at the Inn). **1949** Devil's Daughter. **1950** Francois Villon. **1956** French Can-Can (aka Only the French Can). **1957** Razzle. **1958** Crime et Chatiment (Crime and Punishment, aka The Most Dangerous Sin). **1959** La Vache et le Prisonnier (aka The Cow and I—US 1961); Les Quartre Cents Coups (The 400 Blows). **1960** Tirez sur le Pianiste (Shoot the Piano Player—US 1962); Le Passage du Rhin (aka Tomorrow is My Turn—US 1962). **1962** The Four Horsemen of the Apocalypse; Gigot; La Fayette (US 1963); Le Septieme Jure (The Seventh Juror—US 1964). **1963** Mandrin. **1964** Le Train (The Train—US 1965); Week-end a Zuydcotte (Weekend at Dunkirk—US 1966). **1965** Cent Briques et des Tuiles (aka How Not to Rob a Department Store—US); Mata-Hari Agent H-21 (US 1967). **1966** Grand Prix; Is Paris Burning? **1967** The 25th Hour.

REMY, DICK, SR.
Born: 1873. Died: June 1, 1947, Hollywood, Calif. (heart attack). Screen actor and film director. Appeared in and directed silent films.

RENARD, DAVID
Born: 1921. Died: Aug. 15, 1973, West Hollywood, Calif. (heart attack). Stage and screen actor. Entered films in 1954.

Appeared in: **1961** Frontier Uprising; The Long Rope. **1962** Deadly Duo. **1965** Ship of Fools. **1968** The Counterfeit Killer. **1969** Change of Habit.

RENAVENT, GEORGE (Georges de Cheux)
Born: Apr. 23, 1894, Paris, France. Died: Jan. 2, 1969, Guadalajara, Mexico. Screen, stage actor, stage and film director. Married to actress Selena Royle.

Appeared in: **1919** Erstwhile Susan. **1929** Rio Rita. **1930** Scotland Yard; Le Spectre Vert. **1931** East of Borneo. **1933** Moulin Rouge; Queen Christina. **1934** The Bombay Mail; House of Rothschild. **1935** Follies Bergere; Whipsaw; The White Cockatoo; Front Page Woman; The Last Outpost. **1936** The Invisible Ray; The Sky Parade; Lloyds of London. **1937** History is Made at Night; Seventh Heaven; Cafe Metropole; Love under Fire; Wife, Doctor and Nurse; Charlie Chan at Monte Carlo; Love and Hisses; The Sheik Steps Out; Fight for Your Lady; Artists and Models Abroad; The King and the Chorus Girl. **1938** Jezebel; Gold Diggers in Paris; I'll Give a Million; Suez. **1939** Mr. Moto's Last Warning; Topper Takes a Trip; The Three Musketeers; Pack up Your Troubles. **1940** The House Across the Bay; Son of Monte Cristo; Comrade X; Turnabout. **1941** Sullivan's Travels; That Night in Rio; Road to Zanzibar; The Night of January 16th. **1943** Mission to Moscow; Wintertime; The Desert Song.

1944 Our Hearts Were Young and Gay. **1945** Captain Eddie; Saratoga Trunk. **1946** Tarzan and the Leopard Woman; The Catman of Paris. **1947** Ladies' Man; The Foxes of Harrow. **1951** Secrets of Monte Carlo. **1952** Mara Maru.

RENFRO, RENNIE
Born: 1893. Died: Mar. 2, 1962, Redding, Calif. (heart attack). Screen actor, dog trainer and stuntman. Appeared in early Sennett comedies and trained "Daisy" for the "Blondie" series.

RENN, KATHARINA
Born: 1913, Germany. Died: 1975, Paris, France. Screen, stage and television actress.

Appeared in: **1966** La Prise de Pouvoir par (de) Louis XIV (The Rise of Louis XIV—US 1970).

RENNIE, JAMES
Born: 1889, Toronto, Canada. Died: July 31, 1965, New York, N.Y. Stage and screen actor. Divorced from actress Dorothy Gish (dec. 1968).

Appeared in: **1920** Remodeling Her Husband. **1921** Stardust. **1922** The Dust Follower. **1923** Mighty Lak' a Rose; His Children's Children. **1924** Argentine Love; The Moral Sinner; Restless Wives. **1925** Clothes Make the Pirate; Share and Share Alike. **1930** The Bad Man; Girl of the Golden West; Two Rounds of Love (short). **1931** Illicit; The Lash; Party Husband. **1932** The Little Damozel. **1941** Skylark. **1942** Crossroads; Tales of Manhattan; Now Voyager. **1945** Wilson; A Bell for Adano.

RENNIE, MICHAEL
Born: Aug. 29, 1909, Bradford, Yorkshire, England. Died: June 10, 1971, Harrogate, Yorkshire, England. Screen, stage and television actor.

Appeared in: **1936** The Secret Agent. **1937** Gangway. **1938** The Divorce of Lady X; Bank Holiday (aka Three on a Weekend—US). **1939** This Man in Paris. **1941** Dangerous Moonlight (aka Suicide Squadron—US 1942); The Patient Vanishes (US 1947 aka This Man is Dangerous); The Tower of Terror (US 1942); Turned Out Nice Again; Ships with Wings (US 1942); Pimpernel Smith (aka Mister V—US 1942). **1942** The Big Blockade. **1945** I'll Be Your Sweetheart; The Wicked Lady (US 1946). **1946** Caesar and Cleopatra. **1947** White Cradle (aka High Fury—US 1948); The Root of All Evil. **1948** Idol of Paris; Uneasy Terms. **1949** The Golden Madonna. **1950** Trio; The Black Rose; The Body Said No!; Miss Pilgrim's Progress; Sanitorium. **1951** The House in the Square (aka I'll Never Forget You—US); The 13th Letter; The Day the Earth Stood Still. **1952** Phone Call from a Stranger; Five Fingers; Les Miserables. **1953** Single-Handed (aka Sailor of the King—US); Dangerous Crossing; The Robe; King of the Khyber Rifles. **1954** Demetrius and the Gladiators; Princess of the Nile; Desiree. **1955** Mambo; Seven Cities of Gold; Soldier of Fortune; The Rains of Ranchipur. **1956** Teenage Rebel. **1957** Island in the Sun; Omar Khayyam. **1958** Battle of the V.I. (aka Unseen Heroes—US). **1959** Third Man on the Mountain. **1960** The Lost World. **1963** Mary, Mary. **1965** Night of the Tiger. **1966** Ride Beyond Vengeance. **1967** Hondo and the Apaches; Cyborg 2087; Hotel. **1968** Nude..si Muore (aka The Young, the Evil and the Savage—US); The Power; The Devil's Brigade; Death on the Run; Subterfuge. **1969** Operation Terror; Krakatoa—East of Java.

RENOIR, PIERRE
Born: 1885, France. Died: Mar. 11, 1952, Paris, France. Screen actor. Son of artist Pierre August Renoir.

Appeared in: **1911** La Digue (Ou Pour Sauver la Hollande). **1932** Nuit du carrefour (The Night at the Crossroads). **1934** L'Agonie des Aigles; La Bandera; Madame Bovary. **1938** La Marseillaise; L'Affaire Lafarge; The Patriot; Sacrifice d'Honneur. **1939** Kreutzer Sonata; Le Recif de Corail; Escape from Yesterday; Citadel of Silence. **1941** Hatred; The Mad Emperor; Personal Column. **1944** Les Enfants du Paradis (Children of Paradise—US 1946). **1946** Peleton d'Execution (Resistance); Sirocco. **1948** Foolish Husbands. **1951** Dr. Knock (US 1955).

REPP, STAFFORD (Stafford Alois Repp)
Born: Apr. 26, 1918, Calif. Died: Nov. 5, 1974, Inglewood, Calif. (heart attack). Screen, television and radio actor.

Appeared in: **1955** Not As a Stranger; Man With the Gun. **1956** The Price of Fear; The Steel Jungle. **1957** The Green-Eyed Blonde; Plunder Road. **1958** Hot Spell; I Want to Live. **1961** The Explosive Generation. **1965** A Very Special Favor. **1966** Batman. **1975** Linda Lovelace for President.

RESTA, COL. FRANCIS E.
Born: 1894. Died: Aug. 16, 1968, Bronx, N.Y. Screen actor and leader of U.S. Military Band.

RETTY, WOLF ALBACH
Born: 1908, Austria. Died: Feb. 21, 1967. Screen actor. Father of actress Romy Schneider.

Appeared in: **1935** Winternachtstraum. **1940** Mutterliebe (Mother Love).

REY, ROBERTO (Roberto Colas Iglesias)

Born: 1905, Chile. Died: 1972, Madrid, Spain (heart attack). Stage and screen actor.

Appeared in: **1933** El Principe Gondolero; Gente Alegre; Salga de la Cocina; El Barbero de Sevilla; Cotolay. **1938** La Verbena de la Paloma. **1940** Germina Siempre Asi (It Always Ends That Way). **1963** El Valle de las Espadas (aka The Castilian—US 1963). **1964** Los Pistoleros de Casa Grande (Gunfighters of Casa Grande—US 1965).

REY, ROSA

Died: Apr. 7, 1969. Screen actress.

Appeared in: **1946** Gilda; The Face of Marble. **1948** The Secret Beyond the Door. **1953** The Great Sioux Uprising. **1954** Secret of the Incas. **1955** The Rose Tattoo.

REYES, EFREN

Born: 1924, Philippine Islands. Died: Feb. 11, 1968, Manila, Philippine Islands (heart attack).

Appeared in: **1959** The Scavengers. **1963** Raiders of Leyte Gulf.

REYES, EVA (Adaljina Ardura)

Born: 1915. Died: Mar. 20, 1970, Miami, Fla. (interstitial fibrosis of the lungs). Screen, stage actress and dancer. Was part of dance team of "Paul and Eva Reyes." Also toured with Xavier Cugat's band at one time.

Appeared in: **1947** Copacabana.

REYES, LUCHA

Born: 1908, Mexico. Died: June 25, 1944, Mexico City, Mexico. Singer and screen actress.

Appeared in: **1943** Ay Jalisco no te Rajes.

REYNOLDS, ABE

Born: 1884. Died: Dec. 25, 1955, Hollywood, Calif. Screen, stage, burlesque, vaudeville and radio actor.

Appeared in: **1930** Love at First Sight. **1936** Swing Time. **1949** My Dear Secretary.

REYNOLDS, ADELINE DeWALT

Born: Sept. 19, 1862, Benton County, Iowa. Died: Aug. 13, 1961, Los Angeles, Calif. Stage and screen actress.

Appeared in: **1941** Come Live with Me (film debut); Shadow of the Thin Man. **1942** Tales of Manhattan; Tuttles of Tahiti; Street of Chance. **1943** Behind the Rising Sun; The Human Comedy; Iceland; Happy Land; Son of Dracula. **1944** Going My Way; Old Lady; Since You Went Away. **1945** The Corn Is Green; Counterattack; A Tree Grows in Brooklyn. **1948** The Girl from Manhattan. **1949** Sickle or Cross. **1951** Here Comes the Groom. **1952** Lydia Bailey; Pony Soldier. **1954** Witness to Murder. **1956** The Ten Commandments.

REYNOLDS, CRAIG (Hugh Enfield)

Born: July 15, 1907, Anaheim, Calif. Died: Oct. 22, 1949, Los Angeles, Calif. (result of motorcycle crash). Screen, stage and vaudeville actor. Married to actress Barbara Pepper (dec. 1969).

Appeared in: **1930** Coquette. **1934** Cross Country Cruise; I'll Tell the World; Love Birds. **1935** Four Hours to Kill; Paris in Spring; The Case of the Lucky Legs; Man of Iron; Ceiling Zero. **1936** Broadway Playboy; Brides Are Like That; Times Square Playboy; Jailbreak; Smart Blonde; Here Comes Carter!; The Case of the Black Cat; Treachery Rides the Range; The Golden Arrow; Sons O'Guns; Stage Struck. **1937** The Case of the Stuttering Bishop; Footloose Heiress; Slim; The Great O'Malley; The Great Garrick; Back in Circulation; Under Suspicion; Penrod and Sam; Melody for Two. **1938** House of Mystery; Slander House; Romance on the Run; Gold Mine in the Sky; Making Headlines; Female Fugitive; I am a Criminal. **1939** The Mystery of Mr. Wong; Navy Secrets; Bad Little Angel; The Gentleman from Arizona; Wall Street Cowboy. **1940** The Fatal Hour; Son of the Navy; I Take This Oath. **1944** Nevada. **1945** Divorce; The Strange Affair of Uncle Harry. **1946** Just before Dawn; Queen of Burlesque. **1948** My Dog Shep; The Man from Colorado.

REYNOLDS, HAROLD

Born: 1896. Died: Sept. 21, 1972, Hollywood, Calif. (heart attack). Screen, stage and television actor. Entered films at age 70.

Appeared in: **1971** The Steagle.

REYNOLDS, LAKE

Born: 1889. Died: Feb. 9, 1952, Hollywood, Calif. Screen, stage, minstrel, vaudeville and radio actor.

REYNOLDS, NOAH

Died: Sept. 19, 1948, North Philadelphia, Pa. Screen and stage actor. Appeared in early Lubin Co. and McCurdy Film Co. films.

REYNOLDS, PETER

Born: Aug. 16, 1926, Wilmslow, Cheshire, England. Died: Apr. 22, 1975, Australia. Stage and screen actor.

Appeared in: **1948** The Guinea Pig (US 1949); Adam and Evelyne (aka Adam and Evalyn—US). **1950** Guilt Is My Shadow. **1951** Smart Alec. **1952** The Last Page (aka Manbait—US); A Woman's Angle (US 1954); 24 Hours in a Woman's Life (aka Affair in Monte Carlo (US 1953). **1953** The Robe. **1955** The Silver Chalice. **1957** The Long Haul. **1959** Shake Hands with the Devil. **1960** The Hands of Orlac; The Man Who Couldn't Walk (US 1964); Your Money Or Your Wife (US 1965); It Takes a Thief (aka The Challenge—US 1962). **1962** Murder Can Be Deadly (aka The Painted Smile). **1964** The Great American Car Swindle. **1968** Nobody Runs Forever (aka The High Commissioner—US).

REYNOLDS, QUENTIN

Born: 1903. Died: Mar. 17, 1965. Screen actor, film director, writer and radio newscaster.

Appeared in: **1947** Golden Earrings. **1950** Cassino to Korea (narrator). **1959** Naked Africa (narrator). **1960** Justice and Caryl Chessman (narrator).

REYNOLDS, VERA

Born: Nov. 25, 1905, Richmond, Va. Died: Apr. 22, 1962, Woodland Hills, Calif. Screen actress. Married to actor Robert Ellis (dec. 1935).

Appeared in: **1923** Prodigal Daughters; Woman-Proof. **1924** Feet of Clay; Broken Barriers; Cheap Kisses; Flapper Wives; For Sale; Icebound; Shadows of Paris. **1925** Road to Yesterday; The Golden Bed; The Limited Mail; The Million Dollar Handicap; The Night Club; Without Mercy. **1926** Silence; Corporal Kate; Risky Business; Steel Preferred; Sunny Side Up. **1927** Almost Human; The Little Adventuress; The Main Event. **1928** Divine Sinner; Golf Widows; Jazzland. **1929** Tonight at Twelve. **1930** Back from Shanghai; The Last Dance; Lone Rider; Borrowed Wives. **1931** Hell Bent for Frisco; Lawless Woman; Neck and Neck. **1932** The Gorilla Ship; Dragnet Patrol; The Monster Walks; Tangled Destinies.

RHINE, JACK

Born: 1911. Died: Aug. 21, 1951, San Francisco, Calif. (poliomyelitis). Screen, stage and radio actor.

RHODES, ALFRED "DUSTY"

Died: Feb. 6, 1948, San Francisco, Calif. Screen actor.

RHUDIN, FRIDOLF

Born: 1895, Sweden. Died: Mar. 6, 1935 (brain fever). Stage and screen actor. Appeared in Scandinavian films.

RIANO, RENIE

Died: July 3, 1971, Woodland Hills, Calif. Screen, stage and television actress. Daughter of stage actress Irene Riano (dec. 1940).

Appeared in: **1937** Tovarich; You're a Sweetheart. **1938** Outside of Paradise; Spring Madness; Thanks for Everything; Men Are Such Fools; Four's a Crowd; Nancy Drew, Detective; The Road to Reno. **1939** Wife, Husband and Friend; The Honeymoon's Over; Disputed Passage; Nancy Drew and the Hidden Staircase; The Women; Mr. Moto in Danger Island; Day Time Wife; Nancy Drew, Trouble Shooter. **1940** The Man Who Wouldn't Talk; The Ghost Comes Home; Kit Carson; Remedy for Riches. **1941** You're the One; Adam Had Four Sons; Affectionately Yours; Ice-Capades; You Belong to Me. **1942** Whispering Ghosts; Blondie for Victory. **1943** The Man from Music Mountain; None but the Lonely Heart. **1944** Jam Session; Take It or Leave It; Three Is a Family. **1945** Club Havana; A Song for Miss Julie. **1946** Bringing Up Father; So Goes My Love; Bad Bascomb. **1947** Winter Wonderland. **1948** Jiggs and Maggie in Society; Jiggs and Maggie in Court; The Time of Your Life. **1949** Jackpot Jitters. **1950** Jiggs and Maggie Out West. **1951** As Young as You Feel; The Barefoot Mailman. **1953** Clipped Wings. **1964** Bikini Beach; Pajama Party. **1965** The Family Jewels. **1966** Three on a Couch; Fireball 500.

RIBEIRO, JOY

Born: 1956, New York. Died: Dec. 19, 1972, Los Angeles, Calif. Singer, dancer, television and screen actress.

Appeared in: **1972** Black Gunn; Lady Sings the Blues.

RICE, FLORENCE

Born: Feb. 14, 1911, Cleveland, Ohio. Died: Feb. 22, 1974, Honolulu, Hawaii (lung cancer). Stage and screen actress. Daughter of sports columnist Grantland Rice. Divorced from actor Robert Wilcox (dec. 1955). Married to Fred Butler.

Appeared in: **1932** The Fighting Marshal. **1934** Fugitive Lady. **1935** The Best Man Wins; Carnival; Under Pressure; Death Flies East; Guard That Girl; Escape from Devil's Island; Awakening of Jim Burke. **1936** Superspeed; Panic On the Air; Pride of the Marines; The Blackmailer; Women Are Trouble; Sworn Enemy; The Longest Night. **1937** Under Cover of Night; Man of the People; Married Before Breakfast; Double Wedding; Navy Blue and Gold; Beg, Borrow or Steal; All Is Confusion; Riding On Air. **1938** Sweethearts;

Paradise for Three; Fast Company; Vacation From Love. **1939** The Kid From Texas; At the Circus; Miracles For Sale; Stand Up and Fight; Little Accident; Four Girls in White. **1940** Broadway Melody of 1940; The Secret Seven; Girl in 313; Phantom Raiders; Cherokee Strip. **1941** Doctors Don't Tell; The Blonde from Singapore; Mr. District Attorney; Father Takes a Wife; Borrowed Hero. **1942** Tramp, Tramp, Tramp; Let's Get Tough!; Boss of Big Town; Stand By All Networks. **1943** The Ghost and the Guest.

RICE, FRANK (Frank Thomas Rice)
Born: May 13, 1892, Muskegon, Mich. Died: Jan. 9, 1936, Los Angeles, Calif. (nephritis, hepatitis). Screen actor.

Appeared in: **1923** Blood Test; Desert Rider; The Forbidden Trail; The Red Warning. **1924** The Air Hawk; Dynamite Dan; The Ridin' Kid from Powder River; The Galloping Ace; Wolves of the North (serial). **1925** The Call of Courage; Two-Fisted Jones; Spook Ranch; The Cloud Rider; Moccasins; Riders of Mystery; Ridin' Party; The Speed Demon. **1926** The Border Sheriff; Davy Crockett at the Fall of the Alamo; The Fighting Buckaroo; The Fighting Peacemaker; Flying High. **1927** The Boy Rider; Red Signals; Sky-High Saunders; The Slingshot Kid; Three Miles Up; Tom's Gang; The Wolf's Fangs. **1928** The Bantam Cowboy; Headin' for Danger; The Hound of Silver Creek; Orphan of the Sage; The Pinto Kid; A Thief In the Dark; Rough Ridin' Red; Won in the Clouds; Young Whirlwind. **1929** The Lawless Legion; The Overland Telegraph; Pals of the Prairie; The Royal Rider; Stairs of Sand; The Vagabond Cub; The Wagon Master; Dangerous Females (short); The Forbidden Trail; Faro Nell (aka In Old Californy). **1930** Check and Double Check; On Your Back; So This Is London; Parade of the West; The Fighting Legion. **1931** The Conquering Horde; The Squaw Man; Corsair. **1932** Horse Feathers. **1933** Somewhere In Sonora. **1934** The Last Round-Up. **1935** Ruggles of Red Gap; Hard Rock Harrigan; Stone of Silver Creek; Border Brigands; Powdersmoke Range; Valley of Wanted Men; The Ivory-Handled Gun. **1936** Nevada; The Oregon Trail.

RICE, GRANTLAND
Born: 1881. Died: July 13, 1954, N.Y. (heart attack). Sports writer and screen actor. Appeared as narrator in his sports shorts. Won 1943 Academy Award for best one-reel picture, Amphibious Fighters. Father of actress Florence Rice (dec. 1974).

Appeared in: **1917** Salmon Fishing in New Brunswick and Cane River, Northestern Canada. **1925** Grantland Rice "Sportlights" which included the following shorts: Rough and Tumbling; Brains and Brawn; By Hook or Crook; Sporting Armor; Neptune's Nieces; Traps and Troubles; Action; Beauty Spots; Sporting Judgment; All under One Flag; Dude Ranch Days; Twinkle-Twinkle; Animal Celebrities; Learning How; Why Kids Leave Home; Sons of Swat; Seven Ages of Sport; Barrier Busters; Starting an Argument; Outing for All; Clever Feet; Shooting Time; Walloping Wonders; Then and Now; Fins and Feathers. **1934-35** Grantland Rice "Sportlights." **1935** Nineteen "Sportlights" shorts. **1943** Amphibious Fighters (short).

RICE, JACK (Jack Clifford Rice)
Born: May 14, 1893, Mich. Died: Dec. 14, 1968, Woodland Hills, Calif. (cancer). Stage and screen actor.

Appeared in: **1933** Fits In a Fiddle (short). **1934** The following shorts: A Blasted Event; Odor In the Court; In the Devil's Doghouse; Poisoned Ivory. **1935** The following shorts: Bric-a-Brac; South Seasickness; Sock Me to Sleep; Edgar Hamlet; In Love at 40; Happy 'Tho Married; Alibi Bye Bye. **1936** Walking on Air; plus the following shorts: Gasoloons; Will Power; High Beer Pressure; Dummy Ache. **1938** Arson Racket Squad; Arson Gang Busters; plus the following shorts: Ears of Experience; False Roomers; Men in Fright; The Jitters. **1940** Slightly at Sea (short); Money to Burn; Danger on Wheels. **1941** Men of Timberland; New York Town; plus the following shorts: Westward Ho-Hum; I'll Fix That; A Quiet Fourth; A Polo Pony. **1942** The following shorts: Heart Burn; Interior Decorator; Cooks and Crooks; Two for the Money; Rough on Rents; Duck Soup. **1943** Swing Time Johnny; Reveille With Beverly; Good Morning, Judge; Two Weeks to Live; plus the following shorts: Unlucky Dog; Not On My Account; Hot Foot; Hold Your Temper; Indian Signs. **1944** Lady, Let's Dance!; Goin' to Town; plus the following shorts: Prunes and Politics; Radio Rampage; The Kitchen Cynic; Feather Your Nest. **1945** Leave It to Blondie; The Naughty Nineties; Under Western Skies; Her Lucky Night; plus the following shorts: Sleepless Tuesday; What, No Cigarettes?; It's Your Move; You Drive Me Crazy; The Big Beef; Mother-in-Law's Day. **1946** Blondie Knows Best; Meet Me on Broadway; Life With Blondie; Blondie's Lucky Day; plus the following shorts: Trouble or Nothing; Wall Street Blues; Motor Maniacs; Noisy Neighbors; I'll Build It Myself; Social Terrors. **1947** Blondie's Big Moment; Blondie's Holiday; Blondie's Anniversary; plus the following shorts: Do or Diet; Heading for Trouble; Host to a Ghost; Television Turmoil; Mind Over Mouse. **1948** Blondie's Reward; Variety Time; plus the following shorts: Brother Knows Best; No More Relatives; How to Clean House; Dig That Gold; Home Canning; Contest Crazy. **1949** Blondie's Secret; Blondie's Big Deal; Sweet Cheat (short). **1950** Beware of Blondie. **1951** Corky of Gasoline Alley; So You Want to be a Bachelor (short). **1952** The Pride of St. Louis; Stars and Stripes Forever. **1953** The Marksman; The Silver Whip. **1956** The First Travel-

ing Saleslady; Crashing Las Vegas. **1959** The 30-Foot Bride of Candy Rock. **1963** Son of Flubber.

RICE, JOHN C.
Born: 1858. Died: June 5, 1915, Philadelphia, Pa. (neuraemia, Bright's disease). Stage and screen actor. Married to stage actress Sally Cohen (dec.).

Appeared in: **1896** The Kiss.

RICE, NORMAN
Born: 1910. Died: Nov. 12, 1957, Hollywood, Calif. (heart attack). Screen, television actor, stage director and writer.

Appeared in: **1952** The Miracle of Our Lady of Fatima.

RICE, ROBERT (Robert Lee Rice)
Born: Mar. 4, 1913, Tex. Died: Jan. 8, 1968, Hollywood, Calif.

Appeared in: **1943** The Ghost Ship. **1944** Dragon Seed. **1947** Red Stallion. **1948** Canon City. **1949** In This Corner; Thieves' Highway; Bandit King of Texas. **1950** Under Mexicali Stars; Bells of Coronado. **1951** Government Agents vs. Phantom Legion (serial); Al Jennings of Oklahoma; Gunplay. **1952** Night Stage to Galveston; Junction City; Red Snow; Captain Pirate; Hiawatha. **1953** Captive Women; Tarzan and the She Devil; Paris Model; The Star of Texas; On Top of Old Smoky; The Marksman; Bandits of the West; Border City Rustlers. **1954** The Wild One; The Adventures of Hajii Baba; The Steel Cage. **1955** Three for the Show; Foxfire; Teenage Crime Wave; Dial Red O; The Big Bluff; Bowery to Bagdad; The Gun That Won the West. **1958** It!; The Terror From Beyond Space; Spacemaster X-7.

RICE, SAM (George Samuel O'Hanlon)
Born: 1874. Died: Mar. 12, 1946, Burbank, Calif. Screen, stage, vaudeville and burlesque actor. Known as "The King of Burlesque" in earlier days.

RICH, DICK
Born: 1909. Died: Mar. 29, 1967. Screen actor.

Appeared in: **1937** Headin' East. **1939** Let Freedom Ring; Angels Wash Their Faces. **1940** Lucky Cisco Kid; Murder in the Air; You the People (short); Tear Gas Squad; The Man Who Talked Too Much; Danger Ahead; Brigham Young. **1941** Western Union; Strange Alibi; Dressed to Kill; Rise and Shine; Ride On, Vaquero; Highway West. **1942** Rio Rita; Murder in the Big House; Rubber Racketeers. **1943** The Ox-Bow Incident; Little Miss Pinkerton (short); Secrets of the Underground. **1944** Crime By Night. **1945** The Last Installment (short); Within These Walls. **1947** Violence; Killer at Large; The Burning Cross. **1948** The Walls of Jericho. **1949** Oh, You Beautiful Doll. **1952** The Outcasts of Poker Flat. **1953** The Neanderthal Man; The Fighting Lawman; The Steel Lady. **1954** Overland Pacific; Seven Brides for Seven Brothers. **1955** Black Tuesday. **1956** Ransom!; Inside Detroit.

RICH, FREDDIE
Born: 1898, New York, N.Y. Died: Sept. 8, 1956, Beverly Hills, Calif. Bandleader, songwriter and screen actor.

Appeared in: **1933** Rambling 'Round Radio Row. **1944** A Wave, a Wac and a Marine.

RICH, LILLIAN
Born: 1900, Herne Hill, London, England. Died: Jan. 5, 1954, Woodland Hills, Calif. Screen actress.

Appeared in: **1921** Beyond; The Blazing Trail; Go Straight; Her Social Value; The Millionaire; The Ruse of the Rattler; The Sage Hen. **1922** The Bearcat; Afraid to Fight; Catch My Smoke; The Kentucky Derby; Man to Man; One Wonderful Night. **1924** Cheap Kisses; Empty Hearts; The Love Master; The Man from Wyoming; The Phantom Horseman; Never Say Die. **1925** Braveheart; A Kiss in the Dark; The Love Gamble; Seven Days; Ship of Souls; Simon the Jester; Soft Shoes. **1926** Dancing Days; Exclusive Rights; The Golden Web; The Isle of Retribution; Whispering Smith. **1927** God's Great Wilderness; Snowbound; Wanted a Coward; Web of Fate; Woman's Law. **1928** The Old Code; The Forger; That's My Daddy. **1930** The Eternal Triangle (short). **1931** Once a Lady; Grief Street; The Devil Plays. **1932** Mark of the Spur; Free Wheeling (short); A Lad an'a Lamp (short). **1935** Sprucin' Up (short).

RICH, PHIL
Born: 1896. Died: Feb. 22, 1956, Woodland Hills, Calif. Screen, vaudeville and television actor. Teamed with his wife in vaudeville as "Rich and Adair."

RICHARD, FRIEDA
Born: 1873, Vienna, Austria. Died: Sept. 13, 1946, Salzburg, Austria. Stage and screen actress.

Appeared in: **1925** Peak of Fate. **1926** Manon Lescaut; Faust. **1928** The Two Brothers. **1930** The Burning Heart; Liebe im Ring. **1932** Liebe Ist Liebe. **1935** Unfinished Symphony. **1938** The Affairs of Maupassant.

RICHARDS, ADDISON W. (Addison Whitaker Richards, Jr.)

Born: Oct. 20, 1887 or 1902 (?), Zanesville, Ohio. Died: Mar. 22, 1964, Los Angeles, Calif. (heart attack). Screen, stage and television actor. Entered films in 1933.

Appeared in: 1933 Riot Squad. 1934 Lone Cowboy; Let's Be Ritzy; The Love Captive; The Case of the Howling Dog; Beyond the Law; Our Daily Bread; Gentlemen Are Born; Babbitt; St. Louis Kid; British Agent. 1935 Only Eight Hours; G-Men; Home on the Range; The Eagle's Brood; The Frisco Kid; A Dog of Flanders; Sweet Music; Society Doctor; Here Comes the Band; The White Cockatoo; Front Page Woman; Little Big Shot; Dinky; Alias Mary Dow; The Crusades; Freckles. 1936 Sutter's Gold; Public Enemy's Wife; Trailin' West; Ceiling Zero; Road Gang; Song of the Saddle; The Law in Her Hands; Jail Break; Anthony Adverse; The Case of the Velvet Claws; Hot Money; China Clipper; Smart Blonde; God's Country and the Woman; Man Hunt; Colleen; The Walking Dead. 1937 Draegerman Courage; The Black Legion; Ready, Willing and Able; Her Husband's Secretary; White Bondage; Dance, Charlie, Dance; The Singing Marine; Love Is on the Air; The Barrier. 1938 Flight to Fame; Alcatraz Island; The Black Doll; The Last Express; Accidents Will Happen; Valley of the Giants; Boys Town; Prison Nurse. 1939 Whispering Enemies; They Made Her a Spy; Twelve Crowded Hours; Off the Record; Inside Information; Burn 'Em up O'Connor; Andy Hardy Gets Spring Fever; They All Come Out; Thunder Afloat; Geronimo; Espionage Agent; Nick Carter, Master Detective; Bad Lands; Exile Express; The Gracie Allen Murder Case. 1940 Andy Hardy Meets Debutante; Boom Town; Northwest Passage; The Man from Dakota; The Man from Montreal; The Lone Wolf Strikes; Edison, the Man; Charlie Chan in Panama; South to Karanga; Wyoming; Gangs of Chicago; Girls from Havana; My Little Chickadee; Arizona; Flight Command; Moon over Burma; Black Diamonds; Cherokee Strip; Slightly Honorable. 1941 Western Pacific; Tall, Dark and Handsome; Back in the Saddle; Sheriff of Tombstone; The Great Lie; Men of Boys Town; Mutiny in the Arctic; International Squadron; Texas; Her First Beau; Badlands of Dakota; Andy Hardy's Private Secretary; I Wanted Wings; Strawberry Blonde; The Trial of Mary Dugan. 1942 My Favorite Blonde; The Lady Has Plans; Cowboy Serenade; Pacific Rendezvous; A-Haunting We Will Go; Secrets of a Co-Ed; Man with Two Lives; Secret Agent for Japan; The Pride of the Yankees; Seven Day's Leave; Men of Texas; Top Sergeant; Secret Enemies; Flying Tigers; War Dogs. 1943 Headin' for God's Country; Corvette K-225; Where Are Your Children?; The Mystery of the 13th Guest; Mystery Broadcast; The Deerslayer; Air Force; Underground Agent; A Guy Named Joe. 1944 Smart Guy; The Fighting Seabees; Follow the Boys; Three Men in White; Moon over Las Vegas; Roger Touhy, Gangster; A Night of Adventure; Marriage Is a Private Affair; Since You Went Away; The Mummy's Curse; The Sullivans; Are These Our Parents?; Barbary Coast Gent; Three Little Sisters; Border Town Trail. 1945 Lady on a Train; The Chicago Kid; The Last Installment (short); God Is My Co-Pilot; Betrayal from the East; Rough, Tough and Ready; Bells of Rosarita; Grissly's Millions; Come Out Fighting; I'll Remember April; Black Market Babies; Danger Signal; The Shanghai Cobra; Men in Her Diary; Strange Confession; The Adventures of Rusty; Spellbound; Bewitched; Leave Her to Heaven. 1946 Secrets of a Sorority Girl; Angel on My Shoulder; The Criminal Court; The Hoodlum Saint; Step by Step; Renegades; Don't Gamble with Strangers; The Tiger Woman; The Mummy's Curse; Anna and the King of Siam; Love Laughs at Andy Hardy; Dragonwyck. 1947 The Millerson Case. 1948 Lulu Belle. 1949 The Rustlers; Henry the Rainmaker; Call Northside 777. 1950 Davy Crockett, Indian Scout. 1955 Illegal; High Society; Fort Yuma. 1956 Walk the Proud Land; Reprisal!; Everything but the Truth; When Gangland Strikes; Fury at Gunsight Pass; The Ten Commandments; The Broken Star. 1957 Last of the Badmen; Gunsight Ridge. 1958 The Saga of Hemp Browñ. 1959 The Oregon Trail. 1961 Frontier Uprising; The Gambler Wore a Gun; The Flight That Disappeared. 1962 Saintly Sinners. 1963 The Raiders. 1964 For Those Who Think Young.

RICHARDS, CHARLES

Born: Dec. 16, 1899, Indianapolis, Ind. Died: July 29, 1948, Hollywood, Calif. Screen actor and casting director. Entered films in 1916.

Appeared in: 1923 The Call of the Canyon.

RICHARDS, GORDON

Born: Oct. 27, 1893, Gillingham, Kent, England. Died: Jan. 13, 1964, Hollywood, Calif. Screen, stage and television actor.

Appeared in: 1942 The Wife Takes a Flyer. 1943 Slightly Dangerous. 1944 The Canterville Ghost; The Story of Dr. Wassell; Mrs. Parkington; National Velvet. 1945 Molly and Me; Kitty; White Pongo; Weekend at the Waldorf. 1946 Larceny in Her Heart. 1947 Linda Be Good; The Imperfect Lady; Ladies' Man; Flight to Nowhere. 1948 Won.an in the Night; Thirteen Lead Soldiers. 1950 The Man Who Cheated Himself; The Big Hangover. 1955 High Society.

RICHARDS, GRANT

Born: 1916, New York, N.Y. Died: July 4, 1963, Hollywood, Calif. (leukemia). Screen, stage, radio and television actor.

Appeared in: 1936 Hopalong Cassidy Returns. 1937 A Night of Mystery; On Such a Night. 1938 My Old Kentucky Home; Under the Big Top. 1939 Risky Business; Inside Information. 1940 Isle of Destiny. 1942 Just Off Broadway.

1944 Winged Victory. 1958 Guns, Girls and Gangsters. 1959 The Four Skulls of Jonathan Drake; Inside the Mafia. 1960 Oklahoma Territory; Twelve Hours to Kill; The Music Box Kid. 1961 You Have to Run Fast; Secret of Deep Harbor.

RICHARDS, PAUL E.

Died: Dec. 10, 1974, Los Angeles, Calif. (cancer). Screen and television actor.

Appeared in: 1951 Fixed Bayonets. 1953 War Paint. 1954 Phantom of the Rue Morgue; Playgirl; Pushover; Demetrius and the Gladiators. 1955 Tall Men Riding. 1956 The Houston Story; Scandal, Incorporated; Tension at Table Rock. 1957 The Strange One; Monkey On My Back; Hot Summer Night; The Unknown Terror; The Black Whip. 1958 Blood Arrow. 1959 Four Fast Guns. 1960 All the Young Men. 1967 St. Valentine's Day Massacre. 1970 Beneath the Planet of the Apes.

RICHARDSON, FRANK

Died: Feb. 1913, Murrieta Springs, Calif. Screen actor. Entered films in 1907 with Selig.

Appeared in: 1911 In the Days of Gold.

RICHARDSON, FRANKIE

Born: Sept. 6, 1898, Philadelphia, Pa. Died: Jan. 30, 1962, Philadelphia, Pa. (heart attack). Screen, minstrel and vaudeville actor.

Appeared in: 1925 Don Q.; Seven Sinners. 1926 King of the Pack; Racing Blood. 1928 The Joy Boy of Song (short); Chasing the Blues (short). 1929 Fox Movietone Follies of 1929; Happy Days; Masquerade; Sunny Side Up. 1930 Let's Go Places; New Movietone Follies of 1930.

RICHARDSON, WILLIAM

Born: 1876. Died: Nov. 8, 1937, Los Angeles, Calif. Screen and stage actor.

RICHMAN, AL

Born: 1885. Died: Apr. 20, 1936, Hollywood, Calif. (heart attack). Screen actor.

RICHMAN, CHARLES

Born: 1870, Chicago, Ill. Died: Dec. 1, 1940, Bronx, N.Y. Stage and screen actor.

Appeared in: 1915 The Battle Cry of Peace. 1917 The Secret Kingdom (serial). 1923 Has the World Gone Mad? 1929 The Ninety-Ninth Amendment (short). 1931 The Struggle. 1933 Take a Chance. 1934 His Double Life; The President Vanishes; Woman Haters (short). 1935 In Old Kentucky; George White's 1935 Scandals; The Case of the Curious Bride; The Glass Key; Becky Sharp; Thanks a Million; My Marriage; After Office Hours; Biography of a Bachelor Girl. 1936 The Ex-Mrs. Bradford; Parole; In His Steps; Sing Me a Love Song; Under Your Spell; I'd Give My Life. 1937 The Life of Emile Zola; Make a Wish; Lady Behave; Nothing Sacred. 1938 The Adventures of Tom Sawyer; The Cowboy and the Lady; Blondes at Work. 1939 Torchy Runs for Mayor; Exile Express; Dark Victory. 1940 Devil's Island. 1941 The Sign on the Door; Stranger Than Fiction; Trust Your Wife. 1942 My Friend the Devil.

RICHMAN, HARRY (Henry Richman, Jr.)

Born: Oct. 10, 1895, Cincinnati, Ohio. Died: Nov. 3, 1972, North Hollywood, Calif. Screen, stage, vaudeville, radio actor, singer and songwriter. Divorced from showgirls Yvonne Epstein, Hazel Forbes and Yvonne Day.

Appeared in: 1929 The Song of Broadway. 1930 Putting On the Ritz. 1936 The Music Goes 'Round.

RICHMAN, MARIAN (Marion S. Pearlson)

Born: Apr. 10, 1922, Calif. Died: Feb. 24, 1956, Los Angeles, Calif. (suicide—barbiturates). Screen, radio and television actress.

Appeared in: 1954 Gog.

RICHMOND, KANE (Frederick W. Bowditch)

Born: Dec. 23, 1906, Minneapolis, Minn. Died: Mar. 22, 1973. Stage and screen actor. Entered films in 1930.

Appeared in: 1930 The Leather Pushers (serial). 1931 Politics; Stepping Out; Strangers May Kiss; Cavalier of the West. 1932 Huddle; West of Broadway. 1934 Devil Tiger; Let's Fall in Love; Voice in the Night; Crime of Helen Stanley; I Can't Escape. 1935 The Lost City (serial); Confidential; The Adventures of Rex and Rinty (serial); Circus Shadows; Forced Landing. 1936 Private Number; Born to Fight; Racing Blood; With Love and Kisses. 1937 Nancy Steele Is Missing; Headline Crasher; Tough to Handle; Anything for a Thrill; Young Dynamite; The Reckless Way; Devil Diamond. 1938 Mars Attacks the World. 1939 Tail Spin; The Return of the Cisco Kid; Charlie Chan in Reno; 20,000 Men a Year; The Escape; Winner Take All; Chicken Wagon Family. 1940 Sailor's Lady; Charlie Chan in Panama; Murder Over New York; Knute Rockne—All American. 1941 Play Girl; Great Guns; Hard Guy; Mountain Moonlight; Riders of the Purple Sage; Double Cross. 1942 Spy Smasher (serial—also released as a feature Spy Smasher Returns); A Gentleman at Heart. 1943 Action in the North Atlantic; Three Russian Girls; There's Something About a Soldier. 1944 Ladies Courageous; Bermuda Mystery; Roger Touhy, Gangster; Haunted Harbor (serial). 1945 Jungle Raiders (serial); Brenda Starr,

Reporter (serial); Black Market Babies. **1946** The Tiger Woman; The Mighty McGurk; Behind the Mask; The Missing Lady; The Shadow Returns; Passkey to Danger; Don't Gamble With Strangers; Traffic in Crime. **1947** Black Gold; Brick Bradford (serial). **1948** Stage Struck. **1951** Pirates Harbor (serial rerelease of 1944 serial Haunted Harbor).

RICHMOND, WARNER

Born: Jan. 11, 1895, Culpepper County, Va. Died: June 19, 1948, Los Angeles, Calif. (coronary thrombosis). Screen and stage actor.

Appeared in: **1916** Betty of Graystone. **1918** Sporting Life. **1920** My Lady's Garter. **1921** Tol'able David; Heart of Maryland; The Mountain Woman. **1922** The Challenge; Isle of Doubt; Jan of the Big Snows. **1923** Luck; Mark of the Beast; The Man from Glengarry. **1924** Daughters of the Night; The Speed Spook. **1925** The Crowded Hour; Fear-Bound; The Making of O'Malley; The Pace That Thrills. **1926** Good and Naughty; The Wives of the Prophet. **1927** Slide, Kelly, Slide; The Fire Brigade; Finger Prints; Irish Hearts; White Flannels; Heart of Maryland (and 1921 version). **1928** Hearts of Men; Shadows of the Night; Chicago; Stop That Man; You Can't Beat the Law. **1929** Strange Cargo; Voice of the Storm; The Redeeming Sin; Stark Mad; Fifty-Fifty; Manhattan Madness; Big Brother; The Apache; Big News. **1930** Men without Women; Billy the Kid; Strictly Modern; Remote Control; Vengeance (short). **1931** Quick Millions; Huckleberry Finn. **1932** Hell's Highway; The Woman from Monte Carlo; Beast of the City; Strangers of the Evening; Night Court. **1933** Fast Workers; King of the Jungle; Corruption; Mama Loves Papa; This Day and Age; Police Call; Life in the Raw. **1934** Happy Landing; The Lost Jungle (serial); Gift of Gab. **1935** The Phantom Empire (short); Mississippi; Rainbow's End; Smoky Smith; New Frontier; The Courageous Avenger; Under Pressure; Headline Woman; So Red the Rose; The Singing Vagabond. **1936** Peppery Salt (short); Heart of the West; Below the Deadline; Hearts in Bondage; The White Legion; Song of the Gringo; Headin' for the Rio Grande; In His Steps. **1937** A Lawman Is Born; Wallaby Jim of the Islands; Where Trails Divide; The Gold Racket; Riders of the Dawn; Stars over Arizona; Federal Bullets. **1938** Wolves of the Sea; Six-Shootin' Sheriff; Prairie Moon. **1939** Wild Horse Canyon. **1940** Rainbow over the Range; Rhythm of the Rio Grande; Pals of the Silver Sage; The Golden Trail; Men with Steel Faces. **1946** Colorado Serenade.

RICHTER, PAUL

Born: 1896, Germany. Died: Dec. 30, 1961, Vienna, Austria. Screen, stage and television actor.

Appeared in: **1923** Siegfried (US 1925). **1924** Der Nibelungen. **1926** Human Law. **1927** Peter the Pirate. **1928** Kriemhild's Revenge. **1929** Forbidden Love. **1931** Die Foresterchirstl. **1935** Jungfrau Gegen Moench (Maiden vs. Monk); Drei Kaiserjaeger; Ehestreik. **1936** Der Klosterjaeger; Die Frauen vom Tannhof; Der Wackere Schustermeister; Ein Liebesroman im Hause Habsburg. **1937** Das Schweigen im Walde (The Silence of the Forest). **1939** Der Edelweisskoenig; Starker als die Liebe (Stronger Than Love); Frau Sylvelin. **1940** Waldrausch (Forest Fever).

RICKETTS, THOMAS "TOM"

Born: 1853, London, England. Died: Jan. 20, 1939, Hollywood, Calif. (pneumonia). Screen, stage actor, film director and stage manager.

Appeared in: **1921** The Parish Priest; Puppets of Fate; Sham; Beating the Game; The Killer; The Spenders. **1922** The Eternal Flame; Fools of Fortune; Putting It Over; Shattered Idols; A Tailor-Made Man; The Lavender Bath Lady. **1923** Alice Adams; The Dangerous Maid; Strangers of the Night; Within the Law. **1924** Black Oxen; The Gaiety Girl; Cheap Kisses; Circe, the Enchantress. **1925** The Fate of a Flirt; The Girl Who Wouldn't Work; Never the Twain Shall Meet; Was It Bigamy?; The Business of Love; A Fight to the Finish; My Wife and I; Oh, Doctor; Sealed Lips; Secrets of the Night; Steppin' Out; Wages for Wives; When Husbands Flirt; Bobbed Hair. **1926** Dancing Days; Ladies of Leisure; The Lily; The Nutcracker; The Belle of Broadway; The Cat's Pajamas; Going the Limit; Ladies at Play; Love's Blindness; The Old Soak; Poker Faces; Stranded in Paris; When the Wife's Away. **1927** Sailor's Sweetheart; Broadway Madness; Children of Divorce; In a Moment of Temptation; Too Many Crooks; Venus of Venice. **1928** My Friend from India; Doomsday; Just Married; Dry Martini; Interference; Freedom of the Press; Five and Ten Cent Annie; Law and the Man. **1929** The Glad Rag Doll; Beware of Bachelors; Light Fingers; Skirt Shy (short); Red Hot Speed. **1930** Prince of Diamonds; The Vagabond King; Broken Dishes; Sea Legs. **1931** Man of the World; Side Show; Ambassador Bill; Surrender. **1932** A Farewell to Arms; Forbidden; Thrill of Youth. **1933** He Learned about Women; Women Won't Tell; Mama Loves Papa; Forgotten. **1934** Stolen Sweets; The Curtain Falls; In Love with Life; Little Man, What Now?; No Greater Glory; The Count of Monte Cristo. **1935** Forsaking All Others; Sons of Steel; Now or Never; Cardinal Richelieu; A Tale of Two Cities. **1936** Hi, Gaucho; We Went to College; Pennies from Heaven. **1937** Maid of Salem; The Lady Escapes. **1938** Bluebeard's Eighth Wife; The Young in Heart; Young Fugitives.

RICKS, JAMES

Died: July 2, 1974, New York, N.Y. (heart attack). Black singer and screen actor. Led "Ravens" quartet and was band vocalist with Count Basie.

RICKSON, LUCILLE (aka LUCILLE RICKSEN)

Born: Sept. 2, 1907. Died: Mar. 13, 1925. Screen actress.

Appeared in: **1921** The Old Nest. **1922** Forsaking All Others; The Married Flapper; The Girl Who Ran Wild; Remembrance; The Stranger's Banquet. **1923** Human Wreckage; The Rendezvous; Trimmed in Scarlet; The Social Buccaneer (serial). **1924** Vanity's Price; Behind the Curtain; Galloping Fish; The Hill Billy; Idle Tongues; Judgment of the Storm; The Painted Lady; Those Who Dance; Young Ideas. **1925** The Denial.

RIDDLE, JIM (James Riddle)

Died: Prior to 1976. Screen actor.

Appeared in: **1967** Gentle Giant.

RIDDLE, RICHARD. *See* RICHARD AINLEY

RIDGE, WALTER J.

Born: 1900. Died: Sept. 22, 1968, Los Angeles, Calif. Screen actor, extra and vaudeville actor. Appeared in vaudeville in an act billed as "Mulroy, McNeece and Ridge."

RIDGELY, CLEO

Born: 1894. Died: Aug. 18, 1962, Glendale, Calif. Stage and screen actress. Married to actor James W. Horne (dec. 1942).

Appeared in: **1914** The Spoilers. **1915** The Chorus Lady. **1916** The Yellow Mask; The Yellow Pawn. **1921** Dangerous Pastime. **1922** The Forgotten Law; The Law and the Woman; The Sleepwalker. **1923** The Beautiful and Damned.

RIDGELY, JOHN (John Huntington Rea)

Born: Sept. 6, 1909, Chicago, Ill. Died: Jan. 18, 1968, New York, N.Y. (heart ailment). Screen actor.

Appeared in: **1937** Larger Than Life; They Won't Forget; Submarine D-1. **1938** Forbidden Valley; The Invisible Menace; Torchy Gets Her Man; Secrets of an Actress; Patient in Room 18; He Couldn't Say No; Blondes at Work; Torchy Blane in Panama; Little Miss Thoroughbred; White Banners; Cowboy from Brooklyn; My Bill; Going Places; Hard to Get. **1939** Angels Wash Their Faces; The Cowboy Quarterback; Nancy Drew and the Hidden Staircase; Kid Nightingale; Dark Victory; Secret Service of the Air; Everybody's Hobby; Indianapolis Speedway; Torchy Plays with Dynamite; They Made Me a Criminal; You Can't Get Away with Murder; King of the Underworld; Private Detective; Wings of the Navy; The Return of Dr. X; The Kid from Kokomo. **1940** River's End; Father Is a Prince; The Man Who Talked Too Much; Saturday's Children; Flight Angels; Torrid Zone; Brother Orchid; They Drive by Night. **1941** The Wagons Roll at Night; Million Dollar Baby; International Squadron; The Great Mr. Nobody; The Man Who Came to Dinner; Here Comes Happiness; Strange Alibi; Navy Blues; Highway West. **1942** Bullet Scars; Wings for the Eagle; The Big Shot; Secret Enemies. **1943** Air Force; Northern Pursuit. **1944** Hollywood Canteen; The Doughgirls; Destination Tokyo; Arsenic and Old Lace. **1945** Pride of the Marines; God Is My Co-Pilot; Danger Signal. **1946** My Reputation; Two Guys from Milwaukee; The Big Sleep. **1947** High Wall; The Man I Love; Nora Prentiss; That Way with Women; That's My Man; Cheyenne; Cry Wolf; Possessed. **1948** Night Winds; Luxury Liner; Sealed Verdict; Trouble Makers; The Iron Curtain. **1949** Command Decision; Once More, My Darling; Border Incident; Task Force; Tucson. **1950** Backfire; Beauty on Parade; The Lost Volcano; South Sea Sinner; Petty Girl; Rookie Fireman; Saddle Tramp; Edge of Doom. **1951** The Last Outpost; When the Redskins Rode; Thunder in God's Country; Al Jennings of Oklahoma; Half Angel; A Place in the Sun; The Blue Veil; As You Were. **1952** Fort Osage; The Greatest Show on Earth; Room for One More; The Outcasts of Poker Flat. **1953** Off Limits.

RIDGES, STANLEY

Born: 1892, Southampton, England. Died: Apr. 22, 1951, Westbrook, Conn. Screen, stage and television actor.

Appeared in: **1923** Success. **1930** For Two Cents (short); Let's Merge (short). **1932** The Sign of the Cross. **1934** Crime without Passion. **1935** The Scoundrel. **1936** Winterset; Sinner Take All. **1937** Interns Can't Take Money. **1938** Yellow Jack; They're Always Caught (short); If I Were King; There's That Woman Again; The Mad Miss Manton. **1939** Silver on the Sage; Confessions of a Nazi Spy; Each Dawn I Die; Let Us Live; Union Pacific; I Stole a Million; Dust Be My Destiny; Espionage Agent; Nick Carter, Master Detective. **1940** Black Friday. **1941** The Sea Wolf; Sergeant York; They Died with Their Boots On; Mr. District Attorney. **1942** The Lady Is Willing; Eagle Squadron; To Be or Not to Be; The Big Shot; Eyes in the Night. **1943** Tarzan Triumphs; Air Force; This Is the Army. **1944** Wilson; The Sign of the Cross (revised version of 1932 film); The Story of Dr. Wassell; The Master Race. **1945** The Suspect; God Is My Co-Pilot; Captain Eddie; The Phantom Speaks. **1946** Because of Him; Canyon Passage; Mr. Ace. **1947** Possessed. **1949** Streets of Laredo; Task Force; You're My Everything; An Act of Murder. **1950** No Way Out; Paid in Full; Thelma Jordon; There's a Girl in My Heart. **1951** The Groom Wore Spurs.

RIDGEWAY, FRITZI

Born: 1898, Missoula, Mont. Died: Mar. 29, 1961, Lancaster, Calif. (heart attack). Stage and screen actress. Entered films in 1917.

Appeared in: **1920** Judy of Rogues Harbor. **1921** Bring Him In; The Fatal 30. **1922** Boomerang Justice; Branded Man; The Hate Trail; The Menacing Past; The Old Homestead. **1923** Ruggles of Red Gap; The Cricket on the Hearth; Hollywood; Trifling with Honor. **1927** Man Bait; Face Value; Getting Gertie's Garter; Lonesome Ladies; Nobody's Widow. **1928** The Enemy; Flying Romeos; Son of the Golden West. **1929** Red Hot Speed; This Is Heaven; Hell's Heroes. **1930** Prince of Diamonds. **1931** The Mad Parade. **1932** Ladies of the Big House. **1934** We Will Live Again. **1935** No Ransom.

RIDGEWELL, AUDREY
Born: 1904, London, England. Died: Oct. 27, 1968, Grove Beach, Conn. Stage and screen actress. Daughter of tenor George Ridgewell (dec.)

Appeared in: **1933** His Double Life.

RIDLEY, ROBERT
Born: 1901. Died: Nov. 19, 1958, Hollywood, Calif. Screen actor and extra. One of the founders of Screen Extras Guild.

RIECHERS, HELENE
Born: 1869, Germany. Died: July 24, 1957, Berlin, Germany. Stage and screen actress.

RIEMANN, JOHANNES
Born: 1887, Berlin, Germany. Died: Oct. 8, 1959, Constance, West Germany. Screen actor, film director and screenwriter.

Appeared in: **1932** Sein Scheldungsgrund; Der Falsche Ehemann; Drunter und Drueber. **1933** Heute Nacht-Eventuell; Der Hellscher; Kadetten. **1934** Fraeulein-Falsch Verbunden! **1940** Der Tag Nach der Scheidung (The Day after the Divorce); Ihr Erstes Erlebnis (Her First Experience).

RIES, WILLIAM J.
Born: 1895. Died: Nov. 16, 1955, Hollywood, Calif. Screen actor.

RIETTI, VICTOR
Born: Mar. 1, 1888, Ferrara, Italy. Died: Dec. 4, 1963, London, England (heart ailment). Screen, stage, television actor, stage director and stage producer. Father of actor Robert Rietti.

Appeared in: **1934** Jew Suess (aka Power—US). **1935** Heads We Go; Man of the Moment; Two Hearts in Harmony; Oh, Daddy!; Escape Me Never. **1936** The Ghost Goes West; Dusty Ermine; Juggernaut; London Melody. **1938** First and Last; The Divorce of Lady X; The Viper; Transatlantic Trouble; Secretary in Trouble. **1944** Room for Two; Give Us the Moon; Yellow Canary; Hotel Reserve (US 1946). **1949** A Man about the House. **1950** The Glass Mountain. **1957** The Story of Esther Costello. **1958** Your Past Is Showing (aka The Naked Truth).

RIGA, NADINE
Born: 1909. Died: Dec. 11, 1968, Hollywood, Calif. (cerebral hemorrhage). Screen actress.

Appeared in: **1928** Ramona. **1936** Anthony Adverse. **1943** For Whom the Bell Tolls.

RIGBY, ARTHUR (Arthur Turner)
Born: Sept. 27, 1900, London, England. Died: Apr. 25, 1971, Worthing, England (stroke). Screen, stage and television actor.

Appeared in: **1927** Q Ships (film debut).

RIGBY, EDWARD
Born: 1879, Ashford, Kent, England. Died: Apr. 5, 1951, London, England. Stage and screen actor.

Appeared in: **1935** Lorna Doone; No Limit; Windfall; Gay Old Dog. **1936** Accused; Irish for Luck; Land Without Music (aka Forbidden Music—US 1938); Green Hell (US 1940); The Heirloom Mystery; Queen of Hearts. **1937** Jump for Glory (aka When Thief Meets Thief—US); The Fatal Hour; Mr. Smith Carries On; Young and Innocent (aka A Girl was Young—US 1938); The Show Goes On; Under a Cloud. **1938** A Yank at Oxford; Yellow Sands; Keep Smiling (aka Smiling Along—US 1939); The Ware Case (US 1939); Kicking the Moon Around. **1939** The Stars Look Down (US 1941); Poison Pen (US 1941); There Ain't No Justice; Young Man's Fancy (US 1943). **1940** The Proud Valley; Convoy; Sailors Don't Care; Fingers. **1941** Kipps (aka The Remarkable Mr. Kipps (US 1942); The Common Touch; The Farmer's Wife. **1942** Flying Fortress; Let the People Sing; Penn of Pennsylvania (aka The Courageous Mr. Penn—US 1944); Salute John Citizen; Went the Day Well? (aka 48 Hours—US 1944). **1943** Get Cracking; They Met in the Dark (US 1945). **1944** Perfect Strangers (aka Vacation from Marriage; Murder in Reverse (US 1946); I Live in Grosvenor Square (aka A Yank in London—US 1946); Agitator. **1946** Quiet Weekend (US 1948); The Years Between (US 1947); Piccadilly Incident; Daybreak. **1947** Temptation Harbour (US 1949); Green Fingers; The Loves of Joanne Godden. **1948** Easy Money (US 1949); The Three Weird Sisters; Noose (aka The Silk Noose—US 1950); It's Hard to Be Good (US 1950). **1949** Rover and Me; All Over Town; Christopher Colum-

bus; Don't Ever Leave Me; A Run for Your Money (US 1950). **1950** Double Confession (US 1953); The Happiest Days of Your Life; Tony Draws a Horse (US 1951); What the Butler Saw; The Mudlark. **1951** Into the Blue (aka The Man in the Dinghy—US); Circle of Danger.

RIGGS, TOMMY
Born: Oct. 21, 1908, Pittsburgh, Pa. Died: May 23, 1967, Pittsburgh, Pa. Screen, radio and television actor.

Appeared in: **1938** Goodbye Broadway.

RIGGS, WILLIAM (William Allen Riggs)
Died: Aug. 2, 1975. Screen and television actor.

RIGHTMIRE, WILLIAM H.
Born: 1857. Died: Jan. 14, 1933, Long Beach, Calif. (heart disease). Screen, stage actor and novelist.

RIHANI, NEGUIB
Born: 1891. Died: June 8, 1949, Cairo, Egypt. Stage and screen actor.

RILEY, GEORGE
Born: 1900, Rochester, N.Y. Died: May 30, 1972, Los Angeles, Calif. Vaudeville, tenor soloist, stage and screen actor. Teamed in vaudeville with wife, Helene Heller, as "Heller and Riley."

Appeared in: **1928** Branded Man. **1942** Over My Dead Body. **1946** Night and Day. **1962** Woman Hunt. **1963** The Day Mars Invaded Earth.

RILEY, JACK "SLIM"
Born: 1895. Died: July 9, 1933, Newhall, Calif. Screen actor.

Appeared in: **1921** A Broken Doll.

RIMAC, CIRO CAMPOS
Born: 1894, Peru. Died: Sept. 8, 1973, Miami, Fla. (cancer). Screen and vaudeville actor.

Appeared in: **1945** Dollface.

RIN TIN TIN, SR.
Born: 1916. Died: 1932. Dog screen actor. Father of Rin Tin Tin, Jr. (dec.). Entered films with Warner Bros.

Appeared in: **1922** The Man from Hell's River; My Dad. **1923** Where the North Begins; Shadows of the North. **1924** Find Your Man. **1925** The Lighthouse by the Sea; Clash of the Wolves; Below the Line; Tracked in the Snow Country. **1926** The Night Cry; Hero of the Big Snows; While London Sleeps. **1927** Jaws of Steel; A Dog of the Regiment; Tracked by the Police; Hills of Kentucky. **1928** Rinty of the Desert; Race for Life; Land of the Silver Fox; The Famous Warner Brothers Dog Star (short). **1929** Show of Shows; Frozen River; Million Dollar Collar; Tiger Rose. **1930** Rough Waters; The Man Hunter; On the Border. **1931** Lightning Warrior (serial).

RIN TIN TIN, JR.
Died. Dog screen actor. Son of Rin Tin Tin, Sr. (dec. 1932).

Appeared in: **1927** Hills of Kentucky. **1933** The Wolf Dog (serial); The Big Pay-Off. **1934** Law of the Wild (serial). **1935** Adventures of Rex and Rinty (serial). **1936** Tough Guy.

RING, BLANCHE
Born: 1876, Boston, Mass. Died: Jan. 13, 1961, Santa Monica, Calif. Stage and screen actress. Divorced from actor Charles Winninger (dec. 1969). Sister of actress Frances (dec. 1951) and Julie Ring and actor Cyril Ring (dec. 1967).

Appeared in: **1914** Our Mutual Girl #11. **1915** The Yankee Girl. **1926** It's the Old Army Game. **1940** If I Had My Way.

RING, CYRIL
Born: 1893. Died: July 17, 1967, Hollywood, Calif. Screen and stage actor. For family information, see Blanche Ring.

Appeared in: **1921** The Conquest of Canaan. **1922** Back Home and Broke; Divorce Coupons. **1923** The Exciters; Homeward Bound; The Ne'er-Do-Well. **1924** The Breaking Point; The Guilty One; Hit and Run; Pied Piper Malone; Tongues of Flame; In Hollywood with Potash and Perlmutter. **1926** Mismates. **1928** The News Parade. **1929** The Cocoanuts. **1930** Top Speed; The Social Lion. **1932** Business and Pleasure. **1933** Emergency Call; Too Much Harmony; Neighbors' Wives. **1934** No More Bridge (short); Most Precious Thing in Life; Hollywood Hoodlums. **1936** Border Patrolman; Wedding Present. **1940** One Night in the Tropics. **1941** Hot Spot; Great Guns. **1942** Home in Wyomin'; The Navy Comes Through; Army Surgeon; Over My Dead Body. **1943** Dixie; Melody Parade. **1944** In Society; Hot Rhythm; Follow the Boys; Secret Command; The Bullfighters. **1945** Hollywood and Vine; Beware of Redheads (short); The Naughty Nineties. **1947** Hollywood Barn Dance; Body and Soul; Do or Diet (short).

RING, FRANCES

Born: 1882, N.Y. Died: Jan. 15, 1951, Hollywood, Calif. Screen and stage actress. Married to actor Thomas Meighan (dec. 1936). For family information, see Blanche Ring.

RIORDAN, ROBERT J.

Born: 1913. Died: Jan. 1, 1968, Hollywood, Calif. (heart attack). Screen actor.

Appeared in: 1959 Arson for Hire. 1962 Manchurian Candidate. 1968 Buckskin; The Destructors.

RIOS, LALO

Born: 1927, Mexico. Died: Mar. 7, 1973, Hollywood, Calif. (liver ailment). Screen actor.

Appeared in: 1950 The Lawless (film debut); Bandit Queen. 1952 The Ring. 1953 City Beneath the Sea; Big Leaguer. 1958 Touch of Evil. 1962 Lonely Are the Brave.

RIPLEY, RAYMOND "RAY"

Born: 1891. Died: Oct. 7, 1938, Los Angeles, Calif. Screen actor.

Appeared in: 1920 The Vanishing Dagger (serial). 1921 The Blazing Trail; Why Trust Your Husband? 1922 Turn to the Right. 1925 Heads Up; Smilin' at Trouble. 1926 The Speeding Venus; The Traffic Cop; Western Pluck. 1927 Stolen Pleasures.

RIPLEY, ROBERT L.

Born: Dec. 25, 1893. Died: May 27, 1949, New York, N.Y. (heart attack). Screen, radio actor, author, cartoonist and creator of "Believe It or Not" series that appeared on film, radio and in newspapers.

Appeared in: 1932-33 Vitaphone shorts of his "Believe It or Not" series.

RISCOE, ARTHUR

Born: Nov. 19, 1896, Yorkshire, England. Died: Aug. 6, 1954, London, England. Stage and screen actor.

Appeared in: 1932 For the Love of Mike. 1933 Going Gay (aka Kiss Me Goodbye—US 1935); For Love of You. 1936 Public Nuisance No. 1. 1937 Paradise for Two (aka The Gaiety Girls—US 1938); Street Singer. 1941 Kipps (aka The Remarkable Mr. Kipps—US 1942).

RISDON, ELIZABETH

Born: Apr. 26, 1887, London, England. Died: Dec. 20, 1958, Santa Monica, Calif. (brain hemorrhage). Screen, stage and television actress. Married to actor and director George Loane Tucker (dec. 1921) and later to stage actor Brandon Evans (dec. 1958).

Appeared in: 1913 Maria Marten: Or, The Murder in the Red Barn; Bridegrooms Beware. 1914 The Finger of Destiny; The Cup Final Mystery; The Suicide Club; Beautiful Jim (aka The Price of Justice—US); Her Luck in London; It's a Long Long Way to Tipperary; The Idol of Paris; In the Days of Trafalgar (aka Black-Eyed Susan and The Battling British—US); Inquisitive Ike; The Loss of the Birkenhead; The Sound of Her Voice; The Courage of a Coward; The Bells of Rheims. 1915 The Christian; Florence Nightingale; From Shopgirl to Dutchess; Her Nameless Child; Grip; A Honeymoon for Three; Home; London's Yellow Peril; Midshipman Easy; Another Man's Wife; Charity Ann; Fine Feathers; Love in a Wood; A Will of Her Own; There's Good in Everyone; Gilbert Gets Tiger-Itis. 1916 The Princess of Happy Chance; The Manxman; The Mother of Dartmoor; Meg the Lady; Esther; Driven (aka Desperation—US); Mother Love; A Mother's Influence; The Morals of Weybury (aka The Hypocrites). 1917 Smith. 1919 A Star Overnight. 1935 Guard That Girl; Crime and Punishment. 1936 Don't Gamble with Love; Lady of Secrets; The King Steps Out; Craig's Wife; Theodora Goes Wild; The Final Hour. 1937 The Woman I Love; Make Way for Tomorrow; Mountain Justice; They Won't Forget; Mannequin; Dead End. 1938 Mad about Music; Tom Sawyer, Detective; Cowboy from Brooklyn; My Bill; Girls on Probation; The Affairs of Annabel. 1939 Sorority House; The Girl from Mexico; Full Confession; The Man Who Dared; The Mexican Spitfire; Huckleberry Finn; I Am Not Afraid; The Roaring Twenties; The Forgotten Woman; Disputed Passage; The Great Man Votes; Five Came Back. 1940 The Man Who Wouldn't Talk; Abe Lincoln in Illinois; Honeymoon Deferred; Ma, He's Making Eyes at Me; Saturday's Children; Sing, Dance, Plenty Hot; The Howards of Virginia; The Mexican Spitfire Out West; Slightly Tempered; Let's Make Music. 1941 Nice Girl?; The Mexican Spitfire's Baby; High Sierra; Mr. Dynamite; Footlight Fever. 1942 The Lady Is Willing; Mexican Spitfire at Sea; Mexican Spitfire Sees a Ghost; Jail House Blues; The Man Who Returned to Life; Reap the Wild Wind; I Live on Danger; Are Husbands Necessary?; Mexican Spitfire's Elephant; Journey for Margaret; Random Harvest; Paris Calling. 1943 Never a Dull Moment; Mexican Spitfire's Blessed Event; The Amazing Mrs. Holiday; Higher and Higher. 1944 The Canterville Ghost; Tall in the Saddle; Lost Angel; The Cobra Woman; Weird Woman; In the Meantime, Darling. 1945 Blonde Fever; Grissly's Millions; The Unseen; Song for Miss Julie; The Fighting Guardsman; Mama Loves Papa. 1946 Lover Come Back; Roll on Texas Moon; The Walls Came Tumbling Down; They Made Me a Killer. 1947 Life with Father; The Shocking Miss Pilgrim; Romance of Rosy Ridge; Mourning

Becomes Electra; The Egg and I. 1948 The Bride Goes Wild; Sealed Verdict; Bodyguard; High Wall; Every Girl Should Be Married. 1949 Guilty of Treason; Down Dakota Way. 1950 Bunco Squad; The Milkman; Hills of Oklahoma; The Secret Fury; Sierra. 1951 Bannerline; My True Story; In Old Amarillo. 1952 Scaramouche.

RISHELL, MYRTLE

Born: Sept. 12, 1877, Portland, Ore. Died: Sept. 12, 1942, Los Angeles, Calif. (cancer). Screen actress.

Appeared in: 1920 House of Whispers; Heart of a Child.

RISING, WILLIAM S.

Born: 1851. Died: Oct. 5, 1930, New York, N.Y. (heart trouble). Screen, stage actor and film director.

Appeared in: 1924 America.

RISS, DAN

Born: 1910. Died: Aug. 28, 1970, Hollywood, Calif. (heart attack). Screen and radio actor.

Appeared in: 1949 Pinky. 1950 Kiss Tom Goodbye; Love That Brute; Panic in the Streets; When Willie Comes Marching Home; Wyoming Mail. 1951 Appointment with Danger; Go for Broke; Little Egypt; Only the Valiant. 1952 Carbine Williams; Confidence Girl; Operation Secret; Scarlet Angel; Washington Story. 1953 Man in the Dark; The Miami Story; Vice Squad. 1954 Human Desire; Riders to the Stars; The Three Young Texans; The Yellow Tomahawk. 1957 Man on Fire; Kelly and Me. 1958 Badman's Country. 1960 Ma Barker's Killer Brood; The Story on Page One.

RISSMILLER, LAWSON J.

Born: 1914. Died: Apr. 2, 1953, Oley, Pa. Screen actor and orchestra leader.

Appeared in: 1939 Broadway Buckaroo.

RISSO, ATTILIO

Born: 1913. Died: Oct. 14, 1967, San Francisco, Calif. (liver disease). Screen and television actor. Appeared in films during the 1930s and 1940s with a group called the "Vagabonds."

Appeared in: 1943 It Ain't Hay.

RITCHIE, BILLIE

Born: 1879, Glasgow, Scotland. Died: July 6, 1921, Los Angeles, Calif. Screen and vaudeville actor. Appeared in Universal Films in 1914.

RITCHIE, FRANKLIN

Born: Ritchie, Pa. Died: Jan. 26, 1918, Los Angeles, Calif. (auto accident). Stage and screen actor.

Appeared in: 1914 The Iron Master. 1915 Under Two Flags; Mrs. Van Alden's Jewels; The Barrier Between; The Quicksands of Society; Adam Bebe; Aurora Floyd; The Americano; Dwellers in Glass Houses; After the Storm; To Have and to Lose; The Confession; The Maid O' the Mountains; Man and His Master; The Drab Sister; The Soul of Pierre; The Country Parson; Dora; Harvest; Between Father and Son; The Hungarian Nabob; The Woman of Mystery; The Reproach of Annesley. 1916 The Light; Not My Sister; The Reclamation; Dust; Pique; Lying Lips; Man's Enemy; The Wages of Sin; The Science of Crime; The Honor of the Law; The Undertow. 1917 The Gentle Intruder. 1918 Beloved Rogue.

RITCHIE, TERRY V.

Born: Nov. 28, 1887, Kans. Died: July 27, 1918, Los Angeles, Calif. (suicide—gas asphyxiation). Screen actor.

RITTER, ESTHER

Born: 1902. Died: Dec. 30, 1925, Los Angeles, Calif. (appendicitis). Screen actress. Married to screen actor Cuyler Supplee.

RITTER, GEORGE

Died: Dec. 1919. Screen actor.

RITTER, PAUL J.

Died: Apr. 27, 1962, Dacca, Pakistan. Screen actor and film producer.

RITTER, TEX (Maurice Woodward Ritter)

Born: Jan. 12, 1906, Panola County, Tex. Died: Jan. 2, 1974, Nashville, Tenn. (heart attack). Screen, stage, radio, television actor, singer and musician.

Appeared in: 1936 Song of the Gringo (film debut); Headin' for Rio Grande. 1937 Arizona Days; Trouble in Texas; Hittin' the Trail; Rivers of the Rockies; Tex Rides with the Boy Scouts; The Mystery of the Hooded Horsemen; Sing, Cowboy, Sing. 1938 Frontier Town; Rollin' Plains; The Utah Trail; Starlight Over Texas; Where the Buffalo Roam. 1939 Roll, Wagons, Roll; Song of the Buckaroo; Sundown on the Prairie; Riders of the Frontier; Rollin' Westward; Down the Wyoming Trail; Man From Texas. 1940 Westbound Stage; Rhythm of the Rio Grande; Pals of the Silver Sage; The Golden Trail; The Cowboy from Sundown; Take Me Back to Oklahoma; Rainbow Over the Range; Arizona Frontier; Riding with Buffalo Bill; A-Headin' for Cheyenne; Round-Up Time in the Rockies. **1941** Rolling Home to Texas; Riding the Cherokee Trail; The Pioneers; King of Dodge City; Roaring Frontiers; Lone Star Vigilantes; Bullets for Bandits; The Devil's Trail; North of the Rockies; Prairie Gunsmoke; Vengeance of the West. **1942** Deep in the Heart of Texas; Little Joe the Wrangler; Raiders of the San Joaquin. **1943** The Old Chisholm Trail; The Lone Star Trail; Tenting Tonight on the Old Camp Ground; Cheyenne Roundup; Arizona Trail; Frontier Badmen. **1944** Marshal of Gunsmoke; Oklahoma Raiders; Cowboy Canteen; Gangsters of the Frontier; Dead or Alive; The Whispering Skull; Marked for Murder. **1945** Enemy of the Law; Three in the Saddle; Frontier Fugitives; Flaming Bullets. **1950** Holiday Rhythm. **1952** High Noon. **1953** The Marshal's Daughter. **1954** The Cowboy (narrator). **1955** Apache Ambush; Wichita; The First Badman. **1956** Down Liberty Road. **1957** Trooper Hook. **1966** Nashville Rebel; What's the Country Coming To?; Girl from Tobacco Road. **1967** What Am I Bid?

RITTER, THELMA

Born: Feb. 14, 1905, Brooklyn, N.Y. Died: Feb. 5, 1969, New York, N.Y. (heart attack). Screen, stage, radio and television actress.

Appeared in: **1947** Miracle on 34th Street (film debut). **1949** City Across the River; Father Was a Fullback; A Letter to Three Wives. **1950** Perfect Strangers; All about Eve; I'll Get By. **1951** The Mating Season; The Model and the Marriage Broker; As Young as You Feel. **1952** With a Song in My Heart. **1953** The Farmer Takes a Wife; Pickup on South Street; Titanic. **1954** Rear Window. **1955** Lucy Gallant; Daddy Long Legs. **1956** The Proud and Profane. **1959** A Hole in the Head; Pillow Talk. **1961** The Misfits; The Second Time Around. **1962** Birdman of Alcatraz; How the West Was Won. **1963** A New Kind of Love; Move over, Darling; For Love or Money. **1965** Boeing Boeing. **1967** The Incident. **1968** What's So Bad about Feeling Good?

RITTERBAND, GERHARD

Born: 1905, Germany. Died: Oct. 1959, Berlin, Germany (jaundice). Screen actor. Appeared in early Ernst Lubitsch films and other silents.

RITZ, AL (Al Joachim)

Born: Aug. 27, 1901, Newark, N.J. Died: Dec. 22, 1965, New Orleans, La. (heart attack). Screen, stage, vaudeville and television actor. Brother of actors Harry and Jimmy Ritz. Was member of "Ritz Bros." screen and vaudeville comedy team. All films beginning in 1934 include the three brothers.

Appeared in: **1918** The Avenging Trail (was an extra in this film). **1934** Hotel Anchovy (team film debut—short). **1936** Sing, Baby, Sing. **1937** One in a Million; On the Avenue; You Can't Have Everything; Life Begins in College. **1938** The Goldwyn Follies; Kentucky Moonshine; Straight, Place and Show. **1939** The Three Musketeers; The Gorilla; Pack up Your Troubles. **1940** Argentine Nights. **1942** Behind the Eight Ball. **1943** Hi 'Ya, Chum; Screen Snapshots No. 5 (short); Screen Snapshots No. 8 (short); Never a Dull Moment. **1944** Take It or Leave It (scenes from On the Avenue (1937) in this film). **1945** Everything Happens to Us. **1963** The Sound of Laughter (documentary).

RIVAS, JOSE M. L. (Jose Maria Linares Rivas)

Born: 1901, Mexico. Died: Apr. 13, 1955, Mexico City, Mexico. Stage and screen actor.

Appeared in: **1939** El Romance del Palmar. **1962** The Criminal Life of Archibaldo de la Cruz.

RIVIERE, FRED " CURLY"

Born: 1875. Died: Nov. 6, 1935, Hollywood, Calif. (heart attack). Screen actor.

Appeared in: **1926** The Dangerous Dub.

ROACH, BERT

Born: Aug. 21, 1891, Washington, D.C. Died: Feb. 16, 1971. Stage and screen actor.

Appeared in: **1914** Fatty's Magic Pants. **1916** The Youngest in the Family; The Lawyer's Secret; Dinty's Daring Dash. **1917** Beach Nuts; Roped Into Scandal. **1921** The Millionaire; The Rowdy; A Small Town Idol. **1922** The Black Bag; The Flirt. **1924** Excitement; High Speed; A Lady of Quality; The Storm Daughter. **1925** The Denial; Don't; Excuse Me; Smouldering Fires. **1926** The Flaming Forest; Money Talks; Tin Hats. **1927** The Taxi Dancer; Tillie the Toiler; Twelve Miles Out. **1928** A Certain Young Man; The Crowd; Honeymoon; Paramount-Christie Talking Plays; Riders of the Dark; The Latest from Paris; Telling the World; Under the Black Eagle; Wickedness Preferred. **1929** The Argyle Case; The Desert Rider; The Last Warning; The Show of Shows; So Long Letty; The Time, the Place and the Girl; Young Nowheres; Twin Beds; The Fatal Forceps (short). **1930** So This is Paris Green (short); Captain Thunder; Hold Everything; Lawful Larceny; Liliom; No, No, Nanette; The Princess and the Plumber; Song of the Flame; Viennese Nights; Scrappily Married (short); Down With Husbands (short); For Love or Money (short). **1931** Six Cylinder Love; Compromised; Arrowsmith. **1932** Murder in the Rue Morgue; Hotel Continental; Nigat World; Love Me Tonight; Bird of Paradise; Evenings for Sale. **1933** Hallelujah, I'm a Bum. **1934** Half a Sinner; Paris Interlude. **1935** Traveling Saleslady; Here Comes the Band; Guard That

Girl; Goin' to Town. **1936** Love Before Breakfast; Sons O'Guns; San Francisco; God's Country and the Woman; Hollywood Boulevard. **1937** Sing While You're Able; The Girl Said No; The Emperor's Candlesticks; Double Wedding; Prescription for Romance. **1938** The Jury's Secret; Honolulu; Mad About Music; Stolen Heaven; Romance on the Run; Algiers; Inside Story; The Great Waltz. **1939** Mr. Moto's Last Warning; Rose of Washington Square; The Man in the Iron Mask; Nurse Edith Cavell. **1940** Yesterday's Heroes. **1941** You're The One; Bachelor Daddy. **1942** Fingers at the Window; Dr. Renault's Secret; Quiet Please—Murder. **1943** Hi Diddle Diddle. **1944** Sensations of 1945. **1945** Bedside Manner; Abbott and Costello in Hollywood. **1946** Little Giant; Rendezvous; The Missing Lady; Man from Rainbow Valley; Sing While You Dance. **1947** The Perils of Pauline.

ROACH, MARGARET

Born: Mar. 15, 1921, Los Angeles, Calif. Died: Nov. 22, 1964, Hollywood, Calif. Stage and screen actress. Daughter of film producer Hal Roach.

Appeared in: **1939** Captain Fury; Fast and Furious. **1940** Turnabout. **1941** Road Show; Niagara Falls.

ROACHE, VIOLA

Born: 1886. Died: May 17, 1961, Hollywood, Calif. (heart attack). Stage and screen actress.

Appeared in: **1950** Harriet Craig. **1951** Royal Wedding; Goodbye, My Fancy.

ROBARDS, JASON, SR.

Born: Dec. 31, 1892, Hillsdale, Mich. Died: Apr. 4, 1963, Sherman Oaks, Calif. (heart attack). Stage and screen actor. Father of actor Jason Robards, Jr.

Appeared in: **1921** The Gilded Lily; The Land of Hope. **1925** Stella Maris. **1926** Footloose Widows; The Cohens and the Kellys; The Third Degree. **1927** Casey Jones; Wild Geese; Jaws of Steel; The Heart of Maryland; Hills of Kentucky; Irish Hearts; Polly of the Movies; Tracked by the Police; White Flannels. **1928** Streets of Shanghai; On Trial; The Death Ship (short); Casey Jones; A Bird in the Hand (short). **1929** Paris; The Flying Marine; Trial Marriage; The Isle of Lost Ships; Some Mother's Boy; The Gamblers. **1930** The Last Dance; Jazz Cinderella; Lightnin'; Sisters; Crazy That Way; Peacock Alley; Abraham Lincoln; Trifles (short). **1931** Charlie Chan Carries On; Subway Express; Salvation Nell; Full of Notions; Caught Plastered; Law of the Tongs; Ex-Bad Boy. **1932** Discarded Lovers; Unholy Love; White Eagle; Klondike; Docks of San Francisco; Pride of the Legion; Slightly Married. **1933** Strange Alibi; Corruption; Devil's Mate; Dance Hall Hostess; Ship of Wanted Men; Public Stenographer; Carnival Lady; The Way to Love. **1934** Broadway Bill; One Exciting Adventure; The President Vanishes; The Crimson Romance; Take the Stand; Woman Unafraid; All of Me; Woman Condemned; Super Snooper (short). **1935** The Miracle Rider (serial); Ladies Crave Excitement; The Crusades; Burn 'Em Up Barnes (serial and feature). **1936** The White Legion. **1937** Sweetheart of the Navy; Damaged Lives. **1938** Little Tough Guy; The Clipped Wings; Flight to Fame; Mystery Plane; Cipher Bureau. **1939** Sky Pirate; Stunt Pilot; The Mad Empress; Range War; Danger Flight; I Stole a Million. **1940** The Fatal Hour. **1944** Mlle. Fifi; Bermuda Mystery; The Master Race. **1945** Betrayal from the East; What a Blonde; A Game of Death; Wanderer of the Wasteland; Isle of the Dead; Man Alive; plus the following shorts: What, No Cigarettes?; Let's Go Stepping; It Shouldn't Happen to a Dog. **1946** Bedlam; Ding Dong Williams; The Falcon's Adventure; The Falcon's Alibi; Vacation in Reno; Step by Step; plus the following shorts: I'll Build It Myself; Twin Husbands; I'll Take Milk. **1947** Seven Keys to Baldpate; Under the Tonto Rim; Wild Horse Mesa; Trail Street; Desperate; Thunder Mountain; Riffraff; Do or Diet (short). **1948** Fighting Father Dunne; Guns of Hate; Mr. Blandings Builds His Dream House; Western Heritage; Son of God's Country; Return of the Bad Men. **1949** Rimfire; Post Office Investigator; Alaska Patrol; Impact; Feudin' Rhythm; Horseman of the Sierras; Riders of the Whistling Pines; South of Death Valley. **1951** The Second Woman. **1961** Wild in the Country.

ROBBINS, ARCHIE

Born: 1913. Died: Sept. 26, 1975, New York, N.Y. Vaudeville, stage and screen actor.

Appeared in: **1935** His Night Out. **1936** The Leavenworth Case; Republic. **1944** Winged Victory (stage and film versions). **1954** Roogie's Bump.

ROBBINS, MARCUS B.

Born: 1868. Died: Apr. 7, 1931, Hollywood, Calif. Screen actor and screenwriter.

Appeared in: **1920** Alias Jimmy Valentine. **1922** The Gray Dawn; The Girl Who Ran Wild. **1923** The Marriage Market; The Scarlet Car.

ROBBINS, RICHARD

Born: 1919, Boston, Mass. Died: Oct. 23, 1969, New York, N.Y. (heart attack). Screen, stage and television actor.

Appeared in: **1956** The Wrong Man.

ROBER, RICHARD

Born: May 14, 1906, Rochester, N.Y. Died: May 26, 1952, Santa Monica, Calif. (auto accident). Screen, stage and television actor.

Appeared in: **1947** Call Northside 777 (film debut). **1948** April Showers; Smart Girls Don't Talk; Embraceable You; Larceny. **1949** Illegal Entry; Any Number Can Play; Backfire; I Married a Communist; Port of New York; Task Force. **1950** Thelma Jordan; Deported; Dial 1119; Sierra; The Woman on Pier 13; There's a Girl in My Heart. **1951** The Well; Father's Little Dividend; Passage West; The Tall Target; Watch the Birdie; Man in the Saddle. **1952** The Devil Makes Three; O. Henry's Full House; Outlaw Woman; The Rose Bowl Story; The Savage; Kid Monk Baroni. **1957** Jet Pilot.

ROBERSON, LOU

Born: 1921. Died: Nov. 21, 1966, Hollywood, Calif. Screen actor and stuntman.

ROBERTI, LYDA

Born: 1909, Warsaw, Poland. Died: Mar. 12, 1938, Los Angeles, Calif. (heart ailment). Stage and screen actress.

Appeared in: **1932** Dancers in the Dark; The Kid from Spain; Million Dollar Legs. **1933** Torch Singer; Three-Cornered Moon. **1934** College Rhythm. **1935** George White's 1935 Scandals; The Big Broadcast of 1936. **1937** Nobody's Baby; Pick a Star; Wide Open Faces.

ROBERTS, A. CLEDGE

Born: 1905. Died: June 14, 1957, New York, N.Y. Screen, stage, radio, television actor, film, stage director, film and stage producer.

ROBERTS, ALBERT G.

Born: 1902. Died: May 30, 1941, North Hollywood, Calif. (suicide—gun). Screen actor and cameraman. Married to actress Peggy Shannon (dec. 1941).

ROBERTS, DICK

Born: 1897. Died: Nov. 1, 1966, North Hollywood, Calif. Screen, radio actor and banjoist.

Appeared in: **1936** Banjo on My Knee.

ROBERTS, EDITH (Edith Josephine Roberts)

Born: 1899, New York, N.Y. Died: Aug. 20, 1935, Los Angeles, Calif. Screen, stage and vaudeville actress.

Appeared in: **1917** A Hasty Hazing; Down Went the Key; A Million in Sight; A Bundle of Trouble; Some Specimens; When the Cat's Away; Shot in the West; Mixed Matrimony; The Lost Appetite; Tell Morgan's Girl; What a Clue Will Do; The Home Wreckers; Moving Day; To Be or Not to Be Remarried; Pete the Prowler; The War Bridegroom; Under the Bed; Follow the Tracks; Jilted in Jail; A Burglar by Request; Hot Applications; Treat 'Em Rough; A Macaroni Sleuth; One Thousand Miles an Hour; Practice What You Preach; The Rogue's Nest; Little Moccasins; Her City Beau. **1918** The Vamp Cure; The Love Swindle. **1919** Beans; A Taste of Life; Bill Henry. **1920** The Adorable Savage. **1921** The Fire Cat; The Unknown Wife; White Youth; Thunder Island; Opened Shutters; Luring Lips; In Society. **1922** Saturday Night; Flesh and Blood; A Front Page Story; Pawned; The Son of the Wolf; Thorns and Orange Blossoms. **1923** The Sunshine Trail; Big Brother; Backbone; The Dangerous Age. **1924** An Age of Innocence; The Bowery Bishop; Roaring Rails; Roulette; Thy Name Is Woman; $20 a Week. **1925** Heir-Looms; New Champion; Shattered Lives; Speed Mad; Three Keys; Wasted Lives; Seven Keys to Baldpate; On Thin Ice. **1926** There You Are; The Mystery Club; The Jazz Girl; The Road to Broadway; Shameful Behavior?; The Taxi Mystery. **1928** Man from Headquarters. **1929** The Phantom of the North; The Wagon Master.

ROBERTS, FLORENCE

Born: 1871. Died: July 17, 1927, Hollywood, Calif. Screen actress. Married to screen actor Frederick Vogeding (dec. 1942).

ROBERTS, FLORENCE

Born: Mar. 16, 1861, Frederick, Md. Died: June 6, 1940, Hollywood, Calif. Stage and screen actress. Married to stage actor Walter Gale (dec.). Appeared in "Jones Family" series, 1936-40.

Appeared in: **1912** Sapho. **1925** The Best People. **1930** Grandma's Girl (short); Eyes of the World; Soup to Nuts. **1931** Bachelor Apartment; Fanny Foley Herself; Too Many Cooks; Kept Husband; Everything's Rosie. **1932** Make Me a Star; All American; Westward Passage. **1933** Officer 13; Daring Daughters; Dangerously Yours; Melody Cruise; Torch Singer; Hoopla; Ever In My Heart. **1934** The Cracked Iceman (short); Four Parts (short); Babes in Toyland; Miss Fane's Baby Is Stolen. **1935** Sons of Steel; Les Miserables; The Nut Farm; Rocky Mountain Mystery; Accent on Youth; Harmony Lane; Public Opinion; Your Uncle Dudley. **1936** The Next Time We Love; Nobody's Fool; Every Saturday Night; Educating Father; Back to Nature. **1937** Borrowing Trouble; Nobody's Baby; The Life of Emile Zola; Off to the Races; Big Business; Hot Water. **1938** Love on a Budget; The Storm; A Trip to Paris; Safety in Numbers; Down on the Farm; Personal Secretary. **1939** Everybody's Baby; Jones Family in the Grand Canyon; Jones Family in Hollywood; Too Busy to Work; Quick Millions. **1940** On Their Own; Young as You Feel.

ROBERTS, GEORGE

Born: 1845, England. Died: Apr. 25, 1930, London, England. Stage, screen actor and playwright.

Appeared in: **1925** William Tell.

ROBERTS, GLEN (Leonard Freeman)

Born: 1921. Died: Jan. 20, 1974, Palo Alto, Calif. (following heart surgery). Television, film producer and screen actor.

Appeared in: **1953** Girls in the Night.

ROBERTS, LEONA

Born: 1880. Died: Jan. 30, 1954, Santa Monica, Calif. Screen actress.

Appeared in: **1937** Border Cafe; There Goes the Groom. **1938** Of Human Hearts; Bringing up Baby; Condemned Women; This Marriage Business; Having a Wonderful Time; The Affair of Annabel; Crime Ring; Kentucky; I Stand Accused. **1939** Persons in Hiding; They Made Her a Spy; Bachelor Mother; The Escape; Swanee River; Gone with the Wind. **1940** Sued for Libel; Thou Shalt Not Kill; Queen of the Mob; The Blue Bird; Abe Lincoln in Illinois; Flight Angels; Ski Patrol; Gangs of Chicago; Golden Gloves; Comin' 'Round the Mountain; Wildcat Bus; Blondie Plays Cupid. **1946** The Madonna's Secret. **1947** Boomerang.

ROBERTS, MERRILL

Born: 1885. Died: Dec. 2, 1940, Hollywood, Calif. Screen actor.

ROBERTS, NANCY (Annette Finlay)

Born: 1892. Died: June 25, 1962, London, England. Screen, stage and television actress.

Appeared in: **1915** The Devil's Profession. **1938** Prison Without Bars (US 1939). **1947** Black Narcissus.

ROBERTS, RALPH ARTHUR

Born: 1884, Meerane, Germany. Died: 1940, Berlin, Germany. Screen actor, film director and screenwriter.

Appeared in: **1929** The Headwaiter.

ROBERTS, ROY

Born: 1900. Died: May 28, 1975, Los Angeles, Calif. Screen, stage and television actor.

Appeared in: **1943** Guadalcanal Diary. **1944** The Sullivans; Tampico; Roger Touhy; Gangster; Wilson. **1945** Within These Walls; Circumstantial Evidence; The Caribbean Mystery; A Bell for Adano; Sunset in Eldorado; Colonel Effingham's Raid. **1946** Behind Green Lights; Smoky; It Shouldn't Happen To a Dog; My Darling Clementine; Johnny Comes Flying Home; Strange Triangle. **1947** The Shocking Miss Pilgrim; The Brasher Doubloon; The Foxes of Harrow; Nightmare Alley; Gentleman's Agreement; Daisy Kenyon; Captain from Castile. **1948** Force of Evil; Joan of Arc; Fury at Furnace Creek; The Gay Intruders; He Walked by Night; No Minor Vices; Chicken Every Sunday. **1949** The Reckless Moment; Calamity Jane and Sam Bass; Miss Grant Takes Richmond; Flaming Fury; A Kiss for Corliss. **1950** The Killer That Stalked New York; Chain Lightning; Borderline; Stage to Tucson; Wyoming Mail; The Palomino; Bodyhold; The Second Face. **1951** The Enforcer; I Was a Communist for the FBI; Santa Fe; Fighting Coast Guard; The Man With a Cloak; The Cimarron Kid; The Tanks Are Coming. **1952** The Big Trees; Stars and Stripes Forever; Cripple Creek; Hoodlum Empire; The Man Behind the Gun; Skirts Ahoy. **1953** The Glory Brigade; House of Wax; Lone Hand; Second Chance; Sea of Lost Ships; Tumbleweed; San Antone. **1954** The Outlaw Stallion; Dawn at Socorro; They Rode West. **1955** Big House, USA; The Last Command; Wyoming Renegades; I Cover the Underworld. **1956** The First Texan; The Boss; The King and Four Queens; Yaqui Drums; The White Squaw. **1962** The Chapman Report; The Underwater City. **1963** It's a Mad, Mad, Mad, Mad World. **1965** I'll Take Sweden; Those Calloways. **1967** Hotel; Tammy and the Millionaire. **1969** This Savage Land; Some Kind of a Nut.

ROBERTS, SARA JANE

Born: 1924. Died: Aug. 19, 1968, Hollywood, Calif. Screen actress. Appeared in "Our Gang" comedies.

ROBERTS, STEPHEN

Born: Nov. 23, 1895, Summerville, Va. Died: July 17, 1936, Beverly Hills, Calif. (heart attack). Screen, radio actor, stuntman and film director. Entered films as a stuntman after W.W.I; was in early air films and later became an actor, then a director.

ROBERTS, THAYER

Born: 1903. Died: May 1968, Hollywood, Calif. Screen, stage and vaudeville actor.

Appeared in: **1947** Chinese Ring. **1951** Sky High.

ROBERTS, THEODORE

Born: 1861, San Francisco, Calif. Died: Dec. 14, 1928, Los Angeles, Calif. (uremic poisoning). Stage and screen actor. Married to actress Florence Smythe (dec. 1925).

Appeared in: **1914** Where the Trail Divides. **1915** The Girl of the Golden West; The Wild Goose Chase. **1916** The Sowers; Pudd'n Head Wilson; The Trail of the Lonesome Pine; Honor Thy Name. **1918** M'Liss; We Can't Have Everything; The Source; Such a Little Pirate; The Squaw Man; War Relief (informational services film). **1919** Don't Change Your Husband; Male and Female; Fire of Faith; The Woman Thou Gavest Me; You're Fired; Secret Service; The Lottery Man; Hawthorne of the U.S.A.; The Roaring Road; Everywoman. **1920** Something to Think About; Judy of Rogue's Harbor; Double Speed. **1921** The Affairs of Anatol; Exit the Vamp; Forbidden Fruit; The Love Special; Miss Lulu Bett; Too Much Speed; Sham. **1922** Across the Continent; If You Believe It, It's So; The Man Who Saw Tomorrow; Night Life in Hollywood; The Old Homestead; Our Leading Citizen; Saturday Night; Hail the Woman. **1923** Racing Hearts; Stephen Steps Out; To the Ladies; Prodigal Daughters; The Ten Commandments; Grumpy. **1925** Forty Winks; Locked Doors. **1926** Cat's Pajamas. **1928** The Masks of the Devil. **1929** Noisy Neighbors; Ned McCobb's Daughter.

ROBERTSHAW, JERROLD

Born: 1866, England. Died: 1941. Stage and screen actor.

Appeared in: **1916** The Girl Who Didn't Care. **1917** Dombey and Son. **1920** Build Thy House. **1921** Beside the Bonnie Briar Bush (aka The Bonnie Briar Bush—US). **1922** A Master of Craft. **1923** Don Quixote; Guy Fawkes; A Royal Divorce; Through Fire and Water; The Wandering Jew. **1924** The Sins Ye Do. **1925** The Apache; She. **1927** The Blind Ship; Downhill (aka When Boys Leave Home—US 1928); Huntingtower; My Lord the Chauffeur. **1927** On With the Dance Series. **1928** Bolibar (aka The Marquis of Bolibar); Palais de Danse; Tommy Atkins; You Know What Sailors Are; Glorious Youth (aka Eileen of the Trees). **1929** Power over Men; The Inseparables; Kitty. **1931** The Shadow Between. **1933** The Veteran of Waterloo. **1940** The Great Conway.

ROBERTSON, IMOGENE. *See* MARY NOLAN

ROBERTSON, JAMES "SCOTTY"

Born: 1859. Died: Nov. 13, 1936, Los Angeles, Calif. Screen actor.

ROBERTSON, JEAN

Born: 1894, Australia. Died: Aug. 1967, Sydney, Australia. Stage and screen actress.

Appeared in: **1922** Flesh and Spirit.

ROBERTSON, JOHN S.

Born: June 14, 1878, Ontario, Canada. Died: Nov. 7, 1964, Escondido, Calif. Screen, stage actor and film director.

Appeared in: **1916** An Enemy to the King; The Conflict; His Wife's Good Name; The Combat; Her Right to Live.

ROBERTSON, MARY. *See* MARY NOLAN

ROBERTSON, ORIE O.

Born: 1881. Died: Apr. 14, 1964, Hollywood, Calif. (cancer). Screen actor and stuntman.

Appeared in: **1926** Bucking the Truth.

ROBERTSON, STUART

Born: Mar. 5, 1901, London, England. Died: Dec. 25, 1958, Elstree, Herts, England. Screen, stage, radio actor and singer. Brother of actress Anna Neagle. Married to singer Alice Moxon.

Appeared in: **1933** Bitter Sweet. **1934** The Queen's Affaire (aka Runaway Queen—US 1935). **1935** Peg of Old Drury (US 1936). **1936** As You Like It; Millions; Splinters in the Air; The Gang Show. **1938** Sixty Glorious Years (aka Queen of Destiny—US 1940). **1940** Irene; River's End; No, No, Nanette. **1941** A Yank in the R.A.F.; Confirm or Deny; On the Sunny Side. **1942** This above All; The Black Swan. **1943** Forever and a Day. **1945** Meet the Navy (Canadian Naval film).

ROBERTSON, WILLARD

Born: Jan. 1, 1886, Runnels, Tex. Died: Apr. 5, 1948. Screen, stage actor, author, stage director, playwright and attorney.

Appeared in: **1924** Daughters of the Night. **1930** Last of the Duanes. **1931** Skippy; The Cisco Kid; The Ruling Voice; Fair Warning; Sooky; Upper Underworld; Silence; Murder by the Clock; Graft; Shanghai Love. **1932** The Gay Caballero; The Broken Wing; The Famous Ferguson Case; Behind the Mask; So Big; The Strange Love of Molly Louvain; Doctor X; Guilty as Hell; Virtue; Wild Girl; Call Her Savage; Central Park; Texas Bad Man; Steady Company; Rider of Death Valley; Tom Brown of Culver; If I Had a Million; I Am a Fugitive from a Chain Gang. **1933** The Mad Game; East of 5th Avenue; Lady Killer; Wild Boys of the Road; The World Changes; Tugboat Annie; Another Language; The Whirlpool; Roman Scandals; Central

Airport; Trick for Trick; Destination Unknown; Supernatural; Heroes for Sale. **1934** I'll Tell the World; Have a Heart; Death on the Diamond; Housewife; Gambling Lady; Two Alone; Heat Lightning; Upperworld; Here Comes the Navy; Let's Talk It Over; One Is Guilty; Operator 13; Murder in the Private Car; Dark Hazard; Whirlpool. **1935** Oil for the Lamps of China; Biography of a Bachelor Girl; Dante's Inferno; The Secret Bride; Laddie; Mills of the Gods; O'Shaughnessey's Boy; Straight From the Heart; His Night Out; Black Fury; Million Dollar Baby; Forced Landing; Virginia Judge. **1936** Transient Lady; Dangerous Waters; The Three Godfathers; The Gorgeous Hussy; I Married a Doctor; The First Baby; The Last of the Mohicans; The Man Who Lived Twice; Winterset; That Girl From Paris; Wanted—Jane Turner. **1937** Larceny on the Air; Park Avenue Logger; John Meade's Woman; Exclusive; This Is My Affair; Hot Water; The Go Getter; Roaring Timber. **1938** Gangs of New York; Island In the Sky; You and Me; Men With Wings; Kentucky; Torchy Gets Her Man. **1939** Jesse James; Heritage of the Desert; My Son Is a Criminal; Each Dawn I Die; Range War; Two Bright Boys; Main Street Larceny; Cat and the Canary. **1940** My Little Chickadee; Remember the Night; Castle on the Hudson; Lucky Cisco Kid; Brigham Young—Frontiersman; North West Mounted Police. **1941** The Monster and the Girl; Men of Timberland; Night of January 16th; Texas; I Wanted Wings. **1942** Juke Girl. **1943** Air Force; Background to Danger; No Time for Love. **1944** Nine Girls. **1945** Along Came Jones. **1946** To Each His Own; The Virginian; Perilous Holiday; Renegades; Gallant Journey. **1947** My Favorite Brunette; Deep Valley. **1948** Sitting Pretty; Fury at Furnace Creek.

ROBEY, SIR GEORGE (George Edward Wade)

Born: Sept. 20, 1869, London, England. Died: Nov. 29, 1954, Saltdean, Sussex, England. Screen, stage, radio, television actor, author and screenwriter. Married to stage manager Blanche Littler. Divorced from Ethel Haydon.

Appeared in: **1913** Good Queen Bess; And Very Nice, Too. **1914** George Robey Turns Anarchist. **1916** £ 66.13.9¾ for Every Man, Woman and Child; Blood Tells; Or, the Anti-Frivolity League. **1917** Doing His Bit. **1918** George Robey's Day Off. **1923** The Rest Cure; One Arabian Night (aka Widow Twan-Kee); Don Quixote. **1924** The Prehistoric Man. **1928** Safety First (short); The Barrister (short). **1929** The Bride; Mrs. Mephistopheles. **1932** The Temperance Fete; Marry Me. **1933** Don Quixote (and 1923 version). **1934** Chu Chin Chow. **1935** Birds of a Feather; Royal Cavalcade (aka Regal Cavalcade—US). **1936** Calling the Tune; Southern Roses; Men of Yesterday. **1939** A Girl Must Live (US 1941). **1942** Salute John Citizen. **1943** Variety Jubilee; They Met in the Dark (US 1945). **1945** Henry V (US 1946); Waltz Time. **1946** The Trojan Brothers. **1952** The Pickwick Papers (US 1953). **1953** Ali Baba Nights. **1958** Henry V (rerelease of 1945 film).

ROBINS, EDWARD H.

Born: Oct. 15, 1880, Shamokin, Pa. Died: July 27, 1955, Paramus, N.J. Screen actor.

Appeared in: **1937** Meet the Missus; Music for Madame; Exclusive. **1938** Love on Toast.

ROBINSON, BILL "BOJANGLES"

Born: May 25, 1878, Richmond, Va. Died: Nov. 25, 1949, N.Y. (heart ailment). Black screen, stage, vaudeville actor and dancer.

Appeared in: **1930** Dixiana. **1935** The Little Colonel; In Old Kentucky; Hooray for Love; The Big Broadcast of 1936; The Littlest Rebel; Curly Top. **1936** Dimples. **1937** One Mile from Heaven. **1938** Rebecca of Sunnybrook Farm; Road Demon; Just around the Corner; Up the River; Hot Mikado; Cotton Club Revue. **1943** Stormy Weather.

ROBINSON, DEWEY

Born: 1898, New Haven, Conn. Died: Dec. 11, 1950, Las Vegas, Nev. (heart attack). Stage and screen actor.

Appeared in: **1931** Enemies of the Law. **1932** The Woman from Monte Carlo; Cheaters at Play; Law and Order; The Painted Woman; The Big Broadcast; Hat Check Girl; Blonde Venus; Six Hours to Live; Scarlet Dawn; Women Won't Tell; When Paris Sleeps; Captain's Wife. **1933** She Done Him Wrong; A Lady's Profession; Her Forgotten Past; Diplomaniacs; Soldiers of the Storm; Laughing at Life; Notorious but Nice; Murder on the Campus. **1934** Shadows of Sing Sing; The Big Shakedown; Countess of Monte Cristo; Behold My Wife. **1935** Pursuit; A Midsummer Night's Dream; His Night Out; Too Young to Kill; plus the following shorts: Goin' to Town; Palooka from Paducah; One Run Elmer. **1936** Dangerous Waters; The Return of Jimmy Valentine; All American Chump; Missing Girls; Florida Special; Poppy; Mummy's Boys. **1937** On the Avenue; The Slave Ship; Super Sleuth; Marry the Girl; The Toast of New York; New Faces of 1937; Mama Runs Wild. **1938** Broadway Musketeers; Ride a Crooked Mile; Army Girl. **1939** Forged Passport; Navy Secrets. **1940** The Blue Bird; Diamond Frontier; The Great McGinty; I Can't Give You Anything but Love, Baby; Tin Pan Alley. **1941** The Big Store; Two Yanks in Trinidad; You're the One; Sing for Your Supper. **1942** Rubber Racketeers; Tennessee Johnson; The Palm Beach Story; The Big Street; Blondie for Victory; Jail House Blues; Isle of Missing Men; 'Neath Brooklyn Bridge. **1943** Casablanca; The Ghost Ship; The Woman of the Town. **1944** Wilson; Mrs. Parkington; Alaska; When Strangers Marry; Timber Queen; The Chinese Cat;

Trocadero. **1945** Hollywood and Vine; There Goes Kelly; Fashion Model; Dillinger; The Lady Confesses; Black Market Babies; Stairway to Light (short); Pardon My Past. **1946** Behind the Mask; The Missing Lady. **1947** Mr. Hex; I Wonder Who's Kissing Her Now; The Wistful Widow of Wagon Gap; Stairway to Light (short); The Gangster. **1948** Angels' Alley; Fighting Mad; Let's Live Again; The Checkered Coat. **1949** The Beautiful Blonde from Bashful Bend; Hellfire; Tough Assignment; My Friend Irma. **1950** Buccaneer's Girl; At War with the Army.

ROBINSON, EDWARD G. (Emmanuel Goldenberg)

Born: Dec. 12, 1893, Bucharest, Roumania. Died: Jan. 26, 1973, Hollywood, Calif. (cancer). Screen, stage, television and vaudeville actor. Married to Jane Bodenheimer. Divorced from actress Gladys Lloyd (dec. 1971). Father of actor Edward G. Robinson, Jr. (dec. 1974). Received 1973 Special Academy Award posthumously for lifetime contributions to motion picture arts.

Appeared in: **1923** Bright Shawl. **1929** The Hole in the Wall. **1930** Night Ride; Widow from Chicago; A Lady to Love; Outside the Law; East is West; Little Caesar. **1931** Five Star Final; Smart Money. **1932** Two Seconds; Tiger Shark; Silver Dollar; The Hatchet Man; The Stolen Jools (short—aka The Slippery Pearls). **1933** The Little Giant; I Loved a Woman. **1934** Dark Hazard; The Man with Two Faces. **1935** Barbary Coast; The Whole Town's Talking. **1936** Bullets or Ballots. **1937** Thunder in the City; Kid Galahad; The Last Gangster; Day at Santa Anita (short). **1938** A Slight Case of Murder; The Amazing Dr. Clitterhouse; I Am the Law. **1939** Confessions of a Nazi Spy; Blackmail. **1940** They Knew What They Wanted; The Story of Dr. Ehrlich's Magic Bullet; Brother Orchid; A Dispatch from Reuters. **1941** The Sea Wolf; Manpower; Unholy Partners. **1942** Larceny; Tales of Manhattan. **1943** Destroyer; Flesh and Fantasy. **1944** Tampico; Double Indemnity; Mr. Winkle Goes to War; The Woman in the Window. **1945** Our Vines Have Tender Grapes; Scarlet Street; Journey Together (US 1946). **1946** The Stranger. **1947** The Red House. **1948** All My Sons; Key Largo; Night Has a Thousand Eyes. **1949** House of Strangers; It's a Great Feeling. **1950** My Daughter Joy (Operation X—US 1951). **1952** Actors and Sin. **1953** Vice Squad; Big Leaguer; The Glass Web. **1954** Black Tuesday. **1955** The Violent Men; Tight Spot; A Bullet for Joey; Illegal; Hell on Frisco Bay. **1956** Nightmare; The Ten Commandments. **1959** A Hole in the Head. **1960** Pepe; Seven Thieves. **1962** My Geisha; Two Weeks in Another Town; Sammy Going South (aka A Boy Ten Feet Tall—US 1965). **1963** The Prize. **1964** Good Neighbor Sam; Robin and the 7 Hoods; Cheyenne Autumn; The Outrage. **1965** The Cincinnati Kid. **1967** Die Blonde vom Peking (Peking Blonde—US 1969). **1968** The Biggest Bundle of Them All; Never a Dull Moment; Grand Slam; Operation St. Peter; Mad Checkmate. **1969** McKenna's Gold. **1970** Song of Norway. **1973** Soylent Green.

ROBINSON, EDWARD G., JR.

Born: 1934. Died: Feb. 26, 1974, West Hollywood, Calif. (natural causes). Screen and television actor. Son of actor Edward G. Robinson (dec. 1973) and actress Gladys Lloyd (dec. 1971). Divorced from actresses Frances Robinson and Elaine M. Conte.

Appeared in: **1956** Screaming Eagles. **1958** Tank Battalion. **1959** Some Like It Hot.

ROBINSON, FORREST

Born: 1859. Died: Jan. 1924, Los Angeles, Calif. Screen and stage actor.

Appeared in: **1921** Tol'able David. **1922** Tess of the Storm Country. **1923** Adam's Rib; Ashes of Vengeance; The Meanest Man in the World; Souls for Sale. **1924** Good Bad Boy; When a Man's a Man.

ROBINSON, FRANCES (Marion Frances Ladd)

Born: Apr. 26, 1916, Fort Wadsworth, N.Y. Died: Aug. 15, 1971, Hollywood, Calif. (heart attack). Screen actress.

Appeared in: **1922** Orphans of the Storm. **1937** Forbidden Valley; Tim Tyler's Luck (serial). **1938** A Letter of Introduction; Secrets of a Nurse; Exposed; The Last Warning; His Exciting Night; Service de Luxe. **1939** Risky Business; Tower of London; The Family Next Door. **1940** Riders of Pasco Basin; So You Won't Talk; Glamour for Sale; The Lone Wolf Keeps a Date; The Invisible Man Returns. **1941** Outlaws of the Panhandle; Smilin' Through; Dr. Jekyll and Mr. Hyde. **1946** The Missing Lady. **1947** Suddenly It's Spring. **1949** Backfire (US 1950—aka Somewhere in the City). **1964** Bedtime Story; Kitten with a Whip; The Lively Set. **1967** The Happiest Millionaire.

ROBINSON, GERTRUDE R.

Born: 1891. Died: Mar. 19, 1962, Hollywood, Calif. Screen actress. Divorced from actor James Kirkwood (dec. 1963). Entered films with Biograph.

Appeared in: **1909** Pippa Passes; The Open Gate; The Death Disc. **1910** Gold Is Not All; The Purgation; What the Daisy Said; A Summer Idyll; Examination Day at School. **1913** Judith of Bethulia. **1922** Welcome to Our City. **1925** On Thin Ice.

ROBINSON, JACKIE (Jack Roosevelt Robinson)

Born: Jan. 31, 1919, Cairo, Ga. Died: Oct. 24, 1972, Stamford, Conn. (heart disease). Black professional baseball player, athlete and screen actor.

Appeared in: **1950** The Jackie Robinson Story.

ROBINSON, RUTH "RUTHIE"

Born: 1888. Died: Mar. 17, 1966. Screen actress.

Appeared in: **1911** A Narrow Escape; The Moonshiners. **1912** Wanted—A Wife. **1928** Scarlet Youth; Trial Marriage. **1935** The Story of Louis Pasteur. **1936** The Walking Dead; Sins of Man; China Clipper; The Case of the Velvet Claws. **1937** Midnight Madonna; Outcast; On Such a Night; Lost Horizon. **1938** The Lone Wolf in Paris; Miracle Money (short). **1939** Kansas Terrors; Weather Wizards (short). **1940** Knute Rockne—All American; Covered Wagon Days. **1941** Henry Aldrich for President; Whistling in the Dark; Across the Sierras; One Foot in Heaven; Down Mexico Way; The Corsican Brothers. **1942** Tennessee Johnson. **1943** The Moon is Down; Chatterbox; Shantytown. **1944** The Hairy Ape. **1945** Delightfully Dangerous; Kid Sister. **1946** The Spider Woman Strikes Back. **1947** The Guilty; Stepchild; That Hagen Girl. **1949** Trapped; Impact. **1956** The Search for Bridey Murphy. **1963** Forty Pounds of Trouble; The Miracle of Santa's White Reindeer.

ROBINSON, "SPIKE"

Born: 1884. Died: July 13, 1942, Maywood, Calif. (heart attack). Screen actor.

Appeared in: **1920** Daredevil Jack (serial). **1921** The Foolish Age. **1923** Boston Blackie. **1925** The Fear Fighter.

ROBLES, RICHARD

Born: 1902. Died: Apr. 20, 1940, Los Angeles, Calif. Screen actor.

Appeared in: **1939** Union Pacific.

ROBLES, RUDY

Born: Apr. 28, 1910, Manila, Philippine Islands. Died: Aug. 1970, Manila, Philippine Islands. Stage and screen actor.

Appeared in: **1939** The Real Glory. **1940** South of Pago Pago. **1941** Song of the Islands; Blue, White and Perfect; Blonde from Singapore; The Adventures of Martin Eden. **1942** Submarine Raider; Across the Pacific; Wake Island. **1946** Nocturne. **1947** Singapore; The Son of Rusty. **1949** Rusty Saves a Life; Omoo, Omoo; Flaxy Martin. **1952** Okinawa. **1953** White Goddess.

ROBSON, ANDREW

Born: 1867, Hamilton, Ontario, Canada. Died: Apr. 26, 1921, Los Angeles, Calif. (heart affliction). Screen and stage actor.

Appeared in: **1919** Upstairs and Down. **1920** Alarm Clock Andy; Scratch My Back; Cupid, the Cowpuncher. **1921** All's Fair in Love; Black Roses; Mother O'Mine; One a Minute.

ROBSON, JUNE

Born: 1922. Died: Mar. 16, 1972, Hollywood, Calif. Screen actress.

ROBSON, MAY (Mary Robison)

Born: Apr. 19, 1858, Melbourne, Australia. Miss Robson had her date of birth recorded on casting director's records as 1864. However, at time of her death, birth certificate was found showing she was born in 1858. Died: Oct. 20, 1942, Beverly Hills, Calif. Screen, stage and radio actress.

Appeared in: **1915** How Molly Made Good. **1916** A Night Out. **1919** His Bridal Night; A Broadway Saint; The Lost Battalion. **1926** Pals in Paradise. **1927** The Angel of Broadway; A Harp in Hock; The Rejuvenation of Aunt Mary (stage and film versions); Rubber Tires; King of Kings. **1928** Chicago; The Blue Danube; Turkish Delight. **1931** Mother's Millions (aka The She-Wolf of Wall Street and She-Wolf). **1932** If I Had a Million; Letty Lynton; Two against the World; The Engineer's Daughter; Little Orphan Annie; Red Headed Woman; Strange Interlude. **1933** Men Must Fight; The White Sister; Reunion in Vienna; Dinner at Eight; Beauty for Sale; Broadway to Hollywood; The Solitaire Man; Dancing Lady; Lady for a Day; One Man's Journey; Alice in Wonderland. **1934** You Can't Buy Everything; Straight Is the Way; Lady by Choice. **1935** Vanessa, Her Love Story; Reckless; Age of Indiscretion; Anna Karenina; Grand Old Girl; Strangers All; Mills of the Gods; Three Kids and a Queen (aka The Baxter Millions). **1936** Wife vs. Secretary; The Captain's Kid; Rainbow on the River. **1937** Woman in Distress; A Star Is Born; Rhythm of the River; The Perfect Specimen; Top of the Town. **1938** The Adventures of Tom Sawyer; Bringing up Baby; The Texans; Four Daughters. **1939** They Made Me a Criminal; Yes, My Darling Daughter; That's Right—You're Wrong; Daughters Courageous; The Kid from Kokomo (aka Orphan of the Ring); Four Wives; Nurse Edith Cavell. **1940** Irene; Granny Get Your Gun. **1941** Four Mothers; Million Dollar Baby; Playmates; Texas Rangers Ride Again. **1942** Joan of Paris.

ROBSON, PHILIP

Born: Edinburgh, Scotland. Died: May 6, 1919, New York, N.Y. Stage and screen actor.

Appeared in: **1916** The Conquest of Canaan. **1917** Life's Whirlpool.

ROBYN, GAY

Born: 1912. Died: July 25, 1942, Hollywood, Calif. Screen actress and dancer.

ROBYNS, WILLIAM

Born: 1855. Died: Jan. 22, 1936, Verdugo Hills, Calif. Stage and screen actor.

Appeared in: **1921** Get-Rich-Quick Wallingford. **1923** The Fair Cheat. **1932** The Expert; Hell Fire Austin. **1934** Elmer and Elsie.

ROCCARDI, ALBERT

Born: Paris, France, 1864. Died: May 14, 1934. Screen, stage actor and pantomimist.

Appeared in: **1914** The New Secretary; Buddy's First Call; Mr. Barnes of New York; Wife Wanted; The New Stenographers. **1921** The Inside of the Cup; The Passionate Pilgrim; The Rider of the King Log. **1922** Destiny's Isle; Why Not Marry?; A Pasteboard Crown. **1924** Galloping Hoofs (serial). **1925** The Street of Forgotten Men. **1926** The Belle of Broadway; Fools of Fashion. **1927** Melting Millions (serial). **1928** Partners in Crime. **1929** The Love Parade; Romance of the Rio Grande. **1930** Just Like Heaven.

ROCHA, MIGUEL F.

Born: Argentina. Died: Mar. 6, 1961, Buenos Aires, Argentina. Stage and screen actor.

ROCHE, FRANKLYN D. "FRANK"

Born: 1904. Died: Nov. 20, 1963, Burbank, Calif. Screen and stage actor. Entered films approx. 1930.

Appeared in: **1960** The Prime Time.

ROCHE, JOHN

Born: Feb. 6, 1896, Penn Yan, N.Y. Died: Nov. 10, 1952, Los Angeles, Calif. (stroke). Stage and screen actor.

Appeared in: **1922** The Good Provider. **1923** Bag and Baggage; Lucretia Lombard. **1924** Cornered; Flowing Gold; Her Marriage Vow; K—The Unknown; The Tenth Woman. **1925** Bobbed Hair; The Love Hour; A Lost Lady; A Broadway Butterfly; Kiss Me Again; Marry Me; My Wife and I; Recompense; Scandal Proof. **1926** The Return of Peter Grimm; Don Juan; Her Big Night; The Man Upstairs; Midnight Lovers. **1927** The Truthful Sex; Uncle Tom's Cabin. **1928** Their Hour; Diamond Handcuffs. **1929** Unholy Night; The Dream Melody; The Donovan Affair; The Awful Truth; This Thing Called Love. **1930** Sin Takes a Holiday; Monte Carlo. **1932** Winner Take All; Prosperity; The Cohens and the Kellys in Hollywood. **1933** Beauty for Sale. **1935** Just My Luck. **1946** The Brute Man.

ROCHIN, PAUL

Born: 1889. Died: May 5, 1964, Hollywood, Calif. Screen actor.

ROCK, CHARLES

Born: 1866, Velore, East Indies. Died: July 12, 1919, London, England. Stage and screen actor.

Appeared in: **1913** The House of Temperley. **1914** The Cage; The Black Spot; Clancarty; England's Menace; England Expects; For the Empire (aka For Home and Country—US); Called Back; The King's Minister; Two Little Britons; The Two Columbines; V.C. (aka The Victoria Cross—US 1916); A Christmas Carol; She Stoops to Conquer. **1915** Brother Officers; The King's Outcast (aka His Vindication—US); The Prisoner of Zenda; The Man in the Attic; The Sons of Satan; Whoso Diggeth a Pit; The Third Generation; Jelf's (aka A Man of His Word—US); The Christian; Her Uncle; The Firm of Girdlestone (US 1916); Rupert of Hentzau (US 1916). **1916** You; Esther; The Man Without a Soul (aka I Believe—US 1917); Tatterly; A Fair Imposter; The Morals of Weybury (aka The Hypocrites); Partners at Last; Vice Versa; Some Fish; Beau Brocade; Rescuing an Heiress. **1917** Ultus and the Three-Button Mystery (aka Ultus 6: The Three Button Mystery; Ultus 7). **1918** The Better 'Ole; or, The Romance of Old Bill (aka Carry On—US); A Romany Lass (US 1919); Deception; Big Money. **1919** The Greater Love. **1927** Rilka: or, The Gypsy (reissue of A Romany Lass—1918).

ROCK, WILLIAM T.

Born: 1853. Died: July 27, 1916, Oyster Bay, N.Y. (heart disease). Screen actor and motion picture executive. One of the founders of Vitagraph.

Appeared in: **1912** A Vitagraph Romance.

ROCKWELL, JACK

Died: Nov. 10, 1947. Screen actor.

Appeared in: **1933** The Lone Avenger; Strawberry Roan; The Trail Drive; Gun Justice. **1934** Honor of the Range; In Old Santa Fe; Wheels of Destiny; Smoking Guns. **1935** Lawless Frontier; Justice of the Range; Tumbling Tumbleweeds; Outlawed Guns; Valley of the Wanted Men; Man from Guntown; The Miracle Rider; When a Man Sees Red. **1936** The Lawless Nineties; Heroes of the Range; The Singing Cowboy; Rogue of the Range; Roarin' Guns; The Traitor; Guns and Guitars; Lawless Riders. **1937** Bar Z Badmen; Riders of the Rockies; The Red Robe; Texas Trail; Springtime in the Rockies. **1938** Prairie

Moon; Sunset Trail; Under Western Stars; West of Cheyenne; Law of the Plains; Shine On Harvest Moon; Black Bandit. **1939** Silver on the Sage; The Renegade Trail; Rough Riders' Roundup; Man From Sundown; Days of Jesse James. **1940** Hidden Gold; Stagecoach War; Bullets for Rustlers; Santa Fe Marshall; Cherokee Strip; Pony Post. **1941** Border Vigilantes; Wide Open Town; Secret of the Wasteland; Stick to Your Guns; Twilight On the Trail; The Pinto Kid; Thunder Over the Prairie. **1942** Undercover Man; Tombstone, The Town Too Tough to Die. **1943** Fighting Frontier; Dead Man's Gulch; The Black Hills Express; The Renegade; Wagon Tracks West. **1944** Mystery Man; Forty Thieves; Lumberjack; Gunsmoke Mesa; The Vigilantes Ride; West of the Rio Grande; Trigger Trail. **1945** Flame of the West. **1946** Drifting Along; Frontier Gunlaw; Two–Fisted Stranger; Roaring Rangers; Under Arizona Skies; Cowboy Blues; Gentleman from Texas. **1947** Flashing Guns; Shootin' Irons; Code of the Plains.

ROCKWELL, MARY. *See* MARY ROCKWELL HUMMELL

RODE, WALTER

Died: Feb. 8, 1973. Screen actor.

Appeared in: **1949** Johnny Allegro. **1963** Thirteen Frightened Girls.

RODERICK, LESLIE

Born: 1907. Died: Aug. 16, 1927, Hollywood, Calif. (pneumonia). Screen actress and dancer.

RODGERS, WALTER

Born: 1887. Died: Apr. 24, 1951, Los Angeles, Calif. (following stroke). Screen actor.

Appeared in: **1917** The Fighting Trail (serial); Vengeance and the Woman (serial). **1918** A Fight for Millions (serial). **1919** Smashing Barriers (serial). **1921** Flower of the North; The Secret of the Hills; The Silver Car; The Son of Wallingford; Steelheart. **1922** They Like 'Em Rough. **1925** Rugged Water. **1926** The Flaming Frontier. **1927** The Heart of Maryland; Irish Hearts; Wolf's Clothing.

RODMAN, VICTOR

Born: 1893. Died: June 29, 1965. Screen, television and radio actor. Entered films with Biograph.

Appeared in: **1923** Winter Has Come (short). **1924** Hold Your Breath. **1958** The Long, Hot Summer.

RODNEY, EARLE

Born: 1891. Died: Dec. 16, 1932, Los Angeles, Calif. (pneumonia). Screen, stage, vaudeville actor, screenwriter and film director. Played screen parts with Sennett and Griffith and was a comedy director of Keystone Kop series.

Appeared in: **1915** Crooked to the End. **1916** The Village Vampire (working title The Great Leap); An Oily Scandal. **1917** The Nick of Time Baby; Secrets of a Beauty Parlor. **1920** A Roman Scandal. **1923** Winter Has Came.

RODNEY, JACK

Born: 1916. Died: Feb. 20, 1967, England (rheumatic fever). Screen, stage and television actor.

Appeared in: **1960** The Concrete Jungle (aka The Criminal—US 1962). **1963** The Horse without a Head; The Cracksman. **1964** The Devilship; Pirates.

RODNEY, LYNNE

Died: Sept. 1937 (auto accident). Screen actress and stand-in for actress Grace Moore.

RODRIGUEZ, ESTELITA

Born: July 2, 1915, Guanajay, Cuba. Died: May 12, 1966. Screen, stage, radio actress and night club performer. Divorced from actor Grant Withers (dec. 1959).

Appeared in: **1945** Along the Navajo Trail; Mexicana. **1947** On the Spanish Trail. **1948** The Gay Ranchero; Old Los Angeles. **1949** Susanna Pass; The Golden Stallion. **1950** Belle of Old Mexico; Federal Agent at Large; Sunset in the West; Hit Parade of 1951; California Passage; Twilight in the Sierras. **1951** Cuban Fireball; In Old Amarillo; Havana Rose; Pals of the Golden West. **1952** The Fabulous Senorita; Tropical Heat Wave; South Pacific Trail. **1953** Tropic Zone; Sweethearts on Parade. **1959** Rio Bravo. **1966** Jesse James Meets Frankenstein's Daughter.

RODRIGUEZ, TITO

Born: 1923. Died: Feb. 28, 1973, New York, N.Y. Screen actor, singer and bandleader. Known as "Frank Sinatra of Latin Music."

ROELS, MARCEL

Born: 1893, Belgium. Died: Dec. 27, 1973, Brussels, Belgium. Screen, stage and vaudeville actor. Started career at age 3½.

Appeared in: Un Soir di Joie; Expo, en avant!

ROGERS, CARL D.
Born: 1900. Died: Mar. 1965, Humble, Tex. Child screen actor. Appeared in early "Our Gang" comedies and Keystone comedies.

ROGERS, EUGENE
Born: c. 1867. Died: Mar. 9, 1919, Los Angeles, Calif. (myocarditis and alcoholism). Stage and screen actor.

Appeared in: **1915** Sin on the Sabbath; Silk Hose and High Pressure; Vendetta In a Hospital; Tears and Sunshine. **1916** A September Morning; Phony Teeth and False Friends; Billy's Reformation; Billy's Waterloo; Twenty Minutes at the Fair; False Friends and Fire Alarms; Live Wire and Love Sparks; A Friend, But a Star Boarder; Bill's Narrow Escape; Gambling on the Green; The Jailbirds' Last Flight; The Youngest in the Family; The Scoundrel's Tale. **1917** Stars and Bars; Her Nature Dance.

ROGERS, JOSEPH
Born: 1871. Died: Dec. 29, 1942, Hollywood, Calif. Screen actor.

ROGERS, MILDRED
Born: 1899. Died: Apr. 14, 1973, Hollywood, Calif. Screen actress and singer.

Appeared in: **1932** Fighting Gentlemen; The Forty-Niners. **1935** The Texas Rambler. **1937** The Girl Said No.

ROGERS, RENA
Born: 1901. Died: Feb. 19, 1966, Santa Monica, Calif. Screen and vaudeville actress. Divorced from screenwriter and director Frank Borzage (dec. 1962).

Appeared in: **1915** The Morning After. **1916** Slipping It over on Father; When Papa Died; National Nuts; Nailing on the Lid; Just for a Kid; Bungling Bill's Dream; Bungling Bill's Doctor; His Blowout (aka The Plumber); The Delinquent Bridegrooms; The Iron Mitt; Hired and Fired (aka The Leading Man); A Deep Sea Liar (aka The Landlubbers); Where are My Children?; The Leap; A Mix-Up in Photos; A Mix-Up at Rudolph's. **1917** A Paster Feud; A Vanquished Flirt; The Cricket; An Eight Cylinder Romance.

ROGERS, ROY
Died: Oct. 15, 1967, Calif. Screen, vaudeville and television actor. Do not confuse with cowboy actor Roy Rogers. Married to Olga Alexander, one of the "Alexander Sisters" in vaudeville.

ROGERS, WILL
Born: Nov. 4, 1879, Colagah, U.S. Cherokee Indian Territory. Died: Aug. 15, 1935, near Barrow, Alaska (airplane crash). Screen, vaudeville actor, screenwriter, author and journalist. Father of actor Will Rogers, Jr.

Appeared in: **1918** Laughing Bill Hyde (film debut). **1919** Almost a Husband; Jubilo. **1920** Jes' Call Me Jim; Cupid, the Cowpuncher. **1921** Honest Hutch; Guile of Women; Boys Will Be Boys; An Unwilling Hero; Doubling for Romeo. **1922** A Poor Relation; The Headless Horseman; One Glorious Day. **1923** Hollywood; Fruits of Faith. **1927** Tip Toes; A Texas Steer. **1929** They Had to See Paris. **1930** Happy Days; So This Is London; Lightnin'. **1931** Young as You Feel; A Connecticut Yankee; Ambassador Bill; The Plutocrat. **1932** Business and Pleasure; Down to Earth; Too Busy to Work. **1933** State Fair; Doctor Bull; Mr. Skitch. **1934** Judge Priest; David Harum; Handy Andy; Hollywood on Parade (short). **1935** Life Begins at Forty; The County Chairman; Steamboat 'Round the Bend; In Old Kentucky; Doubting Thomas. **1957** Golden Age of Comedy (documentary).

ROGNAN, JEAN LORRAINE
Born: 1912. Died: Aug. 22, 1969. Screen actress and dancer. Married to actor Rognoni (dec. 1943).

Appeared in: **1938** Generals Without Buttons. **1941** Personal Column. **1942** The Fleet's In.

ROGNONI (Roy Rognan)
Died: Feb. 22, 1943, near Lisbon, Portugal (plane crash). Screen, vaudeville actor and dancer. Married to actress Jean Lorraine Rognan (dec. 1969) with whom he appeared as part of a dancing team called "Lorraine and Rognoni."

Appeared in: **1937** Les Petits. **1938** Generals Without Buttons. **1941** Personal Column. **1942** The Fleet's In.

ROLAND, FREDERICK
Born: 1886. Died: June 2, 1936, Los Angeles, Calif. Stage and screen actor.

Appeared in: **1935** The Rainmakers.

ROLAND, MARION. See MARION ROSS

ROLAND, RUTH
Born: Aug. 26, 1892, San Francisco, Calif. Died: Sept. 22, 1937, Los Angeles, Calif. (cancer). Screen, vaudeville and radio actress. Appeared in "Ruth Roland" series. Maried to actor Ben Bard. Entered films in 1911.

Appeared in: **1911** A Chance Shot. **1912** Ruth Roland, the Kalem Girl; Hypnotic Nell; Ranch Girls on a Rampage. **1913** While Father Telephoned. **1914** Ham, the Piano Mover. **1915** The Red Circle (serial); Comrade John. **1917** The Neglected Wife (serial). **1918** Hands Up; Who Wins? (made in 1916, but released in 1918 retitled Price of Folly). **1919** The Tiger's Trail (serial); The Adventures of Ruth (serial); Love and the Law. **1920** Ruth of the Rockies (serial); What Would You Do? **1921** The Avenging Arrow (serial). **1922** White Eagle (serial); Timber Queen (serial). **1923** Haunted Valley (serial); Ruth of the Range (serial). **1925** Dollar Down; Where the Worst Begins. **1926** The Masked Woman. **1930** Reno. **1936** From Nine to Nine. **1961** Days of Thrills and Laughter (documentary).

ROLDAN, ENRIQUE (Andres Garcia)
Born: 1901, Argentina. Died: Feb. 4, 1954, Buenos Aires, Argentina (accidentally slipped under wheels of train). Stage and screen actor.

Appeared in: **1940** Oro Entre Barro (Gold in Clay)

ROLF, ERIK
Died: May 28, 1957. Screen actor. Divorced from actress Ruth Warwick.

Appeared in: **1942** Atlantic Convoy; Eyes in the Night. **1943** First Comes Courage. **1944** U-Boat Prisoner; None Shall Escape; Secret Command; The Soul of a Monster; She's a Soldier Too; Kansas City Kitty; Strange Affair. **1945** Counter-Attack. **1946** A Close Call for Boston Blackie. **1949** Everybody Does It. **1950** Davy Crockett, Indian Scout.

ROLLAND, JEAN-CLAUDE
Born: 1933. Died: Apr. 1967 (suicide—hanging). Screen, stage and television actor.

ROLLETT, RAYMOND
Born: 1907, England. Died: Dec. 19, 1961, London, England. Stage and screen actor.

Appeared in: **1947** Master of Bankdam (US 1949). **1954** The Angel Who Pawned Her Harp; Men of Sherwood Forest (US 1956). **1957** The Curse of Frankenstein; Blue Murder at St. Trinian's (US 1958).

ROLLIN, GEORGES
Born: France. Died: Mar. 1964, France. Screen actor.

Appeared in: **1939** That They May Live. **1940** Ultimatum. **1943** Hitler's Madmen. **1948** Clandestine; Goupi Mains Rouges (aka It Happened at the Inn—US).

ROLLINS, DAVID
Born: Sept. 2, 1908, Kansas City, Mo. Died: Nov. 10, 1952. Screen actor.

Appeared in: **1927** Win That Girl; High School Hero. **1928** Thanks for the Buggy Ride; The Air Circus; Prep and Pep; Riley the Cop. **1929** Fox Movietone Follies of 1929; Love, Live and Laugh; The Black Watch; Why Leave Home? **1930** Happy Days; The Big Trail. **1931** Young Sinners; Mama Loves Papa (short); The Kickoff (short); Girls Demand Excitement; Morals for Women. **1932** The Phantom Express; Love Pains (short).

ROLLOW, PRESTON J.
Born: 1871. Died: May 1947, N.Y. Stage and screen actor. Appeared in silents.

ROMA, CLARICE (Roma Hann)
Born: 1902. Died: May 3, 1947, Hollywood, Calif. Screen and stage actress.

ROMAIN, GEORGE E.
Born: Bordeaux, France. Died: May 7, 1929, Philadelphia, Pa. (heart trouble). Stage and screen actor.

Appeared in: **1920** The Return of Tarzan. **1921** Diane of Star Hollow. **1924** The Sea Hawk; The Circus Cowboy; The Vagabond Trail.

ROMAN, MURRAY
Died: Nov. 6, 1973. Screen and television actor.

Appeared in: **1969** 2,000 Years Later.

ROMANO, JOHN
Born: 1896. Died: July 24, 1957, Hollywood, Calif. Stage and screen actor.

ROMANOFF, MICHAEL (aka PRINCE DIMITRI ROMANOFF OBOLENSKI, GRAND DUKE MICHAEL ROMANOFF and HARRY GERGUSON)
Born: 1890 or 1893 (?), Russia or Brooklyn, N.Y. (?). Died: Sept. 1, 1971, Los Angeles, Calif. (heart attack). Restaurateur and screen actor.

Appeared in: **1948** Arch of Triumph; An Innocent Affair. **1953** Move Over Darling; Paris Model. **1964** Goodbye, Charlie. **1965** Von Ryan's Express; Do Not Disturb. **1967** A Guide for the Married Man; Caprice; Tony Rome. **1968** Lady in Cement.

ROME, STEWART (Septimus Wernham Ryott)
Born: Jan. 30, 1886, Newbury, Berkshire, England. Died: Feb. 26, 1965, Newbury, England. Stage and screen actor. Was a pioneer silent star in Britain.

Appeared in: **1913** A Throw of the Dice. **1914** The Tragedy of Basil Grieve (aka The Great Poison Mystery); Justice; The Chimes; The Cry of the Captive; The Guest of the Evening; The Girl Who Lived in Straight Street; The Breaking Point; Creatures of Clay; The Stress of Circumstance; Terror of the Air; Only a Flower Girl; Dr. Fenton's Ordeal; The Grip of Ambition; The Schemers: Or, The Jewels of Hate; The Whirr of the Spinning Wheel; The Price of Fame; Thou Shalt Not Steal; What the Firelight Showed; The Heart of Midlothian; The Girl Who Played the Game; Unfit: Or, The Strength of the Weak; So Much Good in the Worst of Us; The Awakening of Nora; The Brothers; Time, the Great Healer; Tommy's Money Scheme; Despised and Rejected; The Double Event; The Man from India; They Say—Let Them Say; John Linworth's Atonement; The Lie; Life's Dark Road; The Bronze Idol; His Country's Bidding (aka The Call); The Quarry Mystery. **1915** Barnaby Rudge; Coward! (aka They Called Him Coward); The Canker of Jealousy (aka Be Sure Your Sins); The Curtain's Secret (aka Behind the Curtain); Courtmartialed (aka The Traitor); The Incorruptible Crown; Spies; The Confession; Schoolgirl Rebels; A Lancashire Lass; The Sweater; Her Boy; Sweet Lavender; The White Hope; The Recalling of John Grey; As the Sun Went Down; Iris; The Nightbirds of London; The Shepherd of Souls; A Moment of Darkness; One Good Turn; Jill and the Old Fiddle; The Bottle; The Baby on the Barge; The Second String; The Golden Pavement. **1916** Annie Laurie; The White Boys; Sowing the Wind; Partners; The Marriage of William Ashe; Molly Bawn; The House of Fortescue; Trelawney of the Wells; The Grand Babylon Hotel; Comin' Thro' the Rye; Love in a Mist; Face to Face. **1917** Her Marriage Lines; The Cobweb; The American Heiress; The Man Behind "The Times"; The Eternal Triangle; A Grain of Sand. **1918** The Touch of a Child. **1919** A Daughter of Eve; The Gentleman Rider (aka Hearts and Saddles—US); A Great Coup; Snow in the Desert. **1920** The Case of Lady Camber; The Romance of a Movie Star; The Great Gay Road. **1921** Christie Johnstone; The Imperfect Lover; Her Penalty (aka The Penalty); In Full Cry; The Penniless Millionaire. **1922** Dicky Monteith; Son of Kissing Cup; When Greek Meets Greek; The White Hope (and 1915 version). **1923** Fires of Fate; The Uninvited Guest; The Woman Who Obeyed; The Prodigal Son. **1924** The Desert Sheik; The Colleen Bawn; The Eleventh Commandment; Nets of Destiny; Reveille; The Shadow of the Mosque; The Stirrup Cup Sensation. **1926** Thou Fool; The Silver Treasure. **1927** Somehow Good. **1928** The Passing of Mr. Quin; The Ware Case (US 1929); Zero; The Man Who Changed His Name. **1929** Dark Red Roses; The Crimson Circle. **1930** The Last Hour; The Price of Things; Kissing Cup's Race. **1931** Deadlock; Rynox; The Great Gay Road; Other People's Sins. **1932** Reunion; Betrayal; The Marriage Bond. **1933** Song of the Plough. **1934** Designing Woman; The Girl in the Flat; Lest We Forget; Temptation; Important People. **1936** Men of Yesterday; Debt of Honour. **1937** The Quaker (aka Murder on Diamond Row—US); Wings of the Morning; Dinner at the Ritz. **1938** The Dance of Death. **1939** Confidential Lady; Shadowed Eyes. **1941** Banana Ridge. **1942** Salute John Citizen; One of Our Aircraft is Missing. **1944** Tom's Ride (short). **1947** The White Unicorn (aka Bad Sister—US 1948). **1948** My Sister and I; Woman Hater (US 1949). **1950** Let's Have a Murder.

ROMEA, ALBERTO
Born: 1883, Spain. Died: Apr. 24, 1960, Madrid, Spain. Screen, stage, radio, television actor and stage manager.

ROMER, LEILA
Born: 1878. Died: Feb. 10, 1944, Hollywood, Calif. (heart attack). Screen, stage and vaudeville actress.

Appeared in: **1919** Anne of Green Gables.

ROMER, TOMI
Born: 1924. Died: July 21, 1969, New York, N.Y. Screen, stage and television actress.

ROMERO, FLORITA
Born: 1931. Died: Feb. 6, 1961, Hollywood, Calif. Screen dancer.

ROMEYN, JANE
Born: 1901. Died: May 5, 1963, Hollywood, Calif. Screen, stage and television actress.

ROOKE, IRENE
Born: England. Died: June 14, 1958, England. Screen and stage actress. Married to actor Milton Rosmer (dec. 1971).

Appeared in: **1916** Lady Windemere's Fan. **1919** Westward Ho! **1920** A Bachelor Husband; Pillars of Society. **1921** The Street of Adventure; Ships That Pass in the Night; The Fruitful Vine; A Romance of Wastdale. **1923** The Loves of Mary, Queen of Scots (aka Marie, Queen of Scots). **1927** Hindle Wakes (aka Fanny Hawthorne—US 1929). **1929** The Woman in White.

ROONER, CHARLES.
Born: 1901, Vienna, Austria. Died: Nov. 22, 1954, Mexico City, Mexico (heart attack). Screen, stage actor and film director. Entered films in 1934.

Appeared in: **1944** La Dama de las Camelias. **1948** The Pear; Sofia. **1953** Plunder of the Sun.

ROONEY, PAT
Born: July 4, 1880, New York, N.Y. Died: Sept. 9, 1962, New York, N.Y. Screen and vaudeville actor. Married to actress Marian Bent (dec. 1940).

Appeared in: **1915** The Busy Bell Boy; He's a Bear; I'll Get You Yet. **1916** The Belle and the Bellhop; He Became a Regular Fellow; Some Medicine Man; Pat's Pasting Ways. **1917** Hell by the Enemy; A Pirate Bold. **1918** Their Sporting Blood; Pat Turns Detective. **1924** Show Business. **1933** Universal shorts. **1948** Variety Time.

ROONEY, PAT (Fred E. Ratsch)
Born: 1891. Died: Jan. 15, 1933, Hollywood, Calif. (lung abscess). Screen, stage and vaudeville actor. Divorced from actress Grace Darling. Entered films with Essanay Company.

ROOPE, FAY
Born: 1893. Died: Sept. 13, 1961, Port Jefferson, N.Y. Screen, stage and television actress.

Appeared in: **1951** You're in the Navy Now (aka U.S.S. Teakettle); The Day the Earth Stood Still; The Frogmen; Callaway Went Thataway. **1952** Young Man with Ideas; Washington Story; Viva Zapata!; The Brigand; Carbine Williams; Deadline U.S.A.; My Six Convicts. **1953** Down among the Sheltering Palms; All Ashore; The Charge at Feather River; The System; Clipped Wings; The Clown. **1954** Alaska Seas; The Atomic Kid; The Black Dakotas; The Lone Gun; Naked Alibi. **1955** Ma and Pa Kettle at Waikiki. **1956** The Proud Ones; The Rack. **1959** The F.B.I. Story.

ROOSEVELT, BUDDY (Kenneth Sanderson)
Born: June 25, 1898, Meeker, Colo. Died: Oct. 6, 1973, Meeker, Colo. Screen actor. Entered films in 1918 as a cowboy extra with Inceville Studios. Doubled for Rudolph Valentino in "The Sheik."

Appeared in: **1924** Biff Bang Buddy; Cyclone Buddy; Battling Buddy; Rip Roarin' Roberts; Rough Ridin'; Walloping Wallace. **1925** Gold and Grit; Galloping Jinx; Action Galore; Fast Fightin'; Reckless Courage; Thundering Through. **1926** The Dangerous Dub; Twin Triggers; Tangled Herds; Easy Going; The Bandit Buster; Hoodoo Ranch; The Ramblin' Galoot. **1927** Ride 'Em High; Smoking Guns; Code of the Cow Country; The Fightin' Comeback; Between Dangers; The Phantom Buster; The Bandit Buster. **1928** Mystery Valley; Lightning Shot; Painted Trail; The Cowboy Cavalier; The Devil's Tower; Trailin' Back. **1929** Trail Riders. **1930** Way Out West. **1931** Westward Bound; Lightnin' Smith's Return. **1932** Wild Horse Mesa. **1933** The Fourth Horseman. **1935** Powdersmoke Range. **1937** The Old Corral. **1938** The Buccaneer. **1946** Boss Cowboy. **1947** Buck Privates Come Home. **1950** Abbott and Costello in the Foreign Legion. **1951** Red Badge of Courage. **1952** The Belle of New York; The Old West. **1956** Flesh and the Spur; Around the World in 80 Days. **1962** The Man Who Shot Liberty Valance.

ROPER, JACK
Born: Mar. 25, 1904, Miss. Died: Nov. 28, 1966, Woodland Hills, Calif. (throat cancer). Screen actor.

Appeared in: **1928** The Red Mark. **1929** The Duke Steps Out. **1938** Fisticuffs (short). **1940** West of Carson City; A Fugitive from Justice; Hold That Woman; Angels Over Broadway; Heroes of the Saddle. **1941** The Pittsburgh Kid; Ring and the Belle (short); Ridin' the Cherokee Trail; North From the Lone Star. **1942** Broadway Big Shot. **1943** Swing Fever; Jack London. **1946** Joe Palooka; Gentleman Joe Palooka. **1947** Joe Palooka in the Knockout. **1948** Fighting Mad; Joe Palooka in Winner Take All. **1949** Joe Palooka in the Big Fight. **1950** Joe Palooka in the Squared Circle. **1951** Stop That Cab.

ROQUEMORE, HENRY
Born: Mar. 13, 1888, Marshall, Tex. Died: June 30, 1943, Beverly Hills, Calif. Stage and screen actor.

Appeared in: **1927** The Fighting Three; For Ladies Only; Is Your Daughter Safe?; Ladies at Ease. **1928** Law and the Man; Branded Man; Gypsy of the North; City of Purple Dreams; The Oklahoma Kid; The Wagon Show. **1929** Sinners in Love; Stocks and Blondes; Anne against the World. **1930** The Last Dance; Beyond the Rio Grande; Second Honeymoon; The Social Lion; Romance of the West; The Parting of the Trails. **1931** Sporting Chance. **1933** Breed of the Border. **1934** City Limits. **1935** Without Regret; Ruggles of Red Gap; The Misses Stooge (short); Nevada; Powdersmoke Range; Racing Luck; The Singing Vagabond. **1936** The Milky Way; Too Many Parents; Hearts in Bondage. **1937** Battle of Greed; Love Takes Flight. **1938** The Arkansas Traveler; Goodbye Broadway; Young Fugitives; Barefoot Boy. **1939** Exile Express; Babes in Arms. **1941** Pot O'Gold; No Greater Sin. **1942** The Postman Didn't Ring; Broadway; Tennessee Johnson; That Other Woman.

ROQUEVERT, NOEL
Born: 1892. Died: Nov. 1973, Paris, France. Screen actor.

Appeared in: **1940** The Mayor's Dilemma. **1947** Carnival of Sinners; The Murderer Lives at Number 21. **1948** Le Corbeau (The Raven); Antoine and Antoinette. **1949** Strangers in the House. **1951** Nana (US 1957). **1952** Fanfan the Tulip (US 1953). **1953** Justice Is Done. **1954** Companions of the Night. **1955** The Sheep Has Five Legs; Diabolique. **1956** Inside a Girls' Dormitory. **1958** La Parisienne; La Moucharde (Woman of Sin—US 1961). **1959** The Law Is the Law; Cantage (Blackmail aka The Lowest Crime—US); Archimede le Clochard (Archimede the Tramp aka The Magnificent Tramp—US 1962). **1960** Babette Goes to War; Marie Octobre; Sexpot (aka Le Desir Mene les Hommes—Desire Leads Men); Un Pied, un Cheval et un Sputnik (A Dog, a Horse and a Sputnik aka Au Pied, au Cheval et par Spoutnik (By Foot, By Horse and By Sputnik)); Crazy for Love; Voulez-Vous Danser Avec Moi (Come Dance With Me); La Francoise et L'Amour (Love and the Frenchwoman—US 1961); Three Murderesses (aka Women Are Weak). **1962** Le Masque de Fer (The Iron Mask); Le Diable et Lex Dix Commandments (The Devil and the 10 Commandments—US 1962); Un Singe en Hiver (Monkey in Winter—US 1963); Cartouche (US 1964). **1964** Patate (aka Friend of the Family—US 1965); Les Barbouzes (aka The Great Spy Chase—US 1966).

RORKE, MARGARET HAYDEN
Born: 1884. Died: Mar. 2, 1969, Hollywood, Calif. Screen and stage actress. Mother of actor Hayden Rorke.

ROSAR, ANNIE
Born: 1888. Died: Aug. 1, 1963, Vienna, Austria (heart ailment). Stage and screen actress.

Appeared in: **1922** Ein Hirsekorn Greift. **1937** The World's in Love. **1938** Liebe im Dreiviertel Takt (Love in Waltz Time); Ihr Leibhusar. **1948** The Mozart Story. **1952** The Devil Makes Three. **1953** Marika. **1958** Corinna Darling (aka Beloved Corinna). **1959** Embezzled Heaven; The Life and Loves of Mozart (aka Give Me Your Hand, My Love). **1962** Am Galgen Hangt die Liebe (Love of the Gallows).

ROSAS, FERNANDO
Born: 1915, Mexico. Died: Mar. 1959, Mexico City, Mexico. Screen, stage actor and singer.

ROSAY, FRANCOISE (Francoise Bandy de Naleche)
Born: Apr. 19, 1891, Paris, France. Died: Mar. 28, 1974, Paris, France. Screen, stage, radio actress, opera singer, author and screenwriter. Married to film director Jacques Feyder (dec. 1948).

Appeared in: **1913** Falstaff (film debut). **1922** Crainquebille. **1925** Gribiche. **1928** Le Bateau de Verre; Les deux Timides; Madame Recamier. **1929** The One Woman Idea; The Trial of Mary Dugan; Buster se Marie (French version of Spite Marriage). **1930** Le Petit Cafe; Si L'Empereur Savait Ca!; Saysons Gais; Echec au roi ou Le Roi S'Ennui. **1931** Jenny Lind; Quand on est Belle; Casanova Wider Willen (German version of Parlor, Bedroom and Bath); Magnificent Lie; La Chance (The Chance); La Femme en Homme. **1932** Papa sans le Savoir; Le Rosier de Madame Husson. **1933** He; La Pouponniere; Tambour Battant; L'abbe Constantin; Tout Pour Rien; La Kermesse Heroique (US 1936); Pension Mimosas (US 1936). **1934** Le Grand Jeu; Die Insel; Vers L'abime. **1935** Coralie et Cie.; Le Billet de Mitte; Marchand D'Amour; Gangster Malgre Lui; Maternite; Marie des Angoisses; The Robber Symphony. **1936** Le Secret de Polichinelle; Die Letzten vier von St. Paul; Jenny. **1937** Drole de Drame; Mein Sohn, der Herr Minister; Un Carnet de Bal; Le Fauteuil 47. **1938** Paix sur le Rhin; Ramuntcho; Les gens du Voyage (Traveling People); Fahrendes Volk. **1939** Serge Panine; Die Hochzeitsreise (The Wedding Journey); Bizarre Bizarre. **1940** Elles Etaient Douze Femmes; Remous (Whirlpool). **1941** Une Femme Disparait. **1944** The Halfway House (US 1945). **1945** Johnny Frenchman (US 1946). **1946** Macadam; La dame de Haut-le-Bois; Portrait of a Woman. **1948** Saraband for Dead Lovers (aka Saraband—US 1949); Quartet (US 1949). **1949** Le Mystere Barton; Les Vagabonds du Reve; Donne Senza Nome. **1950** On N'aime Qu'un Fois; Marie Chapdelaine; The September Affair; The Naked Earth. **1951** L'auberge Rouge (The Red Inn—US); I Figli di Nessumo; Les Sept Peches Capitaux; L'Orgueil; The 13th Letter. **1952** Le Banquet des Frandeurs; Wanda la Peccatrice; Sul Ponte dei Sospiri; Chi e Senza Poccato. **1953** Ramuntcho. **1954** La Reine Margot. **1955** That Lady-Esa Senora; Ragazze D'Oggi; The Naked Heart. **1956** Le Long des Trottoirs. **1957** The Seventh Sin; Interlude. **1958** Me and the Colonel; Le Joueur. **1959** The Sound and the Fury; Du Rififi chez les Femmes (Riff Raff Girls aka Rififi for Girls and Rififi Among the Women); Une Fleur au Fusil; Les Yeux de L'Amour. **1960** Le Bois des Amants; Sans Tambour ni Trompette (aka Die Gans Von Sedan—US 1962); Stefanie in Rio; The Full Treatment. **1961** La Cave se Rebiffe (The Sucker Strikes Back aka The Counterfeiters of Paris and Money, Money, Money—US 1962); Back Streets of Paris; Frau Cheney's Ende; The Full Treatment (aka Stop Me before I Kill—US). **1962** The Longest Day. **1964** Volles Herz und Leere Taschen (A Full Heart and Empty Pockets). **1965** Up From the Beach (aka The Day After). **1966** Cloportes (aka La Metamorphose des Cloportes; The Metamorphosis of the Cockroaches; Metamorphosis of Petty Thieves; Metamorphosis of the Bugs; Metamorphosis of Small-timers). **1967** La 25e Heure (The 25th Hour—US). **1974** The Pedestrian.

ROSCOE, ALAN
Born: Aug. 23, 1888, Memphis, Tenn. Died: Mar. 8, 1933, Hollywood, Calif. Screen actor.

Appeared in: **1921** The Last of the Mohicans. **1923** The Spoilers. **1924** The Mirage; The Chorus Lady; Flirting with Love. **1925** Before Midnight; The Lure of the Wild; The Girl of Gold; Why Women Love (aka Sea Woman and Barriers Aflame); That Devil Quemado. **1926** The Texas Streak; The Wolf Hunters. **1927** Long Pants; Duty's Reward. **1928** Driftwood; The Sawdust Paradise; Marry the Girl; The Mating Call; Modern Mothers. **1929** The Sideshow; Flight; The Vagabond Lover; Seven Keys to Baldpate; Hurricane; Love in the Desert; The Red Sword. **1930** Call of the West; Rain or Shine; Half Shot at Sunrise; The Fall Guy; Danger Lights; The Pay Off. **1931** The Royal Bed; Dirigible; Subway Express; The Public Defender; Hell Divers. **1932** Ladies of the Jury; Strangers of the Evening; The Last Mile; The Last Man. **1933** The Death Kiss.

ROSCOE, ALBERT
Born: 1887, Nashville, Tenn. Died: c. 1925. Screen and stage actor.

Appeared in: **1917** Cleopatra. **1918** Salome. **1919** Evangeline; The Siren's Song; A Man's Country; The City of Comrades; Her Purchase Price. **1920** The Last of the Mohicans; Madame X; The Branding Iron. **1921** The Last Card. **1922** Burning Sands; The Man Who Saw Tomorrow. **1923** Java Head; Lovebound; The Net; The Spoilers; A Wife's Romance. **1924** Pal O'Mine.

ROSE, BLANCHE
Born: 1878, Detroit, Mich. Died: Jan. 5, 1953, Hollywood, Calif. Stage and screen actress. Played in a number of Charlie Chaplin films.

Appeared in: **1921** The Old Swimming Hole. **1922** Smudge; The Barnstormer. **1923** Money, Money, Money. **1928** Satan and the Woman. **1930** Call of the West. **1938** If I Were King. **1948** The Paradine Case.

ROSE, HARRY
Born: c. 1888. Died: Dec. 10, 1962, Hollywood, Calif. Screen, burlesque, vaudeville and television actor.

ROSE, JEWEL
Died: Oct. 21, 1970, Los Angeles, Calif. Screen, radio and television actress.

Appeared in: **1950** The Jackpot.

ROSE, ZELMA
Born: 1873. Died: Nov. 21, 1933, Los Angeles, Calif. (heart attack). Stage and screen actress. Married to actor Col. Reginald Barlow (dec. 1943).

ROSELEIGH, JACK
Born: c. 1887, Tenn. Died: Jan. 5, 1940 (heart attack). Screen, stage and radio actor.

Appeared in: **1921** Bare Knuckles; The Light in the Clearing; That Girl Montana; Singing River.

ROSELLE, WILLIAM
Born: 1878. Died: June 1, 1945, N.Y. Stage and screen actor.

Appeared in: **1916** Gloria's Romance (serial). **1919** The Avalanche. **1921** The Black Panther's Cub; The Man Who; Wedding Bells.

ROSEMOND, CLINTON C.
Born: 1883. Died: Mar. 10, 1966, Los Angeles, Calif. (pneumonia—stroke). Black screen actor.

Appeared in: **1936** Green Pastures. **1937** They Won't Forget; Hollywood Hotel. **1938** The Toy Wife; The Story of Dr. Carver (short); Young Dr. Kildare. **1939** Stand up and Fight; Golden Boy. **1940** Safari; George Washington Carver. **1941** Blossoms in the Dust. **1942** Yankee Doodle Dandy; Syncopation.

ROSEN, JAMES "JIMMY"
Born: 1885, Russia. Died: June 1, 1940, New York, N.Y. Midget screen and stage actor.

Appeared in: **1931** Alice in Wonderland. **1939** The Wizard of Oz.

ROSENBERG, SARAH
Born: 1874. Died: June 16, 1964, Hollywood, Calif. Screen actress. Entered films in 1913.

ROSENBLATT, CANTOR JOSEF
Born: 1882. Died: June 19, 1933, Jerusalem. Screen and stage actor.

Appeared in: **1927** The Jazz Singer; Cantor Josef Rosenblatt (short); Cantor Rosenblatt and Choir. **1934** The Dream of My People.

ROSENTHAL, HARRY
Born: May 15, 1900, New York or Ireland? Died: May 10, 1953, Hollywood, Calif. (heart attack). Screen, stage, radio actor, pianist, orchestra leader and composer.

Appeared in: **1930** The Collegiate Model (short). **1939** Wife, Husband and Friend. **1940** Johnny Apollo; Christmas in July; The Great McGinty. **1941** Unfinished Business; Birth of the Blues. **1944** The Miracle of Morgan's Creek; The Great Moment. **1945** The Horn Blows at Midnight.

ROSING, BODIL (Bodil Hammerich)
Born: 1878, Copenhagen, Denmark. Died: Jan. 1, 1942, Hollywood, Calif. (heart attack). Stage and screen actress.

Appeared in: **1925** Pretty Ladies (film debut); Lights of Old Broadway. **1926** The Sporting Lover; It Must Be Love; The City; The Midnight Kiss; The Return of Peter Grimm. **1927** Sunrise; Wild Geese; Blondes by Choice; Stage Madness. **1928** The Big Noise; Out of the Ruins; Wheel of Chance; The Fleet's In; Ladies of the Mob; The Law of the Range; The Port of Missing Girls; The Woman from Moscow. **1929** Eternal Love; Why Be Good?; Betrayal; Broadway Babies; King of the Rodeo. **1930** The Bishop Murder Case; Hello Sister; A Lady's Morals; Oh, What a Man; Soul Kiss; Part Time Wife; All Quiet on the Western Front. **1931** An American Tragedy; Three Who Loved; Surrender. **1932** Downstairs; The Match King. **1933** The Crime of the Century; Ex-Lady; Hallelujah, I'm a Bum; Reunion in Vienna. **1934** King Kelly of the U.S.A.; The Crimson Romance; Mandalay; Little Man, What Now?; The Painted Veil; Such Women Are Dangerous. **1935** Roberta; Four Hours to Kill; A Night at the Ritz; Let 'Em Have It; Thunder in the Night. **1936** Hearts in Bondage. **1937** Michael O'Halloran; Conquest. **1938** The First Hundred Years; You Can't Take It with You. **1939** Confessions of a Nazi Spy; Beasts of Berlin; The Star Maker; Nurse Edith Cavell. **1941** Reaching for the Sun; Marry the Boss's Daughter; No Greater Sin; Man at Large.

ROSLEY, ADRIAN
Born: 1890, Marseilles, France. Died: Mar. 5, 1937, Hollywood, Calif. (heart attack). Screen, stage actor and opera performer.

Appeared in: **1933** My Weakness; Girl without a Room. **1934** Bum Voyage (short); Handy Andy; Flying Down to Rio; Viva Villa; Of Human Bondage; The Great Flirtation; Notorious Sophie Lang. **1935** Enter Madame; Death Flies East; Roberta; South Seasickness (short); The Girl from Tenth Avenue; Alibi Ike; Here's to Romance; The Misses Stooge (short); Metropolitan. **1936** Sins of Man; The Magnificent Brute; The Gay Desperado; The Garden of Allah; Sing Me a Love Song. **1937** Ready, Willing and Able; The King and the Chorus Girl; A Star Is Born.

ROSMER, MILTON (Arthur Milton Lunt)
Born: Nov. 4, 1881, Southport, Lancashire, England. Died: Dec. 7, 1971, Chesham, England. Screen, stage, radio, television actor, film, stage director and screenwriter. Married to actress Irene Rooke (dec. 1958). Entered films in 1912.

Appeared in: **1915** The Mystery of a Hansom Cab. **1916** Cynthia in the Wilderness; Lady Windermere's Fan; The Man without a Soul (aka I Believe—US 1917); Still Waters Run Deep; Whoso is without Sin; The Greater Need. **1917** Little Women. **1919** A Chinese Puzzle; Odds Against Her. **1920** With All Her Heart; Colonel Newcome the Perfect Gentleman; The Twelve Pound Look; The Golden Web; Torn Sails; Wuthering Heights. **1921** Belphegor the Mountebank; The Amazing Partnership; A Woman of No Importance; General John Regan; A Romance of Wastdale; Demos (aka Why Men Forget—US); The Diamond Necklace; The Will. **1922** The Passionate Friends; The Pointing Finger; Tense Moments with Great Authors Series including David Garrick. **1923** A Gamble with Hearts. **1924** The Shadow of Egypt. **1929** High Treason. **1930** The "W" Plan (US 1931). **1934** Grand Prix. **1935** The Phantom Light. **1937** The Great Barrier (aka Silent Barriers—US). **1938** South Riding. **1939** Goodbye, Mr. Chips; The Stars Look Down (US 1941); The Lion Has Wings (US 1940); Let's Be Famous; Beyond Our Horizon (short). **1940** Return to Yesterday; Dangerous Comment (short). **1941** Atlantic Ferry (aka Sons of the Sea—US); Hatter's Castle. **1946** Daybreak. **1947** Frieda; The End of the River; Fame is the Spur (US 1949). **1948** Who Killed Van Loon?; The Monkey's Paw. **1949** The Small Back Room (US 1952).

ROSS, ANTHONY
Born: 1906, N.Y. Died: Oct. 26, 1955, New York, N.Y. Screen, stage and television actor.

Appeared in: **1947** Kiss of Death. **1950** The Gunfighter; Between Midnight and Dawn; Perfect Strangers; The Skipper Surprised His Wife; The Flying Missile; The Vicious Years. **1952** On Dangerous Ground. **1953** Girls in the Night; Taxi. **1954** Rogue Cop; The Country Girl.

ROSS, BARNEY (Barnet David Rosofsky)
Born: 1907, New York, N.Y. Died: Jan. 18, 1967, Chicago, Ill. (cancer of throat). Professional boxer, screen and vaudeville actor.

Appeared in: **1962** Requiem for a Heavyweight. **1965** The Doctor and the Playgirl.

ROSS, BETTY (aka BETTY ROSS CLARKE)
Born: 1880. Died: Feb. 1, 1947, Hollywood, Calif. Screen actress.

Appeared in: **1920** The Very Idea; If I Were King. **1921** Her Social Value; Lucky Carson. **1922** The Man from Downing Street. **1931** The Age for Love.

1932 Murders in the Rue Morgue. **1938** Judge Hardy's Children; Love Finds Andy Hardy; Woman Against Woman; Too Hot to Handle.

ROSS, CHRISTOPHER "CHRIS"
Born: 1946. Died: May 5, 1970, Hollywood, Calif. Screen, stage, radio and television actor.

Appeared in: **1968** How Sweet It Is; Petulia. **1969** A Session with the Committee; Viva Max.

ROSS, CHURCHILL (Ross Weigle)
Born: Jan. 29, 1901, Lafayette, Ind. Died: May 23, 1961. Screen actor.

Appeared in: **1923** Stephen Steps Out. **1927** The College Hero; Blazing Days. **1928** The Fourflusher. **1929** College Love; King of the Campus. **1930** The King of Jazz; Undertow. **1933** College Humor.

ROSS, CORINNE HEATH SUMNER
Born: 1879. Died: June 22, 1965, Hollywood, Calif. Screen actress.

Appeared in: **1964** My Fair Lady.

ROSS, DAVID
Born: 1891, New York, N.Y. Died: Nov. 12, 1975, New York, N.Y. (heart attack). Radio, television, screen (narrated for movies), vaudeville actor and poet. Married to actress Beatrice Pons.

Appeared in: **1932** Isle of Paradise (narrator). **1933** The Passion of Joan of Arc (narrator); Cuba (short). **1935** The Land of Promise (narrator). **1937** Paramount shorts. **1938** Fight for Peace; Paramount shorts.

ROSS, EARLE
Born: Mar. 29, 1888, Ill. Died: May 21, 1961, North Hollywood, Calif. (cancer). Radio, stage and film actor.

Appeared in: **1936** Cavalry; Stormy Trails. **1937** Riders of the Whistling Skull. **1940** The Courageous Dr. Christian.

ROSS, HERBERT
Born: 1866, England. Died: July 18, 1934, England (following surgery). Stage and screen actor.

Appeared in: **1931** The Skin Game.

ROSS, MARION (aka MARION ROLAND)
Born: 1898. Died: July 23, 1966, Seattle, Wash. (cancer). Screen, stage and vaudeville actress.

Appeared in: **1920** Over the Hill. **1954** Forever Female; Secret of the Incas; The Glenn Miller Story. **1956** The Proud and the Profane. **1957** God Is My Partner; Lizzie. **1958** Teacher's Pet. **1960** Operation Petticoat. **1961** Blueprint for Robbery. **1970** The Forbin Project.

ROSS, MYRNA
Born: 1939. Died: Dec. 26, 1975, near Granby, Colo. (plane crash). Stage and screen actress.

Appeared in: **1965** How to Stuff a Wild Bikini; Beach Blanket Bingo. **1966** The Swinger; The Ghost in the Invisible Bikini. **1968** How Sweet It Is. **1969** 2,000 Years Later.

ROSS, SHIRLEY (Bernice Gaunt)
Born: Jan. 7, 1909 or 1914 (?), Omaha, Nebr. Died: Mar. 9, 1975, Menlo Park, Calif. (cancer). Screen, radio actress and singer.

Appeared in: **1933** Bombshell. **1934** Manhattan Melodrama; The Girl From Missouri; Hollywood Party; The Merry Widow. **1935** Age of Indiscretion; Calm Yourself; Buried Loot (short). **1936** Devil's Squadron; San Francisco; The Big Broadcast of 1937; Anything Goes. **1937** Waikiki Wedding; Blossoms on Broadway; Hideaway Girl. **1938** Prison Farm; Thanks for the Memory; Big Broadcast of 1938. **1939** Paris Honeymoon; Cafe Society; Some Like It Hot; Unexpected Father. **1941** Kisses for Breakfast; Sailors on Leave. **1945** A Song for Miss Julie.

ROSS, THOMAS W.
Born: 1875, Boston, Mass. Died: Nov. 14, 1959, Torrington, Conn. Stage and screen actor.

Appeared in: **1921** Fine Feathers; Without Limit. **1926** The Only Son. **1939** Blondie Takes a Vacation. **1940** Seventeen; Remember the Night; The Saint's Double Trouble; The Mortal Storm; Phantom Raiders. **1942** King's Row; The Remarkable Andrew; Yankee Doodle Dandy.

ROSS, WILLIAM
Born: 1925. Died: Feb. 25, 1963, Pittsburgh, Pa. (heart attack). Screen, stage and radio actor.

ROSSON, ARTHUR H.
Born: Aug. 24, 1889, London, England. Died: June 17, 1960, Los Angeles, Calif. Screen actor, film, stage director, screenwriter and stuntman. Entered films as actor and stuntman.

ROSSON, RICHARD "DICK"
Born: Apr. 4, 1893, New York, N.Y. Died: May 31, 1953, Los Angeles, Calif. (suicide—carbon monoxide poisoning). Screen actor and film director. Divorced from actress Jean Harlow (dec. 1937). Married to Vera Rosson.

Appeared in: **1912** Diamond Cut Diamond; She Cried; O'Hara, Squatter and Philosopher. **1913** Sue Simpkins' Ambition; A Heart of the Forest. **1915** Love, Snow and Ice; Aided by the Movies; Deserted at the Auto; An Auto Bungalow Fracas; Nobody's Home; Cats, Cash and a Cookbook. **1916** Mischief and a Mirror; One by One; Plotters and Papers; Johnny's Jumble; Billy Van Deusen's Muddle; Number Please?; A Trunk and Trouble; Dad's College Widow; Ella Wanted to Elope; Bugs and Bugles; Skelly's Skeleton; Adjusting His Claim; The Coments Come-Back; Billy Van Deusen's Operation; Billy Van Deusen's Egg-spensive Adventure; The House on Hokum Hill; Billy Van Deusen, Masquerader; In the Land of the Tortilla; Seventeen; Gamblers in Greenbacks; Daredevils and Danger; Billy Van Deusen, the Cave Man. **1917** Panthea. **1918** Alias Mary Brown; The Ghost Flower; The Shoes that Danced; A Good Loser; High Stakes; Madame Sphiny. **1919** The Secret Garden; Peggy Does Her Darndest; Poor Boob; Playthings of Passion. **1921** Beating the Game; Her Face Value; For Those We Love; Always the Woman.

ROSWAENGE, HELGE
Born:1896, Denmark. Died: Aug. 1972, Denmark. Screen, stage actor and opera performer.

Appeared in: **1936** Letzte Rose.

ROTH, "SANDY" (Sanford L. Roth)
Born: 1889. Died: Nov. 4, 1943, Beverly Hills, Calif. (heart attack). Screen, vaudeville actor and assistant film director. Entered films as an actor with Mack Sennett in 1916.

Appeared in: **1932** The Beast of the City; Hell's Highways. **1933** Midnight Mary.

ROTMUND, ERNEST
Born: 1887, Germany. Died: Mar. 2, 1955, Munich, Germany. Screen, stage and radio actor.

Appeared in: **1935** Auforderung zum Tanz (Invitation to the Dance).

ROUNESVILLE, ROBERT (aka ROBERT FIELD)
Born: 1914, Attleboro, Mass. Died: Aug. 6, 1974, New York, N.Y. (heart attack). Screen, stage, radio, vaudeville actor and opera performer. Appeared on radio and in vaudeville as Robert Field.

Appeared in: **1951** Tales of Hoffman (film debut). **1956** Carousel.

ROUSE, HALLOCK
Born: 1897. Died: Jan. 2, 1930, over Pacific Ocean (airplane accident). Screen actor and film aviator.

Appeared in: **1929** Behind That Curtain.

ROWAN, DONALD W.
Born: 1906. Died: Feb. 17, 1966, Rocky Hill, Conn. (cerebral hemorrhage). Screen and television actor.

Appeared in: **1935** Whipsaw. **1936** And Sudden Death; The Arizona Raiders; The Return of Sophie Lang; Murder with Pictures; Wives Never Know. **1937** When's Your Birthday?; The Devil's Playground; The Affairs of Cappy Ricks; Sea Racketeers. **1938** Racket Busters; Wanted by the Police. **1939** Nancy Drew and the Hidden Staircase; Tough Kid. **1940** Brother Orchid.

ROWAN, ERNEST
Born: 1886. Died: Sept. 30, 1960, Hampton, Va. Screen and stage actor. Entered films approx. 1925.

ROWLAND, JAMES G.
Died: Nov. 27, 1951, Philadelphia, Pa. Screen, stage, vaudeville and radio actor. Married to actress Ethel Ellet, with whom he appeared in vaudeville.

ROWLANDS, ART
Born: 1898. Died: May 25, 1944, Hollywood, Calif. Screen stunt actor.

Appeared in: **1928** The Black Pearl; Devil's Tower; Mystery Valley; Lightnin' Shot. **1929** Synthetic Sin. **1934** The Live Ghost (short). **1936** Ants in the Pantry (short).

ROY, DAN. *See* ERNEST LOTINGA

ROY, HARRY
Born: 1904. Died: Jan. 30, 1971, London, England. Bandleader, screen actor and song writer.

Appeared in: **1936** Everything Is Rhythm.

ROY, JOHN "JOHNNY"
Born: 1899. Died: May 31, 1975, Hollywood, Calif. (heart attack). Screen actor and stuntman. Father of newscaster John Marshall.

Appeared in: **1940** Brigham Young, Frontiersman.

ROYCE, FORREST "FROSTY"
Born: 1911. Died: May 15, 1965, Hollywood, Calif. (heart attack). Screen stuntman and double for William Boyd in "Hopalong Cassidy" films.

Appeared in: **1940** Oklahoma Renegades.

ROYCE, LIONEL
Born: Mar. 30, 1891, Dolina, Poland. Died: Apr. 1, 1946, Manila, Philippine Islands (touring with U.S.O.). Stage and screen actor.

Appeared in: **1937** Marie Antoinette (film debut). **1938** What Price Safety? (short). **1939** Six Thousand Enemies; Confessions of a Nazi Spy; Pack up Your Troubles; Nurse Edith Cavell; Conspiracy. **1940** The Son of Monte Cristo; The Man I Married; Four Sons; Charlie Chan in Panama; Victory. **1941** So Ends Our Night. **1942** The Lady Has Plans; My Favorite Spy; My Favorite Blonde. **1943** Mission to Moscow; Secret Service in Darkest Africa (serial); Let's Face It; Cross of Lorraine; Bomber's Moon. **1944** Seventh Cross; The Hitler Gang. **1945** Tarzan and the Amazons; White Pongo. **1946** Gilda.

ROYCE, ROSITA
Born: 1918, Lincoln, Nebr. Died: Sept. 24, 1954, Miami, Fla. Screen, vaudeville and burlesque actress.

ROYCE, VIRGINIA
Born: 1932. Died: July 8, 1962, Hollywood, Calif. (cerebral hemorrhage). Screen actress.

Appeared in: **1963** The Caretakers.

ROYER, HARRY "MISSOURI"
Born: 1889. Died: Aug. 1, 1951, Hollywood, Calif. (heart attack). Stage and screen actor.

Appeared in: **1926** The Block Signal; Sky High Corral.

ROYSTON, JULIUS
Died: July 1, 1935, Johannesburg, South Africa (bronchial pneumonia). Stage and screen actor. Appeared in films made in South Africa.

RUARK, ROBERT C. (Robert Chester Ruark)
Born: 1915, Wilmington, N.C. Died: July 1, 1965, London, England. Novelist, screen actor and screenwriter.

Appeared in: **1954** Africa Adventure (narrator). **1955** Target Earth.

RUB, CHRISTIAN
Born: Apr. 13, 1887, Austria. Died: Apr. 14, 1956. Screen actor.

Appeared in: **1932** Silver Dollar; Secrets of the French Police; The Trial of Vivienne Ware; The Man from Yesterday. **1933** Humanity; Mary Stevens, M.D.; The Kiss behind the Mirror. **1934** The Fountain; Music in the Air; Romance in the Rain; The Mighty Barnum; No Ransom; No More Women; No Greater Glory; Man of Two Worlds; Little Man, What Now? **1935** Metropolitan; A Dog of Flanders; We're Only Human; Stolen Harmony; Peter Ibbetson; Oil for the Lamps of China; Hitchhike Lady. **1936** Murder on the Bridal Path; Parole; Sins of Man; Mr. Deeds Goes to Town; Girl's Dormitory; Suzy; Next Time We Love; Dracula's Daughter; Murder with Pictures. **1937** One Hundred Men and a Girl; Cafe Metropole; Outcast; When Love Is Young; Tovarich; Heidi. **1938** You Can't Take It with You; Mad about Music; The Great Waltz; Professor Beware; I'll Give a Million. **1939** Never Say Die; Forged Passport; Everything Happens at Night. **1940** The Swiss Family Robinson; Pinocchio (voice of Gepetto); Four Sons; Earthbound. **1941** Father's Son; Come Back Miss Pipps (short); Henry Aldrich for President; The Big Store. **1942** Berlin Correspondent; Tales of Manhattan; Dangerously They Live. **1944** The Adventures of Mark Twain; Three Is a Family. **1945** Strange Confession. **1948** Fall Guy. **1952** Something for the Birds.

RUBEN, JOSE
Born: 1889, Paris, France. Died: Apr. 28, 1969, N.Y. Screen, stage actor, stage director and playwright. Divorced from actress Mary Nash (dec. 1976).

Appeared in: **1922** The Man from Home. **1923** Dark Secrets. **1925** Salome of the Tenements.

RUBENS, ALMA (Alma Smith)
Born: 1897, San Francisco, Calif. Died: Jan. 23, 1931, Los Angeles, Calif.

(pneumonia). Stage and screen actress. Divorced from actor Ricardo Cortez (dec. 1977).

Appeared in: **1916** Intolerance. **1917** Firefly of Tough Luck. **1918** Madame Sphinx. **1919** Restless Souls. **1920** The World and His Wife; Humoresque. **1921** Thoughtless Women. **1922** Find the Woman; Valley of Silent Men. **1923** Under the Red Robe; The Enemies of Women. **1924** Cytherea; The Price She Paid; Gerald Cranston's Lady; Is Love Everything?; The Rejected Woman; Week-End Husbands. **1925** Fine Clothes; The Dangers; East Lynne; She Wolves; The Winding Stair; A Woman's Faith. **1926** The Gilded Butterfly; Marriage License; Siberia. **1927** The Heart of Salome. **1928** Masks of the Devil. **1929** Showboat; She Goes to War.

RUBIN, PEDRO
Born: Mexico. Died: Apr. 17, 1938, Mexico City, Mexico. Stage and screen actor.

RUBIOLA, JOE
Born: 1906, San Antonio, Tex. Died: Sept. 6, 1939, Mexico City, Mexico. Screen actor.

RUDAMI, ROSA
Born: 1899. Died: Feb. 2, 1966, Albany, N.Y. Screen actress.

Appeared in: **1925** The Wedding Song. **1926** A Poor Girl's Romance; The Lily.

RUFART, CARLOS
Born: 1887, Spain. Died: Apr. 1957, Madrid, Spain. Screen, stage actor and singer.

RUFFO, TITTA (Ruffo Capero Titta)
Born: 1877, Pisa, Italy. Died: July 6, 1953, Florence, Italy (heart attack). Screen actor and opera performer. Appeared in Metro Movietone shorts.

RUGGLES, CHARLES (Charles Sherman Ruggles)
Born: Feb. 8, 1890, Los Angeles, Calif. Died: Dec. 23, 1970, Santa Monica, Calif. (cancer). Screen, stage, vaudeville, radio and television actor. Brother of actor Wesley Ruggles (dec. 1972).

Appeared in: **1915** Peer Gynt. **1923** The Heart Raider. **1928** Wives; Etc. (short). **1929** Gentlemen of the Press; The Lady Lies; The Battle of Paris. **1930** Young Man of Manhattan; Roadhouse Nights; Queen High; Charley's Aunt; Her Wedding Night. **1931** The Girl Habit; The Beloved Bachelor; Honor among Lovers; The Smiling Lieutenant; The Lawyer's Secret. **1932** One Hour with You; This Is the Night; The Night of June 13th; Trouble in Paradise; Evenings for Sale; Love Me Tonight; 70,000 Witnesses; Husband's Holiday; This Reckless Age; Make Me a Star; Madame Butterfly; If I Had a Million. **1933** Murders in the Zoo; Terror Abroad; Mama Loves Papa; Girl without a Room; Alice in Wonderland; Melody Cruise. **1934** Melody in Spring; Murder in the Private Car; Friends of Mr. Sweeney; Six of a Kind; Pursuit of Happiness; Goodbye Love. **1935** Ruggles of Red Gap; People Will Talk; The Big Broadcast of 1936; No More Ladies. **1936** Anything Goes; Early to Bed; Wives Never Know; Mind Your Own Business; Hearts Divided; The Preview Murder Mystery. **1937** Turn off the Moon; Exclusive. **1938** Bringing up Baby; Service de Luxe; His Exciting Night; Breaking the Ice. **1939** Yes, My Darling Daughter; Invitation to Happiness; Boy Trouble; Sudden Money; Night Work; Balalaika. **1940** The Farmer's Daughter; Opened by Mistake; Maryland; Public Deb No. 1; No Time for Comedy. **1941** The Invisible Woman; Model Wife; Honeymoon for Three; The Perfect Snob; Go West, Young Lady; The Parson of Panamint. **1942** Friendly Enemies. **1943** Dixie Dugan. **1944** Our Hearts Were Young and Gay; The Doughgirls; Three Is a Family. **1945** Bedside Manner; Incendiary Blonde. **1946** The Perfect Marriage; Gallant Journey; A Stolen Life; My Brother Talks to Horses. **1947** It Happened on Fifth Avenue; Ramrod. **1948** Give My Regards to Broadway. **1949** The Loveable Cheat; Look for the Silver Lining. **1961** The Pleasure of His Company; The Parent Trap; All in a Night's Work. **1963** Son of Flubber; Papa's Delicate Condition. **1964** I'd Rather Be Rich. **1966** The Ugly Dachshund; Follow Me, Boys!

RUGGLES, WESLEY
Born: June 11, 1889, Los Angeles, Calif. Died: Jan. 8, 1972, Santa Monica, Calif. (stroke). Film director, producer, screen, stage minstrel actor and screenwriter. Brother of actor Charles Ruggles (dec. 1970). Married to actress Marcelle Rogez and divorced from actress Arline Judge (dec. 1974). Entered films as an actor in 1914 with Sennett.

Appeared in: **1915** A Submarine Pirate.

RUICK, BARBARA
Born: 1932, Pasadena, Calif. Died: Mar. 2, 1974, Reno, Nev. (natural causes). Screen, television and radio actress. Daughter of actress Lorene Tuttle. Divorced from actor Robert Horton. Married to composer John Williams.

Appeared in: **1952** Above and Beyond; Apache War Smoke; Fearless Fagan; The Invitation; You for Me. **1953** Confidentially Connie; The Affairs of Dobie Gillis; I Love Melvin. **1956** Carousel.

RUIZ, JOSE RIVERO
Born: 1896. Died: Dec. 27, 1948, Madrid, Spain. Screen and stage actor. Appeared in first talkie in Spain in 1936.

RUMAN, SIEGFRIED (Siegfried Albon Rumann)
Born: 1885, Hamburg, Germany. Died: Feb. 14, 1967, Julian, Calif. (heart attack). Screen, stage and television actor.

Appeared in: **1929** The Royal Box. **1934** Marie Galante; The World Moves On; Servants' Entrance. **1935** The Wedding Night; Under Pressure; Spring Tonic; The Farmer Takes a Wife; A Night at the Opera; East of Java. **1936** The Beloved Rogue; The Princess Comes Across; The Bold Caballero; I Loved a Soldier. **1937** On the Avenue; Dead Yesterday; Seventh Heaven; Midnight Taxi; Think Fast, Mr. Moto; This Is My Affair; Love under Fire; Thin Ice; Lancer Spy; Heidi; Thank You, Mr. Moto; Maytime; A Day at the Races; The Great Hospital Mystery; Nothing Sacred. **1938** Paradise for Three; The Great Waltz; The Saint in New York; I'll Give a Million; Girls on Probation; Suez. **1939** Never Say Die; Honolulu; Remember?; Confessions of a Nazi Spy; Only Angels Have Wings; Ninotchka. **1940** Dr. Ehrlich's Magic Bullet; Outside the Three-Mile Limit; I Was an Adventuress; Four Sons; Victory; So Ends Our Night; That Bitter Sweet; Comrade X. **1941** That Uncertain Feeling; The Man Who Lost Himself; The Wagons Roll at Night; Shining Victory; Love Crazy; World Premiere; This Woman Is Mine. **1942** Remember Pearl Harbor; Crossroads; Enemy Agents Meet Ellery Queen; Berlin Correspondent; China Girl; Desperate Journey; To Be or Not to Be. **1943** Tarzan Triumphs; They Came to Blow up America; Sweet Rosie O'Grady; Government Girl. **1944** Summer Storm; The Devil's Brood; Goodbye My Love; The Hitler Gang; It Happened Tomorrow; The Song of Bernadette. **1945** She Went to the Races; A Royal Scandal; House of Frankenstein; The Dolly Sisters; The Men in Her Diary. **1946** Faithful in My Fashion; Night and Day; A Night in Casablanca. **1947** Mother Wore Tights. **1948** If You Knew Susie; Give My Regards to Broadway; The Emperor Waltz. **1949** Border Incident. **1950** Father Is a Bachelor. **1951** On the Riviera. **1952** O. Henry's Full House; The World in His Arms. **1953** Ma and Pa Kettle on Vacation; Houdini; Stalag 17. **1954** The Glenn Miller Story; White Christmas; Living It Up; Three-Ring Circus. **1955** Many Rivers to Cross; The Spy Chasers; Carolina Cannonball. **1957** The Wings of Eagles. **1962** The Errand Boy. **1964** Robin and the Seven Hoods; 36 Hours. **1966** The Fortune Cookie; The Last of the Secret Agents; Way . . . Way Out.

RUMSEY, BERT (Burtis Harold Rumsey)
Born: Oct. 15, 1892, Montana. Died: July 6, 1968, Woodland Hills, Calif. (lung cancer). Screen actor.

Appeared in: **1953** Botany Bay. **1958** Desert Hell. **1960** The Threat. **1965** Ship of Fools.

RUNNEL, ALBERT F.
Born: 1892, St. Paul, Minn. Died: Jan. 4, 1974, Belleair-Clearwater, Fla. (heart condition). Screen, stage, vaudeville actor and circus performer. Appeared in early Biograph Company films.

RUNYON, DAMON (Alfred Damon Runyon)
Born: Oct. 4, 1844, Manhattan, Kans. Died: Dec. 10, 1946, New York, N.Y. (cancer). Journalist, playwright, screenwriter, author, film producer and screen actor.

Appeared in: **1932** Madison Square Garden.

RUSHING, JIMMY (James Andrew Rushing)
Born: Aug. 26, 1903, Oklahoma City, Okla. Died: June 8, 1972, New York, N.Y. Jazz singer and film actor.

Appeared in: **1944** Funzapoppin'. **1969** The Learning Tree.

RUSS, PAULA (Pauline Ignatiev aka POLA RUSS)
Born: 1893. Died: Mar. 14, 1966, Los Angeles, Calif. Screen actress.

Appeared in: **1956** Around the World in 80 Days.

RUSSELL, ANN (Audrey Ann Dosch)
Died: July 31, 1955, Burbank, Calif. (plane crash, which also killed actor Robert Francis). Screen actress and bit player.

RUSSELL, BILLY
Born: England. Died: Dec. 1956, Ealing, London, England. Screen, stage and vaudeville actor. Noted for his resemblance to Adolph Hitler.

RUSSELL, BYRON
Born: 1884, Ireland. Died: Sept. 1963, New York, N.Y. Screen, stage and television actor.

Appeared in: **1920** The World and His Wife. **1921** The Family Closet. **1922** Determination. **1924** It Is the Law; Janice Meredith. **1935** Mutiny on the Bounty. **1937** Parnell. **1938** A Vitaphone short. **1939** One Third of a Nation.

RUSSELL, EDD X.
Born: 1878. Died: Nov. 17, 1966, Los Angeles, Calif. Screen, stage and vaudeville actor. Stand-in for Robert Benchley.

RUSSELL, GAIL
Born: Sept. 23, 1924, Chicago, Ill. Died: Aug. 26, 1961, Los Angeles, Calif. Screen and television actress. Divorced from actor Guy Madison.

Appeared in: **1943** Henry Aldrich Gets Glamour (film debut). **1944** Lady in the Dark; The Uninvited; Our Hearts Were Young and Gay. **1945** Salty O'Rourke; The Unseen; Duffy's Tavern. **1946** The Bachelor's Daughters; The Virginia; Our Hearts Were Growing Up. **1947** The Angel and the Badman; Variety Girl; Calcutta. **1948** Moonrise; The Night Has a Thousand Eyes; Song of Adventure; Wake of the Red Witch. **1949** El Paso; Song of India; The Great Dan Patch; Captain China. **1950** The Lawless. **1951** Air Cadet. **1953** Devil's Canyon. **1956** Seven Men from Now. **1957** The Tattered Dress. **1958** No Place to Land. **1961** The Silent Call.

RUSSELL, J. GORDON
Born: 1883, Piedmont, Ala. Died: Apr. 21, 1935, Los Angeles, Calif. (heart attack). Screen actor.

Appeared in: **1916-17** American Film Mfg. Co. films. **1921** The Sea Lion; Three Word Brand. **1922** His Back against the Wall; Colleen of the Pines; The Kingdom Within; Trail of Hate. **1923** Kindled Courage; The Spoilers; The Scarlet Lily. **1924** Chastity; Hard Hittin' Hamilton; Singer Jim McKee; The Western Wallop; The No-Gun Man. **1925** Easy Going Gordon; Flying Hoofs; Parisian Love; Galloping Jinx; Quicker'n Lightnin'; Hearts and Spurs; A Roaring Adventure; Tumbleweeds; The Sign of the Cactus. **1926** Looking for Trouble. **1927** The Claw; Spurs and Saddles; Uncle Tom's Cabin; Wild Beauty. **1928** Beyond the Sierras; Saddle Mates.

RUSSELL, JEAN
Died: July 8, 1922, New York, N.Y. (suicide). Screen actress.

RUSSELL, JOHN LOWELL
Born: 1875. Died: Sept. 1937, West Los Angeles, Calif. Screen actor and film producer. Do not confuse with actor John Russell.

Appeared in: **1929** Arizona Days; Manhattan Cowboy.

RUSSELL, LEWIS
Born: 1885. Died: Nov. 12, 1961, Los Angeles, Calif. Stage and screen actor.

Appeared in: **1945** Molly and Me; Hold That Blonde; The Lost Weekend; She Wouldn't Say Yes. **1946** A Night in Casablanca; She Wrote the Book; If I'm Lucky; Cross My Heart. **1947** Jewels of Brandenburg; Ladies' Man; The Trouble with Women; Backlash. **1948** Kiss the Blood off My Hands. **1950** The Underworld Story. **1951** Corky of Gasoline Alley. **1956** The Naked Hills.

RUSSELL, LILLIAN (Helen Louise Leonard)
Born: 1860, Clinton, Iowa. Died: June 5, 1922, Pittsburgh, Pa. Screen, stage, burlesque and vaudeville actress.

Appeared in: **1913** How to Live 100 Years. **1914** Potted Pantomimes. **1915** Wildfire (stage and film versions).

RUSSELL, WILLIAM
Died: c. 1915. Screen, stage and vaudeville actor. Appeared in Essanay films. Do not confuse with actor William Russell (dec. 1929).

Appeared in: **1915** Tag Day; Sealed Lips; The Frame-Up. Prior to 1918: High Play; Lone Star; The Twinkler; Fate and Death; The Torch Bearer; Shackles of Truth; Periwinkle; The Weakness of the Strong; Pride and the Man; The Pagan; Sands of Sacrifice; The Sea Master; Temporary Peter; His Arabian Night; Snap Judgment; Aladdin's Night.

RUSSELL, WILLIAM
Born: Apr. 12, 1886. Died: Feb. 18, 1929, Beverly Hills, Calif. (pneumonia). Screen, stage, vaudeville actor and film producer. Son of stage actress Sarah Russell (dec.). Entered films in 1910 with Griffith.

Appeared in: **1912** The Star of Bethlehem; Lucille. **1913** Robin Hood. **1914** The Straight Road. **1915** The Garden of Lies; The Diamond from the Sky (serial); Tag Day; Sealed Lips; The Flame-Up. **1916** The Sequel to the Diamond from the Sky (serial). **1917** Pride and the Man. **1919** Brass Buttons; Six Feet Four. **1921** High Gear Jeffrey; Bare Knuckles; Challenge of the Law; The Cheater Reformed; Colorado Pluck; Quick Action; The Iron Rider; Children of Night; Singing River; The Roof Tree; Desert Blossoms. **1922** Strength of the Pines; A Self-Made Man; Money to Burn; The Men of Zanzibar; Lady from Longacre; The Great Night; Mixed Faces. **1923** Crusader; Alias the Nightwind; Boston Blackie; Goodbye Girls; Man's Size; Times Have Changed; When Odds Are Even; Anna Christie. **1924** The Beloved Brute. **1925** Before Midnight; Big Pal; My Neighbor's Wife; On Thin Ice; The Way of a Girl. **1926** The Blue Eagle; The Still Alarm; Wings of the Storm. **1927** Brass Knuckles; A Rough Shod Fighter; The Desired Woman; The Girl from Chicago. **1928** Danger Patrol; The Escape; The Head of the Family; The Midnight Taxi; State Street Sadie; Woman Wise. **1929** Girls Gone Wild.

RUTH, BABE (George Herman Ruth)
Born: Feb. 6, 1895, Baltimore, Md. Died: Aug. 16, 1948. Baseball player and screen actor. Married to Helen Woodward (dec. 1929) and later to actress Claire Merritt Ruth (dec. 1976).

Appeared in: **1920** Headin' Home. **1927** Babe Come Home. **1928** Speedy. **1937** A Vitaphone short. **1942** Pride of the Yankees; The Ninth Inning.

RUTH, MARSHALL
Born: Dec. 24, 1898, Marshalltown, Iowa. Died: Jan. 19, 1953, Hollywood, Calif. Screen, stage and radio actor. Entered films in 1922.

Appeared in: **1926** Her Sacrifice. **1927** Ridin' Luck; Wild Born. **1928** Red Wine; Virgin Lips. **1929** Joy Street; Nix on Dames; The Broadway Melody; Wall Street. **1930** Navy Blues. **1935** False Pretenses; Hold 'Em Yale. **1936** Wedding Present.

RUTHERFORD, MARGARET
Born: May 11, 1892, London, England. Died: May 22, 1972, Buckinghamshire, England. Screen, stage, television, radio actress and author. Married to actor Stringer Davis. Won 1963 Academy Award for Best Supporting Actress in The V.I.P.'s. Was made Dame Commander of the Order of the British Empire in 1967.

Appeared in: **1936** Dusty Ermine (aka Hideout in the Alps—US 1938); Talk of the Devil (US 1937). **1937** Beauty and the Barge; Catch as Catch Can; Missing, Believed Married. **1941** Spring Meeting; Quiet Wedding. **1943** Yellow Canary (US 1944); The Demi-Paradise (aka Adventure for Two—US 1945). **1944** English without Tears (aka Her Man Gilbey—US 1949). **1945** Blithe Spirit (stage and film versions). **1947** Atlantic Episode (reissue of 1937 Catch as Catch Can); Meet Me at Dawn (US 1948); While the Sun Shines (US 1950). **1948** Miranda (US 1949). **1949** Passport to Pimlico. **1950** The Happiest Days of Your Life; Her Favorite Husband (aka The Taming of Dorothy—US). **1951** The Magic Box (US 1952). **1952** The Importance of Being Ernest; Castle in the Air; Miss Robin Hood; Curtain Up (US 1953). **1953** Innocents in Paris (US 1955); Trouble in Store (US 1955); The Runaway Bus; The Gay Duellist (reissue of 1947 Meet Me at Dawn). **1954** Aunt Clara; Mad about Men. **1955** An Alligator Named Daisy (US 1957). **1957** The Smallest Show on Earth; Just My Luck. **1959** I'm All Right Jack (US 1960). **1961** Murder She Said (US 1962); On the Double. **1963** The Mouse on the Moon; Murder at the Gallop; The V.I.P.'s. **1964** Murder Most Foul; Murder Ahoy. **1965** The Alphabet Murders (US 1966). **1966** A Countess from Hong Kong (US 1967); Campanadas a Medianoche (aka Falstaff and Chimes at Midnight—US 1967). **1967** The Wacky World of Mother Goose (voice); Arabella (US 1970).

RUTHERFORD, TOM
Died: Jan. 6, 1973, Vienna, Austria. Stage and screen actor.

Appeared in: **1937** The Firefly; Beg, Borrow or Steal; Rosalie. **1938** Vacation from Love; A Desperate Adventure; Anesthesia (short). **1940** Those Were the Days; The Ghost Comes Home. **1941** Virginia.

RUYSDAEL, BASIL
Born: 1888. Died: Oct. 10, 1960, Hollywood, Calif. Screen, stage, radio actor and narrator.

Appeared in: **1929** The Cocoanuts. **1934** Dealers in Death (narr.). **1936** An Educational short. **1937** Vitaphone short. **1949** Colorado Territory; Come to the Stable; Thelma Jordan; The Doctor and the Girl; Pinky. **1950** Broken Arrow; Gambling House; The Dungeon; High Lonesome; There's a Girl in My Heart; One Way Street. **1951** Half Angel; My Forbidden Past; People Will Talk; Raton Pass; The Scarf. **1952** Boots Malone; Carrie. **1954** Prince Valiant; The Shanghai Story. **1955** The Blackboard Jungle; David Crockett, King of the Wild Frontier; Diane; Pearl of the South Pacific; The Violent Men. **1956** Jubal; These Wilder Years. **1958** The Last Hurrah. **1959** The Horse Soldiers. **1960** The Story of Ruth.

RYAN, ANNIE
Born: 1865. Died: Feb. 14, 1943, Hollywood, Calif. Screen and stage actress.

Appeared in: **1927** The Claw.

RYAN, DICK
Born: 1897. Died: Aug. 12, 1969, Burbank, Calif. (protracted illness). Screen, vaudeville, radio and television actor. He and his wife Mary teamed in vaudeville act billed as "Dick and Mary."

Appeared in: **1943** The Constant Nymph. **1948** Mr. Peabody and the Mermaid. **1949** Abandoned; Chicken Every Sunday; Jiggs and Maggie in Jackpot Jitters; Top of the Morning. **1950** Born to Be Bad; For Heaven's Sake. **1951** Guy Who Came Back. **1956** The Search for Bridey Murphy. **1957** The Buster Keaton Story; Wild Is the Wind. **1958** Once upon a Horse. **1961** Ada; Summer and Smoke. **1962** Advise and Consent. **1964** Law of the Lawless.

RYAN, IRENE (Irene Nablett)
Born: 1903, El Paso, Tex. Died: Apr. 26, 1973, Santa Monica, Calif. (stroke). Screen, stage, television, radio and vaudveille actress. Married to actor Tim

Ryan (dec. 1956) with whom she appeared on radio and in vaudeville as "Tim and Irene." Later married and divorced film executive Harold E. Knox.

Appeared in: **1940** Tattle Television (short). **1941** Melody for Three. **1942** Sarong Girl; Hold Your Temper (short); Indian Signs (short). **1944** San Diego, I Love You; Hot Rhythm. **1945** That's the Spirit; That Night With You; The Beautiful Cheat. **1946** The Diary of a Chambermaid; Little Iodine. **1947** The Woman on the Beach; Heading for Heaven. **1948** An Old Fashioned Girl; My Dear Secretary; Texas, Brooklyn and Heaven. **1949** There's a Girl in My Heart. **1951** Meet Me After the Show; Half Angel. **1952** Blackbeard the Pirate; WAC from Walla Walla; Bonzo Goes to College. **1954** Ricochet Romance. **1957** Spring Reunion; Rockabilly Baby. **1960** Desire in the Dust. **1966** Don't Worry, We'll Think of a Title.

RYAN, JOE

Born: 1887. Died: Dec. 23, 1944. Screen actor.

Appeared in: **1914** The Man Who Came Back. **1916** Making Good; Along the Border; The Man Within; The Sheriff's Deputy; Crooked Trails; Going West to Make Good; The Girl of Gold Gulch; Taking a Chance; A Corner in Water; A Close Call; Tom's Sacrifice; The End of the Rainbow. **1917** A Darling in Buckskin; The Tenderfoot; The Fighting Trail (serial); Dead Shot Baker. **1918** A Fight For Millions (serial). **1919** Man of Might (serial). **1920** Hidden Dangers (serial). **1921** The Purple Riders (serial). **1923** Lone Fighter; Smashing Barriers. **1925** The Vanishing American.

RYAN, ROBERT

Born: Nov. 11, 1909, Chicago, Ill. Died: July 11, 1973, New York, N.Y. (cancer). Screen, stage and television actor. Married to actress Jessica Cadwalader (dec. 1972).

Appeared in: **1940** Golden Gloves; Queen of the Mob; Northwest Mounted Police. **1943** Bombardier; Gangway for Tomorrow; The Sky's the Limit; Behind the Rising Sun; The Iron Major; Tender Comrade. **1944** Marine Raiders. **1947** Trail Street; The Woman on the Beach; Crossfire. **1948** Berlin Express; Return of the Badmen; The Boy with Green Hair. **1949** Act of Violence; Caught; The Set-Up; The Woman on Pier 13; I Married a Communist. **1950** The Secret Fury; Born to Be Bad. **1951** Best of the Badmen; Flying Leathernecks; The Racket; On Dangerous Ground; Hard, Fast and Beautiful. **1952** Clash by Night; Beware My Lovely; Horizons West. **1953** City Beneath the Sea; The Naked Spur; Inferno. **1954** Alaska Seas; About Mrs. Leslie; Her Twelve Men; Bad Day at Black Rock. **1955** Escape to Burma; House of Bamboo; The Tall Men. **1956** The Proud Ones; Back from Eternity. **1957** Men in War. **1958** God's Little Acre; Lonelyhearts. **1959** Day of the Outlaw; Odds Against Tomorrow. **1960** Ice Palace. **1961** The Canadians; King of Kings. **1962** The Longest Day; Billy Budd. **1964** The Inheritance (narrator). **1965** The Crooked Road; Battle of the Bulge; Guerre Secrete (aka The Dirty Game—US 1966). **1966** Professionals. **1967** The Busy Body; The Dirty Dozen; Hour of the Gun (aka The Law and the Tombstone); Escondido (aka A Minute to Pray, a Second to Die—US 1968; Dead or Alive; The Prodigal Gun). **1968** Anzio (aka The Battle for Anzio); Custer of the West (aka A Good Day for Fighting). **1969** The Wild Bunch; Captain Nemo and the Underwater City (US 1970 aka Captain Nemo and the Floating City). **1973** Executive Action; The Lolly Madonna War. **1974** The Outfit.

RYAN, SHEILA (Katherine Elizabeth McLaughlin)

Born: June 8, 1921, Topeka, Kans. Died: Nov. 4, 1975, Woodland Hills, Calif. (lung ailment). Screen actress. Married to actor Pat Buttram.

Appeared in: **1940** The Gay Caballero. **1941** Golden Hoofs; Dead Men Tell; Dressed to Kill; Great Guns; We Go Fast; The Gang's All Here. **1942** Pardon My Stripes; The Lone Star Ranger; Who Is Hope Schuyler?; A-Haunting We Will Go; Careful, Soft Shoulders. **1943** Song of Texas. **1944** Ladies of Washington; Something for the Boys. **1945** The Caribbean Mystery; Getting Gertie's Garter. **1946** Lone Wolf in London; Deadline for Murder; Slightly Scandalous. **1947** The Big Fix; Philo Vance's Secret Mission; Railroaded; Heartaches; The Lone Wolf in Mexico. **1948** Cobra Strikes; Caged Fury. **1949** Ring Side; The Cowboy and the Indians; Hideout; Joe Palooka in the Counterpunch. **1950** Mule Train; Western Pacific Agent; Square Dance Katy. **1951** Mask of the Dragon; Fingerprints Don't Lie; Golden Raiders; Jungle Manhunt. **1953** On Top of Old Smoky; Pack Train. **1958** Street of Darkness.

RYAN, TIM

Born: 1899. Died: Oct. 22, 1956, Hollywood, Calif. (heart attack). Screen, radio, vaudeville, television actor and screenwriter. Married to actress Irene Ryan (dec. 1973) with whom he appeared in vaudeville and radio in an act billed as "Tim and Irene."

Appeared in: **1940** Brother Orchid; I'm Nobody's Sweetheart Now; Private Affairs. **1941** Where Did You Get That Girl?; Lucky Devils; A Man Betrayed; Ice Capades; Public Enemies; Harmon of Michigan; Bedtime Story; Mr. and Mrs. North. **1942** The Man in the Trunk; Stand by for Action; Crazy Legs; Sweetheart of the Fleet; Get Hep to Love. **1943** Hit Parade of 1943; Sarong Girl; The Mystery of the 13th Guest; Riding High; The Sultan's Daughter; Two Weeks to Live; True to Life; Melody Parade; Reveille with Beverly. **1944** Hot Rhythm; Hi, Beautiful; Detective Kitty O'Day; Kansas City Kitty; Shadow of Suspicion; Swingtime Johnny; Crazy Knights. **1945** Swingin' on a Rain-

bow; Adventures of Kitty O'Day; Fashion Model; Rockin' in the Rockies. **1946** Bringing up Father; Dark Alibi; Wife Wanted. **1947** News Hounds; Scareheads; Blondie's Holiday; Body and Soul. **1948** Jiggs and Maggie in Court; Luck of the Irish; The Golden Eye; Force of Evil; The Shanghai Chest; Jiggs and Maggie in Society; Angels' Alley. **1949** Ringside; Joe Palooka in the Counterpunch; Jiggs and Maggie in Jackpot Jitters; Shamrock Hill; Stampede; Sky Dragon; Forgotten Women. **1950** Military Academy with That 10th Avenue Gang; The Petty Girl; Maggie and Jiggs Out West; Humphrey Takes a Chance; Military Academy. **1951** The Cuban Fireball; All That I Have; Win, Place and Show; Crazy over Horses. **1952** Here Come the Marines; Fargo; No Holds Barred. **1953** From Here to Eternity; The Marksman; Private Eyes. **1956** Fighting Trouble. **1957** The Buster Keaton Story.

RYCKMAN, CHESTER

Born: 1897. Died: Nov. 6, 1918, Fort Rosecrans, Calif. Screen actor.

Appeared in: **1917** The Nurse of an Aching Heart; Double Dukes.

SABATINI, ERNESTO

Born: 1878, Italy. Died: Oct. 5, 1954, Milan, Italy (heart attack). Screen, stage, radio and television actor.

Appeared in: **1938** Come le Foglie (Like the Leaves). **1940** Between Two Worlds.

SABEL, JOSEPHINE

Born: 1866, Lawrence, Mass. Died: Dec. 24, 1945, Patchogue, N.Y. Screen and vaudeville actress.

Appeared in: **1932** The March of Time (short).

SABIN, CATHERINE JEROME

Born: 1879. Died: May 19, 1943, New York, N.Y. Screen and stage actress.

Appeared in: **1925** New Toys.

SABOURET, MARIE

Born: France. Died: July 23, 1960, St. Jean de Luz, France. Screen actress.

Appeared in: **1956** Rififi. **1960** The Would-Be Gentleman.

SABU (Sabu Dastagir)

Born: Mar. 15, 1924, Karapur, Mysore, India. Died: Dec. 2, 1963, Chatsworth, Calif. (heart attack). Screen actor.

Appeared in: **1937** Elephant Boy. **1938** The Drum. **1940** The Thief of Bagdad. **1942** Arabian Nights; The Jungle Book. **1943** White Savage; Screen Snapshot No. 5 (short). **1944** Cobra Woman. **1946** Tangier. **1947** Black Narcissus. **1948** The End of the River; Man-Eater of Kumaon. **1949** Song of India. **1951** Savage Drums. **1954** Hello, Elephant. **1955** Black Panther. **1956** Jungle Hell; Jaguar. **1957** Sabu and the Magic Ring. **1963** Rampage. **1964** A Tiger Walks.

SACHSE, PETER (Peter Louis Sachse)

Born: 1940. Died: July 12, 1966, LaJolla, Calif. (plane crash). Screen actor, musician and singer. Married to actress Salli Sachse.

Appeared in: **1965** Dr. Goldfoot and the Bikini Machine. **1966** The Ghost and the Invisible Bikini.

SACK, ERNA

Born: 1903, Spandau-Berlin, Germany. Died: Mar. 2, 1972, Wiesbaden, Germany. Screen actress and opera soprano.

Appeared in: **1938** Nanon. **1938** Blumen aus Nizza (Flowers from Nice—US 1939).

SACK, NATHANIEL

Born: 1882. Died: July 2, 1966, New York, N.Y. Screen, stage and television actor.

SACKVILLE, GORDON

Died: Aug. 6, 1926, Los Angeles, Calif. (stroke of apoplexy). Screen actor.

Appeared in: **1911** The Best Man Wins. **1915** The Red Circle (serial). **1921** Dr. Jim; The Fighting Lover. **1922** With Stanley in Africa (serial); Any Night. **1923** Slow as Lightning. **1924** The Snob. **1925** Cowboy Courage.

SADLER, CHARLES R.

Born: 1875. Died: Mar. 23, 1950, Los Angeles, Calif. Screen stuntman.

SADLER, DUDLEY, JR.

Died: Sept. 25, 1951, Santa Monica, Calif. Screen actor.

Appeared in: **1947** Boomerang. **1951** Behave Yourself; Lone Star.

SADLER, IAN

Born: 1902, Glasgow, Scotland. Died: July 1971, London, England. Screen, stage and radio actor.

SADO, KEIJI
Born: 1926, Kyoto, Japan. Died: 1964, Japan (auto accident). Screen actor.

Appeared in: **1947** Phoenix; Red Lips. **1949** Here's to the Girls. **1951** Carmen Comes Home; School of Freedom. **1952** Sad Speech; The Boy Director; Stormy Waters; The First Step of Married Life. **1953** Spring Drum; A Japanese Tragedy; The Journey. **1954** Somewhere Beneath the Wide Sky; Diary of Fallen Leaves; Niizuma No Seiten; A Young Lady as President; A Medal; Family Conference; Shinkon Takuan Fefu; Izuko E; What Is Your Name? **1955** College for Men; The Sun Never Sets; You and Your Friend; The Refuge; Beautiful Days; New Every Day; Distant Clouds. **1956** The White Bridge; Look for Your Bride; Tokyo—Hong Kong Honeymoon; The Fountainhead; Footprints of a Woman. **1957** Ore Wa Sinanai; The Sound of Youth; Hanayome Boshuchu; I'll Buy You; Tears; A Case of Honour; The Embraced Bride; Monkey Business; The Lighthouse (aka Times of Joy and Sorrow); Payoff with Love; Candle in the Wind. **1958** True Love; Triple Betrayal; Boroya no Shunju; Sonokoi Matta Nashi; The Country Boss; Equinox Flower; The Invisible Wall. **1959** Waiting for Spring; No Greater Love; Fufu Gassho; Good Morning; Highteen; Map of the Ocean; Road to Eternity; Tokyo Omnibus; Showdown at Dawn; Fine Fellow. **1960** The Scarlet Flower; Hot Corner Murder; White Pigeon; Of Men and Money; Women of Kyoto; Wild Trio; Study; Late Autumn; The Grave Tells All; Dry Earth. **1961** Hunting Rifle; Uzu; Blue Current; Enraptured; As the Clouds Scatter; The Bitter Spirit (Immortal Love); Tokyo Detective Saga. **1962** Flower in a Storm; Ballad of a Workman; An Autumn Afternoon; Mama I Need You. **1963** Escape from Hell; The Hidden Profile. **1964** A Marilyn of Tokyo; The Assassin; Brand of Evil; Sweet Sweat.

SAGE, FRANCES (Frances Satz aka KATHERINE KEATING)
Born: Feb. 28, 1915, N.Y. Died: Jan. 7, 1963, Malibu, Calif. (suicide). Screen actress. Married to actor Nedrick Young (dec. 1968).

Appeared in: **1936** Without Orders; The Witness Chair.

SAGE, WILLARD (James Willard Sage)
Born: Aug. 13, 1922, Canada. Died: Mar. 17, 1974, Sherman Oaks, Calif. Screen and television actor.

Appeared in: **1954** Dragnet. **1955** It's a Dog's Life; The Tender Trap. **1956** The Brass Legend. **1957** Zero Hour. **1959** Timbukto. **1961** The Great Imposter. **1962** That Touch of Mink. **1963** For Love or Money. **1970** The Forbin Project.

SAHNI, BALRAJ
Born: 1913, India. Died: Apr. 13, 1973, Bombay, India (heart attack). Screen, radio actor and writer. Entered films in 1944.

Appeared in: **1960** Khozhdenie za Tri Morya (The Journey Beyond Three Seas). Other Indian film: Do Bigha Zamin (Two Hectares of Land).

SAIGAL, K. L.
Born: India. Died: Jan. 18, 1947, India. Screen actor and singer.

SAINPOLIS, JOHN. *See* JOHN ST. POLIS

ST. CLAIR, LYDIA
Died: Mar. 28, 1974. Screen actress.

Appeared in: **1945** The House on Ninety-Second Street.

ST. CLAIR, MALCOLM
Born: May 17, 1897, Los Angeles, Calif. Died: June 1, 1952, Pasadena, Calif. Screen actor, film director and screenwriter.

Appeared in: **1916** A La Cabaret; Dollars and Sense; The Three Slims. **1917** Lost—A Cook; Her Circus Knight; The Camera Cure; Their Weak Moments; His Perfect Day; An Innocent Villain; Their Domestic Deception; His Baby Doll. **1921** The Goat. **1926** Fascinating Youth.

ST. CLAIR, MAURICE
Born: 1903. Died: May 9, 1970, Los Angeles, Calif. Screen, vaudeville and television actor. Appeared in vaudeville as part of "St. Clair and Day" team.

Appeared in: **1946** Black Angel.

ST. CLAIR, ROBERT
Born: 1910. Died: June 17, 1967, South Pasadena, Calif. Screen, stage, radio, television actor, screenwriter and playwright.

ST. CLAIR, YVONNE
Born: 1914. Died: Sept. 22, 1971, Seattle, Wash. Screen, vaudeville actress and night club dancer.

Appeared in: **1935** Anna Karenina; A Night at the Opera; A Midsummer Night's Dream. **1936** The Great Ziegfeld.

ST. CLAIRE, ADAH
Born: 1854, N.Y. Died: Aug. 16, 1928, Amityville, N.Y. Screen and stage actress.

ST. CYR, LILLIAN "RED WING"
Born: 1873, Nebr. Died: Mar. 12, 1974, New York, N.Y. Screen actress.

Appeared in: **1912** Red Wing and the Paleface. **1913** The Squaw Man.

ST. DENIS, JOE
Born: 1928. Died: May 15, 1968, Hollywood, Calif. (heart attack). Screen actor.

ST. DENIS, RUTH (Ruth Dennis)
Born: Jan. 20, 1878, Newark, N.J. Died: July 21, 1968, Hollywood, Calif. (heart attack). Dancer, screen and vaudeville actress. Married to actor Ted Shawn (dec. 1972) who was her dancing partner.

Appeared in: **1893** Dance. **1916** Intolerance. **1945** Kitty.

ST. HELIER, IVY (Ivy Aitchison)
Born: England. Died: Nov. 8, 1971, London, England. Screen, stage actress and composer.

Appeared in: **1933** Bitter Sweet. **1945** Henry V (US 1946). **1948** London Belongs to Me (aka Dulcimer Street—US).

ST. JOHN, AL "FUZZY" (aka FUZZY Q. JONES)
Born: Sept. 10, 1893, Santa Ana, Calif. Died: Jan. 21, 1963, Vidalia, Ga. (heart attack). Screen and vaudeville actor. Nephew of actor Roscoe "Fatty" Arbuckle (dec. 1933).

Appeared in: **1914** All at Sea; Bombs and Bangs; Lover's Luck; He Loved the Ladies; In the Clutches of a Gang (aka The Disguised Mayor); Mabel's Strange Predicament; The Knock-Out (aka The Pugilist); Our Country Cousin; The Rounders; The New Janitor (aka The New Porter); Tillie's Punctured Romance. **1915** Our Daredevil Chief; Crossed Love and Swords; Dirty Work in a Laundry (aka A Desperate Scoundrel); Fickle Fatty's Fall; The Village Scandal; Fatty and the Broadway Stars. **1916** Fatty and Mabel Adrift; He Did and He Didn't (aka Love and Lobsters); His Wife's Mistakes; The Other Man; The Moonshiners; The Stone Age (aka Her Cave Man); The Waiters' Ball. **1917** The Butcher Boy; Rough House; His Wedding Night; Fatty at Coney Island; Oh Doctor!; Out West (aka The Sheriff); A Reckless Romeo. **1918** The Bell Boy; Goodnight Nurse; Moonshine; The Cook. **1919** A Desert Hero; Backstage; A Country Hero; The Garage; Camping Out; Love; The Hayseed. **1920** The Scarecrow (short). **1921** The High Sign (short). **1922** All Wet (short). **1924** The Garden of Weeds; plus the following shorts: Stupid, but Brave; His First Car; Never Again; Lovemania. **1925** The following shorts: The Iron Mule; Dynamite Doggie; Curses. **1927** Casey Jones; American Beauty. **1928** Hello Cheyenne; Painted Post. **1929** The Dance of Life; She Goes to War. **1930** Land of Missing Men; The Oklahoma Cyclone; Hell Harbor; Western Knights; Two Fresh Eggs. **1931** Aloha; Son of the Plains; The Painted Desert; plus the following shorts: Marriage Rows; That's My Meat; Honeymoon Trio. **1932** Police Court; Law of the North; Riders of the Desert; Fame Street; Bridge Wives (short). **1933** His Private Secretary; Buzzin' Around (short). **1934** Public Stenographer. **1935** Wanderer of the Wasteland; Bar 20 Rides Again; Law of the 45's. **1936** The Millionaire Kid; West of Nevada; Hopalong Cassidy Returns; Trail Dust. **1937** Love Nest on Wheels (short); A Lawman is Born; Outcasts of Poker Flat; Saturday's Heroes; Melody of the Plains; Sing, Cowboy, Sing. **1938** Song and Bullets; The Rangers Roundup; Knight of the Plains; Call of the Yukon; Frontier Scout. **1939** Trigger Pals; She Goes to War. **1940** Friendly Neighbors; Texas Terrors; Murder on the Yukon; Marked Man. **1941** Billy the Kid's Fighting Pals; The Lone Rider in Ghost Town; Apache Kid; Lone Rider Ambushed; A Missouri Outlaw; Billy the Kid Wanted; Billy the Kid's Round-up; The Lone Rider Fights Back. **1942** Law and Order; Billy the Kid Trapped; Billy the Kid's Smoking Guns; Jesse James, Jr.; Stagecoach Express; Arizona Terrors. **1943** My Son, the Hero; Mysterious Rider; Fugitive of the Plains; The Renegade. **1944** Thundering Gunslingers; The Drifter; Law of the Saddle; Wolves of the Range; Wild Horse Phantom; Oath of Vengeance; Rustler's Hideout; Fuzzy Settles Down; I'm from Arkansas; Frontier Outlaws. **1945** Lightning Raiders; Stagecoach Outlaws; Gangster's Den; Devil Riders; Prairie Rustlers; Fighting Bill Carson; Border Badmen. **1946** His Brother's Ghost; Gentlemen with Guns; Terrors on Horseback; Overland Riders; Ghosts of Hidden Valley; Outlaws of the Plains; Shadows of Death; Prairie Badmen; Blazing Frontiers; Colorado Serenade. **1947** Ghost Town Renegades; Fighting Vigilantes; Return of the Lash; Border Feud; Law of the Lash; Pioneer Justice; Cheyenne Takes Over. **1948** Panhandle Trail; Code of the Plains; My Dog Shep; Mark of the Lash; Raiders of Red Rock; Stage to Mesa City; Frontier Fighters. **1949** Dead Man's Gold; Outlaw Country; Son of a Badman; Son of Billy the Kid; Frontier Revenge. **1960** When Comedy Was King (documentary). **1961** Days of Thrills and Laughter (documentary).

ST. JOHN, HOWARD
Born: 1905. Died: Mar. 13, 1974, New York, N.Y. (heart attack). Screen, stage and television actor. Entered films in 1948.

Appeared in: **1949** Shockproof; The Undercover Man. **1950** David Harding, Counterspy; Counterspy Meets Scotland Yard; Custom's Agent; The Men; Mister 880; Seven Eleven Ocean Drive; Born Yesterday; The Sun Sets at Dawn. **1951** Goodbye, My Fancy; Close to My Heart; Saturday's Hero; Starlift; Strangers on a Train; Big Night. **1952** Stop, You're Killing Me. **1954** Three

Coins in the Fountain. **1955** The Tender Trap; Illegal; I Died a Thousand Deaths. **1956** World in My Corner. **1959** L'il Abner. **1961** Cry for Happy; One, Two, Three; Sanctuary; Lover, Come Back. **1962** Madison Avenue. **1963** Lafayette. **1964** Fate is the Hunter; Sex and the Single Girl; Strait-Jacket; Quick, Before it Melts. **1965** Strange Bedfellows. **1967** Matchless; Banning. **1969** Don't Drink the Water.

ST. MAUR, ADELE
Born: 1888. Died: Apr. 20, 1959, Sunnydale, Calif. (leukemia). Stage and screen actress.

Appeared in: **1933** The Worst Woman in Paris; Broken Dreams. **1935** The Gay Deception; The Melody Lingers On. **1936** The Invisible Ray. **1937** History Is Made at Night. **1943** Farmer for a Day (short). **1952** The Pathfinder. **1953** Little Boy Lost. **1955** Crashout.

ST. PIERRE, CLARA
Born: 1866, Canada. Died: Jan. 30, 1942, Santa Monica, Calif. Stage and screen actress. Entered films approx. 1922.

ST. POLIS, JOHN (aka JOHN SAINPOLIS)
Born: Nov. 24, 1873, New Orleans, La. Died: Oct. 10, 1946. Stage and screen actor.

Appeared in: **1914** Soldiers of Fortune. **1916** The Social Highwayman; The World Against Him. **1917** Sapho; The Mark of Cain; Sleeping Fires. **1920** The Great Lover; Dangerous Business. **1921** Cappy Ricks; The Four Horsemen of the Apocalypse; Old Dad. **1922** Shadows. **1923** Held to Answer; The Hero; A Prince of a King; The Social Code; Souls for Sale; Three Wise Fools; The Untameable; Woman-Proof. **1924** The Folly of Vanity; The Alaskan; A Fool's Awakening; In Every Woman's Life; Three Weeks; Mademoiselle Midnight; The Rose of Paris; Those Who Dance. **1925** The Dixie Handicap; Paint and Powder; My Lady's Lips; The Phantom of the Opera. **1926** The Lily; The Return of Peter Grimm; The Far Cry; The Greater Glory. **1927** Too Many Crooks. **1928** The Grain of Dust; The Gun Runner; Marriage by Contract; A Woman's Way; The Power of Silence; Green Grass Widows. **1929** Coquette; Why Be Good?; Fast Life; The Diplomats. **1930** The Bad One; A Devil with Women; Guilty?; In the Next Room; The Melody Man; Kismet; Party Girl; The Three Sisters. **1931** Doctors' Wives; On the Make; Captain Thunder; Transgression; Men of the Sky; Their Mad Moment; Heartbreak. **1932** Alias the Doctor; Lena Rivers; Symphony of Six Million; Forbidden Company; The Crusader; Gambling Sex. **1933** The World Gone Mad; Sing, Sinner Sing; Notorious but Nice; Terror Trail; King of the Arena. **1934** Guilty Parents. **1935** Death from a Distance; Lady in Scarlet. **1936** The Border Patrolman; Three on the Trail; Magnificent Obsession; Below the Deadline; The Dark Hour. **1937** Rustlers' Valley; The Shadow Strikes; Paradise Isle; Jungle Menace (serial). **1938** Saleslady; International Crime; Phantom Ranger; Mr. Wong, Detective. **1939** Boy's Reformatory; They Shall Have Music. **1940** Rocky Mountain Rangers; On the Spot; The Haunted House.

SAKALL, S. Z. "CUDDLES" (Szdke Szadall and Eugene Gero Szakall)
Born: Feb. 2, 1884, Budapest, Hungary. Died: Feb. 12, 1955, Los Angeles, Calif. (heart attack). Screen, stage, vaudeville actor and author. Appeared in films in Germany, Vienna and Budapest from 1916 to 1936.

Appeared in: **1916** Suszterherceg; Ujszulott Apa. **1922** Der Stumme von Portici. **1929** Grosstadt Schmetterling. **1930** Zwei Herzen im 3/4 Takt (Two Hearts in Waltz Time); Kopfuber ins Gluk; Why Cry at Parting? **1931** Die Faschingsfee; Der Zinker; Die Frau von der man Spricht; Der Unbekannte Gast; Ihr Junge; Die Schwebende Jungfrau; Ich Heirate Meinen Mann (aka Her Wedding Night); Meine Cousine aus Warschau. **1932** Ich will Nicht Wissen; Wer du Bist; Gluk uber Nacht; Melodie der Liebe; Eine Stadt Steht Kopf; Muss Man Sich Gleich Scheiden Lassen? **1933** Eine Frau Wie; Scandal in Budapest; Grossfurstin Alexandra; Mindent a Noert; Az Ellopot Szerda. **1934** Helyet az Oregeknek; Fruhlingsstimmen; Romance in Budapest. **1935** Harom es fel Musketas; Baratsagos Arcot Kerek; Tagebuch der Geliebten; 4-1/2 Musketiere; Smile, Please. **1936** Mircha. **1938** The Affairs of Maupassant. **1940** It's a Date; Spring Parade; The Lilac Domino; Florian; My Love Came Back. **1941** Ball of Fire; The Devil and Miss Jones; The Man Who Lost Himself; That Night in Rio. **1942** Casablanca; Yankee Doodle Dandy; Seven Sweethearts; Broadway. **1943** Wintertime; Thank Your Lucky Stars; The Human Comedy. **1944** Hollywood Canteen; Shine on, Harvest Moon. **1945** The Dolly Sisters; Christmas in Connecticut; Wonder Man; San Antonio. **1946** Two Guys from Milwaukee; Never Say Goodbye; The Time, the Place and the Girl; Cinderella Jones. **1947** Cynthia. **1948** Whiplash; April Showers; Romance on the High Seas; Embraceable You. **1949** Look for the Silver Lining; In the Good Old Summertime; My Dream Is Yours; Oh, You Beautiful Doll; It's a Great Feeling. **1950** Tea for Two; Daughter of Rosie O'Grady; Montana; A Swing of Glory. **1951** Lullaby of Broadway; Sugarfoot; Painting the Clouds with Sunshine; It's a Big Country. **1953** Small Town Girl. **1954** The Student Prince.

SALAS, PACO (Francisco Lago Severino)
Born: 1875. Died: Dec. 24, 1964, Havana, Cuba. Screen, stage, radio and television actor.

SALE, CHARLES "CHIC"
Born: 1885, Huron, South Dakota. Died: Nov. 7, 1936, Los Angeles, Calif. (pneumonia). Screen, stage and vaudeville actor.

Appeared in: **1922** His Nibs. **1924** The New School Teacher. **1929** Marching On. **1931** The Star Witness. **1932** Stranger in Town; When a Feller Needs a Friend; The Expert; The Hurry Call. **1933** The Chief; Men of America; Lucky Day; Lucky Dog; Dangerous Crossroads. **1934** An MGM short; Treasure Island. **1935** An MGM short; Rocky Mountain Mystery. **1936** An MGM short; It's a Great Life; Man Hunt; The Gentleman from Louisiana; The Man I Marry. **1937** You Only Live Once.

SALE, FRANCES
Born: 1892. Died: Aug. 6, 1969, Hollywood, Calif. Screen actress and opera performer. Appeared in silents.

SALISBURY, MONROE
Born: 1876, Angola, N.Y. Died: Aug. 7, 1935, San Bernardino, Calif. (skull fracture from fall). Stage and screen actor.

Appeared in: **1914** The Squaw Man; Rose of the Rancho. **1915** The Goose Girl. **1916** Ramona. **1921** The Barbarian. **1922** The Great Alone. **1930** The Jade Box (serial).

SALMONOVA, LYDA
Born: 1889, Prague, Czechoslovakia. Died: 1968, Prague, Czechoslovakia. Screen actress and dancer. Married to actor Paul Wegener (dec. 1948).

Appeared in: **1925** Monna Vanna. **1928** The Lost Shadow.

SALTER, HAROLD "HAL"
Died: May 1928, Los Angeles, Calif. (influenza). Screen, stage and vaudeville actor.

Appeared in: **1927** The Red Raiders; The Royal American. **1928** The Canyon of Adventure; The Code of the Scarlet.

SALTER, THELMA
Died: Nov. 17, 1953, Hollywood, Calif. Screen actress. Entered films as a child actress in silents. Married to producer Edward Kaufman.

Appeared in: **1914** Curse of Humanity. **1915** The Alien; Matrimony. **1916** The Wasted Years; The Jungle Flashlight. **1917** The Crab; Happiness. **1918** Selfish Yates. **1920** Huckleberry Finn.

SAMBERG, ARNOLD
Born: 1899. Died: May 3, 1936, Alpine, Calif. Screen actor. Appeared in silents. Was stand-in for Joel McCrea.

SAMPSON, TEDDY (aka TEDDY SAMSON)
Born: Aug. 8, 1895, New York, N.Y. Died: Nov. 24, 1970, Woodland Hills, Calif. (cancer). Screen actress. Married to actor Ford Sterling (dec. 1939).

Appeared in: **1916** Triangle films. **1921** Bits of Life; The Chicken in the Case. **1922** Outcast. **1923** The Bad Man.

SAMSON, IVAN
Born: 1895, London, England. Died: May 1, 1963, London, England. Screen, stage, radio and television actor.

Appeared in: **1920** Nance. **1923** I Will Repay (aka Swords and the Woman—US 1924); The Loves of Mary, Queen of Scots (aka Marie, Queen of Scots). **1927** The Fake. **1934** White Ensign; Blossom Time (aka April Romance—US 1937). **1935** Royal Cavalcade (aka Regal Cavalcade—US); Honours Easy (The Student's Romance). **1936** Hail and Farewell. **1945** Waltz Time. **1949** Golden Arrow (aka Three Men and a Girl). **1950** Paul Temple's Triumph (US 1951). **1951** The Browning Version. **1953** Innocents in Paris (US 1955). **1957** You Pay Your Money.

SAMUELS, MAURICE
Born: Jan. 13, 1885, Rumania. Died: Aug. 1, 1964, Los Angeles, Calif. (heart attack). Screen actor.

Appeared in: **1949** Oh You Beautiful Doll; Thieves' Highway. **1950** Black Hand. **1951** Rhythm Inn. **1953** Pickup on South Street.

SANBORN, FRED C.
Born: 1899, Mass. Died: Mar. 9, 1961, Cupertino, Calif. Screen, stage and vaudeville actor. Billed in vaudeville with Ted Healy as "Ted Healy and His Racketeers."

Appeared in: **1930** Soup to Nuts. **1943** Crazy House.

SANCHEZ, JOAQUIN
Born: 1923. Died: Sept. 12, 1966. Screen actor and stuntman.

SANDE, WALTER
Born: 1906, Denver, Colo. Died: Feb. 22, 1972, Chicago, Ill. (heart attack). Screen and television actor.

Appeared in: **1937** Life of the Party. **1938** Tenth Avenue Kid; Ladies in Distress; Arson Gang Buster; Goldwyn Follies. **1939** Eternally Yours; Blondie Meets the Boss; Dad for a Day (short). **1940** You Can't Fool Your Wife. **1941** The Iron Claw (serial); Confessions of Boston Blackie; Parachute Battalion; Great Guns. **1942** Don Winslow of the Navy (serial); Sweetheart of the Fleet; A-Haunting We Will Go; Timber. **1943** Reveille with Beverly; Corvette K-225; The Purple V; After Midnight with Boston Blackie; The Chance of a Lifetime. **1944** To Have and Have Not; I Love a Soldier; The Singing Sheriff. **1945** The Daltons Ride Again; Along Came Jones; What Next, Corporal Hargrove?; The Last Installment (short); The Spider. **1946** The Blue Dahlia; Nocturne; No Leave, No Love. **1947** The Red House; The Woman on the Beach; Wild Harvest; Christmas Eve; In Self Defense; Killer McCoy. **1948** Prince of Thieves; Blonde Ice; Half Past Midnight; Wallflower; Perilous Waters. **1949** Bad Boy; Canadian Pacific; Strange Bargain; Joe Palooka in the Counterpunch; Miss Mink of 1949; Tucson; Rim of the Canyon. **1950** The Kid from Texas; Dark City; Dakota Lil. **1951** Payment on Demand (aka Story of Divorce); Tomorrow is Another Day; A Place in the Sun; The Basketball Fix; The Racket; I Want You; Warpath; Rawhide; Fort Worth; Red Mountain. **1952** Red Planet Mars; Duel at Silver Creek; Mutiny; Bomba and the Jungle Girl; Steel Trap. **1953** The Great Sioux Uprising; War of the Worlds; Powder River; The Kid from Left Field; A Blueprint for Murder. **1954** Overland Pacific; Apache; Bad Day at Black Rock. **1955** Wichita; Texas Lady. **1956** Anything Goes; The Maverick Queen; Gun Brothers; Canyon River. **1957** Johnny Tremain; Drango; The Iron Sheriff. **1959** Last Train from Gun Hill. **1960** Gallant Hours; Sunrise at Campobello; Oklahoma Territory; Noose for a Gunman. **1964** The Quick Gun. **1965** Young Dillinger; I'll Take Sweden. **1966** The Navy vs. the Night Monsters. **1969** Death of a Gunfighter.

SANDERS, GEORGE

Born: July 3, 1906, St. Petersburg, Russia. Died: Apr. 25, 1972, Casteldelfels, Spain (suicide—overdose of barbiturates). Screen, stage, television actor and author. Divorced from Elsie Pool and actresses Zsa Zsa and her sister Magda Gabor. Married to actress Benita Hume (dec. 1967) and after her death married Magda. Brother of actor Tom Conway (dec. 1967). Won 1950 Academy Award as Best Supporting Actor in All About Eve.

Appeared in: **1936** Dishonour Bright; The Man Who Could Work Miracles (US 1937); My Second Wife; Lloyds of London; Things to Come; Find the Lady; Strange Cargo (US 1940). **1937** Love Is News; Slave Ship; The Lady Escapes; Lancer Spy. **1938** International Settlement; Four Men and a Prayer. **1939** So This Is London (US 1940); The Saint Strikes Back; The Saint in London; Nurse Edith Cavell; Allegheny Uprising; Confessions of a Nazi Spy; The Outsider (US 1940); Mr. Moto's Last Warning. **1940** Green Hell; The Saint's Double Trouble; The House of the Seven Gables; Rebecca; Foreign Correspondent; Bitter Sweet; The Son of Monte Cristo; The Saint Takes Over. **1941** Rage in Heaven; The Gay Falcon; Man Hunt; Sundown; A Date with the Falcon; The Saint in Palm Springs. **1942** Her Cardboard Lover; Tales of Manhattan; The Moon and Sixpence; Son of Fury; The Falcon's Brother; The Falcon Takes Over; Quiet Please, Murder!; The Black Swan. **1943** This Land Is Mine; Paris After Dark; They Came to Blow Up America; Appointment in Berlin. **1944** The Lodger; Action in Arabia; Summer Storm. **1945** The Picture of Dorian Gray; Hanover Square; Uncle Harry (aka The Strange Affair of Uncle Harry). **1946** A Scandal in Paris; The Strange Woman; Never Say Goodbye. **1947** Forever Amber; The Ghost and Mrs. Muir; The Private Affairs of Bel Ami; Lured. **1948** Personal Column. **1949** The Fan (aka Lady Windermere's Fan); Samson and Delilah. **1950** All About Eve. **1951** I Can Get it for You Wholesale (aka Only the Best); The Light Touch. **1952** Ivanhoe; Captain Black Jack; Assignment Paris. **1953** Call Me Madame. **1954** Witness to Murder; King Richard and the Crusaders. **1955** Jupiter's Darling; Moonfleet; The Scarlet Coat; The King's Thief; Night Freight. **1956** Never Say Goodbye; While the City Sleeps; That Certain Feeling; Death of a Scoundrel. **1957** The Seventh Sin. **1958** The Whole Truth; From the Earth to the Moon; Outcasts of the City. **1959** That Kind of Woman; A Touch of Larceny (US 1960); Solomon and Sheba. **1960** The Last Voyage; Village of the Damned; Bluebeard's Ten Honeymoons; Cone of Silence (aka Trouble in the Sky—US 1961). **1961** Five Golden Hours; The Rebel (aka Call Me Genius—US). **1962** In Search of the Castaways; Operation Snatch; The Cracksman; Cairo; Mondo di Notte (aka Ecco—US 1966—narrator). **1964** Dark Purpose; A Shot in the Dark. **1965** The Amorous Adventures of Moll Flanders (aka Moll Flanders). **1966** The Quiller Memorandum; Eiser Spielt Falsch (aka Trunk to Cairo—US). **1967** Warning Shot; Good Times; Hurry Sundown; The Jungle Book (voice). **1968** Rey de Africa (King of Africa aka One Step to Hell—US 1969). **1969** Thin Aires (aka Invasion of the Body Stealers and The Body Stealers—US 1970); The Candy Man. **1970** The Kremlin Letter.

SANDERS, HUGH

Born: 1912. Died: Jan. 9, 1966. Screen and television actor.

Appeared in: **1950** Storm Warning; The Magnificent Yankee; The Damned Don't Cry; The Great Rupert; Mister 880; Mrs. O'Malley and Mr. Malone. **1951** Flying Leathernecks; Sugarfoot; Three Guys Named Mike; That's My Boy; Along the Great Divide; Strictly Dishonorable; Tomorrow is Another Day; I Was a Communist for the FBI; Only the Valiant; The Careless Years; The Sellout. **1952** Indian Uprising; The Fighter; Something for the Birds; Boots Malone; The Pride of St. Louis; Montana Territory; The Winning Team; The

First Time; Last of the Comanches. **1953** Thunder over the Plains; City of Bad Men; Here Come the Girls; Gun Belt; Scared Stiff; The Glass Web. **1954** Cattle Queen of Montana; The Wild One; Silver Lode; Shield for Murder; Untamed Heiress. **1955** I Died a Thousand Times; The Last Command; Top Gun; Glory; I Cover the Underworld; Finger Man; The Chicago Syndicate. **1956** One False Step; Glory; The Peacemaker. **1957** Jailhouse Rock; Chain of Evidence; The Phantom Stagecoach; The Guns of Fort Petticoat; The Careless Years. **1958** Going Steady; Voice in the Mirror; Life Begins at 17. **1959** Never Steal Anything Small; The Beat Generation; Don't Give Up the Ship. **1960** The Music Box Kid; Cage of Evil. **1961** Man-Trap. **1962** Panic in Year Zero; The Wild Westerners; To Kill a Mockingbird. **1964** Apache Rifles.

SANDERSON, JULIA (Julia Sackett)

Born: 1888, Springfield, Mass. Died: Jan. 27, 1975, Springfield, Mass. Screen, stage, vaudeville and radio actress. Married to radio actor Frank Crumit (dec. 1943). Daughter of stage actor Albert Sanderson.

Appeared in: **1917** The Runaway.

SANDFORD, "TINY" (Stanley J. Sandford)

Born: Feb. 26, 1894, Osage, Iowa. Died: Oct. 29, 1961. Stage and screen actor. Married to actress Edna Sandford. Entered films in 1910.

Appeared in: **1919** Blind Husbands. **1922** The World's Champion; Don't Shoot. **1923** Breaking into Society. **1924** Paying the Limit. **1927** Ginsberg the Great; Sailors, Beware (short); The Second Hundred Years (short). **1928** The Gate Crasher; The Circus; Flying Elephants (short); From Soup to Nuts (short). **1929** Rio Rita; The Far Call; The Iron Mask; plus the following shorts: Big Business; Double Woopee; The Hoose-Gow. **1930** The following shorts: Blotto; Below Zero; The Laurel-Hardy Murder Case; Fifty Million Husbands; Doctor's Orders. **1931** The following shorts: Pardon Us; High Gear; Come Clean; Bargain Days; Beau Hunks. **1932** The Chimp (short); Too Many Women (short). **1933** The Warrior's Husband; The Devil's Brother; plus the following shorts: Fits in a Fiddle; Midnight Patrol; Beauty and the Bus. **1934** The following shorts: Hi Neighbor; Washee Ironee; I'll Take Vanilla; Another Wild Idea; You Said a Hateful; Woman Haters. **1935** Treasure Blues (short); The Timid Young Man (short). **1936** Our Relations; High Beer Pressure (short); Modern Times. **1940** Trailer Tragedy (short); Slightly at Sea (short). **1965** Laurel and Hardy's Laughing Twenties (doc.).

SANDOW, EUGENE

Born: 1867, Konigsberg, Germany. Died: Oct. 14, 1925, London, England (cerebral hemorrhage). Professional strong man who appeared in at least one pre-1900 film.

SANDROCK, ADELE

Born: 1864, Rotterdam, Holland. Died: 1937, Berlin, Germany. Stage and screen actress.

Appeared in: **1931** Skandal um Eva; Die Foresterchristl; Die Schlacht von Bademuende. **1932** Der Schrecken der Garnison; Keine Feier Ohne Meyer; Das Schoene Abenteuer. **1933** Ihre Majestaet die Liebe; Friederike; Morgenrot (Dawn); Einmal Hoecht' ich Keine Sorgen Haben. **1934** Der Gleuckszylinder; Die Tochter des Regiments; Eine Frau wie Du. **1935** Zigeunerblut; Ich Sing Mich in Dein Herz Hinein; Der Tolle Bomberg; Der Himmel auf Erden. **1936** Alle Tage ist Kein Sonntag; Der Schuechterne Casanova; Ich Sehne Mich Nach Dir; Ein Walzer fuer Dich. **1937** Ein Flascher Fuffziger; Kirschen in Nachbars Garten; Die Grosse Adele. **1938** Eva, das Fabriksmaedel; Rendezvous in Wien; Ein Teufelskerl (A Devil of a Fellow). **1939** Der Favorit der Kaiserin (The Favorite of the Empress).

SANDS, DIANA

Born: 1934, New York. Died: Sept. 21, 1973, New York, N.Y. (cancer). Black screen, stage and television actress.

Appeared in: **1954** Executive Suite. **1957** Garment Jungle. **1961** A Raisin in the Sun (stage and film versions). **1963** An Affair of the Skin. **1964** Ensign Pulver (aka Mr. Pulver and the Captain). **1970** Mr. Landlord. **1971** Doctors' Wives. **1972** Georgia, Georgia. **1974** Willie Dynamite.

SANDS, GEORGE

Born: 1900. Died: Dec. 7, 1933, Hollywood, Calif. Screen actor and screenwriter.

SANFORD, AGNES

Died: Nov. 27, 1955, Staten Island, N.Y. Screen, stage and vaudeville actress.

SANFORD, ALBERT, JR. "BERT"

Born: 1893, New York, N.Y. Died: Feb. 10, 1953, New York, N.Y. Screen actor and film sales executive. Entered films as an actor with D. W. Griffith at Biograph Studios.

SANFORD, RALPH

Born: May 21, 1899, Springfield, Mass. Died: June 20, 1963, Van Nuys, Calif. (heart ailment). Screen actor.

Appeared in: **1937** Sea Racketeers; Escape by Night. **1938** Blondes at Work; If

I Were King; Angels with Dirty Faces; The Great Waltz; The Patient in Room 18; Give Me a Sailor. **1939** Little Accident; The Star Maker; They Asked for It; Kid Nightingale. **1940** Gaucho Serenade; Alias the Deacon; Carolina Moon; Three Cheers for the Irish. **1941** What's a Dummy? (short); High Sierra. **1942** I Live on Danger; My Favorite Spy; Torpedo Boat. **1943** High Explosive; Ladies' Day; Aerial Gunner. **1944** Lost in a Harem. **1945** Thunderhead, Son of Flicka; The Bullfighters; High Powered. **1946** They Made Me a Killer; The Best Years of Our Lives; Girl on the Spot; It Shouldn't Happen to a Dog; Sioux City Sue; My Pal Trigger. **1947** Linda, Be Good; Hit Parade of 1947; Copacabana. **1948** Let's Live Again; French Leave; Shaggy; Winner Take All. **1949** Champion. **1950** Cow Town; Father's Wild Game; So You Think You're Not Guilty (short); The Glass Menagerie; Hi-Jacked; Rogue River; Union Station. **1951** Danger Zone; Behave Yourself; My Favorite Spy; Bright Victory; Fort Defiance; Kentucky Jubilee; Let's Make It Legal. **1952** A Girl in Every Port; Somebody Loves Me; Sea Tiger. **1953** Count the Hours. **1954** The Forty Niners. **1955** The Lieutenant Wore Skirts; Night Freight; Shotgun. **1956** Blackjack Ketchum, Desperado; Uranium Boom. **1957** All Mine to Give. **1958** Alaska Passage. **1959** The Purple Gang; The Remarkable Mr. Pennypacker. **1960** Cage of Evil.

SANGER, BERT
Born: 1894. Died: Sept. 1969, Blackpool, England. Screen and vaudeville actor. Appeared in "Keystone Kop" comedies.

SANTAMARIE, MANUEL
Born: Spain. Died: Mar. 1960, Mexico City, Mexico. Screen and television actor.

SANTANA, VASCO
Born: 1890, Portugal. Died: Aug. 1958, Lisbon, Portugal. Screen, stage, radio and television actor.

SANTINA, BRUNO DELLA
Died: 1968. Screen actor.

Appeared in: **1960** Pay or Die.

SANTLEY, FREDERIC
Born: Nov. 20, 1888, Salt Lake City, Utah. Died: May 14, 1953, Hollywood, Calif. Screen, stage and vaudeville actor. Entered films with Kalem in 1911.

Appeared in: **1930** Leathernecking. **1931** If I Had a Million. **1933** Double Harness; Morning Glory; Walls of Gold. **1934** Such Women Are Dangerous. **1935** George White's 1935 Scandals. **1936** Walking on Air. **1937** This Is My Affair; She's Got Everything. **1938** Topa Topa. **1942** Yankee Doodle Dandy. **1953** The Farmer Takes a Wife.

SANTLEY, JOSEPH (Joseph Mansfield)
Born: Jan. 10, 1889, Salt Lake City, Utah. Died: Aug. 8, 1971, Los Angeles, Calif. Screen, stage, vaudeville child actor, film director and film producer. Married actress Ivy Sawyer.

SANTOS, TIKI
Died: Dec. 10, 1974. Screen actor.

Appeared in: **1962** Advise and Consent.

SANTSCHI, TOM
Born: 1879. Died: Apr. 9, 1931, Hollywood, Calif. (high blood pressure). Stage and screen actor.

Appeared in: **1909** The Power of the Sultan. **1913** The Adventures of Kathlyn (serial). **1914** The Spoilers. **1917** The Garden of Allah. **1918** The Hell Cat. **1919** Shadows; Little Orphan Annie; The Stronger Vow. **1920** The Cradle of Courage; The North Wind's Malice. **1922** Found Guilty; Two Kinds of Women. **1923** Are You a Failure?; Brass Commandments; Tipped Off; Is Divorce a Failure?; Thundering Dawn. **1924** The Street of Tears; The Plunderer; The Storm Daughter; Life's Greatest Game; Little Robinson Crusoe; The Right of the Strongest. **1925** Barriers Burned Away; Paths to Paradise; The Pride of the Force; The Primrose Path; Beyond the Border; My Neighbor's Wife; Frivolous Sal; The Night Ship; Flaming Love. **1926** The Desert's Toll; Hands across the Border; Three Bad Men; Forlorn River; The Hidden Way; Her Honor, the Governor; My Own Pal; Siberia; No Man's Gold. **1927** The Third Degree; The Adventurous Soul; Eyes of the Totem; When a Man Loves; The Cruise of the Hellion; The Haunted Ship; Hills of Kentucky; Jim the Conqueror; The Land beyond the Law; The Overland Stage; Tracked by the Police; Land of the Lawless. **1928** Into No Man's Land; Vultures of the Sea (serial); Crashing Through; Honor Bound; Law and the Man; Land of the Silver Fox; Isle of Lost Men. **1929** The Yellowback; The Shannons of Broadway; The Wagon Master; In Old Arizona. **1930** The Utah Kid; Paradise Island; The Fourth Alarm. **1931** Ten Nights in a Barroom; River's End. **1932** The Last Ride.

SAPELLI, DOMINGO
Born: Argentina. Died: 1961, Argentina. Screen actor.

Appeared in: **1938** El Escuadron Azul (The Blue Squadron).

SARGENT, ALFRED MAXWELL
Born: 1881. Died: Jan. 1949, Kalamazoo, Mich. Stage and screen actor.

SARGENT, SIR MALCOLM
Born: 1895, England. Died: Oct. 2, 1967, England. Musical conductor and screen actor.

Appeared in: **1945** Battle for Music.

SARNO, HECTOR V.
Born: 1880, Naples, Italy. Died: Dec. 16, 1953, Pasadena, Calif. Stage and screen actor. Entered films in 1909.

Appeared in: **1912** The Chief's Blanket. **1921** Cheated Hearts; Diamonds Adrift; The Conflict; The Rough Diamond. **1922** Do and Dare; Arabia; The Wise Kid; While Justice Waits. **1923** Stepping Fast; Girl of the Golden West; Ashes of Vengeance. **1924** The Sea Hawk; The Song of Love; Great Diamond Mystery; Honor among Men. **1925** As Man Desires; Cobra. **1926** Her Sacrifice; The Temptress. **1927** King of Kings; The Climbers. **1928** Sonia. **1929** Lucky Star; Hearts and Hoofs (short); Laughing at Death; Red Hot Speed. **1930** Oklahoma Cyclone. **1937** Easy Living.

SATIE, ERIK (Eric Leslie Satie)
Born: May 17, 1866, Honfleur, France. Died: July 1, 1925, France. Musician and screen actor.

Appeared in: **1924** Entr'Acte.

SATZ, LILLIE
Born: 1896. Died: Apr. 11, 1974, Mamaroneck, N.Y. Screen and stage actress. Married to actor Ludwig Satz (dec. 1944).

SATZ, LUDWIG
Born: 1891, Poland. Died: Aug. 31, 1944, New York, N.Y. Screen, stage actor and film director. Married to actress Lillie Satz (dec. 1974). Appeared in the first Yiddish musical talking film: His Wife's Lover.

SAUERMAN, CARL
Born: 1868, Stockholm, Sweden. Died: Apr. 9, 1924, New York, N.Y. Stage and screen actor.

Appeared in: **1917** The Beautiful Adventure.

SAUM, CLIFFORD
Born: 1883. Died: Mar. 1943, Glendale, Calif. Stage and screen actor.

Appeared in: **1923** Wandering Daughters. **1925** The Bridge of Sighs. **1927** By Whose Hand?; Stage Kisses; The Tigress; The Siren. **1928** Fashion Madness. **1930** Three Sisters. **1937** He Couldn't Say No. **1938** Penrod's Double Trouble; Torchy Gets Her Man. **1939** Nancy Drew—Trouble Shooter. **1940** Ladies Must Live. **1941** The Case of the Black Parrot.

SAUNDERS, JACKIE
Born: 1898. Died: July 14, 1954, Palm Springs, Calif. Screen and stage actress.

Appeared in: **1914** The Square Triangle; Little Sunbeam. **1915** The Woman from the Sea; A Bolt from the Sky; Ill-Starred Bobbie; The Rose among the Briars. **1916** The Grip of Evil (serial); A Slave of Corruption; The Flirting Bride; The Better Instinct. **1917** The Wildcat; The Checkmate; A Bit of Kindling. **1920** Drag Harlan. **1921** The Infamous Miss Ravell; Puppets of Fate. **1923** Shattered Reputations; Defying Destiny. **1924** Broken Laws; Alimony; Flames of Desire; The Great Diamond Mystery; The Courageous Coward. **1925** The People vs. Nancy Preston; Faint Perfume.

SAUNDERS, NELLIE PECK
Born: 1869, Saginaw, Mich. Died: Mar. 3, 1942, Greenwood, S.C. Stage and screen actress.

Appeared in: **1922** Tailor Made Man. **1925** A Little Girl in a Big City; The Mad Dancer. **1926** The Sorrows of Satan. **1927** The Broadway Drifter. **1929** The Hole in the Wall.

SAVAGE, HOUSTON. *See* GENE DeBLASIO

SAVILLE, GUS
Born: 1857. Died: Mar. 25, 1934, Hollywood, Calif. Screen and stage actor.

Appeared in: **1921** The Wolverine. **1922** Tess of the Storm Country. **1923** The Face on the Barroom Floor. **1925** Idaho (serial); Wild West (serial); Fighting Courage. **1926** The High Hand. **1930** The Light of Western Stars.

SAVO, JIMMY
Born: 1866, Bronx, N.Y. Died: Sept. 6, 1960, Teni, Italy (heart attack). Screen, stage actor, pantominist and juggler.

Appeared in: **1926** Exclusive Rights; prior to 1935 The House Dick (short). **1935** Once in a Blue Moon. **1937** Merry-Go-Round of 1938. **1938** Reckless Living.

SAVOY, HOUSTON. *See* GENE DeBLASIO

SAWAMURA, KUNITARO (Tomoichi Kato)
Born: 1905, Japan. Died: Nov. 26, 1974, Tokyo, Japan (stroke). Stage and screen actor. Father of actors Hiroyuki Nagato and Mashiko Tsugawa. Brother of actor Daisuke Kato and actress Sadako Sawamura. Entered films during the 1920s.

SAWYER, LAURA
Born: 1885. Died: Sept. 7, 1970, Matawan, N.J. Screen and stage actress. Entered films with Edison Co.

Appeared in: **1912** The Lighthouse Keeper's Daughter. **1913** The Daughter of the Hills; Christian and Moor; The Question Mark; At Jones' Ferry; A Romance of the Cliff Dwellers; Three of a Kind; The Ironmaster; The Doctor; The Sailor's Love Letter; The Stuff That Dreams are Made Of; Buckskin Jack, the Earl of Gilmore; Leaves of a Romance; The Lighthouse by the Sea; A Perilous Ride; Pull for the Shore, Sailor; The Battle of Trafalgar.

SAXE, TEMPLAR (Templer William Edward Edevein)
Born: Aug. 22, 1865, Redhill, Surrey, England. Died: Mar. 23, 1935, Cincinnati, Ohio. Stage and screen actor.

Appeared in: **1915** The Fates and Flora Fourflush (serial—aka The Ten Billion Dollar Vitaphone Mystery Serial); A Lily in Bohemia; The Starring of Flora Finchurch; Myrtle the Manicurist; The Chief's Goat; The Supreme Temptation; Billy's Wager. **1916** The Devil's Prize; Hesper of the Mountains; Winifred the Shop Girl; The Tarantula; The Secret Runner. **1917** Mary Jane's Pa; In the Balance (aka The Hillman); Intrigue; The Fettered Woman; Bobby Takes a Wife. **1921** Bucking the Tiger; A Millionaire for a Day; The Woman God Changed. **1922** Devil's Angel; How Women Love; What Fools Men Are. **1923** In Search of a Thrill; Sidewalks of New York. **1924** Beau Brummel; Captain Blood; Her Night of Romance; Gerald Cranston's Lady. **1925** The Dancers; The Primrose Path; Time—The Comedian. **1926** The White Black Sheep. **1927** For Ladies Only; The Girl from Gay Paree; When a Man Loves. **1928** Beyond London's Lights; What Price Beauty; Valley of Hunted Men.

SAXON, HUGH A.
Born: Jan. 14, 1869, New Orleans, La. Died: May 14, 1945, Beverly Hills, Calif. Screen actor. Entered films in 1916.

Appeared in: **1920** Sand. **1921** High Heels; Seven Years Bad Luck. **1922** The Guttersnipe; Watch Him Step. **1924** Cytherea. **1925** Fightin' Odds. **1926** Hair Trigger Baxter; The Fighting Boob. **1927** Is Your Daughter Safe?; Bulldog Pluck; King of the Herd. **1928** Tracked; Phantom of the Turf; Gypsy of the North. **1929** One Splendid Hour.

SAXON, MARIE
Born: 1904, Lawrence, Mass. Died: Nov. 12, 1941, Harrison, N.Y. Screen, stage, vaudeville actress and dancer.

Appeared in: **1930** The Broadway Hoofer.

SAYLES, FRANCIS H.
Born: 1892, Buffalo, N.Y. Died: Mar. 19, 1944, Hollywood, Calif. Stage and screen actor. Entered films approx. 1930.

Appeared in: **1932** Strangers of the Evening; Blonde Venus. **1934** Home on the Range; Bum Voyage (short). **1937** Easy Living; The Black Legion. **1938** The Purple Vigilantes.

SAYLOR, SYD (Leo Sailor)
Born: Mar. 24, 1895, Chicago, Ill. Died: Dec. 21, 1962, Hollywood, Calif. (heart attack). Stage and screen actor. Entered films in 1925.

Appeared in: **1926-1927** 54 "Syd Saylor" comedies. **1926** Red Hot Leather. **1928** The Mystery Rider (serial). **1929** Just off Broadway; Shanghai Rose. **1930** Border Legion; Men without Law; The Light of Western Stars. **1931** Unfaithful; Fighting Caravans; Playthings of Hollywood; The Lawyer's Secret; I Take This Woman; Caught; Sidewalks of New York. **1932** Law of the Seas; Million Dollar Legs; Lady and Gent; The Crusader; Tangled Destinies; Horse Feathers. **1933** Justice Takes a Holiday; Man of Sentiment; The Nuisance; Gambling Ship. **1934** Young and Beautiful; The Dude Ranger; The Lost Jungle (serial); When a Man Sees Red; Mystery Mountain (serial). **1935** Headline Woman; Code of the Mounted; Men of Action; Ladies Crave Excitement; Wilderness Mail; Here Comes Cookie. **1936** Hitchhike to Heaven; The Last Assignment; Prison Shadows; The Sky Parade; Nevada; The Three Mesquiteers; Kelly the Second; Headin' for the Rio Grande; Secret Valley. **1937** Guns in the Dark; Wallaby Jim of the Islands; Wild and Woolly; Arizona Days; Forlorn River; Meet the Boy Friend; Sea Racketeers; The Wrong Road; Exiled to Shanghai; House of Secrets. **1938** Born to the West; Passport Husband; There Goes My Heart; Crashin' through Danger; The Black Doll; Little Miss Broadway. **1939** $1,000 a Touchdown; Union Pacific; Geronimo. **1940** Arizona; Abe Lincoln in Illinois. **1941** Sierra Sue; Wyoming Wildcat; The Great American Broadcast; Miss Polly; Borrowed Hero. **1942** Tennessee Johnson; Yankee Doodle Dandy; A Gentleman at Heart; The Man in the Trunk; That Other Woman; Time to Kill; Gentleman Jim; Lady in a Jam; It Happened in Flatbush. **1943** He Hired the Boss; Harvest Melody. **1944** Hey, Rookie!; Swingtime Johnny; Three of a

Kind. **1945** The Navajo Kid; Bedside Manner; Frisco Sal; See My Lawyer. **1946** The Kid from Brooklyn; Six Guns for Hire; Thunder Town; Six Gun Man; Avalanche; Deadline for Murder; The Virginian. **1947** Fun on a Weekend. **1948** Prince of Thieves; Triple Threat; Snake Pit; Racing Luck; Sitting Pretty. **1949** Big Jack; Dancing in the Dark; That Wonderful Urge. **1950** Mule Train; Cheaper by the Dozen; The Jackpot. **1951** Valley of Fire; The Las Vegas Story. **1952** Abbott and Costello Meet Captain Kidd; The Hawk of Wild River; The Old West; Wagon Team; Belles on Their Toes. **1953** The Tall Texan; Abbott and Costello Go To Mars. **1955** Toughest Man Alive. **1956** Crime in the Streets; A Cry in the Night. **1957** Shoot-Out at Medicine Bend; The Spirit of St. Louis. **1959** Escort West. **1963** The Crawling Hand.

SAYRE, BIGELOW
Died: Sept. 14, 1975. Screen actor.

Appeared in: **1950** The Great Jewel Robbery; Union Station; The Jackpot.

SAYRE, JEFFREY
Born: 1901. Died: Sept. 26, 1974, Los Angeles, Calif. (shot). Screen, stage, vaudeville actor and screen extra. Former president and one of the founders of the Screen Extras Guild.

Appeared in: **1938** Major Difficulties (short). **1939** Mutiny in the Big House. **1942** Men of San Quentin. **1944** The Purple Heart; In the Meantime, Darling. **1960** Heller in Pink Tights.

SAZARINA, MARIA
Born: 1914, Germany. Died: Oct. 20, 1959, Hamburg, Germany. Screen actress.

SCADUTO, JOSEPH
Born: 1898. Died: Oct. 19, 1943, Hollywood, Calif. Screen actor.

Appeared in: **1924** Racing Luck.

SCALA, GIA (Giovanna Scoglio)
Born: Mar. 3, 1934, Liverpool, England. Died: Apr. 30, 1972, Hollywood Hills, Calif. (accidental drug overdose). Screen actress.

Appeared in: **1955** All That Heaven Allows (film debut). **1956** The Price of Fear; Four Girls in Town; Never Say Goodbye. **1957** Don't Go Near the Water; The Garment Jungle; Tip on a Dead Jockey; The Big Boodle (aka A Night in Havana). **1958** Ride a Crooked Trail; The Tunnel of Love. **1959** The Two-Headed Spy; Battle of the Coral Sea; The Angry Hills. **1960** I Aim at the Stars. **1961** The Guns of Navarone. **1962** Triumph of Robin Hood. **1966** Operation Delilah.

SCANNELL, WILLIAM J.
Born: 1912, Boston, Mass. Died: July 8, 1963, Hollywood, Calif. (heart attack). Screen, vaudeville and television actor.

Appeared in: **1963** The Greatest Story Ever Told.

SCARDON, PAUL
Born: May 6, 1878, Melbourne, Australia. Died: Jan. 17, 1954, Fontana, Calif. (heart attack). Screen, stage actor, film producer and film director. Entered films as an actor with Majestic in 1911. Married to actress Betty Blythe (dec. 1972).

Appeared in: **1915** The Goddess (serial). **1941** The Son of Davy Crockett; Lady from Louisiana. **1942** Mrs. Miniver; My Favorite Blonde; A Yank at Eton; Tish. **1944** Today I Hang; The Adventures of Mark Twain. **1946** Down Missouri Way. **1947** Magic Town. **1948** Sign of the Ram; Fighting Mad; The Shanghai Chest.

SCHABLE, ROBERT
Born: 1873, Hamilton, Ohio. Died: July 7, 1947, Hollywood, Calif. Stage and screen actor.

Appeared in: **1919** The Test of Honor. **1920** On with the Dance. **1921** Experience; Without Limit; Paying the Piper. **1922** Sherlock Holmes; Sisters; A Daughter of Luxury; The Cowboy and the Lady; The Woman Who Fooled Herself; Love's Masquerade. **1923** Bella Donna; Nobody's Money; The Cheat; In Search of a Thrill; Slander the Woman; The Silent Partner. **1924** The Stranger. **1926** Partners Again; Silken Shackles. **1927** Love of Sunya. **1928** Sailors' Wives. **1929** Careers; Man and the Moment.

SCHACHTER, LEON
Born: 1900. Died: Nov. 9, 1974, New York, N.Y. Screen, stage and vaudeville actor. Married to actress Gitel Stein.

Appeared in: **1950** God, Man and Devil.

SCHAEFER, ALBERT
Born: 1916. Died: Oct. 26, 1942, Hollywood, Calif. Screen actor. An original member of "Our Gang" comedies.

Appeared in: **1926** The Set-Up.

SCHAEFER, CHARLES N.
Born: 1864. Died: Feb. 5, 1939, Hollywood, Calif. Screen and stage actor.

Appeared in: 1927 Ridin' Luck; Wild Born; Gun-Hand Garrison; Man Power. 1929 The Winged Horseman.

SCHARF, HERMAN "BOO-BOO" (aka HERMAN SCHARFF)
Born: 1901. Died: Apr. 8, 1963, Hollywood, Calif. (heart attack). Screen actor and stuntman.

Appeared in: 1955 The Far Horizons.

SCHEFF, FRITZI
Born: 1879, Vienna, Austria. Died: Apr. 8, 1954, New York, N.Y. (natural causes). Screen, stage, vaudeville actress and opera performer.

Appeared in: 1915 The Pretty Mrs. Smith.

SCHEINPFLUGOVA, OLGA
Born: 1902, Czechoslovakia. Died: Apr. 14, 1968, Prague, Czechoslovakia. Screen actress.

Appeared in: 1965 A Paty Jezdec Je Strach (The Fifth Horseman is Fear—US 1968).

SCHENCK, JOSEPH T.
Born: 1891, Brooklyn, N.Y. Died: June 28, 1930, Detroit, Mich. (heart disease). Screen, stage and vaudeville actor. Was part of vaudeville team with Gus Van (dec. 1968) billed as "Van and Schenck." Do not confuse with film producer Joseph Schenck (dec. 1961).

Together they appeared in: 1927 The Pennant Winning Battery of Songland (short). 1929 Metro Movietone (feature with their lives as a background entitled Take It Big); plus several song short subjects. 1930 They Learned about Women.

SCHERMAN, BARBARA
Died: Jan. 29, 1935, Cliffside Park, N.J. (gas poisoning). Screen actress.

SCHEU, JUST
Born: 1903, Germany. Died: Aug. 9, 1956, Bad Mergentheim, West Germany (appendicitis). Screen, radio actor, playwright and composer.

SCHEUER, CONSTANCE
Born: 1910. Died: Nov. 27, 1962, Los Angeles, Calif. (heart attack). Screen actress and dancer.

SCHIESKE, ALFRED
Born: 1909, Stuttgart, Germany. Died: July 14, 1970, West Berlin, Germany. Screen, stage and television actor.

Appeared in: 1949 The Affair Blum. 1951 Odette. 1960 A Day Will Come. 1961 Tomorrow Is My Turn.

SCHILDKRAUT, JOSEPH
Born: Mar. 22, 1896, Vienna, Austria. Died: Jan. 21, 1964, New York, N.Y. (heart attack). Screen, stage and television actor. Son of actor Rudolph Schildkraut (dec. 1930). Won 1937 Academy Award for Best Supporting Actor in The Life of Emile Zola.

Appeared in: 1922 Orphans of the Storm (film debut). 1923 Dust of Desire. 1924 The Song of Love. 1925 The Road to Yesterday. 1926 Meet the Prince; Young April; Shipwrecked. 1927 The Forbidden Woman; His Dog; King of Kings; The Heart Thief. 1928 The Blue Danube; Tenth Avenue. 1929 The Mississippi Gambler; Show Boat. 1930 Die Sehnsucht jeder Frau; Night Ride; Cock of the Walk. 1931 Carnival. 1932 Blue Danube (US 1934 plus 1928 version). 1934 Viva Villa; Sisters under the Skin; Cleopatra. 1935 The Crusades. 1936 The Garden of Allah. 1937 Slave Ship; Lancer Spy; The Life of Emile Zola; Souls at Sea; A Star Is Born; Lady Behave. 1938 The Baroness and the Butler; Suez; Marie Antoinette. 1939 Lady of the Tropics; The Rains Came; Pack up Your Troubles; Mr. Moto Takes a Vacation; Idiot's Delight; The Three Musketeers; The Man in the Iron Mask. 1940 The Shop around the Corner; Rangers of Fortune; Meet the Wildcat; Phantom Raiders. 1941 The Parson of Panamint. 1945 The Cheaters; Flame of the Barbary Coast. 1946 Monsieur Beaucaire; The Plainsman and the Lady. 1947 Northwest Outpost; End of the Rainbow. 1948 Gallant Legion; Old Los Angeles. 1959 The Diary of Anne Frank. 1961 King of the Roaring Twenties. 1964 Dust of Desire; Song of Love. 1965 The Greatest Story Ever Told.

SCHILDKRAUT, RUDOLPH
Born: 1865, Constantinople, Turkey. Died: July 15, 1930, Los Angeles, Calif. (heart disease). Stage and screen actor. Father of actor Joseph Schildkraut (dec. 1964).

Appeared in: 1925 His People; Proud Heart. 1926 Pals in Paradise; Young April. 1927 A Harp in Hock; King of Kings; Turkish Delight; The Main Event; The Country Doctor. 1928 A Ship Comes In. 1929 Christina.

SCHILLING, AUGUST E. "GUS"
Born: June 20, 1908, New York, N.Y. Died: June 16, 1957, Hollywood, Calif. (heart attack). Screen, stage, burlesque and radio actor. Divorced from burlesque actress Betty Rowland.

Appeared in: 1939 Mexican Spitfire. 1940 Mexican Spitfire Out West. 1941 Citizen Kane; Lucky Devils; It Started with Eve; Appointment for Love; Dr. Kildare's Victory; Ice Capades. 1942 The Magnificent Ambersons; Broadway; You Were Never Lovelier; Moonlight in Havana. 1943 Lady Bodyguard; Hi, Buddy; Hers to Hold; Larceny with Music; The Amazing Mrs. Holliday; Chatterbox. 1944 Sing a Jingle. 1945 See My Lawyer; River Gang; A Thousand and One Nights; It's a Pleasure. 1946 Dangerous Business. 1947 Calendar Girl; Stork Bites Man. 1948 Return of October; Macbeth; The Lady from Shanghai; Angel on the Amazon. 1949 Bride for Sale. 1950 Our Very Own; Hit Parade of 1951. 1951 Honeychile; On Dangerous Ground; Gasoline Alley. 1952 One Big Affair. 1954 She Couldn't Say No. 1955 Run for Cover. 1956 Glory; Bigger Than Life.

SCHINDEL, SEYMORE
Born: 1907. Died: Aug. 24, 1948, Hollywood, Calif. Screen and stage actor.

SCHINDELL, CY (Seymore Schindell)
Born: Mar. 4, 1907, Brooklyn, N.Y. Died: Aug. 24, 1948, Van Nuys, Calif. Screen actor.

Appeared in: 1937 Grips, Grunts and Groans (short). 1938 Sue My Lawyer (short); Soul of a Heel (short). 1939 Rattling Romeo (short); Skinny the Moocher (short). 1944 Gold is Where you Lose It (short). 1946 Monkey Businessmen (short). 1947 Fright Night (short).

SCHIPA, TITO
Born: 1889, Lecce, Italy. Died: Dec. 16, 1965, New York, N.Y. (heart attack). Screen actor and opera singer.

Appeared in: 1929 Tito Schipa. 1930 Tito Schipa Concert No. 2. 1932 Tre Womane en Frak. 1937 Vivere (To Live—US 1938); Terre de Feu; Chi e'piu Felice de Me? (Who Is Happier Than I—US 1940). 1943 In Cerca de Felicita. 1944 Rosalba; Vivere an Cora. 1946 Il' Cavaliere del Sogna. 1947 Follie per l'Opera (Mad about Opera—US 1950). 1951 Soho Conspiracy; I Misteri di Venezia. 1952 The Life of Donizetti.

SCHLETTOW, HANS ADELBERT (aka HANS VON SCHLETTOW)
Born: 1888, Frankfurt, Germany. Died: 1945, Berlin, Germany. Stage and screen actor. Entered films in 1919.

Appeared in: 1924 Isn't Life Wonderful. 1925 Siegfried. 1927 The Last Waltz; Aftermath. 1928 Schuldig; Kriemhild's Revenge; Shadows of Fear; Small Town Sinners. 1929 Three Kings. 1930 A Cottage on Dartmoor (aka Escaped from Dartmoor—US). 1931 The Immortal Vagabond; Bockbierfest; Das Maedel von der Reeperbahn. 1932 Der Unsterbliche Lump. 1933 Volga, Volga. 1934 Ja, Treu ist die Soldatenliebe; Der Schlemihl. 1935 Schloss Hubertus; Der Tolle Bomberg; Konjunkturritter; Ich Sing Mich in Dein Herz Hinein. 1936 Alte Kameraden. 1940 Waldrausch (Forest Fever); Anton der Letzte (Anthony the Last); Congo Express.

SCHMITT, JOSEPH
Born: 1871. Died: Mar. 25, 1935, Los Angeles, Calif. Screen actor. Entered films in 1912.

SCHMITZ, LUDWIG
Born: 1884, Germany. Died: July 1954, Munich, Germany (heart attack). Stage and screen actor.

Appeared in: 1938 Der Maulkorb. Other German films: Bruen Ist Die Heide; Am Brunnen vor dem Tore; Pension Schoeller; Der Keusche Josef; Land of Smiles.

SCHMITZ, SYBILLE
Born: 1912, Germany. Died: Apr. 13, 1955, Munich, Germany (suicide—pills). Screen actress. Entered films in early 1930s.

Appeared in: 1935 Der Herr Der Welt. 1936 Oberwachtmeister Schwenke. 1937 Ein Idealer Gatte; Punks Kommt aus Amerika. 1938 Fahrmann Maria (Ferryman Maria). 1939 Hotel Sacher. 1954 The House on the Coast. Other German films: Georges Sand; Stradivari; FBI Does Not Answer; Farewell Waltz.

SCHNEIDER, JAMES
Born: 1882, New York, N.Y. Died: Feb. 14, 1967, Los Angeles, Calif. Screen actor and film director. One of the original Keystone Kops.

SCHNICKELFRITZ. See FREDDIE FISHER

SCHONBERG, ALEXANDER
Born: 1886. Died: Oct. 1, 1945, Hollywood, Calif. Screen and stage actor. Entered films approx. 1930.

Appeared in: **1934** The Mighty Barnum. **1937** Nothing Sacred. **1938** Romance in the Dark. **1939** They Shall Have Music.

SCHONBERG, IB
Born: 1902, Denmark. Died: Sept. 26, 1955, Copenhagen, Denmark. Screen actor.

Appeared in: **1954** We Want a Child.

SCHRECK, MAX
Born: 1879, Berlin, Germany. Died: 1936, Munich, Germany. Stage and screen actor.

Appeared in: **1921** Am Narrenseil. **1922** Der Favorit der Konigin; Nosferatu—Eine Symphonie des Grauens; Pique Ass. **1923** Der Kaufmann von Venedig; Die Strasse; Die Finanzen des Grossherzogs. **1924** Dudu, ein Menschenschicksal (aka Die Geschichte eines Clowns). **1925** Die Gefundene Braut; Krieg im Frieden; Der Rosa Diamant. **1926** Der Sohn der Hagar; Der Alte Fritz; Am Rande der Welt; Dona Juana; Luther. **1928** The Strange Case of Captain Ramper; Das Madchen von der Strasse; Der Kampf der Tertia (aka Jugend von Morgen); Moderne Piraten; Rasputins Liebesabenteuer (aka Rasputin, the Holy Devil—US 1930); Die Republick der Backfische; Ritter der Nacht; Serenissimus und die Letzte Jungfrau; Wolga-Wolga. **1929** Ludwig der Zweite, Konig von Bayern; At the Edge of the World; Nosferatu the Vampire. **1930** Das Land des Lachelns. **1931** Im Banne der Berge (aka Almenrausch). **1932** Muss Man Sich Gleich Scheiden Lassen?; Die Hacht der Versuchung; Ein Mann mit Herz; Die Verkaufte Braut; Furst Seppl (aka Skandal im Grandhotel); Peter Voss, der Millionendieb. **1933** Der Tunnel; Ein Kuss in der Sommernacht; Das Verliebte Hotel; Roman einer Hacht (US 1934); Eine Frau wie Du; Fraulein Hoffmanns Erzahlungen. **1935** Der Schlafwagen Kontrolleur. **1936** Donogoo Tonka; Die Letzten Vier von Santa Cruz.

SCHROFF, WILLIAM
Born: 1889, Stuttgart, Germany. Died: Dec. 5, 1964, Hollywood, Calif. Screen, stage actor, stuntman and circus performer.

SCHUKIN, BORIS
Born: 1894, Russia. Died: Oct. 7, 1939, Moscow, Russia (heart attack). Screen actor. He was holder of the title "People's Artist of the U.S.S.R."

Appeared in: **1938** Lenin in October.

SCHULTZ, MRS. CECIL E.
Born: 1905. Died: Sept. 2, 1953, New York, N.Y. Screen actress.

SCHULTZ, HARRY (Alexander Heinberg)
Born: 1883, Germany. Died: July 5, 1935, Hollywood, Calif. Screen actor.

Appeared in: **1926** Spangles. **1928** Riley the Cop. **1929** One Stolen Night. **1930** High C's (short); The Big House. **1931** Beau Hunks (short); War Mamas (short). **1933** Hypnotized; One Sunday Afternoon; I'm No Angel; His Silent Rachet (short); Arabian Tights (short). **1934** The Pursuit of Happiness; Little Man, What Now?

SCHULZ, FRITZ
Born: 1896, Germany. Died: May 9, 1972, Zurich, Switzerland. Screen, stage, television actor, stage, screen director and screenwriter.

Appeared in: **1931** Die Lindenwirtin vom Rhein; Die Schlacht von Bademuende. **1932** Theaternaechte von Berlin; Der Ungetreue Eckehart; Rendez-Vous; Der Storch Streikt; Dienst ist Dienst; Hurra! Ein Junge!; Pension Schoeller. **1933** Drei Tage Mittelarrest; Heute Nacht—Eventuell; Waltz Time; Der Bettelstudent. **1934** The Constant Nymph; Ja, Treu ist die Soldatenliebe. **1936** Madonna, Wo Bist Du? **1937** Die Schwebende Jungfrau. **1957** Cabaret.

SCHUMACHER, CAPT. MAX (Max Hartmann Schumacher)
Born: May 10, 1925. Died: Aug. 30, 1966, Los Angeles, Calif. (mid-air helicopter collision). KMPC radio traffic helicopter pilot and screen actor.

Appeared in: **1964** The Lively Set.

SCHUMANN-HEINK, ERNESTINE (Ernestine Rossler)
Born: 1861, Prague, Czechoslovakia. Died: Nov. 17, 1936, Los Angeles, Calif. (leukemia). Screen actress and opera performer. Mother of actor Ferdinand Schumann (dec. 1958) and screen technician Henry Schumann.

Appeared in: **1927** The following shorts: Danny Boy; By the Waters of Minnetonka; Der Erlkonig. **1935** Here's to Romance.

SCHUMANN-HEINK, FERDINAND
Born: Aug. 9, 1893, Hamburg, Germany. Died: Sept. 15, 1958, Los Angeles, Calif. (heart attack). Stage and screen actor. Entered films in 1924. Son of actress and opera star Ernestine Schumann-Heink (dec. 1936).

Appeared in: **1925** The Fighting Romeo. **1926** The Gallant Fool. **1928** Four Sons; The Awakening; Riley the Cop. **1930** Hell's Angels; Blaze O'Glory; Worldly Goods; Mamba. **1931** The Seas Beneath; My Pal, the King. **1933** Gigolettes of Paris; The Mad Game. **1934** The World Moves On; Fugitive Road; Orient Express. **1935** Symphony of Living. **1936** Two against the World. **1937** The King and the Chorus Girl. **1938** Romance in the Dark. **1939** Thunder

Afloat; Nurse Edith Cavell; Confessions of a Nazi Spy. **1940** Enemy Agent. **1943** Mission to Moscow.

SCHUMM, HARRY W.
Born: 1878. Died: Apr. 4, 1953, Hollywood, Calif. Screen and stage actor.

Appeared in: **1915** The Broken Coin (serial).

SCHUNZEL, REINHOLD
Born: 1886, Germany. Died: Sept. 11, 1954, Munich, Germany (heart ailment). Screen, stage actor, screenwriter and film director.

Appeared in: **1922** The Last Payment. **1928** Fortune's Fool. **1931** Die Dreigroschenoper (The Beggar's Opera); Ihre Hoheit Befiehlt. **1932** 1914: The Last Days before the War. **1943** First Comes Courage; Hangmen Also Die; Hostages. **1944** The Hitler Gang; The Man in Half Moon Street. **1946** Notorious; Dragonwyck; The Plainsman and the Lady. **1947** Golden Earrings. **1948** Berlin Express; The Vicious Circle; The Woman in Brown. **1952** Washington Story.

SCHWAMM, GEORGE S. "TONY"
Born: 1903. Died: Feb. 15, 1966, Elmendorf, Alaska. Screen stuntman.

SCHWANNEKE, ELLEN
Born: Germany. Died: June 16, 1972, Zurich, Switzerland. Screen and stage actress.

Appeared in: **1932** Maedchen in Uniform. **1933** Kadetten. **1934** Ein Toller Einfall. **1936** The Royal Waltz. **1938** Kein Wort von Liebe (Not a Word About Love); Die Sextanerin—Erste Liebe (First Love).

SCHWARTZ, MAURICE
Born: 1891, Russia. Died: May 10, 1960, near Tel Aviv, Israel (heart attack). Stage and screen actor. Appeared in Yiddish stage productions, etc.

Appeared in: **1926** Broken Hearts. **1932** Uncle Moses. **1939** Tevya the Milkman (filmed for limited circulation). **1951** Bird of Paradise. **1953** Slaves of Babylon; Salome.

SCHWARTZ, WENDIE LEE
Born: 1923. Died: Aug. 23, 1968, Hollywood, Calif. Screen actress.

SCHWEISTHAL, HELEN. *See* LITTLE HELEN ALLERTON

SCOBIE, JAMES
Died: 1968. Screen actor.

Appeared in: **1956** Around the World in 80 Days.

SCOTT, CYRIL
Born: 1866, Ireland. Died: Aug. 16, 1945, Flushing, N.Y. Stage and screen actor.

Appeared in: **1915** How Molly Made Good.

SCOTT, DAVE (James and/or John David Scott)
Born: 1939. Died: Dec. 8, 1964, Pasadena, Calif. (leukemia). Screen, stage and radio actor. Do not confuse with actor Dave Scott born in 1911.

Appeared in: **1963** Night Tide.

SCOTT, DICK
Born: 1903. Died: Sept. 2, 1961, Hollywood, Calif. Screen, stage and radio actor.

SCOTT, FREDERICK T.
Died: Feb. 22, 1942, Staten Island, N.Y. Screen actor and Wild West showman.

Appeared in: **1905** The Great Train Robbery. **1919** Over There. **1936** Romance Rides the Range.

SCOTT, HAROLD
Born: Apr. 21, 1891, Kensington, England. Died: Apr. 15, 1964, London, England. Screen, stage, radio and television actor.

Appeared in: **1943** The Man in Grey (US 1945). **1949** Trottie True (aka Gay Lady—US 1950). **1956** The Spanish Gardener. **1960** The Hand (US 1961); The Brides of Dracula. **1961** The Young Ones (aka Wonderful to be Young—US 1962). **1962** The Man Who Finally Died (US 1967); The Boys (US 1963). **1964** The Yellow Rolls Royce (US 1965).

SCOTT, IVY
Born: 1886, Australia. Died: Feb. 3, 1947, New York, N.Y. Screen, stage and radio actress.

Appeared in: **1940** Too Many Girls. **1943** Higher and Higher.

SCOTT, JAMES D.
Born: 1939. Died: Dec. 8, 1964, Pasadena, Calif. (leukemia). Screen and radio actor. Was Alexander on Blondie and Dagwood radio program.

SCOTT, KAY
Born: 1928. Died: Jan. 1, 1971, Los Angeles, Calif. Screen actress and composer.

Appeared in: 1947 Fear in the Night.

SCOTT, LESLIE (Zakariya Abullah)
Born: 1921. Died: Aug. 20, 1969, New York, N.Y. (cancer). Screen, stage actor and singer.

Appeared in: 1958 Island Women. 1959 Porgy and Bess (screen and European stage versions).

SCOTT, MARK
Born: 1915. Died: July 13, 1960, Burbank, Calif. (heart attack). Screen, radio and television actor.

Appeared in: 1955 Hell's Horizon. 1957 Chicago Confidential.

SCOTT, MARKLE
Born: 1873. Died: July 4, 1958, Hollywood, Calif. Cowboy screen actor. Appeared in silents.

SCOTT, PAUL
Born: 1894. Died: Nov. 24, 1944, Los Angeles, Calif. (heart attack). Stage and screen actor.

SCOTT, WALLACE "WALLY"
Died: May 8, 1970. Screen actor.

Appeared in: 1942 The Big Shot. 1946 The Killers. 1947 Tarzan and the Huntress; The Vigilantes Return. 1950 Captain China.

SCOTT, ZACHARY
Born: Feb. 24, 1914, Austin, Tex. Died: Oct. 3, 1965, Austin, Tex. (brain tumor). Stage and screen actor.

Appeared in: 1944 The Mask of Dimitrios (film debut); Hollywood Canteen. 1945 Mildred Pierce; The Southerner; San Antonio; Danger Signal. 1946 Her Kind of Man. 1947 Stallion Road; Cass Timberlane; The Unfaithful. 1948 Whiplash; Ruthless. 1949 Flamingo Road; Flaxy Martin; South of Saint Louis; Death in a Doll's House; Bed of Roses; One Last Fling. 1950 Born to Be Bad; Thundercloud; Colt .45; Shadow on the Wall; Pretty Baby; Guilty Bystander. 1951 Lightning Strikes Twice; The Secret of Convict Lake; Let's Make It Legal. 1952 Stronghold; Wings of Danger. 1953 Appointment in Honduras. 1955 Shotgun; Flame of the Islands; Treasure of Ruby Hills. 1956 Bandido. 1957 The Counterfeit Plan; Man in the Shadow; Flight into Danger. 1960 Natchez Trace. 1961 The Young One. 1962 It's Only Money.

SEABURY, YNEZ
Born: 1909. Died: Apr. 11, 1973, Sherman Oaks, Calif. (internal complications). Screen, stage, radio and television actress. Known as "The Biograph Baby."

Appeared in: 1915 Billy's Stratagem. 1916 The Sunbeam. 1923 Slander the Woman; Thundergate. 1924 When a Girl Loves. 1925 The Calgary Stampede; Ship of Souls. 1927 Red Clay. 1929 Dynamite. 1930 Madam Satan. 1932 The Drifter. 1936 The Invisible Ray. 1938 The Girl of the Golden West. 1940 Northwest Mounted Police.

SEARLE, KAMUELA C.
Born: Aug. 29, 1890, Hawaii. Died: Feb. 14, 1924, Los Angeles, Calif. (injuries sustained during filming). Sculptor and screen actor.

Appeared in: 1919 Male and Female. 1920 The Son of Tarzan (serial). 1921 Fool's Paradise. 1923 Jungle Trail of the Son of Tarzan (release of 1920 serial Son of Tarzan).

SEARLES, CORA
Born: 1859. Died: Mar. 5, 1935, Los Angeles, Calif. Screen actress.

SEARS, ALLAN
Born: 1887. Died: Aug. 18, 1942, Los Angeles, Calif. Screen actor.

Appeared in: 1920 Rio Grande; Judy of Rogue's Harbor. 1923 Long Live the King. 1924 In Love with Love. 1925 The Scarlet Honeymoon. 1926 Into Her Kingdom. 1928 Into the Night; A Midnight Adventure. 1933 Secrets. 1935 The Singing Vagabond. 1937 Two-Fisted Sheriff.

SEARS, BLANCHE
Born: 1870. Died: Aug. 7, 1939, Los Angeles, Calif. Screen and radio actress.

SEARS, FRED
Born: July 7, 1913, Boston, Mass. Died: Nov. 30, 1957, Hollywood, Calif. (heart attack). Screen, stage, television actor, film, stage, television director and stage producer.

Appeared in: 1947 Down to Earth; The Corpse Came C.O.D.; The Lone Hand Texan; West of Dodge City; Law of the Canyon; Blondie in the Dough; For the Love of Rusty; Blondie's Anniversary. 1948 Gallant Blade; Whirlwind Raiders; Phantom Valley; Adventures in Silverado; Rusty Leads the Way. 1949 Boston Blackie's Chinese Venture; Home in San Antone; Laramie; The Blazing Trail; Frontier Outpost; Renegades of the Sage; Bandits of El Dorado; The Lone Wolf and his Lady; South of Death Valley. 1950 Hoedown; David Harding—Counterspy; Texas Dynamo; Counterspy Meets Scotland Yard. 1951 Bonanza Town; The Kid from Amarillo; The Big Gusher; My True Story; Fort Savage Raider; Cyclone Fury. 1952 Laramie Mountains; The Rough Tough West.

SEARS, ZELDA
Born: 1873, Brockway, Mich. Died: Feb. 19, 1935, Hollywood, Calif. Screen, stage actress, author, playwright and screenwriter.

Appeared in: 1921 The Highest Bidder. 1930 The Bishop Murder Case; The Divorcee. 1931 Inspiration. 1935 A Wicked Woman.

SEASTROM, VICTOR (aka VICTOR SJOSTROM)
Born: Sept. 21, 1879, Varmland, Sweden. Died: Jan. 3, 1960, Stockholm, Sweden. Screen, stage actor, film director and stage director. Married to actress Leli Bech (dec. 1939). Entered films as an actor with Swedish Biograph Co. in 1912.

Appeared in: 1913 Ingeborg Holm. 1916 Terje Vigen. 1920 A Man There Was. 1921 You and I; Ordet (The Word). 1922 The Stroke of Midnight. 1938 John Ericsson, Victor of Hampton Roads. 1949 I Am with You. 1957 Wild Strawberries.

SEATON, SCOTT
Born: Mar. 11, 1878, Sacramento, Calif. Died: June 3, 1968, Hollywood, Calif. Screen, stage and television actor.

Appeared in: 1927 Wild Beauty; Rich Men's Sons; Thumbs Down. 1929 The Greyhound Limited; Leathernecks. 1930 The Other Tomorrow. 1935 Ruggles of Red Gap. 1950 Father of the Bride. 1956 Around the World in 80 Days. 1963 Twilight of Honor; Donovan's Reef.

SEBASTIAN, DOROTHY
Born: Apr. 1903, Birmingham, Ala. Died: Apr. 8, 1957, Hollywood, Calif. Stage and screen actress. Divorced from actor William "Hopalong Cassidy" Boyd (dec. 1972).

Appeared in: 1925 Sackcloth and Scarlet (film debut); Why Women Love (aka Sea Woman and Barriers Aflame); Winds of Chance. 1926 Bluebeard's Seven Wives; You'd Be Surprised. 1927 The Demi-Bride; The Arizona Wildcat; California; The Haunted Ship; Isle of Forgotten Women; On Ze Boulevard; Tea for Three; Twelve Miles Out; The Show. 1928 Our Dancing Daughters; Show People; Their Hour; Wyoming; House of Scandal; The Adventurer. 1929 The Single Standard; Spite Marriage; A Woman of Affairs; The Rainbow; The Spirit of Youth; The Devil's Apple Tree; The Unholy Night; Morgan's Last Raid. 1930 His First Command; Our Blushing Brides; Free and Easy; Hell's Island; Ladies Must Play; Brothers; The Utah Kid; Montana Moon; Officer O'Brien. 1931 The Deceiver; Lightning Flyer; Ships of Hate; The Big Gamble. 1932 They Never Came Back. 1933 Contraband; Ship of Wanted Men. 1934 Allez Oop (short); The Gold Ghost. 1937 The Mysterious Pilot (serial). 1939 Rough Riders' Round-Up; The Women; The Arizona Kid. 1941 Among the Living; Kansas Cyclone. 1942 True to the Army; Reap the Wild Wind.

SEBRING, JAY (Thomas Jay Kummer)
Born: Oct. 10, 1933, Alabama. Died: Aug. 8, 1969, Los Angeles, Calif. (murdered). Hair stylist and screen actor.

Appeared in: 1965 Synanon. 1967 Mondo Hollywood (aka Image and Hippie Hollywood; The Acid-Blasting Freaks).

SEDDON, MARGARET
Born: Nov. 18, 1872, Washington, D.C. Died: Apr. 17, 1968, Philadelphia, Pa. Screen and vaudeville actress. Appeared in vaudeville with Margaret McWade (dec. 1956) in an act billed as the "Pixilated Sisters."

Appeared in: 1915 The Old Homestead. 1917 The Girl Without a Soul. 1919 The Dawn of a Tomorrow; The Unveiling Hand. 1920 Miracle of Money. 1921 The Case of Becky; The Highest Law; The Inside of the Cup; Just Around the Corner; The Man Worth While; A Man's Home; School Days. 1922 Boomerang Bill; The Lights of New York; The Man Who Played God; Timothy's Quest; Women Men Marry; Sonny. 1923 Brass; The Bright Shawl; Little Johnny Jones; The Gold Diggers; Little Church Around the Corner. 1924 The Confidence Man; Snob; Women Who Give; Through the Dark; The Human Terror; A Lady of Quality; The Night Message. 1925 Wages for Wives; Proud Flesh; A Broadway Butterfly; The Lady; The Midshipman; New Lives for Old; On the Threshold. 1926 Blarney; Rolling Home; The Golden Cocoon; A Regular Scout; Wild Oats Lane. 1927 Matinee Ladies; Quality Street; Silk Legs; White Pants Willie; Driven from Home; Home Made. 1928 The Actress; Gentlemen Prefer Blondes. 1929 After the Fog; Bellamy Trial; Dance Hall; She Goes to War. 1930 Dancing Sweeties; The Dude Wrangler. 1931 Divorce Among Friends. 1932 Smilin' Through. 1933 Broadway Bad; Lilly Turner; Heroes for Sale; Midshipman Jack; The Worst Woman in Paris; Walls of Gold. 1935 The Flame Within; The Girl Friend; Two Sinners. 1936 Mr. Deeds Goes to Town; The Big Game; A Woman Rebels; College Holiday. 1937 Let's Make a Million; Danger—Love at Work. **1940** Dr. Kildare's Strangest Case; Raffles; Friendly Neighbors. **1941** Dr. Kildare's Wedding Day. **1942** The Wife Takes a Flyer; Scattergood Survives a Murder. **1943** The Meanest Man in the World. **1950** House by the River. **1951** Three Desperate Men (aka Three Outlaws).

SEDGWICK, EDIE (Edith Sedgwick)
Born: 1943. Died: Nov. 16, 1971, Santa Barbara, Calif. (acute barbitural intoxication).

Appeared in: **1965** Beauty II; Vinyl; Poor Little Rich Girl; Space. **1966** Face; Kitchen; Lupe; Outer and Inner Space. **1967** * * * *. **1968** The Queen. **1969** Diaries, Notes and Sketches. Other films: Restaurant; Chow Manhattan; Afternoon.

SEDGWICK, EDWARD, JR.
Born: Nov. 7, 1889 or 1892 (?), Galveston, Tex. Died: May 7, 1953, North Hollywood, Calif. (heart attack). Screen, stage, vaudeville, burlesque actor, film director and screenwriter. Son of stage actor Edward Sedgwick (dec. 1931) and stage actress Josephine Walker. See Josie Sedgwick for family information.

Appeared in: **1915** Greenbacks and Redskins. **1916** Married a Year; The Fascinating Model. **1917** The Haunted Pajamas; Fat and Foolish; The Yankee Way; The Varmint. **1919** Checkers.

SEDGWICK, JOSIE
Born: 1898, Galveston, Tex. Died: Apr. 30, 1973, Santa Monica, Calif. (stroke). Screen, stage and vaudeville actress. Daughter of stage actor Edward Sedgwick (dec. 1931) and stage actress Josephine Walker. Appeared in vaudeville in a family act billed as the "Five Sedgwicks" which included father, mother, sister Eileen and brother Edward, Jr. (dec. 1953).

Appeared in: **1916** Her Dream Man. **1917** Ashes of Hope; Fighting Back; The Maternal Spark; Indiscreet Corinne; Boss of the Lazy Y. **1918** Camouflage Kiss; Lure of the Circus (serial); Wolves of the Border; Paying His Debt; Wild Life. **1919** Jubilo; The She Wolf. **1920** Daredevil Jack (serial). **1921** Western Hearts; The Duke of Chimney Butte; Double Adventure (serial). **1922** Crimson Clue. **1923** The Sunshine Trail; Michael O'Halloran; Daddy. **1924** The Sawdust Trail; The White Moth. **1925** Daring Days; The Outlaw's Daughter; The Saddle Hawk; Let 'Er Buck. **1932** Son of Oklahoma.

SEEL, JEANNE N.
Born: 1898. Died: Sept. 9, 1964, Hollywood, Calif. (cancer). Stage and screen actress. Married to actor Charles Seel.

SEELOS, ANNETTE (Blanche Wallis)
Born: 1891. Died: Oct. 23, 1918, New York, N.Y. (Spanish influenza). Screen actress. Appeared in Essanay films.

SEELY, BLOSSOM
Born: 1892, San Pablo, Calif. Died: Apr. 17, 1974, New York, N.Y. Screen, stage, vaudeville and television actress. Divorced from theatrical manager Joseph Kane and baseball player Richard Marquard. Later married actor Benny Fields (dec. 1959).

Appeared in: **1933** Mr. Broadway; Blood Money; Broadway Thru a Keyhole.

SEGAR, LUCIA (aka LUCIA SEGER)
Born: 1874. Died: Jan. 17, 1962, New York, N.Y. Screen, stage and television actress.

Appeared in: **1921** The Wild Goose. **1922** The Bond Boy; The Bootleggers. **1923** Fury. **1927** Knockout Reilly. **1929** East Side Sadie. **1947** Boomerang.

SEGURA, LETICIA ESPINOSA
Born: Mexico. Died: Dec. 26, 1956, Mexico City, Mexico (auto accident). Screen and television actress.

SEIDEWITZ, MARIE
Died: Dec. 27, 1929, Baltimore, Md. Screen, stage and vaudeville actress.

SEIDNER, IRENE
Born: Dec. 10, 1880, Austria. Died: Nov. 17, 1959, Los Angeles, Calif. Stage and screen actress.

Appeared in: **1940** We Who are Young. **1942** All Through the Night. **1943** The Purple V. **1956** Miracle in the Rain.

SEITER, WILLIAM A.
Born: June 10, 1892, New York, N.Y. Died: July 26, 1964, Beverly Hills, Calif. (heart attack). Screen actor, film director, television director and film producer. Entered films as an actor with Sennett as a Keystone Kop.

Appeared in: **1913** The Three Wise Men. **1915** The Honeymoon Roll.

SEITZ, GEORGE B.
Born: Jan. 3, 1888, Boston, Mass. Died: July 8, 1944, Hollywood, Calif. Screen, stage actor, film producer, film director, screenwriter and playwright. Wrote the

scenarios, produced, directed and acted in the "Pearl White" Pathe serials. Entered films with Pathe in 1914.

Appeared in the following serials: **1919** The Black Secret; Bound and Gagged. **1920** Pirate Gold; Velvet Fingers. **1921** The Sky Ranger; Rogues and Romance (feature).

SEKELY, IRENE AGAY
Born: 1914, Hungary. Died: Sept. 2, 1950, Hollywood, Calif. Stage and screen actress.

Appeared in: **1946** The Fabulous Suzanne.

SELBIE, EVELYN
Born: July 6, 1882, Louisville, Ky. Died: Dec. 7, 1950, Hollywood, Calif. (heart ailment). Screen, stage and radio actress. Entered films as G. M. Anderson's (Bronco Billy) leading lady in 1912; was known as the original "Bronco Billy Girl."

Appeared in: **1914** The Squaw Man. **1919** The Red Glove (serial). **1921** Devil Dog Dawson; The Devil Within; Without Benefit of Clergy. **1922** Omar the Tentmaker; Thorns and Orange Blossoms; The Half Breed. **1923** The Broken Wing; Snowdrift; The Tiger's Claw. **1924** A Cafe in Cairo; Flapper Wives; Name the Man; Mademoiselle Midnight; Romance Ranch; Poisoned Paradise. **1925** The Prairie Pirate. **1926** The Country Beyond; Hell-Bent for Heaven; Into Her Kingdom; Flame of the Argentine; The Test of Donald Norton; The Silver Treasure; Silken Shackles; Rose of the Tenements; Prisoners of the Storm. **1927** Camille; Wild Geese; King of Kings; Eager Lips. **1928** Freedom of the Press. **1929** Eternal Love; The Mysterious Dr. Fu Manchu. **1930** The Return of Dr. Fu Manchu; Love Comes Along; Dangerous Paradise. **1932** The Hatchet Man. **1935** A Notorious Gentleman. **1938** If I Were King.

SELBY, NORMAN "KID McCOY"
Born: 1874. Died: Apr. 18, 1940, Detroit, Mich. (suicide). Screen actor.

Appeared in: **1921** Bucking the Line; To a Finish; Straight from the Shoulder. **1922** Arabia; Oathbound. **1926** April Showers. **1930** The Painted Angel. **1931** Loose Ankles.

SELK, GEORGE W.
Born: May 15, 1893, Nebr. Died: Jan. 22, 1967, Montrose, Calif. (heart disease). Screen actor.

Appeared in: **1953** City of Bad Men; It Came from Outer Space. **1954** Trader Tom of the China Seas (serial). **1957** The Vampire. **1958** Gun Fever. **1960** Guns of the Timberland.

SELLON, CHARLES
Born: Aug. 24, 1878, Boston, Mass. Died: June 26, 1937, La Crescenta, Calif. Stage and screen actor. Entered films in 1923.

Appeared in: **1923** The Bad Man (stage and film versions); Woman Proof; South Sea Love. **1924** Lover's Lane; The Roughneck; Flowing Gold; Merton of the Movies; Sundown. **1925** The Monster; The Night Ship; Tracked in the Snow Country; Private Affairs; The Calgary Stampede; Lucky Devil; Old Home Week; On the Threshold. **1926** High Steppers; The Speeding Venus; Racing Blood; Whispering Wires. **1927** Painted Ponies; Mysterious Rider; The Prairie King; Easy Pickings; King of Kings; The Valley of the Giants. **1928** Easy Come, Easy Go; Happiness Ahead; Something Always Happens; What a Night!; Feel My Pulse; The Count of Ten; Love Me and the World Is Mine. **1929** The Gamblers; Bulldog Drummond; Hot Stuff; Girl in the Glass Cage; Man and the Moment; The Mighty; The Saturday Night Kid; Big News; Men Are Like That; The Vagabond Lover; Sweetie. **1930** Under a Texas Moon; The Social Lion; Love among the Millionaires; Borrowed Wives; Big Money; For the Love of Lil; Sea Legs; Tom Sawyer; Let's Go Native; Burning Up; Honey. **1931** Man to Man; The Painted Desert; Behind Office Doors; Laugh and Get Rich; Dude Ranch; The Age for Love; Penrod and Sam; The Tip-Off. **1932** The Drifter; Carnival Boat; The Dark Horse; Make Me a Star; Speed Madness; Ride Him, Cowboy!; Central Park. **1933** Employees' Entrance; Strictly Personal; As the Devil Commands; Central Airport; Golden Harvest. **1934** Ready for Love; Private Scandal; Elmer and Elsie; It's a Gift; Bright Eyes. **1935** One Hour Late; Alias Mary Dow; The Devil Is a Woman; Life Begins at 40; It's a Small World; In Old Kentucky; Welcome Home; The Casino Murder Case; Diamond Jim.

SELTEN, MORTON (Morton Stubbs)
Born: Jan. 6, 1860. Died: July 27, 1939, London, England. Stage and screen actor.

Appeared in: **1931** Service for Ladies (aka Reserved for Ladies—US). **1932** Wedding Rehearsal. **1933** Falling for You; The Love Wager. **1934** How's Chances. **1935** His Majesty and Co.; Annie, Leave the Room!; Ten Minute Alibi; Moscow Nights (aka I Stand Condemned—US 1936); Dark World. **1936** The Ghost Goes West; In the Soup; Two's Company; Juggernaut (US 1937). **1937** Fire over England; Action for Slander (US 1938). **1938** The Divorce of Lady X; A Yank at Oxford. **1939** The Diplomatic Lover (reissue of How's Chances—1934); Shipyard Sally; Young Man's Fancy (US 1943). **1940** The Thief of Bagdad.

SELWYN, RUTH

Born: 1905, Tazwell, Va. Died: Dec. 14, 1954, Hollywood, Calif. Screen, stage actress, stage producer and writer.

Appeared in: **1931** Five and Ten. **1932** Speak Easily; Polly of the Circus; The Trial of Vivienne Ware; New Morals for Old. **1933** Men Must Fight. **1934** Fugitive Lovers. **1935** Baby Face Harrington.

SEMELS, HARRY

Born: Nov. 20, 1887, New York, N.Y. Died: Mar. 2, 1946, Los Angeles, Calif. Stage and screen actor. Entered films in 1910.

Appeared in: **1919** A Fallen Idol; Bound and Gagged (serial). **1920** Pirate Gold (serial); Velvet Fingers (serial). **1921** Hurricane Hutch (serial); The Sky Ranger (serial); Rogues and Romance. **1922** Speed (serial). **1923** Plunder (serial). **1924** Into the Net (serial); America. **1925** Play Ball (serial). **1926** The Demon; Moran of the Mounted; Stick to Your Story. **1927** Isle of Forgotten Women. **1928** Beware of Blondes; The Last Command; Out With the Tide; Put 'Em Up; Virgin Lips. **1929** The Delightful Rogue; Hawk of the Hills; The Royal Rider. **1930** Big Money; The Bad Man; Hell's Angels; Those Who Dance. **1931** Subway Express. **1933** Thrill Hunter. **1934** Our Daily Bread. **1935** Revenge Rider; Les Miserables; Sons of Steel; Old Sawbones (short); Stone of Silver Creek; The Last Outpost. **1936** Under Two Flags; The Gay Desperado; The Case of the Velvet Claws; plus the following shorts: Half-Shot Shooters; Disorder in the Court; Movie Maniacs; Am I Having Fun. **1937** Hotel Haywire; Swing It, Professor; Grand Hooter (short). **1938** Swiss Miss; Blockade. **1939** Rovin' Tumbleweeds; King of the Turf; Overland Mail; Three Little Sew and Sews (short). **1941** General Nuisance (short).

SEMON, LARRY

Born: July 16, 1889, West Point, Miss. Died: Oct. 8, 1928, Garcelon Ranch, near Victorville, Calif. (pneumonia). Screen, vaudeville actor, film producer, film director, screenwriter and newspaperman. Married to actress Dorothy Dwan.

Appeared in: **1917** Boasts and Boldness; Worries and Wobbles; Shells and Shivers; Chumps and Chances; Gall and Golf; Slips and Slackers; Risks and Roughnecks; Plans and Pajamas; Plagues and Puppy Love; Sports and Splashes; Toughluck and Tin Lizzies; Rough Toughs and Rooftops; Spooks and Spasms; Noisy Naggers and Nosey Neighbors. **1918** Guns and Greasers; Babes and Boobs; Rooms and Rumors; Meddlers and Moonshine; Stripes and Stumbles; Rummies and Razors; Whistles and Windows; Spies and Spills; Romans and Rascals; Skids and Scalawags; Boodles and Bandits; Hindoos and Hazards; Bathing Beauties and Big Boobs; Dunces and Danger; Mutts and Motors; Huns and Hyphens; Bears and Bad Men; Frauds and Frenzies; Humbus and Husbands; Pluck and Plotters. **1919** The Simple Life; Traps and Tangles; Scamps and Scandals; Soapsuds and Sapheads; Well, I'll Be . . . ; Passing the Buck; The Star Boarder; His Home Sweet Home; Between the Acts; Dull Care; Dew Drop Inn; The Headwaiter. **1920** The following shorts: The Grocery Clerk; The Fly Cop; School Days; Solid Concrete; The Stagehand; The Suitor. **1921** The following shorts: The Sportsman; The Hick; The Rent Collector; The Bakery; The Fall Guy; The Bell Hop. **1922** The following shorts: The Sawmill; The Show; A Pair of Kings; Golf; The Sleuth; The Counter Jumper. **1923** The following shorts: No Wedding Bells; The Barnyard; Midnight Cabaret; The Gown Shop; Lightning Love; Horseshoes. **1924** The Girl in the Limousine; plus the following shorts: Her Boy Friend; Kid Speed. **1925** The Perfect Clown; The Wizard of Oz; Go Straight; plus the following shorts: The Dome Doctor; The Cloudhopper. **1926** Stop, Look and Listen. **1927** Spuds; Underworld; plus the following shorts: The Stuntman; Oh What a Man. **1928** Dummies (short); A Simple Sap (short). **1930** Nuits de Chicago (French release of Underworld—1927).

SENNETT, MACK (Michael Sinnott)

Born: Jan. 17, 1880, Richmond, Quebec, Canada. Died: Nov. 5, 1960, Hollywood, Calif. Screen, stage, burlesque actor, film producer and film director. Entered films as an extra with Griffith. Introduced the Keystone Kops.

Appeared in: **1908** The Vaquero's Vow; Balked at the Altar; Father Gets in the Game; Mr. Jones Had a Card Party; The Curtain Pole; Mr. Jones at the Ball; An Awful Moment; A Wreath in Time; The Salvation Army Lass. **1909** The Slave; The Gibson Goddess; The Song of the Shirt; Politician's Love Story; The Lure of the Gown; Lucky Jim; The Jilt; The Seventh Day; A Convict's Sacrifice; The Better Way; Getting Even; The Awakening; In the Watches of the Night; The Trick That Failed; A Midnight Adventure; In a Hempen Bag; The Dancing Girl of Butte; A Corner in Wheat. **1910** All on Account of the Milk; An Affair of Hearts; A Knot in the Plot; Never Again; A Summer Tragedy; A Gold Necklace; The Passing of a Grouch; Effecting a Cure; His Wife's Sweethearts; The Newlyweds; A Midnight Cupid; A Mohawk's Way; Examination Day at School; An Arcadian Maid. **1911** The Italian Barber; Pricella's Engagement Kiss; Comrades; Paradise Lost; Misplaced Jealousy; The Crooked Road; A Dutch Gold Mine; The Ghost; Mr. Peck Goes Calling; The Dare Devil; The Village Hero; Trailing the Counterfeiter; Caught with the Goods; The $500 Reward. **1912** The Fatal Chocolate; A Message from the Moon; Their First Kidnapping Case; Tomboy Bessie; The Would-Be Shriner; Stern Papa. **1913** The Mistaken Masher; The Battle of Who Run; The Jealous Waiter; The Stolen Purse; Mabel's Heroes; The Sleuth's Last Stand; The Sleuths at the

Floral Parade; A Strong Revenge; The Rube and the Baron; At Twelve O'Clock; Her New Beau; Mabel's Awful Mistake (aka Her Deceitful Lover); Their First Execution; Barney Oldfield's Race for a Life; The Hansom Driver; His Crooked Career; Mabel's Dramatic Career (aka Her Dramatic Debut); Love Sickness at Sea; For Lizzie's Sake; The Chief's Predicament; The Bangville Police. **1914** A False Beauty (aka A Faded Vampire); Mack at It Again; Mabel at the Wheel (aka His Daredevil Queen); The Fatal Mallet; The Knock-Out (aka The Pugilist); In the Clutches of a Gang; Our Country Cousin; The Property Man (aka The Roustabout); His Talented Wife; Tillie's Punctured Romance. **1915** Hearts and Planets; The Little Teacher (aka A Small Town Bully); My Valet; Stolen Magic; Fatty and the Broadway Stars. **1921** Molly O. **1922** Oh, Mabel Behave. **1931** Movie Town (short). **1939** Hollywood Cavalcade. **1955** Abbott and Costello Meet the Keystone Kops. **1961** Days of Thrills and Laughter (documentary).

SERLING, ROD

Born: Dec. 25, 1924, Syracuse, N.Y. Died: June 28, 1975, Rochester, N.Y. (complications after heart surgery). Television producer, writer, narrator, screenwriter, author and screen actor.

Appeared in: **1973** Deadly Fathoms (narrator). **1975** The Outer Space Connection.

SERRANO, VINCENT

Born: 1867. Died: Jan. 10, 1935, New York, N.Y. (heart attack). Stage and screen actor.

Appeared in: **1919** Eyes of Youth. **1920** The Branded Woman. **1927** Convoy.

SERTEL, NEELA

Born: 1901, Turkey. Died: Dec. 1969, Istanbul, Turkey. Screen, stage and radio actress.

SERVOSS, MARY

Born: 1908. Died: Nov. 20, 1968, Los Angeles, Calif. (heart ailment). Stage and screen actress.

Appeared in: **1941** The Lone Wolf Keeps a Date. **1942** The Postman Didn't Ring; In This Our Life. **1943** So Proudly We Hail. **1944** Four Jills in a Jeep; Youth Runs Wild; Mrs. Parkington; Summer Storm; Experiment Perilous; Danger Signal. **1945** Conflict. **1948** Live Today for Tomorrow. **1949** Beyond the Forest.

SESSIONS, ALMIRA

Born: 1888, Washington, D.C. Died: Aug. 3, 1974, Los Angeles, Calif. Screen, stage, vaudeville, radio and television actress.

Appeared in: **1940** Little Nelly Kelly; Chad Hanna. **1941** She Knew All the Answers; Sun Valley Serenade; Three Girls About Town. **1942** Sullivan's Travels. **1943** My Kingdom for a Cook; The Heat's On; Seeing Nellie Home (short); The Ox-Bow Incident. **1944** Dixie Jamboree; Henry Aldrich's Little Secret; Miracle of Morgan's Creek. **1945** The Woman Who Came Back. **1946** Fear; She Wouldn't Say Yes; Diary of a Chambermaid; Do You Love Me?; The Missing Lady. **1947** The Bishop's Wife; Monsieur Verdoux; For the Love of Rusty. **1948** Apartment for Peggy; Arthur Takes Over. **1949** Night Unto Night; Roseanna McCoy; The Fountainhead. **1950** The Blazing Hills (aka The Blazing Sun); The Old Frontier. **1952** Oklahoma Annie; Wagons West. **1953** The Affairs of Dobie Gillis. **1954** Forever Female; Hell's Outpost. **1956** Calling Homicide; The Scarlet Hour. **1961** Summer and Smoke. **1962** Paradise Alley. **1963** Under the Yum Yum Tree. **1968** The Boston Strangler; Rosemary's Baby. **1972** Everything You Always Wanted to Know About Sex But Were Afraid to Ask.

SETON, SIR BRUCE

Born: May 29, 1909, Simla, India. Died: Sept. 17, 1969, London, England. Screen, stage and television actor. Divorced from actress Tamara Desni. Married to actress Antoinette Cellier.

Appeared in: **1935** Blue Smoke; Flame in the Heather. **1936** The Vandergilt Diamond Mystery; Sweeney Todd, the Demon Barber of Fleet Street (US 1939); Wedding Group (aka Wrath of Jealousy—US); Melody of My Heart; Annie Laurie; The Beauty Doctor; Cocktail; The End of the Road. **1937** Cafe Colette (aka Danger in Paris—US); Love from a Stranger; Father Steps Out; Racing Romance; The Green Cockatoo (US 1947 aka Four Dark Hours); Fifty-Shilling Boxer. **1938** If I Were Boss; Weddings Are Wonderful; You're the Doctor; Miracles Do Happen. **1939** The Middle Watch; Lucky to Me; Old Mother Riley Joins Up. **1946** The Curse of the Wraydons. **1948** Bonnie Prince Charlie; Scott of the Antarctic (US 1949); Look Before You Love; The Story of Shirley Yorke. **1949** Whisky Galore! (aka Tight Little Island—US and Mad Little Island). **1950** The Blue Lamp; Paul Temple's Triumph (US 1951); Portrait of Clare. **1951** Take Me to Paris; Blackmailed; Worm's Eye View. **1952** Emergency Call (aka The Hundred Hour Hunt—US 1953). **1953** The Cruel Sea. **1954** Eight O'Clock Walk (US 1955); Delayed Action. **1957** West of Suez (aka Fighting Wildcats—US); There's Always Thursday; The Crooked Sky (US 1959); Morning Call. **1958** The Strange Case of Mr. Manning. **1959** Violent Moment (US 1966); Hidden Homicide (US 1960); Life in Danger (US 1964); John Paul Jones; Make Mine a Million (US 1965). **1960** Operation

Cupid; Trouble with Eve (aka In Trouble with Eve—US 1964). **1961** Gorgo; The Frightened City (US 1962); Greyfriars Bobby.

SEVAL, NEVIN

Born: 1920, Turkey. Died: Nov. 1958, Adana, Turkey. Screen and stage actress.

SEVER, ALFRED

Born: 1891. Died: Mar. 26, 1953, New York, N.Y. Screen actor. Appeared in silent films.

SEVERIN-MARS

Born: France. Died: Sept. 1921 (pneumonia). Stage and screen actor.

Appeared in: **1918** La Dixieme Symphonie. **1921** La Roue.

SEWELL, ALLEN D.

Born: 1883. Died: Jan. 20, 1954, Hollywood, Calif. Screen actor.

Appeared in: **1914** The Squaw Man; The Spoilers. **1927** Between Dangers.

SEYFERTH, WILFRIED

Born: 1908, Germany. Died: Oct. 9, 1954, near Wiesbaden, West Germany (auto accident). Stage and screen actor.

Appeared in: **1933** Schleppzug 17 (film debut). **1951** Decision before Dawn. **1952** The Devil Makes Three. **1953** The Grapes Are Ripe. **1958** Zero Eight One Five (08/15—US 1958). **1959** Das Tanzende Herz (The Dancing Heart). Other German films: Der Froehliche Weimberg; Toxi; Heimweh Nach Dir.

SEYMOUR, CLARINE

Born: 1901. Died: Apr. 25, 1920, New York, N.Y. Screen actress.

Appeared in: **1919** True Heart Susie; The Girl Who Stayed at Home. **1920** The Idol Dancer.

SEYMOUR, HARRY

Born: 1890. Died: Nov. 11, 1967, Hollywood, Calif. (heart attack). Screen, stage, vaudeville actor and composer.

Appeared in: **1925** East Lynne. **1932** The Tenderfoot; You Said a Mouthful; Man against Woman. **1934** The Crosby Case; Service With a Smile (short); The Case of the Howling Dog; Six Day Bike Rider. **1935** Shipmates Forever; Broadway Hostess; Behind Green Lights. **1938** A Slight Case of Murder; Boy Meets Girl. **1939** Kid Nightingale. **1940** A Fugitive from Justice. **1942** Yankee Doodle Dandy. **1947** I Wonder Who's Kissing Her Now. **1948** Give My Regards to Broadway. **1949** It Happens Every Spring. **1950** A Ticket to Tomahawk. **1953** Vicki; Mr. Scoutmaster. **1955** The Girl in the Red Velvet Swing; Daddy Long Legs; How to Be Very, Very Popular; Violent Saturday.

SEYMOUR, JANE

Born: 1899. Died: Jan. 30, 1956, New York, N.Y. Screen, stage, radio and television actress.

Appeared in: **1939** Back Door to Heaven. **1941** Tom, Dick and Harry; Remember the Day.

SHACKLETON, ROBERT W.

Born: 1914, Lawrence, Mass. Died: June 21, 1956, Jacksonville, Fla. (leukemia). Stage and screen actor.

Appeared in: **1951** The Wonder Kid. **1952** Where's Charley? (stage and film versions).

SHADE, JAMESSON

Born: 1895. Died: Apr. 18, 1956, Hollywood, Calif. (heart attack). Screen, stage and telvision actor.

Appeared in: **1943** Santa Fe Scouts; The Woman of the Town. **1944** The Utah Kid. **1945** Wilson. **1949** Treasure of Monte Cristo; Cover-Up. **1955** Ain't Misbehavin'.

SHADOW, BERT

Born: 1890. Died: Nov. 1936, Hollywood, Calif. (heart ailment). Screen and vaudeville actor. Was partner in "Shadow and McNeill" vaudeville team with his wife Lillian McNeill.

SHAFER, MOLLIE B.

Born: 1872. Died: Nov. 19, 1940, Hollywood, Calif. Screen actress.

Appeared in: **1921** The Big Adventure; While the Devil Laughs.

SHAIFFER, "TINY" (Howard Charles Shaiffer)

Born: 1918. Died: Jan. 24, 1967, Burbank, Calif. Screen actor. Member of "Our Gang" comedies.

SHANKLAND, RICHARD

Born: 1904. Died: Jan. 18, 1953, New York, N.Y. Screen, stage and television actor.

Appeared in: **1958** Love Island.

SHANLEY, ROBERT

Died: June 30, 1968, Los Angeles, Calif. Screen, stage, radio, television actor and singer.

Appeared in: **1943** This Is the Army (stage and film versions).

SHANNON, CORA

Born: Jan. 30, 1869 or 1879 (?), Ill. Died: Aug. 27, 1957, Woodland Hills, Calif. (cancer). Stage and screen actress. Entered films in 1912.

Appeared in: **1923** Long Live the King; Held to Answer; The Spanish Dancer; The Good Bad Boy; The Shadows of Paris; The Way Men Love; Her Temporary Husband; Painted People; Cape Cod Folks; Racing Luck; One Law for the Woman; Welcome Stranger; The Last Man; A Woman Who Sinned. **1924** The Dawn of a Tomorrow; Triumph Rose of the Ghetto; The Woman on the Jury; The Silent Stranger; San Francisco; Wanderer of the Wasteland; Hold Your Breath. **1926** Trumpin' Trouble. **1929** Smiling Irish Eyes. **1930** Lummox. **1951** Mr. Belvedere Rings the Bell. **1953** Abbott and Costello Go to Mars.

SHANNON, MRS. DALE

Died: June 1, 1923, New York, N.Y. Stage and screen actress. Appeared in Lubin films.

SHANNON, EFFIE

Born: 1867, Cambridge, Mass. Died: July 24, 1954, Bay Shore, N.Y. Stage and screen actress.

Appeared in: **1914** After the Ball. **1921** Mama's Affair. **1922** The Man Who Played God; The Secrets of Paris; Sure-Fire Flint. **1923** The Tie That Binds; Bright Lights of Broadway; Jacqueline of the Blazing Barriers. **1924** Damaged Hearts; Roulette; Sinners in Heaven; Greater Than Marriage; The Side Show of Life. **1925** Sally of the Sawdust; Soul of Fire; The New Commandment; The Pearl of Love; Wandering Fires. **1932** The Wiser Sex.

SHANNON, ELIZABETH S. (aka BETTY SUNDMARK)

Born: 1914. Died: Aug. 18, 1959, N.Y. Screen actress. Divorced from actor Alan Curtis (dec. 1953).

SHANNON, ETHEL (Ethel Shannon Jackson)

Born: 1898. Died: July 14, 1951, Hollywood, Calif. Screen actress. Married to screenwriter Joe Jackson (dec. 1932).

Appeared in: **1920** An Old Fashioned Boy. **1922** Man's Law and God's; The Top O' the Morning; Watch Him Step. **1923** The Hero; Daughters of the Rich; The Girl Who Came Back; Maytime. **1924** Lightning Romance; Riders Up. **1925** Charley's Aunt; High and Handsome; The Phantom Express; Stop Flirting; The Texas Trail; Speed Wild. **1926** Oh, Baby!; The Speed Limit; The Sign of the Cross; The Silent Power; The High Flyer; The Buckaroo Kid; Danger Quest. **1927** Babe Comes Home; Through Thick and Thin.

SHANNON, FRANK CONNOLLY

Born: 1875. Died: Feb. 1, 1959, Hollywood, Calif. Screen, stage and radio actor.

Appeared in: **1921** The Bride's Play; Perjury. **1922** Boomerang Bill. **1924** Icebound; Monsieur Beaucaire. **1935** G-Men; Men without Names; The Eagle's Brood. **1936** The Prisoner of Shark Island; Flash Gordon (serial); The Texas Rangers. **1937** The Affairs of Cappy Ricks; The Adventurous Blonde. **1938** Blondes at Work; Flash Gordon's Trip to Mars (serial); Mars Attacks the World; Torchy Blane in Panama; Torchy Gets Her Man. **1939** Torchy Plays with Dynamite; Torchy Blane in Chinatown; Torchy Runs for Mayor; The Night of Nights. **1940** Flash Gordon Conquers the Universe (serial); The Return of Frank James; Wildcat Bus; Dancing on a Dime.

SHANNON, HARRY

Born: June 13, 1890, Saginaw, Mich. Died: July 27, 1964; Hollywood, Calif. Stage and screen actor.

Appeared in: **1930** Heads Up. **1933** Poor Fish (short). **1940** Young as You Feel; Parole Fixer; One Crowded Night; Too Many Girls; Gambling on the High Seas; The Girl from Avenue A; Young Tom Edison; City of Chance; Tear Gas Squad; Tugboat Annie Sails Again; Sailor's Lady. **1941** Citizen Kane; The Saint in Palm Springs; Hold Back the Dawn. **1942** The Lady Is Willing; The Big Street; Mrs. Wiggs of the Cabbage Patch; Once upon a Honeymoon; This Gun for Hire; The Falcon Takes Over; In Old California; Random Harvest. **1943** Alaska Highway; Headin' for God's Country; True to Life; Idaho; Someone to Remember; Song of Texas; Gold Town; The Powers Girl. **1944** The Sullivans; The Mummy's Ghost; When the Lights Go on Again; Yellow Rose of Texas; Eve of St. Mark; Ladies of Washington. **1945** Captain Eddie; Crime, Inc.; Nob Hill; Within These Walls. **1946** Night Editor; San Quentin; I Ring Doorbells; Ziegfeld Follies; The Last Crooked Mile. **1947** The Devil Thumbs a Ride; The Farmer's Daughter; Nora Prentiss; The Red House; Time out of Mind; The Invisible Wall; Exposed; Dangerous Years. **1948** The Lady from Shanghai; Mr. Blandings Builds His Dream House; Fighting Father Dunne; Feudin', Fussin' and A-Fightin'. **1949** Tulsa; Rustlers; Champion; Mr. Soft Touch; The Devil's Henchmen. **1950** Mary Ryan, Detective; Tarnished; The Dungeon; Cow Town; The Underworld Story; Singing Guns; Where Danger Lives; Three Little Words; Curtain Call at Cactus Creek; Hunt the Man

Down; The Flying Missile; The Killer That Stalked New York; The Gunfighter. **1951** Pride of Maryland; The Scarf; Al Jennings of Oklahoma; Blue Blood; The Lemon Drop Kid. **1952** High Noon; Boots Malone; Flesh and Fury; The Outcasts of Poker Flat; Lure of the Wilderness. **1953** Cry of the Hunted; Kansas Pacific; Jack Slade; Phantom Stallion; Roar of the Crowd. **1954** Executive Suite; Witness to Murder; Rails into Laramie. **1955** The Tall Men; Violent Men; At Gunpoint; The Marauders. **1956** Come Next Spring; Written on the Wind; The Peacemaker. **1957** The Lonely Man; Duel at Apache Wells; Hell's Crossroads. **1958** The Buccaneer; Man or Gun. **1961** Summer and Smoke; Wild in the Country. **1962** Gypsy.

SHANNON, JACK
Born: 1892. Died: Dec. 1968, Los Angeles, Calif. Screen actor and stuntman. Married to actress Grace Cunard (dec. 1967).

Appeared in: **1935** Stormy.

SHANNON, PEGGY
Born: Jan. 10, 1909, Pine Bluff, Ark. Died: May 11, 1941, North Hollywood, Calif. (natural causes). Stage and screen actress. Married to actor and cameraman Albert Roberts (dec. 1941).

Appeared in: **1931** Silence; The Road to Reno; The Secret Call; Touchdown. **1932** False Faces; This Reckless Age; Hotel Continental; The Painted Woman; Society Girl. **1933** Girl Missing; Devil's Mate; The Deluge; Turn Back the Clock. **1934** Fury of the Jungle; Back Page. **1935** The Fighting Lady; Night Life of the Gods; The Case of the Lucky Legs. **1936** The Man I Marry. **1937** Youth on Parole. **1938** Girls on Probation. **1939** Dad for a Day (short); Blackwell's Island; The Women; The Adventures of Jane Arden; Fixer Dugan. **1940** The House across the Bay; Triple Justice; Cafe Hostess; Street of Missing Women; All About Hash (short).

SHANNON, RAY
Born: 1895. Died: Jan. 1, 1971, Cincinnati, Ohio. Screen, stage, vaudeville and radio actor.

SHANOR, PEGGY
Died: May 30, 1935, New York, N.Y. Screen, stage and vaudeville actress. Featured in vaudeville with Vera Gordon and Sam Selbert.

Appeared in: **1918** The House of Hate (serial). **1919** The Lurking Peril (serial). **1920** The Mystery Mind (serial). **1921** The Sky Ranger (serial). **1922** The Prodigal Judge.

SHARKEY, TOM "SAILOR"
Born: 1873, Dundalk, Ireland. Died: Apr. 17, 1953, San Francisco, Calif. Professional boxer and screen actor.

Appeared in: **1928** Good Morning Judge. **1932** Madison Square Garden.

SHARLAND, REGINALD
Born: 1887, Southend-on-Sea, Essex, England. Died: Aug. 21, 1944, Loma Linda, Calif. Screen, stage and radio actor.

Appeared in: **1929** Show of Shows; Woman to Woman. **1930** Girl of the Port; Scotland Yard; What a Widow; Inside the Lines. **1931** Born to Love. **1934** Long Lost Father.

SHARON, WILLIAM E.
Died: Dec. 26, 1968. Screen actor.

Appeared in: **1962** Experiment in Terror.

SHARP, HENRY (Henry Schacht)
Born: 1887. Died: Jan. 10, 1964, Brooklyn, N.Y. Screen, stage actor and educator. Entered films with D. W. Griffith.

Appeared in: **1945** A Song to Remember. **1956** Singing in the Dark. **1957** A Face in the Crowd; The Violators.

SHARP, LEONARD "LEN"
Born: 1890. Died: Oct. 24, 1958, Waterford, England. Screen, stage and television actor. Married to actress Nora Gordon (dec. 1970).

Appeared in: **1950** The Mudlark. **1952** The Stolen Plans (US 1962). **1954** For Better or Worse (aka Cocktails in the Kitchen—US 1955). **1955** The Ladykillers (US 1956). **1957** At the Stroke of Nine (US 1958).

SHARPE, GYDA
Born: 1908. Died: Jan. 14, 1973, Hollywood, Calif. (cancer). Stage and screen actress.

SHARPE, LESTER (Lester Scharff)
Born: Mar. 21, 1895, New York, N.Y. Died: Nov. 30, 1962, Los Angeles, Calif. (heart attack). Screen actor.

Appeared in: **1940** Remedy for Riches. **1942** Time to Kill. **1943** Hangmen Also Die. **1944** The Mummy's Ghost. **1947** Song of My Heart. **1948** The Gallant Legion; Port Said. **1949** Amazon Quest; I Was a Male War Bride. **1950** The Flying Saucer; Where the Sidewalk Ends; One Too Many; Unmasked. **1952** Carrie. **1954** Princess of the Nile.

SHARPLIN, JOHN
Born: 1916. Died: Apr. 1961, Harrogate, England. Screen, stage and television actor.

SHATTUCK, EDWARD F.
Born: 1890. Died: Jan. 31, 1948, Hollywood, Calif. Screen and vaudeville actor.

SHATTUCK, TRULY
Born: 1876. Died: Dec. 6, 1954, Hollywood, Calif. Screen and stage actress.

Appeared in: **1921** A Wise Fool; The Great Impersonation; The Speed Girl. **1922** The Glory of Clementina; The Hottentot; Beauty's Worth. **1923** Daughters of the Rich. **1927** Rubber Heels. **1935** The Perfect Clue.

SHAW, C. MONTAGUE
Born: Mar. 23, 1884, Adelaide, South Australia. Died: Feb. 6, 1968, Woodland Hills, Calif. Stage and screen actor.

Appeared in: **1926** The Set-Up. **1928** The Water Hole. **1929** Behind That Curtain; Morgan's Last Raid; Square Shoulders. **1932** The Silent Witness; Pack up Your Troubles; Sherlock Holmes; Cynara; Letty Lynton; Rasputin and the Empress. **1933** The Big Brain; The Masquerader; Today We Live; Cavalcade; Gabriel over the White House; Queen Christina. **1934** Shock; Sisters under the Skin; Fog; Riptide; House of Rothschild. **1935** Vanessa, Her Love Story; David Copperfield; Becky Sharp; Two Sinners; I Live for Love. **1936** The Leathernecks Have Landed; Undersea Kingdom (serial); My American Wife; King of Burlesque. **1937** Riders of the Whistling Skull; The Frame Up; Parole Racket; The Sheik Steps Out; A Nation Aflame; Ready, Willing and Able; The King and the Chorus Girl. **1938** Mars Attacks the World; Four Men and a Prayer; Little Miss Broadway; Suez. **1939** Mr. Moto's Last Warning; The Adventures of Sherlock Holmes; The Three Musketeers; The Rains Came; Stanley and Livingstone. **1940** My Son, My Son; The Gay Caballero; Charlie Chan's Murder Cruise. **1941** Hard Guy; Burma Convoy; Charley's Aunt. **1942** Thunder Birds; Random Harvest; Pride of the Yankees. **1944** Faces in the Fog. **1945** An Angel Comes to Brooklyn; Tonight and Every Night. **1946** Road to the Big House. **1947** Thunder in the Valley.

SHAW, DENNIS
Born: 1921. Died: Feb. 28, 1971, London, England (heart attack). Screen and television actor.

Appeared in: **1959** The Mummy; The Night We Dropped a Clanger (aka Make Mine a Double—US 1961); Jack the Ripper (US 1960). **1961** Hellfire Club (US 1963).

SHAW, ELLIOTT
Born: 1887. Died: Aug. 13, 1973. Screen actor and member of the "Shannon Four" and "The Revelers."

Appeared in: Metro short.

SHAW, FRANK M.
Born: 1894. Died: May 7, 1937, Kansas City, Mo. Screen, stage and radio actor.

SHAW, GEORGE BERNARD
Born: July 26, 1856, Dublin, Ireland. Died: Nov. 1, 1950, Ayot St. Lawrence, England (bladder ailment, injuries sustained in fall). Playwright, author, screenwriter and screen performer.

Appeared in: **1918** Masks and Faces.

SHAW, HAROLD M.
Died: Feb. 1926 (auto accident). Screen actor, film producer, director and screenwriter. Married to actress Edna Flugrath. Entered films with Edison Co. in 1909.

Appeared in: **1911** The Three Musketeers; Bob and Rowdy; The Modern Dianas; Mary's Masquerade; The Death of Nathan Hale; Foul Play; Her Wedding Ring; How Mrs. Murray Saved the American Flag; The Kid from the Klondyke; A Conspiracy Against the King; The Awakening of John Bond; The Black Arrow; The Reform Candidate; Home; The Lure of the City; Santa Claus and the Club Man; Freezing Auntie. **1912** Martin Chuzzlewit; Thirty Days at Hard Labor; A Question of Seconds; The Bachelor's Waterloo; The Jewels; Mother and Daughter; The Corsican Brothers; Her Face; For the Commonwealth; The Bank President's Son; The Convict's Parole. **1913** The Wop. **1924** Winning a Continent.

SHAW, OSCAR (Oscar Schwartz)
Born: 1891. Died: Mar. 6, 1967, Little Neck, N.Y. Screen, stage and radio actor.

Appeared in: **1924** The Great White Way. **1925** The King on Main Street. **1926** Going Crooked; Upstage. **1929** The Cocoanuts; Marianne. **1940** Rhythm on the River.

SHAWN, TED (Edwin M. Shawn)
Born: 1892. Died: Jan. 9, 1972, Orlando, Fla. (emphysema). Screen, stage actor, dancer and choreographer. Married to actress and dancer Ruth St. Denis (dec. 1969).

Appeared in: **1919** Don't Change Your Husband.

SHAY, PATRICIA
Died: Aug. 9, 1966. Screen actress.

Appeared in: **1944** To Have and Have Not. **1948** Million Dollar Weekend.

SHEA, BIRD
Died: Nov. 23, 1924, Los Angeles, Calif. Screen actress.

Appeared in: **1925** The Lady.

SHEA, JOHN "JACK"
Born: 1900, Charleston, W.Va. Died: Oct. 13, 1970, Huntington, W.Va. Screen, stage and vaudeville actor.

Appeared in: **1941** Glamour Boy. **1951** Million Dollar Pursuit. **1955** Lucy Gallant. **1958** Satan's Satellites. **1961** Ada; The Last Sunset; The Touchables. **1962** Whatever Happened to Baby Jane?

SHEA, WILLIAM (William James Shea)
Born: Scotland. Died: Nov. 5, 1918, Brooklyn, N.Y. Screen, stage actor and screenwriter. Entered films in 1905 with Vitagraph.

Appeared in: **1911** Intrepid Davy; The Politician's Dream; Vanity Fair. **1912** Pandora's Box; The Little Minister; Her Old Sweetheart; Chumps; Who's to Win?; Aunty's Romance; Too Many Caseys. **1913** An Elopement at Home; O'Hara's Godchild; The Last of the Madisons; The Widow's Might; Classmates; Frolic; Suspicious Henry; The Mouse and the Lion; Dick—The Dead Shot; His Life for His Emperor; She Never Knew; Cupid Through the Keyhole; 'Arriet's Baby. **1914** The Spirit and the Clay; Jerry's Uncle's Namesake; Sweeney's Christmas Bird; Mrs. Maloney's Fortune; The Hero; The Rival Undertakers; The Old Rag Doll; The Vases of Hymen. **1915** A Pair of Queens; Mr. Bixbie's Dilemma; Mr. Jarry's Vacation; Some Duel; Pat Hogan—Deceased; A Wireless Rescue; The Lady of Shalott; Two and Two; Heavy Villains; She Took a Chance; When Hooligan and Dooligan Ran for Mayor; Benjamin Bunter—Booking Agent; Between Two Fires; My Lady's Slipper; No Tickee-No Washee. **1916** Help! Help! Help!; Footlights of Fate; A Night Out; Huey—The Process Server; Putting the Pep in Slowtown; Kernel Nutt, the Piano Tuner; The Blue Envelope Mystery; The Bigamist; The Memory Mill; A Villainous Villain. **1917** Sally in a Hurry; The Doctor's Deception. **1918** A Bachelor's Children.

SHEAN, AL (Alfred Schoenberg)
Born: 1868, Dornum, Germany. Died: Aug. 12, 1949, New York, N.Y. Screen, stage, vaudeville actor and songwriter. Was partner in vaudeville act "Mr. Gallagher and Mr. Shean."

Appeared in: **1923** Around the Town. **1930** Chills and Fever (short). **1934** Music in the Air. **1935** Sweet Music; Page Miss Glory; The Traveling Saleslady; Symphony of Living; It's in the Air. **1936** The Law in Her Hands; San Francisco; Hitchhike to Heaven; At Sea Ashore (short). **1937** The Road Back; It Could Happen to You; 52nd Street; Live, Love and Learn; The Prisoner of Zenda. **1938** Too Hot to Handle; The Great Waltz. **1939** Joe and Ethel Turp Call on the President; Broadway Serenade. **1940** The Blue Bird; Friendly Neighbors. **1941** Ziegfeld Girl. **1942** Tish. **1943** Hitler's Madmen; Crime Doctor. **1944** Atlantic City. **1946** People Are Funny.

SHEARN, EDITH
Born: 1870. Died: May 14, 1968, Hollywood, Calif. Screen actress. Married to actor Warner Oland (dec. 1938).

SHEEHAN, BOBBIE
Died: Oct. 8, 1974. Screen actress and extra.

Appeared in: **1956** Around the World in 80 Days.

SHEEHAN, JOHN J.
Born: Oct. 22, 1890, Oakland, Calif. Died: Feb. 15, 1952, Hollywood, Calif. Screen, stage and vaudeville actor. Entered films with American Film Co. in 1916.

Appeared in: **1930** Swing High; Broken Dishes; Kismet. **1931** Fair Warning; The Criminal Code. **1932** Hold 'Em Jail. **1933** Hard to Handle; The Warrior's Husband; The Past of Mary Holmes; King for a Night; The Gay Nighties (short). **1934** Trimmed in Furs (short); An Old Gypsy Custom (short); The Countess of Monte Cristo; Little Miss Marker; The Circus Clown; Such Women Are Dangerous. **1935** The Murder Man; The Goose and the Gander. **1936** It Had to Happen; Three Godfathers; Laughing Irish Eyes; Ticket to Paradise; The Ex-Mrs. Bradford; The Case of the Black Cat; Smart Blonde; Here Comes Carter. **1937** Join the Marines; All over Town; Mama Runs Wild; On the Avenue; Wake up and Live; Marked Woman; Midnight Court; Love Takes Flight; Night Club Scandal. **1938** Many Sappy Returns (short). **1940** Slightly Honorable; Margie; Young as You Feel. **1941** Broadway Limited. **1942** Yankee

Doodle Dandy; Wake Island. **1943** Swingtime Johnny. **1948** I Wouldn't Be in Your Shoes. **1949** The Doolins of Oklahoma. **1950** Stage to Tucson.

SHEEHAN, TESS (Maria Theresa Sheehan)
Born: 1888. Died: Oct. 29, 1972, Detroit, Mich. Screen, stage, radio and television actress.

SHEERER, WILL E.
Died: Dec. 24, 1915. Stage and screen actor.

Appeared in: **1913** Over the Cliffs.

SHEFFIELD, REGINALD (Reginald Sheffield Cassan)
Born: Feb. 18, 1901, London, England. Died: Dec. 8, 1957, Pacific Palisades, Calif. Stage and screen actor. Entered films in 1913.

Appeared in: **1923** David Copperfield. **1924** Classmates. **1925** The Pinch Hitter. **1926** White Mice. **1927** The Nest; College Widow. **1928** Sweet Sixteen; The Adorable Cheat. **1930** Old English; The Green Goddess. **1931** Partners of the Trail. **1934** The House of Rothschild; Of Human Bondage. **1935** Black Sheep; Cardinal Richelieu; Society Fever; Splendor. **1937** Another Dawn. **1938** Female Fugitive; The Buccaneer. **1939** Gunga Din. **1940** Earthbound. **1941** Suspicion. **1942** Eyes in the Night; Eagle Squadron. **1943** Appointment in Berlin; The Man from Down Under; Tonight We Raid Calais; Bomber's Moon. **1944** Our Hearts Were Young and Gay; The Man in Half Moon Street; Wilson; The Great Moment. **1945** Captain Kidd; Devotion. **1946** Three Strangers; Centennial Summer. **1948** Kiss the Blood off My Hands. **1949** Mr. Belvedere Goes to College; Prison Warden. **1953** Second Chance. **1956** 23 Paces to Baker Street; The Secret of Treasure Mountain. **1957** The Story of Mankind. **1958** The Buccaneer (and 1938 version).

SHELBY, CHARLOTTE (Lily Pearl Miles)
Died: Mar. 13, 1957, Santa Monica, Calif. Screen actress. Mother of actresses Margaret Shelby (dec. 1939) and Mary Miles Minter.

Appeared in: **1915** Always in the Way. **1916** Dimples. **1917** Her Country's Call.

SHELBY, MARGARET
Born: 1900, San Antonio, Tex. Died: 1939. Screen actress. Daughter of actress Charlotte Shelby (dec. 1957) and sister of actress Mary Miles Minter.

Appeared in: **1912** Billie. **1916** Faith. **1917** Her Country's Call; Environment; Peggy Leads the Way. **1918** Rosemary Climbs the Heights; Wives and Other Wives. **1919** A Bachelor's Wife; The Intrusion of Isabel; The Amazing Imposter. **1920** Jenny Be Good.

SHELDON, JEROME
Born: 1891. Died: Apr. 15, 1962, Hollywood, Calif. Screen actor. Appeared in silents.

SHELDON, JERRY (Charles H. Patton)
Born: 1901. Died: Apr. 11, 1962, Hollywood, Calif. Screen and television actor.

Appeared in: **1952** Monkey Business. **1956** Love Me Tender.

SHELDON, MARION W.
Born: 1886. Died: Feb. 28, 1944, Hollywood, Calif. Screen and stage actress. Entered films in 1917.

SHELTON, CONNIE
Born: 1921. Died: Jan. 10, 1947, N.Y. (leukemia). Screen and stage actress.

SHELTON, GEORGE
Born: 1884. Died: Feb. 12, 1971, N.Y. (burns). Screen, stage, vaudeville, burlesque, radio and television actor. Partner in vaudeville and radio with Tom Howard (dec. 1955).

Appeared in: **1932** The Babbling Book (short). **1934-35** Educational shorts. **1945** The House on Ninety-Second Street. **1947** Kiss of Death.

SHELTON, JAMES
Born: 1913, Paducah, Ky. Died: Sept. 2, 1975, Miami, Fla. Screen actor, songwriter and television writer.

Appeared in: **1920** Over the Hill. **1931** City Lights.

SHEPLEY, IDA
Born: England. Died: Mar. 1975, London, England. Screen, stage actress and singer.

SHEPLEY, MICHAEL (Michael Shepley-Smith)
Born: Sept. 29, 1907, Plymouth, England. Died: Sept. 28, 1961, London, England. Stage and screen actor.

Appeared in: **1931** Black Coffee. **1934** Bella Donna (US 1935); Are You a Mason?; The Green Pack. **1935** The Rocks of Valpre (aka High Treason—US 1937); The Lad; The Ace of Spades; The Triumph of Sherlock Holmes; Squibs; Vintage Wine; The Private Secretary. **1936** In the Soup. **1938** Housemaster (US 1939); Crackerjack (aka The Man with a Hundred Faces—US);

It's in the Air (aka George Takes the Air—US 1940). **1939** Goodbye Mr. Chips. **1941** Quiet Wedding. **1942** The Great Mr. Handel (US 1943). **1943** The Demi-Paradise (aka Adventure for Two—US 1945). **1945** Henry V (US 1946); A Place of One's Own (US 1949); I Live in Grosvenor Square (aka A Yank in London—US 1946). **1947** Mine Own Executioner (US 1949). **1949** Maytime in Mayfair (US 1952). **1951** Mr. Denning Drives North (US 1953). **1952** Home at Seven (aka Murder on Monday—US 1953); Secret People. **1954** You Know What Sailors Are; Happy Ever After (aka Tonight's the Night—US). **1955** Where There's a Will; Doctor at Sea (US 1956); An Alligator Named Daisy (US 1957). **1956** My Teenage Daughter (aka Teenage Bad Girl—US 1957); Dry Rot. **1957** The Passionate Stranger (aka A Novel Affair—US); Not Wanted on Voyage. **1958** Henry V (reissue of 1944 film); Gideon's Day (aka Gideon of Scotland Yard—US 1959). **1961** Double Bunk; Don't Bother to Knock.

SHEPLEY, RUTH
Born: 1889, N.Y. Died: Oct. 5, 1951, New York, N.Y. Screen and stage actress.

Appeared in: **1922** When Knighthood Was in Flower.

SHERIDAN, ANN (Clara Lou Sheridan)
Born: Feb. 21, 1915, Denton, Tex. Died: Jan. 21, 1967, Hollywood, Calif. (cancer). Screen, stage, radio and television actress. Divorced from actors Edward Norris and George Brent. Married to actor Scott McKay.

Appeared in: **1927** The Bandit's Son; Casey at the Bat; Casey Jones; Galloping Thunder; The Way of All Flesh; Wedding Bill$. **1933** Search; Bolero. **1934** Ladies Should Listen; Come on, Marines; Notorious Sophie Lang; Limehouse Blues; Kiss and Make Up; Mrs. Wiggs of the Cabbage Patch; Wagon Wheels; Shoot the Works; College Rhythm; You Belong to Me. **1935** Enter Madame; Home on the Range; Behold My Wife; Car No. 99; Rocky Mountain Mystery; The Glass Key; The Crusades; Fighting Youth; Red Blood of Courage; Mississippi; Rumba. **1936** Sing Me a Love Song. **1937** The Great O'Malley; Black Legion; Footloose Heiress; San Quentin; Wine, Women and Horses. **1938** Alcatraz Island; Little Miss Thoroughbred; The Patient in Room 18; She Loved a Fireman; Mystery House; Cowboy from Brooklyn; Angels with Dirty Faces; Letter of Introduction; Broadway Musketeers. **1939** They Made Me a Criminal; Dodge City; Naughty but Nice; Indianapolis Speedway; Winter Carnival; Angels Wash Their Faces. **1940** It All Came True; Castle on the Hudson; Torrid Zone; They Drive by Night; City for Conquest. **1941** Honeymoon for Three; Navy Blues; The Man Who Came to Dinner; King's Row. **1942** Juke Girl; George Washington Slept Here; The Animal Kingdom; Wings for the Eagle. **1943** Edge of Darkness; Thank Your Lucky Stars. **1944** Shine on Harvest Moon; The Doughgirls. **1946** One More Tomorrow. **1947** Nora Prentiss; The Unfaithful. **1948** Good Sam; Treasure of the Sierra Madre; Silver River. **1949** I Was a Male War Bride. **1950** Woman on the Run; Stella. **1952** Steel Town; Just across the Street. **1953** Take Me to Town; Appointment in Honduras. **1956** Come Next Spring; The Opposite Sex. **1957** Woman and the Hunter.

SHERIDAN, DAN (Daniel Marvin Sheridan)
Born: Sept. 3, 1916, Ireland. Died: June 29, 1963, Encino Calif. (suicide—barbiturates). Screen actor.

Appeared in: **1948** California Firebrand. **1949** Horseman of the Sierra. **1958** Hell's Five Hours; Cole Younger—Gunfighter; Bullwhip; Day of the Outlaw; King of the Wild Stallions; Seven Guns to Mesa. **1959** The Young Captives. **1960** Ten Who Dared. **1962** Lonely are the Brave.

SHERIDAN, FRANK
Born: June 11, 1869, Boston, Mass. Died: Nov. 24, 1943, Hollywood, Calif. Stage and screen actor.

Appeared in: **1921** Anne of Little Smoky; The Rider of the King Log; Her Lord and Master. **1922** One Exciting Night. **1923** The Man Next Door. **1924** Two Shall Be Born. **1925** Lena Rivers. **1929** Fast Life. **1930** Side Street; The Other Tomorrow; Danger Lights. **1931** The Public Defender; A Free Soul; Murder by the Clock; Silence; Donovan's Kid; The Ladies of the Big House; The Man I Killed; The Flood. **1932** The Last Mile; Okay America; Afraid to Talk; Washington Merry-Go-Round. **1933** The Man Who Dared; Mama Loves Papa; Deception; The Woman Accused. **1934** Wharf Angel; Upperworld; The Witching Hour; The Cat's Paw. **1935** Whispering Smith Speaks; Nevada; The Payoff. **1936** The Leavenworth Case; The Country Gentleman; Murder with Pictures; Conflict. **1937** The Life of Emile Zola; A Night at the Movies (short); The Great O'Malley; Woman in Distress; A Fight to the Finish. **1938** City Streets.

SHERMAN, FRED E.
Born: 1905. Died: May 20, 1969, Woodland Hills, Calif. Screen, stage and television actor.

Appeared in: **1946** Behind Green Lights; Lady in the Lake. **1950** Chain Lightning. **1951** Valley of Fire. **1957** Dino; The Tall T. **1959** Some Like It Hot. **1961** Twist All Night.

SHERMAN, LOWELL
Born: Oct. 11, 1885, San Francisco, Calif. Died: Dec. 28, 1934, Hollywood, Calif. (pneumonia). Screen, stage, vaudeville, burlesque actor and film director. Son of theatrical manager John Sherman and actress Julia Louise Grey. Di-

vorced from Evelyn Booth, actresses Pauline Garon (dec. 1965) and Helen Costello (dec. 1957).

Appeared in: **1920** The New York Idea; Way Down East; Yes or No. **1921** The Gilded Lily; What No Man Knows; Molly O. **1922** Grand Larceny; The Face in the Fog. **1923** Bright Lights of Broadway. **1924** Monsieur Beaucaire; The Masked Danger; The Truth about Women; The Spitfire. **1925** Satan in Sables. **1926** You Never Know Women; Lost at Sea; The Wilderness Woman; The Reckless Lady; The Love Toy. **1927** The Girl from Gay Paree; Convoy. **1928** The Whip; The Whip Woman; The Ship; Mad Hour; The Divine Woman; The Garden of Eden; The Scarlet Dove; The Heart of a Follies Girl. **1929** Nearly Divorced (short—aka Phipps); Evidence; General Crack; A Lady of Chance. **1930** The Pay Off (aka The Losing Game); Ladies of Leisure; He Knew Women; Midnight Mystery; Lawful Larceny; O Sailor, Behave!; Mammy. **1931** The Royal Bed (aka The Queen's Husband); High Stakes; Bachelor Apartment; Way Down East (reissue of 1920 version). **1932** What Price Hollywood?; False Faces; The Greeks Had a Word for Them; The Slippery Pearls (short).

SHERRY, J. BARNEY (J. Barney Sherry Reeves)
Born: 1872, Germantown, Pa. Died: Feb. 22, 1944, Philadelphia, Pa. Screen, stage, vaudeville and radio actor.

Appeared in: **1905** Raffles, the Amateur Cracksman. **1909-1912** Western series. **1917** Flying Colors; Fuel of Life; Fanatics. **1918** Recording Day; The Secret Code; Evidence; Real Folks; Who Killed Walton?; Her Decision; High Stakes. **1919** The Lion Man (serial); May of Filbert. **1920** Go and Get It; Dinty. **1921** Burn 'Em up Barnes; The Barbarian; Just outside the Door; Man—Woman—Marriage; Thunderclap; The Lotus Eater. **1922** Sure-Fire Flint; Back Pay; The Inner Man; Island Wives; A Woman's Woman; When the Desert Calls; 'Til We Meet Again; Shadows of the Sea; Notoriety; John Smith; What Fools Men Are; The Secrets of Paris; The Broken Silence. **1923** The White Sister; Jacqueline of Blazing Barriers. **1924** Born Rich; Galloping Hoofs (serial); The Warrens of Virginia; Lend Me Your Husband; Miami. **1925** Daughters Who Pay; Play Ball (serial); Crackerjack; Lying Wives; The Live Wire; A Little Girl in a Big City; Enemies of Youth. **1926** The Brown Derby; The Prince of Tempters; Broken Homes; Casey of the Coast Guard (serial). **1927** Spider Webs; The Crimson Flash (serial). **1928** Alex the Great; The Wright Idea; Forgotten Faces. **1929** Jazz Heaven; Broadway Scandals; The Voice Within.

SHERWOOD, MILLIGE G.
Born: 1876. Died: Nov. 12, 1958, Hollywood, Calif. Screen and stage actor.

SHERWOOD, YORKE
Born: 1873. Died: Sept. 27, 1958, Hollywood, Calif. Screen actor.

Appeared in: **1926** The Man in the Saddle. **1928** The Cossacks; A Thief in the Dark; Gentlemen Prefer Blondes. **1930** The Man from Blankley's; Temple Tower. **1931** The Man in Possession. **1933** Eagle and the Hawk. **1936** Lloyds of London. **1944** Jane Eyre. **1956** 23 Paces to Baker Street.

SHIELDS, ARTHUR
Born: 1896, Dublin, Ireland. Died: Apr. 27, 1970, Santa Barbara, Calif. (emphysema). Screen, stage and television actor. Brother of actor Barry Fitzgerald (dec. 1961).

Appeared in: **1932** Sign of the Cross. **1936** The Plough and the Stars. **1939** Drums along the Mohawk. **1940** The Long Voyage Home; Little Nellie Kelly. **1941** Lady Scarface; The Gay Falcon; How Green Was My Valley; Confirm or Deny. **1942** Broadway; This above All; Pacific Rendezvous; Gentleman Jim; Nightmare; The Black Swan. **1943** Lassie Come Home; The Man from Down Under. **1944** Keys of the Kingdom; Youth Runs Wild; National Velvet; The White Cliffs of Dover; The Sign of the Cross (revised version of 1932 film). **1945** Roughly Speaking; Phantoms, Inc. (short); The Corn Is Green; Too Young to Know; The Valley of Decision. **1946** Three Strangers; The Verdict; Gallant Journey. **1947** The Shocking Miss Pilgrim; Easy Come, Easy Go; The Fabulous Dorseys; Seven Keys to Baldpate. **1948** Fighting Father Dunne; Tap Roots; My Own True Love. **1949** She Wore a Yellow Ribbon; The Fighting O'Flynn; Challenge to Lassie; Red Light. **1950** Tarzan and the Slave Girl. **1951** The River; People against O'Hara; Apache Drums; Sealed Cargo; Blue Blood; A Wonderful Life; The Barefoot Mailman. **1952** The Quiet Man. **1953** Scandal at Scourie; South Sea Woman; Main Street to Broadway. **1954** Pride of the Blue Grass; World for Ransom. **1956** The King and Four Queens. **1957** Daughter of Dr. Jekyll. **1958** Enchanted Island. **1959** Night of the Quarter Moon. **1960** For the Love of Mike. **1962** The Pigeon That Took Rome.

SHIELDS, FRANK (Francis X. Shields)
Born: Nov. 18, 1910, New York, N.Y. Died: Aug. 19, 1975. Screen actor.

Appeared in: **1935** Murder in the Fleet; I Live My Life. **1936** Come and Get It. **1937** The Affairs of Cappy Ricks; The Hoosier Schoolboy. **1938** The Goldwyn Follies.

SHIELDS, FREDERICK
Born: 1904. Died: June 30, 1974. Screen, radio actor, writer and radio director.

Appeared in: **1933** The Farmers' Friend (narrator); Her Majesty the Queen Bee (narrator); Queen of the Underworld (narrator).

SHIELDS, HELEN
Died: Aug. 7, 1963, New York, N.Y. Screen, stage and television actress.

Appeared in: **1951** The Whistle at Eaton Falls. **1956** The Wrong Man.

SHIELDS, SANDY
Born: 1873. Died: Aug. 3, 1923, New York, N.Y. Screen and stage actor.

SHIELDS, SYDNEY
Born: 1888. Died: Sept. 19, 1960, Queens, N.Y. Screen and stage actress. Appeared in silents.

SHINE, WILFRED
Born: 1863, Manchester, England. Died: Mar. 14, 1939, Kingston, England. Screen, stage, burlesque, television actor and radio writer. Father of actor Billy Shine.

Appeared in: **1928** The Burgomaster of Stilemode. **1929** Lily of Killarney. **1931** The Hound of the Baskervilles; The Bells.

SHINER, RONALD
Born: June 8, 1903, London, England. Died: June 30, 1966, London, England. Screen, stage and radio actor. His enormous nose was insured for $30,000.

Appeared in: **1934** My Old Dutch (film debut); Doctors Orders. **1935** Royal Cavalcade (aka Regal Cavalcade—US); It's a Bet; Once a Thief; Line Engaged; Gentleman's Agreement; Squibbs. **1936** King of Hearts; Excuse My Glove. **1937** Dreaming Lips; Dinner at the Ritz; Beauty and the Barge. **1938** A Yank at Oxford; Prison without Bars; They Drive by Night. **1939** The Mind of Mr. Reeder (aka The Mysterious Mr. Reeder—US 1940); Trouble Brewing; Flying Fifty Five; The Missing People (US 1940); The Gang's All Here (aka The Amazing Mr. Forrest—US); I Killed the Count (aka Who is Guilty?—US 1940); Discoveries; Come on George; The Middle Watch. **1940** Bulldog Sees It Through; The Case of the Frightened Lady (aka The Frightened Lady—US 1940); Salvage with a Smile; Old Bill and Son. **1941** The Seventh Survivor; South American George. **1942** They Flew Alone (aka Wings and the Woman—US); Those Kids from Town; Sabotage at Sea; King Arthur was a Gentleman; The Balloon Goes Up. **1943** Thursday's Child; Get Cracking; Miss London Ltd.; The Gentle Sex; The Butler's Dilemma. **1944** Bees in Paradise. **1945** I Live in Grosvenor Square (aka A Yank in London—US 1946); The Way to the Stars (aka Johnny in the Clouds—US). **1946** George in Civvy Street; Caesar and Cleopatra. **1947** The Man Within (aka The Smugglers—US 1948); Brighton Rock. **1949** Forbidden. **1951** Worm's Eye View; The Magic Box (US 1952); Reluctant Heroes. **1952** Little Big Shot. **1953** Top of the Form; Innocents in Paris (US 1955); Laughing Anne (US 1954). **1954** Up to His Neck; Aunt Clara. **1955** See How They Run. **1956** My Wife's Family; Dry Rot; Keep It Clean. **1957** Not Wanted on Voyage; Carry on Admiral (aka The Ship was Loaded—US 1959). **1958** Girls at Sea (US 1962). **1959** The Navy Lark; Operation Bullshine (US 1963). **1960** The Night We Got the Bird.

SHIPMAN, NELL
Born: 1893. Died: Jan. 23, 1970. Screen, stage, vaudeville actress, screenwriter and film director.

Appeared in: **1916** Through the Wall. **1918** The Mystery of Lake Lethe. **1921** The Girl from God's Country. **1923** The Grub Stake. **1927** The Golden Yukon.

SHIPSTAD, ROY
Born: 1911. Died: Jan. 20, 1975. Professional ice skater, stage producer and screen actor.

Appeared in: **1939** Ice Follies of 1939.

SHIRART, GEORGIA
Born: 1862. Died: Feb. 1929, Los Angeles, Calif. Screen actress. Entered films with Lubin Co. in 1913.

Appeared in: **1923** The Girl Who Came Back.

SHIRLEY, BOBBIE
Died: Feb. 13, 1970. Screen actress. Appeared in silents.

SHIRLEY, FLORENCE
Born: 1893. Died: May 12, 1967, Hollywood, Calif. Screen and stage actress.

Appeared in: **1939** The Women. **1940** Private Affairs. **1942** A Yank at Eton; Secret Agent of Japan; Her Cardboard Lover; We Were Dancing. **1952** Deadline U.S.A.; Stars and Stripes Forever.

SHIRLEY, TOM (Thomas P. Shirley)
Born: 1900. Died: Jan. 24, 1962, New York, N.Y. Screen, stage, radio and television actor. Entered films as a child with Essanay Films in Chicago.

Appeared in: **1926** Lightning Bill; Red Hot Leather. **1927** King of Kings.

SHOOTING STAR
Born: 1890. Died: June 4, 1966, Hollywood, Calif. (stroke). Sioux Indian screen actor. Entered films approx. 1935.

Appeared in: **1936** Ride, Ranger, Ride. **1949** The Cowboy and the Indians; Laramie.

SHORES, BYRON L.
Born: 1907. Died: Nov. 13, 1957, Kansas City, Mo. (multiple sclerosis). Stage and screen actor.

Appeared in: **1940** You the People (short); Too Many Girls. **1941** Wedding Worries (short); Johnny Eager; Blossoms in the Dust. **1942** Rover's Big Chance (short). **1943** This Is the Army; The Major and the Minor; The Mad Doctor of Market Street. **1943** Air Raid Wardens; Family Trouble (short).

SHORT, ANTRIM
Born: 1900, Cincinnati, Ohio. Died: Nov. 23, 1972, Woodland Hills, Calif. (emphysema). Screen, stage actor, casting director and talent agent. Married to actress Frances Morris. Entered films in 1912 with American Biograph.

Appeared in: **1917** Jewel in Pawn; Tom Sawyer; Pride and the Man. **1918** The Yellow Dog. **1919** Romance and Arabella; Please Get Married. **1920** The Right of Way. **1921** O'Malley of the Mounted; The Son of Wallingford; Rich Girl, Poor Girl; Black Beauty. **1922** Beauty's Worth. **1924** Classmates. **1925** Wildfire; Married? **1926** The Pinch Hitter; The Broadway Boob; Jack O'Hearts. **1936** Movie Maniacs (short). **1937** The Big Show; Artists and Models; Lodge Night (short).

SHORT, FLORENCE
Born: 1889. Died: July 10, 1946, Hollywood, Calif. Screen and stage actress. Sister of actress Gertrude Short (dec. 1968) and daughter of actor Lewis Short (dec. 1958).

Appeared in: **1918** The Eagle's Eye (serial). **1921** Lessons in Love; Woman's Place. **1922** Cardigan; The Lights of New York; Silver Wings. **1923** Does It Pay? **1924** The Enchanted Cottage. **1931** Way Down East.

SHORT, GERTRUDE
Born: Apr. 6, 1902, Cincinnati, Ohio. Died: July 31, 1968, Hollywood, Calif. Screen, stage and vaudeville actress. Sister of actress Florence Short (dec. 1946) and daughter of actor Lewis Short (dec. 1958).

Appeared in: **1913** Uncle Tom's Cabin. **1920** You Never Can Tell. **1922** Rent Free; Boy Crazy; Headin' West; Youth to Youth. **1923** The Gold Diggers; Breaking into Society; Crinoline and Romance; The Prisoner; The Man Life Passed By. **1924** Barbara Frietchie; "The Telephone Girl" series of shorts which included: Julius Sees Her; When Knighthood Was in Power; Money to Burn; Sherlock's Home; King Leary; William Tells; For the Love of Mike; The Square Sex; Bee's Knees; Love and Learn; Faster Foster; Hello and Good Bye. **1925** The Narrow Street; Beggar on Horseback; My Lady's Lips; The Other Woman's Story; Code of the West; Her Market Value; The People vs. Nancy Preston; The Talker; Tessie. **1926** Dangerous Friends; Ladies of Leisure; A Poor Girl's Romance; Sweet Adeline; The Lily. **1927** Ladies at Ease; Tillie the Toiler; Adam and Evil; The Show; The Masked Woman; Polly of the Movies; Women's Wares. **1928** None but The Brave. **1929** Trial Marriage; Gold Diggers of Broadway; The Broadway Hoofer; In Old California; The Three Outcasts. **1930** The Last Dance; Once a Gentleman; The Little Accident. **1931** Laughing Sinners. **1933** The Girl in 419; Son of Kong. **1934** Love Birds; The Key; St. Louis Kid. **1935** G-Men; Helldorado; Woman Wanted; Affairs of Susan. **1937** Park Avenue Logger; Penny Wisdom (short); Stella Dallas. **1938** Tip-Off Girls. **1940** Spots Before Your Eyes (short). **1942** Two for the Money (short); Victory Vittles (short). **1945** Guest Pests (short).

SHORT, HARRY
Born: 1876. Died: Aug. 17, 1943, New York, N.Y. Screen, stage, vaudeville and radio actor.

Appeared in: **1923** Mighty Lak' a Rose. **1926** Just Suppose. **1934** Hotel Anchovy.

SHORT, HASSARD
Born: 1878, England. Died: Oct. 9, 1956, Nice, France. Screen actor, stage director and stage producer.

Appeared in: **1918** The Turn of the Wheel. **1919** The Way of a Woman; The Stronger Vow. **1921** Woman's Place.

SHORT, LEWIS W. "LEW"
Born: Feb. 14, 1875, Dayton, Ohio. Died: Apr. 26, 1958, Hollywood, Calif. Stage and screen actor. Father of actresses Gertrude (dec. 1968) and Florence Short (dec. 1946). Entered films with D.W. Griffith at Biograph in 1908.

Appeared in: **1922** The Black Bag; The Heart of Lincoln. **1926** The Blue Eagle. **1927** The Heart of Maryland. **1928** Black Pearl; Big City. **1929** The Three Outcasts; Is Everybody Happy? **1930** A Girl in the Show. **1942** Tennessee Johnson.

SHOTWELL, MARIE
Born: New York, N.Y. Died: Sept. 18, 1934, Long Island, N.Y. Stage and screen actress.

Appeared in: 1916 The Witching Hour. 1917 Enlighten Thy Daughter; Warfare of the Flesh. 1919 The Thirteenth Chair. 1920 Chains of Evidence; The Harvest Moon; The Evil Eye (serial); Civilian Clothes; The Master Mind; Blackbirds. 1921 Her Lord and Master. 1922 Shackles of Gold. 1923 Does it Pay? 1924 Love of Women. 1925 The Manicure Girl; Shore Leave; Lovers in Quarantine; Sally of the Sawdust. 1927 Running Wild; One Woman to Another.

SHRINER, HERB (Herbert Arthur Schiner)
Born: May 29, 1918, Toledo, Ohio. Died: Apr. 23, 1970, Delray Beach, Fla. (auto accident). Screen, radio and television actor.

Appeared in: 1953 Main Street to Broadway.

SHTRAUKH, MAXIM
Born: 1901, Russia. Died: 1974, Moscow, Russia. Screen actor.

Appeared in: 1925 Stachka (aka Strike—US 1962). 1932 Golden Mountain. 1939 The Man with the Gun; New Horizons. 1947 The Vow. 1948 The Lucky Bride. 1966 Lenin V. Polshe (aka Portrait of Lenin—US 1967).

SHUBERT, EDDIE
Born: July 11, 1898, Milwaukee, Wisc. Died: Jan. 23, 1937, Los Angeles, Calif. Screen, stage, burlesque and vaudeville actor.

Appeared in: 1934 6 Day Bike Rider; Murder in the Clouds; St. Louis Kid; The Case of the Howling Dog. 1935 The Goose and the Gander; Alibi Ike; Black Fury; While the Patient Slept; The Pay-Off; Don't Bet on Blondes. 1936 Song of the Saddle; Road Gang; Man Hunt; The Law in Her Hands; The Case of the Velvet Claws. 1937 Time Out for Romance.

SHUKSHIN, VASILY
Born: 1929, Russia. Died: Oct. 2, 1974, Moscow, Russia (heart attack). Screen actor and film director. Entered films as an actor in the 1950s.

Appeared in: 1962 Kogda Derevya Byli Bolshimi (aka When the Trees Were Tall—US 1965).

SHUMAN, ROY
Born: 1925. Died: July 30, 1973, New York, N.Y. (heart attack). Screen, stage and television actor.

Appeared in: 1958 The Goddess. 1971 The Gang That Couldn't Shoot Straight.

SHUMWAY, LEE (Leonard C. Shumway)
Born: 1884, Salt Lake City, Utah. Died: Jan. 4, 1959. Stage and screen actor.

Appeared in: 1909 She Would Be an Actress. 1914 The Measure of a Man; Sealed Orders; The Candidate for Mayor; Within the Noose; His First Case; The Wolf's Daughter. 1915 Fate and Fugitive; A Question of Conscience; In The Dragon's Claws; When the Range Called; Her Father's Picture; The Red Virgin; The Decoy; Tap! Tap! Tap!; The Dream Dance; The Power of Prayer; The Emerald God; Nell of the Dance Hall; The Strange Unknown; The Wonder Cloth; An Ambassador from the Dead; As the Twig Bent; The Moment Before Death; The Web of Hate; The Convict King; Saved from the Harem; The Sacred Bracelet; Jim West—Gambler; The Secret Room; When War Threatened; The Silent Man; The Inner Chamber; Meg O' the Cliffs; Vengeance of the Oppressed; The Death Web. 1916 The Old Watchman; The Bond Within; The Law's Injustice; Guilty; The Lost Lode; Two News Items; The Dragonman; The Embodied Thought; The Diamond Thieves; Sold to Satan; Behind the Lines; A Song from the Heart; The Conspiracy; The Repentant; The Redemption of Helen; At the Doors of Doom; Soldier's Sons; The Crash; The Rival Pilots; The Candle; The Leap; The Final Payment; Tammy's Tiger; The Usurer's Due; Out of the Flotsam; The Money Lenders; The Human Pendulum; The Half Wit; The Price of Dishonor; The State Witness; Onda of the Orient; A Lesson in Labor; The Avenger. 1917 Honorably Discharged; The Folly of Fanchette; The Gates of Doom; Perils of the Secret Service (serial); Steel Hearts; The Kidnapped Bride; The Phantom's Secret; Helen Grayson's Strategy; Miss Jackie of the Army; The Kingdom of Love. 1918 The Girl with the Champagne Eyes; Confession; The Fallen Angel; The Bird of Prey. 1919 The Siren's Song; The Love Hunger; Rustling a Bride. 1921 The Conflict; The Lure of Jade; Society Secrets; The Torrent; The Big Adventure. 1922 Brawn of the North; Over the Border; Step On It! 1923 The Gunfighter; The Lone Star Ranger; Soft Boiled; Hearts Aflame; Snowdrift. 1924 The Vagabond Trail; The Yankee Consul; The Air Hawk; American Manners; The Bowery Bishop. 1925 The Air Mail; The Bad Lands; The Danger Signal; The Handsome Brute; Introduce Me; The Man from Red Gulch; The Price of Success; Smilin' at Trouble; The Texas Bearcat. 1926 The Bat; The Checkered Flag; Glenister of the Mounted; One Minute to Play; The Sign of the Claw; Whispering Canyon. 1927 The Great Mail Robbery; His Foreign Wife; The Last Trail; Let It Rain; Outlaws of Red River; South Sea Love. 1928 Beyond London's Lights; Hit of the Show; The House of Scandal; A Million for Love; Son of the Golden West. 1929 Evangeline; The Leatherneck; Night Parade; Queen of the Night Clubs; So This is College. 1930 The Lone

Defender (serial); The Lone Star Ranger; The Santa Fe Trail; Showgirl in Hollywood; America or Bust (short); Sweet Mama. 1935 Mysterious Mr. Wong; Million Dollar Baby; Hardrock Harrigan; Outlawed Guns; The Ivory-Handled Gun; Frisco Waterfront. 1936 The Preview Murder Mystery; Song of the Trail; Go Get 'Em Haines. 1937 Hollywood Cowboy; Windjammer; Hollywood Round-Up; Nation Aflame; Nightclub Scandal. 1938 Outlaws of the Prairie; Rawhide; Spawn of the North; Painted Desert. 1939 Rovin' Tumbleweeds. 1940 Deadwood Dick (serial); Prairie Schooners. 1941 Prairie Pioneers; Murder by Invitation; Two-Gun Sheriff; No Greater Sin. 1942 Hold 'Em Jail (short); Home in Wyomin'; Stardust on the Sage; Arizona Terrors; Jesse James Jr.; Prisoners on Parade. 1943 Dead Man's Gulch. 1947 Buck Privates Come Home.

SHUNMUGHAM, T.K.
Born: 1912, Madras, India (?). Died: Mar. 1973, Madras, India. Screen and stage actor.

SHUTTA, JACK
Born: 1899. Died: June 28, 1957, Houston, Tex. (cancer). Screen, stage, vaudeville and burlesque actor.

Appeared in: 1930 Whoopee. 1934 Hello, Prosperity (short); Half-Baked Relations (short). 1935 False Pretenses; The E-Flat Man (short). 1947 The Wistful Widow of Wagon Gap. 1948 The Burning Cross. 1950 Abbott and Costello Go to Mars.

SHY, GUS
Born: 1894, Buffalo, N.Y. Died: June 15, 1945, Hollywood, Calif. Screen, stage, vaudeville actor and film dialog director.

Appeared in: 1930 Good News; New Moon; A Lady's Morals. 1933 A Vitaphone short. 1934 I Sell Anything. 1936 The Captain's Kid. 1937 Once a Doctor.

SHYAM
Born: India. Died: Apr. 26, 1951, India. Screen actor.

SIDNEY, GEORGE (Sammy Greenfield)
Born: Mar. 18, 1876, New York, N.Y. Died: Apr. 29, 1945, Los Angeles, Calif. Screen, stage and vaudeville actor. He was Cohen in "The Cohens and the Kellys" series and Potash in the "Potash and Perlmutter" series.

Appeared in: 1923 Potash and Perlmutter. 1924 In Hollywood with Potash and Permutter. 1925 Classified. 1926 Millionaires; The Cohens and the Kellys; Partners Again; The Prince of Pilsen; Sweet Daddies. 1927 Clancy's Kosher Wedding; The Auctioneer; For the Love of Mike; The Life of Riley; Lost at the Front. 1928 The Flying Romeos; Give and Take; The Cohens and the Kellys in Paris; The Latest from Paris; We Americans. 1929 The Cohens and the Kellys in Atlantic City. 1930 Around the Corner; King of Jazz; The Cohens and the Kellys in Scotland; The Cohens and the Kellys in Africa. 1931 Caught Cheating. 1932 High Pressure; The Cohens and Kellys in Hollywood. 1933 The Cohens and the Kellys in Trouble. 1934 Rafter Romance; Manhattan Melodrama. 1935 Diamond Jim. 1937 The Good Old Soak.

SIDNEY, MABEL
Born: 1884. Died: Oct. 18, 1969, New York, N.Y. Screen, vaudeville and television actress.

SIDNEY, SCOTT (Scott Siggins)
Born: 1872. Died: July 20, 1928, London, England (heart trouble). Screen, stage actor and film director. Entered films as an actor with Thomas Ince Productions.

SIEBEL, PETER
Born: 1884. Died: Mar. 4, 1949, Long Beach, Calif. Screen actor and circus performer.

SIEGEL, BERNARD (aka BERNARD SEGAL)
Born: Apr. 19, 1868, Lemberg, Poland. Died: July 9, 1940, Los Angeles, Calif. (heart attack). Stage and screen actor.

Appeared in: 1921 Heart of Maryland. 1922 The Love Nest; The Madness of Love; The Man Who Paid; A Stage Romance. 1923 None So Blind; Sidewalks of New York; Where Is This West? 1924 Against all Odds; The 40th Door (serial); Emblems of Love; The Next Corner; Romance Ranch. 1925 The Spaniard; The Crimson Runner; The Phantom of the Opera; The Vanishing American; Wild Horse Mesa. 1926 Beau Geste; Desert Gold; Going Crooked. 1927 Blazing Days; Drums of the Desert; King of Kings; Open Range; Ragtime; Ranger of the North. 1928 Freedom of the Press; Laugh, Clown, Laugh; Guardians of the Wild; Stand and Deliver; Divine Sinner. 1929 The Far Call; Redskin; The Rescue; Sea Fury; The Younger Generation. 1930 The Case of Sergeant Grischa; The Phantom of the Opera. 1935 Shadow of Doubt. 1936 The Jungle Princess. 1937 Wells Fargo.

SIEGMANN, GEORGE

Born: 1883. Died: June 22, 1928, Hollywood, Calif. (pernicious anemia). Screen, stage actor and assistant film director.

Appeared in: 1909 The Sealed Room. 1915 Birth of a Nation. 1916 Intolerance. 1918 Hearts of the World; The Great Love. 1919 The Fall of Babylon. 1920 The Hawk's Trail (serial); Little Miss Rebellion. 1921 The Big Punch; A Connecticut Yankee at King Arthur's Court; Partners of Fate; Desperate Trails; The Three Musketeers; Silent Years; The Queen of Sheba; Shame. 1922 Fools First; Hungry Hearts; Monte Cristo; Oliver Twist; A California Romance; The Truthful Liar. 1923 Merry-Go-Round; Lost and Found; Anna Christie; The Eagle's Feather; Hell's Hole; Enemies of Children; The Man Life Passed By; Stepping Fast; Scaramouche; Slander the Woman. 1924 Singer Jim McKee; Jealous Husbands; The Guilty One; Manhattan; On Time; Janice Meredith; Revelation; The Right of the Strongest; A Sainted Devil; The Shooting of Dan McGrew; Stolen Secrets; When a Girl Loves. 1925 Sporting Life; Zander the Great; Manhattan Madness; Pursued; Never the Twain Shall Meet; The Phantom Express; Recompense. 1926 The Old Soak; Born to the West; The Carnival Girl; My Old Dutch; The Midnight Sun; Poker Faces; The Palaces of Pleasure. 1927 King of Kings; The Cat and the Canary; The Red Mill; Uncle Tom's Cabin; The Thirteenth Juror; Hotel Imperial. 1928 Stop That Man; Love Me and the World Is Mine; Man Who Laughs.

SIELANSKI, STANLEY (aka STANLEY STANISLAW)

Born: Poland. Died: Apr. 28, 1955, New York, N.Y. Screen and stage actor.

Appeared in: 1934 Parade Rezerwistow; Maryika. 1936 Manewry Milosne. 1937 Cabman No. 13; Ksiazatko (The Lottery Prince); Krolowa Przedmiescia (Queen of the Market Place). 1938 Pan Redaktor Szaleje (Mr. Editor Is Crazy).

SIGGINS, JULIA WILLIAMS. See JULIA WILLIAMS

SIGNORET, GABRIEL

Born: 1873. Died: Apr. 1937, France (appendicitis). Screen actor.

Appeared in: Bouclette (film debut) and La Reve (both silents); later in Veille d'Arme; 27 Rue de la Paix; Les Hommes Nouveaux.

SIHMADA, IHAMU

Born: Japan. Died: 1965, Japan. Screen actor.

SILBERT, LISA

Born: 1880, Rumania. Died: Nov. 29, 1965, Miami, Fla. Screen, stage and television actress.

Appeared in: 1926 Broken Hearts.

SILETTI, MARIO G.

Born: 1904. Died: Apr. 19, 1964, Los Angeles, Calif. (auto accident). Screen and television actor.

Appeared in: 1949 Thieves' Highway. 1950 Under My Skin; The Man Who Cheated Himself; Black Hand. 1951 The Enforcer; Ann of the Indies; Strictly Dishonorable; Force of Arms; The Great Caruso; House on Telegraph Hill; Stop That Cab. 1952 When in Rome; My Cousin Rachel; Captain Pirate. 1953 Big Leaguer; Wings of the Hawk; Hot News; Kansas City Confidential; So This Is Love; Taxi; Thunder Bay; The Caddy. 1954 Theodora; Slave Empress; Three Coins in the Fountain. 1955 Hell's Island; The Naked Street; Bring Your Serenade. 1958 Man in the Shadow. 1960 Pay or Die. 1966 To Trap a Spy.

SILLS, MILTON

Born: Jan. 10, 1882, Chicago, Ill. Died: Sept. 15, 1930, Santa Monica, Calif. (heart attack). Stage and screen actor.

Appeared in: 1915 The Rack; The Deep Purple. 1917 Patria (serial). 1918 The Hell Cat. 1919 Eyes on Youth; Shadows; The Stronger Vow. 1920 The Week-End; Behold My Wife. 1921 The Marriage Gamble; At the End of the World; The Great Moment; The Faith Healer; Savage; Miss Lulu Bett. 1922 Burning Sands; Borderland; Environment; One Clear Call; The Woman Who Walked Alone; Skin Deep; The Forgotten Law; The Marriage Chance. 1923 Why Women Re-Marry; The Last Hour; Adam's Rib; A Lady of Quality; The Spoilers; Flaming Youth; The Isle of Lost Ships; Legally Dead; Souls for Sale; What a Wife Learned. 1924 Madonna of the Streets; The Sea Hawk; Single Wives; Flowing Gold; The Heart Bandit. 1925 The Unguarded Hour; The Knockout; As Man Desires; I Want My Man; A Lover's Oath; The Making of O'Malley. 1926 Paradise; Men of Steel; Puppets; The Silent Lover. 1927 The Sea Tigers; The Valley of the Giants; Framed; Hard-Boiled Haggerty. 1928 The Barker; Burning Daylight; The Crash; The Hawk's Nest. 1929 His Captive Woman; Love and the Devil. 1930 Man Trouble; The Sea Wolf.

SILVA, ANTONIO JOAO

Born: 1870, Portugal. Died: Jan. 31, 1954, Lisbon, Portugal (result of fall). Stage and screen actor. Entered films in 1930.

SILVA, SIMONE

Born: 1928. Died: Nov. 30, 1957, London, England (natural causes). Screen actress.

Appeared in: 1952 South of Algiers (aka The Golden Mask—US 1954). 1953 Street of Shadows (aka Shadow Man—US); Desperate Moment. 1954 The Weak and the Wicked; Duel in the Jungle. 1955 Third Party Risk (aka The Deadly Game—US). 1956 The Dynamiters.

SILVANI, ALDO

Born: 1891, Italy. Died: Nov. 1964, Milan, Italy. Screen and television actor.

Appeared in: 1947 La Vita Ricomincia (Life Begins Anew); Anything for a Song; To Live in Peace. 1948 Four Steps in the Clouds. 1949 The Golden Madonna; Carmela. 1950 Difficult Years; Mad about Opera. 1951 Teresa; Measure for Measure. 1952 When in Rome; The Thief of Venice. 1953 Stranger on the Prowl; Paolo and Francesca. 1954 La Strada; Beat the Devil; Valley of the Kings. 1959 The Tempest. 1960 Cartagine in Fiamme (Carthage in Flames); Ben Hur. 1961 Five Golden Hours. 1962 Damon and Pythias. 1963 Sodom and Gomorrah. 1964 Robin and the Seven Hoods. 1966 Assault on a Queen.

SILVER, CHRISTINE

Born: 1885. Died: Nov. 23, 1960, London, England. Screen, stage and television actress.

Appeared in: 1920 Judge Not; The Little Welsh Girl. 1938 Dead Men Tell No Tales (US 1939). 1951 Mystery Junction.

SILVER, PAULINE

Born: 1888. Died: Jan. 1, 1969, West Hollywood, Calif. (murdered). Screen actress. Appeared in silents.

SILVERA, FRANK

Born: 1914, Kingston, Jamaica, West Indies. Died: June 11, 1970, Pasadena, Calif. (accidentally electrocuted). Black screen, stage, television actor, stage producer and stage director.

Appeared in: 1951 The Cimarron Kid. 1952 The Fighter; The Miracle of Our Lady of Fatima; Viva Zapata! 1953 Fear and Desire. 1955 Killer's Kiss. 1956 Crowded Paradise; The Mountain; The Lonely Night. 1957 Hatful of Rain. 1958 The Bravados. 1959 Crime and Punishment, U.S.A. 1960 The Mountain Road; Key Witness. 1962 Mutiny on the Bounty. 1963 Lonnie; Toys in the Attic. 1965 The Greatest Story Ever Told. 1966 The Appaloosa. 1967 Hombre; The St. Valentine's Day Massacre. 1968 The Stalking Moon; Betrayal; Up Tight. 1969 Che!; Guns of the Magnificent Seven.

SIMANEK, OTTO

Born: 1901. Died: Oct. 15, 1967, New York, N.Y. Screen, stage and television actor.

Appeared in: 1956 The Wrong Man.

SIMMONDS, ANNETTE (Viscountess Dangan)

Born: 1918, England. Died: Oct. 28, 1959, near London, England (auto accident). Stage and screen actress.

Appeared in: 1950 Blackout. 1951 No Orchids for Miss Blandish.

SIMON, MICHEL (Francois Simon)

Born: Apr. 9, 1895, Geneva, Switzerland. Died: May 30, 1975, near Paris, France (heart failure). Stage and screen actor.

Appeared in: 1925 Feu Mathisa Pascal. 1928 The Passion of Jeanne d'Arc (The Passion of Joan of Arc—US 1929). 1929 Tire au Flanc. 1931 La Chienne; On Purge Bebe. 1932 Jean de la Lune; Boudu Sauve Des Eaux (Boudu Saved from Drowning—US 1967). 1934 L'Atalante (US 1947). 1936 Lac Aux Dames; Le Bonheur; Jeunes Filles de Paris. 1937 Drole de Drame; Razumov. 1938 Les Disparus de Saint-Agil; Le Quay des Brumes (The Foggy Quay). 1939 Fric Frac (US 1948); Bizarre, Bizarre; Port of Shadows; La Fin du Jour (The End of a Day); Circonstances Attenuantes (Extenuating Circumstances—US 1946). 1940 The Kiss of Fire. 1943 Vautrin, the Thief (US 1940). 1944 32 Rue de Montmartre. 1945 Un Ami Viendra Ce Soir (A Friend Will Come Tonight—US 1948); Boule de Suif. 1946 Panique (US 1947); Musiciens du Ciel. 1947 Au Bonheur de Dames (Shop Girls of Paris); The Story of Tosca; The King's Jester. 1948 Not Guilty; Fabiola (US 1951). 1949 La Beaute du Diable (Beauty and the Devil—US 1952). 1952 Full House. 1953 The Strange Desire of Monsieur Bard; Saadia. 1955 Too Bad She's Bad. 1956 La Joyeuse Prison. 1957 The Virtuous Scoundrel. 1959 Die Nackte und der Satan (aka A Head for the Devil; The Screaming Head; The Head—US 1961). 1960 It Happened in Broad Daylight; Candide (US 1962). 1962 Le Diable et Les Dix Commandments (The Devil and the Ten Commandments—US 1963). 1963 Mondo di Notte (Ecco—US 1965). 1964 Cyrano and D'Artagnan. 1965 Two Hours to Kill; The Train. 1967 Le Vieil Homme et L'enfant (The Two of Us—US 1968). 1968 Ce Sacre Grand-Pere (The Marriage Came Tumbling Down—US 1968). 1971 Blanche.

SIMON, SOL S.

Born: 1864. Died: Apr. 24, 1940, Hollywood, Calif. Screen and stage actor. Credited with discovering oil in Kern County, Calif., in 1910.

Appeared in: 1925 Greed. 1928 The Barker; Desperate Courage. 1930 Headin' North; The Land of Missing Men.

SIMONOV, NIKOLAI

Born: 1902, Russia. Died: Apr. 1973, Russia. Screen and stage actor.

Appeared in: 1930 Cain and Artem. 1934 Miracles. 1935 Chapayev. 1937 Peter the First. 1939 The Conquests of Peter the Great. 1949 The First Front. 1950 The Victors and the Vanquished. 1956 The Gadfly.

SIMPSON, GRANT

Born: 1884, Sioux Falls, S.D. Died: Jan. 8, 1932, Asheville, N.C. Screen, stage and vaudeville actor. Married to actress Lulu McConnell (dec. 1962), with whom he teamed in vaudeville.

SIMPSON, IVAN

Born: 1875, Glasgow, Scotland. Died: Oct. 12, 1951, New York, N.Y. Stage and screen actor.

Appeared in: 1915 The Dictator (film debut). 1916 Out of the Drifts. 1922 The Man Who Played God. 1923 Twenty-One; The Green Goddess. 1924 $20 a Week. 1925 Lovers in Quarantine; Miss Bluebeard; Wild, Wild Susan; Womanhandled. 1926 A Kiss for Cinderella. 1929 Disraeli; Evidence. 1930 The Green Goddess (and 1923 version); Old English; The Way of All Men; Manslaughter; The Sea God; Inside the Lines; Isle of Escape. 1931 The Millionaire; The Lady Who Dared; The Reckless Hour; I Like Your Nerve; Safe in Hell. 1932 The Man Who Played God (and 1922 version); A Passport to Hell; The Crash; The Phantom of Crestwood. 1933 The Monkey's Paw; The Past of Mary Holmes; Midnight Mary; Voltaire; Charlie Chan's Greatest Case; The Silk Express; Blind Adventure. 1934 Man of Two Worlds; The Mystery of Mr. X; The House of Rothschild; The World Moves On; British Agent; Among the Missing. 1935 David Copperfield; Shadow of Doubt; Mark of the Vampire; The Bishop Misbehaves; Captain Blood; The Perfect Gentleman; East of Java; Splendor. 1936 Little Lord Fauntleroy; Trouble for Two; Mary of Scotland; Lloyds of London. 1937 Maid of Salem; A Night of Mystery; The Prince and the Pauper; London by Night. 1938 The Baroness and the Butler; Invisible Enemy; Booloo; The Adventures of Robin Hood. 1939 The Hound of the Baskervilles; Made for Each Other; Never Say Die; Adventures of Sherlock Holmes; Ruler of the Seas; The Sun Never Sets. 1940 The Invisible Man Returns; New Moon. 1942 Nazi Agent; The Male Animal; They All Kissed the Bride; Youth on Parade; Nightmare; Random Harvest; The Body Disappears. 1943 My Kingdom for a Cook; Two Weeks to Live; Forever and a Day; This Land Is Mine. 1944 Jane Eyre; The Hour before the Dawn.

SIMPSON, RUSSELL

Born: June 17, 1880, San Francisco, Calif. Died: Dec. 12, 1959, Hollywood, Calif. Screen, stage, radio and television actor. Entered films in 1910.

Appeared in: 1914 The Virginian. 1917 The Barrier. 1918 The Uphill Path; Weaver of Dreams; Blue Jeans. 1919 The Brand. 1920 The Branding Iron. 1921 Godless Men; Shadows of Conscience; Bunty Pulls the Strings; Snowblind; Under the Lash. 1922 Across the Dead Line; Fools of Fortune; The Kingdom Within; Rags to Riches; When Love Is Young; Human Hearts. 1923 Peg O' My Heart; The Girl of the Golden West; The Virginian (and 1914 version); Circus Days; Defying Destiny; Hearts Aflame; The Huntress; Rip Tide. 1924 The Narrow Street; Painted People. 1925 Beauty and the Bad Man; Paint and Powder; Faint Perfume; Old Shoes; Recreation of Brian Kent; Ship of Souls; The Spendid Road; Thunder Mountain; Why Women Love (aka Sea Woman and Barriers Aflame). 1926 The Earth Woman; The Social Highwayman; Lovely Mary; Rustling for Cupid. 1927 Wild Geese; Annie Laurie; The First Auto; The Frontiersman; God's Great Wilderness; Now We're in the Air; The Heart of the Yukon. 1928 Trail of '98; The Bushranger; Life's Mockery; Tropical Nights. 1929 Innocents of Paris; Noisy Neighbors; My Lady's Past; The Kid's Clever; The Sap; After the Fog. 1930 Billy the Kid; Lone Star Ranger; Abraham Lincoln. 1931 Man to Man; The Great Meadow; Susan Lennox, Her Rise and Fall. 1932 Law and Order; Ridin' for Justice; Lean Rivers; Honor of the Press; Riding Tornado; Flames; Cabin in the Cotton; Hello Trouble; Silver Dollar; Call Her Savage. 1933 Face in the Sky; Hello, Everybody! 1934 Three on a Honeymoon; Carolina; The Frontier Marshal; Ever Since Eve; Sixteen Fathoms Deep; The World Moves On. 1935 West of the Pecos; Motive for Revenge; The Hoosier Schoolmaster; Way Down East; Paddy O'Day; The County Chairman. 1936 Man Hunt; The Harvester; Girl of the Ozarks; The Crime of Dr. Forbes; Ramona; San Francisco. 1937 Green Light; That I May Live; Mountain Justice; Wild West Days (serial); Yodelin' Kid from Pine Ridge; Paradise Isle; Maid of Salem. 1938 Gold Is Where You Find It; Valley of the Giants; Hearts of the North. 1939 Western Caravans; Desperate Trails; Drums along the Mohawk; Dodge City; Mr. Smith Goes to Washington; Young Mr. Lincoln; Geronimo. 1940 Girl of the Golden West (and 1923 version); Brigham Young—Frontiersman; Santa Fe Trail; Virginia City; Three Faces West; The Grapes of Wrath. 1941 The Last of the Duanes; Bad Men of Missouri; Wild Bill Hickok Rides; Tobacco Road; Wild Geese Calling; Citadel of Crime; Swamp Water; Outside the Law; Meet John Doe.

1942 Shut My Big Mouth; The Lone Ranger; The Spoilers; Tennessee Johnson. 1943 Woman of the Town; Border Patrol; Moonlight in Vermont. 1944 Texas Masquerade; Man from Frisco. 1945 Along Came Jones; The Big Bonanza; They Were Expendable; Incendiary Blonde. 1946 Bad Bascomb; California Gold Rush; My Darling Clementine. 1947 The Millerson Case; Bowery Buckaroos; The Fabulous Texan; Death Valley; Romance of Rosy Ridge. 1948 Albuquerque; My Dog Shep; Tap Roots; Coroner Creek; Sundown in Santa Fe. 1949 Tuna Clipper; The Beautiful Blonde from Bashful Bend; Free for All; The Gal Who Took the West. 1950 Call of the Klondike; Saddle Tramp; Wagon Master. 1951 Across the Wide Missouri; Comin' 'Round the Mountain. 1952 Feudin' Fools; Lone Star; Ma and Pa Kettle at the Fair; Meet Me at the Fair. 1953 The Sun Shines Bright. 1954 Broken Lance; Seven Brides for Seven Brothers. 1955 The Last Command; The Tall Men. 1956 The Brass Legend; Friendly Persuasion. 1957 The Lonely Man. 1959 The Horse Soldiers.

SINCLAIR, ARTHUR

Born: Aug. 3, 1883, Dublin, Ireland. Died: Dec. 14, 1951, Belfast, Northern Ireland. Stage and screen actor.

Appeared in: 1934 Wild Boy; Irish Hearts (aka Norah O'Neale—US); Sing as We Go; Evensong. 1935 Charing Cross Road; Peg of Old Drury (US 1936). 1937 King Solomon's Mines. 1947 Hungry Hill.

SINCLAIR, DAISY

Born: 1878, N.Y. Died: Jan. 14, 1929, New York, N.Y. Stage and screen actress.

SINCLAIR, HORACE

Born: 1884, Sheffield, England. Died: Feb. 19, 1949, New York, N.Y. Screen, stage, vaudeville actor, stage director and playwright.

Appeared in: 1939 One Third of a Nation.

SINCLAIR, HUGH

Born: May 19, 1903, London, England. Died: Dec. 29, 1962, Slapton, England. Stage and screen actor.

Appeared in: 1935 Escape Me Never. 1936 The Marriage of Corbal (aka Prisoner of Corbal—US 1939); Strangers on a Honeymoon (US 1937). 1939 A Girl Must Live (US 1941); The Four Just Men (aka The Secret Four—US 1940). 1941 The Saint's Vacation; The Saint Meets the Tiger (US 1943). 1942 Alibi; Tomorrow We Live (aka At Dawn We Die—US 1943). 1945 Flight from Folly; They were Sisters (US 1946). 1948 Corridor of Mirrors. 1949 Don't Ever Leave Me; The Rocking Horse Winner (US 1950); Trottie True (aka Gay Lady—US 1950). 1950 No Trace. 1951 Circle of Danger. 1952 Judgment Deferred; The Second Mrs. Tanqueray (US 1954); Never Look Back. 1953 Mantrap (aka Woman in Hiding—US); Three Steps in the Dark.

SINGH, BHOGWAN

Born: Sept. 22, 1883, India. Died: Mar. 6, 1962, Woodland Hills, Calif. (cerebral thrombosis). Screen actor.

Appeared in: 1915 The Arab's Vengeance. 1920 Stronger than Death. 1935 Bonnie Scotland. 1952 Bwana Devil. 1956 Around the World in 80 Days. 1958 The Bride and the Beast; Desert Hell.

SINGH, SARAIN

Born: 1888. Died: Apr. 14, 1952, Hollywood, Calif. Screen actor.

SINGLETON, CATHERINE

Born: 1904. Died: Sept. 9, 1969, Ft. Worth, Tex. Screen and stage actress. Miss Universe of 1926.

SINGLETON, ZUTTY (Arthur James Singleton)

Born: 1898, Bunkie, La. Died: July 14, 1975, New York, N.Y. Black jazz musician (drummer), screen and television actor.

Appeared in: 1943 Stormy Weather. 1947 New Orleans.

SINI'LETTA, VIC (Victor A. Smith)

Died: May 4, 1921, Chicago, Ill. (dropsy and heart ailment). Screen actor and circus performer.

SIN-NUI, HUNG

Born: 1920, China. Died: Oct. 1966, Canton, China (suicide). Screen actress and opera performer. Jumped to her death after Red Guards (teenage militants) had cut off her hair and paraded her through the streets.

SINOEL (Jen Vies)

Born: 1868, France. Died: Aug. 31, 1949, Paris, France. Screen actor.

Appeared in: 1935 Le Dernier Milliardaire. 1947 Francis the First; Vie de Boheme. 1948 Voyage Surprise.

SIODMAK, ROBERT (Robert Siodmark)

Born: 1900, Memphis, Tenn. Died: Mar. 10, 1973, Switzerland (heart attack). Screen actor, film producer, director and author. Appeared in early UFA films in Germany.

SIPPERLEY, RALPH

Born: 1890. Died: Jan. 1928, Bangor, Maine. Stage and screen actor.

Appeared in: 1923 Six Cylinder Love. 1926 The Blue Eagle; The Canyon of Light; Womanpower. 1927 Sunrise.

SISSLE, NOBLE

Born: 1889. Died: Dec. 17, 1975, Tampa, Fla. Black songwriter, orchestra leader, vaudeville and screen actor.

SISSON, VERA

Born: 1891, Salt Lake City, Utah. Died: Aug. 6, 1954. Screen actress.

Appeared in: 1914 Women and Roses; Too Much Married; The Bolted Door; Toilers of the Sea; The Golden Ladder; Value Received; The Sand Hill Lovers; The Proof of a Man; There is a Destiny; Weights and Measures; Little Meg and I. 1915 The Trust; According to Value; Martin Love-Fixer; The Storm; The Guardian of the Flocks; For Cash; The Oyster Dredger; The Laurel of Tears; The Chief Inspector. 1916 Landon's Legacy; The Iron Woman; His Wife's Story; The Man from Nowhere. 1917 Paradise Garden. 1919 The Veiled Adventure. 1920 The Heart of Youth. 1921 The Avenging Arrow (serial). 1926 Love 'Em and Leave 'Em.

SKELLY, HAL (Joseph Harold Skelly)

Born: 1891, Allegheny, Pa. Died: June 16, 1934, West Cornwall, Conn. (auto accident). Screen, stage, circus, minstrel actor, opera performer and stage producer.

Appeared in: 1929 The Dance of Life; Woman Trap. 1930 Behind the Make-up; Men Are Like That. 1931 The Struggle. 1933 Hotel Variety; Shadow Laughs.

SKELLY, JAMES

Born: 1936. Died: Apr. 19, 1969, Palm Springs, Calif. (pneumonia). Screen actor. Entered films approx. 1957.

SKINNER, OTIS

Born: June 28, 1857, Cambridge, Mass. Died: Jan. 5, 1942, New York, N.Y. (uremic poisoning). Screen, stage actor, stage producer and stage director.

Appeared in: 1920 Romance; Kismet. 1922 Mister Antonio. 1930 Kismet (and 1920 version).

SKIPWORTH, ALISON

Born: July 25, 1865, 1870 or 1875 (?), London, England. Died: July 5, 1952, New York, N.Y. Screen, stage and television actress.

Appeared in: 1921 Handcuffs or Kisses. 1930 Strictly Unconventional; Raffles; Outward Bound; Oh, For a Man!; Du Barry, Woman of Passion. 1931 Tonight or Never; Night Angel; Virtuous Husband; The Road to Singapore; Devotion. 1932 Sinners in the Sun; Madame Racketeer; Night after Night; High Pressure; If I Had a Million; Unexpected Father. 1933 Tonight Is Ours; He Learned about Women; A Lady's Profession; Song of Songs; Midnight Club; Tillie and Gus; Alice in Wonderland. 1934 Six of a Kind; Wharf Angel; The Notorious Sophie Lang; Here Is My Heart; Shoot the Works; The Captain Hates the Sea; Coming Out Party. 1935 The Devil Is a Woman; Shanghai; Becky Sharp; Doubting Thomas; The Casino Murder Case; The Girl from Tenth Avenue; Dangerous; Hitch Hike Lady. 1936 Satan Met a Lady; The Princess Comes Across; The Gorgeous Hussy; Two in a Crowd; White Hunter; Stolen Holiday. 1937 Two Wise Maids. 1938 King of the Newsboys; Ladies in Distress; Wide Open Faces.

SKULNIK, MENASHA

Born: 1892. Died: June 4, 1970, New York, N.Y. Yiddish screen and stage actor.

SLACK, FREDDIE

Born: Aug. 7, 1910, La Crosse, Wis. Died: Aug. 10, 1965, Hollywood, Calif. (natural causes). Bandleader and screen actor.

Appeared in: 1943 Reveille with Beverly; The Sky's the Limit. 1944 Hat Check Honey; Follow the Boys; Seven Days Ashore. 1946 High School Hero.

SLATER, JOHN (B. John Slater)

Born: Aug. 22, 1916, London, England. Died: Jan. 9, 1975, London, England (heart attack). Screen, stage, radio and television actor. Married to actress Betty Slater. Entered films in 1939.

Appeared in: 1941 Love on the Dole; Gert and Daisy's Weekend. 1942 Went the Day Well? (aka 48 Hours—US 1944). 1943 Deadlock. 1944 For Those in Peril; A Canterbury Tale. 1945 The Seventh Veil (US 1946); Murder in Reverse (US 1946). 1947 It Always Rains on Sunday (US 1949). 1948 Escape; Noose (aka The Silk Noose—US 1950); Against the Wind (US 1949). 1949 Passport to Pimlico. 1950 Prelude to Fame. 1951 The Third Visitor. 1952 Faithful City. 1953 The Flanagan Boy (aka Bad Blonde—US); The Long Memory. 1954 The Million Pound Note (aka Man with a Million—US); Star of India (US 1956). 1956 Johnny, You're Wanted. 1957 Devil's Pass. 1958 Violent Play-

ground. 1960 The Night We Got the Bird. 1961 Three on a Spree. 1963 A Place to Go.

SLAUGHTER, TOD (N. Carter Slaughter)

Born: Mar. 19, 1885, Newcastle-on-Tyne, England. Died: Feb. 19, 1956. Stage and screen actor.

Appeared in: 1935 Maria Marten: Or, The Murder in the Red Barn. 1936 The Crimes of Stephen Hawke; Sweeney Todd, The Demon Barber of Fleet Street (US 1939). 1937 Song of the Road; Darby and Joan; It's Never Too Late to Mend; The Ticket of Leave Man. 1938 Sexton Blake and the Hooded Terror. 1939 The Face at the Window (US 1940). 1940 Crimes at the Dark House. 1946 Bothered by a Beard (short); The Curse of the Wraydons. 1948 The Greed of William Hart. 1952 King of the Underworld; Murder at Scotland Yard; Murder at the Grange; A Ghost for Sale.

SLEZAK, LEO

Born: 1875. Died: June 6, 1946, Bavaria, Germany. Screen actor and opera performer. Father of actor Walter Slezak and actress Margarete Slezak (dec. 1953).

Appeared in: 1932 Ein Toller Einfall (A Mad Idea—US 1934). 1934 Freut Euch des Lebens. 1935 Tanzmusik; Die Fahrt in Die Jugend; Mein Liebster Ist ein Jaegersmann; La Paloma. 1937 Freuhling im Wien; The World's in Love; The Postillion of Lonjumeau. 1938 Rendezvous in Wien; Gasparone; Husaren Heraus; Eine Nacht an der Donau (A Night on the Danube); Unsterbliche Melodien (Immortal Melodies); Magda; Liebe im Dreiviertel Takt (Love in Waltz Time); Die Gluecklichste Ehe von Wien (The Happiest Married Couple in Vienna). 1939 Ihr Groesster Erfolg (Her Greatest Success); Die Pompadour; Herbst-Monoever (Fall Manoeuvres); Fasching in Wien; Die Blonde Carmen. Other Viennese films: Women's Paradise; Music in the Blood.

SLEZAK, MARGARETE

Born: 1901, Germany. Died: Aug. 30, 1953, Rottach-Egern, Bavaria, Germany (heart attack). Screen actress and opera performer. Daughter of actor Leo Slezak (dec. 1946) and sister of actor Walter Slezak.

Appeared in: 1953 Man on a Tightrope. Other German films: Derby; The Veiled Maja.

SLOANE, EVERETT

Born: Oct. 1, 1909, New York, N.Y. Died: Aug. 6, 1965, Brentwood, Calif. (suicide—sleeping pills). Screen, stage, radio and television actor.

Appeared in: 1941 Citizen Kane. 1942 The Magnificent Ambersons; Journey into Fear. 1945 We Accuse (narr.). 1948 The Lady from Shanghai. 1949 Prince of Foxes. 1950 The Men. 1951 Bird of Paradise; The Enforcer; Sirocco; The Desert Fox; The Blue Veil; The Prince Who Was a Thief; Murder, Inc. 1952 The Sellout; Way of a Gaucho. 1955 The Big Knife. 1956 Massacre at Sand Creek; Patterson; Somebody up There Likes Me; Lust for Life. 1958 Marjorie Morningstar; The Gun Runners. 1960 Home from the Hill. 1961 By Love Possessed. 1962 Brushfire! 1963 The Man from the Diner's Club. 1964 The Patsy; The Disorderly Orderly; Ready for the People. 1970 Mr. Magoo's Holiday Festival (voice).

SLOANE, OLIVE

Born: Dec. 16, 1896. Died: June 28, 1963, London, England. Screen, stage and vaudeville actress. Appeared in vaudeville as "Baby Pearl" and later as a partner in an act billed as "Sisters Love."

Appeared in: 1921 The Door That Has No Key (US 1922); Greatheart. 1922 Trapped by the Mormons; Lonesome Farm. 1923 Rogues of the Turf; Gems of Literature series including: The Dream of Eugene Aram. 1925 Money Isn't Everything. 1928 The Mormon (reissue of Trapped by the Mormons—1922). 1933 The Good Companions; Soldiers of the King (aka The Woman in Command—US 1934). 1934 Sing as We Go; Brides to Be; Faces; Music Hall. 1935 Key to Harmony; Alibi Inn. 1936 The Howard Case; In the Soup. 1937 Dreaming Lips; Mad about Money (aka Stardust and He Loved an Actress—US 1938); Cafe Colette (aka Danger in Paris—US); Overcoat Sam. 1938 Make It Three; Consider Your Verdict. 1939 Inquest. 1941 The Tower of Terror (US 1942). 1942 Those Kids from Town; Let the People Sing. 1945 They Knew Mr. Knight; The Voice Within. 1946 Send for Paul Temple. 1947 Bank Holiday Luck. 1948 The Guinea Pig (US 1949). 1949 Under Capricorn. 1950 Waterfront (aka Waterfront Women—US 1952); Seven Days to Noon. 1951 The Franchise Affair (US 1952). 1952 Curtain Up (US 1953); Tall Headlines; My Wife's Lodger. 1954 The Weak and the Wicked; The Golden Link. 1955 A Prize of Gold. 1956 Alf's Baby; The Man in the Road; The Last Man to Hang? 1957 Brothers in Law. 1959 Serious Charge (aka Immoral Charge—US 1962 and A Touch of Hell—US 1964). 1960 The Price of Silence; Your Money or Your Wife (US 1965). 1963 Heavens Above.

SLOCUM, TEX

Born: 1902. Died: Jan. 18, 1963, Concord, Calif. (heart attack). Screen actor and stuntman who doubled for Tom Mix and Hoot Gibson.

SLOMAN, EDWARD "TED"

Born: 1885, London, England. Died: Sept. 29, 1972, Woodland Hills, Calif. Screen, stage, vaudeville actor and film director. Married to actress Hylda Hollis.

Appeared in: 1914 The Trey O'Hearts (serial). 1915 The Mother Instinct; The Mother Iris; Where Happiness Dwells; The Valley of Regeneration; In the Heart of the Hills; The Markswoman; Vengeance of the Oppressed; The Embodied Thought; Sold to Satan.

SMALL, EDNA

Born: 1898. Died: July 14, 1917, Cincinnati, Ohio. Screen actress. Appeared in early Chaplin films.

SMALLEY, PHILLIPS (Phillips Wendell Smalley)

Born: Aug. 7, 1875, Brooklyn, N.Y. Died: May 2, 1939, Hollywood, Calif. Screen, stage actor, film director and film producer. Appeared in early Rex pictures in 1909.

Appeared in: 1914 The Merchant of Venice; False Colors. 1915 A Cigarette—That's All. 1921 Two Wise Wives. 1922 The Power of a Lie. 1923 The Self-Made Wife; Temptation; Trimmed in Scarlet; Cameo Kirby; Flaming Youth; Nobody's Bride. 1924 Cheap Kisses; For Sale; Single Wives; Daughters of Today. 1925 The Awful Truth; Charley's Aunt; Soul Mates; Wandering Footsteps; Stella Maris; The Fate of a Flirt. 1926 Money Talks; There You Are!; Queen of Diamonds; The Taxi Mystery. 1927 The Broken Gate; Sensation Seekers; Tea for Three; The Dice Woman; The Irresistible Lover; Stage Kisses. 1928 Blindfold; Man Crazy; The Border Patrol; Sinners in Love; Honeymoon Flats; Broadway Daddies. 1929 The Aviator; True Heaven; High Voltage; The Fatal Warning (serial). 1930 Charley's Aunt (and 1925 version); Peacock Alley; The Midnight Special; Drumming It In (short); Liliom. 1931 Lawless Woman; Lady from Nowhere; High Stakes; Get-Rich-Quick Wallingford; A Free Soul. 1932 Murder at Dawn; Hell's Headquarters; Escapade; Sinister Hands; Widow in Scarlet; Face on the Barroom Floor; The Greeks Had a Word for Them. 1933 Midnight Warning; The Cocktail Hour. 1934 The Big Race; Stolen Sweets; Madame Du Barry; Bolero. 1935 Hold 'Em Yale; All The King's Horses; Night Life of the Gods; It's in the Air; A Night at the Opera. 1936 Too Many Parents. 1937 Hotel Haywire. 1938 Booloo.

SMART, J. SCOTT (aka JACK SMART)

Born: 1903. Died: Jan. 15, 1960, Springfield, Ill. Screen and radio actor.

Appeared in: 1947 Kiss of Death. 1951 Fat Man (film and radio).

SMELKER, MARY

Born: 1909. Died: June 2, 1933, Tucson, Ariz. (auto accident). Screen actress.

SMILEY, JOSEPH W.

Born: 1881. Died: Dec. 2, 1945, N.Y. Screen, stage, vaudeville actor and film director. Entered films as actor and director with the Original Imp Co. in 1910.

Appeared in: 1921 Experience; The Old Oaken Bucket; The Woman God Changed; The Rich Slave; The Scarab Ring; The Wild Goose. 1922 The Blonde Vampire; The Face in the Fog. 1925 Old Home Week; Wild, Wild Susan; The Police Patrol. 1926 Aloma of the South Seas; The Show Off; The Untamed Lady. 1927 The Potters.

SMITH, ALBERT E.

Born: 1875, England. Died: Aug. 1, 1958, Hollywood, Calif. One of the founders of Vitagraph Pictures, film producer and screen actor. Do not confuse with actors Albert J. or Al Smith. Married to actress Hazel Neason (dec. 1920); later married and divorced actress Jean Paige, then later married to Lucile Smith.

Appeared in: 1912 A Vitagraph Romance.

SMITH, ALBERT J.

Born: 1894, New York, N.Y. Died: Apr. 12, 1939, Hollywood, Calif. Screen actor.

Appeared in: 1921 Terror Trail (serial). 1923 In the Days of Daniel Boone (serial). 1924 Big Timber; The Measure of a Man; The Sunset Trail; The Fast Express (serial). 1925 The Middler; Straight Through; The Taming of the West; Ace of Spades (serial); Barriers of the Law; Blood and Steel; The Burning Trail; The Circus Cyclone. 1926 The Scarlet Streak (serial); Strings of Steel (serial); Speed Crazed. 1927 Perils of the Jungle (serial); Hills of Peril; Whispering Sage; The Swift Shadow; Hard Fists; Red Clay; Where Trails Begin. 1928 The Law of Fear; The Bullet Mark; Hold 'Em Yale. 1929 The Drifter; Fury of the Wild; "Half Pint Polly" comedies. 1932 The Last Mile. 1934 Honor of the Range.

SMITH, ART (Arthur Gordon Smith)

Born: 1900. Died: Feb. 24, 1973, West Babylon, N.Y. (heart attack). Screen, stage and television actor.

Appeared in: 1942 Native Land. 1943 Edge of Darkness. 1944 None Shall Escape; Uncertain Glory; Mr. Winkle Goes to War; The Black Parachute. 1945 A Tree Grows in Brooklyn. 1946 Moon Over Montana; Trail to Mexico; Six Gun Serenade. 1947 Brute Force; Ride the Pink Horse; Body and Soul;

T-Men. 1948 Oklahoma Blues; Song of the Drifter; Courtin' Trouble; Letter from an Unknown Woman; Mr. Peabody and the Mermaid; The Rangers Ride; Arch of Triumph; A Double Life; Angel in Exile; Range Renegades. 1949 Caught; South of St. Louis; Manhandled; Red, Hot and Blue; Song of Surrender. 1950 South Sea Sinner; In a Lonely Place; Quicksand; The Next Voice You Hear; The Killer That Stalked New York. 1951 Try and Get Me (aka The Sound of Fury); Half Angel; The Painted Hills. 1952 Just for You; The Rose of Cimarron. 1963 The Moving Finger.

SMITH, BEATRICE LIEB

Born: 1862. Died: Aug. 6, 1942, Los Angeles, Calif. Screen and stage actress.

SMITH, BESSIE

Born: Apr. 15, 1894, Chattanooga, Tenn. Died: Sept. 26, 1937, Clarksdale, Miss. (auto accident). Black jazz singer and screen actress.

Appeared in: 1929 St. Louis Blues (short).

SMITH, C. AUBREY

Born: July 21, 1863, London, England. Died: Dec. 20, 1948, Beverly Hills, Calif. (pneumonia). Stage and screen actor.

Appeared in: 1915 Builder of Bridges (film debut). 1916 The Witching Hour. 1918 Red Pottage. 1920 The Face at the Window; The Shuttle of Life; The Bump (short); Castles in Spain. 1922 The Bohemian Girl; Flames of Passion. 1923 The Temptation of Carleton Earle. 1924 The Unwanted; The Rejected Woman. 1930 Such Is the Law; Birds of Prey (aka The Perfect Alibi—US 1931). 1931 Trader Horn; Never the Twain Shall Meet; The Bachelor Father; Daybreak; Son of India; Contraband Love; Just a Gigolo; Man in Possession; The Phantom of Paris; Guilty Hands; Surrender; Dancing Partners. 1932 Polly of the Circus; Tarzan, the Ape Man; But the Flesh Is Weak; Love Me Tonight; Trouble in Paradise; No More Orchids. 1933 They Just Had to Get Married; Luxury Liner; Bombshell; The Barbarian; Secrets; Morning Glory; Adorable; Monkey's Paw; Queen Christina. 1934 The House of Rothschild; Gambling Lady; Riptide; We Live Again; Curtain at Eight; Bulldog Drummond Strikes Back; Cleopatra; Madame Du Barry; One More River; Caravan; The Firebird; The Scarlet Empress. 1935 The Tunnel (aka Trans-Atlantic Tunnel—US); The Right to Live; Lives of a Bengal Lancer; The Florentine Dagger; The Gilded Lily; Clive of India; China Seas; Jalna; The Crusades. 1936 The Story of Papworth (short); Little Lord Fauntleroy; Romeo and Juliet; The Garden of Allah; Lloyds of London. 1937 Wee Willie Winkie; The Prisoner of Zenda; Thoroughbreds Don't Cry; The Hurricane. 1938 Four Men and a Prayer; Kidnapped; Sixty Glorious Years (aka Queen of Destiny—US). 1939 East Side of Heaven; The Four Feathers; Five Came Back; The Sun Never Sets; Eternally Yours; Another Thin Man; The Under-Pup; Balalaika. 1940 Rebecca; City of Chance; A Bill of Divorcement; Waterloo Bridge; Beyond Tomorrow; A Little Bit of Heaven. 1941 Free and Easy; Maisie Was a Lady; Dr. Jekyll and Mr. Hyde. 1943 Forever and a Day; Two Tickets to London; Flesh and Fantasy; Madame Curie. 1944 The White Cliffs of Dover; The Adventures of Mark Twain; Secrets of Scotland Yard; Sensations of 1945. 1945 They Shall Have Faith; And Then There Were None; Scotland Yard Investigator. 1946 Cluny Brown; Rendezvous with Annie. 1947 High Conquest; Unconquered. 1948 An Ideal Husband. 1949 Little Women.

SMITH, CHARLES H.

Born: 1866. Died: July 11, 1942, Hollywood, Calif. Screen and vaudeville actor. Was member of "Smith and Campbell" vaudeville team.

Appeared in: 1921 Nobody; The Silver Lining. 1927 Naughty Nanette. 1929 Clear the Decks; Girl Overboard; The Girl on the Barge. 1930 The Bat Whispers.

SMITH, CHARLOTTE

Born: 1873, Toronto, Canada. Died: Mar. 22, 1928, Beverly Hills, Calif. Stage and screen actress. Mother of actresses Mary and Lottie Pickford (dec. 1936) and actor Jack Pickford (dec. 1933). Appeared in Imp Company films.

SMITH, CYRIL

Born: Apr. 4, 1892, Peterhead, Scotland. Died: Mar. 5, 1963, London, England. Stage and screen actor. Married to actress Anne Rendall.

Appeared in: 1914 Old St. Paul's (aka When London Burned—US). 1919 Pallard, the Punter. 1920 Walls of Prejudice; The Fordington Twins; Will O'Wisp comedies including Sweep; On the Reserve; Cupid's Carnival; Run! Run! Run!; A Broken Contract; Cousin Ebenezer; Souvenirs; The Lightning Liver Cure; A Little Bet; A Pair of Gloves; Home Influence. 1921 The Way of a Man; Class and No Class. 1923 Fires of Fate. 1924 The Desert Sheik. 1932 The Innocents of Chicago (aka Why Saps Leave Home—US); The Major's Nest. 1933 Channel Crossing (US 1934); Friday the Thirteenth (US 1934); The Good Companions. 1934 Waltzes from Vienna (aka Strauss's Great Waltz—US 1935); The Black Abbot; Wild Boy; It's a Cop. 1935 Hello Sweetheart; Key to Harmony; Brown on Resolution (aka Forever England and Born for Glory—US); Bulldog Jack (aka Alias Bulldog Drummond—US); Lend Me Your Wife. 1937 O.H.M.S. (aka You're in the Army Now—US); The Frog (US 1939). 1938 The Challenge (US 1939); No Parking; The Return of the Frog. 1939 Traitor Spy (aka The Torso Murder Mystery—US 1940); Sword of Honor.

1940 The Flying Squad; Law and Disorders. **1943** When We are Married. **1944** One Exciting Night (aka You Can't Do Without Love—US 1946); Meet Sexton Blake. **1945** The Echo Murders; Don Chicago. **1946** School for Secrets; Appointment with Crime (US 1950). **1949** The Rocking Horse Winner (US 1950); Conspirator (US 1950). **1950** The Body Said No!; Old Mother Riley, Headmistress. **1951** The Third Visitor; The Dark Man; Night was Our Friend; Green Grow the Rushes. **1952** Stolen Face; The Lost Hours (aka The Big Frame—US 1953); Women of Twilight (aka Twilight Women—US 1953). **1953** Wheel of Fate. **1954** Svengali; Burnt Evidence; The Strange Case of Blondie. **1956** Sailor Beware! (aka Panic in the Parlour—US 1957); The Angel Who Pawned Her Harp. **1957** Value for Money. **1960** Light Up the Sky. **1961** Over the Odds. **1962** She Knows Y'Know. **1965** Operation Snafu.

SMITH, DWIGHT
Born: 1857, Vevay, Ind. Died: May 30, 1949, Monsey, N.Y. Stage and screen actor. Appeared in silents.

SMITH, G. ALBERT
Born: 1898. Died: Sept. 3, 1959, New York, N.Y. Screen, stage and television actor.

Appeared in: **1931** Stolen Heaven.

SMITH, GEORGE W.
Born: 1899. Died: Nov. 18, 1947, Chicago, Ill. (coronary thrombosis). Stage and screen actor.

Appeared in: **1946** Snafu.

SMITH, GERALD (Gerland Oliver Smith)
Born: June 26, 1896, London, England. Died: May 28, 1974, Woodland Hills, Calif. Screen, stage and radio actor.

Appeared in: **1925** School for Wives. **1936** The Man I Marry; When You're in Love. **1937** Top of the Town; Girl Overboard; One Hundred Men and a Girl; The Lady Fights Back; The Lady Escapes; Behind the Mike. **1938** Invisible Enemy; Gateway. **1939** Bachelor Mother. **1940** West of Pinto Basin; Kiddie Cure (short). **1941** The Singing Hill; Federal Fugitives; Puddin' Head; You're the One. **1942** Beyond the Blue Horizon; Tish; Casablanca. **1943** Forever and a Day; Heaven Can Wait. **1944** Jane Eyre; The Man in Half Moon Street; Knickerbocker Holiday; National Velvet; Mrs. Parkington; Casanova Brown. **1945** Sunbonnet Sue; The Sailor Takes a Wife. **1946** Rainbow over Texas. **1948** Enchantment. **1949** That Forsyte Woman.

SMITH, HOWARD I.
Born: 1893, Attleboro, Mass. Died: Jan. 10, 1968, Hollywood, Calif. (heart attack). Screen, stage, vaudeville, radio and television actor.

Appeared in: **1922** Young America. **1946** Her Kind of Man. **1947** Kiss of Death. **1948** Call Northside 777; State of the Union; Street with No Name. **1950** Cry Murder. **1951** Death of a Salesman. **1952** Never Wave at a WAC. **1953** The Caddy. **1957** Don't Go Near the Water; A Face in the Crowd. **1958** Wind across the Everglades; No Time for Sergeants; I Bury the Living. **1959** Face of Fire. **1960** Murder, Inc. **1962** Bon Voyage! **1963** The Brass Bottle.

SMITH, J. LEWIS
Born: 1906. Died: Sept. 12, 1964, Culver City, Calif. (shot). Screen actor and stuntman.

Appeared in: **1955** The Tall Men. **1956** Around the World in 80 Days. **1959** It Started with a Kiss. **1961** Man-Trap; The Misfits. **1962** How the West Was Won; Jumbo; The Wonderful World of the Brothers Grimm. **1963** Twilight of Honor. **1964** Advance to the Rear.

SMITH, J. STANLEY
Born: Jan. 6, 1905, Kansas City, Mo. Died: Apr. 13, 1974, Pasadena, Calif. Stage and screen actor. Entered films in 1929.

Appeared in: **1929** Sweetie; The Sophomore. **1930** Follow the Leader; Good News; The King of Jazz; Honey; Love Among the Millionaires; Queen High; Soup to Nuts; Paramount on Parade. **1932** Stepping Sisters. **1933** Reform Girl. **1937** A Warner short. **1940** Flight Command. **1941** Buck Privates; Keep 'Em Flying. **1942** Eagle Squadron.

SMITH, JACK
Born: 1896. Died: Jan. 14, 1944, Los Angeles, Calif. Screen actor and songwriter.

Appeared in: **1928** Man in the Rough. **1929** Laughing at Death. **1937** Git Along Little Dogies; Heroes of the Alamo. **1938** Paroled to Die; Frontier Scout. **1939** The Phantom Creeps (serial). **1941** Stick to Your Guns.

SMITH, JOE
Born: 1900. Died: May 5, 1952, Yuma, Ariz. (heart attack). Screen actor and stuntman.

Appeared in: **1952** Desert Song.

SMITH, COL. LEONARD R.
Born: 1889. Died: July 9, 1958, San Antonio, Tex. Screen actor and film director. Did trick riding in silent films for William S. Hart and also worked in Mack Sennett comedies.

SMITH, MABEL. *See* BIG MAYBELLE

SMITH, MARGARET M.
Born: 1881. Died: Dec. 9, 1960, Hollywood, Calif. Screen actress.

Appeared in: **1925** A Roaring Adventure.

SMITH, MARK
Born: 1886. Died: May 10, 1944, New York, N.Y. Screen and stage actor.

SMITH, MATTHEW
Born: 1905. Died: Mar. 16, 1953, New York, N.Y. Screen and stage actor.

Appeared in: **1934** The Barretts of Wimpole Street.

SMITH, PAUL GERALD
Born: Omaha, Neb. Died: 1968. Screen actor, playwright and screenwriter.

Appeared in: **1917** The Mysterious Miss Terry.

SMITH, PLEASANT (aka TOMMY LEE PLEASANT and JIMMY DEE SMITH)
Born: 1886. Died: Mar. 12, 1969, Las Vegas, Nev. Screen actor and wrestler. Appeared in films between 1913 and 1919.

SMITH, SIDNEY
Born: 1892. Died: July 4, 1928, Hollywood, Calif. (possibly effects of bad liquor). Screen actor and comedian.

Appeared in: **1917** Oriental Love; His Uncle Dudley. **1921–1922** The "Hallroom Boys" series. **1923** The Ne'er-Do-Well. **1928** Dugan of the Dugouts; Top Sergeant Mulligan.

SMITH, THOMAS C.
Born: 1892. Died: Dec. 3, 1950, Hollywood, Calif. Screen actor.

Appeared in: **1929** The Invaders.

SMITH, "WHISPERING" JACK
Born: 1898. Died: May 13, 1950, New York, N.Y. (heart attack). Screen, vaudeville, radio, television actor and singer. Known as "The Whispering Baritone."

Appeared in: **1930** Happy Days; The Big Parade; Cheer Up and Smile.

SMITHSON, LAURA
Born: 1878. Died: Dec. 23, 1963. Stage and screen actress.

Appeared in: **1937** Men Are Not Gods.

SMITTERICK, GROVER
Died: Sept. 1914, New York (drowned while filming). Screen actor. Appeared in Progressive Motion Picture Company films.

SMOLLER, DOROTHY
Born: 1901, Memphis, Tenn. Died: Dec. 10, 1926, New York, N.Y. (suicide). Screen actress and dancer.

SMYTHE, FLORENCE
Born: 1878. Died: Aug. 29, 1925, Hollywood, Calif. (heart failure). Stage and screen actress. Married to actor Theodore Roberts (dec. 1928).

Appeared in: **1915** The Wild Goose Chase; The Fighting Hope. **1916** Common Ground. **1917** The Silent Partner; The Winning of Sally Temple.

SNEGOFF, LEONID
Born: May 15, 1883, Russia. Died: Feb. 22, 1974, Los Angeles, Calif. (heart failure—arteriosclerosis). Screen and stage actor.

Appeared in: **1926** Broken Hearts. **1927** The Forbidden Woman. **1933** The Man Who Dared; After Tonight; Girl Without a Room; We Live Again. **1934** Smoky. **1935** The Man Who Broke the Bank at Monte Carlo; The Wedding Night; Dressed to Thrill. **1937** Seventh Heaven; The Three Legionnaires; Cafe Metropole; Dangerously Yours. **1939** Barricade. **1943** For Whom the Bell Tolls; Mission to Moscow. **1947** Song of My Heart. **1953** One Girl's Confession.

SNELLING, MINNETTE
Born: 1878. Died: Dec. 19, 1945, Hollywood, Calif. Screen actress. Entered films in 1917. Appeared in Mack Sennett comedies.

SNITZER, JIMMY
Born: 1926. Died: Mar. 22, 1945, Asbach, Germany. Screen actor.

SNITZER, MIRIAM

Born: 1922. Died: Sept. 6, 1966. Screen actress.

SNOOKUMS. *See* LAWRENCE D. McKEEN, JR.

SNOW, MARGUERITE

Born: 1889. Died: Feb. 17, 1958, Hollywood, Calif. (kidney complications). Screen actress. Married to actor Neely Edwards (dec. 1955).

Appeared in: 1912 Lucille. 1913 Carmen. 1914 Zudora—The Twenty Million Dollar Mystery (serial); Joseph in the Land of Egypt. 1915 The Silent Voice. 1917 Broadway Jones. 1918 The Eagle's Eye (serial). 1921 Lavender and Old Lace. 1922 The Veiled Woman. 1924 Chalk Marks. 1925 Kit Carson over the Great Divide; Savages of the Sea.

SNOW, MORTIMER

Born: 1869. Died: June 20, 1935. Stage and screen actor.

Appeared in: 1922 The Mohican's Daughter; When Knighthood Was in Flower.

SNOWDEN, ELMER "POPS" (Elmer Chester Snowden)

Born: Oct. 9, 1900, Baltimore, Md. Died: May 14, 1973, Philadelphia, Pa. Jazz musician and screen actor. Appeared in Warner Bros. shorts.

SNYDER, MATT

Died: Jan. 17, 1917, San Francisco, Calif. Screen and stage actor.

Appeared in: 1916 The Crisis.

SOBOTKA, RUTH

Born: 1925. Died: June 17, 1967. Stage and screen actress. Divorced from film director Stanley Kubrick.

Appeared in: 1955 Killer's Kiss.

SODDERS, CARL

Died: Dec. 18, 1958, Dayton, Ohio. Screen actor. Appeared in silents.

SODERLING, WALTER

Born: Apr. 13, 1872, Connecticut. Died: Apr. 10, 1948, Los Angeles, Calif. Screen actor.

Appeared in: 1937 Criminals of the Air; Woman Chases Man. 1938 The Story of Dr. Carver (short). 1939 The Gracie Allen Murder Case; St. Louis Blues; Blondie Meets the Boss; Death of a Champion. 1940 When the Daltons Rode; Blondie Has Servant Trouble; Men Without Souls; On Their Own; I'm Nobody's Sweetheart Now; Out West with the Peppers; Ragtime Cowboy Joe; Slightly Tempted. 1941 Penny Serenade; The Return of Daniel Boone; Three Girls About Town; Confessions of Boston Blackie. 1943 The Blocked Trail; True to Life. 1944 The Falcon in Hollywood; The Adventures of Mark Twain; Outlaws of Santa Fe. 1945 Rhapsody in Blue. 1946 King of the Forest Rangers (serial); Danny Boy; The Glass Alibi; In Fast Company; The French Key. 1947 Yankee Fakir. 1948 So Dear to My Heart; Leather Gloves.

SOJIN (Sojin Kamiyama)

Born: Jan. 20, 1891, Sendai, Japan. Died: July 28, 1954, Tokyo, Japan. Stage and screen actor. Appeared in U.S. films from approximately 1913 to 1930 and then appeared in Japanese films. He was one of the six actors to portray "Charlie Chan."

Appeared in: 1924 The Thief of Bagdad. 1925 The White Desert; My Lady's Lips; Proud Flesh; Soft Shoes; East of Suez. 1926 Across the Pacific; Diplomacy; Eve's Leaves; The Lucky Lady; The Lady of the Harem; The Sky Pirate; The Sea Beast; The Bat; The Road to Mandalay; The Wanderer. 1927 All Aboard; The Devil Dancer; Driven from Home; Foreign Devils; King of Kings; The Haunted Ship; Old San Francisco; Streets of Shanghai. 1928 Chinese Parrot; Chinatown Charlie; The Crimson City; The Hawk's Nest; Out With the Tide; Ships of the Night; Something Always Happens; The Man Without a Face (serial); Telling the World; Tropic Madness. 1929 Back from Shanghai; The Rescue; China Slaver; Painted Faces; Seven Footprints to Satan; The Show of Shows; The Unholy Night; Careers. 1930 The Dude Wrangler; Golden Dawn.

SOKOLOFF, VLADIMIR

Born: Dec. 26, 1889, Moscow, Russia. Died: Feb. 14, 1962, Hollywood, Calif. (stroke). Screen, stage actor and stage director.

Appeared in: 1927 Loves of Jeanne Ney. 1930 West Front 1918. 1931 Die Dreigroschenoper (The Beggar's Opera); Der Grosse Tenor. 1932 Niemandsland (No Man's Land); Teilnehmer Antwortet Nicht; L'Atalantide. 1934 Hell on Earth. 1937 The Prisoner of Zenda; The Life of Emile Zola; West of Shanghai; Expensive Husbands; Tovarich; Conquest; Beg, Borrow or Steal; The Lower Depths; Mayerling. 1938 Alcatraz Island; Arsene Lupin Returns; Blockade; The Amazing Dr. Clitterhouse; Spawn of the North; Ride a Crooked Mile. 1939 Juarez; The Real Glory; Song of the Street. 1940 Comrade X. 1941 Compliments of Mr. Flow; Love Crazy. 1942 Crossroads; The Road to Morocco. 1943 Mission to Moscow; Song of Russia; Fom Whom the Bell Tolls; Mr.

Lucky. 1944 Passage to Marseille; The Conspirators; 'Til We Meet Again. 1945 The Blonde from Brooklyn; Paris Underground; Scarlet Street; A Royal Scandal; Back to Bataan. 1946 Two Smart People; Cloak and Dagger; A Scandal in Paris. 1948 To the Ends of the Earth. 1950 The Baron of Arizona. 1952 Macao. 1956 While the City Sleeps. 1957 Istanbul; I Was a Teenage Werewolf; Sabu and the Magic Ring. 1958 The Monster from Green Hill; Twilight for the Gods. 1960 Man on a String; Beyond the Time Barrier; The Magnificent Seven; Cimarron; Confessions of a Counterspy; Die Dreigroschenoper (The Three Penny Opera—also 1931 version). 1961 Mr. Sardonicus. 1962 Taras Bulba; Escape from Zahrain.

SOKOLOW, ETHEL

Died: Dec. 20, 1970. Screen actress.

Appeared in: 1968 Funny Man. 1969 Take the Money and Run.

SOLDANI, CHARLES L.

Born: June 1, 1893, Oklahoma. Died: Sept. 10, 1968, Glendale, Calif. (lung cancer). Screen actor.

Appeared in: 1945 The Cherokee Flash; The Man from Oklahoma. 1949 Apache Chief; Daughter of the Jungle. 1950 Broken Arrow. 1953 Winning of the West. 1956 Around the World in 80 Days. 1959 Escort West.

SOLDI, STEPHEN

Died: Nov. 4, 1974. Screen actor and extra.

Appeared in: 1947 Twilight on the Rio Grande. 1956 Around the World in 80 Days.

SOLER, DOMINGO (Domingo Diaz Pavia)

Born: Apr. 17, 1902, Guerrero, Mexico. Died: June 13, 1961, Acapulco, Mexico (heart attack). Stage and screen actor. Son of actor Domingo Soler, Sr. Brother of actors Andres, Julian and Fernando Soler.

Appeared in: 1935 Corazon Bandolero; Chucho el Roto; Tierra, Amor y Dolor. 1936 La Mujer del Puerto. 1938 Mi Candidato (My Candidate); Hombres de Mar (Men of the Sea); Bajo el Cielo de Mexico (Beneath the Sky of Mexico); Refugidos en Madrid. 1939 Vamonos con Pancho Villa (Let's Go with Pancho Villa); El Senor Alcalde (The Mayor); A lo Macho (In Rough Style); Por Mis Pistolas (By My Pistols); El Latigo (The Whip); La Golondrina (The Swallow). 1940 Corazon de Nino (Heart of a Child); Perfidia (Perfidy); La Bestia Negra (The Black Beast). 1943 The Life of Simon Bolivar; El Conde de Monte Cristo. 1944 Los Miserables. 1950 Hidden River. 1954 La Ilusion Viaja en Tranvia. 1957 Flor ae Mayo (Beyond All Limits—US 1961). 1961 La Maldicion de Nostradamus (The Curse of Nostradamus). 1962 La Sangre de Nostradamus (The Blood of Nostradamus); Nostradamus, El Genio de las Tinieblas (Genii of Darkness); Nostradamus y el Destructor de Monstruos (Monster Demolisher). 1964 La Maldicion de la Llorona (The Curse of the Crying Woman). Other films include: Oro y Plata; El Primo Basilyo.

SOLIS, JAVIER

Born: 1931, Nogales, Sonora, Mexico. Died: Apr. 19, 1966, Mexico City, Mexico (following surgery). Screen actor and singer.

Appeared in: Los 2 Juanes; Juan Pistola.

SOLTZ, ROSE

Died: Sept. 18, 1973. Stage and screen actress.

SOMERS, CAROLE (Judy Cosgrove)

Died: Aug. 2, 1974, Los Angeles, Calif. Screen, stage, radio and television actress.

SOMERS, FRED

Died: Sept. 17, 1970. Screen actor.

Appeared in: 1938 Follow the Arrow (short).

SOMERSET, PAT (Patrick Holme-Somerset)

Born: Feb. 28, 1897, London, England. Died: Apr. 20, 1974, Apple Valley, Calif. (arterial hemorrhage). Stage and screen actor.

Appeared in: 1918 Eve comedies. 1920 Walls of Prejudice. 1921 Serving Two Masters; The White Hen. 1925 One of the Bravest. 1927 One Increasing Purpose. 1928 Mother Machree. 1929 The Black Watch; From Headquarters. 1930 Born Reckless; Good Intentions; Hell's Angels; Up the River; Men Without Women. 1931 Body and Soul; Devotion. 1932 Night World. 1933 Midnight Club. 1934 Murder in Trinidad. 1935 Bonnie Scotland; Clive of India; Cardinal Richelieu; Here's to Romance. 1936 To Mary—With Love. 1937 I Cover the War; Death in the Air; Prisoner of Zenda; Wee Willie Winkie.

SONNEVELD, WIM (aka WILLIAM SONNEVELD)

Born: 1918, Holland? Died: Mar. 8, 1974, Amsterdam, Holland (heart attack). Screen, stage, radio and television actor.

Appeared in: 1957 Silk Stockings.

SOREL, CECILE (Cecile Emilie Seure)
Born: 1874, France. Died: Sept. 3, 1966, Deauville, France (heart attack). Stage and screen actress.

Appeared in: **1937** Les Perles de la Couronne (Pearls of the Crown).

SOREL, GEORGE S.
Born: 1899. Died: Jan. 19, 1948, Hollywood, Calif. Screen actor.

Appeared in: **1936** Sing Me a Love Song. **1937** The Sheik Steps Out. **1938** Swiss Miss. **1939** Three Musketeers. **1942** Ship Ahoy; Once upon a Honeymoon; Casablanca. **1943** The Desert Song; Hitler—Dead or Alive. **1944** Strange Affair; America's Children; To Have and Have Not; The Conspirators. **1947** Northwest Outpost. **1948** All My Sons.

SORIN, LOUIS
Born: 1894. Died: Dec. 14, 1961, New York, N.Y. (pulmonary edema). Screen, stage, radio and television actor.

Appeared in: **1929** Lucky in Love; Mother's Boy. **1930** Animal Crackers. **1937** An Educational short. **1950** With These Hands.

SORKIN, BARNEY
Born: 1903, London, England. Died: Apr. 25, 1973, Los Angeles, Calif. (heart attack). Bandleader and screen actor.

LA SORRENTINA (Mary Frasca)
Died: July 24, 1973, New York. Screen, stage actress and singer.

Appeared in: **1970** Lovers and Other Strangers. **1971** The Gang that Couldn't Shoot Straight. **1972** The Godfather.

SOTHERN, EDWARD H.
Born: Dec. 6, 1859, New Orleans, La. Died: Oct. 28, 1933, New York, N.Y. (pneumonia). Stage and screen actor. Divorced from stage actress Virginia Harned (dec. 1946) and married to actress Julia Marlowe (dec. 1950). Entered films with Vitagraph in 1916.

Appeared in: **1916** An Enemy to the King; The Chattel.

SOTHERN, ETHEL
Born: 1882. Died: Feb. 20, 1957, Hollywood, Calif. Screen and stage actress.

SOTHERN, HARRY
Born: 1884. Died: Feb. 22, 1957, N.Y. Stage and screen actor. Nephew of Shakespearean actor E. H. Sothern (dec. 1933).

Appeared in: **1920** A Tragedy of the East Side. **1922** How Women Love; The Secrets of Paris.

SOTHERN, HUGH (aka ROY SUTHERLAND)
Born: July 20, 1881, Anderson County, Kans. Died: Apr. 13, 1947, Hollywood, Calif. Stage and screen actor. Known as Roy Sutherland on stage.

Appeared in: **1938** The Buccaneer; Dangerous to Know; Border G-Man. **1939** The Oklahoma Kid; The Giant of Norway (short); Juarez. **1940** Northwest Passage; Dispatch from Reuters. **1941** The Mad Doctor; Bad Men of Missouri. **1942** Tennessee Johnson.

SOTHERN, JEAN
Born: 1895, Richmond, Va. Died: Jan. 8, 1924, Chicago, Ill. (cancer). Screen and vaudeville actress.

Appeared in: **1915** The Two Orphans. **1916** The Mysteries of Myra.

SOTO, LUCHY
Born: 1920, Spain. Died: Oct. 1970, Madrid, Spain. Stage and screen actress.

Appeared in: **1938** Morena Clara. Other Spanish film: Garden of Delights.

SOTO, ROBERTO (aka "EL PANZON" [THE BELLY])
Born: 1888, Mexico. Died: July 18, 1960, Mexico City, Mexico (heart attack). Stage and screen actor.

Appeared in: **1938** Tropic Holiday.

SOTOMAYOR, JOSE
Born: 1905, Mexico. Died: Jan. 24, 1967, Mexico City, Mexico (heart attack). Stage and screen actor.

Appeared in: **1919** Juan Soldado. **1941** Carnaval en el Tropico. **1943** Palillo Vargas Heredia.

SOUSSANIN, NICHOLAS
Born: 1909, Yalta, Russia. Died: Apr. 27, 1975, New York, N.Y. (cardiac arrest). Screen, stage actor, playwright, stage director and screenwriter. Divorced from actress Olga Baclanova (dec. 1974).

Appeared in: **1923** Service for Ladies (film debut). **1925** The Swan. **1926** The Midnight Sun. **1927** A Gentleman of Paris; Hotel Imperial; One Increasing Purpose; The Spotlight. **1928** Adoration; The Last Command; The Night Watch; The Woman Disputed; The Yellow Lily. **1929** The Squall; Trent's Last Case. **1930** Are You There? **1931** Daughter of the Dragon; The Criminal Code; White Shoulders. **1932** Parisian Romance. **1936** Under Two Flags. **1939** Those High Grey Walls.

SOUTHARD, HARRY D.
Born: 1881. Died: Apr. 27, 1939, N.Y. Screen, stage and radio actor.

Appeared in: **1922** The Broadway Peacock; Wildness of Youth. **1927** The Winning Oar. **1929** The House of Secrets.

SOUTHERN, SAM
Born: England. Died: Mar. 21, 1920, Los Angeles, Calif. Screen actor.

Appeared in: **1919** The Eyes of Youth.

SOUTHGATE, HOWARD S.
Born: 1895. Died: May 14, 1971, Orlando, Fla. Screen, stage actor, stage director and playwright.

SOUTHWICK, DALE
Born: 1913, Long Beach, Calif. Died: Apr. 29, 1968, Compton, Calif. Screen actor. Appeared in "Our Gang" comedies.

SOVERN, CLARENCE
Born: 1900. Died: Mar. 14, 1929, Burbank, Calif. Screen cowboy actor and stuntman.

SOWARDS, GEORGE ALBERT
Born: 1888, Missouri. Died: Dec. 20, 1975. Screen actor and stuntman. Entered films in 1911.

Appeared in: **1935** The Crimson Trail. **1950** Crooked River; Hostile Country.

SOWARDS, LEN
Born: 1893. Died: Aug. 20, 1962, Los Angeles, Calif. Screen, television actor and stuntman.

SPACEY, CAPT. JOHN G.
Born: 1895. Died: Jan. 2, 1940, Hollywood, Calif. Screen and stage actor.

Appeared in: **1936** The Moon's Our Home; Thank You, Jeeves. **1937** Women of Glamour; Parole Racket. **1938** Four Men and a Prayer; Who Killed Gail Preston? **1939** I'm from Missouri; The Story of Alexander Graham Bell. **1940** British Agent.

SPADARO, ODOARDO
Born: 1894. Died: 1965, Florence, Italy. Screen, stage, television actor and singer.

SPAIN, NANCY
Born: 1918. Died: Mar. 21, 1964, Liverpool, England (plane crash). Screen and television actress.

Appeared in: **1963** Live It Up (aka Sing and Swing—US 1964).

SPANIER, MUGGSY (Francis Joseph Spanier)
Born: 1903. Died: Feb. 12, 1967, Sausalito, Calif. Dixieland cornetist and screen actor.

Appeared in: **1929** Is Everybody Happy? **1935** Here Comes the Band.

SPARKS, NED (Edward A. Sparkman)
Born: 1883, Ontario, Canada. Died: Apr. 2, 1957, Apple Valley, Calif. (intestinal block). Stage and screen actor.

Appeared in: **1922** The Bond Boy; A Wide-Open Town. **1925** Bright Lights; The Only Thing; Seven Keys to Baldpate; Soul Mates; The Boomerang; Faint Perfume; His Supreme Moment. **1926** The Auction Block; Mike; Money Talks; Oh, What a Night!; The Hidden Way; Love's Blindness; When the Wife's Away. **1927** Alias the Lone Wolf; The Secret Studio; The Small Bachelor; Alias the Deacon. **1928** The Magnificent Flirt; The Big Noise; On to Reno. **1929** Nothing but the Truth; The Canary Murder Case; Strange Cargo; Street Girl. **1930** Love Comes Along; The Devil's Holiday; The Fall Guy; Double Cross Roads; Leathernecking; Conspiracy. **1931** The Iron Man; The Secret Call; Corsair; Kept Husbands. **1932** The Miracle Man; Big City Blues; Blessed Event; The Crusader. **1933** 42nd Street; Lady for a Day; Too Much Harmony; Alice in Wonderland; Going Hollywood; Secrets; Gold Diggers of 1933. **1934** Hi, Nellie; Private Scandal; Marie Galante; Sing and Like It; Imitation of Life; Down to Their Last Yacht; Servants' Entrance. **1935** Sweet Adeline; Sweet Music; George White's 1935 Scandals. **1936** Collegiate; The Bride Walks Out; One in a Million. **1937** Wake up and Live; This Way Please; Two's Company. **1938** Hawaii Calls. **1939** The Star Maker. **1941** For Beauty's Sake. **1943** Stage Door Canteen. **1947** Magic Town.

SPAULDING, GEORGE
Born: 1881. Died: Aug. 23, 1959, Hollywood, Calif. Screen, stage, radio, television actor, stage producer and playwright.

Appeared in: **1947** Chinese Ring. **1950** When Willie Comes Marching Home. **1952** Lure of the Wilderness. **1953** The President's Lady.

SPEAR, HARRY

Born: Dec. 16, 1921, Los Angeles, Calif. Died: Feb. 10, 1969, Hollywood, Calif. Screen, stage and vaudeville actor. Entered films at age of three with Big Boy at Educational Studios. Appeared in "Smith Family" and "Our Gang" series and Mack Sennett comedies.

Appeared in: **1929** The following shorts: Small Talk; Railroadin'; Lazy Days; Boxing Gloves; Bouncing Babies.

SPEAR, SAMMY (Sammy Shapiro)

Born: 1910, Brooklyn, N.Y. Died: Mar. 11, 1975, Miami, Fla. (heart attack). Bandleader, musician, television and screen actor.

SPELLMAN, LEORA (aka LEORA SPELLMEYER)

Born: 1891. Died: Sept. 4, 1945, Los Angeles, Calif. (heart attack). Screen, stage and vaudeville actress. Married to actor Charles B. Middleton (dec. 1949) with whom she appeared in vaudeville as "Middleton and Spellmeyer."

Appeared in: **1929** Wise Girls. **1932** Kongo.

SPENCE, RALPH

Born: Nov. 4, 1889, Key West, Fla. or Houston, Tex. Screenwriter, playwright and screen actor. Appeared in Mack Sennett and "Sunshine" comedies.

Appeared in: **1925** Ralph Spence comedies (shorts), incl. Egged On. **1935** Millions in the Air.

SPENCER, DOUGLAS

Born: 1910. Died: Oct. 10, 1960, Hollywood, Calif. (diabetic condition). Screen and television actor.

Appeared in: **1948** The Big Clock. **1949** My Friend Irma; Bride of Vengeance; Follow Me Quietly. **1951** Come Fill the Cup; A Place in the Sun; The Thing; The Redhead and the Cowboy. **1952** Monkey Business; Untamed Frontier. **1953** The Glass Wall; Houdini; Shane; She's Back on Broadway; Trouble along the Way. **1954** The Raid; River of No Return. **1955** The Kentuckian; A Man Alone; Smoke Signal; This Island Earth. **1956** Man from Del Rio; Pardners. **1957** Saddle the Wind; Short Cut to Hell; The Three Faces of Eve; The Unholy Wife. **1958** Cole Younger, Gunfighter. **1959** The Diary of Anne Frank. **1961** The Sins of Rachel Cade.

SPENCER, FRED (Fred Spencer Bretherton)

Died: Oct. 13, 1952, Hollywood, Calif. Screen actor. Appeared in silents for Mack Sennett and others.

SPENCER, KENNETH

Born: 1913, Los Angeles, Calif. Died: Feb. 25, 1964, near New Orleans, La. (plane crash). Black screen, stage, television actor and singer. Appeared in U.S. and German films.

Appeared in: **1943** Cabin in the Sky; Bataan.

SPENCER, TERRY

Born: 1895. Died: Oct. 3, 1954, Hollywood, Calif. Screen actor.

SPENCER, TIM

Born: 1909. Died: Apr. 27, 1974, Los Angeles, Calif. (stroke). Screen actor, singer and composer. Originator of the "Sons of the Pioneers."

Appeared in: **1936** Rhythm on the Range. **1937** The Old Corral. **1946** My Pal Trigger.

SPIKER, RAY

Born: 1902. Died: Feb. 23, 1964, Hollywood, Calif. Screen actor and stuntman.

Appeared in: **1934** Our Daily Bread. **1947** The Brasher Doubloon. **1953** Shane. **1954** Demetrius and the Gladiators; Prince Valiant.

SPINGLER, HARRY

Born: 1890. Died: Apr. 22, 1953, Woodland Hills, Calif. Screen actor.

Appeared in: **1918** A Perfect Lady.

SPIRA, FRANCOISE

Died: Jan. 1965, Paris, France (suicide). Screen, stage actress and stage producer.

SPITALNY, PHIL

Born: 1890. Died: Oct. 11, 1970, Miami Beach, Fla. (cancer). Bandleader, conductor, radio and screen actor. Married to concert mistress Evelyn Kaye, known professionally as "Evelyn and Her Magic Violin."

Appeared in: Prior to 1933 Metro Movietone Act No. 82. **1934** A Vitaphone short. **1935** A Vitaphone short; a Paramount short. **1936** A Vitaphone short. **1945** Here Come the Co-eds.

SPIVY, "MADAME" (Spivy Le Voe)

Born: 1907, Brooklyn, N.Y. Died: Jan. 8, 1971, Woodland Hills, Calif. Screen actress, nightclub entertainer and singer.

Appeared in: **1958** Auntie Mame. **1960** The Fugitive Kind. **1962** Requiem for a Heavyweight; All Fall Down; The Manchurian Candidate.

SPLANE, ELZA K. (Elza Temary)

Born: 1905. Died: Feb. 16, 1968, Tucson, Ariz. Screen actress.

SPONG, HILDA

Born: May 14, 1875, London, England. Died: May 16, 1955, Norwalk, Conn. Stage and screen actress.

Appeared in: **1915** Divorced. **1919** A Star Overnight.

SPORT

Died: California (date not known). Animal screen performer (dog). Was featured in "Our Gang" films.

Appeared in: **1923** Are You a Failure?

SPOTTSWOOD, JAMES

Born: Wash. Died: Oct. 11, 1940, New York, N.Y. (heart attack). Screen, stage and radio actor.

Appeared in: **1929** Thunderbolt. **1938** Hollywood Stadium Mystery.

SPROTTE, BERT

Born: Dec. 9, 1871, Chemnitz, Saxony, Germany. Died: Dec. 30, 1949. Stage and screen actor. Married to actress Anna Ruzena. Entered films in 1917.

Appeared in: **1918** Tyrant Fear. **1920** Jes' Call Me Jim. **1921** Below the Dead Line; Bob Hampton of Placer; The Blazing Trail; Guile of Women; O'Malley of the Mounted; The Night Horsemen; Trailin'; White Oak. **1922** Blue Blazes; Conquering the Woman; The Fighting Streak; Hungry Hearts; For Big Stakes; A Question of Honor; Thelma. **1923** The Miracle Baby; Purple Dawn; Rosita; Snowdrift; Soul of the Beast; Trimmed in Scarlet; Wild Bill Hickok. **1924** His Hour; Little Robinson Crusoe; The Shooting of Dan McGrew; Singer Jim McKee. **1925** Confessions of a Queen; The Human Tornado; Why Women Love. **1927** The Fighting Hombre; Life of an Actress; The Private Life of Helen of Troy; Wild Geese; The Stolen Bride; Shepherd of the Hills. **1929** Married in Hollywood. **1930** A Royal Romance. **1932** A Passport to Hell. **1933** Song of the Eagle. **1934** The Pursuit of Happiness.

SPROULE, RUTH

Born: 1910. Died: Sept. 26, 1968, New York, N.Y. (heart attack). Screen actress and dancer. Was a member of the "Rockettes." Mother of dancer Linda Nostrand.

SQUIRE, RONALD (Ronald Squirl)

Born: Mar. 1886, Tiverton, Devonshire, England. Died: Nov. 16, 1958, London, England. Screen, stage actor, stage producer and stage director.

Appeared in: **1916** Whoso is Without Sin. **1934** The Unfinished Symphony; Wild Boy; Forbidden Territory. **1935** Come Out of the Pantry. **1936** Love in Exile; Dusty Ermine (aka Hideout in the Alps—US 1938). **1937** Action for Slander (US 1938). **1943** The Flemish Farm. **1944** Don't Take It to Heart (US 1949). **1945** Journey Together (US 1946). **1947** While the Sun Shines (US 1950). **1948** The First Gentleman (aka Affairs of a Rogue—US 1949); Woman Hater (US 1949). **1949** The Rocking Horse Winner (US 1950). **1951** No Highway (aka No Highway in the Sky—US); Encore. **1952** It Started in Paradise. **1953** Laxdale Hall (aka Scotch on the Rocks—US 1954); Always a Bride (US 1954); My Cousin Rachel. **1954** The Million Pound Note (aka Man with a Million—US). **1955** Footsteps in the Fog; Raising a Riot (US 1957); Josephine and Men. **1956** Now and Forever; Around the World in 80 Days; The Silent Affair (US 1957). **1957** Seawife; Island in the Sun. **1958** Law and Disorder; The Sheriff of Fractured Jaw; The Inn of the Sixth Happiness. **1959** Count Your Blessings.

SRITRANGE, WANDEE

Born: 1950, Thailand. Died: Aug. 31, 1975, near Bangkok, Thailand. Screen actress.

STAFFORD, HANLEY (John Austin)

Born: Sept. 22, 1898, Staffordshire, England. Died: Sept. 9, 1968, Los Angeles, Calif. (heart attack). Screen, stage, radio and television actor. He was "Daddy" in the Fanny Brice Baby Snooks radio show and "Mr. Dithers" on the Blondie radio show.

Appeared in: **1936** The Great Ziegfeld. **1941** Life With Henry. **1951** Lullaby of Broadway. **1952** Just This Once; A Girl in Every Port; Here Come the Marines. **1953** The Affairs of Dobie Gillis; Francis Covers the Big Town. **1955** The Go-Getter.

STAHL, WALTER O.

Born: 1884. Died: Aug. 6, 1943, Hollywood, Calif. (heart attack). Screen actor and stage producer.

Appeared in: **1937** I'll Take Romance. **1939** Beasts of Berlin. **1942** Once upon a Honeymoon; Woman of the Year. **1943** Watch on the Rhine.

STAHL-NACHBAUR, ERNEST (Ernest Guggenheimer)

Born: 1886, Germany. Died: May 13, 1960, Berlin, Germany. Stage and screen actor.

Appeared in: **1931** Mother Love; Danton; Ein Burschenlied aus Heidelberg. **1933** M.

STALL, KARL

Born: 1871, Cincinnati, Ohio. Died: June 14, 1947, New York, N.Y. Stage and screen actor.

Appeared in: **1931** The Smiling Lieutenant.

STAMP-TAYLOR, ENID

Born: June 12, 1904, Monkseaton, England. Died: Jan. 13, 1946, London, England (injuries from fall). Screen and stage actress.

Appeared in: **1927** Easy Virtue (US 1928); Remembrance; Land of Hope and Glory. **1928** A Little Bit of Fluff (aka Skirts—US); Yellow Stockings; Cocktails. **1929** Broken Melody. **1933** Meet My Sister. **1934** A Political Party; Gay Love; Virginia's Husband; The Feathered Serpent. **1935** Radio Pirates; So You Won't Talk?; Mr. What's-His-Name; Jimmy Boy; While Parents Sleep; Two Hearts in Harmony. **1936** Queen of Hearts; Blind Man's Bluff; House Broken. **1937** Take a Chance; Underneath the Arches; Feather Your Nest; Okay for Sound; Talking Feet; Action for Slander (US 1938). **1938** Blondes for Danger; Stepping Toes; Climbing High (US 1939); Old Iron. **1939** The Lambeth Walk (aka Me and My Girl—US 1940); The Girl Who Forgot. **1941** Spring Meeting; The Farmer's Wife; Hatter's Castle; South American George. **1942** Alibi. **1943** Candlelight in Algeria (US 1944). **1945** The Wicked Lady (US 1946). **1946** Caravan (US 1947).

STANDING, CHARLENE

Born: 1921. Died: Jan. 8, 1957, Dundas, Ontario, Canada. Stage and screen actress. Appeared in U.S. and British films.

STANDING, GORDON

Died: May 22, 1927. Screen actor.

Appeared in: **1921** Man and Woman. **1922** Are Children to Blame? **1923** Outlaws of the Sea. **1925** The Substitute Wife. **1927** Skedaddle Gold; King of the Jungle (serial).

STANDING, SIR GUY, SR.

Born: Sept. 1, 1873, London, England. Died: Feb. 24, 1937, Los Angeles, Calif. (heart attack). Stage and screen actor. Married to stage actress Dorothy Hammond (dec. 1950). Father of actress Kay Hammond and actor Guy Standing, Jr. (dec. 1954) and brother of actor Herbert Standing (dec. 1955).

Appeared in: **1933** The Cradle Song; A Bedtime Story; The Story of Temple Drake; The Eagle and the Hawk; Midnight Club; Hell and High Water. **1934** Imitation of Life; Death Takes a Holiday; The Witching Hour; Double Door; Now and Forever. **1935** Lives of a Bengal Lancer; Car 99; Annapolis Farewell; The Big Broadcast of 1936. **1936** The Return of Sophie Lang; I'd Give My Life; Palm Springs. **1937** Lloyds of London; Bulldog Drummond Escapes.

STANDING, GUY, JR.

Died: Nov. 14, 1954, Reseda, Calif. Stage and screen actor. Son of actor Sir Guy Standing (dec. 1937).

Appeared in: **1953** Titanic.

STANDING, HERBERT, SR.

Born: 1846, England. Died: Dec. 5, 1923, Los Angeles, Calif. Stage and screen actor. Father of actors Herbert, Jr. (dec. 1955), Sir Guy (dec. 1937), Wyndham (dec. 1963), Percy and Aubrey Standing.

STANDING, HERBERT, JR.

Born: 1884, London, England. Died: Sept. 23, 1955, New York, N.Y. Stage and screen actor. Son of actor Herbert Standing, Sr. (dec. 1923) and brother of actors Sir Guy (dec. 1937), Wyndham (dec. 1963), Percy and Aubrey Standing.

Appeared in: **1915** It's No Laughing Matter. **1916** The Right Direction. **1917** A Little Patriot. **1918** Amarilly of Clothes Line; He Comes Up Smiling; Daddy's Girl; The White Man's Law; How Could You, Jean? **1919** My Little Sister; The Home Town Girl; A Rogue's Romance; You Never Saw Such a Girl; Fires of Faith; Through the Wrong Door; Strictly Confidential; Almost a Husband. **1920** Judy of Rogue's Harbor; The Cup of Fury. **1921** Man and Woman; The Infamous Miss Revell; One Wild Week; The Man Worth While. **1922** The Trap; The Masquerader; While Satan Sleeps; The Crossroads of New York; The Impossible Mrs. Bellew. **1923** Jazzmania; Sawdust. **1926** The Brown Derby; Rainbow Riley.

STANDING, JACK

Born: 1886, London, England. Died: Oct. 26, 1917, Los Angeles, Calif. Screen actor. Father of actor Jack Standing, Jr.

Appeared in: **1911** A Good Turn; An Accidental Outlaw; Rescued in Time; Get a Horse; The Easterner's Sacrifice. **1913** Looking for a Mother; The Wiles of Cupid. **1914** The Wasted Years; The Winning Hand. **1915** Fanchon the Cricket; The Love of Women; A Siren of Corsica; Delayed Reformation; Rated at Ten Million Dollars; Road O' Strife (serial); The Inventor's Peril; It Was to Be; The Son; Think Mothers. **1916** The Evangelist. **1917** The Price of Her Soul.

STANDING, WYNDHAM

Born: Aug. 23, 1880, London, England. Died: Feb. 1, 1963, Los Angeles, Calif. Stage and screen actor. Married to actress Winifred Standing. Son of actor Sir Herbert Standing, Sr. (dec. 1923). See Herbert Standing for family information.

Appeared in: **1916** Exile; The Soul of a Magdalen. **1917** The Silence Sellers. **1918** The Hillcrest Mystery (serial); The Life Mask; Rose of the World. **1919** Isle of Conquest; The Marriage Price; Out of the Shadows; Paid in Full; Eyes of the Soul; Miracle of Love; Witness for the Defense. **1920** My Lady's Garter; Earthbound. **1921** The Bride's Play; The Iron Trail; The Marriage of William Ashe; The Journey's End. **1922** The Inner Man; Isle of Doubt; Smilin' Through. **1923** Daytime Wives; The Lion's Mouse; Forgive and Forget; Little Johnny Jones; The Gold Diggers. **1924** Flames of Desire; Pagan Passions; The Rejected Woman; Soiled; Vanity's Price. **1925** The Dark Angel; The Early Bird; The Reckless Sex; The Teaser; The Unchastened Woman. **1926** The Canadian; If Youth But Knew; White Heat. **1927** Thumbs Down; The City Gone Wild. **1928** The Price of Divorce; The Port of Missing Girls; Widecombe Fair. **1929** The Flying Squad; Power Over Men. **1930** Billy the Kid; Hell's Angels. **1932** The Silent Witness. **1933** A Study in Scarlet; Design for Living. **1934** Imitation of Life; Limehouse Blues. **1935** Clive of India. **1936** Mary of Scotland; Beloved Enemy. **1939** Bulldog Drummond's Secret Police; The Man in the Iron Mask; Rulers of the Sea.

STANLEY, EDWIN

Born: 1880. Died: Dec. 24, 1944, Hollywood, Calif. Screen and stage actor.

Appeared in: **1932** Amateur Daddy. **1933** International House; My Woman; No Other Woman. **1934** The Life of Vergie Winters; You Belong to Me. **1936** Hot Money; The Public Pays (short); The Mandarin Mystery. **1937** Alcatraz Island; Easy Living; Marked Woman; Some Blondes Are Dangerous. **1938** Born to Be Wild; Billy the Kid Returns; Little Tough Guy; The Missing Guest; Wives under Suspicion. **1939** Unexpected Father; Eternally Yours; Espionage Agent; Ninotchka; 20,000 Men a Year. **1940** Charlie Chan in Panama; Youth Will Be Served. **1941** Meet John Doe; The Night of January 16th; A Man Betrayed; Arkansas Judge; Scattergood Baines. **1942** The Man Who Came to Dinner; Who Is Hope Schuyler?; Drums of the Congo; The Loves of Edgar Allan Poe; Gentleman Jim. **1944** Buffalo Bill. **1945** Youth on Trial; Conflict.

STANLEY, FORREST

Born: Aug. 21, 1889, New York, N.Y. Died: Aug. 27, 1969, Los Angeles, Calif. (results of fall). Screen and stage actor.

Appeared in: **1915** The Yankee Girl; Jane; Reform Candidate. **1916** Making of Madalina; Heart of Paula; The Code of Marcia Gray. **1918** His Official Fiancee. **1919** Under Suspicion; Thunderbolt. **1920** The Triflers. **1921** Forbidden Fruit; Enchantment; Big Game; The House that Jazz Built; Sacred and Profane Love. **1922** When Knighthood Was in Flower; The Pride of Palomar; Beauty's Worth; The Young Diana. **1923** Tiger Rose; Bavu; Her Accidental Husband. **1924** Through the Dark; The Breath of Scandal; Wine. **1925** Up the Ladder; Beauty and the Bad Man; The Fate of a Flirt; The Girl Who Wouldn't Work; The Unwritten Law; When Husbands Flirt; With This Ring. **1926** Dancing Days; Forest Havoc; The Shadow of the Law. **1927** The Climbers; The Cat and the Canary; The Wheels of Destiny; Great Event Series. **1928** Bare Knees; Into the Night; Jazzland; Phantom of the Turf. **1929** The Drake Case. **1930** The Love Kiss. **1931** Men Are Like That; Arizona. **1932** Racing Youth; Sin's Pay Day; Rider of Death Valley. **1941** Outlaws of the Desert.

STANLEY, RALPH "NICK"

Born: 1914, Mass. Died: May 10, 1972, New York, N.Y. Screen, stage, vaudeville and television actor.

Appeared in: **1953** The Joe Lewis Story. **1957** Mr. Rock and Roll. **1958** Cop Hater. **1970** Jenny. **1971** The Anderson Tapes.

STANLEY, S. VICTOR

Born: 1892. Died: Jan. 29, 1939, London, England. Stage and screen actor.

Appeared in: **1932** The World, the Flesh and the Devil. **1933** Puppets of Fate (aka Wolves of the Underworld—US 1935); The Iron Stair; The Medicine Man; Timbucktoo; The Umbrella; His Grace Gives Notice; The Ghost Camera; The House of Trent. **1934** Four Masked Men; White Ensign. **1935** Gentleman's Agreement; School for Stars.

STANTON, FREDERICK "FRED" R.

Born: 1881. Died: May 27, 1925, Hollywood, Calif. (cancer). Stage and screen actor.

Appeared in: **1917** The Great Secret (serial). **1921** Her Sturdy Oak. **1922** Perils of the Yukon (serial); The Fire Bride; The Son of the Wolf. **1923** Canyon of the Fools; Danger Ahead; Little Church Around the Corner; A Million to Burn; Trifling with Honor. **1924** Find Your Man; When a Man's a Man.

STANTON, LARRY T.

Died: May 9, 1955, Hollywood, Calif. (heart attack). Screen actor. Entered films approx. 1920.

STANTON, PAUL

Born: Dec. 21, 1884. Died: Oct. 9, 1955. Screen actor.

Appeared in: **1918** The Girl and the Judge; Her Pride. **1934** The Most Precious Thing in Life. **1935** Strangers All; Let 'Em Have It; Red Salute; Another Face. **1936** It Had to Happen; Whipsaw; Every Saturday Night; Charlie Chan at the Circus; Sins of Man; Half Angel; Crime of Dr. Forbes; Road to Glory; Poor Little Rich Girl; Private Number; Sing, Baby Sing; The Longest Night; Dimples; Career Woman; Crack-Up; Night Waitress; The Public Pays (short). **1937** City Girl; Midnight Taxi; A Star is Born; It Could Happen to You; Youth on Parole; Portia on Trial; Danger—Love at Work; Paid to Dance; The Black Legion; Love Is News; Man of the People; Make Way for Tomorrow. **1938** Kentucky Moonshine; Rascals; Law of the Underworld; My Lucky Star; Army Girl. **1939** While America Sleeps (short); The Story of Alexander Graham Bell; Rose of Washington Square; Bachelor Mother; Stronger than Desire; 20,000 Men a Year; The Star Maker; Hollywood Cavalcade; Stanley and Livingstone. **1940** The Man Who Wouldn't Talk; And One Was Beautiful; Queen of the Mob; I Love You Again. **1941** Road Show; Strange Alibi; You're in the Army Now; The People vs. Dr. Kildare; The Big Store; Whistling in the Dark; Night of January 16th; Midnight Angel. **1942** The Magnificent Dope; Across the Pacific. **1943** Slightly Dangerous; Air Raid Wardens; So's Your Uncle. **1944** Once Upon a Time; Allergic to Love; Mr. Winkle Goes to War. **1945** She Gets Her Man. **1946** Crime of the Century; Holiday in Mexico; Shadow of a Woman. **1947** That's My Gal; Cry Wolf; Her Husband's Affair; My Wild Irish Rose. **1948** Here Comes Trouble. **1949** The Fountainhead. **1952** Jet Job.

STANTON, WILL (William Sidney Stanton)

Born: Sept. 18, 1885, London, England. Died: Dec. 18, 1969, Santa Monica, Calif. (broncho-pneumonia). Screen, stage and vaudeville actor. Married to actress Rosalind May.

Appeared in: **1927** The following shorts: With Love and Hisses; Sailors, Beware; Do Detectives Think?; Sugar Daddies. **1928** Golf Widows; Sadie Thompson. **1929** True Heaven. **1930** Mamba; Paradise Island; Painted Angel. **1933** Hello Sister; Alice in Wonderland; Cavalcade; Sailor's Luck. **1936** The Last of the Mohicans; Lloyds of London; The White Hunter. **1937** Seventh Heaven; Affairs of Cappy Ricks. **1938** Anesthesia (short); Straight, Place and Show; Four Men and a Prayer. **1939** Weather Wizards (short); The Little Princess; Captain Fury. **1940** Devil's Island. **1941** Charley's Aunt. **1945** A Guy, a Gal and a Pal. **1946** Wife Wanted.

STARBUCK, BETTY

Died: date unknown. Screen, stage actress and dancer.

Appeared in: **1930** The Sap from Syracuse.

STARK, LEIGHTON

Died: July 20, 1924, Mawasquam, N.J. Stage and screen actor.

Appeared in: **1911** The Two Orphans.

STARK, MABEL

Born: 1889. Died: Apr. 29, 1968, Thousand Oaks, Calif. (heart attack). Wild animal trainer and screen actress.

Appeared in: **1922** A Dangerous Adventure.

STARKEY, BERT

Born: 1880, England. Died: June 9, 1939, Los Angeles, Calif. Stage and screen actor.

Appeared in: **1921** The Iron Trail. **1927** Wild Geese; Woman's Law. **1928** Put 'Em Up; You Can't Beat the Law. **1932** Scarface; Hell's Highway.

STARR, FRANCES

Born: 1881, Albany, N.Y. Died: June 11, 1973, New York, N.Y. Stage and screen actress.

Appeared in: **1931** The Star Witness; Five Star Final. **1932** This Reckless Age.

STARR, FREDERICK

Born: 1878, San Francisco, Calif. Died: Aug. 20, 1921, Los Angeles, Calif. Stage and screen actor.

Appeared in: **1919** Elmo, the Mighty (serial). **1920** Daredevil Jack (serial). **1921** The Man of the Forest; Mysterious Rider.

STARR, RANDY (Joseph Randall)

Born: 1931, Ill. Died: Aug. 5, 1970, Los Angeles, Calif. (undetermined illness). Screen stuntman.

Appeared in: **1962** Immoral Charge. **1964** The Creeping Terror; Kissin' Cousins; Roustabout. **1966** Frankie and Johnny; Paradise—Hawaiian Style; Spinout. **1967** Clambake; Double Trouble. **1968** Live a Little, Love a Little. **1969** Hard Trail. **1970** Machismo—40 Graves for 40 Guns.

STEADMAN, VERA

Born: June 23, 1900, Monterey, Calif. Died: Dec. 14, 1966, Long Beach, Calif. Screen actress. Divorced from actor Jack Taylor (dec. 1932). Entered films as a Mack Sennett bathing beauty.

Appeared in: **1917** Hula Hula Land. **1921** Scrap Iron. **1925** Stop Flirting. **1926** Meet the Prince; The Nervous Wreck. **1934** Elmer and Elsie. **1936** Ring around the Moon.

STEDMAN, LINCOLN

Born: 1907, Denver, Colo. Died: Mar. 22, 1948, Los Angeles, Calif. Screen actor and film director. Son of actress Myrtle Stedman (dec. 1938) and actor Marshall Stedman (dec. 1943). Entered films in 1918.

Appeared in: **1920** Nineteen and Phyllis. **1921** Old Swimmin' Hole; Be My Wife; The Charm School; My Lady Friends; Two Minutes to Go; Under the Lash. **1922** The Dangerous Age; A Homespun Vamp; Youth to Youth; The Freshie; White Shoulders. **1923** The Man Life Passed By; The Meanest Man in the World; The Scarlet Lily; The Wanters; The Prisoner; Soul of the Beast. **1924** Captain January; Black Oxen; Cheap Kisses; On Probation; Wife of the Centaur. **1925** The Danger Signal; Sealed Lips; Red Hot Tires. **1926** Dame Chance; Made for Love; Remember; The Warning Signal; One Minute to Play. **1927** The Student Prince in Old Heidelberg; Let It Rain; The Prince of Headwaiters; Rookies; The Little Firebrand; Perch of the Devil. **1928** Farmer's Daughter; Devil's Cage; Green Grass Widows; Harold Teen. **1929** Why Be Good?; The Wild Party; Tanned Legs. **1930** The following shorts: The Bluffer; Grandma's Girl; Don't Bite Your Dentist. **1931** The Woman Between. **1933** Sailor Be Good. **1934** Most Precious Thing in Life.

STEDMAN, MARSHALL

Born: 1874. Died: Dec. 16, 1943, Laguna Beach, Calif. Stage and screen actor. Married to actress Myrtle Stedman (dec. 1938) and father of actor Lincoln Stedman (dec. 1948).

STEDMAN, MYRTLE

Born: Mar. 3, 1889, Chicago, Ill. Died: Jan. 8, 1938, Los Angeles, Calif. (heart attack). Stage and screen actress. Married to actor Marshall Stedman (dec. 1943). Mother of actor Lincoln Stedman (dec. 1948). Entered films in 1913.

Appeared in: **1913** Valley of the Moon. **1915** Peer Gynt. **1920** The Silver Horde; The Tiger's Coat. **1921** Black Roses; The Whistle; Sowing the Wind; The Concert. **1922** Ashes; The Hands of Nara; Nancy from Nowhere; Rich Men's Wives; Reckless Youth. **1923** The Famous Mrs. Fair; Flaming Youth; Dangerous Age; Six Days; Crashin' Thru; Temporary Marriage. **1924** Wine; Lilies of the Field; Bread; The Breath of Scandal; The Age of Desire; The Woman on the Jury. **1925** Chickie; Sally; Tessie; The Mad Whirl; If I Marry Again; The Goose Hangs High. **1926** Don Juan's Three Nights; The Man in the Shadow; The Prince of Pilsen; The Far Cry. **1927** The Black Diamond Express; No Place to Go; Women's Wares; The Life of Riley; The Irresistible Lover; Alias the Deacon. **1928** Sporting Goods; Their Hour. **1929** The Wheel of Life; The Sin Sister; The Jazz Age. **1930** The Truth about Youth; The Love Racket; The Lummox; The Little Accident. **1932** Widow in Scarlet; Alias Mary Smith; Forbidden Company. **1933** One Year Later. **1934** Beggars in Ermine; School for Girls. **1936** Song of the Saddle; Gambling with Souls. **1937** Green Light; Hollywood Hotel; Confession.

STEEL, EDWARD

Born: 1897. Died: Oct. 18, 1965. Screen actor. Father of actor Anthony Steel.

Appeared in: **1966** The Boy Cried Murder.

STEELE, CLIFFORD

Born: 1878. Died: Mar. 5, 1940, Hollywood, Calif. Screen actor. Entered films approx. 1915.

STEELE, MINNIE

Born: 1881, Australia. Died: Jan. 5, 1949, Hollywood, Calif. (stroke). Screen and vaudeville actress. Entered films in 1922.

Appeared in: **1924** "Christie" comedies and "Baby Peggy" pictures; The Darling of New York.

STEELE, VERNON

Born: 1883. Died: July 23, 1955, Los Angeles, Calif. (heart attack). Stage and screen actor.

Appeared in: **1915** Hearts in Exile. **1916** For the Defense. **1921** Beyond Price; Out of the Chorus; The Highest Bidder. **1922** The Danger Point; For the Defense (and 1916 version); A Wonderful Wife; Thelma; When the Devil Drives; The Girl Who Ran Wild; The Hands of Nara. **1923** Alice Adams; The Wanters; What Wives Want; Temptation; Forgive and Forget. **1924** Discontented Husbands; The House of Youth. **1933** Design for Living; The Silk Express. **1934** Where Sinners Meet; The Great Flirtation. **1935** Bonnie Scotland. **1936** Dracula's Daughter. **1937** Time Out for Romance. **1942** Mrs. Miniver. **1945** They Were Expendable. **1949** Madame Bovary.

STEELE, VICKIE FEE
Born: 1947. Died: Dec. 13, 1975, Santa Monica, Calif. Screen actress. Daughter of actress Astrid Allwyn.

STEELE, WILLIAM "BILL" (William A. Gettinger)
Born: 1889, Tex. Died: Feb. 13, 1966, Los Angeles, Calif. Screen actor and stuntman.

Appeared in: **1914** The Voice of the Viola; The Man Within; A Gypsy Romance; 'Cross the Mexican Line; Passing of the Beast. **1916** Across the Rio Grande; The Night Riders; A Knight of the Range. **1917** Blood Money; The Bad Man of Cheyenne; The Outlaw and the Lady; Goin' Straight; The Fighting Gringo; A Marked Man; Hair Trigger Burke; The Secret Man; A 44 Calibre Mystery; The Mysterious Outlaw; The Golden Bullet. **1918** The Phantom Rides. **1921** The Wallop; Riding with Death. **1922** The Fast Mail; Pardon My Nerve!; Bells of San Juan. **1923** Dead Game; Single Handed; Shootin' for Love; Don Quickshot of the Rio Grande. **1924** The Last Man on Earth; Hit and Run; The Ridin' Kid from Powder River; The Sunset Trail. **1925** The Saddle Hawk; Let 'Er Buck; Don Dare Devil; Two-Fisted Jones; The Sagebrush Lady; The Hurricane Kid. **1926** The Flaming Frontier; The Runaway Express; The Wild Horse Stampede; Six Shootin' Romance; Under Western Skies; The Fighting Peacemaker. **1927** Hoof Marks; Rough and Ready; Whispering Sage; The Valley of Hell; Loco Luck; Range Courage. **1928** The Black Ace; Thunder Riders; Call of the Heart; The Fearless Rider. **1930** Doughboys; The Lone Star Ranger. **1935** When a Man Sees Red. **1950** The Showdown.

STEEN, MARGUERITE
Born: 1894, England. Died: Aug. 4, 1975, Blewsbury, Oxfordshire, England. Stage, screen actress and novelist.

STEERS, LARRY (Lawrence Steers)
Born: 1881, Chicago, Ill. Died: Feb. 15, 1951, Woodland Hills, Calif. Stage and screen actor.

Appeared in: **1921** Wealth. **1922** Elope if You Must; South of Suva. **1923** Haunted Valley (serial); Mind over Motor; Soul of the Beast; The Huntress. **1924** Ten Scars Make a Man (serial); A Cafe in Cairo; The Girl in the Limousine. **1925** The Best People; Flattery; New Brooms; The Love Gamble. **1926** Bride of the Storm; The Lodge in the Wilderness; Hearts and Spangles. **1927** The Claw; No Control. **1928** The Terrible People (serial); The Phantom Flyer. **1929** The Fire Detective (serial); In Old California; Dark Skies; Just Off Broadway; Redskin; The Wheel of Life. **1930** The Thoroughbreds; Let's Go Places. **1931** The Secret Call; Grief Street. **1932** If I Had a Million. **1933** The Cocktail Hour. **1936** Navy Born; Pan Handlers (short). **1938** Dummy Owner (short). **1939** Act Your Age (short). **1941** Riding the Wind. **1943** Hands across the Border. **1944** Atlantic City; The Mojave Firebrand. **1945** White Pongo. **1947** The Gangster; Saddle Pals. **1948** Fighting Mad; Docks of New Orleans.

STEFAN, VIRGINIA
Born: 1926. Died: May 5, 1964, New York, N.Y. Screen and television actress.

STEHLI, EDGAR
Born: 1884, France. Died: July 25, 1973, Upper Montclair, N.J. Screen, stage, radio and television actor.

Appeared in: **1954** Executive Suite; Drum Beat. **1955** The Cobweb. **1958** The Brothers Karamazov. **1959** No Name on the Bullet; 4D Man; Cash McCall. **1961** Atlantis, the Lost Continent; Pocketful of Miracles; Parrish. **1962** The Spiral Road. **1963** Twilight of Honor. **1966** Seconds. **1967** The Tiger Makes Out. **1970** Loving.

STEIN, CAROL EDEN
Born: 1927. Died: Oct. 18, 1958, San Francisco, Calif. Screen actress.

STEIN, SAM "SAMMY"
Born: 1906. Died: Mar. 30, 1966. Screen actor.

Appeared in: **1934** The Lost Patrol. **1941** Sierra Sue; The Wildcat of Tucson. **1942** Sing Your Worries Away; Remember Pearl Harbor; Gentleman Jim; Pittsburgh. **1943** Never a Dull Moment. **1945** The Big Show-Off. **1946** The French Key. **1947** Shoot to Kill. **1953** The Veils of Bagdad.

STEINER, ELIO
Born: Mar. 9, 1905, Venice, Italy. Died: Dec. 6, 1965, Rome, Italy. Screen actor. Appeared in Italian, French and German films.

Appeared in: **1928** Vena D'Oro. **1930** La Canzone Dell 'Amore; Corte D'Assisi; Stella Del Cinema. **1931** L'Uomo Dell 'Artiglio; Der Klown. **1932** Pergoleri. **1933** Acqua Cheta; Giallo. **1937** Amore e Dolore. **1942** Giarabub. **1944** Senza Famiglia. **1947** Tombolo. **1952** La Signora senza Camelie.

STEINKE, HANS
Born: 1893, Germany. Died: June 26, 1971, Chicago, Ill. (lung cancer). Screen actor and wrestler.

Appeared in: **1933** Deception; Island of Lost Souls. **1935** People Will Talk. **1936** Once in a Blue Moon. **1938** The Buccaneer.

STEINMETZ, EARL
Born: 1915. Died: May 22, 1942, Los Angeles, Calif. (neck broken by an airplane wing). Screen actor.

STEINRUCK, ALBERT (aka ALBERT STEINRUECK)
Born: 1872, Wettenburg-Waldeck, Germany. Died: 1929, Berlin, Germany. Stage and screen actor.

Appeared in: **1924** Decameron Nights (US 1928). **1929** Eleven Who Were Loyal; At the Edge of the World; The Treasure. **1930** Asphalt.

STENGEL, CASEY (Charles Dillon Stengel)
Born: July 30, 1890, Kansas City, Mo. Died: Sept. 29, 1975, Glendale, Calif. (cancer). Professional baseball player, manager and screen actor.

Appeared in: **1941** Safe at Home.

STEPHEN, JOHN
Born: 1912, Buffalo, N.Y. Died: Apr. 3, 1974, New York, N.Y. Screen, stage, radio and television actor.

Appeared in: **1956** The Wrong Man.

STEPHENS, JUD
Born: 1888. Died: Apr. 18, 1935, Los Angeles, Calif. Screen actor.

STEPHENSON, HENRY (H. S. Garroway)
Born: Apr. 16, 1871, Granada, British West Indies. Died: Apr. 24, 1956, San Francisco, Calif. Screen and stage actor.

Appeared in: **1917** The Spreading Dawn. **1921** The Black Panther's Cub. **1925** Men and Women; Wild, Wild Susan. **1932** Cynara; Red Headed Woman; Guilty as Hell; Animal Kingdom; Bill of Divorcement. **1933** Queen Christina; Blind Adventure; Tomorrow at Seven; Double Harness; My Lips Betray; Little Women; If I Were Free. **1934** One More River; Outcast Lady; She Loves Me Not; All Men Are Enemies; Man of Two Worlds; The Richest Girl in the World; Stingaree; The Mystery of Mr. X; What Every Woman Knows; Thirty Day Princess. **1935** The Night Is Young; Vanessa, Her Love Story; Reckless; The Flame Within; O'Shaughnessey's Boy; Mutiny on the Bounty; Rendezvous; The Perfect Gentleman; Captain Blood. **1936** Little Lord Fauntleroy; Beloved Enemy; Half Angel; Hearts Divided; Give Me Your Heart; Charge of the Light Brigade; Walking on Air. **1937** When You're in Love; The Prince and the Pauper; The Emperor's Candlesticks; Conquest; Wise Girl. **1938** Marie Walewska; The Baroness and the Butler; Suez; Marie Antoinette; Dramatic School; The Young in Heart. **1939** Tarzan Finds a Son; Private Lives of Elizabeth and Essex; The Adventures of Sherlock Holmes. **1940** It's a Date; Spring Parade; Little Old New York; Down Argentine Way. **1941** The Man Who Lost Himself; The Lady from Louisiana. **1942** This above All; Rings on Her Fingers; Half Way to Shanghai. **1943** Mr. Lucky; The Man Trap. **1944** Two Girls and a Sailor; Secrets of Scotland Yard; The Hour before the Dawn; The Reckless Age. **1945** Tarzan and the Amazons. **1946** Heartbeat; The Return of Monte Cristo; The Locket; Night and Day; The Green Years; Of Human Bondage; Her Sister's Secret. **1947** The Homestretch; Ivy; Time out of Mind; Song of Love; Dark Delusion. **1948** Julia Misbehaves. **1949** Challenge to Lassie; Enchantment. **1951** Oliver Twist.

STEPHENSON, JAMES
Born: 1888, Yorkshire, England. Died: July 29, 1941, Pacific Palisades, Calif. (heart attack). Screen and stage actor.

Appeared in: **1937** The Perfect Crime; Take it from Me (aka Transatlantic Trouble); Dangerous Fingers (aka Wanted by Scotland Yard—US); You Live and Learn; The Man Who Made Diamonds. **1938** Dark Stairway; It's in the Blood; Mr. Satan; Cowboy from Brooklyn; White Banners; Heart of the North; When Were You Born?; Boy Meets Girl; Nancy Drew, Detective. **1939** On Trial; Secret Service of the Air; Adventures of Jane Arden; Torchy Blane in Chinatown; The Old Maid; Private Lives of Elizabeth and Essex; Espionage Agent; We Are Not Alone; Confessions of a Nazi Spy; King of the Underworld; Beau Geste. **1940** Devil's Island; Murder in the Air; Wolf of New York; A Dispatch from Reuters; Calling Philo Vance; The Sea Hawk; The Letter; South of Suez; River's End. **1941** Shining Victory; Flight from Destiny; International Squadron.

STEPHENSON, ROBERT ROBINSON
Born: 1901. Died: Sept. 8, 1970, Hollywood, Calif. (cancer). Screen actor.

Appeared in: **1945** The Brighton Strangler; Hotel Berlin. **1951** David and Bathsheba.

STEPPAT, ILSE
Born: 1917, Wuppertal, West Germany. Died: Dec. 22, 1969, West Berlin, Germany. Stage and screen actress.

Appeared in: **1948** Marriage in the Shadows. **1958** The Confessions of Felix Krull. **1959** The Eighth Day of the Week. **1960** The Bridge. **1961** Naked in the

Night (aka Madeleine–TE 136211). **1969** On Her Majesty's Secret Service. Other German films: The Man Who Wanted to Live Twice; The Rabanser Case; Captain Wronski; The Guilt of Dr. Homma.

STEPPLING, JOHN C.

Born: 1869, Germany. Died: Apr. 5, 1932, Hollywood, Calif. Stage and screen actor.

Appeared in: **1913** Bill Mixes with His Relations; The Heiress; Love Through a Lens; Hypnotism in Hicksville; Odd Knots. **1914** Jim; False Gods. **1916-17** American Film Mfg. Co. films. **1917** The Hobo Raid; A Day Out of Jail; Seaside Romeos. **1918** Good Night, Paul. **1919** The Rescuing Angel; The Divorce Trap; Fools and Their Money. **1920** Madame Peacock. **1921** Nobody's Kid; The Silver Car; The Hunch; Black Beauty; Garments of Truth. **1922** Confidence; Extra! Extra!; Too Much Business; The Sin Flood. **1923** Bell Boy 13; Going Up; A Man's Man; What a Wife Learned; The Man Next Door; Let's Go. **1924** Abraham Lincoln; The Fast Worker; The Reckless Age; The Breathless Moment; A Cafe in Cairo; Galloping Fish; Fools in the Dark. **1925** California Straight Ahead; Soft Shoes; Eve's Lover. **1926** The Better Man; Memory Lane; Collegiate; High Steppers. **1927** California or Bust; God's Great Wilderness; The Gay Old Bird; Her Father Said No; Wedding Bill$; By Whose Hands. **1928** Their Hour. **1932** Broken Lullaby.

STERLING, EDYTHE

Born: 1887. Died: June 4, 1962, Hollywood, Calif. Screen and vaudeville actress.

Appeared in: **1921** Vanishing Maid; The Stranger in Canyon Valley. **1923** Crimson Gold; Danger.

STERLING, FORD (George F. Stitch)

Born: Nov. 3, 1880, La Crosse, Wis. Died: Oct. 13, 1939, Los Angeles, Calif. (thrombosis of veins—heart attack). Screen, stage, vaudeville actor and circus performer. Married to actress Teddy Sampson (dec. 1970). Was "Chief" of the original Keystone Kops.

Appeared in: **1912** Cohen Collects a Debt; The Water Nymph; Riley and Schultz; The Beating He Needed; Pedro's Dilemma; Stolen Glory; Ambitious Butler; The Flirting Husband; The Grocery Clerk's Romance; At Coney Island; At It Again; The Deacon's Trouble; A Temperamental Husband; The Rivals; Mr. Fix-It; The New Neighbor; A Bear Escape; Pat's Day Off; A Midnight Elopement; Mabel's Adventures; Hoffmeyer's Legacy. **1913** The Bangville Police; The Walters' Picnic; Out and In; Peeping Pete; His Crooked Career; Rastus and the Game Cock; Safe in Jail; Love and Rubbish; The Peddler; Professor Bean's Removal; Cohen's Outing; A Game of Pool; The Riot; The Firebugs; Baby Day; Mabel's Dramatic Career (aka Her Dramatic Debut); The Faithful Taxicab; When Dreams Come True; The Bowling Match; A Double Wedding; The Cure That Failed; How Hiram Won Out; For Lizzie's Sake; The Mistaken Masher; The Deacon Outwitted; The Elite Ball; The Battle of Who Run; Just Brown's Luck; The Jealous Waiter; The Stolen Purse; Heinze's Resurrection; A Landlord's Troubles; The Professor's Daughter; A Red Hot Romance; The Man Next Door; Love and Pain; The Rube and the Baron; On His Wedding Day; The Sleuths at the Floral Parade; A Strong Revenge; The Two Widows; The Land Salesman; A Game of Poker; Father's Choice; A Life in the Balance; Murphy's IOU; A Fishy Affair; The New Conductor; The Ragtime Band (aka The Jazz Band); His Ups and Downs; Toplitsky and Company; Barney Oldfield's Race for a Life; Schnitz the Tailor; A Healthy Neighborhood; Teddy Telzlaff and Earl Cooper; Speed Kings; Their Husbands; Love Sickness at Sea; A Small Time Act; A Muddy Romance (aka Muddled in Mud); Cohen Saves the Flag; The Gusher; A Bad Game; Zuzu, the Band Leader; Some Nerve; The Speed Queen; The Hansom Driver; Wine (aka Wine Making). **1914** A Dramatic Mistake; Love and Dynamite; In the Clutches of a Gang (aka The Disguised Mayor); Too Many Brides (aka The Love Chase); Double Crossed; A Robust Romeo; Baffles; Gentleman Burglar; Between Showers; A False Beauty (aka A Faded Vampire); Tango Tangles; The Minstrel Man. **1915** That Little Band of Gold (aka For Better or Worse); Our Daredevil Chief; He Wouldn't Stay Down; Court House Crooks; Dirty Work in a Laundry (aka A Desperate Scoundrel); Only a Messenger Boy; His Father's Footsteps; Fatty and the Broadway Stars; The Hunt. **1916** His Pride and Shame; The Now Cure; His Wild Oats; His Lying Heart. **1917** Stars and Bars; Pinched in the Finish; A Maiden's Trust; His Torpedoes Love. **1922** Oh, Mabel Behave. **1923** The Stranger's Banquet; The Brass Bottle; Hollywood; The Spoilers; The Day of Faith; The Destroying Angel. **1924** Wild Oranges; The Woman on the Jury; Love and Glory; He Who Gets Slapped; Galloping Fish. **1925** So Big; Daddy's Gone A-Hunting; The Trouble with Wives; Stage Struck; My Lady's Lips; Steppin' Out. **1926** The Road to Glory; Stranded in Paris; Good and Naughty; Mike; The Show-Off; The American Venus; Miss Brewster's Millions; Everybody's Acting. **1927** For the Love of Mike; Casey at the Bat; Drums of the Desert; The Trunk Mystery. **1928** Sporting Goods; Gentlemen Prefer Blondes; Wife Savers; Figures Don't Lie; Chicken a la King; Oh, Kay! **1929** The Fall of Eve. **1930** Sally; Bride of the Regiment; Spring Is Here; Kismet; The Girl in the Show; Showgirl in Hollywood. **1931** Stout Hearts and Willing Hands; Her Majesty, Love. **1932–1933** Paramount shorts. **1933** Alice in Wonderland. **1935** A Vitaphone short; Behind the Green

Lights; Black Sheep; Headline Woman. **1936** An RKO short. **1961** Days of Thrills and Laughter (documentary).

STERLING, LARRY

Born: 1935. Died: Aug. 25, 1958, Clear Lake, Calif. (water skiing accident). Screen actor.

Appeared in: **1958** The Naked and the Dead.

STERLING, LEE

Born: 1904. Died: Mar. 4, 1951, Santa Monica, Calif. (heart attack). Screen actor.

STERLING, MERTA

Born: 1883. Died: Mar. 14, 1944, Hollywood, Calif. Screen actress.

Appeared in: **1917** Love and Blazes; Nabbing a Noble; A Good Little Bad Boy; Chicken Chased and Henpecked; Fat and Furious; Dry Goods and Damp Deeds. **1918** A Clean Sweep. **1924** The Star Dust Trail; Women First. **1927** Paid to Love.

STERN, BILL

Born: July 1, 1907, Rochester, N.Y. Died: Nov. 19, 1971, Rye, N.Y. (heart attack). Sportscaster on radio and television and screen actor.

Appeared in: **1942** The Pride of the Yankees. **1943** Stage Door Canteen. **1945** Here Come the Co-Eds. **1947** Spirit of West Point. **1954** Go, Man, Go.

STERN, LOUIS

Born: Jan. 10, 1860, New York, N.Y. Died: Feb. 15, 1941, Hollywood, Calif. Screen, stage and vaudeville actor.

Appeared in: **1920** Humoresque. **1925** I Want My Man. **1927** Wedding Bill$. **1929** The Little Wild Cat; Where East Is East; In Old California; The Diamond Master (serial).

STEVEN, BOYD

Born: 1875, Scotland. Died: Dec. 1967, Glasgow, Scotland. Singer and screen actress.

Appeared in: **1947** I Know Where I'm Going.

STEVENS, BYRON E.

Born: 1904. Died: Dec. 15, 1964, Encino, Calif. (heart attack). Screen actor. Entered films approx. 1939. Brother of actress Barbara Stanwyck.

STEVENS, CHARLES

Born: May 26, 1893, Solomansville, Ariz. Died: Aug. 22, 1964, Hollywood, Calif. Screen and vaudeville actor. Appeared in all but one of Douglas Fairbanks' pictures. Was grandson of Apache chief Geronimo.

Appeared in: **1915** Birth of a Nation (film debut). **1921** The Three Musketeers. **1922** Robin Hood; Captain Fly-by-Night. **1923** Where the North Begins. **1924** Empty Hands; The Thief of Bagdad (played 6 roles). **1925** The Vanishing American; Don Q; Recompense; A Son of His Father. **1926** The Black Pirate; Man Trap; Across the Pacific. **1927** The Gaucho; King of Kings; Woman's Law. **1928** Diamond Handcuffs; Stand and Deliver. **1929** The Virginian; The Mysterious Dr. Fu Manchu; The Iron Mask. **1930** The Big Trail; Tom Sawyer. **1931** The Conquering Horde; The Cisco Kid. **1932** South of the Rio Grande; The Stoker; Mystery Ranch. **1933** Drum Taps; When Strangers Marry; California Trail; Police Call. **1934** Fury of the Jungle. **1935** Lives of a Bengal Lancer; Call of the Wild. **1936** Here Comes Trouble; The Beloved Rogue; The Bold Caballero. **1937** Wild West Days (serial); Ebb Tide. **1938** The Crime of Dr. Hallett; Flaming Frontiers (serial). **1939** The Renegade Ranger; Desperate Trails; Frontier Marshal; The Girl and the Gambler. **1940** Kit Carson; Wagons Westward. **1941** The Bad Man; Blood and Sand. **1942** Beyond the Blue Horizon; Tombstone, the Town Too Tough to Die; Pierre of the Plains. **1944** Marked Trails; The Mummy's Curse. **1945** South of the Rio Grande; San Antonio. **1946** Border Bandits; My Darling Clementine. **1947** Buffalo Bill Rides Again. **1948** Fury at Furnace Creek; Belle Starr's Daughter; The Feathered Serpent. **1949** Ambush; The Walking Hills; Roll, Thunder, Roll; The Cowboy and the Indians. **1950** The Showdown; California Passage; Indian Territory; The Savage Horde; A Ticket to Tomahawk. **1951** Oh, Susanna!; Warpath. **1952** Smoky Canyon; The Lion and the Horse. **1953** Savage Mutiny; Ride, Vaquero; Eyes of the Jungle; Jeopardy. **1954** Jubilee Trail; Killer Leopard. **1955** The Vanishing American (and 1925 version). **1956** Partners. **1962** The Outsider.

STEVENS, CYE

Died: June 15, 1974. Screen actor.

Appeared in: **1949** Follow Me Quietly. **1951** The Sellout.

STEVENS, EDWIN

Born: 1860, California. Died: Jan. 2, 1923. Screen, stage and vaudeville actor.

Appeared in: **1916** The Man Inside; The Capital Price; The Yellow Menace (serial); Honor of Mary Blake. **1917** The Boy Girl; Susan's Gentleman; The Brand of Hate. **1919** The Unpardonable Sin; The Crimson Gardenia; Sahara;

The Lottery Man; Hawthorne of the USA. **1921** The Charm School; Crazy to Marry; The Dollar-a-Year Man; Everything for Sale; One Wild Week; The Little Minister; The Snob; What's Worth While?; The Sting of the Lash. **1922** The Game Chicken; The Golden Gallows; The Hands of Nara; The Man Unconquerable; The Ragged Heiress. **1923** Quicksands; The Spider and the Rose; The Voice from the Minaret; The Woman of Bronze.

STEVENS, EMILY
Born: 1882, N.Y. Died: Jan. 2, 1928, New York, N.Y. (overdose of sedatives). Stage and screen actress. Sister of actor Robert Stevens (dec. 1963).

Appeared in: **1915** The Soul of a Woman. **1917** The Slacker.

STEVENS, EVELYN
Born: 1891. Died: Aug. 28, 1938, New York, N.Y. Screen and stage actress. Appeared in early Griffith films.

STEVENS, GEORGE
Born: Dec. 18, 1904, Oakland, Calif. Died: Mar. 8, 1975, Lancaster, Calif. (heart attack). Film director, screenwriter, stage and screen actor. Son of stage actor John Landers Stevens (dec. 1940) and actress Georgie Cooper (dec. 1968). Father of director and producer George Stevens, Jr.

Appeared in: **1915** The Fates and Flora Fourflush (The Ten Billion Dollar Vitagraph Mystery Serial). **1921** Oh Mary Be Careful. **1923** Java Head. **1924** Trail of the Law. **1931** The following shorts: Blood and Thunder; Mama Loves Papa; The Kickoff. **1936** Aces and Eights.

STEVENS, GEORGIA COOPER. *See* GEORGIA COOPER

STEVENS, INGER (Inger Stensland)
Born: Oct. 18, 1935, Stockholm, Sweden. Died: Apr. 30, 1970, Hollywood, Calif. (barbiturate overdose). Screen, stage and television actress.

Appeared in: **1957** Man on Fire. **1958** Cry Terror; The Buccaneer. **1959** The World, the Flesh and the Devil. **1964** The New Interns. **1967** A Time for Killing; A Guide for the Married Man. **1968** Hang 'Em High; House of Cards; Firecreek; Madigan; 5 Card Stud. **1969** A Dream of Kings.

STEVENS, LANDERS (John Landers Stevens)
Born: Feb. 17, 1877, San Francisco, Calif. Died: Dec. 19, 1940, Hollywood, Calif. (heart attack following appendectomy). Screen, stage actor and film producer. Married to actress Georgia Cooper (dec. 1968) and father of actor and director George Stevens (dec. 1975). Entered films in 1920.

Appeared in: **1921** Keeping up with Lizzie; Shadows of Conscience. **1922** The Veiled Woman; A Wonderful Wife; Youth Must Have Love; Wild Honey; Handle with Care. **1925** Battling Bunyon. **1929** Frozen Justice; The Trial of Mary Dugan. **1931** The Gorilla; Hell Divers; The Rainbow Trail. **1935** The Counselitis (short). **1936** We Who are about to Die; Swing Time. **1937** Join the Marines; Bill Cracks Down. **1938** Ears of Experience; Berth Quakes.

STEVENS, LYNN (Franklin Feeney)
Born: 1898. Died: Mar. 28, 1950, Worcester, Mass. Screen and stage actor.

Appeared in: **1926** Men of Steel. **1928** Clothes Make the Woman.

STEVENS, MORTON L.
Born: 1890, Marlboro, Mass. Died: Aug. 5, 1959, Marlboro, Mass. Screen, stage and television actor.

Appeared in: **1914** Perils of Pauline (serial). **1949** Lost Boundaries.

STEVENS, ROBERT
Born: c. 1880. Died: Dec. 19, 1963, Lauderdale-by-the-Sea, Fla. Screen, stage actor and stage director. Brother of actress Emily Stevens (dec. 1928).

Appeared in: **1947** The Millerson Case; Blondie's Big Moment.

STEVENS, VIOLET "VI"
Born: 1892, England. Died: Mar. 22, 1967, London, England. Screen, stage and television actress. Entered films in 1946.

Appeared in: **1951** The Mudlark. **1959** A Cry from the Streets. **1962** Lisa.

STEVENSON, ADLAI E. (Adlai Ewing Stevenson)
Born: Feb. 5, 1900, Los Angeles, Calif. Died: July 14, 1965, London, England (heart attack). Lawyer, public official, writer, diplomat and screen performer.

Appeared in: **1964** A Global Affair.

STEVENSON, CHARLES A. (Charles Alexander Stevenson)
Born: 1851, Dublin, Ireland. Died: July 2, 1929, New York, N.Y. Stage and screen actor. Entered films in 1918.

Appeared in: **1921** Experience. **1922** Her Gilded Cage. **1923** The Bolted Door; The Spanish Dancer; The Woman with Four Faces; Legally Dead; Garrison's Finish. **1924** The Wise Virgin; The Breaking Point. **1927** Aflame in the Sky. **1928** Doomsday.

STEVENSON, CHARLES E.
Born: 1888, Sacramento, Calif. Died: July 4, 1943, Palo Alto, Calif. Screen actor. Entered films with Vitagraph.

Appeared in: **1928** Wallflower. **1929** The Mysterious Dr. Fu Manchu.

STEVENSON, DOUGLAS
Born: 1883. Died: Dec. 31, 1934, Versailles, Ky. Screen, stage actor and dancer.

Appeared in: **1924** Janice Meredith (stage and screen versions).

STEVENSON, HOUSELEY
Born: July 30, 1879, Liverpool or London, England. Died: Aug. 6, 1953, Los Angeles, Calif. Stage and screen actor. Father of actors Onslow Stevens (dec. 1977) and Houseley Stevenson, Jr.

Appeared in: **1936** Law in Her Hands (film debut); Isle of Fury. **1937** Once a Doctor. **1942** Native Land. **1943** Happy Land. **1946** Somewhere in the Night; Little Miss Big. **1947** Dark Passage; The Brasher Doubloon; Time out of Mind; Ramrod; Thunder in the Valley. **1948** Four Faces West; The Challenge; Casbah; Kidnapped; Moonrise; Apartment for Peggy. **1949** Calamity Jane and Sam Bass; Bride of Vengeance; Colorado Territory; Knock on Any Door; The Lady Gambles; Leave It to Henry; Masked Raiders; Sorrowful Jones; Take One False Step; The Walking Hills; You Gotta Stay Happy; The Gal Who Took the West. **1950** All the King's Men; Edge of Doom; Sierra; Gunfighter; Joan of Arc; The Sun Sets at Dawn. **1951** Cave of Outlaws; Hollywood Story; The Secret of Convict Lake; All That I Have. **1952** The Atomic City; Oklahoma Annie; The Wild North.

STEVENSON, JOHN
Born: N.Y. Died: 1922, New York, N.Y. (results of a fall while filming Plunder). Screen actor and stuntman.

Appeared in: **1923** Plunder (serial).

STEVENSON, ROBERT J.
Born: 1915. Died: Mar. 4, 1975, Northridge, Calif. (cardiac arrest). Newscaster, screen, television actor and public official.

Appeared in: **1951** All That I Have. **1952** Radar Men from the Moon (serial). **1954** Fangs of the Wild. **1957** Zero Hour! **1958** Gun Fever; When Hell Broke Loose. **1959** Have Rocket, Will Travel.

STEWART, ANITA
Born: Feb. 17, 1895, Brooklyn, N.Y. Died: May 4, 1961, Beverly Hills, Calif. Screen, stage actress and film producer. Sister of actor George Stewart (dec. 1945).

Appeared in: **1912** The Wood Violet (film debut); Her Choice; The Godmother; Song of the Shell. **1913** The Classmates Frolic; Love Laughs at Blacksmiths (aka Love Finds a Way); The Web; A Fighting Chance; Two's Company, Three's a Crowd; A Regiment of Two; The Forgotten Latchkey; The Song Bird of the North; Sweet Deception; The Moulding; The Prince of Evil; The Tiger; The Lost Millionaire; The Treasure of Desert Island; His Last Fight; Why I am Here; The Wreck; The Swan Girl; His Second Wife. **1914** Diana's Dress Reform; The Right and the Wrong of It; The Lucky Elopement; Lincoln, the Lover; A Million Bid; Back to Broadway; The Girl from Prosperity; He Never Knew; Wife Wanted; The Shadow of the Past; Uncle Bill; The Painted World; Four Thirteen; 'Midst Woodland Shadows. **1915** Two Women; The Sins of the Mothers; The Right Girl; From Headquarters; The Juggernaut; His Phantom Sweetheart; The Awakening; The-Sort-of-Girl-Who-Came-From-Heaven; Count 'Em; The Goddess. **1916** My Lady's Slipper; The Suspect; The Darings of Diana; The Combat. **1917** The Glory of Yolanda; The More Excellent Way; The Message of the Mouse; Clover's Rebellion; The Girl Philippa. **1919** In Old Kentucky; The Mind-the-Paint Girl; Virtuous Wives; A Midnight Romance; Mary Regan; Her Kingdom of Dreams. **1920** Human Desire; The Yellow Typhoon; The Fighting Shepherdess; Harriet and the Piper. **1921** Sowing the Wind; Playthings of Destiny. **1922** Her Mad Bargain; The Invisible Fear; A Question of Honor; The Woman He Married; Rose O' the Sea. **1923** Hollywood; The Love Piker; Mary of the Movies; Souls for Sale. **1924** The Great White Way. **1925** Baree, Son of Kazan; Never the Twain Shall Meet; Go Straight. **1926** The Lodge in the Wilderness; Morganson's Finish; Whispering Wires; The Prince of Pilsen; Rustling for Cupid. **1927** Isle of Sunken Gold; Wild Geese. **1928** Name the Woman; The Romance of a Rogue; Sisters of Eve.

STEWART, ATHOLE
Born: June 24, 1879, Ealing, London, England. Died: Oct. 22, 1940, Buckinghamshire, England. Screen, stage actor and stage director.

Appeared in: **1930** Canaries Sometimes Sing; The Temporary Widow. **1931** The Speckled Band. **1932** Frail Women. **1933** The Little Damozel; Loyalties; The Constant Nymph. **1934** Four Masked Men; The Path of Glory. **1935** The Clairvoyant; While Parents Sleep. **1936** The Amateur Gentleman; Jack of All Trades (aka The Two of Us—US 1937); Where's Sally?; Accused; Dusty Ermine (aka Hideout in the Alps—US 1938); The Tenth Man. **1937** Action for Slander (US 1938); Dr. Syn; Jane Eyre. **1938** The Singing Cop; Thistledown; His Lordship Regrets; Break the News (US 1941); Climbing High. **1939** The

Spy in Black (aka U-Boat 29—US); The Four Just Men (aka The Secret Four—US 1940); Goodbye, Mr. Chips; Poison Pen (US 1941). **1940** Gentleman of Venture (aka It Happened to One Man—US 1941); Tilly of Bloomsbury; Old Mother Riley in Society.

STEWART, BETTY

Born: 1912. Died: Sept. 29, 1944, Hollywood, Calif. Screen actress.

STEWART, BLANCHE

Died: July 25, 1952. Screen and radio actress. Was "Brenda" of "Brenda and Cobina" comedy team.

Appeared in: **1940** A Night at Earl Carroll's. **1941** Swing It Soldier. **1942** Sweetheart of the Fleet.

STEWART, CRAY

Born: 1924. Died: May 30, 1961, Salton Sea, Calif. (heart attack). Stage and screen actor.

STEWART, DANNY (Danny Kalauawa Stewart)

Born: 1907. Died: Apr. 15, 1962, Honolulu, Hawaii. Screen actor and steel guitarist. Appeared in 60 "South Seas" movies.

STEWART, DAVID J. (Abe J. Siegel)

Born: 1914, Omaha, Nebr. Died: Dec. 23, 1966, Cleveland, Ohio (following surgery). Screen, stage and television actor.

Appeared in: **1955** The Silver Chalice. **1960** Murder, Inc. **1961** The Young Savages. **1967** Who's Minding the Mint?

STEWART, DONA JEAN

Born: 1939. Died: July 31, 1961, near Oceanside, Calif. (auto accident). Screen actress.

STEWART, DONALD

Born: 1911, Pa. Died: Mar. 1, 1966, Chertsey, England. Screen, stage and television actor. Married to vaudeville performer Renee Houston.

Appeared in: **1942** Eagle Squadron; Flying Fortress. **1943** Wild Horse Stampede. **1944** One Exciting Night (aka You Can't Do Without Love—US 1946); Arizona Whirlwind. **1955** The Reluctant Bride (aka Two Grooms for a Bride—US 1957); Cross Up (aka Tiger by the Tail). **1958** The Sheriff of Fractured Jaw.

STEWART, FRED

Born: 1907, Ga. Died: Dec. 5, 1970, New York, N.Y. Screen, stage and television actor. Entered films in 1931.

Appeared in: **1932** The Misleading Lady. **1961** Splendor in the Grass. **1964** The World of Henry Orient.

STEWART, GEORGE

Born: 1888. Died: Dec. 25, 1945, Beverly Hills, Calif. Screen actor. Brother of actress Anita Stewart (dec. 1961).

Appeared in: **1921** The Fighter; Gilded Lies; Over the Wire. **1922** The Seventh Day. **1923** Crossed Wires; Hollywood; The Abysmal Brute. **1925** Back to Life; Wings of Youth.

STEWART, JACK

Born: 1914, Larkhall, Scotland. Died: Jan. 2, 1966, London, England. Screen, stage, radio and television actor.

Appeared in: **1952** Hunted (aka The Stranger in Between—US); The Brave Don't Cry. **1954** The Kidnappers (aka The Little Kidnappers—US 1954); The Maggie (aka High and Dry—US). **1957** The Steel Bayonet; The Heart Within. **1961** The Frightened City (US 1962). **1962** Strongroom; Pirates of Blood River; The Amorous Prawn (aka The Playgirl and the War Minister—US 1963). **1963** Tom Jones. **1964** The Three Lives of Thomasina. **1967** I Coltelli del Vendicatore (Knives of the Avenger—US 1968).

STEWART, JULIA

Died: Date unknown, New Jersey. Screen actress.

Appeared in: **1912** It Pays to be Kind; A Living Memory; When an Old Maid Gets Busy; Through Jealous Eyes; The Black Hand; Dick's Wife; The Return of Lady Linda. **1913** Eclaire films.

STEWART, NELLIE

Born: 1858, Australia. Died: June 20, 1931. Screen, stage actress and singer.

Appeared in: **1911** Sweet Nell of Old Drury (her only film).

STEWART, RICHARD

Died: 1938 or 1939? Screen actor. Son of opera performer William G. Stewart (dec. 1941).

Appeared in: **1922** Face to Face.

STEWART, ROY

Born: Oct. 17, 1889, San Diego, Calif. Died: Apr. 26, 1933, Los Angeles, Calif. (heart attack). Screen and stage actor. Entered films in 1913.

Appeared in: **1915** Just Nuts (short). **1916** Liberty, a Daughter of the U.S.A. **1917** Come Through; The Devil Dodger. **1918** Keith of the Border; The Law's Outlaw; Faith Endurin'. **1919** The Westerners. **1920** Riders of the Dawn; Just a Wife. **1921** Prisoners of Love; The Devil to Pay; The Heart of the North; Her Social Value; The Mistress of Shenstone. **1922** Back to the Yellow Jacket; The Innocent Cheat; Life's Greatest Question; A Motion to Adjourn; One Eighth Apache; The Radio King (serial); The Sagebrush Trail; The Snowshoe Trail. **1923** Burning Words; The Love Brand; Pure Grit; Trimmed in Scarlet. **1924** Sundown; The Woman on the Jury. **1925** Kit Carson over the Great Divide; Time, the Comedian; Where the Worst Begins. **1926** General Custer at Little Big Horn; Sparrows; Buffalo Bill on the U. P. Trail; Daniel Boone Thru the Wilderness; You Never Know Women. **1927** The Midnight Watch; One Woman to Another; Roaring Fires. **1928** The Viking; The Candy Kid; Stormy Waters. **1929** Protection; In Old Arizona. **1930** Men without Women; The Great Divide; Born Reckless; Lone Star Ranger; Rough Romance. **1931** Fighting Caravans. **1932** Mystery Ranch; Exposed. **1933** Fargo Express; Come on, Tarzan!; Zoo in Budapest; Rustler's Roundup.

STIEBNER, HANS

Born: 1899, Germany. Died: Mar. 27, 1958, Baden-Baden, West Germany. Screen, stage, television actor and film director.

Appeared in: **1937** Weisse Sklaven. **1938** Mit Versiegelter Order (Under Sealed Orders).

STILLER, MAURITZ

Born: 1883, Helsinki, Finland. Died: 1928, Stockholm, Sweden (infective pleurisy). Screen actor and film director.

Appeared in: **1912** Mother and Daughter. **1914** When Mother-in-Law Reigns.

STIRLING, EDWARD

Born: 1892, Birmingham, England. Died: Jan. 12, 1948, Paris, France (heart attack). Screen, stage, radio actor, playwright and stage producer.

Appeared in: **1948** Eagle with Two Heads.

STITES, FRANK

Born: Feb. 28, 1882, Indiana. Died: Mar. 15, 1915, Universal City, Calif. (plane crash). Screen actor and stuntman.

Appeared in: **1915** The Mysterious Contragrao.

STOCKDALE, CARL (Carlton Stockdale)

Born: Feb. 19, 1874, Worthington, Minn. Died: Mar. 15, 1953, Woodland Hills, Calif. (heart attack). Screen, stage and vaudeville actor. Entered films in 1912.

Appeared in: **1914** Sophie Picks a Dead One; The Calling of Jim Benton; Single-Handed; The Atonement; Broncho Billy Puts One Over; Broncho Billy and the Sheriff; Dan Cupid—Assayer; Broncho Billy—Favorite; The Hills of Peace. **1915** The Bank; My Best Gal. **1916** Intolerance; Atta Boy's Last Race. **1917** Lost and Won; Land of Long Shadows; The Range Boss; Open Places; Men of the Desert; Peggy Leads the Way. **1921** The Fatal 30; Molly O'; Society Secrets. **1922** Bing Bang Boom; Suzanna; The Call of Home; The Half Breed; Red Hot Romance; Oliver Twist; Thorns and Orange Blossoms; Where Is My Wandering Boy Tonight?; Wild Honey. **1923** The Darling of New York; The Grail; The Extra Girl; Man's Size; The Meanest Man in the World; The Tiger's Claw; Money! Money! Money! **1924** The Whispered Name; Try and Get It; Tainted Money; The Beautiful Sinner; A Cafe in Cairo; Gold Heels; The Spirit of the USA. **1925** The Business of Love; The Desert's Price; A Regular Fellow; A Son of His Father; The Trail Rider. **1926** The Man Upstairs; While London Sleeps. **1927** Colleen; King of Kings; See You in Jail; Somewhere in Sonora. **1928** The Air Mail Pilot; Jazzland; My Home Town; The Shepherd of the Hills; The Black Pearl; Broken Barriers; The Terror. **1929** The Love Parade; The Carnation Kid; China Bound. **1930** Abraham Lincoln; The Furies; Hell's Island; Hide-Out; Sisters; All Tied Up (short); Whispering Whoopee (short). **1933** The Vampire Bat. **1935** The Crimson Trail; Circumstantial Evidence; Dr. Socrates; Outlawed Guns; The Ivory-Handled Gun; Ring Around the Moon; Hit and Run Driver (short); Mary Jane's Pa. **1936** The Leavenworth Case; Revolt of the Zombies; Oh, Susannah! **1937** Battle of Greed; Nation Aflame; Courage of the West; Lost Horizon. **1938** Hawaiian Buckaroo; Rawhide; Blockade. **1939** The Story That Couldn't Be Printed (short). **1940** Shooting High; Pioneers of the Frontier; Konga the Wild Stallion; Stage to Chino; Thundering Frontier; Wagon Train. **1941** Scattergood Meets Broadway; Dangerous Lady; All That Money Can Buy (aka Here is a Man); Scattergood Pulls the Strings; Along the Rio Grande; The Return of Daniel Boone. **1953** The Devil and Daniel Webster (reissue of All That Money Can Buy—1941).

STOCKFIELD, BETTY (aka BETTY STOCKFELD)

Born: Jan. 15, 1905, Sydney, Australia. Died: Jan. 27, 1966, London, England (cancer). Stage and screen actress.

Appeared in: **1926** What Price Glory (film debut). **1931** City of Song (aka Farewell to Love—US 1933); Captivation; 77 Park Lane. **1932** Money for Nothing; Life Goes On (aka Sorry You've Been Troubled); The Impassive Footman (aka Woman in Bondage—US); The Maid of the Mountains. **1933** King of the Ritz; Lord of the Manor; Anne One Hundred. **1934** The Man Who Changed His Name; The Battle (aka Thunder in the East—US); Brides to Be. **1935** The Lad; Runaway Ladies. **1936** Under Proof; The Beloved Vagabond; Dishonour Bright. **1937** Who's Your Lady Friend?; Club des Femmes (Girls' Club). **1938** I See Ice; Slipper Episode. **1940** Derriere la Facade (Behind the Facade). **1942** Hard Steel; Flying Fortress; Ils Etaient Heufs Celibataires (Nine Bachelors). **1950** The Girl Who Couldn't Quit; Edouard et Caroline (Edward and Caroline—US 1952). **1956** Guilty. **1957** True as a Turtle. **1958** Forbidden Desire (aka Lover's Net).

STODDARD, BELLE
Born: 1869, Remington, Ohio. Died: Dec. 13, 1950, Hollywood, Calif. Stage and screen actress.

Appeared in: **1925** Kentucky Pride. **1928** Hangman's House. **1929** Anne against the World.

STODDARD, BETSY (Elizabeth S. Zimmerman)
Born: 1884. Died: Sept. 7, 1959, Hollywood, Calif. Screen actress.

STOECKEL, JOE
Born: 1894, Munich, Germany. Died: June 14, 1959, Munich, Germany (circulatory ailment). Screen, stage actor and film director. Entered films in 1916.

Appeared in: **1920** Strong Man. **1934** Der Meisterdetektiv; Die Blonde Cristl; SA Mann Brand; Mit dir Durch Dick und Duenn; Bei der Blonden Kathrein. **1935** Zwischen Himmel und Erde (Between Heaven and Earth); Johannisnacht. **1936** Ein Ganzer Kerl. **1937** Die Grose Adele. **1939** Der Dampf mit dem Drachen (The Fight with the Dragon); 1A in Oberbayern (1A in Upper Bavaria).

STOKER, H. G. (Hew Gordon Dacre Stoker)
Born: Feb. 2, 1885, Dublin, Ireland. Died: Feb. 2, 1966, England. Screen, stage actor and playwright. Also known on stage as Hew Gordon.

Appeared in: **1933** Channel Crossing (US 1934); One Precious Year. **1935** Forever England (aka Brown on Resolution and Born for Glory—US). **1936** First Offence; Rhodes of Africa (aka Rhodes—US); Pot Luck; It's You I Want. **1937** Moonlight Sonata; Non-Stop New York. **1938** Crackerjack (aka The Man with a Hundred Faces—US). **1939** Full Speed Ahead. **1943** The Charmer (reissue of Moonlight Sonata—1937). **1948** Call of the Blood. **1951** Four Days. **1952** Where's Charley?

STOKES, ERNEST L.
Born: 1907. Died: May 26, 1964, Wilson, N.C. Screen and radio actor. Appeared on radio with Frank Rice in a radio team billed as "Mustard and Gravy."

STONE, ARTHUR
Born: 1884, St. Louis, Mo. Died: Sept. 4, 1940, Hollywood, Calif. Screen, stage and vaudeville actor. Entered films in 1924.

Appeared in: **1925** Sherlock Sleuth (short); Change the Needle (short). **1926** It Must Be Love; Miss Nobody; The Silent Lover. **1927** The Patent Leather Kid; The Sea Tigers; An Affair of the Follies; Babe Comes Home; The Valley of the Giants; Hard-Boiled Haggerty. **1928** Chicken a la King; The Farmer's Daughter; Me, Gangster; Burning Daylight. **1929** Through Different Eyes; Captain Lash; The Far Call; Fugitives; New Year's Eve; Red Wine; Frozen Justice; Fox Movietone Follies of 1929. **1930** The Vagabond King; The Bad Man; Arizona Kid; On the Level; Mamba; Girl of the Golden West. **1931** The Lash; The Conquering Horde; Bad Company; The Secret Menace. **1932** The Big Shot; The Broken Wing; So Big; Roar of the Dragon; That's My Boy; plus the following shorts: The Girl in the Tonneau; Lady Please!; The Flirty Sleepwalker; The Line's Busy; Neighbor Trouble; Shopping with Wifie. **1934** She Had to Choose; I'll Tell the World; Love Birds. **1935** Bordertown; Charlie Chan in Egypt; Hot Tip. **1936** Fury. **1938** Go Chase Yourself.

STONE, DOROTHY
Born: 1905. Died: Sept. 24, 1974, Montecito, Calif. Screen, stage and vaudeville actress. Daughter of actor Fred Stone (dec. 1959) and sister of actresses Paula and Carol Stone.

Appeared in: **1924** Broadway after Dark. **1932** Smiling Faces. **1934** Paree, Paree. **1936** Revolt of the Zombies. **1938** A Universal short.

STONE, FRED
Born: Aug. 19, 1873, Denver, Colo. Died: Mar. 6, 1959, North Hollywood, Calif. Father of actresses Dorothy (dec. 1974), Paula and Carol Stone. Screen, stage, vaudeville and circus actor. Appeared in vaudeville as part of "Montgomery and Stone" team. Made a few western films for Lasky in 1917.

Appeared in: **1918** The Goat. **1919** Under the Top; Johnny Get Your Gun. **1921** The Duke of Chimney Butte. **1922** Billy Jim. **1924** Broadway after Dark.

1932 Smiling Faces. **1935** Alice Adams. **1936** The Trail of the Lonesome Pine; My American Wife; The Farmer in the Dell; Jury. **1937** Hideaway; Life Begins in College. **1938** Quick Money. **1939** No Place to Go. **1940** Konga, the Wild Stallion; The Westerner.

STONE, GEORGE
Born: 1877. Died: July 10, 1939, Baldwin, N.Y. Screen, stage and vaudeville actor. Married to actress Etta Pillard with whom he appeared in vaudeville. Do not confuse with actor George E. Stone (dec. 1967).

STONE, GEORGE E. (George Stein)
Born: May 1, 1904, Lodz, Poland. Died: May 26, 1967, Woodland Hills, Calif. (stroke). Screen, stage, vaudeville and television actor. Known for gangster parts in "Boston Blackie" series and other films. Do not confuse with actor George Stone (dec. 1939).

Appeared in: **1918** 'Til I Come Back to You. **1921** Jackie; Penny of Top Hill Trail; The Whistle; White and Unmarried. **1923** The Fourth Musketeer. **1927** Seventh Heaven; Brass Knuckles. **1928** State Street Sadie; Tenderloin; The Racket; Walking Back; Beautiful but Dumb; Clothes Make the Woman; San Francisco Nights; Turn Back the Hours. **1929** Weary River; Skin Deep; Naughty Baby; The Girl in the Glass Cage; Two Men and a Maid; Melody Lane; Redeeming Sin. **1930** Under a Texas Moon; The Medicine Man; The Stronger Sex; So This Is Paris Green; Little Caesar. **1931** Cimarron; Five-Star Final; The Spider; Sob Sister; The Front Page. **1932** The Last Mile; Taxi!; File No. 113; The Woman from Monte Carlo; The World and the Flesh; The Phantom of Crestwood; Slippery Pearls (short). **1933** King for a Night; Vampire Bat; Sailor Be Good!; Song of the Eagle; The Big Brain; Emergency Call; The Wrecker; Sing, Sinner, Sing; Ladies Must Love; Penthouse; He Couldn't Take It; 42nd Street. **1934** Return of the Terror; The Dragon Murder Case; Embarrassing Moments; Frontier Marshal; Viva Villa! **1935** Hold 'Em Yale; Public Hero No. 1; Make a Million; Moonlight on the Prairie; The Frisco Kid; One Hour Late; Secret of the Chateau; Million Dollar Baby. **1936** Man Hunt; Freshman Love; Jailbreak; Anthony Adverse; Bullets or Ballots; The Captain's Kid; Polo Joe; King of Hockey; Here Comes Carter!; Rhythm on the Range. **1937** Don't Get Me Wrong; Clothes and the Woman; Back in Circulation; The Adventurous Blonde. **1938** Alcatraz Island; A Slight Case of Murder; Over the Wall; Mr. Moto's Gamble; Submarine Patrol; The Long Shot; You and Me. **1939** You Can't Get Away with Murder; The Housekeeper's Daughter. **1940** The Night of Nights; I Take This Woman; Island of Doomed Men; Northwest Mounted Police; Slightly Tempted; Cherokee Strip. **1941** Broadway Limited; Last of the Duanes; His Girl Friday; Road Show; The Face behind the Mask; Confessions of Boston Blackie. **1942** Lone Star Ranger; The Affairs of Jimmy Valentine; Little Tokyo, U.S.A.; The Devil with Hitler; Boston Blackie Goes to Hollywood. **1943** The Chance of a Lifetime; After Midnight with Boston Blackie. **1944** Roger Touhy—Gangster; Timber Queen; One Mysterious Night; Strangers in the Night; My Buddy. **1945** One Exciting Night; Boston Blackie's Rendezvous; Scared Stiff; Boston Blackie Booked on Suspicion; Doll Face. **1946** Boston Blackie and the Law; A Close Call for Boston Blackie; The Phantom Thief; Sentimental Journey; Suspense; Abie's Irish Rose. **1948** Trapped by Boston Blackie; Untamed Breed. **1950** Dancing in the Dark. **1952** A Girl in Every Port; Bloodhounds of Broadway. **1953** The Robe; Pickup on South Street; Combat Squad. **1954** Three Ring Circus; The Steel Cage; Broken Lance; The Miami Story. **1955** The Man with the Golden Arm; Guys and Dolls. **1956** Slightly Scarlet. **1957** Sierra Stranger; The Story of Mankind; The Tijuana Story; Baby Face Nelson; Calypso Heat Wave. **1959** Some Like It Hot. **1961** Pocketful of Miracles.

STONE, HARVEY
Born: 1913. Died: Mar. 4, 1974, Bridgetown, Barbados, W.I. (heart attack). Screen, stage, vaudeville and television actor. Married to actress Lois Lee.

STONE, JAMES F.
Born: 1901. Died: Jan. 9, 1969, Calif. Screen, stage and television actor.

Appeared in: **1953** The Glass Web; Gunsmoke; How to Marry a Millionaire. **1954** Black Widow; Broken Lance. **1956** The Scarlet Hour. **1967** Barefoot in the Park.

STONE, LEWIS
Born: Nov. 15, 1879, Worcester, Mass. Died: Sept. 11, 1953, Los Angeles, Calif. (heart attack). Stage and screen actor. Best known for role as "Judge Hardy" in "Andy Hardy" film series.

Appeared in: **1916** Honor Altar (film debut); The Havoc. **1918** Inside the Lines. **1920** Nomads of the North; The Concert; The River's End; Held by the Enemy; Milestones. **1921** The Northern Trail; The Golden Snare; Beau Revel; Pilgrims of the Night; The Child Thou Gavest Me; Don't Neglect Your Wife. **1922** The Prisoner of Zenda; Trifling Women; A Fool There Was; The Rosary. **1923** Scaramouche; The Dangerous Age; You Can't Fool Your Wife. **1924** The Stranger; Why Men Leave Home; Husbands and Lovers; Inez from Hollywood; Cytherea; The Lost World. **1925** The Lady Who Lied; The Talker; Cheaper to Marry; Confessions of a Queen; What Fools Men; Fine Clothes. **1926** Don Juan's Three Nights; Too Much Money; Old Loves and New; Girl from Montmarte; Midnight Lover; The Blonde Saint. **1927** An Affair of the

Follies; Lonesome Ladies; The Prince of Head Waiters; The Notorious Ladies; The Private Life of Helen of Troy. **1928** The Foreign Legion; Freedom of the Press; The Patriot; Inspiration. **1929** The Trial of Mary Dugan; A Woman of Affairs; Wild Orchids; The Circle; Wonder of Women; Madame X. **1930** Their Own Desire; Strictly Unconventional; The Big House; Romance; The Office Wife; Passion Flower; Father's Son. **1931** The Sin of Madelon Claudet; My Past; Inspiration; Always Goodbye; Phantom of Paris; The Bargain; Stolen Heaven; The Secret Six. **1932** Mata Hari; Grand Hotel; The Divorce in the Family; Unashamed; Wet Parade; Night Court; Letty Lynton; New Morals for Old; Red Headed Woman; The Son-Daughter; The Mask of Fu Manchu; Strange Interlude. **1933** The White Sister; Service; Looking Forward; Queen Christina; Bureau of Missing Persons; Men Must Fight. **1934** You Can't Buy Everything; The Girl from Missouri; Treasure Island; The Mystery of Mr. X. **1935** David Copperfield; Vanessa, Her Love Story; West Point of the Air; Public Hero No. 1; Woman Wanted; China Seas; Shipmates Forever. **1936** Three Godfathers; The Unguarded Hour; Small Town Girl; Sworn Enemy; Suzy; Don't Turn 'Em Loose. **1937** Outcast; The Thirteenth Chair; The Man Who Cried Wolf. **1938** You're Only Young Once; Bad Man of Brimstone; Judge Hardy's Children; Stolen Heaven; Love Finds Andy Hardy; Yellow Jack; The Chaser; Out West with the Hardys. **1939** Ice Follies of 1939; The Hardys Ride High; Andy Hardy Gets Spring Fever; The Andy Hardy Family; Judge Hardy and Son; Joe and Ethel Turp Call on the President. **1940** Andy Hardy Meets Debutante; Sporting Blood. **1941** The Bugle Sounds; Andy Hardy's Private Secretary; Life Begins for Andy Hardy. **1942** The Courtship of Andy Hardy; Andy Hardy's Double Life. **1943** Plan for Destruction (short—narration). **1944** Andy Hardy's Blonde Trouble. **1946** Love Laughs at Andy Hardy; The Hoodlum Saint; Three Wise Fools. **1948** State of the Union. **1949** The Sun Comes Up; Any Number Can Play. **1950** Stars in My Crown; Key to the City. **1951** Grounds for Marriage; Night into Morning; Angels in the Outfield; Bannerline; It's a Big Country; The Unknown Man. **1952** Just This Once; Talk About a Stranger; Scaramouche; The Prisoner of Zenda (and 1922 version). **1953** All the Brothers Were Valiant; One Came Home. **1964** Big Parade of Comedy (documentary).

STONE, MAXINE

Born: 1910. Died: Nov. 20, 1964, Hollywood, Calif. Screen, stage and vaudeville actress. Appeared in vaudeville with her husband Benny Ross in act called "Ross and Stone."

Appeared in early Vitaphone shorts and: **1958** South Seas Adventure.

STONE, MRS. ROBERT E.

Died: Nov. 5, 1916. Screen actress.

STONEHOUSE, RUTH

Born: 1893. Died: May 12, 1941, Hollywood, Calif. Screen and stage actress. Was part owner with Billy Anderson of the Essanay studios in Chicago.

Appeared in: **1911** The Papered Door. **1912** Twilight; The End of the Feud; Sunshine; Mr. Hubby's Wife; The Shadow of the Cross Chains; From the Submerged. **1913** The Spy's Defeat; Homespun; The World Above; In Convict Garb. **1914** The Romance of an American Duchess; Blood Will Tell; Nighthawks; The Real Agatha; Let No Man Escape; The Counter-Melody; The Fable of Lutie, the False Alarm; Mother O'Dreams; White Lies; The Darling Young Person; The Other Girl. **1916** The Adventures of Peg O' the Ring (serial). **1919** the Masked Rider (serial); The Master Mystery (serial). **1920** Parlor, Bedroom and Bath. **1921** I Am Guilty; Don't Call Me Little Girl. **1923** Lights Out; The Flash; Flames of Passion; The Way of the Transgressor. **1924** A Girl of the Limberlost; Broken Barriers. **1925** Blood and Steel; The Fugitive; Rough Going; Ermine and Rhinestones; Fifth Avenue Model; The Scarlet West; Straight Through; A Two-Fisted Sheriff. **1926** Broken Homes; The Wives of the Prophet. **1927** Poor Girls; The Ladybird; The Satin Woman. **1928** The Ape; The Devil's Cage.

STOOPNAGLE, COLONEL LEMUEL Q. (F. Chase Taylor)

Born: Oct. 4, 1897, Buffalo, N.Y. Died: May 29, 1950. Screen and radio actor. Was part of radio team of "Stoopnagle and Budd."

Appeared in: **1933** International House. **1934** An Educational short. **1963** The Sound of Laughter (documentary).

STORDAHL, ALEX

Born: Aug. 8, 1913, Staten Island, N.Y. Died: Aug. 30, 1963, Encino, Calif. Bandleader, composer and screen actor. Married to vocalist June Hutton (dec. 1973).

STOSSEL, LUDWIG

Born: Feb. 12, 1883, Austria. Died: Jan. 29, 1973, Beverly Hills, Calif. Screen, stage, television actor, stage director and producer. Married to actress Eleanore Stossel.

Appeared in: **1931** Bockbierfest; Scandal Um Eva; Elisabeth von Oesterreich. **1934** Strich Durch die Rechnung; In Wien Hab' Ich Einmal ein Maedel Geliebt. **1939** O Schwarzwald, O Heimat (Oh Black Forest, Oh Home). **1940** Four Sons; The Man I Married; Jennie; Dance, Girl, Dance. **1941** Man Hunt; Underground; Great Guns; Marry the Boss's Daughter. **1942** All Through the

Night; Woman of the Year; The Pride of the Yankees; Iceland; Casablanca; Who Done It; The Great Impersonation; Pittsburgh. **1943** They Came to Blow up America; Action in the North Atlantic; Hers to Hold; Hitler's Hangman (aka Hitler's Madman); The Strange Death of Adolf Hitler; Above Suspicion. **1944** The Climax; Bluebeard. **1945** Lake Placid Serenade; Dillinger; Her Highness and the Bellboy; House of Dracula; Yolanda and the Thief; Miss Susie Slagle's. **1946** Cloak and Dagger; Temptation; Girl on the Spot. **1947** The Beginning of the End; Song of Love; Escape Me Never; This Time for Keeps. **1948** A Song is Born. **1949** The Great Sinner. **1951** As Young as You Feel; Corky of Gasoline Alley. **1952** The Merry Widow; No Time for Flowers; Somebody Loves Me. **1953** Call Me Madam; White Goddess; The Sun Shines Bright; Geraldine. **1958** Me and the Colonel; From the Earth to the Moon. **1959** The Blue Angel. **1960** G.I. Blues.

STOWE, LESLIE

Born: 1886, Homer, La. Died: July 16, 1949, Englewood, N.J. Stage and screen actor.

Appeared in: **1916** The Closed Road. **1917** The Adopted Son. **1918** Social Quicksands. **1919** Bolshevism on File; The Carter Case (The Craig Kennedy Serial). **1920** The Copperhead. **1921** The Good-Bad Wife; Peggy Puts it Over. **1922** No Trespassing; The Seventh Day. **1923** Columbus; Driven; Jamestown; Second Fiddle. **1924** The Fifth Horseman; Tongues of Flame. **1929** Mother's Boy.

STOWELL, CLARENCE W.

Born: 1878. Died: Nov. 26, 1940, Paterson, N.J. Screen actor.

Appeared in: **1940** The Ramparts We Watch (March of Time's first full-length feature).

STOWELL, WILLIAM H.

Born: Mar. 13, 1885, Boston, Mass. Died: Dec. 1919, Elizabethville, South Africa (train accident). Screen, stage actor and opera performer. Entered films in 1909.

Appeared in: **1911** Two Orphans. **1912** Hypnotized; Sons of the Northwoods; The Redemption of Greek Joe; The Devil, the Servant and the Man; As the Fates Decree; A War Time Romance; The House of His Master; An International Romance; The Fire-Fighter's Love; A Freight Train Drama. **1913** A False Order; The Clue; The Water Rat; The Ex-Convict; A Change of Administration; The Pendulum of Fate; Dixieland; The Devil and Tom Walker; The Ex-Convict's Plunge. **1914** In the Line of Duty; When a Woman's Forty. **1915** The Old Code; The Gentleman Burglar; The Strength of a Samson; The Great Question; The End of the Road; The Tragic Circle; Hartley Merwin's Adventure; The Buzzard's Shadow; Pardoned. **1916** The Other Side of the Door; The Secret Wire; The Gamble; The Man in the Sombrero; Overalls; Lillo of the Sulu Seas; The Blindness; The Overcoat; The Lover Hermit; The Release of Dan Forbes; The Sheriff of Plumas. **1917** Fires of Rebellion; Triumph; The Piper's Price; Bondage; The Flashlight Girl; A Doll's House; Hell Morgan's Girl; The Girl in the Checkered Coat; Fighting Mad. **1918** The Heart of Humanity; The Grand Passion; Broadway Love; The Risky Road. **1919** When a Girl Loves; Paid in Advance. **1920** The Man Who Dared God.

STRADNER, ROSE

Born: July 31, 1913, Vienna, Austria. Died: Sept. 27, 1958, Bedford Village, N.Y. Stage and screen actress. Married to director Joseph L. Mankiewicz.

Appeared in: **1934** Ein Gewisser Herr Gran; Hochzeit am Wolfgangsee. **1936** One Hundred Days of Napoleon. **1937** The Postillion of Lonjumeau. **1938** The Last Gangster. **1939** Blind Alley. **1944** The Keys of the Kingdom.

STRANDMARK, ERIK

Born: 1919, Torsaker, Sweden. Died: 1963, Sweden. Screen, stage actor and writer.

Appeared in: **1955** The People of Hemso. **1956** Unmarried Mothers; Children of the Night. **1958** The Seventh Seal; Med Mord I Bagaget (No Time to Kill—US 1963). Other Swedish films: The Invisible Wall; We Need Each Other; The Royal Rabble; Rolling Sea; U-Boat 39; Love; Barabbas; The Road to Klockrike; Sawdust and Tinsel (aka The Naked Night); Hidden in the Fog; Possessed by Speed; Victory in Darkness; Karin Mansdotter; Salka Valka; Wild Birds; No One is Crazier Than I Am; Kulla-Gulla; The Tough Game; Girl in a Dress Coat; Little Fridolf and I; Stage Entrance; The Way Via Ska; Tarps Elin; Encounters at Dusk; Lights at Night; The Master Detective Leads a Dangerous Life; The Clergyman from Uddarbo; Nothin' But Bones; Woman in a Leopardskin; We on Vaddo; Beautiful Susan and the Old Men.

STRANG, HARRY

Died: Apr. 10, 1972. Screen actor.

Appeared in: **1930** Around the Corner; Hell's Angels. **1931** Hell Bound. **1935** Air Hawks. **1937** Zorro Rides Again (serial). **1938** The Purple Vigilantes; Two Gun Justice; Submarine Patrol. **1939** The Return of the Cisco Kid; Mr. Moto in Danger Island; Mr. Moto Takes a Vacation. **1940** Gaucho Serenade; Calling Philo Vance; Kit Carson. **1941** Buck Privates; The Phantom Submarine. **1942** Who Done It?; My Gal Sal. **1943** It Ain't Hay; Hit the Ice. **1945** Manhunt of

Mystery Island (serial). **1946** King of the Forest Rangers (serial). **1948** Sinister Journey. **1950** When Willie Comes Marching Home. **1957** Looking for Danger. **1958** Toughest Gun in Tombstone.

STRANGE, GLENN (George Glenn Strange)
Born: Aug. 16, 1899, New Mexico. Died: Sept. 20, 1973, Burbank, Calif. (cancer). Screen, radio, television actor, rodeo performer, professional heavyweight boxer and stuntman. Entered films as a stuntman.

Appeared in: **1932** Hurricane Express (serial). **1935** New Frontier; House of Frankenstein. **1937** Arizona Days; Adventure's End. **1938** Black Bandit; The Painted Trail; Pride of the West; In Old Mexico; The Mysterious Rider; Sunset Trail; Border Wolves; The Last Stand; Gun Packer; Call of the Rockies. **1939** Rough Riders' Round-Up; Blue Montana Skies; Range War; Law of the Pampas; Overland Mail; The Llano Kid; Days of Jesse James; The Fighting Gringo; Arizona Legion; Cupid Rides the Range; The Lone Ranger Rides Again (serial). **1940** Land of Six Guns; Pioneer Days; Rhythm of the Rio Grande; Pals of the Silver Sage; Covered Wagon Trails; Stage to Chino; Triple Justice; Wagon Train; Three Men from Texas; Cowboy from Sundown; Fargo Kid. **1941** Riders of Death Valley (serial); Arizona Cyclone; San Francisco Docks; Saddlemates; Wide Open Town; The Kid's Last Ride; The Bandit Trail; Dude Cowboy; Badlands of Dakota; Fugitive Valley; The Driftin' Kid; Billy the Kid Wanted; Billy the Kid's Roundup; Come on, Danger!; In Old Colorado; Westward Ho-Hum (short). **1942** Billy the Kid Trapped; Sunset on the Desert; Romance on the Range; The Mad Monster; Down Texas Way; Little Joe—The Wrangler; Stagecoach Buckaroo; The Ghost of Frankenstein; The Mummy's Tomb. **1943** The Kid Rides Again; The Desperadoes; Wild Horse Stampede; Mission to Moscow; Black Market Rustlers; False Colors; The Woman of the Town. **1944** The Return of the Rangers; The Monster Maker; Silver City Kid; Arizona Trail; The Contender; Forty Thieves; Sonora Stagecoach; Valley of Vengeance; Trail to Gunsight; The San Antonio Kid. **1945** House of Frankenstein; House of Dracula; Renegades of the Rio Grande. **1946** Beauty and the Bandit. **1947** The Wistful Widow of Wagon Gap; Frontier Fighters. **1948** Abbott and Costello Meet Frankenstein; The Far Frontier; Silver Trails; Red River. **1949** Master Minds; Rimfire; Roll Thunder Roll. **1950** Comanche Territory; Double Crossbones. **1951** Comin' Round the Mountain; Texas Carnival; Red Badge of Courage. **1952** The Lawless Breed. **1953** The Veils of Bagdad; The Great Sioux Uprising. **1955** The Vanishing American; The Road to Denver. **1957** Gunfire at Indian Gap; Last Stagecoach West. **1958** Quantrill's Raiders.

STRANGE, ROBERT
Born: 1882. Died: Feb. 22, 1952, Hollywood, Calif. Screen and stage actor.

Appeared in: **1931** The Smiling Lieutenant; The Cheat. **1932** The Misleading Lady. **1934** These Thirty Years; Gambling. **1935** Special Agent; I Found Stella Parish; Frisco Kid. **1936** The Murder of Dr. Harrigan; The Walking Dead; Stolen Holiday; Trapped by Television; Beloved Enemy. **1937** Beware of Ladies; John Meade's Woman; Marked Woman. **1938** Sky Giant; I Stand Accused. **1939** In Name Only; They Made Me a Criminal; Hell's Kitchen; The Saint Strikes Back; The Story of Vernon and Irene Castle; The Spellbinder; Angels Wash Their Faces. **1940** The Castle on the Hudson; The Adventures of Captain Marvel (serial); King of the Royal Mounted. **1941** Robin Hood of the Pecos; High Sierra; Adventures of Captain Marvel (serial); All That Money Can Buy. **1942** Arizona Cyclone; The Yukon Patrol. **1952** The Devil and Daniel Webster (reissue and retitle of All That Money Can Buy—1941).

STRANGIS, JANE
Born: 1932. Died: Jan. 25, 1966, Hollywood, Calif. (leukemia). Screen and television actress.

STRASSBERG, MORRIS
Born: 1898. Died: Feb. 8, 1974, South Laguna Beach, Calif. Screen, stage and television actor.

Appeared in: **1926** Broken Hearts. **1938** Power of Life. **1939** Tevya. **1950** With these Hands. **1970** The Way We Live Now. **1971** Klute.

STRATTON, CHESTER "CHET"
Born: 1913. Died: July 7, 1970, Los Angeles, Calif. Screen, stage and radio actor.

Appeared in: **1937** A Vitaphone Short. **1953** Julius Caesar. **1961** All Hands on Deck; Go Naked in the World. **1962** Lover Come Back; Advise and Consent. **1965** In Harm's Way; Those Calloways; Bus Riley's Back in Town; The Greatest Story Ever Told. **1968** Track of Thunder; Journey to Shiloh; If He Hollers Let Him Go. **1969** Sweet Charity.

STRATTON, HARRY
Born: 1898. Died: Aug. 19, 1955, Hollywood, Calif. (heart attack). Screen and burlesque actor. Stand-in for Bud Abbott.

STRAUB, MARY E.
Born: 1884. Died: Nov. 7, 1951, Hollywood, Calif. Screen actress.

STRAUSS, CLEMENT (aka CLEMENCE STRAUSS)
Born: Sept. 27, 1886, New York. Died: Aug. 8, 1915, Hollywood, Calif. (tuberculosis). Screen actor.

STRAUSS, ROBERT
Born: Nov. 8, 1913, New York, N.Y. Died: Feb. 20, 1975, New York, N.Y. (complications from a stroke). Screen, stage and television actor. Nominated for 1953 Academy Award as Best Supporting Actor in "Stalag 17."

Appeared in: **1942** Native Land. **1951** Sailor Beware (aka At Sea with the Navy). **1952** Jumping Jacks; The Redhead from Wyoming. **1953** Here Come the Girls; Act of Love; Money from Home; Stalag 17 (stage and film versions). **1954** The Atomic Kid. **1955** The Seven Year Itch; The Man with the Golden Arm. **1956** Attack! **1958** Frontier Gun; I, Mobster. **1959** Inside the Mafia; Li'l Abner; 4D Man. **1960** Wake Me When It's Over; September Storm. **1961** Twenty Plus Two; The George Raft Story; The Last Time I Saw Archie; Dondi. **1962** Girls! Girls! Girls! **1963** The Thrill of It All; The Wheeler Dealers. **1964** Stage to Thunder Rock. **1965** The Family Jewels; Harlow; That Funny Feeling. **1966** Frankie and Johnny; Movie Star, American Style or—LSD, I Hate You. **1967** Fort Utah.

STRAUSS, WILLIAM H.
Born: June 13, 1885, New York, N.Y. Died: Aug. 5, 1943, Hollywood, Calif. (heart attack). Screen, stage, vaudeville actor and stage director.

Appeared in: **1920** North Wind's Malice. **1921** Magic Cup; The Barricade. **1922** Other Women's Clothes. **1923** Solomon in Society. **1925** Skinner's Dress Suit. **1926** Private Izzy Murphy; Law of the Snow Country; Millionaires. **1927** Ankles Preferred; For Ladies Only; Sally in Our Alley; The Shamrock and the Rose; The Rawhide Kid; Ladies at Ease; Ragtime; King of Kings; The Show Girl. **1928** So This Is Love; Abie's Irish Rose. **1929** Smiling Irish Eyes; Lucky Boy. **1930** Jazz Cinderella. **1934** Beloved; The House of Rothschild. **1938** Golden Boy.

STREET, DAVID
Born: 1917, Los Angeles, Calif. Died: Sept. 3, 1971, Los Angeles, Calif. Screen, radio, television actor, orchestra leader and singer. Divorced from actress Debra Paget.

Appeared in: **1949** Moonrise. **1950** Holiday Rhythm.

STREET, GEORGE A.
Born: 1869, Montreal, Canada. Died: May 30, 1956, Weston-Super-Mare, England. Screen actor and Wild West showman.

STREET, JULIAN
Born: 1880, Chicago, Ill. Died: Feb. 19, 1947, Lakeville, Conn. (cerebral hemorrhage). Novelist and screen actor.

Appeared in: **1913** Saved by Parcel Post.

STRICKLAND, HELEN
Born: 1863. Died: Jan. 1938, New York, N.Y. Stage and screen actress. Married to actor Robert Conness (dec. 1941).

Appeared in: **1915** Where is My Wandering Boy Tonight?; Clive's Manufactured Mother. **1923** The Steadfast Heart. **1935** The Scoundrel.

STRIKER, JOSEPH
Born: 1900, New York, N.Y. Died: Feb. 24, 1974, Livingston, N.J. Stage and screen actor.

Appeared in: **1920** The Bromley Case; Wall St. Mystery. **1921** Help Yourself; The Matrimonial Web. **1922** The Broadway Peacock; Silver Wings; Queen of the Moulin Rouge; Wildness of Youth; What Fools Men Are. **1923** The Steadfast Heart; The Woman in Chains. **1924** Painted People; I Am the Man. **1925** Scandal Proof; The Best People. **1927** Annie Laurie; The Climbers; The Cradle Snatchers; A Harp in Hock; The Wise Wife; King of Kings. **1928** Paradise; The Wrecker (US 1929). **1929** The House of Secrets.

STRONG, CARL E.
Born: 1907. Died: Jan. 14, 1965, Minneapolis, Minn. Screen, circus, television actor and rodeo rider.

STRONG, JAY
Born: 1896. Died: Dec. 1, 1953, New York, N.Y. Screen, vaudeville actor, stage producer, stage director, television writer, director and producer.

Appeared in: **1919** The Moonshine Trail.

STRONG, PORTER
Born: 1879, St. Joseph, Mo. Died: June 11, 1923, New York, N.Y. Stage and screen actor.

Appeared in: **1915** Safety First. **1916** The Little Life Guard; Martha's Vindication; For Sweet Charity; Ham Agrees with Sherman. **1917** Brainstorm; Even as Him and Her. **1919** A Romance of Happy Valley; I'll Get Him Yet. **1920** Way Down East; The Idol Dancer; Flying Pat. **1921** Dream Street; The Ghost in the Garret. **1922** One Exciting Night. **1923** The White Rose.

STRONG, STEVE
Died: July 14, 1975. Screen actor.

STRONGHEART
Born: 1916, Berlin, Germany. Died: June 1929, Los Angeles, Calif. Screen animal performer (German Shepherd). Mate of "Lady Jule."

Appeared in: 1921 The Silent Call (film debut). 1922 Brawn of the North. 1924 The Love Master. 1925 White Fang. 1926 North Star. 1927 The Return of Boston Blackie.

STROUD, CLARENCE
Born: 1907, Kaufman, Tex. Died: Aug. 15, 1973, Dallas, Tex. (Guillain-Barre syndrome). Screen, vaudeville, radio, television actor and circus performer. Appeared with his twin brother Claude in an act billed as the "Stroud Twins." Father of actor Don Stroud.

Appeared in: 1933 Ace of Aces.

STRYKER, GUSTAVE
Born: 1866, Chicago, Ill. Died: June 3, 1943, New York, N.Y. Screen, stage and radio actor.

STUART, DONALD
Born: 1898, England. Died: Feb. 22, 1944, Hollywood, Calif. (heart attack). Screen and radio actor.

Appeared in: 1926 Beau Geste; Bride of the Storm. 1927 The Lone Eagle; Marriage. 1928 The Cheer Leader; The Girl-Shy Cowboy; The Olympic Hero; Interference. 1929 The Silver King. 1930 Derelict. 1931 Devotion. 1932 In a Monastery Garden; The Man from Yesterday; Cynara. 1933 The Invisible Man; The Woman Accused. 1934 Dancing Man. 1935 First a Girl. 1941 A Yank in the R.A.F. 1942 Eagle Squadron; Destination Unknown. 1943 Immortal Sergeant. 1944 The Hour Before the Dawn; The Canterville Ghost.

STUART, IRIS
Born: 1903. Died: 1936. Screen actress. Was a Wampas Baby Star of 1927.

Appeared in: 1926 Stranded in Paris. 1927 Casey at the Bat; Wedding Bills; Children of Divorce.

STUART, JEAN (Margaret Leisenring)
Born: 1904. Died: Nov. 23, 1926, Hollywood, Calif. (injuries from a fall from a horse). Screen actress.

Appeared in: 1926 The Campus Flirt.

STUART, NICK (Nicholas Pratza)
Born: Apr. 10, 1904, Rumania. Died: Apr. 7, 1973, Biloxi, Miss. (cancer). Screen actor and bandleader. Divorced from actress Sue Carol. Married to Martha Burnett.

Appeared in: 1927 The High School Hero; Cradle Snatchers. 1928 The News Parade; The River Pirate; Why Sailors Go Wrong. 1929 Girls Gone Wild; Why Leave Home; Gold Diggers of Broadway; Happy Days; Joy Street. 1930 Swing High; The Fourth Alarm; Honeymoon Zeppelin; plus the following shorts: Radio Kisses; Hello Television; Goodbye Legs; Campus Crushes; Grandma's Girl. 1931 Sheer Luck; Mystery Train; Sundown Trail. 1933 Secret Sinners; Police Call. 1934 Demon for Trouble. 1935 Secrets of Chinatown. 1936 Rio Grande Romance; Underworld Terror; Put on the Spot. 1937 Blake of Scotland Yard (serial). 1938 An RKO short. 1952 Blackhawk (serial); King of the Congo (serial). 1953 The Great Adventures of Captain Kidd (serial); The Lost Planet (serial); Killer Ape. 1957 High Tide at Noon. 1958 High Hell. 1959 The Sheriff of Fractured Jaw. 1962 We Joined the Navy; The Longest Day. 1963 It's a Mad, Mad, Mad, Mad World. 1966 This Property is Condemned.

STUART, RALPH R.
Born: 1890. Died: Nov. 4, 1952, New York, N.Y. Screen, stage actor and stage director.

Appeared in: 1917 The Mystery of the Double Cross (serial).

STUBBS, HARRY (Harry Oakes Stubbs)
Born: Sept. 7, 1874, England. Died: Mar. 9, 1950, Woodland Hills, Calif. (heart attack). Screen, stage actor, dialogue director and screenwriter.

Appeared in: 1929 Alibi (film debut); The Locked Door; Three Live Ghosts. 1930 Abraham Lincoln; The Bad One; Ladies Must Play; The Truth about Youth; Night Ride. 1931 Gang Buster; Stepping Out; Millie; Fanny Foley Herself; Her Majesty Love. 1932 The Man Who Played God. 1933 The Invisible Man; Mind Reader; When Strangers Marry. 1934 Now and Forever. 1935 Spanish Cape Mystery. 1936 Sutter's Gold; The Girl from Mandalay; The Man I Marry. 1937 On the Avenue; London by Night; Love and Hisses. 1938 In Old Chicago; Dr. Rhythm; Peck's Bad Boy with the Circus; I Stand Accused; Block-heads. 1940 Adventure in Diamonds; Zanzibar; The Invisible Man Returns; The Mummy's Hand. 1941 The Singing Hill; Burma Convoy; The Wolf Man. 1943 Frankenstein Meets the Wolf Man. 1944 The Invisible Man's Revenge.

STURGIS, EDDIE (Josef Edwin Sturgis)
Born: Oct. 22, 1881, Washington, D.C. Died: Dec. 13, 1947, Los Angeles, Calif. (heart disease). Screen actor.

Appeared in: 1921 The Chicken in the Case; Man and Woman. 1923 Legally Dead; Ponjola. 1925 Seven Keys to Baldpate. 1927 Let It Rain; Wolf's Clothing; After Midnight. 1928 The Big City; Fazil; Square Crooks. 1930 Shooting Straight; The Squealer; Outside the Law. 1931 Oh! Oh! Cleopatra (short). 1935 Red Hot Tires; Mississippi.

SUBJECT, EVELYN
Died: Apr. 22, 1975, Temple City, Calif. Stage and screen actress. Appeared in early Vitagraph and Essanay films.

SUDLOW, JOAN
Born: 1892. Died: Feb. 1, 1970, Hollywood, Calif. (result of fall). Screen, stage and television actress.

Appeared in: 1951 Queen for a Day. 1952 Pride of St. Louis. 1966 A Fine Madness.

SUES, LEONARD
Born: 1921. Died: Oct. 24, 1971, Los Angeles, Calif. (cancer). Screen actor and musical director.

Appeared in: 1939 What a Life. 1949 Manhattan Angel.

SULLAVAN, MARGARET (Margaret Brooke Sullavan)
Born: May 16, 1911, Norfolk, Va. Died: Jan. 1, 1960, New Haven, Conn. (suicide—sleeping pills). Screen, stage and television actress. Mother of actress Brooke Hayward.

Appeared in: 1933 Only Yesterday. 1934 Little Man, What Now? 1935 The Good Fairy; So Red the Rose. 1936 Next Time We Love; The Moon's Our Home; I Love a Soldier. 1938 Three Comrades; The Shopworn Angel; The Shining Hour. 1939 When Tomorrow Comes. 1940 The Shop Around the Corner; The Mortal Storm. 1941 So Ends Our Night; Back Street; Appointment for Love. 1944 Cry Havoc. 1950 No Sad Songs for Me.

SULLIVAN, BRIAN (Harry Joseph Sullivan)
Born: Aug. 9, 1919, Oakland, Calif. Died: June 17, 1969, Lake Geneva, Switzerland. Screen, stage actor and opera performer.

Appeared in: 1945 This Man's Navy. 1946 Courage of Lassie.

SULLIVAN, ED (Edward Vincent Sullivan)
Born: Sept. 28, 1902, New York, N.Y. Died: Oct. 13, 1974, New York, N.Y. (cancer). Columnist, television, screen, vaudeville, radio actor, screenwriter and author.

Appeared in: 1933 Mr. Broadway. 1939 Big Town Czar. 1958 Senior Prom. 1963 Bye Bye Birdie. 1964 The Patsy. 1965 The Singing Nun. 1966 Last of the Secret Agents. 1970 The Phynx; What's Happening.

SULLIVAN, ELLIOTT
Born: 1908. Died: June 2, 1974, Los Angeles, Calif. (heart attack). Screen, stage and television actor.

Appeared in: 1937 They Won't Forget. 1938 Accidents Will Happen; Racket Busters; Gangs of New York; Next Time I Marry; Fury Below. 1939 King of the Underworld; I Am Not Afraid; The Spellbinder; Smashing the Money Ring; Angels Wash Their Faces. 1940 The Saint's Double Trouble; Millionaires in Prison; The Man Who Talked Too Much; Calling all Husbands. 1942 Man with Two Lives; Wild Bill Hickok Rides; Yankee Doodle Dandy. 1943 Action in the North Atlantic. 1944 Winged Victory. 1949 The Lady Gambles. 1950 Guilty Bystander. 1953 Taxi. 1956 Crowded Paradise. 1969 The Sergeant; On Her Majesty's Secret Service. 1970 Tropic of Cancer.

SULLIVAN, FRANCIS LOFTUS
Born: Jan. 6, 1903, London, England. Died: Nov. 19, 1956, New York, N.Y. Screen, stage and television actor.

Appeared in: 1932 The Missing Rembrandt; The Chinese Puzzle; When London Sleeps. 1933 F.P.1; The Stickpin; Called Back; The Fire Raisers; The Right to Live; The Wandering Jew (US 1935). 1934 Red Wagon (US 1935); Princess Charming (US 1935); The Return of Bulldog Drummond; Chu Chin Chow; What Happened Then?; Great Expectations; The Warren Case; Cheating Cheaters. 1935 The Mystery of Edwin Drood; Her Last Affaire. 1936 A Woman Alone (aka Two Who Dared—US 1937); Sabotage (aka The Woman Alone—US 1937); Spy of Napoleon (US 1939); The Limping Man; The Interrupted Honeymoon. 1937 Fine Feathers; Action for Slander (US 1938); Non-Stop New York; 21 Days (aka 21 Days Together—US 1940 and The First and the Last); Dinner at the Ritz. 1938 The Gables Mystery; Kate Plus Ten; Climbing High (US 1939); The Citadel; The Ware Case; The Drum (aka Drums—US). 1939 The Four Just Men (aka The Secret Four—US 1940); Young Man's Fancy (US 1943). 1941 Pimpernel Smith (aka Mister V—US 1942). 1942 The Foreman Went to France (aka Somewhere in France—US 1943); The Day Will Dawn (aka The Avengers—US); Lady from Lisbon. 1943 The Butler's Dilemma. 1944 Fiddlers Three. 1946 Caesar and Cleopatra; The

Laughing Lady (US 1950); Great Expectations (US 1947 and 1934 version); The Man Within (aka The Smugglers—US 1948). **1947** Take My Life (US 1948). **1948** Broken Journey; The Winslow Boy (US 1950); Oliver Twist (US 1951); Joan of Arc. **1949** Christopher Columbus; The Red Danube. **1950** Night and the City. **1951** My Favorite Spy; Behave Yourself. **1952** Caribbean. **1953** Plunder of the Sun; Sangaree. **1954** Drums of Tahiti. **1955** Hell's Island; The Prodigal.

SULLIVAN, FREDERICK R. "FRED"
Born: 1872, London, England. Died: July 24, 1937, Los Angeles, Calif. (heart trouble). Stage and screen actor.

Appeared in: **1922** Tailor-Made Man. **1923** The Courtship of Miles Standish; Face on the Barroom Floor. **1925** Winds of Chance; Beggar on Horseback. **1929** The Black Watch. **1930** Around the Corner; Prince of Diamonds. **1931** Murder by the Clock. **1932** If I Had a Million. **1933** Blind Adventure; Duck Soup. **1934** You're Telling Me. **1935** All the King's Horses.

SULLIVAN, JAMES E.
Born: 1864. Died: June 1, 1931. Stage and screen actor.

Appeared in: **1925** The Pinch Hitter.

SULLIVAN, JOE
Born: 1910. Died: Oct. 13, 1971, San Francisco, Calif. Pianist, screen and radio actor. Appeared with Red Nichols' band and others.

SULLIVAN, JOHN MAURICE
Born: 1876. Died: Mar. 8, 1949, Hollywood, Calif. Screen and stage actor. Entered films in 1930.

Appeared in: **1930** Today. **1931** Silence. **1932** Strangers in Love; The Trial of Vivienne Ware; Down to Earth. **1933** Big Executive. **1934** You're Telling Me; Mystery Liner. **1936** Walking on Air. **1938** The Buccaneer. **1946** Blue Skies.

SULLY, FRANK (Frank Sullivan)
Born: 1908. Died: Dec. 17, 1975, Woodland Hills, Calif. Screen, stage, vaudeville and television actor.

Appeared in: **1935** Mary Burns—Fugitive; Fighting Youth. **1937** Daughter of Shanghai; High, Wide and Handsome; Life Begins at College. **1938** Hold that Co-Ed; Thanks for Everything. **1939** Some Like it Hot. **1940** The Grapes of Wrath; The Night of Nights; Lillian Russell; The Doctor Takes a Wife; Cross-Country Romance; Young People; The Return of Frank James; Yesterday's Heroes; Escape to Glory (aka Submarine Zone); Dr. Kildare's Crisis. **1941** A Girl, A Guy and a Gob; Private Nurse; Mountain Moonlight; Let's Go Collegiate. **1942** Two Yanks in Trinidad; Parachute Nurse; My Sister Eileen; Rings on Her Fingers; Sleepytime Gal; The Boogie Man Will Get You; All Through the Night; Inside the Law. **1943** The More the Merrier; Renegades; They Got Me Covered; Thousands Cheer; Dangerous Blondes; Two Senoritas from Chicago. **1944** Secret Command; Two Girls and a Sailor; The Ghost that Walks Alone. **1945** Along Came Jones; Boston Blackie Booked on Suspicion; Boston Blackie's Rendezvous. **1946** Crime Doctor's Man Hunt; A Close Call for Boston Blackie; One Way to Love; Out of the Depths; Talk About a Lady; Throw a Saddle on a Star; The Gentleman Misbehaves; The Phantom Thief; Renegades; It's Great to be Young; Dangerous Business; Boston Blackie and the Law. **1947** South of the Chisholm Trail; Wild Harvest. **1948** Blondie's Reward; Trapped by Boston Blackie. **1949** Boston Blackie's Chinese Venture; Joe Palooka in the Counterpunch. **1950** Bodyhold; Beauty on Parade; Rookie Fireman; Blondie's Hero; Joe Palooka Meets Humphrey; Square Dance Katy; Killer Shark; Joe Palooka in Humphrey Takes a Chance. **1952** No Room for the Groom; With a Song in My Heart; Night Stage to Galveston; Prairie Round-up; Man in the Saddle. **1953** Northern Patrol; Take Me to Town; Pardon My Backfire (short). **1954** Silver Lode; Battle of Rogue River. **1955** The Spoilers; Fling in the Ring (short); Naked Street; The Prodigal; Hell's Island. **1956** Flagpole Sitters (short); You Can't Run Away From It. **1957** Gun A-Poppin (short); The Buckskin Lady; Rockabilly Baby. **1963** Bye Bye Birdie. **1968** Funny Girl.

SUMMERS, ANN
Born: 1920. Died: Jan. 14, 1974, Los Angeles, Calif. Screen, stage and television actress. Married to screenwriter Robert Mann.

Appeared in: **1942** The following shorts: Cooks and Crooks; Dear! Dear!; Pretty Dolly. **1943** Radio Runaround (short); The Avenging Rider; Fighting Frontier. **1970** Glass Houses.

SUMMERS, DOROTHY
Born: England. Died: Jan. 13, 1964, England. Screen actress.

SUMMERVILLE, AMELIA
Born: 1863. Died: Jan. 1934, New York, N.Y. Stage and screen actress.

Appeared in: **1925** Romola. **1926** The Great Deception.

SUMMERVILLE, SLIM (George J. Summerville)
Born: 1896, Albuquerque, N.M. Died: Jan. 6, 1946, Laguna Beach, Calif. (stroke). Screen actor and film director.

Appeared in: **1914** The Knock-Out; Mabel's Busy Day; A Rowboat Romance; Laughing Gas; Gentlemen of Nerve (aka Some Nerve); Cursed by His Beauty; Tillie's Punctured Romance. **1915** Her Winning Punch; The Home Breakers (aka Other People's Wives); Caught in the Act; Gussle's Day of Rest; Their Social Splash; Those College Girls (aka His Bitter Half); The Great Vacuum Robbery; Her Painted Hero; A Game Old Knight. **1916** Cinders of Love; The Winning Punch; Bucking Society (short); Her Busted Trust; The Three Slims; His Bread and Butter. **1917** Villa of the Movies; Her Fame and Shame; A Dog Catcher's Love; His Precious Life; A Pullman Bride. **1918** The Beloved Rogue. **1921** Skirts. **1926** The Texas Streak. **1927** The Beloved Rogue (and 1918 version); The Denver Dude; Painted Ponies; Hey, Hey, Cowboy; The Wreck of the Hesperus. **1928** The Chinese Parrot; Riding for Fame. **1929** King of the Rodeo; Strong Boy; Shannons of Broadway; Tiger Rose; The Last Warning. **1930** See America Thirst; Free Love; Her Man; The Spoilers; One Hysterical Night; Troopers Three; Under Montana Skies; All Quiet on the Western Front; King of Jazz; Little Accident; Hello Russia; We! We! Marie!; Parlez Vous. **1931** Bad Sisters; The Front Page; Arabian Knights; Bless the Ladies; First to Fight; Hotter Than Haiti; Let's Play; Parisian Gaieties; Royal Bluff; Sargie's Playmates; Here's Luck; Reckless Living; Heaven on Earth. **1932** Racing Youth; Unexpected Father; Eyes Have It; In the Bag; Kid Glove Kisses; Meet the Princess; Sea Soldier's Sweeties; Tom Brown of Culver; Air Mail. **1932-33** Universal shorts. **1933** Out All Night; They Just Had to Get Married; Early to Bed; Her First Mate; Love, Honor and Oh, Baby! **1934** Horse Play; The Love Birds; Their Big Moment. **1935** Life Begins at 40; The Farmer Takes a Wife; Way down East. **1936** Captain January; The Country Doctor; Pepper; White Fang; Reunion; Can This Be Dixie? **1937** Off to the Races; Love Is News; Fifty Roads to Town; The Road Back; Five of a Kind. **1939** Charlie Chan in Reno. **1940** Anne of Windy Poplars; Gold Rush Maisie. **1941** Miss Polly; Western Union; Highway West; Tobacco Road. **1942** Niagara Falls; Jesse James; The Spoilers. **1944** I'm from Arkansas; Bride by Mistake. **1946** The Hoodlum Saint.

SUMNER, CORINNE HEATH. *See* CORINNE HEATH SUMNER ROSS

SUMNER, VERLYN
Born: June 7, 1897, Lakefield, Minn. Died: Apr. 10, 1935, Bremerton, Wash. Stage and screen actress.

Appeared in: **1928** Speedy; The Toilers; Excess Baggage.

SUNDERLAND, NAN
Died: Nov. 23, 1973, New York, N.Y. Stage and screen actress. Married to actor Walter Huston (dec. 1950).

Appeared in: **1933** Sweepings. **1947** Unconquered.

SUNDHOLM, WILLIAM "BILL"
Died: Feb. 28, 1971. Screen actor.

Appeared in: **1930** City Girl. **1932** The Last Man. **1949** Loaded Pistols.

SUNDMARK, BETTY. *See* ELIZABETH S. SHANNON

SUNSHINE, "BABY" (Pauline Flood)
Born: Dec. 1, 1915, Calif. Died: Oct. 19, 1917, Los Angeles, Calif. (hit by truck). Known as "Tiniest Star in Films."

SUNSHINE, MARION
Born: 1897. Died: Jan. 25, 1963, New York, N.Y. Screen, stage, vaudeville actress and songwriter.

Appeared in: **1908** The Tavern Keeper's Daughter; The Red Girl. **1909** Her First Biscuits. **1910** In the Season of Buds; Sunshine Sue; Three Sisters; A Decree of Destiny. **1911** The Rose of Kentucky; The Stuff Heroes Are Made Of; Dan the Dandy. **1912** Heredity. **1944** I'm from Arkansas.

SUPPLEE, ESTHER RITTER. *See* ESTHER RITTER

SURATT, VALESKA
Born: 1882, Terre Haute, Ind. Died: July 3, 1962. Screen, stage and vaudeville actress.

Appeared in: **1915** The Immigrant; Soul of Broadway. **1916** Jealousy. **1917** The Victim; She; The Slave; Wife Number Two; The New York Peacock.

SUSANN, JACQUELINE
Born: 1921, Philadelphia, Pa. Died: Sept. 21, 1974, New York, N.Y. (cancer). Screen, stage actress and novelist.

Appeared in: **1967** Valley of the Dolls.

SUSSENGUTH, WALTHER
Born: 1900, Germany. Died: May 1964, Berlin, Germany. Stage and screen actor.

Appeared in: **1935** Der Schimmelreiter (The Rider of the White Horse).

SUTHERLAND, A. EDWARD "EDDIE" (Albert Edward Sutherland)

Born: Jan. 5, 1895, London, England. Died: Dec. 31, 1973, Palm Springs, Calif. Screen, stage actor, film and television director. Son of stage actress Julia Ring (dec.). Divorced from actress Louise Brooks and later married to Edwina Sutherland. Entered films in 1915.

Appeared in: **1916** Love Under Cover; The Telephone Belle; Won by a Foot; Heart Strategy. **1917** Innocent Sinners; The Girl and the Ring; His Foothill Folly; Caught in the End; A Fallen Star; A Toy of Fate; His Cool Nerve; His Saving Grace; Dad's Downfall. **1919** The Viled Adventure. **1920** The Sea Wolf; The Round Up; All of a Sudden Peggy; Conrad in Quest of His Youth. **1921** The Dollar-A-Year Man; The Light in the Clearing; The Witching Hour; Everything for Sale; Just Outside the Door. **1922** The Loaded Door; Elope if You Must; Nancy from Nowhere; Second Hand Rose. **1923** The Woman He Loved; Girl from the West. **1924** Abraham Lincoln. **1929** The Dance of Life.

SUTHERLAND, DICK

Born: 1882, Benton, Ky. Died: Feb. 3, 1934, Hollywood, Calif. Screen, stage and vaudeville actor.

Appeared in: **1921** The Magnificent Brute; God's Gold; Sailor-Made Man. **1922** Gas, Oil and Water; The Deuce of Spades; Rags to Riches; Grandma's Boy. **1923** Hell's Hole; The Rip-Tide; Quicksands; The Shriek of Araby; His Last Race; Masters of Men. **1924** The Dangerous Blonde; The Red Lily; The Tornado; The Mask of Lopez; Battling Mason; Defying the Law; Fighter's Paradise. **1925** The Fighting Demon; Flying Fool; With This Ring; Jimmie's Millions; The Road to Yesterday. **1926** Lloyd Hamilton Comedies; Broken Hearts of Hollywood; Don Juan; The Jazz Girl. **1927** The Claw; Uncle Tom's Cabin; The Beloved Rogue. **1928** Riders of the Dark. **1929** China Slaver; The Hoose Gow (short).

SUTHERLAND, JOHN

Born: 1845, England. Died: Aug. 31, 1921, Brooklyn, N.Y. Stage and screen actor.

Appeared in: **1918** The Lie; Uncle Tom's Cabin; Dodging a Million. **1919** The Silver King; Test of Honor; The Imp. **1920** His House in Order. **1921** Her Lord and Master.

SUTHERLAND, VICTOR

Born: 1889. Died: Aug. 29, 1968, Los Angeles, Calif. Screen, stage and television actor. Divorced from screen actress Pearl White (dec. 1938). Married to actress Linda Barrett.

Appeared in: **1923** The Valley of Lost Souls. **1924** The Love Bandit. **1950** The Sleeping City. **1951** The Whistle at Eaton Falls. **1952** Lone Star; The Pride of St. Louis; The Captive City. **1953** Powder River; Donovan's Brain.

SUTTON, FRANK

Born: 1923, Clarksville, Tenn. Died: June 28, 1974, Shreveport, La. (heart attack). Screen, stage, radio and television actor.

Appeared in: **1955** Marty. **1957** Four Boys and a Gun. **1961** Town Without Pity. **1965** The Satan Bug.

SUTTON, JOHN

Born: Oct. 22, 1908, Rawalpindi, India. Died: 1963. Screen and stage actor.

Appeared in: **1937** Bulldog Drummond's Revenge; Bulldog Drummond Comes Back. **1938** Adventures of Robin Hood; The Blonde Cheat; Booloo; Four Men and a Prayer. **1939** Tower of London; Arrest Bulldog Drummond; Susannah of the Mounties; Bulldog Drummond's Bride; Charlie McCarthy, Detective; Zaza; The Private Lives of Elizabeth and Essex. **1940** Christable Caine; Sandy Is a Lady; I Can't Give You Anything but Love, Baby; South of Karanga; Murder over New York; Hudson Bay; The Invisible Man Returns. **1941** A Very Young Lady; Moon over Her Shoulder; A Yank in the RAF. **1942** Ten Gentlemen from West Point; My Gal Sal; Thunder Birds. **1943** Tonight We Raid Calais. **1944** Jane Eyre; The Hour before the Dawn. **1946** Claudia and David. **1947** Captain from Castile. **1948** The Three Musketeers; The Counterfeiters; Mickey. **1949** The Bride of Vengeance; Bagdad; The Fan. **1950** The Second Face. **1951** The Second Woman; Payment on Demand. **1952** David and Bathsheba; Thief of Damascus; Captain Pirate; The Golden Hawk; My Cousin Rachel; The Lady in the Iron Mask. **1953** Sangaree; East of Sumatra. **1956** The Amazon Trader; Death of a Scoundrel. **1959** The Bat; The Return of the Fly; Beloved Infidel. **1961** The Canadians. **1962** Marizinia. **1964** Of Human Bondage. **1967** The Drums of Tabu; The Lost Safari.

SUTTON, PAUL

Born: 1912. Died: Jan. 31, 1970, Ferndale, Mich. (muscular dystrophy). Screen, radio and television actor.

Appeared in: **1938** The Spy Ring; Air Devils; Bar 20 Justice; In Old Mexico; Shadows Over Shanghai. **1939** Balalaika; The Girl and the Gambler. **1940** Little Old New York. **1941** Ride On, Vaquero; Wild Geese Calling. **1942** Sundown Jim; In Old California; Riders of the Northland.

SUTTON, WILLIAM

Born: 1877. Died: Sept. 10, 1955, West Los Angeles, Calif. Screen, stage actor and magician. Known as the "Great Fontonelle." Appeared in silents.

SVERDLIN, LEV N.

Born: 1902, Russia. Died: Aug. 30, 1969, Moscow, Russia. Screen actor.

Appeared in: **1938** The Defense of Volotchayevsk. **1942** Guerrilla Brigade. **1944** Adventures in Bokhara. **1945** Marriage; Wait for Me. **1946** Great Days; Days and Nights. **1951** Far from Moscow.

SWAIN, MACK

Born: Feb. 16, 1876, Salt Lake City, Utah. Died: Aug. 25, 1935, Tacoma, Wash. Stage and screen actor.

Appeared in: **1914** Caught in a Cabaret (aka The Jazz Waiter); Caught in the Rain; A Busy Day; The Fatal Mallet; The Knock-Out (aka The Pugilist); A Gambling Rube; A Missing Bride; Mabel's Married Life (aka The Squarehead); A Rowboat Romance; Laughing Gas; Gentlemen of Nerve (aka Some Nerve); His Musical Career; His Trysting Place; The Sea Nymphs (aka His Diving Beauty); Among the Mourners; Leading Lizzie Astray; Getting Acquainted; Other People's Business; His Prehistoric Past; Ambrose's First Falsehood; A Dark Lover's Play. **1915** Love, Speed and Thrills; The Home Breakers (aka Other People's Wives); Ye Olden Grafter; Ambrose's Sour Grapes; Willful Ambrose; From Patches to Plenty; Ambrose's Little Hatchet; Ambrose's Fury; Ambrose's Lofty Perch; Ambrose's Nasty Temper; A Human Hound's Triumph; Our Daredevil Chief; Mabel Lost and Won; When Ambrose Dared Walrus; The Battle of Ambrose and Walrus. **1915** Saved by Wireless; The Best of Enemies. **1916** A Movie Star; Love Will Conquer; His Auto Ruination; By Stork Delivery; His Bitter Pill; His Wild Oats; Madcap Ambrose; Vampire Ambrose; Ambrose's Cup of Woe; Ambrose's Rapid Rise; Safety First Ambrose (working title Sheriff Ambrose); A Modern Enoch Arden. **1917** His Naughty Thought; Thirst (rereleased 1923); Lost—A Cook; A Pullman Bride. **1918** "Poppy" series. **1919** Ambrose's Day Off. **1922** The Pilgrim. **1925** The Gold Rush. **1926** Hands Up; Sea Horses; Kiki; Footloose Widows; The Nervous Wreck; Her Big Night; Honesty—the Best Policy; The Torrent; Whispering Wires. **1927** Becky; Finnegan's Ball; The Shamrock and the Rose; The Tired Business Man; The Beloved Rogue; See You in Jail; Mockery; My Best Girl. **1928** Caught in the Fog; Gentlemen Prefer Blondes; A Texas Steer; The Last Warning; Tillie's Punctured Romance; The Cohens and the Kellys. **1929** Marianne; The Cohens and the Kellys in Atlantic City. **1930** Redemption; The Sea Bat; The Locked Door. **1931** Stout Hearts and Willing Hands; Finn and Hattie. **1932** Midnight Patrol. **1932-33** Paramount shorts. **1960** When Comedy Was King (documentary).

SWAN, PAUL

Born: 1884. Died: Feb. 1, 1972, Bedford Hills, N.Y. Screen, stage actor, dancer, painter and sculptor.

Appeared in: **1916** Diana the Huntress. **1923** The Ten Commandments. **1965** Camp. **1968** The Illiac Passion.

SWANWICK, PETER

Born: 1912. Died: Nov. 14, 1968, London, England. Screen, stage actor and singer.

Appeared No in: **1951** The African Queen; Old Mother Riley's Jungle Treasure. **1952** No Haunt for a Gentleman; Circumstantial Evidence; Lady in the Fog (aka Scotland Yard Inspector—US). **1953** Albert RN (aka Break to Freedom—US 1955). **1956** Assignment Redhead (aka Million Dollar Manhunt—US 1962). **1957** The Big Chance; Kill Me Tomorrow (US 1958); You Pay Your Money. **1958** Murder Reported (US 1960); The Two-Headed Spy (US 1959). **1959** Life in Danger (US 1964). **1960** Circus of Horrors. **1961** The Invasion Quartet; The Trunk. **1969** The Looking Glass War (US 1970).

SWARTHOUT, GLADYS

Born: Dec. 25, 1904, Deepwater, Mo. Died: July 7, 1969, Florence, Italy. Opera, screen, stage and radio actress.

Appeared in: **1936** Rose of the Rancho; Give Us This Night. **1937** Champagne Waltz. **1938** Romance in the Dark. **1939** Ambush.

SWARTS, SARA

Born: 1899. Died: Mar. 31, 1949, Woodland Hills, Calif. Screen actress. Entered films approx. 1918.

SWEENEY, EDWARD C.

Born: 1906. Died: Aug. 14, 1967, Miami, Fla. Film producer, lecturer, photographer and founder of the "Explorers Club". He produced and appeared in eleven travel-lecture films.

SWEENEY, FRED C.

Born: 1894. Died: Dec. 10, 1954, Sylmar, Calif. (pulmonary tuberculosis). Screen, stage and vaudeville actor. Appeared in vaudeville team of "Daffy and Sweeney."

SWEENEY, JACK

Born: 1889. Died: Apr. 12, 1950, Hollywood, Calif. Screen actor. Appeared in Sennett films in 1916.

SWEENEY, JOSEPH

Died: Dec. 1963, New York, N.Y. Stage and screen actor.

Appeared in: 1936 Soak the Rich. 1956 The Man in the Gray Flannel Suit; The Fastest Gun Alive. 1957 Twelve Angry Men.

SWEET, HARRY

Born: 1901, Colo. Died: June 18, 1933, near Big Bear, Calif. (plane crash). Screen actor, film director and screenwriter.

Appeared in: 1926 Fascinating Youth. 1928 Homesick. 1930 Hit the Deck; True to the Navy; Her Man. 1932 Carnival Boat.

SWEET, TOM

Born: 1933. Died: Nov. 19, 1967, High Sierras, Calif. (plane crash). Screen, television actor and stuntman. Was the "Galloping White Knight" on television commercials.

Appeared in: 1961 Sniper's Ridge.

SWENSON, ALFRED G.

Born: 1883, Salt Lake City, Utah. Died: Mar. 28, 1941, Staten Island, N.Y. (heart attack). Screen, stage and radio actor.

Appeared in: 1929 The Great Power.

SWICKARD, CHARLES F.

Born: 1861. Died: May 12, 1929, Fresno, Calif. Screen actor and film director. Brother of actor Joseph Swickard (dec. 1940).

SWICKARD, JOSEPH

Born: 1866, Coblenz, Germany. Died: Feb. 29, 1940, Hollywood, Calif. Stage and screen actor. Brother of actor Charles Swickard (dec. 1929). Entered films in 1912.

Appeared in: 1914 A Rowboat Romance; Laughing Gas; The Plumber. 1915 Love, Loot and Crash; A Home Breaking Hound; The Best of Enemies. 1916 Love Will Conquer; The Village Vampire (working title The Great Leap); His Wild Oats; Haystacks and Steeples; Ambrose's Cup of Woe. 1917 Tale of Two Cities. 1921 Beach of Dreams; No Woman Knows; Opened Shutters; Sowing the Wind. 1921 Serenade; Four Horsemen of the Apocalypse; Cheated Hearts; Who Am I? 1922 The Adventures of Robinson Crusoe (serial); Across the Dead Line; Another Man's Shoes; My American Wife; The Golden Gift; Pawned; The Storm; The Young Rajah. 1923 Mr. Billings Spends His Dime; A Prince of a King; Bavu; Maytime; The Cricket on the Hearth; Daughters of the Rich; The Eternal Struggle; Forgive and Forget; Mothers-in-Law. 1924 The Age of Desire; Dante's Inferno; Men; Pal O'Mine; The Shadow of the East; A Boy of Flanders; Defying the Law; Poisoned Paradise; Untamed Youth; North of Nevada. 1925 Off the Highway; The Verdict; She Wolves; The Wizard of Oz; Easy Money; The Mysterious Stranger; Playing with Souls; Northern Code; Fifth Avenue Models; The Keeper of the Bees; The Sign of the Cactus. 1926 Officer Jim; The Unknown Cavalier; The Border Whirlwind; Three Pals; Senor Daredevil; Stop, Look and Listen; Desert Gold; Devil's Dice; Don Juan; The High Flyer; The Night Patrol; Kentucky Handicap; Whispering Canyon. 1927 One Increasing Purpose; Old San Francisco; Senorita; Time to Love; Get Your Man; The Golden Stallion (serial); Compassion; False Morals; King of Kings. 1928 Eagle of the Night (serial); Comrades; Sharp Shooters; Turn Back the Hours. 1929 Bachelor's Club; Dark Skies; Phantoms of the North; Devil's Chaplain; The Eternal Woman; The Veiled Woman; Frozen River; Times Square; Street Corners. 1930 Song of the Caballero; Mamba; Phantom of the Desert. 1934 Hello, Prosperity (short); Beloved; Return of Chandu; Cross Streets. 1935 A Dog of Flanders; The Lost City (serial); The Crusades; Custer's Last Stand (serial). 1936 The Millionaire Kid; Caryl of the Mountains; Boss Rider of Gun Creek. 1937 The Girl Said No; Sandflow. 1938 You Can't Take It with You. 1939 Mexicali Rose.

SWIMMER, BOB

Died: June 26, 1971. Screen actor.

SWINLEY, ION

Born: 1892, England. Died: Sept. 16, 1937, London, England. Screen, stage actor and playwright.

Appeared in: 1920 Bleak House. 1929 The Unwritten Law.

SWITZER, CARL "ALFALFA"

Born: 1926. Died: Jan. 21, 1959, Sepulveda, Calif. (shot). Screen and television actor.

Appeared in: 1935 The following shorts: Southern Exposure; Beginner's Luck; Teacher's Beau; Sprucin' Up; Little Papa; Little Sinner; Our Gang Follies of 1936. 1936 Easy to Take; Right in Your Lap; Kelly the Second; Pick a Star; Too Many Parents; General Spanky; plus the following shorts: Life Hesitates at 40; Pinch Singer; Divot Diggers; The Lucky Corner; Second Childhood; Arbor

Day; Bored of Education; Two Too Young; Pay as You Exit; Spooky Hooky. 1937 Wild and Woolly; plus the following shorts: Reunion in Rhythm; Glove Taps; Three Smart Boys; Hearts are Trumps; Rushin' Ballet; Roamin' Holiday; Night'n Gales; Fishy Tales; Framing Youth; Pigskin Palooka; Mail and Female; Our Gang Follies of 1938. 1938 Scandal Street; plus the following shorts: Canned Fishing; Bear Facts; Three Men in a Tub; Came the Brawn; Feed 'Em and Weep; The Awful Tooth; Hide and Shriek; The Little Ranger; Party Fever; Aladdin's Lantern; Men in Fright; Football Romeo; Practical Jokers. 1939 The following shorts: Alfalfa's Aunt; Tiny Troubles; Duel Personalities; Clown Princes; Cousin Wilbur; Joy Scouts; Dog Daze; Auto Antics; Captain Spanky's Show Boat; Dad for a Day; Time Out for Lessons. 1940 The New Pupil; I Love You Again; Barnyard Follies; plus the following shorts: Alfalfa's Double; The Big Premiere; All about Hash; The New Pupil; Bubbling Trouble; Good Bad Guys; Waldo's Last Stand; Goin' Fishin'; Kiddie Cure. 1941 Reg'lar Fellers. 1942 Johnny Doughboy; Henry and Dizzy; The War against Mrs. Hadley; Mrs. Wiggs of the Cabbage Patch; My Favorite Blonde. 1943 Shantytown. 1944 Rosie the Riveter; The Great Mike; Going My Way. 1946 The Gas House Kids; Courage of Lassie. 1947 The Gas House Kids Go West; The Gas House Kids in Hollywood. 1948 On Our Merry Way; State of the Union; Big Town Scandal; A Letter to Three Wives. 1950 Redwood Forest Trail. 1951 Two Dollar Bettor. 1952 I Dream of Jeanie; Pat and Mike. 1953 Island in the Sky. 1954 The High and the Mighty; Track of the Cat; This Is My Love. 1956 Between Heaven and Hell; Dig That Uranium. 1957 Motorcycle Game. 1958 The Defiant Ones.

SWOGER, HARRY (Harry Edward Swoger)

Born: Mar. 6, 1919, Ohio. Died: June 14, 1970, Van Nuys, Calif. Screen actor.

Appeared in: 1961 Angel Baby. 1964 Robin and the Seven Hoods.

SWOR, BERT

Born: 1878, Paris, Tenn. Died: Nov. 30, 1943, Tulsa, Okla. Screen, stage, vaudeville and minstrel actor. Appeared in vaudeville and films for a short time as Moran in "Moran and Mack" comedy team, usually referred to as the "Two Black Crows." Brother of actor John Swor (dec. 1965).

Appeared in: 1928 Ducks and Deducts (short); A Colorful Sermon (short). 1929 Why Bring That Up; plus the following shorts: The Golfers; A Hollywood Star; The New Halfback; Uppercut O'Brien. 1930 Anybody's War (with Mack).

SWOR, JOHN

Born: Apr. 7, 1883, Paris, Tenn. Died: July 15, 1965, Dallas, Tex. Screen, vaudeville, television and minstrel actor. Appeared for a time in vaudeville team "Moran and Mack" as Moran, usually referred to as the "Two Black Crows." Did not appear in films as part of team. Brother of actor Bert Swor (dec. 1943).

Appeared in: 1930 Up the River. 1931 Charlie Chan Carries On; Quick Millions.

SYDNEY, BASIL

Born: Apr. 23, 1894, St. Osyth, Essex, England. Died: Jan. 10, 1968, London, England. Stage and screen actor. Divorced from actresses Joyce Howard and Doris Keane (dec. 1945).

Appeared in: 1920 Romance (film debut). 1922 Red Hot Romance. 1932 The Midshipmaid. 1934 Dirty Work; The Third Clue. 1935 The Riverside Murder; The Tunnel (aka Transatlantic Tunnel—US); White Lilac. 1936 The Amateur Gentleman; Rhodes of Africa (aka Rhodes—US); Accused; Crime over London (US 1938); Talk of the Devil (US 1937); Blind Man's Bluff. 1939 The Four Just Men (aka The Secret Four—US 1940); Shadowed Eyes. 1941 The Farmer's Wife; Spring Meeting; Ships with Winds (US 1942); The Black Sheep of Whitehall. 1942 The Next of Kin (US 1943); Went the Day Well? (aka 48 Hours—US 1944); They Came in Khaki; Big Blockade (documentary). 1946 Caesar and Cleopatra. 1947 The Man Within (aka The Smugglers—US 1948); Jassy (US 1948). 1948 Hamlet; Meet Me at Dawn (US 1948). 1950 The Angel with the Trumpet; Treasure Island; The Gay Duellist (reissue of Meet Me at Dawn—1947). 1951 The Magic Box (US 1952). 1952 Ivanhoe. 1953 Salome. 1954 Hell Below Zero; Star of India (US 1956). 1955 Simba; The Dam Busters. 1956 Around the World in 80 Days. 1957 Island in the Sun. 1958 A Question of Adultery (US 1959). 1959 John Paul Jones; The Devil's Disciple. 1960 The Three Worlds of Gulliver; A Story of David; The Hands of Orlac.

SYDNEY, BRUCE

Born: 1889. Died: Oct. 18, 1942, Hollywood, Calif. Screen actor.

Appeared in: 1938 Kidnapped.

SYLVA, MARGUERITE

Born: 1876, Brussels, Belgium. Died: Feb. 21, 1957, Glendale, Calif. (auto accident). Stage and screen actress.

Appeared in: 1943 The Seventh Victim. 1945 The Gay Senorita.

SYLVANI, GLADYS

Born: 1885, England. Died: Apr. 20, 1953, Alexandria, Va. Screen actress. One of the first silent film stars in England. Came to U.S. in 1939.

Appeared in: **1911** Jim of the Mounted Police; All's Right with the World; The Three Lovers; Mother's Boy; Harry the Footballer; A Sprained Ankle; A Double Deception; 'Til Death Do Us Part; Twin Roses; The Torn Letter; Wealthy Brother John (aka Our Wealthy Nephew John—US); The Stolen Letters; The Greatest of These; Rachel's Sin; Love and a Sewing Machine. **1912** At the Eleventh Hour; The Bachelor's Ward; The Coiner's Den; The Deception; A Girl Alone; Jimmy Lester; Convict and Gentleman; Mary Has Her Way; Our Bessie; Traitress of Parton's Court; Pamela's Party; Love in a Laundry; Chuck and Stage; Love Wins in the End; The Editor and the Millionaire; A Woman's Wit; Jasmine; A Fisherman's Love Story; Her Only Son. **1913** Fisherman's Luck.

SYLVESTER, FRANK L.
Born: 1868. Died: Dec. 1931, Hollywood, Calif. (heart attack). Screen, stage and vaudeville actor.

SYLVESTER, HENRY
Born: 1882. Died: June 8, 1961. Screen actor.

Appeared in: **1935** Eagle's Blood. **1936** Darkest Africa. **1942** Omaha Trail. **1943** Presenting Lily Mars; Hangmen Also Die.

SYLVIE (Louise Sylvain)
Born: 1882. Died: Jan. 1970, Paris, France. Screen and stage actress.

Appeared in: **1935** Crime et Chatiment (Crime and Punishment). **1939** The End of a Day. **1942** The Pasha's Wives. **1948** Le Corbeau (The Raven); Passionnelle. **1950** Angels of the Streets. **1952** Isle of Sinners (aka God Needs Men—Dieu a Besoin des Hommes); Forbidden Fruit (US 1959); The Little World of Don Camillo (US 1953); Under the Paris Sky. **1955** Ulysses. **1957** The Adulteress (US 1958). **1959** The Mirror Has Two Faces; Anatomy of Love. **1960** Michael Strogoff. **1963** Cronaca Familiare (Family Diary). **1964** Chateau en Suede (Castle in Sweden aka Nutty, Naughty Chateau). **1966** La Vielle Dame Indigne (The Worthless Old Lady aka The Shameless Old Lady). Other French film: Therese Raquin.

SYMONDS, AUGUSTIN
Born: 1869. Died: July 14, 1944. Screen actor.

Appeared in: **1929** Four Feathers.

SZABO, SANDOR
Born: 1906. Died: Oct. 13, 1966. Professional wrestler and screen actor.

Appeared in: **1936** Once in a Blue Moon. **1943** Mission to Moscow. **1952** Dream Boat. **1955** Hell's Island.

SZATHMARY, ALBERT
Born: 1909. Died: June 9, 1975, Hollywood, Calif. (pneumonia). Screen actor.

SZIGETI, JOSEPH
Born: 1893. Died: Feb. 20, 1973. Screen actor.

Appeared in: **1944** Hollywood Canteen.

SZOLD, BERNARD
Born: 1894. Died: Nov. 15, 1960, Victoria, Tex. (heart attack). Screen actor and dramatic coach.

Appeared in: **1951** The Lemon Drop Kid; Flying Leathernecks; The Tanks Are Coming; M; Queen for a Day.

TABER, RICHARD
Born: 1885. Died: Nov. 16, 1957, New York, N.Y. Screen, stage and television actor.

Appeared in: **1929** Lucky in Love. **1935** Two Fisted. **1948** The Naked City. **1950** The Sleeping City. **1951** Under the Gun.

TABLER, P. DEMPSEY (Perce Dempsey Tabler)
Born: 1880, Tenn. Died: 1963, San Francisco, Calif. Screen actor and film producer. The third actor to portray the role of Tarzan.

Appeared in: **1915** Rule G. **1916** The Captive God; The Phantom; The Patriot. **1917** Babes in the Woods. **1919** Love Insurance. **1920** The Son of Tarzan (serial); The Gamesters. **1921** Smiling All the Way. **1923** Jungle Trail of the Son of Tarzan; Spawn of the Desert.

TABOADA, JULIO, JR.
Born: 1926, Mexico. Died: Sept. 15, 1962, Mexico City, Mexico (heart attack). Screen, stage, television actor and stage director.

TABOR, JOAN
Born: 1933. Died: Dec. 18, 1968, Culver City, Calif. Screen, stage and television actress. Divorced from actor Broderick Crawford.

Appeared in: **1960** The Bellboy. **1961** Teenage Millionaire.

TAFT, SARA
Died: Sept. 24, 1973, Los Angeles, Calif. (heart attack). Screen and television actress.

Appeared in: **1943** Cry Havoc. **1951** You Never Can Tell. **1958** Vertigo. **1960** The Story of Ruth. **1961** Parrish. **1962** Tower of London. **1964** The Young Lovers. **1968** Blackbeard's Ghost. **1969** Death of a Gunfighter; The Reivers.

TAGGART, BEN L.
Born: Apr. 5, 1889, Ottawa, Canada. Died: May 17, 1947, Santa Monica, Calif. Stage and screen actor.

Appeared in: **1915** The Woman Next Door; The Sentimental Lady. **1917** Brown of Harvard; She. **1931** Monkey Business; Silence. **1932** Hold 'Em Jail; Horsefeathers; Strangers in Love; Million Dollar Legs. **1934** The Thin Man; The Notorious Sophie Lang. **1935** Unknown Woman; plus the following shorts: Slightly Static; Manhattan Monkey Business; Public Ghost No. 1; Okay Toots!; Poker at Eight; Southern Exposure. **1936** The Count Takes the Count (short); Neighborhood House (short). **1938** A Criminal Is Born (short); The Overland Express. **1939** Rattling Romeo (short); Skinny the Moocher (short); The Green Hornet (serial). **1940** Before I Hang; Nobody's Children. **1941** The Lone Wolf Takes a Chance; Man-Made Monster; The Wildcat of Tucson; The Medico of Painted Springs; I'll Sell My Life; Two in a Taxi; Hard Guy. **1942** The Miracle Kid; Escape from Crime.

TAGGART, HAL
Born: 1892. Died: Dec. 12, 1971. Screen and vaudeville actor. Billed in vaudeville with Tommy Mann as a song and dance act.

Appeared in: **1957** The Monster That Challenged the World. **1962** Advise and Consent.

TAILLON, ANGUS D.
Born: 1888, Ontario, Canada. Died: May 8, 1953, Hollywood, Calif. Screen actor and stand-in for Barry Fitzgerald.

Appeared in: **1949** Top O' the Morning.

TALAZAC, ODETTE
Died: 1948, France. Screen actress. Entered films in 1929.

Appeared in: **1929** Le Collier de la Reine. **1930** Le Sang d'un Poete. **1932** Le Million. **1936** Le Crime de Monsieur Lange (The Crime of Monsieur Lange—US 1964). **1937** Maternite. **1938** L'Esclave Blanche. **1939** La Regle du Jeu. **1947** The Murderer Lives at Number 21.

TALBOT, MAE
Born: 1869. Died: Aug. 4, 1942, Glendale, Calif. (heart attack). Stage and screen actress.

TALBOT, SLIM (Joseph Bovelle Talbot)
Born: 1896. Died: Feb. 1973, Boulevard, Calif. Screen actor, rodeo rider and stuntman.

Appeared in: **1958** The Big Country. **1962** The Man Who Shot Liberty Valance.

TALIAFERRO, EDITH
Born: 1894. Died: Mar. 2, 1958, Newtown, Conn. Sister of screen actress Mabel Taliaferro. Screen, stage, radio and vaudeville actress. Entered films with Lasky Co. in 1915.

TALMADGE, CONSTANCE
Born: Apr. 19, 1898, Brooklyn, N.Y. Died: Nov. 23, 1973, Los Angeles, Calif. (pneumonia). Screen actress and film producer. Sister of actresses Natalie (dec. 1969) and Norma Talmadge (dec. 1957). Entered films in 1914 with Vitagraph as an extra.

Appeared in: **1914** In the Latin Quarter; Bridal Attire. **1915** Billy, the Bear Tamer. **1916** Intolerance; The Matrimaniac. **1917** Scandal; Girl of the Timber Claims; The Honeymoon; Betsy's Burglar. **1918** The Lesson; Up the Road with Sally; A Pair of Silk Stockings; Mrs. Leffingwell's Boots; Sauce for the Goose. **1919** The Veiled Adventure; The Fall of Babylon; A Temperamental Wife; The Love Expert; Happiness a la Mode; A Virtuous Vamp; Romance and Arabella. **1920** The Perfect Woman; Two Weeks; In Search of a Sinner; Good References; Dangerous Business. **1921** Mama's Affair; Lessons in Love; Wedding Bells; Woman's Place. **1922** Polly of the Follies; The Divorcee; East is West; The Primitive Lover. **1923** Dulcy; A Dangerous Maid. **1924** The Goldfish; Her Night of Romance; In Hollywood with Potash and Perlmutter. **1925** Her Sister from Paris; Learning to Love. **1926** The Duchess of Buffalo; Sybil. **1927** Venus of Venice; Breakfast at Sunrise. **1929** Venus.

TALMADGE, NATALIE
Born: 1899, Brooklyn, N.Y. Died: June 19, 1969, Santa Monica, Calif. Screen actress. Divorced from screen actor Buster Keaton (dec. 1966) and mother of screen actor Robert Talmadge. Sister of screen actresses Norma (dec. 1957) and Constance Talmadge (dec. 1973).

Appeared in: **1919** The Isle of Conquest. **1921** The Passion Flower. **1923** Our Hospitality.

TALMADGE, NORMA

Born: May 26, 1893 or 1897, Jersey City, N.J. or Niagara Falls, N.Y.? Died: Dec. 24, 1957, Las Vegas, Nev. (cerebral stroke—pneumonia). Screen, stage, radio and vaudeville actress. Divorced from film producer Joseph Schenck (dec. 1961) and comedian and producer George Jessel. Sister of actresses Natalie (dec. 1969) and Constance Talmadge (dec. 1973).

Appeared in: **1910** A Dixie Mother; Mother by Proxy; Heart O' the Hill; The Household Pest; The Love of the Chrysanthemums. **1911** A Tale of Two Cities; In Neighboring Kingdom; Mrs. 'Enery 'Awkins; Her Hero; Nellie the Model; The Convict's Child; Forgotten; The Child Crusoes; The Wildcat; The Thumb Print; Her Sister's Children; A Broken Spell; Sky Pilot; The General's Daughter; Paola and Francesca. **1912** The First Violin; The Troublesome Stepdaughter; Mr. Butler Butles; The Lovesick Maidens of Cuddleton; Fortunes of a Composer; Omens and Oracles; Mrs. Carter's Necklace; The Midget's Revenge; Mr. Bolter's Sweetheart; O'Hara Helps Cupid; The Extension Table; Squatter and Philosopher; Captain Barnacles' Messmate; Captain Barnacles' Waif; Captain Barnacles' Reformer. **1913** The Other Woman; Casey at the Bat; Wanted—A Strong Hand; The Blue Rose; He Fell in Love With His Mother-In-Law; Counsel for the Defense; 'Arriet's Baby; The Silver Cigarette Case; The Doctor's Secret; Fanny's Conspiracy; Father's Hatband; Plot and Counterplot; A Lady and Her Maid; Sleuthing; The Sacrifice of Kathleen; Officer John Donovan; His Little Page; Country Barber; O'Hara as a Guardian Angel; An Old Man's Love Story; The Tables Turned; Solitaires; Just Show People; His Official Appointment; The Vavasour Ball; Under the Daisies; O'Hara's Godchild; His Silver Bachelorhood; The Honorable Algernon; Counsel for the Defense; An Elopement at Home. **1914** The Hero; Old Reliable; Sawdust and Salome; The Helpful Sisterhood; Cupid vs Money; Mister Murphy's Wedding Present; John Rance, Gentleman; Politics and the Press; The Loan Shark King; A Question of Clothes; Goodbye Summer; Sunshine and Shadows; Memories in Men's Souls; The Hidden Letters; The Peacemaker; A Daughter of Israel; The Curing of Myra May; Fogg's Millions; The Mill of Life; Etta of the Footlights; A Wayward Daughter; Dorothy Danebridge, Militant. **1915** The Barrier of Faith; A Daughter's Strange Inheritance; Elsa's Brother; The Pillar of Flame; The Battle Cry of Peace; The Captivating Mary Carstairs; Janet of the Chorus. **1916** The Missing Links; The Crown Prince's Double; Martha's Vindication; The Children in the House; The Honorable Algy; The Criminal; The Devil's Needle; Going Straight; Fifty-Fifty; The Social Secretary. **1917** Panthea; Poppy; The Secret of Storm Country; The Law of Compensation; The Moth; The Lone Wolf; Under False Colors. **1918** The Forbidden City; The Safety Curtain; The Ghost of Yesterday; By Right of Purchase; De Luxe Annie; Her Only Way; The Heart of Wetona; Salome. **1919** The Probation Wife; The Way of a Woman; The New Moon; The Isle of Conquest. **1920** The Right of Way; The Loves and Lies; A Daughter of Two Worlds; The Woman Gives; Yes or No; The Branded Woman. **1921** The Passion Flower; The Sign on the Door; The Wonderful Thing. **1922** Foolish Wives; The Eternal Flame; Smilin' Through; Love's Redemption; Branded. **1923** Ashes of Vengeance; Dust of Desire; Within the Law; The Voice from the Minaret; Sawdust. **1924** Secrets; The Only Woman; The Song of Love; In Hollywood with Potash and Perlmutter. **1925** The Lady; Graustark. **1926** Kiki. **1927** The Dove; Camille. **1928** Show People; The Woman Disputed. **1930** New York Nights; Du Barry, Woman of Passion.

TALMAN, WILLIAM

Born: Feb. 4, 1915, Detroit, Mich. Died: Aug. 30, 1968, Encino, Calif. (cancer). Screen, stage, television actor and screenwriter. Divorced from actress Barbara Read (dec. 1963).

Appeared in: **1949** Red, Hot and Blue (film debut); I Married a Communist. **1950** The Woman on Pier Thirteen; The Armored Car Robbery; The Kid from Texas. **1951** The Racket. **1952** One Minute to Zero. **1953** The Hitch-Hiker; City that Never Sleeps. **1955** Smoke Signal; Big House, USA; Crashout. **1956** The Man is Armed; Two Gun Lady; Uranium Boom. **1957** The Persuader; Hell on Devil's Island. **1967** The Ballad of Josie.

TAMARA (Tamara Swann)

Died: Feb. 22, 1943, near Lisbon, Portugal (plane crash). Screen, stage actress and singer.

Appeared in: **1928** A Midsummer Night's Dream. **1935** Sweet Surrender. **1937** Roarin' Lead. **1940** No, No, Nanette.

TAMBLYN, EDWARD

Born: 1907, Yonkers, N.Y. Died: June 22, 1957, Hollywood, Calif. Stage and screen actor. Father of actor Russ Tamblyn.

Appeared in: **1931** The Flood. **1933** The Sweetheart of Sigma Chi. **1934** Harold Teen; Money Means Nothing. **1935** A Shot in the Dark. **1936** Palm Springs.

TAMIROFF, AKIM

Born: Oct. 29, 1899, Baku, Russia. Died: Sept. 17, 1972, Palm Springs, Calif. Screen, stage and television actor. Married to actress Tamara Shayne. Nomi-

nated for 1936 Academy Award for Best Supporting Actor for The General Died at Dawn and in 1943 for For Whom the Bell Tolls.

Appeared in: **1932** Okay, America! **1933** Queen Christina; Gabriel Over the White House; Storm at Daybreak. **1934** Fugitive Lovers; Scarlet Empress; The Merry Widow; Chained; Here Is My Heart; The Captain Hates the Sea; Sadie McKee; The Great Flirtation. **1935** Lives of a Bengal Lancer; Naughty Marietta; The Winning Ticket; China Seas; Rumba; The Last Outpost; Black Sleep; Big Broadcast of 1936; Paris in Spring; Two Fisted; Go Into Your Dance; Black Fury; Gay Deception; The Story of Louis Pasteur. **1936** Desire; Woman Trap; The General Died at Dawn; The Jungle Princess; Anthony Adverse. **1937** The Soldier and the Lady (aka Michael Strogoff); Her Husband Lies; King of Gamblers; High, Wide and Handsome; The Great Gambini. **1938** The Buccaneer; Spawn of the North; Dangerous to Know; Ride a Crooked Mile. **1939** Paris Honeymoon; Union Pacific; The Magnificent Fraud; King of Chinatown; Honeymoon in Bali; Disputed Passage; Geronimo. **1940** The Way of All Flesh; Untamed; Northwest Mounted Police; The Great McGinty. **1941** Texas Rangers Ride Again; New York Town; The Corsican Brothers. **1942** Tortilla Flat; Are Husbands Necessary? **1943** Five Graves to Cairo; For Whom the Bell Tolls; His Butler's Sister. **1944** The Bridge of San Luis Rey; Dragon Seed; Miracle of Morgan's Creek; Can't Help Singing; Black Magic. **1946** Pardon My Past; A Scandal in Paris (aka Thieves Holiday). **1947** Fiesta; The Gangster. **1948** My Girl Tisa; 10th Avenue Angel; Relentless. **1949** Black Magic (aka Cagliostro); Outpost in Morocco. **1953** Desert Legion; You Know What Sailors Are (US 1954). **1955** They Who Dare; Confidential Report (aka Mr. Arkadin—US 1962). **1956** Black Sheep; Anastasia. **1957** Battle Hell; The Yangtse Incident; Cartouche. **1958** Touch of Evil; Me and the Colonel. **1959** Desert Desperadoes. **1960** The Tartar Invasion; Ocean's Eleven. **1961** Romanoff and Juliet (aka Dig That Juliet); They Who Dare; Le Baccanti (aka The Bacchantes—US 1963). **1962** Le Proces (aka The Trial—US 1963); The Reluctant Saint; Mr. Arkadin; Don Quixote; Col ferro e col fuoco (aka Daggers of Blood and Invasion 1700—US 1965). **1963** With Fire and Sword; Light and Day. **1964** Topkapi!; Panic Button. **1965** Bambole (aka The Dolls); The Amphaville; La fabuleuse adventure de Marco Polo (aka Marco the Magnificent—US 1966); Lord Jim. **1966** Campanadas a medianoche (aka Chimes at Midnight and Falstaff—US 1967); Lt. Robin Crusoe, USN; Hotel Paradiso; The Liquidator; After the Fox; Funeral in Berlin. **1967** Every Man's Woman; The Vulture; A Rose for Everyone. **1968** Tenderly (aka The Girl Who Couldn't Say No—US 1969); Great Catherine. **1969** 100 Rifles; The Great Bank Robbery. **1970** Venus in Furs.

TAMMY, MARK

Died: July 10, 1975. Screen actor.

TANAKA, SHOJI

Born: 1886. Died: Oct. 20, 1918, New York, N.Y. (Spanish influenza). Screen actor.

TANDY, VALERIE

Born: 1923, England. Died: Apr. 27, 1965, London, England. Stage and screen actress.

TANGUAY, EVA

Born: 1878, Marbleton, Canada. Died: Jan. 11, 1947, Los Angeles, Calif. (heart attack and cerebral hemorrhage). Screen, stage and vaudeville actress. Referred to as the "I Don't Care Girl." Appeared in films for Selznick in 1917.

TANNEN, JULIUS

Born: 1881. Died: Jan. 3, 1965, Hollywood, Calif. Screen and vaudeville actor. Father of actor William Tannen (dec. 1976).

Appeared in: **1935** Collegiate. **1936** Half Angel; The Road to Glory; 36 Hours to Kill; Dimples; Pigskin Parade; Reunion; One in a Million; Stowaway. **1937** Fair Warning; Love Is News; Mama Runs Wild. **1938** Love Is a Headache. **1939** Danger Flight; The Magnificent Fraud. **1940** The Mortal Storm; Christmas in July. **1942** Harvard Here I Come. **1944** The Great Moment. **1945** House of Frankenstein. **1948** Unfaithfully Yours.

TANNER, JAMES J.

Born: 1873. Died: Apr. 3, 1934, Hollywood, Calif. Screen actor and artist.

TANO, GUY (Gaetano Rocco)

Born: 1914. Died: Aug. 19, 1952, New York, N.Y. Screen and stage actor.

TANSEY, MRS. EMMA

Born: 1884. Died: Mar. 23, 1942, Los Angeles, Calif. Screen and stage actress. Entered films approx. 1921.

Appeared in: **1922** Are Children to Blame? **1925** Fast Fightin'. **1930** Beyond the Rio Grande. **1935** Okay Toots! (short). **1938** Knight of the Plains. **1941** Meet John Doe.

TAPLEY, ROSE

Born: June 30, 1883, Petersburg, Va. Died: Feb. 23, 1956, Woodland Hills, Calif. Stage and screen actress. Entered films with Thomas Edison Productions.

Appeared in: **1905** Wanted a Wife (film debut). **1911** Vanity Fair. **1912** As You Like It. **1914** The Christian. **1915** The "Jarr Family" Series. **1922** Her Majesty. **1923** Java Head. **1924** The Man Who Fights Alone. **1925** The Pony Express; The Scarlet Honeymoon; The Redeeming Sin. **1926** The Prince of Pilsen; Morganson's Finish. **1927** It; God's Great Wilderness; Out of the Past. **1929** The Charlatan. **1930** His First Command. **1931** Resurrection.

TAPTUKA, CLARENCE S.
Born: 1898. Died: Nov. 8, 1967, Albuquerque, N.Mex. American Indian screen actor. Appeared in silents.

TARASOVA, ALLA K.
Born: 1898. Died: Apr. 1973, Moscow, Russia. Stage and screen actress.

Appeared in: **1934** Thunderstorm. **1937** Peter the First. **1939** The Conquests of Peter the Great.

TARBAT, LORNA
Born: 1916, England. Died: Apr. 1961, Harrow, Middlesex, England. Screen, stage and television actress.

TARBUTT, FRAZER
Born: 1894. Died: June 16, 1918, France (air crash—killed in action). Screen actor.

TARJAN, GEORGE
Born: 1910, Hungary. Died: Dec. 25, 1973, London, England. Stage actor, director, screen actor and newscaster. Married to actress Etelka Dan.

Appeared in: **1935** Egy ej Velencebzn.

TARKHANOV, MIKHAIL
Born: Russia. Died: Aug. 1948, Moscow, Russia. Screen and stage actor.

Appeared in: **1935** The Youth of Maxim. **1939** The Conquests of Peter the Great.

TASHMAN, LILYAN
Born: Oct. 23, 1900, Brooklyn, N.Y. Died: Mar. 21, 1934, New York, N.Y. (advanced tumorous condition and/or cancer). Stage and screen actress. Married to actor Edmund Lowe (dec. 1971).

Appeared in: **1917** Universal Screen Magazine #21. **1921** Experience. **1922** Head over Heels. **1924** The Garden of Weeds; Manhandled; The Dark Swan; Is Love Everything?; Nellie, the Beautiful Cloak Model; Winner Take All. **1925** Declasse; The Parasite; Ports of Call; Pretty Ladies; Bright Lights; Seven Days; The Girl Who Wouldn't Work; A Broadway Butterfly; I'll Show You the Town. **1926** Rocking Moon; The Skyrocket; Siberia; Whispering Smith; For Alimony Only; Love's Blindness; So This Is Paris. **1927** Don't Tell the Wife; French Dressing; The Prince of Headwaiters; The Texas Steer; Camille; The Stolen Bride; The Woman Who Did Not Care. **1928** Phyllis of the Follies; Craig's Wife; Happiness Ahead; Lady Raffles; Manhattan Cocktail; Take Me Home. **1929** The Lone Wolf's Daughter; The Marriage Playground; Gold Diggers of Broadway; New York Nights; Bulldog Drummond; The Trial of Mary Dugan; Hardboiled. **1930** One Heavenly Night; On the Level; The Cat Creeps; Queen of Scandal; Puttin' on the Ritz; The Matrimonial Bed; Leathernecking; No, No, Nanette; Playing Around. **1931** Girls about Town; Up Pops the Devil; Finn and Hattie; Millie; The Mad Parade; The Road to Reno; Murder by the Clock. **1932** The Wiser Sex; Revolt; Scarlet Dawn; Those We Love. **1933** Mama Loves Papa; Too Much Harmony; Wine, Women and Song; Frankie and Johnny; Style. **1934** Riptide.

TATA, PAUL M., SR.
Born: 1883. Died: Mar. 30, 1962, Memphis, Tenn. Screen actor and fencing instructor.

Appeared in: **1908** The Three Musketeers.

TATE, HARRY (Ronald Macdonald Hutchinson)
Born: July 4, 1872, England. Died: Feb. 14, 1940, London, England (air raid). Screen, stage, vaudeville, radio actor and screenwriter.

Appeared in: **1927** Motoring (US 1929). **1929** The following shorts: The Patent Office; Selling a Car. **1932** Her First Affaire. **1933** Counsel's Opinion; My Lucky Star; I Spy. **1934** Happy. **1935** Royal Cavalcade (aka Regal Cavalcade—US); Look Up and Laugh; Hyde Park Corner; Midshipman Easy (aka Men of the Sea—US). **1936** Keep Your Seats Please; Soft Lights and Sweet Music; Variety Parade. **1937** Wings of the Morning; Take a Chance; Sam Small Leaves Town.

TATE, REGINALD
Born: Dec. 13, 1896, Garforth, England. Died: Aug. 23, 1955, London, England. Screen, stage, television and radio actor.

Appeared in: **1934** Whispering Tongues; Tangled Evidence. **1935** The Phantom Light; The Riverside Murder. **1936** Dark Journey; For Valor. **1939** Too Dangerous to Live; Poison Pen (US 1941). **1940** Gentleman of Venture (aka It

Happened to One Man—US 1941). **1942** The Next of Kin (US 1943). **1943** The Life and Death of Colonel Blimp (US 1945). **1944** The Way Ahead; Madonna of the Seven Moons. **1945** The Man from Morocco; Journey Together (US 1946). **1947** So Well Remembered; Uncle Silas (aka The Inheritance—US 1951). **1948** Noose (aka The Silk Noose—US 1950). **1949** Diamond City. **1950** Midnight Episode (US 1951). **1952** Secret People; The Story of Robin Hood and His Merrie Men. **1953** Escape Route (aka I'll Get You—US); Malta Story (US 1954). **1955** King's Rhapsody.

TATE, SHARON
Born: 1943, Dallas, Tex. Died: Aug. 9, 1969, Bel Air, Calif. (murdered). Screen and television actress. Married to actor and director Roman Polanski.

Appeared in: **1963** The Wheeler Dealers. **1964** The Americanization of Emily. **1965** Vampire Killers; "13"; The Sandpiper. **1967** Don't Make Waves; Eye of the Devil; Valley of the Dolls. **1968** The Fearless Vampire Killers, or, Pardon Me but Your Teeth Are in My Neck. **1969** Thirteen Chairs; The Wrecking Crew; House of Seven Joys.

TATUM, ART (Arthur Tatum)
Born: Oct. 13, 1910, Toledo, Ohio. Died: Nov. 4, 1956, Los Angeles, Calif. (uremia). Pianist, screen and radio actor.

Appeared in: **1947** The Fabulous Dorseys.

TATUM, BUCK
Born: 1897. Died: Oct. 2, 1941, Santa Monica, Calif. Screen actor and cowboy.

TAUBE, MATHIAS
Born: 1876, Lindesburg, Sweden. Died: 1934, Sweden. Screen, stage and radio actor.

Appeared in the following Swedish films: Ships That Meet; Therese; The Gold Spider; Johan; For High Ends; The Girl from Paradise; The People from Simlangen Valley; The Ingmar Inheritance; She, He and Andersson; The Poetry of Adalen (1928); The Land of Rye; The Voice of the Heart; Tomorrow for a Woman; A Night of Love on Oresund; The People of Varmland; We Go Through the Kitchen; Under Notice to Leave.

TAUBER, RICHARD
Born: May 16, 1892, Linz, Austria. Died: Jan. 8, 1948, London, England. Screen actor, opera singer, songwriter and composer. Married to actress Diana Napier.

Appeared in: **1930** Die Grosse Attraktion (The Big Attraction—US 1933); Ich Glaut Nie Mehran Eine Frau (US 1933). **1931** Melodie Der Liebe (The Melody of Love, aka The Right to Happiness). **1933** Das Lockende Ziel. **1934** Blossom Time (aka April Romance—US 1937). **1935** Heart's Desire. **1936** Land Without Music (aka Forbidden Music—US 1938); Pagiacci (aka Clown Must Laugh—US 1938). **1945** Waltz Time. **1946** Lisbon Story. Other films: End of the Rainbow; The Land of Smiles; The Golden Goal.

TAYLOR, ALBERT
Born: Apr. 8, 1871, Montgomery, Ala. Died: Apr. 10, 1940, Hollywood, Calif. Stage and screen actor.

Appeared in: **1934** The Good Fairy; Little Man, What Now? **1935** Reckless; Vanessa, Her Love Story; Times Square Lady; Woman Wanted; College Scandal; The Crusades; The Man on the Flying Trapeze; Accent on Youth. **1936** Nevada; Fury.

TAYLOR, ALMA
Born: Jan. 3, 1895, London, England. Died: Feb. 1974, London, England. Screen and television actress. Entered films in 1907.

Appeared in: **1909** The Little Milliner and the Thief; The Story of a Picture. **1910** The Burglar and Little Phyllis; Tilly the Tomboy Buys Linoleum; Tilly at the Election; Tilly the Tomboy Visits the Poor; A New Hat for Nothing; Tilly the Tomboy Goes Boating. **1911** A Wilful Maid; Tilly's Unsympathetic Uncle; Evicted; When Tilly's Uncle Flirted; Tilly's Party; Tilly at the Seaside; Tilly-Matchmaker; The Veteran's Pension; Tilly and the Mormon Missionary; A Fight With Fire; Tilly and the Fire Engines; The Smuggler's Step-Daughter; A Seaside Introduction; Envy, Hatred and Malice; Tilly and the Smugglers; Tilly and the Dogs; Bill's Reformation; Tilly Works For a Living; The Dear Little Teacher; Oliver Twist; Tilly in a Boarding House; King Robert of Sicily; For Love and Life; Curfew Must Not Ring Tonight. **1912** For a Baby's Sake. **1913** The Real Thing; Winning His Stripes; The Tailor's Revenge; The Mill Girl; Tried in the Fire; The Lover Who Took the Cake; Paying the Penalty; Tilly's Breaking-Up Party; Partners in Crime; Her Little Pet; Adrift on Life's Tide; The Girl at Lancing Mill; David Copperfield; A Midnight Adventure; The Cloister and the Hearth; The Old Curiosity Shop; The Broken Oath; The Curate's Bride; A Little Widow Is a Dangerous Thing; Petticoat Perfidy. **1914** Justice; Blind Faith; The Whirr of the Spinning Wheel; The Price of Fame; An Engagement of Convenience; The Quality of Mercy; The Heart of Midlothian; By Whose Hand? (aka The Mystery of Mr. Marks); The Girl Who Lived in Straight Street; Over the Garden Wall; The Kleptomaniac; The Schemers: Or, The Jewels of Hate; The Hills Are Calling; The Basilisk; His Country's Bidding (aka The Call); In the Shadow of Big Ben; Time the Great Healer; Aladdin: Or, a Lad Out; The Awakening of Nora; Morphia the Death Drug; His Great Opportunity; Oh My Aunt!; The Double Event; Tilly at the Football Match. **1915** The Canker of Jealousy (aka Be Sure of Your Sins); The Painted Lady Betty; Spies; Alma Taylor (film clips from her films 1907–1915); A Lancashire Lass; A Moment of Darkness; Jill and the Old Fiddle; Tilly and the Nut; Courtmartialed (aka The Traitor); The Passing of a Soul; The Baby on the Barge; The Man Who Stayed at Home; Sweet Lavender; The Golden Pavement; The Outrage; Iris. **1916** The Man at the Wheel; Love in a Mist; Trelawney of the Wells; Sowing the Wind; Annie Laurie; The Marriage of William Ashe; The Grand Babylon Hotel; Comin' Thro' the Rye; Molly Bawn. **1917** The Cobweb; The American Heiress; Merely Mrs. Stubbs; Nearer My God to Thee. **1918** The Touch of a Child; Film Tag series including: A New Version; The W.L.A. Girl; The Leopard's Spots; The Refugee; Tares; Boundary House. **1919** Broken in the Wars; The Nature of the Beast; Sunken Rocks; Sheba; The Forest on the Hill. **1920** Anna the Adventuress; Alf's Button; Helen of Four Gates; Mrs. Erricker's Reputation. **1921** The Tinted Venus; Dollars in Surrey; Tansy; The Narrow Valley. **1923** The Pipes of Pan; Mist in the Valley; Strangling Threads; Comin' Thro' the Rye (and 1916 version). **1924** The Shadow of Egypt. **1926** The House of Marney. **1927** Quinneys. **1928** Two Little Drummer Boys; A South Sea Bubble. **1931** Deadlock. **1932** Bachelor's Baby. **1933** House of Dreams. **1935** Things Are Looking Up. **1936** Everybody Dance. **1954** Lilacs in the Spring (aka Let's Make-Up—US 1956). **1955** Stock Car. **1956** Lost (aka Tears for Simon—US 1957). **1957** Blue Murder at St. Trinian's (US 1958).

TAYLOR, BETH

Born: 1889. Died: Mar. 1, 1951, Hollywood, Calif. Screen and stage actress.

TAYLOR, DEEMS

Born: Dec. 22, 1885, New York, N.Y. Died: July 3, 1966, New York, N.Y. (stroke). Music critic, screen, radio, television actor, composer and author.

Appeared in: **1940** Fantasia (narrator). **1947** The Barber of Seville (narrator). **1950** Of Men and Music.

TAYLOR, ESTELLE

Born: May 20, 1899, Wilmington, Del. Died: Apr. 15, 1958, Los Angeles, Calif. (cancer). Screen, stage and vaudeville actress. Divorced from professional fighter Jack Dempsey.

Appeared in: **1920** While New York Sleeps; The Adventurer. **1921** Blind Wives; Footfalls. **1922** Monte Cristo; A Fool There Was; The Lights of New York; Only a Shop Girl; Thorns and Orange Blossoms. **1923** The Ten Commandments; Bavu; Desire; Forgive and Forget; Hollywood; Mary of the Movies. **1924** The Alaskan; Dorothy Vernon of Haddon Hall; Playthings of Desire; Passion's Pathway; Phantom Justice; Tiger Love. **1925** Manhattan Madness; Wandering Footsteps. **1926** Don Juan. **1927** New York. **1928** The Whip Woman; The Singapore Mutiny; Lady Raffles; Honor Bound. **1929** Where East Is East. **1930** Liliom. **1931** Cimarron; Street Scene; The Unholy Garden. **1932** Call Her Savage; The Western Limited. **1938** various shorts. **1945** The Southerner.

TAYLOR, FERRIS

Born: 1893. Died: Mar. 6, 1961, Hollywood, Calif. (heart attack). Screen actor.

Appeared in: **1937** Mr. Dodd Takes the Air. **1938** The Story of Dr. Carver (short); He Couldn't Say No; Santa Fe Stampede; The Daredevil Drivers; The Jury's Secret. **1939** You Can't Cheat an Honest Man; Mexican Spitfire; SOS Tidal Wave; Man of Conquest; The Zero Hour; Mountain Rhythm; Main Street Lawyer. **1940** Chip of the Flying U; Rancho Grande; All About Hash (short); Flight Angels; One Crowded Night; Grand Ole Opry; Ladies Must Live; Always a Bride; Diamond Frontier; Mexican Spitfire Out West. **1941** She Couldn't Say No; Ridin' on a Rainbow; The Saint in Palm Springs; A Man Betrayed; County Fair. **1942** Hello, Annapolis! **1943** Henry Aldrich Haunts a House; Gold Town; Hoosier Holiday; Happy Land. **1944** Wilson; The Town Went Wild; Beautiful but Broke; End of the Road. **1945** Col. Effingham's Raid. **1946** Decoy; Rendezvous 24; Centennial Summer; The Man from Rainbow Valley; Bringing up Father. **1948** Docks of New Orleans; My Dog Rusty. **1950** The Gunfighter; Two Flags West. **1951** The Prince of Peace. **1953** Tricky Dick (short). **1954** The Siege of Red River. **1956** Pardon My Nightshirt (short).

TAYLOR, FORREST (E. Forrest Taylor)

Born: 1884. Died: Feb. 19, 1965. Screen actor.

Appeared in. **1915** Man Afraid of His Wardrobe; The Terror of Twin Mountains; Two Spot Joe; The Sheriff of Willow Creek; The Trail of the Serpent; The Valley Feud; In the Sunset Country; There's Good in the Worst of Us; The Idol. **1916** The Thunderbolt; Wild Jim, Reformer; The White Rosette; April; The Disappearance of Helen Mintern; The Abandonment; The Music Swindlers; The Social Pirates; In the Service of the State; The Madonna of the Night; The Fighting Heiress; Black Magic. **1926** No Man's Gold; A Poor Girl's Romance. **1933** Riders of Destiny. **1934** Terry and the Pirates (serial). **1935** Mississippi; Rider of the Law; Courageous Avenger; Between Men. **1936** Rio Grande Romance; Too Much Beef; Kelly of the Secret Service; West of Nevada; Prison Shadows; Men of the Plains; Put on the Spot; Headin' for Rio Grande; Shadow of Chinatown. **1937** The Mystery of the Hooded Horsemen;

Arizona Days; The Red Rose; Riders of the Dawn; Two Minutes to Play. **1938** Fighting Devil Dogs; Heroes of the Hills; The Painted Trail; The Last Stand; Desert Patrol; Outlaw Express; Gun Packer; Black Bandit; Law of the Texan; Lightning Carson Rides Again; The Story of Dr. Carver. **1939** The Phantom Creeps; Riders of Black River; Rovin' Tumbleweeds. **1940** The Green Hornet; Chip of the Flying U; The Ghost Creeps; Terry and the Pirates; Straight Shooters; Rhythm of the Rio Grande; Wild Horse Range; Frontier Crusader; West of Abilene; The Durango Kid; The Kid from Santa Fe; Trailing Double Trouble. **1941** Flying Wild; The Iron Claw; Ridin' on a Rainbow; Billy the Kid's Fighting Pals; Cyclone Wranglers' Roost; Ridin' on the Cherokee Trail; The Lone Star Vigilantes. **1942** The Spoilers; Perils of the Royal Mounted; Cowboy Serenade; Home in Wyomin'; Sunset in the Desert; A Night for Crime; Sons of the Pioneers; King of the Stallions; The Yanks Are Coming; The Pay-Off. **1943** Air Raid Wardens; Thundering Trails; The Rangers Take Over; Man of Courage; Corregidor; Fighting Buckaroo; Silver Spurs; Sleepy Lagoon. **1944** Haunted Harbor; Mystery Man; Lady in the Death House; Song of Nevada; Shake Hands With Murder; Three Little Sisters; Sundown Valley; The Last Horseman; Sonora Stagecoach; Mojave Firebird; Cyclone Prairie Rangers; Sagebrush Heroes. **1945** Federal Operator 99; Rockin' in the Rockies; Manhunt of Mystery Island; Identity Unknown; Dangerous Intruder; Strange Voyage. **1946** The Caravan Trail; The Glass Alibi; Romance of the West; Colorado Serenade; Texas Panhandle; Santa Fe Uprising; The Crimson Ghost. **1947** The Black Widow; Stagecoach to Denver; Yankee Fakir; The Pretender; Rustlers of Devil's Canyon; Along the Oregon Trail; The Stranger from Ponca City; Buckaroo from Powder River. **1948** The Mystery of the Golden Eye; Four Faces West; Coroner Creek; Tex Granger; The Golden Eye. **1949** Bruce Gentry, Daredevil of the Skies; Deputy Marshal; Navajo Trail Riders; The Lawson Story; Death Valley Gunfighter; Stallion Canyon; The Fighting Redhead. **1950** Cherokee Uprising; The Cowboy and the Prizefighter; Rustlers on Horseback; Forbidden Jungle; The Fighting Stallion; Code of Silver Sage; Rustlers on Horseback. **1951** Prairie Roundup; Wells Fargo Gunmaster; Blazing Bullets; Prince of Peace. **1952** Night Raiders; Smoky Canyon; Border Saddlemates; Park Row; South Pacific Trail. **1953** The Lost Planet; Iron Mountain Trail; The Marshal's Daughter. **1954** Bitter Creek.

TAYLOR, GEORGE

Born: 1889. Died: Nov. 2, 1939, Fillmore, Utah (injuries from auto crash). Screen actor. Do not confuse with stage actor George R. Taylor (dec. 1944).

Appeared in: **1937** Nancy Steele Is Missing; Angel's Holiday.

TAYLOR, HENRY

Born: 1908. Died: Mar. 1, 1969. Screen, radio, vaudeville actor and screenwriter. Member of vaudeville and radio act "The Radio Rogues."

Appeared in: **1930** Beyond the Rio Grande. **1935** Every Night at Eight. **1937** Blossoms on Broadway; You Only Live Once. **1943** Reveille With Beverly.

TAYLOR, JACK

Born: 1896. Died: Oct. 21, 1932, Long Beach, Calif. (stomach disorder). Screen actor and orchestra leader. Divorced from actress Vera Steadman (dec. 1966). Appeared in Warner shorts.

TAYLOR, JOSEPHINE (Josephine Motz)

Born: 1891. Died: Nov. 26, 1964, Calumet City, Ill. Screen actress. Appeared in early Essanay productions.

TAYLOR, LAURETTE (Laurette Cooney)

Born: 1884, New York, N.Y. Died: Dec. 7, 1946, New York, N.Y. (coronary thrombosis). Screen, stage, vaudeville actress and playwright. Married to actor Hartley Manners.

Appeared in: **1923** Peg O' My Heart. **1924** Happiness; One Night in Rome.

TAYLOR, LOUISE

Born: 1908. Died: Mar. 18, 1965, New York, N.Y. Screen, television actress and dancer.

TAYLOR, DR. MARION SAYLE

Born: 1889, Louisville, Ky. Died: Feb. 1, 1942, Hollywood, Calif. (heart attack). Organist, composer, radio commentator and screen actor.

Appeared in: **1937** The Hit Parade.

TAYLOR, ROBERT

Born: 1873. Died: Dec. 9, 1936, New York, N.Y. (gas explosion). Stage and screen actor. Do not confuse with actor with same name (dec. 1969).

TAYLOR, ROBERT (Arlington Spangler Brugh)

Born: Aug. 5, 1911, Filley, Nebr. Died: June 8, 1969, Santa Monica, Calif. (lung cancer). Screen, television and radio actor. Divorced from actress Barbara Stanwyck. Married to actress Ursula Thiess.

Appeared in: **1934** Handy Andy (film debut); Only Eight Hours; There's Always Tomorrow; A Wicked Woman; Crime Does Not Pay. **1935** Lest We Forget (documentary); West Point of the Air; Society Doctor; Times Square Lady; Murder in the Fleet; Broadway Melody of 1936; The Magnificent Obsession;

Buried Loot (short); La Fiesta de Santa Barbara (short). **1936** Small Town Girl; The Gorgeous Hussy; His Brother's Wife; Private Number; Camille. **1937** Personal Property; Broadway Melody of 1938; This Is My Affair. **1938** A Yank at Oxford; Three Comrades; The Crowd Roars. **1939** Stand up and Fight; Lucky Night; Lady of the Tropics; Remember? **1940** Waterloo Bridge; Escape; Flight Command. **1941** Billy the Kid; When Ladies Meet; Johnny Eager. **1942** Her Cardboard Lover; Stand by for Action; Cargo of Innocents. **1943** Song of Russia; Bataan; The Youngest Profession. **1944** The Fighting Lady (narr. documentary). **1946** Undercurrent. **1947** High Wall. **1948** The Secret Land (narr.). **1949** Ambush; The Bribe. **1950** Conspirator; The Devil's Doorway; Big Apple; **1951** Quo Vadis; Westward the Women. **1952** Ivanhoe; Above and Beyond. **1953** Ride, Vaquero; All the Brothers Were Valiant; Knights of the Round Table; I Love Melvin. **1954** Valley of the Kings; Rogue Cop. **1955** Many Rivers to Cross; Quentin Durward. **1956** D-Day, the Sixth of June; The Power and the Prize; The Last Hunt. **1957** Tip on a Dead Jockey. **1958** Saddle the Wind; The Law and Jake Wade; Party Girl. **1959** The Hangman; The House of Seven Hawks. **1960** The Killers of Kilimanjaro. **1963** Cattle King; Guns of Wyoming; The Miracle of the White Stallions. **1964** Big Parade of Comedy (documentary); A House Is Not a Home; The Night Walker. **1966** Johnny Tiger; Return of the Gunfighter. **1967** Hondo and the Apaches; Savage Pampas; As I Rode down to Laredo; The Glass Sphinx. **1968** Where Angels Go . . . Trouble Follows; The Day the Hot Line Got Hot; Devil May Care. **1974** That's Entertainment (film clips).

TAYLOR, WILLIAM DESMOND (William Cunningham Deanne Tanner)
Born: 1877, Carlow, Ireland. Died: Feb. 1, 1922, Los Angeles, Calif. (murdered—shot). Screen actor and film director.

Appeared in: **1914** Millions for Defense. **1917** Captain Alvarez.

TEACHOUT, H. ARTHUR
Born: 1888. Died: Mar. 5, 1939, Cedar Rapids, Iowa. Screen and stage actor.

TEAGARDEN, JACK
Born: 1906. Died: Jan. 15, 1964, New Orleans, La. (pneumonia). Bandleader, screen actor and trombonist. He played with Pete Kelly, Red Nichols, collaborated with Glenn Miller on lyrics for "Basin Street Blues," joined Ben Pollack and Paul Whiteman's band.

Appeared in: **1941** Birth of the Blues. **1952** Glory Alley. **1953** The Glass Wall. **1960** Jazz on a Summer's Day.

TEAGUE, BRIAN
Born: 1937. Died: May 30, 1970, near Lake Isabella, Calif. (auto accident). Screen and television actor. Son of actor Guy Teague (dec. 1970).

TEAGUE, GUY
Died: Jan. 24, 1970, Tex. Screen actor. Father of actor Brian Teague (dec. 1970).

Appeared in: **1950** The Showdown; Vigilante Hideout. **1952** Cattle Town. **1953** The Outlaw Stallion. **1955** Wyoming Renegades. **1956** Fury at Gunsight Pass; The White Squaw.

TEARE, ETHEL
Born: 1894. Died: Mar. 4, 1959, San Mateo, Calif. Screen actress.

Appeared in: **1915** "Ham and Bud" series. **1917** Thirst; Lost—A Cook. **1921** Skirts; The Tomboy. **1923** Thirst (reissue of 1917 film). **1924** A Woman Who Sinned.

TEARLE, CONWAY (Frederick Levy)
Born: May 17, 1878, New York, N.Y. Died: Oct. 1, 1938, Los Angeles, Calif. (heart attack). Stage and screen actor. Married to stage actress Adele Rowland. Half brother of actors Godfrey Tearle (dec. 1953) and Malcolm Tearle (dec. 1935).

Appeared in: **1914** The Nightingale. **1915** Seven Sisters. **1916** The Common Law. **1917** The Fall of Romanoff. **1918** Stella Maris. **1919** Virtuous Wives; The Way of a Woman; The Mind-the-Paint Girl. **1920** A Virtuous Vamp; Two Weeks; The Forbidden Woman. **1921** Bucking the Tiger; Marooned Hearts; The Road of Ambition; Society Snobs; Whispering Devils; The Man of Stone; The Fighter; After Midnight; The Oath. **1922** The Eternal Flame; Love's Masquerade; The Referee; Shadows of the Sea; A Wide Open Town; One Week of Love. **1923** Bella Donna; Ashes of Vengeance; The Dangerous Maid; Woman of Bronze; The Common Law (and 1916 version); The Rustle of Silk. **1924** The White Moth; Black Oxen; Flirting with Love; Lilies of the Field; The Next Corner. **1925** The Mystic; The Great Divide; The Viennese Medley; Bad Company; The Heart of a Siren; Morals for Men; Just a Woman; School for Wives. **1926** Dancing Mothers; My Official Wife; The Dancer of Paris; The Greater Glory; The Sporting Lover. **1927** Altars of Desire; Isle of Forgotten Women; Moulders of Men. **1929** Smoke Bellew; Evidence; Gold Diggers of Broadway. **1930** The Lost Zeppelin; Truth about Youth. **1931** The Lady Who Dared; Morals for Women; Captivation. **1932** Vanity Fair; Pleasure; Her Mad Night; The Man about Town. **1933** Day of Reckoning; Should Ladies Behave? **1934** Fifteen Wives; Stingaree; Sing Sing Nights. **1935** Headline Woman; The

Trail's End; Judgement Book. **1936** The Preview Murder Mystery; Desert Guns; Klondike Annie; Romeo and Juliet.

TEARLE, SIR GODFREY
Born: Oct. 12, 1884, New York, N.Y. Died: June 8, 1953, London, England. Stage and screen actor. Brother of actor Malcolm Tearle (dec. 1935) and half brother of actor Conway Tearle (dec. 1938). Entered films in 1906.

Appeared in: **1908** Romeo and Juliet. **1913** The Fool. **1915** Lochinvar. **1916** Sir James Mortimer's Wager; The Real Thing at Last. **1919** A Sinless Sinner (aka Midnight Gambols—US 1920); Nobody's Child; Queen's Evidence; The March Hare; Fancy Dress. **1925** Salome of the Tenements. **1926** If Youth But Knew; One Colombo Night; The Steve Donoghue series including: Guy of Warwick. **1930** Infatuation. **1931** These Charming People; The Shadow Between. **1933** Puppets of Fate (aka Wolves of the Underworld—US 1935). **1934** Spotting series including: Jade. **1935** The 39 Steps; The Last Journey (US 1936); East Meets West; Tomorrow We Live. **1942** Tomorrow We Live (and 1935 version, aka At Dawn We Die—US 1943); One of Our Aircraft is Missing. **1943** Undercover (aka Underground Guerillas—US 1944); The Lamp Still Burns. **1944** Medal for the General. **1945** The Rake's Progress (aka Notorious Gentleman—US 1946). **1949** Private Angelo. **1951** White Corridors. **1952** I Believe in You (US 1953); Mandy (aka Crash of Silence—US 1953); Decameron Nights. **1953** The Titfield Thunderbolt.

TEARLE, MALCOLM
Born: 1888. Died: Dec. 8, 1935, London, England (suicide). Brother of actor Godfrey Tearle (dec. 1953) and half brother of actor Conway Tearle (dec. 1938).

TEATHER, IDA
Died: Apr. 10, 1954, Ebbw Vale, Wales. Screen, stage and radio actress.

TEEGE, JOACHIM
Born: 1925, Spremberg, Silesia, Poland. Died: Nov. 23, 1969, Munich, Germany. Screen, stage and television actor.

Appeared in: **1967** Those Fantastic Flying Fools. **1968** How to Seduce a Playboy.

TELL, ALMA
Born: 1892. Died: Dec. 30, 1937, San Fernando, Calif. Screen and stage actress. Sister of actress Olive Tell (dec. 1951).

Appeared in: **1916** The Smugglers. **1920** On with the Dance; The Right to Love. **1921** The Iron Trail; Paying the Piper. **1922** Broadway Rose. **1923** The Silent Command. **1928** San Francisco Nights. **1929** Saturday's Children. **1930** Love Comes Along.

TELL, OLIVE
Born: 1894, New York, N.Y. Died: June 8, 1951, New York, N.Y. Stage and screen actress. Sister of actress Alma Tell (dec. 1937). Entered films with Mutual in 1917.

Appeared in: **1918** The Unforseen. **1921** Clothes; Wings of Pride; The Wrong Woman; Worlds Apart. **1925** Chickie. **1926** The Prince of Tempters; Woman-Handled; Summer Bachelors. **1927** Slaves of Beauty. **1928** Sailors' Wives; Soft Living. **1929** Hearts in Exile; The Trial of Mary Dugan; The Very Idea. **1930** Lawful Larceny; Love Comes Along; The Right of Way; Woman Hungry; Devotion; Delicious. **1933** Strictly Personal. **1934** The Scarlet Empress; The Witching Hour; Private Scandal; Baby, Take a Bow. **1935** Four Hours to Kill; Shanghai. **1936** In His Steps; Polo Joe; Yours for the Asking; Brilliant Marriage. **1939** Zaza.

TELLEGEN, LOU (Isidor Louis Bernard Von Dammeler)
Born: Nov. 26, 1881. Died: Nov. 1, 1934, Los Angeles, Calif. (suicide). Stage and screen actor. Divorced from actress Geraldine Farrar (dec. 1967).

Appeared in: **1911** Queen Elizabeth. **1915** The Explorer; The Unknown. **1916** The Victoria Cross; Maria Rosa; The Victory of Conscience. **1917** The Long Trail. **1919** Flame of the Desert; The World and Its Women. **1920** The Woman and the Puppet. **1924** Single Wives; Those Who Judge; Between Friends; The Breath of Scandal; Let Not Man Put Asunder; Greater Than Marriage. **1925** The Redeeming Sin; After Business Hours; East Lynne; The Sporting Chance; Borrowed Finery; Fair Play; Parisian Love; Parisian Nights; The Verdict; With This Ring. **1926** The Outsider; Siberia; The Silver Treasure; Woman-power; Three Bad Men. **1927** The Princess from Hoboken; The Little Firebrand; Married Alive; Stage Madness. **1928** No Other Woman. **1931** Enemies of the Law.

TEMARY, ELZA. See ELZA K. SPLANE

TEMPEST, DAME MARIE (Marie Susan Etherington)
Born: 1864, London, England. Died: Oct. 15, 1942, London, England. Screen, stage actress and opera singer. Married to actor W. Graham Browne (dec. 1937). Was made Dame Commander of the Order of the British Empire in 1937.

Appeared in: **1900** English Nell. **1915** Mrs. Plum's Pudding. **1937** Moonlight

Sonata. **1938** Yellow Sands. **1943** The Charmer (rerelease of 1937 Moonlight Sonata).

TEMPLETON, FAY
Born: Dec. 25, 1866, Little Rock, Ark. Died: Oct. 3, 1939, San Francisco, Calif. Screen, stage and vaudeville actress. Entered films in 1929.

Appeared in: **1932** The March of Time (short). **1933** Broadway to Hollywood.

TENBROOK, HARRY (Henry Olaf Hansen)
Born: Oct. 9, 1887, Norway. Died: Sept. 14, 1960, Woodland Hills, Calif. (lung cancer). Screen actor.

Appeared in: **1923** Kindled Courage. **1924** The Measure of a Man. **1925** The Burning Trail; Manhattan Madness. **1926** The Blue Eagle; Mistaken Orders; The Silent Guardian. **1927** The Outlaw Dog; Speedy Smith; Thunderbolt's Tracks. **1928** Danger Street; The Play Girl. **1929** Eyes of the Underworld; Seven Footprints to Satan. **1930** Men Without Women; On the Level; The Runaway Bride; The Sea Wolf. **1931** Donovan's Kid. **1932** This Reckless Age. **1933** Terror Trail. **1934** The Thin Man. **1935** Millions in the Air. **1937** Hit the Saddle. **1938** Rawhide; A Slight Case of Murder. **1939** Stagecoach; Oklahoma Frontier. **1940** Ragtime Cowboy Joe. **1945** They Were Expendable. **1950** When Willie Comes Marching Home. **1955** Mister Roberts.

TENNBERG, JEAN-MARC
Born: 1924, France. Died: 1971, France. Screen actor.

Appeared in: **1952** Fanfan the Tulip (US 1953). **1954** The Moment of Truth. **1956** Adorable Creatures; French Can-Can (aka Only the French Can). **1962** Les Sept Peches Capitaux (Seven Capital Sins—US 1963); Le Repos du Guerrier (Warrior's Rest aka Love on a Pillow—US 1963). **1964** Une Ravissante Idiote (A Ravishing Idiot—US 1966). **1965** La Traite des Blanches (aka Frustrations—US 1967 and Hot Frustrations).

TERHUNE, MAX
Born: Feb. 12, 1891, Franklin, Ind. Died: June 5, 1973, Cottonwood, Ariz. (heart attack and stroke). Screen, television, vaudeville and radio actor, ventriloquist and magician. Gained fame in Western films as "Alabi and his dummy friend, Elmer."

Appeared in: **1936** The Three Mesquiteers; Ride, Ranger, Ride (debut); Ghost Town Gold. **1937** Hit the Saddle; Heart of the Rockies; Riders of the Whistling Skull; The Hit Parade; Manhattan Merry-Go-Round; Mama Runs Wild; Come On, Cowboys!; Range Defenders; Roarin' Lead; The Big Show; Gunsmoke Ranch; The Trigger Trio. **1938** Call the Mesquiteers; The Purple Vigilantes; Outlaws of Sonora; Ladies in Distress; Riders of the Black Hills; Heroes of the Hills; Pals of the Saddle; Overland Stage Raiders; Wild Horse Rodeo; Santa Fe Stampede; Red River Range. **1939** Man of Conquest; The Night Riders; Three Texas Steers. **1940** The Range Busters; West of Pinto Basin; Trailing Double Trouble. **1941** Tumbledown Ranch in Arizona; Trail of the Silver Spurs; The Kid's Last Ride; Wranglers' Roost; Fugitive Valley. **1942** Trail Riders; Rock River Renegades; Texas to Bataan; Boot Hill Bandits; Texas Trouble Shooters; Saddle Mountain Roundup. **1943** Two-Fisted Justice; Cowboy Commandos; Black Market Rustlers; Haunted Ranch. **1944** Cowboy Canteen; Sheriff of Sundown. **1947** Along the Oregon Trail; White Stallion. **1948** Gunning for Justice; The Sheriff of Medicine Bow. **1949** Square Dance Jubilee; Law of the West; Range Justice; Western Renegades; West of Eldorado; Trail's End. **1951** Rawhide; Jim Thorpe—All American. **1956** Giant. **1957** King and Four Queens.

TERNICK, FRANK
Born: 1895. Died: Oct. 29, 1966. Screen actor and stuntman.

TERR, AL (Albert R. Terr)
Born: May 22, 1893, New York. Died: July 15, 1967, Burbank, Calif. (heart disease). Screen actor and musician.

Appeared in: **1958** Bullwhip. **1960** Lust to Kill.

TERRANOVA, DINO (Corrado Vacirca)
Born: 1904, Italy. Died: Apr. 27, 1969, Miami, Fla. Screen and stage actor.

Appeared in: **1956** The Wrong Man (stage and screen versions). **1963** Flipper. **1968** The Brotherhood.

TERRELL, KEN (Kenneth Jones Terrell)
Born: Apr. 29, 1904, Ga. Died: Mar. 8, 1966, Sherman Oaks, Calif. (arteriosclerosis). Screen actor and stuntman.

Appeared in: **1939** Dick Tracy's G-Men. **1940** Mysterious Dr. Satan. **1941** Jungle Girl. **1942** Perils of Nyoka (serial); Cowboy Serenade. **1944** The Tiger Woman; Captain America (serial). **1945** The Purple Monster Strikes. **1947** Son of Zorro; Robinhood of Texas. **1948** G-Men Never Forget; The Bold Frontiersman; The Gay Ranchero; Grand Canyon Trail. **1949** The Clay Pigeon. **1951** Pals of the Golden West. **1952** Last Train from Bombay; Lydia Bailey. **1953** Port Sinister. **1954** Return to Treasure Island; Drums Across the River. **1956** The Indestructible Man; The Proud Ones. **1957** Attack of the Fifty-Foot Wom-

an; The Brain from Planet Arous; Sabu and the Magic Ring. **1959** Pier 5, Havana. **1961** Master of the World.

TERRISS, ELLALINE
Born: 1871, England. Died: June 16, 1971, London, England. Stage and screen actress. Married to actor Sir Seymour Hicks (dec. 1949).

Appeared in: **1907** My Indian Anna. **1913** David Garrick; Scrooge; Seymour Hicks and Ellaline Terriss (short). **1914** Always Tell Your Wife. **1917** Masks and Face. **1927** Blighty (aka Apres la Guerre); Land of Hope and Glory. **1929** Atlantic. **1931** Glamour; Man of Mayfair. **1935** The Iron Duke; Royal Cavalcade (aka Regal Cavalcade—US). **1939** The Four Just Men (aka The Secret Four—US 1940).

TERRISS, TOM
Born: Sept. 28, 1887, London, England. Died: Feb. 8, 1964, New York, N.Y. Stage and screen actor, film director and screenwriter.

Appeared in: **1914** The Chimes; The Mystery of Edwin Drood. **1915** A Woman of the World; The Pearl of the Antilles; Flame of Passion. **1916** My Country First.

TERRY, DAME ELLEN
Born: 1848, Coventry, England. Died: July 21, 1928, Kent, England (heart trouble). Stage and screen actress. Married to actor James Carew (dec. 1938). Was made Dame Commander of the Order of the British Empire in 1925. Entered films with Triangle in 1919.

Appeared in: **1920** Pillars of Society. **1922** The Bohemian Girl.

TERRY, ETHEL GREY
Born: Oakland, Calif. Died: Jan. 6, 1931, Hollywood, Calif. Stage and screen actress. Married to actor Carl Gerard. Entered films approx. 1917.

Appeared in: **1917** Arsene Lupin. **1919** Hardboiled; The Carter Case (the "Craig Kennedy" serial). **1921** The Breaking Point; Suspicious Wives. **1922** The Crossroads of New York; The Kick Back; Oath-Bound; Shattered Idols; Too Much Business; Travelin' On; Under Two Flags. **1923** Brass; The Self-Made Wife; Garrison's Finish; Wild Bill Hickok; Why Women Remarry; What Wives Want; The Unknown Purple; Peg O' My Heart. **1924** The Fast Worker. **1925** Old Shoes; What Fools Men. **1926** Hard Boiled; The Love Toy. **1927** Cancelled Debts. **1928** Skinner's Big Idea; Modern Mothers; Confessions of a Wife; Sharp Tools (short). **1929** Object Alimony.

TERRY, FRED
Born: England. Died: Apr. 1933, London, England. Screen and stage actor. Married to stage actress Julia Nielson and father of actor Dennis Nielson-Terry (dec. 1932).

Appeared in: **1922** With Wings Outspread.

TERRY, HAZEL (Hazel Neilson-Terry)
Born: Jan. 23, 1918, London, England. Died: Oct. 12, 1974, London, England. Stage and screen actress. Daughter of stage actors Mary Glynne and Denis Neilson-Terry. Entered films in 1935.

Appeared in: **1936** The Marriage of Corbal (aka Prisoner of Corbal—US 1939). **1937** Our Fighting Navy (aka Torpedoed—US 1939); Missing, Believed Married. **1938** Sweet Devil. **1962** Kill or Cure. **1963** The Servant (US 1964).

TERRY, SHEILA (Kay Clark)
Born: Mar. 5, 1910, Warroad, Minn. Died: Jan. 19, 1957. Stage and screen actress.

Appeared in: **1932** Week-End Marriage; Crooner; Big City Blues; I Am a Fugitive From a Chain Gang; Three On a Match; Scarlet Dawn; You Said a Mouthful; Madame Butterfly; Lawyer Man; **1933** Silk Express; Mayor of Hell; Private Detective 62; House on 56th Street; The Sphinx; Convention City; Son of a Sailor; 20,000 Years in Sing Sing; Haunted Gold; Parachute Jumper. **1934** Rocky Rhodes; Take the Stand; When Strangers Meet; 'Neath Arizona Skies. **1935** Lawless Frontier; Rescue Squad; Society Fever. **1936** Murder on a Bridle Path; Special Investigator; Go Get 'Em Haines. **1937** An MGM short.

TETLEY, WALTER (Walter Campbell Tetley)
Born: 1915, New York, N.Y. Died: Sept. 4, 1975. Screen and radio actor.

Appeared in: **1938** Lord Jeff; Prairie Moon. **1939** Spirit of Culver; Tower of London; Boy Slaves; They Shall Have Music. **1940** Military Academy; Under Texas Skies; Let's Make Music. **1942** Thunder Birds; Who Done It?; The Gorilla Man. **1944** Pin Up Girl; The Lodger. **1945** Molly and Me.

TEVIS, CAROL
Born: Mar. 6, 1907, Pa. Died: May 15, 1965, Pacific Palisades, Calif. Screen actress, author and composer.

Appeared in: **1932** Once in a Lifetime; The Millionaire Cat (short). **1935** Sweepstake Annie; The Affaire of Suzan. **1936** Sing, Baby, Sing. **1937** The Big Squirt (short); Love Is News; Love Takes Flight.

THANE, EDWARD

Died: Jan. 1954. Stage and screen actor. Married to actress Louise Hampton (dec. 1954).

Appeared in: **1931** Almost a Honeymoon.

THATCHER, EVELYN "EVA"

Born: 1862, Omaha, Nebr. Died: Sept. 28, 1942, Los Angeles, Calif. Screen, stage and vaudeville actress. Appeared in Mack Sennett comedies. Appeared in vaudeville as "The Irish Lady."

Appeared in: **1916** Haystacks and Steeples. **1917** Her Nature Dance; His Naughty Thought; She Needed a Doctor; Thirst; A Bedroom Blunder. **1923** Thirst (reissue of 1917 film). **1924** Not Built for Runnin'. **1925** Flash O'Lightning; Ranchers and Rascals; The Trouble Buster. **1926** Blind Trail; The Outlaw Express.

THAW, EVELYN NESBIT

Born: 1885. Died: Jan. 18, 1967, Santa Monica, Calif. Screen and vaudeville actress. Known as the "Girl in the Red Velvet Swing."

Appeared in: **1914** Threads of Destiny. **1917** Redemption. **1922** The Hidden Woman.

THAWL, EVELYN

Born: 1915. Died: Nov. 1945, Brooklyn, N.Y. Screen and stage actress.

THEIS, ALFRED

Born: 1899. Died: Sept. 16, 1951, Newfoundland, enroute from Germany (heart attack). Screen and vaudeville actor. Appeared in vaudeville in the "Alfred Theis Tiny Town Revue."

THESIGER, ERNEST

Born: Jan. 15, 1879, London, England. Died: Jan. 14, 1961, London, England. Stage and screen actor.

Appeared in: **1916** The Real Thing at Last. **1918** Nelson; The Life Story of David Lloyd George. **1919** A Little Bit of Fluff. **1921** The Bachelor's Club; The Adventures of Mr. Pickwick. **1928** Weekend Wives (US 1929). **1929** The Vagabond Queen. **1930** Ashes. **1932** The Old Dark House. **1933** The Only Girl (aka Heart Song—US 1934); The Ghoul. **1934** The Night of the Party; My Heart is Calling (US 1935). **1935** Bride of Frankenstein. **1936** The Man Who Could Work Miracles (US 1937). **1938** They Drive by Night; The Ware Case (US 1939); Lightning Conductors. **1943** My Learned Friend; The Lamp Still Burns. **1944** Don't Take it to Heart (US 1949). **1945** Henry V (US 1946); A Place of One's Own (US 1949). **1946** Caesar and Cleopatra; Beware of Pity (US 1947). **1947** The Man Within (aka The Smugglers—US 1948); Jassy (US 1948); The Ghosts of Berkeley Square. **1948** The Winslow Boy (US 1950); Quartet (US 1949); Portrait from Life (aka The Girl in the Painting—US 1949); The Brass Monkey (aka Lucky Mascot—US 1951). **1949** The Bad Lord Byron (US 1952). **1950** Last Holiday. **1951** The Man in the White Suit (US 1952); Scrooge; The Magic Box (US 1952); Laughter in Paradise. **1952** The Woman's Angle (1954). **1953** Meet Mr. Lucifer; The Robe. **1954** The Million Pound Note (aka Man with a Million—US); Father Brown (aka The Detective—US); Make Me an Offer (US 1956). **1955** Quentin Durward; Value for Money (US 1957); An Alligator Named Daisy (US 1957). **1956** Three Men in a Boat (US 1958); Who Done It? **1957** Doctor at Large. **1958** The Truth About Women. **1959** The Horse's Mouth; The Battle of the Sexes (US 1960). **1960** Sons and Lovers. **1962** The Roman Spring of Mrs. Stone. **1963** Invitation to Murder.

THIELE, WILLIAM J.

Born: May 10, 1890, Vienna, Austria. Died: Sept. 7, 1975, Woodland Hills, Calif. Screen, stage actor, film director and writer. Entered films in 1913 as an actor.

THIGPEN, HELEN

Died: Sept. 3, 1966. Black screen actress.

Appeared in: **1959** Porgy and Bess. (stage and film versions).

THIMIG, HELENE

Died: Nov. 7, 1974, Vienna, Austria (heart failure). Screen and stage actress. Married to film producer and director Max Reinhardt (dec. 1943).

Appeared in: **1932** Mensch Ohne Namen. **1942** The Gay Sisters. **1943** The Moon Is Down; Edge of Darkness. **1944** The Hitler Gang; None But the Lonely Heart; Strangers in the Night. **1945** Hotel Berlin; Isle of the Dead; This Love of Ours; Roughly Speaking. **1946** Cloak and Dagger. **1947** The Locket; Cry Wolf; Escape Me Never; High Conquest. **1952** Decision Before Dawn.

THOMAS, EDNA

Born: 1886, Lawrenceville, Va. Died: July 22, 1974, New York, N.Y. (heart condition). Stage and screen actress.

Appeared in: **1951** A Streetcar Named Desire (stage and screen versions).

THOMAS, GRETCHEN

Born: 1897. Died: Nov. 1, 1964, Hollywood, Calif. Screen, stage and television actress.

Appeared in: **1930** Spring Is Here; Young Desire. **1937** Damaged Goods. **1938** Marriage Forbidden. **1957** I Was a Teenage Frankenstein.

THOMAS, GUS

Born: 1865, Toronto, Canada. Died: May 3, 1926, Everett, Wash. Screen, stage and vaudeville actor.

Appeared in: **1922** Alias Julius Caesar.

THOMAS, JAMESON

Born: Mar. 24, 1889. Died: Jan. 10, 1939, Sierra Madre, Calif. (tuberculosis). Screen, stage actor and film director.

Appeared in: **1923** Chu Chin Chow (US 1925). **1924** Decameron Nights (US 1928); The Sins Ye Do. **1925** Afraid of Love; The Apache; A Daughter of Love; The Gold Cure. **1926** The Jungle Woman. **1927** Blighty (aka Apres La Guerre); Pearl of the South Seas; Poppies of Flanders; Roses of Picardy. **1928** The Farmer's Wife (US 1930); The Rising Generation; Tesha; Weekend Wives; The White Sheik (aka King's Mate). **1929** The Feather; High Treason; Piccadilly; Power over Men. **1930** Elstree Calling; The Hate Ship; Extravagance. **1931** Lover Come Back; Night Birds. **1932** Three Wise Girls; Trial of Vivienne Ware; Escapade; No More Orchids; The Phantom President. **1933** Brief Moment; The Invisible Man; Self Defense. **1934** Stolen Sweets; Now and Forever; The Moonstone; A Successful Failure; A Lost Lady; The Curtain Falls; It Happened One Night; Bombay Mail; The Scarlet Empress; A Woman's Man; Beggars in Ermine; Sing Sing Nights; Jane Eyre. **1935** Lives of a Bengal Lancer; Charlie Chan in Egypt; The Last Outpost; The World Accuses; Mr. Dynamite; Coronado; The Lady in Scarlet. **1936** Mr. Deeds Goes to Town; Lady Luck. **1937** The Man Who Cried Wolf; One Hundred Men and a Girl; The League of Frightened Men; House of Secrets. **1938** Death Goes North.

THOMAS, JOHN CHARLES

Born: 1887, Baltimore, Md. Died: Dec. 1960, Apple Valley, Calif. (intestinal cancer). Screen, stage, radio actor and singer.

Appeared in: **1923** Under the Red Robe. **1927** The following shorts: Prologue to I Pagliacci; Danny Deever; Will You Remember Me?

THOMAS, OLIVE

Born: Oct. 29, 1884, Charleroi, Pa. Died: Sept. 10, 1920, Paris, France (suicide). Stage and screen actress. Married to actor Jack Pickford (dec. 1933).

Appeared in: **1916** Beatrice Follies. **1917** Betty Takes a Hand. **1918** Limousine Life. **1919** The Glorious Lady; Upstairs and Down; The Follies Girl. **1920** The Flapper; Footlights and Shadows.

THOMAS, RUTH

Born: 1911. Died: Mar. 23, 1970, Columbus, Ohio. Screen, stage and television actress.

THOMAS, WILLIAM

Born: 1918. Died: May, 1948, Los Angeles, Calif. Screen actor. Do not confuse with William "Buckwheat" Thomas.

Appeared in: **1947** Spirit of West Point; The Big Fix.

THOMASHEFSKY, MAX

Born: 1872. Died: July 24, 1932, New York, N.Y. Screen and stage actor.

THOMPSON, DAVID H.

Born: May 4, 1886, New York, N.Y. Died: May 20, 1957, Hollywood, Calif. Screen, stage actor and film director. Appeared in Edison Film Co. productions in 1910 and in Thanhouser Film Co. productions 1911–14.

THOMPSON, FREDERICK A.

Born: 1870, Montreal, Canada. Died: Jan. 23, 1925, Hollywood, Calif. (heart disease). Stage and screen actor. Entered films in 1910.

Appeared in: **1921** The Heart Line. **1922** A Tailor Made Man.

THOMPSON, GEORGE

Born: 1868. Died: May 29, 1929, Los Angeles, Calif. (following surgery for stomach trouble caused by poisonous facial make-up which started infection). Stage and screen actor.

Appeared in: **1929** Why Bring That Up?

THOMPSON, HAL

Born: 1894. Died: Mar. 3, 1966. Screen actor.

Appeared in: **1925** Who's Your Friend? **1926** Comin' an' Going. **1930** Animal Crackers; Leave It to Lester.

THOMPSON, MOLLY

Born: 1879. Died: Feb. 14, 1928, Culver City, Calif. (brain hemorrhage). Screen actress and casting director. Was an actress with Roach and appeared in nearly all of Harold Lloyd's early comedies.

THOMPSON, POLLY (Hippolita Thompson)

Died: Mar. 8, 1933, New York, N.Y. (suicide—gas). Screen and stage actress.

Appeared in: **1919** Deliverance.

THOMPSON, THERESE

Born: 1876. Died: Sept. 17, 1936, Hollywood, Calif. Screen and stage actress. Sister of actress Trixie Friganza (dec. 1955).

THOMPSON, ULU M.

Born: 1873. Died: Apr. 13, 1957, Hollywood, Calif. (heart ailment). Screen actress.

THOMPSON, WILLIAM "BILL"

Born: 1913. Died: July 15, 1971, Los Angeles, Calif. Screen, radio and television actor. Do not confuse with actor William H. Thompson (dec. 1923), nor stage actor William Thompson (dec. 1929).

Appeared in: **1942** Here We Go Again. **1951** Alice in Wonderland (voice of White Rabbit and Dodo). **1953** Peter Pan (voice). **1955** Lady and the Tramp (voice of Jock, Bull and Dachsie). **1959** Sleeping Beauty (voice only). **1970** The Aristocats (voice only).

THOMPSON, WILLIAM H.

Born: 1852, Glasgow, Scotland. Died: Feb. 4, 1923, New York, N.Y. (pneumonia). Stage and screen actor. Do not confuse with actor William H. Thompson (dec. 1929). Married to stage actress Lillian Dix (dec. 1922).

Appeared in: **1915** Peggy.

THOMSON, FRED

Born: Apr. 28, 1890, Pasadena, Calif. Died: Dec. 25, 1928, Los Angeles, Calif. (following surgery for gallstones). Screen actor, double and stuntman. Married to actress and screenwriter Frances Marion (dec. 1973).

Appeared in: **1921** The Love Light; Just around the Corner. **1922** Oath-Bound; Penrod. **1923** The Eagle's Talons (serial); The Mask of Lopez; A Chapter in Her Life. **1924** The Silent Stranger; The Dangerous Coward; The Fighting Sap; Galloping Gallagher; North of Nevada; Thundering Hoofs; Queniado. **1925** The Wild Bull's Lair; The Bandit's Baby; That Devil Quemado; All around Frying Pan; Ridin' the Wind. **1926** A Regular Scout; Hands across the Border; The Two-Gun Man; The Tough Guy; Lone Hand Saunders. **1927** Silver Comes Through; Jesse James; Arizona Nights; Don Mike. **1928** Kit Carson; The Pioneer Scout.

THOMSON, KENNETH

Born: Jan. 7, 1899, Pittsburgh, Pa. Died: Jan. 27, 1967, Los Angeles, Calif. (emphysema and fibrosis). Screen and stage actor. One of the founders of the Screen Actors Guild.

Appeared in: **1926** Corporal Kate; Man Bait; Risky Business. **1927** White Gold; Almost Human; King of Kings; Turkish Delight. **1928** The Secret Hour; The Street of Illusion. **1929** The Letter; The Bellamy Trial; The Broadway Melody; Say It with Songs; The Careless Age; The Girl from Havana; The Veiled Woman; Song Writer. **1930** Children of Pleasure; Lawful Larceny; Sweethearts on Parade; Doorway to Hell; Just Imagine; Faithful; The Other Tomorrow; A Notorious Affair; Sweet Mama; Wild Company; Reno. **1931** Woman Hungry; Murder at Midnight; Bad Company; Oh! Oh! Cleopatra (short). **1932** By Whose Hands?; Man Wanted; The Famous Ferguson Case; Movie Crazy; 70,000 Witnesses; 13 Women; Her Mad Night; Lawyer Man; Fast Life. **1933** The Little Giant; Female; Son of a Sailor; Daring Daughters; Hold Me Tight; Sitting Pretty; From Headquarters; Jungle Bride. **1934** Change of Heart; Many Happy Returns; Cross Streets; In Old Santa Fe. **1935** Behold My Wife; Behind the Green Lights; Whispering Smith Speaks; Hopalong Cassidy; Manhattan Butterfly. **1936** With Love and Kisses; The Blackmailer. **1937** Jim Hanvey—Detective.

THORBURN, JUNE

Born: 1931, Kashmir, India. Died: Nov. 4, 1967, Fernhurst, Sussex, England (air crash). Screen and television actress.

Appeared in: **1952** The Pickwick Papers (film debut—US 1953). **1953** The Cruel Sea. **1954** Fast and Loose; Delayed Action; Children Galore; Orders Are Orders. **1955** The Hornet's Nest; Touch and Go (aka The Light Touch—US 1956). **1957** True as Turtle. **1958** Rooney; Tom Thumb. **1959** Broth of a Boy. **1960** The Price of Silence; The 3 Worlds of Gulliver; Escort for Hire. **1961** Fury at Smuggler's Bay (US 1963); Transatlantic; Don't Bother to Knock (aka Why Bother to Knock—US 1964). **1963** Master Spy; The Scarlet Blade (aka The Crimson Blade—US 1964).

THORNDIKE, OLIVER

Born: Sept. 12, 1918, Boston, Mass. Died: Apr. 14, 1954, St. Thomas, Virgin Islands. Screen, stage and television actor.

Appeared in: **1932** The Sign of the Cross. **1944** The Sign of the Cross (revised version of 1932 film); The Story of Dr. Wassell.

THORNDIKE, RUSSELL

Died: Nov. 7, 1972, London, England. Stage and screen actor, author and screenwriter. Brother of actress Dame Sybil Thorndike (dec. 1976).

Appeared in: **1916** The Test; The Dream of Eugene Aram. **1918** The Bells. **1922** Tense Moments from Great Plays series including: Macbeth; It's Never Too Late to Mend. **1923** The Audacious Mr. Squire; The Fair Maid of Perth; Heartstrings; Wonder Women of the World series including: Henrietta Maria or, the Queen of Sorrow; Lucrezia Borgia or, Plaything of Power; Gems of Literature series including: The Dream of Eugene Aram; Scrooge; The Bells; The School for Scandal; The Test; The Sins of a Father and Love in an Attic. **1924** Miriam Rozella; Human Desires. **1933** Puppets of Fate (aka Wolves of the Underworld—US 1935); The Roof; A Shot in the Dark (US 1935). **1934** Whispering Tongues. **1936** Fame. **1944** Fiddlers Three. **1945** Henry V (US 1946). **1948** Hamlet. **1955** Richard III (US 1956).

THORNDYKE, LUCYLE

Born: 1885, Seattle, Wash. Died: Dec. 17, 1935, Los Angeles, Calif. Stage and screen actress.

Appeared in: **1924** The Garden of Weeds. **1926** The Speed Limit.

THORNE, DICK

Born: 1905. Died: Jan. 31, 1957, Hollywood, Calif. (heart attack). Screen actor and stuntman. Entered films approx. 1925.

THORNE, ROBERT

Born: 1881. Died: July 3, 1965, New York, N.Y. (heart attack). Stage and screen actor.

Appeared in: **1924** Janice Meredith.

THORNHILL, CLAUDE

Born: 1908, Terre Haute, Ind. Died: July 1, 1965, Caldwell, N.J. (heart attack). Bandleader and screen actor.

THORNTON, GLADYS

Born: 1899. Died: Sept 2, 1964, Hollywood, Calif. Screen, stage and radio actress. Played "Aunt Jemima" on radio.

Appeared in: **1962** If a Man Answers.

THORPE, JIM (James Francis Thorpe)

Born: May 28, 1888, near Prague, Okla. Died: Mar. 28, 1953, Los Angeles, Calif. (heart attack). Screen actor and sports figure. Rated as one of the greatest athletes of all time. Entered films as an extra.

Appeared in: **1932** White Eagle; My Pal, the King; Airmail; Hold 'Em Jail. **1933** Wild Horse Mesa. **1935** Code of the Mounted; Behold My Wife; The Red Rider; Wanderer of the Wasteland; Rustlers of Red Gap (serial); She; Fighting Youth. **1936** Sutter's Gold; Wildcat Trooper; Treachery Rides the Range; Hill Tillies (short). **1937** Big City. **1940** Henry Goes to Arizona; Arizona Frontier; Prairie Schooners. **1944** Outlaw Trail. **1950** Wagonmaster.

THORPE, TED

Born: 1917. Died: Dec. 18, 1970, Honolulu, Hawaii (heart attack). Screen actor.

Appeared in: **1953** Flame of Calcutta; Savage Mutiny; The Lost Planet (serial). **1958** Machine Gun Kelly. **1961** Back Street. **1962** If a Man Answers. **1968** Hang 'Em High.

THUMB, MRS. GENERAL TOM (Lavinia Warren)

Born: 1841, Middleboro, Mass. Died: Nov. 25, 1919. Screen actress and circus midget. Married to circus midget Gen. Tom Thumb (dec. 1883) and later to actor-midget Count Primo Magri (dec. 1920).

Appeared in: **1915** The Lilliputian's Courtship.

THUMB, TOM (Darius Adner Alden)

Died: Sept. 24, 1926, Los Angeles, Calif. (internal hemorrhage). Circus midget and screen actor. Do not confuse with circus midget Gen. Tom Thumb (dec. 1883).

THURBER, J. KENT

Born: 1892. Died: May 26, 1957, St. Petersburg, Fla. Screen, stage actor and stage director.

THURMAN, MARY

Born: 1894, Richmond, Utah. Died: Dec. 23, 1925 (effects of tropical fever). Screen actress.

Appeared in: **1916** Sunshine Dad; His Last Laugh; His First False Step; Bombs; The Scoundrel's Tale; The Stone Age (aka Her Cave Man). **1917** Maggie's First False Step; Pinched in the Finish. **1918** Watch Your Neighbor. **1921** Bare Knuckles; The Sin of Martha Queed; The Lady from Longacre; A Broken Doll; The Primal Law. **1922** The Bond Boy; The Green Temptation. **1923** A Bride for a Knight; Does It Pay?; Wife in Name Only; Zaza; The Tents of Allah. **1924** For another Woman; The Law and the Lady; The Truth about Women; Greater Than Marriage; Love of Woman; Playthings of Desire; Trouping with Ellen; Those Who Judge. **1925** Down upon the Swanee River; The Mad Marriage; The Necessary Evil; Back to Life; The Fool; A Little Girl in a Big City; Wildfire. **1926** The Wives of the Prophet.

THURSTON, CAROL
Born: 1923, Forsyth, Mont. Died: Dec. 31, 1969. Screen and stage actress.

Appeared in: **1944** The Story of Dr. Wassell; The Conspirators. **1945** China Sky. **1946** Swamp Fire. **1947** Jewels of Brandenburg; The Last Round-Up. **1948** Rogue's Regiment. **1949** Arctic Manhunt; Apache Chief. **1951** Flaming Feather. **1952** Arctic Flight. **1953** Conquest of Cochise; Killer Ape. **1954** Yukon Vengeance. **1956** The Women of Pitcairn Island. **1960** The Hypnotic Eye. **1963** Showdown.

THURSTON, CHARLES E.
Born: 1869, Oconto, Wis. Died: Mar. 5, 1940, Hollywood, Calif. Screen, stage and vaudeville actor. Entered films approx. 1917.

Appeared in: **1921** Boys Will Be Boys; Black Sheep. **1922** Doubling for Romeo; The Gray Dawn. **1924** Ridgeway of Montana. **1926** Rolling Home; Is That Nice. **1927** Between Dangers; The Fightin' Comeback; The Broken Gate; Spoilers of the West. **1928** When the Law Rides; The Chaser. **1932** The Big Shot. **1933** Unknown Valley.

THURSTON, HARRY
Died: Sept. 2, 1955. Screen actor.

Appeared in: **1945** And Then There Were None.

THURSTON, MURIEL
Born: 1875, France. Died: May 1, 1943, Hollywood, Calif. Screen actress.

TIBBETT, LAWRENCE
Born: Nov. 16, 1896, Bakersfield, Calif. Died: July 15, 1960, New York, N.Y. Screen, radio actor and opera baritone.

Appeared in: **1930** The Rogue Song; New Moon. **1931** The Prodigal. **1932** Cuban Love Song. **1935** Metropolitan. **1936** Under Your Spell.

TIDBLAD, INGA
Born: 1902, Sweden (?). Died: Sept. 1975, Stockholm, Sweden. Screen and stage actress.

Appeared in: **1930** For Her Sake. **1934** The Song of the Scarlet Flower. **1956** Foreign Intrigue. The following Swedish films: Andersson; Petersson and Lundstrom; Pirates on Lake Malar; The Norrtull Gang; The Counts of Svansta; Man of Destiny; Uncle Frans; Black Rudolf; The General; Longing for the Sea; People of Halsingland; She of Nobody; Jansson's Temptation; Intermezzo; Flames in the Dark; There Burned a Flame; The Invisible Wall; The Royal Hunt; Mandragora; Divorced; House of Women; Gabrielle; The Unicorn; Mother of Pearl.

TIDMARSH, FERDINAND
Born: 1883, Philadelphia, Pa. Died: Nov. 1922, Philadelphia, Pa. Screen, stage and vaudeville actor.

Appeared in: **1915** The Sporting Duchess; The Cowardly Way. **1916** Lovely Mary; The Half Million Bride; The World's Great Snare.

TIEDTKE, JAKOB
Born: June 23, 1875, Berlin, Germany. Died: June 30, 1960, Berlin, Germany. Stage and screen actor.

Appeared in: **1926** The Waltz Dream. **1929** Luther. **1932** Drunter und Drueber; Saison in Kairo. **1934** Fraeulein-Falsch Verbunden!; Tausend Fuer Eine Nacht; Strich Durch die Rechnung; Eines Prinzen Junge Liebe; Ja, Treu Ist die Soldatenliebe; Ein Toller Einfall; Das Blaue Vom Himmel; Heimat am Rhein. **1935** Lockvogel; Die Kalte Mansell; Gretl Zieht das Grosse Los; Die Liebe und die Erste Eisenbahn (Love and the First Railroad); Die Sonne Geht Auf; Der Deppelbraeutigam (The Double Fiancee); Die Grosse Chance; Freuhlingsmaerchen; Der Schuechterne Felix; Frischer Wind aus Kanada; Das Lied vom Gluech (The Song of Happiness); Wenn am Sonntagabend die Dorfmusik Spielt. **1936** Der Vetter aus Dengsda; Der Junge Graf. **1937** Besuch am Abend. **1939** Nanu, Sie Kennen Korff noch Nicht? (So, You Don't Know Korff Yet?); Verwehte Spuren (Covered Tracks). **1940** Peter, Paul und Nanette. **1955** Leave on Parole.

TIGHE, HARRY
Born: approx. 1885. Died: Feb. 10, 1935, Old Lyme, Conn. Screen, stage, vaudeville, radio actor and film director.

Appeared in: **1922** A Wide-Open Town. **1930** Bright Sayings (short).

TILBURY, ZEFFIE
Born: 1863. Died: July 24, 1950, Los Angeles, Calif. Stage and screen actress.

Appeared in: **1919** The Avalanche. **1921** Camille; The Marriage of William Ashe; Big Game. **1924** Another Scandal. **1929** The Single Standard. **1930** The Ship from Shanghai. **1931** Charlie Chan Carries On. **1934** Mystery Liner. **1935** Women Must Dress; The Mystery of Edwin Drood; The Werewolf of London; Alice Adams; The Last Days of Pompeii. **1936** Desire; Vamp Until Ready (short); Second Childhood (short); Give Me Your Heart; The Gorgeous Hussy; The Bohemian Girl. **1937** It Happened in Hollywood; Under Cover of Night; Bulldog Drummond Comes Back; Rhythm in the Clouds; Federal Bullets; Maid of Salem. **1938** Bulldog Drummond's Peril; Hunted Men; Woman against Woman; Josette. **1939** Arrest Bulldog Drummond; Boy Trouble; The Story of Alexander Graham Bell; Tell No Tales; Balalaika. **1940** The Grapes of Wrath; Comin' Round the Mountain. **1941** She Couldn't Say No; Tobacco Road; Sheriff of Tombstone.

TILDEN, BILL (William Tatem Tilden, II)
Died: June 5, 1953, Hollywood, Calif. (heart attack). Former tennis champion, screen, stage actor and playwright.

Appeared in: **1932–33** Universal's Sport shorts. **1935** Commentator for British Lion Shorts.

TILGHMAN, WILLIAM MATTHEW
Born: July 4, 1854, Fort Dodge, Iowa. Died: Nov. 1, 1924, Okla. (shot to death). Police officer and screen actor.

Appeared in: **1908** The Bank Robbery. **1915** The Passing of the Oklahoma Outlaws.

TILLES, KEN (Kenneth A. Tilles)
Born: Apr. 16, 1912, Calif. Died: Jan. 31, 1970, Los Angeles, Calif. (heart attack). Screen actor.

Appeared in: **1969** Stiletto. **1970** Dreams of Glass.

TILTON, EDWIN BOOTH
Born: 1860. Died: Jan. 16, 1926, Hollywood, Calif. Screen, stage actor, film director and screenwriter.

Appeared in: **1920** Love's Harvest; The Little Wanderer. **1921** Bare Knuckles; What Love Will Do; Children of the Night; Bucking the Line; Lovetime; The Mother Heart; While The Devil Laughs; The Primal Law; The Lamplighter. **1922** The Cub Reporter; Winning with Wits; Gleam O'Dawn; The Man under Cover; Hungry Hearts. **1923** Times Have Changed. **1924** The House of Youth; Thundergate; Racing for Life; The Lone Chance; The Midnight Express. **1925** The Taming of the West.

TIMBERG, HERMAN
Born: 1892. Died: Apr. 16, 1952, New York, N.Y. Screen, stage, vaudeville actor, stage producer, songwriter, radio writer and screenwriter.

Appeared in: **1930** The Love Boat (short). **1936–38** Educational shorts.

TIMMONS, JOSEPH
Born: 1897. Died: Mar. 29, 1933, Los Angeles, Calif. (auto accident). Screen actor and stuntman.

TINDALE, FRANKLIN M.
Born: 1871. Died: Feb. 14, 1947, Los Angeles, Calif. Screen actor and film director.

TINDALL, LOREN
Born: 1921. Died: May 10, 1973, Hollywood, Calif. (heart attack). Pianist, screen and stage actor. Piano virtuoso at age of four.

Appeared in: **1944** She's a Sweetheart. **1945** Over 21; Sergeant Mike; Rough, Tough and Ready. **1946** Til the Clouds Roll By; Til the End of Time; Meet Me on Broadway; Out of the Depths; Gallant Journey. **1947** Good News. **1949** Miss Grant Takes Richmond; Francis.

TINSMAN, SYLVIA McKAYE
Born: 1916. Died: Oct. 15, 1975. Screen actress and dancer.

TIRELLA, EDUARDO
Born: 1924. Died: Oct. 7, 1966, Rhode Island (hit by car). Screen actor and interior decorator.

Appeared in: **1965** The Sandpiper. **1967** Don't Make Waves.

TIROFF, JAMES "JIM" (aka JAMES HARPER)
Died: Dec. 18, 1975. Stage and screen actor.

Appeared in: **1965** The Brig.

TISSIER, JEAN
Born: 1896, France. Died: Apr. 1973, Paris, France. Screen and stage actor.

Appeared in: **1938** The Slipper Episode; The Courier of Lyons. **1939** Crossroads. **1946** Symphonie d'Amour. **1947** Her First Affair (aka Children of Paradise); Au Bonheur de Dames (aka Shop-Girls of Paris); The Murderer Lives at Number 21. **1948** Loves of Casanova. **1949** Strangers in the House. **1950** The Naked Woman; Gigi. **1951** Minnie. **1952** The Strollers; Father's Dilemma; L'Ile aux Femmes Nues (aka Naked in the Wind—US 1962 and Naked in the Wind). **1953** The Spice of Life. **1954** The Affairs of Messalina; Crime au Concert Mayol (aka Palace of Nudes—US 1961 and Palace of Shame). **1955** La Mome Pigalle (aka The Maiden—US 1961). **1956** Mama, Papa, the Maid and I. **1957** And God Created Woman; The Hunchback of Notre Dame. **1959** The French Way; Ein Engel auf Erden (Angel on Earth—US 1966). **1960** Candide au L'optimisme au XX Siecle (aka Candide—US 1962). **1961** La Bride sur le Cou (aka Please, Not Now!—US 1963). **1963** Strip-Tease (aka Sweet Skin—US 1965); Un Drole de Paroissien (aka Thank Heaven for Small Favors—US 1965). **1964** Voci Blanche (White Voices—US 1965). **1967** Deux Billets pour Mexico (aka Death Run—US 1969).

TISSOT, ALICE
Born: 1890, France. Died: May 5, 1971, Paris, France (throat cancer). Stage and screen actress.

Appeared in: **1928** La Cousine Bette. **1930** Le Secret du Docteur. **1933** Mirages de Paris. **1935** La Maternelle. **1937** Les Petits. **1938** The Glory of the Faith. **1939** Last Desire. **1945** Les Dames aux Chapeaux Verts (The Women in Green Hats). **1947** Francis the First. **1950** Ignace. **1952** L'Ile aux Femmes Nues (aka Naked in the Wind—US 1962 and Naked in the Mind). **1958** Gates of Paris.

TITHERADGE, DION
Born: 1879, England. Died: Nov. 16, 1934, London, England. Screen, stage actor, author, playwright and screenwriter.

TITHERADGE, MADGE
Born: 1887, England. Died: Nov. 13, 1961, Fetcham, Surrey, England. Stage and screen actress.

Appeared in: **1915** Brigadier Gerard. **1916** A Fair Imposter. **1917** The Woman Who was Nothing. **1918** God Bless Our Red, White and Blue. **1919** Gamblers All. **1920** The Husband Hunter; Love in the Wilderness; A Temporary Gentleman; Her Story (US 1922); David and Jonathan (US 1922).

TITUS, LYDIA YEAMANS
Born: 1866, Australia. Died: Dec. 30, 1929, Glendale, Calif. (paralytic stroke). Screen, stage and vaudeville actress. Married to actor Frederick Titus.

Appeared in: **1918** All Night. **1919** The Peace of Roaring River; Strictly Confidential. **1920** Nurse Marjorie. **1921** Queenie; The Invisible Power; The Mad Marriage; Nobody's Fool; All Dolled Up; Smiling All the Way; The Mistress of Shenstone; Beating the Game; Beau Revel; The Concert; The Freeze Out; The Marriage of William Ashe; His Nibs. **1922** The Glory of Clementina; The Married Flapper; Beauty's Worth; A Girl's Desire; The Lavender Bath Lady; Two Kinds of Women. **1923** Big Dan; The Famous Mrs. Fair; The Footlight Ranger; The Wanters; Winter Has Come; Scaramouche. **1924** Big Timber; In Fast Company; Tarnish; Young Ideas; A Boy of Flanders; Cytherea; The Lullaby. **1925** The Rag Man; Up the Ladder; Head Winds; The Limited Mail; The Talker; The Arizona Romeo. **1926** Irene; The Lily; Sunshine of Paradise Alley. **1927** The Lure of the Night Club; Upstream; Heroes in Blue; Night Life. **1928** The Water Hole; Two Lovers; Sweet Sixteen; While the City Sleeps. **1929** Shanghai Lady; The Voice in the Storm. **1930** Lummox.

TODD, HARRY
Born: 1865, Allegheny, Pa. Died: Feb. 16, 1935, Glendale, Calif. (heart attack). Screen actor. Married to actress Margaret Joslin. Entered films with Essanay.

Appeared in: **1915** "Snakeville" comedies. **1926** Under Western Skies. **1927** The Third Degree; The Riding Rowdy; Skedaddle Gold; The Obligin' Buckaroo; The Bugle Call; Rawhide Kid. **1928** Under the Tonto Rim; The River Woman. **1929** Linda; One Stolen Night. **1930** Under Montana Skies; The Fighting Legion; Lucky Larkin; Sons of the Saddle. **1933** Sucker Money; Gun Law; Her Splendid Folly; Thrill Hunter. **1934** It Happened One Night; One Is Guilty.

TODD, JAMES
Born: July 8, 1908, Chicago, Ill. Died: Feb. 8, 1968, Calif. Stage and screen actor. Entered films in 1931.

Appeared in: **1931** Riders of the Purple Sage. **1932** Charlie Chan's Chance; Disorderly Conduct; Careless Lady. **1948** The Luck of the Irish. **1948** For the Love of Mary; The Velvet Touch; Daredevils of the Skies. **1949** Trapped; The Gal Who Took the West; Fighting Man of the Plains; The Lone Wolf and His Lady; Francis. **1950** Peggy. **1953** Titanic; Torch Song; The Bigamist. **1956** The

Scarlet Hour. **1957** The Wings of Eagles; This Could Be the Night. **1958** The Buccaneer; High School Confidential!

TODD, THELMA
Born: July 29, 1905, Lawrence, Mass. Died: Dec. 18, 1935, Santa Monica, Calif. (carbon monoxide—murder—suicide—accident?). Screen actress. She appeared as part of film comedy team of "Todd and Pitts" with Zasu Pitts (dec. 1963) and "Todd and Kelly" with Patsy Kelly.

Appeared in: **1926** God Gave Me Twenty Cents; Fascinating Youth. **1927** Nevada; The Gay Defender; Rubber Heels; The Shield of Honor. **1928** Vamping Venus; The Crash; The Haunted House; Heart to Heart; The Noose. **1929** Naughty Baby; The Bachelor Girl; Trial Marriage; Careers; Her Private Life; The House of Horror; Look Out Below; Seven Footprints to Satan; plus the following shorts: Snappy Sneezer; Crazy Feet; Stepping Out; Hotter than Hot; Sky Boy; Unaccustomed as We Are; Jack White Talking Comedies. **1930** Hell's Angels; Follow Through; Her Man; plus the following shorts: Another Fine Mess; The Real McCoy; Whispering Whoopee; All Teed Up; Dollar Dizzy; Looser than Loose; High C's; The Head Guy; The Fighting Parson; The Shrimp; The King. **1931** Command Performance; The Maltese Falcon; Broad-Minded; The Hot Heiress; No Limit; Monkey Business; Beyond Victory; Aloha; Swanee River; Corsair; plus the following shorts: Chickens Come Home; The Pip from Pittsburgh; Rough Seas; Love Fever; and the following shorts with Z. Pitts: On the Loose; Let's Do Things; Catch as Catch Can; The Pajama Party; War Mamas. **1932** Call Her Savage; Klondike; Horse Feathers; Speak Easily; Big Timer; This Is the Night; No Greater Love; Cauliflower Alley; The Nickel Nurser (short); plus the following shorts with Z. Pitts: Sneak Easily; Seal Skins; Red Noses; Strictly Unreliable; The Old Bull; Show Business; Alum and Eve; The Soilers. **1933** Air Hostess; Counsellor at Law; Son of a Sailor; Deception; Fra Diablo (The Devil's Brother); Sitting Pretty; Mary Stevens, M.D.; Cheating Blondes; plus the following shorts with Z. Pitts: Asleep in the Fleet; Maids a la Mode; Bargain of the Century; One Track Minds; and the following shorts with P. Kelly: Beauty and the Bus; Backs to Nature; Air Freight. **1934** You Made Me Love You; Hips, Hips, Hooray!; The Cockeyed Cavaliers; Palooka; Bottoms Up; The Poor Rich; Take the Stand; and the following shorts with P. Kelly: Maid in Hollywood; Babes in the Goods; Soup and Fish; I'll Be Suing You; Three Chumps Ahead; One Horse Farmers; Opened by Mistake; Done in Oil; Bum Voyage. **1935** Lightning Strikes Twice; After the Dance; Two for Tonight; and the following shorts with P. Kelly: Treasure Blues; Sing, Sister, Sing; The Tin Man; The Misses Stooge; Slightly Static; Twin Triplets; Hot Money; Top Flat. **1936** The Bohemian Girl; All American Toothache (short with P. Kelly).

TOLER, HOOPER
Born: 1891, Wichita, Kans. Died: June 2, 1922, Los Angeles, Calif. (heart attack). Screen actor.

TOLER, SIDNEY
Born: Apr. 28, 1874, Warrensburg, Mo. Died: Feb. 12, 1947, Beverly Hills, Calif. Screen, stage actor and playwright. He took over role of Charlie Chan in "Charlie Chan" film series after Warner Oland died in 1938.

Appeared in: **1919** Madame X (film debut); In the Nick of Time (short). **1931** Devil's Parade (short); White Shoulders; Strictly Dishonorable. **1932** Strangers in Love; Blonde Venus; The Phantom President; Is My Face Red?; Radio Patrol; Speak Easily; Blondie of the Follies; Tom Brown of Culver. **1933** He Learned about Women; King of the Jungle; The Way to Love; The World Changes; The Billion Dollar Scandal; The Narrow Corner. **1934** Dark Hazard; Massacre; Registered Nurse; Spitfire; The Trumpet Blows; Here Comes the Groom; Upperworld; Operator 13; Romance in Manhattan. **1935** This Is the Life; Call of the Wild; The Daring Young Man; Orchids to You; Champagne for Breakfast. **1936** Three Godfathers; The Gorgeous Hussy; The Longest Night; Our Relations; Give Us This Night. **1937** That Certain Woman; Double Wedding; Quality Street. **1938** Wide Open Faces; Gold is Where You Find It; One Wild Night; Up the River; Charlie Chan in Honolulu; If I Were King; The Mysterious Rider; Three Comrades. **1939** Broadway Cavalier; King of Chinatown; Disbarred; Heritage of the Desert; The Kid from Kokomo; Charlie Chan in Reno; Charlie Chan at Treasure Island; Law of the Pampas; Charlie Chan in City in Darkness. **1940** Charlie Chan in Panama; Charlie Chan's Murder Cruise; Charlie Chan at the Wax Museum; Murder Over New York; **1941** Charlie Chan in Rio; Dead Men Tell. **1942** Castle in the Desert. **1943** A Night to Remember; White Savage; Isle of Forgotten Sins. **1944** Black Magic; Charlie Chan in the Secret Service; The Chinese Cat. **1945** The Scarlet Clue; Jade Mask; It's in the Bag; The Shanghai Cobra; The Red Dragon. **1946** Dark Alibi; Shadows Over Chinatown; Dangerous Money. **1947** The Trap. **1974** That's Entertainment (film clips).

TOLLY, FRANK
Died: Nov. 26, 1924, New York, N.Y. (auto accident). Screen actor, stuntman and circus acrobat. Died while filming stunt for movie "The Great Circus Mystery."

Appeared in: **1925** The Great Circus Mystery (serial).

TOLSTOI, COUNTESS (Sophie Behra)
Born: 1846. Died: Nov. 4, 1919, Trasnaya Polyana, Russia. Screen actress. Married to novelist Leo Tolstoi (dec. 1910).

Appeared in: **1918** George Robey's Day Off.

TOMACK, SID
Born: 1907, Brooklyn, N.Y. Died: Nov. 12, 1962, Palm Springs, Calif. (heart ailment). Screen, television and vaudeville actor. Appeared in vaudeville as part of team of "Sid Tomack and the Reis Bros."

Appeared in: **1944** A Wave, a Wac and a Marine. **1946** The Thrill of Brazil. **1947** Blind Spot; For the Love of Rusty; Blondie's Holiday; Framed. **1948** A Double Life; My Girl Tisa; Hollow Triumph; Homicide for Three. **1949** House of Strangers; Boston Blackie's Chinese Venture; The Crime Doctor's Diary; Make-Believe Ballroom; Abandoned; Force of Evil. **1950** Love That Brute; The Fuller Brush Girl. **1951** Never Trust a Gambler; Joe Palooka in Triple Cross. **1952** Hans Christian Andersen; Somebody Loves Me. **1954** Living It Up. **1955** The Girl Rush. **1956** That Certain Feeling; The Kettles in the Ozarks. **1957** Spring Reunion. **1961** Sail a Crooked Ship.

TOMAMOTO, THOMAS (Tsunetaro Sugimoto)
Born: 1879, Japan. Died: Sept. 28, 1924, New York, N.Y. Stage and screen actor.

TOMARCHIO, LUDOVICO
Born: Jan 6, 1886, Catania, Italy. Died: June 25, 1947, Los Angeles, Calif. (cerebral arteriosclerosis). Screen actor and opera performer.

Appeared in: **1935** The Melody Lingers On; A Night at the Opera. **1936** Millions in the Air; Early to Bed. **1938** Swiss Miss.

TOMBES, ANDREW
Born: Ashtabula, Ohio. Died: date unknown. Screen, vaudeville and stage actor.

Appeared in: **1933** Moulin Rouge. **1934** Born to be Bad. **1935** Doubting Thomas; Here Comes Cookie; Music Is Magic; Thanks a Million. **1936** It Had to Happen; The Country Beyond; Ticket to Paradise; Stage Struck; Hot Money; King of Burlesque; Here Comes Trouble. **1937** Time Out for Romance; The Holy Terror; Fair Warning; Charlie Chan at the Olympics; Turn Off the Moon; Sing and be Happy; Riding On Air; Meet the Boy Friend; The Big City; Easy Living; Borrowing Trouble; 45 Fathers; Checkers. **1938** Sally, Irene and Mary; Battle of Broadway; Romance on the Run; One Wild Night; A Desperate Adventure; Always in Trouble; Thanks for Everything; Five of a Kind; Vacation From Love. **1939** What a Life; Too Busy to Work. **1940** Wolf of New York; Money to Burn; Village Barn Dance; In Old Missouri; Captain Caution; Charter Pilot. **1941** Bedtime Story; Louisiana Purchase; Mountain Moonlight; Meet John Doe; A Dangerous Game; World Premier; Down Mexico Way; Melody for Three; Meet the Chump; The Wild Man of Borneo; Lady Scarface; Last of the Duanes. **1942** Blondie Goes to College; Larceny, Inc.; My Gal Sal; They All Kissed the Bride; Between Us Girls; Road to Morocco. **1943** Crazy House; Swing Fever; Riding High; My Kingdom for a Cook; Reveille With Beverly; It Ain't Hay; The Meanest Man in the World; Coney Island; Let's Face It; Hi Diddle Diddle; I Dood It; His Butler's Sister; A Stranger in Town. **1944** Phantom Lady; Weekend Pass; Reckless Age; San Fernando Valley; The Singing Sheriff; Goin' to Town; Something for the Boys; Murder in the Blue Room; Can't Help Singing. **1945** Patrick the Great; G. I. Honeymoon; Night Club Girl; Bring on the Girls; Lake Placid Serenade; Rhapsody in Blue; You Came Along; Don't Fence Me In; Frontier Gal. **1946** Badman's Territory; Sing While You Dance. **1947** Beat the Band; The Devil Thumbs a Ride; The Fabulous Dorseys; Hoppy's Holiday; Copacabana. **1948** Two Guys From Texas. **1949** Oh, You Beautiful Doll. **1950** Joe Palooka in Humphrey Takes A Chance; The Jackpot. **1951** A Wonderful Life. **1952** I Dream of Jeanie; Oklahoma Annie. **1955** How to Be Very, Very Popular.

TOMEI, LUIGI
Born: 1910. Died: May 15, 1955, San Francisco, Calif. (auto injuries while performing film stunt). Screen actor, stuntman and former Indianapolis Speedway contender.

Appeared in: **1956** Hell on Frisco Bay.

TONE, FRANCHOT (Stanislas Pascal Franchot Tone)
Born: Feb. 27, 1905, Niagara Falls, N.Y. Died: Sept. 18, 1968, New York, N.Y. Screen, stage, television actor, film producer and film director. Divorced from actresses: Joan Crawford (dec. 1977); Jean Wallace; Dolores Dorn-Heft and Barbara Payton (dec. 1967).

Appeared in: **1932** The Wiser Sex (film debut). **1933** Dinner at Eight; Gabriel over the White House; Today We Live; Midnight Mary; The Stranger's Return; Stage Mother; Bombshell; Dancing Lady; Lady of the Night. **1934** Four Walls; Gentlemen Are Born; Moulin Rouge; The World Moves On; Sadie McKee; Straight Is the Way; The Girl from Missouri. **1935** The Lives of a Bengal Lancer; Reckless; One New York Night; No More Ladies; Mutiny on the Bounty; Dangerous. **1936** Exclusive Story; The Unguarded Hour; Suzy; The Gorgeous Hussy; Love on the Run; The King Steps Out; Girl's Dormitory.

1937 Quality Street; They Gave Him a Gun; Between Two Women; The Bride Wore Red. **1938** Man-Proof; Love Is a Headache; Three Comrades; Three Loves Has Nancy. **1939** Fast and Furious; Thunder Afloat; The Girl Downstairs; The Gentle People. **1940** Trail of the Vigilantes. **1941** Virginia; Highly Irregular; Nice Girl?; This Woman Is Mine; She Knew All the Answers. **1942** The Wife Takes a Flyer. **1943** Five Graves to Cairo; Star Spangled Rhythm; Pilot No. 5; His Butler's Sister; True to Life. **1944** Phantom Lady; The Hour before the Dawn; Dark Waters. **1945** That Night with You. **1946** Because of Him. **1947** Her Husband's Affair; Two Men and a Girl; Honeymoon; Army Comes Across; Lost Honeymoon. **1948** I Love Trouble; Every Girl Should Be Married. **1949** Jigsaw; Without Honor; The Man on the Eiffel Tower. **1950** Gun Moll. **1951** Here Comes the Groom. **1958** Uncle Vanya. **1962** Advise and Consent. **1964** La Bonne Soupe (The Good Soup); Big Parade of Comedy (documentary). **1965** In Harm's Way; Mickey One. **1968** The High Commissioner.

TONEY, JAMES
Died: Sept. 19, 1973. Screen actor.

Appeared in: **1935** It's In the Air. **1936** The Lonely Trail. **1937** Fifty Roads to Town. **1939** The Lady and the Mob. **1941** All That Money Can Buy (aka Here Is a Man). **1943** Harrigan's Kid; The Ghost and the Guest. **1950** No Way Out. **1952** The Devil and Daniel Webster (reissue of All That Money Can Buy—1941).

TONG, KAM
Born: 1907. Died: Nov. 8, 1969, Costa Mesa, Calif. Screen and television actor.

Appeared in: **1942** Joan of Ozark; Rubber Racketeers; China Girl; The Hidden Hand; Across the Pacific. **1953** Target Hong Kong. **1954** This Is My Love. **1955** Love Is a Many Splendored Thing. **1960** Who Was That Lady? **1961** Flower Drum Song. **1963** It Happened at the World's Fair. **1966** Dimension #5; Mister Buddwing. **1967** Kill a Dragon.

TONG, SAMMEE
Born: 1901, San Francisco, Calif. Died: Oct. 27, 1964, Palms, Calif. (suicide). Screen and television actor.

Appeared in: **1934** Happiness Ahead (film debut); The Captain Hates the Sea. **1935** Oil for the Lamps of China; Shanghai. **1937** The Good Earth. **1939** Only Angels Have Wings. **1957** Hell Bound. **1958** Suicide Battalion. **1963** It's a Mad, Mad, Mad, Mad World. **1964** For Those Who Think Young. **1965** Fluffy.

TONGE, PHILIP
Born: 1898. Died: Jan. 28, 1959, Hollywood, Calif. Screen and television actor.

Appeared in: **1915** Still Waters. **1933** His Double Life. **1947** Love from a Stranger; Miracle on 34th Street. **1952** Hans Christian Andersen. **1953** House of Wax; Scandal at Scourie; Small Town Girl. **1954** Elephant Walk; Khyber Patrol; Ricochet Romance; Track of the Cat. **1955** Desert Sands; The Prodigal; The Silver Chalice. **1956** Pardners; The Peacemaker. **1957** Les Girls; Witness for the Prosecution. **1958** Darby's Rangers; Macabre. **1959** Invisible Invaders.

TONY (aka TONY THE WONDER HORSE)
Born: 1909. Died: Oct. 12, 1942. Animal performer. (Tom Mix's horse.)

Appeared in: **1922** Four Big Stakes; Just Tony. **1923** Eyes of the Forest; The Lone Star Ranger; Mile-a-Minute Romeo; Soft Boiled; Stepping Fast. **1924** Teeth. **1925** The Best Bad Man. **1926** The Canyon of Light; The Great K&A Train Robbery; Hard Boiled; No Man's Gold; Tony Runs Wild; The Yankee Senor. **1927** The Arizona Wildcat; The Last Trail; Tumbling River; The Broncho Twister; The Circus Ace. **1928** Painted Post; Son of the Golden West; Daredevil's Reward; Hello Cheyenne; A Horseman of the Plains. **1929** The Big Diamond Robbery. **1932** My Pal the King.

TOOKER, WILLIAM H.
Born: 1864, New York, N.Y. Died: Oct. 12, 1936, Hollywood, Calif. Stage and screen actor.

Appeared in: **1921** God's Country and the Law; Worlds Apart; Proxies. **1922** The Power Within; Beyond the Rainbow; My Friend, the Devil; Peacock Alley; The Cradle Buster. **1923** The Woman in Chains; Sinner or Saint; A Bride for a Knight; The Purple Highway; The Net. **1924** Who's Cheating?; The Average Woman; The Lone Wolf. **1925** The Phantom Express. **1926** The Scarlet Letter; The Merry Cavalier; The White Black Sheep. **1927** Two Girls Wanted; Birds of Prey; Ladies Must Dress; The Devil Dancer; Tell It to Sweeney; Jake the Plumber. **1928** Good Morning, Judge; The Look Out Girl; The Night Watch; Sweet Sixteen; Virgin Lips; A Woman against the World. **1929** No Defense; Romance of the Under World; Protection; The Bellamy Trial; Love in the Desert. **1930** Soup to Nuts. **1931** A Woman of Experience. **1935** It's a Gift.

TOPART, LISE
Born: 1930, France. Died: Mar. 3, 1952, Nice, France (plane crash). Screen actress.

TORDESILLA, JESUS

Born: 1893, Spain. Died: Mar. 24, 1973, Madrid, Spain (heart attack). Stage and screen actor.

Appeared in: **1923** Flor de Espana. **1926** Currito de la Cruz. **1950** The Mad Queen. **1958** Spanish Affair. Other Spanish films: Locura de Amor; Agustina de Aragon; Donde vas Alfonso XII? Teresa de Jesus; Los Escondites; Una tumba para el Sheriff.

TOREN, MARTA

Born: May 21, 1926, Stockholm, Sweden. Died: Feb. 19, 1957, Stockholm, Sweden (rare brain disease). Stage and screen actress. Appeared in Swedish, U.S., Italian and Spanish films.

Appeared in: **1948** Casbah (film debut); Rogues' Regiment. **1949** Illegal Entry; Sword in the Desert. **1950** Deported; Mystery Submarine; Spy Hunt; One-Way Street. **1951** Panther's Moon; Sirocco. **1952** Assignment—Paris; The Man Who Watched the Trains Go By. **1953** The Paris Express. **1954** The House of Ricordi (US 1956). **1955** Maddelena.

TORNEK, JACK

Died: Feb. 18, 1974. Screen actor.

Appeared in: **1916** Bombs and Banknotes. **1956** Around the World in 80 Days.

TORRENCE, DAVID (David Thoyson)

Born: Jan. 17, 1864, Edinburgh, Scotland. Died: Dec. 26, 1951. Stage and screen actor. Brother of actor Ernest Torrence (dec. 1933).

Appeared in: **1913** Tess of the D'Urbervilles. **1915** The Prisoner of Zenda. **1921** The Inside of the Cup. **1922** Forsaking All Others; The Power of a Lie; Received Payment; Sherlock Holmes; Tess of the Storm Country; A Virgin's Sacrifice. **1923** The Abysmal Brute; The Drums of Jeopardy; The Light That Failed; The Man Next Door; Railroaded; Trimmed in Scarlet. **1924** The Dawn of a Tomorrow; Idle Tongues; Love's Wilderness; The Sawdust Trail; Surging Seas; Tiger Love; Which Shall It Be? **1925** The Reckless Sex; The Other Woman's Story; Fighting the Flames; He Who Laughs Last; Her Husband's Secret; The Mystic; The Tower of Lies; The Wheel; What Fools Men. **1926** The Auction Block; Brown of Harvard; Forever After; The Isle of Retribution; The King of the Turf; Laddie; The Man in the Shadow; Oh, What a Nurse!; The Wolf Hunters; The Unknown Cavalier; The Third Degree; Sandy; Race Wild. **1927** Annie Laurie; Hazardous Valley; The Midnight Watch; On the Stroke of Twelve; The Mysterious Rider; Rolled Stockings; The World at Her Feet. **1928** The Big Noise; The Cavalier; The City of Dreams (aka City of Purple Dreams); The Little Shepherd of Kingdom Come; Undressed. **1929** Disraeli; The Black Watch; Hearts in Exile; Silks and Saddles; Strong Boy; Untamed Justice. **1930** City Girl; Raffles; River's End; Scotland Yard; The Devil to Pay. **1931** Five Star Final; East Lynne; Bachelor Father. **1932** The Mask of Fu Manchu; A Successful Calamity; Smilin' Through. **1933** Berkeley Square; Voltaire; Queen Christina; Masquerader. **1934** Charlie Chan in London; Madame Spy; Horseplay; Mandalay; What Every Woman Knows; Jane Eyre. **1935** Black Sheep; Bonnie Scotland; Harmony Lane; The Dark Angel; Captain Blood. **1936** The Country Doctor; Mary of Scotland; Beloved Enemy. **1937** The Ebb Tide; Lost Horizon. **1938** Five of a Kind. **1939** Rulers of the Sea; Stanley and Livingstone.

TORRENCE, ERNEST (Ernest Thoyson)

Born: June 16, 1878, Edinburgh, Scotland. Died: May 15, 1933, New York, N.Y. Screen, stage actor and opera performer. Brother of actor David Torrence (dec. 1951).

Appeared in: **1921** Tol'able David (film debut). **1922** Broken Chains; The Kingdom Within; The Prodigal Judge; Singed Wings. **1923** The Trail of the Lonesome Pine; Ruggles of Red Gap; The Covered Wagon; The Hunchback of Notre Dame; The Brass Bottle. **1924** Fighting Coward; The Side Show of Life; West of the Water Tower; The Heritage of the Desert; North of 36. **1925** Peter Pan; The Pony Express; The Dressmaker from Paris; Night Life of New York; Mantrap; The American Venus; The Blood Goddess; The Lady of the Harem; The Rainmaker; The Wanderer. **1927** King of Kings; Captain Salvation; Twelve Miles Out. **1928** Steamboat Bill, Jr.; The Cossacks; Across to Singapore. **1929** Silks and Saddles; The Unholy Night; The Bridge of San Luis Rey; Desert Nights; Speedway; Untamed; Twelve Nights Out. **1930** Sweet Kitty Bellaire; Strictly Unconventional; Officer O'Brien; Call of the Flesh. **1931** Shipmates; The Great Lover; Sporting Blood; The New Adventures of Get-Rich-Quick Wallingford; Fighting Caravans. **1932** Hypnotized; Cuban Love Song; Sherlock Holmes. **1933** The Masquerader; I Cover the Waterfront.

TORRIANI, AIMEE

Born: 1890, New York, N.Y. Died: July 18, 1963, New York, N.Y. Screen, stage and radio actress.

Appeared in: **1955** To Catch a Thief.

TORRUCO, MIGUEL

Born: 1920, Mexico. Died: Apr. 22, 1956, Orizaba, Vera Cruz, Mexico. Screen actor. Married to Mexican screen actress Maria Elena Marques. Entered films in 1949.

Appeared in: **1955** Massacre. Other Mexican film: Horas de Agonia (Agonized Hours).

TORVAY, JOSE

Died: 1973, Mexico. Screen actor.

Appeared in: **1948** Treasure of Sierra Madre; Sofia; Mystery in Mexico. **1949** Border Incident. **1950** Borderline; The Torch. **1951** The Brave Bulls; My Outlaw Brother (aka My Brother the Outlaw). **1952** One Big Affair; My Man and I. **1953** The Hitch-Hiker. **1954** Green Fire. **1955** A Life in the Balance; The Littlest Outlaw; Strange Lady in Town. **1956** Bandido; A Woman's Devotion. **1958** From Hell to Texas. **1961** Code of Silence; The Last Sunset. **1970** Two Mules for Sister Sara.

TOSCANINI, ARTURO

Born: Mar. 25, 1867, Parma, Italy. Died: Jan. 16, 1957, New York, N.Y. (stroke). Conductor and screen actor.

Appeared in: **1946** Hymn of the Nations.

TOSO, OTELLO

Born: Italy. Died: Mar. 15, 1966, Padua, Italy (auto accident). Screen and television actor.

Appeared in: **1950** Le Due Orfanelle (The Two Orphans). **1952** The Cliff of Sin. **1953** What Price Innocence? **1958** Age of Infidelity (aka Muerte de un Ciclista—Death of a Cyclist). Other Italian films: Casanova; Ridi Pagliaccio; 1860.

TOTO (Antonio Furst de Curtis-Gagliardi)

Born: 1897, Italy. Died: Apr. 1967, Rome, Italy. Screen, stage, television actor, author, song writer, playwright and stage producer. Do not confuse with "Toto the Clown" (dec. 1938).

Appeared in: **1936** Fermo con le Mani. **1949** Toto Le Moko. **1953** Cops and Robbers. **1954** Side Street Story; The Gold of Naples (aka The Racketeer—US 1957). **1955** Racconti Romani. **1957** Toto, Vittorio e la Dottoressa (aka The Lady Doctor—US 1963). **1958** Persons Unknown. **1959** The Law Is the Law; The Anatomy of Love. **1960** Risate di Gioia (The Passionate Thief—US 1963). **1961** The Big Deal on Madonna Street. **1963** I due Colonnelli (Two Colonels—US 1966). **1964** South of Tana River. **1965** La Mandragola (aka The Love Root and the Mandragola—US 1966). **1966** Uccellacci e Uccellini (aka The Hawks and the Sparrows—US 1967). **1967** Operazione San Gennaro (Treasure of San Gennaro—US 1968 aka Unser Boss ist Eine Dame); The Commander; Le Streghe (The Witches—US 1968).

TOTO THE CLOWN (Armando Novello)

Born: 1888, Geneva, Switzerland. Died: Dec. 15, 1938, New York, N.Y. Screen, stage, vaudeville actor and circus clown.

Appeared in: **1911** Toto on the Stage; Toto's Little Cart. **1916** Toto of the Byways. **1918** The Dippy Daughter. **1919** Tot's Troubles. **1927** The Junk Man (short); **1936–37** Pathe and educational shorts.

TOUREL, JENNIE (Jennie Davidson)

Born: 1910, Montreal, Canada. Died: Nov. 23, 1973, New York, N.Y. Opera singer and screen actress.

Appeared in: **1968** A Journey to Jerusalem.

TOVER, MAY

Born: 1911. Died: Dec. 20, 1949, Thousand Oaks, Calif. (clawed to death by lion). Screen actress and lion tamer.

Appeared in: **1950** The Reformer and the Redhead.

TOWNSEND, ANNA

Died: Sept. 1923, Los Angeles, Calif. Stage and screen actress.

Appeared in: **1922** Grandma's Boy; Doctor Jack. **1923** Daddy; Safety Last.

TOZERE, FREDERIC

Born: 1901, Brookline, Mass. Died: Aug. 5, 1972, New York, N.Y. Stage, screen, television actor and pantomimist. Married to actress Mary Brady (dec. 1968).

Appeared in: **1939** The Man Who Dared; Everybody's Hobby; Cowboy Quarterback; Nancy Drew and the Hidden Staircase; Confessions of a Nazi Spy; Hell's Kitchen. **1948** The Iron Curtain; An Act of Murder; Live Today for Tomorrow. **1949** Madame Bovary; The Return of October. **1950** Father Is a Bachelor.

TRACEY, THOMAS F.

Born: 1880, County Cork, Ireland. Died: Aug. 27, 1961, New York, N.Y. Screen, stage and television actor.

Appeared in: **1916** Behind Closed Doors. **1917** The Man Hater.

TRACY, LEE (William Lee Tracy)

Born: Apr. 14, 1898, Atlanta, Ga. Died: Oct. 18, 1968, Santa Monica, Calif. (liver cancer). Screen, stage, television and vaudeville actor. Nominated for 1964 Academy Award as Best Actor in The Best Man.

Appeared in: **1929** Big Time (film debut). **1930** She Got What She Wanted; Born Reckless; Liliom; On the Level. **1932** Blessed Event; The Half-Naked Truth; Washington Merry-Go-Round; The Night Mayor; Strange Love of Molly Louvain; Doctor X; Love Is a Racket. **1933** Phantom Fame; The Nuisance; Advice to the Lovelorn; Turn Back the Clock; Dinner at Eight; Private Jones; Bombshell; Clear All Wires. **1934** You Belong to Me; The Lemon Drop Kid; I'll Tell the World. **1935** Carnival; Two Fisted. **1936** Wanted: Jane Turner; Sutter's Gold. **1937** Criminal Lawyer; Behind the Headlines. **1938** Crashing Hollywood. **1939** Fixer Dugan; The Spellbinder. **1940** Millionaires in Prison. **1942** The Payoff. **1943** Power of the Press. **1945** Betrayal from the East; I'll Tell the World (and 1934 version). **1947** High Tide. **1962** Advise and Consent. **1964** Big Parade of Comedy (documentary); The Best Man.

TRACY, SPENCER

Born: Apr. 5, 1900, Milwaukee, Wis. Died: June 10, 1967, Beverly Hills, Calif. (heart attack). Stage and screen actor. Won 1937 Academy Award for Best Actor in Captains Courageous and in 1938 for Boys Town. Was nominated for 1936 Academy Award as Best Actor in San Francisco; in 1950 for Father of the Bride; in 1954 for Bad Day at Black Rock; in 1958 for The Old Man and the Sea; in 1960 for Inherit the Wind; in 1961 for Judgement at Nuremberg; and in 1967 for Guess Who's Coming to Dinner?

Appeared in: **1930** Taxi Talks (short—film debut); The Tough Guy (aka The Hard Guy—short); Up the River. **1931** Quick Millions; Six Cylinder Love; Goldie. **1932** She Wanted a Millionaire; Sky Devils; Disorderly Conduct; Young America; Society Girl; The Painted Woman; Me and My Gal. **1933** 20,000 Years in Sing Sing; Face in the Sky; Shanghai Madness; The Power and the Glory; The Mad Game; A Man's Castle; State Fair. **1934** Looking for Trouble; The Show-Off; Bottoms Up; Now I'll Tell; Marie Galante. **1935** It's a Small World; The Murder Man; Dante's Inferno; Riffraff. **1936** Whipsaw; Fury; Libeled Lady; San Francisco. **1937** They Gave Him a Gun; Captains Courageous; Big City; Mannequin. **1938** Boys Town; Test Pilot. **1939** Stanley and Livingstone. **1940** I Take This Woman; Northwest Passage; Edison, the Man; Boom Town. **1941** Men of Boys Town; Dr. Jekyll and Mr. Hyde. **1942** Tortilla Flat; Keeper of the Flame; Woman of the Year; Ring of Steel (narr.). **1943** A Guy Named Joe. **1944** The Seventh Cross; Battle Stations (short); Thirty Seconds over Tokyo. **1945** Without Love. **1947** The Sea of Grass; Cass Timberlane. **1948** State of the Union. **1949** Edward, My Son; Adam's Rib. **1950** Malaya; Father of the Bride. **1951** Father's Little Dividend; The People against O'Hara. **1952** Pat and Mike; Plymouth Adventure. **1953** The Actress. **1954** Broken Lance; Bad Day at Black Rock. **1956** The Mountain. **1957** Desk Set. **1958** The Old Man and the Sea; The Last Hurrah. **1960** Inherit the Wind. **1961** The Devil at Four O'Clock; Judgement at Nuremberg. **1962** How the West Was Won (narr.). **1963** It's a Mad, Mad, Mad, Mad World. **1964** Big Parade of Comedy (documentary). **1967** Guess Who's Coming to Dinner? **1974** That's Entertainment (film clips).

TRACY, WILLIAM

Born: Dec. 1, 1917, Pittsburgh, Pa. Died: June 18, 1967, Hollywood, Calif. Stage and screen actor.

Appeared in: **1938** Brother Rat; Angels with Dirty Faces. **1939** Jones Family in Hollywood; Million Dollar Legs. **1940** The Amazing Mr. Williams; Terry and the Pirates (serial); The Shop around the Corner; Strike up the Band; Gallant Sons. **1941** Mr. and Mrs. Smith; Tobacco Road; Tillie the Toiler; She Knew All the Answers; Her First Beau; Tanks a Million; Cadet Girl. **1942** Young America; Hayfoot; To the Shores of Tripoli; About Face; Fall In; George Washington Slept Here. **1943** Yanks Ahoy. **1948** Here Comes Trouble; The Walls of Jericho. **1949** Henry, the Rainmaker. **1950** One Too Many. **1951** On the Sunny Side of the Street; As You Were. **1952** Mr. Walkie-Talkie. **1957** The Wings of Eagles.

TRAIN, JACK

Born: 1902. Died: Dec. 19, 1966, London, England. Screen, stage and radio actor.

Appeared in: **1946** Gaiety George (aka Showtime—US 1948). **1964** Catacombs (aka The Woman Who Wouldn't Die—US 1965).

TRAINOR, LEONARD

Born: 1879. Died: July 28, 1940, Los Angeles, Calif. (heart attack). Screen actor. Will Rogers' double and stand-in.

Appeared in: **1922** You Never Know. **1925** Galloping Jinx; Fast Lightnin'. **1926** The Border Sheriff; Hi-Jacking Rustlers. **1928** Headin' for Danger. **1933** Terror Trail.

TRASK, WAYLAND

Born: July 16, 1887, New York. Died: Nov. 11, 1918, Los Angeles, Calif. (Spanish influenza). Screen, stage actor and comedian.

Appeared in: **1915** The Great Vacuum Robbery. **1916** Fatty and Mabel Adrift;

The Great Pearl Tangle; The Judge; His Hereafter (aka Murray's Mix-Up); A Love Riot; The Feathered Nest; Maid Mad; Bombers; Her Marble Heart; Pills of Peril; The Stone Age. **1917** Cactus Nell; That Night; Dodging His Dream; A Maiden's Trust; Her Torpedoed Love; She Needed a Doctor; His Precious Life. **1918** Whose Little Wife Are You?; Her Blighted Love; Watch Your Neighbor.

TRAUBEL, HELEN

Born: 1903, St. Louis, Mo. Died: July 28, 1972, Santa Monica, Calif. (heart attack). Opera singer, screen, television and stage actress.

Appeared in: **1954** Deep In My Heart. **1961** The Ladies' Man. **1967** Gunn.

TRAUTMAN, LUDWIG

Born: 1886, Germany. Died: Jan. 24, 1957, Berlin, Germany. Screen actor. Entered films with Bioscop-Filmgesellshaft in 1912.

TRAVERS, ANTHONY

Born: 1920. Died: Jan. 16, 1959, Hollywood, Calif. Screen actor.

TRAVERS, HENRY (Travers John Geagerty)

Born: March 5, 1874, Berwick-on-Tweed, Northumberland, England. Died: Oct. 18, 1965, Los Angeles, Calif. (complications from arteriosclerosis). Stage and screen actor. Married to stage actress Amy Rhodes Forrest (dec. 1954) and later married to nurse, Ann G. Murphy (dec. 1965).

Appeared in: **1933** Reunion in Vienna (stage and screen versions); Another Language; My Weakness; The Invisible Man. **1934** Born to Be Bad; Ready for Love; The Party's Over; Death Takes a Holiday. **1935** Maybe It's Love; Escapade; Pursuit; After Office Hours; Captain Hurricane; Seven Keys to Baldpate; Four Hours to Kill. **1936** Too Many Parents. **1938** The Sisters. **1939** Dark Victory; You Can't Get Away with Murder; On Borrowed Time; Remember?; Dodge City; Stanley and Livingstone; The Rains Came. **1940** The Primrose Path; Anne of Windy Poplars; Edison, the Man; Wyoming. **1941** High Sierra; The Bad Man; Ball of Fire; A Girl, a Guy and a Gob; I'll Wait for You. **1942** Mrs. Miniver; Pierre of the Plains; Random Harvest. **1943** Shadow of a Doubt; Madame Curie; The Moon Is Down. **1944** Dragon Seed; None Shall Escape; The Very Thought of You. **1945** Thrill of Romance; The Bells of St. Mary's; The Naughty '90's. **1946** Gallant Journey; It's a Wonderful Life; The Yearling. **1947** The Flame. **1948** Beyond Glory. **1949** The Girl from Jones Beach.

TRAVERS, RICHARD C. (Richard Libb)

Born: Apr. 15, 1890, Hudson Bay Post, Northwest Territory, Canada. Died: Apr. 20, 1935, San Diego, Calif. (pneumonia). Stage and screen actor. Entered films with Essanay in 1914.

Appeared in: **1915** The White Sister; In the Palace of the King; The Man Trail. **1916** Captain Jinks of the Horse Marines. **1921** The Mountain Woman; The Single Track; The Rider of the King Long. **1922** White Hell; The Love Nest; Dawn of Revenge; Notoriety. **1923** The Broad Road; The Acquittal; Mary of the Movies; The Rendezvous. **1924** The House of Youth. **1925** Head Winds; Lightnin'. **1926** The Still Alarm; The Dangerous Dude; The Truthful Sex. **1927** Melting Millions (serial). **1929** The Unholy Night; The Black Watch. **1930** The Woman Racket. **1936** Freshman's Love.

TRAVERSE, MADLAINE (Madlaine Businsky)

Born: 1876, Cleveland, Ohio. Died: Jan. 7, 1964, Cleveland, Ohio. Screen actress.

Appeared in: **1913** Leah Kleschna. **1914** Three Weeks. **1916** The Shielding Shadow (serial).

TRAVIS, CHARLES W.

Born: 1861. Died: Aug. 12, 1917, Brooklyn, N.Y. (stroke). Stage and screen actor.

Appeared in: **1913** The Great Ganton Mystery. **1915** The Secret Agent; The House With Nobody In It; The New Adam and Eve. **1916** As a Woman Sows; The Idol of the Stage; I Accuse; The Quality of Faith; Armadale; The Criminal's Thumb; The Hidden Foe.

TREACHER, ARTHUR

Born: July 23, 1894, Brighton, England. Died: Dec. 14, 1975, Manhasset, N.Y. (heart ailment). Screen, stage and television actor. Married to actress Virginia Taylor.

Appeared in: **1929** The Battle of Paris. **1933** Alice in Wonderland; a Vitaphone short. **1934** Madame DuBarry; Here Comes the Groom; Gambling Lady; The Key; The Captain Hates the Sea; Forsaking All Others; Viva Villa; Hollywood Party; Student Tour; Fashion of 1934; Desirable. **1935** The Winning Ticket; David Copperfield; No More Ladies; Bright Lights; I Live My Life; Let's Live Tonight; Cardinal Richelieu; The Woman in Red; The Daring Young Man; Orchids to You; Curly Top; A Midsummer Night's Dream; Remember Last Night?; Hitch-Hike Lady; Magnificent Obsession; Splendor; Vanessa; Go Into Your Dance; I Live for Love; The Nitwits; Bordertown; Personal Maid's Secret. **1936** Anything Goes; Thank You, Jeeves; The Case Against Mrs. Ames; Hearts Divided; Satan Met a Lady; Mister Cinderella; Under Your Spell; Stowaway; Hard Luck Dame. **1937** Step Lively, Jeeves!; She Had to Eat; Thin

Ice; You Can't Have Everything; Heidi. **1938** Mad About Music; Always in Trouble; My Lucky Star; Up the River. **1939** The Little Princess; Bridal Suite; Barricade. **1940** Brother Rat and a Baby; Irene. **1942** Star Spangled Rhythm. **1943** The Amazing Mrs. Holliday; Forever and a Day. **1944** National Velvet; Chip Off the Old Block; In Society. **1945** That's the Spirit; Delightfully Dangerous; Swing Out Sister. **1947** Fun on a Weekend; Slave Girl. **1948** The Countess of Monte Cristo. **1949** That Midnight Kiss. **1950** Love That Brute. **1964** Mary Poppins.

TREACY, EMERSON
Born: Sept. 7, 1905, Philadelphia, Pa. Died: Jan. 10, 1967, Woodland Hills, Calif. Screen, stage, television and radio actor.

Appeared in: **1930** Once a Gentleman. **1931** The Sky Raiders. **1932** O.K. America. **1933** Bedtime Worries (short); Wild Poses (short). **1934** Two Alone. **1937** California Straight Ahead. **1938** Long Shot; Give Me a Sailor. **1939** Gone with the Wind; Invitation to Happiness; They All Come Out. **1949** Adam's Rib. **1950** Wyoming Mail. **1951** Fort Worth; The Prowler. **1955** Prince of Players; Run for Cover. **1960** Dark at the Top of the Stairs. **1961** Return to Peyton Place. **1962** Lover Come Back.

TREADWAY, CHARLOTTE
Born: 1895. Died: Feb. 26, 1963, Hollywood, Calif. Screen and stage actress.

Appeared in: **1937** The Sheik Steps Out. **1938** Female Fugitive. **1939** The Women; A Jed Prouty short; Wrong Room (short). **1941** Life with Henry. **1942** Gentleman Jim.

TREADWELL, LAURA B.
Born: 1879. Died: Nov. 22, 1960, Hollywood, Calif. Screen and stage actress.

Appeared in: **1935** Accent on Youth. **1937** Easy Living; Nobody's Baby. **1939** The Night of Nights; Mr. Smith Goes to Washington. **1946** Bringing up Father. **1947** King of the Bandits. **1951** Strangers on a Train.

TREE, LADY (Helen Maude Holt)
Born: Oct. 5, 1863, London, England. Died: Aug. 7, 1937, London, England (following surgery). Stage and screen actress. Married to actor Sir Herbert Beerbohm Tree (dec. 1917). Mother of actress Viola Tree (dec. 1938).

Appeared in: **1916** Still Waters Run Deep. **1920** Little Dorrit. **1930** Such is the Law. **1932** Wedding Rehearsal. **1933** Early to Bed; The Girl from Maxim's (US 1936); The Private Life of Henry VIII; Her Imaginary Lover. **1936** The Man Who Could Work Miracles (US 1937).

TREE, SIR HERBERT BEERBOHM
Born: Dec. 17, 1852, Kensington, England. Died: July 2, 1917, London, England. Stage and screen actor. Married to actress Lady (Helen Maud Holt) Tree (dec. 1937). Father of actress Viola Tree (dec. 1938).

Appeared in: **1911** Henry VIII. **1914** Trilby. **1916** Macbeth; The Old Folks at Home.

TREE, VIOLA
Born: 1884. Died: Nov. 15, 1938, London, England (pleurisy). British screen, stage actress, author and playwright. Daughter of actor Sir Herbert Beerbohm Tree (dec. 1917) and Lady Tree (dec. 1937).

Appeared in: **1935** Heart's Desire. **1938** Pygmalion.

TRENT, JOHN (aka JACK TRENT)
Born: 1897. Died: Aug. 1, 1961 (fall from horse). Screen actor and stuntman. Do not confuse with actor John Trent (dec. 1966).

TRENT, JOHN (LaVerne Brown)
Born: Dec. 5, 1906, Orange, Calif. Died: May 12, 1966. Aviator and screen actor.

TRESHAM, MRS. JENNIE
Born: 1881. Died: Dec. 18, 1913, Portland, Ore. Screen actress. Appeared in Portland Film Company films.

TRESKOFF, OLGA
Born: 1902. Died: Apr. 23, 1938, New York, N.Y. Screen and stage actress. Appeared in silent films.

TREVI, CHRISTINA (Christina Benitez Trevino)
Born: 1930, Mexico. Died: July 1, 1956, Mexico City, Mexico (following surgery). Screen, television actress and opera soprano.

TREVOR, ANNE
Died: July 1970, England. Stage and screen actress.

Appeared in: **1920** Build Thy House; Wuthering Heights. **1921** Daniel Deronda. **1922** A Rogue In Love. **1936** Murder in the Old Red Barn.

TREVOR, HUGH
Born: Oct. 28, 1903, Yonkers, N.Y. Died: Nov. 10, 1933, Los Angeles, Calif. (complications following appendectomy). Screen actor. Entered films in 1927.

Appeared in: **1927** Rangers of the North. **1928** Skinner's Big Idea; Wallflowers; Beau Broadway; Red Lips; Her Summer Hero; The Pinto Kid. **1929** Dry Martini; Hey, Rube; Taxi 13; Love in the Desert; Night Parade; The Very Idea. **1930** Cuckoos; Midnight Mystery; The Pay-Off; Conspiracy; Half Shot at Sunrise. **1931** The Royal Bed.

TREVOR, NORMAN
Born: 1877, Calcutta, India. Died: Oct. 31, 1929, Norwalk, Calif. Stage and screen actor.

Appeared in: **1917** The Runaway. **1920** Romance. **1921** The Black Panther's Cub; Jane Eyre. **1924** The Wages of Virtue; Roulette. **1925** Dancing Mothers; The Man Who Found Himself. **1926** Beau Geste; The Song and Dance Man; The Ace of Cads. **1927** Afraid to Love; Children of Divorce; The Siren; Sorrell and Son; The Music Master; New York; The Wizard; The Warning. **1928** Mad Hour.

TRICOLI, CARLO
Died: Apr. 1, 1966. Screen actor.

Appeared in: **1950** Black Hand; Lady Without Passport. **1951** Mask of the Avenger. **1952** Wagon Team. **1960** Pay or Die.

TRIGGER
Born: 1932. Died: July 3, 1965. Roy Rogers' Palomino horse. Screen and television performer. Appeared in 87 feature films and 101 half-hour television shows.

Appeared in: **1944** Hollywood Canteen. **1945** Utah. **1946** My Pal Trigger. **1947** Apache Rose. **1949** The Golden Stallion. **1950** Sunset in the West; Trigger, Jr. **1951** Heart of the Rockies.

TRIMBLE, LARRY (Lawrence Trimble)
Born: Feb. 15, 1885, Robbinston, Maine. Died: Feb. 8, 1954, Woodland Hills, Calif. Screen actor, film director and screenwriter. Entered films in 1910 with Vitagraph.

TROTSKY, LEON (Lev Davydovich Bronstein)
Born: Nov. 8, 1879, Yanovka, Kherson Province, Ukraine. Died: Aug. 21, 1940, Mexico City, Mexico (murdered). Politician, philosopher and screen performer.

Appeared in: **1914** My Official Wife.

TROTTER, JOHN SCOTT
Born: 1908, Charlotte, N.C. Died: Oct. 29, 1975, Los Angeles, Calif. (cancer). Musical conductor, arranger, musician and screen, radio and television actor.

Appeared in: **1940** Rhythm On the River. **1941** Kiss the Boys Goodbye.

TROUNCER, CECIL
Born: Apr. 5, 1898, Southport Lanes, England. Died: Dec. 15, 1953. Stage and screen actor.

Appeared in: **1938** Pygmalion. **1947** While the Sun Shines (US 1950). **1948** The Guinea Pig (US 1949); London Belongs to Me (aka Dulcimer Street—US); Saraband for Dead Lovers (aka Saraband—US). **1951** The Magic Box (US 1952); The Lady with the Lamp. **1952** The Pickwick Papers (US 1953). **1954** The Weak and the Wicked.

TROUT, FRANCIS "DINK"
Born: June 18, 1898, Beardstown, Ill. Died: Mar. 26, 1950, Hollywood, Calif. Screen, stage, radio, vaudeville actor and musician. Played with Ben Bernie's band.

Appeared in: **1941** Scattergood Baines. **1943** Gildersleeve's Bad Day. **1944** Up in Arms. **1945** Sudan.

TROW, WILLIAM
Born: 1891. Died: Sept. 2, 1973, Hollywood, Calif. Screen actor. Entered films in 1919.

TROWBRIDGE, CHARLES
Born: Jan. 10, 1882, Vera Cruz, Mexico. Died: Oct. 30, 1967. Stage and screen actor.

Appeared in: **1918** Thais. **1922** Island Wives. **1931** I Take This Woman; Damaged Love; A Secret Call; Silence. **1935** Calm Yourself; Mad Love; It's in the Air; Rendezvous. **1936** Exclusive Story; The Garden Murder Case; We Went to College; Born to Dance; Mother Steps Out; Man of the People; The Gorgeous Hussy; Libeled Lady; The Devil Is a Sissy; Robin Hood of El Dorado; Moonlight Murder; Love on the Run. **1937** Dangerous Number; Espionage; A Day at the Races; A Servant of the People; Fit for a King; Captains Courageous; They Gave Him a Gun; Sea Racketeers; Exiled to Shanghai; That Certain Woman; Without Warning; Saturday's Heroes; The 13th Chair. **1938** Little Tough Guy; Crime School; Nancy Drew, Detective; Alcatraz Island; The Buccaneer; Kentucky; Thanks for Everything; Submarine Patrol; Gang Bullets;

The Last Express; The Invisible Menace; The Patient in Room 18; College Swing; Gangs of New York; Crime Ring. **1939** Angels Wash Their Faces; Risky Business; King of Chinatown; Tropic Fury; King of the Underworld; Boy Trouble; The Story of Alexander Graham Bell; On Trial; Hotel for Women; Swanee River; Each Dawn I Die; While America Sleeps (short); Confessions of a Nazi Spy; The Man They Could Not Hang; Mutiny on the Blackhawk; Joe and Ethel Turp Call on the President; Pride of the Navy; Lady of the Tropics; Cafe Society; Sergeant Madden. **1940** My Love Came Back; House of Seven Gables; The Fighting 69th; Johnny Apollo; The Man with Nine Lives; Knute Rockne—All American; Cherokee Strip; The Mummy's Hand; Dr. Kildare Goes Home; Trail of the Vigilantes; The Fatal Hour. **1941** The Great Lie; The Tell-Tale Heart; Strange Alibi; Dressed to Kill; Blue, White and Perfect; The Nurse's Secret; Rags to Riches; Sergeant York; Hurricane Smith; Great Guns; We Go Fast; The Great Mr. Nobody; Belle Starr; Cadet Girl. **1942** Who Is Hope Schuyler?; Sweetheart of the Fleet; Over My Dead Body; That Other Woman; Ten Gentlemen from West Point; Wake Island; Tennessee Johnson. **1943** Action in the North Atlantic; Wintertime; The Story of Dr. Wassell; Salute to the Marines; Sweet Rosie O'Grady; Mission to Moscow; Adventures of the Flying Cadets (serial). **1944** Faces in the Fog; Summer Storm; Hey Rookie!; Wing and a Prayer; Heavenly Days. **1945** Col. Effingham's Raid; Mildred Pierce; They Were Expendable; The Red Dragon. **1946** Don't Gamble with Strangers; Shock; Undercurrent; Secret of the Whistler; The Hoodlum Saint; Smooth as Silk; Valley of the Zombies. **1947** Key Witness; Buck Privates Come Home; Her Husband's Affairs; The Sea of Grass; The Beginning or the End?; Mr. District Attorney; The Private Affairs of Bel Ami; Tarzan and the Huntress; Song of My Heart; Tycoon; Black Gold; Shoot to Kill. **1948** Stage Struck; Hollow Triumph; The Paleface. **1949** Mr. Soft Touch; Bad Boy. **1950** Unmasked; Peggy. **1952** Bushwhackers. **1957** The Wings of Eagles.

TROY, ELINOR
Died: Nov. 29, 1949 (polio). Stage and screen actress.

Appeared in: **1942** Pride of the Yankees.

TROY, HELEN
Born: 1905. Died: Nov. 1, 1942, Santa Monica, Calif. Screen and radio actress.

Appeared in: **1936** Born to Dance; Song and Dance Man; Human Cargo. **1937** Thoroughbreds Don't Cry; Between Two Women; Broadway Melody of 1938; Big City; Everybody Sing. **1939** Kid Nightingale.

TRUAX, JOHN
Died: June 14, 1969. Screen actor.

Appeared in: **1956** He Laughed Last. **1957** The Fuzzy Pink Nightgown. **1959** Curse of the Undead. **1965** The Great Race.

TRUESDELL, FREDERICK (George Frederick Truesdell)
Born: 1873. Died: May 3, 1937, New York, N.Y. Screen and stage actor.

Appeared in: **1919** Shadows. **1923** The Love Piker; Chastity. **1924** Pleasure Mad; The Beauty Prize.

TRUEX, ERNEST
Born: Sept. 19, 1889, Kansas City, Mo. Died: June 27, 1973, Fallbrook, Calif. (heart attack). Screen, stage, television and vaudeville actor. Married to actress Sally Field. Divorced from actresses Julia Mills and Mary Jane Barrett.

Appeared in: **1914** Good Little Devil. **1917** Artie; Caprice and The American Citizen. **1923** Six Cylinder Love. **1929** Love at First Sight. **1931** The Millionaire. **1933** Whistling in the Dark; The Warrior's Husband. **1936** Everybody Dance. **1937** Mama Runs Wild. **1938** The Adventures of Marco Polo; Start Cheering; Freshman Year; Swing that Cheer; Swing, Sister, Swing. **1939** Ambush; It's a Wonderful World; Bachelor Mother; These Glamour Girls; Little Accident; Island of Lost Men. **1940** Lillian Russell; Christmas in July. **1941** His Girl Friday. **1942** Twin Beds; Private Buckaroo; Star Spangled Rhythm. **1943** The Crystal Ball; Rhythm of the Islands; True to Life; Sleepy Lagoon; Fired Wife. **1944** Chip Off the Old Block; Her Primitive Man. **1945** Pan-Americana; Men in Her Diary. **1946** Life With Blondie. **1948** Always Together. **1956** The Leather Saint. **1957** All Mine to Give. **1958** Twilight For the Gods. **1965** Fluffy.

TRUJILLO, LORENZO L.
Born: 1906, Mexico. Died: Mar. 1962, Mexico City, Mexico (heart attack). Screen, stage and television actor. Appeared in 200 Mexican films including The Exterminating Angel.

TRUPPI, DANNY
Born: July 25, 1919, New York, N.Y. Died: July 6, 1970, Los Angeles, Calif. (heart attack). Screen actor and musician.

Appeared in: **1956** Around the World in 80 Days. **1970** The Trouble With Girls.

TRYON, GLENN
Born: Sept. 14, 1899, Julietta, Idaho. Died: Apr. 18, 1970. Screen, stage actor, film director, producer and screenwriter.

Appeared in: **1924** The Battling Orioles; The White Sheep. **1927** Two Girls

Wanted; A Hero for a Night; The Denver Dude; Painting the Town; The Poor Nut. **1928** Thanks for the Buggy Ride; Hot Heels; How to Handle Women; Lonesome; The Gate Crasher. **1929** Skinner Steps Out; Broadway; Barnum Was Right; It Can be Done; The Kid's Clever. **1930** Dames Ahoy; King of Jazz; The Midnight Special. **1931** Daybreak; The Sky Spider; Neck and Neck; Secret Menace. **1932** Dragnet Patrol; Rule 'Em and Weep (short); Widow in Scarlet; Tangled Destinies; The Pride of the Legion. **1933** Educational shorts. **1934** The Big Pay-Off. **1941** Hold That Ghost; Keep 'Em Flying; Helzapoppin. **1945** George White's Scandals. **1947** Variety Girl. **1965** Laurel and Hardy's Laughing 20's (film clips).

TSIANG, H. T.
Born: 1899. Died: July 16, 1971, Hollywood, Calif. Screen, stage, television actor, poet and author. Entered films in 1928.

Appeared in: **1944** The Purple Heart; Keys of the Kingdom. **1948** Chicken Every Sunday. **1949** State Department File-649. **1950** Panic in the Streets. **1951** Smuggler's Island. **1960** Ocean's 11. **1965** Winter A-Go-Go.

TSUKAMOTO, RAYNUM K.
Born: Mar. 1, 1889, Japan. Died: Aug. 9, 1974, Los Angeles, Calif. (hit by auto). Screen actor.

Appeared in: **1956** The Teahouse of the August Moon. **1966** Operation Bikini.

TUALA, MARIO (Eckard Schulz-Ewerth)
Born: 1924, Samoa, South Sea Islands. Died: July 10, 1961, Berlin, Germany (drowned in boating accident). Screen, radio actor and singer.

TUBBS, WILLIAM
Born: 1908. Died: Jan. 25, 1953, London, England. Screen and stage actor.

Appeared in: **1948** Paisan. **1949** The Pirates of Capri. **1951** Quo Vadis; Three Steps North. **1952** Edward and Caroline. **1953** Singing Taxi Driver. **1954** The Greatest Love; The Golden Coach. **1955** The Wages of Fear.

TUCKER, CY
Born: 1889. Died: July 4, 1952, Hollywood, Calif. Screen actor.

TUCKER, GEORGE LOANE
Born: 1872, Chicago, Ill. Died: June 20, 1921, Los Angeles, Calif. Screen actor, film director and producer. Married to actress Elizabeth Risdon (dec. 1958).

Appeared in: **1911** Uncle's Visit. **1912** A Little Old Woman of Twenty; Next! **1913** Majestic Film Co. films.

TUCKER, HARLAND (aka HARLAN TUCKER)
Died: Mar. 22, 1949, Calif. (heart attack). Screen and stage actor.

Appeared in: **1920** The Loves of Letty. **1921** Beau Revel; The Swamp. **1926** Shameful Behavior?; The Adorable Deceiver. **1927** Stolen Pleasures. **1933** Phantom Broadcast; King for a Night. **1937** Once a Doctor; Racing Lady; Kid Galahad; Slim; Missing Witnesses; Without Warning. **1938** The Invisible Menace; The Patient in Room 18. **1939** King of the Underworld. **1940** The Lone Wolf Strikes. **1941** The Roar of the Press. **1942** Road to Happiness. **1947** Hit Parade of 1947. **1948** A Foreign Affair; Beyond Glory.

TUCKER, RICHARD
Born: 1884, Brooklyn, N.Y. Died: Dec. 5, 1942, Woodland Hills, Calif. (heart attack). Stage and screen actor. Entered films with Edison.

Appeared in: **1913** Her Royal Highness. **1915** While the Tide Was Rising; Vanity Fair. **1917** Threads of Fate; The Law of the North; The Little Chevalier. **1920** Branding Iron. **1921** Roads of Destiny; Don't Neglect Your Wife; The Old Nest; Everything for Sale; What Love Will Do; A Voice in the Dark; A Virginia Courtship; The Night Rose. **1922** Hearts Aflame; The Dangerous Age; A Self-Made Man; Strange Idols; Remembrance; Rags to Riches; Grand Larceny; When the Devil Drives; The Worldly Madonna; Yellow Men and Gold. **1923** Cameo Kirby; The Eleventh Hour; Her Accidental Husband; Poor Men's Wives; Is Divorce a Failure?; Lovebound; The Broken Wing. **1924** Beau Brummell; 40-Horse Hawkins; Helen's Babies; The Fast Worker; The Star Dust Trail; The Tornado. **1925** The Air Mail; The Lure of the Wild; The Man without a Country; The Golden Cocoon; The Bridge of Sighs. **1926** The Blind Goddess; Shameful Behavior?; The Lily; That's My Baby; Devil's Island. **1927** Dearie; Wings; The Girl from Rio; The Lash (short); The Bush Leaguer; The Desired Woman; The Jazz Singer; A Kiss in a Taxi; The World at Her Feet; Matinee Ladies; Women's Wares. **1928** Thanks for the Buggy Ride; Loves of an Actress; On Trial; Captain Swagger; Love over Night; My Man; The Border Patrol; Daughters of Desire; Beware of Married Men; A Bit of Heaven; Show Girl; The Crimson City; The Grain of Dust. **1929** The Dummy; Half Marriage; King of the Kongo (serial); This Is Heaven; Lucky Boy; Synthetic Sin; The Unholy Night; The Squall. **1930** Madonna of the Streets; Brothers; Puttin' on the Ritz; Shadow of the Law; Broken Dishes; Recaptured Love; Safety in Numbers; The Bat Whispers; The Benson Murder Case; Painted Faces; Peacock Alley; Courage; The Man from Blankley's; College Lovers; Manslaughter. **1931** Too Young to Marry; A Holy Terror; Convicted; Devil Plays; Inspiration; Seed; X Marks the Spot; Stepping Out; Hellbound; Maker of Men; The

Deceiver; Graft; Up for Murder; The Black Camel. **1932** Careless Lady; A Successful Calamity; The Stoker; Guilty as Hell; The Crash; Pack up Your Troubles; Flames; Week-End Marriage. **1933** The Iron Master; Her Resale Value; Daring Daughters; The World Gone Mad; Saturday's Millions; Only Yesterday. **1934** Show-Off; Back Page; Take the Stand; Successful Failure; Public Stenographer; The Road to Ruin; Countess of Monte Cristo; A Modern Hero; Handy Andy; Baby Take a Bow; Money Means Nothing; Paris Interlude; Sing Sing Nights. **1935** Buried Loot (short); Diamond Jim; Shadow of Doubt; Murder in the Fleet; Calm Yourself; Here Comes the Band; Sympathy of Living. **1936** In Paris A.W.O.L.; Flash Gordon (serial); The Great Ziegfeld; Ring around the Moon; Flying Hostess; The Plot Thickens; I Loved a Woman; Shall We Dance? **1937** She's Dangerous; Headline Crasher; I Cover the War; The Girl Who Said No; Jungle Menace (serial); Armored Car; Something to Sing About; Make a Wish; The River of Missing Men; Trapped by G-Men. **1938** The Texans; She's Got Everything; The Higgins Family; Sons of the Legion. **1939** Risky Business; The Girl from Rio; The Covered Trailer; The Great Victor Herbert; While America Sleeps (short).

TUCKER, RICHARD (Reuben Ticker)
Born: Aug. 28, 1914, Brooklyn, N.Y. Died: Jan. 8, 1975, Kalamazoo, Mich. (heart attack). Opera tenor and screen actor.

TUCKER, SOPHIE (Sophie Abuza)
Born: Jan. 13, 1884, Boston, Mass. or Russia. Died: Feb. 9, 1966, New York, N.Y. (lung and kidney ailment). Screen, stage, burlesque, vaudeville actress and nightclub entertainer.

Appeared in: **1929** Honky Tonk. **1934** Gay Love. **1937** Broadway Melody of 1938; Thoroughbreds Don't Cry. **1944** Follow the Boys; Sensations of 1945; Atlantic City.

TUFTS, SONNY (Bowen Charleston Tufts, III)
Born: 1912, Boston, Mass. Died: June 5, 1970, Santa Monica, Calif. (pneumonia). Screen, stage, television actor and film producer.

Appeared in: **1939** Ambush. **1943** So Proudly We Hail; Government Girl. **1944** In the Meantime, Darling; I Love a Soldier; Here Comes the Waves. **1945** Bring on the Girls; Duffy's Tavern. **1946** Miss Susie Slagle's; The Virginian; The Well-Groomed Bride. **1947** Swell Guy; Cross My Heart; Easy Come, Easy Go; Blaze of Noon; Variety Girl. **1948** Untamed Breed. **1949** Easy Living; The Crooked Way. **1952** The Gift Horse (aka Glory at Sea—US 1953). **1953** Cat-Women of the Moon; No Escape; Run for the Hills. **1955** The Seven Year Itch. **1956** Come Next Spring. **1957** The Parson and the Outlaw. **1962** All the Way. **1965** The Town Tamer. **1967** Cottonpickin' Chickenpickers.

TULLY, ETHEL
Born: 1898. Died: Oct. 1, 1968, San Antonio, Tex. Screen actress. Model for WW I posters of J. M. Flagg. Entered films with Vitagraph in 1916.

TULLY, JIM
Born: June 3, 1891, near St. Mary's, Ohio. Died: June 22, 1947, Hollywood, Calif. (heart attack). Novelist, screenwriter and screen actor.

Appeared in: **1930** Way for a Sailor.

TUNIS, FAY
Born: 1890. Died: Dec. 4, 1967, Atlantic City, N.J. Screen and stage actress. Appeared in silent films.

TURLEIGH, VERONICA
Born: 1903, England. Died: Sept. 1971, England. Stage and screen actress.

Appeared in: **1952** The Card (aka The Promoter—US). **1958** The Horse's Mouth.

TURNER, EMANUEL
Born: 1884. Died: Dec. 13, 1941, Hollywood, Calif. Screen and stage actor.

Appeared in: **1916** The Redemption of Dave Darcey. **1918** The Love Swindle.

TURNER, F. A. (Fred A. Turner)
Born: 1842 or 1866 (?), Boston, Mass. Died: Feb. 13, 1923. Screen and stage actor.

Appeared in: **1916** Atta Boy's Last Race; Children of the Feud; Intolerance. **1917** Madame Bo-Peep. **1920** The Jack-Knife Man.

TURNER, FLORENCE
Born: 1885, New York, N.Y. Died: Aug. 28, 1946, Woodland Hills, Calif. Screen, stage and vaudeville actress. She began her career on May 17, 1907, at Vitagraph Studios and was known only as "The Vitagraph Girl" and received no billing in early films.

Appeared in: **1910** The New Stenographer; St. Elmo; A Dixie Mother; A Tale of Two Cities. **1911** The Deerslayer; Intrepid Davy; The Wrong Patient; Answer of the Roses; Wig Wag; Auld Lang Syne; One Touch of Nature. **1912** Francesca de Rimini; Indian Romeo and Juliet; Jean Intervenes; How Mr. Bullington Ran the House; The Signal of Distress; Her Diary; Susie to

Suzanne; Two Cinders; When Persistence and Obstinacy Meet; The Price of Silence; A Vitagraph Romance. **1913** Rose of Surrey; Jean's Evidence; The Younger Sister; The Lucky Stone; The Harper Mystery; Sisters All; Stenographer Trouble; Checkmated; Let 'Em Quarrel; Up and Down the Ladder; Pumps; Counselor Bobby; The Wings of a Moth. **1914** Creatures of Habit; The Murdock Trial; The Terrible Twins; Flotilla the Flirt; For Her People; Polly's Progress; Through the Valley of Shadows; The Shepherd Lassie of Argyle; Film Favouriites (aka Florence Turner Impersonates Film Favorites—US); Snobs; Shopgirls—or, The Great Question; Daisy Doodad's Dial; One Thing After Another. **1915** As Ye Repent (aka Redeemed—US); Alone in London; My Old Dutch; Lost and Won (aka Odds Against); Far from the Madding Crowd; A Welsh Singer. **1916** Doorsteps; Grim Justice; East is East. **1920** The Ugly Duckling. **1921** All Dolled Up; Passion Fruit; The Old Wives' Tale. **1922** Was She Justified?; The Little Mother; Famous Poems by George R. Sims Series including: The Lights O'London and the Street Tumblers. **1923** Hornet's Nest; Sally Bishop. **1924** The Boatswain's Mate; Film Favourites (short); Women and Diamonds (aka Conscripts of Misfortune or It Happened in Africa). **1925** The Dark Angel; Never the Twain Shall Meet; The Mad Marriage; The Price of Success. **1926** Flame of the Argentine; The Last Alarm; Padlocked; The Gilded Highway. **1927** The Broken Gate; The Chinese Parrot; The Overland Stage; Stranded; College; The Cancelled Debts; Sally in Our Alley. **1928** Marry the Girl; The Law and the Man; Chinese Parrot; Walking Back; Jazzland; The Pace That Kills; The Road to Ruin. **1929** The Kid's Clever. **1930** The Rampant Age.

TURNER, GEORGE
Born: England. Died: July 27, 1968. Screen actor. Do not confuse with U.S. actor George Turner.

Appeared in: **1920** London Pride; The Biter Bit; The Duchess of Seven Dials. **1921** The Croxley Master. **1922** Running Water; Love's Influence; The Big Strong Man. **1923** Early Birds; Sally Bishop; Mumming Birds; Jail Birds; Woman to Woman (US 1924); M'lord of the White Road. **1924** The Gay Corinthian; The Diamond Man; Nets of Destiny. **1929** White Cargo. **1931** The Lame Duck; A Safe Affair. **1933** The Man from Toronto; In Our Time; Britannia of Billingsgate; Forging Ahead. **1936** Playbox Adventure; Cafe Mascot; Full Speed Ahead; Twin Faces. **1937** Screen Struck. **1938** On the Top of the Underworld series including: Receivers and The Kite Mob. **1940** Two Smart Men.

TURNER, MAIDEL
Born: May 12, 1888, Sherman, Tex. Died: Apr. 12, 1953, Ocean Springs, Miss. Stage and screen actress.

Appeared in: **1926** The Boy Friend. **1933** Another Language; The Worst Woman in Paris; Olsen's Big Moment. **1934** Most Precious Thing in Life; It Happened One Night; The Life of Vergie Winters; Unknown Blonde; Money Means Nothing; Whom the Gods Destroy; A Modern Hero; Transcontinental Bus; The Perfect Clue; The Merry Frinks. **1935** Dante's Inferno; Mutiny Ahead; The Raven; Diamond Jim. **1936** Magnificent Obsession; Palm Springs; And Sudden Death; Make Way for a Lady. **1937** Slim.

TURNER, OTIS "DADDY"
Born: Nov. 29, 1862, Ind. Died: Mar. 28, 1918, Hollywood, Calif. (heart disease). Screen actor and film director.

TURNER, COL. ROSCOE
Born: 1896. Died: June 23, 1970, Indianapolis, Ind. Screen actor, stuntman, aviation pioneer and flying ace.

Appeared in: **1930** Hell's Angels. **1939** Flight at Midnight.

TURNER, WILLIAM H.
Born: 1861, Ireland. Died: Sept. 27, 1942, Philadelphia, Pa. Stage and screen actor. Married to actress Ann Vislaire.

Appeared in: **1916** Perils of Our Girl Reporters (serial). **1923** Blow Your Own Horn; Other Men's Daughters; The Satin Girl; The Darling of New York. **1924** The Enemy Sex; American Manners; The Garden of Weeds; Fast and Fearless; The Measure of a Man; The Gaiety Girl. **1925** The Phantom Bullet; The Pony Express; Gold and Grit; Heir-Loons; Where Was I?; White Thunder; A Woman's Faith. **1926** The Texas Streak; Three Pals; Her Big Adventure; Red Hot Leather; The Warning Signal. **1927** Broadway after Midnight. **1928** Driftin' Sands. **1929** The Trespasser; The Last Performance. **1932** Love Me Tonight.

TURPIN, BEN (Bernard Turpin)
Born: Sept. 17, 1869, New Orleans, La. Died: July 1, 1940, Santa Monica, Calif. (heart disease). Screen, stage, burlesque and vaudeville actor. Married to actress Carrie LeMieux Turpin (dec. 1925) and later married to Babette E. Dietz.

Appeared in: **1907** Ben Gets a Duck and is Ducked. **1909** Midnight Disturbance. **1914** Sweedie and the Lord; Sweedie and the Double Exposure; Sweedie's Skate; Sweedie Springs a Surprise; The Fickleness of Sweedie; She Landed a Big One; Sweedie and the Trouble Maker; Sweedie at the Fair; Madame Double X; Sweedie Learns to Swim. **1915** A Christmas Revenge; His

New Job; A Night Out; Sweedie and her Dog; Sweedie's Suicide; Two Hearts that Beat as Ten; Sweedie's Hopeless Love; Love and Trouble; Sweedie Learns to Ride; Sweedie Goes to College; Sweedie's Hero; Curiosity; The Clubman's Wager; A Coat Tale; Others Started but Sophie Finished; A Quiet Little Game; Sophie and the Fakir; The Merry Models; Snakeville's Hen Medic; Snakeville's Champion; Snakeville's Debutantes; Snakeville's Twins; How Slippery Slim Saw the Show; Two Bold, Bad Men; The Undertaker's Wife; A Bunch of Matches; The Bell Hop; Versus Sledge Hammers; Too Much Turkey; His New Job; By the Sea; A Night Out. **1916** The Delinquent Bridegroom; Carmen; When Papa Died; His Blowout (aka The Plumber); The Iron Mitt; Hired and Fired (aka The Leading Man); A Deep Sea Liar (aka The Landlubber); For Ten Thousand Bucks; Some Liars; The Stolen Booking; Doctoring a Lead (aka A Total Loss); Poultry a la Mode (aka The Harem); Ducking a Discord; He Did and He Didn't; Picture Pirates; Shot in the Fracas; Jealous Jolts; The Wicked City; A Safe Proposition; Some Bravery; A Waiting Game; Taking the Count; National Nuts; Nailing on the Lid (aka Nailing a Lie); Just for a Kid; Lost and Found; Bungling Bill's Dress. **1917** Roping Her Romeo; Are Waitresses Safe?; Taming Target Center; A Circus Cyclone; The Musical Marvels; The Butcher's Nightmare; His Bogus Boast (aka A Cheerful Liar); A Studio Stampede; Frightened Flirts; Sole Mates; Why Ben Bolted (aka He Looked Crooked); Masked Mirth; Bucking the Tiger; Caught in the End; A Clever Dummy; Lost—a Cook; The Pawnbroker's Heart. **1918** She Loved Him Plenty; Sheriff Nell's Tussle; Saucy Madeline; The Battle Royal; Two Tough Tenderfeet; Hide and Seek, Detectives. **1919** Yankee Doodle in Berlin; East Lynne with Variations; Uncle Tom without a Cabin; Salome vs. Shenendoah; Cupid's Day Off; When Love Is Blind; No Mother to Guide Him; Sleuths; Whose Little Wife Are You? **1920** You Wouldn't Believe It (short); The Daredevil; Down on the Farm; Married Life; The Star Boarder (short). **1921** A Small Town Idol; Home Talent; Love's Outcast (short). **1922** Love and Doughnuts (short); Foolish Wives; plus the following shorts: Bright Eyes; Step Forward; Home-Made Movies. **1923** The Shriek of Araby; Hollywood; plus the following shorts: Where's My Wandering Boy Tonight?; Pitfalls of a Big City; Asleep at the Switch. **1924** The following shorts: Romeo and Juliet; Yukon Jake; Ten Dollars or Ten Days; The Hollywood Kid; Three Foolish Weeks; The Reel Virginian. **1925** Hogan's Alley; plus the following shorts: Wild Goose Chaser; Rasberry Romance; The Marriage Circus. **1926** Steele Preferred; plus the following shorts: A Harem Knight; A Blonde's Revenge; When a Man's a Prince; A Prodigal Bridegroom. **1927** The College Hero; A Woman's Way; plus the following shorts: The Pride of Pickeville; Broke in China; A Hollywood Hero; The Jolly Jilter; Love's Languid Lure; Daddy Boy. **1928** The Wife's Relations. **1929** Show of Shows; The Love Parade. **1930** Swing High. **1931** Cracked Nuts; Our Wife (short). **1932** Make Me a Star; Million Dollar Legs; Hypnotized. **1932–33** Paramount shorts. **1934** Law of the Wild (serial). **1935** Keystone Hotel (short); Bring 'Em Back a Lie (short). **1939** Hollywood Cavalcade. **1940** Saps at Sea. **1949** Down Memory Lane (documentary). **1951** Memories of Famous Hollywood Comedians (documentary). **1957** The Golden Age of Comedy (documentary). **1960** When Comedy Was King (documentary). **1961** Days of Thrills and Laughter (documentary). **1968** The Funniest Man in the World (documentary).

TURPIN, CARRIE (Carrie LeMieux)
Born: 1882, Quebec, Canada. Died: Oct. 3, 1925, Beverly Hills, Calif. Stage and screen actress. Married to actor Ben Turpin (dec. 1940).

Appeared in: **1915** Others Started But Sophie Finished; Too Much Turkey; Snakeville's Hen Medic; The Merry Models.

TUTMARC, PAUL H.
Died: Sept. 23, 1972, Seattle, Wash. Musician, singer and screen actor. Reported inventor of the electric guitar.

TWEDDELL, FRANK
Born: 1895, India. Died: Dec. 20, 1971, New Haven, Conn. Stage and screen actor.

Appeared in: **1943** Claudia (stage and screen versions). **1946** Claudia and David. **1949** The Undercover Man. **1950** The Tattooed Stranger. **1951** I'd Climb the Highest Mountain. **1956** Carousel.

TWEED, TOMMY
Born: 1907, Canada. Died: Oct. 12, 1971, Canada. Screen actor and writer.

Appeared in: **1963** The Incredible Journey.

TWELVETREES, HELEN (Helen Jurgens)
Born: Dec. 25, 1908, Brooklyn, N.Y. Died: Feb. 14, 1958, Harrisburg, Pa. (accidental overdose of drugs for kidney ailment). Stage and screen actress.

Appeared in: **1929** The Ghost Talks (film debut); True Heart; Blue Skies; Paris to Bagdad; Words and Music. **1930** Her Man; The Grand Parade; Swing High; The Cat Creeps. **1931** Beyond Victory; The Painted Desert; A Woman of Experience; Bad Company; Millie; Cardigan's Last Case. **1932** Panama Flo; Young Bride; Is My Face Red?; State's Attorney; Unashamed. **1933** A Bedtime Story; Disgraced; My Woman; King for a Night. **1934** All Men Are Enemies; Now I'll Tell; She Was a Lady. **1935** One Hour Late; Times Square Lady; She

Gets Her Man; 'Frisco Waterfront; Spanish Cape Mystery. **1937** Hollywood Round Up. **1939** Persons in Hiding.

TWITCHELL, A. R. "ARCHIE" (Michael Brandon)
Born: Nov. 28, 1906, Pendleton, Ore. Died: Jan. 31, 1957, Pacoima, Calif. (mid-air collision). Screen actor.

Appeared in: **1937** Daughters of Shanghai; Souls at Sea; Partners in Crime; Hold 'Em, Navy; Sophie Lang Goes West. **1938** You and Me; Her Jungle Love; Tip-Off Girls; Cocoanut Grove; Spawn of the North; The Texans; Illegal Traffic; Give Me a Sailor. **1939** Ambush; King of Chinatown; Mickey the Kid; Geronimo. **1940** Granny Get Your Gun; Dr. Kildare Goes Home; Charlie Chan at the Wax Museum; Young Bill Hickok; Behind the News. **1941** I Wanted Wings; West Point Widow; Among the Living; Prairie Stranger; Thundering Hoofs. **1942** Heart Burn (short); Home Work (short); A Tragedy at Midnight. **1945** The Missing Corpse. **1946** Affairs of Geraldine; The French Key; Accomplice. **1947** The Arnelo Affair; Second Chance; Robin Hood in Texas; Web of Danger. **1949** Follow Me Quietly. **1950** Revenue Agent. **1951** Kentucky Jubilee; Yes Sir, Mr. Bones. **1954** The Bounty Hunter.

TYKE, JOHN
Born: 1895. Died: Feb. 23, 1940, Hollywood, Calif. Screen actor and extra. Entered films in 1924.

TYLER, GLADYS C.
Born: 1893. Died: Apr. 14, 1972, Hollywood, Calif. Screen and stage actress. Married to actor Harry Tyler (dec. 1961).

TYLER, HARRY
Born: 1888. Died: Sept. 15, 1961, Hollywood, Calif. (cancer). Screen, stage and television actor. Married to actress Gladys Tyler (dec. 1972).

Appeared in: **1929** The Shannons of Broadway; Oh, Yeah! **1930** Big Money. **1933** Poor Fish (short). **1934** Midnight Alibi; Friends of Mr. Sweeney; Housewife; The Case of the Howling Dog; Babbitt. **1935** The Glass Key; Lady Tubbs; Men without Names; A Night at the Opera. **1936** Two-Fisted Gentlemen; The Man I Marry; Pennies from Heaven; Three Wise Guys; a Vitaphone short. **1937** The Girl Said No; Don't Tell the Wife; Love Takes Flight; Mr. Boggs Steps Out; Jim Hanvey—Detective; Youth on Parole; Midnight Madonna. **1938** Penny's Picnic (short). **1939** The Story of Alexander Graham Bell; Jesse James; The Lady's from Kentucky; 20,000 Men a Year; Young Mr. Lincoln; The Gracie Allen Murder Case. **1940** Andy Hardy Meets a Debutante; Little Old New York; Johnny Apollo; Young People; Meet the Missus; Behind the News; The Grapes of Wrath; Go West. **1941** The Bride Wore Crutches; The Richest Man in Town; Tillie the Toiler; Remember the Day; Tobacco Road. **1942** The Mexican Spitfire Sees a Ghost; Wedded Blitz (short). **1943** True to Life; The Dancing Masters. **1944** Casanova in Burlesque; The Adventures of Mark Twain; Atlantic City; Wilson; Love Your Landlord (short); Movie Pests (short). **1945** Identity Unknown; The Woman Who Came Back; Abbott and Costello in Hollywood. **1946** Behind Green Lights; The Fabulous Suzanne; I Ring Doorbells; Johnny Comes Flying Home; Somewhere in the Night. **1947** Fun on a Weekend; Sarge Goes to College; Winter Wonderland; Heading for Heaven. **1948** Smart Politics; Deep Waters; Strike It Rich; The Untamed Breed; That Wonderful Urge. **1949** Air Hostess; Beautiful Blonde from Bashful Bend; Hellfire. **1950** Lucky Losers; Rider from Tucson; The Traveling Saleswoman; A Woman of Distinction. **1951** Bedtime for Bonzo; Texans Never Cry; Corky of Gasoline Alley; Santa Fe. **1952** Deadline, U.S.A.; The Quiet Man; This Woman Is Dangerous; Wagons West; Lost in Alaska. **1953** The Glass Web. **1954** Witness to Murder. **1955** Jail Busters; A Lawless Street; The Naked Street; Texas Lady; Abbott and Costello Meet the Keystone Kops. **1956** A Day of Fury; Glory. **1957** Plunder Road. **1958** Last Hurrah.

TYLER, JUDY
Born: 1933. Died: July 3, 1957, near Billy-the-Kid, Wyo. (auto crash). Screen actress and singer.

Appeared in: **1957** Bop Girl (aka Bop Girl Goes Calypso); Jailhouse Rock.

TYLER, TOM (Vincent Marko, or Markoski)
Born: Aug. 8, 1903, New York, N.Y. Died: May 1, 1954, Hamtramck, Mich. Screen actor. One of the "Three Mesquiteers." Voted top money-making western star in pictures in Herald–Fame Poll, 1942.

Appeared in: **1925** The Cowboy Musketeer; Let's Go Gallagher; The Wyoming Wildcat. **1926** The Cowboy Cop; Red Hot Hoofs; Born to Battle; The Masquerade Bandit; Out of the West; Tom and His Pals; Wild to Go. **1927** The Sonora Kid; Cyclone of the Range; The Cherokee Kid; The Flying U Ranch; The Desert Pirate; Lightning Lariats; Splitting the Breeze; Tom's Gang. **1928** Phantom of the Range; Terror Mountain; The Avenging Rider; Terror; The Texas Tornado; Tyrant of Red Gulch; When the Law Rides. **1929** The Sorcerer; Trail of the Horse Thieves; Gun Law; Idaho Red; Pride of Pawnee; The Lone Horseman; The Man from Nevada; The Phantom Rider; 'Neath Western Skies; Law of the Plains. **1930** Phantom of the West (serial); Call of the Desert; The Canyon of Missing Men; Pioneers of the West. **1931** A Man from Death Valley; Rider of the Plains; Galloping Through; West of Cheyenne; Rose of the Rio Grande; God's Country and the Man; Battling with Buffalo Bill (serial); Partners of the Trail. **1932** Jungle Mystery (serial); The Tenderfoot; Man from New Mexico; Single-Handed Sanders; Two-Fisted Justice; Honor of the Mounted; Vanishing Men; The Forty-Niners; prior to 1933: Half Pint Polly (short). **1933** War of the Range; When a Man Rides Alone; Deadwood Pass; Clancy of the Mounted (serial); The Phantom of the Air. **1934** Riding Through; Tracy Rides; Riding the Lonesome Trail; Mystery Ranch; Fighting Hero; Terror of the Plains. **1935** The Silent Code; Unconquered Bandit; Powdersmoke Range. **1936** Fast Bullets; Roamin' Wild; The Last Outlaw. **1937** Lost Ranch. **1938** Pinto Rustlers; Orphan of the Pecos; King of Alcatraz. **1939** The Night Riders; Frontier Marshal; The Westerner; Stagecoach; Gone with the Wind. **1940** The Lights of the Western Stars; Brother Orchid; Cherokee Strip; The Mummy's Hand. **1941** Buck Privates; Texas Rangers Ride Again; Border Vigilantes; West of Cimarron; Outlaws of Cherokee Trail; Riders of the Timberline; Gauchos of El Dorado; The Adventures of Captain Marvel (serial). **1942** Code of the Outlaw; Raiders of the Range; Westward, Ho; The Talk of the Town; Valley of the Hunted Men; The Phantom Plainsmen; Valley of the Sun. **1943** The Phantom (serial); Wagon Tracks West; Shadows on the Sage; Thundering Trails; Blocked Trail; Riders of the Rio Grande; Santa Fe Scouts; Sylvester the Great. **1944** Boss of Boomtown; Ladies of Washington. **1945** San Antonio; Sing Me a Song of Texas. **1946** Badmen's Territory. **1947** Cheyenne. **1948** The Dude Goes West; Return of the Bad Men; Blood on the Moon; The Golden Eye. **1949** The Younger Brothers; For Those Who Dare; Hellfire; Beautiful Blonde from Bashful Bend; I Shot Jesse James; Lust for Gold; Masked Raiders; Square Dance Jubilee; She Wore a Yellow Ribbon. **1950** Colorado Ranger; Crooked River; Fast on the Draw; Hostile Country; Marshal of Heldorado; Rio Grande Patrol; West of the Brazos. **1951** The Great Missouri Raid; Best of the Badmen. **1952** What Price Glory?; Road Agent. **1953** Cow Country.

TYNAN, BRANDON

Born: 1879, Dublin, Ireland. Died: Mar. 19, 1967, New York, N.Y. Screen, stage actor and playwright. Married to actress Lily Cahill (dec. 1955).

Appeared in: **1923** Loyal Lives; Success. **1924** Unrestrained Youth. **1937** Parnell; Sh! The Octopus; Wells Fargo. **1938** The Girl of the Golden West; Youth Takes a Fling; Nancy Drew, Detective. **1939** The Great Man Votes; Lady and the Mob; The Lone Wolf Spy Hunt. **1940** It All Came True; Lucky Partners; Rangers of Fortune. **1941** Marry the Boss's Daughter.

UHLIG, MAX E.

Born: 1896. Died: May 1958, North Tarrytown, N.Y. Screen actor. Appeared in silents.

ULMER, EDGAR (Edgar George Ulmer)

Born: Sept. 17, 1900, Vienna, Austria. Died: Sept. 30, 1972, Woodland Hills, Calif. Screen actor, film producer, director, stage designer, screenwriter and author. Made Yiddish and Ukrainian films.

ULRIC, LENORE

Born: 1894, New Ulm, Minn. Died: Dec. 30, 1970, Orangeburg, N.Y. Stage and screen actress. Divorced from actor Sidney Blackmer (dec. 1973).

Appeared in: **1915** Kilmeny; The Better Woman. **1916** Intrigue; The Heart of Paula. **1923** Tiger Rose. **1925** Capital Punishment. **1929** Frozen Justice; South Sea Rose. **1936** Camille. **1940** The Fifth Column. **1946** Temptation; Two Smart People; Notorious. **1947** Northwest Outpost; Anthony and Cleopatra.

UNCLE MURRAY. *See* MURRAY PARKER

UNDERWOOD, LAWRENCE

Born: 1871, Albion, Iowa. Died: Feb. 2, 1939, Los Angeles, Calif. Screen, stage actor, film, stage director and screenwriter.

Appeared in: **1920** Old Lady 31. **1925** Passionate Youth; Thundering Through. **1926** Twisted Triggers. **1927** The Phantom Buster.

UPDEGRAFF, HENRY

Born: 1889. Died: July 29, 1936, Hollywood, Calif. (heart attack). Stage and screen actor.

UPTON, FRANCES

Born: 1904. Died: Nov. 27, 1975, Philadelphia, Pa. Screen and stage actor.

Appeared in: **1930** Night Work.

URBAN, DOROTHY K.

Born: 1869. Died: Oct. 29, 1961, Hollywood, Calif. Screen, stage and vaudeville actress.

Appeared in: **1940** The Fight for Life.

URBANSKY, YEVGENY (aka EVGENY URBANSKY)

Born: 1931, Russia. Died: Nov. 5, 1965, Kyzyl-Kum Desert, Central Asia (auto accident). Stage and screen actor.

Appeared in: **1960** Ballad of a Soldier. **1961** The Letter That Was Never Sent. **1963** Cristoe Nebo (Clear Skies). Other Russian film: Kommunist.

URCELAY, NICOLAS

Born: 1920, Yucatan, Mexico. Died: July 3, 1959, Tampico, Mexico. Screen, stage, television, vaudeville actor and singer.

URE, MARY

Born: Feb. 18, 1933, Glasgow, Scotland. Died: Apr. 3, 1975, London, England (an accidental mixing of alcohol and tranquilizers). Screen, stage and television actress. Divorced from playwright John Osborne and later married to actor-playwright Robert Shaw. Nominated for 1960 Academy Award as Best Supporting Actress in "Sons and Lovers."

Appeared in: **1955** Storm Over the Nile (US 1956—film debut). **1957** Windom's Way (US 1958). **1959** Look Back in Anger. **1960** Sons and Lovers. **1962** The Mind Benders (US 1963). **1964** The Luck of Ginger Coffey. **1968** Where Eagles Dare (US 1969); Custer of the West.

URECAL, MINERVA

Born: 1894. Died: Feb. 1966, Glendale, Calif. (heart attack). Screen, radio and television actress.

Appeared in: **1935** Bonnie Scotland. **1937** Her Husband's Secretary; Love in a Bungalow; Life Begins with Love; The Go Getter; Oh, Doctor; Exiled to Shanghai. **1938** Start Cheering; Prison Nurse; Frontier Scout; Air Devils. **1939** Maid to Order (short). **1940** You Can't Fool Your Wife; Boys of the City. **1941** Man at Large; Arkansas Judge; The Cowboy and the Blonde; Accent on Love; Murder by Invitation; Never Give a Sucker an Even Break. **1942** Henry and Dizzy; Sweater Girl; Quiet Please, Murder; The Corpse Vanishes; That Other Woman; The Living Ghost; Sons of the Pioneers; My Favorite Blonde; Man in the Trunk. **1943** Riding through Nevada; The Ape Man; Kid Dynamite; Ghosts on the Loose; So This Is Washington; Hit the Ice. **1944** Louisiana Hayride; Moonlight and Cactus; County Fair; Crazy Knights; The Bridge of San Luis Rey. **1945** A Medal for Benny; Wanderer of the Wasteland; Alibi Baby (short); The Men in Her Diary; Who's Guilty? (serial); State Fair. **1946** Sioux City Sue; The Virginian; Wake up and Dream; Rainbow over Texas; Dark Corner; Sensation Hunters; The Trap. **1947** The Lost Moment; Ladies Man; Hired Husband (short); Saddle Pals; Apache Rose. **1948** Sitting Pretty; Secret Service Investigator; Variety Time; Good Sam; The Snake Pit; Marshal of Amarillo; Sundown at Santa Fe; The Noose Hangs High. **1949** The Lovable Cheat; Master Minds; Holiday in Havana; Outcasts of the Trail. **1950** Arizona Cowboy; Quicksand; Traveling Saleswoman; My Blue Heaven; The Jackpot. **1951** Blonde Atom Bomb (short); Texans Never Cry; Stop That Cab. **1952** Aaron Slick from Punkin' Crick; Oklahoma Annie; Gobs and Gals; Anything Can Happen; Lost in Alaska; Harem Girl. **1953** The Woman They Almost Lynched; Niagara; Two Gun Marshal. **1955** Sudden Danger; So You Want to Be a V.I.P. (short). **1956** Miracle in the Rain; Tugboat Annie; Crashing Las Vegas. **1960** The Adventures of Huckleberry Finn. **1962** Mr. Hobbs Takes a Vacation. **1964** Seven Faces of Dr. Lao. **1965** That Funny Feeling.

URQUHART, ALASDAIR

Born: 1914, Scotland. Died: Aug. 25, 1954, Glasgow, Scotland. Stage and screen actor. Brother of actress Molly Urquhart.

Appeared in: **1953** Rob Roy; The Highland Rogue.

URQUHART, GORDON (Gordon John Urquhart)

Born: 1922. Died: Oct. 1957, Los Angeles, Calif. (cancer). Screen, radio actor and screenwriter. Married to actress Peggy Middleton.

Appeared in: **1956** Female Jungle.

USHER, GUY

Born: 1875. Died: June 16, 1944, San Diego, Calif. Screen and stage actor.

Appeared in: **1933** This Day and Age (film debut); Fast Worker; The Mystery Man; Face in the Sky. **1934** All of Me; Good Dame; The Witching Hour; The Hell Cat; Kid Millions. **1935** Grand Exit; Mills of the Gods; Hold 'Em Yale; The Crusades; Make a Million; Little Big Shot; The Goose and the Gander; It's a Gift. **1936** Dangerous Waters; Postal Inspector; The President's Mystery; The Case of the Black Cat; King of Hockey; Charlie Chan at the Opera. **1937** Marked Woman; Once a Doctor; White Bondage; Nancy Steele Is Missing; Boots and Saddles; The Mighty Treve; Sophie Lang Goes West; Boy of the Streets. **1938** State Police; Under Western Stars; Romance of the Limberlost; Spawn of the North. **1939** Timber Stampede; Invitation to Happiness; Rovin' Tumbleweeds; The Renegade Ranger; Mister Wong in Chinatown. **1940** Passport to Alcatraz; Doomed to Die. **1941** Lady for a Night; Ridin' on a Rainbow; West of Cimarron; No Greater Sin. **1942** Mummy's Tomb; Bells of Capistrano; Shepherd of the Ozarks; I Was Framed; Bad Men of the Hills. **1943** Lost Canyon.

USHER, HARRY

Born: 1887. Died: Oct. 28, 1950, Hollywood, Calif. (heart attack). Screen and vaudeville actor. Appeared in vaudeville with his wife, Frances Usher.

UTTAL, FRED

Born: 1905. Died: Nov. 28, 1963. Radio announcer and screen extra.

VACKOVA, JARMILA

Born: 1908. Died: Sept. 26, 1971, Santa Monica, Calif. Screen actress. Appeared in U.S. and European films.

VAGUE, VERA (Barbara Jo Allen)

Born: 1904. Died: Sept. 14, 1974, Santa Barbara, Calif. Screen, stage, radio and television actress.

Appeared in: **1940** Sing, Dance, Plenty Hot; Melody and Moonlight; Melody Ranch; Village Barn Dance. **1941** Buy Me That Town; Kiss the Boys Goodbye; The Mad Doctor; Ice-Capades. **1942** Larceny, Inc.; Hi Neighbor; Design for Scandal; Mrs. Wiggs of the Cabbage Patch; Priorities on Parade. **1943** Swing Your Partner; Get Going. **1944** Henry Aldrich Plays Cupid; Rosie the Riveter; Moon Over Las Vegas; Lake Placid Serenade; Girl Rush; Doctor, Feel My Pulse (short); Cowboy Canteen. **1945** Lake Placid Serenade. **1946** Earl Carroll Sketchbook; Snafu. **1950** Square Dance Katy. **1956** Mohawk; The Opposite Sex. **1959** Sleeping Beauty; Born to Be Loved.

VAIL, LESTER

Born: Nov. 28, 1900, Denver, Colo. Died: Nov. 28, 1959, Los Angeles, Calif. Screen, stage, television actor, film and television director.

Appeared in: **1931** Dance, Fools, Dance; It's a Wise Child; Beau Ideal; I Take This Woman; Murder by the Clock; The Woman Between; Consolation Marriage. **1932** Big Town.

VAIL, OLIVE

Born: 1904. Died: June 14, 1951, Cincinnati, Ohio. Screen, stage and vaudeville actress.

Appeared in: **1947** The Spirit of Notre Dame.

VALDEMAR, TANIA

Born: 1904. Died: Nov. 12, 1955, New York, N.Y. Screen, stage actress and ballet dancer.

VALE, LOUISE

Born: New York, N.Y. Died: Oct. 28, 1918, Madison, Wis. Screen and stage actress. Married to actor-director Travers Vale.

Appeared in: **1913** The Code of the U.S.A. **1914** Daybreak; The Iron Master. **1915** Jane Eyre; Dwellers in Glass Houses; The Confession; The Americano; Adam Bede; The Quicksands of Society; The Maid O' the Mountains; Under Two Flags; Man and His Master; The Drab Sister; The Soul of Pierre; Harvest; Between Father and Son; The Reproach of Annesley; The Hungarian Nabob; The Woman of Mystery. **1916** A Beast of Society; The Science of Crime; The Sex Lure; The Honor of the Law. **1917** Easy Money. **1918** The Witch Woman; Journey's End; Vengeance.

VALEDON, LORA

Born: 1884. Died: Sept. 15, 1946, Providence, R.I. Screen, vaudeville, actress, film stuntwoman and circus performer.

VALEN, RITCHIE

Born: 1941. Died: Feb. 3, 1959 (plane crash). Screen actor and singer.

Appeared in: **1959** Go, Johnny, Go!

VALENTINE, ELIZABETH

Died: July 23, 1971. Screen actress.

Appeared in: **1942** Kings Row. **1943** Santa Fe Scouts; The Underdog. **1963** Kiss of the Vampire.

VALENTINE, GRACE

Born: 1890, Springfield, Ohio. Died: Nov. 14, 1964, New York, N.Y. Stage and screen actress. Married to actor Wayne Nunn (dec. 1948).

Appeared in: **1916** The Brand of Cowardice; The Evil Thereof; Dorian's Divorce. **1917** Babbling Tongues. **1921** A Man's Home. **1929** The Phantom in the House. **1932** Silver Lining.

VALENTINO, RUDOLPH (Rudolph Guglielmo)

Born: May 6, 1895, Castellaneta, Italy. Died: Aug. 23, 1926, New York, N.Y. (complications following operation—peritonitis). Screen actor and dancer. Divorced from actresses Jean Acker and Natacha Rambova (aka Winifred Hudnut—dec. 1966).

Appeared in: **1914** My Official Wife. **1916** Patria. **1918** Alimony; A Society Sensation; All Night. **1919** The Delicious Little Devil; A Rogue's Romance; The Homebreaker; Virtuous Sinners; The Big Little Person; Out of Luck; Eyes of Youth. **1920** The Married Virgin; An Adventuress; The Cheater; Once to Every Woman; Passion's Playground; Stolen Moments; The Wonderful Chance. **1921** The Four Horsemen of the Apocalypse; Unchained Seas; Camille; The Conquering Power; The Sheik. **1922** Moran of the Lady Letty; Beyond the Rocks; The Young Rajah; Blood and Sand; The Isle of Love. **1924** Monsieur Beaucaire; A Sainted Devil. **1925** The Eagle; Cobra. **1926** Son of the Sheik.

VALERIO, ALBANO

Born: 1889, San Jose, Calif. Died: Feb. 2, 1961, Los Angeles, Calif. Screen actor.

Appeared in: **1926** The Loves of Ricardo (and 1928 version). **1960** Can-Can.

VALK, FREDERICK

Born: 1901, Germany or Czechoslovakia. Died: July 23, 1956, London, England. Stage and screen actor.

Appeared in: **1940** Gasbags; Night Train to Munich (aka Gestapo and aka Night Train—US); Neutral Port. **1941** The Patient Vanishes (aka This Man Is Dangerous—US 1947); Dangerous Moonlight (aka Suicide Squadron—US 1942). **1942** Thunder Rock (US 1944). **1944** Hotel Reserve (US 1946). **1945** Dead of Night; Latin Quarter. **1947** Mrs. Fitzherbert (US 1950). **1948** Saraband for Dead Lovers (aka Saraband—US 1949). **1949** Dear Mr. Prohack (US 1950). **1951** The Magic Box (US 1952); Outcast of the Islands. **1952** Top Secret (aka Mr. Potts Goes to Moscow—US 1954). **1953** Never Let Me Go; Albert RN (aka Break to Freedom—US 1955); The Flanagan Boy (aka Bad Blonde—US). **1955** The Colditz Story (US 1957); Secret Venture; I Am a Camera. **1956** Wicked as They Come (US 1957); Magic Fire. **1957** Zarak.

VALKYRIEN, VALDA

Born: 1894. Died: Oct. 22, 1953, Los Angeles, Calif. Screen actress and ballet dancer.

Appeared in: **1916** Hidden Valley.

VALLEE, FAY WEBB. *See* FAY WEBB

VALLI, VALLI

Born: 1882, Berlin, Germany. Died: Nov. 4, 1927, London, England. Screen, stage and vaudeville actress.

VALLI, VIRGINIA (Virginia McSweeney)

Born: Jan. 19, 1900, Chicago, Ill. Died: Sept. 24, 1968, Palm Springs, Calif. Screen actress. Married to actor Charles Farrell. Entered films in 1915.

Appeared in: **1917** Efficiency Edgar's Courtship. **1921** The Devil Within; Man Who; The Idle Rich; Sentimental Tommy; A Trip to Paradise; The Silver Lining; Love's Penalty. **1922** The Village Blacksmith; The Black Bag; The Storm; His Back against the Wall; The Right That Failed; Tracked to Earth. **1923** A Lady of Quality; The Shock. **1924** The Signal Tower; K—the Unknown; Wild Oranges; The Confidence Man; In Every Woman's Life. **1925** Siege; The Price of Pleasure; Up the Ladder; The Lady Who Lied; Man Who Found Himself. **1926** The Family Upstairs; Flames; Watch Your Wife; Pleasure Garden. **1927** Ladies Must Dress; Paid to Love; East Side, West Side; Marriage; Judgement of the Hills; Evening Clothes; Stage Madness. **1928** Escape; Street of Illusion. **1929** Beyond Closed Doors; Mister Antonio; Isle of Lost Ships. **1930** Storm; The Lost Zeppelin; Guilty? **1931** Night Life in Reno.

VALLIS, ROBERT "BOB"

Born: England. Died: Dec. 19, 1932, Brighton, England. Screen and stage actor.

Appeared in: **1920** Her Benny; A Son of David. **1921** Hound of the Baskervilles; Gwyneth of the Welsh Hills; The Four Just Men; General John Regan; The Amazing Partnership. **1922** The Card; Little Brother of God; The Peacemaker. **1923** The Convert; What Price Loving Cup?; Rogues of the Turf. **1924** Dixon's Return; Not for Sale; Hurricane Hutch in Many Adventures; The Love Story of Aliette Brunton; The Stirrup Cup Sensation. **1925** Forbidden Cargoes (aka Contraband).

VALSTED, MYRTLE (Myrtle Christine Valsted)

Born: 1910. Died: Sept. 19, 1928, Hollywood, Calif. (following appendicitis operation). Screen actress. Entered films in 1928.

VAN, BILLY (Vito Coppola)

Born: 1912. Died: Aug. 22, 1973, Los Angeles, Calif. (heart attack). Stage and screen actor. Do not confuse with vaudeville actor Billy B. Van (dec. 1972).

VAN, BILLY B.

Born: 1878, Pottstown, Pa. Died: Nov. 16, 1950, Newport, N.H. (heart attack). Screen, stage and vaudeville actor. For a while did a vaudeville act with boxer and actor James J. Corbet (dec. 1933). Married to actress Grace Walsh.

Appeared in: **1922** The Beauty Shop.

VAN, CONNIE

Born: 1909. Died: July 16, 1961, Hollywood, Calif. (cerebral hemorrhage). Screen, stage and radio actress.

Appeared in: **1955** The Far Country.

VAN, GUS

Born: 1888, Brooklyn, N.Y. Died: Mar. 13, 1968, Miami Beach, Fla. (injuries from being hit by auto). Screen, stage, vaudeville, radio and television actor.

Was part of vaudeville team with Joe Schenck (dec. 1930) billed as "Van and Schenck" and later did a single.

Together they appeared in: **1927** The Pennant; Winning Battery of Songland (short). **1929** Metro Movietone Feature with their lives as a background entitled Take It Big, plus several song short subjects. **1930** They Learned about Women; without Schenck in the following: **1931–34** Universal and Columbia shorts. **1935** Gus Van's Music Shoppe (short). **1944** Atlantic City.

VAN AUKER, C. K. (Cecil Van Auker)
Died: Feb. 18, 1938, Prescott, Ariz. (tuberculosis). Screen, stage actor and aviator for silent films.

Appeared in: **1921** Payment Guaranteed; Trailin'; The Girl from God's Country; Cinderella of the Hills; The Mother Heart. **1922** Up and Going; The Ragged Heiress; Youth Must Have Love. **1923** The Gunfighter; The Grub Stake. **1927** The Golden Yukon.

VAN BAILEY, POLLY
Died: Aug. 25, 1952, Hollywood, Calif. Stage and screen actress.

VAN BEERS, STANLEY
Born: 1911, England. Died: May 25, 1961, London, England (heart ailment). Screen, stage and television actor. Married to actress Viviene Burgess.

Appeared in: **1952** So Little Time. **1953** The Fake. **1954** The Dam Busters; Dangerous Voyage (aka Terror Ship—US). **1955** Before I Wake (aka Shadow of Fear—US 1956); The Quatermass Experiment (aka The Creeping Unknown—US 1956). **1959** The Angry Hills.

VANBRUGH, DAME IRENE
Born: 1872, England. Died: Nov. 30, 1949, London, England. Screen, stage actress and novelist. Was made Dame Commander of the Order of the British Empire in 1941. Married to stage actor and playwright Dion Boucicault (dec. 1929) and sister of actress Violet Vanbrugh.

Appeared in: **1917** Masks and Faces; The Gay Lord Quex (stage and film versions). **1934** Head of the Family; Catherine the Great; Youthful Folly; Girls Will Be Boys (US 1935); The Way of Youth. **1935** Escape Me Never. **1937** Wings of the Morning; Knight Without Armour. **1945** I Live in Grosvenor Square (aka A Yank in London—US 1946).

VAN BUREN, MABEL
Born: 1878, Chicago, Ill. Died: Nov. 4, 1947, Hollywood, Calif. Stage and screen actress. Married to actor James Gordon (dec. 1941). Mother of actress Kay Van Buren. Entered films approx. 1914.

Appeared in: **1916** The Victoria Cross. **1920** Conrad in Quest of His Youth. **1921** The Four Horsemen of the Apocalypse; Miss Lulu Bett; A Wise Fool; Moonlight and Honeysuckle. **1922** The Man from Home; Beyond the Rocks; The Woman Who Walked Alone; For the Defense; Pawned; Youth to Youth; Manslaughter; While Satan Sleeps. **1923** In Search of a Thrill; Lights Out; Wandering Daughters; Light That Failed; The Girl of the Golden West. **1924** The Dawn of a Tomorrow. **1925** Smooth as Satin; The Top of the World; His Secretary. **1927** King of Kings; The Meddlin' Stranger. **1928** The Flying Buckaroo; Craig's Wife; Ramona. **1930** His First Command.

VANCE, LUCILLE
Born: 1893. Died: May 10, 1974, Burbank, Calif. Screen, stage and television actress.

Appeared in: **1942** Bowery at Midnight. **1944** Boss of Rawhide. **1947** Thundergap Outlaws.

VANCE, VIRGINIA
Born: 1902. Died: Oct. 13, 1942, Hollywood, Calif. (heart attack). Screen actress.

Appeared in: **1925** Goat Getter. **1926** The Fighting Marine (serial). **1928** Undressed. **1929** New Year's Eve.

VANDERGRIFT, J. MONTE
Born: 1893. Died: July 29, 1939, North Hollywood, Calif. (heart attack). Screen, stage and radio actor.

Appeared in: **1934** Shoot the Works. **1935** G-Men; Private Worlds; Smart Girl; Seven Keys to Baldpate; Hot Money (short). **1936** The Moon's Our Home; Easy Money; The Mandarin Mystery. **1937** California Straight Ahead; Woman Chases Man. **1939** Miracles for Sale.

VAN DYK, JAMES
Born: 1895. Died: Dec. 17, 1951, Montclair, N.J. (heart attack). Screen, stage, radio and television actor.

VAN DYKE, W. S. (Woodbridge Strong Van Dyke II)
Born: Mar. 21, 1887, San Diego, Calif. Died: Feb. 5, 1943, Brentwood, Calif. Screen, stage, vaudeville actor and film director.

Appeared in: **1916** Oliver Twist.

VANE, DENTON
Born: 1890. Died: Sept. 17, 1940, Union Hill, N.J. (heart attack). Stage and screen actor.

Appeared in: **1912** The Adopted Son. **1914** Arthur Truman's Ward. **1915** The Flower of the Hills; Who Killed Joe Merrion?; On Her Wedding Night; Heredity; The Man Who Couldn't Beat God; The Ruling Power; To Cherish and Protect; Green Stockings. **1916** The Wandering Horde; The Ruse; The Island of Surprise; The Hunted Woman; The Ordeal of Elizabeth; Hesper of the Mountains; An Enemy to the King; Green Stockings. **1917** Apartment 29; The Glory of Yolanda; In the Balance; The Soul Master; The Grell Mystery; Transgression. **1918** A Mother's Sin; A Bachelor's Children; A Game with Fate; Love Watches; The Clutch of Circumstance; The Stolen Treaty; Miss Ambition. **1919** Fortune's Child; Beauty Proof; A Girl at Bay; The Bramble Bush. **1921** Women Men Love. **1922** Flesh and Spirit.

VAN EYCK, PETER
Born: July 16, 1913, Germany. Died: July 15, 1969, Zurich, Switzerland. Screen actor.

Appeared in: **1943** Five Graves to Cairo; The Moon Is Down. **1944** Address Unknown; The Imposter; The Hitler Gang. **1950** The Devil's Agent. **1951** The Desert Fox. **1953** Single-Handed (aka Sailor of the King—US); Alerte au Said. **1954** Night People. **1955** Tarzan's Hidden Jungle; Jump into Hell; A Bullet for Joey; Wages of Fear; Mr. Arkadin (US 1962 and aka Confidential Report). **1956** Attack!; The Rawhide Years; Run for the Sun. **1958** The Snorkel; Schwarze Nylons—Heisse Nachte (aka Indecent—US 1962; All Bad; Waylaid Women—US 1968); Flesh and the Woman; Sophie et le Crime (Sophie and the Crime, aka The Girl on the Third Floor); Le Chair et le Diable (The Flesh and the Devil, aka Flesh and Desire); Retour de Manivell (Turn of the Handle aka There's Always a Price Tag). **1959** Verbrechen Nach Schulschluss (aka The Young Go Wild—US 1962); Der Glaserne Turm (The Glass Tower). **1960** Foxhole in Cairo (US 1961); Rosemary; Der Rest ist Schweigen (The Rest is Silence); Die Tausend Augen des Dr. Mabuse (The 1000 Eyes of Dr. Mabuse—US 1966). **1961** An Einem Freitag um Halb Zwolf (The World in My Pocket—US 1962); La Fete Espagnole (aka No Time for Ecstacy—US 1963); Law of War. **1962** The Devil's Agent; Vengeance (aka The Brain—US 1964); Station Six-Sahara (US 1964); The Black Chapel; The Longest Day; Rebel Flight to Cuba. **1963** Das Grosse Liebesspeil (The Big Love Game aka And So to Bed—US 1965); The River Line; Verfuhrung am Meer (Seduction by the Sea—US 1967). **1964** I Misteri della Giungla Nera (The Mystery of Thug Island—US 1966). **1965** Guerre Secrete (aka The Dirty Game—US 1966); An Alibi for Death; The Spy Who Came in from the Cold. **1967** Million Dollar Man. **1968** Shalako; Toview and His Seven Daughters. **1969** Assignment to Kill; The Bridge at Ramagen.

VAN HADEN, ANDERS
Born: 1876. Died: June 19, 1936, Hollywood, Calif. (heart attack). Screen actor, film producer and film director.

Appeared in: **1932** Cheaters at Play; A Passport to Hell. **1933** Best of Enemies; The Secret of the Blue Room; Snug in the Jug (short). **1935** Barbary Coast.

VAN HORN, EMILE
Died: Jan. 1, 1967, New Orleans, La. Screen actor.

Appeared in: **1933** King Kong. **1941** Jungle Girl (serial). **1942** Perils of Nyoka (serial). **1943** The Ape Man. **1948** Are You With It? **1959** A Hole in the Head. **1967** Hotel.

VAN HORN, JAMES "JIMMY"
Born: 1917. Died: Apr. 20, 1966, Hollywood, Calif. (internal hemorrhage). Screen actor and stuntman.

Appeared in: **1927** The Cherokee Kid. **1950** Fast on the Draw; Hostile Country; Marshal of Heldorado. **1951** The Cave of the Outlaws. **1953** Gunsmoke.

VAN LEER, ARNOLD
Born: 1895, London, England. Died: June 3, 1975, Boston, Mass. Screen actor and press agent. Married to stage actress Dorinda Van Leer (dec.). Entered films as an extra and appeared in early Charlie Chaplin films.

VANN, POLLY
Born: July 29, 1882, Scranton, Pa. Died: Aug. 25, 1952, Los Angeles, Calif. (Laennec's cirrhosis). Screen, stage and vaudeville actress.

Appeared in: **1917** To the Death. **1919** Three Black Eyes (aka Scrap Paper); Regular Girl. **1921** Wedding Bells. **1925** Tearin' Loose. **1943** Hers to Hold.

VANNE, MARDA
Born: South Africa. Died: Apr. 27, 1970, London, England. Screen, stage and television actress.

Appeared in: **1968** Joanna.

VAN ROOTEN, LUIS (Luis D'Antin Van Rooten)
Born: Nov. 29, 1906, Mexico City, Mexico. Died: June 17, 1973, Chatham, Mass. Screen, stage, radio, television actor and author.

Appeared in: **1944** The Hitler Gang. **1946** Two Years Before the Mast. **1948** To the Ends of the Earth; Saigon; To the Victor; The Big Clock; Beyond Glory; Night Has a Thousand Eyes; The Gentleman from Nowhere. **1949** City Across the River; Boston Blackie's Chinese Venture; Secret of St. Ives; Cinderella (voice); Champion. **1951** Detective Story; My Favorite Spy. **1952** Lydia Bailey. **1955** The Sea Chase. **1957** The Unholy Wife. **1958** Fraulein; The Curse of the Faceless Man. **1961** Operation Eichmann.

VAN SAHER, LILLA A.
Born: 1912, Hungary. Died: July 15, 1968, New York, N.Y. Screen actress and author.

Appeared in foreign film Grain au Vent.

VAN SLOAN, EDWARD
Born: 1882, San Francisco, Calif. Died: Mar. 6, 1964, San Francisco, Calif. Stage and screen actor.

Appeared in: **1931** Dracula; Frankenstein. **1932** Manhattan Parade; Play Girl; Man Wanted; Behind the Mask; Thunder Below; Forgotten Commandments; The Last Mile; Honeymoon in Bali; The Mummy. **1933** The Death Kiss; Silk Express; The Working Man; Infernal Machine; Trick for Trick; It's Great to Be Alive; The Man Who Reclaimed His Head; The Deluge; Murder on the Campus; Billion Dollar Scandal. **1934** Manhattan Melodrama; I'll Fix It; Death Takes a Holiday; The Scarlet Empress; The Crosby Case; The Life of Vergie Winters. **1935** Air Hawks; Mystery of the Black Room; The Story of Louis Pasteur; Grand Exit; Grand Old Girl; Mills of the Gods; The Woman in Red; A Shot in the Dark; The Last Days of Pompeii. **1936** Road Gang; Sins of Man; Dracula's Daughter. **1937** The Man Who Found Himself. **1938** Penitentiary; Storm over Bengal; Danger on the Air. **1939** The Phantom Creeps (serial). **1940** Abe Lincoln in Illinois; The Doctor Takes a Wife; The Secret Seven; Before I Hang. **1942** Valley of the Hunted Men; A Man's World. **1943** Mission to Moscow; Riders of the Rio Grande; Submarine Alert; The Masked Marvel (serial); End of the Road. **1944** Captain America (serial); The Conspirators; Wing and a Prayer. **1945** I'll Remember April. **1946** The Mask of Dijon. **1947** Betty Coed.

VAN TRESS, MABEL
Born: 1873. Died: Mar. 16, 1962. Screen actress.

VAN TRUMP, JESSALYN
Born: 1885. Died: May 2, 1939, Hollywood, Calif. Screen and stage actress.

Appeared in: **1911–12** American Film Mfg. Co. films.

VAN TUYL, HELEN (Helen Marr Van Tuyl)
Born: 1891. Died: Aug. 22, 1964, Hollywood, Calif. (heart attack). Screen and television actress.

Appeared in: **1952** Stars and Stripes Forever; Confidence Girl. **1953** Titanic. **1955** Daddy Long Legs; The Girl in the Red Velvet Swing.

VAN UPP, VIRGINIA
Born: 1902, Chicago, Ill. Died: Mar. 25, 1970, Hollywood, Calif. (results of a broken hip). Screen actress, film producer and screenwriter. Appeared on screen in features with William Desmond, John Gilbert and others when five years old.

VAN VOORHIS, WESTBROOK
Born: Sept. 21, 1903, New Milford, Conn. Died: July 14, 1968, New Milford, Conn. (cancer). Radio, movie commentator and screen actor. Was voice of "March of Time" in film documentaries.

Appeared in: **1942** We are the Marines (narrator). **1951** Tembo (narrator). **1961** The Ladies' Man. **1962** Castro, Cuba and Communism (narrator—aka Danger on our Doorstep).

VAN ZANDT, PHILIP
Born: Oct. 3, 1904, Amsterdam, Holland. Died: Feb. 16, 1958, Hollywood, Calif. (overdose of sleeping pills). Screen, stage and television actor.

Appeared in: **1939** Those High Grey Walls. **1940** Boobs in Arms (short). **1941** In Old Colorado; City of Missing Girls; So Ends Our Night; Ride on Vaquero; Citizen Kane. **1942** Sherlock Holmes and the Secret Weapon; Wake Island; The Hard Way; Desperate Journey. **1943** Tarzan Triumphs; Murder on the Waterfront; Tarzan's Desert Mystery; Hostages; Deerslayer; Air Raid Wardens. **1944** America's Children; Call of the Jungle; The Big Noise; Swing Hostess; The Unwritten Code. **1945** Outlaws of the Rockies; House of Frankenstein; Sudan; Counter-Attack; A Thousand and One Nights; I Love a Bandleader. **1946** The Avalanche; Below the Deadline; Joe Palooka, Champ; Decoy; Don't Gamble with Strangers; Somewhere in the Night. **1947** Slave Girl; The Last Frontier Uprising. **1948** The Vicious Circle; The Shanghai Chest; Embraceable You; Walk a Crooked Mile; The Loves of Carmen; Street with No Name; Big Clock; April Showers; plus the following shorts: Fiddlers Three; Mummy's Dummies; Squareheads of the Round Table. **1949** The Lady Gambles; Red, Hot and Blue; The Blonde Bandit; Lone Wolf and His Lady; Fuelin' Around (short). **1950** Between Midnight and Dawn; Indian Territory; The Petty Girl; Where Danger Lives; Copper Canyon; Dopey Dicks (short); The Jackpot. **1951**

Submarine Command; The Ghost Chasers; His Kind of Woman; Ten Tall Men; Two Dollar Bettor; Cyrano de Bergerac; Three Arabian Nuts (short). **1952** Viva Zapata; Son of Ali Baba; Thief of Damascus; Yukon Gold. **1953** Prisoners of the Casbah; Capt. John Smith and Pocahontas; Clipped Wings; plus the following shorts: Love's-a-Poppin; So You Want to Be a Musician; So You Want a Television Set; So You Want to Be an Heir; Spooks. **1954** Yankee Pasha; Knock on Wood; Playgirl; Gog; Three Ring Circus; plus the following shorts: Musty Musketeers; So You Want to Go to a Nightclub; Knutzy Knights; Scotched in Scotland. **1955** Untamed; The Big Combo; I Cover the Underworld; plus the following shorts: So You Want to Be a Gladiator; So You Want to Be a V.P.; Bedlam in Paradise. **1956** Our Miss Brooks; Uranium Boom; Around the World in 80 Days; Hot Stuff (short). **1957** Man of a Thousand Faces; The Pride and the Passion; The Crooked Circle; The Lonely Man; Outer Space Jitters (short). **1958** Fifi Blows Her Top (short).

VARDEN, EVELYN
Born: 1895. Died: July 11, 1958. New York, N.Y. Screen, stage, radio and television actress.

Appeared in: **1949** Pinky. **1950** Cheaper by the Dozen; Stella; When Willie Comes Marching Home. **1951** Elopement. **1952** Finders Keepers; Phone Call from a Stranger. **1954** Athena; Desiree; The Student Prince. **1955** The Night of the Hunter. **1956** Hilda Crane; The Bad Seed. **1957** Ten Thousand Bedrooms.

VASS, LULU
Born: 1877. Died: May 6, 1952, Haverstraw, N.Y. Screen, stage and radio actress. Appeared in films from 1941 to 1946.

VASSAR, QUEENIE
Born: Oct. 28, 1870, Glasgow, Scotland. Died: Sept. 11, 1960, Hollywood, Calif. (following surgery). Stage and screen actress. Married to actor Joseph Cawthorne (dec. 1949).

Appeared in: **1940** The Primrose Path. **1942** Lady in a Jam. **1944** None but the Lonely Heart.

VAUGHAN, DOROTHY
Born: Nov. 5, 1889, St. Louis, Mo. Died: Mar. 15, 1955, Hollywood, Calif. (cerebral hemorrhage). Screen, stage, radio and vaudeville actress.

Appeared in: **1935** Annapolis Farewell (film debut). **1936** Love Begins at 20; Times Square Playboy. **1937** The Hoosier Schoolboy; Here's Flash Casey; That Man's Here Again; The Black Legion; Michael O'Halloran. **1938** Little Miss Thoroughbred; Telephone Operator; Little Orphan Annie; Gambling Ship; Slander House; Quick Money. **1939** Unexpected Father; The Man in the Iron Mask; First Love; The Star Maker. **1940** Diamond Frontier; The Old Swimmin' Hole; The Ape. **1941** Secret Evidence; Bad Men of Missouri; Three Girls about Town. **1942** The Magnificent Ambersons; Lady Gangster; Gentleman Jim. **1943** The Iron Major; Sweet Rosie O'Grady; Doughboys in Ireland; Hit the Ice. **1944** The Adventures of Mark Twain; Sweet and Low Down; The Mummy's Ghost; The Town Went Wild; Henry Aldrich's Little Secret. **1945** Dancing in Manhattan; What a Blonde; Those Endearing Young Charms; Ten Cents a Dance. **1946** That Brennan Girl. **1947** Trail to San Antone; The Egg and I; The Bishop's Wife; The Bamboo Blonde; Robin Hood of Texas. **1948** I Wouldn't Be in Your Shoes; Song of Idaho. **1949** Fighting Fools; Home in San Antone; Manhattan Angel. **1950** Chain Gang; Rider from Tucson; Square Dance Katy. **1951** A Wonderful Life.

VAUGHN, ADAMAE
Born: 1906. Died: Sept. 1, 1943, Hollywood, Calif. Screen actress. She was a "Wampas Baby Star" in 1927. Sister of actress Alberta Vaughn.

Appeared in: **1923** The Courtship of Myles Standish. **1925** The Last Edition. **1926** The Arizona Streak; Flashing Fangs. **1929** The Show of Shows. **1930** Dancing Sweeties. **1936** Love before Breakfast.

VAUGHN, HILDA
Born: Dec. 27, 1898, Baltimore, Md. Died: Dec. 28, 1957, Baltimore, Md. Stage and screen actress.

Appeared in: **1929** Three Live Ghosts. **1930** Manslaughter. **1931** It's a Wise Child; A Tailor Made Man; Susan Lennox, Her Rise and Fall. **1932** Ladies of the Big House; The Phantom of Crestwood. **1933** Today We Live; Dinner at Eight; No Marriage Ties; No Other Woman. **1934** Anne of Green Gables. **1935** The Wedding Night; Straight from the Heart; Chasing Yesterday; Men without Names; I Live My Life. **1936** The Trail of the Lonesome Pine; Everybody's Old Man; Half Angel; Banjo on My Knee; The Accusing Finger; The Witness Chair. **1937** Nothing Sacred; Danger—Love at Work. **1938** Maid's Night Out. **1940** Charlie Chan at the Wax Museum.

VAUGHN, VIVIAN (aka GYPSY GOULD)
Born: 1902. Died: Feb. 1, 1966, Hollywood, Calif. Screen, stage actress and singer.

VAUGHN, WILLIAM. *See* WILHELM VON BRINCKEN

VAULTHIER, GEORGES

Born: France. Died: Apr. 1926, Paris, France. Screen actor.

VAVERKA, ANTON

Born: Czechoslovakia. Died: July 2, 1937, Prague, Czechoslovakia. Screen actor.

Appeared in: **1923** Merry Go Round. **1925** The Phantom of the Opera; Secrets of the Night. **1926** The Love Thief; Rolling Home. **1927** On Ze Boulevard. **1928** The Wedding March; Three Sinners. **1929** The Love Parade. **1930** The Melody Man.

VAZQUEZ, MYRNA

Born: 1935, Puerto Rico? Died: Feb. 17, 1975, Boston, Mass. (heart condition). Screen, stage, radio and television actress. Divorced from actor Felix Monclova. Married to Hector Colon Declet.

VEDDER, WILLIAM H.

Born: 1872. Died: Mar. 3, 1961, Hollywood, Calif. (lung cancer). Stage and screen actor.

Appeared in: **1949** Leave It to Henry; Undercover Man. **1950** The Gunfighter. **1951** You Never Can Tell. **1952** O. Henry's Full House; Paula; Stars and Stripes Forever; Boots Malone. **1954** The Wild One. **1955** World without End.

VEIDT, CONRAD

Born: Jan. 22, 1893, Berlin, Germany. Died: Apr. 3, 1943, Los Angeles, Calif. (heart attack). Screen, stage actor, film director and screenwriter. Divorced from music hall artiste Gussy Hall and Felicitas Radke and later married to Lily Barter.

Appeared in: **1917** Der Spion (The Spy) (later released as In Die Wolken Verfolgt); Die Claudi von Geiserhot; Wenn Tote Sprechen; Der Weg des Todes (The Road of Death); Furcht (Fear); Das Ratsel von Bangalor (The Mystery of Bangalor). **1918** Die Serenyi; Das Tagebuch Einer Verlorenen (The Diary of a Lost Woman); Dida Ibsens Geschichte (The Story of Dida Ibsen); Das Dreimaderlhaus (The Three Girls' House); Colomba; Jettchen Geberts Geschichte (Jettchen Gebert's Story); Henriette Jacoby; Sundige Mutter (Sinning Mothers); Opfer der Gesellschaft (Victim of Society); Nocturno der Liebe (Nocturne of Love); Die Japanerin (The Japanese Woman). **1919** Gewitter im Mai; Opium; Die Reise um die Erde in 80 Tagen (Around the World in 80 Days); Peer Gynt; Anders als die Andern (Different from the Others); Die Prostitution (Prostitution); Die Prostitution II (aka Die Sich Verkaufen—Prostitution II—Those Who Sell Themselves); Die Okarina (The Ocarina); Prinz Kuchuck (Prince Cuckoo); Unheimlich Geschichten (Eerie Tales); Wahnsinn (Madness); Nachtgestalten (Figures of the Night); Satanas. **1920** Die Nacht auf Goldenhall (The Night at Goldenhall); Das Kabinett des Dr. Caligari (The Cabinet of Dr. Caligari—US 1921); Der Reigen (The Merry-Go-Round); Patience; Der Januskopf (The Two-Faced Man); Liebestaumel (Love and Passion); Die Augen der Welt (The Eyes of the World); Kurfurstendamm; Moriturus; Abend-Nacht-Morgen (Day, Night and the Morning After); Manolescus Memoiren (The Memoirs of Manolescu); Kunstlerlaunen (Temperamental Artist); Sehnsucht (Desire); Der Gang in die Nacht (aka The Dark Road); Christian Wahnschaffe (Part I: Weltbrand, Part II: Die Flucht aus dem Goldenen Kerker); Der Graf von Cagliostro (The Count of Cagliostro); Das Geheimnis von Bombay (The Secret of Bombay); Menschen im Rausch (Men in Ecstasy). **1921** Die Liebschaften des Hektor Dalmore (The Love Affairs of Hector Dalmore); Der Leidensweg der Inge Krafft (Inge Krafft's Calvary); Landstrasse und Grosstadt (Country Road and Big City); Lady Hamilton; Das Indische Grabmal—Part I: Die Sendung des Yoghi, Part II: Der Tiger von Eschnapur (Mysteries of India aka Above All Law/Truth—US 1922). **1922** Lucrezia Borgia (Lucretia Borgia—US 1929). **1923** Wilhelm Tell (William Tell); Glanz Gegen Gluck (Gold and Luck); Paganini. **1924** Carlos und Elisabeth (Carlos and Elizabeth); Das Wachsfigurenkabinett (Waxworks and aka Three Waxmen—US 1929); Orlacs Hande (The Hands of Orlac—US 1928); Nju; Schicksal (Fate). **1925** Le Comte Kostia (Count Kostia); Ingmarsarvet (aka In Dalarna and Jerusalem and Die Erde Ruft); Liebe Macht Blind (Love is Blind). **1926** Der Geiger von Florenz (The Violinist of Florence aka Impetuous Youth); Die Bruder Schellenberg (The Brothers Schellenberg); Durfen wir Schweigen? (Should We be Silent?); Kreuzzug des Weibes (The Wife's Crusade); Der Student von Prag (The Student of Prague and aka The Man Who Cheated Life—US 1929); Die Flucht in die Nacht (The Flight in the Night). **1927** The Beloved Rogue; A Man's Past; The Man Who Laughs; Husbands or Lovers. **1928** The Last Performance (aka Erik the Great and Illusion); Two Brothers. **1929** Das Land Ohne Frauen (The Land without Women). **1930** Die Letzte Kompagnie (The Last Company and aka Thirteen Men and a Girl—US); Die Grosse Sehnsucht (The Great Desire); Menschen im Kafig (aka Cape Forlorn); Bride 68; Great Power. **1931** Der Mann, der den Mord Beging (The Man Who Committed the Murder); Die Nacht der Entscheidung (The Night of the Decision); Der Kongress Tanzt (Congress Dances); Die Andere Seite (The Other Side); Rasputin. **1932** Der Schwarze Husar (The Black Hussar); Rome Express. **1933** F.P. 1; I was a Spy (US 1934); The Wandering Jew (US 1935); Ich und die Kaiserin (I and the Empress). **1934** Bella Donna (US 1935); Jew Suess (aka Power—US); William Tell (and 1923 version) (aka The Legend of William Tell—US). **1935** The Passing of the Third Floor Back. **1936** King of the Damned. **1937** Under the Red Robe; Dark Journey. **1938** Tempete sur L'Asie (Storm over Asia); Le Joueur d'Echecs (The Chess Player and aka The Devil is an Empress—US 1939). **1939** The Spy in Black (aka U-Boat 29—US); Alex. **1940** Contraband (aka Blackout—US); The Thief of Bagdad; Escape. **1941** A Woman's Face; Whistling in the Dark; The Men in Her Life. **1942** Nazi Agent; All Through the Night. **1943** Casablanca; Above Suspicion.

VEJAR, HARRY J.

Born: Apr. 24, 1890, Los Angeles, Calif. Died: Mar. 1, 1968, Los Angeles, Calif. Stage and screen actor.

Appeared in: **1921** The Sheik. **1926** Mademoiselle Modiste. **1929** Mexicali Rose. **1930** Wings of Adventure. **1932** Scarface. **1935** Mutiny on the Bounty. **1948** The Treasure of Sierra Madre.

VEKROFF, PERRY

Born: 1881, Alexandria, Egypt. Died: Jan. 3, 1937, Hollywood, Calif. (heart disease). Screen, stage actor, film director and screenwriter. Entered films as an actor with Lubin Co.

VELEZ, LUPE (Giadelupe Velez de Villalobos)

Born: July 18, 1908, San Luis Potosi, Mexico. Died: Dec. 14, 1944, Beverly Hills, Calif. (suicide). Screen actress. Divorced from actor and Olympic swimming star Johnny Weissmuller. Star of "Mexican Spitfire" series.

Appeared in: **1927** Sailor Beware! (short); The Gaucho. **1928** Stand and Deliver. **1929** Masquerade; Wolf Song; Lady of the Pavements; Where East Is West; Tiger Rose. **1930** Hell Harbor; The Storm; East Is West. **1931** Resurrection; The Squaw Man; Cuban Love Song; Men in Her Life. **1932** The Broken Wing; Kongo; The Half-Naked Truth. **1933** Mr. Broadway; Hot Pepper. **1934** Palooka; Laughing Boy; Hollywood Party; Strictly Dynamite. **1935** The Morals of Marcus. **1936** Gypsy Melody; Under Your Spell. **1937** High Flyers; Wings. **1938** La Zandunga; He Loved an Actress. **1939** The Girl from Mexico; Mexican Spitfire. **1940** Mexican Spitfire Out West. **1941** Six Lessons from Madame La Zonga; Mexican Spitfire's Baby; Playmates; Honolulu Lu. **1942** Mexican Spitfire at Sea; Mexican Spitfire Sees a Ghost; Mexican Spitfire's Elephant. **1943** Ladies' Day; Redhead from Manhattan; Mexican Spitfire's Blessed Event; Nana. **1964** Big Parade of Comedy (documentary).

VENABLE, REGINALD

Born: 1926. Died: June 28, 1974, Hollywood, Calif. (heart attack). Stage and screen actor. Son of actress Fay Bainter (dec. 1968).

VENESS, AMY

Born: 1876, England. Died: Sept. 22, 1960, Saltdean, England. Stage and screen actress.

Appeared in: **1931** Hobson's Choice; My Wife's Family. **1932** Pyjamas Preferred; Let Me Explain Dear; The Marriage Bond; Self-Made Lady; Money for Nothing; Tonight's the Night. **1933** Their Night Out; Hawley's of High Street; The Love Nest; A Southern Maid. **1934** The Old Curiosity Shop (US 1935); Red Wagon (US 1935). **1935** Brewster's Millions; Lorna Doone; Joy Ride; Play Up the Band; Drake of England (aka Drake the Pirate—US). **1936** King of Hearts; The Beloved Vagabond; Did I Betray?; Skylarks. **1937** Aren't Men Beasts!; The Mill on the Floss (US 1939); Who Killed Markham? (aka The Angelus); The Show Goes On. **1938** Yellow Sands; Thistledown. **1939** Just William. **1940** John Smith Wakes Up. **1941** This England (aka Our Heritage); The Saint Meets the Tiger (US 1943). **1943** The Man in Grey (US 1945); Millions Like Us. **1944** This Happy Breed (US 1947); Fanny by Gaslight (aka Man of Evil—US 1948); Madonna of the Seven Moons; Don't Take it to Heart (US 1949). **1945** Don Chicago; They were Sisters (US 1946). **1946** Carnival. **1947** The Turners of Prospect Road; The Woman in the Hall. **1948** Blanche Fury; My Brother's Keeper; Oliver Twist; Good Time Girl (US 1950); Here Come the Huggetts. **1949** Vote for Huggett; The Huggets Abroad. **1950** Madeleine; The Woman with No Name (aka Her Panelled Door—US 1951); Chance of a Lifetime (US 1951); The Astonished Heart. **1951** Tom Brown's School Days; Captain Horatio Hornblower. **1952** Angels One Five (US 1954). **1954** Doctor in the House (US 1955).

VENKATARAMAYA, RELANGI

Born: 1910, India. Died: 1975, India. Stage and screen actor.

VERDI, JOSEPH

Born: 1885. Died: Dec. 27, 1957, New York, N.Y. Screen, stage, vaudeville and television actor. Billed in vaudeville as part of "Clark and Verdi" team.

Appeared in: **1936** The Crime of Dr. Crespi. **1957** The Vintage.

VERHOEVEN, PAUL

Born: 1901, Unna/Westfalen, Germany. Died: Mar. 22, 1975, Munich, Germany (heart attack). Screen, stage actor, film, stage director, screenwriter, playwright and author. Father of director Michael Verhoeven.

Appeared in: **1959** Menschen im Netz (aka The Unwilling Agent—US 1968). **1968** Hamlet.

VERKOFF, PERRY N.

Born: 1887, Alexandria, Egypt. Died: Jan. 5, 1937. Screen, stage, vaudeville actor, opera performer and film director.

VERMILYEA, HAROLD

Born: Oct. 10, 1889, New York, N.Y. Died: Jan. 8, 1958, New York, N.Y. Screen, stage, radio and television actor.

Appeared in: 1917 The Law that Failed. 1946 O.S.S. 1948 The Emperor Waltz; The Big Clock; The Miracle of the Bells; Gentleman's Agreement; The Sainted Sisters; Beyond Glory; Sorry, Wrong Number. 1949 Chicago Deadline; Manhandled. 1950 Born to Be Bad; Edge of Doom. 1951 Katie Did It. 1952 Finders Keepers.

VERMOYAL, PAUL

Born: France. Died: Oct. 1925, Neuilly, France. Screen and stage actor.

Appeared in: 1924 The Arab.

VERNE, KAREN (Ingeborg Catharine Marie Rose Klinckerfuss—aka KAAR-EN—aka CATHERINE YOUNG and INGABOR KATRINE KLINCK-ERFUSS)

Born: 1918, Berlin, Germany. Died: Dec. 23, 1967, Hollywood, Calif. Screen, stage and television actress. Divorced from actor Peter Lorre (dec. 1964) and married to film historian James Powers.

Appeared in: 1939 Ten Days in Paris (aka Missing Ten Days—US). 1940 Sky Murder. 1941 King's Row; Underground; Missing Ten Days. 1942 All through the Night; The Great Impersonation. 1943 Sherlock Holmes and the Secret Weapon. 1944 The Seventh Cross. 1955 A Bullet for Joey. 1965 Ship of Fools. 1966 Madam X.

VERNEY, GUY

Born: England. Died: Sept. 19, 1970, London, England. Screen, stage actor, television producer and director. Married to actress Margaret Anderson.

Appeared in: 1944 This Happy Breed (US 1947). 1947 Fame Is the Spur (US 1949). 1948 Anna Karenina. 1950 Cage of Gold (US 1951). 1953 Martin Luther.

VERNON, BOBBY

Born: Mar. 9, 1897, Chicago, Ill. Died: June 28, 1939, Hollywood, Calif. (heart attack). Screen, stage actor and screenwriter. Entered films at age 16.

Appeared in: 1913 Mike and Jake at the Beach. 1914 Joker Comedies (shorts). 1915 Fickle Fatty's Fall; The Hunt. 1916 His Pride and Shame; A Dash of Courage; Hearts and Sparks; The Social ʿ ıb; The Danger Girl (working title Love on Skates). 1917 The Nick of Time Baby; Teddy at the Throttle; Dangers of a Bride; Whose Baby?; The Sultan's Wife. 1920 Educational shorts. 1925 The following shorts; French Pastry; Great Guns; Don't Pinch; Air Tight; Watch Out; Slippery Feet; Oo-La-La. 1926 Footloose Widows. 1927–28 Christie Comedies (shorts). 1930 Cry Baby (short). 1931 Stout Hearts and Willing Hands. 1932 Ship A Hooey (short). 1960 When Comedy Was King (documentary).

VERNON, DOROTHY (aka DOROTHY BAIRD and DOROTHY BURNS)

Born: Nov. 11, 1875, Germany. Died: Oct. 28, 1970, Granada Hills, Calif. (heart disease). Screen actress. Married to actor H. B. Irving (dec. 1919). Mother of actor Bobby Vernon (dec. 1939).

Appeared in: 1924 Conductor 1492; Lover's Lane. 1925 Flying Fool; Tricks. 1928 The Manhattan Cowboy; Tenderloin. 1929 Headin' Westward; Should a Girl Marry?; Riders of the Storm. 1930 The Costello Case; Madam Satan. 1934 Woman Haters (short); I Hate Women. 1938 Father O'Flynn.

VERNON, LOU

Born: 1888, Australia. Died: Dec. 22, 1971, Sydney, Australia. Screen, radio actor and singer.

Appeared in: 1959 On the Beach.

VERNON, WALLY

Born: 1904, New York, N.Y. Died: Mar. 7, 1970, Van Nuys, Calif. (hit and run auto accident). Screen, stage, vaudeville, burlesque and minstrel actor.

Appeared in: 1937 Mountain Music; This Way Please; You Can't Have Everything. 1938 Happy Landing; Kentucky Moonshine; Alexander's Ragtime Band; Sharpshooters; Meet the Girls. 1939 Chasing Danger; Tailspin; The Gorilla; Charlie Chan at Treasure Island; Broadway Serenade. 1940 Sailor's Lady; Margie; Sandy Gets Her Man. 1943 Tahiti Honey; Reveille with Beverly; Get Going; Fugitive from Sonora; Here Comes Elmer; Pistol Packin' Mama. 1944 Call of the South Seas; Outlaws of Santa Fe; Silent Partner; Silver City Kid; Stagecoach to Monterey; California Joe. 1948 King of Gamblers, Winner Take All; Fighting Mad. 1949 Always Leave Them Laughing; Square Dance Jubilee. 1950 Beauty on Parade; Border Rangers; Holiday Rhythm; Gunfire; Train to Tombstone; Everybody's Dancing. 1952 What Price Glory?; Bloodhounds of Broadway. 1953 Affair with a Stranger. 1956 Fury at Gunsight Pass; The White Squaw. 1964 What a Way to Go.

VERNON, WILLIAM "BILLY"

Born: June 21, 1912, New York, N.Y. Died: Aug. 19, 1971, Granada Hills, Calif. (heart attack). Screen actor and dialogue coach.

VeSOTA, BRUNO (Bruno William VeSota)

Born: Mar. 25, 1922, Chicago, Ill. Died: Sept. 24, 1976, Culver City, Calif. (heart attack). Screen, stage, radio actor and film director.

Appeared in: 1953 The System. 1954 The Wild One; Bait; Tennessee Champ; Rails into Laramie; The Long Wait; The Egyptian; The Fast and the Furious; The Last Time I Saw Paris. 1955 Jupiter's Darling; Kismet; Dementia. 1956 Female Jungle; The Gunslinger; The Oklahoma Woman. 1957 Carnival Rock; The Undead; Rock All Night; Teenage Doll. 1958 War of the Satellites; Hot Car Girl; The Cry Baby Killer. 1959 Daddy-O; I, Mobster; A Bucket of Blood; Attack of the Giant Leeches (aka The Giant Leeches); The Violent and the Damned; The Wasp Woman. 1960 Valley of the Redwoods; Code of Silence (aka Killer's Cage); The Story of Ruth. 1961 20,000 Eyes; The Cat Burglar; The Choppers. 1962 The Little Bank Robber; The Case of Patty Smith; Invasion of the Star Creatures; The Devil's Hand. 1963 Night Tide; The Haunted Palace. 1964 Attack of the Mayan Mummy; Curse of the Stone Hand (narrator); Your Cheatin' Heart. 1965 The Girls on the Beach; Creature of the Walking Dead. 1966 She Was a Hippy Vampire (aka The Wild World of Batwoman). 1967 Hell's Angels on Wheels; The Perils of Pauline. 1968 A Man Called Dagger; Single Room Furnished. 1971 Wild Rovers; Bunny O'Hare; Million Dollar Duck.

VESPERMANN, KURT

Born: 1887, Kulmsee, West Prussia. Died: July 13, 1957, Berlin, Germany (heart disease). Stage and screen actor.

Appeared in: 1916 The Bear from Baskerville (film debut). 1930 Bride 58. 1932 Der Schrecken der Garnison; Pension Schoeller; Keine Feier Ohne Meyer. 1934 Schuss im Morgengrauen. 1935 Die Kalte Mansell; Konjunkturritter; Die Unschuld vom Lande; Der Unbekannte Gast (The Unknown Guest). 1936 Das Erbe in Pretoria; Die Stimme der Liebe; Ist Mein Mann Nicht Fabelhaft. 1937 Zwei im Sonnenschein. 1938 Wenn Du eine Schwiegermutter Hast (When You Have a Mother-in-Law); Sie und die Drei (She and the Three). 1939 Der Lustige Witwenball (The Merry Widow's Ball); Der Verkannte Lebemann (The Unrecognized Man of the World).

VICKERS, MARTHA (Martha MacVicar)

Born: 1925. Died: Nov. 2, 1971, Van Nuys, Calif. Screen actress. Divorced from actor Mickey Rooney, publicist A. C. Lyles, Jr., and polo player Manuel Rojas.

Appeared in: 1941 The Wolf Man (film debut). 1944 The Mummy's Ghost; The Falcon in Mexico. 1946 The Big Sleep; The Time, the Place and the Girl. 1947 The Man I Love; That Way with Women; Love and Learn. 1948 Ruthless. 1949 Bad Boy; Alimony; Daughter of the West. 1955 The Big Bluff. 1957 The Burglar. 1960 Four Fast Guns.

VICTOR, CHARLES

Born: 1896, England. Died: Dec. 23, 1965, London, England. Stage and screen actor.

Appeared in: 1939 Hell's Cargo (aka Dangerous Cargo—US). 1940 Dr. O'Dowd; Old Mother Riley in Society; Contraband (aka Blackout—US); Old Mother Riley in Business; You Will Remember; Laugh it Off. 1941 East of Piccadilly (aka The Strangler—US 1942); This England (aka Our Heritage); Atlantic Ferry (aka Sons of the Sea—US); The Saint Meets the Tiger (US 1943); He Found a Star; 49th Parallel (aka The Invaders—US 1942); Ships With Wings (US 1942); Breach of Promise (aka Adventure in Blackmail—US 1943). 1942 They Flew Alone (aka Wings and the Woman—US); The Missing Millions; Those Kids from Town; The Next of Kin (US 1943); The Peterville Diamond; Lady from Lisbon; Squadron Leader X; The Foreman Went to France (aka Somewhere in France—US 1943). 1943 The Silver Fleet (US 1945); When We Are Married; Undercover (aka Underground Guerillas—US 1944); Rhythm Serenade; Escape to Danger; My Learned Friend; They Met in the Dark (US 1945); San Demetrio-London. 1944 It Happened one Sunday; Vote for Huggett. 1945 I Live in Grosvenor Square (aka A Yank in London—US 1946); The Way to the Stars (aka Johnny in the Clouds—US); The Rake's Progress (aka Notorious Gentleman—US 1946); The Man from Morocco. 1946 Gaiety George (aka Showtime—US 1948); This Man is Mine; The Magic Bow (US 1947); Woman to Woman. 1947 While the Sun Shines (US 1950); Temptation Harbour (US 1949); Meet Me at Dawn (US 1948); Green Fingers; While I Live. 1948 Broken Journey; The Calendar. 1949 Fools Rush In; Landfall. 1950 The Cure for Love; Waterfront (aka Waterfront Women—US 1952); The Woman in Question (aka Five Angles on Murder—US 1953); The Elusive Pimpernel; Man Who Cheated Himself; Motor Patrol. 1951 The Galloping Major; Encore (US 1952); Calling Bulldog Drummond. 1952 The Frightened Man; Something Money Can't Buy; Made in Heaven; The Ringer. 1953 The Gay Duelist (reissue of 1947 Meet Me at Dawn); Those People Next Door; Appointment in London (US 1955); Street Corner (aka Both Sides of the Law—US 1954); The Girl on the Pier; The Saint's Return (aka The Saint's Girl Friday—US); Meet Mr. Lucifer; The Steel Lady. 1954 The Love Lottery; Fast and Loose; The Embezzler; The Rainbow Jacket; For Better, For Worse (aka Cocktails in the Kitchen—US 1955); Man Crazy. 1955 Police Dog; Value for Money (US 1957); An Alligator Named Daisy (US 1957); Dial 999 (aka The Way Out—US 1956). **1956** Now and Forever; The Extra Day; Eyewitness; Home and Away; Tiger in the Smoke; The Best Things in Life are Free; Charley Moon. **1957** There's Always Thursday; After the Ball; The Prince and the Showgirl. **1958** Twelve Desperate Hours. **1961** The Pit and the Pendulum. **1970** The Psycho Lover (aka Psycho Killer, The Loving Touch and The Lovely Touch).

VICTOR, HENRY

Born: Oct. 2, 1898, London, England. Died: May 15, 1945, Hollywood, Calif. (brain tumor). Screen actor.

Appeared in: **1914** Revolution (aka The King's Romance and aka The Revolutionist—US). **1916** She; The Picture of Dorian Gray. **1917** Ora Pro Nobis. **1918** The Secret Woman. **1919** The Heart of a Rose; The Call of the Sea; A Lass O' the Looms. **1920** Calvary; As God Made Her; John Heriot's Wife; Beyond the Dreams of Avarice. **1921** The Old Wives' Tale; Sheer Bluff. **1922** Bentley's Conscience; A Romance of Old Bagdad; Diana of the Crossways; A Bill for Divorcement; The Crimson Killer. **1923** The Prodigal Son; The Scandal; The Royal Oak. **1924** The Colleen Bawn; The White Shadow (aka White Shadows—US); Henry, King of Navarre; Slaves of Destiny (aka Miranda of the Balcony); His Grace Gives Notice; The Love Story of Aliette Brunton; The Sins Ye Do. **1925** A Romance of Mayfair; Braveheart; The White Monkey. **1926** Crossed Signals; The Fourth Commandment; Mullhall's Great Catch. **1927** The Beloved Rogue; Topsy and Eva; The Luck of the Navy. **1928** The Guns of Loos; Tommy Atkins. **1929** After the Verdict (US 1930); Down Channel; The Hate Ship. **1930** Song of Soho; Are You There?; One Heavenly Night. **1931** Seas Beneath; Suicide Fleet. **1932** The Mummy; Freaks. **1933** I Spy; Tiger Bay; Luxury Liner. **1934** The Scotland Yard Mystery (aka The Living Dead—US); The Way of Youth; Murder at Monte Carlo; Handle with Care; Can You Hear Me Mother? **1936** The Secret Voice; Fame; Conquest of the Air. **1937** Holiday's End; Our Fighting Navy (aka Torpedoed!—US 1939); Fine Feathers; The Great Barrier (aka Silent Barriers—US). **1939** Confessions of a Nazi Spy; Hotel Imperial; Thunder Afloat; Pack Up your Troubles; Nick Carter, Master Detective; Nurse Edith Cavell. **1940** Mystery Sea Raider; Zanzibar. **1941** King of the Zombies; Blue, White and Perfect. **1942** Sherlock Holmes and the Secret Weapon; To Be or Not to Be; Desperate Journey. **1943** That Nazty Nuisance.

VIDACOVICH, IRVING J. "PINKY"

Born: 1905. Died: July 5, 1966, New Orleans, La. Screen actor, musician, radio writer and composer. Known as "Cajun Pete" of radio.

Appeared in: **1950** Panic in the Streets.

VIDAL, HENRI

Born: 1919, France. Died: Dec. 10, 1959, Paris, France (heart attack). Screen actor. Married to actress Michele Morgan.

Appeared in: **1946** Les Maudits (The Damned). **1950** Quai de Grenelle. **1951** Fabiola. **1952** The Seven Capital Sins; The Strollers. **1953** Naughty Martine. **1954** Port du Desir; Desperate Decision. **1955** The Wicked Go to Hell. **1956** Porte Les Lilas. **1958** Gates of Paris; Attila; The House on the Waterfront; La Parisienne; What Price Murder. **1960** Voulez-Vous Danser Avec Moi (Come Dance with Me).

VIGNOLA, ROBERT G.

Born: 1882, Italy. Died: Oct. 25, 1953, Hollywood, Calif. Screen actor and film director. Entered films as an actor with Kalem in 1907.

VIKING, VONCEIL

Died: Dec. 2, 1929, Banning, Calif. (auto accident injuries). Screen and vaudeville actress. "Obtained a picture engagement by riding horseback from New York to Los Angeles in 120 days on a wager of $25,000."

VILA, SABRA DeSHON

Born: 1850. Died: Sept. 20, 1917, Brooklyn, N.Y. Screen and stage actress.

VILAR, JEAN

Born: 1913, France. Died: May 28, 1971, Sete, France (heart attack). Screen, stage actor and stage director.

Appeared in: **1950** Gates of the Night. **1952** The Thirst of Man.

VILCHES, ERNESTO

Born: Spain. Died: Dec. 8, 1954, Barcelona, Spain (auto accident). Stage and screen actor.

Appeared in: **1933** Cascarrabias; La Noche del Pecado. **1936** El Desaparecido. **1938** El 113.

VILLARD, JULIETTE

Born: 1945, France. Died: Mar. 1971, France. Screen actress.

Appeared in: **1967** Le Grand Meaulnes (aka The Wanderer—US 1969). **1970** La Liberte en Croupe.

VILLARET, JOAO

Born: 1914, Portugal. Died: Jan. 23, 1961, Lisbon, Portugal (cancer). Screen, stage, radio and television actor.

VILLARREAL, JULIO

Born: 1885, Mexico. Died: Aug. 4, 1958, Mexico City, Mexico. Screen actor. One of first Spanish speaking actors to make talking films in Hollywood.

Appeared in: **1933** Una Vida Por Otra; El Rey de los Gitanos; La Ley Del Haren; La Noche del Pecado. **1934** Sagrario; Profanacion; Tiburon; La Sangre Manda; Ora y Plata; Tu Hijo; Quien Mato a Eva. **1935** Corazon Bandolero; Chucho el Roto; El Vuelo de la Muerte; Tribu. **1938** El Pasado Acusa (The Accusing Past). **1940** Odio (Hate); Mi Madrecita (My Little Mother). **1943** The Life of Simon Bolivar; El Conde de Monte Cristo. **1947** Honeymoon. **1950** The Torch. **1953** Plunder of the Sun; Eugene Grandet. **1955** Seven Cities of Gold. **1956** The Beast of Hollow Mountain.

VINAYAK, MASTER

Born: India. Died: Aug. 19, 1947. Screen actor, film producer and director.

VINCENOT, LOUIS

Born: 1884. Died: Feb. 25, 1967. Screen actor.

Appeared in: **1934** Limehouse Blues. **1937** The Thirteenth Chair.

VINCENT, GENE

Born: 1935. Died: Oct. 12, 1971, Saugus, Calif. Screen actor, rock-and-roll singer, songwriter and musical group leader.

Appeared in: **1956** The Girl Can't Help It (with "His Blue Caps"). **1958** Hot Rod Gang. **1962** It's Trad, Dad!; Ring-a-Ding Rhythm! **1963** Live it Up (aka Sing and Swing—US 1964). **1970** Naked Hearts.

VINCENT, LARRY

Born: 1925. Died: Mar. 8, 1975, Burbank, Calif. (cancer). Screen, stage and television actor.

Appeared in: **1969** The Witchmaker.

VINCENT, SAILOR BILLY (William J. Vincent)

Born: 1896. Died: July 12, 1966, Toluca Lake, Calif. (heart attack). Screen and television actor, stuntman and professional boxer.

Appeared in: **1929** The Man I Love; Woman Trap; Speakeasy. **1930** Seven Days Leave. **1935** She Gets Her Man. **1944** The Adventures of Mark Twain. **1948** Albuquerque. **1950** Montana; The Fuller Brush Girl; Hot Rod; Blues Busters. **1956** Around the World in 80 Days; The Steel Jungle. **1957** Affair in Reno. **1965** Young Fury.

VINE, BILLY

Born: 1915. Died: Feb. 10, 1958, New York, N.Y. (heart ailment). Screen, stage, vaudeville and television actor.

Appeared in only two films: **1945** The Lucky Stiff. **1956** Vagabond King.

VINTON, ARTHUR ROLFE

Born: Brooklyn, N.Y. Died: Feb. 26, 1963, Guadalajara, Mexico. Screen, stage and radio actor. Best known for portrayal of radio's "The Shadow."

Appeared in: **1931** The Viking. **1932** Washington Merry-Go-Round; Man against Woman; Laughter in Hell. **1933** Gambling Ship; Blondie Johnson; Picture Snatcher; Lilly Turner; Heroes for Sale; Son of a Sailor; When Strangers Marry; This Day and Age; The Avenger; Central Airport. **1934** Gambling Lady; Cross Country Cruise; A Very Honorable Guy; The Personality Kid; Dames; The Man Trailer; Jealousy. **1935** Society Doctor; Unknown Woman; Little Big Shot; Circumstantial Evidence; King Solomon of Broadway; Red Salute; Rendezvous at Midnight.

VISAROFF, MICHAEL

Born: Nov. 18, 1892, Russia. Died: Feb. 27, 1951, Hollywood, Calif. (pneumonia). Stage and screen actor. Married to actress Vina Visaroff (dec. 1938).

Appeared in: **1925** The Swan (film debut). **1926** Paris; Valencia. **1927** The Sunset Derby; Camille; Two Arabian Knights. **1928** The Last Command; The Adventurer; The Night Bird; Plastered in Paris; Tempest; We Americans. **1929** Marquis Preferred; The House of Horror; Illusion; Disraeli; Hungarian Rhapsody; The Exalted Flapper; Four Devils. **1930** Dracula; Morocco. **1931** Arizona Terror; Mata Hari; Freaks; Chinatown after Dark. **1932** The Man Who Played God. **1933** Strange People; The Barbarian; The King of the Arena. **1934** Picture Brides; Fugitive Road; The Marines Are Coming!; The Merry Frinks; The Cat's Paw; Wagon Wheels; We Live Again. **1935** One More Spring; The Mark of the Vampire; The Break of Hearts; Anna Karenina; Paddy O'Day. **1936** The Gay Desperado. **1937** Champagne Waltz; Soldier and the Lady; Angel. **1938** Air Devils; Tropic Holiday; I'll Give a Million. **1939** Paris Honeymoon; Everything Happens at Night; On Your Toes; Juarez and Maximilian. **1940** Charlie Chan at the Wax Museum; The Son of Monte Cristo; Four Sons; Second Chorus. **1943** For Whom the Bell Tolls; Mission to Moscow; Hostages; Paris after Dark. **1945** Song to Remember; Yolanda and the Thief; Her Highness and the Bellboy. **1947** Flight to Nowhere; Intrigue.

VISAROFF, NINA

Born: 1888. Died: Dec. 14, 1938, Beverly Hills, Calif. Stage and screen actress. Married to actor Michael Visaroff (dec. 1951).

Appeared in: **1936** Paddy O'Day.

VITERBO, PATRICIA

Born: 1943, France. Died: Nov. 10, 1966, Paris, France (drowned in car accident). Screen actress.

Appeared in: **1965** You Must Be Joking. **1967** Two for the Road.

VIVIAN, PERCIVAL (Percival Seymoure Vivian)

Born: Mar. 13, 1890, England. Died: Jan. 15, 1961, Burbank, Calif. (arteriosclerosis). Screen actor. Married to stage actress Rene Vivian (dec. 1949). Father of actor Daniel Vivian.

Appeared in: **1945** Kitty; A Letter to Evie. **1946** Susie Steps Out. **1949** A Kiss in the Dark. **1954** Prince Valiant. **1955** Daddy Long Legs; Prince of Players.

VIVIAN, ROBERT

Born: 1859, London, England. Died: Jan. 31, 1944, New York, N.Y. Stage and screen actor.

Appeared in: **1917** Law of the Land. **1918** Under the Greenwood Tree. **1919** Counterfeit; Piccadilly Jim; The Spite Bride; La Belle Russe. **1920** The Plunger; The Restless Sex; The New York Idea. **1939** Back Door to Heaven.

VIVIAN, RUTH

Born: England. Died: Oct. 24, 1949, New York, N.Y. Screen and stage actress.

Appeared in: **1941** The Man Who Came to Dinner (stage and film versions). **1949** A Letter to Three Wives.

VODNOY, MAX (aka MATTHEW VODNOY)

Born: 1892, Russia. Died: May 27, 1939, New York, N.Y. (heart attack). Screen, stage and vaudeville actor.

Appeared in: **1937** The Green Fields. **1938** The Singing Blacksmith.

VOGAN, EMMETT (Charles Emmet Vogan)

Born: Sept. 27, 1893, Ohio. Died: Nov. 13, 1969, Woodland Hills, Calif. (septecemia and pneumonia). Screen actor.

Appeared in: **1934** Love Birds. **1935** Stars over Broadway. **1936** The Public Pays (short); The Big Noise; Two in Revolt; Adventure in Manhattan. **1937** Fly-Away Baby; San Quentin; Let's Get Married. **1938** Sergeant Murphy; Female Fugitive; Beloved Brat; Secret of an Actress; Meet the Girls; What Price Safety?; Rhythm of the Saddle. **1939** The Man Who Dared; The Great Victor Herbert; Romance of the Potato; Angel of Mercy; The Story That Couldn't Be Printed; Tail Spin. **1940** Thou Shalt Not Kill; Margie; Good Bad Guys; Spots Before Your Eyes; Shooting High; The Hidden Master. **1941** The Lady from Cheyenne; Petticoat Politics; Emergency Landing; Hurricane Smith; Redlands of Dakota; Never Give a Sucker an Even Break; Dangerous Lady; Blue, White and Perfect; Robot Wrecks. **1942** Flag of Mercy; Stardust on the Sage; Top Sergeant; The Mummy's Tomb; Whistling in Dixie; The Traitor Within; Don't Lie; Unexpected Riches; Give Out Sisters. **1943** Dixie Dugan; The Crime Smasher; Lady Bodyguard; He Hired the Boss; Chatterbox; Here Comes Kelly; Mystery Broadcast; O, My Darling Clementine; Swingtime Johnny. **1944** Let's Dance; Follow the Boys; Hat Check Honey; Bermuda Mystery; Trocadero; Are These Our Parents?; Song of Nevada; The Mummy's Ghost; Faces in the Fog; Murder in the Blue Room; Tale of a Dog; End of the Road; Enemy of Women. **1945** The Lady Confesses; She Gets Her Man; The Vampire's Ghost; Utah; The Bull Fighters; Night Club Girl; Blood on the Sun; Don Juan Quilligan; Behind City Lights; Senorita from the West; Along the Navajo Trail; The Woman Who Came Back; The Naughty Nineties. **1946** A Close Call for Boston Blackie; Gay Blades; The Shadow Returns; Joe Palooka, Champ; Rendezvous 24; The French Key; Freddie Steps Out; Magnificent Doll; Secrets of a Sorority Girl; Bowery Bombshell; The Jolson Story; Susie Steps Out; Sweetheart of Sigma Chi; Dangerous Money. **1947** I Wonder Who's Kissing Her Now; Last of the Redmen; Smoky River Serenade; Homesteaders of Paradise Valley. **1948** Mary Lou; Docks of New Orleans; Smugglers Cove; The Denver Kid. **1949** Post Office Investigator; Arson, Inc.; Cover Up; Brothers in the Saddle; Sky Dragon; Rusty Saves a Life; Riders of the Whistling Pines; Ladies of the Chorus; South of Rio; Down Dakota Way; Alias the Champ; One Sunday Afternoon (aka The Strawberry Blonde); Sorrowful Jones. **1950** Father's Wild Game. **1951** Pride of Maryland; The Big Gusher; Street Bandits; Pals of the Golden West. **1952** Don't Bother to Knock; My Wife's Best Friend; Something for the Birds. **1953** How to Marry a Millionaire. **1954** Sabrina; Tobor the Great; Red River Shore.

VOGEDING, FREDRIK

Born: Mar. 28, 1890, Nymegen, Netherlands. Died: Apr. 18, 1942, Los Angeles, Calif. (heart attack). Screen, stage and vaudeville actor. Married to actress Florence Roberts (dec. 1927).

Appeared in: **1921** Behind Masks; High Heels. **1933** Below the Sea; My Lips Betray. **1934** Orient Express; Murder on the Blackboard; Fury of the Jungle. **1935** Mills of the Gods; The Woman in Red; Charlie Chan in Shanghai;

Barbary Coast. **1936** The Public Pays (short); The House of a Thousand Candles; A Message to Garcia. **1937** Think Fast, Mr. Moto; Charlie Chan at the Olympics; Cafe Metropole. **1938** Mr. Moto Takes a Chance; Mysterious Mr. Moto; Miracle Money (short); The Cowboy and the Lady; 6,000 Enemies. **1939** Confessions of a Nazi Spy; While America Sleeps (short); Charlie Chan in City in Darkness; The Three Musketeers. **1940** Enemy Agent; British Intelligence; Four Sons; The Man I Married; Man Hunt. **1942** The Great Impersonation.

VOGEL, ELEANORE

Born: 1903. Died: June 26, 1973, Hollywood, Calif. (heart attack). Screen, stage and television actress.

Appeared in: **1963** How the West was Won.

VOGEL, HENRY

Born: 1865. Died: June 17, 1925, New York, N.Y. Screen and stage actor.

VOGEL, PATRICIA

Born: 1909. Died: June 25, 1941, Beverly Hills, Calif. (suicide—hanging). Screen actress.

VOGEL, RUDOLF

Born: 1900, Munich, Germany. Died: 1967, Munich, Germany. Screen, stage and vaudeville actor. Father of actor Peter Vogel.

Appeared in: **1953** The Story of Vicki. **1957** Robinson Soll Nicht Sterben (The Girl and the Legend—US 1966). **1958** Der Bettelstudent (The Beggar Student); Das Wirtshaus im Spessart (The Spessart Inn—US 1961). **1959** Ein Mann geht Durch die Wand (The Man Who Walked Through the Wall—US 1964); Embezzled Heaven. **1965** Heidi (US 1968).

VOGLER, WALTER A.

Born: 1897. Died: Aug. 26, 1955, Los Angeles, Calif. (heart attack). Screen actor and film technical adviser.

Appeared in: **1930** All Quiet on the Western Front.

VOINOFF, ANATOLE

Born: 1896, Russia. Died: Feb. 9, 1965, New York, N.Y. Screen actor. Appeared in silents.

VOLKMAN, IVAN

Died: Oct. 17, 1972, Stockton, Calif. (stroke). Screen actor and assistant film director.

Appeared in: **1967** How to Succeed in Business without Really Trying.

VOLOTSKOY, VLADIMIR

Born: 1853, Russia. Died: Nov. 7, 1927, Hollywood, Calif. Stage and screen actor.

VOLPE, FREDERICK "FRED"

Born: 1873. Died: Mar. 7, 1932, London, England. Screen and stage actor.

Appeared in: **1916** Altar Chains (US 1917); Lifeguardsman (US 1917). **1917** The Profligate. **1918** Les Cloches de Cornville; Once Upon a Time. **1930** The Middle Watch. **1931** Captivation.

VON ALTEN, FERDINAND (Baron von Lamezan auf Altenhofen)

Born: 1885. Died: Mar. 17, 1933, Dessau, Germany (flu). Stage and screen actor.

Appeared in: **1928** Small Town Sinners. **1929** Sajenko, the Soviet; The Man Who Cheated Life.

VON BETZ, MATTHEW. See MATTHEW BETZ

VON BLOCK, BELA

Born: 1889. Died: Mar. 22, 1962, Hollywood, Calif. Screen actor. Appeared in films from 1924 to 1929.

VON BOLVARY, GEZA

Born: 1898, Hungary. Died: Aug. 11, 1961, Munich, West Germany (heart ailment). Screen actor, screenwriter and film director. Appeared in German films shortly after W.W. I; then became director and screenwriter.

VON BRINCKEN, WILHELM (aka ROGER BECKWITH and WILLIAM VAUGHN)

Born: May 27, 1891, Flensburg, Germany. Died: Jan. 18, 1946, Los Angeles, Calif. (ruptured artery). Screen actor and film technical director. Entered films in 1921.

Appeared in: **1930** Mamba; Inside the Lines; Royal Flush; Leathernecking; This Mad World; Hell's Angels. **1932** The Night Club Lady; A Passport to Hell; prior to 1933: Manhattan Comedies (record series). **1933** Private Jones; Shanghai Madness. **1934** I'll Tell the World. **1936** Dracula's Daughter. **1937** The Prisoner of Zenda; Thank You, Mr. Moto; The Life of Emile Zola; Crack

Up; Espionage; They Gave Him a Gun. **1938** International Crime; Bulldog Drummond in Africa. **1939** Confessions of a Nazi Spy; Pack up Your Troubles; Conspiracy. **1940** Four Sons.

VON COLLANDE, GISELA
Born: 1915, Dresden, Germany. Died: Oct. 23, 1960, Pforzheim, West Germany (auto accident). Screen, stage and radio actress.

VON ELTZ, THEODORE
Born: 1894, New Haven, Conn. Died: Oct. 6, 1964, Woodland Hills, Calif. Screen, stage, radio and television actor. Entered films in 1920.

Appeared in: **1923** Tiger Rose. **1924** Being Respectable. **1925** Paint and Powder; On Thin Ice; The Sporting Chance. **1926** The Red Kimono; Sea Wolf; Fools of Fashion. **1927** One Woman to Another; No Man's Law; The Great Mail Robbery. **1928** Way of the Strong; Life's Mockery; Nothing to Wear. **1929** Four Feathers; The Awful Truth; The Voice of the Storm; The Very Idea; The Rescue. **1930** Love among Millionaires; The Furies; The Arizona Kid; The Divorcee; Kismet; The Cat Creeps. **1931** Susan Lennox, Her Rise and Fall; Private Scandal; Heartbreak; The Prodigal; The Secret Six; Up Pops the Devil; Beyond Victory; Wicked; Once a Lady. **1932** Ladies of the Big House; Hotel Continental; The Midnight Lady; Drifting Souls; Strangers of the Evening; The Unwritten Law; Red-Haired Alibi; Breach of Promise; Scarlet Week-End. **1933** Eleventh Commandment; Pleasure Cruise; Arizona to Broadway; High Gear; Jennie Gerhardt; Her Splendid Folly; Dance, Girl, Dance; Master of Men; Luxury Liner. **1934** The Silver Streak; Change of Heart; Call It Luck; Bright Eyes. **1935** Elinore Norton; Streamline Express; Trails of the Wild; Private Worlds; Smart Girl; Behind the Green Lights; Headline Woman; Confidential; His Night Out; The Magnificent Obsession. **1936** Below the Deadline; I Cover Chinatown; Beloved Enemy; The Road to Glory; High Tension; Sussy; Sinner Take All; Mind Your Own Business; Ticket to Paradise. **1937** Clarence; A Man Betrayed; Under Cover of Night; Jim Hanvey, Detective; Youth on Parole; California Straight Ahead; The Westland Case; Topper. **1938** Inside Story; Pardon Our Nerves; Blondes at Work; Smashing the Rackets. **1939** They Made Her a Spy; 5th Avenue Girl; The Sun Never Sets; Legion of Lost Flyers. **1940** The Old Swimmin' Hole; The Great Plane Robbery; The Son of Monte Cristo; Little Old New York; Dr. Ehrlich's Magic Bullet. **1941** Life with Henry; Ellery Queen's Penthouse Mystery; A Shot in the Dark; I'll Wait for You. **1942** The Man in the Trunk; Quiet Please, Murder!; Lady in a Jam. **1944** Follow the Boys; Bermuda Mystery; Hollywood Canteen; Since You Went Away. **1945** Saratoga Trunk; Rhapsody in Blue. **1946** The Big Sleep. **1948** The Devil's Cargo. **1950** Trial without Jury. **1956** The Animal World (narr.).

VON KALTENBORN, HANS
Born: 1879. Died: June 14, 1965, New York, N.Y. (heart ailment). Screen actor and radio announcer.

Appeared in: **1939** Mr. Smith Goes to Washington.

VON LAMBECK, FREDERICK
Born: 1918. Died: Mar. 26, 1950, Rochester, N.Y. Screen actor and horse trainer. Double for actor Tyrone Power (dec. 1958).

VON LEDEBUR, LEOPOLD
Born: 1876, Germany. Died: Sept. 17, 1955, Wankendorf, Germany. Stage and screen actor.

VON MEYERINCK, HUBERT
Born: 1897, Germany. Died: May 13, 1971, Hamburg, Germany. Stage and screen actor. Entered films in 1924.

Appeared in: **1958** Das Wirtshaus in Spessart (The Spessart Inn— 1961). **1959** Ein Mann Geht Durch die Wand (The Man Who Walked Through the Wall— US 1964). **1960** Holiday Island. **1961** One, Two, Three; Secret Ways. **1962** Die Turkischen Gurken (The Turkish Cucumber—US 1963).

VON REMPERT, ALBERT
Born: Germany. Died: Oct. 1958 (injuries sustained filming fight scene in Slave Caravan). Screen actor.

VON SEYFFERTITZ, GUSTAV
Born: 1863, Vienna, Austria. Died: Dec. 25, 1943, Woodland Hills, Calif. Screen, stage actor and film director. During W.W. I he was known as G. Butler Clonblough.

Appeared in: **1918** Old Wives for New. **1922** Sherlock Holmes; When Knighthood Was in Flower. **1924** The Bandolero; The Lone Wolf; Yolanda. **1925** Goose Woman. **1926** Don Juan; Diplomacy; Sparrows; The Bells; Red Dice. **1927** Barbed Wire; The Gaucho; The Magic Flame; The Wizard; Rose of the Golden West; Birds of Prey; The Student Prince. **1928** Yellow Lily; The Woman Disputed; Vamping Venus; Mysterious Lady; Me, Gangster; Docks of New York; The Red Mark. **1929** Chasing through Europe; His Glorious Night; The Canary Murder Case; The Case of Lena Smith; Come Across; Seven Faces. **1930** The Case of Sgt. Grischa; Dangerous Paradise; Are You There? **1931** The Bat Whispers; Dishonored; Ambassador Bill. **1932** Shanghai Express; Road-

house Murder; The Penguin Pool Murder; Rasputin and the Empress; Afraid to Talk; Doomed Battalion. **1933** When Strangers Marry; Queen Christina. **1934** Mystery Liner; The Moonstone; Change of Heart; Little Men. **1935** She; Remember Last Night. **1936** Little Lord Fauntleroy; Murder on the Bridle Path; Mad Holiday. **1938** In Old Chicago; King of Alcatraz; Cipher Bureau. **1939** Nurse Edith Cavell; Juarez and Maximilian.

VON STERNBERG, JOSEF (aka JO STERNBERG and JOE STERN)
Born: 1894, Vienna, Austria. Died: Dec. 22, 1969, Hollywood, Calif. (heart attack). Screen, stage actor, film director, photographer and film narrator.

Narrated: **1954** Ana-Ta-Han (The Devil's Pitchfork).

VON STROHEIM, ERICH, SR. (Erich Oswald Hans Carl Maris Von Nordenwall)
Born: Sept. 22, 1885, Vienna, Austria. Died: May 12, 1957, Paris, France (spinal ailment). Screen actor, film director, film producer and screenwriter. Awarded Legion of Honor by the French government for his contributions to the film industry. Father of actor Erich Von Stroheim, Jr. (dec. 1968).

Appeared in: **1914** Captain McLean. **1915** The Failure; Ghosts; A Bold Impersonation; Old Heidelberg. **1916** Birth of a Nation; Intolerance; The Social Secretary; His Picture in the Papers; Macbeth; Less Than the Dust. **1917** Panthea; In Again—Out Again; Sylvia of the Secret Service; For France. **1918** The Unbeliever; Hearts of the World; Hearts of Humanity; The Hun Within. **1919** Blind Husbands. **1921** Foolish Wives. **1928** Wedding March. **1929** The Great Gabbo. **1930** Three Faces East. **1931** Friends and Lovers. **1932** Lost Squadron; As You Desire Me; Hello Sister. **1934** Crimson Romance; House of Strangers; Fugitive Road. **1935** The Crime of Dr. Crespi. **1936** Marthe Richard au Service de la France; The Devil's Doll. **1937** Les Pirates du Rail; Between Two Women; Mademoiselle Docteur; La Grande Illusion; The Alibi. **1938** Les Desparus de St. Agil; Gibraltar; L'Affaire La Farge. **1939** Boys' School; Tempete sur Paris (Thunder over Paris—US 1940); Macao l'Enfer du Jeu; Paris–New York; Derriere la Facade; Rappel Immediat; Pieges; Le Monde Tremblera. **1940** Ultimatum; I Was an Adventuress. **1941** So Ends Our Night; Personal Column. **1943** Five Graves to Cairo; North Star; Storm over Lisbon; It Happened in Gibraltar; Armored Attack. **1944** The Lady and the Monster; 32 Rue de Montmartre. **1945** The Great Flamarion; Scotland Investigator. **1946** The Mask of Dijon; La Foire aux Chimeres; One Ne Meurt Pas Comme Ca. **1947** La Danse de Mort. **1948** Le Signal Rouge. **1949** Portrait d'un Assassin; The Devil and the Angel. **1950** Sunset Boulevard. **1952** La Maison du Crime; Alraune. **1953** Minuit—Quai de Bercy; Alerte au Sud; L'Envers du Paradis. **1954** Napoleon; Serie Noire. **1955** La Madonna du Sleepings. **1958** L'homme aux Cent Visages.

VON STROHEIM, ERICH, JR.
Born: 1916, Los Angeles, Calif. Died: Oct. 26, 1968, Woodland Hills, Calif. (cancer). Screen actor and assistant film director. Entered films as a child actor. Son of actor and director Erich Von Stroheim, Sr. (dec. 1957).

Appeared in: **1962** Two Weeks in Another Town. **1968** Skidoo.

VON TWARDOWSKI, HANS (Hans Heinrich von Twardowski)
Born: Germany. Died: Nov. 19, 1958, New York, N.Y. Screen, stage, radio, television actor and stage director.

Appeared in: **1932** Scandal for Sale. **1933** Private Jones; Adorable. **1934** The Scarlet Empress. **1935** The Crusades; Storm over the Andes. **1939** Beasts of Berlin; Confessions of a Nazi Spy; Espionage Agent. **1942** Casablanca; Joan of Ozark. **1943** Hangmen Also Die.

VON WINTERSTEIN, EDUARD
Born: 1872, Vienna, Austria. Died: July 22, 1961, East Berlin, Germany. Stage and screen actor.

Appeared in: **1930** Three Faces East. **1931** Friends and Lovers. **1932** Lost Squadron.

VOSBURGH, ALFRED. *See* GAYNE WHITMAN

VOSBURGH, HAROLD
Born: 1870, Penetanguishene, Ont., Canada. Died: Nov. 17, 1926, New Orleans, La. Screen actor.

Appeared in: **1904** The Moonshiner. **1921** If Women Only Knew.

VOSPER, FRANK O.
Born: 1900, England. Died: Mar. 6, 1937, England. Screen, stage actor, playwright and author.

Appeared in: **1932** Rome Express (US 1933). **1934** Jew Suess (aka Power—US); The Man Who Knew Too Much (US 1935); Strauss's Great Waltz (US 1935). **1935** Heart's Desire (US 1937). **1936** Spy of Napoleon (US 1939); The Secret of Stamboul (US 1939). **1940** The Spy in White (reissue of The Secret of Stamboul—1936).

VOSPER, JOHN

Died: Apr. 6, 1954, Hollywood, Calif. (heart attack). Screen, stage, radio and television actor.

Appeared in: **1942** The Wife Takes a Flyer; Undercover Man. **1944** Dark Shadows (short). **1945** Weekend at the Waldorf; Counter-Attack. **1947** A Stolen Life; The Perfect Marriage. **1949** Bride of Vengeance. **1951** The Desert Fox. **1952** Black Hills Ambush. **1953** The Magnetic Monster. **1956** Edge of Hell.

VOSS, FRANK "FATTY"

Born: Oct. 12, 1888, Illinois. Died: Apr. 22, 1917, Los Angeles, Calif. (fatty degeneration of heart). Screen actor.

Appeared in: **1915** In the Claw of the Law; Shot in a Bar Room; A Game of Love; Beach Birds; Greed and Gasoline; Under New Management; Ready for Reno; Lizzie's Shattered Dreams; The Doomed Groom; Pants and Petticoats. **1916** Gertie's Busy Day; Flirtation a la Carte; A Busted Honeymoon; Pirates of the Air; A Bambler's Bambol; Lizzie's Lingering Love; Alice in Society; Unhand Me, Villain. **1917** Fatty's Feature Fillum.

VROOM, FREDERIC WILLIAM

Born: 1858. Died: June 24, 1942, Hollywood, Calif. (heart attack). Stage and screen actor.

Appeared in: **1921** The Millionaire; The Faith Healer; The Great Impersonation; The Heart Line; White and Unmarried. **1922** The Lane That Had No Turning; The Fourteenth Lover; The Woman Who Walked Alone; The Glorious Fool; Tailor-Made Man. **1923** The Acquittal; The Day of Faith; The Tiger's Claw. **1924** The Navigator; His Hour; Hutch of the U.S.A.; Sporting Youth; The Reckless Age; Phantom Justice. **1926** Eyes Right. **1927** The General. **1928** The Terrible People. **1930** The Poor Millionaire. **1932** The Mighty Barnum.

VUOLO, TITO

Born: Mar. 22, 1893, Italy. Died: Sept. 14, 1962, Los Angeles, Calif. (cancer). Screen actor.

Appeared in: **1947** The Web; Mourning Becomes Electra. **1948** Mr. Blandings Builds His Dream House; Cry of the City. **1949** Flamingo Road; House of Strangers; The Great Gatsby; Everybody Does It. **1950** Between Midnight and Dawn; Deported; The Man Who Cheated Himself. **1951** The Enforcer; Up Front; Saturday's Hero; The Racket. **1952** The Racing Tide. **1956** Emergency Hospital. **1957** The Midnight Story; Dragstrip Girl; 20 Million Miles to Earth.

WADE, BESSIE

Born: 1885. Died: Oct. 19, 1966, Dallas, Tex. Screen actress. Entered films in 1916.

Appeared in: **1948** The Velvet Touch.

WADE, JOHN W.

Born: 1876. Died: July 14, 1949, Hollywood, Calif. Screen, stage and vaudeville actor. Toured in "Marse Shelby's Chicken Dinner," vaudeville sketch. Entered films approx. 1924.

Appeared in: **1938** Heroes of the Hills.

WADE, WARREN

Born: 1896, Akron, Ohio. Died: Jan. 14, 1973, Englewood, N.J. Screen, stage, radio, television actor and stage director.

Appeared in: **1959** Heller in Pink Tights. **1960** Song Without End. **1962** The Miracle Worker.

WADHAMS, GOLDEN

Born: 1869. Died: June 26, 1929, Hollywood, Calif. (heart illness). Stage and screen actor.

Appeared in: **1927** Hotel Imperial. **1929** Laughing at Death.

WADKAR, HANSA "SWAN"

Born: 1924, India. Died: Aug. 23, 1971, Bombay, India (cancer). Stage and screen actress.

WADSWORTH, HENRY

Born: 1902, Maysville, Ky. Died: Dec. 5, 1974, New York, N.Y. Screen, stage and vaudeville actor.

Appeared in: **1929** Applause. **1930** Fast and Loose; Slightly Scarlet. **1933** Soldiers of the Storm; The Ghost Train; Luxury Liner; Hold the Press. **1934** This Side of Heaven; Evelyn Prentice; Operator 13; Four Walls; Dangerous Corner; The Show-Off; The Thin Man. **1935** Ceiling Zero; Big Broadcast of 1936; West Point of the Air; Mark of the Vampire. **1936** The Voice of Bugle Ann; Sitting on the Moon. **1938** Dr. Rhythm. **1940** Dr. Kildare Goes Home. **1943** Silver Skates. **1947** Song of the Thin Man.

WADSWORTH, WILLIAM

Born: 1873. Died: June 6, 1950, N.Y. Stage and screen actor.

Appeared in: **1912** What Happened to Mary? (serial). **1913–14** Mr. Wood B.

Wedd's Sentimental Experiences Series including the following: Her Face Was Her Fortune; The Love Senorita; The Beautiful Leading Lady; The Vision in the Window; High Life; A Lady of Spirits; The Revengeful Servant Girl; A Canine Rival; The Busom Country Lass; Love by the Pound; Wood B. Wedd and the Microbes; Wood B. Wedd Goes Snipe Hunting; A Superfluous Baby. **1922** Young America. **1926** White Mice.

WAGENSELLER, WILLIAM H.

Born: 1880. Died: Apr. 25, 1951, North Hollywood, Calif. Stage and screen actor.

WAGNER, JACK

Born: 1897. Died: Feb. 6, 1965, Hollywood, Calif. Screen and stage actor.

Appeared in: **1935** Paris in the Spring. **1939** Nancy Drew—Reporter.

WAGNER, MAX

Born: Nov. 28, 1901, Mexico. Died: Nov. 16, 1975, West Los Angeles, Calif. (heart attack). Screen actor.

Appeared in: **1932** The World and the Flesh. **1933** Arizona to Broadway; Renegades of the West. **1934** Sons of the Desert; Wharf Angel; The Lost Jungle (serial); Hell Bent for Love; The Oil Raider. **1935** Charlie Chan in Shanghai; Under the Pampas Moon; Ladies Crave Excitement. **1936** Two in Revolt; Smart Blonde; The Case Against Mrs. Ames; God's Country and the Woman; The Crime Patrol; Love Begins at Twenty; The Dancing Pirate. **1937** Step Lively, Jeeves; San Quentin; Slim; Border Cafe. **1938** Fool Coverage; Penrod and His Twin Brother; Cocoanut Grove; Painted Desert. **1939** The Roaring Twenties; The Star Maker. **1940** The Trail of the Vigilantes; You Can't Fool Your Wife. **1941** Cyclone on Horseback; Great Guns. **1942** Rough on Rents; True to the Army; Mexican Spitfire's Elephant. **1944** Boss of Boomtown. **1945** A Medal for Benny; The Bull Fighters; Within These Walls; Radio Stars on Parade. **1946** Smoky; The Sin of Harold Diddlebock. **1947** Mad Wednesday. **1949** Bandits of El Dorado. **1951** The Racket; The Secret of Convict Lake. **1952** The Blazing Forest. **1953** Invaders from Mars. **1954** The Country Girl. **1955** Underwater; Lucy Gallant.

WAGNER, WILLIAM

Born: 1885. Died: Mar. 11, 1964, Hollywood, Calif. Screen and stage actor. Entered films approx. 1930.

Appeared in: **1934** Jane Eyre; plus the following shorts: For Pete's Sake; Honkey Donkey; I'll Be Suing You; Done in Oil. **1936** Lloyd's of London; The Lucky Corner (short). **1937** Easy Living. **1938** Rebecca of Sunnybrook Farm.

WAHL, WALTER DARE (Walter Kalwara)

Born: 1896. Died: June 23, 1974, Metamoris, Pa. Screen, stage, vaudeville actor and world's light heavyweight wrestling champion.

Appeared in: **1942** Star Spangled Rhythm. **1954** Top Banana.

WAINWRIGHT, GODFREY

Born: 1879. Died: May 19, 1956, Woodland Hills, Calif. Screen actor.

WAINWRIGHT, HOPE

Born: 1942. Died: 1972, Sigelbach, Germany (auto accident). Screen and television actress.

Appeared in: **1962** Whatever Happened to Baby Jane? **1967** The Graduate.

WAINWRIGHT, MARIE

Born: 1856, Philadelphia, Pa. Died: Aug. 17, 1923, Scranton, Pa. Stage and screen actress.

Appeared in: **1921** Polly with a Past.

WAKEFIELD, DOUGLAS "DUGGIE"

Born: 1900, Hull, England. Died: Apr. 14, 1951, London, England. Screen, stage and vaudeville actor.

Appeared in: **1933** This Week of Grace. **1934** I'll Be Suing You (short). **1935** Look up and Laugh. **1937** The Penny Pool. **1939** Spy for a Day. **1940** Calling All Crooks.

WAKEFIELD, FRANCES. *See* FRANCES WAKEFIELD MANDEL

WAKEFIELD, HUGH

Born: Nov. 10, 1888, Wanstead, England. Died: Dec. 1971, London, England. Stage and screen actor.

Appeared in: **1931** The Sport of Kings; City of Song (aka Farewell to Love—US 1933). **1932** Aren't We All? **1933** The Crime at Blossoms; The Fortunate Fool; King of the Ritz. **1934** The Luck of a Sailor; My Heart is Calling (US 1935); Lady in Danger; The Man Who Knew Too Much. **1935** Marry the Girl; No Monkey Business; 18 Minutes; Runaway Ladies. **1936** The Crimson Circle; Forget-Me-Not (aka Forever Yours—US 1937); The Interrupted Honeymoon; It's You I Want; The Improper Duchess; Dreams Come True. **1937** The Street Singer; The Live Wire; Death Croons the Blues. **1938** Make It Three. **1945** Blithe Spirit; Journey Together (US 1946). **1948** One Night with

You. **1952** Love's a Luxury (aka The Caretaker's Daughter—US). **1954** The Million Pound Note (aka Man with a Million—US).

WAKEFIELD, OLIVER
Born: 1909, England. Died: June 30, 1956, Rye, N.Y. Screen, stage, radio and television actor.

Appeared in: **1933** A Universal Short. **1937** Let's Make a Night of It (US 1938); There Was a Young Man. **1939** Shipyard Sally. **1940** The Briggs Family; George and Margaret. **1942** The Peterville Diamond. **1943** Pictorial Revue of 1943.

WALBROOK, ANTON (Adolph Anton Wilhelm Wohlbrück)
Born: Nov. 19, 1900, Vienna, Austria. Died: Aug. 9, 1967, Munich, West Germany (heart attack). Stage and screen actor.

Appeared in: **1931** Salto Mortale. **1933** Regine; Mond Uber Marvokko; The Waltz War. **1934** Masquerade in Vienna (US 1937); Die Englishe Heirat; Eine Frau die Weisse Was Sie Will. **1935** Zigeunerbaron (Gypsy Baron); The Student of Prague. **1936** Allitria. **1937** Victoria the Great; The Soldier and the Lady; The Rat. **1938** Sixty Glorious Years (aka Queen of Destiny—US). **1940** Gaslight (aka Angel Street—US). **1941** Dangerous Moonlight (aka Suicide Squadron—US 1942); 49th Parallel (aka The Invaders—US 1942); I Give My Life. **1942** Orders from Tokyo. **1943** The Life and Death of Colonel Blimp (aka Colonel Blimp—US 1945). **1945** The Man from Morocco (US 1946). **1948** The Red Shoes. **1949** The Queen of Spades (US 1950). **1950** La Ronde. **1951** Wien Tanzt (Vienna Waltzes—US 1961). **1952** Angel Street. **1955** Oh, Rosalinda!; Lola Montez. **1957** Saint Joan. **1958** I Accuse. Other foreign films (French). L'Affaire Mauricuis; L'Affaire Menrizim.

WALBURN, RAYMOND
Born: Sept. 9, 1887, Plymouth, Ind. Died: July 26, 1969, New York, N.Y. Stage and screen actor.

Appeared in: **1916** The Scarlet Runner (serial). **1930** The Laughing Lady. **1934** The Defense Rests; Jealousy; The Great Flirtation; The Count of Monte Cristo; Broadway Bill; Lady by Choice. **1935** Only Eight Hours; She Married Her Boss; Death Flies East; Mills of the Gods; I'll Love You Always; Redheads on Parade; Society Doctor; It's a Small World; Welcome Home; Thanks a Million. **1936** Mr. Cinderella; Mr. Deeds Goes to Town; The Lone Wolf Returns; The King Steps Out; They Met in a Taxi; Craig's Wife; The Great Ziegfeld; Absolute Quiet; Three Wise Guys; Born to Dance. **1937** Let's Get Married; It Can't Last Forever; Murder in Greenwich Village; Thin Ice; Breezing Home; High, Wide and Handsome; Broadway Melody of 1938. **1938** Start Cheering; Sweethearts; Battle of Broadway; Gateway; Professor Beware. **1939** Let Freedom Ring; It Could Happen to You; The Under-Pup; Eternally Yours. **1940** Heaven with a Barbed-Wire Face; The Dark Command; Millionaires in Prison; Flowing Gold; Third Finger, Left Hand; Christmas in July. **1941** San Francisco Docks; Kiss the Boys Goodbye; Puddin' Head; Bachelor Party; Confirm or Deny; Rise and Shine; Louisiana Purchase. **1942** The Man in the Trunk. **1943** Let's Face It; Dixie Dugan; Lady Bodyguard; Desperadoes; Dixie. **1944** Music in Manhattan; And the Angels Sing; Hail the Conquering Hero; Heavenly Days. **1945** The Cheaters; Honeymoon Ahead; I'll Tell the World. **1946** Affairs of Geraldine; Breakfast in Hollywood; Lover Come Back; The Plainsman and the Lady; Rendezvous with Annie. **1947** Mad Wednesday (aka Sin of Harold Diddlebock). **1948** State of the Union; The World and His Wife. **1949** Henry, the Rainmaker; Leave It to Henry; Red, Hot and Blue. **1950** Riding High; Key to the City; Father's Wild Game; Father Makes Good; Short Grass. **1951** Father Takes the Air; Golden Girl; Excuse My Dust. **1953** Beautiful but Dangerous. **1954** She Couldn't Say No. **1955** The Spoilers.

WALDAU, GUSTAV
Born: 1871, Germany. Died: May 25, 1958, Munich, Germany. Screen actor.

Appeared in: **1932** Der Falsche Ehemann. **1933** Saison in Kairo (Cairo Season). **1934** Eines Prinzen Junge Liebe (A Prince's Young Love). **1935** Klein Dorrit (Little Dorrit). **1937** Das Einmaleins der Liebe (Love's Arithmetic); Drei Maedel um Schubert (Three Girls around Schubert). **1938** Sie und die Drei (She and the Three); Der Schimmelkrieg von Holledau; Eine Nacht an der Donau (A Night on the Danube). **1940** Eine Kleine Nachtmusik. **1951** Eroica (aka The Beethoven Story). **1952** Singing Angels.

WALDEMAR, RICHARD
Born: 1870, Austria. Died: Jan. 1947, Vienna, Austria. Stage and screen actor.

Appeared in: **1932** Hirsekorn Greift Ein.

WALDIS, OTTO
Born: 1906, Germany. Died: Mar. 25, 1974, Hollywood, Calif. (?). (heart attack). Screen actor.

Appeared in: **1947** The Exile. **1948** Letter from an Unknown Woman; Berlin Express; Call Northside 777; The Vicious Circle. **1949** The Fighting O'Flynn (aka The O'Flynn); Border Incident; Bagdad; The Lovable Cheat. **1950** Woman from Headquarters. **1951** Bird of Paradise; Night into Morning; Secrets of Monte Carlo; The Whip Hand. **1952** The Black Castle; Anything Can Happen. **1953** Rebel City; Rogue's March; Flight to Tangier. **1954** Knock on

Wood; Port of Hell; Prince Valiant; The Iron Glove. **1955** Sincerely Yours; Desert Sands; Artists and Models. **1956** Man from Del Rio; Ride the High Iron. **1958** Attack of the 50 Ft. Woman. **1959** Pier 5, Havana. **1961** Judgment at Nuremberg; Nuremberg Trials (aka Hitler's Executioners). **1964** Das Phantom von Soho (The Phantom of Soho—US 1967).

WALDMULLER, LIZZI
Born: 1904, Knitterfeld, Tyrol. Died: 1945, Vienna, Austria (air raid). Screen, stage actress and singer. Entered films in 1931.

Appeared in: **1933** Lachende Erben. Other films: Die Spanische Fliege; Strafsache van Geldern; Liebe auf den Ersten Ton; Peer Gynt; Bel Ami; Casanova Heiratet; Traummusik; Alles fur Gloria; Frau Luna; Liebeskomodie; Die Nacht in Venedig; Ein Walzer mit Dir; Ein Mann wie Maximilian; Es Lebe die Liebe.

WALDOW, ERNST
Born: 1894, Germany. Died: June 5, 1964, Hamburg, Germany (heart attack). Stage and screen actor.

Appeared in: **1936** Wenn der Hahn Kraeht. **1938** Das Meadchen von Gestern Nacht (The Girl of Last Night); Die Kleine Suenderin (The Little Sinner); Streitum den Knaben Jo (Strife over the Boy Jo). **1939** Die Kluge Schwiegermutter (The Wise Mother-in-Law). **1949** The Affair Blum. **1954** Der Zarewitsch (US 1961). **1956** Du Bist Musik (US 1962). **1959** Ein Engel auf Erden (Angel on Earth—US 1966). **1960** Bumerang (aka Cry Double Cross—US 1962). **1963** Schneewittchen und die Sieben Gangler (Snow White and the Seven Jugglers).

WALDRIGE, HAROLD
Born: 1905, New Orleans, La. Died: June 26, 1957, New York, N.Y. Stage and screen actor.

Appeared in: **1922** The Ruling Passion. **1931** Five Star Final; June Moon; Sob Sister. **1932** The Heart of New York; Strangers of the Evening; High Pressure; Alias the Doctor; Play Girl; The Strange Love of Molly Louvain; The All American; False Faces. **1933** She Had to Say Yes; Devil's Mate; The Death Kiss; In the Money. **1934** Manhattan Love Song; Private Scandal; Easy to Love. **1935** Hitch Hike Lady; Slightly Static (short); Gigolette. **1936** Dancing Pirate; Three Men on a Horse. **1937** an Educational short.

WALDRON, CHARLES D.
Born: Dec. 23, 1874, Waterford, N.Y. Died: Mar. 4, 1946, Hollywood, Calif. Stage and screen actor. Father of actor Charles K. Waldron (dec. 1952).

Appeared in: **1921** Everyman's Price. **1935** Mary Burns, Fugitive; Wanderer of the Wasteland; The Great Impersonation; Crime and Punishment. **1936** The Garden of Allah; Career Woman; Ramona. **1937** A Doctor's Diary; My Dear Miss Aldrich; Navy Blue and Gold; It's All Yours; Escape by Night; The Emperor's Candlesticks. **1938** Kentucky; They're Always Caught (short); The Little Adventuress; Marie Antoinette. **1939** On Borrowed Time; The Real Glory. **1940** Three Faces West; Thou Shalt Not Kill; Remember the Night; Dr. Kildare's Strangest Case; The Refugee; Streets of Memories; The Stranger on the Third Floor; Untamed. **1941** The Devil and Miss Jones; The Case of the Black Parrot; The Nurse's Secret; Three Sons O'Guns; Rise and Shine. **1942** Random Harvest; Through Different Eyes; The Gay Sisters. **1943** The Song of Bernadette; The Adventures of Mark Twain; Mlle. Fifi. **1944** Black Parachute. **1946** The Fighting Guardsman; The Big Sleep; Dragonwyck.

WALDRON, CHARLES K.
Born: 1915. Died: Apr. 18, 1952, Los Angeles, Calif. (airplane crash). Screen actor. Son of actor Charles D. Waldron (dec. 1946).

WALDRON, EDNA
Born: 1913. Died: Aug. 24, 1940, Hollywood, Calif. (burns sustained in an attempt to save the life of a child whose clothing was afire). Screen actress.

WALDRON, ISABEL
Born: 1871. Died: Jan. 9, 1950, Mamaroneck, N.Y. Screen and stage actress. Married to stage actor Edward Emery (dec. 1938) and mother of actor John Emery (dec. 1964).

WALDRON, JACK
Born: 1893. Died: Nov. 21, 1969, New York, N.Y. (heart attack). Screen, stage and vaudeville actor.

Appeared in: **1928** A Little Breath of Broadway (short).

WALES, ETHEL
Born: 1881, New York, N.Y. Died: Feb. 15, 1952, Hollywood, Calif. Stage and screen actress. Entered films in 1920.

Appeared in: **1921** Miss Lulu Bett; After the Show. **1922** Nice People; The Old Homestead; Bobbed Hair; Is Matrimony a Failure?; The Bonded Woman; Bought and Paid For; Manslaughter; Our Leading Citizen. **1923** The Covered Wagon; The Marriage Maker; The Fog; Stepping Fast. **1924** The Bedroom Window; Revelation; The White Sin; Icebound; Lovers' Lane; Loving Lies;

Merton of the Movies; Which Shall It Be? **1925** Go Straight; Shattered Lives; Steppin' Out; Begger on Horseback; Don't Let Women Alone; The Overland Limited; When Husbands Flirt; The Wedding Song; Wandering Footsteps; The Monster. **1926** Bertha, the Sewing Machine Girl; Take It from Me; Made for Love; Ladies at Play. **1927** The Cradle Snatchers; The Country Doctor; Almost Human; The Wreck of the Hesperus; Stage Kisses; The Satin Woman; The Girl in the Pullman; My Friend from India. **1928** Tenth Avenue; Craig's Wife; The Masks of the Devil; The Perfect Crime; Ladies' Night in a Turkish Bath; On to Reno; Taxi 13. **1929** Blue Skies; The Saturday Night Kid; The Doctor's Secret; The Donovan Affair. **1930** Loose Ankles; Tom Sawyer; Girl in the Show; The Dude Wrangler; Under Montana Skies. **1931** Subway Express; The Flood; Criminal Code; Honeymoon Lane; Maker of Men. **1932** The Fighting Fool; Love in High Gear; The 13th Guest; Love Me Tonight; Klondike; Tangled Destinies; The Racing Strain; A Man's Land. **1933** The 11th Commandment; The Fighting Parson. **1934** The Mighty Barnum; The Crime Doctor. **1935** Another Face; Bar 20 Rides Again. **1936** Collegiate. **1938** The Gladiator. **1939** In Old Caliente; Days of Jesse James. **1940** Knights of the Range; Hidden Gold; Young Bill Hickok. **1941** Border Vigilantes. **1944** The Lumberjack. **1950** Tarnished.

WALKER, ARLENE
Born: 1919. Died: Apr. 15, 1973, New York. Screen, stage, radio and television actress.

WALKER, AURORA
Born: 1912, Mexico. Died: Jan. 2, 1964, Mexico. Screen actress.

Appeared in: **1940** Odio (Hate); Vivire Otra Vez (I Shall Live Again). **1955** This Strange Passion.

WALKER, CHARLOTTE
Born: 1878, Galveston, Tex. Died: Mar. 24, 1958, Kerville, Tex. Stage and screen actress.

Appeared in: **1915** Kindling. **1916** The Trail of the Lonesome Pine. **1917** Seven Deadly Sins (in one of the seven sequences). **1919** Eve in Exile. **1924** Classmates; The Lone Wolf; The Sixth Commandment. **1925** The Manicure Girl; The Midnight Girl. **1926** The Great Deception; The Savage. **1927** The Clown. **1928** Annapolis. **1929** South Sea Rose; Paris Bound. **1930** Scarlet Pages; Double Crossroads; Three Faces East; Lightnin'. **1931** Millie; Salvation Nell. **1933** Hotel Variety. **1941** Scattergood Meets Broadway.

WALKER, CHERYL
Born: Aug. 1, 1922, South Pasadena, Calif. Died: Oct. 24, 1971 (cancer). Screen actress. Queen of the 1938 Pasadena Tournament of Roses.

Appeared in: **1940** Chasing Trouble. **1943** Stage Door Canteen; Shadows on the Sage. **1944** Three is a Family; Three Little Sisters. **1945** It's a Pleasure; A Song for Miss Julie; Identity Unknown; How Do You Do? **1946** Murder is My Business; Larceny in Her Heart. **1948** Waterfront at Midnight.

WALKER, CHESTER W.
Died: Sept. 16, 1945, Okinawa (typhoon). Screen actor.

WALKER, CHRISTY
Born: 1898. Died: Oct. 29, 1918, New York, N.Y. (influenza). Screen actress.

WALKER, HELEN
Born: 1921, Worcester, Mass. Died: Mar. 10, 1968, North Hollywood, Calif. (cancer). Stage and screen actress.

Appeared in: **1942** Lucky Jordan. **1943** The Good Fellows. **1944** Abroad with Two Yanks; Man in Half-Moon Street. **1945** Duffy's Tavern; Murder, He Says. **1946** Brewster's Millions; Cluny Brown; Her Adventurous Night; Murder in the Music Hall; People Are Funny. **1947** Nightmare Alley; The Homestretch. **1948** Call Northside 777; My Dear Secretary; Nancy Goes to Rio. **1949** Impact. **1951** My True Story. **1952** Heaven Only Knows. **1953** Problem Girls. **1955** The Big Combo.

WALKER, JOHNNIE
Born: 1896, New York, N.Y. Died: Dec. 4, 1949, New York, N.Y. Screen, stage actor, film director, stage and film producer.

Appeared in: **1920** Over the Hill to the Poor House. **1921** Live Wires; The Jolt; Play Square; What Love Will Do. **1922** In the Name of the Law; The Sagebrush Trail; Captain Fly-by-Night; Extra! Extra!; The Third Alarm; My Dad. **1923** Fashionable Fakers; Broken Hearts of Broadway; Children of Dust; Shattered Reputations; Red Lights; The Fourth Musketeer; Mary of the Movies; The Mailman; Souls for Sale. **1924** The Spirit of the U.S.A.; Soiled; The Slanderers; Girls Men Forget; Galloping Hoofs (serial); Life's Greatest Game; Wine of Youth. **1925** The Scarlet West; Reckless Sex; Lilies of the Streets; Children of the Whirlwind; Lena Rivers; The Mad Dancer. **1926** Old Ironsides; So This Is Paris; Honesty—the Best Policy; The Earth Woman; Transcontinental Limited; Fangs of Justice; The Lightning Reporter; Morganson's Finish. **1927** Swell Head; A Boy of the Streets; Cross Breed; Pretty Clothes; The Princess on Broadway; Wolves of the Air; Rose of the Bowery; The Clown; Held by the Law; Snarl of Hate; Where the Trails Begin. **1928** Matinee Idol; So This Is

Love; Bare Knees. **1930** The Melody Man; Ladies in Love; Up the River; Girl of the Golden West; Ladies of Leisure. **1931** Enemies of the Law. **1932** Speaking out of Turn (short). **1934** Fantomas.

WALKER, JUNE
Born: 1904, New York, N.Y. Died: Feb. 3, 1966, Sherman Oaks, Calif. Screen, stage, radio and television actress.

Appeared in: **1921** Coincidence. **1930** War Nurse. **1942** Through Different Eyes. **1960** The Unforgiven. **1963** A Child Is Waiting.

WALKER, LILLIAN "DIMPLES"
Born: Apr. 21, 1888, Brooklyn, N.Y. Died: Oct. 10, 1975, Trinidad, West Indies. Screen, stage, vaudeville actress and film producer.

Appeared in: **1911** The Wager; The Second Honeymoon; Their Charming Mama; The Husking Bee; Testing His Courage. **1912** Alma's Champion; It All Came Out in the Wash; The Diamond Broach; Infatuation; Working for Hubby; Thou Shalt Not Covet; Leap Year Proposals; The Miracle; An Eventful Elopement; The Great Diamond Robbery; Pandora's Box; Mr. Bolter's Infatuation; The Suit of Armor; The Indian Mutiny; How Mr. Bullington Ran the House; An Elephant on Their Hands; Four Days a Widow; Reincarnation of Komar; While She Powdered Her Nose; Troublesome Stepdaughters; Stenographers Wanted. **1913** Love, Luck and Gasoline; The Right Man; The Mouse and the Lion; Those Troublesome Tresses; The Two Purses; The Feudists; Classmates' Frolic; Mr. Ford's Temper; The Final Justice; He Waited; Cutey and the Chorus Girls; Two Hearts that Beat as One; Three to One; Keeping Husbands Home; Which Way Did He Go?; Cutey's Waterloo; The Right Man; The Life Saver. **1914** Cutey's Vacation; Art for a Heart; Doctor Polly; The Speeder's Revenge; Love, Luck and Gasoline; Fanny's Melodrama; Eve's Daughter; The Persistent Mr. Prince; Lillian's Dilemma; Lily of the Valley; A Costume Piece; The Winning Trick; Bread Upon the Waters; The Girl at the Lunch Counter; The New Secretary. **1915** The Love Whip; Arthur Truman's Ward; Peggy of Fifth Avenue; The Capitulation of the Major; Lifting the Ban of Controversy; Breaking In; The Silent W; The Little Doll's Dressmaker; The Honeymoon Pact; Dimples and the Ring; The Guttersnipe; Playing the Ring; Hearts and the Highway; A Lilly in Bohemia; To Save Him for His Wife; Dimples, the Auto Salesgirl; A Keyboard Strategy; The Fire Escape; Green Stockings; Lillian's Husbands; The Shabbies; Save the Coupons. **1916** Mrs. Dane's Danger; Her Bad Quarter of an Hour; The Ordeal of Elizabeth; The Man Behind the Curtain; Hesper of the Mountains; The Dollar and the Law; The Kid; The Blue Envelope Mystery. **1917** Indiscretion; Sally in a Hurry; A Tale of Two Cities; Kitty Mackaye; Princess of Park Row; Lust of the Ages. **1918** A Grain of Dust; The Embarrassment of Riches. **1919** The Love Hunger; The White Man's Chance; The Better Wife; Joyous Liar. **1920** The $1,000,000 Reward (serial). **1921** The Woman God Changed; You and I. **1922** Love's Boomerang. **1934** Enlighten Your Daughter.

WALKER, NELLA
Born: Mar. 6, 1886, Chicago, Ill. Died: Mar. 21, 1971, Los Angeles, Calif. (heart disease). Screen, stage and vaudeville actress. Divorced from actor William Mack, with whom she appeared in vaudeville.

Appeared in: **1929** Seven Keys to Baldpate; The Vagabond Lover; Tanned Legs. **1930** Extravagance; What a Widow! **1931** The Public Defender; The Hot Heiress; Indiscreet; Daughter of the Dragon. **1932** Trouble in Paradise; Lady with a Past; They Call it Sin. **1933** 20,000 Years in Sing Sing; Second Hand Wife; Dangerously Yours; Humanity; Reunion in Vienna; This Day and Age; Going Hollywood; Ever in My Heart; House on 56th Street. **1934** Fashions of 1934; All of Me; Four Frightened People; Elmer and Elsie; The Ninth Guest; Change of Heart; Madame DuBarry; Big Hearted Herbert. **1935** Behold My Wife; The Woman in Red; McFadden's Flats; A Dog of Flanders; Going Highbrow; Red Salute; Coronado; The Right to Love; Bordertown. **1936** Small Town Girl; Captain January; Don't Turn 'em Loose. **1937** Three Smart Girls; Stella Dallas; 45 Fathers. **1938** Young Dr. Kildare; The Crime of Dr. Hallet; The Rage of Paris. **1939** The Saint Strikes Back; Three Smart Girls Grow Up; When Tomorrow Comes; In Name Only; Swanee River. **1940** The Saint Takes Over; Kitty Foyle; I Love You Again. **1941** Hellzapoppin; Repent at Leisure; Buck Privates; Kathleen; Back Street; A Girl, a Guy and a Gob. **1942** Kid Glove Killer; We Were Dancing. **1943** Air Raid Wardens; Hers to Hold; Wintertime. **1944** Take It or Leave It; In Society; Ladies in Washington; Murder in the Blue Room. **1945** A Guy, a Gal and a Pal; Follow That Woman. **1946** Two Sisters from Boston; The Locket. **1947** The Beginning or the End; Undercover Maisie; This Time for Keeps; That Hagen Girl. **1950** Nancy Goes to Rio. **1954** Sabrina.

WALKER, ROBERT "BOB" (Robert Donald Walker)
Born: June 18, 1888, Bethlehem, Pa. Died: Mar. 1954. Stage and screen actor. Do not confuse with actor Robert Walker (dec. 1951). Entered films with Kalem in 1915.

Appeared in: **1915** Children of Eve. **1916** The Light of Happiness; Gates of Eden; The Cossack Whip; The Littlest Magdalene. **1917** The Mortal Sin; Lady Barnacle; Aladdin's Other Lamp; The Girl Without a Soul; Blue Jeans; God's Law and a Man's; A Wife by Proxy. **1919** A Burglar by Proxy; The Lion Man (serial). **1921** White Oak. **1922** Broad Daylight; Reckless Chances. **1923** Itching

Palms; Why Women Remarry; The Drug Traffic. **1924** The Dancing Cheat; Battling Brewster (serial). **1925** A Daughter of the Sioux; Drug Store Cowboy; My Pal; The Outlaw's Daughter; The Rip Snorter; Warrior Gap; Ridin' Comet; Tonio, Son of the Sierras; The Mystery Box (serial). **1926** Deuce High; The Gallant Fool. **1927** Daring Deeds; Roaring Fires; Western Courage. **1928** The Code of the Scarlet; The Cowboy Cavalier; The Upland Rider. **1929** The Dream Melody; The Three Outcasts. **1930** Canyon Hawks; Phantom of the Desert; Ridin' Law; Westward Bound; The Fighting Legion. **1931** The Vanishing Legion (serial). **1935** Captured in Chinatown; Now or Never; Never too Late; The Crimson Trail; Outlawed Guns; The Throwback. **1936** The Black Clin (serial); Hair-Trigger Casey; Fast Bullets; Caryl of the Mountains; The Speed Reporter; The Clutching Hand (serial). **1937** Gunsmoke Ranch; The Mysterious Pilot (serial); Two-Fisted Bullets. **1939** El Diablo Rides. **1947** The Last Round-Up. **1949** Riders in the Sky.

WALKER, ROBERT (Robert Hudson Walker)
Born: Oct. 13, 1914, Utah. Died: Aug. 28, 1951, Santa Monica, Calif. (respiratory failure). Screen, stage and radio actor. Married to Barbara Ford. Divorced from actress Jennifer Jones and father of actor Robert Walker, Jr.

Appeared in: **1939** Winter Carnival. **1941** I'll Sell My Life. **1943** Bataan; Madame Curie. **1944** See Here, Private Hargrove; Since You Went Away; Thirty Seconds over Tokyo. **1945** The Clock; What Next, Corporal Hargrove?; Her Highness and the Bellboy; The Sailor Takes a Wife. **1946** Blue Skies; 'Til the Clouds Roll By. **1947** Song of Love; The Sea of Grass; The Beginning or the End. **1948** One Touch of Venus. **1950** Please Believe Me; The Skipper Surprised His Wife. **1951** Strangers on a Train; Vengeance Valley. **1952** My Son John.

WALKER, ROSE (Rose Walker Dowsey)
Born: 1907. Died: July 29, 1951, Manhasset, N.Y. (injuries from fall from building). Screen actress.

WALKER, SYD
Born: England. Died: Jan. 13, 1945, London, England. Screen, stage and radio actor.

Appeared in: **1924** Old Bill Through the Ages. **1934** Gift of Gab. **1935** Royal Cavalcade (aka Regal Cavalcade—US). **1936** A Universal short. **1937** Over She Goes; Let's Make a Night of It (US 1938). **1938** Oh Boy; Hold My Hand. **1939** What Would You Do, Chums?; The Gang's All Here (aka The Amazing Mr. Forest—US).

WALKER, TEX (Charles Herbert Walker)
Born: 1867. Died: Aug. 22, 1947, Los Angeles, Calif. (pneumonia). Stage and screen actor.

WALKER, VIRGINIA
Born: 1916. Died: Dec. 22, 1946, Hollywood, Calif. Screen actress. Divorced from film producer Howard Hawks.

Appeared in: **1938** Bringing up Baby.

WALKER, WALTER
Born: 1864. Died: Dec. 4, 1947. Screen actor. Do not confuse with Walter "Wally" Walker (dec. 1975).

WALKER, WALTER "WALLY"
Born: 1901. Died: Aug. 7, 1975, Woodland Hills, Calif. (stroke). Screen actor and extra. Entered films in 1920.

Appeared in: **1921** The Chicken in the Case. **1922** The Darling of the Rich. **1926** Black Bird. **1929** Great Power. **1931** Reaching for the Moon; A Tailor Made Man; Annabelle's Affairs; Rebound; Common Law; New Adventures of Get Rich Quick Wallingford. **1932** Tomorrow and Tomorrow; Two Seconds; The Rich are Always With Us; The Woman in Room 13; Letty Lynton; Two Against the World; Life Begins; The Last Mile; You Said a Mouthful; The Conquerers; The Kid from Spain; No Man of Her Own; Fireman, Save My Child; American Madness; Blessed Event. **1933** I Love That Man; Jennie Gerhart; I'm no Angel; Sitting Pretty; Mary Stevens, MD; I Loved a Woman; Female; Flying Down to Rio; The Billion Dollar Scandal; From Hell to Heaven; The Great Jasper; Our Betters; The House on 56th Street. **1934** You Can't Buy Everything; Bedside; A Lost Lady; The Count of Monte Cristo; Mrs. Wiggs of the Cabbage Patch; The Gay Bride; Babbitt. **1935** While the Patient Slept; Sons of Steel; Front Page Woman; Dangerous; Magnificent Obsession. **1936** Everybody's Old Man; Yours for the Asking. **1937** Women Men Marry. **1938** The Cowboy and the Lady. **1946** Ginger. **1948** Docks of New Orleans; I Wouldn't Be in Your Shoes.

WALL, DAVID V.
Born: 1870. Died: June 1, 1938, New York, N.Y. Screen and stage actor.

Appeared in: **1922** When the Desert Calls. **1924** Pied Piper Malone.

WALL, GERALDINE
Born: 1913. Died: June 22, 1970, Woodland Hills, Calif. (pneumonia). Screen, stage and television actress.

Appeared in: **1944** Black Magic; Winged Victory. **1945** Valley of Decision. **1946** Love Laughs at Andy Hardy; Boys' Ranch. **1947** Dark Delusion. **1948** Scudda Hoo!, Scudda Hay!; Green Grass of Wyoming; Beyond Glory. **1949** Alias Nick Beal; Everybody Does It; The Green Promise. **1950** Mister 880; Thelma Jordon; There's a Girl in My Heart. **1951** Appointment with Danger. **1953** By the Light of the Silvery Moon. **1956** The Man in the Gray Flannel Suit. **1957** An Affair to Remember. **1958** This Earth Is Mine; Mardi Gras. **1964** One Man's Way.

WALLACE, BERYL
Born: 1910. Died: June 17, 1948, near Mt. Carmel, Pa. (plane crash). Screen actress. Divorced from actor Milton Berle.

Appeared in: **1934** Murder at the Vanities. **1938** Air Devils. **1939** The Women. **1942** Sunset on the Desert. **1943** The Kansan. **1944** Enemy of Women; The Woman of the Town.

WALLACE, BILL (William Lally)
Born: 1908. Died: Aug. 20, 1956, Hollywood, Calif. (heart attack). Screen actor and film editor.

WALLACE, EDNA. See EDNA WALLACE HOPPER

WALLACE, ETHEL LEE
Born: 1888, Springfield, Mo. Died: Sept. 7, 1956, Springfield, Mo. Stage and screen actress. Appeared in silents.

WALLACE, GEORGE
Born: 1894, Aberdeen, New South Wales. Died: Nov. 1960, Sydney, Australia. Screen, stage, vaudeville, television actor, song writer, screenwriter and playwright. Billed with Dinks Paterson in a vaudeville act known as "Dinks and Onkus." Father of actor George Wallace, Jr. Do not confuse with U.S. actor George Wallace.

Appeared in: **1934** A Ticket in Tatts. **1938** Let George Do It.

WALLACE, GUY
Born: 1913. Died: Aug. 29, 1967. Screen actor and television announcer.

WALLACE, INEZ
Died: June 28, 1966, Cleveland, Ohio. Screen, stage actress and screenwriter. Appeared in silents.

WALLACE, MAUDE
Born: 1894. Died: Apr. 23, 1952, Hollywood, Calif. Screen, vaudeville and television actress. Entered films approx. 1947. Billed in vaudeville with her sister, Myrtle, as the "Hollingsworth Twins" and later billed as part of the "Towers and Wallace" vaudeville team.

Appeared in: **1951** Elopement; Love Nest; People Will Talk. **1952** Scarlet Angel; We're Not Married; Stars and Stripes Forever.

WALLACE, MAY (May Maddox)
Born: 1877. Died: Dec. 11, 1938, Los Angeles, Calif. (heart disease). Screen and vaudeville actress.

Appeared in: **1921** The Cup of Life; My Lady Friends. **1923** Dollar Devils; Gimme. **1924** The Reckless Age; Oh, You Tony! **1929** Painted Faces; Skirt Shy (short). **1931** Love Business (short); Mama Loves Papa (short). **1932** The following shorts: Readin' and Writin'; Free Eats; Pooch; Young Ironsides; You're Telling Me; County Hospital. **1933** What's Your Racket?; Kid from Borneo (short); Twice Two (short—voice). **1934** The Chases of Pimple Street (short). **1935** Beginner's Luck (short); Okay Toots! (short). **1936** The Sky Parade; Arbor Day (short). **1937** Midnight Madonna; Roamin' Holiday (short).

WALLACE, MILTON
Born: 1888. Died: Feb. 16, 1956, Hollywood, Calif. Screen, stage and vaudeville actor.

Appeared in: **1934** Kiss and Make Up; The Mighty Barnum. **1944** None but the Lonely Heart; Seven Doors to Death. **1945** The Lost Weekend. **1947** Kiss of Death.

WALLACE, MORGAN
Born: July 26, 1888, Lompoc, Calif. Died: Dec. 12, 1953, Tarzana, Calif. Screen, stage actor, film, stage producer and playwright.

Appeared in: **1921** Dream Street (film debut). **1922** Orphans of the Storm; One Exciting Night. **1923** The Dangerous Maid; The Fighting Blade. **1924** Daring Love; Reckless Romance; Sandra; Torment; A Woman Who Sinned. **1930** Sisters; Up the River; Big Money. **1931** It Pays to Advertise; Safe in Hell; Alexander Hamilton; Women Go on Forever; Smart Money; The Unholy Garden; Expensive Women. **1932** Hell's House; Grand Hotel; Lady and Gent; Blonde Venus; Wild Girl; Steady Company; Fast Companions; The Final Edition; The Mouthpiece. **1933** Smoke Lightning; Song of Songs; Terror Abroad; Jennie Gerhardt; Mama Loves Papa; Above the Clouds. **1934** The Trumpet Blows; It's a Gift; Cheating Cheaters; Many Happy Returns; The Merry Widow; We Live Again; I Believed in You. **1935** Hit and Run Driver (short); Murder on a Honeymoon; The Devil Is a Woman; Dante's Inferno; Headline Woman; Confidential; Thunder Mountain; $1,000 a Minute. **1936** Mister Cinderella; Love on a Bet; Sutter's Gold; Human Cargo; Fury. **1937** Charlie Chan at the Olympics; The Californian; Under Suspicion; House of Secrets. **1938** Numbered Woman; Gang Bullets; The Lady in the Morgue; Mr. Moto Takes a Vacation; Woman against Woman; Billy the Kid Returns. **1939** Mr. Moto Takes a Vacation The Mystery of Mr. Wong; The Star Maker. **1940** I Love You Again; Three Men from Texas; Ellery Queen, Master Detective. **1941** In Old Colorado; Scattergood Meets Broadway. **1945** I'll Remember April; Song of the Sarong; Dick Tracy. **1946** The Falcon's Alibi.

WALLEN, SIGURD

Born: 1884, Sweden. Died: Mar. 20, 1947, Stockholm, Sweden. Screen, stage actor and film director.

Appeared in: **1931** Brokiga Blad. **1932** Roeda Dagen. **1934** Pattersson and Bendel. **1938** Karl Fredrik Reigns; John Ericsson Victor of Hampton Roads. **1939** Familjen Andersson (The Anderson Family); Med Folket Foer Fosterlandet; Du Gamla, Du Fria (Thou Old, Thou Free). **1945** Crime and Punishment (US 1948).

WALLER, THOMAS "FATS"

Born: 1904, New York, N.Y. Died: Dec. 15, 1943, Kansas City, Mo. (pneumonia). Black pianist, screen, radio, vaudeville actor, bandleader and songwriter.

Appeared in: **1935** Hooray for Love. **1936** King of Burlesque. **1943** Stormy Weather.

WALLING, EFFIE B.

Born: 1879. Died: June 9, 1961, Berkeley, Calif. Screen and stage actress. Entered films with DeMille in 1919.

WALLINGTON, JIMMY (James S. Wallington)

Born: Sept. 15, 1907, Rochester, N.Y. Died: Dec. 22, 1972, Fairfax, Va. Screen actor and radio announcer. Married to dancer Anita Furman (dec. 1935) and later married and divorced actress Betty Jane Cooper. Married to Erna Wallington.

Appeared in: **1932** The Big Broadcast. **1934–35** Stranger Than Fiction (shorts). **1935** A Vitaphone short. **1938** Start Cheering; Hollywood Stadium Mystery. **1951** Joe Palooka in the Triple Cross.

WALLOCK, EDWIN N.

Born: 1878, Council Bluffs, Iowa. Died: Feb. 4, 1951. Stage and screen actor.

Appeared in: **1917** Even as You and I. **1918** The Price Mark. **1921** The Ace of Hearts; Kazan; The Struggle. **1922** Bing Bang Boom; I Can Explain. **1923** Eyes of the Forest; The Hunchback of Notre Dame.

WALLS, TOM

Born: Feb. 18, 1883, Northampton, England. Died: Nov. 27, 1949, Edwell, England. Screen, stage actor, stage producer and film director. Father of actor Tom Walls, Jr.

Appeared in: **1930** Canaries Sometimes Sing; On Approval; Rookery Nook (aka One Embarrassing Night—US). **1931** Plunder. **1932** A Night Like This; Leap Year; Thark. **1933** The Blarney Stone (aka The Blarney Kiss—US); A Cuckoo in the Nest; Just Smith; Turkey Time. **1934** A Cup of Kindness; Lady in Danger. **1935** Fighting Stock; Storm Weather (US 1936); Me and Marlborough; Foreign Affaires. **1936** Pot Luck; Dishonour Bright. **1937** For Valour. **1938** Second Best Bed; Crackerjack (aka The Man with a Hundred Faces—US); Strange Boarders; Old Iron. **1943** They Met in the Dark (US 1945); Undercover (aka Underground Guerillas—US 1944). **1944** Halfway House (US 1945); Love Story (aka A Lady Surrenders—US 1947). **1945** Johnny Frenchman (US 1946). **1946** This Man is Mine. **1947** Master of Bankdam (US 1949); While I Live. **1948** Spring in Park Lane (US 1949). **1949** Maytime in Mayfair (US 1952); The Interrupted Journey (US 1951).

WALLY, GUS (Gustav Wallenberg)

Born: 1904, Stockholm, Sweden. Died: Mar. 3, 1966, Goquete, Panama. Screen, stage actor and stage producer. Entered films with Paramount in 1936.

WALPOLE, HUGH

Born: 1884, Auckland, New Zealand. Died: June 1, 1941, Brackenburn, England (heart attack). Novelist, screen actor and screenwriter.

Appeared in: **1935** David Copperfield.

WALSH, BILLY

Died: June 16, 1952, Brooklyn, N.Y. Screen, vaudeville and radio actor. Appeared in vaudeville as part of acts known as "Walsh, Reed and Walsh," "Walsh, Daly and Walsh," and "Walsh Bros." Entered films with Sennett in 1915 and appeared in Keystone comedies.

WALSH, BLANCHE

Born: 1874. Died: Oct. 31, 1915, Cleveland, Ohio. Screen and stage actress.

Appeared in: **1912** Resurrection.

WALSH, FRANK (Miles Standish March)

Born: 1860. Died: July 19, 1932, New York, N.Y. Screen, stage and vaudeville actor.

Appeared in: **1924** America. **1927** The Joy Girl.

WALSH, THOMAS H.

Born: 1863. Died: Apr. 25, 1925, N.Y. Screen, stage and circus actor.

Appeared in: **1914** The Trey O'Hearts (serial).

WALTER, WILFRID

Born: Mar. 2, 1882, Ripon, England. Died: July 9, 1958, Ashtead, England. Screen, stage actor, playwright and stage producer. Father of actor Richard Walter.

Appeared in: **1938** Owd Bob (aka To the Victor—US); Convict 99. **1939** Dark Eyes of London (aka The Human Monster—US 1940); A Window in London (aka Lady in Distress—US 1942). **1940** Night Train to Munich (aka Gestapo and aka Night Train—US). **1946** Caesar and Cleopatra.

WALTERS, DOROTHY

Born: 1877. Died: Apr. 17, 1934, New York, N.Y. (bronchial pneumonia). Screen, stage and vaudeville actress.

Appeared in: **1918** Little Miss Hoover. **1919** Misleading Widow; Woman, Woman. **1920** Away Goes Prudence; Flying Pat. **1921** Good References; The City of Silent Men; Beyond Price. **1922** The Light in the Dark; Received Payment. **1924** The Confidence Man; The Hoosier Schoolmaster; Pied Piper Malone. **1925** A Man Must Live; The Street of Forgotten Men. **1926** A Kiss for Cinderella.

WALTERS, JACK

Born: 1885, Kans. Died: Jan. 1944, Hollywood, Calif. Screen actor. Entered films in 1913.

Appeared in: **1919** Roped; Ace of the Saddle. **1920** Hitchin' Posts. **1921** A Daughter of the Law; Sure Fire. **1922** Headin' North; The Better Man Wins; Caught Bluffing; The Galloping Kid. **1923** McGuire of the Mounted. **1924** Hoodman Blind. **1928** Wild West Romance.

WALTERS, LAURA

Born: 1894. Died: Apr. 10, 1934, Toledo, Ohio. Screen and stage actress.

WALTERS, MRS. GEORGE B.

Born: England. Died: Feb. 21, 1916, New York, N.Y. Screen and stage actress.

Appeared in: **1912** An Irish Girl's Love.

WALTERS, PATRICIA W.

Died: Dec. 31, 1967, Long Beach, Calif. Stage and screen actress. Daughter of actor Bert Wheeler (dec. 1968).

Appeared in: **1951** The River.

WALTHALL, HENRY B.

Born: Mar. 16, 1878, Shelby City, Ala. Died: June 17, 1936, near Monrovia, Calif. (chronic illness). Stage and screen actor. Married to actress Mary Charleston (dec. 1961).

Appeared in: **1909** In Old Kentucky; A Convict's Sacrifice; The Sealed Room; 1776, or the Hessian Renegades; Pippa Passes; Leather Stocking; Fools of Fate; A Corner in Wheat; In Little Italy; The Call; The Honor of His Family; On the Reef; The Cloister's Touch. **1910** In Old California; The House with Closed Shutters; Ramona; His Last Burglary; The Converts; Gold Is Not All; The Gold Seekers; Thou Shalt Not; The Face at the Window; The Usurer; The Sorrows of the Unfaithful; In Life's Cycle; A Summer Idyll. **1912** The Inner Circle; Oil and Water; A Change of Spirit; Friends; A Feud in the Kentucky Hills; In the Aisles of the Wild; The One She Loved; My Baby; The Informer; The Burglar's Dilemma; The God Within. **1913** Judith of Bethulia; Love in an Apartment Hotel; Broken Ways; Her Mother's Oath; The Sheriff's Baby; The Little Tease; The Wanderer; Death's Marathon; The Battle of Elderberry Gulch; During the Round-Up. **1914** The Avenging Conscience; Home Sweet Home. **1915** Birth of a Nation; The Raven; Ghosts; Great Divide. **1916** The Sting of Victory; The Strange Case of Mary Page. **1918** Robe of Honor; Great Love. **1919** The False Faces. **1920** Splendid Hazard. **1921** Parted Curtains. **1922** The Able Minded Lady; One Clear Call; The Kick Back; The Long Chance; The Marriage Chance; Flowers of the North. **1923** Gimme; Boy of Mine; Face on the Barroom Floor; The Unknown Purple. **1924** Single Wives; The Bowery Bishop; The Woman on the Jury. **1925** The Golden Bed; Simon the Jester. **1926** Road to Mandalay; The Scarlet Letter; The Barrier; Everybody's Acting; The Ice Flood; Three Faces East; The Unknown Soldier; The Plastic Age. **1927** Wings; Fighting Love; London after Midnight. **1928** Love Me and the World Is Mine; Freedom of the Press; Man From Headquarters; Retribution (short). **1929** In Old California (and 1910 version); Speakeasy; The Bridge of San Luis Rey; Blaze O'Glory; Stark Mad; Phantom in the House; Black Magic; The River of Romance; The Jazz Age; Street Corners; The Trespasser. **1930** Abraham Lincoln; The Payoff (short); Temple Tower; Love Trader; Tol'able David. **1931** Is There Justice?; Anybody's Blonde. **1932** Hotel Continental; Police Court; Strange Interlude; Alias Mary Smith; Chandu the Magician; Klondike; Cabin in the Cotton; Central Park; Me and My Gal; Fame Street; Ride Him, Cowboy. **1933** The Sin of Nora Moran; 42nd Street; Laughing at Life; Whispering Shadow (serial); Self Defense; Flaming Signal; Somewhere in Sonora; Headline Shooter; Her Forgotten Past. **1934** Men in White; Judge Priest; Viva, Villa!; The Scarlet Letter (and 1926 version); Change of Heart; Dark Hazard; Beggars in Ermine; Operator 13; Murder in the Museum; A Girl of the Limberlost; The Lemon Drop Kid; Love Time; City Park; Bachelor of Arts. **1935** A Tale of Two Cities; Dante's Inferno; Helldorado. **1936** China Clipper; The Mine with the Iron Door; Hearts in Bondage; The Last Outlaw; The Devil-Doll; The Garden Murder Case.

WALTON, DOUGLAS (J. Douglas Duder)
Born: Woodstock, Toronto, Canada. Died: Nov. 15, 1961, N.Y. Stage and screen actor.

Appeared in: **1931** Over the Hill; Body and Soul. **1933** The Secret of Madame Blanche; Looking Forward; Cavalcade. **1934** The Lost Patrol; Madame Spy; Murder in Trinidad; Shock; The Count of Monte Cristo; Charlie Chan in London. **1935** Captain Hurricane; The Dark Angel; Hitchhike Lady; The Bride of Frankenstein. **1936** The Garden Murder Case; I Conquer the Sea; Mary of Scotland; Thank You, Jeeves; Camille. **1937** Damaged Goods; Wallaby Jim of the Islands; Flight from Glory; A Nation Aflame. **1938** Storm over Bengal. **1939** The Story of Vernon and Irene Castle; The Sun Never Sets; Bad Lands. **1940** Raffles; Northwest Passage; The Long Voyage Home; Too Many Girls. **1941** Singapore Woman; Hurry, Charlie, Hurry! **1942** Jesse James, Jr. **1944** Murder My Sweet. **1945** Bring on the Girls; The Picture of Dorian Gray. **1946** Kitty; Dick Tracy vs. Cueball. **1947** High Conquest; High Tide. **1949** Secret of St. Ives.

WALTON, FRED (Frederick Heming)
Born: 1865, England. Died: Dec. 28, 1936, Los Angeles, Calif. (pneumonia). Stage and screen actor. Entered films in 1924.

Appeared in: **1924** The Fast Set. **1925** New Brooms; She Wolves; Marriage in Transit. **1926** The City; 30 Below Zero; The Splendid Crime. **1927** The Wise Wife; Almost Human; His Dog; The Little Adventuress. **1928** The House of Shame. **1929** Below the Deadline; South of Panama; Circumstantial Evidence; Dynamite. **1930** The Last Dance; Sin Takes a Holiday. **1931** Kiki; The Big Gamble. **1935** Two Sinners. **1936** Little Lord Fauntleroy; The House of a Thousand Candles; Dracula's Daughter.

WALTON, VERA
Born: 1891. Died: Sept. 1, 1965, New York, N.Y. (auto accident). Screen, stage, vaudeville and television actress. Appeared in a song and dance vaudeville act billed as "Now and Then."

Appeared in: **1957** A Face in the Crowd. **1960** Butterfield 8.

WAN, MME. SUL TE (Nellie Conley)
Born: 1873. Died: Feb. 1, 1959, Hollywood, Calif. Black screen actress. Entered films in 1914 with Griffith.

Appeared in: **1958** The Buccaneer.

WANGEL, HEDWIG
Born: 1875, Berlin, Germany. Died: Mar. 12, 1961, Rendsburg, West Germany. Stage and screen actress.

Appeared in: **1929** Rasputin. **1932** Pension Schoeller.

WANZER, ARTHUR
Died: Jan. 1949, Hollywood, Calif. Screen and vaudeville actor. Appeared in vaudeville as part of "Arthur Wanzer and Maybelle Palmer" team.

Appeared in: **1930** Dance with Me. **1933** Soldiers of the Storm; Unknown Valley. **1934** Tomorrow's Children. **1936** The Gentleman from Louisiana.

WARAM, PERCY, C.
Born: 1881, Kent, England. Died: Oct. 5, 1961, Huntington, N.Y. Screen, stage and vaudeville actor.

Appeared in: **1939** One Third of a Nation. **1944** Ministry of Fear. **1947** It Had to Be You; The Late George Apley. **1950** The Big Hangover. **1957** A Face in the Crowd.

WARD, BEATRICE
Born: 1890. Died: Dec. 11, 1964, Hollywood, Calif. Screen actress. Entered films during silents.

WARD, CARRIE (Carrie Clarke-Ward)
Born: 1862, Virginia City, Nev. Died: Feb. 6, 1926, Hollywood, Calif. Stage and screen actress.

Appeared in: **1919** Why Smith Left Home. **1920** Old Lady 31. **1921** One Wild Week; Sham; Black Roses; Her Winning Way; Bob Hampton of Placer; The Love Charm. **1922** Ashes; The Top of New York; Penrod; Through a Glass Window. **1923** Breaking into Society; Soul of the Beast; Scaramouche. **1924** Girls Men Forget; Thundering Hoofs; His Hour. **1925** The Awful Truth; The Eagle; A Fool and His Money; The Man in Blue; Who Cares; Rose of the World; The Only Thing; The Golden Cocoon.

WARD, CLARA
Born: Apr. 21, 1927, Philadelphia, Pa. Died: Jan. 16, 1973, Los Angeles, Calif. (stroke). Screen actress and singer. Do not confuse with actress Clara Clark Ward.

Appeared in: **1967** Spree. **1968** A Time to Sing.

WARD, FANNIE
Born: 1872, St. Louis, Mo. Died: Jan. 27, 1952, New York, N.Y. (cerebral hemorrhage). Screen, stage and vaudeville actress. Married to actor Jack Dean (dec. 1950).

Appeared in: **1915** The Cheat. **1916** Each Hour a Pearl; Tennessee's Pardner. **1917** The School for Husbands; Betty to the Rescue; The Winning of Sally Temple; Unconquered; Her Strange Wedding. **1918** A Japanese Nightingale; The Yellow Ticket. **1919** Our Better Selves; Common Clay. **1921** She Played and Paid. **1922** The Hardest Way. **1929** The Miracle Woman (short).

WARD, "HAP," SR. (John Thomas O'Donnell)
Born: 1868. Died: Jan. 3, 1944, N.Y. Screen, stage and vaudeville actor. Father of actor "Hap" Ward, Jr. (dec. 1940). Was half of vaudeville act billed as "Earl and Ward" (even though his name was O'Donnell, he took name of the original team partner, Ward, whom he replaced in the act). He later teamed with Harry Vokes in a blackface act billed as "Harold and Percy."

Appeared in: **1929** Fugitives.

WARD, "HAP," JR. (John Thomas O'Donnell)
Born: 1899. Died: July 9, 1940. Screen actor. Son of actor "Hap" Ward, Sr. (dec. 1944).

WARD, HARRY (Angelo De Michele)
Born: 1890. Died: Apr. 16, 1952, Los Angeles, Calif. Screen actor. Appeared in vaudeville with brother Anthony in an act known as "Ward and Van."

WARD, KATHERINE CLARE
Born: 1871. Died: Oct. 14, 1938, Hollywood, Calif. Screen, stage and vaudeville actress. Entered films approx. 1923.

Appeared in: **1927** The Magic Garden. **1928** Beyond London Lights. **1929** Drag; The Isle of Lost Ships; Midnight Daddies. **1930** Call of the West; Strictly Modern. **1931** The Conquering Horde; Three Girls Lost. **1932** Three Wise Girls; Make Me a Star; Vanity Street. **1933** Lilly Turner; Son of Kong. **1934** Once to Every Woman; White Lies; an RKO short; an MGM short.

WARD, LUCILLE
Born: 1880. Died: Aug. 8, 1952, Dayton, Ohio. Screen and stage actress.

Appeared in: **1917** American Film Mfg. Co. films. **1921** High Gear Jeffrey; The Traveling Salesman. **1922** The Woman He Loved. **1923** East Side, West Side; Sixty Cents an Hour. **1924** The Girl in the Limousine; Sporting Youth. **1925** Oh, Doctor!; His Majesty, Bunker Bean; California Straight Ahead; A Woman of the World. **1926** Skinner's Dress Suit. **1930** What a Man. **1932** The Purchase Price; Rebecca of Sunnybrook Farm. **1933** Zoo in Budapest; Marriage on Approval; Lilly Turner. **1934** Little Miss Marker. **1935** Old Sawbones (short). **1936** The Leavenworth Case; The Return of Jimmy Valentine; The Harvester. **1938** Mother Carey's Chickens; Sons of the Legion. **1939** First Love. **1940** Christmas in July. **1944** Henry Aldrich's Little Secret.

WARD, PEGGY
Born: 1878. Died: Mar. 8, 1960, Hollywood, Calif. Screen, stage and television actress.

WARD, SAM (George Herman Jacobs)
Born: 1889. Died: May 1, 1952, Los Angeles, Calif. Screen, stage, burlesque and vaudeville actor. Appeared in Hal Roach comedies.

WARD, SOLLY
Born: 1891. Died: May 17, 1942, Hollywood, Calif. Screen, stage, burlesque and radio actor.

Appeared in: **1927** At the Party (short). **1932–33** Paramount shorts. **1937** Flight from Glory; Living on Love; Danger Patrol; She's Got Everything. **1938** Everybody's Doing It; Maid's Night Out; Blind Alibi. **1939** Conspiracy.

WARD, VICTORIA
Born: 1914, Canada. Died: Nov. 6, 1957, Hollywood, Calif. Screen, stage and television actress.

Appeared in: **1956** D Day, the Sixth of June.

WARD, WARWICK (Warwick Mannon)
Born: 1891, St. Ives, England. Died: Dec. 9, 1967. Screen, stage actor and film producer. Appeared in British and German films.

Appeared in: **1919** The Silver Lining. **1920** Mary Latimer, Nun; Wuthering Heights; Build Thy House; The Manchester Man; The Call of the Road. **1921** The Diamond Necklace; Belphegor the Mountebank; Demos (aka Why Men Forget—US); Corinthian Jack; The Mayor of Casterbridge; Little Meg's Children; Handy Andy; The Golden Dawn. **1922** The Lilac Sunbonnet; Tell Your Children; The Call of the East; Petticoat Loose. **1923** The Lady Owner; The Hotel Mouse; Bulldog Drummond. **1924** The Great Turf Mystery; Southern Love (aka A Woman's Secret—US); Hurricane Hutch in Many Adventures; The Prude's Fall; Human Desires; The Money Habit. **1925** Madame Sans-Gene; Variete (Variety—US 1926). **1926** The Woman Tempted (US 1928). **1927** His Supreme Sacrifice (reissue of The Call of the East—1922). **1928** Ara and the Grasshopper; The White Sheik (aka King's Mate—US 1929); Maria Marten. **1929** After the Verdict (US 1930); The Woman He Scorned; Die Wunderbare Luge der Nina Petrowna (The Wonderful Lie of Nina Petrovna—US 1930); The Informer; The Three Kings; Looping the Loop; The Dancer of Barcelona. **1930** The Yellow Mask; Birds of Prey (aka The Perfect Alibi—US 1931); The Strange Case of District Attorney M. **1931** The Loves of Ariane (aka Ariane—US 1934); To Oblige a Lady; Number Please; Deadlock; Stamboul; Man of Mayfair. **1932** The Callbox Mystery; Life Goes On (aka Sorry You've Been Troubled); Blind Spot. **1933** F.P. 1. **1938** Secrets of F.P. 1 (rerelease of F.P. 1 1933). **1952** Elstree Story (narration).

WARDE, ANTHONY
Born: 1909. Died: Jan. 8, 1975, Hollywood, Calif. Screen and stage actor.

Appeared in: **1937** Escape by Night. **1938** Flash Gordon's Trip to Mars (serial); The Affairs of Annabel; Come On, Leathernecks; What Price Safety? (short); Law of the Underworld. **1939** Buck Rogers (serial); Mr. Moto Takes a Vacation; Oklahoma Frontier; Twelve Crowded Hours; Affairs of Annabel. **1940** So You Won't Talk; Chip of the Flying U. **1941** Dick Tracy vs. Crime, Inc. (serial); The Spider Returns (serial); Ridin' on a Rainbow. **1942** King of the Mounties (serial); The Man With Two Lives. **1943** Riders of the Deadline; The Masked Marvel (serial). **1944** The Great Alaskan Mystery (serial); The Mummy's Ghost; The Chinese Cat; Where Are Your Children?; Are These Our Parents?; Dixie Jamboree; Machine Gun Mama; Sensations of 1945; Shadow of Suspicion; Mystery of the River Boat (serial). **1945** Brenda Starr, Reporter (serial); The Monster and the Ape (serial); The Cisco Kid Returns; Here Come the Co-Eds; The Purple Monster Strikes (serial); Allotment Wives; Paris Underground; There Goes Kelly; Captain Tugboat Annie; Who's Guilty? (serial). **1946** Hop Harrigan (serial); King of the Forest Rangers (serial); The Wife of Monte Cristo; Black Market Babies; Dark Alibi; Secrets of a Sorority Girl; Wife Wanted; The Missing Lady; Don Richard Returns. **1947** The Black Widow (serial); King of the Bandits; Killer Dill; High Tide; The 13th Hour; Bells of San Fernando. **1948** Dangers of the Canadian Mounties (serial); Congo Bill (serial); The Big Punch; Stage Struck. **1949** Trail of the Yukon; The Fighting Fools. **1950** Radar Patrol vs. Spy King (serial). **1951** Roaring City. **1952** The Atomic City. **1953** Houdini; Raiders of the Seven Seas. **1954** Rear Window; Day of Triumph. **1955** Strategic Air Command. **1956** The Man Who Knew Too Much. **1959** Inside the Mafia. **1964** The Carpetbaggers.

WARDE, ERNEST C.
Born: 1874, Liverpool, England. Died: Sept. 9, 1923, Los Angeles, Calif. Screen, stage actor and stage director.

Appeared in: **1916** King Lear. **1917** Fires of Youth; The Heart of Ezra Greer. **1923** Ruth of the Range (serial); Blow Your Own Horn.

WARDE, FREDERICK B.
Born: 1872, England. Died: Feb. 7, 1935, Brooklyn, N.Y. (heart trouble). Stage and screen actor.

Appeared in: **1913** Richard III. **1916** King Lear. **1917** Vicar of Wakefield; Under False Colors. **1921** Silas Marner. **1925** A Lover's Oath.

WARDELL, HARRY
Born: 1879. Died: Sept. 17, 1948, Hollywood, Calif. (heart attack). Screen, vaudeville actor and screenwriter. Originated phrases such as: "Life is just a bowl of cherries" and "I'm the matzo ball in the soup of life."

Appeared in: **1934** The Mighty Barnum.

WARE, HELEN
Born: 1877, San Francisco, Calif. Died: Jan. 25, 1939, Carmel, Calif. (throat infection). Stage and screen actress. Married to actor, writer and artist Frederic Burt (dec. 1943).

Appeared in: **1917** The Garden of Allah. **1920** The Deep Purple. **1921** Colorado Pluck. **1922** Fascination. **1923** Mark of the Beast. **1925** Soul Fire. **1928** Napoleon's Barber. **1929** Half Way to Heaven; The Virginian; New Year's Eve; Speakeasy. **1930** Slightly Scarlet; One Night at Susie's; Abraham Lincoln; She's My Weakness; Tol'able David. **1931** I Take This Woman; The Reckless Hour. **1932** Night of June 13th. **1933** Ladies They Talk About; Girl Missing; The Keyhole; She Had to Say Yes; Warrior's Husband. **1934** Sadie McKee; That's Gratitude; Flaming Gold; Romance in Manhattan. **1935** The Raven; Secret of the Chateau.

WARE, WALTER
Born: 1880, Boston, Mass. Died: Jan. 3, 1936, Hollywood, Calif. Stage and screen actor.

Appeared in: **1921** The Family Closet. **1935** Captain Blood; Kind Lady.

WARFIELD, IRENE
Born: 1896. Died: 1961. Stage and screen actress.

Appeared in: **1913** The Boomerang; Autumn Love. **1914** Chains of Bondage; Speak No Evil; Shadows; Life's Weaving; A Vagabond Cupid. **1915** Simon the Jester. **1916** The Voice in the Wilderness; The Three Scratch Clue; A Man for A' That. **1917** The Mirror.

WARING, MARY
Born: 1892. Died: Jan. 10, 1964, Washington, D.C. Screen and radio actress. Appeared in films from 1920–24.

WARNER, GLORIA (Gloria Kelly)
Born: 1915, N.Y. Died: June 8, 1934, Los Angeles, Calif. (anemia). Screen, stage actress and dancer.

Appeared in: School for Romance (short).

WARNER, H. B. (Henry Byran W. Lickford)
Born: Oct. 26, 1876, St. John's Woods, London, England. Died: Dec. 24, 1958, Los Angeles, Calif. Stage and screen actor.

Appeared in: **1900** English Nell. **1916** The Beggar of Cawnpore; The Vagabond Prince; The Raiders; The Market of Vain Desire. **1917** The Danger Trail. **1919** The Man Who Turned White. **1920** One Hour before Dawn. **1921** Below the Deadline; Dice of Destiny; Felix O'Day; When We Were Twenty-One. **1923** Zaza. **1924** Is Love Everything? **1926** The Temptress; Silence; Whispering Smith. **1927** French Dressing; King of Kings; Sorrell and Son. **1928** The Naughty Duchess; Man-Made Women; Romance of a Rogue. **1929** The Divine Lady; Conquest; The Argyle Case; The Doctor's Secret; The Gamblers; Stark Mad; The Trial of Mary Dugan; The Show of Shows; Tiger Rose. **1930** The Furies; Wild Company; The Green Goddess; The Second Floor Mystery; On Your Back; Wedding Rings; The Princess and the Plumber; Liliom. **1931** Five Star Final; A Woman of Experience; The Reckless Hour; Expensive Women. **1932** Tom Brown of Culver; The Son-Daughter; The Menace; The Crusader; Cross Examination; Charlie Chan's Chance; Unholy Love; A Woman Commands; The Phantom of Crestwood. **1933** Christopher Bean; Jennie Gerhardt; Supernatural; Sorrell and Son (and 1927 version); Justice Takes a Holiday. **1934** Grand Canary; In Old Santa Fe. **1935** Behold My Wife; A Tale of Two Cities. **1936** The Garden Murder Case; Mr. Deeds Goes to Town; Moonlight Murder; Rose of the Rancho; The Blackmailer; Along Came Love. **1937** The Lost Horizon; Our Fighting Navy; (aka Torpedoed—US 1939); Victoria the Great. **1938** Army Girl; Bulldog Drummond in Africa; The Adventures of Marco Polo; The Girl of the Golden West; The Toy Wife; You Can't Take It with You; Kidnapped. **1939** The Rains Came; Arrest Bulldog Drummond; Let Freedom Ring; Bulldog Drummond's Secret Police; Bulldog Drummond's Bride; The Gracie Allen Murder Case; Nurse Edith Cavell; Mr. Smith Goes to Washington. **1940** New Moon. **1941** The Corsican Brothers; Topper Returns; City of Missing Girls; Here Is a Man; Ellery Queen and the Perfect Crime; South of Tahiti; All That Money Can Buy. **1942** A Yank in Libya; Boss of Big Town; Crossroads. **1943** Hitler's Children; Women in Bondage; Queen Victoria. **1944** Action in Arabia; Enemy of Women; Faces in the Fog. **1945** Captain Tugboat Annie; Rogues' Gallery. **1946** Gentleman Joe Palooka; It's a Wonderful Life; Strange Impersonation. **1947** Driftwood; Bulldog Drummond Strikes Back. **1948** High Wall; Prince of Thieves. **1949** El Paso; Hellfire; The Judge Steps Out. **1950** Sunset Boulevard. **1951** The First Legion; Journey into Light; Here Comes the Groom; Savage Drums. **1952** The Devil and Daniel Webster (reissue and retitle of All That Money Can Buy—1941). **1956** The Ten Commandments. **1958** Darby's Rangers.

WARNER, J. B.
Born: 1895, Nebraska. Died: Nov. 9, 1924 (tuberculosis). Screen actor.

Appeared in: **1921** Crossing Trails. **1922** Big Stakes; Flaming Hearts. **1923** Crimson Gold; Danger; Lone Fighter. **1924** Behind Two Guns; The Covered Trail; The Hellion; Horseshoe Luck; Treasure Canyon; Wanted by the Law; Wolf Man; Westbound.

WARNOW, HELEN
Born: 1926. Died: Dec. 25, 1970, New York, N.Y. Screen and television actress.

WARREN, C. DENIER
Born: July 29, 1889, Chicago, Ill. Died: Aug. 27, 1971, Torquay, England. Screen, stage, vaudeville, radio actor and screenwriter.

Appeared in: **1933** Counsel's Opinion. **1934** The Great Defender; Kentucky Minstrels. **1935** The Clairvoyant; Heart's Desire; A Fire Has Been Arranged. **1936** A Star Fell from Heaven; Spy of Napoleon; Everybody Dance. **1937** Cotton Queen. **1938** Break the News; Strange Boarders; It's in the Air. **1939** Trouble Brewing. **1940** Lost on the Western Front. **1944** Kiss the Bride Goodbye. **1951** Old Mother Riley, Headmistress. **1952** Old Mother Riley. **1960** Bluebeard's Ten Honeymoons. **1961** The Treasure of Monte Cristo (aka The Secret of Monte Cristo). **1962** Lolita. **1969** The Adding Machine.

WARREN, E. ALYN
Born: 1875. Died: Jan. 22, 1940, Los Angeles, Calif. Screen and stage actor.

Appeared in: 1921 The Millionaire; No Woman Knows; A Tale of Two Worlds; Outside the Law. 1922 East is West; The Truthful Liar; Hungry Hearts. 1923 The Courtship of Myles Standish. 1926 Sweet Rosie O'Grady; Born to the West. 1927 The Opening Night. 1928 The Trail of '98. 1929 Chasing through Europe; Red Wine. 1930 Prince of Diamonds; The Medicine Man; Abraham Lincoln; Son of the Gods; Du Barry, Woman of Passion. 1931 Fighting Caravans; Shipmates; A Free Soul; Daughter of the Dragon; Secret Service; The Hatchet Man. 1932 The Mask of Fu Manchu. 1933 Tarzan the Fearless. 1934 Limehouse Blues. 1935 Chinatown Squad. 1936 The Devil Doll. 1937 They Won't Forget. 1938 Port of Seven Seas.

WARREN, EDWARD
Died: Apr. 3, 1930, Los Angeles, Calif. Stage and screen actor.

Appeared in: 1916 The Little Orphan. 1926 The Belle of Broadway.

WARREN, ELIZA (Eliza Warren Sutton)
Born: 1865. Died: Jan. 20, 1935, Cleveland, Ohio. Screen and stage actress. Entered films with Griffith in 1906.

WARREN, FRED H.
Born: Sept. 16, 1880, Rock Island, Illinois. Died: Dec. 5, 1940, Hollywood, Calif. (ruptured ulcer). Screen and vaudeville actor.

Appeared in: 1916 The Matriamaniac; The Microscope Mystery; Heart o' the Hills. 1917 Her Official Fathers; The Cricket; Nina the Flower Girl. 1918 Kildares of Storm; Sylvia on a Spree. 1919 Johnny-on-the-Spot; A Favor to a Friend; Turning the Tables. 1921 The Man Who Dared. 1922 Little Eva Ascends; Pawn Ticket 210. 1923 The Exiles; The Girl of the Golden West; Stephen Steps Out. 1924 The Shooting of Dan McGrew; The Woman on the Jury. 1925 Capital Punishment; Her Husband's Secret; The Desert Flower; Why Women Love; The Masked Bride; Winds of Chance. 1926 The Bells; Miss Nobody. 1927 California; Eager Lips; Lonesome Ladies; Sitting Bull at the "Spirit Lake Massacre"; Three's a Crowd. 1928 The Noose; The Crash. 1929 The Spieler; In Old Arizona; Synthetic Sin; The Locked Door. 1930 The Girl of the Golden West (and 1923 version); Abraham Lincoln; Rodeo Comedies (shorts); Hearts and Hoofs. 1931 Kiki; Secret Service. 1933 Smoke Lightning. 1934 The Cat's Paw. 1935 The Mysterious Mr. Wong; Ship Cafe. 1936 I Conquer the Sea; The Revolt of the Zombies. 1937 Night Club Scandal. 1938 MGM shorts.

WARREN, KATHERINE
Born: July 12, 1905, Michigan. Died: July 17, 1965, Los Angeles, Calif. (coronary thrombosis and arteriosclerosis). Stage and screen actress.

Appeared in: 1949 The Story of Molly X; Tell It to the Judge; All the King's Men. 1950 Three Secrets; Harriet Craig; Mystery Submarine (aka Submarine); Mary Ryan—Detective; And Baby Makes Three. 1951 Lorna Doone; Night into Morning; The People Against O'Hara; Force of Arms; The Tall Target; The Prowler. 1952 This Woman is Dangerous; Washington Story; Talk About a Stranger; Son of Ali Baba; The Steel Trap. 1953 The Star; The Man Behind the Gun. 1954 The Glenn Miller Story; The Caine Mutiny. 1955 The Violent Men. 1956 Inside Detroit; Fury at Gunsight Pass. 1957 Drango. 1961 I'll Give My Life.

WARREN, LEONARD
Born: Apr. 21, 1911, New York, N.Y. Died: Mar. 4, 1960, New York, N.Y. (heart attack). Opera singer and screen actor.

Appeared in: 1944 Irish Eyes Are Smiling.

WARRENDER, HAROLD
Born: Nov. 15, 1903, London, England. Died: May 6, 1953, Gerrands Cross, England. Screen, stage and radio actor.

Appeared in: 1928 Day Dreams (film debut). 1933 I Spy; Friday the Thirteenth. 1934 Catherine the Great; Lady in Danger. 1935 Mimi; Invitation to the Waltz; Lazybones. 1940 Convoy; Contraband (aka Blackout—US); Sailors Three (aka Three Cockeyed Sailors—US 1941). 1948 Scott of the Antarctic (US 1949); Under the Frozen Falls. 1949 Warning to Wantons; Conspirator (US 1950). 1951 The Six Men; Pandora and the Flying Dutchman; Where No Vultures Fly (aka Ivory Hunter—US 1952). 1952 Ivanhoe. 1953 Intimate Relations (aka Les Parents Terribles); Time Bomb (aka Terror on a Train—US).

WARRENTON, LULE
Born: 1863. Died: May 14, 1932, Laguna Beach, Calif. (operation complications). Screen, stage actress and film director.

Appeared in: 1920 The Sin That Was His. 1921 Blind Hearts; The Dangerous Moment; Ladies Must Live; The Jolt. 1922 Calvert's Valley; Strength of the Pines; Shirley of the Circus.

WARWICK, JOHN (John McIntosh Beattie)
Born: Jan. 4, 1905, Bellengen River, N.S.W. Died: Jan. 10, 1972, Sydney, Australia (heart attack). Screen, stage and television actor.

Appeared in: 1937 Double Alibi; Passenger to London; The Ticket of Leave Man; Riding High (aka Remember When). 1938 Bad Boy; John Halifax—Gentleman; A Yank at Oxford; This Man is News. 1939 The Mind of Mr. Reeder (aka The Mysterious Mr. Reeder—US 1940); The Face at the Window (US 1940); All at Sea. 1940 The Case of the Frightened Lady (aka Frightened Lady—US 1941); Branded (reissue of Bad Boy 1938). 1941 The Saint's Vacation; My Wife's Family. 1942 The Missing Million; The Day Will Dawn (aka The Avengers—US). 1947 Dancing with Crime. 1958 Law and Disorder. 1959 Horrors of the Black Museum.

WARWICK, ROBERT (Robert Taylor Bien)
Born: Oct. 9, 1878, Sacramento, Calif. Died: June 4, 1964, Los Angeles, Calif. Screen, stage and television actor. Married to actress Stella Lattimore (dec. 1960) and divorced from actress Josephine Whittell (dec. 1961).

Appeared in: 1915 The Face in the Moonlight. 1916 Human Driftwood. 1917 The Mad Lover. 1918 The Silent Master. 1919 In Mizzoura; Told in the Hills; Secret Service. 1920 Hunting Trouble; Thou Art the Man; Fourteenth Man. 1924 The Spitfire. 1929 Unmasked. 1931 A Holy Terror; The Royal Bed; Not Exactly Gentlemen; Three Rogues. 1932 So Big; The Dark Horse; The Woman from Monte Carlo; Dr. X.; The Rich Are Always with Us; Unashamed; I Am a Fugitive from a Chain Gang; Silver Dollar; The Girl from Calgary; Afraid to Talk; Secrets of Wu Sin. 1933 Pilgrimage; Charlie Chan's Greatest Case; Frisco Jenny; Ladies They Talk About; Female. 1934 The Dragon Murder Case; Jimmy the Gent; Cleopatra; School for Girls. 1935 Night Life of the Gods; A Thrill for Thelma (short); A Shot in the Dark; The Murder Man; A Tale of Two Cities; Whipsaw; Hopalong Cassidy. 1936 Tough Guy; The Return of Jimmy Valentine; Bulldog Edition; The Beloved Rogue; The Bold Caballero; Sutter's Gold; The Bride Walks Out; Mary of Scotland; Romeo and Juliet; In His Steps; The White Legion; Adventure in Manhattan; Can This Be Dixie?; an MGM short; Timber War. 1937 The Prince and the Pauper; The Life of Emile Zola; Let Them Live; The Road Back; The Awful Truth; Counsel for Crime; Conquest; Trigger Trio. 1938 The Spy Ring; Going Places; The Adventures of Robin Hood; Gangster's Boy; Blockade; Army Girl; Law of the Plains; Come on Leathernecks!; Squadron of Honor. 1939 Devil's Island; Almost a Gentleman; Juarez; The Private Lives of Elizabeth and Essex; The Magnificent Fraud; In Old Monterey. 1940 On the Spot; New Moon; Konga, the Wild Stallion; The Sea Hawk; Murder in the Air. 1941 A Woman's Face; I Was a Prisoner on Devil's Island; Louisiana Purchase; Sullivan's Travels; Spare a Copper. 1942 The Palm Beach Story; Tennessee Johnson; Secret Enemies; Cadets on Parade; Eagle Squadron; I Married a Witch. 1943 Two Tickets to London; Petticoat Larceny; Deerslayer; Dixie. 1944 Man from Frisco; The Princess and the Pirate; Bowery to Broadway; Kismet; Secret Command. 1945 Sudan. 1946 Criminal Court; The Falcon's Adventure. 1947 Gentleman's Agreement; Pirates of Monterey. 1948 Adventures of Don Juan; Fury at Furnace Creek; Million Dollar Weekend; Gun Smugglers. 1949 A Woman's Secret; Impact; Francis. 1950 In a Lonely Place; Tarzan and the Slave Girl; Vendetta. 1951 Sugarfoot; Mark of the Renegade; The Sword of Monte Cristo. 1953 Salome; Mississippi Gambler; Jamaica Run. 1954 Silver Lode; Passion. 1955 Chief Crazy Horse; Lady Godiva; Escape to Burma. 1956 Walk the Proud Land; While the City Sleeps. 1957 Shoot-Out at Medicine Bend. 1958 The Buccaneer. 1959 It Started with a Kiss; Night of the Quarter Moon.

WARWICK, STELLA LATTIMORE
Born: 1905. Died: Dec. 1, 1960, Hollywood, Calif. Screen actress. Married to actor Robert Warwick (dec. 1964).

WASHBURN, ALICE
Born: 1861, Oshkosh, Wis. Died: Nov. 29, 1929, Oshkosh, Wis. (heart ailment). Stage and screen actress.

Appeared in: 1911 Aunt Miranda's Cat; How Father Accomplished His Work; Marjorie's Diamond Ring; Holding the Fort; Bridget's Sudden Wealth; Lazy Bill Hudson; Sally Ann's Strategy; The Totville Eye; The Winking Parson. 1912 A Proposal Under Difficulties. 1913 The Comedian's Downfall; Aunty and the Girls; At Midnight; How Did It Finish?; With the Assistance of Shep. 1914 A Story of Crime; The Sultan and the Roller Skates; On the Lazy Line. 1916 His Dukeship-Mr. Jack; Kernel Nutt, the Janitor; Kernel Nutt Wins a Wife; Kernell Nutt the Footman; Kernel Nutt's One Hundred Dollar Bill; Kernel Nutt's Musical Shirt; Kernel Nutt Flirts with Wifie; Kernel Nutt and High Shoes.

WASHBURN, BRYANT, SR.

Born: Apr. 28, 1889, Chicago, Ill. Died: Apr. 30, 1963, Hollywood, Calif. (heart attack). Screen, stage actor and film producer. Father of actor Bryant Washburn, Jr. (dec. 1960).

Appeared in: 1914 The Promised Land. 1915 The Blindness of Virtue. 1916 The Havoc; The Price of Graustark; Marriage a la Carte. 1917 The Fibbers; Skinner's Dress Suit; Skinner's Baby; Skinner's Bubble; The Golden Idiot. 1918 'Til I Come Back to You; Twenty-One; Kidder and Ko; Ghost of the Rancho; The Gypsy Trail; Venus in the East. 1919 It Pays to Advertise; Way of a Man with a Maid; Why Smith Left Home; Putting It Over; Poor Boob; Very Good Young Man; Something to Do; All Wrong; Love Insurance. 1920 The Six Best Cellars; Too Much Johnson; What Happened to Jones?; Mrs. Temple's Telegram; Sins of St. Anthony; Full House. 1921 An Amateur Devil; Burglar Proof; The Road to London. 1922 Night Life in Hollywood; Hungry Hearts; June Madness; The Woman Conquers; White Shoulders. 1923 Mine to Keep; Rupert of Hentzau; The Common Law; Hollywood; The Love Trap; The Meanest Man in the World; Mary of the Movies; Other Men's Daughters; Temptation. 1924 My Husband's Wives; Try and Get It; The Star Dust Trail. 1925 The Parasite; Passionate Youth; The Wizard of Oz; Wandering Footsteps. 1926 Flames; The Sky Pirate; Young April; Meet the Prince; That Girl Oklahoma; Wet Paint; Sitting Bull at Spirit Lake Massacre. 1927 Her Sacrifice; Breakfast at Sunrise; Beware of Widows; The Love Thrill; Black Tears; In the First Degree; King of Kings; Modern Daughters; Sky Pirates. 1928 Honeymoon Flats; Nothing to Wear; Skinner's Big Idea; A Bit of Heaven; The Chorus Kid; Jazzland; Undressed. 1930 Christmas Knight (short); Niagara Falls (short); Swing High. 1931 Liberty; Kept Husbands; Mystery Train. 1932 The Reckoning; Arm of the Law; Drifting Souls; Exposure; Forbidden Company; Parisian Romance; Thrill of Youth; What Price Hollywood? 1933 What Price Innocence?; Night of Terror; Devil's Mate. 1934 The Curtain Falls; Back Page; The Woman Who Dared; When Strangers Meet; Public Stenographer; The Return of Chandu. 1935 $20 a Week; Swell Head; Danger Ahead; The Throwback; The World Accuses. 1936 The Millionaire Kid; Bridge of Sighs; Gambling with Souls; Preview Murder Mystery; Hollywood Boulevard; Sutter's Gold; Conflict; Three of a Kind; It Couldn't Have Happened; We Who Are about to Die; Jungle Jim (serial). 1937 Sea Racketeers; The Westland Case; Million Dollar Racket. 1938 I Demand Payment. 1939 Stagecoach; Ambush; Sky Patrol. 1941 Paper Bullets; Gangs, Incorporated; Adventures of Captain Marvel (serial). 1942 The Yukon Patrol; Sin Town; Two for the Money (short); War Dogs. 1943 Shadows on the Sage; You Can't Beat the Law; The Law Rides Again; Carson City Cyclone; The Girl from Monterey. 1944 Feather Your Nest (short); The Falcon in Mexico; Nabonga. 1945 Two O'Clock Courage; West of the Pecos. 1947 Do or Diet (short); Sweet Genevieve. 1968 The Further Perils of Laurel and Hardy (documentary).

WASHBURN, BRYANT, JR.

Died: 1960. Screen actor. Son of actor Bryant Washburn, Sr. (dec. 1963).

Appeared in: 1933 Daring Daughters.

WASHBURN, JOHN H.

Died: Dec. 11, 1917, New York, N.Y. Screen actor.

WASHINGTON, DINAH (Ruth Jones)

Born: Aug. 29, 1924, Tuscaloosa, Ala. Died: Dec. 14, 1963, Detroit, Mich. (overdose of sleeping pills). Black singer and screen actress. Married to professional football player Dick "Night Train" Lane. Divorced from musicians Eddie Chamblee and George Jenkins and actor Rafael Campos.

Appeared in: 1960 Jazz on a Summer's Day.

WASHINGTON, KENNY (Kenneth William Washington)

Born: Aug. 31, 1918. Died: June 24, 1971, Los Angeles, Calif. (polyarteritis). Black professional football player and screen actor.

Appeared in: 1947 The Foxes of Harrow. 1948 Rogues' Regiment. 1949 Easy Living; Rope of Sand; Pinky. 1950 The Jackie Robinson Story. 1969 Changes. 1970 Tarzan's Deadly Silence.

WATERMAN, IDA (Ida Shaw Francoeur)

Born: 1852. Died: May 22, 1941, Cincinnati, Ohio. Screen and stage actress.

Appeared in: 1920 Lady Rose's Daughter. 1921 Her Lord and Master; Love's Redemption; The Inner Chamber; The Lotus Eater. 1922 Notoriety. 1924 A Society Scandal; The Enchanted Cottage. 1925 The Swan; That Royle Girl. 1926 Say It Again; A Social Celebrity.

WATKIN, PIERRE

Died: Feb. 3, 1960, Hollywood, Calif. Screen actor.

Appeared in: 1935 Dangerous. 1936 Bunker Bean; Love Letters of a Star; Forgotten Faces; It Had to Happen; The Gentleman from Louisiana; Sitting on the Moon; Country Gentlemen; Nobody's Fool; Counterfeit; Swing Time. 1937 Michael O'Halloran; Interns Can't Take Money; The Californian; The Green Light; The Go-Getter; Ever since Eve; The Singing Marine; The Devil's Playground; Larceny on the Air; Bill Cracks Down; The Hit Parade; Sea Devils; Stage Door; Breakfast for Two; Paradise Isle; Daughters of Shanghai. 1938 Young Dr. Kildare; The Lady Objects; Midnight Intruder; State Police; Mr. Moto's Gamble; Dangerous to Know; Tip-Off Girls; Illegal Traffic; There's Always a Woman; Girls' School; There's That Woman Again; The

Chaser; Mr. Doodle Kicks Off. 1939 Risky Business; The Spirit of Culver; King of the Underworld; Wings of the Navy; Off the Record; Adventures of Jane Arden; The Mysterious Miss X; Wall Street Cowboy; Covered Trailer; They Made Her a Spy; Society Lawyer; Mr. Smith Goes to Washington; Geronimo; Death of a Champion; The Great Victor Herbert. 1940 The Road to Singapore; The Saint Takes Over; Street of Memories; Captain Caution; I Love You Again; Golden Gloves; Out West with the Peppers; Five Little Peppers in Trouble; The Bank Dick; Yesterday's Heroes; Father Is a Prince; Rhythm on the River. 1941 Nevada City; Buy Me That Town; Ellery Queen and the Murder Ring; Ice Capades Revue; Jesse James at Bay; Petticoat Politics; Cheers for Miss Bishop; A Man Betrayed; Meet John Doe; She Knew All the Answers; Adventures in Washington; Life with Henry; The Trial of Mary Dugan; Naval Academy; Great Guns. 1942 Pride of the Yankees; Whistling in Dixie; The Adventures of Martin Eden; Heart of the Rio Grande; Yokel Boy; The Magnificent Dope. 1943 Cinderella Swings It; Mission to Moscow; Old Acquaintance; Jack London; Riding High; Swing Shift Maisie; It Ain't Hay. 1944 Weekend Pass; Bermuda Mystery; Ladies of Washington; South of Dixie; Jubilee Woman; Oh, What a Night!; Atlantic City; The Great Mike; Dead Man's Eyes; Shadow of Suspicion; End of the Road; Song of the Range; Meet Miss Bobby-Socks. 1945 Here Come the Co-Eds; Strange Illusion; The Phantom Speaks; Docks of New York; I'll Remember April; Mr. Muggs Rides Again; Follow That Woman; Keep Your Powder Dry; Three's a Crowd; Allotment Wives; I'll Tell The World; Captain Tugboat Annie; Dakota; Over 21; I Love a Bandleader; Apology for Murder. 1946 Little Giant; So Goes My Love; The Kid from Brooklyn; The Shadow Returns; Murder Is My Business; Swamp Fire; Behind the Mask; High School Hero; The Missing Lady; Claudia and David; Secrets of a Sorority Girl; Sioux City Sue; G.I. War Brides; Her Sister's Secret; I Ring Doorbells; The Madonna's Secret; Shock. 1947 Violence; Hard-Boiled Mahoney; The Red Stallion; Her Husband's Affair; Wild Frontier; The Shocking Miss Pilgrim; Beyond Our Own; Jack Armstrong (serial). 1948 Fighting Back; The Hunted; The Gentleman from Nowhere; Mary Lou; Glamour Girl; State of the Union; Trapped by Boston Blackie; An Innocent Affair; Daredevils of the Clouds; The Counterfeiters; The Shanghai Chest. 1949 Knock on Any Door; Frontier Outpost; Alaska Patrol; Hold That Baby; Zamba; Incident; The Story of Seabiscuit. 1950 The Big Hangover; Frontier Outpost; Last of the Buccaneers; Over the Border; Radar Secret Service; Redwood Forest Trail; Rock Island Trail; The Second Face; Sunset in the West; Blue Grass of Kentucky. 1951 Two Lost Worlds; The Dark Page; In Old Amarillo. 1952 Hold That Line; Scandal Sheet; Thundering Caravans; A Yank in Indo-China. 1953 The Stranger Wore a Gun. 1954 Johnny Dark; About Mrs. Leslie. 1955 The Big Bluff; Sudden Danger; Creature with the Atom Brain. 1956 The Maverick Queen; Shake, Rattle and Rock. 1957 Beginning of the End; Don't Knock the Rock; Pal Joey; Spook Chasers. 1959 The Flying Fontaines.

WATSON, ADELE

Born: 1890, Minn. Died: Mar. 27, 1933, Los Angeles, Calif. (double pneumonia). Screen, stage and vaudeville actress. Entered films in 1918.

Appeared in: 1922 The Lying Truth. 1923 Reno. 1924 Don't Doubt Your Husband. 1925 Welcome Home; Tower of Lies. 1926 Rolling Home. 1927 Good as Gold; A Harp in Hock; Once and Forever; The Broken Gate. 1928 The Black Pearl. 1929 Blue Skies; The Very Idea; Jazz Heaven; This Thing Called Love. 1931 Street Scene; Compromised; Expensive Women; Arrowsmith. 1932 The Purchase Price; Pack up Your Troubles.

WATSON, BENJAMIN T. "BEN"

Died: 1968. Screen actor.

Appeared in: 1951 Across the Wide Missouri.

WATSON, "BOBBY" (Robert Watson Knucher)

Born: 1888, Springfield, Ill. Died: May 22, 1965, Hollywood, Calif. Screen, stage and vaudeville actor. Best known for his portrayals of Hitler.

Appeared in: 1926 That Royle Girl; The Romance of a Million Dollars; The Song and Dance Man. 1929 Syncopation; Maid's Night Out (short); Follow the Leader; plus the following shorts: The Baby Bandit; Contrary Mary; The Stand Up; Nay, Nay, Nero. 1931 Manhattan Parade. 1932 High Pressure. 1933 Moonlight and Pretzels; Going Hollywood; Wine, Women and Song. 1934 Countess of Monte Cristo; I Hate Women. 1935 Society Doctor; The Murder Man. 1936 Mary of Scotland. 1937 Calling All Doctors (short); The Awful Truth; The Adventurous Blonde; You're a Sweetheart. 1938 In Old Chicago; Boys Town; Kentucky; The Story of Alexander Graham Bell. 1939 Everything's on Ice; Dodge City; On Borrowed Time; Blackmail. 1940 Wyoming; Dr. Kildare's Crisis. 1941 Men of Boys Town; Hit the Road. 1942 The Devil with Hitler. 1943 Hitler—Dead or Alive; That Nazty Nuisance; It Ain't Hay. 1944 The Hitler Gang; The Miracle of Morgan's Creek; Practically Yours. 1945 Duffy's Tavern; Hold That Blonde. 1948 The Big Clock; The Paleface. 1949 Red Hot and Blue. 1950 Copper Canyon. 1951 G.I. Jane. 1952 Singing in the Rain. 1957 The Story of Mankind.

WATSON, CAVEN

Born: 1904, Scotland. Died: 1953, Norholt, England. Screen and stage actor. Appeared in Scottish film The Net.

WATSON, FANNY

Born: 1886, Rochester, N.Y. Died: May 17, 1970, Albany, N.Y. Screen, vaudeville, burlesque and radio actress. Appeared with her sister, Kitty (dec. 1967), in vaudeville as the "Watson Sisters."

They appeared in: 1929 Bigger and Better (short).

WATSON, GEORGE A.

Born: 1911. Died: Dec. 5, 1937, Hollywood, Calif. Screen actor.

WATSON, IVORY "DEEK"

Born: 1909. Died: Nov. 4, 1969. Black singer and screen actor. Member of the "Ink Spots" singing group.

Appeared in: 1941 The Great American Broadcast. 1942 Pardon My Sarong. 1947 Sepia Cinderella; Boy! What a Girl.

WATSON, JOSEPH K. (Joseph Koff)

Born: Feb. 12, 1887, Philadelphia, Pa. Died: May 17, 1942, Hollywood, Calif. Screen, stage, vaudeville actor and screenwriter.

Appeared in: 1936 Melody for Two; Cherokee Strip; Bad Man's Territory; Echo Mountain; Champagne Hour.

WATSON, JUSTICE

Born: 1908. Died: July 6, 1962, Hollywood, Calif. Screen, stage and television actor. Entered films approx. 1955.

Appeared in: 1956 Death of a Scoundrel. 1962 Town of London.

WATSON, KITTY (Katherine Watson)

Born: 1887. Died: Mar. 1967, Buffalo, N.Y. Screen, vaudeville and burlesque actress. Appeared with her sister, Fanny (dec. 1970), in vaudeville as the "Watson Sisters."

They appeared in: 1929 Bigger and Better (short). 1942 Mrs. Miniver.

WATSON, LUCILE

Born: May 27, 1879, Quebec, Canada. Died: June 24, 1962, New York, N.Y. Stage and screen actress.

Appeared in: 1916 The Girl with the Green Eyes. 1934 What Every Woman Knows; Men in Black (short). 1935 The Bishop Misbehaves. 1936 A Woman Rebels; The Garden of Allah. 1937 Three Smart Girls. 1938 The Young in Heart; Sweethearts. 1939 Made for Each Other; The Women. 1940 Waterloo Bridge; Florian. 1941 Rage in Heaven; Mr. and Mrs. Smith; Footsteps in the Dark; The Great Lie; Model Wife. 1943 Watch on the Rhine. 1944 'Til We Meet Again; Uncertain Glory; The Thin Man Goes Home. 1946 Song of the South; Tomorrow Is Forever; Never Say Goodbye; The Razor's Edge; My Reputation. 1947 Ivy. 1948 The Emperor Waltz; Julia Misbehaves; That Wonderful Urge. 1949 Everybody Does It; Little Women. 1950 Harriet Craig; Let's Dance. 1951 My Forbidden Past.

WATSON, MINOR

Born: Dec. 22, 1889, Marianna, Ark. Died: July 28, 1965, Alton, Ill. Screen, stage and television actor.

Appeared in: 1913 Rescuing Dave; Love Incognito; Their Waterloo. 1914 No. 28 Diplomat. 1931 24 Hours. 1933 Another Language; Our Betters. 1934 The Pursuit of Happiness; Babbitt. 1935 Charlie Chan in Paris; Mr. Dynamite; Lady Tubbs; Mary Jane's Pa; Age of Indiscretion; Pursuit; Annapolis Farewell. 1936 Rose of the Rancho; The Longest Night. 1937 When's Your Birthday?; The Woman I Love; Saturday's Heroes; Dead End; That Certain Woman; Navy Blue and Gold; Checkers. 1938 Of Human Hearts; Boys Town; Stablemates; While New York Sleeps; Touchdown Army; Love, Honor and Behave; Fast Company. 1939 The Hardys Ride High; Maisie; The Boy Friend; News Is Made at Night; Here I Am a Stranger; Angels Wash Their Faces; The Flying Irishman; Television Spy; Stand up and Fight; Huckleberry Finn. 1940 The Llamo Kid; 20 Mule Team; Hidden Gold; Young People; Rangers of Fortune; Viva, Cisco Kid!; Gallant Sons; Abe Lincoln in Illinois. 1941 The Monster and the Girl; Western Union; The Parson of Panamint; Kiss the Boys Goodbye; Birth of the Blues; They Died with Their Boots On; Moon over Miami; Mr. District Attorney. 1942 The Remarkable Andrew; Yankee Doodle Dandy; Woman of the Year; Frisco Lil; To the Shores of Tripoli; The Big Shot; Gentleman Jim; Flight Lieutenant; Enemy Agent Meets Ellery Queen. 1943 Action in the North Atlantic; Yanks Ahoy!; Secrets in the Dark; The Crime Doctor's Rendezvous; Crash Dive; Mission to Moscow; Princess O'Rourke; Happy Land; Guadalcanal Diary. 1944 Henry Aldrich, Boy Scout; That's My Baby; The Story of Dr. Wassell; Here Come the Waves; The Thin Man Goes Home; The Falcon Out West; Shadows in the Night. 1945 God Is My Co–Pilot; A Bell for Adano; You Came Along; Saratoga Trunk; Bewitched. 1946 Boys' Ranch; Courage of Lassie; The Virginian. 1948 A Southern Yankee. 1949 Beyond the Forest. 1950 Mister 880; The Jackie Robinson Story; There's a Girl in My Heart; Thelma Jordan. 1951 As Young as You Feel; Bright Victory; Little Egypt. 1952 My Son John; Untamed Frontier; Face to Face. 1953 The Star; Roar of the Crowd. 1955 Ten Wanted Men. 1956 Rawhide Years; Trapeze; The Ambassador's Daughter.

WATSON, ROY

Born: 1876. Died: June 7, 1937, Hollywood, Calif. Screen actor. Entered films with Selig.

Appeared in: 1914 The Hazards of Helen (serial). 1920 The Flaming Disc (serial); Elmo, the Fearless (serial). 1921 The Ranger and the Law. 1922 Blue Blazes. 1924 The Loser's End. 1925 Luck and Sand; Win, Lose or Draw; Wolf Blood. 1926 Chasing Trouble. 1927 Cactus Trails; Wanderer of the West. 1928 Restless Youth. 1934 Carolina.

WATSON, WYLIE (John Wylie Robertson)

Born: 1889, Scotland. Died: 1966. Stage and screen actor. Was member of "The Watson Family" on stage.

Appeared in: 1928–31 In U.S. films. 1935 The 39 Steps. 1936 Radio Lover. 1937 Why Pick on Me?; Paradise for Two (aka The Gaiety Girls—US 1938). 1938 Yes, Madam? 1939 Jamaica Inn. 1940 Pack Up Your Troubles. 1941 The Saint Meets the Tiger (US 1943). 1943 The Lamp Still Burns; The Flemish Farm. 1944 Tawny Pipit (US 1947); Don't Take It to Heart (US 1949); Kiss the Bride Goodbye. 1945 Waterloo Road; Strawberry Roan; Waltz Time; Murder in Reverse (US 1946). 1946 The Years Between (US 1947); A Girl in a Million (US 1950). 1947 Fame is the Spur (US 1949); Brighton Rock. 1948 London Belongs to Me (aka Dulcimer Street—US); No Room at the Inn; Things Happen at Night; My Brother Jonathan (US 1949). 1949 The History of Mr. Polly (US 1951); Whisky Galore! (aka Tight Little Island—US and aka Mad Little Island). 1950 Your Witness (aka Eye Witness—US); Morning Departure (aka Operation Disaster—US 1951); The Magnet (US 1951). 1951 Happy-Go-Lovely. 1961 The Sundowners.

WATTIS, RICHARD

Born: 1912, England. Died: Feb. 1, 1975, London, England (heart attack). Screen, stage and television actor.

Appeared in: 1938 A Yank at Oxford (film debut). 1950 The Happiest Days of Your Life. 1951 Appointment with Venus (aka Island Rescue—US 1952). 1952 Song of Paris (aka Bachelor in Paris—US 1953); Stolen Face; The Importance of Being Earnest; Derby Day (aka Four Against Fate—US 1955); Top Secret (aka Mr. Potts Goes to Moscow—US 1954); Mother Riley Meets the Vampire (aka Vampire Over London—US); Made in Heaven. 1953 Innocents in Paris (US 1955); The Intruder (US 1955); Background (aka Edge of Divorce); Park Plaza (aka Norman Conquest—US); Appointment in London (US 1955); Blood Orange; Top of the Form. 1954 Hobson's Choice; Doctor in the House (US 1955); Lease of Life; The Crowded Day. 1955 The Colditz Story (US 1957); See How they Run; The Time of His Life; I Am a Camera; A Yank in Ermine; Simon and Laura (US 1956); An Alligator Named Daisy (US 1957). 1956 Jumping for Joy; The Man Who Never Was; Around the World in 80 Days; The Man Who Knew Too Much; Eyewitness; It's a Wonderful World (US 1961); The Silken Affair (US 1957); The Iron Petticoat; A Touch of the Sun. 1957 The Prince and the Showgirl; Second Fiddle; The Abominable Snowman; High Flight (US 1958); Barnacle Bill (aka All at Sea—US 1958); Blue Murder at St. Trinian's (US 1958). 1958 The Inn of the Sixth Happiness. 1959 The Captain's Table (US 1960); Left, Right and Centre (US 1961); Ten Seconds to Hell; The Ugly Duckling; Follow a Star (US 1961); Libel. 1960 Follow that Horse (US 1962); Your Money or Your Wife (US 1965). 1961 Very Important Person (aka A Coming-Out-Party—US 1962); Nearly a Nasty Accident (US 1962); Dentist on the Job (aka Get On With It!—US 1963). 1962 The Longest Day; Play it Cool (US 1963); I Thank a Fool; Bon Voyage! 1963 The Vip's; Come Fly with Me. 1964 Carry on Spying. 1965 The Liquidator; The Battle of the Villa Fiorita; The Amorous Adventures of Moll Flanders; Operation Crossbow; Up Jumped a Swagman; The Alphabet Murders (US 1966); Bunny Lake is Missing; You Must be Joking! 1966 The Great St. Trinian's Train Robbery (US 1967). 1967 Casino Royale. 1968 Wonderwall; Chitty Chitty Bang Bang. 1969 Those Daring Young Men in Their Jaunty Jalopies; Monte Carlo or Bust. 1970 Game that Lovers Play. 1973 That's Your Funeral; Diamonds of Wheels; Hot Property.

WATTS, CHARLES

Died: Dec. 13, 1966, Nashville, Tenn. (cancer). Screen, stage and television actor.

Appeared in: 1952 Wait Till the Sun Shines Nellie; Just This Once; Million Dollar Mermaid; Something for the Birds. 1953 Silver Whip. 1954 Boy from Oklahoma; Ricochet Romance. 1955 Tall Man Riding; The View from Pompey's Head (aka Secret Interlude). 1956 Giant. 1957 An Affair to Remember; Don't Go Near the Water; The Lone Ranger and the Lost City of Gold; The Spirit of St. Louis; The Big Land. 1959 The Big Circus; No Name on the Bullet. 1961 Ada; Summer and Smoke; Something Wild. 1962 Days of Wine and Roses; Jumbo; Lover, Come Back. 1963 The Wheeler Dealers. 1964 Apache Rifles; Dead Ringer. 1965 Baby, the Rain Must Fall.

WATTS, CHARLES H. "COTTON"

Born: 1902. Died: Mar. 5, 1968, Atlanta, Ga. Black screen and minstrel actor.

Appeared in: 1951 Yes Sir, Mr. Bones.

WATTS, GEORGE
Born: 1877. Died: July 1, 1942, Hollywood, Calif. (heart attack). Screen, stage and vaudeville actor. Appeared in vaudeville as part of "Watts and Hawley" team.

Appeared in: **1936** Soak the Rich. **1940** One Crowded Night; Sky Murder; Angels over Broadway. **1941** Mr. District Attorney; Wild Geese Calling; Hurry, Charlie, Hurry; No Hands on the Clock. **1942** The Remarkable Andrew; The Talk of the Town.

WATTS, PEGGY
Born: 1906. Died: Apr. 27, 1966. Screen actress.

Appeared in: **1932** Cock of the Air.

WAYNE, JUSTINA
Died: Dec. 2, 1951, Freeport, N.Y. Screen, stage and radio actress.

WAYNE, NAUNTON
Born: June 22, 1901, Llanwonno, South Wales. Died: Nov. 17, 1970, Subiton, England. Screen, stage, vaudeville and television actor.

Appeared in: **1932** The First Mrs. Fraser. **1933** Going Gay (aka Kiss Me Goodbye—US 1935); For Love of You. **1938** The Lady Vanishes. **1939** A Girl Must Live (US 1941). **1940** Night Train to Munich (aka Night Train—US and aka Gestapo); Crooks Tour. **1942** Partners in Crime. **1943** Millions Like Us. **1944** Dead of Night. **1946** A Girl in a Million (US 1950). **1948** Quartet. **1949** It's Not Cricket; Passport to Pimlico; Stop Press Girl; Obsession (aka The Hidden Room—US 1950). **1950** Double Confession (US 1953); Trio; Highly Dangerous (US 1951). **1951** Circle of Danger. **1952** The Happy Family (aka Mr. Lord Says No—US); Tall Headlines; Treasure Hunt. **1953** The Titfield Thunderbolt. **1954** You Know What Sailors Are. **1959** Operation Bullshine (US 1963). **1961** Nothing Barred; Double Bunk.

WAYNE, PATRICIA. See PATRICIA CUTTS

WAYNE, RICHARD
Died: Mar. 15, 1958, Hollywood, Calif. Screen actor.

Appeared in: **1921** Whatever She Wants; Wealth; The Snob; The Traveling Salesman. **1922** The Impossible Mrs. Bellew; Minnie; Her Husband's Trademark. **1923** Reno; Unknown Purple; Broadway Gold; The Cheat; Truxton King; Wasted Lives. **1924** Good Bad Boy. **1925** Cheaper to Marry.

WAYNE, ROBERT
Born: Oct. 28, 1864 or 1867 (?), Pittsburgh, Pa. Died: Sept. 26, 1946, Los Angeles, Calif. Stage and screen actor. Entered films in 1915.

Appeared in: **1929** Fashions in Love. **1930** The Love Racket. **1933** The Bitter Tea of General Yen. **1939** Dick Tracy's G-Men.

WEATHERFORD, TAZWELL
Born: 1889, Indiana. Died: July 22, 1917, Los Angeles, Calif. (suicide—poison). Screen actor.

WEAVER, CHARLEY. See CLIFF ARQUETTE

WEAVER, LEON (Leon Abner Weaver)
Born: 1883. Died: May 27, 1950, Hollywood, Calif. Screen actor and singer. Brother of singer and actor Frank and singer and actress Elvira Weaver with whom he appeared as part of the "Weaver Family."

Appeared in: **1938** Swing Your Lady; Romance on the Run; Down in Arkansas. **1939** Jeepers Creepers. **1940** In Old Missouri; Grand Ole Opry; Friendly Neighbors. **1941** Arkansas Judge; Mountain Moonlight. **1942** Shepherd of the Ozarks; The Old Homestead; Mountain Rhythm. **1949** Loaded Pistols; Riders of the Whistling Pines. **1951** Disc Jockey.

WEBB, CLIFTON (Webb Parmelee Hollenbeck)
Born: Nov. 19, 1889 or 1896 (?), Indianapolis, Ind. Died: Oct. 13, 1966, Beverly Hills, Calif. (heart attack). Stage and screen actor. Nominated for 1944 Academy Award as Best Supporting Actor in Laura and in 1946 for The Razor's Edge and nominated for 1948 Academy Award for Best Actor in Sitting Pretty.

Appeared in: **1920** Polly with a Past. **1924** New Toys. **1925** The Heart of a Siren. **1930** Still Alarm (short). **1944** Laura. **1946** The Razor's Edge; Dark Corner. **1948** Sitting Pretty; Julie. **1949** Mr. Belvedere Goes to College. **1950** Cheaper by the Dozen; For Heaven's Sake. **1951** Mr. Belvedere Rings the Bell; Elopement. **1952** Dreamboat; Stars and Stripes Forever. **1953** Titanic; Mr. Scoutmaster. **1954** Woman's World; Three Coins in the Fountain. **1956** The Man Who Never Was. **1957** Boy on a Dolphin. **1959** The Remarkable Mr. Pennypacker; Holiday for Lovers. **1962** Satan Never Sleeps.

WEBB, FAY (aka FAY WEBB VALLEE)
Born: 1906. Died: Nov. 18, 1936, Santa Monica, Calif. (following abdominal operation). Screen actress. Divorced from actor Rudy Vallee.

WEBB, FRANK
Died: Dec. 20, 1974 (auto accident). Screen actor.

Appeared in: **1969** The Bridge at Remagen. **1970** The Computer Wore Tennis Shoes; Too Late the Hero.

WEBB, GEORGE
Born: Oct. 3, 1887, Indianapolis, Ind. Died: May 24, 1943. Stage and screen actor.

Appeared in: **1916** The Secret of the Submarine (serial); Lying Lips; The Wolf Woman. **1917** The Stolen Actress; The Little Orphan; Come Through; Because of the Woman; The Charmer; The Idolaters; Bond of Fear. **1920** Alarm Clock Andy; Below the Surface; Home Spun Folks. **1921** Black Beauty; Fifty Candles; First Love; The Son of Wallingford. **1922** The Crusader; The Man Under Cover. **1923** Little Johnny Jones; Romance Land. **1924** My Man. **1925** Lucky Devil. **1931** Dude Ranch.

WEBB, MILLARD
Born: Dec. 6, 1893, Clay City, Ky. Died: Apr. 21, 1935, Los Angeles, Calif. (intestinal ailment). Screen, stage actor, film director and screenwriter. Entered films as an extra with D.W. Griffith in 1915.

WEBER, JOE (Morris Weber)
Born: 1867, N.Y. Died: May 10, 1942, Los Angeles, Calif. Screen, stage, vaudeville, burlesque and minstrel actor. Was partner with Lou Fields (dec. 1941) in comedy team of "Weber and Fields."

The team appeared in: **1914** The Fatal Mallet. **1915** Two of the Finest; Two of the Bravest; Fatty and the Broadway Stars; The Best of Enemies; Old Dutch. **1916** The Worst of Friends. **1918** The Corner Grocer. **1925** Friendly Enemies. **1927** Mike and Meyer (short). **1936** March of Time. **1937** Blossoms on Broadway. **1939** The Story of Vernon and Irene Castle. **1940** Lillian Russell.

WEBER, JOSEPH W.
Born: 1861. Died: Apr. 4, 1943. Stage and screen actor.

WEBER, LOIS
Born: 1883, Allegheny, Pa. Died: Nov. 13, 1939, Los Angeles, Calif. (stomach ailment). Screen actress, film producer, film director and screenwriter. Entered films with Rex Pictures approx. 1906.

Appeared in: **1914** The Merchant of Venice; False Colors. **1919** A Midnight Romance.

WEBER, REX
Born: 1889, Lexington, Ky. Died: Dec. 8, 1918, Chicago, Ill. (Spanish influenza). Screen, stage actor, film director and producer.

WEBSTER, BEN
Born: June 2, 1864, London, England. Died: Feb. 26, 1947, Hollywood, Calif. (after operation). Stage and screen actor. Married to actress Dame May Whitty (dec. 1948). Father of actress Margaret Webster (dec. 1973).

Appeared in: **1900** English Nell. **1913** The House of Temperley. **1914** Bottle's Baby; Enoch Arden; V.C. (aka The Victoria Cross—US); Lil O'London; Liberty Hall. **1915** In the Blood; A Garret in Bohemia. **1916** The Two Roads; His Daughter's Dilemma; Cynthia in the Wilderness; The Vicar of Wakefield (US 1917). **1917** Masks and Faces; The Profligate; The Gay Lord Quex; If Thou Wert Blind. **1918** Because. **1919** 12-10; Nobody's Child. **1920** The Call of Youth (US 1921). **1924** Miriam Rozella. **1925** The Only Way. **1927** Downhill (aka When Boys Leave Home—US 1928). **1931** The Lyons Mail. **1932** Threads. **1933** One Precious Year. **1934** The Old Curiosity Shop (US 1935). **1935** Drake of England (aka Drake the Pirate—US). **1936** Eliza Comes to Stay; Conquest of the Air. **1937** The Prisoner of Zenda; Two Women. **1942** Mrs. Miniver. **1943** Lassie Come Home.

WEBSTER, MARGARET
Born: Mar. 15, 1905, New York, N.Y. Died: Nov. 13, 1972, London, England. Stage actress, director, producer and screen actress. Daughter of actress Dame May Whitty (dec. 1948) and actor Ben Webster (dec. 1947).

WEED, LELAND T. See BOB BAKER

WEEKS, MARION
Born: 1887. Died: Apr. 20, 1968, New York, N.Y. Screen, stage and vaudeville actress. Entered films with Edison in 1912.

Appeared in: **1912–13** The Office Boy's Birthday.

WEEMS, TED
Born: 1901, Pitcairn, Pa. Died: May 6, 1963, Tulsa, Okla. (emphysema). Bandleader and screen actor.

Appeared in: **1938** Swing, Sister, Swing.

WEGENER, PAUL

Born: 1874, Germany. Died: Sept. 13, 1948, Berlin, Germany. Screen, stage actor, film director and film producer. Married to actress Lyda Salmonova (dec. 1968).

Appeared in: **1913** The Student of Prague. **1914** The Golem. **1921** One Arabian Night; The Golem (and 1914 version). **1922** The Loves of Pharaoh. **1923** Monna Vanna. **1927** Svengali; Lucrezia Borgia. **1926** The Magician. **1928** The Lost Shadow; Vanina; Alraune; The Strange Case of Captain Ramper. **1929** The Weavers. **1930** Survival. **1934** Inge und die Millionen. **1936** Ein Liebestroman im Hause Habsburg. **1939** Horst Wessel; Starker als die Liebe (Stronger Than Love). **1940** Das Recht auf Liebe (The Right to Love); The Living Dead. **1941** Der Grosse Konig. **1948** Der Grosse Mandarin.

WEIDLER, VIRGINIA

Born: Mar. 21, 1927, Hollywood, Calif. Died: July 1, 1968. Screen actress.

Appeared in: **1933** After Tonight. **1934** Long Lost Father; Stamboul Quest; Mrs. Wiggs of the Cabbage Patch. **1935** Big Broadcast of 1936; Peter Ibbetson; Laddie; Freckles. **1936** Suicide Club; Timothy's Quest; Trouble for Two; Girl of the Ozarks; Big Broadcast of 1937. **1937** Maid of Salem; Outcasts of Poker Flat; Souls at Sea. **1938** Out West with the Hardy's; Scandal Street; Love is a Headache; Mother Carey's Chickens; Men with Wings; Too Hot to Handle. **1939** The Great Man Votes; The Lone Wolf Spy Hunt; Fixer Dugan; The Under-Pup; Bad Little Angel; The Women. **1940** Henry Goes to Arizona; Bad Little Angel; Young Tom Edison; All This and Heaven Too; Gold Rush Maisie; The Philadelphia Story. **1941** I'll Wait for You; Barnacle Bill; Babes on Broadway. **1942** This Time for Keeps; Born to Sing; Once Upon a Thursday. **1943** The Youngest Profession; Best Foot Forward.

WEIGEL, PAUL

Born: Feb. 18, 1867, Halle, Germany. Died: May 25, 1951. Screen, stage and vaudeville actor.

Appeared in: **1916** Each Pearl a Tear; Naked Hearts; Witchcraft. **1917** The Winning of Sally Temple; Each to His Kind; Pride and the Man; Forbidden Paths. **1918** The Claim; Her Body in Bond; The Only Road; Me und Gott. **1919** Evangeline; The Parisian Tigress. **1920** The Breath of the Gods. **1921** Bring Him In; They Shall Pay. **1922** Up and Going. **1923** Bag and Baggage; Bluebeard's Eighth Wife. **1924** The Fatal Mistake; The Folly of Vanity; Fighting for Justice; Honor Among Men; Mademoiselle Midnight; The Silent Accuser; Tainted Money; Which Shall It Be? **1925** Declassee; Excuse Me; Soft Shoes; A Lover's Oath; The Verdict; Folly of Vanity. **1926** For Heaven's Sake; The Speed Limit. **1927** Blonde or Brunette; Broadway after Midnight; Hidden Aces; The King of Kings; Sinews of Steel. **1928** Code of the Air; Isle of Lost Men; Marry the Girl; The Wagon Show. **1929** The Leatherneck. **1932** Back Street. **1933** The Vampire Bat. **1934** The Black Cat. **1936** The Invisible Ray. **1940** The Great Dictator. **1942** Joan of Paris. **1943** Miss V from Moscow; Happy Land. **1944** The Hairy Ape.

WEIL, HARRY

Born: 1878. Died: Jan. 23, 1943, Los Angeles, Calif. Screen and stage actor.

WEIL, HARRY

Born: 1890. Died: July 30, 1974, Syracuse, N.Y. Screen and vaudeville actor. Was member of vaudeville team of Adler, Herman and Weil and was one of the original Yacht Club Boys vocal group. Do not confuse with actor Harry Weil (dec. 1943) or director and writer of same name.

Appeared in: **1935** Thanks a Million. **1936** Stagestruck; Pigskin Parade. **1937** Artists and Models; Thrill of a Lifetime. **1938** Cocoanut Grove.

WEILER, CONSTANCE

Born: 1918. Died: Dec. 10, 1965, San Francisco, Calif. (result of fall). Stage and screen actress. Entered films in 1938.

WEINBERG, GUS

Born: 1866. Died: Aug. 11, 1952, Portland, Maine. Screen, stage actor, playwright and songwriter.

Appeared in: **1921** The Frontier of the Stars. **1923** The Ne'er-Do-Well; Homeward Bound; Jacqueline of Blazing Barriers. **1925** Coming Through; Soul Fire.

WEINGARTEN, LAWRENCE

Born: 1898, Chicago, Ill. Died: Feb. 5, 1975, Los Angeles, Calif. (leukemia). Screen producer, director and actor.

Appeared in: **1916** Bittersweet.

WEIR, JANE

Born: 1916, Davenport, Iowa. Died: Aug. 21, 1937, Los Angeles, Calif. (appendectomy). Screen actress.

WEISER, GRETHE

Born: 1903, Germany. Died: Oct. 2, 1970, near Bad Toeiz, Bavaria, Germany (auto accident). Screen, stage and television actress. Married to film producer and lawyer Hermann Schwerin (died in same accident).

Appeared in: **1935** Frischer Wind aus Kanada. **1936** Einer zu viel an Bord; Lotzte Rose. **1937** The Divine Jetta; Liebe auf Umwegen (Love by Indirection). **1938** Meine Fuer Veronika; Familie Schimek. **1939** Der Verkannte Lebemann (The Unrecognized Man of the World). **1940** Our Little Wife. **1952** Tromba, the Tiger Man. **1955** Die Stadt ist Voller Geheimnisse (aka City of Secrets—US 1963). **1956** Du Bist Musik (US 1962).

WEISSBURG, EDWARD

Born: 1876. Died: Aug. 30, 1950, Hollywood, Calif. (heart attack). Screen actor.

WEISSE, HANNI

Born: 1892, Germany. Died: Dec. 1967, Liebenzell, Black Forest, Germany. Screen actress. Appeared in films from 1909 to 1939.

Appeared in: **1913** The Golden Bed. **1929** Berlin after Dark.

WEISSMAN, DORA

Died: May 21, 1974, New York, N.Y. Screen, stage, television and radio actress. Married to playwright Anshel Schorr (dec.).

Appeared in: **1935** Shir Hashirim. **1953** The Gorilla Girl. **1959** Middle of the Night.

WEITZ, EMILE

Born: 1883. Died: May 12, 1951, Hollywood, Calif. Screen actor.

WELCH, EDDIE

Born: 1900. Died: Jan. 15, 1963, Miami, Fla. (diabetes). Screen actor and stuntman. Married to actress Charlotte Delaney. Doubled for Tom Mix and Buck Jones.

WELCH, HARRY FOSTER

Born: 1899. Died: Aug. 16, 1973, Blowing Rock, N.C. Screen actor. Voice of cartoon character, "Popeye the Sailor Man" for almost 40 years, also did the voices of Bluto and Olive Oyl.

Appeared in: **1936** King of Burlesque.

WELCH, JAMES T.

Born: 1869. Died: Apr. 6, 1949, Hollywood, Calif. Screen, stage and minstrel actor.

Appeared in: **1921** The Broken Spur. **1922** Two-Fisted Jefferson; The Sheriff of Sun-Dog; The Marshal of Moneymint. **1924** Abraham Lincoln; The Iron Horse; Behind Two Guns; The Tornado. **1925** Tonio, Son of the Sierras; Warrior Gap. **1926** Speedy Spurs; West of the Rainbow's End. **1927** The Heart of Maryland. **1928** Rough Ridin' Red; Wizard of the Saddle; The Little Buckaroo. **1936** The Trail of the Lonesome Pine. **1935** Ruggles of Red Gap.

WELCH, JOSEPH N.

Born: Oct. 22, 1891. Died: Oct. 6, 1960, Hyannis, Mass. Attorney, screen and television actor. Won 1959 Academy Award nomination for Best Supporting Actor in Anatomy of a Murder.

Appeared in: **1959** Anatomy of a Murder.

WELCH, MARY

Born: 1923. Died: May 31, 1958, New York, N.Y. Screen, stage and television actress. Married to actor David White.

Appeared in: **1952** Park Row.

WELCHMAN, HARRY

Born: Feb. 24, 1886, Barnstable, Devon, England. Died: Jan. 3, 1966, Penzance, England (coronary thrombosis). Screen, stage, radio and television actor.

Appeared in: **1915** The Verdict of the Heart. **1916** The Lyons Mail. **1920** The House on the Marsh. **1932** The Maid of the Mountains. **1933** A Southern Maid. **1936** The Last Waltz. **1945** Waltz Time. **1954** Eight O'Clock Walk (US 1955).

WELDON, LILLIAN (Elizabeth Martin)

Born: 1869. Died: Aug. 22, 1941, Los Angeles, Calif. Screen, vaudeville and burlesque actress. Appeared in vaudeville as part of "Murray and Martin" team.

WELFORD, DALLAS

Born: 1872, England. Died: Sept. 28, 1946, Santa Monica, Calif. Stage and screen actress.

Appeared in: **1921** Wedding Bells.

WELLES, MERI

Born: c. 1930. Died: Aug. 1973, Dallas, Tex. (heart attack). Screen actress. Divorced from actor and director Mel Welles.

Appeared in: **1960** The Little Shop of Horrors. **1961** The Errand Boy; The Ladies' Man. **1964** A House is Not a Home; The Pink Panther.

WELLESLEY, CHARLES

Born: 1875, London, England. Died: July 24, 1946, Amityville, N.Y. Stage and screen actor.

Appeared in: **1921** The Silver Lining; Stardust; His Greatest Sacrifice; It Isn't Being Done This Season; Nobody. **1922** Just a Song at Twilight; Outcast. **1923** Don't Marry for Money; The Acquittal; Does It Pay?; Enemies of Children; Legally Dead; Alias the Night Wind. **1924** The Wolf Man; Cytherea; Traffic in Hearts; The Perfect Flapper. **1925** The Half-Way Girl; The Lost World; The Unholy Three. **1926** College Days. **1927** The Stolen Bride; Sinews of Steel. **1928** Skinner's Big Idea.

WELLINGTON, BABE

Born: 1897. Died: Dec. 28, 1954, New York, N.Y. Screen, stage, vaudeville and burlesque actress. Appeared in silents as a child actress and later was in vaudeville as part of dancing team billed as "The Dancing Kellers."

WELLMAN, EMILY ANN

Died: Mar. 19, 1946. Stage and screen actress.

WELLMAN, WILLIAM A. (William Augustus Wellman)

Born: Feb. 29, 1896, Brookline, Mass. Died: Dec. 9, 1975, Los Angeles, Calif. (leukemia). Screen director, actor, producer, screenwriter and author. Divorced from actresses Helen Chadwick, Marjorie Chapin and Marjorie Crawford. Married to actress Dorothy Coonan.

Appeared in: **1919** The Knickerbocker Buckaroo; Evangeline.

WELLS, "BOMBARDIER" BILLY

Born: 1888. Died: June 11, 1967, London, England. Screen actor and British heavyweight boxing champion. He used to sound the gong in Rank films as their trademark.

Appeared in: **1913** Carpentier vs. Bombardier Wells Fight. **1916** Kent, the Fighting Man. **1918** The Great Game (aka The Straight Game). **1919** Silver Lining. **1927** The Ring. **1937** Make Up; Concerning Mr. Martin.

WELLS, DEERING

Born: 1896. Died: Sept. 29, 1961, London, England. Stage and screen actor.

Appeared in: **1955** Richard III (US 1956). **1958** The Two-Headed Spy (US 1959).

WELLS, H. G.

Born: 1866, England. Died: Aug. 13, 1946, London, England. Author, screenwriter and screen actor.

Appeared in: **1922** The Jungle Goddess (serial).

WELLS, L. M.

Born: 1862. Died: Jan. 1, 1923, Screen actor.

Appeared in: **1915** Graft (serial). **1916** Liberty, A Daughter of the U.S.A. (serial). **1917** The Red Ace (serial). **1920** Vanishing Trails (serial). **1921** Forgotten Woman; The Girl from God's Country; A Virginia Courtship; The Witching Hour. **1922** The Forest King.

WELLS, MAI

Born: 1862. Died: Aug. 1, 1941, Los Angeles, Calif. Screen and stage actress.

Appeared in: **1921** Opened Shutters. **1922** The Pilgrim. **1925** Excuse Me. **1927** Blondes by Choice.

WELLS, MARIE

Born: 1894. Died: July 2, 1949, Hollywood, Calif. (overdose of sleeping pills—suicide). Stage and screen actress.

Appeared in: **1923** The Love Brand; The Man from New York. **1929** The Desert Song. **1930** The Song of the West. **1934** Service with a Smile (short); The Scarlet Empress; Elmer and Elsie. **1935** Old Sawbones (short). **1936** Cain and Mabel.

WENCK, EDUARD

Born: 1894. Died: May 17, 1954, Berlin, Germany (suicide because of heart ailment). Stage and screen actor.

Appeared in: **1939** Der Lustige Witwenball (The Merry Widow's Ball); Der Biberpelz (The Beaver Coat).

WENDELL, HOWARD D. (Howard David Wendell).

Born: 1908, Johnstown, Pa. Died: Aug. 11, 1975, Oregon City, Ore. Screen, stage and television actor.

Appeared in: **1952** Affair in Trinidad; You for Me. **1953** By the Light of the Silvery Moon; The Big Heat; Captain Scarface; Gentlemen Prefer Blondes. **1954** Prince Valiant; The Black Dakotas; Athena. **1955** The Fighting Chance; The View from Pompey's Head. **1956** Wiretappers; Storm Center; Never Say Goodbye; Day of Fury. **1959** Stranger in My Arms; The Four Skulls of Jonathan Drake; It Happened to Jane. **1962** Sail a Crooked Ship. **1965** The Cincinnati Kid; My Blood Runs Cold.

WENDORFF, LAIOLA

Born: 1895. Died: Jan. 21, 1966, Hollywood, Calif. Screen and television actress.

Appeared in: **1950** No Way Out. **1960** The Little Shop of Horrors; Song without End.

WENGRAF, JOHN E.

Born: 1897, Vienna, Austria. Died: May 4, 1974, Santa Barbara, Calif. Screen, stage actor and stage director.

Appeared in: **1941** Convoy. **1942** Lucky Jordan. **1943** Song of Russia; Mission to Moscow; Sahara; Paris After Dark. **1944** The Seventh Cross; 'Til We Meet Again; U-Boat Prisoner; Strange Affair. **1945** Weekend at the Waldorf. **1946** Tomorrow is Forever; The Razor's Edge. **1947** T-Men. **1948** Sofia. **1949** The Lovable Cheat. **1952** Five Fingers. **1953** The Desert Rats; Call Me Madam; Flight to Tangier; Tropic Zone. **1954** The French Line; The Gambler from Natchez; Gog; Paris Playboys; Hell and High Water. **1955** The Racers. **1957** Oh Men! Oh Women!; The Pride and the Passion; The Disembodied; Valerie. **1958** The Return of Dracula. **1960** Portrait in Black; Twelve to the Moon. **1961** Judgment at Nuremberg. **1962** Hitler. **1963** The Prize. **1965** Ship of Fools.

WENTWORTH, MARTHA (Verna "Martha" Wentworth)

Born: New York, N.Y. Died: Mar. 8, 1974, Sherman Oaks, Calif. Screen, stage, television and radio actress. Known as the "actress of 100 voices" in radio.

Appeared in: **1940** Waterloo Bridge. **1941** Bowery Blitzkrieg. **1943** Clancy Street Boys. **1945** Fallen Angel; A Tree Grows in Brooklyn. **1946** Santa Fe Uprising (serial); The Stranger. **1947** Vigilantes Boomtown (serial); Oregon Trail; Marshal of Cripple Creek; Rustlers of Devil Canyon; Homesteaders of Paradise Valley; Stagecoach to Denver. **1951** Love Nest. **1952** Young Man with Ideas; O. Henry's Full House (aka Full House). **1953** One Girl's Confession. **1955** Artists and Models; Good Morning Miss Dove; Jupiter's Darling; The Man with the Golden Arm. **1957** Daughter of Dr. Jekyll. **1961** One Hundred and One Dalmations. **1963** The Sword and the Stone (voice).

WERBESIK, GISELA

Born: 1875. Died: Apr. 15, 1956, Hollywood, Calif. Screen and stage actress. Appeared in U.S., British and German films.

Appeared in: **1944** The Hairy Ape. **1945** Wonder Man. **1946** A Scandal in Paris.

WERKMEISTER, LOTTE

Born: 1886, Germany. Died: July 1970, Bergholz-Rehbruecke, East Germany. Stage and screen actress.

Appeared in: **1931** Der Hampelmann. **1934** Zu Befehl Herr Unteroffizier. **1935** Die Toerichte Jungfrau.

WERNER, BUD

Born: Feb. 28, 1936. Died: Apr. 12, 1964, St. Moritz, Switzerland (avalanche). American ski champion and screen actor killed while making a sports documentary.

WERNER, WALTER

Born: 1884, Germany. Died: Jan. 8, 1956, Berlin, Germany (pneumonia). Stage and screen actor.

Appeared in: **1938** The Kreutzer Sonata. **1948** Marriage in the Shadows.

WERNER-KAHLE, HUGO

Born: 1883, Germany. Died: May 1, 1961, Berlin, Germany. Stage and screen actor.

Appeared in: **1931** Mother Love. **1935** Gruen ist die Heide. Other German films: Der Maulkorb; Traummusik; Affair Roedern.

WERNICKE, OTTO

Born: 1893, Osterode/Harz, Germany. Died: 1965, Munich, Germany. Stage and screen actor.

Appeared in: **1932** Stuerme der Leidenschaft. **1933** M. **1934** Die Blonde Christl; Die Verkaufte Braut; S A Mann Brand. **1935** Zwischen Himmel und Erde (Between Heaven and Earth). **1936** Knock-Out. **1937** Stimme des Blutes (Blood Bond). **1938** Gleisdrejeck. **1940** Henker Fraven und Soldaten (Hangman, Women and Soldiers); Die Neue Deutsche Luftwaffe Greift an (The New German Air Force Attacks); Johannis Fever (St. John's Fire); Maria Lilona. **1948** Long is the Road. **1959** Himmel Ohne Sterne (Sky without Stars).

WERTZ, CLARENCE

Died: Dec. 25, 1935, Hollywood, Calif. (following operation). Screen actor and stuntman.

Appeared in: **1922** The Three Must-Get-There's. **1926** Spangles.

WERY, CARL

Born: 1898, Bavaria, Germany. Died: Mar. 14, 1975, Munich, Germany (acute pneumonia and chronic cerebral sclerosis). Stage and screen actor.

Appeared in: **1953** Heidi. **1954** Desires; Angelika. **1955** Heidi and Peter. **1958** Ballerina. **1959** Kriegsgericht (Court Martial—US 1962). **1962** Am Galgen Hangt die Liebe (Love of the Gallows).

WESS, OTTO FRANCIS
Born: 1914. Died: Mar. 18, 1969, Youngstown, Ohio. Screen, vaudeville, radio actor and dancer. Appeared on stage as Ray Ravelle.

WESSEL, DICK (Richard Wessel)
Born: 1913. Died: Apr. 20, 1965, Studio City, Calif. (heart attack). Screen, stage, radio and television actor.

Appeared in: **1935** In Spite of Danger. **1937** Round-up Time in Texas; The Game That Kills; Slim; Borrowing Trouble. **1938** Arson Gang Busters. **1939** Beasts of Berlin; Dust Be My Destiny; Missing Daughters; They Made Me a Criminal. **1940** Cafe Hostess; Brother Orchid; So You Won't Talk; The Border Legion. **1941** The Great Train Robbery; Desert Bandit; Tanks a Million. **1942** Bells of Capistrano; X Marks the Spot; Dudes are Pretty People; Yankee Doodle Dandy; The Traitor Within; You Can't Escape Forever; Gentleman Jim; Highways by Night. **1943** Silver Spurs; Action in the North Atlantic. **1946** In Old Sacramento; Dick Tracy vs. Cueball; In Fast Company; Noisy Neighbors (short). **1947** Merton of the Movies; plus the following shorts: Wife to Spare; Do or Diet; In Room 303; Blondes Away; Fright Night. **1948** Pitfall; Unknown Island; When My Baby Smiles at Me; Badmen of Tombstone; Eight-Ball Andy (short); Dig That Gold (short). **1949** Thieves' Highway; Blondie Hits the Jackpot; Slattery's Hurricane; Frontier Outpost; Canadian Pacific; Billie Gets Her Man (short). **1950** Blondie's Hero; The Dungeon; Wabash Avenue; Beware of Blondie; Watch the Birdie; Punchy Cowpunchers (short). **1951** The Scarf; Reunion in Reno; Texas Carnival; Corky of Gasoline Alley; Honeychile. **1952** Love Is Better Than Ever; The Belle of New York; Blackbeard the Pirate; Wac from Walla Walla; Young Man with Ideas. **1953** Gentlemen Prefer Blondes; Champ for a Day; Let's Do It Again; The Caddy; Fresh Painter (short). **1955** Bowery to Bagdad; Fling in the Ring (short). **1956** Around the World in 80 Days; Andy Goes Wild (short). **1960** The Gazebo. **1963** Wives and Lovers; Pocketful of Miracles; Who's Minding the Store? **1966** The Ugly Dachshund.

WESSELHOEFT, ELEANOR (Elinor Wesselhoeft)
Born: 1873, Cambridge, Mass. Died: Dec. 9, 1945, Hollywood, Calif. Stage and screen actress.

Appeared in: **1931** Street Scene (film debut). **1932** Madame Racketeer. **1933** The Great Jasper; Cradle Song. **1934** All Men Are Enemies; Thirty Day Princess; Black Moon. **1935** Country Chairman; The Wedding Night; The Woman in Red. **1936** Boulder Dam; A Son Comes Home; Ladies in Love. **1938** Miracle Money (short); The Baroness and the Butler. **1939** Intermezzo; The Story of Alfred Nobel (short); Everything Happens at Night. **1940** Four Sons. **1941** More Trifles of Importance (short).

WESSON, GENE
Born: 1921. Died: Aug. 22, 1975, New York, N.Y. (heart attack). Screen, stage and television actor. Brother of Dick Wesson with whom he appeared in a comedy act known as "The Wesson Brothers."

Appeared in: **1955** Wichita. **1965** Satan's Bed. **1967** The Battle of Algiers; The Hunt. **1968** The Uninhibited.

WEST, BILLY (Roy B. Weisberg)
Born: Sept. 21, 1893, Russia. Died: July 21, 1975, Hollywood, Calif. (heart attack). Screen and vaudeville actor, screen director, screenwriter and cartoonist. Entered films in 1909. Starred in a series of "Billy West Comedies."

Appeared in: **1914** For Her Father's Sin; A Mother's Influence; The Niggard; At Dawn; Bright and Early. **1915** The Comeback. **1917** Dough-Nuts; The Prospector; The Chief Cook. **1918** The Orderly; The Rogue; His Day Out; The Stranger; Playmates; King Solomon (aka Ol King Sol); The Slave. **1920** Beauties in Distress. **1925** Billy West series, including: Copper Butt-Ins; West is West; Fiddlin' Around; The Joke's on You; So Long Billy. **1926** Thrilling Youth. **1927** Lucky Fool. **1933** The Diamond Trail. **1934** Perfectly Mismated (short). **1935** Motive for Revenge. **1968** The Further Perils of Laurel and Hardy (doc.).

WEST, CHARLES H.
Born: Nov. 30, 1885, Pittsburgh, Pa. Died: Oct. 10, 1943, Los Angeles, Calif. Stage and screen actor. Entered films with Biograph in 1910.

Appeared in: **1912** The Goddess of Sagebrush Gulch. **1917** Betty to the Rescue; The American Consul; The Little Pirate; Little Miss Optimist; The Trouble Buster. **1921** Bob Hampton of Placer; Not Guilty; The Witching Hour. **1922** The Lane That Had No Turning; Love in the Dark; Manslaughter. **1923** The Eternal Three; Held to Answer; Red Lights; Times Have Changed. **1925** The Fate of a Flirt; The Overland Limited; The Part Time Wife; The Road to Yesterday; The Talker. **1926** The Skyrocket; House without a Key (serial). **1927** King of Kings; Nobody's Widow; On the Stroke of Twelve. **1928** Man from Headquarters. **1929** Acquitted; Handcuffed. **1930** Along Came Youth; For the Defense. **1933** Police Car 17. **1934** The Man Trailer. **1935** The Bride Comes Home. **1937** Don't Tell Your Wife.

WEST, EDNA RHYS
Born: 1887. Died: Feb. 7, 1963, Middletown, N.Y. Screen and stage actress.

Appeared in: **1929** Half Way to Heaven.

WEST, JAMES "BUSTER"
Born: 1902, Philadelphia, Pa. Died: Mar. 19, 1966, Encino, Calif. (brain tumor). Screen, stage and vaudeville actor. Appeared in vaudeville with his parents in an act billed as "Wells, Virginia and West."

Appeared in the following Christie shorts prior to 1933: The Dancing Gob (film debut); Marching to Georgie; Don't Give Up. **1934–38** Educational shorts. **1938** Radio City Revels. **1949** Make Mine Laughs.

WEST, KATHERINE (aka LILLIAN WESTNER)
Born: 1883. Died: Sept. 26, 1936, Los Angeles, Calif. (heart attack). Stage and screen actress. Appeared as Katherine West, Lillian Westner and Maxine Morton.

WEST, PAT (Arthur Pat West)
Born: 1889. Died: Apr. 1944, Hollywood, Calif. Screen, stage and vaudeville actor. Appeared in vaudeville with his wife Lucille in an act billed as "Arthur and Lucille West."

Appeared in: **1929** Ship Ahoy (short). **1930** Russian Around (short); Gates of Happiness (short). **1935** Red Morning. **1936** Cain and Mabel; Ceiling Zero; Song of the Saddle; Three of a Kind; On the Wrong Trek (short). **1937** Turn Off the Moon. **1938** Bringing Up Baby; If I Were King; Thanks for the Memory. **1939** Geronimo; Only Angels Have Wings; Some Like It Hot. **1940** His Girl Friday. **1942** Madame Spy; Invisible Agent. **1944** To Have and to Have Not.

WEST, THOMAS
Born: 1859. Died: July 28, 1932, Philadelphia, Pa. (liver ailment). Screen, stage and vaudeville actor. Was known as "Chinese Tommy" for his interpretations of oriental characters. Entered films with Lubin.

WEST, WILLIAM
Died: Sept. 23, 1918, New York, N.Y. (injuries sustained from a fall). Screen actor. Entered films with the Edison Company.

Appeared in: **1911** The Stuff That Dreams are Made Of; The Minute Man; The New Church Carpet; Money to Burn; The Stolen Dog; Uncle Hiram's List; The Professor and the New Hat; The Declaration of Independence; An Unknown Language; Eugene Wrayburn; Foul Play; Her Wedding Ring; Mike's Hero; The Rise and Fall of Weary Willie; Ludwig from Germany; The Living Peach; The Lure of the City; How Sir Andrew Lost His Vote; Freezing Auntie. **1912** Von Weber's Last Waltz; The Harbinger of Peace; Blinks and Jinks; Attorneys-at-law; In His Father's Steps; The Grandfather; A Romance of the Rails; The Windking Parson; The Old Reporter; The Sunset Gun; How Father Accomplished His Work; The Green-Eyed Monster. **1913** For Her; The Mountaineers; A Will and a Way; Kathleen Mavourneen; The Elder Brother; The Inventor's Sketch; With the Eyes of the Blind; The Golden Wedding; Scenes from Other Days; A Mutual Understanding; The Awakening of a Man. **1914** The Birth of the Star Spangled Banner; A Question of Identity; The Perfect Truth; The Man in the Dark; On Christmas Eve; The Powers of the Air; Tango in Tuckerville; The Active Life of Dollie of the Dailies (serial); Grand Opera in Rubeville; The Resurrection of Caleb Worth; The Borrowed Finery; Frederick the Great. **1915** On the Stroke of Twelve; On the Wrong Track; What Happened on the Barbuda; The Magistrate's Story; The Ploughshare; The Magic Skin.

WEST, WILLIAM HERMAN
Born: 1860. Died: Aug. 28, 1915, Glendale, Calif. Screen actor.

Appeared in: **1912** The Plot That Failed; The Peril of the Cliffs; The Power of a Hymn; The Indian Uprising at Santa Fe; The Skinflint; Red Wing and the Paleface; The Flower Girl's Revenge; The Driver of the Deadwood Coach. **1913** On the Brink of Ruin; The Struggle; The Big Horn Massacre; Perils of the Sea; The Last Blockhouse; Red Sweeney's Mistake; The Poet and the Soldier; The Pride of Angry Bear; The Redemption; Missing Bonds. **1914** The Barrister of Ignorance; The Fatal Opal; The Smugglers of Lone Isle; Who Goes There? **1915** The Vanishing Vases; The Strangler's Cord; The Affair of the Deserted House (serial); The Apartment House Mystery (serial); In the Shadow of Death; The Writing on the Wall; The Tattooed Hand; The Accomplice; The Vivisectionist; The Money-Leechers; The Wolf's Prey; The Man on Watch; The Dream Seekers.

WESTCOTT, GORDON
Born: 1903, near St. George, Utah. Died: Oct. 31, 1935, Hollywood, Calif. (injuries suffered in polo-playing fall). Stage and screen actor.

Appeared in: **1931** Enemies of the Law. **1932** Guilty as Hell; Devil and the Deep; Hot Saturday; Love Me Tonight. **1933** The Crime of the Century; He Learned about Women; Heritage of the Desert; The Working Man; Lilly Turner; Heroes for Sale; Convention City; Private Detective 62; Footlight Parade; Voltaire; The World Changes. **1934** Fashions of 1934; Fog over Frisco; I've Got Your Number; Call It Luck; The Circus Clown; Registered Nurse; Six

Day Bike Rider; The Case of the Howling Dog; Kansas City Princess; Murder in the Clouds; Dark Hazard; We're in the Money. **1935** The White Cuckatoo; A Night at the Ritz; Go into Your Dance; Going Highbrow; Bright Lights; Front Page Woman; This Is the Life; Two-Fisted; Ceiling Zero.

WESTERFIELD, JAMES "JIM"

Born: 1913. Died: Sept. 20, 1971, Woodland Hills, Calif. (heart attack). Screen, stage and television actor. Married to actress Fay Tracy.

Appeared in: **1941** Highway West. **1946** Undercurrent; The Chase. **1951** The Whistle at Eaton Falls; The Human Jungle. **1954** Three Hours to Kill; On the Waterfront. **1955** Chief Crazy Horse; The Violent Men; The Cobweb; The Scarlet Coat; Lady Gallant; Man with the Gun. **1957** Three Brave Men; Jungle Heat; Decision at Sundown. **1958** Cowboy; The Proud Rebel. **1959** The Shaggy Dog; The Gunfight at Dodge City. **1960** Wild River; The Plunderers. **1961** The Absent-Minded Professor; Homicidal. **1962** Birdman of Alcatraz; The Scarface Mob. **1963** Son of Flubber. **1964** Man's Favorite Sport?; Bikini Beach. **1965** The Sons of Katie Elder; That Funny Feeling. **1966** Dead Heat on a Merry-Go-Round. **1968** Blue; Hang 'Em High. **1969** Smith!; A Man Called Gannon; The Love God; True Grit; Recent Mexican film: Arde (Burn).

WESTLEY, HELEN (Henrietta Remson Meserole Maney Conroy)

Born: 1879, Brooklyn, N.Y. Died: Dec. 12, 1942, Franklin Township, N.J. Stage and screen actress. Divorced from actor John Westley (dec. 1948).

Appeared in: **1934** Death Takes a Holiday; The House of Rothschild; Moulin Rouge; The Age of Innocence; Anne of Green Gables. **1935** Splendor; Roberta; Captain Hurricane; Chasing Yesterday; The Melody Lingers On. **1936** Showboat; Half Angel; Dimples; Banjo on My Knee; Stowaway. **1937** Sing and Be Happy; Cafe Metropole; Heidi; I'll Take Romance. **1938** Keep Smiling; Rebecca of Sunny Brook Farm; The Baroness and the Butler; Alexander's Ragtime Band; She Married an Artist; Wife, Husband and Friend. **1939** Zaza. **1940** All This and Heaven Too; The Captain Is a Lady; Lady with Red Hair; Lillian Russell. **1941** Henry Aldrich for President; Adam Had Four Sons; The Smiling Ghost; Bedtime Story; Million Dollar Baby; Sunny; Lady from Louisiana. **1942** My Favorite Spy.

WESTLEY, JOHN (John Conroy)

Died: Dec. 26, 1948, Hollywood, Calif. Stage and screen actor. Divorced from actress Helen Westley (dec. 1942).

WESTMAN, NYDIA

Born: 1902. Died: May 23, 1970, Burbank, Calif. (cancer). Screen, stage and television actress.

Appeared in: **1932** Strange Justice; Manhattan Tower. **1933** Bondage; The Way to Love; The Cradle Song; Little Women; King of the Jungle; From Hell to Heaven. **1934** Two Alone; Success at Any Price; Ladies Should Listen; The Trumpet Blows; One Night of Love; Manhattan Love Song. **1935** Captain Hurricane; Dressed to Thrill; Sweet Adeline; A Feather in Her Hat. **1936** The Georgeous Hussy; Craig's Wife; The Rose Bowl; The Invisible Ray; Pennies from Heaven; Three Live Ghosts. **1937** When Love Is Young; Bulldog Drummond's Revenge. **1938** The Goldwyn Follies; The First Hundred Years; Bulldog Drummond's Peril. **1939** The Cat and the Canary; When Tomorrow Comes. **1940** Forty Little Mothers; Hullabaloo. **1941** The Bad Man; The Chocolate Soldier. **1942** They All Kissed the Bride; The Remarkable Andrew. **1943** Princess O'Rourke; Hers to Hold. **1944** Her Primitive Man. **1947** The Late George Apley. **1948** The Velvet Touch. **1962** For Love or Money; Don't Know the Twist. **1966** The Chase; The Ghost of Mr. Chicken; The Swinger. **1967** The Reluctant Astronaut. **1968** The Horse in the Gray Flannel Suit. **1969** Nobody Loves Flapping Eagle; Run Rabbit Run.

WESTMORELAND, PAULINE

Born: 1910. Died: Jan. 28, 1947, Los Angeles, Calif. Screen actress.

WESTNER, LILLIAN. See KATHERINE WEST

WESTON, DORIS (Doris Wester)

Born: Sept. 9, 1917, Chicago, Ill. Died: July 27, 1960, N.Y. (cancer). Screen and radio actress.

Appeared in **1937** Submarine D-1; The Singing Marine. **1938** Born to Be Wild. **1940** Chip of the Flying U.

WESTON, GEORGE

Died: Apr. 7, 1923, N.Y. Stage and screen actor.

WESTON, JOSEPH J.

Born: 1888. Died: May 1, 1972, Los Angeles, Calif. Screen actor.

Appeared in: **1942** Bashful Bachelor; Over My Dead Body.

WESTON, MAGGIE

Died: Nov. 3, 1926, New York, N.Y. Stage and screen actress.

WESTON, RUTH

Born: Aug. 31, 1906, Boston, Mass. Died: Nov. 5, 1955, East Orange, N.J. Stage and screen actress.

Appeared in: **1931** The Public Defender; Devotion; Smart Woman; The Woman Between. **1932** This Sporting Age. **1935** Splendor. **1938** That Certain Age. **1939** Made for Each Other.

WESTON, SAMMY

Born: 1889. Died: Feb. 1, 1951, Hollywood, Calif. Screen and stage actor.

WESTWOOD, MARTIN F.

Born: 1883. Died: Dec. 19, 1928, Glendale, Calif. (pneumonia). Screen actor.

WETHERELL, M. A.

Born: 1887. Died: Feb. 25, 1939, Johannesburg, South Africa. Screen actor, film producer and film director.

Appeared in: **1921** The Buried City. **1922** The Wee Macgregor's Sweetheart; The Vulture's Prey. **1923** Through Fire and Water. **1924** Women and Diamonds (aka Conscripts of Misfortune or It Happened in Africa). **1925** Livingstone (aka Livingstone in Africa—US 1929). **1927** Robinson Crusoe.

WHALEN, MICHAEL (Joseph Kenneth Shovlin)

Born: 1902, Wilkes Barre, Pa. Died: Apr. 14, 1974, Woodland Hills, Calif. (bronchial pneumonia). Screen, stage, radio, television actor and singer.

Appeared in: **1935** Professional Soldier. **1936** The Man I Marry; Sing, Baby, Sing; Song and Dance Man; The Country Doctor; The Poor Little Rich Girl; White Fang; Career Woman. **1937** Woman Wise; Time Out for Romance; The Lady Escapes; Wee Willie Winkie. **1938** Time Out for Murder; Change of Heart; Walking Down Broadway; Island in the Sky; Speed to Burn; While New York Sleeps; Inside Story; Pardon Our Nerve; Meridian 7-1212. **1939** The Mysterious Miss X; They Asked for It. **1940** Ellery Queen, Master Detective. **1941** Sign of the Wolf; I'll Sell My Life. **1942** Nazi Spy Ring. **1943** Tahiti Honey. **1947** Gas House Kids in Hollywood. **1948** Highway 13; Thunder in the Pines; Blonde Ice. **1949** Shep Comes Home; Omoo, Omoo, the Shark God (aka Omoo, Omoo); Sky Liner; Son of a Badman; Tough Assignment; Treasure of Monte Cristo; Parole, Inc. **1950** Sarumba. **1951** Mask of the Dragon; Kentucky Jubilee; According to Mrs. Hoyle; Fingerprints Don't Lie; G. I. Jane. **1952** Waco. **1955** The Silver Star. **1956** The Phantom from 10,000 Leagues. **1957** She Shoulda Said No. **1958** Missile to the Moon. **1960** Elmer Gantry.

WHALEY, BERT

Died: Jan. 17, 1973. Screen actor.

WHEAT, LAWRENCE "LARRY" (aka LAURENCE WHEAT)

Born: 1876. Died: Aug. 7, 1963. Screen actor.

Appeared in: **1921** Hush Money; The Land of Hope. **1922** Our Leading Citizen; The Bachelor Daddy; Back Home and Broke; The Beauty Shop; The Man Who Saw Tomorrow. **1923** The Ne'er-Do-Well; Hollywood; The Song of Love. **1924** The Confidence Man; Inez from Hollywood. **1925** Not So Long Ago; Coming Through; Old Home Week. **1926** Irene. **1934** The Loud Speaker; Peck's Bad Boy. **1935** Public Hero Number One; It's In the Air; The Big Broadcast of 1936; Postal Inspector. **1945** It's Your Move (short); What a Blonde.

WHEATCROFT, STANHOPE (Stanhope Nelson Wheatcroft)

Born: May 11, 1888, New York. Died: Feb. 12, 1966, Woodland Hills, Calif. (heart attack). Stage and screen actor.

Appeared in: **1915** Bought. **1916** Camille; Broken Chains; East Lynne; Under Two Flags; Sins of Men; The Madness of Helen. **1917** The Corner Grocer; A Modern Cinderella; The Runaway; Maternity; Courage of the Commonplace. **1919** Secret Service. **1921** Cold Steel; Dr. Jim; Greater Than Love. **1922** The Hottentot; The Sign of the Rose; Two Kinds of Women. **1923** Blow Your Own Horn; Breaking Into Society. **1924** Broadway or Bust; The Iron Horse; Laughing at Danger; No More Women; The Yankee Consul. **1925** Keep Smiling; Madame Behave; Ridin' Pretty. **1927** The King of Kings; Women's Wares. **1934** The Notorious Sophie Lang.

WHEELER, BERT (Albert Jerome Wheeler)

Born: 1895, Paterson, N.J. Died: Jan. 18, 1968, New York, N.Y. (emphysema). Screen, stage, vaudeville, television actor and screenwriter. Father of actress Patricia Walters (dec. 1967). Was partner with Robert Woolsey (dec. 1938) in vaudeville and film comedy team of "Wheeler and Woolsey." Unless otherwise noted, the films listed are for the team.

Appeared in: **1922** Captain Fly-by-Night. **1929** The Voice of Hollywood (Wheeler only—short); Rio Rita (stage and film versions); Small Timers (Wheeler only—short). **1930** The Cuckoos; Dixiana; Half Shot at Sunrise; Hook, Line and Sinker; Caught Plastered; Oh! Oh! Cleopatra (short); Peach O'Reno; Too Many Cooks (Wheeler only). **1932** Girl Crazy; The Slippery Pearls (short); Hold 'Em Jail; Hollywood Handicap (Wheeler only—short). **1933** So This Is Africa; Diplomaniacs. **1934** Hips, Hips, Hooray; Cockeyed Cavaliers; Kentucky Kernels. **1935** The Nitwits; The Rainmakers; A Night at the Biltmore Bowl (Wheeler only—short). **1936** Silly Billies; Mummy's Boys. **1937** On Again, Off Again; High Flyers. **1939** Cowboy Quarterback (Wheeler only). **1941** Las Vegas Nights (Wheeler only). **1951** The Awful Sleuth (Wheeler only—short).

WHEELER, BURRITT (Burritt Nash Wheeler)
Born: Dec. 25, 1883, Ill. Died: Nov. 11, 1957, Los Angeles, Calif. (cancer). Screen actor and radio producer.

Appeared in: **1950** Stella.

WHEELER, TERESA (aka CABARET TESS)
Died: Dec. 26, 1975. Screen and vaudeville actress. Appeared in silent films.

WHELAN, LEO M.
Born: 1876, Bridgeport, Conn. Died: Oct. 15, 1952, Arlington, N.J. Silent screen and vaudeville actor. Appeared in vaudeville with members of his family in an act billed as "Four Happy Whelans."

WHELAN, RON
Born: 1905, England. Died: Dec. 8, 1965, Los Angeles, Calif. (leukemia). Screen, stage actor and film director.

Appeared in: **1937** Wild Innocence. **1950** Massacre Hill. **1953** Kangaroo. **1963** Gun Hawk; The Three Stooges Go around the World in a Daze. **1965** Greatest Story Ever Told.

WHELAN, TIM
Born: Nov. 2, 1893, Ind. Died: Aug. 12, 1957, Beverly Hills; Calif. Screen, stage actor, film director, film producer and screenwriter. Entered films as an actor in 1922.

WHELAR, LANGOIS M.
Born: 1898. Died: Oct. 17, 1918, France. Screen actor.

WHIFFEN, MRS. THOMAS (Blanche Galton)
Born: Mar. 12, 1845, London, England. Died: Nov. 26, 1936, Montvale, Va. Screen, stage actress and opera performer.

Appeared in: **1915** Barbara Frietchie.

WHIPPER, LEIGH, SR. (aka LEE WHIPPER)
Born: 1877, Charleston, S.C. Died: July 26, 1975, Harlem, N.Y. Black screen, stage and television actor.

Appeared in: **1939** Of Mice and Men. **1941** Robin Hood of the Pecos; Virginia; King of the Zombies; Bahama Passage; The Vanishing Virginian. **1942** White Cargo; Heart of the Golden West. **1943** Happy Land; Mission to Moscow; The Oxbow Incident; Bahama Passage. **1944** The Imposter. **1946** Undercurrent. **1947** Untamed Fury (narration). **1949** Lost Boundaries. **1955** The Shrike. **1956** The Harder They Fall. **1957** The Young Don't Cry. **1958** Marjorie Morningstar.

WHIPS, ANDREA. See ANDREA FELDMAN

WHISTLER, MARGARET
Born: 1892. Died: Aug. 23, 1939, Hollywood, Calif. Screen actress.

WHITAKER, CHARLES "SLIM" (Charles Orbie Whitaker)
Born: July 29, 1893. Died: June 27, 1960 (heart attack). Screen actor. Do not confuse with screenwriter Charles E. Whittaker.

Appeared in: **1925** Galloping On; On the Go; Hurricane Horseman; Tearin' Loose. **1926** Ace of Action; The Bandit Buster; The Bonanza Buckaroo; The Fighting Cheat; Rawhide; Trumpin' Trouble; Twin Triggers. **1927** The Desert of the Lost; The Ridin' Rowdy; Soda Water Cowboy; The Obligin' Buckaroo; The Phantom Buster. **1928** The Canyon of Adventure; The Flying Buckaroo; Desperate Courage; Saddle Mates. **1930** Shadow Ranch; Dawn Trail. **1931** Rider of the Plains; Desert Vengeance. **1932** The Man from New Mexico. **1933** Drum Taps; Deadwood Pass; Smoking Guns; Dawn Trail. **1934** The Law of the Wild (serial); Man From Hell; Terror on the Plains. **1935** Unconquered Bandit; Rustlers' Paradise; Tumbling Tumbleweeds. **1936** Ghost Patrol; Riding. **1937** Melody of the Plains. **1938** Rawhide; Frontier Scout; Under Western Stars. **1939** Rollin' Westward; Legion of the Lawless; New Frontier. **1940** Bullet Code; Prairie Law; Marshal of Mesa City; Legion of the Lawless. **1941** Along the Rio Grande; Arizona Bound; Cyclone on Horseback. **1942** The Mad Monster; The Silver Bullet; Billy the Kid's Smoking Guns. **1943** The Mysterious Rider; The Kid Rides Again; Fighting Frontier. **1944** The Laramie Trail; The Drifter; Oklahoma Raiders; Marshal of Gunsmoke. **1946** Overland Riders; Outlaw of the Plains; Panhandle Trail; Law of the Lash. **1948** The Westward Trail.

WHITBECK, FRANK
Born: 1882, Rochester, N.Y. Died: Dec. 23, 1963. Film director, screen actor, publicist and screenwriter. Narrated numerous MGM trailers.

WHITE, ALFRED H. (Alfred Weisman)
Born: 1883. Died: Aug. 22, 1972, Fort Lauderdale, Fla. Stage, vaudeville and screen actor.

Appeared in: **1933** Don't Bet on Love.

WHITE, BILL (William A. Rattenberry)
Born: 1857. Died: Apr. 21, 1933, Los Angeles, Calif. (heart attack). Stage and screen actor.

Appeared in: **1921** A Motion to Adjourn. **1922** Two-Fisted Jefferson; The Sheriff of Sun-Dog. **1923** The Fighting Skipper (serial); At Devil's Gorge; The Devil's Dooryard. **1924** Western Yesterdays; Western Feuds.

WHITE, EDWARD J. (Edward Jocelyn White)
Born: Mar. 15, 1902, New York, N.Y. Died: Sept. 24, 1973, Culver City, Calif. Film, television producer and screen actor.

WHITE, FRANCES
Born: 1898. Died: Feb. 24, 1969, Los Angeles, Calif. Singer and screen actress. Was a Ziegfeld Follies girl. Divorced from actor Frank Fay (dec. 1961).

Appeared in: **1922** Face to Face. **1934** The Mighty Barnum. **1936** The Great Ziegfeld.

WHITE, GEORGE
Born: 1890, Toronto, Ontario, Canada. Died: Oct. 11, 1968, Los Angeles, Calif. (leukemia). Stage, film producer, stage, film director, screen and stage actor.

Appeared in: **1920** Scandals. **1930** Scandals. **1934** George White's Scandals of 1934. **1935** George White's 1935 Scandals. **1946** Rhapsody in Blue.

WHITE, HUGH "HUEY"
Born: 1896. Died: June 23, 1938, Hollywood, Calif. (injuries from auto accident). Stage and screen actor.

Appeared in: **1931** Hush Money. **1933** Female; Convention City. **1934** Gambling Lady; The Hell Cat; The Million Dollar Ransom. **1935** G-Men. **1936** Crash Donovan. **1938** When G-Men Step In.

WHITE, J. IRVING
Born: 1865. Died: Apr. 17, 1944, Los Angeles, Calif. Stage and screen actor.

Appeared in: **1930** The Spoilers; Girl of the Golden West. **1932** Sign of the Cross (and revised version made in 1944).

WHITE, LEE ROY "LASSES"
Born: Aug. 28, 1888, Wills Point, Tex. Died: Dec. 16, 1949, Hollywood, Calif. Screen, stage, vaudeville, minstrel and radio actor. Entered films in 1938.

Appeared in: **1939** Rovin' Tumbleweeds. **1940** Oklahoma Renegades; Grandpa Goes to Town. **1941** Scattergood Pulls the Strings; Dude Cowboy; Riding the Wind; The Bandit Trail; Come On, Danger!; Sergeant York; Scattergood Baines; Thundering Hoofs; The Roundup; Cyclone on Horseback. **1942** Talk of the Town. **1943** Cinderella Swings It!; The Unknown Guest. **1943** Something to Shout About; The Outlaw. **1944** The Minstrel Man; The Adventures of Mark Twain; Alaska; When Strangers Marry; Song of the Range. **1945** Red Rock Outlaws; In Old Mexico; The Lonesome Trail; Saddle Serenade; Springtime in Texas; Three's a Crowd; Dillinger. **1946** Moon over Montana; Trail to Mexico; West of the Alamo. **1947** Rainbow over the Rockies; Six Gun Serenade; Song of the Sierras; Louisiana; The Wistful Widow of Wagon Gap. **1948** The Dude Goes West; The Golden Eye; Indian Agent; The Valiant Hombre. **1949** Mississippi Rhythm. **1950** The Texan Meets Calamity Jane.

WHITE, LEO
Born: 1880, Manchester, England. Died: Sept. 21, 1948, Hollywood, Calif. Stage and screen actor. Entered films with Essanay Co. in 1914. Appeared in early Charlie Chaplin comedies.

Appeared in: **1914** "Swedie" series. **1921** Keeping up with Lizzie; The Rookie's Return; Her Sturdy Oak; The Rage of Paris. **1922** Blood and Sand; Headin' West; Fools First. **1923** Breaking into Society; The Rustle of Silk; Why Worry?; In Search of a Thrill; Vanity Fair. **1924** The Brass Bowl; When a Girl Loves; The Woman on the Jury; Wine; A Lady of Quality; Sporting Youth; The Goldfish. **1925** Ben-Hur; The Masked Bride; One Year to Live; American Pluck; The Lady Who Lied. **1926** Devil's Island; The Lady of the Harem; The Blonde Saint; The Truthful Sex; A Desperate Moment; The Far Cry. **1927** See You in Jail; Beauty Shoppers; The Girl from Gay Paree; The Slaver; A Bowery Cinderella; McFadden's Flats; The Ladybird. **1928** Breed of the Sunsets; What Price Beauty?; Thunder Riders; How to Handle Women; Manhattan Knights. **1929** Campus Knights; Smilin' Guns; Born to the Saddle. **1930** Roaring Ranch. **1931** Along Came Youth; Monkey Business. **1933** Only Yesterday. **1934** Madame Du Barry; Done in Oil (short). **1935** Pop Goes the Easel (short); All the King's Horses; A Night at the Opera. **1936** Cain and Mabel. **1937** Tovarich. **1940** The Great Dictator. **1942** Gentleman Jim. **1946** So You Want to Play the Horses (short). **1947** My Wild Irish Rose. **1949** The Fountainhead.

WHITE, MARJORIE (aka MARJORIE TIERNEY)

Born: July 22, 1908, Winnipeg, Canada. Died: Aug. 20, 1935, Los Angeles, Calif. (auto accident). Screen, stage and vaudeville actress. Married to actor Eddie Tierney with whom she appeared in vaudeville. Entered films in 1929.

Appeared in: **1929** Happy Days; Sunny Side Up. **1930** Oh, for a Man!; The Golden Calf; Fox Movietone Follies of 1930; Just Imagine. **1931–32** "Voice of Hollywood" series. **1931** Women of All Nations; Charlie Chan Carries On; The Black Camel; Possessed. **1933** Diplomaniacs; Her Bodyguard. **1934** Woman Haters (short).

WHITE, PEARL

Born: Mar. 4, 1889, 1893 or 1897 (?), Green Ridge, Mo. Died: Aug. 4, 1938, Paris, France (liver ailment). Screen and stage actress. Divorced from actor Wallace McCutcheon (dec. 1928).

Appeared in: **1911** Through the Window; Helping Him Out; The Power of Love; The Lost Necklace. **1912** Mayblossom; Her Dressmaker's Bills; The Gypsy Flirt; Locked out; A Tangled Marriage; His Birthday; The Girl in the Next Room. **1913** Where Charity Begins; Hearts Entangled; Pearl's Mistake; Dress Reform; The Woman and the Law; Robert's Lesson; Girls Will Be Boys; His Rich Uncle; Hubby's New Coat; A Woman's Revenge; Pearl's Hero; The Cabaret Singer The Convict's Daughter. **1914** The Exploits of Elaine (serial); The Perils of Pauline (serial). **1915** The New Exploits of Elaine (serial); The Romance of Elaine (serial). **1916** Hazel Kirke; The Iron Claw (serial); Pearl of the Army (serial). **1917** The Fatal Ring (serial). **1919** The Black Secret (serial); The Lightning Raider (serial). **1920** The White Moll. **1921** Know Your Men; A Virgin Paradise; Tiger's Cub; The Thief; The Mountain Women; Beyond Price. **1922** Without Fear; The Breadway Peacock; Any Wife. **1923** Plunder (serial). **1924** Parisian Nights. **1925** Perils of Paris. **1961** Days of Thrills and Laughter (documentary).

WHITE, RUTH

Born: 1914, Perth Amboy, N.J. Died: Dec. 3, 1969, Perth Amboy, N.J. (cancer). Screen, stage and television actress.

Appeared in: **1956** Rumpus in the Harem (short). **1957** Muscle up a Little Closer (short); A Merry Mix-Up (short); Edge of the City. **1959** The Nun's Story. **1962** To Kill a Mockingbird. **1965** A Rage to Live; Baby, the Rain Must Fall. **1966** Cast a Giant Shadow. **1967** The Tiger Makes Out; Up the Down Staircase; Hang 'Em High; No Way to Treat a Lady; Charley. **1968** A Lovely Way to Die. **1969** Midnight Cowboy; The Reivers. **1971** The Pursuit of Happiness.

WHITE, SAMMY

Born: May 28, 1896, Providence, R.I. Died: Mar. 3, 1960, Beverly Hills, Calif. Screen, stage, vaudeville and television actor. First teamed in vaudeville with Lou Clayton and later with his wife Eva Puck (later divorced).

Appeared in: **1936** Show Boat; Cain and Mabel. **1937** The Hit Parade. **1938** Swing Your Lady. **1950** 711 Ocean Drive. **1951** Half Breed. **1952** Pat and Mike. **1953** Remains to Be Seen; The Bad and the Beautiful. **1954** About Mrs. Leslie; Living It Up. **1956** Somebody up There Likes Me. **1957** The Helen Morgan Story.

WHITE, VALERIE

Born: 1915, South Africa. Died: Dec. 3, 1975, London, England. Stage and screen actress.

Appeared in: **1944** The Halfway House (US 1945). **1947** Hue and Cry (US 1950).

WHITEFORD, JOHN P. "BLACKIE"

Born: 1873. Died: Mar. 21, 1962, Hollywood, Calif. Screen actor.

Appeared in: **1929** The Hoose Gow (short). **1931** Cyclone Kid. **1932** Shopping With Wifie; Mark of the Spur; Scarlet Brand; Man from New Mexico. **1933** Deadwood Pass. **1934** West of the Divide; Demon for Trouble. **1935** Toll of the Desert. **1936** Share the Wealth (short); Peppery Salt (short); The Last of the Warrens. **1937** Pardon Us; Grips, Grunts and Groans (short). **1945** Rough, Tough and Ready. **1946** Uncivil Warbirds (short); Three Troubledoers (short). **1947** The Last Round-Up. **1950** Marinated Mariner (short); Cow Town.

WHITELAW, BARRETT

Born: c. 1897. Died: Oct. 3, 1947, Los Angeles, Calif. (cerebral hemorrhage). Screen actor and extra.

Appeared in: **1946** The Kid from Brooklyn.

WHITEMAN, PAUL

Born: 1890, Denver, Colo. Died: Dec. 29, 1967, Doylestown, Pa. (heart attack). Bandleader, screen, stage, radio actor and composer.

Appeared in: **1924** Broadway after Dark. **1930** King of Jazz. **1935** Thanks a Million. **1940** Strike up the Band. **1944** Atlantic City. **1945** Rhapsody in Blue. **1947** The Fabulous Dorseys.

WHITESIDE, WALKER

Born: 1869, Logansport, Ind. Died: Aug. 18, 1942, Hastings-on-Hudson, N.Y. Screen, stage actor, stage producer and playwright.

Appeared in: **1915** The Melting Pot.

WHITFIELD, JORDAN

Born: 1917, Pittsburgh, Pa. Died: Nov. 11, 1967, Hollywood, Calif. (heart attack). Black screen and television actor.

Appeared in: **1938** You Can't Take It with You. **1946** Swamp Fire; Three Little Girls in Blue. **1948** Another Part of the Forest. **1950** Right Cross. **1954** Carmen Jones. **1958** The Cry Baby Killer. **1965** That Funny Feeling.

WHITFIELD, DR. WALTER W.

Born: 1888. Died: Jan. 13, 1966, Cleveland, Ohio. Black screen, stage actor, singer and dentist. Sang background music for films.

Appeared in: **1936** Green Pastures (stage and film versions).

WHITFORD, ANNABELLE. *See* "PEERLESS ANNABELLE"

WHITING, JACK

Born: June 22, 1901, Philadelphia, Pa. Died: Feb. 15, 1961, N.Y. Screen, stage and vaudeville actor.

Appeared in: **1930** Top Speed (film debut); College Lovers; The Life of the Party. **1933** Take a Chance. **1935** Broadway Brevities (short). **1938** Sailing Along; Give Me a Sailor.

WHITLEY, CRANE (Clem Wilenchick)

Died: Feb. 28, 1958. Screen actor.

Appeared in: **1938** The Last Warning. **1939** Beasts of Berlin; The Flying Deuces. **1942** My Favorite Blonde; Who Done It?; They Raid by Night. **1943** Girls in Chains. **1944** Enemy of Women. **1945** You Came Along. **1946** The Wife of Monte Cristo. **1947** The Return of Monte Cristo. **1948** Walk a Crooked Mile. **1949** Outpost in Morocco; The Crooked Way. **1950** The Crime Doctor's Diary. **1950** The Savage Horde. **1951** Insurance Investigator; Red Mountain. **1952** Mutiny. **1953** Treasure of the Golden Condor.

WHITLOCK, T. LLOYD

Born: Jan. 2, 1891, Springfield, Mo. Died: Jan. 8, 1966. Stage and screen actor.

Appeared in: **1916** The Masked Woman; The Diamond Lure; The Shadow Sinister. **1917** June Madness; The Man Who Took a Chance; The College Boys' Special; A Daughter of Daring (serial); The Edge of the Law (aka A Gentle Ill Wind). **1919** The Love Call; The Boomerang. **1920** Rouge and Riches; Scratch My Back. **1921** Courage; Face of the World; False Kisses; The Love Special; Not Guilty; One Man in a Million; A Private Scandal; See My Lawyer; They Shall Pay; White and Unmarried. **1922** Domestic Relations; The Flirt; The Girl Who Ran Wild; Kissed; The Ninety and Nine; The Snowshoe Trail; The Truthful Liar; Wild Honey. **1923** Cordelia the Magnificent; The Man Who Won; An Old Sweetheart of Mine; Slippy McGee; The Thrill Chaser; When Odds Are Even; The Woman of Bronze. **1924** The Foolish Virgin; The Midnight Express; The Price She Paid; The Triflers; Unmarried Wives; Women First. **1925** The Air Mail; Dollar Down; The Ancient Highway; The Great Sensation; The Prairie Pirate; New Champion; Speed Mad; Who Cares. **1926** The Fighting Buckaroo; The Man in the Saddle; Paradise; Peril of the Rail; Sparrows. **1927** A Hero for a Night; On the Stroke of Twelve; The Perfect Sap; Poor Girls; Pretty Clothes; The Thirteenth Juror; The War Horse. **1928** Hot Heels; Man from Headquarters; The Michigan Kid; Queen of the Chorus; House of Shame. **1929** The Kid's Clever; The Leatherneck; One Hysterical Night; Skinner Steps Out; The Fatal Warning (serial). **1930** The Cohens and Kellys in Africa; The Cohens and the Kellys in Scotland; See America Thirst; Young Eagles. **1931** Honeymoon Lane. **1932** Tangled Destinies. **1935** Behind the Green Lights. **1936** Night Cargo; Navy Born; The Dark House; Ride, Ranger, Ride. **1938** Arson Gang Busters; International Crime.

WHITMAN, ERNEST

Born: 1893. Died: Aug. 5, 1954, Hollywood, Calif. (heart attack). Black screen, radio and television actor. Known as Bill Jackson on radio and television "Beulah" shows.

Appeared in: **1936** The Prisoner of Shark Island; White Hunter; The Green Pastures. **1937** Daughter of Shanghai. **1939** Jesse James. **1940** Congo Maisie; Maryland; The Return of Frank James; Third Finger, Left Hand. **1941** The Get-Away; The Pittsburgh Kid; Among the Living. **1942** The Bugle Sounds; Drums of the Congo. **1943** Cabin in the Sky; Stormy Weather. **1947** My Brother Talks to Horses; Blonde Savage.

WHITMAN, ESTELLE

Died: July 14, 1970, Los Angeles, Calif. Screen actress. Entered films with Triangle Films during silents.

WHITMAN, GAYNE (aka ALFRED VOSBURGH)

Born: Mar. 19, 1890, Chicago, Ill. Died: Aug. 31, 1958, Hollywood, Calif.

(heart attack). Screen, stage, radio, television actor and screenwriter. Was radio's original "Chandu, the Magician."

Appeared in: **1925** The Wife Who Wasn't Wanted; His Majesty, Bunker Bean; The Love Hour; The Pleasure Buyers. **1926** Exclusive Rights; Three Weeks in Paris; Oh, What a Nurse!; Hell Bent for Heaven; The Love Toy; The Night Cry; Sunshine of Paradise Alley; A Woman's Heart; A Woman of the Sea; His Jazz Bride. **1927** Backstage; Wolves of the Air; The Woman on Trial; Stolen Pleasures; Too Many Crooks; In the First Degree. **1928** The Adventurer; Sailors' Wives. **1929** Lucky Boy. **1930** Reno. **1935** Little America (narr.); Wings over Ethiopia (narr.). **1940** Misbehaving Husbands. **1941** Parachute Battalion. **1942** Tennessee Johnson; Phantom Killer. **1944** My Gal Loves Music. **1949** The Sickle or the Cross. **1952** Strange Fascination; Big Jim McLain. **1953** Dangerous Crossing; One Girl's Confession.

WHITMAN, WALT
Born: 1868. Died: Mar. 27, 1928, Santa Monica, Calif. Screen and stage actor.

Appeared in: **1918** The Heart of Humanity. **1920** Mark of Zorro. **1921** The Three Musketeers; His Nibs; The Home Stretch; The New Disciple; Mysterious Rider; The Girl from God's Country. **1922** The Fire Bride; A Question of Honor; The Girl from Rocky Point. **1923** Hearts Aflame; Long Live the King; The Grub Stake; The Love Letter; Wasted Lives. **1924** Missing Daughters.

WHITNEY, CLAIRE
Born: 1890. Died: Aug. 27, 1969, Sylmar, Calif. Screen actress. Married to actor Robert Emmett Keane.

Appeared in: **1914** Life's Shop Window. **1915** The Nigger. **1918** Kaiser's Finish. **1919** The Isle of Conquest. **1921** Fine Feathers; The Leech; The Passionate Pilgrim. **1926** The Great Gatsby. **1928** Innocent Love. **1929** Gossip (short); Room 909 (short). **1931** A Free Soul. **1934** Enlighten Thy Daughter. **1939** Three Smart Girls Grow Up; When Tomorrow Comes. **1940** Chip of the Flying U. **1941** In the Navy. **1942** The Silver Bullet; Silver Queen; Frisco Lil. **1944** The Mummy's Ghost. **1945** She Gets Her Man; Under Western Skies; G.I. Honeymoon; A Guy, a Gal and a Pal. **1949** Frontier Investigator; An Old Fashioned Girl; Roaring Westward.

WHITNEY, PETER (Peter King Engle)
Born: 1916, Long Branch, N.J. Died: Mar. 30, 1972, Santa Barbara, Calif. (heart attack). Screen, stage and television actor.

Appeared in: **1941** Underground; Blues in the Night; 9 Lives Are Not Enough. **1942** Rio Rita; Valley of the Sun; Spy Ship; Whistling in Dixie; Busses Roar. **1943** Action in the North Atlantic; Destination Tokyo; Reunion in France. **1944** Mr. Skeffington. **1945** Bring on the Girls; Murder, He Says; Hotel Berlin. **1946** Blonde Alibi; The Notorious Lone Wolf; The Brute Man; Three Strangers. **1947** Violence; Northwest Outpost. **1948** The Iron Curtain. **1953** All the Brothers Were Valiant; The Big Heat; The Great Sioux Uprising. **1954** The Black Dakotas; Day of Triumph; Gorilla at Large. **1955** The Sea Chase; The Last Frontier. **1956** Man from Del Rio; Great Day in the Morning; The Cruel Tower. **1957** Domino Kid. **1958** Buchanan Rides Alone. **1962** The Wonderful World of the Brothers Grimm. **1965** The Sword of Ali Baba. **1967** In the Heat of the Night. **1968** Chubasco. **1969** The Great Bank Robbery. **1970** The Ballad of Cable Hogue.

WHITNEY, RALPH
Born: 1874. Died: June 14, 1928, Los Angeles, Calif. (injuries from fall). Screen actor and stuntman.

WHITNEY, ROBERT, II
Born: 1945, Los Angeles, Calif. Died: Jan. 6, 1969, Los Angeles, Calif. Screen actor. Entered films approx. 1963.

WHITSON, FRANK
Born: 1876, New York, N.Y. Died: Mar. 19, 1946. Screen, stage and vaudeville actor.

Appeared in: **1916** The Mark of Cain; The Isle of Life; The Price of Silence. **1917** The Clock; Sudden Jim; The Woman Who Would Not Pay. **1921** Gilded Lies; The Adventures of Tarzan (serial). **1922** Fortune's Mask; Headin' West; The Man from Hell's River. **1923** The Bolted Door; Flames of Passion; Tango Cavalier; The Way of the Transgressor. **1924** Captain Blood; $50,000 Reward; Her Man; Racing for Life; The Valley of Hate; The White Panther. **1925** Fighting Courage. **1926** Bad Man's Bluff; The Fighting Boob; Walloping Kid. **1927** Hidden Aces. **1928** The Texas Tornado.

WHITTELL, JOSEPHINE
Born: San Francisco, Calif. Died: June 1, 1961, Hollywood, Calif. Stage and screen actress. Divorced from actor Robert Warwick (dec. 1964).

Appeared in: **1919** The Climbers. **1921** The Inner Chamber. **1931** False Roomers (short); Caught Plastered (short); Peach O'Reno. **1932** Symphony of Six Million; What Price Hollywood? **1933** Infernal Machine; Zoo in Budapest; Baby Face. **1934** The Life of Vergie Winters; Servants' Entrance; Love Time. **1935** It's a Gift; Shanghai. **1936** Follow Your Heart. **1937** Hotel Haywire; Larceny on the Air; Beware of Ladies. **1938** Women Are Like That. **1939** The

Women. **1940** Kiddie Cure (short). **1941** Glamour Boy. **1942** The Magnificent Dope. **1944** Standing Room Only. **1945** State Fair; The Enchanted Cottage. **1946** The Virginian; Easy to Wed. **1948** An Act of Murder. **1949** Adventure in Baltimore. **1951** Molly. **1954** Forever Female.

WHITTINGTON, MARGERY
Born: 1904. Died: Oct. 1957. Screen actress.

Appeared in: **1925** Stagestruck.

WHITTY, DAME MAY
Born: June 19, 1865, Liverpool, England. Died: May 29, 1948, Beverly Hills, Calif. Stage and screen actress. Was made Dame Commander of the Order of the British Empire in 1918. Married to actor Ben Webster (dec. 1947). Mother of actress Margaret Webster (dec. 1973).

Appeared in: **1914** Enoch Arden. **1915** The Little Minister. **1920** Colonel Newcome, the Perfect Gentleman. **1937** Night Must Fall; Thirteenth Chair; Conquest (aka Marie Walewska). **1938** The Lady Vanishes; I Met My Love Again. **1939** Raffles. **1940** Return to Yesterday; A Bill of Divorcement. **1941** Suspicion; One Night in Lisbon. **1942** Mrs. Miniver; Thunder Birds. **1943** Madame Curie; Slightly Dangerous; Crash Dive; Flesh and Fantasy; Lassie Come Home; Stage Door Canteen. **1944** The White Cliffs of Dover; Gaslight. **1945** My Name Is Julia Ross. **1946** Devotion. **1947** This Time for Keeps; If Winter Comes; Green Dolphin Street. **1948** The Return of October; The Sign of the Ram.

WHORF, RICHARD
Born: 1906, Winthrop, Mass. Died: Dec. 14, 1966, Santa Monica, Calif. (heart attack). Screen, stage actor, film and television director and television producer.

Appeared in: **1934** Midnight. **1941** Blues in the Night. **1942** Juke Girl; Yankee Doodle Dandy. **1943** Keeper of the Flame; Assignment in Brittany; The Cross of Lorraine. **1944** The Imposter; Christmas Holiday; Strange Confession. **1945** Champion of Champions; The Hidden Eye. **1947** Love from a Stranger; Call It Murder (reissue and retitle of Midnight—1934). **1948** Luxury Liner. **1950** Champagne for Caesar; Chain Lightning. **1951** The Groom Wore Spurs. **1954** Autumn Fever.

WICHART, LITA BELLE
Born: 1907. Died: Jan. 24, 1929, near Newhall, Calif. (attempting parachute jump from plane). Screen stunt double. Married to stuntman Floyd Bowman.

Appeared in: **1929** Winged Horseman (died while filming).

WICKLAND, LARRY
Born: June 28, 1898, Kansas City, Mo. Died: Apr. 18, 1938, Los Angeles, Calif. Screen actor, film director and screenwriter. Appeared in early Universal Jesse Lasky Feature Play Company and DeMille productions.

Appeared in: **1916** Trail of the Lonesome Pine.

WIEMAN, MATHIAS
Born: 1902, Germany. Died: Dec. 3, 1969, Zurich, Switzerland. Stage and screen actor. Entered films during early films.

Appeared in: **1929** The Jolly Peasant. **1930** Bride 68. **1931** Rosenmontag (Monday's Roses—US 1932). **1932** Avalanche; Mensch Ohne Namen; Die Graeffin von Monte Christo (The Countess of Monte Cristo). **1933** Anna Und Elizabeth (Anna and Elizabeth—US 1936). **1935** Klein Dorrit. **1936** Das Verlorene Tal. **1937** Togger; Patriots; The Eternal Mask. **1938** Winter Stuerme (Winter Storms); Wir Sind vom K u K Infanterie-Regiment. **1939** Die Hochzeitsreise (The Wedding Journey). **1956** As Long as You're Near Me; Fear. **1957** Robinson soll Nicht Sterben (aka The Girl and the Legend—US 1966); If All the Guys in the World. **1958** Eine Liebesgeschichte (A Love Story). **1963** Der Sittlichkeitsverbrecher (The Molesters—US 1964).

WIERE, SYLVESTER
Born: 1910, Prague, Germany. Died: July 7, 1970, Hidden Hills, Calif. (kidney ailment). Screen, stage, vaudeville and television actor. Was member of comedy team "The Wiere Bros." with his brothers, Herbert and Harry.

They appeared in: **1941** The Great American Broadcast. **1943** Swing Shift Maisie; Hands across the Border. **1947** Road to Rio. **1967** Double Trouble.

WIETH, MOGENS
Born: 1920, Denmark. Died: Sept. 10, 1962, London, England. Stage and screen actor.

Appeared in: **1950** The Invisible Army. **1951** The Tales of Hoffman. **1956** The Man Who Knew Too Much. **1960** De Sista Stegen (A Matter of Morals—US 1961).

WIFSTRAND, NAIMA
Born: 1890, Stockholm, Sweden. Died: 1968, Sweden. Screen, stage actress and opera performer.

Appeared in: **1948** The Poetry of Adalen; Musik i Morker (Night Is My Future—US 1963). **1951** The Wind Is My Lover (aka Singoalla/Singoalla The Saga of Singoalla/ and aka Gypsy Fury—US). **1952** Kvinnors Vantan (Secrets of Women—US 1961). **1955** The True and the False. **1956** Girl in a Dress-coat; La Sorciere (The Sorceress—US aka Blonde Witch). **1957** Smiles of a Summer Night. **1959** Ansiket (The Face aka The Magician—US); Wild Strawberries. **1960** Journey Into Autumn (aka Kvinnodrom and Dreams). **1966** Nattlck (Night Games—US). **1968** Vargtimmen (Hour of the Wolf—US). Other Swedish films: Madame Visits Oslo; King's Street; Watch Out for Spies; Born: A Daughter; Sten Stensson Comes to Town; Girls in the Harbour; Hotell Kakbrinken; Handsome Augusta; I Love You You Vixen; The Long Road; Nights in the Djurgard; The Art of Love; Life in the Depths of the Forest; A Guest Came; Two Women; The Nightwatchman's Wife; People of the Simlang Valley; Lapp Blood; Private Bom; The Roar of Hammar Rapids; Miss Sun-Beam; Revue at the Sodran Theatre; Gentlemen of the Navy; That Woman Drives Me Crazy; Plaything Truant; The Devil and the Man from Smaland; Thrist (aka Three Strange Loves); The Wing Is my Lover; My Name Is Puck; A Fiancee for Hire; Because of my Hot Youth; Say It With Flowers; Dull Clang; The Road to Klockrike; Wing-beats in the Night; Ursula—the Girl from the Forest Depths; Gentle Thief of Love; The Dance Hall; Paradise; My Hot Desire; The Witch; Seventeen Years Old; The Judge; The Brig "Three Lilies"; The Myth; Waltz of Sex.

WIGGINS, MARY L.
Born: 1910. Died: Dec. 1945, North Hollywood, Calif. (shot herself). Screen stunt woman.

WILBUR, CRANE
Born: Nov. 17, 1889, Athens, N.Y. Died: Oct. 18, 1973, North Hollywood, Calif. (following a stroke). Screen, stage, radio actor, screenwriter, film director, playwright and film producer. Divorced from actresses Edna Hermance, Suzanne Caubert and Beatrice Blinn. Married to actress Lenita Lane.

Appeared in: **1914** The Perils of Pauline (serial). **1915** The Road O' Strife (serial). **1917** The Painted Lie; The Eye of Envy; The Blood of His Fathers. **1919** Unto the End; Devil McCare; Breezy Jim; Stripped for a Million. **1921** Something Different; The Heart of Maryland. **1934** Tomorrow's Children; Name the Woman. **1935** High School Girl; Public Opinion; Unknown Woman; Invincible. **1936** Yellow Cargo; Captain Calamity.

WILCOX, FRANK
Born: Mar. 13, 1907, DeSoto, Mo. Died: Mar. 3, 1974, Northridge, Calif. Screen, stage, television actor and stage director.

Appeared in: **1940** The Fighting 69th; Santa Fe Trail; 'Til We Meet Again; Tear Gas Squad; River's End; Murder in the Air; Virginia City. **1941** The Wagons Roll at Night; They Died With Their Boots On; Affectionately Yours; Navy Blues; Highway West; A Shot in the Dark; Wild Bill Hickok Rides. **1942** Across the Pacific; Busses Roar; Lady Gangster; The Hidden Hand; Bullet Scars; Murder in the Big House; Wings for the Eagle; Escape from Crime; Secret Enemies. **1943** North Star; Juke Girl; Truck Busters. **1944** In the Meantime, Darling; The Adventures of Mark Twain; The Imposter. **1945** Conflict. **1946** Night Editor; The Devil's Mask; Strange Triangle. **1947** Philo Vance Returns; Cass Timberlane; Gentleman's Agreement; The Beginning or the End; Something in the Wind; Blondie's Anniversary; I Cover Big Town. **1948** The Miracle of the Bells. **1949** Samson and Delilah; All the King's Men; The Mysterious Desperado; Masked Raiders; The Clay Pigeon. **1950** The Kid from Texas; Blondie's Hero; Chain Gang; Mister 880. **1952** The Greatest Show on Earth; Ruby Gentry; The Half-Breed; The Treasure of Lost Canyon; Trail Guide. **1953** Those Redheads from Seattle; China Venture; Pony Express. **1954** Three Young Texans; Naked Alibi; The Black Dakotas. **1955** Abbott and Costello Meet the Keystone Kops; Carolina Cannonball. **1956** A Strange Adventure; Dance With Me Henry; Hollywood or Bust; Never Say Goodbye; The First Traveling Saleslady; The Man in the Gray Flannel Suit; Earth versus the Flying Saucers; Seventh Cavalry; Uranium Boom. **1957** Kelly and Me; Hell's Crossroads; New Day at Sundown; Pal Joey; Beginning of the End. **1958** Johnny Rocco; Man from God's Country. **1959** Go, Johnny, Go! **1961** Double Trouble. **1962** A Majority of One; The Scarface Mob; Swingin' Along. **1965** I'll Take Sweden.

WILCOX, HARLOW
Born: 1900. Died: Sept. 24, 1960, Hollywood, Calif. Screen and radio actor.

Appeared in: **1941** Look Who's Laughing.

WILCOX, ROBERT
Born: May 19, 1910, Rochester, N.Y. Died: June 11, 1955, near Rochester, N.Y. (heart attack on train). Stage and screen actor. Diorced from actress Florence Rice (dec. 1974). Married to actress Diana Barrymore (dec. 1960).

Appeared in: **1936** The Cop; The Stones Cry Out. **1937** Let Them Live; The Man in Blue; Armored Car; Carnival Queen; Wild and Woolly. **1938** City Girl; Reckless Living; Rascals; Young Fugitives; Little Tough Guy; Swing That Cheer; Gambling Ship. **1939** Undercover Doctor; Blondie Takes a Vacation; The Man They Could Not Hang; The Kid from Texas. **1940** Island of Doomed Men; Dreaming Out Loud; The Lone Wolf Strikes; Buried Alive; Gambling on the High Seas; Father Is a Prince; Mysterious Dr. Satan (serial). **1946** The Unknown; Wild Beauty. **1947** The Vigilantes Return. **1954** Day of Triumph.

WILCOX, VIVIAN
Born: 1912. Died: Jan. 5, 1945, Hollywood, Calif. Screen actress.

WILDER, MARSHALL P.
Born: 1860, Geneva, N.Y. Died: Jan. 10, 1915, St. Paul, Minn. Screen and vaudeville actor.

Appeared in: **1912** Chumps; The Five Senses; The Pipe; The Widow's Might; The Greatest Thing in the World; Professor Optimo; Mockery; The Godmother; The Curio Hunters.

WILDHACK, ROBERT
Born: 1882. Died: June 19, 1940, Montrose, Calif. (pulmonary ailment). Screen and radio actor. Known on radio as the man of "Sneezes and Snores."

Appeared in: **1935** Broadway Melody of 1936. **1937** Broadway Melody of 1938. **1939** Back Door to Heaven.

WILEY, JOHN A.
Born: 1884. Died: Sept. 30, 1962, San Antonio, Tex. Screen actor.

Appeared in: **1923** The Covered Wagon. **1926** The Winning of Barbara Worth; Chasing Trouble.

WILHELM, THEODORE
Born: 1909, Germany. Died: Nov. 30, 1971, London, England. Screen, stage and television actor.

Appeared in: **1956** Assignment Redhead (aka Million Dollar Manhunt—US 1962). **1958** The Trollenberg Terror (aka The Crawling Eye—US). **1961** Circle of Deception.

WILKERSON, GUY
Born: 1898. Died: July 15, 1971, Hollywood, Calif. (cancer). Screen, stage and television actor.

Appeared in: **1937** Paradise Express; Mountain Justice; The Yodelin' Kid from Pine Ridge; Our Neighbors, the Carters; Untamed. **1941** Spooks Run Wild. **1942** Swamp Woman. **1943** The Rangers Take Over; Border Buckaroos. **1944** Boss of Rawhide; Brand of the Devil; Gangsters of the Frontier; Guns of the Law; Gunsmoke Mesa; The Pinto Bandit; Trail of Terror; Return of the Rangers; Spooktown; Outlaw Roundup; The Whispering Skull; Dead or Alive. **1945** Captain Tugboat Annie; Bus Pests (short); Enemy of the Law; Three in the Saddle. **1946** Frontier Fugitives. **1947** The Michigan Kid; Thundergap Outlaws. **1948** Fury at Furnace Creek. **1949** Texas, Brooklyn and Heaven. **1950** The Great Missouri Raid; Ticket to Tomahawk. **1951** Comin' 'Round the Mountain. **1952** The Big Sky. **1953** The Last Posse; The Stranger Wore a Gun. **1955** Foxfire. **1956** Jubal. **1957** The Buster Keaton Story; Decision at Sundown. **1958** Cowboy; Wild Heritage; Man of the West. **1960** The Walking Target. **1961** Susan Slade. **1962** To Kill a Mockingbird. **1963** The Haunted Palace. **1965** Black Spurs; War Party. **1969** True Grit. **1970** Monte Walsh.

WILKERSON, HERBERT
Born: 1881. Died: Aug. 19, 1943, Hollywood, Calif. Screen and stage actor.

WILKERSON, WILLIAM (William Penn Wilkerson)
Born: 1903, Okla. Died: Mar. 3, 1966, Hollywood, Calif. Indian screen actor.

Appeared in: **1939** Juarez. **1940** Dr. Cyclops. **1947** Robin Hood of Texas. **1950** Davy Crockett, Indian Scout; The Rock Island Trail; Broken Arrow. **1951** Jungle Manhunt. **1952** Brave Warrior. **1953** Saginaw Trail.

WILLARD, JESS
Born: Dec. 29, 1881, Pottawatomie Indian Reservation, Kans. Died: Dec. 15, 1968, Los Angeles, Calif. (cerebral hemorrhage). World Heavyweight Champion Boxer and screen actor.

Appeared in: **1919** The Heart Punch; The Challenge of Chance. **1968** The Legendary Champions (documentary).

WILLENZ, MAX
Born: 1888. Died: Nov. 10, 1954, Hollywood, Calif. (heart attack). Stage and screen actor.

Appeared in: **1942** Pride of the Yankees; Pierre of the Plains; I Married an Angel. **1945** Yolanda and the Thief. **1953** Gentlemen Prefer Blondes.

WILLEY, LEONARD (Leonard Louis Willey)
Born: Dec. 15, 1882, England. Died: June 30, 1964, Los Angeles, Calif. (arteriosclerosis). Stage and screen actor.

Appeared in: **1937** The Prince and the Pauper; Night Club Scandal. **1938** Invisible Enemy; The Adventures of Robin Hood. **1940** Tom Brown's School Days. **1941** Penny Serenade.

WILLIAM, JOSEPH "RANGER BILL"
Born: 1878. Died: Nov. 12, 1939. Screen actor and cowboy. Appeared in silents.

WILLIAM, WARREN (William Krech)

Born: Dec. 2, 1895, Aitkens, Minn. Died: Sept. 24, 1948, Encino, Calif. (multiple myeloma, blood disease). Screen, stage and radio actor. Star of "Lone Wolf" film series.

Appeared in: 1920 The Town that Forgot God. 1923 Plunder (serial). 1927 Twelve Miles Out. 1930 Let Us Be Gay. 1931 Expensive Women; Honor of the Family; Those Who Love. 1932 Woman from Monte Carlo; Beauty and the Boss; Dark Horse; Under Eighteen; Skyscraper Souls; The Mouthpiece; The Match King; Three on a Match. 1933 The Mind Reader; Employees' Entrance; The Great Jasper; Gold Diggers of 1933; Goodbye Again; Lady for a Day. 1934 Smarty; Upper World; The Case of the Howling Dog; The Secret Bride; Bedside; Dr. Monica; The Dragon Murder Case; Imitation of Life; Cleopatra. 1935 Living on Velvet; The Case of the Curious Bride; The Case of the Lucky Legs; Don't Bet on Blondes. 1936 The Widow from Monte Carlo; The Case of the Velvet Claws; Stage Struck; Satan Met a Lady; Times Square Playboy; Go West, Young Man. 1937 Outcast; Midnight Madonna; The Firefly; Madame X. 1938 Arsene Lupin Returns; The First Hundred Years; Wives under Suspicion. 1939 The Lone Wolf Spy Hunt; Gracie Allen Murder Case; The Man in the Iron Mask; Daytime Wife. 1940 Lillian Russell; The Lone Wolf Strikes; The Lone Wolf Meets a Lady; Arizona; Trail of the Vigilantes. 1941 The Lone Wolf Takes a Chance; The Wolf Man; Wild Geese Calling; The Lone Wolf Keeps a Date. 1942 Counter Espionage; Eyes of the Underworld; Wild Bill Hickok Rides. 1943 One Dangerous Night; Passport to Suez. 1945 Strange Illusion. 1946 Fear. 1947 The Private Affairs of Bel Ami.

WILLIAMS, ANNABELLE (Annabelle Rucker)

Born: 1904, Oklahoma City, Okla. Died: Dec. 26, 1967, Hollywood, Calif. Stage and screen actress.

WILLIAMS, BERESFORD

Born: 1904, England. Died: Apr. 22, 1966, England. Screen, stage and television actor.

WILLIAMS, BERT (Egbert Austins Williams)

Born: 1877, New Providence, Nassau, British West Indies. Died: Mar. 4, 1922, New York, N.Y. (pneumonia). Black screen, stage, minstrel and vaudeville actor. Appeared in vaudeville and minstrel shows in team of "Williams and Walker."

Appeared in: 1916 A Natural Born Gambler.

WILLIAMS, BILL

Born: 1921. Died: Nov. 14, 1964, Gallup, N.M. Screen and television stuntman.

Appeared in: 1961 The Comancheros; Two Rode Together. 1964 Cheyenne Autumn. 1965 The Hallelujah Trail (killed while filming).

WILLIAMS, BILLY

Born: 1910. Died: Oct. 12, 1972, Chicago, Ill. Black screen, television actor and singer. Member of the "Charioteers" and the "Billy Williams Quartet."

WILLIAMS, BRANSBY (Eric Bransby Williams)

Born: Aug. 14, 1870, London, England. Died: Dec. 3, 1961, London England. Screen, stage, vaudeville and television actor.

Appeared in: 1914 The Seven Ages of Man; Bernardo's Confession; Grimaldi. 1915 Hard Times. 1918 Adam Bede; The Greatest Wish in the World. 1921 The Adventures of Mr. Pickwick. 1924 His Grace Gives Notice; The Sins Ye Do. 1925 The Secret Kingdom; Confessions; The Gold Cure; The Wonderful Wooing. 1926 The Jungle Woman. 1927 Easy Virtue (US 1928); Pearl of the South Seas. 1928 Scrooge; Grandfather Smallweed; Hell Cat; Troublesome Wives (aka Summer Lightning). 1929 Little Miss London; When Knights were Bold. 1932 The Wonderful Story. 1933 Soldiers of the King (aka The Woman in Command—US 1934). 1936 Hearts of Humanity. 1937 Song of the Road. 1941 The Common Touch. 1942 Those Kids from Town; Tomorrow We Live (aka At Dawn We Die—US 1943). 1946 The Trojan Brothers.

WILLIAMS, CHARLES B.

Born: Sept. 27, 1898, Albany, N.Y. Died: Jan. 3, 1958, Hollywood, Calif. Screen, stage actor, playwright, screenwriter and television writer. Entered films as an actor with Paramount in N.Y.

Appeared in: 1922 The Old Homestead. 1925 Action Galore. 1932 Dance Team; Strangers of the Evening; The Devil Is Driving. 1933 Gambling Ship; The Gay Nineties (short). 1934 Search for Beauty; Woman in the Dark. 1936 Rhythm on the Range; Wedding Present. 1937 Four Days' Wonder; Love Is News; Wake up and Live; Charlie Chan on Broadway; Love and Hisses; Turn off the Moon; Jim Hanvey, Detective; Merry-Go-Round of 1938. 1938 Born to Be Wild; Hollywood Stadium Mystery; Mr. Moto's Gamble; Alexander's Ragtime Band; Little Miss Broadway; Just around the Corner. 1939 Wife, Husband and Friend; The Flying Irishman; Undercover Doctor. 1941 Convoy; Flying Cadets. 1942 Isle of Missing Men; Time to Kill. 1943 Sarong Girl; The Girl From Monterrey. 1944 End of the Road; Where Are Your Children? 1945 Guest Wife; Identity Unknown; Love on the Dole. 1946 Our Hearts Were Growing Up; Doll Face; Passkey to Danger; Heldorado; It's a Wonderful Life. 1948 Marshal of Amarillo; The Dude Goes West. 1949 Grand Canyon. 1950

The Missourians. 1951 According to Mrs. Hoyle; Corky of Gasoline Alley; Kentucky Jubilee. 1955 A Lawless Street. 1956 Fighting Trouble.

WILLIAMS, CLARA

Born: 1891, Seattle, Wash. Died: May 8, 1928, Los Angeles, Calif. Screen actress. Entered films with Selig in 1910.

Appeared in: 1916 Hell's Hinges. 1917 Paws of the Bear. 1918 Carmen of the Klondike.

WILLIAMS, CORA

Born: 1871. Died: Dec. 1, 1927, Los Angeles, Calif. (heart trouble). Stage and screen actress.

Appeared in: 1919 His Parisian Wife. 1925 His Buddy's Wife; Womanhandled. 1926 The Adorable Deceiver. 1927 Temptations of a Shop Girl; The Great Mail Robbery; Sensation Seekers.

WILLIAMS, CRAIG

Born: 1877, Germany. Died: July 5, 1941, New York, N.Y. Stage and screen actor.

WILLIAMS, DOUGLAS

Died: Dec. 24, 1968. Screen actor.

WILLIAMS, EARLE

Born: Feb. 28, 1895, Sacramento, Calif. Died: Apr. 25, 1927, Los Angeles, Calif. (bronchial pneumonia). Screen, stage actor and film producer. Entered films with Vitagraph approx. 1910.

Appeared in: 1911 Saving an Audience. 1912 Happy Go Lucky. 1913 The Artist's Madonna. 1914 Two Women; The Christian; My Official Wife. 1915 The Goddess (serial); My Lady's Slipper. 1916 The Scarlet Runner (serial). 1917 Arsene Lupin. 1918 The Seal of Silence. 1919 A Rogue's Romance. 1920 The Fortune Hunter. 1921 The Silver Car; A Master Stroke; The Purple Cipher; The Romance Promoters; Diamonds Adrift; It Can Be Done; Lucky Carson. 1922 The Man from Downing Street; Bring Him In; Restless Souls; Fortune's Mask; You Never Know. 1923 The Eternal Struggle; Masters of Men. 1924 Jealous Husbands; Borrowed Husbands. 1925 Lena Rivers; Was It Bigamy?; The Adventurous Sex; The Ancient Mariner. 1926 Diplomacy; You'd Be Surprised; The Skyrocket. 1927 Red Signals; Say It with Diamonds; She's My Baby.

WILLIAMS, FRED J.

Born: 1875. Died: May 29, 1942, Los Angeles, Calif. Screen actor and film producer. Entered films approx. 1917.

Appeared in: 1925 A Modern Cain.

WILLIAMS, GEORGE

Born: 1854. Died: Feb. 21, 1936, Los Angeles, Calif. Screen actor.

Appeared in: 1922 Foolish Wives; Little Miss Smiles. 1924 Geared to Go; The Fighting Sap; The Silent Stranger. 1925 Super Speed; The Rattler. 1926 The Winner.

WILLIAMS, GEORGE B.

Born: 1866. Died: Nov. 17, 1931, Santa Monica, Calif. (auto accident). Screen actor.

Appeared in: 1921 Cheated Love; A Poor Relation; Danger Ahead; Her Mad Bargain; One Man in a Million. 1922 Second Hand Rose; The Golden Gallows; Her Night of Nights; The Siren Call. 1923 The Ghost Patrol. 1924 The Gaiety Girl; A Lady of Quality; Captain Blood. 1925 Fifth Avenue Models; The Phantom of the Opera. 1926 The Midnight Sun.

WILLIAMS, GUINN "BIG BOY"

Born: Apr. 26, 1899, Decatur, Tex. Died: June 6, 1962, Hollywood, Calif. (uremic poisoning). Screen and television actor. For a time was U.S. Congressman from Texas. Father of actor Malcolm (aka "Big Boy") Williams.

Appeared in: 1919 Almost a Husband (as an extra). 1921 The Jack Rider; The Vengeance Trail; Western Firebrands. 1922 Trail of Hate; Across the Border; Blaze Away; Rounding up the Law; The Cowboy King. 1923 Freshie; End of the Rope; Cyclone Jones; $1,000 Reward; Riders at Night. 1924 The Avenger; The Eagle's Claw. 1925 Red Blood and Blue; Whistling Jim; Black Cyclone; Bad Man from Bodie; Big Stunt; Courage of Wolfheart; Fangs of Wolfheart; Riders of the Sand Storm; Rose of the Desert; Wolfheart's Revenge; Sporting West. 1926 Brown of Harvard; The Desert's Toll. 1927 Quarantined Rivals; Slide, Kelly, Slide; The College Widow; The Down Grade; Backstage; Lightning; Snowbound; The Woman Who Did Not Care. 1928 My Man; Burning Daylight; Vamping Venus; Ladies' Night in a Turkish Bath. 1929 Noah's Ark; Lucky Star; From Headquarters; The Forward Pass. 1930 The Big Fight; The Bad Man; College Lovers; Liliom; City Girl. 1931 The Great Meadow; The Bachelor Fathers; Catch as Catch Can (short); War Mamas (short). 1932 Polly of the Circus; Drifting Souls; 70,000 Witnesses; You Said a Mouthful; Ladies of the Jury; The Devil Is Driving. 1933 Heritage of the Desert; Man of the Forest; College Coach; Laughing at Life. 1934 Romance in the Rain; Palooka; The

Mystery Squadron (serial); Half a Sinner; Flirtation Walk; One in a Million; Here Comes the Navy; The Silver Streak; The Cheaters; Rafter Romance. **1935** Society Fever; Cowboy Holiday; Private Worlds; Gun Play; The Glass Key; Village Tale; Powdersmoke Range; The Littlest Rebel; Miss Pacific Fleet; Law of the 45's; Here Comes Cookie. **1936** The Vigilantes Are Coming (serial); Muss 'Em Up; Grand Jury; The Big Game; Kelly the Second; End of the Trail; North of Nome; Career Woman. **1937** You Only Live Once; A Star Is Born; Don't Tell the Wife; The Singing Marine; Dangerous Holiday; She's No Lady; Big City; My Dear Miss Aldrich; Wise Girl. **1938** I Demand Payment; Flying Fists; The Marines Are Here; Crashing Through; Hold That Co-ed; Everybody's Doing It; The Bad Men of Brimstone; Army Girl; Down in "Arkansaw"; You and Me; Professor Beware! **1939** 6,000 Enemies; Blackmail; Fugitive at Large; Street of Missing Men; Mutiny on the Blackhawk; Legion of Lost Flyers; Badlands; Dodge City; Pardon Our Nerve. **1940** The Fighting 69th; Castle on the Hudson; Virginia City; Money and the Woman; Santa Fe Trail; Alias the Deacon; Dulcy; Wagons Westward. **1941** Six Lessons from Madame La Zonga; Country Fair; Billy the Kid; You'll Never Get Rich; Swamp Water; The Bugle Sounds; Riders of Death Valley (serial). **1942** Between Us Girls; Mr. Wise Guy; Lure of the Islands; American Empire; Silver Queen. **1943** Hands across the Border; Buckskin Frontier; Minesweeper; The Desperadoes. **1944** The Cowboy and the Senorita; The Cowboy Canteen; Thirty Seconds over Tokyo; Belle of the Yukon; Swing in the Saddle; Song of the Prairie. **1945** The Man Who Walked Alone; Rhythm Roundup; Sing Me a Song of Texas. **1946** Cowboy Blues; Singing on the Trail; Throw a Saddle on a Star; That Texas Jubilee. **1947** King of the Wild Horses; Singin' in the Corn; Road to the Big House. **1948** Bad Men of Tombstone; Station West. **1949** Brimstone. **1950** Hoedown; Rocky Mountain. **1951** Al Jennings of Oklahoma; Man in the Saddle. **1952** Springfield Rifle; Hangman's Knot. **1954** Massacre Canyon; Southwest Passage; The Outlaws' Daughter. **1956** Hidden Guns; Man from Del Rio. **1957** The Hired Gun. **1960** The Alamo; Five Bold Women. **1962** The Comancheros.

WILLIAMS, HANK
Born: 1924. Died: Jan. 1, 1953, near Oak Hill, W.Va. (heart attack). Country singer, composer, instrumentalist and screen, radio and television actor.

WILLIAMS, HARCOURT
Born: Mar. 30, 1880, Croyden, Surrey, England. Died: Dec. 13, 1957. Stage and screen actor.

Appeared in: **1945** Henry V (US 1946). **1947** Brighton Rock. **1948** Vice Versa; Hamlet; No Room at the Inn. **1949** Third Time Lucky (US 1950); The Lost People; Trottie True (aka Gay Lady—US 1950); Under Capricorn. **1950** Your Witness (aka Eye Witness—US); Cage of Gold (US 1951). **1951** The Late Edwina Black (aka Obsessed—US); The Magic Box (US 1952). **1953** Time Bomb (aka Terror on a Train—US); Quentin Durward. **1956** Around the World in 80 Days.

WILLIAMS, HERB (Herbert Schussler Billerbeck)
Born: 1874, Philadelphia, Pa. Died: Oct. 1, 1936, Freeport, N.Y. (internal hemorrhages). Screen, stage and vaudeville actor. Appeared in vaudeville with his wife Hulda in an act billed "Williams and Wolfus."

Appeared in: **1936** Rose of the Rancho.

WILLIAMS, HUGH (Brian Williams)
Born: Mar. 6, 1904, Boxhill-on-Sea, England. Died: Dec. 7, 1969, London, England. Screen, stage actor, screenwriter and playwright. Divorced from Gwyne Whitby. Married to actress and playwright Margaret Vyner. Father of actor Simon Williams.

Appeared in: **1930** Charley's Aunt (film debut). **1931** A Night in Montmartre; A Gentleman of Paris. **1932** Down Our Street; White Face; Insult; Rome Express; After Dark. **1933** Bitter Sweet; Sorrell and Son; The Jewel; This Acting Business. **1934** All Men are Enemies; Elinor Norton; Outcast Lady. **1935** The Last Journey (US 1936); Lieutenant Daring, RN; Her Last Affaire; David Copperfield; Let's Live Tonight. **1936** The Amateur Gentleman; The Man Behind the Mask; The Happy Family. **1937** Gypsy; The Windmill; Side Street Angel; The Perfect Crime; Brief Ecstacy. **1938** Bank Holiday (aka Three on a Weekend—US); The Dark Stairway; Dead Men Tell No Tales (US 1939); His Lordship Goes to Press; Premiere (aka One Night in Paris—US 1940). **1939** Wuthering Heights; Inspector Hornleigh; Dark Eyes of London (aka The Human Monster—US 1940). **1941** Ships with Wings (US 1942). **1942** One of Our Aircraft is Missing; The Day Will Dawn (aka The Avengers—US); Talk about Jacqueline; Secret Mission. **1946** A Girl in a Million (US 1950). **1947** Take My Life (US 1948). **1948** The Blind Goddess (US 1949); An Ideal Husband. **1949** Elizabeth of Ladymead; Paper Orchid; The Romantic Age (aka Naughty Arlette—US 1951). **1952** The Gift Horse (aka Glory at Sea—US 1953); The Holly and the Ivy. **1953** Twice Upon a Time; The Fake; The Intruder (US 1955). **1954** Star of My Night. **1966** Khartoum. **1967** Doctor Faustus (US 1968).

WILLIAMS, JEFFREY
Born: 1860. Died: Dec. 27, 1938, Los Angeles, Calif. Screen and stage actor.

Appeared in: **1921** The Saphead. **1934** Old Fashioned Way.

WILLIAMS, JOHN J.
Born: 1856, Lynn, Mass. Died: Oct. 5, 1918, New York, N.Y. (heart failure). Screen, stage, vaudeville actor and comedian.

Appeared in: **1915** Marse Covington.

WILLIAMS, JULIA
Born: 1879. Died: Feb. 7, 1936, New York, N.Y. Screen, stage, opera and vaudeville actress. Entered films during silents, appearing in early Pathe and Biograph films.

WILLIAMS, KATHLYN
Born: 1872 or 1888, Butte, Mont. Died: Sept. 23, 1960, Hollywood, Calif. Screen actress.

Appeared in: **1908** Harbor Island. **1910** The Fire Chief's Daughter. **1911** The Two Orphans; Back to the Primitive. **1913** A Mansion of Misery; The Adventures of Kathlyn (serial). **1914** The Spoilers; Chip of the Flying U. **1916** Sweet Lady Peggy; The Ne'er-Do-Well. **1917** Redeeming Love; Big Timber. **1918** The Highway of Hope; We Can't Have Everything. **1920** Just a Wife; Conrad in Quest of His Youth. **1921** Everything for Sale; Hush; A Man's Home; Morals; Forbidden Fruit; A Private Scandal; A Virginia Courtship. **1922** Clarence. **1923** The Spanish Dancer; Broadway Gold; Souls for Sale; Trimmed in Scarlet; The World's Applause. **1924** Single Wives; The City That Never Sleeps; The Enemy Sex; The Painted Flapper; Wanderer of the Wasteland; When a Girl Lives. **1925** The Best People; Locked Doors. **1926** The Wanderer. **1927** Sally in Our Alley. **1928** Our Dancing Daughters; We Americans; Honeymoon Flats. **1929** A Single Man; The Single Standard. **1930** Road to Paradise; Wedding Rings. **1931** Daddy Long Legs. **1932** Unholy Love. **1933** Blood Money. **1935** Rendezvous at Midnight. **1947** The Other Love.

WILLIAMS, LAWRENCE "LARRY"
Born: 1890. Died: Mar. 30, 1956, Hollywood, Calif. (heart attack). Screen actor. Married to screen actress Helen Dickson. Entered films approx. 1931.

Appeared in: **1938** Torchy Blane in Panama; Garden of the Moon; Girls on Probation; Brother Rat. **1939** Going Places; Nancy Drew—Reporter; Torchy Plays With Dynamite; Wings of the Navy; Secret Service of the Air; On Trial; Waterfront. **1940** Brother Rat and a Baby. **1941** Sky Raiders (serial). **1942** Flight Lieutenant; Hello Annapolis.

WILLIAMS, MACK
Born: 1907. Died: July 29, 1965, Hollywood, Calif. (heart attack). Stage and screen actor.

Appeared in: **1949** Trapped; Command Decision. **1950** Destination Big House; No Way Out; Where the Sidewalk Ends; Whirlpool. **1951** The Blue Veil; Force of Arms; Flying Leathernecks; Try and Get Me; Call Me Mister. **1953** The Bigamist. **1955** Unchained; Violent Saturday. **1956** The Monster That Challenged the World. **1958** Ten North Frederick; As Young as We Are. **1960** Chartroose Caboose. **1962** Cape Fear; A Public Affair.

WILLIAMS, MALCOLM
Born: 1870. Died: June 10, 1937, New York, N.Y. (heart attack). Stage and screen actor.

Appeared in: **1928** The First Kiss.

WILLIAMS, MARIE
Born: 1921. Died: July 5, 1967, Encino, Calif. (heart attack). Screen actress.

WILLIAMS, MARJORIE ROSE
Born: 1913. Died: July 18, 1933, Los Angeles, Calif. (suicide—gun). Screen actress.

WILLIAMS, MOLLY
Born: England. Died: Nov. 1, 1967, Halifax, Nova Scotia, Canada. Screen, stage, vaudeville, radio and television actress.

WILLIAMS, RHYS
Born: 1892, England. Died: May 28, 1969, Santa Monica, Calif. Screen, stage and television actor.

Appeared in: **1941** How Green Was My Valley. **1942** This above All; Eagle Squadron; Remember Pearl Harbor; Cairo; Random Harvest; Gentleman Jim; Mrs. Miniver. **1943** No Time for Love. **1945** The Corn Is Green; You Came Along; Blood on the Sun; The Bells of St. Mary's. **1946** So Goes My Love; The Strange Woman; The Spiral Staircase; Voice of the Whistler. **1947** Cross My Heart; Easy Come, Easy Go; The Trouble with Women; If Winter Comes; Moss Rose; The Farmer's Daughter; The Imperfect Lady. **1948** Black Arrow; Tenth Avenue Angel; Hills of Home. **1949** Fighting Man of the Plains; Bad Boy; The Crooked Way; The Inspector General; Tokyo Joe. **1950** The Showdown; Tyrant of the Sea; One Too Many; California Passage; Devil's Doorway; Kiss Tomorrow Goodbye. **1951** Sword of Monte Cristo; Million Dollar Pursuit; The Law and the Lady; The Light Touch; The Son of Dr. Jekyll; Never Trust a Gambler; Lightning Strikes Twice. **1952** Okinawa; Mutiny; The World in His Arms; Carbine Williams; Les Miserables; Meet Me at the Fair;

Plymouth Adventure. **1953** Scandal at Scourie; Julius Caesar; Bad for Each Other. **1954** Man in the Attic; The Black Shield of Falworth; Johnny Guitar; There's No Business Like Show Business; Battle Cry. **1955** The Scarlet Coat; How to Be Very, Very Popular; The King's Thief; The Kentuckian; Battle Cry; Many Rivers to Cross. **1956** The Desperadoes Are in Town; Nightmare; The Boss; Mohawk; The Fastest Gun Alive. **1957** The Restless Breed; Raintree County; Lure of the Swamp. **1958** Merry Andrew. **1960** Midnight Lace. **1965** The Sons of Katie Elder. **1966** Our Man Flint. **1970** Skullduggery.

WILLIAMS, ROBERT
Born: Sept. 15, 1899, Morganton, N.C. Died: Nov. 3, 1931, Hollywood, Calif. (peritonitis following appendectomy). Stage and screen actor.

Appeared in: **1931** Rebound (stage and film versions); The Common Law; Platinum Blonde; Devotion.

WILLIAMS, SCOTT T. *See* CHIEF THUNDERCLOUD

WILLIAMS, SPENCER
Born: 1893, British West Indies. Died: Dec. 13, 1969, Los Angeles, Calif. (kidney aliment). Black radio, television and screen actor. The Andy of television's "Amos 'n Andy" program during the 1950s.

Appeared in: **1928** Tenderfeet. **1930** Georgia Rose. **1935** The Virginia Judge. **1937** Harlem on the Prairie. **1939** Harlem Rides the Range. **1944** Go Down Death. **1947** Juke Joint.

WILLIAMS, WILLIAM A. (William Albert Williams)
Born: 1870. Died: May 4, 1942, Hollywood, Calif. Screen actor.

Appeared in: **1930** La Grande Mare.

WILLIAMSON, MELVIN E.
Born: 1900, Memphis, Tenn. Died: Feb. 15, 1959, Scott Air Force Base, Ill. Screen, radio actor, film director, television producer and director.

Appeared in: **1929** Wings.

WILLIAMSON, ROBERT (aka BOB WILLIAMSON)
Born: 1885, Glasgow, Scotland. Died: Mar. 13, 1949, Amityville, N.Y.

Appeared in: **1922** The Bond Boy. **1924** The Fighting Sap; Headin' Through. **1925** Don X. **1926** The Haunted Range; Lawless Trails.

WILLIAMSON, ROBIN E.
Born: June 30, 1889, Denver, Colo. Died: Feb. 21, 1935, Los Angeles, Calif. (heart attack). Screen, stage, vaudeville actor and film director.

Appeared in: **1916** What'll You Have?; The Reward; Side-Tracked; Stranded; The Man Hunters; The Great Safe Tangle; Help! Help!; Furnished Rooms; The Tryout. **1928** The Apache Raider.

WILLINGHAM, HARRY G.
Born: 1881. Died: Nov. 17, 1943, North Hollywood, Calif. (suicide—gun). Screen actor. Entered films during silents.

WILLIS, DAVE
Born: 1895. Died: Jan. 1, 1973, Peebles, Scotland. Stage, vaudeville and screen actor. Father of comedian Denny Willis. Appeared in act known as "Willis and Richards."

WILLIS, LOUISE
Born: 1880. Died: Jan. 2, 1929, Chicago, Ill. Stage and screen actress.

WILLS, BEVERLY
Born: 1934. Died: Oct. 24, 1963, Palm Springs, Calif. (fire). Screen, radio and television actress. Daughter of actress Joan Davis (dec. 1961).

Appeared in: **1938** Anesthesia (short). **1945** George White's Scandals. **1948** Mickey. **1952** Skirts Ahoy. **1953** Small Town Girl. **1959** Some Like It Hot. **1961** The Ladies' Man. **1963** Son of Flubber.

WILLS, BOB
Born: 1905. Died: May 13, 1975, Ft. Worth, Tex. (bronchial pneumonia). Screen actor, singer and composer.

Appeared in: **1941** Go West, Young Lady. **1944** The Vigilantes Ride; Wyoming Hurricane; The Last Horseman. **1946** Lawless Empire. **1965** Thunder in Dixie. **1967** Country Western Hoedown.

WILLS, DRUSILLA
Born: Nov. 14, 1884, London, England. Died: Aug. 11, 1951, London, England. Stage and screen actress.

Appeared in: **1932** Old Spanish Customers; The Lodger (aka The Phantom Fiend—US 1935). **1933** The Medicine Man; Little Miss Nobody; Britannia of Billingsgate. **1934** Night Club Queen; The Black Abbot. **1935** The Big Splash; Squibs. **1937** Non-Stop New York; The High Command. **1938** Quiet Please; Yellow Sands; A Spot of Bother; Sixty Glorious Years (aka Queen of Destiny—US); Luck of the Navy (aka North Sea Patrol—US 1940). **1939** A Girl Must

Live (US 1941). **1939** Inspector Hornleigh on Holiday. **1944** Champagne Charlie. **1949** The Queen of Spades.

WILLS, NAT (Louis MacGrath Wills)
Born: July 11, 1873, Fredericksburg, Va. Died: Dec. 9, 1917, Woodcliff, N.J. (accidental carbon monoxide poisoning). Screen, stage and vaudeville actor.

Appeared in: **1911** Nat Wills as King of Kazam.

WILLS, WALTER
Born: 1881. Died: Jan. 18, 1967, Hollywood, Calif. Screen and stage actor and dancer.

Appeared in: **1923** In Search of a Thrill. **1938** Santa Fe Stampede. **1939** The Night Riders; Cowboys from Texas. **1941** Ye Olde Minstrels (short). **1942** Melodies Old and New (short); Doin' Their Bit (short).

WILLSON, RINI. *See* RINI ZAROVA

WILMER-BROWN, MAISIE
Born: 1893. Died: Feb. 13, 1973, London, England. Screen and vaudeville actress. Appeared in silents.

WILMOT, LEE
Born: 1899. Died: Mar. 9, 1938, Hollywood, Calif. (suicide—fall from building). Screen and radio actor.

WILSON, AL
Born: Harrisburgh, Ky. Died: 1932. Screen actor, aviator and stuntman.

Appeared in: **1923** The Eagle's Talons (serial); Ghost City (serial). **1924** The Air Hawk. **1925** The Cloud Rider; The Crackerjack; Flyin' Thru; Fighting Ranger (serial). **1926** The Brown Derby; The Flying Mail. **1927** Home Made; Three Miles Up; Sky-High Saunders. **1928** The Air Patrol; Chinatown Charlie; The Cloud Dodger; The Phantom Flyer; Won in the Clouds; The Wright Idea. **1929** The Sky Skidder. **1930** Hell's Angels.

WILSON, ALAN C.
Born: 1943. Died: Sept. 2, 1970, Los Angeles, Calif. Screen actor and musician. Member of "Canned Heat" rock group.

Appeared in: **1969** Monterey Pop. **1970** Woodstock; The Naked Zoo.

WILSON, BENJAMIN F.
Born: 1876, Clinton, Iowa. Died: Aug. 25, 1930, Glendale, Calif. (heart ailment). Screen actor, film director and producer. Entered films as an actor with Edison and Nestor film companies, approx. 1912.

Appeared in: **1912** What Happened to Mary (serial); The Passing of J. B. Randall and Co.; At the Point of the Sword; A Chase Across the Continent; Believe Me If All Those Endearing Young Charms; For Valor; 'Ostler Joe; In His Father's Steps; Treasure Island; The Close of the American Revolution. **1914** Edison series. **1917** The Mystery Ship (serial); The Voice on the Wire. **1919** Trail of the Octopus (serial). **1920** Screaming Shadow (serial); The Branded Four (serial). **1921** The Mysterious Pearl (serial); Dangerous Paths. **1924** The Desert Hawk; His Majesty the Outlaw; Notch Number One. **1925** The Power God (serial); The Fugitive; A Daughter of the Sioux; The Man from Lone Mountain; Renegade Holmes, M.D.; Sand Blind; Tonio, Son of the Sierras; Fort Frayne; Warrior Gap; The Mystery Box (serial); Vic Dyson Pays. **1926** Officer 444 (serial); Baited Trap; Rainbow Riley; West of the Law; Wolves of the Desert; Sheriff's Girl. **1927** The Mystery Brand; A Yellow Streak; Riders of the West; The Range Riders. **1929** Bye, Bye Buddy; China Slaver; Girls Who Dare. **1930** Shadow Ranch.

WILSON, CHARLES CAHILL
Born: 1894. Died: Jan. 7, 1948 (esophagal hemorrhage). Screen actor.

Appeared in: **1929** Lucky Boy; Acquitted; Broadway Scandals; Song of Love. **1933** Female; Havana Widows; Elmer the Great; The Mayor of Hell; Mary Stevens, M.D.; Footlight Parade; The Kennel Murder Case; College Coach. **1934** Here Is My Heart; Dragon Murder Case; Miss Fane's Baby Is Stolen; Roman Scandals; I've Got Your Number; Harold Teen; St. Louis Kid; Murder in the Clouds; The Circus Clown; Broadway Bill; The Hell Cat; Affairs of a Gentleman; The Lemon Drop Kid; Death on the Diamond; It Happened One Night; Fog Over Frisco; The Human Side. **1935** Behold My Wife; Great Hotel Murder; The Gilded Lily; Four Hours to Kill; The Glass Key; Smart Girl; Mary Burns, Fugitive; Car 99; The Nitwits; Another Face; Fighting Youth; The Public Menace; Hitch Hike Lady; I'd Give My Life; Men of the Hour; Murder in the Fleet; The Case of the Lucky Legs; Music is Magic; Show Them No Mercy; Waterfront Lady; Port of Lost Dreams; The Perfect Clue. **1936** We're Only Human; Strike Me Pink; The Return of Jimmy Valentine; Gentleman from Louisiana; Grand Jury; They Wanted to Marry; Big Brown Eyes; Three Married Men; Mind Your Own Business; The Mine With the Iron Door; Panic on the Air; Legion of Terror; Pennies from Heaven; Showboat; The Magnificent Brute; Educating Father; Earthworm Tractors; Down the Stretch; Ticket to Paradise; Satan Met a Lady; I'd Give My Life. **1937** Woman in Distress; The Devil is Driving; Roaring Timber; Life Begins in College; The Adventurous Blonde; They Wanted to Marry; Murder Goes to College; Find the Witness; Partners in Crime; Merry-Go-Round of 1938; Charlie Chan on Broadway. **1938** State Police; Sally, Irene and Mary; When Were You Born?; Tenth Avenue Kid; Little Miss Thoroughbred; Night Hawk; Hold That Coed; The Spider's Web (serial). **1939** Fighting Thoroughbreds; Rose of Washington Square; Desperate Trails; Hotel for Women; Smashing the Money Ring; The Return of Dr. X; The Cowboy Quarterback; Here I Am a Stranger. **1940** He Married His Wife; Sandy Is a Lady; The Girl in 313; Knute Rockne—All American; Public Deb No. 1; Charter Pilot. **1941** The Face Behind the Mask; Meet John Doe; Federal Fugitives; Broadway Limited; Dressed to Kill; The Officer and the Lady; Blues in the Night. **1942** Lady Gangster; Rings on Her Finger; Escape from Crime. **1943** Silver Spurs; Two Senoritas from Chicago. **1944** Crime by Night; Hey, Rookie; Kansas City Kitty; The Big Noise; Shadows in the Night. **1945** Incendiary Blonde. **1946** Suspense; I Ring Doorbells; Passkey to Danger; Larceny in Her Heart; Crime of the Century; If I'm Lucky; Blonde for a Day; Bringing Up Father; Gas House Kids. **1947** Her Husband's Affair. **1948** Crime on Their Hands (short).

WILSON, CLARENCE H. (Clarence Hummel Wilson)
Born: 1877, Cincinnati, Ohio. Died: Oct. 5, 1941, Hollywood, Calif. Stage and screen actor. Entered films approx. 1920.

Appeared in: **1927** Mountains of Manhattan; The Silent Avenger. **1928** Phantom of the Turf. **1930** Dangerous Paradise; Love in the Rough. **1931** Front Page; Night Life in Reno; Sea Ghost; Her Majesty, Love. **1932** Amateur Daddy; Winner Take All; Young Ironsides (short); Purchase Price; Down to Earth; The Phantom of Crestwood; The Penguin Pool Murder; The All American; The Jewel Robbery. **1933** Smoke Lightning; Pick-Up Girl; A Shriek in the Night; Flaming Guns; The Mysterious Rider; The Girl in 419; Terror Abroad; Tilli and Gus; King for a Night; Son of Kong. **1934** Shrimps for a Day (short); You Said a Hateful (short); Count of Monte Cristo; Successful Failure; The Lemon Drop Kid; Wake up and Dream; I'll Fix It; Love Birds; I Like It That Way; Now I'll Tell; Unknown Blonde; Bachelor Bait; The Old-Fashioned Way. **1935** Ruggles of Red Gap; Let 'Em Have It!; Champagne for Breakfast; Waterfront Lady; Great Hotel Murder; When a Man's a Man; One Frightened Night; plus the following shorts: Little Sinner; Nurse to You!; Public Ghost No. 1; and The Tin Man. **1936** Little Miss Nobody; Love Begins at Twenty; The Case of the Black Cat; On the Wrong Trek (short); Rainbow on the River; Hats Off. **1937** Two Wise Maids; Damaged Goods; Small Town Boy; Westland Case. **1938** Rebecca of Sunnybrook Farm; Kentucky Moonshine; Little Miss Broadway; Having a Wonderful Time; You Can't Take It with You. **1939** Drums Along the Mohawk; East Side of Heaven; Clown Princes (short); Desperate Trails. **1940** Little Old New York; Melody Ranch. **1941** Angels with Broken Wings; Road Show; You're the One.

WILSON, DOOLEY
Born: Apr. 3, 1894, Tyler, Tex. Died: May 30, 1953, Los Angeles, Calif. Black screen, stage, vaudeville, radio actor and bandleader. Toured Europe with his own band from 1919 to 1930.

Appeared in: **1942** Casablanca (film debut); Night in New Orleans; Take a Letter, Darling; Cairo; My Favorite Blonde. **1943** Two Tickets to London; Stormy Weather; Higher and Higher. **1944** Seven Days Ashore. **1948** Racing Luck. **1949** Come to the Stable; Free for All. **1951** Passage West.

WILSON, ED
Born: 1916. Died: Feb. 6, 1975. Screen actor.

Appeared in: **1926** The Flaming Frontier. **1934** I Like It That Way.

WILSON, EDNA
Born: 1880. Died: July 23, 1960, N.Y. Stage and screen actress. One of the original "Gibson Girls" in early films.

WILSON, FRANCIS
Born: Feb. 1854, Philadelphia, Pa. Died: Oct. 7, 1935, N.Y. Screen, stage, minstrel actor and author. Appeared in Sennett's comedies in 1915.

WILSON, FRANK H.
Born: 1886, N.Y. or Jacksonville, Fla. Died: Feb. 16, 1956, Queens, N.Y. Black screen, stage, vaudeville, radio and television actor.

Appeared in: **1933** Emperor Jones. **1936** Green Pastures (stage and film versions). **1937** The Devil Is Driving; The Awful Truth; All American Sweetheart; A Dangerous Adventure; Life Begins with Love. **1938** Extortion. **1943** Watch on the Rhine.

WILSON, GEORGE (Alfred Ensom)
Born: 1854, England. Died: July 30, 1954, London, England. Screen actor, "England's oldest."

Appeared in: **1943** The Life and Death of Colonel Blimp (aka Colonel Blimp—US 1945). **1945** Henry V (US 1946). **1946** Caesar and Cleopatra.

WILSON, HAL
Born: Oct. 2, 1887, New York, N.Y. Died: May 22, 1933, Los Angeles, Calif. (paralytic stroke). Stage and screen actor. Entered films with Vitagraph in 1907.

Appeared in: **1908** The Clown's Adventures. **1921** The Secret Four (serial); Charge It; The Unknown Wife. **1922** Lady Godiva; Nan of the North (serial); Blaze Away; According to Hoyle; Forget-Me-Not. **1923** Main Street. **1924** Sundown; The Love Master. **1925** Don Q; Smilin' at Trouble. **1929** Iron Mask; Divorce Made Easy. **1930** Big House. **1931** Guilty Hands.

WILSON, IMOGENE "BUBBLES." *See* MARY NOLAN

WILSON, JACK
Born: 1917. Died: Dec. 18, 1966, Los Angeles, Calif. (cerebral hemorrhage). Stage and screen actor.

Appeard in: **1951** Francis Goes to the Races. **1953** Son of the Renegade.

WILSON, M. K.
Born: 1890. Died: Oct. 9, 1933, Long Beach, Calif. (auto accident injuries). Stage and screen actor.

Appeared in: **1930** The Costello Case.

WILSON, MARIE (Kathleen Elizabeth White)
Born: Aug. 19, 1916, Anaheim, Calif. Died: Nov. 23, 1972, Hollywood Hills, Calif. (cancer). Screen, television, radio actress, night club entertainer and stage actress. Divorced from actor Allen Nixon. Married to producer and writer Robert Fallon.

Appeared in: **1934** Babes in Toyland; My Girl Sally. **1935** Slide, Kelly, Slide; Stars Over Broadway; Miss Pacific Fleet; Broadway Hostess. **1936** Colleen; Satan Met a Lady; The Great Ziegfeld; China Clipper; King of Hockey; The Big Noise. **1937** The Great Garrick; Without Warning; Melody for Two; Public Wedding. **1938** Fools for Scandal; Boy Meets Girl; The Invisible Menace; Broadway Musketeers. **1939** Should Husbands Work?; Waterfront; The Sweepstakes Winner; The Cowboy Quarterback. **1941** Virginia; Flying Blind; Rookies on Parade. **1942** Harvard, Here I Come; She's In the Army; Broadway. **1944** Shine on Harvest Moon; You Can't Ration Love; Music for Millions. **1946** No Leave, No Love; Young Widow. **1947** The Hal Roach Comedy Carnival; Linda Be Good; The Private Affairs of Bel Ami; Fabulous Joe. **1949** My Friend Irma. **1950** My Friend Irma Goes West. **1952** A Girl in Every Port. **1953** Never Wave at a WAC; Marry Me Again. **1957** The Story of Mankind. **1962** Mr. Hobbs Takes a Vacation.

WILSON, ROBERTA
Born: 1904. Died: Feb. 2, 1972, Hollywood, Calif. (stroke). Screen actress and singer.

WILSON, WARD (Harry Warden Wilson)
Born: 1904, Trenton, N.J. Died: Mar. 21, 1966, West Palm Beach, Fla. Screen, stage, radio and television actor. He narrated numerous shorts for Paramount, Columbia, etc.

Appeared in: **1957** The Golden Age of Comedy (narr.).

WILSON, WAYNE
Born: 1899. Died: Jan. 1970, San Antonio, Tex. Screen, stage, radio and television actor.

WILSON, WENDELL C.
Born: 1889. Died: Jan. 9, 1927, Vancouver, B.C., Canada (pneumonia). Screen, stage actor, stage manager and stage director.

WILSON, WHIP
Born: 1915. Died: Oct. 23, 1964, Hollywood, Calif. (heart attack). Screen actor and rodeo performer.

Appeared in: **1948** Silver Trails (film debut). **1949** Crshing Thru; Haunted Trails; Range Land; Riders of the Dusk; Shadows of the West. **1950** Arizona Territory; Canyon Raiders; Cherokee Uprising; Fence Riders; Gunslingers; Outlaw of Texas; Silver Raiders. **1951** Abilene Trail; Lawless Cowboys; Montana Incident; Nevada Badmen; Stagecoach Driver. **1952** Gunman; Hired Gun; Night Raiders; Wyoming Roundup.

WILSON, WILLIAM
Died: July 9, 1972. Screen actor. Do not confuse with screen actor William F. Wilson (dec. 1956).

WILSON, WILLIAM F.
Born: 1894. Died: May 10, 1956, Woodland Hills, Calif. Screen and stage actor.

Appeared in: **1927** The Bush Leaguer.

WILTON, ERIC
Born: 1883. Died: Feb. 23, 1957. Screen actor.

Appeared in: **1932** The Silent Witness. **1933** The Masquerader. **1934** Midnight Alibi. **1936** Forbidden Heaven. **1937** Beware of Ladies. **1939** The Adventures of Sherlock Holmes. **1940** Johnny Apollo. **1942** They Raid by Night; Rings on Her Fingers. **1945** Molly and Me. **1946** Three Strangers; Claudia and David.

1948 Appointment with Murder; Docks of New Orleans. **1950** Jolson Sings Again. **1951** Valentino. **1953** How to Marry a Millionaire. **1954** Woman's World. **1956** Three Bad Sisters.

WILTSIE, SIMEON S.

Born: 1853, New York. Died: Jan. 13, 1918, Englewood, N.J. Screen actor.

Appeared in: **1915** The Secret Agent.

WINCHELL, WALTER

Born: Apr. 7, 1897, Harlem, N.Y. Died: Feb. 20, 1972, Los Angeles, Calif. Journalist, Broadway columnist, screen, television, vaudeville and radio actor.

Appeared in: **1933** Universal short. **1937** Wake Up and Live; Love and Hisses. **1957** The Helen Morgan Story. **1960** College Confidential. **1961** Dondi; Wild Harvest. **1962** The Scarface Mob. **1968** Wild in the Streets.

WINCHESTER, BARBARA

Born: c. 1895. Died: Apr. 20, 1968, New York, N.Y. Screen, stage, radio and television actress.

Appeared in: **1962** The Connection.

WINCOTT, ROSALIE AVOLO

Born: 1873. Died: Nov. 1951, Los Angeles, Calif. Screen and stage actress.

WINDHEIM, MAREK

Born: 1895, Poland. Died: Dec. 1, 1960. Screen actor, television producer and opera performer.

Appeared in: **1937** Something to Sing About; I'll Take Romance. **1938** She Married an Artist; Say It in French; Dramatic School. **1939** Ninotchka; On Your Toes; Hotel Imperial. **1941** Marry the Boss's Daughter. **1942** Holiday Inn; I Married an Angel; Mrs. Miniver; Crossroads. **1943** Mission to Moscow; Hi Diddle Diddle. **1944** In Our Time; Allergic to Love; Kismet; Mrs. Parkington; Our Hearts Were Young and Gay. **1945** Yolanda and the Thief; Weekend at the Waldorf. **1946** Tarzan and the Leopard Woman; The Best Years of Our Lives.

WINDSOR, CLAIRE (Claire Viola Cronk)

Born: Apr. 14, 1897, Coffee City, Kans. Died: Oct. 24, 1972, Los Angeles, Calif. (heart attack). Screen actress. Divorced from actor Bert Lytell (dec. 1954). Entered films as an extra with Lasky.

Appeared in: **1921** To Please One Woman; Dr. Jim; The Blot; The Raiders; What Do Men Want?; Too Wise Wives; What's Worth While? **1922** Broken Chains; Grand Larceny; Fools First; Brothers Under the Skin; One Clear Call; The Stranger's Banquet; Rich Men's Wives. **1923** The Acquittal; Little Church Around the Corner; The Eternal Three; Souls for Sale; Rupert of Hentzau. **1924** Nellie, The Beautiful Cloak Model; Born Rich; For Sale; A Son of the Sahara. **1925** Souls for Sables; The Dixie Handicap; The Denial; Just a Woman; The White Desert. **1926** Dance Madness; Money Talks; Tin Hats. **1927** Blondes by Choice; The Claw; A Little Journey; The Bugle Call; Foreign Devils; The Frontiersman; The Opening Night. **1928** The Grain of Dust; Domestic Meddlers; Fashion Madness; Satan and the Woman; Nameless Men. **1929** Captain Lash; Midstream. **1932** Hollywood on Parade (short). **1933** Sister to Judas; Self Defense; Constant Woman. **1934** Cross Streets. **1938** Barefoot Boy. **1945** How Do You Do? **1952** The Last Act.

WING, DAN

Born: 1923. Died: June 14, 1969, Fresno, Calif. (heart attack). Screen, stage and television actor.

WINN, GODFREY

Born: 1909, England. Died: June 19, 1971, England (heart attack). Screen, stage, radio actor and journalist.

Appeared in: **1927** Blight (aka Apres La Guerre). **1961** Very Important Person (aka A Coming-Out-Party—US 1962). **1963** Billy Liar. **1964** The Bargee. **1966** The Great St. Trinian's Train Robbery (US 1967).

WINNINGER, CHARLES

Born: May 26, 1884, Athens, Wis. Died: Jan. 1969, Palm Springs, Calif. Screen, stage, vaudeville, radio and television actor. Appeared in vaudeville with his parents, brothers and sisters. Married to stage actress Gertrude Walker and divorced from actress Blanche Ring (dec. 1931). Entered films with Elko Comedy Co.

Appeared in: **1915** The Doomed Groom. **1924** Pied Piper Malone. **1926** The Canadian; Summer Bachelors. **1930** Soup to Nuts. **1931** God's Gift to Women; Fighting Caravans; Gun Smoke; Children of Dreams; The Sin of Madelon Claudet; Bad Sister; Gambling Daughters; The Devil Was Sick; Night Nurse; Flying High. **1932** Husband's Holiday. **1934** Social Register. **1936** White Fang; Show Boat (stage and film versions). **1937** Dancing for Love; Three Smart Girls; You're a Sweetheart; Woman Chases Man; Nothing Sacred; Cafe Metropole; You Can't Have Everything; The Go-Getter; Every Day's a Holiday. **1938** Goodbye Broadway; Hard to Get. **1939** Barricade; Three Smart Girls Grow Up; Babes in Arms; Destry Rides Again; First Love; Fifth Avenue Girl.

1940 If I Had My Way; My Love Came Back; When Lovers Meet; Beyond Tomorrow; Little Nellie Kelly. **1941** The Get-Away; My Life with Caroline; Pot O'Gold; Ziegfeld Girl. **1942** Friendly Enemies. **1943** Coney Island; A Lady Takes A Chance; Flesh and Fantasy; Hers to Hold. **1944** Broadway Rhythm; Belle of the Yukon; Sunday Dinner for a Soldier. **1945** She Wouldn't Say Yes; State Fair. **1946** Lover Come Back. **1947** Living in a Big Way; Something in the Wind. **1948** Inside Story; Give My Regards to Broadway. **1950** Father Is a Bachelor. **1953** The Sun Shines Bright; Torpedo Alley; Perilous Journey; Champ for a Day. **1955** Las Vegas Shakedown. **1960** Raymie.

WINSCOTT, EDWIN C. See TEDDY V. ARMAND

WINSTON, BRUCE (Charles Bruce Winston)

Born: Mar. 4, 1879, Liverpool, England. Died: Sept. 27, 1946, at sea enroute to N.Y. (heart attack). Screen, stage actor and stage producer. Entered films in 1919.

Appeared in: **1931** Children of Dreams. **1933** The Private Life of Henry VIII. **1934** Blossom Time (aka April Romance—US 1937); My Song for You; The Private Life of Don Juan. **1935** Heat Wave. **1936** The Man Who Could Work Miracles; Everybody Dance. **1937** Intimate Relations. **1938** Alf's Button Afloat. **1940** The Thief of Bagdad. **1945** Flight from Folly. **1946** Carnival.

WINSTON, IRENE

Born: 1920. Died: Sept. 1, 1964, Hollywood, Calif. (pneumonia complications). Screen, stage actress and television writer.

Appeared in: **1951** Dear Brat. **1952** My Son, John. **1954** Rear Window. **1957** The Delicate Delinquent.

WINSTON, JACKIE

Born: 1915. Died: Nov. 9, 1971, N.Y. Screen, stage, television actor and comedian. Entered show business when nine years old, winning a singing stint with Will Osborne's band.

Appeared in: **1967** The Happening.

WINTER, CHARLES R.

Born: 1876. Died: June 29, 1952, Redondo Beach, Fla. Screen, vaudeville and radio actor. Appeared in vaudeville as part of "Williams and Charles" team (formerly entitled "Deltorelli and Glissandos"; then "Del and Gliss," and finally as "Williams and Charles").

WINTER, WILLIAM. See WILLIAM WINTER JEFFERSON

WINTER, WINONA

Born: 1891. Died: Apr. 27, 1940, Hollywood, Calif. Screen, stage and vaudeville actress.

WINTHROP, JOY (Josephine Williams)

Born: 1864. Died: Apr. 1, 1950, Hollywood, Calif. Screen and stage actress.

Appeared in: **1921** The Blazing Trail. **1922** Man's Law and God's. **1923** Her Fatal Millions. **1928** Stolen Love. **1930** The First Seven Years (short).

WINTON, JANE

Born: Oct. 10, 1905, Philadelphia, Pa. Died: Sept. 22, 1959, New York, N.Y. Screen, stage actress and opera performer. Entered films in 1925.

Appeared in: **1925** Tomorrow's Love. **1926** Why Girls Go Back Home; Don Juan; Across the Pacific; Footloose Widows; The Honeymoon Express; The Love Toy; Millionaires; My Old Dutch; My Official Wife; The Passionate Quest. **1927** Sunrise; The Beloved Rogue; The Gay Old Bird; The Crystal Cup; The Fair Co-Ed; Upstream; Lonesome Ladies; The Monkey Talks; The Poor Nut; Perch of the Devil. **1928** Burning Daylight; The Yellow Lily; The Patsy; Melody of Love; Nothing to Wear; Bare Knees; Honeymoon Flats. **1929** Scandal; Captain Lash; The Bridge of San Luis Rey. **1930** In the Next Room; The Furies; Hell's Angels. **1934** The Hired Wife.

WISE, JACK

Born: 1893. Died: Mar. 6, 1954, Hollywood, Calif. (heart attack). Screen and vaudeville actor.

Appeared in: **1929** Smilin' Guns; In the Headlines. **1935** Bright Lights. **1936** The Captain's Kid. **1938** Penrod's Double Trouble; Comet over Broadway. **1942** Gentleman Jim; Yankee Doodle Dandy.

WISE, TOM (Thomas A. Wise)

Born: 1865, England. Died: Mar. 21, 1928, New York, N.Y. (heart and asthma complications). Stage and screen actor.

Appeared in: **1922** Father Tom. **1924** The Great White Way.

WISMER, HARRY

Born: 1911. Died: Dec. 4, 1967. Screen actor.

Appeared in: **1947** The Spirit of West Point. **1948** The Babe Ruth Story; Triple Threat. **1956** Somebody Up There Likes Me.

WITHERS, CHARLES

Born: 1889, Louisville, Ky. Died: July 10, 1947, Bayside, N.Y. Screen, stage and vaudeville actor. Married to actress May Withers with whom he appeared in vaudeville.

Appeared in: 1936 Gasoloons (short). 1937 Hideaway.

WITHERS, GRANT

Born: June 17, 1904, Pueblo, Colo. Died: Mar. 27, 1959, Hollywood, Calif. (suicide). Screen and television actor. Divorced from actress Loretta Young and singer Estelita Rodriquez (dec. 1966). Entered films as an extra for Douglas McLean.

Appeared in: 1926 The Gentle Cyclone. 1927 College; The Final Extra; In a Moment of Temptation; Upstream. 1928 Bringing up Father; Tillie's Punctured Romance; Golden Shackles; The Road to Ruin. 1929 Tiger Rose; The Madonna of Avenue A; The Time, the Place and the Girl; In the Headlines; Hearts in Exile; Show of Shows; Saturday's Children; The Greyhound Limited. 1930 Broken Dishes; Scarlet Pages; Soldiers and Women; So Long Letty; Back Pay; The Other Tomorrow; Dancing Sweeties; The Second Floor Mystery; Sinners' Holiday; The Steel Highway. 1931 Other Men's Women; Too Young to Marry; Swanee River; In Strange Company; First Aid. 1932 Gambling Sex; Red Haired Alibi. 1933 Secrets of Wu Sin. 1934 The Red Rider (serial); Tailspin Tommy (serial). 1935 Rip Roaring Riley; The Fighting Marines (serial); Valley of Wanted Men; Skybound; Hold 'Em Yale; Goin' to Town; Ship Cafe; Storm over the Andes; Waterfront Lady; Society Fever. 1936 The Sky Parade; Three on a Limb (short); Border Flight; Lady Be Careful; The Arizona Raiders; Let's Sing Again; Jungle Jim (serial). 1937 Paradise Express; Bill Cracks Down; Radio Patrol (serial); Hollywood Round-Up. 1938 Telephone Operator; Held for Ransom; The Secret of a Treasure Island (serial); Three Loves Has Nancy; Touchdown Army; Mr. Wong, Detective. 1939 Irish Luck; Navy Secrets; Mexican Spitfire; Boys' Dormitory; Mr. Wong in Chinatown; Mutiny in the Big House; Mystery of Mr. Wong; Daughter of the Tong. 1940 The Fatal Hour; Son of the Navy; On the Spot; Tomboy; Doomed to Die; Phantom of Chinatown; Men against the Sky; The Mexican Spitfire Out West. 1941 Let's Make Music; Country Fair; Billy the Kid; The People vs. Dr. Kildare; You'll Never Get Rich; Swamp River; The Bugle Sounds; The Get-Away; Parachute Battalion; The Masked Rider. 1942 Between Us Girls; Woman of the Year; Lure of the Islands; Butch Minds the Baby; Northwest Rangers; Tennessee Johnson; Captive Wild Woman. 1943 In Old Oklahoma; Gildersleeve's Bad Day; Petticoat Larceny; No Time for Love; The Apache Trail; A Lady Takes a Chance. 1944 The Cowboy and the Senorita; Cowboy Canteen; The Fighting Seabees; The Girl Who Dared; Goodnight, Sweetheart; Silent Partners; The Yellow Rose of Texas. 1945 Utah; Bring on the Girls; Dangerous Partners; Road to Alcatraz; Dakota; Bells of Rosarita; The Vampire's Ghost. 1946 In Old Sacramento; Affairs of Geraldine; Throw a Saddle on a Star; That Texas Jamboree; Singing on the Trail; Cowboy Blues; Singin' in the Corn; My Darling Clementine. 1947 Gunfighters; King of the Wild Horses; Over the Santa Fe Trail; The Ghost Goes Wild; The Trespasser; Wyoming; Blackmail; Tycoon. 1948 Bad Men of Tombstone; Station West; Old Los Angeles; Gallant Legion; Daredevils of the Clouds; Sons of Adventure; Angel in Exile; The Plunderers; Homicide for Three; Night Time in Nevada; Wake of the Red Witch; Fort Apache. 1949 Brimstone; Hellfire; The Fighting Kentuckian; The Last Bandit; Duke of Chicago. 1950 Rocky Mountain; Hoedown; Bells of Coronado; Rio Grande; Rock Island Trail; The Savage Horde; Trigger, Jr.; Tripoli; Hit Parade of 1951. 1951 Man in the Saddle; Al Jennings of Oklahoma; Million Dollar Pursuit; The Sea Hornet; Spoilers of the Plains; Utah Wagon Train. 1952 Captive of Billy the Kid; Tropical Heatwave; Springfield Rifle; Hangman's Knot; Hoodlum Empire; Leadville Gunslinger; Oklahoma Annie; Women in the North Country. 1953 Champ for a Day; Fair Wind to Java; Iron Mountain Trail; The Sun Shines Bright; Tropic Zone. 1954 Massacre Canyon; Southwest Passage; Outlaw's Daughter. 1955 Lady Godiva; Run for Cover. 1956 Hidden Guns; The Man from Del Rio; The White Squaw. 1957 The Hired Gun; Hell's Crossroads; The Last Stagecoach West. 1958 I, Mobster.

WITHERS, ISABEL

Born: Jan. 20, 1896, Frankton, Ind. Died: Sept. 3, 1968, Hollywood, Calif. Screen, stage and television actress. Entered films in 1916 with Pagent Film Co. in Kansas City.

Appeared in: 1930 Paid. 1932 The Tenderfoot; Mother-In-Law's Day (short). 1933 Women Won't Tell; Baby Face. 1938 Brother Rat. 1941 Manpower. 1942 Behind Prison Walls; George Washington Slept Here; Lady of Burlesque. 1943 Mission to Moscow; Salute for Three. 1944 Beautiful But Broke; Law Men; Tahiti Nights; Together Again; Practically Yours; Casanova Brown. 1945 The Missing Corpse; I Love a Mystery; Kiss and Tell; The Gay Senorita; A Sporting Chance. 1946 To Each His Own; Tomorrow Is Forever; The Undercover Woman. 1947 Suddenly It's Spring; Possessed; A Likely Story. 1948 You Gotta Stay Happy. 1949 Manhattan Angel; Riders in the Sky; Mr. Belvedere Goes to College; The Fountainhead. 1950 Beware of Blondie; My Blue Heaven; The Fuller Brush Girl; Perfect Strangers. 1951 A Wonderful Life; Ma and Pa Kettle Back on the Farm. 1952 Monkey Business. 1953 Tonight We Sing.

WITHERSPOON, CORA

Born: Jan. 5, 1890, New Orleans, La. Died: Nov. 17, 1957, Las Cruces, N.Mex. Stage and screen actress. Entered films in 1931.

Appeared in: 1931 Night Angel; Peach O'Reno. 1932 Ladies of the Jury. 1934 Midnight; Gambling. 1935 An Educational short; Frankie and Johnnie. 1936 Piccadilly Jim; Libeled Lady. 1937 Dangerous Number; Personal Property; Madame X; Beg, Borrow or Steal; On the Avenue; The Lady Escapes; Quality Street; Big Shot. 1938 He Couldn't Say No; Port of Seven Seas; Marie Antoinette; Three Loves Has Nancy; Professor, Beware!; Just around the Corner. 1939 Woman Doctor; Dodge City; For Love or Money; The Women; Dark Victory; The Flying Irishman. 1940 Charlie Chan's Murder Cruise; I Was an Adventuress; The Bank Dick. 1943 Follies Girl. 1945 Over 21; Colonel Effingham's Raid; This Love of Ours. 1946 I've Always Loved You; Dangerous Business; Young Widow. 1951 The Mating Season. 1952 The First Time; Just for You.

WITT, WASTL

Born: 1890. Died: Dec. 21, 1955, Harlachinger, West Germany. Stage and screen actor.

WITTING, ARTHUR EUGENE

Born: 1868, Prairie du Chien, Wis. Died: Feb. 1, 1941. Stage and screen actor.

Appeared in: 1916 The Fall of a Nation; Two Men of Sandy Bar. 1927 Gun-Hand Garrison; Wild Born.

WIX, FLORENCE E.

Born: 1883, England. Died: Nov. 23, 1956, Woodland Hills, Calif. (cancer). Stage and screen actress.

Appeared in: 1924 The Female; Secrets. 1925 Enticement. 1927 Ladies Beware; The Return of Boston Blackie; Naughty Nanette. 1928 Beyond London Lights. 1929 She Goes to War. 1937 Easy Living. 1938 Romance in the Dark; The Missing Guest. 1942 Mrs. Miniver.

WOEGERER, OTTO

Born: 1907. Died: July 1966, Schwanenstadt, Austria. Screen and stage actor.

Appeared in: 1937 Die Nacht mit dem Kaiser. 1956 The Last Ten Days.

WOLBERT, DOROTHEA

Born: 1874, Philadelphia, Pa. Died: Sept. 16, 1958, Hollywood, Calif. (arteriosclerosis). Screen actress.

Appeared in: 1921 Action; The Ruse of the Rattler. 1922 The Flirt; The Ninety and Nine; The Little Minister. 1923 The Abysmal Brute. 1924 The Galloping Ace; A Lady of Quality; The Guilty One. 1925 A Woman of the World; Duped. 1926 The College Boob; Pleasures of the Rich. 1927 Sailor's Sweetheart; Snowbound. 1928 Anybody Here Seen Kelly?; Love and Learn. 1929 Universal shorts. 1930 The Medicine Man; Dangerous Paradise; Borrowed Wives. 1931 Friends and Lovers. 1932 The Expert; Two Seconds. 1933 Hallelujah, I'm a Bum. 1934 Autobuyography (short); The Scarlet Letter. 1935 Paris in Spring. 1938 If I Were King. 1950 Three Husbands. 1951 Little Egypt.

WOLBERT, WILLIAM

Born: 1884. Died: Dec. 12, 1918, Los Angeles, Calif. (pneumonia/influenza). Screen actor and film director.

Appeared in: 1914 Bess the Detectress or, The Old Mill at Midnight; Willie Walrus, Detective; Willie Walrus and the Baby; Cupid Incognito; The Skeleton; The Quack; The Den of Thieves; Willie Walrus and the Awful Confession; Bess the Detectress in the Dog Watch. 1915 Treasure Seekers. 1916 The Dumb Girl of Portici. 1917 Willie Walrus Pays Alimony.

WOLD, DAVID

Born: 1890. Died: June 3, 1953, Hollywood, Calif. (heart attack). Screen actor.

"WOLF II" (Wolf Cheechako)

Died: July 1932, Santa Ana, Calif. Screen animal performer (Alaskan Husky).

WOLFE, BUD

Died: Apr. 13, 1960. Screen actor.

Appeared in: 1942 Cowboy Serenade. 1947 Blackmail. 1948 Lightnin' in the Forest; The Fuller Brush Man. 1950 The Man Who Cheated Himself. 1954 Naked Alibi. 1956 Around the World in 80 Days.

WOLFF, FRANK (Frank Hermann)

Born: 1928, San Francisco, Calif. Died: Dec. 12, 1971, Rome, Italy (suicide). Screen actor.

Appeared in: 1959 Beast from a Haunted Cave; The Wild and Innocent. 1960 Ski Troop Attack. 1961 Atlas. 1963 The Four Days of Naples; The Demon; America, America. 1964 Salvatore Guiliano. 1965 Situation Hopeless—but Not Serious. 1966 Judith. 1968 Villa Rides; A Stranger in Town; Anyone Can Play; Treasure of San Gennaro. 1969 God Forgives—I Don't; The Libertine; Once Upon a Time in the West. 1970 Kill Them All and Come Back Alone; The Lickerish Quartet.

WOLFIT, SIR DONALD

Born: Apr. 20, 1902, Newmark-on-Trent, England. Died: Feb. 17, 1968, London, England (heart attack). Screen, stage and television actor. Divorced from Chris Frances Castor and Susan Katherine Anthony. Married to actress Rosalind Iden.

Appeared in: **1934** The Wigan Express (aka Death at Broadcasting House—film debut). **1935** Drake of England (aka Drake the Pirate—US); The Silent Passenger; Checkmate; The Guv'nor (aka Mister Hobo—US 1936); Hyde Park Corner; Late Extra. **1936** Calling the Tune. **1937** Knight Without Armour. **1952** The Ringer; The Pickwick Papers (US 1953). **1953** Isn't Life Wonderful! **1954** Svengali. **1955** A Prize of Gold. **1956** Guilty?; Satellite in the Sky; The Man in the Road. **1957** The Traitor (aka The Accursed). **1958** I Accuse!; Blood of the Vampire. **1959** Room at the Top; The Angry Hills; The Rough and the Smooth (aka Portrait of a Sinner—US 1961). **1960** The Hands of Orlac. **1961** The Mark. **1962** Dr. Crippen (US 1964); Lawrence of Arabia. **1964** Becket. **1965** Life at the Top; Tricet Jedna ve Stinu (90 Degrees in the Shade—US 1966). **1966** The Sandwich Man. **1968** The Charge of the Light Brigade; Decline and Fall . . . of a Birdwatcher (US 1969).

WOLFSON, BILLY

Born: 1898. Died: Jan. 15, 1973, Miami, Fla. (heart attack). Screen actor.

Appeared in: **1937** Penrod and Sam. **1938** Penrod and His Twin Brother; Penrod's Double Trouble.

WOLHEIM, LOUIS

Born: Mar. 23, 1880, New York, N.Y. Died: Feb. 18, 1931, Los Angeles, Calif. (cancer). Stage and screen actor.

Appeared in: **1916** The Brand of Cowardice; Dorian's Divorce; The Sunbeam. **1917** The Avenging Trail; The Eternal Mother; The Carter Case (serial). **1918** A Pair of Cupids. **1920** Dr. Jekyll and Mr. Hyde. **1921** Orphans of the Storm; Experience. **1922** Sherlock Holmes; Determination; The Face in the Fog. **1923** Little Old New York; The Go-Getter; The Last Moment; Love's Old Sweet Song; Unseeing Eyes. **1924** America; The Story Without a Name; The Uninvited Guest. **1925** Lover's Island. **1927** Two Arabian Knights; Sorrell and Son. **1928** Tempest; The Awakening; The Racket. **1929** Wolf Song; Square Shoulders; Condemned; Frozen Justice; The Shady Lady. **1930** Danger Lights; The Silver Horde; The Ship from Shanghai; All Quiet on the Western Front. **1931** Gentlemen's Fate; Sin Ship.

WONG, ANNA MAY (Lu Tsong Wong)

Born: Jan. 3, 1907, Los Angeles, Calif. Died: Feb. 3, 1961, Santa Monica, Calif. (heart attack). Screen actress.

Appeared in: **1919** Red Lantern. **1921** Bits of Life; Shame. **1922** The Toll of the Sea. **1923** Drifting; Thundering Dawn. **1924** The Thief of Bagdad; Alaskan; Peter Pan; The Fortieth Door. **1925** Forty Winks. **1926** The Desert's Toll; Fifth Avenue; The Silk Bouquet; A Trip to Chinatown. **1927** The Chinese Parrot; Old San Francisco; Mr. Wu; Driven from Home; Streets of Shanghai; The Devil Dancer. **1928** Across to Singapore; Show Life; Chinatown Charlie; The Crimson City; Song. **1929** Piccadilly. **1930** Elstree Calling; On the Spot; Wasted Love; The Flame of Love; L'Amour Maitre des Choses. **1931** Daughter of the Dragon. **1932** Shanghai Express. **1933** A Study in Scarlet; Tiger Bay. **1934** Chu Chin Chow; Limehouse Blues. **1935** Java Head. **1937** Daughter of Shanghai. **1938** Dangerous to Know; When Were You Born? **1939** King of Chinatown; Island of Lost Men. **1941** Ellery Queen's Penthouse Mystery. **1942** Bombs over Burma; Lady from Chungking. **1949** Impact. **1953** Ali Baba Nights. **1960** Portrait in Black; The Savage Innocents.

WONG, BRUCE

Born: 1906. Died: Nov. 1, 1953, Hollywood, Calif. (heart attack). Screen actor.

Appeared in: **1942** Time to Kill.

WONG, MARY (Mary Liu H. Wong)

Born: Mar. 11, 1915, Los Angeles, Calif. Died: July 25, 1940, Los Angeles, Calif. (suicide—hanging). Screen actress.

Appeared in: **1937** The Good Earth.

WONG, W. BEAL

Born: May 11, 1906, Wong Chong Sai, China. Died: Feb. 6, 1962, Hollywood, Calif. (cerebral hemorrhage). Screen actor.

Appeared in: **1936** The Leathernecks Have Landed. **1942** Prisoner of Japan; Little Tokyo USA; China Girl. **1943** Lady of Burlesque; China. **1944** The Purple Heart; The Big Noise. **1945** Nob Hill. **1951** Peking Express. **1955** The Big Bluff; The Left Hand of God; Soldier of Fortune. **1958** Hong Kong Confidential; Guns, Girls and Gangsters. **1961** Flower Drum Song. **1962** Brushfire!

WONTNER, ARTHUR

Born: Jan. 21, 1875, London, England. Died: July 10, 1960, London, England. Screen, stage and television actor. Entered films in 1915.

Appeared in: **1916** Lady Windermere's Fan; The Bigamist; Frailty (aka Temptation's Hour). **1923** Bonnie Prince Charlie; The Jose Collins Drama series including: Shadow of Death; The Velvet Woman; The Battle of Love; The Courage of Despair; The Last Stake; and Secret Mission. **1924** Eugene Aram; The Diamond Man. **1928** The Infamous Lady. **1930** The Message (short). **1931** A Gentleman of Paris; The Sleeping Cardinal (aka Sherlock Holmes' Fatal Hour—US). **1932** The Missing Rembrandt; Condemned to Death; The Sign of Four. **1935** The Triumph of Sherlock Holmes; Line Engaged. **1936** Dishonour Bright; Second Bureau. **1937** Thunder in the City; Storm in a Teacup; The Live Wire; Silver Blaze (aka Murder at the Baskervilles—US 1941). **1938** Kate Plus Ten; Just Like a Woman; Old Iron; 13 Men and a Gun; The Terror. **1943** The Life and Death of Colonel Blimp (aka Colonel Blimp—US 1945). **1948** Blanche Fury. **1950** The Elusive Pimpernel. **1952** Brandy for the Parson. **1953** Sea Devils; Genevieve. **1955** Three Cases of Murder.

WOOD, ALLAN

Born: 1892. Died: Mar. 26, 1947, St. Petersburg, Fla. Screen, stage, vaudeville, radio actor, screenwriter and playwright. Appeared in vaudeville with "Doc" Rockwell in a team called "Rockwell and Wood."

Appeared in: **1933** From Hell to Heaven. **1934** The Gridiron Flash. **1935** Home on the Range; The Pay-Off. **1940** Buck Benny Rides Again. **1942** Heart of the Rio Grande. **1943** Harrigan's Kid.

WOOD, BRITT

Born: 1885. Died: Apr. 13, 1965, Hollywood, Calif. Screen and vaudeville actor.

Appeared in: **1927** The Boob and His Harmonica (short). **1936** Trail Dust. **1937** Adventure's End. **1939** Range War. **1940** Santa Fe Marshal; The Showdown; Hidden Gold; Stagecoach War. **1941** Border Vigilantes; Pirates on Horseback. **1947** Square Dance Jubilee. **1949** Riders of the Whistling Pines. **1950** Return of the Frontiersman. **1962** The Choppers.

WOOD, CARL "BUDDY"

Born: 1905. Died: Apr. 17, 1948, Los Angeles, Calif. Screen and stage actor.

WOOD, DONNA

Born: 1918. Died: Apr. 9, 1947, Hollywood, Calif. (heart ailment). Singer and screen actress. Vocalist with Kay Kyser orchestra.

Appeared in: **1941** Pot O'Gold.

WOOD, DOUGLAS

Born: 1880, New York, N.Y. Died: Jan. 13, 1966, Woodland Hills, Calif. Stage and screen actor. Son of actress Ida Jeffreys.

Appeared in: **1934** The President Vanishes; Bottoms Up; The Trumpet Blows; The Fountain. **1935** The Wedding Night; Love in Bloom; College Scandal; Dangerous. **1936** Two in a Crowd; Hearts in Bondage; The Prisoner of Shark Island; Dracula's Daughter; Parole; Navy Born; Wedding Present; Two against the World. **1937** Great Guy; On the Avenue; This Is My Affair; Over the Goal; Dangerously Yours; West of Shanghai; Ali Baba Goes to Town. **1938** I Am the Law. **1939** Off the Record; East Side of Heaven; Eternally Yours; 20,000 Men a Year. **1940** The Man Who Wouldn't Talk; Dr. Ehrlich's Magic Bullet; Private Affair. **1941** Glamour Boy; Honky Tonk; H. M. Pullman, Esq.; Buck Privates; In the Navy. **1942** Murder in the Big House; Parachute Nurse. **1943** What a Woman; Never a Dull Moment. **1944** I'm from Arkansas; America's Children; Meet Miss Bobby Socks; The Adventures of Mark Twain. **1945** Big Show-Off; Eadie Was a Lady; Come Out Fighting; Boston Blackie Booked on Suspicion. **1946** Because of Him; Voice of the Whistler; Tomorrow is Forever. **1947** My Wild Irish Rose; Blondie's Big Moment; It Had to Be You; Two Blondes and a Redhead. **1948** An Old Fashioned Girl; Shamrock Hill. **1950** The Petty Girl; Harriet Craig; Border Outlaws. **1955** No Man's Woman. **1956** That Certain Feeling.

WOOD, ERNEST

Born: Apr. 17, 1892, Atchison, Kans. Died: July 13, 1942, Hollywood, Calif. (heart attack). Screen, stage and vaudeville actor. Entered films in 1923.

Appeared in: **1925** Passionate Youth. **1926** Atta Boy. **1927** Horse Shoes; Out of the Past; Woman's Law; The Princess on Broadway. **1928** A Perfect Gentleman; A Certain Young Man; Take Me Home. **1929** Red Wine. **1930** Not Damaged; Scotch (short); Sweethearts on Parade; Dining Out (short). **1931** June Moon; Annabelle's Affairs; Sob Sister; Ambassador Bill. **1933** Parole Girl; A Bedtime Story; International House; Jennie Gerhardt. **1934** Call It Luck; For Love or Money. **1935** Fugitive Lady; False Pretenses. **1937** Roaring Timber.

WOOD, EUGENE

Born: 1904. Died: Jan. 22, 1971, West Palm Beach, Fla. (heart attack). Screen, stage and television actor.

Appeared in: **1964** Nothing But a Man. **1970** Diary of a Mad Housewife; Dirtymouth; The Way We Live Now.

WOOD, FRANKER

Born: 1883, Stromsburg, Nebr. Died: Nov. 13, 1931, Farmingdale, N.Y. Screen, stage and vaudeville actor. Appeared with his wife Bunnee Wyde in an act billed "Wood and Wyde."

Appeared in: **1930** Hit the Deck.

WOOD, FREEMAN N.

Born: 1897, Denver, Colo. Died: Feb. 19, 1956, Hollywood, Calif. Stage and screen actor.

Appeared in: **1919** The Adventure Shop. **1921** Made in Heaven; Diane of Star Hollow; High Heels; The Rage of Paris. **1922** White Hands; Electric House. **1923** Gossip; Innocence; Broken Hearts of Broadway; Divorce; The Man Alone; The Wild Party; Out of Luck; Fashion Row. **1924** Butterfly; The Female; The Price She Paid; One Glorious Night; The Girl on the Stairs; The Gaiety Girl. **1925** The Dancers; Raffles, The Amateur Cracksman; Hearts and Spurs; The Part Time Wife; Scandal Proof; Wings of Youth. **1926** Josselyn's Wife; Mannequin; The Lone Wolf Returns; A Social Celebrity; The Prince of Broadway. **1927** McFadden's Flats; Taxi, Taxi; The Coward. **1928** Little Yellow House; Half a Bride; Scarlet Youth; The Legion of the Condemned; The Garden of Eden. **1929** Chinatown Nights; Why Bring That Up? **1930** Only the Brave; Young Eagles; Ladies in Love; Lilies of the Field; The Swellhead. **1931** Kept Husbands. **1932** Lady with a Past. **1936** Hollywood Boulevard.

WOOD, G. D. *See* GORDON DeMAIN

WOOD, MARJORIE

Born: 1888. Died: Nov. 8, 1955, Hollywood, Calif. Screen and stage actress.

Appeared in: **1939** The Women; They Shall Have Music. **1940** Pride and Prejudice. **1941** Look Who's Laughing. **1942** Saboteur; Klondike Fury. **1951** The Company She Keeps; Excuse My Dust; Texas Carnival. **1953** Sweethearts on Parade. **1954** Seven Brides for Seven Brothers.

WOOD, MICKEY

Born: 1898. Died: Nov. 20, 1963, London, England. Screen actor and stuntman.

Appeared in: **1960** Circle of Deception (US 1961).

WOOD, PHILIP

Born: 1896. Died: Mar. 3, 1940, Hollywood, Calif. (heart attack). Screen, stage actor, playwright and author.

Appeared in: **1938** Room Service. **1940** Our Town.

WOOD, ROLAND

Born: 1897. Died: Feb. 3, 1967, New York, N.Y. (heart attack). Stage and screen actor.

Appeared in: **1967** The Tiger Makes Out.

WOOD, SAM

Born: July 10, 1883, Philadelphia, Pa. Died: Sept. 22, 1949, Hollywood, Calif. (heart attack). Screen, stage actor and film director. Entered films as an actor with DeMille in 1910.

WOOD, SUZANNE

Died: Sept. 12, 1934, Hollywood, Calif. Screen, stage actress and author.

WOOD, VICTOR

Born: 1914. Died: Oct. 1958, London, England. Screen, stage and television actor.

Appeared in: **1947** Moss Rose. **1948** If Winter Comes; The Iron Curtain; Hills of Home. **1950** Joan of Arc. **1951** The Desert Fox; Kind Lady. **1952** My Cousin Rachel. **1953** Scandal at Scourie; The Snows of Kilimanjaro. **1959** The Lock.

WOODBRIDGE, GEORGE

Born: Feb. 16, 1907, Exeter, Devonshire, England. Died: Mar. 31, 1973. Stage, screen and television actor.

Appeared in: **1941** The Tower of Terror (US 1942). **1942** The Big Blockade. **1946** Green for Danger. **1948** Blanche Fury; Escape; The Fallen Idol (US 1949); Bonnie Prince Charlie. **1949** Silent Dust; The Queen of Spades; Children of Chance. **1950** Double Confession (US 1953). **1951** Cloudburst (US 1952). **1952** Murder in the Cathedral; The Flanagan Boy (aka Bad Blonde—US). **1953** The Story of Gilbert and Sullivan (aka The Great Gilbert and Sullivan—US). **1954** For Better, For Worse (aka Cocktails in the Kitchen—US 1955); The Green Buddha (US 1955). **1955** Third Party Risk (aka Deadly Game—US); The Constant Husband; An Alligator Named Daisy (US 1957); Richard III (US 1956); The Naked Heart. **1956** Three Men in a Boat (US 1958). **1957** The Passionate Stranger (aka A Novel Affair—US); The Good Companions; Day of Grace; High Flight (US 1958). **1958** Dracula (aka Horror of Dracula—US); The Revenge of Frankenstein; Son of Robin Hood (US 1959). **1959** Jack the Ripper (US 1960). **1960** Two-Way Stretch (US 1961); The Flesh and the Fiends (aka Mania—US 1961). **1961** The Curse of the Werewolf; No Place Like Homicide (aka What a Carve Up!—US 1962); Raising the Wind (aka Roommates—US 1962). **1963** Nurse on Wheels (US 1964); Heavens Above! **1964** Carry On Jack. **1965** Dracula—Prince of Darkness (US

1966); The Reptile (US 1966). **1969** Where's Jack?; Take a Girl Like You (US 1970).

WOODBURY, DOREEN

Born: 1927, Australia. Died: Feb. 6, 1957, New York, N.Y. (suicide—pills). Screen and television actress.

Appeared in: **1957** Space Ship Sappy (short); The Shadow on the Window.

WOODFORD, JOHN

Born: 1862, Tex. Died: Apr. 17, 1927, Saranac Lake, N.Y. Stage and screen actor.

Appeared in: **1921** Get-Rich-Quick-Wallingford; The Rider of the King Log. **1922** Ten Nights in a Bar Room. **1923** Success. **1925** The Mad Dancer.

WOODHOUSE, TODD

Born: 1902. Died: June 19, 1958, Hollywood, Calif. Screen actor and stuntman.

WOODRUFF, EDNA

Born: 1874. Died: Oct. 16, 1947, Los Angeles, Calif. Screen actress and novelist.

WOODRUFF, HENRY

Born: 1870. Died: Oct. 6, 1916, New York, N.Y. Stage and screen actor.

Appeared in: **1915** A Man and His Mate. **1916** The Beckoning Flame.

WOODRUFF, WILLIAM H. "BURT"

Born: 1856. Died: June 14, 1934, Los Angeles, Calif. Stage and screen actor. Appeared in Charles Ray films.

WOODS, AL (Frederick Ludwig Dreeke)

Born: 1895. Died: June 3, 1946, Pasadena, Calif. (heart attack). Stage and screen actor.

Appeared in: **1936** Easy Money.

WOODS, ERCELL

Born: 1916. Died: Apr. 23, 1948, Los Angeles, Calif. (auto crash). Screen actress.

WOODS, GRANT

Died: Oct. 31, 1968. Screen actor.

Appeared in: **1966** The Silencers.

WOODS, HARRY LEWIS, SR.

Born: 1889. Died: Dec. 28, 1968, Los Angeles, Calif. (uremia). Screen actor.

Appeared in: **1921** "Ruth Roland" serials. **1923** The Steel Trail (serial); Don Quickshot of the Rio Grande. **1924** The Fast Express (serial); Ten Scars Make a Man (serial); Wolves of the North (serial); Dynamite Dan. **1925** The Bandit's Baby; A Cafe in Cairo. **1926** A Regular Scout; A Trip to Chinatown; Man Four Square. **1927** Cyclone of the Range; Jesse James; Tom's Gang; Splitting the Breeze; Silver Comes Thru. **1928** The Candy Kid; When the Law Rides; Red Riders of Canada; Tyrant of Red Gulch; The Sunset Legion. **1929** China Bound; The Desert Rider; The Viking; Gun Law; The Phantom Rider; 'Neath Western Skies. **1930** The Lone Rider; Men without Law; Ranch House Blues; Pardon My Gun. **1931** West of Cheyenne; Texas Ranger; In Old Cheyenne; Palmy Days; Range Fed; Monkey Business; Pardon Us. **1932** Night World; I Am a Fugitive from a Chain Gang; Radio Patrol; Haunted Gold; Law and Order. **1933** Shadows of Sing Sing. **1934** St. Louis Kid; The President Vanishes; Belle of the Nineties; School for Girls; Devil Tiger; The Crosby Case; The Scarlet Empress; Wonder Bar; The Circus Clown. **1935** Let 'Em Have It; Robin Hood of El Dorado; Heir to Trouble; When a Man's a Man; Rustlers of Red Gap; The Call of the Savage (serial); Gallant Defender; Ship Cafe. **1936** The Lawless Nineties; Silly Billies; Human Cargo; The Unknown Ranger; Conflict; Rose of the Rancho; The Plainsman; Ticket to Paradise; Heroes of the Range. **1937** Courage of the West; Land Beyond the Law; Outcast; I Promise to Pay; Range Defenders. **1938** Hawaiian Buckaroo; The Arizona Wildcat; Come on, Rangers; Penamint's Bad Man; Blockheads; The Buccaneer; The Spy Ring; Crime Takes a Holiday. **1939** Frontier Marshal; Union Pacific; Days of Jesse James; Mr. Moto in Danger Island; The Man in the Iron Mask; In Old California; Blue Montana Skies; Beau Geste. **1940** South of Pago Pago; Isle of Destiny; Bullet Code; West of Carson City; The Ranger and the Lady; Triple Justice; Meet the Missus; Winners of the West (serial). **1941** Petticoat Politics; Sheriff of Tombstone; Forbidden Passage (short); Last of the Duanes. **1942** Today I Hang; Romance on the Range; Down Texas Way; Riders of the West; Deep in the Heart of Texas; West of the Law; Forest Rangers; Reap the Wild Wind; Jackass Mail; Dawn on the Great Divide. **1943** Outlaws of Stampede Pass; Cheyenne Roundup; The Ghost Rider; Bordertown Gunfighters; Beyond the Last Frontier. **1944** Call of the Rockies; Marshal of Gunsmoke; Nevada; Westward Bound; The Adventures of Mark Twain; Tall in the Saddle. **1945** Wanderer of the Wasteland; West of the Pecos; Radio Stars on Parade. **1946** Trouble or Nothing (short); South of Monterey; My Darling Clementine. **1947** Wild Rose Mesa; Wyoming; Tycoon; Trail Street; Thunder Mountain; Code of the West. **1948** Western Heritage; The Gallant Legion;

Indian Agent. **1949** Colorado Territory; The Fountainhead; Hellfire; Masked Raiders; She Wore a Yellow Ribbon. **1950** Traveling Saleswoman; Short Grass; Law of the Badlands. **1952** Lone Star; Rancho Notorious. **1954** Hell's Outpost. **1956** Ten Commandments.

WOODS, JOSEPH A.
Born: 1860, N.Y. Died: Feb. 13, 1926, New York, N.Y. (heart disease). Stage and screen actor. He often impersonated President Woodrow Wilson because of the marked resemblance.

WOODS, NICK (Nicholas Schaber)
Born: 1858. Died: Mar. 21, 1936, New Rochelle, N.Y. Screen and stage actor. Was billed on stage as "N. S. Woods, the Boy Actor."

WOODTHROPE, GEORGIA
Born: 1859. Died: Aug. 25, 1927, Glendale, Calif. Stage and screen actress.

Appeared in: **1919** The Midnight Man (serial). **1921** Four Horsemen of the Apocalypse; Bunty Pulls the Strings. **1922** The Song of Life. **1923** Gimme; Thundering Dawn; Rouged Lips. **1924** Daddies.

WOODWARD, H. GUY
Born: 1858, Minneapolis, Minn. Died: Aug. 20, 1919, Detroit, Mich. (heart disease). Screen, stage actor and circus performer. Appeared in "Sunshine" Comedies.

Appeared in: **1915** Fickle Fatty's Fall; The Best of Enemies; The Hunt; Double Trouble. **1916** Because He Loved Her; His Pride and Shame; A Dash of Courage; His Wild Oats; A Tugboat Romeo. **1917** Dodging His Doom; A Shanghaied Jonah; Hula Hula Land.

WOODWARD, ROBERT "BOB"
Born: 1909. Died: Feb. 7, 1972, Hollywood, Calif. (heart attack). Screen actor. Doubled for many Western stars such as Buck Jones and Dick Foran.

Appeared in: **1938** Frontier Scout. **1939** Home on the Prairie. **1947** Stage to Mesa City; Cheyenne Takes Over. **1948** The Westward Trail; The Tioga Kid; Crossed Trails; Triggerman; Range Renegades; Frontier Agent; Overland Trails; Gunning for Justice; Courtin' Trouble; Silver Trails; The Sheriff of Medicine Bow; Hidden Danger; Cowboy Cavalier; The Rangers Ride; Song of the Drifter; The Fighting Ranger; Back Trail. **1949** Gun Runner; Crashin' Thru; Law of the West; West of El Dorado; Shadows of the West; Range Justice; Brand of Fear; Roaring Westward; Across the Rio Grande. **1950** The Blazing Hills (aka The Blazing Sun); Radar Secret Service. **1951** Hills of Utah. **1952** The Old West; Night Stage to Galveston; Barbed Wire; Junction City; Blue Canadian Rockies. **1953** Winning of the West. **1955** Wyoming Renegade. **1958** Apache Territory. **1961** Gun Fight. **1963** Red Runs the River.

WOOLDRIDGE, DORIS
Born: 1890. Died: July 17, 1921, Los Angeles, Calif. (appendix operation). Stage and screen actress.

WOOLF, BARNEY
Born: 1877. Died: Feb. 10, 1972, Hollywood, Calif. Screen and television actor and extra.

WOOLF, MRS. YETTI
Born: 1882. Died: Nov. 27, 1965, Hollywood, Calif. Screen actress.

WOOLLCOTT, ALEXANDER
Born: Jan. 19, 1887, Phalanx, N.J. Died: Jan. 23, 1943, New York, N.Y. Drama critic, playwright, screen, stage and radio actor.

Appeared in: **1934** Gift of Gab. **1935** The Scoundrel. **1937** RKO shorts. **1942** Babes on Broadway.

WOOLLEY, MONTY (Edgar Montillion Wooley)
Born: Aug. 17, 1888, New York, N.Y. Died: May 6, 1963, Albany, N.Y. (kidney and heart ailment). Stage and screen actor. Entered films in 1931.

Appeared in: **1937** Live, Love and Learn; Nothing Sacred. **1938** Everybody Sing; Arsene Lupin Returns; The Girl of the Golden West; Three Comrades; Lord Jeff; Artists and Models Abroad; Young Dr. Kildare; Vacation from Love. **1939** Zaza; See Your Doctor (short); Dancing Co-ed; Man about Town; Midnight; Never Say Die. **1941** The Man Who Came to Dinner. **1942** The Pied Piper; Life Begins at 8:30. **1943** The Light of Heart; Holy Matrimony. **1944** Since You Went Away; Irish Eyes Are Smiling. **1945** Molly and Me. **1946** Night and Day. **1947** The Bishop's Wife. **1948** Miss Tatlock's Millions; Will You Love Me in December? **1950** Paris 1950 (narr.). **1951** As Young as You Feel. **1955** Kismet.

WOOLSEY, ROBERT
Born: Aug. 14, 1889, Oakland, Calif. Died: Oct. 1938, Malibu Beach, Calif. (kidney ailment). Screen, stage and vaudeville actor. Was partner in vaudeville and film comedy team of "Wheeler and Woolsey." See Bert Wheeler for films they made together.

Appeared without Wheeler in: **1930** The Voice of Hollywood (short). **1931** Everything's Rosie. **1933** Hollywood on Parade (short).

WORLOCK, FREDERICK
Born: 1886. Died: Aug. 1, 1973, Woodland Hills, Calif. (cerebral ischemia). Stage and screen actor. Divorced from actress Elsie Ferguson (dec. 1961).

Appeared in: **1939** Miracles for Sale; Lady of the Tropics; Balalaika; The Story That Couldn't Be Printed (short). **1940** Strange Cargo; Moon Over Burma; The Sea Hawk; Murder Over New York; South of Suez; Hudson's Bay; Northwest Passage; The Earl of Chicago. **1941** Rage in Heaven; Free and Easy; Man Hunt; Dr. Jekyll and Mr. Hyde; A Yank in the R A F; How Green Was My Valley; International Lady. **1942** Captains of the Clouds; Eagle Squadron; Pacific Rendezvous; Pierre of the Plains; The Black Swan; London Blackout Murders; Random Harvest; Madero (short); Pier 29 (short). **1943** Air Raid Wardens; Appointment in Berlin; Sherlock Holmes Faces Death; Thumbs Up; Madame Curie. **1944** The Lodger; Jane Eyre; Secrets of Scotland Yard; National Velvet. **1945** Hangover Square; The Woman in Green; Pursuit to Algiers; Captain Kidd; Fatal Witness; Scotland Yard Investigator; The Picture of Dorian Gray. **1946** Terror by Night; She-Wolf of London; Dressed to Kill. **1947** The Imperfect Lady; Last of the Redmen; Singapore; The Lone Wolf in London; Love From a Stranger; Forever Amber; A Woman's Vengeance; The Macomber Affair. **1948** Joan of Arc; Hills of Home; A Double Life; The Woman in White; Johnny Belinda. **1958** Jet Over the Atlantic (US 1960); Spartacus. **1961** One Hundred and One Dalmations (voice). **1962** The Notorious Landlady. **1966** Spinout.

WORTH, BILL
Born: 1884. Died: May 2, 1951, Westwood, Calif. (heart attack). Screen actor.

WORTH, CONSTANCE (Jocelyn Howarth)
Born: 1915, Sydney, Australia. Died: Oct. 18, 1963. Screen actress. Divorced from actor George Brent.

Appeared in: **1919** The Non-Conformist Parson; Wisp O' the Woods. **1920** Fate's a Plaything. **1921** The Education of Nicky. **1922** A Bachelor's Baby; No. 7 Brick Row. **1923** Within the Maze. **1924** Love in the Welsh Hills. **1937** China Passage; Windjammer. **1940** Angels Over Broadway. **1941** Meet Boston Blackie; Borrowed Hero. **1943** Crime Doctor; G-Men vs. the Black Dragon (serial); Crime Doctor's Strangest Case. **1944** Cyclone Prairie Rangers; Sagebrush Heroes. **1945** Why Girls Leave Home; Kid Sister. **1946** Deadline at Dawn; Sensation Hunters. **1949** Western Renegades.

WORTH, PEGGY
Born: 1891. Died: Mar. 23, 1956, New York, N.Y. Screen and stage actress.

Appeared in: **1921** You Find It Everywhere.

WORTHING, HELEN LEE
Born: 1905. Died: Aug. 25, 1948, Los Angeles, Calif. Stage and screen actress.

Appeared in: **1924** Janice Meredith. **1925** The Crowded Hour; Flower of the Night; Night Life of New York; The Swan; The Other Woman's Story. **1926** Don Juan; The County of Luxembourg; Lew Tyler's Wives; Watch Your Wife. **1927** Vanity; Thumbs Down.

WORTHINGTON WILLIAM J.
Born: 1872, Troy, N.Y. Died: Apr. 9, 1941, Beverly Hills, Calif. Screen, stage, vaudeville actor, opera performer, film director and film producer. Former president and treasurer of Multicolor Films. Entered films as an actor in 1915.

Appeared in: **1915** Damon and Pythias; The Black Box (serial). **1921** High Heels. **1923** Red Lights; The Green Goddess. **1926** Her Honor, the Governor; Return of Boston Blackie; Kid Boots. **1928** Good Morning Judge; Half a Bride. **1930** The Climax; Shipmates; Laughing Sinners; Susan Lenox, Her Rise and Fall; Possessed; The Man Who Came Back. **1933** Duck Soup; No More Orchids. **1934** The Gold Ghosts (short); One Exciting Adventure. **1935** $20 a Week; Cardinal Richelieu; The Keeper of the Bees. **1936** Can This Be Dixie? **1937** Battle of Greed. **1938** Angels with Dirty Faces.

WRAY, ALOHA
Born: 1928. Died: Apr. 28, 1968, Hollywood, Calif. Screen actress and dancer. Divorced from actor Frankie Darro (dec. 1976).

Appeared in: **1935** George White's 1935 Scandals.

WRAY, JOHN GRIFFITH (John Griffith Malloy)
Born: Feb. 13, 1888, Philadelphia, Pa. Died: Apr. 5, 1940, Los Angeles, Calif. Screen, stage actor, playwright and film director. Entered films in 1929.

Appeared in: **1930** New York Nights; All Quiet on the Western Front; The Czar of Broadway. **1931** Quick Millions; Silence; Safe in Hell. **1932** High Pressure; The Woman from Monte Carlo; The Miracle Man; The Mouthpiece; The Rich Are Always with Us; Miss Pinkerton; Doctor X; Central Park; The Match King; I Am a Fugitive from a Chain Gang. **1933** The Death Kiss; After Tonight; I'll Fix It; Lone Cowboy; Bombay Mail; The Crosby Case; The Love Captive; Embarrassing Moments; The Big Shakedown; The Most Precious Thing in Life; The Defense Rests; Green Eyes; Fifteen Wives; The

Captain Hates the Sea. **1935** I Am a Thief; Ladies Love Danger; Atlantic Adventure; Bad Boy; The Great Hotel Murder; The Whole Town's Talking; Stranded; Frisco Kid; Men without Names. **1936** Mr. Deeds Goes to Town; The Poor Little Rich Girl; Sworn Enemy; A Son Comes Home; Valiant Is the Word for Carrie; The President's Mystery; We Who Are about to Die. **1937** A Man Betrayed; You Only Live Once; Outcast; On Such a Night; The Devil Is Driving; The Women Men Marry; Circus Girl. **1938** House of Mystery; What Price Safety? (short); Making the Headlines; The Black Doll; Crime Takes a Holiday; Gangs of New York; A Man to Remember; Pacific Lines; Spawn of the North; Tenth Avenue Kid; Golden Boy. **1939** Risky Business; Pacific Liner; The Amazing Mr. Williams; Smuggled Cargo; Each Dawn I Die; Blackmail; The Cat and the Canary. **1940** The Man from Dakota; Remember the Night; Swiss Family Robinson; Know Your Money (short).

WRAY, TED
Born: 1909. Died: Jan. 26, 1950, near Big Bear, Calif. (heart attack). Screen actor.

WREN, SAM
Born: 1897, Brooklyn, N.Y. Died: Mar. 15, 1962, Hollywood, Calif. Screen, stage, television actor and stage director. Married to screen actress Virginia Sale.

Appeared in: **1935** Dr. Socrates. **1936** I Married a Doctor. **1937** Marked Woman. **1942** Over My Dead Body. **1943** Dixie Dugan.

WRIGHT, ARMAND VINCENT "CURLY"
Born: June 6, 1896, New York, N.Y Died: Mar. 28, 1965, North Hollywood, Calif. (cancer). Screen actor.

Appeared in: **1932** Lawyer Man. **1933** Sailor's Luck; Fits in a Fiddle (short). **1938** Panamint's Bad Man. **1942** To Be or Not to Be.

WRIGHT, ED
Died: Mar. 31, 1975. Screen actor.

Appeared in: **1958** Gang War; Showdown at Boot Hill. **1959** The Oregon Trail.

WRIGHT, FRED
Born: England? Died: Dec. 12, 1928, New York, N.Y. Screen actor.

Appeared in: **1916** The Grand Babylon Hotel; Molly Bawn. **1920** La Poupee. **1922** The Glorious Adventure; The Further Adventures of Sherlock Holmes series including: The Norwood Builder. **1923** Hornet's Nest; M'Lord of the White Road. **1926** Cinders.

WRIGHT, HAIDEE
Born: 1898, London, England. Died: Jan. 29, 1943, London, England. Stage and screen actress.

Appeared in: **1915** Evidence. **1919** In Bondage (aka Faith). **1920** Colonel Newcome the Perfect Gentleman; Aunt Rachel; The Winning Goal. **1921** Demos (aka Why Men Forget—US); The Old Country. **1922** The Glorious Adventure; A Bachelor's Baby. **1923** Paddy the Next Best Thing. **1926** The Sea Urchin. **1927** The Cabaret Kid. **1933** Strange Evidence; The Blarney Stone (aka The Blarney Kiss—US). **1934** Jew Suess (aka Power—US). **1936** Tomorrow We Live.

WRIGHT, HARRY WENDELL "WEN"
Born: 1916. Died: June 17, 1954, Humboldt, Nev. (auto accident). Screen actor and stuntman.

WRIGHT, HENRY OTHO
Born: 1892. Died: June 7, 1940, San Bernardino, Calif. Screen actor.

WRIGHT, HUGH E.
Born: Apr. 13, 1879, Cannes, France. Died: Feb. 13, 1940, Windsor, England. Screen, stage actor, playwright, screenwriter and lyricist.

Appeared in: **1918** The Kiddies in the Ruins; Where's Watling?; The Bette 'Ole, Or, The Romance of Old Bill (aka Carry On—US). **1920** Garry Owen; Nothing Else Matters. **1921** The Old Curiosity Shop; Mary-Find-The-Gold; Squibs; The Corner Man. **1922** A Sailor Tramp; Squibs Wins the Calcutta Sweep. **1923** The Romany; Squibs, MP; Squibs' Honeymoon. **1929** Auld Lang Syne; The Silver King. **1931** Down River; The Great Gay Road; East Lynne on the Western Front; Stranglehold. **1932** Brother Alfred; Lord Camber's Ladies. **1933** The Good Companions; Cash (aka For Love or Money—US 1934); Oh What a Duchess! (aka My Old Duchess); You Made Me Love You; A Shot in the Dark (US 1935). **1934** On the Air; Crazy People; Adventure Limited; Radio Parade of 1935 (US 1935). **1935** Widow's Might; Scrooge. **1936** Royal Eagle.

WRIGHT, HUNTLEY
Born: 1870, England. Died: July 10, 1941, Bangor, Wales (heart attack). Screen, stage and radio actor.

Appeared in: **1933** The Only Girl (aka Heart Song—US 1935). **1935** Look Up and Laugh.

WRIGHT, MACK V. "MAC"
Died: Aug. 14, 1965, Boulder City, Nev. Screen actor, screenwriter and film director.

Appeared in: **1915** The Black Box. **1919** The Lion Man (serial). **1921** Red Courage. **1922** Perils of the Yukon (serial). **1923** Single Handed. **1924** Crossed Trails; Western Vengeance. **1925** Blood and Steel; Border Intrigue; Border Justice; Moccasins; Riders of Mystery. **1926** Mistaken Orders; Silver Fingers. **1928** The Manhattan Cowboy; Silent Trail. **1929** Headin' Westward; Arizona Days; The Law of the Mounted; West of Santa Fe; The Lone Horseman. **1930** Pioneers of the West; Hunted Men; The Oklahoma Sheriff.

WRIGHT, WILL
Born: Mar. 26, 1891, San Francisco, Calif. Died: June 19, 1962, Hollywood, Calif. (cancer). Screen, stage, vaudeville, radio and television actor.

Appeared in: **1936** China Clipper. **1939** Silver on the Sage. **1940** Blondie Plays Cupid. **1941** The Richest Man in Town. **1942** Shut My Big Mouth; True to the Army; Night in New Orleans; Wildcat; A Parachute Nurse; Sweetheart of the Fleet; Tennessee Johnson; The Daring Young Man; A Man's World; The Postman Didn't Ring. **1943** A Night to Remember; In Old Oklahoma; Reveille with Beverly; Lucky Legs; Murder in Times Square; Cowboy in Manhattan; Practically Yours. **1945** Eve Knew Her Apples; Road to Utopia; Rhapsody in Blue; Gun Smoke; Sleepy Lagoon; Blonde Fever; Grissly's Millions; Bewitched; Eadie Was a Lady; The Strange Affair of Uncle Harry; You Came Along; Salome, Where She Danced. **1946** Hot Cargo; The Inner Circle; Johnny Comes Flying Home; The Madonna's Secret; Rendezvous with Annie; One Exciting Week; The Blue Dahlia. **1947** Along the Oregon Trail; Keeper of the Bees; Wild Harvest; Mother Wore Tights; Blaze of Noon; Cynthia. **1948** Relentless; They Live By Night (aka The Twisted Road and Your Red Wagon); The Inside Story; Green Grass of Wyoming; The Walls of Jericho; Disaster; Whispering Smith; California's Golden Beginning; Black Eagle; Act of Violence; Act of Murder. **1949** Big Jack; Brimstone; For Those Who Dare; Mrs. Mike; All the King's Men; Adam's Rib; Lust for Gold; Miss Grant Takes Richmond. **1950** House by the River; The Savage Horde; Sunset in the West; A Ticket to Tomahawk; No Way Out; Dallas. **1951** My Forbidden Past; Vengeance Valley; Excuse My Dust; The Tall Target; People Will Talk. **1952** Lydia Bailey; The Las Vegas Story; Paula; Lure of the Wilderness; O. Henry's Full House; Happy Time; Holiday for Sinners. **1953** Niagara; The Last Posse. **1954** Johnny Guitar; The Wild One; River of No Return; The Raid. **1955** The Man with the Golden Arm; The Tall Men; The Court Martial of Billy Mitchell. **1956** These Wilder Years. **1957** The Iron Sheriff; Johnny Tremain; The Wayward Bus. **1958** The Missouri Traveler; Quantrille's Raiders; Gunman's Walk. **1959** Alias Jesse James; The Thirty Foot Bride of Candy Rock. **1961** The Deadly Companions; Twenty Plus Two. **1962** Cape Fear. **1964** Fail Safe.

WRIGHT, WILLIAM
Born: 1912, Ogden, Utah. Died: Jan. 19, 1949, Ensenada, Mexico (cancer). Stage and screen actor.

Appeared in: **1941** Rookies on Parade; Nothing but the Truth; World Premiere; Glamour Boy; The Devil Pays Off. **1942** Parachute Nurse; True to the Army; Night in New Orleans; Sweetheart of the Fleet. **1943** A Night to Remember; Here Comes Elmer. **1944** Dancing in Manhattan; One Mysterious Night. **1945** Eadie Was a Lady; State Fair; Escape in the Fog. **1946** Down Missouri Way; Lover Come Back; The Mask of Dijon. **1947** Philo Vance Returns; The Gas House Kids Go West. **1948** King of Gamblers. **1949** Daughter of the Jungle; Impact; Air Hostess; Rose of the Yukon.

WU, HONORABLE
Born: 1903, San Francisco, Calif. Died: Mar. 1, 1945, Hollywood, Calif. Screen, stage, vaudeville and radio actor.

Appeared in: **1936** Stowaway. **1938** Mr. Moto; The Crime of Dr. Hallett; Mr. Moto Takes a Vacation. **1939** North of Shanghai. **1941** Ellery Queen and the Perfect Crime.

WUEST, IDA
Born: 1884, Wiesbaden, Germany. Died: Nov. 2, 1958, Berlin, Germany. Stage and screen actress. Married to actor Bruno Kastner (dec.).

Appeared in: **1929** The Last Waltz. **1930** The Burning Heart. **1931** Bockbierfest; Das Alte Lied; Ein Burschenlied aus Heidelberg; Die Lindenwirtin vom Rhein; Bomben auf Monte Carlo (The Bombardment of Monte Carlo). **1932** Die Csikos Baroness; Mein Leopold; Hurra! Ein Junge!; Schoen ist die Manoeverzeit (Beautiful Maneuver Time); Wenn die Soldaten; Man Braucht Kein Geld; Der Walzerkoenig; Das Schoene Abenteuer. **1933** Namensheirat; Friederike; Drei Tage Mittelarrest; Lachende Erben. **1934** Wie Sag' Ich's Meinem Mann?; Eines Prinzen Junge Liebe; Ja, Treu ist die Soldatenliebe; Zu Befehl; Herr Unteroffizier; Melodie der Liebe; Es War Einmal ein Walzer; Fleuchtlinge; Einmal Eine Grosse Dame Sein; Freut Euch des Lebens. **1935** Die Liebe und die Erste Eisenbahn (Love and the First Railroad); Jungfrau Gegen Moench (Maiden vs. Monk); Csardasfuerstin (The Czardas Duchess); Fruehlingsmaerchen; So ein Maedel Vergisst Man Nicht. **1936** The Private Life of

Louis XIV; Die Marquise von Pompadour; Annette in Paradise; Der Bettelstudent. **1937** The World's in Love. **1938** Wenn Du eine Schwiegermutter Hast (When You Have a Mother-in-Law); Husaren Heraus; Kater Lampe; Eine Seefahrt die ist Lustig (A Merry Sea Trip); Eine Nacht an der Donau (A Night on the Danube). **1939** Kleines Bezirksgericht (Little Country Court); Diskretion-Ehrensache (Discretion with Honor); Herbst-Monoever (Fall Manoeuvres); Der Lustige Witwenball (The Merry Widow's Ball); Die Blonde Carmen; Die Kluge Schwiegermutter (The Wise Mother-in-Law).

WUNDERLEE, FRANK
Born: 1875, St. Louis, Mo. Died: Dec. 11, 1925 (apoplexy). Stage and screen actor.

Appeared in: **1919** The Carter Case (serial); The Fatal Fortune (serial). **1921** A Divorce of Convenience. **1922** One Exciting Night; Reported Missing. **1923** No Mother to Guide Her. **1924** The Great White Way.

WYATT, EUSTACE (Eustace George William Wyatt)
Born: Mar. 5, 1882, Bath, England. Died: Oct. 25, 1944, Los Angeles, Calif. (heart failure). Screen actor.

Appeared in: **1942** Journey into Fear; Nightmare. **1944** The Man in Half Moon Street; Ministry of Fear.

WYCHERLY, MARGARET
Born: 1881, London, England. Died: June 6, 1956, New York, N.Y. Screen, stage, vaudeville and television actress.

Appeared in: **1929** Thirteenth Chair (film debut). **1934** Midnight. **1938** Wanderlust (short). **1940** Victory. **1941** Sergeant York. **1942** Crossroads; Random Harvest; Keeper of the Flame. **1943** The Moon Is Down; Assignment in Brittany; Hangmen also Die. **1944** Experiment Perilous. **1945** Johnny Angel. **1946** Enchanted Cottage. **1947** Something in the Wind; The Yearling; Forever Amber. **1948** The Loves of Carmen. **1949** White Heat. **1951** The Man with a Cloak. **1953** The President's Lady; That Man from Tangier. **1956** Richard III.

WYMAN, ELEANORE
Born: 1914. Died: Sept. 1, 1940, Lancaster, Calif. (auto accident). Screen actress.

WYMARK, PATRICK (Patrick Cheeseman)
Born: 1926, Grimsby, England. Died: Oct. 20, 1970, Melbourne, Australia (heart attack). Screen, stage and television actor.

Appeared in: **1960** The Criminal (aka The Concrete Jungle—US 1962); The League of Gentlemen (US 1961). **1964** The Finest Hours (voice of Churchill); The Secret of Blood Island (US 1965). **1965** Repulsion; Operation Crossbow (aka The Great Spy Mission); The Skull. **1966** The Psychopath; A King's Story (US 1967) **1967** Sept fois Femme (Woman Times Seven—US). **1968** Witchfinder General (aka The Conqueror Worm—US); Where Eagles Dare (US 1969); Tell Me No Lies. **1969** Battle of Britain; Doppelganger (aka The Far Side of the Sun—US). **1970** Cromwell.

WYNARD, DIANA (Dorothy Cox)
Born: Jan. 16, 1906, London, England. Died: May 13, 1964, London, England (kidney ailment). Stage and screen actress. Divorced from film director Sir Carol Reed (dec. 1976).

Appeared in: **1932** Rasputin and the Empress (film debut). **1933** Cavalcade; Men Must Fight; Reunion in Vienna. **1934** Where Sinners Meet; Let's Try Again; One More River; Hollywood on Parade (short). **1939** On the Night of the Fire (aka The Fugitive—US 194). **1940** Gaslight (aka Angel Street—US). **1941** Freedom Radio (aka A Voice in the Night—US); The Prime Minister; Kipps (aka The Remarkable Mr. Kipps—US 1942). **1948** An Ideal Husband. **1951** Tom Brown's School Days. **1956** The Feminine Touch (aka The Gentle Touch—US 1957). **1957** Island in the Sun.

WYNN, BESSIE
Born: 1876. Died: July 8, 1968, Towaco, N.Y. Screen and stage actress.

Appeared in: **1913** Animated Weekly No. 53.

WYNN, DORIS (Doris Rink)
Born: 1910. Died: July 14, 1925, Los Angeles, Calif. (pneumonia). Screen actress. Appeared in Christie films.

WYNN, ED (Edward Leopold)
Born: Nov. 9, 1886, Philadelphia, Pa. Died: June 19, 1966, Los Angeles, Calif. (cancer). Screen, stage, vaudeville, radio and television actor. Won 1959 Academy Award for Best Supporting Actor in The Diary of Anne Frank. Father of actor Keenan Wynn.

Appeared in: **1927** Rubber Heels. **1930** Follow the Leader; Manhattan Mary. **1933** The Chief. **1943** Stage Door Canteen. **1951** Alice in Wonderland (voice only). **1956** The Great Man. **1958** Marjorie Morningstar. **1959** The Diary of Anne Frank. **1960** The Absent-Minded Professor; Cinderfella. **1961** Babes in Toyland. **1963** Son of Flubber. **1964** Those Calloways; Mary Poppins; The Sound of Laughter (documentary); Patsy; Erasmus with Freckles. **1965** That Darn Cat; Dear Brigitte; The Greatest Story Ever Told. **1966** The Daydreamer (voice only). **1967** Warning Shot; The Gnome Mobile.

WYNN, NAN
Born: 1916. Died: Mar. 21, 1971, Santa Monica, Calif. (cancer). Screen, stage actress and singer. Her voice was dubbed for Rita Hayworth in several singing films.

Appeared in: **1941** A Shot in the Dark; Million Dollar Baby. **1942** Pardon My Sarong. **1943** Princess O'Rourke. **1944** Jam Session.

YACONELLI, FRANK
Born: Oct. 2, 1898, Italy. Died: Nov 19, 1965, Los Angeles, Calif. (lung cancer). Screen actor.

Appeared in: **1927** I'll Be There. **1929** Senor Americano. **1930** Firebrand Jordan; Parade of the West. **1933** Strawberry Roan; The Barber Shop (short); Kickin' the Crown Around (short). **1934** Perfectly Mismated (short); Death Takes A Holiday. **1935** Awakening of Jim Burke; Western Frontier; Gun Play; I'm a Father (short); A Night at the Opera; Here Comes Cookie. **1936** Blazing Justice; Down to the Sea; Romance Rides the Range; The Three Mesqueteers; Lawless Riders. **1937** It Could Happen to You; Wild West Days (serial). **1939** Wild Horse Canyon. **1940** East Side Kids; Dr. Cyclops; Pioneer Days; Torrid Zone; Wild Horse Range. **1941** Forced Landing; Riding the Sunset Trail; The Driftin' Kid; Two In a Taxi. **1942** Fiesta. **1943** Man of Courage. **1946** South of Monterey; Beauty and the Bandit; Slightly Scandalous. **1947** Riding the California Trail. **1949** Alias the Champ. **1950** September Affair; The Baron of Arizona. **1952** Abbott and Costello Meet Captain Kidd. **1953** Cash Stashers (short). **1954** Dragon's Gold. **1955** The Racers. **1956** Serenade.

YAKOVLEV, YASHA
Born: 1912, Russia. Died: May 17, 1970, New York, N.Y. (heart attack). Screen actor and dancer.

Appeared in: **1960** L'Idiot (The Idiot).

YAMAMOTO, KAJIRO
Born: 1902, Japan. Died: Sept. 28, 1974, Japan (cirrhosis of the liver). Screen actor and film director. Entered films during silents.

YANAGIYA, KINGORO
Born: Japan. Died: Oct. 22, 1972, Tokyo, Japan (cancer). Stage and screen actor. Appeared in films in 1920 as a popular comedian and "rakugo" (storyteller).

Appeared in: **1961** The Poem of the Blue Star. **1968** Onsen Gerira dai Shogeki (aka Kigeki dai Shogeki) (Hotsprings Holiday—US 1970).

YARBOROUGH, BARTON
Born: 1900. Died: Dec. 19, 1951, Hollywood, Calif. Screen, radio and television actor.

Appeared in: **1941** They Meet Again; Let's Go Collegiate. **1942** The Ghost of Frnkenstein; Saboteur. **1945** Red Dragon; Captain Tugboat Annie; I Love a Mystery. **1946** The Devil's Mask; Wife Wanted; The Unknown. **1947** Kilroy Was Here. **1949** Henry the Rainmaker.

YARDE, MARGARET
Born: Apr. 2, 1878, Dartmouth, England. Died: Mar. 11, 1944, London, England. Screen, stage actress and opera performer.

Appeared in: **1913** A Cigarette Maker's Romance. **1923** Gems of Literature series including: Falstaff the Tavern Knight; Wonder Women of the World series including: Madame Recamier—or the Price of Virtue. **1925** The Only Way; The Art of Love series including: The Weakness of Men (aka The Lady in Silk Stockings); and Sables of Death (aka The Lady in Furs). **1926** London. **1929** The Crooked Billet. **1930** Night Birds. **1931** Michael and Mary (US 1932); Uneasy Virtue; The Woman Between (aka The Woman Decides—US 1932); Third Time Lucky; Let's Love and Laugh (aka Bridegroom for Two—US 1932). **1933** A Shot in the Dark (US 1935); The Good Companions; The Man from Toronto; Matinee Idol; Tiger Bag; Enemy of the People. **1934** Trouble in Store; Sing as We Go; Father and Son; A Glimpse of Paradise; Nine Forty-Five; The Broken Rosary; Guest of Honour. **1935** Widow's Might; The Crouching Beast; 18 Minutes; Scrooge; The Deputy Drummer; Jubilee Window; Squibs; That's My Uncle; Who's Your Father?; Handle With Care; Full Circle; It Happened in Paris. **1936** Queen of Hearts; What the Puppy Said; Faithful; In the Soup; Gypsy Melody; No Escape; Fame. **1937** Beauty and the Barge; The Compulsory Wife; The Biter Bit (aka Calling All Ma's); French Leave; You Live and Learn. **1938** You're the Doctor; Prison Without Bars (US 1939). **1939** The Face at the Window (US 1940); French Without Tears (US 1940). **1940** Crimes at the Dark House; George and Margaret; Two Smart Men; Henry Steps Out. **1942** Tomorrow We Live (aka At Dawn We Die—US 1943). **1943** Thursday's Child. **1944** The Two Fathers.

YARNELL, BRUCE
Born: 1938. Died: Nov. 30, 1973, Calif. (plane accident). Screen, stage, television actor and singer. Married to soprano Joan Patenaude.

Appeared in: **1963** Irma La Douce. **1968** The Road Hustlers.

YASSIN, ISMAIL
Born: 1912. Died: 1972 (heart attack). Screen actor.

Appeared in: **1951** Little Miss Devil.

YBARRA, ROCKY
Born: 1900. Died: Dec. 12, 1965, Hollywood, Calif. (heart attack). Screen cowboy actor.

Appeared in: **1960** The Third Voice. **1965** The Reward.

YEARSLEY, RALPH
Born: 1897. Died: Dec. 4, 1928, Hollywood, Calif. (suicide). Screen actor.

Appeared in: **1921** Tol'able David; Pardon My French. **1922** Arabia; Why Not Marry?; The Village Blacksmith. **1923** The Call of the Canyon; A Chapter in Her Life; Anna Christie. **1924** The Fighting Sap; One Night in Rome; The Valley of Hate; The Hill Billy. **1925** The Gambling Fool. **1926** Desert Gold. **1927** The Kid Brother. **1928** The Big Killing; Rose Marie; The Little Shepherd of Kingdom Come. **1929** Show Boat.

YEATS, MURRAY F.
Born: 1910. Died: Jan. 27, 1975, Sepulveda, Calif. (pneumonia and other complications). Stage and screen actor.

YENSEN, ULA
Born: 1940, Denmark. Died: Aug. 26, 1959, Mexico City, Mexico (suicide—pills). Screen and television actress.

Appeared in: Senoritas; Sube y Baja (Up and Down).

YEOMAN, GEORGE
Born: 1869. Died: Nov. 2, 1936, Hollywood, Calif. Screen, stage and vaudeville actor. Appeared in vaudeville in an act billed as "George Yeoman and Lizzie."

YIP, WILLIAM
Died: Oct. 18, 1968. Screen actor.

Appeared in: **1949** Bad Men of Tombstone. **1954** Hell and High Water. **1956** The King and I. **1958** Twilight for the Gods.

YORK, DUKE
Born: 1902. Died: Jan. 24, 1952, Hollywood, Calif. (suicide—gun). Screen actor.

Appeared in: **1934** Elmer and Elsie; Pursuit of Happiness. **1935** Here Comes Cookie. **1936** All American Toothache (short); Strike Me Pink; Ticket to Paradise; The Three Mesquiteers; Mind Your Own Business; Flash Gordon (serial). **1937** Midnight Madonna. **1938** A Slight Case of Murder; Topper Takes a Trip. **1941** Sky Raiders (serial). **1942** All Work and No Pay (short); Who Done It? **1943** Three Little Twerps (short). **1944** Idle Roomers (short). **1949** Stampede; Mississippi Rhythm. **1950** Call of the Klondike; Fortunes of Captain Blood; Rogue River; Snow Dog; Hit Parade of 1951. **1951** Texans Never Cry; Silver Canyon; Valley of Fire. **1952** Night Stage to Galveston; Barbed Wire. **1953** Trail Blazers. **1956** For Crimin' Out Loud (short).

YORKE, CAROL (Carol Bjorkman)
Born: 1929. Died: July 5, 1967, New York, N.Y. (leukemia). Screen actress.

Appeared in: **1948** Letter from an Unknown Woman (film debut).

YORKE, EDITH (Edithe Byard aka EDITHE YORKE)
Born: Croyden, England. Died: July 28, 1934. Stage and screen actress.

Appeared in: **1921** Passing Thru; Chickens; Lying Lips. **1922** A Daughter of Luxury; One Clear Call; Step On It! **1923** The Age of Desire; Burning Words; The Fourth Musketeer; Merry-Go-Round; Mothers-in-Law; The Miracle Makers; Sawdust; Souls for Sale; Slippy McGee; Thru the Flames. **1924** Husbands and Lovers; The Beauty Prize; Happiness; My Man; The Other Kind of Love; Pride of Sunshine Alley; Riders Up; The Slanderers; The Tenth Woman. **1925** Seven Keys to Baldpate; Below the Line; Capital Punishment; Excuse Me; Silent Sanderson; Souls for Sables; Wild Horse Mesa; The Thoroughbred. **1926** The Belle of Broadway; Born to the West; The Heart of a Coward; His New York Wife; Oh, What a Nurse!; Rustlers' Ranch; Red Dice; Rustling for Cupid; The Timid Terror; Volcano; Transcontinental Limited; The Silent Flyer (serial). **1927** The Bachelor's Baby; The Western Whirlwind; Sensation Seekers. **1928** Making the Varsity; The Port of Missing Girls; Satan and the Woman. **1929** Fugitives; The Love Racket; Seven Keys to Baldpate (and 1925 version); The Valiant. **1930** City Girl; Phantom of the Opera.

YORKE, OSWALD
Born: London, England. Died: Jan. 25, 1943, New York, N.Y. Stage and screen actor.

Appeared in: **1924** Monsieur Beaucaire.

YORKNEY, JOHN C.
Born: 1871, Argentina. Died: Aug. 20, 1941, Fort Lee, N.Y. (heart attack). Stage and screen actor. Entered films during silents.

YOST, HERBERT A.
Born: 1880, Harrison, Ohio. Died: Oct. 23, 1945, New York, N.Y. Stage and screen actor. Herbert A. Yost was his stage name, but he appeared in some films as Barry O'Moore. Entered films with Biograph Studios in 1908 and later appeared in Edison series films in 1914.

Appeared in: **1909** The Deception; Edgar Allan Poe. **1912** What Happened to Mary (serial); Every Rose Has Its Stem. **1914** The Man Who Disappeared (serial). **1929** Love, Honor and Oh, Baby (short). **1930** Fast and Loose. **1934** Age of Innocence.

YOUNG, ARTHUR
Born: 1898. Died: 1959. Stage and screen actor.

Appeared in: **1935** Radio Parade of 1935; No Limit. **1937** Victoria the Great. **1940** 21 Days Together. **1941** Murder by Invitation. **1948** My Brother Jonathan. **1951** The Lady with a Lamp. **1954** An Inspector Calls; Paid to Kill. **1956** Dynamiters; The Gelignite Gang.

YOUNG, BULL (John W. Young)
Died: Aug. 2, 1913, Los Angeles, Calif. (concussion and hemorrhages after fighting). Professional boxer and screen actor.

Appeared in: **1913** One Round O'Brien Comes Back.

YOUNG, CAPTAIN JACK
Died: Oct. 28, 1966. Screen actor. Do not confuse with photographer Jack Young.

Appeared in: **1942** Yankee Doodle Dandy. **1943** Mission to Moscow.

YOUNG, CARLETON G.
Born: 1907. Died: July 11, 1971, Hollywood, Calif. (cancer). Screen, radio and television actor. Father of actor Tony Young.

Appeared in: **1936** Happy Go Lucky; A Man Betrayed. **1937** Join the Marines; Git Along Little Dogies; Navy Blues; Dangerous Holiday; Dick Tracy (serial). **1938** The Old Barn Dance; Heroes of the Hills; Cassidy of Bar 20; Gang Bullets. **1939** Convict's Code. **1941** Buck Privates; Keep 'Em Flying; Pride of the Bowery. **1942** Code of the Outlaw; SOS Coastguard. **1944** Ladies of Washington; Take It or Leave It; In the Meantime, Darling. **1945** Thunderhead, Son of Flicka; Thrill of a Romance; Abbott and Costello in Hollywood. **1947** Smash-Up, the Story of a Woman. **1948** The Kissing Bandit. **1950** American Guerilla in the Philippines; Double Deal. **1951** The Mob; People Will Talk; Red Mountain; Flying Leathernecks; Hard, Fast and Beautiful; Anne of the Indies; Gene Autry and the Mountains; Chain of Circumstance; Best of the Bad Men; The Day the Earth Stood Still; His Kind of Woman. **1952** The Brigand; Diplomatic Courier; Deadline U.S.A.; Last of the Comanches; My Six Convicts; Battle Zone. **1953** The Glory Brigade; A Blueprint for Murder; Goldtown Ghost Riders; Mexican Manhunt; Niagara; Torpedo Alley. **1954** Arrow in the Dust; Prince Valiant; Bitter Creek; Riot in Cell Block 11; 20,000 Leagues under the Sea. **1955** The Court Martial of Billy Mitchell; Artists and Models; Battle Cry; Phantom of the Jungle; The Racers. **1956** Battle Hymn; The Bottom of the Bottle; Julie; Beyond a Reasonable Doubt; Flight to Hong Kong. **1957** The Spirit of St. Louis. **1958** Cry Terror; The Last Hurrah. **1959** The Horse Soldiers; Here Come the Jets. **1960** Sergeant Rutledge; Gallant Hours; The Music Box Kid. **1961** Armored Command; Twenty Plus Two; The Big Show. **1962** The Man Who Shot Liberty Valance. **1964** Cheyenne Autumn.

YOUNG, CLARA KIMBALL
Born: 1890, Benton Harbor, Mich. Died: Oct. 15, 1960, Woodland Hills, Calif. Daughter of actress Pauline Kimball (dec. 1919). Screen, stage, vaudeville, television actress and film producer.

Appeared in: **1910** Ransomed; The Sepoy's Wife. **1912** Cardinal Wolsey; The Haunted Rockery; The Violin of Monsieur; Happy-Go-Lucky; Put Yourself in Their Place; Rock of Ages; Ann Boleyn. **1913** Beau Brummell; The Hindoo Charm; The Mystery of the Stolen Jewels; The Old Guard; The Little Minister; Love's Sunset. **1914** Goodness Gracious; The Flat Above. **1915** Camille; Trilby; Heart's in Exile; The Heart of the Blueridge; Lola; The Deep Purple; Marrying Money; The Fates and Flora Four-Flush (The Ten Billion Dollar Vitagraph Mystery Serial). **1916** The Common Law; The Feast of Life; The Yellow Passport; My Official Wife. **1917** The Easiest Way; The Foolish Virgin; Magda; The Marionettes; The Price She Paid; Shirley Kaye. **1918** The Savage Woman; The Road Through the Dark; The Claw; House of Glass; The Reason Why. **1919** Cheating Cheaters; The Eyes of Youth; The Better Wife. **1920** Mid Channel; The Forbidden Woman; Silk Husbands and Calico Wives; Possession. **1921** Charge It; Hush; Straight from Paris; Who No Man Knows.

1922 Enter Madame; The Hands of Nara; The Worldly Madonna. 1923 Cordelia the Magnificent; A Wife's Romance; The Woman of Bronze. 1925 Lying Wives. 1930 Mother and Son. 1931 Kept Husbands; Women Go on Forever. 1932 File No. 113; Probation; Love Bound. 1933 Souls for Sables. 1934 Return of Chandu (serial); I Can't Escape. 1935 Fighting Youth; His Night Out; She Married Her Boss. 1936 Three on the Trail; Love in September (short); The Last Assignment; Rouge's Tavern; Oh, Susannah!; Ants in the Pantry (short). 1937 The Mysterious Pilot (serial); The Hills of Old Wyoming. 1938 The Frontiersman. 1941 Mr. Celebrity; The Roundup.

YOUNG, CLIFTON
Born: 1917. Died: Sept. 10, 1951, Los Angeles, Calif. (smoke asphyxiation). Screen, vaudeville and radio actor.

Appeared in: 1924 "Our Gang" comedies. 1946 So You Want to Play the Horses (short). 1947 Pursued; Possessed; My Wild Irish Rose; Dark Passage; So You're Going on a Vacation (short). 1948 Blood on the Moon; plus the following shorts: So You Want an Apartment; So You Want to Build a House; So You Want to be a Detective; So You Want to be in Politics. 1949 Abandoned Woman; Calamity Jane and Sam Bass; Illegal Entry; So You Want to be Popular (short); So You're Having In-Law Trouble (short). 1950 The Return of Jesse James; Salt Lake Raiders; Trail of Robin Hood; A Woman of Distinction; Bells of Coronado.

YOUNG, DESMOND
Born: 1892. Died: June 27, 1966, Sark, Channel Islands. Author and screen actor.

Appeared in: 1951 The Desert Fox.

YOUNG, GLADYS
Born: 1905, England. Died: Aug. 18, 1975, Eastbourne, England. Screen, stage, radio and television actress.

Appeared in: 1952 Kathy's Love Affairs. 1956 One Wish Too Many (US 1962).

YOUNG, LUCILLE
Born: 1892. Died: Aug. 2, 1934, Hollywood, Calif. (following surgery). Screen actress. Entered films approx. 1914.

Appeared in: 1917 American Film Mfg. Co. films. 1926 Quicker'n Lightnin'. 1930 Lightnin'.

YOUNG, MARY
Born: 1857. Died: Nov. 13, 1934, Los Angeles, Calif. Screen actress.

Appeared in: 1922 The Angel of Crooked Street; Ninety and Nine. 1925 After Marriage.

YOUNG, MARY MARSDEN
Born: 1879. Died: June 23, 1971, La Jolla, Calif. Screen, stage and television actress.

YOUNG, NEDRICK "NED"
Born: Philadelphia, Pa. Died: Sept. 16, 1968, Los Angeles, Calif. (heart attack). Screen actor and screenwriter. Married to actress Frances Sage (dec. 1963).

Appeared in: 1942 Bombs over Burma. 1943 Ladies Day. 1946 The Devil's Playground; Unexpected Guest. 1947 The Swordsman. 1948 Gallant Blade. 1949 Deadly Is the Female. 1950 A Lady without a Passport; Gun Crazy. 1952 The Iron Mistress; Retreat, Hell!; Springfield Rifle. 1953 Captain Scarlet. 1958 Terror in a Texas Town. 1966 Seconds.

YOUNG, NORMA. See "PRUDENCE PENNY"

YOUNG, OLIVE
Born: June 21, 1907, St. Joseph, Mo. Died: Oct. 4, 1940, Bayonne, N.J. (internal hemorrhages). Screen, stage and vaudeville actress.

Appeared in: 1930 Trailing Trouble; Ridin' Law. 1931 The Man Who Came Back.

YOUNG, ROLAND
Born: Nov. 11, 1887 (or 1903), London, England. Died: June 5, 1953, New York, N.Y. Screen, stage, radio, television actor and author. Divorced from Marjorie Kummer. Married to actress Dorothy Patience.

Appeared in: 1922 Sherlock Holmes (film debut); Moriarty. 1923 Fog Bound. 1924 Grit. 1929 The Unholy Night; Her Private Life. 1930 The Bishop Murder Case; Wise Girls; Madam Satan; New Moon. 1931 Sin of Madelon Claudet; Don't Bet on Women; The Prodigal; Annabelle's Affairs; The Squaw Man; The Guardsman; Pagan Lady; He Met a French Girl. 1932 This Is the Night; One Hour with You; A Woman Commands; William and Mary; Wedding Rehearsal; Lovers Courageous; Street of Women. 1933 His Double Life; Pleasure Cruise; A Lady's Profession; Blind Adventure; They Just Had to Get Married. 1934 Here Is My Heart. 1935 David Copperfield; Ruggles of Red Gap. 1936 The Unguarded Hour; One Rainy Afternoon; Give Me Your Heart. 1937 The Man Who Could Work Miracles; Gypsy; Call It a Day; King Solomon's Mines; Ali Baba Goes to Town; Topper. 1938 Sailing Along; The

Young in Heart. 1939 Topper Takes a Trip; Yes, My Darling Daughter; The Night of Nights; Here I Am a Stranger. 1940 He Married His Wife; Irene; Star Dust; Private Affairs; Dulcy; No, No, Nanette; Philadelphia Story. 1941 Topper Returns; Two-Faced Woman; Flame of New Orleans. 1942 The Lady Has Plans; They All Kissed the Bride; Tales of Manhattan. 1943 Forever and a Day. 1944 Standing Room Only. 1945 And Then There Were None. 1948 Bond Street (US 1950); You Gotta Stay Happy. 1949 The Great Lover. 1950 Let's Dance. 1951 St. Benny the Dip. 1953 That Man from Tangier.

YOUNG, TAMMANY
Born: 1887. Died: Apr. 26, 1936, Hollywood, Calif. (heart attack). Stage and screen actor. Was W. C. Fields' stooge in some of his films.

Appeared in: 1917 The Great Secret (serial). 1919 Checkers; A Regular Girl. 1921 Bits of Life; The Man Who; Rainbow; The Right Way; The Man Worth While. 1922 John Smith; The Seventh Day; 'Til We Meet Again; Women Men Marry; When the Desert Calls. 1923 A Bride for a Knight. 1924 The Great White Way. 1925 Camille of the Barbary Coast; The Wrongdoers; The White Monkey; New Toys; The Unguarded Hour; The Police Patrol. 1927 The Perfect Sap; Blind Alleys. 1930 The Rube (short); Roadhouse Nights. 1933 She Done Him Wrong; Tugboat Annie; Heroes for Sale; The Bowery; Hallelujah, I'm a Bum; Gold Diggers of 1933. 1934 Search for Beauty; Little Miss Marker; The Lemon Drop Kid; The Mighty Barnum; Six of a Kind; You're Telling Me; Old Fashioned Way; It's a Gift; Gift of Gab. 1935 The Glass Key; Champagne for Breakfast; Little Big Shot; Wanderer of the Wasteland; The Man on the Flying Trapeze. 1936 Poppy.

YOUNG, WALTER
Born: 1878. Died: Apr. 18, 1957, New York, N.Y. Screen, stage actor and stage and film director.

Appeared in: 1937 The Adventurous Blonde; Alcatraz Island.

YULE, JOE
Born: Apr. 30, 1894, Scotland. Died: Mar. 30, 1950, Hollywood, Calif. (heart attack). Screen, stage and burlesque actor. Father of actor Mickey Rooney.

Appeared in: 1939 Sudden Money; Idiot's Delight; Fast and Furious; Judge Hardy and Son; They All Come Out; The Secret of Dr. Kildare. 1940 Broadway Melody of 1940; Go West; New Moon; Boom Town. 1941 The Big Store; I'll Wait for You; Billy the Kid; Kathleen. 1942 Born to Sing; Jackass Mail. 1943 Air Raid Wardens. 1944 Two Girls and a Sailor; Nothing but Trouble. 1946 Bringing up Father. 1949 Jiggs and Maggie in Jackpot Jitters. 1950 Jiggs and Maggie Out West.

YURKA, BLANCHE
Born: 1887, Czechoslovakia. Died: June 6, 1974, New York, N.Y. (arteriosclerosis). Stage and screen actress. Divorced from actor Ian Keith (dec. 1960).

Appeared in: 1935 A Tale of Two Cities. 1940 Queen of the Mob; City for Conquest; Escape. 1941 Ellery Queen and the Murder Ring. 1942 Lady of the Night; Pacific Rendezvous. 1943 Tonight We Raid Calais; The Song of Bernadette; A Night to Remember; Hitler's Madman (aka Hitler's Hangman). 1944 Cry of the Werewolf; One Body Too Many; The Bridge of San Luis Rey. 1945 The Southerner. 1947 13 Rue Madeleine; The Flame. 1950 The Furies. 1952 At Sword's Point (aka Sons of the Musketeers). 1953 Taxi. 1959 Thunder in the Sun.

ZABELLE, FLORA
Born: 1880. Died: Oct. 7, 1968, Manhattan, N.Y. Screen and stage actress. Married to actor Raymond Hitchcock (dec. 1929).

Appeared in: 1916 The Red Widow.

ZACCHINI, HUGO
Born: 1898. Died: Oct. 20, 1975, San Bernardino, Calif. (stroke). Screen actor and circus performer. Was originator of "Human Cannonball" act. Father of actor Hugo and Parchay Elsa Zacchini.

ZAMBA
Died: 1964, Calif. Screen animal performer (lion).

Appeared in: 1962 The Lion. 1965 Fluffy.

ZAMPI, MARIO
Born: Nov. 1, 1903, Rome, Italy. Died: Dec. 2, 1963, London, England. Film producer, director and screen actor. Appeared in early Italian silents.

ZANETTE, GUY
Born: 1907. Died: July 11, 1962, Hollywood, Calif. (cancer). Screen actor and dancer.

Appeared in: 1950 Snow Dog; Under My Skin. 1951 Yellow Fin.

ZANY, KING
Died: Feb. 19, 1939, Mojave, Calif. Screen actor and poet.

Appeared in: 1923 Hollywood. 1924 Broadway or Bust; The Garden of Weeds. 1927 The City Gone Wild. 1928 The Danger Rider. 1929 The Rainbow.

ZAROVA, RINI (aka RINI WILLSON)

Born: 1912, Russia. Died: Dec. 6, 1966, Santa Monica, Calif. Screen, stage, opera, radio and television actress. Married to conductor and composer Meredith Wilson.

ZAYAS, ALFONSO

Born: 1910, Mexico. Died: Feb. 1961, Mexico City, Mexico (heart attack). Screen actor. Entered films approx. 1945.

Appeared in: I, Too, Was a Champion.

ZBYSKO, STANISLAUS

Born: 1879, Poland. Died: Sept. 22, 1967, St. Joseph, Mo. Professional wrestler and screen actor.

Appeared in: **1932** Madison Square Garden. **1950** Night and the City.

ZEARS, MARJORIE

Born: 1911. Died: Mar. 9, 1952, Hollywood, Calif. (murdered). Screen actress. Was a Mack Sennett bathing beauty. Appeared in silent films.

ZEERS, FRED C.

Born: 1895. Died: Aug. 1946, Hollywood, Calif. (injuries following assault by bandits). Screen actor.

ZEGEL, FERDINAND

Born: 1895. Died: June 1973. Screen, stage and television actor and opera performer. Appeared in silents.

ZELAYA, DON ALFONSO

Born: 1894, Nicaragua. Died: Dec. 14, 1951, Hollywood, Calif. (heart attack). Screen actor and pianist.

Appeared in: **1940** Girl from God's Country. **1944** The Hairy Ape. **1949** Amazon Quest. **1952** Macao.

ZELLMAN, TOLLIE

Born: 1887. Died: Oct. 9, 1964, Stockholm, Sweden. Screen and stage actress.

Appeared in: **1911** The Judgment of the Society. **1932** Roeda Dagen. **1933** Vi Som Gar Koksvagen. **1936** Ungdom Av I Dag; Vaaran Pojke. **1939** Rena Rama Sanningen (Nothing but the Truth). **1947** While the Doors Are Closed.

ZIMINA, VALENTINA

Born: 1899, Russia. Died: Dec. 3, 1928, Hollywood, Calif. (influenza). Screen actress.

Appeared in: **1925** A Son of His Father. **1926** La Boheme; Rose of the Tenements. **1927** The Woman on Trial. **1928** The Scarlet Lady.

ZIMMERMAN, ED

Born: 1933. Died: July 6, 1972, York, Maine. Stage, screen, television actor and author.

Appeared in: **1971** Who Is Harry Kellerman and Why Is He Saying Those Terrible Things About Me?

ZUCCO, FRANCES

Born: 1933. Died: Mar. 15, 1962. Screen actress. Daughter of actor George Zucco (dec. 1960).

Appeared in: **1952** Top Secret; The Miracle of Our Lady of Fatima. **1953** Never Wave at a WAC.

ZUCCO, GEORGE

Born: Jan. 11, 1886, Manchester, England. Died: May 28, 1960, Hollywood, Calif. Screen, stage and vaudeville actor. Father of actress Frances Zucco (dec. 1962). Appeared in vaudeville in an act billed "The Suffragette."

Appeared in: **1931** Dreyfus (aka The Dreyfus Case—US film debut). **1932** There Goes the Bride. **1933** The Good Companions; The Man from Toronto; The Roof. **1934** What's in a Name?; What Happened Then?; Autumn Crocus (stage and film versions). **1935** It's a Bet. **1936** After the Thin Man; Sinner Take All; The Man Who Could Work Miracles (US 1937). **1937** Parnell; The Firefly; Saratoga; London by Night; Madame X; The Bride Wore Red; Conquest; Rosalie; Souls at Sea. **1938** Arsene Lupin Returns; Marie Antoinette; Lord Jeff; Fast Company; Vacation from Love; Suez; Charlie Chan in Honolulu. **1939** Arrest Bulldog Drummond; The Magnificent Fraud; Captain Fury; Here I Am a Stranger; The Cat and the Canary; The Hunchback of Notre Dame; The Adventures of Sherlock Holmes. **1940** Green Hell; Arise My Love; The Mummy's Hand; New Moon; Dark Streets of Cairo. **1941** The Monster and the Girl; Topper Returns; Ellery Queen and the Murder Ring; A Woman's Face; International Lady. **1942** Dr. Renault's Secret; The Mad Monster; The Mummy's Tomb; My Favorite Blonde; The Black Swan; Halfway to Shanghai. **1943** Holy Matrimony; Never a Dull Moment; Sherlock Holmes in Washington; The Mad Ghoul; The Black Raven; Dead Men Walk. **1944** The Devil's Brood; The Seventh Cross; The Mummy's Ghost; Return of the Ape Man; The Voodoo Man; One Body Too Many; Shadows in the Night. **1945** Hold That Blonde; The Woman in Green; One Exciting Night; Weekend at the Waldorf; House of Frankenstein; Having a Wonderful Crime; Sudan; Confidential Agent; Midnight Manhunt. **1946** Flying Serpent. **1947** The Imperfect Lady; Lured; Desire Me; Moss Rose; Where There's Life; Captain from Castile. **1948** The Pirate; Tarzan and the Mermaids; Who Killed "Doc" Robbin?; Secret Service Investigator. **1949** Madame Bovary; The Secret Garden; The Barkleys of Broadway. **1950** Joan of Arc; Let's Dance; Harbor of Missing Men. **1951** The First Legion; Flame of Stamboul; David and Bathsheba.

SELECTED BIBLIOGRAPHY

Aaronson, Charles S., ed. International Motion Picture Almanac. New York: Quigley Publications, 1933–1976.

Alicoate, Charles A., ed. The Film Daily Year Book of Motion Pictures. New York: Wid's Films & Film Folk, 1926–1971.

Barbour, Alan G. Days of Thrills and Adventure. London: Collier-Macmillan, 1971.

Barbour, Alan G. The Thrill of It All. London: Collier-Macmillan, 1971.

Blesh, Rudi. Keaton. New York: Macmillan, 1966.

Blum, Daniel. A New Pictorial History of the Talkies. New York: Grosset & Dunlap, 1970.

Blum, Daniel. A Pictorial History of the Silent Screen. New York: Grosset & Dunlap, 1953.

Blum, Daniel. A Pictorial History of the Talkies. New York: Grosset & Dunlap, 1958.

Brownlow, Kevin. The Parade's Gone By. New York: Alfred A. Knopf, 1968.

Catalog of Copyright Entries, 1912–1960. Washington, D.C.: Copyright Office of the Library of Congress.

Christopher, Milbourne. Houdini: The Untold Story. New York: Pocketbooks, 1970.

Cowie, Peter, ed. Focus on Film. London: Tantivy Press. Quarterly. Various issues through Winter 1976.

Dannenberg, Joseph. Film Year Book, 1922–1927. New York & Hollywood: Joseph Dannenberg.

Deschner, Donald. The Films of W. C. Fields. New York: Citadel Press, 1964.

Dimmitt, Richard Bertrand. An Actor Guide to the Talkies. Vols. 1 & 2. Metuchen, N.J.: Scarecrow Press, 1968.

Everson, William K. The Bad Guys. New York: Citadel Press, 1964.

Fenin, George N., and William K. Everson. The Western. New York: Bonanza Books, 1962.

Filmlexicon degli Autori e delle Opere. Italy: Edizioni di Bianco e Nero, 1958.

Griffith, Richard, and Arthur Mayer. The Movies. New York: Simon & Schuster, 1957.

Halliwell, Leslie. The Filmgoer's Companion. New York: Hill & Wang. 1st ed. 1965. Rev. & expanded ed. 1967. 3rd ed. 1970. 4th ed. 1974.

Henderson, Robert M. D. W. Griffith—The Years at Biograph. New York: Farrar, Straus & Giroux, 1970.

Johns, Eric. Dames of the Theatre. New Rochelle, N.Y.: Arlington House Publishers, 1974.

Krafsur, Richard P., exec ed. American Film Institute Catalog: Feature Films, 1961–1970. New York & London: R. R. Bowker Co., 1976. Indexes in separate volume.

Lahue, Kalton C. Continued Next Week. Norman, Okla.: University of Oklahoma Press, 1964.

Lahue, Kalton C. Kops and Custards. Norman, Okla.: University of Oklahoma Press, 1967.

Lahue, Kalton C. World of Laughter. Norman, Okla.: University of Oklahoma Press, 1966.

Lebel, Jean. Buster Keaton. London: Zwemmer, 1967.

Limbacher, James L., ed. Remakes, Series and Sequels on Film and Television. 3rd ed. Dearborn, Mich.: Audio-Visual Division, Henry Ford Centennial Library, 1970.

Low, Rachel. The History of the British Film. Vols. 2–4. Old Woking, Eng.: Unwin Brothers. Vols. 2 & 3 1948. Vol. 4 1971.

Low, Rachel, and Roger Manvell. The History of the British Film. Vol. 1. Old Woking, Eng.: Unwin Brothers, 1948.

Maltin, Leonard. The Great Movie Shorts: Those Wonderful One- and Two-Reelers of the Thirties and Forties. New York: Bonanza Books, 1972.

Maltin, Leonard. Movie Comedy Teams. New York: New American Library, 1970.

Michael, Paul. Humphrey Bogart: The Man and His Films. Indianapolis: Bobbs-Merrill Co., 1965.

Michael, Paul, ed. The American Movies Reference Book: The Sound Era. Englewood Cliffs, N.J.: Prentice-Hall, 1969.

Motion Picture Studio Directory & Trade Annual, 1920–1921. New York: Motion Picture News.

Munden, Kenneth W., ed. American Film Institute Catalog: Feature Films, 1921–1930. New York & London: R. R. Bowker Co., 1971. Indexes in separate volume.

New York Times Directory of the Film. New York: Arno Press, 1953.

New York Times Directory of the Theater. New York: Arno Press, 1973.

Parker, John. Who's Who in the Theatre, 1936–1967. Vols. 8–14. London: Isaac Pitman & Sons, 1972.

Robinson, Edward G., and Leonard Spigelgass. All My Yesterdays: An Autobiography. New York: Hawthorn Books, 1973.

Silverman, Syd, ed. Variety. Weekly. Jan. 1920–Dec. 1976.

Springer, John. All Talking! All Singing! All Dancing! New York: Citadel Press, 1966.

Stuart, Ray, ed. Immortals of the Screen. New York: Bonanza Books, 1965.

Thomas, William F., ed. Los Angeles Times. Various issues 1930–1976.

Twomey, Alfred E., and Arthur F. McClure. The Versatiles. New York: A. S. Barnes & Co., 1969.

Weaver, John T. Forty Years of Screen Credits, 1929–1969. Vols. I & II. Metuchen, N.J.: Scarecrow Press, 1970.

Young, William C. Famous Actors and Actresses of the American Stage: Documents of American Theater History. Vols. I & II. New York & London: R. R. Bowker Co., 1975.